The Longman Anthology of British Literature

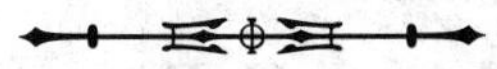

VOLUME 1B

THE EARLY MODERN PERIOD

David Damrosch
COLUMBIA UNIVERSITY

Christopher Baswell
BARNARD COLLEGE

Clare Carroll
QUEENS COLLEGE, CITY UNIVERSITY OF NEW YORK

Kevin J. H. Dettmar
CLEMSON UNIVERSITY

Heather Henderson
MOUNT HOLYOKE COLLEGE

Constance Jordan
CLAREMONT GRADUATE UNIVERSITY

Peter J. Manning
UNIVERSITY OF SOUTHERN CALIFORNIA

Anne Howland Schotter
WAGNER COLLEGE

William Chapman Sharpe
BARNARD COLLEGE

Stuart Sherman
FORDHAM UNIVERSITY

Jennifer Wicke
UNIVERSITY OF VIRGINIA

Susan J. Wolfson
PRINCETON UNIVERSITY

The Longman Anthology of British Literature

David Damrosch
General Editor

VOLUME 1B

THE EARLY MODERN PERIOD

Constance Jordan *and* Clare Carroll

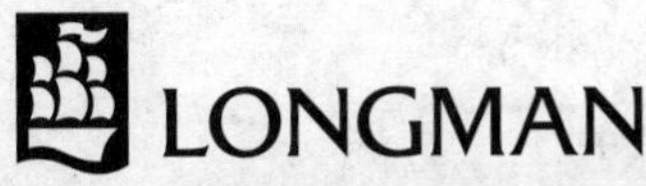

An imprint of Addison Wesley Longman, Inc.

New York • Reading, Massachusetts • Menlo Park, California • Harlow, England
Don Mills, Ontario • Sydney • Mexico City • Madrid • Amsterdam

Editor-in-Chief: *Patricia Rossi*
Senior Editor: *Lisa Moore*
Development Editor: *Mark Getlein*
Marketing Manager: *Melanie Goulet*
Supplements Editor: *Donna Campion*
Project Coordination and Text Design: *York Production Services*
Cover Designer: *Kay Petronio*
Cover Design Manager: *Nancy Danahy*
On the Cover: *Hans Holbein.* The Ambassadors. *1553. © National Portrait Gallery, London.*
Photo Researcher: *Julie Tesser*
Full Service Production Manager: *Valerie Zaborski*
Publishing Services Manager: *Al Dorsey*
Senior Print Buyer: *Hugh Crawford*
Electronic Page Makeup: *York Production Services*
Printer and Binder: *R.R. Donnelley and Sons Company*
Cover Printer: *The Lehigh Press, Inc.*

For permission to use copyrighted material, grateful acknowledgment is made to the copyright holders on page xxvii, which are hereby made part of this copyright page.

Library of Congress Cataloging-in-Publication Data

The Longman anthology of British literature. Early modern period.
[compiled by] Constance Jordan and Clare Carroll.
p. cm.
Includes bibliographical references (p. 2009) and indexes.
ISBN 0-321-06763-0
1. English literature—Early modern, 1500–1700. 2. Great Britain—History—Tudors, 1485–1603 Literary collections. 3. Great Britain—History—Early Stuarts, 1603–1640 Literary collections. 4. Great Britain—History—Commonwealth and Protectorate, 1649–1660 Literary collections. I. Jordan, Constance. II. Carroll, Clare, 1955– . III. Title—Early modern period
PR1121.L66 1999
820.8'003—dc21 98-35637
CIP

ISBN 0-321-06763-0

1234567890–DOC–010099

CONTENTS

PREFACE

This is an exciting time to be reading British literature. Literary studies are experiencing a time of transformation, involving lively debate about the nature of literature itself, its relations to the wider culture, and the best ways to read and understand it. These questions have been sharpened by the "culture wars" of recent years, in which traditionalists have debated advocates of fundamental reform, close readers have come up against cultural theorists who may seem more interested in politics than in aesthetic questions, and lovers of canonical texts have found themselves sharing the stage with multiculturalists who typically focus on ethnic and minority literatures, usually contemporary and often popular in nature, rather than on earlier and more elite literary productions.

The goal of this anthology is to present the wealth of British literature, old and new, classic and newly current, in ways that will respond creatively to these debates. We have constructed this anthology in the firm belief that it is important to attend both to aesthetic and to cultural questions as we study literature, and to continue to read the great classics even as we discover or rediscover new or neglected works. Admittedly, it is difficult to do all this at once, especially within the pages of a single anthology or the time constraints of a survey course. To work toward these goals, it has been necessary to rethink the very form of an anthology. This preface can serve as a kind of road map to the pages that follow.

A New Literary Geography

Let us begin by defining our basic terms: What is "British" literature? What is literature itself? And just what is the function of an anthology at the present time? The term "British" can mean many things, some of them contradictory, some of them even offensive to people on whom the name has been imposed. If the term has no ultimate essence, it does have a history. The first British were Celtic people who inhabited the British Isles and the northern coast of France (still called Brittany), before various Germanic tribes of Angles and Saxons moved onto the islands in the fifth and sixth centuries. Gradually the Angles and Saxons amalgamated into the Anglo-Saxon culture that became dominant in the southern and eastern regions of Britain and then spread outward; the old British people were pushed west, toward what became known as Cornwall, Wales, and Ireland, which remained independent kingdoms for centuries, as did Celtic Scotland to the north. By an ironic twist of linguistic fate, the Anglo-Saxons began to appropriate the term British from the Britons they had displaced, and they took as a national hero the legendary Welsh King Arthur. By the seventeenth century, English monarchs had extended their sway over Wales, Ireland, and Scotland, and they began to refer to their holdings as "Great Britain." Today, Great Britain includes England, Wales, Scotland, and Northern Ireland, but does not include the Republic of Ireland, which has been independent from England since 1922.

This anthology uses "British" in a broad sense, as a geographical term encompassing the whole of the British Isles. For all its fraught history, it seems a more satisfactory term than to speak simply of "English" literature, for two reasons. First: most speakers of English live in countries that are not the focus of this anthology; second, while the English language and its literature have long been dominant in the British Isles, other cultures in the region have always used other languages and have produced great literature in these languages. Important works by Irish, Welsh, and Scots writers appear regularly in the body of this anthology, some of them written directly in their languages and presented here in translation, others written in an English inflected by the rhythms, habits of thought, and modes of expression characteristic of these other languages and the people who use them. Important works, moreover, have often been written in the British Isles by recent arrivals, from Marie de France in the twelfth century to T. S. Eliot and Salman Rushdie in the twentieth; in a very real sense, their writings too are part of British literary production.

We use the term "literature" itself in a similarly capacious sense, to refer to a range of artistically shaped works written in a charged language, appealing to the imagination at least as much as to discursive reasoning. It is only relatively recently that creative writers have been able to make a living composing poems, plays, and novels purely "for art's sake," and only in the past hundred years or so have "belles lettres" or works of high literary art been thought of as sharply separate from other sorts of writing that the same authors would regularly produce. Sometimes, Romantic poets wrote sonnets to explore the deepest mysteries of individual perception and memory; at other times, they wrote sonnets the way a person might now write an Op-Ed piece, and such a sonnet would be published and read along with parliamentary debates and letters to the editor on the most pressing contemporary issues.

Great literature is double in nature: it is deeply rooted in its cultural moment, and yet it transcends this moment as well, speaking to new readers in distant times and places, long after the immediate circumstances of its production have been forgotten. The challenge today is to restore our awareness of cultural contexts without trapping our texts within them. Great writers create imaginative worlds that have their own compelling internal logic, built around the stories they tell using formal patterns of genre, literary reference, imagery, and style. At the same time, as Virginia Woolf says in *A Room of One's Own*, the gossamer threads of the artist's web are joined to reality "with bands of steel." To understand where a writer is taking us imaginatively, it is helpful to know where we are supposed to be starting from in reality: any writer assumes a common body of current knowledge, which this anthology attempts to fill in by means of detailed period introductions, full introductions to the individual authors, and notes and glosses to each text. Many of the greatest works of literature, moreover, have been written in response to the most sharply contested issues of the authors' own times. This anthology presents and groups selections in such a way as to suggest the literary and cultural contexts in which, and for which, they were created.

Women's Writing, and Men's

Literary culture has always involved an interplay between central and marginal regions, groups, and individuals. At a given time, some will seem dominant; in retrospect, some will remain so and others will be eclipsed, for a time or permanently, while formerly neglected writers may achieve a new currency. A major emphasis in literary study in recent years has been the recovery of writing by a range of women writers, some of them little read until recently, others major figures in their time and now again fascinating to read. Attending to the voices of such compelling writers as Margery Kempe, Elizabeth Cary, Mary Wollstonecraft, Mary Shelley, and Edith Nesbit often involves a shift in our understanding of the literary landscape, giving a new and lively perspective on much-read works. Thus, Shakespeare's *Othello* can fruitfully be read together with Elizabeth Cary's *Tragedy of Mariam, the Fair Queen of Jewry*, which tells a tale of jealousy and betrayal from a woman's point of view. On a larger scale, the first third of the nineteenth century can be defined more broadly than as a "Romantic Age" dominated by six male poets; looking closely at women's writing as well as men's, and at prose writing as well as poetry, we can deepen our understanding of the period as a whole—including the specific achievements of Blake, William Wordsworth, Coleridge, Keats, Percy Shelley, and Byron, all of whom continue to have a major presence in these pages as most of them did during the nineteenth century.

Historical Periods in Perspective

Overall, we have sought to give a varied presentation of the major periods of literary history, as customarily construed by scholars today: the Middle Ages (punctuated by the Norman Conquest in 1066); the early modern period or Renaissance; the Restoration and the eighteenth century; the era of the Romantics and their contemporaries; the Victorian age; and the twentieth century. These names mix chronology, politics, and literary movements: each period is of course a mixture of all of these elements and many others. Further, the boundaries of all these periods are fluid. Milton should be thought of in the context of Restoration politics as well as of early modern humanism; what is more, selections from *Paradise Lost* will also be found in Volume 2, in a Context section showing Milton's influence on the Romantics and their contemporaries. Reflecting the division of Thomas Hardy's literary life, Hardy appears in the Victorian section as a prose writer, and in the Twentieth Century as a poet. In general, one of the great pleasures of a survey of centuries of British literary production is the opportunity to see the ways texts speak to one another both across periods and within them, and indeed several layers of time may coexist within a single era: many writers consciously or unconsciously hearken back to earlier values (there were medievalists in the nineteenth century), while other writers cast "shadows of futurity" before them, in Percy Shelley's phrase.

Within periods, we have sought a variety of means to suggest the many linkages that make up a rich literary culture, which is something more than a sequence of individual writers all producing their separate bodies of work. In this anthology, each period includes several groupings called "Perspectives," with texts that address an important literary or social issue of the time. These Perspective sections typically illuminate underlying issues in a variety of the major works of their time, as with a section on Government and Self-Government that relates broadly to Sir Thomas More's *Utopia*, to Spenser's *Faerie Queene*, and to Milton's *Paradise Lost*. Most of the writers included in Perspective sections are important period figures, less well known today, who might be neglected if they were listed on their own with just a few pages each; grouping them together should be useful pedagogically as well as intellectually. Perspective sections may also include writing by a major author whose primary listing appears elsewhere in the period: thus, a Perspective section on the abolition of slavery and the slave trade—a hotly debated issue in England from the 1790s through the 1830s—includes poems and essays by Wordsworth, Byron, and Barbauld, so as to give a rounded presentation of the issue in ways that can inform the reading of those authors in their individual sections.

Works in Context

Periodically throughout the anthology we also present major works "In Context," to show the terms of a specific debate to which an author is responding. Thus Sir Philip Sidney's great *The Apology for Poetry* is accompanied by a context section to show the controversy that was raging at the time concerning the nature and value of poetry. Similarly, Thomas Dekker and Thomas Middleton's hilarious seventeenth-century comedy *The Roaring Girl: Or, Moll Cut-Purse* is accompanied by a Context section giving several readings on the virtues and vices of city life. Some of the writers in that context section are not classically literary figures, but all have produced lively and intriguing works, from King James I's *Counterblast to Tobacco* to Thomas Deloney's satiric account of *How Simon's Wife . . . Being Wholly Bent to Pride and Pleasure, Requested Her Husband to See London*.

Additionally, we include "Companion Readings" to present specific prior texts to which a work is responding: when Sir Thomas Wyatt creates a beautiful poem, *Whoso List to Hunt*, by making a free translation of a Petrarch sonnet, we include Petrarch's original (and a more literal translation) as a companion reading. For Conrad's *Heart of Darkness*, companion texts include Conrad's diary of the Congo journey on which he based his novella, and a bizarre lecture by Sir Henry Morton Stanley, the explorer-adventurer whose travel writings Conrad parodies.

Illustrating Visual Culture

Literature has always been a product of cultures that are visual as well as verbal. We include a hundred illustrations in the body of the anthology, presenting artistic and cultural images that figured importantly for literary creation. Sometimes, a poem refers to a specific painting, or more generally emulates qualities of a school of visual art. At other times, photographs, advertisements, or political cartoons can set the stage for literary works. In some cases, visual and literary creation have merged, as in Hogarth's series *A Rake's Progress*, included in Volume 1, or Blake's engravings of his *Songs of Innocence and Experience*, several of whose plates are reproduced in Volume 2.

Aids to Understanding

We have tried to contextualize our selections in a suggestive rather than an exhaustive way, wishing to enhance rather than overwhelm the experience of reading the texts themselves. Our introductions to periods and authors are intended to open up ways of reading rather than dictating a particular interpretation, and the suggestions presented here should always be seen as points of departure rather than definitive pronouncements. We have striven for clarity and ease of use in our editorial matter.

Thus, when difficult or archaic words need defining in poems, we use glosses in the margins, in all periods, so as to disrupt the reader's eye as little as possible; footnotes are intended to be concise and informative, rather than massive or interpretive. Spelling and punctuation are modernized in Volume 1, except when older forms are important for meter or rhyme, and with general exceptions for certain major writers, like Chaucer and Spenser, whose specific usages are crucial to their understanding. Important literary and social terms are defined when they are used; for convenience of reference, there is also an extensive glossary of literary and cultural terms at the end of each volume, and we provide summaries of British political and religious orders, and of money, weights, and measures. For further reading, we give carefully selected bibliographies for each period and for each author.

A New and Varied Format

For this printing, we introduce a choice of form: the anthology is available in the classic two-volume version, and also in six separate parts, one for each of the historical periods into which the anthology is divided. To preserve full freedom of choice, we have kept the paging the same in both versions, so that either can be used within a single course. The three sections of Volume 1 are thus available separately as Volumes 1A, 1B, and 1C, and the individual sections of Volume 2 can similarly be purchased as Volumes 2A, 2B, and 2C. When bought together, these sets are available at the same price as the two-volume version. The two-volume format keeps more material together, for ease of comparison and cross-reference; the six-volume version greatly increases the portability of the individual sections, and also enables them to be purchased individually for use in period courses. We hope that this innovative format will greatly increase the convenience and flexibility of the anthology; it is a physical embodiment of the variousness of British literature itself.

Varieties of Literary Experience

Above all, we have striven to give as full a presentation as possible to the varieties of great literature produced over the centuries in the British Isles, by women as well as by men, in outlying regions as well as in the metropolitan center of London, and in prose, drama, and verse alike. This is, in fact, the most capacious anthology of British literature ever assembled in a form suited to a survey course.

We hope that this anthology will show that the great works of earlier centuries can also speak to us compellingly today, their value only increased by the resistance they offer to our views of ourselves and our world. To read and reread the full sweep of this literature is to be struck anew by the degree to which the most radically new works are rooted in centuries of prior innovation. Even this preface can close in no better way than by quoting the words written eighteen hundred years ago by Apuleius—both a consummate artist and a kind of anthologist of extraordinary tales—when he concluded the prologue to his masterpiece *The Golden Ass:* Attend, reader, and pleasure is yours.

David Damrosch

ACKNOWLEDGMENTS

Throughout the extended collaborative process that has produced these volumes, the editors have benefited enormously from advice and counsel of many kinds. Our first and greatest debt is to our editor, Lisa Moore, who inspired us to begin this project, and whose enthusiasm and good judgment have seen us through. She and her associates Roth Wilkofsky, Richard Wohl, and Patricia Rossi have supported us in every possible way throughout the process, ably assisted by Lynn Huddon and Christopher Narozny. We have also been fortunate to enjoy the constant aid of Mark Getlein, the Platonic ideal of a developmental editor, whose literary and visual sensitivity have benefited every page of this anthology.

The best table of contents in the world would be of little use without actual texts following it. For these we are first of all indebted to the eloquence and cajolery of permissions wizards Kathy Smeilis and Robert Ravas, who negotiated hundreds of permissions with often recalcitrant publishers and occasionally unbalanced heirs. Julie Tesser traced and cleared our illustrations. Kevin Bradley, Candice Carta, and the staff of York Production Services then performed miracles in producing a beautiful and highly accurate text out of incredible masses of tearsheets, sometimes involving semilegible texts of works that hadn't been republished for centuries. The canny copyediting of Stephanie Argeros-Magean and her colleagues did much to bring clarity and consistency to the work of a dozen editors across thirteen thousand pages of copyedited manuscript. Through these stages and as the book went to press, Valerie Zaborski, Paula Soloway, and Patti Brecht oversaw a production process of Joycean complexity, with an edgy good humor that kept everyone focused on a constantly endangered schedule.

At every stage of the project, our plans and our prose were thoughtfully reviewed and assessed by colleagues at institutions around the country. Their advice helped us enormously in selecting our materials and in refining our presentation of them. We owe hearty thanks to Lucien Agosta (California State University, Sacramento), Anne W. Astell (Purdue University), Derek Attridge (Rutgers University), Linda Austin (Oklahoma State University), Joseph Bartolomeo (University of Massachusetts, Amherst), Todd Bender (University of Wisconsin, Madison), Bruce Boehrer (Florida State University), Joel J. Brattin (Worcester Polytechnic Institute), James Campbell (University of Central Florida), J. Douglas Canfield (University of Arizona), Paul A. Cantor (University of Virginia), George Allan Cate (University of Maryland, College Park), Eugene R. Cunnar (New Mexico State University), Earl Dachslager (University of Houston), Elizabeth Davis (University of California, Davis), Andrew Elfenbein (University of Minnesota), Margaret Ferguson (University of California, Davis), Sandra K. Fisher (State University of New York, Albany), Allen J. Frantzen (Loyola University, Chicago), Kate Garder Frost (University of Texas), Leon Gottfried (Purdue University), Mark L. Greenberg (Drexel University), James Hala (Drew University), Wayne Hall (University of Cincinnati), Wendell Harris (Pennsylvania State University), Richard H. Haswell (Washington State University), Susan Sage Heinzelman (University of Texas, Austin), Standish Henning (University of Wisconsin, Madison), Jack W. Herring (Baylor University),

Maurice Hunt (Baylor University), Colleen Juarretche (University of California, Los Angeles), R. B. Kershner (University of Florida), Lisa Klein (Ohio State University), Rita S. Kranidis (Radford University), Elizabeth B. Loizeaux (University of Maryland), John J. Manning (University of Connecticut), Michael B. McDonald (Iowa State University), Celia Millward (Boston University), Thomas C. Moser, Jr. (University of Maryland), Jude V. Nixon (Baylor University), Violet O'Valle (Tarrant County Junior College, Texas), Richard Pearce (Wheaton College), Renée Pigeon (California State University, San Bernardino), Tadeusz Pioro (Southern Methodist University), Deborah Preston (Dekalb College), Elizabeth Robertson (University of Colorado), Deborah Rogers (University of Maine), Brian Rosenberg (Allegheny College), Charles Ross (Purdue University), Harry Rusche (Emory University), Kenneth D. Shields (Southern Methodist University), Clare A. Simmons (Ohio State University), Sally Slocum (University of Akron), Phillip Snyder (Brigham Young University), Isabel Bonnyman Stanley (East Tennessee University), Margaret Sullivan (University of California, Los Angeles), Herbert Sussmann (Northeastern University), Ronald R. Thomas (Trinity College), Theresa Tinkle (University of Michigan), William A. Ulmer (University of Alabama), Jennifer A. Wagner (University of Memphis), Anne D. Wallace (University of Southern Mississippi), Jackie Walsh (McNeese State University, Louisiana), John Watkins (University of Minnesota), Martin Wechselblatt (University of Cincinnati), Arthur Weitzman (Northeastern University), Bonnie Wheeler (Southern Methodist University), Dennis L. Williams (Central Texas College), and Paula Woods (Baylor University).

Other colleages brought our developing book into the classroom, teaching from portions of the work-in-progress while it was still in page proof. Our thanks for classroom testing to Lisa Abney (Northwestern State University), Charles Lynn Batten (University of California, Los Angeles), Brenda Riffe Brown (College of the Mainland, Texas), John Brugaletta (California State University, Fullerton), Dan Butcher (Southeastern Louisiana University), Lynn Byrd (Southern University at New Orleans), David Cowles (Brigham Young University), Sheila Drain (John Carroll University), Lawrence Frank (University of Oklahoma), Leigh Garrison (Virginia Polytechnic Institute), David Griffin (New York University), Rita Harkness (Virginia Commonwealth University), Linda Kissler (Westmoreland County Community College, Pennsylvania), Brenda Lewis (Motlow State Community College, Tennessee), Paul Lizotte (River College), Wayne Luckman (Green River Community College, Washington), Arnold Markely (Pennsylvania State University, Delaware County), James McKusick (University of Maryland, Baltimore), Eva McManus (Ohio Northern University), Manuel Moyrao (Old Dominion University), Kate Palguta (Shawnee State University, Ohio), Paul Puccio (University of Central Florida), Sarah Polito (Cape Cod Community College), Meredith Poole (Virginia Western Community College), Tracy Seeley (University of San Francisco), Clare Simmons (Ohio State University), and Paul Yoder (University of Arkansas, Little Rock).

As if all this help weren't enough, the editors also drew directly on friends and colleagues in many ways, for advice, for information, sometimes for outright contributions to headnotes and footnotes, even (in a pinch) for aid in proofreading. In particular, we wish to thank James Cain, Michael Coyle, Pat Denison, Andrew Fleck, Laurie Glover, Lisa Gordis, Joy Hayton, Jean Howard, David Kastan, Stanislas Kemper, Ron Levao, Carol Levin, David Lipscomb, Denise MacNeil, Jackie Maslowski, Richard Matlak, Anne Mellor, James McKusick, Michael North, David Paroissien, Stephen M. Parrish, Peter Platt, Cary Plotkin, Gina Renee, Alan Richardson, Esther Schor, Catherine Siemann, Glenn Simshaw, David Tresilian, Shasta Turner, Nicholas Watson, Michael Winckleman, and Gillen Wood for all their guidance and assistance.

The pages on the Restoration and the eighteenth century are the work of many collaborators, diligent and generous. Michael F. Suarez, S. J. (Campion Hall, Oxford) edited the Swift and Pope sections; Mary Bly (Washington University) edited Etherege and Sheridan; Michael Caldwell (University of Chicago) edited the portions of "Reading Papers" on *The Craftsman* and the South Sea Bubble. Steven N. Zwicker (Washington University) co-wrote the period introduction, and the headnotes for the Dryden section. Bruce Redford (Boston University) crafted the footnotes for Dryden, Gay, Johnson, and Boswell. Susan Brown, Christine Coch, and Paige Reynolds helped with texts, footnotes, and other matters throughout; William Pritchard gathered texts, wrote notes, and prepared bibliography. To all, abiding thanks.

It has been a pleasure to work with all of these colleagues, and this is, after all, only the beginning of what we hope will be a long-term collaboration with those who use this anthology, as teachers, students, and general readers. This book exists for its readers, whose reactions and suggestions we warmly welcome, as these will in turn reshape this book for later users in the years to come.

CREDITS

TEXT CREDITS

Cary, Elizabeth: Excerpt from ELIZABETH CARY, TRAGEDY OF MIRIAM: THE FAIR QUEEN OF JEWRY, WITH THE LADY FALKLAND: HER LIFE, BY ONE OF HER DAUGHTERS, edited by Barry Weller and Margaret W. Ferguson. Copyright © 1994 The Regents of the University of California. Reprinted by permission of The University of California Press.

Dekker, Thomas: From "Lantern and Candlelight" by Thomas Dekker from THOMAS DEKKER: SELECTED WRITINGS edited by E. D. Pendry. Copyright © 1968 by E. D. Pendry. Reprinted by permission of Harvard University Press and Edward Arnold Publishers Ltd.

Deloney, Thomas: Excerpt from "Thomas of Reading" by Thomas Deloney from THE NOVELS OF THOMAS DELONEY edited by Merritt E. Lawlis, 1961, pp. 294-303. Reprinted by permission of Indiana University Press.

Glossary of Literary and Cultural Terms: Excerpts from THE HARPER HANDBOOK TO LITERATURE, 2/E by Northrop Frye, et al. Copyright © 1997 by Addison -Wesley Educational Publishers Inc. Reprinted by permission of the publisher.

Milton, John: Adapted and abridged excerpts from Alastair Fowler's notes from PARADISE LOST by Milton. Copyright © 1968 Longman Group Limited. Reprinted by permission of Addison Wesley Longman, Essex, England.

Petrarch: Sonnets 140, 190 and 164 from PETRARCH'S LYRIC POEMS translated and edited by Robert M. Durling. Copyright © 1976 by Robert M. Durling. Reprinted by permission of the publisher, Harvard University Press, Cambridge, MA.

Shakespeare, William: Notes for "Othello" from THE COMPLETE WORKS OF SHAKESPEARE edited by David Bevington, 4/E. Copyright © 1992 by HarperCollins Publishers, Inc.

Wroth, Lady Mary: THE POEMS OF LADY MARY WROTH, edited, with and Introduction and Notes, by Josephine A. Roberts. Copyright © 1983 by Louisiana State University Press. Reprinted by permission of Louisiana State University Press.

ILLUSTRATION CREDITS

Cover: By permission of the National Portrait Gallery, London. Page 568: By permission of the Folger Shakespeare Library. Page 572: By permission of the National Portrait Gallery, London. Page 573: Copyright © The British Museum. Page 580: Stock Montage. Page 587: The British Library. Page 707: Rare Book Collection, Cornell University Library, Ithaca, NY. Pages 1022–1023: Sherborne Castle Estate. Page 1067: British Library. Page 1097: Victoria & Albert Museum, London/Art Resource, NY. Page 1262: Devonshire Collection, Chatsworth. Reproduced by permission of the Chatsworth Settlement Trustees. Page 1329: By permission of the Folger Shakespeare Library. Page 1426–1427: Copyright © The British Museum. Page 1598: The British Library. Page 1599: By permission of the Folger Shakespeare Library. Page 1698: National Portrait Gallery. Page 1700: The National Gallery, London.

The Longman Anthology of British Literature

VOLUME 1B

THE EARLY MODERN PERIOD

Frontispiece from Saxton's *Atlas*. 1579.

The Early Modern Period

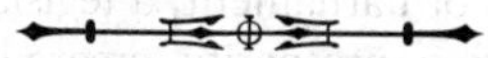

We see the past through lenses that show us something of the world we are living in. How we mark periods in history depends less on an objective evaluation of evidence than on our sense of its relation to our own present. The centuries between 1500 and 1700 have been termed the "Renaissance" and, more recently, "the early modern period." What do these two names mean and what do they tell us about our understanding of this single and continuous stretch of time?

However we describe these centuries, they encompassed events that changed profoundly the way people lived and thought. In 1500, the English church was part of a united Western Christendom led by the Pope, and people around the country prayed according to a common liturgy. It was understood that the earth was the center of the universe; that the human body was a balance of the four elements—earth, air, fire, and water; and that nature, read like a book, could reveal a moral order. English men and women had a deep respect for law, which they assumed would protect them from tyranny as well as anarchy. These beliefs had been challenged in the preceding century and a half by the natural calamities of plague and famine, by the political upheaval of the Rising of 1381, and more generally by the growth of towns, trade, and a degree of social mobility. Yet for most people in 1500 the old beliefs held fast, as did the traditional way of life that sustained them. And outside the growing merchant class, a person's place tended to be fixed at birth; the majority of folk lived in country villages, worked the land, and traded in regional markets.

By the end of the seventeenth century, much of this way of life had vanished. England had broken away from Roman religious authority; in addition to the Church of England and the Presbyterian churches of Scotland, Protestantism had created a variety of sects: Anabaptists, Puritans, and Quakers. Worship was conducted in English, not in the Latin that had been used for centuries. Catholics, suspected of subversive intentions, were barely tolerated. A natural philosophy based on experimental methods had begun to reshape the disciplines of physics, medicine, and biology; such ancient authorities as Aristotle, Galen, and Pliny were no longer unquestioned. Sketched in principle by Sir Francis Bacon in his treatise on scientific inquiry, *Novum Organum* (literally, "the new instrument"), published in 1620, a systematic investigation of nature had not begun before the restoration of the Stuart monarchy in 1660. But the world view it would help to confirm was already evident early in the seventeenth century: the work of the Italian physicist Galileo Galilei on gravitational force had demonstrated that the most elementary laws of nature were mathematical; the German astronomer Johannes Kepler had confirmed that the universe was heliocentric; and in England, William Harvey had established that the body was energized not by the eccentric flow of "humors" but by a circulation of blood to and from the heart. Scientists would consolidate their status as intellectuals by forming the Royal Society for the Advancement of Science in 1660—a foundation that was vigorously supported by the new Stuart king, Charles II.

Political life had taken a new direction as well. A civil war, interrupting the peace of over a century, had created a new kind of monarchy. The war had been fought over social and economic issues but also over a matter of principle: England was to be governed by a monarch whose authority and power were not absolute but limited by law and the actions of Parliament, a legislative assembly representing his subjects. The cities, enjoying a prosperity created by international commerce, became crowded even as they expanded with new streets, marketplaces, and buildings for private as well as public use. Country folk flocked to these burgeoning urban centers. Succumbing to diseases spread by filth and overcrowding, they often died younger than did their rural relatives. But England was becoming a nation of city dwellers, and everyone knew of "citizens" who had gained wealth and station in these exciting, if also terrifying, cities.

The Humanist Renaissance and Early Modern Society

The tumultuous character of the age has been described as a "renaissance"—literally a "rebirth." Nineteenth-century historians attributed the intellectual and social energy that initiated the reform of the medieval world to a revival of interest in the classical past. By 1400, Italian scholars had begun to reread the works of Greek and Roman authors—Plato and Aristotle, Virgil, Ovid, and Horace—and to look with fresh eyes at the physical monuments of the ancient world that were still so prominent in their landscapes. Their movement traveled north and west to France, the Low Countries, Germany, the Iberian peninsula, and eventually England. What was "reborn" as a result was a sense of the meanings to be discovered in the here and now, in the social, political and economic everyday world. Writing about the intellectual vitality of the age, the French humanist François Rabelais had his amiable giant Gargantua confess that his own education had been "darksome, obscured with clouds of ignorance." Gargantua knows, however, that his son will be taught differently:

> Good literature has been restored unto its former light and dignity, and with such amendment and increase of knowledge, that now hardly should I be admitted unto the first form of the little grammar-school boys . . . I see robbers, hangmen, freebooters, tapsters, ostlers, and such like, of the very rubbish of the people, more learned now than the doctors and preachers were in my time.

These comically overstated remarks nevertheless convey the spirit of the Renaissance: learning was no longer only to be devoted to securing salvation, but should address the conditions of ordinary life as well. The pre-Christian cultures of the ancient Mediterranean had introduced Europeans to philosophies that valued human society and its future generations; studying classical texts afresh, thinkers began to attend in new ways to the world around them. The writers and scholars responsible for the rebirth of a secular culture have been known as "humanists," because they read "humane" as well as "sacred" letters; and their intellectual and artistic practices have been termed "humanism."

The humanists cultivated certain habits of thought that became widely adopted by early modern thinkers of all kinds: skill in using language analytically, attentiveness to public and political affairs as well as private and moral ones, and an acute appreciation for differences between peoples, regions, and times. It was, after all, the humanists who began to realize that the classical past required *understanding*; they recognized the past as unfamiliar, neither Christian nor European, and they knew, therefore, that it had to be studied, interpreted, and, in a sense, reborn.

At the same time, changes were occurring for which there were no precedents. During these years, the modern world was born as much as an older world was reborn, and for this reason the sixteenth and seventeenth centuries have also been called the "early modern period." Its modernity was registered in many ways. Instruments for measuring time and space provided a knowledge of physical nature, a mapping of land, sea, and even the sky that began to permit global travel. Means had to be designed to compute the wealth that was being created by manufacture and trade, and new methods were employed by a people keen to exploit all kinds of resources, including the labor of individuals. Money was used in new and complex ways, its flow managed through such innovations as double-entry bookkeeping and letters of exchange that registered debt and credit in interregional markets. The capital that accumulated as a result of these kinds of transactions fueled merchant banks, joint-stock companies, and—notably in England—trading companies that sponsored colonies abroad. In England especially, wealth was increasingly based on money, not land, and the change encouraged a social mobility that reflected but also exploited the old hierarchy. Riches could and did make it possible for an artisan's son to purchase a coat of arms and become a gentleman, as William Shakespeare did. More important, moneyed wealth supported the artistic and scholarly institutions that allowed the stepson of a bricklayer to go to the best school in London, to profit from the business of the theater, and to compose literary works of sufficient brilliance to make him poet laureate, as Ben Jonson did. "Ambition is like choler," warned Francis Bacon; it makes men "active, earnest, full of alacrity and stirring." But if ambition "be stopped and cannot have his way, it becommeth adust, and thereby maligne and venomous." Early modern society was certainly both active and stirring; but the very energy that gave it momentum could also lead to hardship, distress, and personal tragedy.

Urban life flourished in conditions that were increasingly hospitable to commerce; rural existence became precarious as small farms failed. During the fifteenth century the nobility had begun to enlarge their estates by the incorporation or "enclosing" of what had formerly been public or common land. They sought to profit from a new activity: sheep farming. Thousands of men and women who had worked the land on modest estates lost their livelihoods as a result. Many came to the cities, particularly London; others traveled through the country, looking for odd work, begging, and thieving. The situation got worse when Henry VIII broke England's tie to the Catholic Church, for Henry added to the property of the very rich by giving them the land he had confiscated from the church. On the other hand, the great centers of commerce—Bristol, Norwich, and London—sustained not only trade but also many kinds of manufacture. One of the most important was printing. The invention of movable type in 1436 by a German printer, Johann Gutenberg, revolutionized the dissemination of texts. A single illuminated manuscript took years to produce and provided what was often a unique version of a text, an item that might cost as much as a small farm; a printing press could quickly produce multiple copies of identical versions of a text for as little as a few shillings.

Both the mentality of the "Renaissance" and the more comprehensive culture of the early modern period are illustrated by the history of the most frequently disseminated and contested text of these centuries: the Bible. It was the work of humanists to establish what that text was (after centuries of corrupted versions) and then to translate it into the vernacular languages. Desiderius Erasmus provided accurate Hebrew and Greek texts and translated them into Latin. Printed English translations

Hans Holbein. *The Ambassadors.* 1533. National Portrait Gallery, London.

begin with William Tyndale's New Testament, introduced to England in the 1520s. Later versions included the Geneva Bible with its Calvinist commentary; the Bishops' Bible, repudiating much of that commentary; and the King James Bible, or "Authorized Version," a work by forty-seven translators that was published in 1611. Protestant doctrine emphasized the importance of reading Scripture as a means to spiritual enlightenment, and the preface to the King James Bible insists that for this purpose a translation is as good as the original: "No cause why the word translated should be denied to be the word." But the importance of the Bible went beyond its status as the basis for religious belief.

People from various walks of life, not only humanists, found the Bible a source of inspiration for social reform, a means to link together religious conviction and political practice. Drawing on the Bible to justify their ideas of government, writers as different as the radical Bishop of Winchester, John Ponet, and the scholarly King James VI of Scotland, eventually James I of England, presented arguments for distinctive kinds of monarchy. Ponet insisted that a monarch was obliged to obey the law of the land and thus to adhere to a "constitution"; James thought that a monarch should respect only divine law and be considered "absolute." Other writers, inspired by their

19.
SCVLPTVRA IN ÆS.
Sculptor noua arte, bracteata in lamina Scalpit figuras, atque prælis imprimit.

Hans Collaert, after Jan van der Straet, called Stradanus. *The Printmaker's Workshop* (detail).

own understanding of God's word, forged new concepts of the state, the subject, and sovereignty that would continue to shape political philosophy to the American War of Independence.

The Bible and the attitudes it prompted were also factors in the establishment of an English church. The English people had been forced to break formally and definitively from the Catholic Church because their king, Henry VIII, wished to be independent of the papacy and its government in Rome. His reasons were many and complex. Certainly responsive to the demand for changes in church government, doctrine, and liturgy, Henry was motivated by personal and political interests as well. In love with a lady of the court, Anne Boleyn, he was persuaded that his marriage to Catherine of Aragon, the widow of his older brother, Prince Arthur, violated divine law. Catherine, mother of the girl who would become Mary I, had failed to give Henry a son, and he saw in his frustrated hopes for the dynastic stability that would come from having a male heir a sign that God was displeased with his marriage. He sought a divorce from the Pope and was refused. In 1533, however, his pliable Archbishop of Canterbury, Thomas Cranmer, defying the Pope out of loyalty to his king, pronounced Henry's marriage to Catherine invalid. The following year, Parliament passed the Act of Supremacy; besides making the monarch of England head of an English church, it made Henry immediately free from the Pope's jurisdiction. English clergy who had promoted the idea of a reformation began to institute the changes they had envisaged. But the socially destabilizing effects of the English reformation, far from abating, grew more profound as time went on.

Huge numbers of the faithful would suffer, Protestants as well as Catholics. The creation of an English church not only separated England from most of the continent, it disturbed the religious peace that had prevailed for centuries. The story is a grim one: Catholics in the north of England unsuccessfully resisted Henry's imposition of Protestantism in their Pilgrimage of Grace in 1536; Protestants were in turn persecuted by Mary I throughout her reign; Catholics were suppressed by Elizabeth I; and sectarians of various denominations were required to adhere to Anglican forms of worship and obey episcopal power under the Stuarts.

The prodigiously revolutionary changes in early modern England were vividly reflected in its profuse and varied literature. Topics and issues that for centuries had been considered by relatively small numbers of literate people were now registered in general debate. New and evolving conditions of religious, intellectual, and political life provided writers with a vast subject matter, and their work shed light on the world that they saw unfolding before them. They showed its potential for prosperous development through all kinds of human activity; they represented its long and varied history as proof of providential direction; and they praised its myriad forms as the expression of a divine and beneficent artificer.

As late twentieth-century readers, we come to the literature of this period with our own perspectives on what is modern and what we understand as postmodern. Many features of early modern culture are again in transition today: the printed book, which once superseded the manuscript, is now being challenged by computer-generated hypertext; the nation-state, which once eclipsed the feudal domain and divided "Christendom," is now qualified by an international economy; and the belief in human progress, which was once applauded as an advance over the medieval faith in divine providence, is now subject to criticism, in large part because of such kinds of injustice and inequity as slavery, colonialism, and the exploitation of wage labor—all factors in the growth of early modern England and of other states in Europe. As modern and postmodern readers, we have a special affinity with our early modern counterparts. Like them, we study change.

History and Epic

The political life of the sixteenth century was dominated by the genius of a single dynasty: the Tudors. Its founder was Owen Tudor, a squire of an ancient Welsh family who was employed at the court of Henry V and eventually married his widow, Catherine of Valois. Its first monarch was Owen Tudor's grandson, Henry, Earl of Richmond, who defeated Richard III at Bosworth Field in 1485 to become Henry VII. He married Elizabeth, daughter of Edward IV, whom Richard III had succeeded—a fortunate event for the people of England, as it united the two parties by whom the crown had been disputed for many decades. Once Henry, who represented the House of Lancaster (whose emblem was a white rose), was joined to Elizabeth, a member of the House of York (signified by a red rose), the "Wars of the Roses" were at an end. Henry VII's bureaucratic skills then settled the kingdom in ways that allowed it to grow and become identified as a single nation, however much it also comprised different peoples: the midlands and the north were distinguished from the more populous south by dialectal forms of speech; and to the west, in Cornwall and Wales, many English subjects still spoke Gaelic. More thoroughly Gaelic were Scotland to the north and Ireland across the sea to the west. Although the Anglo-Normans had invaded Ireland in the twelfth century, it was not until the reign of Elizabeth that the English pursued the subjugation of Ireland by establishing colonizing plantations and conducting a brutal military campaign that produced famine, massacres, and the forced relocation of people. But this supposed English fiefdom remained rebellious and effectively unconquered for Elizabeth's entire reign. Its resistance to English rule was crushed only in 1603, an event that marked the end of an independent Ireland for three hundred years. Scotland, to the far north, was a separate and generally unfriendly kingdom with strong ties to France until James VI of Scotland became James I of England. His accession to the English throne in 1603 began a process that would end with the complete union of the two kingdoms in 1707. There were also more remote regions to consider: England's colonization of the Americas began under Elizabeth I, progressed under James I, and allowed the English to think of themselves as an imperial power.

Writing history offered a way to reinforce the developing sense of nationhood, a project that was all the more appealing after the creation of an English church and the beginnings of a British empire. Medieval historians had concentrated on the actions of ambitious men and women whose lives reflected their good or bad qualities; early modern historians wrote about events and their manifold causes. William Camden's *Britannia* and Raphael Holinshed's *Chronicles of England, Scotland, and Ireland* (the source for many of Shakespeare's plays) celebrate the deeds and the character of the early peoples of the British Isles, including the ancient origins of the English kingdom, its exemplars of heroism and villainy, its struggle for unity realized under the Tudors, and the sturdy resistance of its subjects to absolute monarchic power. The land itself became the subject of comment: William Harrison wrote a description of the English counties (included in Holinshed), and John Stow surveyed the neighborhoods of London; Michael Drayton, a Stuart poet, wrote a mythopoetic account of England's towns and countryside entitled *Poly-Olbion;* and Richard Hakluyt's collection of travel histories, *The Principal Navigations, Voyages and Discoveries of the English Nation,* reported in magnificent detail the exploration of the New World. Accounts of this wild and fruitful land fired the imaginations of English readers, who, it was hoped, would decide to promote and even participate in the laborious task of colonization. Describing landfall on the coast of Virginia, Arthur Barlow wrote:

> we found shoal water, where we smelled so sweet and so strong a smell as if we had been in the midst of some delicate garden abounding with all kind of odoriferous flowers. . . . I think in all the world the like abundance is not to be found. And my selfe having seen those parts of Europe that most abound, find such difference as were incredible to be written.

All these works comprising history, the description of various regions, and reports of travel have been loosely described as *epic,* but none of them conforms to the genre as contemporary poetics represented it—expressing heroic grandeur not only in action but also in the musical verse form and elevated language of the epic tradition.

The masterpieces of the early modern English epic are Edmund Spenser's *The Faerie Queene* and John Milton's *Paradise Lost.* Spenser imitated continental models to create an English Protestant epic-romance, an optimistic projection of Elizabethan culture. The realities of Elizabeth I's reign, though far from the poet's vision of things, were nonetheless very impressive. England's cities had grown to be centers of commerce, her navy controlled the principal routes of trade, and her people pursued lucrative interests in Europe and the Americas, successfully resisting Spanish efforts to dominate world settlement and trade. The defeat of the Spanish Armada in 1588 and the bold explorations of such men as Sir Francis Drake and Sir Walter Raleigh testified to the nation's seafaring power. In the figures of his poem, Spenser embodied the energies producing this expansive growth. His virtuous knights overcome monstrous threats to order, peace, and tranquillity. Aspects of the queen's own genius are reflected in his heroines. Like the warrior maiden Britomart, Elizabeth I assumed a martial character when England was in danger from abroad; like his Queen Mercilla, she could be gracious to her enemies; like the virgin Una, she stood for what the poet and most of his readers believed was the one true faith: Protestantism. And like Spenser's enigmatic and distant Queen Gloriana, the Faerie Queene of the title, Elizabeth exercised her authority and power in unpredictable ways: secrecy and dissimulation were her stock in trade. To her subjects, her majesty was awful and sometimes terrifying. But she was also mortal, and at her death, few could have foreseen the new and divided nation that came into being with the accession of James I. The new king was greeted with mixed feelings: on the one hand, his claim to the throne was not disputed; on the other hand, he came from Scotland, long an enemy of England and always the source of anxiety to those who sought dominion over the British Isles as a whole. Although he was educated by the humanist George Buchanan, whose treatises praising republican government were widely known and read, James favored absolute rule and believed that a monarch should be *lex loquens*, the living spirit of the law, beyond the control of Parliament and indifferent to the rights of his subjects. His personal conduct appeared to be dubious: his critics represented him as frequently unkempt and claimed that he preferred to hunt deer rather than to take charge of matters of state. Disputes with the House of Commons over money to support the Crown's activities were frequent. Reports of intrigue with Catholic Spain shattered the nation's sense of security; an attempt in 1605 to blow up the Houses of Parliament, revealed as the Gunpowder Plot, caused a near panic. These and other kinds of unrest grew more intense when James's heir, Charles I, proved to be even more autocratic than his father. Charles's queen, Henrietta Maria, the daughter of Henry IV of France, was a Catholic, and it was rumored that she was treacherous. Religious controversy raged throughout the British Isles, and the struggle over the authority and power of the monarch culminated in a series of bloody civil wars. Across England and Scotland, forces loyal the king fought the army of Parliament, led by Oliver Cromwell, a Puritan Member of the Commons. The war, which lasted from 1642 to 1651, ended with the defeat of the royalists.

In 1649, Charles I was captured and executed by order of Parliament, and England began to be governed as a republic. She was no longer a kingdom but a Commonwealth, and this period in her history is known as the Interregnum, the period between kingdoms. The long-advocated change, now a reality, could hardly have begun in a more shocking way. The monarchy had always been regarded as a sacred office and institution, as Shakespeare's Richard II had said:

> Not all the water in the rough rude sea
> Can wash the balm off from an anointed king;
> The breath of worldly men cannot depose
> The deputy elected by the Lord.

But in the course of half a century, the people had proved themselves to be a sovereign power, and it was politically irrelevant that Charles, on the block, exemplified regal self-control. As the Parliamentarian poet Andrew Marvell later wrote of the king's execution:

> He nothing common did or mean
> Upon that memorable scene,
>   But with his keener eye
>   The ax's edge did try,

Nor called the gods with vulgar spite
To vindicate his helpless right;
But bowed his comely head
Down as upon a bed.

The conflict itself, its causes, and its outcome have been variously interpreted. As a revolution in government, it was defined by common lawyers, energized by Puritan enthusiasm, and motivated by widespread hatred of Stuart autocracy. As a religious and cultural struggle, it has been described as the War of Three Kingdoms, comprising the resistance of Scots Presbyterians and Irish Catholics to the centralizing control of the English church and government. But whatever its historical character, the Civil War marked England's transition to a society in which the absolute rule of a monarch was no longer a possibility. The people themselves had acquired a political voice. To some extent, this was a religious voice: Puritans who professed a belief in congregational church government were generally proponents of republican rule. Their dedication to the ideal of a society of equals under the law was shared by men and women of other sects: the Levellers, led by John Lilburne, who argued for a written constitution, universal manhood suffrage, and religious toleration; the Diggers, led by Gerrard Winstanley, who proposed to institute a communistic society in the wastelands they were ploughing and cultivating; the Quakers, led by George Fox, who rejected all forms of church order in deference to the inner light of an individual conscience and, insisting on social equality, refused to take off their hats before gentry or nobility; and the Ranters, who denied the authority of Scripture and saw God everywhere in nature. Without widespread acceptance of the egalitarian concept that had initiated the Protestant reformation—all believers are members of a real though invisible priesthood—it is hard to see how the move from a monarchy to a representative and republican government could have taken place.

The most comprehensive contemporary history of the Civil War, *The True Historical Narrative of the Rebellion and Civil Wars in England,* by Edward Hyde, Earl of Clarendon, was not published before 1704, but the troubled period found an oblique commentary in what is arguably England's greatest and certainly most humanistic epic poem: Milton's *Paradise Lost,* in print by 1667. Milton's career was inextricably bound up with the fate of the Commonwealth. Educated at Cambridge and with his reputation as a poet well established, Milton had begun to contribute to a defense of Puritanism and the creation of a republican government by 1649. Despite worsening eyesight, he published *The Tenure of Kings and Magistrates*, a sustained and eloquent apology for tyrannicide, after the execution of Charles I; and in his *Eikonoklastes* ("image-breaker"), written after he was made Latin secretary to the new executive, the Council of State, Milton derided attempts by royalists to celebrate Charles I in their pamphlet *Eikon Basilike* ("image of a king"). In 1660, disturbed by the proposed restoration of Charles Stuart, soon to be Charles II, Milton—now completely blind—published his last political treatise, *The Ready and Easy Way to Establish a Commonwealth.* It represented the case for a republicanism that had already lost most of its popularity: the government of the Commonwealth had adopted measures that resembled the autocratic rule of the monarchy it had overthrown. Meanwhile, the composition of *Paradise Lost* was underway. Indebted to many of Spenser's themes in *The Faerie Queene*, Milton infused his subject—the fall of the rebellious angels and the exile from paradise of the disobedient Adam and Eve—with the spirit of the account in Genesis. His poem is the product of a doubly dark vision of life. Sightless and suffering again what he felt were the constraints of a monarchy, Milton shaped his story of exile from Paradise to speak of his own and England's loss of innocence and painful acquisition of the knowledge of good and evil during the Civil War, the Interregnum, and the Restoration. His *Paradise Lost* and its sequel, *Paradise Regained*, are poems that express the most provocative ambiguities of contemporary English culture; they were—and still are—praised as rivaling the epics of Homer, Virgil, and Dante in their power and scope.

Drama and Social Satire

Drama provided another perspective on English life. While epic depicted the grander aspirations of the nation, its human character was expressed in stage plays, masques or speaking pageants, and dramatic processions. These forms exploited the material of chronicle so that it illustrated not only the virtues of heroes, but also their foibles and limitations; history's villains warned viewers that evil was punished, if not by civil authority then by providence. Writing tragedy based on history and legend, Christopher Marlowe and Shakespeare complicated the direct moralism of medieval drama. Rather than portraying characters who became victims of their own misdoings, rising to power only to fall to disgrace, the early modern stage showed virtue and vice as intertwined—a hero's tragic error could also be at the heart of his greatness. The origins of evil were seen to be mysterious, even obscure. Some sense of this moral ambiguity can be traced to the tragedies of the Roman philosopher Seneca, which were translated into English and published in 1581. English drama reproduced many of their features: the five-act structure; rapid-fire dialogue punctuated by pithy maxims; and images of tyranny, revenge, and fate illustrated by haunting dreams and echoing curses. Shakespeare's *Richard III*, the most frequently performed of his plays in his own time, and Elizabeth Cary's *Tragedy of Mariam*, the first tragedy in English by a woman, powerfully exemplify the qualities of early modern tragedy.

If tragedy turned away from straightforward piety, so did comedy. The medieval drama of Christian salvation, in which the hero's struggle against sin was ended by his acknowledgment of grace, was replaced with plays about the wars between the sexes and between parents and children. Much of this material was modeled on the comedies of Plautus, a Roman playwright, and on the tales or *novellas* of contemporary Italian writers. Playwrights such as Ben Jonson also found a wealth of material in the improvisatory Italian *commedia dell'arte*, with its stock characters of the old dotard, the cuckolded husband, the damsel in distress, and the mountebank or quack. An even more topical form of comedy combined some of these continental traditions with themes and figures specifically drawn from London life: Thomas Dekker and Thomas Middleton's *The Roaring Girl* dramatizes the urban culture of guildsmen, shopkeepers, city wives, and coney-catchers (con artists) as they encounter the city gentry and their servants. The social critique implicit in these plays was, of course, one reason why they were so popular; their pointed criticisms of various kinds of behaviors, including religious practices, appeared in various genres from city presses, and their popularity showed just how ready audiences were to imagine a reform of their society. The end of the century saw a brilliant example of satire in a series of pamphlets secretly published by an anonymous author, known as Martin Marprelate, who disparaged all aspects of the episcopacy and promoted in its place a frankly Presbyterian church, in which authority would reside in Scripture and in congregations rather than in a church hierarchy. These expressions of a new kind of self-consciousness revealed an understanding of the whole social order that appeared anarchic to some, particularly moralists opposed to stage plays. As Stephen Gosson wrote in *Plays Confuted in Five Actions:*

> If private men be suffered to forsake their calling because they desire to talk gentlemen-like in satin & velvet, with a buckler at their heels, proportion is so broken, unity dissolved, harmony confounded, that the whole body must be dismembered, and the prince or head cannot choose but sicken.

The fear was not only that the tricksters of drama would be the objects of emulation rather than scorn, but also that the actors' masquerade of identities would spur social instability in the public theater's audience from the "groundlings of the pit" (crowded in front of the stage) to the gentry in the higher-priced seats. Only in 1633 did Parliament repeal the strict sumptuary laws that determined which styles and fabrics were allowed to nobility but denied to everyone else. Although some, like the playwright Thomas Heywood, praised plays as a form of instruction of the unschooled, others, like the Puritan pamphleteer Philip Stubbes, asserted that plays "maintain bawdry, insinuate foolery, and revive the remembrance of heathen idolatry."

Londoners enjoyed two kinds of theater: public and private. The public theaters were open to all audiences for a fee and were generally immune from oversight because they were located outside the City of London in an area referred to as the Liberties, notorious for prostitution and the sport of bearbaiting. London's two biggest theaters were located there: the Fortune and the more famous Globe, home to Shakespeare's company. Private theaters—open only to invited guests—were located in the large houses of the gentry, the Inns of Court (the schools of common law), and the guildhalls; the best-known, Blackfriars, was housed in an old monastery. Their performances were acted almost exclusively by boy actors. The popularity of these companies was short-lived; James I, annoyed by the send-up of the Scots court in *Eastward Ho!*, a play that Ben Jonson had a part in writing, dissolved his queen's own company, known as the Queen's Revels Children. The most private and prestigious stage of all remained the royal court. Shakespeare's *Othello* was first acted at James's court in 1604. Of exclusive interest to this audience was the masque, a speaking pageant accompanied by music and dancing, staged with elaborate sets and costumes, and acted by members of the court, including the Queens Anne (wife of James I) and Henrietta Maria (wife of Charles I). But in 1649 a Puritan Parliament, disgusted by what it considered the immorality of the drama, banned all stage plays, and the theaters remained closed until the Restoration in 1660.

LYRIC POETRY AND ROMANCE

In early modern England, epic narratives, stage plays, and satire in all forms were genres designed for audiences and readers the writer did not know, a general public with varied tastes and background. Lyric poetry, prose romances, and tales were more often written for a closed circle of friends. Circulated in manuscript, works in these genres allowed a writer's wit to play on personal or coterie matters. Here writers could speak of the pain of love or the thrill of ambition, and both reveal and, in a sense, create their own identities in and through language. By imitating and at the same time changing the conventions of lyric, particularly as they were illustrated by the Italian poet Francesco Petrarch, English poets were able to represent a persona or fictive self that became, in turn, a model for others. Unlike Petrarch, who saw his

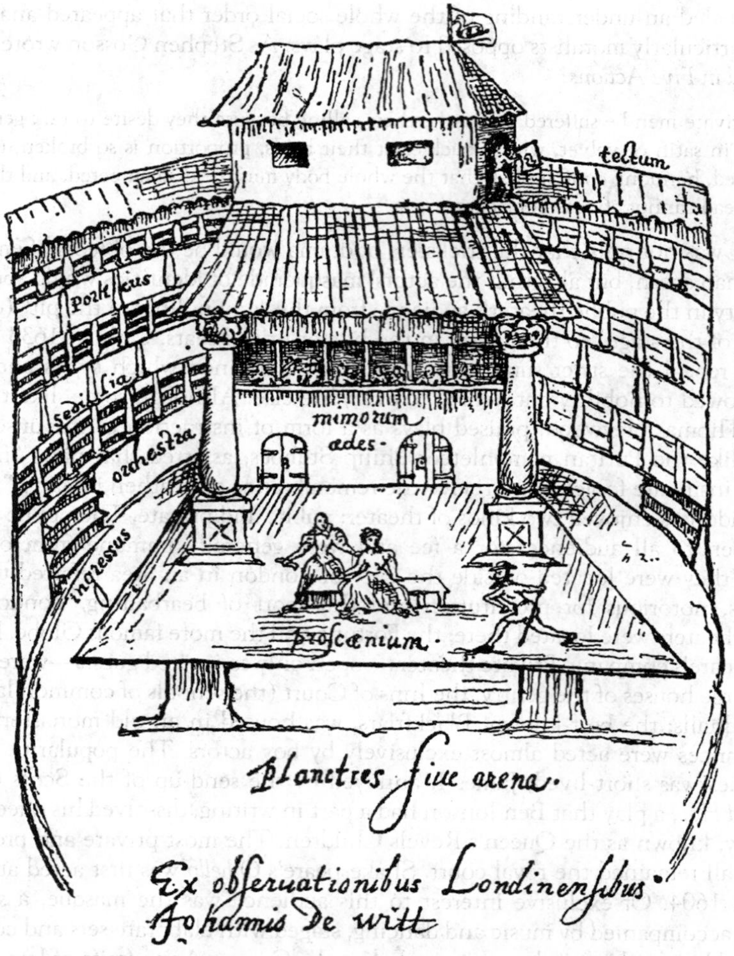

Arend von Buchell. *The Swan Theater,* after Johannes de Witt. c. 1596. The only extant drawing of a public theater in 1590s London, this sketch shows what Shakespeare's Globe must have looked like. The round playhouse centered on the curtainless platform of the stage (*proscenium*), which projected into the yard (*planities sive arena*). Raised above the stage by two pillars, the roof (*tectum*) stored machinery. At the back of the stage, the tiring house (*mimorum aedes*), where the actors dressed, contained two doors for entrances and exit. There were no stage sets and only moveable props such as thrones, tables, beds, and benches, like the one shown here. Other documents on the early modern stage are the contract of the Fortune Theatre, where *The Roaring Girl* was performed, and stage directions in the plays themselves. Modelled on The Globe, although square in shape, The Fortune featured a stage forty-three feet broad and twenty-seven and a half feet deep. Stage directions include further clues: sometimes a curtained booth made "discovery" scenes possible; trapdoors allowed descents; and a space "aloft," such as the gallery above the stage doors, represented a room above the street. Eyewitness accounts fill out the picture. In the yard stood the groundlings who paid a penny for standing room, exposed to the sky, which provided natural lighting. For those willing to pay a penny or two more, three galleries (*orchestra, sedilia, and porticulus*) provided seats—the most expensive of which were cushioned. Spectators could buy food and drink during the performance. The early modern theater held an audience of roughly eight hundred standing in the yard, and fifteen hundred more seated in the galleries. According to Thomas Platter, who had seen Shakespeare's *Julius Caesar* in 1599, "everyone has a good view."

lady as imbued with numinous power before which he could only submit, such poets as Sir Thomas Wyatt, Sir Philip Sidney, Shakespeare, Ben Jonson, John Donne, and Andrew Marvell imagined love in social and very human terms; in the struggle to gain affection and power, their subjectivity took strength from their conquests as well as their resistance to defeat. Women poets, such as Mary Herbert, Amelia Lanyer, Lady Mary Wroth, and Katherine Philips reworked the conventions of love lyric to encompass a feminine perspective on passion and, equally important, on friendship. Sonnet sequences were popular and, reflecting a taste for narrative romance, often dramatized a conflict between lovers. Shakespeare wrote the best-known sonnets of the period; his cast of characters, including the poet as principal speaker, his beloved male friend, a rival poet, and a fickle lady, appear as protagonists in a drama of love, betrayal, devotion, and despair. Some poets embedded their love poetry in prose narratives that told a story, as the Italian poet Dante Alighieri had in his sequence of songs and sonnets to the lady Beatrice, entitled *The New Life*. A brilliant tale of seduction frames George Gascoigne's lyrics in his *Adventures of Master F.J.*, and Sidney's eclogues or pastoral poems punctuate the long and complicated narrative of his romance *Arcadia*.

Prose romances also provided images of new kinds of identity. Stories of marvels surrounded the lives of the powerful and exotic—such as Robert Greene's *Pandosto* (the source for Shakespeare's *The Winter's Tale*) and Thomas Lodge's *Rosalind*—while the tales of lower-class artisan-adventurers illustrate the enthusiasm with which early modern writers and readers embraced a freedom to reinvent themselves. The romantic notion of the "marvelous" gained a new meaning in the tales of tricksters as well as of sturdy entrepreneurs who survived against all odds—they illustrated the creative energies possessed by plain folk. The short fiction of Thomas Nashe, Thomas Deloney, and the hilarious (and anonymous) *Life and Pranks of Long Meg of Westminster* conclusively broke with the delicate sentimentality of pure romance and, appealing to a taste for the ordinarily wonderful, pointed the way for such later novelists as Daniel Defoe, Henry Fielding, and Charles Dickens. Finally, the spirit of romance infused narratives of travel, many of which made little distinction between fact and fantasy.

Sir John Mandeville's fifteenth-century *Travels*, in print throughout the sixteenth century, responded to Europeans' growing curiosity about the wonders of nature in distant lands, which harbored whole peoples who were pictured as utterly different from anything known at home. The wonders reported in popular collections of travel narratives—such as Richard Hakluyt's *Principal Navigations, Voyages, and Discoveries of the English Nation* (1589) and Samuel Purchas's *Purchas his Pilgrimage, or Relations of the World and the Religions observed in all Ages* (1613)—were designed to attract not repel readers, but a horror of "the other" was nevertheless implied in many of these accounts. Shakespeare's Othello both embodies foreignness himself and shares the European love of the exotic: confusing fact with fantasy, he tells the Venetian senate that parts of the globe are inhabited by "Cannibals that each other eat, / The Anthropophagi," as well as "men whose heads / Do grow beneath their shoulders." But the lure of distant lands could also attract the social critic who sought to devise images of an ideal world in order to better the real world. Sir Thomas More's *Utopia* projects a fantasy of a communal state that does double duty by pointing to both the inequities of English society and the absurdities of reforms that assume men and women can be consistently reasonable. Literally describing a *utopia*, or a "nowhere," More's treatise is effectively also a "dystopia," or a work describing a "bad place." Neither Sir Francis Bacon's *New Atlantis* (1627) nor James Harrington's *Commonwealth of Oceana* (1656)—true utopias suggesting a radical reform of political and intellectual life—emulates More's embrace of both utopian and dystopian perspectives. But the dystopias of later writers, such as Jonathan Swift's *Gulliver's Travels* (1726), Samuel Butler's *Erewhon*, an anagram for "nowhere" (1872), and George Orwell's *Nineteen-Eighty-Four* (1949) impressively illustrate the hazards of idealistic and visionary social thought.

The situation for women was somewhat different. Ancient philosophy and medieval theology had insisted that womankind was essentially and naturally different from *man*kind, distinguished by physical weakness, intellectual passivity, and an aptitude for housework, childcare, and the minor decorative arts. The fact that women had distinguished themselves in occupations traditionally reserved for men was understood to signal an exception, and in general social doctrine imposed rigid codes of behavior on men and women. But early modern life was changing in this respect, too. Contemporary treatises devoted to pro-woman argument or the defense of womankind drew on evidence that supported a revolution in ideas of sex and gender. The Bible, they pointed out, stated that woman, like man, was made in the image of God and therefore had the same degree of reason as man; history, they insisted, revealed that women had undertaken all kinds of activity and therefore had same range of talents as man. In short, they maintained that the absolute difference between man and woman was not naturally part of things, but rather was conventional and subject to modification. Social practice reflected and substantiated some of this argument. Early modern women who were classified as legally independent or *femes soles* (literally, women alone) could own and manage property and businesses as men did; educated women, such as Mary Herbert, Aemilia Lanyer, and Katherine Philips, contributed to all the literary genres and got their work published; and during the Civil War, sectarian women registered political protest in public places, including the House of Commons.

These novel ways of understanding women found corresponding changes in attitudes toward men. Departing from medieval social norms, humanists had stressed that men should be educated in the arts as well as arms, and writers such as Sir Philip Sidney, illustrating the sensitivity of men to emotional life, devised characters whose masculinity was amplified by attributes that were conventionally associated with women: passion, sympathy, and an aptitude for creative deception. The central figure in Sidney's *Arcadia* is the prince Pyrocles who appears as an Amazonian warrior through most of the narrative; as the androgynous Cleophila, he is always referred to as "she." Flexibility with respect to categories of gender is also a feature of much lyric poetry; the male poet's beloved is sometimes another man. Shakespeare's sonnets include striking examples of homoerotic verse in this period, and homoerotic innuendo, often suggested as a feature of a love triangle, is common in all genres of writing. In Marlowe's poem *Hero and Leander* the youth Leander loves the girl Hero, and Leander attracts the sexual attentions of the sea-god Neptune.

Ideas as well as social forms and practices were also changing. The repeated shifts in religious practice, from medieval Catholicism to Henrician Protestantism back to the Catholicism dictated by Queen Mary I and then on to the Anglican Church of Queen Elizabeth I, revealed that divine worship could alter its form without bringing on the apocalypse. More subtly, the emerging capitalist economy produced a conceptual model for cultural exchange. Just as material goods flowed through regional and national markets, entering a particular locale to move elsewhere, sometimes great distances, so might ideas, styles, and artistic sensibilities. Drama especially conveyed how fluid were the customs, codes, and practices that gave society its sense of identity. The enthusiasm for stage plays was motivated, in part, by an interest in role-playing: If an actor who in real life might have been born a servant could perform the part of a king in a play, then might he not also perform the part of a king indeed? Was there more to being than performing? This mutability was both liberating and dangerous, as Shakespeare showed by dramatizing the protean powers of Othello's false friend, Iago, who chillingly boasts: "I am not what I am."

The Business of Literature

It was the business of early modern literature to ask these questions. The idea that social convention was established on a natural order of things was no longer accepted. As Shakespeare's bastard Edmund declares, rejecting the customary inferiority of a person who is born out of wedlock, "Why bastard, Wherefore base? / When my dimensions are as well compact . . . As honest madam's issue." Writers were certainly supposed to educate their readers in virtuous ways. Spenser intended that his epic would "fashion a gentleman or noble person in vertuous and gentle discipline." And Sidney believed that poetry, at its finest, could "take naughtiness away and plant goodness even in the secretest cabinet of our souls." But literature also questioned matters of being and identity because writers themselves were in the forefront of a class that was in the process of changing its way of life and its means of support.

During the early modern period an educated man who sought employment as a writer was the object of patronage by the gentry or nobility, often functioning as a tutor or secretary in a prosperous household. The poet John Skelton taught the future Henry VIII; John Donne accompanied his patron Sir William Drury on his European journeys and dedicated his *Anniversaries* to Drury's deceased daughter Elizabeth; and Andrew Marvell educated Lord Fairfax's daughter Mary. Men who were employed in other ways—in diplomacy, law, or some aspect of commerce—might be rewarded for their writing by stipends from the rich. Elizabeth I gave Spenser, one of her administrators in Ireland, a single grant of fifty pounds for *The Faerie Queene*; and Ben Jonson, thanks to the generosity of James I, was able to make a successful career for himself as a poet. As a young man, Milton was patronized by the noble Egerton family, for whom he wrote a masque called *Comus*. But as the seventeeth century progressed, writers discovered that they could be supported by a broader public; after the Restoration the talented playwright Aphra Behn gained a living by selling her literary work to producers and printers. Increasingly, the forces of the market had moved to include the business of printing and thus to both liberate and captivate the energies of the nation's writers.

It was obvious to those in power and authority that the printing press was an agent of change; the question they had to answer was how to control it. Under Elizabeth I, all printing was regulated (in effect, subject to censorship) by the Stationer's Company, which had the exclusive right to print and sell literary work. The theater was also controlled. From 1574, all plays had to be licensed by the Master of Revels, a servant and appointee of the monarch, before they could be produced. These conditions bound writers to observe royal and ecclesiastical policy, at least in their direct statements. Some resorted to coded critique; others openly defied custom. In 1579 John Stubbs wrote a pamphlet against the Queen's proposed marriage to the French king's brother, the Duke of Alençon, entitled *The Discoverie of a Gaping Gulf wherein-to England is like to be Swallowed;* he was arrested and had his hand cut off as punishment. This situation, in which publication was officially regulated, was altered early in the seventeenth century by the development of a new institution: journalism.

By the middle of James I's reign, there was a market for a periodical news pamphlet known as a "coranto," or current of news, which contained foreign intelligence taken from foreign papers: the first was actually printed in Amsterdam and shipped to England. Within a short time, English printers were publishing their own news in the form of sixteen-page "newsbooks" or Diurnalls, and by 1646, Londoners could read fourteen different papers in English. The rapid growth of the news industry promoted a public readership increasingly informed of political affairs. Parliament grew alarmed and discussed imposing stringent forms of licensing; in 1649 it approved the publication of only two newspapers, both dedicated to printing official news. Underground presses continued to publish on current affairs, however; some of them took a royalist point of view and others endorsed Parliament's position. Their writers enjoyed a risky freedom, but it was still a freedom. The boldest of them was Marchamont Nedham, a supporter of Parliament and the chief author of the *Mercurius Britanicus* (still an important source of information about the Civil War and the Interregnum); he had to flee to Holland at the Restoration, although he subsequently was pardoned and returned to England. But journalism did more than provide news; it also created a basis for the freedom of writers in general. The most eloquent attack on a state-controlled press was by Milton, whose *Areopagitica* protested the practice of licensing books before their publication—that is, before readers had a chance to make up their minds about what these books contained. Milton drew on ideas of democracy from ancient Athens and on the Puritan notion that good emerges only in contact with evil: "I cannot praise a fugitive and cloistered virtue," he announced; no true virtue is untested, unchallenged, unexamined—it is valid only when it has deliberately and consciously rejected what is false. The journalistic enterprise of this period fostered the right to free speech and a free press that is now the bedrock of modern democracies.

The Languages of Literature: The New Science and the Old Nature

Changing ideas of identity, both personal and political, were reflected in changes in the English language, which responded to popular as well as learned culture. An accomplished classicist, Ben Jonson closely modeled his verses on Latin poems and their syntax; at the same time the language of his poetry and plays often echoes the cadences of the English spoken by ordinary folk. Authors of popular comic pamphlets, such as Dekker and Robert Greene, conveyed the lively language of London rogues and vagabonds, combining local slang with parodic Latin. The writing of English prose was further changed by the study of Latin grammar and rhetoric in the humanist curriculum that was inspired by the pedagogical reforms of Erasmus and his English followers, John Colet, Roger Ascham (tutor to Elizabeth I), and Richard Mulcaster. Many words of Latin origin were introduced into English vocabulary; many writers experimented with analytic prose by adapting Latin syntax, which allowed them to show relations of cause and effect by resorting to clauses beginning with "if," "when," "because," and so forth. The first Latin-English dictionary on humanist principles was compiled by Sir Thomas Elyot; and one of the most important English grammars, Ascham's *The Schoolmaster* (1570), instructed readers in the merits of an eloquent style.

This enrichment of language from various sources inevitably caused debate. Prose composition was especially affected. Proponents of the so-called Ciceronian style (after the Roman orator Cicero) liked long sentences of many clauses exhibiting variation and restatement. Practitioners of the Senecan style favored short, direct, and uncomplicated sentences. Francis Bacon in particular criticized Ciceronian rhetoric for its emphasis on decorative "tropes and figures" rather than descriptive substance or "weight of matter"; he argued for a language that would accurately denote what he considered "scientific" data: the measures of the physical world. Bacon's reforms influenced English pedagogy and were further realized in the enterprise of the Royal Academy of Science, founded in 1660 by Charles II, who was determined to give his monarchy a new look and a new purpose. The terse, clear, pointed language of Bacon's *Essays* (1597) resembles more what we might think of as modern than does, for example, the florid style that Robert Burton used a quarter of a century later for his mythological-historical, medical discourse *The Anatomy of Melancholy*.

Language and style were changing notions of the world and God's design in creating it. Habits of thought that had prevailed during the medieval period now seemed to be incompatible with knowledge that derived from experience of nature. Europeans had inherited from classical philosophy an idea of creation as a vast aggregate of layered systems or spheres, supposedly centered on the densest matter at the earth's core, that emanated out and up to end, finally, in the sphere of pure spirit or the ethereal presence of divinity. The entities in these layered spheres had assigned places that determined their natures both within their particular sphere and in relation to other spheres. Thus gold, the most precious metal, was superior to silver, but it was at the same time analogous to a lion, a king, and the sun, each also representing the peak of perfection within its particular class of beings. Human nature was also systematized, the body and personality alike being regulated by a balanced set of "humors," each of which consisted of a primary element. The earth, water, air, and fire that made up the great world, or macrocosm, of nature also composed the small universe, or microcosm, of the individual man or woman, whose personality was ideally balanced between impulses that were melancholic (caused by a kind of bile), phlegmatic (brought on by a watery substance), sanguine or bloody, and choleric or hot-tempered. Excessive learning, the contemplation of death, the darkness of night, and isolation were all associated with melancholia, a diseased condition that in more or less severe form is represented in such disparate texts as Marlowe's *Dr. Faustus*, Milton's *Il Penseroso*, and Sir Thomas Browne's *Religio Medici* (literally, "the religion of a doctor").

This view of creation was important for artists and writers because it gave them a symbolic language of correspondences by which they could refer to creatures in widely differing settings and conditions. In a sense, it made nature hospitable to poetry by seeing creation as a divine work of art, designed to inspire awe but also a kind of familiarity. Things were the likenesses of other things. In the poetry of Donne, Herbert, Henry Vaughan, and Marvell, human emotional experience is compared to the realms of astronomy, geography, medicine, Neoplatonic philosophy, and Christian theology. These correspondences are created through strikingly unusual metaphors, which some have called metaphysical conceits, from the Italian *concetto* ("concept"). The result is a pervasive sense of a universal harmony in all human experience.

Such analogies were not always respected, however; increasingly, they were questioned by proponents of a kind of vision that depended on a quantitative or denotative sense of identity or difference. Poetic metaphor might not be able to account for creation in all its complexity; instead, nature had to be understood through the abstractions of science. By the seventeenth century it was becoming difficult to regard creation as a single and comprehensive whole; natural philosophers and scientists in the making wanted to analyze it piece by individual piece. As John Donne wrote of the phenomenon of uniqueness in his elegy for Elizabeth Drury, *The First Anniversary:*

> The element of fire is quite put out;
> The Sun is lost, and th' earth, and no man's wit
> Can well direct him, where to look for it.
> And freely men confess, that this world's spent,
> When in the Planets, and the Firmament
> They seek so many new; they see that this
> Is crumbled out again to his Atomies.
> Tis all in pieces, all coherence gone;
> All just supply, and all Relation:
> Prince, Subject, Father, Son, are things forgot,
> For every man alone thinks he has got
> To be a Phoenix, and that there can be
> None of that kind, of which he is, but he.

The earth had been decentered by the insights of the astronomer Nicholas Copernicus, who in the 1520s deduced that the earth orbits the sun. This "Copernican revolution" was confirmed by the calculations of Tycho Brahe and Johannes Kepler, and our solar system itself was revealed as one among many. With traditional understandings of the natural order profoundly shaken, many thinkers feared for the survival of the human capacity to order and understand society as well. Ironically, Donne complains of radical individualism by invoking the emblem of the phoenix, the very sort of traditional metaphor that constituted the coherence that he claims has "gone." But whereas the symbol in a devotional book would carry with it the myth of the bird's Christlike death and rebirth, the image of the rare bird takes on a newly skeptical and even satirical meaning in *The Anniversary:* it becomes the sign of a dangerous fragmentation within nature's order. Donne's audience would have been familiar with such symbols from emblem books, which presented images along with poems and mottoes, as well as in interior decoration, clothing, coats of arms, and the printers' marks on title pages of books. They were also featured on the standards or flags carried in the Civil War—antique signs in a decidedly modern conflict.

The Civil War and the Modern Order of Things

The Civil War, or the War of Three Kingdoms, ended with the restoration of the Stuart monarchy, but the society to which Charles II was heir in 1660 was very different from the one his grandfather, James I, had come from Scotland to rule in 1603. The terms of modern life were formulated during this period, even though they were only partially and inconsistently realized. They helped to shape these essentially modern institutions: a representative government under law, a market economy fueled by concentrations of capital, and a class system determined by wealth and the power it conferred. They supported a culture in which extreme and opposing points of view were usual. Milton's republican *Tenure of Kings and Magistrates* (1649) was followed by Thomas Hobbes's defense of absolute rule, *The Leviathan, or the Matter, Form, and Power of a Commonwealth, Ecclesiastical and Civil* (1651). Hobbes rejected

The Souldiers in their passage to York turn unto reformers pull down Popish pictures, break down rayles, turn altars into Tables,

Wenceslaus Hollar. *Parliamentarian soldiers in Yorkshire destroying "Popish" paintings, etc.* Illustration to *Sight of the Transactions of these latter yeares,* by John Vicars. 1646.

the assumption that had determined all previous political thought—based on Aristotle's idea that man was naturally sociable—by characterizing the natural condition of human life as "solitary, poor, nasty, brutish and short." A civil state, said Hobbes, depended on the willingness of each and every citizen to relinquish all his or her rights to the sovereign, which is the Commonwealth. The vigorous language of Puritan sermons, preached and published during the 1640s and 1650s, underlay such topical writing as Oliver Cromwell's letters from his campaign to subdue Ireland on behalf of Parliament, the Leveller John Lilburne's pamphlets supporting the common man (for God, he wrote, "doth not choose many rich, nor many wise"), and the corantoes, newsbooks, and Diurnalls of the period. These new forms would eventually lead to the sophisticated commentary of eighteenth-century journalism. Nationalism, however problematic, was registered in history and epic, as well as in attempts to colonize the Americas and to subdue the Gaelic peoples to the west and the north. Irish poems supporting the Stuarts and lamenting the losses of the Cromwellian wars would become rallying cries in the late seventeenth- and eighteenth-century nationalist risings against English control, eventually to result in Ireland's inclusion in the 1801 Union of Great Britain.

Intellectual thought, mental attitudes, religious practices, and the customs of the people fostered new relations to the past and a new sense of self. While Milton was perhaps the greatest humanist of his time, able to read and write Hebrew, Greek, Latin, Italian, and French, his contemporaries witnessed the disappearance of the culture of Petrarch, Erasmus, and More—humanists who had fashioned the disciplines of humanism. Much seventeenth-century literature reflected personal experience; the diary of Ralph Josselin, a prosperous country squire, and the printed testimony of the trial of Anna Trapnel, a Quaker woman accused of witchcraft, convey the details of social life with an immediacy that avoids the studied figures of earlier

Renaissance prose. Such personal reckonings are comparable to the spiritual interiority revealed in John Bunyan's allegorical novel about his conversion to faith in God, *The Pilgrim's Progress*, and the first-person narrative of Daniel Defoe's *Robinson Crusoe*, the story of a sailor shipwrecked on an island somewhere off the coast of South America, which was actually modeled on the history of a Scotsman, Alexander Selkirk, who was similarly marooned.

As more particularized portraits of individual life emerged, new philosophical trends promoted abstract figurations of the world. The modern organization of Europe was based on new modes of representation, such as schematic outlines of arguments, the grids sectioning the world maps of Gerardus Mercator (facilitating the circumnavigation of the globe), and the discourses of political economy characterized by an interest in quantitative analysis. Shortly after the Restoration of Charles II, the Royal Academy of Science would form "a committee for improving the English language," an attempt to design a universal grammar and an ideal philosophical language. This project, inspired by the intellectual reforms of Francis Bacon, would have been uncongenial to the skeptical casts of mind exhibited by Erasmus and More. The abstract rationalism of the new science, the growth of an empire overseas, a burgeoning industry and commerce at home, and a print culture spreading news throughout Europe and across the Atlantic would continue to be features of life in the British Isles through the eighteenth century.

John Skelton

1460?–1529

The first great Tudor satirist, John Skelton illustrates the appeal of the unorthodox. When he took holy orders at the age of thirty-eight, Skelton already enjoyed an impressive reputation as a writer of satire and love lyrics. His poems must have appealed to Henry VII, who made him responsible for the education of his second son, the future Henry VIII, and they would eventually prompt Erasmus to call Skeleton "a light and ornament of British literature." In 1502, following the death of Henry's older brother Arthur, Skelton lost his employment as royal tutor; Henry, now heir apparent to the English throne, was obliged to trade Skelton's gentle instruction in humane and sacred letters for practical training in statecraft and the art of war. At forty-two already an old man (by contemporary reckoning), Skelton undertook pastoral duties, although he lived away from his rectory for much of the rest of his life. His satires of the clergy in *Colin Clout* and of Cardinal Wolsey in *Why Come Ye Not to Court* may have placed him in some jeopardy; it is said that a threat from the Cardinal forced Skelton to take refuge on the grounds of Westminster Abbey in London. Skelton never got the satisfaction of witnessing Wolsey's disgrace; he died just a few months before Wolsey lost the office of Lord Chancellor for failing to procure a divorce for the king.

Skelton's poetry is as unusual as was his career. His favorite verse form has become known as "skeltonics"; it consists of a series of lines of two or three stresses whose end rhyme repeats itself for an unspecified number of lines. The lines themselves show alliteration and move at a headlong pace. In *Colin Clout,* Skelton excused his practice by noting the "pith" or substance it conveys:

> For though my rhyme be ragged,
> Tattered and jagged,
> Rudely rain-beaten,
> Rusty and moth-eaten,
> If ye take well therewith,
> It hath in it some pith.

Skelton's satires poke fun at the pretensions that characterize all forms of public life, including the ways of courtiers and vagabonds. His dream poem, *The Bowge of Court,* and his morality play about wealth and power, *Magnificence,* provide a witty view of court corruption. His elegy *Philip Sparrow,* on a pet sparrow mauled and eaten by its young mistress's cat, weaves themes and figures from liturgy and the Office of the Dead to create an extraordinary burlesque of sacred elegy that manages to be at once tender and cutting.

The poem falls into three parts. Between passages of prayer for the soul of Philip, assumed to be in a Christian heaven, the bereaved girl, Jane Scrope, expresses her grief in terms that recall the lamentations of women who mourn dead lovers in classical legend. Jane addresses her sparrow as her beloved, even while she defends the propriety of her affection for him. A thematics of erotic love—announced by the poet speaking in his own voice—features in the second part of the poem. It transforms Jane into the unattainable lady of courtly lyric, and in an apparent allusion to Dante's angelic Beatrice, the beloved lady of his sonnet sequence, *The New Life,* compares her to a divine creature. The poem ends with *The Addition,* which instructs the reader to overlook Jane's innocently frivolous devotion to Philip and defends (in Latin) the poet's own celebration of her grief on the death of her pet.

Philip Sparrow[1]

Pla ce bo,[2]
Who is there, who?
Di le xi,
Dame Margery;
Fa, re, mi, mi,° — *notes of the musical scale*
Wherefore and why, why?
For the soul of Philip Sparrow,
That was late slain at Carrow,[3]
Among the Nuns Black,
For that sweet soul's sake,
And for all sparrows' souls,
Set in our beadrolls,[4]
Pater noster qui,° — *Our Father who*
With an *Ave Marie,*° — *Hail Mary*
And with the corner of a Creed,
The more shall be your meed.° — *reward*
When I remember again
How my Philip was slain,
Never half the pain
Was between you twain,
Pyramus and Thisbe,[5]
As then befell to me:
I wept and I wailed,
The tears down hailed;
But nothing it availed
To call Philip again,
Whom Gib our cat hath slain.
Gib, I say, our cat
Worried her on that
Which I loved best:
It cannot be expressed
My sorrowful heaviness,
But all without redress;
For within that stound,° — *moment*
Half slumbering, in a sound
I fell down to the ground.
Unneth° I cast mine eyes — *scarcely*
Toward the cloudy skies:
But when I did behold
My sparrow dead and cold,
No creature but that wold° — *would*
Have rued° upon me, — *taken pity*
To behold and see

1. This poem, usually dated 1505–1507, echoes phrases from the funeral liturgy known as Office for the Dead and its sequel, the Order for Commendations (lines 1–844 and 845–1268, respectively). It is spoken by Skelton's character, Jane Scrope, but closes with an "Addition" in Skelton's own voice (in print in 1523), his response to the criticism of Alexander Barclay, a contemporary Scots poet.
2. *Placebo:* "I shall please"; *Dilexi:* "I have loved" (Psalm 114.9 and 1).
3. Carrow Abbey, a Benedictine nunnery. Benedictines, who wore black habits, followed the rule of St. Benedict, the first of the monastic orders.
4. Lists of souls for whom prayers, signified by the beads of the rosary, were offered.
5. Unfortunate lovers who die in each other's arms (Ovid, *Metamorphoses* 4.55ff.).

What heaviness did me pang;
Wherewith my hands I wrang,° *wrung*
That my sinews cracked,
As though I had been racked,
So pained and so strained,
That no life wellnigh° remained. *nearly*
I sighed and I sobbed,
For that I was robbed
Of my sparrow's life.
O maiden, widow, and wife,
Of what estate you be,
Of high or low degree,
Great sorrow than you might see,
And learn to weep at me!
Such pains did me fret,
That mine heart did beat,
My visage pale and dead,
Wan, and blue as lead;
The pangs of hateful death
Wellnigh had stopped my breath.
Heu, heu, me,
That I am woe for thee!
Ad Dominum, cum tribularer, clamavi:[6]
Of God nothing else crave I
But Philip's soul to keep
From the marees° deep *marshes*
Of Acherontes well,[7]
That is a flood of hell;
And from the great Pluto,
The prince of endless woe;
And from foul Alecto,
With visage black and blo;° *blue*
And from Medusa, that mare,° *specter*
That like a fiend doth stare;
And from Megaera's udders,
For ruffling of Philip's feathers,
And from her fiery sparklings,
For burning of his wings;
And from the smokes sour
Of Proserpina's bower;
And from the dens dark,
Where Cerberus doth bark,
Whom Theseus did affray,° *frighten*
Whom Hercules did outray,° *overcome*
As famous poets say;
From that hell hound,

6. "I cried out to the Lord when I suffered" (Psalm 119.1).

7. The well of Acheron, source of one of the mythical rivers of hell. In the following lines, Skelton names mythological figures associated with hell: Pluto, god of the underworld; Alecto, a fury or spirit of wrathful revenge; Medusa, a monster who turns whoever looks at her to stone; Megaera, another Fury, whose hair (like Medusa's) is composed of adders or poisonous snakes; Proserpina, goddess of spring who descends to the underworld every autumn; Cerberus, the three-headed dog who guards the gates of hell; Theseus, the legendary hero who frightened Cerberus as he descended to hell to rescue his friend, Pirithous; Hercules, the legendary hero who dragged Cerberus out of hell.

That lieth in chains bound,
With ghastly heads three,
To Jupiter° pray we   *king of the gods*
That Philip preserved may be!
Amen, say you with me!
  Do mi nus,°   *Lord*
Help now, sweet Jesus!
Levavi oculos meos in montes:[8]
Would God I had Zenophontes,[9]
Or Socrates the wise,
To show me their devise,°   *instruction*
Moderately to take
This sorrow that I make
For Philip Sparrow's sake!
So fervently I shake,
I feel my body quake;
So urgently I am brought
Into careful thought.
Like Andromach, Hector's wife,[1]
Was weary of her life,
When she had lost her joy,
Noble Hector of Troy;
In like manner also
Encreaseth my deadly woe,
For my sparrow is go.
  It was so pretty a fool,
It would sit on a stool,
And learned after my school
For to keep his cut,°   *place*
With, Philip, keep your cut!
  It had a velvet cap,
And would sit upon my lap,
And seek after small worms,
And sometime white bread crumbs;
And many times and oft
Between my breasts soft
It would lie and rest;
It was proper and pressed.°   *lively*
  Sometimes he would gasp
When he saw a wasp;
A fly or a gnat,
He would fly at that;
And prettily he would pant
When he saw an ant;
Lord, how he would pry
After the butterfly!
Lord, how he would hop
After the gressop!°   *grasshopper*

8. "I lifted my eyes to the mountains" (Psalm 120.1).
9. Xenophon, a Greek historian; Socrates: a Greek philosopher whose teaching is represented in the dialogues of the philosopher Plato.

1. Homer decribes Andromache's grief when Achilles, the Greek hero, kills her husband, the principal defender of Troy (*Iliad* 24.725ff.).

And when I said, Phip, Phip,
Than he would leap and skip,
And take me by the lip.
Alas, it will me slo,° *slay*
That Philip is gone me fro!° *from*
Si in i qui ta tes,[2]
Alas, I was evil at ease!
De pro fun dis cla ma vi,[3]
When I saw my sparrow die!
Now, after my dome,° *judgment*
Dame Sulpicia at Rome,[4]
Whose name registered was
For ever in tables of brass,
Because that she did pass
In poesy to endite,° *write*
And eloquently to write,
Though she would pretend
My sparrow to commend,
I trowe° she could not amend *trust*
Reporting the virtues all
Of my sparrow royal.
For it would come and go,
And fly so to and fro;
And on me it would leap
When I was asleep,
And his feathers shake,
Wherewith he would make
Me often for to wake,
And for to take him in
Upon my naked skin;
God wot,° we thought no sin: *knows*
What though he crept so low?
It was no hurt, I trowe,
He did nothing perde° *indeed*
But sit upon my knee:
Philip, though he were nice,° *wanton, fresh*
In him it was no vice;
Philip had leave to go
To pick my little toe;
Philip might be bold
And do what he would;
Philip would seek and take
All the fleas black
That he could there espy
With his wanton eye.
O pe ra,[5]
La, sol, fa, fa,

2. "If iniquities" (Psalm 129.3).
3. "Out of the depths I have cried" (Psalm 129.1).
4. There were two women poets in ancient Rome who were named Sulpicia; Skelton has combined them in a single figure.
5. Works; i.e., "works of your hand I have not despised" (Psalm 137.8).

Confitebor tibi, Domine, in toto corde meo.[6]
Alas, I would ride and go
A thousand mile of ground!
If any such might be found,
It were worth an hundred pound
Of king Croesus's gold,
Or of Attalus the old,
The rich prince of Pargame,[7]
Who so list° the story to see. *wishes*
Cadmus, that his sister sought,[8]
And he should be bought
For gold and fee,
He should over the sea,
To weet° if he could bring *know*
Any of the offspring,
Or any of the blood.
But whoso understood
Of Medea's art,[9]
I would I had a part
Of her crafty magic!
My sparrow then should be quick
With a charm or twain,
And play with me again.
But all this is in vain
Thus for to complain.
I took my sampler once,
Of purpose, for the nonce,° *occasion*
To sew with stitches of silk
My sparrow white as milk,
That by representation
Of his image and fashion,
To me it might import
Some pleasure and comfort
For my solace and sport:
But when I was sewing his beak,
Methought, my sparrow did speak,
And opened his pretty bill,
Saying, Maid, you are in will
Again me for to kill,
You prick me in the head!
With that my needle waxed red,
Methought, of Philip's blood;
Mine hair right upstood,
And was in such a fray,° *fright*
My speech was taken away.
I cast down that there was,
And said, Alas, alas,

6. "I shall confess to you, Lord, with all my heart" (Psalm 137.1).
7. Croesus, king of Lydia, 560–546 B.C.; Attalus, ancient king of Pergamum in Asia Minor, known for extraordinary wealth. Jane emphasizes how valuable Philip was.
8. Cadmus, son of Agenor, mythological king of Tyre, was sent to find his sister Europa; she had been carried off by Jupiter, who had taken the form of a bull (Ovid, *Metamorphoses* 3.1ff.).
9. Medea, a mythological sorceress, restored youth to Jason, the hero who secured the golden fleece.

How cometh this to pass?
My fingers, dead and cold,
Could not my sampler hold;
My needle and thread
I threw away for dread.
The best now that I may,
Is for his soul to pray:
A porta inferi,[1]
Good Lord, have mercy
Upon my sparrow's soul,
Written in my beadroll!
   Au di vi vo cem,[2]
Japhet, Cam, and Sem,
Mag gni fi cat,
Show me the right path
To the hills of Armony,[3]
Wherefore the boards yet cry
Of your father's boat,
That was sometime afloat,
And now they lie and rot;
Let some poets write
Deucalion's flood[4] it hight:° *was called*
But as verily as you be
The natural sons three
Of Noah the patriarch,
That made that great ark,
Wherein he had apes and owls,
Beasts, birds, and fowls,
That if you can find
Any of my sparrow's kind,
God send the soul good rest!
I would have yet a nest
As pretty and as pressed
As my sparrow was.
But my sparrow did pass
All sparrows of the wood
That were since Noah's flood,
Was never none so good;
King Philip of Macedony[5]
Had no such Philip as I,
No, no, sir, hardly.
   That vengeance I ask and cry,
By way of exclamation,
On all the whole nation
Of cats wild and tame;
God send them sorrow and shame!
That cat specially

1. From the gates of hell; Jane Scrope prays that Philip's soul be delivered from the underworld.
2. "I have heard a voice" (Revelation 14.13). Jane Scrope, calling on the sons of Noah—Shem, Ham, and Japhet—concludes with the first word of the *Magnificat,*"My soul magnifies the Lord," Mary's hymn of thanks when God makes her pregnant with Jesus (Luke 1.46).
3. Armenia, where Noah's ark ("your father's boat") was said to have come to rest after the flood.
4. Deucalion was the survivor of the flood according to Greek mythology.
5. Father of the Emperor Alexander the Great.

That slew so cruelly
My little pretty sparrow
That I brought up at Carrow.
O cat of carlish° kind, *churlish*
The fiend was in thy mind
When thou my bird untwined!° *destroyed*
I would thou hadst been blind!
The leopards savage,
The lions in their rage,
Might catch thee in their paws,
And gnaw thee in their jaws!
The serpents of Lybany° *Libya*
Might sting thee venomously!
The dragons with their tongues
Might poison thy liver and lungs!
The manticors of the mountains° *monsters*
Might feed them on thy brains!
Melanchates,[6] that hound
That plucked Actaeon to the ground,
Gave him his mortal wound,
Changed to a deer,
The story doth appear,
Was changed to an hart:
So thou, foul cat that thou art,
The selfsame hound
Might thee confound,
That his own lord bote,° *bit*
Might bite assunder thy throat!
Of Inde° the greedy gripes° *India/griffins*
Might tear out all thy tripes!
Of Arcady the bears
Might pluck away thine ears!
The wild wolf Lycaon
Bite asunder thy back bone!
Of Etna the brennyng° hill, *burning*
That day and night brenneth still,
Set in thy tail ablaze,
That all the world may gaze
And wonder upon thee,
From Occya° the great sea *Ocean*
Unto the Iles of Orchady,° *Orkney*
From Tilbury[7] ferry
To the plain of Salisbury!
So traiterously my bird to kill
That never ought° thee evil will! *showed*
Was never bird in cage
More gentle of corage° *spirit*
In doing his homage

6. A hound that devoured his master, Actaeon, who had been turned into a deer by the goddess Diana. Jane Scrope continues to inveigh against her cat by citing animals that attack human beings: griffins (mythical birds) of India; bears of Arcady, a region in Greece; Lycaon, a king who was turned into a wolf.

7. A town on the Channel coast, near London.

Unto his sovereign.
Alas, I say again,
Death hath departed us twain!
The false cat hath thee slain:
Farewell, Philip, adieu!
Our Lord thy soul rescue!
Farewell without restore,
Farewell for evermore!
And it were a Jew,
It would make one rue,° *pity*
To see my sorrow new.
These villainous false cats
Were made for mice and rats,
And not for birds small.
Alas, my face waxeth° pale, *grows*
Telling this piteous tale,
How my bird so fair,
That was wont to repair,
And go in at my spare,° *pocket*
And creep in at my gore° *opening*
Of my gown before,
Flickering with his wings!
Alas, my heart it stings,
Remembering pretty things!
Alas, mine heart is sleth° *slain*
My Philip's doleful death,
When I remember it,
How prettily it would sit,
Many times and oft,
Upon my finger aloft!
I played with him tittle tattle,
And fed him with my spittle,
With his bill between my lips;
It was my pretty Phips!
Many a pretty kusse° *kiss*
Had I of his sweet musse;° *mouth*
And now the cause is thus,
That he is slain me fro,
To my great pain and woe.
Of fortune this the chance
Standeth on variance:
Oft time after pleasance
Trouble and grievance;
No man can be sure
Allway° to have pleasure: *always*
As well perceive you may
How my disport and play
From me was taken away
By Gib, our cat savage,
That in a furious rage
Caught Philip by the head,
And slew him there stark dead.

Kyrie, eleison,
Christe, eleison,
Kyrie, eleison![8]
For Philip Sparrow's soul,
Set in our beadroll,
Let us now whisper
A *Pater noster*.
Lauda, anima mea, Dominum![9]
To weep with me look that you come,
All manner of birds in your kind;
See none be left behind.
To mourning look that you fall
With dolorous songs funeral,
Some to sing, and some to say,
Some to weep, and some to pray,
Every bird in his lay.° *own voice*
The goldfinch, the wagtail;
The jangling jay to rail,
The flecked pie° to chatter *magpie*
Of this dolorous matter;
And robin redbreast,
He shall be the priest
The requiem mass to sing,
Softly warbling,
With help of the red sparrow,
And the chattering swallow,
This hearse for to hallow;
The lark with his long toe;
The spink,° and the martinet also; *finch*
The shovelar° with his broad beak; *spoonbill*
The doterel,° that foolish peak,° *plover / silly bird*
And also the mad coot,
With a bald face to toot;° *look carefully*
The feldefare,° and the snite;° *thrush / snipe*
The crow, and the kite;° *hawk*
The raven, called Rolf,
His plain song to solfe;° *sing*
The partridge, the quail;
The plover with us to wail;
The woodhack,° that singeth "chur" *woodpecker*
Hoarsely, as he had the mur;° *a cold*
The lusty chanting nightingale;
The popingay° to tell her tale, *parrot*
That toteth° oft in a glass, *looks*
Shall read the Gospel at mass;
The mavys° with her whistle *thrush*
Shall read there the 'pistle.
But with a large and a long° *correct rhythm*
To keep just plain song,

8. Lord have mercy, Christ have mercy; phrases from the Mass.
9. Jane Scrope intends to say "Our Father," i.e., the Lord's Prayer. But she continues with "Praise the Lord, my soul" (Psalm 145.1).

Our chanters° shall be the cuckoo, *singers*
The culver, the stockdove,
With "peewit," the lapwing
The versicles shall sing.
  The bitter° with his "bump," *bittern*
The crane with his "trump,"
The swan of Menander,
The goose and the gander,
The duck and the drake,
Shall watch at this wake;
The peacock so proud,
Because his voice is loud,
And hath a glorious tail,
He shall sing the grail;[1]
The owl, that is so foul,
Must help us to howl;
The heron so gaunce,° *gaunt, thin*
And the cormoraunce,° *cormorant*
With the pheasant,
And the gagling gaunte,° *goose*
And the churlish chough;° *crow*
The knoute° and the rough;° *kinds of sandpipers*
The barnacle,° the buzzard, *goose*
With the wild mallard;
The dyvendop° to sleep; *waterbird*
The water hen to weep;
The puffin and the teal° *a duck*
Money they shall deal
To poor folk at large,
That shall be their charge;
The seamew and the titmouse;
The woodcock with the longe nose;
The threstle° with her warbling; *thrush*
The starling with her brabbling;
The rook, with the osprey
That putteth fishes to a fraye;° *fright*
And the dainty curlew,
With the turtle most true.
  At this *Placebo*
We may not well forgo
The countering of the coe:[2]
The stork also,
That maketh his nest
In chimneys to rest;
Within those walls
No broken galls° *sores*
May there abide
Of cuckoldry side,
Or else philosophy

1. A book of prayers to be used on the church steps, also known as the gradual.

2. The accompaniment of the jackdaw.

Maketh a great lie.[3]
The estrige,° that will eat — *ostrich*
An horseshoe so great,
In the stead of meat,
Such fervent heat
His stomach doth freat;° — *consume*
He cannot well fly,
Nor sing tunably,
Yet at a braid° — *in an outburst*
He hath well assayed
To solfe above ela,[4]
Fa, lorell, fa, fa;
Ne quando
Male cantando,[5]
The best that we can,
To make him our bellman,
And let him ring the bells;
He can do nothing else.
Chaunteclere, our cock,
Must tell what is of the clock
By the astrology
That he hath naturally
Conceived and caught,
And was never taught
By Albumazar[6]
The astronomer,
Nor by Ptolomy
Prince of astronomy,
Nor yet by Haly;
And yet he croweth daily
And nightly the tides
That no man abides,
With Partlot his hen,
Whom now and then
He plucketh by the head
When he doth her tread.° — *mate with her*
The bird of Araby,
That potentially
May never die,
And yet there is none
But one alone;[7]
A phoenix it is
This hearse that must blys° — *bless*
With armatycke° gums — *aromatic*
That cost great sums,
The way of thurifycation° — *burning incense*
To make a fumigation,

3. Jane Scrope believes that the stork protects a household from cuckoldry, according to "philosophy," if it does not lie.

4. The ostrich, in a sudden burst of energy, has tried to sing fa, a note above ela.

5. Lest when, singing badly. This makes no literal sense; Jane Scrope suggests that the ostrich, because he sings badly, can only be employed as a bell ringer.

6. Jane Scrope mentions several famous astronomers: Albumazar, Ptolemy, and Haly Aben Ragel.

7. The phoenix, a mythical bird, was as Jane Scrope describes it: unique in the world, both self-consuming and self-regenerating.

Sweet of reflayre,° *smell*
And redolent of air,
This corse° for to cense° *body/perfume*
With great reverence,
As patriarch or pope
In a black cope;° *cape*
Whiles he censeth the hearse,
He shall sing the verse,
Libera me,[8]
In de, la, sol, re,
Softly bemole[9]
For my sparrow's soul.
Pliny[1] showeth all
In his story natural,
What he doth find
Of the phoenix kind;
Of whose incineration
There riseth a new creation
Of the same fashion
Without alteration,
Saving that old age
Is turned into corage
Of fresh youth again;
This matter true and plain,
Plain matter indeed,
Who so list to read.
But for the eagle doth fly
Highest in the sky,
He shall be the sedeane,° *subdean*
The choir to demean,
As provost principal,
To teach them their ordinal;° *order of service*
Also the noble falcon,[2]
With the gyrfalcon,
The tarsel° gentle, *small falcon*
They shall mourn soft and still
In their amysse° of gray; *robe*
The sacre° with them shall say *large falcon*
Dirige[3] for Philip's soul;
The goshawk shall have a role
The choristers to control;
The lanners° and the marlyons° *falcons/merlin*
Shall stand in their mourning gowns;
The hobby° and the muskette° *falcon/hawk*
The censers° and the cross shall fet;° *incense holders/fetch*
The kestrel in all this work,
Shall be holy water clerk.

8. Free me; the first words of the response in the service of the Mass.
9. I.e., sing softly the notes indicated in the preceding line.
1. Roman philosopher who wrote *Historia Naturalis*, an account of the natural world.
2. Jane lists different kinds of falcon—the gyrfalcon, the tarsel, the sacre, the lanner, and the hobby (lines 556–567)—all of which participate in Philip's funeral.
3. Proceed; a word indicating the beginning of the service for the dead.

And now the dark cloudy night
Chaseth away Phoebus° bright, *the sun*
Taking his course toward the west,
God send my sparrow's soul good rest!
Requiem aeternam dona eis, Domine![4]
Fa, fa, fa, mi, re,
A *por ta in fe ri*,
Fa, fa, fa, mi, mi.
Credo videre bona Domini,
I pray God, Philip to heaven may fly!
Domine, exaudi orationem meam!
To heaven he shall, from heaven he came!
Do mi nus vo bis cum!
Of all good prayers God send him some!
Oremus:
Deus, cui proprium est misereri et parcere,
On Philip's soul have pity!
For he was a pretty cock,
And came of a gentle stock,
And wrapped in a maiden's smock,
And cherished full daintily,
Till cruel fate made him to die:
Alas, for doleful destiny!
But whereto should I
Longer mourn or cry?
To Jupiter I call,
Of heaven imperial,
That Philip may fly
Above the starry sky,
To tread the pretty wren,
That is our Lady's hen:
Amen, amen, amen!
Yet one thing is behind,
That now cometh to mind;
An epitaph I would have
For Philip's grave:
But for I am a maid,
Timorous, half afraid,
That never yet assayed
Of Elyconys well,
Where the Muses dwell;[5]
Though I can read and spell,
Recount, report, and tell
Of the Tales of Canterbury,[6]
Some sad stories, some merry;
As Palamon and Arcet,° *Arcite*
Duke Theseus, and Partelet;° *Pertelot*
And of the Wife of Bath,

4. Lord, grant them eternal rest. Translations of subsequent lines follow: I believe I shall see the good things of the Lord (line 579); Lord, hear my prayer (line 581); The Lord be with you (line 583); Let us pray; O Lord, who alone can pity and pardon (lines 585–586).

5. The Muses were said to live on Mount Helicon in Greece.

6. Jane Scrope, having said she is unlearned, states that she knows Geoffrey Chaucer's *Canterbury Tales*; she names characters from *The Knight's Tale*, *The Nun's Priest's Tale*, and *The Wife of Bath's Tale*.

That worketh much scath° harm
When her tale is told
Among huswives° bold, wives
How she controlled
Her husbands as she wolde,° would
And them to despise
In the homeliest wise,
Bring other wives in thought
Their husbands to set at nought:
And though that read have I
Of Gawain and sir Guy,[7]
And tell can a great piece
Of the Golden Fleece,
How Jason it wan,° won
Like a valiant man;
Of Arthur's round table,
With his knights commendable,
And dame Gaynour,° his queen, Guinevere
Was somewhat wanton, I ween;° think
How sir Launcelot de Lake
Many a spear brake° broke
For his ladies' sake;
Of Tristram, and king Mark,
And all the whole warke° work
Of Belle Isold his wife,
For whom was much strife;
Some say she was light,
And made her husband knight
Of the common hall,
That cuckolds men call;
And of sir Libius,
Named Desconius;
Of Quater Fylz Amund,° Four Sons of Aymon
And how they were summoned
To Rome, to Charlemagne,
Upon a great pain,
And how they rode each one
On Bayard Mountalbon;
Men see him now and then
In the forest of Arden:
What though I can frame
The stories[8] by name

7. Jane Scrope lists the romances she has read: the stories of Gawain; Guy of Warwick; Jason and the Golden Fleece; King Arthur and his Round Table; Lancelot and Queen Guinevere; Tristram and Isolde, wife of King Mark; Libius or Libaeus Desconus, son of Gawain; the four sons of Aymon, who rode on the " bayard" or horse called Montalbon; see lines 628–658.

8. Jane Scrope also knows stories from classical epic and history: She cites accounts of Judas Maccabeus and Julius Caesar (two of nine "worthies"); Paris and Helen (Vyene); Hannibal, the Carthaginian general who invaded Rome by crossing the Alps from France; Scipio Africanus Minor, who sacked Carthage in 146 B.C.; Hector and Achilles, the great warriors of the Trojan War; the Trojan Troilus, who, through the mediation of Pandarus, fell in love with Cressida, who eventually sided with the Greeks; Penelope, who waited years for the return of Ulysses; Marcus Marcellus, the Roman consul who triumphed in Gaul and fought Hannibal in Sicily; Antiochus, King of Antioch and ally of Hannibal. She has also read Josephus's *Jewish Antiquities*; The Book of Esther (Hester) telling of Mordecai (Mardocheus), Ahasuerus (Assuerus), and Vashti (Vesca); the histories of Alexander the Great; King Evander who ruled the region that would become Rome before Aeneas arrived (*Aeneid* 8.126ff.); and King Porsena, King of Etruria; see lines 659–748.

Of Judas Maccabeus,
And of Caesar Julius;
And of the love between
Paris and Vyene;
And of the duke Hannibal,
What made the Romans all
Fordrede° and to quake; *fear*
How Scipio did wake
The city of Carthage,
Which by his merciful rage
He beat down to the ground:
And though I can expound
Of Hector of Troy,
That was all their joy,
Whom Achilles slew,
Wherefore all Troy did rue;
And of the love so hote° *hot*
That made Troilus to dote
Upon fair Cresseyde,
And what they wrote and said,
And of their wanton wills
Pandar bare the bills° *letters*
From one to the other;
His master's love to further,
Sometimes a precious thing,
An ouche,° or else a ring; *brooch*
From her to him again
Sometimes a pretty chain,
Or a bracelet of her hair,
Prayed Troilus for to wear
That token for her sake;
How hartely° he did it take, *lovingly*
And much thereof did make;
And all that was in vain,
For she did but feign;
The story telleth plain,
He could not obtain,
Though his father were a king,
Yet there was a thing
That made the male to wring;[9]
She made him to sing
The song of lovers' lay;° *story*
Musing night and day,
Mourning all alone,
Comfort had he none,
For she was quite gone;
Thus in conclusion,
She brought him in abusion;° *deception*
In earnest and in game
She was much to blame;

9. An obscure phrase that seems to mean "to bring about trouble."

Disparaged is her fame,
And blemished is her name,
In manner half with shame;
Troilus also hath lost
On her much love and cost,
And now must kiss the post;° *pay the price*
Pandara, that went between,
Hath won nothing, I ween,° *think*
But light° for summer green; *light clothing*
Yet for a special laud° *praise*
He is named Troilus's bawd,
Of that name he is sure
While the world shall dure:° *last*
  Though I remember the fable
Of Penelope most stable,
To her husband most true,
Yet long time she ne knew° *did not know*
Whether he were on live or dead;
Her wit stood her in stead,[1]
That she was true and just
For any bodily lust
To Ulysses her make,° *mate*
And never would him forsake:
  Of Marcus Marcellus
A process I could tell us;
And of Antiochus;
And of Josephus
De Antiquitatibus;
And of Mardocheus,
And of great Assuerus,
And of Vesca his queen,
Whom he forsook with teen,° *anger*
And of Hester his other wife,
With whom he led a pleasant life;
Of King Alexander;
And of King Evander;
And of Porsena the great,
That made the Romans to sweat:
  Though I have enrolled
A thousand new and old
Of these historious tales,
To fill bougets° and males° *bags / trunks*
With books that I have read,
Yet I am nothing sped,
And can but little skill
Of Ovid or Virgil,[2]
Or of Plutarch,
Or Francis Petrarch,
Alcaeus or Sappho,

1. I.e., her wit informed her.
2. Jane Scrope confesses that she is not skilled in Latin, Greek, or Italian (despite having referred to classical mythology and history). Among Greek authors whom she mentions she does not know are Alcaeus, Sappho, Linus, Euphorion, Arion, Philemon, Simonides, Philistion, and Phorocides.

Or such other poets mo,° *more*
As Linus and Homerus,
Euphorion and Theocritus,
Anacreon and Arion,
Sophocles and Philemon,
Pindarus and Simonides,
Philistion and Phorocides;
These poets of auncyente,° *antiquity*
They are too diffuse for me:
For, as I tofore° have said, *before*
I am but a young maid,
And cannot in effect
My style as yet direct
With English words elect:
Our natural tongue is rude,
And hard to be enneude° *revived*
With polished terms lusty;
Our language is so rusty,
So cankered, and so full
Of frowards,° and so dull, *additities*
That if I would apply
To write ornately,
I wot not where to find
Terms to serve my mind.
Gower's[3] English is old,
And of no value told;
His matter° is worth gold, *content*
And worthy to be enrolled.
In Chaucer I am sped,° *acquainted*
His tales I have read:
His matter is delectable,
Solacious,° and commendable; *salacious*
His English well allowed,
So as it is enprowed,[4]
For as it is employed,
There is no English void,
At those days much commended;
And now men would have amended
His English, whereat they bark,
And mar all they warke:° *write*
Chaucer, that famous clerk,
His terms were not dark,
But pleasant, easy, and plain;
Ne word he wrote in vain.
Also John Lydgate
Writeth after an higher rate;
It is diffuse° to find *difficult*

3. Jane refers to the poet John Gower, who wrote a popular collection of love stories, the *Confessio Amantis* (literally, "the confession of lovers"); to Chaucer and later to John Lydgate who wrote (among many other works) an English translation of Giovanni Boccaccio's *Concerning the Fall of Famous Men*, entitled *The Fall of Princes;* see lines 784–812.

4. I.e., as long as it is used to advantage. Jane Scrope praises Chaucer's English, which is not "void" (empty) and was much commended in his own time.

The sentence° of his mind, *meaning*
Yet writeth he in his kind,
No man that can amend
Those matters that he hath penned;
Yet some men find a faute,° *fault*
And say he writeth too haute.° *abstractly*
Wherefore hold me excused
If I have not well perused
Mine English half abused;
Though it be refused,
In worth I shall it take,
And fewer words make.
But, for my sparrow's sake,
Yet as a woman may,
My wit I shall assay
An epitaph to write
In Latin plain and light,
Whereof the elegy
Followeth by and by:
Flos volucrum formose, vale![5]
Philippe, sub isto
Marmore jam recubas,
Qui mihi carus eras.
Semper erunt nitido
Radiantia sidera cœlo;
Impressusque meo
Pectore semper eris.
Per me laurigerum
Britonum Skeltonida vatem
Hæc cecinisse licet
Ficta sub imagine texta.
Cujus eris volucris,
Præstanti corpore virgo:
Candida Nais erat,
Formosior ista Joanna est;
Docta Corinna fuit,
Sed magis ista sapit.
Bien m'en souvient.

The Commendations

Beati im ma cu la ti in via,
O gloriosa foemina![6]
Now mine whole imagination

5. The following Latin elegy is represented up to line 833 as being by Jane Scrope. The remaining lines disclose that their actual author is Skelton, writing in the persona of Jane, who nevertheless continues to mourn for Philip. "O flower of birds, fair one, farewell! Philip, now you lie under this marble, you who were dear to me. The shining stars will always be in the bright sky; you will always be held in my heart. By me, Skelton, the British poet laureate, it has been permitted to sing these things, composed in the guise of her whose bird you were; [she is] a maiden with a lovely body: Nais was fair, but this Joanna is more beautiful; Corinna was learned, but this girl knows more." Skelton concludes with a French phrase: "I remember it well."

6. Skelton continues the remainder of the poem in his own voice, commending Jane Scrope for her devotion to Philip: "Blessed are the pure, in the course [of this life], O glorious woman."

And studious meditation
Is to take this commendation
In this consideration;
And under patient toleration
Of that most goodly maid
That *Placebo* hath said,
And for her sparrow prayed
In lamentable wise,
Now will I enterprise,° *undertake*
Through the grace divine
Of the Muses nine,
Her beauty to commend,
If Arethusa° will send *a fountain in Sicily*
Me influence to endite,
And with my pen to write;
If Apollo° will promise *god of music*
Melodiously it to devise
His tunable harp strings
With harmony that sings
Of princes and of kings
And of all pleasant things,
Of lust° and of delight, *pleasure*
Through his godly might;
To whom be the laud° ascribed *praise*
That my pen hath imbibed
With the aureat° drops, *golden*
As verily my hope is,
Of Tagus,[7] that golden flood,
That passeth all earthly good;
And as that flood doth pass
All floods that ever was
With his golden sands,
Who so that understands
Cosmography, and the stremes° *rivers*
And the floods in strange remes,° *kingdoms*
Right so she doth exceed
All other of whom we read,
Whose fame by me shall spread
Into Perce° and Mede,° *Persia/Medea*
From Britons' Albion° *British Isles*
To the Tower of Babylon.
I trust it is no shame,
And no man will me blame,
Though I register her name
In the court of Fame;
For this most goodly flower,[8]
This blossom of fresh color,

7. A river in Spain whose sands were apparently golden.

8. "For this most goodly flower . . . In beauty and virtue": a refrain throughout the rest of the poem. In subsequent lines, Skelton renders "flower" as "floure"; the words were probably pronounced the same, rhyming with "colór" (accented on second syllable).

So Jupiter me succor,° *help*
She flourisheth new and new
In beauty and virtue:
Hac claritate gemina[9]
O gloriosa fœmina,
Retribue servo tuo, vivifica me!
Labia mea laudabunt te.
   But enforced am I
Openly to askry,° *protest*
And to make an outcry
Against odious Envy,
That evermore will lie,
And say cursedly;
With his ledder° eye, *leather*
And cheeks dry;
With visage wan,
As swart° as tan; *dark*
His bones crake,° *crack*
Lean as a rake;
His gums rusty
Are full unlusty;° *useless*
His heart withal
Bitter as gall;
His liver, his lung
With anger is wrung;
His serpent's tongue
That many one hath stung;
He frowneth ever;
He laugheth never,
Even nor morrow,
But other men's sorrow
Causeth him to grin
And rejoice therein;
No sleep can him catch,
But ever doth watch,
He is so bete° *agitated*
With malice, and frete° *worn out*
With anger and ire,
His foul desire
Will suffer no sleep
In his head to creep;
His foul semblaunt° *appearance*
All displeasaunt;
When other are glad,
Then is he sad;
Frantic and mad;
His tongue never still
For to say ill,

9. "With this twin brightness, O glorious woman, deal bountifully with your servant, give me life! My lips will praise you" (Psalm 62.3).

Writhing and wringing,
Biting and stinging;
And thus this elf
Consumeth himself,
Himself doth slo° *slay*
With pain and woe.
This false Envy
Sayeth that I
Use great folly
For to endite,
And for to write,
And spend my time
In prose and rhyme,
For to express
The nobleness
Of my mistress,
That causeth me
Studious to be
To make a relation
Of her commendation;
And there again
Envy doth complain,
And hath disdain;
But yet certain
I will be plain,
And my style dress° *suit*
To this process.
Now Phoebus° me ken° *Apollo/teach*
To sharp my pen,
And lead my fist
As him best list,
That I may say
Honor alway
Of womankind!
Truth doth me bind
And loyalty
Ever to be
Their true bedell,° *herald*
To write and tell
How women excel
In nobleness;
As my mistress,
Of whom I think
With pen and ink
For to compile
Some goodly style;
For this most goodly floure,
This blossom of fresh color,
So Jupiter me succor,
She flourisheth new and new
In beauty and virtue:

Hac claritate gemina
O gloriosa fœmina,
Legem pone mihi, domina, in viam justificationum tuarum!
Quemadmodum desiderat cervus ad fontes aquarum.[1]
How shall I report
All the goodly sort
Of her features clear,
That hath none earthly peer?
Her favor of her face
Ennewed° all with grace, — *enlivened*
Comfort, pleasure, and solace,
Mine heart doth so embrace,
And so hath ravished me
Her to behold and see,
That in words plain
I cannot me refrain
To look on her again:
Alas, what should I fain?° — *desire*
It were a pleasant pain
With her aye to remain.
Her eyen gray and stepe° — *arched*
Causeth mine heart to leap;
With her brows bent
She may well represent
Fair Lucres,[2] as I ween,
Or else fair Polexene,
Or else Calliope,
Or else Penelope;
For this most goodly floure,
This blossom of fresh color,
So Jupiter me succor,
She flourisheth new and new
In beauty and virtue:
Hac claritate gemina
O gloriosa fœmina,
Memor esto verbi tui servo tuo!
Servus tuus sum ego.[3]
The Indy° sapphire blue — *India*
Her veins doth ennew;° — *ornament*
The orient pearl so clear,
The whiteness of her lere;° — *face*
The lusty ruby ruddes° — *complexion*
Resemble the rose buds;
Her lips soft and merry
Emblomed° like the cherry, — *blooming*
It were an heavenly bliss

1. "Teach me the law, O my lady, the way of your statutes! As the deer pants after the water brooks" (Psalm 41.2). Scripture addresses a *dominus* or lord, not a *domina* or lady.
2. Skelton compares Jane to Lucrece, i.e., Lucretia and Polyxena (both legendary heroines); Caliope: the muse of epic poetry.
3. "Remember thy word to thy servant; I am your servant" (Psalm 118.49 and 125).

Her sugared mouth to kiss.
Her beauty to augment,
Dame Nature hath her lent
A wart upon her cheek,
Whoso list to seek
In her visage a scar,
That seemeth from afar
Like to the radiant star,
All with favor fret,° *beauty adorned*
So properly it is set:
She is the violet,
The daisy delectable,
The columbine commendable,
The jelofer° amiable; *gilly flower*
For this most goodly floure,
This blossom of fresh color,
So Jupiter me succor,
She flourisheth new and new
In beauty and virtue:
Hac claritate gemina
O *gloriosa fœmina,*
Bonitatem fecisti cum servo tuo, domina,
Et ex praecordiis sonant praeconia![4]
And when I perceived
Her wart and conceived,
It cannot be denayd° *denied*
But it was well conveyed,
And set so womanly,
And nothing wantonly,
But right conveniently,
And full congruently,
As Nature could devise,
In most goodly wise;
Whoso list, behold,
It maketh lovers bold
To her to sue for grace,
Her favor to purchase;
The scar upon her chin,
Enhached° on her fair skin, *inlaid*
Whiter than the swan,
It would make any man
To forget deadly sin
Her favor to win;
For this most goodly floure,
This blossom of fresh color,
So Jupiter me succor,
She flourisheth new and new
In beauty and virtue:
Hac claritate gemina

4. "Thou hast dealt bountifully with thy servant, O Lady, and from the heart praises sound" (Psalm 118).

O gloriosa fœmina,
Defecit in salutatione tua anima mea;
Quid petis filio, mater dulcissima? babae![5]
  Soft, and make no din,
For now I will begin
To have in remembrance
Her goodly dalliance,
And her goodly pastaunce:° *pastime*
So sad and so demure,
Behaving her so sure,
With words of pleasure
She would make to the lure° *draw to her*
And any man convert
To give her his whole heart.
She made me sore amazed
Upon her whan I gazed,
Me thought mine heart was crazed,
My eyne° were so dazed; *eyes*
For this most goodly floure,
This blossom of fresh color,
So Jupiter me succor,
She flourisheth new and new
In beauty and virtue:
Hac claritate gemina
O gloriosa fœmina,
Quomodo dilexi legem tuam, domina!
Recedant vetera, nova sint omnia.[6]
  And to amend her tale,
When she list to avale,[7]
And with her fingers small,
And hands soft as silk,
Whiter than the milk,
That are so quickly veined,
Wherewith my hand she strained,
Lord, how I was pained!
Unneth° I me refrained, *unless*
How she me had reclaimed,
And me to her retained,
Embracing therewithal
Her goodly middle small
With sides long and straight;
To tell you what conceit
I had then in a trice,
The matter were too nice,
And yet there was no vice,
Nor yet no villainy,

5. "My soul faints as it greets you; what do you ask for your son, sweetest mother?" (Psalm 118.81).
6. "How I loved thy law, O Lady; old things pass away, everything is new" (Psalm 118.97 and 2 Corinthians 5.17).
7. Skelton proposes to "amend" or improve upon her "tale" or the account of her excellence. He states that when she desires to "avale" or condescend to take his hand, he suffers pain.

But only fantasy;
For this most goodly floure,
This blossom of fresh color,
So Jupiter me succor,
She flourisheth new and new
In beauty and virtue:
Hac claritate gemina
O gloriosa fœmina,
Iniquos odio habui!
Non calumnientur me superbi.[8]
But whereto should I note
How often did I tote
Upon her pretty fote?° *foot*
It raised mine heart rote° *root*
To see her tread the ground
With heels short and round.
She is plainly express° *exactly*
Egeria,[9] the goddess,
And like to her image,
Emportured° with corage, *painted(?)*
A lover's pilgrimage;
There is no beast savage,
Nor no tiger so wood,° *furious*
But she would change his mood,
Such relucent grace
Is formed in her face;
For this most goodly floure,
This blossom of fresh color,
So Jupiter me succor,
She flourisheth new and new
In beauty and virtue:
Hac claritate gemina
O gloriosa fœmina,
Mirabilia testimonia tua!
Sicut novellæ plantationes in juventute sua.[1]
So goodly as she dresses,
So properly she presses
The bright golden tresses
Of her hair so fine,
Like Phoebus beams shine.
Whereto should I disclose
The gartering of her hose?
It is for to suppose
How that she can were° *wear*
Gorgeously her gere;° *garments*
Her fresh habiliments° *clothes*
With other implements

8. "I hate vain thoughts; let not the proud oppress me" (Psalm 118.113 and 122).

9. A nymph who counseled the legendary King Numa Pompilius, the successor to Romulus, supposed to be the first king of Rome.

1. "Wonderful are thy testimonies; that our sons may be as plants grown up in their youth" (Psalms 118.129 and 143.12).

To serve for all intents,
Like dame Flora,° queen *goddess of spring*
Of lusty summer green;
For this most goodly floure,
This blossom of fresh color,
So Jupiter me succor,
She flourisheth new and new
In beauty and virtue:
Hac claritate gemina
O gloriosa fœmina,
Clamavi in toto corde, exaudi me!
Misericordia tua magna est super me.[2]
Her kirtle° so goodly laced, *skirt*
And under that is braced
Such pleasures that I may
Neither write nor say;
Yet though I write not with ink,
No man can let me think,
For thought hath liberty,
Thought is frank and free;
To think a merry thought
It cost me little nor nought.
Would God mine homely style
Were polished with the file
Of Cicero's eloquence,
To praise her excellence!
For this most goodly floure,
This blossom of fresh color,
So Jupiter me succor,
She flourisheth new and new
In beauty and virtue:
Hæ claritate gemina
O gloriosa fœmina,
Principes persecuti sunt me gratis!
Omnibus consideratis,
Paradisus voluptatis
Hæc virgo est dulcissima.[3]
   My pen it is unable,
My hand it is unstable,
My reason rude and dull
To praise her at the full;
Goodly mistress Jane,
Sober, demure Diane;[4]
Jane this mistress hight
The lode star of delight,
Dame Venus of all pleasure,
The well of worldly treasure;

2. "I have cried with all my heart, hear me; great is thy mercy toward me" (Psalms 118.145 and 85.13).
3. "Princes have persecuted me unjustly" (Psalm 118.161); "All things considered, this girl is the sweetest of heavenly pleasures."
4. By naming Jane Scrope "Diane" here and "Venus" and "Pallas" (Athena) later, Skelton transforms her into a composite of goddesses.

She doth exceed and pass
In prudence dame Pallas;
For this most goodly floure,
This blossom of fresh color,
So Jupiter me succor,
She flourisheth new and new
In beauty and virtue:
Hac claritate gemina
O gloriosa foemina!
Requiem aeternam dona eis, Domine![5]
With this psalm, *Domine, probasti me,*[6]
Shall° sail over the sea, — *I shall*
With *Tibi, Domine, commendamus,*[7]
On pilgrimage to saint James,[8]
For shrimps, and for pranys,° — *prawns*
And for stalking cranys;° — *cranes*
And where my pen hath offended,
I pray you it may be amended
By discrete consideration
Of your wise reformation;
I have not offended, I trust,
If it be sadly discussed.
It were no gentle guise° — *fashion*
This treatise to despise
Because I have written and said
Honor of this fair maid;
Wherefore should I be blamed,
That I Jane have named,
And famously proclaimed?
She is worthy to be enrolled
With letters of gold.
Car elle vault.[9]
Per me laurigerum Britonum Skeltonida vatem[1]
Laudibus eximiis merito hæc redimita puella est:
Formosam cecini, qua non formosior ulla est;
Formosam potius quam commendaret Homerus.
Sic juvat interdum rigidos recreare labores,
Nec minus hoc titulo tersa Minerva mea est:
Rien que playsere.

Thus endeth the boke of Philip Sparow, and here followeth an addition made by master Skelton.

The guise nowadays
Of some jangling jays° — *i.e., raucous critics*
Is to discommend

5. Grant them eternal rest, O Lord.
6. Lord, you have tested me.
7. We commend ourselves to thee, O Lord.
8. The shrine of St. James was in Compostela, in northern Spain.
9. Because she is deserving.
1. Through me, Skelton, laureate poet of Britain, this girl is honored with praise for her merit; I have sung of her beauty, she of whom none is more beautiful; Homer would praise no beauty more. Thus it is delightful to recreate demanding labor now and then. Nor is my Minerva [i.e., my art] less free from error than this title: Nothing but to please.

That they cannot amend,
Though they would spend
All the wits they have.
  What ail them to deprave° *vilify*
Philip Sparrow's grave?
His *Dirige*, her Commendation
Can be no derogation,
But mirth and consolation
Made by protestation,
No man to miscontent
With Philip's interment.
  Alas, that goodly maid,
Why should she be afraid?
Why should she take shame
That her goodly name,
Honorably reported,
Should be set and sorted,
To be matriculate° *enrolled*
With ladies of estate?
  I conjure thee, Philip Sparrow,
By Hercules that hell did harrow,[2]
And with a venomous arrow
Slew of the Epidaures[3]
One of the Centaurs,° *half man, half horse*
Or Onocentaurs,° *half man, half ass*
Or Hippocentaurs;° *centaur*
By whose might and main
An heart was slain
With horns twain
Of glittering gold;
And the apples of gold
Of Hesperides[4] withhold,
And with a dragon kept
That never more slept,
By martial strength
He won at length;
And slew Gerion[5]
With three bodies in one;
With mighty corage
Adauntid° the rage *subdued*
Of a lion savage;
Of Diomedes' stable[6]
He brought out a rabble
Of coursers° and rounces° *war horses / riding horses*
With leaps and bounces;
And with mighty lugging,

2. Skelton describes the labors of Hercules; see lines 1291–1322.
3. Men of the region in Greece known as Epidaurus.
4. Mythical daughters of the evening, who lived far to the west.
5. A three-headed monster who owned oxen that Hercules was required to steal.
6. Diomedes, a mythical king of Thrace whose horses ate human flesh.

Wrestling and tugging,
He plucked the bull
By the horned skull,
And offered to Cornucopia;° *horn of plenty*
And so forth *per cetera:*
Also by Ecate's[7] bower
In Pluto's ghastly tower;
By the ugly Eumenides,
That never have rest nor ease;
By the venomous serpent,
That in hell is never brent,° *burned*
In Lerna, the Greeks' fen,
That was engendered then;
By Chimera's flames,
And all the deadly names
Of infernal posty,° *power*
Where souls fry and rousty;° *roast*
By the Stygyal° flood, *of Styx*
And the streams wood° *mad waters*
Of Cocytus's bottomless well;
By the ferryman of hell,
Charon with his beard hoar,° *white, frosted*
That roweth with a rude oar
And with his frounced foretop° *wrinkled forehead*
Guideth his boat with a prop:° *pole*
I conjure Philip, and call
In the name of king Saul,[8]
Primo Regum express;° *specifically*
He bad the Phitoness° *Pythoness*
To witchcraft her to dress,
And by her abusions,° *abusive actions*
And damnable illusions
Of marvelous conclusions,
And by her superstitions
Of wonderful conditions,
She raised up in that stead
Samuel that was dead;
But whether it were so,
He were *idem in numero*,° *in the same body*
The selfsame Samuel,
How be it to Saul did he tell
The Philistines should him ascry,° *assail*
And the next day he should die,
I will myself discharge

7. Skelton invokes mythological figures associated with the underworld. "Ecate," or Hecate, and Pluto were deities who presided over the underworld; the Eumenides were the Furies, who tormented the dead as well as the living; Lerna was the home of the many-headed Hydra; the Chimera was a fire-breathing beast. The Styx and Cocytus were rivers in the underworld; Charon was the boatman who ferried souls across the Styx.

8. Skelton refers to passages in 1 Samuel (or the book that was known as *Primum Regum*, or First Kings) in which King Saul orders the Pythoness, a witch, to raise King Samuel from the dead; Samuel then prophecies the death of Saul at the hands of the Philistines.

To lettered men at large:
  But, Philip, I conjure thee
Now by these names three,
Diana[9] in the woods green,
Luna that so bright doth shene,° *shine*
Proserpina in hell,
That thou shortly tell,
And show now unto me
What the cause may be
Of this perplexity!

Inferias, Philippe, tuas Scroupe pulchra Joanna
Instanter petiit: cur nostri carminis illam
Nunc pudet? est sero; minor est infamia vero.[1]

  Than such as have disdained
And of this work complained,
I pray God they be pained
No worse than is contained
In verses two or three
That follow as you may see.
Luride, cur, livor, volucris pia funera damnas?
Talia te rapiant rapiunt quæ fata volucrem!
Est tamen invidia mors tibi continua.[2]

Sir Thomas Wyatt
1503–1542

A gifted poet and diplomat, Sir Thomas Wyatt exemplified the ambitious mixture of social and artistic skills that later ages would see as the ideal of the "Renaissance man." Having entered the household of King Henry VIII immediately after his education at Cambridge, Wyatt promoted English interests on missions to France, Venice, Rome, Spain, and the Low Countries. His career was to prove more precarious at home, where he became involved in court politics. He was deeply attached to the Lady Anne Boleyn, who, by 1527, was the object of Henry's affections and a probable pretext for the King's divorce from Catherine of Aragon and England's break from the Roman Catholic Church. Made Henry's queen in 1533 but out of favor by 1536, Anne implicated by association those who were supposed to have been her lovers. Wyatt was lucky to suffer no more than imprisonment; the Queen's other favorites were executed. Wyatt subsequently regained political status both at home and abroad, although not without periods of disappointment: his verse letter *Mine Own John Poyns* praises the security of a country life away from London and its intrigues. Wyatt's most protracted mission was from 1537 to 1539, as the King's ambassador to the court of the Holy Roman Emperor in Spain: he tells of his anticipated return to England in the hauntingly brief lyric *Tagus, Farewell*. Despite

9. Luna (or Lucina), Proserpina: the two other aspects of Diana who, as the goddess of the moon, also represents the cycles of life: virginity, procreation, and death.

1. "O Philip, the beautiful Joanna Scrope urgently desires your obsequies. Why is she ashamed of our song? It is too late. Shame is less than truth."

2. "Why, ghastly envy, do you condemn the sacred funeral of a bird? May such fates seize you as seized the bird. Yet envy is a continual death to you."

the execution of his powerful patron Sir Thomas Cromwell and a second prison term in 1541 for suspected treason, Wyatt obtained Henry's goodwill at the end of his short life. He died from a fever at the age of thirty-nine while on a diplomatic mission for the king.

By any poetic reckoning, Wyatt is to be valued as a pioneer of English verse. Although many of his poems exhibit irregular meters, they have been praised for their remarkable texture and sense of surprise. His translations of Francesco Petrarch's sonnets established the principal forms of English lyric, the rhyming sonnet with its pentameter line and the more loosely configured song derived from the Italian *canzone*. Wyatt's own poems change the spirit of their Petrarchan themes by giving erotic subjects a satirical and even bitter twist, and political topics an inward and personal reference. In one of his best-known sonnets, *Whoso List to Hunt*, he writes of vainly pursuing a "hind" or "deer" (a dear or beloved lady) belonging to "Caesar" (King Henry VIII). Long understood to be a reference to Anne Boleyn, Wyatt's "deer" is quite a different figure than the "deer" in his source, Petrarch's sonnet to a "white doe," who represents his lady, Laura, whom he met in 1327 and loved from a distance until her death in 1350. While Petrarch's lady is imagined as chastely devoted to a heavenly Caesar or God, and therefore as inspiring a religious awe, Wyatt's beloved is the possession of an earthly Caesar, King Henry VIII, and thus the cause of his immediate frustration.

Wyatt's verse was circulated in manuscript during his lifetime and probably read only by his friends and his acquaintances at court. A few poems were published in 1540, in a collection entitled *The Court of Venus*, but the majority—ninety-seven poems in all—appeared in 1557, in a massive anthology called *Songs and Sonnets*, published by the printer Richard Tottel. This volume, which includes poems by Henry Howard, Earl of Surrey and others, was a milestone in the history of literature. Unlike the earlier sixteenth-century poetry of the British Isles, which remained relatively simple in its genres and diction, *Tottel's Miscellany* (as it has come to be known), exhibited a range of new forms and meters: the sonnet, the song (or *canzone*), the epigram, and rhyming and blank verse. Familiar to writers and readers of Italian and French, these forms allowed poets (now writing a recognizably modern English) to develop a stylistic flexibility and thematic richness previously achieved only by the Middle English poet Geoffrey Chaucer. Before presenting his anthology to the public, however, Tottel did some fairly drastic editing: smoothing out metrical irregularities by adding, subtracting, or changing words, he obviously sought to impress readers with what he judged to be the elegant and up-to-date styles represented by the works in his collection. The poems reprinted here are based not on the *Songs and Sonnets* but on Wyatt's original texts.

The Long Love, That in My Thought Doth Harbor

The long love, that in my thought doth harbor
And in mine heart doth keep his residence,
Into my face presseth with bold pretence,
And therein campeth, spreading his banner.
She that me learneth° to love and suffer, *teaches*
And will that my trust and lust's negligence
Be reined by reason, shame and reverence,
With his hardiness° taketh displeasure. *boldness*
Wherewithal, unto the heart's forest he fleeth,
Leaving his enterprise with pain and cry,
And there him hideth and not appeareth.
What may I do when my master feareth
But in the field with him to live and die?
For good is the life, ending faithfully.

Companion Reading

Petrarch, Sonnet 140[1]

Amor, che nel penser mio vive et regna
e 'l suo seggio maggior nel mio cor tene,
talor armato ne la fronte vene;
ivi si loca et ivi pon sua insegna.
Quella ch' amare et sofferir ne 'nsegna
e vol che 'l gran desio, l'accesa spene
ragion, vergogna, et reverenza affrene,
di nostro ardir fra se stessa si sdegna.
Onde Amor paventoso fugge al core,
lasciando ogni sua impresa, et piange et trema;
ivi s'asconde et non appar più fore.
Che poss' io far, temendo il mio signore,
se non star seco infin a l'ora estrema?
ché bel fin fa chi ben amando more.

Petrarch, Sonnet 140: A Translation

Love, who lives and reigns in my thought and keeps his principal seat in my heart, sometimes comes forth all in armor into my forehead, there camps, and there sets up his banner.

She who teaches us to love and to be patient, and wishes my great desire, my kindled hope, to be reined in by reason, shame, and reverence, at our boldness is angry within herself.

Wherefore Love flees terrified to my heart, abandoning his every enterprise, and weeps and trembles; there he hides and no more appears outside.

What can I do, when my lord is afraid, except stay with him until the last hour? For he makes a good end who dies loving well.

Whoso List to Hunt

Who so list° to hunt, I know where is an hind,° *wishes / doe*
But as for me, helas, I may no more:
The vain travail° hath wearied me so sore. *idle labor*
I am of them that farthest cometh behind.
Yet may I by no means my wearied mind
Draw from° the deer: but as she fleeth afore, *forget*
Fainting I follow. I leave off therefore,
Since in a net I seek to hold the wind.
Who list her hunt I put him out of doubt,
As well as I may spend his time in vain:
And, graven° with diamonds, in letters plain *engraved*
There is written her fair neck round about:

1. Petrarch (1304–1374), known to his fellow Italians as Francesco Petrarca, was the virtual inventor of modern lyric poetry. Comprising sonnets, songs (*canzone*), and odes, his *Rime sparse* or "various poems"—widely circulated during and after his lifetime—were translated and imitated by poets throughout Europe. Petrarch's verse demonstrated to his early modern readers that a lyric poet could invest subjects with a spirituality and a seriousness previously attributed to the epic, the ode, and to philosophical poems. Translations by Robert M. Durling.

Noli me tangere,[1] for Caesar's I am,
And wild for to hold though I seem tame.

COMPANION READING

Petrarch, Sonnet 190

Una candida cerva sopra l'erba
verde m'apparve con duo corna d'oro,
fra due riviere all' ombra d'un alloro,
Levando 'l sole a la stagione acerba.
Era sua vista sì dolce superba
ch' i'lasciai per seguirla ogni lavoro,
come l'avaro che 'n cercar tesoro
con diletto l'affanno disacerba.
"Nessun mi tocchi," al bel collo d'intorno
scritto avea di diamanti et di topazi.
"Libera farmi al mio Cesare parve."
Et era 'l sol già vòlto al mezzo giorno,
gli occhi miei stanchi di mirar, non sazi,
quand' io caddi ne l'acqua et ella sparve.

Petrarch, Sonnet 190: A Translation

A white doe on the green grass appeared to me, with two golden horns, between two rivers, in the shade of a laurel, when the sun was rising in the unripe season.

Her look was so sweet and proud that to follow her I left every task, like the miser who as he seeks treasure sweetens his trouble with delight.

"Let no one touch me," she bore written with diamonds and topazes around her lovely neck. "It has pleased my Caesar to make me free."

And the sun had already turned at midday; my eyes were tired by looking but not sated, when I fell into the water, and she disappeared.

My Galley

My galley charged° with forgetfulness — *loaded*
Through sharp seas in winter nights doth pass
'Tween rock and rock; and eke° mine enemy, alas, — *also*
That is my lord, steereth with cruelness;
And every hour a thought in readiness,
As though that death were light° in such a case. — *easy*
An endless wind doth tear the sail apace.
Of forced sights and trusty fearfulness.
A rain of tears, a cloud of dark disdain
Hath done the wearied cords° great hindrance, — *worn rigging*
Wreathed with error and eke with ignorance.
The stars be hid that led me to this pain,
Drowned is reason that should me comfort,
And I remain despairing of the port.

1. "Touch me not," the words the resurrected but not yet risen Christ spoke to Mary Magdalene before his tomb (John 20.17). The "deer" of the poem has often been identified with Anne Boleyn and "Caesar" with Henry VIII.

They Flee from Me

They flee from me that sometime did me seek
With naked foot stalking in my chamber.
I have seen them gentle tame and meek
That now are wild and do not remember
That sometime they put themself in danger
To take bread at my hand; and now they range
Busily seeking with a continual change.
Thanked be fortune, it hath been otherwise
Twenty times better; but once in special,
In thine array after a pleasant guise,° *manner*
When her loose gown from her shoulders did fall,
And she me caught in her arms long and small;
Therewithal sweetly did me kiss,
And softly said, "dear heart, how like you this?"
It was no dream: I lay broad waking.
But all is turned through my gentleness
Into a strange fashion of forsaking;
And I have leave to go of her goodness,
And she also to use new fangledness.
But since that I so kindly am served,
I would fain° know what she hath deserved. *wish to*

Some Time I Fled the Fire[1]

Some time I fled the fire that me brent° *burned*
By sea, by land, by water and by wind;
And now I follow the coals that be quent° *quenched*
From Dover to Calais against my mind.
Lo! how desire is both sprung and spent!
And he may see that whilom° was so blind; *formerly*
And all his labor now he laugh to scorn,
Mashed in the breers° that erst° was all to torn.° *briars / once / torn up*

My Lute, Awake!

My lute, awake! perform the last
Labor that thou and I shall waste
  And end that I have now begun,
For when this song is sung and past,
  My lute be still, for I have done.

As to be heard where ere is none,° *there is no one*
As lead to grave in marble stone,
  My song may pierce her heart as sone;° *soon*
Should we then sigh, or sing, or moan?
  No, no, my lute, for I have done.

1. This poem appears to record Wyatt's attitude as he attended Anne Boleyn on her way to Calais in October 1532. Having been burned by her "fire" (a possible reference to a love affair), he now follows the dead coals of that fire against his will.

The rocks do not so cruelly
Repulse the waves continually,
As she my suit and affection,
So that I am past remedy,
Whereby my lute and I have done.

Proud of the spoil that thou hast got
Of simple hearts through love's shot,
By whom, unkind, thou has them won,
Think not he hath his bow forgot,
Although my lute and I have done.

Vengeance shall fall on thy disdain,
That makest but game on earnest pain;
Think not alone under the sun
Unquit° to cause thy lover's plain,° *freely / lament*
Although my lute and I have done.

Perchance thee lie weathered and old,
The winter nights that are so cold,
Plaining in vain unto the mone;° *moon*
Thy wishes then dare not be told,
Care then who list,° for I have done. *wishes*

And then may chance thee to repent
The time that thou hast lost and spent
To cause thy lover's sigh and swoon;
Then shalt thou know beauty but lent
And wish and want as I have done.

Now cease, my lute, this is the last
Labor that thou and I shall wast,° *waste*
And ended is that we begun;
Now is this song both sung and past,
My lute be still, for I have done.

Tagus, Farewell

Tagus,[1] farewell, that westward with thy streams
Turns up the grains of gold already tried:
With spur and sail for I go seek the Thames,
Gainward° the sun that showeth her wealthy pride; *toward*
And to the town which Brutus[2] sought by dreams
Like bended moon doth lend her lusty side.
My King, my country, alone for whom I live,
Of mighty love the wings for this me give.

Forget Not Yet

Forget not yet the tried° intent *proven*
Of such a truth as I have meant,

1. The Tagus, or Tajo, River is the longest on the Iberian peninsula and empties into the Atlantic at Portugal. Wyatt was sent to Spain as a diplomat but returned to England in 1539.

2. The legendary Trojan hero Brutus was supposed to have settled the British Isles and founded London, to which he was led by a series of dreams sent to him by the goddess Diana.

My great travail° so gladly spent *effort*
Forget not yet.

Forget not yet when first began
The weary life ye know since whan,° *when*
The suit, the service none tell can,
Forget not yet.

Forget not yet the great assays,° *trials*
The cruel wrong, the scornful ways,
The painful patience in denays,° *denials*
Forget not yet.

Forget not yet, forget not this,
How long ago hath been and is
The mind that never meant amiss,
Forget not yet.

Forget not then thine own aprovyd,[1]
The which so long hath thee so lovyd,
Whose steadfast faith yet never movyd,
Forget not this.

Blame Not My Lute

Blame not my lute for he must sound
Of this or that as liketh me,
For lack of wit the lute is bound
To give such tunes as pleaseth me:
Though my songs be somewhat strange,
And speaks such words as touch thy change,[1]
Blame not my lute.

My lute, alas, doth not offend,
Though that perforce he must agree
To sound such tunes as I intend
To sing to them that heareth me;
Then though my songs be somewhat plain,
And toucheth some that used to fain,[2]
Blame not my lute.

My lute and strings may not deny,
But as I strike they must obey;
Break not them then so wrongfully,
But wreak° thyself some wiser way: *revenge*
And though the songs which I endite° *write*
Do quit° thy change with rightful spite, *discharge, answer*
Blame not my lute.

Spite asketh spite and changing change,
And falsed° faith must needs be known; *betrayed*

1. The poet himself, her "approved" lover.

1. I.e., the lady's change of heart, probably also to be signified by a change of tone in the music to which this lyric was supposedly set.

2. Who used to be desirous or who used to feign desire.

The fault so great, the case so strange,
  Of right it must abroad be blown:
Then since that by thine own desart° *desert*
My songs do tell how true thou art,
    Blame not my lute.

Blame but the self that hast misdone
  And well deserved to have blame;
Change thou thy way, so evil begun,
  And then my lute shall sound that same:
But if till then my fingers play
By thy desart their wonted way,
    Blame not my lute.

Farewell, unknown, for though thou break
  My strings in spite with great disdain,
Yet have I found out for thy sake
  Strings for to string my lute again;
And if perchance this folys° rhyme *foolish*
Do make thee blush at any time,
    Blame not my lute.

Lucks, My Fair Falcon, and Your Fellows All

Lucks, my fair falcon, and your fellows all,
How well pleasant it were your liberty!
Ye not forsake me that fair might ye befall.[1]
But they that sometime liked my company,
Like lice away from dead bodies they crawl:
Lo, what a proof in light adversity![2]
But ye my birds I swear by all your bells,
Ye be my friends, and so be but few else.

Stand Whoso List

Stand whoso list° upon the slipper° top *wishes / slippery*
Of courts' estates, and let me here rejoice;
And use me° quiet without let° or stop, *my / hindrance*
Unknown in court, that hath such brackish joys:
In hidden place, so let my days forth pass,
That when my years be done, withouten noise,
I may die aged after the common trace.[1]
For him death greep' the° right hard by the crop° *grips / throat*
That is much known of other; and of himself alas,
Doth die unknown, dazed with dreadful face.

1. I.e., "You do not forsake me so that good luck may come your way." Wyatt states that despite the falcon's name, which suggests that he seeks good fortune, Lucks is loyal to his master.
2. Wyatt may have written this poem during one of his imprisonments; in any event, he complains here that in prison only his falcons visit and befriend him. Falcons wore bells on their legs to let their masters know where they were.

1. In the common or usual manner; from age and sickness rather than murder. Wyatt alludes to the perilous existence of a man in public life.

Mine Own John Poyns

Mine own John Poyns,[1] since ye delight to know
The cause why that homeward I me draw,
And flee the press of courts[2] where so they° go, *courtiers*
Rather then to live thrall° under the awe *enslaved*
Of lordly looks, wrapped within my cloak,
To will and lust learning to set a law;
It is not for because I scorn or mock
The power of them to whom fortune hath lent
Charge over us, of right, to strike the stroke.
But true it is that I have always meant
Less to esteem them than the common sort
Of outward things that judge in their intent
Without regard what doth inward resort.
I grant sometime that of glory the fire
Doth touch my heart: me list° not to report *wish*
Blame by honor and honor to desire.
But how may I this honor now attain
That cannot dye the color black a liar?[3]
My Poyns, I cannot frame my tongue to feign,
To cloak the truth for praise, without desert,
Of them that list all vice for to retain.[4]
I cannot honor them that sets their part
With Venus and Bacchus[5] all their life long;
Nor hold my piece of them although I smart.
I cannot crouch nor kneel nor do so great a wrong,
To worship them like God on earth alone,
That are as wolves these sely° lambs among. *innocent*
I cannot with my words complain and moan
And suffer nought, nor smart without complaint,
Nor turn the word that from my mouth is gone.
I cannot speak and look like a saint,
Use wiles for wit and make deceit a pleasure,
And call craft counsel, for profit still to paint.[6]
I cannot wrest the law to fill the coffer,
With innocent blood to feed myself fat,
And do most hurt where most help I offer.
I am not he that can allow the state
Of high Caesar and damn Cato to die,[7]
That with his death did scape out of the gate
From Caesar's hands, if Livy do not lie,

1. John Poyns, or Poynz, a friend of Wyatt, spent time at court in the 1520s.
2. Here Wyatt's posing as a retired courtier critical of the court may illustrate his attitude during one of the periods in which he was out of favor with Henry VIII. He had extensive holdings in Kent, to which he could retire and from which he was elected to Parliament shortly before his death.
3. I.e., who cannot change (dye) black another color and hence call black a liar.
4. I.e., to lie by praising those who wish to retain vicious ways and therefore do not deserve praise.
5. Venus: the goddess of love; Bacchus: the god of wine (also known as Dionysius). Together they represented lust and excess.
6. I.e., to represent a falsehood as the truth for profit.
7. I.e., I cannot condone the rule of Caesar and damn Cato. Livy: a Roman historian of the republican period; he records the story of Cato of Utica, who opposed the tyrannical impulses of Julius Caesar and committed suicide rather than live under tyranny.

And would not live where liberty was lost:
So did his heart the common weal° apply.° *state / value*
I am not he such eloquence to boast,
To make the crow singing as the swan,
Nor call the lion of coward beasts the most
That cannot take a mouse as the cat can:
And he that dieth for hunger of the gold
Call him Alessaundre;[8] and say that Pan
Passeth Apollo in music manifold;° *many times*
Praise Sir Thopas[9] for a noble tale,
And scorn the story that the knight told.
Praise him for counsel that is drunk of ale;
Grin when he laugheth that beareth all the sway,
Frown when he frowneth and groan when he is pale;
On others lust to hang both night and day:
None of these points would ever frame in me;
My wit is nought, I cannot learn the way.
And much the less of things that greater be,
That asken help of colors of device° *kinds of deception*
To join the mean with each extremity,
With the nearest virtue to cloak alway the vice:
And as to purpose likewise it shall fall,[1]
To press° the virtue that it may not rise; *suppress*
As drunkenness good fellowship to call;
The friendly foe with his double face
Say he is gentle and courteous therewithal;
And say that Favel° hath a goodly grace *Flattery, a character*
In eloquence, and cruelty to name
Zeal of justice and change in time and place;
And he that suffereth offence without blame
Call him pitiful; and him true and plain
That raileth reckless° to every man's shame. *carelessly criticizes*
Say he is rude that cannot lie and feign,
The lecher a lover, and tyranny
To be the right of a prince's reign.
I cannot, I. No, no, it will not be.
This is the cause that I could never yet
Hang on their sleeves that weigh as thou mayst see
A chip of chance more than a pound of wit.[2]
This maketh me at home to hunt and to hawk
And in foul weather at my book to sit.
In frost and snow then with my bow to stalk;
No man doth mark whereso I ride or go;
In lusty lees at liberty I walk,
And of these news I feel nor weal° nor woe, *happiness*

8. I.e., flatter as Alexander the Great a man so greedy for gold that he dies of hunger. Wyatt continues to list the flattery he cannot give: Pan—half-man, half-goat—was god of shepherds and famous for his music on his reed pipe, but the undisputed god of music was Apollo.
9. *The Tale of Sir Thopas*, one of Chaucer's *Canterbury Tales*, was composed to illustrate how not to tell a story; *The Knight's Tale*, by contrast, exemplified the high style of poetic narrative.
1. Also, when occasion permits.
2. I.e., follow those who value a little good fortune more than a lot of intelligence.

Sauf° that a clog doth hang yet at my heel: *except*
No force for that, for it is ordered so
That I may leap both hedge and dike full well.
I am not now in France to judge the wine,
With saffry° sauce the delicates to feel; *saffron*
Nor yet in Spain where one must him incline
Rather than to be, outwardly to seem.
I meddle not with wits that be so fine,
Nor Flanders' cheer[3] letteth° not my sight to deem° *hinders / judge*
Of black and white, nor taketh my wit away
With beastliness, they beasts do so esteem;[4]
Nor I am not where Christ is given in prey° *in exchange*
For money, poison and treason at Rome,
A common practice used night and day:
But here I am in Kent and Christendom
Among the muses where I read and rhyme;
Where if thou list, my Poyns, for to come,
Thou shalt be judge how I do spend my time.

Henry Howard, Earl of Surrey

1517?–1545

To belong to a rich and powerful family was no guarantee of a secure and prosperous life. Henry Howard, son of the Duke of Norfolk, was one of the most gifted young men in the court of King Henry VIII, yet he was embroiled in factionalism from a very early age. As a boy, he was the companion of Henry Fitzroy, Duke of Richmond, the king's illegitimate son. They spent a year together as guests of the King of France and, after their return to England, continued their friendship at Windsor Castle. After Richmond's death in 1536, Surrey apparently ran afoul of the law and found himself again at Windsor Castle, this time the king's prisoner. Playing up the irony of his situation in *So Cruel Prison,* he memorializes Windsor, formerly a "place of bliss" but now the site of his sorrow at the loss of his freedom and the greater loss of his friend. Surrey was imprisoned again five years later in London, ostensibly for breaking windows. This punishment occasioned a satire, *London, Thou Hast Accused Me*, on the real corruption in the city. At twenty-seven, Surrey took part in the war against the French, was wounded, and, a year later, was made commander of Boulogne. But he fell from favor when he opposed his sister's marriage to the brother of his rival, Edward Seymour, Lord Hertford, and denounced Seymour as guardian of Prince Edward, Henry's heir. Angered beyond all reconciliation, Henry had Surrey tried and executed for treason in 1545.

As a poet, Surrey is often coupled with Wyatt, who was actually a generation older. Many of his poems (like Wyatt's) emulated Petrarchan forms, themes, and imagery, and were published initially by Richard Tottel in 1557 in a volume entitled *Songs and Sonnets*. But Surrey's own accomplishments were unique. He perfected English blank or unrhymed verse, characterized by the pentameter or five-stress line, and he was the likely inventor of the form that became the standard for the English sonnet: three quatrains followed by a couplet, rhyming *ababcdcdefefgg*. Some of his poems on social subjects adopt a satirical tone and convey his vigorous rejection of contemporary manners and morals.

3. The Flemish were reputed to love drinking.

4. The Flemish esteem beasts, i.e., drunks.

Love That Doth Reign and Live within My Thought

Love that doth reign and live within my thought,
And built his seat within my captive breast,
Clad in the arms wherein with me he fought
Oft in my face he doth his banner rest.
But she that taught me love and suffer pain,
My doubtful hope and eke° my hot desire *also*
With shamefast° cloak to shadow and refrain, *ashamed*
Her smiling grace converteth straight to ire.
And coward love then to the heart apace
Taketh his flight, where he doth lurk and plain° *complain*
His purpose lost, and dare not show his face.
For my lord's guilt thus faultless bide° I pain; *suffer*
Yet from my lord shall not foot remove:
Sweet is the death that taketh end by love.

Th'Assyrians' King, in Peace with Foul Desire

Th'Assyrian's king,[1] in peace with foul desire
And filthy lusts that stained his regal heart,
In war that should set princely hearts afire
Vanquished did yield for want of martial art.
The dent of swords from kisses seemed strange,[2]
And harder than his lady's side his targe;° *shield*
From glutton feasts to soldiers' fare a change,
His helmet, far above a garland's charge.[3]
Who scarce the name of manhood did retain,
Drenched in sloth and womanish delight;
Feeble of sprite,° unpatient of pain, *spirit*
When he had lost his honor and his right—
Proud time of wealth, in storms appalled with dread—
Murdered himself to show some manful deed.

Set Me Whereas the Sun Doth Parch the Green

Set me whereas the sun doth parch the green,
Or where his beams may not dissolve the ice,
In temperate heat where he is felt and seen;
With proud people, in presence sad and wise;
Set me in base, or yet in high degree,
In the long night or in the shortest day,
In clear weather or where mists thickest be,
In lusty youth, or when my hairs be grey;
Set me in earth, in heaven, or yet in hell,
In hill, in dale, or in the foaming flood;
Thrall,° or at large, alive whereso I dwell, *captive*
Sick, or in health, in ill fame or in good:

1. The king was Sardanapalus, often regarded as dissolute. He committed suicide by self-immolation.

2. I.e., the dent of swords seemed distasteful compared to kisses.

3. I.e., his helmet was a greater burden than a garland.

Yours will I be, and with that only thought
Comfort myself when that my hap° is nought. *fortune*

The Soote Season

The soote° season, that bud and bloom forth brings, *sweet*
With green hath clad the hill and eke the vale:
The nightingale with feathers new she sings:
The turtle to her make° hath told her tale: *mate*
Summer is come, for every spray now springs,
The hart° hath hung his old head° on the pale:° *stag / horns / stake*
The buck in brake° his winter coat he flings: *thicket*
The fishes float with new repaired scale:
The adder all her slough away she slings:
The swift swallow pursueth the flies small:
The busy bee her honey now she minges:° *remembers*
Winter is worn° that was the flowers' bale:° *passed / evil*
And thus I see among these pleasant things
Each care decays, and yet my sorrow springs.

Alas, So All Things Now Do Hold Their Peace

Alas, so all things now do hold their peace.
Heaven and earth disturbed in nothing:
The beasts, the air, the birds their song do cease:
The night's chair° the stars about doth bring: *Ursa Major*
Calm is the sea, the waves work less and less:
So am not I, whom love alas doth wring,
Bringing before my face the great increase
Of my desires, whereat I weep and sing
In joy and woe as in a doubtful ease.
For my sweet thoughts sometime do pleasure bring:
But by and by the cause of my disease
Gives me a pang, that inwardly doth sting,
When that I think what grief it is again,
To live and lack the thing should rid my pain.

COMPANION READING

Petrarch, Sonnet 164

Or che 'l ciel et la terra e 'l vento tace
et le fere e gli augelli il sonno affrena,
notte il carro stellato in giro mena
et nel suo letto il mar senz' onda giace,

vegghio, penso, ardo, piango; et chi mi sface
sempre m'è inanzi per mia dolce pena:
guerra è 'l mio stato, d'ira e di duol piena,
et sol di lei pensando ò qualche pace.

Così sol d'una chiara fonte viva
move 'l dolce et l'amaro ond' io mi pasco,

una man sola mi risana et punge;
et perché 'l mio martir non giunga a riva,
mille volte il dì moro et mille nasco,
tanto da la salute mia son lunge.

Petrarch, Sonnet 164: A Translation[1]

Now that the heavens and the earth and the wind are silent, and sleep reins in the beasts and the birds, Night drives her starry car about, and in its bed the sea lies without a wave,

I am awake, I think, I burn, I weep; and she who destroys me is always before me, to my sweet pain: war is my state, full of sorrow and suffering, and only thinking of her do I have any peace.

Thus from one clear living fountain alone spring the sweet and the bitter on which I feed; one hand alone heals me and pierces me.

And that my suffering may not reach an end, a thousand times a day I die and a thousand am born, so distant am I from health.

So Cruel Prison

So cruel prison, how could betide,° alas, — *it happen*
As proud Windsor,[1] where I in lust and joy
With a king's son my childish years did pass,
In greater feast than Priam's sons of Troy;[2]

Where° each sweet place returns a taste full sour. — *that*
The large green courts, where we were wont to hove,° — *accustomed to linger*
With eyes cast up unto the maidens' tower,
And easy sighs, such as folk draw in love.

The stately sales,° the ladies bright of hue, — *halls*
The dances short, long tales of great delight,
With words and looks that tigers could but rue,
Where each of us did plead the other's right.

The palm play,[3] where, despoiled for the game,
With dazed eyes oft we by gleams of love
Have missed the ball and got sight of our dame
To bait her eyes which kept the leads° above. — *roofs*

The graveled ground,° with sleeves tied on the helm,[4] — *jousting arena*
On foaming horse, with swords and friendly hearts,
With cheer,° as° though the one should overwhelm, — *joyfully / even*
Where we have fought and chased oft with darts.

With silver drops the meads yet spread for ruth,° — *pity*
In active games of nimbleness and strength
Where we did strain, trailed by swarms of youth,
Our tender limbs, that yet shot up in length.

1. For Petrarch, see the introductory footnote to the Wyatt companion reading, page 621. This translation is also by Durling.

1. Surrey was imprisoned in Windsor Castle in 1537; in this poem his distress at his imprisonment is augmented by his memories of Henry Fitzroy, the Earl of Richmond and bastard son of Henry VIII, with whom he spent time at Windsor when they were young. Richmond married Surrey's sister in 1533; he died in 1536.

2. Priam, King of Troy, was defeated by the Greeks in the Trojan War.

3. Surrey refers to court tennis, a game resembling modern tennis but played against the walls of a court; he remembers that as players, he and Fitzroy watched the ladies who followed the game from the "leads," sheets of metal used to cover roofs.

4. When jousting, a man would tie the sleeve of a lady's garment to his helmet as a sign of her favor.

The secret groves, which oft we made resound
Of pleasant plaint° and of our ladies' praise, *complaint*
Recording soft what grace each one had found,
What hope of speed, what dread of long delays.

The wild forest, the clothed holts° with green, *woods*
With reins avaled° and swift ybreathed° horse, *slackened/panting*
With cry of hounds and merry blasts between,
Where we did chase the fearful hart a force.° *ran it down*

The void° walls eke, that harbored us each night; *empty*
Wherewith, alas, revive within my breast
The sweet accord, such sleeps as yet delight,
The pleasant dreams, the quiet bed of rest,

The secret thoughts imparted with such trust,
The wanton talk, the divers change of play,
The friendship sworn, each promise kept so just,
Wherewith we passed the winter nights away.

And with this thought the blood forsakes my face,
The tears berain my cheeks of deadly hue;
The which, as soon as sobbing sighs, alas,
Upsupped° have, thus I my plaint renew: *absorbed*

O place of bliss! renewer of my woes!
Give me accompt where is my noble fere,° *companion*
Whom in thy walls thou didst each night enclose,
To other lief,° but unto me most dear. *dear*

Each wall, alas, that doth my sorrow rue,
Returns thereto a hollow sound of plaint.
Thus I, alone, where all my freedom grew,
In prison pine with bondage and restraint,

And with remembrance of the greater grief,
To banish the less, I find my chief relief.

London, Hast Thou Accused Me

London, hast thou accused me
Of breach of laws, the root of strife?[1]
Within whose breast did boil to see,
(So fervent hot) thy dissolute life,
That even the hate of sins, that grow
Within thy wicked walls so rife,
For to break forth did convert so
That terror could it not repress.
The which, by words, since preachers know
What hope is left for to redress,
By unknown means it liked me
My hidden burden to express,

1. Surrey was accused of breaking windows with his bow in the city of London in 1543. He states that he was moved to this action by his hatred of the dissolute life within the city (line 4) and that he was responding to an idea of Justice (line 15).

Whereby it might appear to thee
That secret sin hath secret spite;
From Justice° rod no fault is free; *Justice's*
But that all such as works unright
In most quiet are next ill rest.[2]
In secret silence of the night
This made me, with a reckless breast,
To wake thy sluggards with my bow;
A figure of the Lord's behest,[3]
Whose scourge for sin the scriptures show.
That, as the fearful thunder clap
By sudden flame at hand we know,
Of pebble stones the soundless rap,
The dreadful plage° might make thee see *shore*
Of God's wrath, that doth thee enwrap;[4]
That pride might know, from conscience free,
How lofty works may her defend;[5]
And envy find, as he hath sought,
How other seek him to offend;
And wrath taste of each cruel thought
The just shapp hire in the end;[6]
And idle sloth, that never wrought,
To heaven his spirit lift° may begin; *to lift*
And greedy lucre live in dread
To see what hate ill-got goods win;
The lechers, ye that lusts do feed,
Perceive what secrecy is in sin;
And gluttons' hearts for sorrow bleed,
Awaked when their fault they find.
In loathsome vice, each drunken wight° *man*
To stir to God, this was my mind.
Thy windows had done me no spite;
But proud people that dread no fall,
Clothed with falsehed° and unright *falsehood*
Bred in the closures of thy wall,
But wrested to wrath in fervent zeal
Thou hast to strife my secret call.[7]
Endured° hearts no warning feel. *hardened*
Oh shameless whore! is dread then gone
By such thy foes as meant thy weal?[8]
Oh member of false Babylon!
The shop of craft! the den of ire!

2. I.e., all those who act wrongly, if they are resting quietly, are nearest to being disturbed.
3. Surrey imagines that he is like a prophet who does the Lord's command (cf. Isaiah 47.11).
4. The phrase is obscure: "just as we know lightening by thunder, so the soundless rap of pebble stones might make you see the dreadful shore of God's wrath, that surrounds you."
5. Surrey becomes ironic: "Pride, free from conscience, might know how lofty works may defend her"—i.e., important or prodigious works do not defend from punishment the proud, who are (by definition) without a conscience.
6. I.e., wrath receives, for each of its cruel thoughts, the justly shaped or appointed hire or payment in the end.
7. I.e., you have heard my secret call to strife or struggle.
8. Surrey addresses London as the whore of Babylon, the epitome of iniquity, and asks, "Do you no longer fear those enemies that complain of your happiness?"

Thy dreadful dome° draws fast upon; *judgment*
Thy martyrs' blood, by sword and fire,
In heaven and earth for Justice call.
The Lord shall hear their just desire;
The flame of wrath shall on thee fall;
With famine and pest lamentably
Stricken shall be thy lechers all;
Thy proud towers and turrets high,
Enemies to God, beat° stone from stone; *beaten*
Thine idols burnt that wrought iniquity.
When none thy ruin shall bemoan,
But render unto the right wise Lord,
That so hath judged Babylon,
Immortal praise with one accord.

Wyatt Resteth Here

Wyatt resteth here, that quick° could never rest;[1] *alive*
Whose heavenly gifts increased by disdain
And virtue sank the deeper in his breast:
Such profit he of envy could obtain.

A head, where wisdom mysteries did frame;
Whose hammers beat still in that lively brain
As on a stith,° where some work of fame *anvil*
Was daily wrought, to turn to Britain's gain.

A visage, stern and mild; where both did grow,
Vice to condemn, in virtues to rejoice;
Amid great storms whom grace assured so
To live upright and smile at fortune's choice.

A hand that taught what might be said in rhyme;
That reft° Chaucer the glory of his wit; *took from*
A mark the which (unperfited, for time)[2]—
Some may approach, but never none shall hit.

A tongue that served in foreign realms his king;
Whose courteous talk to virtue did enflame
Each noble heart, a worthy guide to bring
Our English youth, by travail[3] unto fame.

An eye whose judgment no affect° could blind, *feeling*
Friends to allure, and foes to reconcile;
Whose piercing look did represent a mind
With virtue fraught, reposed, void of guile.

A heart where dread yet never so impressed
To hide the thought that might the truth avaunce;° *advance*

1. This elegy for the poet Thomas Wyatt was published in 1542, shortly after his death.
2. I.e., was left unperfected for lack of time.
3. Work, but also travel, in that Surrey describes Wyatt as a "guide."

In neither fortune lift, nor so repressed,[4]
To swell in wealth, or yield unto mischance.

A valiant corps,° where force and beauty met, *body*
Happy, alas! too happy, but for foes,
Lived, and ran the race that nature set;
Of manhood's shape, where she the mold did lose.

But to the heavens that simple soul is fled;
Which left with such, as covet° Christ to know *desire*
Witness to faith that never shall be dead:
Sent for our wealth, but not received so.

Thus, for our guilt, this jewel have we lost;
The earth his bones, the heavens possess his ghost.
Amen.

My Radcliffe, When Thy Reckless Youth Offends

My Radcliffe,[1] when thy reckless youth offends:
Receive thy scourge by others' chastisement.
For such calling, when it works none° amends: *no*
Then plagues are sent without advertisement.
Yet Salomon[2] said, the wronged shall recure:° *recover*
But Wyatt said true, the scar doth aye endure.

Sir Thomas More

1477?–1535

After fifteen years of loyal and distinguished service as a government minister and finally Lord Chancellor, Sir Thomas More refused to do the King's bidding. He declined to take the Oath of Allegiance that Henry VIII required of all his subjects, a token of their repudiation of the Pope and recognition of the king as "Defender of the Faith" in England. More's stubborn fidelity to the only church he had ever known drove Henry to extreme measures. He ordered More to the Tower of London and, a year later, had him executed for treason. More may not have been surprised by the decision; he once observed that "If my head should win [Henry] a castle in France, it should not fail to go." It is reported that More's parboiled severed head was fastened to a pole on London Bridge for all to see. By displaying this pathetic remnant of the most conspicuously brilliant man in England, Henry signaled his iron determination to control not only the religious destiny of his kingdom but also its intellectual life.

More's beginnings were auspicious. The son of Agnes and John More, a barrister, he was sent to be a page in the household of Thomas Morton, Archbishop of Canterbury and Lord Chancellor, and then to Oxford, where he met John Colet (1467?–1519), who became, in More's words, "the director of my life." Colet was in many respects a paradoxical source of

4. I.e., neither raised up by fortune to get rich, nor so depressed (by ill fortune) as to yield to a temptation that will lead to misfortune.

1. This epigram is probably addressed to Thomas Radcliffe, third Earl of Essex.

2. Surrey concludes by contrasting an optimistic sentence of King Solomon, which he probably associated with the book of Ecclesiasticus, with the dour reflection of Wyatt.

inspiration for More. A schoolmaster and later a university don, Colet was identified with the scholarship of a Christian humanism that had as its purpose a return to the practices of the primitive and apostolic church. More would end his life professing the authority of the Pope and affirming the Catholic faith as the only true way to salvation.

More was called to the bar and, in 1504, was elected to Parliament. Married that year to Jane Colte and soon the father of four, More organized his household in Chelsea as a center of intellectual activity; there his guests included Desiderius Erasmus and even the King himself. In 1526 the painter Holbein began the first of several visits; his portrait of Thomas More surrounded by numerous family members, including More's gifted daughter Margaret, testifies to the highly conscientious civility that More cultivated in domestic life.

Busy with state and diplomatic affairs from 1504 on, More was knighted and made subtreasurer to the king in 1521. As Lord Chancellor from 1529 to 1532, More was known for his wit, his judicial acumen, and his deft treatment of parties to a case. A popular jingle suggests how swiftly he saw justice done:

When More some time had Chancellor been,
  No more suits did remain;
The like will never more be seen,
  Till More be there again.

Perhaps More's dispatch in matters of law gave him some leisure for literature. In any case his talent as a writer was obvious in his first works: Latin translations of Lucian's dialogues, the *Life of Johan Picus, Earl of Mirandula, Utopia* (in Latin), and the *History of Richard III*. Later works reflect the passion for religious orthodoxy that drove him to oppose reforms proposed by Luther, Calvin, and their followers. In 1528 he published *A Dialogue of Sir Thomas More* against the opinions of the English reformer William Tyndale, whose "Englishing" of the Bible had resolved many of its readers to espouse the new faith. *Supplication of Souls* and *The Confutation of Tyndale's Answer*—similarly directed against the reformation—appeared in 1529 and 1532. More's religious enthusiasm was also expressed in punitive action against those he decided were enemies of the church. John Foxe, whose *Acts and Monuments of These Latter Perilous Days* chronicles the persecution of Christians from the earliest days of the church to his present moment, described More as "blinded in the zeal of popery to all humane considerations." Blinded More was not, however, when he cast an eye to the future. Foreseeing the consequences of Henry's divorce from Catherine of Aragon and his intention to marry again, More resigned his chancellorship in 1532, the year that Parliament published the *Supplication Against the Ordinaries*, a list of grievances against the Catholic Church, and the English church accepted the king as its head. More wrote two more works, the first while still a free (although suspect) man and the second as the King's prisoner: *The Apology of Sir Thomas More* (1533) denounces the reformation, and *A Dialogue of Comfort Against Tribulation* (1533) testifies to the courage that faith could instill in a man who, once possessed of great authority and power, finally found himself in desperate circumstances.

Utopia

When More published his account of a hitherto unknown island republic in 1516, Europeans were still largely ignorant of the world beyond their continent. The exploration that would open up so much of the globe was just getting underway, and accounts of voyages to places hardly dreamed of were yet to constitute a literary genre. What travel writing there was catered to readers who loved reports of "marvels" and had no clear appreciation for what later centuries would call a "fact." Sir John Mandeville, whose still popular account of his travels was first circulated in 1356, described the peoples, customs, and wild life of lands in the East in utterly fantastic terms. But when More called his newly discovered land *Utopia*, literally "nowhere" in Greek, he did so only half in fun. Although his island republic was clearly a figment of More's imagination, the political order that he gave it challenged many of the ideals and practices of contemporary monarchies in Europe, especially in England. His *Utopia* is therefore deceptive: apparently a report of a new people and their society, it was also a critique of the habits of thought and the government that had sustained European and English society for centuries. More composed this work, in Latin, between late September 1515 and September 3, 1516, when he sent it to Erasmus, who helped arrange for the book's first publication in Holland; the first English translation, by Ralph Robinson, appeared in 1551. *Utopia*'s text reflects the international scope of its own production. In fact, More the author did, like "More" the character, visit Peter Giles in Antwerp while on a diplomatic mission; and John Clement was More's "pupil-servant"—a tutor to his children and eventually one of the king's physicians.

The second book of the *Utopia*, written before the first, describes a government in which administrative and legal authority rotates among the elders of the society, a society in which all property is common, and a culture supported by citizens who have identical tastes, aspirations, and outlooks on life. In the words of the aged philosopher and world traveler, a character More names Hythlodaeus (literally "learned in nonsense"), Utopian society is populated entirely by rational beings. Each citizen is trained in a trade, is guaranteed employment, and will get what he or she needs from cradle to grave. The economy is one in which exchange is by barter, not money; clothing is uniform; education and medical care are free to everyone; and defense is conducted by foreigners whom the Utopians hire to protect them. Utopians who protest or rebel against these policies and practices are seen as unreasonable. The first book, evidently an afterthought, establishes a perspective by which to view the extraordinary claims of the second; it shows why Hythlodaeus can be considered an idealistic dreamer as well as an acute critic. Here More prefaces the praise he will have Hythlodaeus give Utopian society by having the philosopher point out the social ills of contemporary England. Refusing to compromise the ideals he says were practiced in Utopia, Hythlodaeus maintains that he must withdraw from societies like those in England and Europe because he can do them no good. His critique of governments is supported by his denunciation of enclosures and capital punishment for minor felonies and of kings and magistrates who are driven by greed and a lust for power.

More's account of Utopia, as reported by his character Hythlodaeus, has convinced some readers that he meant his treatise to be taken as a model for the future. Others have given more weight to its elaborate framing as a report from "nowhere" and have seen it rather as a satire on the idea of a wholly rational society. Whatever balance the reader finds in More's brilliant distinctions, his images of an ideal and imaginary society find analogues in those later represented by Jonathan Swift in *Gulliver's Travels*, Samuel Butler in *Erewhon*, and William Morris in *News from Nowhere*.

Utopia[1]

The Best State of a Commonwealth and the New Island Of Utopia

A Truly Golden Handbook, No Less Beneficial Than Entertaining, by the Distinguished and Eloquent Author

1. Translated by Edward Surtz, S. J.

THOMAS MORE
Citizen and Sheriff of the Famous City of London
Thomas More to Peter Giles,[2] *Greetings.*

I am almost ashamed, my dear Peter Giles, to send you this little book about the state of Utopia after almost a year, when I am sure you looked for it within a month and a half. Certainly you know that I was relieved of all the labor of gathering materials for the work and that I had to give no thought at all to their arrangement. I had only to repeat what in your company I heard Raphael[3] relate. Hence there was no reason for me to take trouble about the style of the narrative, seeing that his language could not be polished. It was, first of all, hurried and impromptu and, secondly, the product of a person who, as you know, was not so well acquainted with Latin as with Greek. Therefore the nearer my style came to his careless simplicity the closer it would be to the truth, for which alone I am bound to care under the circumstances and actually do care.

I confess, my dear Peter, that all these preparations relieved me of so much trouble that scarcely anything remained for me to do. Otherwise the gathering or the arrangement of the materials could have required a good deal of both time and application even from a talent neither the meanest nor the most ignorant. If it had been required that the matter be written down not only accurately but eloquently, I could not have performed the task with any amount of time or application. But, as it was, those cares over which I should have had to perspire so hard had been removed. Since it remained for me only to write out simply what I had heard, there was no difficulty about it.

Yet even to carry through this trifling task, my other tasks left me practically no leisure at all. I am constantly engaged in legal business, either pleading or hearing, either giving an award as arbiter or deciding a case as judge. I pay a visit of courtesy to one man and go on business to another. I devote almost the whole day in public to other men's affairs and the remainder to my own. I leave to myself, that is to learning, nothing at all.

When I have returned home, I must talk with my wife, chat with my children, and confer with my servants. All this activity I count as business when it must be done—and it must be unless you want to be a stranger in your own home. Besides, one must take care to be as agreeable as possible to those whom nature has supplied, or chance has made, or you yourself have chosen, to be the companions of your life, provided you do not spoil them by kindness, or through indulgence make masters out of your servants.

Amid these occupations that I have named, the day, the month, the year slip away. When, then, can we find time to write? Nor have I spoken a word about sleep, nor even of food, which for many people takes up as much time as sleep—and sleep takes up almost half a man's life! So I get for myself only the time I filch from sleep and food. Slowly, therefore, because this time is but little, yet finally, because this time *is* something, I have finished *Utopia* and sent it to you, my dear Peter, to read—and to remind me of anything that has escaped me.

2. More was made undersheriff of London in 1510, sitting as judge and representing the sheriff's cases in the city court. His friend Peter Giles (c. 1486–1533) was a classical scholar, a member of Erasmus's circle, and city clerk of Antwerp, where he oversaw commercial business.

3. Raphael Hythlodaeus, the fictional traveler who tells the character Sir Thomas More about Utopia.

In this respect I do not entirely distrust myself. (I only wish I were as good in intelligence and learning as I am not altogether deficient in memory!) Nevertheless, I am not so confident as to believe that I have forgotten nothing. As you know, John Clement,[4] my pupil-servant, was also present at the conversation. Indeed I do not allow him to absent himself from any talk which can be somewhat profitable, for from this young plant, seeing that it has begun to put forth green shoots in Greek and Latin literature, I expect no mean harvest some day. He has caused me to feel very doubtful on one point.

According to my own recollection, Hythlodaeus[5] declared that the bridge which spans the river Anydrus at Amaurotum is five hundred paces in length. But my John says that two hundred must be taken off, for the river there is not more than three hundred paces in breadth. Please recall the matter to mind. If you agree with him, I shall adopt the same view and think myself mistaken. If you do not remember, I shall put down, as I have actually done, what I myself seem to remember. Just as I shall take great pains to have nothing incorrect in the book, so, if there is doubt about anything, I shall rather tell an objective falsehood than an intentional lie—for I would rather be honest than wise.

Nevertheless, it would be easy for you to remedy this defect if you ask Raphael himself by word of mouth or by letter. You must do so on account of another doubt which has cropped up, whether more through my fault or through yours or Raphael's I do not know. We forgot to ask, and he forgot to say, in what part of the new world Utopia lies. I am sorry that point was omitted, and I would be willing to pay a considerable sum to purchase that information, partly because I am rather ashamed to be ignorant in what sea lies the island of which I am saying so much, partly because there are several among us, and one in particular, a devout man and a theologian by profession, burning with an extraordinary desire to visit Utopia. He does so not from an idle and curious lust for sight-seeing in new places but for the purpose of fostering and promoting our religion, begun there so felicitously.

To carry out his plan properly, he has made up his mind to arrange to be sent by the pope and, what is more, to be named bishop for the Utopians. He is in no way deterred by any scruple that he must sue for this prelacy, for he considers it a holy suit which proceeds not from any consideration of honor or gain but from motives of piety.

Therefore I beg you, my dear Peter, either by word of mouth if you conveniently can or by letter if he has gone, to reach Hythlodaeus and to make sure that my work includes nothing false and omits nothing true. I am inclined to think that it would be better to show him the book itself. No one else is so well able to correct any mistake, nor can he do this favor at all unless he reads through what I have written. In addition, in this way you will find out whether he accepts with pleasure or suffers with annoyance the fact that I have composed this work. If he himself has decided to put down in writing his own adventures, perhaps he may not want me to do so. By making known the commonwealth of Utopia, I should certainly dislike to forestall him and to rob his narrative of the flower and charm of novelty.

Nevertheless, to tell the truth, I myself have not yet made up my mind whether I shall publish it at all. So varied are the tastes of mortals, so peevish the characters of some, so ungrateful their dispositions, so wrongheaded their judgments, that those

4. John Clement (d. 1572), who tutored More's children, was also a distinguished humanist: a Reader at Oxford; co-editor of the first Greek edition of Galen (c. 130–200), a celebrated physician whose works on medicine remained authoritative through the early modern period; and physician to Henry VIII.

5. This reference introduces the play on Greek words that will characterize the description of Utopia in Book II. Hythlodaeus means "learned in nonsense"; the river Anydrus and the city Amaurotum mean "waterless" and "made dark or dim," respectively.

persons who pleasantly and blithely indulge their inclinations seem to be very much better off than those who torment themselves with anxiety in order to publish something that may bring profit or pleasure to others, who nevertheless receive it with disdain or ingratitude.

Very many men are ignorant of learning; many despise it. The barbarian rejects as harsh whatever is not positively barbarian. The smatterers despise as trite whatever is not packed with obsolete expressions. Some persons approve only of what is old; very many admire only their own work. This fellow is so grim that he will not hear of a joke; that fellow is so insipid that he cannot endure wit. Some are so dull-minded that they fear all satire as much as a man bitten by a mad dog fears water. Others are so fickle that sitting they praise one thing and standing another thing.

These persons sit in taverns, and over their cups criticize the talents of authors. With much pontificating, just as they please, they condemn each author by his writings, plucking each one, as it were, by the hair. They themselves remain under cover and, as the proverb goes, out of shot. They are so smooth and shaven that they present not even a hair of an honest man by which they might be caught.

Besides, others are so ungrateful that, though extremely delighted with the work, they do not love the author any the more. They are not unlike discourteous guests who, after they have been freely entertained at a rich banquet, finally go home well filled without thanking the host who invited them. Go now and provide a feast at your own expense for men of such dainty palate, of such varied taste, and of such unforgetful and grateful natures!

At any rate, my dear Peter, conduct with Hythlodaeus the business which I mentioned. Afterwards I shall be fully free to take fresh counsel on the subject. However, since I have gone through the labor of writing, it is too late for me to be wise now. Therefore, provided it be done with the consent of Hythlodaeus, in the matter of publishing which remains I shall follow my friends' advice, and yours first and foremost. Good-by, my sweetest friend, with your excellent wife. Love me as you have ever done, for I love you even more than I have ever done.

The Best State of a Commonwealth, The Discourse of the Extraordinary Character, Raphael Hythlodaeus, as Reported by the Renowned Figure, THOMAS MORE, Citizen and Sheriff of the Famous City of Great Britain, London

Book 1

The most invincible King of England, Henry, the eighth of that name, who is distinguished by all the accomplishments of a model monarch, had certain weighty matters[6] recently in dispute with His Serene Highness, Charles, Prince of Castile.[7] With

6. The "weighty matters" that took More to Flanders concerned the payment of tolls to Flemish ports by the English merchant fleet.

7. The future Charles I of Spain and Charles V, Holy Roman emperor; he ruled the Spanish kingdoms, Spanish America, Naples, Sicily, the Low Countries, and parts of Austria.

a view to their discussion and settlement, he sent me as a commissioner to Flanders—as a companion and associate of the peerless Cuthbert Tunstal, whom he has just created Master of the Rolls[8] to everyone's immense satisfaction. Of the latter's praises I shall say nothing, not because I fear that the testimony of a friend should be given little credit but because his integrity and learning are too great for it to be possible, and too well-known for it to be necessary, for me to extol them—unless I should wish to give the impression, as the proverb goes, of displaying the sun with a lamp!

We were met at Bruges, according to previous arrangement, by those men put in charge of the affair by the Prince—all outstanding persons. Their leader and head was the Burgomaster[9] of Bruges, a figure of magnificence, but their chief speaker and guiding spirit was Georges de Themsecke,[1] Provost of Cassel, a man not only trained in eloquence but a natural orator—most learned, too, in the law and consummately skillful in diplomacy by native ability as well as by long experience. When after one or two meetings there were certain points on which we could not agree sufficiently, they bade farewell to us for some days and left for Brussels to seek an official pronouncement from the Prince.

Meanwhile, as my business led me, I made my way to Antwerp. While I stayed there, among my other visitors, but of all of them the most welcome, was Peter Giles, a native of Antwerp, an honorable man of high position in his home town yet worthy of the very highest position, being a young man distinguished equally by learning and character; for he is most virtuous and most cultured, to all most courteous, but to his friends so open-hearted, affectionate, loyal, and sincere that you can hardly find one or two anywhere to compare with him as the perfect friend on every score. His modesty is uncommon; no one is less given to deceit, and none has a wiser simplicity of nature. Besides, in conversation he is so polished and so witty without offense that his delightful society and charming discourse largely took away my nostalgia and made me less conscious than before of the separation from my home, wife, and children to whom I was exceedingly anxious to get back, for I had then been more than four months away.

One day I had been at divine service in Notre Dame, the finest church in the city and the most crowded with worshippers. Mass being over, I was about to return to my lodging when I happened to see him in conversation with a stranger, a man of advanced years, with sunburnt countenance and long beard and cloak hanging carelessly from his shoulder, while his appearance and dress seemed to me to be those of a ship's captain.

When Peter had espied me, he came up and greeted me. As I tried to return his salutation, he drew me a little aside and, pointing to the man I had seen him talking with, said:

"Do you see this fellow? I was on the point of taking him straight to you."

"He would have been very welcome," said I, "for your sake."

"No," said he, "for his own, if you knew him. There is no mortal alive today who can give you such an account of unknown peoples and lands, a subject about which I know you are always most greedy to hear."

"Well, then," said I, "my guess was not a bad one. The moment I saw him, I was sure he was a ship's captain."

8. The principal clerk of the Chancery Court, a court of appeals from decisions by the common-law courts.
9. Mayor.

1. A Flemish diplomat, employed on numerous missions, who died in 1536.

"But you are quite mistaken," said he, "for his sailing has not been like that of Palinurus but that of Ulysses or, rather, of Plato.[2] Now this Raphael—for such is his personal name, with Hythlodaeus as his family name—is no bad Latin scholar, and most learned in Greek. He had studied that language more than Latin because he had devoted himself unreservedly to philosophy, and in that subject he found that there is nothing valuable in Latin except certain treatises of Seneca and Cicero.[3] He left his patrimony at home—he is a Portuguese—to his brothers, and, being eager to see the world, joined Amerigo Vespucci[4] and was his constant companion in the last three of those four voyages which are now universally read of, but on the final voyage he did not return with him. He importuned and even wrested from Amerigo permission to be one of the twenty-four who at the farthest point of the last voyage were left behind in the fort. And so he was left behind that he might have his way, being more anxious for travel than about the grave. These two sayings are constantly on his lips: 'He who has no grave is covered by the sky,' and 'From all places it is the same distance to heaven.' This attitude of his, but for the favor of God, would have cost him dear.[5] However, when after Vespucci's departure he had traveled through many countries with five companions from the fort, by strange chance he was carried to Ceylon, whence he reached Calicut.[6] There he conveniently found some Portuguese ships, and at length arrived home again, beyond all expectation."

When Peter had rendered this account, I thanked him for his kindness in taking such pains that I might have a talk with one whose conversation he hoped would give me pleasure; then I turned to Raphael. After we had greeted each other and exchanged the civilities which commonly pass at the first meeting of strangers, we went off to my house. There in the garden, on a bench covered with turfs of grass, we sat down to talk together.

He recounted how, after the departure of Vespucci, he and his friends who had stayed behind in the fort began by degrees through continued meetings and civilities to ingratiate themselves with the natives till they not only stood in no danger from them but were actually on friendly terms and, moreover, were in good repute and favor with a ruler (whose name and country I have forgotten). Through the latter's generosity, he and his five companions were supplied with ample provision and travel resources and, moreover, with a trusty guide on their journey (which was partly by water on rafts and partly over land by wagon) to take them to other rulers with careful recommendations to their favor. For, after traveling many days, he said, they found towns and cities and very populous commonwealths with excellent institutions.

To be sure, under the equator and on both sides of the line nearly as far as the sun's orbit extends, there lie waste deserts scorched with continual heat. A gloomy and dismal region looms in all directions without cultivation or attractiveness, inhabited by wild beasts and snakes or, indeed, men no less savage and harmful than

2. Palinurus: the pilot of the ship sailed by Aeneas from Troy to Italy in Virgil's *Aeneid;* he fell overboard while sleeping at the helm. Ulysses: the Latin name for Odysseus, the hero of Homer's epic poem, the *Odyssey*, who returns to his kingdom, Ithaka, after years of wandering. Plato: the Greek philosopher who is said to have traveled throughout the Mediterranean world.

3. Two Roman writers who composed works on moral and political philosophy.

4. Florentine merchant adventurer (1451–1512), whose accounts of his voyages to the New World were reprinted in many editions.

5. More's paraphrases of two classical authors indicate his humanist training. From Lucan's epic *Pharsalia* he takes: "Mother Earth has room for all her children, and he who lacks an urn has the sky to cover him" (8.819); and from Cicero's *Tusculan Disputations* he takes: "There is a fine remark of Anaxagoras. He was dying at Lampasacus, and his friends asked if he wanted to be taken home. . . . 'There's no need,' he said, 'it's the same distance from anywhere to the underworld'" (1.43.104).

6. Seaport on the west coast of India.

are the beasts. But when you have gone a little farther, the country gradually assumes a milder aspect, the climate is less fierce, the ground is covered with a pleasant green herbage, and the nature of living creatures becomes less wild. At length you reach peoples, cities, and towns which maintain a continual traffic by sea and land not only with each other and their neighbors but also with far-off countries.

Then they had opportunity of visiting many countries in all directions, for every ship which was got ready for any voyage made him and his companions welcome as passengers. The ships they saw in the parts first traveled were flat-bottomed and moved under sails made of papyrus or osiers[7] stitched together and sometimes under sails made of leather. Afterwards they found ships with pointed keels and canvas sails, in fact, like our own in all respects.

Their mariners were skilled in adapting themselves to sea and weather. But he reported that he won their extraordinary favor by showing them the use of the magnetic needle[8] of which they had hitherto been quite ignorant so that they had hesitated to trust themselves to the sea and had boldly done so in the summer only. Now, trusting to the magnet, they do not fear wintry weather, being dangerously confident. Thus, there is a risk that what was thought likely to be a great benefit to them may, through their imprudence, cause them great mischief.

What he said he saw in each place would be a long tale to unfold and is not the purpose of this work. Perhaps on another occasion we shall tell his story, particularly whatever facts would be useful to readers, above all, those wise and prudent provisions which he noticed anywhere among nations living together in a civilized way. For on these subjects we eagerly inquired of him, and he no less readily discoursed; but about stale travelers' wonders we were not curious. Scyllas and greedy Celaenos and folk-devouring Laestrygones[9] and similar frightful monsters are common enough, but well and wisely trained citizens are not everywhere to be found.

To be sure, just as he called attention to many ill-advised customs among these new nations, so he rehearsed not a few points from which our own cities, nations, races, and kingdoms may take example for the correction of their errors. These instances, as I said, I must mention on another occasion. Now I intend to relate merely what he told us of the manners and customs of the Utopians, first, however, giving the talk which drew and led him on to mention that commonwealth.

Raphael had touched with much wisdom on faults in this hemisphere and that, of which he found very many in both, and had compared the wiser measures which had been taken among us as well as among them; for he remembered the manners and customs of each nation as if he had lived all his life in places which he had only visited. Peter expressed his surprise at the man as follows:

"Why, my dear Raphael, I wonder that you do not attach yourself to some king. I am sure there is none of them to whom you would not be very welcome because you are capable not only of entertaining a king with this learning and experience of men and places but also of furnishing him with examples and of assisting him with counsel. Thus, you would not only serve your own interests excellently but be of great assistance in the advancement of all your relatives and friends."

"As for my relatives and friends," he replied, "I am not greatly troubled about them, for I think I have fairly well performed my duty to them already. The possessions, which other men do not resign unless they are old and sick and even then

7. Papyrus: reed paper. Osiers: willow twigs.
8. Compass.
9. Fabulous monsters from the *Odyssey* and the *Aeneid:* Scylla is a six-headed sea monster; Celaeno, a harpy, is a bird with a woman's face; the Lestrygonians were gigantic cannibals.

resign unwillingly when incapable of retention, I divided among my relatives and friends when I was not merely hale and hearty but actually young. I think they ought to be satisfied with this generosity from me and not to require or expect additionally that I should, for their sakes, enter into servitude to kings."

"Fine words!" declared Peter. "I meant not that you should be in servitude but in service to kings."

"The one is only one syllable less than the other," he observed.

"But my conviction is," continued Peter, "whatever name you give to this mode of life, that it is the very way by which you can not only profit people both as private individuals and as members of the commonwealth but also render your own condition more prosperous."

"Should I," said Raphael, "make it more prosperous by a way which my soul abhors? As it is, I now live as I please, which I surely fancy is very seldom the case with your grand courtiers. Nay, there are plenty of persons who court the friendship of the great, and so you need not think it a great loss if they have to do without me and one or two others like me."

"Well," I then said, "it is plain that you, my dear Raphael, are desirous neither of riches nor of power. Assuredly, I reverence and look up to a man of your mind no whit less than to any of those who are most high and mighty. But it seems to me you will do what is worthy of you and of this generous and truly philosophic spirit of yours if you so order your life as to apply your talent and industry to the public interest, even if it involves some personal disadvantages to yourself. This you can never do with as great profit as if you are councilor to some great monarch and make him follow, as I am sure you will, straightforward and honorable courses. From the monarch, as from a never-failing spring, flows a stream of all that is good or evil over the whole nation. You possess such complete learning that, even had you no great experience of affairs, and such great experience of affairs that, even had you no learning, you would make an excellent member of any king's council."

"You are twice mistaken, my dear More," said he, "first in me and then in the matter in question. I have no such ability as you ascribe to me and, if I had ever so much, still, in disturbing my own peace and quiet, I should not promote the public interest. In the first place almost all monarchs prefer to occupy themselves in the pursuits of war—with which I neither have nor desire any acquaintance—rather than in the honorable activities of peace, and they care much more how, by hook or by crook, they may win fresh kingdoms than how they may administer well what they have got.

"In the second place, among royal councilors everyone is actually so wise as to have no need of profiting by another's counsel, or everyone seems so wise in his own eyes as not to condescend to profit by it, save that they agree with the most absurd sayings of, and play the parasite to, the chief royal favorites whose friendliness they strive to win by flattery. To be sure, it is but human nature that each man favor his own discoveries most—just as the crow and the monkey like their own off-spring best.

"If anyone, when in the company of people who are jealous of others' discoveries or prefer their own, should propose something which he either has read of as done in other times or has seen done in other places, the listeners behave as if their whole reputation for wisdom were jeopardized and as if afterwards they would deserve to be thought plain blockheads unless they could lay hold of something to find fault with in the discoveries of others. When all other attempts fail, their last resource is a remark such as this: 'Our forefathers were happy with that sort of thing, and would to heaven we had their wisdom.' And then, as if that comment were a brilliant conclusion to the whole business, they take their seats—implying, of course, that it would be a dangerous thing to be found with more wisdom on any point than our forefathers. And yet, no matter what excellent ideas our forefathers may have had, we very serenely bid them a curt farewell. But if in any situation they failed to take the wiser course, that defect gives us a handle which we greedily grab and never let go. Such proud, ridiculous, and obstinate prejudices I have encountered often in other places and once in England too."

"What," I asked, "were you ever in our country?"

"Yes," he answered, "I spent several months there, not long after the disastrous end of the insurrection of western Englishmen against the king, which was put down with their pitiful slaughter.[1] During that time I was much indebted to the Right Reverend Father, John Cardinal Morton, Archbishop of Canterbury, and then also Lord Chancellor of England.[2] He was a man, my dear Peter (for More knows about him and needs no information from me), who deserved respect as much for his prudence and virtue as for his authority. He was of middle stature and showed no sign of his advanced age. His countenance inspired respect rather than fear. In conversation he was agreeable, though serious and dignified. Of those who made suit to him he enjoyed making trial by rough address, but in a harmless way, to see what mettle and what presence of mind a person would manifest. Provided it did not amount to impudence, such behavior gave him pleasure as being akin to his own disposition and excited his admiration as being suited to those holding public office. His speech was polished and pointed. His knowledge of law was profound, his ability incomparable, and his memory astonishingly retentive, for he had improved his extraordinary natural qualities by learning and practice.

"The king placed the greatest confidence in his advice, and the commonwealth seemed much to depend upon him when I was there. As one might expect, almost in earliest youth he had been taken straight from school to court, had spent his whole life in important public affairs, and had sustained numerous and varied vicissitudes of fortune, so that by many and great dangers he had acquired a statesman's sagacity which, when thus learned, is not easily forgotten.

"It happened one day that I was at his table when a layman, learned in the laws of your country, was present. Availing himself of some opportunity or other, he began to speak punctiliously of the strict justice which was then dealt out to thieves. They were everywhere executed, he reported, as many as twenty at a time being hanged on one gallows, and added that he wondered all the more, though so few escaped execution, by what bad luck the whole country was still infested with them. I dared be free in expressing my opinions without reserve at the Cardinal's table, so I said to him:

"'You need not wonder, for this manner of punishing thieves goes beyond justice and is not for the public good. It is too harsh a penalty for theft and yet is not a sufficient deterrent. Theft alone is not a grave offense that ought to be punished with death, and no penalty that can be devised is sufficient to restrain from acts of robbery those who have no other means of getting a livelihood. In this respect not your country alone but a great part of our world resembles bad schoolmasters, who would rather

1. In 1497 the people of Cornwall rebelled against taxation by the crown; they were defeated by the king's army outside London, in the Battle of Blackheath.

2. More served for two years as a page in the household of Cardinal Morton (1420–1500).

beat than teach their scholars. You ordain grievous and terrible punishments for a thief when it would have been much better to provide some means of getting a living, that no one should be under this terrible necessity first of stealing and then of dying for it.'

"'We have,' said the fellow, 'made sufficient provision for this situation. There are manual crafts. There is farming. They might maintain themselves by these pursuits if they did not voluntarily prefer to be rascals.'

"'No,' I countered, 'you shall not escape so easily. We shall say nothing of those who often come home crippled from foreign or civil wars, as recently with you Englishmen from the battle with the Cornishmen and not long ago from the war in France.[3] They lose their limbs in the service of the commonwealth or of the king, and their disability prevents them from exercising their own crafts, and their age from learning a new one. Of these men, I say, we shall take no account because wars come sporadically, but let us consider what happens every day.

"'Now there is the great number of noblemen who not only live idle themselves like drones on the labors of others, as for instance the tenants of their estates whom they fleece to the utmost by increasing the returns[4] (for that is the only economy they know of, being otherwise so extravagant as to bring themselves to beggary!) but who also carry about with them a huge crowd of idle attendants who have never learned a trade for a livelihood. As soon as their master dies or they themselves fall sick, these men are turned out at once, for the idle are maintained more readily than the sick, and often the heir is not able to support as large a household as his father did, at any rate at first.

"'In the meantime the fellows devote all their energies to starving, if they do not to robbing. Indeed what can they do? When by a wandering life they have worn out their clothes a little, and their health to boot, sickly and ragged as they are, no gentleman deigns to engage them and the farmers dare not do so either. The latter know full well that a man who has been softly brought up in idleness and luxury and has been wont[5] in sword and buckler to look down with a swaggering face on the whole neighborhood and to think himself far above everybody will hardly be fit to render honest service to a poor man with spade and hoe, for a scanty wage, and on frugal fare.'

"'But this,' the fellow retorted, 'is just the sort of man we ought to encourage most. On them, being men of a loftier and nobler spirit than craftsmen and farmers, depend the strength and sinews of our army when we have to wage war.'

"'Of course,' said I, 'you might as well say that for the sake of war we must foster thieves. As long as you have these men, you will certainly never be without thieves. Nay, robbers do not make the least active soldiers, nor do soldiers make the most listless robbers, so well do these two pursuits agree. But this defect, though frequent with you, is not peculiar to you, for it is common to almost all peoples.

"'France in particular is troubled with another more grievous plague. Even in peacetime (if you can call it peacetime) the whole country is crowded and beset with mercenaries hired because the French follow the train of thought you Englishmen take in judging it a good thing to keep idle retainers. These wiseacres think that the public safety depends on having always in readiness a strong and reliable garrison, chiefly of veterans, for they have not the least confidence in tyros.[6] This attitude

3. Hythlodaeus refers to actual battles at Dixmude in 1489 and in Boulogne in 1492.
4. Rents.
5. Accustomed.
6. Raw recruits.

obliges them always to be seeking for a pretext for war just so they may not have soldiers without experience, and men's throats must be cut without cause lest, to use Sallust's witty saying, "the hand or the mind through lack of practice become dulled." Yet how dangerous it is to rear such wild beasts France has learned to its cost, and the examples of Rome, Carthage, Syria, and many other nations show.[7] Not only the supreme authority of the latter countries but their land and even their cities have been more than once destroyed by their own standing armies.

"'Now, how unnecessary it is to maintain them is clearly proved by this consideration: not even the French soldiers, assiduously trained in arms from infancy, can boast that they have very often got the better of it face to face with your draftees.[8] Let me say no more for fear of seeming to flatter you barefacedly. At any rate, your town-bred craftsmen or your rough and clodhopper farmers are not supposed to be much afraid of those idle attendants on gentlemen, except those of the former whose build of body is unfitted for strength and bravery or those whose stalwart spirit is broken by lack of support for their family. Consequently there is no danger that those attendants whose bodies, once strong and vigorous (for it is only the picked men that gentlemen deign to corrupt), are now either weakened by idleness or softened by almost womanish occupations, should become unmanned if trained to earn their living in honest trades and exercised in virile labors!

"'However the case may be, it seems to me by no means profitable to the common weal to keep for the emergency of a war a vast multitude of such people as trouble and disturb the peace. You never have war unless you choose it, and you ought to take far more account of peace than of war. Yet this is not the only situation that makes thieving necessary. There is another which, as I believe, is more special to you Englishmen.'

"'What is that?' asked the Cardinal.

"'Your sheep,' I answered, 'which are usually so tame and so cheaply fed, begin now, according to report, to be so greedy and wild that they devour human beings themselves and devastate and depopulate fields, houses, and towns.[9] In all those parts of the realm where the finest and therefore costliest wool is produced, there are noblemen, gentlemen, and even some abbots, though otherwise holy men, who are not satisfied with the annual revenues and profits which their predecessors used to derive from their estates. They are not content, by leading an idle and sumptuous life, to do no good to their country; they must also do it positive harm. They leave no ground to be tilled; they enclose every bit of land for pasture; they pull down houses and destroy towns, leaving only the church to pen the sheep in. And, as if enough of your land were not wasted on ranges and preserves of game, those good fellows turn all human habitations and all cultivated land into a wilderness.

"'Consequently, in order that one insatiable glutton and accursed plague of his native land may join field to field and surround many thousand acres with one fence, tenants are evicted. Some of them, either circumvented by fraud or overwhelmed by violence, are stripped even of their own property, or else, wearied by unjust acts, are driven to sell. By hook or by crook the poor wretches are compelled to leave their

7. The Romans, Carthaginians, and Syrians used mercenary armies but suffered mutinies as a result.
8. Hythlodaeus refers to English soldiers who won victories over French forces in such battles as Crecy (1346), Poitiers (1356), and Agincourt (1415).
9. Hythlodaeus criticizes the management of the English wool trade. The potential for profit from sheep's wool led landlords to fence off or enclose vast open spaces that had previously been shared in common and farmed by peasants. Many of these displaced people sought work in the cities or became migrant day-laborers throughout the country.

homes—men and women, husbands and wives, orphans and widows, parents with little children and a household not rich but numerous, since farm work requires many hands. Away they must go, I say, from the only homes familiar and known to them, and they find no shelter to go to. All their household goods which would not fetch a great price if they could wait for a purchaser, since they must be thrust out, they sell for a trifle.

"'After they have soon spent that trifle in wandering from place to place, what remains for them but to steal and be hanged—justly, you may say!—or to wander and beg. And yet even in the latter case they are cast into prison as vagrants for going about idle when, though they most eagerly offer their labor, there is no one to hire them. For there is no farm work, to which they have been trained, to be had, when there is no land for plowing left. A single shepherd or herdsman is sufficient for grazing livestock on that land for whose cultivation many hands were once required to make it raise crops.

"'A result of this situation is that the price of food has risen steeply in many localities. Indeed, the price of raw wools has climbed so high that your poor people who used to make cloth cannot possibly buy them, and so great numbers are driven from work into idleness. One reason is that, after the great increase in pasture land, a plague carried off a vast multitude of sheep as though God were punishing greed by sending upon the sheep a murrain[1]—which should have fallen on the owners' heads more justly! But, however much the number of sheep increases, their price does not decrease a farthing because, though you cannot brand that a monopoly which is a sale by more than one person, yet their sale is certainly an oligopoly,[2] for all sheep have come into the hands of a few men, and those already rich, who are not obligated to sell before they wish and who do not wish until they get the price they ask.

"'By this time all other kinds of livestock are equally high-priced on the same account and still more so, for the reason that, with the pulling down of farmsteads and the lessening of farming, none are left to devote themselves to the breeding of stock. These rich men will not rear young cattle as they do lambs, but they buy them lean and cheap abroad and then, after they are fattened in their pastures, sell them again at a high price. In my estimation, the whole mischief of this system has not yet been felt. Thus far, the dealers raise the prices only where the cattle are sold, but when, for some time, they have been removing them from other localities faster than they can be bred there, then, as the supply gradually diminishes in the markets where they are purchased, great scarcity must needs be here.

"'Thus, the unscrupulous greed of a few is ruining the very thing by virtue of which your island was once counted fortunate in the extreme. For the high price of food is causing everyone to get rid of as many of his household as possible, and what, I ask, have they to do but to beg, or—a course more readily embraced by men of mettle—to become robbers?

"'In addition, alongside this wretched need and poverty you find wanton luxury. Not only the servants of noblemen but the craftsmen and almost the clodhoppers themselves, in fact all classes alike, are given to much ostentatious sumptuousness of dress and to excessive indulgence at table. Do not dives, brothels, and those other places as bad as brothels, to wit, taverns, wine shops and ale-houses—do not all those crooked games of chance, dice, cards, backgammon, ball, bowling, and quoits, soon drain the purses of their votaries[3] and send them off to rob someone?

1. A disease of livestock.
2. Control of a commercial market by a small number of companies or merchants.
3. Devotees.

"'Cast out these ruinous plagues. Make laws that the destroyers of farmsteads and country villages should either restore them or hand them over to people who will restore them and who are ready to build. Restrict this right of rich individuals to buy up everything and this license to exercise a kind of monopoly for themselves. Let fewer be brought up in idleness. Let farming be resumed and let cloth-working be restored once more that there may be honest jobs to employ usefully that idle throng, whether those whom hitherto pauperism has made thieves or those who, now being vagrants or lazy servants, in either case are likely to turn out thieves. Assuredly, unless you remedy these evils, it is useless for you to boast of the justice you execute in the punishment of theft. Such justice is more showy than really just or beneficial. When you allow your youths to be badly brought up and their characters, even from early years, to become more and more corrupt, to be punished, of course, when, as grown-up men, they commit the crimes which from boyhood they have shown every prospect of committing, what else, I ask, do you do but first create thieves and then become the very agents of their punishment?'

"Even while I was saying these things, the lawyer had been busily preparing himself to reply and had determined to adopt the usual method of disputants who are more careful to repeat what has been said than to answer it, so highly do they regard their memory.

"'Certainly, sir,' he began, 'you have spoken well, considering that you are but a stranger who could hear something of these matters rather than get exact knowledge of them—a statement which I shall make plain in a few words. First, I shall repeat, in order, what you have said; then I shall show in what respects ignorance of our conditions has deceived you; finally I shall demolish and destroy all your arguments. So, to begin with what I promised first, on four points you seemed to me—'

"'Hold your peace,' interrupted the Cardinal, 'for you hardly seem about to reply in a few words if you begin thus. So we shall relieve you of the trouble of making your answer now, but we shall reserve your right unimpaired till your next meeting, which I should like to set for tomorrow, provided neither you nor Raphael here is hindered by other business.

"'But now I am eager to have you tell me, my dear Raphael, why you think that theft ought not to be punished with the extreme penalty, or what other penalty you yourself would fix, which would be more beneficial to the public. I am sure that not even you think it ought to go unpunished. Even as it is, with death as the penalty, men still rush into stealing. What force and what fear, if they once were sure of their lives, could deter the criminals? They would regard themselves as much invited to crime by the mitigation of the penalty as if a reward were offered.'

"'Certainly,' I answered, 'most reverend and kind Father, I think it altogether unjust that a man should suffer the loss of his life for the loss of someone's money. In my opinion, not all the goods that fortune can bestow on us can be set in the scale against a man's life. If they say that this penalty is attached to the offense against justice and the breaking of the laws, hardly to the money stolen, one may well characterize this extreme justice as extreme wrong. For we ought not to approve such stern Manlian rules of law[4] as would justify the immediate drawing of the sword when they

4. Manlius Torquatus, a Roman general of the 4th century B.C., who, having made a law against single encounters, executed his own son for fighting and defeating an enemy warrior.

are disobeyed in trifles nor such Stoical[5] ordinances as count all offenses equal so that there is no difference between killing a man and robbing him of a coin when, if equity has any meaning, there is no similarity or connection between the two cases.[6]

"'God has said, "Thou shalt not kill," and shall we so lightly kill a man for taking a bit of small change? But if the divine command against killing be held not to apply where human law justifies killing, what prevents men equally from arranging with one another how far rape, adultery, and perjury are admissible? God has withdrawn from man the right to take not only another's life but his own. Now, men by mutual consent agree on definite cases where they may take the life of one another. But if this agreement among men is to have such force as to exempt their henchmen from the obligation of the commandment, although without any precedent set by God they take the life of those who have been ordered by human enactment to be put to death, will not the law of God then be valid only so far as the law of man permits? The result will be that in the same way men will determine in everything how far it suits them that God's commandments should be obeyed.

"'Finally, the law of Moses,[7] though severe and harsh—being intended for slaves, and those a stubborn breed—nevertheless punished theft by fine and not by death. Let us not suppose that God, in the new law of mercy in which He gives commands as a father to his sons, has allowed us greater license to be cruel to one another.

"'These are the reasons why I think this punishment unlawful. Besides, surely everyone knows how absurd and even dangerous to the commonwealth it is that a thief and a murderer should receive the same punishment. Since the robber sees that he is in as great danger if merely condemned for theft as if he were convicted of murder as well, this single consideration impels him to murder the man whom otherwise he would only have robbed. In addition to the fact that he is in no greater danger if caught, there is greater safety in putting the man out of the way and greater hope of covering up the crime if he leaves no one left to tell the tale. Thus, while we endeavor to terrify thieves with excessive cruelty, we urge them on to the destruction of honest citizens.

"'As to the repeated question about a more advisable form of punishment, in my judgment it is much easier to find a better than a worse. Why should we doubt that a good way of punishing crimes is the one which we know long found favor of old with the Romans, the greatest experts in managing the commonwealth? When men were convicted of atrocious crimes they condemned them for life to stone quarries and to digging in metal mines, and kept them constantly in chains.

"'Yet, as concerns this matter, I can find no better system in any country than that which, in the course of my travels, I observed in Persia among the people commonly called the Polylerites,[8] a nation that is large and well-governed and, except that it pays an annual tribute to the Persian padishah [emperor], otherwise free and autonomous in its laws. They are far from the sea, almost ringed round by mountains, and satisfied with the products of their own land, which is in no way infertile. In consequence they rarely pay visits to other countries or receive them. In accordance with their long-standing national policy, they do not try to enlarge their territory and easily protect what they have from all aggression by their mountains and by the tribute

5. Austere.

6. Hythlodaeus alludes to an important feature of the law: Cases in which the law invoked to cover them is too general to do justice to their complexity are decided by addressing the circumstances in which the alleged violation was committed, the condition of the disputants, and the remedies apart from the law that might serve to settle the case. Such a mitigated justice was known as equity.

7. The Decalogue or Ten Commandments, one of which is "Thou shalt not kill" (Exodus 20.13).

8. "People of Much Nonsense."

paid to their overlord. Being completely free from militarism, they live a life more comfortable than splendid and more happy than renowned or famous, for even their name, I think, is hardly known except to their immediate neighbors.

"'Now, in their land, persons who are convicted of theft repay to the owner what they have taken from him, not, as is usual elsewhere, to the prince, who, they consider, has as little right to the thing stolen as the thief himself. But if the object is lost, the value is made up out of the thieves' goods, and the balance is then paid intact to their wives and children. They themselves are condemned to hard labor. Unless the theft is outrageous, they neither are confined to prison nor wear shackles about their feet but, without any bonds or restraints, are set to public works. Convicts who refuse to labor or are slack are not put in chains but urged on by the lash. If they do a good day's work, they need fear no insult or injury. The only check is that every night, after their names are called over, they are locked in their sleeping quarters.

"'Except for the constant toil, their life has no hardship. For example, as serviceable to the common weal, they are fed well at the public's expense, the mode varying from place to place. In some parts, what is spent on them is raised by almsgiving. Though this method is precarious, the Polylerite people are so kindhearted that no other is found to supply the need more plentifully. In other parts, fixed public revenues are set aside to defray the cost. Elsewhere, all pay a specified personal tax for these purposes. Yes, and in some localities the convicts do no work for the community, but, whenever a private person needs a hired laborer, he secures in the market place a convict's service for that day at a fixed wage, a bit lower than what he would have paid for free labor. Moreover, the employer is permitted to chastise with stripes a hired man if he be lazy. The result is that they are never out of work and that each one, besides earning his own living, brings in something every day to the public treasury.

"'All of them wear clothes of a color not worn by anyone else. Their hair is not shaved but cropped a little above the ears, from one of which the tip is cut off. Food and drink and clothes of the proper color may be given them by their friends. The gift of money is a capital offense, both for the donor and the receiver. It is no less dangerous for a free man to receive a penny for any reason from a condemned person, or for slaves (which is the name borne by the convicts) to touch weapons. The slaves of each district are distinguished by a special badge, which it is a capital offense to throw away, as it is to appear beyond their own bounds or to talk to a slave from another district. Further, it is no safer to plot escape than actually to run away. Yes, and the punishment for connivance in such a plan is death for the slave and slavery for the free man. On the other hand, rewards are appointed for an informer: money for a free man, liberty for a slave, and pardon and immunity for both for their complicity. The purpose is never to make it safer to follow out an evil plan than to repent of it.

"'This is the law and this the procedure in the matter, as I have described it to you. You can easily see how humane and advantageous it is. The object of public anger is to destroy the vices but to save the persons and so to treat them that they necessarily become good and that, for the rest of their lives, they repair all the damage done before.

"'Further, so little is it to be feared that they may sink back into their old evil ways, even travelers who have to go on a journey think themselves most safe if they secure as guides these slaves, who are changed with each new district. For the latter have nothing suitable with which to commit robbery. They bear no arms; money would merely insure the detection of the crime; punishment awaits the man who is caught; and there is absolutely no hope of escaping to a safe place. How could a man so cover his flight as to elude observation when he resembles ordinary people in no part of his attire—unless he were to run away naked? Even then his ear would betray him in his flight!

"'But, of course, would there not at least be risk of their taking counsel together and conspiring against the commonwealth? As if any district could conceive a hope of success without having first sounded and seduced the slave gangs of many other districts! The latter are so little able to conspire together that they may not even meet and converse or greet one another. Much less will they boldly divulge to their own fellow slaves the plot, which they know is dangerous to those concealing it and very profitable to those betraying it. On the other hand, no one is quite without hope of gaining his freedom eventually if he accepts his punishment in a spirit of obedience and resignation and gives evidence of reforming his future life; indeed, every year a number of them are granted their liberty which they have merited by their submissive behavior.'

"When I had finished this speech, I added that I saw no reason why this method might not be adopted even in England and be far more beneficial in its working than the justice which my legal opponent had praised so highly. The lawyer replied: 'Never could that system be established in England without involving the commonwealth in a very serious crisis.' In the act of making this statement, he shook his head and made a wry face and so fell silent. And all who were present gave him their assent.

"Then the Cardinal remarked: 'It is not easy to guess whether it would turn out well or ill inasmuch as absolutely no experiment has been made. If, after pronouncement of the sentence of death, the king were to order the postponement of its execution and, after limitation of the privileges of sanctuary,[9] were to try this system, then, if success proved its usefulness, it would be right to make the system law. In case of failure, then and there to put to death those previously condemned would be no less for the public good and no more unjust than if execution were done here and now. In the meantime no danger can come of the experiment. Furthermore, I am sure that vagrants might very well be treated in the same way for, in spite of repeated legislation against them, we have made no progress.'

"When the Cardinal had finished speaking, they all vied in praising what they all had received with contempt when suggested by me, but especially the part relating to vagrants because this was the Cardinal's addition.

"I am at a loss as to whether it were better to suppress what followed next, for it was quite absurd. But I shall relate it since it was not evil in itself and had some bearing on the matter in question.

"There happened to be present a hanger-on, who wanted to give the impression of imitating a jester but whose imitation was too close to the real thing. His ill-timed witticisms were meant to raise a laugh, but he himself was more often the object of laughter than his jests. The fellow, however, sometimes let fall observations which were to the point, thus proving the proverb true, that if a man throws the dice often he will sooner or later make a lucky throw. One of the guests happened to say:

"'Raphael's proposal has made good provision for thieves. The Cardinal has taken precautions also for vagrants. It only remains now that public measures be devised for persons whom sickness or old age has brought to want and made unable to work for their living.'

9. From the 7th century until the Reformation, English churches and sometimes their surrounding precincts provided limited asylum for fugitives from judicial authority.

"'Give me leave,' volunteered the hanger-on. 'I shall see that this situation, too, be set right. I am exceedingly anxious to get this sort of person out of my sight. They have often harassed me with their pitiful whinings in begging for money—though they never could pitch a tune which would get a coin out of my pocket. For one of two things always happens: either I do not want to give or I cannot, since I have nothing to give. Now they have begun to be wise. When they see me pass by, they say nothing and spare their pains. They no longer expect anything from me—no more, by heaven, than if I were a secular priest! As for me, I should have a law passed that all those beggars be distributed and divided among the Benedictine monasteries and that the men be made so-called lay brothers.[1] The women I should order to become nuns.'

"The Cardinal smiled and passed it off in jest, but the rest took it in earnest. Now a certain theologian who was a friar[2] was so delighted by this jest at the expense of secular priests and of monks that he also began to make merry, though generally he was serious almost to the point of being dour.

"'Nay,' said he, 'not even so will you be rid of mendicants unless you make provision for us friars too.'

"'But this has been taken care of already,' retorted the hanger-on. 'His Eminence made excellent provision for you when he determined that tramps should be confined and made to work, for you are the worst tramps of all.'

"When the company, looking at the Cardinal, saw that he did not think this jest any more amiss than the other, they all proceeded to take it up with vigor—but not the friar. He—and I do not wonder—deluged by these taunts, began to be so furious and enraged that he could not hold back even from abusing the joker. He called him a rascal, a slanderer, and a 'son of perdition,' quoting the while terrible denunciations out of Holy Scripture. Now the scoffer began to scoff in earnest and was quite in his element:

"'Be not angry, good friar. It is written: "In your patience shall you possess your souls."'[3]

"Then the friar rejoined—I shall repeat his very words: 'I am not angry, you gallows bird, or at least I do not sin, for the psalmist says: "Be angry, and sin not."'[4]

"At this point the Cardinal gently admonished the friar to calm his emotions, but he replied:

"'No, my lord, I speak motivated only by a good zeal—as I should. For holy men have had a good zeal; wherefore Scripture says, "The zeal of Thy house has eaten me up,"[5] and churches resound with the hymn: "The mockers of Eliseus[6] as he went up to the house of God felt the zeal of the baldhead"—just as this mocking, scorning, ribald fellow will perhaps feel it.'

"'Maybe,' said the Cardinal, 'you behave with proper feeling, but I think that you would act, if not more holily, at any rate more wisely, if you would not set your wits against those of a silly fellow and provoke a foolish duel with a fool.'

1. Members of the regular religious orders who performed manual labor and sometimes administrative or temporal functions within the monastery. They were distinct from those men who had taken monastic vows and devoted their lives entirely to following the word of God.
2. Friars were members of the mendicant orders who lived solely off alms in return for their prayers and preaching.
3. Luke 21.19.
4. Psalms 4.4.
5. Psalms 69.9.
6. Elisha, the son of the prophet Elijah. Hythlodaeus refers to a hymn ascribed to the medieval writer Adam of St. Victor. It alludes to the story of Elisha, who, when mocked by children for his baldness, curses them "in the name of the Lord"; this causes two bears to emerge from the woods and rip forty-two of the children to pieces (2 Kings 2.23–4).

"'No, my lord,' he replied, 'I should not do more wisely. Solomon himself, the wisest of men, says: "Answer a fool according to his folly"[7]—as I do now. I am showing him the pit into which he will fall if he does not take good heed, for, if many scorners of Eliseus, who numbered only one baldhead, felt the zeal of the baldhead, how much more will one scorner of many friars, among whom are numbered many baldheads! And, besides, we have a papal bull[8] by which all who scoff at us are excommunicated!'

"When the Cardinal realized there was no making an end, he sent away the hanger-on by a motion of his head and tactfully turned the conversation to another subject. Soon afterwards he rose from the table and, going to hear the petitions of his suitors, dismissed us.

"Look, my dear More, with how lengthy a tale I have burdened you. I should have been quite ashamed to protract it if you had not eagerly called for it and seemed to listen as if you did not want any part of the conversation to be left out. Though I ought to have related this conversation more concisely, still I felt bound to tell it to exhibit the attitude of those who had rejected what I had said first yet who, immediately afterward, when the Cardinal did not disapprove of it, also gave their approval, flattering him so much that they even smiled on and almost allowed in earnest the fancies of the hanger-on, which his master in jest did not reject. From this reaction you may judge what little regard courtiers would pay to me and my advice."

"To be sure, my dear Raphael," I commented, "you have given me great pleasure, for everything you have said has been both wise and witty. Besides, while listening to you, I felt not only as if I were at home in my native land but as if I were become a boy again, by being pleasantly reminded of the very Cardinal in whose court I was brought up as a lad. Since you are strongly devoted to his memory, you cannot believe how much more attached I feel to you on that account, attached exceedingly as I have been to you already. Even now, nevertheless, I cannot change my mind but must needs think that, if you could persuade yourself not to shun the courts of kings, you could do the greatest good to the common weal by your advice. The latter is the most important part of your duty as it is the duty of every good man. Your favorite author, Plato, is of opinion that commonwealths will finally be happy only if either philosophers become kings or kings turn to philosophy.[9] What a distant prospect of happiness there will be if philosophers will not condescend even to impart their counsel to kings!"

"They are not so ungracious," he rejoined, "that they would not gladly do it—in fact, many have already done it in published books—if the rulers would be ready to take good advice. But, doubtless, Plato was right in foreseeing that if kings themselves did not turn to philosophy, they would never approve of the advice of real philosophers because they have been from their youth saturated and infected with wrong ideas. This truth he found from his own experience with Dionysius.[1] If I proposed beneficial measures to some king and tried to uproot from his soul the seeds of evil and corruption, do you not suppose that I should be forthwith banished or treated with ridicule?

"Come now, suppose I were at the court of the French king and sitting in his privy council. In a most secret meeting, a circle of his most astute councilors over which he personally presides is setting its wits to work to consider by what crafty

7. Proverbs 26.5.
8. Edict.
9. *Republic*, 5.473d.

1. Having tried to instruct Dionysius II, King of Syracuse, in the art of ruling as a philosopher, Plato became a virtual prisoner of the court.

machinations he may keep his hold on Milan and bring back into his power the Naples which has been eluding his grasp; then overwhelm Venice and subjugate the whole of Italy; next bring under his sway Flanders, Brabant, and finally, the whole of Burgundy—and other nations, too, whose territory he has already conceived the idea of usurping.

"At this meeting, one advises that a treaty should be made with the Venetians to last just as long as the king will find it convenient, that he should communicate his intentions to them, and that he should even deposit in their keeping part of the booty, which, when all has gone according to his mind, he may reclaim. Another recommends the hiring of German *Landsknechte* [infantry], and another the mollification of the Swiss with money, and another the propitiation of the offended majesty of the emperor with gold as an acceptable offering. Another thinks that a settlement should be made with the King of Aragon and that, as a guarantee of peace, someone else's kingdom of Navarre should be ceded him! Another proposes that the Prince of Castile be caught by the prospect of a marriage alliance and that some nobles of his court be drawn to the French side by a fixed pension.

"Meanwhile the most perplexing question of all comes up: what is to be done with England? They agree that negotiations for peace should be undertaken, that an alliance always weak at best should be strengthened with the strongest bonds, and that the English should be called friends but suspected as enemies. The Scots therefore must be posted in readiness, prepared for any opportunity to be let loose on the English if they make the slightest movement. Moreover, some exiled noble must be fostered secretly—for treaties prevent it being done openly—to maintain a claim to the throne, that by this handle France may keep in check a king in whom it has no confidence.

"In such a meeting, I say, when such efforts are being made, when so many distinguished persons are vying with each other in proposals of a warlike nature, what if an insignificant fellow like myself were to get up and advise going on another tack? Suppose I expressed the opinion that Italy should be left alone. Suppose I argued that we should stay at home because the single kingdom of France by itself was almost too large to be governed well by a single man so that the king should not dream of adding other dominions under his sway. Suppose, then, I put before them the decisions made by the people called the Achorians[2] who live on the mainland to the south-southeast of the island of Utopia.

"Once upon a time they had gone to war to win for their king another kingdom to which he claimed to be the rightful heir by virtue of an old tie by marriage. After they had secured it, they saw they would have no less trouble in keeping it than they had suffered in obtaining it. The seeds of rebellion from within or of invasion from without were always springing up in the people thus acquired. They realized they would have to fight constantly for them or against them and to keep an army in continual readiness. In the meantime they were being plundered, their money was being taken out of the country, they were shedding their blood for the little glory of someone else, peace was no more secure than before, their morals at home were being corrupted by war, the lust for robbery was becoming second nature, criminal recklessness was emboldened by killings in war, and the laws were held in contempt—all because the king, being distracted with the charge of two kingdoms, could not properly attend to either.

2. A people "without place, region, or district."

"At length, seeing that in no other way would there be any end to all this mischief, they took counsel together and most courteously offered their king his choice of retaining whichever of the two kingdoms he preferred. He could not keep both because there were too many of them to be ruled by half a king, just as no one would care to engage even a muleteer whom he had to share with someone else. The worthy king was obliged to be content with his own realm and to turn over the new one to one of his friends, who was driven out soon afterwards.

"Furthermore, suppose I proved that all this war-mongering, by which so many nations were kept in a turmoil on the French king's account, would, after draining his resources and destroying his people, at length by some mischance end in naught and that therefore he had better look after his ancestral kingdom and make it as prosperous and flourishing as possible, love his subjects and be loved by them, live with them and rule them gently, and have no designs upon other kingdoms since what he already possessed was more than enough for him. What reception from my listeners, my dear More, do you think this speech of mine would find?"

"To be sure, not a very favorable one," I granted.

"Well, then, let us proceed," he continued. "Picture the councilors of some king or other debating with him and devising by what schemes they may heap up treasure for him. One advises crying up the value of money when he has to pay any and crying down its value below the just rate when he has to receive any—with the double result that he may discharge a large debt with a small sum and, when only a small sum is due to him, may receive a large one. Another suggests a make-believe war under pretext of which he would raise money and then, when he saw fit, make peace with solemn ceremonies to throw dust in his simple people's eyes because their loving monarch in compassion would fain avoid human bloodshed.

"Another councilor reminds him of certain old and moth-eaten laws, annulled by long non-enforcement, which no one remembers being made and therefore everyone has transgressed. The king should exact fines for their transgression, there being no richer source of profit nor any more honorable than such as has an outward mask of justice! Another recommends that under heavy penalties he prohibit many things and especially such as it is to the people's advantage not to allow. Afterwards for money he should give a dispensation to those with whose interests the prohibition has interfered. Thus favor is won with the people and a double profit is made: first, by exacting fines from those whose greed of gain has entangled them in the snare and, second, by selling privileges to others—and, to be sure, the higher the price the better the king, since he hates to give any private citizen a privilege which is contrary to the public welfare and will not do so except at a great price!

"Another persuades him that he must bind to himself the judges, who will in every case decide in favor of the king's side. In addition, he must summon them to the palace and invite them to debate his affairs in his presence. There will be no cause of his so patently unjust in which one of them will not, either from a desire to contradict or from shame at repeating another's view or to curry favor, find some loophole whereby the law can be perverted. When through the opposite opinions of the judges a thing in itself as clear as daylight has been made a subject of debate, and when truth has become a matter of doubt, the king is opportunely furnished a handle to interpret the law in his own interest. Everyone else will acquiesce from shame or from fear. Afterwards the decision is boldly pronounced from the Bench. Then, too, a pretext can never be wanting for deciding on the king's side. For such a judge it is enough that either equity be on his side or the letter of the law or the twisted meaning of the written word or, what finally outweighs all law with conscientious judges, the indisputable royal prerogative![3]

"All the councilors agree and consent to the famous statement of Crassus:[4] no amount of gold is enough for the ruler who has to keep an army. Further, the king, however much he wishes, can do no wrong; for all that all men possess is his, as they themselves are, and so much is a man's own as the king's kindness has not taken away from him. It is much to the king's interest that the latter be as little as possible, seeing that his safeguard lies in the fact that the people do not grow insolent with wealth and freedom. These things make them less patient to endure harsh and unjust commands, while, on the other hand, poverty and need blunt their spirits, make them patient, and take away from the oppressed the lofty spirit of rebellion.

"At this point, suppose I were again to rise and maintain that these counsels are both dishonorable and dangerous for the king, whose very safety, not merely his honor, rests on the people's resources rather than his own. Suppose I should show that they choose a king for their own sake and not for his—to be plain, that by his labor and effort they may live well and safe from injustice and wrong. For this very reason, it belongs to the king to take more care for the welfare of his people than for his own, just as it is the duty of a shepherd, insofar as he is a shepherd, to feed his sheep rather than himself.[5]

"The blunt facts reveal that they are completely wrong in thinking that the poverty of the people is the safeguard of peace. Where will you find more quarreling than among beggars? Who is more eager for revolution than he who is discontented with his present state of life? Who is more reckless in the endeavor to upset everything, in the hope of getting profit from some source or other, than he who has nothing to lose? Now if there were any king who was either so despicable or so hateful to his subjects that he could not keep them in subjection otherwise than by ill usage, plundering, and confiscation and by reducing them to beggary, it would surely be better for him to resign his throne than to keep it by such means—means by which, though he retain the name of authority, he loses its majesty. It is not consistent with the dignity of a king to exercise authority over beggars but over prosperous and happy subjects. This was certainly the sentiment of that noble and lofty spirit, Fabricius,[6] who replied that he would rather be a ruler of rich people than be rich himself.

"To be sure, to have a single person enjoy a life of pleasure and self-indulgence amid the groans and lamentations of all around him is to be the keeper, not of a kingdom, but of a jail. In fine, as he is an incompetent physician who cannot cure one

3. Conditions in which the principle of equity is subverted: The law, rather than being applied in such a way as to respect the conditions and circumstances of a particular case, is bent or twisted to suit the interest of a particular party. In England the courts of equity were often devoted to matters of state and were susceptible to corruption in the interest of promoting royal business. The prerogative was the absolute power of the monarch only in special categories of activity (i.e., the import and export trade), and it was exempt from any legal restrictions.

4. Marcus Licinius Crassus (d. 53 B.C.), a man of great wealth who, together with Julius Caesar and Pompey, formed a coalition known as the first triumvirate.

5. A king who did not care for the welfare of his people was usually identified as a tyrant. As Aristotle stated, a tyranny is a perversion of a monarchy and it is characterized by "irresponsible rule over subjects . . . with a view to its own private interest and not in the interest of the persons ruled" (*Politics*, 4.8.3).

6. Roman commander of the republican period; whether he actually made the statement attributed to him is unclear. In any case it outlines a critique of monarchy common in antityrannical literature of the early modern period.

disease except by creating another, so he who cannot reform the lives of citizens in any other way than by depriving them of the good things of life must admit that he does not know how to rule free men.

"Yea, the king had better amend his own indolence or arrogance, for these two vices generally cause his people either to despise him or to hate him. Let him live harmlessly on what is his own. Let him adjust his expenses to his revenues. Let him check mischief and crime, and, by training his subjects rightly, let him prevent rather than allow the spread of activities which he will have to punish afterwards. Let him not be hasty in enforcing laws fallen into disuse, especially those which, long given up, have never been missed. Let him never take in compensation for violation anything that a private person would be forbidden in court to appropriate for the reason that such would be an act of crooked craftiness.

"What if then I were to put before them the law of the Macarians,[7] a people not very far distant from Utopia? Their king, on the day he first enters into office, is bound by an oath at solemn sacrifices that he will never have at one time in his coffer more than a thousand pounds of gold or its equivalent in silver. They report that this law was instituted by a very good king, who cared more for his country's interest than his own wealth, to be a barrier against hoarding so much money as would cause a lack of it among his people. He saw that this treasure would be sufficient for the king to put down rebellion and for his kingdom to meet hostile invasions. It was not large enough, however, to tempt him to encroach on the possessions of others. The prevention of the latter was the primary purpose of his legislation. His secondary consideration was that provision was thus made to forestall any shortage of the money needed in the daily business transactions of the citizens. He felt, too, that since the king had to pay out whatever came into his treasury beyond the limit prescribed by law, he would not seek occasion to commit injustice. Such a king will be both a terror to the evil and beloved by the good. To sum it all up, if I tried to obtrude these and like ideas on men strongly inclined to the opposite way of thinking, to what deaf ears should I tell the tale!"

"Deaf indeed, without doubt," I agreed, "and, by heaven, I am not surprised. Neither, to tell the truth, do I think that such ideas should be thrust on people, or such advice given, as you are positive will never be listened to. What good could such novel ideas do, or how could they enter the minds of individuals who are already taken up and possessed by the opposite conviction? In the private conversation of close friends this academic philosophy is not without its charm, but in the councils of kings, where great matters are debated with great authority, there is no room for these notions."

"That is just what I meant," he rejoined, "by saying there is no room for philosophy with rulers."

"Right," I declared, "that is true—not for this academic philosophy which thinks that everything is suitable to every place. But there is another philosophy, more practical for statesmen, which knows its stage, adapts itself to the play in hand, and performs its role neatly and appropriately. This is the philosophy which you must employ. Otherwise we have the situation in which a comedy of Plautus is being performed and the household slaves are making trivial jokes at one another and then you come on the stage in a philosopher's attire and recite the passage

7. "Happy Ones."

from the *Octavia* where Seneca is disputing with Nero.[8] Would it not have been preferable to take a part without words than by reciting something inappropriate to make a hodgepodge of comedy and tragedy? You would have spoiled and upset the actual play by bringing in irrelevant matter—even if your contribution would have been superior in itself. Whatever play is being performed, perform it as best you can, and do not upset it all simply because you think of another which has more interest.

"So it is in the commonwealth. So it is in the deliberations of monarchs. If you cannot pluck up wrongheaded opinions by the root, if you cannot cure according to your heart's desire vices of long standing, yet you must not on that account desert the commonwealth. You must not abandon the ship in a storm because you cannot control the winds.

"On the other hand, you must not force upon people new and strange ideas which you realize will carry no weight with persons of opposite conviction. On the contrary, by the indirect approach you must seek and strive to the best of your power to handle matters tactfully. What you cannot turn to good you must at least make as little bad as you can. For it is impossible that all should be well unless all men were good, a situation which I do not expect for a great many years to come!"

"By this approach," he commented, "I should accomplish nothing else than to share the madness of others as I tried to cure their lunacy. If I would stick to the truth, I must needs speak in the manner I have described. To speak falsehoods, for all I know, may be the part of a philosopher, but it is certainly not for me. Although that speech of mine might perhaps be unwelcome and disagreeable to those councilors, yet I cannot see why it should seem odd even to the point of folly. What if I told them the kind of things which Plato creates in his republic or which the Utopians actually put in practice in theirs? Though such institutions were superior (as, to be sure, they are), yet they might appear odd because here individuals have the right of private property, there all things are common.

"To persons who had made up their minds to go headlong by the opposite road, the man who beckons them back and points out dangers ahead can hardly be welcome. But, apart from this aspect, what did my speech contain that would not be appropriate or obligatory to have propounded everywhere? Truly, if all the things which by the perverse morals of men have come to seem odd are to be dropped as unusual and absurd, we must dissemble among Christians almost all the doctrines of Christ. Yet He forbade us to dissemble them to the extent that what He had whispered in the ears of His disciples He commanded to be preached openly from the housetops.[9] The greater part of His teaching is far more different from the morals of mankind than was my discourse. But preachers, crafty men that they are, finding that men grievously disliked to have their morals adjusted to the rule of Christ and following I suppose your advice, accommodated His teaching to men's morals as if it

8. More's character "More" illustrates the poor social skills of the philosopher by imagining a situation in which the philosopher quotes lines from Seneca's tragedy while everyone else is enjoying a comedy by Plautus. "More" asks not only that the philosopher observe conditions of time and place, but also that—in political situations in which the philosopher might like to instruct his people in moral action but finds that they do not want to listen to him—he not give up his civic obligations and go into retirement. The predicament was one that More and many of his contemporary humanist statesmen actually confronted when they attempted to give advice to their political superiors.

9. Hythlodaeus paraphrases Matthew 10.27 and Luke 12.3; he proposes that the practical and accommodating flexibility that "More" advocates finds its limits in the absolute moral doctrine preached by Jesus Christ and therefore to be followed by Christians.

were a rule of soft lead that at least in some way or other the two might be made to correspond.[1] By this method I cannot see what they have gained, except that men may be bad in greater comfort.

"And certainly I should make as little progress in the councils of princes. For I should hold either a different opinion, which would amount to having none at all, or else the same, and then I should, as Mitio says in Terence, help their madness.[2] As to that indirect approach of yours, I cannot see its relevancy; I mean your advice to use my endeavors, if all things cannot be made good, at least to handle them tactfully and, as far as one may, to make them as little bad as possible. At court there is no room for dissembling, nor may one shut one's eyes to things. One must openly approve the worst counsels and subscribe to the most ruinous decrees. He would be counted a spy and almost a traitor, who gives only faint praise to evil counsels.

"Moreover, there is no chance for you to do any good because you are brought among colleagues who would easily corrupt even the best of men before being reformed themselves. By their evil companionship, either you will be seduced yourself or, keeping your own integrity and innocence, you will be made a screen for the wickedness and folly of others. Thus you are far from being able to make anything better by that indirect approach of yours.

"For this reason, Plato by a very fine comparison shows why philosophers are right in abstaining from administration of the commonwealth. They observe the people rushing out into the streets and being soaked by constant showers and cannot induce them to go indoors and escape the rain. They know that, if they go out, they can do no good but will only get wet with the rest. Therefore, being content if they themselves at least are safe, they keep at home, since they cannot remedy the folly of others.[3]

"Yet surely, my dear More, to tell you candidly my heart's sentiments, it appears to me that wherever you have private property and all men measure all things by cash values, there it is scarcely possible for a commonwealth to have justice or prosperity—unless you think justice exists where all the best things flow into the hands of the worst citizens or prosperity prevails where all is divided among very few—and even they are not altogether well off, while the rest are downright wretched.

"As a result, when in my heart I ponder on the extremely wise and holy institutions of the Utopians, among whom, with very few laws, affairs are ordered so aptly that virtue has its reward, and yet, with equality of distribution, all men have abundance of all things, and then when I contrast with their policies the many nations elsewhere ever making ordinances and yet never one of them achieving good order—nations where whatever a man has acquired he calls his own private property, but where all these laws daily framed are not enough for a man to secure or to defend or

1. The "rule of soft lead," or the Lesbian rule (after the leaden measure used in architecture on the island of Lesbos in the Aegean), is the figure Aristotle uses to illustrate the concept of equity. The measure, supposedly a rule or an absolute, corresponds to the idea of a written law; but because it is flexible, it is also a written law that is always interpreted in such a way as to fit the particulars of a case.

2. Hythlodaeus insists that for a philosopher to cross a person in authority and with power will only make the philosopher appear nonsensical and therefore render the ruler less reasonable than he was at first; that is, both philosopher and ruler will appear to be madmen. He instances Mitio, a character in Terence's play *The Brothers*, who declares: "Still, if I inflamed or even fell in with his passionate temper, I should surely give him another madman for company" (1.145–147).

3. Cf. *Republic* 6.496d: "he keeps quiet and minds his own business—as a man in a storm . . . stands aside under a little wall. Seeing others filled with lawlessness, he is content if somehow he himself can live his life here pure of injustice and unholy deeds."

even to distinguish from someone else's the goods which each in turn calls his own, a predicament readily attested by the numberless and ever new and interminable law-suits—when I consider, I repeat, all these facts, I become more partial to Plato and less surprised at his refusal to make laws for those who rejected that legislation which gave to all an equal share in all goods.

"This wise sage, to be sure, easily foresaw that the one and only road to the general welfare lies in the maintenance of equality in all respects. I have my doubts that the latter could ever be preserved where the individual's possessions are his private property. When every man aims at absolute ownership of all the property he can get, be there never so great abundance of goods, it is all shared by a handful who leave the rest in poverty. It generally happens that the one class preeminently deserves the lot of the other, for the rich are greedy, unscrupulous, and useless, while the poor are well-behaved, simple, and by their daily industry more beneficial to the commonwealth than to themselves. I am fully persuaded that no just and even distribution of goods can be made and that no happiness can be found in human affairs unless private property is utterly abolished.[4] While it lasts, there will always remain a heavy and inescapable burden of poverty and misfortunes for by far the greatest and by far the best part of mankind.

"I admit that this burden can be lightened to some extent, but I contend that it cannot be removed entirely. A statute might be made that no person should hold more than a certain amount of land and that no person should have a monetary income beyond that permitted by law. Special legislation might be passed to prevent the monarch from being overmighty and the people overweening; likewise, that public offices should not be solicited with gifts, nor be put up for sale, nor require lavish personal expenditures. Otherwise, there arise, first, the temptation to recoup one's expenses by acts of fraud and plunder and, secondly, the necessity of appointing rich men to offices which ought rather to have been administered by wise men. By this type of legislation, I maintain, as sick bodies which are past cure can be kept up by repeated medical treatments, so these evils, too, can be alleviated and made less acute. There is no hope, however, of a cure and a return to a healthy condition as long as each individual is master of his own property. Nay, while you are intent upon the cure of one part, you make worse the malady of the other parts. Thus, the healing of the one member reciprocally breeds the disease of the other as long as nothing can so be added to one as not to be taken away from another."[5]

"But," I ventured, "I am of the contrary opinion. Life cannot be satisfactory where all things are common. How can there be a sufficient supply of goods when each withdraws himself from the labor of production? For the individual does not have the motive of personal gain and he is rendered slothful by trusting to the indus-

4. It was thought that primordial humans did not understand that property could be private and belong to one party only. With the congregation of men and women into tribes, however, private property was established by markers: boundary lines, signs and emblems, and distinctive styles of manufacture. This moment also saw the institution of a civil society characterized by religion and law. By advocating a state in which there is no private property, Hythlodaeus posits a political and economic situation that his contemporaries would have recognized in such limited societies as those under monastic or some other kind of religious rule.

5. The trope of the body politic is ubiquitous in early modern political thought. In *The Education of a Christian Prince*, Erasmus argues: "[A monarch] should consider his kingdom as a great body of which he is the most outstanding member and remember that they who have entrusted all their fortunes and their very safety to the good faith of one man are deserving of consideration. He should keep constantly in mind the example of those rulers to whom the welfare of their people was dearer than their own lives; for it is obviously impossible for a prince to do violence to the state without injuring himself." See also Plato's *Republic*, 5.462.

try of others. Moreover, when people are goaded by want and yet the individual cannot legally keep as his own what he has gained, must there not be trouble from continual bloodshed and riot? This holds true especially since the authority of magistrates and respect for their office have been eliminated, for how there can be any place for these among men who are all on the same level I cannot even conceive."

"I do not wonder," he rejoined, "that it looks this way to you, being a person who has no picture at all, or else a false one, of the situation I mean. But you should have been with me in Utopia and personally seen their manners and customs as I did, for I lived there more than five years and would never have wished to leave except to make known that new world. In that case you unabashedly would admit that you had never seen a well-ordered people anywhere but there."

"Yet surely," objected Peter Giles, "it would be hard for you to convince me that a better-ordered people is to be found in that new world than in the one known to us. In the latter I imagine there are equally excellent minds, as well as commonwealths which are older than those in the new world. In these commonwealths long experience has come upon very many advantages for human life—not to mention also the chance discoveries made among us, which no human mind could have devised."

"As for the antiquity of commonwealths," he countered, "you could give a sounder opinion if you had read the historical accounts of that world. If we must believe them, there were cities among them before there were men among us. Furthermore, whatever either brains have invented or chance has discovered hitherto could have happened equally in both places. But I hold for certain that, even though we may surpass them in brains, we are far inferior to them in application and industry.

"According to their chronicles, up to the time of our landing they had never heard anything about our activities (they call us the Ultra-equinoctials) except that twelve hundred years ago a ship driven by a tempest was wrecked on the island of Utopia. Some Romans and Egyptians were cast on shore and remained on the island without ever leaving it. Now mark what good advantage their industry took of this one opportunity. The Roman empire possessed no art capable of any use which they did not either learn from the shipwrecked strangers or discover for themselves after receiving the hints for investigation—so great a gain was it to them that on a single occasion some persons were carried to their shores from ours.

"But if any like fortune has ever driven anyone from their shores to ours, the event is as completely forgotten as future generations will perhaps forget that I had once been there. And, just as they immediately at one meeting appropriated to themselves every good discovery of ours, so I suppose it will be long before we adopt anything that is better arranged with them than with us. This trait, I judge, is the chief reason why, though we are inferior to them neither in brains nor in resources, their commonwealth is more wisely governed and more happily flourishing than ours."

"If so, my dear Raphael," said I, "I beg and beseech you, give us a description of the island. Do not be brief, but set forth in order the terrain, the rivers, the cities, the inhabitants, the traditions, the customs, the laws, and, in fact, everything which you think we should like to know. And you must think we wish to know everything of which we are still ignorant."

"There is nothing," he declared, "I shall be more pleased to do, for I have the facts ready to hand. But the description will take time."

"In that case," I suggested, "let us go in to dine. Afterwards we shall take up as much time as we like."

"Agreed," he replied.

So we went in and dined. We then returned to the same place, sat down on the same bench, and gave orders to the servants that we should not be interrupted. Peter Giles and I urged Raphael to fulfill his promise. As for him, when he saw us intent and eager to listen, after sitting in silent thought for a time, he began his tale as follows.

THE END OF BOOK ONE

Book 2

The island of the Utopians extends in the center (where it is broadest) for two hundred miles and is not much narrower for the greater part of the island, but toward both ends it begins gradually to taper. These ends form a circle five hundred miles in circumference and so make the island look like a new moon, the horns of which are divided by straits about eleven miles across. The straits then unfold into a wide expanse. As the winds are kept off by the land which everywhere surrounds it, the bay is like a huge lake, smooth rather than rough, and thus converts almost the whole center of the country into a harbor which lets ships cross in every direction to the great convenience of the inhabitants.

The mouth of this bay is rendered perilous here by shallows and there by reefs. Almost in the center of the gap stands one great crag which, being visible, is not dangerous. A tower built on it is occupied by a garrison. The other rocks are hidden and therefore treacherous. The channels are known only to the natives, and so it does not easily happen that any foreigner enters the bay except with a Utopian pilot. In fact, the entrance is hardly safe even for themselves, unless they guide themselves by landmarks on the shore. If these were removed to other positions, they could easily lure an enemy's fleet, however numerous, to destruction.

On the outer side of the island, harbors are many. Everywhere, however, the landing is so well defended by nature or by engineering that a few defenders can prevent strong forces from coming ashore.

As the report goes and as the appearance of the ground shows, the island once was not surrounded by sea. But Utopus,[6] who as conqueror gave the island its name (up to then it had been called Abraxa[7]) and who brought the rude and rustic people to such a perfection of culture and humanity as makes them now superior to almost all other mortals, gained a victory at his very first landing. He then ordered the excavation of fifteen miles on the side where the land was connected with the continent and caused the sea to flow around the land. He set to the task not only the natives but, to prevent them from thinking the labor a disgrace, his own soldiers also. With the work divided among so many hands, the enterprise was finished with incredible speed and struck the neighboring peoples, who at first had derided the project as vain, with wonder and terror at its success.

The island contains fifty-four city-states,[8] all spacious and magnificent, identical in language, traditions, customs, and laws. They are similar also in layout and everywhere, as far as the nature of the ground permits, similar even in appearance. None of them is separated by less than twenty-four miles from the nearest, but none is so isolated that a person cannot go from it to another in a day's journey on foot. From each

6. Ruler over no place.
7. The name for the highest of 365 heavens, according to the Gnostic philosopher Basilides.
8. When More wrote *Utopia*, England consisted of fifty-three counties and the City of London, its principal urban center. This allusion to England establishes a connection between Books 1 and 2 and suggests that More intended aspects of Utopia to be understood in relation to life in England.

city three old and experienced citizens meet to discuss the affairs of common interest to the island once a year at Amaurotum, for this city, being in the very center of the country, is situated most conveniently for the representatives of all sections. It is considered the chief as well as the capital city.

The lands are so well assigned to the cities that each has at least twelve miles of country on every side, and on some sides even much more, to wit, the side on which the cities are farther apart. No city has any desire to extend its territory, for they consider themselves the tenants rather than the masters of what they hold.

Everywhere in the rural districts they have, at suitable distances from one another, farmhouses well equipped with agricultural implements. They are inhabited by citizens who come in succession to live there. No rural household numbers less than forty men and women, besides two serfs attached to the soil.[9] Over them are set a master and a mistress, serious in mind and ripe in years. Over every group of thirty households rules a phylarch.[1]

Twenty from each household return every year to the city, namely, those having completed two years in the country. As substitutes in their place, the same number are sent from the city. They are to be trained by those who have been there a year and who therefore are more expert in farming; they themselves will teach others in the following years. There is thus no danger of anything going wrong with the annual food supply through want of skill, as might happen if all at one time were newcomers and novices at farming. Though this system of changing farmers is the rule, to prevent any individual's being forced against his will to continue too long in a life of rather hard work, yet many men who take a natural pleasure in agricultural pursuits obtain leave to stay several years.

The occupation of the farmers is to cultivate the soil, to feed the animals, and to get wood and convey it to the city either by land or by water, whichever way is more convenient. They breed a vast quantity of poultry by a wonderful contrivance. The hens do not brood over the eggs, but the farmers, by keeping a great number of them at a uniform heat, bring them to life and hatch them. As soon as they come out of the shell, the chicks follow and acknowledge humans as their mothers!

They rear very few horses, and these only high-spirited ones, which they use for no other purpose than for exercising their young men in horsemanship. All the labor of cultivation and transportation is performed by oxen, which they admit are inferior to horses in a sudden spurt but which are far superior to them in staying power and endurance and not liable to as many diseases. Moreover, it requires less trouble and expense to feed them. When they are past work, they finally are of use for food.

They sow grain only for bread. Their drink is wine or cider or perry,[2] or it is even water. The latter is sometimes plain and often that in which they have boiled honey or licorice, whereof they have a great abundance.

Though they are more than sure how much food the city with its adjacent territory consumes, they produce far more grain and cattle than they require for their own use: they distribute the surplus among their neighbors. Whenever they need things

9. According to feudal practice in medieval Europe, a serf was a person who was in servitude for life and could not leave the land whose lord he served. Unlike most slaves, however, who were generally men or women taken captive in the course of a war and who could buy their freedom, a serf was never freed from his connection to an estate. Hythlodaeaus refers to other kinds of Utopian slaves later in his account of how Utopians organize their society.

1. Chief.

2. Pear liqueur.

not found in the country, they send for all the materials from the city and, having to give nothing in exchange, obtain it from the municipal officials without the bother of bargaining. For very many go there every single month to observe the holyday.

When the time of harvest is at hand, the agricultural phylarchs inform the municipal officials what number of citizens they require to be sent. The crowd of harvesters, coming promptly at the appointed time, dispatch the whole task of harvesting almost in a single day of fine weather.

The Cities, Especially Amaurotum

The person who knows one of the cities will know them all, since they are exactly alike insofar as the terrain permits. I shall therefore picture one or other (nor does it matter which), but which should I describe rather than Amaurotum? First, none is worthier, the rest deferring to it as the meeting place of the national senate; and, secondly, none is better known to me, as being one in which I had lived for five whole years.

To proceed. Amaurotum is situated on the gentle slope of a hill and is almost four-square in outline. Its breadth is about two miles starting just below the crest of the hill and running down to the river Anydrus; its length along the river is somewhat more than its breadth.

The Anydrus rises eighty miles above Amaurotum from a spring not very large; but, being increased in size by several tributaries, two of which are of fair size, it is half a mile broad in front of the city. After soon becoming still broader and after running farther for sixty miles, it falls into the ocean. Through the whole distance between the city and the sea, and even above the city for some miles, the tide alternately flows in for six whole hours and then ebbs with an equally speedy current. When the sea comes in, it fills the whole bed of the Anydrus with its water for a distance of thirty miles, driving the river back. At such times it turns the water salt for some distance farther, but above that point the river grows gradually fresh and passes the city uncontaminated. When the ebb comes, the fresh and pure water extends down almost to the mouth of the river.[3]

The city is joined to the opposite bank of the river not by a bridge built on wooden pillars or piles but by one magnificently arched with stonework. It is situated in the quarter which is farthest from the sea so that ships may pass along the whole of that side of the city without hindrance.

They have also another river, not very large, but very gentle and pleasant, which rises out of the same hill whereon the city is built and runs down through its middle into the river Anydrus. The head and source of this river just outside the city has been connected with it by outworks, lest in case of hostile attack the water might be cut off and diverted or polluted. From this point the water is distributed by conduits made of baked clay into various parts of the lower town. Where the ground makes that course impossible, the rain water collected in capacious cisterns is just as useful.

The city is surrounded by a high and broad wall with towers and ravelins at frequent intervals. A moat, dry but deep and wide and made impassable by thorn hedges, surrounds the fortifications on three sides; on the fourth the river itself takes the place of the moat.

The streets are well laid out both for traffic and for protection against the winds. The buildings, which are far from mean, are set together in a long row, continuous through the block and faced by a corresponding one. The house fronts of the respec-

3. These features of the Anydrus resemble those of London's Thames River.

tive blocks are divided by an avenue twenty feet broad. On the rear of the houses, through the whole length of the block, lies a broad garden enclosed on all sides by the backs of the blocks. Every home has not only a door into the street but a back door into the garden. What is more, folding doors, easily opened by hand and then closing of themselves, give admission to anyone. As a result, nothing is private property anywhere. Every ten years they actually exchange their very homes by lot.

The Utopians are very fond of their gardens. In them they have vines, fruits, herbs, flowers, so well kept and flourishing that I never saw anything more fruitful and more tasteful anywhere. Their zest in keeping them is increased not merely by the pleasure afforded them but by the keen competition between blocks as to which will have the best kept garden. Certainly you cannot readily find anything in the whole city more productive of profit and pleasure to the citizens. Therefore it would seem their founder attached the greatest importance to these gardens.

In fact, they report that the whole plan of the city had been sketched at the very beginning by Utopus himself. He left to posterity, however, to add the adornment and other improvements for which he saw one lifetime would hardly suffice. Their annals, embracing the history of 1760 years, are preserved carefully and conscientiously in writing. Here they find stated that at first the houses were low, mere cabins and huts, haphazardly made with any wood to hand, with mud-plastered walls. They had thatched the ridged roofs with straw.

But now all the homes are of handsome appearance with three stories. The exposed faces of the walls are made of stone or cement or brick, rubble being used as filling for the empty space between the walls. The roofs are flat and covered with a kind of cement which is cheap but so well mixed that it is impervious to fire and superior to lead in defying the damage caused by storms. They keep the winds out of their windows by glass (which is in very common use in Utopia) or sometimes by thin linen smeared with translucent oil or amber. The advantage is twofold: the device results in letting more light in and keeping more wind out.

The Officials

Every thirty families choose annually an official whom in their ancient language they call a syphogrant[4] but in their newer a phylarch. Over ten syphogrants with their families is set a person once called a tranibor but now a protophylarch.[5] The whole body of syphogrants, in number two hundred, having sworn to choose the man whom they judge most useful, by secret balloting appoint a governor, specifically one of the four candidates named to them by the people, for one is selected out of each of the four quarter of the city to be commended to the senate.

The governor holds office for life, unless ousted on suspicion of aiming at a tyranny. The tranibors are elected annually but are not changed without good reason. The other officials all hold their posts for one year.

The tranibors enter into consultation with the governor every other day and sometimes, if need arises, oftener. They take counsel about the commonwealth. If there are any disputes between private persons—there are very few—they settle them without loss of time. They always admit to the senate chamber two syphogrants, and different ones every day. It is provided that nothing concerning the commonwealth be ratified if it has not been discussed in the senate three days before the passing of the decree. To take counsel on matters of common interest outside the senate or the

4. Wise old man.

5. Tranibor: glutton; protophylarch: principal chief.

popular assembly is considered a capital offense. The object of these measures, they say, is to prevent it from being easy, by a conspiracy between the governor and the tranibors and by tyrannous oppression of the people, to change the order of the commonwealth. Therefore whatever is considered important is laid before the assembly of the syphogrants who, after informing their groups of families, take counsel together and report their decision to the senate. Sometimes the matter is laid before the council of the whole island.

In addition, the senate has the custom of debating nothing on the same day on which it is first proposed but of putting it off till the next meeting. This is their rule lest anyone, after hastily blurting out the first thought that popped into his head, should afterwards give more thought to defending his opinion than to supporting what is for the good of the commonwealth, and should prefer to jeopardize the public welfare rather than to risk his reputation through a wrongheaded and misplaced shame, fearing he might be thought to have shown too little foresight at the first—though he should have been enough foresighted at the first to speak with prudence rather than with haste!

Occupations

Agriculture is the one pursuit which is common to all, both men and women, without exception. They are all instructed in it from childhood, partly by principles taught in school, partly by field trips to the farms closer to the city as if for recreation. Here they do not merely look on, but, as opportunity arises for bodily exercise, they do the actual work.

Besides agriculture (which is, as I said, common to all), each is taught one particular craft as his own. This is generally either wool-working or linen-making or masonry or metal-working or carpentry. There is no other pursuit which occupies any number worth mentioning. As for clothes, these are of one and the same pattern throughout the island and down the centuries, though there is a distinction between the sexes and between the single and married. The garments are comely to the eye, convenient for bodily movement, and fit for wear in heat and cold. Each family, I say, does its own tailoring.

Of the other crafts, one is learned by each person, and not the men only, but the women too. The latter as the weaker sex have the lighter occupations and generally work wool and flax. To the men are committed the remaining more laborious crafts. For the most part, each is brought up in his father's craft, for which most have a natural inclination. But if anyone is attracted to another occupation, he is transferred by adoption to a family pursuing that craft for which he has a liking. Care is taken not only by his father but by the authorities, too, that he will be assigned to a grave and honorable householder. Moreover, if anyone after being thoroughly taught one craft desires another also, the same permission is given. Having acquired both, he practices his choice unless the city has more need of the one than of the other.

The chief and almost the only function of the syphogrants is to manage and provide that no one sit idle, but that each apply himself industriously to his trade, and yet that he be not wearied like a beast of burden with constant toil from early morning till late at night. Such wretchedness is worse than the lot of slaves, and yet it is almost everywhere the life of workingmen—except for the Utopians. The latter divide the day and night into twenty-four equal hours and assign only six to work. There are three before noon, after which they go to dinner. After dinner, when they have rested for two hours in the afternoon, they again give three to work and finish up with supper. Counting one o'clock as the first hour after noon, they go to bed about eight o'clock, and sleep claims eight hours.

The intervals between the hours of work, sleep, and food are left to every man's discretion, not to waste in revelry or idleness, but to devote the time free from work to some other occupation according to taste. These periods are commonly devoted to intellectual pursuits. For it is their custom that public lectures are daily delivered in the hours before daybreak. Attendance is compulsory only for those who have been specially chosen to devote themselves to learning. A great number of all classes, however, both males and females, flock to hear the lectures, some to one and some to another, according to their natural inclination. But if anyone should prefer to devote this time to his trade, as is the case with many minds which do not reach the level for any of the higher intellectual disciplines, he is not hindered; in fact, he is even praised as useful to the commonwealth.

After supper they spend one hour in recreation, in summer in the gardens, in winter in the common halls in which they have their meals. There they either play music or entertain themselves with conversation. Dice and that kind of foolish and ruinous game they are not acquainted with. They do play two games not unlike chess. The first is a battle of numbers in which one number plunders another. The second is a game in which the vices fight a pitched battle with the virtues. In the latter is exhibited very cleverly, to begin with, both the strife of the vices with one another and their concerted opposition to the virtues; then, what vices are opposed to what virtues, by what forces they assail them openly, by what stratagems they attack them indirectly, by what safeguards the virtues check the power of the vices, by what arts they frustrate their designs; and, finally, by what means the one side gains the victory.

But here, lest you be mistaken, there is one point you must examine more closely. Since they devote but six hours to work, you might possibly think the consequence to be some scarcity of necessities. But so far is this from being the case that the aforesaid time is not only enough but more than enough for a supply of all that is requisite for either the necessity or the convenience of living. This phenomenon you too will understand if you consider how large a part of the population in other countries exists without working. First, there are almost all the women, who constitute half the whole; or, where the women are busy, there as a rule the men are snoring in their stead. Besides, how great and how lazy is the crowd of priests and so-called religious! Add to them all the rich, especially the masters of estates, who are commonly termed gentlemen and noblemen. Reckon with them their retainers—I mean, that whole rabble of good-for-nothing swashbucklers. Finally, join in the lusty and sturdy beggars who make some disease an excuse for idleness. You will certainly find far less numerous than you had supposed those whose labor produces all the articles that mortals require for daily use.

Now estimate how few of those who do work are occupied in essential trades. For, in a society where we make money the standard of everything, it is necessary to practice many crafts which are quite vain and superfluous, ministering only to luxury and licentiousness. Suppose the host of those who now toil were distributed over only as few crafts as natural needs and conveniences require. In the great abundance of commodities which must then arise, the prices set on them would be too low for the craftsmen to earn their livelihood by their work. But suppose all those fellows who are now busied with unprofitable crafts, as well as all the lazy and idle throng, any one of whom now consumes as much of the fruits of other men's labors as any two of the workingmen, were all set to work and indeed to useful work. You can easily see how small an allowance of time would be enough and to spare for the production of all that is required by necessity or comfort (or even pleasure, provided it be genuine and natural).

The very experience of Utopia makes the latter clear. In the whole city and its neighborhood, exemption from work is granted to hardly five hundred of the total of men and women whose age and strength make them fit for work. Among them the syphogrants, though legally exempted from work, yet take no advantage of this privilege so that by their example they may the more readily attract the others to work. The same exemption is enjoyed by those whom the people, persuaded by the recommendation of the priests, have given perpetual freedom from labor through the secret vote of the syphogrants so that they may learn thoroughly the various branches of knowledge. But if any of these scholars falsifies the hopes entertained of him, he is reduced to the rank of workingman. On the other hand, not seldom does it happen that a craftsman so industriously employs his spare hours on learning and makes such progress by his diligence that he is relieved of his manual labor and advanced into the class of men of learning. It is out of this company of scholars that they choose ambassadors, priests, tranibors, and finally the governor himself, whom they call in their ancient tongue Barzanes but in their more modern language Ademus.[6]

Nearly all the remaining populace being neither idle nor busied with useless occupations, it is easy to calculate how much good work can be produced in a very few hours. Besides the points mentioned, there is this further convenience that in most of the necessary crafts they do not require as much work as other nations. In the first place the erection or repair of buildings requires the constant labor of so many men elsewhere because what a father has built, his extravagant heir allows gradually to fall into ruin. As a result, what might have been kept up at small cost, his successor is obliged to erect anew at great expense. Further, often even when a house has cost one man a large sum, another is so fastidious that he thinks little of it. When it is neglected and therefore soon becomes dilapidated, he builds a second elsewhere at no less cost. But in the land of the Utopians, now that everything has been settled and the commonwealth established, a new home on a new site is a rare event, for not only do they promptly repair any damage, but they even take care to prevent damage. What is the result? With the minimum of labor, buildings last very long, and masons and carpenters sometimes have scarcely anything to do, except that they are set to hew out timber at home and to square and prepare stone meantime so that, if any work be required, a building may the sooner be erected.

In the matter of clothing, too, see how little toil and labor is needed. First, while at work, they are dressed unpretentiously in leather or hide, which lasts for seven years. When they go out in public, they put on a cape to hide their comparatively rough working clothes. This garment is of one color throughout the island and that the natural color. Consequently not only is much less woolen cloth needed than elsewhere, but what they have is much less expensive. On the other hand, since linen cloth is made with less labor, it is more used. In linen cloth only whiteness, in woolen cloth only cleanliness, is considered. No value is set on fineness of thread. So it comes about that, whereas elsewhere one man is not satisfied with four or five woolen coats of different colors and as many silk shirts, and the more fastidious not even with ten, in Utopia a man is content with a single cape, lasting generally for two years. There is no reason, of course, why he should desire more, for if he had them he would not be better fortified against the cold nor appear better dressed in the least.

6. Barzanes: "son of Zeus"; Ademus, "peopleless." These names indicate that the governor of Utopia, although considered a divinity in the primitive period of the state, is so impartial in his efforts to rule that he seems to belong to no family, region, or people.

Wherefore, seeing that they are all busied with useful trades and are satisfied with fewer products from them, it even happens that when there is an abundance of all commodities, they sometimes take out a countless number of people to repair whatever public roads are in bad order. Often, too, when there is nothing even of this kind of work to be done, they announce publicly that there will be fewer hours of work. For the authorities do not keep the citizens against their will at superfluous labor since the constitution of their commonwealth looks in the first place to this sole object: that for all the citizens, as far as the public needs permit, as much time as possible should be withdrawn from the service of the body and devoted to the freedom and culture of the mind. It is in the latter that they deem the happiness of life to consist.

Social Relations

But now, it seems, I must explain the behavior of the citizens toward one another, the nature of their social relations, and the method of distribution of goods. Since the city consists of households, households as a rule are made up of those related by blood. Girls, upon reaching womanhood and upon being settled in marriage, go to their husbands' domiciles. On the other hand, male children and then grandchildren remain in the family and are subject to the oldest parent, unless he has become a dotard with old age. In the latter case the next oldest is put in his place.

But that the city neither be depopulated nor grow beyond measure, provision is made that no household shall have fewer than ten or more than sixteen adults; there are six thousand such households in each city, apart from its surrounding territory. Of children under age, of course, no number can be fixed.[7] This limit is easily observed by transferring those who exceed the number in larger families into those that are under the prescribed number. Whenever all the families of a city reach their full quota, the extra persons help to make up the deficient population of other cities.

And if the population throughout the island should happen to swell above the fixed quotas, they enroll citizens out of every city and, on the mainland nearest them, wherever the natives have much unoccupied and uncultivated land, they found a colony under their own laws. They join with themselves the natives if they are willing to dwell with them. When such a union takes place, the two parties gradually and easily merge and together absorb the same way of life and the same customs, much to the great advantage of both peoples. By their procedures they make the land sufficient for both, which previously seemed poor and barren to the natives. The inhabitants who refuse to live according to their laws, they drive from the territory which they carve out for themselves. If they resist, they wage war against them. They consider it a most just cause for war when a people which does not use its soil but keeps it idle and waste nevertheless forbids the use and possession of it to others who by the rule of nature ought to be maintained by it.

If ever any misfortune so diminishes the number in any of their cities that it cannot be made up out of other parts of the island without bringing other cities below their proper strength (this has happened, they say, only twice in all the ages on account of the raging of a fierce pestilence), they are filled up by citizens returning from colonial territory. They would rather that the colonies should perish than that any of the cities of the island should be enfeebled.

7. In England, women came of age at 18, men at 22.

But to return to the dealings of the citizens. The oldest, as I have said, rules the household. Wives wait on their husbands, children on their parents, and generally the younger on their elders.

Every city is divided into four equal districts. In the middle of each quarter is a market of all kinds of commodities. To designated market buildings the products of each family are conveyed. Each kind of goods is arranged separately in storehouses. From the latter any head of a household seeks what he and his require and, without money or any kind of compensation, carries off what he seeks. Why should anything be refused? First, there is a plentiful supply of all things and, secondly, there is no underlying fear that anyone will demand more than he needs. Why should there be any suspicion that someone may demand an excessive amount when he is certain of never being in want? No doubt about it, avarice and greed are aroused in every kind of living creature by the fear of want, but only in man are they motivated by pride alone—pride which counts it a personal glory to excel others by superfluous display of possessions. The latter vice can have no place at all in the Utopian scheme of things.

Next to the market place that I have mentioned are the food markets. Here are brought not only different kinds of vegetables, fruit, and bread but also fish and whatever is edible of bird and four-footed beast. Outside the city are designated places where all gore and offal may be washed away in running water. From these places they transport the carcasses of the animals slaughtered and cleaned by the hands of slaves. They do not allow their citizens to accustom themselves to the butchering of animals, by the practice of which they think that mercy, the finest feeling of our human nature, is gradually killed off. In addition, they do not permit to be brought inside the city anything filthy or unclean for fear that the air, tainted by putrefaction, should engender disease.

To continue, each street has spacious halls, located at equal distance from one another, each being known by a special name of its own. In these halls live the syphogrants. To each hall are assigned thirty families, fifteen on either side, to take their meals in common. The managers of each hall meet at a fixed time in the market and get food according to the number of person in their individual charge.

Special care is first taken of the sick who are looked after in public hospitals. They have four at the city limits, a little outside the walls. These are so roomy as to be comparable to as many small towns. The purpose is twofold: first, that the sick, however numerous, should not be packed too close together in consequent discomfort and, second, that those who have a contagious disease likely to pass from one to another may be isolated as much as possible from the rest.[8] These hospitals are very well furnished and equipped with everything conducive to health. Besides, such tender and careful treatment and such constant attendance of expert physicians are provided that, though no one is sent to them against his will, there is hardly anybody in the whole city who, when suffering from illness, does not prefer to be nursed there rather than at home.

After the supervisor for the sick has received food as prescribed by the physicians, then the finest of everything is distributed equally among the halls according to the number in each, except that special regard is paid to the governor, the high

8. The germ theory of disease dates from the 19th century and the work of Louis Pasteur. Here More seems to be basing his idea of contagion on the experience of the bubonic plague, or Black Death, a major 14th-century European epidemic that killed roughly three-quarters of the population in 20 years.

priest, and the tranibors, as well as to ambassadors and all foreigners (if there are any, but they are few and far between). Yet the latter, too, when they are in Utopia, have definite homes got ready for them.

To these halls, at the hours fixed for dinner and supper, the entire syphograncy assembles, summoned by the blast of a brazen trumpet, excepting persons who are taking their meals either in the hospitals or at home. No one is forbidden, after the halls have been served, to fetch food from the market to his home: they realize that no one would do it without good reason. For, though nobody is forbidden to dine at home, yet no one does it willingly since the practice is considered not decent and since it is foolish to take the trouble of preparing an inferior dinner when an excellent and sumptuous one is ready at hand in the hall nearby.

In this hall all menial offices which to some degree involve heavy labor or soil the hands are performed by slaves. But the duty of cooking and preparing the food and, in fine, of arranging the whole meal is carried out by the women alone, taking turns for each family. Persons sit down at three or more tables according to the number of the company. The men sit with their backs to the wall, the women on the outside, so that if they have any sudden pain or sickness, such as sometimes happens to women with child, they may rise without disturbing the arrangements and go to the nurses.

The nurses sit separately with the infants in a dining room assigned for the purpose, never without a fire and a supply of clean water nor without cradles. Thus they can both lay the infants down and, when they wish, undo their wrappings and let them play freely by the fire. Each woman nurses her own offspring, unless prevented by either death or disease. When that happens, the wives of the syphogrants quickly provide a nurse and find no difficulty in doing so. The reason is that women who can do the service offer themselves with the greatest readiness since everybody praises this kind of pity and since the child who is thus fostered looks on his nurse as his natural mother. In the nurses' quarters are all children up to five years of age. All other minors, among whom they include all of both sexes below the age of marriage, either wait at table on the diners or, if they are not old and strong enough, stand by—and that in absolute silence. Both groups eat what is handed them from the table and have no other separate time for dining.

The syphogrant and his wife sit in the middle of the first table, which is the highest place and which allows them to have the whole company in view, for it stands crosswise at the farthest end of the dining room. Alongside them are two of the eldest, for they always sit four by four at all tables. But if there is a temple in the syphograncy, the priest and his wife so sit with the syphogrant as to preside. On both sides of them sit younger people, and next to them old people again, and so through the house those of the same age sit together and yet mingle with those of a different age. The reason for this practice, they say, is that the grave and reverend behavior of the old may restrain the younger people from mischievous freedom in word and gesture, since nothing can be done or said at table which escapes the notice of the old present on every side.

The trays of food are not served in order from the first place and so on, but all the old men, who are seated in conspicuous places, are served first with the best food, and then equal portions are given to the rest. The old men at their discretion give a share of their delicacies to their neighbors when there is not enough to go around to everybody in the house. Thus, due respect is paid to seniority, and yet all have an equal advantage.

They begin every dinner and supper with some reading which is conducive to morality but which is brief so as not to be tiresome. Taking their cue from the reading, the elders introduce approved subjects of conversation, neither somber nor dull. But they do not monopolize the whole dinner with long speeches: they are ready to hear the young men too, and indeed deliberately draw them out that they may test each one's ability and character, which are revealed in the relaxed atmosphere of a feast.

Their dinners are somewhat short, their suppers more prolonged, because the former are followed by labor, the latter by sleep and a night's rest. They think the night's rest to be more efficacious to wholesome digestion. No supper passes without music, nor does the dessert course lack delicacies. They burn spices and scatter perfumes and omit nothing that may cheer the company. For they are somewhat more inclined to this attitude of mind: that no kind of pleasure is forbidden, provided no harm comes of it.

This is the common life they live in the city. In the country, however, since they are rather far removed from their neighbors, all take their meals in their own homes. No family lacks any kind of edible inasmuch as all the food eaten by the city dwellers comes from those who live in the country.

UTOPIAN TRAVEL, [ETC.]

Now if any citizens conceive a desire either to visit their friends who reside in another city or to see the place itself, they easily obtain leave from their syphogrants and tranibors, unless some good reason prevents them. Accordingly a party is made up and dispatched carrying a letter from the governor which bears witness to the granting of leave to travel and fixes the day of their return. A wagon is granted them with a public slave to conduct and see to the oxen, but, unless they have women in their company, they dispense with the wagon, regarding it as a burden and hindrance. Throughout their journey, though they carry nothing with them, yet nothing is lacking, for they are at home everywhere. If they stay longer than a day in any place, each practices his trade there and is entertained very courteously by workers in the same trade.

If any person gives himself leave to stray out of his territorial limits and is caught without the governor's certificate, he is treated with contempt, brought back as a runaway, and severely punished. If he dares to repeat the offense, he is punished with slavery.

If anyone is seized with the desire of exploring the country belonging to his own city, he is not forbidden to do so, provided he obtain his father's leave and his wife's consent. In any district of the country to which he comes, he receives no food until he has finished the morning share of the day's work or the labor that is usually performed there before supper. If he keep to this condition, he may go where he pleases within the territory belonging to his city. In this way he will be just as useful to the city as if he were in it.

Now you can see how nowhere is there any license to waste time, nowhere any pretext to evade work—no wine shop, no alehouse, no brothel anywhere, no opportunity for corruption, no lurking hole, no secret meeting place. On the contrary, being under the eyes of all, people are bound either to be performing the usual labor or to be enjoying their leisure in a fashion not without decency. This universal behavior must of necessity lead to an abundance of all commodities. Since the latter are distributed evenly among all, it follows, of course, that no one can be reduced to poverty or beggary.

In the senate at Amaurotum (to which, as I said before, three are sent annually from every city), they first determine what commodity is in plenty in each particular place and again where on the island the crops have been meager. They at once fill up the scarcity of one place by the surplus of another. This service they perform without payment, receiving nothing in return from those to whom they give. Those who have given out of their stock to any particular city without requiring any return from it receive what they lack from another to which they have given nothing. Thus, the whole island is like a single family.

But when they have made sufficient provision for themselves (which they do not consider complete until they have provided for two years to come, on account of the next year's uncertain crop), then they export into other countries, out of their surplus, a great quantity of grain, honey, wool, linen, timber, scarlet and purple dyestuffs, hides, wax, tallow, leather, as well as livestock. Of all these commodities they bestow the seventh part on the poor of the district and sell the rest at a moderate price.

By this trade they bring into their country not only such articles as they lack themselves—and practically the only thing lacking is iron—but also a great quantity of silver and gold. This exchange has gone on day by day so long that now they have everywhere an abundance of these metals, more than would be believed. In consequence, they now care little whether they sell for ready cash or appoint a future day for payment, and in fact have by far the greatest amount out on credit. In all transactions on credit, however, they never trust private citizens but the municipal government, the legal documents being drawn up as usual. When the day for payment comes, the city collects the money due from private debtors and puts it into the treasury and enjoys the use of it until the Utopians claim payment.

The Utopians never claim payment of most of the money. They think it hardly fair to take away a thing useful to other people when it is useless to themselves. But if circumstances require that they should lend some part of it to another nation, then they call in their debts—or when they must wage war. It is for that single purpose that they keep all the treasure they possess at home: to be their bulwark in extreme peril or in sudden emergency. They use it above all to hire at sky-high rates of pay foreign mercenaries (whom they would jeopardize rather than their own citizens), being well aware that by large sums of money even their enemies themselves may be bought and set to fight one another either by treachery or by open warfare.

For these military reasons they keep a vast treasure, but not as a treasure. They keep it in a way which I am really quite ashamed to reveal for fear that my words will not be believed. My fears are all the more justified because I am conscious that, had I not been there and witnessed the phenomenon, I myself should have been with difficulty induced to believe it from another's account. It needs must be almost always the rule that, as far as a thing is unlike the ways of the hearers, so far is it from obtaining their credence. An impartial judge of things, however, seeing that the rest of their institutions are so unlike ours, will perhaps wonder less that their use of silver and gold should be adapted to their way of life rather than to ours. As stated, they do not use money themselves but keep it only for an emergency, which may actually occur, yet possibly may never happen.

Meanwhile, gold and silver, of which money is made, are so treated by them that no one values them more highly than their true nature deserves. Who does not see that they are far inferior to iron in usefulness since without iron mortals cannot live any more than without fire and water? To gold and silver, however, nature has given no use that we cannot dispense with, if the folly of men had not made them valuable because they are rare. On the other hand, like a most kind and indulgent mother, she has exposed to view all that is best, like air and water and earth itself, but has removed as far as possible from us all vain and unprofitable things.

If in Utopia these metals were kept locked up in a tower, it might be suspected that the governor and the senate—for such is the foolish imagination of the common folk—were deceiving the people by the scheme and they themselves were deriving some benefit therefrom. Moreover, if they made them into drinking vessels and other such skillful handiwork, then if occasion arose for them all to be melted down again and applied to the pay of soldiers, they realize that people would be unwilling to be deprived of what they had once begun to treasure.

To avoid these dangers, they have devised a means which, as it is consonant with the rest of their institutions, so it is extremely unlike our own—seeing that we value gold so much and are so careful in safeguarding it—and therefore incredible except to those who have experience of it. While they eat and drink from earthenware and glassware of fine workmanship but of little value, from gold and silver they make chamber pots and all the humblest vessels for use everywhere, not only in the common halls but in private homes also. Moreover, they employ the same metals to make the chains and solid fetters which they put on their slaves. Finally, as for those who bear the stigma of disgrace on account of some crime, they have gold ornaments hanging from their ears, gold rings encircling their fingers, gold chains thrown around their necks, and, as a last touch, a gold crown binding their temples. Thus by every means in their power they make gold and silver a mark of ill fame. In this way, too, it happens that, while all other nations bear the loss of these metals with as great grief as if they were losing their very vitals, if circumstances in Utopia ever required the removal of all gold and silver, no one would feel that he were losing as much as a penny.[9]

They also gather pearls by the seashore and diamonds and rubies on certain cliffs. They do not look for them purposely, but they polish them when found by chance. With them they adorn little children, who in their earliest years are proud and delighted with such decorations. When they have grown somewhat older and perceive that only children use such toys, they lay them aside, not by any order of their parents, but through their own feeling of shame, just as our own children, when they grow up, throw away their marbles, rattles, and dolls.

What opposite ideas and feelings are created by customs so different from those of other people came home to me never more clearly than in the case of the Anemolian ambassadors. They arrived in Amaurotum during my stay there. Because they came to treat of important matters, the three representatives of each city had assembled before their appearance. Now all the ambassadors of neighboring nations, who had previously visited the land, were well acquainted with the manners of the Utopians and knew that they paid no respect to costly clothes but looked with contempt on silk and regarded gold as a badge of disgrace. These persons usually came in the simplest possible dress. But the Anemolians, living farther off and having had fewer dealings with them, since they heard that in Utopia all were dressed alike, and in a homespun fashion at that, felt sure that they did not possess what they made no use of. Being more proud than wise, they determined by the grandeur of their apparel to represent the gods themselves and by their splendid adornment to dazzle the eyes of the poor Utopians.

9. Hythlodaeus distinguishes first between the use value and the exchange value of an object: Gold, a soft metal, is useless except as decoration; but as a scarce commodity, it can be exchanged for other objects that do have a use value. He then places a moral construction on precious (or scarce) metals because they are used to indicate wealth and promote ostentation.

Consequently the three ambassadors made a grand entry with a suite of a hundred followers, all in parti-colored clothes and most in silk. The ambassadors themselves, being noblemen at home, were arrayed in cloth of gold, with heavy gold necklaces and earrings, with gold rings on their fingers, and with strings of gleaming pearls and gems upon their caps; in fact, they were decked out with all those articles which in Utopia are used to punish slaves, to stigmatize evil-doers, or to amuse children. It was a sight worth seeing to behold their cockiness when they compared their grand clothing with that of the Utopians, who had poured out into the street to see them pass. On the other hand, it was no less delightful to notice how much they were mistaken in their sanguine[1] expectations and how far they were from obtaining the consideration which they had hoped to get. To the eyes of all the Utopians, with the exception of the very few who for a good reason had visited foreign countries, all this gay show appeared disgraceful. They therefore bowed to the lowest of the party as to the masters but took the ambassadors themselves to be slaves because they were wearing gold chains, and passed them over without any deference whatever.

Why, you might have seen also the children who had themselves discarded gems and pearls, when they saw them attached to the caps of the ambassadors, poke and nudge their mothers and say to them:

"Look, mother, that big rascal is still wearing pearls and jewels as if he were yet a little boy!"

But the mother, also in earnest, would say:

"Hush, son, I think it is one of the ambassadors' fools."

Others found fault with the golden chains as useless, being so slender that a slave could easily break them or, again, so loose that at his pleasure he could throw them off and escape anywhere scot-free.

After spending one or more days there, the ambassadors saw an immense quantity of gold held as cheaply and in as great contempt there as in honor among themselves. They saw, too, that more gold and silver were amassed to make the chains and fetters of one runaway slave than had made up the whole array of the three of them. They then were crestfallen and for shame put away all the finery with which they had made themselves haughtily conspicuous, especially when, after familiar talk with the Utopians, they had learned their ways and opinions.

The Utopians wonder that any mortal takes pleasure in the uncertain sparkle of a tiny jewel or precious stone when he can look at a star or even the sun itself. They wonder that anyone can be so mad as to think himself more noble on account of the texture of a finer wool, since, however fine the texture is, a sheep once wore the wool and yet all the time was nothing more than a sheep.

They wonder, too, that gold, which by its very nature is so useless, is now everywhere in the world valued so highly that man himself, through whose agency and for whose use it got this value, is priced much cheaper than gold itself. This is true to such an extent that a blockhead who has no more intelligence than a log and who is as dishonest as he is foolish keeps in bondage many wise men and good men merely for the reason that a great heap of gold coins happens to be his. Yet if some chance or some legal trick (which is as apt as chance to confound high and low) transfers it from this master to the lowest rascal in his entire household, he will surely very soon pass into the service of his former servant—as if he were a mere appendage of and

1. Optimistic.

addition to the coins! But much more do they wonder at and abominate the madness of persons who pay almost divine honors to the rich, to whom they neither owe anything nor are obligated in any other respect than that they are rich. Yet they know them to be so mean and miserly that they are more than sure that of all that great pile of cash, as long as the rich men live, not a single penny will ever come their way.

These and similar opinions they have conceived partly from their upbringing, being reared in a commonwealth whose institutions are far removed from follies of the kind mentioned, and partly from instruction and reading good books. Though there are not many in each city who are relieved from all other tasks and assigned to scholarship alone, that is to say, the individuals in whom they have detected from childhood an outstanding personality, a first-rate intelligence, and an inclination of mind toward learning, yet all children are introduced to good literature. A large part of the people, too, men and women alike, throughout their lives, devote to learning the hours which, as we said, are free from manual labor.

They learn the various branches of knowledge in their native tongue. The latter is copious in vocabulary and pleasant to the ear and a very faithful exponent of thought. It is almost the same as that current in a great part of that side of the world, only that everywhere else its form is more corrupt, to different degrees in different regions.

Of all those philosophers whose names are famous in the part of the world known to us, the reputation of not even a single one had reached them before our arrival. Yet in music, dialectic, arithmetic, and geometry they have made almost the same discoveries as those predecessors of ours in the classical world. But while they measure up to the ancients in almost all other subjects, still they are far from being a match for the inventions of our modern logicians. In fact, they have discovered not even a single one of those very ingeniously devised rules about restrictions, amplifications, and suppositions which our own children everywhere learn in the *Small Logicals*. In addition, so far are they from ability to speculate on second intentions that not one of them could see even man himself as a so-called universal—though he was, as you know, colossal and greater than any giant, as well as pointed out by us with our finger.[2]

They are most expert, however, in the courses of the stars and the movements of the celestial bodies. Moreover, they have ingeniously devised instruments in different shapes, by which they have most exactly comprehended the movements and positions of the sun and moon and all the other stars which are visible in their horizon. But of the agreements and discords of the planets and, in sum, of all that infamous and deceitful divination by the stars, they do not even dream.

They forecast rains, winds, and all the other changes in weather by definite signs which they have ascertained by long practice. But as to the causes of all these phenomena, and of the flow of the sea and its saltiness, and, in fine, of the origin and nature of the heavens and the universe, they partly treat of them in the same way as our ancient philosophers and partly, as the latter differ from one another, they, too, in introducing new theories disagree with them all and yet do not in all respects agree with fellow Utopians.

In that part of philosophy which deals with morals, they carry on the same debates as we do. They inquire into the good: of the soul and of the body and of external gifts. They ask also whether the name of good may be applied to all three or

2. In logic a first intention is the conception gained from the apprehension of an object as a whole; a second intention is the abstracted conception gained by generalizing upon a first intention and as such exists only in the mind. The Utopians cannot conceive of second intentions because they are themselves second intentions; they are the product of More's reflection upon the particular European governments he has studied.

simply belongs to the endowments of the soul. They discuss virtue and pleasure, but their principal and chief debate is in what thing or things, one or more, they are to hold that happiness consists. In this matter they seem to lean more than they should to the school that espouses pleasure as the object by which to define either the whole or the chief part of human happiness.

What is more astonishing is that they seek a defense for this soft doctrine from their religion, which is serious and strict, almost solemn and hard. They never have a discussion of happiness without uniting certain principles taken from religion as well as from philosophy, which uses rational arguments. Without these principles they think reason insufficient and weak by itself for the investigation of true happiness. The following are examples of these principles. The soul is immortal and by the goodness of God born for happiness. After this life rewards are appointed for our virtues and good deeds, punishment for our crimes. Though these principles belong to religion, yet they hold that reason leads men to believe and to admit them.[3]

Once the principles are eliminated, the Utopians have no hesitation in maintaining that a person would be stupid not to realize that he ought to seek pleasure by fair means or foul, but that he should only take care not to let a lesser pleasure interfere with a greater nor to follow after a pleasure which would bring pain in retaliation. To pursue hard and painful virtue and not only to banish the sweetness of life but even voluntarily to suffer pain from which you expect no profit (for what profit can there be if after death you gain nothing for having passed the whole present life unpleasantly, that is, wretchedly?)—this policy they declare to be the extreme of madness.

As it is, they hold happiness rests not in every kind of pleasure but only in good and decent pleasure. To such, as to the supreme good, our nature is drawn by virtue itself, to which the opposite school alone attributes happiness. The Utopians define virtue as living according to nature since to this end we were created by God. That individual, they say, is following the guidance of nature who, in desiring one thing and avoiding another, obeys the dictates of reason.[4]

Now reason first of all inflames men to a love and veneration of the divine majesty, to whom we owe both our existence and our capacity for happiness. Secondly, it admonishes and urges us to lead a life as free from care and as full of joy as possible and, because of our natural fellowship, to help all other men, too, to attain that end. No one was ever so solemn and severe a follower of virtue and hater of pleasure that he, while imposing on you labors, watchings, and discomforts, would not at the same time bid you do your best to relieve the poverty and misfortunes of others. He would bid you regard as praiseworthy in humanity's name that one man should provide for another man's welfare and comfort—if it is especially humane (and humanity is the virtue most peculiar to man) to relieve the misery of others and, by taking away all sadness from their life, restore them to enjoyment, that is, to pleasure. If so, why should not nature urge everyone to do the same for himself also?

3. By believing in the immortality of the soul, an afterlife of rewards or punishments, and the goodness of God, the Utopians show that they are aware of "natural law," held to be apprehensible by reason.

4. The Utopians represent a people for whom religion is manifest in nature, as it was for the Greeks and the Romans, rather than revealed by God, as it was for the ancient Israelites and, after them, the disciples of Christ. The Utopian is typically reasonable, follows the dictates of reason, and is guided by a beneficent nature that has not been revealed as fallen from an Edenic state of purity and excellence. Hence in Utopia there is no harm in seeking and enjoying pleasure. Nothing in this conception of human nature admits that humankind is inherently corrupted by original sin, a point of doctrine for Christians.

For either a joyous life, that is, a pleasurable life, is evil, in which case not only ought you to help no one to it but, as far as you can, should take it away from everyone as being harmful and deadly, or else, if you not only are permitted but are obliged to win it for others as being good, why should you not do so first of all for yourself, to whom you should show no less favor than to others? When nature bids you to be good to others, she does not command you conversely to be cruel and merciless to yourself. So nature herself, they maintain, prescribes to us a joyous life or, in other words, pleasure, as the end of all our operations. Living according to her prescription they define as virtue.

To pursue this line. Nature calls all men to help one another to a merrier life. (This she certainly does with good reason, for no one is raised so far above the common lot of mankind as to have his sole person the object of nature's care, seeing that she equally favors all whom she endows with the same form.) Consequently nature surely bids you take constant care not so to further your own advantages as to cause disadvantages to your fellows.[5]

Therefore they hold that not only ought contracts between private persons to be observed but also public laws for the distribution of vital commodities, that is to say, the matter of pleasure, provided they have been justly promulgated by a good king or ratified by the common consent of a people neither oppressed by tyranny nor deceived by fraud. As long as such laws are not broken, it is prudence to look after your own interests, and to look after those of the public in addition is a mark of devotion. But to deprive others of their pleasure to secure your own, this is surely an injustice. On the contrary, to take away something from yourself and to give it to others is a duty of humanity and kindness which never takes away as much advantage as it brings back. It is compensated by the return of benefits as well as by the actual consciousness of the good deed. Remembrance of the love and good will of those whom you have benefited gives the mind a greater amount of pleasure than the bodily pleasure which you have forgone would have afforded. Finally—and religion easily brings this home to a mind which readily assents—God repays, in place of a brief and tiny pleasure, immense and never-ending gladness. And so they maintain, having carefully considered and weighed the matter, that all our actions, and even the very virtues exercised in them, look at last to pleasure as their end and happiness.

By pleasure they understand every movement and state of body or mind in which, under the guidance of nature, man delights to dwell. They are right in including man's natural inclinations. For just as the senses as well as right reason aim at whatever is pleasant by nature—whatever is not striven after through wrong-doing, nor involves the loss of something more pleasant, nor is followed by pain—so they hold that whatever things mortals imagine by a futile consensus to be sweet to them in spite of being against nature (as though they had the power to change the nature of things as they do their names) are all so far from making for happiness that they are even a great hindrance to it. The reason is that they possess the minds of persons in whom they have once become deep-seated with a false idea of pleasure so that no room is left anywhere for true and genuine delights. In fact, very many are the things which, though of their own nature they contain no sweetness, nay, a good part of

5. Hythlodaeus describes the classical notion of a benefit, an action that furthers the welfare of a community of persons rather than that of a particular person. The logic of a benefit dictates that an individual can act to confer an advantage not only to himself but also to the community of which he is a part; correspondingly, an action that is to the disadvantage of another individual or his community may not be beneficial to him, however profitable it may seem in the short run.

them very much bitterness, still are, through the perverse attraction of evil desires, not only regarded as the highest pleasures but also counted among the chief reasons that make life worth living.

In the class that follow this spurious pleasure, they put those whom I mentioned before, who think themselves the better men, the better the coat they wear. In this one thing they make a twofold mistake: they are no less deceived in thinking their coat better than in thinking themselves better. If you consider the use of the garment, why is wool of finer thread superior to that of thicker? Yet, as if it were by nature and not by their own mistake that they had the advantage, they hold their heads high and believe some extra worth attaches to themselves thereby. Thus, the honor which, if ill-clad, they would not have ventured to hope for, they require as if of right for a smarter coat. If passed by with some neglect, they are indignant.

Again, does it not show the same stupidity to think so much of empty and unprofitable honors? What natural and true pleasure can another's bared head or bent knees afford you? Will this behavior cure the pain in your own knees or relieve the lunacy in your own head? In this conception of counterfeit pleasure, a strange and sweet madness is displayed by men who imagine themselves to be noble and plume themselves on it and applaud themselves because their fortune has been to be born of certain ancestors of whom the long succession has been counted rich—for that is now the only nobility—and especially rich in landed estates. They consider themselves not a whit less noble even if their ancestors have not left them a square foot or if they themselves have consumed in extravagant living what was left them.

With these persons they class those who, as I said, dote on jewels and gems and who think they become a species of god if ever they secure a fine specimen, especially of the sort which at the period is regarded as of the highest value in their country. It is not everywhere or always that one kind of stone is prized. They will not purchase it unless taken out of its gold setting and exposed to view, and not even then unless the seller takes an oath and gives security that it is a true gem and a true stone, so anxious are they lest a spurious stone in place of a genuine one deceive their eyes. But why should a counterfeited one give less pleasure to your sight when your eye cannot distinguish it from the true article? Both should be of equal value to you, even as they would be, by heaven, to a blind man!

What can be said of those who keep superfluous wealth to please themselves, not with putting the heap to any use but merely with looking at it?[6] Do they feel true pleasure, or are they not rather cheated by false pleasure? Or, what of those who have the opposite failing and hide the gold, which they will never use and perhaps never see again, and who, in their anxiety not to lose it, thereby do lose it? What else but loss is it to deprive yourself of its use, and perhaps all other men too, and to put it back in the ground? And yet you joyfully exult over your hidden treasure as though your mind were now free from all anxiety. Suppose that someone removed it by stealing it and that you died ten years afterwards knowing nothing of the theft. During the whole decade which you lived after the money was stolen, what did it matter to you whether it was stolen or safe? In either case it was of just as little use to you.

Among those who indulge such senseless delights they reckon dicers (whose madness they know not by experience but by hearsay only), as well as hunters and hawkers. What pleasure is there, they ask, in shooting dice upon a table? You have

6. Hythlodaeus implies that money is useful because it can be exchanged for goods in a market. Money exchange is more efficient than barter, as it can always find a commensurable value.

shot them so often that, even if some pleasure had been in it, weariness by now could have arisen from the habitual practice. Or what sweetness can there be, and not rather disgust, in hearing the barking and howling of dogs? Or what greater sensation of pleasure is there when a dog chases a hare than when a dog chases a dog? The same thing happens in both cases: there is racing in both if speed gives you delight.

But if you are attracted by the hope of slaughter and the expectation of a creature being mangled under your eyes, it ought rather to inspire pity when you behold a weak, fugitive, timid, and innocent little hare torn to pieces by a strong, fierce, and cruel dog. In consequence the Utopians have imposed the whole activity of hunting, as unworthy of free men, upon their butchers—a craft, as I explained before, they exercise through their slaves. They regard hunting as the meanest part of the butcher's trade and its other functions as more useful and more honorable, seeing that they do much more positive good and kill animals only from necessity, whereas the hunter seeks nothing but pleasure from the killing and mangling of a poor animal. Even in the case of brute beasts, this desire of looking on bloodshed, in their estimation, either arises from a cruel disposition or degenerates finally into cruelty through the constant practice of such brutal pleasure.

Although the mob of mortals regards these and all similar pursuits—and they are countless—as pleasures, yet the Utopians positively hold them to have nothing to do with true pleasure since there is nothing sweet in them by nature. The fact that for the mob they inspire in the senses a feeling of enjoyment—which seems to be the function of pleasure—does not make them alter their opinion. The enjoyment does not arise from the nature of the thing itself but from their own perverse habit. The latter failing makes them take what is bitter for sweet, just as pregnant women by their vitiated taste suppose pitch and tallow sweeter than honey. Yet it is impossible for any man's judgment, depraved either by disease or by habit, to change the nature of pleasure any more than that of anything else.

The pleasures which they admit as genuine they divide into various classes, some pleasures being attributed to the soul and others to the body. To the soul they ascribe intelligence and the sweetness which is bred of contemplation of truth. To these two are joined the pleasant recollection of a well-spent life and the sure hope of happiness to come.

Bodily pleasure they divide into two kinds. The first is that which fills the sense with clearly perceptible sweetness. Sometimes it comes from the renewal of those organs which have been weakened by our natural heat. These organs are then restored by food and drink. Sometimes it comes from the elimination of things which overload the body. This agreeable sensation occurs when we discharge feces from our bowels or perform the activity generative of children or relieve the itching of some part by rubbing or scratching. Now and then, however, pleasure arises, not in process of restoring anything that our members lack, nor in process of eliminating anything that causes distress, but from something that tickles and affects our senses with a secret but remarkable moving force and so draws them to itself. Such is that pleasure which is engendered by music.

The second kind of bodily pleasure they claim to be that which consists in a calm and harmonious state of the body. This is nothing else than each man's health undisturbed by any disorder. Health, if assailed by no pain, gives delight of itself, though there be no motion arising from pleasure applied from without. Even though it is less obvious and less perceptible by the sense than that overblown craving for eating and drinking, yet none the less many hold it to be the greatest of pleasures. Almost all the Utopians regard it as great and as practically the foundation and basis of all pleasures. Even by itself it can make the state of life peaceful and desirable, whereas without it absolutely no place is left for any pleasure. The absence of pain without the presence of health they regard as insensibility rather than pleasure.

They long ago rejected the position of those who held that a state of stable and tranquil health (for this question, too, had been actively discussed among them) was not to be counted as a pleasure because its presence, they said, could not be felt except through some motion from without. But on the other hand now they almost all agree that health is above all things conducive to pleasure. Since in disease, they query, there is pain, which is the bitter enemy of pleasure no less than disease is of health, why should not pleasure in turn be found in the tranquillity of health? They think that it is of no importance in the discussion whether you say that disease is pain or that disease is accompanied with pain, for it comes to the same thing either way. To be sure, if you hold that health is either a pleasure or the necessary cause of pleasure, as fire is of heat, in both ways the conclusion is that those who have permanent health cannot be without pleasure.

Besides, while we eat, say they, what is that but health, which has begun to be impaired, fighting against hunger, with food as its comrade in arms? While it gradually gains strength, the very progress to the usual vigor supplies the pleasure by which we are thus restored. Shall the health which delights in conflict not rejoice when it has gained the victory? When at length it has successfully acquired its former strength, which was its sole object through the conflict, shall it immediately become insensible and not recognize and embrace its own good? The assertion that health cannot be felt they think to be far wide of the truth. Who in a waking state, ask they, does not feel that he is in good health—except the man who is not? Who is bound fast by such insensibility or lethargy that he does not confess that health is agreeable and delightful to him? And what is delightful except pleasure under another name?

To sum up, they cling above all to mental pleasures, which they value as the first and foremost of all pleasures. Of these the principal part they hold to arise from the practice of the virtues and the consciousness of a good life. Of these pleasures which the body supplies, they give the palm to health. The delight of eating and drinking, and anything that gives the same sort of enjoyment, they think desirable, but only for the sake of health. Such things are not pleasant in themselves but only in so far as they resist the secret encroachment of ill health. Just as a wise man should pray that he may escape disease rather than crave a remedy for it and that he may drive pain off rather than seek relief from it, so it would be better not to need this kind of pleasure rather than to be soothed by it.

If a person thinks that his felicity consists in this kind of pleasure, he must admit that he will be in the greatest happiness if his lot happens to be a life which is spent in perpetual hunger, thirst, itching, eating, drinking, scratching, and rubbing. Who does not see that such a life is not only disgusting but wretched? These pleasures are surely the lowest of all as being most adulterated, for they never occur unless they are coupled with the pains which are their opposites. For example, with the pleasure of eating is united hunger—and on no fair terms, for the pain is the stronger and lasts the longer. It comes into existence before the pleasure and does not end until the pleasure dies with it. Such pleasures they hold should not be highly valued and only insofar as they are necessary. Yet they enjoy even these pleasures and gratefully acknowledge the kindness of mother nature who, with alluring sweetness, coaxes her offspring to that which of necessity they must constantly do. In what discomfort should we have to live if, like all other sicknesses which less frequently assail us, so also these daily diseases of hunger and thirst had to be expelled by bitter poisons and drugs?

Beauty, strength, and nimbleness—these as special and pleasant gifts of nature they gladly cherish. Nay, even those pleasures entering by the ears, eyes, or nostrils, which nature intended to be peculiarly characteristic of man (for no other species of living creature either takes in the form and fairness of the world or is affected by the pleasantness of smell, except in choice of food, or distinguishes harmonious and dissonant intervals of sound)—these, too, I say, they follow after as pleasant seasonings of life.[7] But in all they make this limitation: that the lesser is not to interfere with the greater and that pleasure is not to produce pain in aftermath. Pain they think a necessary consequence if the pleasure is base.

But to despise the beauty of form, to impair the strength of the body, to turn nimbleness into sluggishness, to exhaust the body by fasts, to injure one's health, and to reject all the other favors of nature, unless a man neglects these advantages to himself in providing more zealously for the pleasure of other persons or of the public, in return for which sacrifice he expects a greater pleasure from God—but otherwise to deal harshly with oneself for a vain and shadowy reputation of virtue to no man's profit or for preparing oneself more easily to bear adversities which may never come—this attitude they think is extreme madness and the sign of a mind which is both cruel to itself and ungrateful to nature, to whom it disdains to be indebted and therefore renounces all her benefits.

This is their view of virtue and pleasure. They believe that human reason can attain to no truer view, unless a heaven-sent religion inspire man with something more holy. Whether in this stand they are right or wrong, time does not permit us to examine—nor is it necessary. We have taken upon ourselves only to describe their principles, and not also to defend them. But of this I am sure, that whatever you think of their ideas, there is nowhere in the world a more excellent people nor a happier commonwealth. They are nimble and active of body, and stronger than you would expect from their stature. The latter, however, is not dwarfish. Though they have not a very fertile soil or a very wholesome climate, they protect themselves against the atmosphere by temperate living and make up for the defects of the land by diligent labor. Consequently, nowhere in the world is there a more plentiful supply of grain and cattle, nowhere are men's bodies more vigorous and subject to fewer diseases. Not only may you behold the usual agricultural tasks carefully administered there, whereby the naturally barren soil is improved by art and industry, but you may also see how a whole forest has been uprooted in one place by the hands of the people and planted in another. Herein they were thinking not so much of abundance as of transport, that they might have wood closer to the sea or the rivers or the cities themselves. For it takes less labor to convey grain than timber to a distance by land.

The people in general are easygoing, good-tempered, ingenious, and leisure-loving. They patiently do their share of manual labor when occasion demands, though otherwise they are by no means fond of it. In their devotion to mental study they are unwearied. When they had heard from us about the literature and learning of the

7. Just as the Utopians imagine humankind without original sin, so they cannot imagine any point in ascetic discipline of the body for the sake of curbing or controlling its inherent tendency to sin.

Greeks (for in Latin there was nothing, apart from history and poetry, which seemed likely to gain their great approval), it was wonderful to see their extreme desire for permission to master them through our instruction.

We began, therefore, to give them public lessons, more at first that we should not seem to refuse the trouble than that we expected any success. But after a little progress, their diligence made us at once feel sure that our own diligence would not be bestowed in vain. They began so easily to imitate the shapes of the letters, so readily to pronounce the words, so quickly to learn by heart, and so faithfully to reproduce what they had learned that it was a perfect wonder to us. The explanation was that most of them were scholars picked for their ability and mature in years, who undertook to learn their tasks not only fired by their own free will but acting under orders of the senate. In less than three years they were perfect in the language and able to peruse good authors without any difficulty unless the text had faulty readings. According to my conjecture, they got hold of Greek literature more easily because it was somewhat related to their own. I suspect that their race was derived from the Greek because their language, which in almost all other respects resembles the Persian, retains some traces of Greek in the names of their cities and officials.

When about to go on the fourth voyage, I put on board, in place of wares to sell, a fairly large package of books,[8] having made up my mind never to return rather than to come back soon. They received from me most of Plato's works, several of Aristotle's, as well as Theophrastus on plants, which I regret to say was mutilated in parts. During the voyage an ape found the book, left lying carelessly about, and in wanton sport tore out and destroyed several pages in various sections. Of grammarians they have only Lascaris, for I did not take Theodore with me. They have no dictionaries except those of Hesychius and Dioscorides. They are very fond of the works of Plutarch and captivated by the wit and pleasantry of Lucian. Of the poets they have Aristophanes, Homer, and Euripides, together with Sophocles in the small Aldine type. Of the historians they possess Thucydides and Herodotus, as well as Herodian.

In medicine, moreover, my companion Tricius Apinatus had carried with him some small treatises of Hippocrates and the *Ars medica* of Galen, to which books they attribute great value. Even though there is scarcely a nation in the whole world that needs medicine less, yet nowhere is it held in greater honor—and this for the reason that they regard the knowledge of it as one of the finest and most useful branches of philosophy. When by the help of this philosophy they explore the secrets of nature, they appear to themselves not only to get great pleasure in doing so but also to win

8. Hythlodaeus has given the Utopians only works in Greek, even though they cover topics in the history of Rome. By this, More clearly intended to emphasize what he thought was the intellectual superiority of Greek over Roman culture. Beyond the works of Plato and Aristotle, Hythlodaeus's library contains the works of Theophrastus (3rd century B.C.), who wrote a history of plants; Constantine Lascaris and Theodore of Gaza, both grammarians of the 15th century; Hesychius, a Greek lexicographer of the 4th century B.C.; Dioscurides, a Greek physician of the 1st century, who wrote a medical textbook, known and used through the early modern period; Plutarch, a Greek biographer and moralist of the 2nd century; Lucian, a Greek rhetorician of the 2nd century, who wrote satirical dialogues; Aristophanes, a Greek dramatist of the 4th century B.C., who wrote comic drama; Homer, the name given the author or authors of the Greek epics, the *Iliad* and the *Odyssey*, committed to writing about 800 B.C.; and Euripides and Sophocles, both Greek tragedians of the 5th century B.C.. Herodotus and Thucydides lived during the 5th century B.C.; Herodotus wrote of the wars between the kingdoms of the near east and the Greek states in his *Histories*, Thucydides of the tragic fall of the Athenian state in his *Peloponnesian Wars*. Herodian, a Syrian historian, wrote, in Greek, of the Roman emperors from the death of Marcus Aurelius in A.D. 180 to 238. "Tricius Apinatus" is a fictitious author, but Hippocrates and Galen were Greek physicians of the 5th century B.C. and the 2nd century, respectively, whose medical treatises were popular until the end of the 17th century. "Aldine type" was the particular typeface used by the early 16-century Venetian printer Aldus Manutius, who was famous for his publication of fine editions of Greek authors.

the highest approbation of the Author and Maker of nature. They presume that, like all other artificers, He has set forth the visible mechanism of the world as a spectacle for man, whom alone He has made capable of appreciating such a wonderful thing. Therefore He prefers a careful and diligent beholder and admirer of His work to one who like an unreasoning brute beast passes by so great and so wonderful a spectacle stupidly and stolidly.

Thus, trained in all learning, the minds of the Utopians are exceedingly apt in the invention of the arts which promote the advantage and convenience of life. Two, however, they owe to us, the art of printing and the manufacture of paper—though not entirely to us but to a great extent also to themselves. When we showed them the Aldine printing in paper books, we talked about the material of which paper is made and the art of printing without giving a detailed explanation, for none of us was expert in either art. With the greatest acuteness they promptly guessed how it was done. Though previously they wrote only on parchment, bark, and papyrus, from this time they tried to manufacture paper and print letters. Their first attempts were not very successful, but by frequent experiment they soon mastered both. So great was their success that if they had copies of Greek authors, they would have no lack of books. But at present they have no more than I have mentioned, but by printing books they have increased their stock by many thousands of copies.

Whoever, coming to their land on a sight-seeing tour, is recommended by any special intellectual endowment or is acquainted with many countries through long travel, is sure of a hearty welcome, for they delight in hearing what is happening in the whole world. On this score our own landing was pleasing to them. Few persons, however, come to them in the way of trade. What could they bring except iron, or what everybody would rather take back home with him—gold and silver! And as to articles of export, the Utopians think it wiser to carry them out of the country themselves than to let strangers come to fetch them. By this policy they get more information about foreign nations and do not forget by disuse their skill in navigation.

Slavery, [Etc.]

Prisoners of war are not enslaved unless captured in wars fought by the Utopians themselves; nor are the sons of slaves,[9] nor anyone who was in slavery when acquired of slaves, nor anyone whom they could acquire from slavery in other countries. Their slaves are either such or such as have been condemned to death elsewhere for some offense. The greater number are of this latter kind. They carry away many of them; sometimes they buy them cheaply; but often they ask for them and get them for nothing. These classes of slaves they keep not only continually at work but also in chains. Their own countrymen are dealt with more harshly, since their conduct is regarded as all the more regrettable and deserving a more severe punishment as an object lesson because, having had an excellent rearing to a virtuous life, they still could not be restrained from crime.

There is yet another class of slaves, for sometimes a hard-working and poverty-stricken drudge of another country voluntarily chooses slavery in Utopia. These individuals are well treated and, except that they have a little more work assigned to

9. More uses the Latin word *servus*, which means servant, slave, and serf. Most commonly captives in war, slaves were also persons punished for crime, as in Utopia. Voluntary slavery, aside from indentured servitude (for a term), was rare except in theory; presumably such persons chose to work as slaves in exchange for a subsistence living.

them as being used to it, are dealt with almost as leniently as citizens. If anyone wishes to depart, which seldom happens, they do not detain him against his will nor send him away empty-handed.

The sick, as I said, are very lovingly cared for, nothing being omitted which may restore them to health, whether in the way of medicine or diet. They console the incurable diseased by sitting and conversing with them and by applying all possible alleviations. But if a disease is not only incurable but also distressing and agonizing without any cessation, then the priests and the public officials exhort the man, since he is now unequal to all life's duties, a burden to himself, and a trouble to others, and is living beyond the time of his death, to make up his mind not to foster the pest and plague any longer nor to hesitate to die now that life is torture to him but, relying on good hope, to free himself from this bitter life as from prison and the rack, or else voluntarily to permit others to free him.[1] In this course he will act wisely, since by death he will put an end not to enjoyment but to torture. Because in doing so he will be obeying the counsels of the priests, who are God's interpreters, it will be a pious and holy action.

Those who have been persuaded by these arguments either starve themselves to death or, being put to sleep, are set free without the sensation of dying. But they do not make away with anyone against his will, nor in such a case do they relax in the least their attendance upon him. They do believe that death counseled by authority is honorific. But if anyone commits suicide without having obtained the approval of priests and senate, they deem him unworthy of either fire or earth and cast his body ignominiously into a marsh without proper burial.

Women do not marry till eighteen, men not till they are four years older. If before marriage a man or woman is convicted of secret intercourse, he or she is severely punished, and they are forbidden to marry altogether unless the governor's pardon remits their guilt. In addition, both father and mother of the family in whose house the offense was committed incur great disgrace as having been neglectful in doing their duties. The reason why they punish this offence so severely is their foreknowledge that, unless persons are carefully restrained from promiscuous intercourse, few will contract the tie of marriage, in which a whole life must be spent with one companion and all the troubles incidental to it must be patiently borne.

In choosing mates, they seriously and strictly espouse a custom which seemed to us very foolish and extremely ridiculous. The woman, whether maiden or widow, is shown naked to the suitor by a worthy and respectable matron, and similarly the suitor is presented naked before the maiden by a discreet man. We laughed at this custom and condemned it as foolish. They, on the other hand, marvelled at the remarkable folly of all other nations. In buying a colt, where there is question of only a little money, persons are so cautious that though it is almost bare they will not buy until they have taken off the saddle and removed all the trappings for fear some sore lies concealed under these coverings. Yet in the choice of a wife, an action which will cause either pleasure or disgust to follow them the rest of their lives, they are so careless that, while the rest of her body is covered with clothes, they estimate the value of the whole woman from hardly a single handbreadth of her, only the face being visible, and clasp her to themselves not without great danger of their agreeing ill together if something afterwards gives them offense.

1. Neither suicide nor euthanasia was considered immoral in Greek and Roman society.

All are not so wise as to regard only the character of the spouse, and even in the marriages of the wise, bodily attractions also are no small enhancement to the virtues of the mind. Certainly such foul deformity may be hidden beneath these coverings that it may quite alienate a man's mind from his wife when bodily separation is no longer lawful. If such a deformity arises by chance after the marriage has been contracted, each person must bear his own fate, but beforehand the laws ought to protect him from being entrapped by guile.

This provision was the more necessary because the Utopians are the only people in those parts of the world who are satisfied with one spouse and because matrimony there is seldom broken except by death, unless it be for adultery or for intolerable offensiveness of character. When husband or wife is thus offended, leave is granted by the senate to take another mate.[2] The other party perpetually lives a life of disgrace as well as of celibacy. But they cannot endure the repudiation of an unwilling wife, who is in no way to blame, because some bodily calamity has befallen her. They judge it cruel that a person should be abandoned when most in need of comfort and that old age, since it both entails disease and is a disease itself, should have only an unreliable and weak fidelity.

It sometimes happens, however, that when a married couple agree insufficiently in their dispositions and both find others with whom they hope to live more agreeably, they separate by mutual consent and contract fresh unions, but not without the sanction of the senate. The latter allows of no divorce until its members and their wives have carefully gone into the case. Even then they do not readily give consent because they know that it is a very great drawback to cementing the affection between husband and wife if they have before them the easy hope of a fresh union.

Violators of the conjugal tie are punished by the strictest form of slavery. If both parties are married, the injured parties, provided they consent, are divorced from their adulterous mates and couple together, or else are allowed to marry whom they like. But if one of the injured parties continues to feel affection for so undeserving a mate, it is not forbidden to have the marriage continue in force on condition that the party is willing to accompany and share the labor of the other who has been condemned to slavery. Now and then it happens that the penance of the one and the dutiful assiduity of the other move the compassion of the governor and win back their liberty. Relapse into the same offense, however, involves the penalty of death.

For all other crimes there is no law prescribing any fixed penalty, but the punishment is assigned by the senate according to the atrocity, or veniality, of the individual crime. Husbands correct their wives, and parents their children, unless the offense is so serious that it is to the advantage of public morality to have it punished openly. Generally the worst offenses are punished by the sentence of slavery since this prospect, they think, is no less formidable to the criminal and more advantageous to the state than if they make haste to put the offenders to death and get them out of the way at once. Their labor is more profitable than their death, and their example lasts longer to deter others from like crimes. But if they rebel and kick against this treatment, they are thereupon put to death like untameable beasts that cannot be restrained by prison or chain. If they are patient, however, they are not entirely deprived of all hope. When tamed by long and hard punishment, if they

2. In England, divorce was granted only on the grounds of adultery. By contrast, the Utopians grant divorce for incompatibility and extend the privilege to the wife as well as the husband. Adultery, however, is punished with slavery.

show such repentance as testifies that they are more sorry for their sin than for their punishment, then sometimes by the prerogative of the governor and sometimes by the vote of the people their slavery is either lightened or remitted altogether.

To tempt another to an impure act is no less punishable than the commission of that impure act. In every crime the deliberate and avowed attempt is counted equal to the deed, for they think that failure ought not to benefit one who did everything in his power not to fail.

They are very fond of fools.[3] It is a great disgrace to treat them with insult, but there is no prohibition against deriving pleasure from their foolery. The latter, they think, is of the greatest benefit to the fools themselves. If anyone is so stern and morose that he is not amused with anything they either do or say, they do not entrust him with the care of a fool. They fear that he may not treat him with sufficient indulgence since he would find in him neither use nor even amusement, which is his sole faculty.

To deride a man for a disfigurement or the loss of a limb is counted as base and disfiguring, not to the man who is laughed at but to him who laughs, for foolishly upbraiding a man with something as if it were a fault which he was powerless to avoid. While they consider it a sign of a sluggish and feeble mind not to preserve natural beauty, it is, in their judgment, disgraceful affectation to help it out by cosmetics. Experience itself shows them how no elegance of outward form recommends wives to husbands as much as probity and reverence. Some men are attracted only by a handsome shape, but no man's love is kept permanently except by virtue and obedience.

Not merely do they discourage crime by punishment but they offer honors to invite men to virtue. Hence, to great men who have done conspicuous service to their country they set up in the market place statues to stand as a record of noble exploits and, at the same time, to have the glory of forefathers serve their descendants as a spur and stimulus to virtue.

The man who solicits votes to obtain any office is deprived completely of the hope of holding any office at all. They live together in affection and good will. No official is haughty or formidable. They are called fathers and show that character. Honor is paid them willingly, as it should be, and is not exacted from the reluctant. The governor himself is distinguished from citizens not by a robe or a crown but by the carrying of a handful of grain, just as the mark of the high priest is a wax candle borne before him.

They have very few laws because very few are needed for persons so educated. The chief fault they find with other peoples is that almost innumerable books of laws and commentaries are not sufficient. They themselves think it most unfair that any group of men should be bound by laws which are either too numerous to be read through or too obscure to be understood by anyone.

Moreover, they absolutely banish from their country all lawyers, who cleverly manipulate cases and cunningly argue legal points. They consider it a good thing that every man should plead his own cause and say the same to the judge as he would tell his counsel. Thus there is less ambiguity and the truth is more easily elicited when a man, uncoached in deception by a lawyer, conducts his own case and the judge skillfully weighs each statement and helps untutored minds to defeat the false accusations of the crafty. To secure these advantages in other countries is difficult, owing to the

3. In early modern Europe, a "fool" could be a professional jester; usually, he was employed at a royal or noble court and had special license to amuse and even criticize his master.

immense mass of extremely complicated laws. But with the Utopians each man is expert in law. First, they have, as I said, very few laws and, secondly, they regard the most obvious interpretation of the law as the most fair interpretation.

This policy follows from their reasoning that, since all laws are promulgated to remind every man of his duty, the more recondite interpretation reminds only very few (for there are few who can arrive at it) whereas the more simple and obvious sense of the laws is open to all. Otherwise, what difference would it make for the common people, who are the most numerous and also most in need of instruction, whether you framed no law at all or whether the interpretation of the law you framed was such that no one could elicit it except by great ingenuity and long argument? Now, the untrained judgment of the common people cannot attain to the meaning of such an interpretation nor can their lives be long enough, seeing that they are wholly taken up with getting a living.

These virtues of the Utopians have spurred their neighbors (who are free and independent since many of them were long ago delivered from tyrants by the Utopians) to obtain officials from them, some for one year and others for five years. On the expiration of their office they escort them home with honor and praise and bring back successors with them to their own country. Certainly these peoples make very good and wholesome provision for the commonwealth. Seeing that the latter's prosperity or ruin depends on the character of officials, of whom could they have made a wiser choice than of those who cannot be drawn from the path of honor by any bribe since it is no good to them as they will shortly return home, nor influenced by crooked partiality or animosity toward any since they are strangers to the citizens? These two evils, favoritism and avarice, wherever they have settled in men's judgments, instantly destroy all justice, the strongest sinew of the commonwealth. The nations who seek their administrators from Utopia are called allies by them; the name of friend is reserved for all the others whom they have benefited.

Treaties which all other nations so often conclude among themselves, break, and renew, they never make with any nation. "What is the use of a treaty," they ask, "as though nature of herself did not sufficiently bind one man to another? If a person does not regard nature, do you suppose he will care anything about words?"

They are led to this opinion chiefly because in those parts of the world treaties and alliances between kings are not observed with much good faith. In Europe, however, and especially in those parts where the faith and religion of Christ prevails, the majesty of treaties is everywhere holy and inviolable, partly through the justice and goodness of kings, partly through the reverence and fear of the Sovereign Pontiffs. Just as the latter themselves undertake nothing which they do not most conscientiously perform, so they command all other rulers to abide by their promises in every way and compel the recalcitrant by pastoral censure and severe reproof.[4] Popes are perfectly right, of course, in thinking it a most disgraceful thing that those who are specially called the faithful should not faithfully adhere to their commitments.

But in that new world, which is almost as far removed from ours by the equator as their life and character are different from ours, there is no trust in treaties. The more numerous and holy the ceremonies with which a treaty is struck the more quickly is it broken. They find some defect in the wording, which sometimes they cunningly devise of set purpose, so that they can never be held by such strong bonds

4. More is being ironic in extolling the faithful observance of treaties by the papacy. Pope Julius II, who died a few years before the publication of More's treatise, was notorious for breaking his word.

as not somehow to escape from them and break both the treaty and their faith. If this cunning, nay fraud and deceit, were found to have occurred in the contracts of private persons, the treaty-makers with great disdain would exclaim against it as sacrilegious and meriting the gallows—though the very same men plume themselves on being the authors of such advice when given to kings.

In consequence men think either that all justice is only a plebeian and low virtue which is far below the majesty of kings or that there are at least two forms of it: the one which goes on foot and creeps on the ground, fit only for the common sort and bound by many chains so that it can never overstep its barriers; the other a virtue of kings, which, as it is more august than that of ordinary folk, is also far freer so that everything is permissible to it—except what it finds disagreeable.

This behavior, as I said, of rulers there who keep their treaties so badly is, I suppose, the reason why the Utopians make none; if they lived here, they would perhaps change their minds. Nevertheless they believe that, though treaties are faithfully observed, it is a pity that the custom of making them at all had grown up. The result (as though peoples which are divided by the slight interval of a hill or a river were joined by no bond of nature) is men's persuasion that they are born one another's adversaries and enemies and that they are right in aiming at one another's destruction except in so far as treaties prevent it. What is more, even when treaties are made, friendship does not grow up but the license of freebooting continues to the extent that, for lack of skill in drawing up the treaty, no sufficient precaution to prevent this activity has been included in the articles. But the Utopians, on the contrary, think that nobody who has done you no harm should be accounted an enemy, that the fellowship created by nature takes the place of a treaty, and that men are better and more firmly joined together by good will than by pacts, by spirit than by words.

Military Affairs

War, as an activity fit only for beasts and yet practiced by no kind of beast so constantly as by man, they regard with utter loathing. Against the usage of almost all nations they count nothing so inglorious as glory sought in war. Nevertheless men and women alike assiduously exercise themselves in military training on fixed days lest they should be unfit for war when need requires. Yet they do not lightly go to war. They do so only to protect their own territory or to drive an invading enemy out of their friends' lands or, in pity for a people oppressed by tyranny, to deliver them by force of arms from the yoke and slavery of the tyrant, a course prompted by human sympathy.

They oblige their friends with help, not always indeed to defend them merely but sometimes also to requite and avenge injuries previously done to them. They act, however, only if they themselves are consulted before any step is taken and if they themselves initiate the war after they have approved the cause and demanded restitution in vain. They take the final step of war not only when a hostile inroad has carried off booty but also much more fiercely when the merchants among their friends undergo unjust persecution under the color of justice in any other country, either on the pretext of laws in themselves unjust or by the distortion of laws in themselves good.

Such was the origin of the war which the Utopians had waged a little before our time on behalf of the Nephelogetes[5] against the Alaopolitans. The Nephelogetic traders suffered a wrong, as they thought, under pretence of law, but whether right or

5. "Cloud born" (insubstantial) people; the Alaopolitans are "citizens without a people or a country"—that is, stateless.

wrong, it was avenged by a fierce war. Into this war the neighboring nations brought their energies and resources to assist the power and to intensify the rancor of both sides. Most flourishing nations were either shaken to their foundations or grievously afflicted. The troubles upon troubles that arose were ended only by the enslavement and surrender of the Alaopolitans. Since the Utopians were not fighting in their own interest, they yielded them into the power of the Nephelogetes, a people who, when the Alaopolitans were prosperous, were not in the least comparable to them.

So severely do the Utopians punish wrong done to their friends, even in money matters—but not wrongs done to themselves. When they lose their goods anywhere through fraud, but without personal violence, their anger goes no further than abstention from trade with that nation until satisfaction is made. The reason is not that they care less for their citizens than their allies. They are more grieved at their allies' pecuniary loss than their own because their friends' merchants suffer severely by the loss as it falls on their private property, but their own citizens lose nothing but what comes from the common stock and what was plentiful and, as it were, superfluous at home—or else it would not have been exported. As a result, the loss is not felt by any individual. They consider it excessively cruel to avenge such a loss by the death of many when the disadvantage of the loss affects neither the life nor the subsistence of any of their own people.

If a Utopian citizen, however, is wrongfully disabled or killed anywhere, whether the plot is due to the government or to a private citizen, they first ascertain the facts by an embassy and then, if the guilty persons are not surrendered, they cannot be appeased but forthwith declare war. If the guilty persons are surrendered, they are punished either with death or with enslavement.

They not only regret but blush at a victory that has cost much bloodshed, thinking it folly to purchase wares, however precious, too dear. If they overcome and crush the enemy by stratagem and cunning, they feel great pride and celebrate a public triumph over the victory and put up a trophy as for a strenuous exploit. They boast themselves as having acted with valor and heroism whenever their victory is such as no animal except man could have won, that is, by strength of intellect; for, by strength of body, say they, bears, lions, boars, wolves, dogs, and other wild beasts are wont to fight. Most of them are superior to us in brawn and fierceness, but they are all inferior in cleverness and calculation.

Their one and only object in war is to secure that which, had it been obtained beforehand, would have prevented the declaration of war. If that is out of the question, they require such severe punishment of those on whom they lay the blame that for the future they may be afraid to attempt anything of the same sort. These are their chief interests in the enterprise, which they set about promptly to secure, yet taking more care to avoid danger than to win praise or fame.

The moment war is declared, they arrange that simultaneously a great number of placards, made more effective by bearing their public seal, should be set up secretly in the most prominent spots of enemy territory. Herein they promise huge rewards to anyone who will kill the enemy king. Further, they offer smaller sums, but those considerable, for the heads of the individuals whose names they specify in the same proclamations. These are the men whom, next to the king himself, they regard as responsible for the hostile measures taken against them. Whatever reward they fix for an assassin, they double for the man who brings any of the denounced parties alive to them. They actually offer the same rewards, with a guarantee of personal safety, to the persons proscribed, if they will turn against their fellows.

So it swiftly comes about that their enemies suspect all outsiders and, in addition, neither trust nor are loyal to one another. They are in a state of utter panic and no less peril. It is well known that it has often happened that many of them, and especially the king himself, have been betrayed by those in whom they had placed the greatest trust, so easily do bribes incite men to commit every kind of crime. They are boundless in their offers of reward. Remembering, however, what a risk they invite the man to run, they take care that the greatness of the peril is balanced by the extent of the rewards. In consequence they promise and faithfully pay down not only an immense amount of gold but also landed property with high income in very secure places in the territory of friends.

This habit of bidding for and purchasing an enemy, which is elsewhere condemned as the cruel deed of a degenerate nature, they think reflects great credit, first on their wisdom because they thus bring to a conclusion great wars without any battle at all, and secondly on their humanity and mercy because by the death of a few guilty people they purchase the lives of many harmless persons who would have fallen in battle, both on their own side and that of the enemy. They are almost as sorry for the throng and mass of the enemy as for their own citizens. They know that the common folk do not go to war of their own accord but are driven to it by the madness of kings.

If this plan does not succeed, they sow the seeds of dissension broadcast and foster strife by leading a brother of the king or one of the noblemen to hope that he may obtain the throne. If internal strife dies down, then they stir up and involve the neighbors of their enemies by reviving some forgotten claims to dominion such as kings have always at their disposal. Promising their own assistance for the war, they supply money liberally but are very chary of sending their own citizens. They hold them so singularly dear and regard one another of such value that they would not care to exchange any of their own people for the king of the opposite party. As to gold and silver, since they keep it all for this one use, they pay it out without any reluctance, for they would live just as well if they spent it all. Moreover, in addition to the riches which they keep at home, they have also a vast treasure abroad in that many nations, as I said before, are in their debt.

With the riches, they hire and send to war soldiers from all parts, but especially from among the Zapoletans.[6] These people live five hundred miles to the east of Utopia and are fearsome, rough, and wild. They prefer their own rugged woods and mountains among which they are bred. They are a hard race, capable of enduring heat, cold, and toil, lacking all refinements, engaging in no farming, careless about the houses they live in and the clothes they wear, and occupied only with their flocks and herds. To a great extent they live by hunting and plundering. They are born for warfare and zealously seek an opportunity for fighting. When they find it, they eagerly embrace it. Leaving the country in great force, they offer themselves at a cheap rate to anyone who needs fighting men. The only trade they know in life is that by which they seek their death.

They fight with ardor and incorruptible loyalty for those from whom they receive their pay. Yet they bind themselves for no fixed period but take sides on such terms that the next day when higher pay is offered them, even by the enemy, they take his side, and then the day after, if a trifle more is offered to tempt them back, return to the side they took at first.

6. "Busy sellers," that is, of their services.

In almost every war that breaks out there are many of them in both armies. It is a daily occurrence that men connected by ties of blood, who were hired on the same side and so became intimate with one another, soon afterward are separated into two hostile forces and meet in battle. Forgetting both kinship and friendship, they run one another through with the utmost ferocity. They are driven to mutual destruction for no other reason than that they are hired by opposing kings for a tiny sum of which they take such careful account that they are readily induced to change sides by the addition of a penny to their daily rate of pay. So have they speedily acquired a habit of avarice which nevertheless profits them not one whit. What they get by exposing their lives they spend instantly in debauchery and that of a dreary sort.

This people will battle for the Utopians against any mortals whatsoever because their service is hired at a rate higher than they could get anywhere else. The Utopians, just as they seek good men to use them, so enlist these villains to abuse them. When need requires, they thrust them under the tempting bait of great promises into greatest perils. Generally a large proportion never returns to claim payment, but the survivors are honestly paid what has been promised them to incite them again to like deeds of daring. The Utopians do not care in the least how many Zapoletans they lose, thinking that they would be the greatest benefactors to the human race if they could relieve the world of all the dregs of this abominable and impious people.

Next to them they employ the forces of the people for whom they are fighting and then auxiliary squadrons of all their other friends. Last of all they add a contingent of their own citizens out of which they appoint some man of tried valor to command the whole army. For him they have two substitutes who hold no rank as long as he is safe. But if he is captured or killed, the first of the two becomes as it were his heir and successor, and he, if events require, is succeeded by the third. They thus avoid the disorganization of the whole army through the endangering of the commander, the fortunes of war being always incalculable.

In each city a choice is made among those who volunteer. No one is driven to fight abroad against his will because they are convinced that if anyone is somewhat timorous by nature, he not only will not acquit himself manfully but will throw fear into his companions. Should any war, however, assail their own country, they put the fainthearted, if physically fit, on shipboard mixed among the braver sort or put them here and there to man the walls where they cannot run away. Thus, shame at being seen to flinch by their own side, the close quarters with the enemy, and the withdrawal of hope of escape combine to overpower their timidity, and often they make a virtue of extreme necessity.

Just as no one of the men is made to go to a foreign war against his will, so if the women are anxious to accompany their husbands on military service, not only do they not forbid them but actually encourage them and incite them by expressions of praise. When they have gone out, they are placed alongside their husbands on the battle front. Each man is surrounded by his own children and relations by marriage and blood so that those may be closest and lend one another mutual assistance whom nature most impels to help one another. It is the greatest reproach for one spouse to return without the other or for a son to come back having lost his parent. The result is that, when it comes to hand-to-hand fighting, if the enemy stands his ground, the battle is long and anguished and ends with mutual extermination.

As I have said, they take every care not to be obliged to fight in person as long as they can finish the war by the assistance of hired substitutes. When personal service is inevitable, they are as courageous in fighting as they were ingenious in avoiding it as long as they might. They are not fierce in the first onslaught, but their strength increases by degrees through their slow and hard resistance. Their spirit is so stubborn that they would rather be cut to pieces than give way. The absence of anxiety about livelihood at home, as well as the removal of that worry which troubles men about the future of their families (for such solicitude everywhere breaks the highest courage), makes their spirit exalted and disdainful of defeat.

Moreover, their expert training in military discipline gives them confidence. Finally, their good and sound opinions, in which they have been trained from childhood both by teaching and by the good institutions of their country, give them additional courage. So they do not hold their life so cheap as recklessly to throw it away and not so immoderately dear as greedily and shamefully to hold fast to it when honor bids them give it up.

While the battle is everywhere most hot, a band of picked youths who have taken an oath to devote themselves to the task hunt out the opposing general. They openly attack him; they secretly ambush him. They assail him both from far and from near. A long and continuous wedge of men, fresh comers constantly taking the place of those exhausted, keeps up the attack. It seldom happens, unless he look to his safety by running away, that he is not killed or does not fall alive into the enemy's hands.

If the victory rests with them, there is no indiscriminate carnage, for they would rather take the routed as prisoners than kill them. They never pursue the fleeing enemy without keeping one division all the time drawn up ready for engagement under their banners. To such an extent is this the case that if, after the rest of the army has been beaten, they win the victory by this last reserve force, they prefer to let all their enemies escape rather than get into the habit of pursuing them with their own ranks in disorder. They remember that more than once it has happened to themselves that, when the great bulk of their army has been beaten and routed and when the enemy, flushed with victory, has been chasing the fugitives in all directions, a few of their number, held in reserve and ready for emergencies, have suddenly attacked the scattered and straying enemy who, feeling themselves quite safe, were off their guard. Thereby they have changed the whole fortune of the battle and, wresting out of the enemy's hands a certain and undoubted victory, have, though conquered, conquered their conquerors in turn.

It is not easy to say whether they are more cunning in laying ambushes or more cautious in avoiding them. You would think they contemplated flight when that is the very last thing intended; but, on the other hand, when they do determine to flee, you would imagine that they were thinking of anything but that. If they feel themselves to be inferior in number or in position, either by night they noiselessly march and move their camp or evade the enemy by some stratagem, or else by day they retire so imperceptibly and in such regular order that it is as dangerous to attack them in retreat as it would be in advance. They protect their camp most carefully by a deep and broad ditch, the earth taken out of it being thrown inside. They do not utilize the labor of the lowest workmen for the purpose, but the soldiers do it with their own hands. The whole army is set at work, except those who watch under arms in front of the rampart in case of emergencies. Thus, through the efforts of so many, they complete great fortifications, enclosing a large space, with incredible speed.

They wear armor strong enough to turn blows but easily adapted to all motions and gestures of the body. They do not feel any awkwardness even in swimming, for they practice swimming under arms as part of their apprenticeship in military discipline. The weapons they use at a distance are arrows, which they shoot with great strength and sureness of aim not only on foot but also on horseback. At close quarters they use not swords but battle-axes which, because of their sharp point and great weight, are deadly weapons, whether employed for thrusting or hacking. They are very clever in inventing war machines. They hide them, when made, with the greatest care lest, if made known before required by circumstances, they be rather a laughingstock than an instrument of war. In making them, their first object is to have them easy to carry and handy to pivot.

If a truce is made with the enemy, they keep it so religiously as not to break it even under provocation. They do not ravage the enemy's territory nor burn his crops. Rather, they do not even allow them to be trodden down by the feet of men or horses, as far as can be, thinking that they grow for their own benefit. They injure no noncombatant unless he is a spy. When cities are surrendered to them, they keep them intact. They do not plunder even those which they have stormed but put to death the men who prevented surrender and make slaves of the rest of the defenders. They leave unharmed the crowd of noncombatants. If they find out that any persons recommended the surrender of the town, they give them a share of the property of the condemned. They present their auxiliaries with the rest of the confiscated goods, but not a single one of their own men gets any of the booty.

When the war is over, they do not charge the expense against their friends, for whom they have borne the cost, but against the conquered. Under this head they make them not only pay money, which they lay aside for similar warlike purposes, but also surrender estates, from which they may enjoy forever a large annual income. In many countries they have such revenues which, coming little by little from various sources, have grown to the sum of over seven hundred thousand ducats a year.[7] To these estates they dispatch some of their own citizens under the title of Financial Agents to live there in great style and to play the part of magnates. Yet much is left over to put into the public treasury, unless they prefer to give the conquered nation credit. They often do the latter until they need to use the money, and even then it scarcely ever happens that they call in the whole sum. From these estates they confer a share on those who at their request undertake the dangerous mission which I have previously described.

If any king takes up arms against them and prepares to invade their territory, they at once meet him in great strength beyond their borders. They never lightly make war in their own country nor is any emergency so pressing as to compel them to admit foreign auxiliaries into their island.

Utopian Religions

There are different kinds of religion not only on the island as a whole but also in each city. Some worship as god the sun, others the moon, others one of the planets. There are some who reverence a man conspicuous for either virtue or glory in the past not only as god but even as the supreme god. But by far the majority, and those by far the wiser, believe in nothing of the kind but in a certain single being, unknown, eternal, immense, inexplicable, far above the reach of the human mind, diffused throughout the universe not in mass but in power. Him they call father. To him alone they attribute the beginnings, the growth, the increase, the changes, and the ends of all things as they have perceived them. To no other do they give divine honors.

In addition, all the other Utopians too, though varying in their beliefs, agree with them in this respect that they hold there is one supreme being, to whom are due both the creation and the providential government of the whole world. All alike call him Mithras[8] in their native language, but in this respect they disagree, that he is

7. A vast sum of money; by today's reckoning, the amount would equal several million dollars.

8. Persian sun god.

looked on differently by different persons. Each professes that whatever that is which he regards as supreme is that very same nature to whose unique power and majesty the sum of all things is attributed by the common consent of all nations. But gradually they are all beginning to depart from this medley of superstitions and are coming to unite in that one religion which seems to surpass the rest in reasonableness. Nor is there any doubt that the other beliefs would all have disappeared long ago had not whatever untoward event, that happened to anyone when he was deliberating on a change of religion, been construed by fear as not having happened by chance but as having been sent from heaven as if the deity whose worship he was forsaking were thus avenging an intention so impious against himself.

But after they had heard from us the name of Christ, His teaching, His character, His miracles, and the no less wonderful constancy of the many martyrs whose blood freely shed had drawn so many nations far and wide into their fellowship, you would not believe how readily disposed they, too, were to join it, whether through the rather mysterious inspiration of God or because they thought it nearest to that belief which has the widest prevalence among them. But I think that this factor, too, was of no small weight, that they had heard that His disciples' common way of life had been pleasing to Christ and that it is still in use among the truest societies of Christians. But whatever it was that influenced them, not a few joined our religion and were cleansed by the holy water of baptism.

But because among us four (for that was all that was left, two of our group having succumbed to fate) there was, I am sorry to say, no priest, they were initiated in all other matters, but so far they lack those sacraments which with us only priests administer. They understand, however, what they are, and desire them with the greatest eagerness. Moreover, they are even debating earnestly among themselves whether, without the dispatch of a Christian bishop, one chosen out of their own number might receive the sacerdotal character. It seemed that they would choose a candidate, but by the time of my departure they had not yet done so.

Even those who do not agree with the religion of Christ do not try to deter others from it. They do not attack any who have made their profession. Only one of our company, while I was there, was interfered with. As soon as he was baptized, in spite of our advice to the contrary, he spoke publicly of Christ's religion with more zeal than discretion. He began to grow so warm in his preaching that not only did he prefer our worship to any other but he condemned all the rest outright. He proclaimed them to be profane in themselves and their followers to be impious and sacrilegious and worthy of everlasting fire. When he had long been preaching in this style, they arrested him, tried him, and convicted him not for despising their religion but for stirring up a riot among the people. His sentence after the verdict of guilty was exile. Actually, they count this principle among their most ancient institutions, that no one should suffer for his religion.

Utopus had heard that before his arrival the inhabitants had been continually quarreling among themselves about religion. He had observed that the universal dissensions between the individual sects who were fighting for their country had given him the opportunity of overcoming them all. From the very beginning, therefore, after he had gained the victory, he especially ordained that it should be lawful for every man to follow the religion of his choice, that each might strive to bring others over to his own, provided that he quietly and modestly supported his own by reasons nor bitterly demolished all others if his persuasions were not successful nor used any violence and refrained from abuse. If a person contends too vehemently in expressing his views, he is punished with exile or enslavement.

Utopus laid down these regulations not merely from regard for peace, which he saw to be utterly destroyed by constant wrangling and implacable hatred, but because he thought that this method of settlement was in the interest of religion itself. On religion he did not venture rashly to dogmatize. He was uncertain whether God did not desire a varied and manifold worship and therefore did not inspire different people with different views. But he was certain in thinking it both insolence and folly to demand by violence and threats that all should think to be true what you believe to be true. Moreover, even if it should be the case that one single religion is true and all the rest are false, he readily foresaw that, provided the matter was handled reasonably and moderately, truth by its own natural force would finally emerge sooner or later and stand forth conspicuously. But if the struggle were decided by arms and riots, since the worst men are always the most unyielding, the best and holiest religion would be overwhelmed because of the conflicting false religions, like grain choked by thorns and underbrush.

So he made the whole matter of religion an open question and left each one free to choose what he should believe. By way of exception, he conscientiously and strictly gave injunction that no one should fall so far below the dignity of human nature as to believe that souls likewise perish with the body or that the world is the mere sport of chance and not governed by any divine providence. After this life, accordingly, vices are ordained to be punished and virtue rewarded. Such is their belief, and if anyone thinks otherwise, they do not regard him even as a member of mankind, seeing that he has lowered the lofty nature of his soul to the level of a beast's miserable body—so far are they from classing him among their citizens whose laws and customs he would treat as worthless if it were not for fear. Who can doubt that he will strive either to evade by craft the public laws of his country or to break them by violence in order to serve his own private desires when he has nothing to fear but laws and no hope beyond the body?

Therefore an individual of this mind is tendered no honor, is entrusted with no office, and is put in charge of no function. He is universally regarded as of a sluggish and low disposition. But they do not punish him in any way, being convinced that it is in no man's power to believe what he chooses, nor do they compel him by threats to disguise his views, nor do they allow in the matter any deceptions or lies which they hate exceedingly as being next door to calculated malice. They forbid him to argue in support of his opinion in the presence of the common people, but in private before the priests and important personages they not only permit but also encourage it, being sure that such madness will in the end give way to reason.

There are others, too, and these not a few, who are not interfered with because they do not altogether lack reason for their view and because they are not evil men. By a much different error, these believe that brute animals also have immortal souls, but not comparable to ours in dignity or destined to equal felicity. Almost all Utopians are absolutely certain and convinced that human bliss will be so immense that, while they lament every man's illness, they regret the death of no one but him whom they see torn from life anxiously and unwillingly. This behavior they take to be a very bad omen as though the soul, being without hope and having a guilty conscience, dreaded its departure through a secret premonition of impending punishment. Besides, they suppose that God will not be pleased with the coming of one who, when summoned, does not gladly hasten to obey but is reluctantly drawn against his will. Persons who behold this kind of death are filled with horror and therefore carry the dead out to burial in melancholy silence. Then, after praying God to be merciful to their shades and graciously to pardon their infirmities, they cover the corpse with earth.

On the other hand, when men have died cheerfully and full of good hope, no one mourns for them, but they accompany their funerals with song, with great affection commending their souls to God. Then, with reverence rather than with sorrow, they cremate the bodies. On the spot they erect a pillar on which are inscribed the good points of the deceased. On returning home they recount his character and his deeds. No part of his life is more frequently or more gladly spoken of than his cheerful death.

They judge that this remembrance of uprightness is not only a most efficacious means of stimulating the living to good deeds but also a most acceptable form of attention to the dead. The latter they think are present when they are talked about, though invisible to the dull sight of mortals. It would be inconsistent with the lot of the blessed not to be able to travel freely where they please, and it would be ungrateful of them to reject absolutely all desire of revisiting their friends to whom they were bound during their lives by mutual love and charity. Charity, like all other good things, they conjecture to be increased after death rather than diminished in all good men. Consequently they believe that the dead move about among the living and are witnesses of their words and actions. Hence they go about their business with more confidence because of reliance on such protection. The belief, moreover, in the personal presence of their forefathers keeps men from any secret dishonorable deed.

They utterly despise and deride auguries and all other divinations of vain superstition, to which great attention is paid in other countries. But miracles, which occur without the assistance of nature, they venerate as operations and witnesses of the divine power at work.[9] In their country, too, they say, miracles often occur. Sometimes in great and critical affairs they pray publicly for a miracle, which they very confidently look for and obtain.

They think that the investigation of nature, with the praise arising from it, is an act of worship acceptable to God. There are persons, however, and these not so very few, who for religious motives eschew learning and scientific pursuit and yet allow themselves no leisure. It is only by keeping busy and by all good offices that they are determined to merit the happiness coming after death. Some tend the sick. Others repair roads, clean out ditches, rebuild bridges, dig turf and sand and stone, fell and cut up trees, and transport wood, grain, and other things into the cities in carts. Not only for the public but also for private persons they behave as servants and as more than slaves.

If anywhere there is a task so rough, hard, and filthy that most are deterred from it by the toil, disgust, and despair involved, they gladly and cheerfully claim it all for themselves. While perpetually engaged in hard work themselves, they secure leisure for the others and yet claim no credit for it. They neither belittle insultingly the life of others nor extol their own. The more that these men put themselves in the position of slaves the more are they honored by all.

Of these persons there are two schools. The one is composed of celibates who not only eschew all sexual activity but also abstain from eating flesh meat and in

9. Christian doctrine held that a miracle was an intervention by God into the natural order of things. God can perform miracles among non-Christians as well as Christians.

some cases from eating all animal food. They entirely reject the pleasures of this life as harmful. They long only for the future life by means of their watching and sweat. Hoping to obtain it very soon, they are cheerful and active in the meantime.

The other school is just as fond of hard labor, but regards matrimony as preferable, not despising the comfort which it brings and thinking that their duty to nature requires them to perform the marital act and their duty to the country to beget children. They avoid no pleasure unless it interferes with their labor. They like flesh meat just because they think that this fare makes them stronger for any work whatsoever. The Utopians regard these men as the saner but the first-named as the holier. If the latter based upon arguments from reason their preference of celibacy to matrimony and of a hard life to a comfortable one, they would laugh them to scorn. Now, however, since they say they are prompted by religion, they look up to and reverence them. For there is nothing about which they are more careful than not lightly to dogmatize on any point of religion. Such, then, are the men whom in their language they call by a special name of their own, Buthrescae, a word which may be translated as "religious par excellence."

They have priests of extraordinary holiness, and therefore very few. They have no more than thirteen in each city—with a like number of churches—except when they go to war. In that case, seven go forth with the army, and the same number of substitutes is appointed for the interval. When the regular priests come back, everyone returns to his former duties. Then those who are above the number of thirteen, until they succeed to the places of those who die, attend upon the high priest in the meantime. One, you see, is appointed to preside over the rest.They are elected by the people, just as all the other officials are, by secret ballot to avoid party spirit. When elected, they are ordained by their own group.

They preside over divine worship, order religious rites, and are censors of morals. It is counted a great disgrace for a man to be summoned or rebuked by them as not being of upright life. It is their function to give advice and admonition, but to check and punish offenders belongs to the governor and the other civil officials. The priests, however, do exclude from divine services persons whom they find to be unusually bad. There is almost no punishment which is more dreaded: they incur very great disgrace and are tortured by a secret fear of religion. Even their bodies will not long go scot-free. If they do not demonstrate to the priests their speedy repentance, they are seized and punished by the senate for their impiety.

To the priests is entrusted the education of children and youths. They regard concern for their morals and virtue as no less important than for their advancement in learning. They take the greatest pains from the very first to instill into children's minds, while still tender and pliable, good opinions, which are also useful for the preservation of their commonwealth. When once they are firmly implanted in children, they accompany them all through their adult lives and are of great help in watching over the condition of the commonwealth. The latter never decays except through vices which arise from wrong attitudes.

The feminine sex[1] is not debarred from the priesthood, but only a widow advanced in years is ever chosen, and that rather rarely. Unless they are women, the priests have for their wives the very finest women of the country.

1. In Greek and Roman religious practice, women could perform priestly functions. As these were the peoples whom More identified as understanding natural law, he must have thought that natural law did not limit a woman's role in religion.

To no other office in Utopia is more honor given, so much so that, even if they have committed any crime, they are subjected to no tribunal, but left only to God and to themselves. They judge it wrong to lay human hands upon one, however guilty, who has been consecrated to God in a singular manner as a holy offering. It is easier for them to observe this custom because their priests are very few and very carefully chosen.

Besides, it does not easily happen that one who is elevated to such dignity for being the very best among the good, nothing but virtue being taken into account, should fall into corruption and wickedness. Even if it does happen, human nature being ever prone to change, yet since they are but few and are invested with no power except the influence of honor, it need not be feared that they will cause any great harm to the state. In fact, the reason for having but few and exceptional priests is to prevent the dignity of the order, which they now reverence very highly, from being cheapened by communicating the honor to many. This is especially true since they think it hard to find many men so good as to be fit for so honorable a position for the filling of which it is not enough to be endowed with ordinary virtues.

They are not more esteemed among their own people than among foreign nations. This can easily be seen from a fact which, I think, is its cause. When the armies are fighting in battle, the priests are to be found separate but not very far off, settled on their knees, dressed in their sacred vestments. With hands outstretched to heaven, they pray first of all for peace, next for a victory to their own side—but without much bloodshed on either side. When their side is winning, they run among the combatants, and restrain the fury of their own men against the routed enemy. Merely to see and to appeal to them suffices to save one's life; to touch their flowing garments protects one's remaining goods from every harm arising from war.

This conduct has brought them such veneration among all nations everywhere and has given them so real a majesty that they have saved their own citizens from the enemy as often as they have protected the enemy from their own men. The following is well known. Sometimes their own side had given way, their case had been desperate, they were taking to flight, and the enemy was rushing on to kill and to plunder. Then the carnage had been averted by the intervention of the priests. After the armies had been parted from each other, peace had been concluded and settled on just terms. Never had there been any nation so savage, cruel, and barbarous that it had not regarded their persons as sacred and inviolable.

They celebrate as holydays the first and the last day of each month and likewise of each year. The latter they divide into months, measured by the orbit of the moon just as the course of the sun rounds out the year. In their language they call the first days Cynemerni and the last days Trapemerni. These names have the same meaning as if they were rendered "First-Feasts" and "Final-Feasts."

Their temples are fine sights, not only elaborate in workmanship but also capable of holding a vast throng, and necessarily so, since there are so few of them. The temples are all rather dark. This feature, they report, is due not to an ignorance of architecture but to the deliberate intention of the priests. They think that excessive light makes the thoughts wander, whereas scantier and uncertain light concentrates the mind and conduces to devotion.

In Utopia, as has been seen, the religion of all is not the same, and yet all its manifestations, though varied and manifold, by different roads as it were, tend to the same end, the worship of the divine nature. Therefore nothing is seen or heard in the temples which does not seem to agree with all in common. If any sect has a rite of its own, it is performed within the walls of each man's home. Public worship is conducted according to a ritual which does not at all detract from any of the private devotions. Therefore no image of the gods is seen in the temple so that the individual may be free to conceive of God with the most ardent devotion in any form he pleases. They invoke God by no special name except that of Mithras. By this word they agree to represent the one nature of the divine majesty whatever it be. The prayers formulated are such as every man may utter without offense to his own belief.

On the evening of the Final-Feasts, they gather in the temple, still fasting. They thank God for the prosperity they have enjoyed in the month or year of which that holyday is the last day. Next day, which is the First-Feast, they flock to the temples in the morning. They pray for good luck and prosperity in the ensuing year or month, of which this holyday is the auspicious beginning.

On the Final-Feasts, before they go to the temple, wives fall down at the feet of their husbands, children at the feet of their parents. They confess that they have erred, either by committing some fault or by performing some duty carelessly, and beg pardon for their offense. Hence, if any cloud of quarrel in the family has arisen, it is dispelled by this satisfaction so that with pure and clear minds they may be present at the sacrifices, for they are too scrupulous to attend with a troubled conscience. If they are aware of hatred or anger against anyone they do not assist at the sacrifices until they have been reconciled and have cleansed their hearts, for fear of swift and great punishment.

When they reach the temple, they part, the men going to the right side and the women to the left. Then they arrange their places so that the males in each home sit in front of the head of the household and the womenfolk are in front of the mother of the family. They thus take care that every gesture of everyone abroad is observed by those whose authority and discipline govern them at home. They also carefully see to it that everywhere the younger are placed in the company of the elder. If children were trusted to children, they might spend in childish foolery the time in which they ought to be conceiving a religious fear toward the gods, the greatest and almost the only stimulus to the practice of virtues.

They slay no animal in their sacrifices. They do not believe that the divine clemency delights in bloodshed and slaughter, seeing that it has imparted life to animate creatures that they might enjoy life. They burn incense and other fragrant substances and also offer a great number of candles. They are not unaware that these things add nothing to the divine nature, any more than do human prayers, but they like this harmless kind of worship. Men feel that, by these sweet smells and lights, as well as the other ceremonies, they somehow are uplifted and rise with livelier devotion to the worship of God.

The people are clothed in white garments in the temple. The priest wears vestments of various colors, of wonderful design and shape, but not of material as costly as one would expect. They are not interwoven with gold or set with precious stones but wrought with the different feathers of birds so cleverly and artistically that no costly material could equal the value of the handiwork. Moreover, in these birds' feathers and plumes and the definite order and plan by which they are set off on the priest's vestment, they say certain hidden mysteries are contained. By knowing the meaning as it is carefully handed down by the priests, they are reminded of God's benefits toward them and, in turn, of their own piety toward God and their duty toward one another.

As soon as the priest thus arrayed appears from the vestibule, all immediately fall on the ground in reverence. The silence all around is so deep that the very appearance of the congregation strikes one with awe as if some divine power were really present. After remaining a while on the ground, at a signal from the priest they rise.

At this point they sing praises to God, which they diversify with musical instruments, largely different in shape from those seen in our part of the world. Very many of them surpass in sweetness those in use with us, but some are not even comparable with ours. But in one respect undoubtedly they are far ahead of us. All their music, whether played on instruments or sung by the human voice, so renders and expresses the natural feelings, so suits the sound to the matter (whether the words be supplicatory, or joyful, or propitiatory, or troubled, or mournful, or angry), and so represents the meaning by the form of the melody that it wonderfully affects, penetrates, and inflames the souls of the hearers.

At the end, the priest and the people together repeat solemn prayers fixed in form, so drawn up that each individual may apply to himself personally what all recite together. In these prayers every man recognizes God to be the author of creation and governance and all other blessings besides. He thanks Him for all the benefits received, particularly that by the divine favor he has chanced on that commonwealth which is the happiest and has received that religion which he hopes to be the truest. If he errs in these matters or if there is anything better and more approved by God than that commonwealth or that religion, he prays that He will, of His goodness, bring him to the knowledge of it, for he is ready to follow in whatever path He may lead him. But if this form of a commonwealth be the best and his religion the truest, he prays that then He may give him steadfastness and bring all other mortals to the same way of living and the same opinion of God—unless there be something in this variety of religions which delights His inscrutable will.

Finally, he prays that God will take him to Himself by an easy death, how soon or late he does not venture to determine. However, if it might be without offense to His Majesty, it would be much more welcome to him to die a very hard death and go to God than to be kept longer away from Him even by a very prosperous career in life.[2]

After this prayer has been said, they prostrate themselves on the ground again. Then shortly they rise and go away to dinner. The rest of the day they pass in games and in exercises of military training.

Now I have described to you, as exactly as I could, the structure of that commonwealth which I judge not merely the best but the only one which can rightly claim the name of a commonwealth. Outside Utopia, to be sure, men talk freely of the public welfare—but look after their private interests only. In Utopia, where nothing is

2. The Utopians do not pray for forgiveness of the sins they have committed in the past, although they do pray for divine guidance in avoiding the errors they may commit in the future.

private, they seriously concern themselves with public affairs. Assuredly in both cases they act reasonably. For, outside Utopia, how many are there who do not realize that, unless they make some separate provision for themselves, however flourishing the commonwealth, they will themselves starve? For this reason, necessity compels them to hold that they must take account of themselves rather than of the people, that is, of others.

On the other hand, in Utopia, where everything belongs to everybody, no one doubts, provided only that the public granaries are well filled, that the individual will lack nothing for his private use. The reason is that the distribution of goods is not niggardly. In Utopia there is no poor man and no beggar. Though no man has anything, yet all are rich.

For what can be greater riches for a man than to live with a joyful and peaceful mind, free of all worries—not troubled about his food or harassed by the querulous demands of his wife or fearing poverty for his son or worrying about his daughter's dowry, but feeling secure about the livelihood and happiness of himself and his family: wife, sons, grandsons, great-grandsons, great-great-grandsons, and all the long line of their descendants that gentlefolk anticipate? Then take into account the fact that there is no less provision for those who are now helpless but once worked than for those who are still working.

At this point I should like anyone to be so bold as to compare this fairness with the so-called justice prevalent in other nations, among which, upon my soul, I cannot discover the slightest trace of justice and fairness. What brand of justice is it that any nobleman whatsoever or goldsmith-banker or moneylender or, in fact, anyone else from among those who either do no work at all or whose work is of a kind not very essential to the commonwealth, should attain a life of luxury and grandeur on the basis of his idleness or his nonessential work? In the meantime, the common laborer, the carter, the carpenter, and the farmer perform work so hard and continuous that beasts of burden could scarcely endure it and work so essential that no commonwealth could last even one year without it. Yet they earn such scanty fare and lead such a miserable life that the condition of beasts of burden might seem far preferable. The latter do not have to work so incessantly nor is their food much worse (in fact, sweeter to their taste) nor do they entertain any fear for the future. The workmen, on the other hand, not only have to toil and suffer without return or profit in the present but agonize over the thought of an indigent old age. Their daily wage is too scanty to suffice even for the day: much less is there an excess and surplus that daily can be laid by for their needs in old age.

Now is not this an unjust and ungrateful commonwealth? It lavishes great rewards on so-called gentlefolk and banking goldsmiths and the rest of that kind, who are either idle or mere parasites and purveyors of empty pleasures. On the contrary, it makes no benevolent provision for farmers, colliers, common laborers, carters, and carpenters without whom there would be no commonwealth at all. After it has misused the labor of their prime and after they are weighed down with age and disease and are in utter want, it forgets all their sleepless nights and all the great benefits received at their hands and most ungratefully requites them with a most miserable death.

What is worse, the rich every day extort a part of their daily allowance from the poor not only by private fraud but by public law. Even before they did so it seemed unjust that persons deserving best of the commonwealth should have the worst return. Now they have further distorted and debased the right and, finally, by making laws, have palmed it off as justice. Consequently, when I consider and turn over in my mind the state of all commonwealths flourishing anywhere today, so help me God, I can see nothing else than a kind of conspiracy of the rich, who are aiming at their own interests under the name and title of the commonwealth.[3] They invent and devise all ways and means by which, first, they may keep without fear of loss all that they have amassed by evil practices and, secondly, they may then purchase as cheaply as possible and abuse the toil and labor of all the poor. These devices become law as soon as the rich have once decreed their observance in the name of the public—that is, of the poor also!

Yet when these evil men with insatiable greed have divided up among themselves all the goods which would have been enough for all the people, how far they are from the happiness of the Utopian commonwealth! In Utopia all greed for money was entirely removed with the use of money. What a mass of troubles was then cut away! What a crop of crimes was then pulled up by the roots! Who does not know that fraud, theft, rapine, quarrels, disorders, brawls, seditions, murders, treasons, poisonings, which are avenged rather than restrained by daily executions, die out with the destruction of money? Who does not know that fear, anxiety, worries, toils, and sleepless nights will also perish at the same time as money? What is more, poverty, which alone money seemed to make poor, forthwith would itself dwindle and disappear if money were entirely done away with everywhere.

To make this assertion clearer, consider in your thoughts some barren and unfruitful year in which many thousands of men have been carried off by famine. I emphatically contend that at the end of that scarcity, if rich men's granaries had been searched, as much grain could have been found as, if it had been divided among the people killed off by starvation and disease, would have prevented anyone from feeling that meager return from soil and climate. So easily might men get the necessities of life if that blessed money, supposedly a grand invention to ease access to those necessities, was not in fact the only barrier to our getting what we need.

Even the rich, I doubt not, have such feelings. They are not unaware that it would be a much better state of affairs to lack no necessity than to have abundance of superfluities—to be snatched from such numerous troubles rather than to be hemmed in by great riches. Nor does it occur to me to doubt that a man's regard for his own interests or the authority of Christ our Savior—who in His wisdom could not fail to know what was best and who in His goodness would not fail to counsel what He knew to be best—would long ago have brought the whole world to adopt the laws of the Utopian commonwealth, had not one single monster, the chief and progenitor of all plagues, striven against it—I mean, Pride.

Pride measures prosperity not by her own advantages but by others' disadvantages.[4] Pride would not consent to be made even a goddess if no poor wretches were left for her to domineer over and scoff at, if her good fortune might not dazzle by

3. Hythlodaeus condemns practices associated with the accumulation of wealth as capital and the corresponding exploitation of workers in the interest of increasing capital. This goal is promoted by various legal "devices," particularly involving estates, that preserve capital within the upper ranks of society. But capital cannot be accumulated in a barter economy, where goods are exchanged for goods rather than for money. Hence Hythlodaeus eliminates money as a way of preventing the formation of capital.

4. Pride therefore prevents a society based on benefits, which typically redound to the welfare of a community rather than to that of particular individuals.

comparison with their miseries, if the display of her riches did not torment and intensify their poverty. This serpent from hell entwines itself around the hearts of men and acts like the suckfish in preventing and hindering them from entering on a better way of life.

Pride is too deeply fixed in men to be easily plucked out. For this reason, the fact that this form of a commonwealth—which I should gladly desire for all—has been the good fortune of the Utopians at least, fills me with joy. They have adopted such institutions of life as have laid the foundations of the commonwealth not only most happily, but also to last forever, as far as human prescience can forecast. At home they have extirpated the roots of ambition and factionalism, along with all the other vices. Hence there is no danger of trouble from domestic discord, which has been the only cause of ruin to the well-established prosperity of many cities. As long as harmony is preserved at home and its institutions are in a healthy state, not all the envy of neighboring rulers, though it has rather often attempted it and has always been repelled, can avail to shatter or to shake that nation.

When Raphael had finished his story, many things came to my mind which seemed very absurdly established in the customs and laws of the people described—not only in their method of waging war, their ceremonies and religion, as well as their other institutions, but most of all in that feature which is the principal foundation of their whole structure. I mean their common life and subsistence—without any exchange of money. This latter alone utterly overthrows all the nobility, magnificence, splendor, and majesty which are, in the estimation of the common people, the true glories and ornaments of the commonwealth.

I knew, however, that he was wearied with his tale, and I was not quite certain that he could brook any opposition to his views, particularly when I recalled his censure of others on account of their fear that they might not appear to be wise enough, unless they found some fault to criticize in other men's discoveries. I therefore praised their way of life and his speech and, taking him by the hand, led him in to supper. I first said, nevertheless, that there would be another chance to think about these matters more deeply and to talk them over with him more fully. If only this were some day possible!

Meanwhile, though in other respects he is a man of the most undoubted learning as well as of the greatest knowledge of human affairs, I cannot agree with all that he said. But I readily admit that there are very many features in the Utopian commonwealth which it is easier for me to wish for in our countries than to have any hope of seeing realized.

END OF BOOK TWO

THE END OF THE AFTERNOON DISCOURSE OF RAPHAEL HYTHLODAEUS ON THE LAWS AND CUSTOMS OF THE ISLAND OF UTOPIA, HITHERTO KNOWN BUT TO FEW, AS REPORTED BY THE MOST DISTINGUISHED AND MOST LEARNED MAN, MR. THOMAS MORE, CITIZEN AND SHERIFF OF LONDON

FINIS

Perspectives

Government and Self-Government

In a period marked by an increasingly centralized monarchy and a corresponding resistance to its bureaucratic reforms, ideas on government were debated in a variety of discourses. Political philosophers, such as More, described ideal forms of rule; historians reported events that actually happened and attempted to explain what followed as a result. A writer's point of view was clearly important; philosophers constructed models of order that reflected their belief in a certain kind of creation and the deity overseeing its development, while historians tried to interpret the actions of a person or a group in relation to the social interests they judged were at stake. Inevitably, the practice of government demonstrated the limits of a theory, while theory suggested the implications of a practice.

The selections included here reveal how comprehensive were these concerns, understood both in theory and in relation to daily life. Political thinkers sought to determine the proper business of state and also the conduct required of individual persons. Of course, they identified men and women as particular characters, each with his or her habits of mind and behavior, but they also recognized that every person had a specific office, a place and a role in life that was governed by expectations created by custom and, to a lesser extent, by common law. A man

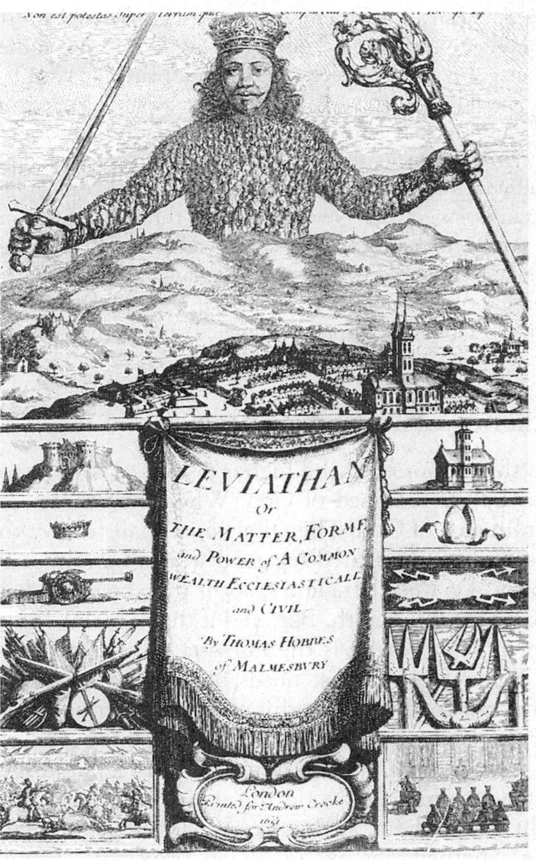

Frontispiece to *Leviathan,* by Thomas Hobbes. 1651. This engraving illustrates the author's idea of government in a "commonwealth." Rising above the countryside is the mystical figure of the body politic. It consists of a crowned head—perhaps a dictator, perhaps a monarch—who has sovereign authority, and a body comprising the people, his subjects. The sovereign wields two powers: a civil power, symbolized by the sword in his right hand, and an ecclesiastical power, symbolized by the crozier in his left. Cells in the lower register of the engraving depict the mechanisms that support these powers, with scenes and symbols of the military on the left and of the church on the right. Published in 1651, *Leviathan* attempted to articulate conditions of rule proclaimed two years earlier, after the execution of Charles I. Hobbes believed that government was created by men who, rejecting the warlike state of nature in which they had originated, had handed over their natural rights to a sovereign in a kind of "contract" which traded their obedience for his protection. The idea of a body politic regularly was featured in early modern political thought and was discussed by writers as different as Bishop John Ponet and James I.

was primarily understood in terms of his work—as servant, artisan, yeoman, merchant, magistrate, or lord. A woman had fewer options and was usually identified according to her marital status—as a maid, a mother, or a widow. Over the course of the century, these categories became subject to challenge. Controversy grew as to the very basis of social order, the fundamental authority and power of the superior (whatever the office) over his or her subordinates. Protestant notions of the primacy of the individual conscience over collective authority were particularly effective in upsetting customary hierarchies of rule. On the one hand, they were used to justify individual rights; on the other, they supplied a rationale for those claiming such rights to protest as a group or a social body. There was a general agreement that states and persons should be governed by rules, but what these rules ought to be was becoming a contentious topic. Discussions of the power and authority of monarchs and magistrates generally emphasized that their power and authority were not absolute but limited by divine, natural, and positive law or the law of the land. This emphasis is matched by a pervasive fear of the tyrant—the ruler who not only makes and unmakes the law but does so in his own interest rather than for his people's welfare.

William Tyndale

c. 1495–1536

William Tyndale was perhaps the foremost of early English Protestants. Best known as the first translator of the Bible into English, he was active in political disputes as well, insisting on the absolute authority and power of the secular arm of government. He was motivated, in part, by his belief that no European monarch should have to obey the Pope in Rome. To him a monarch and his magistrates were God's ministers on earth. In its later formulations under the Stuarts, this view of government was criticized for its toleration of tyranny. Tyndale found allies in Protestant Europe, and especially in Martin Luther whom he visited in Wittenberg. He travelled extensively, seeing his translation of the New Testament through presses in Cologne and Worms, settling finally in Antwerp. As the popularity of Tyndale's work grew, he became increasingly the target of criticism. Denounced by bishops in England and particularly by Sir Thomas More, then a privy counsellor to Henry VIII, Tyndale was eventually arrested for heresy by officers of the Holy Roman Empire, imprisoned, strangled, and burned at the stake at Vilvorde in 1535.

from The Obedience of a Christian Man

Let every soul submit himself unto the authority of the higher powers. There is no power but of God; the powers that be are ordained of God. Whosoever therefore resisteth the power, resisteth the ordinance of God. They that resist shall receive to themselves damnation. For rulers are not to be feared for good works, but for evil. Wilt thou be without fear of the power? Do well then, and so shalt thou be praised of the same, for he is the minister of God for thy wealth. But, and if thou do evil, then fear, for he beareth not a sword for nought, for he is the minister of God, to take vengeance on them that do evil. Wherefore ye must needs obey, not for fear of vengeance only, but also because of conscience. Even for this cause pay ye tribute: for they are God's ministers serving for the same purpose. * * *

God therefore hath given laws unto all nations, and in all lands hath put kings, governors, and rulers in his own stead, to rule the world through them. And hath commanded all causes to be brought before them, as thou readest (Exod. 22). In all causes (saith he) of injury or wrong, whether it be ox, ass, sheep, or vesture, or any lost thing which another challengeth, let the cause of both parties be brought unto the gods; whom the gods condemn, the same shall pay double unto his neighbor. Mark, the judges are called gods in the Scriptures, because they are in God's room,[1] and execute the commandments of God. And in another place of the said chapter, Moses chargeth saying, See that thou rail not on[2] the gods, neither speak evil of the ruler of thy people. Whosoever therefore resisteth them, resisteth God (for they are in the room of God) and they that resist shall receive the damnation.

Such obedience unto father and mother, master, husband, emperor, king, lords, and rulers, requireth God of all nations, yea of the very Turks and infidels. * * *

Neither may the inferior person avenge himself upon the superior, or violently resist him for whatsoever wrong it be. If he do, he is condemned in the deed doing, inasmuch as he taketh upon him that which belongeth to God only, which saith, Vengeance is mine, and I will reward (Deut. 32). And Christ sayeth (Mat. 26), All they that take the sword shall perish with the sword. Taketh thou a sword to avenge thyself? So givest thou not room unto God to avenge thee, but robbest him of his most high honor, in that thou wilt not let him be judge over thee.

1528

Juan Luis Vives

1492–1540

A Spanish philosopher educated in Valencia, Paris, and Bruges, Vives lectured at Oxford and attended the court of Henry VIII between 1523 and 1528. His treatise on the education of women was composed for Mary Tudor while she was still a child, at the request of her mother, Catherine of Aragon, wife of Henry VIII. It was published in Latin in 1523; the English translation, by Richard Hyrde, was published in 1540. It illustrates the way in which the idea of government comprised doctrine on matters of individual conduct. Vives clearly believed that the subordination of a wife to a husband was an expression of the natural order of things, not a social convention; he thought it depended on the innate characteristics of the female in contrast to the male.

from Instruction of a Christian Woman

Chastity is the principal virtue of a woman, and counterepayseth with[1] all the rest. If she have that, no man will look for any other, and if she lack that, no man will regard other. * * * She that is chaste is fair, well-favored, rich, fruitful, noble, and all best things that can be named, and contrary, she that is unchaste is a sea and treasure of all illness. Now shamefastness[2] and soberness be the inseparable companions of chastity, insomuch that she cannot be chaste that is not ashamed.[3] * * *

Of shamefastness cometh demureness and measureableness, that whether she think ought, or say, or do, nothing shall be outrageous, neither in passions of mind, nor words, nor deeds; nor presumptuous; nor nice,[4] wanton, pert; nor boasting; nor ambitious; and as for honors she will neither think herself worthy nor desire them but rather flee them, and if they chance unto her, she will be ashamed of them, as of a

1. Place.
2. Complain against.

1. Outweighs.
2. Modesty.
3. I.e., good manners and temperance derive from modesty.
4. Fastidious.

thing not deserved; nor be for nothing high-minded, neither for beauty, nor properness,[5] nor kindred, nor riches, being sure that they shall soon perish and that pride shall have everlasting pain.

The man getteth, that woman saveth and keepeth. Therefore he hath stomach given to him to gather lustily,[6] and she hath it taken from her, that she may warily keep.[7] And of this soberness of body cometh soberness of mind. * * * Let her apply herself to virtue and be content with a little, and take in worth that[8] she hath nor seek for other that she hath not, nor for [the wealth of] other folks, whereof riseth envy, hate, or curiosity of other folks' matters.

Forth she must go sometimes, but I would it should be as seldom as may be for many causes. Principally because as often as a maid goeth forth among people, so often she cometh in judgment and extreme peril of her beauty, honesty, demureness, wit, shamefastness, and virtue. For nothing is more tender than is the fame and estimation of women, nor nothing more in danger of wrong, insomuch that it hath been said, and not without a cause, to hang by a cobweb.

Let the woman understand that if she will not spend all her substance to save her husband from never so little harms, she is not worthy to bear the name neither of a good nor Christian woman, nor once to be called wife. * * * I will that she shall give him great worship, reverence, great obedience, and service also, which thing not only the example of the old world teacheth us, but also all laws, both spiritual and temporal, and nature herself cryeth and commandeth that the woman shall be subject and obedient to the man. And in all kinds of beasts the females obey the males and wait upon them and fawn upon them and suffer themselves to be corrected of them, which thing nature showeth must be and is convenient[9] to be done. * * * Nature showeth that the male's duty is to succor and defend, and the female's to follow and wait upon the male and to creep under his aid and obey him, that she may live the better.

Let the authority and rule be reserved unto thy husband and be thou an example to all thine house what sovereignty they owe unto him. Do thou prove him to be lord by thine obedience, and make him great with thine humility, for the more honor thou givest unto him, the [more] honorable thou shalt be thyself.

That thou mayest better obey thy husband and do all things after his mind, first thou must learn all his manners and consider well his dispositions and state, for there be many kinds of husbands and all ought to be loved, honored and worshipped and obeyed, but all must not be entreated under one manner. * * * If thou have one after thine appetite, thou mayest be glad, * * * but if he be ill, either find some craft to make him good or at the leastwise better to deal with.

Sir Thomas Elyot

c. 1490–1546

To support his defense of monarchy in his treatise on government, Sir Thomas Elyot—a humanist and Henry VIII's ambassador to Emperor Charles V—drew on popular analogies with what he saw as the hierarchical order of the heavens and the natural world. He also insisted that a monarchy—in which the king (or queen) held a patriarchal kind of power—

5. Station in life.
6. Energetically.
7. Carefully conserve.
8. Value what.
9. Appropriate.

preserved security within society and yet, by observing custom and established law, avoided tyranny or anarchy. His later work continued to engage political topics. His dialogue supporting women's rule may have been composed in the anticipation of Mary Tudor's queenship; its argument drew on a literature debating the nature of womankind as it was represented in both the medieval *querelle des femmes*, or "controversy on the subject of womankind," and the classical and humanist histories of famous women. His character Candidus ("honest and open-minded") represents the affirmative case; Caninius ("snarling and spiteful") states his objections to it.

from The Book Named the Governor

Like as to a castle or fortress sufficeth one owner or sovereign, and where any more be of like power and authority seldom cometh the work to perfection; or being already made, where the one diligently overseeth and the other neglecteth, in that contention all is subverted and cometh to ruin, in semblable wise[1] doth a public weal[2] that hath more chief governors than one. Example we may take of the Greeks, among whom in divers cities were divers forms of public weals governed by multitudes. Wherein one was most tolerable where the governance and rule was always permitted to them which excelled in virtue, and was in the Greek tongue called *Aristocratia*, in Latin *Optimorum Potentia*, in the English rule of men of best disposition, which the Thebans of long time observed.

Another public weal was among the Athenians, where equality was of estate among[3] the people, and only by their whole consent their city and dominions were governed: which might well be called a monster with many heads. Nor never was it certain nor stable, and often times they banished or slew the best citizens, which by their virtue and wisdom had most profited to the public weal. This manner of governance was called in Greek *Democratia*, in Latin *Popularis Potentia*, in English the rule of the commonalty. Of these two governances none of them may be sufficient. For in the first, which consisteth of good men, virtue is not so constant in a multitude, but that some, being once in authority be incensed with a glory, some with ambition, other with covetousness and desire of treasure or possessions. Whereby they fall into contention, and finally, where any achieveth the superiority, the whole government is reduced unto a few in number, which fearing the multitude and their mutability, to the intent to keep them in dread to rebel, ruleth by terror and cruelty, thinking thereby to keep themselves in surety.[4] Nothwithstanding, rancour, coarcted[5] and long detained in a narrow room, at the last bursteth out with intolerable violence and bringeth all to confusion. For the power that is practised to the hurt of many cannot continue. The popular estate,[6] if it anything do vary from equality of substance or estimation, or that the multitude of people have overmuch liberty, of necessity one of these inconveniences must happen: either tyranny, where he that is too much in favor would be elevate and suffer none equality, or else into the rage of a commonalty,[7] which of all rules is most to be feared. For like as the commons, if they feel some severity, they do humbly serve and obey, so where they embracing a license refuse to be bridled, they fling[8] and plunge. And if they once throw down their governor, they order everything without justice, only with vengeance and cruelty, and

1. The same way.
2. State.
3. Endorsed by.
4. Elyot argues against democracy because he believes that it leads to various forms of tyranny: Among the many, a few will gain ascendancy and, to keep their fellow citizens from rebelling, will rule by terror and think themselves secure.
5. Confined.
6. Common people.
7. Democracy also leads to the tyranny of a single man or of the mob: either the single man manages to take charge and allows no "equality" among the ruled, or the many degenerate into a mob.
8. Rear.

with incomparable difficulty and unneth[9] by any wisdom [can they] be pacified and brought again into order. Wherefore undoubtedly the best and most sure governance is by one king or prince, which ruleth only for the weal[1] of his people to him subject; and that manner of governance is best approved, and hath longest continued, and is most ancient. For who can deny but that all thing in heaven and earth is governed by one God, by one perpetual order, by one providence? One sun ruleth over the day, and one moon over the night. And to descend down to the earth, in a little beast, which of all other is most to be marveled at, I mean the bee, is left to man by nature, as it seemeth, a perpetual figure of a just governance or rule, who hath among them one principal bee for their governor, who excelleth all other in greatness, yet hath he no prick or sting, but in him is more knowledge than in the residue.[2] For if the day following shall be fair and dry, and that the bees may issue out of their stalls without peril of rain or vehement wind, in the morning early he calleth them, making a noise as it were the sound of the horn or a trumpet; and with that all the residue prepare them to labor, and flyeth abroad, gathering nothing but that shall be sweet and profitable, although they sit often times on herbs and other things that be venomous and stinking.

The captain himself laboreth not for his sustenance, but all the other for him; he only seeth that if any drone or other unprofitable bee entereth into the hive and consumeth the honey gathered by other, that he be immediately expelled from that company. And when there is another number of bees increased, they semblably[3] have also a captain, which be not suffered to continue with the other. Wherefore this new company gathered into a swarm, having their captain among them and environing[4] him to preserve him from harm, they issue forth seeking a new habitation, which they find in some tree, except with some pleasant noise they be lured and conveyed unto another hive. I suppose who seriously beholdeth this example, and hath any commendable wit, shall thereof gather much matter to the forming of a public weal.

1531

from The Defence of Good Women

CANDIDUS [to Caninius, detractor of women] And so ye conclude,[1] that the power of reason is more in the prudent and diligent keeping than in the valiant or politic getting, and that discretion, election, and prudence, which is all and in every part reason, do excel strength, wit, and hardiness.[2] And consequently, they in whom be those virtues, in that, that they have them, do excel in just estimation them that be strong, hardy, or politic in getting of anything.

CANINIUS Ye have well gathered together all that conclusion.

CANDIDUS Behold Caninius, where ye be now: ye have so much extolled reason, that in the respect thereof bodily strength remaineth as nothing. Forasmuch as the corporal powers with powers of the soul can make no comparison. And ye have

9. Scarcely.
1. Good.
2. Elyot did not realize that the bee that ruled the hive was in fact female.
3. Similarly.
4. Surrounding.
1. Candidus reminds Caninius that they have reached a conclusion: Reason is more manifest in the arts that conserve resources than in those that acquire them. The effect of this conclusion will then prove decisive to the debate between the two men: By putting reason above any other attribute, Caninius has unwittingly established a basis for Candidus's claim that women, conventionally held to excel in virtues associated with introspection, are superior to men, who were rather praised for excelling in virtues associated with physical strength. The notion of a woman's function as conservative is expressed in treatises on domestic economy by Xenophon and Aristotle.
2. Courage.

not denied but that this word *Man*, unto whom reason pertaineth, doth imply in it both man and woman.[3] And agreeing unto Aristotle's saying ye have confirmed that prudence which in effect is more aptly applied to the woman, whereby she is more circumspect in keeping, as strength is to the man, that he may be more valiant in getting. And likewise ye have preferred the prudence in keeping, for the utility thereof, before the valiantness in getting, and seemingly them which be prudent in keeping before them that be only strong and hardy in getting. And so ye have concluded that women, which are prudent in keeping, be more excellent than men in reason, which be only strong and valiant in getting. And where excellency is, there is most perfection. Wherefore a woman is not a creature unperfect, but as it seemeth is more perfect than man.

CANINIUS Why, have ye dallied herefore with me all this long season?

CANDIDUS Surely I have used neither dalliance nor sophistry, but if ye consider it well, ye shall find it but a natural induction, and plain to all them that have any capacity. But yet have I somewhat more to say to you. Ye said moreover Caninius, that the wits of women were apt only to trifles and shrewdness and not to wisdom and civil policy. I will be plain to you, I am sorry to find in your words such manner of lewdness, I cry you mercy, I would have said so much ungentleness, and in your own words so much forgetfulness.

CANINIUS What mean ye thereby?

CANDIDUS Ye have twice granted that natural reason is in women as well as in men.

CANINIUS Yes and what then?

CANDIDUS Then have women also discretion, election, and prudence, which do make that wisdom which pertaineth to governance. And perdy,[4] many arts and necessary occupations have been invented by women, as I will bring now some unto your remembrance.

1540

John Ponet
1514–1556

Ponet was among the most articulate and thoughtful of the Protestants who wrote against tyranny. Made Bishop of Winchester under Henry VIII, he fled to Frankfurt after the accession of Mary I; his treatise on government was composed in 1556 while he was abroad and is one of several such works produced during this period by writers who have been called the Marian exiles. Ponet's argument supporting tyrannicide is grounded in his belief that the monarch has authority and power by virtue of his office not his person; once he fails to rule according to the requirements of office, he is no longer a monarch and therefore can be deposed and even tried for crimes like any other subject. Many of the points in Ponet's treatise were rehearsed in arguments against the rule of Charles I.

from A Short Treatise of Political Power

Forasmuch as those that be the rulers in the world and would be taken for gods (that is, the ministers and images of God here in earth, the examples and mirrors of all godliness, justice, equity, and other virtues) claim and exercise an absolute power, which

3. A reminder that man and woman were alike in being made in the image of God (Genesis 1.27).

4. Indeed.

also they call a fullness of power, or prerogative to do what they lust, and none may gainsay them; to dispense with the laws as pleaseth them, and freely and without correction or offence do contrary to the law of nature, and other [of] God's laws and the positive laws and customs of their countries, or break them; and use their subjects as men do their beasts, and as lords do their villeins and bondmen, getting their goods from them by hook and by crook, with *Sic voio, Sic jubeo* [As I wish, so I command], and spending it to the destruction of their subjects, the misery of this time requireth to examine whether they do it rightfully or wrongfully; that if it be rightful, the people may the more willingly obey and receive the same; if it be wrongful, that then those that use it may the rather for the fear of God leave it. For (no doubt) God will come, and judge the world with equity, and revenge the cause of the oppressed. * * *

True it is, that in matters indifferent, that is, that of themselves be neither good nor evil, hurtful, or profitable, but for a decent order, kings and princes (to whom the people have given their authority) may make such laws, and dispense with them. But in matters not indifferent, but godly and profitably ordained for the commonwealth, there can they not (for all their authority) break them or dispense with them. For princes are ordained to do good, not to do evil; to take away evil, not to increase it; to give example of well doing, not to be procurers of evil; to procure the wealth and benefit of their subjects, and not to work their hurt or undoing. * * *

Antiochus the third, King of Syria, wrote thus to all the cities of his dominion, that if he did command anything that should be contrary to the laws, they should not pass thereon, but that rather they should think it was stolen or forged without his knowledge, considering that the prince or governor is nothing else but the minister of the laws. And this same saying of this most noble king seemed to be so just and reasonable that it is taken for a common principle, how subjects should know when they should do that they be commanded, and when they ought not.

Likewise a bishop of Rome, called Alexander the third,[1] wrote to an archbishop to do a thing which seemed to the archbishop to be unreasonable and contrary to the laws. The pope perceiving that the archbishop was offended with his writing and would not do that he required, desired him not to be offended, but that if there were cause why he thought he should not do that he required, he would advertise him and therewith would be satisfied.[2]

This is a pope's saying, which who is so hardy daring to deny to be of less authority than a law? Yea, not below, but above God's word?[3] Whereupon this is a general rule, that the pope is not to be obeyed, but in lawful and honest things, and so by good argument from the more to the less, that princes (being but footstools and stirrup holders to popes) commanding their subjects [to do] that [which] is not godly, not just, not lawful, or hurtful to their country, ought not to be obeyed, but withstood. For the subjects ought not (against nature) to further their own destruction, but to seek their own salvation, not to maintain evil but to suppress evil. For not only the doers but also the consentors to evil shall be punished, say both God's and man's laws. And men ought to have more respect to their country, than to their prince; to the commonwealth, than to any one person. For the country and commonwealth is a degree above the king. Next unto God, men ought to love their country, and the

1. I.e., Pope Alexander III. As a Protestant, Ponet could not consider that the Pope was anything more than the Bishop of Rome.

2. The Pope would reconsider his order to determine whether it was lawful.

3. The law is above not only the word of the Pope but even the word of God expressed in Scripture. Ponet understands the law as positive law, the aggregate of the common law and statute; it is, in other words, law made by the people.

whole commonwealth before any member of it, as kings and princes (be they never so great) are but members, and commonwealths may stand well enough and flourish, albeit there be no kings, but contrarywise, without a commonwealth there can be no king. Commonwealths and realms may live when the head is cut off, and may put on a new head, that is, make them a new governor, when they see their old head seek too much his own will and not the wealth of the whole body, for the which he was only ordained. And by that justice and law that lately hath been executed in England (if it may be called justice and law), it should appear that the ministers of civil power do sometimes command that, that the subjects ought not to do.

When the innocent Lady Jane, contrary to her will, yea by force, with tears dropping down her cheeks, suffered herself to be called Queen of England, yet ye see, because she consented to that which was not by civil justice lawful, she and her husband for company suffered the pains of traitors, both headless, buried in one pit. * * *

But thou wilt say, whereof cometh this common saying: all things be the kaiser's, all things be the king's?[4] It cannot come of nothing. But by that that is already said, ye see that every man may keep his own and none may take it from him, so that it cannot be interpreted that all things be the kaiser's or king's, as his own proper,[5] or that they may take them from their subjects at their pleasure, but it is thus to be expounded, that they ought to defend that[6] every man hath, that he may quietly enjoy his own, and to see that they be not robbed or spoiled thereof. For as in a great man's house all things be said to be the steward's, because it is committed to his charge to see that every man in the house behave himself honestly and do his duty to see that all things be well kept and preserved; and may take nothing away from any man, nor misspend, or waste; and of his doings he must render account to his lord for all, so in a realm or other dominion, the realm and country are God's. He is the lord, the people are his servants, and the king or governor is but God's minister or steward, ordained not to misuse the servants, that is the people, neither to spoil them of what they have, but to see the people do their duty to their lord God, that the goods of this world be not abused but spent to God's glory, to the maintenance and defense of the commonwealth, and not to the destruction of it. The prince's watch ought to defend the poor man's house, his labor the subject's ease, his diligence the subject's pleasure, his trouble the subject's quietness. And as the sun never standeth still but continually goeth about the world, doing his office, with his heat refreshing and comforting all natural things in the world, so ought a good prince to be continually occupied in his ministry, not seeking his own profit, but the wealth of those that be committed to his charge.

John Foxe
1516–1587

Like John Ponet, Foxe was a Protestant scholar who left England after the accession of Mary I. He went to live in Basel, where he (barely) supported himself as a proofreader. In Basel he began the work that would eventually result in his major history of the Christian church and its martyrs. He returned to London after the Protestant Queen Elizabeth ascended the throne, and in 1563 published his book under the title *Acts and Monuments of these latter and perilous*

4. Cf. Matthew 22.21: "Render unto Caesar the things which are Caesar's, and unto God the things that are God's."

5. Property.

6. That which.

days; it soon became known as *The Book of Martyrs*. Like many of his fellow Marian exiles, Foxe believed that the authority and power of the monarchy should be limited, especially with respect to church doctrine and matters of faith. His accounts of martyrs to Catholicism testify not only to the gruesome persecutions the state enacted and the formidable courage of those who resisted the power of the secular arm of government, but also to his own skillful use of images, reported speech, and descriptive detail, as he shapes the reader's sympathies toward his cause. His book was enormously popular, a fact that illustrates how ready contemporary readers were to take sides in religious conflict and how effectively historical narrative, however polemical and one-sided, could be used to advance or discredit a particular political or religious position.

from The Book of Martyrs

There was a certain act of parliament made in the government of the lord Hamilton, earl of Arran, and governor of Scotland, giving privilege to all men of the realm of Scotland, to read the Scriptures in their mother tongue and language, secluding nevertheless all reasoning, conference, convocation of people to hear the Scriptures read or expounded. Which liberty of private reading being granted by public proclamation, lacked not its own fruit, so that in sundry parts of Scotland thereby were opened the eyes of the elect of God to see the truth, and abhor the papistical abominations, amongst whom were certain persons in St. John's-town, as after is declared.

At this time there was a sermon made by friar Spence, in St. John's-town, otherwise called Perth, affirming prayer made to saints to be so necessary that without it there could be no hope of salvation to man. This blasphemous doctrine a burgess of the said town, called Robert Lamb, could not abide, but accused him in open audience of erroneous doctrine, and adjured[1] him, in God's name, to utter the truth. This the friar, being stricken with fear, promised to do; but the trouble, tumult, and stir of the people increased so, that the friar could have no audience, and yet the said Robert, with great danger of his life, escaped the hands of the multitude, namely of the women who, contrary to nature, addressed them to extreme cruelty against him.

At this time, A.D. 1543, the enemies of the truth procured John Charterhouse, who favored the truth and was provost of the said city and town of Perth, to be deposed from his office by the said governor's authority, and a papist, called Master Alexander Marbeck, to be chosen in his room, that they might bring the more easily their wicked and ungodly enterprise to an end.

After the deposing of the former provost and election of the other, in the month of January the year aforesaid, on St. Paul's day came to St. John's-town the governor, the cardinal, the Earl of Argyle, Justice Sir John Campbell of Lundie, knight, and Justice Defort, the Lord Borthwicke, the bishops of Dunblane and Orkney, with certain other of the nobility. And although there were many accused for the crime of heresy (as they term it), yet these persons only were apprehended upon the said St. Paul's day: Robert Lamb, William Anderson, James Hunter, James Raveleson, James Finlason, and Helen Stirke his wife, and were cast that night in the Spay Tower of the said city, the morrow after to abide judgment.

Upon the morrow, when they appeared and were brought forth to judgment in the town, were laid in general to all their charge the violating of the act of parliament before expressed and their conference and assemblies in hearing and expounding of Scripture against the tenor of the said act. Robert Lamb was accused, in spe-

1. Charged.

cial, for interrupting of the friar in the pulpit; which he not only confessed, but also affirmed constantly, that it was the duty of no man who understood and knew the truth to hear the same impugned without contradiction, and therefore sundry who were there present in judgment, who hid the knowledge of the truth, should bear the burden in God's presence for consenting to the same.

The said Robert also, with William Anderson and James Raveleson, were accused for hanging up the image of St. Francis in a cord, nailing of rams' horns to his head, and a cow's rump to his tail, and for eating of a goose on Allhallow-even.

James Hunter, being a simple man and without learning, and a flesher[2] by occupation, so that he could be charged with no great knowledge in the doctrine, yet because he often used that suspected company of the rest, he was accused.

The woman Helen Stirke was accused, for that in her childbed she was not accustomed to call on the name of the Virgin Mary, being exorted thereto by her neighbors, but only on God for Jesus Christ's sake; and because she said, in like manner, that if she herself had been in the time of the Virgin Mary, God might have looked to her humility and base estate as he did to the Virgin's in making her the mother of Christ, thereby meaning that there were no merits in the Virgin which procured her that honor, to be made the Mother of Christ and to be preferred before other women, but that only God's free mercy exalted her to that estate, which words were counted most execrable in the face of the clergy, and of the whole multitude.

James Raveleson aforesaid, building a house, set upon the round of his fourth stair the three-crowned diadem of Peter carved out of tree, which the cardinal took as done in mockage of his cardinal's hat; and this procured no favor to the said James at their hands.

These aforesaid persons, upon the morrow after St. Paul's day, were condemned and judged to death, and that by an assize, for violating (as was alleged) the act of parliament, in reasoning and conferring upon Scripture, for eating flesh upon days forbidden, for interrupting the holy friar in the pulpit, for dishonoring of images, and for blaspheming of the Virgin Mary, as they alleged.

After sentence was given, their hands were bound and the men cruelly treated, which thing the woman beholding, desired likewise to be bound by the sergeants with her husband for Christ's sake.

There was great intercession made by the town in the mean season, for the life of these persons aforenamed, to the governor, who of himself was willing so to have done that they might have been delivered, but the governor was so subject to the appetite of the cruel priests that he could not do that which he would. Yea, they menaced to assist his enemies and to depose him, except that he assisted their cruelty.[3]

There were certain priests in the city, who did eat and drink before these honest men's houses, to whom the priests were much bounden. These priests were earnestly desired to entreat for their hosts at the cardinal's hands, but they altogether refused, desiring rather their death than their preservation.[4] So cruel are these beasts, from the lowest to the highest.

Then after, they were carried by a great band of armed men (for they feared rebellion in the town except they had their men of war) to the place of execution, which was common to all thieves, and that to make their cause appear more odious to the people.

2. Butcher.
3. If the governor did not agree with the priests, they would turn to his enemies and attempt to depose him.
4. I.e., the priests discounted the hospitality they had enjoyed and agreed to the persecution of their hosts.

Robert Lamb, at the gallows' foot, made his exortation to the people, desiring them to fear God, and leave the leaven of papistical abominations,[5] and manifestly there prophesied of the ruin and plague which came upon the cardinal thereafter. So every one comforting another, and assuring themselves they should sup together in the kingdom of heaven that night, they commended themselves to God, and died constantly in the Lord.

The woman desired earnestly to die with her husband, but she was not suffered; yet, following him to the place of execution, she gave him comfort, exorting him to perseverance and patience for Christ's sake, and, parting from him with a kiss, said on this manner, "Husband, rejoice, for we have lived together many joyful days; but this day, in which we must die, ought to be most joyful unto us both, because we must have joy forever. Therefore I will not bid you good night, for we shall suddenly meet with joy in the kingdom of heaven." The woman, after that, was taken to a place to be drowned, and albeit she had a child sucking on her breast, yet this moved nothing the unmerciful hearts of the enemies. So, after she had commended her children to the neighbors of the town for God's sake, and the sucking bairn was given to the nurse, she sealed up the truth by her death.

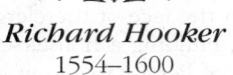

Richard Hooker
1554–1600

Richard Hooker was a theologian and a professor of Hebrew at Oxford whose *Laws of Ecclesiastical Polity* embraced a wide range of topics as it explored on the moral and political foundations of the Church of England. One of the great masters of English prose, Hooker began his book as a final reply to a controversy that had been stirred up by *An Admonition to the Parliament*, which had been secretly published in 1572 by Puritans who denied Queen Elizabeth's right to lead a national church. Hooker worked on his book from 1591 to the end of his life; it was published in sections from 1593 through 1614. In his work, he defended the newly established church against both Roman Catholics and Puritans, arguing for a middle position that would give weight both to the individual reading of Scripture and to the authority of a national church, headed by the monarch rather than the Pope. His discussions of national and church governance entailed probing basic concepts of law itself. Hooker distinguished between natural law—unwritten, universally recognized, and discoverable by reason—on the one hand, and positive law or "laws politic"—the written law of a particular people or state—on the other. He valued human reason and its capacity to discern "goodness" and natural law, but he also believed that human beings harbored a "wild beast" within themselves which had to be controlled by positive law. The first selection is from Book 1; the second is from Book 8.

from The Laws of Ecclesiastical Polity

Signs and tokens to know good by are of sundry kinds; some more certain and some less. The most certain token of evident goodness is if the general persuasion of all men do so account it. And therefore a common received error is never utterly overthrown, till such time as we go from signs unto causes, and show some manifest root or fountain thereof common unto all, whereby it may clearly appear how it hath come to pass that so many have been overseen. In which case surmises and slight

5. Lamb imagines that Catholic doctrine is the "leaven" or corruption (as in fermentation) of Christianity.

probabilities will not serve, because the universal consent of men is the perfectest and strongest in this kind, which comprehendeth only the signs and tokens of goodness. Things casual do vary, and that which a man doth but chance to think well of cannot still have the like hap.[1] Wherefore although we know not the cause, yet thus much we may know; that some necessary cause there is, whensoever the judgments of all men generally or for the most part run one and the same way, especially in matters of natural discourse. For of things necessarily and naturally done there is no more affirmed but this, "They keep either always or for the most part one tenure."[2] The general and perpetual voice of men is as the sentence of God himself.[3] For that which all men have at all times learned, nature herself must needs have taught; and God being the author of nature, her voice is but his instrument. By her from Him we receive whatsoever in such sort we learn. Infinite duties there are, the goodness whereof is by this rule sufficiently manifested, although we had no other warrant besides to approve them. The Apostle St. Paul having speech concerning the heathen saith of them, "They are a law unto themselves" (Rom. 2:14). His meaning is, that by force of the light of reason, wherewith God illuminateth every one which cometh into the world, men being enabled to know truth from falsehood and good from evil, do thereby learn in many things what the will of God is; which will, himself not revealing by any extraordinary means unto them, but they by natural discourse attaining the knowledge thereof, seem the makers of those laws which indeed are his, and they but only the finders of them out. * * *

We see then how nature itself teacheth laws and statutes to live by. The laws which have been hitherto mentioned do bind men absolutely even as they are men, although they have never any settled fellowship, never any solemn agreement amongst themselves what to do or not to do. But forasmuch as we are not by ourselves sufficient to furnish ourselves with competent store of things needful for such a life as our nature doth desire, a life fit for the dignity of man; therefore to supply those defects and imperfections which are in us living single and solely by ourselves, we are naturally induced to seek communion and fellowship with others.[4] This was the cause of men's uniting themselves at the first in politic societies, which societies could not be without government, nor government without a distinct kind of law from that which hath been already declared. Two foundations there are which bear up public societies; the one, a natural inclination, whereby all men desire sociable life and fellowship; the other, an order expressly or secretly agreed upon touching the manner of their union in living together. The latter is that which we call the law of a commonweal, the very soul of a politic body, the parts whereof are by law animated, held together, and set on work in such actions as the common good requireth. Laws politic, ordained for external order and regiment amongst men, are never framed as they should be, unless presuming the will of man to be inwardly obstinate, rebellious, and adverse from all obedience unto the sacred laws of his nature; in a word, unless presuming man to be in regard of his depraved mind little better than a wild beast, they do accordingly provide notwithstanding so to frame his outward actions, that they be no hindrance unto the common good for which societies are instituted. Unless they do this, they are not perfect.

1. Cannot always have the same outcome.
2. Condition.
3. Hooker identifies the law of nature in human beings, the law they know by virtue of being human, with the law of God. He further identifies the source of this law as reason.
4. The following sentences describe the origins of government in man's natural instinct to gather into societies. The classic statement of this idea of a political society is Aristotle's; see *Politics*, 1.1252b1–1253a1.

[THE RULE OF LAW]

Many of the ancients in their writings do speak of kings with such high and ample terms, as if universality of power, even in regard of things and not of persons only, did appertain[5] to the very being of a king. The reason is because their speech concerning kings they frame according to the state of those monarchs to whom unlimited authority was given, which some not observing imagine that all kings, even in that they are kings, ought to have whatsoever power they find any sovereign ruler lawfully to have enjoyed. But that most judicious philosopher,[6] whose eye scarce anything did escape which was to be found in the bosom of nature, he considering how far the power of one sovereign ruler may be different from another regal authority, noteth in Spartan kings, "that of all others they were most tied to law, and so had the most restrained power." A king which hath not supreme power in the greatest things, is rather entitled a king, than invested with real sovereignty. We cannot properly term him a king, of whom it may not be said, at the leastwise as touching certain the very chiefest affairs of state, "his right in them is to have rule, not subject to any other predominant."[7] I am not of opinion that simply always in kings the most, but the best limited power is best. The most limited is that which may deal in fewest things; the best, that which in dealing is tied unto the soundest, perfectest, and most indifferent rule, which rule is the law.[8] I mean not only the law of nature and of God, but very national or municipal law consonant thereunto. Happier that people whose law is their king in the greatest of things, than that whose king is himself their law. Where the king doth guide the state, and the law the king, that commonwealth is like an harp or melodious instrument, the strings whereof are tuned and handled all by one hand, following as laws the rules and canons of musical science. Most divinely therefore Archytas[9] maketh unto public felicity these four steps, every later whereof doth spring from the former, as from a mother cause: "The king ruling by law, the magistrate following, the subject free, and the whole society happy"; adding on the contrary side, that "where this order is not, it cometh by transgression thereof to pass that the king grows a tyrant; he that ruleth under him abhorreth to be guided and commanded by him; the people subject under both, have freedom under neither; and the whole community is wretched."

James I (James VI of Scotland)

1567–1625

James VI of Scotland, eventually James I of England, wrote his treatise on monarchy to curb the enthusiasm of his subjects for a government under the law rather than by an all-powerful ruler. He had ascended his throne in highly uncertain circumstances. His father died when James was eight months old; a few months later his mother Mary was forced from the throne, and James became king of Scotland in 1567 at the age of one. Mary left the kingdom the following year; James never saw her again. He grew up reading widely, writing poetry, harrassed

5. Belong.
6. Aristotle; see *Politics*, 3.1284b–1285b.
7. Power.
8. Hooker states that a king's "best" power is not the most power but rather the "best limited" power; that is, it is limited not because it deals with only a few things, but rather it is limited by law—it therefore comprehends what law does, the workings of the entire body politic. Hooker goes on to argue for a monarchy under positive law, much as Ponet did.
9. A mathematician and friend of Plato, to whom is attributed the treatise *On Law and Justice*. (c. 400 B.C.)

by fears of the devil but enjoying the fellowship of a few trusted Scottish lords. He published a work on devils entitled *Daemonologie* in 1597; *The True Law of Free Monarchies* was published the next year, following conflicts with the Scottish parliament and church authorities. In his book, James insisted that the people had no rights of resistance, even against monarchs who broke divine and natural law; at the same time, he acknowledged that a good king, obeying the law, would not give his subjects a reason to dispute his rule. In theory, James was unequivocally committed to the proposition that Scripture and moral law justified absolute monarchy; in practice, however, he conceded authority and power to Parliament and the common law.

from The True Law of Free Monarchies

Kings are called gods by the prophetical King David, because they sit upon God's Throne in the earth and have the count of their administration to give unto him. Their office is to minister justice and judgment to the people, as the same David saith; to advance the good and punish the evil, as he likewise saith; to establish good laws to his people, and procure obedience to the same, as divers good kings of Judah did; to procure the peace of the people, as the same David saith; to decide all controversies that can arise among them, as Solomon did; to be the minister of God for the weal[1] of them that do well, and as the minister of God, to take vengeance upon them that do evil, as St. Paul saith. And finally, as a good pastor, to go out and in before his people as is said in the first of Samuel; that through the prince's prosperity, the people's peace may be procured, as Jeremy saith. * * *

By the law of nature the king becomes a natural father to all his lieges at his coronation and as the father, of his fatherly duty, is bound to care for the nourishing, education, and virtuous government of his children, even so is the king bound to care for all his subjects.[2] As all the toil and pain that the father can take for his children will be thought light and well-bestowed by him, so that the effect thereof redound to their profit and weal, so ought the prince to do towards his people. As the kindly father ought to foresee all inconveniences and dangers that may arise towards his children, and though with the hazard of his own person press to prevent the same, so ought the king towards his people. As the father's wrath and correction upon any of his children that offendeth ought to be by a fatherly chastisement seasoned with pity, as long as there is any hope of amendment in them, so ought the king towards any of his lieges that offend in that measure. * * *

The kings therefore in Scotland were before any estates or ranks of men within the same, before any Parliaments were holden or laws made, and by them was the land distributed (which at the first was wholly theirs), states erected and discerned, and forms of government devised and established. And so it follows of necessity that the kings were the authors and makers of the laws and not the laws of the kings. And to prove this my assertion more clearly, it is evident by the rolls of our chancellery (which contain our eldest and fundamental Laws) that the king is *Dominus omnium honorum*, and *Dominus directus totius Dominii*,[3] the whole subjects being but his vassals and from him holding all their lands as their overlord, who according to good services done unto him, changeth their holdings from tack to fee, from ward to blanch,[4]

1. Benefit.
2. James's identification of royal with paternal or patriarchal power—that is, the power of the father over his children, or the head of the family over its members—is modeled after what was thought to be Roman law and custom, in which the male head of the household ruled absolutely over it.
3. The lord of the manor, the first lord of all lords.
4. These are legal terms relating to the conditions of feudal tenure. James notes that the king can change what is required of his tenants from knightly service to the payment of rent and can change the nature of the rent his tenants pay from goods to coin.

erecteth new baronies and uniteth old, without advice or authority of either Parliament or any other subaltern judicial seat. So as if wrong might be admitted in play (albeit I grant wrong should be wrong in all persons), the king might have a better color for his pleasure, without further reason, to take the land from his lieges,[5] as overlord of the whole, and do with it as pleaseth him, since all that they hold is of him, then, as foolish writers say, the people might unmake the king and put in another in his room; but either of them, as unlawful and against the ordinance of God, ought to be alike odious to be thought, much less put in practice. * * *

The king is overlord of the whole land, so is he master over every person that inhabiteth the same, having power over the life and death of every one of them. For although a just prince will not take the life of any of his subjects without a clear law, yet the same laws whereby he taketh them are made by himself, or his predecessors, and so the power flows always from himself; as by daily experience we see, good and just princes will from time to time make new laws and statutes, adjoining the penalties to the breakers thereof, which before the law was made, had been no crime to the subject to have committed. Not that I deny the old definition of a king, and of a law, which makes the king to be a speaking law, and the law a dumb king, for certainly a king that governs not by his law can neither be countable to God for his administration nor have a happy and established reign. For albeit be true that I have at length proved that the king is above the law, as both the author and giver of strength thereto, yet a good king will not only delight to rule his subjects by the law, but even will conform himself in his own actions thereto, always keeping that ground that the health of the commonwealth be his chief law. And where he sees the law doubtsome or rigorous, he may interpret or mitigate the same, lest otherwise *Summum jus be summa injuria*.[6] And therefore general laws, made publicly in Parliament, may upon known respects to the king by his authority be mitigated and suspended upon causes only known to him.

Baldassare Castiglione

1478–1529

A courtier at Urbino, the ducal seat of the Gonzaga family, Castiglione wrote his book of advice for men and women seeking advancement in court society. Published in 1528, it proved popular not only with Italian readers but throughout Europe. It was translated into English in 1561 by the diplomat Sir Thomas Hoby. One of the most influential prose stylists of his generation. Hoby belonged to a group of writers who sought to create a clear and forceful English prose free of ornate Latinisms. Written in dialogue form, *The Book of the Courtier* sketched the principles of self-government as they applied to those who sought favor and patronage from rich and powerful nobility; chiefly, it specified how a courtier could gain and keep his lord's attention. One of Castiglione's best-known directives concerns the manner in which the courtier should perform his duties: it will only be impressive, Castiglione insists, if it seems to be completely unlearned, unrehearsed, and natural. Castiglione's arguments influenced many writers, including Shakespeare; the courtier and writer Sir Philip Sidney "never stirred abroad without a copy in his pocket."

5. Lords.
6. The most exacting enforcement of the law may be an injustice. Here James invokes the principle of equity, which allows a magistrate discretion to moderate the effect of the law in certain cases.

from The Book of the Courtier

Whoso mindeth to be gracious or to have a good grace in the exercises of the body (presupposing first that he be not of nature unapt) ought to begin betimes and to learn his principles of cunning men. The which thing how necessary a matter Philip King of Macedonia thought it, a man may gather in that his will was that Aristotle, so famous a philosopher and perhaps the greatest that hath ever been in the world, should be the man that should instruct Alexander his son in the first principles of letters. * * *

He therefore that will be a good scholar, beside the practicing of good things must evermore set all his diligence to be like his master, and (if it were possible) change himself into him. And when he hath had some entry, it profiteth him much to behold sundry men of that profession, and governing himself with that good judgment that must always be his guide, go about to pick out, sometime of one and sometime of another, sundry matters. And even as the bee in the green meadows fleeth always about the grass choosing out flowers, so shall our courtier steal this grace from them that to his seeming have it, and from each one that parcel that shall be most worthy praise. And not do, as a friend of ours, whom you all know, that thought he resembled much King Ferdinand the younger of Aragon, and regarded not to resemble him in any other point but in the often lifting up his head, wrying therewithall a part of his mouth, the which custom the king had gotten by infirmity. And many such there are that think they do much, so they resemble a great man in somewhat, and take many times the thing in him that worst becometh him. But I, imagining with myself oftentimes how this grace cometh, leaving apart such as have it from above, find one rule that is most general which in this part (methink) taketh place in all things belonging to man in word or deed above all other. And that is to eschew as much as a man may, and as a sharp and dangerous rock, affectation or curiosity and (to speak a new word) to use in everything a certain recklessness, to cover art withall, and seem whatsoever he doth and sayeth to do it without pain and (as it were) not minding it. And of this do I believe grace is much derived, for in rare matters and well brought to pass every man knoweth the hardness[1] of them, so that a readiness therein maketh great wonder. And contrariwise to use force, and (as they say) to haul by the hair, giveth a great disgrace, and maketh every thing how great soever it be, to be little esteemed. Therefore that may be said to be a very art that appeareth not to be art, neither ought a man to put more diligence in anything than in covering it, for in case it be open, it loseth credit clean, and maketh a man little set by. And I remember that I have read in my days that there were some most excellent orators, which among other their cares, enforced themselves to make every man believe that they had no sight in letters, and dissembling their cunning, made semblant[2] their orations to be made very simply, and rather as nature and truth lead them than study and art, the which if it had been openly known would have put a doubt in the people's mind, for fear least he beguiled them. You may see then how to show art and such bent[3] study taketh away the grace of every thing.

1. Difficulty.
2. Made it apparent that.
3. Dedicated.

Roger Ascham
1515–1568

Secretary to both Queen Mary and Queen Elizabeth, Ascham was convinced that the education of children was crucial to the prosperity of the state; for him, education was not a private concern but a public matter. Adopting humanist methods of instruction, teachers in this period had become increasingly committed to preparing students not only to understand what they read but also why it was important. In short, the value of rote learning, which depends on a quick memory and a willing acceptance of authority, had become debatable. Ascham favored an education based on discussion, questioning, and criticism, and he preferred teaching in English rather than Latin. In 1545 he had published the first book written in English on the subject of archery; *The Schoolmaster,* published posthumously in 1570, embodies Ascham's ideals in a lively and emphatic style. In the following excerpt, he defends a "hard-witted" student, one who learns slowly but thoroughly, thereby highlighting the importance of character in the process of learning; by stressing character, Ascham turns the attention of the reader from the formal aspects of education and toward its role in the formation of the individual citizen.

from The Schoolmaster

If your scholar do miss sometimes in marking rightly these foresaid six things, chide not hastily, for that shall both dull his wit and discourage his diligence; but monish[1] him gently, which shall make him both willing to amend and glad to go forward in love and hope of learning.

I have now wished, twice or thrice, this gentle nature to be in a schoolmaster, and that I have done so neither by chance nor without some reason I will now declare at large, why, in mine opinion, love is fitter than fear, gentleness better than beating, to bring up a child rightly in learning.

With the common use of teaching and beating in common schools of England I will not greatly contend, which if I did, it were but a small grammatical controversy, neither belonging to heresy nor treason, nor greatly touching God nor the prince; although in very deed, in the end the good or ill bringing up of children doth as much serve to the good or ill service of God, our prince, and our whole country, as any one thing doth beside.

I do gladly agree with all good schoolmasters in these points: to have children brought to good perfectness in learning, to all honesty in manners, to have all faults rightly amended, to have every vice severally corrected; but for the order and way that leadeth rightly to these points, we somewhat differ. For commonly, many schoolmasters, some, as I have seen, more, as I have heard tell, be of so crooked a nature as when they meet with a hard-witted scholar, they rather break him than bow him, rather mar him than mend him. For when the schoolmaster is angry with some other matter, then will he soonest fall to beat his scholar, and though he himself should be punished for his folly, yet must he beat some scholar for his pleasure though there be no cause for him to do so nor yet fault in the scholar to deserve so. These will ye say be fond schoolmasters, and few they be

1. Admonish.

that be found to be such. They be found indeed, but surely over-many such be found everywhere. But this will I say, that even the wisest of your great beaters do as oft punish nature as they do correct faults. Yea, many times, the better nature is sorer punished, for if one by quickness of wit take his lesson readily, another, by hardness of wit taketh it not so speedily; the first is always commended, the other is commonly punished, when a wise schoolmaster should rather discreetly consider the right disposition of both their natures and not so much weigh what either of them is able to do now, as what either of them is likely to do hereafter. For this I know, not only by reading of books in my study, but also by experience of life abroad in the world, that those which be commonly the wisest, the best learned and best men also, when they be old, were never commonly the quickest of wit when they were young. The causes why, amongst other, which be many, that move me thus to think be these few which I will reckon. Quick wits commonly be apt to take, unapt to keep; soon hot and desirous of this and that; as cold and soon weary of the same again; more quick to enter speedily than able to pierce far; even like some over-sharp tools, whose edges be very soon turned. Such wits delight themselves in easy and pleasant studies and never pass far forward in high and hard sciences. And therefore the quickest wits commonly may prove the best poets, but not the wisest orators; ready of tongue to speak boldly, not deep of judgment, either for good counsel or wise writing. Also, for manners and life, quick wits commonly be in desire newfangled; in purpose, unconstant; light to promise anything, ready to forget everything, both benefit and injury; and thereby neither fast to friend nor fearful to foe; inquisitive of every trifle, not secret in greatest affairs; bold with any person; busy in any matter; soothing such as be present, nipping any that is absent; of nature also, always flattering their betters, envying their equals, despising their inferiors; and by quickness of wit, very quick and ready to like none so well as themselves.

Moreover, commonly, men very quick of wit be also very light of conditions, and thereby very ready of disposition, to be carried over quickly by any light company to any riot and unthriftiness when they be young, and therefore seldom either honest of life or rich in living when they be old. For, quick in wit and light in manners be either seldom troubled or very soon weary in carrying a heavy purse. Quick wits also be, in most part of all their doings, over-quick, hasty, rash, heady, and brainsick. These last two words, heady and brainsick, be fit and proper words, rising naturally of the matter and termed aptly by the condition of overmuch quickness of wit. In youth also they be ready scoffers, privy mockers, and ever over-light and merry. In age, soon testy, very waspish, and always over-miserable, and yet few of them come to any great age, by reason of their misordered life when they were young; but a great deal fewer of them come to show any great countenance or bear any great authority abroad in the world, but either live obscurely, men know not how, or die obscurely, men mark not when. They be like trees that show forth fair blossoms and broad leaves in springtime, but bring out small and not long lasting fruit in harvest time; and that only such as fall and rot before they be ripe and so never or seldom come to any good at all. For this ye shall find most true by experience, that amongst a number of quick wits in youth, few be found in the end either very fortunate for themselves or very profitable to serve the commonwealth, but decay and vanish men know not which way, except a very few, to whom peradventure blood and happy parentage may perchance purchase a long standing upon the stage. The which felicity, because it cometh by others' procuring, not by their own deserving, and stand by other men's feet, and not by their own, what outward brag so ever is born by them, is indeed, of itself and in wise men's eyes, of no great estimation. * * *

Contrariwise, a wit in youth, that is not over dull, heavy, knotty, and lumpish, but hard, rough and though somewhat staffish, as Tully wisheth *otium, quietum, non languidum*, and *negotium cum labore, non cum periculo*,[2] such a wit, I say, if it be first well handled by the mother and rightly smoothed and wrought as it should, not overthwartly and against the wood by the schoolmaster, both for learning and whole course of living, proveth always the best. In wood and stone, not the softest, but hardest be always aptest for portraiture, both fairest for pleasure and most durable for profit. Hard wits be hard to receive, but sure to keep; painful without weariness, heedful without wavering, constant without newfangledness; bearing heavy things, though not lightly, yet willingly; entering hard things, though not easily, yet deeply; and so come to that perfectness of learning in the end that quick wits seem in hope, but do not in deed, or else very seldom ever attain unto. Also, for manners and life, hard wits commonly are hardly carried either to desire every new thing or else to marvel at every strange thing, and therefore they be careful and diligent in their own matters, not curious or busy in other men's affairs; and so they become wise themselves and also are counted honest by others. They be grave, steadfast, silent of tongue, secret of heart; not hasty in making, but constant in keeping any promise; not rash in uttering, but wary in considering every matter; and thereby, not quick in speaking, but deep of judgment, whether they write or give counsel in all weighty affairs. And these be the men that become in the end both most happy for themselves and always best esteemed abroad in the world.

Richard Mulcaster

1530–1611

One of the best-known humanists of the early Tudor period, Mulcaster remained a schoolteacher all his life, first at Merchant Taylors' School and then at Saint Paul's, both in London. Like Ascham, he rejected methods of teaching that did not result in a thoughtful and open-minded student. Early in the second of his two treatises on education, *The Elementary* (1582), he identifies ignorance and prejudice as impediments to learning; of the two, he insists, prejudice is worse.

from The First Part of the Elementary

What greater enemies hath learning even in nature than prejudice and ignorance? Whence is there more open show of implacable hostility to knowledge than from prejudice and ignorance? Ignorance knoweth nothing, and therefore is no friend to an unknown good, prejudice knoweth and will not, and therefore is a great foe to a not-favored good. Ignorance yet in part deserveth some excuse for all her disfriendship, because infirmity is her fault, not bolstered with ill will, and the worst is her own, an ordinary case, where even enmity pitieth.[1] But prejudice is a poison to any commonweal, so far as it stretcheth, which being at the first infected with the incur-

2. Ascham refers to Cicero, who desires "a quiet not a languid leisure" and "an occupation that entails work not danger."

1. I.e., ignorance does not imply ill will; its effects are limited by its own failure to seek knowledge; even his enemies pity the ignorant man.

able disease of a cankered and a corrupt opinion gathered by confluence of sundry ill humors, will neither itself yield to a right judgment, nor will suffer any other, where her persuasion can take place. For by yielding herself she feareth the impairing of her misconceived estimation, and by suffering other to yield, she feareth the increase of knowledge's friends, whereby herself shall come in danger to be oppressed, both with truth of matter and number of patrons. Wherefore she opposeth herself, she bendeth all her eloquence, she mureth up[2] all passages, so much as she may, both by persuasion and entreaty, that none shall judge right which will hear her speak and regard her authority, but shall take that music to sound the sweetest which cometh from her, though she be but a mermaid, which by offering of delight endeavoreth to destroy.

Ignorance is violent and like unto a lion, when it encountereth with knowledge, still in fury without feeling, in rage without reason, and riseth of two causes, either infirmity in nature or negligence in labor. Whereof the one could not, the other would not conceive at the first when knowledge was in dealing. Both enemies to knowledge, but negligence the greater,[3] which, either fearing disdain for her first refusal or envying him which loveth where she left, will not seem to favor where she once forsook and stomacheth[4] him which embraceth her leavings, wreaking her malice in show upon knowledge, indeed upon folly. Which folly, being lodged within her own breast beside that negligent ignorance, useth to call in a dangerous opinion the contempt of that good, which she ought to commend, rather than she will by change of opinion and altering her hue, bewray her own error, which all men see saving she that should.[5] Being at defiance with knowledge, not by simplicity of nature, which offered, but by naughtiness of choice, which refused the attaining thereof.

Now natural infirmity the other and more gentle mean of ignorance would perhaps, nay would indeed change her blind opinion, if she could once change her ingenerate heaviness. She would reverence learning if she might see her beauty wherewith to be ravished, being enemy unto her, not of malice but of weakness. * * *

But that same perverse prejudice is a subtle foe to knowledge like a many-headed hydra, and as the venom of his authority is gathered of diverse grounds, so the sting of his poison infecteth diverse ways. The person himself which is thus carried away by a peevish opinion is commonly no heavy head,[6] but either superfically learned and yet loath to seem so, or enviously affected and still carping at[7] his better; or ambitiously given and presumeth upon countenance;[8] or he measureth knowledge by gain, and setteth naught by any more than he himself shall need to compass that [which] he coveteth, where a little cunning will compass much more than reason thinks enough in corruption of minds.[9] * * * The party so corrupted will seek by all means to continue his credit, so much the more a deadly enemy to knowledge, because prejudice must give place if knowledge come in place, and therefore that it may not come, he employeth all his forces, by all cunning and all well-colored shifts[1] to shoulder it out: a professed foe, and so much the shrewder, because he supplanteth knowledge under the opinion of knowledge.

[END OF PERSPECTIVES: GOVERNMENT AND SELF-GOVERNMENT]

2. Walls up.
3. Negligence is a greater enemy to knowledge than "infirmity in nature" because it will not seem to favor the knowledge it has rejected or to tolerate the person who picks up that knowledge; negligence acts with malice toward knowledge, acting foolishly.
4. Will not tolerate.
5. Folly persists in condemning what is good lest others see her error—as they do anyway.
6. Slow learner.
7. Criticizing.
8. Appearance.
9. I.e., cleverness will do more than reason thinks is necessary to corrupt minds.
1. Persuasive arguments.

George Gascoigne

c. 1534–1577

Satire may produce ambiguous results, particularly when it is directed at the author's own life and work. To judge from his candidly witty self-portraits in *Alexander Neville's Theme* and *Woodmanship*, Gascoigne saw a good subject in his own career. The events of his life indicate that whatever ventures he attempted, he failed "to hit the whites [bulls-eyes] which live with all good luck." Educated at Cambridge and trained as a lawyer at Gray's Inn, Gascoigne went into debt trying to keep up with fashionable life in London. His election to Parliament was voided by the claims of his creditors, and in 1561 he compounded his legal difficulties by a bigamous marriage to Elizabeth Boyes, the widow of Willam Breton and the estranged wife of Edward Boyes. His service in the Low Countries was no more successful. He commanded English troops against the Spanish but, after several miscalculated maneuvers, surrendered to the Spanish at Leiden and spent four months as a prisoner of Spain. Upon returning to England he found himself under yet another kind of attack, this time for poetry that was supposed to report the scandalous behavior of certain figures at court. It had been published in 1573 in his absence (and perhaps without his knowledge) in a volume entitled *A Hundreth Sundrie Flowres*. After augmenting the collection—and reworking much of its material so that it conformed to more conventional standards of propriety, he reissued the volume as *The Posies of George Gascoigne* (1575), the version used here. The same volume also contains a prose romance, *The Adventures of Master F.J.*, a racy account of seduction and betrayal, opportunistic lovers, and resourceful ladies.

As Sir Thomas Wyatt had shown, the conventions that had dictated modes of self-expression in lyric poetry were capable of great transformation. Professions of virtuous love and devotion to patriotic ideals in the manner of Petrarch and his followers were no longer the only topics a poet was supposed to address, and Gascoigne, like Wyatt and such later poets as Sir Philip Sidney and John Donne, retuned the lyric voice so that it became capable of illustrating a sense of self charged not only with desire, but also with chagrin, dismay, bitterness, and even revulsion. At the same time, Gascoigne's vision of society remained essentially humorous; throughout his verse he is more committed to castigating himself than those who may have exploited him. Rarely has an author plagued by so many reversals represented as mellow a vision of society. As a rule, satire flattens its subjects to achieve pointed and deliberate effects; Gascoigne's satire gives his subjects a complexity that makes them seem less outrageous than familiar.

Seven Sonnets to Alexander Neville

Alexander Neville delivered him this theme, *Sat cito, si sat bene,* whereupon he compiled these seven sonnets in sequence, therein bewraying his own *Nimis cito,* and therewith his *Vix bene,* as followeth.[1]

1

In haste, post haste, when first my wand'ring mind,
Beheld the glist'ring court with gazing eye,

1. Gascoigne states that he composed these sonnets at the request of Alexander Neville (a poet, translator of Seneca, and secretary to Archbishop Matthew Parker). He was given a theme, *sat cito, si sat bene*, "if it be [done] well, let it be quickly," which he developed to satirize his own fault of acting too quickly: *nimis cito, vix bene*, or "if it be [done] very quickly, it is hardly well."

Such deep delights I seemed therein to find,
As might beguile a graver guest than I.
The stately pomp of princes and their peers,
Did seem to swim in floods of beaten gold,
The wanton world of young delightful years,
Was not unlike a heaven for to behold.
Wherin did swarm (for every saint) a dame,
So fair of hue, so fresh of their attire,
As might excel dame Cynthia[2] for fame,
Or conquer Cupid with his own desire.
These and such like were baits that blazed still
Before mine eye to feed my greedy will.

2

Before mine eye to feed my greedy will,
'Gan° muster eke° mine old acquainted mates, *began to / also*
Who helped the dish (of vain delight) to fill
My empty mouth with dainty delicates:
And foolish boldness took the whip in hand,
To lash my life into this trustless trace,° *harness*
Till all in haste I leaped aloof° from land, *aloft*
And hoist° up sail to catch a courtly grace: *hoisted*
Each ling'ring day did seem a world of woe,
Till in that hapless haven my head was brought:
Waves of wanhope° so tossed me to and fro, *discouragement*
In deep despair to drown my dreadful thought:
Each hour a day, each day a year did seem,
And every year a world my will did deem.

3

And every year a world my will did deem,
Till lo, at last, to court now am I come,
A seemly swaine, that might the place beseem,
A gladsome guest embraced of all and some:
Not there content with common dignity,
My wand'ring eye in haste, (yea post post haste)
Beheld the blazing badge of bravery,
For want whereof, I thought myself disgraced:
Then peevish pride puffed up my swelling heart,
To further forth so hot an enterprise:
And comely cost began to play his part,
In praising patterns of mine own devise.° *devising*
Thus all was good that might be got in haste,
To prink° me up, and make me higher placed. *dress*

4

To prink me up and make me higher placed,
All came too late that taried any time,
Pill of provision[3] pleased not my taste,
They made my heels too heavy for to climb:
Me thought it best that boughs of boist'rous oak,

2. The goddess of the moon, an aspect of the goddess Diana, the goddess of chastity.

3. The property his family had provided him as his inheritance. Requiring greater wealth, he began to cut the trees on his estate.

Should first be shred to make my feathers gay.
Till at the last a deadly dinting stroke,
Brought down the bulk with edgetools of decay:
Of every farm I then let fly a lease,
To feed the purse that paid for peevishness,
Till rent and all were fall'n in such disease,
As scarce could serve to maintain cleanliness:
They bought the body, fine,° farm, lease, and land, *recorded grant*
All were too little for the merchant's hand.[4]

5

All were too little for the merchant's hand,
And yet my bravery bigger than his book:
But when this hot accompt° was coldly scanned, *account*
I thought high time about me for to look:
With heavy cheer I cast my head aback,
To see the fountain of my furious race.
Compared my loss, my living, and my lack,
In equal balance with my jolly grace.
And saw expenses grating on the ground
Like lumps of lead to press my purse full oft,
When light reward and recompense were found,
Fleeting like feathers in the wind aloft:
These thus compared, I left the court at large,
For why? the gains doth seldom quit° the charge. *compensate for*

6

For why? the gains doth seldom quit the charge,
And so say I, by proof too dearly bought,
My haste made waste, my brave and brainsick barge,
Did float too fast, to catch a thing of naught:
With leisure, measure, mean, and many mo,° *more*
I mought° have kept a chair of quiet state, *might*
But hasty heads cannot be settled so,
Till crooked Fortune give a crabbed mate:[5]
As busy brains must beat on tickle° toys, *fickle*
As rash invention breeds a raw device,
So sudden falls do hinder hasty joys,
And as swift baits do fleetest fish entice.
So haste makes waste, and therefore now I say,
No haste but good, where wisdom makes the way.

7

No haste but good, where wisdom makes the way,
For proof whereof, behold the simple snail,
(Who sees the soldier's carcass cast away,
With hot assault the castle to assail,)
By line and leisure climbs the lofty wall,

4. Having leased his farms, he could no longer sell what they produced; in all, none of the financial arrangements he made to acquire more money proved adequate to meet what the merchant charged for his apparel and upkeep.
5. Fortune will give those who act in haste an outcome that is unsatisfactory.

And wins the turret's top more cunningly,
Than doughty Dick, who lost his life and all,
With hoisting up his head too hastily.
The swiftest bitch brings forth the blindest whelps,
The hottest fevers coldest cramps ensue,
The naked'st need hath over latest helps:[6]
With Neville then I find this proverb true,
That haste makes waste, and therefore still I say,
No haste but good, where wisdom makes the way.

Sic tuli[7]

Woodmanship[1]

Gascoigne's woodmanship written to the Lord Grey of Wilton upon this occasion, the said Lord Grey delighting (amongst many other good qualities) in choosing of his winter deer, and killing the same with his bow, did furnish the author with a crossbow *cum pertinenciis* [with accessories] and vouchsafed to use his company in the said exercise, calling him one of his woodmen. Now the author shooting very often, could never hit any deer, yea and oftentimes he let the herd pass by as though he had not seen them. Whereat when this noble lord took some pastime, and had often put him in remembrance of his good skill in choosing, and readiness in killing of a winter deer, he thought good thus to excuse it in verse.

My worthy Lord, I pray you wonder not,
To see your woodman shoot so oft awry,
Nor that he stands amazed like a sot,
And lets the harmless deer (unhurt) go by.
Or if he strike a doe which is but carren,° *pregnant*
Laugh not good Lord, but favor such a fault,
Take will in worth, he would fain hit the barren,
But though his heart be good, his hap is naught:
And therefore now I crave your Lordship's leave,
To tell you plain what is the cause of this:
First, if it please your honour to perceive,
What makes your woodman shoot so oft amiss,
Believe me, Lord, the case is nothing strange,
He shoots awry almost at every mark,
His eyes have been so used for to range,
That now, God knows, they be both dim and dark.
For proof, he bears the note of folly now,
Who shot sometimes to hit philosophy,[2]
And ask you why? forsooth I make avow,
Because his wanton wit went all awry.
Next that, he shot to be a man of law,

6. Gascoigne alludes to the ironies of Fortune; in sum, the most dire need is met with help, but that help comes too late.
7. Thus I have persevered.
1. This enigmatic satire is Gascoigne's reflection on his experience of hunting deer on the estate of Lord Grey of Wilton. Grey was the queen's Chief Deputy in Ireland, one of the most prominent of her officers overseeing the colonization of that country. Gascoigne reacts to Grey's description of his own lack of skill in hunting deer. "Winter deer" were to be shot selectively, avoiding pregnant deer who would give birth during the coming spring.
2. Gascoigne lists the various professions he has tried: philosophy, law, etc.

And spent sometime with learned Littleton,[3]
Yet in the end, he proved but a daw,° *fool*
For law was dark and he had quickly done.
Then could he with Fitzherbert[4] such a brain,
As Tully had, to write the law by art,
So that with pleasure or with little pain,
He might perhaps have caught a truant's part.
But all to late, he most misliked the thing,
Which most might help to guide his arrow straight:
He winked° wrong, and so let slip the string, *aimed*
Which cast him wide, for all his quaint conceit.° *foolish fancy*
From thence he shot to catch a courtly grace,
And thought even there to wield the world at will,
But out, alas, he much mistook the place,
And shot awrie at every rover° still. *random mark*
The blazing baits which draw the gazing eye,
Unfeathered there his first affection,
No wonder then although° he shot awry, *that*
Wanting the feathers of discretion.
Yet more than them, the marks of dignity,
He much mistook and shot the wronger way,
Thinking the purse of prodigality,
Had been best mean to purchase such a prey.
He thought the flatt'ring face which fleareth° still, *smiles*
Had been full fraught with all fidelity,
And that such words as courtiers use at will,
Could not have varied from the verity.
But when his bonnet buttoned with gold,
His comely cape beguarded all with gay,° *lavishly decorated*
His bombast hose,° with linings manifold, *upper stockings*
His knit silk stocks° and all his quaint array, *lower stockings*
Had picked his purse of all the Peter pence,[5]
Which might have paid for his promotion,
Then (all to late) he found that light expense,
Had quite quenched out the court's devotion.
So that since then the taste of misery,
Hath been always full bitter in his bit,
And why? forsooth because he shot awry,
Mistaking still the marks which others hit.
But now behold what mark the man doth find,
He shoots to be a soldier in his age,
Mistrusting all the virtues of the mind,
He trusts the power of his personage.

3. Written by Sir Thomas Littleton in the 15th century and always referred to as "Littleton," this was the principal text used in the practice of common law.
4. Sir Anthony Fitzherbert wrote an abridgment of the common law in 1514; Gascoigne states that if he had had a brain like that of Fitzherbert or "Tully" (Cicero), he would have been able to reduce the law to a set of basic principles and to play truant at law school. As it happened, he took aim badly and missed the mark by a wide margin.
5. An annual tax paid to Rome before the Reformation. Gascoigne alludes to it as a symbol of bribery, what was needed to pay for his advancement.

As though long limbs led by a lusty heart,
Might yet suffice to make him rich again;
But Flushing frays° have taught him such a part,[6] *battles*
That now he thinks the war yield no such gain.
And sure I fear, unless your Lordship deign,
To train him yet into some better trade,
It will be long before he hit the vein,
Whereby he may a richer man be made.
He cannot climb as other catchers can,
To lead a charge before himself be led;
He cannot spoil the simple sakeless° man, *innocent*
Which is content to feed him with his bread.
He cannot pinch the painful soldier's pay,
And shear° him out his share in ragged sheets, *dole*
He cannot stoop to take a greedy pray
Upon his fellows groveling in the streets.
He cannot pull the spoil from such as pill,° *steal*
And seem full angry at such foul offence,
Although the gain content his greedy will,
Under the cloak of contrary pretense:
And nowadays, the man that shoots not so,
May shoot amiss, even as your woodman doth:
But then you marvel why I let them go,
And never shoot, but say farewell forsooth:
Alas my Lord, while I do muse hereon,
And call to mind my youthful years misspent,
They give me such a bone to gnaw upon,
That all my senses are in silence pent.
My mind is rapt in contemplation,
Wherein my dazzled eyes only behold,
The black hour of my constellation,[7]
Which framed me so luckless on the mold:° *on earth*
Yet therewithal I cannot but confess,
That vain presumption makes my heart to swell,
For thus I think, not all the world (I guess)
Shoots bet° than I, nay some shoots not so well.[8] *better*
In Aristotle somewhat did I learn,
To guide my manners all by comeliness,
And Tully taught me somewhat to discern
Between sweet speech and barbarous rudeness.
Old Parkins, Rastell, and Dan Bracton's books,[9]
Did lend me somewhat of the lawless law;
The crafty courtiers with their guileful looks,

6. Gascoigne was deployed as a soldier in Flushing in 1572.

7. I.e., the unfortunate alignment of the stars at his birth.

8. Gascoigne's argument is complex and somewhat ironic; he states he cannot cheat (lines 73ff.) as if to establish his moral rectitude, but then he declares that his behavior is the result of a poor configuration of the stars at his birth (lines 95ff.) as if to denigrate that moral rectitude. Finally, he asserts that he is not the worst shot; some hunters are even less able to exploit others than he is.

9. Gascoigne lists various moral and legal authorities, including the lawyers John Parkins, John Rastell, and Henry Bracton, all of whom published books on the common law. None has made him a successful shot.

Must needs put some experience in my maw:° *stomach*
Yet cannot these with many maistries mo,° *more skills*
Make me shoot straight at any gainful prick,° *point on a target*
Where some that never handled such a bow,
Can hit the white,° or touch it near the quick,° *center/heart*
Who can nor speak, nor write in pleasant wise,
Nor lead their life by Aristotle's rule,[1]
Nor argue well on questions that arise,
Nor plead a case more than my Lord Mayor's mule;
Yet can they hit the marks that I do miss,
And win the mean which may the man maintain.
Now when my mind doth mumble upon this,
No wonder then although I pine for pain:
And whiles mine eyes behold this mirror thus,
The herd goeth by, and farewell gentle does:
So that your Lordship quickly may discuss
What blinds mine eyes so oft (as I suppose).
But since my Muse can to my Lord rehearse
What makes me miss, and why I do not shoot,
Let me imagine in this worthless verse,
If right before me, at my standing's foot° *hunting position*
There stood a doe, and I should strike her dead,
And then she prove a carrion carcass too,
What figure might I find within my head,
To 'scuse the rage which ruled me so to do?
Some might interpret by plain paraphrase,
That lack of skill or fortune led the chance,
But I must otherwise expound the case.
I say Jehovah did this doe advance,
And made her bold to stand before me so,
Till I had thrust mine arrow to her heart
That by the sudden of her overthrow,
I might endeavor to amend my part,
And turn mine eyes that they no more behold,
Such guileful markes as seem more than they be:
And though they glister° outwardly like gold, *glisten*
Are inwardly but brass, as men may see:
And when I see the milk hang in her teat,
Methinks it saith: old babe, now learn to suck,
Who in thy youth couldst never learn the feat
To hit the whites which live with all good luck.[2]
Thus have I told my Lord, (God grant in season)
A tedious tale in rhyme, but little reason.

Haud ictus sapio[3]

1. Probably the rule of the virtuous mean between behavioral extremes.
2. Gascoigne extracts an ironic moral from his suppositious story of yet another failure: Jehovah or God sent him this pregnant doe not to warn him against hunting or hoping to get lucky, but rather to teach him to "suck," to take advantage of the circumstances in which he finds himself, however unlucky they may appear to be. With this reflection, Gascoigne avoids the temptation to attribute his lack of success to a superior morality and instead admits that he wants to be like everyone else: interested in his own advancement.
3. Not having been completely defeated, I [now] know.

Edmund Spenser

1552?–1599

A man whose poetry has come to be known as a monument to Queen Elizabeth's England began life modestly enough. Attending Cambridge as a "sizar," or "poor scholar," he worked as a servant to pay for his fees. Allegiance to the English church was expected of all subjects, and Spenser showed his support of the faith while still a student by contributing anti-Catholic verses to the first emblem book published in England. The genre, consisting of emblems or symbolic scenes explained by clever captions, acquainted the aspiring poet with elements of the mode he was later to master: allegory. Literally a writing that conveys "other" (from the Greek *allos*, "other") than literal meanings, the allegory that Spenser would eventually perfect for his epic poem *The Faerie Queene* produced narrative verse of great flexibility and verve. Building on powerful images, his verse allegories of education in a "virtuous" chivalry convey the challenges he saw attending the creation of a civil society in early modern England.

Shortly after leaving Cambridge in 1576, Spenser found employment as a secretary in the London household of the rich and influential Earl of Leicester, a favorite courtier of Queen Elizabeth and an ardent defender of international Protestantism. There he met Leicester's already famous nephew, Sir Philip Sidney, to whom Spenser dedicated his first work, the deliberately archaic, neo-Chaucerian *The Shepheardes Calendar*, a sequence of twelve eclogues or poems on pastoral subjects, one for each month of the year. A work of a paradoxically innovative style, *The Shepheardes Calendar* demonstrated a range of metrical forms that had yet to be seen in English poetry; probably more compelling to the general reader was Spenser's use of pastoral motifs and settings to represent opinions on love, poetry, and social order. Sidney's response to the poem was, nevertheless, somewhat ambivalent. While recognizing that Spenser's eclogues had "much poetry" in them, he stated that he disliked verse composed in an "old rustic language"; among earlier and model poets of pastoral, "neither Theocritus in Greek, Virgil in Latin, nor Sannazaro in Italian did affect it." But precisely because this "old rustic language" could be recognized as purely English and independent of European traditions, Spenser would use a modified form of it in *The Faerie Queene*; in this way he hoped to demonstrate that English literature had as rich a past as any in Europe. He probably began the poem while in Leicester's service; the seventeenth-century biographer John Aubrey reported the discovery of "an abundance of cards, with stanzas of the *Faerie Queene* written on them" in the wainscoting of Spenser's London lodging.

From 1580 to the end of his life, Spenser lived in Ireland, serving as secretary to the Lord Deputy of Ireland, Arthur Grey. At such a distance from Queen Elizabeth's court, Spenser could not have secured royal favor. He was rescued from obscurity in 1589 by Sir Walter Raleigh, who, impressed with the first three books of *The Faerie Queene*, invited Spenser to present his poem to the queen. Beside the gallant and charismatic Raleigh, the poet—said to have been a "little man, who wore short hair, little bands (collars) and little cuffs"—must have cut a poor figure. But the queen liked the poem that illustrated her majesty in so many ways, "desired at timely hours to hear" it, and rewarded Spenser with a life pension of £50 a year. When Spenser returned to Ireland in 1590, he met and fell in love with Elizabeth Boyle, a woman much his junior. They were married in 1594, and Spenser celebrated their courtship and wedding in the *Amoretti*, a sonnet sequence describing the poet's quest for his "deer" or dear, and *Epithalamion*, a hymn to each of the twenty-four hours of their wedding day. The second three books of *The Faerie Queene*, published in 1596, proved as popular with readers as the first three, although James VI of Scotland (later James I of England) thought slanderous its portrait of the evil queen Duessa, whom he identified as his mother, Mary, Queen of Scots. He demanded that Spenser be "duly tried and punished"; fortunately, however, Spenser's friends at court intervened, and nothing came of the king's displeasure.

The last years of the poet's life were full of grief and bitter disappointment. In 1598 the Irish in the province of Munster, rebelling against the English colonial authorities, burned the castle in which Spenser lived. The poet and his wife fled; their newborn child was reported to have perished in the flames. In December of that year, Spenser went to London to deliver letters to the queen from the Governor of Ireland concerning the uprising. He included a note describing his own assessment of the situation—a note that may have included material in a treatise entitled *A View of the Present State of Ireland*, supporting a militaristic policy to colonize the people of Ireland, which he is supposed to have written. He died a month after arriving in London in January of 1599 and was buried in Westminster Abbey near Geoffrey Chaucer, whose poetry had meant so much to him. The monument placed on his grave is inscribed with these words: "Prince of poets in his time, whose Divine Spirit needs no other witness than the works which he left behind."

Consciously aspiring both to Chaucer's humane dignity and to his vividly colloquial style, Spenser saw himself as fashioning and refashioning a tradition of English and possibly British poetry. As he made a point of using older terms and spelling, his poems are presented here unmodernized. Spenser's choice of language parallels his use of the motifs of knightly romance: turning to the past, he sought a vital perspective on the present. John Milton would later describe him as a "sage and serious" poet, who, in *The Faerie Queene,* wrote of the struggle of good against evil and the triumph of faith over falsehood. The subject, treated by weaving different story lines together to form a vast tapestry, interested not only Milton, who was clearly inspired by Spenser's complex understanding of human psychology, but also the next generation of poets in England, especially Ben Jonson, John Donne, and George Herbert, who turned to Spenser for a poetry of satirical vigor and spiritual insight. Yet other readers have been moved by Spenser's lyrics. His shorter poems and occasional verse show his skillful use of repetitive sounds or verbal echoes and reveal his unerring sense of language as a musical medium.

The Shepheardes Calender

The genre of pastoral, which originated with Greek and Latin poets, especially Virgil, was popular with early modern writers of lyric verse. Because the genre represents its subjects from the idealized perspectives of rural life, it gave writers who were critical of the more sophisticated manners of the city a chance to praise the virtues of simplicity and artlessness. In fact, Spenser's eclogues are rhetorically complex. Composed as dialogues, they exhibit a consciously archaic diction and a demanding rhyme scheme. *October* is "eclogue the tenth" (*aegloga decima*) in a series of twelve eclogues or pastoral poems, published in 1579. Each eclogue was composed for a month of the year and as a whole they formed a "calendar." The subject of *October* is the poet's craft; it presents an argument between Cuddie, a shepherd and also a piper who wants to renounce his art as unremunerative, and Piers, a shepherd who tells Cuddie that the purpose of his music is to lead its listeners in better ways.

from The Shepheardes Calender

October

Aegloga decima

Argument[1]

In Cuddie is set out the perfecte paterne of a Poete, whiche finding no maintenaunce of his state and studies, complayneth of the contempte of Poetrie, and the causes

1. This "Argument" is a prose synopsis of the following dialogue and was written by "E.K.," thought to be Edward Kirke, a friend of Spenser.

thereof: Specially having bene in all ages, and even amongst the most barbarous alwayes of singular accounpt and honor, and being indede so worthy and commendable an arte: or rather no arte, but a divine gift and heavenly instinct not to bee gotten by laboure and learning, but adorned with both: and poured into the witte by a certaine ἐνθουσιασμὸς [enthusiasm] and celestiall inspiration, as the Author hereof els where at large discourseth, in his booke called the English Poete, which booke being lately come to my hands, I mynde also by Gods grace upon further advisement to publish.

PIERS

Cuddie, for shame hold up thy heavye head,
And let us cast with what delight to chace,
And weary thys long lingring Phoebus race.[2]
Whilome° thou wont the shepheards laddes to leade, *formerly*
In rymes, in ridles, and in bydding base:° *simple requests*
Now they in thee, and thou in sleepe art dead.

CUDDIE

Piers, I have pyped erst° so long with payne, *first*
That all mine Oten reedes° bene rent and wore: *shepherd's pipe*
And my poore Muse hath spent her spared store,
Yet little good hath got, and much lesse gayne.
Such pleasaunce makes the Grashopper so poore,
And ligge so layd,[3] when Winter doth her straine:

The dapper ditties, that I wont devise,
To feede youthes fancie, and the flocking fry,° *children*
Delighten much: what I the bett for thy?[4]
They han the pleasure, I a sclender prise.
I beate the bush, the byrds to them doe flye:[5]
What good thereof to Cuddie can arise?

PIERS

Cuddie, the prayse is better, then the price,° *prize*
The glory eke° much greater then the gayne: *also*
O what an honor is it, to restraine
The lust of lawlesse youth with good advice:
Or pricke them forth with pleasaunce of thy vaine,° *poetic vein*
Whereto thou list° their trayned willes entice.[6] *wish*

Soone as thou gynst to sette thy notes in frame,
O how the rurall routes° to thee doe cleave: *crowds*
Seemeth thou dost their soule of sence bereave,
All as the shepheard, that did fetch his dame
From Plutoes balefull bowre withouten leave:
His musicks might the hellish hound did tame.[7]

2. The race of Apollo, god of the sun, through the day.
3. Having sung all summer, the grasshopper lies in poverty when winter comes.
4. What am I the better for this?
5. I rouse game that flies to others.
6. Piers advises Cuddie that a poet must entice the educated wills of his readers by the pleasure his subject matter gives them.
7. Orpheus, mythic father of poetry, rescued his wife from hell, kingdom of the underworld god Pluto, using his music to charm Pluto's savage guard dog Cerberus.

CUDDIE

So praysen babes the Peacoks spotted traine,
And wondren at bright Argus[8] blazing eye:
But who rewards him ere° the more for thy?° *ever / this*
Or feedes him once the fuller by a graine?
Sike° prayse is smoke, that sheddeth in the skye, *such*
Sike words bene wynd, and wasten soone in vayne.

PIERS

Abandon then the base and viler clowne,° *bumpkin*
Lyft up thy selfe out of the lowly dust:
And sing of bloody Mars,° of wars, of giusts,° *god of war / jousts*
Turne thee to those, that weld° the awful crowne. *wield*
To doubted° Knights, whose woundlesse armour rusts, *undefeated*
And helmes unbruzed wexen° dayly browne. *grow*

There may thy Muse display her fluttryng wing,
And stretch her selfe at large from East to West:
Whither thou list in fayre Elisa[9] rest,
Or if thee please in bigger notes to sing,
Advaunce the worthy whome shee loveth best,
That first the white beare to the stake did bring.[1]

And when the stubborne stroke of stronger stounds,° *times*
Has somewhat slackt the tenor of thy string:
Of love and lustihead tho° mayst thou sing, *then*
And carrol lowde, and leade the Myllers rownde,
All° were Elisa one of thilke° same ring. *although / that*
So mought° our Cuddies name to Heaven sownde. *might*

CUDDIE

Indeede the Romish Tityrus, I heare,
Through his Mecoenas left his Oaten reede,[2]
Whereon he earst had taught his flocks to feede,
And laboured lands to yield the timely eare,
And eft° did sing of warres and deadly drede, *often*
So as the Heavens did quake his verse to here.

But ah Mecoenas is yclad in claye,
And great Augustus long ygoe is dead:
And all the worthies liggen° wrapt in leade, *lie*
That matter made for Poets on to play:
For ever, who in derring doe° were dreade,° *bold action / feared*
The loftie verse of hem° was loved aye.° *about them / ever*

But after vertue gan for age to stoupe,
And mighty manhode brought a bedde of ease:
The vaunting Poets found nought worth a pease,
To put in preace° emong the learned troupe. *public*

8. Mythical herdsman who had eyes all over his body.
9. Queen Elizabeth. Piers suggests that Cuddie may wish to take the queen for his poetic subject.
1. "He meaneth (as I guesse) the most honorable and renowned the Erle of Leycester" (E.K.). Leicester's emblem was a bear and staff.
2. Cuddie explains that when Tityrus (the name the poet Virgil assumes in his *Eclogues*) was patronized by Mecoenas, or Maecenas, a liberal patron of letters during the reign of the Roman Emperor Augustus, he could afford to write epic, that is, a long verse narrative that describes a heroic action.

Tho gan the streames of flowing wittes to cease,
And sonnebright honour pend in shamefull coupe.° *pen*

And if that any buddes of Poesie,
Yet of the old stocke gan to shoote agayne:
Or it° mens follies mote be forst to fayne,° *poetry / represent*
And rolle with rest in rymes of rybaudrye:
Or as it sprong, it wither must agayne:
Tom Piper makes us better melodie.[3]

PIERS

O pierlesse Poesye, where is then thy place?
If nor° in Princes pallace thou doe sitt: *neither*
(And yet is Princes pallace the most fitt)
Ne° brest of baser birth doth thee embrace. *nor*
Then make thee winges of thine aspyring wit,
And, whence thou camst, flye backe to heaven apace.

CUDDIE

Ah Percy it is all to weake and wanne,
So high to sore, and make so large a flight:
Her peeced pyneons bene not so in plight,[4]
For Colin[5] fittes° such famous flight to scanne: *it suits*
He, were he not with love so ill bedight,° *afflicted*
Would mount as high, and sing as soote° as Swanne. *sweet*

PIERS

Ah fon,° for love does teach him climbe so hie, *fool*
And lyftes him up out of the loathsome myre:
Such immortall mirrhor, as he doth admire,
Would rayse ones mynd above the starry skie.
And cause a caytive° corage to aspire, *cowardly*
For lofty love doth loath a lowly eye.

CUDDIE

All otherwise the state of Poet stands,
For lordly love is such a Tyranne fell:° *terrible*
That where he rules, all power he doth expell.
The vaunted verse a vacant head demaundes,
Ne wont° with crabbed care the Muses dwell. *used*
Unwisely weaves, that takes two webbes in hand.

Who ever casts to compasse° weightye prise, *gain*
And thinks to throwe out thondring words of threate:
Let powre in lavish cups and thriftie° bitts of meate, *good*
For Bacchus° fruite is frend to Phoebus wise. *god of wine*
And when with Wine the braine begins to sweate,
The nombers flowe as fast as spring doth ryse.

Thou kenst not Percie howe the ryme should rage.
O if my temples were distaind with wine,
And girt in girlonds of wild Yvie twine,

3. Cuddie states that because the present age has no virtuous subjects, such poetry as epic is no longer written. To be revived, it must either represent the folly of the present time or wither again for lack of a subject; for the present, a "Tom Piper" or popular singer will produce better songs than poets can.

4. I.e., the mended wings of Poetry are not in such a condition.

5. Another of the shepherds who participate in the eclogues' dialogues.

How I could reare the Muse on stately stage,
And teache her tread aloft in bus-kin° fine, *high boots*
With queint Bellona° in her equipage. *goddess of war*

But ah my corage cooles ere it be warme,
For thy,° content us in thys humble shade: *now*
Where no such troublous tydes han us assayde,° *tried*
Here we our slender pipes may safely charme.

PIERS

And when my Gates° shall han their bellies layd:° *she-goats/borne kids*
Cuddie shall have a Kidde to store° his farme. *enrich*

Cuddies Embleme

Agitante calescimus illo &c.[6]

The Faerie Queene

In 1583 Spenser told guests at a dinner he was attending that he proposed to write a poem in which he would "represent all the moral virtues, assigning to every virtue a knight in whose actions and chivalry the operations of that virtue are to be expressed, and the vices and unruly appetites that oppose themselves to be beaten down." The project, obviously ambitious, recalls the great epics of classical antiquity: the twenty-four books of Homer's *Iliad*, the twelve books of Virgil's *Aeneid*. Spenser must have believed he was prepared for such an undertaking; like Virgil, he had served his apprenticeship by writing pastoral poetry, with the composition of *The Shepheardes Calendar*. But whatever his intention, he realized his great work only in part. He depicted the first six virtues in the "legends" of Holiness, Temperance, Chastity, Friendship, Justice, and Courtesy, in which each virtue is perfected by the trials of a particular knight fighting the evil that most threatens his character. He published the first three books in 1590, adding the next three in a second edition in 1596. His plan for a second set of six books resulted in only two cantos—on the virtue of Constancy.

Spenser's moral chivalry is sponsored and sustained by the court of Gloriana, the Faerie Queene, in whom is reflected the imposing figure of Queen Elizabeth. Gloriana's story is illustrated by the actions of a character called Prince Arthur, who intervenes at crucial moments to assist Gloriana's knights and is otherwise bent on seeking out Gloriana herself, the bride he has chosen in a dream. In the mythical genealogy of the Tudors, King Arthur (known to Spenser's readers through Sir Thomas Malory's *Morte Darthur*) was identified as the dynasty's progenitor; thus, in the allegorical schema of the poem, the prospective marriage of the Faerie Queene and Prince Arthur, also the champion of Magnificence, signifies the perfect union of monarch and state.

Book 1 relates the adventures of the knight of Holiness, known as the Redcrosse Knight from the sign on his shield and identified as Saint George, England's patron saint. His mission is to overcome the machinations of spiritual error menacing the English church and to deliver the parents of Una, his lady, who is the Truth, from the demons of false faith. The foes of the Redcrosse Knight are many: the fiendish wizard Archimago, who stands for corrupt doctrine; the cunning queen Duessa, who, as the embodiment of duplicity, is never what she seems; the bloated giant Orgoglio, or Pride; and the loathsome many-headed dragon who is supposed to wield the institutional power of the Catholic Church. The Redcrosse Knight kills Pride and the dragon but, although he at last understands that they are thoroughly sinister, fails to capture Duessa and Archimago. They return in later books to trouble Gloriana's other knights.

Book 2 tells of the adventures of the knight of Temperance, Sir Guyon, who must destroy a garden of surpassing beauty, known as the Bower of Bliss, presided over by a brilliantly seductive witch called Acrasia. He is accompanied on his quest by the Palmer, who as the embodi-

6. "When he stirs, we glow, etc." From Ovid's *Fasti* 6.5, referring to "Deus in nobis," (the god [of poetry] within us).

ment of reason, informs and guides him in achieving the perfection of his virtue. In Canto 12, perhaps the best-known canto in the entire poem, Guyon sails to Acrasia's island garden in the company of the Palmer, is tempted by the illusionistic pleasures Acrasia provides her suitors, but finally rejects her in a massive act of defiance, tearing down all the beguiling structures of her island in a salutary rage.

The verse form of *The Faerie Queene* is virtually unique to Spenser. It features a sequence of stanzas each (known to later readers as "Spenserian") comprising nine lines, of which the first eight contain five feet or accented syllables and the last contains six feet. They are rhymed in a pattern—*ababbcbcc*—particularly difficult for poets writing in English. Unlike the Romance languages (French, Italian, and Spanish), English has relatively few words ending in vowel sounds, which are easily rhymed. Spenser's ear for the sound of English allowed him to compose verse of a musicality comparable to what was possible in the Romance languages, itself an extraordinary accomplishment. The narrative units of Spenser's epic poem achieve a dramatic coherence by his constructive use of imagery in particular story lines that continuously develop new contexts for their subjects. In other words, a character signifying a special quality in one canto will not signify precisely that quality in another canto: Spenser will change his or her role with the setting the story demands. This gives the reader an active role in the poem's interpretation; in a sense, the reader finds the meaning of the poem in the process of reading it.

FROM The Faerie Queene

A Letter of the Authors[1]

A letter of the Authors expounding his whole intention in the course of this worke: which for that it giveth great light to the Reader, for the better understanding is hereunto annexed.

To the Right noble, and Valorous, Sir Walter Raleigh knight, Lo. Wardein of the Stanneryes, and her Majesties liefetenaunt of the County of Cornewayll.

Sir knowing how doubtfully all Allegories may be construed, and this booke of mine, which I have entituled the Faery Queene, being a continued Allegory, or darke conceit,[2] I have thought good aswell for avoyding of gealous opinions and misconstructions, as also for your better light in reading thereof, (being so by you commanded,) to discover unto you the general intention and meaning, which in the whole course thereof I have fashioned, without expressing of any particular purposes or by-accidents therein occasioned. The generall end therefore of all the booke is to fashion a gentleman or noble person in vertuous and gentle discipline: Which for that I conceived shoulde be most plausible and pleasing, being coloured with an historicall fiction, the which the most part of men delight to read, rather for variety of matter, then for profite of the ensample:[3] I chose the historye of king Arthure,[4] as most fitte for the excellency of his person, being made famous by many mens former workes, and also furthest from

1. Spenser addressed this letter explaining the purpose and plot of *The Faerie Queene* to Sir Walter Raleigh, who had agreed to bring the poem to the attention of Elizabeth I.

2. In Spenser's poetics a series of images or figures that are to be interpreted as metaphor. The narrative understood literally thus implies a second level whose meaning or meanings the reader is to infer.

3. Example.

4. Spenser states that he chose material from the legendary past of Britain: the story of King Arthur and his knights. In fact, apart from a few characters such as Prince Arthur and the magician Merlin, Spenser represented virtually nothing of the Arthurian cycle, known to his readers from Sir Thomas Malory's prose narrative *Morte Darthur*. More important in a structural and thematic sense were the poets mentioned subsequently: Homer and Virgil; Lodovico Ariosto (1474–1533), who wrote *Orlando Furioso;* and Torquato Tasso (1544–1595), who wrote *Jerusalem Delivered*. From these models, Spenser derived the idea of a hero in whom a particular virtue would be exemplified. His division of virtues into moral or ethical on the one hand and political on the other is indebted to Aristotle, who considered the actions of a private person in his *Ethics* and the organization of a whole society in his *Politics*.

the daunger of envy, and suspition of present time. In which I have followed all the antique Poets historicall, first Homere, who in the Persons of Agamemnon and Ulysses hath ensampled a good governour and a vertuous man, the one in his Ilias, the other in his Odysseis: then Virgil, whose like intention was to doe in the person of Aeneas: after him Ariosto comprised them both in his Orlando: and lately Tasso dissevered[5] them againe, and formed both parts in two persons, namely that part which they in Philosophy call Ethice, or vertues of a private man, coloured in his Rinaldo: The other named Politice in his Godfredo. By ensample of which excellente Poets, I labour to pourtraict in Arthure, before he was king, the image of a brave knight, perfected in the twelve private morall vertues, as Aristotle hath devised, the which is the purpose of these first twelve bookes: which if I finde to be well accepted, I may be perhaps encoraged, to frame the other part of polliticke vertues in his person, after that hee came to be king. To some I know this Methode will seeme displeasaunt, which had rather have good discipline delivered plainly in way of precepts, or sermoned at large, as they use,[6] then thus clowdily enwrapped in Allegoricall devises.[7] But such, me seeme, should be satisfide with the use of these dayes, seeing all things accounted by their showes, and nothing esteemed of, that is not delightfull and pleasing to commune sence. For this cause is Xenophon preferred before Plato,[8] for that the one in the exquisite depth of his judgement, formed a Commune welth such as it should be, but the other in the person of Cyrus and the Persians fashioned a governement such as might best be: So much more profitable and gratious is doctrine by ensample, then by rule. So have I laboured to doe in the person of Arthure: whome I conceive after his long education by Timon, to whom he was by Merlin delivered to be brought up, so soone as he was borne of the Lady Igrayne, to have seene in a dream or vision the Faery Queen, with whose excellent beauty ravished,[9] he awaking resolved to seeke her out, and so being by Merlin armed, and by Timon throughly instructed, he went to seeke her forth in Faerye land. In that Faery Queene I meane glory in my generall intention,[1] but in my particular I conceive the most excellent and glorious person of our soveraine the Queene, and her kingdome in Faery land. And yet in some places els, I doe otherwise shadow her.[2] For considering she beareth two persons, the one of a most royall Queene or Empresse, the other of a most vertuous and beautifull Lady, this latter part in some places I doe expresse in Belphoebe, fashioning her name according to your owne excellent conceipt of Cynthia, (Phoebe and Cynthia being both names of Diana.) So in the person of Prince Arthure[3] I sette forth magnificence in particular, which vertue for that (according to Aristotle and the rest) it is the perfection of all the rest, and conteineth in it them all, therefore in the whole course I mention the deedes of Arthure applyable to that vertue, which I write of in that booke. But of the xii. other vertues, I make xii. other knights the patrones, for the more variety of the history: Of which these three

5. Revealed.
6. Are accustomed to.
7. Figures.
8. Xenophon: the Greek historian (c. 430–355 B.C.), whose account of the Persian king Cyrus creates memorable characters for the reader to emulate; Plato: the Greek philosopher (c. 427–348 B.C.), whose works comprise ethics, politics, and metaphysics. Spenser repeats a conventional excuse for fiction or poetic representation in contrast to philosophy.
9. Overcome.
1. I.e., in the figure of the Faerie Queene Spenser intends to represent glory in general and Queen Elizabeth in particular. He goes on to say that the queen is also represented by the figure of Belphoebe, a nymph who has attributes of Cynthia, or the goddess of the moon, who is herself an aspect of Diana, also the goddess of chastity and the hunt.
2. Represent.
3. Legendary king of the Britons. Spenser's character is to represent "magnificence," i.e, a splendid and comprehensive generosity, traditionally the virtue most appropriate to royalty. The remaining characters Spenser mentions—the Redcrosse Knight, Sir Guyon, and Britomartis (or Britomart)—represent other virtues and are his own creations.

bookes contayn three, The first of the knight of the Redcrosse, in whome I expresse Holynes: The seconde of Sir Guyon, in whome I sette forth Temperaunce: The third of Britomartis a Lady knight, in whome I picture Chastity. But because the beginning of the whole worke seemeth abrupte and as depending upon other antecedents, it needs that ye know the occasion of these three knights severall adventures. For the Methode of a Poet historical is not such, as of an Historiographer.[4] For an Historiographer discourseth of affayres orderly as they were donne, accounting as well the times as the actions, but a Poet thrusteth into the middest, even where it most concerneth him, and there recoursing[5] to the thinges forepaste,[6] and divining of thinges to come, maketh a pleasing Analysis of all. The beginning therefore of my history, if it were to be told by an Historiographer should be the twelfth booke, which is the last, where I devise[7] that the Faery Queene kept her Annuall feaste xii. dayes, uppon which xii. severall dayes, the occasions of the xii. severall adventures hapned, which being undertaken by xii. severall knights, are in these xii books severally handled and discoursed. The first was this. In the beginning of the feast, there presented him selfe a tall clownishe[8] younge man, who falling before the Queen of Faries desired a boone[9] (as the manner then was) which during that feast she might not refuse: which was that hee might have the atchievement of any adventure, which during that feaste should happen, that being graunted, he rested him on the floore, unfitte through his rusticity for a better place. Soone after entred a faire Ladye in mourning weedes,[1] riding on a white Asse, with a dwarfe behind her leading a warlike steed, that bore the Armes of a knight, and his speare in the dwarfes hand. Shee falling before the Queene of Faeries, complayned that her father and mother an ancient King and Queene, had bene by an huge dragon many years shut up in a brasen[2] Castle, who thence suffred them not to yssew:[3] and therefore besought the Faery Queene to assygne her some one of her knights to take on him that exployt. Presently that clownish person upstarting, desired that adventure: whereat the Queene much wondering, and the Lady much gainesaying,[4] yet he earnestly importuned[5] his desire. In the end the Lady told him that unlesse that armour which she brought, would serve him (that is the armour of a Christian man specified by Saint Paul v. Ephes.)[6] that he could not succeed in that enterprise, which being forthwith put upon him with dewe furnitures[7] thereunto, he seemed the goodliest man in al that company, and was well liked of the Lady. And eftesoones[8] taking on him knighthood, and mounting on that straunge Courser,[9] he went forth with her on that adventure: where beginneth the first booke, vz.

A gentle knight was pricking on the playne. &c.

4. History represents sequential narratives of real events revealing relations of cause and effect; by contrast, poetry constructs narratives governed by the poet's wish to pick and choose among a variety of sources and to speculate on outcomes that may or may not ever come to pass.
5. Having recourse.
6. Passed.
7. Imagine.
8. Countrified.
9. Wish.
1. Clothes.
2. Brass.
3. Get out.
4. Protesting.
5. Begged for.
6. St. Paul's Letter to the Ephesians, often used to justify the spiritual symbolism that from the late Middle Ages had become associated with the practices of chivalry. "Wherefore take unto you the whole armour of God, that ye may be able to withstand in the evil day, and having done all, to stand. Stand therefore, having your loins girt about with truth, and having on the breastplate of righteousness; And your feet shod with the preparation of the gospel of peace; Above all, taking the shield of faith, wherewith ye shall be able to quench all the fiery darts of the wicked. And take the helmet of salvation, and the sword of the Spirit, which is the word of God" (Ephesians 6.13–17).
7. Equipment.
8. Immediately.
9. Warhorse.

The second day ther came in a Palmer[1] bearing an Infant with bloody hands, whose Parents he complained to have bene slayn by an Enchaunteresse called Acrasia: and therfore craved of the Faery Queene, to appoint him some knight, to performe that adventure, which being assigned to Sir Guyon, he presently went forth with that same Palmer: which is the beginning of the second booke and the whole subject thereof. The third day there came in, a Groome who complained before the Faery Queene, that a vile Enchaunter called Busirane had in hand a most faire Lady called Amoretta, whom he kept in most grievous torment, because she would not yield him the pleasure of her body. Whereupon Sir Scudamour the lover of that Lady presently tooke on him that adventure. But being unable to performe it by reason of the hard Enchauntments, after long sorrow, in the end met with Britomartis, who succoured[2] him, and reskewed his love.

But by occasion hereof, many other adventures are intermedled, but rather as Accidents, then intendments.[3] As the love of Britomart, the overthrow of Marinell, the misery of Florimell, the vertuousnes of Belphoebe, the lasciviousnes of Hellenora, and many the like.

Thus much Sir, I have briefly overronne[4] to direct your understanding to the welhead[5] of the History, that from thence gathering the whole intention of the conceit, ye may as in a handfull gripe[6] al the discourse, which otherwise may happily seeme tedious and confused. So humbly craving the continuaunce of your honorable favour towards me, and th'eternall establishment of your happines, I humbly take leave.

23. January, 1589.

Yours most humbly affectionate.

ED. SPENSER.

The First Booke of the Faerie Queene
Contayning The Legende of the Knight of the Red Crosse,
or
Of Holinesse.

1

Lo I the man, whose Muse whilome° did maske,[1] — *formerly*
As time her taught, in lowly Shepheards weeds,° — *clothing*
Am now enforst a far unfitter taske,
For trumpets sterne to chaunge mine Oaten reeds,
And sing of Knights and Ladies gentle deeds;
Whose prayses having slept in silence long,
Me, all too meane,° the sacred Muse areeds° — *lowly/commands*
To blazon broad° emongst her learned throng: — *proclaim abroad*
Fierce warres and faithfull loves shall moralize my song.

2

Helpe then, O holy Virgin chiefe of nine,[2]
Thy weaker Novice to performe thy will,

1. A pilgrim who carries a palm leaf signifying that he has been to the Holy Land; hence any pilgrim.
2. Helped.
3. I.e., they are not central to the principal development of the allegory.
4. Outlined.
5. Source.
6. Gather

1. In this stanza and in the rest of the Proem (introduction), Spenser is announcing his intention to write an epic poem. His earlier *Shepheardes Calender* had been written in the more modest pastoral style, characterized by the "oaten reed" of the shepherd's pipe. Here, he casts off the guise of the shepherd to undertake the lofty subject of *The Faerie Queene*.
2. Spenser calls on a muse to inspire him; he may be referring to Clio, the muse of history, or to Calliope, the muse of epic poetry. Tanaquill was a Roman woman famous for her chaste and noble character; here Spenser establishes a symbolic relation between Tanaquill, the Faerie Queene (whom Arthur seeks in the poem), and Queen Elizabeth I, much as he will later refer to other characters—most prominently, Britomart, Gloriana, and Mercilla—as figuring aspects of the queen, her power and attributes.

Lay forth out of thine everlasting scryne° (*treasure chest*)
The antique rolles,° which there lye hidden still, (*scrolls*)
Of Faerie knights and fairest Tanaquill,
Whom that most noble Briton Prince° so long (*Arthur*)
Sought through the world, and suffered so much ill,
That I must rue° his undeserved wrong: (*regret*)
O helpe thou my weake wit, and sharpen my dull tong.

3

And thou most dreaded impe° of highest Jove,[3] (*child*)
Faire Venus sonne,° that with thy cruell dart (*Cupid, god of love*)
At that good knight° so cunningly didst rove,° (*Arthur*)
That glorious fire it kindled in his hart,
Lay now thy deadly Heben° bow apart, (*ebony*)
And with thy mother milde come to mine ayde:[4]
Come both, and with you bring triumphant Mart,° (*Mars*)
In loves and gentle jollities arrayd,
After his murdrous spoiles and bloudy rage allayd.° (*quelled*)

4

And with them eke, O Goddesse heavenly bright,[5]
Mirrour of grace and Majestie divine,
Great Lady of the greatest Isle, whose light
Like Phoebus lampe throughout the world doth shine,
Shed thy faire beames into my feeble eyne,
And raise my thoughts too humble and too vile,
To thinke of that true glorious type° of thine, (*the Faerie Queene*)
The argument of mine afflicted stile:
The which to heare, vouchsafe,° O dearest dread° a-while. (*grant/power*)

Canto 1

The Patron of true Holinesse,
Foule Errour doth defeate:
Hypocrisie him to entrapp;
Doth to his home entreate.

1

A Gentle Knight[6] was pricking° on the plaine, (*riding*)
Y cladd in mightie armes and silver shielde,
Wherein old dints of deepe wounds did remaine,
The cruell markes of many a bloudy fielde;
Yet armes till that time did he never wield:
His angry steede did chide his foming bitt,
As much disdayning to the curbe to yield:
Full jolly knight he seemd, and faire did sitt,
As one for knightly giusts° and fierce encounters fitt. (*joust*)

3. The king of the pagan gods. Like all the poets of the period who were not writing religious verse, Spenser refers to the classical pantheon as a way of alluding to God and to his various expressions of power.

4. Spenser also invokes Cupid, who combines the loving nature of Venus and the warlike spirit of Mars, to illustrate the mood of his poem.

5. Spenser celebrates the nature of Elizabeth I in grandiose terms: She is a "goddess" whose eyes, like the lamp of Phoebus Apollo (the sun), shine throughout the world and must now illuminate the poet's mind.

6. This gentle or well-born knight, soon to be identified as the Redcrosse Knight from the sign on his shield, wears the armor of Christianity. The armor itself has been worn by many who fought for the faith, but the Redcrosse Knight is new to the spiritual battlefield and will have to prove himself.

2

But on his brest a bloudie Crosse[7] he bore,
The deare remembrance of his dying Lord,
For whose sweete sake that glorious badge he wore,
And dead as living ever him ador'd:
Upon his shield the like was also scor'd,° *represented*
For soveraine hope, which in his° helpe he had: *his Lord's*
Right faithfull true he was in deede and word,
But of his cheere° did seeme too solemne sad; *demeanor*
Yet nothing did he dread,° but ever was ydrad.° *fear / feared*

3

Upon a great adventure he was bond,
That greatest Gloriana[8] to him gave,
That greatest Glorious Queene of Faerie lond,
To winne him worship, and her grace to have,
Which of all earthly things he most did crave;
And ever as he rode, his hart did earne
To prove his puissance° in battell brave *power*
Upon his foe, and his new force to learne;
Upon his foe, a Dragon horrible and stearne.

4

A lovely Ladie[9] rode him faire beside,
Upon a lowly Asse more white then snow,
Yet she much whiter, but the same did hide
Under a vele, that wimpled° was full low, *gathered*
And over all a blacke stole she did throw,
As one that inly mournd: so was she sad,
And heavie sat upon her palfrey[1] slow:
Seemed in heart some hidden care she had,
And by her in a line a milke white lambe she lad.

5

So pure an innocent, as that same lambe,
She was in life and every vertuous lore,
And by descent from Royall lynage came
Of ancient Kings and Queenes, that had of yore
Their scepters stretcht from East to Westerne shore,
And all the world in their subjection held;[2]
Till that infernall feend with foule uprore
Forwasted all their land, and them expeld:
Whom to avenge, she had this Knight from far compeld.

7. The red cross is Spenser's figure for the salvation offered by Christ to humankind through his death on the cross, the sacrifice of his blood, and his resurrection. It was also the badge traditionally worn by St. George, the patron saint of England, with whom the Redcrosse Knight will later be identified.

8. The character Spenser most frequently invokes when he alludes to Elizabeth I. Gloriana presides over the action of the poem, although she does not take part in it herself.

9. Later revealed to be Una or ("one"). The undivided truth (as opposed to "two," that is, doubleness or duplicity), she is associated with the one true Church. The snow-white ass she rides signifies Christ's humility; her veil is emblematic of the veil that stands between Truth and fallen humanity; and the lamb symbolizes innocence and Christian sacrifice. The mourning garb she wears suggests her sorrow over the captivity of her parents, later understood to be Adam and Eve, trapped by the dragon that embodies the forces of evil that have conspired to corrupt the true Church.

1. A horse suitable for a woman.

2. The Lady traces her lineage to Adam and Eve, who held dominion over Eden before the Fall. The "infernall feend," or Satan, is represented as the destroyer of their realm, which stretched from East to West and was therefore truly universal, unlike the regions dominated by Rome or by the Catholic Church. By designating the Knight as the avenger of Adam and Eve, Spenser identifies him with Christ.

6

Behind her farre away a Dwarfe[3] did lag,
That lasie seemd in being ever last,
Or wearied with bearing of her bag
Of needments at his backe. Thus as they past,
The day with cloudes was suddeine overcast,
And angry Jove an hideous storme of raine
Did poure into his Lemans[4] lap so fast,
That every wight to shrowd° it did constrain,° *shelter / impel*
And this faire couple eke° to shroud themselves were fain.° *also / desirous*

7

Enforst to seeke some covert° nigh at hand, *hiding place*
A shadie grove not far away they spide,
That promist ayde the tempest to withstand:
Whose loftie trees yclad with sommers pride,
Did spred so broad, that heavens light did hide,
Not perceable with power of any starre:
And all within were pathes and alleies wide,
With footing worne, and leading inward farre:
Faire harbour that them seemes; so in they entred arre.

8

And foorth they passe, with pleasure forward led,
Joying to heare the birdes sweete harmony,
Which therein shrouded from the tempest dred,
Seemd in their song to scorne the cruell sky.
Much can they prayse the trees so straight and hy,
The sayling° Pine, the Cedar proud and tall, *soaring*
The vine-prop Elme, the Poplar never dry,
The builder Oake, sole king of forrests all,
The Aspine good for staves,° the Cypresse funerall. *poles*

9

The Laurell, meed° of mightie Conquerours *reward*
And Poets sage, the Firre that weepeth still,
The Willow worne of forlorne Paramours,° *forsaken lovers*
The Eugh obedient to the benders will,
The Birch for shaftes, the Sallow° for the mill, *willow*
The Mirrhe sweete bleeding in the bitter wound,
The warlike Beech, the Ash for nothing ill,
The fruitfull Olive, and the Platane° round, *sycamore*
The carver Holme,° the Maple seeldom inward sound. *holly*

10

Led with delight, they thus beguile° the way, *make pleasant*
Untill the blustring storme is overblowne;
When weening° to returne, whence they did stray, *thinking*
They cannot finde that path, which first was showne,
But wander too and fro in wayes unknowne,
Furthest from end then, when they neerest weene,
That makes them doubt, their wits be not their owne:

3. The servant who serves the Lady, a source of prudence, common sense, and wariness.

4. I.e., his lady love's, or the earth's.

So many pathes, so many turnings seene,
That which of them to take, in diverse doubt they been.

11

At last resolving forward still to fare,
Till that some end° they finde or° in or out, *way / either*
That path they take, that beaten seemd most bare,
And like to lead the labyrinth about;
Which when by tract they hunted had throughout,
At length it brought them to a hollow cave,
Amid the thickest woods. The Champion stout
Eftsoones dismounted from his courser brave,
And to the Dwarfe a while his needlesse spere he gave.

12

Be well aware, quoth then that Ladie milde,
Least suddaine mischiefe ye too rash provoke:
The danger hid, the place unknowne and wilde,
Breedes dreadful doubts: Oft fire is without smoke,
And perill without show: therefore your stroke
Sir knight with-hold, till further triall made.
Ah Ladie (said he) shame were to revoke
The forward footing for an hidden shade:
Vertue gives her selfe light, through darkenesse for to wade.[5]

13

Yea but (quoth she) the perill of this place
I better wot° then you, though now too late *know*
To wish you backe returne with foule disgrace,
Yet wisedome warnes, whilest foot is in the gate,
To stay° the steppe, ere forced to retrate.° *halt / retreat*
This is the wandring wood, this Errours den,
A monster vile, whom God and man does hate:
Therefore I read beware. Fly fly (quoth then
The fearefull Dwarfe:) this is no place for living men.

14

But full of fire and greedy hardiment,
The youthfull knight could not for ought° be staide, *anything*
But forth unto the darksome hole he went,
And looked in: his glistring armor made
A litle glooming light, much like a shade,
By which he saw the ugly monster plaine,
Halfe like a serpent horribly displaide,
But th'other halfe did womans shape retaine,[6]
Most lothsom, filthie, foule, and full of vile disdaine.

15

And as she lay upon the durtie ground,
Her huge long taile her den all overspred,

5. Lacking humility and overly confident of his own virtue, the Redcrosse Knight believes he is strong enough to withstand the dangers of the wood. In fact, as we learn in the next stanza, he has stepped into the den of a monster who personifies Error, one of Satan's many manifestations in the poem.

6. Spenser follows traditional treatments of Error in giving her a woman's face and a serpent's body.

Yet was in knots and many boughtes° upwound, *coils*
Pointed with mortall sting. Of her there bred
A thousand yong ones, which she dayly fed,
Sucking upon her poisonous dugs, eachone
Of sundry shapes, yet all ill favored:
Soone as that uncouth° light upon them shone, *strange*
Into her mouth they crept, and suddain all were gone.

16

Their dam upstart, out of her den effraide,
And rushed forth, hurling her hideous taile
About her cursed head, whose folds displaid
Were stretcht now forth at length without entraile.° *coiling*
She lookt about, and seeing one in mayle° *armor*
Armed to point, sought backe to turne againe;
For light she hated as the deadly bale,° *injury*
Ay wont° in desert darknesse to remaine, *ever used*
Where plaine° none might her see, nor she see any plaine. *plainly*

17

Which when the valiant Elfe° perceiv'd, he lept *Redcrosse Knight*
As Lyon fierce upon the flying pray,
And with his trenchand blade her boldly kept
From turning backe, and forced her to stay:
Therewith enrag'd she loudly gan to bray,
And turning fierce, her speckled taile advaunst,
Threatning her angry sting, him to dismay:
Who nought aghast, his mightie hand enhaunst:° *raised up*
The stroke down from her head unto her shoulder glaunst.

18

Much daunted with that dint, her sence was dazd,
Yet kindling rage, her selfe she gathered round,
And all attonce her beastly body raizd
With doubled forces high above the ground:
Tho wrapping up her wrethed sterne° arownd, *tail*
Lept fierce upon his shield, and her huge traine° *tail*
All suddenly about his body wound,
That hand or foot to stirre he strove in vaine:
God helpe the man so wrapt in Errours endlesse traine.

19

His Lady sad to see his sore constraint,° *predicament*
Cride out, Now now Sir knight, shew what ye bee,
Add faith unto your force, and be not faint:
Strangle her, else she sure will strangle thee.
That when he heard, in great perplexitie,
His gall did grate° for griefe and high disdaine, *anger was aroused*
And knitting all his force got one hand free,
Wherewith he grypt her gorge with so great paine,
That soone to loose her wicked bands did her constraine.

20

Therewith she spewd out of her filthy maw° *stomach*
A floud of poyson horrible and blacke,
Full of great lumpes of flesh and gobbets raw,

Which stunck so vildly, that it forst him slacke
His grasping hold, and from her turne him backe:
Her vomit full of bookes and papers was,[7]
With loathly frogs and toades, which eyes did lacke,
And creeping sought way in the weedy gras:
Her filthy parbreake° all the place defiled has. *vomit*

21

As when old father Nilus° gins to swell *the river Nile*
With timely pride aboue the Aegyptian vale,
His fattie° waves do fertile slime outwell,° *fertile / pour forth*
And overflow each plaine and lowly dale:
But when his later spring° gins to avale,° *last waters / subside*
Huge heapes of mudd he leaves, wherein there breed
Ten thousand kindes of creatures, partly male
And partly female of his fruitfull seed;
Such ugly monstrous shapes elswhere may no man reed.° *know*

22

The same so sore annoyed has the knight,
That welnigh choked with the deadly stinke,
His forces faile, ne can no longer fight.
Whose corage when the feend perceiv'd to shrinke,
She poured forth out of her hellish sinke° *womb*
Her fruitfull cursed spawne° of serpents small, *offspring*
Deformed monsters, fowle, and blacke as inke,
Which swarming all about his legs did crall,
And him encombred sore, but could not hurt at all.

23

As gentle Shepheard in sweete even-tide,
When ruddy Phoebus gins to welke° in west, *sink*
High on an hill, his flocke to vewen wide,
Markes which do byte their hasty supper best;
A cloud of combrous gnattes do him molest,
All striving to infixe their feeble stings,
That from their noyance he no where can rest,
But with his clownish hands their tender wings
He brusheth oft, and oft doth mar their murmurings.

24

Thus ill bestedd,° and fearefull more of shame, *situated*
Then of the certaine perill he stood in,
Halfe furious unto his foe he came,
Resolv'd in minde all suddenly to win,
Or soone to lose, before he once would lin;° *surrender*
And strooke at her with more then manly force,
That from her body full of filthie sin
He raft° her hatefull head without remorse; *cut off*
A streame of cole black bloud forth gushed from her corse.

25

Her scattred brood, soone as their Parent deare
They saw so rudely° falling to the ground, *violently*

7. Error's vomit is a figurative depiction of the falsehoods that corrupt religion. The vehicles of such lies are both the spoken and written word; hence the material issuing from Error's mouth includes books as well as other poisonous things.

Groning full deadly, all with troublous feare,
Gathred themselves about her body round,
Weening their wonted entrance to have found
At her wide mouth: but being there withstood
They flocked all about her bleeding wound,
And sucked up their dying mothers blood,
Making her death their life, and eke her hurt their good.

26

That detestable sight him much amazde,
To see th'unkindly Impes° of heaven accurst, *unnatural offspring*
Devoure their dam; on whom while so he gazd,
Having all satisfide their bloudy thurst,
Their bellies swolne he saw with fulnesse burst,
And bowels gushing forth: well worthy end
Of such as drunke her life, the which them nurst;
Now needeth him no lenger labour spend,
His foes have slaine themselves, with whom he should contend.

27

His Ladie seeing all, that chaunst, from farre
Approcht in hast to greet his victorie,
And said, Faire knight, borne under happy starre,
Who see your vanquisht foes before you lye:
Well worthy be you of that Armorie,[8]
Wherein ye have great glory wonne this day,
And proov'd your strength on a strong enimie,
Your first adventure: many such I pray,
And henceforth ever wish, that like succeed it may.

28

Then mounted he upon his Steede againe,
And with the Lady backward sought to wend;
That path he kept, which beaten was most plaine,
Ne ever would to any by-way bend,
But still did follow one unto the end,
The which at last out of the wood them brought.
So forward on his way (with God to frend)
He passed forth, and new adventure sought;
Long way he travelled, before he heard of ought.

29

At length they chaunst to meet upon the way
An aged Sire, in long blacke weedes yclad,
His feete all bare, his beard all hoarie gray,
And by his belt his booke he hanging had;
Sober he seemde, and very sagely sad,
And to the ground his eyes were lowly bent,
Simple in shew, and voyde of malice bad,
And all the way he prayed, as he went,
And often knockt his brest, as one that did repent.

8. The Lady is proclaiming that by conquering Error, the Redcrosse Knight has become worthy to wear the armor of Christ; the episode foreshadows the knight's final triumph over the many-headed dragon that represents false faith.

30

He faire the knight saluted, louting° low, *bowing*
Who faire him quited,° as that courteous was: *answered*
And after asked him, if he did know
Of straunge adventures, which abroad did pas.
Ah my deare Sonne (quoth he) how should, alas,
Silly° old man, that lives in hidden cell, *simple*
Bidding° his beades all day for his trespas, *telling*
Tydings of warre and worldly trouble tell?
With holy father sits not with such things to mell.° *meddle*

31

But if of daunger which hereby doth dwell,
And homebred evill ye desire to heare,
Of a straunge man I can you tidings tell,
That wasteth° all this countrey farre and neare. *destroys*
Of such (said he)° I chiefly do inquere, *Redcrosse Knight*
And shall you well reward to shew the place,
In which that wicked wight his dayes doth weare°: *spend*
For to all knighthood it is foule disgrace,
That such a cursed creature lives so long a space.

32

Far hence (quoth he)° in wastfull wildernesse *the aged Sire*
His dwelling is, by which no living wight
May ever passe, but thorough° great distresse. *through*
Now (sayd the Lady) draweth toward night,
And well I wote,° that of your later fight *know*
Ye all forwearied° be: for what so strong, *exhausted*
But wanting rest will also want of might?
The Sunne that measures heaven all day long,
At night doth baite° his steedes the Ocean waves emong. *nourish*

33

Then with the Sunne take Sir, your timely rest,
And with new day new worke at once begin:
Untroubled night they say gives counsell best.
Right well Sir knight ye have advised bin,
(Quoth then that aged man;) the way to win
Is wisely to advise: now day is spent;
Therefore with me ye may take up your In
For this same night. The knight was well content:
So with that godly father to his home they went.

34

A little lowly Hermitage it was,[9]
Downe in a dale, hard by° a forests side, *next to*
Far from resort of people, that did pas
In travell to and froe: a little wyde
There was an holy Chappell edifyde,° *built*

9. This stanza illustrates the use of symbol in allegory; taken as a whole, its imagery suggests that the Redcrosse Knight has met the hermit because he suffers from a failing that the hermit will exploit. The hermitage is down in a dale, or valley, because the knight has begun to descend into a false faith; it is isolated because he is traveling in a strange and unusual direction; and it is by a fountain that appears to be sacred but that will be revealed as the antithesis of the Well of Life that will later restore him.

Wherein the Hermite dewly wont to say
His holy things each morne and eventyde:
Thereby a Christall streame did gently play,
Which from a sacred fountaine welled forth alway.

35

Arrived there, the little house they fill,
Ne looke for entertainement, where none was:
Rest is their feast, and all things at their will;
The noblest mind the best contentment has.
With faire discourse the evening so they pas:
For that old man of pleasing wordes had store,
And well could file his tongue as smooth as glas;
He told of Saintes and Popes, and evermore
He strowd° an Ave-Mary after and before.[1] *recited*

36

The drouping Night thus creepeth on them fast,
And the sad humour° loading their eye liddes, *moisture*
As messenger of Morpheus° on them cast *god of sleep*
Sweet slombring deaw, the which to sleepe them biddes.
Unto their lodgings then his guestes he° riddes: *the aged Sire*
Where when all drownd in deadly sleepe he findes,
He to his study goes, and there amiddes
His Magick bookes and artes of sundry kindes,
He seekes out mighty charmes, to trouble sleepy mindes.

37

Then choosing out few wordes most horrible,
(Let none them read) thereof did verses frame,° *compose*
With which and other spelles like terrible,
He bad awake blacke Plutoes griesly Dame,[2]
And cursed heaven, and spake reprochfull shame
Of highest God, the Lord of life and light;
A bold bad man, that dar'd to call by name
Great Gorgon,[3] Prince of darknesse and dead night,
At which Cocytus quakes, and Styx is put to flight.[4]

38

And forth he cald out of deepe darknesse dred
Legions of Sprights,° the which like little flyes *spirits*
Fluttring about his ever damned hed,
A-waite whereto their service he applyes,
To aide his friends, or fray° his enimies: *frighten*
Of those he chose out two, the falsest twoo,
And fittest for to forge true-seeming lyes;
The one of them he gave a message too,
The other by him selfe staide other worke to doo.

1. Despite his pious demeanor, the old man's discourse of saints and popes and his recital of Ave Marias indicate his affiliation with Catholicism; they are therefore intended to signal his corrupt and duplicitous character. The Redcrosse Knight is intended to represent English Protestantism and the true Church; by contrast, Spenser rejects Catholicism as a corruption of that Church.

2. Persephone, Pluto's wife and sometimes goddess of the underworld.

3. One of a family of monsters, daughters of the primitive gods of antiquity; Spenser, making her male, identifies the Gorgon with Pluto and also Satan.

4. The Cocytus and the Styx were rivers in the classical underworld.

39

He making speedy way through spersed° ayre, *empty*
And through the world of waters wide and deepe,
To Morpheus[5] house doth hastily repaire.
Amid the bowels of the earth full steepe,
And low, where dawning day doth never peepe,
His dwelling is; there Tethys his wet bed
Doth ever wash, and Cynthia still doth steepe
In silver deaw his ever-drouping hed,
Whiles sad Night over him her mantle black doth spred.

40

Whose double gates he findeth locked fast,
The one faire fram'd of burnisht Yvory,
The other all with silver overcast;
And wakefull dogges before them farre do lye,
Watching to banish Care their enimy,
Who oft is wont to trouble gentle Sleepe.
By them the Sprite doth passe in quietly,
And unto Morpheus comes, whom drowned deepe
In drowsie fit° he findes: of nothing he takes keepe.° *stupor/notice*

41

And more, to lulle him in his slumber soft,
A trickling streame from high rocke tumbling downe
And ever-drizling raine upon the loft,
Mixt with a murmuring winde, much like the sowne
Of swarming Bees, did cast him in a swowne°: *faint*
No other noyse, nor peoples troublous cryes,
As still are wont t'annoy the walled towne,
Might there be heard: but carelesse Quiet lyes,
Wrapt in eternall silence farre from enemyes.

42

The messenger approching to him spake,
But his wast wordes returnd to him in vaine:
So sound he° slept, that nought mought him awake. *Morpheus*
Then rudely he him thrust, and pusht with paine,
Whereat he gan to stretch: but he againe
Shooke him so hard, that forced him to speake.
As one then in a dreame, whose dryer braine
Is tost with troubled sights and fancies weake,
He mumbled soft, but would not all his silence breake.

43

The Sprite then gan more boldly him to wake,
And threatned unto him the dreaded name
Of Hecate:[6] whereat he gan to quake,
And lifting up his lumpish head, with blame
Halfe angry asked him, for what he came.

5. God of sleep, who lives in the depths of the dark earth: Tethus or the sea washes him; Cynthia or the moon bedews him, and Night covers him.

6. The dark aspect of Cynthia, the moon, and thus also of Diana; Hecate figures the underworld, death, and darkness.

Hither (quoth he) me Archimago[7] sent,
He that the stubborne Sprites can wisely tame,
He bids thee to him send for his intent
A fit false dreame, that can delude the sleepers sent.° *senses*

44

The God obayde, and calling forth straight way
A diverse dreame out of his prison darke,
Delivered it to him, and downe did lay
His heavie head, devoide of carefull carke,° *sorrowful anxiety*
Whose sences all were straight benumbd and starke.° *paralyzed*
He backe returning by the Yvorie dore,
Remounted up as light as chearefull Larke,
And on his litle winges the dreame he bore
In hast unto his Lord, where he him left afore.

45

Who all this while with charmes and hidden artes,
Had made a Lady of that other Spright,
And fram'd of liquid ayre her tender partes
So lively, and so like in all mens sight,
That weaker sence it° could have ravisht quight: *the spright*
The maker selfe for all his wondrous witt,
Was nigh beguiled with so goodly sight:
Her all in white he clad, and over it
Cast a blacke stole, most like to seeme for Una[8] fit.

46

Now when that ydle dreame was to him brought,
Unto that Elfin knight he° bad him° fly, *Archimago / the spright*
Where he slept soundly void of evill thought,
And with false shewes abuse his fantasy,
In sort as he him schooled privily:
And that new creature borne without her dew,° *unnaturally*
Full of the makers guile, with usage sly
He taught to imitate that Lady trew,
Whose semblance she did carrie under feigned hew.

47

Thus well instructed, to their worke they hast,
And comming where the knight in slomber lay,
The one upon his hardy head him plast,
And made him dreame of loves and lustfull play,
That nigh his manly hart did melt away,
Bathed in wanton blis and wicked joy:
Then seemed him his Lady by him lay,
And to him playnd, how that false winged boy° *Cupid*
Her chast hart had subdewd, to learne Dame pleasures toy.

7. The sage Sire is named Archimago, an "arch (or chief) magus (or magician)" and hence a forger or architect of images rather than real things. Because these images are clever and deceptive imitations of reality, Archimago is associated with hypocrisy and magic, an art that Christians were forbidden to practice.

8. Here the Lady is named Una; she is to symbolize the ideal unity of Truth and the Church whose faith the Redcrosse Knight defends. She is named only when her false double appears.

48

And she her selfe of beautie soveraigne Queene,
Faire Venus seemde unto his bed to bring
Her,[9] whom he waking evermore did weene
To be the chastest flowre, that ay did spring
On earthly braunch, the daughter of a king,
Now a loose Leman to vile service bound:
And eke the Graces seemed all to sing,
Hymen iõ Hymen,[1] dauncing all around,
Whilst freshest Flora her with Yvie girlond crownd.

49

In this great passion of unwonted lust,
Or wonted feare of doing ought amis,
He° started up, as seeming to mistrust *Redcrosse Knight*
Some secret ill, or hidden foe of his:
Lo there before his face his Lady is,
Under blake stole hyding her bayted hooke,
And as halfe blushing offred him to kis,
With gentle blandishment and lovely looke,
Most like that virgin true, which for her knight him took.

50

All cleane° dismayd to see so uncouth sight, *fully*
And halfe enraged at her shamelesse guise,
He thought have slaine her in his fierce despight:° *indignation*
But hasty heat tempring with sufferance° wise, *patience*
He stayde his hand, and gan himselfe advise
To prove his sense,° and tempt° her faigned truth.[2] *what he saw / test*
Wringing her hands in wemens pitteous wise,
Tho° can she weepe, to stirre up gentle ruth, *then*
Both for her noble bloud, and for her tender youth.

51

And said, Ah Sir, my liege Lord and my love,
Shall I accuse the hidden cruell fate,
And mightie causes wrought in heaven above,
Or the blind God, that doth me thus amate,° *dismay*
For hoped love to winne me certaine hate?
Yet thus perforce he bids me do, or die.
Die is my dew:° yet rew° my wretched state *due / pity*
You, whom my hard avenging destinie
Hath made judge of my life or death indifferently.

52

Your owne deare sake forst me at first to leave
My Fathers kingdome, There she stopt with teares;

9. I.e., she, impersonating Una, seemed also a Venus; this composite queen of beauty appears to the Redcrosse Knight to have come into his bed.

1. A Roman chant praising Hymen, the god of marriage, sung here by the Graces, handmaids of Venus, who personify the arts of courtesy and courtship. The union they celebrate in this case is not, however, a lawful Christian marriage but rather one provoked by lust and sexuality. In Roman mythology, Flora is the goddess of flowers, but early modern poets often gave her the role of a harlot. This entire scene uses the imagery of the Roman Bacchanalia (celebration of the god Bacchus) to suggest the mood of an orgy.

2. The Redcrosse Knight unwisely tests his senses rather than his faith. In doing so, he succumbs to the sensuality of the false Una and thus proves himself false to the true Una. The episode illustrates the danger inherent in powerful illusion; in such cases the false and the true may be indistinguishable.

Her swollen hart her speach seemd to bereave,
And then againe begun, My weaker yeares
Captiv'd to fortune and frayle worldly feares,
Fly to your faith for succour and sure ayde:
Let me not dye in languor and long teares.
Why Dame (quoth he) what hath ye thus dismayd?
What frayes° ye, that were wont to comfort me affrayd? *frightens*

53

Love of your selfe, she said, and deare° constraint° *dire / danger*
Lets me not sleepe, but wast the wearie night
In secret anguish and unpittied plaint,
Whiles you in carelesse sleepe are drowned quight.
Her doubtfull words made that redoubted knight
Suspect her truth: yet since no'untruth he knew,
Her fawning love with foule disdainefull spight
He would not shend,° but said, Deare dame I rew, *reproach*
That for my sake unknowne such griefe unto you grew.

54

Assure your selfe, it fell not all to ground;
For all so deare as life is to my hart,
I deeme your love, and hold me to you bound;
Ne let vaine feares procure your needlesse smart,° *pain*
Where cause is none, but to your rest depart.
Not all content, yet seemd she to appease
Her mournefull plaintes, beguiled of her art,
And fed with words, that could not chuse but please,
So slyding softly forth, she turnd as to her ease.

55

Long after lay he musing at her mood,
Much griev'd to thinke that gentle Dame so light,
For whose defence he was to shed his blood.
At last dull wearinesse of former fight
Having yrockt a sleepe his irkesome spright,
That troublous dreame gan freshly tosse his braine,
With bowres, and beds, and Ladies deare delight:
But when he saw his labour all was vaine,
With that misformed spright he backe returnd againe.

Canto 2

The guilefull great Enchaunter parts
The Redcrosse Knight from Truth:
Into whose stead faire falshood steps,
And workes him wofull ruth.

1

By this the Northerne wagoner had set
His sevenfold teme behind the stedfast starre,[1]

1. Spenser is referring to a constellation that includes Ursa Major, which contemporary English readers envisioned as a ploughman drawing a wagon. The "stedfast starre" is the Pole Star; it remains at the center of the stars in Ursa Major, which revolve around it and is "never wet" because it never sets into the ocean. The brightest star in this constellation is Arcturus, which the English associated with the mythical King Arthur.

That was in Ocean waves yet never wet,
But firme is fixt, and sendeth light from farre
To all, that in the wide deepe wandring arre:
And chearefull Chaunticlere° with his note shrill *a rooster*
Had warned once, that Phoebus fiery carre° *chariot*
In hast was climbing up the Easterne hill,
Full envious that night so long his roome° did fill. *the sky*

2

When those accursed messengers of hell,
That feigning dreame, and that faire-forged Spright
Came to their wicked maister, and gan° tell *did*
Their bootelesse paines,° and ill succeeding night: *fruitless efforts*
Who all in rage to see his skilfull might
Deluded so, gan threaten hellish paine
And sad Proserpines wrath, them to affright.
But when he saw his threatning was but vaine,
He cast about, and searcht his balefull° bookes againe. *evil*

3

Eftsoones° he tooke that miscreated faire, *soon after*
And that false other Spright, on whom he spred
A seeming body of the subtile aire,
Like a young Squire, in loves and lusty-hed° *lechery*
His wanton dayes that ever loosely led,
Without regard of armes and dreaded fight:
Those two he tooke, and in a secret bed,
Covered with darknesse and misdeeming° night, *deceiving*
Them both together laid, to joy in vaine delight.

4

Forthwith he runnes with feigned faithfull hast
Unto his guest, who after troublous sights
And dreames, gan° now to take more sound repast, *began*
Whom suddenly he wakes with fearefull frights,
As one aghast with feends or damned sprights,
And to him cals, Rise rise unhappy Swaine,° *youth*
That here wex old in sleepe, whiles wicked wights
Have knit themselves in Venus shamefull chaine;
Come see, where your false Lady doth her honour staine.

5

All in amaze he suddenly up start
With sword in hand, and with the old man went;
Who soone him brought into a secret part,
Where that false couple were full closely ment° *joined*
In wanton lust and lewd embracement:
Which when he saw, he burnt with gealous fire,
The eye of reason was with rage yblent,° *blinded*
And would have slaine them in his furious ire,
But hardly was restreined of that aged sire.

6

Returning to his bed in torment great,
And bitter anguish of his guiltie sight,

He could not rest, but did his stout heart eat,
And wast his inward gall° with deepe despight,° *irritation/malice*
Yrkesome° of life, and too long lingring night. *tired*
At last faire Hesperus[2] in highest skie
Had spent his lampe, and brought forth dawning light,
Then up he rose, and clad him hastily;
The Dwarfe him brought his steed: so both away do fly.

7

Now when the rosy-fingred Morning faire,
Weary of aged Tithones[3] saffron bed,
Had spred her purple robe through deawy aire,
And the high hils Titan[4] discovered,
The royall virgin shooke off drowsy-hed,
And rising forth out of her baser bowre,
Lookt for her knight, who far away was fled,
And for her Dwarfe, that wont to wait° each houre; *used to attend*
Then gan she waile and weepe, to see that woefull stowre.° *plight*

8

And after him she rode with so much speede
As her slow beast could make; but all in vaine:
For him so far had borne his light-foot steede,
Pricked with wrath and fiery fierce disdaine,
That him to follow was but fruitlesse paine;
Yet she her weary limbes would never rest,
But every hill and dale, each wood and plaine
Did search, sore grieved in her gentle brest,
He so ungently left her, whom she loved best.

9

But subtill Archimago, when his guests
He saw divided into double parts,
And Una wandring in woods and forrests,
Th'end of his drift,° he praisd his divelish arts, *intention*
That had such might over true meaning harts;
Yet rests not so, but other meanes doth make,
How he may worke unto her further smarts:
For her he hated as the hissing snake,
And in her many troubles did most pleasure take.

10

He then devisde himselfe how to disguise;
For by his mightie science he could take
As many formes and shapes in seeming wise,
As ever Proteus[5] to himselfe could make:
Sometime a fowle, sometime a fish in lake,
Now like a foxe, now like a dragon fell,° *deadly*
That of himselfe he oft for feare would quake,

2. The evening and morning star, the planet Venus.
3. Husband of the dawn.
4. The sun. I.e., when the sun revealed the high hills.
5. A sea-god, son of two other deities of the sea, Oceanus and Tethys; Proteus could change his shape at will.

And oft would flie away. O who can tell
The hidden power of herbes, and might of Magicke spell?

11

But now seemde best, the person to put on
Of that good knight, his late beguiled° guest: *deceived*
In mighty armes he was yclad anon,° *presently*
And silver shield: upon his coward brest
A bloudy crosse, and on his craven crest° *cowardly head*
A bounch of haires discolourd diversly:
Full jolly knight he seemde, and well addrest,
And when he sate upon his courser free,
Saint George himself ye would have deemed him to be.[6]

12

But he the knight, whose semblaunt° he did beare, *likeness*
The true Saint George was wandred far away,
Still flying from his thoughts and gealous feare;
Will was his guide, and griefe led him astray.
At last him chaunst to meete upon the way
A faithlesse Sarazin[7] all arm'd to point,
In whose great shield was writ with letters gay
Sans-Foy:° full large of limbe and every joint *faithless*
He was, and cared not for God or man a point.° *bit*

13

He had a faire companion of his way,
A goodly Lady[8] clad in scarlot° red, *a royal cloth*
Purfled with gold and pearle of rich assay,° *quality*
And like a Persian mitre° on her hed *papal hat*
She wore, with crownes and owches° garnished, *jewels*
The which her lavish lovers to her gave;
Her wanton palfrey all was overspred
With tinsell trappings, woven like a wave,
Whose bridle rung with golden bels and bosses brave.° *splendid ornaments*

14

With faire disport° and courting dalliaunce° *teasing/play*
She intertainde her lover all the way:
But when she saw the knight his speare advaunce,
She soone left off her mirth and wanton play,
And bad her knight addresse him to the fray:° *face the challenge*
His foe was nigh at hand. He prickt° with pride *spurred on*
And hope to winne his Ladies heart that day,
Forth spurred fast: adowne his coursers side
The red bloud trickling staind the way, as he did ride.

6. Here, Archimago assumes the appearance of the Redcrosse Knight; incidentally, he reveals that the true knight is actually Saint George.

7. A Saracen, or follower of Islam. Early modern Europeans commonly represented believers in a non-Christian faith as infidels or nonbelievers. Sans-Foy (as this knight is later named—literally, "without faith") is therefore not actually without a faith, but he is a Saracen and not a Christian.

8. The description of this Lady associates her with the Whore of Babylon (Revelation 17.4), who was identified by 16th-century Protestants with the Antichrist, i.e., the Pope and his retinue.

15

The knight of the Redcrosse when him he spide,
Spurring so hote with rage dispiteous,° *cruel*
Gan fairely couch his speare, and towards ride:
Soone meete they both, both fell and furious,
That daunted° with their forces hideous, *dazed*
Their steeds do stagger, and amazed stand,
And eke themselves too rudely rigorous,
Astonied° with the stroke of their owne hand, *stunned*
Do backe rebut,° and each to other yeeldeth land. *recoil*

16

As when two rams stird with ambitious pride,
Fight for the rule of the rich fleeced flocke,
Their horned fronts so fierce on either side
Do meete, that with the terrour of the shocke
Astonied both, stand sencelesse as a blocke,
Forgetfull of the hanging victory:
So stood these twaine, unmoved as a rocke,
Both staring fierce, and holding idely
The broken reliques of their former cruelty.

17

The Sarazin sore daunted with the buffe° *blow*
Snatcheth his sword, and fiercely to him flies;
Who well it wards, and quyteth° cuff° with cuff: *repays/blow*
Each others equall puissaunce° envies, *power*
And through their iron sides with cruell spies
Does seeke to perce: repining° courage yields *exhausted*
No foote to foe. The flashing fier flies
As from a forge out of their burning shields,
And streames of purple bloud new dies the verdant fields.

18

Curse on that Crosse (quoth then the Sarazin)
That keepes thy body from the bitter fit;° *pangs of death*
Dead long ygoe I wote thou haddest bin,
Had not that charme from thee forwarned° it: *prevented*
But yet I warne thee now assured sitt,
And hide thy head. Therewith upon his crest
With rigour so outrageous he smitt,° *struck*
That a large share it hewd out of the rest,
And glauncing downe his shield, from blame° him fairely blest.° *injury/protected*

19

Who thereat wondrous wroth,° the sleeping spark *angry*
Of native vertue gan eftsoones revive,
And at his haughtie helmet making mark,
So hugely stroke, that it the steele did rive,° *cut*
And cleft his head. He tumbling downe alive,
With bloudy mouth his mother earth did kis,
Greeting his grave: his grudging ghost did strive
With the fraile flesh; at last it flitted is,
Whither the soules do fly of men, that live amis.

20

The Lady when she saw her champion fall,
Like the old ruines of a broken towre,
Staid not to waile his woefull funerall,
But from him° fled away with all her powre; *Redcrosse Knight*
Who after her as hastily gan scowre,° *pursue*
Bidding the Dwarfe with him to bring away
The Sarazins shield, signe of the conqueroure.
Her soone he overtooke, and bad° to stay, *commanded*
For present cause was none of dread her to dismay.[9]

21

She turning backe with ruefull° countenaunce, *pitiful*
Cride, Mercy mercy Sir vouchsafe to show
On silly Dame, subject to hard mischaunce,
And to your mighty will. Her humblesse low
In so ritch weedes and seeming glorious show,
Did much emmove his stout heroïcke heart,
And said, Deare dame, your suddein overthrow
Much rueth me;° but now put feare apart, *I regret*
And tell, both who ye be, and who that tooke your part.

22

Melting in teares, then gan she thus lament;
The wretched woman, whom unhappy howre
Hath now made thrall to your commandement,
Before that angry heavens list to lowre,° *scowl*
And fortune false betraide me to your powre,
Was, (O what now availeth° that I was!) *does it help*
Borne the sole daughter of an Emperour,
He that the wide West under his rule has,[1]
And high hath set his throne, where Tiberis° doth pas. *Tiber River, in Rome*

23

He in the first flowre of my freshest age,
Betrothed me unto the onely haire
Of a most mighty king, most rich and sage;
Was never Prince so faithfull and so faire,
Was never Prince so meeke and debonaire;° *gentle*
But ere my hoped day of spousall° shone, *marriage*
My dearest Lord fell from high honours staire,
Into the hands of his accursed fone,° *foe*
And cruelly was slaine, that shall I ever mone.

24

His blessed body spoild of lively breath,
Was afterward, I know not how, convaid
And fro me hid: of whose most innocent death
When tidings came to me unhappy maid,

9. I.e., he did not mean to frighten her.

1. The Lady's story in this and the next two stanzas allegorically describes the corruption of the Holy Roman Empire and its separation from true Christianity. The Lady's father, an emperor, reigned in Rome, the seat of Catholicism (cf. Una's father, who is Adam), and the prince she was to marry was Christ. The Lady's quest to find his corpse suggests that she denies the doctrine of the resurrection of the body. In any case, Protestants in this period were critical of the Catholic emphasis on Christ's dead body in religious art and literature and contrasted it to the Protestant celebration of his resurrection.

O how great sorrow my sad soule assaid.° *afflicted*
Then forth I went his woefull corse to find,
And many yeares throughout the world I straid,
A virgin widow, whose deepe wounded mind
With love, long time did languish as the striken hind.° *doe*

25

At last it chaunced this proud Sarazin
To meete me wandring, who perforce° me led *forcibly*
With him away, but yet could never win
The Fort, that Ladies hold in soveraigne dread.
There lies he now with foule dishonour dead,
Who whiles he liv'de, was called proud Sans-Foy,
The eldest of three brethren, all three bred
Of one bad sire, whose youngest is Sans-Joy,
And twixt them both was borne the bloudy bold Sans-Loy.[2]

26

In this sad plight, friendlesse, unfortunate,
Now miserable I Fidessa[3] dwell,
Craving of you in pitty of my state,
To do none ill, if please ye not do well.
He in great passion all this while did dwell,
More busying his quicke eyes, her face to view,
Then his dull eares, to heare what she did tell;
And said, Faire Lady hart of flint would rew
The undeserved woes and sorrowes, which ye shew.

27

Henceforth in safe assuraunce may ye rest,
Having both found a new friend you to aid,
And lost an old foe, that did you molest:
Better new friend then an old foe is said.
With chaunge of cheare the seeming simple maid
Let fall her eyen,° as shamefast to the earth, *eyes*
And yeelding soft, in that she nought gain-said,° *denied*
So forth they rode, he feining seemely merth,
And she coy lookes: so dainty they say maketh derth.[4]

28

Long time they thus together traveiled,
Till weary of their way, they came at last,
Where grew two goodly trees, that faire did spred
Their armes abroad, with gray mosse overcast,
And their greene leaves trembling with every blast,
Made a calme shadow far in compasse round:
The fearefull Shepheard often there aghast° *frightened*
Under them never sat, ne wont there sound
His mery oaten pipe, but shund th'unlucky ground.

2. Sans-Loy ("without law") and Sans-Joy ("without joy") illustrate other aspects of the infidel attacking the spiritual well-being of the Redcrosse Knight. Spenser draws on Galatians 5.22–23: "But the fruit of the spirit is love, joy . . . faith . . . temperance; against such there is no Law."

3. The Lady in Persian dress calls herself Fidessa, a name that can mean "faithful" in a corrupted kind of Latin. From her association with Sans-Foy, however, the reader knows that she is not representative of the true faith and so only puts on the appearance of fidelity.

4. I.e., such daintiness is costly.

29

But this good knight soone as he them can spie,
For the coole shade him thither hastly got:
For golden Phoebus now ymounted hie,
From fiery wheeles of his faire chariot
Hurled his beame so scorching cruell hot,
That living creature mote° it not abide; *might*
And his new Lady it endured not.
There they alight, in hope themselves to hide
From the fierce heat, and rest their weary limbs a tide.° *while*

30

Faire seemely pleasaunce each to other makes,
With goodly purposes there as they sit:
And in his falsed fancy he her takes
To be the fairest wight,° that lived yit; *creature*
Which to expresse, he bends his gentle wit,
And thinking of those braunches greene to frame
A girlond for her dainty forehead fit,
He pluckt a bough; out of whose rift there came
Small drops of gory bloud, that trickled downe the same.[5]

31

Therewith a piteous yelling voyce was heard,
Crying, O spare with guilty hands to teare
My tender sides in this rough rynd embard,° *enclosed*
But fly, ah fly far hence away, for feare
Least to you hap, that happened to me heare,
And to this wretched Lady, my deare love,
O too deare love, love bought with death too deare.
Astond he stood, and up his haire did hove,
And with that suddein horror could no member move.

32

At last whenas the dreadfull passion
Was overpast, and manhood well awake,
Yet musing at the straunge occasion,
And doubting much his sence, he thus bespake;
What voyce of damned Ghost from Limbo lake,° *the pit of hell*
Or guilefull spright wandring in empty aire,
Both which fraile men do oftentimes mistake,
Sends to my doubtfull eares these speaches rare,
And ruefull plaints, me bidding guiltlesse bloud to spare?

33

Then groning deepe, Nor damned Ghost, (quoth he,)
Nor guilefull sprite to thee these wordes doth speake,
But once a man Fradubio,[6] now a tree,
Wretched man, wretched tree; whose nature weake,

5. Following Dante and Ariosto, Spenser imitates a well-known episode in Virgil's *Aeneid* in which the hero Aeneas, thinking he might have reached the country in which he was to found a new Troy, is warned by a bleeding bush that he must continue his quest. Spenser probably expected that his readers would take pleasure in his own inventive transformation of this powerful image.

6. Brother Doubt (Italian). Since loss of faith through doubt is dehumanizing, Fradubio is cast into the form of a plant. He is intended to convey to the Redcrosse Knight how dangerous a creature Fidessa is.

A cruell witch her cursed will to wreake,
Hath thus transformd, and plast in open plaines,
Where Boreas° doth blow full bitter bleake, *the north wind*
And scorching Sunne does dry my secret vaines:
For though a tree I seeme, yet cold and heat me paines.

34

Say on Fradubio then, or man, or tree,
Quoth then the knight, by whose mischievous arts
Art thou misshaped thus, as now I see?
He oft finds med'cine, who his griefe imparts;
But double griefs afflict concealing harts,
As raging flames who striveth to suppresse.
The author then (said he) of all my smarts,° *pains*
Is one Duessa[7] a false sorceresse,
That many errant knights hath brought to wretchednesse.

35

In prime of youthly yeares, when corage° hot *spirit*
The fire of love and joy of chevalree° *chivalry*
First kindled in my brest, it was my lot
To love this gentle Lady, whom ye see,
Now not a Lady, but a seeming tree;
With whom as once I rode accompanyde,
Me chaunced of a knight encountred bee,
That had a like faire Lady by his syde,
Like a faire Lady, but did fowle Duessa hyde.

36

Whose forged° beauty he did take in hand, *artificial*
All other Dames to have exceeded farre;
I in defence of mine did likewise stand,
Mine, that did then shine as the Morning starre:
So both to battell fierce arraunged° arre, *engaged*
In which his harder fortune was to fall
Under my speare: such is the dye° of warre: *hazard*
His Lady left as a prise martiall,
Did yield her comely person, to be at my call.

37

So doubly lov'd of Ladies unlike° faire, *differently*
Th'one seeming such, the other such indeede,
One day in doubt I cast° for to compare, *sought*
Whether in beauties glorie did exceede;
A Rosy girlond was the victors meede:
Both seemde to win, and both seemde won to bee,
So hard the discord was to be agreede.
Fraelissa[8] was as faire, as faire mote bee,
And ever false Duessa seemde as faire as shee.

7. Double-being (Italian), i.e., two-faced or duplicitous. The name contrasts with Una, or the undivided truth. Duessa wears a mask of beauty, although she is actually hideous and evil. Spenser places Duessa, who is not what she appears to be, in opposition to Una, whose beauty is hidden beneath a veil but who signifies wholeness or integrity.

8. Fradubio's lady is Fraelissa, "frail nature" (Italian); she, like Fradubio, is Duessa's victim.

38

The wicked witch now seeing all this while
  The doubtfull ballaunce equally to sway,
  What not by right, she cast to win by guile,
  And by her hellish science raisd streight way
  A foggy mist, that overcast the day,
  And a dull blast, that breathing on her face,
  Dimmed her° former beauties shining ray, *Fraelissa's*
  And with foule ugly forme did her disgrace:° *disfigure*
Then was she faire alone, when none was faire in place.

39

Then cride she out, Fye, fye, deformed wight,
  Whose borrowed beautie now appeareth plaine
  To have before bewitched all mens sight;
  O leave her soone, or let her soone be slaine.[9]
  Her loathly visage viewing with disdaine,
  Eftsoones I thought her such, as she me told,
  And would have kild her; but with faigned paine,
  The false witch did my wrathfull hand with-hold;
So left her, where she now is turnd to treen mould.° *a treelike shape*

40

Thens forth I tooke Duessa for my Dame,
  And in the witch unweeting° joyd long time, *without knowing*
  Ne ever wist, but that she was the same,
  Till on a day (that day is every Prime,° *first (of the month)*
  When Witches wont do penance for their crime)
  I chaunst to see her in her proper hew,
  Bathing her selfe in origane° and thyme: *oregano*
  A filthy foule old woman I did vew,
That ever to have toucht her, I did deadly rew.

41

Her neather° partes misshapen, monstruous, *lower*
  Were hidd in water, that I could not see,
  But they did seeme more foule and hideous,
  Then womans shape man would beleeve to bee.
  Thens forth from her most beastly companie
  I gan refraine, in minde to slip away,
  Soone as appeard safe opportunitie:
  For danger great, if not assur'd decay
I saw before mine eyes, if I were knowne to stray.

42

The divelish hag by chaunges of my cheare
  Perceiv'd my thought, and drownd in sleepie night,
  With wicked herbes and ointments did besmeare
  My bodie all, through charmes and magicke might,
  That all my senses were bereaved° quight: *departed*
  Then brought she me into this desert waste,
  And by my wretched lovers side me pight,° *planted*

9. Duessa ironically condemns Fraelissa as a witch and tells Fradubio to abandon her.

Where now enclosd in wooden wals full faste,
Banisht from living wights, our wearie dayes we waste.

43

But how long time, said then the Elfin knight,
Are you in this misformed house to dwell?
We may not chaunge (quoth he) this evil plight,
Till we be bathed in a living well;[1]
That is the terme prescribed by the spell.
O how, said he, mote I that well out find,
That may restore you to your wonted well?
Time and suffised fates to former kynd
Shall us restore, none else from hence may us unbynd.

44

The false Duessa, now Fidessa hight,° *called*
Heard how in vaine Fradubio did lament,
And knew well all was true. But the good knight
Full of sad feare and ghastly dreriment,° *terror*
When all this speech the living tree had spent,° *finished*
The bleeding bough did thrust into the ground,
That from the bloud he might be innocent,
And with fresh clay did close the wooden wound:
Then turning to his Lady, dead with feare her found.

45

Her seeming dead he found with feigned feare,
As all unweeting of that well she knew,
And paynd himselfe with busie care to reare
Her out of carelesse° swowne. Her eylids blew *unconscious*
And dimmed sight with pale and deadly hew° *color*
At last she up gan lift: with trembling cheare
Her up he tooke, too simple and too trew,[2]
And oft her kist. At length all passed feare,
He set her on her steede, and forward forth did beare.

Canto 3

Forsaken Truth long seekes her love,
And makes the Lyon mylde,
Marres blind Devotions mart, and fals
In hand of leachour vylde.

1

Nought is there under heav'ns wide hollownesse,
That moves more deare compassion of mind,
Then beautie brought t'unworthy wretchednesse
Through envies snares or fortunes freakes unkind:
I, whether lately through her brightnesse blind,

1. The Well of Life: a spring of constantly flowing water, figured in the water of baptism that promises eternal life to the faithful (John 4.14).

2. The Redcrosse Knight fails to connect Fradubio's story to his own; he does not follow the model presented by Virgil's Aeneas, and therefore he remains deceived and on the wrong course.

Or through alleageance and fast fealtie,° *loyalty*
Which I do owe unto all woman kind,
Feele my heart perst° with so great agonie, *pierced*
When such I see, that all for pittie I could die.

2

And now it is empassioned° so deepe, *moved*
For fairest Unaes sake, of whom I sing,
That my fraile eyes these lines with teares do steepe,° *soak*
To thinke how she through guilefull handeling,
Though true as touch, though daughter of a king,
Though faire as ever living wight was faire,
Though nor in word nor deede ill meriting,
Is from her knight divorced° in despaire *separated*
And her due loves° deriv'd to that vile witches share. *the love due her*

3

Yet she most faithfull Ladie all this while
Forsaken, wofull, solitarie mayd
Farre from all peoples prease,° as in exile, *crowds*
In wildernesse and wastfull deserts strayd,
To seeke her knight; who subtilly betrayd
Through that late vision, which th'Enchaunter wrought,
Had her abandond. She of nought affrayd,
Through woods and wastnesse wide him daily sought;
Yet wished tydings none of him unto her brought.

4

One day nigh wearie of the yrkesome way,
From her unhastie beast she did alight,
And on the grasse her daintie limbes did lay
In secret shadow, farre from all mens sight:
From her faire head her fillet she undight,
And laid her stole aside. Her angels face
As the great eye of heaven shyned bright,
And made a sunshine in the shadie place;
Did never mortall eye behold such heavenly grace.

5

It fortuned out of the thickest wood
A ramping Lyon[1] rushed suddainly,
Hunting full greedie after salvage° blood; *savage*
Soone as the royall virgin he did spy,
With gaping mouth at her ran greedily,
To have attonce devour'd her tender corse:
But to the pray when as he drew more ny,
His bloudie rage aswaged with remorse,
And with the sight amazd, forgat his furious forse.

6

In stead thereof he kist her wearie feet,
And lickt her lilly hands with fawning tong,
As° he her wronged innocence did weet. *as if*

1. This is the typical heraldic posture of the lion: standing on its hind legs with its paws in the air. A symbol of royal power, the lion was believed to protect virgins and weary pilgrims.

O how can beautie maister the most strong,
And simple truth subdue avenging wrong?
Whose yeelded pride and proud submission,
Still dreading death, when she had marked long,
Her hart gan melt in great compassion,
And drizling teares did shed for pure affection.

7

The Lyon Lord of everie beast in field,
Quoth she, his princely puissance° doth abate, *strength*
And mightie proud to humble weake does yield,
Forgetfull of the hungry rage, which late
Him prickt, in pittie of my sad estate:
But he° my Lyon, and my noble Lord, *Redcrosse Knight*
How does he find in cruell hart to hate
Her that him lov'd, and ever most adord,
As the God of my life? why hath he me abhord?

8

Redounding teares did choke th'end of her plaint,
Which softly ecchoed from the neighbour wood;
And sad to see her sorrowfull constraint
The kingly beast upon her gazing stood;
With pittie calmd, downe fell his angry mood.
At last in close hart shutting up her paine,
Arose the virgin borne of heavenly brood,
And to her snowy Palfrey got againe,
To seeke her strayed Champion, if she might attaine.° *overtake him*

9

The Lyon would not leave her desolate,
But with her went along, as a strong gard
Of her chast person, and a faithfull mate
Of her sad troubles and misfortunes hard:
Still when she slept, he kept both watch and ward,
And when she wakt, he waited diligent,
With humble service to her will prepard:
From her faire eyes he tooke commaundement,
And ever by her lookes conceived° her intent. *understood*

10

Long she thus traveiled through deserts wyde,
By which she thought her wandring knight shold pas,
Yet never shew of living wight espyde;
Till that at length she found the troden gras,
In which the tract° of peoples footing was, *trace*
Under the steepe foot of a mountaine hore;° *barren*
The same she followes, till at last she has
A damzell spyde slow footing her before,
That on her shoulders sad a pot of water bore.

11

To whom approching she to her gan call,
To weet, if dwelling place were nigh at hand;
But the rude wench her answer'd nought at all,
She could not heare, nor speake, nor understand;

Till seeing by her side the Lyon stand,
With suddaine feare her pitcher downe she threw,
And fled away: for never in that land
Face of faire Ladie she before did vew,
And that dread Lyons looke her cast in deadly hew.

12

Full fast she fled, ne° ever lookt behynd, *nor*
As if her life upon the wager lay,
And home she came, whereas her mother blynd
Sate in eternall night: nought could she say,
But suddaine catching hold, did her dismay
With quaking hands, and other signes of feare:
Who full of ghastly fright and cold affray,° *terror*
Gan shut the dore. By this arrived there
Dame Una, wearie Dame, and entrance did requere.° *request*

13

Which when none yeelded, her unruly Page
With his rude clawes the wicket° open rent, *small gate*
And let her in; where of his cruell rage
Nigh dead with feare, and faint astonishment,
She found them both in darkesome corner pent;
Where that old woman day and night did pray
Upon her beades devoutly penitent;
Nine hundred *Pater nosters* every day,
And thrise nine hundred *Aves* she was wont to say.[2]

14

And to augment her painefull pennance more,
Thrise every weeke in ashes she did sit,
And next her wrinkled skin rough sackcloth wore,
And thrise three times did fast from any bit:° *bit of food*
But now for feare her beads she did forget.
Whose needlesse dread for to remove away,
Faire Una framed words and count'nance fit:
Which hardly doen,° at length she gan them pray, *done*
That in their cotage small, that night she rest her may.

15

The day is spent, and commeth drowsie night,
When every creature shrowded is in sleepe;
Sad Una downe her laies in wearie plight,
And at her feet the Lyon watch doth keepe:
In stead of rest, she does lament, and weepe
For the late losse of her deare loved knight,
And sighes, and grones, and evermore does steepe
Her tender brest in bitter teares all night,
All night she thinks too long, and often lookes for light.

16

Now when Aldeboran was mounted hie
Above the shynie Cassiopeias chaire,[3]

2. Spenser's readers would have identified Pater Nosters and Ave Marias as Catholic prayers.

3. Aldeboran and Cassiopeia are stars that appear at midnight during the winter solstice; the references to winter and midnight reflect Una's distress.

And all in deadly sleepe did drowned lie,
One knocked at the dore, and in would fare;
He knocked fast, and often curst, and sware,
That readie entrance was not at his call:
For on his backe a heavy load he bare
Of nightly stelths° and pillage severall, *thefts*
Which he had got abroad by purchase criminall.

17

He was to weete° a stout and sturdie thiefe,[4] *wit*
Wont to robbe Churches of their ornaments,
And poore mens boxes of their due reliefe,
Which given was to them for good intents;
The holy Saints of their rich vestiments
He did disrobe, when all men carelesse slept,
And spoild the Priests of their habiliments,° *holy things*
Whiles none the holy things in safety kept;
Then he by cunning sleights° in at the window crept. *tricks*

18

And all that he by right or wrong could find,
Unto this house he brought, and did bestow
Upon the daughter of this woman blind,
Abessa daughter of Corceca slow,[5]
With whom he whoredome usd, that few did know,
And fed her fat with feast of offerings,
And plentie, which in all the land did grow;
Ne spared he to give her gold and rings:
And now he to her brought part of his stolen things.

19

Thus long the dore with rage and threats he bet,
Yet of those fearefull women none durst rize,
The Lyon frayed° them, him in to let: *frightened*
He would no longer stay him to advize,° *consider*
But open breakes the dore in furious wize,
And entring is; when that disdainfull° beast *indignant*
Encountring fierce, him suddaine doth surprize,
And seizing cruell clawes on trembling brest,
Under his Lordly foot him proudly hath supprest.

20

Him booteth not° resist, nor succour call, *it did no good to*
His bleeding hart is in the vengers hand,
Who streight him rent° in thousand peeces small, *tore*
And quite dismembred hath: the thirstie land
Drunke up his life; his corse left on the strand.[6]
His fearefull friends weare out the wofull night,
Ne dare to weepe, nor seeme to understand

4. This thief is later named Kirkrapine, literally "church robber" (see stanza 22). Spenser's Protestant contemporaries complained that the Roman Catholic Church had used English abbeys and monasteries as a means of amassing wealth at the expense of the spiritual well-being of the people that they were supposed to serve.

5. Corceca means "blind of heart"; her daughter, Abessa, who is both deaf and mute, is the offspring of ignorant superstition. Through her name, Spenser associates Abessa with Catholic abbeys and monasteries, which he criticizes in this and the previous two stanzas.

6. Kirkrapine's death signifies a step toward the purification of the Church and thereby an approach to the true Church, which Una represents.

The heavie hap,° which on them is alight, *event*
Affraid, least to themselves the like mishappen might.

21

Now when broad day the world discovered has,
Up Una rose, up rose the Lyon eke,
And on their former journey forward pas,
In wayes unknowne, her wandring knight to seeke,
With paines farre passing that long wandring Greeke,[7]
That for his love refused deitie;
Such were the labours of this Lady meeke,
Still seeking him, that from her still did flie,
Then furthest from her hope, when most she weened nie.

22

Soone as she parted thence, the fearefull twaine,
That blind old woman and her daughter deare
Came forth, and finding Kirkrapine° there slaine, *church-robber*
For anguish great they gan to rend their heare,
And beat their brests, and naked flesh to teare.
And when they both had wept and wayld their fill,
Then forth they ranne like two amazed deare,
Halfe mad through malice, and revenging will,° *desire to revenge*
To follow her, that was the causer of their ill.

23

Whom overtaking, they gan loudly bray,
With hollow howling, and lamenting cry,
Shamefully at her rayling° all the way, *accusing*
And her accusing of dishonesty,
That was the flowre of faith and chastity;
And still amidst her rayling, she did pray,
That plagues, and mischiefs, and long misery
Might fall on her, and follow all the way,
And that in endlesse error she might ever stray.

24

But when she saw her prayers nought prevaile,
She backe returned with some labour lost;
And in° the way as she did weepe and waile, *along*
A knight her met in mighty armes embost,
Yet knight was not for all his bragging bost,° *display*
But subtill Archimag, that Una sought
By traynes° into new troubles to have tost: *tricks*
Of that old woman tydings he besought,
If that of such a Ladie she could tellen ought.

25

Therewith she gan her passion to renew,
And cry, and curse, and raile,° and rend her heare, *accuse*
Saying, that harlot she too lately knew,
That causd her shed so many a bitter teare,
And so forth told the story of her feare:
Much seemed he to mone her haplesse chaunce,

7. Una is compared to Ulysses, whose love for his wife Penelope caused him to reject the goddess Calypso and the promise of immortality she offered him.

And after for that Ladie did inquere;° *inquire*
Which being taught, he forward gan advaunce
His fair enchaunted steed, and eke his charmed launce.

26

Ere long he came, where Una traveild slow,
And that wilde Champion wayting her besyde:
Whom seeing such, for dread he° durst not show *Archimago*
Himselfe too nigh at hand, but turned wyde
Unto an hill; from whence when she him spyde,
By his like seeming shield, her knight by name
She weend it was, and towards him gan ryde:[8]
Approching nigh, she wist it was the same,
And with faire fearefull humblesse towards him shee came.

27

And weeping said, Ah my long lacked° Lord, *lost*
Where have ye bene thus long out of my sight?
Much feared I to have bene quite abhord,
Or ought have done, that ye displeasen might,
That should as death unto my deare hart light:° *come*
For since mine eye your joyous sight did mis,
My chearefull day is turnd to chearelesse night,
And eke my night of death the shadow is;
But welcome now my light, and shining lampe of blis.

28

He thereto meeting said, My dearest Dame,
Farre be it from your thought, and fro° my will, *from*
To thinke that knighthood I so much should shame,
As you to leave,° that have me loved still, *lose*
And chose in Faery court of meere goodwill,
Where noblest knights were to be found on earth:
The earth shall sooner leave her kindly skill° *natural art*
To bring forth fruit, and make eternall derth,° *famine*
Then I leave you, my liefe, yborne of heavenly berth.

29

And sooth° to say, why I left you so long, *truly*
Was for to seeke adventure in strange place,
Where Archimago said a felon strong
To many knights did daily worke disgrace;
But knight he now shall never more deface:
Good cause of mine excuse; that mote° ye please *might*
Well to accept, and evermore embrace
My faithfull service, that by land and seas
Have vowd you to defend, now then your plaint appease.

30

His lovely words her seemd due recompence
Of all her passed paines: one loving howre
For many yeares of sorrow can dispence:° *compensate*
A dram of sweet is worth a pound of sowre:
She has forgot, how many a wofull stowre° *hardship*

8. Una recognizes the arms of the Redcrosse Knight but is deceived by appearances; she is actually greeting Archimago.

For him she late endur'd; she speakes no more
Of past: true is, that true love hath no powre
To looken backe; his eyes be fixt before.
Before her stands her knight, for whom she toyld so sore.

31

Much like, as when the beaten marinere,
That long hath wandred in the Ocean wide,
Oft soust° in swelling Tethys° saltish teare, *drenched / a sea-goddess*
And long time having tand his tawney hide
With blustring breath of heaven, that none can bide,
And scorching flames of fierce Orions hound,[9]
Soone as the port from farre he has espide,
His chearefull whistle merrily doth sound,
And Nereus° crownes with cups;° his mates him pledg around. *a sea-god / of wine*

32

Such joy made Una, when her knight she found;
And eke th'enchaunter joyous seemd no lesse,
Then° the glad marchant, that does vew from ground *than*
His ship farre come from watrie wildernesse,
He hurles out vowes,° and Neptune oft doth blesse: *makes promises*
So forth they past, and all the way they spent
Discoursing of her dreadfull late distresse,
In which he askt her, what the Lyon ment:
Who° told her all that fell° in journey as she went. *Una / had happened*

33

They had not ridden farre, when they might see
One pricking towards them with hastie heat,
Full strongly armd, and on a courser free,
That through his fiercenesse fomed all with sweat,
And the sharpe yron° did for anger eat, *iron bit*
When his hot ryder spurd his chauffed side;
His looke was sterne, and seemed still to threat
Cruell revenge, which he in hart did hyde,
And on his shield Sans-Loy in bloudie lines was dyde.

34

When nigh he drew unto this gentle payre
And saw the Red-crosse, which the knight did beare,
He burnt in fire, and gan eftsoones prepare
Himselfe to battell with his couched° speare. *lowered*
Loth was that other,° and did faint through feare, *Archimago*
To taste th'vntryed dint of deadly steele;
But yet his Lady did so well him cheare,
That hope of new good hap he gan to feele;
So bent his speare, and spurnd° his horse with yron heele. *spurred*

35

But that proud Paynim° forward came so fierce,[1] *pagan*
And full of wrath, that with his sharp-head speare

9. Sirius, the Dog Star, which marks the hottest days of the year. Nereus is the eldest child of Tethys, a sea-goddess.

1. The double deception registered in this episode is characteristic of Spenser's complex allegories: mistaken in his sense of identity, Sans-Loy attacks the very person who is best able to protect him. Archimago, having assumed the guise of the Redcrosse Knight, finds that the cross that should protect him from harm does not in fact do so. In this instance his shield is "vainely crossed."

Through vainely crossed shield he quite did pierce,
And had his staggering steede not shrunke for feare,
Through shield and bodie eke he should him beare:
Yet so great was the puissance of his push,
That from his saddle quite he did him beare:
He tombling rudely downe to ground did rush,
And from his gored wound a well of bloud did gush.

36

Dismounting lightly from his loftie steed,
He to him lept, in mind to reave° his life, *take*
And proudly said, Lo there the worthie meed
Of him, that slew Sans-Foy with bloudie knife;
Henceforth his ghost freed from repining° strife, *fretting*
In peace may passen° over Lethe lake,[2] *pass*
When morning altars° purgd with enemies life, *altars of mourning*
The blacke infernall Furies doen aslake:° *satisfy*
Life from Sans-Foy thou tookst, Sans-Loy shall from thee take.

37

Therewith in haste his helmet gan unlace,
Till Una cride, O hold that heavie hand,
Deare Sir, what ever that thou be in place:
Enough is, that thy foe doth vanquisht stand
Now at thy mercy: Mercie not withstand:° *oppose*
For he is one the truest° knight alive, *the one truest*
Though conquered now he lie on lowly land,
And whilest him fortune favourd, faire did thrive
In bloudie field: therefore of life him not deprive.

38

Her piteous words might not abate his rage,
But rudely° rending up his helmet, would *violently*
Have slaine him straight: but when he sees his age,
And hoarie head of Archimago old,
His hastie hand he doth amazed hold,
And halfe ashamed, wondred at the sight:
For the old man well knew he, though untold,° *i.e., by sight*
In charmes and magicke to have wondrous might,
Ne ever wont in field, ne in round lists° to fight. *tournament arenas*

39

And said, Why Archimago, lucklesse syre,
What doe I see? what hard mishap is this,
That hath thee hither brought to taste mine yre?
Or thine the fault, or mine the error is,
In stead of foe to wound my friend amis?
He answered nought, but in a traunce still lay,
And on those guilefull dazed eyes of his
The cloud of death did sit. Which doen away,° *having passed*
He left him lying so, ne would no lenger stay.

40

But to the virgin comes, who all this while
Amased stands, her selfe so mockt to see

2. The lake of forgetfulness in the underworld.

By him, who has the guerdon° of his guile, *reward*
For so misfeigning her true knight to bee:
Yet is she now in more perplexitie,° *distress*
Left in the hand of that same Paynim bold,
From whom her booteth° not at all to flie; *it helped her*
Who by her cleanly° garment catching hold, *pure*
Her from her Palfrey pluckt, her visage to behold.

41

But her fierce servant full of kingly awe
And high disdaine, whenas his soveraine Dame
So rudely handled by her foe he sawe,
With gaping jawes full greedy at him came,
And ramping on° his shield, did weene the same *charging at*
Have reft away with his sharpe rending clawes:
But he was stout, and lust did now inflame
His corage more, that from his griping pawes
He hath his shield redeem'd,° and foorth his swerd he drawes. *retained*

42

O then too weake and feeble was the forse
Of salvage beast, his puissance to withstand:
For he was strong, and of so mightie corse,
As ever wielded speare in warlike hand,
And feates of armes did wisely understand.
Eftsoones he perced through his chaufed° chest *angered*
With thrilling° point of deadly yron brand, *piercing*
And launcht° his Lordly hart: with death opprest *pierced*
He roar'd aloud, whiles life forsooke his stubborne brest.

43

Who now is left to keepe the forlorne maid
From raging spoile of lawlesse victors will?[3]
Her faithful gard remov'd, her hope dismaid,° *thwarted*
Her selfe a yeelded pray to save or spill.° *destroy*
He now Lord of the field, his pride to fill,
With foule reproches, and disdainfull spight
Her vildly entertaines,° and will or nill, *treats*
Beares her away upon his courser light:
Her prayers nought prevaile, his rage is more of might.

44

And all the way, with great lamenting paine,
And piteous plaints she filleth his dull eares,
That stony hart could riven have in twaine,
And all the way she wets with flowing teares:
But he enrag'd with rancor, nothing heares.
Her servile beast yet would not leave her so,
But followes her farre off, ne ought he feares,
To be partaker of her wandring woe,
More mild in beastly kind,° then that her beastly foe. *animal nature*

3. I.e., who will now protect Una from becoming the spoil or booty of the lawless victor's raging will?

Canto 4

To sinfull house of Pride,[1] Duessa
guides the faithfull knight,
Where brothers death to wreak° Sans-Joy — *avenge*
doth chalenge him to fight.

1

Young knight, what ever° that dost armes professe, — *whoever*
And through long labours huntest after fame,
Beware of fraud, beware of ficklenesse,
In choice, and change of thy deare loved Dame,
Least° thou of her beleeve° too lightly blame, — *lest/faith*
And rash misweening° doe thy hart remove: — *rashly mistrusting*
For unto knight there is no greater shame,
Then lightnesse and inconstancie in love;
That doth this Redcrosse knights ensample° plainly prove. — *example*

2

Who after that he had faire Una lorne,° — *lost*
Through light misdeeming of her loialtie,
And false Duessa in her sted had borne,
Called Fidess', and so supposd to bee;
Long with her traveild, till at last they see
A goodly building, bravely garnished,
The house of mightie Prince it seemd to bee:
And towards it a broad high way that led,
All bare° through peoples feet, which thither traveiled. — *worn bare*

3

Great troupes of people traveild thitherward
Both day and night, of each degree and place,
But few returned, having scaped hard,
With balefull° beggerie, or foule disgrace, — *wretched*
Which ever after in most wretched case,
Like loathsome lazars,° by the hedges lay. — *lepers*
Thither Duessa bad him bend° his pace: — *direct*
For she is wearie of the toilesome way,
And also nigh consumed is the lingring day.

4

A stately Pallace built of squared bricke,[2]
Which cunningly was without morter laid,
Whose wals were high, but nothing strong, nor thick,
And golden foile all over them displaid,
That purest skye with brightnesse they dismaid:° — *shamed*
High lifted up were many loftie towres,
And goodly galleries farre over laid,° — *built high above*
Full of faire windowes, and delightfull bowres;° — *chambers*
And on the top a Diall° told the timely howres. — *sundial*

1. An extended metaphor for the consequences of the sin of Pride. Like the Tower of Babel, which Spenser invokes in this passage, the house of Pride is the product of humanity's art, ambition, and vanity but is devoid of Christian values.

2. The house of Pride offers a dazzling facade, but its construction is weak, much like the sin of Pride itself, which places outward appearances over inner substance. It is surmounted by a sundial to tell the hours, a sign that Pride has no sense of eternity but lives only for the moment.

5

It was a goodly heape° for to behould, *structure*
And spake the praises of the workmans wit;
But full great pittie, that so faire a mould
Did on so weake foundation ever sit:
For on a sandie hill, that still did flit,° *shift*
And fall away, it mounted was full hie,
That every breath of heaven shaked it:
And all the hinder° parts, that few could spie, *rear*
Were ruinous and old, but painted cunningly.

6

Arrived there they passed in forth right;
For still° to all the gates stood open wide, *always*
Yet charge of them was to a Porter hight° *called*
Cald Malvenù,° who entrance none denide: *welcome to evil*
Thence to the hall, which was on every side
With rich array and costly arras dight:° *furnished*
Infinite sorts of people did abide
There waiting long, to win the wished sight
Of her, that was the Lady of that Pallace bright.

7

By them they passe, all gazing on them round,
And to the Presence mount; whose glorious vew
Their frayle amazed senses did confound:° *confuse*
In living Princes court none ever knew
Such endlesse richesse, and so sumptuous shew;
Ne° Persia selfe, the nourse° of pompous pride *not even / nurse*
Like ever saw. And there a noble crew
Of Lordes and Ladies stood on every side,
Which with their presence faire, the place much beautifide.

8

High above all a cloth of State was spred,
And a rich throne, as bright as sunny day,
On which there sate most brave embellished
With royall robes and gorgeous array,
A mayden Queene,[3] that shone as Titans ray,
In glistring gold, and peerelesse pretious stone:
Yet her bright blazing beautie did assay° *strive*
To dim the brightnesse of her glorious throne,
As envying her selfe, that too exceeding shone.

9

Exceeding shone, like Phoebus fairest childe,[4]
That did presume his fathers firie wayne,
And flaming mouthes of steedes unwonted° wilde *unaccustomed*
Through highest heaven with weaker hand to rayne;° *guide*
Proud of such glory and advancement vaine,
While flashing beames do daze his feeble eyen,
He leaves the welkin° way most beaten plaine, *well-known*

3. "The maiden queen": a reference to the "virgin daughter of Babylon" (Isaiah 47.1). She is later identified as Lucifera, a feminine form of Lucifer, literally "light bringer," but also Satan's name when he was still an angel. Hence the queen shines as brightly as the sun (Titan).

4. Phaeton (son of the sun god Apollo), who stole his father's chariot and perished because he could not manage the horses. He is a figure for the sin of Pride.

And rapt with whirling wheeles, inflames the skyen,
With fire not made to burne, but fairely for to shyne.

10

So proud she shyned in her Princely state,
Looking to heaven; for earth she did disdayne,
And sitting high; for lowly she did hate:
Lo underneath her scornefull feete, was layne
A dreadfull Dragon with an hideous trayne,
And in her hand she held a mirrhour bright,
Wherein her face she often vewed fayne,
And in her selfe-lov'd semblance° tooke delight; *image*
For she was wondrous faire, as any living wight.

11

Of griesly Pluto she the daughter was,[5]
And sad Proserpina the Queene of hell;
Yet did she thinke her pearelesse° worth to pas *unequaled*
That parentage, with pride so did she swell,
And thundring Jove, that high in heaven doth dwell,
And wield the world, she claymed for her syre,
Or if that any else did Jove excell:
For to the highest she did still aspyre,
Or if ought higher were then° that, did it desyre. *than*

12

And proud Lucifera men did her call,
That made her selfe a Queene, and crownd to be,
Yet rightfull kingdome she had none at all,
Ne heritage° of native° soveraintie, *inheritance / rightful*
But did ysurpe° with wrong and tyrannie *usurp*
Upon the scepter, which she now did hold:
Ne ruld her Realmes with lawes, but pollicie,° *political cunning*
And strong advizement of six wisards old,
That with their counsels bad her kingdome did uphold.

13

Soone as the Elfin knight in presence came,
And false Duessa seeming Lady faire,
A gentle Husher,° Vanitie by name *usher*
Made rowme, and passage for them did prepaire:
So goodly brought them to the lowest staire
Of her high throne, where they on humble knee
Making obeyssance,° did the cause declare, *submissive bows*
Why they were come, her royall state to see,
To prove° the wide report of her great Majestee. *confirm*

14

With loftie eyes, halfe loth° to looke so low, *disdaining*
She thanked them in her disdainefull wise,
Ne other grace vouchsafed° them to show *condescended*
Of Princesse worthy, scarse them bad arise.
Her Lordes and Ladies all this while devise

5. Lucifera is identified as the daughter of Pluto, king of the underworld, and Proserpina, goddess of the seasons, who is obliged to spend half the year underground with her husband Pluto. The conflation of mythologies represented in this description of Lucifera is characteristic of Spenser's allegory; here he associates the biblical figure of the daughter of Babylon with the pagan figures of Pluto and Proserpina. Their "daughter" Lucifera is his own invention.

Themselves to setten forth to straungers sight:
Some frounce° their curled haire in courtly guise, *arrange*
Some prancke° their ruffes, and others trimly dight *adjust*
Their gay attire: each others greater pride does spight.

15

Goodly they all that knight do entertaine,
Right glad with him to have increast their crew:
But to Duess' each one himselfe did paine
All kindnesse and faire courtesie to shew;
For in that court whylome° her well they knew: *previously*
Yet the stout Faerie[6] mongst the middest crowd
Thought all their glorie vaine in knightly vew,
And that great Princesse too exceeding prowd,
That to strange knight no better countenance° allowd. *reception*

16

Suddein upriseth from her stately place
The royall Dame, and for her coche doth call:
All hurtlen° forth, and she with Princely pace, *rush*
As faire Aurora° in her purple pall, *goddess of the dawn*
Out of the East the dawning day doth call:
So forth she comes: her brightnesse brode° doth blaze; *abroad*
The heapes of people thronging in the hall,
Do ride each other, upon her to gaze:
Her glorious glitterand° light doth all mens eyes amaze. *glittering*

17

So forth she comes, and to her coche does clyme,
Adorned all with gold, and girlonds gay,
That seemd as fresh as Flora° in her prime, *goddess of spring*
And strove to match, in royall rich array,
Great Junoes golden chaire, the which they say
The Gods stand gazing on, when she does ride
To Joves high house through heavens bras-paved way
Drawne of faire Pecocks, that excell in pride,
And full of Argus[7] eyes their tailes dispredden° wide. *spread out*

18

But this was drawne of six unequall beasts,
On which her six sage Counsellours[8] did ryde,
Taught to obay their bestiall beheasts,° *urges*
With like conditions to their kinds° applyde: *natures*
Of which the first, that all the rest did guyde,
Was sluggish Idlenesse the nourse of sin;
Upon a slouthfull Asse he chose to ryde,
Arayd in habit blacke, and amis° thin, *monk's hood*
Like to an holy Monck, the service to begin.

19

And in his hand his Portesse° still he bare, *prayer book*
That much was worne, but therein little red,

6. The Redcrosse Knight. He is designated as a faerie because he is an inhabitant of Faerie Land but also to distinguish him from the inhabitants of the house of Pride.

7. A mythical herdsman with 100 eyes. When Argus died, Juno—goddess of marriage and wife to Jupiter or Jove, king of the gods—set his eyes in the tail of a peacock.

8. The following stanzas describe the procession of Lucifer's wise counsellors, actually the Seven Deadly Sins: Pride (in the person of Lucifera), Idleness, Gluttony, Lechery, Avarice (greed), Envy, and Wrath.

For of devotion he had little care,
Still drownd in sleepe, and most of his dayes ded;
Scarse could he once uphold his heavie hed,
To looken, whether it were night or day:
May seeme° the wayne was very evill led, *it may seem that*
When such an one had guiding of the way,
That knew not, whether right he went, or else astray.

20

From worldly cares himselfe he did esloyne,° *withdraw*
And greatly shunned manly exercise,
From every worke he chalenged essoyne,° *claimed exception*
For contemplation sake: yet otherwise,
His life he led in lawlesse riotise;° *unruly conduct*
By which he grew to grievous malady;
For in his lustlesse limbs through evill guise
A shaking fever raignd° continually: *ruled*
Such one was Idlenesse, first of this company.

21

And by his side rode loathsome Gluttony,
Deformed creature, on a filthie swyne,
His belly was up-blowne with luxury,
And eke with fatnesse swollen were his eyne,° *eyes*
And like a Crane his necke was long and fyne,
With which he swallowd up excessive feast,
For want whereof poore people oft did pyne;
And all the way, most like a brutish beast,
He spued up his gorge,° that all did him deteast. *vomited his food*

22

In greene vine leaves he was right fitly clad;
For other clothes he could not weare for heat,
And on his head an ivie girland had,
From under which fast trickled downe the sweat:
Still as he rode, he somewhat still did eat,
And in his hand did beare a bouzing° can, *drinking*
Of which he supt so oft, that on his seat
His dronken corse he scarse upholden can,
In shape and life more like a monster, then a man.

23

Unfit he was for any worldly thing,
And eke unhable once to stirre or go,
Not meet to be of counsell to a king,
Whose mind in meat and drinke was drowned so,
That from his friend he seldome knew his fo:
Full of diseases was his carcas blew,
And a dry dropsie[9] through his flesh did flow:
Which by misdiet daily greater grew:
Such one was Gluttony, the second of that crew.

24

And next to him rode lustfull Lechery,
Upon a bearded Goat, whose rugged haire,

9. A disease characterized by bloating.

And whally° eyes (the signe of gelosy,) *glaring*
Was like the person selfe,° whom he did beare: *himself*
Who rough, and blacke, and filthy did appeare,
Unseemely man to please faire Ladies eye;
Yet he of Ladies oft was loved deare,
When fairer faces were bid standen by:
O who does know the bent of womens fantasy?

25

In a greene gowne he clothed was full faire,
Which underneath did hide his filthinesse,
And in his hand a burning hart he bare,
Full of vaine follies, and new fanglenesse:
For he was false, and fraught with ficklenesse,
And learned had to love with secret lookes,
And well could daunce, and sing with ruefulnesse,° *melancholy*
And fortunes tell, and read in loving bookes,° *books of love*
And thousand other wayes, to bait his fleshly hookes.

26

Inconstant man, that loved all he saw,
And lusted after all, that he did love,
Ne would his looser life be tide to law,
But joyd weake wemens hearts to tempt and prove° *test*
If from their loyall loves he might them move;
Which lewdnesse fild him with reprochfull paine
Of that fowle evill, which all men reprove,
That rots the marrow, and consumes the braine:
Such one was Lecherie, the third of all this traine.

27

And greedy Avarice by him did ride,
Upon a Camell loaden all with gold;
Two iron coffers hong on either side,
With precious mettall full, as they might hold,
And in his lap an heape of coine he told;° *counted*
For of his wicked pelfe° his God he made, *profits*
And unto hell him selfe for money sold;
Accursed usurie was all his trade,[1]
And right and wrong ylike in equall ballaunce waide.

28

His life was nigh unto deaths doore yplast,° *i.e., nearly over*
And thred-bare cote, and cobled° shoes he ware, *patched*
Ne scarse good morsell all his life did tast,
But both from backe and belly still did spare,
To fill his bags, and richesse to compare;[2]
Yet chylde ne kinsman living had he none
To leave them to; but thorough daily care

1. Usury (lending money for profit) was forbidden by Scripture but was nevertheless practiced—with certain restrictions—in early modern Europe and England. High rates of interest were generally forbidden, but loans could be made as forms of investment in commerce or industry.

2. I.e., he wore rags and starved himself.

To get, and nightly feare to lose his owne,° *his own wealth*
He led a wretched life unto him selfe unknowne.

29

Most wretched wight, whom nothing might suffise,
Whose greedy lust did lacke in greatest store,
Whose need had end, but no end covetise,° *coveteousness*
Whose wealth was want, whose plenty made him pore,
Who had enough, yet wished ever more;
A vile disease, and eke in foote and hand
A grievous gout tormented him full sore,
That well he could not touch, nor go, nor stand:
Such one was Avarice, the fourth of this faire band.

30

And next to him malicious Envie rode,
Upon a ravenous wolfe, and still did chaw° *chew*
Betweene his cankred° teeth a venemous tode, *infected*
That all the poison ran about his chaw;° *mouth*
But inwardly he chawed his owne maw° *guts*
At neighbours wealth, that made him ever sad;
For death it was, when any good he saw,
And wept, that cause of weeping none he had,
But when he heard of harme, he wexed° wondrous glad. *grew*

31

All in a kirtle° of discolourd say° *gown/fine cloth*
He clothed was, ypainted full of eyes;
And in his bosome secretly there lay
An hatefull Snake, the which his taile uptyes
In many folds, and mortall sting implyes.[3]
Still as he rode, he gnasht his teeth, to see
Those heapes of gold with griple Covetyse,[4]
And grudged at the great felicitie
Of proud Lucifera, and his owne companie.

32

He hated all good workes and vertuous deeds,
And him no lesse, that any like did use,° *perform*
And who with gracious bread the hungry feeds,
His almes for want of faith he doth accuse;° *misrepresent*
So every good to bad he doth abuse:[5]
And eke the verse of famous Poets witt
He does backebite, and spightfull poison spues
From leprous mouth on all, that ever writt:
Such one vile Envie was, that fifte in row did sitt.

3. Envy's clothing symbolically displays the envious and covetous eyes with which he views the world. The snake he carries in his bosom was a traditional symbol of envy; its "mortall sting" is deadly to Envy himself as well as to others.

4. Grasping Avarice; Envy is envious of Avarice's gold.

5. Envy believes that good deeds reveal a lack of faith. Here Spenser attacks doctrine associated with radical Protestant sects that, rejecting Catholic belief in the merit of good works as a means to salvation, insist that it is only through faith and God's grace that a Christian is saved.

33

And him beside rides fierce revenging Wrath,
Upon a Lion, loth for° to be led; *reluctant*
And in his hand a burning brond° he hath, *brand*
The which he brandisheth about his hed;
His eyes did hurle forth sparkles fiery red,
And stared sterne on all, that him beheld,
As ashes pale of hew and seeming ded;
And on his dagger still his hand he held,
Trembling through hasty rage, when choler° in him sweld. *anger*

34

His ruffin° raiment all was staind with blood, *ruffianly*
Which he had spilt, and all to rags yrent,
Through unadvized rashnesse woxen wood;° *grown mad*
For of his hands he had no governement,° *control*
Ne car'd for bloud in his avengement:
But when the furious fit was overpast,
His cruell facts° he often would repent; *deeds*
Yet wilfull man he never would forecast,° *foresee*
How many mischieves° should ensue his heedlesse hast. *evil consequences*

35

Full many mischiefes follow cruell Wrath;
Abhorred bloudshed, and tumultuous strife,
Unmanly murder, and unthrifty scath,° *wasteful harm*
Bitter despight,° with rancours rusty knife, *malice*
And fretting griefe the enemy of life;
All these, and many evils moe haunt ire,
The swelling Splene,° and Frenzy raging rife, *temper*
The shaking Palsey, and Saint Fraunces fire:[6]
Such one was Wrath, the last of this ungodly tire.° *procession*

36

And after all, upon the wagon beame° *shaft*
Rode Sathan, with a smarting whip in hand,
With which he forward lasht the laesie teme,
So oft as Slowth still in the mire did stand.
Huge routs of people did about them band,
Showting for joy, and still° before their way *always*
A foggy mist had covered all the land;
And underneath their feet, all scattered lay
Dead sculs and bones of men, whose life had gone astray.

37

So forth they marchen in this goodly sort,
To take the solace of the open aire,
And in fresh flowring fields themselves to sport;
Emongst the rest rode that false Lady faire,

6. Erysipelas or, as it was actually known, St. Anthony's fire. A common disease of the period, it was characterized by a disfiguring and painful skin rash.

The fowle Duessa, next unto the chaire
Of proud Lucifera, as one of the traine:
But that good knight would not so nigh repaire,° *follow*
Him selfe estraunging from their joyaunce vaine,
Whose fellowship seemd far unfit for warlike swaine.

38

So having solaced themselves a space
With pleasaunce of the breathing fields yfed,[7]
They backe returned to the Princely Place;
Whereas° an errant° knight in armes ycled, *where / wandering*
And heathnish shield, wherein with letters red
Was writ Sans-Joy, they new arrived find:
Enflam'd with fury and fiers hardy-hed,° *boldness*
He seemd in hart to harbour thoughts unkind,
And nourish bloudy vengeaunce in his bitter mind.

39

Who when the shamed shield of slaine Sans-Foy
He spide with that same Faery champions page,
Bewraying° him, that did of late destroy *revealing*
His eldest brother, burning all with rage
He to him leapt, and that same envious gage° *envious token*
Of victors glory from him snatcht away:
But th'Elfin knight, which ought° that warlike wage, *owned*
Disdaind to loose° the meed° he wonne in fray, *give up / reward*
And him recountring° fierce, reskewd the noble pray.[8] *combatting*

40

Therewith they gan to hurtlen° greedily, *fight*
Redoubted battaile ready to darrayne,° *wage*
And clash their shields, and shake their swords on hy,
That with their sturre they troubled all the traine;
Till that great Queene upon eternall paine
Of high displeasure, that ensewen° might, *follow*
Commaunded them their fury to refraine,
And if that either to that shield had right,
In equall lists° they should the morrow next it fight. *tournament*

41

Ah dearest Dame, (quoth then the Paynim bold,)
Pardon the errour of enraged wight,
Whom great griefe made forget the raines° to hold *reins*
Of reasons rule, to see this recreant° knight, *cowardly*
No knight, but treachour full of false despight° *indignation*
And shamefull treason, who through guile hath slayn
The prowest knight, that ever field did fight,

7. I.e., having fed themselves with fresh air from the fields, where they momentarily escape the stench of sin.

8. By striving to recover Sans-Foy's shield instead of pursuing his quest to free Una's parents, the Redcrosse Knight exhibits pride and exemplifies a false chivalry.

Even stout Sans-Foy (O who can then refrayn?)
Whose shield he beares renverst,° the more to heape disdayn. *upside down*

42

And to augment the glorie of his guile,
His dearest love the faire Fidessa loe° *look*
Is there possessed of° the traytour vile,[9] *by*
Who reapes the harvest sowen by his foe,
Sowen in bloudy field, and bought with woe:
That brothers hand shall dearely well requight° *repay*
So be, O Queene, you equall favour showe.
Him litle answerd th'angry Elfin knight;
He never meant with words, but swords to plead his right.° *cause*

43

But threw his gauntlet° as a sacred pledge, *glove*
His cause in combat the next day to try:
So been they parted both, with harts on edge,
To be aveng'd each on his enimy.
That night they pas in joy and jollity,
Feasting and courting both in bowre and hall;
For Steward was excessive Gluttonie,
That of his plenty poured forth to all;
Which doen, the Chamberlain° Slowth did to rest them call. *master of bedchambers*

44

Now whenas° darkesome night had all displayd *when*
Her coleblacke curtein over brightest skye,
The warlike youthes on dayntie couches layd,
Did chace away sweet sleepe from sluggish eye,
To muse on meanes of hoped victory.
But whenas Morpheus had with leaden mace
Arrested° all that courtly company, *i.e., put to sleep*
Up-rose Duessa from her resting place,
And to the Paynims lodging comes with silent pace.

45

Whom broad awake she finds, in troublous fit,
Forecasting, how his foe he might annoy,° *injure*
And him amoves° with speaches seeming fit: *arouses*
Ah deare Sans-Joy, next dearest to Sans-Foy,
Cause of my new griefe, cause of my new joy,
Joyous, to see his ymage in mine eye,
And greev'd, to thinke how foe did him destroy,
That was the flowre of grace and chevalrye;
Lo his Fidessa to thy secret faith I flye.

46

With gentle wordes he can° her fairely greet, *did*
And bad° say on the secret of her hart. *commanded*
Then sighing soft, I learne that little sweet
Oft tempred is (quoth she) with muchell smart:° *much pain*

9. Sans-Joy accused the Redcrosse Knight of absconding with Fidessa (i.e., Duessa), who actually belonged to his brother, Sans-Foy.

For since my brest was launcht° with lovely dart *pierced*
Of deare Sans-Foy, I never joyed howre,
But in eternall woes my weaker hart
Have wasted, loving him with all my powre,
And for his sake have felt full many an heavie stowre.° *sorrowful time*

47

At last when perils all I weened past,
And hop'd to reape the crop of all my care,
Into new woes unweeting I was cast,
By this false faytor,° who unworthy ware° *deceiver / wore*
His° worthy shield, whom he with guilefull snare *Sans-Foy's*
Entrapped slew, and brought to shamefull grave.
Me silly maid away with him he bare,
And ever since hath kept in darksome cave,
For that° I would not yeeld, that to Sans-Foy I gave. *that which*

48

But since faire Sunne hath sperst° that lowring° clowd, *dispersed / threatening*
And to my loathed life now shewes some light,
Under your beames I will me safely shrowd,° *take shelter*
From dreaded storme of his° disdainfull spight: *Redcrosse Knight's*
To you th'inheritance belongs by right
Of brothers prayse, to you eke longs his love.
Let not his love, let not his restlesse spright
Be unreveng'd, that calles to you above
From wandring Stygian° shores, where it doth endlesse move. *underworld*

49

Thereto said he, Faire Dame be nought dismaid
For sorrowes past; their griefe is with them gone:
Ne yet of present perill be affraid;
For needlesse feare did never vantage none,° *benefit anyone*
And helplesse hap it booteth° not to mone. *helps*
Dead is Sans-Foy, his vitall paines° are past, *troubles in life*
Though greeved ghost for vengeance deepe do grone:
He lives, that shall him pay his dewties last,° *final debts*
And guiltie Elfin bloud shall sacrifice in hast.

50

O but I feare the fickle freakes° (quoth shee) *accidents*
Of fortune false, and oddes of armes in field.
Why dame (quoth he) what oddes can ever bee,
Where both do fight alike, to win or yield?
Yea but (quoth she) he beares a charmed shield,
And eke enchaunted armes, that none can perce,
Ne none can wound the man, that does them wield.
Charmd or enchaunted (answerd he then ferce)
I no whit reck,° ne you the like need to reherce.° *care nothing / mention*

51

But faire Fidessa, sithens° fortunes guile, *since*
Or enimies powre hath now captived you,
Returne from whence ye came, and rest a while
Till morrow next, that I the Elfe subdew,
And with Sans-Foyes dead dowry you endew.° *give*

Ay me, that is a double death (she said)
With proud foes sight my sorrow to renew:
Where ever yet I be, my secrete aid
Shall follow you. So passing forth she him obaid.

Canto 5

The faithfull knight in equall field
subdewes his faithlesse foe,
Whom false Duessa saves, and for
his cure to hell does goe.

1

The noble hart, that harbours vertuous thought,
And is with child° of glorious great intent, *pregnant*
Can never rest, untill it forth have brought
Th'eternall brood of glorie excellent:
Such restlesse passion did all night torment
The flaming corage of that Faery knight,
Devizing, how that doughtie° turnament *worthy*
With greatest honour he atchieven might;
Still did he wake, and still did watch for dawning light.

2

At last the golden Orientall° gate *eastern*
Of greatest heaven gan to open faire,
And Phoebus fresh, as bridegrome to his mate,
Came dauncing forth, shaking his deawie haire:
And hurld his glistring° beames through gloomy aire. *glistening*
Which when the wakeful Elfe perceiv'd, streight way
He started up, and did him selfe prepaire,
In sun-bright armes, and battailous° array: *warlike*
For with that Pagan proud he combat will that day.

3

And forth he comes into the commune hall,
Where earely waite him many a gazing eye,
To weet° what end to straunger knights may fall. *know*
There many Minstrales maken melody,
To drive away the dull melancholy,
And many Bardes, that to the trembling chord
Can tune their timely voyces cunningly,
And many Chroniclers, that can record
Old loves, and warres for Ladies doen by many a Lord.

4

Soone after comes the cruell Sarazin,
In woven maile all armed warily,° *carefully*
And sternly lookes at him, who not a pin
Does care for looke of living creatures eye.
They bring them wines of Greece and Araby,° *Arabia*
And daintie spices fetcht from furthest Ynd,° *India*
To kindle heat of corage privily:° *internally*
And in the wine a solemne oth they bynd
T'observe the sacred lawes of armes, that are assynd.

5

At last forth comes that far renowmed° Queene, *famed*
With royall pomp and Princely majestie;
She is ybrought unto a paled greene,° *enclosed field*
And placed under stately canapee,
The warlike feates of both those knights to see.
On th'other side in all mens open vew
Duessa placed is, and on a tree
Sans-Foy his shield is hangd with bloudy hew:
Both those the lawrell girlonds to the victor dew.[1]

6

A shrilling trompet sownded from on hye,
And unto battaill bad them selves addresse:
Their shining shieldes about their wrestes they tye,
And burning blades about their heads do blesse,[2]
The instruments of wrath and heavinesse:
With greedy force each other doth assayle,
And strike so fiercely, that they do impresse
Deepe dinted furrowes in the battred mayle;
The yron walles° to ward their blowes are weake and fraile. *of the armor*

7

The Sarazin was stout, and wondrous strong,
And heaped blowes like yron hammers great:
For after bloud and vengeance he did long.
The knight was fiers, and full of youthly heat:
And doubled strokes, like dreaded thunders threat:
For all for prayse and honour he did fight.
Both stricken strike, and beaten both do beat,
That from their shields forth flyeth firie light,
And helmets hewen deepe,° shew marks of eithers might. *deeply cut*

8

So th'one for wrong, the other strives for right:
As when a Gryfon[3] seized of his pray,
A Dragon fiers encountreth in his flight,
Through widest ayre making his ydle way,
That would his rightfull ravine° rend away: *spoil*
With hideous horrour both together smight,
And souce° so sore, that they the heavens affray: *attack*
The wise Southsayer seeing so sad sight,
Th'amazed vulgar tels of warres and mortall fight.

9

So th'one for wrong, the other strives for right,
And each to deadly shame would drive his foe:
The cruell steele so greedily doth bight
In tender flesh, that streames of bloud down flow,

1. I.e., the victor will receive both Sans-Foy's shield and Duessa as his prize.

2. Brandish: they make the sign of the cross in the air with their swords.

3. A lion with eagle's wings. Dante used the gryfon as a symbol for the dual nature of Christ, as both spirit and flesh. However, in traditional iconography the gryfon also appeared as a creature who guarded gold and was thus emblematic of greed. The image suggests that the Redcrosse Knight is foolish to engage in a contest for material prizes.

With which the armes, that earst° so bright did show, *first*
Into a pure vermillion now are dyde:
Great ruth° in all the gazers harts did grow, *pity*
Seeing the gored woundes to gape so wyde,
That victory they dare not wish to either side.

10

At last the Paynim chaunst to cast his eye,
His suddein eye, flaming with wrathfull fyre,
Upon his brothers shield, which hong thereby:
Therewith redoubled was his raging yre,
And said, Ah wretched sonne of wofull syre,° *Sans-Foy*
Doest thou sit wayling by black Stygian° lake, *by the river Styx*
Whilest here thy shield is hangd for victors hyre,
And sluggish german° doest thy forces slake, *kinsman*
To after-send his foe, that him may overtake?[4]

11

Goe caytive Elfe,[5] him quickly overtake,
And soone redeeme from his long wandring woe;
Goe guiltie ghost, to him my message make,
That I his shield have quit° from dying foe. *recovered*
Therewith upon his crest he stroke him so,
That twise he reeled, readie twise to fall;
End of the doubtfull battell deemed tho
The lookers on, and lowd to him gan call
The false Duessa, Thine the shield, and I, and all.[6]

12

Soone as the Faerie heard his Ladie speake,
Out of his swowning dreame he gan awake,
And quickning faith, that earst was woxen° weake, *had grown*
The creeping deadly cold away did shake:
Tho mou'd with wrath, and shame, and Ladies sake,
Of all attonce he cast avengd to bee,
And with so'exceeding furie at him strake,° *struck*
That forced him to stoupe upon his knee;
Had he not stouped so, he should have cloven° bee. *cut in half*

13

And to him said, Goe now proud Miscreant,° *heathen*
Thy selfe thy message doe to german deare,
Alone he wandring thee too long doth want:° *lack*
Goe say, his foe thy shield with his doth beare.
Therewith his heavie hand he high gan reare,° *began to raise*
Him to have slaine; when loe a darkesome clowd
Upon him fell: he no where doth appeare,
But vanisht is. The Elfe him cals alowd,
But answer none receiues: the darknes him does shrowd.

4. Sans-Joy is addressing the dead Sans-Foy, asking if Sans-Foy grieves because his shield is a prize and the strength of his brother, Sans-Joy, which should be wielded to dispatch the Redcrosse Knight to the shores of the Styx, is actually slackening, growing weak.

5. Sans-Joy addresses the Redcrosse Knight. The epithet "caytive," meaning "servile," was especially insulting in the context of chivalry, since it implied weakness and lack of valor.

6. Duessa is calling to Sans-Joy; however, the Redcrosse Knight assumes that she is cheering him on and therefore redoubles his force.

14

In haste Duessa from her place arose,
And to him running said, O prowest° knight, *most valiant*
That ever Ladie to her love did chose,
Let now abate the terror of your might,
And quench the flame of furious despight,
And bloudie vengeance; lo th'infernall powres
Covering your foe with cloud of deadly night,
Have borne him hence to Plutoes balefull° bowres. *deadly*
The conquest yours, I yours, the shield, and glory yours.

15

Not all so satisfide, with greedie eye
He sought all round about, his thirstie blade
To bath in bloud of faithlesse enemy;
Who all that while lay hid in secret shade:
He standes amazed, how he thence should fade.
At last the trumpets Triumph sound on hie,
And running Heralds humble homage made,
Greeting him goodly with new victorie,
And to him brought the shield, the cause of enmitie.

16

Wherewith he goeth to that soveraine Queene,
And falling her before on lowly knee,
To her makes present of his service seene:
Which she accepts, with thankes, and goodly gree,° *courteous goodwill*
Greatly advauncing his gay chevalree.
So marcheth home, and by her takes the knight,
Whom all the people follow with great glee,
Shouting, and clapping all their hands on hight,° *high*
That all the aire it fils, and flyes to heaven bright.

17

Home is he brought, and laid in sumptuous bed:
Where many skilfull leaches° him abide, *doctors*
To salve° his hurts, that yet still freshly bled. *dress*
In wine and oyle they wash his woundes wide,
And softly can embalme on every side.
And all the while, most heavenly melody
About the bed sweet musicke did divide,° *modulate*
Him to beguile of griefe and agony:
And all the while Duessa wept full bitterly.

18

As when a wearie traveller that strayes
By muddy shore of broad seven-mouthed Nile,
Unweeting of the perillous wandring wayes,
Doth meet a cruell craftie Crocodile,
Which in false griefe hyding his harmefull guile,
Doth weepe full sore, and sheddeth tender teares:
The foolish man, that pitties all this while
His mournefull plight, is swallowd up unwares,
Forgetfull of his owne, that mindes° anothers cares. *attends to*

19

So wept Duessa untill eventide,
That shyning lampes in Joves high house were light:
Then forth she rose, ne lenger° would abide, *no longer*
But comes unto the place, where th'Hethen knight
In slombring swownd nigh voyd of vitall spright,° *living spirit*
Lay cover'd with inchaunted cloud all day:
Whom when she found, as she him left in plight,
To wayle his woefull case she would not stay,
But to the easterne coast of heaven makes speedy way.

20

Where griesly Night, with visage deadly sad,
That Phoebus chearefull face durst never vew,
And in a foule blacke pitchie mantle clad,
She findes forth comming from her darkesome mew,° *den*
Where she all day did hide her hated hew.
Before the dore her yron charet stood,
Alreadie harnessed for journey new;
And coleblacke steedes yborne of hellish brood,
That on their rustie bits did champ, as they were wood.° *mad*

21

Who when she saw Duessa sunny bright,
Adornd with gold and jewels shining cleare,
She greatly grew amazed at the sight,
And th'unacquainted light began to feare:
For never did such brightnesse there appeare,
And would have backe retyred to her cave,
Untill the witches speech she gan to heare,
Saying, Yet O thou dreaded Dame, I crave
Abide,° till I have told the message, which I have. *wait*

22

She stayd, and foorth Duessa gan proceede,
O thou most auncient Grandmother of all,[7]
More old then Jove, whom thou at first didst breede,
Or that great house of Gods caelestiall,
Which wast begot in Daemogorgons° hall, *chaos's*
And sawst the secrets of the world unmade,° *not yet made*
Why suffredst thou thy Nephewes deare to fall
With Elfin sword, most shamefully betrade?
Lo where the stout° Sans-Joy doth sleepe in deadly shade. *sturdy*

23

And him before, I saw with bitter eyes
The bold Sans-Foy shrinke underneath his speare;
And now the pray of fowles in field he lyes,
Nor wayld of friends, nor laid on groning beare,° *bier*
That whylome was to me too dearely deare.
O what of Gods then boots° it to be borne, *benefits*
If old Aveugles[8] sonnes so evill heare?

7. Invoking Night, Duessa recalls that Jove was raised in a dark cave to escape being eaten by his father, Saturn; here, Spenser is implying that darkness gave birth to Jove.

8. Blind (French). Duessa uses the name "Aveugle" to refer to either Night herself or her husband; "Aveugles sonne" is Sans-Joy.

Or who shall not great Nightes children scorne,
When two of three her Nephews are so fowle forlorne?° *foully abandoned*

24

Up then, up dreary Dame, of darknesse Queene,
Go gather up the reliques° of thy race, *remains*
Or else goe them avenge, and let be seene,
That dreaded Night in brightest day hath place,° *highest rank*
And can the children of faire light deface.
Her feeling speeches some compassion moved
In hart, and chaunge in that great mothers face:
Yet pittie in her hart was never proved° *experienced*
Till then: for evermore she hated, never loved.

25

And said, Deare daughter rightly may I rew
The fall of famous children borne of mee,
And good successes, which their foes ensew:
But who can turne the streame of destinee,
Or breake the chayne of strong necessitee,
Which fast is tyde to Joves eternall seat?[9]
The sonnes of Day he favoureth, I see,
And by my ruines thinkes to make them great:
To make one great by others losse, is bad excheat.° *exchange*

26

Yet shall they not escape so freely all;
For some shall pay the price of° others guilt: *for*
And he the man that made Sans-Foy to fall,
Shall with his owne bloud price that he hath spilt.
But what art thou, that telst of Nephews kilt?° *killed*
I that do seeme not I, Duessa am,
(Quoth she) how ever now in garments gilt,
And gorgeous gold arayd I to thee came;
Duessa I, the daughter of Deceipt and Shame.

27

Then bowing downe her aged backe, she kist
The wicked witch, saying; In that faire face
The false resemblance of Deceipt, I wist
Did closely° lurke; yet so true-seeming grace *secretly*
It carried, that I scarse in darkesome place
Could it discerne, though I the mother bee
Of falshood, and root of Duessaes race.
O welcome child, whom I have longd to see,
And now have seene unwares.° Lo now I go with thee. *unknowingly*

28

Then to her yron wagon she betakes,
And with her beares the fowle welfavourd witch:[1]
Through mirkesome° aire her readie way she makes. *murky*
Her twyfold° Teme, of which two blacke as pitch, *twofold*
And two were browne, yet each to each unlich,° *unlike*
Did softly swim away, ne ever stampe,

9. Night reveals her fatalism and therefore her ignorance of Christian grace. God can forgive a repentant sinner; hence for Christians there is no "chain of necessity" prior to God's decision to send the sinner to eternal damnation.

1. Duessa is a foul creature disguised as a beautiful woman.

Unlesse she chaunst their stubborne mouths to twitch;
Then foming tarre, their bridles they would champe,
And trampling the fine element,° would fiercely rampe.° *air/rear up*

29

So well they sped, that they be come at length
Unto the place, whereas the Paynim lay,
Devoid of outward sense, and native° strength, *natural*
Coverd with charmed cloud from vew of day,
And sight of men, since his late luckelesse fray.° *fight*
His cruell wounds with cruddy bloud congealed,
They binden up so wisely, as they may,
And handle softly, till they can be healed:
So lay him in her charet, close° in night concealed. *hidden*

30

And all the while she stood upon the ground,
The wakefull dogs did never cease to bay,° *howl*
As giving warning of th'unwonted° sound, *unaccustomed*
With which her yron wheeles did them affray,
And her darke griesly looke them much dismay;
The messenger of death, the ghastly Owle
With drearie shriekes did also her bewray;° *expose*
And hungry Wolves continually did howle,
At her abhorred face, so filthy and so fowle.

31

Thence turning backe in silence soft they stole,
And brought the heavie corse with easie pace
To yawning gulfe of deepe Avernus° hole. *a lake in hell*
By that same hole an entrance darke and bace° *low*
With smoake and sulphure hiding all the place,
Descends to hell: there creature never past,
That backe returned without heavenly grace;
But dreadfull Furies,[2] which their chaines have brast,
And damned sprights sent forth to make ill° men aghast. *bad*

32

By that same way the direfull° dames doe drive *dreadful*
Their mournefull charet, fild° with rusty blood, *defiled*
And downe to Plutoes house are come bilive:° *quickly*
Which passing through, on every side them stood
The trembling ghosts with sad amazed mood,
Chattring their yron teeth, and staring wide
With stonie eyes; and all the hellish brood
Of feends infernall flockt on every side,
To gaze on earthly wight, that with the Night durst° ride. *dared*

33

They pas the bitter waves of Acheron,[3]
Where many soules sit wailing woefully,
And come to fiery flood of Phlegeton,
Whereas the damned ghosts in torments fry,

2. The three mythical female spirits who live in the underworld and punish people for their crimes; they personified the forces of revenge.

3. Acheron and Phlegeton are two of the four rivers of the underworld.

And with sharpe shrilling shriekes doe bootlesse° cry, *futilely*
Cursing high Jove, the which them thither sent.
The house of endlesse paine is built thereby,
In which ten thousand sorts of punishment
The cursed creatures doe eternally torment.

34

Before the threshold dreadfull Cerberus[4]
His three deformed heads did lay along,
Curled with thousand adders venemous,
And lilled forth° his bloudie flaming tong: *stuck out*
At them he gan to reare his bristles strong,
And felly gnarre,° untill dayes enemy *deadly snarl*
Did him appease; then downe his taile he hong
And suffered them to passen quietly:
For she in hell and heaven had power equally.

35

There was Ixion[5] turned on a wheele,
For daring tempt the Queene of heaven to sin;
And Sisyphus an huge round stone did reele
Against an hill, ne might from labour lin;
There thirstie Tantalus hong by the chin;
And Tityus fed a vulture on his maw;
Typhoeus joynts were stretched on a gin,
Theseus condemned to endlesse slouth by law,
And fifty sisters water in leake vessels draw.

36

They all beholding worldly wights in place,
Leave off their worke, unmindfull of their smart,° *pain*
To gaze on them; who forth by them doe pace,
Till they be come unto the furthest part:
Where was a Cave ywrought° by wondrous art, *built*
Deepe, darke, uneasie, dolefull, comfortlesse,
In which sad Aesculapius[6] farre a part
Emprisond was in chaines remedilesse,
For that Hippolytus rent corse he did redresse.° *restore*

37

Hippolytus a jolly huntsman was,
That wont° in charet chace the foming Bore; *often*
He all his Peeres in beautie did surpas,
But Ladies love as losse of time forbore:° *abstained from*
His wanton stepdame° loved him the more, *stepmother*
But when she saw her offred sweets refused
Her love she turnd to hate, and him before

4. The fierce, three-headed dog who guards the entrance to the underworld.

5. This stanza describes various mythological figures who suffer in the underworld. Ixion, king of Thessaly, sought the love of Juno and was punished by being bound forever on a revolving wheel. Sisyphus, a greedy king of Corinth, was condemned forever to roll up a hill a heavy stone, which always rolled back down again. Tantalus was doomed to stand up to his neck in water with fruit hanging at his fingertips, yet could never reach the fruit or drink the water. Tityus's punishment was to have a vulture constantly feed on his liver, which grew back as soon as it was devoured. Theseus, hero and eventually king of Athens, was famous for a multitude of exploits and adventures; he was condemned to sit forever in the chair of forgetfulness. The 50 sisters were the daughters of Danaus, king of Argos; they were condemned to collect water in leaky pots because they had murdered their husbands on their wedding night.

6. The god of medicine. In the following stanzas, Spenser tells the story of how Aesculapius revived the corpse of Hippolytus and was punished for exceeding the limits of medical art.

His father fierce of treason false accused,
And with her gealous termes his open eares abused.

38

Who ail in rage his Sea-god syre besought,
Some cursed vengeance on his sonne to cast:
From surging gulf two monsters straight were brought,
With dread whereof his chasing steedes aghast,° *terrified*
Both charet swift and huntsman overcast.
His goodly corps on ragged cliffs yrent,
Was quite dismembred, and his members chast° *virgin, virtuous*
Scattered on every mountaine, as he went,
That of Hippolytus was left no moniment.° *trace*

39

His cruell stepdame seeing what was donne,
Her wicked dayes with wretched knife did end,
In death avowing th'innocence of her sonne.
Which hearing his rash Syre, began to rend° *tear*
His haire, and hastie tongue, that did offend:
Tho gathering up the relicks of his smart° *pain*
By Dianes° meanes, who was Hippolyts frend, *goddess of the hunt*
Them brought to Aesculape, that by his art
Did heale them all againe, and joyned every part.

40

Such wondrous science in mans wit to raine° *rule*
When Jove avizd,° that could the dead revive, *found out*
And fates expired could renew againe,
Of endlesse life he might him not deprive,
But unto hell did thrust him downe alive,
With flashing thunderbolt ywounded sore:
Where long remaining, he did alwaies strive
Himselfe with salves to health for to restore,
And slake° the heavenly fire, that raged evermore. *put out*

41

There auncient Night arriving, did alight
From her nigh wearie waine, and in her armes
To Aesculapius brought the wounded knight:
Whom having softly disarayd of armes,
Tho gan to him discover all his harmes,° *injuries*
Beseeching him with prayer, and with praise,
If either salves, or oyles, or herbes, or charmes
A fordonne° wight from dore of death mote raise, *dying*
He would at her request prolong her nephews daies.

42

Ah Dame (quoth he) thou temptest me in vaine,
To dare the thing, which daily yet I rew,
And the old cause of my continued paine
With like attempt to like end to renew.[7]
Is not enough, that thrust from heaven dew
Here endlesse penance for one fault I pay,
But that redoubled crime with vengeance new

7. I.e., to repeat the actions which caused his punishment in the first place and thus to renew the punishment itself.

Thou biddest me to eeke?° Can Night defray° *increase / appease*
The wrath of thundring Jove, that rules both night and day?

43

Not so (quoth she) but sith that heavens king
From hope of heaven hath thee excluded quight,
Why fearest thou, that canst not hope for thing,° *anything*
And fearest not, that more thee hurten might,
Now in the powre of everlasting Night?
Goe to then, O thou farre renowmed sonne
Of great Apollo, shew thy famous might
In medicine, that else hath to thee wonne
Great paines, and greater praise, both never to be donne.° *surpassed*

44

Her words prevaild: And then the learned leach° *doctor*
His cunning hand gan to his wounds to lay,
And all things else, the which his art did teach:
Which having seene, from thence arose away
The mother of dread darknesse, and let stay
Aveugles sonne there in the leaches cure,
And backe returning tooke her wonted way,
To runne her timely race, whilst Phoebus pure
In westerne waves his wearie wagon did recure.° *renew*

45

The false Duessa leaving noyous° Night, *noxious*
Returnd to stately pallace of dame Pride;
Where when she came, she found the Faery knight
Departed thence, albe° his woundes wide *although*
Not throughly heald, unreadie were to ride.
Good cause he had to hasten thence away;
For on a day his wary Dwarfe had spide,
Where in a dongeon deepe huge numbers lay
Of caytive wretched thrals,° that wayled night and day. *prisoners*

46

A ruefull sight, as could be seene with eie;
Of whom he learned had in secret wise° *manner*
The hidden cause of their captivitie,
How mortgaging their lives to Covetise,° *greed*
Through wastfull Pride, and wanton Riotise,° *idle abandon*
They were by law of that proud Tyrannesse
Provokt with Wrath, and Envies false surmise,° *suspicion*
Condemned to that Dongeon mercilesse,
Where they should live in woe, and die in wretchednesse.[8]

47

There was that great proud king of Babylon,° *Nebuchadnezzar*
That would compell all nations to adore,
And him as onely° God to call upon, *the only*

8. Spenser lists some of the inhabitants of the underworld, the domain of Night, implying that they were damned for their evil deeds and were therefore in a Christian hell. The theology supporting this image is problematic: While Spenser names individuals who were considered to have been proud and malicious, they were also not people who could have known the salutary message of Christianity. Nebuchadnezzar, king of Babylon, set up a golden image to be worshipped as God and was transformed into an ox as a punishment (Daniel 3–6); Croesus was the vastly rich king of Lydia; Antiochus, king of Antioch, was supposed scornfully to have danced on an altar; Nimrod was the first tyrant to emerge after the Flood; Ninus, the founder of Nineveh, conquered India and was the first to make war. "That mightie Monarch" was Alexander the Great, who rejected his father to claim descent from Jove or Jupiter, sometimes called Jupiter Ammon.

Till through celestiall doome° throwne out of dore, *heavenly judgment*
Into an Oxe he was transform'd of yore:° *in ancient times*
There also was king Croesus, that enhaunst
His heart too high through his great riches store;
And proud Antiochus, the which advaunst
His cursed hand gainst God, and on his altars daunst.

48

And them long time before, great Nimrod was,
That first the world with sword and fire warrayd;° *ravaged*
And after him old Ninus farre did pas
In princely pompe, of all the world obayd;
There also was that mightie Monarch layd
Low under all, yet above all in pride,
That name of native syre° did fowle upbrayd,° *natural father / denounce*
And would as Ammons sonne be magnifide,
Till scornd of God and man a shamefull death he dide.

49

All these together in one heape were throwne,
Like carkases of beasts in butchers stall.
And in another corner wide were strowne° *strewn*
The antique ruines of the Romaines fall:[9]
Great Romulus the Grandsyre of them all,
Proud Tarquin, and too lordly Lentulus,
Stout Scipio, and stubborne Hanniball,
Ambitious Sylla, and sterne Marius,
High Caesar, great Pompey, and fierce Antonius.

50

Amongst these mighty men were wemen mixt,[1]
Proud wemen, vaine, forgetfull of their yoke:° *place*
The bold Semiramis, whose sides transfixt
With sonnes owne blade, her fowle reproches spoke;
Faire Sthenoboea, that her selfe did choke
With wilfull cord, for wanting of her will;
High minded Cleopatra, that with stroke
Of Aspes° sting her selfe did stoutly kill: *snakes'*
And thousands moe the like, that did that dongeon fill.

51

Besides the endlesse routs° of wretched thralles, *crowds*
Which thither were assembled day by day,
From all the world after their wofull falles,
Through wicked pride, and wasted wealthes decay.° *loss*
But most of all, which in that Dongeon lay
Fell from high Princes courts, or Ladies bowres,

9. Spenser lists men who figured prominently in the history of ancient Rome; some were heroes, others were tyrants or wrongdoers. Romulus was the founder and first king of Rome; Tarquin was the last king of Rome before it became a republic; Lentulus attempted to set fire to Rome; Scipio was a Roman general who conquered Africa; Hannibal constantly waged war against Rome; Sylla was a Roman dictator who was engaged in civil war with Marius; Caesar, Pompey, and Antonius fought among themselves for rulership of Rome and its colonies, Caesar eventually winning the office only to be assassinated shortly thereafter.

1. The women in the underworld, like the men, were figures from ancient history and mythology; those that are listed were judged to have been evil. After the death of her husband, King Ninus, Semiramis disguised herself as her son to gain the throne. Her son killed her when she tried to sleep with him. Sthenoboea lusted after her brother-in-law, Bellerophon, and committed suicide when he refused her advances. After Egypt had been defeated by the Roman forces of Octavius (later the Emperor Augustus), Cleopatra, the queen of Egypt, committed suicide by allowing herself to be bitten by asps, a kind of poisonous snake.

Where they in idle pompe, or wanton play,
Consumed had their goods, and thriftlesse howres,
And lastly throwne themselves into these heavy stowres.° *afflictions*

52

Whose case when as the carefull Dwarfe had tould,
And made ensample° of their mournefull sight *description*
Unto his maister, he no lenger° would *longer*
There dwell in perill of like° painefull plight, *similar*
But early rose, and ere that dawning light
Discovered had the world to heaven wyde,
He by a privie Posterne° tooke his flight, *secret back door*
That of no envious eyes he mote he spyde:
For doubtlesse death ensewd, if any him descryde.° *discovered*

53

Scarse could he footing find in that fowle way,
For° many corses, like a great Lay-stall° *because of/open grave*
Of murdred men which therein strowed lay,° *lay strewn*
Without remorse, or decent funerall:
Which all through that great Princesse pride did fall
And came to shamefull end. And them beside
Forth ryding underneath the castell wall,
A donghill° of dead carkases he spide, *garbage heap*
The dreadfull spectacle of that sad house of Pride.

Canto 6

From lawlesse lust by wondrous grace
fayre Una is releast:
Whom salvage nation does adore,
and learnes her wise beheast.° *teaching*

1

As when a ship, that flyes faire under saile,
An hidden rocke escaped hath unwares,
That lay in waite her wrack° for to bewaile, *destruction*
The Marriner° yet halfe amazed stares *sailor*
At perill past, and yet in doubt ne dares° *dares not*
To joy at his foole-happie° oversight: *lucky*
So doubly is distrest twixt joy and cares
The dreadlesse courage of this Elfin knight,
Having escapt so sad ensamples° in his sight. *warnings*

2

Yet sad he was that his too hastie speed
The faire Duess' had forst him leave behind;
And yet more sad, that Una his deare dreed° *revered one*
Her truth had staind with treason so unkind;° *unnatural*
Yet crime in her could never creature find,
But for his love, and for her owne selfe sake,
She wandred had from one to other Ynd,° *throughout the world*
Him for to seeke, ne ever would forsake,
Till her unwares the fierce Sans-Loy did overtake.

3

Who after Archimagoes fowle defeat,
Led her away into a forrest wilde,
And turning wrathfull fire to lustfull heat,
With beastly sin thought° her to have defilde, *decided*
And made the vassall° of his pleasures vilde. *slave*
Yet first he cast by treatie,° and by traynes,° *treaty/tricks*
Her to perswade, that stubborne fort° to yilde: *i.e., her chastity*
For greater conquest of hard love he gaynes,
That workes it to his will, then he that it constraines.° *forces*

4

With fawning wordes he courted her a while,
And looking lovely,° and oft sighing sore, *amorously*
Her constant hart did tempt with diverse guile:° *various deceits*
But wordes, and lookes, and sighes she did abhore,
As rocke of Diamond stedfast evermore.
Yet for to feed his fyrie lustfull eye,
He snatcht the vele, that hong her face before;
Then gan her beautie shine, as brightest skye,
And burnt his beastly hart t'efforce° her chastitye. *to force*

5

So when he saw his flatt'ring arts to fayle,
And subtile engines bet from batteree,[1]
With greedy force he gan the fort assayle,° *attack*
Whereof he weend° possessed soone to bee, *believed*
And win rich spoile of ransackt chastetee.
Ah heavens, that do this hideous act behold,
And heavenly virgin thus outraged° see, *violated*
How can ye vengeance just so long withhold,
And hurle not flashing flames upon that Paynim bold?

6

The pitteous maiden carefull° comfortlesse, *grief-stricken*
Does throw out thrilling° shriekes, and shrieking cryes, *piercing*
The last vaine helpe of womens great distresse,
And with loud plaints° importuneth the skyes, *laments*
That molten° starres do drop like weeping eyes; *melting*
And Phoebus flying so most shamefull sight,
His blushing face in foggy cloud implyes,° *hides*
And hides for shame. What wit of mortall wight
Can now devise to quit a thrall from such a plight?

7

Eternall providence exceeding thought,
Where none appeares can make her selfe a way:
A wondrous way it for this Lady wrought,
From Lyons clawes to pluck the griped° pray. *trapped*
Her shrill outcryes and shriekes so loud did bray,
That all the woodes and forestes did resownd;
A troupe of Faunes and Satyres° far away *woodland deities*

1. I.e., Sans-Loy's clever devices are overcome by the success of Una's "battery" or repulses.

Within the wood were dauncing in a rownd,° *circle*
Whiles old Sylvanus° slept in shady arber sownd.° *a wood god/soundly*

8

Who when they heard that pitteous strained voice,
In hast forsooke° their rurall meriment, *abandoned*
And ran towards the far rebownded° noyce, *reverberating*
To weet,° what wight so loudly did lament. *discover*
Unto the place they come incontinent:° *headlong*
Whom when the raging Sarazin espide,
A rude, misshapen, monstrous rablement,
Whose like he never saw, he durst° not bide,° *dared/stay*
But got his ready steed, and fast away gan ride.

9

The wyld woodgods arrived in the place,
There find the virgin dolefull desolate,
With ruffled rayments, and faire blubbred° face, *tear-stained*
As her outrageous foe had left her late,° *recently*
And trembling yet through feare of former hate;
All stand amazed at so uncouth° sight, *strange*
And gin to pittie her unhappie state,
All stand astonied° at her beautie bright, *amazed*
In their rude eyes unworthie of so wofull plight.

10

She more amaz'd, in double dread doth dwell;
And every tender part for feare does shake:
As when a greedie Wolfe through hunger fell° *deadly*
A seely° Lambe farre from the flocke does take, *innocent*
Of whom he meanes his bloudie feast to make,
A Lyon spyes fast running towards him,
The innocent pray in hast he does forsake,
Which quit° from death yet quakes in every lim° *rescued/limb*
With chaunge of feare, to see the Lyon looke so grim.

11

Such fearefull fit assaid° her trembling hart, *assailed*
Ne word to speake, ne joynt to move she had:
The salvage° nation[2] feele her secret smart, *wild*
And read her sorrow in her count'nance sad;
Their frowning forheads with rough hornes yclad,
And rusticke horror all a side doe lay,° *put away*
And gently grenning,° shew a semblance° glad *grinning/expression*
To comfort her, and feare to put away,
Their backward bent knees teach her humbly to obay.[3]

12

The doubtfull Damzell dare not yet commit
Her single person to their barbarous truth,° *allegiance*
But still twixt feare and hope amazd does sit,

2. I.e., the wood gods.
3. The fauns and satyrs have goat legs, so when they kneel before Una, their legs bend backward. It is not clear who teaches whom to obey in this line: their own act of kneeling may be teaching the fauns and satyrs to obey Una, or their awkward gestures may be teaching Una to obey them and put away her fear.

Late° learnd what harme to hastie trust ensu'th,° *recently/follows*
They in compassion of her tender youth,
And wonder of her beautie soveraine,
Are wonne with pitty and unwonted° ruth, *unaccustomed*
And all prostrate upon the lowly plaine,° *ground*
Do kisse her feete, and fawne on her with count'nance faine.° *glad expressions*

13

Their harts she ghesseth by their humble guise,
And yieldes her to extremitie of time;[4]
So from the ground she fearelesse doth arise,
And walketh forth without suspect° of crime:° *fear/evil*
They all as glad, as birdes of joyous Prime,° *spring*
Thence lead her forth, about her dauncing round,
Shouting, and singing all a shepheards ryme,
And with greene braunches strowing° all the ground, *strewing*
Do worship her, as Queene, with olive girlond cround.

14

And all the way their merry pipes they sound,
That all the woods with doubled Eccho ring,
And with their horned feet do weare° the ground, *tread*
Leaping like wanton° kids in pleasant Spring. *playful*
So towards old Sylvanus they her bring;
Who with the noyse awaked, commeth out,
To weet° the cause, his weake steps governing,° *discover/guiding*
And aged limbs on Cypresse stadle stout,[5]
And with an yvie twyne° his wast is girt° about. *vine/wrapped*

15

Far off he wonders, what them makes so glad,
Or° Bacchus[6] merry fruit° they did inuent, *whether/grapes*
Or Cybeles[7] franticke rites have made them mad;
They drawing nigh, unto their God° present *Sylvanus*
That flowre of faith and beautie excellent.
The God himselfe vewing that mirrhour rare,
Stood long amazd, and burnt in his intent;
His owne faire Dryope[8] now he thinkes not faire,
And Pholoe fowle, when her to this he doth compaire.

16

The woodborne° people fall before her flat, *born of the woods*
And worship her as Goddesse of the wood;
And old Sylvanus selfe bethinkes not,° what *cannot tell*
To thinke of wight so faire, but gazing stood,
In doubt to deeme° her borne of earthly brood; *believe*
Sometimes Dame Venus selfe he seemes to see,

4. I.e., she submits to the necessities imposed on her by circumstances and loses her fear of the fauns and satyrs.

5. Sylvanus uses a cane made from the trunk of a cypress tree.

6. The Roman god of wine; he is associated with both riot and fertility. Sylvanus suspects the fauns and satyrs of having discovered and drunk too much wine.

7. The goddess of grain and the harvest; the spring festival held in her honor was a fertility rite that resembled a bacchanalia.

8. At this point, Una is still unveiled from her encounter with Sans-Loy. When Sylvanus views her, he sees a mirror reflecting heavenly faith and beauty and hence considers his beloved nymphs, Dryope and Pholoe, ugly by comparison.

But Venus never had so sober° mood; *serious*
Sometimes Diana he her takes to bee,
But misseth bow, and shaftes,° and buskins° to her knee. *arrows/boots*

17

By vew of her he ginneth to revive
His ancient love, and dearest Cyparisse,[9]
And calles to mind his pourtraiture aliue,° *living image*
How faire he was, and yet not faire to this,
And how he slew with glauncing dart amisse
A gentle Hynd, the which the lovely boy
Did love as life, above all worldly blisse;
For griefe whereof the lad n'ould after° joy, *would never afterward*
But pynd° away in anguish and selfe-wild° annoy. *wasted/self-willed*

18

The wooddy Nymphes, faire Hamadryades° *tree spirits*
Her to behold do thither runne apace,
And all the troupe of light-foot Naiades,° *water nymphs*
Flocke all about to see her lovely face:
But° when they vewed have her heavenly grace, *except for*
They envie her in their malitious mind,
And fly away for feare of fowle disgrace:
But all the Satyres scorne their woody kind,
And henceforth nothing faire, but her on earth they find.

19

Glad of such lucke, the luckelesse lucky maid,
Did her content to please their feeble eyes,
And long time with that salvage people staid,
To gather breath in many miseries.
During which time her gentle wit she plyes,° *employs*
To teach them truth, which worshipt her in vaine,
And made her th'Image of Idolatryes;
But when their bootlesse° zeale she did restraine *misguided*
From her own worship, they her Asse would worship fayn.° *gladly*

20

It fortuned° a noble warlike knight *happened*
By just occasion to that forrest came,
To seeke his kindred, and the lignage right,° *proper lineage*
From whence he tooke his well deserved name:
He had in armes abroad wonne muchell° fame, *much*
And fild far landes with glorie of his might,
Plaine, faithfull, true, and enimy of shame,
And ever lou'd to fight for Ladies right,
But in vaine glorious frayes° he litle did delight. *battles*

21

A Satyres sonne yborne in forrest wyld,
By straunge adventure as it did betyde,° *happen*

9. Cyparisse was a boy whom Sylvanus loved. Here Spenser recounts how Sylvanus accidentally killed Cyparisse's doe, after which the boy became so sad that Apollo turned him into a cypress to relieve his distress.

And there begotten of a Lady myld,
Faire Thyamis the daughter of Labryde,[1]
That was in sacred bands of wedlocke tyde
To Therion, a loose unruly swayne;° *fellow*
Who had more joy to raunge the forrest wyde,
And chase the salvage beast with busie payne,° *painstakingly*
Then° serve his Ladies love, and wast in pleasures vayne. *than*

22

The forlone mayd did with loves longing burne,
And could not lacke° her lovers company, *do without*
But to the wood she goes, to serve her turne,° *satisfy her desire*
And seeke her spouse, that from her still° does fly, *always*
And followes other game and venery:
A Satyre chaunst her wandring for to find,
And kindling coles of lust in brutish eye,
The loyall links of wedlocke did unbind,
And made her person thrall° unto his beastly kind. *prisoner*

23

So long in secret cabin there he held
Her captive to his sensuall desire,
Till that with timely fruit her belly sweld,
And bore a boy unto that salvage sire:
Then home he suffred her for to retire,° *return*
For ransome leaving him the late borne childe;
Whom till to ryper yeares he gan aspire,° *began to grow*
He noursled up° in life and manners wilde, *raised*
Emongst wild beasts and woods, from lawes of men exilde.

24

For all he taught the tender ymp,° was but *child*
To banish cowardize and bastard feare;
His trembling hand he would him force to put
Upon the Lyon and the rugged Beare,
And from the she Beares teats her whelps° to teare; *cubs*
And eke wyld roring Buls he would him make
To tame, and ryde their backes not made to beare;° *be ridden*
And the Robuckes° in flight to overtake, *bucks*
That every beast for feare of him did fly and quake.

25

Thereby so fearelesse, and so fell° he grew, *deadly*
That his owne sire and maister of his guise° *behavior*
Did often tremble at his horrid vew,
And oft for dread of hurt would him advise,
The angry beasts not rashly to despise,
Nor too much to provoke; for he would learne° *teach*
The Lyon stoup° to him in lowly wise, *to bow*
(A lesson hard) and make the Libbard° sterne *leopard*
Leave roaring, when in rage he for revenge did earne.° *yearn*

1. The Greek names reveal the natures of these characters: Thyamis means "passion"; Labryde means "turbulence" or "greed"; and Therion means "wild beast."

26

And for to make his powre approved° more, *apparent*
Wyld beasts in yron yokes he would compell;° *command*
The spotted Panther, and the tusked Bore,
The Pardale° swift, and the Tigre cruell; *female leopard*
The Antelope, and Wolfe both fierce and fell;
And them constraine in equall teme to draw.° *harness together*
Such joy he had, their stubborne harts to quell,° *subdue*
And sturdie courage tame with dreadfull aw,
That his beheast° they feared, as a tyrans° law. *command/tyrant's*

27

His loving mother came upon a day
Unto the woods, to see her little sonne;
And chaunst unwares to meet him in the way,
After his sportes, and cruell pastime donne,
When after him a Lyonesse did runne,
That roaring all with rage, did lowd requere° *demand*
Her children deare, whom he away had wonne:° *taken*
The Lyon whelpes she saw how he did beare,
And lull° in rugged° armes, withouten childish feare. *cradle/hairy*

28

The fearefull Dame° all quaked at the sight, *his mother*
And turning backe, gan fast to fly away,
Untill with love revokt° from vaine affright, *restrained*
She hardly yet perswaded was to stay,
And then to him these womanish words gan say;
Ah Satyrane,[2] my dearling, and my joy,
For love of me leave off° this dreadfull play; *stop*
To dally thus with death, is no fit toy,° *pastime*
Go find some other play-fellowes, mine own sweet boy.

29

In these and like delights of bloudy game
He trayned was, till ryper yeares he raught,° *reached*
And there abode,° whilst any beast of name° *lived/known*
Walkt in that forest, whom he had not taught
To feare his force: and then his courage haught° *haughty*
Desird of forreine foemen to be knowne,
And far abroad for straunge° adventures sought: *foreign*
In which his might was never overthrowne,
But through all Faery lond his famous worth was blown.° *broadcast*

30

Yet evermore it was his manner faire,
After long labours and adventures spent,
Unto those native woods for to repaire,
To see his sire and ofspring auncient.
And now he thither came for like intent;
Where he unwares the fairest Una found,
Straunge Lady, in so straunge habiliment,° *surroundings*

2. Like a satyr.

Teaching the Satyres, which her sat around,
Trew sacred lore, which from her sweet lips did redound.

31

He wondred at her wisedome heavenly rare,
Whose like in womens wit he never knew;
And when her curteous deeds he did compare,
Gan her admire, and her sad sorrowes rew,
Blaming of Fortune, which such troubles threw,
And joyd to make proofe of° her° crueltie *test/Fortune's*
On gentle Dame, so hurtlesse, and so trew:
Thenceforth he kept her goodly company,
And learnd her discipline of faith and veritie.

32

But she all vowd unto the Redcrosse knight,
His wandring perill closely did lament,
Ne in this new acquaintaunce could delight,
But her deare heart with anguish did torment,
And all her wit in secret counsels spent,
How to escape. At last in privie wise° *secretly*
To Satyrane she shewed her intent;
Who glad to gain such favour, gan devise,
How with that pensive Maid he best might thence arise.° *depart*

33

So on a day when Satyres all were gone,
To do their service to Sylvanus old,
The gentle virgin left behind alone
He led away with courage stout and bold.
Too late it was, to Satyres to be told,
Or ever hope recover her againe:
In vaine he seekes that having cannot hold.
So fast he carried her with carefull paine,° *skill*
That they the woods are past, and come now to the plaine.

34

The better part now of the lingring day,
They traveild had, when as they farre espide
A wearie wight forwandring° by the way, *wandering*
And towards him they gan in hast to ride,
To weet° of newes, that did abroad betide,° *learn/occur*
Or tydings of her knight of the Redcrosse.
But he them spying, gan to turne aside,
For feare as seemd, or for some feigned losse;
More greedy they of newes, fast towards him do crosse.

35

A silly° man, in simple weedes forworne,° *simple/old clothes*
And soild with dust of the long dried way;
His sandales were with toilesome travell torne,
And face all tand with scorching sunny ray,
As he had traveild many a sommers day,
Through boyling sands of Arabie and Ynde;° *India*
And in his hand a Iacobs staffe,° to stay *pilgrim's staff*

His wearie limbes upon: and eke behind,
His scrip° did hang, in which his needments he did bind. *bag*

36

The knight approching nigh, of him inquerd° *asked*
Tydings of warre, and of adventures new;
But warres, nor new adventures none he herd.
Then Una gan to aske, if ought he knew,
Or heard abroad of that her champion trew,
That in his armour bare a croslet° red. *small cross*
Aye me, Deare dame (quoth he) well may I rew
To tell the sad sight, which mine eies have red:° *seen*
These eyes did see that knight both living and eke ded.

37

That cruell word her tender hart so thrild,° *pierced*
That suddein cold did runne through every vaine,
And stony horrour all her sences fild
With dying fit,° that downe she fell for paine. *deathlike swoon*
The knight her lightly° reared° up againe, *quickly / lifted*
And comforted with curteous kind reliefe:
Then wonne° from death,[3] she bad° him tellen plaine *brought back / ordered*
The further processe of her hidden griefe;
The lesser pangs can beare, who hath endur'd the chiefe.° *greater*

38

Then gan the Pilgrim thus, I chaunst this day,
This fatall day, that shall I ever rew,
To see two knights in travell° on my way *traveling*
(A sory sight) arraung'd° in battell new,[4] *engaged*
Both breathing vengeaunce, both of wrathfull hew:
My fearefull flesh did tremble at their strife,
To see their blades so greedily imbrew,° *stain themselves*
That drunke with bloud, yet thristed after life:
What more? the Redcrosse knight was slaine with Paynim knife.

39

Ah dearest Lord (quoth she) how might that bee,
And he the stoutest° knight, that ever wonne? *sturdiest*
Ah dearest dame (quoth he) how might° I see *could*
The thing, that might not be, and yet was donne?
Where is (said Satyrane) that Paynims sonne,
That him of life, and us of joy hath reft?° *deprived*
Not far away (quoth he) he hence doth wonne° *stay*
Foreby° a fountaine, where I late him left *nearly*
Washing his bloody wounds, that through° the steele were cleft.° *by / cut*

40

Therewith the knight thence marched forth in hast,
Whiles Una with huge heavinesse opprest,° *overcome*

3. Recovered from her swoon, Una asks the old man to continue telling her the details of the tale as yet unknown to her that will cause her further grief.

4. The old man (who is, in fact, Archimago) is telling the story of Archimago's battle with Sans-Loy; however, he fabricates a second round of the battle here.

Could not for sorrow follow him so fast;
And soone he came, as he the place had ghest,° *guessed*
Whereas° that Pagan proud him selfe did rest, *where*
In secret shadow by a fountaine side:
Even he it was, that earst° would have supprest *previously*
Faire Una: whom when Satyrane espide,
With fowle reprochfull words he boldly him defide.° *challenged*

41

And said, Arise thou cursed Miscreaunt,° *heathen*
That hast with knightlesse guile and trecherous train° *tricks*
Faire knighthood fowly shamed, and doest vaunt° *boast*
That good knight of the Redcrosse to have slain:
Arise, and with like treason° now maintain° *treachery / defend*
Thy guilty wrong, or else thee guilty yield.° *admit*
The Sarazin this hearing, rose amain,° *at once*
And catching up in hast his three square° shield, *triangular*
And shining helmet, soone him buckled° to the field. *prepared*

42

And drawing nigh him said, Ah misborne Elfe,
In evill houre thy foes thee hither sent,
Anothers wrongs to wreake upon° thy selfe: *bring down*
Yet ill° thou blamest me, for having blent° *wrongly / defiled*
My name with guile and traiterous intent;
That Redcrosse knight, perdie,° I never slew, *by God*
But had he beene, where earst° his armes were lent,° *previously / borrowed*
Th'enchaunter vaine his errour should not rew:
But thou his errour shalt, I hope now proven trew.[5]

43

Therewith they gan, both furious and fell,
To thunder blowes, and fiersly to assaile
Each other bent° his enimy to quell,° *intending / subdue*
That with their force they perst both plate and maile,° *types of armor*
And made wide furrowes in their fleshes fraile,
That it would pitty° any living eie. *inspire pity in*
Large floods of bloud adowne their sides did raile;° *pour*
But floods of bloud could not them satisfie:
Both hungred after death: both chose to win, or die.

44

So long they fight, and fell revenge pursue,
That fainting each, themselves to breathen let,° *to catch their breath*
And oft refreshed, battell oft renue:
As when two Bores with rancling malice met,
Their gory° sides fresh bleeding fiercely fret,° *gored / wound*
Til breathlesse both them selves aside retire,
Where foming wrath, their cruell tuskes they whet,° *sharpen*
And trample th'earth, the whiles they may respire;° *so they can breathe*
Then backe to fight againe, new breathed and entire.° *refreshed*

5. Sans-Loy refers to the action in 3.33–39. He denies killing the Redcrosse Knight, but he also states that had the Redcrosse Knight, and not Archimago, been wearing his own armor, then Sans-Loy would have killed him, and Archimago would not have to regret his, Sans-Loy's, error. But Sans-Loy will make good this error by engaging in judicial combat with Satyrane.

45

So fiersly, when these knights had breathed° once, *rested*
They gan to fight returne, increasing more
Their puissant° force, and cruell rage attonce,° *powerful/at once*
With heaped° strokes more hugely, then before, *increased*
That with their drerie° wounds and bloudy gore *bloody*
They both deformed,° scarsely could be known. *disfigured*
By this sad Una fraught° with anguish sore, *afflicted*
Led with their noise, which through the aire was thrown,
Arriv'd, where they in erth° their fruitles° bloud had sown. *on the ground/futile*

46

Whom all so soone as that proud Sarazin
Espide, he gan revive the memory
Of his lewd lusts, and late attempted sin,
And left the doubtfull° battell hastily, *undecided*
To catch her, newly offred to his eie:
But Satyrane with strokes him turning, staid,
And sternely bad him other businesse plie,° *attend*
Then hunt the steps of pure unspotted Maid:
Wherewith he° all enrag'd, these bitter speaches said. *Sans-Loy*

47

O foolish faeries sonne, what furie mad
Hath thee incenst,° to hast thy dolefull fate? *enraged*
Were it not better, I that Lady had,
Then that thou hadst repented° it too late? *regretted*
Most sencelesse man he, that himselfe doth hate,
To love another. Lo then for thine ayd
Here take thy lovers token on thy pate.° *head*
So they to fight; the whiles the royall Mayd
Fled farre away, of that proud Paynim sore afrayd.

48

But that false Pilgrim, which that leasing° told, *lie*
Being in deed old Archimage, did stay
In secret shadow, all this to behold,
And much rejoyced in their bloudy fray:
But when he saw the Damsell passe away
He left his stond,° and her pursewd apace,° *place/awhile*
In hope to bring her to her last decay.° *death*
But for to tell her lamentable cace,° *situation*
And eke this battels end, will need another place.

Canto 7

The Redcrosse knight is captive made
By Gyaunt proud opprest,
Prince Arthur meets with Una greatly
with those newes distrest.

1

What man so wise, what earthly wit so ware,° *alert*
As to descry° the crafty cunning traine,° *perceive/guile*
By which deceipt doth maske in visour° faire, *mask*

And cast her colours dyed deepe in graine,
To seeme like Truth, whose shape she well can faine,
And fitting gestures to her purpose frame,° *suit*
The guiltlesse man with guile to entertaine?
Great maistresse of her art was that false Dame,
The false Duessa, cloked with Fidessaes name.[1]

2

Who when returning from the drery Night,
She fownd not in that perilous house of Pryde,
Where she had left, the noble Redcrosse knight,
Her hoped pray,° she would no lenger bide,° *victim / stay*
But forth she went, to seeke him far and wide.
Ere long she fownd, whereas he wearie sate,
To rest him selfe, foreby a fountaine side,
Disarmed all of yron-coted Plate,° *armor*
And by his side his steed the grassy forage ate.

3

He feedes upon the cooling shade, and bayes° *bathes*
His sweatie forehead in the breathing wind,
Which through the trembling leaves full gently playes
Wherein the cherefull birds of sundry kind
Do chaunt sweet musick, to delight his mind:
The Witch approching gan him fairely greet,
And with reproch of carelesnesse unkind
Upbrayd,° for leaving her in place unmeet, *accused*
With fowle words tempring faire, soure gall° with hony sweet. *anger*

4

Unkindnesse past, they gan of solace treat,° *speak of pleasure*
And bathe in pleasaunce of the joyous shade,
Which shielded them against the boyling heat,
And with greene boughes decking a gloomy glade,
About the fountaine like a girlond made;
Whose bubbling wave did ever freshly well,
Ne ever would through fervent sommer fade:° *dry up*
The sacred Nymph, which therein wont to dwell,
Was out of Dianes favour, as it then befell.° *so happened*

5

The cause was this: one day when Phoebe[2] fayre
With all her band was following the chace,
This Nymph, quite tyr'd with heat of scorching ayre
Sat downe to rest in middest of the race:
The goddesse wroth gan fowly her disgrace,
And bad the waters, which from her did flow,
Be such as she her selfe was then in place.
Thenceforth her waters waxed dull and slow,
And all that drunke thereof, did faint and feeble grow.[3]

1. Duessa (duplicity) falsely bears the name Fidessa (fidelity).

2. An aspect or persona of Diana. As Diana, she is goddess of the hunt, but as Phoebe she is also goddess of the moon.

3. The nymph is transformed into a fountain whose waters cause fatigue rather than rejuvenation; paradoxically, this is a fountain that is never dry.

6

Hereof° this gentle knight unweeting was, *of this*
And lying downe upon the sandie graile,° *gravel*
Drunke of the streame, as cleare as cristall glas;
Eftsoones his manly forces gan to faile,
And mightie strong was turnd to feeble fraile.
His chaunged powres at first them selves not felt,
Till crudled° cold his corage° gan assaile, *congealing / vital powers*
And chearefull bloud in faintnesse chill did melt,
Which like a fever fit[4] through all his body swelt.° *raged*

7

Yet goodly court° he made still to his Dame, *advances*
Pourd out in loosnesse° on the grassy grownd, *licentiousness*
Both carelesse of his health, and of his fame:
Till at the last he heard a dreadfull sownd,
Which through the wood loud bellowing, did rebownd,
That all the earth for terrour seemd to shake,
And trees did tremble. Th'Elfe therewith astownd,
Upstarted lightly from his looser make,° *mate*
And his unready weapons gan in hand to take.

8

But ere he could his armour on him dight,° *put*
Or get his shield, his monstrous enimy
With sturdie steps came stalking in his sight,
An hideous Geant horrible and hye,° *tall*
That with his talnesse seemd to threat the skye,
The ground eke groned under him for dreed;
His living like saw never living eye,
Ne durst° behold:[5] his stature did exceed *nor dared*
The hight of three the tallest sonnes of mortall seed.° *men*

9

The greatest Earth his uncouth° mother was, *unnatural*
And blustring Aeolus° his boasted sire, *god of the winds*
Who with his breath, which through the world doth pas,
Her hollow womb did secretly inspire,° *impregnate*
And fild her hidden caues with stormie yre,
That she conceiv'd; and trebling° the dew time, *tripling*
In which the wombes of women do expire,° *give birth*
Brought forth this monstrous masse of earthly slime,
Puft up with emptie wind, and fild with sinfull crime.

10

So growen great through arrogant delight
Of th'high descent, whereof he was yborne,
And through presumption of his matchlesse might,
All other powres and knighthood he did scorne.[6]

4. Heat is usually associated with strength, but here, the weakening effect of the fountain, associated with coldness, turns its forces against the Knight's strength, causing him to suffer both chill and fever.

5. I.e., no living person had ever seen anything like the giant nor would even have dared to look at such a creature.

6. I.e., the giant's ancestry has caused him to grow both extremely tall and extremely proud.

Such now he marcheth to this man forlorne,
And left to losse: his stalking steps are stayde° *supported*
Upon a snaggy Oke, which he had torne
Out of his mothers bowelles, and it made
His mortall° mace,° wherewith his foemen he dismayde. *deadly/club*

11

That when the knight he spide, he gan advance
With huge force and insupportable° mayne,° *irresistible/force*
And towardes him with dreadfull fury praunce;
Who haplesse, and eke hopelesse, all in vaine
Did to him pace, sad battaile to darrayne,° *engage*
Disarmd, disgrast, and inwardly dismayde,
And eke so faint in every joynt and vaine,
Through that fraile fountaine, which him feeble made,
That scarsely could he weeld° his bootlesse° single blade. *raise/useless*

12

The Geaunt strooke so maynly° mercilesse, *forcefully*
That could have overthrowne a stony towre,
And were not heavenly grace, that him did blesse,° *preserve*
He had beene pouldred° all, as thin as flowre:° *pulverized/flour*
But he was wary of that deadly stowre,° *attack*
And lightly lept from underneath the blow:
Yet so exceeding was the villeins powre,
That with the wind it did him overthrow,
And all his sences stound,° that still he lay full low. *stunned*

13

As when that divelish yron Engin° wrought *the cannon*
In deepest Hell, and framd by Furies skill,[7]
With windy Nitre and quick Sulphur fraught,
And ramd with bullet round, ordaind to kill,
Conceiveth° fire, the heavens it doth fill *catches*
With thundring noyse, and all the ayre doth choke,
That none can breath, nor see, nor heare at will,
Through smouldry cloud of duskish° stincking smoke, *dusky*
That th'onely breath him daunts, who hath escapt the stroke.[8]

14

So daunted when the Geaunt saw the knight,[9]
His heavie hand he heaved up on hye,
And him to dust thought to have battred quight,
Untill Duessa loud to him gan crye;
O great Orgoglio,[1] greatest under skye,
O hold° thy mortall hand for Ladies sake, *stop*
Hold for my sake, and do him not to dye,

7. According to Renaissance tradition, the cannon was invented by the devil in hell. "Nitre" (potassium nitrate) and sulfur are the main ingredients of gunpowder; they are "windy" because they produce the blast that propels the cannonball through the air.

8. I.e., those who are not struck by the cannonball are overcome by the smoke.

9. I.e., when the Giant saw that the Knight was overcome by the smoke, he raised his heavy hand to beat him down completely.

1. Pride, haughtiness, disdain (Italian).

But vanquisht thine eternall bondslave make,
And me thy worthy meed unto° thy Leman° take. *as/beloved*

15

He hearkned, and did stay from further harmes,
To gayne so goodly guerdon,° as she spake: *prize*
So willingly she came into his armes,
Who her as willingly to grace did take,
And was possessed of his new found make.
Then up he tooke the slombred sencelesse corse,
And ere he could out of his swowne° awake, *swoon*
Him to his castle brought with hastie forse,
And in a Dongeon deepe him threw without remorse.

16

From that day forth Duessa was his deare,
And highly honourd in his haughtie° eye, *proud*
He gave her gold and purple pall° to weare, *robe*
And triple crowne set on her head full hye,
And her endowd with royall majestye:
Then for to make her dreaded more of men,
And peoples harts with awfull terrour tye,° *enthrall*
A monstrous beast ybred° in filthy fen° *born/swamp*
He chose, which he had kept long time in darksome den.

17

Such one it was, as that renowmed° Snake *famous*
Which great Alcides in Stremona slew,[2]
Long fostred in the filth of Lerna lake,
Whose many heads out budding ever new,
Did breed him endlesse labour to subdew:
But this same Monster much more ugly was;
For seven great heads out of his body grew,
An yron brest, and backe of scaly bras,
And all embrewd° in bloud, his eyes did shine as glas. *stained*

18

His tayle was stretched out in wondrous length,
That to the house of heavenly gods it raught,° *reached*
And with extorted° powre, and borrow'd strength, *wrongfully obtained*
The ever-burning lamps from thence it brought,
And prowdly threw to ground, as things of nought;° *worthless*
And underneath his filthy feet did tread
The sacred things, and holy heasts foretaught.° *previously taught*
Upon this dreadfull Beast with sevenfold head
He set the false Duessa, for more aw and dread.[3]

2. The "snake" Spenser is referring to is the hydra, a creature from Greek mythology with a hundred heads, that lived in the lake of Lerna and was killed by Hercules (Alcides) as one of his 12 labors. The hydra was particularly difficult for Hercules to kill because each time he cut off one of its heads, several new ones grew in its place. Hercules eventually burnt the hydra's neck after each decapitation, thus preventing new heads from sprouting up. Stremona is a river in Thrace.

3. Spenser compares the hydra with the Roman Catholic Church. The seven heads of this monster refer to the seven hills on which Rome was built, as well as the seven deadly sins. Orgoglo mounts Duessa upon the seven-headed monster to make her more dreaded and awe-inspiring. This gesture also associates Duessa with the corrupt Roman Catholic Church, which, represented by the monster, has gained its power through tyranny and defiles true Christian doctrine.

19

The wofull Dwarfe, which saw his maisters fall,
Whiles he had keeping of his grasing steed,
And valiant knight become a caytive thrall,
When all was past, tooke up his forlorne weed,° *abandoned armor*
His mightie armour, missing most at need;
His silver shield, now idle maisterlesse;
His poynant° speare, that many made to bleed, *sharp*
The ruefull moniments of heavinesse,° *tokens of grief*
And with them all departes, to tell his great distresse.

20

He had not travaild° long, when on the way *traveled*
He wofull Ladie, wofull Una met,
Fast flying from the Paynims greedy pray,[4]
Whilest Satyrane him from pursuit did let:° *hinder*
Who when her eyes she on the Dwarfe had set,
And saw the signes, that deadly tydings spake,
She fell to ground for sorrowfull regret,
And lively breath° her sad brest did forsake, *breath of life*
Yet might her pitteous hart be seene to pant and quake.

21

The messenger of so unhappie newes
Would faine° have dyde: dead was his hart within, *rather*
Yet outwardly some little comfort shewes:
At last recovering hart, he does begin
To rub her temples, and to chaufe° her chin, *rub*
And every tender part does tosse and turne:
So hardly° he the flitted life does win, *with difficulty*
Unto her native prison to retourne:[5]
Then gins° her grieved ghost thus to lament and mourne. *begins*

22

Ye dreary instruments of dolefull° sight,[6] *sorrowful*
That doe this deadly spectacle behold,
Why do ye lenger° feed on loathed light, *longer*
Or liking find to gaze on earthly mould,° *shapes*
Sith cruell fates[7] the carefull threeds° unfould, *threads*
The which my life and love together tyde?
Now let the stony dart of senselesse cold
Perce to my hart, and pas through every side,
And let eternall night so sad sight fro° me hide. *from*

23

O lightsome day, the lampe of highest Jove,
First made by him, mens wandring wayes to guyde,
When darknesse he in deepest dongeon drove,
Henceforth thy hated face for ever hyde,

4. I.e., Una is flying from Sans-Loy, who greedily has made her his prey or victim (see 6.42–47). The Dwarf meets Una at this point, while Satyrane is distracting Sans-Loy from his pursuit of her.

5. The native prison of Una's spirit is her body.

6. Here Una is addressing her eyes.

7. Mythical arbiters of human life, who measure out the life (or fate) of every individual in threads mounted on spinning wheels.

And shut up heavens windowes shyning wyde:
For earthly sight can nought but sorrow breed,
And late repentance, which shall long abyde.° *persist*
Mine eyes no more on vanitie shall feed,
But seeled up with death, shall have their deadly meed.° *reward of death*

24

Then downe againe she fell unto the ground;
But he her quickly reared° up againe: *raised*
Thrise did she sinke adowne in deadly swownd,
And thrise he her reviv'd with busie paine:
At last when life recover'd had the raine,° *rein, control*
And over-wrestled his strong enemie,
With foltring tong,° and trembling every vaine, *faltering tongue*
Tell on (quoth she) the wofull Tragedie,
The which these reliques sad present unto mine eie.

25

Tempestuous fortune hath spent all her spight,
And thrilling sorrow throwne his utmost dart;
Thy sad tongue cannot tell more heavy plight,
Then that I feele, and harbour in mine hart:
Who hath endur'd the whole, can beare each part.
If death it be, it is not the first wound,[8]
That launched° hath my brest with bleeding smart.° *pierced/wound*
Begin, and end the bitter balefull stound;° *wretched situation*
If lesse, then° that I feare, more favour I have found.[9] *than*

26

Then gan the Dwarfe the whole discourse° declare, *story*
The subtill traines° of Archimago old; *tricks*
The wanton loves of false Fidessa faire,
Bought with the bloud of vanquisht Paynim bold:
The wretched payre° transform'd to treen mould;° *pair/tree shape*
The house of Pride, and perils round about;
The combat, which he with Sans-Joy did hould;
The lucklesse conflict with the Gyant stout,° *sturdy*
Wherein captiv'd, of life or death he stood in doubt.

27

She heard with patience all unto the end,
And strove to maister sorrowfull assay,° *grief*
Which greater grew, the more she did contend,° *struggle*
And almost rent her tender hart in tway;° *two*
And love fresh coles unto her fire did lay:
For greater love, the greater is the losse.
Was never Ladie loved dearer day,
Then she did love the knight of the Redcrosse;[1]
For whose deare sake so many troubles her did tosse.° *suffer*

8. I.e., if the Redcrosse Knight has met his death, this would not be the first knight who died attempting to help Una with her quest, and therefore this would not be the first time that Una has felt the pain of learning of such a death.

9. I.e., if what the Dwarf has to tell is less terrible than Una fears, she will consider herself lucky.

1. I.e., there was never a lady who loved life itself more than Una loved the Redcrosse Knight.

28

At last when fervent° sorrow slaked° was, *burning/quenched*
She up arose, resolving him to find
A live or dead: and forward forth doth pas,° *proceed*
All as the Dwarfe the way to her assynd:° *indicated*
And evermore in constant carefull mind
She fed her wound with fresh renewed bale;° *bitterness*
Long tost with stormes, and bet° with bitter wind, *beat*
High over hils, and low adowne the dale,° *valley*
She wandred many a wood, and measurd° many a vale.° *crossed/valley*

29

At last she chaunced by good hap° to meet *luck*
A goodly knight, faire marching by the way
Together with his Squire, arayed meet:° *well-dressed*
His glitterand armour shined farre away,
Like glauncing° light of Phoebus brightest ray; *dazzling*
From top to toe no place appeared bare,
That deadly dint° of steele endanger may: *stroke*
Athwart° his brest a bauldrick brave° he ware, *across/splendid belt*
That shynd, like twinkling stars, with stons most pretious rare.

30

And in the midst thereof one pretious stone
Of wondrous worth, and eke of wondrous mights,° *powers*
Shapt like a Ladies head, exceeding shone,
Like Hesperus[2] emongst the lesser lights,
And strove for to amaze° the weaker sights; *dazzle*
Thereby his mortall° blade full comely hong *deadly*
In yvory sheath, ycarv'd with curious slights;° *strange designs*
Whose hilts were burnisht° gold, and handle strong *polished*
Of mother pearle, and buckled with a golden tong.° *pin*

31

His haughtie° helmet, horrid° all with gold, *tall/encrusted*
Both glorious brightnesse, and great terrour bred;
For all the crest a Dragon did enfold
With greedie pawes, and over all did spred
His golden wings: his dreadfull hideous hed
Close couched° on the bever,° seem'd to throw *crouched/visor*
From flaming mouth bright sparkles fierie red,
That suddeine horror to faint° harts did show; *weak*
And scaly tayle was stretcht adowne his backe full low.

32

Upon the top of all his loftie crest,
A bunch of haires discolourd diversly,° *of many colors*
With sprincled pearle, and gold full richly drest,
Did shake, and seem'd to daunce for jollity,
Like to an Almond tree ymounted hye
On top of greene Selinis[3] all alone,

2. The evening star, associated with Venus. The comparison of the stone on Arthur's breast to Venus suggests that love is central in his quest.

3. From *palmosa Selinis* ("palmy Selinis"), a town in Italy. Spenser suggests that the knight's helmet is topped with palms, signifying victory in battle. This helmet, decorated with a dragon, identifies the knight as Prince Arthur, whose father, Uther Pendragon, was so named because he carried a golden dragon to war with him. "Pendragon" literally means "dragon's head."

With blossomes brave bedecked° daintily; *splendidly ornamented*
Whose tender locks do tremble every one
At every little breath, that under heaven is blowne.

33

His warlike shield all closely cover'd° was, *hidden*
Ne might of mortall eye be ever seene;
Not made of steele, nor of enduring bras,
Such earthly mettals soone consumed bene:[4]
But all of Diamond perfect pure and cleene
It framed was, one massie entire mould,° *solid piece*
Hewen° out of Adamant° rocke with engines keene,° *cut/diamond/sharp*
That point of speare it never percen could,
Ne dint° of direfull° sword divide the substance would. *stroke/dreadful*

34

The same to wight° he never wont disclose,[5] *creature*
But when as monsters huge he would dismay,
Or daunt° unequall armies of his foes, *vanquish*
Or when the flying heavens he would affray;° *frighten*
For so exceeding shone his glistring ray,
That Phoebus golden face it did attaint,
As when a cloud his beames doth over-lay;
And silver Cynthia wexed pale and faint,
As when her face is staynd with magicke arts° constraint. *witchcraft*

35

No magicke arts hereof had any might,
Nor bloudie wordes of bold Enchaunters call,
But all that was not such, as seemd in sight,
Before that shield did fade, and suddeine fall:[6]
And when him list the raskall routes appall,[7]
Men into stones therewith he could transmew,° *transform*
And stones to dust, and dust to nought at all;
And when him list the prouder lookes subdew,
He would them gazing blind, or turne to other hew.[8]

36

Ne let it seeme, that credence this exceedes,[9]
For he that made the same, was knowne right well
To have done much more admirable deedes.
It Merlin[1] was, which whylome° did excell *formerly*
All living wightes in might° of magicke spell: *power*
Both shield, and sword, and armour all he wrought
For this young Prince, when first to armes he fell;

4. I.e., steel or brass would soon have been destroyed or disintegrated. The diamond will last forever.
5. Arthur never shows his diamond to anyone except when he uses it to overcome his enemies, since it is too dazzling. In this respect, Arthur's diamond functions much like Una's face, whose truth and beauty are so brilliant that she wears a veil to cover it.
6. All that was false, i.e., that was not what it appeared to be, was vanquished in the presence of Arthur's shield.
7. When Arthur wished to subdue vulgar mobs, he would turn them to stone.
8. When Arthur wished to subdue his more elevated opponents, he would blind them.
9. Let it not be thought that this is beyond belief.
1. A magician and prophet in the court of Arthur's father. He created the shield, sword, and armor worn by the young Prince Arthur. By commenting that Arthur's armor still exists in Faerie Land, Spenser suggests that Arthur's virtue lives on in England and may be discovered through faith.

But when he dyde, the Faerie Queene it brought
To Faerie lond, where yet it may be seene, if sought.

37

A gentle youth, his dearely loved Squire
His speare of heben wood° behind him bare, *ebony*
Whose harmefull head,° thrice heated in the fire, *point*
Had riven many a brest with pikehead° square;° *spear tip / accurately*
A goodly person, and could menage° faire *manage a horse*
His stubborne steed with curbed canon° bit, *a kind of bit*
Who under him did trample as the aire,
And chauft,° that any on his backe should sit; *annoyed*
The yron rowels° into frothy fome he bit. *part of the bit*

38

When as this knight nigh to the Ladie drew,
With lovely court° he gan her entertaine; *attention*
But when he heard her answeres loth,° he knew *reluctant*
Some secret sorrow did her heart distraine:° *afflict*
Which to allay,° and calme her storming paine, *sooth*
Faire feeling words he wisely gan display,
And for her humour fitting purpose faine,[2]
To tempt the cause it selfe for to bewray;° *reveal*
Wherewith emmou'd, these bleeding words she gan to say.

39

What worlds delight, or joy of living speach
Can heart, so plung'd in sea of sorrowes deepe,
And heaped with so huge misfortunes, reach?
The carefull cold beginneth for to creepe,
And in my heart his yron arrow steepe,° *immerse*
Soone as I thinke upon my bitter bale:° *sorrows*
Such helplesse harmes yts° better hidden keepe, *it is*
Then rip up griefe, where it may not availe,° *avail*
My last left comfort is, my woes to weepe and waile.

40

Ah Ladie deare, quoth then the gentle knight,
Well may I weene,° your griefe is wondrous great; *know*
For wondrous great griefe groneth in my spright,
Whiles thus I heare you of your sorrowes treat.° *tell*
But wofull Ladie let me you intrete,° *entreat*
For to unfold the anguish of your hart:
Mishaps are maistred° by advice discrete, *mastered*
And counsell° mittigates the greatest smart; *advice*
Found never helpe, who never would his hurts impart.[3]

41

O but (quoth she) great griefe will not be tould,
And can more easily be thought, then said.
Right so; (quoth he) but he, that never would,
Could never: will to might gives greatest aid.[4]
But griefe (quoth she) does greater grow displaid,° *when displayed*

2. Arthur chooses words more appropriate to Una's sadness.
3. He who never tells his woes will never find a remedy.
4. Desire to overcome adversity is the greatest help. Arthur is preventing Una from falling into a state of hopeless despair and helping her to reaffirm her faith.

If then it find not helpe, and breedes despaire.
Despaire breedes not (quoth he) where faith is staid.° *strong*
No faith so fast° (quoth she) but flesh does paire.° *firm/weaken*
Flesh may empaire° (quoth he) but reason can repaire. *impair*

42

His goodly reason, and well guided speach
So deepe did settle in her gratious thought,
That her perswaded to disclose the breach,° *wound*
Which love and fortune in her heart had wrought,
And said; Faire Sir, I hope good hap° hath brought *luck*
You to inquire the secrets of my griefe,
Or that your wisedome will direct my thought,
Or that your prowesse° can me yield reliefe: *valor*
Then heare the storie sad, which I shall tell you briefe.

43

The forlorne Maiden, whom your eyes have seene
The laughing stocke of fortunes mockeries,
Am th'only daughter of a King and Queene,
Whose parents deare, whilest equall° destinies *impartial*
Did runne about,° and their felicities *run their course*
The favourable heavens did not envy,
Did spread their rule through all the territories,
Which Phison and Euphrates floweth by,
And Gehons golden waves doe wash continually.[5]

44

Till that their cruell cursed enemy,
An huge great Dragon[6] horrible in sight,
Bred in the loathly lakes of Tartary,° *Hell*
With murdrous ravine,° and devouring might *violence*
Their kingdome spoild, and countrey wasted quight:
Themselves, for feare into his jawes to fall,
He forst to castle strong to take their flight,
Where fast embard° in mightie brasen° wall, *imprisoned/brass*
He has them now foure yeres besiegd to make them thrall.

45

Full many knights adventurous and stout
Have enterprizd° that Monster to subdew; *undertaken*
From every coast that heaven walks about,
Have thither come the noble Martiall[7] crew,
That famous hard atchievements still pursew,
Yet never any could that girlond win,
But all still shronke, and still he greater grew:
All they for want of faith, or guilt of sin,
The pitteous pray of his fierce crueltie have bin.[8]

5. Una's parents are Adam and Eve, and the territory that they govern is Eden. The Phison, Euphrates, and Gehon are three of the four rivers surrounding Eden and were thought to water the entire world.

6. The dragon is Satan. After the Fall, Adam and Eve were exiled from Eden. The "four years" that Spenser refers to may figuratively represent the 4,000 years that, according to the Geneva Bible, passed between the Fall and the birth of Christ.

7. This stanza refers to the many knights ("the noble Martiall crew") who have undertaken to assist Una in her quest to overcome the Dragon and rescue her parents.

8. Until now, the knights have all failed in their quest because they have lacked faith or have succumbed to sin and have thus become victims of the Dragon's cruelty.

46

At last yledd° with farre reported praise, *led by*
Which flying fame throughout the world had spred,
Of doughtie° knights, whom Faery land did raise, *worthy*
That noble order hight of Maidenhed,° *virginity*
Forthwith to court of Gloriane I sped,
Of Gloriane great Queene of glory bright,
Whose kingdomes seat Cleopolis[9] is red,° *named*
There to obtaine some such redoubted° knight, *formidable*
That Parents deare from tyrants powre deliver might.

47

It was my chance (my chance was faire and good)
There for to find a fresh unproved° knight, *untried in battle*
Whose manly hands imbrew'd° in guiltie blood *stained*
Had never bene, ne ever by his might
Had throwne to ground the unregarded right:[1]
Yet of his prowesse° proofe he since hath made *virtue*
(I witnesse am) in many a cruell fight;
The groning ghosts of many one dismaide° *defeated*
Have felt the bitter dint of his avenging blade.

48

And ye[2] the forlorne reliques of his powre,
His byting sword, and his devouring speare,
Which have endured many a dreadfull stowre,° *conflict*
Can speake his prowesse, that did earst° you beare, *formerly*
And well could rule: now he hath left you heare,
To be the record of his ruefull losse,
And of my dolefull disaventurous° deare: *unfortunate*
O heavie record of the good Redcrosse,
Where have you left your Lord, that could so well you tosse?° *brandish*

49

Well hoped I, and faire beginnings had,
That he my captive langour[3] should redeeme,
Till all unweeting,° an Enchaunter bad *unknown to the knight*
His sence abusd,° and made him to misdeeme° *distorted/misjudge*
My loyalty, not such as it did seeme;[4]
That rather death desire, then° such despight.° *than/outrage*
Be judge ye heavens, that all things right esteeme,
How I him lov'd, and love with all my might,
So thought I eke of him, and thinke I thought aright.

50

Thenceforth me desolate he quite forsooke,
To wander, where wilde fortune would me lead,
And other bywaies he himselfe betooke,
Where never foot of living wight did tread,

9. The city of fame or glory where the Faerie Queene lives. The knights of her court belong to the order of the "Maidenhed," or virginity, an order that reflects the Faerie Queene's own virtue as well as that of Queen Elizabeth I, who was known as the "virgin queen."

1. The right for which he had no regard or respect; on the contrary, the Redcrosse Knight promotes and protects the right.

2. Here Una is addressing the Redcrosse Knight's armor.

3. Una is referring to her parents' languishment in captivity but also the symbolic captivity of humankind whom the Redcrosse Knight, as a figure of Christ, will redeem.

4. The Redcrosse Knight misjudged Una's loyalty, thinking that it was not what it appeared to be.

That brought not backe the balefull° body dead; *wretched*
In which him chaunced false Duessa meete,
Mine onely foe, mine onely deadly dread,
Who with her witchcraft and misseeming sweete,
Inveigled° him to follow her desires unmeete.° *tricked/unsuitable*

51

At last by subtill sleights° she him betraid *tricks*
Unto his foe, a Gyant huge and tall,
Who him disarmed, dissolute,° dismaid,° *weakened/vanquished*
Unwares surprised, and with mightie mall° *weapon*
The monster mercilesse him made to fall,
Whose fall did never foe before behold;[5]
And now in darkesome dungeon, wretched thrall,
Remedilesse,° for aie° he doth him hold; *helpless/ever*
This is my cause of griefe, more great, then° may be told. *than*

52

Ere she had ended all, she gan° to faint: *began*
But he her comforted and faire bespake,
Certes,° Madame, ye have great cause of plaint, *certainly*
That stoutest heart, I weene,° could cause to quake. *believe*
But be of cheare, and comfort to you take:
For till I have acquit° your captive knight, *avenged*
Assure your selfe, I will you not forsake.
His chearefull words reviv'd her chearelesse spright,
So forth they went, the Dwarfe them guiding ever right.

Canto 8

Faire virgin to reedeme her deare
brings Arthur to the fight:
Who slayes the Gyant, wounds the beast,
and strips Duessa quight.

1

Ay me, how many perils doe enfold
The righteous man, to make him daily fall?
Were not,° that heavenly grace doth him uphold,[1] *were it not*
And stedfast truth acquite° him out of all. *absolve*
Her love is firme, her care continuall,
So oft as he through his owne foolish pride,
Or weaknesse is to sinfull bands made thrall:
Else° should this Redcrosse knight in bands have dyde, *otherwise*
For whose deliverance she this Prince doth thither guide.

2

They sadly traveild thus, untill they came
Nigh to a castle builded strong and hie:
Then cryde the Dwarfe, lo yonder is the same,
In which my Lord my liege° doth lucklesse lie, *master*
Thrall to that Gyants hatefull tyrannie:

5. The Redcrosse Knight had never yet been defeated in battle.

1. In this stanza, Una is overtly equated with heavenly grace. The Redcrosse Knight originally undertook the quest to help Una redeem her parents, but in this canto it is she who delivers the Redcrosse Knight from captivity.

Therefore, deare Sir, your mightie powres assay.° *prove*
The noble knight alighted by and by
From loftie steede, and bad the Ladie stay,
To see what end of fight should him befall that day.

3

So with the Squire, th'admirer of his might,
He marched forth towards that castle wall;
Whose gates he found fast shut, ne living wight
To ward° the same, nor answere commers° call. *guard / visitor's*
Then tooke that Squire an horne of bugle small,
Which hong adowne his side in twisted gold,
And tassels gay. Wyde wonders over all
Of that same hornes great vertues weren told,[2]
Which had approved bene in uses manifold.° *many*

4

Was never wight, that heard that shrilling sound,
But trembling feare did feele in every vaine;
Three miles it might be easie heard around,
And Ecchoes three answerd it selfe againe:
No false enchauntment, nor deceiptfull traine° *deception*
Might once abide° the terror of that blast, *tolerate*
But presently was voide and wholly vaine:° *ineffectual*
No gate so strong, no locke so firme and fast,
But with that percing noise flew open quite, or brast.° *burst*

5

The same before the Geants gate he blew,
That all the castle quaked from the ground,
And every dore of freewill° open flew. *itself*
The Gyant selfe dismaied with that sownd,
Where he with his Duessa dalliance fownd,[3]
In hast came rushing forth from inner bowre,° *chamber*
With staring° countenance sterne, as one astownd,° *glaring / confused*
And staggering steps, to weet, what suddein stowre° *uproar*
Had wrought that horror strange, and dar'd° his dreaded powre. *defied*

6

And after him the proud Duessa came,
High mounted on her manyheaded beast,
And every head with fyrie tongue did flame,
And every head was crowned on his creast,[4]
And bloudie mouthed with late cruell feast.
That when the knight beheld, his mightie shild
Upon his manly arme he soone addrest,° *made ready*
And at him fiercely flew, with courage fild,
And eger greedinesse through every member thrild.

7

Therewith the Gyant buckled° him to fight, *engaged*
Inflam'd with scornefull wrath and high disdaine,
And lifting up his dreadfull club on hight,

2. Wonderful stories of the horn's powers were told everywhere.
3. The sound of the horn reached the chamber where the Giant and Duessa were engaged in lovemaking.
4. Each head of Duessa's many-headed beast had a crown on it.

All arm'd° with ragged snubbes° and knottie graine, *covered / roots*
Him thought at first encounter to have slaine.
But wise and warie was that noble Pere,
And lightly leaping from so monstrous maine,° *force*
Did faire° avoide the violence him nere; *easily*
It booted nought,° to thinke, such thunderbolts to beare. *it was useless*

8

Ne shame° he thought to shunne so hideous might: *not shameful*
The idle stroke, enforcing furious way,
Missing the marke of his misaymed sight
Did fall to ground, and with his heavie sway° *force*
So deepely dinted° in the driven° clay, *struck / packed*
That three yardes deepe a furrow up did throw:
The sad earth wounded with so sore assay,° *attack*
Did grone full grievous underneath the blow,
And trembling with strange feare, did like an earthquake show.

9

As when almightie Jove in wrathfull mood,
To wreake the guilt of mortall sins is bent,° *determined*
Hurles forth his thundring dart with deadly food,° *hatred*
Enrold° in flames, and smouldring dreriment, *engulfed*
Through riven cloudes and molten firmament;° *sky*
The fierce threeforked engin° making way, *the thunderbolt*
Both loftie towres and highest trees hath rent,
And all that might his angrie passage stay,° *hinder*
And shooting in the earth, casts up a mount° of clay. *mountain*

10

His boystrous° club, so buried in the ground, *enormous*
He could not rearen° up againe so light,° *raise / easily*
But° that the knight him at avantage found, *so*
And whiles he strove his combred° clubbe to quight° *encumbered / free*
Out of the earth, with blade all burning bright
He smote° off his left arme, which like a blocke *struck*
Did fall to ground, depriv'd of native might;
Large streames of bloud out of the truncked stocke° *truncated stump*
Forth gushed, like fresh water streame from riven rocke.

11

Dismaied with so desperate deadly wound,
And eke impatient of unwonted paine,
He loudly brayd with beastly yelling sound,
That all the fields rebellowed° againe; *echoed his bellows*
As great a noyse, as when in Cymbrian plaine[5]
An heard of Bulles, whom kindly rage doth sting,
Do for the milkie mothers want° complaine, *absence*
And fill the fields with troublous bellowing,
The neighbour woods around with hollow murmur ring.

12

That when his deare Duessa heard, and saw
The evill stownd°, that daungerd her estate,° *peril / situation*
Unto his aide she hastily did draw

5. The Cimbri were a savage tribe that invaded Europe in the first century B.C.

Her dreadfull beast, who swolne with bloud of late
Came ramping° forth with proud presumpteous gate, *bounding*
And threatned all his heads like flaming brands.
But him the Squire made quickly to retrate,° *retreat*
Encountring fierce with single sword in hand,
And twixt° him and his Lord did like a bulwarke° stand. *between / barrier*

13

The proud Duessa full of wrathfull spight,
And fierce disdaine, to be affronted so,
Enforst° her purple beast with all her might *spurred on*
That stop° out of the way to overthroe, *obstacle*
Scorning the let° of so unequall° foe: *hindrance / inferior*
But nathemore° would that courageous swayne° *not at all / fellow*
To her yeeld passage, gainst his Lord to goe,
But with outrageous strokes did him restraine,
And with his bodie bard° the way atwixt them twaine.° *barred / between*

14

Then tooke the angrie witch her golden cup,
Which still she bore, replete° with magick artes; *filled*
Death and despeyre did many thereof sup,° *drink*
And secret poyson through their inner parts,
Th'eternall bale° of heavie wounded harts; *destruction*
Which after charmes and some enchauntments said,
She lightly sprinkled on his weaker parts;
Therewith his sturdie courage soone was quayd,° *quelled*
And all his senses were with suddeine dread dismayd.° *overcome*

15

So downe he fell before the cruell beast,
Who on his necke his bloudie clawes did seize,
That life nigh crusht out of his panting brest:
No powre he had to stirre, nor will to rize.
That when the carefull knight gan well avise,° *notice*
He lightly left the foe, with whom he fought,
And to the beast gan turne his enterprise;° *attack*
For wondrous anguish in his hart it wrought,
To see his loved Squire into such thraldome brought.

16

And high advauncing° his bloud-thirstie blade, *lifting up*
Stroke one of those deformed heads so sore,
That of his puissance° proud ensample made; *strength*
His monstrous scalpe downe to his teeth it tore,
And that misformed shape mis-shaped more:
A sea of bloud gusht from the gaping wound,
That her gay garments staynd with filthy gore,
And overflowed all the field around;
That over shoes in bloud he waded on the ground.[6]

17

Thereat he roared for exceeding paine,
That to have heard, great horror would have bred,[7]

6. The pool of blood is so deep that it reaches over Arthur's shoes.

7. The beast roars so loudly from the pain that anyone who heard it would have been struck with horror.

And scourging° th'emptie ayre with his long traine,° *tearing/tail*
Through great impatience of his grieved hed
His gorgeous ryder from her loftie sted° *place*
Would have cast downe, and trod in durtie myre,
Had not the Gyant soone her succoured;° *rescued*
Who all enrag'd with smart° and franticke yre, *pain*
Came hurtling in full fierce, and forst the knight retyre.° *to back off*

18

The force, which wont° in two to be disperst, *usually*
In one alone left hand he now unites,[8]
Which is through rage more strong then both were erst;° *before*
With which his hideous club aloft he dites,° *raises*
And at his foe with furious rigour° smites, *violence*
That strongest Oake might seeme to ouerthrow:
The stroke upon his shield so heavie lites,° *falls*
That to the ground it doubleth° him full low: *collapse*
What mortall wight could ever beare so monstrous blow?

19

And in his fall his shield, that covered was,
Did loose his vele° by chaunce, and open flew: *its covering*
The light whereof, that heavens light did pas,° *surpass*
Such blazing brightnesse through the aier threw,
That eye mote° not the same endure to vew. *could*
Which when the Gyaunt spyde with staring eye,
He downe let fall his arme, and soft withdrew
His weapon huge, that heaved° was on hye *raised*
For to have slaine the man, that on the ground did lye.

20

And eke the fruitfull-headed° beast, amaz'd *many-headed*
At flashing beames of that sunshiny shield,
Became starke blind, and all his senses daz'd,
That downe he tumbled on the durtie field,
And seem'd himselfe as conquered to yield.[9]
Whom when his maistresse proud perceiv'd to fall,
Whiles yet his feeble feet for faintnesse reeld,
Unto the Gyant loudly she gan call,
O helpe Orgoglio, helpe, or else we perish all.

21

At her so pitteous cry was much amoov'd
Her champion stout, and for to ayde his frend,
Againe his wonted° angry weapon proov'd:° *usual/tried*
But all in vaine: for he has read his end° *death*
In that bright shield, and all their forces spend
Themselves in vaine: for since that glauncing° sight, *dazzling*
He hath no powre to hurt, nor to defend;
As where th'Almighties lightning brond° does light, *bolt*
It dimmes the dazed eyen, and daunts° the senses quight. *stuns*

8. The strength that has been divided in the Giant's two hands is now concentrated in his remaining hand.

9. By falling down, the beast seems not only to be conquered, but also to submit himself ("yield") to Arthur.

22

Whom when the Prince, to battell new addrest,
And threatning high his dreadfull stroke did see,[1]
His sparkling blade about his head he blest,° *brandished*
And smote off quite his right leg by the knee,
That downe he tombled; as an aged tree,
High growing on the top of rocky clift,
Whose hartstrings with keene steele nigh hewen be,° *are nearly cut off*
The mightie trunck halfe rent, with ragged rift° *splitting*
Doth roll adowne the rocks, and fall with fearefull drift.° *force*

23

Or as a Castle reared° high and round, *built*
By subtile° engins and malitious slight *clever*
Is undermined from the lowest ground,
And her° foundation forst,° and feebled quight, *the castle's / broken*
At last downe falles, and with her heaped hight
Her hastie ruine does more heavie make,
And yields it selfe unto the victours might;
Such was this Gyaunts fall, that seemd to shake
The stedfast globe of earth, as it for feare did quake.

24

The knight then lightly leaping to the pray,° *victim*
With mortall steele him smot° againe so sore, *struck*
That headlesse his unweldy bodie lay,
All wallowd in his owne fowle bloudy gore,
Which flowed from his wounds in wondrous store.° *amounts*
But soone as breath out of his breast did pas,
That huge great body, which the Gyaunt bore,
Was vanisht quite,° and of that monstrous mas *completely*
Was nothing left, but like an emptie bladder was.[2]

25

Whose grievous fall, when false Duessa spide,
Her golden cup she cast unto the ground,
And crowned mitre° rudely threw aside; *papal crown*
Such percing griefe her stubborne hart did wound,
That she could not endure that dolefull stound,° *dismal situation*
But leaving all behind her, fled away:
The light-foot Squire her quickly turnd around,
And by hard meanes enforcing her to stay,
So brought unto his Lord, as his deserved pray.

26

The royall Virgin, which beheld from farre,
In pensive plight, and sad perplexitie,
The whole atchievement° of this doubtfull° warre, *progress / fearful*
Came running fast to greet his victorie,
With sober gladnesse, and myld modestie,
And with sweet joyous cheare him thus bespake;
Faire braunch of noblesse, flowre of chevalrie,

1. The Giant is already overcome by the sight of Arthur's shield, but when Arthur sees him raising his weapon to defend Duessa, Arthur renews the battle.

2. A bladder or balloon can be blown up to a great size, although it is actually empty, that is, full of hot air.

That with your worth the world amazed make,
How shall I quite° the paines, ye suffer for my sake? *repay*

27

And you fresh bud of vertue springing fast,
Whom these sad eyes saw nigh unto deaths dore,
What hath poore Virgin for such perill past,
Wherewith you to reward? Accept therefore
My simple selfe, and service evermore;
And he that high does sit, and all things see
With equall° eyes, their merites to restore, *impartial*
Behold what ye this day have done for mee,
And what I cannot quite, requite with usuree.[3]

28

But sith° the heavens, and your faire handeling° *since/skill*
Have made you maister of the field this day,
Your fortune maister eke with governing,
And well begun end all so well, I pray,[4]
Ne let that wicked woman scape° away; *escape*
For she it is, that did my Lord bethrall,° *seduce, enslave*
My dearest Lord, and deepe in dongeon lay,
Where he his better dayes hath wasted all.
O heare, how piteous he to you for ayd does call.

29

Forthwith he gave in charge unto his Squire,
That scarlot whore to keepen carefully;
Whiles he himselfe with greedie° great desire *eager*
Into the Castle entred forcibly,
Where living creature none he did espye;
Then gan he lowdly through the house to call:
But no man car'd to answere to his crye.
There raignd a solemne silence over all,
Nor voice was heard, nor wight was seene in bowre or hall.

30

At last with creeping crooked pace forth came
An old old man, with beard as white as snow,
That on a staffe his feeble steps did frame,° *support*
And guide his wearie gate° both too and fro: *steps*
For his eye sight him failed long ygo,° *ago*
And on his arme a bounch of keyes he bore,
The which unused rust did overgrow:
Those were the keyes of every inner dore,
But he could not them use, but kept them still in store.° *handy*

31

But very uncouth° sight was to behold, *strange*
How he did fashion his untoward° pace, *awkward*
For as he forward moov'd his footing old,

3. What Una cannot completely repay, God will repay with interest. Unlike Duessa, who offers herself as a mistress to those who are victorious in battle, Una, a virgin, can offer only her loyalty and service. She goes on to call on God to restore her champions to a state of grace, with "merites" referring to all that was lost through the Fall of humankind.

4. While the heavens and skill have made you the "maister of the field this day," now you must also master your fortune through governance, and I pray that what has begun well will also end well.

So backward still was turnd his wrincled face,
Unlike to men, who ever as they trace,
Both feet and face one way are wont to lead.[5]
This was the auncient keeper of that place,
And foster father of the Gyant dead;
His name Ignaro did his nature right aread.

32

His reverend haires and holy grauitie
The knight much honord, as beseemed well,[6]
And gently askt, where all the people bee,
Which in that stately building wont° to dwell. *accustomed*
Who answerd him full soft, he could not tell.
Againe he askt, where that same knight was layd,
Whom great Orgoglio with his puissaunce fell° *deadly strength*
Had made his caytive thrall;° againe he sayde, *wretched prisoner*
He could not tell: ne ever other answere made.

33

Then asked he, which way he in might pas:° *enter*
He could not tell, againe he answered.
Thereat the curteous knight displeased was,
And said, Old sire, it seemes thou hast not red° *perceived*
How ill it sits° with that same silver hed *unsuitable*
In vaine to mocke, or mockt in vaine to bee:
But if thou be, as thou art pourtrahed
With natures pen, in ages grave degree,
Aread° in graver wise, what I demaund of thee.[7] *declare*

34

His answere likewise was, he could not tell.
Whose sencelesse speach, and doted° ignorance *stupid*
When as the noble Prince had marked well,
He ghest° his nature by his countenance,° *guessed/behavior*
And calmd his wrath with goodly temperance.
Then to him stepping, from his arme did reach
Those keyes, and made himselfe free enterance.
Each dore he opened without any breach;° *breaking in*
There was no barre to stop, nor foe him to empeach.° *hinder*

35

There all within full rich arayd he found,
With royall arras and resplendent gold.
And did with store of every thing abound,
That greatest Princes presence might behold.[8]
But all the floore (too filthy to be told)
With bloud of guiltlesse babes, and innocents trew,
Which there were slaine, as sheepe out of the fold,
Defiled was, that dreadfull was to vew,
And sacred ashes[9] over it was strowed new.° *newly scattered*

5. The steward and doorkeeper of Orgoglio's castle, Ignaro (Ignorance), walks forward but keeps his face turned backward, unlike humans, who look where they go.
6. Arthur treats Ignaro with the respect that his appearance of advanced age warrants.
7. If you are as old and wise as you appear, respond more seriously to what I ask of you.
8. The castle is equipped with everything worthy of the greatest prince.
9. The ashes of martyred saints used here to soak up the blood of innocent Christians. The newly strewn ashes appear to be evidence of a recently performed pagan ritual, as is suggested by the altar in the next stanza.

36

And there beside of marble stone was built
An Altare, carv'd with cunning imagery,
On which true Christians bloud was often spilt,
And holy Martyrs often doen to dye,
With cruell malice and strong tyranny:
Whose blessed sprites from underneath the stone
To God for vengeance cryde continually,
And with great griefe were often heard to grone,
That hardest heart would bleede, to heare their piteous mone.

37

Through every rowme he sought, and every bowr,
But no where could he find that wofull thrall:° *Redcrosse Knight*
At last he came unto an yron doore,
That fast was lockt, but key found not at all
Emongst that bounch, to open it withall;
But in the same a little grate was pight,° *placed*
Through which he sent his voyce, and lowd did call
With all his powre, to weet, if living wight
Were housed therewithin, whom he enlargen° might. *release*

38

Therewith an hollow, dreary, murmuring voyce
These piteous plaints and dolours° did resound; *laments*
O who is that, which brings me happy choyce
Of death, that here lye dying every stound,° *moment*
Yet live perforce° in balefull° darkenesse bound? *constrained/wretched*
For now three Moones have changed thrice their hew,° *shape*
And have beene thrice hid underneath the ground,
Since I the heavens chearefull face did vew,
O welcome thou, that doest of death bring tydings trew.[1]

39

Which when that Champion heard, with percing point
Of pitty deare his hart was thrilled° sore, *pierced*
And trembling horrour ran through every joynt,
For ruth of gentle knight so fowle forlore:° *forlorn*
Which shaking off, he rent that yron dore,
With furious force, and indignation fell;° *deadly*
Where entred in, his foot could find no flore,
But all a deepe descent, as darke as hell,
That breathed ever forth a filthie banefull° smell. *poisonous*

40

But neither darkenesse fowle, nor filthy bands,
Nor noyous° smell his purpose could withhold, *noxious*
(Entire affection hateth nicer hands)[2]
But that with constant zeale, and courage bold,
After long paines and labours manifold,
He found the meanes that Prisoner up to reare;[3]

1. Three moons have changed their shape three times; in other words, nine months have passed. The voice they hear rings with despair, wishing for death rather than rescue or salvation.

2. A perfect love disdains great fastidiousness; Prince Arthur could overlook the filth of Orgoglio's prison because he cares so much for the Redcrosse Knight.

3. The Prisoner's legs are too weak to hold him up, so Arthur has to lift him out of the dungeon. The "light" is also a reference to Una.

Whose feeble thighes, unhable° to uphold — *unable*
His pined corse,° him scarse to light could beare, — *wasted body*
A ruefull spectacle of death and ghastly drere.° — *misery*

41

His sad dull eyes deepe sunck in hollow pits,
Could not endure th'unwonted° sunne to view; — *unaccustomed*
His bare thin cheekes for want° of better bits,° — *lack/food*
And empty sides deceived° of their dew, — *deprived*
Could make a stony hart his hap° to rew; — *situation*
His rawbone° armes, whose mighty brawned bowrs° — *thin/brawny muscles*
Were wont to rive steele plates, and helmets hew,
Were cleane consum'd, and all his vitall powres
Decayd, and all his flesh shronk up like withered flowres.

42

Whom when his Lady saw,[4] to him she ran
With hasty joy: to see him made her glad,
And sad to view his visage pale and wan,° — *thin*
Who earst in flowres of freshest youth was clad.° — *dressed*
Tho when her well of teares she wasted had,
She said, Ah dearest Lord, what evill starre
On you hath found, and pourd his influence bad,[5]
That of your selfe ye thus berobbed arre,
And this misseeming hew° your manly looks doth marre? — *appearance*

43

But welcome now my Lord, in wele° or woe, — *prosperity*
Whose presence I have lackt too long a day;
And fie° on Fortune mine avowed foe, — *shame*
Whose wrathfull wreakes° them selves do now alay.° — *vengeances/abate*
And for these wrongs shall treble penaunce° pay — *penance*
Of treble good: good growes of evils priefe.° — *trial*
The chearelesse man, whom sorrow did dismay,° — *overcome*
Had no delight to treaten° of his griefe; — *tell*
His long endured famine needed more reliefe.

44

Faire Lady, then said that victorious knight,
The things, that grievous were to do, or beare,
Them to renew,° I wote, breeds no delight; — *repeat*
Best musicke breeds delight in loathing eare:
But th'onely good, that growes of passed feare,
Is to be wise, and ware° of like agein. — *wary*
This dayes ensample° hath this lesson deare° — *example/dire*
Deepe written in my heart with yron pen,
That blisse may not abide in state of mortall men.

45

Henceforth sir knight, take to you wonted strength,
And maister these mishaps° with patient might; — *misfortunes*
Loe where your foe lyes stretcht in monstrous length,
And loe that wicked woman in your sight,

4. Una recognizes the Prisoner as the Redcrosse Knight.

5. The Redcrosse Knight has ended up in the dungeon through his own folly; however, Una insists here that it must have been an "evill starre," i.e., misfortune, that was responsible for his imprisonment.

The roote of all your care,° and wretched plight, *trouble*
Now in your powre, to let her live, or dye.
To do her dye (quoth Una) were despight,° *malice*
And shame t'avenge so weake an enimy;
But spoile her of her scarlot robe, and let her fly.[6]

46

So as she bad,° that witch they disaraid,° *commanded / undressed*
And robd of royall robes, and purple pall,° *cloak*
And ornaments that richly were displaid;
Ne spared they to strip her naked all.
Then when they had despoild her tire and call,° *attire and headdress*
Such as she was, their eyes might her behold,
That her misshaped parts did them appall,
A loathly, wrinckled hag, ill favoured, old,
Whose secret filth good manners biddeth not be told.

47

Her craftie head was altogether bald,
And as in hate of honorable eld,[7]
Was overgrowne with scurfe° and filthy scald;[8] *scabs*
Her teeth out of her rotten gummes were feld,° *fallen*
And her sowre breath abhominably smeld;
Her dried dugs,° like bladders lacking wind, *breasts*
Hong downe, and filthy matter from them weld;° *oozed*
Her wrizled° skin as rough, as maple rind,[9] *wrinkled*
So scabby was, that would have loathd all womankind.

48

Her neather° parts, the shame of all her kind, *lower*
My chaster Muse for shame doth blush to write;
But at her rompe° she growing had behind *rump*
A foxes taile, with dong all fowly dight;
And eke her feete most monstrous were in sight;
For one of them was like an Eagles claw,
With griping talaunts° armd to greedy fight, *talons*
The other like a Beares uneven° paw: *rough*
More ugly shape yet never living creature saw.

49

Which when the knights beheld, amazd they were,
And wondred at so fowle deformed wight.
Such then (said Una) as she seemeth here,
Such is the face of falshood, such the sight
Of fowle Duessa, when her borrowed light
Is laid away, and counterfesaunce° knowne. *falsity*
Thus when they had the witch disrobed quight,
And all her filthy feature° open showne, *body*
They let her goe at will, and wander wayes unknowne.

6. Like Christ, who seeks to destroy the works of the devil rather than the devil himself (1 John 3.8), Una seeks to destroy Duessa's ability to do evil.

7. I.e., Duessa's ugly head is a hateful mockery of old people whose baldness is usually a sign of honorable "eld" or old age.

8. Scall, a disease that causes scabs to form on the scalp.

9. Maples were often thought to be hard on the outside but rotten inside. Duessa's diseased appearance also suggests syphilis.

50

She flying fast from heavens hated face,
And from the world that her discovered wide,
Fled to the wastfull° wildernesse apace, *desolate*
From living eyes her open shame to hide,
And lurkt in rocks and caves long unespide.
But that faire crew of knights, and Una faire
Did in that castle afterwards abide,
To rest them selves, and weary powres repaire,
Where store° they found of all, that dainty was and rare. *supplies*

Canto 9

His loves and lignage Arthur tells:
The knights knit friendly bands:
Sir Trevisan flies from Despayre,
Whom Redcrosse knight withstands.

1

O Goodly golden chaine, wherewith yfere° *together*
The vertues linked are in lovely wize:
And noble minds of yore allyed were,
In brave poursuit of chevalrous emprize,° *adventure*
That none did others safety despize,° *disregard*
Nor aid envy to him, in need that stands,
But friendly each did others prayse devize
How to advaunce with favourable hands,
As this good Prince redeemd the Redcrosse knight from bands.° *captivity*

2

Who when their powres, empaird° through labour long, *weakened*
With dew° repast they had recured° well, *suitable/recovered*
And that weake captive wight now wexed° strong, *grown*
Them list no lenger there at leasure dwell,
But forward fare, as their adventures fell,
But ere they parted, Una faire besought
That straunger knight his name and nation tell;
Least so great good, as he for her had wrought,
Should die unknown, and buried be in thanklesse thought.

3

Faire virgin (said the Prince) ye me require
A thing without the compas of my wit:[1]
For both the lignage° and the certain Sire, *lineage*
From which I sprong, from me are hidden yit.
For all so soone as life did me admit
Into this world, and shewed heavens light,
From mothers pap° I taken was unfit: *breast*
And streight delivered to a Faery knight,
To be upbrought in gentle thewes° and martiall might. *manners*

1. I.e., your question is beyond my ability to answer.

4

Unto old Timon[2] he me brought bylive,° *immediately*
Old Timon, who in youthly yeares hath beene
In warlike feates th'expertest man alive,
And is the wisest now on earth I weene;° *believe*
His dwelling is low in a valley greene,
Under the foot of Rauran[3] mossy hore,
From whence the river Dee[4] as silver cleene
His tombling billowes rolls with gentle rore:
There all my dayes he traind me up in vertuous lore.

5

Thither the great Magicien Merlin came,
As was his use,° ofttimes to visit me: *custom*
For he had charge my discipline to frame,[5]
And Tutours nouriture to oversee.
Him oft and oft I askt in privitie,° *privately*
Of what loines and what lignage I did spring:
Whose aunswere bad me still assured bee,
That I was sonne and heire unto a king,
As time in her just terme° the truth to light should bring. *due course*

6

Well worthy impe,° said then the Lady gent,° *offspring / noble*
And Pupill fit for such a Tutours hand.
But what adventure, or what high intent
Hath brought you hither into Faery land,
Aread° Prince Arthur, crowne of Martiall band?[6] *declare*
Full hard it is (quoth he) to read aright
The course of heavenly cause, or understand
The secret meaning of th'eternall might,
That rules mens wayes, and rules the thoughts of living wight.

7

For whither° he through fatall deepe foresight *whether*
Me hither sent, for cause to me unghest,° *unguessed*
Or that fresh bleeding wound, which day and night
Whilome° doth rancle in my riven° brest, *constantly / wounded*
With forced° fury following his behest,° *forceful / command*
Me hither brought by wayes yet never found,
You to have helpt I hold my selfe yet blest.
Ah curteous knight (quoth she) what secret wound
Could ever find, to grieve the gentlest hart on ground?[7]

8

Deare Dame (quoth he) you sleeping sparkes awake,
Which troubled once, into huge flames will grow,[8]
Ne ever will their fervent fury slake,° *cease*
Till living moysture[9] into smoke do flow,

2. Honor (Greek).
3. A hill in Wales, hoary with moss.
4. A river marking the boundary between England and Wales.
5. Merlin was in charge of Arthur's education and made sure Arthur's tutor was properly recompensed.
6. Although Arthur does not declare his name, Una is able to recognize him.
7. I.e., what injury could ever find a way to hurt the gentlest heart "on ground" (in the world)?
8. Prince Arthur addresses Una; she reminds him of his hidden pain, which once reawakened will continue to grow.
9. A reference to the Renaissance medical theory of the humors that compose the human body.

And wasted life do lye in ashes low.
Yet sithens° silence lesseneth not my fire, *since*
But told it flames, and hidden it does glow,
I will revele, what ye so much desire:
Ah Love, lay downe thy bow,[1] the whiles I may respire.° *breathe*

9

It was in freshest flowre of youthly yeares,
When courage first does creepe in manly chest,
Then first the coale of kindly heat appeares
To kindle love in every living brest;
But me had warnd old Timons wise behest,° *warning*
Those creeping flames° by reason to subdew, *of love*
Before their rage grew to so great unrest,
As miserable lovers use to rew,
Which still wex old in woe, whiles woe still wexeth new.[2]

10

That idle name of love, and lovers life,
As losse of time, and vertues enimy
I ever scornd, and joyd to stirre up strife,
In middest of° their mournfull Tragedy, *in the midst of*
Ay wont to laugh, when them I heard to cry,
And blow the fire, which them to ashes brent:° *burned*
Their God himselfe,° griev'd at my libertie, *Cupid*
Shot many a dart at me with fiers intent,
But I them warded all with wary government.° *cautious self-control*

11

But all in vaine: no fort can be so strong,
Ne fleshly brest can armed be so sound,° *completely*
But will at last be wonne with battrie° long, *battery*
Or unawares at disavantage found;[3]
Nothing is sure, that growes on earthly ground:
And who most trustes in arme of fleshly might,
And boasts, in beauties chaine not to be bound,
Doth soonest fall in disaventrous° fight, *unfortunate*
And yeeldes his caytive° neck to victours most despight.° *servile / malice*

12

Ensampel° make of him your haplesse joy, *example*
And of my selfe now mated,° as ye see; *checked*
Whose prouder vaunt° that proud avenging boy *boast*
Did soone pluck downe, and curbd my libertie.
For on a day prickt forth with jollitie
Of looser life, and heat of hardiment,[4]
Raunging the forest wide on courser° free, *horse*
The fields, the floods, the heavens with one consent
Did seeme to laugh on me, and favour mine intent.

1. Cupid shoots arrows of love at people and causes them to fall in love with the first person they see.
2. Sorrow makes lovers grow old while their sorrow remains forever young.
3. No fort is so strong, or flesh so well protected, that it cannot be overcome by continual battering.
4. Inspired by the joy of a life of freedom and the heat of boldness.

13

For-wearied° with my sports, I did alight *tired*
From loftie steed, and downe to sleepe me layd;
The verdant° gras my couch did goodly dight,° *green/adorn*
And pillow was my helmet faire displayd:
Whiles every sence the humour° sweet embayd,° *dew of sleep/bathed*
And slombring soft my hart did steale away,
Me seemed,° by my side a royall Mayd *it seemed to me*
Her daintie limbes full softly down did lay:
So faire a creature yet saw never sunny day.

14

Most goodly glee° and lovely blandishment *entertainment*
She to me made, and bad me love her deare,
For dearely sure her love was to me bent,
As when just time expired should appeare.[5]
But whether dreames delude, or true it were,
Was never hart so ravisht with delight,
Ne living man like° words did ever heare, *similar*
As she to me delivered all that night;
And at her parting said, She Queene of Faeries hight.° *was called*

15

When I awoke, and found her place devoyd,° *empty*
And nought° but pressed gras, where she had lyen,° *nothing/lain*
I sorrowed all so much, as earst° I joyd, *at first*
And washed all her place with watry eyen.
From that day forth I lov'd that face divine;
From that day forth I cast° in carefull mind, *resolved*
To seeke her out with labour, and long tyne,° *suffering*
And never vow to rest, till her I find,
Nine monethes I seeke in vaine yet ni'll° that vow unbind. *never will*

16

Thus as he spake, his visage wexed pale,
And chaunge of hew great passion did bewray;° *betray*
Yet still he strove to cloke his inward bale,° *sorrow*
And hide the smoke, that did his fire display,
Till gentle Una thus to him gan° say; *did*
O happy Queene of Faeries, that hast found
Mongst many, one that with his prowesse may
Defend thine honour, and thy foes confound:
True Loves are often sown, but seldom grow on ground.° *on this earth*

17

Thine, O then, said the gentle Redcrosse knight,
Next to that Ladies love, shalbe the place,
O fairest virgin, full of heavenly light,
Whose wondrous faith, exceeding earthly race,° *people*
Was firmest fixt in mine extremest case.
And you, my Lord, the Patrone° of my life, *protector*
Of that great Queene may well gaine worthy grace:

5. Her love was directed as it would appear in the due course of time. Arthur's dream is both lifelike and prophetic.

For onely worthy you through prowes priefe[6]
If living man mote° worthy be, to be her liefe.° *might/beloved*

18

So diversly° discoursing of their loves, *variously*
The golden Sunne his glistring head gan shew,
And sad remembraunce now the Prince amoves,° *compels*
With fresh desire his voyage to pursew:
Als Una earnd her traveill° to renew. *quest*
Then those two knights, fast° friendship for to bynd, *firm*
And love establish each to other trew,
Gave goodly gifts, the signes of gratefull mynd,
And eke° as pledges firme, right hands together joynd. *also*

19

Prince Arthur gave a boxe of Diamond sure,
Embowd° with gold and gorgeous ornament, *encircled*
Wherein were closd few drops of liquor pure,[7]
Of wondrous worth, and vertue excellent,
That any wound could heale incontinent:° *immediately*
Which to requite, the Redcrosse knight him gave
A booke, wherein his Saveours testament° *the Gospels*
Was writ with golden letters rich and brave;
A worke of wondrous grace, and able soules to save.

20

Thus beene they parted, Arthur on his way
To seeke his love, and th'other for to fight
With Unaes foe, that all her realme did pray.° *molest*
But she now weighing the decayed plight,
And shrunken synewes of her chosen knight,
Would not a while her forward course pursew,
Ne bring him forth in face of dreadfull fight,
Till he recovered had his former hew:
For him to be yet weake and wearie well she knew.

21

So as they traveild, lo they gan espy
An armed knight towards them gallop fast,
That seemed from some feared foe to fly,
Or other griesly thing, that him agast.
Still as he fled, his eye was backward cast,
As if his feare still followed him behind;
Als flew his steed, as he his bands had brast,° *burst*
And with his winged heeles did tread the wind,
As he had beene a fole° of Pegasus[8] his kind. *foal*

22

Nigh as he drew, they might perceive his head
To be unarmd, and curld uncombed heares
Upstaring° stiffe, dismayd with uncouth° dread; *standing/unknown*
Nor drop of bloud in all his face appeares

6. The test of your valor shows that you are the only one worthy of her grace.
7. The blood of Christ, the wine of the Eucharist.
8. A winged horse, belonging to the mythological hero Perseus.

Nor life in limbe: and to increase his feares,
In fowle reproch of knighthoods faire degree,
About his neck an hempen rope he weares,
That with his glistring armes° does ill agree; *armor*
But he of rope or armes has now no memoree.

23

The Redcrosse knight toward him crossed fast,
To weet,° what mister° wight was so dismayd: *know / manner of*
There him he finds all sencelesse and aghast,
That of him selfe he seemd to be afrayd;
Whom hardly he from flying forward stayd,[9]
Till he these wordes to him deliver might;
Sir knight, aread who hath ye thus arayd,° *clothed*
And eke from whom make ye this hasty flight:
For never knight I saw in such misseeming° plight. *unseemly*

24

He answerd nought° at all, but adding new *not*
Feare to his first amazment, staring wide
With stony° eyes, and hartlesse hollow hew, *staring*
Astonisht stood, as one that had aspide
Infernall furies, with their chaines untide.
Him yet againe, and yet againe bespake
The gentle knight; who nought to him replide,
But trembling every joynt did inly quake,
And foltring° tongue at last these words seemd forth to shake. *stammering*

25

For Gods deare love, Sir knight, do me not stay;° *detain*
For loe° he comes, he comes fast after mee. *here*
Eft° looking backe would faine° have runne away; *again / rather*
But he him forst to stay, and tellen free° *freely tell*
The secret cause of his perplexitie:
Yet nathemore° by his bold hartie speach, *not at all*
Could his bloud-frosen hart emboldned bee,[1]
But through his boldnesse rather feare did reach,
Yet forst, at last he made through silence suddein breach.° *break*

26

And am I now in safetie sure (quoth he)
From him, that would have forced me to dye?
And is the point of death now turnd fro° mee, *from*
That I may tell this haplesse° history? *unlucky*
Feare nought: (quoth he) no daunger now is nye.
Then shall I you recount a ruefull cace,° *sad situation*
(Said he) the which with this unlucky eye
I late beheld, and had not greater grace
Me reft° from it, had bene partaker of the place.[2] *torn*

9. The Redcrosse Knight could hardly keep the frightened knight (earlier identified as Sir Trevisan) from trying to flee.

1. The Redcrosse Knight's bold words do not encourage Sir Trevisan; in the end, however, the Redcrosse Knight forces him to speak.

2. Had not greater grace torn me from the unfortunate events I beheld, I would have been a victim of those events myself.

27

I lately chaunst (Would I had never chaunst)
With a faire knight to keepen companee,
Sir Terwin hight, that well himselfe advaunst
In all affaires, and was both bold and free,
But not so happie as mote happie bee:
He lov'd, as was his lot, a Ladie gent,° *gentle*
That him againe° lov'd in the least degree: *in return*
For she was proud, and of too high intent,° *ambition*
And joyd to see her lover languish and lament.

28

From whom° returning sad and comfortlesse, *Terwin's lady*
As on the way together we did fare,° *travel*
We met that villen (God from him me blesse)
That cursed wight, from whom I scapt° whyleare,° *escaped/earlier*
A man of hell, that cals himselfe Despaire:
Who first us greets, and after faire areedes° *tells*
Of tydings strange, and of adventures rare:
So creeping close, as Snake in hidden weedes,
Inquireth of our states, and of our knightly deedes.

29

Which when he knew, and felt our feeble harts
Embost° with bale,° and bitter byting griefe, *encrusted/sorrow*
Which love had launched with his deadly darts,
With wounding words and termes of foule repriefe° *scorn*
He pluckt from us all hope of due reliefe,
That earst° us held in love of lingring life; *recently*
Then hopelesse hartlesse, gan the cunning thiefe
Perswade us die, to stint° all further strife: *stop*
To me he lent this rope, to him a rustie knife.

30

With which sad instrument of hastie death,
That wofull lover, loathing lenger° light, *longer*
A wide way° made to let forth living breath. *cut*
But I more fearefull, or more luckie wight,° *creature*
Dismayd with that deformed dismall sight,
Fled fast away, halfe dead with dying feare:° *fear of dying*
Ne yet assur'd of life by you, Sir knight,
Whose like infirmitie like chaunce may beare:
But God you never let his charmed speeches heare.[3]

31

How may a man (said he) with idle speach
Be wonne,° to spoyle the Castle of his health? *convinced*
I wote° (quoth he) whom triall late did teach, *would not*
That like would not for all this worldes wealth:[4]
His subtill tongue, like dropping honny, mealt'th° *melteth*
Into the hart, and searcheth every vaine,

3. May God prevent you from hearing his seductive speeches.

4. I would not undergo such a test for all the wealth in the world.

That ere° one be aware, by secret stealth *before*
His powre is reft,° and weaknesse doth remaine. *broken*
O never Sir desire to try° his guilefull traine.° *test/trickery*

32

Certes° (said he) hence shall I never rest, *indeed*
Till I that treachours° art have heard and tride;° *traitor's/tested*
And you Sir knight, whose name mote I request,
Of grace do me unto his cabin° guide. *cave*
I that hight° Trevisan (quoth he) will ride *am called*
Against my liking backe, to doe you grace:° *a favor*
But nor for gold nor glee will I abide
By you, when ye arrive in that same place;
For lever° had I die, then° see his deadly face. *rather/than*

33

Ere long they come, where that same wicked wight
His dwelling has, low in an hollow cave,
Farre underneath a craggie clift ypight,° *pitched*
Darke, dolefull, drearie, like a greedie grave,
That still° for carrion carcases doth crave: *always*
On top whereof aye° dwelt the ghastly Owle, *ever*
Shrieking his balefull° note, which ever drave *sorrowful*
Farre from that haunt all other chearefull fowle;
And all about it wandring ghostes did waile and howle.

34

And all about old stockes and stubs of trees,
Whereon nor fruit, nor leafe was ever seene,
Did hang upon the ragged rocky knees;° *hillsides*
On which had many wretches hanged beene,
Whose carcases were scattered on the greene,
And throwne about the cliffs. Arrived there,
That bare-head knight for dread and dolefull teene,° *grief*
Would faine have fled, ne durst° approchen neare, *dared*
But th'other forst him stay, and comforted in feare.

35

That darkesome cave they enter, where they find
That cursed man, low sitting on the ground,
Musing full sadly in his sullein mind;
His griesie lockes, long growen, and unbound,
Disordred hong about his shoulders round,
And hid his face; through which his hollow eyne
Lookt deadly dull, and stared as astound;
His raw-bone cheekes through penurie° and pine,° *poverty/starvation*
Were shronke into his jawes, as he did never dine.

36

His garment nought but many ragged clouts,° *rags*
With thornes together pind and patched was,
The which his naked sides he wrapt abouts;
And him beside there lay upon the gras
A drearie° corse,° whose life away did pas, *gory/body*
All wallowd in his owne yet luke-warme blood,

That from his wound yet welled fresh alas;
In which a rustie knife fast fixed stood,
And made an open passage for the gushing flood.

37

Which piteous spectacle, approving° trew *proving*
The wofull tale that Trevisan had told,
When as the gentle Redcrosse knight did vew,
With firie zeale he burnt in courage bold,
Him to avenge, before his bloud were cold,
And to the villein said, Thou damned wight,
The author of this fact, we here behold,
What justice can but judge against thee right,
With thine owne bloud to price° his bloud, here shed in sight? *pay for*

38

What franticke fit (quoth he) hath thus distraught
Thee, foolish man, so rash a doome° to give? *judgment*
What justice ever other judgement taught,
But he should die, who merites not to live?
None° else to death this man despayring drive,° *nothing/drove*
But his owne guiltie mind deserving death.
Is then unjust to each his due to give?
Or let him die, that loatheth living breath?
Or let him die at ease, that liveth here uneath?° *unhappily*

39

Who travels by the wearie wandring way,
To come unto his wished home in haste,
And meetes a flood, that doth his passage stay,
Is not great grace to helpe him over past,
Or free his feet, that in the myre sticke fast?
Most envious man, that grieves at neighbours good,
And fond,° that joyest in the woe thou hast, *foolish*
Why wilt not let him passe, that long hath stood
Upon the banke, yet wilt thy selfe not passe the flood?

40

He there does now enjoy eternall rest
And happie ease, which thou doest want and crave,
And further from it daily wanderest:
What if some litle paine the passage have,
That makes fraile flesh to feare the bitter wave?
Is not short paine well borne, that brings long ease,
And layes the soule to sleepe in quiet grave?
Sleepe after toyle, port after stormie seas,
Ease after warre, death after life does greatly please.

41

The knight much wondred at his suddeine wit,
And said, The terme of life is limited,
Ne may a man prolong, nor shorten it;
The souldier may not move from watchfull sted,° *post*
Nor leave his stand, untill his Captaine bed.° *command*
Who life did limit by almightie doome,
(Quoth he) knowes best the termes established;

And he, that points the Centonell his roome,
Doth license him depart at sound of morning droome.° *drum*

42

Is not his deed, what ever thing is donne,
In heaven and earth? did not he all create
To die againe? all ends that was begonne.
Their times in his eternall booke of fate
Are written sure, and have their certaine date.
Who then can strive with strong necessitie,
That holds the world in his still chaunging state,
Or shunne the death ordaynd by destinie?
When houre of death is come, let none aske whence, nor why.

43

The lenger life, I wote the greater sin,[5]
The greater sin, the greater punishment:
All those great battels, which thou boasts to win,
Through strife, and bloud-shed, and avengement,
Now praysd, hereafter deare° thou shalt repent: *dearly*
For life must life, and bloud must bloud repay.
Is not enough thy evill life forespent?° *wasted*
For he, that once hath missed the right way,
The further he doth goe, the further he doth stray.

44

Then do no further goe, no further stray,
But here lie downe, and to thy rest betake,
Th'ill° to prevent, that life ensewen° may. *evil/continue*
For what hath life, that may it loved make,
And gives not rather cause it to forsake?° *leave*
Feare, sicknesse, age, losse, labour, sorrow, strife,
Paine, hunger, cold, that makes the hart to quake;
And ever fickle fortune rageth rife
All which, and thousands mo° do make a loathsome life. *more*

45

Thou wretched man, of death hast greatest need,
If in true ballance thou wilt weigh thy state:° *condition*
For never knight, that dared warlike deede,
More lucklesse disaventures did amate:° *meet*
Witnesse the dongeon deepe, wherein of late
Thy life shut up, for death so oft did call;
And though good lucke prolonged hath thy date,
Yet death then, would the like mishaps forestall,
Into the which hereafter thou maiest happen fall.[6]

46

Why then doest thou, O man of sin, desire
To draw thy dayes forth to their last degree?
Is not the measure of thy sinfull hire° *employment*
High heaped up with huge iniquitie,° *sinfulness*
Against the day of wrath, to burden thee?

5. The longer the life, the greater the sin.

6. If death had come when you called for it, then the misfortunes that await you might have been prevented.

Is not enough, that to this Ladie milde
Thou falsed° hast thy faith with perjurie, *violated*
And sold thy selfe to serve Duessa vilde,° *vile*
With whom in all abuse thou hast thy selfe defilde?

47

Is not he just, that all this doth behold
From highest heaven, and beares an equall eye?
Shall he thy sins up in his knowledge fold,
And guiltie be of thine impietie?
Is not his law, Let every sinner die:
Die shall all flesh? what then must needs be donne,
Is it not better to doe willinglie,
Then° linger, till the glasse be all out ronne? *than*
Death is the end of woes: die soone, O faeries sonne.

48

The knight was much enmoved° with his speach, *moved*
That as a swords point through his hard did perse,° *pierce*
And in his conscience made a secret breach,[7]
Well knowing true all, that he did reherse,
And to his fresh remembrance did reverse° *recall*
The ugly vew of his deformed crimes,
That all his manly powres it did disperse,
As° he were charmed with inchaunted rimes, *as if*
That oftentimes he quakt, and fainted oftentimes.

49

In which amazement, when the Miscreant° *misbeliever (Despair)*
Perceived him to waver weake and fraile,
Whiles trembling horror did his conscience dant,° *overcome*
And hellish anguish did his soule assaile,
To drive him to despaire, and quite to quaile,
He shew'd him painted in a table° plaine,° *picture/clearly*
The damned ghosts, that doe in torments waile,
And thousand feends that doe them endlesse paine
With fire and brimstone, which for ever shall remaine.

50

The sight whereof so throughly him dismaid,
That nought° but death before his eyes he saw, *nothing*
And ever burning wrath before him laid,
By righteous sentence of th'Almighties law:
Then gan the villein him to overcraw,° *triumph over*
And brought unto him swords, ropes, poison, fire,
And all that might him to perdition draw;
And bad him choose, what death he would desire:
For death was due to him, that had provokt Gods ire.

51

But when as none of them he saw him take,
He to him raught° a dagger sharpe and keene, *handed*
And gave it him in hand: his hand did quake,
And tremble like a leafe of Aspin greene,

7. Despair's words disrupt the Redcrosse Knight's inner knowledge of God's grace.

And troubled bloud through his pale face was seene
To come, and goe with tydings from the hart,
As it a running messenger had beene.
At last resolv'd to worke his finall smart,° *pain*
He lifted up his hand, that backe againe did start.

52

Which when as Una saw, through every vaine
The crudled cold ran to her well of life,° *her heart*
As in a swowne: but soone reliv'd° againe, *revived*
Out of his hand she snatcht the cursed knife,
And threw it to the ground, enraged rife,° *uncontrollably*
And to him said, Fie, fie,° faint harted knight, *shame*
What meanest thou by this reprochfull strife?
Is this the battell, which thou vauntst° to fight *boast*
With that fire-mouthed Dragon, horrible and bright?

53

Come, come away, fraile, feeble, fleshly wight,
Ne let vaine words bewitch thy manly hart,
Ne divelish thoughts dismay thy constant spright.
In heavenly mercies hast thou not a part?
Why shouldst thou then despeire, that chosen art?
Where justice growes, there grows eke greater grace,
The which doth quench the brond of hellish smart,
And that accurst hand-writing doth deface.[8]
Arise, Sir knight arise, and leave this cursed place.

54

So up he rose, and thence amounted streight.° *immediately*
Which when the carle° beheld, and saw his guest *villain*
Would safe depart, for all his subtill sleight,° *trickery*
He chose an halter° from among the rest, *noose*
And with it hung himselfe, unbid unblest.
But death he could not worke himselfe thereby;
For thousand times he so himselfe had drest,
Yet nathelesse° it could not doe° him die, *nevertheless / make*
Till he should die his last, that is eternally.

Canto 10

Her faithfull knight faire Una brings
to house of Holinesse,
Where he is taught repentance, and
the way to heavenly blesse.

1

What man is he, that boasts of fleshly might,
And vaine° assurance of mortality, *empty*
Which all so soone, as it doth come to fight,
Against spirituall foes, yeelds by and by,
Or from the field most cowardly doth fly?

8. Una alludes to heavenly grace and God's mercy toward repentent sinners—an allowance that Despair had omitted from his argument.

Ne let the man ascribe it to his skill,
That thorough° grace hath gained victory. *through*
If any strength we have, it is to ill,
But all the good is Gods, both power and eke will.

2

By that, which lately hapned, Una saw,
That this her knight was feeble, and too faint;
And all his sinews woxen° weake and raw, *grown*
Through long enprisonment, and hard constraint,
Which he endured in his late restraint,
That yet he was unfit for bloudie fight:
Therefore to cherish° him with diets daint,° *nourish/dainty foods*
She cast to bring him, where he chearen° might, *be cheered*
Till he recovered had his late decayed plight.

3

There was an auntient° house not farre away, *ancient*
Renowmd throughout the world for sacred lore,° *wisdom*
And pure unspotted life: so well they say
It governd was, and guided evermore,
Through wisedome of a matrone grave and hore;° *venerable*
Whose onely joy was to relieve the needes
Of wretched soules, and helpe the helpelesse pore:
All night she spent in bidding of her bedes,° *saying prayers*
And all the day in doing good and godly deedes.

4

Dame Caelia° men did her call, as thought *heavenly*
From heaven to come, or thither to arise,
The mother of three daughters, well upbrought
In goodly thewes,° and godly exercise: *manners*
The eldest two most sober, chast, and wise,
Fidelia° and Speranza° virgins were, *Faith/Hope*
Though spousd, yet wanting wedlocks solemnize;[1]
But faire Charissa° to a lovely fere° *Charity/loving husband*
Was lincked, and by him had many pledges° dere. *children*

5

Arrived there, the dore they find fast° lockt; *tightly*
For it was warely° watched night and day, *carefully*
For feare of many foes: but when they knockt,
The Porter opened unto them streight way:° *right away*
He was an aged syre, all hory gray,
With lookes full lowly cast,[2] and gate° full slow, *pace*
Wont on a staffe his feeble steps to stay,° *support*
Hight Humiltá.° They passe in stouping low; *named Humility*
For streight and narrow was the way, which he did show.

6

Each goodly thing is hardest to begin,
But entred in a spacious court they see,

1. Faith and Hope are each engaged to be married, but their marriages have not yet taken place. The implication is that Faith and Hope are not fulfilled in this life but will be fulfilled in the hereafter through God's promise of salvation.

2. The porter casts his eyes down in an expression of humility.

Both plaine, and pleasant to be walked in,
Where them does meete a francklin[3] faire and free,
And entertaines with comely° courteous glee, *appropriate*
His name was Zele,[4] that him right well became,
For in his speeches and behaviour hee
Did labour lively to expresse the same,
And gladly did them guide, till to the Hall they came.

7

There fairely them receives a gentle Squire,
Of milde demeanure,° and rare courtesie, *manner*
Right cleanly clad in comely sad attire;
In word and deede that shew'd great modestie,
And knew his good to all of each degree,[5]
Hight Reverence. He them with speeches meet
Does faire entreat; no courting nicetie,° *flattery*
But simple true, and eke unfained° sweet, *honest*
As might become a Squire so great persons to greet.

8

And afterwards them to his Dame he leades,
That aged Dame, the Ladie of the place:
Who all this while was busie at her beades:
Which doen,° she up arose with seemely grace, *done*
And toward them full matronely did pace.° *walk*
Where when that fairest Una she beheld,
Whom well she knew to spring from heavenly race,
Her hart with joy unwonted inly° sweld, *inwardly*
As feeling wondrous comfort in her weaker eld.° *age*

9

And her embracing said, O happie earth,
Whereon thy innocent feet doe ever tread,
Most vertuous virgin borne of heavenly berth,
That to redeeme thy woeful parents head,
From tyrans° rage, and ever-dying dread, *tyrant's*
Hast wandred through the world now long a day;
Yet ceasest not thy wearie soles° to lead, *feet, souls*
What grace hath thee now hither brought this way?
Or doen° thy feeble feet unweeting hither stray? *do*

10

Strange thing it is an errant° knight to see *wandering*
Here in this place, or any other wight,
That hither turnes his steps. So few there bee,
That chose the narrow path, or seeke the right:
All keepe the broad high way, and take delight
With many rather for to go astray,
And be partakers of their evill plight,
Then with a few to walke the rightest° way; *righteous*
O foolish men, why haste ye to your owne decay?

3. A person who owns his own land and is therefore his own master.
4. The franklin's zeal or enthusiasm is an attribute of his Christian freedom.
5. He knows how to behave courteously toward members of each social rank.

11

Thy selfe to see, and tyred limbs to rest,
O matrone sage° (quoth she) I hither came, — *wise*
And this good knight his way with me addrest,° — *directed*
Led with thy prayses and broad-blazed° fame, — *widely reported*
That up to heaven is blowne. The auncient Dame
Him goodly greeted in her modest guise,
And entertaynd them both, as best became,
With all the court'sies, that she could devise,° — *think of*
Ne wanted ought, to shew her bounteous° or wise. — *generous*

12

Thus as they gan of sundry things devise,
Loe two most goodly virgins came in place,
Ylinked° arme in arme in lovely wise,[6] — *linked*
With countenance° demure,° and modest grace, — *expression / modest*
They numbred even steps and equall pace:
Of which the eldest, that Fidelia hight,
Like sunny beames threw from her Christall face,
That could have dazd the rash° beholders sight, — *foolish*
And round about her head did shine like heavens light.

13

She was araied° all in lilly white, — *dressed*
And in her right hand bore a cup of gold,[7]
With wine and water fild up to the hight,° — *brim*
In which a Serpent did himselfe enfold,° — *coil*
That horrour made to all, that did behold;
But she no whit° did chaunge her constant mood: — *not a bit*
And in her other hand she fast° did hold — *tightly*
A booke, that was both signd and seald with blood,
Wherein darke things were writ, hard to be understood.

14

Her younger sister, that Speranza hight,° — *was called*
Was clad in blew,[8] that her beseemed° well; — *suited*
Not all so chearefull seemed she of sight,
As was her sister; whether dread° did dwell, — *fear*
Or anguish in her hart, is hard to tell:
Upon her arme a silver anchor lay,[9]
Whereon she leaned ever, as befell:° — *it happened*
And ever up to heaven, as she did pray,
Her stedfast eyes were bent, ne swarved° other way. — *turned*

15

They seeing Una, towards her gan wend,
Who them encounters° with like courtesie; — *greets*
Many kind speeches they betwene them spend,
And greatly joy each other well to see:

6. Faith and Hope enter the room harmoniously linked, unlike in the House of Pride, where the inhabitants are joined by a yoke of servitude.

7. The sacramental cup of the Holy Communion; it contains the healing blood and baptismal water that poured from Christ's wounds when he was crucified. The serpent here is a symbol of healing and redemption, and the book Fidelia holds is the New Testament, which is sealed with Christ's blood in the sense that Christ's crucifixion assures salvation for all humankind.

8. Blue is the color of the Virgin Mary.

9. Cf. Hebrews 6.19: "which hope we have as an anchor of the soul, both sure and steadfast." Silver is a symbol of purity.

Then to the knight with shamefast° modestie *humble*
They turne themselves, at Unaes meeke request,
And him salute with well beseeming glee;
Who faire them quites,° as him beseemed best, *greets*
And goodly gan discourse° of many a noble gest.° *speak / deed*

16

Then Una thus; But she your sister deare,
The deare Charissa where is she become?[1]
Or wants° she health, or busie is elsewhere? *lacks*
Ah no, said they, but forth she may not come:
For she of late is lightned of her wombe,° *recently gave birth*
And hath encreast° the world with one sonne more, *increased*
That her to see should be but troublesome.
Indeede (quoth she) that should her trouble sore,
But thankt be God, and her encrease so evermore.[2]

17

Then said the aged Caelia, Deare dame,
And you good Sir, I wote° that of your toyle, *believe*
And labours long, through which ye hither came,
Ye both forwearied° be: therefore a whyle *tired*
I read you rest, and to your bowres recoyle.° *retire*
Then called she a Groome, that forth him led
Into a goodly lodge, and gan despoile° *remove*
Of puissant armes, and laid in easie bed;
His name was meeke Obedience rightfully ared.° *understood*

18

Now when their wearie limbes with kindly rest,
And bodies were refresht with due repast,
Faire Una gan Fidelia faire request,
To have her knight into her schoolehouse plaste,
That of her heavenly learning he might taste,
And heare the wisedome of her words divine.
She graunted, and that knight so much agraste,° *graced*
That she him taught celestiall discipline,
And opened his dull eyes, that light mote° in them shine. *might*

19

And that her sacred Booke, with bloud ywrit,° *written*
That none could read, except° she did them teach, *unless*
She unto him disclosed every whit,° *bit*
And heavenly documents thereout did preach,
That weaker wit of man could never reach,
Of God, of grace, of justice, of free will,
That wonder was to heare her goodly speach:
For she was able, with her words to kill,
And raise againe to life the hart,[3] that she did thrill.° *pierce*

20

And when she list° poure out her larger spright, *chose to*
She would commaund the hastie Sunne to stay,° *stop*

1. What has become of her?
2. May God give her more children.
3. Cf. 2 Corinthians 3.6: "for the letter killeth, but the Spirit giveth life."

Or backward turne his course from heavens hight;
Sometimes great hostes of men she could dismay,° *defeat*
Dry-shod to passe, she parts the fluds in tway;° *two*
And eke huge mountaines from their native seat
She would commaund, themselves to beare away,
And throw in raging sea with roaring threat.° *threatening roar*
Almightie God her gave such powre, and puissance great.[4]

21

The faithfull knight now grew in litle space,
By hearing her, and by her sisters lore,
To such perfection of all heavenly grace,
That wretched world he gan for to abhore,
And mortall life gan loath,° as thing forlore,° *despise / lost*
Greev'd with remembrance of his wicked wayes,
And prickt° with anguish of his sinnes so sore, *wounded*
That he desirde to end his wretched dayes:
So much the dart of sinfull guilt the soule dismayes.° *overwhelms*

22

But wise Speranza gave him comfort sweet,
And taught him how to take assured hold
Upon her silver anchor, as was meet;
Else had his sinnes so great, and manifold
Made him forget all that Fidelia told.
In this distressed doubtfull agonie,
When him his dearest Una did behold,
Disdeining life, desiring leave° to die, *permission*
She found her selfe assayld with great perplexitie.

23

And came to Caelia to declare her smart,° *pain*
Who well acquainted with that commune plight,
Which sinfull horror workes in wounded hart,
Her wisely comforted all that she might,
With goodly counsell and advisement° right; *advice*
And streightway sent with carefull diligence,
To fetch a Leach,° the which had great insight *doctor*
In that disease of grieved conscience,
And well could cure the same; His name was Patience.

24

Who comming to that soule-diseased knight,
Could hardly him intreat,° to tell his griefe:[5] *convince*
Which knowne, and all that noyd° his heavie spright *troubled*
Well searcht,° eftsoones he gan apply reliefe *explored*
Of salves and med'cines, which had passing priefe,° *surpassing efficacy*
And thereto added words of wondrous might:
By which to ease he him recured briefe,° *quickly cared*
And much asswag'd° the passion° of his plight, *soothed / suffering*
That he his paine endur'd, as seeming now more light.

4. These miracles were attested in Scripture: stopping the sun, Joshua 10.12–13; turning back the sun, 2 Kings 20.10–11; defeating great hosts, Judges 1.21; parting the sea, Exodus 14.22; and moving mountains, Matthew 21.21.

5. Confession is a necessary element of the Redcrosse Knight's recovery.

25

But yet the cause and root of all his ill,
Inward corruption, and infected sin,
Not purg'd° nor heald, behind remained still, *cleansed*
And festring sore did rankle yet within,
Close creeping twixt the marrow° and the skin. *bone*
Which to extirpe,° he laid him privily° *remove / privately*
Downe in a darkesome lowly place farre in,
Whereas he meant his corrosives to apply,
And with streight° diet tame his stubborne malady.[6] *strict*

26

In ashes and sackcloth he did array° *dress*
His daintie corse,[7] proud humors to abate,[8]
And dieted with fasting every day,
The swelling of his wounds to mitigate,
And made him pray both earely and eke late:
And ever as superfluous flesh did rot
Amendment readie still at hand did wayt,
To pluck it out with pincers firie whot,° *hot*
That soone in him was left no one corrupted jot.° *bit*

27

And bitter Penance with an yron whip,
Was wont him once to disple° every day: *discipline*
And sharpe Remorse his hart did pricke° and nip, *pierce*
That drops of bloud thence° like a well did play; *from his heart*
And sad Repentance used to embay° *drench*
His bodie in salt water smarting sore,
The filthy blots of sinne to wash away.
So in short space they did to health restore
The man that would not live, but earst lay at deathes dore.

28

In which his torment often was so great,
That like a Lyon he would cry and rore,
And rend his flesh, and his owne synewes° eat. *muscles*
His owne deare Una hearing evermore
His ruefull shriekes and gronings, often tore
Her guiltlesse garments, and her golden heare,
For pitty of his paine and anguish sore;
Yet all with patience wisely she did beare;
For well she wist, his crime could else be never cleare.° *cleansed*

29

Whom thus recover'd by wise Patience,
And trew Repentance they to Una brought:
Who joyous of his cured conscience,
Him dearely kist, and fairely eke besought
Himselfe to chearish, and consuming thought

6. To heal the Redcrosse Knight, Patience returns him to Orgoglio's dungeon. Patience intends to use corrosive medication to remove his "inward corruption."

7. Patience has the Redcrosse Knight assume the role of a penitent.

8. According to Renaissance medicine, the humors, or bodily fluids, must be in balance to achieve good health; here Patience wants to "abate" or diminish them. The Redcrosse Knight's adventure in the House of Pride has left him with an excess of pride, which the doctor seeks to remove through penance and prayer.

To put away out of his carefull° brest. *worried*
By this Charissa, late in child-bed brought,[9]
Was woxen strong, and left her fruitfull nest;
To her faire Una brought this unacquainted guest.

30

She was a woman in her freshest age,
Of wondrous beauty, and of bountie° rare, *generosity*
With goodly grace and comely° personage, *attractive*
That was on earth not easie to compare;
Full of great love, but Cupids wanton snare
As hell she hated, chast in worke and will;
Her necke and breasts were ever open bare,
That ay° thereof her babes might sucke their fill; *always*
The rest was all in yellow robes arayed still.° *always*

31

A multitude of babes about her hong,
Playing their sports, that joyd her to behold,
Whom still° she fed, whiles they were weake and young, *always*
But thrust them forth still, as they wexed° old: *grew*
And on her head she wore a tyre° of gold, *crown*
Adornd with gemmes and owches° wondrous faire, *jewels*
Whose passing price uneath° was to be told;[1] *scarcely*
And by her side there sate a gentle paire
Of turtle doves, she sitting in an yvorie chaire.

32

The knight and Una entring, faire her greet,
And bid her joy of that her happie brood;
Who them requites° with court'sies seeming meet,° *repays/suitable*
And entertaines with friendly chearefull mood.
Then Una her besought,° to be so good, *requested*
As in her vertuous rules to schoole her knight,
Now after all his torment well withstood,
In that sad house of Penaunce, where his spright
Had past the paines of hell, and long enduring night.

33

She was right joyous of her just° request, *reasonable*
And taking by the hand that Faeries sonne,
Gan him instruct in every good behest,° *command*
Of love, and righteousnesse, and well to donne,° *good deeds*
And wrath, and hatred warely° to shonne, *carefully*
That drew on men Gods hatred, and his wrath,
And many soules in dolours had fordonne:° *overcome*
In which when him she well instructed hath,
From thence to heaven she teacheth him the ready° path. *direct*

34

Wherein his weaker wandring steps to guide,
An auncient matrone she to her does call,
Whose sober lookes her wisedome well descride:° *revealed*

9. Charissa, who had recently given birth.

1. Whose surpassing value was incalculable.

Her name was Mercie, well knowne over all,
To be both gratious, and eke liberall:
To whom the carefull charge of him she gave,
To lead aright, that he should never fall
In all his wayes through this wide worldes wave,° *currents*
That Mercy in the end his righteous soule might save.

35

The godly Matrone by the hand him beares° *leads*
Forth from her presence, by a narrow way,
Scattred with bushy thornes, and ragged breares,° *briars*
Which still° before him she remov'd away, *ever*
That nothing might his ready° passage stay:° *direct / stop*
And ever when his feet encombred were,
Or gan to shrinke,° or from the right to stray, *pull back*
She held him fast,° and firmely did upbeare,° *firmly / support*
As carefull Nourse her child from falling oft does reare.° *raise*

36

Eftsoones unto an holy Hospitall,° *hostel*
That was fore° by the way, she did him bring, *close*
In which seven Bead-men° that had vowed all *men of prayer*
Their life to service of high heavens king
Did spend their dayes in doing godly thing:
Their gates to all were open evermore,° *always*
That by the wearie way were traveiling,
And one sate° wayting ever them before, *sat*
To call in commers-by,° that needy were and pore. *passers-by*

37

The first of them that eldest was, and best,
Of all the house had charge and governement,
As Guardian and Steward of the rest:
His office° was to give entertainment° *duty / provisions*
And lodging, unto all that came, and went:
Not unto such, as could him feast againe,
And double quite,° for that he on them spent, *repay*
But such, as want° of harbour did constraine:[2] *lack*
Those for Gods sake his dewty was to entertaine.

38

The second was as Almner[3] of the place,
His office was, the hungry for to feed,
And thristy give to drinke, a worke of grace:
He feard not once him selfe to be in need,
Ne car'd to hoord° for those, whom he did breede:° *hoard / his children*
The grace of God he layd up still in store,
Which as a stocke he left unto his seede;
He had enough, what need him care for more?
And had he lesse, yet some he would give to the pore.[4]

2. He did not provide for those who could return the favor with an even more lavish reception, but provided only for those who were destitute.

3. One who provides charitable relief to the poor.

4. He did not accumulate worldly goods for the wealth of his family, but gave to the poor, which made him rich in the virtue of charity.

39

The third had of their wardrobe custodie,
  In which were not rich tyres,° nor garments gay,° *clothes/trashy*
  The plumes of pride, and wings of vanitie,
  But clothes meet to keepe keene could° away, *sharp cold*
  And naked nature seemely° to aray; *suitably*
  With which bare wretched wights he dayly clad,
  The images of God in earthly clay;
  And if that no spare cloths to give he had,
His owne coate he would cut, and it distribute glad.

40

The fourth appointed by his office was,
  Poore prisoners to relieve with gratious ayd,° *aid*
  And captives to redeeme° with price of bras, *ransom*
  From Turkes and Sarazins, which them had stayd;° *imprisoned*
  And though they faultie were,[5] yet well he wayd,° *judged*
  That God to us forgiveth every howre
  Much more then that, why° they in bands° were layd, *for which/chains*
  And he that harrowd hell with heavie stowre,° *sorrow*
The faultie soules from thence brought to his heavenly bowre.[6]

41

The fift had charge sicke persons to attend,
  And comfort those, in point° of death which lay; *at the brink*
  For them most needeth comfort in the end,
  When sin, and hell, and death do most dismay
  The feeble soule departing hence away.
  All is but lost, that living we bestow,
  If not well ended at our dying day.[7]
  O man have mind of that last bitter throw;° *agony*
For as the tree does fall, so lyes it ever low.

42

The sixt had charge of them now being dead,
  In seemely sort their corses to engrave,° *bury*
  And deck with dainty flowres their bridall bed,
  That to their heavenly spouse[8] both sweet and brave
  They might appeare, when he their soules shall save.
  The wondrous workemanship of Gods owne mould,° *image*
  Whose face he made, all beasts to feare, and gave
  All in his hand, even dead we honour should.
Ah dearest God me graunt, I dead be not defould.° *defiled*

43

The seventh now after death and buriall done,
  Had charge the tender Orphans of the dead
  And widowes ayd, least° they should be undone:° *lest/ruined*
  In face of judgement he their right would plead,

5. Christian prisoners of pagans were "faultie" if they had given up their faith, even if they had been tortured in the process. But although succumbing to pagan force was strictly speaking a sin, the fourth Beadman considers that God forgives much greater sins all the time.

6. According to a medieval story, after his crucifixion Christ descended into Hell to release good people who had lived before him and thus had not been able to enter heaven.

7. A lifetime of faith is lost if one gives in to despair at the time of death.

8. In Revelation 21.2, the redeemed are "prepared as a bride adorned for her husband."

Ne ought° the powre of mighty men did dread — *not at all*
In their defence,[9] nor would for gold or fee
Be wonne° their rightfull causes downe to tread: — *bribed*
And when they stood in most necessitee,
He did supply their want, and gave them° ever° free. — *to them/always*

44

There when the Elfin knight arrived was,
The first and chiefest of the seven, whose care° — *duty*
Was guests to welcome, towardes him did pas:° — *go*
Where seeing Mercie, that his steps up bare,° — *supported*
And alwayes led, to her with reverence rare
He humbly louted° in meeke lowlinesse, — *bowed*
And seemely° welcome for her did prepare: — *suitable*
For of their order she was Patronesse,° — *protector*
Albe° Charissa were their chiefest founderesse. — *although*

45

There she awhile him stayes, him selfe to rest,
That to the rest° more able he might bee: — *remainder*
During which time, in every good behest° — *deed*
And godly worke of Almes and charitee
She him instructed with great industree;
Shortly therein so perfect he became,
That from the first unto the last degree,
His mortall life he learned had to frame° — *conduct*
In holy righteousnesse,[1] without rebuke or blame.

46

Thence forward by that painfull way they pas,° — *go*
Forth to an hill, that was both steepe and hy;
On top whereof a sacred chappell was,
And eke a litle Hermitage thereby,
Wherein an aged holy man did lye,
That day and night said his devotion,
Ne other worldly busines did apply;° — *conduct*
His name was heavenly Contemplation;
Of God and goodnesse was his meditation.

47

Great grace that old man to him given had;
For God he often saw from heavens hight,° — *height*
All were his earthly eyen both blunt° and bad, — *blurred*
And through great age had lost their kindly° sight, — *natural*
Yet wondrous quick and persant° was his spright, — *piercing*
As Eagles eye, that can behold the Sunne:
That hill they scale° with all their powre and might, — *climb*
That his frayle thighes nigh° wearie and fordonne — *all but*
Gan faile, but by her° helpe the top at last he wonne.° — *Mercy's/reached*

48

There they do finde that godly aged Sire,
With snowy lockes adowne his shoulders shed,

9. He would plead their causes in court and did not fear the power of mighty men.

1. Spenser emphasizes that holy righteousness is not just an inner moral state but is achieved through the active practice of charity.

As hoarie frost with spangles° doth attire — *icicles*
The mossy braunches of an Oke halfe ded.
Each bone might through his body well be red,° — *seen*
And every sinew° seene through his long fast: — *muscle*
For nought he car'd his carcas long unfed;[2]
His mind was full of spirituall repast,
And pyn'd° his flesh, to keepe his body low and chast. — *starred*

49

Who when these two approching he aspide,° — *saw*
At their first presence grew agrieved sore,° — *very upset*
That forst him lay his heavenly thoughts aside;
And had he not that Dame respected more,
Whom highly he did reverence and adore,
He would not once have moved for the knight.
They him saluted standing far afore;° — *at a distance*
Who well them greeting, humbly did requight,° — *return the greeting*
And asked, to what end they clomb that tedious height.

50

What end (quoth° she) should cause us take such paine, — *said*
But that same end, which every living wight
Should make his marke,° high heaven to attaine? — *aim*
Is not from hence the way, that leadeth right
To that most glorious house, that glistreth° bright — *shines*
With burning starres, and everliuing fire,
Whereof the keyes[3] are to thy hand behight° — *delivered*
By wise Fidelia? she doth thee require,
To shew it to this knight, according° his desire. — *granting*

51

Thrise° happy man, said then the father grave, — *thrice*
Whose staggering steps thy steady hand doth lead,
And shewes the way, his sinfull soule to save.
Who better can the way to heaven aread,° — *show*
Then thou thy selfe, that was both borne and bred
In heavenly throne, where thousand Angels shine?
Thou doest the prayers of the righteous sead° — *the redeemed*
Present before the majestie divine,
And his avenging wrath to clemencie incline.[4]

52

Yet since thou bidst, thy pleasure shalbe donne.
Then come thou man of earth, and see the way,
That never yet was seene of Faeries sonne,
That never leads the traveiler astray,
But after labours long, and sad delay,
Brings them to joyous rest and endlesse blis.
But first thou must a season fast and pray,
Till from her bands° the spright assoiled° is,[5] — *bonds/released*
And have her strength recur'd° from fraile infirmitis. — *restored*

2. He did not care about the hunger of his body.
3. The keys to the kingdom of heaven.
4. Contemplation is addressing Mercy, who turns the Almighty's wrath into forgiveness.
5. The bonds that Contemplation is referring to are the bonds of the flesh.

53

That done, he leads him to the highest Mount;[6]
Such one,[7] as that same mighty man of God,
That bloud-red billowes[8] like a walled front
On either side disparted with his rod,
Till that his army dry-foot through them yod,° *went*
Dwelt fortie dayes upon; where writ in stone
With bloudy letters by the hand of God,
The bitter doome of death and balefull mone° *moan*
He did receive, whiles flashing fire about him shone.[9]

54

Or like that sacred hill, whose head full hie,
Adornd with fruitfull Olives all arownd,[1]
Is, as it were for endlesse memory
Of that deare Lord, who oft thereon was fownd,
For ever with a flowring girlond crownd:
Or like that pleasaunt Mount, that is for ay
Through famous Poets verse each where renownd,[2]
On which the thrise three learned Ladies[3] play
Their heavenly notes, and make full many a lovely lay.

55

From thence, far off he unto him did shew
A litle path, that was both steepe and long,
Which to a goodly Citie[4] led his vew;
Whose wals and towres were builded high and strong
Of perle and precious stone, that earthly tong
Cannot describe, nor wit of man can tell;
Too high a ditty for my simple song;
The Citie of the great king hight it well,° *it is well named*
Wherein eternall peace and happinesse doth dwell.[5]

56

As he thereon stood gazing, he might see
The blessed Angels to and fro descend[6]
From highest heaven, in gladsome° companee,° *happy/friendship*
And with great joy into that Citie wend,
As commonly as friend does with his frend.
Whereat he wondred much, and gan enquere,° *asked*
What stately building durst° so high extend *dared*
Her loftie towres unto the starry sphere,° *heavens*
And what unknowen nation there empeopled were.° *inhabited it*

6. This is the "great and high mountain" of Revelation 21.10, from which God showed John the New Jerusalem.
7. Such a mountain—Sinai—Moses climbed to spend 40 days before receiving the Ten Commandments.
8. Spenser is referring to the Red Sea, which Moses parted to allow the Israelites to escape from Egypt without drowning.
9. Referring to the burning bush through which God appeared to Moses (Deuteronomy 4.11).
1. The Mount of Olives, where Jesus taught.
2. Parnassus, the home of the Greek gods and celebrated by the Greek poets.
3. The nine Muses, goddesses of the arts and sciences.
4. The New Jerusalem, the promised home of the faithful in eternity (Revelation 20.10–21).
5. Cf. Psalms 48.2: "the joy of the whole earth is Mount Zion . . . the city of the great king."
6. The image recalls Jacob's vision of the ladder that extended from earth to heaven (Genesis 28.12).

57

Faire knight (quoth he) Hierusalem that is,
The new Hierusalem, that God has built
For those to dwell in, that are chosen his,
His chosen people purg'd from sinfull guilt,
With pretious bloud,[7] which cruelly was spilt
On cursed tree, of that unspotted lam,° *lamb*
That for the sinnes of all the world was kilt:
Now are they Saints all in that Citie sam,° *same*
More deare unto their God, then younglings to their dam.

58

Till now, said then the knight, I weened well,
That great Cleopolis,[8] where I have beene,
In which that fairest Faerie Queene doth dwell,
The fairest Citie was, that might be seene;
And that bright towre all built of christall cleene,
Panthea, seemd the brightest thing, that was:
But now by proofe all otherwise I weene;
For this great Citie that does far surpas,
And this bright Angels towre quite dims that towre of glas.

59

Most trew, then said the holy aged man;
Yet is Cleopolis for earthly frame,[9]
The fairest peece, that eye beholden can:
And well beseemes all knights of noble name,
That covet in th'immortall booke of fame
To be eternized, that same to haunt,
And doen their service to that soveraigne Dame,[1]
That glorie does to them for guerdon° graunt: *reward*
For she is heavenly borne, and heaven may justly vaunt.[2]

60

And thou faire ymp,° sprong out from English race, *child*
How ever now accompted° Elfins sonne, *considered*
Well worthy doest thy service for her grace,
To aide a virgin desolate foredonne.° *in distress*
But when thou famous victorie hast wonne,
And high emongst all knights hast hong thy shield,
Thenceforth the suit° of earthly conquest shonne,° *pursuit/shun*
And wash thy hands from guilt of bloudy field:
For bloud can nought but sin, and wars but sorrowes yield.

61

Then seeke this path, that I to thee presage,° *foretell*
Which after all to heaven shall thee send;
Then peaceably thy painefull pilgrimage

7. The blood spilled by Christ when he was crucified and by which the faithful are redeemed from sin.

8. The Redcrosse Knight compares the New Jerusalem with Cleopolis, the city ruled by the Faerie Queene and Panthea—literally, in Greek, all sights or the best of sights—each a perfect representation of a political state (as realized by Spenser and perhaps by Plato and others in their political treatises). He finds that the transcendent brilliance of the angels' city surpasses that of the other cities of "glass," that is, products of a merely human power of reflection.

9. As an earthly as opposed to a heavenly structure.

1. It is fitting that noble knights who seek glory serve in the Faerie Queene's court.

2. Since the Faerie Queene was born in Heaven, Heaven may rightfully boast ("vaunt") that it is her home.

To yonder same Hierusalem do bend,° *go*
Where is for thee ordaind a blessed end:
For thou emongst those Saints, whom thou doest see,
Shalt be a Saint, and thine owne nations frend
And Patrone: thou Saint George shalt called bee,
Saint George of mery England, the signe of victoree.

62

Unworthy wretch (quoth he°) of so great grace, *Redcrosse Knight*
How dare I thinke such glory to attaine?
These that have it attaind, were in like cace
(Quoth he°) as wretched, and liv'd in like paine. *Contemplation*
But deeds of armes must I[3] at last be faine,° *willing*
And Ladies love to leave so dearely bought?
What need of armes, where peace doth ay° remaine, *ever*
(Said he) and battailes none are to be fought?
As for loose loves are vaine,° and vanish into nought. *false*

63

O let me not (quoth he) then turne againe
Backe to the world, whose joyes so fruitlesse are;
But let me here for aye° in peace remaine, *ever*
Or streight way° on that last long voyage fare,[4] *immediately*
That nothing may my present hope empare.° *diminish*
That may not be (said he) ne maist thou yit
Forgo° that royall maides bequeathed care, *give up*
Who did her cause into thy hand commit,[5]
Till from her cursed foe thou have her freely quit.

64

Then shall I soone, (quoth he) so God me grace,
Abet° that virgins cause disconsolate, *assist*
And shortly backe returne unto this place,
To walke this way in Pilgrims poore estate.° *condition*
But now aread,° old father, why of late° *tell me / just now*
Didst thou behight° me borne of English blood, *call*
Whom all a Faeries sonne doen nominate?[6]
That word shall I (said he) avouchen° good, *prove*
Sith to thee is unknowne the cradle of thy brood.° *girth*

65

For well I wote, thou springst from ancient race
Of Saxon kings, that have with mightie hand
And many bloudie battailes fought in place° *in that place*
High reard° their royall throne in Britane land, *erected*
And vanquisht them,° unable to withstand: *the Britons*
From thence a Faerie thee unweeting reft,° *took*
There as thou slepst in tender swadling band,

3. The Redcrosse Knight asks himself whether he can abandon chivalry and then understands that in the New Jerusalem there are neither wars nor loves.
4. The Redcrosse Knight is referring to death.
5. He may not yet give up Una's quest to which he is committed; he must avenge and free her from her enemy.
6. The Redcrosse Knight believes he is an inhabitant of Faerie Land, the fictional ground of the poem as Spenser names it to his readers. When Contemplation tells the Redcrosse Knight that he is actually English, Spenser is alerting readers to the fact that Saint George (as Spenser apparently believed) was a historical figure, represented in historical record, and not merely a figment of the poet's imagination.

And her base Elfin brood° there for the thee left.[7] — *child*
Such men do Chaungelings° call, so chaungd° by Faeries theft. — *changelings / switched*

66

Thence° she thee brought into this Faerie lond, — *from there*
And in an heaped furrow did thee hyde,
Where thee a Ploughman all unweeting fond,
As he his toylesome teme° that way did guyde, — *toiling oxen*
And brought thee up in ploughmans state to byde,
Whereof Georgos° he thee gave to name; — *farmer*
Till prickt° with courage, and thy forces pryde, — *moved*
To Faery court thou cam'st to seeke for fame,
And prove thy puissaunt armes, as seemes thee best became.[8]

67

O holy Sire (quoth he) how shall I quight° — *repay*
The many favours I with thee have found,
That hast my name and nation red aright,° — *correctly*
And taught the way that does to heaven bound?
This said, adowne he looked to the ground,
To have returnd, but dazed were his eyne,
Through passing brightnesse, which did quite confound° — *bewilder*
His feeble sence, and too exceeding shyne.[9]
So darke are earthly things compard to things divine.

68

At last whenas himselfe he gan to find,
To Una back he cast him° to retire; — *decided*
Who him awaited still with pensive mind.
Great thankes and goodly meed° to that good syre, — *reward*
He thence departing gave for his paines hyre.[1]
So came to Una, who him joyd to see,
And after litle rest, gan him desire,
Of her adventure° mindfull for to bee. — *quest*
So leave they take of Caelia, and her daughters three.

Canto 11

The knight with that old Dragon fights
two dayes incessantly:
The third him overthrowes, and gayns
most glorious victory.

1

High time now gan it wex° for Una faire, — *grow*
To thinke of those her captive Parents deare,
And their forwasted° kingdome to repaire: — *desolated*

7. I.e., unknown to you, a fairy took you from your cradle and put its own child in your place.
8. The qualities that prompted the Redcrosse Knight to leave the farm—i.e., pride in his chivalric skill—are qualities his faith will have had to modify to conform to a Christian mode of life.
9. The Redcrosse Knight glances down, intending to look back up, but the force of revelation overwhelms him.
1. The hire of his pains, the trouble Contemplation took to instruct the Redcrosse Knight.

Whereto whenas they now approched neare,
With hartie words her knight she gan to cheare,
And in her modest manner thus bespake;° *said*
Deare knight, as deare, as ever knight was deare,
That all these sorrowes suffer for my sake,
High heaven behold the tedious toyle, ye for me take.[1]

2

Now are we come unto my native soyle,
And to the place, where all our perils dwell;
Here haunts° that feend, and does his dayly spoyle,° *lurks / evil*
Therefore henceforth be at your keeping well,° *on your guard*
And ever ready for your foeman fell.° *dangerous enemy*
The sparke of noble courage now awake,
And strive your excellent selfe to excell;° *outdo yourself*
That shall ye evermore renowmed make,
Above all knights on earth, that batteill undertake.

3

And pointing forth, lo yonder is (said she)
The brasen towre in which my parents deare
For dread of that huge feend emprisond be,
Whom I from far see on the walles appeare,
Whose sight my feeble soule doth greatly cheare:
And on the top of all I do espye
The watchman wayting tydings glad to heare,[2]
That O my parents might I happily
Unto you bring, to ease you of your misery.

4

With that they heard a roaring hideous sound,
That all the ayre with terrour filled wide,
And seemd uneath° to shake the stedfast ground. *almost*
Eftsoones that dreadfull Dragon they espide,
Where stretcht he lay upon the sunny side
Of a great hill, himselfe like a great hill.
But all so soone, as he from far descride° *saw*
Those glistring armes, that heaven with light did fill,
He rousd himselfe full blith,° and hastned them untill.° *joyfully / toward them*

5

Then bad the knight his Lady yede aloofe,° *stand aside*
And to an hill her selfe with draw aside,
From whence she might behold that battailles proof
And eke be safe from daunger far descryde:° *seen from a distance*
She him obayd, and turnd a little wyde.° *moved aside*
Now O thou sacred Muse, most learned Dame,[3]
Faire ympe of Phoebus, and his aged bride,
The Nourse of time, and everlasting fame,
That warlike hands ennoblest with immortall name;

1. Una asks the heavens to witness the difficult task that the Redcrosse Knight undertakes for her.
2. Waiting to hear good news. In the next line, Una addresses her parents, expressing her wish to bring them the good news of their rescue herself.
3. Spenser is calling upon Clio, the muse of history, who preserves great events and records glorious deeds.

6

O gently come into my feeble brest,
Come gently, but not with that mighty rage,
Wherewith the martiall troupes thou doest infest,° *inspire*
And harts of great Heroës doest enrage,
That nought their kindled courage may aswage,° *diminish*
Soone as they dreadfull trompe° begins to sownd; *trumpet*
The God of warre with his fiers equipage° *weapons*
Thou doest awake, sleepe never he so sownd,
And scared nations doest with horrour sterne astownd.° *astonish*

7

Faire Goddesse lay that furious fit aside,[4]
Till I of warres and bloudy Mars do sing,
And Briton fields with Sarazin bloud bedyde,
Twixt that great faery Queene and Paynim king,
That with their horrour heaven and earth did ring,
A worke of labour long, and endlesse prayse:[5]
But now a while let downe that haughtie string,
And to my tunes thy second tenor° rayse, *accompaniment*
That I this man of God his godly armes may blaze.° *proclaim*

8

By this the dreadful Beast drew nigh to hand,° *near*
Halfe flying, and halfe footing in his hast,
That with his largenesse measured much land,
And made wide shadow under his huge wast;° *bulk*
As mountaine doth the valley overcast.
Approching nigh, he reared high afore
His body monstrous, horrible, and vast,
Which to increase his wondrous greatnesse more,
Was swolne with wrath, and poyson, and with bloudy gore.

9

And over, all with brasen scales was armd,
Like plated coate of steele, so couched neare,° *closely set*
That nought mote perce, ne might his corse be harmd
With dint of sword, nor push of pointed speare;
Which as an Eagle, seeing pray appeare,
His aery plumes doth rouze, full rudely dight,° *violently arranged*
So shaked he, that horrour was to heare,
For as the clashing of an Armour bright,
Such noyse his rouzed scales did send unto the knight.

10

His flaggy° wings when forth he did display, *drooping*
Were like two sayles, in which the hollow wynd
Is gathered full,[6] and worketh speedy way:
And eke the pennes,[7] that did his pineons° bynd, *feathers*
Were like mayne-yards,° with flying canvas lynd, *mainsail ropes*
With which whenas him list the ayre to beat,

4. The muse's "furious fit" is music that rouses men to war.
5. The song of war that Spenser refers to here may be some part of the poem he plans to write in the future.
6. The force of the wind fills the sails and makes them billow out.
7. The bones in the Dragon's wings.

And there by force unwonted passage find,[8]
The cloudes before him fled for terrour great,
And all the heavens stood still amazed with his threat.

11

His huge long tayle wound up in hundred foldes,
Does overspred his long bras-scaly backe,
Whose wreathed boughts° when ever he unfoldes, *wound-up coils*
And thicke entangled knots adown does slacke,
Bespotted as with shields of red and blacke,
It sweepeth all the land behind him farre,
And of three furlongs does but litle lacke;[9]
And at the point two stings in-fixed arre,
Both deadly sharpe, that sharpest steele exceeden farre.

12

But stings and sharpest steele did far exceed
The sharpnesse of his cruell rending clawes;
Dead was it sure, as sure as death in deed,
What ever thing does touch his ravenous pawes,
Or what within his reach he ever drawes.
But his most hideous head my toung to tell
Does tremble: for his deepe devouring jawes
Wide gaped, like the griesly mouth of hell,
Through which into his darke abisse° all ravin° fell. *pit / prey*

13

And that more wondrous was, in either jaw
Three ranckes of yron teeth enraunged were,
In which yet trickling bloud and gobbets° raw *chunks*
Of late devoured bodies did appeare,
That sight thereof bred cold congealed feare:
Which to increase, and all atonce° to kill, *suddenly*
A cloud of smoothering smoke and sulphur seare° *burning*
Out of his stinking gorge forth steemed still,
That all the ayre about with smoke and stench did fill.

14

His blazing eyes, like two bright shining shields,
Did burne with wrath, and sparkled living fyre;
As two broad Beacons, set in open fields,
Send forth their flames farre off to every shyre,° *district*
And warning give, that enemies conspyre,
With fire and sword the region to invade;
So flam'd his eyne with rage and rancorous yre:
But farre within, as in a hollow glade,
Those glaring lampes were set, that made a dreadfull shade.

15

So dreadfully he towards him did pas,
Forelifting° up aloft his speckled brest, *raising*
And often bounding on the brused gras,
As for great joyance of his newcome guest.

8. Although the Dragon cannot fly normally, he does so through the sheer force with which he beats his wings.

9. The Dragon's tail measures nearly three furlongs, 660 yards, a third of a mile.

Eftsoones he gan advance his haughtie crest,
As chauffed Bore° his bristles doth upreare, *angry boar*
And shoke his scales to battell readie drest;[1]
That made the Redcrosse knight nigh quake for feare,
As bidding° bold defiance to his foeman neare. *inciting*

16

The knight gan fairely couch his steadie speare,
And fiercely ran at him with rigorous might:
The pointed steele arriving rudely theare,
His harder hide would neither perce, nor bight,
But glauncing by forth passed forward right;
Yet sore amoved with so puissant push,
The wrathfull beast about him turned light,° *quickly*
And him so rudely passing by, did brush
With his long tayle, that° horse and man to ground did rush.° *so that/fall*

17

Both horse and man up lightly rose againe,
And fresh encounter towards him addrest:
But th'idle stroke° yet backe recoyld in vaine, *futile swordstroke*
And found no place his deadly point to rest.
Exceeding rage enflam'd the furious beast,
To be avenged of so great despight;
For never felt his imperceable brest
So wondrous force, from hand of living wight;
Yet had he prov'd° the powre of many a puissant knight. *tested*

18

Then with his waving wings displayed wyde,
Himselfe up high he lifted from the ground,
And with strong flight did forcibly divide
The yielding aire, which nigh° too feeble found *almost*
Her flitting partes, and element unsound,
To beare so great a weight:[2] he cutting way
With his broad sayles, about him soared round:
At last low stouping with unweldie sway,° *awkward force*
Snatcht up both horse and man, to beare them quite away.

19

Long he them bore above the subject plaine,
So farre as Ewghen° bow a shaft may send, *made of yew*
Till struggling strong did him at last constraine,
To let them downe before his flightes end:
As hagard hauke° presuming to contend *untamed hawk*
With hardie fowle, above his hable° might, *natural*
His wearie pounces° all in vaine doth spend, *claws*
To trusse° the pray too heavie for his flight; *carry off*
Which comming downe to ground, does free it selfe by fight.

20

He so disseized° of his gryping grosse,° *freed/heavy grasp*
The knight his thrillant speare againe assayd

1. He shook his scales into position for battle.
2. The air is almost too weak to support the Dragon; in other words, the Dragon is almost too heavy to fly, given the strength of his wings in relation to his overall weight.

In his bras-plated body to embosse,° *embed*
And three mens strength unto the stroke he layd;
Wherewith the stiffe beame° quaked, as affrayd, *shaft*
And glauncing from his scaly necke, did glyde
Close under his left wing, then broad displayd.
The percing steele there wrought a wound full wyde,
That with the uncouth smart° the Monster lowdly cryde. *pain*

21

He cryde, as raging seas are wont to rore,
When wintry storme his wrathfull wreck does threat,
The rolling billowes beat the ragged shore,
As they the earth would shoulder from her seat,
And greedie gulfe does gape, as he would eat
His neighbour element° in his revenge: *the earth*
Then gin the blustring brethren boldly threat,
To move the world from off his stedfast henge,° *hinge*
And boystrous battell make, each other to avenge.

22

The steely head stucke fast° still in his flesh, *firmly*
Till with his cruell clawes he snatcht the wood,° *shaft*
And quite a sunder broke. Forth flowed fresh
A gushing river of blacke goarie blood,
That drowned all the land, whereon he stood;
The streame thereof would drive a water-mill.
Trebly augmented was his furious mood
With bitter sense of his deepe rooted ill,
That flames of fire he threw forth from his large nosethrill.° *nostril*

23

His hideous tayle then hurled he about,
And therewith all enwrapt the nimble thyes° *thighs*
Of his froth-fomy steed, whose courage stout
Striving to loose the knot, that fast him tyes,
Himselfe in streighter bandes° too rash implyes, *tighter bondage*
That to the ground he is perforce° constraynd *thereby*
To throw his rider: who can quickly ryse
From off the earth, with durty bloud distaynd,° *stained*
For that reprochfull fall right fowly he disdaynd.

24

And fiercely tooke his trenchand° blade in hand, *sharp*
With which he stroke so furious and so fell,
That nothing seemd the puissance could withstand:
Upon his crest the hardned yron fell,
But his more hardned crest was armd so well,
That deeper dint therein it would not make;
Yet so extremely did the buffe° him quell,° *blow/overwhelm*
That from thenceforth he shund the like to take,
But when he saw them come, he did them still forsake.° *avoid*

25

The knight was wrath to see his stroke beguyld,° *foiled*
And smote againe with more outrageous might;
But backe againe the sparckling steele recoyld,
And left not any marke, where it did light;° *land*

As if in Adamant° rocke it had bene pight. *hardest*
The beast impatient of his smarting wound,
And of so fierce and forcible despight,° *injury*
Thought with his wings to stye° above the ground; *fly*
But his late wounded wing unserviceable found.

26

Then full of griefe and anguish vehement,
He lowdly brayd, that like was never heard,
And from his wide devouring oven° sent *mouth*
A flake of fire, that flashing in his° beard, *Redcrosse Knight's*
Him all amazd, and almost made affeard:
The scorching flame sore swinged° all his face, *singed*
And through his armour all his bodie seard,° *burned*
That he could not endure so cruell cace,° *situation*
But thought his armes to leave, and helmet to unlace.

27

Not that great Champion[3] of the antique world,
Whom famous Poetes verse so much doth vaunt,° *celebrate*
And hath for twelve huge labours high extold,° *praised*
So many furies and sharpe fits did haunt,
When him the poysoned garment did enchaunt
With Centaures bloud, and bloudie verses charm'd,
As did this knight twelve thousand dolours daunt,° *defy*
Whom fyrie steele now burnt, that earst° him arm'd, *recently*
That erst° him goodly arm'd, now most of all him harm'd. *at first*

28

Faint, wearie, sore, emboyled, grieved, brent
With heat, toyle, wounds, armes, smart, and inward fire
That never man such mischiefes did torment;
Death better were, death did he oft desire,
But death will never come, when needes require.
Whom so dismayd when that his foe° beheld, *the Dragon*
He cast to suffer him no more respire,[4]
But gan his sturdie sterne° about to weld, *tail*
And him° so strongly stroke, that to the ground him feld. *Redcrosse Knight*

29

It fortuned (as faire it then befell)
Behind his backe unweeting, where he stood,
Of auncient time there was a springing well,
From which fast trickled forth a silver flood,
Full of great vertues, and for med'cine good.
Whylome, before that cursed Dragon got
That happie land, and all with innocent blood
Defyld those sacred waves, it rightly hot
The well of life, ne yet his vertues had forgot.

30

For unto life the dead it could restore,
And guilt of sinfull crimes cleane wash away,

3. Hercules. After successfully completely his 12 impossible labors, the hero was plagued ("haunted") by "furies": his wife gave him a tunic soaked in the poison blood of a centaur. The blood was meant to work as a love charm but instead burned Hercules' flesh, and he died in agony.

4. The Dragon, seeing how desperate the Redcrosse Knight is, determines to kill him.

Those that with sicknesse were infected sore,
It could recure,° and aged long decay *cure*
Renew, as one were borne that very day.
Both Silo this,[5] and Jordan did excell,
And th'English Bath, and eke the german Spau,
Ne can Cephise, nor Hebrus match this well:
Into the same the knight backe overthrowen, fell.

31

Now gan the golden Phoebus for to steepe
His fierie face in billowes of the west,
And his faint steedes watred in Ocean deepe,
Whiles from their journall° labours they did rest, *daily*
When that infernall Monster, having kest° *cast*
His wearie foe into that living well,
Can high advance his broad discoloured brest,
Above his wonted pitch, with countenance fell,
And clapt his yron wings, as victor he did dwell.° *remain*

32

Which when his pensive° Ladie saw from farre, *worried*
Great woe and sorrow did her soule assay,
As weening that the sad end of the warre,
And gan to highest God entirely pray,
That feared chance from her to turne away;[6]
With folded hands and knees full lowly bent
All night she watcht, ne once adowne would lay
Her daintie limbs in her sad dreriment,° *plight*
But praying still did wake, and waking did lament.

33

The morrow next gan early to appeare,
That Titan rose to runne his daily race;
But early ere the morrow next gan reare
Out of the sea faire Titans deawy face,
Up rose the gentle virgin from her place,
And looked all about, if she might spy
Her loved knight to move his manly pace:
For she had great doubt° of his safety, *fear*
Since late she saw him fall before his enemy.

34

At last she saw, where he upstarted brave
Out of the well, wherein he drenched lay;
As Eagle fresh out of the Ocean wave,
Where he hath left his plumes all hoary gray,
And deckt himselfe with feathers youthly gay,
Like Eyas hauke[7] up mounts unto the skies,
His newly budded pineons° to assay, *wings*

5. Silo, Jordan, Bath, Spau, Cephise, and Hebrus: all waters reputed to have healing powers. The blind man is cured by bathing in the waters of Siloam (John 9.7), and John baptized Christ in the River Jordan (Matthew 3.16). Cephise and Hebrus are mentioned in classical mythology. Spenser probably wanted his readers to associate the water from "the well of life" with baptism, as in John 4.14.

6. She prayed to God to prevent the event she fears, the death of the Redcrosse Knight.

7. A young, untamed hawk; a symbol of victory.

And marveiles at himselfe, still as he flies:
So new this new-borne knight to battell new did rise.

35

Whom when the damned feend so fresh did spy,
No wonder if he wondred at the sight,
And doubted, whether his late enemy
It were, or other new supplied knight.
He,° now to prove his late renewed might, *Redcrosse Knight*
High brandishing his bright deaw-burning blade,[8]
Upon his crested scalpe so sore did smite,
That to the scull a yawning wound it made:
The deadly dint his dulled senses all dismaid.

36

I wote not, whether the revenging steele
Were hardned with that holy water dew,
Wherein he fell, or sharper edge did feele,
Or his baptized hands now greater grew;
Or other secret vertue did ensew;° *result*
Else never could the force of fleshly arme,
Ne molten mettall in his° bloud embrew:° *the Dragon's / soak*
For till that stownd° could never wight him harme,[9] *moment*
By subtilty, nor slight, nor might, nor mighty charme.

37

The cruell wound enraged him so sore,
That loud he yelded for exceeding paine;
As hundred ramping Lyons seem'd to rore,
Whom ravenous hunger did thereto constraine:° *torment*
Then gan he tosse aloft his stretched traine,
And therewith scourge the buxome° aire so sore, *yielding*
That to his force to yeelden it was faine;
Ne ought° his sturdie strokes might stand afore,° *nor anything / before*
That high trees overthrew, and rocks in peeces tore.

38

The same° advauncing high above his head, *the Dragon*
With sharpe intended sting so rude him smot,
That to the earth him drove, as stricken dead,
Ne living wight would have him life behot:° *predicted*
The mortall sting his angry needle shot
Quite through his shield, and in his shoulder seasd,° *pierced*
Where fast it stucke, ne would there out be got:
The griefe thereof him wondrous sore diseasd,
Ne might his ranckling paine with patience be appeasd.

39

But yet more mindfull of his honour deare,
Then of the grievous smart, which him did wring,° *afflict*
From loathed soile he can° him lightly reare, *did*
And strove to loose the farre infixed sting:
Which when in vaine he tryde with struggeling,
Inflam'd with wrath, his raging blade he heft,° *lifted*
And strooke so strongly, that the knotty string

8. The Redcrosse Knight's sword is like the sun, which burns up the dew.

9. Until that moment, neither human strength nor human weapons could succeed in piercing the Dragon's flesh.

Of his huge taile he quite a sunder cleft,
Five joynts thereof he hewd,° and but the stump him left. *cut*

40

Hart cannot thinke, what outrage, and what cryes,
With foule enfouldred[1] smoake and flashing fire,
The hell-bred beast threw forth unto the skyes,
That all was covered with darknesse dire:
Then fraught with rancour,° and engorged ire, *malice*
He cast at once him to avenge for all,
And gathering up himselfe out of the mire,
With his uneven wings did fiercely fall
Upon his sunne-bright shield, and gript it fast withall.° *as well*

41

Much was the man encombred with his hold,
In feare to lose his weapon in his paw,
Ne wist yet, how his talants to unfold;
Nor harder was from Cerberus[2] greedie jaw
To plucke a bone, then from his cruell claw
To reave°by strength the griped gage[3] away: *pry*
Thrise he assayd it from his foot to draw,
And thrise in vaine to draw it did assay,
It booted nought to thinke, to robbe him of his pray.

42

Tho when he saw no power might prevaile,
His trustie sword he cald to his last aid,
Wherewith he fiercely did his foe assaile,
And double blowes about him stoutly laid,
That glauncing fire out of the yron plaid;° *leaped*
As sparckles from the Anduile° use to fly, *anvil*
When heavie hammers on the wedge° are swaid;° *metal / struck*
Therewith at last he forst him to unty
One of his grasping feete, him° to defend thereby. *himself*

43

The other foot, fast fixed on his shield,
Whenas no strength, nor stroks mote him° constraine *the Dragon*
To loose, ne yet the warlike pledge to yield,
He° smot thereat with all his might and maine, *Redcrosse Knight*
That nought° so wondrous puissance might sustaine; *nothing*
Upon the joynt the lucky steele did light,
And made such way, that hewd it quite in twaine;
The paw yet missed not his minisht might,° *diminished strength*
But hong still on the shield, as it at first was pight.° *fixed*

44

For griefe thereof, and divelish despight,
From his infernall fournace forth he threw
Huge flames, that dimmed all the heavens light,
Enrold in duskish smoke and brimstone[4] blew;
As burning Aetna° from his boyling stew *a volcano in Sicily*
Doth belch out flames, and rockes in peeces broke,

1. Like a thundercloud filled with lightning bolts.
2. The mythological three-headed dog guarding the gates of Hell.
3. The prize over which a battle is fought; here, the Redcrosse Knight's shield.
4. Sulfur, which burns blue.

And ragged ribs of mountaines molten new,° *newly molten*
Enwrapt in coleblacke clouds and filthy smoke,
That all the land with stench, and heaven with horror choke.

45

The heate whereof, and harmefull pestilence° *destruction*
So sore him noyd,° that forst him to retire *injured*
A little backward for his best defence,
To save his bodie from the scorching fire,
Which he° from hellish entrailes did expire. *the Dragon*
It chaunst (eternall God that chaunce did guide)
As he recoyled° backward, in the mire *shrank*
His nigh forwearied° feeble feet did slide, *tired*
And downe he fell, with dread of shame sore terrifide.

46

There grew a goodly tree him faire beside,
Loaden with fruit and apples rosie red,
As they in pure vermilion had beene dide,
Whereof great vertues over all were red:
For happie life to all, which thereon fed,
And life eke everlasting did befall:
Great God it planted in that blessed sted° *place*
With his almightie hand, and did it call
The tree of life,[5] the crime of our first fathers fall.

47

In all the world like was not to be found,
Save in that soile, where all good things did grow,
And freely sprong out of the fruitfull ground,
As incorrupted Nature did them sow,
Till that dread Dragon° all did overthrow. *Satan, the serpent*
Another like faire tree eke grew thereby,[6]
Whereof who so did eat, eftsoones did know
Both good and ill: O mornefull memory:
That tree through one mans fault hath doen us all to dy.

48

From that first tree forth flowd, as from a well,
A trickling streame of Balme, most soveraine
And daintie deare,° which on the ground still fell, *very precious*
And overflowed all the fertill plaine,
As it had deawed° bene with timely raine: *sprinkled*
Life and long health that gratious ointment gave,
And deadly woundes could heale, and reare againe
The senseless corse appointed for the grave.[7]
Into that same he fell: which did from death him save.

49

For nigh thereto the ever damned beast
Durst° not approch, for he was deadly made,[8] *dared*
And all that life preserved, did detest:

5. The tree of life was denied to Adam for his "crime"—his defiance of God's commandment not to eat the fruit of the tree of knowledge of good and evil. As a result, God expelled him from the Garden of Eden where the tree of life grew.
6. The tree of knowledge of good and evil.
7. The balm from the tree of life heals the Redcrosse Knight; its function follows that of the water in baptism. Having been freed of the consequences of original sin in baptism, the baptized are constantly open to restorations of faith in pursuit of good works. Cf. Revelation 22.2: "The leaves of the tree [of life] served to heale the nations."
8. He was allied with Death, not Life.

Yet he it° oft adventur'd° to invade.° *the tree/tried/destroy*
By this the drouping day-light gan to fade,
And yeeld his roome° to sad succeeding night, *place*
Who with her sable mantle gan to shade
The face of earth, and wayes of living wight,
And high her burning torch set up in heaven bright.

50

When gentle Una saw the second fall
Of her deare knight, who wearie of long fight,
And faint through losse of bloud, mov'd not at all,
But lay as in a dreame of deepe delight,
Besmeard with pretious Balme, whose vertuous might
Did heale his wounds, and scorching heat alay,
Againe she stricken was with sore affright,
And for his safetie gan devoutly pray;
And watch the noyous° night, and wait for joyous day. *sorrowful*

51

The joyous day gan early to appeare,
And faire Aurora[9] from the deawy bed
Of aged Tithone gan her selfe to reare,
With rosie cheekes, for shame as blushing red;
Her golden lockes for haste were loosely shed
About her eares, when Una her did marke
Clymbe to her charet, all with flowers spred,
From heaven high to chase the chearelesse darke;
With merry note her° loud salutes the mounting larke. *Una*

52

Then freshly up arose the doughtie knight,
All healed of his hurts and woundes wide,
And did himselfe to battell readie dight;
Whose early foe awaiting him beside
To have devourd, so soone as day he spyde,
When now he saw himselfe so freshly reare,
As if late fight had nought him damnifyde,° *harmed*
He woxe° dismayd, and gan his fate to feare; *grew*
Nathlesse° with wonted rage he him advaunced neare. *nonetheless*

53

And in his first encounter, gaping wide,
He thought attonce° him to have swallowd quight, *at once*
And rusht upon him with outragious pride;
Who him r'encountring fierce, as hauke in flight,
Perforce° rebutted° backe. The weapon bright *necessarily/attacked*
Taking advantage of his open jaw,
Ran through his mouth with so importune° might, *violent*
That deepe emperst his darksome hollow maw,° *mouth*
And back retyrd,° his life bloud forth with all did draw. *retracted*

54

So downe he fell, and forth his life did breath,[1]
That vanisht into smoke and cloudes swift;
So downe he fell, that th'earth him underneath

9. The goddess of the dawn, married to Tithone or Tithonus.

1. The blood that flows from the Dragon takes his life with it.

Did grone, as feeble so great load to lift;
So downe he fell, as an huge rockie clift,
Whose false foundation waves have washt away,
With dreadfull poyse° is from the mayneland rift, *force*
And rolling downe, great Neptune doth dismay;
So downe he fell, and like an heaped mountaine lay.

55

The knight himselfe even trembled at his fall,
So huge and horrible a masse it seem'd;
And his deare Ladie, that beheld it all,
Durst not approch for dread, which she misdeem'd,
But yet at last, when as the direfull feend
She saw not stirre, off-shaking vaine affright,° *empty fear*
She nigher drew, and saw that joyous end:
Then God she praysd, and thankt her faithfull knight,
That had atchiev'd so great a conquest by his might.

Canto 12

Faire Una to the Redcrosse knight
betrouthed is with joy:
Though false Duessa it to barre° *prevent*
her false sleights doe imploy.

1

Behold I see the haven° nigh at hand, *harbor*
To which I meane my wearie course to bend;
Vere° the maine shete, and beare up with° the land, *loosen/steer toward*
The which afore is fairely to be kend,° *recognized*
And seemeth safe from stormes, that may offend;
There this faire virgin wearie of her way
Must landed be, now at her journeyes end:
There eke my feeble barke° a while may stay, *ship*
Till merry wind and weather call her thence away.

2

Scarsely had Phoebus in the glooming° East *glowing*
Yet harnessed his firie-footed teeme,
Ne reard above the earth his flaming creast,
When the last deadly smoke aloft did steeme,
That signe of last outbreathed life did seeme
Unto the watchman on the castle wall;
Who thereby dead that balefull Beast did deeme,
And to his Lord and Ladie lowd gan call,
To tell, how he had seene the Dragons fatall fall.

3

Uprose with hastie joy, and feeble speed
That aged Sire,° the Lord of all that land, *Una's father*
And looked forth, to weet, if true indeede
Those tydings were, as he did understand,
Which whenas true by tryall° he out fond, *investigation*
He bad to open wyde his brazen gate,
Which long time had bene shut, and out of hond° *immediately*

Proclaymed joy and peace through all his state;
For dead now was their foe, which them forrayed° late.° *plundered/lately*

4

Then gan triumphant Trompets sound on hie,
That sent to heaven the ecchoed report
Of their new joy, and happie victorie
Gainst him, that had them long opprest with tort,° *wrong*
And fast imprisoned in sieged fort.
Then all the people, as in solemne feast,
To him assembled with one full consort,° *in unison*
Rejoycing at the fall of that great beast,
From whose eternall bondage now they were releast.

5

Forth came that auncient Lord and aged Queene,
Arayd° in antique robes downe to the ground, *dressed*
And sad habiliments right well beseene;[1]
A noble crew° about them waited round *crowd*
Of sage and sober Peres, all gravely gownd;
Whom farre before did march a goodly band
Of tall young men, all hable° armes to sownd,° *able/wield*
But now they laurell braunches bore in hand;
Glad signe of victorie and peace in all their land.

6

Unto that doughtie° Conquerour they came, *worthy*
And him before themselves prostrating low,
Their Lord and Patrone loud did him proclame,
And at his feet their laurell boughes did throw.
Soone after them all dauncing on a row
The comely virgins came, with girlands dight,° *prepared*
As fresh as flowres in medow greene do grow,
When morning deaw upon their leaves doth light:° *land*
And in their hands sweet Timbrels° all upheld on hight. *tambourines*

7

And them before, the fry° of children young *group*
Their wanton sports and childish mirth did play,
And to the Maydens sounding tymbrels sung
In well attuned notes, a joyous lay,
And made delightfull musicke all the way,
Untill they came, where that faire virgin stood;
As faire Diana in fresh sommers day
Beholds her Nymphes, enraung'd° in shadie wood, *spread out*
Some wrestle, some do run, some bathe in christall flood.° *clear waters*

8

So she beheld those maydens meriment
With chearefull vew; who when to her they came,
Themselves to ground with gratious humblesse bent,
And her ador'd by honorable name,
Lifting to heaven her everlasting fame:
Then on her head they set a girland greene,

1. Their somber clothes were appropriate.

And crowned her twixt earnest and twixt game;[2]
Who in her selfe-resemblance well beseene,[3]
Did seeme such, as she was, a goodly maiden Queene.

9

And after, all the raskall many° ran, *playful crowd*
Heaped together in rude rablement,° *confusion*
To see the face of that victorious man:° *Redcrosse Knight*
Whom all admired, as from heaven sent,
And gazd upon with gaping wonderment.
But when they came, where that dead Dragon lay,
Stretcht on the ground in monstrous large extent,
The sight with idle feare did them dismay,
Ne durst° approch him nigh, to touch, or once assay.[4] *nor dared*

10

Some feard, and fled; some feard and well it faynd;° *hid it well*
One that would wiser seeme, then° all the rest, *than*
Warnd him not touch, for yet perhaps remaynd
Some lingring life within his hollow brest,
Or in his wombe might lurke some hidden nest
Of many Dragonets, his fruitfull seed;
Another said, that in his eyes did rest
Yet sparckling fire, and bad thereof take heed;° *care*
Another said, he saw him move his eyes indeed.

11

One mother, when as her foolehardie chyld
Did come too neare, and with his talants° play, *claws*
Halfe dead through feare, her litle babe revyld,
And to her gossips gan in counsell say;
How can I tell, but that his talants may
Yet scratch my sonne, or rend his tender hand?
So diversly themselves in vaine they fray;° *frighten*
Whiles some more bold, to measure him nigh stand,
To prove how many acres he did spread of land.

12

Thus flocked all the folke him round about,
The whiles that hoarie° king, with all his traine, *aged*
Being arrived, where that champion stout
After his foes defeasance° did remaine, *defeat*
Him goodly greetes, and faire does entertaine,
With princely gifts of yvorie and gold,
And thousand thankes him yeelds° for all his paine. *gives*
Then when his daughter deare he does behold,
Her dearely doth imbrace, and kisseth manifold.° *many times*

13

And after to his Pallace he them brings,
With shaumes,° and trompets, and with Clarions° sweet; *oboes/trumpets*
And all the way the joyous people sings,
And with their garments strowes the paved street:
Whence mounting up, they find purveyance meet° *suitable refreshment*

2. Half seriously, half playfully.
3. Una appears appropriately like herself (unlike Duessa, for instance, who appeared to be something other than what she was).
4. They did not dare to approach the dragon, to touch it, or even to try to touch it.

Of all, that royall Princes court became,
And all the floore was underneath their feet
Bespred with costly scarlot° of great name, *cloth*
On which they lowly sit, and fitting purpose frame.° *converse nicely*

14

What needs me tell their feast and goodly guize,° *behavior*
In which was nothing riotous nor vaine?
What needs of daintie dishes to devize,° *describe*
Of comely services, or courtly trayne?
My narrow leaves cannot in them containe
The large discourse of royall Princes state.
Yet was their manner then but bare° and plaine: *simple*
For th'antique world excesse and pride did hate;
Such proud luxurious pompe is swollen up but late.° *only recently*

15

Then when with meates and drinkes of every kinde
Their fervent appetites they quenched had,
That auncient Lord gan fit occasion finde,
Of straunge adventures, and of perils sad,
Which in his travell him befallen had,
For to demaund of his renowmed° guest: *renowned*
Who then with utt'rance° grave, and count'nance sad, *expression*
From point to point, as is before exprest,
Discourst° his voyage long, according his request. *related*

16

Great pleasure mixt with pittifull regard,° *compassion*
That godly King and Queene did passionate,° *empathize*
Whiles they his pittifull adventures heard,
That oft they did lament his lucklesse state,
And often blame the too importune° fate, *cruel*
That heapd on him so many wrathfull wreakes:° *injuries*
For never gentle knight, as he of late,° *recently*
So tossed was in fortunes cruell freakes;° *accidents*
And all the while salt teares bedeawd° the hearers cheaks. *wetted*

17

Then said that royall Pere in sober wise;
Deare Sonne, great beene the evils, which ye bore
From first to last in your late enterprise,
That I note, whether prayse, or pitty more:
For never living man, I weene, so sore
In sea of deadly daungers was distrest;
But since now safe ye seised° have the shore, *reached*
And well arrived are, (high God be blest)
Let us devize° of ease and everlasting rest. *speak*

18

Ah dearest Lord, said then that doughty° knight, *worthy*
Of ease or rest I may not yet devize;
For by the faith, which I to armes have plight,
I bounden am streight after this emprize,° *enterprise*
As that your daughter can ye well advize,
Backe to returne to that great Faerie Queene,
And her to serve six yeares in warlike wize,° *manner*

Gainst that proud Paynim king, that workes her teene:° *sorrow*
Therefore I ought crave pardon, till I there have beene.

19

Unhappie falles that hard necessitie,
(Quoth he) the troubler of my happie peace,
And vowed foe of my felicitie;
Ne I against the same can justly preace:° *argue*
But since that band° ye cannot now release, *bond*
Nor doen undo; (for vowes may not be vaine)
Soone as the terme of those six yeares shall cease,
Ye then shall hither backe returne againe,
The marriage to accomplish vowd° betwixt you twain. *promised*

20

Which for my part I covet° to performe, *desire*
In sort as through the world I did proclame,
That who so kild that monster most deforme,
And him in hardy battaile overcame,
Should have mine onely daughter to his Dame,
And of my kingdome heire apparaunt bee:
Therefore since now to thee perteines the same,
By dew desert of noble chevalree,
Both daughter and eke kingdome, lo I yield to thee.

21

Then forth he called that his daughter faire,
The fairest Un' his onely daughter deare,
His onely daughter, and his onely heyre;
Who forth proceeding with sad sober cheare,
As bright as doth the morning starre appeare
Out of the East, with flaming lockes bedight,
To tell that dawning day is drawing neare,
And to the world does bring long wished light;
So faire and fresh that Lady shewd her selfe in sight.

22

So faire and fresh, as freshest flowre in May;
For she had layd her mournefull stole° aside, *dark cloak*
And widow-like sad wimple throwne away,
Wherewith her heavenly beautie she did hide,
Whiles on her wearie journey she did ride;
And on her now a garment she did weare,
All lilly white, withoutten° spot, or pride, *without a*
That seemd like silke and silver woven neare,
But neither silke nor silver therein did appeare.

23

The blazing brightnesse of her beauties beame,
And glorious light of her sunshyny face
To tell, were as to strive against the streame.
My ragged rimes° are all too rude and bace, *rhymes*
Her heavenly lineaments° for to enchace.° *features/display*
Ne wonder; for her owne deare loved knight,
All were she dayly with himselfe in place,° *by his side*
Did wonder much at her celestiall sight:
Oft had he seene her faire, but never so faire dight.

24

So fairely dight, when she in presence came,
She to her Sire made humble reverence,
And bowed low, that her right well became,
And added grace unto her excellence:
Who with great wisedome, and grave eloquence
Thus gan to say. But eare he thus had said,
With flying speede, and seeming great pretence,° *purpose*
Came running in, much like a man dismaid,° *overwhelmed*
A Messenger with letters, which his message said.

25

All in the open hall amazed stood,
At suddeinnesse of that unwarie° sight, *unexpected*
And wondred at his breathlesse hastie mood.
But he for nought would stay his passage right,° *stop*
Till fast before° the king he did alight;° *in front of/arrive*
Where falling flat, great humblesse he did make,
And kist the ground, whereon his foot was pight;° *placed*
Then to his hands that writ° he did betake,° *message/deliver*
Which he disclosing,° red thus, as the paper spake.° *unfolding/said*

26

To thee, most mighty king of Eden faire,
Her greeting sends in these sad lines addrest,
The wofull daughter, and forsaken heire
Of that great Emperour of all the West;
And bids thee be advized for the best,
Ere thou thy daughter linck° in holy band *join*
Of wedlocke to that new unknowen guest:
For he already plighted° his right hand *promised*
Unto another love, and to another land.

27

To me sad mayd, or rather widow sad,
He was affiaunced° long time before, *engaged*
And sacred pledges he both gave, and had,
False erraunt° knight, infamous, and forswore:° *erring/lying*
Witnesse the burning Altars, which° he swore,[5] *by which*
And guiltie heavens of his bold perjury,° *lie*
Which though he hath polluted oft of yore,
Yet I to them for judgement just do fly,
And them conjure° t'avenge this shamefull injury.[6] *implore*

28

Therefore since mine he is, or free or bond,
Or false or trew, or living or else dead,
Withhold, O soveraine Prince, your hasty hond
From knitting league with him, I you aread;° *advise*
Ne weene my right with strength adowne to tread,[7]
Through weakenesse of my widowhed,° or woe: *widowhood*
For truth is strong, her rightfull cause to plead,

5. Referring to a pagan marriage ritual in which sacrifices are burned on an altar to confirm the marriage vows.

6. Although the Redcrosse Knight has polluted the heavens with his lies, the author of the message nonetheless looks to them for judgment against him.

7. Do not try to overcome my rights by force.

And shall find friends, if need requireth soe,
So bids thee well to fare,° Thy neither friend, nor foe. *farewell*

29

When he° these bitter byting words had red,° *the king / heard*
The tydings° straunge did him abashed make, *news*
That still he sate long time astonished
As in great muse,° ne word to creature spake. *astonishment*
At last his solemne silence thus he brake,
With doubtfull eyes fast fixed on his guest;
Redoubted° knight, that for mine onely sake *formidable*
Thy life and honour late adventurest,
Let nought be hid from me, that ought to be exprest.

30

What meane these bloudy vowes, and idle threats,
Throwne out from womanish impatient mind?
What heavens? what altars? what enraged heates° *rantings*
Here heaped up with termes of love unkind,
My conscience cleare with guilty bands would bind?
High God be witnesse, that I guiltlesse ame.
But if your selfe, Sir knight, ye faultie° find, *guilty*
Or wrapped be in loves of former Dame,
With crime° do not it cover, but disclose the same. *lies*

31

To whom the Redcrosse knight this answere sent,
My Lord, my King, be nought hereat dismayd,
Till well ye wote by grave intendiment,° *careful consideration*
What woman, and wherefore° doth me upbrayd *why*
With breach of love, and loyalty betrayd.
It was in my mishaps, as hitherward° *on my way here*
I lately traveild, that unwares I strayd
Out of my way, through perils straunge and hard;
That day should faile me, ere I had them all declard.

32

There did I find, or rather I was found
Of this false woman, that Fidessa hight,
Fidessa hight the falsest Dame on ground,
Most false Duessa, royall richly dight,
That easie° was t'invegle° weaker sight: *eager / blind*
Who by her wicked arts, and wylie skill,
Too false and strong for earthly skill or might,
Unwares° me wrought unto her wicked will, *unknowingly*
And to my foe betrayd, when least I feared ill.

33

Then stepped forth the goodly royall Mayd,
And on the ground her selfe prostrating° low, *bowing*
With sober countenaunce thus to him sayd;
O pardon me, my soveraigne Lord, to show
The secret treasons, which of late° I know *recently*
To have bene wroght° by that false sorceresse. *committed*
She onely she it is, that earst did throw

This gentle knight into so great distresse,
That death him did awaite in dayly wretchednesse.

34

And now it seemes, that she suborned° hath *bribed*
This craftie messenger with letters vaine,° *false*
To worke new woe and improvided° scath, *unforeseen*
By breaking of the band betwixt us twaine;
Wherein she used hath the practicke paine° *crafty labor*
Of this false footman, clokt° with simplenesse, *cloaked*
Whom if ye please for° to discover plaine, *wish*
Ye shall him Archimago find, I ghesse,
The falsest man alive; who° tries shall find no lesse. *whoever*

35

The king was greatly moved at her speach,
And all with suddein indignation fraight,° *filled*
Bad on that Messenger rude hands to reach.
Eftsoones the Gard, which on his state did wait,
Attacht° that faitor false, and bound him strait: *seized*
Who seeming sorely chauffed° at his band, *annoyed*
As chained Beare, whom cruell dogs do bait,
With idle force did faine° them to withstand, *attempt*
And often semblaunce made° to scape out of their hand.[8] *pretended*

36

But they him layd full low in dungeon deepe,
And bound him hand and foote with yron chains.
And with continuall watch did warely° keepe; *carefully*
Who then would thinke, that by his subtile trains
He could escape fowle death or deadly paines?
Thus when that Princes wrath was pacifide,
He gan renew the late forbidden banes,° *banns*
And to the knight his daughter deare he tyde,
With sacred rites and vowes for ever to abyde.[9]

37

His owne two hands the holy knots did knit,
That none but death for ever can devide;
His owne two hands, for such a turne most fit,
The housling° fire[1] did kindle and provide, *domestic*
And holy water thereon sprinckled wide;
At which the bushy Teade° a groome did light, *torch*
And sacred lampe in secret chamber hide,
Where it should not be quenched day nor night,
For feare of evill fates, but burnen ever bright.

38

Then gan they sprinckle all the posts with wine,[2]
And made great feast to solemnize that day;

8. Since Archimago himself is false, his efforts to escape are also false.

9. The King recommences the announcement of marriage that had been recently forbidden by Duessa's false charges against the Redcrosse Knight.

1. Originally Roman marriage rituals, the fire and water used by the King here also suggest baptism and the sanctification of married love.

2. Roman brides sprinkled the doorposts of their new homes with wine in a ritual symbolizing joy and fertility.

They all perfumde with frankincense divine,
And precious odours fetcht from far away,
That all the house did sweat with great aray:° *ceremony*
And all the while sweete Musicke did apply
Her curious skill, the warbling notes to play,
To drive away the dull Melancholy;
The whiles one sung a song of love and jollity.

39

During the which there was an heavenly noise
Heard sound through all the Pallace pleasantly,
Like as it had bene many an Angels voice,
Singing before th'eternall majesty,
In their trinall triplicities[3] on hye;
Yet wist no creature, whence that heavenly sweet
Proceeded, yet eachone felt secretly
Himselfe thereby reft of his sences meet,° *ordinary*
And ravished with rare impression in his sprite.

40

Great joy was made that day of young and old,
And solemne feast proclaimd throughout the land,
That their exceeding merth° may not be told: *joy*
Suffice it heare by signes to understand[4]
The usuall joyes at knitting of loves band.
Thrise° happy man the knight himselfe did hold, *thrice*
Possessed of his Ladies hart and hand,
And ever, when his eye did her behold,
His heart did seeme to melt in pleasures manifold.

41

Her joyous presence and sweet company
In full content he there did long enjoy,
Ne wicked envie, ne vile gealosy
His deare delights were able to annoy:
Yet swimming in that sea of blisfull joy,
He nought forgot, how he whilome had sworne,
In case he could that monstrous beast destroy,
Unto his Faerie Queene backe to returne:
The which he shortly did, and Una left to mourne.

42

Now strike your sailes ye jolly Mariners,
For we be come unto a quiet rode,° *haven*
Where we must land some of our passengers,
And light this wearie vessell of her lode.
Here she a while may make her safe abode,
Till she repaired have her tackles spent,° *worn out fittings*
And wants supplide. And then againe abroad
On the long voyage whereto she is bent:
Well may she speede° and fairely finish her intent. *continue*

3. The triple triad or the nine orders of angels. The music that they play is the music of the spheres, which humankind had been unable to hear since the Fall.

4. Since the happiness of the occasion is beyond the ability of words to express, let it be sufficient to understand it through symbols.

from The Second Booke of the Faerie Queene

Contayning The Legend of Sir Guyon or Temperaunce

Canto 12

Guyon, by Palmers governance,
passing through perils great,
Doth overthrow the Bowre of blisse,
and Acrasie defeat.

1

Now gins° this goodly frame of Temperance — *begins*
Fairely to rise, and her adorned hed
To pricke of highest praise forth to advance,
Formerly° grounded, and fast setteled — *previously*
On firme foundation of true bountihed;[1]
And this brave knight, that for that vertue fights,
Now comes to point of that same perilous sted,° — *dangerous place*
Where Pleasure dwelles in sensuall delights,
Mongst thousand dangers, and ten thousand magick mights.° — *powers*

2

Two dayes now in that sea he sayled has,
Ne ever land beheld, ne living wight,
Ne ought° save perill, still as he did pas: — *nor anything*
Tho when appeared the third Morrow bright,
Upon the waves to spred her trembling light,
An hideous roaring farre away they heard,
That all their senses filled with affright,
And streight they saw the raging surges reard
Up to the skyes, that them of drowning made affeard.

3

Said then the Boteman, Palmer stere aright,
And keepe an even course; for yonder way
We needes must passe (God do us well acquight,)° — *deliver*
That is the Gulfe° of Greedinesse, they say, — *whirlpool*
That deepe engorgeth° all this worldes pray: — *swallows*
Which having swallowd up excessively,
He soone in vomit up againe doth lay,
And belcheth forth his superfluity,° — *excess*
That all the seas for feare do seeme away to fly.

4

On th'other side an hideous Rocke is pight,° — *placed*
Of mightie Magnes° stone, whose craggie clift — *magnet*
Depending from on high, dreadfull to sight,
Over the waves his rugged armes doth lift,
And threatneth downe to throw his ragged rift° — *rocks*
On who so commeth nigh; yet nigh it drawes

1. The spirit of temperance begins to be inspired to celebrate and highly praise temperance, now that this virtue is established on goodness ("bountihed").

All passengers, that none from it can shift:
For whiles they fly that Gulfes devouring jawes,
They on this rock are rent, and sunck in helplesse waves.° *waves*

5

Forward they passe, and strongly he them rowes,
Untill they nigh unto that Gulfe arrive,
Where streame more violent and greedy growes:
Then he with all his puissance° doth strive *power*
To strike his oares, and mightily doth drive
The hollow vessell through the threatfull wave,
Which gaping wide, to swallow them alive,
In th'huge abysse of his engulfing grave,
Doth rore at them in vaine, and with great terror rave.

6

They passing by, that griesly mouth did see,
Sucking the seas into his entralles° deepe, *bowels*
That seem'd more horrible then hell to bee,
Or that darke dreadfull hole of Tartare[2] steepe,
Through which the damned ghosts doen often creepe
Backe to the world, bad livers to torment:
But nought that falles into this direfull deepe,
Ne that approcheth nigh the wide descent,
May backe returne, but is condemned to be drent.° *drowned*

7

On th'other side, they saw that perilous Rocke,
Threatning it selfe on them to ruinate,° *fall*
On whose sharpe clifts the ribs of vessels broke,
And shivered ships, which had bene wrecked late,
Yet stuck, with carkasses exanimate° *dead*
Of such, as having all their substance spent
In wanton joyes, and lustes intemperate,
Did afterwards make shipwracke violent,
Both of their life, and fame for ever fowly blent.° *destroyed*

8

For thy,° this hight The Rocke of vile Reproch, *therefore*
A daungerous and detestable place,
To which nor fish nor fowle did once approch,
But yelling Meawes,° with Seagulles hoarse and bace, *gulls*
And Cormoyrants, with birds of ravenous race,
Which still sate waiting on that wastfull clift,
For spoyle of wretches, whose unhappie cace,
After lost credite and consumed thrift,° *savings*
At last them driven hath to this despairefull drift.° *end*

9

The Palmer seeing them in safetie past,
Thus said; Behold th'ensamples° in our sights, *examples*
Of lustfull luxurie and thriftlesse wast:
What now is left of miserable wights,
Which spent their looser daies in lewd delights,

2. Tartarus, the lowest region of hell in Greek mythology.

But shame and sad reproch, here to be red,° *seen*
By these rent reliques, speaking their ill plights?
Let all that live, hereby be counselled,
To shunne Rocke of Reproch, and it as death to dred.

10

So forth they rowed, and that Ferryman
With his stiffe oares did brush the sea so strong,
That the hoare° waters from his frigot° ran, *foaming/boat*
And the light bubbles daunced all along,
Whiles the salt brine out of the billowes sprong.
At last farre off they many Islands spy,
On every side floting the floods emong:° *in the water*
Then said the knight, Loe I the land descry,° *see*
Therefore old Syre thy course do thereunto apply.° *steer*

11

That may not be, said then the Ferryman
Least° we unweeting hap to be fordonne:° *lest/destroyed*
For those same Islands, seeming now and than,° *then*
Are not firme lande, nor any certein wonne,° *dwelling place*
But straggling plots, which to and fro do ronne
In the wide waters: therefore are they hight
The wandring Islands. Therefore doe them shonne;
For they have oft drawne many a wandring wight
Into most deadly daunger and distressed plight.

12

Yet well they seeme to him,° that farre° doth vew, *Guyon/afar*
Both faire and fruitfull, and the ground dispred° *covered*
With grassie greene of delectable hew,
And the tall trees with leaves apparelled,
Are deckt with blossomes dyde in white and red,
That mote the passengers thereto allure;
But whosoever once hath fastened
His foot thereon, may never it recure,° *recover*
But wandreth ever more uncertein and unsure.

13

As th'Isle of Delos[3] whylome men report
Amid th' Aegaean sea long time did stray,
Ne made for shipping any certaine port,
Till that Latona traveiling that way,
Flying from Junoes wrath and hard assay,
Of her faire twins was there delivered,° *gave birth*
Which afterwards did rule the night and day;
Thenceforth it firmely was established,
And for Apolloes honor highly herried.° *praised*

14

They to him hearken,° as beseemeth meete, *listen*
And passe on forward: so their way does ly,
That one of those same Islands, which doe fleet° *float*

3. An island in the Aegean Sea that was associated with Eden. Latona, or Leda, after being impregnated by Zeus in the form of a swan, fled Juno's wrath to the island of Delos and there gave birth to Apollo and Artemis.

In the wide sea, they needes must passen by,
Which seemd so sweet and pleasant to the eye,
That it would tempt a man to touchen there:
Upon the banck they sitting did espy
A daintie damzell, dressing of her heare,° *hair*
By whom a little skippet,° floting did appeare. *small boat*

15

She them espying, loud to them can call,
Bidding them nigher draw unto the shore;
For she had cause to busie them withall;[4]
And therewith loudly laught: But nathemore
Would they once turne, but kept on as afore:
Which when she saw, she left her lockes undight,° *undone*
And running to her boat withouten ore
From the departing land[5] it launched light,° *quickly*
And after them did drive with all her power and might.

16

Whom overtaking, she in merry sort° *manner*
Them gan to bord,° and purpose diversly,[6] *confront*
Now faining dalliance° and wanton sport,° *flirting/sexual play*
Now throwing forth lewd words immodestly;
Till that the Palmer gan full bitterly
Her to rebuke, for being loose and light:
Which not abiding, but more scornefully
Scoffing at him, that did her justly wite,° *rightfully accuse*
She turnd her bote about, and from them rowed quite.° *away*

17

That was the wanton Phaedria,[7] which late
Did ferry him over the Idle lake:
Whom nought regarding, they kept on their gate,° *way*
And all her vaine allurements did forsake,
When them the wary Boateman thus bespake;
Here now behoveth° us well to avyse,° *profits/consider*
And of our safetie good heede° to take; *care*
For here before a perlous passage lyes,
Where many Mermayds haunt,° making false melodies. *live*

18

But by the way, there is a great Quicksand,
And a whirlepoole of hidden jeopardy,
Therefore, Sir Palmer, keepe an even hand;
For twixt them both the narrow way doth ly.
Scarse had he said, when hard at hand they spy
That quicksand nigh with water covered;
But by the checked wave they did descry
It plaine, and by the sea discoloured:
It called was the quicksand of Unthriftyhed.° *extravagance*

4. She had a reason to cause them to be interested in her. The phrase may have a double meaning: "cause" is a pun on the word "case," which was Elizabethan slang for "vagina."
5. She launched her boat from the island that was floating away.
6. Intentionally to behave in various ways.
7. Glittering one (Greek). This character was identified in Book 2, Canto 6, as beguilingly licentious; on that occasion, Guyon managed to escape from her island.

19

They passing by, a goodly Ship did see,
Laden from far with precious merchandize,
And bravely° furnished, as ship might bee, *splendidly*
Which through great disaventure,° or mesprize,° *bad luck/poor judgment*
Her selfe had runne into that hazardize;° *hazard*
Whose mariners and merchants with much toyle,
Labour'd in vaine, to have recur'd° their prize, *recovered*
And the rich wares to save from pitteous spoyle,° *ruin*
But neither toyle nor travell might her backe recoyle.° *retrieve*

20

On th'other side they see that perilous Poole,
That called was the Whirlepoole of decay,
In which full many had with haplesse doole° *grief*
Beene suncke, of whom no memorie did stay:
Whose circled waters rapt° with whirling sway, *caught*
Like to a restlesse wheele, still running round,
Did covet,° as they passed by that way, *desire*
To draw their boate within the utmost bound
Of his wide Labyrinth, and then to have them dround.

21

But th'heedfull Boateman strongly forth did stretch
His brawnie armes, and all his body straine,
That th'utmost sandy breach° they shortly fetch,° *beach/reach*
Whiles the dred daunger does behind remaine.
Suddeine they see from midst of all the Maine,° *sea*
The surging waters like a mountaine rise,[8]
And the great sea puft up with proud disdaine,
To swell above the measure of his guise,° *custom*
As threatning to devoure all, that his powre despise.

22

The waves come rolling, and the billowes rore
Outragiously, as they enraged were,
Or wrathfull Neptune did them drive before
His whirling charet, for exceeding feare:
For not one puffe of wind there did appeare,
That all the three thereat woxe much afrayd,
Unweeting, what such horrour straunge did reare.
Eftsoones they saw an hideous hoast° arrayd, *army*
Of huge Sea monsters, such as living sence dismayd.° *overwhelmed*

23

Most ugly shapes, and horrible aspects,° *appearances*
Such as Dame Nature selfe mote feare to see,
Or shame, that ever should so fowle defects
From her most cunning hand escaped bee;
All dreadfull pourtraicts° of deformitee: *portraits*
Spring-headed Hydraes,[9] and sea-shouldring Whales,[1]

8. They encounter a tidal wave. This is later described as full of sea monsters.
9. In Greek mythology, sea monsters with many heads. When one head is cut off, another one springs back in its place.
1. The whale "shoulders" or raises up the sea by exhaling a spout of water up into the air and creating whirlpools.

Great whirlpooles, which all fishes make to flee,
Bright Scolopendraes,[2] arm'd with silver scales,
Mighty Monoceroses,[3] with immeasured tayles.

24

The dreadfull Fish,[4] that hath deserv'd the name
Of Death, and like him lookes in dreadfull hew,
The griesly Wasserman,° that makes his game — *merman*
The flying ships with swiftnesse to pursew,
The horrible Sea-satyre, that doth shew
His fearefull face in time of greatest storme,
Huge Ziffius,° whom Mariners eschew — *swordfish*
No lesse, then rockes, (as travellers informe,)
And greedy Rosmarines° with visages deforme. — *seahorses*

25

All these, and thousand thousands many more,
And more deformed Monsters thousand fold,
With dreadfull noise, and hollow rombling rore,
Came rushing in the fomy waves enrold,° — *rolling*
Which seem'd to fly for feare, them to behold:
Ne wonder, if these did the knight appall;
For all that here on earth we dreadfull hold,
Be but as bugs° to fearen babes withall, — *bugaboos*
Compared to the creatures in the seas entrall.° — *depths*

26

Feare nought, (then said the Palmer well aviz'd;)
For these same Monsters are not these in deed,
But are into these fearefull shapes disguiz'd
By that same wicked witch,[5] to worke us dreed,
And draw from on this journey to proceede.
Tho lifting up his vertuous staffe[6] on hye,
He smote the sea, which calmed was with speed,
And all that dreadfull Armie fast gan flye
Into great Tethys° bosome, where they hidden lye. — *goddess of the sea*

27

Quit° from that daunger, forth their course they kept, — *free*
And as they went, they heard a ruefull cry
Of one, that wayld and pittifully wept,
That through the sea the resounding plaints did fly:
At last they in an Island did espy
A seemely Maiden, sitting by the shore,
That with great sorrow and sad agony,
Seemed some great misfortune to deplore,° — *lament*
And lowd° to them for succour° called evermore. — *loudly / help*

28

Which Guyon hearing, streight° his Palmer bad, — *immediately*
To stere the boate towards that dolefull Mayd,

2. Fantastic fish.
3. Literally, one-horned fish, narwhales.
4. A walrus or "morse" (from the Latin *mors*, "death").
5. Acrasia, the spirit presiding over the Bower of Bliss, which Guyon must destroy to be perfect in temperance.
6. The Palmer calms the sea with his powerful or "vertuous" staff, which resembles both the herald's staff or caduceus of Hermes or Mercury, which was given to him by Zeus or Jupiter as a sign of power and respect, and Moses' rod, which divided the Red Sea (Exodus 14.16).

That he might know, and ease her sorrow sad:
Who° him avizing better, to him sayd; *the Palmer*
Faire Sir, be not displeasd, if disobayd:
For ill it were to hearken to her cry;
For she is inly nothing ill apayd,[7]
But onely womanish fine forgery,° *deceit, trick*
Your stubborne hart t'affect with fraile infirmity.

29

To which when she your courage hath inclind
Through foolish pitty, then her guilefull bayt
She will embosome° deeper in your mind, *bury*
And for your ruine at the last° awayt. *in the end*
The knight was ruled,° and the Boateman strayt *convinced*
Held on his course with stayed° stedfastnesse, *constant*
Ne ever shruncke, ne ever sought to bayt° *rest*
His tyred armes for toylesome wearinesse,
But with his oares did sweepe the watry wildernesse.

30

And now they nigh approched to the sted,° *place*
Where as those Mermayds[8] dwelt: it was a still
And calmy bay, on th'one side sheltered
With the brode shadow of an hoarie° hill, *mossy*
On th'other side an high rocke toured° still, *towered*
That twixt them both a pleasaunt port they made,
And did like an halfe Theatre[9] fulfill:
There those five sisters had continuall trade,° *residence*
And usd to bath themselves in that deceiptfull shade.

31

They were faire Ladies, till they fondly striv'd
With th'Heliconian maides[1] for maistery;
Of whom they over-comen, were depriv'd
Of their proud beautie, and th'one moyity
Transform'd to fish, for their bold surquedry,° *arrogance*
But th'upper halfe their hew° retained still, *shape*
And their sweet skill in wonted melody;
Which ever after they abusd to ill,
T'allure weake travellers, whom gotten they did kill.

32

So now to Guyon, as he passed by,
Their pleasaunt tunes they sweetly thus applide;
O thou faire sonne of gentle Faery,
That art in mighty armes most magnifide
Above all knights, that ever battell tride,
O turne thy rudder hither-ward a while:

7. Inwardly she is not at all distressed; the fact that she seems to be complaining about something illustrates her feminine guile, designed to induce you to lose your sense of yourself and so become ineffectual.

8. The Sirens from Homer's *Odyssey* whose beautiful songs tempt sailors to throw themselves overboard. Guyon, like Odysseus before him, does not succumb to the sirens' music. Traditionally only three in number, Spenser's sirens are five, corresponding to the five senses.

9. The bay is in the shape of a semicircle, like half of an amphitheater.

1. The nine Muses. In Greek mythology the Sirens engaged in a contest with the Muses to see who could sing the best. The Sirens lost and were punished by being turned into sea creatures.

Here may thy storme-bet° vessell safely ride; *storm-beaten*
This is the Port of rest from troublous toyle,
The worlds sweet In,° from paine and wearisome turmoyle. *inn*

33

With that the rolling sea resounding soft,
In his big base them fitly answered,
And on the rocke the waves breaking aloft,
A solemne Meane unto them measured,
The whiles sweet Zephirus° lowd whisteled *the west wind*
His treble, a straunge kinde of harmony;[2]
Which Guyons senses softly tickeled,° *enticed*
That he the boateman bad row easily,° *slowly*
And let him heare some part of their rare melody.

34

But him the Palmer from that vanity,° *folly*
With temperate advice discounselled,° *counseled*
That they it past, and shortly gan descry° *see*
The land, to which their course they leveled;
When suddeinly a grosse fog over spred
With his dull vapour all that desert has,
And heavens chearefull face enveloped,° *covered*
That all things one, and one as nothing was,
And this great Universe seemd one confused mas.

35

Thereat they greatly were dismayd, ne wist
How to direct their way in darkenesse wide,
But feard to wander in that wastfull mist,
For tombling into mischiefe unespide.
Worse is the daunger hidden, then descride.° *exposed*
Suddeinly an innumerable flight
Of harmefull fowles° about them fluttering, cride, *birds*
And with their wicked wings them oft did smight,
And sore annoyed, groping in that griesly night.

36

Even all the nation° of unfortunate *every type*
And fatall birds about them flocked were,
Such as by nature men abhorre and hate,
The ill-faste° Owle, deaths dreadfull messengere, *evil-faced*
The hoars Night-raven, trump° of dolefull drere,° *trumpet/misery*
The lether-winged Bat, dayes enimy,
The ruefull Strich,° still waiting on the bere, *screech-owl*
The Whistler° shrill, that who so heares, doth dy, *a nocturnal bird*
The hellish Harpies,[3] prophets of sad destiny.

37

All those, and all that else does horrour breed,
About them flew, and fild their sayles with feare:
Yet stayd they not, but forward did proceed,

2. This forms a four-part harmony: the sirens take the alto part, the sea provides the bass, the waves the mean or tenor, and the West Wind the treble or soprano.

3. Fictional creatures—half vulture, half woman—who defile and consume food set out for human consumption.

Whiles th'one did row, and th'other stifly° steare;[4] *steadily*
Till that at last the weather gan to cleare,
And the faire land it selfe did plainly show.
Said then the Palmer, Lo where does appeare
The sacred soile, where all our perils grow;
Therefore, Sir knight, your ready armes about you throw.° *put on*

38

He hearkned, and his armes about him tooke,
The whiles the nimble boate so well her sped,
That with her crooked keele° the land she strooke,° *curved prow/struck*
Then forth the noble Guyon sallied,° *leaped*
And his sage Palmer, that him gouerned;
But th'other by his boate behind did stay.
They marched fairly forth, of nought ydred,° *afraid*
Both firmely armd for every hard assay,° *trial*
With constancy and care, gainst daunger and dismay.

39

Ere long they heard an hideous bellowing
Of many beasts,[5] that roard outrageously,
As if that hungers point, or Venus sting° *i.e., sexual desire*
Had them enraged with fell surquedry;° *dangerous arrogance*
Yet nought they feard, but past on hardily,
Untill they came in vew of those wild beasts:
Who all attonce, gaping full greedily,
And rearing fiercely their upstarting crests,
Ran towards, to devoure those unexpected guests.

40

But soone as they approcht with deadly threat,
The Palmer over them his staffe upheld,
His mighty staffe, that could all charmes defeat:
Eftsoones their stubborne courages° were queld, *spirits*
And high advaunced crests downe meekely feld,
In stead of fraying,° they them selves did feare, *frightening*
And trembled, as them passing they beheld:
Such wondrous powre did in that staffe appeare,
All monsters to subdew to him, that did it beare.

41

Of that same wood it fram'd was cunningly,
Of which Caduceus[6] whilome° was made, *formerly*
Caduceus the rod of Mercury,
With which he wonts the Stygian° realmes invade, *underworld*
Through ghastly horrour, and eternall shade;
Th' infernall feends with it he can asswage,
And Orcus° tame, whom nothing can perswade, *Pluto, hell's ruler*

4. The Boatman rowed; the Palmer steered.

5. These beasts are the creatures of Acrasia, the lady governor of the Bower of Bliss; they resemble the beasts ruled by Circe on her island, Aeaea, as depicted in the *Odyssey*. Formerly men, they had been transformed by Circe's witchcraft.

6. The winged staff carried by Hermes or Mercury, the messenger god; see line 231.

And rule the Furyes,[7] when they most do rage:
Such vertue in his staffe had eke this Palmer sage.

42

Thence passing forth, they shortly do arrive,
Whereas the Bowre of Blisse was situate;
A place pickt out by choice of best alive,
That natures worke by art can imitate
In which what ever in this worldly state
Is sweet, and pleasing unto living sense,
Or that may dayntiest fantasie aggrate,° *please*
Was poured forth with plentifull dispence,° *abundance*
And made there to abound with lavish affluence.° *extravagance*

43

Goodly it was enclosed round about,
Aswell their entred° guestes to keepe within, *entered*
As those unruly beasts to hold without;° *keep out*
Yet was the fence thereof but weake and thin;
Nought° feard their force, that fortilage° to win, *nothing / fortress*
But wisedomes powre, and temperaunces might,
By which the mightiest things efforced bin:[8]
And eke the gate was wrought of substaunce light,
Rather for pleasure, then for battery° or fight. *physical assault*

44

Yt framed was of precious yvory,
That seemd a worke of admirable wit;° *skill*
And therein all the famous history
Of Jason and Medaea[9] was ywrit;
Her mighty charmes, her furious loving fit,
His goodly conquest of the golden fleece,
His falsed° faith, and love too lightly flit,° *violated / fickle*
The wondred Argo, which in venturous peece° *adventurous ship*
First through the Euxine seas bore all the flowr of Greece.

45

Ye might have seene the frothy billowes fry
Under the ship,° as thorough them she went, *the Argo*
That seemd the waves were into yvory,
Or yvory into the waves were sent;
And other where° the snowy substaunce sprent° *elsewhere / sprinkled*
With vermell, like the boyes bloud therein shed,[1]
A piteous spectacle did represent,
And otherwhiles° with gold besprinkeled; *elsewhere*
Yt seemd th'enchaunted flame, which did Creüsa[2] wed.

7. Spirits of vengeance, traditionally imagined as female, who pursue the victims of crime to compel them to take revenge.

8. Acrasia did not fear beasts but only the power of wisdom and temperance, which can control the mightiest things.

9. Jason sailed in the Argo, the first oceangoing ship, to capture the golden fleece, a Greek treasure, which belonged to King Aeetes of Colchis. The king's daughter, Medea, assisted Jason with her magical powers. When Jason abandoned her, betraying the fidelity he had promised her, Medea took revenge. Medea was said to have inherited her magical powers from Circe, her aunt.

1. A reference to Medea's murder of her brother, whose body she threw into the sea to distract her father as she and Jason fled from Colchis with the golden fleece.

2. The woman for whom Jason abandoned Medea. In revenge, Medea sent Creüsa an enchanted dress, which burned her to death with its own fire; hence Creüsa could be said to have wed a flame.

46

All this, and more might in that goodly gate
Be red;° that ever open stood to all, *seen*
Which thither came: but in the Porch there sate
A comely personage of stature tall,
And semblaunce pleasing, more then naturall,
That travellers to him seemd to entize;° *entice*
His looser garment to the ground did fall,
And flew about his heeles in wanton wize,° *manner*
Not fit for speedy pace, or manly exercize.

47

They in that place him Genius[3] did call:
Not that celestiall powre, to whom the care
Of life, and generation of all
That lives, pertaines in charge particulare,° *as a special charge*
Who wondrous things concerning our welfare,
And straunge phantomes° doth let us oft forsee, *images*
And oft of secret ill bids us beware:
That is our Selfe, whom though we do not see,
Yet each doth in him selfe it well perceive to bee.

48

Therefore a God him sage Antiquity
Did wisely make, and good Agdistes call:
But this same was to that quite contrary,
The foe of life, that good envyes to all,
That secretly doth us procure° to fall, *cause*
Through guilefull semblaunts,° which he makes us see. *deceitful images*
He of this Gardin had the governall,° *management*
And Pleasures porter was devizd° to bee, *appointed*
Holding a staffe in hand for more formalitee.

49

With diverse flowres he daintily was deekt,
And strowed° round about, and by his side *strewn*
A mighty Mazer° bowle of wine was set, *maple*
As if it had to him bene sacrifide;[4]
Wherewith all new-come guests he gratifide:
So did he eke Sir Guyon passing by:
But he his idle curtesie defide,
And overthrew his bowle disdainfully;
And broke his staffe, with which he charmed semblants sly.

50

Thus being entred, they behold around
A large and spacious plaine, on every side
Strowed with pleasauns,° whose faire grassy ground *small parks*
Mantled° with greene, and goodly beautifide *cloaked*
With all the ornaments of Floraes° pride, *goddess of flowers*

3. Not what he is traditionally, that is, the spirit, associated with heavenly power, who has a specific duty to care for each individual man or woman. Identified as a "self" or ego, genius also has the force of a moral consciousness. Although we do not see this genius, each of us has a sense of it. Spenser specifies that genius is called Agdistes. However, the figure at Acrasia's gate is his diabolical double.

4. As if it were a sacrificial offering.

Wherewith her mother Art, as halfe in scorne
Of niggard Nature, like a pompous bride
Did decke her, and too lavishly adorne,[5]
When forth from virgin bowre she comes in th'early morne.

51

There to the Heavens alwayes Joviall,° *joyful*
Lookt on them lovely, still° in stedfast° state, *always/constant*
Ne suffred° storme nor frost on them to fall, *allowed*
Their tender buds or leaves to violate,
Nor scorching heat, nor cold intemperate
T'afflict the creatures, which therein did dwell,
But the milde aire with season moderate
Gently attempred,° and disposd so well, *temperate*
That still it breathed forth sweet spirit and holesome smell.

52

More sweet and holesome, then the pleasaunt hill
Of Rhodope,[6] on which the Nimphe, that bore
A gyaunt babe, her selfe for griefe did kill;
Or the Thessalian Tempe, where of yore
Faire Daphne Phoebus hart with love did gore;
Or Ida, where the Gods lov'd to repaire,° *retire*
When ever they their heavenly bowres forlore;
Or sweet Parnasse, the haunt of Muses faire;
Or Eden selfe, if ought° with Eden mote compaire. *anything*

53

Much wondred Guyon at the faire aspect° *appearance*
Of that sweet place, yet suffred° no delight *allowed*
To sincke into his sence, nor mind affect,
But passed forth, and lookt still forward right,° *straight ahead*
Bridling his will, and maistering his might:
Till that he came unto another gate;
No gate, but like one, being goodly dight° *decorated*
With boughes and braunches, which did broad dilate° *extend*
Their clasping armes, in wanton wreathings intricate.

54

So fashioned a Porch[7] with rare device,° *design*
Archt over head with an embracing vine,
Whose bounches° hanging downe, seemed to entice *bunches*
All passers by, to tast their lushious wine,
And did themselves into their hands incline,° *hang*
As freely offering to be gathered:
Some deepe empurpled as the Hyacint,[8]
Some as the Rubine,° laughing sweetly red, *ruby*
Some like faire Emeraudes,° not yet well ripened. *emeralds*

5. Flora's mother, Art, scorns the simplicity of Nature and dresses Flora in showy clothing.

6. Spenser compares the Bower of Bliss with five Greek landscapes, all of which (except for Parnassus) were also the scenes of montrosity and tragedy. Rhodope was the hill where Orpheus sang and was torn to pieces by the Maenads, also the name of a nymph who gave birth to a giant child whose father was Neptune. Daphne was the first love of Phoebus or Apollo, who could be said to have wounded his heart by her disdain of him; Mount Ida was the site of the beauty contest between Hera (Juno), Aphrodite (Venus), and Athena (Minerva) that led to the Trojan War.

7. The branches created a sort of porch.

8. Hyacinth or jacinth, a blue stone.

55

And them° amongst, some were of burnisht gold, *the grapes*
So made by art, to beautifie the rest,
Which did themselves emongst the leaves enfold,
As lurking from the vew of covetous° guest, *greedy*
That the weake bowes,° with so rich load opprest, *boughs*
Did bow adowne, as over-burdened.
Under that Porch a comely dame did rest,
Clad in faire weedes, but fowle disordered,° *sloppy*
And garments loose, that seemd unmeet for womanhed.[9]

56

In her left hand a Cup of gold she held,
And with her right the riper fruit did reach,
Whose sappy liquor, that with fulnesse sweld,
Into her cup she scruzd,° with daintie breach° *squeezed/crushing*
Of her fine fingers, without fowle empeach,[1]
That so faire wine-presse made the wine more sweet:
Thereof she usd to give to drinke to each,
Whom passing by she happened to meet:
It was her guise, all Straungers goodly so to greet.

57

So she to Guyon offred it to tast;
Who taking it out of her tender hond,
The cup to ground did violently cast,
That all in peeces it was broken fond,
And with the liquor stained all the lond:
Whereat Excesse[2] exceedingly was wroth,
Yet no'te° the same amend, ne yet withstond,° *could not/prevent*
But suffered him to passe, all were she loth;° *reluctant*
Who nought regarding her displeasure forward goth.

58

There the most daintie Paradise on ground,
It selfe doth offer to his sober eye,
In which all pleasures plenteously abound,
And none does others happinesse envye:
The painted flowres, the trees upshooting hye,
The dales for shade, the hilles for breathing space,
The trembling groves, the Christall running by;
And that, which all faire workes doth most aggrace,° *add grace to*
The art, which all that wrought, appeared in no place.[3]

59

One would have thought, (so cunningly, the rude,
And scorned parts were mingled with the fine,)
That nature had for wantonesse ensude° *imitated*
Art, and that Art at nature did repine;° *fret*
So striving each th'other to undermine,
Each did the others worke more beautifie;
So diff'ring both in willes, agreed in fine:

9. Unsuitable for womanhood.
1. She used her own fingers to squeeze the grapes without soiling her fingers or ruining the grapes.
2. The lady at the Porch.
3. The scene appears natural, and the art that created it is invisible.

So all agreed through sweete diversitie,° *disagreement*
This Gardin to adorne with all varietie.

60

And in the midst of all, a fountaine stood,
Of richest substaunce, that on earth might bee,
So pure and shiny, that the silver flood
Through every channell running one might see;
Most goodly it with curious imageree
Was over-wrought, and shapes of naked boyes,
Of which some seemd with lively jollitee,
To fly about, playing their wanton toyes,
Whilest others did them selves embay° in liquid joyes. *bathe*

61

And over all, of purest gold was spred,
A trayle° of yvie in his native hew: *vine*
For the rich mettall was so coloured,
That wight, who did not well avis'd° it vew, *carefully*
Would surely deeme it to be yvie trew:
Low his° lascivious armes adown did creepe, *the ivy's*
That themselves dipping in the silver dew,
Their fleecy flowres they tenderly did steepe,
Which drops of Christall seemd for wantones to weepe.

62

Infinit streames continually did well
Out of this fountaine, sweet and faire to see,
The which into an ample laver° fell, *basin*
And shortly grew to so great quantitie,
That like a little lake it seemd to bee;
Whose depth exceeded not three cubits° hight, *about four feet*
That through the waves one might the bottom see,
All pav'd beneath with Jaspar° shining bright, *green stone*
That seemd the fountaine in that sea did sayle upright.[4]

63

And all the margent° round about was set, *edge*
With shady Laurell trees, thence to defend
The sunny beames, which on the billowes bet,° *beat*
And those which therein bathed, mote offend.[5]
As Guyon hapned by the same to wend,
Two naked Damzelles he therein espyde,
Which therein bathing, seemed to contend,
And wrestle wantonly,° ne car'd to hyde, *lewdly*
Their dainty parts from vew of any, which them eyde.

64

Sometimes the one would lift the other quight
Above the waters, and then downe againe
Her plong,° as over maistered by might, *plunge*
Where both awhile would covered remaine,
And each the other from to rise restraine;

4. The jet of water rose up in the fountain so that it resembled a ship sailing on the sea.

5. The beams of the sun might bother bathers.

The whiles their snowy limbes, as through a vele,
So through the Christall waves appeared plaine:
Then suddeinly both would themselves unhele,° *release*
And th'amarous sweet spoiles to greedy eyes revele.

65

As that faire Starre, the messenger of morne,
His deawy face out of the sea doth reare:
Or as the Cyprian goddesse, newly borne
Of th'Oceans fruitfull froth, did first appeare:[6]
Such seemed they, and so their yellow heare
Christalline humour° dropped downe apace. *water of the fountain*
Whom such when Guyon saw, he drew him neare,
And somewhat gan relent his earnest° pace, *brisk*
His stubborn brest gan secret pleasaunce° to embrace. *pleasure*

66

The wanton Maidens him espying, stood
Gazing a while at his unwonted° guise;° *unfamiliar/manner*
Then th'one her selfe low ducked in the flood,
Abasht, that her a straunger did a vise:° *view*
But th'other rather higher did arise,
And her two lilly paps° aloft displayd, *breasts*
And all, that might his melting hart entise
To her delights, she unto him bewrayd:° *revealed*
The rest hid underneath, him more desirous made.

67

With that, the other likewise up arose,
And her faire lockes,° which formerly were bownd *hair*
Up in one knot, she low adowne did lose:
Which flowing long and thick, her cloth'd arownd,
And th'yvorie in golden mantle gownd:° *draped*
So that faire spectacle from him was reft,° *taken*
Yet that, which reft it, no lesse faire was fownd:
So hid in lockes and waves from lookers theft,
Nought but her lovely face she for his looking left.

68

Withall she laughed, and she blusht withall,
That blushing to her laughter gave more grace,
And laughter to her blushing, as did fall:
Now when they spide the knight to slacke his pace,
Them to behold, and in his sparkling face
The secret signes of kindled lust appeare,
Their wanton meriments they did encreace,
And to him beckned, to approch more neare,
And shewd him many sights, that courage cold could reare.[7]

69

On which when gazing him the Palmer saw,
He much rebukt those wandring eyes of his,
And counseld well, him forward thence did draw.° *move*

6. Both star and the Cyprian goddess signify Venus.

7. They showed Guyon many things that could arouse his lust.

Now are they come nigh to the Bowre of blis
Of° her° fond favorites so nam'd amis:° *by/Acrasia's/wrongly*
When thus° the Palmer; Now Sir, well avise; *thus spoke*
For here the end of all our travell is:
Here wonnes° Acrasia,[8] whom we must surprise, *dwells*
Else she will slip away, and all our drift° despise. *purpose*

70

Eftsoones they heard a most melodious sound,
Of all° that mote delight a daintie eare, *everything*
Such as attonce might not on living ground,
Save in this Paradise, be heard elswhere:
Right hard it was, for wight, which did it heare,
To read,° what manner musicke that mote bee: *understand*
For all that pleasing is to living eare,
Was there consorted° in one harmonee, *joined*
Birdes, voyces, instruments, windes, waters, all agree.

71

The joyous birdes shrouded° in chearefull shade, *hidden*
Their notes unto the voyce° attempred° sweet, *harmony/attuned*
Th'Angelicall soft trembling voyces made
To th'instruments° divine respondence° meet: *of the Bower/answer*
The silver sounding instruments did meet
With the base murmure of the waters fall:
The waters fall with difference discreet,
Now soft, now loud, unto the wind did call:
The gentle warbling wind low answered to all.

72

There, whence that Musick seemed heard to bee,
Was the faire Witch her selfe now solacing,° *relaxing*
With a new Lover, whom through sorceree
And witchcraft, she from farre did thither bring:
There she had him now layd a slombering,
In secret shade, after long wanton joyes:
Whilst round about them pleasauntly did sing
Many faire Ladies, and lascivious boyes,
That ever mixt their song with light licentious toyes.° *pastimes*

73

And all that while, right over him she hong,
With her false eyes fast fixed in his sight,
As seeking medicine, whence she was stong,
Or greedily depasturing° delight: *grazing on*
And oft inclining downe with kisses light,
For feare of waking him, his lips bedewd,° *wet*
And through his humid eyes did sucke his spright,
Quite molten° into lust and pleasure lewd; *melted*
Wherewith she sighed soft, as if his case she rewd.

74

The whiles some one did chaunt° this lovely lay;° *sing/song*
Ah see, who so faire thing doest faine° to see, *wish*

8. Ill-temper, incontinence, impotence (medieval Latin).

In springing flowre the image of thy day;° *life*
Ah see the Virgin Rose, how sweetly shee
Doth first peepe forth with bashfull modestee,
That fairer seemes, the lesse ye see her may;[9]
Lo see soone after, how more bold and free
Her bared bosome she doth broad° display; *openly*
Loe see soone after, how she fades, and falles away.

75

So passeth,° in the passing of a day, *passes*
Of mortall life the leafe, the bud, the flowre,
Ne more doth flourish after first decay,° *withering*
That earst was sought to decke° both bed and bowre, *adorn*
Of many a Ladie, and many a Paramowre:° *lover*
Gather therefore the Rose, whilest yet is prime,[1]
For soone comes age, that will her pride deflowre:
Gather the Rose of love, whilest yet is time,
Whilest loving thou mayst loved be with equall crime.

76

He ceast, and then gan all the quire° of birdes *choir*
Their diverse notes t'attune unto his lay,
As in approvance° of his pleasing words. *as if approving*
The constant paire heard all, that he did say,
Yet swarved,° but kept their forward way, *turned*
Through many covert groves, and thickets close,
In which they creeping did at last display° *discover*
That wanton Ladie, with her lover lose,
Whose sleepie head she in her lap did soft dispose.° *lay*

77

Upon a bed of Roses she was layd,
As faint through heat, or dight to° pleasant sin, *prepared for*
And was arayd, or rather disarayd,
All in a vele of silke and silver thin,
That hid no whit her alablaster° skin, *white*
But rather shewd more white, if more might bee:
More subtile web Arachne[2] cannot spin,
Nor the fine nets, which oft we woven see
Of scorched° deaw, do not in th'aire more lightly flee.° *dried/float*

78

Her snowy brest was bare to readie spoyle° *easy view*
Of hungry eies, which n'ote° therewith be fild, *could not*
And yet through languour° of her late sweet toyle, *weariness*
Few drops, more cleare then Nectar, forth distild,° *gathered*
That like pure Orient perles adowne it trild,° *trickled*
And her faire eyes sweet smyling in delight,
Moystened their fierie beames, with which she thrild° *pierced*

9. The less you see of her, the fairer she seems.
1. A figure common in love lyrics; the woman is compared to a flower that is to be picked just as it is about to bloom—an argument against moderation and temperance and for gratification and pleasure. Spenser concludes his version of the figure uncharacteristically, with a reminder that in the life of a temperate man or woman this kind of passion is a "crime."
2. A princess whose skill in the art of weaving surpassed that of the goddess Athena, who became jealous and transformed Arachne into a spider.

Fraile harts, yet quenched not; like starry light
Which sparkling on the silent waves, does seeme more bright.

79

The young man sleeping by her, seemd to bee
Some goodly swayne of honorable place,
That certes it great pittie was to see
Him his nobilitie so foule deface;° *horribly disgrace*
A sweet regard, and amiable grace,
Mixed with manly sternnesse did appeare
Yet sleeping, in his well proportiond face,
And on his tender lips the downy heare° *hair*
Did now but freshly spring, and silken blossomes beare.

80

His warlike armes,° the idle instruments *armor*
Of sleeping praise, were hong upon a tree,
And his brave shield, full of old moniments,° *marks of battle*
Was fowly ra'st,° that none the signes might see; *erased*
Ne for them, ne for honour cared hee,
Ne ought, that did to his advauncement tend,
But in lewd loves, and wastfull luxuree,
His dayes, his goods, his bodie he did spend:
O horrible enchantment, that him so did blend.° *blind*

81

The noble Elfe, and carefull Palmer drew
So nigh them, minding nought, but lustfull game,° *pleasures*
That suddein° forth they on them rusht, and threw *suddenly*
A subtile net, which onely for the same
The skilfull Palmer formally° did frame. *especially*
So held them under fast, the whiles the rest[3]
Fled all away for feare of fowler° shame. *fouler*
The faire Enchauntresse, so unwares opprest,
Tryde all her arts, and all her sleights, thence out to wrest.° *escape*

82

And eke her lover strove: but all in vaine;
For that same net so cunningly was wound,° *woven*
That neither guile, nor force might it distraine.° *destroy*
They tooke them both, and both them strongly bound
In captive bandes, which there they readie found:
But her in chaines of adamant° he tyde; *hard stone*
For nothing else might keepe her safe and sound;
But Verdant[4] (so he hight) he soone untyde,
And counsell sage in steed° thereof to him applyde. *stead*

83

But all those pleasant bowres and Pallace brave,
Guyon broke downe, with rigour° pittilesse; *violence*
Ne ought their goodly workmanship might save
Them from the tempest of his wrathfulnesse,
But that their blisse he turn'd to balefulnesse:° *misery*

3. The Bower's other inhabitants.

4. Greening, growing green; here, one who is young and at the beginning of his maturity.

Their groves he feld, their gardins did deface,
Their arbers spoyle, their Cabinets° suppresse, *bowers*
Their banket° houses burne, their buildings race,° *banquet/raze*
And of the fairest late, now made the fowlest place.

84

Then led they her away, and eke that knight
They with them led, both sorrowfull and sad:
The way they came, the same retourn'd they right,
Till they arrived, where they lately had
Charm'd those wild-beasts, that rag'd with furie mad.
Which now awaking, fierce at them gan fly,
As in their mistresse reskew, whom they lad;[5]
But them the Palmer soone did pacify.
Then Guyon askt, what meant those beastes, which there did ly.

85

Said he, These seeming beasts are men indeed,
Whom this Enchauntresse hath transformed thus,
Whylome° her lovers, which her lusts did feed, *formerly*
Now turned into figures hideous,
According to their mindes like monstruous.
Sad end (quoth he) of life intemperate,
And mournefull meed of joyes delicious:
But Palmer, if it mote thee so aggrate,° *please*
Let them returned be unto their former state.

86

Streight way he with his vertuous staffe them strooke,
And streight of beasts they comely men became;
Yet being men they did unmanly looke,
And stared ghastly, some for inward shame,
And some for wrath, to see their captive Dame:
But one above the rest in speciall,
That had an hog beene late, hight Grille[6] by name,
Repined° greatly, and did him miscall,° *raged/insult*
That had from hoggish forme him brought to naturall.

87

Said Guyon, See the mind of beastly man,
That hath so soone forgot the excellence
Of his creation, when he life began,
That now he chooseth, with vile difference,
To be a beast, and lacke intelligence.
To whom the Palmer thus, The donghill kind
Delights in filth and foule incontinence:
Let Grill be Grill, and have his hoggish mind,
But let us hence depart, whilest wether serves and wind.[7]

---

5. The beasts attack Guyon and the Palmer as if to rescue their mistress, whom Guyon and the Palmer are leading.
6. Hog (Greek). Here Spenser follows the Odyssey: Grille is one of Ulysses's men whom Circe had transformed into a hog; he later refused to be returned to his human state.
7. While the weather and the wind are in our favor.

from Amoretti[1]

1

Happy ye leaves° when as those lilly hands, *of the book*
Which hold my life in their dead doing° might, *death-dealing*
Shall handle you and hold in loves soft bands,° *bonds*
Lyke captives trembling at the victors sight.
And happy lines, on which with starry light,
Those lamping° eyes will deigne sometimes to look *flashing*
And reade the sorrowes of my dying spright,° *spirit*
Written with teares in harts close bleeding book.
And happy rymes bath'd in the sacred brooke,[2]
Of Helicon whence she derived is,
When ye behold that Angels blessed looke,
My soules long lacked foode, my heavens blis.
Leaves, lines, and rymes, seeke her to please alone,
Whom if ye please, I care for other none.

4

New yeare forth looking out of Janus[3] gate,
Doth seeme to promise hope of new delight:
And bidding th'old Adieu, his passed date
Bids all old thoughts to die in dumpish spright° *low spirits*
And calling forth out of sad Winters night,
Fresh love, that long hath slept in cheerlesse bower:
Wils him awake, and soone about him dight
His wanton wings and darts of deadly power.
For lusty spring now in his timely howre,
Is ready to come forth him to receive:
And warnes the Earth with divers colord flowre,
To decke hir selfe, and her faire mantle weave.
Then you faire flowre, in whom fresh youth doth raine,° *reign*
Prepare your selfe new love to entertaine.

13

In that proud port,° which her so goodly graceth,[4] *bearing*
Whiles her faire face she reares up to the skie:
And to the ground her eie lids low embaseth° *casts down*
Most goodly temperature° ye may descry,° *temperament/perceive*

1. "Little loves," a sonnet sequence apparently written for Elizabeth Boyle, whom Spenser married in 1594, though he may have written some of the sonnets much earlier and for another woman. The *Amoretti* were published in 1595 together with the *Epithalamion*, Spenser's marriage hymn upon his wedding. Both the sonnets and the hymn, each referring to regular moments in the passage of time, can be read as one continuous narrative.

2. Aganippe, which rises (or is "derived") from Helicon, a mountain that is home to the Muses, goddesses of all the arts but known especially for their inspiration of poets.

3. A Roman god of the new year who has two faces; one looks back at December, the other ahead to January. For Christians the liturgical new year began on March 25, the Feast of the Annunciation, when the Angel Gabriel was thought to have announced the coming of Jesus Christ to the Virgin Mary. Throughout the sequence, Spenser plays with these two concepts of the year, juxtaposing the time dictated by nature, figured by the Roman calendar, with time according to Christian history and celebrated by the fasts and feasts of the church.

4. Spenser describes the lady to whom the sonnet is addressed.

Myld humblesse° mixt with awfull° majesty, *humility / awesome*
For looking on the earth whence she was borne:
Her minde remembreth her mortalitie,
What so is fayrest shall to earth returne.
But that same lofty countenance seemes to scorne
Base thing, and thinke how she to heaven may clime:
Treading downe earth as lothsome and forlorne,
That hinders heavenly thoughts with drossy° slime. *heavy*
Yet lowly still vouchsafe° to looke on me, *condescend*
Such lowlinesse shall make you lofty be.

22

This holy season fit to fast and pray,[5]
Men to devotion ought to be inclynd:
Therefore, I lykewise on so holy day,
For my sweet Saynt some service fit will find.
Her temple fayre is built within my mind,
In which her glorious ymage placed is,
On which my thoughts doo day and night attend
Lyke sacred priests that never thinke amisse.
There I to her as th'author of my blisse,
Will builde an altar to appease her yre:° *anger*
And on the same my hart will sacrifise,
Burning in flames of pure and chast desyre:
The which vouchsafe O goddesse to accept,
Amongst thy deerest relicks to be kept.

62

The weary yeare his race now having run,
The new[6] begins his compast° course anew: *encompassed*
With shew of morning mylde he hath begun,
Betokening peace and plenty to ensew.
So let us, which this chaunge of weather vew,
Chaunge eeke° our mynds and former lives amend, *also*
The old yeares sinnes forepast° let us eschew,° *gone by / avoid*
And fly the faults with which we did offend.
Then shall the new yeares joy forth freshly send,
Into the glooming° world his gladsome ray: *gloomy*
And all these stormes which now his beauty blend,° *dim*
Shall turne to caulmes and tymely cleare away.
So likewise love cheare you your heavy spright,
And chaunge old yeares annoy° to new delight. *grief*

65

The doubt° which ye misdeeme,° fayre love, is vaine, *fear / misconceive*
That fondly° feare to loose° your liberty, *foolishly / lose*

5. The holy season is Lent; the holy day is Ash Wednesday. The sonnet celebrates the poet's admission that his love has a spiritual dimension; complimenting his heart's desire is the worship he gives to his lady's image in the temple of his mind.

6. The Christian new year, the Feast of the Annunciation.

When loosing one, two liberties ye gayne,
And make him bond that bondage earst dyd fly.
Sweet be the bands, the which true love doth tye,
Without constraynt or dread of any ill:
The gentle birde feeles no captivity
Within her cage, but singes and feeds her fill.
There pride dare not approch, nor discord spill
The league twixt them, that loyal love hath bound:
But simple truth and mutuall good will,
Seekes with sweet peace to salve° each others wound: *heal*
There fayth doth fearlesse dwell in brasen towre,
And spotlesse pleasure builds her sacred bowre.

66

To all those happy blessings which ye have,
With plenteous hand by heaven upon you thrown:
This one disparagement they to you gave,
That ye your love lent to so meane a one.[7]
Yee whose high worths surpassing paragon,
Could not on earth have found one fit for mate,
Ne but in heaven matchable to none,
Why did ye stoup unto so lowly state.
But ye thereby much greater glory gate,° *got*
Then° had ye sorted° with a princes pere:° *than/consorted/peer*
For now your light doth more it selfe dilate,° *spread*
And in my darknesse greater doth appeare.
Yet since your light hath once enlumind° me, *illuminated*
With my reflex° yours shall encreased be. *reflected light*

68

Most glorious Lord of lyfe that on this day,[8]
Didst make thy triumph over death and sin:
And having harrowd hell, didst bring away
Captivity thence captive us to win.[9]
This joyous day, deare Lord, with joy begin,
And grant that we for whom thou diddest dye
Being with thy deare blood clene washt from sin,
May live for ever in felicity.
And that thy love we weighing worthily,
May likewise love thee for the same againe:
And for thy sake that all lyke deare° didst buy, *at the same cost*
With love may one another entertayne.
So let us love, deare love, lyke as we ought,
Love is the lesson which the Lord us taught.

7. Working forward from Sonnet 62 and counting each sonnet as representing a day of love and devotion, Sonnet 66 corresponds to Good Friday. Spenser exploits the idea of humility, consistent with the passion of Christ, to express his own sense of devotion to his lady's virtue.

8. The sonnet addresses the "dear Lord" of the Passion on Easter Day to harmonize the poet's love for his lady and his obligation to follow the lesson of Christ.

9. Christians believed that after his Resurrection, Christ descended into hell to rescue Adam and Eve and the patriarchs and prophets of the Hebrew Bible. The event is often described as the harrowing of hell.

75

One day I wrote her name upon the strand,° *beach*
But came the waves and washed it away:
Agayne I wrote it with a second hand,
But came the tyde, and made my paynes his pray.
Vayne man, sayd she, that doest in vaine assay,° *attempt*
A mortall thing so to immortalize.
For I my selve shall lyke to this decay,
And eek my name bee wyped out lykewize.
Not so, (quod I) let baser things devize,° *consent*
To dy in dust, but you shall live by fame:
My verse your vertues rare shall eternize,° *make eternal*
And in the hevens wryte your glorious name:
Where whenas death shall all the world subdew,
Our love shall live, and later life renew.

Epithalamion[1]

Ye learned sisters[2] which have oftentimes
Beene to me ayding, others to adorne:
Whom ye thought worthy of your gracefull rymes,
That even the greatest did not greatly scorne
To heare theyr names sung in your simple layes,° *verses*
But joyed° in theyr prayse. *took pleasure*
And when ye list° your owne mishaps to mourne, *wish*
Which death, or love, or fortunes wreck did rayse,
Your string could soone to sadder tenor turne,
And teach the woods and waters to lament
Your dolefull dreriment.° *misfortune*
Now lay those sorrowfull complaints aside,
And having all your heads with girland° crownd, *garlands*
Helpe me mine owne loves prayses to resound,
Ne let the same of any be envide:
So Orpheus[3] did for his owne bride,
So I unto my selfe alone will sing,
The woods shall to me answer and my Eccho ring.

Early before the worlds light giving lampe,
His golden beame upon the hils doth spred,
Having disperst the nights unchearefull dampe,
Doe ye awake and with fresh lusty hed,° *merriment*
Go to the bowre of my beloved love,
My truest turtle dove

1. An epithalamion (meaning "at the bedroom" in Greek) was a poem written in celebration of a marriage. Spenser's epithalamion is unusual in that he wrote it for his own marriage to the lady of the *Amoretti,* Elizabeth Boyle; epithalamia (the plural form of the word) were usually written by a professional for a family with whom he had no personal connection. Each of the 24 sections of Spenser's poem describes a hour in the wedding day, which begins at one in the morning and continues to 12 midnight. The temporal structure of the *Epithalamion* recalls the calendrical structure of the *Amoretti*.

2. The nine Muses, the creative spirits presiding over the arts and sciences. The "others" Spenser refers to include Queen Elizabeth, whom he celebrates in various figures throughout *The Faerie Queene*.

3. The founder of poetry, according to Greek mythology; he was often invoked as a model by lyric poets of the early modern period.

Bid her awake; for Hymen° is awake, *god of marriage*
And long since ready forth his maske° to move, *masque*
With his bright Tead° that flames with many a flake, *torch*
And many a bachelor to waite on him,
In theyr fresh garments trim.
Bid her awake therefore and soone her dight,° *dress*
For lo the wished day is come at last,
That shall for al the paynes and sorrowes past,
Pay to her usury of long delight,
And whylest she doth her dight,
Doe ye to her joy and solace sing,
That all the woods may answer and your eccho ring.

Bring with you all the Nymphes[4] that you can heare° *here*
Both of the rivers and the forrests greene:
And of the sea that neighbours to her neare,
Al with gay girlands goodly wel beseene.° *appearing*
And let them also with them bring in hand,
Another gay girland
For my fayre love of lillyes and of roses,
Bound truelove wize with a blew silke riband.
And let them make great store of bridale poses,° *posies*
And let them eeke bring store of other flowers
To deck the bridale bowers.
And let the ground whereas her foot shall tread,
For feare the stones her tender foot should wrong
Be strewed with fragrant flowers all along,
And diapred lyke the discolored mead.[5]
Which done, doe at her chamber dore awayt,
For she will waken strayt,° *immediately*
The whiles doe ye this song unto her sing,
The woods shall to you answer and your Eccho ring.

Ye Nymphes of Mulla[6] which with carefull heed,° *attention*
The silver scaly trouts doe tend full well,
And greedy pikes which use therein to feed,
(Those trouts and pikes all others doo excell)
And ye likewise which keepe the rushy lake,
Where none doo fishes take,
Bynd up the locks° the which hang scatterd light, *of the nymphs*
And in his waters which your mirror make,
Behold your faces as the christall bright,
That when you come whereas my love doth lie,
No blemish she may spie.
And eke ye lightfoot mayds which keepe the deere,
That on the hoary mountayne use to towre,° *soar*
And the wylde wolves which seeke them to devoure,
With your steele darts doo chace from comming neer

4. The spirits in nature, generally associated with trees and streams.
5. Variegated like the many-colored fields.
6. Spenser's name for the Awbeg, a river in the county of Munster in Ireland, where he was serving as a deputy for the English crown at the time of his marriage to Elizabeth Boyle.

Be also present heere,
To helpe to decke her and to help to sing,
That all the woods may answer and your eccho ring.

Wake now my love, awake; for it is time,
The Rosy Morne long since left Tithones[7] bed,
All ready to her silver coche° to clyme, *coach*
And Phoebus[8] gins to shew his glorious hed.
Hark how the cheerefull birds do chaunt° theyr laies° *sing/songs*
And carroll of loves praise.
The merry Larke hir mattins sings aloft,
The thrush replyes, the Mavis° descant° playes, *thrush/accompaniment*
The Ouzell° shrills, the Ruddock° warbles soft, *blackbird/redbreast*
So goodly all agree with sweet consent,
To this dayes merriment.
Ah my deere love why doe ye sleepe thus long,
When meeter° were that ye should now awake, *more fitting*
T'awayt the comming of your joyous make,° *mate*
And hearken to the birds lovelearned song,
The deawy leaves among.
For they of joy and pleasance to you sing,
That all the woods them answer and theyr eccho ring.

My love is now awake out of her dreame,
And her fayre eyes like stars that dimmed were
With darksome cloud, now shew theyr goodly beams
More bright then Hesperus[9] his head doth rere.
Come now ye damzels, daughters of delight,
Helpe quickly her to dight,
But first come ye fayre houres which were begot
In loves sweet paradice, of Day and Night,
Which doe the seasons of the yeare allot,
And al that ever in this world is fayre
Doe make and still° repayre.[1] *forever*
And ye three handmayds of the Cyprian Queene,[2]
The which doe still adorne her beauties pride,
Helpe to addorne my beautifullest bride.
And as ye her array, still throw betweene
Some graces to be seene,
And as ye use to Venus, to her sing,
The whiles the woods shal answer and your eccho ring.

Now is my love all ready forth to come,
Let all the virgins therefore well awayt,
And ye fresh boyes that tend upon her groome
Prepare your selves; for he is comming strayt.
Set all your things in seemely good aray
Fit for so joyfull day,

7. The mythical lover of the goddess of the dawn.
8. Apollo, the god of the sun.
9. Venus, the evening or morning star.
1. The hours or time both create and recreate everything in the world.
2. Venus, whose handmaids are the Graces, attributes of courtesy and artistic expression.

The joyfulst day that ever sunne did see.
Faire Sun, shew forth thy favourable ray,
And let thy lifull° heat not fervent be *full of life*
For feare of burning her sunshyny face,
Her beauty to disgrace.
O fayrest Phoebus,[3] father of the Muse,
If ever I did honour thee aright,
Or sing the thing, that mote° thy mind delight, *could*
Doe not thy servants simple boone° refuse, *favor*
But let this day let this one day be myne,
Let all the rest be thine.
Then I thy soverayne prayses loud wil sing,
That all the woods shal answer and theyr eccho ring.

Harke how the Minstrels gin to shrill aloud
Their merry Musick that resounds from far,
The pipe, the tabor, and the trembling Croud,° *violin*
That well agree withouten breach° or jar. *discord*
But most of all the Damzels doe delite,
When they their tymbrels° smyte, *tambourines*
And thereunto doe daunce and carrol sweet,
That all the sences they doe ravish quite,
The whyles the boyes run up and downe the street,
Crying aloud with strong confused noyce,
As if it were one voyce.
Hymen[4] io Hymen, Hymen they do shout,
That even to the heavens theyr shouting shrill
Doth reach, and all the firmament doth fill,
To which the people standing all about,
As in approvance° doe thereto applaud *approval*
And loud advaunce her laud,° *praise*
And evermore they Hymen Hymen sing,
That al the woods them answer and theyr eccho ring.

Loe where she comes along with portly° pace, *dignified*
Lyke Phoebe[5] from her chamber of the East,
Arysing forth to run her mighty race,
Clad all in white, that seemes a virgin best.
So well it her beseemes° that ye would weene° *befits/think*
Some angell she had beene.
Her long loose yellow locks lyke golden wyre,
Sprinckled with perle, and perling° flowres a tweene,° *rippling/between*
Doe lyke a golden mantle her attyre,
And being crowned with a girland greene,
Seeme lyke some mayden Queene.
Her modest eyes abashed to behold
So many gazers, as on her do stare,
Upon the lowly ground affixed are.

3. Apollo, god of the sun and music, hence the father of the Muses and the muse of lyric poetry.
4. The god of marriage who was invoked as part of the marriage ceremony.
5. Diana, goddess of the moon.

Ne dare lift up her countenance too bold,
But blush to heare her prayses sung so loud,
So farre from being proud.
Nathlesse° doe ye still loud her prayses sing, *nevertheless*
That all the woods may answer and your eccho ring.

Tell me ye merchants daughters did ye see
So fayre a creature in your towne before,
So sweet, so lovely, and so mild as she,
Adornd with beautyes grace and vertues store,
Her goodly eyes lyke Saphyres shining bright,
Her forehead yvory white,
Her cheekes lyke apples which the sun hath rudded,° *reddened*
Her lips lyke cherryes charming men to byte,
Her brest like to a bowle of creame uncrudded,° *uncurdled*
Her paps lyke lyllies budded,
Her snowie necke lyke to a marble towre,
And all her body like a pallace fayre,
Ascending uppe with many a stately stayre,
To honors seat and chastities sweet bowre.
Why stand ye still ye virgins in amaze,
Upon her so to gaze,
Whiles ye forget your former lay to sing,
To which the woods did answer and your eccho ring.

But if ye saw that which no eyes can see,
The inward beauty of her lively spright,
Garnisht with heavenly guifts of high degree,
Much more then would ye wonder at that sight,
And stand astonisht lyke to those which red° *looked at*
Medusaes[6] mazeful hed.
There dwels sweet love and constant chastity,
Unspotted fayth and comely womanhood,
Regard of honour and mild modesty,
There vertue raynes as Queene in royal throne,
And giveth lawes alone.
The which the base affections doe obay,
And yeeld theyr services unto her will,
Ne thought of thing uncomely° ever may *improper*
Thereto approch to tempt her mind to ill.
Had ye once seene these her celestial threasures,
And unrevealed pleasures,
Then would ye wonder and her prayses sing,
That al the woods should answer and your echo ring.

Open the temple gates unto my love,
Open them wide that she may enter in,
And all the postes adorne as doth behove,
And all the pillours deck with girlands trim,

6. One of three mythological monstrous women, the Gorgons; Medusa, whose hair consisted of snakes (hence her head is "mazeful"), turned anyone who looked at her to stone.

For to recyve° this Saynt with honour dew, *receive*
That commeth in to you.
With trembling steps and humble reverence,
She commeth in, before th'almighties vew,
Of her ye virgins learne obedience,
When so ye come into those holy places,
To humble your proud faces:
Bring her up to th'high altar that she may,
The sacred ceremonies there partake,
The which do endlesse matrimony make,
And let the roring Organs loudly play;
The praises of the Lord in lively notes,
The whiles with hollow throates
The Choristers the joyous Antheme sing,
That al the woods may answere and their eccho ring.

Behold whiles she before the altar stands
Hearing the holy priest that to her speakes
And blesseth her with his two happy hands,
How the red roses flush up in her cheekes,
And the pure snow with goodly vermill° stayne, *vermilion*
Like crimsin dyde in grayne,° *fast dyed*
That even th'Angels which continually,
About the sacred Altare doe remaine,
Forget their service and about her fly,
Ofte peeping in her face that seemes more fayre,
The more they on it stare.
But her sad eyes still fastened on the ground,
Are governed with goodly modesty,
That suffers not one looke to glaunce awry,
Which may let in a little thought unsownd.° *suspicions*
Why blush ye love to give to me your hand,
The pledge of all our band?
Sing ye sweet Angels, Alleluya sing,
That all the woods may answere and your eccho ring.

Now al is done; bring home the bride againe,
Bring home the triumph of our victory,
Bring home with you the glory of her gaine,
With joyance bring her and with jollity.° *merriment*
Never had man more joyfull day then this,
Whom heaven would heape with blis.
Make feast therefore now all this live long day,
This day for ever to me holy is,
Poure out the wine without restraint or stay,
Poure not by cups, but by the belly full,
Poure out to all that wull,° *will*
And sprinkle all the postes and wals with wine,
That they may sweat, and drunken be withall.
Crowne ye God Bacchus[7] with a coronall,° *garland*

7. The god of wine.

And Hymen also crowne with wreathes of vine,
And let the Graces daunce unto the rest;
For they can doo it best:
The whiles the maydens doe theyr carroll sing,
To which the woods shal answer and theyr eccho ring.

Ring ye the bels, ye yong men of the towne,
And leave your wonted labors for this day:
This day is holy; doe ye write it downe,
That ye for ever it remember may.
This day the sunne is in his chiefest hight,
With Barnaby the bright,[8]
From whence declining daily by degrees,
He somewhat loseth of his heat and light,
When once the Crab[9] behind his back he sees.
But for this time it ill ordained was,
To chose the longest day in all the yeare,
And shortest night, when longest fitter weare:° *were*
Yet never day so long, but late would passe.
Ring ye the bels, to make it weare away,
And bonefiers° make all day, *bonfires*
And daunce about them, and about them sing:
That all the woods may answer, and your eccho ring.

Ah when will this long weary day have end,
And lende me leave to come unto my love?
How slowly do the houres theyr numbers spend?
How slowly does sad Time his feathers° move? *wings*
Hast thee O fayrest Planet[1] to thy home
Within the Westerne fome:° *the sea*
Thy tyred steedes long since have need of rest.
Long though it be, at last I see it gloome,
And the bright evening star with golden creast
Appeare out of the East.
Fayre childe of beauty, glorious lampe of love
That all the host of heaven in rankes doost lead,
And guydest lovers through the nightes dread,
How chearefully thou lookest from above,
And seemst to laugh atweene° thy twinkling light *between*
As joying in the sight
Of these glad many which for joy doe sing,
That all the woods them answer and their echo ring.

Now ceasse ye damsels your delights forepast;
Enough is it, that all the lay was youres:
Now day is doen, and night is nighing° fast: *approaching*
Now bring the Bryde into the brydall boures.° *chambers*

8. Spenser's wedding took place on St. Barnabas day, June 11, the solstice or longest day of the year in the Elizabethan calendar.

9. The constellation Cancer, through which the sun passes in late July.

1. The sun, according to Ptolomaic astronomy.

Now night is come, now soone her disaray,° *undress*
And in her bed her lay;
Lay her in lillies and in violets,
And silken courteins over her display,
And odourd sheetes, and Arras[2] coverlets.
Behold how goodly my faire love does ly
In proud humility;
Like unto Maia,[3] when as Jove her tooke,
In Tempe, lying on the flowry gras,
Twixt sleepe and wake, after she weary was,
With bathing in the Acidalian brooke.
Now it is night, ye damsels may be gon,
And leave my love alone,
And leave likewise your former lay to sing:
The woods no more shal answere, nor your echo ring.

Now welcome night, thou night so long expected,
That long daies labour doest at last defray,° *repay*
And all my cares, which cruell love collected,
Hast sumd in one, and cancelled for aye:° *ever*
Spread thy broad wing over my love and me,
That no man may us see,
And in thy sable mantle us enwrap,
From feare of perrill and foule horror free.
Let no false treason seeke us to entrap,
Nor any dread disquiet once annoy
The safety of our joy:
But let the night be calme and quietsome,
Without tempestuous storms or sad afray:
Lyke as when Jove with fayre Alcmena[4] lay,
When he begot the great Tirynthian groome:
Or lyke as when he with thy selfe did lie,
And begot Majesty.
And let the mayds and yongmen cease to sing:
Ne let the woods them answer, nor theyr eccho ring.

Let no lamenting cryes, nor dolefull teares,
Be heard all night within nor yet without:
Ne let false whispers breeding hidden feares,
Breake gentle sleepe with misconceived dout.
Let no deluding dreames, nor dreadful sights
Make sudden sad affrights;
Ne let housefyres, nor lightnings helpelesse harmes,
Ne let the Pouke,° nor other evill sprights, *a house fairy*
Ne let mischivous witches with theyr charmes,
Ne let hob Goblins, names whose sence we see not,

2. A town in France, famous for its textiles.
3. The daughter of Atlas and the mother of Mercury by Jupiter, i.e., Jove.
4. The mother of Hercules, the "Tirynthian groom," who was supposed to have taken three nights to beget.

Fray° us with things that be not. *frighten*
Let not the shriech Oule,° nor the Storke be heard: *screech owl*
Nor the night Raven that still deadly yels,
Nor damned ghosts cald up with mighty spels,
Nor griesly vultures make us once affeard:
Ne let th'unpleasant Quyre° of Frogs still croking *choir*
Make us to wish theyr choking.
Let none of these theyr drery accents sing;
Ne let the woods them answer, nor theyr eccho ring.

But let stil Silence trew night watches keepe,
That sacred peace may in assurance rayne,
And tymely sleep, when it is tyme to sleepe,
May poure his limbs forth on your pleasant playne,° *complaint of love*
The whiles an hundred little winged loves,
Like divers° fethered doves, *many*
Shall fly and flutter round about your bed,
And in the secret darke, that none reproves,
Their prety stealthes shal worke, and snares shal spread
To filch away sweet snatches of delight,
Conceald through covert night.
Ye sonnes of Venus, play your sports at will,
For greedy pleasure, carelesse of your toyes,
Thinks more upon her paradise of joyes,
Then what ye do, albe it good or ill.
All night therefore attend your merry play,
For it will soone be day:
Now none doth hinder you, that say or sing,
Ne will the woods now answer, nor your Eccho ring.

Who is the same, which at my window peepes?
Or whose is that faire face, that shines so bright,
Is it not Cinthia,° she that never sleepes, *the moon*
But walkes about high heaven al the night?
O fayrest goddesse, do thou not envy
My love with me to spy:
For thou likewise didst love, though now unthought,
And for a fleece of woll, which privily,
The Latmian shephard[5] once unto thee brought,
His pleasures with thee wrought.
Therefore to us be favorable now;
And sith of wemens labours thou hast charge,
And generation goodly dost enlarge,
Encline thy will t'effect our wishfull vow,
And the chast wombe informe° with timely seed, *implant*
That may our comfort breed:

5. Endymion, beloved of Diana, goddess of the moon, chastity, and childbirth, also known as Cynthia.

Till which we cease our hopefull hap° to sing, *condition*
Ne let the woods us answere, nor our Eccho ring.

And thou great Juno,[6] which with awful might
The lawes of wedlock still dost patronize,
And the religion of the faith first plight
With sacred rites hast taught to solemnize:
And eeke for comfort often called art
Of women in their smart,
Eternally bind thou this lovely band,
And all thy blessings unto us impart.
And thou glad Genius,[7] in whose gentle hand,
The bridale bowre and geniall° bed remaine, *generative*
Without blemish or staine,
And the sweet pleasures of theyr loves delight
With secret ayde doest succour and supply,
Till they bring forth the fruitfull progeny,
Send us the timely fruit of this same night.
And thou fayre Hebe,[8] and thou Hymen free,
Grant that it may so be.
Til which we cease your further prayse to sing,
Ne any woods shal answer, nor your Eccho ring.

And ye high heavens, the temple of the gods,
In which a thousand torches flaming bright
Doe burne, that to us wretched earthly clods:
In dreadful darknesse lend desired light;
And all ye powers which in the same remayne,
More than we men can fayne,° *represent*
Poure out your blessing on us plentiously,
And happy influence upon us raine,
That we may raise a large posterity,
Which from the earth, which they may long possesse,
With lasting happinesse,
Up to your haughty° pallaces may mount, *high*
And for the guerdon° of theyr glorious merit *reward*
May heavenly tabernacles there inherit,
Of blessed Saints for to increase the count.
So let us rest, sweet love, in hope of this,
And cease till then our tymely joyes to sing,
The woods no more us answer, nor our eccho ring.

Song made in lieu of many ornaments,
With which my love should duly have bene dect,° *bedecked*
Which cutting off through hasty accidents,
Ye would not stay your dew time to expect,
But promist both to recompens,
Be unto her a goodly ornament,
And for short time an endlesse moniment.

6. Wife of Jupiter, goddess of marriage.
7. In Roman religion, the spirit of paternity who protected the family.
8. Handmaid to the gods, daughter of Jupiter and Juno.

Sir Philip Sidney

1554–1586

Reality is often stranger but hardly ever more perfect than fiction. As Sir Philip Sidney tells us, the poets bring forth a "golden world." Exempt from judgments about its truth or falsehood, "poetry" (by which Sidney meant fiction) should construct forms of the ideal to mitigate our suffering and move us to good action. Sidney's own work comments brilliantly on contemporary moral and political issues: his sonnet sequence *Astrophil and Stella* illustrates the lover's paradox (love may require chastity); his prose romance *The Arcadia* describes the politics of love and sexuality; and his *Apology for Poetry* defends poetic and dramatic art from critics who would dismiss it in favor of philosophy and history. Yet to his countrymen, Sidney's most important achievement may have been a life dedicated to a public heroism and shaped by a sense of personal honor.

History has portrayed him as a prodigy. As his friend Fulke Greville wrote, "though I knew him from a child, yet I never knew him other than a man, . . . his very play tending to enrich his mind, so that even his teachers found something in him to observe and learn above that which they had usually read or taught." Play—understood in the Renaissance manner as "serious play"—took up much of Sidney's early career. Leaving Oxford at the age of seventeen but without a degree, Sidney embarked on what in later centuries was known as the Grand Tour. He visited Europe's major cities, seeking men and women who were fashioning the political goals and aesthetic sensibilities of the age. They included the philosopher Hubert Languet, whose Protestantism was linked to a fiercely antityrannical politics; the artists Tintoretto and Paolo Veronese, whose luminous realism was to determine painterly style for more than a generation; and, finally, Henry of Navarre (later King Henry IV of France) and his wife, Margaret of Valois, whose reign would see the worst of the religious wars in Europe. Back in England by 1575, Sidney espoused a politics that challenged authority. Siding with his father, Henry Sidney, Queen Elizabeth's Lord Deputy Governor of Ireland, he argued for imposing a land tax on the Anglo-Irish nobility, citing their "unreasonable and arrogant pretensions" as a cause of civil unrest. And in 1580, seeking to protect the monarchy from foreign influences, he wrote to the Queen cautioning her against a match with Francis, Duke of Alençon and brother to the French king, Henry III. She was furious at his temerity and ordered him to the country, where he was to remain out of touch with court affairs. By 1584 she had relented, sending Sidney to the Netherlands to assess the Protestant resistance to Spanish rule. There, in 1586, fighting for the Queen's interest and the Protestant cause she championed, he died of an abscessed bullet wound in his thigh.

Sidney's first literary work was a brief pastoral masque entitled *The Lady of May*, composed in honor of the Queen in 1578. His subsequent exile from court provided him with extensive time to write. He was often at Wilton, the estate of his sister, Mary Herbert, Countess of Pembroke; it was there that he wrote the first two of his major works, in all likelihood with his sister and her circle as his first readers and critics. *The Apology for Poetry*, a work defending what Sidney called his "unelected vocation," answers attacks on art, poetry, and the theater by such censorious writers as Stephen Gosson. But its argument exceeds the limits of antitheatrical debate to embrace questions about the uses of history and the effectiveness of philosophy—a subject that bears comparison with the poetics of Aristotle and Horace. Readers have remembered most its insistence that "poetry" goes beyond nature to fashion an ideal; it works "not only to make a Cyrus, which had been but a particular excellency as nature might have done, but to bestow a Cyrus upon the world to make many Cyruses." Poetry's creatures—whether heroes, heroines, or villains—cannot misrepresent fact because they exist only in the imagination of readers and listeners: "for the poet," Sidney declared, "he nothing affirms, and therefore never lieth."

The marvelous world of Sidney's *Arcadia* vividly dramatizes the chief points of his poetics. An early version of this satirical pastoral, written during Sidney's exile from Elizabeth's court and finished in 1581, depicts the willfulness of a superstitious and lazy duke, Basilius, who sequesters his marriageable daughters, Pamela and Philoclea, in the country where no suitor can meet them. His plans are foiled by two foreign princes, Pyrocles and Musidorus, who, disguised as a woman and a shepherd, manage to court and win the love of these ladies. Sidney's treatment of sex and gender is provocative: Pyrocles, disguised as a woman, attracts the interest of Basilius, who thinks "she" is female; at the same time, Pyrocles causes Gynecia, Basilius's wife, who senses that "she" is male, to fall in love with "her." Philoclea also falls in love with the disguised Pyrocles but represses that love because she thinks that Pyrocles is female. The encounters that follow challenge customary assumptions of sex as strictly linked to gender and suggest the extent to which social behavior between men and women is conventional. Interspersed throughout the prose narrative of these events are poems, termed *eclogues*, expressing the joys and sorrows of pastoral life, one of which, *As I my little flock on Ister bank*, has persuaded many readers that Sidney was arguing for a radical, essentially republican politics.

A second version of the *Arcadia*, apparently written two or three years later, very explicitly introduces politics to the plot: Sidney sketches the characters of several rulers, magnificent and tyrannical; includes arguments for resistance and rebellion; and illustrates the nature of justice and equity. This version, revised and readied for publication after Sidney's death by his sister, Mary Herbert, Countess of Pembroke, contains splendid portraits of queens both good and bad. Especially memorable is the wicked Cecropia, who plots to capture and kill the Arcadian princesses. The mother of Amphialus, who is a kind of moving target for misfortune's arrows, Cecropia has sometimes been understood to figure Catherine de'Medici, the powerful French queen, who many maintained had helped plan the massacre of hundreds of Protestants on Saint Bartholomew's Day, 1572.

Sidney's last work, *Astrophil and Stella*, has often been understood as self-satire. Its principal character, the young Astrophil, is frustrated by the marriage of his beloved Stella to a man who is characterized as "rich," an apparent reference to Sidney's disappointment when Penelope Devereux, whom he had courted for several years, married Lord Rich. Sidney mocks the young lover's passionate complaints while at the same time transforming the courtly figure of the distant yet beloved lady to reveal a paradox: as "absent," Stella may be present to Astrophil in spirit; as "present," she can only deny him her intimate friendship. The sequence is a marvelously witty reconceptualization of the principal themes of English Petrarchanism, a style that by the 1580s had become rather trite. Addressing his Stella, Sidney's Astrophil ends a sonnet with these lines:

And not content to be Perfection's heir
Thyself, doest strive all minds that way to move:
Who mark in thee what is in thee most fair.
So while thy beauty draws the heart to love,
As fast thy virtue bends that love to good:
But ah, Desire still cries, give me some food.

Conventionally Petrarchan in his depiction of the lady as a model and inspiration to a moral virtue that would seem to rule out any physical expressions of love, Sidney is at last very unconventional: he refuses to renounce "Desire" and its "food," or sexual gratification. A more imitative poet would not have so rejected Petrarch's idealistic asceticism. But just as Sidney had challenged the authority of church and state to promote better government (as he saw it), so did he exploit the process of "invention," the discovery of new meaning in old matter, to revitalize literary forms and expression.

The Apology for Poetry

When the right virtuous Edward Wotton[1] and I were at the Emperor's court together, we gave ourselves to learn horsemanship of John Pietro Pugliano, one that with great commendation had the place of an esquire in his stable. And he, according to the fertileness of the Italian wit, did not only afford us the demonstration of his practice, but sought to enrich our minds with the contemplations therein, which he thought most precious. But with none I remember mine ears were at that time more laden, than when (either angered with slow payment, or moved with our learner-like admiration) he exercised his speech in the praise of his faculty. He said soldiers were the noblest estate of mankind, and horsemen the noblest of soldiers. He said they were the masters of war and ornaments of peace, speedy goers and strong abiders, triumphers both in camps and courts. Nay, to so unbelieved a point he proceeded as that no earthly thing bred such wonder to a prince as to be a good horseman—skill of government was but a *pedanteria* [pedantry] in comparison. Then would he add certain praises, by telling what a peerless beast the horse was, the only serviceable courtier without flattery, the beast of most beauty, faithfulness, courage, and such more, that if I had not been a piece of a logician before I came to him, I think he would have persuaded me to have wished myself a horse. But thus much at least with his no few words he drave into me, that self-love is better than any gilding to make that seem gorgeous wherein ourselves be parties. Wherein, if Pugliano's strong affection and weak arguments will not satisfy you, I will give you a nearer example of myself, who (I know not by what mischance) in these my not old years and idlest times having slipped into the title of a poet, am provoked to say something unto you in the defense of that my unelected vocation,[2] which if I handle with more good will than good reasons, bear with me, since the scholar is to be pardoned that followeth the steps of his master. And yet I must say that, as I have more just cause to make a pitiful defense of poor poetry, which from almost the highest estimation of learning is fallen to be the laughingstock of children, so have I need to bring some more available proofs: since the former is by no man barred of his deserved credit, the silly latter hath had even the names of philosophers used to the defacing of it, with great danger of civil war among the Muses.[3]

And first, truly, to all them that, professing learning, inveigh against poetry may justly be objected that they go very near to ungratefulness, to seek to deface that which, in the noblest nations and languages that are known, hath been the first light-giver to ignorance, and first nurse, whose milk by little and little enabled them to feed afterwards of tougher knowledges. And will they now play the hedgehog that, being received into the den, drive out his host? Or rather the vipers, that with their birth kill their parents?

Let learned Greece in any of his manifold sciences be able to show me one book before Musaeus, Homer, and Hesiod, all three nothing else but poets.[4] Nay, let any history be brought that can say any writers were there before them, if they were not

1. Edward Wotton (1548–1626), half-brother of Henry Wotton who saw diplomatic service under James I. Edward Wotton and Sidney undertook a mission to the court of the Emperor Maximilian at Vienna in 1574–1575.

2. Sidney refers to writing poetry as his "unelected vocation" because he would have readers believe that he undertook it only after Elizabeth I had exiled him from court.

3. Mythological figures who were thought to inspire the liberal arts.

4. Musaeus was in fact a poet of the 5th century A.D., reported to be a pupil of the mythical Orpheus, the first musician. Homer was the legendary author of the *Iliad*, an epic poem telling of the seige of Troy by the army of the Greeks led by the hero, Achilles; and of the *Odyssey*, recounting the return of the hero, Odysseus, from Troy to his homeland in Ithaka. Hesiod is known as the poet of the *Theogony*, which tells the story of the gods in Greece; and of *Works and Days*, which describes the rituals and practices of the agricultural year. Both Homer and Hesiod lived in the 8th century B.C.

men of the same skill, as Orpheus, Linus,[5] and some other are named, who, having been the first of that country that made pens deliverers of their knowledge to the posterity, may justly challenge to be called their fathers in learning: for not only in time they had this priority (although in itself antiquity be venerable) but went before them, as causes to draw with their charming sweetness the wild untamed wits to an admiration of knowledge. So, as Amphion[6] was said to move stones with his poetry to build Thebes, and Orpheus to be listened to by beasts—indeed stony and beastly people—so among the Romans were Livius Andronicus and Ennius. So in the Italian language the first that made it aspire to be a treasure-house of science were the poets Dante, Boccaccio, and Petrarch. So in our English were Gower and Chaucer, after whom, encouraged and delighted with their excellent fore-going,[7] others have followed, to beautify our mother tongue, as well in the same kind as in other arts.

This did so notably show itself, that the philosophers of Greece durst not a long time appear to the world but under the masks of poets. So Thales, Empedocles, and Parmenides[8] sang their natural philosophy in verses; so did Pythagoras and Phocylides their moral counsels; so did Tyrtaeus in war matters, and Solon in matters of policy: or rather they, being poets, did exercise their delightful vein in those points of highest knowledge, which before them lay hid to the world. For that wise Solon was directly a poet it is manifest, having written in verse the notable fable of the Atlantic Island, which was continued by Plato. And truly even Plato[9] whosoever well considereth shall find that in the body of his work, though the inside and strength were philosophy, the skin, as it were, and beauty depended most of[1] poetry: for all standeth upon dialogues, wherein he feigneth many honest burgesses of Athens to speak of such matters, that, if they had been set on the rack, they would never have confessed them, besides his poetical describing the circumstances of their meetings, as the well ordering of a banquet,[2] the delicacy of a walk, with interlacing mere tales, as Gyges' ring and others, which who knoweth not to be flowers of poetry did never walk into Apollo's garden.[3]

And even historiographers (although their lips sound of things done, and verity[4] be written in their foreheads) have been glad to borrow both fashion and, perchance, weight of the poets. So Herodotus entitled his History by the name of the nine Muses;[5] and both he and all the rest that followed him either stale[6] or usurped of poetry

5. Supposed to have been the teacher of Orpheus.

6. Sidney lists historical and legendary poets to illustrate his claim that they were the founders of civilization and culture. Amphion was supposed to have moved stones by playing his music and thus to have built the walls of Troy; Livius Andronicus (c. 284–204 B.C.) was believed to have been the first Latin poet; Ennius (c. 239–169 B.C.) was traditionally regarded as the greatest of the early Latin poets. Dante, Boccaccio, and Petrarch were the first of the great Italian poets of the early Renaissance; Chaucer and Gower were the most important of the late medieval poets who wrote in English.

7. Example.

8. Sidney lists the best-known of the Greek philosophers before Plato: Thales, a geometrician; Empedocles, who studied the concepts of change and permanence; Parmeneides, who investigated the nature of being; Pythagoras, a mathematician and astronomer; Phocylides, a moralist; and Tyrtaeus, a poet. Solon (c. 640–558 B.C.) was an Athenian statesman, poet, and constitutional reformer. No trace remains of a poem by Solon telling of Atlantis, an island beyond the pillars of Hercules that vanishes beneath the sea; Sidney recalls Plato's dialogue (*Timaeus*, 21–24), in which Critias tells Socrates that the story of Atlantis originates in an unfinished poem of Solon.

9. Author of many works of philosophy in dialogue form, notably *The Republic*, on the construction of an ideal state, and *The Symposium*, on the nature of love and its association with beauty and truth. He was a key influence on Renaissance thinkers.

1. On.

2. A banquet is the setting of *The Symposium*; speakers take a walk in the *The Phaedrus*; and the story of Gyges' ring is told in *The Republic*.

3. Apollo was the god of poetry.

4. Truth.

5. Herodotus, a Greek historian (480–425) B.C.), wrote about the struggle between Asia and Greece; later classical editors divided his work, which he entitled simply *History*, into nine books named after the nine Muses: Calliope, Clio, Euterpe, Melpomene, Terpsichore, Erato, Polyhymnia, Urania, and Thalia.

6. Stole.

their passionate describing of passions, the many particularities of battles, which no man could affirm; or, if that be denied me, long orations put in the mouths of great kings and captains, which it is certain they never pronounced.

So that truly neither philosopher nor historiographer could at the first have entered into the gates of popular judgments, if they had not taken a great passport of poetry, which in all nations at this day where learning flourisheth not, is plain to be seen; in all which they have some feeling of poetry.

In Turkey, besides their law-giving divines, they have no other writers but poets. In our neighbor country Ireland, where truly learning goeth very bare, yet are their poets held in a devout reverence. Even among the most barbarous and simple Indians where no writing is, yet have they their poets who make and sing songs, which they call *areytos*,[7] both of their ancestors' deeds and praises of their gods: a sufficient probability that, if ever learning come among them, it must be by having their hard dull wits softened and sharpened with the sweet delights of poetry—for until they find a pleasure in the exercises of the mind, great promises of much knowledge will little persuade them that know not the fruits of knowledge. In Wales, the true remnant of the ancient Britons, as there are good authorities to show the long time they had poets, which they called bards, so through all the conquests of Romans, Saxons, Danes, and Normans, some of whom did seek to ruin all memory of learning from among them, yet do their poets even to this day last; so as it is not more notable in soon beginning than in long continuing.

But since the authors of most of our sciences[8] were the Romans, and before them the Greeks, let us a little stand upon their authorities, but even so far as to see what names they have given unto this now scorned skill.

Among the Romans a poet was called *vates*, which is as much as a diviner, foreseer, or prophet, as by his conjoined words *vaticinium* [prediction] and *vaticinari* [to foretell] is manifest: so heavenly a title did that excellent people bestow upon this heart-ravishing knowledge. And so far were they carried into the admiration thereof, that they thought in the chanceable hitting upon any such verses great foretokens of their following fortunes were placed. Whereupon grew the word of *Sortes Virgilianae*,[9] when by sudden opening Virgil's book they lighted upon any verse of his making, whereof the histories of the emperors' lives are full: as of Albinus, the governor of our island, who in his childhood met with this verse

Arma amens capio nec sat rationis in armis[1]

and in his age performed it. Which, although it were a very vain and godless superstition, as also it was to think spirits were commanded by such verses—whereupon this word charms, derived of *carmina* [songs], cometh—so yet serveth it to show the great reverence those wits were held in; and altogether not without ground, since both the oracles of Delphos and Sibylla's prophecies were wholly delivered in verses.[2] For that same exquisite observing of number and measure[3] in the words, and that high flying liberty of conceit proper to the poet, did seem to have some divine force in it.

7. A West Indian dance, recorded by José de Acosta in his *Natural and Moral History of the West Indies* (translated into English in 1604).
8. Any body of knowledge, typically natural philosophy and also including ethics and politics.
9. The Virgilian lots, or fortune as it is implied in lines from the *Aeneid*, which the reader chose at random and then subjects to interpretation.
1. "I seize arms madly, nor is there reason in arming" (2.314).
2. The shrine of Apollo at Delphi was presided over by a priestess who was believed to know the god's thoughts about the future; the Sibyls were supposed to be ancient prophetesses whose words were collected in the *Sibylline Books*.
3. Meter and rhythm.

And may not I presume a little further, to show the reasonableness of this word *vates*, and say that the holy David's Psalms are a divine poem? If I do, I shall not do it without the testimony of great learned men, both ancient and modern. But even the name of Psalms will speak for me, which being interpreted, is nothing but songs; then that it is fully written in meter, as all learned Hebricians agree, although the rules be not yet fully found; lastly and principally, his handling his prophecy, which is merely poetical: for what else is the awaking his musical instruments, the often and free changing of persons, his notable *prosopopoeias* [personifications], when he maketh you, as it were, see God coming in His majesty, his telling of the beasts' joyfulness and hills leaping,[4] but a heavenly poesy, wherein almost he showeth himself a passionate lover of that unspeakable and everlasting beauty to be seen by the eyes of the mind, only cleared by faith? But truly now having named him, I fear me I seem to profane that holy name, applying it to poetry, which is among us thrown down to so ridiculous an estimation. But they that with quiet judgments will look a little deeper into it, shall find the end and working of it such as, being rightly applied, deserveth not to be scourged out of the Church of God.

But now let us see how the Greeks named it, and how they deemed of it. The Greeks called him a "poet," which name hath, as the most excellent, gone through other languages. It cometh of this word ποιεῖν, which is, to make: wherein, I know not whether by luck or wisdom, we Englishmen have met with the Greeks in calling him a maker: which name, how high and incomparable a title it is, I had rather were known by marking the scope of other sciences than by any partial allegation.

There is no art delivered to mankind that hath not the works of nature for his principal object, without which they could not consist, and on which they so depend, as they become actors and players, as it were, of what nature will have set forth. So doth the astronomer look upon the stars, and, by that he seeth, set down what order nature hath taken therein. So doth the geometrician and arithmetician in their diverse sorts of quantities. So doth the musicians in time tell you which by nature agree, which not. The natural philosopher thereon hath his name, and the moral philosopher standeth upon the natural virtues, vices, or passions of man; and follow nature (saith he) therein, and thou shalt not err. The lawyer saith what men have determined; the historian what men have done. The grammarian speaketh only of the rules of speech; and the rhetorician and logician, considering what in nature will soonest prove and persuade, thereon give artificial rules, which still are compassed within the circle of a question according to the proposed matter. The physician weigheth the nature of man's body, and the nature of things helpful or hurtful unto it. And the metaphysic,[5] though it be in the second and abstract notions, and therefore be counted supernatural, yet doth he indeed build upon the depth of nature. Only the poet, disdaining to be tied to any such subjection, lifted up with the vigor of his own invention, doth grow in effect another nature, in making things either better than nature bringeth forth, or, quite anew, forms such as never were in nature, as the Heroes, Demigods, Cyclops, Chimeras, Furies,[6] and such like: so as he

4. Psalm 29.

5. A philosopher who considered abstractions and aspects of mental and spiritual life entertained in a state of contemplation rather than of action.

6. Furies: supernatural forces figured as mad goddesses pursuing revenge; demigods: male offspring of a god and a mortal, having some divine powers; cyclops: a one-eyed giant; chimeras: imaginary monsters made up of grotesquely disparate parts.

goeth hand in hand with nature, not enclosed within the narrow warrant[7] of her gifts, but freely ranging only within the zodiac of his own wit. Nature never set forth the earth in so rich tapestry as divers poets have done; neither with so pleasant rivers, fruitful trees, sweet-smelling flowers, nor whatsoever else may make the too much loved earth more lovely. Her world is brazen, the poets only deliver a golden.

But let those things alone, and go to man—for whom as the other things are, so it seemeth in him her uttermost cunning is employed—and know whether she have brought forth so true a lover as Theagenes, so constant a friend as Pylades, so valiant a man as Orlando, so right a prince as Xenophon's Cyrus, so excellent a man every way as Virgil's Aeneas.[8] Neither let this be jestingly conceived, because the works of the one be essential, the other in imitation or fiction; for any understanding knoweth the skill of each artificer standeth in that *idea* or fore-conceit[9] of the work, and not in the work itself. And that the poet hath that *idea* is manifest, by delivering them forth in such excellency as he had imagined them. Which delivering forth also is not wholly imaginative, as we are wont to say by them that build castles in the air; but so far substantially it worketh, not only to make a Cyrus, which had been but a particular excellency as nature might have done, but to bestow a Cyrus upon the world to make many Cyruses, if they will learn aright why and how that maker made him.

Neither let it be deemed too saucy a comparison to balance the highest point of man's wit with the efficacy of nature; but rather give right honor to the heavenly Maker of that maker, who having made man to His own likeness, set him beyond and over all the works of that second nature: which in nothing he showeth so much as in poetry, when with the force of a divine breath he bringeth things forth surpassing her doings—with no small arguments to the credulous of that first accursed fall of Adam, since our erected wit maketh us know what perfection is, and yet our infected will keepeth us from reaching unto it. But these arguments will by few be understood, and by fewer granted. This much (I hope) will be given me, that the Greeks with some probability of reason gave him the name above all names of learning.

Now let us go to a more ordinary opening of him, that the truth may be the more palpable: and so I hope, though we get not so unmatched a praise as the etymology of his names will grant, yet his very description, which no man will deny, shall not justly be barred from a principal commendation.

Poesy therefore is an art of imitation,[1] for so Aristotle termeth it in the word μίμησις—that is to say, a representing, counterfeiting, or figuring forth—to speak metaphorically, a speaking picture—with this end, to teach and delight.

7. Authority.

8. Sidney cites men recognized for their virtues. Theagenes exemplifies the true lover in Heliodorus's romance, the *Aethiopica;* Pylades, who helped Orestes avenge his father Agamemnon's murder, was cited by Renaissance commentators as a perfect friend; Orlando (modeled on Roland, the knight who fought for Charlemagne against the Basques at the battle of Roncesvalles, A.D. 778) was the hero of Ariosto's *Orlando Furioso* and illustrated the Renaissance idea of valor. The *Anabasis* of Xenophon (himself a general in Cyrus's army) relates how Cyrus the Younger, a Persian prince, helped the Peloponnesians resist the army of Athens and then died in an attempt to take the Persian throne from his brother Artaxerxes in the fifth century B.C. Aeneas, the hero of Virgil's *Aeneid* and the mythical founder of the Roman Empire, was generally considered to be the epitome of the statesman.

9. The element of the literary work that determines how and to what end its subject is conveyed. Sidney later states that an *Idea* works "substantially" because it makes readers want to imitate the virtuous characters represented in a literary work.

1. Aristotle stated that poetry was a mimetic (from *mimesis*) or imitative art; Sidney (following Horace, who sees that poetry is like painting) adds that this imitation is (in some sense) pictorial.

Of this have been three general kinds. The chief, both in antiquity and excellency, were they that did imitate the unconceivable excellencies of God. Such were David in his Psalms; Solomon in his Song of Songs, in his Ecclesiastes, and Proverbs; Moses and Deborah in their Hymns; and the writer of Job: which, beside other, the learned Emanuel Tremellius and Franciscus Junius[2] do entitle the poetical part of the Scripture. Against these none will speak that hath the Holy Ghost in due holy reverence. (In this kind, though in a full wrong divinity, were Orpheus, Amphion, Homer in his Hymns, and many other, both Greeks and Romans.)[3] And this poesy must be used by whosoever will follow St. James's counsel in singing psalms when they are merry, and I know is used with the fruit of comfort by some, when, in sorrowful pangs of their death-bringing sins, they find the consolation of the never-leaving goodness.

The second kind is of them that deal with matters philosophical, either moral, as Tyrtaeus,[4] Phocylides, Cato, or natural, as Lucretius and Virgil's *Georgics;* or astronomical, as Manilius and Pontanus; or historical, as Lucan: which who mislike, the fault is in their judgment quite out of taste, and not in the sweet food of sweetly uttered knowledge.

But because this second sort is wrapped within the fold of the proposed subject, and takes not the course of his own invention, whether they properly be poets or no let grammarians dispute, and go to the third, indeed right poets, of whom chiefly this question ariseth: betwixt whom and these second is such a kind of difference as betwixt the meaner sort of painters, who counterfeit only such faces as are set before them, and the more excellent, who having no law but wit, bestow that in colors upon you which is fittest for the eye to see: as the constant though lamenting look of Lucretia,[5] when she punished in herself another's fault, wherein he painteth not Lucretia whom he never saw, but painteth the outward beauty of such a virtue. For these third be they which most properly do imitate to teach and delight, and to imitate borrow nothing of what is, hath been, or shall be; but range, only reined with learned discretion, into the divine consideration of what may be and should be. These be they that, as the first and most noble sort may justly be termed *vates,* so these are waited on in the excellentest languages and best understandings with the fore-described name of poets. For these indeed do merely make to imitate, and imitate both to delight and teach; and delight, to move men to take that goodness in hand, which without delight they would fly as from a stranger; and teach, to make them know that goodness whereunto they are moved—which being the noblest scope to which ever any learning was directed, yet want there not idle tongues to bark at them.

2. Sixteenth-century translators of the Hebrew and Greek Bible into Latin who considered the books here mentioned (all in the Hebrew Bible) to be poetry.

3. Sidney distinguishes the mystical works of Hellenic antiquity as erroneous in their depiction and understanding of divinity.

4. Sidney lists poets who he considers wrote some kind of philosophy and are not altogether "right," that is, pure poets. Tyrtaeus: mid-7th century B.C. Greek poet known for his praise of valor; Phocylides: a moralist of the 6th century B.C.; Cato: Dionysius Cato (c. A.D. 300), a moralist of whom little is known, who wrote a collection of moral sayings in verse couplets, published by Erasmus for use in schools; Lucretius: the Roman poet of the first century B.C. who wrote about the creation of the physical world; Virgil: the poet who stated the principles of farming in his *Georgics;* Manilius: the poet of the first century A.D. who wrote a versified treatise on astronomy; Pontanus: Joannes Jovius Pontanus, a late 15th-century poet who wrote a work on astronomy; and Lucan: the Roman poet of the first century A.D. who wrote the epic *Pharsalia,* which describes the events in the civil war between Caesar and Pompey up to Caesar's seduction of the Egyptian queen, Cleopatra.

5. Legendary heroine of the ancient Roman republic who committed suicide rather than live in shame after being raped by the tyrant Sextus Tarquinius. Her story was told in versions by Ovid, Livy, Chaucer, Christine de Pisan, Shakespeare, and others.

These be subdivided into sundry more special denominations. The most notable be the heroic, lyric, tragic, comic, satiric, iambic, elegiac, pastoral,[6] and certain others, some of these being termed according to the matter they deal with, some by the sorts of verses they liked best to write in; for indeed the greatest part of poets have apparelled their poetical inventions in that numbrous kind of writing which is called verse—indeed but apparelled, verse being but an ornament and no cause to poetry, since there have been many most excellent poets that never versified, and now swarm many versifiers that need never answer to the name of poets. For Xenophon, who did imitate so excellently as to give us *effigiem iusti imperii,* the portraiture of a just empire, under the name of Cyrus (as Cicero saith of him), made therein an absolute heroical poem.[7] So did Heliodorus in his sugared invention of that picture of love in Theagenes and Chariclea;[8] and yet both these wrote in prose: which I speak to show that it is not rhyming and versing that maketh a poet—no more than a long gown maketh an advocate, who though he pleaded in armor should be an advocate and no soldier. But it is that feigning notable images of virtues, vices, or what else, with that delightful teaching, which must be the right describing note to know a poet by; although indeed the senate of poets hath chosen verse as their fittest raiment, meaning, as in matter they passed all in all, so in manner to go beyond them: not speaking (table-talk fashion or like men in a dream) words as they chanceably fall from the mouth, but peising[9] each syllable of each word by just proportion according to the dignity of the subject.

Now therefore it shall not be amiss first to weigh this latter sort of poetry by his works, and then by his parts; and if in neither of these anatomies he be condemnable, I hope we shall obtain a more favorable sentence.

This purifying of wit—this enriching of memory, enabling of judgment, and enlarging of conceit—which commonly we call learning, under what name soever it come forth, or to what immediate end soever it be directed, the final end is to lead and draw us to as high a perfection as our degenerate souls, made worse by their clayey lodgings, can be capable of.

This, according to the inclination of the man, bred many-formed impressions. For some that thought this felicity principally to be gotten by knowledge, and no knowledge to be so high or heavenly as acquaintance with the stars, gave themselves to astronomy; others, persuading themselves to be demigods if they knew the causes of things, became natural and supernatural philosophers; some an admirable delight drew to music; and some the certainty of demonstration to the mathematics. But all, one and other, having this scope: to know, and by knowledge to lift up the mind from the dungeon of the body to the enjoying his own divine essence.

But when by the balance of experience it was found that the astronomer, looking to the stars, might fall in a ditch, that the inquiring philosopher might be blind in himself, and the mathematician might draw forth a straight line with a crooked heart, then lo, did proof, the overruler of opinions, make manifest that all these are but serving sciences, which, as they have each a private end in themselves, so yet are they all directed to the highest end of the mistress-knowledge, by the Greeks

6. Sidney lists the eight genres of poetry; "iambic" was a kind of satiric verse written in iambics, a meter made up of units or feet, each of which consists of a lightly stressed syllable followed by a heavily stressed syllable.
7. Sidney refers to Xenophon's *Cyropaedia*, his history of Cyrus, the emperor of Persia, a work that he thinks has a heroic quality because it deals with the fate of an empire.
8. Characters in Heliodorus's romance, *Aethiopica*.
9. Weighing.

called ἀρχιτεκτονική, which stands (as I think) in the knowledge of a man's self, in the ethic and politic consideration, with the end of well-doing and not of well-knowing only—even as the saddler's next end is to make a good saddle, but his further end to serve a nobler faculty, which is horsemanship, so the horseman's to soldiery, and the soldier not only to have the skill, but to perform the practice of a soldier. So that, the ending end of all earthly learning being virtuous action, those skills that most serve to bring forth that have a most just title to be princes over all the rest.

Wherein, if we can, show we the poet's nobleness, by setting him before his other competitors. Among whom as principal challengers step forth the moral philosophers, whom, me thinketh, I see coming towards me with a sullen gravity, as though they could not abide vice by daylight, rudely clothed for to witness outwardly their contempt of outward things, with books in their hands against glory, whereto they set their names, sophistically speaking against subtlety, and angry with any man in whom they see the foul fault of anger. These men casting largess as they go, of definitions, divisions, and distinctions, with a scornful interrogative do soberly ask whether it be possible to find any path so ready to lead a man to virtue as that which teacheth what virtue is; and teach it not only by delivering forth his very being, his causes and effects, but also by making known his enemy, vice, which must be destroyed, and his cumbersome servant, passion, which must be mastered; by showing the generalities that containeth it, and the specialities that are derived from it; lastly, by plain setting down how it extendeth itself out of the limits of a man's own little world to the government of families and maintaining of public societies.

The historian scarcely giveth leisure to the moralist to say so much, but that he, laden with old mouse-eaten records, authorizing himself (for the most part) upon other histories, whose greatest authorities are built upon the notable foundation of hearsay; having much ado to accord differing writers and to pick truth out of their partiality; better acquainted with a thousand years ago than with the present age, and yet better knowing how this world goeth than how his own wit runneth; curious for antiquities and inquisitive of novelties; a wonder to young folks and a tyrant in table talk, denieth, in a great chafe,[1] that any man for teaching of virtue, and virtuous actions is comparable to him. "I am *testis temporum, lux veritatis, vita memoriae, magistra vitae, nuntia vetustatis*.[2] The philosopher," saith he, "teacheth a disputative virtue, but I do an active. His virtue is excellent in the dangerless Academy of Plato,[3] but mine showeth forth her honorable face in the battles of Marathon, Pharsalia, Poitiers, and Agincourt.[4] He teacheth virtue by certain abstract considerations, but I only bid you follow the footing of them that have gone before you. Old-aged experience goeth beyond the fine-witted philosopher, but I give the experience of many ages. Lastly, if he make the songbook, I put the learner's hand to the lute; and if he be the guide, I am the light." Then would he allege you innumerable examples, confirming story by stories, how much the wisest senators and princes have been directed by

1. Heat, fury.
2. Sidney quotes Cicero in his *De Oratore* (*Concerning the Orator*): "I am the witness of time, the light of truth, the life of memory, the governess of life, the herald of antiquity."
3. The olive grove near Athens, where Plato and his successors taught philosophy.
4. Sidney mentions some memorable battles: The Athenians defeated the invading Persians at Marathon in 490 B.C.; Caesar defeated Pompey at Pharsalus in 48 B.C.; the Franks, under Charles Martel, defeated the Moors, led by Spanish emir Abd al-Rahman Ghafiqi in 732; the English, under Edward, the Black Prince, overcame the French army and captured their king, John II in 1356, each time at Poitiers; finally, Henry V defeated the French in 1415 at Agincourt.

the credit of history, as Brutus, Alphonsus of Aragon,[5] and who not, if need be? At length the long line of their disputation maketh a point in this, that the one giveth the precept, and the other the example.

Now whom shall we find (since the question standeth for the highest form in the school of learning) to be moderator? Truly, as me seemeth, the poet; and if not a moderator, even the man that ought to carry the title from them both, and much more from all other serving sciences. Therefore compare we the poet with the historian and with the moral philosopher; and if he go beyond them both, no other human skill can match him. For as for the divine, with all reverence it is ever to be excepted, not only for having his scope as far beyond any of these as eternity exceedeth a moment, but even for passing each of these in themselves. And for the lawyer, though *Ius* [Right] be the daughter of Justice, and justice the chief of virtues, yet because he seeketh to make men good rather *formidine poenae* than *virtutis amore;*[6] or, to say righter, doth not endeavor to make men good, but that their evil hurt not others; having no care, so he be a good citizen, how bad a man he be: therefore as our wickedness maketh him necessary, and necessity maketh him honorable, so is he not in the deepest truth to stand in rank with these who all endeavor to take naughtiness away and plant goodness even in the secretest cabinet of our souls. And these four are all that any way deal in that consideration of men's manners, which being the supreme knowledge, they that best breed it deserve the best commendation.

The philosopher, therefore, and the historian are they which would win the goal, the one by precept, the other by example. But both, not having both, do both halt.[7] For the philosopher, setting down with thorny arguments the bare rule, is so hard of utterance and so misty to be conceived, that one that hath no other guide but him shall wade in him till he be old before he shall find sufficient cause to be honest. For his knowledge standeth so upon the abstract and general, that happy is that man who may understand him, and more happy that can apply what he doth understand. On the other side, the historian, wanting the precept, is so tied, not to what should be but to what is, to the particular truth of things and not to the general reason of things, that his example draweth no necessary consequence, and therefore a less fruitful doctrine.

Now doth the peerless poet perform both: for whatsoever the philosopher saith should be done, he giveth a perfect picture of it in someone by whom he presupposeth it was done, so as he coupleth the general notion with the particular example. A perfect picture I say, for he yieldeth to the powers of the mind an image of that whereof the philosopher bestoweth but a wordish description, which doth neither strike, pierce, nor possess the sight of the soul so much as that other doth. For as in outward things, to a man that had never seen an elephant or a rhinoceros, who should tell him most exquisitely all their shapes, color, bigness, and particular marks, or of a gorgeous palace, an *architector* [architect], with declaring the full beauties, might well make the hearer able to repeat, as it were by rote, all he had heard, yet should never satisfy his inward conceit[8] with being witness to itself of a true lively

5. Brutus: Roman statesman, one of Caesar's assassins, who is said to have spent the night before the battle of Pharsalus reading history; Alphonsus: King of Aragon and Sicily who encouraged his soldiers to seize the libraries of those they conquered and to bring their books to him.

6. I.e., rather "from fear of punishment" than "from love of virtue" (Horace, *Epistles* 1.2.62). Sidney distinguishes between staying within the law and moral behavior.

7. Limp.

8. The listener's mental picture or image.

knowledge; but the same man, as soon as he might see those beasts well painted, or the house well in model, should straightways grow, without need of any description, to a judicial comprehending of them: so no doubt the philosopher with his learned definitions—be it of virtue, vices, matters of public policy or private government—replenisheth the memory with many infallible grounds of wisdom, which, notwithstanding, lie dark before the imaginative and judging power, if they be not illuminated or figured forth by the speaking picture of poesy.

Tully[9] taketh much pains, and many times not without poetical helps, to make us know the force love of our country hath in us. Let us but hear old Anchises speaking in the midst of Troy's flames,[1] or see Ulysses in the fullness of all Calypso's delights bewail his absence from barren and beggarly Ithaca. Anger, the Stoics said, was a short madness: let but Sophocles bring you Ajax on a stage, killing or whipping sheep and oxen, thinking them the army of Greeks, with their chieftains Agamemnon and Menelaus, and tell me if you have not a more familiar insight into anger than finding in the schoolmen his *genus* [race] and difference.[2] See whether wisdom and temperance in Ulysses and Diomedes, valor in Achilles, friendship in Nisus and Euryalus, even to an ignorant man carry not an apparent shining; and, contrarily, the remorse of conscience in Oedipus, the soon repenting pride in Agamemnon, the self-devouring cruelty in his father Atreus, the violence of ambition in the two Theban brothers, the sour-sweetness of revenge in Medea; and, to fall lower, the Terentian Gnatho and our Chaucer's Pandar so expressed that we now use their names to signify their trades:[3] and finally, all virtues, vices, and passions so in their own natural seats laid to the view, that we seem not to hear of them, but clearly to see through them.

But even in the most excellent determination of goodness, what philosopher's counsel can so readily direct a prince, as the feigned Cyrus in Xenophon; or a virtuous man in all fortunes, as Aeneas in Virgil; or a whole commonwealth, as the way of Sir Thomas More's *Utopia?* I say the way, because where Sir Thomas More erred, it was the fault of the man and not of the poet, for that way of patterning a commonwealth was most absolute, though he perchance hath not so absolutely performed it. For the question is, whether the feigned image of poetry or the regular instruction of philosophy hath the more force in teaching: wherein if the philosophers have more rightly showed themselves philosophers than the poets have attained to the high top of their profession, as in truth

Mediocribus esse poetis,
Non dii, non homines, non concessere columnae;[4]

it is, I say again, not the fault of the art, but that by few men that art can be accomplished.

Certainly, even our Savior Christ could as well have given the moral commonplaces of uncharitableness and humbleness as the divine narration of Dives and Lazarus;[5] or of disobedience and mercy, as that heavenly discourse of the lost child

9. Cicero.

1. In the remainder of this paragraph, Sidney refers to exemplary moments in the lives of mythical figures as illustrated in the literature of antiquity, especially the works of Virgil, Homer, and the Greek and Roman dramatists.

2. Species.

3. Gnatho: a parasite and flatterer in the Roman playwright Terence's *Eunuchus;* Pandar: the go-between for the lovers in Chaucer's *Troilus and Creseyde*.

4. Neither gods, nor men, nor booksellers permit poets to be mediocre; a statement adapted from Horace's *Art of Poetry*.

5. Sidney cites several parables from scripture. The rich man, Dives, refused to help the beggar Lazarus; Dives was condemned to hell, Lazarus went to heaven (Luke 16.19–31). He then cites the story of the Prodigal Son, welcomed home by his father after a period of dissolution (Luke 15.11–32).

and the gracious father; but that His through-searching wisdom knew the estate of Dives burning in hell, and of Lazarus in Abraham's bosom, would more constantly (as it were) inhabit both the memory and judgment. Truly, for myself, meseems I see before mine eyes the lost child's disdainful prodigality, turned to envy a swine's dinner: which by the learned divines[6] are thought not historical acts, but instructing parables.

For conclusion, I say the philosopher teacheth, but he teacheth obscurely, so as the learned only can understand him, that is to say, he teacheth them that are already taught; but the poet is the food for the tenderest stomachs, the poet is indeed the right popular philosopher, whereof Aesop's tales[7] give good proof: whose pretty allegories, stealing under the formal tales of beasts, make many, more beastly than beasts, begin to hear the sound of virtue from these dumb speakers.

But now may it be alleged that if this imagining of matters be so fit for the imagination, then must the historian needs surpass, who bringeth you images of true matters, such as indeed were done, and not such as fantastically or falsely may be suggested to have been done. Truly, Aristotle himself, in his discourse of poesy, plainly determineth this question, saying that poetry is φιλοσοφώτερον and σπουδαιότερον, that is to say, it is more philosophical and more studiously serious than history. His reason is, because poesy dealeth with καθόλου, that is to say, with the universal consideration, and the history with καθέκαστον, the particular: now, saith he, the universal weighs what is fit to be said or done, either in likelihood or necessity (which the poesy considereth in his imposed names), and the particular only marks whether Alcibiades did, or suffered, this or that.[8] Thus far Aristotle: which reason of his (as all his) is most full of reason. For indeed, if the question were whether it were better to have a particular act truly or falsely set down, there is no doubt which is to be chosen, no more than whether you had rather have Vespasian's picture[9] right as he was, or, at the painter's pleasure, nothing resembling. But if the question be for your own use and learning, whether it be better to have it set down as it should be, or as it was, then certainly is more doctrinable the feigned Cyrus in Xenophon than the true Cyrus in Justin, and the feigned Aeneas in Virgil than the right Aeneas in Dares Phrygius:[1] as to a lady that desired to fashion her countenance to the best grace, a painter should more benefit her to portrait a most sweet face, writing Canidia upon it, than to paint Canidia as she was, who, Horace sweareth, was full ill-favored.[2]

If the poet do his part aright, he will show you in Tantalus, Atreus, and such like,[3] nothing that is not to be shunned; in Cyrus, Aeneas, Ulysses, each thing to be followed; where the historian, bound to tell things as things were, cannot be liberal (without he will be poetical) of a perfect pattern, but, as in Alexander or Scipio himself, show doings, some to be liked, some to be misliked. And then how will you discern what to follow but by your own discretion, which you had without reading

6. Theologians.

7. Moralistic fables reputedly by a Greek slave who lived about 570 B.C.; numerous translations into English of his work were available in the 16th century.

8. Sidney paraphrases Aristotle's *Poetics* (9, 1451b). Alcibiades was a talented if unscrupulous Greek statesman.

9. A Roman emperor (A.D. 70–79) who was described by the historian Suetonius as very ugly.

1. Justinus (c. 4th century A.D.), and Dares Phrygius (5th century) wrote histories that some readers thought were more accurate than the more literary accounts by Xenophon, Homer, and Virgil.

2. Canidia was a prostitute who jilted the Roman poet, Horace; he then attacked her in his poems.

3. Evil figures (Tantalus served the flesh of his son, Pelops, to the gods; Atreus served his nephews' flesh to their father Thyestes).

Quintus Curtius?[4] And whereas a man may say, though in universal consideration of doctrine the poet prevaileth, yet that the history, in his saying such a thing was done, doth warrant a man more in that he shall follow—the answer is manifest: that, if he stand upon that[5] was (as if he should argue, because it rained yesterday, therefore it should rain today), then indeed hath it some advantage to a gross conceit; but if he know an example only informs a conjectured likelihood, and so go by reason, the poet doth so far exceed him as he is to frame his example to that which is most reasonable (be it in warlike, politic, or private matters), where the historian in his bare *Was* hath many times that which we call fortune to overrule the best wisdom. Many times he must tell events whereof he can yield no cause; or, if he do, it must be poetically.

For that a feigned example hath as much force to teach as a true example (for as for to move, it is clear, since the feigned may be tuned to the highest key of passion), let us take one example wherein an historian and a poet did concur. Herodotus and Justin do both testify that Zopyrus, King Darius's faithful servant, seeing his master long resisted by the rebellious Babylonians, feigned himself in extreme disgrace of his king: for verifying of which, he caused his own nose and ears to be cut off, and so flying to the Babylonians, was received, and for his known valor so sure credited, that he did find means to deliver them over to Darius.[6] Much like matter doth Livy record of Tarquinius and his son. Xenophon excellently feigneth such another stratagem performed by Abradatas in Cyrus's behalf.[7] Now would I fain know, if occasion be presented unto you to serve your prince by such an honest dissimulation, why you do not as well learn it of Xenophon's fiction as of the other's verity; and truly so much the better, as you shall save your nose by the bargain: for Abradatas did not counterfeit so far. So then the best of the historian is subject to the poet; for whatsoever action, or faction, whatsoever counsel, policy, or war stratagem the historian is bound to recite, that may the poet (if he list[8]) with his imitation make his own, beautifying it both for further teaching, and more delighting, as it please him: having all, from Dante's heaven to his hell, under the authority of his pen.[9] Which if I be asked what poets have done so, as I might well name some, so yet say I, and say again, I speak of the art, and not of the artificer.

Now, to that which commonly is attributed to the praise of history, in respect of the notable learning is got by marking the success, as though therein a man should see virtue exalted and vice punished—truly that commendation is particular to poetry, and far off from history. For indeed poetry ever sets virtue so out in her best colors, making Fortune her well-waiting handmaid, that one must needs be enamored of her. Well may you see Ulysses in a storm, and in other hard plights; but they are but exercises of patience and magnanimity, to make them shine the more in the near-following prosperity. And of the contrary part, if evil men come to the stage, they ever go out (as the tragedy writer answered to one that misliked the show of such persons) so manacled as they little animate folks to follow them. But the history, being captived to the truth of a foolish world, is many times a terror from well-doing, and an encour-

4. Quintus Curtius (1st century A.D.) wrote a history of Alexander the Great.
5. What.
6. The story of Zopyrus is told in Herodotus's *Histories* (3.153–58) and in Justin's *Histories* (1.10.15–22).
7. Tarquinius Superbus was the last of the Roman kings: his son, Sextus Tarquinius, passed himself off as an ally of the Gabians to spy for Rome (Livy, *Histories* 1, 3–4). Abradates (actually Araspes), acted in the same way for the Persian king, Cyrus (Xenophon, *Cyropaedia* 6.1.39).
8. Wishes.
9. Dante's *Divine Comedy* describes his journey through hell, purgatory, and paradise.

agement to unbridled wickedness. For see we not valiant Miltiades rot in his fetters?[1] The just Phocion and the accomplished Socrates put to death like traitors? The cruel Severus live prosperously? The excellent Severus miserably murdered? Sulla and Marius dying in their beds? Pompey and Cicero slain then when they would have thought exile a happiness? See we not virtuous Cato driven to kill himself, and rebel Caesar so advanced that his name yet, after 1600 years, lasteth in the highest honor? And mark but even Caesar's own words of the aforenamed Sulla (who in that only did honestly, to put down his dishonest tyranny), *literas nescivit,*[2] as if want of learning caused him to do well. He meant it not by poetry, which, not content with earthly plagues, deviseth new punishments in hell for tyrants, nor yet by philosophy, which teacheth *occidendos esse;* but no doubt by skill in history, for that indeed can afford you Cypselus, Periander, Phalaris, Dionysius, and I know not how many more of the same kennel, that speed well enough in their abominable injustice of usurpation.

I conclude, therefore, that he excelleth history, not only in furnishing the mind with knowledge, but in setting it forward to that which deserveth to be called and accounted good: which setting forward, and moving to well-doing, indeed setteth the laurel crown upon the poets as victorious, not only of the historian, but over the philosopher, howsoever in teaching it may be questionable.

For suppose it be granted (that which I suppose with great reason may be denied) that the philosopher, in respect of his methodical proceeding, doth teach more perfectly than the poet, yet do I think that no man is so much φιλοφιλόσοφος [a lover of philosophy] as to compare the philosopher in moving with the poet. And that moving is of a higher degree than teaching, it may by this appear, that it is well nigh both the cause and effect of teaching. For who will be taught, if he be not moved with desire to be taught? And what so much good doth that teaching bring forth (I speak still of moral doctrine) as that it moveth one to do that which it doth teach? For, as Aristotle saith, it is not γνῶσις [knowing] but πρᾶξις [doing] must be the fruit. And how πρᾶξις can be, without being moved to practice, it is no hard matter to consider.[3]

The philosopher showeth you the way, he informeth you of the particularities, as well of the tediousness of the way, as of the pleasant lodging you shall have when your journey is ended, as of the many by-turnings that may divert you from your way. But this is to no man but to him that will read him, and read him with attentive studious painfulness; which constant desire whosoever hath in him, hath already passed

1. Sidney demonstrates that the study of history is not conducive to good morals because it does not show virtue rewarded or vice punished. Miltiades: unsuccessful against the Persians in his seige of Paros, he was imprisoned by his own people, the Athenians (Herodotus, *Histories* 6, 136). Phocion: an Athenian statesman wrongly put to death for a supposed conspiracy (Plutarch, *Phocion* 38). Plato's teacher Socrates had been put to death for supposed impiety. Lucius Septimius Severus, Emperor of Rome (193–211), was able but termed "most cruel" by his biographer, Aelius Spartianus; by contrast, his virtuous successor Marcus Aurelius Alexander Severus was murdered by mutinous soldiers. Lucius Cornelius Sulla was a dictator of Rome, who tyrannized his subjects and yet died peacefully in his bed in 78 B.C.; Caius Marius was also a tyrant and never punished. Pompey opposed Caesar and was murdered after his defeat at Pharsalus; Marcus Tullius Cicero, the most accomplished of Roman lawyers and orators, was murdered by the order of Marcus Antonius in 43 B.C. Marcus Portius Cato committed suicide after his defeat at the battle of Thapsus rather than be captured by Caesar. Sidney calls Caesar a "rebel" because he invaded the territory of the Roman state (crossing the river Rubicon) without permission from the Roman Senate.

2. He knew no literature. Sidney indicates that the learning Sulla lacked was not of poetry, which reveals the punishments of hell; or of philosophy, which teaches *occidendum esse*—that is, when someone should be put to death, or the punishments inflicted by the state. Sidney argues that Sulla learned his misgovernment from history, which instructed him in the profitable ways of tyrants: Cipselus and Periander, both tyrants of Corinth; Phalaris, tyrant of Agrigentum; and Dionysius, tyrant of Syracuse.

3. *Nicomachean Ethics*, 1.1.

half the hardness of the way, and therefore is beholding to the philosopher but[4] for the other half. Nay truly, learned men have learnedly thought that where once reason hath so much overmastered passion as that the mind hath a free desire to do well, the inward light each mind hath in itself is as good as a philosopher's book; since in nature we know it is well to do well, and what is well, and what is evil, although not in the words of art which philosophers bestow upon us; for out of natural conceit the philosophers drew it. But to be moved to do that which we know, or to be moved with desire to know, *hoc opus, hic labor est.*[5]

Now therein of all sciences (I speak still of human, and according to the human conceit[6]) is our poet the monarch. For he doth not only show the way, but giveth so sweet a prospect into the way, as will entice any man to enter into it. Nay, he doth, as if your journey should lie through a fair vineyard, at the first give you a cluster of grapes, that full of that taste, you may long to pass further. He beginneth not with obscure definitions, which must blur the margin with interpretations, and load the memory with doubtfulness; but he cometh to you with words set in delightful proportion, either accompanied with, or prepared for, the well enchanting skill of music; and with a tale forsooth he cometh unto you, with a tale which holdeth children from play, and old men from the chimney corner. And, pretending no more, doth intend the winning of the mind from wickedness to virtue—even as the child is often brought to take most wholesome things by hiding them in such other as have a pleasant taste, which, if one should begin to tell them the nature of *aloes* or *rhabarbarum*[7] they should receive, would sooner take their physic at their ears than at their mouth. So is it in men (most of which are childish in the best things, till they be cradled in their graves): glad they will be to hear the tales of Hercules, Achilles, Cyrus, Aeneas; and, hearing them, must needs hear the right description of wisdom, valor, and justice; which, if they had been barely, that is to say philosophically, set out, they would swear they be brought to school again.

That imitation whereof poetry is, hath the most conveniency to nature of all other, insomuch that, as Aristotle saith, those things which in themselves are horrible, as cruel battles, unnatural monsters, are made in poetical imitation delightful.[8] Truly, I have known men that even with reading *Amadis de Gaule*[9] (which God knoweth wanteth much of a perfect poesy) have found their hearts moved to the exercise of courtesy, liberality, and especially courage. Who readeth Aeneas carrying old Anchises on his back, that wisheth not it were his fortune to perform so excellent an act? Whom doth not these words of Turnus move, the tale of Turnus having planted his image in the imagination,

Fugientem haec terra videbit?
Usque adeone mori miserum est?[1]

Where the philosophers, as they scorn to delight, so must they be content little to move—saving wrangling whether *virtus* [virtue] be the chief or the only good, whether the contemplative or the active life do excel—which Plato and Boethius well knew, and therefore made mistress Philosophy very often borrow the masking

4. Merely.
5. "This is the task, this the work"; the words of the Cumaean sybil to the hero Aeneas, who intends to return to earth from the underworld (*Aeneid* 6.128).
6. Way of thinking.
7. Medicines.
8. *Poetics*, 4.14486.
9. Chivalric romance in Spanish by Vasco de Lobeyra, c. 1325. It appeared in English translation in 1567.
1. In Virgil, Turnus unsuccessfully defended his native Latium (the region around Rome) against the invading Trojans led by Aeneas. Taking his last stand, Turnus cries: "Shall this ground see [Turnus] fleeing? Is it so hard, then, to die?" (*Aeneid* 12.645–46).

raiment of poesy.[2] For even those hard-hearted evil men who think virtue a school name, and know no other good but *indulgere genio* [self-indulgence], and therefore despise the austere admonitions of the philosopher, and feel not the inward reason they stand upon, yet will be content to be delighted—which is all the good-fellow poet seemeth to promise—and so steal to see the form of goodness (which seen they cannot but love) ere themselves be aware, as if they took a medicine of cherries.

Infinite proofs of the strange effects of this poetical invention might be alleged; only two shall serve, which are so often remembered as I think all men know them. The one of Menenius Agrippa,[3] who, when the whole people of Rome had resolutely divided themselves from the senate, with apparent show of utter ruin, though he were (for that time) an excellent orator, came not among them upon trust of figurative speeches or cunning insinuations, and much less with far-fet[4] maxims of philosophy, which (especially if they were Platonic) they must have learned geometry before they could well have conceived; but forsooth he behaves himself like a homely and familiar poet. He telleth them a tale, that there was a time when all the parts of the body made a mutinous conspiracy against the belly, which they thought devoured the fruits of each other's labor; they concluded they would let so unprofitable a spender starve. In the end, to be short (for the tale is notorious, and as notorious that it was a tale), with punishing the belly they plagued themselves. This applied by him wrought such effect in the people, as I never read that only words brought forth but then so sudden and so good an alteration; for upon reasonable conditions a perfect reconcilement ensued. The other is of Nathan the prophet,[5] who, when the holy David had so far forsaken God as to confirm adultery with murder, when he was to do the tenderest office of a friend in laying his own shame before his eyes, sent by God to call again so chosen a servant, how doth he it but by telling of a man whose beloved lamb was ungratefully taken from his bosom: the application most divinely true, but the discourse itself feigned; which made David (I speak of the second and instrumental cause) as in a glass see his own filthiness, as that heavenly psalm of mercy well testifieth.

By these, therefore, examples and reasons, I think it may be manifest that the poet, with that same hand of delight, doth draw the mind more effectually than any other art doth. And so a conclusion not unfitly ensue: that, as virtue is the most excellent resting place for all worldly learning to make his end of, so poetry, being the most familiar to teach it, and most princely to move towards it, in the most excellent work is the most excellent workman.

But I am content not only to decipher him[6] by his works (although works, in commendation or dispraise, must ever hold a high authority), but more narrowly will examine his parts; so that (as in a man) though all together may carry a presence full of majesty and beauty, perchance in some one defectuous piece we may find blemish.

Now in his parts, kinds, or species (as you list to term them), it is to be noted that some poesies have coupled together two or three kinds, as the tragical and comical, whereupon is risen the tragicomical. Some, in the manner, have mingled prose and verse, as Sannazaro and Boethius.[7] Some have mingled matters heroical and pastoral. But that cometh all to one in this question, for, if severed they be good, the

2. The philosophers Plato and Boethius both argued that a retired and contemplative life was superior to the active life or the life in public service. By contrast, the Roman orator Cicero asserted the value of prudence and the importance of contributing to the public good.

3. Roman consul who calmed rebellious commoners in 494 B.C. (Livy, *Histories* 2.32).

4. Far-fetched.

5. 2 Samuel 12.1–7.

6. Poetry.

7. Sannazaro: Italian poet (1458–1530) whose pastoral of mixed prose and verse, the *Arcadia*, influenced Sidney's work of the same name. Boethius (480?–524?): the Roman and Christian philosopher whose work *The Consolation of Philosophy* contains passages of prose and poetry.

conjunction cannot be hurtful. Therefore, perchance forgetting some and leaving some as needless to be remembered, it shall not be amiss in a word to cite the special kinds, to see what faults may be found in the right use of them.

Is it then the Pastoral poem which is misliked? (For perchance where the hedge is lowest they will soonest leap over.) Is the poor pipe disdained, which sometime out of Meliboeus's mouth can show the misery of people under hard lords or ravening soldiers, and again, by Tityrus, what blessedness is derived to them that lie lowest from the goodness of them that sit highest;[8] sometimes, under the pretty tales of wolves and sheep, can include the whole considerations of wrongdoing and patience; sometimes show that contentions for trifles can get but a trifling victory: where perchance a man may see that even Alexander and Darius, when they strave who should be cock of this world's dunghill, the benefit they got was that the after-livers may say

Haec memini et victum frustra contendere Thirsin:
Ex illo Corydon, Corydon est tempore nobis.[9]

Or is it the lamenting Elegiac;[1] which in a kind heart would move rather pity than blame; who bewails with the great philosopher Heraclitus, the weakness of mankind and the wretchedness of the world; who surely is to be praised, either for compassionate accompanying just causes of lamentations, or for rightly painting out how weak be the passions of woefulness? Is it the bitter but wholesome Iambic,[2] who rubs the galled mind, in making shame the trumpet of villainy, with bold and open crying out against naughtiness? Or the Satiric, who

Omne vafer vitium ridenti tangit amico;[3]

who sportingly never leaveth till he make a man laugh at folly, and at length shamed, to laugh at himself, which he cannot avoid without avoiding the folly; who, while

circum praecordia ludit,[4]

giveth us to feel how many headaches a passionate life bringeth us to; how, when all is done,

Est Ulubris, animus si nos non deficit aequus?[5]

No, perchance it is the Comic, whom naughty playmakers and stage-keepers have justly made odious. To the arguments of abuse I will answer after. Only this much now is to be said, that the comedy is an imitation of the common errors of our life, which he representeth in the most ridiculous and scornful sort that may be, so as it is impossible that any beholder can be content to be such a one. Now, as in geometry the oblique must be known as well as the right, and in arithmetic the odd as well as the even, so in the actions of our life who seeth not the filthiness of evil wanteth a great foil to perceive the beauty of virtue. This doth the comedy handle so in our private and domestical matters as with hearing it we get as it were an experience what is

8. Meliboeus and Tityrus are characters in Virgil's *Eclogues*. Sidney responds to the idea that pastoral is the least elevated of the poetic genres; here he declares that it is capable of conveying political and moral ideas.

9. "These things I remember, how vanquished Thrysis tried in vain. Since then it has been Coridon, only Coridon, with us" (Virgil, *Eclogues*, 7.69–70). These lines suggest the futility of ambition.

1. A kind of poetry lamenting loss or remembering what no longer exists. Heraclitus: a philosopher of conflict and flux, who lived about 500 B.C.

2. A verse form used in satire.

3. "The sly man probes every one of his friend's faults while making his friend laugh" (Persius, *Satires*, 1.116–17).

4. "He plays around the heart" (Persius, *Satires* 1.117).

5. "[Contentment] is at Ulubrae, if a well-balanced mind doesn't fail us" (Horace, *Epistles*, 1.11.30). Ulubrae was a notoriously disagreeable small town.

to be looked for of a niggardly Demea, of a crafty Davus, of a flattering Gnatho, of a vainglorious Thraso;[6] and not only to know what effects are to be expected, but to know who be such, by the signifying badge given them by the comedian. And little reason hath any man to say that men learn the evil by seeing it so set out, since, as I said before, there is no man living but, by the force truth hath in nature, no sooner seeth these men play their parts, but wisheth them *in pistrinum*;[7] although perchance the sack of his own faults lie so hidden behind his back that he seeth not himself dance the same measure; whereto yet nothing can more open his eyes than to find his own actions contemptibly set forth.

So that the right use of comedy will (I think) by nobody be blamed; and much less of the high and excellent Tragedy, that openeth the greatest wounds, and showeth forth the ulcers that are covered with tissue; that maketh kings fear to be tyrants, and tyrants manifest their tyrannical humors; that, with stirring the affects of admiration and commiseration, teacheth the uncertainty of this world, and upon how weak foundations gilden roofs are builded; that maketh us know

> *Qui sceptra saevus duro imperio regit*
> *Timet timentes; metus in auctorem redit.*[8]

But how much it can move, Plutarch yieldeth a notable testimony of the abominable tyrant Alexander Pheraeus,[9] from whose eyes a tragedy, well made and represented, drew abundance of tears, who without all pity had murdered infinite numbers, and some of his own blood: so as he, that was not ashamed to make matters for tragedies, yet could not resist the sweet violence of a tragedy. And if it wrought no further good in him, it was that he, in despite of himself, withdrew himself from hearkening to that which might mollify his hardened heart. But it is not the tragedy they do mislike; for it were too absurd to cast out so excellent a representation of whatsoever is most worthy to be learned.

Is it the Lyric that most displeaseth, who with his tuned lyre and well-accorded voice, giveth praise, the reward of virtue, to virtuous acts; who gives moral precepts, and natural problems; who sometimes raiseth up his voice to the height of the heavens, in singing the lauds of the immortal God? Certainly, I must confess my own barbarousness, I never heard the old song of Percy and Douglas[1] that I found not my heart moved more than with a trumpet; and yet is it sung but by some blind crowder,[2] with no rougher voice than rude style; which, being so evil apparelled in the dust and cobwebs of that uncivil age, what would it work trimmed in the gorgeous eloquence of Pindar?[3] In Hungary I have seen it the manner at all feasts, and other such meetings, to have songs of their ancestors' valor, which that right soldierlike nation think one of the chiefest kindlers of brave courage. The incomparable Lacedemonians[4] did not only carry that kind of musicever with them to the field, but even at home, as such songs were made, so were they all content to be singers of them—when the lusty men were to tell what they did, the old men what they had done, and the young what they would do. And where a man may say that Pindar many times praiseth highly

6. Stock characters from the Roman comedies of Terence.
7. At a mill; a customary punishment for criminals and unruly slaves.
8. "The cruel man (i.e., the tyrant) who rules his people with a harsh government fears his fearful people; terror returns to its author" (Seneca, *Oedipus*, 3.705–6).
9. Tyrant of Pherae in Thessaly (369–357), described by Plutarch in his *Life of Pelopidas*.

1. Sidney refers to the ballad *Chevy Chase*, which describes the conflict between the Earls of Percy and Douglas.
2. Fiddler.
3. The most famous of Greek lyric poets (c. 522–402 B.C.), whose metrically complex odes celebrate victories in the Panhellenic games, the most famous of which was held every four years at Olympia.
4. Spartans.

victories of small moment, matters rather of sport than virtue; as it may be answered, it was the fault of the poet, and not of the poetry, so indeed the chief fault was in the time and custom of the Greeks, who set those toys at so high a price that Philip of Macedon[5] reckoned a horserace won at Olympus among his three fearful[6] felicities. But as the unimitable Pindar often did, so is that kind most capable and most fit to awake the thoughts from the sleep of idleness to embrace honorable enterprises.

There rests the Heroical—whose very name (I think) should daunt all backbiters: for by what conceit can a tongue be directed to speak evil of that which draweth with him no less champions than Achilles, Cyrus, Aeneas, Turnus, Tydeus, and Rinaldo?[7]—who doth not only teach and move to a truth, but teacheth and moveth to the most high and excellent truth; who maketh magnanimity and justice shine through all misty fearfulness and foggy desires; who, if the saying of Plato and Tully be true, that who could see virtue would be wonderfully ravished with the love of her beauty—this man sets her out to make her more lovely in her holiday apparel, to the eye of any that will deign not to disdain until they understand. But if anything be already said in the defense of sweet poetry, all concurreth to the maintaining the heroical, which is not only a kind, but the best and most accomplished kind of poetry. For as the image of each action stirreth and instructeth the mind, so the lofty image of such worthies most inflameth the mind with desire to be worthy, and informs with counsel how to be worthy. Only let Aeneas be worn in the tablet of your memory, how he governeth himself in the ruin of his country; in the preserving his old father, and carrying away his religious ceremonies; in obeying God's commandment to leave Dido, though not only all passionate kindness, but even the human consideration of virtuous gratefulness, would have craved other of him; how in storms, how in sports, how in war, how in peace, how a fugitive, how victorious, how besieged, how besieging, how to strangers, how to allies, how to enemies, how to his own; lastly, how in his inward self, and how in his outward government—and I think, in a mind not prejudiced with a prejudicating humor, he will be found in excellency fruitful, yea, even as Horace saith,

> *melius Chrysippo et Crantore*.[8]

But truly I imagine it falleth out with these poet-whippers, as with some good women, who often are sick, but in faith they cannot tell where; so the name of poetry is odious to them, but neither his cause nor effects, neither the sum that contains him, nor the particularities descending from him, give any fast handle to their carping dispraise.

Since then poetry is of all human learning the most ancient and of most fatherly antiquity, as from whence other learnings have taken their beginnings; since it is so universal that no learned nation doth despise it, nor barbarous nation is without it; since both Roman and Greek gave such divine names unto it, the one of prophesying, the other of making, and that indeed that name of making is fit for him, considering that where all other arts retain themselves within their subject, and receive, as

5. Father of Alexander the Great, himself a conquering general and hero. Olympus: Sidney's error for Olympia, site of the Olympian Games.
6. Wonderful.
7. Epic heroes and moral exemplars. Tydeus fought to bring Polyneices, the son of Oedipus, to the throne of Thebes (see Statius's *Thebaid*); Rinaldo was one of the French king Charlemagne's knights who fought against the Saracens in Italy (see Ludovico Ariosto's *Orlando Furioso* and Torquato Tasso's *Jerusalem Delivered*).
8. "Better than [the philosophers] Chrysippus and Crantor" (Horace, *Epistles*, 1.4).

it were, their being from it, the poet only bringeth his own stuff, and doth not learn a conceit out of a matter,[9] but maketh matter for a conceit; since neither his description nor end containing any evil, the thing described cannot be evil; since his effects be so good as to teach goodness and to delight the learners; since therein (namely in moral doctrine, the chief of all knowledges) he doth not only far pass the historian, but, for instructing, is well nigh comparable to the philosopher, for moving leaves him behind him; since the Holy Scripture (wherein there is no uncleanness) hath whole parts in it poetical, and that even our Savior Christ vouchsafed to use the flowers of it; since all his kinds are not only in their united forms but in their severed dissections fully commendable; I think (and think I think rightly) the laurel crown appointed for triumphant captains doth worthily (of all other learnings) honor the poet's triumph.

But because we have ears as well as tongues, and that the lightest reasons that may be will seem to weigh greatly, if nothing be put in the counterbalance, let us hear, and, as well as we can, ponder what objections be made against this art, which may be worthy either of yielding or answering.

First, truly I note not only in these μισόμουσοι, poet-haters, but in all that kind of people who seek a praise by dispraising others, that they do prodigally spend a great many wandering words in quips and scoffs, carping and taunting at each thing which, by stirring the spleen, may stay the brain from a through-beholding the worthiness of the subject. Those kind of objections, as they are full of a very idle easiness, since there is nothing of so sacred a majesty but that an itching tongue may rub itself upon it, so deserve they no other answer, but, instead of laughing at the jest, to laugh at the jester. We know a playing wit can praise the discretion of an ass, the comfortableness of being in debt, and the jolly commodities of being sick of the plague. So of the contrary side, if we will turn Ovid's verse

Ut lateat virtus proximitate mali,[1]

that good lie hid in nearness of the evil, Agrippa will be as merry in showing the vanity of science as Erasmus was in the commending of folly. Neither shall any man or matter escape some touch of these smiling railers. But for Erasmus and Agrippa,[2] they had another foundation than the superficial part would promise. Marry, these other pleasant faultfinders, who will correct the verb before they understand the noun, and confute others' knowledge before they confirm their own—I would have them only remember that scoffing cometh not of wisdom. So as the best title in true English they get with their merriments is to be called good fools; for so have our grave forefathers ever termed that humorous kind of jesters.

But that which giveth greatest scope to their scorning humor is rhyming and versing. It is already said (and, as I think, truly said), it is not rhyming and versing that maketh poesy. One may be a poet without versing, and a versifier without poetry. But yet, presuppose it were inseparable (as indeed it seemeth Scaliger[3] judgeth), truly it were an inseparable commendation. For if *oratio* next to *ratio*, speech next to

9. Does not take his theme from his material.
1. "That virtue may lie next to evil" (Cf. Ovid, *The Art of Love*, 2.662).
2. Henry Cornelius Agrippa of Nettesheim (1486–1533), a German philosopher, and Desiderius Erasmus of Rotterdam (1467–1536), the greatest humanist scholar of the early modern period. Sidney refers to their most popular works, *The Uncertainty and Vanity of Knowledge* and *The Praise of Folly*, respectively, both written to satirize human pretensions.
3. Julius Caesar Scaliger (1484–1558), an Italian scholar who wrote a treatise, *Seven Books on Poetry*.

reason, be the greatest gift bestowed upon mortality, that cannot be praiseless which doth most polish that blessing of speech; which considers each word, not only (as a man may say) by his most forcible quality, but by his best measured quantity, carrying even in themselves a harmony—without, perchance, number, measure, order, proportion be in our time grown odious. But lay aside the just praise it hath, by being the only fit speech for music (music, I say, the most divine striker of the senses), thus much is undoubtedly true, that if reading be foolish without remembering, memory being the only treasure of knowledge, those words which are fittest for memory are likewise most convenient for knowledge. Now, that verse far exceedeth prose in the knitting up of memory, the reason is manifest: the words (besides their delight, which hath a great affinity to memory) being so set as one cannot be lost but the whole work fails; which accusing itself, calleth the remembrance back to itself, and so most strongly confirmeth it. Besides, one word so, as it were, begetting another, as, be it in rhyme or measured verse, by the former a man shall have a near guess to the follower. Lastly, even they that have taught the art of memory have showed nothing so apt for it as a certain room divided into many places well and thoroughly known. Now, that hath the verse in effect perfectly, every word having his natural seat, which seat must needs make the word remembered. But what needeth more in a thing so known to all men? Who is it that ever was a scholar that doth not carry away some verses of Virgil, Horace, or Cato, which in his youth he learned, and even to his old age serve him for hourly lessons? But the fitness it hath for memory is notably proved by all delivery of arts: wherein for the most part, from grammar to logic, mathematics, physic, and the rest, the rules chiefly necessary to be borne away are compiled in verses. So that, verse being in itself sweet and orderly, and being best for memory, the only handle of knowledge, it must be in jest that any man can speak against it.

Now then go we to the most important imputations laid to the poor poets. For aught I can yet learn, they are these. First, that there being many other more fruitful knowledges, a man might better spend his time in them than in this. Secondly, that it is the mother of lies. Thirdly, that it is the nurse of abuse, infecting us with many pestilent desires; with a siren's sweetness drawing the mind to the serpent's tail of sinful fancies (and herein, especially, comedies give the largest field to ear,[4] as Chaucer saith); how, both in other nations and in ours, before poets did soften us, we were full of courage, given to martial exercises, the pillars of manlike liberty, and not lulled asleep in shady idleness with poets' pastimes. And lastly, and chiefly, they cry out with open mouth as if they had overshot Robin Hood,[5] that Plato banished them out of his commonwealth. Truly, this is much, if there be much truth in it.

First, to the first. That a man might better spend his time, is a reason indeed; but it doth (as they say) but *petere principium* [beg the question]. For if it be as I affirm, that no learning is so good as that which teacheth and moveth to virtue; and that none can both teach and move thereto so much as poetry: then is the conclusion manifest that ink and paper cannot be to a more profitable purpose employed. And certainly, though a man should grant their first assumption, it should follow (methinks) very unwillingly, that good is not good, because better is better. But I still and utterly deny that there is sprong out of earth a more fruitful knowledge.

4. Sidney refers to an expression in Chaucer's *Canterbury Tales:* "a large feeld to ere," *The Knight's Tale*, 1.28.

5. The medieval folk hero, who is said to have lived in Sherwood Forest. Plato banishes poets in his treatise on the ideal state (*The Republic* 3.392).

To the second, therefore, that they should be the principal liars, I answer paradoxically, but truly, I think truly, that of all writers under the sun the poet is the least liar, and, though he would, as a poet can scarcely be a liar. The astronomer, with his cousin the geometrician, can hardly escape, when they take upon them to measure the height of the stars. How often, think you, do the physicians lie, when they aver things good for sicknesses, which afterwards send Charon[6] a great number of souls drowned in a potion before they come to his ferry? And no less of the rest, which take upon them to affirm. Now, for the poet, he nothing affirms, and therefore never lieth. For, as I take it, to lie is to affirm that to be true which is false. So as the other artists, and especially the historian, affirming many things, can, in the cloudy knowledge of mankind, hardly escape from many lies. But the poet (as I said before) never affirmeth. The poet never maketh any circles about your imagination, to conjure you to believe for true what he writes. He citeth not authorities of other histories, but even for his entry calleth the sweet Muses to inspire into him a good invention; in truth, not laboring to tell you what is or is not, but what should or should not be. And therefore, though he recount things not true, yet because he telleth them not for true, he lieth not—without we will say that Nathan lied in his speech before-alleged to David; which as a wicked man durst scarce say, so think I none so simple would say that Aesop lied in the tales of his beasts; for who thinks that Aesop wrote it for actually true were well worthy to have his name chronicled among the beasts he writeth of. What child is there, that, coming to a play, and seeing *Thebes* written in great letters upon an old door, doth believe that it is Thebes? If then a man can arrive to that child's age to know that the poets' persons and doings are but pictures what should be, and not stories what have been, they will never give the lie to things not affirmatively but allegorically and figuratively written. And therefore, as in history, looking for truth, they may go away full fraught with falsehood, so in poesy, looking but for fiction, they shall use the narration but as an imaginative ground-plot of a profitable invention. But hereto is replied, that the poets give names to men they write of, which argueth a conceit of an actual truth, and so, not being true, proves a falsehood. And doth the lawyer lie then, when under the names of *John-a-stiles* and *John-a-nokes*[7] he puts his case? But that is easily answered. Their naming of men is but to make their picture the more lively, and not to build any history: painting men, they cannot leave men nameless. We see we cannot play at chess but that we must give names to our chessmen; and yet, methinks, he were a very partial champion of truth that would say we lied for giving a piece of wood the reverend title of a bishop. The poet nameth Cyrus or Aeneas no other way than to show what men of their fames, fortunes, and estates should do.

Their third is, how much it abuseth men's wit, training it to wanton sinfulness and lustful love: for indeed that is the principal, if not only, abuse I can hear alleged.[8] They say, the comedies rather teach than reprehend amorous conceits. They say the lyric is larded with passionate sonnets; the elegiac weeps the want of his mistress; and that even to the heroical, Cupid hath ambitiously climbed. Alas, Love, I would thou couldst as well defend thyself as thou canst offend others. I would those on whom thou dost attend could either put thee away, or yield good reason why they keep thee. But grant love of beauty to be a beastly fault (although it be very hard, since

6. According to Greek myth, Charon ferries souls across the River Styx to the underworld.
7. I.e., John Doe, or John Roe of ancient law courts.
8. Sidney refers to contemporary criticism of the drama, the best known of which was Stephen Gosson's *School of Abuse* (1579); see page 946.

only man, and no beast, hath that gift to discern beauty); grant that lovely name of Love to deserve all hateful reproaches (although even some of my masters the philosophers spent a good deal of their lamp-oil in setting forth the excellency of it); grant, I say, whatsoever they will have granted, that not only love, but lust, but vanity, but (if they list) scurrility, possesseth many leaves of the poets' books; yet think I, when this is granted, they will find their sentence may with good manners put the last words foremost, and not say that poetry abuseth man's wit, but that man's wit abuseth poetry.

For I will not deny but that man's wit may make poesy, which should be εἰκαστική [representing real things] (which some learned have defined: figuring forth good things), to be φανταστική [representing imaginary things] (which doth, contrariwise, infect the fancy with unworthy objects), as the painter, that should give to the eye either some excellent perspective, or some fine picture, fit for building or fortification, or containing in it some notable example (as Abraham sacrificing his son Isaac, Judith killing Holofernes, David fighting with Goliath),[9] may leave those, and please an ill-pleased eye with wanton shows of better hidden matters. But what, shall the abuse of a thing make the right use odious? Nay truly, though I yield that poesy may not only be abused, but that being abused, by the reason of his sweet charming force, it can do more hurt than any other army of words: yet shall it be so far from concluding that the abuse should give reproach to the abused, that, contrariwise, it is a good reason that whatsoever, being abused, doth most harm, being rightly used (and upon the right use each thing conceiveth his title), doth most good. Do we not see the skill of physic, the best rampire[1] to our often-assaulted bodies, being abused, teach poison, the most violent destroyer? Doth not knowledge of law, whose end is to even and right all things, being abused, grow the crooked fosterer of horrible injuries? Doth not (to go to the highest) God's word abused breed heresy, and His name abused become blasphemy? Truly, a needle cannot do much hurt, and as truly (with leave of ladies be it spoken) it cannot do much good: with a sword thou mayst kill thy father, and with a sword thou mayst defend thy prince and country. So that, as in their calling poets fathers of lies they said nothing, so in this their argument of abuse they prove the commendation.

They allege herewith, that before poets began to be in price our nation had set their hearts' delight upon action, and not imagination: rather doing things worthy to be written, than writing things fit to be done. What that before-time was, I think scarcely Sphinx[2] can tell, since no memory is so ancient that hath not the precedent of poetry. And certain it is that, in our plainest homeliness, yet never was the Albion[3] nation without poetry. Marry, this argument, though it be levelled against poetry, yet is it indeed a chainshot[4] against all learning, or bookishness as they commonly term it. Of such mind were certain Goths,[5] of whom it is written that, having in the spoil of a famous city taken a fair library, one hangman (belike fit to execute the fruits of their wits) who had murdered a great number of bodies, would have set fire in it: no, said another very gravely, take heed what you do, for while they are busy about these toys, we shall with more leisure conquer their countries. This indeed is the ordinary doctrine of ignorance, and many words sometimes I have heard spent in

9. Sidney refers to episodes in the Bible (Genesis 22, 1 Samuel 17, Judith 2–14).
1. Rampart.
2. In Greek mythology a monster with a woman's head and a lion's body who posed riddles to human beings.
3. British.
4. Two cannonballs joined by a chain; it was deployed in naval warfare, usually against the rigging on enemy ships.
5. Northern European tribes, often described as uncivilized by ancient historians. The fate of "a fair library" is told by Michel de Montaigne in his essay *Of Pedantry* (*Essays* 1.24.)

it. But because this reason is generally against all learning as well as poetry, or rather, all learning but poetry; because it were too large a digression to handle it, or at least too superfluous (since it is manifest that all government of action is to be gotten by knowledge, and knowledge best by gathering many knowledges, which is reading), I only, with Horace, to him that is of that opinion

jubeo stultum esse libenter;[6]

for as for poetry itself, it is the freest from this objection.

For poetry is the companion of camps. I dare undertake, Orlando Furioso, or honest King Arthur, will never displease a soldier; but the quiddity of *ens* and *prima materia* will hardly agree with a corselet;[7] and therefore, as I said in the beginning, even Turks and Tartars are delighted with poets. Homer, a Greek, flourished before Greece flourished. And if to a slight conjecture a conjecture may be opposed, truly it may seem, that as by him their learned men took almost their first light of knowledge, so their active men received their first motions of courage. Only Alexander's example may serve, who by Plutarch is accounted of such virtue, that Fortune was not his guide but his footstool; whose acts speak for him, though Plutarch did not: indeed the phoenix of warlike princes.[8] This Alexander left his schoolmaster, living Aristotle, behind him, but took dead Homer with him. He put the philosopher Callisthenes to death for his seeming philosophical, indeed mutinous, stubbornness, but the chief thing he was ever heard to wish for was that Homer had been alive. He well found he received more bravery of mind by the pattern of Achilles than by hearing the definition of fortitude. And therefore, if Cato misliked Fulvius for carrying Ennius with him to the field,[9] it may be answered that, if Cato misliked it, the noble Fulvius liked it, or else he had not done it; for it was not the excellent Cato Uticensis (whose authority I would much more have reverenced), but it was the former, in truth a bitter punisher of faults (but else a man that had never well sacrificed to the Graces: he misliked and cried out against all Greek learning, and yet, being eighty years old, began to learn it, belike fearing that Pluto understood not Latin). Indeed, the Roman laws allowed no person to be carried to the wars but he that was in the soldiers' roll; and therefore, though Cato misliked his unmustered person, he misliked not his work.[1] And if he had, Scipio Nasica, judged by common consent the best Roman, loved him. Both the other Scipio brothers, who had by their virtues no less surnames than of Asia and Afric, so loved him that they caused his body to be buried in their sepulture. So as Cato's authority, being but against his person, and that answered with so far greater than himself, is herein of no validity.

But now indeed my burden is great; now Plato's name is laid upon me, whom, I must confess, of all philosophers I have ever esteemed most worthy of reverence, and with good reason: since of all philosophers he is the most poetical. Yet if he will

6. "I order [him] to be stupid cheerfully" (Horace, *Satires,* 1.1.63).

7. Soldiers will enjoy reading about knights like Ariosto's Orlando Furioso or Malory's King Arthur, but will balk at philosophers' concerns with "quiddities" (subtleties), "*ens*" (being), and "*prima materia*" (the original matter of the universe).

8. Sidney cites various episodes from Plutarch's accounts of Alexander the Great in his *Lives* (c. A.D. 100), which was translated into English by Sir Thomas North in 1579. The phoenix was a mythic bird thought to be eternally reborn in the ashes of its own funeral pyre.

9. Marcus Portius Cato the Censor (234–184 B.C.), criticized the general Marcus Flavius Nobilior for carrying the poetry of Quintus Ennius (239–169 B.C.) on a battle campaign. Sidney goes on to distinguish Cato the Censor from his great-grandson, Marcus Porcius Cato, the chief political antagonist of Julius Caesar.

1. In fact, as Sidney states, the poet Ennius in person actually accompanied Flavius; he was "unmustered" in that he was not on the army payroll. Sidney continues to praise Ennius by saying that he was loved by various Scipios: Publius Cornelius Scipio Nasica, Publius Cornelius Scipio Africanus, and Lucius Cornelius Scipio Asiaticus, all notable patriots and generals.

defile the fountain out of which his flowing streams have proceeded, let us boldly examine with what reasons he did it. First, truly, a man might maliciously object that Plato, being a philosopher, was a natural enemy of poets. For indeed, after the philosophers had picked out of the sweet mysteries of poetry the right discerning true points of knowledge, they forthwith putting it in method, and making a school-art of that which the poets did only teach by a divine delightfulness, beginning to spurn at their guides, like ungrateful prentices, were not content to set up shops for themselves, but sought by all means to discredit their masters; which by the force of delight being barred them, the less they could overthrow them, the more they hated them. For indeed, they found for Homer seven cities strave who should have him for their citizen; where many cities banished philosophers as not fit members to live among them. For only repeating certain of Euripides' verses,[2] many Athenians had their lives saved of the Syracusans, where the Athenians themselves thought many philosophers unworthy to live. Certain poets, as Simonides and Pindar, had so prevailed with Hiero the First,[3] that of a tyrant they made him a just king; where Plato could do so little with Dionysius, that he himself of a philosopher was made a slave. But who should do thus, I confess, should requite the objections made against poets with like cavillations[4] against philosophers; as likewise one should do that should bid one read *Phaedrus* or *Symposium* in Plato, or the discourse of love in Plutarch, and see whether any poet do authorize abominable filthiness, as they do. Again, a man might ask out of what commonwealth Plato did banish them:[5] in sooth, thence where he himself alloweth community of women—so as belike this banishment grew not for effeminate wantonness, since little should poetical sonnets be hurtful when a man might have what woman he listed.[6] But I honor philosophical instructions, and bless the wits which bred them: so as they be not abused, which is likewise stretched to poetry.

St. Paul himself (who yet, for the credit of poets, twice citeth poets, and one of them by the name of "their prophet") setteth a watchword upon philosophy—indeed upon the abuse.[7] So doth Plato upon the abuse, not upon poetry. Plato found fault that the poets of his time filled the world with wrong opinions of the gods, making light tales of that unspotted essence, and therefore would not have the youth depraved with such opinions. Herein may much be said. Let this suffice: the poets did not induce such opinions, but did imitate those opinions already induced. For all the Greek stories can well testify that the very religion of that time stood upon many and many-fashioned gods, not taught so by the poets, but followed according to their nature of imitation. Who list may read in Plutarch the discourses of Isis and Osiris,[8] of the cause why oracles ceased, of the divine providence, and see whether the theology of that nation stood not upon such dreams

2. Plutarch states that Greek slaves living outside Greece had won their release by teaching their masters the poetry of Euripides (*Life of Nicias*, c. 29).
3. Tyrant of Syracuse (478–476 B.C.), who patronized Greek poets. Aeschylus was a playwright; Bacchylides a lyric poet; and Simonides a writer of satire. Dionysius the Elder of Syracuse was said to have sold Plato to the Spartan ambassador Pollis as a slave, a situation from which he was later liberated.
4. Objections.
5. I.e., poets. Plato argued that in his ideal republic, all women should be common, that is, not married to a single man but sexually available to all men (*Republic* 5, 449–462). Sidney observes that Plato banishes poets not because poetry makes men licentious, an impossibility in a state in which women are readily available, but for some other reason.
6. Desired.
7. Paul rejects the assessment of poets by philosophers (Acts 17.18, Colossians 2.8); and he castigates false prophets (Titus 1.12).
8. Isis, the Egyptian goddess of fertility, was sister and wife of Osiris, civilizer of Egypt, god of the dead, and source of life.

which the poets indeed superstitiously observed—and truly (since they had not the light of Christ) did much better in it than the philosophers, who, shaking off superstition, brought in atheism. Plato therefore (whose authority I had much rather justly construe than unjustly resist) meant not in general of poets, in those words of which Julius Scaliger saith *Qua authoritate barbari quidam atque hispidi abuti velint ad poetas e republica exigendos;*[9] but only meant to drive out those wrong opinions of the Deity (whereof now, without further law, Christianity hath taken away all the hurtful belief) perchance (as he thought) nourished by the then esteemed poets. And a man need go no further than to Plato himself to know his meaning: who, in his dialogue called *Ion*, giveth high and rightly divine commendation unto poetry. So as Plato, banishing the abuse, not the thing, not banishing it, but giving due honor unto it, shall be our patron, and not our adversary. For indeed I had much rather (since truly I may do it) show their mistaking of Plato (under whose lion's skin they would make an ass-like braying against poesy) than go about to overthrow his authority; whom, the wiser a man is, the more just cause he shall find to have in admiration; especially since he attributeth unto poesy more than myself do, namely, to be a very inspiring of a divine force, far above man's wit, as in the forenamed dialogue is apparent.

Of the other side, who would show the honors have been by the best sort of judgments granted them, a whole sea of examples would present themselves: Alexanders, Caesars, Scipios, all favorers of poets; Laelius, called the Roman Socrates, himself a poet, so as part of *Heautontimorumenos*[1] in Terence was supposed to be made by him; and even the Greek Socrates, whom Apollo confirmed to be the only wise man, is said to have spent part of his old time in putting Aesop's fables into verses. And therefore, full evil should it become his scholar Plato to put such words in his master's mouth against poets. But what need more? Aristotle writes the Art of Poesy;[2] and why, if it should not be written? Plutarch teacheth the use to be gathered of them; and how, if they should not be read? And who reads Plutarch's either history or philosophy, shall find he trimmeth both their garments with guards of poesy. But I list not to defend poesy with the help of his underling historiography. Let it suffice to have showed it is a fit soil for praise to dwell upon; and what dispraise may be set upon it, is either easily overcome, or transformed into just commendation.

So that, since the excellencies of it may be so easily and so justly confirmed, and the low-creeping objections so soon trodden down: it not being an art of lies, but of true doctrine; not of effeminateness, but of notable stirring of courage; not of abusing man's wit, but of strengthening man's wit; not banished, but honored by Plato: let us rather plant more laurels for to engarland the poets' heads (which honor of being laureate, whereas besides them only triumphant captains were, is a sufficient authority to show the price they ought to be held in) than suffer the ill-favored breath of such wrong-speakers once to blow upon the clear springs of poesy.

9. By abuse of whose authority, barbarous and crude men wish to expel poets from the Republic; Scaliger is commenting on Plato's expulsion of poets from an ideal republic in his own treatise on poetry.

1. Gaius Laelius was said to have written parts of a play called *Heautontimorumenos* (*The Self-Tormenter*), reputed to be by the Roman playwright Terence. Plato reports that Socrates turned Aesop's fables into verse.

2. Sidney refers to Aristotle's *Poetics*.

But since I have run so long a career in this matter, methinks, before I give my pen a full stop, it shall be but a little more lost time to inquire why England, the mother of excellent minds, should be grown so hard a stepmother to poets, who certainly in wit ought to pass all other, since all only proceedeth from their wit, being indeed makers of themselves, not takers of others. How can I but exclaim

Musa, mihi causas memora, quo numine laeso?[3]

Sweet poesy, that hath anciently had kings, emperors, senators, great captains, such as, besides a thousand others, David, Adrian, Sophocles, Germanicus, not only to favor poets, but to be poets;[4] and of our nearer times can present for her patrons a Robert, king of Sicily, the great King Francis of France, King James of Scotland; such cardinals as Bembus and Bibbiena; such famous preachers and teachers as Beza and Melanchthon; so learned philosophers as Fracastorius and Scaliger; so great orators as Pontanus and Muretus; so piercing wits as George Buchanan; so grave counselors as, beside many, but before all, that Hospital of France,[5] than whom (I think) that realm never brought forth a more accomplished judgment, more firmly builded upon virtue: I say these, with numbers of others, not only to read others' poesies, but to poetize for others' reading—that poesy, thus embraced in all other places, should only find in our time a hard welcome in England, I think the very earth lamenteth it, and therefore decketh our soil with fewer laurels than it was accustomed. For heretofore poets have in England also flourished, and, which is to be noted, even in those times when the trumpet of Mars[6] did sound loudest. And now that an overfaint quietness should seem to strew[7] the house for poets, they are almost in as good reputation as the mountebanks[8] at Venice. Truly even that, as of the one side it giveth great praise to poesy, which like Venus (but to better purpose) had rather be troubled in the net with Mars than enjoy the homely quiet of Vulcan:[9] so serves it for a piece of a reason why they are less grateful to idle England, which now can scarce endure the pain of a pen.

Upon this necessarily followeth, that base men with servile wits undertake it, who think it enough if they can be rewarded of the printer. And so as Epaminondas[1] is said with the honor of his virtue to have made an office, by his exercising it, which before was contemptible, to become highly respected; so these men, no more but setting their names to it, by their own disgracefulness disgrace the most graceful poesy. For now, as if all the Muses were got with child to bring forth bastard poets, without any commission they do post over the banks of Helicon,[2] till they make the readers more weary than post-horses; while, in the meantime, they

Queis meliore luto finxit praecordia Titan

3. "Muse, tell me the cause, by what wounded divinity. . . ." (*Aeneid* 1.8).

4. King David of Israel composed psalms; the emperor Adrian (i.e., Hadrian) wrote verse and prose; Germanicus Caesar, conqueror of Germany, is supposed to have written poetry and plays. Sidney goes on to list a range of modern statesmen-poets.

5. Michel de L'Hôpital (1505–1573), a statesman who favored religious toleration, wrote Latin poems.

6. God of war.

7. Be scattered over.

8. Itinerant quacks peddling fake medicines.

9. Roman god of fire and smiths who caught his adulterous wife, Venus, and Mars, the god of war, in a net he had forged.

1. Theban general (4th century B.C.).

2. Not a very clear paragraph. The mountain named Helicon is sacred to the muses. Here it represents the inspirational springs that are being "post[ed] over," that is, bypassed, by contemporary "bastard poets" eager to publish, while better writers "whose hearts the Titan [Prometheus] molded out of better clays" (Juvenal, *Satires* 14.36) keep their works private rather than be lumped in with their inferiors. Sidney himself claims, perhaps with false modesty, that as a poet he is classed with the mediocrities, and declares that the reason for poets low esteem is "want of desert" or lack of worth: They have not been helped by Pallas Athena, goddess of wisdom.

are better content to suppress the outflowings of their wit, than, by publishing them, to be accounted knights of the same order. But I that, before ever I durst aspire unto the dignity, am admitted into the company of the paper-blurrers, do find the very true cause of our wanting estimation is want of desert—taking upon us to be poets in despite of Pallas.

Now, wherein we want desert were a thankworthy labor to express; but if I knew, I should have mended myself. But I, as I never desired the title, so have I neglected the means to come by it. Only, overmastered by some thoughts, I yielded an inky tribute unto them. Marry, they that delight in poesy itself should seek to know what they do, and how they do; and especially look themselves in an unflattering glass of reason, if they be inclinable unto it. For poesy must not be drawn by the ears; it must be gently led, or rather it must lead—which was partly the cause that made the ancient-learned affirm it was a divine gift, and no human skill: since all other knowledges lie ready for any that hath strength of wit. A poet no industry can make, if his own genius be not carried into it; and therefore it is an old proverb, *orator fit, poeta nascitur* [the orator is made, the poet born].

Yet confess I always that as the fertilest ground must be manured, so must the highest-flying wit have a Daedalus to guide him.[3] That Daedalus, they say, both in this and in other, hath three wings to bear itself up into the air of due commendation: that is, art, imitation, and exercise. But these, neither artificial rules nor imitative patterns, we much cumber ourselves withal. Exercise indeed we do, but that very fore-backwardly: for where we should exercise to know, we exercise as having known; and so is our brain delivered of much matter which never was begotten by knowledge. For there being two principal parts, matter to be expressed by words and words to express the matter, in neither we use art or imitation rightly. Our matter is *quodlibet* [what you will] indeed, though wrongly performing Ovid's verse,

> *Quicquid conabor dicere, versus erit;*[4]

never marshalling it into any assured rank, that almost the readers cannot tell where to find themselves.

Chaucer, undoubtedly, did excellently in his *Troilus and Criseyde;*[5] of whom, truly, I know not whether to marvel more, either that he in that misty time could see so clearly, or that we in this clear age go so stumblingly after him. Yet had he great wants, fit to be forgiven in so reverent an antiquity. I account the *Mirror of Magistrates* meetly furnished of beautiful parts, and in the Earl of Surrey's lyrics many things tasting of a noble birth, and worthy of a noble mind. The *Shepherds' Calendar* hath much poetry in his eclogues, indeed worthy the reading, if I be not deceived. (That same framing of his style to an old rustic language I dare not allow, since neither Theocritus in Greek, Virgil in Latin, nor Sannazaro in Italian did affect it.) Besides these I do not remember to have seen but few (to speak boldly) printed that have poetical sinews in them; for proof whereof, let but most of the

3. The mythical artisan Daedalus built wings so that he and his son Icarus could escape from Crete, where Minos had confined him in the maze of his own making; but Icarus flew too near the sun, the wax in his wings melted, and he fell into the Aegean Sea and drowned. He is often cited as a figure of ambition.

4. "Whatever I shall try to say shall become verse" (*Tristia* 4.10.26).

5. Sidney gives grudging praise to a number of poets of the early modern period: Chaucer's romance *Troilus and Creseyde* relates the unhappy love affair of two Trojans; the *Mirror of* [*i.e., for*] *Magistrates*, a poem by various authors and added to at intervals during the 16th century, illustrated exemplary tragedies; the Earl of Surrey is Henry Howard; *The Shepherd's Calendar* was written by Edmund Spenser. Theocritus, Virgil, and Sannazzaro were poets of pastoral.

verses be put in prose, and then ask the meaning, and it will be found that one verse did but beget another, without ordering at the first what should be at the last; which becomes a confused mass of words, with a tingling sound of rhyme, barely accompanied with reason.

Our tragedies and comedies (not without cause cried out against), observing rules neither of honest civility nor skilful poetry—excepting *Gorboduc*[6] (again, I say, of those that I have seen), which notwithstanding as it is full of stately speeches and well-sounding phrases, climbing to the height of Seneca's style, and as full of notable morality, which it doth most delightfully teach, and so obtain the very end of poesy, yet in truth it is very defectuous[7] in the circumstances, which grieveth me, because it might not remain as an exact model of all tragedies. For it is faulty both in place and time, the two necessary companions of all corporal actions. For where the stage should always represent but one place, and the uttermost time presupposed in it should be, both by Aristotle's precept and common reason, but one day, there is both many days, and many places, inartificially[8] imagined.

But if it be so in *Gorboduc*, how much more in all the rest, where you shall have Asia of the one side, and Afric of the other, and so many other under-kingdoms, that the player, when he cometh in, must ever begin with telling where he is, or else the tale will not be conceived? Now you shall have three ladies walk to gather flowers: and then we must believe the stage to be a garden. By and by we hear news of shipwreck in the same place: and then we are to blame if we accept it not for a rock. Upon the back of that comes out a hideous monster with fire and smoke: and then the miserable beholders are bound to take it for a cave. While in the meantime two armies fly in, represented with four swords and bucklers: and then what hard heart will not receive it for a pitched field?

Now, of time they are much more liberal: for ordinary it is that two young princes fall in love; after many traverses, she is got with child, delivered of a fair boy; he is lost, groweth a man, falls in love, and is ready to get another child; and all this in two hours' space: which, how absurd it is in sense, even sense may imagine, and art hath taught, and all ancient examples justified—and at this day, the ordinary players in Italy will not err in. Yet will some bring in an example of *Eunuchus* in Terence, that containeth matter of two days, yet far short of twenty years. True it is, and so was it to be played in two days, and so fitted to the time it set forth. And though Plautus have in one place done amiss, let us hit with him, and not miss with him.[9]

But they will say: How then shall we set forth a story which containeth both many places and many times? And do they not know that a tragedy is tied to the laws of poesy, and not of history; not bound to follow the story, but having liberty either to feign a quite new matter or to frame the history to the most tragical conveniency? Again, many things may be told which cannot be showed, if they know the difference betwixt reporting and representing. As, for example, I may speak (though I am here) of Peru, and in speech digress from that to the description of Calicut;[1] but in action I cannot represent it without Pacolet's horse;[2] and so was the manner the ancients took, by some *Nuntius* [messenger] to recount things done in former time or

6. A tragedy by Thomas Sackville and Thomas Norton (1561).
7. Defective.
8. Inartistically.
9. Terence, Plautus: two well-known writers of Roman comedies who influenced the drama in early modern England; Shakespeare took the plot of *The Comedy of Errors* from Plautus's *Menaechmi*.
1. Seaport on the west coast of India.
2. A magic horse in the French romance *Valentine and Orson*.

other place. Lastly, if they will represent a history, they must not (as Horace saith) begin *ab ovo* [from the beginning], but they must come to the principal point of that one action which they will represent.

By example this will be best expressed. I have a story of young Polydorus,[3] delivered for safety's sake, with great riches, by his father Priam to Polymnestor, king of Thrace, in the Trojan war time; he, after some years, hearing the overthrow of Priam, for to make the treasure his own, murdereth the child; the body of the child is taken up by Hecuba; she, the same day, findeth a sleight to be revenged most cruelly of the tyrant. Where now would one of our tragedy writers begin, but with the delivery of the child? Then should he sail over into Thrace, and so spend I know not how many years, and travel numbers of places. But where doth Euripides? Even with the finding of the body, leaving the rest to be told by the spirit of Polydorus. This need no further to be enlarged; the dullest wit may conceive it.

But besides these gross absurdities, how all their plays be neither right tragedies, nor right comedies, mingling kings and clowns, not because the matter so carrieth it, but thrust in the clown by head and shoulders to play a part in majestical matters with neither decency nor discretion, so as neither the admiration and commiseration, nor the right sportfulness, is by their mongrel tragicomedy obtained. I know Apuleius did somewhat so,[4] but that is a thing recounted with space of time, not represented in one moment; and I know the ancients have one or two examples of tragicomedies, as Plautus hath *Amphitryo;*[5] but, if we mark them well, we shall find that they never, or very daintily, match hornpipes and funerals. So falleth it out that, having indeed no right comedy, in that comical part of our tragedy, we have nothing but scurrility, unworthy of any chaste ears, or some extreme show of doltishness, indeed fit to lift up a loud laughter, and nothing else: where the whole tract of a comedy should be full of delight, as the tragedy should be still maintained in a well-raised admiration.

But our comedians think there is no delight without laughter; which is very wrong, for though laughter may come with delight, yet cometh it not of delight, as though delight should be the cause of laughter; but well may one thing breed both together. Nay, rather in themselves they have, as it were, a kind of contrariety: for delight we scarcely do but in things that have a conveniency to ourselves or to the general nature; laughter almost ever cometh of things most disproportioned to ourselves and nature. Delight hath a joy in it, either permanent or present. Laughter hath only a scornful tickling.

For example, we are ravished with delight to see a fair woman, and yet are far from being moved to laughter; we laugh at deformed creatures, wherein certainly we cannot delight. We delight in good chances, we laugh at mischances: we delight to hear the happiness of our friends, or country, at which he were worthy to be laughed at that would laugh; we shall, contrarily, laugh sometimes to find a matter quite mistaken and go down the hill against the bias in the mouth of some such men—as for the respect of them one shall be heartily sorry, he cannot choose but laugh, and so is rather pained than delighted with laughter.

3. Sidney praises the narrative of the hero Polydorus as told by Euripides, who avoids a lengthy plot in his play on the subject, *Hecuba*.

4. In his prose romance *The Golden Ass* (c. 155 A.D.); William Adlington translated the work into English in the 16th century.

5. In this play the tragic element is represented by the heroine Alcmena, tricked into sleeping with the god Jupiter, who is disguised as her husband Amphitrion, and the comic element by the burlesque behavior of the gods who arrange the deception.

Yet deny I not but that they may go well together. For as in Alexander's picture well set out we delight without laughter,[6] and in twenty mad antics we laugh without delight; so in Hercules, painted with his great beard and furious countenance, in a woman's attire, spinning at Omphale's commandment, it breedeth both delight and laughter: for the representing of so strange a power in love procureth delight, and the scornfulness of the action stirreth laughter. But I speak to this purpose, that all the end of the comical part be not upon such scornful matters as stir laughter only, but, mixed with it, that delightful teaching which is the end of poesy. And the great fault even in that point of laughter, and forbidden plainly by Aristotle, is that they stir laughter in sinful things, which are rather execrable than ridiculous, or in miserable, which are rather to be pitied than scorned. For what is it to make folks gape at a wretched beggar and a beggarly clown; or, against law of hospitality, to jest at strangers, because they speak not English so well as we do? What do we learn, since it is certain

Nil habet infelix paupertas durius in se,
Quam quod ridiculos homines facit?[7]

But rather, a busy loving courtier and a heartless threatening Thraso;[8] a self-wise-seeming schoolmaster; an awry-transformed traveler. These if we saw walk in stage names, which we play naturally, therein were delightful laughter, and teaching delightfulness—as in the other, the tragedies of Buchanan[9] do justly bring forth a divine admiration.

But I have lavished out too many words of this play matter. I do it because, as they are excelling parts of poesy, so is there none so much used in England, and none can be more pitifully abused; which, like an unmannerly daughter showing a bad education, causeth her mother Poesy's honesty to be called in question.

Other sort of poetry almost have we none, but that lyrical kind of songs and sonnets: which, Lord, if He gave us so good minds, how well it might be employed, and with how heavenly fruit, both private and public, in singing the praises of the immortal beauty: the immortal goodness of that God who giveth us hands to write and wits to conceive; of which we might well want words, but never matter; of which we could turn our eyes to nothing, but we should ever have new-budding occasions. But truly many of such writings as come under the banner of unresistible love, if I were a mistress, would never persuade me they were in love: so coldly they apply fiery speeches, as men that had rather read lovers' writings—and so caught up certain swelling phrases which hang together like a man that once told my father that the wind was at northwest and by south, because he would be sure to name winds enough—than that in truth they feel those passions, which easily (as I think) may be bewrayed by that same forcibleness or *energia* (as the Greeks call it) of the writer. But let this be a sufficient though short note, that we miss the right use of the material point of poesy.

Now, for the outside of it, which is words, or (as I may term it) diction, it is even well worse. So is that honey-flowing matron Eloquence appareled, or rather disguised, in a courtesan-like painted affectation: one time, with so far-fet words that

6. Sidney distinguishes reactions to different kinds of descriptions: Alexander's portrait delights; mad antics provoke laughter; Hercules, captive and dressed as a woman by Queen Omphale of Lydia, both delights and provokes laughter.

7. "Unfortunate poverty has nothing in itself harder to bear than that it makes men ridiculous" (Juvenal, *Satires* 3.152–3).

8. The braggart soldier of Terence's comedy *Eunuchus*.

9. A Scots humanist (1506—1582) who wrote four tragedies on biblical and classical themes.

may seem monsters but must seem strangers to any poor Englishman; another time, with coursing[1] of a letter, as if they were bound to follow the method of a dictionary; another time, with figures and flowers, extremely winter-starved. But I would this fault were only peculiar to versifiers, and had not as large possession among prose-printers; and (which is to be marveled) among many scholars; and (which is to be pitied) among some preachers. Truly I could wish, if at least I might be so bold to wish in a thing beyond the reach of my capacity, the diligent imitators of Tully and Demosthenes[2] (most worthy to be imitated) did not so much keep Nizolian paper-books[3] of their figures and phrases, as by attentive translation (as it were) devour them whole, and make them wholly theirs: for now they cast sugar and spice upon every dish that is served to the table—like those Indians, not content to wear ear-rings at the fit and natural place of the ears, but they will thrust jewels through their nose and lips, because they will be sure to be fine. Tully, when he was to drive out Catiline, as it were with a thunderbolt of eloquence, often used the figure of repetition, as *Vivit. Vivit? Imo in senatum venit, & c.*[4] Indeed, inflamed with a well-grounded rage, he would have his words (as it were) double out of his mouth, and so do that artificially which we see men in choler do naturally. And we, having noted the grace of those words, hale them in sometimes to a familiar epistle, when it were too too much choler to be choleric. How well store of *similiter cadences* [similar cadences] doth sound with the gravity of the pulpit, I would but invoke Demosthenes' soul to tell, who with a rare daintiness useth them. Truly they have made me think of the sophister[5] that with too much subtlety would prove two eggs three, and though he might be counted a sophister, had none for his labor. So these men bringing in such a kind of eloquence, well may they obtain an opinion of a seeming finesse, but persuade few—which should be the end of their finesse. Now for similitudes, in certain printed discourses, I think all herbarists, all stories of beasts, fowls, and fishes are rifled up,[6] that they come in multitudes to wait upon any of our conceits; which certainly is as absurd a surfeit to the ears as is possible. For the force of a similitude not being to prove anything to a contrary disputer, but only to explain to a willing hearer, when that is done, the rest is a most tedious prattling, rather over-swaying the memory from the purpose whereto they were applied, than any whit informing the judgment, already either satisfied, or by similitudes not to be satisfied. For my part, I do not doubt, when Antonius and Crassus,[7] the great forefathers of Cicero in eloquence, the one (as Cicero testifieth of them) pretended not to know art, the other not to set by it, because with a plain sensibleness they might win credit of popular ears (which credit is the nearest step to persuasion, which persuasion is the chief mark of oratory), I do not doubt (I say) but that they used these knacks very sparingly; which who doth generally use, any man may see doth dance to his own music, and so be noted by the audience more careful to speak curiously than to speak truly. Undoubtedly (at least to my opinion undoubtedly), I have found in divers smally

1. Alliteration.
2. Athenian statesman and orator (383–322 B.C.).
3. Marius Nizolius, a 16th-century Italian rhetorician and lexicographer, published a collection of phrases by Cicero (i.e., Tully). Sidney complains that contemporary writers use them too often. Cicero, when he prosecuted the traitor Catiline, employed repetition skillfully to heighten the effect of his argument, but writers in Sidney's time are not as discriminating.
4. "He lives. He lives? He still comes into the Senate. . . ." The sentences paraphrase the opening of Cicero's first oration against Catiline.
5. One who argues by specious reasons.
6. Sidney suggests that the figures in beast fables are all "rifled" or taken by many writers; hence they have become trite.
7. Antonius: Marcus Antonius, consul in 99 B.C.; Crassus: Publius Licinius Crassus Dives Mucianus, consul in 175 B.C. Both men were famous orators.

learned courtiers a more sound style than in some professors of learning; of which I can guess no other cause, but that the courtier, following that which by practice he findeth fittest to nature, therein (though he know it not) doth according to art, though not by art: where the other, using art to show art, and not to hide art (as in these cases he should do), flieth from nature, and indeed abuseth art.

But what? Methinks I deserve to be pounded for straying from poetry to oratory. But both have such an affinity in the wordish consideration, that I think this digression will make my meaning receive the fuller understanding: which is not to take upon me to teach poets how they should do, but only, finding myself sick among the rest, to show some one or two spots of the common infection grown among the most part of writers, that, acknowledging ourselves somewhat awry, we may bend to the right use both of matter and manner: whereto our language giveth us great occasion, being indeed capable of any excellent exercising of it. I know some will say it is a mingled language.[8] And why not so much the better, taking the best of both the other? Another will say it wanteth grammar. Nay truly, it hath that praise, that it wants not grammar: for grammar it might have, but it needs it not, being so easy in itself, and so void of those cumbersome differences of cases, genders, moods, and tenses, which I think was a piece of the Tower of Babylon's curse,[9] that a man should be put to school to learn his mother-tongue. But for the uttering sweetly and properly the conceits of the mind (which is the end of speech), that hath it equally with any other tongue in the world; and is particularly happy in compositions of two or three words together, near the Greek, far beyond the Latin, which is one of the greatest beauties can be in a language.

Now of versifying there are two sorts, the one ancient, the other modern: the ancient marked the quantity of each syllable, and according to that framed his verse; the modern, observing only number (with some regard of the accent), the chief life of it standeth in that like sounding of the words, which we call rhyme. Whether of these be the more excellent, would bear many speeches: the ancient (no doubt) more fit for music, both words and time observing quantity, and more fit lively to express diverse passions, by the low or lofty sound of the well-weighed syllable; the latter likewise, with his rhyme, striketh a certain music to the ear, and, in fine, since it doth delight, though by another way, it obtains the same purpose: there being in either sweetness, and wanting in neither majesty. Truly the English, before any vulgar language I know, is fit for both sorts. For, for the ancient, the Italian is so full of vowels that it must ever be cumbered with elisions;[1] the Dutch so, of the other side, with consonants, that they cannot yield the sweet sliding, fit for a verse; the French in his whole language hath not one word that hath his accent in the last syllable saving two, called *antepenultima* [third from last]; and little more hath the Spanish, and therefore very gracelessly may they use dactyls.[2] The English is subject to none of these defects. Now for the rhyme, though we do not observe quantity, yet we observe the accent very precisely, which other languages either cannot do, or will not do so absolutely. That *caesura,* or breathing place in the midst of the verse, neither Italian nor Spanish have, the French and we never almost fail of. Lastly, even the very

8. Sidney describes English as a "mingled" language because it is derived from Anglo-Saxon, brought over by the invading Germanic tribes during the 6th century, and Norman-French, introduced by William the Conqueror in 1066.

9. Early modern writers identified Babylon with Babel (see Genesis 10.10).

1. The suppression of a vowel at the end of a word when the next word begins with a vowel.

2. A metric foot in classical poetry, consisting of one long and two short syllables, as in the words "murmuring," "sensible."

rhyme itself, the Italian cannot put it in the last syllable, by the French named the masculine rhyme, but still in the next to the last, which the French call the female, or the next before that, which the Italian term *sdrucciola* [three-syllable rhyme]. The example of the former is *buono: suono*, of the *sdrucciola* is *femina: semina*. The French, of the other side, hath both the male, as *bon: son*, and the female, as *plaise: taise*, but the *sdrucciola* he hath not: where the English hath all three, as *due: true*, *father: rather*, *motion: potion*[3]—with much more which might be said, but that already I find the triflingness of this discourse is much too much enlarged.

So that since the ever-praiseworthy Poesy is full of virtue-breeding delightfulness, and void of no gift that ought to be in the noble name of learning; since the blames laid against it are either false or feeble; since the cause why it is not esteemed in England is the fault of poet-apes, not poets; since, lastly, our tongue is most fit to honor poesy, and to be honored by poesy; I conjure you all that have had the evil luck to read this ink-wasting toy of mine, even in the name of the nine Muses, no more to scorn the sacred mysteries of poesy; no more to laugh at the name of poets, as though they were next inheritors to fools; no more to jest at the reverent title of a rhymer; but to believe, with Aristotle, that they were the ancient treasurers of the Grecians' divinity; to believe, with Bembus, that they were first bringers-in of all civility; to believe, with Scaliger, that no philosopher's precepts can sooner make you an honest man than the reading of Virgil; to believe, with Clauserus,[4] the translator of Cornutus, that it pleased the heavenly Deity, by Hesiod and Homer, under the veil of fables, to give us all knowledge, logic, rhetoric, philosophy natural and moral, and *quid non?* [what not]; to believe, with me, that there are many mysteries contained in poetry, which of purpose were written darkly, lest by profane wits it should be abused; to believe, with Landino,[5] that they are so beloved of the gods that whatsoever they write proceeds of a divine fury; lastly, to believe themselves, when they tell you they will make you immortal by their verses. Thus doing, your name shall flourish in the printers' shops; thus doing, you shall be of kin to many a poetical preface; thus doing, you shall be most fair, most rich, most wise, most all, you shall dwell upon superlatives; thus doing, though you be *libertino patre natus* [son of freed slave], you shall suddenly grow *Herculea proles* [a descendant of Hercules],

Si quid mea carmina possunt;[6]

thus doing, your soul shall be placed with Dante's Beatrice, or Virgil's Anchises. But if (fie of such a but) you be born so near the dull-making cataract of Nilus[7] that you cannot hear the planet-like music of poetry; if you have so earth-creeping a mind that it cannot lift itself up to look to the sky of poetry, or rather, by a certain rustical disdain, will become such a mome as to be a Momus[8] of poetry; then, though I will not wish unto you the ass's ears of Midas, nor to be driven by a poet's verses, as

3. *Motion* and *potion* presumably retained three syllables, as the Middle English spelling "mocioun" reveals.
4. Conrad Clauser, a 16th-century German scholar who translated the works of Lucius Annaeus Cornutus, a first-century Greek slave who wrote commentaries on Aristotle and Virgil.
5. Cristofor Landino (1424–1504), an Italian humanist who wrote moral dialogues.
6. "If my songs can do anything" (*Aeneid*, 9.446).
7. Cicero claimed that hearing the sound of the cataracts of the Nile river in Egypt caused deafness; the Neoplatonists thought the movement of the planets produced heavenly music, the music of the spheres.
8. Momus personified the faultfinder in Greek literature; a mome is a blockhead. Apollo changed Midas's ears to those of an ass to signal his stupidity after Midas judged Pan's flute playing to be superior to Apollo's (Ovid, *Metamorphosis* 11.146).

Bubonax[9] was, to hang himself, nor to be rhymed to death, as is said to be done in Ireland; yet thus much curse I must send you, in the behalf of all poets, that while you live, you live in love, and never get favor for lacking skill of a sonnet; and, when you die, your memory die from the earth for want of an epitaph.

1579–80 1595

The Apology in Context

The Art of Poetry

After the spread of Reformation doctrine on the importance of moral discipline, English readers often encountered denunciations of poetry and especially drama. The issues that Sidney took up when he defended poetry were the subject of sharp dispute. Stephen Gosson represented the opinions of many of poetry's detractors. As he declares in *The School of Abuse*, published shortly before Sidney wrote his *Apology*, poetry provides frivolous distraction from the serious business of life and, what is worse, temptations to godlessness. But others, like Sidney, took a more optimistic view of the subject. In *The Art of English Poesy*, George Puttenham states that poets were the first lawgivers (as Sidney had) and focuses particularly on epic poetry, which, he says, give readers images of a truth beyond history as well as consistently inspiring models of action to imitate. His popular treatise contains a wealth of practical advice for aspiring writers and even today remains a useful sourcebook for information on rhetorical figures of thought and speech.

In addition to the challenge posed by moralists such as Gosson, defenders of English poetry also had to confront purely practical problems. Unlike the Romance languages—Italian, French, and Spanish—sixteenth-century English had lost almost all its feminine endings, the accented vowel sounds that made rhyming fairly easy. English was also a language in which words of one syllable were quite common, and poets had trouble creating the metrical harmonies usual in poetry written in languages rich in polysyllables. George Gascoigne's brief treatise *Certain Notes of Instruction concerning the making of verse or rhyme in English* deals with these conditions directly. He warns against trying to achieve euphony or a musical quality by "rolling in pleasant words," as in the sequence "Rim, Ram, Ruff," and he insists that the "truer Englishman" uses words of one syllable. Critics could differ in what they valued, of course; in *A Defence of Rhyme*, Samuel Daniel justified rhyme as "pleasing to nature," which desires form and closures, not chaos and infinity. More important, he defended English writers against the claim that they could never match their classical precursors. He reminded readers that imputations of barbarism and ignorance are based on relative, not absolute, judgments.

Stephen Gosson

from *The School of Abuse*[1]

The Syracusans used such variety of dishes in their banquets that when they were set and their boards furnished,[2] they were many times in doubt which they should touch first or taste last. And in my opinion the world giveth every writer so large a field to walk in that before he set pen to the book, he shall find himself feasted at Syracuse,

9. Sidney conflates Hipp*onax*, a Greek poet, with *Bu*palus, a sculptor. The latter had made an unflattering portrait of the former, who took revenge with deadly verses. Irish poets claimed their verses could kill man or beast.

1. Stephen Gosson was a playwright who turned against the stage, and then wrote Puritanical critiques of what he considered its immorality. His *School of Abuse* was published in 1579.

2. Tables set.

uncertain where to begin or when to end. This caused Pindarus[3] to question with his Muse whether he were better with his art to decipher the life of Nimpe Melia, or Cadmus's encounter with the dragon, or the wars of Hercules at the walls of Thebes, or Bacchus's cups, or Venus's juggling? He saw so many turnings laid open to his feet, that he knew not which way to bend his pace.

Therefore, as I cannot but commend his wisdom which in banqueting feeds most upon that that doth nourish best, so must I dispraise his method in writing which, following the course of amorous poets, dwelleth longest on those points that profit least, and like a wanton whelp,[4] leaveth the game[5] to run riot. The scarab flies over many a sweet flower and lights in a cowsherd.[6] It is the custom of the fly to leave the sound places of the horse and suck at the botch,[7] the nature of colloquintida[8] to draw the worst humors to itself, the manner of swine to forsake the fair fields and wallow in the mire, and the whole practice of poets, either with fables to show their abuses or with plain terms to unfold their mischief, discover their shame, discredit themselves, and disperse their poison through the world. Virgil sweats in describing his gnat, Ovid bestirreth him to paint out his flea; the one shows his art in the lust of Dido, the other his cunning in the incest of Myrrha and that trumpet of bawdry, the craft of love.[9]

I must confess that poets are the whetstones of wit, notwithstanding that wit is dearly bought. Where honey and gall are mixed, it will be hard to sever the one from the other. The deceitful physician giveth sweet syrups to make his poison go down the smoother, the juggler casteth a mist to work the closer, the siren's song is the sailor's wrack,[1] the fowler's whistle the bird's death, the wholesome bait the fish's bane. The Harpies[2] have virgin faces, and the vultures, talents; Hyena speaks like a friend and devours like a foe; the calmest seas hide dangerous rocks; the wolf jets in wether's fells.[3] Many good sentences are spoken by David to shadow his knavery,[4] and written by poets as ornaments to beautify their works and set their trumpery to sale without suspect.

But if you look well to Epaeus's horse,[5] you shall find in his bowels the destruction of Troy; open the sepulchre of Semiramis,[6] whose title promiseth such wealth to the kings of Persia, you shall see nothing but dead bones; rip up the golden ball that Nero consecrated to Jupiter Capitolinus,[7] you shall [find] it stuffed with the shavings of his beard; pull off the visor that poets mask in, you shall disclose their reproach, bewray[8] their vanity, loathe their wantonness, lament their folly, and perceive their

3. Pindar, the most difficult and obscure of Greek poets, famous for his odes. The story of Cadmus's encounter with the dragon is a fragment of a cycle of legends about the city of Thebes; the legendary hero Hercules delivered the city of Thebes from the burden of paying tribute to the foreign king Orchomenus; Bacchus was the Roman god of wine; and Venus's "juggling" refers to her erotic escapades.

4. Unruly puppy.

5. Hunt.

6. Cow dung.

7. Ulcer.

8. A wild cucumber, used as an herbal medicine.

9. Dido, Queen of Carthage, with whom the legendary Trojan hero Aeneas stayed on his way to founding Rome; Virgil's *Aeneid* provides the best-known account of this episode. According to legend, Myrrha was the mother of the Greek god of vegetation, Adonis, by her father, King Cinyras, who, when he learned of his incest, changed her into a myrtle; the story is told by Ovid in his *Metamorphoses*, a poem describing erotic transformations. Gosson condemns Ovid's poem *Ars Amatoria*, or "the craft (or art) of love," as an immoral work ("bawdry" is licentiousness).

1. The mermaid's song is the sailor's shipwreck.

2. Monstrous and filthy birds whom Aeneas and his companions encounter.

3. The wolf strolls in sheep's clothing.

4. King of the ancient Israelites and poet of the psalms, David was guilty of adulterous love for Bathsheba, whose husband he murdered.

5. The Trojan horse.

6. Mythical queen of Assyria, who is supposed to have built the city of Babylon.

7. The Emperor Nero is said to have consecrated a golden ball to Jupiter in his temple on the Capitoline Hill in Rome.

8. Expose.

sharp sayings to be placed as pearls in dunghills, fresh pictures on rotten walls, chaste matrons' apparel on common courtesans. These are the cups of Circe,[9] that turn reasonable creatures into brute beasts; the balls of Hippomenes,[1] that hinder the course of Atalanta; and the blocks of the Devil, that are cast in our ways to cut off the race of toward wits. No marvel though Plato shut them out of his school and banished them quite from his commonwealth as effeminate writers,[2] unprofitable members, and utter enemies to virtue.

George Puttenham
from *The Art of English Poesie*[1]

How Poets were the first Philosophers, the first Astronomers and Historiographers, and Orators and Musicians of the world.[2]

Utterance also and language is given by nature to man for persuasion of others and aid of themselves, I mean the first ability to speak. For speech itself is artificial and made by man, and the more pleasing it is, the more it prevaileth to such purpose as it is intended for. But speech by meter is a kind of utterance more cleanly couched and more delicate to the ear than prose is, because it is more current and slipper upon the tongue and withal tunable and melodious as a kind of music and therefore may be termed a musical speech or utterance which cannot but please the hearer very well. Another cause is for that[3] is briefer and more compendious and easier to bear away and be retained in memory than that which is contained in multitude of words and full of tedious ambage and long periods.[4] It is beside a manner of utterance more eloquent and rhetorical than the ordinary proof which we use in our daily talk, because it is decked and set out with all manner of fresh colors and figures, which maketh that it sooner inveigleth[5] the judgment of man and carryeth his opinion this way and that, whither soever the heart by impression of the ear shall be most affectionately bent and directed. The utterance in prose is not of so great efficacy because not only it is daily used, and by that occasion the care is over-glutted with it, but is also not so voluble and slipper on the tongue, being wide and loose, and nothing numerous nor contrived into measures and founded with so gallant and harmonical accents, nor in fine allowed that figurative conveyance[6] nor so great license in choice of words and phrases as meter is. So as the poets were also from the beginning the best persuaders and their eloquence the first rhetoric of the world, even so it became[7] that the high mysteries of the gods should be revealed and taught by a manner of utterance and language of extraordinary phrase and brief and compendious and above all others sweet and civil as the metrical is. The same also was meetest to register the lives and noble gifts of princes, and of the great monarchs of the world and all other memo-

9. In Homer's *Odyssey*, the goddess who transformed the companions of Odysseus into swine.
1. The legendary suitor of Atalanta, who refused to marry anyone she could defeat in a footrace. Hippomenes won the race by dropping golden apples on the race track. Atalanta could not resist stopping to pick them up, and her delay allowed Hippomenes victory.
2. Plato exiles poets from his ideal republic (see *The Republic* 3, 398A).
1. George Puttenham has always been assumed to be the author of *The Art of English Poesy*, a critical treatise that appeared in 1589. Dividing his work into three books: *Of Poets and Poesy*, *Of Proportion*, and *Of Ornament*, Puttenham discusses the works of English poets, poetic forms and genres, and figures of speech and thought respectively. The work as a whole is a compendium of contemporary ideas and practices illustrating the proper way to compose and appreciate poetry.
2. In his *Apology for Poetry*, Sidney also claims that poets were the first human beings to express feeling, thought, and a sense of the higher purposes of life.
3. I.e., poetry.
4. Dull indirection and long sentences.
5. Appeals to.
6. Expression.
7. Was appropriate.

rable accidents of time, so as the poet was also the first historiographer. Then forasmuch as they were the first observers of all natural causes and effects in the things generable and corruptable, and from thence mounted up to search after the celestial courses and influences and yet penetrated further to know the divine essences and substances separate,[8] as is said before, they were the first astronomers and philosophists and metaphysics. Finally, because they did altogether endeavor themselves to reduce[9] the life of man to a certain method of good manners, and made the first differences between virtue and vice, and then tempered all these knowledges and skills with the exercise of a delectable music by melodious instruments, which withall served them to delight their hearers and to call the people together by admiration to a plausible and virtuous conversation, therefore were they the first philosophers ethic[1] and the first artificial musicians of the world. Such was Linus, Orpheus, Amphion, and Musaeus,[2] the most ancient poets and philosophers, of whom there is left any memory by the profane writers. King David also and Solomon his son and many other of the holy prophets wrote in meters and used to sing them to the harp,[3] although to many of us ignorant of the Hebrew language and phrase and not observing it, the same seem but a prose. It cannot be therefore that any scorn or indignity should justly be offered to so noble, profitable, ancient, and divine a science as Poesie is. * * *

Of historical poesie,[4] by which the famous acts of Princes and the virtuous and worthy lives of our forefathers were reported.

There is nothing in man of all the potential parts of his mind (reason and will excepted) more noble or more necessary to the active life than memory. Because it maketh[5] most to a sound judgment and perfect worldly wisdom, examining and comparing the times past with the present and by them both considering the time to come, [it] concludeth with a steadfast resolution what is the best course to be taken in all his actions and advices in this world. It came upon this reason: experience [is] to be so highly commended in all consultations of importance and preferred before any learning or science, and yet experience is no more than a mass of memories assembled, that is, such trials as man hath made in time before. Right so, no kind of argument in all the oratory craft doth better persuade and more universally satisfy than example, which is but the representation of old memories and like successes [that have] happened in times past. For these regards, the poesie historical is of all other, next[6] the divine, most honorable and worthy, as well for the common benefit as for the special comfort every man receiveth by it. No one thing in the world with more delectation [is] reviving our spirits than to behold, as it were in a glass, the lively image of our dear forefathers, their noble and virtuous manner of life, with other things authentic, which because we are not able otherwise to attain to the knowledge of by any of our fences,[7] we apprehend them by memory, whereas the present time and things so swiftly pass away [so] as they give us no leisure almost to look into them

8. I.e., to know the divine essences and the particular objects present in the heavens.
9. Abstract.
1. I.e., philosophers who consider ethics.
2. Puttenham names legendary figures who were thought to be among the first poets: Linus, a poet and the teacher of Hercules, who later killed him with his own lyre; Orpheus, commonly considered the first poet, whose music charmed even the animals; Amphion, the poet whose music moved stones to build Thebes; and Musaeus, said to have been a pupil of Orpheus.
3. Scripture provides accounts of King David, supposed to be the author of the psalms, and Solomon, to whom the Song of Songs is attributed.
4. Epic poetry.
5. Benefits.
6. After.
7. Ways of arguing.

and much less to know and consider of them thoroughly. The things future, being also events very uncertain, and such as cannot possibly be known because they be not yet, cannot be used for example nor for delight otherwise than by hope, though many promise the contrary, by vain and deceitful arts taking upon them to reveal the truth of accidents to come, which if it were so as they surmise, are yet but sciences merely conjectural and not of any benefit to man or to the commonwealth where they be used or professed. Therefore the good and exemplary things and actions of the former ages were reserved only to the historical reports of wise and grave men; those of the present time [were] left to the fruition and judgment of our senses; the future as hazards and uncertain events [were] utterly neglected and laid aside for magicians and mockers to get their livings by, such manner of men as by negligence of magistrates and remisses of laws every country breedeth great store of. These historical men nevertheless used not the matter so precisely to wish that all they wrote should be accounted true,[8] for that was not needful nor expedient to the purpose, namely to be used either for example or for the pleasure, considering that many times it is seen a feigned matter or altogether fabulous, besides that it maketh more mirth than any other, works no less good conclusions for example than the most true and veritable, but oftentimes more, because the poet hath the handling of them[9] to fashion at his pleasure, but not so of the other[1] which must go according to their verity and none otherwise without the writers' great blame. Again as ye know, more and more excellent examples may be feigned in one day by a good wit than many ages through man's frailty are able to put in ure,[2] which made the learned and witty men of those times to devise many historical matters of no verity at all, but with purpose to do good and no hurt, as using them for a manner of discipline and precedent of commendable life. Such was the commonwealth of Plato, and Sir Thomas More's *Utopia,* resting all in device,[3] but never [to be] put in execution and easier wished than to be performed. And you shall perceive that histories were of three sorts, wholly true and wholly false, and a third holding part of either, but for honest recreation and good example they were all of them.[4]

George Gascoigne
from *Certain Notes of Instruction*[1]

The first and most necessary point that ever I found meet to be considered in making of a delectable poem is this, to ground it upon some fine invention.[2] For it is not enough to roll in pleasant words, nor yet to thunder in Rim, Ram, Ruff, by letter (quoth my master Chaucer) nor yet to abound in apt vocables or epithets, unless the invention have in it also *aliquid salis* [something salty]. By this *aliquid salis* I mean some good and fine device, showing the quick capacity of a writer, and where I say some good and fine invention, I mean that I would have it both fine and good. For many inventions are so superfine that they are *Vix* [scarcely] good. And again many

8. Puttenham identifies epic poets as historical, in that they represent the past, but not as historians, in that they do not represent it entirely truthfully.
9. His poetic subjects.
1. I.e., the historian who must try to discover the factual truth of the past.
2. Use.
3. Conception.
4. I.e., they were all equally good for recreation and good moral example.

1. George Gascoigne's *Certain Notes* was published in 1575 as part of his second work, containing both poetry and prose, entitled *The Posies of George Gascoigne*. Gascoigne's principal listing begins on page 728.
2. In early modern treatises on the art of writing poetry, "invention" meant the discovery and development of "matter," the topics and ideas that the poet will then represent. After "invention," he draws on a knowledge of rhetoric, the techniques by which "matter" is made interesting and memorable.

inventions are good, and yet not finely handled. And for a general forewarning: what theme soever you do take in hand, if you do handle it but *tanquam in oratione perpetua* [as a perpetual sermon], and never study for some depth of device in your invention and some figures also in the handling thereof, it will appear to the skillful reader but a tale of a tub. To deliver unto you general examples it were almost impossible, since the occasions of inventions are (as it were) infinite. Nevertheless, take in worth mine opinion and perceive my further meaning in these few points. If I should undertake to write in praise of a gentlewoman, I would neither praise her crystal eye nor her cherry lip, etc., for these things are *trita et obvia* [trite and obvious]. But I would either find some supernatural cause whereby my pen might walk in superlative degree, or else I would undertake to answer for any imperfection that she hath, and thereupon raise the praise of her commendation.[3] Likewise, if I should disclose my pretense in[4] love, I would either make a strange discourse of some intolerable passion, or find occasion to plead by the example of some history, or discover[5] my disquiet in shadows *per allegoriam* [through allegory], or use the covertest mean that I could to avoid the uncomely customs of common writers. Thus much I adventure to deliver unto you (my friend) upon [the] rule of invention, which of all other rules is most to be marked and hardest to be prescribed in certain and infallible rules. Nevertheless, to conclude therein, I would have you stand most upon the excellency of your invention and stick[6] not to study deeply for some fine device. For that being found, pleasant words will follow well enough and fast enough.

Your invention being once devised, take heed that neither pleasure of rhyme nor variety of device do carry you from it. For as to use obscure and dark phrases in a pleasant[7] sonnet is nothing delectable, so to intermingle merry jests in a serious matter is an indecorum.[8]

I will next advise you that you hold the just measure wherewith you begin your verse. I will not deny but this may seem a preposterous order, but because I covet rather to satisfy you particularly than to undertake a general tradition, I will not so much stand upon the manner as the matter of my precepts. I say then, remember to hold the same measure wherewith you begin, whether it be in a verse of six syllables, eight, ten, twelve, etc., and though this precept might seem ridiculous unto you, since every young scholar can conceive that he ought to continue in the same measure wherewith he beginneth, yet do I see and read many men's poems nowadays which beginning with the measure of twelve in the first line and fourteen in the second (which is the common kind of verse), they will yet (by that time they have passed over a few verses) fall into fourteen and fourteen and *sic de similibus* [so on], the which is either forgetfulness or carelessness. * * *

I think it not amiss to forewarn you that you thrust as few words of many syllables into your verse as may be, and hereunto I might allege many reasons. First, the most ancient English words are of one syllable, so that the more monosyllables that you use, the truer Englishman you shall seem, and the less you shall smell of the inkhorn.[9] Also, words of many syllables do cloy a verse and make it unpleasant, whereas words of one syllable will more easily fall to be short or long as occasion requireth, or will be adapted to become circumflex[1] or of an indifferent[2] sound.

3. My compliment to her.
4. Profession of.
5. Reveal.
6. Hesitate.
7. Lighthearted.
8. Improper act.
9. Inkpot.
1. Accentuated.
2. Soft.

I would exhort you also to beware of rhyme without reason. My meaning is hereby that your rhyme lead you not from your first invention, for many writers when they have laid the platform of their invention are yet drawn sometimes (by rhyme) to forget it or at least to alter it, as when they cannot readily find out a word which may rhyme to the first (and yet continue their determinate invention) they do then either botch it up with a word that will rhyme (how small reason soever it carry with it) or else they alter their first word and so perhaps decline or trouble their former invention. But do you always hold your first determined invention, and do rather search the bottom of your brains for apt words than change good reason for rumbling rhyme.

* * *

Also as much as may be, eschew strange words or *obsoleta et inusitata* [obsolete and rare], unless the theme do give just occasion. Marry, in some places a strange word doth draw attentive reading, but yet I would have you therein to use discretion.

And as much as you may, frame your style to perspicuity and to be sensible, for the haughty obscure verse doth not much delight and the verse that is too easy is like a tale of a rusted[3] horse. But let your poem be such as may both delight and draw attentive reading and therewithal may deliver such matter as be worth the marking.

Samuel Daniel
from *A Defense of Rhyme*[1]

Such affliction doth laborsome curiosity[2] still lay upon our best delights (which ever must be made strange and variable) as if art were ordained to afflict nature and that we could not go but in fetters. Every science, every profession, must be so wrapped up in unnecessary intrications, as if it were not to fashion but to confound the understanding, which makes me much to distrust man and fear that our presumption goes beyond our ability and our curiosity is more than our judgment, laboring ever to seem to be more than we are or laying greater burdens upon our minds than they are well able to bear, because we would not appear like other men.

And indeed I have wished there were not that multiplicity of rhymes as is used by many in sonnets, which yet we see in some so happily to succeed and hath been so far from hindering their inventions as it hath begot conceit[3] beyond expectation and comparable to the best inventions of the world. For sure in an eminent spirit whom nature hath fitted for that mystery, rhyme is no impediment to his conceit, but rather gives him wings to mount and carries him, not out of his course, but as it were beyond his power to a far happier flight. All excellencies being sold us at the hard price of labor, it follows, where we bestow most thereof, we buy the best success, and rhyme being far more laborious than loose measures (whatsoever is objected), must needs, meeting with wit and industry, breed greater and worthier effects in our language. So that if our labors have wrought out a manumission[4] from bondage and that we go at liberty, notwithstanding these ties, we are no longer the slaves of rhyme but we make it a most excellent instrument to serve us. Nor is this certain limit observed in sonnets any tyrannical bounding of the conceit,[5] but rather a reducing it in *girum*

3. Restless.

1. Samuel Daniel, a poet and playwright, published a variety of works throughout his long career, notably: a collection of sonnets, *Delia* (1592); two tragedies, *Cleopatra* (1594) and *Philotas* (1604); an epic poem of the Wars of the Roses, *Civil Wars* (1595, 1609); and several masques. His essay on poetry, *A Defence of Rhyme*, was published in 1603.
2. Daniel's criticism of "laborsome curiosity" is comparable to Gascoigne's criticism of an "inkhorn" style: both poets reject pedantry.
3. Created conceptions.
4. Release.
5. I.e., the conception informing the poem.

[in bounds], and a just form, neither too long for the shortest project nor too short for the longest, being but only employed for a present passion. For the body of our imagination, being as an unformed chaos without fashion, without day, if by the divine power of the spirit it be wrought into an orb of order and form, is it not more pleasing to nature that desires a certainty and comports not with that which is infinite, to have these closes[6] rather than not to know where to end or how far to go, especially seeing our passions are often without measure. And we find in the best of the Latins many times either not concluding or else otherwise in the end than they began. Besides, is it not most delightful to see much excellently ordered in a small room, or little gallantly disposed and made to fill up a space of like capacity, in such sort that the one would not appear so beautiful in a larger circuit nor the other do well in a less, which often we find to be so, according to the powers of nature, in the workman. And these limited proportions and rests of stanzas, consisting of six, seven, or eight lines, are of that happiness, both for the disposition of the matter, the apt planting the sentence where it may best stand to hit, the certain close of delight with the full body of a just period well-carried,[7] is such as neither the Greeks or Latins ever attained unto. For their boundless running on often so confounds the reader that having once lost himself must either give off unsatisfied or certainly cast back to retrieve the escaped sense and to find way again into his matter.

Methinks we should not so soon yield our consents captive to the authority of antiquity unless we saw more reason. All our understandings are not to be built by the square of Greece and Italy. We are the children of nature as well as they, we are not so placed out of the way of judgment but that the same sun of discretion shineth upon us, we have our portion of the same virtues as well as of the same vices. * * *

It is not the observing of trochaics nor their iambics[8] that will make our writings aught the wiser. All their poesie, all their philosophy is nothing unless we bring the discerning light of conceit[9] with us to apply it to use. It is not books, but only that great book of the world and the all-overspreading grace of heaven that makes men truly judicial.[1] Nor can it be but a touch of arrogant ignorance to hold this or that nation barbarous, these or those times gross, considering how this manifold creature man, wheresoever he stand in the world, hath always some disposition of worth, entertains the order of society, affects that which is most in use, and is eminent in some one thing or other that fits his humor and the times. The Grecians held all other nations barbarous but themselves, yet Pyrrhus when he saw the well-ordered marching of the Romans, which made them see their presumptuous error, could say it was no barbarous manner of preceding. The Goths, Vandals, and Longobards,[2] whose coming down like an innundation overwhelmed, as they say, all the glory of learning in Europe, have yet left us still their laws and customs as the originals of most of the provincial constitutions of Christendom, which well-considered with their other course of government may serve to clear them from this imputation of ignorance. And though the vanquished never yet spoke well of the conqueror,[3] yet even through the unsound coverings of malediction appear those monuments of truth as argue well their worth and proves them not without judgment, though without Greek and Latin.

6. Endings, as in rhyme.
7. A well-constructed sentence.
8. Meters used in classical poetry.
9. Imagination.
1. Discriminating.
2. Lombards.
3. Daniels refers to the culture of conquered peoples without specifying which conquests or peoples he has in mind. But he acknowledges that even in the curses of these peoples, as they complain about their conquerors, there are "monuments of truth" that reveal worth and judgment.

from The Arcadia

Book 1

To My Dear Lady and Sister
The Countess of Pembroke[1]

Here now have you (most dear, and most worthy to be most dear, lady) this idle work of mine, which I fear (like the spider's web) will be thought fitter to be swept away than worn to any other purpose. For my part, in very truth (as the cruel fathers among the Greeks were wont to do to the babes they would not foster) I could well find in my heart to cast out in some desert of forgetfulness this child which I am loath to father. But you desired me to do it, and your desire to my heart is an absolute commandment. Now it is done only for you, only to you; if you keep it to yourself, or to such friends who will weigh errors in the balance of goodwill, I hope, for the father's sake, it will be pardoned, perchance made much of, though in itself it have deformities. For indeed, for severer eyes it is not, being but a trifle, and that triflingly handled. Your dear self can best witness the manner, being done in loose sheets of paper, most of it in your presence, the rest by sheets sent unto you as fast as they were done. In sum, a young head not so well stayed[2] as I would it were (and shall be when God will) having many many fancies begotten in it, if it had not been in some way delivered, would have grown a monster, and more sorry might I be that they came in than that they gat[3] out. But his chief safety shall be the not walking abroad; and his chief protection the bearing the livery of your name which (if much much goodwill do not deceive me) is worthy to be a sanctuary for a greater offender.[4] This say I because I know the virtue so; and this say I because it may be ever so; or, to say better, because it will be ever so. Read it then at your idle times, and the follies your good judgment will find in it, blame not, but laugh at. And so, looking for no better stuff than, as in a haberdasher's shop, glasses or feathers, you will continue to love the writer who doth exceedingly love you, and most most heartily prays you may long live to be a principal ornament to the family of the Sidneys.

Your loving brother,
Philip Sidney

The First Book or Act of The Countess of Pembroke's Arcadia

Arcadia[5] among all the provinces of Greece was ever had in singular reputation, partly for the sweetness of the air and other natural benefits, but principally for the moderate and well tempered minds of the people who (finding how true a contentation[6] is gotten by following the course of nature, and how the shining title of glory, so much affected by other nations, doth indeed help little to the happiness of life) were the only people which, as by their justice and providence gave neither cause nor

1. Sidney originally composed the *Arcadia* for his sister, Mary Herbert, the Countess of Pembroke. The work was begun about 1580, at Wilton, the Pembroke estate. Sidney completed a first version in 1581; he began but did not complete a revision in 1583–1584. His sister published the unfinished revision in 1590, then published a new edition in 1593, completing the work by adding in the last two books of the first version.
2. Balanced.
3. Got.
4. Sidney indicates that he wants his romance to be circulated privately and not published; additionally, it is protected from criticism by being dedicated to his sister.
5. A region located in the middle of the Peloponnesian peninsula, surrounded by mountains and very fertile; it was considered to be the place in which pastoral poetry originated.
6. Contentment.

hope to their neighbors to annoy them, so were they not stirred with false praise to trouble others' quiet, thinking it a small reward for the wasting of their own lives in ravening[7] that their posterity should long after say they had done so. Even the muses seemed to approve their good determination by choosing that country as their chiefest repairing place, and by bestowing their perfections so largely there that the very shepherds themselves had their fancies opened to so high conceits[8] as the most learned of other nations have been long time since content both to borrow their names and imitate their cunning. In this place some time there dwelled a mighty duke named Basilius,[9] a prince of sufficient skill to govern so quiet a country where the good minds of the former princes had set down good laws, and the well bringing up of the people did serve as a most sure bond to keep them. He married Gynecia,[1] the daughter of the king of Cyprus; a lady worthy enough to have had her name in continual remembrance if her latter time had not blotted her well governed youth, although the wound fell more to her own conscience than to the knowledge of the world, fortune something supplying her want of virtue. Of her the duke had two fair daughters, the elder Pamela,[2] the younger Philoclea,[3] both so excellent in all those gifts which are allotted to reasonable creatures as they seemed to be born for a sufficient proof that nature is no stepmother to that sex, how much soever the rugged disposition of some men, sharp-witted only in evil speaking, hath sought to disgrace them. And thus grew they on in each good increase till Pamela, a year older than Philoclea, came to the point of seventeen years of age. At which time the duke Basilius—not so much stirred with the care for his country and children as with the vanity which possesseth many who, making a perpetual mansion of this poor baiting place of man's life,[4] are desirous to know the certainty of things to come, wherein there is nothing so certain as our continual uncertainty—Basilius, I say, would needs undertake a journey to Delphos,[5] there by the oracle to inform himself whether the rest of his life should be continued in like tenor of happiness as thitherunto it had been, accompanied with the wellbeing of his wife and children, whereupon he had placed greatest part of his own felicity. Neither did he long stay; but the woman appointed to that impiety, furiously inspired, gave him in verse this answer:

Thy elder care shall from thy careful face
By princely mean be stolen and yet not lost;
Thy younger shall with nature's bliss embrace
An uncouth love, which nature hateth most.
Thou with thy wife adult'ry shalt commit,
And in thy throne a foreign state shall sit.
All this on thee this fatal year shall hit.

Which, as in part it was more obscure than he could understand, so did the whole bear such manifest threatenings, that his amazement was greater than his fore[6] curiosity—both passions proceeding out of one weakness: in vain to desire to know that of which in vain thou shalt be sorry after thou hast known it. But thus the duke answered though not satisfied, he returned into his country with a countenance well

7. Plundering.
8. Conceptions.
9. "King."
1. "Womanly."
2. "All sweetness."
3. "Lover of glory."
4. A place in which human beings are "baited" or tempted by the prospect of learning the future.
5. A town in Greece famous for its oracle of Apollo. Its priestess, called the Pythia, uttered obscure prophecies, which were interpreted by a priest.
6. Earlier.

witnessing the dismayedness of his heart; which notwithstanding upon good considerations he thought not good to disclose, but only to one chosen friend of his named Philanax, whom he had ever found a friend not only in affection but judgment, and no less of the duke than dukedom[7]—a rare temper, whilst most men either servilely yield to all appetites, or with an obstinate austerity, looking to that they fancy good, wholly neglect the prince's person. But such was this man; and in such a man had Basilius been happy if his mind, corrupted with a prince's fortune, had not resolved to use a friend's secrecy rather for confirmation of fancies than correcting of errors, which in this weighty matter he well showed. For having with many words discovered unto him both the cause and success of his Delphos journey, in the end he told him that, to prevent all these inconveniences of the loss of his crown and children (for as for the point of his wife, he could no way understand it), he was resolved for this fatal year to retire himself with his wife and daughters into a solitary place where, being two lodges built of purpose, he would in the one of them recommend his daughter Pamela to his principal herdman—a place in that world, not so far gone into painted vanities, of some credit—by name Dametas, in whose blunt truth he had great confidence, thinking it a contrary salve against the destiny threatening her mishap by a prince to place her with a shepherd. In the other lodge he and his wife would keep their younger jewel, Philoclea; and because the oracle touched some strange love of hers, have the more care of her, in especial keeping away her nearest kinsmen, whom he deemed chiefly understood, and therewithal all other likely to move any such humor.[8] And so for himself, being so cruelly menaced by fortune, he would draw himself out of her way by this loneliness, which he thought was the surest mean to avoid her blows; where for his pleasure he would be recreated with all those sports and eclogues[9] wherein the shepherds of that country did much excel. As for the government of the country, and in especial manning of his frontiers (for that only way he thought a foreign prince might endanger his crown), he would leave the charge to certain selected persons; the superintendence of all which he would commit to Philanax. And so ended he his speech, for fashion's sake asking him his counsel. But Philanax, having forthwith taken into the depth of his consideration both what the duke said and with what mind he spake it, with a true heart and humble countenance in this sort answered:

"Most redoubted[1] and beloved prince, if as well it had pleased you at your going to Delphos, as now, to have used my humble service, both I should in better season and to better purpose have spoken, and you perhaps at this time should have been, as no way more in danger, so undoubtedly much more in quietness. I would then have said unto you that wisdom and virtue be the only destinies appointed to man to follow, wherein one ought to place all his knowledge, since they be such guides as cannot fail which, besides their inward comfort, do make a man see so direct a way of proceeding as prosperity must necessarily ensue. And, although the wickedness of the world should oppress it, yet could it not be said that evil happened to him who should fall accompanied with virtue; so that, either standing or falling with virtue, a man is never in evil case. I would then have said the heavenly powers to be reverenced and not searched into, and their mercy rather by prayers to be sought than their hidden counsels by curiosity; these kinds of soothsaying sorceries (since the

7. Philanax ("lover of lordship") was a friend not only to the duke, Basilius, but also to Basilius's dukedom, the province of Arcadia.

8. Mood.

9. Pastoral poems.

1. Dreaded.

heavens have left us in ourselves sufficient guides) to be nothing but fancies wherein there must either be vanity or infallibleness, and so either not to be respected or not to be prevented. But since it is weakness too much to remember what should have been done, and that your commandment stretcheth to know what shall be done, I do, most dear lord, with humble boldness say that the manner of your determination doth in no sort better please me than the cause of your going.[2] These thirty years past have you so governed this realm that neither your subjects have wanted justice in you, nor you obedience in them; and your neighbors have found you so hurtlessly strong that they thought it better to rest in your friendship than make new trial of your enmity. If this, then, have proceeded out of the good constitution of your state, and out of a wise providence generally to prevent all those things which might encumber your happiness, why should you now seek new courses, since your own example comforts you to continue on, and that it is most certain no destiny nor influence whatsoever can bring man's wit to a higher point than wisdom and goodness? Why should you deprive yourself of governing your dukedom for fear of losing your dukedom, like one that should kill himself for fear of death? Nay rather, if this oracle be to be accounted of, arm up your courage the more against it; for who will stick to him that abandons himself? Let your subjects have you in their eyes, let them see the benefits of your justice daily more and more; and so must they needs rather like of present sureties[3] than uncertain changes. Lastly, whether your time call you to live or die, do both like a prince. And even the same mind hold I as touching my ladies, your daughters, in whom nature promiseth nothing but goodness, and their education by your fatherly care hath been hitherto such as hath been most fit to restrain all evil, giving their minds virtuous delights, and not grieving them for want of well ruled liberty: now to fall to a sudden straitening them, what can it do but argue suspicion, the most venomous gall to virtue? Leave women's minds, the most untamed that way of any; see whether any cage can please a bird, or whether a dog grow not fiercer with tying. What doth jealousy else but stir up the mind to think what it is from which they are restrained? For they are treasures or things of great delight which men use to hide for the aptness they have to catch men's fancies; and the thoughts once awaked to that, harder sure it is to keep those thoughts from accomplishment than it had been before to have kept the mind (which, being the chief part, by this means is defiled) from thinking. Now, for the recommending so principal a charge of her, whose mind goes beyond the governing of many hundreds of such, to such a person as Dametas is, besides that the thing in itself is strange, it comes of a very ill ground that ignorance should be the mother of faithfulness. O no, he cannot be good that knows not why he is good, but stands so far good as his fortune may keep him unassayed. But coming to that, his rude[4] simplicity is either easily changed or easily deceived; and so grows that to be the last excuse of his fault which seemed to have been the first foundation of his faith.[5] Thus far hath your commandment and my zeal drawn me to speak; which I, like a man in a valley may discern hills, or like a poor passenger may spy a rock, so humbly submit to your gracious consideration, beseeching you to stand wholly upon your own virtue as the surest way to maintain you in that you are, and to avoid any evil which may be imagined."

2. Philanax advises Basilius that he should neither be curious to know the future nor abandon his dukedom for a new way of life, in this case, in the country and away from his subjects.
3. Certainties.
4. Rural.
5. Dametas has been chosen to guard Pamela because he is simple; but he may fail to guard her well because he is simple.

Whilst Philanax used these words, a man might see in the duke's face that, as he was wholly wedded to his own opinion, so was he grieved to have any man say that which he had not seen. Yet did the goodwill he bare to Philanax so far prevail with him that he passed into no further choler,[6] but with short manner asked him: "And would you, then," said he, "that in change of fortune I shall not change my determination,[7] as we do our apparel according to the air, and as the ship doth her course with the wind?"

"Truly sir," answered he, "neither do I as yet see any change; and though I did, yet would I think a constant virtue,[8] settled, little subject unto it. And, as in great necessity I would allow a well proportioned change,[9] so in the sight of an enemy to arm himself the lighter, or at every puff of wind to strike sail, is such a change as either will breed ill success or no success."

"To give place to blows", said the duke, "is thought no small wisdom."

"That is true," said Philanax, "but to give place before they come takes away the occasion, when they come, to give place."

"Yet the reeds stand with yielding," said the duke.

"And so are they but reeds, most worthy prince," said Philanax, "but the rocks stand still and are rocks."

But the duke, having used thus much dukely sophistry to deceive himself, and making his will wisdom, told him resolutely he stood upon his own determination; and therefore willed him, with certain other he named, to take the government of the state, and especially to keep narrow watch of the frontiers. Philanax, acknowledging himself much honored by so great trust, went with as much care to perform his commandment as before he had with faith yielded his counsel, which in the latter short disputations he had rather proportioned to Basilius's words than to any towardness[1] of argument. And Basilius, according to his determination, retired himself into the solitary place of the two lodges, where he was daily delighted with the eclogues and pastimes of shepherds. In the one of which lodges he himself remained with his wife and the beauty of the world, Philoclea; in the other, near unto him, he placed his daughter Pamela with Dametas, whose wife was Miso and daughter Mopsa, unfit company for so excellent a creature, but to exercise her patience and to serve for a foil to her perfections.

Now, newly after that the duke had begun this solitary life, there came (following the train their virtues led them) into this country two young princes: the younger, but chiefer, named Pyrocles, only son to Euarchus, king of Macedon; the other his cousin german,[2] Musidorus, duke of Thessalia;[3] both like in virtues, near in years, near in blood, but nearest of all in friendship. And because this matter runs principally of them, a few more words how they came hither will not be superfluous. Euarchus, king of Macedon, a prince of such justice that he never thought himself privileged by being a prince, nor did measure greatness by anything but by goodness; as he did thereby root an awful[4] love in his subjects towards him, so yet could he not avoid the assaults of envy—the enemy and yet the honor of virtue. For the kings of Thrace, Pannonia, and Epirus,[5] not being able to attain his perfections, thought in their base

6. Anger.
7. Way of life.
8. Resolute mind.
9. I.e., a change in a way of life must suit the challenge that confronts it.
1. Aptness.
2. First cousin.
3. Pyrocles: first glory; Euarchus: good ruler; Musidorus: gift of the Muses. Macedon and Thessalia, or Thessaly, were regions in northern Greece.
4. Full of awe.
5. Regions in Greece to the north and west of Arcadia; their kings do not wish to be compared unfavorably to Euarchus.

wickedness best to take away so odious a comparison, lest his virtues, joined now to the fame and force of the Macedonians, might in time both conquer the bodies and win the minds of their subjects. And thus conspiring together, they did three sundry ways enter into his kingdom at one time. Which sudden and dangerous invasions, although they did nothing astonish Euarchus, who carried a heart prepared for all extremities (as a man that knew both what ill might happen to a man never so prosperous, and withal[6] what the uttermost of that ill was), yet were they cause that Euarchus did send away his young son Pyrocles, at that time but six years old, to his sister, the dowager and regent of Thessalia, there to be brought up with her son Musidorus. Which, though it proceeded of necessity, yet was not the counsel in itself unwise, the sweet emulation that grew being an excellent nurse of the good parts in these two princes, two princes indeed born to the exercise of virtue. For they, accompanying the increase of their years with the increase of all good inward and outward qualities, and taking very timely into their minds that the divine part of man was not enclosed in this body for nothing, gave themselves wholly over to those knowledges which might in the course of their life be ministers to well doing. And so grew they on till Pyrocles came to be seventeen and Musidorus eighteen years of age; at which time Euarchus, having after ten years' war conquered the kingdom of Thrace and brought the other two to be his tributaries, lived in the principal city of Thrace called at that time Byzantium,[7] whither he sent for his son and nephew to delight his aged eyes in them and to make them enjoy the fruits of his victories. But so pleased it God, who reserved them to greater traverses,[8] both of good and evil fortune, that the sea, to which they committed themselves, stirred with terrible tempest, forced them to fall far from their course upon the coast of Lydia[9] where, what befell unto them, what valiant acts they did, passing in one year's space through the lesser Asia, Syria, and Egypt, how many ladies they defended from wrongs, and disinherited persons restored to their rights, it is a work for a higher style than mine. This only shall suffice: that their fame returned so fast before them into Greece that the king of Macedon received that as the comfort of their absence, although accompanied with so much more longing as he found the manifestation of their worthiness greater. But they, desirous more and more to exercise their virtues and increase their experience, took their journey from Egypt towards Greece. Which they did, they two alone, because, that being their native country they might have the most perfect knowledge of it; wherein they that hold the countenances of princes have their eyes most dazzled.

And so, taking Arcadia in their way, for the fame of the country, they came thither newly after that this strange solitariness had possessed Basilius. Now so fell it unto them that they, lodging in the house of Kerxenus, a principal gentleman in Mantinea, so was the city called, near to the solitary dwelling of the duke, it was Pyrocles' either evil or good fortune walking with his host in a fair gallery that he perceived a picture, newly made by an excellent artificer, which contained the duke and duchess with their younger daughter Philoclea, with such countenance and fashion as the manner of their life held them in, both the parents' eyes cast with a loving care upon their beautiful child, she drawn as well as it was possible art should counterfeit so perfect a workmanship of nature. For therein, besides the show of her beauties, a man might judge even the nature of her countenance, full of bashfulness, love, and reverence—and all by the cast of her eye—, mixed with a sweet grief to find her

6. Also.
7. A city on the Bosporus, today the site of Istanbul.
8. Adventures.
9. Western Asia Minor.

virtue suspected. This moved Pyrocles to fall into questions of her; wherein being answered by the gentleman as much as he understood, which was of her strange kind of captivity; neither was it known how long it should last; and there was a general opinion grown the duke would grant his daughters in marriage to nobody. As the most noble heart is most subject unto it,[1] from questions grew to pity; and when with pity once his heart was made tender, according to the aptness of the humor, it received straight a cruel impression of that wonderful passion which to be defined is impossible, by reason no words reach near to the strange nature of it. They only know it which inwardly feel it. It is called love. Yet did not the poor youth at first know his disease, thinking it only such a kind of desire as he was wont to have to see unwonted sights, and his pity to be no other but the fruits of his gentle nature. But even this arguing with himself came of a further thought; and the more he argued, the more his thought increased. Desirous he was to see the place where she remained, as though the architecture of the lodges would have been much for his learning; but more desirous to see herself, to be judge, forsooth, of the painter's cunning—for thus at the first did he flatter himself, as though his wound had been no deeper. But when within short time he came to the degree of uncertain wishes, and that those wishes grew to unquiet longings; when he could fix his thoughts upon nothing but that, within a little varying, they should end with Philoclea; when each thing he saw seemed to figure out some part of his passions, and that he heard no word spoken but that he imagined it carried the sound of Philoclea's name; then did poor Pyrocles yield to the burden, finding himself prisoner before he had leisure to arm himself, and that he might well, like the spaniel, gnaw upon the chain that ties him, but he should sooner mar his teeth than procure liberty. Then was his chief delight secretly to draw his dear friend a-walking to the desert[2] of the two lodges where he saw no grass upon which he thought Philoclea might hap to tread but that he envied the happiness of it; and yet, with a contrary folly, would sometimes recommend his whole estate unto it. Till at length love, the refiner of invention, put in his head a way how to come to the sight of his Philoclea; for which he with great speed and secrecy prepared everything that was necessary for his purpose, but yet would not put it in execution till he had disclosed it to Musidorus, both to perform the true laws of friendship and withal to have his counsel and allowance. And yet, out of the sweetness of his disposition, was bashfully afraid to break it with him to whom (besides other bonds), because he was his elder, he bare a kind of reverence, until some fit opportunity might, as it were, draw it from him. Which occasion time shortly presented unto him.

For Musidorus, having informed himself fully of the strength and riches of the country; of the nature of the people, and of the manner of their laws; and seeing the duke's court could not be visited, and that they came not without danger to that place, prohibited to all men but to certain shepherds, grew no less weary of his abode there than marvelled of the great delight Pyrocles took in that place. Whereupon one day, at Pyrocles' earnest request being walked thither again, began in this manner to say unto him:

"A mind well trained and long exercised in virtue, my sweet and worthy cousin, doth not easily change any course it once undertakes but upon well grounded and well weighed causes; for being witness to itself of his own inward good, it finds nothing without it of so high a price for which it should be altered. Even the very countenance and behavior of such a man doth show forth images of the same constancy by

1. I.e., pity.

2. Barren countryside.

maintaining a right harmony betwixt it and the inward good in yielding itself suitable to the virtuous resolutions of the mind. This speech I direct to you, noble friend Pyrocles, the excellency of whose mind and well chosen course in virtue, if I do not sufficiently know, having seen such rare demonstrations of it, it is my weakness and not your unworthiness. But as indeed I do know it, and knowing it, most dearly love both it and him that hath it, so must I needs say that since our late[3] coming into this country I have marked in you, I will not say an alteration, but a relenting, truly, and slacking of the main career you had so notably begun and almost performed; and that, in such sort as I cannot find sufficient reasons in my great love towards you how to allow it. For, to leave off other secreter arguments which my acquaintance with you makes me easily find, this in effect to any man may be manifest: that, whereas you were wont, in all the places you came, to give yourself vehemently to knowledge of those things which might better your mind; to seek the familiarity of excellent men in learning and soldiery; and lastly, to put all these things in practice both by continual wise proceeding and worthy enterprises, as occasions fell for them; you now leave all these things undone; you let your mind fall asleep, besides your countenance troubled (which surely comes not out of virtue; for virtue, like the clear heaven, is without clouds); and lastly, which seemeth strangest unto me, you haunt greatly this place, wherein, besides the disgrace that might fall of it (which, that it hath not already fallen upon you, is rather luck than providence, this duke having sharply forbidden it), you subject yourself to solitariness, the sly enemy that doth most separate a man from well doing."

These words, spoken vehemently and proceeding from so dearly an esteemed friend as Musidorus, did so pierce poor Pyrocles that his blushing cheeks did witness with him he rather could not help, than did not know, his fault. Yet, desirous by degrees to bring his friend to a gentler consideration of him, and beginning with two or three broken sighs, answered him to this

"Excellent Musidorus, in the praises you gave me in the beginning of your speech, I easily acknowledge the force of your goodwill unto me; for neither could you have thought so well of me if extremity of love had not something[4] dazzled your eyes, nor you could have loved me so entirely if you had not been apt to make so great, though undeserved, judgment of me. And even so must I say of those imperfections, to which though I have ever through weakness been subject, yet you by the daily mending of your mind have of late been able to look into them, which before you could not discern; so that the change you spake of falls not out by my impairing but by your bettering. And yet, under the leave of your better judgment, I must needs say thus much, my dear cousin, that I find not myself wholly to be condemned because I do not with a continual vehemency follow those knowledges which you call the bettering of my mind; for both the mind itself must, like other things, sometimes be unbent, or else it will be either weakened or broken, and these knowledges, as they are of good use, so are they not all the mind may stretch itself unto. Who knows whether I feed not my mind with higher thoughts? Truly, as I know not all the particularities, so yet see I the bounds of all those knowledges; but the workings of the mind, I find, much more infinite than can be led unto by the eye or imagined by any that distract their thoughts without[5] themselves. And in such contemplations, or, as I think, more excellent, I enjoy my solitariness; and my solitariness, perchance,

3. Recent.
4. Somewhat.
5. Beyond.

is the nurse of these contemplations. Eagles, we see, fly alone; and they are but sheep which always herd together. Condemn not, therefore, my mind sometimes to enjoy itself, nor blame not the taking of such times as serve most fit for it!"

And here Pyrocles suddenly stopped, like a man unsatisfied in himself, though his wit might well have served to have satisfied another. And so, looking with a countenance as though he desired he should know his mind without hearing him speak, and yet desirous to speak to breathe out some part of his inward evil, sending again new blood to his face, he continued his speech in this manner:

"And lord! dear cousin," said he, "doth not the pleasantness of this place carry in itself sufficient reward for any time lost in it, or for any such danger that might ensue? Do you not see how everything conspires together to make this place a heavenly dwelling? Do you not see the grass, how in color they excel the emeralds, everyone striving to pass his fellow—and yet they are all kept in an equal height? And see you not the rest of all these beautiful flowers, each of which would require a man's wit to know, and his life to express? Do not these stately trees seem to maintain their flourishing old age with the only happiness of their seat, being clothed with a continual spring because no beauty here should ever fade? Doth not the air breathe health, which the birds, delightful both to the ear and eye, do daily solemnize with the sweet concent of their voices? Is not every echo here a perfect music? And these fresh and delightful brooks, how slowly they slide away, as loath to leave the company of so many things united in perfection! And with how sweet a murmur they lament their forced departure! Certainly, certainly, cousin, it must needs be that some goddess this desert belongs unto, who is the soul of this soil; for neither is any less than a goddess worthy to be shrined in such a heap of pleasures, nor any less than a goddess could have made it so perfect a model of the heavenly dwellings."

And so he ended, with a deep sigh, ruefully casting his eye upon Musidorus, as more desirous of pity than pleading. But Musidorus had all this while held his look fixed upon Pyrocles' countenance, and with no less loving attention marked how his words proceeded from him. But in both these he perceived such strange diversities that they rather increased new doubts than gave him ground to settle any judgment; for, besides his eyes sometimes even great with tears, the oft changing of his color, with a kind of shaking unstaidness[6] over all his body, he might see in his countenance some great determination mixed with fear, and might perceive in him store of thoughts rather stirred than digested, his words interrupted continually with sighs which served as a burden to each sentence, and the tenor of his speech (though of his wonted phrase) not knit together to one constant end but rather dissolved in itself, as the vehemency of the inward passion prevailed: which made Musidorus frame his answer nearest to that humor which should soonest put out the secret. For, having in the beginning of Pyrocles' speech which defended his solitariness framed in his mind a reply against it in the praise of honorable action (in showing that such kind of contemplation is but a glorious title to idleness; that in action a man did not only better himself but benefit others; that the gods would not have delivered a soul into the body which hath arms and legs (only instruments of doing) but that it were intended the mind should employ them; and that the mind should best know his own good or evil by practice; which knowledge was the only way to increase the one and correct the other; besides many other better arguments which the plentifulness of the matter yielded to the sharpness of his wit), when he found Pyrocles leave that, and fall to

6. Unsteadiness.

such an affected praising of the place, he left it likewise, and joined therein with him because he found him in that humor utter most store of passion.[7] And even thus, kindly embracing him, he said:

"Your words are such, noble cousin, so sweetly and strongly handled in the praise of solitariness, as they would make me likewise yield myself up unto it, but that the same words make me know it is more pleasant to enjoy the company of him that can speak such words than by such words to be persuaded to follow solitariness. And even so do I give you leave, sweet Pyrocles, ever to defend solitariness so long as, to defend it, you ever keep company. But I marvel at the excessive praises you give to this desert. In truth, it is not unpleasant; but yet, if you would return into Macedon, you should see either many heavens or find this no more than earthly. And even Tempe[8], in my Thessalia, where you and I (to my great happiness) were brought up together, is nothing inferior unto it. But I think you will make me see that the vigor of your wit can show itself in any subject; or else you feed sometimes your solitariness with the conceits[9] of the poets whose liberal pens can as easily travel over mountains as mole-hills, and so (like well disposed men) set up everything to the highest note[1]—especially when they put such words in the mouth of one of these fantastical mind-infected people that children and musicians call lovers."

This word of "lover" did no less pierce poor Pyrocles than the right tune of music toucheth him that is sick of the tarantula.[2] There was not one part of his body that did not feel a sudden motion, the heart drawing unto itself the life of every part to help it, distressed with the sound of that word. Yet, after some pause, lifting up his eyes a little from the ground, and yet not daring to place them in the face of Musidorus, armed with the very countenance of the poor prisoner at the bar[3] whose answer is nothing but "guilty," with much ado he brought forth this question:

"And alas," said he, "dear cousin, what if I be not so much the poet, the freedom of whose pen can exercise itself in anything, as even that very miserable subject of his cunning whereof you speak?"

"Now the eternal gods forbid," mainly[4] cried out Musidorus. But Pyrocles, having broken the ice, pursued on in this manner:

"And yet such a one am I," said he, "and in such extremity as no man can feel but myself, nor no man believe; since no man ever could taste the hundredth part of that which lies in the inwardmost part of my soul. For since it was the fatal overthrow of all my liberty to see in the gallery of Mantinea the only Philoclea's picture, that beauty did pierce so through mine eyes to my heart that the impression of it doth not lie but live there, in such sort as the question is not now whether I shall love or no, but whether loving, I shall live or die."

Musidorus was no less astonished with these words of his friend than if, thinking him in health, he had suddenly told him that he felt the pangs of death oppress him. So that, amazedly looking upon him (even as Apollo is painted when he saw Daphne suddenly turned to a laurel),[5] he was not able to say one word; but gave Pyrocles occasion, having already made the breach, to pass on in this sort:

7. Musidorus stops reasoning with Pyrocles because he realizes that Pyrocles' mood is such that he can express only passion.
8. A valley in Thessaly known for its abundant vegetation and mild climate.
9. Images.
1. Musidorus remarks that poets, who describe their subjects in exaggerated terms, can provoke a desire for solitude in impressionable audiences, such as lovers and children.
2. Poisonous spider.
3. On trial.
4. Vigorously.
5. Apollo loved the nymph Daphne, who, rejecting his attentions, fled from him; just before he caught up with her, the gods turned her into a laurel tree.

"And because I have laid open my wound, noble cousin," said he, "I will show you what my melancholy hath brought forth for the preparation at least of a salve, if it be not in itself a medicine. I am resolved, because all direct ways are barred me of opening my suit to the duke, to take upon me the estate of an Amazon lady[6] going about the world to practise feats of chivalry and to seek myself a worthy husband. I have already provided all furniture[7] necessary for it; and my face, you see, will not easily discover[8] me. And hereabout will I haunt till, by the help of this disguising, I may come to the presence of her whose imprisonment darkens the world, that my own eyes may be witnesses to my heart it is great reason why he should be thus captived. And then, as I shall have attained to the first degree of my happiness, so will fortune, occasion, and mine own industry put forward the rest. For the principal point is to set in a good way the thing we desire; for then will time itself daily discover new secret helps. As for my name, it shall be Cleophila,[9] turning Philoclea to myself, as my mind is wholly turned and transformed into her. Now therefore do I submit myself to your counsel, dear cousin, and crave your help."

And thus he ended, as who should say, "I have told you all, have pity on me." But Musidorus had by this time gathered his spirits together, dismayed to see him he loved more than himself plunged in such a course of misery. And so, when Pyrocles had ended, casting a ghastful[1] countenance upon him, as if he would conjure some strange spirit he saw possess him, with great vehemency uttered these words:

"And is it possible that this is Pyrocles, the only young prince in the world, formed by nature and framed by education to the true exercise of virtue? Or is it, indeed, some Amazon Cleophila that hath counterfeited the face of my friend in this sort to vex me? For likelier, sure, I would have thought it that any outward face might have been disguised than that the face of so excellent a mind could have been thus blemished. O sweet Pyrocles, separate yourself a little, if it be possible, from yourself, and let your own mind look upon your own proceedings; so shall my words be needless, and you best instructed. See with yourself how fit it will be for you in this your tender youth (born so great a prince, of so rare, not only expectation, but proof, desired of your old father, and wanted of your native country, now so near your home) to divert your thoughts from the way of goodness to lose, nay to abuse, your time; lastly, to overthrow all the excellent things you have done, which have filled the world with your fame (as if you should drown your ship in the long-desired haven, or like an ill player should mar the last act of his tragedy). Remember (for I know you know it) that, if we will be men, the reasonable part of our soul is to have absolute commandment, against which if any sensual weakness arise, we are to yield all our sound forces to the overthrowing of so unnatural a rebellion; wherein, how can we want courage, since we are to deal against so weak an adversary that in itself is nothing but weakness? Nay, we are to resolve that if reason direct it, we must do it; and if we must do it, we will do it; for to say I cannot is childish, and I will not womanish. And see how extremely every way you endanger your mind; for to take this woman's habit, without you frame your behavior accordingly, is wholly vain; your behavior can never come kindly[2] from you but as the mind is proportioned unto it. So that you must resolve, if you will play your part to any purpose, whatsoever peevish imperfections are in that sex, to soften your heart to receive them—the very first

6. A race of female warriors alleged to exist in ancient Scythia (now in Russia); hence any female warrior.
7. Equipment.
8. Identify.
9. "Glory of love."
1. Ghostlike.
2. Naturally.

down step to all wickedness. For do not deceive yourself, my dear cousin; there is no man suddenly either excellently good or extremely evil, but grows either as he holds himself up in virtue or lets himself slide to viciousness. And let us see what power is the author of all these troubles: forsooth, love; love, a passion, and the basest and fruitlessest of all passions. Fear breedeth wit; anger is the cradle of courage; joy openeth and enableth the heart; sorrow, as it closeth it, so yet draweth it inward to look to the correcting of itself. And so all of them generally have power towards some good, by the direction of reason. But this bastard love (for, indeed, the name of love is unworthily applied to so hateful a humor as it is, engendered betwixt lust and idleness), as the matter it works upon is nothing but a certain base weakness, which some gentle fools call a gentle heart; as his adjoined companions be unquietness, longings, fond comforts, faint discomforts, hopes, jealousies, ungrounded rages, causeless yieldings; so is the highest end it aspires unto a little pleasure, with much pain before, and great repentance after. But that end, how endlessly it runs to infinite evils, were fit enough for the matter we speak of; but not for your ears, in whom, indeed, there is so much true disposition to virtue. Yet thus much of his worthy effects in yourself is to be seen: that it utterly subverts the course of nature in making reason give place to sense, and man to woman. And truly, I think, hereupon it first gat the name of love. For, indeed, the true love hath that excellent nature in it, that it doth transform the very essence of the lover into the thing loved, uniting and, as it were, incorporating it with a secret and inward working. And herein do these kinds of love imitate the excellent; for, as the love of heaven makes one heavenly, the love of virtue, virtuous, so doth the love of the world make one become worldly. And this effeminate love of a woman doth so womanize a man that, if you yield to it, it will not only make you a famous Amazon, but a launder, a distaff-spinner,[3] or whatsoever other vile occupation their idle heads can imagine and their weak hands perform. Therefore, to trouble you no longer with my tedious but loving words, if either you remember what you are, what you have been, or what you must be; if you consider what it is that moves you, or for what kind of creature you are moved, you shall find the cause so small, the effects so dangerous, yourself so unworthy to run into the one or to be driven by the other, that I doubt not I shall quickly have occasion rather to praise you for having conquered it than to give you any further counsel how to do it."

Pyrocles' mind was all this while so fixed upon another devotion that he no more attentively marked his friend's discourse than the child that hath leave to play marks the last part of his lesson, or the diligent pilot in a dangerous tempest doth attend to the unskillful words of the passenger. Yet, the very sound having left the general points of his speech in his mind, the respect he bare to his friend brought forth this answer, having first paid up his late-accustomed tribute of sighs:

"Dear and worthy friend, whatsoever good disposition nature hath bestowed on me, or howsoever that disposition hath been by bringing up confirmed, this must I confess: that I am not yet come to that degree of wisdom to think lightly of the sex of whom I have my life; since, if I be anything (which your friendship rather finds than I acknowledge), I was to come to it born of a woman and nursed of a woman.[4] And certainly (for this point of your speech doth nearest touch me) it is strange to see the unmanlike cruelty of mankind who, not content with their tyrannous ambition to have brought the others' virtuous patience under them, like childish masters, think

3. A person who washes clothes or spins thread—occupations usually reserved for women.

4. In the speech that follows, Pyrocles rehearses many of the arguments proposed in contemporary defenses of women.

their masterhood nothing without doing injury to them who (if we will argue by reason) are framed of nature with the same parts of the mind for the exercise of virtue as we are. And, for example, even this estate[5] of Amazons, which I now for my greatest honor do seek to counterfeit, doth well witness that, if generally the sweetness of their disposition did not make them see the vainness of these things which we account glorious, they neither want[6] valor of mind, nor yet doth their fairness take away their force. And truly, we men and praisers of men should remember that, if we have such excellencies, it is reason to think them excellent creatures of whom we are, since a kite[7] never brought forth a good flying hawk. But to tell you true, I do both disdain to use any more words of such a subject which is so praised in itself as it needs no praises; and withal fear lest my conceit (not able to reach unto them) bring forth words which for their unworthiness may be a disgrace to them I so inwardly honor. Let this suffice: that they are capable of virtue. And virtue, you yourself say, is to be loved; and I, too, truly. But this I willingly confess: that it likes me much better when I find virtue in a fair lodging than when I am bound to seek it in an ill-favored creature, like a pearl in a dunghill."

And here Pyrocles stayed as to breathe himself, having been transported with a little vehemency because it seemed him Musidorus had over bitterly glanced against the reputation of womankind. But then quieting his countenance, as well as out of an unquiet mind it might be, he thus proceeded on:

"And poor love," said he, "dear cousin, is little beholding unto you, since you are not contented to spoil it of the honor of the highest power of the mind (which notable men have attributed unto it), but you deject it below all other passions—in truth, something strangely since, if love receive any disgrace, it is by the company of those passions you prefer unto it. For those kinds of bitter objections (as that lust, idleness, and a weak heart should be, as it were, the matter and form of love), rather touch me, dear Musidorus, than love. But I am good witness of mine own imperfections, and therefore will not defend myself. But herein, I must say, you deal contrary to yourself; for, if I be so weak, then can you not with reason stir me up, as you did, by the remembrance of mine own virtue. Or if indeed I be virtuous, then must you confess that love hath his working in a virtuous heart. And so no doubt hath it, whatsoever I be.[8] For, if we love virtue, in whom shall we love it but in virtuous creatures?—Without[9] your meaning be I should love this word of virtue when I see it written in a book. Those troublesome effects you say it breeds be not the fault of love, but of him that loves, as an unable vessel to bear such a power—like ill eyes, not able to look on the sun, or like a weak brain, soonest overthrown with the best wine. Even that heavenly love you speak of is accompanied in some hearts with hopes, griefs, longings, and despairs. And in that heavenly love, since there are two parts (the one, the love itself; the other, the excellency of the thing loved), I (not able at the first leap to frame both in myself) do now, like a diligent workman, make ready the chief instrument and first part of that great work, which is love itself. Which, when I have a while practised in this sort, then you shall see me turn it to greater matters. And thus gently you may, if it please you, think of me. Neither doubt you, because I wear a woman's apparel, I will be the more womanish; since, I assure you, for all my apparel, there is nothing I desire more than fully to prove myself a man in this enterprise.

5. Condition.
6. Lack.
7. Small hawk.
8. Pyrocles asserts if love had filled him with vice, Musidorus would have converted him to reason; as he is virtuous, the cause is love, for virtue acquires its character by loving virtue in another person.
9. Unless.

Much might be said in my defence, much more for love, and most of all for that divine creature which hath joined me and love together. But these disputations are fitter for quiet schools than my troubled brains, which are bent rather in deeds to perform, than in words to defend, the noble desire that possesseth me."

"O lord," said Musidorus, "how sharp-witted you are to hurt yourself!"

"No," answered he, "but it is the hurt you speak of which makes me so sharp-witted."

"Even so," said Musidorus, "as every base occupation makes one sharp in that practice and foolish in all the rest."

"Nay rather," answered Pyrocles, "as each excellent thing, once well learned, serves for a measure of all other knowledges."

"And is that become," said Musidorus, "a measure for other things, which never received measure in itself?"

"It is counted without measure," answered Pyrocles, "because the workings of it are without measure; but otherwise in nature it hath measure, since it hath an end allotted unto it."

"The beginning being so excellent, I would gladly know the end."

"Enjoying," answered Pyrocles, with a deep sigh.

"O," said Musidorus, "now set you forth the baseness of it since, if it end in enjoying, it shows all the rest was nothing."

"You mistake me," answered Pyrocles, "I spake of the end to which it is directed; which end ends not no sooner than the life."

"Alas! Let your own brain disenchant you," said Musidorus.

"My heart is too far possessed," said Pyrocles.

"But the head gives you direction."

"And the heart gives me life," answered Pyrocles.

But Musidorus was so grieved to see his beloved friend obstinate, as he thought to his own destruction, that it forced him, with more than accustomed vehemency, to speak these words:

"Well, well," said he, "you list[1] to abuse yourself. It was a very white and red virtue which you could pick out by the sight of a picture. Confess the truth, and you shall find the uttermost was but beauty; a thing which, though it be in as great excellency in yourself as may be in any, yet am I sure you make no further reckoning of it than of an outward fading benefit nature bestowed upon you. And yet, such is your want of a true-grounded virtue (which must be like itself in all points) that what you wisely count a trifle in yourself, you fondly become a slave unto in another. For my part, I now protest I have left nothing unsaid which my wit could make me know, or my most entire friendship to you requires of me. I do now beseech you, even for the love betwixt us (if this other love have left any in you towards me), and for the remembrance of your old careful father (if you can remember him, that forgets yourself), lastly, for Pyrocles' own sake (who is now upon the point of falling or rising), to purge your head of this vile infection. Otherwise, give me leave rather in absence to bewail your mishap than to bide the continual pang of seeing your danger with mine eyes."

The length of these speeches before had not so much cloyed Pyrocles (though he were very impatient of long deliberations) as this last farewell of him he loved as his own life did wound his soul—as, indeed, they that think themselves afflicted are apt to conceive unkindness deeply—; insomuch that, shaking his head, and delivering some show of tears, he thus uttered his griefs:

1. Wish.

"Alas," said he, "Prince Musidorus, how cruelly you deal with me! If you seek the victory, take it; and if you list, triumph. Have you all the reason of the world, and with me remain all the imperfections; yet such as I can no more lay from me than the crow can be persuaded by the swan to cast off his blackness. But truly, you deal with me like a physician that, seeing his patient in a pestilent fever, should chide him instead of ministering help, and bid him be sick no more; or rather, like such a friend that, visiting his friend condemned to perpetual prison and loaden with grievous fetters, should will him to shake off his fetters, or he would leave him. I am sick, and sick to the death. I am prisoner; neither is there any redress but by her to whom I am slave. Now, if you list, leave him that loves you in the highest degree; but remember ever to carry this with you: that you abandon your friend in his greatest need."

And herewith, the deep wound of his love being rubbed afresh with this new unkindness, began, as it were, to bleed again, in such sort that he was unable to bear it any longer; but, gushing out abundance of tears and crossing his arms over his woeful heart, he sank down to the ground. Which sudden trance went so to the heart of Musidorus that, falling down by him, and kissing the weeping eyes of his friend, he besought him not to make account of his speech which, if it had been over vehement, yet was it to be borne withal, because it came out of a love much more vehement; that he had never thought fancy could have received so deep a wound, but now finding in him the force of it, he would no further contrary it, but employ all his service to medicine it in such sort as the nature of it required. But even this kindness made Pyrocles the more melt in the former unkindness, which his manlike tears well showed, with a silent look upon Musidorus, as who should say, "and is it possible that Musidorus should threaten to leave me?" And this strook Musidorus's mind and senses so dumb, too, that for grief not being able to say anything, they rested with their eyes placed one upon another, in such sort as might well paint out the true passion of unkindness, which is never aright but betwixt them that most dearly love.

And thus remained they a time, till at length Musidorus, embracing him, said, "And will you thus shake off your friend?"

"It is you that shake off me," said Pyrocles, "being, for my unperfectness, unworthy of your friendship."

"But this," said Musidorus, "shows you much more unperfect, to be cruel to him that submits himself unto you. But since you are unperfect," said he, smiling, "it is reason you be governed by us wise and perfect men. And that authority will I begin to take upon me with three absolute commandments: the first, that you increase not your evil with further griefs; the second, that you love Philoclea with all the powers of your mind; and the last commandment shall be that you command me to do you what service I can towards the attaining of your desires."

Pyrocles' heart was not so oppressed with the two mighty passions of love and unkindness but that it yielded to some mirth at this commandment of Musidorus that he should love Philoclea. So that, something clearing his face from his former shows of grief, "Well," said he, "dear cousin, I see by the well choosing of your commandments that you are far fitter to be a prince than a councillor. And therefore I am resolved to employ all my endeavor to obey you, with this condition: that the commandments you command me to lay upon you shall only be that you continue to love me, and look upon my imperfections with more affection than judgment."

"Love you," said he, "alas, how can my heart be separated from the true embracing of it without it burst by being too full of it? But," said he, "let us leave off these flowers of new-begun friendship; and since you have found out that way as your readiest remedy, let us go put on your transforming apparel. For my part, I will ever remain hereabouts, either to help you in any necessity or, at least, to be partaker of any evil may fall unto you."

Pyrocles, accepting this as a most notable testimony of his long-approved friendship, and returning to Mantinea where, having taken leave of their host (who, though he knew them not, was in love with their virtue), and leaving with him some apparel and jewels, with opinion they would return after some time unto him, they departed thence to the place where he had left his womanish apparel which, with the help of his friend, he had quickly put on in such sort as it might seem love had not only sharpened his wits but nimbled his hands in anything which might serve to his service. And to begin with his head, thus was he dressed: his hair (which the young men of Greece ware[2] very long, accounting them most beautiful that had that in fairest quantity) lay upon the upper part of his forehead in locks, some curled and some, as it were, forgotten, with such a careless care, and with an art so hiding art, that he seemed he would lay them for a paragon whether nature simply, or nature helped by cunning, be the more excellent. The rest whereof was drawn into a coronet of gold, richly set with pearls, and so joined all over with gold wires, and covered with feathers of divers colors, that it was not unlike to a helmet, such a glittering show it bare, and so bravely it was held up from the head. Upon his body he ware a kind of doublet[3] of sky-color satin, so plated over with plates of massy gold that he seemed armed in it; his sleeves of the same, instead of plates, was covered with purled[4] lace. And such was the nether part of his garment; but that made so full of stuff, and cut after such a fashion that, though the length fell under his ankles, yet in his going one might well perceive the small of the leg which, with the foot, was covered with a little short pair of crimson velvet buskins,[5] in some places open (as the ancient manner was) to show the fairness of the skin. Over all this he ware a certain mantle of like stuff, made in such manner that, coming under his right arm, and covering most part of that side, it touched not the left side but upon the top of the shoulder where the two ends met, and were fastened together with a very rich jewel, the device[6] whereof was this: an eagle covered with the feathers of a dove, and yet lying under another dove, in such sort as it seemed the dove preyed upon the eagle, the eagle casting up such a look as though the state he was in liked[7] him, though the pain grieved him. Upon the same side, upon his thigh he ware a sword (such as we now call scimitars), the pommel whereof was so richly set with precious stones as they were sufficient testimony it could be no mean personage that bare it. Such was this Amazon's attire: and thus did Pyrocles become Cleophila—which name for a time hereafter I will use, for I myself feel such compassion of his passion that I find even part of his fear lest his name should be uttered before fit time were for it; which you, fair ladies that vouchsafe to read this, I doubt not will account excusable.[8] But Musidorus, that had helped to dress his friend, could not satisfy himself with looking upon him, so did he find his excellent beauty set out with this new change, like a diamond set in a more advantageous sort. Insomuch that he could not choose, but smiling said unto him:

2. Wore.
3. Jacket.
4. Embroidered.
5. Boots.
6. Emblem.
7. Pleased.
8. The narrator declares he will rename Pyrocles Cleophila, because he shares "her" fear that she will be unmasked before she has had time to court and win Philoclea.

"Well," said he, "sweet cousin, since you are framed of such a loving mettle, I pray you, take heed of looking yourself in a glass lest Narcissus's[9] fortune fall unto you. For my part, I promise you, if I were not fully resolved never to submit my heart to these fancies, I were like enough while I dressed you to become a young Pygmalion."[1]

"Alas," answered Cleophila, "if my beauty be anything, then will it help me to some part of my desires; otherwise I am no more to set by it than the orator by his eloquence that persuades nobody."

"She is a very invincible creature, then," said he, "for I doubt me much, under your patience, whether my mistress, your mistress, have a greater portion of beauty."

"Speak not that blasphemy, dear friend," said Cleophila, "for if I have any beauty, it is the beauty which the imagination of her strikes into my fancies, which in part shines through my face into your eyes."

"Truly," said Musidorus, "you are grown a notable philosopher of fancies."

"Astronomer," answered Cleophila, "for they are heavenly fancies."

In such friendly speeches they returned again to the desert of the two lodges, where Cleophila desired Musidorus he would hide himself in a little grove where he might see how she could play her part; for there, she said, she was resolved to remain till, by some good favor of fortune, she might obtain the sight of her whom she bare continually in the eyes of her mind. Musidorus obeyed her request, full of extreme grief to see so worthy a mind thus infected; besides he could see no hope of success, but great appearance of danger. Yet, finding it so deeply grounded that striving against it did rather anger than heal the wound, and rather call his friendship in question than give place to any friendly counsel, he was content to yield to the force of the present stream, with hope afterwards, as occasion fell out, to prevail better with him; or at least to adventure his life in preserving him from any injury might be offered him. And with the beating of those thoughts, remained he in the grove till, with a new fullness, he was emptied of them—as you shall after hear.

In the mean time, Cleophila walking up and down in that solitary place, with many intricate determinations, at last wearied both in mind and body, sat her down, and beginning to tune her voice, with many sobs and tears, sang this song which she had made since her first determination thus to change her estate:

Transformed in show, but more transformed in mind,
I cease to strive, with double conquest foiled;
For (woe is me) my powers all I find
With outward force and inward treason spoiled.

For from without came to mine eyes the blow,
Whereto mine inward thoughts did faintly yield;
Both these conspired poor reason's overthrow;
False in myself, thus have I lost the field.

And thus mine eyes are placed still in one sight,
And thus my thoughts can think but one thing still;
Thus reason to his servants gives his right;

9. A youth who fell in love with his own reflection in a pool and pined away; finally, he was changed into the flower that bears his name.

1. A king of Cyprus who fell in love with a statue of a beautiful young woman he had sculpted; subsequently, Venus brought her to life.

Thus is my power transformed to your will.
What marvel, then, I take a woman's hue,
Since what I see, think, know, is all but you?

I might entertain you, fair ladies, a great while, if I should make as many interruptions in the repeating as she did in the singing. For no verse did pass out of her mouth but that it was waited on with such abundance of sighs, and, as it were, witnessed with her flowing tears, that, though the words were few, yet the time was long she employed in uttering them; although her pauses chose so fit times that they rather strengthened a sweeter passion than hindered the harmony. Musidorus himself (that lay so as he might see and hear these things) was yet more moved to pity by the manner of Cleophila's singing than with anything he had ever seen—so lively an action doth the mind, truly touched, bring forth. But so fell it out that, as with her sweet voice she recorded once or twice the last verse of her song, it awakened the shepherd Dametas, who at that time had laid his sleepy back upon a sunny bank not far thence, gaping as far as his jaws would suffer him. But being troubled out of his sleep (the best thing his life could bring forth) his dull senses could not convey the pleasure of the excellent music to his rude mind, but that he fell into a notable rage. Insomuch that, taking a hedging bill[2] lay by him, he guided himself by the voice till he came to the place where he saw Cleophila sitting, wringing her hands, and with some few words to herself, breathing out part of the vehemency of that passion which she had not fully declared in her song. But no more were his eyes taken with her beauty than his ears with her music. But beginning to swear by the pantable[3] of Pallas, Venus's waistcoat, and such other oaths as his rustical bravery could imagine, leaning his hands upon his bill, and his chin upon his hands, he fell to mutter such railings and cursings against her as a man might well see he had passed through the discipline of an alehouse. And because you may take the better into your fancies his mannerliness, the manner of the man shall in few words be described. He was a short lean fellow, of black hair, and notably backed for a burden, one of his eyes out, his nose turned up to take more air, a seven or eight long black hairs upon his chin, which he called his beard; his breast he ware always unbuttoned for heat, and yet a stomacher[4] before it for cold; ever untrussed, yet points[5] hanging down, because he might be trussed if he list; ill gartered for a courtlike carelessness; only well shod for his father's sake, who had upon his death bed charged him to take heed of going wet. He had for love chosen his wife Miso, yet so handsome a beldam[6] that she was counted a witch only for her face and her splay foot. Neither inwardly nor outwardly was there anything good in her but that she observed decorum, having in a wretched body a froward[7] mind. Neither was there any humor in which her husband and she could ever agree, but in disagreeing. Betwixt these two issued forth mistress Mopsa, a fit woman to participate of both their perfections. But because Alethes, an honest man of that time, did her praises in verse, I will only repeat them and spare mine own pen, because she bare the sex of a woman; and these they were:

What length of verse can serve brave Mopsa's good to show,
Whose virtues strange, and beauties such, as no man them may know?
Thus shrewdly burdened then, how can my muse escape?
The gods must help and precious things must serve to show her shape.

2. Pruning tool.
3. From the French *pantofle*, slipper.
4. Waistcoat.
5. Cords for attaching stockings to a doublet.
6. Hag.
7. Perverse.

Like great god Saturn[8] fair, and like fair Venus chaste;
As smooth as Pan, as Juno mild, like goddess Iris fast.
With Cupid she foresees, and goes god Vulcan's pace;
And for a taste of all these gifts, she borrows Momus' grace.
Her forehead jacinth[9] like, her cheeks of opal hue,
Her twinkling eyes bedecked with pearl, her lips of sapphire blue;
Her hair pure crapal[1] stone; her mouth O heav'nly wide;
Her skin like burnished gold, her hands like silver ore untried.
As for those parts unknown, which hidden sure are best,
Happy be they which will believe, and never seek the rest.

The beginning of this Dametas's credit with Basilius was by the duke's straying out of his way one time a-hunting where, meeting this fellow, and asking him the way, and so falling into other questions, he found some of his answers touching husbandry[2] matters (as a dog sure, if he could speak, had wit enough to describe his kennel) not unsensible; and all uttered with such a rudeness, which the duke interpreted plainness (although there be great difference betwixt them), that the duke, conceiving a sudden delight in his entertainment, took him to his court, with apparent show of his good opinion; where the flattering courtier had no sooner taken the prince's mind but that there were straight reasons to confirm the duke's doing, and shadows of virtues found for Dametas. His silence grew wit, his bluntness integrity, his beastly ignorance virtuous simplicity; and the duke (according to the nature of great persons, in love with that he had done himself) fancied that the weakness was in him, with his presence, would grow wisdom. And so, like a creature of his own making, he liked him more and more. And thus gave he him first the office of principal herdman. And thus lastly did he put his life into his hands—although he grounded upon a great error; for his quality was not to make men, but to use men according as men were, no more than an ass will be taught to manage, a horse to hunt, or a hound to bear a saddle, but each to be used according to the force of his own nature.

But Dametas, as I said, suddenly awaked, remembering the duke's commandment, and glad he might use his authority in chiding, came swearing to the place where Cleophila was, with a voice like him that plays Hercules[3] in a play and, God knows, never had Hercules' fancy in his head. The first word he spake, after his railing oaths, was "Am not I Dametas? Why, am not I Dametas?"

These words made Cleophila lift up her eyes upon him, and seeing what manner of man he was, the height of her thoughts would not suffer her to yield any answer to so base a creature; but casting again down her eyes, leaning upon the ground, and putting her cheek in the palm of her hand, fetched a great sigh, as if she had answered him, "my head is troubled with greater matters." Which Dametas (as all persons witnesses of their own unworthiness are apt to think they are contemned[4]) took in so heinous a chafe that, standing upon his tiptoes, and staring as if he would have had a mote[5] pulled out of his eye, "Why," said he, "thou woman or boy, or both, or whatsoever thou be, I tell thee, here is no place for thee; get thee gone, I tell thee, it is the duke's pleasure. I tell thee, it is master Dametas's pleasure."

8. Saturn: god of agriculture, remarkable for his ugliness; Venus: goddess of love (and not at all chaste); Pan: god of shepherds and flocks, whose lower body is that of a goat; Juno: goddess of marriage, Jupiter's Queen, and notoriously given to jealousy; Iris: messenger of the gods, identified as a rainbow and thus subject to change or not "fast," i.e., steadfast; Cupid: the blind god of love; Vulcan: the lame god of fire and metalworking; Momus: the god of ridicule and criticism; hence not one who exhibits grace or overlooks the faults of others.

9. Orange.

1. Tortoise shell.

2. Agricultural.

3. Legendary hero known for his prodigious feats of strength and daring.

4. Scorned.

5. Speck of dust.

Cleophila could not choose but smile at him, and yet, taking herself with the manner, spake these words to herself:

"O spirit," said she, "of mine, how canst thou receive any mirth in the midst of thine agonies? And thou, mirth, how darest thou enter into a mind so grown of late thy professed enemy?"

"Thy spirit," said Dametas, "dost thou think me a spirit? I tell thee I am the duke's officer, and have the charge of him and his daughters."

"O pearl," said sobbing Cleophila, "that so vile an oyster should keep thee!"

"By the combcase of Diana!" sware Dametas, "this woman is mad; oysters and pearls; dost thou think I will buy oysters? I tell thee, get thee packing, or else I must needs be offended."

"O sun," said Cleophila, "how long shall this cloud live to darken thee, and the poor creatures that live only by thee be deprived of thee?"

These speeches to herself put Dametas out of all patience; so that, hitting her upon the breast with the blunt end of his bill, "Maid Marian,"[6] said he, "am not I a personage to be answered?"

But Cleophila no sooner felt the blow but that, the fire sparkling out of her eyes, and rising up with a right Pyrocles countenance in a Cleophila face, "Vile creature," said she, laying her hand upon her sword, "force me not to defile this sword in thy base blood!"

Dametas, that from his childhood had ever feared the blade of a sword, ran back backwards, with his hands above his head, at least twenty paces, gaping and staring with the very countenance of those clownish churls that by Latona's[7] prayer were turned into frogs. At length staying, he came a little nearer her again, but still without the compass of blows, holding one leg, as it were, ready to run away; and then fell to scolding and railing, swearing it was but a little bashfulness in him that had made him go back; and that if she stayed any longer he would make her see his blood came out of the eldest shepherd's house in that country. But seeing her walk up and down without marking what he said, he went for more help to his own lodge where, knocking a good while, at length he cried to his wife Miso that in a whore's name she should come out to him. But instead of that, he might hear a hollow rotten voice that bid him let her alone, like a knave as he was, for she was busy about my lady Pamela. This dashed poor Dametas more than anything, for old acquaintance had taught him to fear that place; and therefore, calling with a more pitiful voice to his daughter, he might see a face look out of a window, enough to have made any blind man in love. It was mistress Mopsa that, instead of answer, asked him whether he were mad to forget his duty to her mother. Dametas shrunk down his shoulders, like the poor ass that lays down his ears when he must needs yield to the burden; and yet his tongue, the valiantest part of him, could not forbear to say these words: "Here is foreign wars abroad, and uncivil wars at home—and all with women. Now," said he, "the black jaundice and the red flix[8] take all the warbled kind of you!"

And with this prayer, he went to the other lodge where the duke lay at that time sleeping, as it was in the heat of the day. And there he whistled, and stamped, and knocked, crying "Ho! my liege!" with such faces as might well show what a deformity a passion can bring a man unto when it is not governed with reason; till at length the

6. The companion of Robin Hood, legendary outlaw of medieval England.

7. The goddess and daughter of the Titans, primeval gods in the Greek pantheon, who turned into frogs the fools who insulted her.

8. Dametas wishes that all warbling or babbling women would sicken with jaundice (darkening the skin) or severe (bloody) dysentery.

fair Philoclea came down in such loose apparel as was enough to have bound any man's fancies, and with a sweet look asking him what he would have. Dametas, without any reverence, commanded her in the duke's name she should tell the duke he was to speak with the duke, for he forsooth[9] had things to tell the duke that pertained to the duke's service. She answered him he should be obeyed, since such was the fortune of her and her sister. And so went she to tell her father of Dametas's being there, leaving him chafing at the door and whetting his bill, swearing if he met her again neither she nor the tallest woman in the parish should make him run away any more.

But the duke, understanding by his jewel Philoclea that something there was which greatly troubled Dametas's conscience, came presently down unto him to know the matter; where he found Dametas, talking to himself, and making faces like an ape that had newly taken a purgation,[1] pale, shaking, and foaming at the mouth. And a great while it was before the duke could get any word of him. At length, putting his leg before him (which was the manner of his curtsy), he told the duke that, saving the reverence of his duty, he should keep himself from thenceforward, he would take no more charge of him. The duke, accustomed to take all well at his hands, did but laugh to see his rage, and, stroking his head, desired him of fellowship to let him know the matter.

"I tell you," saith Dametas, "it is not for me to be an officer without I may be obeyed."

"But what troubles thee, my good Dametas?" said the duke.

"I tell you," said Dametas, "I have been a man in my days, whatsoever I be now."

"And reason," answered the duke, "but let me know that I may redress thy wrongs."

"Nay," says Dametas, "no wrongs neither. But thus falls out the case, my liege; I met with such a mankind creature yonder, with her sword by her hip, and with such a visage as, if it had not been for me and this bill, God save it, she had come hither and killed you and all your house."

"What, strike a woman!" said the duke.

"Indeed," said Dametas, "I made her but a little weep, and after I had pity of her."

"It was well and wisely done," said the duke, "but I pray thee show me her."

"I pray you," said Dametas, "first call for more company to hold me from hurting her; for my stomach riseth against her."

"Let me but see the place," said the duke, "and then you shall know whether my words or your bill be the better weapon."

Dametas went stalking on before the duke as if he had been afraid to wake his child; and then, pointing with his bill towards her, was not hasty to make any nearer approaches. But the duke no sooner saw Cleophila but that he remained amazed at the goodliness of her stature and the stateliness of her march (for at that time she was walking with a countenance well setting forth an extreme distraction of her mind), and, as he came nearer her, at the excellent perfection of her beauty; insomuch that, forgetting any anger he conceived in Dametas's behalf, and doing reverence to her, as to a lady in whom he saw much worthy of great respect, "Fair lady," said he "it is nothing strange that such a solitary place as this should receive solitary persons; but much do I marvel how such a beauty as yours is could be suffered to be thus alone."

She, looking with a grave majesty upon him, as if she found in herself cause why she should be reverenced, "They are never alone," said she, "that are accompanied with noble thoughts."

9. Truly.

1. Emetic.

"But those thoughts," said the duke (replying for the delight he had to speak further with her), "cannot in this your loneliness neither warrant you from suspicion in others nor defend you from melancholy in yourself."

Cleophila, looking upon him as though he pressed her further than needed, "I seek no better warrant," said she, "than mine own conscience, nor no greater pleasure than mine own contentation."[2]

"Yet virtue seeks to satisfy others," said Basilius.

"Those that be good," answered Cleophila, "and they will be satisfied as long as they see no evil."

"Yet will the best in this country," said the duke, "suspect[3] so excellent a beauty, being so weakly guarded."

"Then are the best but stark naught," answered Cleophila, "for open suspecting others comes of secret condemning themselves. But in my country," said she, continuing her speech with a brave vehemency, "whose manners I am in all places to maintain and reverence, the general goodness which is nourished in our hearts makes everyone think that strength of virtue in another whereof they find the assured foundation in themselves."

But Basilius, who began to feel the sparkles of those flames which shortly after burned all other thoughts out of his heart, felt such a music, as he thought, in her voice, and such an eye-pleasing in her face, that he thought his retiring into this solitary place was well employed if it had been only to have met with such a guest. And therefore, desirous to enter into nearer points with her, "Excellent lady," said he, "you praise so greatly, and yet so wisely, your country that I must needs desire to know what the nest is out of which such birds do fly."

"You must first deserve that knowledge," said she, "before you obtain it."

"And by what means," said Basilius, "shall I deserve to know your estate?"

"By letting me first know yours," answered she.

"To obey you," said he, "I will do it; although it were so much more reason yours should be known first, as you do deserve in all points to be preferred. Know you, fair lady," said he, "that my name is Basilius, unworthy duke of this country; the rest, either fame hath already brought to your ears, or, if it please you to make this place happy by your presence, at more leisure you shall understand of me."

Cleophila (who had from the beginning suspected it should be he, but would not seem she did so, to keep her majesty the better), making some reverence unto him, "Mighty prince," said she, "let my not knowing of you serve for the excuse of my boldness, and the little reverence I do you, impute it to the manner of my country, which is the invincible land of the Amazons, myself niece to Senicia, queen thereof, lineally descended of the famous Penthesilea,[4] slain before Troy by the bloody hand of Pyrrhus. I, having in this my youth determined to make the world see the Amazons' excellencies, as well in private as in public virtues, have passed many dangerous adventures in divers countries, till the unmerciful sea deprived me of all my company; so that shipwrack brought me to this realm, and uncertain wandering guided me to this place."

Whoever saw a man to whom a beloved child long lost did, unlooked for, return might easily figure unto his fancy the very fashion of Basilius's countenance—so far had love become his master. And so had this young siren[5] charmed his old ears, insomuch that, with more vehement importunancy than any greedy host would use to

2. Contentment.
3. Mistrust.
4. An Amazon killed by Phyrrus or Neoptolemus, son of Achilles, in the Trojan War.
5. A mythical sea-nymph or mermaid whose singing enchanted sailors.

well acquainted passengers, he fell to entreat her abode there for some time. She, although nothing could come fitter to the very point of her desire, yet had she already learned that womanish quality to counterfeit backwardness in that she most wished; so that he, desirous to prove whether intercession coming out of fitter mouths might better prevail, called to Dametas, and commanded him to bring forth his wife and two daughters—three ladies, although of diverse, yet all of excellent beauty: the duchess Gynecia, in grave matronlike attire, with a countenance and behaviour far unlike to fall into those inconveniences she afterwards tasted of. The fair Pamela, whose noble heart had long disdained to find the trust of her virtue reposed in the hands of a shepherd, had yet, to show an obedience, taken on a shepherdish apparel, which was of russet velvet, cut after their fashion, with a straight body, open breasted, the nether part full of pleats, with wide open sleeves, hanging down very low; her hair at the full length, only wound about with gold lace—by the comparison to show how far her hair did excel in colour; betwixt her breasts, which sweetly rase up like two fair mountainets in the pleasant vale of Tempe, there hanged down a jewel which she had devised as a picture of her own estate.[6] It was a perfect white lamb tied at a stake with a great number of chains, as it had been feared lest the silly creature should do some great harm; neither had she added any word unto it, but even took silence as the word of the poor lamb, showing such humbleness as not to use her own voice for complaint of her misery.

But when the ornament of the earth, young Philoclea, appeared in her nymphlike apparel, so near nakedness as one might well discern part of her perfections, and yet so apparelled as did show she kept the best store of her beauties to herself; her excellent fair hair drawn up into a net made only of itself (a net indeed to have caught the wildest disposition); her body covered with a light taffeta garment, so cut as the wrought smock came through it in many places (enough to have made a very restrained imagination have thought what was under it); with the sweet cast of her black eye which seemed to make a contention whether that in perfect blackness, or her skin in perfect whiteness, were the most excellent; then, I say, the very clouds seemed to give place to make the heaven more fair. At least, the clouds of Cleophila's thoughts quite vanished, and so was her brain fixed withal that her sight seemed more forcible and clear than ever before or since she found it, with such strange delight unto her (for still, fair ladies, you remember that I use the she-title to Pyrocles, since so he would have it) that she stood like a well wrought image, with show of life, but without all exercise of life, so forcibly had love transferred all her spirits into the present contemplation of the lovely Philoclea. And so had it been like enough she would have stayed long time but that by chance Gynecia stepped betwixt her sight and the lady Philoclea, and the change of the object made her recover her senses; so that she could with good manner receive the salutation of the duchess and the princess Pamela, doing them yet no further reverence than one princess useth to another. But when she came to the lady Philoclea, she fell down on her knees, taking by force her fair hands and kissing them with great show of extreme affection, and with a bowed-down countenance began this speech unto her: "Divine lady," said she, "let not the world nor these great princes marvel to see me contrary to my manner do this especial honour unto you, since all, both men and women, owe this homage to the perfection of your beauty."

6. Situation.

Philoclea's blushing cheeks quickly witnessed how much she was abashed to see this singularity used to herself; and therefore, causing Cleophila to rise, "Noble lady," said she, "it is no marvel to see your judgment much mistaken in my beauty, since you begin with so great an error as to do more honor unto me than to them to whom I myself owe all service."

"Rather," answered Cleophila, "that shows the power of your beauty which hath forced me to fall into such an error, if it were an error."

"You are so acquainted," said Philoclea, sweetly smiling, "with your own beauty that it makes you easily fall into the discourse of beauty."

"Beauty in me!" said Cleophila, deeply sighing, "Alas! if there be any, it is in mine eyes, which your happy presence hath imparted unto them."

Basilius was even transported with delight to hear these speeches betwixt his well beloved daughter and his better loved lady; and so made a sign to Philoclea that she should entreat her to remain with them; which she willingly obeyed, for already she conceived delight in Cleophila's presence, and therefore said unto her: "It is a great happiness, I must confess, to be praised of them that are themselves most praiseworthy. And well I find you are an invincible Amazon, since you will overcome in a wrong matter. But if my beauty be anything," said she, "then let it obtain thus much of you: that you will remain in this company some time, to ease your own travail, and our solitariness."

"First let me die," said Cleophila, "before any word spoken by such a mouth should come in vain. I yield wholly to your commandment, fearing nothing but that you command that which may be troublesome to yourself."

Thus, with some other words of entertaining, her staying was concluded, to the unspeakable joy of the duke—although, perchance, with some little envy in the other ladies, to see young Philoclea's beauty so greatly advanced. You ladies know best whether sometimes you feel impression of that passion; for my part, I would hardly think that the affection of a mother and the noble mind of Pamela could be overthrown with so base a thing as envy is—especially Pamela, to whom fortune had already framed another, who no less was dedicated to her excellencies than Cleophila was to Philoclea's perfections, as you shall shortly hear. For the duke going into the lodge with his wife and daughters, Cleophila desired them to excuse her for a while, for that she had thoughts to pass over with herself; and that shortly after she would come in to them—indeed meaning to find her friend Musidorus, and to glory with him of the happiness of her choice. But when she looked in the grove and could nowhere find him, marveling something at it, she gave herself to feed those sweet thoughts which now had the full possession of her heart, sometimes thinking how far Philoclea herself passed her picture, sometimes fore-imagining with herself how happy she should be if she could obtain her desires; till, having spent thus an hour or two, she might perceive afar off one coming towards her, in the apparel of a shepherd, with his arms hanging down, going a kind of languishing pace, with his eyes sometimes cast up to heaven as though his fancies strave to mount up higher, sometimes thrown down to the ground as if the earth could not bear the burden of his pains. At length she heard him, with a lamentable tune, sing these few verses:

Come shepherd's weeds,° become your master's mind: *garments*
Yield outward show, what inward change he tries:
Nor be abashed, since such a guest you find,
Whose strongest hope in your weak comfort lies.

Come shepherd's weeds, attend my woeful cries:
Disuse yourselves from sweet Menalcas'° voice: *a shepherd*
For other be those tunes which sorrow ties
From those clear notes which freely may rejoice.
Then pour out plaint,° and in one word say this: *complaint*
Helpless his plaint who spoils° himself of bliss. *robs*

And having ended, she might see him strike himself upon the breast, uttering these words: "O miserable wretch, whither do thy destinies guide thee?"

It seemed to Cleophila that she knew the voice; and therefore drawing nearer, that her sight might receive a perfect discerning, she saw plainly, to her great amazement, it was her dear friend Musidorus. And now having named him, methinks it reason I should tell you what chance brought him to this change. I left him lately, if you remember, fair ladies, in the grove by the two lodges, there to see what should befall to his dear new-transformed friend. There heard he all the complaints (not without great compassion) that his friend made to himself; and there (not without some laughter) did he see what passed betwixt him and Dametas, and how stately he played the part of Cleophila at the duke's first coming. And falling into many kind fancies towards him, sometimes pitying his case, sometimes praising his behavior, he would often say to himself: "O sweet Pyrocles, how art thou bewitched! Where is thy virtue? Where is the use of thy reason? Much am I inferior to thee in all the powers of the mind; and yet know I that all the heavens cannot bring me to such a thraldom."

Scarcely, think I, he had spoken those words but that the duchess, being sent for to entertain Cleophila, came out with her two daughters; where the beams of the princess Pamela's beauty had no sooner stricken into his eyes but that he was wounded with more sudden violence of love than ever Pyrocles was. Whether indeed it were that this strange power would be bravely revenged of him for the bitter words he had used, or that his very resisting made the wound the crueler (as we see the harquebus[7] doth most endamage the stiffest metal), or rather that the continual healthfulness of his mind made this sudden ill the more incurable (as the soundest bodies, once infected, are most mortally endangered); but howsoever the cause was, such was the effect that, not being able to bear the vehement pain, he ran away through the grove, like a madman, hoping perchance (as the fever-sick folks do) that the change of places might ease his grief. But therein was his luck indeed better than his providence; for he had not gone a little but that he met with a shepherd (according to his estate, handsomely appareled) who was as then going to meet with other shepherds (as upon certain days they had accustomed) to do exercises of activity and to play new-invented eclogues before the duke. Which, when Musidorus had learned of him (for love is full of desire, and desire is always inquisitive), it came straight into his head that there were no better way for him to come by the often enjoying of the princess Pamela's sight than to take the apparel of this shepherd upon him. Which he quickly did, giving him his own much richer; and withal, lest the matter by him might be discovered, hired him to go without stay into Thessalia, writing two or three words by him, in a pair of tables[8] well closed up, to a servant of his that he should, upon the receipt, arrest and keep him in good order till he heard his further pleasure. Yet before Menalcas departed (for so was his name), he learned of him both his own estate and the manner of their pastimes and eclogues. And thus furnished, he

7. Gun.

8. Writing tablets.

returned again to the place where his heart was pledged, so oppressed in mind that it seemed to him his legs were uneath[9] able to bear him. Which grief he uttered in the doleful song I told you of before, and was cause that his dear he-she friend, Cleophila, came unto him; who, when she was assured it was he (with wonted entireness embracing him), demanded of him what sudden thing had thus suddenly changed him; whether the goddess of those woods had such a power to transform everybody; or whether, indeed, as he had always in all enterprises most faithfully accompanied her, so he would continue to match her in this new metamorphosis. But Musidorus, looking dolefully upon her, wringing his hands, and pouring out abundance of tears, began to recount unto her all this I have already told you, but with such passionate dilating of it that, for my part, I have not a feeling insight enough into the matter to be able lively to express it. Sufficeth it that whatsoever a possessed heart with a good tongue, to a dear friend, could utter was at that time largely set forth. The perfect friendship Cleophila bare him, and the great pity she (by good experience) had of his case could not keep her from smiling at him, remembering how vehemently he had cried out against the folly of lovers; so that she thought good a little to punish him, playing with him in this manner: "Why, how now, dear cousin," said she, "you that were even now so high in the pulpit against love, are you now become so mean an auditor?[1] Remember that love is a passion, and that a worthy man's reason must ever have the masterhood."

"I recant, I recant!" cried Musidorus, and withal falling down prostrate, "O thou celestial, or infernal, spirit of love," said he, "or what other heavenly or hellish title thou list to have, for both those effects I find in myself, have compassion of me, and let thy glory be as great in pardoning them that be submitted to thee as in conquering those that were rebellious!"

"No, no!" said Cleophila, yet further to urge him, "I see you well enough; you make but an interlude of my mishaps, and do but counterfeit thus to make me see the deformity of my passions. But take heed," said she, "cousin, that this jest do not one day turn into earnest."

"Now I beseech thee," said Musidorus, taking her fast by the hand, "even by the truth of our friendship (of which, if I be not altogether an unhappy man, thou hast some remembrance), and by those sacred flames (which I know have likewise nearly touched thee), make no jest of that which hath so earnestly pierced me through; nor let that be light to thee which is to me so burdenous that I am not able to bear it."

Musidorus did so lively deliver out his inward griefs that Cleophila's friendly heart felt a great impression of pity withal—as certainly all persons that find themselves afflicted easily fall to compassion of them who taste of like misery, partly led by the common course of humanity, but principally because, under the image of them, they lament their own mishaps; and so the complaints the others make seem to touch the right tune of their own woes. Which did mutually work so in these two young princes that, looking ruefully one upon the other, they made their speech a great while nothing but doleful sighs. Yet sometimes they would yield out suchlike lamentations: "Alas! What further evil hath fortune reserved for us, or what shall be the end of this our tragical pilgrimage? Shipwracks, daily dangers, absence from our country, have at length brought forth this captiving of us within ourselves which hath transformed the one in sex, and the other in state, as much as the uttermost work of changeable fortune can be extended unto."

9. Scarcely.

1. Listener.

And then would they kiss one another, vowing to continue partakers of all either good or evil fortune. And thus perchance would they have forgotten themselves some longer time, but that Basilius, whose heart was now set on fire with his new mistress, finding her absence long, sent out Dametas to her to know if she would command anything, and to invite her to go with his wife and daughters to a fair meadow thereby to see the sports and hear the eclogues of his country shepherds. Dametas came out with two or three swords about him, his hedging bill on his neck, and a chopping knife under his girdle,[2] armed only behind, as fearing most the blows that might fall upon the reins of his back; for, indeed, Cleophila had put such a sudden fear into his head that from thenceforth he was resolved never to come out any more ill provided. Yet had his blunt brains perceived some favor the duke bare to this new-come lady; and so framing himself thereunto (as without doubt the most servile flattery is most easy to be lodged in the most gross capacity; for their ordinary conceit draws a yielding to their greatness, and then have they not wit to discern right degrees of goodness),[3] he no sooner saw her but, with head and arms, he laid his reverence before her, enough to have made a man forswear all courtesy. And then, in the duke's name, did he require her she would take pains to see their pastorals (for so their sports were termed); but when he spied Musidorus standing by her (for his eye had been placed all this while upon her), not knowing him, he would fain have persuaded himself to have been angry but that he durst not. Yet, muttering and champing as though his cud troubled him, he gave occasion to Musidorus to come nearer him, and to feign a tale of his own life: that he was a younger brother of the shepherd Menalcas, by name Dorus,[4] sent by his father in his tender age to Athens, there to learn some cunning more than ordinary for to excel his fellow shepherds in their eclogues; and that his brother Menalcas, lately gone thither to fetch him home, was deceased; where, upon his deathbed, he had charged him to seek the service of Dametas, and to be wholly and only guided by his counsel, as one in whose judgement and integrity the duke had singular confidence; for token whereof he gave him a sum of gold in ready coin which Menalcas had bequeathed him upon condition he should receive this poor Dorus into his service, that his mind and manners might grow the better by his daily example. Dametas no sooner saw the gold but that his heart was presently infected with the self-conceit he took of it; which, being helped with the tickling of Musidorus's praises, so turned the brain of good Dametas that he became slave to that which he that would be his servant bestowed on him, and gave in himself an example for ever that the fool can never be honest since, not being able to balance what points virtue stands upon, every present occasion catches his senses, and his senses are masters of his silly mind. Yet, for countenance's sake, he seemed very squeamish, in respect he had the charge of the princess Pamela, to accept any new servant into his house. But such was the secret operation of the gold, helped with the persuasions of the Amazon Cleophila, who said it was pity so proper a young man should be anywhere else than with so good a master, that in the end he agreed to receive him for his servant, so as that day in their pastorals he proved himself active in mind and body.

And thus went they to the lodge, with greater joy to Musidorus (now only poor shepherd Dorus) than all his life before had ever brought forth unto him—so manifest it is that the greatest point outward things can bring a man unto is the content-

2. Belt.
3. Those who, like Dametas, have poor powers of reason flatter the great, for their ordinary powers of conception make them inclined to yield to the great, and they do not have the intelligence to see any degrees of goodness.
4. "Gift."

ment of the mind, which once obtained, no state is miserable; and without that, no prince's seat restful. There found they Gynecia, with her two daughters, ready to go to the meadow; whither also they went. For, as for Basilius, he desired to stay behind them to debate a little with himself of this new guest that had entered and possessed his brains. There, it is said, the poor old Basilius, now alone (for, as I said, the rest were gone to see the pastorals), had a sufficient eclogue in his own head betwixt honor, with the long experience he had had of the world, on the one side, and this new assault of Cleophila's beauty on the other side. There hard by the lodge walked he, carrying this unquiet contention about him. But passion ere long had gotten the absolute masterhood, bringing with it the show of present pleasure, fortified with the authority of a prince whose power might easily satisfy his will against the far-fet[5] (though true) reasons of the spirit—which, in a man not trained in the way of virtue, have but slender working. So that ere long he utterly gave himself over to the longing desire to enjoy Cleophila, which finding an old broken vessel of him, had the more power in him than, perchance, it would have had in a younger man. And so, as all vice is foolish, it wrought in him the more absurd follies. But thus, as I say, in a number of intermixed imaginations, he stayed solitary by the lodge, waiting for the return of his company from the pastorals, some good space of time, till he was suddenly stirred out of his deep muses[6] by the hasty and fearful running unto him of most part of the shepherds who came flying from the pastoral sports, crying to one another to stay and save the duchess and young ladies. But even whilst they cried so they ran away as fast as they could; so that the one tumbled over the other, each one showing he would be glad his fellow should do valiantly, but his own heart served him not. The duke, amazed to see such extreme shows of fear, asked the matter of them. But fear had so possessed their inward parts that their breath would not serve to tell it him, but after such a broken manner that I think it best not to trouble you, fair ladies, with their panting speeches; but to make a full declaration of it myself. And thus it was: Gynecia, with her two daughters, Cleophila, the shepherds Dorus and Dametas, being parted from the duke whom they left solitary at the lodge, came into the fair meadow appointed for their shepherdish pastimes. It was, indeed, a place of great delight, for through the midst of it there ran a sweet brook which did both hold the eye open with her beautiful streams and close the eye with the sweet purling[7] noise it made upon the pebble-stones it ran over; the meadow itself yielding so liberally all sorts of flowers that it seemed to nourish a contention betwixt the colour and the smell whether in his kind were the more delightful. Round about the meadow, as if it had been to enclose a theater, grew all such sorts of trees as either excellency of fruit, stateliness of growth, continual greenness, or poetical fancies have made at any time famous. In most part of which trees there had been framed by art such pleasant arbors that it became a gallery aloft, from one tree to the other, almost round about, which below yielded a perfect shadow, in those hot countries counted a great pleasure.

In this place, under one of the trees, the ladies sat down, inquiring many questions of young Dorus (now newly perceived of them), whilst the other shepherds made them ready to the pastimes. Dorus, keeping his eye still upon the princess Pamela, answered with such a trembling voice and abashed countenance, and oftentimes so far from the matter, that it was some sport to the ladies, thinking it had been want of education which made him so discountenanced with unwonted presence. But Cleophila (that saw in him the glass[8] of her own misery), taking the fair hand of

5. Far-fetched.
6. Musings.
7. Murmurings.
8. Mirror.

Philoclea, and with more than womanish ardency kissing it, began to say these words: "O love, since thou art so changeable in men's estates, how art thou so constant in their torments?"—when suddenly there came out of the wood a monstrous lion, with a she-bear of little less fierceness, which, having been hunted in forests far off, had by chance come to this place where such beasts had never before been seen. Which, when the shepherds saw, like silly wretches that think all evil is ever next themselves, ran away in such sort as I told you till they came to the duke's presence. There might one have seen at one instant all sorts of passions lively painted out in the young lovers' faces—an extremity of love shining in their eyes; fear for their mistresses; assured hope in their own virtue; anger against the beasts; joy that occasion employed their service; sorrow to see their ladies in agony. For, indeed, the sweet Philoclea no sooner espied the ravenous lion but that, opening her arms, she fell so right upon the breast of Cleophila, sitting by her, that their faces at unawares closed together, which so transported all whatsoever Cleophila was that she gave leisure to the lion to come very near them before she rid herself from the dear arms of Philoclea. But necessity, the only overruler of affections, did force her then gently to unfold herself from those sweet embracements; and so drawing her sword, waited the present assault of the lion who, seeing Philoclea fly away, suddenly turned after her. For, as soon as she had risen up with Cleophila, she ran as fast as her delicate legs would carry her towards the lodge after the fugitive shepherds. But Cleophila, seeing how greedily the lion went after the prey she herself so much desired, it seemed all her spirits were kindled with an unwonted fire; so that, equaling the lion in swiftness, she overtook him as he was ready to have seized himself of his beautiful chase, and disdainfully saying "are you become my competitor?"—strake him so great a blow upon the shoulder that she almost cleaved him asunder. Yet the valiant beast turned withal so far upon the weapon, that with his paw he did hurt a little the left shoulder of Cleophila; and mortal it would have been had not the death wound Cleophila, with a new thrust, gave unto him taken away the effect of his force. But therewithal he fell down, and gave Cleophila leisure to take off his head to carry it for a present to her lady Philoclea, who all this while, not knowing what was done behind her, kept on her course, as Arethusa when she ran from Alpheus,[9] her light nymphlike apparel being carried up with the wind, that much of those beauties she would at another time have willingly hidden were presented to the eye of the twice-wounded Cleophila; which made Cleophila not follow her over hastily lest she should too soon deprive herself of that pleasure. But, carrying the lion's head in her hand, did not fully overtake her till they came both into the presence of Basilius, at that time examining the shepherds of what was passed, and preparing himself to come to their succor. Neither were they long there but that Gynecia came to them; whose look had all this while been upon the combat, eyeing so fixedly Cleophila's manner of fighting that no fear did prevail over her but, as soon as Cleophila had cut off his head, and ran after Philoclea, she could not find in her heart but to run likewise after Cleophila. So that it was a new sight fortune had prepared to those woods, to see these three great personages thus run one after the other, each carried away with the violence of an inward evil: the sweet Philoclea, with such fear that she thought she was still in the lion's mouth; Cleophila, with a painful delight she had to see without hope of enjoying; Gynecia, not so much with the love she bare to her best beloved daughter as with a new wonderful passionate love had possessed her heart of the goodly Cleophi-

9. The nymph Arethusa, pursued by the river-god Alpheus, was metamorphosed into a fountain.

la. For so the truth is that, at the first sight she had of Cleophila, her heart gave her she was a man thus for some strange cause disguised, which now this combat did in effect assure her of, because she measured the possibility of all women's hearts out of her own. And this doubt framed in her a desire to know, and desire to know brought forth shortly such longing to enjoy that it reduced her whole mind to an extreme and unfortunate slavery—pitifully, truly, considering her beauty and estate; but for a perfect mark of the triumph of love who could in one moment overthrow the heart of a wise lady, so that neither honor long maintained, nor love of husband and children, could withstand it. But of that you shall after hear; for now, they being come before the duke, and the fair Philoclea scarcely then stayed from her fear, Cleophila, kneeling down, presented the head of the lion unto her with these words: "Only lady," said she, "here see you the punishment of that unnatural beast which, contrary to his own kind, would have wronged prince's blood; neither were his eyes vanquished with the duty all eyes bear to your beauty."

"Happy am I and my beauty both," answered the fair Philoclea (the blood coming again to her cheeks, pale before for fear), "that you, excellent Amazon, were there to teach him good manners."

"And even thank that beauty," said Cleophila, "which forceth all noble swords to be ready to serve it."

Having finished these words, the lady Philoclea perceived the blood that ran abundantly down upon Cleophila's shoulder; so that starting aside, with a countenance full of sweet pity, "Alas," said she, "now perceive I my good hap[1] is waited on with great misfortune, since my safety is wrought with the danger of a much more worthy person."

"Noble lady," answered she, "if your inward eyes could discern the wounds of my soul, you should have a plentifuller cause to exercise your compassion."

But it was sport to see how in one instant both Basilius and Gynecia (like a father and mother to a beloved child) came running to see the wound of Cleophila; into what rages Basilius grew, and what tears Gynecia spent—for so it seemed that love had purposed to make in those solitary woods a perfect demonstration of his unresistible force, to show that no desert place can avoid his dart. He must fly from himself that will shun his evil. But so wonderful and in effect incredible was the passion which reigned as well in Gynecia as Basilius (and all for the poor Cleophila, dedicated another way) that it seems to myself I use not words enough to make you see how they could in one moment be so overtaken. But you, worthy ladies, that have at any time feelingly known what it means, will easily believe the possibility of it. Let the ignorant sort of people give credit to them that have passed the doleful passage, and daily find that quickly is the infection gotten which in long time is hardly cured. Basilius sometimes would kiss her forehead, blessing the destinies that had joined such beauty and valour together. Gynecia would kiss her more boldly, by the liberty of her womanish show, although her heart were set of nothing less; for already was she fallen into a jealous envy against her daughter Philoclea, because she found Cleophila showed such extraordinary dutiful favor unto her; and even that settled her opinion the more of her manhood. And this doubtful jealousy served as a bellows to kindle the violent coals of her passion. But as the over kind nurse may sometimes with kissing forget to give the child suck so had they, with too much kindness, unkindly forgotten the wound of Cleophila, had not Philoclea, whose heart had not

1. Fortune.

yet gone beyond the limits of a right goodwill, advised herself, and desired her mother to help her to dress the wound of Cleophila. For both those great ladies were excellently seen in that part of surgery—an art in that age greatly esteemed because it served as a minister to virtuous courage, which in those worthy days was even by ladies more beloved than any outward beauty. So to the great comfort of Cleophila, more to feel the delicate hands of Philoclea than for the care she had of her wound, these two ladies had quickly dressed it, applying so precious a balm as all the heat and pain was presently assuaged, with apparent hope of soon amendment. In which doing, I know not whether Gynecia took some greater conjectures of Cleophila's sex. But even then, and not before, did Cleophila remember herself of her dear friend Musidorus; for having only had care of the excellent Philoclea, she never missed neither her friend nor the princess Pamela—not so much to be marveled at in her, since both the duke and duchess had forgotten their daughter, so were all their thoughts plunged in one place. Besides Cleophila had not seen any danger was like to fall unto him, for her eye had been still fixed upon Philoclea, and that made her the more careless. But now, with a kind of rising in her heart, lest some evil should be fallen to her chosen friend, she hastily asked what was become of the princess Pamela, with the two shepherds, Dametas and Dorus. And then the duke and Gynecia remembered their forgetfulness, and with great astonishment made like[2] inquiry for her. But of all the company of the shepherds (so had the lion's sight put them from themselves), there was but one could say anything of her; and all he said was this: that as he ran away he might perceive a great bear run directly towards her. Cleophila (whose courage was always ready without deliberation) took up the sword lying by her, with mind to bestow her life for the succor or revenge of her Musidorus and the gracious Pamela. But as she had run two or three steps, they might all see Pamela coming betwixt Dametas and Dorus, Pamela having in her hand the paw of the bear which the shepherd Dorus had newly presented unto her, desiring her to keep it, as of such a beast which, though she was to be punished for her over great cruelty, yet was her wit to be esteemed, since she could make so sweet a choice. Dametas for his part came piping and dancing, the merriest man of a parish; but when he came so near as he might be heard of the duke, he sang this song for joy of their success:

Now thanked be the great god Pan
That thus preserves my loved life:
Thanked be I that keep a man
Who ended hath this fearful strife:
So if my man must praises have,
What then must I that keep the knave?

For as the moon the eye doth please
With gentle beams not hurting sight,
Yet hath sir sun the greatest praise,
Because from him doth come her light:
So if my man must praises have,
What then must I that keep the knave?

It were a very superfluous thing to tell you how glad each party was of the happy returning from these dangers, and doubt you not, fair ladies, there wanted no questioning how things had passed; but because I will have the thanks myself, it shall be I

2. Similar.

you shall hear it of. And thus the ancient records of Arcadia say it fell out: the lion's presence had no sooner driven away the heartless shepherds, and followed, as I told you, the excellent Philoclea, but that there came out of the same woods a monstrous she-bear which, fearing to deal with the lion's prey, came furiously towards the princess Pamela who, whether it were she had heard that such was the best refuge against that beast, or that fear (as it fell out most likely) brought forth the effects of wisdom, she no sooner saw the bear coming towards her but she fell down flat upon her face. Which when the prince Musidorus saw (whom, because such was his pleasure, I am bold to call the shepherd Dorus), with a true resolved magnānimity, although he had no other weapon but a great shepherd's knife, he leaped before the head of his dear lady, and saying these words unto her, "Receive here the sacrifice of that heart which is only vowed to your service," attended with a quiet courage the coming of the bear which, according to the manner of that beast's fight, especially against a man that resists them, rase up upon her hinder feet, so to take him in her ugly paws. But, as she was ready to give him a mortal[3] embracement, the shepherd Dorus, with a lusty strength and good fortune, thrust his knife so right into the heart of the beast that she fell down dead without ever being able to touch him. Which being done, he turned to his lady Pamela (at that time in a swoon with extremity of fear), and softly taking her in his arms, he took the advantage to kiss and re-kiss her a hundred times, with such exceeding delight that he would often after say he thought the joy would have carried his life from him, had not the grief he conceived to see her in such case something diminished it. But long in that delightful agony he was not; for the lady Pamela, being come out of her swoon, opened her fair eyes, and seeing herself in the hands of this new-come shepherd, with great disdain put him from her. But when she saw the ugly bear lying hard by her, starting aside (for fear gave not reason leave to determine whether it were dead or no), she forgot her anger, and cried to Dorus to help her. Wherefore he, cutting off the forepaw of the bear, and showing unto her the bloody knife, told her she might well by this perceive that there was no heart so base, nor weapon so feeble, but that the force of her beauty was well able to enable them for the performance of great matters. She, inquiring the manner, and whether himself were hurt, gave him great thanks for his pains, with promise of reward. But being ashamed to find herself so alone with this young shepherd, looked round about if she could see anybody; and at length they both perceived the gentle Dametas, lying with his head and breast as far as he could thrust himself into a bush, drawing up his legs as close unto him as he could. For, indeed, as soon as he saw the bear coming towards him (like a man that was very apt to take pity of himself), he ran headlong into this bush, with full resolution that, at the worst hand, he would not see his own death. And when Dorus pushed him, bidding him be of good courage, it was a great while before they could persuade him that Dorus was not the bear; so that he was fain to pull him out by the heels, and show him her as dead as he could wish her—which, you may believe me, was a very joyful sight unto him. And yet, like a man of a revengeful spirit, he gave the dead body many a wound, swearing by much it was pity such beasts should be suffered in a commonwealth. And then, with as immoderate joy as before with fear (for his heart was framed never to be without a passion), he went by his fair charge, dancing, piping, and singing; till they all came to the presence of the careful company, as before I told you. Thus now this little, but noble, company united again together, the first thing was done was the

3. Deadly.

yielding of great thanks and praises of all sides to the virtuous Cleophila. The duke told with what a gallant grace she ran after Philoclea with the lion's head in her hand, like another Pallas with the spoils of Gorgon.[4] Gynecia sware she saw the very face of young Hercules killing the Nemean lion;[5] and all, with a grateful assent, confirmed the same praises. Only poor Dorus, though of equal desert,[6] yet not proceeding from equal estate, should have been left forgotten, had not Cleophila (partly to put by the occasion of her own excessive praises, but principally for the true remembrance she had of her professed friend), with great admiration, spoken of his hazardous act, asking afresh (as if she had never before known him) what he was, and whether he had haunted that place before, protesting that, upon her conscience, she could not think but that he came of some very noble blood—so noble a countenance he bare, and so worthy an act he had performed. This Basilius took (as the lover's heart is apt to receive all sudden sorts of impression) as though his mistress had given him a secret reprehension that he had not showed more gratefulness to the valiant Dorus. And therefore, as nimbly as he could, began forthwith to inquire of his estate, adding promise of great rewards—among the rest offering to him that, if he would exercise his valor in soldiery, he would commit some charge[7] unto him under Philanax, governor of his frontiers. But Dorus, whose ambition stretched a quite other way, having first answered (touching his estate) that he was brother to the shepherd Menalcas whom the duke had well known, and excused his going to soldiery by the unaptness he found in himself that way, told the duke that his brother, in his last testament, had commanded him to dedicate his service to Dametas; and therefore, as well for due obedience thereto as for the satisfaction of his own mind (which was wholly set upon pastoral affairs), he would think his service greatly rewarded if he might obtain by that means to live in the sight of the duke more than the rest of his fellows, and yet practise that his chosen vocation. The duke, liking well of his modest manner, charged Dametas to receive him like a son in his house, telling him, because of his tried valor, he would have him be as a guard to his daughter Pamela, to whom likewise he recommended him, sticking not to say such men were to be cherished since she was in danger of some secret misadventure.

All this while Pamela said little of him, and even as little did Philoclea of Cleophila; although everybody else filled their mouths with their praises. Whereof seeking the cause that they which were most bound said least, I note this to myself, fair ladies, that even at this time they did begin to find they themselves could not tell what kind of inclination towards them; whereof feeling a secret accusation in themselves, and in their simplicity not able to warrant it, closed up all such motion in secret, without daring scarcely to breathe out the names of them who already began to breed unwonted war in their spirits. For, indeed, fortune had framed a very stage-play of love among these few folks, making the old age of Basilius, the virtue of Gynecia, and the simplicity of Philoclea, all affected to one; but by a three-headed kind of passion: Basilius assuring himself she was, as she pretended, a young lady, but greatly despairing for his own unworthiness's sake; Gynecia hoping her judgment to be right of his disguising, but therein fearing a greater sore if already his heart were pledged to

4. One of three mythical monsters, with snakes for hair, who turned those who looked at them to stone; the most famous of the Gorgons was Medusa. After she was decapitated by the hero Perseus, she was flayed by Pallas, that is, Pallas Athene, the goddess of wisdom, who carried her skin about as a breastplate.

5. This lion had a skin that could not be penetrated, so Hercules choked him to death—the first of his twelve prodigious labors.

6. Merit.

7. Basilius promises that Dorus will have command of a unit of soldiers in an army led by Philanax.

her daughter. But sweet Philoclea grew shortly after of all other into worst terms; for taking her to be such as she professed, desire she did, but she knew not what; and she longed to obtain that whereof she herself could not imagine the mean, but full of unquiet imaginations rested only unhappy because she knew not her good hap. Cleophila hath (I think) said enough for herself to make you know, fair ladies, that she was not a little enchanted; and as for Dorus, a shepherd's apparel upon a duke of Thessalia will answer for him. Pamela was the only lady that would needs make open war upon herself, and obtain the victory; for, indeed, even now find she did a certain working of a new-come inclination to Dorus. But when she found perfectly in herself whither it must draw her, she did overmaster it with the consideration of his meanness. But how therein Dorus sought to satisfy her you shall after hear; for now the day being closed up in darkness the duke would fain have had Cleophila gone to rest, because of her late-received wound. But she (that found no better salve than Philoclea's presence) desired first that by torchlight they might see some of the pastorals the lion's coming had disordered. Which accordingly was done; whereof I will repeat you a few to ease you, fair ladies, of the tediousness of this long discourse.

Here ends the first book or act.

from Astrophil and Stella[1]

1

Loving in truth, and fain° in verse my love to show, *wishing*
That she (dear she) might take some pleasure of my pain:
Pleasure might cause her read, reading might make her know,
Knowledge might pity win, and pity grace obtain,
I sought fit words to paint the blackest face of woe,
Studying inventions[2] fine, her wits to entertain:
Oft turning others' leaves, to see if thence would flow
Some fresh and fruitfull showers upon my sun-burned brain.
But words came halting forth, wanting Invention's stay,° *support*
Invention Nature's child, fled step-dame Study's blows,
And others' feet still seemed but strangers in my way.
Thus great with child to speak, and helpless in my throes,° *agonies*
Biting my trewand° pen, beating my self for spite, *truant*
Fool, said my Muse to me, look in thy heart and write.

31

With how sad steps, O Moon, thou climb'st the skies,
How silently, and with how wan° a face, *pale*
What may it be, that even in heavenly place
That busy archer° his sharp arrows tries? *Cupid*
Sure if° that long with Love acquainted eyes *surely if those*
Can judge of Love, thou feel'st a lover's case;
I read it in thy looks, thy languished grace
To me that feel the like, thy state descries.° *reveals*
Then ev'n of fellowship, O Moon, tell me

1. This sonnet sequence was composed in 1582, published in 1591.
2. "Invention" was the term early modern rhetoricians used to designate the choice of a literary subject and its development as an argument, in contrast to the forms of expression, figures of thought and speech, and imagery by which that subject was conveyed. As Sidney suggests, "invention" depended on the writer's imaginative intelligence, not on his literary education.

Is constant Love deemed there but want of wit?
Are Beauties there as proud as here they be?
Do they above love to be loved, and yet
Those lovers scorn whom that Love doth possess?
Do they call Virtue there ungratefulness?

39

Come sleep, O sleep, the certain knot of peace,
The baiting° place of wit, the balm of woe, *resting*
The poor man's wealth, the prisoner's release,
Th'indifferent judge between the high and low;
With shield of proof° shield me from out the prease° *proven shield/throng*
Of those fierce darts, despair at me doth throw:
O make in me those civil wars to cease;
I will good tribute pay if thou do so.
Take thou of me smooth pillows, sweetest bed,
A chamber deaf to noise, and blind to light:
A rosy garland, and a weary head:
And if these things, as being thine by right,
Move not thy heavy grace, thou shalt in me
Livelier then elsewhere Stella's image see.

45

Stella oft sees the very face of woe
Painted in my beclouded stormy face:
But cannot skill° to pity my disgrace, *does not know how*
Not though thereof the cause herself she know:
Yet hearing late a fable, which did show
Of Lovers never known, a grievous case,° *situation*
Pity thereof gate° in her breast such place, *got*
That from that sea derived tears' spring did flow.[3]
Alas, if Fancy drawn by imag'd° things, *imagined*
Though false, yet with free scope more grace doth breed
Than servants' wrack, where new doubts honor brings;[4]
Then think my dear, that you in me do read
Of Lovers' ruin some sad Tragedy:
I am not I, pity the tale of me.

60

When my good Angel guides me to the place,
Where all my good I do in Stella see,
That heav'n of joys throws only down on me
Thundered disdains and lightnings of disgrace:
But when the ruggedst step of Fortune's race° *course*
Makes me fall from her sight, then sweetly she
With words, wherein the Muses' treasures be,
Shows love and pity to my absent case.[5]
Now I wit-beaten long by hardest Fate,

3. I.e., derived from that sea [of pity], a spring of tears did flow.

4. I.e., Fancy with free scope breeds more grace or sympathy than the actual destruction of a servant, a situation in which a sense of honor provokes new doubts about that person's worth.

5. I.e., when a good angel or good fortune guides the poet to Stella, heaven throws at him only the "joys" of disdain and disgrace. On the other hand, when he is away from her, she shows him love and pity.

So dull am, that I cannot look into
The ground of this fierce Love and lovely hate:
Then some good body tell me how I do,
Whose presence, absence, absence presence is;[6]
Blist° in my curse, and cursed in my bliss. *blessed*

71

Who will in fairest book of Nature[7] know,
How Virtue may best lodged in beauty be,
Let him but learn of Love to read in thee
Stella, those fair lines, which true goodness show.
There shall he find all vices overthrow,° *overthrown*
Not by rude force, but sweetest sovereignty
Of reason, from whose light those night-birds fly;
That inward sun in thine eyes shineth so.
And not content to be Perfection's heir
Thyself, doest strive all minds that way to move:
Who mark in thee what is in thee most fair.
So while thy beauty draws the heart to love,
As fast thy Virtue bends that love to good:
But ah, Desire still cries, give me some food.

Fourth song

Only joy, now here you° are, *Stella*
Fit to hear and ease my care:
Let my whispering voice obtain,
Sweet reward for sharpest pain:
Take me to thee, and thee to me.
No, no, no, no, my Dear, let be.[8]

Night hath closed all in her cloak,
Twinkling stars Love-thoughts provoke:
Danger hence good care doth keep,[9]
Jealousy itself doth sleep:
Take me to thee, and thee to me.
No, no, no, no, my Dear, let be.

Better place no wit can find,
Cupid's yoke to loose or bind:
These sweet flowers on fine bed too,
Us in their best language woo:
Take me to thee, and thee to me.
No, no, no, no, my Dear, let be.

This small light the Moon bestows,
Serves thy beams but to disclose,

6. This paradox is repeated in stanzas 106 and 108.
7. All of creation, in effect the second "book" of God and a supplement to the Bible. It was a philosophical commonplace that Nature was the repository of natural law, which all human beings could discover through reason, just as the Bible held divine law, which was revealed to the faithful through grace.
8. The last line of each stanza is Stella's reply to Astrophil's entreaties in the preceding five lines. An earlier sonnet has suggested that logically two negatives are the same as a positive; thus it is possible to read a certain ambiguity into Stella's rejection of Astrophil here.
9. I.e., good care keeps danger away.

So to raise my hap more high;[1]
Fear not else, none can us spy:
Take me to thee, and thee to me.
No, no, no, no, my Dear, let be.

That you heard was but a mouse,
Dumb sleep holdeth all the house:
Yet a sleep, me thinks they say,
Young folks, take time while you may:
Take me to thee, and thee to me.
No, no, no, no, my Dear, let be.

Niggard° Time threats, if we miss *miserly*
This large offer of our bliss:
Long stay ere[2] he grant the same:
Sweet then, while each thing doth frame:° *suit*
Take me to thee, and thee to me.
No, no, no, no, my Dear, let be.

Your fair mother is abed,
Candles out, and curtains spread:
She thinks you do letters write:
Write, but let me first endite:° *speak*
Take me to thee, and thee to me.
No, no, no, no, my Dear, let be.

Sweet alas, why strive you thus?
Concord better fitteth us:
Leave to Mars the force of hands,
Your power in your beauty stands:
Take thee to me, and me to thee.
No, no, no, no, my Dear, let be.

Woe to me, and do you swear
Me to hate, but I forbear,
Cursed be my destines° all, *destinies*
That brought me so high to fall:
Soon with my death I will please thee.
No, no, no, no, my Dear, let be.

Eighth song

In a grove most rich of shade,
Where birds wanton music made,
May then young his pied weeds showing,[3]
New perfumed with flowers fresh growing,

Astrophil with Stella sweet,
Did for mutual comfort meet,

1. Astrophil states that the moon reveals Stella's beauty and thus raises his fortune. Writers and artists in this period imagined fortune as a goddess or as a kind of fatal force that turned a wheel to which a person's prosperity was tied; when one was at the top of Fortune's wheel, pleasure and power were within one's grasp. In the last stanza, Astrophil declares that Stella's hate will signal his fall and foresees his death. The images of rising and dying also have a sexual meaning.

2. I.e., it will be long before Time will give us another chance.

3. I.e., May, young then, showed his many-colored garments.

Both within themselves oppressed,
But each in the other blessed.

Him great harms had taught much care,
Her fair neck a foul yoke[4] bare,
But her sight his cares did banish,
In his sight her yoke did vanish.

Wept they had, alas the while,
But now tears themselves did smile,
While their eyes by love directed,
Interchangeably reflected.

Sigh they did, but now betwixt° *between*
Sighs of woes were glad sighs mixed,
With arms crossed, yet testifying
Restless rest, and living dying.

Their ears hungry of each word,
Which the dear tongue would afford,
But their tongues restrained from walking,
Till their hearts had ended talking.

But when their tongues could not speak,
Love itself did silence break;
Love did set his lips asunder,
Thus to speak in love and wonder:

Stella, sovereign of my joy,
Fair triumpher of° annoy,° *over/despair*
Stella, star of heavenly fire,
Stella, loadstar° of desier. *magnet*

Stella, in whose shining eyes,
Are the lights of Cupid's skies,
Whose beams where they once are darted,
Love therewith is straight imparted.

Stella, whose voice when it speaks,
Senses all asunder breaks;
Stella, whose voice when it singeth,
Angels to acquaintance bringeth.

Stella, in whose body is
Writ° each character of bliss, *written*
Whose face all, all beauty passeth,
Save thy mind which yet surpasseth.

Grant, O grant, but speech alas,
Fails me fearing on to pass,
Grant, O me, what am I saying?
But no fault there is in praying.

4. The "yoke" Stella wears is her marriage to Lord Rich; it is "foul" to Astrophil, since it means that he can no longer court her, at least openly.

Grant, O dear, on knees I pray,
(Knees on ground he then did stay)
That not I but since I love you,
Time and place for me may move you.

Never season was more fit,
Never room more apt for it;
Smiling air allows my reason,
These birds sing; now use the season.

This small wind which so sweet is,
See how it the leaves doth kiss,
Each tree in his best attiring,
Sense of love to love inspiring.

Love makes earth the water drink,
Love to earth makes water sink;
And if dumb things be so witty,
Shall a heavenly grace want pity?

There his hands in their speech fain
Would have made tongue's language plain;[5]
But her hands his hands repelling,
Gave repulse all grace excelling.[6]

Then she spake; her speech was such,
As not ears but heart did touch:
While such wise she love denied,
As yet love she signified.

Astrophil said she, my love
Cease in these effects to prove:
Now be still, yet still believe me,
Thy grief more than death would grieve me.

If that any thought in me,
Can taste comfort but of thee,° *except from you*
Let me feed with hellish anguish,
Joyless, hopeless, endless languish.

If those eyes you praised, be
Half so dear as you to me,
Let me home return, stark blinded
Of those eyes, and blinder minded.[7]

If to secret° of my heart, *the secrets*
I do any wish impart,
Where thou art not foremost placed,
Be both wish and I defaced.

If more may be said, I say,
All my bliss in thee I lay;

5. I.e., he would have had the language of his hands make plain what he had spoken.
6. I.e., she rejected him in a way that excelled all the grace that would have accompanied her acceptance of him.
7. I.e., even blinder in my mind.

If thou love, my love content thee,
For all love, all faith is meant thee,

Trust me while I thee deny,
In myself the smart° I try,° *pain / feel*
Tyran° honor doth thus use thee, *tyrant*
Stella's self might not refuse thee.

Therefore, Dear, this no more move,
Lest, though I leave not thy love,
Which too deep in me is framed,
I should blush when thou art named.

Therewithal away she went,
Leaving him so passion rent,
With what she had done and spoken,
That therewith my song is broken.

106

O absent presence, Stella is not here;
False flattering hope, that with so fair a face,
Bare° me in hand, that in this orphan place, *took*
Stella, I say my Stella, should appear.
What sayest thou now, where is that dainty cheer,° *food*
Thou toldst mine eyes should help their famist° case? *famished*
But thou art gone now that self felt disgrace,
Doth make me most to wish thy comfort near.[8]
But here I do store of fair ladies meet,
Who may with charm of conversation sweet,
Make in my heavy mold new thoughts to grow:
Sure they prevail as much with me, as he
That bad his friend but then new maimed,° to be *wounded*
Merry with him, and not think of his woe.

108

When sorrow (using mine own fire's might)
Melts down his lead into my boiling breast,
Through that dark furnace to heart oppressed,
There shines a joy from thee my only light;
But soon as thought of thee breeds my delight,
And my young soul flutters to thee his nest,
Most rude despair my daily unbidden guest,
Clips straight my wings, straight wraps me in his night,
And makes me then bow down my head, and say,
Ah what doth Phoebus' gold that wretch avail,
Whom iron doors do keep from use of day?
So strangely (alas) thy works[9] in me prevail,
That in my woes for thee thou art my joy,
And in my joys for thee my only annoy.

8. I.e., you are gone now that that self (my own self) has felt the disgrace of rejection; this makes me wish you here.

9. I.e., "your works," what you have done and meant, affect me strangely.

Isabella Whitney

fl. 1567–1573

Little is known about the life of Isabella Whitney. Biographers agree that she was the sister of Geoffrey Whitney, the author of the first emblem book in England, and that, like him, she was born in Cheshire. The rest is to be deduced from her poetry, which points to an author with little formal education, a sharp eye for the details of urban life, and some knowledge of classical mythology. The modesty of Whitney's literary background sets her off from such later and accomplished poets as Mary Herbert and Aemilia Lanyer, and her poems on the challenges of love, friendship, and survival in a large city distinguish her from women who wrote devotional verse. Her poems follow the form and conventions of broadside ballads, a feature that may have made them popular with readers who were drawn to stories that gave advice on affairs of the heart and matters of the purse. Of "the middling sort," Whitney probably came to London for employment and diversion, but she seems to have had difficulty supporting herself. In any case, after publishing two collections of verse, *The Copy of a Letter* (c. 1567) and *A Sweet Nosegay* (1573), she left the city, having lived out the dreams as well as the disappointments of many English villagers who went to London to find work. Poems like *The Manner of Her Will* provide a detailed sketch of the delights and horrors of urban life as it was experienced by a talented woman of limited means.

I.W. To Her Unconstant Lover

As close° as you your wedding[1] kept *quiet*
  yet now the truth I hear,
Which you (ere now) might me have told
  what need you nay to swear?

You know I always wished you well,
  so will I during life,
But since you shall a husband be,
  God send you a good wife.

And this (whereso you shall become)
  full boldly may you boast:
That once you had as true a love
  as dwelt in any coast.

Whose constantness had never quailed
  if you had not begun,
And yet it is not so far past,
  but might again be won.

If you so would; yea and not change
  so long as life should last,
But if that needs you marry must?
  then farewell, hope is past.

And if you cannot be content
  to lead a single life?

1. The formal announcement of an impending marriage; he is not yet actually married.

(Although the same right quiet be)
then take me to your wife.

So shall the promises be kept,
that you so firmly made;
Now choose whether ye will be true,
or be of Sinon's trade.[2]

Whose trade if that you long shall use,
it shall your kindred stain;
Example take by many a one
whose falsehood now is plain.

As by Aeneas[3] first of all,
who did poor Dido leave,
Causing the Queen by his untruth
with sword her heart to cleave.

Also I find that Theseus did
his faithful love forsake,
Stealing away within the night,
before she did awake.

Jason that came of noble race
two ladies did beguile;
I muse how he durst show his face
to them that knew his wile.° *cunning*

For when he by Medea's art
had got the fleece of gold
And also had of her that time
all kind of things he would,

He took his ship and fled away
regarding not the vows,
That he did make so faithfully
unto his loving spouse.

How durst he trust the surging seas
knowing himself forsworn?
Why did he scape safe to the land
before the ship was torn?

I think King Aeolus° stayed the winds *god of the winds*
and Neptune° ruled the sea; *god of the sea*
Then might he boldly pass the waves
no perils could him slay.

But if his falsehood had to them
been manifest before,

2. Posing as a deserter from the Greek army, Sinon persuaded the beseiged Trojans to open the city gates to him and a large wooden horse that he pretended was a gift from Athena but in fact hid Greek warriors in its belly.

3. Whitney lists unfaithful lovers recorded in myth: Aeneas, the Trojan hero and founder of Rome, who deserted Dido, queen of Carthage, after expressing love for her; Theseus, the hero and king of Athens, who left Ariadne, the daughter of Minos, king of Crete, on a island in the sea, even though she had saved him from the monster, Minotaur; Jason, the leader of the Argonauts who captured the golden fleece—a Greek treasure—with the help of Medea, and then abandoned her in favor of Glauce, daughter of Creon, king of Corinth.

They would have rent the ship as soon
as he had gone from shore.

Now may you hear how falseness is
made manifest in time,
Although they that commit the same
think it a venial crime.

For they, for their unfaithfulness,
did get perpetual fame.
Fame? Wherefore did I term it so?
I should have called it shame.

Let Theseus be, let Jason pass,
let Paris[4] also 'scape,° *escape*
That brought destruction unto Troy
all through the Grecian rape,

And unto me a Troilus[5] be,
if not you may compare,
With any of these persons that
above expressed are.

But if I cannot please your mind,
for wants that rest in me,
Wed whom you list,° I am content, *wish*
your refuse for to be.

It shall suffice me simple soul
of thee to be forsaken,
And it may chance, although not yet,
you wish you had me taken.

But rather than you should have cause
to wish this through° your wife, *because of*
I wish to her, ere her you have,
no more but loss of life.

For she that shall so happy be,
of thee to be elect,
I wish her virtues to be such,
she need not be suspect.

I rather wish her Helen's face,
than one of Helen's trade,
With chasteness of Penelope[6]
the which did never fade.

A Lucrece for her constancy,
and Thisby for her truth;

4. Son of Priam, king of Troy; he stole Helen, the wife of King Menelaus of Sparta, a theft that brought about the invasion of Troy by Menelaus and the Greeks.
5. Son of Priam, king of Troy; his fidelity to Cressida, who deserted him in favor of Diomedes, a Greek warrior, is recounted in a 4th century addition to the stories of the Trojan War.
6. Whitney alludes to women who exemplify fidelity: Penelope, who waited for the return of Odysseus from the Trojan War; Lucrece or Lucretia, who killed herself after confessing to her husband that she had been raped; and Thisby or Thisbe, who killed herself when she saw her dying lover, Pyramus.

If such thou have, then Peto[7] be,
not Paris, that were ruth.

Perchance, ye will think this thing rare
in one woman to find;
Save Helen's beauty, all the rest
the gods have me assigned.

These words I do not speak, thinking
from thy new love to turn thee.
Thou knowest by proof what I deserve;
I need not to inform thee.

But let that pass. Would God I had
Cassandra's gift[8] me lent;
Then either thy ill chance or mine
my foresight might prevent.

But all in vain for this I seek,
wishes may not attain it;
Therefore may hap° to me what shall, *happen*
and I cannot refrain it.

Wherefore I pray God be my guide
and also thee defend;
No worser than I wish myself,
until thy life shall end.

Which life I pray God may again
King Nestor's[9] life renew,
And after that your soul may rest
amongst the heavenly crew.

Thereto I wish King Xerxes'[1] wealth,
or else King Croesus's gold,
With as much rest and quietness
as man may have on mold.° *in the world*

And when you shall this letter have
let it be kept in store.
For she that sent the same hath sworn
as yet to send no more.

And now farewell, for why at large
my mind is here expressed?
The which you may perceive, if that
you do peruse the rest.

Finis.

c. 1567

7. The source of this name is unknown.
8. Daughter of Priam, king of Troy; she had prophetic powers, though her prophecies of the city's fall were not believed.
9. King of Pylos and wise counselor to all the Greeks during their seige of Troy.
1. Whitney names men of legendary wealth: Xerxes, king of the Persians, who, with enormous resources gathered from all Asia Minor, attacked Athens and was defeated there by Themistocles; and Croesus, king of Lydia, who was defeated by Cyrus, king of the Persians.

The Admonition by the Author
to All Young Gentlewomen, and to All Other Maids Being in Love

Ye virgins that from Cupid's tents
do bear away the foil,[1]
Whose hearts as yet with raging love
most painfully do boil.

To you I speak, for you be they
that good advice do lack;
Oh, if I could good counsel give,
my tongue should not be slack.

But such as I can give, I will.
here in few words express,
Which if you do observe, it will
some of your care redress.

Beware of fair and painted talk,
beware of flattering tongues;
The mermaids do pretend no good
for all their pleasant songs.

Some use the tears of crocodiles
contrary to their heart,
And if they cannot always weep,
they wet their cheeks by art.

Ovid, within his art of love,[2]
doth teach them this same knack,
To wet their hand and touch their eyes,
so oft as tears they lack.

Why have ye such deceit in store?
have you such crafty wile?
Less craft than this, God knows, would soon
us simple souls beguile.

And will ye not leave off? But still
delude us in this wise?
Since it is so, we trust we shall
take heed to feigned lies.

Trust not a man at the first sight,
but try him well before;
I wish all maids within their breasts
to keep this thing in store:

For trial shall declare his truth,
and show what he doth think,

1. The reference is obscure. Cupid's weapons were traditionally a bow and arrows; Whitney describes him rather as a fencer who wounds his victims with a foil or sword. By bearing his foil away, Whitney's virgins appear to have experienced but not acquiesced to love.

2. The *Ars Amatoria*, a facetious treatise in which the poet advises men how to court and make love to women. Here, Whitney implies that her readers either imitate or avoid the examples of legendary women whose stories she tells.

Whether he be a lover true,
or do intend to shrink.

If Scylla[3] had not trust too much
before that she did try,
She could not have been clean forsake° *forsaken*
when she for help did cry.

Or if she had had good advice,
Nisus had lived long;
How durst she trust a stranger, and
do her dear father wrong?

King Nisus had a hair by fate
which hair while he did keep
He never should be overcome
neither on land nor deep.

The stranger that the daughter loved
did war against the King,
And always sought how that he might
them in subjection bring.

This Scylla stole away the hair
for to obtain her will,
And gave it to the stranger that
did straight her father kill.

Then she, who thought herself most sure
to have her whole desire,
Was clean reject,° and left behind *rejected*
when he did home retire.

Or if such falsehood had been once
unto Oenone[4] known,
About the fields of Ida wood
Paris had walked alone.

Or if Demophoon's deceit
to Phyllis[5] had been told,
She had not been transformed so,
as poets tell of old.

Hero did try Leander's[6] truth
before that she did trust,
Therefore she found him unto her
both constant, true, and just.

3. Daughter of the mythical Nisus, king of Megara, Scylla trusted the love of Minos, king of Crete, who was beseiging her father's city. For love of Minos (whom Whitney refers to as "the stranger"), Scylla betrayed her father by stealing a lock of his hair, a guarantee that Megara would remain free. According to Virgil, Minos, having taken Megara, captured Scylla, tied her to his ship, and dragged her through the sea. She was eventually transformed into a ciris, or sea-bird.

4. A nymph of Mount Ida, who was abandoned by Paris, son of Priam, king of Troy.

5. A mythical princess of Thrace and loved by the Greek warrior Demophon (or Demophoon); believing that he would not return to her after the Trojan War, she hanged herself.

6. Hero's lover, Leander, drowned while swimming across the Hellespont to be with her, whereupon she, too, threw herself into the sea.

For always did he swim the sea
when stars in sky did glide,
Till he was drowned by the way
near hand unto the side.

She scratched her face, she tore her hair
(it grieveth me to tell)
When she did know the end of him,
that she did love so well.

But like Leander there be few,
therefore in time take heed;
And always try before ye trust,
so shall you better speed.

The little fish that careless is
within the water clear,
How glad is he, when he doth see
a bait for to appear.

He thinks his hap° right good to be, *luck*
that he the same could spy,
And so the simple fool doth trust
too much before he try.

O little fish what hap hadst thou,
to have such spiteful fate,
To come into one's cruel hands
out of so happy state?

Thou didst suspect no harm, when thou
upon the bait didst look;
O that thou hadst had Linceus's[7] eyes
for to have seen the hook.

Then hadst thou with thy pretty mates
been playing in the streams,
Whereas Sir Phoebus° daily doth *the sun god Apollo*
show forth his golden beams.

But since thy fortune is so ill
to end thy life on shore,
Of this thy most unhappy end
I mind to speak no more.

But of thy fellow's chance that late
such pretty shift did make,
That he from fisher's hook did sprint
before he could him take.

And now he pries on every bait,
suspecting still that prick
(For to lie hid in every thing)
wherewith the fishers strick.° *strike*

7. A sharp-eyed mythical warrior of Greece.

And since the fish that reason lacks
 once warned doth beware,
Why should not we take heed to that
 that turneth us to care?

And I who was deceived late
 by one's unfaithful tears
Trust now for to beware, if that
 I live this hundred years.

Finis.

c. 1567

A Careful Complaint by the Unfortunate Author

Good Dido[1] stint thy tears,
 and sorrows all resign
To me that born was to augment
 misfortune's luckless line.
Or using still the same,
 good Dido do thy best,
In helping to bewail the hap
 that furthereth mine unrest.
For though thy Troyan mate,
 that Lord Aeneas hight,
Requiting all thy steadfast love,
 from Carthage took his flight,
And foully broke his oath,
 and promise made before,
Whose falsehood finished thy delight,
 before thy hairs were hoar.
Yet greater cause of grief
 compels me to complain,
For Fortune fell° converted hath *evil*
 my health to heaps of pain.
And that she[2] swears my death,
 too plain it is (alas),
Whose end let malice still attempt
 to bring the same to pass.
O Dido, thou hadst lived
 a happy woman still,
If fickle fancy had not thralled° *enslaved*
 thy wits to reckless will.
For as the man by whom
 thy deadly dolors bred,
Without regard of plighted troth
 from Carthage city fled,
So might thy cares in time
 be banished out of thought,

1. Queen of Carthage, seduced and then abandoned by Aeneas on his way from Troy to Italy.

2. I.e., Fortune, whose end or purpose, Whitney's death, malice will bring to pass.

His absence might well salve the sore
that erst° his presence wrought. *first*
For fire no longer burns
than faggots° feed the flame, *except when sticks*
The want of things that breed annoy
may soon redress the same.[3]
But I, unhappy most,
and gripped with endless griefs,
Despair (alas) amid my hope,
and hope without relief.
And as the swelt'ring heat
consumes the war away,
So do the heaps of deadly harms
still threaten my decay.
O death delay not long
thy duty to declare.
Ye Sisters three[4] dispatch my days
and finish all my care.

The Manner of Her Will

The Author (though loath to leave the City) upon her friend's procurement is constrained to depart, wherefore she feigneth as she would die and maketh her will and testament, as followeth, with large legacies of such goods and riches which she most abundantly hath left behind her, and thereof maketh London sole executor to see her legacies performed.

A communication which the Author had to London, before she made her will.

The time is come I must depart
from thee, ah famous city.
I never yet to rue my smart,
did find that thou hadst pity.
Wherefore small cause there is that I
should grieve from thee go.
But many women foolishly,
like me, and other mo'e,
Do such a fixed fancy set,
on those which least deserve,
That long it is ere° wit we get, *before*
away from them to swerve.° *turn*
But time with pity oft will tell
to those that will her try,
Whether it best be more to mell,° *associate with*
or utterly defy.
And now hath time me put in mind,
of thy great cruelness,
That never once a help would find,
to ease me in distress.
Thou never yet wouldst credit give
to board me for a year,
Nor with apparel me relieve

3. I.e., "want," which breeds annoyance, will also end annoyance, as it will eventually result in death.

4. I.e., the three Fates, who determine the length of life and the time of death.

except thou paid were.
No, no, thou never didst me good,
nor ever wilt, I know;
Yet I am in no angry mood
but will, or ere I go
In perfect love and charity,
my testament here write,
And leave to thee such treasury
as I in it recite.
Now stand aside and give me leave
to write my latest will,
And see that none you do deceive
of that I leave them till.[1]

The manner of her will, and what she left to London and to all those in it at her departing.

I whole in body, and in mind,
but very weak in purse,
Do make, and write my testament
for fear it will be worse.
And first I wholly do commend,
my soul and body eke,° *also*
To God the Father and the Son,
so long as I can speak.
And after speech, my soul to him,
and body to the grave,
Till time that all shall rise again,
their judgment for to have.
And then I hope they both shall meet,
to dwell for aye° in joy *ever*
Whereas I trust to see my friends
released from all annoy.
Thus have you heard touching my soul,
and body what I mean,
I trust you all will witness bear,
I have a steadfast brain.
And now let me dispose such things,
as I shall leave behind,
That those which shall receive the same,
may know my willing mind.
I first of all to London leave
because I there was bred,
Brave buildings rare, of churches store,
and Paul's to the head.[2]
Between the same, fair streets there be
and people goodly store;
Because their keeping craveth° cost, *requires*

1. I.e., you must not deceive my inheritors by taking what I leave them until I leave them.
2. St. Paul's Cathedral, in the heart of the City of London; Whitney describes it as the foremost or "head" of London's public buildings.

I yet will leave him[3] more.
First for their food, I butchers leave,
that every day shall kill;
By Thames you shall have brewers store,
and bakers at your will.
And such as orders do observe,° *clergymen*
and eat fish thrice a week,
I leave two streets, full fraught therewith,
they need not far to seek.
Watling Street, and Canwick Street,
I full of woolen leave,
And linen store in Friday Street,
if they me not deceive.
And those which are of calling such,
that costlier they require,
I mercers leave, with silk so rich,
as any would desire.
In cheap of them, they store shall find,
and likewise in that street,[4]
I goldsmiths leave, with jewels such
as are for ladies meet.
And plate to furnish cupboards with,
full brave there shall you find,
With purl° of silver and of gold. *cord*
to satisfy your mind.
With hoods, bongraces,° hats or caps, *sunshades*
such store are in that street,
As if on one side you should miss,
the other serves you feat.
For nets of every kind of sort,
I leave within the pawn,
French ruffs, high purls,° gorgets° and sleeves, *ruffs / collars*
of any kind of lawn.° *thin cloth*
For purse or knives, for comb or glass,
or any needful knack,
I by the stocks have left a boy
will ask you what you lack.
I hose do leave in Birchin Lane,
of any kind of size,
For women stitched, for men both trunks
and those of Gascoigne guise,
Boots, shoes, or pantables° good store, *slippers*
Saint Martin's hath for you;
In Cornwall, there I leave you beds,
and all that 'longs° thereto. *belongs*
For women shall you tailors have,
by Bow, the chiefest dwell,
In every lane you some shall find,
can do indifferent well.

3. St. Paul's, to whose district Whitney will leave "more" than the "goodly store" already there.

4. I.e., they shall also find much cheap cloth in that street.

And for the men, few streets or lanes,
but bodymakers° be, *suitmakers*
And such as make the sweeping cloaks,
with guards° beneath the knee. *ornamental borders*
Artillery at Temple Bar,
and dagges° at Tower Hill, *pistols*
Swords and bucklers of the best,
are nigh the Fleet until.[5]
Now when thy folk are fed and clad
with such as I have named,
For dainty mouths, and stomachs weak
some junkets° must be framed. *milk puddings*
Wherefore I 'pothecaries° leave, *apothecaries*
with banquets in their shop,
Physicians also for the sick,
diseases for to stop.
Some roisters° still, must bide in thee, *thugs*
and such as cut it out,
That with the guiltless quarrel will,
to let their blood about.[6]
For them I cunning surgeons leave,
some plasters° to apply, *bandages*
That ruffians may not still be hanged,
nor quiet persons die.
For salt, oatmeal, candles, soap,
or what you else do want,
In many places, shops are full,
I left you nothing scant.
If they that keep what you I leave,
ask money, when they sell it,
At mint,° there is such store, it is *the mint*
unpossible to tell it.
At stillyard° store of wines there be, *the distillery*
your dulled minds to glad,
And handsome men, that must not wed
except they leave their trade.[7]
They oft shall seek for proper girls,
and some perhaps shall find,
That need compels, or lucre lures
to satisfy their mind.
And near the same, I houses leave
for people to repair,
To bathe themselves, so to prevent
infection of the air.
On Saturdays I wish that those,
which all the week do drug,° *drudge*
Shall thither trudge, to trim them up
on Sundays to look smug.

5. I.e., near the Temple Bar up to Fleet Street.
6. I.e., those who assault men who have done them no harm must remain in London.
7. I.e., because they deal in liquor, they are not fit husbands.

If any other thing be lacked
  in thee, I wish them look,
For there it is, I little brought
  but nothing from thee took.
Now for the people in thee left,
  I have done as I may,
And that the poor, when I am gone,
  have cause for me to pray.
I will to prisons portions leave,
  what though but very small,
Yet that they may remember me,
  occasion be it shall,
And first the counter they shall have,
  lest they should go to wrack,° *ruin*
Some coggers,° and some honest men, *crooks*
  that sergeants draw aback.[8]
And such as friends will not them bail,
  whose coin is very thin,
For them I leave a certain hole,
  and little ease within.
The Newgate once a month shall have
  a sessions° for his share, *court trials*
Lest being heaped, infection might
  procure a further care.[9]
And at those sessions some shall 'scape,
  with burning near the thumb,
And afterward to beg their fees,
  till they have got the sum.
And such whose deeds deserveth death,
  and twelve° have found the same, *a jury*
They shall be drawn up Holborn Hill
  to come to further shame.
Well, yet to such I leave a nag
  shall soon their sorrows cease,
For he shall either break their necks
  or gallop from the preace.° *crowd*
The Fleet, not in their circuit is,[1]
  yet if I give him nought,
It might procure his curse, ere I
  unto the ground be brought.
Wherefore I leave some papist old
  to underprop his roof,
And to the poor within the same,
  a box for their behoof.° *benefit*
What makes you standers-by to smile,

8. Whitney seems to wish to endow prisons with a "counter," a device to keep track of accounts, lest the prisoners be ruined by tradesmen, both crooks and honest men, who sell goods to prisoners and who are also restrained in their commerce by sergeants.

9. I.e., Newgate prison shall hold trials once a month to avoid overcrowding and disease. Some prisoners, marked by a burn on the thumb, will be freed to beg for bail money.

1. In the 16th century the Fleet was a prison for people convicted of crimes by the Star Chamber, a court dealing with affairs of conscience, such as treason and differences of faith; hence it is where one would find a Catholic, a papist. It is not a prison for people convicted by the common law; hence it is not in the same "circuit" as Newgate.

and laugh so in your sleeve,
I think it is, because that I
to Ludgate° nothing give. *a debtors' prison*
I am not now in case to lie,
here is no place of jest;
I did reserve that for myself,
if I my health possessed.
And ever came in credit so
a debtor for to be,
When days of payment did approach,
I thither meant to flee.
To shroud myself amongst the rest,
that choose to die in debt;
Rather than any creditor,
should money from them get.
Yet 'cause° I feel myself so weak *because*
that none me credit° dare, *give me credit*
I here revoke, and do it leave,
some bankrupts to his° share. *their*
To all the bookbinders by Paul's° *St. Paul's Cathedral*
because I like their art,
They every week shall money have,
when they from books depart.° *sell their books*
Amongst them all, my printer must,
have somewhat to his share;
I will my friends these books to buy
of him, with other ware.
For maidens poor, I widowers rich
do leave, that oft shall dote,
And by that means shall marry them,
to set the girls afloat.
And wealthy widows will I leave,
to help young gentlemen,
Which when you° have, in any case *i.e., gentlemen*
be courteous to them° then. *i.e., widows*
And see their plate and jewels eke
may not be marred with rust,
Nor let their bags too long be full,
for fear that they do burst.
To every gate under the walls
that compass thee about,
I fruit wives leave to entertain
such as come in and out.
To Smithfield° I must something leave, *the meat market*
my parents there did dwell;
So careless for to be of it,
none would account it well.
Wherefore it thrice a week shall have,
of horse and neat° good store, *beef*
And in his spittle,[2] blind and lame,

2. In the hospital at Smithfield the blind and lame are always to dwell or find refuge.

to dwell for evermore.
And Bedlam[3] must not be forgot,
for that was oft my walk,
I people there too many leave,
that out of tune do talk.
At Bridewell[4] there shall beadles be,
and matrons that shall still
See chalk well-chopped, and spinning plied,
and turning of the mill.
For such as cannot quiet be,
but strive for house or land,
At th'Inns of Court,[5] I lawyers leave
to take their cause in hand.
And also leave I at each Inn,
of Court or Chancery,
Of gentlemen, a youthful root,
full of activity,
For whom I store of books have left,
at each bookbinder's stall,
And part of all that London hath
to furnish them withal.° *with*
And when they are with study cloyed,° *tired*
to recreate their mind,
Of tennis courts, of dancing schools,
and fence they store shall find.
And every Sunday at the least,
I leave to make them sport,
In divers places players that
of wonder shall report.
Now London have I (for thy sake)
within thee, and without,
As comes into my memory,
dispersed round about
Such needful things, as they should have
here left now unto thee,
When I am gone, with conscience
let them dispersed be.
And though I nothing named have
to bury me withal,
Consider that above the ground
annoyance be I shall.° *I shall be*
And let me have a shrouding sheet
to cover me from shame,
And in oblivion bury me
and never more me name.
Ringings° nor other ceremonies *of church bells*
use you not for cost,
Nor at my burial, make no feast,

3. Asylum for the insane.
4. A prison for persons convicted for minor offenses; it also served as a workhouse for the unemployed.
5. The offices of those practicing common law; also the schools teaching common law.

your money were but lost.
Rejoice in God that I am gone,
out of this vale so vile.
And that of each thing, left such store,
as may your wants exile.
I make thee sole executor, because
I loved thee best.
And thee I put in trust, to give
the goods unto the rest.
Because thou shalt a helper need,
in this so great a charge,
I wish good Fortune be thy guide, lest
thou shouldst run at large.
The happy days and quiet times,
they both her servants be,
Which well will serve to fetch and bring,
such things as need° to thee. *are needed*
Wherefore (good London) not refuse,° *do not refuse*
for helper her to take,
Thus being weak, and weary both
an end here will I make.
To all that ask what end I made,
and how I went away,
Thou answer mayest like those which here
no longer tarry may.
And unto all that wish me well,
or rue that I am gone,
Do me commend, and bid them cease
my absence for to moan.
And tell them further, if they would,
my presence still have had,
They should have sought to mend my luck,
which ever was too bad.
So fare thou well a thousand times,
God shield thee from thy foe,
And still make thee victorious
of those that seek thy woe.
And though I am persuade° that I *persuaded*
shall never more thee see,
Yet to the last, I shall not cease
to wish much good of thee.
This twenty of October, I,
in Anno Domini,
A thousand five hundred seventy three,
as almanacs descry,
Did write this will with mine own hand
and it to London gave,
In witness of the standers-by,
whose names if you will have,
Paper, Pen, and Standish° were, *inkstand*
at that same present by,
With Time, who promised to reveal,

so fast as she could hie,
The same, lest of my nearer kin,
for any thing should vary,
So finally I make an end
no longer can I tarry.
Finis.

1573

Mary Herbert, Countess of Pembroke

1561–1621

Mary Herbert was like many women of her time in having two phases to her life: a period of service to men, followed by a phase of independent activity. Deeply attached to her brother, Sir Philip Sidney, she spent much of her young adulthood in his company. The estate she presided over as wife to Henry Herbert, Earl of Pembroke, was Sidney's place of refuge after Queen Elizabeth had exiled him from court. At Wilton House and in his sister's company he wrote *The Apology for Poetry* and the first version of his prose romance, *The Arcadia*. Mary Herbert was an interested party in yet another project, his translation of the psalms, and when he died in 1586, she resolved to finish the project. Picking up where he had left off, at Psalm 43, she completed the cycle. Her work was encouraged by the circle of friends that gathered frequently at Wilton House and included such writers and musicians as Francis Mere, Edmund Spenser, Samuel Daniel, Nicholas Breton, Fulke Greville, and Abraham Fraunce. The seventeenth-century biographer John Aubrey spoke of the group as a "college."

Translations of the psalms were popular among Protestant writers of the period; they fulfilled the obligation to know both the Word and the indwelling spirit of God. Poets of religious lyric in the next century, especially George Herbert, would seek and represent a similar knowledge. Mary Herbert dedicated her work to Queen Elizabeth in a poem entitled *Even Now That Care*, which was followed by an elegy for her brother Philip, *To Thee Pure Sprite*. Although riddled with ellipses or words that have been deliberately omitted, they convey the spiritual intensity that characterizes her translations. Some critics think that she did not write a second elegy (here attributed to her), *The Lay of Clorinda*; it is, however, what we might expect a woman of her station and training to have written about the death of a beloved friend. Milton would later give a profoundly political and religious dimension to the genre in his *Lycidas*, an elegy that is as much for an age and its temperament as it is for a person.

Even Now That Care[1]

Even now that care which on thy crown attends,
And with thy happy greatness daily grows,
Tells me, thrice sacred Queen, my Muse offends,
And of respect to thee the line outgoes.[2]
One instant will, or willing can she° lose *Queen Elizabeth*
I say not reading, but receiving rhymes,

1. This poem prefaces Mary Herbert's translation of the psalms, dedicated to Queen Elizabeth.

2. I.e., my Muse oversteps the boundary of respect that your status demands.

On whom in chief dependeth to dispose
What Europe acts in these most active times?[3]

Yet dare I so, as humbleness may dare
Cherish some hope they shall acceptance find;
Not weighing less thy state, lighter thy care,
But knowing more thy grace, abler thy mind.
What heavenly powers thee highest throne assigned,
Assigned thee goodness suiting that degree,
And by thy strength thy burden so defined;
To others' toil, is exercise to thee.[4]

Cares though still great, cannot be greatest still;
Business must ebb, though leisure never flow.
Then these the posts of duty and goodwill
Shall press to offer what their senders owe,
Which once in two, now in one subject go,[5]
The poorer left, the richer reft away,
Who better might (O might! Ah, word of woe)
Have given for me what I for him defray.° *pay*

How can I name whom sighing sighs extend,° *wordlessly amplify*
And not unstop my tears' eternal spring?
But he did warp, I weaved this web to end.[6]
The stuff not ours, our work no curious thing,
Wherein yet well we thought the psalmist king,
Now English denizened though Hebrew born,
Would to thy music undispleased sing,
Oft having worse, without repining worn.[7]

And I the cloth in both our names present,
A livery robe to be bestowed by° thee, *on*
Small parcel of that undischarged rent,
From which nor pains, nor payments can us free.
And yet enough to cause our neighbors see
We will our best, though scanted° in our will; *deficient*
And those nigh fields where sown thy favors be
Unwealthy do, not else unworthy till.[8]

For in our work what bring we but thine own?
What English is, by many names is thine.
There humble laurels in thy shadows grown
To garland others' world, themselves repine.° *are sorrowful*
Thy breast the cabinet, thy seat the shrine,
Where Muses hang their vowed memories,
Where wit, where art, where all that is divine
Conceived best, and best defended lies.

3. I.e., will she or can she lose an instant receiving rhymes—she, who is governing Europe?
4. I.e., thy burden, defined by thy strength, is to others toil, [but] to thee exercise.
5. I.e., Herbert and Sidney; the latter is the richer of the two subjects, the one who could better have offered the queen duty and good will.
6. I.e., he laid the warp of this web (placed its threads lengthwise); I wove it to completion (after his death).
7. I.e., you often had worse stuff than our web to wear (or our poems to listen to), which you did without complaining.
8. I.e., those near fields where thy favors are sown (as seed) we, not wealthy but not unworthy, cultivate. Herbert thanks the queen for her support.

Which if men did not (as they do) confess,
And wronging worlds would otherwise consent,[9]
Yet here° who minds° so meet a patroness — *in England / finds*
For author's state or writing's argument?
A king° should only to a queen be sent. — *King David*
God's loved choice unto his chosen love,
Devotion to devotion's president;° — *chief object*
What all applaud, to her whom none reprove.

And who sees aught,° but sees how justly square° — *anything / suitable*
His° haughty ditties to thy glorious days? — *King David's*
How well beseeming thee his triumphs are?
His hope, his zeal, his prayer, plaint,° and praise, — *complaint*
Needless thy person to their height to raise,
Less need to bend them down to thy degree;
These holy garments each good soul assays,° — *tries on*
Some sorting° all, all sort to none but thee. — *fitting*

For ev'n thy rule is painted° in his reign, — *illustrated*
Both clear in right, both nigh° by wrong oppressed. — *closely*
And each at length (man crossing God in vain)
Possessed of place,° and each in peace possessed. — *office, rule*
Proud Philistines did interrupt his rest,
The foes of heav'n no less have been thy foes;
He with great conquest, thou with greater blessed;
Thou sure to win, and he secure to lose.° — *secure against loss*

Thus hand in hand with him thy glories walk,
But who can trace them where alone they go?
Of thee two hemispheres on honor talk,
And hands and seas thy trophies jointly show.
The very winds did on thy party° blow, — *ally*
And rocks in arms thy foemen eft defy;[1]
But soft my muse, thy pitch is earthly low,
Forbear this heaven, where only eagles fly.

Kings on a queen enforced their states to lay,
Mainlands for empire waiting on an isle;
Men drawn by worth a woman to obey,
One moving all, herself unmoved the while.[2]
Truth's restitution, vanity's exile,
Wealth sprung of want, war held without annoy;
Let subject be of some inspired style,
Till then the object of her subject's joy.[3]

Thy utmost can but offer to her sight
Her handmaid's task, which most her will endears,

9. I.e., if men did not confess that your breast is the shrine of the Muses, even unfair worlds would otherwise agree that this was the case.

1. I.e., winds blew to help your allies; rocks defied your enemies who were up in arms. Herbert then protests that the level of her poetic skill is low; it must not aspire to a height that only "eagles," or poets of great power, attain.

2. I.e., kings are forced to place their "states" (authority and power) on a queen; mainlands anticipating empire are forced to lay their "states" (conditions, resources) on an island, i.e., England.

3. Herbert defines the subjects of an inspired style of poetry: the restitution of truth, the exile of vanity, a "wealth" created by necessity (i.e., moral virtue), war without harm.

And pray unto thy pains life from that light
Which lively light some court and kingdom cheers.
What[4] wish she° may (far past her living peers *the Queen*
And rival still to Judah's faithful king,
In more than he and more triumphant years),
Sing what God doth, and do what men may sing.

c. 1590

To Thee Pure Sprite[1]

To thee pure sprite,° to thee alone's addressed *spirit*
this coupled work, by double interest thine:
first raised by thy blessed hand, and what is mine
Inspired by thee, thy secret power impressed.° *informed by*
so dared my Muse with thine itself combine,
as mortal stuff with that which is divine.
Thy lightening beams give lustre to the rest,

That heaven's king may deign his own transformed
in substance no, but superficial tire° *attire*
by thee° put on to praise,[2] not to aspire *Sidney*
To those high tones so in themselves adorned,
which angels sing in their celestial choir,
and all of tongues with soul and voice admire.
These sacred hymns thy kingly prophet formed.

Oh, had that soul which honor brought to rest
too soon not left, and reft the world of all
what man could show, which we perfection call,
This half-maimed piece had sorted with° the best. *matched*
deep wounds enlarged, long festered in their gall,
fresh bleeding smart; not eye- but heart-tears fall.
Ah memory, what needs this new arrest?° *delay*

Yet here behold, (oh, wert thou to behold!)
this[3] finished now, thy matchless Muse begun,
the rest but pieced, as left by thee undone.
Pardon (oh, blessed soul) presumption too too bold,
if love and zeal such error ill-become,
'tis zealous love, love which hath never done,
Nor can enough in world of words unfold.

And since it hath no further scope to go,
nor other purpose but to honor thee,
thee in thy works, where all the Graces[4] be
As little streams with all their all do flow
to their great sea, due tribute's grateful fee;[5]

4. I.e., court and kingdom.

1. Herbert's elegy is for her brother, Sir Philip Sidney. In it she acknowledges his part in the translations.

2. I.e., your intelligence informs this verse not so that the king of heaven will consider his own light transformed substantially; rather it is that your own attire, clothing, is put over that light to praise him. Herbert returns to the idea, expressed earlier in her dedicatory poem to Elizabeth, that the psalms are a web or woven cloth.

3. I.e., the translation.

4. Personifications of the elements of courtesy and courteous expression; typically, they are attributes of poetic and artistic work.

5. I.e., the streams are a tribute to the sea.

so press my thoughts, my burdened thoughts, in me,
To pay the debt of infinites I owe

To thy great worth. Exceeding nature's store,
wonder of men, sole° born perfection's kind, *alone*
phoenix[6] thou wert. So rare thy fairest mind,
Heav'nly adorned, Earth justly might adore,
where truthful praise in highest glory shined,
for there alone was praise to truth confined;
And where but there, to live for ever more?

Oh! When to this account, this cast up sum,
this reckoning made, this audit of my woe,
I call my thoughts, whence so strange passions flow,
How works my heart, my senses stricken dumb?
that° would thee more than ever heart could show, *my thoughts*
and all too short,° who knew thee best doth know, *inadequate*
There lives no wit that may thy praise become.° *express*

Truth I invoke (who scorn elsewhere to move
or here in aught my blood should partialize),[7]
Truth, sacred Truth, thee sole to solemnize.
Those precious rights well known best mind's approve;
and who but doth, hath wisdom's open eyes,
not owly° blind the fairest light still° flies, *owl-like/always*
Confirm no less?[8] At least 'tis sealed above.

Where thou art fixed among my fellow lights,
my day put out, my life in darkness cast,
thy angel's soul, with highest angels placed,
There blessed sings enjoying heaven, delights° *delights in*
thy maker's praise, as far from earthly taste
as here thy works so worthily embraced
By all of worth, where never envy bites.

As goodly buildings to some glorious end
cut off by fate, before the Graces had
each wond'rous part in all their beauties clad,
Yet so much done, as art would not amend;
so thy rare works to which no wit can add,
in all men's eyes, which are not blindly mad,
Beyond compare, above all praise extend.

Immortal monuments of thy fair fame,
though not complete, nor in the reach of thought,
how on that passing peacetime would have wrought
Had Heav'n so spared the life of life to frame
the rest?[9] But ah, such loss! Hath this world aught
can equal it? Or which like grievance brought?
Yet there will live thy ever-praised name.

6. A mythical bird, unique in the world, which is miraculously reborn from the ashes of its own funeral pyre.

7. I.e., I scorn that my blood (passion, temperament) should favor anything in a partial or prejudicial way.

8. I.e., who that has wisdom's open eyes and is not owlishly blind, fleeing strong light, does not confirm this?

9. I.e., had Heaven so spared your life so that you could frame the life of the rest of mankind.

To which these dearest offerings of my heart,
dissolved to ink, while pen's impressions move
the bleeding veins of never dying love,
I render here; these wounding lines of smart,
sad characters indeed of simple love,
not art nor skill which abler wits do prove,
Of my full soul receive the meanest part.

Receive these hymns, these obsequies receive,
if any mark of thy sweet sprite appear,
well are they born,[1] no title else shall bear.
I can no more. Dear soul, I take my leave;
sorrow still strives, would mount thy highest sphere
presuming so just cause might meet thee there.[2]
Oh happy change! Could so I take my leave.

c. 1590

Psalm 71: In Te Domini Speravi

On thee my trust is grounded.
Lord, let me never be
With shame confounded,
But set me free
And in thy justice rescue me;
Thy gracious ear to meward° bend *toward me*
And me defend.

Be thou my rock, my tower,
My ever safe resort,
Whose saving power
Hath not been short° *deficient*
To work my safety, for my fort
On thee alone is built; in thee
My strongholds be.

Me, O my God, deliver
From wicked, wayward hand.
God, my help-giver,
On whom I stand
And stood since I could understand,
Nay, since by life I first became
What now I am.

Since prisoned in my mother,
By thee I prison brake,° *broke from*
I trust no other,
No other make
My stay, no other refuge take,
Void of thy praise no time doth find
My mouth and mind.

1. I.e, the hymns are of good parentage.
2. I.e., my sorrow would climb to your sphere in heaven, presuming that so just a cause would allow my sorrow to be there.

Men for a monster took me,
Yet hope of help from thee
Never forsook me.
Make then by me
All men, with praise extolled, may see
Thy glory,[1] thy magnificence,
Thy excellence.

When feeble years do leave me
No stay of other sort,
Do not bereave me
Of thy support,
And fail not then to be my fort,
When weakness, in me killing might,° *strength*
Usurps his right.[2]

For now against me banded,
My foes have talked of me;
Now unwithstanded,° *not withstood*
Who° their spies be *whoever*
Of me have made a firm decree:
(Lo!) God to him hath bid adieu,
Now then pursue.[3]

Pursue, say they, and take him;
No succor can he win,
No refuge make him.
O God, begin
To bring with speed thy forces in.
Help me, my God, my God, I say
Go not away.

But let them be confounded
And perish by whose hate
My soul is wounded;
And in one rate,° *as a class*
Let them all share in shameful state
Whose counsels, as their farthest end,° *goal*
My wrong intend.

For I will still persevere
My hopes on thee to raise,
Augmenting ever
Thy praise with praise.
My mouth shall utter forth always
Thy truths, thy helps, whose sum surmounts
My best accounts.

1. I.e., cause all men to see, by my aid, thy glory magnified with praise.
2. I.e., when weakness, having overcome strength, takes the place of strength in my soul.
3. I.e., my enemies' spies have decreed: God has said goodbye to him, so now hunt him down.

Thy force keeps me from fearing,
Nor ever dread I aught;
Thy justice bearing
In mindful thought
And glorious acts which thou hast taught
Me from my youth;[4] and I have shown
What I have known.

Now age doth overtake me
And paint my head with snow;
Do not forsake me
Until I show
The ages which succeeding grow,
And every afterliving wight,° *generation of men*
Thy power and might.

How is thy justice raised
Above the height of thought;
How highly praised
What thou hast wrought.
Sought let be all that can be sought,
None shall be found, nay none shall be,
O God, like thee.

What if thou down didst drive me
Into the gulf of woes;
Thou wilt revive me
Again from those
And from the deep, which deepest goes;
Exalting me again will make
Me comfort take.

My greatness shall be greater
By thee; by comfort thine
My good state better.
O lute of mine,
To praise his truth thy tunes incline;
My harp extol the Holy One
In Judah known.

My voice to my harp join thee,[5]
My soul saved from decay,
My voice conjoin° thee, *join with*
My tongue each day,
In all men's view his justice lay,° *reveal*
Who° hath disgraced and shamed so, *those who*
Who work my woe.

c. 1590

4. I.e., bearing thy justice and glorious acts in mindful thought.

5. I.e., let my voice, joined to my harp, join thee.

COMPANION READING

Miles Coverdale: Psalm 71[1]

In thee, O Lord, is my trust, let me never be put to confusion, but rid me and deliver me through thy righteousness. Incline thine ear unto me and help me. Be thou my stronghold (whereunto I may always fly), thou that hast promised to help me; for thou art my house of defense and my castle. Deliver me (O my God) out of the hand of the ungodly, out of the hand of the unrighteous and cruel man. For thou (O Lord God) art the thing that I long for, thou art my hope even from my youth. I have leaned upon thee ever since I was born, thou art he that took me out of my mother's womb, therefore is my praise always of thee. I am become a wonder unto the multitude, but my sure trust is in thee. Oh, let my mouth be filled with thy praise and honor all the day long. Cast me not away in mine old age, forsake me not when my strength faileth me. For mine enemies speak against me, and they that lay wait for my soul take their counsel together, saying, God hath forsaken him; persecute him, take him, for there is none to help him. Go not far from me, O God; my God haste thee to help me. Let them be confounded and perish that are against my soul; let them be covered with shame and dishonor that seek to do me evil. As for me, I will patiently abide always and will ever increase thy praise. My mouth shall speak of thy righteousness and saving health all the day long, for I know no end thereof. Let me go in (O Lord God) and I will make mention of thy power and righteousness only. Thou (O God) hast learned me from my youth up until now, therefore will I tell of thy wondrous works. Forsake me not (O God) in mine old age, when I am grey-headed; until I have showed thine arm unto children's children, and thy power to all them that are yet for to come. Thy righteousness (O God) is very high, thou that doest great things, O God, who is like unto thee? O what great troubles and adversity hast thou showed me, and yet didst thou turn and refresh me; yea, and broughtest me from the deep of the earth again. Thou hast brought me to great honor and comforted me on every side. Therefore will I praise thee and thy faithfulness (O God), playing upon the lute, unto thee will I sing upon the harp, O thou holy one of Israel. My lips would fain sing praises unto thee and so would my soul, whom thou hast delivered.

My tongue talketh of thy righteousness all the day long, for they are confounded and brought unto shame that sought to do me evil.

Psalm 121: Levavi Oculos

Unto the hills, I now will bend
    And list° with joy my hopeful sight; *incline*
To him who me doth comfort send,
    My gracious God, the Lord of might.
        Even he (who ever blessed be he named)
        Who Heaven and Earth and all therein hath framed.

By him thy foot, from slip shall stay,° *prevent*
    Nor will he sleep who thee sustains;
Israel's great God by night or day
    To sleep or slumber aye° disdains. *always*

1. Miles Coverdale published his English translation of the Bible (using earlier translations into Latin and German as well as the English translation of William Tyndale) in 1535. Although the Authorized Version, commissioned by James I in 1604 and published in 1611, essentially reproduced Tyndale's translation of the New Testament and portions of the Hebrew Bible, the Prayer Book text of the psalms is considered to be Coverdale's work.

For he is still thy guard forever waking,
On thy right hand thy safety undertaking.

So undertakes that neither sun
By day with heat shall thee molest,
Nor moon by night, when day is done,
Offend thee, or disturb thy rest.
Yea, from all evil thou still in his protection
Shalt safely dwell from harm or ill infection.

This Lord (who never fails his flock)
Shall thee in all thy ways attend
At home, abroad, thy fort, thy rock
From all annoy shall thee defend.
Yea, from this time from age to age for ever
Will be thy God, and thee forsaking never.

c. 1590

The Doleful Lay° of Clorinda

ballad

Ay me, to whom shall I my case complain
That may compassion° my impatient grief? *sympathize with*
Or where shall I unfold my inward pain,
That my enriven° ear may find relief? *dismayed*
Shall I unto the heavenly powers it show?
Or unto earthly men that dwell below?

To heavens? Ah they, alas, the authors were
And workers of my unremedied woe;
For they foresee what to us happens here,
And they foresaw, yet suffered this be so.
From them comes good, from them comes also ill;
That which they made, who can them warn to spill.° *destroy*

To men? Ah they, alas, like wretched be
And subject to the heavens' ordinance;
Bound to abide whatever they decree,
Their best redress is their best sufferance.[1]
How then can they, like wretched, comfort me,
The which no less, need comforted to be?[2]

Then to myself will I my sorrow mourn,
Since none alive like sorrowful remains;
And to myself my plaints shall back return,
To pay their usury with doubled pains.
The woods, the hills, the rivers shall resound
The mournful accent of my sorrow's ground.° *cause*

Wood, hills, and rivers now are desolate,
Since he is gone the which them all did grace;
And all the fields do wail their widow state,

1. I.e., the best recourse for men subject to heaven is to tolerate its decrees.

2. I.e., how can they comfort me, wretched as I am, who themselves need to be comforted?

Since death their fairest flower did late deface.
The fairest flower in field that ever grew,
Was Astrophel;[3] that was, we all may rue.

What cruel hand of cursed fate unknown,
Hath cropped the stalk which bore so fair a flower?
Untimely cropped, before it were well grown,
And clean defaced in untimely hour.
Great loss to all that ever him did see,
Great loss to all, but greatest loss to me.

Break now your garlands, O ye shepherds' lasses,
Since the fair flower which them adorned is gone;
The flower which them adorned is gone to ashes,
Never again let lass put garland on.
Instead of garland, wear sad cypress now,
And bitter elder, broken from the bow.

Nor ever sing the love-lays which he made,
Who ever made such lays of love as he?
Nor ever read the riddles which he said
Unto yourselves to make you merry glee.
Your merry glee is now laid all abed,
Your merry maker now, alas, is dead.

Death, the devourer of all world's delight,
Hath robbed you and reft from me my joy;
Both you and me and all the world he quite
Hath robbed of joyance and left sad annoy.
Joy of the world, and shepherds' pride was he,
Shepherds' hope, never like again to see.

Oh death, that hast us of such riches reft,
Tell us at least, what hast thou with it done?
What is become of him whose flower here left
Is but the shadow of his likeness gone,
Scarce like the shadow of that which he was,
Naught° like, but that he like a shade did pass? *nothing*

But that immortal spirit, which was decked
With all the dowries of celestial grace,
By sovereign choice from the heavenly choirs select,
And lineally derived from angel's race,
O what is now of it become, aread—° *tell*
Ay me, can so divine a thing be dead?

Ah no, it is not dead, nor can it die,
But lives for aye° in blissful paradise, *ever*
Where like a newborn babe it soft doth lie,
In bed of lilies wrapped in tender wise.° *manner*

3. Astrophel or Astrophil: the principal speaker and the lover of "Stella," the figure representing the beloved woman, in Sir Philip Sidney's sonnet sequence *Astrophil and Stella*.

And compassed all about with roses sweet,
And dainty violets from head to feet.

There thousand birds all of celestial brood,
To him do sweetly carol day and night,
And with strange notes, or him well understood,
Lull him asleep in angel-like delight,
While in sweet dream to him presented be
Immortal beauties which no eye may see.

But he them sees and takes exceeding pleasure
Of their divine aspects, appearing plain,
And kindling love in him above all measure,
Sweet love still joyous, never feeling pain.
For what so goodly form he there doth see,
He may enjoy from jealous rancor free.

There liveth he in everlasting bliss,
Sweet spirit never fearing more to die,
Nor dreading harm from any foes of his,
Nor fearing salvage° beasts more cruelty. *savage*
While we here, wretches, wail his private lack,
And with vain vows do often call him back.

But live thou there still happy, happy spirit,
And give us leave thee here thus to lament.
Not thee that dost thy heaven's joy inherit,
But our own selves that here in dole are drent.° *drenched*
Thus do we weep and wail and wear our eyes,
Mourning others, our own miseries.

Elizabeth I

1533–1602

No British monarch has left posterity a more dazzling record of accomplishments than Elizabeth Tudor, second daughter of Henry VIII. In the course of her reign, England became a nation to rival France and Spain; England's cities became centers of commerce, her navy controlled the principal routes of trade, and her people pursued lucrative interests in Europe and the New World. Having ruled England for almost half a century, Elizabeth has lived on as a figure of compelling power in the history of her people. What Shakespeare said of his character Cleopatra—"Age cannot wither her, nor custom stale her infinite variety"—conveys something of the fascination the memory of this extraordinary woman has had for the English people as well as for others around the globe. Age did, of course, eventually touch her being; doubtless, too, the brilliant strategies by which she governed subjects who were ever jealous of her royal prerogative must finally have become predictable. But Elizabeth was brought up in the atmosphere of a volatile politics, given to shifts in the winds of chance, susceptible to the heat of violent controversy and even to the flames of rebellion. She did what she had to do to remain on the throne; her father's example, if nothing else, taught her how fragile was the rule

Robert Peake (attr.). *Queen Elizabeth Going in Procession to Blackfriars in 1600. This splendid painting is linked to no particular event. Its arrangement of figures suggests a Roman imperial triumph, and evokes the success of the queen's monarchy. She appears to be in a litter, but is actually in a chair on wheels pushed by attendants, and protected by a canopy held by courtiers. She is preceded by a knight, perhaps Gilbert Talbot, Earl of Shrewsbury, who carries the sword of state. Though Elizabeth was sixty-eight when this painting was made in 1601, she is shown as a much younger woman. Her wish to be recognized as always desirable and ever the object of courtly devotion is well illustrated by her pale, unlined face, her highly dressed hair and her stylized body, clothed in a bejeweled dress whose puffed sleeves and intricate lace ruff suggest an etherial and even divine creature. She is attended by six Knights of the Garter; the knight standing directly beside her (with a bald head and stiff grey beard) has been identified as her current favorite, Edward Somerset, Earl of Worcester; his two principal castles, Raglan and Chepstow, are probably those in the background of the painting.*

of a monarch who depended much more on the loyalty of subjects than on the authority of office or the power of the law.

Elizabeth's birth was itself a disappointment, at least to Henry VIII, who had hoped for a son. Her mother was the king's second wife, the charming Anne Boleyn, whom he married after divorcing Catherine of Aragon, the mother of his first daughter, Mary Tudor. The divorce precipitated the king's break with the Catholic Church, made Mary Tudor illegitimate, and effectively defined Anne's politics as unequivocally Protestant. But the new queen's influence was short-lived. Supporters of Catholicism, those who remained faithful to the memory of Catherine and respected the claims of Mary Tudor, may have been responsible for convincing the king that Anne had been unfaithful to him; in any case he ordered her execution. Ten days later, he married Jane Seymour, declared Elizabeth illegitimate, and again waited for the birth of a son. Elizabeth's half-brother, the future Edward VI, was born in 1537, when Elizabeth was four years old. Fortunately, at the age of ten, Elizabeth at last acquired a loving stepmother: Henry's sixth wife, Catherine

Parr, looked after her interests and education. An excellent student, fluent in Latin, French, and Italian and versed in history, Elizabeth was raised to be the subject of her brother, who became king after Henry's death in 1547. When he died in 1553, she became a pawn in a long and vicious struggle for the crown. Imprisoned in the Tower and then in Woodstock Castle in Oxfordshire by the Catholic supporters of her sister's claim to the throne, Elizabeth wrote lyrics that testify to both her fears and her faith during this dangerous time.

In 1558, Queen Mary died, and Elizabeth was crowned with much rejoicing; in the historian William Camden's words: "neither did the people ever embrace any other Prince with more willing and constant mind." Once on the throne, Elizabeth pursued a policy of exemplary discretion; she rewarded those who were loyal to her and punished those who showed signs of disobedience. In 1568, when her cousin Mary, Queen of Scots, abdicated the throne of Scotland in favor of her son, James VI, Elizabeth granted Mary refuge in England. Yet evidence later suggested that Mary, an ardent Catholic, had plotted to kill Elizabeth and restore Catholicism in England, and in 1587, Elizabeth ordered her execution with great regret. Reflecting on this action, also the subject of a speech to Parliament, the queen declared: "This death will wring my heart as long as I live."

A woman and reigning monarch, Elizabeth's position was anomalous. As a woman, she retained an important kind of social power only as long as she was an object of desire, to be courted and won; as a reigning monarch, she was expected not only to govern but also to secure the succession. In her speech to Parliament on the subject of marriage early in her reign, Elizabeth provided reasons why she would delay taking a husband. She probably never intended to take one. Continuing the fiction of courtship well past the age at which she could be expected to have a child, she saw to it that she remained at once attractive and unavailable. Most important, she succeeded in commanding the attention of her subjects by transforming her court into a center of literary and artistic activity. Late in life, she met her most serious suitor, the Duke of Alençon, brother to the French king, Henry III. A dwarf whose face was disfigured by smallpox, he was her "little frog," a man she is said to have loved dearly. The problem of succession required another kind of temporizing. She refused to name James VI of Scotland as the next king of England until shortly before she died—a silence that she maintained was necessary to preserve the peace.

Throughout her long reign she cultivated two personas. As a monarch, she could speak courageously (as she did to her soldiers at Tilbury on the Devon coast while they waited for the Spanish to invade); as a woman, she could convey understanding (as she did to her critics in her so-called Golden Speech curtailing her prerogative to create monopolies). Her government remained a conscientious one to its very end. She cultivated a habit of mind that must have helped to ensure its stability: as her translation of Boethius's *Consolation of Philosophy* (made when she was sixty years old) reminds us, she never allowed herself to forget the vicissitudes of fortune and her own mortality.

Written with a Diamond on Her Window at Woodstock[1]

Much suspected by° me, *to have been done by*
Nothing proved can be,
    Quoth Elizabeth prisoner.

1. Elizabeth was imprisoned at Woodstock Castle, near Oxford, from May 23, 1554, to sometime late in April 1555. The queen, Mary I, Elizabeth's half-sister, suspected her of treason. This and the following poem are thought to have been written at this time.

Written on a Wall at Woodstock

Oh fortune, thy wresting wavering state
Hath fraught with cares my troubled wit,
Whose witness this present prison late
Could bear, where once was joy's loan quit.[1]
Thou causedst the guilty to be loosed
From bands° where innocents were inclosed, *bonds*
And caused the guiltless to be reserved,° *bound*
And freed those that death had well deserved.
But all herein° can be nothing wrought, *in prison*
So God send to my foes all they have thought.[2]

The Doubt of Future Foes

The doubt° of future foes exiles my present joy, *fear*
And wit me warns to shun such snares as threaten mine annoy;[1]
For falsehood now doth flow, and subjects' faith doth ebb,
Which should not be if reason ruled or wisdom weaved the web.
But clouds of joys untried° do cloak aspiring minds, *untested*
Which turn to rain of late repent by changed course of winds.[2]
The top of hope supposed the root upreared shall be,
And fruitless all their grafted guile, as shortly ye shall see.[3]
The dazzled eyes with pride, which great ambition blinds,
Shall be unsealed by worthy wights[4] whose foresight falsehood finds.
The daughter of debate that discord aye° doth sow *ever*
Shall reap no gain where former rule[5] still peace hath taught to know.
No foreign banished wight[6] shall anchor in this port;
Our realm brooks not seditious sects, let them elsewhere resort.
My rusty sword through rest shall first his edge employ
To poll their tops[7] that seek such change or gape[8] for future joy.

On Monsieur's Departure[1]

I grieve and dare not show my discontent,
I love and yet am forced to seem to hate,
I do, yet dare not say I ever meant,
I seem stark mute but inwardly do prate.
  I am and not,° I freeze and yet am burned, *am not*
  Since from myself another self I turned.

My care is like my shadow in the sun,
Follows me flying, flies when I pursue it,

1. I.e., this prison could bear witness recently to fortune's wavering state, where once it did not have to borrow joy [as it does now].
2. I.e., nothing can be done by one who is in prison, so may God send to my foes what they have suspected me of planning.
1. My harm.
2. I.e., because of a change of wind, my enemies' clouds of joy can turn to the rain of repentance.
3. I.e., at their most hopeful, my enemies supposed that the tree of my monarchy would be uprooted, but their grafted limbs of guile will bear no fruit.
4. Men.
5. The rule of Elizabeth's father, Henry VIII, and brother, Edward VI, both Protestants.
6. Any supporter of Philip II, king of Spain and consort of Mary I.
7. Cut their heads off.
8. Smile.
1. The poem expresses Elizabeth's regret at the departure of the Duke d'Alençon, who had sought her hand in marriage. After four years of visits and inconclusive negotiations, the courtship ended in 1583.

Stands and lies by me, doth what I have done.
His too familiar care doth make me rue° it. *regret*
No means I find to rid him from my breast,
Till by the end of things° it be supprest. *death*

Some gentler passion slide into my mind,
For I am soft and made of melting snow;
Or be more cruel, love, and so be kind.
Let me or° float or sink, be high or low. *either*
Or let me live with some more sweet content,
Or die and so forget what love ere meant.

Psalm 13

Fools that true faith yet never had
Saith in their hearts, there is no God.
Filthy they are in their practice,
Of them not one is godly wise.
From heaven the Lord on man did look
To know what ways he undertook.
All they were vain and went astray,
Not one he found in the right way.
In heart and tongue have they deceit,
Their lips throw forth a poisoned bait.
Their minds are mad, their mouths° are wode,° *speech/empty*
And swift they be in shedding blood.
So blind they are, no truth they know,
No fear of God in them will grow.
How can that cruel sort be good,
Of God's dear flock which suck the blood?
On him rightly shall they not call,
Despair will so their hearts appall.
At all times God is with the just,
Because they put in him their trust.
Who shall therefore from Sion[1] give
That health which hangeth in our belief?
When God shall take from his the smart,
Then will Jacob rejoice in heart.
Praise to God

from The Metres of Boethius's *Consolation of Philosophy*[1]

Book 1, No. 2

O in how headlong depth the drowned mind is dim!
And losing light her own, to others' darkness drawn,
As oft as driven with earthly flaws the harmful care upward grows.[2]
Once this man free in open field used the skies to view,

1. Zion, the heavenly city, source and object of salvation.

1. These poems are Elizabeth's translations, undertaken late in her life, of portions of the *De consolatione philosophiae* (*On the Consolation of Philosophy*) by the Christian martyr Anicius Manlius Severinus Boethius (475–525), written while Boethius was in prison, awaiting execution. The treatise's representation of a heavenly perspective from which earthly concerns appear trivial made it a favorite work of moral philosophy through the Middle Ages and early modern period. Even at the height of her power, Elizabeth was attracted by Boethius's Stoic rejection of worldly ambition.

2. I.e., losing her own light, the mind is drawn to the darkness of others, just as care grows with the faults of others.

Of rosie sun the light beheld,
Of frosty moon the planets saw,
And what star else runs her wonted° course. *accustomed*
Bending by many circles this man had wone° *used to*
By number to know them all;[3]
Yea, causes each whence roaring winds the seas perturb.
Acquainted with the spirit that rolls the steady world,
And why the star that falls to the Hesperia's waters[4]
From his reddy° root doth raise herself.[5] *reddish*
Who that gives the spring's mild hours their temper,
That with rosy flowers the earth bedeckt,
Who made the fertile autumn at fullest of the year
Abound with grape all swollen with ripest fruits.
He, wonted to search and find sundry causes of hidden nature,
Down lies of mind's light bereaved,[6]
With bruised neck by overheavy chains,
A bowed low look by weight bearing,
Driven, alas, the silly° earth behold. *insignificant*

Book 1, No. 7

Dim clouds,
Sky close
Light none
Can afford.
If roiling seas
Boisterous soweth,° *scatters*
Mix his° foam, *its*
Greeny° once *greenish*
Like the clearest
Days, the water—
Straight mud,
Stirred up all foul—
The sight gainsays.° *prevents*
Running stream
That pours
From highest hills,
Oft is stayed
By slaked° *cool*
Stone of rock.
Thou, if thou wilt
In clearest light
The truth behold,
By straight line
Hit in the path.[1]
Chase joys,

3. I.e., this man was accustomed to know all the "circles" (cycles and epicycles of the stars and planets).
4. The sea to the west of the Hesperides, mythical islands located beyond the known horizon.
5. "His root" and "herself" both refer to the star that sinks in the west, perhaps the planet Mars, known for its reddish tinge.
6. I.e., happiness comes to the man who studies and knows nature; but when he contemplates the insignificance of the earth, he is weighed down with care.
1. I.e., keep to the path in a straight line.

Repulse fear,
Thrust out hope,
Woe not retain.
Cloudy is the mind
With snaffle° bound — *bridle-bit*
Where they reign.[2]

Book 2, No. 3

In pool when Phoebus with reddy wain[1]
The light to spread begins,
The star,[2] dimmed with flames° uprising, — *of the sun*
Pales her whitty° looks. — *whitish*
When wood° with Siphirus'[3] milding blast — *vegetation*
Blusheth with the springing° roses, — *budding*
And cloudy soweth his blustering blasts,
Away from stalk° the beauty goes. — *of the flower*
Some time with calmy fair° the sea — *a fair calm*
Void of waves doth run;
Oft boisterous tempests the north
With foaming seas turns up.[4]
If rarely steady be the world's form,
If turns so many it makes,
Believe slippar° mens' lucks, — *slippery*
Trust that sliding° be their goods. — *impermanent*
Certain, and in eternal law is writ,
Sure standeth naught° is made. — *nothing that*

SPEECHES

The speeches of Elizabeth I exemplify early modern public oratory at its most effective. But they are also marked by features uniquely derived from her sense of herself as a monarch who wished (and probably needed) to convince her subjects that their welfare was more important to her than her own. In the excerpts that follow, Elizabeth emphasizes that although nature made her a woman and therefore of the weaker sex, divine right has made her a "prince," a person endowed with a masculine persona whose function it is to command not obey. She further emphasizes that her principal care is for her subjects, who are her charges and in some sense her children. In her public dealings throughout her reign, she played the gender card for all it was worth; in so doing, she transformed the fact that she was a woman, potentially a liability, into an instrument of policy.

On Marriage[1]

I may say unto you that from my years of understanding, sith[2] I first had consideration of myself to be born a servitor of Almighty God, I happily chose this kind of life in which

2. Boethius extols the extreme indifference to fortune and the emotions that Stoic philosophers believed was necessary for the good life.

1. I.e., when Phoebus, or Apollo, god of the sun with his red chariot, spreads his light over the deep.

2. Venus, who as the morning star is known as Lucifer, or the light-bearer.

3. Zephyrus, god of the west wind.

4. This series of alterations in states of being—from darkness to light, from a breeze to a gale, and from a calm to a foaming sea—illustrate the "eternal law" of change.

1. In 1559, a year after she had acceded to the throne at the age of twenty-five, Elizabeth addressed Parliament on the subject of marriage. Because the monarchy passed on by inheritance, it was expected that a monarch would marry and have children. In this speech, Elizabeth hints that she will never marry and also that she trusts God to provide for her successor who, she guesses, may be more "beneficial" to the kingdom than any child of her own would be. She probably intended to convey to her subjects that she would never abandon the kingdom either to the rule of a foreign prince (as Mary I had) or to a succession crisis.

2. Since.

I yet live, which I assure you for mine own part hath hitherto best contented myself and I trust hath been most acceptable to God. From the which, if either ambition of high estate offered to me in marriage by the pleasure and appointment of my prince[3]—whereof I have some records in this presence, as you our Lord Treasurer[4] well know; or if the eschewing of the danger of mine enemies or the avoiding of the period of death, whose messenger or rather continual watchman, the prince's indignation, was not little time daily before mine eyes—by whose means, although I know or justly may suspect, yet I will not now utter; or if the whole cause were in my sister herself, I will not now burthen her therewith, because I will not charge the dead: if any of these I say, I had not now remained in this estate wherein you see me. But so constant have I always continued in this determination—although my youth and words may seem to some hardly to agree together—yet is it most true that at this day I stand free from any other meaning that either I have had in times past or have at this present. With which trade of life I am so thoroughly acquainted that I trust God, who hath hitherto therein preserved and led me by the hand, will not now of His goodness suffer me to go alone. * * *

Nevertheless—if any of you be in suspect—whensoever it may please God to incline my heart to another kind of life, ye may well assure yourselves my meaning is not to do or determine anything wherewith the realm may or shall have just cause to be discontented. And therefore put that clean out of your heads.[5] For I assure you—what credit my assurance may have with you I cannot tell, but what credit it shall deserve to have the sequence shall declare—I will never in that matter conclude anything that shall be prejudicial to the realm, for the weal, good, and safety whereof I will never shun to spend my life. And whomsoever my chance shall be to light upon, I trust he shall be as careful for the realm and you—I will not say as myself, because I cannot so certainly determine of any other; but at the least ways, by my good will and desire he shall be such as shall be as careful for the preservation of the realm and you as myself.

And albeit it might please Almightly God to continue me still in this mind to live out of the state of marriage, yet it is not to be feared but He will so work in my heart and in your wisdoms as good provision by His help may be made in convenient time, whereby the realm shall not remain destitute of an heir that may be a fit governor, and peradventure more beneficial to the realm than such offspring as may come of me. For, although I be never so careful of your well doings and mind ever so to be, yet may my issue grow out of kind and become perhaps ungracious. And in the end, this shall be for me sufficient, that a marble stone shall declare that a Queen, having reigned such a time, lived and died a virgin.

On Mary, Queen of Scots,[1]

The bottomless graces and immeasurable benefits bestowed upon me by the Almighty are and have been such, as I must not only acknowledge them but admire

3. The "prince" Elizabeth refers to is probably not Philip II, the consort of Mary I, but rather Mary herself, who in her official capacity as queen regnant might have offered her sister's hand in marriage to a suitable consort. Elizabeth can refer to Mary as her "sister" when she alludes to a "cause" that had no implications for the state but is rather personal, "in my sister herself."

4. The Marquis of Winchester.

5. Elizabeth emphasizes that her subjects and their representatives in Parliament have no authority to force her into marriage, however desirable they may think marriage is for the future of the kingdom.

1. The text is Elizabeth's answer to a petition from Parliament to execute Mary, Queen of Scots, who was reported to have conspired to depose her cousin Elizabeth and who had been a prisoner of the English queen for ten years. In August 1586, evidence of a new plot came to light, and the conspirators, led by Sir Thomas Babington, were executed. On the evidence in letters to Babington, Mary was then formally tried and convicted of treason by a special court of peers, counsellors, and judges. Elizabeth answered Parliament in October by asking for delay and divine enlightenment.

them, accounting them as well miracles as benefits; not so much in respect of His Divine Majesty—with whom nothing is more common than to do things rare and singular—as in regard of our weakness, who cannot sufficiently set forth His wonderful works and graces, which to me have been so many, so diversely folded and embroidered one upon another, as in no sort am I able to express them.

And although there liveth not any that may more justly acknowledge themselves infinitely bound unto God than I, whose life He hath miraculously preserved at sundry times (beyond my merit) from a multitude of perils and dangers, yet is not that the cause for which I count myself the deepliest bound to give Him my humblest thanks, or to yield Him greatest recognition; but this which I shall tell you hereafter, which will deserve the name of wonder, if rare things and seldom seen be worthy of account. Even this it is: that as I came to the crown with the willing hearts of subjects, so do I now, after twenty-eight years' reign, perceive in you no diminution of good wills, which, if haply I should want, well might I breathe but never think I lived.

And now, albeit I find my life hath been full dangerously sought, and death contrived by such as no desert procured it, yet am I thereof so clear from malice—which hath the property to make men glad at the falls and faults of their foes, and make them seem to do for other causes, when rancor is the ground—as I protest it is and hath been my grievous thought that one, not different in sex, of like estate, and my near kin, should be fallen into so great a crime. Yea, I had so little purpose to pursue her with any color of malice, that as it is not unknown to some of my Lords here—for now I will play the blab—I secretly wrote her a letter upon the discovery of sundry treasons, that if she would confess them, and privately acknowledge them by her letters unto myself, she never should need be called for them into so public question. Neither did I it of mind to circumvent her, for then I knew as much as she could confess; and so did I write.

And if, even yet, now the matter is made but too apparent, I thought she truly would repent—as perhaps she would easily appear in outward show to do—and that for her none other would take the matter upon them; or that we were but as two milk-maids, with pails upon our arms; or that there were no more dependency upon us, but mine own life were only in danger, and not the whole estate of your religion and well doings; I protest—wherein you may believe me, for although I may have many vices, I hope I have not accustomed my tongue to be an instrument of untruth—I would most willingly pardon and remit this offence. Or if by my death other nations and kingdoms might truly say that this realm had attained an ever prosperous and flourishing estate, I would (I assure you) not desire to live, but gladly give my life, to the end my death might procure you a better prince. And for your sakes it is that I desire to live: to keep you from a worse. For, as for me, I assure you I find no great cause I should be fond to live. I take no such pleasure in it that I should much wish it, nor conceive such terror in death that I should greatly fear it. And yet I say not but, if the stroke were coming, perchance flesh and blood would be moved with it, and seek to shun it.

I have had good experience and trial of this world. I know what it is to be a subject, what to be a sovereign, what to have good neighbors, and sometime meet evil-willers. I have found treason in trust, seen great benefits little regarded, and instead of gratefulness, courses[2] of purpose to cross. These former remembrances, present feeling, and future expectation of evils, (I say), have made me think an evil is much the better the less while it dureth,[3] and so them happiest that are soonest

2. Plans.

3. Lasts.

hence;[4] and taught me to bear with a better mind these treasons, than is common to my sex—yea, with a better heart perhaps than is in some men. Which I hope you will not merely impute to my simplicity or want of understanding, but rather that I thus conceived—that had their purposes taken effect, I should not have found the blow, before I had felt it; nor, though my peril should have been great, my pain should have been but small and short. Wherein, as I would be loath to die so bloody a death, so doubt I not but God would have given me grace to be prepared for such an event; which, when it shall chance, I refer to His good pleasure.

And now, as touching their treasons and conspiracies, together with the contriver of them. I will not so prejudicate myself and this my realm as to say or think that I might not, without the last statute, by the ancient laws of this land have proceeded against her; which[5] was not made particularly to prejudice her, though perhaps it might then be suspected in respect of the disposition of such as depend that way. It was so far from being intended to entrap her, that it was rather an admonition to warn the danger thereof. But sith it is made, and in the force of a law, I thought good, in that which might concern her, to proceed according thereunto rather than by course of common law. Wherein, if you the judges have not deceived me, or that the books you brought me were not false—which God forbid—I might as justly have tried her by the ancient laws of the land.

But you lawyers are so nice and so precise in sifting and scanning every word and letter, that many times you stand more upon form than matter, upon syllables than the sense of the law. For, in this strictness and exact following of common form, she must have been indicted in Staffordshire, been arraigned at the bar, holden up her hand, and then been tried by a jury: a proper course, forsooth, to deal in that manner with one of her estate! I thought it better, therefore, for avoiding of these and more absurdities, to commit the cause to the inquisition of a good number of the greatest and most noble personages of this realm, of the judges and others of good account, whose sentence I must approve.[6]

And all little enough: for we Princes, I tell you, are set on stages, in the sight and view of all the world duly observed. The eyes of many behold our actions; a spot is soon spied in our garments, a blemish quickly noted in our doings. It behoveth us, therefore, to be careful that our proceedings be just and honorable.

But I must tell you one thing more: that in this late Act of Parliament you have laid an hard hand on me—that I must give direction for her death, which cannot be but most grievous, and an irksome burden to me. And lest you might mistake mine absence from this Parliament—which I had almost forgotten: although there be no cause why I should willingly come amongst multitudes (for that amongst many, some may be evil), yet hath it not been the doubt of any such danger or occasion that kept me from thence, but only the great grief to hear this cause spoken of, especially that such one of state and kin should need so open a declaration, and that this nation should be so spotted with blots of disloyalty. Wherein, the less is my grief for that I hope the better part is mine; and those of the worse not much to be accounted of, for that in seeking my destruction they might have spoiled their own souls.

And even now could I tell you that which would make you sorry. It is a secret; and yet I will tell it you (although it be known I have the property to keep counsel but too well, often times to mine own peril). It is not long since mine eyes did see it

4. I.e., out of this world.
5. I.e., the Parliamentary statute of 1584–85, known as the Act for the Queen's Surety, which provided for the trial of Mary, Queen of Scots, should she be accused of treason.
6. Elizabeth claims that Mary could have been tried as a criminal in a common law court but that this would have been an improper way to proceed as Mary remained a Queen of Scotland and therefore was not liable under English law.

written that an oath was taken within few days either to kill me or to be hanged themselves; and that to be performed ere one month were ended. Hereby I see your danger in me, and neither can or will be so unthankful or careless of your consciences as to take no care for your safety.

I am not unmindful of your oath made in the Association,[7] manifesting your great good wills and affections, taken and entered into upon good conscience and true knowledge of the guilt, for safeguard of my person; done (I protest to God) before I ever heard it, or ever thought of such a matter, till a thousand hands, with many obligations, were showed me at Hampton Court, signed and subscribed with the names and seals of the greatest of this land. Which, as I do acknowledge as a perfect argument of your true hearts and great zeal to my safety, so shall my bond be stronger tied to greater care for all your good.

But, for that this matter is rare, weighty and of great consequence, and I think you do not look for any present resolution—the rather for that, as it is not my manner in matters of far less moment to give speedy answer without due consideration, so in this of such importance—I think it very requisite with earnest prayer to beseech His Divine Majesty so to illuminate mine understanding and inspire me with His grace, as I may do and determine that which shall serve to the establishment of His Church, preservation of your estates, and prosperity of this Commonwealth under my charge. Wherein, for that I know delay is dangerous, you shall have with all conveniency our resolution delivered by our message. And what ever any prince may merit of their subjects, for their approved testimony of their unfeigned sincerity, either by governing justly, void of all partiality, or sufferance of any injuries done (even to the poorest), that do I assuredly promise inviolably to perform, for requital of your so many deserts.

On Mary's Execution[1]

Full grievous is the way whose going on and end breeds cumber[2] for the hire of a laborious journey. I have strived more this day than ever in my life whether I should speak or use silence. If I speak and not complain, I shall dissemble; if I hold my peace, your labor taken were full vain.

For me to make my moan were strange and rare, for I suppose you shall find few that, for their own particular, will cumber you with such a care. Yet such, I protest, hath been my greedy desire and hungry will that of your consultation might have fallen out some other means to work my safety, joined with your assurance, than that for which you are become so earnest suitors, as I protest I must needs use complaint[3]—though not of you, but unto you, and of the cause; for that I do perceive, by your advices, prayers, and desires, there falleth out this accident, that only my injurer's bane must be my life's surety.

But if any there live so wicked of nature to suppose that I prolonged this time only pro forma, to the intent to make a show of clemency, thereby to set my praises to the wire-drawers[4] to lengthen them the more, they do me so great a wrong as they can hardly recompense. Or if any person there be that think or imagine that the least vain-

7. The Oath (or Bond) of Association was taken by the Queen's Council in October 1582. It provided for Mary's arrest and execution without a trial; in essence, it sanctioned a lynching.

1. Parliament had determined that Elizabeth's safety and the future of Protestantism in England could be secured only by Mary's execution; it sent a delegation to Elizabeth asking for her approval. Again Elizabeth demurred. It was only in February 1587, after a new conspiracy was discovered, that Elizabeth signed Mary's death warrant.

2. Distress.

3. Express regret.

4. One who draws metal into wire.

glorious thought hath drawn me further herein, they do me as open injury as ever was done to any living creature—as He that is the maker of all thoughts knoweth best to be true. Or if there be any that think that the Lords, appointed in commission, durst do no other, as fearing thereby to displease or to be suspected to be of a contrary opinion to my safety, they do but heap upon me injurious conceits. For, either those put in trust by me to supply my place have not performed their duty towards me, or else they have signified unto you all that my desire was that every one should do according to his conscience, and in the course of these proceedings should enjoy both freedom of voice and liberty of opinion, and what they would not openly, they might privately to myself declare. It was of a willing mind and great desire I had, that some other means might be found out, wherein I should have taken more comfort than in any other thing under the sun.

And since now it is resolved that my surety cannot be established without a princess's head, I have just cause to complain that I, who have in my time pardoned so many rebels, winked at so many treasons, and either not produced[5] them or altogether slipped them over with silence, should now be forced to this proceeding, against such a person. I have besides, during my reign, seen and heard many opprobrious books and pamphlets against me, my realm and state, accusing me to be a tyrant. I thank them for their alms. I believe therein their meaning was to tell me news: and news it is to me indeed. I would it were as strange to hear of their impiety. What will they not now say, when it shall be spread that for the safety of her life a maiden queen could be content to spill the blood even of her own kinswoman? I may therefore full well complain that any man should think me given to cruelty; whereof I am so guiltless and innocent as I should slander God if I should say He gave me so vile a mind. Yea, I protest, I am so far from it that for mine own life I would not touch her. Neither hath my care been so much bent how to prolong mine, as how to preserve both: which I am right sorry is made so hard, yea so impossible.

I am not so void of judgment as not to see mine own peril; nor yet so ignorant as not to know it were in nature a foolish course to cherish a sword to cut mine own throat; nor so careless as not to weigh that my life daily is in hazard. But this I do consider, that many a man would put his life in danger for the safeguard of a king. I do not say that so will I; but I pray you think that I have thought upon it.

But sith so many hath both written and spoken against me, I pray you give me leave to say somewhat for myself, and, before you return to your countries, let you know for what a one you have passed so careful thoughts. And, as I think myself infinitely beholding unto you all that seek to preserve my life by all the means you may, so I protest that there liveth no prince—nor ever shall be—more mindful to requite so good deserts. Wherein, as I perceive you have kept your old wont[6] in a general seeking the lengthening of my days, so am I sure that never shall I requite it, unless I had as many lives as you all; but for ever I will acknowledge it while there is any breath left me. Although I may not justify, but may justly condemn, my sundry faults and sins to God, yet for my care in this government let me acquaint you with my intents.

When first I took the sceptre, my title made me not forget the giver, and therefore [I] began as it became me, with such religion as both I was born in, bred in, and, I trust, shall die in; although I was not so simple as not to know what danger and peril so great an alteration might procure me—how many great princes of the contrary opinion would attempt all they might against me, and generally what enmity I should thereby breed unto myself. Which all I regarded not, knowing that He, for whose sake I did it,

5. Acted upon.

6. Desire.

might and would defend me. Rather marvel that I am, than muse that I should not be if it were not God's holy hand that continueth me beyond all other expectation.

I was not simply trained up, nor in my youth spent my time altogether idly; and yet, when I came to the crown, then entered I first into the school of experience, bethinking myself of those things that best fitted a king—justice, temper, magnanimity, judgment. As for the two latter, I will not boast. But for the two first, this may I truly say: among my subjects I never knew a difference of person, where right was one;[7] nor never to my knowledge preferred for favor what I thought not fit for worth; nor bent mine ears to credit a tale that first was told me; nor was so rash to corrupt my judgment with my censure, ere I heard the cause. I will not say but many reports might fortune[8] be brought me by such as must hear the matter, whose partiality might mar the right; for we princes cannot hear all causes ourselves. But this dare I boldly affirm: my verdict went with the truth of my knowledge.

But full well wished Alcibiades[9] his friend, that he should not give any answer till he had recited the letters of the alphabet. So have I not used over-sudden resolutions in matters that have touched me full near: you will say that with me, I think. And therefore, as touching your counsels and consultations, I conceive them to be wise, honest, and conscionable; so provident and careful for the safety of my life (which I wish no longer than may be for your good), that though I never can yield you of recompense your due, yet shall I endeavor myself to give you cause to think your good will not ill bestowed, and strive to make myself worthy for such subjects. And as for your petition: your judgment I condemn not, neither do I mistake your reasons, but pray you to accept my thankfulness, excuse my doubtfulness, and take in good part my answer-answerless. Wherein I attribute not so much to my own judgment, but that I think many particular persons may go before me, though by my degree I go before them. Therefore, if I should say, I would not do what you request, it might peradventure be more than I thought; and to say I would do it, might perhaps breed peril of that you labor to preserve, being more than in your own wisdoms and discretions would seem convenient,[1] circumstances of place and time being duly considered.

To the English Troops at Tilbury, Facing the Spanish Armada[1]

My loving people, we have been persuaded by some that are careful of our safety, to take heed how we commit ourselves to armed multitudes, for fear of treachery. But I assure you, I do not desire to live to distrust my faithful and loving people. Let tyrants fear. I have always so behaved myself that, under God, I have placed my chiefest strength and safeguard in the loyal hearts and good will of my subjects; and therefore I am come amongst you, as you see, at this time, not for my recreation and disport,[2] but being at this time resolved, in the midst and heat of the battle, to live or die amongst you all, to lay down for my God, and for my kingdom, and for my people, my honor and my blood, even in the dust. I know I have the body of a weak and feeble woman, but I have the heart and stomach of a king, and of a king of England too, and think

7. I.e., my justice was impartial; it did not regard rank, occupation, or property as factors in determining what was right.

8. By chance.

9. An Athenian statesman who took part in the Peloponnesian War; changed sides to support Athen's enemy, Sparta; and was finally assassinated by Persians with whom he sought an alliance. The source of Elizabeth's reference is unknown.

1. Elizabeth equivocates nicely. She refuses to disagree with Parliament, lest she not respect her own misgivings; she refuses to agree with Parliament, lest its policy not be in her own interest.

1. In 1588, with the Spanish fleet threatening the south coast of England, Elizabeth went to Tilbury, in Dorset, to speak to the troops who were guarding England against an invasion.

2. Amusement.

foul scorn[3] that Parma or Spain, or any prince of Europe should dare to invade the border of my realm; to which rather than any dishonor shall grow[4] by me, I myself will take up arms, I myself will be your general, judge, and rewarder of every one of your virtues in the field. I know, already for your forwardness[5] you have deserved rewards and crowns;[6] and we do assure you, in the word of a prince, they shall be duly paid you.

The Golden Speech[1]

Mr. Speaker, we have heard your declaration and perceive your care of our estate, by falling into a consideration of a grateful acknowledgment of such benefits as you have received; and that your coming is to present thanks to us, which I accept with no less joy than your loves can have desire to offer such a present.

I do assure you there is no prince that loves his subjects better, or whose love can countervail our love. There is no jewel, be it of never so rich a price, which I set before this jewel: I mean your love. For I do esteem it more than any treasure or riches; for that we know how to prize, but love and thanks I count unvaluable. And, though God hath raised me high, yet this I count the glory of my crown, that I have reigned with your loves. This makes me that I do not so much rejoice that God hath made me to be a queen, as to be a queen over so thankful a people. Therefore, I have cause to wish nothing more than to content the subject; and that is a duty which I owe. Neither do I desire to live longer days than I may see your prosperity; and that is my only desire. And as I am that person that still yet under God hath delivered you, so I trust, by the almighty power of God, that I shall be His instrument to preserve you from every peril, dishonor, shame, tyranny and oppression; partly by means of your intended helps which we take very acceptably, because it manifesteth the largeness of your good loves and loyalties unto your sovereign.

Of myself I must say this: I never was any greedy, scraping grasper, nor a strait, fast-holding prince, nor yet a waster. My heart was never set on any worldly goods, but only for my subjects' good. What you bestow on me, I will not hoard it up, but receive it to bestow on you again. Yea, mine own properties I account yours, to be expended for your good; and your eyes shall see the bestowing of all for your good. Therefore, render unto them, I beseech you, Mr. Speaker, such thanks as you imagine my heart yieldeth, but my tongue cannot express.

Since I was queen, yet did I never put my pen to any grant but that, upon pretext and semblance made unto me, it was both good and beneficial to the subject in general, though a private profit to some of my ancient servants who had deserved well at my hands. But the contrary being found by experience, I am exceedingly beholding to such subjects as would move the same at the first. And I am not so simple to suppose, but that there be some of the Lower House whom these grievances never touched: and for them, I think they spake out of zeal to their countries,[2] and not out of spleen or malevolent affection as being parties grieved; and I take it exceeding gratefully from them, because it gives us to know that no respects or interest had moved them, other than the minds they have to suffer no diminution of our

3. Shameful.
4. Be caused.
5. Courage.
6. Recompense.
1. The queen had the prerogative or absolute power to grant favored subjects a patent for an exclusive manufacture. But the monopolies so created were disliked by those who would otherwise have competed for business, and a move to limit them was begun in Parliament. In response, in 1601, Elizabeth met with a committee of the House of Commons, led by the Speaker, thanked them for the subsidies recently granted the crown by the Commons, and promised to reform her practice.
2. I.e, those members who protested monopolies in behalf of their constituents, or "countries," and not on their own account.

honor and our subjects' love unto us. The zeal of which affection, tending to ease my people and knit their hearts unto me, I embrace with a princely care, for above all earthly treasure I esteem my people's love, more than which I desire not to merit.

That my grants should be grievous to my people and oppressions privileged under color of our patents, our kingly dignity shall not suffer[3] it. Yea, when I heard it, I could give no rest unto my thoughts until I had reformed it. Shall they, think you, escape unpunished that have thus oppressed you, and have been respectless of their duty, and regardless of our honor?[4] No, I assure you, Mr. Speaker, were it not more for conscience' sake than for any glory or increase of love that I desire, these errors, troubles, vexations and oppressions, done by these varlets and lewd persons, not worthy the name of subjects, should not escape without condign punishment. But I perceive they dealt with me like physicians who, ministering a drug, make it more acceptable by giving it a good aromatical savor, or when they give pills do gild them all over.[5]

I have ever used to set the Last-Judgment Day before mine eyes, and so to rule as I shall be judged to answer before a higher Judge, to whose judgment seat I do appeal, that never thought was cherished in my heart that tended not unto my people's good. And now, if my kingly bounties have been abused, and my grants turned to the hurt of my people, contrary to my will and meaning, and if any in authority under me have neglected or perverted what I have committed to them, I hope God will not lay their culps[6] and offences to my charge; who, though there were danger in repealing our grants, yet what danger would I not rather incur for your good, than I would suffer them still to continue?

I know the title of a king is a glorious title; but assure yourself that the shining glory of princely authority hath not so dazzled the eyes of our understanding, but that we well know and remember that we also are to yield an account of our actions before the great Judge. To be a king and wear a crown is a thing more glorious to them that see it, than it is pleasant to them that bear it. For myself, I was never so much enticed with the glorious name of a king or royal authority of a queen, as delighted that God hath made me His instrument to maintain His truth and glory, and to defend this kingdom (as I said) from peril, dishonor, tyranny and oppression.

There will never queen sit in my seat with more zeal to my country, care for my subjects, and that will sooner with willingness venture her life for your good and safety, than myself. For it is my desire to live nor reign no longer than my life and reign shall be for your good. And though you have had and may have many princes more mighty and wise sitting in this seat, yet you never had nor shall have any that will be more careful and loving.

Shall I ascribe anything to myself and my sexly weakness? I were not worthy to live then; and, of all, most unworthy of the mercies I have had from God, who hath given me a heart that yet never feared any foreign or home enemy. And I speak it to give God the praise, as a testimony before you, and not to attribute anything to myself. For I, oh Lord! what am I, whom practices and perils past should not fear? Or what can I do? That I should speak for any glory, God forbid.

This, Mr. Speaker, I pray you deliver unto the House, to whom heartily recommend me. And so I commit you all to your best fortunes and further counsels. And I pray you, Mr. Comptroller,[7] Mr. Secretary,[8] and you of my Council, that before these gentlemen go into their countries, you bring them all to kiss my hand.

3. Allow.
4. I.e., those who benefited from a monopoly without regard to the welfare of the general public.
5. Elizabeth compares unscrupulous patentees to physicians who coat bitter pills with sugar; in this case she is the patient who did not realize what was being given to her.
6. Sins.
7. Sir William Knollys.
8. Sir Robert Cecil.

Aemilia Lanyer

1569–1645

Aemilia Lanyer was born Aemilia Bassano, the daughter of Queen Elizabeth's court musician, Baptista Bassano. Acquaintance with the nobility surrounding the Queen allowed her an education that was typically reserved for women of high station. At eighteen, shortly after her mother's death, she became the mistress of Henry Cary Hunsdon, the Lord Chancellor. Her position increased her presence at court until, at twenty-three, she became pregnant and was forced to marry a court musician. Their son, conspicuously named Henry, was born three months after the wedding. The first years of her married life were not auspicious. Alfonso Lanyer was a spendthrift, and the money Aemilia had acquired as Hunsdon's mistress was soon exhausted. Desperate for reassurance, she visited the astrologer Simon Forman to learn whether the stars indicated that Alfonso would gain a knighthood. The disreputable Forman appears to have had other ideas. His casebook records that on one occasion, he "went and supped with her and stayed all night, and she was familiar and friendly to him in all things. But only she would not halek [have intercourse] . . . he never obtained his purpose and she was a whore and dealt evil with him."

Lanyer's character is more accurately represented in the record of her long friendship with Margaret Clifford, Countess of Cumberland, and her daughter Anne. In 1610, partly in tribute to the loyal support of her patroness, Lanyer published a volume of poetry entitled *Salve Deus Rex Judaeorum;* this included a verse defense of women and a poem to Cookham, a country house leased by Margaret Clifford's brother, William Russell, and visited frequently by Lanyer until 1605. She particularly records two critical transformations in her sense of herself: a spiritual awakening, inspired by the piety of the Countess, and a confirmation of herself as a poet. Her impressions of Cookham express a unity among aesthetic elements that are usually opposed and antithetical: pagan culture and Christian vision, temporal experience and spiritual knowledge, and the erotic pleasure in the discipline of chastity.

The Description of Cookham

Farewell (sweet Cookham) where I first obtained
Grace from that Grace where perfit° grace remained; *perfect*
And where the Muses[1] gave their full consent,
I should have power the virtuous to content;
Where princely Palace willed me to indite,° *write*
The sacred story[2] of the soul's delight.
Farewell (sweet place) where virtue then did rest,
And all delights did harbor in her breast;
Never shall my said eyes again behold
Those pleasures which my thoughts did then unfold:
Yet you (great Lady),[3] Mistress of that place,
From whose desires did spring this work of grace;
Vouchsafe° to think upon those pleasures past, *agree*
As fleeting worldly joys that could not last,
Or, as dim shadows of celestial pleasures,
Which are desired above all earthly treasures.
Oh how (me thought) against you thither came,[4]

1. Divinities who presided over the arts and courtesy.
2. Possibly the story of the Passion, recounted in the poem *Salve Deus Rex Judaeorum*.
3. Margaret Clifford, the Countess of Cumberland.
4. In preparation for your arrival.

Each part did seem some new delight to frame!
The house received all ornaments to grace it,
And would endure no foulness to deface it.
The walks put on their summer liveries,° *uniforms*
And all things else did hold like similies:° *comparisons*
The trees with leaves, with fruits, with flowers clad,
Embraced each other, seeming to be glad,
Turning themselves to beauteous canopies,
To shade the bright sun from your brighter eyes.
The crystal streams with silver spangles graced,
While by the glorious sun they were embraced,
The little birds in chirping notes did sing,
To entertain both you and that sweet spring.
And Philomela[5] with her sundry lays,° *songs*
Both you and that delightful place did praise.
Oh, how me thought each plant, each flower, each tree
Set forth their beauties then to welcome thee:
The very hills right humbly did descend,
When you to tread upon them did intend.
And as you set your feet, they still did rise,
Glad that they could receive so rich a prize.
The gentle winds did take delight to be
Among those woods that were so graced by thee.
And in sad° murmur uttered pleasing sound, *deep*
That pleasure in that place might more abound:
The swelling banks delivered all their pride,
When such a Phoenix[6] once they had espied.
Each arbor, bank, each seat, each stately tree,
Thought themselves honored in supporting thee.
The pretty birds would oft come to attend thee,
Yet fly away for fear they should offend thee:
The little creatures in the burrow by° *nearby*
Would come abroad to sport them in your eye;
Yet fearful of the bow in your fair hand,
Would run away when you did make a stand.
Now let me come unto that stately tree,
Wherein such goodly prospects you did see;
That oak that did in height his fellows pass,
As much as lofty trees, low growing grass
Much like a comely cedar straight and tall,
Whose beauteous stature far exceeded all.
How often did you visit this fair tree,
Which seeming joyful in receiving thee,
Would like a palm tree spread his arms abroad,
Desirous that you there should make abode:
Whose fair green leaves much like a comely veil,
Defended Phoebus when he would assail:[7]

5. In Greek mythology a woman who was transformed into a swallow; in Latin versions of her story she becomes a nightingale.

6. A mythical bird, always unique on earth, that regenerates itself in its own funeral pyre and therefore signifies eternity; here it figures the Countess.

7. The leaves of the palm tree protected the Countess from Phoebus, the god of the sun.

Whose pleasing boughs did yield a cool fresh air,
Joying his happiness when you were there.
Where being seated, you might plainly see,
Hills, vales, and woods, as if on bended knee
They had appeared, your honor to salute,
Or to prefer some strange unlooked for suit:
All interlaced with brooks and crystal springs,
A prospect fit to please the eyes of kings:
And thirteen shires appeared all in your sight,
Europe could not afford much more delight.
What was there then but gave you all content,
While you the time in meditation spent,
Of their Creator's power, which there you saw,
In all his creatures held a perfit law;
And in their beauties did you plain descry,° *discern*
His beauty, wisdom, grace, love, majesty.
In these sweet woods how often did you walk,
With Christ and his apostles there to talk;
Placing his holy writ in some fair tree,
To meditate what you therein did see:
With Moses you did mount his holy hill,[8]
To know his pleasure, and perform his will.
With lovely David[9] you did often sing
His holy hymns to heaven's eternal king.
And in sweet music did your soul delight,
To sound his praises, morning, noon, and night.
With blessed Joseph you did often feed
Your pined° brethren, when they stood in need.[1] *poor*
And that sweet lady sprung from Clifford's race,[2]
Of noble Bedford's blood, fair steam of grace,
To honorable Dorset now espoused,
In whose fair breast true virtue then was housed.
Oh, what delight did my weak spirits find
In those pure parts of her well framed mind,
And yet it grieves me that I cannot be
Near unto her, whose virtues did agree
With those fair ornaments of outward beauty,
Which did enforce from all both love and duty.
Unconstant Fortune, thou art most to blame,
Who casts us down into so low a frame,
Where our great friends we cannot daily see,
So great a diffrence is there in degree.
Many are placed in those orbs of state,
Parters° in honor, so ordained by Fate; *participants*
Nearer in show, yet farther off in love,

8. Moses climbed Mount Sinai to receive the law of God (Exodus 24, 25).
9. King David the psalmist.
1. Sold by his jealous brothers into slavery, Joseph became Pharoah's right-hand man and granted these same brothers food and money during a famine many years later (Genesis 42.1–28).
2. The Lady is the Countess's daughter Anne, descended from Margaret Russell of Bedford and her father George Clifford, Duke of Cumberland. Anne married the Earl of Dorset in 1609 and is thus referred to as Dorset.

In which, the lowest always are above.[3]
But whither am I carried in conceit?° *imagination*
My wit too weak to conster of° the great. *understand*
Why not? although we are but born of earth,
We may behold the heavens, despising death;
And loving heaven that is so far above,
May in the end vouchsafe us entire love.
Therefore sweet memory do thou retain
Those pleasures past, which will not turn again;
Remember beauteous Dorset's former sports,
So far from being touched by ill reports;
Wherein myself did always bear a part,
While reverend Love presented my true heart.
Those recreations let me bear in mind,
Which her sweet youth and noble thoughts did find,
Whereof deprived, I evermore must grieve,
Hating blind Fortune, careless to relieve.
And you sweet Cookham, whom these ladies leave,
I now must tell the grief you did conceive
At their departure; when they went away,
How everything retained a sad dismay;
Nay long before, when once an inkling came,
Methought each thing did unto sorrow frame:
The trees that were so glorious in our view,
Forsook both flowers and fruit, when once they knew
Of your depart,° their very leaves did wither, *departure*
Changing their colors as they grew together.
But when they saw this had no power to stay you,
They often wept, though speechless, could not pray[4] you;
Letting their tears in your fair bosoms fall,
As if they said, "Why will ye leave us all?"
This being vain, they cast their leaves away,
Hoping that pity would have made you stay,
Their frozen tops like age's hoary hairs,
Shows their disasters, languishing in fears;
A swarthy riveled rine° all overspread, *bark*
Their dying bodies half alive, half dead.
But your occasions called you so away,
That nothing there had power to make you stay:
Yet did I see a noble grateful mind,
Requiting each according to their kind,
Forgetting not to turn and take your leave
Of these sad creatures, powerless to receive
Your favor when with grief you did depart,
Placing their former pleasures in your heart;
Giving great charge to noble memory,
There to preserve their love continually:
But specially the love of that fair tree,

3. I.e., persons of low station or rank love more than those who are of the gentry or nobility.

4. Beg.

That first and last you did vouchsafe to see:
In which it pleased you oft to take the air,
With noble Dorset, then a virgin fair:
Where many a learned book was read and scanned
To this fair tree, taking me by the hand,
You did repeat the pleasures which had passed,
Seeming to grieve they could no longer last.
And with a chaste, yet loving kiss took leave,
Of which sweet kiss I did it soon bereave:[5]
Scorning a senseless creature should possess
So rare a favor, so great happiness.
No other kiss it could receive from me,
For fear to give back what it took of thee:
So I ungrateful creature did deceive it,
Of that which you vouchsafed in love to leave it.
And though it oft° had given me much content, *often*
Yet this great wrong I never could repent:
But of the happiest made it most forlorn,
To show that nothing's free from Fortune's scorn,
While all the rest with this most beauteous tree,
Made their sad consort° sorrow's harmony. *music*
The flowers that on the banks and walks did grow,
Crept in the ground, the grass did weep for woe.
The winds and waters seemed to chide together,
Because you went away they know not whither:
And those sweet brooks that ran so fair and clear,
With grief and trouble wrinkled did appear.
Those pretty birds that wonted° were to sing, *accustomed*
Now neither sing, nor chirp, nor use their wing;
But with their tender feet on some bare spray,
Warble forth sorrow, and their own dismay.
Fair Philomela leaves her mournful ditty,
Drowned in dead sleep, yet can procure no pity:
Each arbor, bank, each seat, each stately tree,
Looks bare and desolate now for want of thee;
Turning green tresses into frosty gray,
While in cold grief they wither all away.
The sun grew weak, his beams no comfort gave,
While all green things did make the earth their grave;
Each briar, each bramble, when you went away,
Caught fast your clothes, thinking to make you stay;
Delightful Echo[6] wonted° to reply *used*
To our last words, did now for sorrow die:
The house cast off each garment that might grace it,
Putting on dust and cobwebs to deface it.
All desolation then there did appear,
When you were going whom they held so dear.
This last farewell to Cookham here I give,

5. I.e., I took their kiss from the tree on which they had put it.

6. A nymph who can only repeat what she has heard; in the absence of voices she dies.

When I am dead thy name in this may live,
Wherein I have performed her noble hest,° *request*
Whose virtues lodge in my unworthy breast,
And ever shall, so long as life remains,
Tying my heart to her by those rich chains.

from Salve Deus Rex Judaeorum

To the Doubtful Reader

Gentle reader, if thou desire to be resolved, why I give this title, *Salve Deus Rex Judaeorum,* know for certain; that it was delivered unto me in sleep many years before I had any intent to write in this manner, and was quite out of my memory, until I had written the Passion of Christ, when immediately it came into my remembrance, what I had dreamed long before; and thinking it a significant token, that I was appointed to perform this work, I gave the very same words I received in sleep as the fittest title I could devise for this book.

To the Virtuous Reader[1]

Often have I heard, that it is the property of some women, not only to emulate the virtues and perfections of the rest, but also by all their powers of ill speaking, to eclipse the brightness of their deserved fame. Now contrary to this custom, which men I hope unjustly lay to their charge, I have written this small volume, or little book, for the general use of all virtuous ladies and gentlewomen of this kingdom; and in commendation of some particular persons of our own sex, such as for the most part are so well known to myself, and others, that I dare undertake fame dares not to call any better. And this have I done, to make known to the world that all women deserve not to be blamed, though some—forgetting they are women themselves and in danger to be condemned by the words of their own mouths—fall into so great an error as to speak unadvisedly against the rest of their sex; which if it be true, I am persuaded they can show their own imperfection in nothing more: and therefore could wish (for their own ease, modesties, and credit) they would refer[2] such points of folly to be practiced by evil disposed men, who forgetting they were born of women, nourished of women, and that if it were not by the means of women, they would be quite extinguished out of the world and a final end of them all, do like vipers deface the wombs wherein they were bred, only to give way and utterance to their want of discretion and goodness. Such as these, were they that dishonored Christ his apostles and prophets, putting them to shameful deaths. Therefore we are not to regard any imputations, that they undeservedly lay upon us, no[3] otherwise than to make use of them to our own benefits as spurs to virtue, making us fly all occasions that may color their unjust speeches to pass current,[4] especially considering that they have tempted even the patience of God himself, who gave power to wise and virtuous women, to bring down their pride and arrogance: As was cruel *Caesar* by the discreet counsel of noble

1. This preface is Lanyer's general introduction to her poem *Salve Deus Rex Judaeorum* (Hail, Lord God, King of the Jews). Three excerpts follow: the invocation, an argument against beauty without virtue, and Pilate's apology for Eve.

2. Assign.

3. Not.

4. To avoid occasions in which their unjust speeches might appear to have some truth.

Deborah,[5] judge and prophetess of Israel; and resolution of *Jael*, wife of *Heber* the Kenite; wicked *Haman*, by the divine prayers and prudent proceedings of beautiful *Hester*; blasphemous *Holofernes*, by the invincible courage, rare wisdom, and confident carriage of *Judith*; and the unjust judges, by the innocence of chaste *Susanna*; with infinite others, which for brevity's sake I will omit. As also in respect it pleased our Lord and Savior Jesus Christ, without the assistance of man, being free from original and all other sins from the time of his conception till the hour of his death, to be begotten of a woman, born of a woman, nourished of a woman, obedient to a woman; and that he healed woman,[6] pardoned women, comforted women; yea, even when he was in his greatest agony and bloody sweat, going to be crucified, and also in the last hour of his death, took care to dispose of a woman;[7] after his resurrection, appeared first to a woman, sent a woman to declare his most glorious resurrection to the rest of his disciples.[8] Many other examples I could allege of divers faithful and virtuous women, who have in all ages, not only been confessors, but also endured most cruel martyrdom for their faith in Jesus Christ. All which is sufficient to enforce all good Christians and honorable-minded men to speak reverently of our sex, and especially of all virtuous and good women. To the modest censures of both which, I refer these my imperfect endeavors, knowing that according to their own excellent dispositions, they will rather, cherish, nourish, and increase the least spark of virtue where they find it, by their favorable and best interpretations, than quench it by wrong constructions. To whom I wish all increase of virtue, and desire their best opinions.

[INVOCATION]

Sith *Cynthia*[9] is ascended to that rest
Of endless joy and true eternity,
That glorious place that cannot be expressed
By any wight° clad in mortality, *person*
In her almighty love so highly blest,
And crowned with everlasting sovereignty;
  Where saints and angels do attend her throne,
  And she gives glory unto God alone.

To thee great Countess[1] now I will apply
My pen, to write thy never dying fame;
That when to heaven thy blessed soul shall fly,
These lines on earth record thy reverend name:
And to this task I mean my muse to tie,
Though wanting skill I shall but purchase blame:

5. Lanyer lists virtuous women who benefited their people: Deborah, a wise judge and prophet of Israel, who urged the warrior Barak to attack their enemy, Sisera [Cesarus]; Jael, who killed Sisera with a blow to the head (both figures from Judges 4); Hester [Esther], the queen of the Israelites, who hanged Haman (Esther 5–7); the Jewish heroine Judith, who saved her town by killing King Nebuchadnezzar's general Holofernes (the Apocryphal Book of Judith 8–12); and Susanna, whose chastity was proved by the prophet Daniel (the Apocryphal History of Daniel and Susanna).

6. Womankind.

7. Jesus, from the cross, ordered a disciple (traditionally understood to be John) to care for his mother (John 19.25–27).

8. After his resurrection, Jesus appeared first to Mary Magdalene and "the other Mary," who then told the other disciples of this event (Matthew 28.8–10).

9. Goddess of the moon, also known as Diana; here she represents Queen Elizabeth I.

1. Lady Margaret Clifford, the Countess of Cumberland. Lanyer declares that the poem she is writing will be a memorial to her.

Pardon (dear Lady) want of woman's wit
To pen thy praise, when few can equal it.

[Against Beauty Without Virtue]

That outward beauty which the world commends
Is not the subject I will write upon,
Whose date expired, that tyrant Time soon ends;
Those gaudy colors soon are spent and gone;
But those fair virtues which on thee attends,
Are always fresh, they never are but one:
They make thy beauty fairer to behold,
Than was that queen's[2] for whom proud Troy was sold.

As for those matchless colors red and white,
Or perfit° features in a fading face, *perfect*
Or due proportion pleasing to the sight;
All these do draw but dangers and disgrace;
A mind enriched with virtue, shines more bright,
Adds everlasting beauty, gives true grace,
Frames an immortal goddess on the earth,
Who though she dies, yet fame gives her new birth.

That pride of nature which adorns the fair,
Like blazing comets to allure all eyes,
Is but the thread, that weaves their web of care,
Who glories most, where most their danger lies;
For greatest perils do attend the fair,
When men do seek, attempt, plot and devise,
How they may overthrow the chastest dame,
Whose beauty is the white[3] whereat they aim.

'Twas beauty bred in Troy the ten years' strife,
And carried *Helen* from her lawful lord;
'Twas beauty made chaste *Lucrece*[4] lose her life,
For which proud *Tarquin's* fact° was so abhorr'd: *deed*
Beauty the cause *Antonius*[5] wronged his wife,
Which could not be decided but by sword:
Great *Cleopatra's* beauty and defects
Did work *Octavia's* wrongs, and his neglects.

What fruit did yield that fair forbidden tree,
But blood, dishonor, infamy, and shame?
Poor blinded queen,[6] could'st thou no better see,
But entertain disgrace, instead of fame?

2. Helen of Troy, wife of King Menelaus of Sparta. Renowned for her beauty, she was kidnapped by Paris, son of Priam, King of Troy. This brought about the Trojan War.
3. The "white" at which hunters aim is the breast of the deer (or dear), a common figure for the beloved lady.
4. Wife of the Roman nobleman Collatinus. She was raped by Sextus Tarquinius, son of Superbus, King of Rome. The crime aroused the people of Rome to overthrow the tyranny of the Tarquins and institute a republic.
5. Marc Antony, who married Octavia, sister to Octavius, who would become the Emperor Augustus; Antony later abandoned her in favor of Cleopatra, queen of Egypt.
6. Cleopatra, figuratively blinded by her passion for Marc Antony. The couple committed suicide after Marc Antony's defeat by Octavius at the battle of Actium.

Do these designs with majesty agree?
To stain thy blood, and blot thy royal name.
That heart that gave consent unto this ill,
Did give consent that thou thyself should'st kill.

[Pilate's Wife Apologizes for Eve]

Now *Pontius Pilate*[7] is to judge the cause
Of faultless *Jesus*, who before him stands;
Who neither hath offended prince, nor laws,
Although he now be brought in woeful bands:° *bonds*
"O noble governor, make thou you a pause,
Do not in innocent blood imbrue° thy hands; *stain*
But hear the words of thy most worthy wife,
Who sends to thee, to beg her Saviour's life.

Let barbarous cruelty far depart from thee,
And in true justice take affliction's part;
Open thine eyes, that thou the truth mayest see;
Do not the thing that goes against thy heart,
Condemn not him that must thy Saviour be;
But view his holy life, his good desert.
Let not us women glory in men's fall,
Who had power given to overrule us all.

Till now your indiscretion sets us free,
And makes our former fault much less appear;[8]
Our Mother *Eve*, who tasted of the tree,
Giving to *Adam* what she held most dear,
Was simply good, and had no power to see,
The after-coming harm did not appear:[9]
The subtle serpent that our sex betrayed,
Before our fall so sure a plot had laid.

That undiscerning ignorance° perceived *i.e., of Eve*
No guile, or craft that was by him intended;
For had she known, of what we were bereaved,
To his request she had not condescended.
But she (poor soul) by cunning was deceived,
No hurt therein her harmless heart intended:
For she alleged God's word, which he denies,
That they should die, but even as gods, be wise.

But surely *Adam* cannot be excused,
Her fault though great, yet he was most to blame;
What weakness offered, strength might have refused,

7. The Roman governor of Jerusalem, A.D. 26–36. He was the judge at the trial of Jesus, who was accused of violating the laws of Rome. His wife warned him against condemning Jesus, saying, "Have thou nothing to do with that just man: for I have suffered many things this day in a dream because of him" (Matthew 27.19).

8. Lanyer recapitulates points raised by many writers who denied that Eve should have all the blame for the loss of Eden and paradise. Lanyer stresses Eve's innocence, and emphasizes that Adam should have exercised authority over Eve. This latter point is central to Milton's representation of Adam's sin in *Paradise Lost*, exonerating Eve while also making her Adam's subordinate.

9. She could not foresee the harm that would follow her disobedience.

Being Lord of all, greater was his shame:
Although the serpent's craft had her abused,
God's holy word ought all his actions frame,
For he was lord and king of all the earth,
Before poor *Eve* had either life or breath.

Who being framed by God's eternal hand,
The perfectest man that ever breathed on earth;
And from God's mouth received that strait° command, *stern*
The breach whereof he knew was present death:
Yea, having power to rule both sea and land,
Yet with one apple won to lose that breath
Which god had breathed in his beauteous face,
Bringing us all in danger and disgrace.

And then to lay the fault on Patience° back, *Patience's*
That we (poor women) must endure it all;
We know right well he did discretion lack,
Being not persuaded thereunto at all;
If *Eve* did err, it was for knowledge sake,
The fruit being fair, persuaded him to fall:
No subtle serpent's falsehood did betray him,
If he would eat it, who had power to stay him?

Not *Eve,* whose fault was only too much love,
Which made her give this present to her dear,
That what she tasted, he likewise might prove,
Whereby his knowledge might become more clear;
He never sought her weakness to reprove,
With those sharp words, which he of God did hear:
Yet men will boast of knowledge, which he took
From *Eve's* fair hand, as from a learned book.

If any evil did in her remain,
Being made of him, he was the ground of all;
If one of many worlds[1] could lay a stain
Upon our sex, and work so great a fall
To wretched man, by Satan's subtle train;
What will so foul a fault amongst you all?
Her weakness did the serpent's words obey;
But you in malice God's dear Son betray.

Whom, if unjustly you condemn to die,
Her sin was small, to what you do commit;
All mortal sins that do for vengeance cry,
Are not to be compared unto it:
If many worlds would altogether try,
By all their sins the wrath of God to get;
This sin of yours, surmounts them all as far
As doth the sun, another little star.

1. I.e., Adam who, as the father of all humankind, was of many people.

Then let us have our liberty again,
And challenge° to your selves no sovereignty;[2] *attribute*
You came not in the world without our pain:
Make that a bar against your cruelty;
Your fault being greater, why should you disdain
Our being your equals, free from tyranny?
  If one weak woman simply did offend,
  This sin of yours, hath no excuse, nor end.

To which (poor souls) we never gave consent,
Witness thy wife (O *Pilate*) speaks for all,
Who did but dream, and yet a message sent,
That thou should'st have nothing to do at all
With that just man; which, if thy heart relent,
Why wilt thou be a reprobate° with *Saul?* *sinner*
  To seek the death of him that is so good,
  For thy soul's health to shed his dearest blood.

Sir Walter Raleigh

c. 1554–1618

Born in South Devon, a region in which ports and shipyards testified to the importance of England's world trade and colonies abroad, Sir Walter Raleigh spent a considerable part of his life outside his native land. As a boy, he fought with Huguenot armies in France; at twenty-four he led an expedition to the West Indies with his half-brother, Sir Humphrey Gilbert; and two years later, he commanded a contingent of English troops in Ireland. He is reported to have been a great favorite of Elizabeth, at least until in 1592, when he secretly married one of her ladies-in-waiting, Elizabeth Throckmorton; the queen, furious that she had had no say in the match, imprisoned Raleigh in the Tower of London for a period that summer.

Raleigh was famous for his travels. His most challenging expedition was intended to locate the legendary gold mines of El Dorado in South America. In 1595 he set out for the Spanish colony of Guiana, penetrating the interior of that land by venturing up the Orinoco. He described his trip in the brilliantly detailed *Discovery of the Large, Rich and Beautiful Empire of Guiana,* and although he returned to England without the gold he had gone for, his leadership of an expedition to sack the harbor of Cadiz in 1596 was enough to restore him to royal favor. But Raleigh was to encounter real trouble with the accession of James I. His enemies at court convinced the king that Raleigh had committed treason, and in 1603 he was tried, convicted, and once again confined to the Tower of London, this time with his wife and family. He remained there for thirteen years. His release was finally granted on the condition that he lead another expedition to Guiana. He had informed the king that on his earlier trip he had discovered an actual gold mine, and he now claimed that his new adventure would be successful. In fact, it was a disaster. Not only did he find no gold; the mine to whose existence he had sworn was revealed to be a fabrication. On this occasion the grounds for proving treason were stronger than they had been in 1603. Raleigh was executed in 1618.

2. Because men are afflicted with the weakness of Adam, they forfeit their original sovereignty over creation; their rule over woman is therefore a tyranny.

During his long imprisonment, Raleigh began to write a complete history of the world, managing only to cover events in ancient history to 168 B.C. Entitled *The History of the World* and published in 1614, the work is primarily remembered for the stunning reflection on death that appears on its last page: "O eloquent, just and mighty Death! Whom none could advise, thou hast persuaded; what none hath dared, thou hast done; and whom all the world hath flattered, thou only hast cast out of the world and despised; thou hast drawn together all the far stretched greatness, all the pride, cruelty, and ambition of man, and covered it all over with those two narrow words, *Hic iacet*."

Much of Raleigh's poetry is occasional, written to address the circumstances and the moment in which he found himself. It possesses the quality Castiglione celebrated in his treatise on court life: a brilliance of self-expression that contemporary Italians termed *sprezzatura*, created by the supposedly artless use of artifice showing not the courtier's education, but rather his native wit and talent. Raleigh exploits images of common life but with an unusual intensity, adding sensuous detail to expressions of affection and reminders of mortality to celebrations of love. His longest and greatest poem, *The 21st and Last Book of the Ocean to Cynthia*, remained fragmentary at the time of his death. Occasioned when Queen Elizabeth imprisoned him for his marriage, the poem illustrates Raleigh's fury at the queen's inconsistent treatment of her "Ocean" or "Water," as Raleigh pronounced his first name. It ends in an equivocation: Raleigh professes his devotion to Elizabeth, instancing his good will that "knit up by faith shall ever last"; but he also concludes that despite this, they will not be reconciled: "Her love hath end; my woe must ever last."

Nature That Washed Her Hands in Milk

Nature that washed her hands in milk
    And had forgot to dry them,
Instead of earth took snow and silk,[1]
    At love's request to try them,
If she a mistress could compose
To please love's fancy out of those.

Her eyes he would should be of light,
    A violet breath and lips of jelly,
Her hair not black nor over-bright,
    And of the softest down her belly;
As for her inside he would have it
Only of wantonness and wit.

At love's entreaty, such a one
    Nature made, but with her beauty
She hath framed a heart of stone,
    So as love by ill destiny
Must die for her whom nature gave him
Because her darling would not save him.

But time, which nature doth despise,
    And rudely gives her love the lie,
Makes hope a fool, and sorrow wise,
    His hands doth neither wash nor dry,

1. "And the Lord God formed man of the dust of the ground" (Genesis 2.7).

But being made of steel and rust,
Turns snow, and silk, and milk to dust.

The light, the belly, lips, and breath
He dims, discolors, and destroys,
With those he feeds, but fills not death,
Which sometimes were the food of joys;
Yea, time doth dull each lively wit
And dries all wantonness with it.

Oh cruel time which takes in trust
Our youth, our joys, and all we have,
And pays us but with age and dust,
Who in the dark and silent grave,
When we have wandered all our ways,
Shuts up the story of our days.[2]

c. 1592

To the Queen[1]

Our passions are most like to floods and streams,
The shallow murmur, but the deep are dumb.
So when affections yield discourse, it seems
The bottom is but shallow whence they come.
They that are rich in words must needs discover
That they are poor in that which makes a lover.

Wrong not, dear empress of my heart,
The merit of true passion,
With thinking that he feels no smart,
That sues for no compassion.
Since, if my plaints serve not to prove
The conquest of your beauty,
It comes not from defect of love,
But from excess of duty.

For knowing that I sue to serve
A saint of such perfection,
As all desire, but none deserve,
A place in her affection;
I rather choose to want relief
Than venture the revealing,
When glory recommends the grief,
Despair distrusts the healing.

Thus those desires that aim too high
For any mortal lover,

2. With one slight change and the addition of a final couplet, the last stanza of this poem is also Raleigh's *Epitaph*.

1. This elaborate compliment is typical of the courtly expressions of devotion Elizabeth I often inspired. Its respectful complaint can be compared to the bitter regret in Raleigh's later poem *The Shepherd of the Ocean to Cynthia*.

When reason cannot make them die,
Discretion will them cover.
Yet when discretion doth bereave
The plaints that they should utter,
Then your discretion may perceive
That silence is a suitor.

Silence in love bewrays more woe
Than words, though ne'er so witty,
A beggar that is dumb, you know,
Deserveth double pity.
Then misconceive not (dearest heart)
My true, though secret passion,
He smarteth most that hides his smart,
And sues for no compassion.

c. 1590

On the Life of Man

What is our life? A play of passion,
Our mirth the music of division,
Our mothers' wombs the tiring houses be,
Where we are dressed for this short comedy,
Heaven the judicious sharp spectator is,
That sits and marks still who doth act amiss,
Our graves that hide us from the searching sun,
Are like drawn curtains when the play is done;
Thus march we playing to our latest rest,
Only we die in earnest, that's no jest.

1612

The Author's Epitaph, Made by Himself

Even such is time, which takes in trust
Our youth, our joys, and all we have,
And pays us but with age and dust,
Who in the dark and silent grave,
When we have wandered all our days,
Shuts up the story of our days;
And from which earth, and grave, and dust,
The Lord shall raise me up, I trust.

As You Came from the Holy Land

As you came from the holy land
Of Walsingham[1]

1. A district in the county of Norfolk and site of Walsingham Abbey, one of the great shrines of medieval England.

Met you not with my true love
  By the way as you came?[2]

How shall I know your true love
  That have met many one?
As I went to the holy land
  That have come, that have gone.

She is neither white nor brown
  But as the heavens, fair.
There is none hath a form so divine
  In the earth or the air.

Such a one did I meet good sir,
  Such an angelic face,
Who like a queen, like a nymph did appear
  By her gait, by her grace.

She hath left me here all alone,
  All alone as unknown,
Who sometimes did me lead with herself,
  And me loved as her own.

What's the cause that she leaves you alone
  And a new way doth take,
Who loved you once as her own,
  And her joy did you make?

I have loved her all my youth,
  But now old, as you see;
Love likes not the falling fruit
  From the withered tree.

Know that love is a careless child
  And forgets promise past;
He is blind, he is deaf, when he list,° *wishes*
  And in faith never fast.

His desire is a dureless content
  And a trustless joy;
He is won with a world of despair
  And is lost with a toy.

Of womankind such indeed is the love
  Or the word love abused,
Under which many childish desires
  And conceits are excused.

But love is a durable fire
  In the mind ever burning;
Never sick, never old, never dead,
  From itself never turning.

2. This stanza is the first in the dialogue that constitutes the poem. Its first seven stanzas alternate statements between two speakers. Stanzas 7, 8, and 9 are spoken by the lover, the first speaker; the final two stanzas are spoken by the traveler.

from The 21st and Last Book of the Ocean to Cynthia[1]

Sufficeth to you, my joys interred,
In simple words that I my woes complain;
You that then died when first my fancy erred—[2]
Joys under dust that never live again.

If to the living were my muse addressed,
Or did my mind her own spirit still inhold,
Were not my living passion so repressed
As to the dead° the dead did these unfold, *i.e., joys*

Some sweeter words, some more becoming verse
Should witness my mishap in higher kind;
But my love's wounds, my fancy in the hearse,
The idea but resting of a wasted mind,

The blossoms fallen, the sap gone from the tree,
The broken monuments of my great desires—
From these so lost what may the affections° be? *passions*
What heat in cinders of extinguished fires?

Lost in the mud of those high-flowing streams,
Which through more fairer fields their courses bend,
Slain with self-thoughts, amazed in fearful dreams,
Woes without date, discomforts without end.

From fruitless trees I gather withered leaves,
And glean° the broken ears° with miser's hand, *harvest / of grain*
Who sometime did enjoy the weighty sheaves;
I seek fair flowers amid the brinish° sand. *salty*

All in the shade, even in the fair sun days,
Under those healthless trees I sit alone,
Where joyful birds sing neither lovely lays,
Nor Philomen° recounts her direful moan. *the nightingale*

No feeding flocks, no shepherd's company,
That might renew my dolorous conceit,° *imagination*
While happy then, while love and fantasy
Confined my thoughts on that fair flock to wait;

No pleasing streams fast to the ocean wending,
The messengers sometimes of my great woe;
But all on earth, as from the cold storms bending,
Shrink from my thoughts in high heavens or below.

1. This lyric complaint, a fragment of what was projected as a much longer work, is the most important of Raleigh's poems. It tells of his despair at losing the Queen's favor and reproaches her for indifference to his devoted service. Adopting the conventions of pastoral, Raleigh styles himself "The Shepherd of the Ocean," perhaps to draw attention to his first name, which he pronounced "Water." "Cynthia" is, of course, Elizabeth, figured here (as she was so often) as the moon, ever changeful, as well as Diana, the goddess of the moon and of chastity. Characterizing Cynthia as the moving force in his life, Raleigh's verse illustrates how conventions of courtly love could acquire a political reference: both Elizabeth and her courtiers were accustomed to conveying their hopes and desires in the coded language of erotic compliment. Spenser's poem *Colin Clout's Come Home Again* (1591) notes that the subject of Raleigh's "Cynthia" is "the great unkindness" and "usage hard" of the "Lady of the Sea," who has "from her presence faultless him (i.e., the Shepherd) debarred."

2. The poet complains to his own "joys" that are now dead and buried.

Oh, hopeful love, my object and invention,
Oh, true desire, the spur of my conceit,
Oh, worthiest spirit, my mind's impulsion,° *force*
Oh, eyes transpersant,° my affection's bait, *that penetrate*

Oh princely form, my fancy's adamant,° *magnet*
Divine conceit,° my pains' acceptance, *image*
Oh, all in one! Oh, heaven on earth transparent!
The seat of joys and love's abundance!

Out of that mass of miracles, my muse
Gathered those flowers, to her pure senses pleasing;
Out of her eyes, the store of joys, did choose
Equal delights, my sorrow's counterpoising.

Her regal looks my vigorous sighs suppressed,
Small drops of joys sweetened great worlds of woes,
One gladsome day a thousand cares redressed—
Whom love defends, what fortune overthrows?

When she did well, what did there else amiss?
When she did ill, what empires would have pleased?
No other power affecting woe or bliss,
She gave, she took, she wounded, she appeased.

The honor of her love, love still devising,
Wounding my mind with contrary conceit,
Transferred itself sometime to her aspiring,
Sometime the trumpet of her thought's retreat.[3]

To seek new worlds for gold, for praise, for glory,
To try° desire, to try love severed far, *test*
When I was gone, she sent her memory,
More strong than were ten thousand ships of war,

To call me back; to leave great honor's thought;
To leave my friends, my fortune, my attempt;
To leave the purpose[4] I so long had sought,
And hold both cares and comforts in contempt.

Such heat in ice, such fire in frost remained,
Such trust in doubt, such comfort in despair,
Which, like the gentle lamb, though lately weaned,
Plays with the dug, though finds no comfort there.

But as a body, violently slain,
Retaineth warmth although the spirit be gone,
And by a power in nature moves again
Till it be laid below the fatal stone;

3. The honor of being loved by her creating love (in me), wounding me with a contrary (twofold) conception, sometimes aspiring to (please) her, sometimes heralding the withdrawal of her attention. In other words, the poet is constantly aware that his love makes him have a conflicted conception of how to approach Cynthia: sometimes he pleases her, sometimes what he does causes her disdain.

4. Raleigh's "purpose" was to find gold for England in the wilderness of the New World; he continued to hope for success in this venture until 1617, when his last voyage to Guiana ended in nothing.

Or as the earth, even in cold winter days,
Left for a time by her life-giving sun,
Doth by the power remaining of his rays
Produce some green, though not as it hath done;

Or as a wheel, forced by the falling stream,
Although the course be turned some other way,
Doth for a time go round upon the beam,
Till, wanting strength to move, it stands at stay;

So my forsaken heart, my withered mind—
Widow of all the joys it once possessed,
My hopes clean out of sight with forced wind—
To kingdoms strange, to lands far off, addressed,

Alone, forsaken, friendless, on the shore
With many wounds, with death's cold pangs embraced,
Writes in the dust, as one that could no more,
Whom love, and time, and fortune, had defaced,

Of things so great, so long, so manifold,
With means so weak, the soul even then depicting
The weal, the woe, the passages of old,
And worlds of thoughts descried° by one last sighing. *discerned*

As if, when after Phoebus° is descended, *the sun*
And leaves a light much like the past day's dawning,
And every toil and labor wholly ended,
Each living creature draweth to his resting,

We should begin by such a parting light
To write the story of all ages past,
And end the same before approaching night.

Such is again the labor of my mind,
Whose shroud, by sorrow woven now to end,
Hath seen that ever shining sun declined,
So many years that so could not descend,

But that the eyes of my mind held her beams
In every part transferred by love's swift thought,
Far off or near, in waking or in dreams,
Imagination strong in lustre brought.

Such force her angelic appearance had
To master distance, time, or cruelty,
Such art to grieve, and after to make glad,
Such fear in love, such love in majesty.

My weary lines her memory embalmed;
My darkest ways her eyes make clear as day.
What storms so great but Cynthia's beams appeased?
What rage so fierce, that love could not allay?

Twelve years entire I wasted in this war,[5]
Twelve years of my most happy younger days;
But I in them, and they now wasted are,
"Of all which past, the sorrow only stays."

. . .

Yet as the air in deep caves underground
Is strongly drawn when violent heat hath vent
Great clefts therein, till moisture do abound,
And then the same, imprisioned and up-pent,° *pent up*

Breaks out in earthquakes, tearing all asunder,
So in the center of my cloven heart—
My heart, to whom her beauties were such wonder—
Lies the sharp, poisoned head of that love's dart

Which, till all break and dissolve to dust,
Thence drawn it cannot be, or therein known,
There, mixed with my heart-blood, the fretting rust
The better part hath eaten and outgrown.

But what of those or these? Or what of aught
Of that which was, or that which is, to treat?
What I possess is but the same I sought;
My love was false, my labors were deceit.

Nor less than such they are esteemed to be,
A fraud bought at the price of many woes,
A guile, whereof the profits unto me—
Could it be thought premediate° for those? *plead*

Witness those withered leaves left on the tree,
The sorrow-worn face, the pensive mind,
The external shows, what may the internal be;
Cold care hath bitten both the root and rind.

But stay, my thoughts, make end, give fortune way;
Harsh is the voice of woe and sorrow's sound;
Complaints cure not, and tears do but allay
Griefs for a time, which after more abound.

To seek for moisture in the Arabian sand
Is but a loss of labor and of rest,
The links which time did break of hearty bands
Words cannot knit, or wailings make anew,
Seek not the sun in clouds when it is set. . . .
On highest mountains, where those cedars[6] grew,
Against whose banks the troubled ocean beat,

And were the marks to find thy hoped port,
Into a soil far off themselves remove.
On Sestos' shore, Leander's late resort,
Hero hath left no lamp to guide her love.[7]

5. The 12 years of service to Elizabeth began with his command of troops in Ireland in 1580 and ended, in the terms the poem supplies, with his marriage and imprisonment in 1592. Raleigh was only 36 at the time.

6. The cedar was identified as a tree of royalty; so Raleigh can speak of the ocean beating against banks over which the cedar presides.

7. Leander and Hero were two lovers who lived on opposite shores of the Hellespont. When Leander swam at night from Abydos to visit Hero in Sestos, she hung out a lantern to guide him.

Thou lookest for light in vain, and storms arise,
She sleeps thy death, that erst thy danger sighed,
Strive then no more, bow down thy weary eyes—
Eyes which to all these woes thy heart have guided.

She is gone, she is lost, she is found, she is ever fair;
Sorrow draws weakly where love draws not too,
Woe's cries sound nothing, but only in love's ear.
Do then by dying what life cannot do.

Unfold thy flocks and leave them to the fields,
To feed on hills or dales, where likes them best,
Of what the summer or the springtime yields,
For love and time hath given thee leave to rest.

Thy heart which was their fold, now in decay
By often storms and winter's many blasts,
All torn and rent, becomes misfortune's prey,
False hope, my shepherd's staff, now age hath brast.° *broken*

My pipe, which love's own hand gave my desire
To sing her praises and my woe upon—
Despair hath often threatened to the fire,
As vain to keep now all the rest are gone.

Thus home I draw, as death's long night draws on,
Yet every foot, old thoughts turn back mine eyes;
Constraint me guides, as old age draws a stone
Against a hill, which over-weighty lies
For feeble arms or wasted strength to move.
My steps are backward, gazing on my loss,
My mind's affection and my soul's sole love,
Not mixed with fancy's chaff or fortune's dross.
To God I leave it,° who first gave it me, *my soul*
And I her gave, and she returned again,
As it was hers; so let His mercies be
Of my last comforts the essential mean.° *factor*
But be it so or not, the effects are past;
Her love hath end, my woes must ever last.

from The Discovery of the Large, Rich and Beautiful Empire of Guiana[1]

from *Epistle Dedicatory*

To the Right Honorable my singular good lord and kinsman, Charles Howard,[2] Knight of the Garter, Baron, and Chancellor, and of the Admirals of England the most reknowned, and to the Right Honorable Sir Robert Cecil, Knight, Counselor in Her Highness's Privy Councils.[3]

1. A region in Venezuela. The full title of Raleigh's report is *The Discovery of the Large, Rich and Beautiful Empire of Guiana, with a relation of the Great and Golden City of Manoa (which the Spaniards call El Dorado) and the provinces of Emeria, Arromaia, Amapaia and other Countries, with their rivers, adjoining.* It was written and published in London in 1596, a year after Raleigh undertook his expedition.

2. Charles Howard (1536–1624) was Baron Howard of Effingham and Earl of Nottingham, commander of the Queen's navy at the defeat of the Armada and the capture of Cadiz.

3. Sir Robert Cecil was the first Earl of Salisbury, son of a principal advisor to Elizabeth I. Robert Cecil became Elizabeth's secretary of state in 1589 and was a key figure in the administration of James I, in which he eventually held the office of Lord Treasurer.

For your Honors' many honorable and friendly parts, I have hitherto only returned promises, and now for answer of both your adventures, I have sent you a bundle of papers which I have divided between your Lordship and Sir Robert Cecil in these two respects chiefly. First, for it is reasonable that wasteful factors,[4] when they have consumed such stocks as they had in trust, do yield some color for the same in their account; secondly, for that I am assured that whatsoever shall be done or written by me shall need a double protection and defense. The trial that I had of both your loves, when I was left of all but of malice and revenge, makes me still presume that you will be pleased (knowing what little power I had to perform aught, and the great advantage of forewarned enemies) to answer that out of knowledge which others shall but object out of malice.[5] In my more happy times as I did especially honor you both, so I found that your loves sought me out in the darkest shadow of adversity, and the same affection which accompanied my better fortune, soared not away from me in my many miseries. All which, though I cannot requite, yet I shall ever acknowledge, and the great debt which I have no power to pay, I can do no more for a time but confess to be due. It is true that as my errors were great, so they have yielded very grievous effects, and if aught might have been deserved in former times to have counterpoised any part of offenses, the fruit thereof (as it seemeth) was long before fallen from the tree and the dead stock[6] only remained.[7] I did therefore even in the winter of my life undertake these travels, fitter for boys less blasted with misfortunes, for men of greater ability, and for minds of better encouragement, that thereby if it were possible I might recover but the moderation of excess and the least taste of the greatest plenty formerly possessed. If I had known other way to win, if I had imagined how greater adventures might have regained, if I could conceive what further means I might yet use but even to appease so powerful displeasure, I would not doubt but for one year more to hold fast my soul in my teeth til it were performed. Of that little remain I had, I have wasted in effect all therein,[8] I have undergone many constructions,[9] I have been accompanied with many sorrows, with labor, hunger, heat, sickness, and peril. It appeareth notwithstanding that I made no other bravado of going to sea than was meant, and that I was neither hidden in Cornwall or elsewhere, as was supposed.[1] They have grossly belied me, that forejudged that I would rather become a servant to the Spanish king than return; and the rest were much mistaken who would have persuaded that I was too easeful and sensual to undertake a journey of so great travel. But if what I have done receive the gracious construction[2] of a painful pilgrimage and purchase the least remission, I shall think all too little, and that there were wanting to the rest, many miseries.[3] But if both the times past, the present, and what may be in the future do all by one grain of gall continue in an eternal distaste, I do not then know whether I should bewail myself either for my too much travel and expense, or condemn myself for doing less than that which can

4. Raleigh refers to himself as a "factor," an agent who is commissioned to perform a certain function. Factors who exhausted the resources at their disposal had to account for their expenditures.

5. Raleigh presumes that Howard and Cecil will be able to answer his detractors (who speak from malice) with knowledge gained from this account of his travels to Guiana.

6. Trunk.

7. Raleigh admits that he has made errors and that the successes he had earlier in his career, which might have compensated for these errors, can no longer serve this purpose.

8. I.e., of what was left of my resources, I have effectually wasted everything.

9. Trials.

1. I.e., it is apparent that I made no other boast of going to sea than to state that I intended to do it and that I was not hidden in Cornwall or elsewhere. Here Raleigh addresses the rumor that he had never gone to Guiana but rather had waited for his men to return from there, then claimed that his expedition was a success.

2. Interpretation.

3. I.e., if I could get some credit for having taken this painful pilgrimage, I would wish that my miseries had been more severe.

deserve nothing.[4] From myself I have deserved no thanks, for I am returned a beggar, and withered, but that I might have bettered my poor estate it shall appear by the following discourse, if I had not only respected Her Majesty's future honor and riches. It became not the former fortune in which I once lived, to go journeys of picorie,[5] and it had sorted ill with the offices of honor which by Her Majesty's grace I hold this day in England to run from Cape to Cape and from place to place for the pillage of ordinary prizes. Many years since, I had knowledge by relation of that mighty, rich and beautiful Empire of Guiana and of that great and golden city which the Spaniards call El Dorado, and the naturals,[6] Manoa, which city was conquered, re-edified, and enlarged by a younger son of Guainacapa, Emperor of Peru, at such time as Francisco Pizarro[7] and others conquered the said empire from his two elder brethren, Guascar and Atabalipa, both then contending for the same, the one being favored by the Oreiones of Cuzco, the other by the people of Caximalca. I sent my servant Jacob Whiddon the year before to get knowledge of the passages, and I had some light from Captain Parker, sometime my servant and now attending on your Lordship, that such a place there was to the southward of the great bay of Charuas, or Guanipa, but I found that it was six hundred miles farther off than they supposed, and many other impediments to them unknown and unheard. After I had displanted[8] Don Antonio de Berreo, who was upon the same enterprise, leaving my ships at Trinidad, at the port called Curiapan, I wandered four hundred miles into the said country by land and river, the particulars I will leave to the following discourse.[9] The country hath more quantity of gold by manifold than the best parts of the Indies or Peru; all the most of the kings of the borders are already become Her Majesty's vassals and seem to desire nothing more than Her Majesty's protection and the return of the English nation.

To the Reader

Because there have been diverse opinions conceived of the gold ore brought from Guiana, and for that an alderman of London and an officer of Her Majesty's Mint hath given out that the same is of no price, I have thought good by the addition of these lines to give answer as well to the said malicious slander, as to other objections. It is true that while we abode at the Island of Trinidad, I was informed by an Indian that not far from the port where we were anchored there were found certain mineral stones which they esteemed to be gold and were thereunto persuaded the rather for that they had seen both English and French men gather and embark some quantities thereof. Upon this likelihood I sent forty men and gave order that each one should bring a stone of that mine to make trial of the goodness, which being performed, I assured them at their return that the same was marcasite[1] and of no riches or value.

4. I.e., if everything continues to go badly, I do not know whether I should regret my travel or condemn myself for doing less than what can deserve nothing (what is not enough to deserve anything).
5. Suitable for the *picaro,* or rogue in Spanish.
6. Indigenous people.
7. Pizarro (1475–1541) conquered Peru by capturing the Incan king Atahualpa, whom Raleigh refers to as Atabalipa. Atahualpa was the son of Guainacapa and the brother of Guascar, whom he killed to get the throne. This passage suggests that Guianacapa had three sons; Raleigh later states that he had only two sons. Pizarro captured Cuzco, the principal city of the Incas, in 1533. The Oreiones were the native people of Cuzco; Caximalca or Casimarca was another large city in Peru.
8. Dislodged.
9. Here Raleigh claims that a Captain Parker told him that El Dorado was south of the bay of Guanipa (which opens onto the Gulf of Paria and has no connection with the Orinoco), but he discovered that it was 600 miles in the interior of the country and away from the shore. Don Antonio de Berreo was the Spanish Governor of Trinidad and Guiana; Trinidad is an island just off the Venezuelan coast. Presumably, Raleigh marched from that coast 400 miles inland.
1. Pyrite.

Notwithstanding, diverse,[2] trusting more to their own sense than to my opinion, kept of the said marcasite and have tried thereof, since my return, in diverse places. In Guiana itself I never saw marcasite, but all the rocks, mountains, all stones in the plains, in woods, and by the rivers' sides are in effect thereof shining, and appear marvelous rich, which being tried[3] to be no marcasite, are the true signs of rich minerals, but[4] are no other than *el madre del oro* (as the Spaniards term them), which is the mother of gold, or as it is said by others, the scum of gold. Of diverse sorts of these, many of my company brought also into England, every one taking the fairest for the best, which is not general.[5] For mine own part, I did not countermand any man's desire or opinion, and I could have afforded them little if I should have denied them the pleasing of their own fancies therein. But I was resolved that gold must be found either in grains separate from the stone (as it is in most of all the rivers in Guiana) or else in a kind of hard stone, which we call the white spar, of which I saw diverse hills and in sundry places but had neither time, nor men, nor instruments fit to labor. Near unto one of the rivers I found of the said white spar or flint a very great ledge or bank which I endeavored to break by all means I could, because there appeared on the outside some small grains of gold, but finding no means to work the same upon the upper part, seeking the sides and circuit of the said rock, I found a cleft in the same from whence with daggers and with the head of an ax we got out some small quantity thereof, of which kind of white stone (wherein gold is engendered) we saw diverse hills and rocks in every part of Guiana wherein we traveled. Of this there hath been made many trials, and in London it was first assayed by Master Westwood, a refiner dwelling in Wood Street, and it was held after the rate of 12,000 or 13,000 pounds a ton. Another sort was afterward tried by Master Bulmar and Master Dimoke, assay master, and it held after the rate of 23,000 pounds a ton. There was some of it again tried by Master Palmer, comptroller of the mint, and Master Dimoke in Goldsmith's Hall, and it held after 26,900 pounds a ton. There was also at the same time and by the same persons a trial made of the dust of the said mine, which held eight pounds, six ounces weight of gold in the hundred. There was likewise at the same time a trial made of an image of copper made in Guiana which held a third part gold, besides diverse trials made in the country and by others in London.[6] But because there came of ill with the good, and belike the said alderman was not presented with the best, it hath pleased him therefore to scandal[7] all the rest, and to deface[8] the enterprises as much as in him lieth. It hath also been concluded by diverse that if there had been any such ore in Guiana and the same discovered, that I would have brought home a greater quantity thereof. First, I was not bound to satisfy any man of the quantity, but such only as adventured, if any store had been returned thereof. But it is very true that had all their mountains been of massy gold, it was impossible for us to have made any longer stay to have wrought the same, and whosoever hath seen with what strength of stone the best gold is environed,[9] he will not think it easy to be had out in heaps and especially by us who had neither men, instruments, nor time (as it is said before) to perform the same. There were, on this discovery, no less than one hundred persons, who can all witness that when we passed any

2. Some men.
3. Discovered.
4. And.
5. I.e., the fairest mineral is judged to be best, provided that it is also rare or "not general."
6. Raleigh reports that the ore he broughht back from Guiana was tested by several goldsmiths, who were experts at refining the metal, and that it was found to be substantially gold. Throughout his address to the reader, Raleigh argues that he actually discovered gold and that this gold will allow England to rival Spain.
7. Disparage.
8. Criticize.
9. Embedded.

branch of the river to view the land within, and stayed from our boats but six hours, we were driven to wade to the eyes at our return, and if we attempted the same the day following, it was impossible either to ford it or to swim it,[1] both by reason of the swiftness and also for that the borders were so pestered[2] with fast[3] woods as neither boat nor man could find place either to land or to embark. For in June, July, August, and September, it is impossible to navigate any of those rivers, for such is the fury of the current and there are so many trees and woods overflowed as if any boat but touch upon any tree or stake, it is impossible to save any one person therein, and ere we departed the land, it ran with that swiftness as[4] we drove down most commonly against the wind little less than one hundred miles a day. Besides, our vessels were no other than wherries,[5] one little barge, a small cockboat,[6] and a bad galiota,[7] which we framed in haste for that purpose at Trinidad, and those little boats had nine or ten men apiece, with all their victuals and arms. It is further true that we were about four hundred miles from our ships and had been a month from them, which also we left weakly manned in an open road[8] and had promised our return in fifteen days. Others have devised that the same ore was had from Barbary,[9] and that we carried it with us into Guiana. Surely the singularity of that device I do not well comprehend; for my own part, I am not so much in love with these long voyages as to devise, thereby to cozen myself, to lie hard, to fare worse, to be subjected to perils, to diseases, to ill savors, to be parched and withered, and withal to sustain the care and labor of such an enterprise, except the same had more comfort than the fetching of marcasite in Guiana or buying of gold ore in Barbary.[1] But I hope the better sort will judge me by themselves, and that the way of deceit is not the way of honor or good opinion. I have herein consumed much time and many crowns, and I had no other respect or desire than to serve Her Majesty and my country thereby. If the Spanish nation had been of like belief to these detractors, we should little have feared or doubted their attempts wherewith we now are daily threatened.[2] But if we now consider of the actions both of Charles the Fifth,[3] who had the maidenhead of Peru and the abundant treasures of Atabalipa, together with the affairs of the Spanish king now living,[4] what territories he hath purchased, what he hath added to the acts of predecessors, how many kingdoms he hath endangered, how many armies, garrisons, and navies he hath and doth maintain, the great losses which he hath repaired, as in 1588, above one hundred sail of great ships with their artillery, and that no year is less unfortunate but that many vessels, treasures, and people are devoured, and yet notwithstanding he beginneth again like a storm to threaten shipwreck to us all, we shall find that these abilities rise not from the trades of sacks[5] and Seville oranges, nor from aught else that either Spain, Portugal, or any of his other provinces produce. It is his Indian gold that endangereth and disturbeth all the nations of Europe, it purchaseth intelligence, creepeth into councils, and setteth bound loyalty at liberty in the greatest monarchies of Europe. If the Spanish king can keep us from foreign enterprises and

1. The river Orinoco, which Raleigh describes as tidal.
2. Crowded.
3. Thick.
4. That.
5. Small barges.
6. Rowboat.
7. A small sailing ship, also equipped with oars.
8. An exposed anchorage, outside the protection of a harbor.
9. The regions along the coast of North Africa.
1. I.e., I would not have undergone such trials to bring marcasite from Guiana or to buy gold in Barbary.
2. Raleigh uses the Spaniards' interest in American gold as proof that his detractors are wrong.
3. Charles V (1500–1558) was the Holy Roman Emperor under whose rule the Spanish empire in the Americas was enormously enlarged.
4. Philip II (1527–1598). Raleigh alludes to the expenditures of that king—including the repair of his Armada, which was defeated by the English fleet in 1588—none of which stood in the way of his harrassing English interests and property. Spanish affluence and influence, Raleigh claims, are sustained by "Indian gold."
5. Wines.

from the empeachment of his trades, either by offer of invasions or by besieging us in Britain, Ireland, or elsewhere, he hath then brought the work of our peril in great forwardness.[6] Those princes which abound in treasure have great advantages over the rest, if they once constrain them[7] to a defensive war, where they are driven once a year or oftener to cast lots for their own garments, and from such shall all trades and intercourse be taken away, to the general loss and impoverishment of the kingdom and commonweal so reduced. Besides, when men are constrained to fight, it hath not the same hope as when they are pressed and encouraged by the desire of spoil and riches. Further, it is to be doubted how those that in time of victory seem to affect[8] their neighbor nations will remain after the first view of misfortunes or ill success. To trust also to the doubtfulness of a battle is but a fearful and uncertain adventure, seeing therein fortune is as likely to prevail as virtue. It shall not be necessary to allege all that might be said, and therefore I will thus conclude that whatsoever kingdom shall be enforced to defend itself may be compared to a body dangerously diseased, which for a season may be preserved with vulgar[9] medicines, but in a short time and by little and little, the same must needs fall to the ground and be dissolved. I have therefore labored all my life, both according to my small power and persuasion, to advance all those attempts that might either promise return of profit for ourselves or at least be a let[1] and empeachment to the quiet course and plentiful trades of the Spanish nation, who[2] in my weak judgment by such a war were as easily endangered and brought from his powerfulness as any prince in Europe, if it be considered from how many kingdoms and nations his revenues are gathered, and those so weak in their own beings and so far severed from mutual succour. But because such a preparation and resolution are not to be hoped for in haste, and that the time which our enemies embrace cannot be had again to advantage, I will hope that these provinces and that empire now by me discovered shall suffice to enable Her Majesty and the whole kingdom with no less quantities of treasure than the King of Spain hath in all the Indies, east and west, which he possesseth; which if the same be considered and followed ere the Spaniards enforce the same, and if Her Majesty will undertake it, I will be contented to lose Her Highness's favor and good opinion forever, and my life withal, if the same be not found rather to exceed than to equal whatsoever is in this discourse promised or declared. I will now refer the reader to the following discourse with the hope that the perilous and chargeable labors and endeavors of such as thereby seek the profit and honor of Her Majesty and the English nation shall by men of quality and virtue receive such construction and good acceptance as themselves would look to be rewarded withal in the like.

[The Amazons]

I made inquiry amongst the most ancient and best traveled of the Orenoqueponi, and I had knowledge of all the rivers between Orenoque and [the river of the] Amazons, and was very desirous to understand the truth of those warlike women, because of some it is believed, of others not.[1] And though I digress from my purpose, yet I will set down what hath been delivered me for truth of those women, and I spake with a

6. I.e., he has advanced the work of our destruction.
7. I.e., the rest.
8. Support.
9. Ordinary.
1. Hindrance.
2. I.e., Philip II.

1. Raleigh takes his account of the Amazons from a native of Guiana. He associates this race of women, whose presence has never been verified, with a comparable people described in Greek mythology who are also warlike and consort with men only to conceive children.

Casique or Lord of people that told me he had been in the river, and beyond it also. The nations of these women are on the south side of the river in the provinces of Topago, and their chiefest strengths and retreats are in the Islands situated on the south side of the entrance, some 60 leagues within the mouth of the said river. The memories of the like women are very ancient as well in Africa as in Asia. In Africa those that had Medusa[2] for Queen: others in Scithia near the rivers of Tanais and Thermadon: we find also that Lampedo and Marthesia[3] were Queens of the Amazons: in many histories they are verified to have been, and in diverse ages and provinces. But they which are not far from Guiana do accompany with men but once a year, and for the time of one month, which I gather by their relation to be in April. At that time all the kings of the borders assemble, and the queens of the Amazons, and after the queens have chosen, the rest cast lots for their Valentines. This one month, they feast, dance, and drink of their wines in abundance, and the moon being done, they all depart to their own provinces. If they conceive, and be delivered of a son, they return him to the father, if of a daughter they nourish it, and retain it, and as many as have daughters send unto the begetters a present, all being desirous to increase their own sex and kind, but that they cut off the right dug of the breast I do not find to be true. It was further told me, that if in the wars they took any prisoners that they used to accompany with those also at what time soever, but in the end for certain they put them to death: for they are said to be very cruel and bloodthirsty, especially to such as offer to invade their territories.

[THE ORINOCO]

The great river of Orenoque or Baraquan hath nine branches which fall out on the north side of his own main mouth. On the south side it hath seven other fallings into the sea, so it disemboqueth[1] by sixteen arms in all, between islands and broken ground, but the islands are very great, many of them as big as the Isle of Wight[2] and bigger, and many less. From the first branch on the north to the last of the south it is at least one hundred leagues, so as the river's mouth is no less than three hundred miles wide at his entrance into the sea, which I take to be far bigger than that of [the] Amazons. All those that inhabit in the mouth of this river upon the several north branches are these Tiuitiuas,[3] of which there are two chief lords which have continual wars one with the other. The islands which lie on the right hand are called Pallamos, and the land on the left, Hororotomaka, and the river by which John Douglas returned within the land from Amana to Capuri, they call Macuri.

These Tiuitiuas are a very goodly people and very valiant, and have the most manly speech and most deliberate that ever I heard of, what nation so ever. In the summer they have houses on the ground as in other places, where they build very artificial towns and villages, as it is written in the Spanish story of the West Indies, that those people do in the low lands near the gulf of Uraba. For between May and September, the river of Orenoque riseth thirty foot upright, and then those islands overflow twenty foot high above the level of the ground, saving some few raised grounds in the middle of them, and for this cause they are enforced to live in this

2. A mythical monstrous woman, one of the Gorgons, who turned to stone whoever looked at her.
3. The legendary queen of the Amazons who fought in the Trojan war.
1. Discharges.
2. Island off the southern coast of England.
3. The Waraus, an indigenous people who live on the delta of the Orinoco and adjoining coasts. Spanish historians refer to them as the Guaraunos or Guaraunu.

manner. They never eat of anything that is set or sown, and as at home they use neither planting nor other manurance, so when they come abroad they refuse to feed of aught but of that which nature without labor bringeth forth.[4] They use the tops of *palmitos* [palm trees] for bread and kill deer, fish, and porks for the rest of their sustenance; they also have many sorts of fruits that grow in the woods and a great variety of birds and fowl.

And if to speak of them were not tedious and vulgar, surely we saw in those passages of very rare colors and forms not elsewhere to be found, for as much as I have either seen or read. Of these poeple, those that dwell upon the branches of the Orenoque called Capuri and Macureo are for the most part carpenters of *canoas* [canoes], for they make the most and fairest houses and sell them into Guiana for gold, and into Trinidad for tobacco, in the excessive taking whereof they exceed all nations, and notwithstanding the moistness of the air in which they live, the hardness of their diet, and the great labors they suffer to hunt, fish, and fowl for their living, in all my life either in the Indies or in Europe did I never behold a more goodly or better-favored people, or a more manly. They were wont to make war upon all nations and especially on the Cannibals, so as none durst without a good strength trade by those rivers; but of late they are at peace with their neighbors, all holding the Spaniards for a common enemy.[5] When their commanders die, they use great lamentation, and when they think the flesh of their bodies is putrified and fallen from the bones, then they take up the carcass again and hang it in the Casique's house that died, and deck his skull with feathers of all colors and hang all his gold plates about the bones of his arms, thighs, and legs. Those nations which are called Arwacas,[6] which dwell on the south of Orenoque (of which place and nation our Indian pilot was), are dispersed in many other places and do use to beat the bones of their lords into powder, and their wives and friends drink it all in their several sorts of drinks.

[The King of Aromaia]

The next day we arrived at the port of Morequito,[1] and anchored there, sending away one of our pilots to seek the king of Aromaia, uncle to Morequito, slain by Berreo as aforesaid. The next day following, before noon he came to us on foot from his house, which was fourteen English miles (himself being 110 years old), and returned on foot the same day, and with him many of the borderers,[2] with many women and children that came to wonder at our nation and to bring us down victual, which they did in great plenty, as venison, pork, hens, chickens, fowl, fish, with diverse sorts of excellent fruits and roots, and great abundance of *pinas* [pineapples], the princess of fruits that grow under the sun, especially those of Guiana. They brought us also store of

4. As people that do not farm, the Tiuitiuas would have been categorized by many Europeans as having no conception of property and therefore incapable of being dispossessed.

5. Here and throughout the narrative, Raleigh portrays the people of the region as desiring the protection of the English against the Spanish, whose mistreatment of the natives of the Americas was well publicized. Raleigh could claim that by making these natives vassals of the English monarch, England could acquire an empire to rival Spain's.

6. Known today as Arawaks, these people were neighbors of the Tiuitiuas.

1. A king whose territory bordered Guiana. He was captured and executed by the Spanish Governor of Trinidad, Antonio de Berreo, for having killed a Spanish garrison. His uncle, here described as the king of Aromaia and later named Topiawari, succeeded Morequito. His people are later identified as the Orenoqueponi, because they live on the shores of the Orinoco. The king's dignified report testifies to both his status as royalty and the culture of the Orenoqueponi, who are conscious of their history as one among many peoples of the territory which is now northern Venezuela.

2. People living on the borders of Aromaia.

bread, and of their wine, and a sort of *paraquitos* [parakeets], no bigger than wrens, and of all other sorts both small and great. One of them gave me a beast called by the Spaniards *armadilla* [armadillo] which they call *cassacam*, which seemeth to be all barred over with small plates somewhat like to a *renocero* [rhinoceros], with a white horn growing in his hinder parts as big as a great hunting horn, which they use to wind[3] instead of a trumpet. Monadarus writeth that a little of the powder of that horn put into the ear cureth deafness.

After this old king had rested a while in a little tent that I caused to be set up, I began by my interpretor to discourse with him of the death of Morequito his predecessor and afterward of the Spaniards, and ere I went any farther I made him know the cause of my coming thither, whose servant I was, and that the Queen's pleasure was I should undertake the voyage for their defense and to deliver them from the tyranny of the Spaniards, dilating[4] at large (as I had done before to those of Trinidad) Her Majesty's greatness, her justice, her charity to all oppressed nations, with as many of the rest of her beauties and virtues as either I could express or they conceive, all which being with great admiration attentively heard and marvellously admired, I began to sound the old man as touching Guiana and the state thereof, what sort of commonwealth it was, how governed, of what strength and policy, how far it extended, and what nations were friends or enemies adjoining, and finally of the distance and the way to enter the same; he told me that himself and his people, with all those down the river towards the sea, as far as Emeria, the province of Carapana, were of Guiana, but that they called themselves Orenoqueponi, because they bordered the great river of Orenoque, and that all the nations between the river and those mountains in sight called Wacarima were of the same cast and appellation, and that on the other side of the the mountains of Wacarima there was a large plain (which after I discovered in my return) called the valley of Amariocapana, in all that valley the people were also of the ancient Guianans. I asked what nations those were which inhabited on the further side of those mountains, beyond the valley of Amariocapana, he answered with a great sigh (as a man which had inward feeling of the loss of his country and liberty, especially for that his eldest son was slain in a battle on that side of the mountains, whom he most entirely loved) that he remembered in his father's lifetime, when he was very old and himself a young man, that there came down into that large valley of Guiana, a nation from so far off as the sun slept (for such were his own words) with so great a multitude as they could not be numbered or resisted, and that they wore large coats and hats of crimson color, which color he expressed by showing a piece of red wood wherewith my tent was supported, and that they were called Oreiones and Epuremei,[5] those that had slain and rooted out so many of the ancient people as there were leaves in the wood upon all the trees, and had now made themselves lords of all, even to that mountain foot called Curaa, saving only of two nations, the one called Iwarawaqueri, and the other Cassipagotos, and that in the last battle fought between the Epuremei and the Iwarawaqueri, his eldest son was chosen to carry to the aide of the Iwarawaqueri a great troop of the Orenoqueponi and was there slain with all his people and friends, and that he now had remaining but one son; and further told me that those Epuremei had built a great town called Macureguarai at the said mountain foot, at the beginning of the great plains of Guiana, which have no end, and that their houses have many rooms, one

3. Blow.
4. Describing.
5. The King of Aromaia describes a conquest of the Orenoqueponi by the Oreiones, a "nation from so far off as the sun slept," i.e., Peru. His son, he reports, was killed in a battle with the Oreiones.

over the other, and that therein the great king of the Oreiones and Epuremei kept three thousand men to defend the borders against them and withal daily to invade and slay them; but that of late years, since the Christians offered to invade his territories and those frontiers, they were all at peace and traded one with another, saving only the Iwarawaqueri and those other nations upon the head of the river Caroli called Cassipagotos, which we afterwards discovered, each one holding the Spaniard for a common enemy.

After he had answered thus far, he desired leave to depart, saying that he had far to go, that he was old, and weak, and was every day called for by death, which was also his own phrase. I desired him to rest with us that night, but I could not entreat him. But he told me that at my return from the country above he would again come to us and in the mean time provide for us the best he could of all that his country yielded. The same night he returned to Orocotona, his own town, so as he went that day 28 miles, the weather being very hot, the country being situated between four and five degrees of the equator. This Topiawari is held for the proudest and wisest of all the Orenoqueponi, and so he behaved himself towards me in all his answers at my return, as I marvelled to find a man of that gravity and judgment and of so good discourse that had no help of learning or breed.

[THE NEW WORLD OF GUIANA]

To conclude, Guiana is a country that hath yet her maidenhead, never sacked, turned, nor wrought; the face of the earth hath not been torn, nor the virtue and salt of the soil spent by manurance, the graves have not been opened for gold, the mines not broken with sledges, nor their images pulled down out of their temples. It hath never been entered by any army of strength and never conquered or possessed by any Christian prince. It is besides so defensible that if two forts be builded in one of the provinces which I have seen, the flood setteth in so near the bank where the channel also lieth that no ship can pass but within a pike's length of the artillery, first of the one and afterwards of the other. Which two forts will be a sufficient guard both to the empire of *Inga* [Inca] and to an hundred other several kingdoms lying within the said river, even to the city of Quito in Peru.

There is therefore a great difference between the easiness of the conquest of Guiana and the defense of it being conquered, and the West or East Indies. Guiana hath but one entrance by the sea (if it have that) for any vessels of burden, so as whosoever shall first possess it, it shall be found inaccessible for any enemy except he come in wherries, barges, or *canoas*, or else in flat-bottomed boats; and if he do offer to enter it in that manner, the woods are so thick two hundred miles together upon the rivers of such entrance as a mouse cannot sit in a boat unhit from the bank. By land it is more impossible to approach, for it hath the strongest situation of any region under the sun, and is so environed with impassable mountains on every side as it is impossible to victual any company in the passage, which hath been well-proved by the Spanish nation, who, since the conquest of Peru have never left five years free from attempting this empire or discovering some way into it, and yet of twenty-three several gentlemen, knights, and noblemen, there was never any that knew which way to lead an army by land or to conduct ships by sea anything near the said country. Oreliano, of which the river of the Amazons taketh name, was the first, and Don Anthonio de Berreo (whom we displanted), the last; and I doubt much whether he himself or any of his yet know the best way into the said empire. It can therefore hardly be regained if any strength be formerly set down but in one or two places, and but two or three crumsters or galleys built and furnished upon the river within. The West Indies hath many ports, watering places, and landings, and nearer than three hundred miles to Guiana no man can harbor a ship, except he know one only place which is not learned in haste, and which I will undertake there is not any one of my companies that knoweth, whosoever hearkened after it.

Besides by keeping one good fort or building one town of strength, the whole empire is guarded, and whatsoever companies shall be afterwards planted within the land, although in twenty several provinces, those shall be able all to reunite themselves upon any occasion either by the way of one river or be able to march by land without either wood, bog, or mountain; whereas in the West Indies there are few towns or provinces that can succour or relieve one the other, either by land or sea. By land the countries are either desert, mountainous, or strong enemies. By sea, if any man invade to the eastward, those to the west cannot in many months turn against the breeze and east wind, besides the Spaniards are therein so dispersed as they are nowhere strong but in *Nueva Hispania* [New Spain] only. The sharp mountains, the thorns, the poisoned prickles, the sandy and deep ways in the valleys, the smothering heat and air, and want of water in other places are their only and best defense, which (because those nations that invade them are not victualled or provided to stay, neither have any place to friend adjoining) do serve them instead of good arms and great multitudes.

The West Indies were first offered Her Majesty's grandfather by Columbus,[1] a stranger in whom there might be doubt of deceit, and besides it was then thought incredible that there were such and so many lands and regions never written of before. This empire is made known to Her Majesty by her own vassal, and by him that oweth to her more duty than an ordinary subject, so that it shall ill sort with the many graces and benefits which I have received to abuse Her Highness either with fables or imaginations. The country is already discovered,[2] many nations won to Her Majesty's love and obedience, and those Spaniards which have latest and longest labored about the conquest, beaten out, discouraged and disgraced, which among these nations were thought invincible. Her Majesty may in this enterprise employ all those soldiers and gentlemen that are younger brethren, and all captains and chieftains that want employment, and the charge will be only the first setting out in victualling and arming them, for after the first or second year I doubt not but to see in London a contratation house of more receipt for Guiana than there is now in Seville for the West Indies.[3]

And I am resolved that if there were but a small army afoot in Guiana, marching towards Manoa, the chief city of *Inga,* he would yield Her Majesty by composition so many hundred thousand pounds yearly as should both defend all enemies abroad and defray all expenses at home and that he would besides pay a garrison of three or four thousand soldiers very royally to defend him against other nations. For he cannot but know how his predecessors, yea, how his own great uncles Guascar and Atibalipa,

1. The brother of Christopher Columbus, Bartholomew Columbus, who invited Henry VII, King of England and grandfather of Elizabeth I, to accept his brother's services in his effort to find a continent west of England. Henry is reported to have accepted this offer but not before Christopher Columbus had contracted his services to Queen Isabella of Spain. Therefore the West Indies were not ever offered to Henry VII; they were and remained Spanish through the 19th century.

2. The continent of which Guiana is a part.

3. Raleigh states that there will be a trading house or mercantile exchange for investors in Guiana that will exceed in its volume of business the comparable institution for the West Indian trade in Seville.

sons to Guanacapa, Emperor of Peru, were (while they contended for the empire) beaten out by the Spaniards and that both of late years and ever since the said conquest, the Spaniards have sought the passages and entry of his country; and of their cruelties used to the borderers he cannot be ignorant. In which respects no doubt but he will be brought to tribute with great gladness, if not, he hath neither shot nor iron weapon in all his empire and therefore may be easily conquered.

And I further remember that Berreo confessed to me and others (which I protest before the majesty of God to be true) that there was found among the prophecies of Peru (at such time as the empire was reduced to Spanish obedience) in their chiefest temples, among diverse others, which foreshadowed the loss of the said empire, that from *Inglatierra* [England] those *Ingas* should be again in time to come restored and delivered from the servitude of the said conquerors. And I hope, as we with these few hands have displanted the first garrison and driven them out of the said country, so Her Majesty will give order for the rest and either defend it and hold it as tributary, or conquer and keep it as Empress of the same. For whatsoever Prince shall possess it shall be greatest, and if the king of Spain enjoy it, he will become unresistable. Her Majesty hereby shall confirm and strengthen the opinions of all nations as touching her great and princely actions. And where the south border of Guiana reacheth to the dominion and empire of the Amazons, those women shall hereby hear the name of a virgin which is not only able to defend her own territories and her neighbors, but also to invade and conquer so great empires so far removed.[4]

To speak more at this time I fear would be but troublesome. I trust in God, this being true will suffice, and that he which is King of all Kings and Lord of all Lords will put it into her heart which is Lady of Ladies to possess it, if not, I will judge those men worthy to be kings thereof that by her grace and leave will undertake of it themselves.

The Discovery in Context
Voyage Literature

During the second half of the sixteenth century in England, descriptions of the land and peoples of the New World increasingly found their way into print. Much of this material, including translations of treatises written in Spanish, French, and Portuguese, was gathered by Richard Hakluyt and published in volumes under the general title of *The Principal Navigations, Voyages, and Discoveries of the English Nation* (1598–1600). In some respects the observations and opinions of these adventurers to the Caribbean, Virginia, Newfoundland, and other points on the Atlantic coast can be appreciated as a kind of anthropology; the accounts Hakluyt collected by writers such as Arthur Barlow, Thomas Hariot, and René Landonnière convey their fascination with the cultures of the New World. In other respects their writing is obviously self-interested, motivated by a desire for wealth. Treatises encouraging trade with the natives of the New World were often punctuated with apologies for the use of violence, justifications for dispossession of native property, and professions of faith in a providence that allowed Europeans a chance to convert the heathen to Christianity and to civilize peoples that many judged to be "barbarians." In contrast, the great French essayist Michel de Montaigne, having declared that the term "barbarian" originally meant foreign rather than uncivilized, slyly drew on reports of cannibalism among the Indians in Brazil to condemn the European practice of torture as less humane than cannibalism.

4. This reference to the Amazons allows Raleigh to pay tribute to Elizabeth I, who represented herself as a powerful virgin queen.

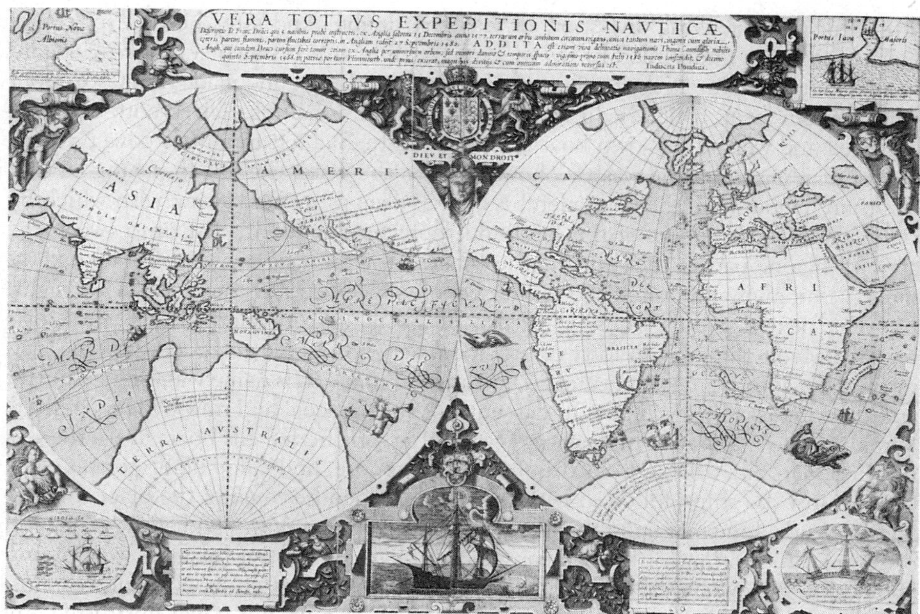

Hondius. *Sir Francis Drake's Map of the World.* ca. 1590.

Arthur Barlow
from *The First Voyage Made to the Coasts of America*[1]

This island had many goodly woods full of deer, coneys,[2] hares, and fowl, even in the midst of summer in incredible abundance. The woods are not such as you find in Bohemia, Muscovy, or Hercynia,[3] barren and fruitless, but the highest and reddest cedars of the world, far bettering the cedars of the Azores, of the Indies; or lybanus,[4] pines, cypress, sassafras, the lentisk, or the tree that beareth the mastic,[5] the tree that beareth the rind of black cinnamon, of which Master Winter brought from the straits of Magellan; and many other of excellent smell and quality. We remained by the side of this island two whole days before we saw any people of the country. The third day we espied one small boat rowing toward us, having in it three persons. This boat came to the island side, four harquebus[6]-shot from our ships, and there two of the people remaining, the third came along the shore side toward us, and, and we being then all within board, he walked up and down upon the point of the land next unto us. Then the master and the pilot of the Admiral,[7] Simon Ferdinando, and Captain Philip Amadas, myself, and others rowed to the land, whose coming this fellow

1. Published in 1600 in Hakluyt's third volume, Arthur Barlow's account describes events in a voyage he took to North America in the summer of 1584. His company landed on the coast of what is now Virginia on July 4 and, by a verbal declaration of "the right of the Queen's most excellent Majesty, as rightful Queen and Princess of the same," took possession of all the land that they could see on July 13. Barlow's account is notable for its picture of the Indians as hospitable people who were prepared to engage in trade with the English on the fairest of terms, although in general his judgments reflect his own Anglo-European experience. Describing the Indians' reliance on prophecy, for example, Barlow compares it to the Romans' dependence on the oracle of Apollo.
2. Rabbits.
3. The woods of Virginia are described by what they are not like: those in Bohemia (now a region comprising portions of Hungary and the Czech Republic), Muscovy (the western portions of modern Russia), and Hercynia (now the Bavarian Alps in modern Germany).
4. Known for its incense.
5. Gum.
6. Gun.
7. The ship on which the admiral of the fleet sails.

attended, never making any show of fear and doubt. And after he had spoken of many things not understood by us, we brought him with his own good liking aboard the ship and gave him a shirt, a hat, and some other things, and made him taste of our wine and our meat, which he liked very well. And after having viewed both barks, he departed and went to his own boat again, which he had left in a little cove or creek adjoining. As soon as he was two bowshot into the water, he fell to fishing, and in less than half an hour, he had laden his boat as deep as it could swim, with which he came again to the point of the land and there he divided his fish into two parts, appointing one part to the ship and the other to the pinnace, which, after he had (as much as he might) requited the former benefits received, departed out of our sight.

The next day there came to us diverse boats, and in one of them the King's brother, accompanied with forty or fifty men, very handsome and goodly people, and in their behavior as mannerly and civil as any of Europe. His name was Granganimeo, and the king is called Wingina, the country Wingandacoa, and now by Her Majesty, Virginia. The manner of his coming was in this sort: he left his boats altogether, as the first man did, a little from the ships by the shore, and came along to the place over against the ships, followed with forty men. When he came to the place, his servants spread a long mat upon the ground, on which he sat down, and at the other end of the mat four others of his company did the like; the rest of his men stood round about him, somewhat afar off. When we came to the shore to him with our weapons, he never moved from his place, nor any of the other four, nor never mistrusted any harm to be offered from us, but sitting still, he beckoned us to come and sit by him, which we performed. And being set, he made all signs of joy and welcome, striking on his head with his breast and afterwards on ours, to show we were all one, smiling and making show the best he could of all love and familiarity. After he had made a long speech unto us, we presented him with diverse things, which he received very joyfully and thankfully. None of the company durst speak one word all the time, only the four which were at the other end spake one in the other's ear very softly.

The king is greatly obeyed, and his brothers and children reverenced. The king himself in person was, at our being there, sore wounded in a fight which he had with the king of the next country, called Wingina, and was shot in two places through the body, and once clean through the thigh, but yet he recovered. By reason whereof and for that he lay at the chief town of the country, being six days' journey off, we saw him not at all.

After we presented this his brother with such things as we thought he liked, we likewise gave somewhat to the other that sat with him on the mat. But presently he arose and took all from them and put it into his own basket, making signs and tokens that all things ought to be delivered unto him, and the rest were but his servants and followers. A day or two after this, we fell to trading with them, exchanging some things that we had for chamois, buff, and deerskins. When we showed him all our packet of merchandise, of all things that he saw, a bright tin dish most pleased him, which he presently took up and clapped it before his breast, and after made a hole in the brim thereof and hung it about his neck, making signs that it would defend him against his enemies' arrows; for those people maintain a deadly and terrible war, with the people and the king adjoining. We exchanged our tin dish for twenty skins, worth twenty crowns or twenty nobles, and a copper kettle for fifty skins worth fifty crowns. They offered us good exchange for our hatchets and axes, and for knives, and would have given anything for swords, but we would not depart with any. After two or three days the king's brother came aboard the ships and drank wine and eat of our meat and of our bread, and liked exceedingly thereof; and after a few days had overpassed, he brought his wife with him to the ships, his daughter, and two or three children. His wife was very well-favored, of mean stature and very bashful; she had on her back a long cloak of leather with the fur side next to her body and before her a piece of the same. About her forehead she had a band of white coral, and so had her husband many times. In her ears she had bracelets of pearls hanging to her middle (whereof we delivered your worship a little bracelet) and those were of the bigness of good peas. The rest of her women of the better sort had pendants of copper hanging in either ear, and some of the children of the king's brother and other noblemen have five or six in either ear. He himself had upon his head a broad plate of gold or copper, for being unpolished we knew not what metal it would be, neither would he by any means suffer us to take it off his head, but feeling it, it would bow very easily. His apparel was as his wife's, only the women wear their hair long on both sides and the men but on one. They are of color yellowish, and their hair black for the most part, and yet we saw children that had very fine auburn- and chestnut-colored hair.

After that these women had been there, there came down from all parts great store of people, bringing with them leather, coral, diverse kinds of dyes very excellent, and exchanged with us; but when Granganimeo the king's brother was present, none durst trade but himself, except such as wear red pieces of copper on their heads like himself, for that is the difference between the noblemen and the governors of countries, and the meaner sort. And we both noted there and you have understood since by these men which we have brought home, that no people in the world carry more respect to their king, nobility, and governors than these do. The king's brother's wife, when she came to us (as she did many times) was allowed with forty or fifty women always, and when she came into the ship, she left them all on land, saving her two daughters, her nurse, and one or two more. The king's brother always kept this order, as many boats as he would come withal to the ships, so many fires would he make on the shore afar off, to the end we might understand with what strength and company he approached. Their boats are made of one tree, either of pine or pitch trees, a wood not commonly known to our people, nor found growing in England. They have no edge tools to make them withal; if they have any, they are very few and those it seems they had twenty years since, which, as those two men declared, was out of a wreck which happened upon their coast of some Christian ship, being beaten that way by some storm and outrageous weather, whereof none of the people were saved, but only the ship, or some part of her being cast upon the sand out of whose sides they drew the nails and the spikes and with those they made their best instruments. The manner of making their boats is thus: They burn down some great tree, or take such as are windfallen, and putting gum and rosin upon one side thereof, they set fire into it, and when it hath burnt it hollow, they cut out the coal with their shells and everywhere they would burn it deeper or wider they lay on gums which burn away the timber and by this means they fashion very fine boats and such as will transport twenty men. Their oars are like scoops, and many times they set[8] with long poles as the depth serveth.

The king's brother had great liking of our armor, a sword, and diverse other things which we had, and offered to lay a great box of pearl in gage[9] for them; but we refused it for this time, because we would not make them know that we esteemed thereof until we had understood in what places of the country the pearl grew, which now your worship doth very well understand.

He was very just of his promise; for many times we delivered him merchandise upon his word, but ever he came within the day and performed his promise. He sent us everyday a brace or two of fat bucks, coneys, hares, fish, the best of the world. He

8. Punt.

9. Payment.

sent us diverse kinds of fruits, melons, walnuts, cucumbers, gourds, peas, and diverse roots, and fruits very excellent good, and of their country, corn,[1] which is very white, fair, and well-tasted, and growth three times in five months. In May they sow, in July they reap; in June they sow, in August they reap; in July they sow, in September they reap. Only they cast the corn into the ground, breaking a little of the soft turf with a wooden mattock or pickaxe. Ourselves proved the soil and put some of our peas in the ground, and in ten days they were of fourteen inches high. They have also beans very fair of diverse colors and wonderful plenty, some growing naturally and some in their gardens, and so have they wheat and oats.

The soil is the most plentiful, sweet, fruitful, and wholesome of all the world. There are above fourteen several sweet-smelling timber trees, and the most part of their underwoods are bays and such like. They have those oaks that we have, but far greater and better. After they had been diverse times aboard our ships, myself with seven more went twenty miles into the river that runneth toward the city of Skicoak, which river they call Occam; and the evening following, we came to an island which they call Raonoak,[2] distant from the harbor by which we entered seven leagues. And at the north end thereof was a village of nine houses, built of cedar and fortified round about with sharp trees to keep out their enemies, and the entrance into it made like a turnpike, very artificially. When we came toward it, standing near unto the water's side, the wife of Granganimeo, the king's brother, came running out to meet us very cheerfully and friendly; her husband was not then in the village. Some of her people she commanded to draw our boat on shore for the beating of the billow, others she appointed to carry us on their backs to the dry ground, and others to bring our oars into the house for fear of stealing. When we were come into the outer room, having five rooms in her house, she caused us to sit down by a great fire, and took off our clothes and washed them and dried them again. Some of the women plucked off our stockings and washed them, some washed our feet in warm water, and she herself took great pains to see all things ordered in the best manner she could, making great haste to dress some meat for us to eat.

After we had thus dried ourselves, she brought us into the inner room, where she set on the board standing along the house some wheat like fermenty,[3] sodden[4] venison and roasted; fish, sodden, boiled and roasted; melons raw and sodden; roots of diverse kinds, and diverse fruits. Their drink is commonly water, but while the grape lasteth, they drink wine, and for want of casks to keep it, all the year after they drink water, but it is sodden with ginger in it, and black cinnamon, and sometimes sassafras and diverse other wholesome and medicinable herbs and trees. We were entertained with all love and kindness, and with as much bounty (after their manner) as they could possibly devise. We found the people most gentle, loving and faithful, void of all guile and treason, and such as live after the manner of the golden age.[5] The people could only care how to defend themselves from the cold in their short winter, and to feed themselves with such meat as the soil affordeth. Their meat is very well sodden and they make broth very sweet and savory. Their vessels are earthen pots, very large,

1. Possibly buckwheat. The English used the term "maize" for the grain that in the United States is now known as corn.

2. Roanoke. A year later, this island in what is now North Carolina was to be the site of the first English colony in North America. Sir Walter Raleigh sent out settlers in 1585, who returned to England in 1586; another group, who tried to revive the colony in 1587, had vanished without a trace by 1591, when ships from England reached them with additional settlers and supplies.

3. Porridge.

4. Boiled.

5. The Indians of the Americas were sometimes compared with the people who were supposed to have lived during the mythical golden age, a period in which nature provided food without toil, property was common, and human society was free of conflict.

white, and sweet; their dishes are wooden platters of sweet timber. Within the place where they feed was their lodging, and within that, their idol which they worship, of whom they speak incredible things. While we were at meat, there came in at the gates two or three men with their bows and arrows from hunting, whom when we espied, we began to look one toward another and offered to reach our weapons; but as soon as she spied our mistrust, she was very much moved and caused some of her men to run out and take away their bows and arrows and break them and withal beat the poor fellows out of the gate again. When we departed in the evening and would not tarry all night, she was very sorry and gave us into our boat our supper half dressed, pots and all, and brought us to our boat's side, in which we lay all night, removing the same a pretty distance from the shore. She, perceiving our jealousy,[6] was much grieved, and sent diverse men and thirty women to sit all night on the bank side by us and sent us into our boats five mats to cover us from the rain, using many words to entreat us to rest in their houses. But because we were few men and if we had miscarried, the voyage had been in very great danger, we durst not adventure of anything, though there was no cause of doubt; for a more kind and loving people there cannot be found in the world, as far as we have hitherto had trial.

* * *

They wondered marvelously when we were amongst them at the whiteness of our skins, ever coveting[7] to touch our breast and to view the same. Besides they had our ships in marvelous admiration and all things else were so strange unto them as it appeared that none of them had ever seen the like. When we discharged any piece, were it but an harquebus, they would tremble thereat for very fear and for the strangeness of the same. For the weapons which themselves use are bows and arrows; the arrows are but of small canes, headed with a sharp shell or tooth of a fish sufficient enough to kill a naked man. Their swords be of wood hardened, likewise they use wooden breastplates for their defense. They have besides a kind of club, in the end whereof they fasten the sharp horns of a stag or other beast. When they go to wars they carry about with them their idol, of whom they ask counsel, as the Romans were wont of the Oracle of Apollo. They sing songs as they march toward the battle, instead of drums and trumpets. Their wars are very cruel and bloody by reason whereof, and of their civil dissensions which have happened of late years among them, the people are marvelously wasted,[8] and in some places the country left desolate.

Thomas Hariot

from ***A Brief and True Report of the Newfound Land of Virginia***[1]

It resteth I speak a word or two of the natural inhabitants, their natures and manners, leaving large discourse thereof until time more convenient hereafter; now only so far forth as that you may know how they in respect of troubling our inhabiting and planting are not to be feared, but that they shall have cause both to fear and love us that shall inhabit with them.

6. Fear.
7. Wishing.
8. Reduced in numbers.
1. Thomas Hariot, an astronomer and mathematician, was a member of Sir Walter Raleigh's household. This account, published by Hakluyt in 1598, reports on his voyage to Virginia in 1586. He tells of an unanticipated yet terrible consequence of European colonization: the death of numbers of Indians from diseases—brought by colonists—to which the Indians had no immunity. As a scientific matter, the phenomenon was not at all understood, and Hariot describes attempts by the English to explain what it meant in supposedly moral terms and also to take advantage of its practical effect—the reduction of the Indian population—as a way to colonize the region further.

They are a people clothed with loose mantles made of deerskins, and aprons of the same round about their middles, all else naked; of such a difference of statures only as we in England;[2] having no edge tools or weapons of iron or steel to offend us withal, neither know they how to make any. Those weapons that they have are only bows made of witch hazel and arrows of reeds, flat-edged truncheons also of wood about a yard long; neither have they anything to defend themselves but targets[3] made of barks and some armors made of sticks wickered together with thread. * * *

Their manner of war amongst themselves is either by sudden surprising one another, most commonly about the dawning of the day or moonlight, or else by ambushes or some subtle devices. Set battles are very rare, except it fall out where there are many trees, where either part may have some hope of defense after the delivery of every arrow, in leaping behind some or other.[4]

If there fall out any wars between us and them, what their fight is likely to be, we having advantages against them so many manner of ways, as by our discipline, our strong weapons and devices else, especially ordinance[5] great and small, it may easily be imagined. By the experience we have had in some places, the turning up of their heels against us in running away was their best defense.

In respect of us they are a people poor, and for want of skill and judgment in the knowledge and use of our things do esteem our trifles before things of greater value. Nothwithstanding, in their proper manner (considering the want of such means as we have), they seem very ingenious. For although they have no such tools, nor any such crafts, sciences, and arts as we, yet in those things they do, they show excellency of wit. And by how much they upon due consideration shall find our manner of knowledges and crafts to exceed theirs in perfection and speed for doing or execution, by so much the more is it probable that they should desire our friendship and love and have the greater respect for pleasing and obeying us. Whereby may be hoped, if means of good government be used, that they may in a short time be brought to civility and the embracing of true religion.

Some religion they have already, which although it be far from the truth, yet being as it is, there is hope that it may be the easier and sooner reformed.

They believe that there are many gods, which they call Mantoac, but of different sorts and degrees, one only chief and great God, which hath been from all eternity, who, as they affirm, when he purposed to make the world, made first other gods of a principal order to be as means and instruments to be used in the creation and government to follow, and after, the sun, moon, and stars as petty gods and the instruments of the other more principal. First (they say) were made waters, out of which by the gods was made all diversity of creatures that are visible or invisible.

For mankind, they say a woman was made first, which by the working of one of the gods, conceived and brought forth children; and in such sort they say they had their beginning. But how many years or ages have passed since, they say they can make no relation, having no letters or other such means as we to keep records of the particularities of times past, but only tradition from father to son.

2. I.e., the Indians are generally of the same stature as the English and have the same range of differences in height as the English.

3. Shields.

4. Europeans fought each other in "set battles." Typically, an army was led by its cavalry and supported by its infantry, who marched to a distance from which they could fire their guns and cannons at the enemy. Indians waged what is known in the modern period as guerilla warfare, attacking the enemy by surprise maneuvers and defending themselves in quick retreats.

5. Artillery.

* * *

Most things they saw with us, as mathematical instruments, sea compasses, the virtue of the loadstone[6] in drawing[7] iron, a perspective glass[8] whereby was showed many strange sights, burning glasses,[9] wild fireworks, guns, hooks, writing and reading, springclocks that seem to go of themselves, and many other things that we had were so strange unto them and so far exceeded their capacities to comprehend the reason and means how they should be made and done that they thought they were rather the works of gods than of men, or at the leastwise they had been given and taught us of the gods. Which made many of them to have such opinion of us as that if they knew not the truth of God and religion already, it was rather to be had from us whom God so specially loved than from a people that were so simple as they found themselves to be in comparison of us. Whereupon greater credit was given unto that we spoke of, concerning such matters. * * *

There could at no time happen any strange sickness, losses, hurts, or any other cross unto them but that they would impute to us the cause or means thereof, for offending or not pleasing us. One other rare and strange accident, leaving others, will I mention before I end, which moved the whole country that either knew or heard of us, to have us in wonderful admiration.

There was no town where we had any subtle devise[1] practiced against us, we leaving it unpunished or not revenged (because we sought by all means possible to win them by gentleness) but that within a few days after our departure from every such town, the people began to die very fast, and many in short space; in some towns about twenty, in some forty, and in one six score, which in truth was very many in respect of their numbers. This happened in no place that we could learn but where we had been where they used some practice against us, and after such time.[2] The disease also was so strange that they neither knew what it was, nor how to cure it, the like by report of the oldest men in the country never happened before, time out of mind. * * *

This marvelous accident in all the country wrought so strange opinions of us that some people could not tell whether to think us gods or men, and the rather because that all the space of their sickness, there was no man of ours known to die or that was especially sick; they noted also that we had no women among us, neither that we did care for any of theirs.

Some therefore were of opinion that we were not born of women, and therefore not mortal, but that we were men of an old generation many years past, then risen again to immortality.

Some would likewise seem to prophecy that there were more of our generation yet to come to kill theirs and take their places, as some thought the purpose was, by that which was already done. Those that were immediately to come after us they imagined to be in the air, yet invisible and without bodies, and that they by our entreaty and for the love of us did make the people to die in that sort as they did by shooting invisible bullets into them.

To confirm this opinion, their physicians (to excuse their ignorance in curing the disease) would not be ashamed to say but earnestly make the simple people believe that the strings of blood that they sucked out of the sick bodies were the

6. Magnet.
7. Attracting.
8. Telescope.
9. Magnifying glasses.
1. Trick.
2. Hariot moralizes the phenomenon of immunity by stating that Indian villages that came down with disease were those that had resisted or "used some practice against" the English.

strings wherewithal the invisible bullets were tied and cast. Some also thought that we shot them ourselves out of our pieces from the place where we dwelt and killed the people in any town that had offended us, as we listed, how far distant from us so ever it were. And other some said that it was the special work of God for our sakes as we ourselves have cause in some sort to think no less, whatsoever some do or may imagine to the contrary, specially some astrologers, knowing of the eclipse of the sun which we saw the same year before in our voyage thitherward, which unto them appeared very terrible. And also of a comet which began to appear but a few days before the beginning of the said sickness.[3] But to exclude them[4] from being the special causes of so special an accident, there are further reasons than I think fit at this present to be alleged. These their[5] opinions I have set down the more at large that it may appear unto you that there is good hope that they may be brought through discreet dealing and government to the embracing of the truth and consequently to honor, obey, fear, and love us.

And although some of our company toward the end of the year showed themselves too fierce in slaying some of the people in some towns, upon causes that on our part might easily enough have been born withal; yet notwithstanding, because it was on their part justly deserved, the alteration of their opinions generally and for the most part concerning us is the less to be doubted.[6] And whatsoever else they may be, by carefulness[7] of ourselves need nothing at all to be feared.

René Landonnière

from *A Notable History Containing Four Voyages Made to Florida*[1]

My Lord Admiral of Chastillion, a nobleman more desirous of the public than of his private benefit, understanding the pleasure of the King his prince, which was to discover new and strange countries, caused vessels fit for this purpose to be made ready with all diligence and men to be levied meet for such an enterprise, among whom he chose Captain John Ribault, a man in truth expert in sea causes, which having received his charge, set himself to sea in the year 1562, the eighteenth of February, accompained only with two of the king's ships, but so well furnished with gentlemen (of whose number I myself was one) and with old soldiers that he had means to achieve some notable thing and worthy of eternal memory. Having therefore sailed two months, never holding the usual course of the Spaniards, he arrived in Florida.

* * *

Having sailed twelve leagues at the least, we perceived a troop of Indians, which as soon as ever they espied the pinnaces[2] were so afraid that they fled into the woods leaving behind them a young lucerne[3] which they were turning upon a spit, for

3. The Indians attributed their disease to God's favor toward the English. Hariot observes that the English concurred in this opinion, despite the warnings of astrologers who saw a recent eclipse of the sun and the arrival of a comet as bad omens. He concludes that the Indians' sense of a divine power backing the English enterprise could be the basis for their further peaceful subjugation.
4. The eclipse and the comet.
5. I.e., the Indians'.
6. Hariot admits that the English were "too fierce" in killing Indians for insufficient reason; at the same time he states, without further explanation, that as these actions were "justly deserved," the English need fear no change in the Indians' attitude toward them.
7. Taking care.

1. Landonnière set sail with John (Jean) Ribault, a French captain under the command of the Admiral of Chastillon in 1562. This account of their adventures was translated from French into English and published in 1600 in Hakluyt's third volume.
2. Small sailing ships, often used to scout along rivers and bays.
3. Wildcat.

which cause the place was called Cape Lucerne. Proceeding forth on our way, we found another arm of the river, which ran toward the east, up which the Captain determined to sail and to leave the great current. A little while after, they began to espy diverse other Indians, both men and women, half hidden within the woods, who, knowing not that we were such as desired their friendship were dismayed at the first but soon after were emboldened, for the Captain caused store of merchandise to be showed them openly whereby they knew that we meant nothing but well unto them. And then they made a sign that we should come on land, which we would not refuse. At our coming on shore, diverse of them came to salute our general according to their barbarous fashion. Some of them gave him skins of chamois;[4] others, little baskets made of palm leaves. Some presented him with pearls, but no great number. Afterwards they went about to make an arbor to defend us in that place from the parching heat of the sun; but we would not stay as then. Wherefore the Captain thanked them much for their good will and gave presents to each of them, wherewith he pleased them so well before he went thence that his sudden departure was nothing pleasant unto them. For knowing him to be so liberal, they would have wished him to have stayed a little longer, seeking by all means to give him occasion to stay, showing him by signs that he should stay but that day only, and that they desired to advertise a great Indian lord which had pearls in great abundance and silver also, all which things should be given unto him at the king's[5] arrival, saying further that in the meantime while that this great lord came thither, they would lead him to their houses and show him there a thousand pleasures in shooting and seeing the stag killed, therefore they prayed him not to deny them their request. Notwithstanding, we returned to our ships. * * *

A few days afterward, John Ribault determined to return once again toward the Indians which inhabited that arm of the river which runneth toward the west, and to carry with him good store of soldiers. For his meaning was to take two Indians of this place to bring them into France, as the queen had commanded him. With this deliberation again we took our former course so far forth that at the last we came into the selfsame place where at the first we found the Indians, from thence we took two Indians by permission of the king, which thinking they were more favored than the rest thought themselves very happy to stay with us. But these two Indians, seeing we made no show at all that we would go on land but rather that we followed in the midst of the current, began to be somewhat offended and would by force have leapt into the water, for they are so good swimmers that immediately they would have gotten into the forests.[6] Nevertheless, being acquainted with their humor, we watched them narrowly and sought by all means to appease them, which we could not by any means do for that time, though we offered them things which they much esteemed, which things they disdained to take and gave back again whatever was given them, thinking that such gifts should have altogether bound them and that in restoring them they should be restored unto their liberty. In fine, perceiving that all that they did availed them nothing, they prayed us to give them those things which they had restored, which we did incontinent. Then they approached one toward the other and began to sing, agreeing so sweetly together that in hearing their song it seemed that they lamented the absence of their friends. They continued their songs all night

4. Deerskin.
5. I.e., of the Indians.
6. In effect, the Indians found that they were prisoners.

without ceasing, all which time we were constrained to lie at anchor by reason that the tide was against us; but we hoisted sail the next day very early in the morning and returned to our ships.[7] As soon as we were come to our ships, every one sought to gratify these two Indians and to show them the best countenance that was possible, to the intent that by such courtesies they might perceive the good desire and affection which we had to remain their friends in time to come. Then we offered them meat to eat, but they refused it and made us to understand that they were accustomed to wash their face and to stay until the sun were set before they did eat, which is a ceremony common to all the Indians of New France. Nevertheless in the end they were constrained to forget their superstitions and to apply themselves to our nature, which was somewhat strange to them at the first. They became therefore more jocund, every hour made us a thousand discourses, being marvelous sorry that we could not understand them. A few days after, they began to bear so goodwill toward me that, as I think, they would rather have taken perished with hunger and thirst than have taken their refection at any man's hand but mine. Seeing this their goodwill, I sought to learn some Indian words and began to ask them questions, showing them the thing whereof I desired to know the name and how they called it. They were very glad to tell it me and, knowing the desire that I had to learn their language, they encouraged me afterward to ask them everything. So that putting down in writing the words and phrases of the Indian speech, I was able to understand the greatest part of their discourses. Every day they did nothing but speak unto me of the desire that they had to use me well, if we returned unto their houses, and cause me to receive all the pleasures that they could devise, as well in hunting as in seeing their very strange and superstitious ceremonies at a certain feast which they call Toya, which feast they observe as straightly as we observe the Sunday. They gave me to understand that they would bring me to see the greatest lord of this country, which they call Chicola, who exceedeth them in height (as they told me) a good foot and a half. They said unto me that he dwelt within the land in a very large place and enclosed exceeding high, but I could not learn wherewith. And as far as I can judge, this place whereof they spoke unto me was a very fair city. For they said unto me that within the enclosure there was great store of houses which were built very high, wherein there was an infinite number of men like unto themselves which made none account of gold, of silver, nor of pearls, seeing they had thereof in abundance. * * * After they had stayed awhile in our ships, they began to be sorry and still demanded of me when they should return. I made them to understand that the Captain's will was to send them home again, but that first he would bestow apparel of them, which a few days after was delivered unto them. But seeing he would not give them license to depart, they resolved themselves to steal away by night and to get a little boat which we had, and by the help of the tide to sail home toward their dwellings and by this means to save themselves; which thing they failed not to do, and put their enterprise in execution, yet leaving behind them the apparel which the Captain had given them and carrying away nothing but that which was their own, showing well hereby that they were not void of reason. The Captain cared not greatly for their departure, considering they had not been used otherwise than well and that therefore they should not estrange themselves from the Frenchmen.

7. These "ships" were the larger sailing vessels, or galleons, having three masts, five or six sails, and three or four decks, on which most settlers crossed the ocean.

Michel de Montaigne
from *Of Cannibals*[1]

All [the Brazilians'] moral discipline containeth but these two articles; first, an undismayed resolution to war, then an inviolable affection to their wives. * * * They war against the nations that lie beyond their mountains, to which they go naked, having no other weapons than bows or wooden swords, sharp at one end, as our broaches are. It is an admirable thing to see the constant resolution of their combats, which never end but by effusion of blood and murder, for they know not what fear or routs are. Every victor brings home the head of the enemy he hath slain as a trophy of his victory, and fasteneth the same at the entrance of his dwelling place. After they have long time used and entreated their prisoners well and with all commodities they can devise, he that is the master of them, summoning a great assembly of his acquaintance, tieth a cord to one of his prisoner's arms, by the end whereof they hold him fast, with some distance from him for fear he might offend him, and giveth the other arm, bound in like manner, to the dearest friend he hath, and both in the presence of all the assembly kill him with swords. Which done, they roast and then eat him in common and send slices of him to such friends as are absent. It is not, as some imagine, to nourish themselves with it (as anciently the Scythians were wont to do), but to represent an extreme and inexpiable revenge. Which we prove thus: some of them perceiving the Portuguese, who had confederated themselves with their adversaries, to use another kind of death when they took them to be prisoners, which was to bury them up to the middle and against the upper part of the body to shoot arrows and then, being almost dead, to hang them up, they supposed that these people of the other world (as they who had sowed the knowledge of many vices amongst their neighbors and were much more cunning in all kinds of evils and michief than they) undertook not this manner of revenge without cause and that consequently it was more smartful and cruel than theirs, and thereupon began to leave their old fashion to follow this. I am not sorry we note the barbarous manner of such an action, but grieved that prying so narrowly into their faults we are so blinded in ours. I think there is more barbarism in eating men alive than to feed upon them, being dead; to mangle by tortures and torments a body full of lively sense, to roast him in pieces, to make dogs and swine to gnaw and tear him in mammocks[2] (as we have not only read but seen very lately, yea, and in our own memory, not amongst ancient enemies but our neighbors and fellow citizens and, which is worse, under the pretence of piety and religion) than to roast and eat him after he is dead. Chrysippus and Zeno,[3] arch-pillars of the Stoic sect, have supposed that it was no hurt at all, in time of need and to what end so ever, to make use of our carrion bodies and to feed upon them, as did our forefathers who, being beseiged by Caesar in the city of Alexia, resolved to sustain the famine of the seige with the bodies of old men, women, and other persons unserviceable and unfit to fight.

1. The great French humanist Michel de Montaigne virtually invented the modern essay, and actually coined the term *Essais* ("trials, attempts") for his collection, first published in 1580 and again in 1588 and 1595, each time with additions and revisions. The selection given here is from the first English translation (1603), by John Florio. This essay reflects on the account of French travelers to Brazil who reported on the manners and customs of the natives there. Montaigne comments especially on the Brazilians' practice of cannibalism, which consisted of a ritual eating of their dead prisoners of war, and compares it to the torture of prisoners in the religious wars that were being waged in France at that time. He concludes by declaring that the Brazilian practice is, in his view, less "barbarous," strange, and inhuman than the European.

2. Pieces.

3. Zeno was the founder of the Stoic school of philosophy in Athens, c. 315 B.C.; Stoics believed that happiness derived from a life in tune with nature and free from emotional attachments. Zeno was followed by Chrysippus (c. 204 B.C.).

Vascones (fama est) alimentis talibus usi
Produxere animas.
Gascoynes (as fame reports)
Lived with meats of such sorts.

And physicians fear not, in all kinds of compositions availful to our health, to make use of it, be it for outward or inward applications. But there was never any opinion found so unnatural and immodest that would excuse treason, treachery, disloyalty, tyranny, cruelty, and suchlike, which are our ordinary faults. We may then well call them barbarous, in regard of reason's rules, but not in respect of us that exceed them in all kind of barbarism. Their wars are noble and generous and have as much excuse and beauty as this human infirmity may admit. They aim at naught so much and have no other foundation amongst them but the mere jealousy of virtue. They contend not for the gaining of new lands, for to this day they yet enjoy that natural uberty[4] and fruitfulness which without laboring toil doth in such plenteous abundance furnish them with all necessary things that they need not enlarge their limits. They are yet in that happy estate as they desire no more than what their natural necessities direct them; whatsover is beyond it is to them superfluous.

Richard Barnfield

1577–1627

Richard Barnfield, a precocious yet only briefly productive poet, published four books of verse before his twenty-fifth birthday but then nothing else; we know merely that he lived to the age of fifty-two, comfortably settled on his Staffordshire estate, a husband and the father of a son, Robert. As a poet, he chose to follow the conventions of the amorous pastoral, fashionable for the ease with which they allowed the representation of lovers' intrigues. His frankly homoerotic verses express the love of a shepherd, Daphnis, for a boy called Ganimede or Ganymede, the mythological cup-bearer to Jupiter, the king of the gods. *The Tears of an Affectionate Shepherd* describes two phases to Daphnis's love; in *The Complaint* he offers Ganimede gifts from the pastoral world; in *The Lamentation*, claiming that what is fair is not necessarily good, he specifies steps to moral virtue. Complicating his narrative is the story of Ganimede's love for a woman, Queen Guendolen, whom Daphnis accuses of promiscuity. This rival threesome can be compared with the central figures of Shakespeare's (virtually contemporaneous) sonnet sequence: the poet, the young man, and the so-called dark lady. Finally, however, Barnfield creates his own poetic character, playing with occasional irony on the semantic and biblical association between shepherds and pastors. Barnfield's second collection of poems, published as *Cynthia*, continues to describe the competition for Ganimede's affection.

Slight as his total output was, Barnfield got the attention of readers. Francis Meres, his fellow student at Oxford and later critic of contemporary literature, placed him with Spenser, Sidney, and Abraham Fraunce as "best for pastoral." Barnfield's style is more vividly sensuous than theirs, however; his poems are best compared with the erotic pastoral verse of Theocritus, a Greek poet of the third century B.C., the first of its kind in Europe and a model for all subsequent examples of that genre.

4. Abundance.

The Affectionate Shepherd

To the Right Excellent and Most Beautiful Lady,
The Lady Penelope Rich[1]

Fair lovely Lady, whose angelic eyes
Are vestal candles of sweet beauty's treasure,
Whose speech is able to enchant the wise,
Converting joy to pain, and pain to pleasure;
Accept this simple toy of my soul's duty,
Which I present unto thy matchless beauty,

And albeit the gift be all too mean,
Too mean an offering for thine ivory shrine;
Yet must thy beauty my just blame susteane,° *sustain*
Since it is mortal, but thyself divine.
Then (noble lady) take in gentle worth,
This newborn babe which here my muse brings forth.

Your honors most affectionate
and perpetually devoted shepherd:
Daphnis.[2]

The Tears of an Affectionate Shepherd Sick for Love
or
The Complaint of Daphnis for the Love of Ganimede

Scarce had the morning star hid from the light
Heaven's crimson canopy with stars bespangled,
But I began to rue th'unhappy sight
Of that fair boy° that had my heart entangled; *Ganimede*
Cursing the time, the place, the sense, the sin;
I came, I saw, I viewed, I slipped in.

If it be sin to love a sweet-faced boy,
(Whose amber locks trussed up in golden trammels,° *braids*
Dangle adown his lovely cheeks with joy,
When pearl and flowers his fair hair enamels)
If it be sin to love a lovely lad;
Oh then sin I, for whom my soul is sad.

His ivory-white and alabaster[3] skin
Is stained throughout with rare vermilion red,
Whose twinkling starry lights do never blin° *cease*
To shine on lovely Venus (Beauty's bed):
But as the lily and the blushing rose,
So white and red on him in order grows.

1. Lady Penelope Rich (1562–1607) was the sister of Robert Devereux, Earl of Essex, the wife of Lord Rich, and the model for Sir Philip Sidney's "Stella."

2. A name conventionally assigned to a shepherd in pastoral poetry; Ganimede was frequently represented as his lover. Barnfield's Daphnis typifies the naive lover of pastoral who offers his beloved only the simple gifts of the countryside.

3. A white stone, prized for fine statuary.

Upon a time the nymphs bestirred themselves
To try who could his beauty soonest win:
But he accounted them but all as elves,
Except it were the fair Queen Guendolen,[4]
Her he embraced, of her was beloved,
With plaints he proved,° and with tears he moved. *succeeded*

But her an old man had been suitor too,
That in his age began to dote again;
Her would he often pray, and often woo,
When through old age enfeebled was his brain:
But she before had loved a lusty youth
That now was dead, the cause of all her ruth.

And thus it happened, Death and Cupid met
Upon a time at swilling Bacchus'° house, *the god of wine*
Where dainty cates° upon the board were set, *cakes*
And goblets full of wine to drink carouse:° *riotously*
Where Love and Death did love the liquor so,
That out they fall and to the fray° they go. *to combat*

And having both their quivers at their back
Filled full of arrows; th'one of fatal steel,
The other all of gold; Death's shaft was black,
But Love's was yellow: Fortune turned her wheel;
And from Death's quiver fell a fatal shaft,
That under Cupid by the wind was waft.° *blown*

And at the same time by ill hap° there fell *misfortune*
Another arrow out of Cupid's quiver;
The which was carried by the wind at will,
And under Death the amorous shaft did shiver:
They being parted, Love took up Death's dart,
And Death took up Love's arrow (for his part.)

Thus as they wandered both about the world,
At last Death met with one of feeble age:
Wherewith he drew a shaft and at him hurled
The unknown arrow (with a furious rage),
Thinking to strike him dead with Death's black dart,
But he (alas) with Love did wound his heart.

This was the doting fool, this was the man
That loved fair Guendolena, Queen of Beauty;
She cannot shake him off, do what she can,
For he hath vowed to her his soul's last duty:
Making him trim upon the holy-days;
And crowns his love with garlands made of bays.

Now doth he stroke his beard; and now (again)
He wipes the drivel from his filthy chin;
Now offers he a kiss; but high disdain

4. In Arthurian legend, Guendolen is a fay, or elf, who seduces King Arthur.

Will not permit her heart to pity him:
Her heart more hard than adamant° or steel, *hard stone*
Her heart more changeable than Fortune's wheel.

But leave we him in love (up to the ears),
And tell how Love behaved himself abroad;
Who seeing one that mourned still in tears
(A young man groaning under Love's great load),
Thinking to ease his burden, rid his pains:
For men have grief as long as life remains.

Alas (the while) that unawares he drew
The fatal shaft that death had dropped before;
By which deceit great harm did then ensue,
Staining his face with blood and filthy gore.
His face, that was to Guendolen more dear
Than love of lords, or any lordly peer.

This was that fair and beautiful young man,
Whom Guendolena so lamented for;
This is that love whom she doth curse and ban,
Because she doth that dismal chance abhor:
And if it were not for his mother's[5] sake,
Even Ganimede himself she would forsake.

Oh would she would forsake my Ganimede,
Whose surged love is full of sweet delight,
Upon whose forehead you may plainly read
Love's pleasure, graved in ivory tables bright:
In whose fair eyeballs you may clearly see
Base Love still stained with foul indignity.

Oh, would to God he would but pity me,
That love him more than any mortal wight;
Then he and I with love would soon agree,
That now cannot abide his suitor's° sight. *Guendolen's*
O would to God (so I might have my fee)° *rightful reward*
My lips were honey, and thy mouth a bee.

Then shouldst thou suck my sweet and my fair flower
That now is ripe, and full of honey-berries:
Then would I lead thee to my pleasant bower
Filled full of grapes, of mulberries, and cherries;
Then shouldst thou be my wasp or else my bee,
I would thy hive, and thou my honey be.

I would put amber bracelets on thy wrists,
Crownets° of pearl about thy naked arms: *little crowns*
And when thou sitst at swilling° Bacchus's feasts *drinking greedily*
My lips with charms should save thee from all harms:

5. Ganimede's mother is the mythological Callirrhoe, wife of Tros, King of Troy. Why this character is introduced at this point in the poem is unclear.

And when in sleep thou tookst thy chiefest pleasure,
Mine eyes should gaze upon thine eyelids' treasure.

And every morn by dawning of the day,
When Phoebus° riseth with a blushing face, *the sun*
Silvanus'° chapel-clerks shall chant a lay,° *a wood god / song*
And play thee hunts-up° in thy resting place: *a game*
My cote° thy chamber, my bosom thy bed; *shed*
Shall be appointed for thy sleepy head.

And when it pleaseth thee to walk abroad,
(Abroad into the fields to take fresh air):
The meads with Flora's° treasure should be strowd,° *goddess of spring / strewn*
(The mantled° meadows and the fields so fair). *flower-covered*
And by a silver well (with golden sands)
I'll sit me down, and wash thine ivory hands.

And in the sweltering heat of summertime,
I would make cabinets° for thee (my love:) *shelters*
Sweet-smelling arbors made of eglantine
Should be thy shrine, and I would be thy dove.
Cool cabinets of fresh green laurel boughs
Should shadow us, ore-set° with thick-set yews. *overlaid*

Or if thou list to bathe thy naked limbs,
Within the crystal of a pearl-bright brook,
Paved with dainty pebbles to the brims;
Or clear, wherein thyself thyself mayst look;
We'll go to Ladon,[6] whose still trickling noise,
Will lull thee fast asleep amidst thy joys.

Or if thou'lt go unto the river side,
To angle for the sweet fresh-water fish;
Arm'd with thy implements that will abide
(Thy rod, hook, line) to take a dainty dish;
Thy rods shall be of cane, thy lines of silk,
Thy hooks of silver, and thy baits of milk.

Or if thou lovest to hear sweet melody,
Or pipe a round upon an oaten reed,
Or make thyself glad with some mirthful glee,
Or play them music whilst thy flock doth feed;
To Pan's[7] own pipe I'll help my lovely lad,
(Pan's golden pipe) which he of Syrinx had.

Or if thou darest to climb the highest trees
For apples, cherries, medlars, pears, or plums,
Nuts, walnuts, filberts, chestnuts, cervices,[8]
The hoary peach, when snowy winter comes;
I have fine orchards full of mellowed fruit;
Which I will give thee to obtain my suit.

6. A river in Arcadia, the land of pastoral.
7. A woodland god, half man, half goat. He loved a nymph, Syrinx, who, wishing to escape his attentions, was changed into a reed by the gods. Pan named his pipe of seven reeds after her.
8. The small edible fruit of a rose tree.

Not proud Alcynous[9] himself can vaunt,° *boast*
Of goodlier orchards or of braver trees
Than I have planted; yet thou wilt not grant
My simple suit; but like the honeybees
  Thou suckest the flower till all the sweet be gone;
  And lovest me for my coin till I have none.

Leave Guendolen (sweet heart), though she be fair
Yet is she light; not light in virtue shining:
But light in her behavior, to impair
Her honor in her chastity's declining;
  Trust not her tears, for they can wantonize,° *arouse you*
  When tears in pearl are trickling from her eyes.

If thou wilt come and dwell with me at home;
My sheepcote shall be strowed° with new green rushes: *strewn*
We'll haunt the trembling prickets° as they roam *young buck*
About the fields, along the hawthorn bushes;
  I have a piebald cur to hunt the hare:
  So we will live with dainty forest fare.

Nay more than this, I have a garden plot,
Wherein there wants nor herbs, nor roots, nor flowers;
(Flowers to smell, roots to eat, herbs for the pot),
And dainty shelters when the welkin° lowers: *heaven*
  Sweet-smelling beds of lilies and of roses,
  Which rosemary banks and lavender encloses.

There grows the gilliflower, the mint, the daisy
(Both red and white), the blew-veined-violet:
The purple hyacinth, the spike° to please thee, *lavender*
The scarlet-dyed carnation bleeding yet;
  The sage, the savory, and sweet marjoram,
  Hyssop, thyme, and eyebright,° good for the blind and dumb. *figwort*

The pink, the primrose, cowslip, and daffadilly,
The harebell blue, the crimson columbine,
Sage, lettuce, parsley, and the milkwhite lily,
The rose, and speckled flower called sops-in-wine,
  Fine pretty kingcups, and the yellow boots,° *buttercups*
  That grows by rivers, and by shallow brooks.

And many thousand more (I cannot name)
Of herbs and flowers that in gardens grow,
I have for thee; and coneys° that be tame, *rabbits*
Yong rabbits, white as swan, and black as crow,
  Some speckled here and there with dainty spots:
  And more I have two milch° and milkwhite goats. *milk*

All these, and more, I'll give thee for thy love;
If these, and more, may 'tice° thy love away: *entice*

9. King of the Phaeacians, who gave Odysseus hospitality on his journey home from Troy to Ithaca. His gardens were reputed to be wonderful.

I have a pigeonhouse, in it a dove,
Which I love more than mortal tongue can say:
And last of all, I'll give thee a little lamb
To play withal, new weaned from her dam.

But if thou wilt not pity my complaint,
My tears, nor vows, nor oaths, made to thy beauty;
What shall I do? But languish, die, or faint,
Since thou dost scorn my tears, and my soul's duty:
And tears contemned,° vows and oaths must fail; *scorned*
For where tears cannot, nothing can prevail.

Compare the love of fair Queen Guendolen
With mine, and thou shalt see how she doth love thee:
I love thee for thy qualities divine,
But she doth love another swain above thee:
I love thee for thy gifts, she for her pleasure;
I for thy virtue, she for beauty's treasure.

And always (I am sure) it cannot last,
But sometime nature will deny those dimples:
Instead of beauty (when thy blossom's past)
Thy face will be deformed, full of wrinkles:
Then she that loved thee for thy beauty's sake,
When age draws on, thy love will soon forsake.

But I that loved thee for thy gifts divine,
In the December of thy beauty's waning,
Will still admire (with joy) those lovely eyne,° *eyes*
That now behold me with their beauty's baning:° *poisoning*
Though January will never come again,
Yet April years[1] will come in showers of rain.

When will my May come, that I may embrace thee?
When will the hour be of my soul's joying?
Why dost thou seek in mirth still to disgrace me?
Whose mirth's° my health, whose grief's my heart's annoying. *mirth is*
Thy bane my bale,° thy bliss my blessedness, *misfortune*
Thy ill my hell, thy weal my welfare is.

Thus do I honor thee that love thee so,
And love thee so, that so do honor thee,
Much more than any mortal man doth know,
Or can discern by love or jealousy:
But if that thou disdainest my loving ever;
Oh happy I, if I had loved never.

Finis.

Plus fellus quam mellis Amor.[2]

1. The time of love when tears follow frustration, after the January of indifference and before the May of pleasure.

2. More bitter than sweet is Love.

The Second Day's Lamentation of the Affectionate Shepherd.[1]

Next morning when the golden sun was risen,
And new had bid good morrow to the mountains;
When night her silver light had locked in prison,
Which gave a glimmering on the crystal fountains:
Then ended sleep: and then my cares began,
Even with the uprising of the silver Swan.[2]

O glorious sun, quoth I (viewing the sun),
That lightenest everything but me alone:
Why is my summer season almost done?
My springtime past, and age's autumn gone?
My harvest's come, and yet I reaped no corn:
My love is great, and yet I am forlorn.

Witness these wat'ry eyes my sad lament
(Receiving cisterns° of my ceaseless tears), *tanks*
Witness my bleeding heart, my soul's intent,
Witness the weight distressed Daphnis bears:
Sweet Love, come ease me of thy burthen's pain;[3]
Or else I die, or else my heart is slain.

And thou love-scorning boy, cruel, unkind;
Oh let me once again entreat some pity:
May be thou wilt relent thy marble mind,
And lend thine ears unto my doleful ditty:
Oh pity him, that pity craves so sweetly:
Or else thou shalt be never named meekly.

If thou wilt love me, thou shalt be my boy,
My sweet delight, the comfort of my mind,
My love, my dove, my solace, and my joy:
But if I can no grace nor mercy find,
I'll go to Caucasus to ease my smart,
And let a vulture gnaw upon my heart.[4]

Yet if thou wilt but show me one kind look,
(A small reward for my so great affection)
I'll grave thy name in beauty's golden book,
And shroud thee under Helicon's[5] protection;
Making the muses chant thy lovely praise:
(For they delight in shepherds' lowly lays.)

And when th'art weary of thy keeping sheep
Upon a lovely down (to please thy mind),
I'll give thee fine ruff-footed doves to keep,

1. This poem is distinguished from its earlier counterpart by being a lamentation or expression of grief, rather than a complaint or protest that love has not been returned. It is presented on a "second day" in the sense that it is a reflection of a first day or an earlier time. In fact, the poet represents himself on the second day as an old man who has had ample time to consider matters of vice and virtue overlooked in his complaint.

2. Cygnus, a constellation.

3. I.e., ease me of the pain of loving you, a burden, because you do not love me.

4. An allusion to the fate of Prometheus, who, for having stolen fire from the gods to give to humans, was chained to the Caucasus Mountains to be eaten by a vulture.

5. A mountain in northern Greece, sacred to the muses.

And pretty pigeons of another kind:
A robin-red-breast shall thy minstrel be,
Chirping thee sweet, and pleasant melody.

Or if thou wilt go shoot at little birds
With bow and boult° (the thrustle-cock and sparrow) *crossbow arrow*
Such as our country hedges can afford's;° *afford us*
I have a fine bow, and an ivory arrow:
And if thou miss, yet meat thou shalt not lack,
I'll hang a bag and a bottle at thy back.

Wilt thou set springes° in a frosty night, *traps*
To catch the long-billed woodcock and the snipe?
(By the bright glimmering of the starry light),
The partridge, pheasant, or the greedy gripe?° *vulture*
I'll lend thee lime-twigs, and fine sparrow calls,
Wherewith the fowler silly birds enthrals.

Or in a misty morning if thou wilt
Make pit-falls for the lark and pheldifare;
Thy prop and sweak shall be both over-gilt:[6]
With Cyparissus'[7] self thou shalt compare
For gins° and wiles, the ouzels° to beguile; *traps / blackbirds*
Whilst thou under a bush shalt sit and smile.

Or with hare-pipes (set in a muset° hole) *hedge*
Wilt thou deceive the deep-earth-delving coney?° *rabbit*
Or wilt thou in a yellow boxen° bowl *box tree*
Taste with a wooden splint° the sweet lithe honey? *a flat spoon*
Clusters of crimson grapes I'll pull thee down;
And with vine-leaves make thee a lovely crown.

Or wilt thou drink a cup of new-made wine
Frothing at top, mixed with a dish of cream;
And strawberries, or bilberries in their prime,
Bathed in a melting sugar-candy stream:
Bunnell and Perry° I have for thee (alone) *apple and pear liqueur*
When vines are dead, and all the grapes are gone.

I have a pleasant-noted nightingale,
(That sings as sweetly as the silver swan),
Kept in a cage of bone; as white as whale,
Which I with singing of Philemon[8] wan:
Her shalt thou have, and all I have beside;
If thou wilt be my boy, or else my bride.

Then will I lay out all my lardary° *dairy food*
(Of cheese, of cracknells,° curds and clotted-cream) *biscuits*
Before thy malcontent ill-pleasing eye:

6. Prop and sweak are parts of a trap to catch wild fowl; Ganimede's trap will be gilded, in keeping with his arrows, which are ivory.

7. A shepherd boy, beloved of Apollo, who killed him accidently with a discus; he was changed into a cypress tree.

8. The legendary husband of Baucis. Together this old couple were hospitable to Jupiter and Mercury; the gods rewarded them by saving them from a universal deluge.

But why do I of such great follies dream?
Alas, he will not see my simple cote;
For all my speckled lamb, nor milk-white goat.

Against° my birthday thou shalt be my guest: *for*
We'll have green cheeses and fine syllabubs;° *puddings*
And thou shalt be the chief of all my feast.
And I will give thee two fine pretty cubs,° *young foxes*
With two young whelps,° to make thee sport withal, *puppies*
A golden racket and a tennis ball

A gilded nutmeg and a race° of ginger, *root*
A silken girdle and a drawn-work band,° *woven bracelet*
Cuffs for thy wrists, a gold ring for thy finger,
And sweet rose-water for thy lily-white hand,
A purse of silk, bespanged with spots of gold,
As brave a one as ere thou didst behold.

A pair of knives, a green hat and a feather,
New gloves to put upon thy milk-white hand
I'll give thee, for to keep thee from the weather;
With Phoenix[9] feathers shall thy face be fanned,
Cooling those cheeks, that being cooled wax° red, *grow*
Like lilies in a bed of roses shed.

Why do thy coral lips disdain to kiss,
And suck that sweet, which many have desired?
That balm my bane, that means would mend my miss:[1]
Oh let me then with thy sweet lips b'inspired;
When thy lips touch my lips, my lips will turn
To coral too, and being cold ice will burn.

Why should thy sweet lovelock hang dangling down,
Kissing thy girdle-steed° with falling pride? *waist*
Although thy skin be white, thy hair is brown:
Oh let not then thy hair thy beauty hide;
Cut off thy lock, and sell it for gold wire:
(The purest gold is tried in hottest fire).

Fair-long-hair-wearing Absolon[2] was killed,
Because he wore it in a bravery:° *boastingly*
So that which graced his beauty, beauty spilled,
Making him subject to vile slavery,
In being hanged: a death for him too good,
That sought his own shame, and his father's blood.

Again, we read of old King Priamus,[3]
(The hapless sire of valiant Hector slain)
That his hair was so long and odious

9. A legendary bird that regenerates itself.
1. I.e., that balm of your lips would cure my misfortune; that means or way would repair my miss or lack.
2. Having led a failed revolt against his father King David, Absalom fled but was caught when his long hair tangled in a tree (2 Samuel 18).
3. King of Troy, father of the hero Hector. Barnfield relates Priam's murder by the Greek hero Pyrrhus, also known as Neoptolemus, the son of Achilles.

In youth, that in his age it bred his pain:
For if his hair had not been half so long,
His life had been, and he had had no wrong.

For when his stately city was destroyed
(That monument of great antiquity)
When his poor heart (with grief and sorrow cloyed)
Fled to his wife (last hope in misery);
Pyrrhus (more hard than adamantine rocks)
Held him and hauled him by his aged locks.

These two examples by the way I show,
To prove th'indecency of men's long hair:
Though I could tell thee of a thousand moe,° *more*
Let these suffice for thee (my lovely fair)
Whose eye's my star; whose smiling is my sun;
Whose love did end before my joys begun.

Fond love is blind, and so art thou (my dear),
For thou seest not my love, and great desart;° *deserving*
Blind love is fond, and so thou dost appear;
For fond, and blind, thou grievest my grieving heart:
Be thou fond-blind, blind-fond, or one, or all;
Thou art my love, and I must be thy thrall.° *slave*

Oh lend thine ivory forehead for love's book,
Thine eyes for candles to behold the same;
That when dim-sighted ones therein shall look
They may discern that proud disdainful dame;[4]
Yet clasp that book, and shut that casement light;
Lest th'one obscured, the other shine too bright.

Sell thy sweet breath to'th'dainty musk-ball-makers;[5]
Yet sell it so as thou mayst soon redeem it:
Let others of thy beauty be partakers;
Else none but Daphnis will so well esteem it:
For what is beauty except it be well known?
And how can it be known, except first shown?

Learn of the gentlewomen of this age,[6]
That set their beauties to the open view,
Making disdain their lord, true love their page;
A custom zeal doth hate, desert doth rue:
Learn to look red, anon wax pale and wan,
Making a mock of love, a scorn of man.

A candle light, and covered with a veil,
Doth no man good, because it gives no light;
So beauty of her beauty seems to fail,
When being not seen it cannot shine so bright.

4. Barnfield personifies Ganimede's disdain for him by the figure of a proud lady.
5. Musk was a kind of perfume; a muskball was a receptacle to hold it.
6. This and the next stanza are ironic; Daphnis instructs Ganimede to show himself so that he will recognize his own pride.

Then show thyself and know thyself withal,
Lest climbing high thou catch too great a fall.

Oh, foul eclipser[7] of that fair sunshine,
Which is entitled beauty in the best;
Making that mortal, which is else divine,
That stains the fair which women 'steem not least:
Get thee to Hell again (from whence thou art)
And leave the center of a woman's heart.

Ah, be not stained (sweet boy) with this vile spot,° *pride*
Indulgence daughter,° mother of mischance; *daughter of indulgence*
A blemish that doth every beauty blot;
That makes them loathed, but never doth advance
Her clients, fautors,° friends; or them that love her; *patrons*
And hates them most of all, that most reprove her.

Remember age, and thou canst not be proud,
For age pulls down the pride of every man;
In youthful years by nature 'tis allowed
To have self-will, do nurture what she can;
Nature and nurture once together met,
The soul and shape° in decent order set. *body*

Pride looks aloft, still staring on the stars,
Humility looks lowly on the ground;
Th'one menaceth the gods with civil wars,
The other toils till he have virtue found:
His thoughts are humble, not aspiring high;
But pride looks haughtily with scornful eye.

Humility is clad in modest weeds,
But pride is brave and glorious to the show;
Humility his friends with kindness feeds,
But pride his friends (in need) will never know:
Supplying not their wants, but them disdaining;
Whilst they to pity never need complaining.

Humility in misery is relieved,
But pride in need of no man is regarded;
Pity and mercy weep to see him grieved
That in distress had them so well rewarded:
But Pride is scorned, contemned, disdained, derided,
Whilst humbleness of all things is provided.

Oh then be humble, gentle, meek, and mild;
So shalt thou be of every mouth commended;
Be not disdainful, cruel, proud, (sweet child)
So shalt thou be of no man much condemned;
Care not for them that virtue do despise;
Virtue is loathed of fools; loved of the wise.

7. The pride of Queen Guendolen, whom the poet chastizes for seducing Ganimede.

O fair boy, trust not to thy beauty's wings,
They cannot carry thee above the sun:
Beauty and wealth are transitory things,
(For all must end that ever was begun)
But fame and virtue never shall decay;
For fame is tombless, virtue lives for aye.

The snow is white, and yet the pepper's black,
The one is bought, the other is contemned:
Pebbles we have, but store of jeat° we lack; *a black stone*
So white compared to black is much condemned:
We do not praise the swan because she's white,
But for she doth in music much delight.

And yet the silver-noted nightingale,
Though she be not so white is more esteemed;
Sturgeon is dun of hue, white is the whale,
Yet for the daintier dish the first is deemed;
What thing is whiter than the milk-bred lily?
Thou knows it not for naught, what man so silly?[8]

Yea what more noisomer° unto the smell *vivid*
Than lilies are? What's sweeter than the sage?
Yet for pure white the lily bears the bell
Till it be faded through decaying age;
Housedoves are white, and ouzels blackbirds be;
Yet what a difference in the taste, we see.

Compare the cow and calf with ewe and lamb,
Rough hairy hides with softest downy fell;° *wool*
Heifer and bull with wether and with ram,
And you shall see how far they do excel;
White kine with black, black coney-skins with gray,
Kine, nesh° and strong; skin, dear° and cheap alway. *weak/expensive*

The whitest silver is not always best,
Lead, tin, and pewter are of base esteem;
The yellow burnished gold, that comes from th'East,
And West (of late invented) may beseem
The world's rich treasury, or Midas'[9] eye;
(The rich man's god, poor man's felicity).

Bugle° and jeat, with snow and alablaster *black glass*
I will compare: white damascene° with black; *inlaid metal*
Bullas and wheaton plums[1] (to a good taster),
The ripe red cherries have the sweetest smack;
When they be green and young, th'are sour and naught;
But being ripe, with eagerness th'are bought.

8. I.e., you do not know it because it is worthless; what man would be so silly as to give it value. Barnfield continues with his series of comparisons showing that unattractive objects are often valuable and vice versa. These comparisons introduce in turn a series of moral instructions that play on the concept of the shepherd as pastor, or clergyman.

9. Legendary King of Phrygia, who wished that all he touched were gold.

1. Bullas and wheaton plums are two varieties of plum.

Compare the wildcat to the brownish beaver,
Running for life, with hounds pursued sore;
When huntsmen of her precious stones bereave her
(Which with her teeth sh'had bitten off before):
Restoratives, and costly curious felts
Are made of them, and rich embroidered belts.

To what use serves a piece of crumbling chalk?
The agate stone is white, yet good for nothing;
Fie, fie, I am ashamed to hear thee talk;
Be not so much of thine on image doting:
So fair Narcissus[2] lost his love and life.
(Beauty is often with itself at strife).

Right diamonds are of a russet hue,
The brightsome carbuncles° are red to see too, *garnets*
The sapphire stone is of a watchet° blue, *deep*
(To this thou canst not choose but soon agree too):
Pearls are not white but gray, rubies are red:
In praise of black, what can be better said?

For if we do consider of each thing
That flies in welkin,° or in water swims, *heaven*
How everything increaseth with the spring,
And how the blacker still the brighter dims:
We cannot choose but needs we must confess,
Sable excels milkwhite in more or less.

As for example, in the crystal clear
Of a sweet stream or pleasant running river,
Where thousand forms of fishes will appear,
(Whose names to thee I cannot now deliver):
The blacker still the brighter have disgraced,
For pleasant profit, and delicious taste.

Salmon and trout are of a ruddy color,
Whiting and dare is of a milkwhite hue:
Nature by them (perhaps) is made the fuller,
Little they nourish, be they old or new:
Carp, loach, tench, eels (though black and bred in mud)
Delight the tooth with taste, and breed good blood.

Innumerable be the kinds, if I could name them;
But I a shepherd, and no fisher am:
Little it skills whether I praise or blame them,
I only meddle with my ewe and lamb:
Yet this I say, that black the better is,
In birds, beasts, fruit, stones, flowers, herbs, metals, fish.

And last of all, in black there doth appear
Such qualities, as not in ivory;

2. The mythical youth, who, falling in love with his own image in a pool, died from grief that he could not possess it.

Black cannot blush for shame, look pale for fear,
Scorning to wear another livery.° *servant's uniform*
Black is the badge of sober modesty,
The wonted wear of ancient gravity.

The learned sisters suit themselves in black,
Learning abandons white and lighter hues:
Pleasure and pride light colors never lack;
But true religion doth such toys refuse:
Virtue and gravity are sisters grown,
Since black by both and both by black are known.

White is the color of each paltry miller,
White is the ensign° of each common woman; *sign*
White, is white virtue's for black vice's pillar;[3]
White makes proud fools inferior unto no man:
White is the white of body, black of mind,
(Virtue we seldom in white habit find).

Oh, then be not so proud because th'art fair,
Virtue is only the rich gift of God:
Let not self-pride thy virtue's name impair,
Beat not green youth with sharp repentance rod;
(A fiend, a monster, a misshapen devil;
Virtue's foe, vice's friend, the root of evil.)

Apply thy mind to be a virtuous man,
Avoid ill company (the spoil of youth);
To follow virtue's lore, do what thou can
(Whereby great profit unto thee ensueth):
Read books, hate ignorance (the foe to art,
The dam° of error, envy of the heart). *mother*

Serve Jove (upon thy knees) both day and night,
Adore his name above all things on earth:
So shall thy vows be gracious in his sight,
So little babes are blessed in their birth;
Think on no worldly woe, lament thy sin:
(For lesser cease, when greater griefs begin).

Swear no vain oaths; hear much but little say;
Speak ill of no man, tend thine own affairs,
Bridle thy wrath, thine angry mood delay;
(So shall thy mind be seldom cloyed with cares):
Be mild and gentle in thy speech to all,
Refuse no honest gain when it doth fall.

Be not beguiled with words, prove not ungrateful,
Relieve thy neighbor in this greatest need,
Commit no action that to all is hateful,
Their want with wealth, the poor with plenty feed:
Twit° no man in the teeth with what th'hast done; *taunt*
Remember flesh is frail and hatred shun.

3. White virtues support black vices by masking their true nature.

Leave wicked things, which men to mischief move,
(Least cross mishap° may thee in danger bring), *evil chance*
Crave no preferment of thy heavenly Jove,
Nor any honor of thy earthly king:
  Boast not thyself before th'Almighty's sight,
  (Who knows thy heart and any wicked wight).

Be not offensive to the people's eye,
See that thy prayers heart's true zeal affords,
Scorn not a man that's fallen in misery,
Esteem no tattling tales, nor babbling words;
  That reason is exiled always think,
  When as a drunkard rails amidst his drink.

Use not thy lovely lips to loathsome lies,
By crafty means increase no worldly wealth;
Strive not with mighty men (whose fortune flies)
With temp'rate diet nourish wholesome health;
  Place well thy words, leave not thy friend for gold;
  First try, then trust; in vent'ring° be not bold. *adventuring*

In Pan[4] repose thy trust; extol his praise
(That never shall decay, but ever lives):
Honor thy parents (to prolong thy days),
Let not thy left hand know what right hand gives:
  From needy men turn not thy face away,
  (Though charity be now yclad in clay).

Hear shepherds oft (thereby great wisdom grows),
With good advice a sober answer make:
Be not removed with every wind that blows,
(That course do only sinful sinners take).
  Thy talk will show thy fame or else thy shame;
  (A prattling tongue doth often purchase blame).

Obtain a faithful friend that will not fail thee,
Think on thy mother's pain in her childbearing,
Make no debate, lest quickly thou bewail thee,
Visit the sick with comfortable cheering;
  Pity the prisoner, help the fatherless,
  Revenge the widow's wrongs in her distress.

Think on thy grave, remember still thy end,
Let not thy winding sheet be stained with guilt,
Trust not a feigned reconciled friend,
More than an open foe (that blood hath spilt)
  (Who toucheth pitch, with pitch shall be defiled),
  Be not with wanton company beguiled.

Take not a flattering woman to thy wife,
A shameless creature, full of wanton words,
(Whose bad, thy good; whose lust will end thy life,

4. The god of flocks and shepherds; sometimes understood to refer to Christ.

Cutting thy heart with sharp two-edged swords):
Cast not thy mind on her whose looks allure,
But she that shines in truth and virtue pure.

Praise not thyself, let other men commend thee:
Bear not a flattering tongue to glaver° any, *wheedle*
Let parents' due correction not offend thee;
Rob not thy neighbor, seek the love of many;
Hate not to hear good counsel given thee,
Lay not thy money unto usury.

Restrain thy steps from too much liberty,
Fulfill not th'envious man's malicious mind;
Embrace thy wife, live not in lechery;
Content thyself with what Fates have assigned:
Be ruled by reason, warning dangers save;
True age is reverend worship to thy grave.

Be patient in extreme adversity,
(Man's chiefest credit grows by doing well),
Be not highminded in prosperity;
Falsehood abhor, no lying fable tell.
Give not thyself to sloth (the sink of shame,
The moth of time, the enemy to fame).

This leare° I learned of a Beldame Trot, *wisdom*
(When I was young and wild as now thou art):
But her good counsel I regarded not;
I marked it with my ears, not with my heart:
But now I find it too-too true (my son),
When my age-withered spring is almost done.

Behold my gray head, full of silver hairs,
My wrinkled skin, deep furrows in my face:
Cares bring old age, old age increaseth cares;
My time is come, and I have run my race;
Winter hath snowed upon my hoary head,
And with my winter all my joys are dead.

And thou love-hating boy (whom once I loved),
Farewell, a thousand-thousand times farewell:
My tears the marble stones to ruth° have moved; *pity*
My sad complaints the babbling echoes tell:
And yet thou wouldst take no compassion on me,
Scorning that cross which love hath laid upon me.

The hardest steel with fire doth mend his miss,
Marble is mollified° with drops of rain; *softened*
But thou (more hard than steel or marble is)
Dost scorn my tears and my true love disdain,
Which for thy sake shall everlasting be,
Wrote in the annals of eternity.

By this, the night (with darkness overspread)
Had drawn the curtains of her coal-black bed;

And Cynthia° muffling her face with a cloud, *the moon*
(Lest all the world of her should be too proud)
Had taken *congé*° of the sable night, *leave*
(That wanting her cannot be half so bright);

When I poor forlorn man and outcast creature
(Despairing of my love, despised of° beauty) *by*
Grew malcontent, scorning his lovely feature
That had disdained my ever zealous duty:
I hied me homeward by the moonshine light;
Forswearing love and all his fond delight.
Finis.

1594

Sonnets from *Cynthia*

1

Sporting at fancy, setting light by love,
There came a thief and stole away my heart,
(And therefore robbed me of my chiefest part)
Yet cannot reason him a felon prove.
For why his beauty (my heart's thief) affirmeth,
Piercing no skin (the body's fensive° wall) *defensive*
And having leave, and free consent withal,
Himself not guilty, from love guilty termeth,[1]
Conscience the judge, twelve reasons are the jury,
They find mine eyes the beauty t'have let in,
And on this verdict given, agreed they been,
Wherefore, because his beauty did allure ye,[2]
Your doom is this: in tears still to be drowned,
When his fair forehead with disdain is frowned.

5

It is reported of fair Thetis'[3] son,
(Achilles, famous for his chivalry,
His noble mind and magnanimity),
That when the Trojan wars were new begun,
Whos'ever was deep-wounded with his spear,
Could never be recurred° of his maim,° *cured / wound*
Nor ever after be made whole again;
Except with that spear's rust he holpen were.° *could be helped*
Even so it fareth with my fortune now,
Who being wounded with his piercing eye,
Must either thereby find a remedy,
Or else to be relieved, I know not how,
Then if thou hast a mind still to annoy me,
Kill me with kisses, if thou wilt destroy me.

1. Himself not guilty, he puts a limit or term to guilty love.
2. You, i.e., the speaker addresses himself.
3. The mother of Achilles, the great Greek hero of the Trojan War.

9

Diana° (on a time) walking the wood, *goddess of the hunt*
To sport herself, of her fair train forlorn,
Chancest for to prick her foot against a thorn,
And from thence issued out a stream of blood.
No sooner she was vanished out of sight,
But love's fair Queen° came there by chance, *Venus*
And having of this hap a glimmering glance,
She put the blood into a crystal bright,
When being now come unto Mount Rhodope,
With her fair hands she forms a shape of snow,
And blends it with this blood; from whence doth grow
A lovely creature, brighter than the day.
And being christened in fair Paphos'[4] shrine,
She called him Ganimede: as all divine.

11

Sighing, and sadly sitting by my love,
He asked the cause of my heart's sorrowing,
Conjuring me by heaven's eternal king
To tell the cause which me so much did move.
Compelled (quoth I) to thee will I confess,
Love is the cause; and only love it is
That doth deprive me of my heavenly bliss.
Love is the pain that doth my heart oppress.
And what is she (quoth he) whom thou dost love?
Look in this glass (quoth I) there shalt thou see
The perfect form of my felicity.
When, thinking that it would strange magic prove,
He opened it; and taking off the cover,
He straight perceived himself to be my lover.

13

Speak, Echo, tell; how may I call my love? *Love*[5]
But how his lamps that are so crystalline? *Eyne*° *eyes*
Oh, happy stars that make your heavens divine:
And happy gems that admiration move.
How term'st his golden tresses waved with air? *Hair*
Oh, lovely hair of your more lovely master,
Image of love, fair shape of alabaster,
Why dost thou drive thy lover to despair?
How dost thou call the bed where beauty grows? *Rose*
Fair virgin rose, whose maiden blossoms cover
The milk-white lily, thy embracing lover:
Whose kisses makes thee oft thy red to love.
And blushing oft for shame, when he hath kissed thee,
He vades° away, and thou rangest° where it list thee. *fades/wander*

4. Cyprus, sacred to Venus.
5. This poem exploits a rhetorical figure called *paronomasia*, in which sounds are repeated; in this case the repetition is of the last syllable of a line, which produces the effect of an echo.

Nicholas Hilliard. *The Young Man amongst Roses*. ca. 1597.

19

Ah no; nor I myself: though my pure love
(Sweet Ganimede) to thee hath still been pure,
And even till my last gasp shall aye endure,
Could ever thy obdurate beauty move:
Then cease, oh goddess' son (for sure thou are,
A goddess' son that canst resist desire)
Cease thy hard heart, and entertain love's fire,
Within thy sacred breast: by nature's art.
And as I love thee more than any creature,
(Love thee, because thy beauty is divine;
Love thee because thyself, my soul, is thine:
Wholly devoted to thy lovely feature)
Even so of all the vowels, I and U,
Are dearest unto me, as doth ensue.

1595

Christopher Marlowe

1564–1593

When Christopher Marlowe began his career as a dramatist, the Elizabethan stage was at the height of its popularity and sophistication. Marlowe's plays were an immediate success, fascinating audiences with dazzling characters, exotic settings, and controversial subjects. Throughout his career—and even after his sudden death at the age of twenty-nine—Marlowe was Shakespeare's principal commercial and artistic rival.

A shoemaker's son, Marlowe went to Cambridge on a scholarship that was intended to prepare him for holy orders. His interests proved to be literary rather than religious, however, and he left Cambridge for London. As a student, he had composed a number of poems, notably the brilliant but unfinished *Hero and Leander*, a narrative of heterosexual and homosexual passion, but public recognition came with the production of his first play, *Tamburlaine the Great*, in 1587. This was followed by *The Second Part of Tamburlaine the Great*, *The Jew of Malta*, *Edward II*, *Dr. Faustus*, *Dido, Queen of Carthage*, and finally *The Massacre at Paris*, all composed within a period of six years. Marlowe's bold and inventive language captivated audiences; his blank verse, in which the sense of a sentence is not interrupted at the end of each line by the constraints of rhyme, brought the rhythms of natural speech to the language of theater. His characterizations of heroes were equally astonishing: driven by an incandescent desire that no conquest could satisfy, they revealed the torment and tragedy that were occasioned by pride.

Marlowe himself may have been employed in subversive activities. While still at Cambridge, he became a spy for Queen Elizabeth's secret service, dedicated to the infiltration and exposure of Catholic groups in England and abroad. How much activity he was responsible for remains guesswork. At the very least, the manner in which he died suggests his involvement in clandestine politics. In May 1593, the Queen's Privy Council issued a warrant for his arrest. The charge against him—blasphemy—seems to have come from Thomas Kyd, a fellow playwright with whom Marlowe shared lodgings. While in London waiting for a hearing, Marlowe, who was drinking in an alehouse, got into a fight with three men (all government spies), one of whom was Ingram Friser. Marlowe raised a dagger to stab Friser, but Friser, warding off the blow, managed to turn the dagger against Marlowe. It pierced his eye "in such sort that his brains coming out at the dagger point, he shortly after died." The affair did not end there; two days after Marlowe's death, Richard Baines (himself a former spy) accused him before the Privy Council of atheism, treason, and the opinion "that they that love not tobacco and boys were fools." Whether or not these accusations held any truth, they referred to views that were not unusual in the circles Marlowe traveled in; they indicate a skepticism in matters of religion and an indifference to social decorum that authorities responsible for political order would have considered dangerous. Some scholars think that Marlowe was murdered by government command. Although the mystery surrounding his death may never be solved, the mercurial brilliance of his work remains undisputed.

With the exception of the two parts of *Tamburlaine*, published in 1590, Marlowe's works were published after his death: *Edward II* and *Dido, Queen of Carthage* in 1594; *Hero and Leander* in 1598; *Dr. Faustus* in 1604; and *The Jew of Malta* in 1633. The celebrated lyric entitled *The Passionate Shepherd to His Love* first appeared in 1599 in an unauthorized collection of verse called *The Passionate Pilgrim* published by William Jaggard.

The Passionate Shepherd to His Love

Come live with me, and be my love,
And we will all the pleasures prove,
That valleys, groves, hills, and fields,
Woods, or steepy mountain yields.

And we will sit upon the rocks,
Seeing the shepherds feed their flocks,
By shallow rivers, to whose falls,
Melodious birds sing madrigals.

And I will make thee beds of roses,
And a thousand fragrant poesies,
A cap of flowers, and a kirtle,
Embroidered all with leaves of myrtle.

A gown made of the finest wool,
Which from our pretty lambs we pull,
Fair lined slippers for the cold,
With buckles of the purest gold.

A belt of straw, and ivy buds,
With coral clasps and amber studs,
And if these pleasures may thee move,
Come live with me, and be my love.

The shepherd swains shall dance and sing,
For thy delight each May morning,
If these delights thy mind may move,
Then live with me and be my love.

Companion Reading

Sir Walter Raleigh: The Nymph's Reply to the Shepherd[1]

If all the world and love were young,
And truth in every shepherd's tongue,
These pretty pleasures might me move,
To live with thee, and be thy love.

Time drives the flocks from field to fold,
When rivers rage, and rocks grow cold,
And Philomel° becometh dumb, *the nightingale*
The rest complain of cares to come.

The flowers do fade, and wanton fields,
To wayward winter reckoning yields,
A honey tongue, a heart of gall,
Is fancy's spring, but sorrow's fall.

Thy gowns, thy shoes, thy beds of roses,
Thy cap, thy kirtle, and thy poesies,
Soon break, soon wither, soon forgotten;
In folly ripe, in reason rotten.

Thy belt of straw and ivy buds,
Thy coral clasps and amber studs,
All these in me no means can move,
To come to thee, and be thy love.

1. Raleigh's *Reply* was published together with Marlowe's poem in Jaggard's collection.

But could youth last, and love still breed,
Had joys no date, nor age no need,
Then these delights my mind might move,
To live with thee, and be thy love.

Hero and Leander[1]

On Hellespont,[2] guilty of true love's blood,
In view and opposite, two cities stood,
Seaborders,° disjoined by Neptune's might. *seaports*
The one Abydos, the other Sestos hight.
As Sestos, Hero dwelt, Hero the fair,
Whom young Apollo° courted for her hair, *god of the sun*
And offered as a dower° his burning throne, *wedding gift*
Where she should sit for men to gaze upon.
The outside of her garments were of lawn,° *fine cloth*
The lining, purple silk, with gilt stars drawn,
Her wide sleeves green, and bordered with a grove,
Where Venus° in her naked glory strove, *goddess of love*
To please the careless and disdainful eyes,
Of proud Adonis° that before her lies. *Venus's lover*
Her kirtle° blue, whereon was many a stain, *gown*
Made with the blood of wretched lovers slain.
Upon her head she wore a myrtle wreath,
From whence her veil reached to the ground beneath.
Her veil was artificial flowers and leaves,
Whose workmanship both man and beast deceives.
Many would praise the sweet smell as she passed,
When t'was the odor which her breath forth cast,
And there for honey, bees have fought in vain,
And beat from thence, have lighted there again.
About her neck hung chains of pebble stone,
Which, lightened by her neck, like diamonds shone.
She wore no gloves, for neither sun nor wind
Would burn or parch her hands, but to her mind,
Or warm or cool them, for they took delight
To play upon those hands, they were so white.
Buskins° of shells all silvered, used she, *boots*
And branched° with blushing coral to the knee. *decorated*
Where sparrows perched, of hollow pearl and gold,
Such as the world would wonder to behold.
Those with sweet water oft her handmaid fills,
Which as she went would chirrup through the° bills.[3] *their*
Some say, for her the fairest Cupid pined,
And looking in her face, was strucken° blind. *struck*
But this is true, so like was one the other,

1. In the early modern period the story of the lovers Hero and Leander was attributed to the legendary poet Musaeus; in fact, it appears to be the work of an anonymous Greek poet of the 4th or 5th century A.D.
2. The straits separating Asia Minor from Thracian Greece, now the Dardanelles.
3. A fantastic costume: Hero's boots are decorated with shells that are filled with water on which mechanical sparrows made of pearl and gold perch and chirp.

As he imagined Hero was his mother.
And oftentimes into her bosom flew,
About her naked neck his bare arms threw.
And laid his childish head upon her breast,
And with still panting rocked, there took his rest.
So lovely fair was Hero, Venus' nun,
As nature wept, thinking she was undone,
Because she took more from her than she left,
And of such wondrous beauty her bereft.
Therefore in sign° her treasure suffered wrack,° *to signify / loss*
Since Hero's time, hath half the world been black.
Amorous Leander, beautiful and young,
(Whose tragedy divine Musaeus sung)
Dwelt at Abidos, since him dwelt there none
For whom succeeding times make greater moan.
His dangling tresses that were never shorn,
Had they been cut and unto Colchis[4] borne,
Would have allured the vent'rous° youth of Greece, *adventurous*
To hazard more than for the golden fleece.
Fair Cynthia° wished his arms might be her sphere, *goddess of the moon*
Grief makes her pale, because she moves not there.
His body was straight as Circe's[5] wand,
Jove might have sipped out nectar from his hand.
Even as delicious meat is to the taste,
So was his neck in touching, and surpassed
The white of Pelops'[6] shoulder; I could tell ye
How smooth his breast was, and how white his belly,
And whose immortal fingers did imprint,
That heavenly path with many a curious dint
That runs along his back, but my rude pen
Can hardly blazon° forth the loves of men,[7] *list*
Much less of powerful gods. Let it suffice,
That my slack muse sings of Leander's eyes.
Those orient° cheeks and lips, exceeding his *shining*
That leapt into the water for a kiss
Of his own shadow, and despising many,
Died ere he could enjoy the love of any.
Had wild Hippolytus[8] Leander seen,
Enamored of his beauty had he been,
His presence made the rudest peasant melt,
That in the vast uplandish° country dwelt; *rustic*
The barbarous Thracian[9] soldier, moved with nought,

4. A country at the east end of the Black Sea, to which the legendary golden fleece—a Greek treasure—had been taken. Colchis was raided by the Greek hero Jason and his men, the Argonauts, who carried the fleece back to their homeland.
5. The Greek divinity who with her magic wand turned the companions of Odysseus into swine (*Odyssey* 10).
6. A legendary figure whose father, Tantalus, had him cooked and served to the gods. Only his shoulder was eaten, however, and that was restored with a piece of ivory.
7. The homoerotic element in Marlowe's description of Leander becomes explicit here and continues to be prominent later in the poet's account of Neptune's love for Leander.
8. A legendary hero, vowed to hunting and chastity; at the command of Phaedra, his stepmother, he was consumed by a sea-monster for having refused to return her love for him.
9. Thrace was a mountainous region in northeastern Greece.

Was moved with him, and for his favor fought.
Some swore he was a maid in man's attire,
For in his looks were all that men desire,
A pleasant, smiling cheek, a speaking eye,
A brow for love to banquet royally,
And such as knew he was a man would say,
Leander, thou art made for amorous play;
Why art thou not in love, and loved of all?
Though thou be fair, yet be not thine own thrall.° *slave*

The men of wealthy Sestos, every year
(For his sake whom their goddess° held so dear, *Venus*
Rose-cheeked Adonis), kept a solemn feast;
Thither resorted many a wandering guest
To meet their loves; such as had none at all
Came lovers home from this great festival.
For every street like to a firmament° *sky*
Glistered with breathing stars, who where they went,
Frighted the melancholy earth, which deemed,
Eternal heaven to burn, for so it seemed
As if another Phaeton[1] had got
The guidance of the sun's rich chariot.
But far above, the loveliest Hero shined,
And stole away th'enchanted gazer's mind,
For like sea-nymphs inveigling harmony,
So was her beauty to the standers-by.
Nor that night-wandering pale and watery star,[2]
(When yawning dragons draw her thirling° car, *spinning*
From Latmos' mount up to the gloomy sky,
Where crowned with blazing light and majesty,
She proudly sits) more over-rules the flood,
Than she the hearts of those that near her stood.
Even as, when gaudy nymphs pursue the chase,
Wretched Ixion's shaggy-footed race,[3]
Incensed with savage heat, gallop amain,
From steep pine-bearing mountains to the plain,
So ran the people forth to gaze upon her,
And all that viewed her were enamored on her.
And as in fury of a dreadful fight,
Their fellows being slain or put to flight,
Poor soldiers stand with fear of death strucken,
So at her presence all surprised and tooken° *taken*
Await the sentence of her scornful eyes;
He whom she favors lives, the other dies.
There might you see one sigh, another rage,
And some (their violent passions to assuage)
Compile sharp satires; but alas too late,
For faithful love will never turn to hate.

1. Apollo's son, who drove his father's chariot too near the earth and was struck down by Jove's thunderbolt.
2. The moon, or Cynthia, whose seat is Mount Latmos.

3. Centaurs, creatures who were half-man, half-horse. The sons of Ixion, they were punished for loving Juno, the queen of the gods, by being bound on a wheel of fire.

And many, seeing great princes were denied,
Pined as they went and thinking on her, died.
On this feast day, O cursed day and hour,
Went Hero through Sestos, from her tower
To Venus' temple, where unhappily,
As after chanced, they did each other spy.
So fair a church as this had Venus none,
The walls were of discolored jasper stone,
Wherein was Proteus[4] carved, and o'erhead,
A lively vine of green sea agate spread,
Where by one hand, light-headed Bacchus° hung, *god of wine*
And with the other, wine from grapes out-wrung.
Of crystal shining fair the pavement was,
The town of Sestos called it Venus' glass.
There might you see the gods in sundry shapes
Committing heady riots, incest, rapes.
For know that underneath this radiant flower
Was Danae's statue[5] in a brazen tower;
Jove, stealing from his sister's bed
To dally with Idalian Ganymede,
And for his love, Europa, bellowing loud,
And tumbling with the rainbow in a cloud;
Blood-quaffing Mars, heaving the iron net,
Which limping Vulcan and his Cyclops set;
Love kindling fire to burn such towns as Troy;
Sylvanus weeping for the lovely boy
That now is turned into a cypress tree,
Under whose shade the wood gods love to be.
And in the midst a silver altar stood,
There Hero, sacrificing turtle's° blood, *dove's*
Veiled to the ground, veiling her eyelids close,
And modestly they opened as she rose;
Thence flew Love's arrow with the golden head,
And thus Leander was enamored.
Stone still he stood, and evermore he gazed,
Till with the fire that from his count'nance blazed,
Relenting Hero's gentle heart was struck,
Such force and virtue hath an amorous look.

It lies not in our power to love or hate,
For will in us is overruled by fate.
When two are stripped long ere the course begin,
We wish that one should lose, the other win.
And one especially do we affect,
Of two gold ingots like in each respect.
The reason no man knows, let it suffice,

4. A sea-god, who could change his shape at will.

5. The figure of the mythical woman Danae, whose father shut her up in a tower to keep her from suitors; Jupiter visited her there in a shower of gold. Marlowe continues his description of "Venus' glass" by allusions to popular mythological figures: Ganymede, Jove's cup-bearer and lover; Europa, carried off by Jove disguised as a bull; the lover of Venus, Mars, who was caught in the net of Vulcan, Venus' husband, assisted by his one-eyed helpers, the Cyclops; and Sylvanus, a wood god, who wept for his lover, Cyparissus, who had been turned into a tree.

What we behold is censured° by our eyes. *judged*
Where both deliberate, the love is slight,
Who ever loved that loved not at first sight?

He kneeled, but unto her devoutly prayed.
Chaste Hero to herself thus softly said,
Were I the saint he worships, I would hear him,
And as she spoke those words, came somewhat near him.
He started up, she blushed as one ashamed,
Wherewith Leander much more was inflamed.
He touched her hand, in touching it she trembled,
Love deeply grounded, hardly is dissembled.
These lovers parled° by the touch of hands; *spoke*
True love is mute, and oft amazed stands.
Thus while dumb signs their yielding hearts entangled,
The air with sparks of living fire was spangled,
And Night, deep-drenched in misty Acheron,° *a river in hell*
Heaved up her head, and half the world upon
Breathed darkness forth (dark night is Cupid's day)
And now begins Leander to display
Love's holy fire with words, with sighs and tears,
Which like sweet music entered Hero's ears,
And yet at every word she turned aside,
And always cut him off as he replied.
At last, like to a bold, sharp sophister,° *false reasoner*
With cheerful hope thus he accosted her.

Fair creature, let me speak without offence,
I would my rude words had the influence
To lead thy thoughts, as thy fair looks do mine,
Then shouldst thou be his prisoner who is thine.
Be not unkind and fair, misshapen stuff° *ungainly persons*
Are of behavior boisterous and rough.
O shun me not, but hear me ere you go,
God knows I cannot force love, as you do.
My words shall be as spotless as my youth,
Full of simplicity and naked truth.
This sacrifice (whose sweet perfume descending
From Venus' altar to your footsteps bending)
Doth testify that you exceed her far,
To whom you offer, and whose nun you are.
Why should you worship her, her you surpass,
As much as sparkling diamonds flaring° glass. *flashing*
A diamond set in lead his worth retains,
A heavenly nymph, beloved of human swains,° *suitors*
Receives no blemish, but oft times more grace,
Which makes me hope, although I am but base,
Base in respect of thee, divine and pure,
Dutiful service may thy love procure,
And I in duty will excel all other,
As thou in beauty dost exceed Love's mother.
Nor heaven, nor thou, were made to gaze upon,

As heaven preserves all things, so save thou one.° *Leander*
A stately builded ship, well-rigged and tall,
The ocean maketh more majestical.
Why vowest thou then to live in Sestos here,
Who on Love's seas more glorious wouldst appear?
Like untuned golden strings all women are,
Which, long time lie untouched, will harshly jar.
Vessels of brass oft handled brightly shine,
What difference betwixt the richest mine
And basest mold, but use? For both not used
Are of like worth. Then treasure is abused
When misers keep it; being put to loan,
In time it will return us two for one.
Rich robes, themselves and others do adorn,
Neither themselves nor others, if not worn.
Who builds a palace and rams up the gate,
Shall see it ruinous and desolate.
Ah, simple Hero, learn thyself to cherish,
Lone women, like to empty houses, perish.
Less sins the poor rich man that starves himself,
In heaping up a mass of drossy pelf,° *worthless booty*
Than such as you; his golden earth remains,
Which, after his decease, some other gains.
But this fair gem, sweet in the loss alone,
When you fleet hence, can be bequeathed to none.
Or if it could, down from th'enamelled sky,
All heaven would come to claim this legacy,
And with intestine broils° the world destroy, *civil wars*
And quite confound nature's sweet harmony.
Well therefore by the gods decreed it is,
We human creatures should enjoy that bliss.
One is no number, maids are nothing then,
Without the sweet society of men.
Wilt thou live single still? One shalt thou be,
Though never-singling Hymen[6] couple thee.
Wild savages, that drink of running springs,
Think water far excels all earthly things.
But they that daily taste neat° wine, despise it. *unwatered*
Virginity, albeit some highly prize it,
Compared with marriage, had you tried them both,
Differs as much as wine and water doth.
Base boullion° for the stamp's sake we allow,[7] *metal*
Even so for men's impression do we you.
By which alone, our reverend fathers say,
Women receive perfection every way.
This idol which you term virginity,
Is neither essence subject to the eye,

6. Marlowe turns to paradox: Although Hero is coupled by Hymen, the god of marriage, she can also remain "one" or single.

7. Just as a coin has the value stamped on it, so a person is valued according to the impression she (or he) gives.

No, nor to any one exterior sense,
Nor hath it any place of residence,
Nor is't of earth or mold celestial,
Or capable of any form at all.
Of that which hath no being do not boast,
Things that are not at all are never lost.
Men foolishly do call it virtuous,
What virtue is it, that is born with us?
Much less can honor be ascribed thereto;
Honor is purchased by the deeds we do.
Believe me, Hero, honor is not won,
Until some honorable deed be done.
Seek you for chastity, immortal fame,
And know that some have wronged Diana's name?
Whose name is it, if she be false or not,
So she be fair, but some vile tongues will blot?
But you are fair (aye me), so wondrous fair,
So young, so gentle, and so debonair,° *courteous*
As Greece will think if thus you live alone,
Some one or other keeps you as his own.
Then, Hero, hate me not, nor from me fly,
To follow swiftly blasting infamy.
Perhaps thy sacred priesthood makes thee loath,
Tell me, to whom mad'st thou that heedless oath?

To Venus, answered she, and as she spoke,
Forth from those two translucent cisterns broke
A stream of liquid pearl, which down her face
Made milk-white paths, whereon the gods might trace
To Jove's high court. He thus replied: the rites
In which love's beauteous empress most delights
Are banquets, Doric[8] music, midnight revel,
Plays, masques, and all that stern age counteth evil.
Thee as a holy Idiot doth she scorn,
For thou, in vowing chastity, hast sworn
To rob her name and honor, and thereby
Commit'st a sin far worse than perjury,
Even sacrilege against her deity,
Through regular and formal purity.
To expiate which sin, kiss and shake hands,
Such sacrifice as this Venus demands.

Thereat she smiled, and did deny him so,
As put thereby, yet might he hope for mo'e.
Which makes him quickly re-enforce his speech,
And her in humble manner thus beseech.

Though neither gods nor men may thee deserve,
Yet for her sake whom you have vowed to serve,
Abandon fruitless, cold virginity,

8. Pertaining to the Greek region of Doris, noted for the simplicity of its culture.

The gentle Queen of Love's sole enemy.
Then shall you most resemble Venus' nun,
When Venus' sweet rites are performed and done.
Flint-breasted Pallas[9] joys in single life,
But Pallas and your mistress are at strife.
Love, Hero, then, and be not tyrannous,
But heal the heart that thou has wounded thus,
Nor stain thy youthful years with avarice,
Fair fools delight to be accounted nice.° *coy*
The richest corn° dies if it be not reaped, *grain*
Beauty alone is lost, too warily kept.
These arguments he used, and many more,
Wherewith she yielded, that was won before,
Hero's looks yielded, but her words made war;
Women are won when they begin to jar.° *quarrel*
Thus having swallowed Cupid's golden hook,
The more she strived, the deeper was she struck.
Yet evilly feigning anger, strove she still,
And would be wrought to grant against her will.
So having paused a while, at last she said:
Who taught thee rhetoric to deceive a maid?
Aye me, such words as these should I abhor,
And yet I like them for the orator.

With that Leander stooped, to have embraced her,
But from his spreading arms away she cast her,
And thus bespake him: Gentle youth, forbear
To touch the sacred garments which I wear.

Upon a rock, and underneath a hill,
Far from the town (where all is whist° and still, *quiet*
Save that sea playing on yellow sand
Sends forth a rattling murmur to the land,
Whose sound allures the golden Morpheus,° *god of sleep*
In silence of the night to visit us)
My turret stands, and there God knows I play
With Venus' swans and sparrows all the day,
A dwarfish beldame° bears° me company, *old woman / keeps*
That hops about the chamber where I lie,
And spends the night (that might be better spent)
In vain discourse and apish merriment.
Come thither; as she spake this, her tongue tripped,
For unawares (Come thither) from her slipped,
And suddenly her former color changed,
And here and there her eyes through anger ranged,
And like a planet, moving several ways,
At one self instant, she, poor soul, assays,
Loving, not to love at all, and every part,
Strove to resist the motions of her heart.
And hands so pure, so innocent, nay such,

9. Athena or Minerva, goddess of wisdom, justice, and war.

As might have made heaven stoop to have a touch,
Did she uphold to Venus, and again,
Vowed spotless chastity, but all in vain.
Cupid beat down her prayers with his wings,
Her vowes above the empty air he flings.
All deep enraged, his sinewy bow he bent,
And shot a shaft that burning from him went,
Wherewith she, stroocken,° looked so dolefully, *struck*
As made Love sigh to see his tyranny.
And as she wept, her tears to pearl he turned,
And wound them on his arm, and for her mourned.
Then towards the palace of the Destinies,° *the Fates*
Laden with languishment and grief, he flies.
And to those stern nymphs humbly made request,
Both might enjoy each other, and be blessed.
But with a ghastly dreadful countenance,
Threatening a thousand deaths at every glance,
They answered Love, nor would vouchsafe so much
As one poor word, their hate to him was such.
Harken a while, and I will tell you why:
Heaven's winged herald, Jove-born Mercury,[1]
The selfsame day that he asleep had laid
Enchanted Argus, spied a country maid,
Whose careless hair, instead of pearl t'adorn it,
Glistered with dew, as one that seemed to scorn it,
Her breath as fragrant as the morning rose,
Her mind pure and her tongue untaught to glose.° *deceive*
Yet proud she was (for lofty pride that dwells
In towered courts, is oft in shepherd's cells),° *cottages*
And too too well the fair vermillion knew,
And silver tincture of her cheeks, that drew
The love of every swain. On her, this god
Enamored was, and with his snakey rod,° *Mercury's staff*
Did charm her nimble feet, and made her stay,
The while upon a hillock down he lay,
And sweetly on his pipe began to play,
And with his smooth speech, her fancy to assay,° *attempt*
Till in his twining arms he locked her fast,
And then he wooed her with kisses and at last,
As shepherds do, her on the ground he laid,
And tumbling in the grass, he often strayed
Beyond the bounds of shame, in being bold
To eye those parts, which no eye should behold,
And like an insolent commanding lover,
Boasting his parentage, would needs discover
The way to new Elysium; but she,
Whose only dower° was her chastity, *dowry, wealth*
Having striven in vain, was now about to cry,

1. The messenger god; he enchanted the many-eyed herdsman Argus (or Argos), whom Juno had ordered to guard the heifer Io, beloved of Jupiter.

And crave the help of the shepherds that were nigh.
Herewith he stayed his fury, and began
To give her leave to rise; away she ran,
After went Mercury, who used such cunning,
As she to hear his tale, left off running.
Maids are not wooed by brutish force and might,
But speeches full of pleasure and delight.
And knowing Hermes° courted her, was glad *Mercury*
That she such loveliness and beauty had
As could provoke his liking, yet was mute,
And neither would deny, nor grant his suit.
Still vowed he love, she wanting no excuse
To feed him with delays, as women use,
Or thirsting after immortality,
All women are ambitious naturally,
Imposed upon her lover such a task,
As he ought not perform, nor yet she ask.
A draught of flowing nectar, she requested,
Wherewith the king of the gods and men is feasted.
He ready to accomplish what she willed,
Stole some from Hebe° (Hebe, Jove's cups filled) *a goddess*
And gave it to his simple rustic love,
Which being known (as what is hid from Jove?)
He inly stormed, and waxed more furious
Than for the fire filched by Prometheus[2],
And thrusts him down from heaven; he wandering here,
In mournful terms, with sad and heavy cheer
Complained to Cupid. Cupid, for his° sake, *Prometheus'*
To be revenged on Jove, did undertake,
And those on whom heaven, earth, and hell relies,
I mean the adamantine° Destinies, *implacable*
He wounds with love, and forced them equally,
To dote upon deceitful Mercury.
They offered him the deadly, fatal knife,
That shears the slender threads of human life,
At his fair feathered feet, the engines laid,
Which th'earth from ugly Chaos'[3] den up-weighed:
These he regarded not, but did entreat
That Jove, usurper of his father's° seat, *Saturn's*
Might presently be banished into hell,
And aged Saturn in Olympus dwell.
They granted what he craved, and once again,
Saturn and Ops° began their golden reign. *Wealth (Saturn's wife)*
Murder, rape, war, lust, and treachery
Were, with Jove, closed in Stygian Emprie.° *empire of hell*
But long this blessed time continued not,
As soon as he his wished purpose got;
He reckless of his promise, did despise

2. In Greek mythology the figure of "forethought"; he made mankind out of clay and, when Jupiter deprived them of fire, stole it from heaven.
3. The infinite space that precedes creation.

The love of the everlasting Destinies.
They seeing it, both Love and him abhorred,
And Jupiter unto his place restored.
And but that learning, in despite of Fate,
Will mount aloft and enter heaven's gate,
And to the seat of Jove itself advance,
Hermes[4] had slept in hell with ignorance.
Yet as a punishment they added this,
That he and Poverty should always kiss.
And to this day is every scholar poor,
Gross gold from them runs headlong to the boor.
Likewise the angry sisters° thus deluded, *the Destinies*
To venge themselves on Hermes have concluded
That Midas' brood[5] shall sit in honor's chair,
To which the Muses' sons are only heir.
And fruitful wits that in aspiring° are, *ambitious*
Shall, discontent, run into regions far,
And few great lords in virtuous deeds shall joy,
But be surprised with every garish toy.
And still enrich the lofty° servile clown, *proud*
Who with encroaching guile keeps learning down.
Then muse not Cupid's suit no better sped,° *succeeded*
Seeing in their loves the Fates were injured.

By this, sad Hero, with love unacquainted
Viewing Leander's face, fell down and fainted.
He kissed her and breathed life into her lips,
Wherewith as one displeased, away she trips.
Yet as she went full often looked behind,
And many poor excuses did she find
To linger by the way, and once she stayed,
And would have turned again, but was afraid,
In offering parley,° to be counted light. *speech*
So on she goes, and in her idle flight,
Her painted fan of curled plumes let fall,
Thinking to train° Leander therewithal. *tempt*
He, being a novice, knew not what she meant,
But stayed, and after her a letter sent.
Which joyful Hero answered in such sort,
As he had hope to scale the beauteous fort,
Wherein the liberal graces locked their wealth,
And therefore to her tower he got by stealth.
Wide open stood the door, he need not climb,
And she herself before the pointed° time, *appointed*
Had spread the board, with roses strewed the room,
And oft looked out and mused he did not come.

4. Hermes (or Mercury), as Learning (or the messenger god), must rise to a god's status; he cannot therefore be imprisoned in ignorance for long. Marlowe's unprecedented mythology is complicated: he describes "deceitful Mercury" as instituting a new golden age, then as losing it because he neglects "the Destinies," and finally as regaining divine favor because of what he signifies.

5. Like their father, the children of Midas would have the golden touch, that is, money; ironically, the Destinies decree that money is also honor.

At last he came, O who can tell the greeting,
These greedy lovers had at their first meeting.
He asked, she gave, and nothing was denied,
Both to each other quickly were affied.° *betrothed*
Look how their hands, so were their hearts united,
And what he did, she willingly requited.
(Sweet are the kisses, the embracements sweet,
When like desires and affections meet
For from the earth to heaven, is Cupid raised,
Where fancy is in equal balance paised),° *poised*
Yet she this rashness suddenly repented,
And turned aside and to herself lamented.
As if her name and honor had been wronged,
By being possessed of him for whom she longed.
I, and she wished, albeit not from her heart,
That he would leave her turret and depart.
The mirthful god of amorous pleasure smiled,
To see how he this captive nymph beguiled.
For hitherto he did but fan the fire,
And kept it down that it might burn the higher.
Now waxed she jealous, lest his love abated,
Fearing her own thoughts made her to be hated.[6]
Therefore unto him hastily she goes,
And like light Salmacis,[7] her body throws
Upon his bosom, where with yielding eyes,
She offers up herself a sacrifice,
To slake his anger, if he were displeased,
O what god would not therewith be appeased?
Like Aesop's cock,[8] this jewel he enjoyed,
And as a brother with his sister toyed,
Supposing nothing else was to be done,
Now he her favor and good will had won.
But know you not that creatures wanting sense° *inanimate*
By nature have a mutual appetence,° *desire*
And wanting organs to advance a step,
Moved by Love's force, unto each other leap?
Much more in subjects having intellect,
Some hidden influence breeds like effect.
Albeit Leander, rude in love and raw,
Long dallying with Hero, nothing saw
That might delight him more, yet he suspected
Some amorous rites or other were neglected.
Therefore unto his body, hers he clung,° *clasped*
She fearing on the rushes° to be flung, *a floor covering*
Strived with redoubled strength; the more she strived,
The more a gentle pleasing heat revived,

6. I.e., fearing that she was hated, she imagined that she was hated.
7. A nymph who pursued the boy Hermaphroditus; when she embraced him they became one, half-girl, half-boy.
8. According to Aesop, a writer of animal fables supposed to have lived in Thrace in the 6th century B.C., his cock found a precious jewel in the barnyard but rejected it because it was not a barleycorn. In the context of Marlowe's story the comparison is ambiguous.

Which taught him all that elder lovers know,
And now the same 'gan° so to scorch and glow, *began*
As in plain terms (yet cunningly) he craved it,
Love always makes those eloquent that have it.
She, with a kind of granting, put him by it,
And ever as he thought himself most nigh it,
Like to the tree of Tantalus[9] she fled,
And seeming lavish, saved her maidenhead.
Ne'er king more sought to keep his diadem
Than Hero this inestimable gem.
Above our life we love a steadfast friend,
Yet when a token of great wealth we send,
We often kiss it, often look thereon,
And stay the messenger that would be gone;
No marvel then, though Hero would not yield
So soon to part from that she dearly held.
Jewels being lost are found again; this, never.
T'is lost but once, and once lost, lost for ever.

Now had the morn° espied her lover's° steeds, *Aurora/Apollo*
Whereat she starts, puts on her purple weeds,
And red for anger that he stayed so long,
All headlong throws herself the clouds among,
And now Leander, fearing to be missed,
Embraced her suddenly, took leave, and kissed,
Long was he taking leave, and loath to go,
And kissed again, as lovers use to do,
Sad Hero wrung him by the hand and wept,
Saying, let your vows and promises be kept.
Then standing at the door, she turned about,
As loath to see Leander going out.
And now the sun that through th'orizon peeps,
As pitying these lovers, downward creeps.
So that in silence of the cloudy night,
Though it was morning, did he take his flight.
But what the secret trusty night concealed,
Leander's amorous habit soon revealed,
With Cupid's myrtle was his bonnet crowned,
About his arms the purple ribbon wound,
Wherewith she wreathed her largely spreading hair.
Nor could the youth abstain, but he must wear
The sacred ring wherewith she was endowed
When first religious chastity she vowed,
Which made his love through Sestos to be known,
And thence to Abydos sooner blown
Than he could sail, for incorporeal Fame,° *i.e., Rumor*
Whose weight consists of nothing but her name,
Is swifter than the wind, whose tardy plumes
Are reeking° water and dull earthly fumes. *vaporizing*

9. Punished in hell for revealing the secrets of the gods, Tantalus was doomed to reach for fruit from a tree whose branches were always beyond his grasp.

Home when he came, he seemed not to be there,
But like exiled air thrust from his sphere,
Set in a foreign place, and straight from thence,
Alcides-like,° by mighty violence, *like Heracles*
He would have chased away the swelling main,
That him from her unjustly did detain.
Like as the sun in a diameter[1]
Fires and enflames objects removed far,
And heateth kindly,° shining lat'rally, *gently*
So beauty sweetly quickens when 'tis nigh.
But being separated and removed,
Burns where it cherished, murders where it loved.
Therefore even as an index to a book,
So to his mind was young Leander's look.° *appearance*
O none but gods have power their love to hide,
Affection by the countenance is descried.
The light of hidden fire itself discovers,
And love that is concealed betrays poor lovers.
His secret flame apparently was seen,
Leander's father knew where he had been,
And for the same mildly rebuked his son,
Thinking to quench the fire new begun.
But love resisted once grows passionate,
And nothing more than counsel, lovers hate.
For as a hot, proud horse lightly disdains
To have his head controlled, but breaks the reins,
Spits forth the ringled bit° and with his hooves *the bit with rings*
Checks the submissive ground, so he that loves,
The more he is restrained, the worse he fares,
What is it now but mad Leander dares?
O Hero, Hero, thus he cried full oft,
And then he got him to a rock aloft.
Where having spied her tower, long stared he on't,
And prayed the narrow toiling Hellespont
To part in twain, that he might come and go,
But still the rising billows answered no.
With that he stripped him to the ivory skin,
And crying, Love I come!, leapt lively° in. *quickly*
Whereat the sapphire-visaged god[2] grew proud,
And made his capr'ing triton sound aloud,
Imagining that Ganymede, displeased,
Had left the heavens, therefore on him he seized.
Leander strived, the waves about him wound,
And pulled him to the bottom, where the ground
Was strewed with pearl and in low coral groves,
Sweet singing mermaids sported with their loves
On heaps of heavy gold, and took great pleasure
To spurn the careless sort, the shipwrack° treasure. *shipwrecked*

1. I.e., directly (as opposed to obliquely) above the earth.

2. Neptune, whose son, Triton, is both a shell and the creature who blows upon it.

For here the stately azure palace stood,
Where kingly Neptune and his train abode,
The lusty god embraced him, called him love,
And swore he never should return to Jove.
But when he knew it was not Ganymede,
For underwater he was almost dead,
He heaved him up, and looking on his face,
Beat down the gold waves with his triple mace,
Which mounted up, intending to have kissed him,
And fell in drops like tears because they missed him.
Leander, being up, began to swim,
And looking back, saw Neptune follow him.
Whereat aghast, the poor soul 'gan to cry,
O let me visit Hero ere I die!
The god put Helle's[3] bracelet on his arm,
And swore the sea should never do him harm.
He clapped his plump cheeks, with his tresses played,
And smiling wantonly, his love bewrayed.° *revealed*
He watched his arms, and as they opened wide,
At every stroke, betwixt them would he slide,
And steal a kiss, and then run out and dance,
And as he turned, cast many a lustful glance,
And threw him gaudy toys to please his eye,
And dive into the water, and there pry
Upon his breast, his thighs, and every limb,
And up again, and close beside him swim
And talk of love. Leander made reply,
You are deceived, I am no woman I.
Thereat smiled Neptune, and then told a tale,
How that a shepherd sitting in a vale,
Played with a boy so fair and kind,
As for his love both earth and heaven pined,
That of the cooling river durst not drink,
Lest water nymphs should pull him from the brink.
And when he sported in the fragrant lawns,
Goat-footed satyrs and up-staring fawns,[4]
Would steal him thence. Ere half this tale was done,
Aye me, Leander cried, th'enamored sun,
That now should shine on Thetis' glassy bower,[5]
Descends upon my radiant Hero's tower.
O that these tardy arms of mine were wings,
And as he spake, upon the waves he springs.
Neptune was angry that he gave no ear,
And in his heart, revenging malice bore.
He flung at him his mace, but as it went,
He called it in, for love made him repent.
The mace, returning back, his own hand hit,

3. The daughter of the mythical Athamas and Nephele, who had to escape from the wrath of her stepmother, Ino, on a flying ram; she fell off its back into the part of the sea called the Hellespont. Neptune is said to have rescued her; the bracelet the god puts on Leander's arm signifies divine protection.

4. Fauns, spirits who are guided by the heavens.

5. The bower of Thetis, a sea nymph, is the sea.

As meaning to be venged for darting it.
When this fresh-bleeding wound Leander viewed,
His color went and came, as if he rued
The grief which Neptune felt. In gentle breasts,
Relenting thoughts, remorse, and pity rests.
And who have hard hearts, and obdurate minds,
But vicious, harebrained, and illit'rate hinds?° *rustics*
The god, seeing him with pity to be moved,
Thereon concluded that he was beloved.
(Love is too full of faith, too credulous,
With folly and false hope deluding us.)
Wherefore Leander's fancy to surprise,
To the rich ocean for gifts he flies.
'Tis wisdom to give much, a gift prevails,
When deep, persuading oratory fails.
By this, Leander, being near the land,
Cast down his weary feet and felt the sand.
Breathless albeit he were, he rested not,
Till to the solitary tower he got.
And knocked and called, at which celestial noise,
The longing heart of Hero much more joys
Than nymphs and shepherds when the timbrell° rings, *tambourine*
Or crooked dolphin when the sailor sings.[6]
She stayed not her robes, but straight arose,
And drunk with gladness, to the door she goes,
Where seeing a naked man, she screeched for fear,
Such sighs as this to tender maids are rare.
And ran into the dark herself to hide;
Rich jewels in the dark are soonest spied.
Unto her he was led, or rather drawn,
By those white limbs which sparkled through the lawn.
The nearer he came, the more she fled,
And seeking refuge, slipped into her bed.
Whereon Leander sitting, thus begin,
Though numbing cold, all feeble, faint, and wan:

If not for love, yet love, for pity's sake,
Me in thy bed and maiden bosom take,
At least vouchsafe these arms some little room,
Who hoping to embrace thee cheerily swome.° *swam*
This head was beat with many a churlish billow,
And therefore let it rest upon thy pillow.
Herewith, afrighted, Hero shrunk away,
And in her lukewarm place Leander lay.
Whose lively head like fire from heaven fet,° *fetched*
Would animate gross clay, and higher set
The drooping thoughts of base declining souls,
Than dreary° Mars, carousing nectar bowls.° *bloody / bowls of nectar*
His hands he cast upon her like a snare,

6. The sailor is the musician Arion, who was saved by dolphins ("crooked" because of their curved backs) when they heard him sing.

She, overcome with shame and sallow fear,
Like chaste Diana when Actaeon spied her,
Being suddenly betrayed, dived down to hide her.
And as her silver body downward went,
With both her hands she made the bed a tent,
And in her own mind thought herself secure,
O'ercast with dim and darksome coverture.° *covering*
And now she lets him whisper in her ear,
Flatter, entreat, promise, protest, and swear,
Yet ever as he greedily assayed
To touch those dainties, she the Harpy[7] played
And every limb did as a soldier stout,
Defend the fort, and keep the foe-man out.
For though the rising iv'ry mount he scaled,
Which is with azure circling lines empaled,
Much like a globe (a globe may I term this,
By which love sails to regions full of bliss),
Yet there with Sisyphus[8] he toiled in vain,
Till gentle parley° did the truce obtain. *speech*
She trembling strove, this strife of hers (like that
Which made the world) another world begat,
Of unknown joy. Treason was in her thought,
And cunningly to yield herself she sought.
Seeming not won, yet won she was at length,
In such wars women use but half their strength.
Leander now like Thebian Hercules,[9]
Entered the orchard of Th'esperides.
Whose fruit none rightly can describe, but he
That pulls or shakes it from the golden tree.
Wherein Leander on her quivering breast,
Breathless spoke some thing and sighed out the rest,
Which so prevailed, as he with small ado,
Enclosed her in his arms and kissed her too.
And every kiss to her was as a charm,
And to Leander as a fresh alarm.
So that the truce was broke, and she alas,
(Poor silly maiden) at his mercy was.
Love is not full of pity (as men say)
But deaf and cruel, where he means to prey,
Even as a bird, which in our hands we wring,
Forth plungeth and oft flutters with her wing.
And now she wished this night were never done,
And sighed to think upon th'approaching sun,
For much it grieved her that the bright daylight
Should know the pleasure of this blessed night.
And then like Mars and Ericine° displayed, *Venus*

7. One of the fierce birds who snatched food from the Trojan companions of Aeneas on their way from Troy to Italy (*Aeneid* 3.225ff.).

8. The legendary king of Corinth, who in the underworld was eternally condemned to roll a large stone to the top of a hill, only to have it roll down again.

9. The eleventh labor of Hercules was to steal the golden apples of the Hesperides, daughters of the evening, who watched over their orchard on an island in a distant western sea.

Both in each others' arms, chained as they laid,
Again she knew not how to frame her look,
Or speak to him who in a moment took
That which so long, so charily she kept,
And feign by stealth away she would have crept,
And to some corner secretly have gone,
Leaving Leander in the bed alone.
But as her naked feet were whipping out,
He on the sudden clinged her so about,
That mermaid-like unto the floor she slid,
One half appeared, the other half was hid.
Thus near the bed she blushing stood upright,
And from her countenance behold ye might,
A kind of twilight break, which through the hair,
As from an orient cloud, glimpse here and there.
And round about the chamber this false morn
Brought forth the day before the day was born,
So Hero's ruddy cheek, Hero betrayed,
And her all naked to his sight displayed.
Whence his admiring eyes more pleasure took
Than Dis on heaps of gold fixing his look.
By this Apollo's golden harp began,
To sound forth music to the ocean,
Which watchful Hesperus[1] no sooner heard,
But he the day bright-bearing car prepared
And ran before, as harbinger of light,
And with his flaming beams mocked ugly Night,
Till she, o'ercome with anguish, shame, and rage,
Danged° down to Hell her loathsome carriage. *hurled*
Desunt nonnulla.[2]

The Tragical History of Dr. Faustus

Marlowe's play is the first dramatic rendition of the medieval legend of a man who sold his soul to the devil. Sixteenth-century readers associated him with a necromancer named Dr. Faustus, and Marlowe exploited this identification when he reworked the medieval plot for his play. Rejecting the usual learning available to ambitious men—philosophy, medicine, law, and theology—Marlowe's Faustus signs a contract with the devil, represented in this case by his servant, Mephostophilis; in exchange for his soul, Faustus gains superhuman powers for twenty-four years. He uses these powers to conjure the Pope in Rome into giving the Protestant Emperor Charles V authority over the church through a surrogate Pope, Bruno; but his powers are also deployed in the banal trickery of simple and even criminal characters. The play is enigmatic on points of doctrine. Mephostophilis describes hell not as a locale but rather as the state of mind of one who has rejected God—a description that Milton will later amplify—telling Faustus: "this is hell, nor am I out of it." And Faustus, having worshipped the devil, is nevertheless offered a chance to repent and find salvation even at the very end of his alloted life. But he rejects God's love in favor of a night with Helen of Troy, praising her in lines that

1. Marlowe mistakes the evening star, Hesperus, for the morning star, Venus.
2. "Some things are missing." Added in 1598 by Marlowe's printer, Edward Blunt, who believed the poem was unfinished.

are now famous: "Was this the face that launched a thousand ships, / And burnt the topless towers of Ilium?" The play concludes with a report of Faustus' mangled body, torn to bits by the demon to whom he had given his soul.

A short version of the play, in thirteen scenes, was published in 1604; known as the A text, it was probably used by touring companies. The longer B text, given here, was published in 1616, probably based on Marlowe's original manuscript but also incorporating revisions and additions by Marlowe or others, as (typically in this period) the play continued to evolve in performance.

The Tragical History of Dr. Faustus

Dramatis Personae

CHORUS
FAUSTUS
WAGNER, *Servant to Faustus*
GOOD ANGEL AND EVIL ANGEL
VALDES } *Friends to Faustus*
CORNELIUS }
MEPHOSTOPHILIS
LUCIFER
BELZEBUB
THE SEVEN DEADLY SINS
CLOWN/ROBIN
DICK
RAFE
VINTNER
CARTER
HOSTESS
THE POPE
BRUNO
RAYMOND, *King of Hungary*
CHARLES, *the German Emperor*
MARTINO
FREDERICK
BENVOLIO
SAXONY
DUKE OF VANHOLT
DUCHESS OF VANHOLT
SPIRITS IN THE SHAPES OF ALEXANDER THE GREAT, DARIUS, PARAMOUR, AND HELEN
AN OLD MAN
SCHOLARS, SOLDIERS, DEVILS, COURTIERS, CARDINALS, MONKS, CUPIDS

[*Enter Chorus.*]

CHORUS Not marching in the fields of Thrasimene,[1]
Where Mars did mate the warlike Carthigens,
Nor sporting in the dalliance of love
In courts of kings where state is overturned,
Nor in the pomp of proud audacious deeds,
Intends our muse to vaunt his heavenly verse.[2]
Only this, gentles: we must now perform
The form of Faustus' fortunes, good or bad.
And now to patient judgments we appeal,
And speak for Faustus in his infancy.
Now is he born, of parents base of stock,
In Germany, within a town called Rhodes.
At riper years to Wittenberg he went,
Whereas his kinsmen chiefly brought him up.
So much he profits in divinity,
The fruitful plot° of scholarism graced, *field*

1. Trasimeno, a lake in Italy near Rome. The Carthaginian general Hannibal conquered Roman forces at Trasimeno in 217 B.C.; Marlowe's "Mars" is probably a reference to the Roman army, which "mated" or engaged the enemy opposition there.

2. These lines may refer to plays Marlowe had previously staged and whose subjects were war (*Tamburlaine*) and love (*Edward II, Dido, Queen of Carthage*).

That shortly he was graced with Doctor's name,
Excelling all; and sweetly can dispute
In th' heavenly matters of theology.
Till swol'n with cunning of a self-conceit,
His waxen wings did mount above his reach,
And melting, heavens conspired his overthrow.[3]
For falling to a devilish exercise,
And glutted now with learning's golden gifts,
He surfeits upon cursed necromancy.
Nothing so sweet as magic is to him,
Which he prefers before his chiefest bliss:
And this the man that in his study sits.

Act 1

Scene One

[*Faustus in his study*.]

FAUSTUS Settle thy studies, Faustus, and begin
To sound the depth of that thou wilt profess.
Having commenced, be a divine in show,
Yet level at the end of every art
And live and die in Aristotle's works.
Sweet Analytics, 'tis thou hast ravished me.[4]
Bene disserere est finis logices.
Is "to dispute well logic's chiefest end"?
Affords this art no greater miracle?
Then read no more: thou hast attained that end.
A greater subject fitteth Faustus' wit.
Bid *on cai me on*° farewell. And Galen,[5] come. *being and non-being*
Seeing, *ubi desinit philosophus, ibi incipit medicus*.
Be a physician, Faustus: heap up gold
And be eternized for some wondrous cure.
Summum bonum medicinae sanitas:
"The end of physic is our body's health."
Why, Faustus, hast thou not attained that end?
Is not thy common talk sound aphorisms?° *wise sayings*
Are not thy bills hung up as monuments,
Whereby whole cities have escaped the plague,
And thousand desperate maladies been cured?
Yet art thou still but Faustus and a man.
Couldst thou make men to live eternally,
Or being dead, raise them to life again,
Then this profession were to be esteemed.

3. Faustus is compared to the legendary figure of Icarus, whose father, the master craftsman Daedalus, made him a pair of wings that were attached to his body with wax. Icarus flew too near the sun, the wax supporting his wings melted, and he fell to the sea. The legend is generally understood to signify the consequences of pride and presumption.

4. Aristotle (384–22 B.C.), the best known of the Greek philosophers, wrote on the natural and social sciences. His *Analytics* dealt with logic.

5. Greek physician (130–200) whose works on medicine were studied through the early modern period. Faustus welcomes his change of authorities with "where the philosopher ends, the physician begins."

Physic, farewell. Where is Justinian?[6]
Si una eademque res legatur duobus,
Alter rem, alter valorem rei etc.,
A petty case of paltry legacies!
Exhaereditare filium non potest pater, nisi—
Such is the subject of the institute
And universal body of the law.
This study fits a mercenary drudge,
Who aims at nothing but external trash,
Too servile and illiberal for me.
When all is done Divinity is best.
Jerome's Bible![7] Faustus, view it well.
Stipendium peccati mors est. Ha! Stipendium etc.,
"The reward of sin is death."[8] That's hard.
Si pecasse negamus, fallimur, et nulla est in nobis veritas.
"If we say that we have no sin
We deceive ourselves, and there is no truth in us."[9]
Why then, belike, we must sin,
And so consequently die.
Ay, we must die, an everlasting death.
What doctrine call you this? *Che sera, sera.*
"What will be, shall be." Divinity, adieu!
These necromantic books are heavenly,
Lines, circles, scenes, letters and characters:
Ay, these are those that Faustus most desires.
Oh, what a world of profit and delight,
Of power, of honor, of omnipotence,
Is promised to the studious artisan!
All things that move between the quiet poles
Shall be at my command. Emperors and kings
Are but obeyed in their several provinces.
Nor can they raise the wind or rend the clouds.
But his dominion that exceeds in this
Stretcheth as far as doth the mind of man:
A sound magician is a demi-god.
Here, tire° my brains to get° a deity. *use / engender*

[*Enter Wagner.*]

Wagner, commend me to my dearest friends,
The German Valdes and Cornelius.
Request them earnestly to visit me.

WAGNER I will, sir. [*Exit.*]

FAUSTUS Their conference will be a greater help to me
Than all my labors, plod I ne'er so fast.

6. Justinian, Emperor of Byzantium (483–565), codified all of Roman law; his *Institutes* provided the basis for civil law in England as well as on the continent. Faustus cites a principle of estate law: "if one and the same thing is bequeathed to two people, one of them should have the thing itself, and the other the value of it"; and "the father may not disinherit the son."

7. Jerome (347–420), a theologian who translated the Greek Bible and some of the Hebrew Bible into Latin, also wrote on Christian doctrine.

8. Romans 6.23.

9. 1 John 1.8.

[*Enter the Good and Evil Angels*.]

GOOD ANGEL Oh Faustus, lay that damned book aside,
And gaze not on it lest it tempt thy soul
And heap God's heavy wrath upon thy head.
Read, read the scriptures: that is blasphemy.

EVIL ANGEL Go forward, Faustus, in that famous art
Wherein all nature's treasure is contained.
Be thou on earth as Jove[1] is in the sky,
Lord and commander of these elements. [*Exeunt Angels*.]

FAUSTUS How am I glutted with conceit° of this! *idea*
Shall I make spirits fetch me what I please,
Resolve me of all ambiguities,
Perform what desperate enterprise I will?
I'll have them fly to India for gold,
Ransack the ocean for orient pearl,
And search all corners of the new-found world
For pleasant fruits and princely delicates.
I'll have them read me strange philosophy,
And tell the secrets of all foreign kings.
I'll have them wall all Germany with brass,
And make swift Rhine circle fair Wittenberg.
I'll have them fill the public schools° with silk, *college lecture halls*
Wherewith the students shall be bravely clad.
I'll levy soldiers with the coin they bring,
And chase the Prince of Parma from our land,
And reign sole king of all the provinces.
Yea, stranger engines for the brunt of war
Than was the fiery keel[2] at Antwerp's bridge
I'll make my servile spirits to invent.
Come, German Valdes and Cornelius,
And make me blest with your sage conference.

[*Enter Valdes and Cornelius*.]

Valdes, sweet Valdes and Cornelius!
Know that your words have won me at the last
To practice magic and concealed arts.
Yet not your words only but mine own fantasy
That will receive no object° for my head, *idea*
But ruminates on necromantic skill.
Philosophy is odious and obscure.
Both law and physic are for petty wits.
Divinity is basest of the three,
Unpleasant, harsh, contemptible and vile.
'Tis magic, magic that hath ravished me.
Then, gentle friends, aid me in this attempt,
And I, that have with subtle syllogisms
Gravelled the pastors of the German Church

1. Roman god of the heavens and king of the gods.

2. In 1585 a fireship destroyed the Duke of Parma's bridge across the river Scheldt in the city of Antwerp.

And made the flowering pride of Wittenberg
Swarm to my problems as the infernal spirits
On sweet Musaeus[3] when he came to hell,
Will be as cunning as Agrippa was,
Whose shadow made all Europe honor him.

VALDES Faustus, these books, thy wit and our experience
Shall make all nations to canonize us,
As Indian moors obey their Spanish lords.
So shall the spirits of every element
Be always serviceable to us three.
Like lions shall they guard us when we please;
Like Almain rutters° with their horsemen's staves; *German knights*
Or Lapland giants trotting by our sides.
Sometimes like women or unwedded maids,
Shadowing more beauty in their airy brows
Than has the white breasts of the queen of love.
From Venice shall they drag huge argosies,° *merchant ships*
And from America the golden fleece[4]
That yearly stuffs old Philip's treasury
If learned Faustus will be resolute.

FAUSTUS Valdes, as resolute am I in this
As thou to live, therefore object° it not. *reject*

CORNELIUS The miracles that magic will perform
Will make thee vow to study nothing else.
He that is grounded in Astrology,
Enriched with tongues,° well seen° in minerals, *languages / educated*
Hath all the principles magic doth require.
Then doubt not, Faustus, but to be renowned,
And more frequented° for this mystery *sought after*
Than heretofore the Delphian oracle.[5]
The spirits tell me they can dry the sea,
And fetch the treasure of all foreign wracks,° *wrecks*
Yea, all the wealth that our forefathers hid
Within the massy° entrails of the earth. *massive*
Then tell me, Faustus, what shall we three want?

FAUSTUS Nothing, Cornelius! Oh, this cheers my soul.
Come, show me some demonstrations magical,
That I may conjure in some bushy grove,
And have these joys in full possession.

VALDES Then haste thee to some solitary grove,
And bear wise Bacon's and Albanus'[6] works,

3. Faustus wants to model himself on Musaeus, a legendary poet, said to have been a student of Orpheus, and Cornelius Agrippa of Nettesheim (1486–1535), a philosopher known for his works on scepticism and the occult.

4. The "golden fleece" refers to the treasure (the gold wool of a divine ram) sought and won by the legendary hero, Jason, and his companions, known as the Argonauts (from the name of their ship, the Argo). Faustus alludes to this treasure when he refers to the gold the King of Castile, Philip II, was taking from lands in the New World.

5. A shrine of Apollo, the god of the sun, music, and medicine, in his temple at Delphi, where his priestess, called the Pythia, spoke incoherent phrases that a priest later interpreted as prophecies.

6. Roger Bacon (1214–1294) was an English Franciscan monk and a lecturer at Oxford University who was interested in natural science, particularly alchemy. Albanus is perhaps Pietro D'Abano (1250–1360), who was supposed to be a sorcerer and was burned in effigy by the Inquisition after his death.

The Hebrew Psalter and New Testament;
And whatsoever else is requisite
We will inform thee e're our conference cease.

CORNELIUS Valdes, first let him know the words of art,
And then, all other ceremonies learned,
Faustus may try his cunning by himself.

VALDES First I'll instruct thee in the rudiments,
And then wilt thou be perfecter than I.

FAUSTUS Then come and dine with me, and after meat
We'll canvass every quiddity° thereof, *question*
For ere I sleep, I'll try what I can do.
This night I'll conjure, though I die therefore. [*Exeunt.*]

Scene Two

[*Enter two Scholars.*]

FIRST SCHOLAR I wonder what's become of Faustus, that was wont to make our schools ring with *sic probo.*[7]

[*Enter Wagner.*]

SECOND SCHOLAR That shall we presently know. Here comes his boy.

FIRST SCHOLAR How now, sirrah, where's thy master?

WAGNER God in heaven knows.

SECOND SCHOLAR Why, dost not thou know then?

WAGNER Yes, I know, but that follows not.

FIRST SCHOLAR Go to, sirrah. Leave your jesting and tell us where he is.

WAGNER That follows not by force of argument, which you, being licentiates,[8] should stand upon. Therefore, acknowledge your error and be attentive.

SECOND SCHOLAR Then you will not tell us?

WAGNER You are deceived, for I will tell you. Yet if you were not dunces, you would never ask me such a question. For is he not *Corpus naturale*?[9] And is not that *mobile*? Then wherefore should you ask me such a question? But that I am by nature phlegmatic, slow to wrath and prone to lechery (to love, I would say), it were not for you to come within forty foot of the place of execution, although I do not doubt but to see you both hanged the next sessions. Thus, having triumphed over you, I will set my countenance like a precision,[1] and begin to speak thus: "Truly, my dear brethren, my master is within at dinner with Valdes and Cornelius, as this wine, if it could speak, would inform your worships. And so the Lord bless you, preserve you and keep you, my dear brethren." [*Exit.*]

FIRST SCHOLAR Oh Faustus, then I fear that which I have long suspected:
That thou art fallen into that damned art
For which they two are infamous through the world.

SECOND SCHOLAR Were he a stranger, not allied to me,
The danger of his soul would make me mourn.
But come, let us go, and inform the Rector.
It may be his grave counsel may reclaim him.

FIRST SCHOLAR I fear me nothing will reclaim him now.

SECOND SCHOLAR Yet let us see what we can do. [*Exeunt.*]

7. "Thus I prove."
8. Postgraduates.
9. A natural body.
1. Puritan.

Scene Three

[*Thunder. Enter Lucifer and Four Devils. Faustus to them with this speech.*]

FAUSTUS Now that the gloomy shadow of the night,
Longing to view Orion's drizzling look,
Leaps from th'Antarctic world unto the sky,
And dims the welkin° with her pitchy breath, *heaven*
Faustus, begin thine incantations
And try if devils will obey thy hest,° *command*
Seeing thou hast prayed and sacrificed to them.
Within this circle is Jehovah's name
Forward and backward anagrammatized:
The abbreviated names of holy saints,
Figures of every adjunct to the heavens,
And characters of signs and evening stars,
By which the spirits are enforced to rise.
Then fear not, Faustus, to be resolute
And try the utmost magic can perform.[2]

[*Thunder.*]

Sint mihi dei acherontis propitii, valeat numen triplex Jehovae, ignei areii, aquatani spiritus salvete: orientis princeps Belzebub, inferni ardentis monarcha et demigorgon, propitiamus vos, ut appareat, et surgat Mephostophilis *(Dragon)*[3] *quod tumeraris: per Jehovam, gehennam, et consecratam aquam quam nunc spargo; signumque crucis quod nunc facio; et per vota nostra ipse nunc surgat nobis dicatus Mephostophilis.*

[*Enter a Devil.*]

I charge thee to return and change thy shape.
Thou art too ugly to attend on me.
Go, and return an old Franciscan friar:
That holy shape becomes a devil best. [*Exit Devil.*]
I see there's virtue in my heavenly words.
Who would not be proficient in this art?
How pliant is this Mephostophilis!
Full of obedience and humility,
Such is the force of magic and my spells.
Now, Faustus, thou art conjuror laureate:[4]
Thou canst command great Mephostophilis.
Quin redis Mephostophilis fratris imagine.

[*Enter Mephostophilis.*]

MEPHOSTOPHILIS Now, Faustus, what wouldst thou have me do?

FAUSTUS I charge thee wait upon me whilst I live,
To do whatever Faustus shall command,

2. Faustus styles himself an accomplished magician. He now repeats, in Latin, his command to Mephostophilis to appear in the guise of a friar: "May the gods of the underworld be kind to me; may the triple deity of Jehovah be gone; to the spirits of fire, air, and water, greetings. Prince of the east, Beelzebub, monarch of the fires below, and Demogorgon, we appeal to you so that Mephostophilis may appear and rise. Why do you delay? By Jehovah, hell and the hallowed water which I now sprinkle, and the sign of the cross, which I now make, and by our vows, let Mephostophilis himself now arise to serve us."

3. This appears to be a stage direction that was inserted into the playtext; it probably indicates that at this point the figure of a dragon should come on stage.

4. Faustus, stating he is a "conjurer laureate" or honored magician, asks again, in Latin: "Why do you not return, Mephostophilis, in the guise of a friar?"

Be it to make the moon drop from her sphere,
Or the ocean to overwhelm the world.
MEPHOSTOPHILIS I am a servant to great Lucifer,
And may not follow thee without his leave.
No more than he commands must we perform.
FAUSTUS Did not he charge thee to appear to me?
MEPHOSTOPHILIS No, I came now hither of mine own accord.
FAUSTUS Did not my conjuring speeches raise thee? Speak.
MEPHOSTOPHILIS That was the cause, but yet *per accidens*;° *by accident*
For when we hear one rack the name of God,
Abjure the scriptures and his saviour Christ,
We fly in hope to get his glorious soul.
Nor will we come unless he use such means
Whereby he is in danger to be damned.
Therefore the shortest cut for conjuring
Is stoutly to abjure all godliness
And pray devoutly to the price of hell.
FAUSTUS So Faustus hath already done, and holds this principle:
There is no chief but only Belzebub,
To whom Faustus doth dedicate himself.
This word "damnation" terrifies not me,
For I confound hell in elysium.° *heaven*
My ghost be with the old philosophers.
But leaving these vain trifles of men's souls,
Tell me, what is that Lucifer, thy lord?
MEPHOSTOPHILIS Arch-regent and commander of all spirits.
FAUSTUS Was not that Lucifer an angel once?
MEPHOSTOPHILIS Yes, Faustus, and most dearly loved of God.
FAUSTUS How comes it then that he is prince of devils?
MEPHOSTOPHILIS Oh, by aspiring pride and insolence,
For which God threw him from the face of heaven.
FAUSTUS And what are you that live with Lucifer?
MEPHOSTOPHILIS Unhappy spirits that fell with Lucifer,
Conspired against our God with Lucifer,
And are for ever damned with Lucifer.
FAUSTUS Where are you damned?
MEPHOSTOPHILIS In hell.
FAUSTUS How comes it then that thou art out of hell?
MEPHOSTOPHILIS Why, this is hell, nor am I out of it.
Think'st thou that I that saw the face of God
And tasted the eternal joys of heaven,
Am not tormented with ten thousand hells
In being deprived of everlasting bliss?
Oh, Faustus, leave these frivolous demands,
Which strike a terror to my fainting soul.
FAUSTUS What, is great Mephostophilis so passionate
For being deprived of the joys of heaven?
Learn thou of Faustus manly fortitude,
And scorn those joys thou never shalt possess.

Go, bear these tidings to great Lucifer,
Seeing Faustus hath incurred eternal death
By desperate thoughts against Jove's deity.
Say he surrenders up to him his soul,
So he will spare him four and twenty years,
Letting him live in all voluptuousness,
Having thee ever to attend on me,
To give me whatsoever I shall ask,
To tell me whatsoever I demand,
To slay mine enemies and to aid my friends
And always be obedient to my will.
Go, and return to mighty Lucifer,
And meet me in my study at midnight,
And then resolve me of thy master's mind.

MEPHOSTOPHILIS I will, Faustus. [*Exit.*]

FAUSTUS Had I as many souls as there be stars,
I'd give them all for Mephostophilis.
By him I'll be great emperor of the world,
And make a bridge through the air
To pass the ocean. With a band of men
I'll join the hills that bind the Affrick shore,
And make that country continent to Spain,
And both contributory to my crown.
The Emperor shall not live but by my leave,
Nor any potentate of Germany.
Now that I have obtained what I desired,
I'll live in speculation of this art
Till Mephostophilis return again. [*Exit.*]

Scene Four

[*Enter Wagner and the Clown.*]

WAGNER Come hither, sirrah boy.

CLOWN Boy? Oh, disgrace to my person! Zounds! "Boy" in your face! You have seen many boys with beards, I am sure.

WAGNER Sirrah, hast thou no comings in?

CLOWN Yes, and goings out too, you may see, sir.

WAGNER Alas, poor slave. See how poverty jests in his nakedness. I know the villain's out of service and so hungry that I know he would give his soul to the devil for a shoulder of mutton though it were blood-raw.

CLOWN Not so neither. I had need to have it well roasted, and good sauce to it, if I pay so dear, I can tell you.

WAGNER Sirrah, wilt thou be my man and wait on me? And I will make thee go like *Qui mihi discipulus*.[5]

CLOWN What, in verse?

WAGNER No, slave, in beaten silk and stavesacre.[6]

CLOWN Stavesacre? That's good to kill vermin. Then belike, if I serve you I shall be lousy.

5. One who is my disciple.

6. A poison.

WAGNER Why, so thou shalt be whether thou dost it or no. For, sirrah, if thou dost not presently bind thyself to me for seven years, I'll turn all the lice about thee into familiars,[7] and make them tear thee in pieces.

CLOWN Nay, sir, you may save yourself a labor, for they are as familiar with me as if they paid for their meat and drink, I can tell you.

WAGNER Well, sirrah, leave your jesting and take these guilders.[8]

CLOWN Yes, marry, sir, and I thank you too.

WAGNER So, now thou art to be at an hour's warning, whensoever and wheresoever the devil shall fetch thee.

CLOWN Here, take your guilders.

WAGNER Truly, I'll none of them.

CLOWN Truly but you shall.

WAGNER Bear witness I gave them him.

CLOWN Bear witness I give them you again.

WAGNER Not I. Thou art pressed. Prepare thyself, for I will presently raise up two devils, to carry thee away: Banio, Belcher!

CLOWN Belcher? And Belcher come here, I'll belch him! I am not afraid of a devil.

[*Enter Two Devils and the Clown runs up and down crying*.]

WAGNER How now, sir, will you serve me now?

CLOWN Ay, good Wagner. Take away the devil then.

WAGNER Baliol and Belcher, spirits, away! [*Exeunt Devils*.]

CLOWN What, are they gone? A vengeance on them! They have vile long nails. There was a he-devil and a she-devil. I'll tell you how you shall know them: all he-devils has horns, and all she-devils has clifts[9] and cloven feet.

WAGNER Well, sirrah, follow me.

CLOWN But, do you hear, if I should serve you, would you teach me to raise up Banio's and Belcheo's?

WAGNER I will teach thee to turn thyself to anything, to a dog, or a cat, or a mouse, or a rat, or anything.

CLOWN How? A Christian fellow to a dog or a cat, a mouse or a rat? No, no, sir, if you turn me into anything, let it be in the likeness of a little pretty frisking flea, that I may be here and there and everywhere. Oh, I'll tickle the pretty wenches' plackets![1] I'll be amongst them, i'faith.

WAGNER Well, sirrah, come.

CLOWN But do you hear, Wagner?

WAGNER How? Baliol and Belcher!

CLOWN Oh Lord, I pray, sir, let Banio and Belcher go sleep.

WAGNER Villain, call me Master Wagner, and see that you walk attentively and let your right eye be always diametrically fixed upon my left heel, that thou mayest *Quasi vestigias nostras insistere*.[2] [*Exit*.]

CLOWN God forgive me, he speaks Dutch fustian![3] Well, I'll follow him. I'll serve him, that's flat. [*Exit*.]

Scene Five

[*Enter Faustus in his study*.]

FAUSTUS Now, Faustus, must thou needs be damned?

7. Spirits.
8. Coins.
9. Clefts.
1. Petticoats.
2. Wagner mocks the Clown by telling him to walk "as if to tread in our footsteps," knowing that the clown's magic will never be as powerful as his own.
3. Nonsense.

And canst thou not be saved?
What boots it then to think on God or heaven?
Away with such vain fancies and despair,
Despair in God and trust in Belzebub.° *the Devil*
Now go not backward. No, Faustus, be resolute.
Why waverest thou? Oh, something soundeth in mine ears
Abjure this magic, turn to God again.
Ay, and Faustus will turn to God again.
To God? He loves thee not.
The God thou servest is thine own appetite,
Wherein is fixed the love of Belzebub.
To him I'll build an altar and a church,
And offer lukewarm blood of new-born babes.

[*Enter the Good and Evil Angels.*]

GOOD ANGEL Sweet Faustus, leave that execrable art.
FAUSTUS Contrition, prayer, repentance, what of these?
GOOD ANGEL Oh, they are means to bring thee unto heaven.
EVIL ANGEL Rather illusions, fruits of lunacy,
That make men foolish that do trust them most.
GOOD ANGEL Sweet Faustus, think of heaven and heavenly things.
EVIL ANGEL No, Faustus, think of honor and of wealth. [*Exeunt Angels.*]
FAUSTUS Of wealth!
Why, the signory of Emden[4] shall be mine!
When Mephostophilis shall stand by me,
What God can hurt thee, Faustus? Thou art safe.
Cast no more doubts. Come, Mephostophilis,
And bring glad tidings from great Lucifer.
Is't not midnight? Come Mephostophilis!
Veni, veni,° *Mephostophile!* *come, come*

[*Enter Mephostophilis.*]

Now tell me, what saith Lucifer, thy lord?
MEPHOSTOPHILIS That I shall wait on Faustus whilst he lives,
So he will buy my service with his soul.
FAUSTUS Already Faustus hath hazarded that for thee.
MEPHOSTOPHILIS But now thou must bequeath it solemnly,
And write a deed of gift with thine own blood,
For that security craves great Lucifer.
If thou deny it, I will back to hell.
FAUSTUS Stay, Mephostophilis, and tell me
What good will my soul do thy lord?
MEPHOSTOPHILIS Enlarge his kingdom.
FAUSTUS Is that the reason why he tempts us thus?
MEPHOSTOPHILIS *Solamen miseris, socios habuisse doloris.*[5]
FAUSTUS Why, have you any pain, that torture others?
MEPHOSTOPHILIS As great as have the human souls of men.
But tell me, Faustus, shall I have thy soul?

4. At this point in his career, Faustus aspires to the governorship of Emden, an important trading town in Germany, a pathetic exchange for his immortal soul.

5. Mephostophilis states that misery loves company in hell: "It is a comfort in wretchedness to have companions in woe."

And I will be thy slave and wait on thee,
And give thee more than thou hast wit to ask.
FAUSTUS Ay, Mephostophilis, I'll give it thee.
MEPHOSTOPHILIS Then, Faustus, stab thy arm courageously,
And bind thy soul, that at some certain day
Great Lucifer may claim it as his own,
And then be thou as great as Lucifer.
FAUSTUS Lo, Mephostophilis, for love of thee
I cut mine arm, and with my proper blood
Assure my soul to be great Lucifer's,
Chief lord and regent of perpetual night.
View here the blood that trickles from mine arm,
And let it be propitious for my wish.
MEPHOSTOPHILIS But, Faustus, thou must write it in manner of a deed of gift.
FAUSTUS Ay, so I will. But, Mephostophilis,
My blood congeals and I can write no more!
MEPHOSTOPHILIS I'll fetch thee fire to dissolve it straight. [*Exit.*]
FAUSTUS What might the staying of my blood portend?
Is it unwilling I should write this bill?
Why streams it not that I may write afresh?
"Faustus gives to thee his soul": ah, there it stayed!
Why shouldst thou not? Is not thy soul thine own?
Then write again: "Faustus gives to thee his soul."
[*Enter Mephostophilis with a chafer of coals.*]
MEPHOSTOPHILIS Here's fire. Come, Faustus, set it on.
FAUSTUS So, now my blood begins to clear again.
Now will I make an end immediately.
MEPHOSTOPHILIS Oh what will not I do to obtain his soul!
FAUSTUS *Consummatum est:*[6] this bill is ended,
And Faustus hath bequeathed his soul to Lucifer.
But what is this inscription on mine arm?
Homo fuge!° Whither should I flee? *Flee, O man*
If unto heaven, he'll throw me down to hell.
My senses are deceived: here's nothing writ!
Oh, yes, I see it plain. Even here is writ
Homo fuge. Yet shall not Faustus fly.
MEPHOSTOPHILIS I'll fetch him somewhat to delight his mind. [*Exit.*]
[*Enter Devils, giving crowns and rich apparel to Faustus; they dance and then depart. Enter Mephostophilis.*]
FAUSTUS What means this show? Speak, Mephostophilis.
MEPHOSTOPHILIS Nothing, Faustus, but to delight thy mind,
And let thee see what magic can perform.
FAUSTUS But may I raise such spirits when I please?
MEPHOSTOPHILIS Ay, Faustus, and do greater things than these.
FAUSTUS Then there's enough for a thousand souls.
Here, Mephostophilis, receive this scroll,
A deed of gift, of body and of soul:

6. Faustus speaks the last words of Jesus on the cross: "It is finished" (John 19.30), and then realizes he must try to avoid the consequences: "Flee, O man."

But yet conditionally, that thou perform
All covenants and articles between us both.
MEPHOSTOPHILIS Faustus, I swear by hell and Lucifer
To effect all promises between us both.
FAUSTUS Then hear me read it, Mephostophilis.
On these conditions following:
First, that Faustus may be a spirit in form and substance.
Secondly, that Mephostophilis shall be his servant, and be by him commanded.
Thirdly, that Mephostophilis shall do for him, and bring him whatsoever.
Fourthly, that he shall be in his chamber or house invisible.
Lastly, that he shall appear to the said John Faustus at all times, in what shape and form soever he please.
I, John Faustus of Wittenberg Doctor, by these presents, do give both body and soul to Lucifer, Prince of the East, and his minister Mephostophilis, and furthermore grant unto them that four and twenty years being expired, and these articles above written being inviolate, full power to fetch or carry the said John Faustus, body and soul, flesh, blood or goods, into their habitation wheresoever.
By me, John Faustus.
MEPHOSTOPHILIS Speak, Faustus, do you deliver this as your deed?
FAUSTUS Ay, take it, and the devil give thee good of it.
MEPHOSTOPHILIS So now, Faustus, ask me what thou wilt.
FAUSTUS First I will question with thee about hell.
Tell me, where is the place that men call hell?
MEPHOSTOPHILIS Under the heavens.
FAUSTUS Ay, so are all things else; but whereabouts?
MEPHOSTOPHILIS Within the bowels of these elements,
Where we are tortured and remain for ever.
Hell hath no limits, nor is circumscribed
In one self place. But where we are is hell,
And where hell is there must we ever be.
And to be short, when all the world dissolves
And every creature shall be purified,
All places shall be hell that is not heaven.
FAUSTUS Come, I think hell's a fable.
MEPHOSTOPHILIS Ay, think so still, till experience change thy mind.
FAUSTUS Why, dost thou think that Faustus shall be damned?
MEPHOSTOPHILIS Ay, of necessity, for here's the scroll
In which thou hast given thy soul to Lucifer.
FAUSTUS Ay, and body too, but what of that?
Think'st thou that Faustus is so fond to imagine
That after this life there is any pain?
Tush, these are trifles and old wives' tales.
MEPHOSTOPHILIS But Faustus, I am an instance to prove the contrary,
For I tell thee I am damned, and now in hell.
FAUSTUS How? Now in hell? Nay, and this be hell, I'll willingly be damned here. What! Sleeping, eating, walking and disputing? But leaving this, let me have a wife, the fairest maid in Germany, for I am wanton and lascivious, and can not live without a wife.
MEPHOSTOPHILIS How, a wife? I prithee, Faustus, talk not of a wife.

FAUSTUS Nay, sweet Mephostophilis, fetch me one, for I will have one.

MEPHOSTOPHILIS Well, thou wilt have one. Sit there till I come: I'll fetch thee a wife in the devil's name.

[*Enter a Devil dressed like a woman, with fireworks.*]

FAUSTUS What sight is this?

MEPHOSTOPHILIS Tell, Faustus, how dost thou like thy wife?

FAUSTUS A plague on her for a hot whore.

MEPHOSTOPHILIS Tut, Faustus, marriage is but a ceremonial toy.
If thou lovest me, think no more of it.
I'll cull thee out the fairest courtesans
And bring them every morning to thy bed.
She whom thine eye shall like, thy heart shall have,
Be she as chaste as was Penelope,[7]
As wise as Saba, or as beautiful
As was bright Lucifer before his fall.
Here, take this book, and peruse it well.
The iterating° of these lines brings gold, *repetition*
The framing of this circle on the ground
Brings thunder, whirlwinds, storm and lightning.
Pronounce this thrice devoutly to thyself
And men in harness shall appear to thee,
Ready to execute what thou commandest.

FAUSTUS Thanks, Mephostophilis. Yet fain would I have a book wherein I might behold all spells and incantations, that I might raise up spirits when I please.

MEPHOSTOPHILIS Here they are in this book. [*There turn to them.*]

FAUSTUS Now would I have a book where I might see all characters and planets of the heavens, that I might know their motions and dispositions.

MEPHOSTOPHILIS Here they are too. [*Turn to them.*]

FAUSTUS Nay, let me have one book more, and then I have done, wherein I might see all plants, herbs and trees that grow upon the earth.

MEPHOSTOPHILIS Here they be.

FAUSTUS Oh thou art deceived.

MEPHOSTOPHILIS Tut, I warrant thee. [*Turn to them.*]

Act 2

Scene One

[*Enter Faustus in his study, and Mephostophilis.*]

FAUSTUS When I behold the heavens then I repent,
And curse thee, wicked Mephostophilis,
Because thou hast deprived me of those joys.

MEPHOSTOPHILIS 'Twas thine own seeking, Faustus, thank thyself.
But thinkst thou heaven is such a glorious thing?
I tell thee, Faustus, it is not half so fair
As thou or any man that breathes on earth.

FAUSTUS How prov'st thou that?

MEPHOSTOPHILIS 'Twas made for man; then he's more excellent.

7. Mephostophilis compares the ideal woman to Penelope, the wife of Odysseus, who waited 20 years for him to return from the Trojan wars, and to Saba, the wise Queen of Sheba, who taught King Solomon, known himself for his wisdom (1 Kings).

FAUSTUS If heaven was made for man, 'twas made for me.
I will renounce this magic and repent.
[*Enter the Good and Evil Angels*.]
GOOD ANGEL Faustus, repent. Yet God will pity thee.
EVIL ANGEL Thou art a spirit. God cannot pity thee.
FAUSTUS Who buzzeth in mine ears I am a spirit?
Be I a devil, yet God may pity me.
Yea, God will pity me if I repent.
EVIL ANGEL Ay, but Faustus never shall repent. [*Exeunt*.]
FAUSTUS My heart's so hardened I cannot repent.
Scarce can I name salvation, faith or heaven,
But fearful echoes thunder in mine ears
"Faustus, thou art damned." Then swords and knives,
Poison, guns, halters and envenomed steel
Are laid before me to dispatch myself.
And long ere this I should have done the deed,
Had not sweet pleasure conquered deep despair.
Have not I made blind Homer sing to me
Of Alexander's love and Oenon's death?[1]
And hath not he that built the walls of Thebes
With ravishing sound of his melodious harp
Made music with my Mephostophilis?[2]
Why should I die then, or basely despair?
I am resolved, Faustus shall not repent.
Come, Mephostophilis, let us dispute again,
And reason of divine astrology.
Speak, are there many spheres above the moon?
Are all celestial bodies but one globe,
As is the substance of this centric earth?[3]
MEPHOSTOPHILIS As are the elements, such are the heavens,
Even from the moon unto the empyrial orb,
Mutually folded in each other's spheres,
And jointly move upon one axle-tree,
Whose termine° is termed the world's wide pole. *end point*
Nor are the names of Saturn, Mars or Jupiter
Feigned, but are erring stars.
FAUSTUS But have they all one motion, both *situ et tempore*?[4]
MEPHOSTOPHILIS All move from east to west in four and twenty hours upon the poles of the world, but differ in their motions upon the poles of the zodiac.
FAUSTUS Tush, these slender trifles Wagner can decide. Hath Mephostophilis no greater skill? Who knows not the double motion of the planets? That the first is finished in a natural day? The second thus, as Saturn in thirty years,

1. Faustus claims he has made the poet Homer sing to him of the love of Alexander the Great (356–323 B.C.), who was married to Statira, daughter of the Emperor Darius of Persia; and of Oenone, a nymph of Mount Ida, who died from grief when her lover, Paris of Troy, deserted her for Helen, the wife of King Menalaus of Sparta.
2. Faustus further claims that the legendary Amphion, whose music built the walls of Thebes, also made music with Mephostophilis, now Faustus's servant.
3. Faustus alludes to the Ptolemaic universe in which the earth, at the center, is surrounded by concentric spheres, beginning with the moon. Beyond the spheres of the stars that were thought to move (the constellations) were the spheres of the fixed stars.
4. In place and in time.

Jupiter in twelve, Mars in four, the sun, Venus and Mercury in twenty-eight days. Tush, these are freshmen's suppositions. But tell me, hath every sphere a dominion or *intelligentia*?[5]

MEPHOSTOPHILIS Ay.

FAUSTUS How many heavens or spheres are there?

MEPHOSTOPHILIS Nine, the seven planets, the firmament, and the empyrial heaven.

FAUSTUS But is there not *coelum igneum et cristallinum?*

MEPHOSTOPHILIS No, Faustus, they be but fables.[6]

FAUSTUS Resolve me then in this one question. Why are not conjunctions, oppositions, aspects, eclipses, all at one time, but in some years we have more, in some less?

MEPHOSTOPHILIS *Per inaequalem motum, respectu totius.*[7]

FAUSTUS Well, I am answered. Now tell me, who made the world?

MEPHOSTOPHILIS I will not.

FAUSTUS Sweet Mephostophilis, tell me.

MEPHOSTOPHILIS Move me not, Faustus.

FAUSTUS Villain, have not I bound thee to tell me anything?

MEPHOSTOPHILIS Ay, that is not against our kingdom, but this is.
Think on hell, Faustus, for thou art damned.

FAUSTUS Think, Faustus, upon God, that made the world.

MEPHOSTOPHILIS Remember this— [*Exit*.]

FAUSTUS Ay, go, accursed spirit to ugly hell.
'Tis thou hast damned distressed Faustus' soul.
Is't not too late?

[*Enter the Good and Evil Angels*.]

EVIL ANGEL Too late.

GOOD ANGEL Never too late, if Faustus will repent.

EVIL ANGEL If thou repent devils will tear thee in pieces.

GOOD ANGEL Repent, and they shall never raze° thy skin. *shave*

[*Exeunt Angels*.]

FAUSTUS Ah, Christ my savior,
Seek to save distressed Faustus' soul.

[*Enter Lucifer, Belzebub and Mephostophilis*.]

LUCIFER Christ cannot save thy soul, for he is just.
There's none but I have interest in the same.

FAUSTUS Oh what art thou that look'st so terribly?

LUCIFER I am Lucifer, and this is my companion prince in hell.

FAUSTUS Oh Faustus, they are come to fetch away thy soul.

BELZEBUB We are come to tell thee thou dost injure us.

LUCIFER Thou call'st on Christ contrary to thy promise.

BELZEBUB Thou shouldst not think on God.

LUCIFER Think on the devil.

BELZEBUB And his dam too.

FAUSTUS Nor will I henceforth. Pardon me in this,
And Faustus vows never to look to heaven,

5. Guiding spirit.

6. Faustus asks whether there is a "fiery and crystalline heaven" beyond the "empyrial heaven" Mephostophilis has mentioned, and he is told it is a fiction.

7. Faustus asks why planetary and astral events do not occur uniformly, and Mephostophilis answers that they do "with respect to the whole" but each "by unequal motion."

Never to name God or to pray to him,
To burn his scriptures, slay his ministers,
And make my spirits pull his churches down.

LUCIFER Do so, and we will highly gratify thee.

BELZEBUB Faustus, we are come from hell in person to show thee some pastime. Sit down and thou shalt behold the seven deadly sins appear to thee in their own proper shapes and likeness.

FAUSTUS That sight will be as pleasant to me as Paradise was to Adam the first day of his creation.

LUCIFER Talk not of Paradise or Creation, but mark this show. Talk of the devil and nothing else. Go, Mephostophilis, fetch them in.

[*Enter the Seven Deadly Sins.*]

BELZEBUB Now, Faustus, question them of their names and dispositions.

FAUSTUS That shall I soon. What art thou, the first?

PRIDE I am Pride. I disdain to have any parents. I am like to Ovid's flea.[8] I can creep into every corner of a wench. Sometimes like a periwig I sit upon her brow. Next, like a necklace I hang about her neck. Then, like a fan of feathers, I kiss her. And then turning myself to a wrought smock do what I list. But fie, what a smell is here! I'll not speak a word for a king's ransome, unless the ground be perfumed and covered with cloth of Arras.[9]

FAUSTUS Thou art a proud knave indeed. What art thou, the second?

COVETOUSNESS I am Covetousness. Begotten of an old churl in a leather bag. And might I now obtain my wish, this house, you and all, should turn to gold, that I might lock you safe into my chest. Oh, my sweet gold!

FAUSTUS And what art thou, the third?

ENVY I am Envy, begotten of a chimney-sweeper and an oyster-wife. I cannot read and therefore wish all books were burnt. I am lean with seeing others eat. Oh, that there would come a famine over all the world, that all might die, and I live alone, then thou should'st see how fat I'd be. But must thou sit and I stand? Come down, with a vengeance!

FAUSTUS Out, envious wretch. But what art thou, the fourth?

WRATH I am Wrath. I had neither father nor mother. I leapt out of a lion's mouth when I was scarce an hour old, and ever since have run up and down the world with this case of rapiers, wounding myself when I could get none to fight withal. I was born in hell, and look to it, for some of you shall be my father.

FAUSTUS And what art thou, the fifth?

GLUTTONY I am Gluttony. My parents are all dead, and the devil a penny they have left me, but a small pension and that buys me thirty meals a day and ten bevers:[1] a small trifle to suffice nature. I come of a royal pedigree; my father was a gammon of bacon and my mother was a hog's head of claret wine. My godfathers were these: Peter Pickle-herring and Martin Martlemas-beef. But my godmother, oh, she was an ancient gentlewoman, and well-beloved in every good town and city. Her name was Mistress Margery March-beer. Now, Faustus, thou hast heard all my progeny, wilt thou bid me to supper?

8. One of the poems of the Roman poet Ovid (43 B.C.–A.D. 18) describes the journey of a flea around a woman's body.

9. Flemish cloth for tapestries.

1. Snacks.

FAUSTUS No, I'll see thee hanged. Thou wilt eat up all my victuals.

GLUTTONY Then the devil choke thee.

FAUSTUS Choke thyself, Glutton. What art thou, the sixth?

SLOTH Hey ho, I am Sloth. I was begotten on a sunny bank where I have lain ever since, and you have done me great injury to bring me from thence. Let me be carried thither again by Gluttony and Lechery. I'll not speak another word for a king's ransom.

FAUSTUS And what are you, Mistress Minx, the seventh and last?

LECHERY Who, I sir? I am one that loves an inch of raw mutton better than an ell of fried stockfish,[2] and the first letter of my name begins with Lechery.

FAUSTUS Away to hell! Away, on, piper! [*Exeunt the Seven Deadly Sins.*]

LUCIFER Now, Faustus, how dost thou like this?

FAUSTUS Oh, this feeds my soul.

LUCIFER Tut, Faustus, in hell is all manner of delight.

FAUSTUS Oh, might I see hell and return again safe, how happy were I then!

LUCIFER Faustus, thou shalt. At midnight I will send for thee. Meanwhile, peruse this book and view it throughly, and thou shalt turn thyself into what shape thou wilt.

FAUSTUS Thanks, mighty Lucifer. This will I keep as chary as my life.

LUCIFER Now, Faustus, farewell, and think on the devil.

FAUSTUS Farewell, great Lucifer. Come, Mephostophilis.

[*Exeunt omnes, several ways.*]

Scene Two

[*Enter the Clown.*]

CLOWN What, Dick, look to the horses there till I come again. I have gotten one of Doctor Faustus' conjuring books, and now we'll have such knavery as't passes.

[*Enter Dick.*]

DICK What, Robin, you must come away and walk the horses.

ROBIN I walk the horses? I scorn't, faith. I have other matters in hand. Let the horses walk themselves and they will. A *per se a, t.h.e. the: o per se o deny orgon, gorgon.*[3] Keep further from me, O thou illiterate and unlearned hostler.

DICK 'Snails![4] What hast thou got there? A book? Why, thou canst not tell ne'er a word on't.

ROBIN That thou shalt see presently. Keep out of the circle, I say, lest I send you into the ostry[5] with a vengeance.

DICK That's like, faith. You had best leave your foolery, for, an my master come, he'll conjure you, faith!

ROBIN My master conjure me? I'll tell thee what, an my master come here, I'll clap as fair a pair of horns[6] on's head as e'er thou sawest in thy life.

DICK Thou need'st not do that, for my mistress hath done it.

ROBIN Ay, there be of us here, that have waded as deep into matters as other men, if they were disposed to talk.

2. Lechery implies that she would prefer a short but energetic penis to a yard-long but dry one.

3. Barely literate, Robin is trying to parse a Latin phrase, *atheo Demigorgon* ("godless Demigorgon").

4. Christ's nails.

5. Inn.

6. Sign of a cuckold.

DICK A plague take you! I thought you did not sneak up and down after her for nothing. But I prithee tell me, in good sadness, Robin, is that a conjuring book?

ROBIN Do but speak what thou't have me to do, and I'll do't. If thou't dance naked, put off thy clothes and I'll conjure thee about presently. Or if thou't go but to the tavern with me, I'll give thee white wine, red wine, claret wine, sack, muskadine, malmesey and whippincrust.[7] Hold, belly, hold; and we'll not pay one penny for it.

DICK Oh brave! Prithee, let's to it presently, for I am as dry as a dog.

ROBIN Come, then, let's away. *[Exeunt.]*

Act 3

Scene One

[Enter the Chorus.]

CHORUS Learned Faustus,
To find the secrets of astronomy,
Graven in the book of Jove's high firmament,
Did mount him up to scale Olympus' top,
Where sitting in a chariot burning bright,
Drawn by the strength of yoked dragons' necks,
He views the clouds, the planets, and the stars,
The tropic, zones, and quarters of the sky,
From the bright circle of the horned moon,
Even to the height of *Primum Mobile*.[1]
And whirling round with this circumference,
Within the concave compass of the pole,
From east to west his dragons swiftly glide,
And in eight days did bring him home again.
Not long he stayed within his quiet house,
To rest his bones after his weary toil,
But new exploits do hale him out again,
And mounted then upon a dragon's back,
That with his wings did part the subtle air,
He now is gone to prove cosmography,
That measures coasts and kingdoms of the earth;
And as I guess will first arrive at Rome,
To see the Pope and manner of his court,
And take some part of holy Peter's feast,
The which this day is highly solemnized. *[Exit.]*

Scene Two

[Enter Faustus and Mephostophilis.]

FAUSTUS Having now, my good Mephostophilis,
Passed with delight the stately town of Trier,
Environed round with airy mountain tops,

7. Robin lists various kinds of wine; "whippencrust" is probably a corruption of "hippocras," a kind of sweet wine.

1. The outermost of the heavenly spheres. Faustus is pictured as viewing the heavens from Mount Olympus to the circle of the moon and beyond, to the *primum mobile*.

With walls of flint, and deep entrenched lakes,
Not to be won by any conquering prince,
From Paris next coasting the realm of France
We saw the river Main fall into Rhine,
Whose banks are set with groves of fruitful vines;
Then up to Naples, rich Campania,
Whose buildings fair and gorgeous to the eye,
The streets straight forth and paved with finest brick,
Quarters the town in four equivolence.° *parts*
There saw we learned Maro's golden tomb,[2]
The way he cut an English mile in length,
Thorough a rock of stone in one night's space.
From thence to Venice, Padua and the rest,
In midst of which a sumptuous temple stands,
That threats the stars with her aspiring top,
Whose frame is paved with sundry colored stones,
And roofed aloft with curious work in gold.
Thus hitherto hath Faustus spent his time.
But tell me now, what resting place is this?
Hast thou, as erst I did command,
Conducted me within the walls of Rome?

MEPHOSTOPHILIS I have, my Faustus, and for proof thereof,
This is the goodly palace of the Pope;
And cause we are no common guests,
I choose his privy chamber for our use.

FAUSTUS I hope his Holiness will bid us welcome.

MEPHOSTOPHILIS All's one, for we'll be bold with his venison.
But now, my Faustus, that thou may'st perceive
What Rome contains for to delight thine eyes,
Know that this city stands upon seven hills
That underprop the groundwork of the same.
Just through the midst runs flowing Tiber's stream,
With winding banks that cut it in two parts,
Over the which four stately bridges lean,
That make safe passage to each part of Rome.
Upon the bridge called Ponto Angelo
Erected is a castle passing strong,
Where thou shalt see such store of ordinance
As that the double cannons forged of brass
Do match the number of the days contained
Within the compass of one complete year.
Beside the gates and high pyramides,
That Julius Caesar brought from Africa.[3]

FAUSTUS Now by the kingdoms of infernal rule,
Of Styx, or Acheron, and the fiery lake

2. Faustus' fiery chariot cut through rocks to go from Naples, where the Roman poet Publius Virgilius Maro, or Virgil, is buried, to Padua and Venice.

3. The Emperor Caligula brought an obelisk back from Heliopolis in Egypt, which stands before St. Peter's in Rome.

Of ever-burning Phlegethon,° I swear *rivers in hell*
That I do long to see the monuments
And situation of bright splendent Rome.
Come, therefore, let's away.

MEPHOSTOPHILIS Now, stay, my Faustus. I know you'd see the Pope,
And take some part of holy Peter's feast,
The which in state and high solemnity
This day is held through Rome and Italy
In honor of the Pope's triumphant victory.

FAUSTUS Sweet Mephostophilis, thou pleasest me.
Whilst I am here on earth let me be cloyed
With all things that delight the heart of man.
My four and twenty years of liberty
I'll spend in pleasure and in dalliance,
That Faustus' name, whilst this bright frame doth stand,
May be admired through the furthest land.

MEPHOSTOPHILIS 'Tis well said, Faustus. Come then, stand by me,
And thou shalt see them come immediately.

FAUSTUS Nay stay, my gentle Mephostophilis,
And grant me my request, and then I go.
Thou know'st within the compass of eight days
We viewed the face of heaven, of earth and hell.
So high our dragons soared into the air,
That looking down, the earth appeared to me
No bigger than my hand in quantity.
There did we view the kingdoms of the world,
And what might please mine eye, I there beheld.
Then in this show let me an actor be,
That this proud Pope may Faustus' cunning see.

MEPHOSTOPHILIS Let it be so, my Faustus, but first stay
And view their triumphs° as they pass this way. *procession*
And then devise what best contents thy mind
By cunning in thine art to cross the Pope,
Or dash the pride of this solemnity,
To make his monks and abbots stand like apes,
And point like antics° at his triple crown, *clowns*
To beat the beads about the friars' pates,
Or clap huge horns upon the cardinals' heads,
Or any villainy thou canst devise,
And I'll perform it, Faustus. Hark, they come!
This day shall make thee be admired in Rome.

[*Enter the Cardinals and Bishops, some bearing crosiers, some the pillars, Monks and Friars, singing their procession. Then the Pope and Raymond, King of Hungary with Bruno*[4] *led in chains.*]

POPE Cast down our footstool.

RAYMOND Saxon Bruno, stoop,

4. This character has no apparent historical counterpart or model.

Whilst on thy back his Holiness ascends
Saint Peter's chair and state pontifical.

BRUNO Proud Lucifer, that state belongs to me:
But thus I fall to Peter, not to thee.

POPE To me and Peter shalt thou grovelling lie,
And crouch before the papal dignity.
Sounds trumpets then, for thus Saint Peter's heir
From Bruno's back ascends Saint Peter's chair.

[*A flourish while he ascends*.]

Thus, as the gods creep on with feet of wool
Long ere with iron hands they punish men,
So shall our sleeping vengeance now arise,
And smite with death thy hated enterprise.
Lord cardinals of France and Padua,
Go forthwith to our holy consistory,
And read amongst the statutes decretal,
What by the holy council held at Trent[5]
The sacred synod hath decreed for them
That doth assume the papal government,
Without election and a true consent.
Away, and bring us word with speed!

FIRST CARDINAL We go, my lord. [*Exeunt Cardinals*.]

POPE Lord Raymond.

FAUSTUS Go, haste thee, gentle Mephostophilis,
Follow the cardinals to the consistory,
And as they turn their superstitious books,
Strike them with sloth and drowsy idleness,
And make them sleep so sound that in their shapes
Thyself and I may parly° with this Pope, *speak*
This proud confronter of the Emperor,[6]
And in despite of all his holiness
Restore this Bruno to his liberty
And bear him to the states of Germany.

MEPHOSTOPHILIS Faustus, I go.

FAUSTUS Dispatch it soon,
The Pope shall curse that Faustus came to Rome.

[*Exeunt Faustus and Mephostophilis*.]

BRUNO Pope Adrian,[7] let me have some right of law:
I was elected by the Emperor.

POPE We will depose the Emperor for that deed,
And curse the people that submit to him.
Both he and thou shalt stand excommunicate,
And interdict from Church's privilege

5. The council of Trent, called to meet the challenges posed by the Protestant Reformation, was held between 1545 and 1563.

6. The Holy Roman Emperor, Charles V, Emperor from 1519.

7. Possibly Marlowe means Hadrian VI (1522–23), although he was Pope before the Council of Trent, after which the action of the play is supposed to have taken place.

And all society of holy men.
He grows too proud in his authority,
Lifting his lofty head above the clouds
And like a steeple overpeers the Church.
But we'll pull down his haughty insolence,
And, as Pope Alexander, our progenitor,
Stood on the neck of German Frederick,[8]
Adding this golden sentence to our praise,
That Peter's heirs should tread on emperors
And walk upon the dreadful adder's back,
Treading the lion and the dragon down,
And fearless spurn the killing basilisk,[9]
So will we quell that haughty schismatic,
And by authority apostolical
Depose him from his regal government.

BRUNO Pope Julius swore to princely Sigismond[1]
For him and the succeeding popes of Rome,
To hold the emperors their lawful lords.

POPE Pope Julius did abuse the Church's rites,
And therefore none of his decrees can stand.
Is not all power on earth bestowed on us?
And therefore though we would we cannot err.
Behold this silver belt, whereto is fixed
Seven golden seals fast sealed with seven seals,
In token of our seven-fold power from heaven,
To bind or loose, lock fast, condemn or judge,
Resign or seal, or what so pleaseth us.
Then he and thou, and all the world, shall stoop,
Or be assured of our dreadful curse,
To light as heavy as the pains of hell.

[*Enter Faustus and Mephostophilis, like the cardinals.*]

MEPHOSTOPHILIS Now tell me, Faustus, are we not fitted well?

FAUSTUS Yes, Mephostophilis, and two such cardinals
Ne'er served a holy Pope as we shall do.
But whilst they sleep within the consistory,
Let us salute his reverend fatherhood.

RAYMOND Behold, my lord, the cardinals are returned.

POPE Welcome, grave fathers, answer presently
What have our holy council there decreed
Concerning Bruno and the Emperor,
In quittance of their late conspiracy
Against our state and papal dignity?

FAUSTUS Most sacred patron of the Church of Rome,
By full consent of all the synod
Of priests and prelates, it is thus decreed:

8. Pope Alexander III (1159–81) forced Emperor Frederick Barbarossa to acknowledge his authority.
9. A mythical creature whose glance was lethal.

1. It is unclear to whom Marlowe refers; there was no Pope Julius during the reign of the Emperor Sigismund (1368–1436).

That Bruno and the German Emperor
Be held as lollards[2] and bold schismatics
And proud disturbers of the Church's peace.
And if that Bruno by his own assent,
Without enforcement of the German peers,
Did seek to wear the triple diadem
And by your death to climb Saint Peter's chair,
The statutes decretal have thus decreed:
He shall be straight condemned of heresy
And on a pile of faggots burnt to death.

POPE It is enough. Here, take him to your charge,
And bear him straight to Ponto Angelo,
And in the strongest tower enclose him fast.
Tomorrow, sitting in our consistory
With all our college of grave cardinals,
We will determine of his life or death.
Here, take his triple crown along with you,
And leave it in the Church's treasury.
Make haste again, my good lord cardinals,
And take our blessing apostolical.

MEPHOSTOPHILIS So, so, was never devil thus blessed before.

FAUSTUS Away, sweet Mephostophilis, be gone:
The cardinals will be plagued for this anon.

[*Exeunt Faustus and Mephostophilis.*]

POPE Go presently, and bring a banquet forth
That we may solemnize Saint Peter's feast,
And with Lord Raymond, King of Hungary,
Drink to our late and happy victory. [*Exeunt.*]

Scene Three

[*A sennet*[3] *while the banquet is brought in, and then enter Faustus and Mephostophilis in their own shapes.*]

MEPHOSTOPHILIS Now, Faustus, come prepare thyself for mirth.
The sleepy cardinals are hard at hand
To censure Bruno that is posted° hence, *ridden*
And on a proud paced steed as swift as thought
Flies o'er the Alps to fruitful Germany,
There to salute the woeful Emperor.

FAUSTUS The Pope will curse them for their sloth today,
That slept both Bruno and his crown away.
But now, that Faustus may delight his mind,
And by their folly make some merriment,
Sweet Mephostophilis, so charm me here,
That I may walk invisible to all,
And do what e'er I please unseen of any.

MEPHOSTOPHILIS Faustus, thou shalt. Then kneel down presently:

2. Heretics; in England, followers of John Wycliffe (1328?–1384).

3. A trumpet call.

Whilst on thy head I lay my hand,
And charm thee with this magic wand.
First wear this girdle, then appear
Invisible to all are here.
The planets seven, the gloomy air,
Hell and the Furies'[4] forked hair,
Pluto's[5] blue fire and Hecate's[6] tree,
With magic spells so compass thee,
That no eye may thy body see.
So, Faustus, now for all their holiness,
Do what thou wilt, thou shalt not be discerned.

FAUSTUS Thanks, Mephostophilis. Now, friars, take heed
Lest Faustus make your shaven crowns to bleed.

MEPHOSTOPHILIS Faustus, no more. See where the cardinals come.

[Enter the Pope and all the Lords. Enter the Cardinals with a book.]

POPE Welcome, lord cardinals. Come, sit down.
Lord Raymond, take your seat. Friars, attend
And see that all things be in readiness
As best beseems this solemn festival.

FIRST CARDINAL First, may it please your sacred Holiness,
To view the sentence of the reverend synod
Concerning Bruno and the Emperor?

POPE What needs this question? Did I not tell you
Tomorrow we would sit i'the consistory
And there determine of his punishment?
You brought us word even now, it was decreed
That Bruno and the cursed Emperor
Were by the holy Council both condemned
For loathed lollards and base schismatics.
Then wherefore would you have me view that book?

FIRST CARDINAL Your Grace mistakes. You gave us no such charge.

RAYMOND Deny it not. We all are witnesses
That Bruno here was late delivered you,
With his rich triple crown to be reserved
And put into the Church's treasury.

BOTH CARDINALS By holy Paul, we saw them not.

POPE By Peter, you shall die
Unless you bring them forth immediately.
Hale° them to prison, lade their limbs with gyves!° *take / chains*
False prelates, for this hateful treachery,
Cursed be your souls to hellish misery.

FAUSTUS So, they are safe. Now Faustus, to the feast.
The Pope had never such a frolic guest.

POPE Lord Archbishop of Rheims, sit down with us.

BISHOP I thank your Holiness.

FAUSTUS Fall to, and the devil choke you an you spare.

4. Greek divinities instigating revenge.
5. The Roman god of the underworld.
6. Goddess representing death and the dark side of the moon.

POPE Who's that spoke? Friars, look about.
FRIARS Here's nobody, if it like your Holiness.
POPE Lord Raymond, pray fall to. I am beholding
To the Bishop of Milan for this so rare a present.
FAUSTUS I thank you, sir. [*Snatches it.*]
POPE How now? Who snatched the meat from me?
Villains, why speak you not?
My good Lord Archbishop, here's a most dainty dish
Was sent me from a cardinal in France.
FAUSTUS I'll have that too. [*Snatches it.*]
POPE What lollards do attend our Holiness
That we receive such great indignity? Fetch me some wine.
FAUSTUS Ay, pray do, for Faustus is a-dry.
POPE Lord Raymond, I drink unto your grace.
FAUSTUS I pledge your grace. [*Snatches the glass.*]
POPE My wine gone too? Ye lubbers,° look about *louts*
And find the man that doth this villainy,
Or by our sanctitude you all shall die.
I pray, my lords, have patience at this
Troublesome banquet.
BISHOP Please it your Holiness, I think it be some ghost crept out of Purgatory, and now is come unto your Holiness for his pardon.
POPE It may be so.
Go, then, command our priests to sing a dirge
To lay the fury of this same troublesome ghost.
[*The Pope crosseth himself.*]
FAUSTUS How now? Must every bit be spiced with a cross?
Nay then, take that.
[*Faustus hits him a box of the ear.*]
POPE Oh, I am slain! Help me, my lords.
Oh come, and help to bear my body hence.
Damned be this soul for ever for this deed!
[*Exeunt the Pope and his train.*]
MEPHOSTOPHILIS Now, Faustus, what will you do now?
For I can tell you, you'll be cursed with bell, book and candle.
FAUSTUS Bell, book and candle, candle, book and bell,
Forward and backward, to curse Faustus to hell.
[*Enter the Friars with bell, book and candle, for the dirge.*]
FIRST FRIAR Come, brethren, let's about our business with good devotion.
[*sing*] Cursed be he that stole his Holiness' meat from the table. *Maledicat dominus.*[7]
Cursed be he that took his Holiness a blow on the face. *Maledicat dominus.*
Cursed be he that struck Friar Sandelo a blow on the pate. *Maledicat dominus.*
Cursed be he that disturbeth our holy dirge. *Maledicat dominus.*
Cursed be he that took away his Holiness' wine. *Maledicat dominus.*
Et omnes sancti.[8] Amen.

7. May God curse you.

8. And all the saints.

[*Faustus and Mephostophilis beat the Friars, fling fireworks among them and exeunt. Enter Chorus.*]

CHORUS When Faustus had with pleasure ta'en the view
Of rarest things and royal courts of kings,
He stayed his course and so returned home;
Where such as bear his absence but with grief,
I mean his friends and nearest companions,
Did gratulate his safety with kind words,
And in their conference of what befell,
Touching his journey through the world and air,
They put forth questions of astrology,
Which Faustus answered with such learned skill
As they admired and wondered at his wit.
Now is his fame spread forth in every land;
Amongst the rest, the Emperor is one,
Carolus the Fifth, at whose palace now
Faustus is feasted 'mongst his noblemen.
What there he did in trial of his art,
I leave untold: your eyes shall see performed.

Scene Four

[*Enter Robin the ostler*[9] *with a book in his hand.*]

ROBIN Oh this is admirable! Here I ha' stol'n one of Doctor Faustus' conjuring books, and, i'faith, I mean to search some circles for my own use. Now will I make all the maidens in our parish dance at my pleasure stark naked before me. And so by that means I shall see more than ere I felt or saw yet.

[*Enter Rafe calling Robin.*]

RAFE Robin, prithee come away! There's a gentleman tarries to have his horse, and he would have his things rubbed and made clean. He keeps such a chafing with my mistress about it, and she has sent me to look thee out. Prithee, come away!

ROBIN Keep out, keep out, or else you are blown up. You are dismembered, Rafe, keep out, for I am about a roaring piece of work.

RAFE Come, what dost thou with that same book? Thou canst not read?

ROBIN Yes, my master and mistress shall find that I can read, he for his forehead, she for her private study. She's born to bear with me, or else my art fails.

RAFE Why, Robin, what book is that?

ROBIN What book? Why, the most intolerable book for conjuring that ere was invented by any brimstone devil.

RAFE Canst thou conjure with it?

ROBIN I can do all these things easily with it. First, I can make thee drunk with ippocras at any tavern in Europe, for nothing. That's one of my conjuring works!

RAFE Our master parson says that's nothing.

ROBIN True, Rafe. And more, Rafe, if thou hast any mind to Nan Spit, our kitchen maid, then turn her and wind her to thy own use as often as thou wilt, and at midnight.

9. Stableman.

RAFE Oh brave Robin! Shall I have Nan Spit, and to mine own use? On that condition, I'll feed thy devil with horsebread as long as he lives, of free cost.

ROBIN No more, sweet Rafe. Let's go and make clean our boots which lie foul upon our hands, and then to our conjuring, in the devil's name.

[*Exeunt. Re-enter Robin and Rafe with a silver goblet.*]

ROBIN Come, Rafe, did I not tell thee we were for ever made by this Doctor Faustus' book? *Ecce signum,*[1] here's a simple purchase for horse-keepers. Our horses shall eat no hay as long as this lasts.

[*Enter the Vintner.*]

RAFE But, Robin, here comes the vintner.

ROBIN Hush, I'll gull[2] him supernaturally. Drawer, I hope all is paid. God be with you. Come, Rafe.

VINTNER Soft, sir, a word with you. I must yet have a goblet paid from you ere you go.

ROBIN I, a goblet? Rafe, I a goblet? I scorn you, and you are but a etc. I, a goblet? Search me.

VINTNER I mean so, sir, with your favor.

ROBIN How say you now?

VINTNER I must say somewhat to your fellow—you, sir.

RAFE Me, sir? Me, sir? Search your fill. Now, sir, you may be ashamed to burden honest men with a matter of truth.

VINTNER Well, t'one of you hath this goblet about you.

ROBIN You lie, drawer. 'Tis afore me! Sirrah, you! I'll teach ye to impeach honest men. Stand by, I'll scour you for a goblet. Stand aside, you were best. I charge you in the name of Belzebub. Look to the goblet, Rafe.

VINTNER What mean you, sirrah?

ROBIN I'll tell you what I mean. [*He reads*] *Sanctobolorum Periphrasticon.*[3] Nay, I'll tickle you, vintner—look to the goblet, Rafe. *Polypragmos Belseborams framanto pacostiphos tostu Mephostophilis, Etc.*

[*Enter Mephostophilis, who sets squibs*[4] *at their backs. They run about.*]

VINTNER *O nomine Domine*[5] what mean'st thou, Robin? Thou hast no goblet.

RAFE *Peccatum peccatorum*[6] here's thy goblet, good vintner.

ROBIN *Misericordia pro nobis*[7] what shall I do? Good devil, forgive me now and I'll never rob thy library more.

[*Enter to them Mephostophilis.*]

MEPHOSTOPHILIS Vainish villains! Th'one like an ape, another like a bear, the third an ass, for doing this enterprise.

Monarch of hell, under whose black survey
Great potentates do kneel with awful fear,
Upon whose altars thousand souls do lie,
How am I vexed with these villains' charms?
From Constantinople am I hither come,
Only for pleasure of these damned slaves.

ROBIN How, from Constantinople? You have had a great journey. Will you take six pence in your purse to pay for your supper, and be gone?

1. "Behold, the sign"; i.e., of the truth.
2. Trick.
3. Gibberish.
4. Firecrackers.
5. In God's name.
6. Sin of sins.
7. Mercy on us.

MEPHOSTOPHILIS Well, villains, for your presumption I transform thee into an ape and thee into a dog, and so be gone. [*Exit.*]

ROBIN How, into an ape? That's brave! I'll have fine sport with the boys. I'll get nuts and apples enow.

RAFE And I must be a dog!

ROBIN I'faith thy head will never be out of the potage pot. [*Exeunt.*]

Act 4

Scene One

[*The Emperor's Court. Enter Martino and Frederick at several doors.*]

MARTINO What ho, officers, gentlemen!
Hie to the presence to attend the Emperor.
Good Frederick, see the rooms be voided straight.
His Majesty is coming to the hall;
Go back, and see the state in readiness.

FREDERICK But where is Bruno, our elected Pope,
That on a fury's back came post from Rome?
Will not his grace consort° the Emperor? *greet*

MARTINO Oh yes, and with him comes the German conjuror,
The learned Faustus, fame of Wittenberg,
The wonder of the world for magic art.
And he intends to show great Carolus
The race of all his stout progenitors,
And bring in presence of his Majesty
The royal shapes and warlike semblances
Of Alexander and his beauteous paramour.[1]

FREDERICK Where is Benvolio?

MARTINO Fast asleep, I warrant you.
He took his rouse with stoups° of Rhenish wine *large cups*
So kindly yesternight to Bruno's health,
That all this day the sluggard keeps his bed.

FREDERICK See, see, his window's ope. We'll call to him.

MARTINO What ho, Benvolio?

[*Enter Benvolio above at a window in his nightcap, buttoning.*]

BENVOLIO What a devil ail you two?

MARTINO Speak softly, sir, lest the devil hear you;
For Faustus at the court is late arrived,
And at his heels a thousand furies wait
To accomplish whatsoever the Doctor please.

BENVOLIO What of this?

MARTINO Come, leave thy chamber first, and thou shalt see
This conjuror perform such rare exploits
Before the Pope and royal Emperor
As never yet was seen in Germany.

BENVOLIO Has not the Pope enough of conjuring yet?
He was upon the devil's back late enough,

1. Alexander the Great and his wife, Roxana.

And if he be so far in love with him,
I would he would post with him to Rome again.

FREDERICK Speak, wilt thou come and see this sport?

BENVOLIO Not I.

MARTINO Wilt thou stand in thy window and see it, then?

BENVOLIO Ay, and I fall not asleep i' the meantime.

MARTINO The Emperor is at hand, who comes to see
What wonders by black spells may compassed be.

BENVOLIO Well, go you, attend the Emperor. I am content for this once to thrust my head out at a window, for they say if a man be drunk over night the devil cannot hurt him in the morning. If that be true, I have a charm in my head shall control him as well as the conjuror, I warrant you.

[*Exeunt Martino and Frederick.*]

Scene Two

[*Sennet. Charles, the German Emperor, Bruno, Saxony, Faustus, Mephostophilis, Frederick, Martino, and Attendants. Benvolio still at the window.*]

EMPEROR Wonder of men, renowned magician,
Thrice-learned Faustus, welcome to our court.
This deed of thine, in setting Bruno free
From his and our professed enemy,
Shall add more excellence unto thine art,
Than if by powerful necromantic spells
Thou couldst command the world's obedience.
For ever be beloved of Carolus;
And if this Bruno thou hast late redeemed,
In peace possess the triple diadem
And sit in Peter's chair, despite of chance,
Thou shalt be famous through all Italy,
And honored of the German Emperor.

FAUSTUS These gracious words, most royal Carolus,
Shall make poor Faustus to his utmost power
Both love and serve the German Emperor,
And lay his life at holy Bruno's feet.
For proof whereof, if so your Grace be pleased,
The Doctor stands prepared, by power of art,
To cast his magic charms that shall pierce through
The ebon° gates of ever-burning hell, *ebony*
And hale the stubborn furies from their caves,
To compass whatsoe'er your Grace commands.

BENVOLIO [*Aside*] Blood, he speaks terribly! But for all that, I do not greatly believe him. He looks as like a conjuror as the Pope to a coster-monger.[2]

EMPEROR Then, Faustus, as thou late didst promise us,
We would behold that famous conqueror,
Great Alexander, and his paramour,
In their true shapes and state majestical,

2. Vegetable seller.

That we may wonder at their excellence.
FAUSTUS Your Majesty shall see them presently.
Mephostophilis, away!
And with a solemn noise of trumpets' sound,
Present before this royal Emperor
Great Alexander and his beauteous paramour.
MEPHOSTOPHILIS Faustus, I will.
BENVOLIO Well, Master Doctor, an your devils come not away quickly, you shall have me asleep presently. Zounds, I could eat myself for anger, to think I have been such an ass all this while, to stand gaping after the devil's governor, and can see nothing.
FAUSTUS I'll make you feel something anon, if my art fail me not.
My lord, I must forwarn your Majesty
That when my spirits present the royal shapes
Of Alexander and his paramour,
Your Grace demand no questions of the King,
But in dumb silence let them come and go.
EMPEROR Be it as Faustus please, we are content.
BENVOLIO Ay, ay, and I am content too. And thou bring Alexander and his paramour before the Emperor, I'll be Actaeon[3] and turn myself to a stag.
FAUSTUS And I'll play Diana, and send you the horns presently.
[*Sennet. Enter at one the Emperor Alexander, at the other Darius. They meet. Darius is thrown down; Alexander kills him, takes off his crown, and, offering to go out, his Paramour meets him. He embraceth her and sets Darius' crown upon her head, and coming back, both salute the Emperor, who, leaving his state, offers to embrace them, which Faustus seeing, suddenly stays him. Then trumpets cease and music sounds.*]
My gracious lord, you do forget yourself.
These are but shadows, not substantial.
EMPEROR Oh pardon me, my thoughts are so ravished
With sight of this renowned Emperor,
That in mine arms I would have compassed him.
But, Faustus, since I may not speak to them,
To satisfy my longing thoughts at full,
Let me this tell thee: I have heard it said
That this fair lady, whilst she lived on earth,
Had on her neck a little wart or mole.
How may I prove that saying to be true?
FAUSTUS Your Majesty may boldly go and see.
EMPEROR Faustus, I see it plain,
And in this sight thou better pleasest me
Than if I gained another monarchy.
FAUSTUS Away, be gone. [*Exit Show.*]
See, see, my gracious lord, what strange beast is yon, that thrusts his head out at window?
EMPEROR Oh, wondrous sight! See, Duke of Saxony,

3. Mythical hunter, changed by the goddess Diana into a stag because he had seen her naked as she bathed after a hunt; he was then devoured by his own dogs.

Two spreading horns most strangely fastened
Upon the head of young Benvolio![4]

SAXONY What, is he asleep? Or dead?

FAUSTUS He sleeps, my lord: but dreams not of his horns.

EMPEROR This sport is excellent. We'll call and wake him.
What ho, Benvolio!

BENVOLIO A plague upon you! Let me sleep awhile.

EMPEROR I blame thee not to sleep much, having such a head of thine own.

SAXONY Look up, Benvolio, 'tis the Emperor calls.

BENVOLIO The Emperor? Where? Oh, zounds, my head!

EMPEROR Nay, and thy horns hold, 'tis no matter for thy head, for that's armed sufficiently.

FAUSTUS Why, how now, Sir Knight? What, hanged by the horns? This most horrible! Fie, fie! Pull in your head for shame; let not all the world wonder at you.

BENVOLIO Zounds, Doctor, is this your villainy?

FAUSTUS Oh, say not so, sir. The Doctor has no skill,
No art, no cunning, to present these lords
Or bring before this royal Emperor
The mighty monarch, warlike Alexander.
If Faustus do it, you are straight resolved
In bold Actaeon's shape to turn a stag.
And therefore, my lord, so please your majesty,
I'll raise a kennel of hounds shall hunt him so
As all his footmanship shall scarce prevail
To keep his carcass from their bloody fangs.
Ho, Belimote, Argiron, Asterote!

BENVOLIO Hold, hold! Zounds, he'll raise up a kennel of devils, I think anon. Good my lord, entreat for me. 'Sblood, I am never never able to endure these torments.

EMPEROR Then, good Master Doctor,
Let me entreat you to remove his horns:
He has done penance now sufficiently.

FAUSTUS My gracious lord, not so much for injury done to me, as to delight your majesty with some mirth, hath Faustus justly requited this injurious knight; which being all I desire, I am content to remove his horns. Mephostophilis, transform him. And hereafter, sir, look you speak well of scholars.

BENVOLIO [*Aside*] Speak well of ye? 'Sblood, and scholars be such cuckold-makers to clap horns of honest men's heads o' this order, I'll ne'er trust smooth faces and small ruffs more. But an I be not revenged for this, would I might be turned to a gaping oyster and drink nothing but salt water.

EMPEROR Come, Faustus, while the Emperor lives,
In recompense of this thy high desert,° *merit*
Thou shalt command the state of Germany,
And live beloved of mighty Carolus. [*Exeunt omnes.*]

4. To be "horned" was to be cuckolded. Benvolio, who has insulted scholars, is given horns by Faustus, who takes a scholar's revenge. The insult is introduced as a reflection on the myth of Diana and Actaeon.

Scene Three

[*Enter Benvolio, Martino, Frederick and Soldiers.*]

MARTINO Nay, sweet Benvolio, let us sway thy thoughts
From this attempt against the conjuror.
BENVOLIO Away, you love me not, to urge me thus.
Shall I let slip° so great an injury, *overlook*
When every servile groom jests at my wrongs,
And in their rustic gambols proudly say
Benvolio's head was graced with horns today?
Oh, may these eyelids never close again
Till with my sword I have that conjuror slain.
If you will aid me in this enterprise,
Then draw your weapons and be resolute.
If not, depart. Here will Benvolio die,
But Faustus' death shall quit my infamy.
FREDERICK Nay, we will stay with thee, betide what may,
And kill that Doctor if he come this way.
BENVOLIO Then, gentle Frederick, hie° thee to the grove, *take*
And place our servants and our followers
Close in an ambush there behind the trees.
By this I know the conjuror is near:
I saw him kneel and kiss the Emperor's hand,
And take his leave, laden with rich rewards.
Then, soldiers, boldly fight. If Faustus die,
Take you the wealth, leave us the victory.
FREDERICK Come, soldiers, follow me unto the grove.
Who kills him shall have gold and endless love.
[*Exit Frederick with the Soldiers.*]
BENVOLIO My head is lighter than it was by th'horns,
But yet my heart more ponderous than my head,
And pants until I see that conjuror dead.
MARTINO Where shall we place ourselves, Benvolio?
BENVOLIO Here will we stay to bide the first assault.
Oh, were that damned hell-hound but in place,
Thou soon shouldst see me quit my foul disgrace.

[*Enter Frederick.*]

FREDERICK Close, close! The conjuror is at hand,
And all alone comes walking in his gown.
Be ready then, and strike the peasant down.
BENVOLIO Mine be that honor, then. Now sword, strike home.
For horns he gave, I'll have his head anon.

[*Enter Faustus with a false head.*]

MARTINO See, see, he comes.
BENVOLIO No words. This blow ends all.
Hell take his soul; his body thus must fall. [*Attacks Faustus.*]
FAUSTUS Oh!
FREDERICK Groan you, Master Doctor?
BENVOLIO Break may his heart with groans! Dear Frederick, see,
Thus will I end his griefs immediately. [*Cuts off his head.*]

MARTINO Strike with a willing hand: his head is off.
BENVOLIO The devil's dead! The Furies now may laugh.
FREDERICK Was this that stern aspect, that awful frown,
Made the grim monarch of infernal spirits
Tremble and quake at his commanding charms?
MARTINO Was this that damned head, whose heart conspired
Benvolio's shame before the Emperor?
BENVOLIO Ay, that's the head, and here the body lies,
Justly rewarded for his villainies.
FREDERICK Come, let's devise how we may add more shame
To the black scandal of his hated name.
BENVOLIO First, on his head, in quittance° of my wrongs, *payment*
I'll nail huge forked horns, and let them hang
Within the window where he yoked° me first, *overcame*
That all the world may see my just revenge.
MARTINO What use shall we put his beard to?
BENVOLIO We'll sell it to a chimney-sweeper: it will wear out ten birching° brooms, I warrant you. *birch-twig*
FREDERICK What shall eyes do?
BENVOLIO We'll put out his eyes, and they shall serve for buttons to his lips, to keep his tongue from catching cold.
MARTINO An excellent policy! And now, sirs, having divided him, what shall the body do?
[*Faustus rises*.]
BENVOLIO Zounds, the devil's alive again!
FREDERICK Give him his head, for God's sake!
FAUSTUS Nay, keep it. Faustus will have heads and hands.
I call your hearts to recompense this deed.
Knew you not, traitors, I was limited
For four and twenty years to breathe on earth?
And had you cut my body with your swords,
Or hewed this flesh and bones as small as sand,
Yet in a minute had my spirit returned,
And I had breathed a man made free from harm.
But wherefore do I dally° my revenge? *delay*
Asteroth, Belimoth, Mephostophilis!
[*Enter Mephostophilis and other Devils*.]
Go, horse these traitors on your fiery backs,
And mount aloft with them as high as heaven;
Thence pitch them headlong to the lowest hell.
Yet stay, the world shall see their misery,
And hell shall after plague their treachery.
Go, Belimoth, and take this caitiff° hence, *coward*
And hurl him in some lake of mud and dirt.
Take thou this other: drag him through the woods
Amongst the pricking thorns and sharpest briars,
Whilst with my gentle Mephostophilis,
This traitor flies unto some steepy rock,
That rolling down may break the villain's bones,

As he intended to dismember me.
Fly hence, dispatch my charge immediately.

FREDERICK Pity us, gentle Faustus! Save our lives!

FAUSTUS Away!

FREDERICK He must needs go that the devil drives.

[*Exeunt Spirits with the Knights. Enter the Ambush Soldiers.*]

FIRST SOLDIER Come, sirs, prepare yourselves in readiness.
Make haste to help these noble gentlemen.
I heard them parley with the conjuror.

SECOND SOLDIER See, where he comes. Dispatch and kill the slave.

FAUSTUS What's here? An ambush to betray my life!
Then Faustus, try thy skill. Base peasants, stand!
For lo, these trees remove at my command,
And stand as bulwarks twixt yourselves and me,
To shield me from your hated treachery.
Yet, to encounter this your weak attempt,
Behold an army comes incontinent.° *rapidly*

[*Faustus strikes the door, and enter a devil playing on a drum; after him another bearing an ensign;*[5] *and divers with weapons; Mephostophilis with fireworks. They set upon the soldiers and drive them out.*]

Scene Four

[*Enter at several doors Benvolio, Frederick and Martino, their heads and faces bloody and besmeared with mud and dirt, all having horns on their heads.*]

MARTINO What ho, Benvolio!

BENVOLIO Here! What, Frederick, ho!

FREDERICK Oh help me, gentle friend. Where is Martino?

MARTINO Dear Frederick, here,
Half smothered in a lake of mud and dirt,
Through which the Furies dragged me by the heels.

FREDERICK Martino, see Benvolio's horns again!

MARTINO Oh misery! How now, Benvolio?

BENVOLIO Defend me, heaven! Shall I be haunted still?

MARTINO Nay, fear not, man; we have no power to kill.

BENVOLIO My friends transformed thus! Oh hellish spite!
Your heads are all set with horns!

FREDERICK You hit it right:
It is your own you mean. Feel on your head.

BENVOLIO Zounds, horns again!

MARTINO Nay, chafe not, man. We all are sped.° *done for*

BENVOLIO What devil attends this damned magician,
That, spite of spite, our wrongs are doubled?

FREDERICK What may we do, that we may hide our shames?

BENVOLIO If we should follow him to work revenge,
He'd join long asses' ears to these huge horns,
And make us laughing stocks to all the world.

5. Flag.

MARTINO What shall we then do, dear Benvolio?
BENVOLIO I have a castle joining near these woods,
And thither we'll repair and live obscure,
Till time shall alter these our brutish shapes.
Sith° black disgrace hath thus eclipsed our fame, *since*
We'll rather die with grief, than live with shame. [*Exeunt omnes*.]

Scene Five

[*Enter Faustus and Mephostophilis*.]

FAUSTUS Now, Mephostophilis, the restless course
That time doth run with calm and deadly foot,
Shortening my days and thread of vital life,
Calls for the payment of my latest years.
Therefore, sweet Mephostophilis, let us
Make haste to Wittenberg.
MEPHOSTOPHILIS What, will you go on horseback, or on foot?
FAUSTUS Nay, till I am past this fair and pleasant green
I'll walk on foot.

[*Enter a Horse-Courser*.][6]

HORSE-COURSER I have been all this day seeking one master Fustian.[7] Mass, see where he is! God save you, Master Doctor.

FAUSTUS What, horse-courser! You are well met.

HORSE-COURSER Do you hear, sir? I have brought you forty dollars for your horse.

FAUSTUS I cannot sell him so. If thou likest him for fifty, take him.

HORSE-COURSER Alas, sir, I have no more. I pray you, speak for me.

MEPHOSTOPHILIS I pray you, let him have him. He is an honest fellow, and he has a great charge, neither wife nor child.

FAUSTUS Well, come, give me your money. My boy will deliver him to you. But I must tell you one thing before you have him: ride him not into the water at any hand.

HORSE-COURSER Why, sir, will he not drink of all waters?

FAUSTUS Oh yes, he will drink of all waters; but ride him not into the water. Ride him over hedge or ditch or where thou wilt, but not into the water.

HORSE-COURSER Well, sir, now I am a made man for ever. I'll not leave my horse for forty. If he had but the quality of hey ding ding, hey ding ding, I'd make a brave living on him. He has a buttock as slick as an eel. Well, God bye, sir. Your boy will deliver him me. But hark ye sir: if my horse be sick or ill at ease, if I bring his water to you, you'll tell me what is?

FAUSTUS Away, you villain! What, dost think I am a horse-doctor?

[*Exit Horse-Courser*.]

What art thou, Faustus, but a man condemned to die?
Thy fatal time doth draw to final end:
Despair doth drive distrust into my thoughts.
Confound these passions with a quiet sleep.
Tush, Christ did call the thief upon the cross;

6. Horse trader.

7. Bombast.

Then rest thee, Faustus, quiet in conceit.

[*Sleeps in his chair. Enter Horse-Courser all wet, crying.*]

HORSE-COURSER Alas, alas, Doctor Fustian quotha! Mass, Doctor Lopus[8] was never such a doctor. Has given me a purgation has purged me of forty dollars: I shall never see them more. But yet like an ass as I was, I would not be ruled by him, for he bade me I should ride him into no water. Now I, thinking my horse had had some rare quality that he would not have had me known of, I, like a venturous youth, rid him into the deep pond at the town's end. I was no sooner in the middle of the pond but my horse vanished away, and I sat upon a bottle of hay, never so near drowning in my life. But I'll seek out my Doctor and have my forty dollars again, or I'll make it the dearest horse. Oh, yonder is his snipper-snapper. Do you hear? You! Hey-pass, where's your master?

MEPHOSTOPHILIS Why, sir, what would you? You cannot speak with him.

HORSE-COURSER But I *will* speak with him.

MEPHOSTOPHILIS Why, he's fast asleep. Come some other time.

HORSE-COURSER I'll speak with him now, or I'll break his glass windows about his ears.

MEPHOSTOPHILIS I tell thee he has not slept this eight nights.

HORSE-COURSER And he have not slept this eight weeks I'll speak with him.

MEPHOSTOPHILIS See where he is fast asleep.

HORSE-COURSER Ay, this is he. God save ye, Master Doctor. Master Doctor! Master Doctor Fustian! Forty dollars, forty dollars for a bottle of hay!

MEPHOSTOPHILIS Why, thou seest he hears thee not.

HORSE-COURSER So, ho, ho! So, ho, ho! [*Hollows in his ear.*]
No, will you not wake? I'll make you wake e'er I go.

[*He pulls him by the leg, and pulls it away.*]

Alas, I am undone! What shall I do?

FAUSTUS Oh, my leg, my leg! Help, Mephostophilis. Call the officers. My leg, my leg!

MEPHOSTOPHILIS Come, villain, to the Constable.

HORSE-COURSER Oh lord, sir, let me go and I'll give you forty dollars more.

MEPHOSTOPHILIS Where be they?

HORSE-COURSER I have none about me. Come to my hostry and I'll give them you.

MEPHOSTOPHILIS Be gone, quickly!

[*Horse-Courser runs away.*]

FAUSTUS What, is he gone? Farewell he. Faustus has his leg again, and the horse-courser, I take it, a bottle of hay for his labor. Well, this trick shall cost him forty dollars more.

[*Enter Wagner.*]

FAUSTUS How now, Wagner, what news with thee?

WAGNER If it please you, the Duke of Vanholt[9] doth earnestly entreat your company, and hath sent some of his men to attend you with provision for your journey.

FAUSTUS The Duke of Vanholt's an honorable gentleman, and one to whom I must be no niggard[1] of my cunning. Come, away. [*Exeunt.*]

8. Dr. Lopez, Queen Elizabeth's physician, who was executed in 1594 for alleged complicity in an attempt to murder the Queen. Marlowe died in 1593, so the reference is not his but one of a later editor.

9. The Duchy of Anholt in Germany.

1. Miser.

Scene Six

[*Enter Clown, Dick, Horse-Courser and a Carter.*]

CARTER Come, my masters, I'll bring you to the best beer in Europe. What ho, hostess. Where be these whores?

[*Enter Hostess.*]

HOSTESS How now, what lack you? What, my old guests, welcome!

CLOWN Sirrah Dick, dost thou know why I stand so mute?

DICK No, Robin, why is't?

CLOWN I am eighteen pence on the score.[2] But say nothing. See if she have forgotten me.

HOSTESS Who's this, that stands so solemnly by himself? What, my old guest?

CLOWN Oh, hostess, how do you? I hope my score stands still.

HOSTESS Ay, there's no doubt of that, for methinks you make no haste to wipe it out.

DICK Why, hostess, I say, fetch us some beer.

HOSTESS You shall presently. Look up into the hall there, ho! [*Exit.*]

DICK Come, sirs, what shall we do now till mine hostess comes?

CARTER Marry, sir, I'll tell you the bravest tale how a conjuror served me. You know Doctor Faustus?

HORSE-COURSER Ay, a plague take him. Here's some on's have cause to know him. Did he conjure thee too?

CARTER I'll tell you how he served me. As I was going to Wittenberg t'other day, with a load of hay, he met me and asked me what he should give me for as much hay as he could eat. Now, sir, I, thinking that a little would serve his turn, bade him take as much as he would for three-farthings. So he presently gave me my money and fell to eating. And, as I am a cursen man, he never left eating till he had eat up all my load of hay.

ALL Oh monstrous! Eat a whole load of hay?

CLOWN Yes, yes, that may be, for I have heard of one that has eat a load of logs.

HORSE-COURSER Now, sirs, you shall hear how villainously he served me. I went to him yesterday to buy a horse of him, and he would by no means sell him under forty dollars. So, sir, because I knew him to be such a horse as would run over hedge and ditch and never tire, I gave him his money. So when I had my horse, Doctor Fauster bade me ride him night and day and spare him no time. But, quoth he, in any case ride him not into the water. Now, sir, I thinking the horse had some quality that he would not have me know of, what did I but ride him into a great river, and when I came just in the midst, my horse vanished away, and I sat straddling upon a bottle of hay.

ALL Oh brave Doctor!

HORSE-COURSER But you shall hear how bravely I served him for it: I went me home to his house, and there I found him asleep. I kept a-hallowing and whooping in his ears, but all could not wake him. I, seeing that, took him by the leg and never rested pulling, till I had pulled me his leg quite off, and now 'tis at home in mine hostry.

CLOWN And has the Doctor but one leg, then? That's excellent, for one of his devils turned me into the likeness of an ape's face.

CARTER Some more drink, hostess.

2. Eighteen pence in debt.

CLOWN Hark you, we'll into another room and drink a while, and then we'll go seek out the Doctor. [*Exeunt omnes.*]

Scene Seven

[*Enter the Duke of Vanholt, his Duchess, Faustus and Mephostophilis.*]

DUKE Thanks, Master Doctor, for these pleasant sights. Nor know I how sufficiently to recompense your great deserts in erecting that enchanted castle in the air, the sight whereof so delighted me, as nothing in the world could please me more.

FAUSTUS I do think myself, my good lord, highly recompensed in that it pleaseth your grace to think but well of that which Faustus hath performed. But, gracious lady, it may be that you have taken no pleasure in those sights. Therefore, I pray you tell me, what is the thing you most desire to have. Be it in the world, it shall be yours. I have heard that great-bellied women do long for things are rare and dainty.

LADY True, Master Doctor, and since I find you so kind, I will make known unto you what my heart desires to have; and were it now summer, as it is January, a dead time of the winter, I would request no better meat than a dish of ripe grapes.

FAUSTUS This is but a small matter. Go, Mephostophilis, away.

[*Exit Mephostophilis.*]

Madame, I will do more than this for your content.

[*Enter Mephostophilis again with the grapes.*]

Here, now taste ye these. They should be good, for they come from a far country, I can tell you.

DUKE This makes me wonder more than all the rest, that at this time of the year, when every tree is barren of his fruit, from whence you had these ripe grapes.

FAUSTUS Please it your grace, the year is divided into two circles over the whole world, so that when it is winter with us, in the contrary circle it is likewise summer with them, as in India, Saba and such countries that lie far East, where they have fruit twice a year. From whence, by means of a swift spirit that I have, I had these grapes brought as you see.

LADY And trust me, they are the sweetest grapes that e'er I tasted.

[*The Clowns bounce at the gate within.*]

DUKE What rude disturbers have we at the gate?
Go, pacify their fury. Set it ope,
And then demand of them what they would have.

[*They knock again and call out to talk with Faustus.*]

A SERVANT Why, how now, masters? What a coil[3] is there?
What is the reason you disturb the Duke?

DICK We have no reason for it, therefore a fig for him.

SERVANT Why, saucy varlets, dare you be so bold?

HORSE-COURSER I hope, sir, we have wit enough to be more bold than welcome.

SERVANT It appears so. Pray be bold elsewhere,
And trouble not the Duke.

DUKE What would they have?

SERVANT They all cry out to speak with Doctor Faustus.

CARTER Ay, and we will speak with him.

3. Disturbance.

DUKE Will you, sir? Commit the rascals.
DICK Commit with us! He were as good commit with his father as commit with us.
FAUSTUS I do beseech your grace let them come in.
They are good subject for a merriment.
DUKE Do as thou wilt, Faustus; I give thee leave.
FAUSTUS I thank your grace.
[*Enter the Clown, Dick, Carter and Horse-Courser.*]
Why, how now, my good friends?
Faith, you are too outrageous, but come near.
I have procured your pardons. Welcome all.
CLOWN Nay, sir, we will be welcome for our money, and we will pay for what we take. What ho! Give's half-a-dozen of beer here, and be hanged.
FAUSTUS Nay, hark you. Can you tell me where you are?
CARTER Ay, marry can I. We are under heaven.
SERVANT Ay, but, sir sauce-box, know you in what place?
HORSE-COURSER Ay, ay, the house is good enough to drink in. Zounds, fill us some beer or we'll break all the barrels in the house and dash out all your brains with your bottles.
FAUSTUS Be not so furious. Come, you shall have beer.
My lord, beseech you give me leave awhile.
I'll gage my credit, 'twill content your Grace.
DUKE With all my heart, kind Doctor; please thyself.
Our servants and our court's at thy command.
FAUSTUS I humbly thank your Grace. Then fetch some beer.
HORSE-COURSER Ay, marry. There spake a doctor indeed, and faith, I'll drink a health to thy wooden leg for that word.
FAUSTUS My wooden leg? What dost thou mean by that?
CARTER Ha, ha, ha! Dost thou hear him, Dick? He has forgot his leg.
HORSE-COURSER Ay, ay, he does not stand much upon that.
FAUSTUS No, faith. Not much upon a wooden leg.
CARTER Good lord! That flesh and blood should be so frail with your worship. Do not you remember a horse-courser you sold a horse to?
FAUSTUS Yes, I remember I sold one a horse.
CARTER And do you remember you bid he should not ride into the water?
FAUSTUS Yes, I do very well remember that.
CARTER And do you remember nothing of your leg?
FAUSTUS No, in good sooth.
CARTER Then I pray remember your courtesy.[4]
FAUSTUS I thank you, sir.
CARTER 'Tis not so much worth. I pray you, tell me one thing.
FAUSTUS What's that?
CARTER Be both your legs bedfellows every night together?
FAUSTUS Wouldst thou make a colossus[5] of me, that thou askest me such questions?
CARTER No, truly, sir. I would make nothing of you, but I would fain know that.
[*Enter Hostess with drink.*]
FAUSTUS Then I assure thee certainly they are.
CARTER I thank you, I am fully satisfied.
FAUSTUS But wherefore dost thou ask?

4. Kindness

5. Huge statue.

CARTER For nothing, sir: but methinks you should have a wooden bedfellow of one of 'em.

HORSE-COURSER Why, do you hear, sir? Did not I pull off one of your legs when you were asleep?

FAUSTUS But I have it again now I am awake. Look you here, sir.

ALL Oh horrible! Had the Doctor three legs?

CARTER Do you remember, sir, how you cozened[6] me and eat up my load of—

[*Faustus charms him dumb.*]

DICK Do you remember how you made me wear an ape's—

HORSE-COURSER You whoreson conjuring scab, do you remember how you cozened me with a ho—

CLOWN Ha'you forgotten me? You think to carry it away with your hey-pass and re-pass. Do you remember the dog's fa—

[*Faustus has charmed each dumb in turn; exeunt Clowns.*]

HOSTESS Who pays for the ale? Hear you, Master Doctor, now you have sent away my guests, I pray who shall pay me for my a—? [*Exit Hostess.*]

LADY My lord,
We are much beholding to this learned man.

DUKE So are we, madam, which we will recompense
With all the love and kindness that we may.
His artful sport drives all sad thoughts away. [*Exeunt.*]

Act 5

Scene One

[*Thunder and lightning. Enter Devils with covered dishes. Mephostophilis leads them into Faustus' study. Then enter Wagner.*]

WAGNER I think my master means to die shortly.
He hath made his will, and given me his wealth,
His house, his goods, and store of golden plate,
Besides two thousand ducats ready coined.
And yet methinks, if that death were near,
He would not banquet and carouse and swill
Amongst the students, as even now he doth,
Who are at supper with such belly-cheer
As Wagner ne'er beheld in all his life.
See where they come; belike the feast is ended. [*Exit.*]

[*Enter Faustus, Mephostophilis and two or three Scholars.*]

FIRST SCHOLAR Master Doctor Faustus, since our conference about fair ladies, which was the beautifullest in all the world, we have determined with ourselves that Helen of Greece[1] was the admirablest lady that ever lived. Therefore Master Doctor, if you will do us so much favor, as to let us see that peerless dame of Greece, whom all the world admires for majesty, we should think ourselves much beholding unto you.

FAUSTUS Gentlemen, for that I know your friendship is unfeigned,
It is not Faustus' custom to deny
The just request of those that wish him well.
You shall behold that peerless dame of Greece,

6. Tricked.

1. The mythical queen of Menelaus, King of Sparta, who was abducted by Paris, son of King Priam of Troy. The action began the Trojan War.

No otherwise for pomp of majesty,
Than when Sir Paris crossed the seas with her,
And brought the spoils to rich Dardania.° *Troy*
Be silent then, for danger is in words.

[*Music sounds. Mephostophilis brings in Helen; she passeth over the stage.*]

SECOND SCHOLAR Was this fair Helen, whose admired worth
Made Greece with ten years wars afflict poor Troy?

THIRD SCHOLAR Too simple is my wit to tell her worth
Whom all the world admires for majesty.

FIRST SCHOLAR Now we have seen the pride of nature's work,
We'll take our leaves, and for this blessed sight
Happy and blest be Faustus evermore.

[*Enter an Old Man.*]

FAUSTUS Gentlemen, farewell: the same wish I to you.
[*Exeunt Scholars.*]

OLD MAN Oh gentle Faustus, leave this damned art,
This magic, that will charm thy soul to hell,
And quite bereave thee of salvation.
Though thou hast now offended like a man,
Do not persever in it like a devil.
Yet, yet, thou hast an amiable° soul, *lovable*
If sin by custom grow not into nature:
Then, Faustus, will repentance come too late,
Then thou art banished from the sight of heaven;
No mortal can express the pains of hell.
It may be this my exhortation
Seems harsh and all unpleasant; let it not,
For, gentle son, I speak it not in wrath,
Or envy of thee, but in tender love,
And pity of thy future misery.
And so have hope, that this my kind rebuke,
Checking thy body, may amend thy soul.

FAUSTUS Where art thou, Faustus? Wretch, what hast thou done?
Damned art thou, Faustus, damned: despair and die.
Hell claims his right, and with a roaring voice
Says "Faustus, come, thine hour is almost come"

[*Mephostophilis gives him a dagger.*]

And Faustus now will come to do thee right.

OLD MAN Oh stay, good Faustus, stay thy desperate steps.
I see an angel hover o'er thy head,
And with a vial full of precious grace,
Offers to pour the same into thy soul.
Then call for mercy and avoid despair.

FAUSTUS Ah my sweet friend, I feel thy words
To comfort my distressed soul.
Leave me awhile to ponder on my sins.

OLD MAN I leave thee, but with grief of heart,
Fearing the ruin of thy hopeless soul. [*Exit.*]

FAUSTUS Accursed Faustus, wretch, what hast thou done?
I do repent, and yet I do despair.

Hell strives with grace for conquest in my breast.
What shall I do to shun the snares of death?

MEPHOSTOPHILIS Thou traitor, Faustus, I arrest thy soul
For disobedience to my sovereign lord.
Revolt,[2] or I'll in piecemeal tear thy flesh.

FAUSTUS I do repent I e'er offended him.
Sweet Mephostophilis, entreat thy lord
To pardon my unjust presumption,
And with my blood again I will confirm
The former vow I made to Lucifer.

MEPHOSTOPHILIS Do it then, Faustus, with unfeigned heart,
Lest greater dangers do attend thy drift.

FAUSTUS Torment, sweet friend, that base and crooked age
That durst dissuade me from thy Lucifer,
With greatest torment that our hell affords.

MEPHOSTOPHILIS His faith is great: I cannot touch his soul.
But what I may afflict his body with
I will attempt, which is but little worth.

FAUSTUS One thing, good servant, let me crave of thee,
To glut the longing of my heart's desire,
That I may have unto my paramour
That heavenly Helen which I saw of late,
Whose sweet embraces may extinguish clear
Those thoughts that do dissuade me from my vow,
And keep my vow I made to Lucifer.

MEPHOSTOPHILIS This, or what else my Faustus shall desire,
Shall be performed in twinkling of an eye.

[*Enter Helen again, passing over between two Cupids.*]

FAUSTUS Was this the face that launched a thousand ships,
And burnt the topless towers of Ilium?
Sweet Helen, make me immortal with a kiss.
Her lips suck forth my soul: see where it flies.
Come, Helen, come, give me my soul again.
Here will I dwell, for heaven is in those lips,
And all is dross that is not Helena.

[*Enter Old Man.*]

I will be Paris,[3] and for love of thee
Instead of Troy shall Wittenberg be sacked,
And I will combat with weak Menelaus,
And wear thy colors on my plumed crest.
Yea, I will wound Achilles in the heel,
And then return to Helen for a kiss.
Oh, thou art fairer than the evening's air,
Clad in the beauty of a thousand stars.
Brighter art thou than flaming Jupiter,
When he appeared to hapless Semele:[4]

2. I.e., return to the terms of your bargain with the devil.

3. Faustus imagines he will be not only Paris, Helen's lover, but also the victor in combat with her husband, King Menelaus, as well as with the greatest of the Greek warriors, Achilles.

4. The mortal woman to whom Jupiter appeared as lightening.

More lovely than the monarch of the sky,
In wanton Arethusa's[5] azure arms,
And none but thou shalt be my paramour. [*Exeunt.*]

OLD MAN Accursed Faustus, miserable man,
That from thy soul exclud'st the grace of heaven,
And fliest the throne of his tribunal seat.

[*Enter the Devils.*]

Satan begins to sift° me with his pride, *scrutinize*
As in this furnace God shall try my faith.
My faith, vile hell, shall triumph over thee.
Ambitious fiends, see how the heavens smiles
At your repulse, and laughs your state to scorn.
Hence, hell, for hence I fly unto my God. [*Exeunt.*]

Scene Two

[*Thunder. Enter Lucifer, Belzebub and Mephostophilis.*]

LUCIFER Thus from infernal Dis° do we ascend *hell*
To view the subjects of our monarchy,
Those souls which sin seals the black sons of hell,
'Mong which as chief, Faustus, we come to thee,
Bringing with us lasting damnation
To wait upon thy soul. The time is come
Which makes it forfeit.

MEPHOSTOPHILIS And this gloomy night,
Here in this room will wretched Faustus be.

BELZEBUB And here we'll stay,
To mark him how he doth demean himself.

MEPHOSTOPHILIS How should he, but in desperate lunacy?
Fond worldling, now his heart blood dries with grief.
His conscience kills it, and his laboring brain
Begets a world of idle fantasies
To overreach the devil. But all in vain:
His store of pleasures must be sauced with pain.
He and his servant Wagner are at hand.
Both come from drawing Faustus' latest will.
See where they come.

[*Enter Faustus and Wagner.*]

FAUSTUS Say, Wagner, thou hast perused my will:
How dost thou like it?

WAGNER Sir, so wondrous well
As in all humble duty I do yield
My life and lasting service for your love.

[*Enter the Scholars.*]

FAUSTUS Gramercies, Wagner. Welcome, gentlemen.

FIRST SCHOLAR Now, worthy Faustus, methinks your looks are changed.

FAUSTUS Oh gentlemen!

SECOND SCHOLAR What ails Faustus?

FAUSTUS Ah, my sweet chamber-fellow, had I lived with thee

5. A nymph beloved by the river-god Alpheus; no myth describes her as Jupiter's lover.

Then had I lived still, but now must die eternally.
Look, sirs, comes he not? Comes he not?

FIRST SCHOLAR Oh, my dear Faustus, what imports this fear?

SECOND SCHOLAR Is all our pleasure turned to melancholy?

THIRD SCHOLAR He is not well with being oversolitary.

SECOND SCHOLAR If it be so, we'll have physicians, and Faustus shall be cured.

THIRD SCHOLAR 'Tis but a surfeit, sir; fear nothing.

FAUSTUS A surfeit of deadly sin, that hath damned both body and soul.

SECOND SCHOLAR Yet Faustus, look up to heaven, and remember mercy is infinite.

FAUSTUS But Faustus' offence can ne'er be pardoned, The serpent that tempted Eve may be saved, but not Faustus. Oh gentlemen, hear with patience and tremble not at my speeches. Though my heart pant and quiver to remember that I have been a student here these thirty years, oh would I had never seen Wittenberg, never read book. And what wonders I have done all Germany can witness, yea all the world, for which Faustus hath lost both Germany and the world, yea heaven itself, heaven, the seat of God, the throne of the blessed, the kingdom of joy, and must remain in hell for ever. Hell, oh hell for ever. Sweet friends, what shall become of Faustus, being in hell for ever?

SECOND SCHOLAR Yet Faustus, call on God.

FAUSTUS On God, whom Faustus hath abjured? On God, whom Faustus hath blasphemed? Oh my God, I would weep, but the devil draws in my tears. Gush forth blood instead of tears, yea, life and soul. Oh, he stays my tongue. I would lift up my hands, but see, they hold them, they hold them.

ALL Who, Faustus?

FAUSTUS Why, Lucifer and Mephostophilis: Oh gentlemen, I gave them my soul for my cunning.

ALL Oh, God forbid.

FAUSTUS God forbade it indeed, but Faustus hath done it. For vain pleasure of four and twenty years hath Faustus lost eternal joy and felicity. I writ them a bill with mine own blood, the date is expired: this is the time, and he will fetch me.

FIRST SCHOLAR Why did not Faustus tell us of this before, that divines might have prayed for thee?

FAUSTUS Oft have I thought to have done so, but the devil threatened to tear me in pieces if I named God; to fetch me body and soul if I once gave ear to divinity, and now 'tis too late. Gentlemen, away, lest you perish with me.

SECOND SCHOLAR Oh what may we do to save Faustus?

FAUSTUS Talk not of me, but save yourselves and depart.

THIRD SCHOLAR God will strengthen me. I will stay with Faustus.

FIRST SCHOLAR Tempt not God, sweet friend, but let us into the next room and pray for him.

FAUSTUS Ay, pray for me, pray for me. And what noise soever you hear, come not unto me, for nothing can rescue me.

SECOND SCHOLAR Pray thou, and we will pray, that God may have mercy upon thee.

FAUSTUS Gentlemen, farewell. If I live till morning, I'll visit you. If not, Faustus is gone to hell.

ALL Faustus, farewell. [*Exeunt Scholars.*]

MEPHOSTOPHILIS Ay, Faustus, now thou hast no hope of heaven,
Therefore despair, think only upon hell,
For that must be thy mansion, there to dwell.

FAUSTUS Oh, thou bewitching fiend, 'twas thy temptation

Hath robbed me of eternal happiness.
MEPHOSTOPHILIS I do confess it, Faustus, and rejoice.
'Twas I that, when thou were't i' the way to heaven,
Dammed up thy passage; when thou took'st the book
To view the scriptures, then I turned the leaves
And led thine eye.
What, weep'st thou? 'Tis too late, despair. Farewell.
Fools that will laugh on earth, must weep in hell. [*Exit.*]
[*Enter the Good and the Evil Angel at several doors.*]
GOOD ANGEL Oh Faustus, if thou hadst given ear to me,
Innumerable joys had followed thee.
But thou didst love the world.
EVIL ANGEL Gave ear to me,
And now must taste hell's pains perpetually.
GOOD ANGEL Oh, what will all thy riches, pleasures, pomps,
Avail thee now?
EVIL ANGEL Nothing but vex thee more,
To want in hell, that had on earth such store.
[*Music while the throne descends.*]
GOOD ANGEL Oh, thou hast lost celestial happiness,
Pleasures unspeakable, bliss without end.
Hadst thou affected sweet divinity,
Hell, or the devil, had had no power on thee.
Hadst thou kept on that way, Faustus, behold
In what resplendent glory thou hadst sat
In yonder throne, like those bright shining saints,
And triumphed over hell. That thou hast lost,
And now, poor soul, must thy good angel leave thee:
The jaws of hell are open to receive thee. [*Exit.*]
[*Hell is discovered.*]
EVIL ANGEL Now, Faustus, let thine eyes with horror stare
Into that vast perpetual torture-house.
There are the furies tossing damned souls
On burning forks. Their bodies broil in lead.
There are live quarters broiling on the coals
That ne'er can die. This ever-burning chair
Is for o'er-tortured souls to rest them in.
These, that are fed with sops of flaming fire,
Were gluttons, and loved only delicates,
And laughed to see the poor starve at their gates.
But yet all these are nothing. Thou shalt see
Ten thousand tortures that more horrid be.
FAUSTUS Oh, I have seen enough to torture me.
EVIL ANGEL Nay, thou must feel them, taste the smart of all:
He that loves pleasure must for pleasure fall.
And so I leave thee, Faustus, till anon.
Then wilt thou tumble in confusion. [*Exit.*]
[*The clock strikes eleven.*]
FAUSTUS Ah Faustus,
Now hast thou but one bare hour to live,

And then thou must be damned perpetually.
Stand still, you ever-moving spheres of heaven,
That time may cease and midnight never come.
Fair nature's eye, rise, rise again, and make
Perpetual day. Or let this hour be but
A year, a month, a week, a natural day,
That Faustus may repent and save his soul.
O lente, lente, currite noctis equi.[6]
The stars move still, time runs, the clock will strike.
The devil will come, and Faustus must be damned.
Oh, I'll leap up to my God: who pulls me down?
See, see, where Christ's blood streams in the firmament.
One drop would save my soul, half a drop. Ah, my Christ!
Ah, rend not my heart for naming of my Christ!
Yet will I call on him. Oh, spare me, Lucifer!
Where is it now? 'Tis gone:
And see where God stretcheth out his arm,
And bends his ireful brows.
Mountains and hills, come, come, and fall on me,
And hide me from the heavy wrath of God.
No, no. Then will I headlong run into the earth.
Earth, gape! Oh no, it will not harbor me.
You stars that reigned at my nativity,
Whose influence hath allotted death and hell,
Now draw up Faustus like a foggy mist
Into the entrails of yon laboring cloud,
That when you vomit forth into the air
My limbs may issue from your smoky mouths,
So that my soul may but ascend to heaven.
[*The watch strikes.*]
Ah! half the hour is past,
'Twill all be past anon.° *soon*
Oh God, if thou wilt not have mercy on my soul,
Yet, for Christ's sake whose blood hath ransomed me,
Impose some end to my incessant pain.
Let Faustus live in hell a thousand years,
A hundred thousand, and at last be saved.
Oh, no end is limited to damned souls.
Why wert thou not a creature wanting soul?
Or why is this immortal that thou hast?
Ah, Pythagoras' *metempsychosis*,[7] were that true
This soul should fly from me, and I be changed
Unto some brutish beast.
All beasts are happy, for when they die
Their souls are soon dissolved in elements,
But mine must live still to be plagued in hell.
Cursed be the parents that engendered me!

6. Faustus quotes from Ovid's *Amores* 1.13.40: "O slowly, slowly run, horses of the night."

7. The transmigration of souls. The Greek philosopher Pythagoras speculated that souls were reborn in other bodies in an endless progression.

No, Faustus, curse thyself, curse Lucifer,
That hath deprived thee of the joys of heaven.
[*The clock strikes twelve.*]
Oh, it strikes, it strikes! Now body turn to air,
Or Lucifer will bear thee quick to hell.
[*Thunder and lightning.*]
Oh soul, be changed into little water drops
And fall into the ocean, ne'er be found.
[*Thunder. Enter the Devils.*]
My God, my God, look not so fierce on me.
Adders and serpents, let me breathe awhile.
Ugly hell, gape not, come not, Lucifer!
I'll burn my books. Ah, Mephostophilis! [*Exeunt with him.*]

Scene Three

[*Enter the Scholars.*]

FIRST SCHOLAR Come, gentlemen, let us go visit Faustus,
For such a dreadful night was never seen
Since first the world's creation did begin.
Such fearful shrieks and cries were never heard.
Pray heaven the Doctor have escaped the danger.
SECOND SCHOLAR Oh help us, heaven! See, here are Faustus' limbs,
All torn asunder by the hand of death.
THIRD SCHOLAR The devils whom Faustus served have torn him thus:
For twixt the hours of twelve and one, methought
I heard him shriek and call aloud for help,
At which self time the house seemed all on fire
With dreadful horror of these damned fiends.
SECOND SCHOLAR Well, gentlemen, though Faustus' end be such.
As every Christian heart laments to think on,
Yet, for he was a scholar once admired
For wondrous knowledge in our German schools,
We'll give his mangled limbs due burial,
And all the students clothed in mourning black
Shall wait upon his heavy funeral. [*Exeunt.*]

Epilogue

[*Enter the Chorus.*]

CHORUS Cut is the branch that might have grown full straight,
And burned is Apollo's laurel bough,
That sometime grew within this learned man.
Faustus is gone. Regard his hellish fall,
Whose fiendful fortune may exhort the wise
Only to wonder at unlawful things,
Whose deepness doth entice such forward wits,
To practice more than heavenly power permits.

Terminat hora diem, Terminat Author opus.[8]

Finis.

8. The hour ends the day, the author ends the work.

William Shakespeare

1564–1616

English colonists venturing to the New World carried with them an English Bible; if they owned a single secular book, it was probably the works of Shakespeare. A humanist scripture of sorts, his works have never hardened into doctrine; rather, they have lent themselves to a myriad range of interpretations, each shaped by particular interests, tastes, and expectations. Ben Jonson's line—"He was not of an age, but for all time!"—describes the appeal Shakespeare has had for speakers of English and the many other languages into which his works have been translated.

Shakespeare was born in the provincial town of Stratford-on-Avon, a three-day journey from London by horse or carriage. His father, John Shakespeare, was a glover and local justice of the peace; his mother, Mary Arden, came from a family that owned considerable land in the county. He probably went to a local grammar school where he learned Latin and read histories of the ancient world. Jonson's disparaging comment, that Shakespeare knew "small Latin and less Greek," must not be taken too seriously. Shakespeare (unlike Jonson) was not classically inclined, but his mature works reveal a mind that was extraordinarily well informed and acutely aware of rhetorical techniques and logical argument. At eighteen, Shakespeare married Anne Hathaway, who was twenty-six; in the next three years they had a daughter, Susanna, and then twins, Hamnet and Judith. Six years later, perhaps after periods of teaching school in Stratford, he went to London, eventually (in 1594) to join one of the great theatrical companies of the day, the Chamberlain's Men. It was with this company that he began his career as actor, manager, and playwright. In 1599 the troupe began to put on plays at the Globe, an outdoor theater in Southwark, not far from the other principal theaters of the day—the Rose, the Bear Garden, and the Swan—and across the river from the city of London itself. Because these theaters were outside city limits, in a district known as "the liberties," they were free from the control of authorities responsible for civic order; in effect, the theater provided a place in which all kinds of ideas and ways of life, whether conventional or not, could be represented, examined, and criticized. When James I acceded to the throne in 1603, Shakespeare's company became the King's Men and played also at court and at Blackfriars, an indoor theater in London. Some critics think that the change in venue necessitated a degree of allusiveness and innuendo that was not evident in earlier productions.

During the years Shakespeare was writing for the theater, the populations of Europe were periodically devastated by the plague, and city authorities were obliged to close places of public gathering, including theaters. Shakespeare provided plays for seasons in which the theaters in London were open, composing them at lightning speed and helping to stage productions on very short notice. The plays that we now accept as Shakespeare's fall roughly into several general categories: first, the histories, largely based on the chronicles of the Tudor historian Raphael Holinshed, and the Roman plays, inspired by Plutarch's *Lives of the Ancient Romans*, written in Greek and translated by Sir Thomas North; second, the comedies, often set in the romantic world of the English countryside or an Italian town; third, the tragedies, some of which explore the dark legends of the past; and fourth, a group in the mixed genre of tragicomedy but also called, after critics in the nineteenth century, the romances. A fifth somewhat anomalous group—*All's Well That Ends Well*, *Measure for Measure*, and *Troilus and Cressida*—falls between comedy and satire; these plays are usually termed "problem comedies."

The early phase of Shakespeare's career, the decade beginning in the late 1580s, saw the first cycle of his English histories. In four plays (known as the first tetralogy) this cycle depicted events in the reigns of Henry VI and Richard III and concluded by dramatizing the accession of the first Tudor monarch, Henry VII. Fascinated by the fate of peoples governed by feeble or oppressive rulers, Shakespeare expressed his loathing of tyranny by showing how the misgovernment of a weak king can lead to despotic rule. The cycle ends with the death of the tyrant, Richard III, and the accession of the Duke of Richmond, later Henry VII (Elizabeth's grandfather)—an action that celebrates the founder of the Tudor dynasty and the providence that had selected this family to bring peace to England. A later play, *King John,* concerns an earlier monarch whose claim to the throne is suspect; here divine right, having validated the succession of the Tudor monarchy in the first tetralogy, is made doubtful by a monarch's own viciousness. The play implies a question that Shakespeare continues to ask of history for the rest of his career: in what sense may divine right to be understood as a principle of monarchic rule? History, as Shakespeare will go on to represent it, no longer clearly demonstrates the triumph of justice, but rather shows the interrelatedness of good and evil motives that end in morally ambiguous action. The first of the Roman plays, *The Tragedy of Titus Andronicus,* which tells of the Roman general's revenge for the rape of his daughter Lavinia, and the early comedies, *The Taming of the Shrew, The Comedy of Errors, Two Gentlemen of Verona,* and *Love's Labor's Lost,* which depicts the effects of mistaken identity and misunderstood speech, illustrate other themes that Shakespeare will continue to represent: the terrible consequences of the search for revenge and the unfortunate, as well as salutary, self-deceptions of love.

The second phase, culminating in productions around 1600, is marked by more and subtler comedy: *A Midsummer Night's Dream, The Merchant of Venice, The Merry Wives of Windsor, Much Ado About Nothing, As You Like It, and Twelfth Night.* These plays insert into plots that focus primarily on the courtship of young couples a dramatic commentary on darker kinds of human desire: a longing for possessions; a wish to control others, particularly children; and a self-love so intense that it leads to fantasy and delusion. A romantic tragedy of this period, *Romeo and Juliet,* shows how the gross unreason sustaining a family feud and a mysteriously malevolent fate combine to destroy the future of lovers. A second cycle of four English histories, beginning with the deposition of Richard II and ending in the triumphs of Henry V and the birth of Henry VI, reveals how Shakespeare complicates the genre. An ostensible motive for the second tetralogy was the celebration of an English monarchy that had been preserved through the ages by God's will. Yet the actions of even the least controversial of its kings are questionable: Henry V's conquest of France is driven by greed as much as by his claim to the French throne, which is represented as dubious even in the playtext. A second Roman play, *The Tragedy of Julius Caesar,* takes up the question of tyranny in relation to the liberty inherent in a republic; the play seems most tragic when its action suggests that the Roman people do not recognize the sacrifices that are necessary to preserve such freedom and even regard freedom itself as negligible. As a whole, these plays demonstrate the characteristics of Shakespeare's mature style. Certain recurring images unify the plays thematically and, more important, link them to contemporary habits of speech as well as to the intellectual discourse of the period. Visual images—the I and the eye of the lover—often clarify the language of love, and figures denoting the well-being of different kinds of "corporation," including the human body, the family, and the body politic, signal the comprehensive order that was supposed to govern relations among all the elements of creation.

Incorporating many of the themes in the "problem comedies," the tragedies of the same period preoccupied Shakespeare for the seven years following the accession of James I: *Hamlet, Othello, King Lear, Macbeth, Antony and Cleopatra,* and *Coriolanus,* together with *Timon of Athens,* a play that was apparently written in collaboration with Thomas Middleton. *All's Well That Ends Well* and *Measure for Measure* illustrate societies that contain rather than reject sordid or unregenerate characters, both noble and common, and thus provide opportunities for comic endings to situations that might otherwise have ended in tragedy. And making much of the need for order but exemplifying the deep disorder of the military societies of Greece and Troy, the characters in *Troilus and Cressida* reveal the extent to which Shakespeare could imagine language as ironic and the human spirit as utterly possessed by a cynical need to turn every occasion to its own advantage. These plays serve to introduce tragedies of unprecedented scope.

Featuring heroes who overreach the limits of their place in life and so fail to fulfill their obligations to themselves and their dependents, Shakespeare's later tragedies embrace a wider range of human experience than can be explained by traditional conceptions of sin and fate. Profoundly complex in their treatment of motivation and the operations of the will, the tragedies entertain the idea of a beneficent deity who both permits terrible suffering and infuses, to use Hamlet's words, a "special providence in the fall of a sparrow." They reveal the blinding egotism that causes fatal misperceptions of character, motive, and action; their heroes are at once terribly in error and also strangely sympathetic. The human capacity for evil is perhaps most fully realized in the characters of women: the bestial daughters of King Lear, Goneril and Regan; the diabolical Lady Macbeth; the shamelessly duplicitous Cleopatra. Yet even they are not entirely unsympathetic; in many ways their behavior responds to the challenges that other, essentially more authoritative characters represent. The romances—*Pericles*, *Cymbeline*, *The Winter's Tale*, and *The Tempest*—round out the final phase of Shakespeare's dramatic career, representing (like the comedies) the restoration of family harmony and (like the histories) the return of good government. The deeply troubling divisions within families and states that characterize the tragedies are the basis for the restorative unions in the romances. Their depiction of passages of time and space that allow providential recoveries of health and prosperity to both individual characters and whole bodies politic are largely owing to the intervention of women. Unlike the women of the tragedies, the daughters and wives of the romances are generative in the broadest sense. They heal their fathers and husbands by restoring to their futures the possibility of descendents and therefore of dynastic continuity. Their agency is, in turn, sustained by forces identified as divine and outside history. *Henry VIII*, a history, and *Two Noble Kinsmen*, a romance, both probably composed jointly with John Fletcher, conclude Shakespeare's career as a dramatist.

Shakespeare also wrote narrative and lyric poems of great power, notably *Venus and Adonis*, *The Rape of Lucrece*, and a cycle of 154 sonnets. In a bold departure from tradition the sonnets celebrate the poet's steadfast love for a young man (never identified), his competitive rivalry with another poet (sometimes identified as Christopher Marlowe), and his troubled relationship with a woman who has dark features. The cycle encourages an interpretation that accounts for its romantic elements, but it also thwarts any obvious construction of events. It is thought that most of the sonnets were composed in the mid-1590s, although they were not published until 1609, apparently without Shakespeare's oversight. Their order therefore cannot be assigned to Shakespeare, and for this reason alone their function as narrative must remain problematic. Still, the reader can trace their representation of successive relations between persons and themes: the young man, although himself derelict in the duties of friendship, will remain beloved by the poet and made immortal by his verse, while the dark lady, who is unscrupulous and afflicted with venereal disease, receives only expressions of desire and lust, shadowed by the poet's disdain and self-loathing.

In a sense, Shakespeare has always been up to date. True, his language is not what is heard today, and his characters are shaped by forces within his culture, not ours. Yet we continue to see his plays on stage and in film, sometimes as recreations of the productions that historians of theater think he knew and saw but more often as reconceived with the addition of modern costumes, settings, and music as well as some strategic cutting of the dramatic text. Earlier periods produced their own kinds of Shakespeare. The Restoration stage, with scenery that allowed audiences to imagine they were looking through a window to life itself, put on plays that were embellished and trimmed to satisfy the taste of the time. Some producers omitted characters who were considered superfluous (the porter in *Macbeth*); others added characters who were judged essential for balance (Miranda's sister, Dorinda, in *The Tempest*). *King Lear* acquired a happy ending when Edgar married Cordelia. No one production of any period has defined a play entirely; every director has had his or her vision of what Shakespeare meant an audience to see. These reinterpretations testify to the perennial vitality of a playwright who was indeed, as Jonson said, "for all time."

THE SONNETS

The entire sequence numbers 154 sonnets. The first fourteen encourage a young man to marry and have children and may have been commissioned by his family. Neither the young man nor his family has been identified, although some readers have thought Henry Wriosthesley, Earl of Southampton, a possible subject. In Sonnet 15, Shakespeare turns to a related topic: the young man will be made eternal not only by his descendants but by the poet's praise of him in verse. Sonnet 20 initiates a long sequence of sonnets addressed to a young man as the poet's lover; whether he is the man who featured in the earlier sonnets on procreation is unclear, but it has generally been assumed so. Beginning with Sonnet 78, the poet complains that a rival poet is stealing his subject—the young man's virtue and grace—to the detriment of his own poetry. Who Shakespeare's rival is (or whether he is in fact a single person) is not known, although some readers have considered Christopher Marlowe a possibility. A final set of twenty-eight sonnets introduces a new character to the sequence, a figure often referred to as "the dark lady," who is the lover of both the poet and the young man. The threesome make up a dramatic unity that is fraught with tension and anguish.

SONNETS

1

From fairest creatures we desire increase,
That thereby beauty's rose might never die,
But as the riper° should by time decease, *the older person*
His tender heir might bear his memory;
But thou, contracted° to thine own bright eyes, *engaged, shrunk*
Feed'st thy light's flame with self-substantial fuel,
Making a famine where abundance lies,
Thyself thy foe, to thy sweet self too cruel.
Thou that art now the world's fresh ornament
And only herald to the gaudy spring,
Within thine own bud buriest thy content,
And, tender churl, mak'st waste in niggarding.° *hoarding*
Pity the world, or else this glutton be:
To eat the world's due, by the grave and thee.[1]

12

When I do count the clock that tells the time,
And see the brave day sunk in hideous night;
When I behold the violet past prime,
And sable° curls all silvered o'er with white; *dark*
When lofty trees I see barren of leaves
Which erst from heat did canopy the herd,
And summer's green, all girded up in sheaves,
Borne on the bier with white and bristly beard,[2]
Then of thy beauty do I question make
That thou among the wastes of time must go,
Since sweets and beauties do themselves forsake[3]

1. Have pity on the world and do not consume your own substance, refusing to engender the child you owe now to the world and finally to the grave.
2. The harvest of grain, once green, is gathered in bundles; each stalk ends in clusters of kernels protected by husks that resemble a white and bristling beard, which, like a bier or coffin, suggests mortality.
3. Beauties fade, seeming to forsake themselves.

And die as fast as they see others grow;
  And nothing 'gainst Time's scythe can make defense
  Save breed, to brave° him when he takes thee hence. *defy*

15

When I consider every thing that grows
Holds in perfection but a little moment,
That this huge stage presenteth naught but shows
Whereon the stars in secret influence comment;[4]
When I perceive that men as plants increase,
Cheerèd and checked even by the selfsame sky,
Vaunt° in their youthful sap, at height decrease, *boast*
And wear their brave state out of memory;° *until forgotten*
Then the conceit° of this inconstant stay *idea*
Set you most rich in youth before my sight,
Where wasteful Time debateth with Decay
To change your day of youth to sullied° night, *dark*
  And all in war with Time for love of you,
  As he takes from you, I ingraft you new.[5]

18

Shall I compare thee to a summer's day?
Thou art more lovely and more temperate.
Rough winds do shake the darling buds of May,
And summer's lease hath all too short a date.° *duration*
Sometimes too hot the eye of heaven shines,
And often is his gold complexion dimmed;
And every fair from fair sometimes declines,
By chance or nature's changing course untrimmed.° *stripped bare*
But thy eternal summer shall not fade
Nor lose possession of that fair thou ow'st;° *own*
Nor shall Death brag thou wanderest in his shade,
When in eternal lines° to time thou grow'st. *of verse*
  So long as men can breathe or eyes can see,
  So long lives this, and this gives life to thee.

20

A woman's face with Nature's own hand painted
Hast thou, the master-mistress of my passion;[6]
A woman's gentle heart, but not acquainted
With shifting change, as is false women's fashion;
An eye more bright than theirs, less false in rolling,° *straying*
Gilding the object whereupon it gazeth;
A man in hue, all hues in his controlling,[7]
Which steals men's eyes and women's souls amazeth.

4. Human action is a kind of show, influenced by the stars or heavenly forces.
5. Renew by grafting, implanting new beauty in verse.
6. Feminine in appearance, the young man is both a master and a mistress of the poet's passion. This is the first of a series of sonnets in which Shakespeare addresses the young man in clearly erotic language.
7. A man in appearance, he determines the nature of what he sees, what is apparent to him.

And for a woman wert thou first created,
Till Nature, as she wrought thee, fell a-doting,° *in love*
And by addition me of thee defeated,[8]
By adding one thing to my purpose nothing.
  But since she pricked thee out for women's pleasure,
  Mine be thy love and thy love's use their treasure.

29

When, in disgrace with fortune and men's eyes,
I all alone beweep my outcast state,
And trouble deaf heaven with my bootless° cries, *unavailing*
And look upon myself and curse my fate,
Wishing me like to one more rich in hope,
Featured like him, like him with friends possessed,
Desiring this man's art and that man's scope,° *powers*
With what I most enjoy contented least;
Yet in these thoughts myself almost despising,
Haply° I think on thee, and then my state, *perhaps*
Like to the lark at break of day arising
From sullen earth, sings hymns at heaven's gate;
  For thy sweet love remembered such wealth brings
  That then I scorn to change° my state with kings. *exchange*

31

Thy bosom is endearèd with all hearts,
Which I by lacking have supposèd dead,
And there reigns love and all love's loving parts,
And all those friends which I thought burièd.[9]
How many a holy and obsequious° tear *mournful*
Hath dear religious love stol'n from mine eye
As interest of the dead, which now appear
But things removed that hidden in thee lie!
Thou art the grave where buried love doth live,
Hung with the trophies of my lovers gone,
Who all their parts° of me to thee did give; *shares*
That due of many now is thine alone.
  Their images I loved I view in thee,[1]
  And thou, all they, hast all the all of me.

33

Full many a glorious morning have I seen
Flatter the mountaintops with sovereign eye,
Kissing with golden face the meadows green,

8. The last four lines of the sonnet are full of double meanings: the thing loving nature adds to the young man is a penis; this points or "pricks" him out for women's pleasure or "use" (with the added suggestion that his body is capital, which through usury generates interest); but the poet reserves for himself the young man's love, which is beyond commerce and has no price.

9. I.e., my past loves seem to live again in your bosom; the affection they had is now made over to you.

1. Here Shakespeare plays with a convention of courtly love: the virtues of all previous loves are said to be summed up in a present love, who embodies a universal perfection.

Gilding pale streams with heavenly alchemy;
Anon° permit the basest clouds to ride *soon*
With ugly rack° on his celestial face, *driven clouds*
And from the forlorn world his visage hide,
Stealing unseen to west with this disgrace.
Even so my sun one early morn did shine
With all-triumphant splendor on my brow.
But out, alack! He was but one hour mine;
The region° cloud hath masked him from me now. *of the upper air*
  Yet him for this my love no whit disdaineth;
  Suns of the world may stain when heaven's sun staineth.[2]

35

No more be grieved at that which thou hast done.
Roses have thorns, and silver fountains mud,
Clouds and eclipses stain both moon and sun,
And loathsome canker° lives in sweetest bud. *worm*
All men make faults, and even I in this,
Authorizing thy trespass with compare,° *comparisons*
Myself corrupting, salving thy amiss,
Excusing thy sins more than thy sins are.
For to thy sensual fault I bring in sense°— *reason*
Thy adverse party° is thy advocate— *accuser*
And 'gainst myself a lawful plea commence.
Such civil war is in my love and hate
  That I an accessary needs must be
  To that sweet thief which sourly robs from me.

55

Not marble nor the gilded monuments
Of princes shall outlive this powerful rhyme,
But you shall shine more bright in these contents
Than unswept stone besmeared with sluttish° time. *dirty*
When wasteful war shall statues overturn,
And broils° root out the work of masonry, *uprisings*
Nor° Mars his sword nor war's quick fire shall burn *neither*
The living record of your memory.
'Gainst death and all-oblivious° enmity *casting into oblivion*
Shall you pace forth; your praise shall still find room
Even in the eyes of all posterity
That wear this world out to the ending doom.° *judgment day*
  So, till the judgment that yourself° arise, *when you yourself*
  You live in this, and dwell in lovers' eyes.

60

Like as the waves make towards the pebbled shore,
So do our minutes hasten to their end;

2. If the sun may be covered by clouds, so too the suns (or sons) of the world may dim in their affections. This is the first of the poet's laments for his lover's insincerity.

Each changing place with that which goes before,
In sequent° toil all forwards do contend.° *successive / strive*
Nativity, once in the main° of light, *sea*
Crawls to maturity, wherewith being crowned,
Crookèd eclipses 'gainst his glory fight,
And Time that gave doth now his gift confound.° *destroy*
Time doth transfix° the flourish set on youth *puncture*
And delves° the parallels in beauty's brow, *digs*
Feeds on the rarities of nature's truth,
And nothing stands but for his scythe to mow.
And yet to times in hope my verse shall stand,
Praising thy worth despite his cruel hand.

73

That time of year thou mayst in me behold
When yellow leaves, or none, or few, do hang
Upon those boughs which shake against the cold,
Bare ruined choirs[3] where late the sweet birds sang.
In me thou seest the twilight of such day
As after sunset fadeth in the west,
Which by and by black night doth take away,
Death's second self, that seals up all in rest.
In me thou seest the glowing of such fire
That on the ashes of his youth doth lie
As the deathbed whereon it must expire,
Consumed with that which it was nourished by.
This thou perceiv'st, which makes thy love more strong,
To love that well which thou must leave ere long.

80

O, how I faint when I of you do write,
Knowing a better spirit° doth use your name, *the rival poet*
And in the praise thereof spends all his might
To make me tongue-tied, speaking of your fame!
But since your worth, wide as the ocean is,
The humble as° the proudest sail doth bear, *as well as*
My saucy bark, inferior far to his,
On your broad main° doth willfully appear. *sea*
Your shallowest° help will hold me up afloat, *slightest*
Whilst he upon your soundless° deep doth ride; *unfathomable*
Or, being wrecked, I am a worthless boat,
He of tall building° and of goodly pride. *construction*
Then if he thrive and I be cast away,
The worst was this: my love was my decay.° *ruin*

86

Was it the proud full sail of his great verse,
Bound for the prize° of all-too-precious you, *captive booty*

3. The choir is the section of a church reserved for the singers in the choir. "Choir" puns on "quire," the gathering of pages in a book, and thus recalls the "leaves" in line 2.

That did my ripe thoughts in my brain inhearse,° *entomb*
Making their tomb the womb wherein they grew?
Was it his spirit,° by spirits taught to write *genius*
Above a mortal pitch, that struck me dead?[4]
No, neither he, nor his compeers by night
Giving him aid, my verse astonishèd.
He, nor that affable familiar ghost° *spirit*
Which nightly gulls him with intelligence,
As victors of my silence cannot boast;
I was not sick of any fear from thence.
  But when your countenance filled up his line,[5]
  Then lacked I matter; that enfeebled mine.° *my verse*

87

Farewell! Thou art too dear for my possessing,
And like enough thou know'st thy estimate.° *value*
The charter of thy worth gives thee releasing;[6]
My bonds in thee are all determinate.° *ended*
For how do I hold thee but by thy granting,
And for that riches where is my deserving?
The cause of this fair gift in me is wanting,
And so my patent[7] back again is swerving.
Thyself thou gav'st, thy own worth then not knowing,
Or me, to whom thou gav'st it, else mistaking;
So thy great gift, upon misprision° growing, *error*
Comes home again, on better judgment making.
  Thus have I had thee as a dream doth flatter,
  In sleep a king, but waking no such matter.

93

So shall I live, supposing thou art true,
Like a deceivèd husband; so love's face
May still seem love to me, though altered new,
Thy looks with me, thy heart in other place.
For there can live no hatred in thine eye,
Therefore in that I cannot know thy change.° *infidelity*
In many's looks the false heart's history
Is writ in moods and frowns and wrinkles strange,
But heaven in thy creation did decree
That in thy face sweet love should ever dwell;
Whate'er thy thoughts or thy heart's workings be,
Thy looks should nothing thence but sweetness tell.
  How like Eve's apple doth thy beauty grow,
  If thy sweet virtue answer not thy show![8]

4. Shakespeare ironically suggests that the rival poet writes with supernatural help, or at least what he claims is supernatural help. Shakespeare later implies that this help is actually no more than a gull's (trickster's) intelligence or gossip.
5. When you became his subject.
6. You are worth so much that you can pay off all obligations you owe me; in other words, I have no right to you.
7. Deed granting a monopoly.
8. Like Eve's deceptively attractive apple, the young man's beauty is a kind of temptation that leads to the death of him who succumbs to it.

104

To me, fair friend, you never can be old,
For, as you were when first your eye I eyed,
Such seems your beauty still. Three winters cold
Have from the forests shook three summers' pride,
Three beauteous springs to yellow autumn turned
In process of the seasons have I seen,
Three April perfumes in three hot Junes burned,
Since first I saw you fresh, which yet are green.
Ah, yet doth beauty, like a dial[9] hand,
Steal from his figure and no pace perceived.
So your sweet hue, which methinks still doth stand,
Hath motion, and mine eye may be deceived,
  For fear of which, hear this, thou age unbred:° *unborn*
  Ere you were born was beauty's summer dead.

106

When in the chronicle of wasted° time *past*
I see descriptions of the fairest wights,° *people*
And beauty making beautiful old rhyme
In praise of ladies dead and lovely knights,
Then, in the blazon° of sweet beauty's best, *catalogue*
Of hand, of foot, of lip, of eye, of brow,
I see their antique pen would have expressed
Even such a beauty as you master° now. *possess*
So all their praises are but prophecies
Of this our time, all you prefiguring;
And, for° they looked but with divining eyes, *because*
They had not skill enough your worth to sing.
  For we, which now behold these present days,
  Have eyes to wonder, but lack tongues to praise.[1]

107

Not mine own fears nor the prophetic soul
Of the wide world dreaming on things to come[2]
Can yet the lease of my true love control,
Supposed as forfeit to a confined doom.° *at a set time*
The mortal moon hath her eclipse endured,
And the sad augurs mock their own presage;
Incertainties now crown themselves assured,
And peace proclaims olives of endless age.[3]

9. Beauty is like the hand of a clock, a dial; it moves slowly but inexorably away from the height of the hour.
1. The poets of antiquity could not describe your perfection because they could only guess at it; we recognize your perfection but lack but the skill to describe it.
2. Shakespeare may have had in mind the ancient concept of *anima mundi* (literally, a world soul), which was imagined as breathing life into all creation.
3. A supposedly dangerous lunar eclipse has passed, and those who predicted disaster now mock their own predictions. The moon may be Elizabeth I, who died in 1603; the endless peace to follow may be the one that James I negotiated with the Spanish in 1604. Or the moon's eclipse may figure Elizabeth's sixty-third year, a numerologically suspect period; in this case the ensuing peace describes a time in which anxiety over the future of the kingdom diminished, or "uncertainties" were "assured," i.e., became certainties.

Now with the drops of this most balmy time[4]
My love looks fresh, and Death to me subscribes,° *yields*
Since, spite of him, I'll live in this poor rhyme,
While he insults° o'er dull and speechless tribes; *triumphs*
  And thou in this shalt find thy monument,
  When tyrants' crests and tombs of brass are spent.° *worn away*

116

Let me not to the marriage of true minds
Admit impediments. Love is not love
Which alters when it alteration finds,° *in the beloved*
Or bends with the remover to remove.
O, no, it is an ever-fixèd mark° *landmark*
That looks on tempests and is never shaken;
It is the star to every wandering bark,
Whose worth's unknown, although his height be taken.[5]
Love's not Time's fool, though rosy lips and cheeks
Within his bending sickle's compass° come; *range*
Love alters not with his brief hours and weeks,
But bears it out even to the edge of doom.° *judgment day*
  If this be error and upon me proved,
  I never writ, nor no man ever loved.

123

No, Time, thou shalt not boast that I do change.
Thy pyramids[6] built up with newer might
To me are nothing novel, nothing strange;
They are but dressings of a former sight.
Our dates are brief, and therefore we admire
What thou dost foist upon us that is old,
And rather make them born to our desire
Than think that we before have heard them told.
Thy registers° and thee I both defy, *records*
Not wondering at the present nor the past,
For thy records and° what we see doth lie, *and also*
Made more or less by thy continual haste.
  This I do vow and this shall ever be:
  I will be true, despite thy scythe and thee.

124

If my dear love were but the child of state,
It might for Fortune's bastard be unfathered,
As subject to Time's love or to Time's hate,

4. A time that is restorative, as from the application of a medicinal ointment; a possible reference to the coronation of James I, celebrated by anointing the monarch with balm and other rituals.
5. The star by which ships navigate by measuring its altitude from the horizon (known values) is itself beyond valuation.
6. Any imposing structure; those built recently, "with newer might," are reconceptions, "dressings," of former structures.

Weeds among weeds, or flowers with flowers gathered.[7]
No, it was builded far from accident;
It suffers not in smiling pomp, nor falls
Under the blow of thrallèd° discontent, *enslaved*
Whereto th' inviting time our fashion° calls. *manner*
It fears not Policy,° that heretic, *expediency*
Which works on leases of short-numbered hours,
But all alone stands hugely politic,[8]
That it nor grows with heat nor drowns with showers.
  To this I witness call the fools of Time,
  Which die for goodness, who have lived for crime.[9]

126

O thou, my lovely boy, who in thy power
Dost hold Time's fickle glass,° his sickle hour; *hourglass*
Who hast by waning grown, and therein show'st
Thy lovers withering as thy sweet self grow'st;
If Nature, sovereign mistress over wrack,° *destruction*
As thou goest onwards, still will pluck thee back,
She keeps thee to this purpose, that her skill
May Time disgrace and wretched minutes kill.[1]
Yet fear her, O thou minion° of her pleasure! *slave*
She may detain, but not still keep, her treasure.
Her audit, though delayed, answered must be,
And her quietus° is to render thee.[2] *settlement*

130[3]

My mistress' eyes are nothing like the sun;
Coral is far more red than her lips' red;
If snow be white, why then her breasts are dun;° *brown*
If hairs be wires, black wires grow on her head.
I have seen roses damasked,° red and white, *mingled*
But no such roses see I in her cheeks;
And in some perfumes is there more delight
Than in the breath that from my mistress reeks.
I love to hear her speak, yet well I know
That music hath a far more pleasing sound.
I grant I never saw a goddess go;
My mistress, when she walks, treads on the ground.

7. If my love for you were merely a product of circumstance, it would be no more than Fortune's bastard and not have a father; it would be subject to accidents, both good and bad.
8. His love is beyond the expedient maneuvers of mere "policy" because it is itself "politic" or a state.
9. This enigmatic couplet may mean that those who have lived as criminals and then die for goodness are Time's fools because deathbed repentance is folly; or that those who have lived as criminals and then die in a good cause are Time's fools in the sense that everyone who resists the temporizing ways of the world is a fool.
1. His lover's power can hold back time and prevent his sickle from mowing down his green youth; paradoxically, while others grow old, he grows young. Nature permits this expressly to defy Time.
2. Yet Nature owes you to Time and will pay her debt by handing you over at last. The sonnet ends short of the 14 lines the form demands, as if to emphasize the idea of brevity.
3. Sonnet 127 was the first to have a woman, not a man, as its principal subject; she is described as a woman of dark complexion.

And yet, by heaven, I think my love as rare
As any she belied with false compare.[4]

138

When my love swears that she is made of truth
I do believe her, though I know she lies,
That she might think me some untutored youth,
Unlearnèd in the world's false subtleties.
Thus vainly thinking that she thinks me young,
Although she knows my days are past the best,
Simply I credit her false-speaking tongue;
On both sides thus is simple truth suppressed.
But wherefore says she not she is unjust?
And wherefore say not I that I am old?
O, love's best habit is in seeming° trust, *apparent*
And age in love loves not to have years told.
Therefore I lie with her, and she with me,[5]
And in our faults by lies we flattered be.

144

Two loves I have, of comfort and despair,
Which like two spirits do suggest° me still: *tempt*
The better angel is a man right fair,
The worser spirit a woman colored ill.
To win me soon to hell, my female evil
Tempteth my better angel from my side,
And would corrupt my saint to be a devil,
Wooing his purity with her foul pride.
And whether that my angel be turned fiend
Suspect I may, yet not directly tell;
But being both from me, both to each friend,
I guess one angel in another's hell.
Yet this shall I ne'er know, but live in doubt
Till my bad angel fire my good one out.[6]

152

In loving thee thou know'st I am forsworn,° *faithless*
But thou art twice forsworn, to me love swearing:
In act thy bed-vow° broke, and new faith torn *marriage vow*
In vowing new hate after new love bearing.[7]
But why of two oaths' breach do I accuse thee,
When I break twenty? I am perjured most,
For all my vows are oaths but to misuse° thee, *deceive*

4. The couplet suggests ironic or hyperbolic compliment: my mistress is exceptional in that she has set new standards for true beauty by a comparison that defies its standards.

5. We deceive each other; we have sex with each other.

6. The couplet suggests several interpretations. The poet's lady or bad angel could fire or dismiss his "fair" friend; she could infect him with a venereal disease, a condition that would cause a fever; finally, she could be the cause of his descent into hellfire, a consequence of sin.

7. You have broken your marriage vow and your vow to love me.

And all my honest faith in thee is lost.
For I have sworn deep oaths of thy deep kindness,
Oaths of thy love, thy truth, thy constancy,
And, to enlighten thee, gave eyes to blindness,[8]
Or made them swear against the thing they see;
For I have sworn thee fair. More perjured eye,
To swear against the truth so foul a lie!

Othello

Othello (1604) is a tragedy both of its time and ahead of its time. Basing *Othello* on a novella from Giraldi Cinthio's *Hecatommithi* (1565), Shakespeare takes an Italian Renaissance tale of greed, lust, and brutality and turns it into a timeless tragedy of ingenious evil spiraling toward destruction, and love haunted by demonic jealousy. A brief plot synopsis of the novella will make the point. Lusting after Desdemona and resenting Cassio for being given the position of lieutenant by Othello, Iago sets about convincing Othello that his wife has been unfaithful with Cassio. When Desdemona meets with Othello's suspicious jealousy, she concludes that she should never have married a Moor. Iago and Othello together plot to kill her. Bludgeoning her to death with sandbags, they pull down the plaster from the ceiling to make it look like an accident. The remorseful Othello betrays Iago, who then fingers Othello. Desdemona's family catches up with Othello and gets their revenge.

Although Shakespeare gives Iago the twin motives of sexual jealousy (he suspects his wife Emilia of having slept with Othello) and resentment, the intelligence and cunning of Iago make him resemble a politically calculating reader of Machiavelli's *Prince* rather than a brutal thug. To match this villain, Shakespeare creates a noble hero—not only a great general and war hero but a man enthralled by his wife, reluctant to believe her guilty, and manipulated into blaming her by the false evidence of the handkerchief. Faced with the protean shape-shifting ability of Iago to make not only himself but also the people around him appear to be what they are not, Othello is less a coconspirator than a victim. He is also a victim of his own status as outsider, an element that the tragedy plays up from the very first scene, where Iago shouts in the streets to Brabantio, Desdemona's father, "the black ram is tupping your white ewe." Othello loves Desdemona with a passionate intensity that is only equalled by the terrifying jealousy by which he undoes them both, "when I love thee not, / Chaos is come again." Shakespeare's Desdemona is also far more complex than her counterpart in the Italian novella. Portrayed from the outset of the play as a woman unafraid of incurring her father's wrath for marrying the man she loves, she loves Othello to the end—preferring to die rather than to live without his love.

Shakespeare makes his audience question preconceptions about sex, race, and identity in ways that are still urgent today. The play represents the sexual relation between Othello and Desdemona as one that is both passionate and yet somehow, at least from the point of view of Iago and Brabantio, obscene. The only time we see the couple in the bedroom together is in the final scene, where they both meet their deaths at Othello's hand. He likens himself to the "base Indian" ("Judean" in the Folio) who "sacrificed all his tribe for a pearl of great price." Othello sees himself as a cultural other, like the Turk he has been fighting throughout the play. There is no getting around the play's obsession with Othello's blackness; the language and imagery repeatedly impress upon us the issue of the hero's race.

Finally, identity itself is a central theme of *Othello*. The play abounds in incongruities of identity. Othello the Moor of Venice is a bit like Nanook of Las Vegas. And Venice, a city known for its decadent courtesans, is here the home of a woman of complete faithfulness. From the first act, where Iago declares "I am not what I am," to his declaration of love for Othello at

8. To make you seem fair, I saw what was not there or did not see what was there.

the moment where the audience knows he is enacting the greatest hatred, Shakespeare allows his audience to see the deceptively manipulative role-playing involved in the struggle for power. But rather than achieving power, Iago destroys not only Othello and Desdemona but also Emilia and himself. Whether Iago's evil is unfathomable or not, there is certainly something about it that is beyond the control of his own amazing powers of strategy and improvisation. It is an evil strong enough to overtake and inhabit even a man as noble as Othello.

Othello, the Moor of Venice

The Names of the Actors

OTHELLO, *the Moor*
BRABANTIO, *a senator, father to Desdemona*
CASSIO, *an honorable lieutenant to Othello*
IAGO, *Othello's ancient, a villain*
RODERIGO, *a gulled gentleman*
DUKE OF VENICE
SENATORS *of Venice*
MONTANO, *Governor of Cyprus*
GENTLEMEN *of Cyprus*
LODOVICO AND GRATIANO, *kinsmen to Brabantio, two noble Venetians*
SAILORS
CLOWN
DESDEMONA, *daughter to Brabantio and wife to Othello*
EMILIA, *wife to Iago*
BIANCA, *a courtesan and mistress to Cassio*
A MESSENGER
A HERALD
A MUSICIAN
SERVANTS, ATTENDANTS, OFFICERS, SENATORS, MUSICIANS, GENTLEMEN

Scene: *Venice; a seaport in Cyprus*

Act 1[1]

Scene 1

[*Location: Venice. A street. Enter Roderigo and Iago.*]

RODERIGO Tush, never tell me! I take it much unkindly
That thou, Iago, who hast had my purse
As if the strings were thine, shouldst know of this.[2]
IAGO 'Sblood,[3] but you'll not hear me.
If ever I did dream of such a matter,
Abhor me.
RODERIGO Thou toldst me thou didst hold him in thy hate.
IAGO Despise me
If I do not. Three great ones of the city,
In personal suit to make me his lieutenant,
Off-capped to him;° and by the faith of man, *Othello*
I know my price, I am worth no worse a place.
But he, as loving his own pride and purposes,
Evades them with a bombast circumstance[4]
Horribly stuffed with epithets of war,
And, in conclusion,
Nonsuits° my mediators. For, "Certes,"° says he, *rejects / certainly*
"I have already chose my officer."
And what was he?

1. Our text is taken, and the notes are adapted, from David Bevington, ed., *The Complete Works of Shakespeare*.
2. I.e., Desdemona's elopement.
3. By His (Christ's) blood.
4. Wordy evasion. *Bombast* is cotton padding.

Forsooth, a great arithmetician,[5]
One Michael Cassio, a Florentine,
A fellow almost damned in a fair wife,[6]
That never set a squadron in the field
Nor the division of a battle knows
More than a spinster[7]—unless the bookish theoric,° *theory*
Wherein the togaed consuls° can propose° *senators/discuss*
As masterly as he. Mere prattle without practice
Is all his soldiership. But he, sir, had th'election;
And I, of whom his° eyes had seen the proof *Othello's*
At Rhodes, at Cyprus, and on other grounds
Christened° and heathen, must be beleed and calmed[8] *Christian*
By debitor and creditor.[9] This countercaster,[1]
He, in good time,° must his lieutenant be, *opportunely*
And I—God bless the mark![2]—his Moorship's ancient.° *ensign*

RODERIGO By heaven, I rather would have been his hangman.

IAGO Why, there's no remedy. 'Tis the curse of service;
Preferment° goes by letter and affection,[3] *promotion*
And not by old gradation,[4] where each second
Stood heir to th' first. Now, sir, be judge yourself
Whether I in any just term° am affined° *respect/bound*
To love the Moor.

RODERIGO I would not follow him then.

IAGO O sir, content you.[5]
I follow him to serve my turn upon him.
We cannot all be masters, nor all masters
Cannot be truly° followed. You shall mark *faithfully*
Many a duteous and knee-crooking knave
That, doting on his own obsequious bondage,
Wears out his time, much like his master's ass,
For naught but provender, and when he's old, cashiered.° *dismissed*
Whip me[6] such honest knaves. Others there are
Who, trimmed in forms and visages of duty,[7]
Keep yet their hearts attending on themselves,
And, throwing but shows of service on their lords,
Do well thrive by them, and when they have lined their coats,[8]
Do themselves homage.[9] These fellows have some soul,
And such a one do I profess myself. For, sir,
It is as sure as you are Roderigo,
Were I the Moor I would not be Iago.[1]

5. A man whose military knowledge is merely theoretical, based on books of tactics.
6. Cassio does not seem to be married, but his counterpart in Shakespeare's source does have a woman in his house.
7. A housewife, one whose regular occupation is spinning.
8. Left to leeward without wind, becalmed (a sailing metaphor).
9. A name for a system of bookkeeping, here used as a contemptuous nickname for Cassio.
1. Bookkeeper, one who tallies with *counters,* or "metal disks." Said contemptuously.
2. Perhaps originally a formula to ward off evil; here an expression of impatience.
3. Personal influence and favoritism.
4. Step-by-step seniority, the traditional way.
5. Don't you worry about that.
6. Whip, as far as I'm concerned.
7. Dressed up in the mere form and show of dutifulness.
8. Stuffed their purses.
9. Attend to self-interest solely.
1. If I were able to assume command, I certainly would not choose to remain a subordinate, or, I would keep a suspicious eye on a flattering subordinate.

In following him, I follow but myself—
Heaven is my judge, not I for love and duty,
But seeming so for my peculiar° end. *particular*
For when my outward action doth demonstrate
The native° act and figure° of my heart *innate/intent*
In compliment extern,[2] 'tis not long after
But I will wear my heart upon my sleeve
For daws[3] to peck at. I am not what I am.[4]
RODERIGO What a full° fortune does the thick-lips[5] owe° *swelling/own*
If he can carry 't thus!° *carry this off*
IAGO Call up her father.
Rouse him, make after him, poison his delight,
Proclaim him in the streets; incense her kinsmen,
And, though he in a fertile climate dwell,
Plague him with flies.[6] Though that his joy be joy,[7]
Yet throw such changes of vexation° on 't *vexing changes*
As it may lose some color.[8]
RODERIGO Here is her father's house. I'll call aloud.
IAGO Do, with like timorous° accent and dire yell *frightening*
As when, by night and negligence, the fire
Is spied in populous cities.
RODERIGO What ho, Brabantio! Signor Brabantio, ho!
IAGO Awake! What ho, Brabantio! Thieves, thieves, thieves!
Look to your house, your daughter, and your bags!
Thieves, thieves!
[*Brabantio enters above at a window.*][9]
BRABANTIO What is the reason of this terrible summons?
What is the matter° there? *your business*
RODERIGO Signor, is all your family within?
IAGO Are your doors locked?
BRABANTIO Why, wherefore ask you this?
IAGO Zounds,[1] sir, you're robbed. For shame, put on your gown!
Your heart is burst; you have lost half your soul.
Even now, now, very now, an old black ram
Is tupping your white ewe.[2] Arise, arise!
Awake the snorting° citizens with the bell, *snoring*
Or else the devil[3] will make a grandsire of you.
Arise, I say!
BRABANTIO What, have you lost your wits?
RODERIGO Most reverend signor, do you know my voice?
BRABANTIO Not I. What are you?
RODERIGO My name is Roderigo.
BRABANTIO The worser welcome.

2. Outward show (conforming in this case to the inner workings and intention of the heart).
3. Small crowlike birds, proverbially stupid and avaricious.
4. I am not one who wears his heart on his sleeve.
5. Elizabethans often applied the term "Moor" to Negroes.
6. Though he seems prosperous and happy now, vex him with misery.
7. Although he seems fortunate and happy.
8. That may cause it to lose some of its fresh gloss.
9. This stage direction, from the Quarto, probably calls for an appearance on the gallery above and rearstage.
1. By His (Christ's) wounds.
2. Covering, copulating with (said of sheep).
3. The devil was conventionally pictured as black.

I have charged thee not to haunt about my doors.
In honest plainness thou hast heard me say
My daughter is not for thee; and now, in madness,
Being full of supper and distempering° drafts, *intoxicating*
Upon malicious bravery[4] dost thou come
To start° my quiet. *disrupt*

RODERIGO Sir, sir, sir—

BRABANTIO But thou must needs be sure
My spirits and my place[5] have in° their power *have it in*
To make this bitter to thee.

RODERIGO Patience, good sir.

BRABANTIO What tell'st thou me of robbing? This is Venice;
My house is not a grange.° *country house*

RODERIGO Most grave Brabantio,
In simple° and pure soul I come to you. *sincere*

IAGO Zounds, sir, you are one of those that will not serve God if the devil bid you. Because we come to do you service and you think we are ruffians, you'll have your daughter covered with a Barbary[6] horse; you'll have your nephews[7] neigh to you; you'll have coursers for cousins and jennets for germans.[8]

BRABANTIO What profane wretch art thou?

IAGO I am one, sir, that comes to tell you your daughter and the Moor are now making the beast with two backs.

BRABANTIO Thou art a villain.

IAGO You are—a senator.[9]

BRABANTIO This thou shalt answer.[1] I know thee, Roderigo.

RODERIGO Sir, I will answer anything. But I beseech you,
If 't be your pleasure and most wise° consent— *well-informed*
As partly I find it is—that your fair daughter,
At this odd-even[2] and dull watch o' the night,
Transported with° no worse nor better guard *by*
But with a knave of common hire,[3] a gondolier,
To the gross clasps of a lascivious Moor—
If this be known to you and your allowance° *permission*
We then have done you bold and saucy° wrongs. *insolent*
But if you know not this, my manners tell me
We have your wrong rebuke. Do not believe
That, from° the sense of all civility,° *contrary to / decency*
I thus would play and trifle with your reverence.[4]
Your daughter, if you have not given her leave,
I say again, hath made a gross revolt,
Tying her duty, beauty, wit,° and fortunes *intelligence*
In an extravagant° and wheeling° stranger[5] *expatriate / vagabond*
Of here and everywhere. Straight° satisfy yourself. *straightway*

4. With hostile intent to defy me.
5. My temperament and my authority of office.
6. From northern Africa (and hence associated with Othello).
7. I.e., grandsons.
8. You'll have stallions for kinsmen and ponies for relatives.
9. Said with mock politeness, as though the word itself were an insult.
1. Be held accountable for.
2. Between one day and the next, i.e., about midnight.
3. Than by a low fellow, a servant.
4. The respect due to you.
5. Foreigner.

If she be in her chamber or your house,
Let loose on me the justice of the state
For thus deluding you.

BRABANTIO Strike on the tinder,[6] ho!
Give me a taper! Call up all my people!
This accident° is not unlike my dream. *event*
Belief of it oppresses me already.
Light, I say, light! *[Exit above.]*

IAGO Farewell, for I must leave you.
It seems not meet° nor wholesome to my place° *fitting/position*
To be producted[7]—as, if I stay, I shall—
Against the Moor. For I do know the state,
However this may gall° him with some check,° *oppress/rebuke*
Cannot with safety cast° him, for he's embarked° *dismiss/engaged*
With such loud reason[8] to the Cyprus wars,
Which even now stands in act,° that, for their souls,[9] *are going on*
Another of his fathom[1] they have none
To lead their business; in which regard,[2]
Though I do hate him as I do hell pains,
Yet for necessity of present life° *livelihood*
I must show out a flag and sign of love,
Which is indeed but sign. That you shall surely find him,
Lead to the Sagittary[3] the raisèd search,[4]
And there will I be with him. So farewell. *[Exit]*

[Enter below, Brabantio in his nightgown[5] with servants and torches.]

BRABANTIO It is too true an evil. Gone she is;
And what's to come of my despisèd time[6]
Is naught but bitterness. Now, Roderigo,
Where didst thou see her?—O unhappy girl!—
With the Moor, sayst thou?—Who would be a father!—
How didst thou know 'twas she?—O, she deceives me
Past thought!—What said she to you?—Get more tapers.
Raise all my kindred.—Are they married, think you?

RODERIGO Truly, I think they are.

BRABANTIO O heaven! How got she out? O treason of the blood!
Fathers, from hence trust not your daughters' minds
By what you see them act. Is there not charms° *spells*
By which the property° of youth and maidhood *nature*
May be abused?° Have you not read, Roderigo, *deceived*
Of some such thing?

RODERIGO Yes, sir, I have indeed.

BRABANTIO Call up my brother.—O, would you had had her!—
Some one way, some another.—Do you know
Where we may apprehend her and the Moor?

6. Charred linen ignited by a spark from flint and steel, used to light torches or *tapers*.
7. Produced (as a witness).
8. Unanimous shout of confirmation (in the Senate).
9. To save themselves.
1. I.e., ability, depth of experience.
2. Out of regard for which.
3. An inn or house where Othello and Desdemona are staying, named for its sign of Sagittarius, or Centaur.
4. Search party roused out of sleep.
5. Dressing gown. (This costuming is specified in the Quarto text.)
6. I.e., remainder of life.

RODERIGO I think I can discover° him, if you please *reveal*
To get good guard and go along with me.
BRABANTIO Pray you, lead on. At every house I'll call;
I may command° at most.—Get weapons, ho! *demand aid*
And raise some special officers of night.—
On, good Roderigo. I will deserve° your pains. *reward*
[*Exeunt.*]

Scene 2

[*Location: Venice. Another street. Before Othello's lodgings. Enter Othello, Iago, attendants with torches.*]

IAGO Though in the trade of war I have slain men,
Yet do I hold it very stuff[7] o' the conscience
To do no contrived° murder. I lack iniquity *premeditated*
Sometimes to do me service. Nine or ten times
I had thought t' have yerked° him° here under the ribs. *stabbed / Roderigo*
OTHELLO 'Tis better as it is.
IAGO Nay, but he prated,
And spoke such scurvy and provoking terms
Against your honor
That, with the little godliness I have,
I did full hard forbear him.[8] But, I pray you, sir,
Are you fast married? Be assured of this,
That the magnifico[9] is much beloved,
And hath in his effect° a voice potential° *command / powerful*
As double as the Duke's. He will divorce you,
Or put upon you what restraint or grievance
The law, with all his might to enforce it on,
Will give him cable.° *scope*
OTHELLO Let him do his spite.
My services which I have done the seigniory° *government*
Shall out-tongue his complaints. 'Tis yet to know°— *not yet known*
Which, when I know that boasting is an honor,
I shall promulgate—I fetch my life and being
From men of royal siege,° and my demerits° *rank / deserts*
May speak unbonneted[1] to as proud a fortune
As this that I have reached. For know, Iago,
But that I love the gentle Desdemona,
I would not my unhousèd° free condition *unconfined*
Put into circumscription and confine° *confinement*
For the sea's worth.[2] But look, what lights come yond?
[*Enter Cassio and certain officers*[3] *with torches.*]
IAGO Those are the raisèd father and his friends.
You were best go in.
OTHELLO Not I. I must be found.

7. Essence, basic material (continuing the metaphor of *trade* from line 1).
8. I restrained myself with great difficulty from assaulting him.
9. Venetian grandee, i.e., Brabantio.
1. Without removing the hat, i.e., on equal terms (or "with hat off," "in all due modesty").
2. All the riches at the bottom of the sea.
3. The Quarto text calls for "Cassio with lights, officers with torches."

My parts, my title, and my perfect soul[4]
Shall manifest me rightly. Is it they?
IAGO By Janus,[5] I think no.
OTHELLO The servants of the Duke? And my lieutenant?
The goodness of the night upon you, friends!
What is the news?
CASSIO The Duke does greet you, General,
And he requires your haste-post-haste appearance
Even on the instant.
OTHELLO What is the matter,° think you? *business*
CASSIO Something from Cyprus, as I may divine.° *guess*
It is a business of some heat.° The galleys *urgency*
Have sent a dozen sequent° messengers *successive*
This very night at one another's heels,
And many of the consuls,° raised and met, *senators*
Are at the Duke's already. You have been hotly called for;
When, being not at your lodging to be found,
The Senate hath sent about[6] three several° quests *separate*
To search you out.
OTHELLO 'Tis well I am found by you.
I will but spend a word here in the house
And go with you. [*Exit.*]
CASSIO Ancient, what makes° he here? *does*
IAGO Faith, he tonight hath boarded[7] a land carrack.° *merchant ship*
If it prove lawful prize,° he's made forever. *booty*
CASSIO I do not understand.
IAGO He's married.
CASSIO To who?
[*Enter Othello.*]
IAGO Marry,[8] to—Come, Captain, will you go?
OTHELLO Have with you.[9]
CASSIO Here comes another troop to seek for you.
[*Enter Brabantio, Roderigo, with officers and torches.*][1]
IAGO It is Brabantio. General, be advised.[2]
He comes to bad intent.
OTHELLO Holla! Stand there!
RODERIGO Signor, it is the Moor.
BRABANTIO Down with him, thief!
[*They draw on both sides.*]
IAGO You, Roderigo! Come, sir, I am for you.
OTHELLO Keep up° your bright swords, for the dew will rust them. *sheathe*
Good signor, you shall more command with years
Than with your weapons.

4. My natural gifts, my position or reputation, and my unflawed conscience.
5. Roman two-faced god of beginnings.
6. All over the city.
7. Gone aboard and seized as an act of piracy (with sexual suggestion).
8. An oath, originally "by the Virgin Mary"; here used with wordplay on *married*.
9. Let's go.
1. The Quarto text calls for "others with lights and weapons."
2. Be on your guard.

BRABANTIO O thou foul thief, where hast thou stowed my daughter?
Damned as thou art, thou hast enchanted her!
For I'll refer me to all things of sense,[3]
If she in chains of magic were not bound
Whether a maid so tender, fair, and happy,
So opposite to marriage that she shunned
The wealthy curlèd darlings of our nation,
Would ever have, t' incur a general mock,
Run from her guardage[4] to the sooty bosom
Of such a thing as thou—to fear, not to delight.
Judge me the world if 'tis not gross in sense° *obvious*
That thou hast practiced on her with foul charms,
Abused her delicate youth with drugs or minerals° *poisons*
That weakens motion.[5] I'll have 't disputed on;[6]
'Tis probable and palpable to thinking.
I therefore apprehend and do attach° thee *arrest*
For an abuser of the world, a practicer
Of arts inhibited° and out of warrant.°— *black magic / illegal*
Lay hold upon him! If he do resist,
Subdue him at his peril.

OTHELLO Hold your hands,
Both you of my inclining° and the rest. *following*
Were it my cue to fight, I should have known it
Without a prompter.—Whither will you that I go
To answer this your charge?

BRABANTIO To prison, till fit time
Of law and course of direct session[7]
Call thee to answer.

OTHELLO What if I do obey?
How may the Duke be therewith satisfied,
Whose messengers are here about my side
Upon some present business of the state
To bring me to him?

OFFICER 'Tis true, most worthy signor.
The Duke's in council, and your noble self,
I am sure, is sent for.

BRABANTIO How? The Duke in council?
In this time of the night? Bring him away.° *right along*
Mine's not an idle° cause. The Duke himself, *trifling*
Or any of my brothers of the state,
Cannot but feel this wrong as 'twere their own;
For if such actions may have passage free,[8]
Bondslaves and pagans shall our statesmen be.
[*Exeunt*.]

3. Submit my case to creatures possessing common sense.
4. My guardianship of her.
5. Impair the vital faculties.
6. Argued in court by professional counsel, debated by experts.
7. Regular or specially convened legal proceedings.
8. Are allowed to go unchecked.

Scene 3

[*Location: Venice. A council chamber. Enter Duke and Senators and sit at a table, with lights, and Officers. The Duke and Senators are reading dispatches.*][9]

DUKE There is no composition° in these news — *consistency*
That gives them credit.
FIRST SENATOR Indeed, they are disproportioned.° — *inconsistent*
My letters say a hundred and seven galleys.
DUKE And mine, a hundred forty.
SECOND SENATOR And mine, two hundred.
But though they jump° not on a just° account— — *agree / exact*
As in these cases, where the aim° reports — *conjecture*
'Tis oft with difference—yet do they all confirm
A Turkish fleet, and bearing up to Cyprus.
DUKE Nay, it is possible enough to judgment.
I do not so secure me in the error
But the main article I do approve[1]
In fearful sense.
SAILOR [*within*] What ho, what ho, what ho!
[*Enter Sailor.*]
OFFICER A messenger from the galleys.
DUKE Now, what's the business?
SAILOR The Turkish preparation[2] makes for Rhodes.
So was I bid report here to the state
By Signor Angelo.
DUKE How say you by° this change? — *about*
FIRST SENATOR This cannot be
By no assay° of reason. 'Tis a pageant° — *test / mere show*
To keep us in false gaze.[3] When we consider
Th' importancy of Cyprus to the Turk,
And let ourselves again but understand
That, as it more concerns the Turk than Rhodes,
So may he with more facile question bear it,[4]
For that° it stands not in such warlike brace,° — *since / state*
But altogether lacks th' abilities° — *means of defense*
That Rhodes is dressed in°—if we make thought of this, — *equipped with*
We must not think the Turk is so unskillful° — *careless*
To leave that latest° which concerns him first, — *last*
Neglecting an attempt of ease and gain
To wake° and wage° a danger profitless. — *stir up / risk*
DUKE Nay, in all confidence, he's not for Rhodes.
OFFICER Here is more news.
[*Enter a Messenger.*]
MESSENGER The Ottomites, reverend and gracious,
Steering with due course toward the isle of Rhodes,

9. The Quarto text calls for the Duke and senators to "sit at a table with lights and attendants."
1. I do not take such (false) comfort in the discrepancies that I fail to perceive the main point, i.e., that the Turkish fleet is threatening.
2. Fleet prepared for battle.
3. Looking the wrong way.
4. So also he (the Turk) can more easily capture it (Cyprus).

Have there injointed them[5] with an after° fleet. *following*
FIRST SENATOR Ay, so I thought. How many, as you guess?
MESSENGER Of thirty sail; and now they do restem
Their backward course,[6] bearing with frank° appearance *undisguised*
Their purposes toward Cyprus. Signor Montano,
Your trusty and most valiant servitor,° *officer*
With his free duty[7] recommends[8] you thus,
And prays you to believe him.
DUKE 'Tis certain then for Cyprus.
Marcus Luccicos, is not he in town?
FIRST SENATOR He's now in Florence.
DUKE Write from us to him, post-post-haste. Dispatch.
FIRST SENATOR Here comes Brabantio and the valiant Moor.
[*Enter Brabantio, Othello, Cassio, Iago, Roderigo, and officers.*]
DUKE Valiant Othello, we must straight° employ you *straightway*
Against the general enemy[9] Ottoman.
[*To Brabantio.*] I did not see you; welcome, gentle° signor. *noble*
We lacked your counsel and your help tonight.
BRABANTIO So did I yours. Good Your Grace, pardon me;
Neither my place° nor aught I heard of business *official position*
Hath raised me from my bed, nor doth the general care
Take hold on me, for my particular° grief *personal*
Is of so floodgate[1] and o'erbearing nature
That it engluts° and swallows other sorrows *engulfs*
And it is still itself.[2]
DUKE Why, what's the matter?
BRABANTIO My daughter! O, my daughter!
DUKE AND SENATORS Dead?
BRABANTIO Ay, to me.
She is abused,° stol'n from me, and corrupted *deceived*
By spells and medicines bought of mountebanks;
For nature so preposterously to err,
Being not deficient,° blind, or lame of sense, *defective*
Sans° witchcraft could not. *without*
DUKE Whoe'er he be that in this foul proceeding
Hath thus beguiled your daughter of herself,
And you of her, the bloody book of law
You shall yourself read in the bitter letter
After your own sense[3]—yea, though our proper° son *my own*
Stood in your action.[4]
BRABANTIO Humbly I thank Your Grace.
Here is the man, this Moor, whom now it seems
Your special mandate for the state affairs
Hath hither brought.
ALL We are very sorry for 't.

5. Joined themselves.
6. Retrace their original course.
7. Freely given and loyal service.
8. Commends himself and reports to.
9. Universal enemy to all Christendom.

1. Overwhelming (as when floodgates are opened).
2. Remains undiminished.
3. According to your own interpretation.
4. Were under your accusation.

DUKE [*to Othello*]
What, in your own part, can you say to this?
BRABANTIO Nothing, but this is so.
OTHELLO Most potent, grave, and reverend signors,
My very noble and approved° good masters: *esteemed*
That I have ta'en away this old man's daughter,
It is most true; true, I have married her.
The very head and front[5] of my offending
Hath this extent, no more. Rude° am I in my speech, *unpolished*
And little blessed with the soft phrase of peace;
For since these arms of mine had seven years' pith,[6]
Till now some nine moons wasted,[7] they have used
Their dearest° action in the tented field; *most valuable*
And little of this great world can I speak
More than pertains to feats of broils and battle,
And therefore little shall I grace my cause
In speaking for myself. Yet, by your gracious patience,
I will a round° unvarnished tale deliver *plain*
Of my whole course of love—what drugs, what charms,
What conjuration, and what mighty magic,
For such proceeding I am charged withal,° *with*
I won his daughter.
BRABANTIO A maiden never bold;
Of spirit so still and quiet that her motion
Blushed at herself;[8] and she, in spite of nature,
Of years,[9] of country, credit,° everything, *reputation*
To fall in love with what she feared to look on!
It is a judgment maimed and most imperfect
That will confess° perfection so could err *concede (that)*
Against all rules of nature, and must be driven
To find out practices° of cunning hell *plots*
Why this should be. I therefore vouch° again *assert*
That with some mixtures powerful o'er the blood,° *passions*
Or with some dram conjured to this effect,[1]
He wrought upon her.
DUKE To vouch this is no proof,
Without more wider° and more overt test° *fuller / testimony*
Than these thin habits[2] and poor likelihoods° *weak inferences*
Of modern seeming[3] do prefer° against him. *bring forth*
FIRST SENATOR But Othello, speak.
Did you by indirect and forcèd courses[4]
Subdue and poison this young maid's affections?
Or came it by request and such fair question° *conversation*
As soul to soul affordeth?
OTHELLO I do beseech you,

5. Height and breadth, entire extent.
6. Since I was seven.
7. Until some nine months ago (since when Othello has evidently not been on active duty, but in Venice).
8. She blushed easily at herself. (*Motion* can suggest the impulse of the soul or of the emotions, or physical movement.)
9. I.e., difference in age.
1. Dose made by magical spells to have this effect.
2. Garments, i.e., appearances.
3. Commonplace assumption.
4. Means used against her will.

Send for the lady to the Sagittary
And let her speak of me before her father.
If you do find me foul in her report,
The trust, the office I do hold of you
Not only take away, but let your sentence
Even fall upon my life.

DUKE Fetch Desdemona hither.

OTHELLO Ancient, conduct them. You best know the place.
[*Exeunt Iago and attendants*.]
And, till she come, as truly as to heaven
I do confess the vices of my blood,° *passions*
So justly° to your grave ears I'll present *accurately*
How I did thrive in this fair lady's love,
And she in mine.

DUKE Say it, Othello.

OTHELLO Her father loved me, oft invited me,
Still° questioned me the story of my life *continually*
From year to year—the battles, sieges, fortunes
That I have passed.
I ran it through, even from my boyish days
To th' very moment that he bade me tell it,
Wherein I spoke of most disastrous chances,
Of moving accidents° by flood and field, *stirring happenings*
Of hairbreadth scapes i' th' imminent deadly breach,[5]
Of being taken by the insolent foe
And sold to slavery, of my redemption thence,
And portance° in my travels' history, *conduct*
Wherein of antres° vast and deserts idle,° *caverns / barren*
Rough quarries,° rocks, and hills whose heads touch heaven, *rock formations*
It was my hint° to speak—such was my process— *opportunity*
And of the Cannibals that each other eat,
The Anthropophagi,[6] and men whose heads
Do grow beneath their shoulders. These things to hear
Would Desdemona seriously incline;
But still the house affairs would draw her thence,
Which ever as she could with haste dispatch
She'd come again, and with a greedy ear
Devour up my discourse. Which I, observing,
Took once a pliant° hour, and found good means *well-suiting*
To draw from her a prayer of earnest heart
That I would all my pilgrimage dilate,° *relate in detail*
Whereof by parcels° she had something heard, *piecemeal*
But not intentively.° I did consent, *continuously*
And often did beguile her of her tears,
When I did speak of some distressful stroke
That my youth suffered. My story being done,
She gave me for my pains a world of sighs.
She swore, in faith, 'twas strange, 'twas passing° strange, *exceedingly*

5. Death-threatening gaps made in a fortification.

6. Man-eaters (a term from Pliny's *Natural History*).

'Twas pitiful, 'twas wondrous pitiful.
She wished she had not heard it, yet she wished
That heaven had made her° such a man. She thanked me, *created her to be*
And bade me, if I had a friend that loved her,
I should but teach him how to tell my story,
And that would woo her. Upon this hint° I spake. *opportunity*
She loved me for the dangers I had passed,
And I loved her that she did pity them.
This only is the witchcraft I have used.
Here comes the lady. Let her witness it.
[*Enter Desdemona, Iago, and attendants.*]

DUKE I think this tale would win my daughter too.
Good Brabantio,
Take up this mangled matter at the best.[7]
Men do their broken weapons rather use
Than their bare hands.

BRABANTIO I pray you, hear her speak.
If she confess that she was half the wooer,
Destruction on my head if my bad blame
Light on the man!—Come hither, gentle mistress.
Do you perceive in all this noble company
Where most you owe obedience?

DESDEMONA My noble Father,
I do perceive here a divided duty.
To you I am bound for life and education;° *upbringing*
My life and education both do learn° me *teach*
How to respect you. You are the lord of duty;[8]
I am hitherto your daughter. But here's my husband,
And so much duty as my mother showed
To you, preferring you before her father,
So much I challenge° that I may profess *claim*
Due to the Moor my lord.

BRABANTIO God be with you! I have done.
Please it Your Grace, on to the state affairs.
I had rather to adopt a child than get° it. *beget*
Come hither, Moor. [*He joins the hands of Othello and Desdemona.*]
I here do give thee that with all my heart[9]
Which, but thou hast already, with all my heart° *gladly*
I would keep from thee.—For your sake,° jewel, *on your account*
I am glad at soul I have no other child,
For thy escape° would teach me tyranny, *elopement*
To hang clogs[1] on them.—I have done, my lord.

DUKE Let me speak like yourself,[2] and lay a sentence[3]
Which, as a grice° or step, may help these lovers *step*
Into your favor.
When remedies° are past, the griefs are ended *hopes of remedy*

7. Make the best of a bad bargain.
8. To whom duty is due.
9. Wherein my whole affection has been engaged.
1. Blocks of wood fastened to the legs of criminals or convicts to inhibit escape.
2. As you would, in your proper temper.
3. Apply a maxim.

By seeing the worst, which late on hopes depended.[4]
To mourn a mischief° that is past and gone *misfortune*
Is the next° way to draw new mischief on. *nearest*
What° cannot be preserved when fortune takes, *whatever*
Patience her injury a mockery makes.[5]
The robbed that smiles steals something from the thief;
He robs himself that spends a bootless grief.[6]

BRABANTIO So let the Turk of Cyprus us beguile,
We lose it not, so long as we can smile.
He bears the sentence well that nothing bears
But the free comfort which from thence he hears,
But he bears both the sentence and the sorrow
That, to pay grief, must of poor patience borrow.[7]
These sentences, to sugar or to gall,
Being strong on both sides, are equivocal.[8]
But words are words. I never yet did hear
That the bruised heart was piercèd through the ear.[9]
I humbly beseech you, proceed to th' affairs of state.

DUKE The Turk with a most mighty preparation makes for Cyprus. Othello, the fortitude[1] of the place is best known to you; and though we have there a substitute[2] of most allowed[3] sufficiency, yet opinion, a sovereign mistress of effects, throws a more safer voice on you.[4] You must therefore be content to slubber[5] the gloss of your new fortunes with this more stubborn[6] and boisterous expedition.

OTHELLO The tyrant custom, most grave senators,
Hath made the flinty and steel couch of war
My thrice-driven° bed of down. I do agnize[7] *thrice sifted*
A natural and prompt alacrity
I find in hardness,° and do undertake *hardship*
These present wars against the Ottomites.
Most humbly therefore bending to your state,[8]
I crave fit disposition for my wife,
Due reference of place and exhibition,[9]
With such accommodation° and besort° *provision/attendance*
As levels° with her breeding.° *suits/upbringing*

DUKE Why, at her father's.

BRABANTIO I will not have it so.

OTHELLO Nor I.

DESDEMONA Nor I. I would not there reside,
To put my father in impatient thoughts

4. Which griefs were sustained until recently by hopeful anticipation.
5. Patience laughs at the injury inflicted by fortune (and thus eases the pain).
6. Indulges in unavailing grief.
7. A person well bears out your maxim who can enjoy its platitudinous comfort, free of all genuine sorrow, but anyone whose grief bankrupts his poor patience is left with your saying and his sorrow, too. (*Bears the sentence* also plays on the meaning, "receives judicial sentence.")
8. These fine maxims are equivocal, either sweet or bitter in their application.
9. I.e., surgically lanced and cured by mere words of advice.
1. Strength.
2. Deputy.
3. Acknowledged.
4. General opinion, an important determiner of affairs, chooses you as the best man.
5. Soil, sully.
6. Harsh, rough.
7. Know in myself, acknowledge.
8. Bowing to your authority.
9. Provision of appropriate place to live and allowance of money.

By being in his eye. Most gracious Duke,
To my unfolding° lend your prosperous° ear, *proposal/propitious*
And let me find a charter° in your voice, *authorization*
T' assist my simpleness.

DUKE What would you, Desdemona?

DESDEMONA That I did love the Moor to live with him,
My downright violence and storm of fortunes[1]
May trumpet to the world. My heart's subdued
Even to the very quality of my lord.[2]
I saw Othello's visage in his mind,
And to his honors and his valiant parts° *qualities*
Did I my soul and fortunes consecrate.
So that, dear lords, if I be left behind
A moth[3] of peace, and he go to the war,
The rites[4] for why I love him are bereft me,
And I a heavy interim shall support
By his dear[5] absence. Let me go with him.

OTHELLO Let her have your voice.° *consent*
Vouch with me, heaven, I therefor beg it not
To please the palate of my appetite,
Nor to comply with heat°—the young affects° *sexual passion/desires*
In me defunct—and proper° satisfaction, *personal*
But to be free° and bounteous to her mind. *generous*
And heaven defend° your good souls that you think° *forbid/should think*
I will your serious and great business scant
When she is with me. No, when light-winged toys
Of feathered Cupid seel[6] with wanton dullness
My speculative and officed instruments,[7]
That my disports corrupt and taint my business,[8]
Let huswives make a skillet of my helm,
And all indign° and base adversities *unworthy, shameful*
Make head° against my estimation!° *rise up/reputation*

DUKE Be it as you shall privately determine,
Either for her stay or going. Th' affair cries haste,
And speed must answer it.

A SENATOR You must away tonight.

DESDEMONA Tonight, my lord?

DUKE This night.

OTHELLO With all my heart.

DUKE At nine i' the morning here we'll meet again.
Othello, leave some officer behind,
And he shall our commission bring to you,
With such things else of quality and respect[9]

1. My plain and total breach of social custom, taking my future by storm and disrupting my whole life.
2. My heart is brought wholly into accord with Othello's virtues; I love him for his virtues.
3. I.e., one who consumes merely.
4. Rites of love (with a suggestion, too, of "rights," sharing).
5. Heartfelt. Also, costly.
6. I.e., make blind (as in falconry, by sewing up the eyes of the hawk during training).
7. Eyes and other faculties used in the performance of duty.
8. So that my sexual pastimes impair my work.
9. Of importance and relevance.

As doth import° you. *concern*
OTHELLO So please Your Grace, my ancient;
A man he is of honesty and trust.
To his conveyance I assign my wife,
With what else needful Your Good Grace shall think
To be sent after me.
DUKE Let it be so.
Good night to everyone. [*To Brabantio.*] And, noble signor,
If virtue no delighted° beauty lack, *delightful*
Your son-in-law is far more fair than black.
FIRST SENATOR Adieu, brave Moor. Use Desdemona well.
BRABANTIO Look to her, Moor, if thou hast eyes to see.
She has deceived her father, and may thee.
[*Exeunt Duke, Brabantio, Cassio, Senators, and officers.*]
OTHELLO My life upon her faith! Honest Iago,
My Desdemona must I leave to thee.
I prithee, let thy wife attend on her,
And bring them after in the best advantage.[1]
Come, Desdemona. I have but an hour
Of love, of worldly matters and direction,° *instructions*
To spend with thee. We must obey the time.[2]
[*Exit with Desdemona.*]
RODERIGO Iago—
IAGO What sayst thou, noble heart?
RODERIGO What will I do, think'st thou?
IAGO Why, go to bed and sleep.
RODERIGO I will incontinently° drown myself. *immediately*
IAGO If thou dost, I shall never love thee after. Why, thou silly gentleman?
RODERIGO It is silliness to live when to live is torment; and then have we a prescription[3] to die when death is our physician.
IAGO O villainous![4] I have looked upon the world for four times seven years, and, since I could distinguish betwixt a benefit and an injury, I never found man that knew how to love himself. Ere I would say I would drown myself for the love of a guinea hen,[5] I would change my humanity with a baboon.
RODERIGO What should I do? I confess it is my shame to be so fond,[6] but it is not in my virtue[7] to amend it.
IAGO Virtue? A fig![8] 'Tis in ourselves that we are thus or thus. Our bodies are our gardens, to the which our wills are gardeners; so that if we will plant nettles or sow lettuce, set hyssop[9] and weed up thyme, supply it with one gender[1] of herbs or distract it with[2] many, either to have it sterile with idleness[3] or manured with industry—why, the power and corrigible authority[4] of this lies in our wills.

1. At the most favorable opportunity.
2. The urgency of the present crisis.
3. Right based on long-established custom. Also, doctor's prescription
4. I.e., what perfect nonsense.
5. A slang term for a prostitute.
6. Infatuated.
7. Strength, nature.
8. To give a fig is to thrust the thumb between the first and second fingers in a vulgar and insulting gesture.
9. An herb of the mint family.
1. Kind.
2. Divide it among.
3. Want of cultivation.
4. Power to correct.

If the beam[5] of our lives had not one scale of reason to poise[6] another of sensuality, the blood[7] and baseness of our natures would conduct us to most preposterous conclusions. But we have reason to cool our raging motions,[8] our carnal stings, our unbitted[9] lusts, whereof I take this that you call love to be a sect or scion.[1]

RODERIGO It cannot be.

IAGO It is merely a lust of the blood and a permission of the will. Come, be a man. Drown thyself? Drown cats and blind puppies. I have professed me thy friend, and I confess me knit to thy deserving with cables of perdurable[2] toughness. I could never better stead[3] thee than now. Put money in thy purse. Follow thou the wars; defeat thy favor[4] with an usurped[5] beard. I say, put money in thy purse. It cannot be long that Desdemona should continue her love to the Moor—put money in thy purse—nor he his to her. It was a violent commencement in her, and thou shalt see an answerable sequestration[6]—put but money in thy purse. These Moors are changeable in their wills[7]—fill thy purse with money. The food that to him now is as luscious as locusts[8] shall be to him shortly as bitter as coloquintida.[9] She must change for youth; when she is sated with his body, she will find the error of her choice. She must have change, she must. Therefore put money in thy purse. If thou wilt needs damn thyself, do it a more delicate way than drowning. Make[1] all the money thou canst. If sanctimony[2] and a frail vow betwixt an erring[3] barbarian and a supersubtle Venetian be not too hard for my wits and all the tribe of hell, thou shalt enjoy her. Therefore make money. A pox of drowning thyself! It is clean out of the way.[4] Seek thou rather to be hanged in compassing[5] thy joy than to be drowned and go without her.

RODERIGO Wilt thou be fast[6] to my hopes if I depend on the issue?[7]

IAGO Thou art sure of me. Go, make money. I have told thee often, and I retell thee again and again, I hate the Moor. My cause is hearted;[8] thine hath no less reason. Let us be conjunctive[9] in our revenge against him. If thou canst cuckold him, thou dost thyself a pleasure, me a sport. There are many events in the womb of time which will be delivered. Traverse,[1] go, provide thy money. We will have more of this tomorrow. Adieu.

RODERIGO Where shall we meet i' the morning?

IAGO At my lodging.

RODERIGO I'll be with thee betimes.° [*He starts to leave.*] *early*

IAGO Go to, farewell.—Do you hear, Roderigo?

RODERIGO What say you?

5. Balance.
6. Counterbalance.
7. Natural passions.
8. Appetites.
9. Unbridled, uncontrolled.
1. Cutting or offshoot.
2. Very durable.
3. Assist.
4. Disguise your face.
5. The suggestion is that Roderigo is not man enough to have a beard of his own.
6. A corresponding separation or estrangement.
7. Carnal appetites.
8. Fruit of the carob tree (see Matthew 3:4), or perhaps honeysuckle.
9. Colocynth or bitter apple, a purgative.
1. Raise, collect.
2. Sacred ceremony.
3. Wandering, vagabond, unsteady.
4. Entirely unsuitable as a course of action.
5. Encompassing, embracing.
6. True.
7. Successful outcome.
8. Fixed in the heart, heartfelt.
9. United.
1. A military marching term.

IAGO No more of drowning, do you hear?
RODERIGO I am changed.
IAGO Go to, farewell. Put money enough in your purse.
RODERIGO I'll sell all my land. [*Exit.*]
IAGO Thus do I ever make my fool my purse;
For I mine own gained knowledge should profane
If I would time expend with such a snipe[2]
But for my sport and profit. I hate the Moor;
And it is thought abroad° that twixt my sheets *rumored*
He's done my office.[3] I know not if 't be true;
But I, for mere suspicion in that kind,
Will do as if for surety.[4] He holds me well;[5]
The better shall my purpose work on him.
Cassio's a proper° man. Let me see now: *handsome*
To get his place and to plume[6] up my will
In double knavery—How, how?—Let's see:
After some time, to abuse° Othello's ear *deceive*
That he° is too familiar with his wife. *Cassio*
He hath a person and a smooth dispose° *disposition*
To be suspected, framed to make women false.
The Moor is of a free° and open° nature, *frank / unsuspicious*
That thinks men honest that but seem to be so,
And will as tenderly° be led by the nose *readily*
As asses are.
I have 't. It is engendered. Hell and night
Must bring this monstrous birth to the world's light.
[*Exit.*]

Act 2

Scene 1

[*A seaport in Cyprus. An open place near the quay. Enter Montano and two Gentlemen.*]

MONTANO What from the cape can you discern at sea?
FIRST GENTLEMAN Nothing at all. It is a high-wrought flood.° *agitated sea*
I cannot, twixt the heaven and the main,° *ocean*
Descry a sail.
MONTANO Methinks the wind hath spoke aloud at land;
A fuller blast ne'er shook our battlements.
If it hath ruffianed° so upon the sea, *raged*
What ribs of oak, when mountains° melt on them, *of water*
Can hold the mortise?[7] What shall we hear of this?
SECOND GENTLEMAN A segregation° of the Turkish fleet. *dispersal*
For do but stand upon the foaming shore,
The chidden[8] billow seems to pelt the clouds;
The wind-shaked surge, with high and monstrous mane,[9]

2. Woodcock, i.e., fool.
3. My sexual function as husband.
4. Act as if on certain knowledge.
5. Regards me favorably.
6. Put a feather in the cap of, i.e., glorify, gratify.
7. Hold their joints together.
8. I.e., rebuked, repelled (by the shore), and thus shot into the air.
9. The surf is like the mane of a wild beast.

Seems to cast water on the burning Bear[1]
And quench the guards of th' ever-fixèd pole.
I never did like molestation° view *such a disturbance*
On the enchafèd° flood. *angry*

MONTANO If that° the Turkish fleet *if*
Be not ensheltered and embayed,° they are drowned; *in a harbor*
It is impossible to bear it out.° *survive*

Enter a [Third] Gentleman.

THIRD GENTLEMAN News, lads! Our wars are done.
The desperate tempest hath so banged the Turks
That their designment° halts.° A noble ship of Venice *enterprise / is lame*
Hath seen a grievous wreck° and sufferance° *shipwreck / damage*
On most part of their fleet.

MONTANO How? Is this true?

THIRD GENTLEMAN The ship is here put in,
A Veronesa;[2] Michael Cassio,
Lieutenant to the warlike Moor Othello,
Is come on shore; the Moor himself at sea,
And is in full commission here for Cyprus.

MONTANO I am glad on 't. 'Tis a worthy governor.

THIRD GENTLEMAN But this same Cassio, though he speak of comfort
Touching the Turkish loss, yet he looks sadly° *gravely*
And prays the Moor be safe, for they were parted
With foul and violent tempest.

MONTANO Pray heaven he be,
For I have served him, and the man commands
Like a full° soldier. Let's to the seaside, ho! *perfect*
As well to see the vessel that's come in
As to throw out our eyes for brave Othello,
Even till we make the main and th' aerial blue[3]
An indistinct regard.[4]

THIRD GENTLEMAN Come, let's do so,
For every minute is expectancy° *gives expectation*
Of more arrivance.° *arrival*

[Enter Cassio.]

CASSIO Thanks, you the valiant of this warlike isle,
That so approve° the Moor! O, let the heavens *honor*
Give him defense against the elements,
For I have lost him on a dangerous sea.

MONTANO Is he well shipped?

CASSIO His bark is stoutly timbered, and his pilot
Of very expert and approved allowance;° *tested reputation*
Therefore my hopes, not surfeited to death,[5]
Stand in bold cure.[6]

[A cry within:] "A sail, a sail, a sail!"

1. The constellation Ursa Minor or the Little Bear, which includes the polestar (and hence regarded as the *guards of th' ever-fixed pole* in the next line; sometimes the term *guards* is applied to the two "pointers" of the Big Bear or Dipper, which may be intended here.)
2. Fitted out in Verona for Venetian service, or possibly *Verennessa* (the Folio spelling), i.e., *verrinessa*, a cutter (from *verrinare*, "to cut through").
3. The sea and the sky.
4. Indistinguishable in our view.
5. Overextended, worn thin through repeated application or delayed fulfillment.
6. In strong hopes of fulfillment.

CASSIO What noise?
A GENTLEMAN The town is empty. On the brow o' the sea[7]
Stand ranks of people, and they cry "A sail!"
CASSIO My hopes do shape him for[8] the governor.
[*A shot within.*]
SECOND GENTLEMAN They do discharge their shot of courtesy;[9]
Our friends at least.
CASSIO I pray you, sir, go forth,
And give us truth who 'tis that is arrived.
SECOND GENTLEMAN I shall. [*Exit.*]
MONTANO But, good Lieutenant, is your general wived?
CASSIO Most fortunately. He hath achieved a maid
That paragons° description and wild fame,° — *surpasses / rumor*
One that excels the quirks° of blazoning[1] pens, — *witty conceits*
And in th' essential vesture of creation
Does tire the enginer.[2]
[*Enter Second Gentleman.*][3]
How now? Who has put in?° — *to harbor*
SECOND GENTLEMAN 'Tis one Iago, ancient to the General.
CASSIO He's had most favorable and happy speed.
Tempests themselves, high seas, and howling winds,
The guttered° rocks and congregated sands— — *jagged*
Traitors ensteeped° to clog the guiltless keel— — *lying under water*
As° having sense of beauty, do omit° — *as if / suspend*
Their mortal° natures, letting go safely by — *deadly*
The divine Desdemona.
MONTANO What is she?
CASSIO She that I spake of, our great captain's captain,
Left in the conduct of the bold Iago,
Whose footing° here anticipates our thoughts — *landing*
A se'nnight's° speed. Great Jove, Othello guard, — *week's*
And swell his sail with thine own powerful breath,
That he may bless this bay with his tall° ship, — *splendid*
Make love's quick pants in Desdemona's arms,
Give renewed fire to our extincted spirits,
And bring all Cyprus comfort!
[*Enter Desdemona, Iago, Roderigo, and Emilia.*]
O, behold,
The riches of the ship is come on shore!
You men of Cyprus, let her have your knees.
[*The gentlemen make curtsy to Desdemona.*]
Hail to thee, lady! And the grace of heaven
Before, behind thee, and on every hand
Enwheel thee round!
DESDEMONA I thank you, valiant Cassio.
What tidings can you tell me of my lord?

7. Cliff-edge.
8. I hope it is.
9. Fire a salute in token of respect and courtesy.
1. Setting forth as though in heraldic language.
2. In her real, God-given, beauty, (she) defeats any attempt to praise her. The engineer [engineer] is the poet, one who devises.
3. So identified in the Quarto text here and in lines 57, 60, 67 and 95; the Folio calls him a gentleman.

CASSIO He is not yet arrived, nor know I aught
But that he's well and will be shortly here.
DESDEMONA O, but I fear—How lost your company?
CASSIO The great contention of the sea and skies
Parted our fellowship.
[*Within: "A sail, a sail!" A shot.*]
But hark. A sail!
SECOND GENTLEMAN They give their greeting to the citadel.
This likewise is a friend.
CASSIO See for the news.
[*Exit Second Gentleman.*]
Good Ancient, you are welcome. [*Kissing Emilia.*]
Welcome, mistress.
Let it not gall your patience, good Iago,
That I extend° my manners; 'tis my breeding[4] *give scope to*
That gives me this bold show of courtesy.
IAGO Sir, would she give you so much of her lips
As of her tongue she oft bestows on me,
You would have enough.
DESDEMONA Alas, she has no speech![5]
IAGO In faith, too much.
I find it still,° when I have list° to sleep. *always / desire*
Marry, before your ladyship, I grant,
She puts her tongue a little in her heart
And chides with thinking.[6]
EMILIA You have little cause to say so.
IAGO Come on, come on. You are pictures out of doors,[7]
Bells[8] in your parlors, wildcats in your kitchens,[9]
Saints° in your injuries, devils being offended, *martyrs*
Players° in your huswifery,° and huswives[1] in your beds. *idlers / housekeeping*
DESDEMONA O, fie upon thee, slanderer!
IAGO Nay, it is true, or else I am a Turk.[2]
You rise to play, and go to bed to work.
EMILIA You shall not write my praise.
IAGO No, let me not.
DESDEMONA What wouldst write of me, if thou shouldst praise me?
IAGO O gentle lady, do not put me to 't,
For I am nothing if not critical.° *censorious*
DESDEMONA Come on, essay.°—There's one gone to the harbor? *try*
IAGO Ay, madam.
DESDEMONA I am not merry, but I do beguile
The thing I am[3] by seeming otherwise.
Come, how wouldst thou praise me?

4. Training in the niceties of etiquette.
5. She's not a chatterbox, as you allege.
6. In her thoughts only.
7. Silent and well-behaved in public.
8. Jangling, noisy, and brazen.
9. In domestic affairs. (Ladies would not do the cooking.)
1. Hussies (i.e., women are "busy" in bed, or unduly thrifty in dispensing sexual favors).
2. An infidel, not to be believed.
3. My anxious self.

To change the cod's head for the

She that could think and ne'er disclose her mind,
See suitors following and not look behind,
She was a wight, if ever such wight were—

DESDEMONA To do what?

IAGO To suckle fools and chronicle small beer.[8]

DESDEMONA O most lame and impotent conclusion! Do not learn of him, Emilia, though he be thy husband. How say you, Cassio? Is he not a most profane and liberal[9] counselor?

CASSIO He speaks home,[1] madam. You may relish[2] him more in[3] the soldier than in the scholar.

[*Cassio and Desdemona stand together, conversing intimately*.]

4. Sticky substance used to catch small birds.
5. Exerts herself. Also, prepares to deliver a child (with a following pun on "*delivered*" in line 130).
6. Her cleverness will make use of her beauty.
7. Dark-complexioned, brunette.
8. A fair person (with wordplay on "wight," a person).
9. With sexual suggestion of mating.
1. With added meaning of "lechery, wantonness."
2. Foolish.
3. Ugly.

4. Compel the approval.
5. Avoided temptation where the choice was hers.
6. Resolved to put up with her injury patiently.
7. To exchange a lackluster husband for a sexy lover(?) (*Cod's head* is slang for "penis.")
8. To nurse babies and keep petty household accounts.
9. Ribald and licentious.
1. Right to the target (a term from fencing).
2. Appreciate.
3. In the character of.

f. With as little a web
hile upon her, do; I will
tis so, indeed. If such tricks
been better you had not kissed
u are most apt to play the sir[8] in.
tesy! 'Tis so, indeed. Yet again your
clyster pipes[9] for your sake! [*Trumpet*
et.

and receive him.

.]

.

My dear Othello!
wonder great as my content
e before me. O my soul's joy,
tempest come such calms,
winds blow till they have weakened death,
the laboring bark climb hills of seas
mpus-high, and duck again as low
s hell's from heaven! If it were now to die,
'Twere now to be most happy, for I fear
My soul hath her content so absolute
That not another comfort like to this
Succeeds in unknown fate.[1]

DESDEMONA The heavens forbid
But that our loves and comforts should increase
Even as our days do grow!

OTHELLO Amen to that, sweet powers!
I cannot speak enough of this content.
It stops me here; it is too much of joy.
And this, and this, the greatest discords be
[*They kiss.*][2]
That e'er our hearts shall make!

IAGO [*aside*] O, you are well tuned now!
But I'll set down[3] the pegs that make this music,
As honest as I am.[4]

OTHELLO Come, let us to the castle.
News, friends! Our wars are done, the Turks are drowned.
How does my old acquaintance of this isle?—
Honey, you shall be well desired° in Cyprus; *welcomed*
I have found great love amongst them. O my sweet,
I prattle out of fashion,° and I dote *incoherently*

4. Well done.
5. Fetter, shackle.
6. Courtesy, show of courtly manners.
7. That's right, go ahead.
8. The fine gentleman.
9. Tubes used for enemas and douches.
1. Can follow in the unknown future.
2. The direction is from the Quarto.
3. Loosen (and hence untune the instrument).
4. For all my supposed honesty.

In mine own comforts.—I prithee, good Iago,
Go to the bay and disembark my coffers.° *chests*
Bring thou the master° to the citadel; *ship's captain*
He is a good one, and his worthiness
Does challenge° much respect.—Come, Desdemona.— *deserve*
Once more, well met at Cyprus!

[*Exeunt Othello and Desdemona and all but Iago and Roderigo.*]

IAGO [*to an attendant*] Do thou meet me presently at the harbor. [*To Roderigo.*] Come hither. If thou be'st valiant—as, they say, base men[5] being in love have then a nobility in their natures more than is native to them—list[6] me. The Lieutenant tonight watches on the court of guard.[7] First, I must tell thee this: Desdemona is directly in love with him.

RODERIGO With him? Why, 'tis not possible.

IAGO Lay thy finger thus,[8] and let thy soul be instructed. Mark me with what violence she first loved the Moor, but[9] for bragging and telling her fantastical lies. To love him still for prating? Let not thy discreet heart think it. Her eye must be fed; and what delight shall she have to look on the devil? When the blood is made dull with the act of sport,[1] there should be, again to inflame it and to give satiety a fresh appetite, loveliness in favor,[2] sympathy[3] in years, manners, and beauties—all which the Moor is defective in. Now, for want of these required conveniences,[4] her delicate tenderness will find itself abused,[5] begin to heave the gorge,[6] disrelish and abhor the Moor. Very nature[7] will instruct her in it and compel her to some second choice. Now, sir, this granted—as it is a most pregnant[8] and unforced position—who stands so eminent in the degree[9] of this fortune as Cassio does? A knave very voluble,[1] no further conscionable[2] than in putting on the mere form of civil and humane[3] seeming for the better compassing of his salt[4] and most hidden loose affection.[5] Why, none, why, none. A slipper[6] and subtle knave, a finder out of occasions, that has an eye can stamp[7] and counterfeit advantages,[8] though true advantage never present itself; a devilish knave. Besides, the knave is handsome, young, and hath all those requisites in him that folly[9] and green[1] minds look after. A pestilent complete knave, and the woman hath found him[2] already.

RODERIGO I cannot believe that in her. She's full of most blessed condition.[3]

IAGO Blessed fig's end! The wine she drinks is made of grapes. If she had been blessed, she would never have loved the Moor. Blessed pudding![4] Didst thou not see her paddle with the palm of his hand? Didst not mark that?

5. Even lowly born men.
6. Listen to.
7. Guardhouse. (Cassio is in charge of the watch.)
8. I.e., on your lips
9. Only.
1. Sex.
2. Appearance.
3. Correspondence, similarity.
4. Things conducive to sexual compatibility.
5. Cheated, revolted.
6. Experience nausea.
7. Her very instincts.
8. Evident, cogent.
9. As next in line for.
1. Facile, glib.
2. Conscientious, conscience-bound.
3. Polite, courteous.
4. Licentious.
5. Passion.
6. Slippery.
7. An eye that can coin, create.
8. Favorable opportunities.
9. Wantonness.
1. Immature.
2. Sized him up, perceived his intent.
3. Disposition.
4. Sausage.

RODERIGO Yes, that I did; but that was but courtesy.

IAGO Lechery, by this hand. An index[5] and obscure prologue to the history of lust and foul thoughts. They met so near with their lips that their breaths embraced together. Villainous thoughts, Roderigo! When these mutualities[6] so marshal the way, hard at hand[7] comes the master and main exercise, th' incorporate[8] conclusion. Pish! But, sir, be you ruled by me. I have brought you from Venice. Watch you[9] tonight; for the command, I'll lay 't upon you.[1] Cassio knows you not. I'll not be far from you. Do you find some occasion to anger Cassio, either by speaking too loud, or tainting[2] his discipline, or from what other course you please, which the time shall more favorably minister.[3]

RODERIGO Well.

IAGO Sir, he's rash and very sudden in choler,[4] and haply[5] may strike at you. Provoke him that he may, for even out of that will I cause these of Cyprus to mutiny,[6] whose qualification[7] shall come into no true taste[8] again but by the displanting of Cassio. So shall you have a shorter journey to your desires by the means I shall then have to prefer[9] them, and the impediment most profitably removed, without the which there were no expectation of our prosperity.

RODERIGO I will do this, if you can bring it to any opportunity.

IAGO I warrant[1] thee. Meet me by and by[2] at the citadel. I must fetch his necessaries ashore. Farewell.

RODERIGO Adieu. [*Exit.*]

IAGO That Cassio loves her, I do well believe 't;
That she loves him, 'tis apt° and of great credit.° *probable / credibility*
The Moor, howbeit that I endure him not,
Is of a constant, loving, noble nature,
And I dare think he'll prove to Desdemona
A most dear husband. Now, I do love her too,
Not out of absolute lust—though peradventure
I stand accountant° for as great a sin— *accountable*
But partly led to diet° my revenge *feed*
For that I do suspect the lusty Moor
Hath leaped into my seat, the thought whereof
Doth, like a poisonous mineral, gnaw my innards;
And nothing can or shall content my soul
Till I am evened with him, wife for wife,
Or failing so, yet that I put the Moor
At least into a jealousy so strong
That judgment cannot cure. Which thing to do,
If this poor trash of Venice, whom I trace[3]
For[4] his quick hunting, stand[5] the putting on,

5. Table of contents.
6. Exchanges, intimacies.
7. Closely following.
8. Carnal.
9. Stand watch.
1. I'll arrange for you to be appointed, given orders.
2. Disparaging.
3. Provide.
4. Wrath.
5. Perhaps.
6. Riot.
7. Appeasement.
8. Acceptable state
9. Advance.
1. Assure.
2. Immediately.
3. Train, or follow (?), or perhaps *trash*, a hunting term, meaning to put weights on a hunting dog to slow him down.
4. To make more eager.
5. Respond properly when I incite him to quarrel.

I'll have our Michael Cassio on the hip,[6]
Abuse° him to the Moor in the rank garb°— *slander / coarse manner*
For I fear Cassio with my nightcap[7] too—
Make the Moor thank me, love me, and reward me
For making him egregiously an ass
And practicing upon° his peace and quiet *plotting against*
Even to madness. 'Tis here, but yet confused.
Knavery's plain face is never seen till used. [*Exit.*]

Scene 2

[*Location: Cyprus. A street. Enter Othello's Herald with a proclamation.*]

HERALD It is Othello's pleasure, our noble and valiant general, that, upon certain tidings now arrived, importing the mere perdition[8] of the Turkish fleet, every man put himself into triumph:[9] some to dance, some to make bonfires, each man to what sport and revels his addiction[1] leads him. For, besides these beneficial news, it is the celebration of his nuptial. So much was his pleasure should be proclaimed. All offices[2] are open, and there is full liberty of feasting from this present hour of five till the bell have told eleven. Heaven bless the isle of Cyprus and our noble general Othello!

[*Exit.*]

Scene 3

[*Location: Cyprus. The citadel. Enter Othello, Desdemona, Cassio, and attendants.*]

OTHELLO Good Michael, look you to the guard tonight.
Let's teach ourselves that honorable stop° *restraint*
Not to outsport° discretion. *celebrate beyond*

CASSIO Iago hath direction what to do,
But notwithstanding, with my personal eye
Will I look to 't.

OTHELLO Iago is most honest.
Michael, good night. Tomorrow with your earliest[3]
Let me have speech with you. [*To Desdemona.*] Come, my dear love,
The purchase made, the fruits are to ensue;
That profit's yet to come 'tween me and you.[4]—
Good night.

[*Exit Othello, with Desdemona and attendants.*]

[*Enter Iago.*]

CASSIO Welcome, Iago. We must to the watch.

IAGO Not this hour,[5] Lieutenant; 'tis not yet ten o' the clock. Our general cast[6] us thus early for the love of his Desdemona; who[7] let us not therefore blame. He hath not yet made wanton the night with her, and she is sport for Jove.

CASSIO She's a most exquisite lady.

IAGO And, I'll warrant her, full of game.

6. At my mercy, where I can throw him (a wrestling term).
7. As a rival in my bed, as one who gives me cuckold's horns.
8. Complete destruction.
9. Public celebration.
1. Inclination.
2. Rooms where food and drink are kept.
3. At your earliest convenience.
4. Though married, we haven't yet consummated our love.
5. Not for an hour yet.
6. Dismissed.
7. Othello.

CASSIO Indeed, she's a most fresh and delicate creature.

IAGO What an eye she has! Methinks it sounds a parley[8] to provocation.

CASSIO An inviting eye, and yet methinks right modest.

IAGO And when she speaks, is it not an alarum[9] to love?

CASSIO She is indeed perfection.

IAGO Well, happiness to their sheets! Come, Lieutenant, I have a stoup[1] of wine, and here without[2] are a brace[3] of Cyprus gallants that would fain have a measure[4] to the health of black Othello.

CASSIO Not tonight, good Iago. I have very poor and unhappy brains for drinking. I could well wish courtesy would invent some other custom of entertainment.

IAGO O, they are our friends. But one cup! I'll drink for you.[5]

CASSIO I have drunk but one cup tonight, and that was craftily qualified[6] too, and behold what innovation[7] it makes here.[8] I am unfortunate in the infirmity and dare not task my weakness with any more.

IAGO What, man? 'Tis a night of revels. The gallants desire it.

CASSIO Where are they?

IAGO Here at the door. I pray you, call them in.

CASSIO I'll do't, but it dislikes me.[9] [*Exit.*]

IAGO If I can fasten but one cup upon him,
With that which he hath drunk tonight already,
He'll be as full of quarrel and offense[1]
As my young mistress' dog. Now, my sick fool Roderigo,
Whom love hath turned almost the wrong side out,
To Desdemona hath tonight caroused° *drunk off*
Potations pottle-deep;[2] and he's to watch.° *stand watch*
Three lads of Cyprus—noble swelling° spirits, *proud*
That hold their honors in a wary distance,[3]
The very elements° of this warlike isle— *typical sort*
Have I tonight flustered with flowing cups,
And they watch° too. Now, 'mongst this flock of drunkards *are on guard*
Am I to put our Cassio in some action
That may offend the isle.—But here they come.

[*Enter Cassio, Montano, and gentlemen; servants following with wine.*]

If consequence do but approve my dream,[4]
My boat sails freely both with wind and stream.° *current*

CASSIO 'Fore God, they have given me a rouse° already. *large drink*

MONTANA Good faith, a little one; not past a pint, as I am a soldier.

IAGO Some wine, ho!
[*He sings.*] "And let me the cannikin° clink, clink, *cup*
And let me the cannikin clink.

8. Calls for a conference, issues an invitation.
9. Signal calling men to arms (continuing the military metaphor of *parley*, line 21).
1. Measure of liquor, two quarts.
2. Outside.
3. Pair.
4. Gladly drink a toast.
5. In your place. (Iago will do the steady drinking to keep the gallants company while Cassio has only one cup.)
6. Diluted.
7. Disturbance, insurrection.
8. I.e., in my head.
9. I'm reluctant.
1. Readiness to take offense.
2. To the bottom of the tankard.
3. Are extremely sensitive of their honor.
4. If subsequent events will only substantiate my scheme.

A soldier's a man,
O, man's life's but a span;[5]
Why, then, let a soldier drink."

Some wine, boys!

CASSIO 'Fore God, an excellent song.

IAGO I learned it in England, where indeed they are most potent in potting.[6] Your Dane, your German, and your swag-bellied Hollander—drink, ho!—are nothing to your English.

CASSIO Is your Englishman so exquisite in his drinking?

IAGO Why, he drinks you,[7] with facility, your Dane dead drunk; he sweats not[8] to overthrow your Almain;[9] he gives your Hollander a vomit ere the next pottle can be filled.

CASSIO To the health of our general!

MONTANO I am for it, Lieutenant, and I'll do you justice.[1]

IAGO O sweet England! [*He sings.*]

"King Stephen was and-a worthy peer,
His breeches cost him but a crown;
He held them sixpence all too dear,
With that he called the tailor lown.° *lout*

He was a wight of high renown,
And thou art but of low degree.
'Tis pride[2] that pulls the country down;
Then take thy auld° cloak about thee." *old*

Some wine, ho!

CASSIO 'Fore God, this is a more exquisite song than the other.

IAGO Will you hear 't again?

CASSIO No, for I hold him to be unworthy of his place that does those things. Well, God's above all; and there be souls must be saved, and there be souls must not be saved.

IAGO It's true, good Lieutenant.

CASSIO For mine own part—no offense to the General, nor any man of quality[3]—I hope to be saved.

IAGO And so do I too, Lieutenant.

CASSIO Ay, but, by your leave, not before me; the lieutenant is to be saved before the ancient. Let's have no more of this; let's to our affairs.—God forgive us our sins!—Gentlemen, let's look to our business. Do not think gentlemen, I am drunk. This is my ancient; this is my right hand, and this is my left. I am not drunk now. I can stand well enough, and speak well enough.

GENTLEMEN Excellent well.

CASSIO Why, very well then; you must not think then that I am drunk. [*Exit.*]

MONTANO To th' platform, masters. Come, let's set the watch.[4]

5. Brief span of time. (Cf. Psalm 39.5 as rendered in the Book of Common Prayer: "Thou hast made my days as it were a span long.")
6. Drinking.
7. Drinks.
8. Need not exert himself.
9. German.
1. I'll drink as much as you.
2. Extravagance in dress.
3. Rank.
4. Mount the guard.

[*Exeunt Gentlemen*.]

IAGO You see this fellow that is gone before.
He's a soldier fit to stand by Caesar
And give direction; and do but see his vice.
'Tis to his virtue a just equinox,[5]
The one as long as th' other. 'Tis pity of him.
I fear the trust Othello puts him in,
On some odd time of his infirmity,
Will shake this island.
MONTANO But is he often thus?
IAGO 'Tis evermore the prologue to his sleep.
He'll watch the horologe a double set,[6]
If drink rock not his cradle.
MONTANO It were well
The General were put in mind of it.
Perhaps he sees it not, or his good nature
Prizes the virtue that appears in Cassio
And looks not on his evils. Is not this true?
[*Enter Roderigo*.]
IAGO [*aside to him*] How now, Roderigo?
I pray you, after the Lieutenant; go. [*Exit Roderigo*.]
MONTANO And 'tis great pity that the noble Moor
Should hazard such a place as his own second
With[7] one of an engraffed° infirmity. *inveterate*
It were an honest action to say so
To the Moor.
IAGO Not I, for this fair island.
I do love Cassio well and would do much
To cure him of this evil. [*Cry within*: "Help! Help!"]
But, hark! What noise?
[*Enter Cassio, pursuing Roderigo*.][8]
CASSIO Zounds, you rogue! You rascal!
MONTANO What's the matter, Lieutenant?
CASSIO A knave teach me my duty? I'll beat the knave into a twiggen[9] bottle.
RODERIGO Beat me?
CASSIO Dost thou prate, rogue? [*He strikes Roderigo*.]
MONTANO Nay, good Lieutenant. [*Restraining him*.] I pray you, sir, hold your hand.
CASSIO Let me go, sir, or I'll knock you o'er the mazard.[1]
MONTANO Come, come, you're drunk.
CASSIO Drunk? [*They fight*.]
IAGO [*aside to Roderigo*]
Away, I say. Go out and cry a mutiny.[2]
[*Exit Roderigo*.]
Nay, good Lieutenant—God's will, gentlemen—

5. Exact counterpart. (*Equinox* is an equal length of days and nights.)
6. Stay awake twice around the clock or *horologe*.
7. Risk giving such an important position as his second in command to.
8. The Quarto text reads, "driving in."
9. Wicker-covered. (Cassio vows to assail Roderigo until his skin resembles wickerwork or until he has driven Roderigo through the holes in a wickerwork.)
1. Head (literally, a drinking vessel).
2. Riot.

Help, ho!—Lieutenant—sir—Montano—sir—
Help, masters!°—Here's a goodly watch indeed! *sirs*
[*A bell rings*.][3]
Who's that which rings the bell?—Diablo,° ho! *the devil*
The town will rise.° God's will, Lieutenant, hold! *grow riotous*
You'll be ashamed forever.
[*Enter Othello and attendants with weapons*].

OTHELLO What is the matter here?

MONTANO Zounds, I bleed still.
I am hurt to th' death. He dies! [*He thrusts at Cassio*.]

OTHELLO Hold, for your lives!

IAGO Hold, ho! Lieutenant—sir—Montano—gentlemen—
Have you forgot all sense of place and duty?
Hold! The General speaks to you. Hold, for shame!

OTHELLO Why, how now, ho! From whence ariseth this?
Are we turned Turks, and to ourselves do that
Which heaven hath forbid the Ottomites?[4]
For Christian shame, put by this barbarous brawl!
He that stirs next to carve for[5] his own rage
Holds his soul light;[6] he dies upon his motion.[7]
Silence that dreadful bell. It frights the isle
From her propriety.° What is the matter, masters? *proper state*
Honest Iago, that looks dead with grieving,
Speak. Who began this? On thy love, I charge thee.

IAGO I do not know. Friends all but now, even now,
In quarter[8] and in terms° like bride and groom *on good terms*
Devesting them° for bed; and then, but now— *undressing*
As if some planet had unwitted men—
Swords out, and tilting one at others' breasts
In opposition bloody. I cannot speak° *explain*
Any beginning to this peevish odds;° *quarrel*
And would in action glorious I had lost
Those legs that brought me to a part of it!

OTHELLO How comes it, Michael, you are thus forgot?[9]

CASSIO I pray you, pardon me. I cannot speak.

OTHELLO Worthy Montano, you were wont° be civil; *accustomed to be*
The gravity and stillness° of your youth *sobriety*
The world hath noted, and your name is great
In mouths of wisest censure.° What's the matter *judgment*
That you unlace[1] your reputation thus
And spend your rich opinion° for the name *reputation*
Of a night-brawler? Give me answer to it.

MONTANO Worthy Othello, I am hurt to danger.
Your officer, Iago, can inform you—
While I spare speech, which something° now offends° me— *somewhat/pains*

3. This direction is from the Quarto, as are *Exit Roderigo* at line 130, *They fight* at line 129, and *with weapons* at line 136.
4. Inflict on ourselves the harm that heaven has prevented the Turks from doing (by destroying their fleet).
5. Indulge, satisfy with his sword.
6. Places little value on his life.
7. If he moves.
8. In friendly conduct, within bounds.
9. Have forgotten yourself thus.
1. Undo, lay open (as one might loose the strings of a purse containing reputation).

Of all that I do know; nor know I aught
By me that's said or done amiss this night,
Unless self-charity be sometimes a vice,
And to defend ourselves it be a sin
When violence assails us.

OTHELLO Now, by heaven,
My blood[2] begins my safer guides[3] to rule,
And passion, having my best judgment collied,° *darkened*
Essays° to lead the way. Zounds, if I stir, *undertakes*
Or do but lift this arm, the best of you
Shall sink in my rebuke. Give me to know
How this foul rout° began, who set it on; *riot*
And he that is approved in° this offense, *found guilty of*
Though he had twinned with me, both at a birth,
Shall lose me. What? In a town of[4] war
Yet wild, the people's hearts brim full of fear,
To manage° private and domestic quarrel? *undertake*
In night, and on the court and guard of safety?[5]
'Tis monstrous. Iago, who began 't?

MONTANO [*to Iago*] If partially affined,[6] or leagued in office,[7]
Thou dost deliver more or less than truth,
Thou art no soldier.

IAGO Touch me not so near.
I had rather have this tongue cut from my mouth
Than it should do offense to Michael Cassio;
Yet, I persuade myself, to speak the truth
Shall nothing wrong him. Thus it is, General.
Montano and myself being in speech,
There comes a fellow crying out for help,
And Cassio following him with determined sword
To execute[8] upon him. Sir, this gentleman [*indicating Montano*.]
Steps in to Cassio and entreats his pause.° *him to stop*
Myself the crying fellow did pursue,
Lest by his clamor—as it so fell out—
The town might fall in fright. He, swift of foot,
Outran my purpose, and I returned, the rather° *sooner*
For that I heard the clink and fall of swords
And Cassio high in oath, which till tonight
I ne'er might say before. When I came back—
For this was brief—I found them close together
At blow and thrust, even as again they were
When you yourself did part them.
More of this matter cannot I report.
But men are men; the best sometimes forget.° *forget themselves*
Though Cassio did some little wrong to him,
As men in rage strike those that wish them best,[9]
Yet surely Cassio, I believe, received
From him that fled some strange indignity,

2. Passion (of anger).
3. I.e., reason.
4. Town garrisoned for.
5. At the main guardhouse or headquarters and on watch.
6. Made partial by some personal relationship.
7. In league as fellow officers.
8. Give effect to (his anger).
9. Even those who are well disposed.

Which patience could not pass.° *overlook*

OTHELLO I know, Iago,
Thy honesty and love doth mince this matter,
Making it light to Cassio. Cassio, I love thee,
But nevermore be officer of mine.

[*Enter Desdemona, attended.*]

Look if my gentle love be not raised up.
I'll make thee an example.

DESDEMONA What is the matter, dear?

OTHELLO All's well now, sweeting;
Come away to bed. [*To Montano.*] Sir, for your hurts,
Myself will be your surgeon.[1]—Lead him off.

[*Montano is led off.*]

Iago, look with care about the town
And silence those whom this vile brawl distracted.
Come, Desdemona. 'Tis the soldiers' life
To have their balmy slumbers waked with strife.

[*Exit with all but Iago and Cassio.*]

IAGO What, are you hurt, Lieutenant?

CASSIO Ay, past all surgery.

IAGO Marry, God forbid!

CASSIO Reputation, reputation, reputation! O, I have lost my reputation! I have lost the immortal part of myself, and what remains is bestial. My reputation, Iago, my reputation!

IAGO As I am an honest man, I thought you had received some bodily wound; there is more sense in that than in reputation. Reputation is an idle and most false imposition,[2] oft got without merit and lost without deserving. You have lost no reputation at all, unless you repute yourself such a loser. What, man, there are more ways to recover[3] the General again. You are but now cast in his mood[4]—a punishment more in policy[5] than in malice, even so as one would beat his offenseless dog to affright an imperious lion.[6] Sue[7] to him again and he's yours.

CASSIO I will rather sue to be despised than to deceive so good a commander with so slight,[8] so drunken, and so indiscreet an officer. Drunk? And speak parrot?[9] And squabble? Swagger? Swear? And discourse fustian with one's own shadow? O thou invisible spirit of wine, if thou hast no name to be known by, let us call thee devil!

IAGO What was he that you followed with your sword? What had he done to you?

CASSIO I know not.

IAGO Is 't possible?

CASSIO I remember a mass of things, but nothing distinctly; a quarrel, but nothing wherefore.[1] O God, that men should put an enemy in their mouths to steal away their brains! That we should, with joy, pleasance, revel, and applause[2] transform ourselves into beasts!

IAGO Why, but you are now well enough. How came you thus recovered?

1. Make sure you receive medical attention.
2. Thing artificially imposed and of no real value.
3. Regain favor with.
4. Dismissed in a moment of anger.
5. Done for expediency's sake and as a public gesture.
6. Would make an example of a minor offender to deter more important and dangerous offenders.
7. Petition.
8. Worthless.
9. Talk nonsense, rant. (*Discourse fustian*, in the next line, has much the same meaning.)
1. Why.
2. Desire for applause.

CASSIO It hath pleased the devil drunkenness to give place to the devil wrath. One unperfectness shows me another, to make me frankly despise myself.

IAGO Come, you are too severe a moraler.[3] As the time, the place, and the condition of this country stands, I could heartily wish this had not befallen; but since it is as it is, mend it for your own good.

CASSIO I will ask him for my place again; he shall tell me I am a drunkard. Had I as many mouths as Hydra,[4] such an answer would stop them all. To be now a sensible man, by and by a fool, and presently a beast! O, strange! Every inordinate cup is unblessed, and the ingredient is a devil.

IAGO Come, come, good wine is a good familiar creature, if it be well used. Exclaim no more against it. And, good Lieutenant, I think you think I love you.

CASSIO I have well approved[5] it, sir. I drunk!

IAGO You or any man living may be drunk at a time,[6] man. I'll tell you what you shall do. Our general's wife is now the general—I may say so in this respect, for that[7] he hath devoted and given up himself to the contemplation, mark, and denotement[8] of her parts[9] and graces. Confess yourself freely to her; importune her help to put you in your place again. She is of so free,[1] so kind, so apt, so blessed a disposition, she holds it a vice in her goodness not to do more than she is requested. This broken joint between you and her husband entreat her to splinter;[2] and, my fortunes against any lay[3] worth naming, this crack of your love shall grow stronger than it was before.

CASSIO You advise me well.

IAGO I protest,[4] in the sincerity of love and honest kindness.

CASSIO I think it freely;[5] and betimes in the morning I will beseech the virtuous Desdemona to undertake for me. I am desperate of my fortunes if they check[6] me here.

IAGO You are in the right. Good night, Lieutenant. I must to the watch.

CASSIO Good night, honest Iago. *[Exit Cassio.]*

IAGO And what's he then that says I play the villain,
When this advice is free[7] I give, and honest,
Probal° to thinking, and indeed the course *reasonable*
To win the Moor again? For 'tis most easy
Th' inclining° Desdemona to subdue° *willing / persuade*
In any honest suit; she's framed as fruitful[8]
As the free elements.[9] And then for her
To win the Moor—were 't to renounce his baptism,
All seals and symbols of redeemèd sin—
His soul is so enfettered to her love
That she may make, unmake, do what she list,
Even as her appetite[1] shall play the god
With his weak function.[2] How am I then a villain,

3. Moralizer.
4. The Lernaean Hydra, a monster with many heads and the ability to grow two heads when one was cut off, slain by Hercules as the second of his twelve labors.
5. Proved.
6. At one time or another.
7. In view of this fact, that.
8. Both words mean "observation."
9. Qualities.
1. Generous.
2. Bind with splints.
3. Stake, wager.
4. Insist, declare.
5. Unreservedly.
6. Repulse.
7. Free from guile. Also, freely given.
8. Created as generous.
9. I.e., earth, air, fire, and water, unrestrained and spontaneous.
1. Her desire, or, perhaps, his desire for her.
2. Exercise of faculties (weakened by his fondness for her).

To counsel Cassio to this parallel[3] course
Directly to his good? Divinity of hell![4]
When devils will the blackest sins put on,° *instigate*
They do suggest° at first with heavenly shows, *tempt*
As I do now. For whiles this honest fool
Plies Desdemona to repair his fortune,
And she for him pleads strongly to the Moor,
I'll pour this pestilence into his ear,
That she repeals him[5] for her body's lust;
And by how much she strives to do him good,
She shall undo her credit with the Moor.
So will I turn her virtue into pitch,[6]
And out of her own goodness make the net
That shall enmesh them all.

[*Enter Roderigo.*]

How now, Roderigo?

RODERIGO I do follow here in the chase, not like a hound that hunts, but one that fills up the cry.[7] My money is almost spent; I have been tonight exceedingly well cudgeled; and I think the issue will be I shall have so much[8] experience for my pains, and so, with no money at all and a little more wit, return again to Venice.

IAGO How poor are they that have not patience!
What wound did ever heal but by degrees?
Thou know'st we work by wit, and not by witchcraft,
And wit depends on dilatory time.
Does 't not go well? Cassio hath beaten thee,
And thou, by that small hurt, hast cashiered° Cassio. *dismissed*
Though other things grow fair against the sun,
Yet fruits that blossom first will first be ripe.[9]
Content thyself awhile. By the Mass, 'tis morning!
Pleasure and action make the hours seem short.
Retire thee; go where thou art billeted.
Away, I say! Thou shalt know more hereafter.
Nay, get thee gone. [*Exit Roderigo.*]
Two things are to be done.
My wife must move° for Cassio to her mistress; *plead*
I'll set her on;
Myself the while to draw the Moor apart
And bring him jump° when he may Cassio find *precisely*
Soliciting his wife. Ay, that's the way.
Dull not device° by coldness° and delay. [*Exit.*] *plot/lack of zeal*

Act 3

Scene 1

[*Location: Before the chamber of Othello and Desdemona. Enter Cassio and Musicians.*]

3. Corresponding to these facts and to his best interests.
4. Inverted theology of hell (which seduces the soul to its damnation).
5. Attempts to get him restored.
6. Foul blackness. Also a snaring substance.
7. Merely takes part as one of the pack.
8. Just so much and no more.
9. Plans that are well prepared and set expeditiously in motion will soonest ripen into success.

CASSIO Masters, play here—I will content your pains[1]—
Something that's brief, and bid "Good morrow, General." [*They play.*]
[*Enter Clown.*]

CLOWN Why, masters, have your instruments been in Naples, that they speak i' the nose[2] thus?

A MUSICIAN How, sir, how?

CLOWN Are these, I pray you, wind instruments?

A MUSICIAN Ay, marry, are they, sir.

CLOWN O, thereby hangs a tail.

A MUSICIAN Whereby hangs a tale, sir?

CLOWN Marry, sir, by many a wind instrument[3] that I know. But, masters, here's money for you. [*He gives money.*] And the General so likes your music that he desires you, for love's sake,[4] to make no more noise with it.

A MUSICIAN Well, sir, we will not.

CLOWN If you have any music that may not[5] be heard, to 't again; but, as they say, to hear music the General does not greatly care.

A MUSICIAN We have none such, sir.

CLOWN Then put up your pipes in your bag, for I'll away.[6] Go, vanish into air, away! [*Exeunt Musicians.*]

CASSIO Dost thou hear, mine honest friend?

CLOWN No, I hear not your honest friend; I hear you.

CASSIO Prithee, keep up[7] thy quillets.[8] There's a poor piece of gold for thee. [*He gives money.*] If the gentlewoman that attends the General's wife be stirring, tell her there's one Cassio entreats her a little favor of speech.[9] Wilt thou do this?

CLOWN She is stirring, sir. If she will stir[1] hither, I shall seem[2] to notify unto her.

CASSIO Do, good my friend. [*Exit Clown.*]
[*Enter Iago.*]
In happy time,[3] Iago.

IAGO You have not been abed, then?

CASSIO Why, no. The day had broke
Before we parted. I have made bold, Iago,
To send in to your wife. My suit to her
Is that she will to virtuous Desdemona
Procure me some access.

IAGO I'll send her to you presently;
And I'll devise a means to draw the Moor
Out of the way, that your converse and business
May be more free.

CASSIO I humbly thank you for 't. [*Exit Iago.*]
I never knew

1. Reward your efforts.
2. Sound nasal. Also sound like one whose nose has been attacked by syphilis. (Naples was popularly supposed to have a high incidence of venereal disease.)
3. With a joke on flatulence. The *tail* that hangs nearby the *wind instrument* suggests the penis.
4. Out of friendship and affection. Also, for the sake of lovemaking in Othello's marriage.
5. Cannot.
6. (Possibly a misprint, or a snatch of song?)
7. Do not bring out.
8. Quibbles, puns.
9. The favor of a brief talk.
1. Bestir herself (with a play on *stirring*, "rousing herself from rest").
2. Deem it good, think fit.
3. I.e., well met.

A Florentine[4] more kind and honest.
[*Enter Emilia.*]
EMILIA Good morrow, good Lieutenant. I am sorry
For your displeasure;° but all will sure be well. *fall from favor*
The General and his wife are talking of it,
And she speaks for you stoutly.° The Moor replies *spiritedly*
That he you hurt is of great fame° in Cyprus *importance*
And great affinity,° and that in wholesome wisdom *family connection*
He might not but refuse you; but he protests° he loves you *insists*
And needs no other suitor but his likings
To take the safest occasion by the front[5]
To bring you in again.
CASSIO Yet I beseech you,
If you think fit, or that it may be done,
Give me advantage of some brief discourse
With Desdemon alone.
EMILIA Pray you, come in.
I will bestow you where you shall have time
To speak your bosom° freely. *thoughts*
CASSIO I am much bound to you. [*Exeunt.*]

Scene 2

[*Location: The citadel. Enter Othello, Iago, and Gentlemen.*]
OTHELLO [*giving letters*] These letters give, Iago, to the pilot,
And by him do my duties° to the Senate. *give my respects*
That done, I will be walking on the works;° *fortifications*
Repair° there to me. *return*
IAGO Well, my good lord, I'll do 't.
OTHELLO This fortification, gentlemen, shall we see 't?
GENTLEMEN We'll wait upon° your lordship. [*Exeunt.*] *attend*

Scene 3

[*Location: The garden of the citadel. Enter Desdemona, Cassio, and Emilia.*]
DESDEMONA Be thou assured, good Cassio, I will do
All my abilities in thy behalf.
EMILIA Good madam, do. I warrant it grieves my husband
As if the cause were his.
DESDEMONA O, that's an honest fellow. Do not doubt, Cassio,
But I will have my lord and you again
As friendly as you were.
CASSIO Bounteous madam,
Whatever shall become of Michael Cassio,
He's never anything but your true servant.
DESDEMONA I know 't. I thank you. You do love my lord;
You have known him long, and be you well assured
He shall in strangeness° stand no farther off *aloofness*

4. I.e., even a fellow Florentine. (Iago is a Venetian; Cassio is a Florentine.)

5. Opportunity by the forelock.

Than in a politic[6] distance.
CASSIO Ay, but, lady,
That policy may either last so long,
Or feed upon such nice and waterish diet,[7]
Or breed itself so out of circumstance,[8]
That, I being absent and my place supplied,[9]
My general will forget my love and service.
DESDEMONA Do not doubt° that. Before Emilia here *fear*
I give thee warrant° of thy place. Assure thee, *guarantee*
If I do vow a friendship I'll perform it
To the last article. My lord shall never rest.
I'll watch him tame[1] and talk him out of patience;[2]
His bed shall seem a school, his board° a shrift;° *table/confessional*
I'll intermingle everything he does
With Cassio's suit. Therefore be merry, Cassio,
For thy solicitor° shall rather die *advocate*
Than give thy cause away.° *up*
Enter Othello and Iago at a distance].
EMILIA Madam, here comes my lord.
CASSIO Madam, I'll take my leave.
DESDEMONA Why, stay, and hear me speak.
CASSIO Madam, not now. I am very ill at ease,
Unfit for mine own purposes.
DESDEMONA Well, do your discretion.[3] [*Exit Cassio*.]
IAGO Ha? I like not that.
OTHELLO What dost thou say?
IAGO Nothing, my lord; or if—I know not what.
OTHELLO Was not that Cassio parted from my wife?
IAGO Cassio, my lord? No, sure, I cannot think it,
That he would steal away so guiltylike,
Seeing you coming.
OTHELLO I do believe 'twas he.
DESDEMONA How now, my lord?
I have been talking with a suitor here,
A man that languishes in your displeasure.
OTHELLO Who is 't you mean?
DESDEMONA Why, your lieutenant, Cassio. Good my lord,
If I have any grace or power to move you,
His present reconciliation take;[4]
For if he be not one that truly loves you,
That errs in ignorance and not in cunning,° *wittingly*
I have no judgment in an honest face.
I prithee, call him back.
OTHELLO Went he hence now?
DESDEMONA Yes, faith, so humbled

6. Required by wise policy.
7. Or sustain itself at length upon such trivial and meager technicalities.
8. Continually renew itself so out of chance events, or yield so few chances for my being pardoned.
9. Filled by another person.
1. Tame him by keeping him from sleeping (a term from falconry).
2. Past his endurance.
3. Act according to your own discretion.
4. Let him be reconciled to you right away.

That he hath left part of his grief with me
To suffer with him. Good love, call him back.

OTHELLO Not now, sweet Desdemon. Some other time.

DESDEMONA But shall 't be shortly?

OTHELLO The sooner, sweet, for you.

DESDEMONA Shall 't be tonight at supper?

OTHELLO No, not tonight.

DESDEMONA Tomorrow dinner,° then? *noontime*

OTHELLO I shall not dine at home.
I meet the captains at the citadel.

DESDEMONA Why, then, tomorrow night, or Tuesday morn,
On Tuesday noon, or night, on Wednesday morn.
I prithee, name the time, but let it not
Exceed three days. In faith, he's penitent;
And yet his trespass, in our common reason°— *judgments*
Save that, they say, the wars must make example
Out of her best[5]—is not almost° a fault *scarcely*
T' incur a private check.[6] When shall he come?
Tell me, Othello. I wonder in my soul
What you would ask me that I should deny,
Or stand so mammering on.° What? Michael Cassio, *wavering about*
That came a-wooing with you, and so many a time,
When I have spoke of you dispraisingly,
Hath ta'en your part—to have so much to do
To bring him in!° By 'r Lady, I could do much— *restore him to favor*

OTHELLO Prithee, no more. Let him come when he will;
I will deny thee nothing.

DESDEMONA Why, this is not a boon.
'Tis as I should entreat you wear your gloves,
Or feed on nourishing dishes, or keep you warm,
Or sue to you to do a peculiar° profit *personal*
To your own person. Nay, when I have a suit
Wherein I mean to touch° your love indeed, *test*
It shall be full of poise[7] and difficult weight,
And fearful to be granted.

OTHELLO I will deny thee nothing.
Whereon,° I do beseech thee, grant me this, *in return*
To leave me but a little to myself.

DESDEMONA Shall I deny you? No. Farewell, my lord.

OTHELLO Farewell, my Desdemona. I'll come to thee straight.° *straightway*

DESDEMONA Emilia, come.—Be as your fancies° teach you; *inclinations*
Whate'er you be, I am obedient. [*Exit with Emilia.*]

OTHELLO Excellent wretch![8] Perdition catch my soul
But I do love thee! And when I love thee not,
Chaos is come again.[9]

5. Were it not that, as the saying goes, military discipline requires making an example of the very best men. (*Her* refers to *wars* as a singular concept.)
6. Even a private reprimand.
7. Weight, heaviness; or equipoise, delicate balance involving hard choice.
8. A term of affectionate endearment.
9. I.e., My love for you will last forever, until the end of time when chaos will return. (But with an unconscious, ironic suggestion that, if anything should induce Othello to cease loving Desdemona, the result would be chaos.)

IAGO My noble lord—
OTHELLO What dost thou say, Iago?
IAGO Did Michael Cassio, when you wooed my lady,
Know of your love?
OTHELLO He did, from first to last. Why dost thou ask?
IAGO But for a satisfaction of my thought;
No further harm.
OTHELLO Why of thy thought, Iago?
IAGO I did not think he had been acquainted with her.
OTHELLO O, yes, and went between us very oft.
IAGO Indeed?
OTHELLO Indeed? Ay, indeed. Discern'st thou aught in that?
Is he not honest?
IAGO Honest, my lord?
OTHELLO Honest. Ay, honest.
IAGO My lord, for aught I know.
OTHELLO What dost thou think?
IAGO Think, my lord?
OTHELLO "Think, my lord?" By heaven, thou echo'st me,
As if there were some monster in thy thought
Too hideous to be shown. Thou dost mean something.
I heard thee say even now, thou lik'st not that,
When Cassio left my wife. What didst not like?
And when I told thee he was of my counsel° *in my confidence*
In my whole course of wooing, thou criedst "Indeed?"
And didst contract and purse° thy brow together *knit*
As if thou then hadst shut up in thy brain
Some horrible conceit.° If thou dost love me, *fancy*
Show me thy thought.
IAGO My lord, you know I love you.
OTHELLO I think thou dost;
And, for° I know thou'rt full of love and honesty, *because*
And weigh'st thy words before thou giv'st them breath,
Therefore these stops° of thine fright me the more; *pauses*
For such things in a false disloyal knave
Are tricks of custom,° but in a man that's just *customary*
They're close dilations,[1] working from the heart
That passion cannot rule.[2]
IAGO For° Michael Cassio, *as for*
I dare be sworn I think that he is honest.
OTHELLO I think so too.
IAGO Men should be what they seem;
Or those that be not, would they might seem none![3]
OTHELLO Certain, men should be what they seem.
IAGO Why, then, I think Cassio's an honest man.
OTHELLO Nay, yet there's more in this.
I prithee, speak to me as to thy thinkings,

1. Secret or involuntary expressions or delays.
2. I.e., that are too passionately strong to be restrained (referring to the workings), or that cannot rule its own passions (referring to the heart).
3. I.e., not to be men, or not seem to be honest.

As thou dost ruminate, and give thy worst of thoughts
The worst of words.

IAGO Good my lord, pardon me.
Though I am bound to every act of duty,
I am not bound to that° all slaves are free to.[4] *that which*
Utter my thoughts? Why, say they are vile and false,
As where's that palace whereinto foul things
Sometimes intrude not? Who has that breast so pure
But some uncleanly apprehensions
Keep leets and law days,[5] and in sessions sit
With° meditations lawful?° *along with / innocent*

OTHELLO Thou dost conspire against thy friend,[6] Iago,
If thou but think'st him wronged and mak'st his ear
A stranger to thy thoughts.

IAGO I do beseech you,
Though I perchance am vicious° in my guess— *wrong*
As I confess it is my nature's plague
To spy into abuses, and oft my jealousy° *suspicious nature*
Shapes faults that are not—that your wisdom then,° *on that account*
From one[7] that so imperfectly conceits,° *conjectures*
Would take no notice, nor build yourself a trouble
Out of his scattering° and unsure observance. *random*
It were not for your quiet nor your good,
Nor for my manhood, honesty, and wisdom,
To let you know my thoughts.

OTHELLO What dost thou mean?

IAGO Good name in man and woman, dear my lord,
Is the immediate° jewel of their souls. *essential*
Who steals my purse steals trash; 'tis something, nothing;
'Twas mine, 'tis his, and has been slave to thousands;
But he that filches from me my good name
Robs me of that which not enriches him
And makes me poor indeed.

OTHELLO By heaven, I'll know thy thoughts.

IAGO You cannot, if° my heart were in your hand, *even if*
Nor shall not, whilst 'tis in my custody.

OTHELLO Ha?

IAGO O, beware, my lord, of jealousy.
It is the green-eyed monster which doth mock
The meat it feeds on.[8] That cuckold lives in bliss
Who, certain of his fate, loves not his wronger;[9]
But O, what damnèd minutes tells° he o'er *counts*
Who dotes, yet doubts, suspects, yet fondly loves!

OTHELLO O misery!

IAGO Poor and content is rich, and rich enough,[1]

4. Free with respect to.
5. I.e., hold court, set up their authority in one's heart. *Leets* are a kind of manor court; *law days* are the days courts sit in session, or those sessions.
6. I.e., Othello.
7. I.e., myself, Iago.
8. Mocks and torments the heart of its victim, the man who suffers jealously.
9. I.e., his faithless wife. (The unsuspecting cuckold is spared the misery of loving his wife only to discover she is cheating on him.)
1. To be content with what little one has is the greatest wealth of all (proverbial).

But riches fineless° is as poor as winter *boundless*
To him that ever fears he shall be poor.
Good God, the souls of all my tribe defend
From jealousy!

OTHELLO Why, why is this?
Think'st thou I'd make a life of jealousy,
To follow still the changes of the moon
With fresh suspicions?[2] No! To be once in doubt
Is once° to be resolved.[3] Exchange me for a goat *once and for all*
When I shall turn the business of my soul
To such exsufflicate and blown[4] surmises
Matching thy inference.° 'Tis not to make me jealous *allegation*
To say my wife is fair, feeds well, loves company,
Is free of speech, sings, plays, and dances well;
Where virtue is, these are more virtuous.
Nor from mine own weak merits will I draw
The smallest fear or doubt of her revolt,[5]
For she had eyes, and chose me. No, Iago,
I'll see before I doubt; when I doubt, prove;
And on the proof, there is no more but this—
Away at once with love or jealousy.

IAGO I am glad of this, for now I shall have reason
To show the love and duty that I bear you
With franker spirit. Therefore, as I am bound,
Receive it from me. I speak not yet of proof.
Look to your wife; observe her well with Cassio.
Wear your eyes thus, not° jealous nor secure.° *neither / certain*
I would not have your free and noble nature,
Out of self-bounty,[6] be abused.° Look to 't. *deceived*
I know our country disposition well;
In Venice they do let God see the pranks
They dare not show their husbands; their best conscience
Is not to leave 't undone, but keep 't unknown.

OTHELLO Dost thou say so?

IAGO She did deceive her father, marrying you;
And when she seemed to shake and fear your looks,
She loved them most.

OTHELLO And so she did.

IAGO Why, go to,[7] then!
She that, so young, could give out such a seeming,° *false appearance*
To seel[8] her father's eyes up close as oak,[9]
He thought 'twas witchcraft! But I am much to blame.
I humbly do beseech you of your pardon
For too much loving you.

OTHELLO I am bound[1] to thee forever.

2. To be constantly imagining new causes for suspicion, changing incessantly like the moon.
3. Free of doubt, having settled the matter.
4. Inflated and blown up, rumored about, or, spat out and flyblown, hence loathsome, disgusting.
5. Fear of her unfaithfulness.
6. Inherent or natural goodness and generosity.
7. An expression of impatience.
8. Blind (a term from falconry).
9. A close-grained wood.
1. Indebted (but perhaps with the ironic sense of "tied").

IAGO I see this hath a little dashed your spirits.
OTHELLO Not a jot, not a jot.
IAGO I' faith, I fear it has.
I hope you will consider what is spoke
Comes from my love. But I do see you're moved.
I am to pray you not to strain my speech
To grosser issues° nor to larger reach° *significances/scope*
Than to suspicion.
OTHELLO I will not.
IAGO Should you do so, my lord,
My speech should fall into such vile success° *effect*
Which my thoughts aimed not. Cassio's my worthy friend.
My lord, I see you're moved.
OTHELLO No, not much moved.
I do not think but Desdemona's honest.° *chaste*
IAGO Long live she so! And long live you to think so!
OTHELLO And yet, how nature erring from itself—
IAGO Ay, there's the point! As—to be bold with you—
Not to affect° many proposèd matches *prefer*
Of her own clime, complexion, and degree,[2]
Whereto we see in all things nature tends—
Foh! One may smell in such a will° most rank, *sensuality*
Foul disproportion,° thoughts unnatural. *abnormality*
But pardon me. I do not in position° *argument*
Distinctly speak of her, though I may fear
Her will, recoiling° to her better[3] judgment, *reverting*
May fall to match you with her country forms[4]
And happily repent.[5]
OTHELLO Farewell, farewell!
If more thou dost perceive, let me know more.
Set on thy wife to observe. Leave me, Iago.
IAGO [*going*] My lord, I take my leave.
OTHELLO Why did I marry? This honest creature doubtless
Sees and knows more, much more, than he unfolds.
IAGO [*returning*] My Lord, I would I might entreat your honor
To scan° this thing no farther. Leave it to time. *scrutinize*
Although 'tis fit that Cassio have his place—
For, sure, he fills it up with great ability—
Yet, if you please to hold him off awhile,
You shall by that perceive him and his means.[6]
Note if your lady strain his entertainment[7]
With any strong or vehement importunity;
Much will be seen in that. In the meantime,
Let me be thought too busy° in my fears— *interfering*
As worthy cause I have to fear I am—
And hold her free,[8] I do beseech your honor.

2. Country, color, and social position.
3. I.e., more natural and reconsidered.
4. Undertake to compare you with Venetian norms of handsomeness.
5. Perhaps repent her marriage.
6. The method he uses (to regain his post).
7. Urge his reinstatement.
8. Regard her as innocent.

OTHELLO Fear not my government.° *conduct*
IAGO I once more take my leave. [*Exit.*]
OTHELLO This fellow's of exceeding honesty,
And knows all qualities,° with a learnèd spirit, *natures*
Of human dealings. If I do prove her haggard,[9]
Though that her jesses[1] were my dear heartstrings,
I'd whistle her off and let her down the wind[2]
To prey at fortune.[3] Haply, for[4] I am black
And have not those soft parts of conversation[5]
That chamberers° have, or for I am declined *gallants*
Into the vale of years—yet that's not much—
She's gone. I am abused,° and my relief *deceived*
Must be to loathe her. O curse of marriage,
That we can call these delicate creatures ours
And not their appetites! I had rather be a toad
And live upon the vapor of a dungeon
Than keep a corner in the thing I love
For others' uses. Yet, 'tis the plague of great ones;
Prerogatived[6] are they less than the base.[7]
'Tis destiny unshunnable, like death.
Even then this forkèd[8] plague is fated to us
When we do quicken.[9] Look where she comes.
[*Enter Desdemona and Emilia.*]
If she be false, O, then heaven mocks itself!
I'll not believe 't.
DESDEMONA How now, my dear Othello?
Your dinner, and the generous° islanders *noble*
By you invited, do attend° your presence. *await*
OTHELLO I am to blame.
DESDEMONA Why do you speak so faintly?
Are you not well?
OTHELLO I have a pain upon my forehead here.
DESDEMONA Faith, that's with watching.° 'Twill away again. *too little sleep*
[*She offers her handkerchief.*]
Let me but bind it hard, within this hour
It will be well.
OTHELLO Your napkin° is too little. *handkerchief*
Let it alone.° Come, I'll go in with you. *never mind*
[*He puts the handkerchief from him, and it drops.*]
DESDEMONA I am very sorry that you are not well.
[*Exit with Othello.*]
EMILIA [*picking up the handkerchief*]
I am glad I have found this napkin.

9. Wild (like a wild female hawk).
1. Straps fastened around the legs of a trained hawk.
2. I'd let her go forever. (To release a hawk downwind was to invite it not to return.)
3. Fend for herself in the wild.
4. Perhaps because.
5. Pleasing graces of social behavior.
6. Privileged (to have honest wives).
7. Ordinary citizens. (Socially prominent men are especially prone to the unavoidable destiny of being cuckolded and to the public shame that goes with it.)
8. An allusion to the horns of the cuckold.
9. Receive life. *Quicken* may also mean to swarm with maggots as the body festers, in which case these lines suggest that *even then*, in death, we are cuckolded by *forkèd* worms.

This was her first remembrance from the Moor.
My wayward° husband hath a hundred times *capricious*
Wooed me to steal it, but she so loves the token—
For he conjured her she should ever keep it—
That she reserves it evermore about her
To kiss and talk to. I'll have the work ta'en out,[1]
And give 't Iago. What he will do with it
Heaven knows, not I;
I nothing but to please his fantasy.° *whim*
[*Enter Iago.*]
IAGO How now? What do you here alone?
EMILIA Do not you chide. I have a thing for you.
IAGO You have a thing for me? It is a common thing[2]—
EMILIA Ha?
IAGO To have a foolish wife.
EMILIA O, is that all? What will you give me now
For that same handkerchief?
IAGO What handkerchief?
EMILIA What handkerchief?
Why, that the Moor first gave to Desdemona;
That which so often you did bid me steal.
IAGO Hast stolen it from her?
EMILIA No, faith. She let it drop by negligence,
And to th' advantage[3] I, being here, took 't up.
Look, here 'tis.
IAGO A good wench! Give it me.
EMILIA What will you do with 't, that you have been so earnest
To have me filch it?
IAGO [*snatching it*] Why, what is that to you?
EMILIA If it be not for some purpose of import,
Give 't me again. Poor lady, she'll run mad
When she shall lack° it. *miss*
IAGO Be not acknown on 't.[4]
I have use for it. Go, leave me. [*Exit Emilia.*]
I will in Cassio's lodging lose[5] this napkin
And let him find it. Trifles light as air
Are to the jealous confirmations strong
As proofs of Holy Writ. This may do something.
The Moor already changes with my poison.
Dangerous conceits° are in their natures poisons, *ideas*
Which at the first are scarce found to distaste,° *be distasteful*
But with a little act° upon the blood *action*
Burn like the mines of sulfur.
[*Enter Othello.*]
I did say so.
Look where he comes! Not poppy nor mandragora[6]

1. Design of the embroidery copied.
2. With bawdy suggestion; *common* suggests coarseness and availability to all comers, and *thing* is a slang term for the genitals.
3. Taking the opportunity.
4. Do not confess knowledge of it.
5. The Folio spelling, *loose*, is a normal spelling for "lose," but it may also contain the idea of "let go," "release."
6. An opiate made of the mandrake root.

Nor all the drowsy syrups of the world
Shall ever medicine thee to that sweet sleep
Which thou owedst° yesterday. *you did own*

OTHELLO Ha, ha, false to me?

IAGO Why, how now, General? No more of that.

OTHELLO Avaunt! Begone! Thou hast set me on the rack.
I swear 'tis better to be much abused
Than but to know 't a little.

IAGO How now, my lord?

OTHELLO What sense had I of her stolen hours of lust?
I saw 't not, thought it not, it harmed not me.
I slept the next night well, fed well, was free° and merry; *carefree*
I found not Cassio's kisses on her lips.
He that is robbed, not wanting° what is stolen, *missing*
Let him not know 't and he's not robbed at all.

IAGO I am sorry to hear this.

OTHELLO I had been happy if the general camp,
Pioners[7] and all, had tasted her sweet body,
So° I had nothing known. O, now, forever *provided*
Farewell the tranquil mind! Farewell content!
Farewell the plumèd troops and the big° wars *stately*
That makes ambition virtue! O, farewell!
Farewell the neighing steed and the shrill trump,
The spirit-stirring drum, th' ear-piercing fife,
The royal banner, and all quality,° *character*
Pride,° pomp, and circumstance° of glorious war! *display / pageantry*
And O, you mortal engines,[8] whose rude throats
Th' immortal Jove's dread clamors° counterfeit, *thunder*
Farewell! Othello's occupation's gone.

IAGO Is 't possible, my lord?

OTHELLO Villain, be sure thou prove my love a whore!
Be sure of it. Give me the ocular proof,
Or, by the worth of mine eternal soul,
Thou hadst been better have been born a dog
Than answer my waked wrath!

IAGO Is 't come to this?

OTHELLO Make me to see 't, or at the least so prove it
That the probation° bear no hinge nor loop *proof*
To hang a doubt on, or woe upon thy life!

IAGO My noble lord—

OTHELLO If thou dost slander her and torture me,
Never pray more; abandon all remorse;° *pity*
On horror's head horrors accumulate;
Do deeds to make heaven weep, all earth amazed;
For nothing canst thou to damnation add
Greater than that.

IAGO O grace! O heaven forgive me!
Are you a man? Have you a soul or sense?

7. Diggers of mines, the lowest grade of soldiers.

8. Cannon. (*Mortal* means "deadly.")

God b' wi' you; take mine office. O wretched fool,[9]
That lov'st to make thine honesty a vice!° *failing*
O monstrous world! Take note, take note, O world,
To be direct and honest is not safe.
I thank you for this profit,° and from hence° *instruction/henceforth*
I'll love no friend, sith° love breeds such offense.[1] *since*
OTHELLO Nay, stay. Thou shouldst be honest.[2]
IAGO I should be wise, for honesty's a fool
And loses that° it works for. *what*
OTHELLO By the world,
I think my wife be honest and think she is not;
I think that thou art just and think thou art not.
I'll have some proof. My name, that was as fresh
As Dian's[3] visage, is now begrimed and black
As mine own face. If there be cords, or knives,
Poison, or fire, or suffocating streams,
I'll not endure it. Would I were satisfied!
IAGO I see, sir, you are eaten up with passion.
I do repent me that I put it to you.
You would be satisfied?
OTHELLO Would? Nay, and I will.
IAGO And may; but how? How satisfied, my lord?
Would you, the supervisor,° grossly gape on? *onlooker*
Behold her topped?
OTHELLO Death and damnation! O!
IAGO It were a tedious difficulty, I think,
To bring them to that prospect. Damn them then,[4]
If ever mortal eyes do see them bolster[5]
More° than their own.° What then? How then? *other/own eyes*
What shall I say? Where's satisfaction?
It is impossible you should see this,
Were they as prime° as goats, as hot as monkeys, *wanton*
As salt° as wolves in pride,° and fools as gross *lustful/heat*
As ignorance made drunk. But yet I say,
If imputation[6] and strong circumstances
Which lead directly to the door of truth
Will give you satisfaction, you might have 't.
OTHELLO Give me a living reason she's disloyal.
IAGO I do not like the office.
But sith° I am entered in this cause so far, *since*
Pricked° to 't by foolish honesty and love, *spurred*
I will go on. I lay with Cassio lately,
And being troubled with a raging tooth
I could not sleep. There are a kind of men
So loose of soul that in their sleeps will mutter

9. Iago addresses himself as a fool for having carried honesty too far.
1. Harm to the one who offers help and friendship.
2. It appears that you are. (But Iago replies in the sense of "ought to be.")
3. Diana, goddess of the moon and of chastity.
4. They would have to be really incorrigible.
5. Go to bed together, share a bolster.
6. Strong circumstantial evidence.

Their affairs. One of this kind is Cassio.
In sleep I heard him say, "Sweet Desdemona,
Let us be wary, let us hide our loves!"
And then, sir, would he grip and wring my hand,
Cry "O sweet creature!", then kiss me hard,
As if he plucked up kisses by the roots
That grew upon my lips; then laid his leg
Over my thigh, and sighed, and kissed, and then
Cried, "Cursèd fate that gave thee to the Moor!"

OTHELLO O monstrous! Monstrous!

IAGO Nay, this was but his dream.

OTHELLO But this denoted a foregone conclusion.[7]
'Tis a shrewd doubt,[8] though it be but a dream.

IAGO And this may help to thicken other proofs
That do demonstrate thinly.

OTHELLO I'll tear her all to pieces.

IAGO Nay, but be wise. Yet we see nothing done;
She may be honest yet. Tell me but this:
Have you not sometimes seen a handkerchief
Spotted° with strawberries in your wife's hand? *embroidered*

OTHELLO I gave her such a one. 'Twas my first gift.

IAGO I know not that; but such a handkerchief—
I am sure it was your wife's—did I today
See Cassio wipe his beard with.

OTHELLO If it be that—

IAGO If it be that, or any that was hers,
It speaks against her with the other proofs.

OTHELLO O, that the slave° had forty thousand lives! *Cassio*
One is too poor, too weak for my revenge.
Now do I see 'tis true. Look here, Iago,
All my fond[9] love thus do I blow to heaven.
'Tis gone.
Arise, black vengeance, from the hollow hell!
Yield up, O love, thy crown and hearted° throne *fixed in the heart*
To tyrannous hate! Swell, bosom, with thy freight,° *burden*
For 'tis of aspics'° tongues! *venomous serpents'*

IAGO Yet be content.° *calm*

OTHELLO O, blood, blood, blood!

IAGO Patience, I say. Your mind perhaps may change.

OTHELLO Never, Iago. Like to the Pontic Sea,[1]
Whose icy current and compulsive course
Ne'er feels retiring ebb, but keeps due on
To the Propontic[2] and the Hellespont,[3]
Even so my bloody thoughts with violent pace
Shall ne'er look back, ne'er ebb to humble love,

7. Concluded experience or action.
8. Suspicious circumstance.
9. Foolish (but also suggesting "affectionate").
1. Black Sea.
2. Sea of Marmora, between the Black Sea and the Aegean.
3. Dardanelles, straits where the Sea of Marmora joins with the Aegean.

Till that a capable° and wide revenge *ample*
Swallow them up. Now, by yond marble[4] heaven,
[*Kneeling*.] In the due reverence of a sacred vow
I here engage my words.

IAGO Do not rise yet.
[*He kneels*.][5] Witness, you ever-burning lights above,
You elements that clip° us round about, *encompass*
Witness that here Iago doth give up
The execution° of his wit,° hands, heart, *exercise / mind*
To wronged Othello's service. Let him command,
And to obey shall be in me remorse,[6]
What bloody business ever.° [*They rise*.] *soever*

OTHELLO I greet thy love,
Not with vain thanks, but with acceptance bounteous,
And will upon the instant put thee to 't.[7]
Within these three days let me hear thee say
That Cassio's not alive.

IAGO My friend is dead;
'Tis done at your request. But let her live.

OTHELLO Damn her, lewd minx!° O, damn her, damn her! *wanton*
Come, go with me apart. I will withdraw
To furnish me with some swift means of death
For the fair devil. Now art thou my lieutenant.

IAGO I am your own forever. [*Exeunt*.]

Scene 4

[*Location: Before the citadel. Enter Desdemona, Emilia, and Clown*.]

DESDEMONA Do you know, sirrah,[8] where Lieutenant Cassio lies?

CLOWN I dare not say he lies[9] anywhere.

DESDEMONA Why, man?

CLOWN He's a soldier, and for me to say a soldier lies, 'tis stabbing.

DESDEMONA Go to. Where lodges he?

CLOWN To tell you where he lodges is to tell you where I lie.

DESDEMONA Can anything be made of this?

CLOWN I know not where he lodges, and for me to devise a lodging and say he lies here, or he lies there, were to lie in mine own throat.[1]

DESDEMONA Can you inquire him out, and be edified by report?

CLOWN I will catechize the world for him; that is, make questions, and by them answer.

DESDEMONA Seek him, bid him come hither. Tell him I have moved[2] my lord on his behalf and hope all will be well.

CLOWN To do this is within the compass of man's wit, and therefore I will attempt the doing it. [*Exit Clown*.]

DESDEMONA Where should I lose that handkerchief, Emilia?

4. I.e., gleaming like marble and unrelenting.
5. In the Quarto text, Iago kneels here after Othello has knelt at line 460.
6. Pity (for Othello's wrongs).
7. To the proof.
8. A form of address to an inferior.
9. Lodges. (But the Clown makes the obvious pun.)
1. Lie egregiously and deliberately. Also, use the windpipe to speak a lie.
2. Petitioned.

EMILIA I know not, madam.
DESDEMONA Believe me, I had rather have lost my purse
Full of crusadoes;° and but my noble Moor *gold coins*
Is true of mind and made of no such baseness
As jealous creatures are, it were enough
To put him to ill thinking.
EMILIA Is he not jealous?
DESDEMONA Who, he? I think the sun where he was born
Drew all such humors[3] from him.
EMILIA Look where he comes.
[*Enter Othello.*]
DESDEMONA I will not leave him now till Cassio
Be called to him.—How is 't with you, my lord?
OTHELLO Well, my good lady. [*Aside.*] O, hardness to dissemble!—
How do you, Desdemona?
DESDEMONA Well, my good lord.
OTHELLO Give me your hand. [*She gives her hand.*] This hand is moist, my lady.
DESDEMONA It yet hath felt no age nor known no sorrow.
OTHELLO This argues fruitfulness and liberal heart.[4]
Hot, hot, and moist. This hand of yours requires
A sequester° from liberty, fasting and prayer, *separation*
Much castigation,° exercise° devout; *discipline/prayer*
For here's a young and sweating devil here
That commonly rebels. 'Tis a good hand,
A frank[5] one.
DESDEMONA You may indeed say so,
For 'twas that hand that gave away my heart.
OTHELLO A liberal hand. The hearts of old gave hands,[6]
But our new heraldry is hands, not hearts.[7]
DESDEMONA I cannot speak of this. Come now, your promise.
OTHELLO What promise, chuck?[8]
DESDEMONA I have sent to bid Cassio come speak with you.
OTHELLO I have a salt and sorry rheum[9] offends me;
Lend me thy handkerchief.
DESDEMONA Here, my lord. [*She offers a handkerchief.*]
OTHELLO That which I gave you.
DESDEMONA I have it not about me.
OTHELLO Not?
DESDEMONA No, faith, my lord.
OTHELLO That's a fault. That handkerchief
Did an Egyptian to my mother give.
She was a charmer,° and could almost read *sorceress*
The thoughts of people. She told her, while she kept it
'Twould make her amiable° and subdue my father *desirable*

3. Refers to the four bodily fluids thought to determine temperament.
4. Gives evidence of amorousness, fecundity, and sexual freedom.
5. Generous, open (with sexual suggestion).
6. In former times, people would give their hearts when they gave their hands to something.
7. In our decadent times, the joining of hands is no longer a badge to signify the giving of hearts.
8. A term of endearment.
9. Distressful head cold or watering of the eyes.

Entirely to her love, but if she lost it
Or made a gift of it, my father's eye
Should hold her loathèd and his spirits should hunt
After new fancies.° She, dying, gave it me, *loves*
And bid me, when my fate would have me wived,
To give it her.[1] I did so; and take heed on 't;
Make it a darling like your precious eye.
To lose 't or give 't away were such perdition° *loss*
As nothing else could match.

DESDEMONA Is 't possible?

OTHELLO 'Tis true. There's magic in the web° of it. *weaving*
A sibyl, that had numbered in the world
The sun to course two hundred compasses,[2]
In her prophetic fury[3] sewed the work;° *embroidered pattern*
The worms were hallowed that did breed the silk,
And it was dyed in mummy[4] which the skillful
Conserved of[5] maidens' hearts.

DESDEMONA I' faith! Is 't true?

OTHELLO Most veritable. Therefore look to 't well.

DESDEMONA Then would to God that I had never seen 't!

OTHELLO Ha? Wherefore?

DESDEMONA Why do you speak so startingly and rash?[6]

OTHELLO Is 't lost? Is 't gone? Speak, is 't out o' the way?° *misplaced*

DESDEMONA Heaven bless us!

OTHELLO Say you?

DESDEMONA It is not lost; but what an if° it were? *if*

OTHELLO How?

DESDEMONA I say it is not lost.

OTHELLO Fetch 't, let me see 't.

DESDEMONA Why, so I can, sir, but I will not now.
This is a trick to put me from my suit.
Pray you, let Cassio be received again.

OTHELLO Fetch me the handkerchief! My mind misgives.

DESDEMONA Come, come,
You'll never meet a more sufficient° man. *able*

OTHELLO The handkerchief!

DESDEMONA I pray, talk° me of Cassio. *talk to*

OTHELLO The handkerchief!

DESDEMONA A man that all his time[7]
Hath founded his good fortunes on your love,
Shared dangers with you—

OTHELLO The handkerchief!

DESDEMONA I' faith, you are to blame.

OTHELLO Zounds! [*Exit Othello.*]

EMILIA Is not this man jealous?

DESDEMONA I ne'er saw this before.

1. I.e., to my wife.
2. Annual circlings. (The *sibyl*, or prophetess, was 200 years old.)
3. Frenzy of prophetic inspiration.
4. Medicinal or magical preparation drained from mummified bodies.
5. Prepared or preserved out of.
6. Disjointedly and impetuously, excitedly.
7. Throughout his career.

Sure, there's some wonder in this handkerchief.
I am most unhappy in the loss of it.

EMILIA 'Tis not a year or two shows us a man.[8]
They are all but° stomachs, and we all but food; *nothing but*
They eat us hungerly,° and when they are full *hungrily*
They belch us.

[*Enter Iago and Cassio.*]

Look you, Cassio and my husband.

IAGO [*to Cassio*]
There is no other way; 'tis she must do 't.
And, lo, the happiness![9] Go and importune her.

DESDEMONA How now, good Cassio? What's the news with you?

CASSIO Madam, my former suit. I do beseech you
That by your virtuous° means I may again *efficacious*
Exist and be a member of his love
Whom I, with all the office° of my heart, *loyal service*
Entirely honor. I would not be delayed.
If my offense be of such mortal° kind *fatal*
That nor° my service past, nor present sorrows, *neither*
Nor purposed merit in futurity
Can ransom me into his love again,
But to know so must be my benefit;[1]
So shall I clothe me in a forced content,
And shut myself up in[2] some other course,
To fortune's alms.[3]

DESDEMONA Alas, thrice-gentle Cassio,
My advocation° is not now in tune. *advocacy*
My lord is not my lord; nor should I know him,
Were he in favor° as in humor° altered. *appearance / mood*
So help me every spirit sanctified
As I have spoken for you all my best
And stood within the blank[4] of his displeasure
For my free speech! You must awhile be patient.
What I can do I will, and more I will
Than for myself I dare. Let that suffice you.

IAGO Is my lord angry?

EMILIA He went hence but now,
And certainly in strange unquietness.

IAGO Can he be angry? I have seen the cannon
When it hath blown his ranks into the air,
And like the devil from his very arm
Puffed his own brother—and is he angry?
Something of moment[5] then. I will go meet him.
There's matter in 't indeed, if he be angry.

DESDEMONA I prithee, do so. [*Exit Iago.*]

8. You can't really know a man even in a year or two of experience (?), or, real men come along seldom (?).
9. In happy time, fortunately met.
1. Merely to know that my case is hopeless will have to content me (and will be better than uncertainty).
2. Confine myself to.
3. Throwing myself on the mercy of fortune.
4. Within pointblank range. (The *blank* is the center of the target.)
5. Of immediate importance, momentous.

Something, sure, of state,° *state affairs*
Either from Venice, or some unhatched practice[6]
Made demonstrable here in Cyprus to him,
Hath puddled° his clear spirit; and in such cases *muddied*
Men's natures wrangle with inferior things,
Though great ones are their object. 'Tis even so;
For let our finger ache, and it indues° *induces*
Our other, healthful members even to a sense
Of pain. Nay, we must think men are not gods,
Nor of them look for such observancy° *attentiveness*
As fits the bridal.[7] Beshrew me[8] much, Emilia,
I was, unhandsome° warrior as I am, *unskillful*
Arraigning his unkindness with[9] my soul;
But now I find I had suborned the witness,[1]
And he's indicted falsely.

EMILIA Pray heaven it be
State matters, as you think, and no conception
Nor no jealous toy° concerning you. *fancy*

DESDEMONA Alas the day! I never gave him cause.

EMILIA But jealous souls will not be answered so;
They are not ever jealous for the cause,
But jealous for° they're jealous. It is a monster *do because*
Begot upon itself,[2] born on itself.

DESDEMONA Heaven keep that monster from Othello's mind!

EMILIA Lady, amen.

DESDEMONA I will go seek him. Cassio, walk hereabout.
If I do find him fit, I'll move your suit
And seek to effect it to my uttermost.

CASSIO I humbly thank your ladyship.

[*Exit Desdemona with Emilia*.]

[*Enter Bianca*.]

BIANCA Save° you, friend Cassio! *God save*

CASSIO What make° you from home? *do*
How is 't with you, my most fair Bianca?
I' faith, sweet love, I was coming to your house.

BIANCA And I was going to your lodging, Cassio.
What, keep a week away? Seven days and nights?
Eightscore-eight[3] hours? And lovers' absent hours
More tedious than the dial[4] eightscore times?
O weary reckoning!

CASSIO Pardon me, Bianca.
I have this while with leaden thoughts been pressed;
But I shall, in a more continuate° time, *uninterrupted*
Strike off this score[5] of absence. Sweet Bianca,

6. As yet unexecuted or undiscovered plot.
7. Wedding (when a bridegroom is newly attentive to his bride).
8. A mild oath.
9. Before the bar of.
1. Induced the witness to give false testimony.
2. Generated solely from itself.
3. One hundred sixty-eight, the number of hours in a week.
4. A complete revolution of the clock.
5. Settle this account.

[*Giving her Desdemona's handkerchief.*]
Take me this work out.[6]
BIANCA O Cassio, whence came this?
This is some token from a newer friend.° *mistress*
To the felt absence now I feel a cause.
Is 't come to this? Well, well.
CASSIO Go to, woman!
Throw your vile guesses in the devil's teeth,
From whence you have them. You are jealous now
That this is from some mistress, some remembrance.
No, by my faith, Bianca.
BIANCA Why, whose is it?
CASSIO I know not, neither. I found it in my chamber.
I like the work well. Ere it be demanded°— *inquired for*
As like° enough it will—I would have it copied. *likely*
Take it and do 't, and leave me for this time.
BIANCA Leave you? Wherefore?
CASSIO I do attend here on the General,
And think it no addition,[7] nor my wish,
To have him see me womaned.
BIANCA Why, I pray you?
CASSIO Not that I love you not.
BIANCA But that you do not love me.
I pray you, bring° me on the way a little, *accompany*
And say if I shall see you soon at night.
CASSIO 'Tis but a little way that I can bring you,
For I attend here; but I'll see you soon.
BIANCA 'Tis very good. I must be circumstanced.[8]
[*Exeunt omnes.*]

Act 4

Scene 1

[*Location: Before the citadel. Enter Othello and Iago.*]
IAGO Will you think so?
OTHELLO Think so, Iago?
IAGO What,
To kiss in private?
OTHELLO An unauthorized kiss!
IAGO Or to be naked with her friend in bed
An hour or more, not meaning any harm?
OTHELLO Naked in bed, Iago, and not mean harm?
It is hypocrisy against the devil.
They that mean virtuously and yet do so,
The devil their virtue tempts, and they tempt heaven.
IAGO If they do nothing, 'tis a venial° slip. *pardonable*
But if I give my wife a handkerchief—
OTHELLO What then?

6. Copy this embroidery for me.
7. I.e., addition to my reputation.
8. Be governed by circumstance, yield to your conditions.

IAGO Why then, 'tis hers, my lord, and being hers,
She may, I think, bestow 't on any man.
OTHELLO She is protectress of her honor too.
May she give that?
IAGO Her honor is an essence that's not seen;
They have it[9] very oft that have it not.
But, for the handkerchief—
OTHELLO By heaven, I would most gladly have forgot it.
Thou saidst—O, it comes o'er my memory
As doth the raven o'er the infectious house,[1]
Boding to all—he had my handkerchief.
IAGO Ay, what of that?
OTHELLO That's not so good now.
IAGO What
If I had said I had seen him do you wrong?
Or heard him say—as knaves be such abroad,° *around about*
Who having, by their own importunate suit,
Or voluntary dotage[2] of some mistress,
Convincèd or supplied[3] them, cannot choose
But they must blab—
OTHELLO Hath he said anything?
IAGO He hath, my lord; but, be you well assured,
No more than he'll unswear.
OTHELLO What hath he said?
IAGO Faith, that he did—I know not what he did.
OTHELLO What? What?
IAGO Lie—
OTHELLO With her?
IAGO With her, on her; what you will.
OTHELLO Lie with her? Lie on her? We say "lie on her" when they belie[4] her. Lie with her? Zounds, that's fulsome.[5]—Handkerchief—confessions—handkerchief!—To confess and be hanged for his labor—first to be hanged and then to confess.[6]—I tremble at it. Nature would not invest herself in such shadowing passion without some instruction.[7] It is not words[8] that shakes me thus. Pish! Noses, ears, and lips.—Is 't possible?—Confess—handkerchief!—O devil!
[*Falls in a trance.*]
IAGO Work on, My medicine, work! Thus credulous fools are caught,
And many worthy and chaste dames even thus,
All guiltless, meet reproach.—What, ho! My lord!
My lord! I say! Othello!
[*Enter Cassio.*]
How now, Cassio?
CASSIO What's the matter?

9. They enjoy a reputation for it.
1. Allusion to the belief that the raven hovered over a house of sickness or infection, such as one visited by the plague.
2. Willing infatuation.
3. Seduced or sexually gratified.
4. Slander.
5. Foul.
6. Othello reverses the proverbial *confess and be hanged;* Cassio is to be given no time to confess before he dies.
7. I.e., without some foundation in fact, nature would not have dressed herself in such an overwhelming passion that comes over me now and fills my mind with images, or in such a lifelike fantasy as Cassio had in his dream of lying with Desdemona.
8. Mere words.

IAGO My lord is fall'n into an epilepsy.
This is his second fit. He had one yesterday.
CASSIO Rub him about the temples.
IAGO No, forbear.
The lethargy° must have his° quiet course. *coma/its*
If not, he foams at mouth, and by and by
Breaks out to savage madness. Look, he stirs.
Do you withdraw yourself a little while.
He will recover straight. When he is gone,
I would on great occasion speak with you.
[*Exit Cassio.*]
How is it, General? Have you not hurt your head?
OTHELLO Dost thou mock me?[1]
IAGO I mock you not, by heaven.
Would you would bear your fortune like a man!
OTHELLO A hornèd man's a monster and a beast.
IAGO There's many a beast then in a populous city,
And many a civil° monster. *city-dwelling*
OTHELLO Did he confess it?
IAGO Good sir, be a man.
Think every bearded fellow that's but yoked[2]
May draw with you.[3] There's millions now alive
That nightly lie in those unproper° beds *shared*
Which they dare swear peculiar.° Your case is better.[4] *their own*
O, 'tis the spite of hell, the fiend's arch-mock,
To lip° a wanton in a secure couch *kiss*
And to suppose her chaste! No, let me know,
And knowing what I am,[5] I know what she shall be.[6]
OTHELLO O, thou art wise. 'Tis certain.
IAGO Stand you awhile apart;
Confine yourself but in a patient list.[7]
Whilst you were here o'erwhelmèd with your grief—
A passion most unsuiting such a man—
Cassio came hither. I shifted him away,[8]
And laid good 'scuse upon your ecstasy,° *trance*
Bade him anon return and here speak with me,
The which he promised. Do but encave° yourself *conceal*
And mark the fleers,° the gibes, and notable° scorns *sneers/obvious*
That dwell in every region of his face;
For I will make him tell the tale anew,
Where, how, how oft, how long ago, and when
He hath and is again to cope° your wife. *have sex with*
I say, but mark his gesture. Marry, patience!
Or I shall say you're all-in-all in spleen,[9]
And nothing of a man.

1. Othello takes Iago's question about hurting his head to be a mocking reference to the cuckold's horns.
2. Married. Also, put into the yoke of infamy and cuckoldry.
3. Pull as you do, like oxen who are yoked, i.e., share your fate as cuckold.
4. I.e., because you know the truth.
5. I.e., a cuckold.
6. Will happen to her.
7. Within the bounds of patience.
8. Used a dodge to get rid of him.
9. Utterly governed by passionate impulses.

OTHELLO Dost thou hear, Iago?
I will be found most cunning in my patience;
But—dost thou hear?—most bloody.
IAGO That's not amiss;
But yet keep time[1] in all. Will you withdraw?
[*Othello stands apart*.]
Now will I question Cassio of Bianca,
A huswife° that by selling her desires *hussy*
Buys herself bread and clothes. It is a creature
That dotes on Cassio—as 'tis the strumpet's plague
To beguile many and be beguiled by one.
He, when he hears of her, cannot restrain° *refrain*
From the excess of laughter. Here he comes.
[*Enter Cassio*.]
As he shall smile, Othello shall go mad;
And his unbookish° jealousy must conster° *uninstructed / construe*
Poor Cassio's smiles, gestures, and light behaviors
Quite in the wrong.—How do you now, Lieutenant?
CASSIO The worser that you give me the addition° *title*
Whose want[2] even kills me.
IAGO Ply Desdemona well and you are sure on 't.
[*Speaking lower*.] Now, if this suit lay in Bianca's power,
How quickly should you speed!
CASSIO [*laughing*] Alas, poor caitiff!° *wretch*
OTHELLO [*aside*] Look how he laughs already!
IAGO I never knew a woman love man so.
CASSIO Alas, poor rogue! I think, i' faith, she loves me.
OTHELLO Now he denies it faintly, and laughs it out.
IAGO Do you hear, Cassio?
OTHELLO Now he importunes him
To tell it o'er. Go to![3] Well said,° well said. *well done*
IAGO She gives it out that you shall marry her.
Do you intend it?
CASSIO Ha, ha, ha!
OTHELLO Do you triumph, Roman?[4] Do you triumph?
CASSIO I marry her? What? A customer?[5] Prithee, bear some charity to my wit;[6] do not think it so unwholesome. Ha, ha, ha!
OTHELLO So, so, so, so! They laugh that win.[7]
IAGO Faith, the cry goes that you shall marry her.
CASSIO Prithee, say true.
IAGO I am a very villain else.[8]
OTHELLO Have you scored me?[9] Well.
CASSIO This is the monkey's own giving out. She is persuaded I will marry her out of her own love and flattery,[1] not out of my promise.

1. Keep yourself steady (as in music).
2. The lack of which.
3. An expression of remonstrance.
4. The Romans were noted for their *triumphs* or triumphal processions.
5. Prostitute.
6. Be more charitable to my judgment.
7. I.e., they that laugh last laugh best.
8. Call me a complete rogue if I'm not telling the truth.
9. Scored off me, beaten me, made up my reckoning, branded me.
1. Self-flattery, self-deception.

OTHELLO Iago beckons° me. Now he begins the story. *signals*

CASSIO She was here even now; she haunts me in every place. I was the other day talking on the seabank[2] with certain Venetians, and thither comes the bauble,[3] and, by this hand,[4] she falls me thus about my neck—

[*He embraces Iago.*]

OTHELLO Crying, "O dear Cassio!" as it were; his gesture imports it.

CASSIO So hangs and lolls and weeps upon me, so shakes and pulls me. Ha, ha, ha!

OTHELLO Now he tells how she plucked him to my chamber. O, I see that nose of yours, but not that dog I shall throw it to.[5]

CASSIO Well, I must leave her company.

IAGO Before me,[6] look where she comes.

[*Enter Bianca with Othello's handkerchief.*]

CASSIO 'Tis such another fitchew![7] Marry, a perfumed one.—What do you mean by this haunting of me?

BIANCA Let the devil and his dam[8] haunt you! What did you mean by that same handkerchief you gave me even now? I was a fine fool to take it. I must take out the work? A likely piece of work,[9] that you should find it in your chamber and know not who left it there! This is some minx's token, and I must take out the work? There; give it your hobbyhorse.[1] [*She gives him the handkerchief.*] Wheresoever you had it, I'll take out no work on 't.

CASSIO How now, my sweet Bianca? How now? How now?

OTHELLO By heaven, that should be[2] my handkerchief!

BIANCA If you'll come to supper tonight, you may; if you will not, come when you are next prepared for.[3]

[*Exit.*]

IAGO After her, after her.

CASSIO Faith, I must. She'll rail in the streets else.

IAGO Will you sup there?

CASSIO Faith, I intend so.

IAGO Well, I may chance to see you, for I would very fain speak with you.

CASSIO Prithee, come. Will you?

IAGO Go to. Say no more. [*Exit Cassio.*]

OTHELLO [*advancing*] How shall I murder him, Iago?

IAGO Did you perceive how he laughed at his vice?

OTHELLO O, Iago!

IAGO And did you see the handkerchief?

OTHELLO Was that mine?

IAGO Yours, by this hand. And to see how he prizes the foolish woman your wife! She gave it him, and he hath given it his whore.

OTHELLO I would have him nine years a-killing. A fine woman! A fair woman! A sweet woman!

2. Seashore.
3. Plaything.
4. I make my vow.
5. Othello imagines himself cutting off Cassio's nose and throwing it to a dog.
6. On my soul.
7. What a polecat she is! Just like all the others. (Polecats were often compared with prostitutes because of their rank smell and presumed lechery.)
8. Mother.
9. A fine story.
1. Harlot.
2. Must be.
3. When I'm ready for you (i.e., never).

IAGO Nay, you must forget that.

OTHELLO Ay, let her rot and perish, and be damned tonight, for she shall not live. No, my heart is turned to stone; I strike it, and it hurts my hand. O, the world hath not a sweeter creature! She might lie by an emperor's side and command him tasks.

IAGO Nay, that's not your way.[4]

OTHELLO Hang her! I do but say what she is. So delicate with her needle! An admirable musician! O, she will sing the savageness out of a bear. Of so high and plenteous wit and invention![5]

IAGO She's the worse for all this.

OTHELLO O, a thousand, a thousand times! And then, of so gentle a condition![6]

IAGO Ay, too gentle.[7]

OTHELLO Nay, that's certain. But yet the pity of it, Iago! O, Iago, the pity of it, Iago!

IAGO If you are so fond[8] over her iniquity, give her patent[9] to offend, for if it touch not you it comes near nobody.

OTHELLO I will chop her into messes.[1] Cuckold me?

IAGO O, 'tis foul in her.

OTHELLO With mine officer?

IAGO That's fouler.

OTHELLO Get me some poison, Iago, this night. I'll not expostulate with her, lest her body and beauty unprovide[2] my mind again. This night, Iago.

IAGO Do it not with poison. Strangle her in her bed, even the bed she hath contaminated.

OTHELLO Good, good! The justice of it pleases. Very good.

IAGO And for Cassio, let me be his undertaker.[3] You shall hear more by midnight.

OTHELLO Excellent good. [*A trumpet within.*] What trumpet is that same?

IAGO I warrant, something from Venice.

[*Enter Lodovico, Desdemona, and attendants.*]

'Tis Lodovico. This comes from the Duke.
See, your wife's with him.

LODOVICO God save you, worthy General!

OTHELLO With all my heart, sir.[4]

LODOVICO [*giving him a letter*] The Duke and the senators of Venice greet you.

OTHELLO I kiss the instrument of their pleasures.

[*He opens the letter, and reads.*]

DESDEMONA And what's the news, good cousin Lodovico?

IAGO I am very glad to see you, signor.
Welcome to Cyprus.

LODOVICO I thank you. How does Lieutenant Cassio?

IAGO Lives, sir.

DESDEMONA Cousin, there's fall'n between him and my lord
An unkind[5] breach; but you shall make all well.

4. I.e., the way you should think of her.
5. Imagination.
6. Wellborn and well-bred.
7. Generous, yielding (to other men).
8. Foolish.
9. License.

1. Portions of meat, i.e., bits.
2. Weaken, render unfit.
3. Undertake to dispatch him.
4. I thank you most heartily.
5. Unnatural, contrary to their natures; hurtful.

OTHELLO Are you sure of that?
DESDEMONA My lord?
OTHELLO [*reads*] "This fail you not to do, as you will—"
LODOVICO He did not call; he's busy in the paper.
Is there division twixt my lord and Cassio?
DESDEMONA A most unhappy one. I would do much
T' atone° them, for the love I bear to Cassio. *reconcile*
OTHELLO Fire and brimstone!
DESDEMONA My lord?
OTHELLO Are you wise?
DESDEMONA What, is he angry?
LODOVICO Maybe the letter moved him;
For, as I think, they do command him home,
Deputing Cassio in his government.° *office*
DESDEMONA By my troth, I am glad on 't.° *of it*
OTHELLO Indeed?
DESDEMONA My lord?
OTHELLO I am glad to see you mad.[6]
DESDEMONA Why, sweet Othello—
OTHELLO [*striking her*] Devil!
DESDEMONA I have not deserved this.
LODOVICO My lord, this would not be believed in Venice,
Though I should swear I saw 't. 'Tis very much.° *outrageous*
Make her amends; she weeps.
OTHELLO O devil, devil!
If that the earth could teem° with woman's tears, *breed*
Each drop she falls° would prove a crocodile.[7] *lets fall*
Out of my sight!
DESDEMONA I will not stay to offend you. [*Going.*]
LODOVICO Truly, an obedient lady.
I do beseech your lordship, call her back.
OTHELLO Mistress!
DESDEMONA [*returning*] My lord?
OTHELLO What would you with her, sir?
LODOVICO Who, I, my lord?
OTHELLO Ay, you did wish that I would make her turn.[8]
Sir, she can turn, and turn, and yet go on
And turn again; and she can weep, sir, weep;
And she's obedient,[9] as you say, obedient,
Very obedient.—Proceed you in your tears.—
Concerning this, sir—O well-painted passion!—° *grief*
I am commanded home.—Get you away;
I'll send for you anon.—Sir, I obey the mandate
And will return to Venice.—Hence, avaunt!

[*Exit Desdemona.*]

Cassio shall have my place. And, sir, tonight

6. I.e., I am glad to see that you are insane enough to rejoice in Cassio's promotion. (Othello bitterly plays on Desdemona's *I am glad*.)
7. Crocodiles were supposed to weep hypocritical tears for their victims.
8. Othello implies that Desdemona is pliant and will do a *turn* for any man.
9. With much the same sexual connotation as *turn*.

I do entreat that we may sup together.
You are welcome, sir, to Cyprus.—Goats and monkeys![1]

LODOVICO Is this the noble Moor whom our full Senate
Call all in all sufficient? Is this the nature
Whom passion could not shake? Whose solid virtue
The shot of accident nor dart of chance
Could neither graze nor pierce?

IAGO He is much changed.

LODOVICO Are his wits safe? Is he not light of brain?

IAGO He's that he is. I may not breathe my censure
What he might be. If what he might he is not,
I would to heaven he were![2]

LODOVICO What, strike his wife?

IAGO Faith, that was not so well; yet would I knew
That stroke would prove the worst!

LODOVICO Is it his use?° *custom*
Or did the letters work upon his blood° *passions*
And new-create his fault?

IAGO Alas, alas!
It is not honesty in me to speak
What I have seen and known. You shall observe him,
And his own courses will denote[3] him so
That I may save my speech. Do but go after,
And mark how he continues.

LODOVICO I am sorry that I am deceived in him. [*Exeunt.*]

Scene 2

[*Location: The Citadel. Enter Othello and Emilia.*]

OTHELLO You have seen nothing then?

EMILIA Nor ever heard, nor ever did suspect.

OTHELLO Yes, you have seen Cassio and she together.

EMILIA But then I saw no harm, and then I heard
Each syllable that breath made up between them.

OTHELLO What, did they never whisper?

EMILIA Never, my lord.

OTHELLO Nor send you out o' the way?

EMILIA Never.

OTHELLO To fetch her fan, her gloves, her mask, nor nothing?

EMILIA Never, my lord.

OTHELLO That's strange.

EMILIA I durst, my lord, to wager she is honest,
Lay down my soul at stake.° If you think other, *as the wager*
Remove your thought; it doth abuse your bosom.° *deceive you*
If any wretch have put this in your head,
Let heaven requite it with the serpent's curse![4]

1. The most lustful animals.

2. I dare not venture an opinion as to whether he's of unsound mind, as you suggest, but, if he isn't, then it might be better to wish he were in fact insane, since only that could excuse his wild behavior.

3. Actions will reveal.

4. The curse pronounced by God on the serpent for deceiving Eve, just as some man has done to Othello and Desdemona. (See Genesis 3.14.)

For if she be not honest, chaste, and true,
There's no man happy; the purest of their wives
Is foul as slander.

OTHELLO Bid her come hither. Go.
[*Exit Emilia.*]
She says enough; yet she's a simple bawd
That cannot say as much.[5] This° is a subtle whore, *Desdemona*
A closet lock and key of villainous secrets.
And yet she'll kneel and pray; I have seen her do 't.
[*Enter Desdemona and Emilia.*]

DESDEMONA My lord, what is your will?

OTHELLO Pray you, chuck, come hither.

DESDEMONA What is your pleasure?

OTHELLO Let me see your eyes.
Look in my face.

DESDEMONA What horrible fancy's this?

OTHELLO [*to Emilia*] Some of your function,[6] mistress.
Leave procreants° alone and shut the door; *mating couples*
Cough or cry "hem" if anybody come.
Your mystery,° your mystery! Nay, dispatch. *trade*
[*Exit Emilia.*]

DESDEMONA [*kneeling*] Upon my knees, what doth your speech import?
I understand a fury in your words,
But not the words.

OTHELLO Why, what art thou?

DESDEMONA Your wife, my lord, your true
And loyal wife.

OTHELLO Come, swear it, damn thyself,
Lest, being like one of heaven,[7] the devils themselves
Should fear to seize thee. Therefore be double damned:
Swear thou art honest.

DESDEMONA Heaven doth truly know it.

OTHELLO Heaven truly knows that thou art false as hell.

DESDEMONA To whom, my lord? With whom? How am I false?

OTHELLO [*weeping*] Ah, Desdemon! Away, away, away!

DESDEMONA Alas the heavy day! Why do you weep?
Am I the motive° of these tears, my lord? *cause*
If haply you my father do suspect
An instrument of this your calling back,
Lay not your blame on me. If you have lost him,
I have lost him too.

OTHELLO Had it pleased heaven
To try me with affliction, had they[8] rained
All kinds of sores and shames on my bare head,
Steeped me in poverty to the very lips,
Given to captivity me and my utmost hopes,
I should have found in some place of my soul

5. Any procuress or go-between who couldn't make up as plausible a story as Emilia's would have to be pretty stupid.
6. I.e., practice your chosen profession, that of bawd (by guarding the door).
7. Looking like an angel.
8. I.e., heavenly powers.

A drop of patience. But, alas, to make me
A fixèd figure for the time of scorn[9]
To point his° slow and moving finger[1] at! *its*
Yet could I bear that too, well, very well.
But there where I have garnered° up my heart, *stored*
Where either I must live or bear no life,
The fountain° from the which my current runs *spring*
Or else dries up—to be discarded thence!
Or keep it as a cistern° for foul toads *cesspool*
To knot° and gender° in! Turn thy complexion there,[2] *couple/engender*
Patience, thou young and rose-lipped cherubin—
Ay, there look grim as hell![3]

DESDEMONA I hope my noble lord esteems me honest.° *chaste*

OTHELLO O, ay, as summer flies are in the shambles,° *slaughterhouse*
That quicken° even with blowing.[4] O thou weed, *come to life*
Who art so lovely fair and smell'st so sweet
That the sense aches at thee, would thou hadst ne'er been born!

DESDEMONA Alas, what ignorant sin[5] have I committed?

OTHELLO Was this fair paper, this most goodly book,
Made to write "whore" upon? What committed?
Committed? O thou public commoner!° *prostitute*
I should make very forges of my cheeks,
That would to cinders burn up modesty,
Did I but speak thy deeds. What committed?
Heaven stops the nose at it and the moon winks;[6]
The bawdy[7] wind, that kisses all it meets,
Is hushed within the hollow mine[8] of earth
And will not hear 't. What committed?
Impudent strumpet!

DESDEMONA By heaven, you do me wrong.

OTHELLO Are not you a strumpet?

DESDEMONA No, as I am a Christian.
If to preserve this vessel° for my lord *body*
From any other foul unlawful touch
Be not to be a strumpet, I am none.

OTHELLO What, not a whore?

DESDEMONA No, as I shall be saved.

OTHELLO Is 't possible?

DESDEMONA O, heaven forgive us!

OTHELLO I cry you mercy,° then. *beg you pardon*
I took you for that cunning whore of Venice
That married with Othello. [*Calling out.*] You, mistress,
That have the office opposite to Saint Peter
And keep the gate of hell!
[*Enter Emilia.*]

9. Scornful world.
1. I.e., hour hand of the clock, moving so slowly it seems hardly to move at all. (Othello envisages himself as being eternally pointed at by the scornful world as the numbers on a clock are pointed at by the hour hand.)
2. Change your color, grow pale, at such a sight.
3. Even Patience, that rose-lipped cherub, will look grim and pale at this spectacle.
4. I.e., with the puffing up of something rotten in which maggots are breeding.
5. Sin in ignorance.
6. Closes her eyes. (The moon symbolizes chastity.)
7. Kissing one and all.
8. Cave (where the winds were thought to dwell).

You, you, ay, you!
We have done our course.[9] There's money for your pains. [*He gives money.*]
I pray you, turn the key and keep our counsel. [*Exit.*]
EMILIA Alas, what does this gentleman conceive?° *suppose*
How do you, madam? How do you, my good lady?
DESDEMONA Faith, half asleep.[1]
EMILIA Good madam, what's the matter with my lord?
DESDEMONA With who?
EMILIA Why, with my lord, madam.
DESDEMONA Who is thy lord?
EMILIA He that is yours, sweet lady.
DESDEMONA I have none. Do not talk to me, Emilia.
I cannot weep, nor answers have I none
But what should go by water.[2] Prithee, tonight
Lay on my bed my wedding sheets, remember;
And call thy husband hither.
EMILIA Here's a change indeed! [*Exit.*]
DESDEMONA 'Tis meet° I should be used so, very meet. *fitting*
How have I been behaved, that he might stick° *attach*
The small'st opinion° on my least misuse?° *censure / misconduct*
[*Enter Iago and Emilia.*]
IAGO What is your pleasure, madam? How is 't with you?
DESDEMONA I cannot tell. Those that do teach young babes
Do it with gentle means and easy tasks.
He might have chid me so, for, in good faith,
I am a child to chiding.
IAGO What is the matter, lady?
EMILIA Alas, Iago, my lord hath so bewhored her,
Thrown such despite and heavy terms upon her,
That true hearts cannot bear it.
DESDEMONA Am I that name, Iago?
IAGO What name, fair lady?
DESDEMONA Such as she said my lord did say I was.
EMILIA He called her whore. A beggar in his drink
Could not have laid such terms upon his callet.° *whore*
IAGO Why did he so?
DESDEMONA [*weeping*]
I do not know. I am sure I am none such.
IAGO Do not weep, do not weep. Alas the day!
EMILIA Hath she forsook so many noble matches,
Her father and her country and her friends,
To be called whore? Would it not make one weep?
DESDEMONA It is my wretched fortune.
IAGO Beshrew° him for 't! *curse*
How comes this trick° upon him? *delusion*
DESDEMONA Nay, heaven doth know.
EMILIA I will be hanged if some eternal° villain, *inveterate*

9. Business (with an indecent suggestion of "trick," turn at sex).

1. I.e., dazed.

2. Be expressed by tears.

Some busy and insinuating° rogue, *wheedling*
Some cogging,° cozening° slave, to get some office, *cheating/defrauding*
Have not devised this slander. I will be hanged else.

IAGO Fie, there is no such man. It is impossible.

DESDEMONA If any such there be, heaven pardon him!

EMILIA A halter° pardon him! And hell gnaw his bones! *hangman's noose*
Why should he call her whore? Who keeps her company?
What place? What time? What form?° What likelihood? *appearance*
The Moor's abused by some most villainous knave,
Some base notorious knave, some scurvy fellow.
O heaven, that such companions thou'dst unfold,[3]
And put in every honest hand a whip
To lash the rascals naked through the world
Even from the east to th' west!

IAGO Speak within door.[4]

EMILIA O, fie upon them! Some such squire° he was *fellow*
That turned your wit the seamy side without° *wrong side out*
And made you to suspect me with the Moor.

IAGO You are a fool. Go to.[5]

DESDEMONA Alas, Iago,
What shall I do to win my lord again?
Good friend, go to him; for, by this light of heaven,
I know not how I lost him. Here I kneel. [*She kneels*.]
If e'er my will did trespass 'gainst his love,
Either in discourse of thought or actual deed,
Or that° mine eyes, mine ears, or any sense *if*
Delighted them° in any other form; *took delight*
Or that I do not yet,° and ever did, *still*
And ever will—though he do shake me off
To beggarly divorcement—love him dearly,
Comfort forswear[6] me! Unkindness may do much,
And his unkindness may defeat° my life, *destroy*
But never taint my love. I cannot say "whore."
It does abhor[7] me now I speak the word;
To do the act that might the addition° earn *title*
Not the world's mass of vanity° could make me. *showy splendor*
[*She rises*.]

IAGO I pray you, be content. 'Tis but his humor.° *mood*
The business of the state does him offense,
And he does chide with you.

DESDEMONA If 'twere no other—

IAGO It is but so, I warrant. [*Trumpets within*.]
Hark, how these instruments summon you to supper!
The messengers of Venice stays the meat.° *wait to dine*
Go in, and weep not. All things shall be well.

[*Exeunt Desdemona and Emilia*.]

[*Enter Roderigo*.]

3. If only you would expose such fellows.
4. I.e., not so loud.
5. I.e., that's enough.
6. May heavenly comfort forsake.
7. Fill me with abhorrence. Also, make me whorelike.

How now, Roderigo?

RODERIGO I do not find that thou deal'st justly with me.

IAGO What in the contrary?

RODERIGO Every day thou daff'st me[8] with some device,[9] Iago, and rather, as it seems to me now, keep'st from me all conveniency[1] than suppliest me with the least advantage[2] of hope. I will indeed no longer endure it, nor am I yet persuaded to put up[3] in peace what already I have foolishly suffered.

IAGO Will you hear me, Roderigo?

RODERIGO Faith, I have heard too much, for your words and performances are no kin together.

IAGO You charge me most unjustly.

RODERIGO With naught but truth. I have wasted myself out of my means. The jewels you have had from me to deliver[4] Desdemona would half have corrupted a votarist.[5] You have told me she hath received them and returned me expectations and comforts of sudden respect[6] and acquaintance, but I find none.

IAGO Well, go to, very well.

RODERIGO "Very well"! "Go to"! I cannot go to,[7] man, nor 'tis not very well. By this hand, I think it is scurvy, and begin to find myself fopped[8] in it.

IAGO Very well.

RODERIGO I tell you 'tis not very well.[9] I will make myself known to Desdemona. If she will return me my jewels, I will give over my suit and repent my unlawful solicitation; if not, assure yourself I will seek satisfaction[1] of you.

IAGO You have said now?[2]

RODERIGO Ay, and said nothing but what I protest intendment[3] of doing.

IAGO Why, now I see there's mettle in thee, and even from this instant do build on thee a better opinion than ever before. Give me thy hand, Roderigo. Thou hast taken against me a most just exception; but yet I protest I have dealt most directly in thy affair.

RODERIGO It hath not appeared.

IAGO I grant indeed it hath not appeared, and your suspicion is not without wit and judgment. But, Roderigo, if thou hast that in thee indeed which I have greater reason to believe now than ever—I mean purpose, courage, and valor—this night show it. If thou the next night following enjoy not Desdemona, take me from this world with treachery and devise engines[4] for my life.

RODERIGO Well, what is it? Is it within reason and compass?

IAGO Sir, there is especial commission come from Venice to depute Cassio in Othello's place.

RODERIGO Is that true? Why, then Othello and Desdemona return again to Venice.

IAGO O, no; he goes into Mauritania and takes away with him the fair Desdemona, unless his abode be lingered here by some accident; wherein none can be so determinate[5] as the removing of Cassio.

8. You put me off.
9. Excuse, trick.
1. Advantage, opportunity.
2. Increase.
3. Submit to, tolerate.
4. Deliver to.
5. Nun.
6. Immediate consideration.
7. Roderigo changes Iago's *go to*, an expression urging patience, to *I cannot go to*, "I have no opportunity for success in wooing."
8. Fooled, duped.
9. Roderigo changes Iago's *very well*, "all right, then," to *not very well*, "not at all good."
1. Repayment. (The term normally means settling of accounts in a duel.)
2. Have you finished?
3. Intention.
4. Plots against.
5. Conclusive.

RODERIGO How do you mean, removing of him?

IAGO Why, by making him uncapable of Othello's place—knocking out his brains.

RODERIGO And that you would have me to do?

IAGO Ay, if you dare do yourself a profit and a right. He sups tonight with a harlotry,[6] and thither will I go to him. He knows not yet of his honorable fortune. If you will watch his going thence, which I will fashion to fall out[7] between twelve and one, you may take him at your pleasure. I will be near to second your attempt, and he shall fall between us. Come, stand not amazed at it, but go along with me. I will show you such a necessity in his death that you shall think yourself bound to put it on him. It is now high[8] suppertime, and the night grows to waste.[9] About it.

RODERIGO I will hear further reason for this.

IAGO And you shall be satisfied. [*Exeunt.*]

Scene 3

[*Location: The Citadel. Enter Othello, Lodovico, Desdemona, Emilia, and attendants.*]

LODOVICO I do beseech you, sir, trouble yourself no further.

OTHELLO O, pardon me; 'twill do me good to walk.

LODOVICO Madam, good night. I humbly thank your ladyship.

DESDEMONA Your honor is most welcome.

OTHELLO Will you walk, sir?
O, Desdemona!

DESDEMONA My lord?

OTHELLO Get you to bed on th' instant. I will be returned forthwith. Dismiss your attendant there. Look 't be done.

DESDEMONA I will, my lord.

[*Exit Othello, with Lodovico and attendants.*]

EMILIA How goes it now? He looks gentler than he did.

DESDEMONA He says he will return incontinent,° *immediately*
And hath commanded me to go to bed,
And bid me to dismiss you.

EMILIA Dismiss me?

DESDEMONA It was his bidding. Therefore, good Emilia,
Give me my nightly wearing, and adieu.
We must not now displease him.

EMILIA I would you had never seen him!

DESDEMONA So would not I. My love doth so approve him
That even his stubbornness,° his checks,° his frowns— *roughness/rebukes*
Prithee, unpin me—have grace and favor in them.

[*Emilia prepares Desdemona for bed.*]

EMILIA I have laid those sheets you bade me on the bed.

DESDEMONA All's one.[1] Good faith, how foolish are our minds!
If I do die before thee, prithee shroud me
In one of these same sheets.

EMILIA Come, come, you talk.° *prattle*

6. Slut.
7. Occur.
8. Fully.
9. Wastes away.
1. All right. It doesn't really matter.

DESDEMONA My mother had a maid called Barbary.
She was in love, and he she loved proved mad° *wild*
And did forsake her. She had a song of "Willow."
An old thing 'twas, but it expressed her fortune,
And she died singing it. That song tonight
Will not go from my mind; I have much to do
But to go hang[2] my head all at one side
And sing it like poor Barbary. Prithee, dispatch.
EMILIA Shall I go fetch your nightgown?° *dressing gown*
DESDEMONA No, unpin me here.
This Lodovico is a proper° man. *handsome*
EMILIA A very handsome man.
DESDEMONA He speaks well.
EMILIA I know a lady in Venice would have walked barefoot to Palestine for a touch of his nether lip.
DESDEMONA [*singing*] "The poor soul sat sighing by a sycamore tree,
Sing all a green willow;[3]
Her hand on her bosom, her head on her knee,
Sing willow, willow, willow.
The fresh streams ran by her and murmured her moans;
Sing willow, willow, willow;
Her salt tears fell from her, and softened the stones—"
Lay by these.
[*Singing*.] "Sing willow, willow, willow—"
Prithee, hie thee.° He'll come anon.° *hurry/right away*
[*Singing*.] "Sing all a green willow must be my garland.
Let nobody blame him; his scorn I approve—"
Nay, that's not next.—Hark! Who is 't that knocks?
EMILIA It's the wind.
DESDEMONA [*singing*] "I called my love false love; but what said he then?
Sing willow, willow, willow;
If I court more women, you'll couch with more men."
So, get thee gone. Good night. Mine eyes do itch;
Doth that bode weeping?
EMILIA 'Tis neither here nor there.
DESDEMONA I have heard it said so. O, these men, these men!
Dost thou in conscience think—tell me, Emilia—
That there be women do abuse° their husbands *deceive*
In such gross kind?
EMILIA There be some such, no question.
DESDEMONA Wouldst thou do such a deed for all the world?
EMILIA Why, would not you?
DESDEMONA No, by this heavenly light!
EMILIA Nor I neither by this heavenly light;
I might do 't as well i' the dark.
DESDEMONA Wouldst thou do such a deed for all the world?
EMILIA The world's a huge thing. It is a great price

2. I can scarcely keep myself from hanging.

3. A conventional emblem of disappointed love.

For a small vice.

DESDEMONA Good troth, I think thou wouldst not.

EMILIA By my troth, I think I should, and undo 't when I had done. Marry, I would not do such a thing for a joint ring,[4] nor for measures of lawn,[5] nor for gowns, petticoats, nor caps, nor any petty exhibition.[6] But for all the whole world! Uds[7] pity, who would not make her husband a cuckold to make him a monarch? I should venture purgatory for 't.

DESDEMONA Beshrew me if I would do such a wrong
For the whole world.

EMILIA Why, the wrong is but a wrong i' the world, and having the world for your labor, 'tis a wrong in your own world, and you might quickly make it right.

DESDEMONA I do not think there is any such woman.

EMILIA Yes, a dozen, and as many
To th' vantage[8] as would store° the world they played[9] for. *populate*
But I do think it is their husbands' faults
If wives do fall. Say that they slack their duties° *marital duties*
And pour our treasures into foreign laps,[1]
Or else break out in peevish jealousies,
Throwing restraint upon us?[2] Or say they strike us,
Or scant our former having in despite?[3]
Why, we have galls,[4] and though we have some grace,
Yet have we some revenge. Let husbands know
Their wives have sense° like them. They see, and smell, *physical sense*
And have their palates both for sweet and sour,
As husbands have. What is it that they do
When they change us for others? Is it sport?° *sexual pastime*
I think it is. And doth affection° breed it? *passion*
I think it doth. Is 't frailty that thus errs?
It is so, too. And have not we affections,
Desires for sport, and frailty, as men have?
Then let them use us well; else let them know,
The ills we do, their ills instruct us so.

DESDEMONA Good night, good night. God me such uses° send *practice*
Not to pick bad from bad, but by bad mend![5]

[*Exeunt.*]

Act 5

Scene 1

[*Location: A street in Cyprus. Enter Iago and Roderigo.*]

IAGO Here stand behind this bulk.[6] Straight will he come.
Wear thy good rapier bare,° and put it home. *unsheathed*
Quick, quick! Fear nothing. I'll be at thy elbow.

4. A ring made in separate halves.
5. Fine linen.
6. Gift.
7. God's.
8. In addition, to boot.
9. Gambled. Also, sported sexually.
1. I.e., are unfaithful, give what is rightfully ours (semen) to other women.
2. I.e., jealously restricting our freedom to see other men.
3. Reduce our allowance to spite us.
4. Are capable of resenting injury and insult.
5. Not to learn bad conduct from others' badness (as Emilia has suggested women learn from men), but to mend my ways by perceiving what badness is, making spiritual benefit out of evil and adversity.
6. Framework projecting from the front of a shop.

It makes us or it mars us. Think on that,
And fix most firm thy resolution.
RODERIGO Be near at hand. I may miscarry in 't.
IAGO Here, at thy hand. Be bold, and take thy stand.
[*Iago stands aside. Roderigo conceals himself.*]
RODERIGO I have no great devotion to the deed;
And yet he hath given me satisfying reasons.
'Tis but a man gone. Forth, my sword! He dies.
[*He draws.*]
IAGO I have rubbed this young quat° almost to the sense,° *pimple/raw*
And he grows angry. Now, whether he kill Cassio
Or Cassio him, or each do kill the other,
Every way makes my gain. Live Roderigo,[7]
He calls me to a restitution large
Of gold and jewels that I bobbed° from him *swindled*
As gifts to Desdemona.
It must not be. If Cassio do remain,
He hath a daily beauty in his life
That makes me ugly; and besides, the Moor
May unfold° me to him; there stand I in much peril. *expose*
No, he must die. Be 't so. I hear him coming.
[*Enter Cassio.*]
RODERIGO [*coming forth*] I know his gait, 'tis he.—Villain, thou diest!
[*He attacks Cassio.*]
CASSIO That thrust had been mine enemy indeed,
But that my coat[8] is better than thou know'st.
I will make proof° of thine. *a test*
[*He draws, and wounds Roderigo.*]
RODERIGO O, I am slain! [*He falls.*]
[*Iago, from behind, wounds Cassio in the leg, and exit.*]
CASSIO I am maimed forever. Help, ho! Murder! Murder!
[*Enter Othello.*]
OTHELLO The voice of Cassio! Iago keeps his word.
RODERIGO O, villain that I am!
OTHELLO It is even so.
CASSIO O, help, ho! Light! A surgeon!
OTHELLO 'Tis he. O brave Iago, honest and just,
That hast such noble sense of thy friend's wrong!
Thou teachest me. Minion,[9] your dear lies dead,
And your unblest fate hies.° Strumpet, I come. *hastens on*
Forth of° my heart those charms, thine eyes, are blotted; *from out*
Thy bed, lust-stained, shall with lust's blood be spotted. [*Exit Othello.*]
[*Enter Lodovico and Gratiano.*]
CASSIO What ho! No watch? No passage?° Murder! Murder! *passers-by*
GRATIANO 'Tis some mischance. The voice is very direful.
CASSIO O, help!
LODOVICO Hark!

7. If Roderigo lives.
8. Possibly a garment of mail under the outer clothing, or simply a tougher coat than Roderigo expected.
9. Hussy (i.e., Desdemona).

RODERIGO O wretched villain!
LODOVICO Two or three groan. 'Tis heavy° night; *thick, dark*
These may be counterfeits. Let's think 't unsafe
To come in° to the cry without more help. *approach*
[*They remain near the entrance.*]
RODERIGO Nobody come? Then shall I bleed to death.
[*Enter Iago in his shirtsleeves, with a light.*]
LODOVICO Hark!
GRATIANO Here's one comes in his shirt, with light and weapons.
IAGO Who's there? Whose noise is this that cries on° murder? *cries out*
LODOVICO We do not know.
IAGO Did not you hear a cry?
CASSIO Here, here! For heaven's sake, help me!
IAGO What's the matter?
[*He moves toward Cassio.*]
GRATIANO [*to Lodovico*] This is Othello's ancient, as I take it.
LODOVICO [*to Gratiano*] The same indeed, a very valiant fellow.
IAGO [*to Cassio*] What° are you here that cry so grievously? *who*
CASSIO Iago? O, I am spoiled,° undone by villains! *ruined*
Give me some help.
IAGO O me, Lieutenant! What villains have done this?
CASSIO I think that one of them is hereabout,
And cannot make° away. *get*
IAGO O treacherous villains!
[*To Lodovico and Gratiano.*] What are you there? Come in, and
give some help. [*They advance.*]
RODERIGO O, help me there!
CASSIO That's one of them.
IAGO O murderous slave! O villain!
[*He stabs Roderigo.*]
RODERIGO O damned Iago! O inhuman dog!
IAGO Kill men i' the dark?—Where be these bloody thieves?—
How silent is this town!—Ho! Murder, murder!—
[*To Lodovico and Gratiano.*]
What may you be? Are you of good or evil?
LODOVICO As you shall prove us, praise° us. *appraise*
IAGO Signor Lodovico?
LODOVICO He, sir.
IAGO I cry you mercy.[1] Here's Cassio hurt by villains.
GRATIANO Cassio?
IAGO How is 't, brother?
CASSIO My leg is cut in two.
IAGO Marry, heaven forbid!
Light, gentlemen! I'll bind it with my shirt.
[*He hands them the light and tends to Cassio's wound.*]
[*Enter Bianca.*]
BIANCA What is the matter, ho? Who is 't that cried?

1. I beg your pardon.

IAGO Who is 't that cried?
BIANCA O my dear Cassio!
My sweet Cassio! O Cassio, Cassio, Cassio!
IAGO O notable strumpet! Cassio, may you suspect
Who they should be that have thus mangled you?
CASSIO No.
GRATIANO I am sorry to find you thus. I have been to seek you.
IAGO Lend me a garter. [*He applies a tourniquet.*] So.—O, for a chair,° *litter*
To bear him easily hence!
BIANCA Alas, he faints! O Cassio, Cassio, Cassio!
IAGO Gentlemen all, I do suspect this trash
To be a party in this injury.—
Patience awhile, good Cassio.—Come, come;
Lend me a light. [*He shines the light on Roderigo.*]
Know we this face or no?
Alas, my friend and my dear countryman
Roderigo! No.—Yes, sure.—O heaven! Roderigo!
GRATIANO What, of Venice?
IAGO Even he, sir. Did you know him?
GRATIANO Know him? Ay.
IAGO Signor Gratiano? I cry your gentle° pardon. *noble*
These bloody accidents° must excuse my manners *sudden events*
That so neglected you.
GRATIANO I am glad to see you.
IAGO How do you, Cassio? O, a chair, a chair!
GRATIANO Roderigo!
IAGO He, he, 'tis he. [*A litter is brought in.*] O, that's well said;[2] the chair.
Some good man bear him carefully from hence;
I'll fetch the General's surgeon. [*To Bianca.*] For you, mistress,
Save you your labor.[3] He that lies slain here, Cassio,
Was my dear friend. What malice° was between you? *enmity*
CASSIO None in the world, nor do I know the man.
IAGO [*to Bianca*] What, look you pale?—O, bear him out o' th' air.[4]
[*Cassio and Roderigo are borne off.*]
Stay you,[5] good gentlemen.—Look you pale, mistress?—
Do you perceive the gastness° of her eye?— *terror*
Nay, if you stare,[6] shall hear more anon.—
Behold her well; I pray you, look upon her.
Do you see, gentlemen? Nay, guiltiness
Will speak, though tongues were out of use.
[*Enter Emilia.*]
EMILIA 'Las, what's the matter? What's the matter, husband?
IAGO Cassio hath here been set on in the dark
By Roderigo and fellows that are scaped.
He's almost slain, and Roderigo dead.
EMILIA Alas, good gentleman! Alas, good Cassio!
IAGO This is the fruits of whoring. Prithee, Emilia,

2. Well done.
3. Never you mind tending Cassio.
4. Fresh air was thought to be dangerous for a wound.
5. Lodovico and Gratiano are evidently about to leave.
6. Iago pretends to interpret Bianca's wild looks as an involuntary confession of guilt.

Go know° of Cassio where he supped tonight. *learn*
[*To Bianca.*] What, do you shake at that?
BIANCA He supped at my house, but I therefore shake not.
IAGO O, did he so? I charge you go with me.
EMILIA O, fie upon thee, strumpet!
BIANCA I am no strumpet, but of life as honest° *chaste*
As you that thus abuse me.
EMILIA As I? Faugh! Fie upon thee!
IAGO Kind gentlemen, let's go see poor Cassio dressed.[7]—
Come, mistress, you must tell 's another tale.
Emilia, run you to the citadel
And tell my lord and lady what hath happed.—
Will you go on afore? [*Aside.*] This is the night
That either makes me or fordoes° me quite. [*Exeunt.*] *ruins*

Scene 2

[*Location: A bedchamber in the citadel.*
Enter Othello with a light, and Desdemona in her bed.][8]
OTHELLO It is the cause,[9] it is the cause, my soul.
Let me not name it to you, you chaste stars!
It is the cause. Yet I'll not shed her blood,
Nor scar that whiter skin of hers than snow,
And smooth as monumental alabaster.[1]
Yet she must die, else she'll betray more men.
Put out the light, and then put out the light.[2]
If I quench thee, thou flaming minister,[3]
I can again thy former light restore,
Should I repent me;° but once put out thy light, *change my mind*
Thou cunning'st pattern[4] of excelling nature,
I know not where is that Promethean heat[5]
That can thy light relume.° When I have plucked thy rose, *rekindle*
I cannot give it vital growth again;
It needs must wither. I'll smell thee on the tree.
[*He kisses her.*]
O balmy breath, that dost almost persuade
Justice to break her sword! One more, one more.
Be thus when thou art dead, and I will kill thee,
And love thee after. One more, and that's the last.
[*He kisses her.*]
So sweet was ne'er so fatal. I must weep,
But they are cruel° tears. This sorrow's heavenly; *unrelenting*
It strikes where it doth love.[6] She wakes.
DESDEMONA Who's there? Othello?
OTHELLO Ay, Desdemona.

7. Cassio's wounds dressed.
8. Either the curtains are drawn back to reveal the bed in a recessed area backstage or the bed is "thrust out" onstage as the scene begins.
9. Cause of justice, the offense itself, which Othello must correct as an agent of justice.
1. Used in making tombs and funeral monuments.
2. The torch or lamp . . . Desdemona's life.
3. Torch or lamp that serves me.
4. You skillfully wrought perfect example.
5. Divine fire (alluding to the theft of fire from heaven by Prometheus).
6. Compare Hebrews 12.6: "For whom the Lord loveth he chasteneth."

DESDEMONA Will you come to bed, my lord?
OTHELLO Have you prayed tonight, Desdemon?
DESDEMONA Ay, my lord.
OTHELLO If you bethink yourself of any crime° *sin*
Unreconciled as yet to heaven and grace,
Solicit° for it straight.° *pray / immediately*
DESDEMONA Alack, my lord, what may you mean by that?
OTHELLO Well, do it, and be brief. I will walk by.
I would not kill thy unpreparèd spirit.
No, heaven forfend!° I would not kill thy soul. *forbid*
DESDEMONA Talk you of killing?
OTHELLO Ay, I do.
DESDEMONA Then heaven
Have mercy on me!
OTHELLO Amen, with all my heart!
DESDEMONA If you say so, I hope you will not kill me.
OTHELLO Humh!
DESDEMONA And yet I fear you; for you're fatal then
When your eyes roll so. Why I should fear I know not,
Since guiltiness I know not; but yet I feel I fear.
OTHELLO Think on thy sins.
DESDEMONA They are loves I bear to you.[7]
OTHELLO Ay, and for that thou diest.
DESDEMONA That death's unnatural that kills for loving.
Alas, why gnaw you so your nether lip?
Some bloody passion shakes your very frame.
These are portents; but yet I hope, I hope,
They do not point on[8] me.
OTHELLO Peace, and be still!
DESDEMONA I will so. What's the matter?
OTHELLO That handkerchief which I so loved and gave thee
Thou gav'st to Cassio.
DESDEMONA No, by my life and soul!
Send for the man and ask him.
OTHELLO Sweet soul, take heed, take heed of perjury.
Thou art on thy deathbed.
DESDEMONA Ay, but not yet to die.
OTHELLO Yes, presently.° *immediately*
Therefore confess thee freely of thy sin;
For to deny each article with oath
Cannot remove nor choke the strong conception[9]
That I do groan withal.[1] Thou art to die.
DESDEMONA Then Lord have mercy on me!
OTHELLO I say, amen.
DESDEMONA And have you mercy too! I never did
Offend° you in my life; never loved Cassio *wrong*
But with such general warranty° of heaven *sanction*

7. If I sinned, it was in loving you more than my father or more than God.
8. Point at, predict what is to happen to.
9. Belief in your guilt. Also, plan in my mind.
1. Groan at in sorrow. Also, as in giving birth.

As I might love. I never gave him token.
OTHELLO By heaven, I saw my handkerchief in 's hand.
O perjured woman! Thou dost stone° heart, *harden*
And makes me call what I intend to do
A murder, which I thought a sacrifice.
I saw the handkerchief.
DESDEMONA He found it, then.
I never gave it him. Send for him hither;
Let him confess a truth.
OTHELLO He hath confessed.
DESDEMONA What, my lord?
OTHELLO That he hath used thee.
DESDEMONA How? Unlawfully?
OTHELLO Ay.
DESDEMONA He will not say so.
OTHELLO No, his mouth is stopped;
Honest Iago hath ta'en order° for 't. *taken measures*
DESDEMONA O, my fear interprets. What, is he dead?
OTHELLO Had all his hairs been lives, my great revenge
Had stomach for them all.
DESDEMONA Alas, he is betrayed and I undone! [*She weeps.*]
OTHELLO Out, strumpet! Weep'st thou for him to my face?
DESDEMONA O, banish me, my lord, but kill me not!
OTHELLO Down, strumpet!
DESDEMONA Kill me tomorrow; let me live tonight!
OTHELLO Nay, if you strive—
DESDEMONA But half an hour!
OTHELLO Being done,[2] there is no pause.
DESDEMONA But while I say one prayer!
OTHELLO It is too late. [*Smothers her.*]
EMILIA [*at the door*] My lord, my lord! What, ho! My lord, my lord!
OTHELLO What noise is this? Not dead? Not yet quite dead?
I that am cruel am yet merciful;
I would not have thee linger in thy pain. [*He dispatches her.*]
So, so.
EMILIA [*within*] What, ho! My lord, my lord!
OTHELLO Who's there?
EMILIA [*within*] O, good my lord, I would speak a word with you!
OTHELLO Yes, 'tis Emilia.—By and by.—She's dead.
'Tis like° she comes to speak of Cassio's death.— *likely that*
The noise was here.[3] Ha! No more moving?
Still as the grave. Shall she come in? Were 't good?—
I think she stirs again. No. What's best to do?
If she come in, she'll sure speak to my wife.
My wife! My wife! What wife? I have no wife.
O, insupportable! O heavy hour!
Methinks it should be now a huge eclipse
Of sun and moon, and that th' affrighted globe

2. Since justice has begun its relentless course.

3. The Folio's *high* is possible, suggesting that the commotion of the attack on Cassio was loud.

Should yawn[4] at alteration.[5]
EMILIA [*within*] I do beseech you
That I may speak with you, O, good my lord!
OTHELLO I had forgot thee. O, come in, Emilia.—
Soft,° by and by. Let me the curtains draw.— *wait a minute*
[*He closes the bed-curtains and opens the door.*]
Where art thou?
[*Enter Emilia.*]
What's the matter with thee now?
EMILIA O, my good lord, yonder's foul murders done!
OTHELLO What, now?
EMILIA But now, my lord.
OTHELLO It is the very error° of the moon; *aberration, irregularity*
She comes more nearer earth than she was wont,
And makes men mad.
EMILIA Cassio, my lord, hath killed a young Venetian
Called Roderigo.
OTHELLO Roderigo killed?
And Cassio killed?
EMILIA No, Cassio is not killed.
OTHELLO Not Cassio killed? Then murder's out of tune,
And sweet revenge grows harsh.
DESDEMONA O, falsely, falsely murdered!
EMILIA O Lord, what cry is that?
OTHELLO That? What?
EMILIA Out[6] and alas, that was my lady's voice.
[*She opens the bed-curtains.*]
Help, help, ho, help! O lady, speak again!
Sweet Desdemona! O sweet mistress, speak!
DESDEMONA A guiltless death I die.
EMILIA O, who hath done this deed?
DESDEMONA Nobody; I myself. Farewell.
Commend me to my kind lord. O, farewell! [*She dies.*]
OTHELLO Why, how should she be murdered?
EMILIA Alas, who knows?
OTHELLO You heard her say herself it was not I.
EMILIA She said so. I must needs report the truth.
OTHELLO She's like a liar gone to burning hell!
'Twas I that killed her.
EMILIA O, the more angel she,
And you the blacker devil!
OTHELLO She turned to folly,[7] and she was a whore.
EMILIA Thou dost belie° her, and thou art a devil. *slander*
OTHELLO She was false as water.

4. Gape in amazement, i.e., move in an earthquake. (According to Pliny, earthquakes often happen during eclipses.)
5. At these cataclysmic events in nature, well suited to express the horror of Desdemona's death.
6. A cry of dismay, intensifying *alas*.
7. I.e., wantonness, fleshly sin.

EMILIA Thou art rash as fire to say
That she was false. O, she was heavenly true!
OTHELLO Cassio did top her. Ask thy husband else.[8]
O, I were damned beneath all depth in hell
But that I did proceed upon just grounds
To this extremity. Thy husband knew it all.
EMILIA My husband?
OTHELLO Thy husband.
EMILIA That she was false to wedlock?
OTHELLO Ay, with Cassio. Nay, had she been true,
If heaven would make me such another world
Of one entire and perfect chrysolite,° *precious topaz*
I'd not have sold her for it.
EMILIA My husband?
OTHELLO Ay, 'twas he that told me on her first.
An honest man he is, and hates the slime
That sticks on filthy deeds.
EMILIA My husband?
OTHELLO What needs this iterance,° woman? I say thy husband. *repetition*
EMILIA O mistress, villainy hath made mocks° with love! *made sport*
My husband say she was false?
OTHELLO He, woman;
I say thy husband. Dost understand the word?
My friend, thy husband, honest, honest Iago.
EMILIA If he say so, may his pernicious soul
Rot half a grain a day! He lies to th' heart.
She was too fond of her most filthy bargain.
OTHELLO Ha? [*He draws.*]
EMILIA Do thy worst!
This deed of thine is no more worthy heaven
Than thou wast worthy her.
OTHELLO Peace, you were best.[9]
EMILIA Thou hast not half that power to do me harm
As I have to be hurt.° O gull!° O dolt! *to endure hurt/dupe*
As ignorant as dirt! Thou hast done a deed—
I care not for thy sword; I'll make thee known,
Though I lost twenty lives.—Help! Help, ho, help!
The Moor hath killed my mistress! Murder, murder!
[*Enter Montano, Gratiano, and Iago.*]
MONTANO What is the matter? How now, General?
EMILIA O, are you come, Iago? You have done well,
That men must lay their murders on your neck.
GRATIANO What is the matter?
EMILIA [*to Iago*]
Disprove this villain, if thou be'st a man.
He says thou toldst him that his wife was false.
I know thou didst not; thou'rt not such a villain.
Speak, for my heart is full.

8. I.e., if you don't believe me.

9. It would be best for you.

IAGO I told him what I thought, and told no more
Than what he found himself was apt° and true. *plausible*
EMILIA But did you ever tell him she was false?
IAGO I did.
EMILIA You told a lie, an odious, damnèd lie!
Upon my soul, a lie, a wicked lie.
She false with Cassio? Did you say with Cassio?
IAGO With Cassio, mistress. Go to, charm[1] your tongue.
EMILIA I will not charm my tongue; I am bound to speak.
My mistress here lies murdered in her bed—
ALL O heavens forfend!
EMILIA And your reports have set the murder on.
OTHELLO Nay, stare not, masters. It is true indeed.
GRATIANO 'Tis a strange truth.
MONTANO O monstrous act!
EMILIA Villainy, villainy, villainy!
I think upon 't—I think I smell 't! O villainy!
I thought so then[2]—I'll kill myself for grief—
O villainy, villainy!
IAGO What, are you mad? I charge you, get you home.
EMILIA Good gentlemen, let me have leave to speak.
'Tis proper I obey him, but not now.
Perchance, Iago, I will ne'er go home.
OTHELLO O! O! O! [*Othello falls on the bed.*][3]
EMILIA Nay, lay thee down and roar,
For thou hast killed the sweetest innocent
That e'er did lift up eye.[4]
OTHELLO [*rising*] O, she was foul!
I scarce did know you, uncle. There lies your niece,
Whose breath indeed these hands have newly stopped.
I know this act shows° horrible and grim. *looks*
GRATIANO Poor Desdemon! I am glad thy father's dead.
Thy match was mortal to him, and pure grief
Shore his old thread[5] in twain. Did he live now,
This sight would make him do a desperate turn,° *deed*
Yea, curse his better angel from his side,
And fall to reprobance.[6]
OTHELLO 'Tis pitiful. But yet Iago knows
That she with Cassio hath the act of shame
A thousand times committed. Cassio confessed it;
And she did gratify° his amorous works *reward*
With that recognizance° and pledge of love *token*
Which I first gave her. I saw it in his hand;
It was a handkerchief, an antique token
My father gave my mother.
EMILIA O God! O heavenly God!
IAGO Zounds, hold your peace.

1. Keep silent (as though by a magic spell).
2. Perhaps in 3.3 and 4.2.
3. This direction is from the Quarto.
4. Lift her eyes to heaven.
5. Sheared the thread of his old age (as Atropos, one of the three Fates, was thought to do).
6. Damnation, i.e., suicide.

EMILIA 'Twill out, 'twill out! I peace?
No, I will speak as liberal as the north.[7]
Let heaven and men and devils, let them all,
All, all, cry shame against me, yet I'll speak.

IAGO Be wise, and get you home.

EMILIA I will not.

[*Iago threatens Emilia.*]

GRATIANO Fie,
Your sword upon a woman?

EMILIA O thou dull Moor! That handkerchief thou speak'st of
I found by fortune and did give my husband;
For often, with a solemn earnestness,
More than indeed belonged° to such a trifle, *was appropriate*
He begged of me to steal 't.

IAGO Villainous whore!

EMILIA She give it Cassio? No, alas! I found it,
And I did give 't my husband.

IAGO Filth, thou liest!

EMILIA By heaven, I do not, I do not, gentlemen.
O murderous coxcomb![8] What should such a fool
Do with so good a wife?

OTHELLO Are there no stones[9] in heaven
But what serves for the thunder?—Precious° villain! *utter*

[*He runs at Iago; Montano disarms Othello. Iago, from behind, stabs Emilia.*][1]

GRATIANO The woman falls! Sure he hath killed his wife.

EMILIA Ay, ay. O, lay me by my mistress' side.

[*Exit Iago.*]

GRATIANO He's gone, but his wife's killed.

MONTANO 'Tis a notorious villain. Take you this weapon,
Which I have here recovered from the Moor.
Come, guard the door without. Let him not pass,
But kill him rather. I'll after that same villain,
For 'tis a damnèd slave.

[*Exit with all but Othello and Emilia, who has been laid by Desdemona's side.*]

OTHELLO I am not valiant neither,
But every puny whipster[2] gets my sword.
But why should honor[3] outlive honesty?° *integrity*
Let it go all.

EMILIA What did thy song bode, lady?
Hark, canst thou hear me? I will play the swan,
And die in music. [*She sings.*] "Willow, willow, willow."
Moor, she was chaste. She loved thee, cruel Moor.
So come my soul to bliss as I speak true.
So speaking as I think, alas, I die. [*She dies.*]

OTHELLO I have another weapon in this chamber;

7. Freely as the north wind (blows).
8. Fool (addressed to Othello).
9. Bolts, such as those used for thunderbolts.
1. The Quarto text reads, "The Moor runs at Iago. Iago kills his wife." The Quarto also specifies the exit of Iago below.
2. Contemptible fellow (one who is always ready to whip out his sword).
3. The bravery for which one enjoys a soldier's reputation.

It was a sword of Spain, the ice-brook's temper[4]—
O, here it is. [*He finds a sword.*] Uncle, I must come forth.

GRATIANO [*within*] If thou attempt it, it will cost thee dear.
Thou hast no weapon, and perforce must suffer.

OTHELLO Look in upon me then and speak with me,
Or, naked° as I am, I will assault thee. *unarmed*

[*Enter Gratiano.*]

GRATIANO What is the matter?

OTHELLO Behold, I have a weapon;
A better never did itself sustain
Upon a soldier's thigh. I have seen the day
That, with this little arm and this good sword,
I have made my way through more impediments
Than twenty times your stop.[5] But O, vain boast!
Who can control his fate? 'Tis not so now.
Be not afraid, though you do see me weaponed;
Here is my journey's end, here is my butt[6]
And very seamark[7] of my utmost sail.

[*Gratiano steps back.*]

Do you go back dismayed? 'Tis a lost° fear; *wasted*
Man but a rush[8] against Othello's breast
And he retires. Where should Othello go?

[*He turns to Desdemona.*]

Now, how dost thou look now? O ill-starred wench!
Pale as thy smock! When we shall meet at compt,° *Judgment Day*
This look of thine will hurl my soul from heaven,
And fiends will snatch at it. Cold, cold, my girl?
Even like thy chastity. O cursèd, cursèd slave![9]
Whip me, ye devils,
From the possession of this heavenly sight!
Blow me about in winds! Roast me in sulfur!
Wash me in steep-down gulfs of liquid fire!
O Desdemon! Dead, Desdemon! Dead! O! O!

[*Enter Lodovico, Cassio (carried in a litter),*[1] *Montano, and Iago (prisoner), with officers.*]

LODOVICO Where is this rash and most unfortunate man?

OTHELLO That's he that was Othello. Here I am.

LODOVICO Where is that viper? Bring the villain forth.

[*Iago is led forward.*]

OTHELLO I look down towards his feet;[2] but that's a fable.
If that thou be'st a devil, I cannot kill thee.

[*He wounds Iago.*]

LODOVICO Wrench his sword from him. [*Othello is disarmed.*]

IAGO I bleed, sir, but not killed.

OTHELLO I am not sorry neither. I'd have thee live,
For in my sense[3] 'tis happiness to die.

4. Tempered in ice-cold water.
5. Power (to stop).
6. Goal, limit (an archery term).
7. Beacon (marking his destination or limit).
8. Wield no more than a reed.
9. Othello himself.
1. The Quarto specifies that Cassio is "in a chair."
2. I.e., to see if they are cloven, as the devil's are fabled to be.
3. To one who feels as I do.

LODOVICO O thou Othello, that was once so good,
Fall'n in the practice[4] of a cursèd slave,° *villain*
What shall be said to thee?
OTHELLO Why, anything.
An honorable murderer, if you will,
For naught I did in hate, but all in honor.
LODOVICO This wretch hath part confessed his villainy.
Did you and he consent° in Cassio's death? *agree*
OTHELLO Ay.
CASSIO Dear General, I never gave you cause.
OTHELLO I do believe it, and I ask your pardon.
Will you, I pray, demand that demi-devil
Why he hath thus ensnared my soul and body?
IAGO Demand me nothing. What you know, you know.
From this time forth I never will speak word.
LODOVICO What, not to pray?
GRATIANO Torments° will ope your lips. *torture*
OTHELLO Well, thou dost best.
LODOVICO Sir, you shall understand what hath befall'n,
Which, as I think, you know not. Here is a letter
Found in the pocket of the slain Roderigo;
And here another. [*He produces letters.*] The one of them imports
The death of Cassio, to be undertook
By Roderigo.
OTHELLO O villain!
CASSIO Most heathenish and most gross!° *monstrous*
LODOVICO [*showing another paper*] Now here's another discontented paper
Found in his pocket too. And this, it seems,
Roderigo meant t' have sent this damnèd villain;
But that belike° Iago in the interim *most likely*
Came in and satisfied him.[5]
OTHELLO O thou pernicious caitiff!—
How came you, Cassio, by that handkerchief
That was my wife's?
CASSIO I found it in my chamber;
And he himself confessed but even now
That there he dropped it for a special purpose
Which wrought to his desire.[6]
OTHELLO O fool, fool, fool!
CASSIO There is besides in Roderigo's letter
How he upbraids Iago, that he made him
Brave° me upon the watch, whereon it came[7] *defy*
That I was cast;° and even but now he spake, *dismissed*
After long seeming dead, Iago hurt him,
Iago set him on.
LODOVICO [*to Othello*] You must forsake this room and go with us.
Your power and your command is taken off,° *taken away*

4. Through the plotting, into the snare.
5. Interposed and gave him satisfactory explanation.
6. Worked out as he wished, fitted in with his plan.
7. Whereof it came about.

And Cassio rules in Cyprus. For this slave,
If there be any cunning cruelty
That can torment him much and hold him long,[8]
It shall be his. You shall close prisoner rest° *remain*
Till that the nature of your fault be known
To the Venetian state.—Come, bring away.

OTHELLO Soft you;° a word or two before you go. *one moment*
I have done the state some service, and they know't.
No more of that. I pray you, in your letters,
When you shall these unlucky° deeds relate, *unfortunate*
Speak of me as I am; nothing extenuate,
Nor set down aught in malice. Then must you speak
Of one that loved not wisely but too well;
Of one not easily jealous but, being wrought,[9]
Perplexed° in the extreme; of one whose hand, *distraught*
Like the base Indian,[1] threw a pearl away
Richer than all his tribe; of one whose subdued[2] eyes,
Albeit unusèd to the melting mood,
Drops tears as fast as the Arabian trees
Their medicinable gum.° Set you down this; *myrrh*
And say besides that in Aleppo once,
Where a malignant and a turbaned Turk
Beat a Venetian and traduced the state,
I took by th' throat the circumcisèd dog
And smote him, thus. [*He stabs himself.*][3]

LODOVICO O bloody period!° *end, conclusion*

GRATIANO All that is spoke is marred.

OTHELLO I kissed thee ere I killed thee. No way but this,
Killing myself, to die upon a kiss.
[*He kisses Desdemona and dies.*]

CASSIO This did I fear, but thought he had no weapon;
For he was great of heart.

LODOVICO [*to Iago*] O Spartan dog,[4]
More fell° than anguish, hunger, or the sea! *cruel*
Look on the tragic loading of this bed.
This is thy work. The object poisons sight;
Let it be hid.[5] Gratiano, keep° the house, *remain in*
[*The bed curtains are drawn*]
And seize upon the fortunes of the Moor,
For they succeed on you.[6] [*To Cassio.*] To you, Lord Governor,
Remains the censure° of this hellish villain, *sentencing*
The time, the place, the torture. O, enforce it!
Myself will straight aboard, and to the state
This heavy act with heavy heart relate. [*Exeunt.*]

8. Keep him alive a long time (during his torture).
9. Worked upon, worked into a frenzy.
1. This reading from the Quarto pictures an ignorant savage who cannot recognize the value of a precious jewel. The Folio reading, *Iudean* or *Judean*, i.e., infidel or disbeliever, may refer to Herod, who slew Mariam in a fit of jealousy, or to Judas Iscariot, the betrayer of Christ.
2. I.e., overcome by grief.
3. This direction is in the Quarto text.
4. Spartan dogs were noted for their savagery and silence.
5. I.e., draw the bed curtains. (No stage direction specifies that the dead are to be carried offstage at the end of the play.)
6. Take legal possession of Othello's property, which passes as though by inheritance to you.

Othello in Context

Ethnography in the Literature of Travel and Colonization

What would Shakespeare's audience have thought of the description of Othello as "the Moor"? Both the play itself and the literature on Africa that was available in English in the early modern period show that "Moor" was a synonym for "Negro." Two kinds of accounts of the Moors and North Africans were available to Shakespeare's audience: a kind of mythical travel literature inherited from such classical authors as Herodotus, Pliny, and Diodorus Siculus and more recent eyewitness accounts by seamen and traders who had traveled to Africa. While there were still many completely fantastical notions about non-European peoples such as Moors, Africans, and Turks, Leo Africanus's *History of Africa* enlightened sixteenth- and seventeenth-century European and English audiences about the peoples and customs of Africa.

This kind of writing, describing the physical features and social customs of a people, is called ethnography. The word comes from two Greek roots: *ethnos* ("nation") and *graphia* ("writing"). Rather than stressing the history of a people through time, ethnography reads as a timeless description of a people in space. Not surprisingly, ethnography was deployed mainly to describe cultural others, from the Scythians (the wild Northern Europeans of Book Four of Herodotus' *Histories*) to the Ethiopes of Philemon Holland's *Description of Africa*. Even within the British Isles, Spenser and other authors portrayed the Irish as barbarians because their language, customs, and religion were different from those of the English, who settled as colonists in Ireland.

Ethnography was also used to describe the people of the Caribbean. Columbus's description of the Caribes, or Canibes, gave rise to the word "cannibal." At the same time that Europeans traveled to and colonized the Americas, they also embarked on trade and took slaves in Africa. With the explorations of Portuguese navigators of the African coast came the exploitation of Africans as slaves in the plantations of the Caribbean. The British brought the first African slaves to Virginia in 1619. Leo Africanus himself was taken as a slave by Italian pirates. He was a learned man and was able to win his freedom through conversion. His accounts and those of eyewitnesses began to change the view of Africa as a place of such fantastical creatures as "men whose heads / Do grow beneath their shoulders" (*Othello* 1.3.145–46) to a place of prosperous kings and traders.

Peter Martyr

The Italian humanist Peter Martyr (Pietro Martire d'Anghiera, 1457?–1526) came to the court of Isabella and Ferdinand of Spain some time after 1480. Martyr became part of an intellectual movement that celebrated the consolidation of the monarchy's power over Spain and their conquests in the Americas. Although Martyr deplored the interventions of the French into Italy, he celebrated Spanish exploration and colonization around the world in *De Orbe Novo Decades* (1530). The style of this book has something in common with the tradition of travel writing and ethnography going back to Book 4 of Herodotus's *Histories* as well as Italian humanist letter writing as a method of disseminating information. Martyr himself never traveled beyond Europe, basing his accounts upon the reports of eyewitnesses.

Like Martyr, his English translator Richard Eden (1521?–1576) had a humanist education. Studying at Cambridge with Sir Thomas Smith prepared Eden for a life in government, in which he used his scholarship. He served as private secretary to Sir William Cecil in 1552 and gained a position in the English treasury of the Prince of Spain in 1554.

Eden added two eyewitness accounts of English voyages to Africa to his English translation of Martyr's work, *Decades of the New World* (1555). Although two papal bulls had given a monopoly over the West African coast to the Portuguese, two English seamen defied the ban: Thomas Windham voyaged to Guinea in 1553 and John Lok to Mina

Inigo Jones. *A Negro Nymph,* from the costume designs for Ben Jonson's *Masque of Blackness,* 1605. A designer of sets and costumes, Inigo Jones collaborated with Ben Jonson on many of his masques. In his notes on *The Masque of Blackness,* Jonson mentions Leo Africanus as a source. The ladies of the court painted their faces black to play the Negro Nymphs—among them Lady Mary Wroth, who would deploy metaphors of darkness and night to great effect in her poetry. Jones was also patronized by Lady Wroth's lover, William Herbert, the Earl of Pembroke, who financed the artist's journey to Italy where he studied Roman ruins and Palladio's buildings and writing on architecture. Jones became the first great English architect, designing such buildings as the earliest part of the Greenwich Hospital (1635) and the Church of Saint Paul, Covent Garden, with its square (1631–1638). In 1619 James I commissioned Jones to design the Banqueting House at Whitehall, the first English building to embody Palladian features such as rows of columns and symmetrical classical proportions. (See the engraving of the execution of Charles I before Jones's Banqueting House, page 1698.)

(Elmina) in 1554–1555. The account of Windham's voyage is the source for the first excerpt here, a description of the court of Benin, a kingdom in what is now Nigeria. Eden introduces these two accounts with his own "brief description of Africa" and interjects his comments throughout the eyewitness reports, as in the next excerpted passage taken from "Second Voyage." Eden mixes his informants' observations with fanciful fables about the mythical Christian king of Ethiopia, Preseter John, derived from medieval legend, and outlandish and bizarre ethnographic fictions, from Pliny's *Historia Naturalis*. Eden's accounts of Africa were later republished in Richard Haklyut's monumental *Principal Navigations* (1589).

from *Decades of the New World*

[The Court of Benin]

When they came they were brought with a great company to the presence of the king [of Benin], who being a black Moor[1] (although not so black as the rest) sat in a great huge hall, long and wide, the walls made of earth without windows, the roof of thin boards, open in sundry places, like unto louvers to let in the air.

And here to speak of the great reverence they give to their king being such that if we would give as much to our Savior Jesus Christ, we should remove from our heads many plagues which we daily deserve for our contempt and impiety. * * *

And now to speak somewhat of the communication that was between the king and our men, you shall first understand that he himself could speak the Portugal tongue, which he had learned of a child. Therefore after that he had commanded our men to stand up and demanded of them the cause of their coming into that country, they answered by Pinteado[2] that they were merchants traveling into those parts for the commodities of his country for exchange of wares which they had brought from their countries, being such as should be no less commodious for him and his people.

[The People of Africa]

Now therefore I will speak somewhat of the people and their manners and manner of living, with also another brief description of Africa. It is to understand that the people which now inhabit the regions of the coast of Guinea, and the mid parts of Africa, as Libya the inner, and Nubia,[3] with diverse other great and large regions about the same, were in old time called Ethiopes and Nigrite, which we now call Moors, Moorens, or Negros, a people of beastly living, without a god, law, religion, or commonwealth, and so scorched and vexed with the heat of the sun, that in many places they curse it when it riseth.[4] * * *

But to speak somewhat more of Ethiopia. Although there are many nations of people so named, yet is Ethiopia chiefly divided into two parts, whereof the one is called Ethiopia under Egypt, a great and rich region. To this pertaineth the Island of Meroe, embraced round about with the streams of the river Nilus.[5] In this island women reigned in old time. Josephus writeth, that it was sometime

1. Inhabitants of northwestern Africa (Morocco and Algeria), who were Islamic. From the Middle Ages to the 17th century, Europeans thought of the Moors primarily as blacks, and so the word became a synonym for Negro; hence the term "Blackamoor."

2. Captain Antonianes Pinteado was a Portuguese mariner and guide whom Windham used as translator. Once a member of the King of Portugal's household, Pinteado was "forced by poverty" into England. Eden portrays Pinteado as "a man worthy to serve any prince most vilely used." Both Windham and the crew derisively called him "a Jew," and after Windham's death, Pinteado was made a prisoner and died on board ship.

3. Nubia is in northeastern Africa. At its height the kingdom stretched from the first cataract of the Nile in Egypt to Khartoum in Sudan. During the time of the Roman Emperor Diocletian, the Negro tribe the Nobatae settled in Nubia. The Nubian kingdom was converted to Christianity in the 6th century. After the Moslems moved into Nubia in 1366, Nubia was divided into smaller states.

4. Many Greek and Roman as well as early modern authors believed that Africans had black skin because of the intense heat of the sun. Sir Thomas Browne was one of the first to show this "common opinion" was an "error" in *Pseudodoxia Epidemica* (1646); see 6.10: "Of the Blackness of Negroes."

5. When the Nubians were expelled from Egypt in the 7th century B.C., they moved their capital to Meroe, which the Ethiopians conquered in A.D. 350. The site of ancient pyramids, Meroe, is on the Nile in Northern Sudan.

called Saba, and that the queen of Saba came from thence to Jerusalem to hear the wisdom of Solomon.[6] From hence toward the East reigneth the said Christian Emperor Prester John,[7] whom some call Papa Johannes, and others say that he is called Pean Juan (that is) great John, whose empire reacheth far beyond Nilus and is extended to the coasts of the Red Sea and Indian Sea. The middle of the region is almost in the 66 degrees of longitude, and 12 degrees of latitude. About this region inhabit the people called Clodii, Risophagi, Babilonii, Axiunite, Mosili, and Molibe. After these is the region called Trogloditica, whose inhabitants dwell in caves and dens, for these are their houses, and the flesh of serpents their meat, as writeth Pliny and Diodorus Siculus.[8] They have no speech, but rather a grinning and chattering. There are also people without heads, called Blemines, having their eyes and mouth in their breast. Likewise Strucophagi, and naked Ganphasantes; Satyrs also, which have nothing of men but only shape. Moreover Oripei, great hunters. Mennones also, and the region of Smyrnophara, which bringeth forth myrrh. After these is the region of Azania, in the which many elephants are found. A great part of the other regions of Africa that are beyond the equinoctial line, are now ascribed to the kingdom of Melinde,[9] whose inhabitants are accustomed to traffic with the nations of Arabie, and their kind is joined in friendship with the king of Portugal, and payeth tribute to Prester John.

The other Ethiope, called Ethiopia Interior (that is) the inner Ethiope, is not yet known for the greatness thereof, but only by the seacoasts. Yet is it described in this manner. First from the equinoctial toward the south is a great region of Ethiopians, which bringeth forth white elephants, tigers, and the beasts called Rhinocerontes. Also a region that bringeth forth plenty of cinnamon, lying between the branches of Nilus. Also the kingdom of Habech or Habassia,[1] a region of Christian men, lying both on this side and beyond Nilus. Here are also the Ethiopians, called Ichthiophagi (that is) such as live only by fish, and were sometimes subdued by the wars of great Alexander. Furthermore the Ethiopians calleth Rhapsii, and Anthropophagi, that are accustomed to man's flesh, inhabit the regions near unto the mountains called Montes Lunae (that is) the Mountains of the Moon.[2] Gazatia is under the Tropic of Capricorn.[3] After this followeth the front of Africa, the Cape of Buena Speranza, or Caput Bonae Spei (that is) the Cape of Good Hope,[4] by the which they pass that sail from Spain to Calicut. But by what names the capes and gulfs are called, for as much as the same are in every globe and card, it were here superfluous to rehearse them.

6. For the visit of the Queen of Sheba (Saba) to Solomon, see 1 Kings 10. See also *Antiquities of the Jews* by the Jewish historian Flavius Josephus (37–c. 95).

7. The medieval legend of Prester John placed this Christian king in either Asia or Africa. Marco Polo said that Prester John ruled over the Tartars, and some European writers thought of him as King of a Christian kingdom in either Ethiopia or India.

8. For Pliny, see *The History of the World* below. Diodorus Siculus (d. 21 B.C.) was a Sicilian author of a world history, including Ethiopia and North Africa, which is today considered unreliable.

9. Said to be in Arabia, 90 miles from Persia (Introduction to Martyr's *Decades*).

1. Possibly Abyssinia, another name for Ethiopia. In the 4th century the king of Northern Ethiopia was converted to Coptic Christianity, but later, in 451, the Alexandrian patriarch refused to recognize the Ethopian Christians as part of the Church. They believe that Christ has one nature in which his humanity is subsumed under his divinity.

2. This fantastical passage comes from Pliny.

3. The Southern Tropic.

4. The southern tip of Africa, around which the Portuguese sailed to India.

Pliny the Elder
from *The History of the World*[1]

All Ethiopia in general was in old time called Aetheria, afterwards Atlantia, and finally of Vulcan's son Aethops, it took the name Ethiopia. No wonder it is, that about the coasts thereof there be found both men and beasts of strange and monstrous shapes, considering the agility of the sun's fiery heat, so strong and powerful in those countries, which is able to frame bodies artificially of sundry proportions, and to imprint and grave[2] in them diverse forms. Certes, reported it is, that far within the country eastward there are a kind of people without any nose at all on their face, having their visage all plain and flat. Others again without any upper lip, and some tongueless. Moreover, there is a kind of them that want a mouth, framed apart from their nostrils, and at one and the same hole, and no more, taketh in breath, receiveth drink by drawing it in with an oaten straw; yea, and after the same manner feed themselves with the grains of oats, growing of their own accord without man's labor and tillage, for their only food. And others there be, who instead of speech and words, make signs, as well with nodding their heads, as moving their other members. There are also among them, that before the time of Ptolomaeus Lathyrus king of Egypt,[3] knew no use at all of fire.

Furthermore, writers there be, who have reported, that in the country near unto the mires and marshes from whence Nilus issueth, there inhabit those little dwarves called Pygmies * * * But then he [Dalion, the historian] telleth fabulous and incredible tales of those countries. Namely, that westward there are people called Nigroi, whose king hath but one eye, and that in the midst of his forehead. Also he talketh of the Agriophagi, who live most of panthers and lions flesh. Likewise of the Pomphagi, who eat all things whatsoever. Moreover, of the Anthopophagi, that feed on man's flesh. Furthermore, of the Cynamolgi,[4] who have heads like dogs. Over and besides, the Artabatites who wander and go up and down in the forests like four-footed savage beasts. Beyond whom, as he saith, be the Hesperioi and Perorsi, who, as we said before, were planted in the confines of Mauritania. In certain parts also of Ethiopia the people live off locusts only, which they powder with salt and hang up in smoke to harden, for their yearly provision, and these live not above 40 years at the most.

Leo Africanus

Born in Moorish Granada in the late 1480s and educated in Fez, to which his Moslem family fled in 1497, Al Hassan ibn Mohammed Al-Wezaz, Al-Fasi (Leo Africanus, 1488?–1552) was the first to write accurately about the interior of Africa. Captured by Italian pirates in the Mediterranean, he was at first enslaved and then presented to Pope Leo X, who freed him once he had converted to Christianity. In Rome, Leo Africanus learned Latin and taught Arabic. He wrote his history of Africa in 1526, but it was published in Venice only in 1550, when, according to one contemporary, Leo was living in Tunis, where he returned to his Moslem faith.

1. Pliny the Elder (Caius Plinius Secundus, A.D. 23–79) was a Roman naturalist from Cisalpine Gaul. His sole remaining work, the *Historia Naturalis*, is an encyclopedia of natural science, divided into 37 books, dealing with everything from the nature of the universe to geography, anthropology, and a history of the arts. Like the Greek historian Herodotus, Pliny knew more about Egypt than he did about the rest of Africa and had to rely on stories and legends for his accounts. The European view of Africa and Africans as wild, exotic, and unnatural derives from such accounts as the following from Book 6 of *The History of the World* (1601), the English translation of Pliny by Philemon Holland. This passage was Shakespeare's source for Othello's description of the "Anthropophagi" (man-eaters) in Othello 1.3.144–46.

2. Engrave.

3. Ptolomeus Lathyrus (d. 81 B.C.), King of Ancient Egypt of the Macedonian dynasty.

4. Dog-milkers.

Encouraged by Richard Haklyut, who called Leo's work "the very best," John Pory first translated it into English as *A Geographical History of Africa* in 1600. Leo's history, which first appeared in Italian, was already known in England through Latin and French editions. Sir Thomas Smith owned a French translation, and Ben Jonson mentions Leo's work as a source for his *Masque of Blackness*. According to Lois Whitney and Eldred Jones, strong circumstantial evidence suggests that Shakespeare knew Leo's *Geographical History* and that it provided the background material for references to Africa in *Othello* and *Antony and Cleopatra*.

Pory prefaced his translation with Leo's biography, excerpted here, which makes for fascinating reading. There are some parallels between Leo's life and Othello's. A North African Moor, Leo had visited many parts of Africa but lived much of his life in Italy. Leo was not only a scholar and traveler but also a soldier; as Pory relates, Leo "did . . . personally serve king Mahumet of Fez in his wars." Like Leo who often recited poems and stories, Othello told his "travel's history." Both Leo and many of the African kingdoms that he describes emerge from his work as civilized, learned, and prosperous in contrast to the stereotyped ethnographies, which had portrayed Africans as barbarous, ignorant, and poor. While Leo's account of Africa was well known to Shakespeare's generation and even the generation that followed, subsequent scholarship chose either to misrepresent it, as in Peter Heylyn's highly selective choice of uncomplimentary passages, or to ignore it, as in Samuel Coleridge's false assertion that "at that time . . . negroes were not known except as slaves."

from *The History and Description of Africa*

from JOHN PORY'S PREFACE

Give me leave (gentle readers) if not to present unto your knowledge, because some perhaps may as well be informed as myself; yet, to call to your remembrance, some few particulars, concerning this geographical history and John Leo the author thereof.

Who albeit by birth a Moor, and by religion for many years a Mahumetan; yet if you consider his parentage, wit, education, learning, employments, travels, and his conversion to Christianity, you shall find him not altogether unfit to undertake such an enterprise, not unworthy to be regarded.

First therefore his parentage seemeth not to have been ignoble, seeing (as in his second book himself testifieth) an uncle of his was so honorable a person and so excellent an orator and poet, that he was sent as a principal ambassador, from the king of Fez to the king of Tombuto.[1]

And whether this our author were born at Granada in Spain (as it is most likely) or in some part of Africa,[2] certain it is, that in natural sharpness and vivacity of wit, he most lively resembled those great and classical authors, Pomponius Mela, Justinus Historicus, Columella, Seneca, Quintilian, Orosius, Prudentius, Martial, Juvenal, Avicen, etc., reputed all for Spanish writers, as likewise Terentius Afer, Tertullian, Saint Augustine, Victor, Optatus, etc. known to be writers of Africa.[3] But amongst great variety which are to be found in the process of this notable discourse, I will here

1. Timbuktu, near the Niger, with the Sahara to the north. Settled in 1087, Timbuktu was a center for trade and Moslem culture.

2. Pory's hesitation is due to a passage in the Latin translation (Antwerp 1556) that can be translated as "Africa, unto which country I stand indebted for my birth." But in the original Italian edition, this passage simply states that Africa was his "nurse," where he spent the early part of his life.

3. Pomponius Mela . . . Juvenal: Roman historians and rhetoricians; Avicen: the Arabic translator of Aristotle; Terentius Afer: a Roman writer of comedies, born in Carthage; Tertullian, Saint Augustine: the Church Fathers of late antiquity; Victorinus: a Neoplatonist convert to Christianity.

lay before your view our only pattern of his surpassing wit. In his second book therefore, if you peruse the description of Mount Teneves, you shall there find the learned and sweet Arabian verses of John Leo, not being then fully sixteen years of age, so highly esteemed by the prince of the same mountain that in recompense thereof, after bountiful entertainment, he dismissed him with gifts of great value.

Neither wanted he the best education that all Barbary could afford. For being even from his tender years trained up at the University of Fez, in grammar, poetry, rhetoric, philosophy, history, Cabala, astronomy, and other ingenuous sciences,[4] and having so great acquaintance and conversation in the king's court, how could he choose but prove in his kind a most accomplished and absolute man? So as I may justly say (if the comparison be tolerable) that as Moses was learned in all the wisdom of the Egyptians, so likewise was Leo, in that of the Arabians and Moors.

And that he was not meanly, but extraordinarily learned; let me keep silence, that the admirable fruits of his rare learning and this geographical history among the rest may bear record. Besides which, he wrote an Arabian grammar, highly commended by a great linguist of Italy who had the sight and examination thereof, as likewise a book of the lives of the Arabian philosophers and a discourse of the religion of Mahumet, with diverse excellent poems and other monuments of his industry, which are not come to light.

Now as concerning his employments, were they not such as might well beseem a man of good worth? For (to omit how many courts and camps of princes he had frequented) did not he, as himself in his third book witnesseth, personally serve king Mahumet of Fez in his wars against Arzilla?[5] And was he not at another time, as appeareth out of his second book, in service and honorable place under the same king of Fez, and sent ambassador by him to the king of Morocco? Yea, how often in regard of his singular knowledge and judgment in the laws of those countries, was he appointed and sometimes constrained at diverse strange cities and towns through which he traveled, to become a judge and arbiter in matters of greatest moment?

Moreover as touching his exceeding great travels, had he not at the first been a Moor and a Mahumetan in religion, and most skillful in the languages and customs of the Arabians and Africans, and for the most part traveled in caravans or under the authority, safe conduct, and commendation of great princes? I marvel much how ever he should have escaped so many thousands of imminent dangers. And (all the former notwithstanding) I marvel much more, how ever he escaped them. For how many desolate cold mountains and huge, dry, and barren deserts passed he? How often was he in hazard to have been captived or to have had his throat cut by the prowling Arabians and wild Moors? And how hardly many times escaped he the lion's greedy mouth and the devouring jaws of the crocodile? But if you will needs have a brief journal of his travels, you may see in the end of his eighth book, what he writeth for himself. Wherefore (saith he) if it shall please God to vouchsafe me longer life, I purpose to describe all the regions of Asia which I have traveled—to wit, Arabia Deserta, Arabia Petrea, Arabia Felix,[6] the Asian part of Egypt, Armenia, and some part of Tartaria—all which countries I saw and passed through in the time of my youth. Likewise I will describe my last voyages from Constantinople to Egypt and from

4. The University of Fez dated from the 13th-century Merinid dynasty. The Cabala, or Kabbala, was a system of occult wisdom and mystical interpretation of the Scriptures.

5. Leo served the Sultan Mohammed VI, who reigned in Fez (1508–1527), both in war and in diplomacy.

6. The ancients divided Arabia into three parts based on its principle place Petra, the desert, and the fertile area.

thence unto Italy, etc. Besides all which places he had also been at Tauris in Persia; and of his own country and other African regions adjoining and remote, he was so diligent a traveler that there was no kingdom, province, signory, or city, or scarcely any town, village, mountain, valley, river, or forest, etc. which he left unvisited. And so much the more credit and commendation deserveth this worthy history of his, in that it is (except the antiquities and certain other incidents) nothing else but a large itinerarium or journal of his African voyages, neither describeth he almost any one particular place, where himself had not sometime been an eyewitness.

But, not to forget his conversion to Christianity, amidst all these his busy and dangerous travels, it pleased the divine providence, for the discovery and manifestation of God's wonderful works and of his dreadful and just judgments performed in Africa (which before the time of John Leo, were either utterly concealed or unperfectly and fabulously reported both by ancient and late writers) to deliver this author of ours, and this present geographical history into the hands of certain Italian pirates about the isle of Gerbi, situated in the Gulf of Capes, between the cities of Tunis and Tripolis in Barbary. Being thus taken, the pirates presented him and his book unto Pope Leo the Tenth, who, esteeming of him as of a most rich and invaluable prize, greatly rejoiced at his arrival and gave him most kind entertainment and liberal maintenance, til such time as he had won him to be baptized in the name of Christ, and to be called John Leo, after the Pope's own name. And so during his abode in Italy, learning the Italian tongue, he translated this book thereinto, being before written in Arabic. Thus much of John Leo.

[On the Customs of the African People in Libya]

Those five kinds of people before rehearsed, to wit, the people of Zenega, of Gansiga, of Terga, of Leuta, and of Bardeoa, are called of the Latins Numidae;[7] and they live all after one manner, that is to say, without all law and civility. Their garment is a narrow and base piece of cloth, wherewith scarce half their body is covered. Some of them wrap their heads in a kind of black cloth, as it were with a scarf, such as the Turks use, which is commonly called a turbant.[8] Such as well be discerned from the common sort, for gentlemen wear a jacket made of blue cotton with wide sleeves. And cotton cloth is brought unto them by certain merchants from the land of negros. They have no beasts fit to ride upon except their camels, unto whom nature, between the bunch standing upon the hinder part of their backs and their necks, hath allotted a place, which may fitly serve to ride upon, instead of a saddle. Their manner of riding is most ridiculous. For sometimes they lay their legs across upon the camel's neck, and sometimes again (having no knowledge nor regard of stirrups) they rest their feet upon a rope, which is cast over his shoulders. Instead of spurs they use a truncheon of a cubit's length, having at the one end thereof a goad, wherewith they prick only the shoulders of their camels. Those camels which they use to ride upon have a hole bored through the gristles of their nose, in the which a ring of leather is fastened, whereby as with a bit, they are more easily curbed and mastered, after which manner I have seen buffles[9] used in Italy. For beds, they lie upon mats made of sedge and bul-

7. Numidia, an ancient kingdom in North Africa, north of the Sahara, was at one time a province of the Roman Empire. Leo here gives a description of the Tuareg, a pastoral people on the western and central Sahara, now located in Algeria, Mali, and Niger. The alphabet of the Tuareg is related to ancient Phoenician script.

8. Tuareg men traditionally wore dark blue robes and turbans.

9. Buffaloes.

rushes. Their tents are covered for the most part with coarse chamlet[1] or with a harsh kind of wool which commonly groweth upon the boughs of their date trees. As for their manner of living, it would seem to any man incredible what hunger and scarcity this nation will endure. Bread they have none at all, neither use they any seething or roasting; their food is camel's milk only, and they desire no other dainties. For their breakfast they drink off a great cup of camel's milk; for supper they have certain dried flesh steeped in butter and milk, whereof each man, taking his share, eateth it out of his fist. And that this their meat may not stay long undigested in their stomachs, they sup off the foresaid broth wherein their flesh was steeped; for which purpose they use the palms of their hands as a most fit instrument framed by nature to the same end. After that, each one drinks his cup of milk, & so their supper hath an end. These Numidians, while they have any store of milk, regard water nothing at all, which for the most part happeneth in the spring of the year, all which time you shall find some among them that will neither wash their hands nor their faces. Which seemeth not altogether to be unlikely; for (as we said before) while their milk lasteth, they frequent not those places where water is common; yea, and their camels, so long as they may feed upon grass, will drink no water at all. They spend their whole days in hunting and thieving; for all their endeavor and exercise is to drive away the camels of their enemies; neither will they remain above three days in one place, by reason that they have not pasture any longer for the sustenance of their camels. And albeit (as is aforesaid) they have no civility at all, nor any laws prescribed unto them, yet have they a certain governor or prince placed over them, unto whom they render obedience and due honor, as unto their king. They are not only ignorant of all good learning and liberal sciences, but are likewise altogether careless and destitute of virtue, insomuch that you shall find scarce one amongst them all which is a man of judgment or counsel. And if any injured party will go to the law with his adversary, he must ride continually five or six days before he can come to the speech of any judge. This nation hath all learning and good disciplines in such contempt that they will not once vouchsafe to go out of their deserts for the study and attaining thereof; neither, if any learned man shall chance to come among them, can they love his company and conversation, in regard of their most rude and detestable behavior. Howbeit, if they can find any judge, which can frame himself to live and continue among them, to him they give [a] most large yearly allowance. Some allow their judge a thousand ducats yearly, some more, and some less, according as themselves think good. They that will seem to be accounted of the better sort, cover their heads (as I said before) with a piece of black cloth, part whereof, like a vizard or mask, reacheth down over their faces, covering all their countenance except their eyes; and this is their daily kind of attire. And so often as they put meat into their mouths they remove the said mask, which being done, they forthwith cover their mouths again, alleging this fond reason: for (say they) as it is unseemly for a man, after he hath received meat into his stomach, to vomit it out of his mouth again and to cast it upon the earth; even so it is an undecent part to eat meat with a man's mouth uncovered.

The women of this nation be gross, corpulent, and of a swart[2] complexion. They are fattest upon their breast and paps, but slender about the girdle-stead.[3] Very civil they are, after their manner, both in speech and gestures. Sometimes they will accept

1. Chamlet, a fabric made from a mixture of silk and camel's hair.

2. Dark.

3. Waist.

of a kiss; but whoso tempteth them farther, putteth his own life in hazard. For by reason of jealousy you may see them daily one to be the death and destruction of another, and that in such savage and brutish manner that in this case they will show no compassion at all. And they seem to be more wise in this behalf than diverse of our people, for they will by no means match themselves unto a harlot.

The liberality of this people hath at all times been exceeding great. And when any travelers may pass through their dry and desert territories, they will never repair unto their tents, neither will they themselves travel upon the common highway. And if any caravan or multitude of merchants will pass those deserts, they are bound to pay certain custom unto the prince of the said people, namely, for every camel's load a piece of cloth worth a ducat. Upon a time I remember that traveling in the company of certain merchants over the desert called by them Araoan, it was our chance there to meet with the prince of Zanaga; who, after he had received his due custom, invited the said company of merchants, for their recreation, to go and abide with him in his tents four or five days. Howbeit, because his tents were too far out of our way, and for that we should have wandered farther than we thought good, esteeming it more convenient for us to hold on our direct course, we refused his gentle offer, and for his courtesy gave him great thanks. But not being satisfied therewith, he commanded that our camels should proceed on forward, but the merchants he carried along with him and gave them very sumptuous entertainment at his place of abode. Where we were no sooner arrived but this good prince caused camels of all kinds and ostriches, which he had hunted and taken by the way, to be killed for his household provision. Howbeit we requested him not to make such daily slaughters of his camels, affirming moreover that we never used to eat the flesh of a gelt[4] camel, but when all other victuals failed us. Whereunto he answered that he should deal uncivilly, if he welcomed so worthy and so seldom seen guests with the killing of small cattle only. Wherefore he wished us to fall to such provision as was set before us. Here might you have seen great plenty of roasted and sudden flesh. Their roasted ostriches were brought to the table in wicker platters, being seasoned with sundry kinds of herbs and spices. Their bread made of mill and panick[5] was of a most savory and pleasant taste; and always at the end of dinner or supper we had plenty of dates and great store of milk served in. Yea, this bountiful and noble prince, that he might sufficiently show how welcome we were unto him, would together with his nobility always bear us company; howbeit we ever dined and supped apart by ourselves. Moreover he caused certain religious and most learned men to come unto our banquet, who, all the time we remained with the said prince, used not to eat any bread at all, but fed only upon flesh and milk. Whereat we being somewhat amazed, the good prince gently told us that they all were born in such places whereas no kind of grain would grow, howbeit that himself, for the entertainment of strangers, had great plenty of corn laid up in store. Wherefore he bade us to be of good cheer, saying that he would eat only of such things as his own native soil afforded, affirming moreover, that bread was yet in use among them at their feast of passover, and at other feasts also, whereupon they used to offer sacrifice. And thus we remained with him for the space of two days, all which time, what wonderful and magnificent cheer we had made us, would seem incredible to report. But the third day, being desirous to take our leave, the prince accompanied us to that place where we overtook our camels and company sent before. And this I dare most deeply take mine oath on, that we spent the said prince

4. Gelded, castrated.

5. Varieties of millet, or grain.

ten times more than our custom which he received came to.[6] We thought it not amiss here to set down this history to declare in some sort the courtesy and liberality of the said nation. Neither could the prince aforesaid understand our language nor we his, but all our speech to and fro was made by an interpreter. And this which we have here recorded as touching this nation is likewise to be understood of the other four nations above mentioned, which are dispersed over the residue of the Numidian deserts.

Edmund Spenser

In addition to writing some of the greatest English poetry, Edmund Spenser wrote a colonialist tract promoting England's subjugation of Ireland. Spenser first came to Ireland as secretary to Lord Grey de Wilton, Lord Deputy of Ireland, in 1580. Through government service, Spenser acquired his land and house in Kilcoman, property confiscated from Sir John of Desmond, an "Old English" aristocrat who had rebelled against English rule. The Old English had been Anglo-Normans who settled in Ireland in the twelfth century. In *A View of the Present State of Ireland,* Spenser writes about the customs of the Irish, among whom he finds the Old English to be the most troublesome because they have gone native and become "more Irish than O'Hanlon's breech." Drawing heavily on the ethnographic stereotypes of the medieval *Topography of Ireland* by Gerald of Wales, Spenser wrote his text as a dialogue between Irenius, ("Peaceful") a veteran of English service in Ireland, and Eudoxus ("Of good opinion"), a younger man who questions why English policy in Ireland has not worked. In the 1590s, when Spenser was writing this text, another Irish rebellion had broken out under the command of Hugh O'Neill. Spenser and his family were driven out of Kilcoman. Creating a view of the Irish as a separate race, Spenser compares Irish customs with those of Africans and Moors. The description of the Irish as barbarous prepares for the conclusion of the text in which he recommends a military solution to the colonization of Ireland. Though not published until 1633, *A View of the Present State of Ireland* was entered in the Stationer's Register in 1598 and circulated widely in manuscript.

from *A View of the Present State of Ireland*

Eudoxus. Believe me, this observation of yours, Irenius,[1] is very good and delightful; far beyond the blind conceit of some, who (I remember) have upon the same word *Farragh*, made a very blunt conjecture, as namely Master Stanyhurst,[2] who though he be the same countryman born, that should search more nearly into the secret of these things, yet hath strayed from the truth all the heavens wide (as they say), for he thereupon groundeth a very gross imagination, that the Irish should descend from the Egyptians which came into that island, first under the leading of one Scota the daughter of Pharaoh, whereupon they use (saith he) in all their battles to call upon the name of Pharaoh, crying Ferragh, Ferragh.[3] Surely he shoots wide on the bow hand and very far from the mark. For I would first know of him what ancient ground of authority he hath for such a senseless fable, and if he have any of the rude Irish

6. Leo is saying that the prince gave them much more than they paid in tribute.

1. Irenius, who has greater experience of Ireland then Eudoxus, has just asserted that the Irish battle cry "Ferragh" is from the Scottish word "Fergus," which means that the Irish are Scots. The 17th-century Irish language historian Geoffrey Keating points out in his *History of Ireland* that the Irish etymology of "Ferragh" is "faire ó" or "ó faire" ("take care").

2. Richard Stanyhurst (1547–1618), a Dubliner and Catholic, wrote *Description of Ireland* in Holinshed's *Chronicles*, as well as *De rebus in Hibernia gestis*, in which he dismisses the Egyptian origin of the Irish war cry.

3. The notion that the Irish were descended from the Egyptian Scota dates back to the 8th-century life of St. Abban and is repeated in the medieval Irish *Book of Invasions (Leabhar gabhála)*.

books, as it may be he hath, yet (me seems) that a man of his learning should not so lightly have been carried away with old wives' tales, from approvance of his own reason; for whether it be a smack of any learned judgment to say that Scota is like an Egyptian word, let the learned judge. But his Scota rather comes of the Greek *scotos*, that is, darkness, which hath not let him see the light of the truth.

Irenius. You know not, Eudoxus, how well Master Stanyhurst could see in the dark; perhaps he hath owls' or cats' eyes. But well I wot he seeth not well the very light in matters of more weight. * * * There be other sorts of cries also used among the Irish, which savor greatly of the Scythian barbarism,[4] as their lamentations at their burials, with despairful outcries, and immoderate wailings, the which Master Stanyhurst might also have used for an argument to prove them Egyptians. For so in scripture it is mentioned, that the Egyptians lamented for the death of Joseph.[5] Others think this custom to come from the Spaniards, for that they do immeasurably likewise bewail their dead. But the same is not proper Spanish, but altogether heathenish, brought in thither first either by the Scythians, or the Moors that were Africans and long possessed that country. For it is the manner of all pagans and infidels to be intemperate in their wailings of their dead, for that they had no faith nor hope of salvation. And this ill custom also is specially noted by Diodorus Siculus,[6] to have been in the Scythians, and is yet amongst the Northern Scots at this day, as you may read in their chronicles.

Eudoxus. This is sure an ill custom also, but yet doth not so much concern civil reformation, as abuse in religion.[7]

* * *

Eudoxus. It seemeth strange to me that the English should take more delight to speak that language than their own, whereas they should (me thinks) rather take scorn to acquaint their tongues thereto. For it hath ever been the use of the conqueror to despise the language of the conquered and to force him by all means to learn his. So did the Romans always use, insomuch that there is almost no nation in the world but is sprinkled with their language. It were good therefore (me seems) to search out the original cause of this evil; for, the same being discovered, a redress thereof will the more easily be provided. For I think it very strange that the English being so many, and the Irish so few, as they then were left, the fewer should draw the more unto their use.

Irenius. I suppose that the chief cause of bringing in the Irish language amongst them was especially their fostering[8] and marrying with the Irish, the which are two most dangerous infections; for first the child that sucketh the milk of the nurse must of necessity learn his first speech of her, the which being the first inured to his tongue, is ever after most pleasing unto him insomuch as though he afterwards be taught English, yet the smack of the first will always abide with him, and not only of speech but also of the manners and conditions. For besides that young children be like apes, which will affect and imitate what they see done before them, especially by their nurses whom they love so well, they moreover draw into themselves together with their suck even the nature and disposition of their nurses; for the mind fol-

4. Spenser claims both Irish and Scots are descended from the Scythians, described by Herodotus as a nomadic, barbarous people to the northwest of Greece.

5. Jacob, not Joseph (see Genesis 50.3).

6. Diodorus Siculus (d. 21 B.C.), a Sicilian author of a world history in Greek.

7. Irenius continues to discuss the Scythian, i.e., barbarous, character of Irish customs including going into battle naked, wearing glibs (masses of hair), and the women's riding facing right in the "old Spanish and as some say African" fashion, drinking blood and speaking the Irish language.

8. Gaelic custom of having children raised by clients, friends, or relatives to cement alliances.

loweth much the temperature of the body, and also the words are the image of the mind, so as they proceeding from the mind, the mind must needs be affected with the words. So that the speech being Irish, the heart must needs be Irish; for out of the abundance of the heart the tongue speaketh. The next is the marrying with the Irish, which how dangerous a thing it is in all commonwealths, appeareth to every simplest sense. And though some great ones have perhaps used such matches with their vassals and have of them nevertheless raised worthy issue, as Telamon did with Tocmissa, Alexander the Great with Roxanne, and Julius Caesar with Cleopatra,[9] yet the example is so perilous, as it is not to be adventured; for instead of those few good, I could count unto them infinite many evil. And indeed how can such matching but bring forth an evil race, seeing that commonly the child taketh most of his nature of the mother, besides speech, manners, and inclination, which are (for the most part) agreeable to the conditions of their mothers; for by them they are first framed and fashioned, so as what they receive once from them, they will hardly ever after forgo. Therefore are these evil customs of fostering and marrying with the Irish most carefully to be restrained; for of them two, the third evil, that is the custom of language (which I spake of), chiefly proceedeth.

Sir John Smith
from *The General History of Virginia, New England and the Summer Isles*[1]

Being thus satisfied with Europe and Asia, understanding of the wars in Barbary, he went from Gibraltar to Guta and Tanger, thence to Safee,[2] where growing into acquaintance with a French man-of-war,[3] the captain and some twelve more went to Morocco, to see the ancient monuments of that large renowned city. It was once the principal city in Barbary, situated in a goodly plain country, 14 miles from the great Mount Atlas and sixty miles from the Atlantic Sea, but now little remaining but the king's palace, which is like a city of itself, and the Christian church, on whose flat square steeple is a great brooch of iron, whereon is placed the three golden balls of Africa. The first is near three ells[4] in circumference, the next above it somewhat less, the uppermost the least over them, as it were, an half ball, and over all a pretty gilded pyramid. Against those golden balls hath been shot many a shot, their weight is recorded 700 weight of pure gold, hollow within, yet no shot did ever hit them, nor could ever any conspirator attain that honor as to get them down. They report the prince of Morocco betrothed himself to the king's daughter of Ethiopia, he dying before their marriage, she caused those three golden balls to be set up for his monument, and vowed virginity all her life. The Alfantica is also a place of note because it

9. All examples of interracial or cross-cultural marriages: the Phrygian Tecmessa with Greek Ajax, the Bactrian Roxana with the Macedonian Alexander, the Egyptian Cleopatra with the Roman Caesar.

1. Sir John Smith (1580–1631) spent his youth as a merchant's apprentice and then, at his father's death, set off to travel. He fought against the Turks in eastern Europe and was enslaved for a time in Turkey. On returning to England, he invested in the Virginia Company in 1606 and was appointed a member of the government council for the Jamestown settlement. He is probably best known for the much romanticized story of his being rescued from captivity by Pocahontas, the Indian princess and daughter of King Powhatan. After years of sea voyaging, warfare, and exploration, Smith returned to England. Among his many works of travel writing are *A Map of Virginia* (1612), *A Description of New England* (1616), and *The Generall Historie of Virginia New-England and the Summer Isles* (1624), from which the following passage describing the Barbary Coast (Tunisia and Morocco) is taken. Note Smith's mention of "that most excellent statesman, John de Leo,"—further evidence of how well known Leo Africanus' history of Africa was in early modern England.

2. From Gibraltar at the southern tip of Spain to Tangier in Morocco.

3. A large sailing ship equipped for warfare.

4. Twelve feet.

is environed with a great wall, wherein lie the goods of all the merchants securely guarded. The Juderea is also (as it were) a city of itself, where dwell the Jews. The rest for the most part is defaced, but by the many pinnacles and towers, with balls on their tops, hath much appearance of much sumptuousness and curiosity. There have been many famous universities, which are now but stables for fowls and beasts, and the houses in most parts lie tumbled one above another; the walls of earth are with the great fresh floods washed to the ground, nor is there any village in it, but tents for strangers, Larbes and Moors. Strange tales they will tell of a great garden, wherein were all sorts of birds, fishes, beasts, fruits and fountains, which for beauty, art and pleasure, exceeded any place known in the world, though now nothing but dunghills, pigeon houses, shrubs and bushes. There are yet many excellent fountains adorned with marble, and many arches, pillars, towers, ports and temples, but most only relics of lamentable ruins and sad desolution.

When Mully Hamet[5] reigned in Barbary he had three sons, Mully Sheck, Mully Sidan, and Mully Befferes—he, a most good and noble king that governed well with peace and plenty, til his empress, more cruel than any beast in Africa, poisoned him, her own daughter, Mully Sheck his eldest son born of a Portugal Lady, and his daughter, to bring Mully Sidan to the crown now reigning, which was the cause of all those brawls and wars that followed betwixt those brothers, their children, and a saint that start up, but he played the Devil.[6]

King Mully Hamet was not black, as many suppose, but Molata, or tawny, as are the most of his subjects, in every way noble, kind and friendly, very rich and pompous in state and majesty, though he sitteth not upon a throne nor chair of estate, but cross-legged upon a rich carpet, as doth the Turk, whose religion of Mahomet, with an incredible miserable curiosity they observe. His ordinary guard is at least 5,000 but in progress he goeth not with less than 20,000 horsemen, himself as rich in all his equipage as any prince in Christendom, and yet a contributor to the Turk. In all his kingdom were so few good artificers that he entertained from England, goldsmiths, plumbers, carvers and polishers of stone, and watchmakers, so much he delighted in the reformation of workmanship he allowed each of them ten shillings a day standing fee, linen, woolen, silks, and what they would for diet and apparel, and custom-free to transport or import what they would; for there were scare any of those qualities in his kingdoms, but those of which there are diverse of them living at this present in London. Amongst the rest, one Mr. Henry Archer, a watchmaker, walking in Morocco from the Alfantica to the Juderea, the way being very foul, met a great priest, or a Sante (as they call all great clergymen) who would have thrust him into the dirt for the way. But Archer, not knowing what he was, gave him a box on the ear; presently he was apprehended and condemned to have his tongue cut out and his hand cut off; but no sooner it was known at the king's court but 300 of his guard came and broke open the prison and delivered him, although the fact was next degree to treason. * * *

Fez also is a most large and plentiful country, the chief city is called Fez, divided into two parts, old Fez, containing about 80 thousand households, the other 4,000 pleasantly situated upon a river in the heart of Barbary, part upon hills, part upon plains, full of people and all sorts of merchandise. The great temple is called Carucer,

5. Sultan of Morocco.

6. A reference to the "battle of the three kings" (1578) in Alcazarquivir, in which the Moroccan sultan (whose army was victorious), his Portuguese-supported rival, and Sebastian of Portugal (a religiously fervent prince who led an army of mercenaries to disaster) all perished.

in breadth seventeen arches, in length 120 born up with 2,500 white marble pillars. Under the chief arch, where the tribunal is kept, hangeth a most huge lamp, compassed with 110 lesser; under the other also hang great lamps, and about some are burning fifteen hundred lights. They say they were all made of the bells the Arabians brought from Spain. It hath three gates of notable height, priests and officers so many that the circuit of the church, the yard, and other houses is little less than a mile and an half in compass. There are in this city 200 schools, 200 inns, 400 water mills, 600 water conduits, 700 temples and oratories, but fifty of them most stately and richly furnished. Their Alcazer[7] or Burse is walled about; it hath twelve gates and fifteen walks covered with tents to keep the sun from the merchants and them that come there. The king's palace, both for strength and beauty is excellent, and the citizens have many great privileges. Those two countries of Fez and Morocco are the best part of Barbary, abounding with people, cattle, and all good necessaries for man's use. For the rest, as the Larbes, or Mountainers, the kingdoms of Cocow, Algier, Tripoly, Tunis, and Egypt, there are so many large histories of them in diverse languages, especially that writ by that most excellent statesman, John de Leo [Africanus], who afterward turned Christian. The unknown countries of Ginny and Binne[8] this six and twenty years have been frequented with a few English ships only to trade, especially the river of Senega, by Captain Brimstead, Captain Brockit, Mr. Crump, and diverse others. Also the great river of Gambra, by Captain Jobson, who is returned in thither again in the year 1626 with Mr. William Grent and thirteen or fourteen others, to stay in the country, to discover some way to those rich mines of Gago or Tumbatu,[9] from whence is supposed the Moors of Barbary have their gold, and the certainty of those supposed descriptions and relations of those interior parts, which daily the more they are sought into, the more they are corrected. For surely, those interior parts of Africa are little known to either English, French, or Dutch, though they use much the coast; therefore we will make a little bold with the observations of the Portugals.

Elizabeth Cary

1585?–1639

Elizabeth Cary was the first English woman to write and publish an original play, *The Tragedy of Mariam, The Fair Queen of Jewry*. She was also the first English woman to be the subject of a biography, her daughter's *The Lady Falkland: Her Life*. When we consider that the French poet Louise Labé was called a "common whore" by Calvin because she published her love poems and that Mary Wroth was forced to withdraw her work from publication, we can begin to get an idea of how unusual it was for Elizabeth Cary to publish her work. She showed similar independence by separating from her husband, by converting to Catholicism, and by translating controversial theological works. A prodigious scholar, a committed Catholic, and mother of eleven children, Elizabeth Cary was the extraordinary author of an extraordinary play.

6. A palace formed around a courtyard, here compared to a "Burse," or trading place.

7. Guinea and Benin, on the west coast of Africa.

8. Timbuktu, near the Niger with the Sahara to the north, a center of trade and Moslem culture.

Born Elizabeth Tanfield, the daughter of a wealthy lawyer, she had an independent mind and a passion for learning even as a child. Once, when the young Elizabeth observed her father hearing a case of witchcraft, the girl intervened, whispering in his ear the crucial question that exposed the evidence against the accused woman as a fraud. The precocious Elizabeth studied French, Spanish, and Italian, and she also studied the ancient languages of Latin and Hebrew, normally restricted to male students; she even translated some of Seneca's *Epistles* when she was only seven years old. She also translated Abraham Ortelius's *Le Miroir du Monde*, which described such places as China, India, and America. When Elizabeth was only twelve, the poet Michael Drayton praised her learning in his *Englands Heroicall Epistles*. She was such an avid reader that when her parents forbade her to read at night, she borrowed candles from the servants.

Her family arranged her marriage to Henry Cary in 1602. Master of the Queen's jewels and later made Viscount Falkland, Henry supplied the title and gentry status to the marriage, while Elizabeth supplied the money. Separated by Henry's military duty in the Protestant war against Spain in Holland during the early years of their marriage, they had their first child in 1609. Elizabeth's attempts to aid Henry's career by mortgaging her joint ownership of family property angered her father, who disinherited her.

In 1622 her husband became Lord Deputy of Ireland, and sharp disagreements arose between them. While he directed the colonial administration of Ireland, she studied the Irish language and set up a trade school for poor children in Dublin. While her husband attempted to enforce conformity to Protestantism in Catholic Ireland, Elizabeth's own desire to convert to Catholicism strengthened. From childhood she had found Calvinism inimical because of its emphasis on predestination, and she was also critical of Anglicanism. She returned to England at her husband's orders in 1625, and in 1626 she publicly converted to Catholicism. Nonconformity to the official church was dangerous for anyone in early modern England, but Elizabeth's open declaration of it was particularly dangerous for her husband, who was in government service. Henry was outraged and completely distanced himself from her. She complained to King Charles I that her husband did not support her financially; Henry excused himself by charging her with refusing to live "quietly." Their daughter claimed, nevertheless, that her parents were reconciled at Henry's deathbed in 1633.

Elizabeth moved to a small village outside London, where she continued to write until her death in 1639. She lived modestly, giving much of her income to charity. She arranged for her two youngest sons and four daughters, who had also converted, to live in Catholic France, where her daughters became Benedictine nuns. Her son Lucius, made famous by Ben Jonson's ode, remained behind in England. Not sharing his mother's religion, he was able to inherit his grandmother's money. He did, however, share his mother's love of languages and of theological dispute, which she continued to pursue. She translated the reply of a French theologian, Jacques Du Perron, to King James I's attack on Catholicism. A comment she made in the preface to her translation shows how thoroughly she rejected the conventional aristocratic and feminine stance of shunning publication: "I will not make use of the worn out form of saying I printed it against my will, moved by the importunity of friends; I was moved to it by my belief that it might make those English that understand not French . . . read Perron." She dedicated this work to the Catholic wife of Charles I, Queen Henrietta Maria. Published on the Continent, this work was immediately confiscated and burned when it was smuggled into England. At the time she died, Elizabeth was translating the Hebrew and Latin writings of the Flemish mystic Blosius.

During the early years of her marriage, Elizabeth Cary wrote a verse life of Tamberlain. Two texts about Edward II are now often attributed to her; one of these, *The History of the Life, Reign, and Death of Edward II*, contains the initials of Elizabeth Falkland on its title page. In addition to her numerous translations, she wrote occasional poetry which circulated in manuscript. Her former tutor Sir John Davies wrote verses praising two of her plays: a lost play set in Greece and *The Tragedy of Mariam*.

Though not published until 1613, *Mariam* was probably written sometime between 1604 and 1609. The play portrays Mariam's struggle between her own integrity and her loyalty to her husband Herod when confronted with his tyranny and tragically mistaken jealousy. The play also includes a subplot of political intrigue in which two minor characters, the sons of Baba, attempt to resist King Herod's tyranny. The story is taken from a pair of ancient sources, Josephus's *Jewish War* and *Antiquities of the Jews*, first translated into English in 1602. The dramatic influences may include Shakespeare's *Antony and Cleopatra* and *Othello*, although some would argue that Cary's *Mariam* could have influenced Shakespeare. Cary frequently attended the theater, and though her work was a closet drama—like Seneca's tragedies, meant to be read rather than performed—it is full of high emotion and dramatic action. In fact, *Othello* and *Mariam* have much in common. Both concern marriages that defy the expectations of the status quo, a husband's irrational jealousy, and the proper behavior of women. Cary surrounds the chaste yet outspoken Mariam with a range of vivid female characters: Salome, who promotes divorce for women; Graphina, who remains quiet and obedient; and Alexandra, who objects to her daughter's marriage.

Some of the conflicts in *The Tragedy of Mariam* can be related to those in Elizabeth Cary's own life. For example, the disparity between the royal Mariam and her upstart husband may reflect the social and financial disparity between Cary and her husband. The heroine's struggle between obedience to her husband and fidelity to herself may be related to the author's own crisis of conscience. Mariam's questioning of her "public voice" may be read as the text's questioning of the author's publication of her work. More generally, the play illustrates conflicts in the larger social context. The dissent of English Catholics, a long overlooked aspect of early modern English culture, surfaces in the figure of Herod. Catholics saw Herod as an allegorical figure for Henry VIII, because both kings killed their wives and imposed arbitrary dictates on their subjects. Cary's work can also be read as a comment on the norms of chastity, silence, and obedience for women of her time. Dramatic tension arises from the contrasts between the conventional pronouncements of the chorus on women's conduct and the perspectives of the female characters.

In her own time Elizabeth Cary was praised by her son's biographer, Edward Clarendon, as "a lady of a most masculine understanding," but she is now appreciated for representing a woman's subjectivity in the genre of tragedy. With its unique blend of popular Shakespearian and learned Senecan tragic style, *Mariam* gives us insight into the history of English drama. Along with the interracial couple of *Othello*, the mixed marriage of Cary's *Mariam* looks forward to a similar theme in Aphra Behn's *Oroonoko* (1688). For its questioning of power relationships, Elizabeth Cary's *Tragedy of Mariam* is a trenchant comment on perennial problems. In its emotional depth, *Mariam* can play a role in our understanding not only of the past but of ourselves.

The Tragedy of Mariam, The Fair Queen of Jewry[1]

To Diana's Earthly Deputess and My Worthy Sister, Mistress Elizabeth Cary[2]

When cheerful Phoebus[3] his full course hath run,
His sister's fainter beams our hearts doth cheer;

1. The sole early modern edition, of 1613, contains some obvious misprints, and inconsistencies in spelling and punctuation, which this edition silently corrects. More problematic errors that have been corrected by modern editors are mentioned in the footnotes.

2. Two extant copies of the play contain this sonnet dedicated to the author's sister-in-law.

3. Apollo, the sun god, twin brother of Diana.

So your fair brother is to me the sun,
And you his sister as my moon appear.

You are my next beloved, my second friend,
For when my Phoebus' absence makes it night,
Whilst to the Antipodes[4] his beams do bend,
From you my Phoebe,[5] shines my second light.

He like to Sol,[6] clear-sighted, constant, free,
You Luna-like, unspotted, chaste, divine;
He shone on Sicily, you destined be,
To illumine the now obscurèd Palestine.
My first[7] was consecrated to Apollo,
My second to Diana now shall follow.

E.C.

The names of the speakers

Herod, *King of Judea*
Doris, *his first wife*
Mariam, *his second wife*
Salome, *Herod's sister*
Antipater, *his son by Doris*
Alexandra, *Mariam's mother*
Silleus, *Prince of Arabia*
Constabarus, *husband to Salome*
Pheroras, *Herod's brother*
Graphina, *his love*
Babas' first son
Babas' second son
Ananell, *the high Priest*
Sohemus, *a counselor to Herod*
Nuntio
Butler, *another messenger*
Chorus, *a company of Jews*

The Argument

Herod the son of Antipater (an Idumean[8]), having crept by the favor of the Romans into the Jewish monarchy, married Mariam the granddaughter of Hircanus, the rightful king and priest; and for her (besides her high blood, being of singular beauty) he repudiated Doris, his former wife, by whom he had children.

This Mariam had a brother called Aristobolus, and next him and Hircanus his grandfather, Herod in his wife's right had the best title. Therefore to remove them, he charged Hircanus with treason, and put him to death, and drowned Aristobolus under color of sport. Alexandra, daughter to the one and mother to the other, accused him for their deaths before Anthony.

So when he was forced to go answer this accusation at Rome, he left the custody of his wife to Josephus, his uncle that had married his sister Salome, and out of a violent affection (unwilling any should enjoy her after him) he gave strict and private commandment, that if he were slain, she should be put to death. But he returned with much honor, yet found his wife extremely discontented, to whom Josephus had (meaning it for the best, to prove Herod loved her) revealed his charge.

So by Salome's accusation he put Josephus to death, but was reconciled to Mariam, who still bare the death of her friends[9] exceeding hardly.

In the meantime Herod was again necessarily to revisit Rome, for Caesar, having overthrown Anthony his great friend, was likely to make an alteration of Herod's fortune.

4. The opposite end of the earth.
5. Diana, or Luna, the moon.
6. The sun.
7. Cary's first play, which is now lost.
8. People of Edom, south of Judea, who had converted to Judaism but were not considered fully Jewish.
9. Family.

In his absence, news came to Jerusalem that Caesar had put him to death. Their willingness it should be so, together with the likelihood, gave this rumor so good credit, as Sohemus that had succeeded Josephus' charge,[1] *succeeded him likewise in revealing it. So at Herod's return, which was speedy and unexpected, he found Mariam so far from joy that she showed apparent signs of sorrow. He, still desiring to win her to a better humor, she being very unable to conceal her passion, fell to upbraiding him with her brother's death. As they were thus debating, came in a fellow with a cup of wine, who, hired by Salome, said first, it was a love potion, which Mariam desired to deliver to the king; but afterwards he affirmed that it was a poison and that Sohemus had told her somewhat, which procured the vehement hate in her.*

The king, hearing this, more moved with jealousy of Sohemus than with this intent of poison, sent her away; and presently after, by the instigation of Salome, Mariam was beheaded. Which rashness was afterward punished in him, with an intolerable and almost frantic passion for her death.

Act 1

Scene 1

[*Mariam alone.*]

MARIAM How oft have I with public voice run on?
To censure Rome's last hero for deceit;
Because he wept when Pompey's life was gone,
Yet when he lived, he thought his name too great.
But now I do recant,° and, Roman lord,[2] *renounce my error*
Excuse too rash a judgment in a woman;
My sex pleads pardon, pardon then afford,
Mistaking is with us, but too too common.
Now do I find by self-experience taught,
One object yields both grief and joy;
You wept indeed, when on his worth you thought,
But joyed that slaughter did your foe destroy.
So at his death your eyes true drops did rain,
Whom dead, you did not wish alive again.
When Herod lived, that now is done to death,
Oft have I wished that I from him were free;
Oft have I wished that he might lose his breath;
Oft have I wished his carcass dead to see.
Then rage and scorn had put my love to flight,
That love which once on him was firmly set;
Hate hid his true affection from my sight,
And kept my heart from paying him his debt.
And blame me not, for Herod's jealousy
Had power even constancy itself to change;
For he, by barring me from liberty,
To shun° my ranging, taught me first to range. *prevent*
But yet too chaste a scholar was my heart,
To learn to love another than my lord;

1. Who had taken on Josephus' duties.
2. Mariam addresses the absent Julius Caesar ("Rome's last hero"), who was said by Plutarch to have wept when he saw the head of his slain rival Pompey. The characters frequently speak in apostrophe to an imagined or absent figure.

To leave his love, my lesson's former part,
I quickly learned, the other I abhorred.
But now his death to memory doth call,
The tender love, that he to Mariam bare;
And mine to him, this makes those rivers fall,
Which by another thought unmoistened are.
For Aristobolus the lowliest youth
That ever did in angel's shape appear,
The cruel Herod was not moved to ruth;° *pity*
Then why grieves Mariam Herod's death to hear?
Why joy I not the tongue no more shall speak,
That yielded forth my brother's latest doom;
Both youth and beauty might thy° fury break, *Herod's*
And both in him did ill befit a tomb.
And worthy grandsire ill did he requite,[3]
His high assent alone by thee procured,
Except he murdered thee to free the sprite° *spirit*
Which still he thought on earth too long immured.° *confined*
How happy was it that Sohemus' mind
Was moved to pity my distressed estate!
Might Herod's life a trusty servant find,[4]
My death to his had been unseparate.
These thoughts have power, his death to make me bear,
Nay more, to wish the news may firmly hold;
Yet cannot this repulse some falling tear,
That will against my will some grief unfold.
And more I owe him for his love to me,
The deepest love that ever yet was seen;
Yet had I rather much a milkmaid be,
Than be the monarch of Judea's queen.
It was for naught but love, he wished his end
Might to my death but the vaunt-courier° prove; *forerunner*
But I had rather still be foe than friend,
To him that saves for hate, and kills for love.[5]
Hard-hearted Mariam, at thy discontent,
What floods of tears have drenched his manly face?
How canst thou then so faintly now lament,
Thy truest lover's death, a death's disgrace;[6]
Ay, now, mine eyes you do begin to right
The wrongs of your admirer and my lord.[7]
Long since you should have put your smiles to flight,
Ill doth a widowed eye with joy accord.
Why now methinks the love I bore him then,
When virgin freedom left me unrestrained,
Doth to my heart begin to creep again,
My passion now is far from being feigned.
But tears fly back, and hide you in your banks,[8]

3. Lines 43–46 are addressed to her dead grandfather Hircanus.
4. If Herod had been trustworthy while alive.
5. See *Othello*, 5.2.44, page 1252.
6. Her lack of grief dishonors his death.
7. Herod.
8. Her eyes.

You must not be to Alexandra seen;
For if my moan be spied, but little thanks
Shall Mariam have, from that incensèd queen.

Scene 2

[*Mariam, Alexandra.*]

ALEXANDRA What means these tears? My Mariam doth mistake,
The news we heard did tell the tyrant's end;
What° weepst thou for thy brother's murd'rer's sake, *why*
Will ever wight° a tear for Herod spend? *a person*
My curse pursue his breathless trunk and spirit,
Base Edomite the damnèd Esau's heir;
Must he ere Jacob's child the crown inherit?[9]
Must he, vile wretch, be set in David's chair°? *throne*
No David's soul within the bosom placed,
Of our forefather Abram was ashamed;
To see his seat with such a toad disgraced,
That seat that hath by Judah's race been famed.
Thou fatal enemy to royal blood,[1]
Did not the murder of my boy suffice,
To stop thy cruel mouth that gaping stood?
But must thou dim the mild Hircanus' eyes?
My gracious father, whose too ready hand
Did lift this Idumean from the dust;[2]
And he ungrateful caitiff° did withstand,° *wretch / oppose*
The man that did in him most friendly trust.
What kingdom's right could cruel Herod claim,
Was he not Esau's issue, heir of hell?
Then what succession can he have but shame?
Did not his ancestor his birthright sell?
O yes, he doth from Edom's name derive
His cruel nature which with blood is fed;[3]
That made him me of sire and son deprive,
He ever thirsts for blood, and blood is red.
Weep'st thou because his love to thee was bent?
And read'st thou love in crimson characters?
Slew he thy friends to work thy heart's content?
No; hate may justly call that action hers.
He gave the sacred priesthood for thy sake
To Aristobolus, yet doomed him dead;
Before his back the ephod warm could make,
And ere the miter settled on his head;[4]
Oh, had he given my boy no less than right,
The double oil should to his forehead bring
A double honor, shining double bright;
His birth anointed him both priest and king.
And say my father and my son he slew

9. The Edomites descended from Esau, who sold his birthright to his brother Jacob (Genesis 25.29–34).

1. Lines 13–16 are addressed to Herod.

2. Hircanus raised Herod's station by permitting his marriage to Miriam.

3. The root meaning of Edom is "red."

4. The ephod and the miter were Jewish priestly vestments.

To royalize by right your prince-born breath;[5]
Was love the cause, can Mariam deem it true,
That Mariam gave commandment for her death?
I know by fits he showed some signs of love,
And yet not love, but raging lunacy;
And this his hate to thee may justly prove,
That sure he hates Hircanus' family.
Who knows if he unconstant wavering lord,
His love to Doris[6] had renewed again?
And that he might his bed to her afford,
Perchance he wished that Mariam might be slain.

MARIAM Doris, alas her time of love was past,
Those coals were raked in embers long ago
Of Mariam's love, and she was now disgraced,[7]
Nor did I glory in her overthrow.
He not a whit his first-born son esteemed,
Because as well as his he was not mine;
My children only for his own he deemed,
These boys that did descend from royal line.
These did he style his heirs to David's throne,
My Alexander if he live, shall sit
In the majestic seat of Solomon,
To will it so, did Herod think it fit.

ALEXANDRA Why? Who can claim from Alexander's brood[8]
That gold-adornèd, lion-guarded chair?
Was Alexander not of David's blood?
And was not Mariam Alexander's heir?
What more than right could Herod then bestow,
And who will think except for more than right,
He did not raise them, for they were not low,[9]
But born to wear the crown in his despite.
Then send those tears away that are not sent
To thee by reason, but by passion's power;
Thine eyes to cheer, thy cheeks to smiles be bent,
And entertain with joy this happy hour.
Felicity, if when she comes, she finds
A mourning habit and a cheerless look,
Will think she is not welcome to thy mind,
And so perchance her lodging will not brook.° *put up with*
Oh, keep her whilst thou hast her; if she go
She will not easily return again.
Full many a year have I endured in woe,
Yet still have sued her presence to obtain;
And did not I to her as presents send
A table,° that best art did beautify *picture*

5. To make Mariam's son inherit royal power.

6. Herod's first wife.

7. "If" in the 1613 text is emended to "Of." "Mariam's love" (either Herod's love for Mariam or Mariam's for Herod) covers the coals of Doris's love with ashes.

8. Alexander was Mariam's father.

9. How could Herod grant Mariam's children anything more than what they were already entitled to? Whoever thinks Herod granted them "more than right" should know that "he did not raise them" since "they were not low" in the first place.

Of two, to whom heaven did best feature lend,
To woo her love by winning Anthony?
For when a prince's favor we do crave,
We first their minions'° loves do seek to win; *favorites'*
So I, that sought felicity to have,
Did with her minion Anthony begin.
With double slight I sought to captivate
The warlike lover, but I did not right;
For if my gift had born but half the rate,
The Roman had been overtaken quite.
But now he farèd like a hungry guest,
That to some plenteous festival is gone;
Now this, now that, he deems to eat were best,
Such choice doth make him let them all alone.
The boy's large forehead first did fairest seem,
Then glanced his eye upon my Mariam's cheek;
And that without comparison did deem,
What was in either but he most did seek.
And, thus distracted, either's beauty's might
Within the other's excellence was drowned;
Too much delight did bare him from delight,
For either's love, the other's did confound.
Where if thy portraiture had only gone,
His life from Herod, Anthony had taken;
He would have lovèd thee, and thee alone,
And left the brown Egyptian clean forsaken.
And Cleopatra then to seek had been,[1]
So firm a lover of her wanèd° face; *dark, gloomy*
Then great Antonius' fall we had not seen,
By her that fled to have him hold the chase.
Then Mariam in a Roman's chariot set,
In place of Cleopatra might have shown;
A mart of beauties in her visage met,
And part in this, that they were all her own.

MARIAM Not to be empress of aspiring Rome,
Would Mariam like to Cleopatra live;
With purest body will I press my tomb,
And wish no favors Anthony could give.[2]

ALEXANDRA Let us return us, that we may resolve
How now to deal in this reversèd state;
Great are the affairs that we must now revolve,
And great affairs must not be taken late.

Scene 3

[*Mariam, Alexandra, Salome.*]

SALOM More plotting yet? Why, now you have the thing
For which so oft you spent your suppliant° breath; *humbly begging*

1. Cleopatra would have been left seeking.

2. Mariam disdains Cleopatra's quest for power through her affairs with Julius Caesar and Mark Antony.

And Mariam hopes to have another king.
Her eyes do sparkle joy for Herod's death.
ALEXANDRA If she desired another king to have,
She might before she came in Herod's bed
Have had her wish. More kings than one did crave,
For leave to set a crown upon her head.
I think with more than reason she laments,
That she is freed from such a sad annoy;
Who is't will weep to part from discontent,
And if she joy, she did not causeless joy.[3]
SALOME You durst not thus have given your tongue the rein,
If noble Herod still remained in life;
Your daughter's betters far I dare maintain,
Might have rejoiced to be my brother's wife.
MARIAM My betters far! Base woman, 'tis untrue,
You scarce have ever my superiors seen;
For Mariam's servants were as good as you,
Before she came to be Judea's queen.
SALOME Now stirs the tongue that is so quickly moved,
But more then once your choler° have I borne; *anger*
Your fumish° words are sooner said than proved, *hot-tempered*
And Salome's reply is only scorn.
MARIAM Scorn those that are for thy companions held.
Though I thy brother's face had never seen,
My birth, thy baser birth so far excelled,
I had to both of you the princess been.
Thou parti-Jew, and parti-Edomite,[4]
Thou mongrel, issued from rejected race,
Thy ancestors against the heavens did fight,[5]
And thou like them wilt heavenly birth disgrace.
SALOME Still twit° you me with nothing but my birth, *blame*
What odds betwixt your ancestors and mine?
Both born of Adam, both were made of earth,
And both did come from holy Abraham's line.
MARIAM I favor thee when nothing else I say,
With thy black acts I'll not pollute my breath;
Else to thy charge I might full justly lay
A shameful life, besides a husband's death.
SALOME 'Tis true indeed, I did the plots reveal,
That passed betwixt your favorites and you;[6]
I meant not, I, a traitor to conceal;
Thus Salome your minion° Joseph slew. *favorite*
MARIAM Heaven, dost thou mean this infamy to smother?
Let slandered Mariam open thy closèd ear;
Self-guilt hath ever been suspicion's mother,[7]
And therefore I this speech with patience bear.

3. If she were delighted, it would be with good reason.
4. Part Jewish, part Edomite.
5. In resisting the power of Israel, the Edomites were portrayed as opposing God (Ezekiel 25.13,35).
6. Salome accused her first husband, Josephus, and Mariam of adultery. Herod judged Josephus's telling Mariam about the secret order that she be killed in the event of Herod's death as proof of Josephus's guilt, and so ordered his execution.
7. Your own guilt makes you suspicious of me.

No, had not Salome's unsteadfast heart,
In Josephus' stead her Constabarus placed[8]
To free herself, she had not used the art,
To slander hapless Mariam for unchaste.

ALEXANDRA Come Mariam, let us go: it is no boot° *use*
To let the head contend against the foot.

Scene 4

[*Salome alone.*]

SALOME Lives Salome, to get so base a style° *name*
As foot, to the proud Mariam? Herod's spirit
In happy time for her endured exile,[9]
For did he live she should not miss her merit;[1]
But he is dead; and though he were my brother,
His death such store of cinders cannot cast
My coals of love to quench; for though they smother
The flames a while, yet will they out at last.
Oh blest Arabia, in best climate placed,
I by the fruit will censure of the tree;
'Tis not in vain, thy happy name thou hast,
If all Arabians like Silleus[2] be;
Had not my fate been too too contrary,
When I on Constabarus first did gaze,
Silleus had been object to mine eye,
Whose looks and personage must always amaze.
But now ill-fated Salome, thy tongue
To Constabarus by itself is tied;
And now except I do the Hebrew wrong
I cannot be the fair Arabian bride;
What childish lets° are these? Why stand I now *hindrances*
On honorable points? 'Tis long ago
Since shame was written on my tainted brow;[3]
And certain 'tis, that shame is honor's foe.
Had I upon my reputation stood,
Had I affected an unspotted life,
Josephus' veins had still been stuffed with blood,
And I to him had lived a sober wife.
Then had I never cast an eye of love
On Constabarus' now detested face,
Then had I kept my thoughts without remove
And blushed at motion of the least disgrace;[4]
But shame is gone, and honor wiped away,
And Impudency on my forehead sits;
She bids me work my will without delay,
And for my will I will employ my wits.
He loves, I love; what then can be the cause
Keeps me from being the Arabian's wife?

8. Mariam claims that she was accused of adultery by Salome because Salome wanted to get rid of her husband so that she could marry Constabarus.

9. Separation of the soul from the body, i.e., death.

1. If he were alive, she would get what she deserves.

2. Salome's lover and minister to King Obodas of Arabia.

3. Since she showed any sign of shame.

4. Compare *Othello*, 1.3.96–97, page 1190.

It is the principles of Moses' laws;
For Constabarus still remains in life;
If he to me did bear as earnest hate
As I to him, for him there were an ease,
A separating bill[5] might free his fate
From such a yoke that did so much displease.
Why should such privilege to man be given?
Or given to them, why barred from women then?
Are men than we in greater grace with Heaven?
Or cannot women hate as well as men?[6]
I'll be the custom-breaker, and begin
To show my sex the way to freedom's door,
And with an offering will I purge my sin,
The law was made for none but who are poor.
If Herod had lived, I might to him accuse
My present lord. But for the future's sake
Then would I tell the king he did refuse
The sons of Baba in his power to take.[7]
But now I must divorce him from my bed,
That my Silleus may possess his room.
Had I not begged his life he had been dead,[8]
I curse my tongue the hinderer of his doom;
But then my wandering heart to him was fast,
Nor did I dream of change. Silleus said,
He would be here, and see he comes at last,
Had I not named him longer had he stayed.

Scene 5

[*Salome, Silleus.*]

SILLEUS Well found fair Salome, Judea's pride!
Hath thy innated° wisdom found the way *inborn*
To make Silleus deem him deified,
By gaining thee a more than precious prey?

SALOME I have devised the best I can devise:
A more imperfect means was never found;
But what cares Salome? It doth suffice
If our endeavors with their end be crowned.
In this our land we have an ancient use,
Permitted first by our law-giver's° head; *Moses'*
Who hates his wife, though for no just abuse,
May with a bill divorce her from his bed.
But in this custom women are not free,
Yet I for once will wrest it; blame not thou
The ill I do, since what I do's for thee,
Though others blame, Silleus should allow.

5. A bill of divorce, which only men could sue for.
6. Compare *Othello*, 4.3.88–99, page 1247.
7. Constabarus was supposed to have captured Herod's political enemies, the sons of Babas, but instead hid them on his own estate in hope that they might be useful to him in usurping power.
8. When Herod found out that Constabarus, as governor of Idumea, had tried to take over the kingdom, only Salome was able to convince Herod to spare his life.

SILLEUS Thinks Salome, Silleus hath a tongue
To censure her fair actions? Let my blood
Bedash my proper brow,[9] for such a wrong,
The being yours, can make even vices good;
Arabia, joy, prepare thy earth with green,
Thou never happy wert indeed 'til now;
Now shall thy ground be trod by beauty's queen,
Her foot is destined to depress thy brow.
Thou shalt fair Salome command as much
As if the royal ornament were thine;
The weakness of Arabia's king is such,
The kingdom is not his so much as mine.
My mouth is our Obodas' oracle,
Who thinks not aught but what Silleus will.
And thou rare creature, Asia's miracle,
Shalt be to me as it: Obodas' still.[1]
SALOME 'Tis not for glory I thy love accept,
Judea yields me honor's worthy store;
Had not affection in my bosom crept,
My native country should my life deplore.[2]
Were not Silleus he with whom I go,
I would not change my Palestine for Rome;
Much less would I a glorious state to show,
Go far to purchase an Arabian tomb.
SILLEUS Far be it from Silleus so to think,
I know it is thy gratitude requites
The love that is in me, and shall not shrink
'Til death do sever me from earth's delights.
SALOME But whist;° methinkes the wolf is in our talk,[3] *be silent*
Be gone Silleus, who doth here arrive?
'Tis Constabarus that doth hither walk,
I'll find a quarrel, him from me to drive.
SILLEUS Farewell, but were it not for thy command,
In his despite Silleus here would stand.

Scene 6

[*Salome, Constabarus.*]
CONSTABARUS Oh Salome, how much you wrong your name,
Your race, your country, and your husband most!
A stranger's private conference is shame;[4]
I blush for you, that have your blushing lost.
Oft have I found, and found you to my grief,
Comforted with this base Arabian here;
Heaven knows that you have been my comfort chief,
Then do not now my greater plague appear.
Now by the stately carved edifice

9. Splash against my own forehead.
1. Even though Obodas rules the Kingdom, he follows my judgment as I follow yours, Salome.
2. If it weren't for love of you, Silleus, I would regret leaving my country my whole life long.
3. In discussing our plot for power, we are in danger of being overheard.
4. Talking privately with a stranger is shameful.

That on Mount Sion makes so fair a show,[5]
And by the altar fit for sacrifice,
I love thee more than thou thyself dost know.
Oft with a silent sorrow have I heard
How ill Judea's mouth doth censure thee;
And did I not thine honor much regard,
Thou shouldst not be exhorted thus for me.
Didst thou but know the worth of honest fame,
How much a virtuous woman is esteemed,
Thou wouldst like hell eschew deservèd shame,
And seek to be both chaste and chastely deemed.
Our wisest prince did say, and true he said,
A virtuous woman crowns her husband's head.[6]

SALOME Did I for this uprear thy low estate?
Did I for this requital beg thy life,
That thou hadst forfeited to hapless fate,
To be to such a thankless wretch the wife?
This hand of mine hath lifted up thy head,
Which many a day ago had fall'n full low,
Because the sons of Babas are not dead;
To me thou dost both life and fortune owe.

CONSTABARUS You have my patience often exercised,
Use make my choler keep within the banks;[7]
Yet boast no more, but be by me advised,
A benefit upbraided, forfeits thanks.[8]
I prithee Salome, dismiss this mood,
Thou dost not know how ill it fits thy place:
My words were all intended for thy good,
To raise thine honor and to stop disgrace.

SALOME To stop disgrace? Take thou no care for me,
Nay, do thy worst, thy worst I set not by;[9]
No shame of mine is like to light on thee,
Thy love and admonitions I defy.
Thou shalt no hour longer call me wife,
Thy jealousy procures my hate so deep;
That I from thee do mean to free my life,
By a divorcing bill before I sleep.

CONSTABARUS Are Hebrew women now transformed to men?
Why do you not as well our battles fight,
And wear our armor? Suffer this, and then
Let all the world be topsy-turvèd° quite. *upside down*
Let fishes graze, beasts, swine, and birds descend,
Let fire burn downwards whilst the earth aspires;
Let winter's heat and summer's cold offend,
Let thistles grow on vines, and grapes on briars,
Set us to spin or sow, or at the best

5. The temple of Jerusalem.
6. Proverbs 12.4; attributed to Solomon.
7. May habit control my anger.
8. If you blame someone for having granted him a benefit, you lose his gratitude.
9. I couldn't care less about the worst you could do to me.

Make us wood-hewers, water-bearing wights;
For sacred service let us take no rest,
Use us as Joshua did the Gibonites.[1]

SALOME Hold on your talk, 'til it be time to end,
For me I am resolved it shall be so;
Though I be first that to this course do bend,
I shall not be the last full well I know.

CONSTABARUS Why then be witness heaven, the judge of sins,
Be witness spirits that eschew the dark;
Be witness angels, witness cherubins,
Whose semblance sits upon the holy Ark;
Be witness earth, be witness Palestine,
Be witness David's city, if my heart
Did ever merit such an act of thine;
Or if the fault be mine that makes us part,
Since mildest Moses, friend unto the Lord,
Did work his wonders in the land of Ham,[2]
And slew the first-born babes without a sword,
In sign whereof we eat the holy lamb;[3]
'Til now that fourteen hundred years are past,
Since first the Law[4] with us hath been in force;
You are the first, and will, I hope, be last,
That ever sought her husband to divorce.

SALOME I mean not to be led by precedent,
My will shall be to me instead of Law.

CONSTABARUS I fear me much you will too late repent,
That you have ever lived so void of awe;
This is Silleus' love that makes you thus
Reverse all order; you must next be his.
But if my thoughts aright the cause discuss,
In winning you, he gains no lasting bliss;
I was Silleus, and not long ago
Josephus then was Constabarus now;
When you became my friend° you proved his° foe, *lover/Josephus's*
As now for him° you break to me your vow. *Silleus*

SALOME If once I loved you, greater is your debt;
For certain 'tis that you deserve it not.
And undeserved love we soon forget,
And therefore that to me can be no blot.
But now fare ill my once belovèd lord,
Yet never more beloved than now abhorred.

CONSTABARUS Yet Constabarus biddeth thee farewell.
Farewell light creature. Heaven forgive thy sin;
My prophesying spirit doth foretell
Thy wavering thoughts do yet but new begin.
Yet I have better 'scaped than Joseph did;
But if our Herod's death had been delayed,
The valiant youths[5] that I so long have hid

1. Joshua enslaved the Gibonites (Joshua 9).
2. Egypt.
3. During the Passover celebration commemorating the Israelites' deliverance from Egypt (Exodus 12).
4. The law of Moses.
5. Babas's sons.

Had been by her, and I for them betrayed.
Therefore in happy hour did Caesar give
The fatal blow to wanton Anthony;
For had he lived, our Herod then should live,
But great Anthonius' death made Herod die.
Had he enjoyed his breath, not I alone
Had been in danger of a deadly fall;
But Mariam had the way of peril gone,
Though by the tyrant most beloved of all.
The sweet-faced Mariam as free from guilt
As heaven from spots, yet had her lord come back
Her purest blood had been unjustly spilt.
And Salome it was would work her wrack.° *destruction*
Though all Judea yield her innocent,
She often hath been near to punishment. [*Exit.*]

CHORUS Those minds that wholly dote upon delight,
Except° they only joy in inward good, *unless*
Still hope at last to hop upon the right,[6]
And so from sand they leap in loathsome mud.
Fond wretches, seeking what they cannot find,
For no content attends a wavering mind.

If wealth they do desire, and wealth attain,
Then wondrous fain° would they to honor leap; *gladly*
Of mean degree they do in honor gain,
They would but wish a little higher step.
Thus step to step, and wealth to wealth they add,
Yet cannot all their plenty make them glad.

Yet oft we see that some in humble state,
Are cheerful, pleasant, happy, and content;
When those indeed that are of higher state,
With vain additions do their thoughts torment.
Th' one would to his mind his fortune bind,
Th' other to his fortune frames his mind.

To wish variety is sign of grief,
For if you like your state as now it is,
Why should an alteration bring relief?
Nay change would then be feared as loss of bliss.
That man is only happy in his fate,
That is delighted in a settled state.

Still Mariam wished she from her lord were free,
For expectation of variety;
Yet now she sees her wishes prosperous be,
She grieves, because her lord so soon did die.
Who can those vast imaginations feed,
Where in a property contempt doth breed?[7]

6. To hop on to land on the right side meant to achieve a good outcome.

7. Where what is possessed is despised.

Were Herod now perchance to love again,
She would again as much be grieved at that;
All that she may,[8] she ever doth disdain,
Her wishes guide her to she knows not what.
And sad must be their looks, their honor sour,
That care for nothing being in their power.

Act 2

Scene 1

[*Pheroras and Graphina.*][9]

PHERORAS 'Tis true Graphina, now the time draws nigh
Wherein the holy priest with hallowed right,
The happy long-desired knot shall tie,
Pheroras and Graphina to unite;
How oft have I with lifted hands implored
This blessed hour, 'til now implored in vain,
Which hath my wished liberty restored,
And made my subject self my own again.
Thy love, fair maid, upon mine eye doth sit,
Whose nature hot doth dry the moisture all,
Which were in nature, and in reason fit
For my monarchal brother's death to fall;
Had Herod lived, he would have plucked my hand
From fair Graphina's palm perforce; and tied
The same in hateful and despisèd band,
For I had had a baby to my bride;[1]
Scarce can her infant tongue with easy voice
Her name distinguish to another's ear;[2]
Yet had he lived, his power, and not my choice
Had made me solemnly the contract swear.
Have I not cause in such a change to joy?
What? Though she be my niece, a princess born;
Near-blood's without respect: high birth a toy,
Since love can teach us blood and kindred's scorn.
What booted it[3] that he did raise my head,
To be his realm's copartner, kingdom's mate?
Withall, he kept Graphina from my bed,
More wished by me than thrice Judea's state.
Oh, could not he be skilful judge in love,
That doted so upon his Mariam's face?
He, for his passion, Doris did remove;
I needed not a lawful wife displace.
It could not be but he had power to judge,
But he that never grudged a kingdom's share,
This well-known happiness to me did grudge,

8. All that she may have or do.

9. From the minor figure of a nameless slave girl in Josephus's *Jewish War*, Cary created Graphina, derived from *graphesis*, the Greek word for writing.

1. Herod would have ordered a marriage between his oldest daughter ("a baby") and Pheroras.

2. She is so young she can hardly say her own name clearly; "infant" from Latin *infans*, speechless.

3. What use was it?

And meant to be therein without compare.
Else had I been his equal in love's host,° *army*
For though the diadem on Mariam's head
Corrupt the vulgar judgments, I will boast
Graphina's brow's as white, her cheeks as red.
Why speaks thou not fair creature? Move thy tongue,
For silence is a sign of discontent;
It were to both our loves too great a wrong
If now this hour do find thee sadly bent.

GRAPHINA Mistake me not my lord, too oft have I
Desired this time to come with wingèd feet,
To be enwrapped with grief when 'tis too nigh,
You know my wishes ever yours did meet;
If I be silent, 'tis no more but fear
That I should say too little when I speak;
But since you will my imperfections bear,
In spite of doubt I will my silence break;
Yet might amazement tie my moving tongue,
But that I know before Pheroras' mind.
I have admired° your affection long, *marvelled at*
And cannot yet therein a reason find.
Your hand hath lifted me from lowest state,
To highest eminency's wondrous grace,
And me your handmaid have you made your mate,
Though all but you alone do count me base.
You have preserved me pure at my request,
Though you so weak a vassal[4] might constrain
To yield to your high will; then last not best
In my respect a princess you disdain;
Then need not all these favors study crave,
To be requited by a simple maid?[5]
And study still you know must silence have,
Then be my cause for silence justly weighed,
But study cannot boot nor I requite,
Except your lowly handmaid's steadfast love
And fast obedience may your mind delight,
I will not promise more then I can prove.

PHERORAS That study needs not let Graphina smile,
And I desire no greater recompense;
I cannot vaunt° me in a glorious style, *boast, proclaim*
Nor show my love in far-fetched eloquence;
But this believe me, never Herod's heart
Hath held his prince-born beauty-famèd wife
In nearer place than thou, fair virgin, art,
To him that holds the glory of his life.
Should Herod's body leave the sepulcher,
And entertain the severed ghost again;[6]

4. The feudal relation between lord and subordinate with a pun on "vessel," as in woman as "the weaker vessel" (1 Peter 3.7).

5. All these favors will require effort for a simple maid to repay them.

6. The spirit separated from the body, an image of death.

He should not be my nuptial hinderer,
Except he hindered it with dying pain.
Come fair Graphina, let us go in state,
This wish-endearèd time to celebrate.

Scene 2

[*Constabarus and Babas' Sons.*]

FIRST SON Now valiant friend you have our lives redeemed,
Which lives as saved by you, to you are due;
Command and you shall see yourself esteemed,
Our lives and liberties belong to you.
This twice six years with hazard of your life,
You have concealed us from the tyrant's sword;
Though cruel Herod's sister were your wife,
You durst in scorn of fear this grace afford.
In recompense we know not what to say,
A poor reward were thanks for such a merit,[7]
Our truest friendship at your feet we lay,
The best requital to a noble spirit.

CONSTABARUS Oh how you wrong our friendship valiant youth,
With friends there is not such a word as debt,
Where amity is tied with bond of truth,
All benefits are therein common set.
Then is the golden age with them renewed,
All names of properties are banished quite;[8]
Division and distinction are eschewed;
Each hath to what belongs to other's right.[9]
And 'tis not sure so full a benefit,
Freely to give, as freely to require;
A bounteous act hath glory following it,
They cause the glory that the act desire.
All friendship should the pattern imitate,
Of Jesse's son and valiant Jonathan;[1]
For neither sovereign's nor father's hate,
A friendship fixed on virtue sever can.
Too much of this, 'tis written in the heart,
And need no amplifying with the tongue;
Now may you from your living tomb depart,
Where Herod's life hath kept you overlong.
Too great an injury to a noble mind,
To be quick buried;[2] you had purchased fame,
Some years ago, but that you were confined,
While thousand meaner did advance their name.
Your best of life the prime of all your years,
Your time of action is from you bereft.
Twelve winters have you overpassed in fears;

7. Thanks would be a poor reward for your saving our lives.
8. All individual ownership is forbidden.
9. Each one has a right to what belongs to the other.

1. See 1 Samuel 20 for how David (Jesse's son) was saved by Jonathan (Saul's son) from death at the hands of King Saul.
2. Buried alive.

Yet if you use it well, enough is left.
And who can doubt but you will use it well?
The sons of Babas have it by descent;
In all their thoughts each action to excel,
Boldly to act, and wisely to invent.

SECOND SON Had it not like the hateful cuckoo been,
Whose riper age his infant nurse doth kill;[3]
So long we had not kept ourselves unseen,
But Constabarus safely crossed our will;
For had the tyrant fixed his cruel eye,
On our concealèd faces wrath had swayed
His justice so, that he had forced us die.
And dearer price than life we should have paid;
For you our truest friend had fallen with us,
And we much like a house on pillars set,
Had clean depressed our prop, and therefore thus
Our ready will with our concealment met.
But now that you, fair lord, are dangerless,
The sons of Babas shall their rigor show;
And prove it was not baseness did oppress
Our hearts so long, but honor kept them low.

FIRST SON Yet do I fear this tale of Herod's death,
At last will prove a very tale indeed;
It gives me strongly in my mind, his breath
Will be preserved to make a number bleed;
I wish not therefore to be set at large,
Yet peril to myself I do not fear;
Let us for some days longer be your charge,° *care*
'Til we of Herod's state the truth do hear.

CONSTABARUS What art thou turned a coward, noble youth,
That thou beginn'st to doubt undoubted truth?

FIRST SON Were it my brother's tongue that cast this doubt
I from his heart would have the question out
With this keen falchion,° but 'tis you my lord *curved sword*
Against whose head I must not lift a sword:
I am so tied in gratitude.

CONSTABARUS Believe
You have no cause to take it ill,
If any word of mine your heart did grieve
The word descended from the speaker's will;
I know it was not fear the doubt begun,
But rather valor and your care of me,
A coward could not be your father's son,
Yet know I doubts unnecessary be;
For who can think that in Anthonius' fall,
Herod his bosom friend should 'scape unbruised.[4]
Then, Caesar, we might thee an idiot call,

3. The cuckoo lays its eggs in other birds' nests, and when grown the chicks kill their foster parents.

4. The victory of Octavian over Anthony and Cleopatra in the battle of Actium made it seem unlikely that Herod would remain in power.

If thou by him should'st be so far abused.
SECOND SON Lord Constabarus, let me tell you this,
Upon submission Caesar will forgive;
And therefore though the tyrant did amiss,
It may fall out that he will let him live.
Not many years agone it is since I
Directed thither by my father's care,
In famous Rome for twice twelve months did live,
My life from Hebrew's cruelty to spare,
There though I were but yet of boyish age,
I bent mine eye to mark, mine ears to hear.
Where I did see Octavius then a page,
When first he did to Julius' sight appear;[5]
Methought I saw such mildness in his face,
And such a sweetness in his looks did grow,
Withall, commixed with so majestic grace,
His phis'nomy his fortune did foreshow;[6]
For this I am indebted to mine eye,
But then mine ear received more evidence,
How he with hottest choler° could dispense. *anger*
CONSTABARUS But we have more than barely heard the news,
It hath been twice confirmed. And though some tongue
Might be so false, with false report t'abuse,
A false report hath never lasted long.
But be it so that Herod have his life,
Concealment would not then a whit avail;
For certain 'tis, that she that was my wife,
Would not to set her accusation fail.
And therefore now as good the venture give,
And free ourselves from blot of cowardice,
As show a pitiful desire to live,
For, who can pity but they must despise?
FIRST SON I yield, but to necessity I yield;
I dare upon this doubt engage mine arm:[7]
That Herod shall again this kingdom wield,
And prove his death to be a false alarm.
SECOND SON I doubt° it too. God grant it be an error, *fear*
'Tis best without a cause to be in terror;
And rather had I, though my soul be mine,
My soul should lie, than prove a true divine.[8]
CONSTABARUS Come, come, let fear go seek a dastard's nest,
Undaunted courage lies in noble breast.

Scene 3

[*Doris and Antipater.*]
DORIS You royal buildings bow your lofty side,

5. Octavius (63 B.C.–A.D. 14), Julius Caesar's great-nephew and adopted heir, later became Augustus Caesar.
6. Octavius' courteous manners and graceful appearance (physiognomy) foretold his greatness.
7. I am willing to take up arms on the suspicion that Herod is still alive and will return to power.
8. I would rather that my suspicions be found false than that I be confirmed as a prophet.

And stoop to her that is by right your queen;
Let your humility upbraid the pride
Of those in whom no due respect is seen;
Nine times have we with trumpets' haughty sound,
And banishing sour leaven from our taste,
Observed the feast that takes the fruit from ground.[9]
Since I, fair city, did behold thee last,
So long it is since Mariam's purer cheek
Did rob from mine the glory.[1] And so long
Since I returned my native town to seek,
And with me nothing but the sense of wrong,
And thee my boy, whose birth though great it were,
Yet have thy after fortunes proved but poor;
When thou wert born how little did I fear
Thou shouldst be thrust from forth thy father's door.
Art thou not Herod's right begotten son?
Was not the hapless Doris, Herod's wife?
Yes: ere he had the Hebrew kingdom won,
I was companion to his private life.
Was I not fair enough to be a queen?
Why, ere thou wert to me false monarch tied,
My lake of beauty might as well be seen,
As after I had lived five years thy bride.
Yet then thine oath came powering like the rain,
Which all affirmed my face without compare,
And that if thou might'st Doris love obtain,
For all the world besides thou didst not care.
Then was I young, and rich, and nobly borne,
And therefore worthy to be Herod's mate;
Yet thou ungrateful cast me off with scorn,
When heaven's purpose raised your meaner fate.
Oft have I begged for vengeance for this fact,° *action*
And with dejected° knees, aspiring hands *bent down*
Have prayed the highest power to enact
The fall of her that on my trophy[2] stands.
Revenge I have according to my will,
Yet where I wished this vengeance did not light.
I wished it should high-hearted Mariam kill,
But it against my whilom° lord did fight. *former*
With thee, sweet boy, I came, and came to try
If thou before his bastards might be placed
In Herod's royal seat and dignity.
But Mariam's infants here are only graced,
And now for us there doth no hope remain;
Yet we will not return 'til Herod's end
Be more confirmed, perchance he is not slain.
So glorious fortunes may my boy attend,
For if he° live, he'll think it doth suffice, *Herod*

9. The feast of first fruits was observed on the day after Passover (the feast of unleavened bread).

1. It had been nine years since Herod's divorce of Doris.

2. The spoils of my defeat.

That he to Doris shows such cruelty;
For as he did my wretched life despise,
So do I know I shall despisèd die.
Let him but prove as natural to thee,
As cruel to thy miserable mother;
His cruelty shall not upbraided be
But in thy fortunes.[3] I his faults will smother.

ANTIPATER Each mouth within the city loudly cries
That Herod's death is certain. Therefore we
Had best some subtle hidden plot devise,
That Mariam's children might subverted be,
By poisons drink, or else by murderous knife,
So we may be advanced, it skills not° how; *makes no difference*
They are but bastards, you were Herod's wife,
And foul adultery blotteth Mariam's brow.

DORIS They are too strong to be by us removed,
Or else revenge's foulest spotted face;
By our detested wrongs might be approved,
But weakness must to greater power give place.
But let us now retire to grieve alone,
For solitariness best fitteth moan. [*They exit.*]

Scene 4

[*Silleus and Constabarus.*]

SILLEUS Well met Judean lord, the only wight° *person*
Silleus wished to see. I am to call
Thy tongue to strict account.

CONSTABARUS For what despite
I ready am to hear, and answer all.
But if directly at the cause I guess
That breeds this challenge, you must pardon me;[4]
And now some other ground of fight profess,
For I have vowed, vows must unbroken be.

SILLEUS What may be your exception? Let me know.[5]

CONSTABARUS Why? Aught concerning Salome, my sword
Shall not be wielded for a cause so low,
A blow for her my arm will scorn t'afford.

SILLEUS It is for slandering her unspotted name,[6]
And I will make thee in thy vows despite,
Suck up the breath that did my mistress blame,
And swallow it again to do her right.

CONSTABARUS I prithee give some other quarrel ground
To find beginning, rail against my name;
Or strike me first, or let some scarlet wound
Inflame my courage, give me words of shame,
Do thou our Moses' sacred laws disgrace,

3. I won't criticize his cruelty except in so far as it affects your fortunes.

4. If I am right in guessing why you want to fight me, you'll have to excuse me from responding to your challenge.

5. "Expectation" in the 1613 text has been emended "exception," the reason why you will not fight.

6. I challenge you because you have slandered Salome.

Deprave our nation, do me some despite;
I'm apt enough to fight in any case,
But yet for Salome I will not fight.

SILLEUS Nor I for aught but Salome. My sword
That owes his service to her sacred name
Will not an edge for other cause afford;
In other fight I am not sure of fame.

CONSTABARUS For her,[7] I pity thee enough already,
For her, I therefore will not mangle thee;
A woman with a heart so most unsteady,
Will of herself sufficient torture be.
I cannot envy for so light a gain,
Her mind with such inconstancy doth run;
As with a word thou didst her love obtain,
So with a word she will from thee be won.
So light as her possessions for most day
Is her affections lost, to me 'tis known;[8]
As good go hold the wind as make her stay,
She never loves, but 'til she call her own.[9]
She merely is a painted sepulcher,[1]
That is both fair, and vilely foul at once;
Though on her outside graces garnish her,
Her mind is filled with worse than rotten bones.
And ever ready lifted is her hand,
To aim destruction at a husband's throat;
For proofs, Josephus and myself do stand,
Though once on both of us she seemed to dote.
Her mouth though serpentlike it never hisses,
Yet like a serpent, poisons where it kisses.

SILLEUS Well Hebrew well, thou bark'st, but wilt not bite.

CONSTABARUS I tell thee still for her I will not fight.

SILLEUS Why then I call thee coward.

CONSTABARUS From my heart
I give thee thanks. A coward's hateful name,
Cannot to valiant minds a blot impart,
And therefore I with joy receive the same.
Thou know'st I am no coward. Thou wert by
At the Arabian battle th'other day,
And saw'st my sword with daring valiancy
Amongst the faint Arabians cut my way.
The blood of foes no more could let it shine,
And 'twas enamelèd with some of thine.
But now have at thee;[2] not for Salome
I fight, but to discharge a coward's style;° *name*
Here 'gins the fight that shall not parted be,
Before a soul or two endure exile. [*They fight.*]

7. Because of her.
8. You value her affection so little when you have it that it is a light loss when you lose it.
9. She loves only up to the point when she gets what she wants.
1. See Matthew 23.27: "Woe unto you, scribes and Pharisees, hypocrites! for ye are like unto whited sepulchres."
2. I'll fight you.

SILLEUS Thy sword hath made some windows for my blood,
To show a horrid crimson phis'nomy;° *face*
To breathe° for both of us methinks 'twere good, *catch breath*
The day will give us time enough to die.
CONSTABARUS With all my heart take breath, thou shalt have time,
And if thou list° a twelve month: let us end; *wish*
Into thy cheeks there doth a paleness climb,
Thou canst not from my sword thyself defend.
What needest thou for Salome to fight?
Thou hast her, and may'st keep her, none strives for her;
I willingly to thee resign my right,
For in my very soul I do abhor her.
Thou seest that I am fresh, unwounded yet,
Then not for fear I do this offer make;
Thou art with loss of blood, to fight unfit.
For here is one, and there another take.[3]
SILLEUS I will not leave, as long as breath remains
Within my wounded body. Spare your words,
My heart in blood's stead, courage entertains,
Salome's love no place for fear affords.
CONSTABARUS Oh, could thy soul but prophesy like mine,
I would not wonder thou should'st long to die;
For Salome, if I aright divine,
Will be than death a greater misery.
SILLEUS Then list, I'll breathe no longer.[4]
CONSTABARUS Do thy will,
I hateless fight, and charitably kill. [*They fight.*] Aye, aye,
Pity thyself Silleus, let not death
Intrude before his time into thy heart;
Alas it is too late to fear, his breath
Is from his body now about to part.
How farest thou brave Arabian?
SILLEUS Very well,
My leg is hurt, I can no longer fight;
It only grieves me, that so soon I fell,
Before fair Salom's wrongs[5] I came to right.
CONSTABARUS Thy wounds are less than mortal. Never fear,
Thou shalt a safe and quick recovery find;
Come, I will thee unto my lodging bear,
I hate thy body, but I love thy mind.
SILLEUS Thanks, noble Jew, I see a courteous foe,
Stern enmity to friendship can no art;[6]
Had not my heart and tongue engaged me so,
I would from thee no foe, but friend depart.
My heart to Salome is tied too fast
To leave her love for friendship, yet my skill
Shall be employed to make your favor last,

3. In this fight, each of us gives and takes.
4. Then listen, I won't pause or live any longer.
5. The wrong done to Salome.
6. Enmity doesn't know a way to friendship.

And I will honor Constabarus still.
CONSTABARUS I ope my bosom to thee, and will take
Thee in, as friend, and grieve for thy complaint;
But if we do not expedition make,
Thy loss of blood I fear will make thee faint. [*They exit.*]

CHORUS To hear a tale with ears prejudicate,° *prejudiced*
It spoils the judgment and corrupts the sense;
That human error given to every state,
Is greater enemy to innocence.[7]
It makes us foolish, heady, rash, unjust,
It makes us never try before we trust.[8]

It will confound the meaning, change the words,
For it our sense of hearing much deceives;
Besides no time to judgment it affords,
To weigh the circumstance our ear receives.
The ground of accidents[9] it never tries,
But makes us take for truth ten thousand lies.

Our ears and hearts are apt to hold for good,
That we ourselves do most desire to be;
And then we drown objections in the flood
Of partiality, 'tis that[1] we see
That makes false rumors long with credit passed,
Though they like rumors must conclude at last.

The greatest part of us prejudicate,° *judge too soon*
With wishing Herod's death do hold it true;
The being once deluded doth not bate,° *lessen*
The credit to a better likelihood due.[2]
Those few that wish it not, the multitude
Do carry headlong, so they doubts conclude.[3]

They° not object the weak uncertain ground, *the few*
Whereon they built this tale of Herod's end;
Whereof the author scarcely can be found,
And all because their wishes that way bend.
They think not of the peril that ensu'th,° *comes about*
If this should prove the contrary to truth.

On this same doubt, on this so light a breath,
They pawn their lives and fortunes. For they all
Behave them as the news of Herod's death,
They did of most undoubted credit call;
But if their actions now do rightly hit,° *succeed*
Let them commend their fortune, not their wit.

7. The naive are more vulnerable to human error.
8. It makes us jump to conclusions before we test them.
9. Basis or cause of appearances.
1. I.e., partiality.
2. Having been once deceived before about Herod's death doesn't lessen the belief that it might be true this time.
3. Those who do not wish for Herod's death are swayed by the majority and so stop doubting.

Act 3

Scene 1

[*Pheroras, Salome.*]

PHERORAS Urge me no more Graphina to forsake,
Not twelve hours since I married her for love;
And do you think a sister's power can make
A resolute decree, so soon remove?
SALOME Poor minds they are that honor not affects.
PHERORAS Who hunts for honor, happiness neglects.
SALOME You might have been both of felicity,
And honor too in equal measure seized.
PHERORAS It is not you can tell so well as I,
What 'tis can make me happy, or displeased.
SALOME To match for neither beauty nor respects
One mean of birth, but yet of meaner mind,
A woman full of natural defects,
I wonder what your eye in her could find.
PHERORAS Mine eye found loveliness, mine ear found wit,
To please the one, and to enchant the other;
Grace on her eye, mirth on her tongue doth sit,
In looks a child, in wisdom's house a mother.
SALOME But say you thought her fair, as none thinks else,
Knows not Pheroras, beauty is a blast;[4]
Much like this flower which today excels,
But longer than a day it will not last.
PHERORAS Her wit exceeds her beauty.
SALOME Wit may show
The way to ill as well as good you know.
PHERORAS But wisdom is the porter of her head,
And bars all wicked words from issuing thence.
SALOME But of a porter, better were you sped,° *provided*
If she against their entrance made defense.[5]
PHERORAS But wherefore comes the sacred Ananell,[6]
That hitherward his hasty steps doth bend?
Great sacrificer y'are arrived well,
Ill news from holy mouth I not attend.° *expect*

Scene 2

[*Pheroras, Salome, Ananell.*]

ANANELL My lips, my son, with peaceful tidings bless'd,
Shall utter honey to your list'ning ear;
A word of death comes not from priestly breast,
I speak of life: in life there is no fear.
And for the news I did the Heavens salute,
And filled the temple with my thankful voice;

4. A brief gust of wind.
5. See *Othello*, 3.3.136–41, page 1219.
6. Herod first had made Ananelus high priest, but then, he gave the position to Mariam's brother Aristobolus. After a year, jealous of Aristobulus' popularity, Herod had him killed and made Ananelus high priest again.

For though that mourning may not me pollute,[7]
At pleasing accidents I may rejoice.
PHERORAS Is Herod then revived from certain death?
SALOME What? Can your news restore my brother's breath?
ANANELL Both so, and so, the king is safe and sound,
And did such grace in royal Caesar meet;
That he with larger style than ever crowned,
Within this hour Jerusalem will greet.
I did but come to tell you, and must back
To make preparatives for sacrifice;
I knew his death, your hearts like mine did rack,
Though to conceal it, proved you wise. [*Exit.*]
SALOME How can my joy sufficiently appear?
PHERORAS A heavier tale did never pierce mine ear.
SALOME Now Salome of happiness may boast.
PHERORAS But now Pheroras is in danger most.
SALOME I shall enjoy the comfort of my life.
PHERORAS And I shall lose it, losing of my wife.
SALOME Joy heart, for Constabarus shall be slain.
PHERORAS Grieve soul, Graphina shall from me be ta'en.
SALOME Smile, cheeks, the fair Silleus shall be mine.
PHERORAS Weep, eyes, for I must with a child combine.
SALOME Well, brother, cease your moans, on one condition
I'll undertake to win the King's consent;
Graphina still shall be in your tuition,° *care*
And her with you be ne'er the less content.
PHERORAS What's the condition? Let me quickly know,
That I as quickly your command may act;
Were it to see what herbs in Ophir grow,
Or that the lofty Tyrus might be sacked.[8]
SALOME 'Tis not so hard a task; it is no more,
But tell the king that Constabarus hid
The sons of Babas, done to death before;[9]
And 'tis no more than Constabarus did.
And tell him more that he for Herod's sake,
Not able to endure his brother's foe,
Did with a bill our separation make,
Though loath from Constabarus else to go.
PHERORAS Believe this tale for told, I'll go from hence,
In Herod's ear the Hebrew to deface;
And I that never studied eloquence,
Do mean with eloquence this tale to grace. [*Exit.*]
SALOME This will be Constabarus' quick dispatch,
Which from my mouth would lesser credit find;
Yet shall he not decease without a match,
For Mariam shall not linger long behind.
First, jealousy, if that avail not, fear

7. Priests had to avoid ritually defiling contact with corpses in mourning rites (Leviticus 21.1–2).
8. Ophir, on the west coast of Arabia or India, was a source of gold. Tyre, on the coast of Lebanon, was the greatest city of ancient Phoenicia.
9. Assumed to have been put to death.

Shall be my minister to work her end.
A common error moves not Herod's ear,
Which doth so firmly to his Mariam bend.
She shall be charged with so horrid crime,
As Herod's fear shall turn his love to hate;
I'll make some swear that she desires to climb,
And seeks to poison him for his estate.° *royal position*
I scorn that she should love my birth t'upbraid,
To call me base and hungry Edomite;
With patient show her choler I betrayed,[1]
And watched the time to be revenged by slight.
Now tongue of mine with scandal load her name,
Turn hers to fountains, Herod's eyes to flame;
Yet first I will begin Pheroras' suit,
That he my earnest business may effect;
And I of Mariam will keep me mute,
'Till first some other doth her name detect.° *accuse*
Who's there, Silleus' man? How fares your lord
That your aspects do bear the badge of sorrow?

SILLEUS' MAN He hath the marks of Constabarus' sword,
And for a while desires you sight to borrow.

SALOME My heavy curse the hateful sword pursue;
My heavier curse on the more hateful arm
That wounded my Silleus. But renew
Your tale again. Hath he no mortal harm?

SILLEUS' MAN No sign of danger doth in him appear,
Nor are his wounds in place of peril seen;
He bids you be assured you need not fear,
He hopes to make you yet Arabia's queen.

SALOME Commend my heart to be Silleus' charge.
Tell him my brother's sudden coming now
Will give my foot no room to walk at large,
But I will see him yet ere night I vow.

Scene 3

[*Mariam and Sohemus.*]

MARIAM Sohemus, tell me what the news may be
That makes your eyes so full, your cheeks so blue?

SOHEMUS I know not how to call them. Ill for me
'Tis sure they are; not so, I hope, for you.
Herod—

MARIAM Oh what of Herod?

SOHEMUS Herod lives.

MARIAM How! Lives? What, in some cave or forest hid?

SOHEMUS Nay, back returned with honor. Caesar gives
Him greater grace than ere Anthonius did.

MARIAM Foretell the ruin of my family,
Tell me that I shall see our city burned,

1. By pretending patience, I provoked her to anger.

Tell me I shall a death disgraceful die,
But tell me not that Herod is returned.

SOHEMUS Be not impatient madam, be but mild,
His love to you again will soon be bred.

MARIAM I will not to his love be reconciled,
With solemn vows I have forsworn his bed.

SOHEMUS But you must break those vows.

MARIAM I'll rather break
The heart of Mariam. Cursed is my fate.
But speak no more to me, in vain ye speak° *tell me*
To live with him I so profoundly hate.

SOHEMUS Great Queen, you must to me your pardon give,
Sohemus cannot now your will obey;
If your command should me to silence drive,
It were not to obey, but to betray.
Reject and slight my speeches, mock my faith,
Scorn my observance, call my counsel nought
Though you regard not what Sohemus saith,
Yet will I ever freely speak my thought.
I fear ere long I shall fair Mariam see
In woeful state and by herself undone;
Yet for your issue's sake more temp'rate be,
The heart by affability is won.

MARIAM And must I to my prison turn again?
Oh, now I see I was an hypocrite;
I did this morning for his death complain,
And yet do mourn, because he lives ere night.
When I his death believed, compassion wrought,
And was the stickler° 'twixt my heart and him; *mediator*
But now that curtain's drawn from off my thought,
Hate doth appear again with visage grim,
And paints the face of Herod in my heart,
In horrid colors with detested look.
Then fear would come, but scorn doth play her part,
And saith that scorn with fear can never brook.° *put up with*
I know I could enchain him with a smile,
And lead him captive with a gentle word;
I scorn my look should ever man beguile,
Or other speech, than meaning° to afford. *what I mean*
Else Salome in vain might spend her wind,
In vain might Herod's mother whet her tongue,
In vain had they complotted and combined,
For I could overthrow them all ere long.
Oh what a shelter is mine innocence,
To shield me from the pangs of inward grief,
'Gainst all mishaps it is my fair defense,
And to my sorrows yields a large relief.
To be commandress of the triple earth,
And sit in safety from a fall secure:
To have all nations celebrate my birth,
I would not that my spirit were impure.

Let my distressed state unpitied be,
Mine innocence is hope enough for me. [*Exit.*]

SOHEMUS Poor guiltless Queen. Oh that my wish might place
A little temper° now about thy heart; *moderation*
Unbridled speech is Mariam's worst disgrace,
And will endanger her without desert.[2]
I am in greater hazard. O'er my head,
The fatal ax doth hang unsteadily;
My disobedience once discovered
Will shake it down: Sohemus so shall die.
For when the king shall find we thought his death
Had been as certain as we see his life,
And marks withall I slighted so his breath,° *order*
As to preserve alive his matchless wife.
Nay more, to give to Alexander's hand[3]
The regal dignity. The sovereign power,
How I had yielded up at her command
The strength of all the city, David's Tower.
What more than common death may I expect,
Since I too well do know his cruelty?
'Twere death, a word of Herod's to neglect,
What then to do directly contrary?
Yet life I quit thee with a willing spirit,
And think thou could'st not better be employed;
I forfeit thee for her that more doth merit,
Ten such° were better dead than she destroyed. *such as I*
But fare thee well chaste Queen, well may I see
The darkness palpable and rivers part,
The sun stand still, nay more, retorted° be, *turned backward*
But never woman with so pure a heart.
Thine eyes' grave majesty keeps all in awe,
And cuts the wings of every loose desire;
Thy brow is table° to the modest law, *tablet*
Yet though we dare not love, we may admire.
And if I die, it shall my soul content,
My breath in Mariam's service shall be spent.

CHORUS 'Tis not enough for one that is a wife
To keep her spotless from an act of ill;
But from suspicion she should free her life,[4]
And bare herself of power as well as will.
'Tis not so glorious for her to be free,
As by her proper° self restrained to be. *own*

When she hath spacious ground to walk upon,
Why on the ridge should she desire to go?
It is no glory to forebear alone° *only*
Those things that may her honor overthrow.

2. Without her deserving it.
3. To Mariam's son.
4. Conduct books for women stressed that they should be pure not only in deed but also in reputation.

But 'tis thank-worthy, if she will not take
All lawful liberties for honor's sake.

That wife her hand against her fame doth rear,
That more than to her lord alone will give
A private word to any second ear,
And though she may with reputation live,
Yet though most chaste, she doth her glory blot,
And wounds her honor, though she kills it not.

When to their husbands they themselves do bind,
Do they not wholly give themselves away?
Or give they but their body not their mind,
Reserving that though best, for other's prey?
No sure, their thoughts no more can be their own,
And therefore should to none but one be known.

Then she usurps upon another's right,
That seeks to be by public language graced;
And though her thoughts reflect with purest light,
Her mind if not peculiar° is not chaste. *kept private*
For in a wife it is no worse to find,
A common° body, than a common mind. *shared, public*

And every mind though free from thought of ill,
That out of glory[5] seeks a worth to show;
When any's ears but one therewith they fill,
Doth in a sort her pureness overthrow.
Now Mariam had (but that to this she bent)[6]
Been free from fear, as well as innocent.

Act 4

Scene 1

[*Enter Herod and his attendants*.]

HEROD Hail happy city, happy in thy store,° *abundance*
And happy that thy buildings such we see;
More happy in the temple where w'adore,
But most of all that Mariam loves in thee. [*Enter Nuntio*.]
Art thou returned? How fares my Mariam? How?[7]

NUNTIO She's well my Lord, and will anon be here
As you commanded.

HEROD Muffle up thy brow,
Thou day's dark taper.[8] Mariam will appear.
And where she shines, we need not thy dim light.
Oh haste thy steps rare creature, speed thy pace,
And let thy presence make the day more bright,
And cheer the heart of Herod with thy face.

5. Out of a desire for glory.
6. Except that she wanted to speak about herself to more than one person.
7. Modern editors have added "How?" to correct the rhyme scheme.
8. Candle, "day's dark taper," as a metaphor for the sun.

It is an age since I from Mariam went,
Methinks our parting was in David's days;[9]
The hours are so increased by discontent,
Deep sorrow, Joshua-like the season stays;[1]
But when I am with Mariam, time runs on,
Her sight can make months minutes, days of weeks;
An hour is then no sooner come than gone,
When in her face mine eye for wonders seeks.
You world-commanding city, Europe's grace,
Twice hath my curious eye your streets surveyed,
And I have seen the statue-fillèd place,
That once if not for grief had been betrayed.
I all your Roman beauties have beheld,
And seen the shows your ediles° did prepare, *Roman magistrates*
I saw the sum of what in you excelled,
Yet saw no miracle like Mariam rare.
The fair and famous Livia,[2] Caesar's love,
The world's commanding mistress did I see,
Whose beauties both the world and Rome approve,
Yet Mariam, Livia is not like to thee.
Be patient but a little, while mine eyes
Within your compassed limits be contained;
That object straight shall your desires suffice,
From which you were so long a while restrained.
How wisely Mariam doth the time delay,
Least sudden joy my sense should suffocate;
I am prepared, thou needst no longer stay.
Who's there, my Mariam, more than happy fate?
Oh no, it is Pheroras, welcome brother,
Now for a while, I must my passion smother.

Scene 2

[*Herod, Pheroras.*]

PHERORAS All health and safety wait upon my Lord,
And may you long in prosperous fortunes live
With Rome-commanding Caesar at accord,
And have all honors that the world can give.

HEROD Oh brother, now thou speakst not from thy heart;
No, thou hast struck a blow at Herod's love
That cannot quickly from my memory part,
Though Salome did me to pardon move.
Valiant Phasaelus,[3] now to thee farewell,
Thou wert my kind and honorable brother;
Oh hapless hour, when you self-stricken fell,
Thou father's image, glory of thy mother.
Had I desired a greater suit of thee

9. A thousand years before.

1. Joshua ordered the sun to keep shining so the Israelites could finish a battle (Joshua 10.12–14).

2. Wife of the Emperor Augustus.

3. Herod's brother Phasaelus killed himself to escape the disgrace of being executed by his enemies, who captured him in the war against Herod's rival, Antigonus.

Than to withhold thee from a harlot's bed,
Thou shouldst have granted it; but now I see
All are not like that in a womb are bred.
Thou wouldst not, hadst thou heard of Herod's death,
Have made his burial time, thy bridal hour;
Thou wouldst with clamors, not with joyful breath,
Have showed the news to be not sweet but sour.

PHERORAS Phasaelus' great worth I know did stain
Pheroras' petty valor; but they lie
(Excepting you yourself) that dare maintain
That he did honor Herod more than I.
For what I showed, love's power constrained me show,
And pardon loving faults[4] for Mariam's sake.

HEROD Mariam, where is she?

PHERORAS Nay, I do not know,
But absent use of her fair name I make;
You have forgiven greater faults than this,
For Constabarus that against your will
Preserved the sons of Baba, lives in bliss,
Though you commanded him the youths to kill.

HEROD Go, take a present order for his death,
And let those traitors feel the worst of fears;
Now Salome will whine to beg his breath,
But I'll be deaf to prayers and blind to tears.

PHERORAS He is my lord from Salome divorced,
Though her affection did to leave him grieve;
Yet was she by her love to you enforced
To leave the man that would your foes relieve.

HEROD Then haste them to their death. I will requite
Thee gentle Mariam—Salome, I mean—
The thought of Mariam doth so steal my spirit,
My mouth from speech of her I cannot wean. [*Exit.*]

Scene 3

[*Herod, Mariam.*]

HEROD And here she comes indeed. Happily met
My best and dearest half. What ails my dear?
Thou doest the difference certainly forget
'Twixt dusky habits and a time so clear.[5]

MARIAM My lord, I suit my garment to my mind,
And there no cheerful colors can I find.

HEROD Is this my welcome? Have I longed so much
To see my dearest Mariam discontent?
What is't that is the cause thy heart to touch?
Oh speak, that I thy sorrow may prevent.
Art thou not Jewry's queen and Herod's too?
Be my commandress, be my sovereign guide;

4. Errors motivated by love.

5. You have forgotten how inappropriate dark clothes are for such a bright and joyful day.

To be by thee directed I will woo,
For in thy pleasure lies my highest pride.
Or if thou think Judea's narrow bound
Too strict a limit for thy great command,
Thou shalt be Empress of Arabia crowned,
For thou shalt rule, and I will win the land.
I'll rob the holy David's sepulcher
To give thee wealth, if thou for wealth do care;
Thou shalt have all they did with him inter,
And I for thee will make the temple bare.

MARIAM I neither have of power nor riches want,
I have enough, nor do I wish for more;
Your offers to my heart no ease can grant,
Except they could my brother's life restore.
No, had you wished the wretched Mariam glad,
Or had your love to her been truly tied,
Nay, had you not desired to make her sad,
My brother nor my grandsire had not died.

HEROD Wilt thou believe no oaths to clear thy lord?
How oft have I with execration° sworn *curses*
Thou art by me beloved, by me adored;
Yet are my protestations heard with scorn.
Hircanus plotted to deprive my head
Of this long-settled honor that I wear.
And therefore I did justly doom him dead,
To rid the realm from peril, me from fear.
Yet I for Mariam's sake do so repent
The death of one whose blood she did inherit;
I wish I had a kingdom's treasure spent,
So I had ne'er expelled Hircanus' spirit.
As I affected that same noble youth,[6]
In lasting infamy my name enroll,
If I not mourned his death with hearty truth.
Did I not show to him my earnest love,
When I to him the priesthood did restore?
And did for him a living priest remove,
Which never had been done but once before.

MARIAM I know that moved by importunity,
You made him priest, and shortly after die.

HEROD I will not speak, unless to be believed,
This froward° humor will not do you good; *perverse*
It hath too much already Herod grieved,
To think that you on terms of hate have stood.
Yet smile my dearest Mariam, do but smile,
And I will all unkind conceits° exile. *thoughts*

MARIAM I cannot frame disguise, nor never taught
My face a look dissenting from my thought.

HEROD By heaven, you vex me, build not on my love.

6. Since I was fond of Aristobolus ("that same noble youth"), Mariam's young brother, whom Herod had murdered. There may be a missing line just before this one, since the rhyme scheme is interrupted here.

MARIAM I will not build on so unstable ground.
HEROD Nought is so fixed, but peevishness may move.
MARIAM 'Tis better slightest cause than none were found.
HEROD Be judge yourself, if ever Herod sought
Or would be moved a cause of change to find;
Yet let your look declare a milder thought,
My heart again you shall to Mariam bind.
How oft did I for you my mother chide,
Revile my sister, and my brother 'rate,° *berate*
And tell them all my Mariam they belied,° *told lies about*
Distrust me still, if these be signs of hate.

Scene 4

[*Enter Butler.*]
HEROD What hast thou here?
BUTLER A drink procuring love
The queen desired me to deliver it.
MARIAM Did I? Some hateful practice° this will prove, *intrigue*
Yet can it be no worse than heaven's permit.
HEROD [*To the Butler.*] Confess the truth thou wicked instrument
To her outrageous will, 'tis poison sure;[7]
Tell true, and thou shalt 'scape the punishment,
Which, if thou do conceal, thou shalt endure.
BUTLER I know not, but I doubt it be no less,
Long since the hate of you her heart did seize.
HEROD Know'st thou the cause thereof?
BUTLER My Lord I guess
Sohemus told the tale that did displease.
HEROD Oh heaven! Sohemus false! Go let him die,
Stay not to suffer him to speak a word;
Oh damned villain, did he falsify
The oath he swore ev'n of his own accord?
Now did I know thy falsehood, painted devil,
Thou white enchantress.[8] Oh thou art so foul
That hyssop[9] cannot cleanse thee, worst of evil.
A beauteous body hides a loathsome soul,
Your love Sohemus moved by his affection,
Though he have ever heretofore been true
Did blab forsooth, that I did give direction,
If we were put to death to slaughter you.
And you in black revenge attended° now *waited*
To add a murther to your breach of vow.
MARIAM Is this a dream?
HEROD Oh heaven, that 'twere no more
I'll give my realm to who can prove it so;
I would I were like any beggar poor,

7. The text reads "passion," but editors have emended this to "poison" to make sense of the plot and to follow Cary's source, Josephus's *Antiquities*.
8. "White," appearing to be good, with a possible allusion to the Renaissance notion of a "white devil," a hypocritical woman.
9. An herb used to treat lepers.

So I for false my Mariam did not know.
Foul pith contained in the fairest rind,
That ever graced a cedar. Oh thine eye
Is pure as heaven, but impure thy mind,
And for impurity shall Mariam die.
Why didst thou love Sohemus?

MARIAM They can tell
That say I loved him, Mariam says not so.

HEROD Oh cannot impudence the coals expel,
That for thy love in Herod's bosom glow?
It is as plain as water, and denial
Makes of thy falsehood but a greater trial.
Hast thou beheld thyself, and couldst thou stain
So rare perfection. Even for love of thee
I do profoundly hate thee. Wert thou plain,
Thou shouldst the wonder of Judea be.
But oh thou art not. Hell itself lies hid
Beneath thy heavenly show. Yet never wert thou chaste;
Thou might'st exalt, pull down, command, forbid,
And be above the wheel of fortune placed.[1]
Hadst thou complotted Herod's massacre,
That so thy son a monarch might be styled,
Not half so grievous such an action were,
As once to think, that Mariam is defiled.
Bright workmanship of nature sullied o'er,
With pitched darkness now thine end shall be.
Thou shalt not live fair fiend to cozen° more, trick
With heavy[2] semblance, as thou cozenest me.
Yet must I love thee in despite of death,
And thou shalt die in the despite of love;
For neither shall my love prolong thy breath,
Nor shall thy loss of breath my love remove.
I might have seen thy falsehood in thy face,
Where couldst thou get thy stars that served for eyes?
Except by theft, and theft is foul disgrace.
This had appeared before were Herod wise,
But I'm a sot,° a very sot, no better; fool
My wisdom long ago a-wandering fell,
Thy face encountering it, my wit did fetter,
And made me for delight my freedom sell.
Give me my heart, false creature, 'tis a wrong,
My guiltless heart should now with thine be slain;
Thou hadst no right to lock it up so long,
And with usurper's name I Mariam stain.

[Enter Butler.]

HEROD Have you designed Sohemus to his end?

BUTLER I have my Lord.

HEROD Then call our royal guard
To do as much for Mariam. *[Exit Butler.]* They offend

1. Free from reversals of fortune.

2. Perhaps an error for "heavenly."

Leave[3] ill unblamed, or good without reward. [*Enter soldiers.*]
Here, take her to her death. Come back, come back,
What meant I to deprive the world of light;
To muffle Jewry in the foulest black,
That ever was an opposite to white?
Why whither would you carry her?

SOLDIER You bade
We should conduct her to her death my Lord.

HEROD Why, sure I did not, Herod was not mad.
Why should she feel the fury of the sword?
Oh now the grief returns into my heart,
And pulls me piecemeal. Love and hate do fight,
And now hath love acquired the greater part,
Yet now hath hate affection conquered quite.
And therefore bear her hence: and, Hebrew, why
Seize you with lion's paws the fairest lamb
Of all the flock? She must not, shall not, die.
Without her I most miserable am.
And with her more than most. Away, away,
But bear her but to prison not to death;
And is she gone indeed? Stay, villains, stay,
Her looks alone preserved your sovereign's breath.
Well, let her go, but yet she shall not die;
I cannot think she meant to poison me;
But certain 'tis she lived too wantonly,
And therefore shall she never more be free. [*They exit.*]

Scene 5

BUTLER Foul villain, can thy pitchy-colored soul
Permit thine ear to hear her causeless doom?° *fate*
And not enforce thy tongue that tale control,[4]
That must unjustly bring her to her tomb?
Oh Salome thou hast thyself repaid
For all the benefits that thou hast done;
Thou art the cause I have the queen betrayed,
Thou hast my heart to darkest falsehood won.
I am condemned, Heav'n gave me not my tongue
To slander innocents, to lie, deceive,
To be that hateful instrument to wrong,
The earth of greatest glory to bereave.
My sin ascends and doth to Heav'n cry,
It is the blackest deed that ever was,
And there doth fit an angel notary,
That doth record it down in leaves of brass.
Oh how my heart doth quake. Achitophel,
Thou founds° a means thyself from shame to free;[5] *foundest*

3. Who leave.
4. And not compel your tongue to hold back the tale.
5. When King David's son Absalom rebelled against his father, his counselor Achitophel urged a decisive quick strike. Absalom rejected this advice; knowing their cause would be doomed by delay, Achitophel went home and hanged himself.

And sure my soul approves° thou didst not well, *judges*
All follow some, and I will follow thee. [*He exits*.]

Scene 6

[*Constabarus, Babas' sons, and their guard*.]

CONSTABARUS Now here we step our last, the way to death;
We must not tread this way a second time;
Yet let us resolutely yield our breath,
Death is the only ladder, heaven to climb.

FIRST SON With willing mind I could myself resign,
But yet it grieves me with a grief untold;
Our death should be accompanied with thine,
Our friendship we to thee have dearly sold.

CONSTABARUS Still wilt thou wrong the sacred name of friend?
Then shouldst thou never style it friendship more,
But base mechanic traffic[6] that doth lend;
Yet will be sure they shall the debt restore.
I could with needless complement return,
'Tis for thy ceremony I could say;
'Tis I that made the fire your house to burn,
For but for me she would not you betray.
Had not the damned woman sought mine end,
You had not been the subject of her hate.
You never did her hateful mind offend,
Nor could your deaths have freed her nuptial fate.
Therefore fair friends, though you were still unborn,
Some other subtlety devised should be,
Whereby my life, though guiltless should be torn;
Thus have I proved, 'tis you that die for me,
And therefore should I weakly now lament,
You have but done your duties; friends should die
Alone their friends' disaster to prevent,[7]
Though not compelled by strong necessity.
But now farewell, fair city, never more
Shall I behold your beauty shining bright;
Farewell, of Jewish men the worthy store,
But no farewell to any female wight.° *creature*
You wavering crew: my curse to you I leave,
You had but one to give you any grace;
And you yourselves will Mariam's life bereave,
Your commonwealth doth innocency chase.° *drive out*
You creatures made to be the human curse,
You tigers, lionesses, hungry bears,
Tear massacring hyenas:[8] nay far worse,
For they for prey do shed their feigned tears.
But you will weep, (you creatures cross° to good) *opposed*

6. Base business; "mechanics" are manual laborers, "traffic" is the exchange of goods or services.

7. Friends should be willing to die to save their friends' lives.

8. Hyenas were said to pretend to weep over their victims as they tore them to shreds. (See Pliny, *Natural History*, 8.44).

For your unquenchèd thirst of human blood;
You were the angels cast from Heav'n for pride,
And still do keep your angel's outward show,
But none of you are inly° beautified, *inwardly*
For still your heaven-depriving pride doth grow.
Did not the sins of man[9] require a scourge,
Your place on earth had been by this withstood;[1]
But since a flood no more the world must purge,
You stayed in office of a second flood.[2]
You giddy creatures, sowers of debate,
You'll love today, and for no other cause,
But for you yesterday did deeply hate,
You are the wreck of order, breach of laws.
Your best are foolish, froward,° wanton, vain, *perverse*
Your worst adulterous, murderous, cunning, proud;[3]
And Salome attends° the latter train,° *follows/set*
Or rather she their leader is allowed.
I do the sottishness° of men bewail, *foolishness*
That do with following you enhance your pride;
'Twere better that the human race should fail,
Than be by such a mischief multiplied.
Cham's servile curse to all your sex was given,
Because in Paradise you did offend;[4]
Then do we not resift the will of Heaven,
When on your wills like servants we attend?
You are to nothing constant but to ill,
You are with nought but wickedness indued,° *endowed*
Your loves are set on nothing but your will,
And thus my censure I of you conclude.
You are the least of goods, the worst of evils,
Your best are worse than men; your worst than devils.

SECOND SON Come, let us to our death: are we not bless'd?
Our death will freedom from these creatures give;
Those trouble-quiet° sowers of unrest, *peace-disturbing*
And this I vow that had I leave to live,
I would for ever lead a single life,
And never venture° on a devilish wife. *take a risk*

Scene 7

[Herod and Salome.]

HEROD Nay, she shall die. Die quoth you? That she shall.
But for the means. The means! Methinks 'tis hard

9. The text reads "many," but as Weller and Ferguson point out, both the meter and the meaning of the line call for the emendation to "man."
1. By this time denied.
2. As God promised never to send another worldwide flood, women had to perform the function of "scourge" to mankind.
3. For the tradition of misogyny such as this, see the work of Joseph Swetnam in Perspectives: Tracts on Women and Gender, pages 1335–1338.
4. A combination of the pain of childbirth, the curse upon Eve after the fall (Genesis 3), with slavery, the curse upon Canaan (the son of Cham or Ham) after Ham brought his brothers to see their father Noah's nakedness. (Genesis 9).

To find a means to murther her withall,
Therefore I am resolved she shall be spared.
SALOME Why? Let her be beheaded.
HEROD That were well,
Think you that swords are miracles like you?
Her skin will ev'ry curtlax° edge refell,° *heavy sword/repel*
And then your enterprise you well may rue.
What if the fierce Arabian notice take
Of this your wretched weaponless estate;
They[5] answer when we bid resistance make,
That Mariam's skin their falchions° did rebate.° *broadswords/blunt*
Beware of this, you make a goodly hand,
If you of weapons do deprive our land.
SALOME Why, drown her then.
HEROD Indeed, a sweet device,
Why? Would not ev'ry river turn her course
Rather than do her beauty prejudice?° *harm*
And be reverted° to the proper source? *driven back*
So not a drop of water should be found
In all Judea's quondam° fertile ground. *once*
SALOME Then let the fire devour her.
HEROD 'Twill not be;
Flame is from her derived° into my heart; *drawn off*
Thou nursest flame, flame will not murther thee,
My fairest Mariam, fullest of desert.
SALOME Then let her live for me.[6]
HEROD Nay, she shall die.
But can you live without her?
SALOME Doubt you that?
HEROD I'm sure I cannot; I beseech you try;
I have experience but I know not what.[7]
SALOME How should I try?
HEROD Why, let my love be slain,
But if we cannot live without her sight
You'll find the means to make her breathe again,
Or else you will bereave my comfort quite.
SALOME Oh I, I warrant° you. [*Exit.*] *assure*
HEROD What is she gone?
And gone to bid the world be overthrown?
What? Is her heart's composure hardest stone?
To what a pass are cruel women grown? [*Re-enter Salome.*]
She is returned already: have you done?
Is't possible you can command so soon
A creature's heart to quench the flaming sun,
Or from the sky to wipe away the moon?
SALOME If Mariam be the sun and moon, it is;

5. The people of Jerusalem.
6. As far as I am concerned.
7. I know not either what to do in this instance or what to do in the event of Mariam's death.

For I already have commanded this.
HEROD But have you seen her cheek?
SALOME A thousand times.
HEROD But did you mark it too?
SALOME Aye, very well.
HEROD What is't?
SALOME A crimson bush, that ever limes[8]
The soul whose foresight doth not much excel.
HEROD Send word she shall not die. Her cheek a bush,
Nay, then I see indeed you marked it not.
SALOME 'Tis very fair, but yet will never blush,
Though foul dishonors do her forehead blot.
HEROD Then let her die, 'tis very true indeed,
And for this fault alone shall Mariam bleed.
SALOME What fault my Lord?
HEROD What fault is't? You that ask,
If you be ignorant I know of none,
To call her back from death shall be your task,
I'm glad that she for innocent is known.
For on the brow of Mariam hangs a fleece,
Whose slenderest twine is strong enough to bind
The hearts of kings, the pride and shame of Greece,
Troy-flaming Helen's not so fairly shined.[9]
SALOME 'Tis true indeed, she lays them[1] out for nets,
To catch the hearts that do not shun a bait.
'Tis time to speak: for Herod sure forgets
That Mariam's very tresses hide deceit.
HEROD Oh do they so? Nay, then you do but well,
In sooth I thought it had been hair.
Nets call you then? Lord, how they do excel,
I never saw a net that showed so fair.
But have you heard her speak?
SALOME You know I have.
HEROD And were you not amazed?
SALOME No, not a whit.
HEROD Then 'twas not her you heard; her life I'll save,
For Mariam hath a world-amazing wit.
SALOME She speaks a beauteous language, but within
Her heart is false as powder, and her tongue
Doth but allure the auditors to sin,
And is the instrument to do you wrong.
HEROD It may be so: nay, 'tis so: she's unchaste,
Her mouth will ope° to ev'ry stranger's ear; *open*
Then let the executioner make haste,
Lest she enchant him, if her words he hear.

8. Entraps.
9. Mariam's hair is compared to the golden fleece, sought by Jason and the Argonauts, and the hair of Helen, the great beauty whose abduction was the cause of the Trojan War.
1. Strands of her hair.

Let him be deaf, lest she do him surprise
That shall to free her spirit be assigned.
Yet what boots° deafness if he have his eyes, *good is*
Her murtherer must be both deaf and blind.
For if he see, he needs must see the stars
That shine on either side of Mariam's face,
Whose sweet aspect will terminate the wars,
Wherewith he should a soul so precious chase.
Her eyes can speak, and in their speaking move;
Oft did my heart with reverence receive
The world's mandates. Pretty tales of love
They utter, which can humane bondage weave.
But shall I let this Heaven's model die?
Which for a small self-portraiture she° drew? *Heaven*
Her eyes like stars, her forehead like the sky,
She is like Heaven, and must be heavenly true.

SALOME Your thoughts do rave with doting on the queen,
Her eyes are ebon-hued,° and you'll confess, *dark black*
A sable star hath been but seldom seen;
Then speak of reason more, of Mariam less.

HEROD Yourself are held a goodly creature here,
Yet so unlike my Mariam in your shape
That when to her you have approached near,
Myself hath often ta'en you for an ape.
And yet you prate of beauty: go your ways,
You are to her a sun-burnt blackamoor;[2]
Your paintings[3] cannot equal Mariam's praise,
Her nature is so rich, you are so poor.
Let her be stayed from death, for if she die,
We do we know not what to stop her breath.[4]
A world cannot another Mariam buy,
Why stay you lingering? countermand her death.

SALOME Then you'll no more remember what hath past,
Sohemus' love, and hers shall be forgot;
'Tis well in truth, that fault may be her last,
And she may mend, though yet she love you not.

HEROD Oh God, 'tis true. Sohemus! Earth and heaven,
Why did you both conspire to make me curs'd,
In coz'ning° me with shows and proofs unev'n?° *tricking/unjust*
She showed the best, and yet did prove the worst.
Her show was such as had our singing king,
The holy David, Mariam's beauty seen,
The Hittite had then felt no deadly sting,
Nor Bathsheba had never been a queen.[5]

2. Female vice was often portrayed in terms of blackness. The Moors were thought of as black in the medieval and early modern periods.
3. Your face made up with cosmetics.
4. Compare with Luke 23.34, when Christ says of his executioners "they know not what they do."
5. When Bathsheba became pregnant by David, he ordered her husband Uriah the Hittite to go to war, where he would be killed in battle (2 Samuel 11).

Or had his son the wisest man of men,
Whose fond delight did most consist in change,[6]
Beheld her face, he had been stayed again;
No creature having her, can wish to range.
Had Asuerus seen my Mariam's brow,
The humble Jew, she might have walked alone,[7]
Her beauteous virtue should have stayed below,
Whiles Mariam mounted to the Persian throne.
But what avails it all? For in the weight° *balance*
She is deceitful, light as vanity.
Oh, she was made for nothing but a bait,
To train° some hapless man to misery. *mislead*
I am the hapless man that have been trained
To endless bondage. I will see her yet;
Methinks I should discern her if she feigned;
Can human eyes be dazed by woman's wit?
Once more these eyes of mine with hers shall meet,
Before the headsman° do her life bereave. *executioner*
Shall I forever part from thee, my sweet,
Without the taking of my latest leave?

SALOME You had as good resolve to save her now.
I'll stay her death, 'tis well determined;
For sure she nevermore will break her vow,
Sohemus and Josephus both are dead.

HEROD She shall not live, nor will I see her face;
A long-healed wound, a second time doth bleed;
With Joseph I remember her disgrace,
A shameful end ensues° a shameful deed. *follows*
Oh that I had not called to mind anew
The discontent of Mariam's wavering heart!
'Twas you, you foul-mouthed Até,[8] none but you,
That did the thought hereof to me impart.
Hence from my sight, my black tormenter hence,
For hadst not thou made Herod unsecure
I had not doubted Mariam's innocence,
But still had held her in my heart for pure.

SALOME I'll leave you to your passion; 'tis no time
To purge me now, though of a guiltless crime. [*Exit.*]

HEROD Destruction take thee; thou hast made my heart
As heavy as revenge, I am so dull,
Methinks I am not sensible of smart,
Though hideous horrors at my bosom pull.
My head weighs downwards; therefore will I go
To try if I can sleep away my woe. [*Exit.*]

Scene 8

[*Mariam.*]

MARIAM Am I the Mariam that presumed so much,

6. David's son Solomon was known for his wisdom and his many concubines (1 Kings 4.11).

7. See Esther 2 for how Ahasuerus made Esther (the humble Jew) queen.

8. "Até" in Greek means blindness or delusion and is goddess of discord.

And deemed my face must needs preserve my breath?
Ay, I it was that thought my beauty such,
As it alone could countermand my death.
Now death will teach me: he can pale as well
A cheek of roses as a cheek less bright,
And dim an eye whose shine doth most excel,
As soon as one that casts a meaner light.
Had not myself against myself conspired,
No plot, no adversary from without
Could Herod's love from Mariam have retired,
Or from his heart have thrust my semblance out.
The wanton queen that never loved for love,
False Cleopatra, wholly set on gain,
With all her flights did prove, yet vainly prove,° *try*
For her the love of Herod to obtain.
Yet her allurements, all her courtly guile,
Her smiles, her favors, and her smooth deceit
Could not my face from Herod's mind exile,
But were with him of less than little weight.
That face and person that in Asia late
For beauty's goddess, Paphos' queen[9] was ta'en,
That face that did captive° great Julius'[1] fate, *capture*
That very face that was Anthonius'[2] bane.° *ruin*
That face that to be Egypt's pride was born,
That face that all the world esteemed so rare.
Did Herod hate, despise, neglect, and scorn
When with the same, he Mariam's did compare?
This made that I improvidently wrought,
And on the wager even my life did pawn,
Because I thought, and yet but truly thought,
That Herod's love could not from me be drawn.
But now, though out of time, I plainly see
It could be drawn, though never drawn from me;
Had I but with humility been graced
As well as fair, I might have proved me wise;
But I did think because I knew me chaste,
One virtue for a woman might suffice.
That mind for glory of our sex might stand,
Wherein humility and chastity
Doth march with equal paces, hand in hand.
But one if single seen, who setteth by?° *values*
And I had singly one, but 'tis my joy,
That I was ever innocent, though sour.
And therefore can they but my life destroy;
My soul is free from adversary's power. [*Enter Doris.*]
You princes great in power and high in birth,
Be great and high, I envy not your hap;° *fortune*
Your birth must be from dust, your power on earth,

9. Aphrodite or Venus.
1. Julius Caesar.
2. Mark Antony.

In heaven shall Mariam sit in Sarah's lap.[3]

DORIS In heaven! Your beauty cannot bring you thither,
Your soul is black and spotted, full of sin;
You in adult'ry lived nine year together,
And Heav'n will never let adult'ry in.[4]

MARIAM What art thou that dost poor Mariam pursue?
Some spirit sent to drive me to despair,
Who sees for truth that Mariam is untrue?
If fair she be, she is as chaste as fair.

DORIS I am that Doris that was once beloved,
Beloved by Herod, Herod's lawful wife.
'Twas you that Doris from his side removed,
And robbed from me the glory of my life.

MARIAM Was that adult'ry? Did not Moses say,
That he that being matched did deadly hate
Might by permission put his wife away
And take a more beloved to be his mate?

DORIS What did he hate me for: for simple truth?
For bringing° beauteous babes for love to him, *giving birth to*
For riches, noble birth, or tender youth?
Or for no stain did Doris' honor dim?
Oh tell me Mariam, tell me if you know,
Which fault of these made Herod Doris' foe?
These thrice three years have I with hands held up,
And bowèd knees fast nailed to the ground,
Besought for thee the dregs of that same cup,
That cup of wrath that is for sinners found.
And now thou art to drink it: Doris' curse
Upon thyself did all this while attend,
But now it shall pursue thy children worse.

MARIAM Oh, Doris, now to thee my knees I bend,
That heart that never bowed to thee doth bow;
Curse not mine infants, let it thee suffice,
That Heav'n doth punishment to me allow.
Thy curse is cause that guiltless Mariam dies.

DORIS Had I ten thousand tongues, and ev'ry tongue
Inflamed with poison's power and steeped in gall,
My curses would not answer for my wrong,
Though I in cursing thee employed them all.
Hear thou that didst mount Gerizim[5] command,
To be a place whereon with cause to curse;
Stretch thy revenging arm, thrust forth thy hand,
And plague the mother much, the children worse.
Throw flaming fire upon the base-born heads
That were begotten in unlawful[6] beds.

3. With the wife of Abraham.
4. The charge of adultery against Mariam makes her analogous to Anne Boleyn, who was seen as an adulteress by some who objected to Henry VIII's divorce.
5. Weller and Ferguson emend Gerarim to Gerizim, named as the place of blessing in Deuteronomy 11, here confused with the twin mountain Ebal, a place of cursing.
6. Outside of marriage.

But let them live 'til they have sense to know
What 'tis to be in miserable state;
Then be their nearest friends their overthrow,
Attended be they by suspicious hate.
And, Mariam, I do hope this boy of mine
Shall one day come to be the death of thine.[7] [*Exit.*]

MARIAM Oh! Heaven forbid. I hope the world shall see,
This curse of thine shall be returned on thee.
Now earth farewell, though I be yet but young;
Yet I, methinks, have known thee too too long. [*Exit.*]

CHORUS The fairest action of our human life
Is scorning to revenge an injury;
For who forgives without a further strife,
His adversary's heart to him doth tie.
And 'tis a firmer conquest truly said,
To win the heart than overthrow the head.

If we a worthy enemy do find,
To yield to worth, it must be nobly done;[8]
But if of baser metal be his mind,
In base revenge there is no honor won.
Who would a worthy courage overthrow,
And who would wrestle with a worthless foe?

We say our hearts are great and cannot yield;
Because they cannot yield it proves them poor;
Great hearts are tasked beyond their power, but seld,° *seldom*
The weakest lion will the loudest roar.
Truths schooled for certain doth this same allow,
High-heartedness doth sometimes teach to bow.

A noble heart doth teach a virtuous scorn,
To scorn to owe a duty over-long,[9]
To scorn to be for benefits foreborn,[1]
To scorn to lie, to scorn to do a wrong.
To scorn to bear an injury in mind,
To scorn a free-born heart slave-like to bind.

But if for wrongs we needs revenge must have,
Then be our vengeance of the noblest kind;[2]
Do we his body from our fury save,
And let our hate prevail against our mind?[3]

7. Doris foretells the future, in which her son Antipater turns Herod against Mariam's sons.
8. We act nobly when we concede victory to a worthy enemy.
9. To delay in fulfilling an obligation.
1. Not being required to fulfill an obligation because of previous good deeds.
2. Forgiveness.
3. Do we allow our enemy to escape injury from our anger but then turn that anger against ourselves by holding a grudge?

What can ’gainst him a greater vengeance be,
Then make his foe more worthy far than he?

Had Mariam scorned to leave a due unpaid,
She would to Herod then have paid her love,
And not have been by sullen passion swayed.
To fix her thoughts all injury above
Is virtuous pride. Had Mariam thus been proved,[4]
Long, famous life to her had been allowed.

Act 5

Scene 1

[*Nuntio.*]

NUNTIO When, sweetest friend, did I so far offend
Your heavenly self, that you my fault to quit
Have made me now relator of your end,
The end of beauty, chastity and wit?[5]
Was none so hapless in the fatal place,
But I, most wretched, for the queen t’ choose,
’Tis certain I have some ill-boding face
That made me culled° to tell this luckless news. *picked*
And yet no news to Herod; were it new,
To him unhappy it had not been at all;[6]
Yet do I long to come within his view,
That he may know his wife did guiltless fall.
And here he comes. Your Mariam greets you well.

[*Enter Herod.*]

HEROD What? Lives my Mariam? Joy, exceeding joy,
She shall not die.

NUNTIO Heaven doth your will repel.

HEROD Oh, do not with thy words my life destroy,
I prithee tell no dying-tale; thine eye
Without thy tongue doth tell but too too much;
Yet let thy tongue’s addition make me die,
Death welcome, comes to him whose grief is such.

NUNTIO I went amongst the curious gazing troop,
To see the last of her that was the best:
To see if death had heart to make her stoop,
To see the sun admiring phoenix’[7] nest.
When there I came, upon the way I saw
The stately Mariam not debased by fear;
Her look did seem to keep the world in awe,
Yet mildly did her face this fortune bear.

HEROD Thou dost usurp my right, my tongue was framed

4. Had Mariam proved to be virtuously proud.
5. These lines are addressed to Mariam.
6. If Herod had been ignorant of (and not responsible for) Mariam’s death, the news of it would not be tragic to him.
7. A mythical bird, which burnt itself every 500 years only to emerge from its ashes renewed. The phoenix symbolized Christ’s resurrection. See the entry on the phoenix from Geoffrey Whitney’s *Choice of Emblems* in Perspectives: Emblem, Style, and Metaphor, page 1599.

To be the instrument of Mariam's praise;
Yet speak: she cannot be too often famed,
All tongues suffice not her sweet name to raise.
NUNTIO But as she came she Alexandra met,
Who did her death (sweet queen) no whit bewail,
But as if nature she did quite forget,
She did upon her daughter loudly rail.° *utter abuse*
HEROD Why stopped you not her mouth? Where had she words
To darken that, that heaven made so bright?
Our sacred tongue no epithet affords
To call her other than the world's delight.
NUNTIO She told her that her death was too too good,
And that already she had lived too long;
She said, she shamed to have a part in blood
Of her that did the princely Herod wrong.
HEROD Base pick-thank° devil. Shame, 'twas all her glory *flattering*
That she to noble Mariam was the mother;
But never shall it live in any story—
Her name, except to infamy I'll smother.
What answer did her princely daughter make?
NUNTIO She made no answer, but she looked the while,
As if thereof she scarce did notice take,
Yet smiled, a dutiful, though scornful smile.
HEROD Sweet creature, I that look to mind do call,
Full oft hath Herod been amazed withall.
Go on.
NUNTIO She came unmoved with pleasant grace,
As if to triumph her arrival were,
In stately habit, and with cheerful face;
Yet ev'ry eye was moist, but Mariam's there.
When justly opposite to me she came,
She picked me out from all the crew;
She beckoned to me, called me by my name,
For she my name, my birth, and fortune knew.
HEROD What, did she name thee? Happy, happy man,
Wilt thou not ever love that name the better?
But what sweet tune did this fair dying swan[8]
Afford thine ear. Tell all, omit no letter.
NUNTIO Tell thou my Lord, said she.
HEROD Me, meant she me?
Is't true, the more my shame: I was her lord;
Were I not mad, her lord I still should be;
But now her name must be by me adored.
Oh say, what said she more? Each word she said
Shall be the food whereon my heart is fed.
NUNTIO "Tell thou my Lord thou saw'st me loose[9] my breath."
HEROD Oh that I could that sentence now control![1]

8. The swan was said to sing at its death. See *Othello*, 5.2.253–57, page 1257.

9. Meaning "let go of" or "lose."

1. If only I could overturn her death sentence.

NUNTIO If guiltily eternal be my death,
HEROD I hold her chaste ev'n in my inmost soul.
NUNTIO By three days hence if wishes could revive,
I know himself would make me oft alive.[2]
HEROD Three days, three hours, three minutes, not so much,
A minute in a thousand parts divided,
My penitency for her death is such,
As in the first[3] I wished she had not died.
But forward in thy tale.
NUNTIO Why on she went,
And after she some silent prayer had said.
She did as if to die she were content,
And thus to Heav'n her heavenly soul is fled.
HEROD But art thou sure there doth no life remain?
Is't possible my Mariam should be dead?
Is there no trick to make her breathe again?
NUNTIO Her body is divided from her head.
HEROD Why, yet methinks there might be found by art
Strange ways of cure, 'tis sure rare things are done
By an inventive head and willing heart.
NUNTIO Let not, my Lord, your fancies idly run.
It is as possible it should be seen
That we should make the holy Abraham live,
Though he entombed two thousand years had been,
As breath again to slaughtered Mariam give.
But now for more assaults prepare your ears.
HEROD There cannot be a further cause of moan;
This accident shall shelter me from fears.
What can I fear? Already Mariam's gone.
Yet tell ev'n what you will.
NUNTIO As I came by,
From Mariam's death I saw upon a tree
A man that to his neck a cord did tie,
Which cord he had designed his end to be.
When me he once discerned, he downward bowed,
And thus with fearful voice, he cried aloud:
"Go tell the king he trusted ere he tried,
I am the cause that Mariam causeless died."
HEROD Damnation take him, for it was the slave
That said she meant with poison's deadly force
To end my life that she the crown might have,[4]
Which tale did Mariam from herself divorce.
Oh pardon me thou pure unspotted ghost,
My punishment must needs sufficient be,
In missing that content I valued most,
Which was thy admirable face to see.

2. The "three days" may allude to the time between Christ's death and resurrection.
3. The first thousandth of a minute.
4. The Butler's accusation that Mariam was attempting to take over the throne is not in Cary's source, Josephus's *Antiquities*.

I had but one inestimable jewel,[5]
Yet one I had no monarch had the like,
And therefore may I curse myself as cruel,
'Twas broken by a blow myself did strike.
I gazed thereon and never thought me bless'd,
But when on it my dazzled eye might rest,
A precious mirror made by wonderous art,
I prized it ten times dearer than my crown,
And laid it up fast-folded in my heart.
Yet I in sudden choler cast it down,
And pashed° it all to pieces. 'Twas no foe *smashed*
That robbed me of it; no Arabian host,
Nor no Armenian guide hath used me so;
But Herod's wretched self hath Herod crossed.
She was my graceful moiety;° me accursed, *half*
To slay my better half and save my worst.
But sure she is not dead, you did but jest,
To put me in perplexity a while;
'Twere well indeed if I could so be dressed:° *treated*
I see she is alive, methinks you smile.

NUNTIO If sainted Abel yet deceased be,[6]
'Tis certain Mariam is as dead as he.

HEROD Why then go call her to me, bid her now
Put on fair habit, stately ornament,
And let no frown o'ershade her smoothest brow;
In her doth Herod place his whole content.

NUNTIO She'll come in stately weeds° to please your sense, *clothes*
If now she come attired in robe of Heav'n.
Remember you yourself did send her hence,
And now to you she can no more be given.

HEROD She's dead, hell take her murderers, she was fair,
Oh what a hand she had, it was so white,
It did the whiteness of the snow impair.
I never more shall see so sweet a sight.

NUNTIO 'Tis true, her hand was rare.

HEROD Her hand? Her hands.
She had not singly one of beauty rare,
But such a pair as here where Herod stands;
He dares the world to make to both compare.[7]
Accursed Salome, hadst thou been still,° *silent*
My Mariam had been breathing by my side.
Oh never had I, had I had my will,
Sent forth command that Mariam should have died!
But Salome thou didst with envy vex,
To see thyself out-matchèd in thy sex;

5. See *Othello*, 5.2.353–55; "one whose hand / Like the base Indian, threw a pearl away / Richer than all his tribe", page 1260. The folio text reads "Judean" for "Indian" and thus may allude to Herod.

6. The death of innocent Abel in Genesis 4 was read as a prefiguration of Christ's death in the New Testament.

7. To find a pair of hands as beautiful as Mariam's.

Upon your sex's forehead Mariam sat,
To grace you all like an imperial crown;
But you, fond fool, have rudely pushed thereat,
And proudly pulled your proper glory down.
One smile of hers—nay—not so much—a look
Was worth a hundred thousand such as you;
Judea how canst thou the wretches brook,° *put up with*
That robbed from thee the fairest of the crew?
You dwellers in the now deprived land,
Wherein the matchless Mariam was bred,
Why grasp not each of you a sword in hand,
To aim at me our cruel sovereign's head.
Oh, when you think of Herod as your king,
And owner of the pride of Palestine,
This act to your remembrance likewise bring,
'Tis I have overthrown your royal line.
Within her purer veins the blood did run,
That from her grandam Sarah she derived,
Whose beldam° age the love of kings hath won; *old woman's*
Oh that her issue had as long been lived.
But can her eye be made by death obscure?° *dull*
I cannot think but it must sparkle still;
Foul sacrilege to rob those lights so pure,
From out a temple made by heavenly skill.
I am the villain that have done the deed,
The cruel deed, though by another's hand;
My word though not my sword made Mariam bleed,
Hircanus' grandchild did at my command—
That Mariam that I once did love so dear,
The partner of my now detested bed,
Why shine you sun with an aspect so clear?
I tell you once again my Mariam's dead.
You could but shine, if some Egyptian blowse
Or Ethiopian dowdy lose her life;[8]
This was—then wherefore bend you not your brows?—
The King of Jewry's fair and spotless wife.
Deny thy beams, and moon refuse thy light,
Let all the stars be dark, let Jewry's eye
No more distinguish which is day and night;
Since her best birth did in her bosom die.
Those fond idolaters, the men of Greece,
Maintain these orbs are falsely governèd;[9]
That each within themselves have gods a piece
By whom their steadfast course is justly led.
But were it so, as so it cannot be,

8. A "blowse" was a beggar's prostitute; a "dowdy" was a shabbily dressed woman. "Egyptian" here probably refers to Cleopatra.

9. In Ptolemaic astronomy the orbs are the hollow spheres that surround the earth and within which the planets revolve around the earth. Each was thought to be governed by one of the gods, each of whom embodied human qualities.

They all would put their mourning garments on;
Not one of them would yield a light to me,
To me that is the cause that Mariam's gone.
For though they feign their Saturn melancholy,
Of sour behaviors and of angry mood,
They feign him likewise to be just and holy,
And justice needs must seek revenge for blood.
Their Jove, if Jove he were, would sure desire,
To punish him that slew so fair a lass;
For Leda's beauty set his heart on fire,[1]
Yet she not half so fair as Mariam was.
And Mars would deem his Venus had been slain,[2]
Sol[3] to recover her would never stick;° *hesitate*
For if he want the power her life to gain,
Then physic's god is but an empiric.° *quack*
The Queen of Love would storm for beauty's sake,
And Hermes too, since he bestowed her wit;
The night's pale light for angry grief would shake,
To see chaste Mariam die in age unfit.
But, oh, I am deceived, she pass'd° them all *surpassed*
In every gift, in every property.° *quality*
Her excellencies wrought her timeless fall,
And they rejoiced, not grieved to see her die.
The Paphian goddess did repent her waste[4]
When she to one such beauty did allow;
Mercurius thought her wit his wit surpassed,
And Cynthia envied Mariam's brighter brow.[5]
But these are fictions, they are void of sense;
The Greeks but dream, and dreaming falsehoods tell.
They neither can offend nor give defense,
And not by them it was my Mariam fell.
If she had been like an Egyptian black[6]
And not so fair, she had been longer lived;
Her overflow of beauty turned back,
And drowned the spring from whence it was derived.
Her heavenly beauty 'twas that made me think
That it with chastity could never dwell;
But now I see that heaven in her did link
A spirit and a person° to excel. *appearance*
I'll muffle up myself in endless night,
And never let mine eyes behold the light.
Retire thyself vile monster, worse than he
That stained the virgin earth with brother's blood;[7]
Still in some vault or den enclosèd be,

1. Jove (or Jupiter) turned himself into a swan to rape Leda.
2. Mars, the god of war, was the lover of Venus, goddess of love and beauty.
3. Sol, or Apollo, was the god of the sun and of medicine.
4. The "Paphian goddess," Venus, would have regretted having given so much beauty to Mariam.
5. Cynthia, or Diana, goddess of chastity and of the moon.
6. Another allusion to Cleopatra.
7. Herod compares himself to Cain, who murdered Abel.

Where with thy tears thou mayst beget a flood,
Which flood in time may drown thee. Happy day
When thou at once shalt die and find a grave,
A stone upon the vault, someone shall lay,
Which monument shall an inscription have.
And these shall be the words it shall contain:
"Here Herod lies, that hath his Mariam slain." [*Exit.*]

CHORUS Who ever hath beheld with steadfast eye
The strange events of this one only day?[8]
How many were deceived? How many die,
That once today did grounds of safety lay?
It will from them all certainty bereave,
Since twice six hours so many can deceive.

This morning Herod held for surely dead,
And all the Jews on Mariam did attend;
And Constabarus rise from Salom's bed,
And neither dreamed of a divorce or end.
Pheroras joyed that he might have his wife,
And Babas' sons for safety of their life.

Tonight our Herod doth alive remain,
The guiltless Mariam is deprived of breath;
Stout Constabarus both divorced and slain,
The valiant sons of Babas have their death.
Pheroras sure his love to be bereft,
If Salome her suit unmade had left.[9]

Herod this morning did expect with joy
To see his Mariam's much belovèd face;
And yet ere night he did her life destroy,
And surely thought she did her name disgrace.
Yet now again so short do humors last,
He both repents her death and knows her chaste.

Had he with wisdom now her death delayed,
He at his pleasure might command her death;
But now he hath his power so much betrayed,
As all his woes cannot restore her breath.
Now doth he strangely lunaticly rave,
Because his Mariam's life he cannot save.

This day's events were certainly ordained,
To be the warning to posterity;
So many changes are therein contained,
So admirably strange variety.
This day alone, our sagest Hebrews shall
In after-times the school of wisdom call.

8. The play follows the unity of time, "one day," as required by neoclassical critics.

9. Pheroras would have lost Graphina if Salome had not interceded on his behalf with Herod.

PERSPECTIVES

Tracts on Women and Gender

What is the nature of woman? Is she meant to be subordinate to man or an equal partner? What virtues is she capable of? Does she have intellectual ability, and if so, is it appropriate for her to write? How should she behave toward her husband? What are his responsibilities to her? What is the difference between a good woman and a bad one? What is the difference between manly behavior and womanly behavior? These are some of the questions that early modern English tracts on women and gender ask. Although we would not ask all of these questions in precisely the same way today, they are still of burning interest. The debate over these questions in early modern tracts on women sheds light on the representation of sex and gender in the poetry and drama of the period. By *sex* is meant the representation of biological difference; by *gender* is meant the representation of sex difference as it is socially constructed.

In the Middle Ages there were both attacks on women and defenses of them by both women and men, but intellectual and social changes modified the debate in the early modern period. One of the prominent medieval genres that continued to be imitated in the early mod-

Title page from *The English Gentlewoman,* by Richard Brathwaite. 1631.

ern period was the praise of exemplary women, such as Boccaccio's *De Claris Mulieribus* ("concerning famous women"), Chaucer's *Legend of Good Women*, and Christine de Pisan's *Le Livre de la Cité des Dames* (translated into English in 1521 as *The Book of the City of Ladies*). Renaissance humanism brought a new intellectual rigor to the genre. The German humanist Heinrich Cornelius Agrippa (1486–1535) stands out in the early Tudor controversy of the 1540s. Agrippa's *De Nobilitate et Praecellentia Foemenei Sexus* (translated in 1542 as *A Treatise of the Nobilitie and Excellencye of Woman Kynde*) not only lists Biblical and classical heroines but also examines how the place of women in society is determined by culture rather than nature: "And thus by these lawes, the women being subdued as it were by force of arms, are constrained to give place to men, and to obey their subduers, not by natural, nor divine necessity or reason, but by custom, education, fortune, and a certain tyrannical occasion." However, even a humanist author such as Erasmus, who had enlightened views on other social issues, had very strict views about the absolute subordination of wife to husband. Indeed, this subordination seems to have increased in intensity in the early modern period as the nuclear family headed by the father superseded the extended family, in which power was more dispersed throughout the network of kinship.

Among the learned, the new classical humanist education was still largely reserved for young men. Such changes moved the historian Joan Kelly Gadol to ask, "Did women have a Renaissance?" At the same time, some early modern women were educated enough to represent themselves in the debate on the nature of women, and they brought new perspectives to it. Margaret Tyler was one of the first English women to speak in defense of women as writers. Rachel Speght, the first polemical or argumentative woman writer in English, wrote her defense of women in response to a controversy set in motion by the publication of Joseph Swetnam's *An Arraignment of Lewd, Idle, Froward, and Unconstant Women* (1615). Swetnam was a misogynist (woman hater), but his tract had the virtue of eliciting defenses of women. Among these responses were *A Muzzle for Melastomus*, written from the theological perspective of Rachel Speght, and *Ester Hath Hanged Haman*, written from the more secular outlook of "Esther Sowernam" (a pen-name adopted to counter the "sweet" in the name Swetnam). Two other tracts of the 1620s, *Hic Mulier* ("the mannish woman") and *Haec Vir* ("the womanish man") humorously raised the problem of the blurring of genders and carried on a debate about the style of dress and behavior that men and women should adopt.

Whether these tracts take the form of an oration, a speech by one person, or a dialogue between two people (as in *Haec Vir*), they are all in lively conversation with each other, either directly or indirectly. They are also in a lively conversation with other texts in this period. Questions about marriage and a wife's relations with people other than her husband as well as a woman's speech and silence are dealt with directly in *Othello* and *The Tragedy of Mariam*. Representing only a fraction of the early modern literature on women and gender, these tracts attest to heightened interest in questions of gender, such as those posed by the speakers in Lady Mary Wroth's and Katherine Philips's poems and the cross-dressing, independent Moll Cutpurse of Thomas Dekker and Thomas Middleton's *The Roaring Girl*.

Desiderius Erasmus

1469?–1536

Erasmus was the author not only of the humorous *Encomium Morae* (*The Praise of Folly*), dedicated to his friend Thomas More, but also of numerous works on Christian morals. Although *The Praise of Folly* was translated into English only in 1551, Erasmus's *Coniugium* (c. 1523), a text on marriage, appeared in English as *A Mery Dialogue, Declaringe the Propertyes of Shrewde Shrewes, and Honest Wyves* as early as 1542. This text advocated wifely submissiveness but also domesticity for both men and women—concepts that influenced the English bourgeois notion of marriage. Richard Tavernour also translated Erasmus's writing on marriage as *A Ryght Frutefull Epystle Devised in Laude and Praise of Matrimony* (1534). The following passage from this text demonstrates a view of marriage as the closest possible bond between human beings—and, more than that, as a sacrament calling for the wife's sole loyalty to her husband and lasting even beyond death.

from In Laude and Praise of Matrimony

* * * if the most part of things (yea which be also bitter) are of a good man to be desired for none other purpose, but because they be honest, matrimony doubtless is chiefly to be desired whereof a man may doubt whether it hath more honesty than pleasure. For what thing is sweeter than with her to live, with whom ye may be most straightly coupled, not only in the benevolence of the mind, but also in the conjunction of the body? If a great delectation of mind be taken of the benevolence of our other kinsmen, since it is an especial sweetness to have one with whom ye may communicate the secret affections of your mind, with whom ye may speak even as it were with your own self, whom ye may safely trust, which supposeth your chances to be his, what felicity (think ye) have the conjunction of man and wife, than which no thing in the universal world may be found either greater or firmer. For with our other friends we be conjoined only with the benevolence of minds, with our wife we be coupled with most high love, with permixtion[1] of bodies, with the confederate band of the sacrament, and finally with the fellowship of all chances. Furthermore, in other friendships, how great simulation is there, how great falsity? Yea, they whom we judge our best friends, like as the swallows flee away when summer is gone, so they forsake us when fortune turneth her wheel. And sometime the fresher friend casts out the old. We hear of few whose fidelity endure till their lives' end. The wife's love is with no falsity corrupted, with no simulation obscured, with no chance of things minished,[2] finally with death only (nay not with death neither) withdrawn. She, the love of her parents, she, the love of her sisters, she, the love of her brethren, despiseth for the love of you, her only respect is to you, of you she hangeth,[3] with you she coveteth to die. * * *

* * * Do ye judge any pleasure to be compared with this so great a conjunction? If ye tarry at home there is at hand which shall drive away the tediousness of solitary being. If from home ye have one that shall kiss you when ye depart, long for you when ye be absent, receive you joyously when ye return. A sweet companion of youth, a kind solace of age. By nature yea any fellowship is delectable to man, as whom nature hath created to benevolence and friendship. This fellowship then how shall it not be most sweet, in which everything is common to them both? And contrarily, if we see the savage beasts also abhor[4] solitary living and delighted in fellowship, in my mind he is not once to be supposed a man, which abhoreth from[5] this fellowship most honest and pleasant of all. For what is more hateful than the man which (as though he were born only to himself) liveth for himself, seeketh for himself, spareth for himself, doth cost to himself, loveth no person, is loved of no person? Shall not such a monster be adjudged worthy to be cast out of all men's company into the mid sea with Timon the Athenian,[6] which because he fled all men's company, was called Misanthropus that is to say hate man * * *

1. A thorough mixture or mingling.
2. Diminished, lessened in power.
3. In the sense of clinging, holding fast, adhering.
4. Hate.
5. Shrink with horror from.
6. The story of how Timon shunned society after his friends abandoned him when he lost his wealth is told by Plutarch (the source for Shakespeare's *Timon of Athens*).

But I know well enough what among these, ye murmur against me. A blessed thing is wedlock, if all prove according to the desire, But what if a wayward wife chanceth?[7] What if an unchaste? What if unnatural children? There will run in your mind the examples of those whom wedlock have brought to utter destruction. Heap up as much as ye can, but yet these be the vices of men and not of wedlock. Believe me, an evil wife is not wont to chance, but to evil husbands. Put this unto it, that it lieth in you to choose out a good one. But what if after the marriage she be marred?[8] Of an evil husband (I will well) a good wife may be marred, but of a good, the evil is wont to be reformed and mended. We blame wives falsely. No man (if ye give any credence to men) had ever a shrew to his wife, but through his own default.[9]

Barnabe Riche
1542–1617

A veteran of wars in the Low Countries and Ireland and author of twenty-six books, Barnabe Riche led a life as fraught with contention as his writing. Best known as the author of *His Farewell to Military Profession* (1581), which contains the source for Shakespeare's *Twelfth Night*, Riche was both a keen observer of contemporary social life and a spy. Alongside his attacks on shameless city women in *My Lady's Looking Glass* (1616) and *A New Description of Ireland* (1610), he also portrays Dublin ladies as critics of his work in *A True and Kind Excuse* (1612)—an interesting episode documenting women's literacy in this period. His writing has the zealous spirit of reforming Protestantism and looks forward to the impassioned prose of radical dissenters in the Civil War. *My Lady's Looking Glass* was published by Thomas Adams, London, in 1616, and dedicated to Lady Saint Jones, wife of the Lord Deputy of Ireland. This text bears comparison with Riche's *Excellency of Good Women* (London, 1613), as well as numerous other Jacobean tracts on the conduct of women.

from My Lady's Looking Glass

But my promise was to give rules how to distinguish between a good woman and a bad, and promise is debt, but I must be well advised how I take the matter in hand; for we were better to charge a woman with a thousand defects in her soul, than with that one abuse of her body; and we must have two witnesses, besides our own eyes, to testify, or we shall not be believed: but I myself have thought of a couple that I hope will carry credit.

The first is the prophet Isaiah, that in his days challenged the daughters of Zion for their stretched-out necks, their wandering eyes, at their mincing and wanton demeanor as they passed through the streets: these signs and shows have ever been thought to be the special marks whereby to know a harlot.[1] But Solomon in a more particular manner better furnishes us with more assured notes, and to the end that we might the better distinguish the good woman from the bad, he delivereth their several qualities, and wherein they are opposite: and speaking of a good woman he saith, *She seeketh out wool and flax, and laboreth cheerfully with her hands: she overseeth the ways of her household, and eateth not the bread of idleness.*[2]

7. Comes about by chance.
8. Injured.
9. Fault.

1. See Isaiah 3.16.
2. See Proverbs 31.13, 27.

Solomon thinketh that a good woman should be a home *housewife*, he pointeth her out her housework. *She overseeth the ways of her household*, she must look to her children, her servants and family; but *the paths of a harlot* (he saith) *are movable, for now she is in the house, now in the streets, now she lies in wait in every corner*, she is still gadding from place to place, from person to person, from company to company; from custom to custom, she is evermore wandering: her feet are wandering, her eyes are wandering, her wits are wandering, *Her ways are like the ways of a serpent:* hard to be found out.[3]

A good woman (again) *opens her mouth with wisdom, the law of grace is in her tongue*: but *a harlot is full of words, she is loud and babbling*, saith Solomon.

She is bold, she is impudent, she is shameless, she cannot blush: and she that hath lost all these virtues hath lost her evidence of honesty: for the ornaments of a good woman are temperance in her mind, silence in her tongue, and bashfulness in her countenance.

It is not she that can lift up her heels highest in the dancing of a galliard,[4] she that is lavish of her lips or loose of her tongue.

Now if Solomon's testimony be good, the woman that is impudent, immodest, shameless, insolent, audacious, a night-walker, a company-keeper, a gadder from place to place, a reveller, a ramper, a roister, a rioter: she that has these properties, has the certain signs and marks of a harlot, as Solomon has avowed. Now what credit his words will carry in the Commissaries' court, I leave to those that be advocates, and proctors in women's causes.[5]

I have hitherto presented to your view the true resemblance of a harlot, as well what she is, as how she might be discerned: I would now give you the like notice of that notable *Strumpet, the whore of Babylon*,[6] that has made so many Kings and Emperors drunk with the cup of abominations, by whom the nations of the earth have so defiled themselves by their spiritual fornication, called in the Scripture by the name of *idolatry* (but now within the last five hundred years, amongst Christians) shadowed under the title of Popery. This harlot has her agents, Popes, Cardinals, Bishops, Abbots, Monks, Friars, Jesuits, Priests, with a number of other like, and all of them factors in her bands,[7] the professed enemies of the Gospel of Jesus Christ, that do superstitiously adore the crucifix, and are indeed enemies of the cross of Christ, and do tread his holy blood under their scornful feet: that build up devotion with ignorance, and do ring out their hot alarms in the ears of the unlearned, teaching that the light can be no light, that the Scriptures can be no Scriptures, nor the truth can be no truth, but by their allowance, and if they will say that high noon is midnight, we must believe them, and make no more ado but get us to bed.

Margaret Tyler

flourished 1578

Margaret Tyler is best known today for the preface to her translation of Diego Ortunez de Calahorra's Spanish prose romance *The Mirrour of Princely Deedes and Knighthood*, Book I (1578), in which she argues that women have the ability to write on any subject. She was a

3. See Proverbs 7.10–12.
4. A lively dance in triple time.
5. Commissaries' court: the court of a bishop's representative, which had jurisdiction over divorce and probate; advocates: pleaders, legal counselors; proctors: attorneys.
6. An image from Revelation 17, taken by Protestants to symbolize the Roman Catholic Church.
7. Agents in her leagues, or covenants.

waiting woman in the Catholic household of the Duke of Norfolk in the 1560s, where she may have read her translation aloud to the Duchess and her circle. In the preface to her translation, Tyler refers both to the "friends" who wanted her to return to her "old reading" and defends herself against potential critics who might object to her translating "matter more manlike than becometh my sex." She argues that she is more interested in virtue than in war and that, in any case, war affects women as much as it does men. The sixteenth-century humanist Vives had viewed romances as unsuitable for women readers, while male authors of romances often dedicated their work to women. Arguing for women's right to an education, Tyler reasons that if men can dedicate their texts to women, then women can read them, and that if women can read texts on such subjects as war and government, then they can write them.

from Preface to The First Part of the Mirror of Princely Deeds

Thou hast here, gentle Reader, the history of Trebatio, an Emperor in Greece: whether a true history of him indeed, or a feigned fable, I wot[1] not, neither did I greatly seek after it in the translation, but by me it is done into English for thy profit and delight. The chief matter therein contained, is of exploits of wars, and the parties therein named are especially renowned for their magnanimity and courage. * * * Such delivery as I have made I hope thou wilt friendly accept, the rather for that it is a woman's work, though in a story profane, and a matter more manlike than becometh my sex. But as for any manliness of the matter, thou knowest that it is not necessary for every trumpeter or drumstare[2] in the war to be a good fighter. They take wages only to incite others, though themselves have privy maims,[3] and are thereby recureless.[4] So, gentle reader, if my travail in Englishing this author may bring thee to a liking of the virtues herein commended, and by example thereof in thy princes' and countries' quarrel to hazard thy person, and purchase good name, as for hope of well deserving myself that way, I neither bend my self thereto, nor yet fear the speech of people if I be found backward. I trust every man holds not the plough, which would that the ground were tilled, and it is no sin to talk of Robin Hood, though you never shot in his bow. Or be it that the attempt were bold to intermeddle in arms, as the ancient Amazons[5] did, and in this story Claridiana doth, and in other stories not a few, yet to report of arms is not so odious, but that it may be borne withall, not only in you men which yourselves are fighters, but in us women, to whom the benefit in equal part appertains of your victories, either the matter is so commendable that it carries no discredit from the homeliness of the speaker, or that it is so generally known, that it fits every man to speak thereof. * * * But my defense is by example of the best, amongst which, many have dedicated their labors, some stories, some of war, some physic, some law, some as concerning government, some divine matters, unto diverse ladies and gentlewomen. And if men may and do bestow such of their travails upon gentlewomen, then may we women read such of their works as they dedicate to us, and if we may read them, why not further wade in them to the search of truth. * * * But to return to whatever the truth is, whether that women may not at all discourse in learning, for men late in their claim to being sole possessioners of knowledge, or whether they may in some manner, that is by limitation or appointment in some kind of learning, my persuasion hath been thus, that it is all one for a

1. Know.
2. Drummer.
3. Secret weaknesses.
4. Irrecoverable.
5. A tribe of female warriors described by Herodotus and other ancient Greek authors as living in Scythia.

woman to pen a story, as for a man to address his story to a woman. But amongst all my ill-willers, some I hope are not so straight that they would enforce me necessarily either not to write or to write of divinity. Whereas neither durst I trust mine own judgment sufficiently, if matter of controversy were handled, nor yet could I find any book in any tongue, which would not breed offense to some. But I perceive some may be rather angry to see their Spanish delight turned to all English pastime: they could well allow the story in Spanish, but they may not afford it so cheap, or they would have it proper to themselves. What natures such men be of, I list[6] not greatly to dispute, but my meaning hath been to make others partners of my liking, as I doubt not gentle reader, but if it shall please thee after serious matters to sport thyself with this Spaniard, that thou shalt find in him the just reward of malice and cowardice, with the good speed of honesty and courage, being able to furnish thee with sufficient store of foreign examples to both purposes. And as in such matters which have been rather devised to beguile time, than to breed matter of sad learning, he hath ever borne away any price which could season such delights with some profitable reading: so shalt thou have this stranger an honest man when need serveth, and at other times either a good companion to drive out a weary night, or a merry jest at thy board. And this much concerning this present story, that it is neither unseemly for a woman to deal in, neither greatly requiring a less staid age than mine is. But of these two points, gentle reader, I thought to give thee warning, lest perhaps understanding my name and years, there mightest be a wrong suspect[7] of my boldness and rashness, from which I would gladly free myself by this plain excuse, and if I may deserve thy good favor by like labor, when the choice is my own, I will have a special regard of thy liking. So I wish thee well.

Thine to use, M.T.[8]

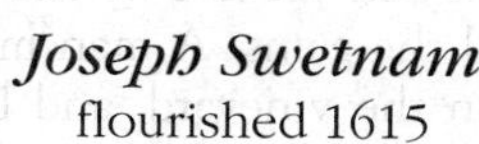

Joseph Swetnam
flourished 1615

Little is known about Joseph Swetnam other than that he stirred up an enormous controversy over the question of women when he wrote *An Arraignment of Lewd, Idle, Froward, and Unconstant Women* (1615). The work was published anonymously with an introductory letter signed by "Thomas Tel-troth." Trotting out all the negative stereotypes of women he could jumble together, Swetnam constructed his mock treatise as a piece of raucous comedy, aimed at the lowest common denominator. Reading Swetnam's work as a serious diatribe against women, Rachel Speght and the pseudonymous Esther Sowernam and Constantia Munda produced critiques of misogyny. Speght unmasked Swetnam's authorship and identified him as a fencing master in Bristol. An anonymous comedy, *Swetnam the Woman-hater, Arraigned by Women* (1620), possibly by Thomas Heywood, dramatized the debate as a court trial with Swetnam prosecuting his case against women and the Amazon Atlanta (a soldier disguised as a woman) defending them. Swetnam is finally turned over to a court of women, who find him guilty and muzzle him (an obvious reference to Speght's *Muzzle for Melastomus*).

6. Wish.
7. Suspicion.
8. Margaret Tyler.

from The Arraignment of Lewd, Idle, Froward, and Inconstant Women

from *Chapter 2. The Second Chapter showeth the manner of such women as live upon evil report: it also showeth that the beauty of women has been the bane of many a man, for it hath overcome valiant and strong men, eloquent and subtle men. And in a word it hath overcome all men, as by examples following shall appear.*

First, that of Solomon unto whom God gave singular wit and wisdom, yet he loved so many women that he quite forgot his God which always did guide his steps, so long as he lived godly and ruled justly, but after he had glutted himself with women, then he could say, vanity of vanity all is but vanity. He also in many places of his book of Proverbs exclaims most bitterly against lewd women calling them all that naught is, and also displayeth their properties, and yet I cannot let men go blameless although women go shameless; but I will touch them both, for if there were not receivers then there would not be so many stealers: if there were not some knaves there would not be so many whores, for they both hold together to bolster each other's villainy, for always birds of a feather will flock together hand in hand to bolster each other's villainy.

Men, I say, may live without women, but women cannot live without men. For Venus, whose beauty was excellent fair, yet when she needeth man's help she took Vulcan, a clubfooted smith. And therefore if a woman's face glister,[1] and her gesture pierce the marble wall, or if her tongue be as smooth as oil or as soft as silk, and her words so sweet as honey, or if she were a very ape for wit, or a bag of gold for wealth, or if her personage have stolen away all that nature can afford, and if she be decked up in gorgeous apparel, then a thousand to one but she will love to walk where she may get acquaintance, and acquaintance bringeth familiarity, and familiarity setteth all follies abroach,[2] and twenty to one that if a woman love gadding but that she will pawn her honor to please her fantasy.

Man must be at all the cost and yet live by the loss. A man must take all the pains and women will spend all the gains. A man must watch and ward, fight and defend, till the ground, labor in the vineyard, and look what he getteth in seven years; a woman will spread it abroad with a fork in one year, and yet little enough to serve her turn but a great deal too little to get her good will. Nay, if thou give her ever so much and yet if thy person please not her humor, then will I not give a halfpenny for her honesty at the year's end.

For then her breast will be the harborer of an envious heart, and her heart the storehouse of poisoned hatred; her head will devise villainy, and her hands are ready to practice that which their heart desireth. Then who can but say that women are sprung from the devil, whose heads, hands and hearts, minds and souls are evil, for women are called the hook of all evil, because men are taken by them as a fish is taken in with the hook.

For women have a thousand ways to entice thee, and ten thousand ways to deceive thee, and all such fools as are suitors unto them; some they keep in hand with promises, and some they feed with flattery, and some they delay with dalliances, and some they please with kisses. They lay out the folds of their hair to entangle men into their love; betwixt their breasts is the vale of destruction, and in their beds there is

1. Glitter, shine.

2. Flowing abroad.

hell, sorrow and repentance. Eagles do not eat men till they are dead, but women devour them alive, for a woman will pick thy pocket and empty thy purse, laugh in thy face and cut thy throat. They are ungrateful, perjured, full of fraud, flouting and deceit, unconstant, waspish,[3] toyish,[4] light, sullen, proud, discourteous and cruel, and yet they were by God created, and by nature formed, and therefore by policy and wisdom to be avoided, for good things abused are to be refused. Or else for a month's pleasure, she may make thee go stark naked. She will give thee roast meat, but she will beat thee with the spit. If thou hast crowns in thy purse, she will be thy heart's gold until she leave thee not a whit of white money. They are like summer birds, for they will abide no storm, but flock about thee in the pride of thy glory, and fly from thee in the storms of affliction; for they aim more at thy wealth than at thy person, and esteem more thy money than any man's virtuous qualities; for they esteem of a man without money as a horse does a fair stable without meat. They are like eagles which will always fly where the carrion is.

They will play the horse-leech to suck away thy wealth, but in the winter of thy misery, she will fly away from thee. Not unlike the swallow, which in the summer harboreth herself under the eaves of a house, and against winter flieth away, leaving nothing but dirt behind her.

Solomon saith, he that will suffer himself to be led away or to take delight in such women's company is like a fool which rejoiceth when he is led to the stocks. *Proverbs* 7.

Hosea, by marrying a lewd woman of light behavior was brought unto idolatry, *Hosea* 1. Saint Paul accounteth fornicators so odious, that we ought not to eat meat with them. He also showeth that fornicators shall not inherit the kingdom of Heaven, *1 Corinthians* the 9th and 11th verse.

And in the same chapter Saint Paul excommunicateth fornicators, but upon amendment he receiveth them again. Whoredom punished with death, *Deuteronomy* 22.21 and *Genesis* 38.24. Phineas a priest thrust two adulterers, both the man and the woman, through the belly with a spear, *Numbers* 25.

God detests the money or goods gotten by whoredom, *Deuteronomy* 23.17, 18. Whores called by diverse names, and the properties of whores, *Proverbs* 7.6 and 21. A whore envieth an honest woman, *Esdras* 16 and 24. Whoremongers God will judge, *Hebrews* 13 and 42. They shall have their portions with the wicked in the lake that burns with fire and brimstone, *Revelation* 21.8.

Only for the sin of whoredom God was sorry at heart, and repented that he ever made man, *Genesis* 6.67.

Saint Paul saith, to avoid fornication every man may take a wife, 1 *Corinthians* 6.9.

Therefore he which hath a wife of his own and yet goeth to another woman is like a rich thief which will steal when he has no need.

There are three ways to know a whore: by her wanton looks, by her speech, and by her gait. *Ecclesiasticus* 26.[5] and in the same chapter he saith, that we must not give our strength unto harlots, for whores are the evil of all evils, and the vanity of all vanities, they weaken the strength of a man and deprive the body of his beauty, it furroweth his brows and maketh the eyes dim, and a whorish woman causeth the fever and the gout; and at a word, they are a great shortening to a man's life.

3. Spiteful
4. Frivolous, wanton.
5. Apocryphal book of the Old Testament.

For although they seem to be as dainty as sweet meat, yet in trial not so wholesome as sour sauce. They have wit, but it is all in craft; if they love it is vehement, but if they hate it is deadly.

Plato saith, that women are either angels or devils, and that they either love dearly or hate bitterly, for a woman hath no mean in her love, nor mercy in her hate, no pity in revenge, nor patience in her anger; therefore it is said, that there is nothing in the world which both pleases and displeases a man more than a woman, for a woman most delighteth a man and yet most deceiveth him, for as there is nothing more sweet to a man than a woman when she smiles, even so there is nothing more odious than the angry countenance of a woman.

Solomon in his 20th chapter of *Ecclesiastes*[6] saith, that an angry woman will foam at the mouth like a boar. If all this be true as most true it is, why shouldest thou spend one hour in the praise of women as some fools do, for some will brag of the beauty of such a maid, another will vaunt of the bravery of such a woman, that she goeth beyond all the women in the parish. Again, some study their fine wits how they may cunningly swooth[7] women, and with logic how to reason with them, and with eloquence to persuade them. They are always tempering their wits as fiddlers do their strings, who wrest them so high, that many times they stretch them beyond time, tune and reason.

Again, there are many that weary themselves with dallying, playing, and sporting with women, and yet they are never satisfied with the unsatiable desire of them; if with a song thou wouldest be brought asleep, or with a dance be led to delight, then a fair woman is fit for thy diet. If thy head be in her lap she will make thee believe that thou are hard by[8] God's seat, when indeed thou are just at hell gate.

Rachel Speght

1597?–?

The daughter of the rector of two London churches and the wife of a minister, Rachel Speght was only about nineteen years old when she wrote *A Muzzle for Melastomus, the Cynical Baiter of, and Foul-Mouthed Barker Against Evah's Sex, or an Apologetical Answer to the Irreligious and Illiterate Pamphlet made by Io. Swu. and by him Intituled The Arraignment of Women*. Speght interpreted Swetnam's *Arraignment* as a serious attack on women in order to show the faulty logic underpinning misogyny. Her title indicates the dual thrust of her analysis: the *irreligious* Swetnam has misinterpreted Scripture, and the *illiterate* pamphlet is logically confused and rhetorically flawed. She argues for a view of marriage as a mutual partnership and the relation between the sexes as one of greater equality. Modern critics have debated the implications of Speght's work: Barbara Lewalski has called Rachel Speght "the first self-proclaimed and positively identified female polemicist in England" while Ann Rosalind Jones has questioned whether Speght's work can be considered as feminist in the twentieth-century sense. All critics of early modern gender studies agree, however, that Speght was a learned and committed author. She alone of the participants in the Jacobean controversy about women affixed her own name to the title page. And she reiterated her authorship with the publication of her poetic dream-vision *Mortalities Memorandum* (1621), in which she defends women's education.

6. A faulty citation: in Ecclesiasticus 25, an angry woman is compared to a bear.

7. Sway, woo.

8. Close to.

from A Muzzle for Melastomus

Of Woman's Excellency, with the causes of her creation, and of the sympathy which ought to be in man and wife each toward other

The work of creation being finished, this approbation thereof was given by God himself, that "All was very good."[1] If all, then woman, who—except man—is the most excellent creature under the canopy of heaven. But if it be objected by any:

First, that woman, though created good, yet by giving ear to Satan's temptations brought death and misery upon all her posterity.

Secondly, that "Adam was not deceived, but that the woman was deceived and was in the transgression."[2]

Thirdly, that St. Paul says "It were good for a man not to touch a woman."[3]

Fourthly and lastly, that of Solomon, who seems to speak against all of our sex: "I have found one man of a thousand, but a woman among them all I have not found,"[4] whereof in its due place.

To the first of these objections, I answer: that Satan first assailed the woman because where the hedge is lowest, most easy it is to get over, and she being the weaker vessel[5] was with more facility to be seduced—like as a crystal glass sooner receives a crack than a strong stone pot. Yet we shall find the offense of Adam and Eve almost to parallel; for as an ambitious desire to be made like God was the motive which caused her to eat, so likewise was it his, as may plainly appear by that *ironia:* "Behold, man is become as one of us"[6]—not that he was so indeed, but hereby his desire to attain a greater perfection than God had given him was reproved. Woman sinned, it is true, by her infidelity in not believing the word of God but giving credit to Satan's fair promises that "she should not die";[7] but so did the man, too. And if Adam had not approved of that deed which Eve had done, and been willing to tread the steps where she had gone, he—being her head—would have reproved her and have made the commandment a bit to restrain him from breaking his Maker's injunction. For if a man burn his hand in the fire, the bellows that blew the fire is not to be blamed, but himself rather for not being careful to avoid the danger. Yet if the bellows had not blown, the fire had not burned; no more is woman simply to be condemned for man's transgression. For by the free will which before his fall he enjoyed, he might have avoided and been free from being burned or singed with that fire which was kindled by Satan and blown by Eve. It therefore served not his turn a whit afterwards to say: "The woman which thou gavest me gave me of the tree, and I did eat."[8] For a penalty was inflicted upon him as well as on the woman, the punishment of her transgression being particular to her own sex and to none but the female kind, but for the sin of man the whole earth was cursed.[9] And he being better able than the woman to have resisted temptation, because the stronger vessel, was first called to account, to show that to whom much is given, of them much is required; and that he who was the sovereign of all creatures visible should have yielded greatest obedience to God.

1. Genesis 1.31. References to the Bible are indicated in the margins of Speght's text.
2. 1 Timothy 2.14.
3. 1 Corinthians 7.1.
4. Ecclesiastes 7.28.
5. "The weaker vessel," a phrase taken from 1 Peter 3.7, is frequently used in early modern English sermons to describe woman.
6. Genesis 3.22. "Ironia," or irony, is a figure of speech in which the meaning is the opposite of that of the words used and the tone of which is often mocking.
7. Genesis 3.4.
8. Genesis 3.12.
9. Genesis 3.17.

True it is (as is already confessed) that woman first sinned, yet find we no mention of spiritual nakedness till man had sinned. Then it is said "Their eyes were opened,"[1] the eyes of their mind and conscience; and then perceived they themselves naked, that is, not only bereft of that integrity which they originally had, but felt the rebellion and disobedience of their members in the disordered motions of their now corrupt nature, which made them for shame to cover their nakednesse. Then (and not afore) it is said that they saw it, as if sin were imperfect and unable to bring a deprivation of a blessing received, or death on all mankind, till man (in whom lay the active power of generation) had transgressed. The offense, therefore, of Adam and Eve is by St. Austin[2] thus distinguished: "the man sinned against God and himself, the woman against God, herself and her husband"; yet in her giving of the fruit to eat had she no malicious intent towards him, but did therein show a desire to make her husband partaker of that happiness, which she thought by their eating they should both have enjoyed. This her giving Adam of that sauce, wherewith Satan had served her, whose sourness, afore he had eaten, she did not perceive, was that which made her sin to exceed his. Wherefore, that she might not of him who ought to honor her be abhorred,[3] the first promise that was made in Paradise, God makes to woman, that by her seed should the serpent's head be broken.[4] Whereupon Adam calls her *Hevah,* Life, that as the woman had been an occasion of his sin so should woman bring forth the Savior from sin, which was in the fullness of time accomplished.[5] By which was manifested that he is a Savior of believing women no less than of men, that so the blame of sin may not be imputed to his creature, which is good, but to the will by which Eve sinned; and yet by Christ's assuming the shape of man was it declared that his mercy was equivalent to both sexes. So that by Hevah's blessed seed, as St. Paul affirms, it is brought to pass that "male and female are all one in Christ Jesus."[6]

To the second objection I answer: that the Apostle does not hereby exempt man from sin, but only giveth to understand that the woman was the primary transgressor, and not the man; but that man was not at all deceived was far from his meaning. For he afterwards expressly saith that "in Adam all die, so in Christ shall all be made alive."[7]

For the third objection, "It is good for a man not to touch a woman": the Apostle makes it not a positive prohibition but speaks it only because of the Corinth[ian]s' present necessity,[8] who were then persecuted by the enemies of the church. For which cause, and no other, he saith: "Art thou loosed from a wife? Seek not a wife"—meaning whilst the time of these perturbations should continue in their heat; "but if thou are bound, seek not to be loosed; if thou marriest, thou sinnest not," only increase thy care: "for the married careth for the things of this world. And I wish that you were without care that ye might cleave fast to the Lord without separation: for the time remaineth, that they which have wives be as though they had none, for the persecutors shall deprive you of them either by imprisonment, banishment or death." So that manifest it is, that the Apostle does not hereby forbid marriage, but only adviseth the Corinth[ian]s to forbear a while, till God in mercy should curb the fury of their adversaries. For (as Eusebius[9] writeth) Paul was afterward married himself,

1. Genesis 3.7.
2. Saint Augustine; this commonplace echoes parts of his sermon on Adam and Eve.
3. 1 Peter 3.7.
4. Genesis 3.15.
5. Galatians 4.4.
6. Galatians 3.28.
7. 1 Corinthians 15.22.
8. 1 Corinthians 7.
9. Eusebius (A.D. 260–340) was Bishop of Caesarea and a church historian. See *Ecclesiastical History* 3.30.

the which is very probable, being that interrogatively he saith: "Have we not power to lead about a wife being a sister, as well as the rest of the Apostles, and as the brethren of the Lord, and Cephas?"[1]

The fourth and last objection is that of Solomon: "I have found one man among a thousand, but a woman among them all have I not found.[2] For answer of which, if we look into the story of his life, we shall find therein a commentary upon this enigmatical[3] sentence included. For it is there said that Solomon had seven hundred wives and three hundred concubines, which number connected make one thousand. These women turning away his heart from being perfect with the Lord his God,[4] sufficient cause had he to say, that among the said thousand women found he not one upright. He saith not, that among a thousand women never any man found one worthy of commendation, but speaks in the first person singularly "I have not found," meaning in his own experience. For this assertion is to be held a part of the confession of his former follies, and no otherwise, his repentance being the intended drift of *Ecclesiastes*.

Thus having (by God's assistance) removed those stones whereat some have stumbled, others broken their shins, I will proceed toward the period of my intended task, which is to decipher the excellency of women. Of whose creation I will, for order's sake, observe: first, the efficient cause,[5] which was God; secondly, the material cause, or whereof she was made; thirdly, the formal cause, or fashion and proportion of her feature; fourthly and lastly, the final cause, the end or purpose for which she was made. To begin with the first.

The efficient cause of woman's creation was Jehovah the Eternal, the truth of which is manifest in Moses his narration of the six days' works, where he says, "God created them male and female."[6] And David, exhorting all "the earth to sing to the Lord" (meaning, by a metonymy,[7] "earth": all creatures that live on the earth, of whatever sex or nation) gives this reason: "For the Lord has made us."[8] That work then cannot choose but be good, yea very good, which is wrought by so excellent a workman as the Lord; for he, being a glorious Creator, must effect a worthy creature. Bitter water cannot proceed from a pleasant sweet fountain, nor bad work from that workman which is perfectly good—and, in propriety, none but he.[9]

Secondly, the material cause, or matter whereof woman was made, was of a refined mold, if I may so speak. For man was created of the dust of the earth,[1] but woman was made of a part of man after that he was a living soul. Yet she was not produced from Adam's foot, to be his too low inferior; nor from his head to be his superior; but from his side, near his heart, to be his equal: that where he is lord, she may be lady. And therefore saith God concerning man and woman jointly: "Let them rule over the fish of the sea, and over the fowls of the heaven, and over every beast that moves upon the earth."[2] By which words he makes their authority equal, and all creatures to be in subjection to them both. This, being rightly considered, doth teach men to make such account of their wives as Adam did of Eve: "This is bone of my bone, and flesh of my flesh."[3] As also, that they neither do or wish any more hurt

1. 1 Corinthians 9.5.
2. Ecclesiastes 7.30.
3. Mysterious.
4. 1 Kings 11.3.
5. The agent who makes something; see Aristotle's *Physics* 2.3.
6. Genesis 1.28 [27].
7. A figure of speech that substitutes one term for another to which it is closely related.
8. Psalms 100.3.
9. Psalms 100.5; Matthew 19.7.
1. Genesis 2.7.
2. Genesis 1.26.
3. Genesis 2.23.

unto them, than unto their own bodies. For men ought to love their wives as themselves, because he that loves his wife loves himself;[4] and never did man hate his own flesh (which the woman is) unless a monster in nature.

Thirdly, the formal cause, fashion and proportion, of woman was excellent. For she was neither like the beasts of the earth, fowls of the air, fishes of the sea, or any other inferior creature; but man was the only object which she did resemble. For as God gave man a lofty countenance that he might look up toward Heaven, so did he likewise give unto woman. And as the temperature of man's body is excellent, so is woman's. For whereas other creatures, by reason of their gross humors, have excrements for their habit—as fowls their feathers, beasts their hair, fishes their scales—man and woman only have their skin clear and smooth.[5] And (that more is) in the image of God were they both created; yea and to be brief, all the parts of their bodies, both external and internal, were correspondent and meet each for other.

Fourthly and lastly, the final cause or end for which woman was made was to glorify God, and to be a collateral companion for man to glory God, in using her body and all the parts, powers and faculties thereof as instruments for his honor. As with her voice to sound forth his praises, like Miriam, and the rest of her company;[6] with her tongue not to utter words of strife, but to give good counsel unto her husband, the which he must not despise. For Abraham was bidden to give ear to Sarah his wife.[7] Pilate was willed by his wife not to have any hand in the condemning of Christ;[8] and a sin it was in him that he listened not to her; Leah and Rachel counseled Jacob to do according to the word of the Lord;[9] and the Shunamite put her husband in mind of harboring the prophet Elisha.[1] Her hands should be open, according to her ability, in contributing towards God's service and distressed servants, like to that poor widow who cast two mites into the treasury;[2] and as Mary Magdalene, Susanna and Joanna, the wife of Herod's steward, with many others which of their substance ministered unto Christ.[3] Her heart should be a receptacle for God's word, like Mary that treasured the sayings of Christ in her heart.[4] Her feet should be swift in going to seek the Lord in his sanctuary, as Mary Magdalene made haste to seek Christ at his sepulcher.[5] Finally, no power external or internal ought woman to keep idle, but to employ it in some service of God, to the glory of her creator and comfort of her own soul.

The other end for which woman was made was to be a companion and helper for man; and if she must be a *helper*, and but a *helper*, then are those husbands to be blamed, which lay the whole burden of domestical affairs and maintenance on the shoulders of their wives. For, as yoke-fellows they are to sustain part of each other's cares, griefs and calamities. But as if two oxen be put into one yoke, the one being bigger than the other, the greater bears most weight; so the husband, being the stronger vessel, is to bear a greater burden than his wife. And therefore the Lord said to Adam: "In the sweat of your face shall you eat your bread, till you return to the dust."[6] And St. Paul says that "he that provideth not for his household is worse than

4. Ephesians 5.28.
5. Genesis 1.26
6. Exodus 15.20.
7. Genesis 21.12.
8. Matthew 27.19.
9. Genesis 31.16.

1. 2 Kings 4.9.
2. Mark 12.43.
3. Luke 8.
4. Luke 1.45.
5. John 20.1.
6. Genesis 3.19.

an infidel."[7] Nature hath taught senseless creatures to help one another: as the male pigeon, when his hen is weary with sitting on her eggs and comes off from them, supplies her place, that in her absence they may receive no harm, until such time as she is fully refreshed. Of small birds, the cock always helps his hen to build her nest; and while she sits upon her eggs he flies abroad to get meat for her, who cannot then provide any for herself. The crowing cockerel helps his hen to defend her chickens from peril, and will endanger himself to save her and them from harm. Seeing then, that these unreasonable creatures by the instinct of nature bear such affection to each other, that without any grudge they willingly according to their kind help one another, I may reason, *a minore ad maius*,[8] that much more should man and woman, which are reasonable creatures, be helpers to each other in all things lawful, they having the law of God to guide them, his word to be a lantern to their feet and a light unto their paths, by which they are excited to a far more mutual participation of each other's burden than other creatures. So that neither the wife may say to her husband nor the husband to his wife: "I have no need of thee,"[9] no more than the members of the body may say to each other, between whom there is such a sympathy that if one member suffer, all suffer with it. Therefore though God bade Abraham forsake his country and kindred, yet he bade him not forsake his wife who, being "Flesh of his flesh, and bone of his bone," was to be copartner with him of whatsoever did betide him, whether joy or sorrow. Wherefore Solomon says "woe to him that is alone";[1] for when thoughts of discomfort, troubles of this world and fear of dangers do possess him, he wants a companion to lift him up from the pit of perplexity into which he is fallen.[2] For a good wife, saith Plautus, is the wealth of the mind and the welfare of the heart; and therefore a meet associate for her husband. And "woman," saith Paul, "is the glory of the man."[3]

Marriage is a merri-age, and this world's paradise, where there is mutual love. Our blessed Savior vouchsafed to honor a marriage with the first miracle that he wrought,[4] unto which miracle matrimonial estate may not unfitly be resembled. For as Christ turned water into wine, a far more excellent liquor (which, as the Psalmist saith, "Makes glad the hearts of man";[5] so the single man is changed by marriage from a bachelor to a husband, a far more excellent title: from a solitary life to a joyful union and conjunction with such a creature as God had made meet for man, for whom none was fit till she was made. The enjoying of this great blessing made Pericles more unwilling to part from his wife than to die for his country; and Antonius Pius to pour forth that pathetic exclamation against death for depriving him of his dearly beloved wife: "O cruel hard-hearted death in bereaving me of her whom I esteemed more than my own life!"[6] "A virtuous woman," saith Solomon, "is the crown of her husband";[7] by which metaphor he shows both the excellency of such a wife and what account her husband is to make of her. For a king does not trample his crown under his feet, but highly esteems it, gently handles it and carefully lays it up as the evidence of his kingdom; and therefore when David destroyed Rabbah[8] he

7. 1 Timothy 5.8.
8. From the lesser to the greater.
9. 1 Corinthians 12.21.
1. Ecclesiastes 4.10.
2. Ecclesiastes 4.10.
3. 1 Corinthians 11.7.
4. John 2.
5. Psalms 104.15.
6. Antonius Pius (A.D. 86–161) Roman emperor, founded a charity for orphaned girls in honor of his wife. Plutarch writes about how Pericles (495–429 B.C.), ruler of Athens, greatly loved Aspasia.
7. Proverbs 7.4.
8. 1 Chronicles 20.2. Joab destroyed Rabbah, while David took the king's crown.

took off the crown from their king's head. So husbands should not account their wives as their vassals but as those that are "heirs together of the grace of life,"[9] and with all lenity and mild persuasions set their feet in the right way if they happen to tread awry, bearing with their infirmities, as Elkanah did with his wife's barrenness.[1]

The kingdom of God is compared to the marriage of a king's son;[2] John calleth the conjunction of Christ and his chosen a marriage;[3] and not few but many times does our blessed Savior in the Canticles[4] set forth his unspeakable love towards his church under the title of a husband rejoicing with his wife, and often vouchsafeth to call her his sister a spouse—by which is showed that with God "is no respect of persons," nations, or sexes.[5] For whosoever, whether it be man or woman, that doth "believe in the lord Jesus, such shall be saved."[6] And if God's love, even from the beginning, had not been as great toward woman as to man, then he would not have preserved from the deluge of the old world as many women as men. Nor would Christ after his resurrection have appeared to a woman first of all other, had it not been to declare thereby, that the benefits of his death and resurrection are as available, by belief, for women as for men; for he indifferently died for the one sex as well as the other.

"Esther Sowernam"

The pen name Esther Sowernam comes from the Old Testament heroine Esther, who defended her people against Haman, and the antithesis of Joseph Swetnam's last name (sweet/sour). The full title of her text also parodies Swetnam's: *Ester Hath Hanged Haman; or An Answer to a Lewd Pamphlet, Entitled The Arraignment of Women. With the Arraignment of Lewd, Idle, Froward and Unconstant Men, and Husbands* (1617). On the whole the author of this pamphlet presents herself in a more secular light than Rachel Speght does. Sowernam's criticisms of misogyny are more psychological and social than moral and logical. Trained in classics as well as Scripture and a keen observer, Esther Sowernam finds that Swetnam has incorrectly stated that the Bible is the source of the statement that women are a necessary evil and finds that the true source is in Euripides' *Medea*. The occasion for Sowernam's writing is a dinner party at which Swetnam's book and Speght's response were discussed. Sowernam finds fault with both—Swetnam because he "damns all women" and Speght because she "undertaking to defend women doth rather charge and condemn them." Sowernam cites the double standard by which men are excused for what women are judged harshly for in order to assert women's superiority. She argues that women are judged more severely because they are thought to be more virtuous in the first place. The second half of her pamphlet may have helped to inspire the comedy that spoofed the entire controversy, *Swetnam the Woman-Hater Arraigned By Women* (1620).

from **Ester Hath Hanged Haman**

from *Chapter 7. The answer to all objections which are material made against women*

As for that crookedness and frowardness[1] with which you charge women, look from whence they have it. For of themselves and their own disposition it doth not proceed, which is proved directly by your own testimony. For in your 46th page, line

9. 1 Peter 3.7.
1. 1 Samuel 1.17.
2. Matthew 22.
3. Revelation 19.7.
4. The Song of Songs.
5. Romans 2.11.
6. John 3.18.
1. Perversity, unreasonableness.

15[16], you say: "A young woman of tender years is flexible, obedient, and subject to do anything, according to the will and pleasure of her husband." How cometh it then that this gentle and mild disposition is afterwards altered? Yourself doth give the true reason, for you give a great charge not to marry a widow. But why? Because, say you in the same page, "A widow is framed to the conditions[2] of another man." Why then, if a woman have froward conditions, they be none of her own, she was framed to them. Is not our adversary ashamed of himself to rail against women for those faults which do all come from men? Doth not he most grievously charge men to learn[3] their wives bad and corrupt behavior? For he saith plainly: "Thou must unlearn a widow, and make her forget and forego her former corrupt and disordered behavior." Thou must unlearn her; *ergo*, what fault she hath learned: her corruptness comes not from her own disposition but from her husband's destruction.

Is it not a wonder that your pamphlets are so dispersed? Are they not wise men to cast away time and money upon a book which cutteth their own throats? 'Tis pity but that men should reward you for your writing (if it be but as the Roman Sertorius[4] did the idle poet: he gave him a reward, but not for his writing—but because he should never write more). As for women, they laugh that men have no more able a champion. This author cometh to bait women or, as he foolishly saith, the "Bear-baiting of Women," and he bringeth but a mongrel cur who doth his kind[5] to brawl and bark, but cannot bite. The mild and flexible disposition of a woman is in philosophy proved in the composition of her body, for it is a maxim: *Mores animi sequntur temperaturam corporis* (the disposition of the mind is answerable to the temper of the body). A woman in the temperature of her body is tender, soft and beautiful, so doth her disposition in mind correspond accordingly: she is mild, yielding and virtuous. What disposition accidentally happeneth unto her is by the contagion of a froward husband, as Joseph Swetnam affirmeth.

And experience proveth. It is a shame for a man to complain of a froward woman—in many respects all concerning himself. It is a shame he hath no more government over the weaker vessel.[6] It is a shame he hath hardened her tender sides and gentle heart with his boisterous and Northern blasts. It is a shame for a man to publish and proclaim household secrets—which is a common practice amongst men, especially drunkards, lechers, and prodigal spendthrifts. These when they come home drunk, or are called in question for their riotous misdemeanors, they presently show themselves the right children of Adam. They will excuse themselves by their wives and say that their unquietness and frowardness at home is the cause that they run abroad: an excuse more fitter for a beast than a man. If thou wert a man thou wouldst take away the cause which urgeth a woman to grief and discontent, and not by thy frowardness increase her distemperature.[7] Forbear thy drinking, thy luxurious riot, thy gaming and spending, and thou shalt have thy wife give thee as little cause at home as thou givest her great cause of disquiet abroad. Men which are men, if they chance to be matched with froward wives—either of their own making or others' marring[8]—they would make a benefit of the discommodity:[9] either try his skill to make her mild or exercise his patience to endure her cursedness; for all crosses are inflicted either for punishment of sins or for exercise of virtues. But humorous[1] men will sooner mar a thousand women than out of a hundred make one good.

2. Circumstances, character traits.
3. Teach.
4. Quintus Sertorius, Roman general, appointed governor of Farther Spain in 83 B.C.
5. Nature.
6. From 1 Peter 3.7.
7. Disorder in mind and body.
8. Spoiling.
9. Inconvenience, disadvantageousness.
1. Moody.

And this shall appear in the imputation which our adversary chargeth upon our sex: to be lascivious, wanton and lustful. He saith: "Women tempt, allure and provoke men." How rare a thing is it for women to prostitute and offer themselves? How common a practice is it for men to seek and solicit women to lewdness? What charge do they spare? What travail do they bestow? What vows, oaths and protestations do they spend to make them dishonest? They hire panders, they write letters, they seal them with damnations and execrations to assure them of love when the end proves but lust. They know the flexible disposition of women, and the sooner to overreach them some will pretend they are so plunged in love that, except they obtain their desire, they will seem to drown, hang, stab, poison, or banish themselves from friends and country. What motives are these to tender dispositions? Some will pretend marriage, another offer continual maintenance; but when they have obtained their purpose, what shall a woman find?—just that which is her everlasting shame and grief: she hath made herself the unhappy subject to a lustful body and the shameful stall[2] of a lascivious tongue. Men may with foul shame charge woman with this sin which she had never committed, if she had not trusted; nor had ever trusted, if she had not been deceived with vows, oaths and protestations. To bring a woman to offend in one sin, how many damnable sins do they commit? I appeal to their own consciences. The lewd disposition of sundry men doth appear in this: if a woman or maid will yield to lewdness, what shall they want?[3]—but if they would live in honesty, what help shall they have? How much will they make of the lewd? How base an account of the honest? How many pounds will they spend in bawdy houses? But when will they bestow a penny upon an honest maid or woman, except it be to corrupt them?

Our adversary bringeth many examples of men which have been overthrown by women. It is answered before: the fault is their own. But I would have him, or anyone living, to show any woman that offended in this sin of lust, but that she was first solicited by a man.

Helen was the cause of Troy's burning: first, Paris did solicit her; next, how many knaves and fools of the male kind had Troy, which to maintain whoredom would bring their city to confusion?

When you bring in examples of lewd women and of men which have been stained by women, you show yourself both frantic and a profane irreligious fool to mention Judith,[4] for cutting off Holofernes' head, in that rank.

You challenge women for untamed and unbridled tongues; there was never woman was ever noted for so shameless, so brutish, so beastly a scold as you prove yourself in this base and odious pamphlet. Your blaspheme God, you rail at his creation, you abuse and slander his creatures; and what immodest or impudent scurrility is it which you do not express in this lewd and lying pamphlet?

Hitherto I have so answered all your objections against women that, as I have not defended the wickedness of any, so I have set down the true state of the question. As Eve did not offend without temptation of a serpent, so women do seldom offend but it is by provocation of men. Let not your impudency, nor your consorts' dishonesty, charge our sex hereafter with those sins of which you yourselves were the first procurers. I have, in my discourse, touched you, and all yours, to the quick. I have taxed you with bitter speeches; you will, perhaps, say I am a railing scold. In this

2. Target.
3. Lack, need.
4. A wealthy, attractive widow who saved her people from Holofernes, an Assyrian general, by attracting and then killing him. (See The Book of Judith, part of the Catholic Bible, but viewed as apocryphal by Jews and Protestants.)

objection, Joseph Swetnam, I will teach you both wit and honesty. The difference between a railing scold and an honest accuser is this: the first rageth upon passionate fury without bringing cause or proof, the other bringeth direct proof for what she allegeth. You charge women with clamorous words, and bring no proof; I charge you with blasphemy, with impudency, scurrility, foolery and the like. I show just and direct proof for what I say. It is not my desire to speak so much; it is your dessert to provoke me upon just cause so far. It is not railing to call a crow black, or a wolf a ravenor,[5] or a drunkard a beast; the report of the truth is never to be blamed: the deserver of such a report deserves the shame.

Now, for this time, to draw to an end. Let me ask according to the question of Cassian, *cui bono?*[6]—what have you gotten by publishing your pamphlet? Good I know you can get none. You have, perhaps, pleased the humors of some giddy, idle, conceited persons. But you have dyed yourself in the colors of shame, lying, slandering, blasphemy, ignorance, and the like.

The shortness of time and the weight of business call me away, and urge me to leave off thus abruptly; but assure yourself, where I leave now I will by God's grace supply the next term, to your small content. You have exceeded in your fury against widows, whose defense you shall hear of at the time aforesaid. In the mean space, recollect your wits; write out of deliberation, not out of fury; write out of advice, not out of idleness: forbear to charge women with faults which come from the contagion of masculine serpents.

Hic Mulier and *Haec Vir*

Hic Mulier and *Haec Vir* were published anonymously within a week of each other in February 1620. *Hic Mulier*, the first of the two pamphlets to appear, begins with the complaint that "since the days of Adam women were never so masculine." The title introduces this theme by a gender switch of its own: *Hic Mulier*, Latin for "This Woman," uses the masculine form *hic* instead of the feminine *haec*. The title page contains illustrations of two such mannish women—one wearing a man's hat, which she admires in a mirror, and another sitting in a barber's chair to get her hair cut. Structured as a "brief declamation," or oration, the text argues that such activities as hair bobbing and wearing men's clothes are immoral and unnatural for women. Furthermore, such gender crossing is also a threat to the entire political order: "most pernicious to the commonwealth for she hath power by example to do it a world of injury."

As its subtitle boasts, *Haec Vir* was "an answer to the late book intituled *Hic Mulier*" and was represented as "a brief dialogue between Haec Vir the Womanish Man, and Hic Mulier the Man-Woman." The effeminate man and the hermaphroditic woman first misrecognize each other's gender. Once that is cleared up, the foppish man launches into a diatribe against the woman, who defends herself by arguing that "custom is an idiot." The first half of the dialogue reads like a proclamation of the equality of the sexes, with the bare-breasted, dagger-swinging Hic Mulier exclaiming, "We are as free-born as men, have as free election, and as free spirits, we are compounded of like parts and may with like liberty make benefit of our creations." Despite this bold challenge, the text as a whole makes a rather conservative case for

5. An animal who seizes in order to devour.

6. "To whose benefit," a phrase attributed by Cicero to Lucius Cassius.

the need for gender distinctions, the overturning of which was seen as an assault on hierarchy. The dialogue ends with both participants agreeing to exchange clothes and Latin pronouns so that men will again be manly and women subservient to them.

These pamphlets display the early modern fascination with, and loathing of, transvestism. Not only did the fashionable young male favorites of King James I's court resemble the womanish man of *Haec Vir,* but there were more than a few documented cases of women wearing breeches on the streets. One of these women, the notorious Mary Frith, was immortalized in Dekker and Middleton's comedy, *The Roaring Girl*. A few women were actually brought before ecclesiastical courts for "shamefully" putting on "man's apparel."

While conforming to the comic pattern of disrupting and then reestablishing the status quo, these pamphlets show that questions about custom, nature, and sex and gender roles were being asked in the early seventeenth century.

from **Hic Mulier; or, The Man-Woman**

So I present these masculine women in their deformities as they are, that I may call them back to the modest comeliness in which they were.

The modest comeliness in which they were? Why, did ever these mermaids, or rather mere-monsters,[1] that wear the Car-man's block,[2] the Dutchman's feather *upse-van-muffe*, the poor man's pate pouled by a Treene dish, the French doublet trussed with points, to Mary Aubries' light nether skirts, the fool's baldric, and the devil's poniard. Did they ever know comeliness or modesty? Fie, no, they never walked in those paths, for these at the best are sure but rags of gentry, torn from better pieces for their foul stains, or else the adulterate branches of rich stocks,[3] that taking too much sap from the root, are cut away, and employed in base uses; or, if not so, they are the stinking vapors drawn from dunghills, which nourished in the higher regions of the air, become meteors and false fires blazing and flashing therein, and amazing men's minds with their strange proportions, till the substance of their pride being spent, they drop down again to the place from whence they came, and there rot and consume unpitied, and unremembered.

And questionless it is true, that such were the first beginners of these last deformities, for from any purer blood would have issued a purer birth; there would have been some spark of virtue: some excuse for imitation; but this deformity has no agreement with goodness, nor any difference against the weakest reason: it is all base, all barbarous. Base, in the respect it offends men in the example, and God in the most unnatural use: barbarous, in that it is exorbitant from nature, and an antithesis to kind,[4] going astray (with ill-favored affectation) both in attire, in speech, in manners, and (it is to be feared) in the whole courses and stories of their actions. What can be more true and curious consent of the most fairest colors and the wealthy gardens which fill the world with living plants? Do but you receive virtuous inmates (as what palaces are more rich to receive heavenly messengers?) and you shall draw men's souls to you with that severe, devout, and holy adoration, that you shall never want praise, never love, never reverence.

But now methinks I hear the witty-offending great ones reply in excuse of their deformities: What, is there no difference amongst women? no distinction of places, no respect of honors, nor no regard of blood, or alliance? Must but a bare pair of

1. Pure monsters.
2. A merchant's hat. Descriptions of ridiculous fashions follow: the *upse-van-muffe* is an elaborate feathered hat; the pate pouled by a Treene dish is hair cut short to the shape of a wooden dish; the French doublet is a man's close-fitting upper body garment tied with laces; baldric: fancy belt; poniard: dagger.
3. Trunks or stems.
4. The opposite of what is natural to the gender.

shears pass between noble and ignoble, between the generous spirit and the base mechanic; shall we be all co-heirs of one honor, one estate, and one habit? O men, you are then too tyrannous, and not only injure nature, but also break the laws and customs of the wisest princes. Are not bishops known by their miters, princes by their crowns, judges by their robes, and knights by their spurs? But poor women have nothing (how great soever they be) to divide themselves from the enticing shows or moving images which do furnish most shops in the city. What is it that either the laws have allowed to the greatest ladies, custom found convenient, or their bloods or places challenged, which hath not been engrossed into the city with as great greediness, and pretense of true title; as if the surcease[5] from the imitation were the utter breach of their charter everlastingly.

For this cause, these apes of the city have enticed foreign nations to the cells, and there committing gross adultery with their gewgaws,[6] have brought out such unnatural conceptions, that the whole world is not able to make a *Democritus* big enough to laugh at their foolish ambitions.[7] Nay, the very art of painting (which to the last age shall ever be held in detestation) they have so cunningly stolen and hidden amongst their husbands' hoards of treasure, that the decayed stock of prostitution (having little other revenues) are hourly in bringing their action of *detinue*[8] against them. Hence (being thus troubled with these *Popeniars*,[9] and loath still to march in one rank with fools and *zanies*[1]) have proceeded these disguised deformities, not to offend the eyes of goodness, but to tire with ridiculous contempt the never to be satisfied appetites of these gross and unmannerly intruders. Nay, look if this very last edition of disguise, this which is so full of faults, corruptions, and false quotations, this bait which the devil had laid to catch the souls of wanton women, be not as frequent in the demi-palaces of burghers and citizens as it is either at masque, triumph, tilt-yard, or playhouse. Call but to account the tailors that are contained within the circumference of the walls of the city, and let but their heels and their hard reckonings be justly summed together, and it will be found they have raised more new foundations of this new disguise, and metamorphosed more modest old garments, to this new manner of short base and French doublet (only for the use of freemen's wives[2] and their children) in one month, than has been worn in court, suburbs, or country, since the unfortunate beginning of the first devilish invention.

Let therefore the powerful Statute of Apparel[3] but lift his battle-axe, and crush the offenders in pieces, so as every one may be known by the true badge of their blood, or fortune; and then these *Chimeras* of deformity will be sent back to hell, and there burn to cinders in the flames of their own malice.

Thus, methinks, I hear the best offenders argue, nor can I blame a high blood to swell when it is coupled and counter-checked with baseness and corruption; yet this shows an anger passing near akin to envy, and alludes much to the saying of an excellent poet:

Women never
Love beauty in their sex, but envy ever.

5. Cessation, stop.
6. Showy decorations.
7. Seneca recounts how Democritus laughed rather than cried at human life (*De tranquilitate animi* 15.2).
8. Legal action to recover personal property.
9. Popinjays, vain and empty people.
1. Parasites, those who play the fool for amusement.
2. Women married to men possessing the freedom of a city, borough, or corporation.
3. Laws governing dress that were intended to differentiate the aristocracy from the common people had been ennacted from the Middle Ages through to the early modern period.

They have Caesar's ambition, and desire to be one and one alone, but yet to offend themselves, to grieve others, is a revenge dissonant to reason, and as *Euripides* says, a woman of that malicious nature is a fierce beast, and most pernicious to the commonwealth, for she has power by example to do it a world of injury. But far be such cruelty from the softness of their gentle dispositions: O let them remember what the poet saith:

> Women be
> Fram'd with the same parts of the mind as men
> Nay Nature triumph'd in their beauty's birth,
> And women made the glory of the earth,
> The life of beauty, in whose simple breast,
> (As in her fair lodging) Virtue rests:
> Whose towering thoughts attended with remorse,
> Do make their fairness be of greater force.

But when they thrust virtue out of doors, and give a shameless liberty to every loose passion, that either their weak thoughts engender, or the discourse of wicked tongues can charm into their yielding bosoms (much too apt to be opened with any pick-lock of flattering and deceitful insinuation) then they turn maskers, mummers, nay monsters in their disguises, and so they may catch the bridle in their teeth, and run away with their rulers, they care not into what dangers they plunge either their fortunes or reputations, the disgrace of the whole sex, or the blot and obloquy of their private families, according to the saying of the poets

> Such is the cruelty of women-kind,
> When they have shaken off the shamefac'd band
> With which wise nature did them strongly bind,
> T'obey the bests of man's well-ruling hand
> That then all rule and reason they withstand
> To purchase a licentious liberty;
> But virtuous women wisely understand,
> That they were born to mild humility,
> Unless the heavens them lift to lawful sovereignty.[4]

To you therefore that are fathers, husbands, of sustainers of these new hermaphrodites, belongs the cure of this impostume;[5] it is you that give fuel to the flames of their wild indiscretion. You add the oil which makes their stinking lamps defile the whole house with filthy smoke, and your purses purchase these deformities at rates both dear and unreasonable. Do you but hold close your liberal hands, or take a strict account of the employment of the treasure you give to their necessary maintenance, and these excesses will either cease, or else die smothered in prison in the tailors' trunks for want of redemption.

from Haec Vir; or, The Womanish Man

Hic-Mulier: Well, then to the purpose: first, you say, I am base in being a slave to novelty. What flattery can there be in freedom of election? Or what baseness to crown my delights with those pleasures which are most suitable to mine affections? Bondage or slavery is a restraint from those actions, which the mind (of its own

4. Description of the tyranny of the Amazonian ruler Radigund in Spenser's *Faerie Queene* 5.5.25.

5. Abcess.

accord) doth most willingly desire: to perform the intents and purposes of another's disposition, and that not but by mansuetude[1] or sweetness of entreaty; but by the force of authority and strength of compulsion. Now for me to follow change, according to the limitation of my own will and pleasure, there cannot be a greater freedom. Nor do I in my delight of change otherwise than as the whole world doth, or as becometh a daughter of the world to do. For what is the world, but a very shop or warehouse of change? Sometimes winter, sometimes summer; day and night: they hold sometimes riches, sometimes poverty, sometimes health, sometimes sickness: now pleasure; presently anguish; now honor; then contempt: and to conclude, there is nothing but change, which doth surround and mix with all our fortunes. And will you have poor woman such a fixed star, that she shall not so much as move or twinkle in her own sphere? That would be true slavery indeed, and a baseness beyond the chains of the worst servitude. Nature to everything she hath created hath given a singular delight in change, as to herbs, plants, and trees a time to wither and shed their leaves, a time to bud and bring forth their leaves, and a time for their fruits and flowers; to worms and creeping things a time to hide themselves in the pores and hollows of the earth, and a time to come abroad and suck the dew; to beasts liberty to choose their food, liberty to delight in their food, and liberty to feed and grow fat with their food. The birds have the air to fly in, the waters to bathe in, and the earth to feed on. But to man, both these and all things else, to alter, frame, and fashion, according to his will and delight shall rule him. Again, who will rob the eye of the variety of objects, the ear of the delight of sounds, the nose of smells, the tongue of taste, and the hand of feeling? And shall only woman, excellent woman, so much better in that she is something purer, be only deprived of this benefit? Shall she be the bondslave of time, the handmaid of opinion, or the strict observer of every frosty or cold benumbed imagination? It would be a cruelty beyond the rack or strapado.[2]

But you will say it is not change, but novelty, from which you deter us: a thing that doth avert the good, and erect the evil; prefer the faithless, and confound desert; that with the change of opinions breeds the change of states, and with continual alterations thrusts headlong forward both ruin and subversion. Alas (soft Sir) what can you christen by that new imagined title, when the words of a wise man are: *that what was done, is but done again: all things do change, and under the cope of heaven there is no new thing.*[3] So that whatsoever we do or imitate, it is neither slavish, base, nor a breeder of novelty.

Next, you condemn me of unnaturalness, in forsaking my creation, and contemning[4] custom. How do I forsake my creation, that do all the right and offices due to my creation? I was created free, born free, and live free: what lets me then so to spin out my time, that I may die free?

To alter creation were to walk on my hands with my heels upward, to feed myself with my feet, or to forsake the sweet sound of sweet words, for the hissing noise of the serpent: but I walk with a face erected, with a body clothed, with a mind busied, and with a heart full of reasonable and devout cogitations; only offensive in attire, inasmuch as it is a stranger to the curiosity of the present times, and an enemy to custom. Are we then bound to be the flatterers of time, or the dependents on custom? O miserable servitude chained only to baseness and folly! For then custom, nothing is more absurd, nothing more foolish. * * *

1. Gentleless, meekness.
2. Rack: a frame with a roller at either end on which a person would be tortured; strapado: a form of torture in which the victim's hands would be hands tied behind his or her back and the victim would then be suspended by a pulley with a sharp jolt.
3. Ecclesiastes 1.9.
4. Disdaining, despising.

Cato Iunior held it for a custom, never to eat meat but sitting on the ground. The Venetians kiss one another ever at the first meeting; and even in this day it is a general received custom amongst our English, that when we meet or overtake any man in our travel or journeying, to examine him whither he rides, how far, to what purpose, and where he lodgeth? Nay, and with that unmannerly boldness of inquisition, that it is a certain ground of a most insufficient quarrel, not to receive a full satisfaction of those demands which go far astray from good manners, or comely civility; and will you have us to marry ourselves to these mimic and most fantastic customs? It is a fashion or custom with us to mourn in black, yet the Argian[5] and Roman ladies ever mourned in white; and (if we will tie the action upon the signification of colors) I see not but we may mourn in green, blue, red or any simple color used in heraldry. For us to salute strangers with a kiss is counted but civility, but with foreign nations immodesty; for you to cut the hair of your upper lips, familiar here in England, everywhere else almost thought unmanly. To ride on side-saddles at first was counted here abominable pride, and et cetera. I might instance in a thousand things that only custom and not reason hath approved. To conclude, Custom is an idiot, and whoever dependeth wholly upon him, without the discourse of reason, will take from him his pied[6] coat, and become a slave indeed to contempt and censure.

But you say we are barbarous and shameless and cast off all softness, to run wild through a wilderness of opinions. In this you express more cruelty than in all the rest, because I do not stand with my hands on my belly like a baby[7] at Bartholomew Fair,[8] that move not my whole body when I should but only stir my head like Jack of the clock house[9] which has no joints, that is not dumb when wantons court me, as if asslike I were ready for all burdens, or because I weep not when injury gripes me, like a worried deer in the fangs of many curs. Am I therefore barbarous or shameless? He is much injurious that so baptized us; we are as free-born as men, have as free election, and as free spirits, we are compounded of like parts, and may with like liberty make benefit of our creations; my countenance shall smile on the worthy, and frown on the ignoble, I will hear the wise, and be deaf to idiots, give counsel to my friend, but be dumb to flatterers, I have hands that shall be liberal to reward desert, feet that shall move swiftly to do good offices, and thoughts that shall ever accompany freedom and severity. If this be barbarous, let me leave the city and live with creatures of like simplicity.

* * *

Hic-Mulier: Therefore to take your proportion in a few lines, (my dear Feminine-Masculine) tell me what Charter, prescription or right of claim you have to those things you make our absolute inheritance? Why do you curl, frizzle and powder your hair, bestowing more hours and time in dividing lock from lock, and hair from hair, in giving every thread his posture, and every curl his true fence and circumference than ever Caesar did in marshalling his army, either at Pharsalia, in Spain, or Britain? Why do you rob us of our ruffs, our earrings, carkanets,[1] and mamillions,[2] of our fans and feathers, our busks and French bodies, nay, of our masks, hoods, shadows, and shapynas,[3] not so much as the very art of painting, but you have so greedily engrossed it, that were it not for that little fantastical sharp pointed dagger that

5. Of Argos.
6. Spotted, motley.
7. Doll.
8. A popular carnival fair held every year from 1133 to 1865 at West Smithfield on August 24, the feast day of Saint Bartholomew.
9. Figure that strikes the bell of a clock.
1. A jeweled or gold necklace.
2. Rounded protuberances (from French *mamelon*, nipple).
3. Disguises.

hangs at your chins, and the cross hilt which guards your upper lip, hardly would there be any difference between the fair mistress and the foolish servant. But is this theft the uttermost of our spoil? Fie, you have gone a world further, and even ravished from us our speech, our actions, sports, and recreations. Goodness leave me, if I have not heard a man court his mistress with the same words that Venus did Adonis, or as near as the book could instruct him;[4] where are the tilts and tourneys, and lofty galliards[5] that were danced in the days of old, when men capered in the air like wanton kids on the tops of mountains, and turned above ground as if they had been compact of fire or a purer element?[6] Tut, all's forsaken, all's vanished, those motions showed more strength than art, and more courage than courtship; it was much too robustious, and rather spent the body than prepared it, especially where any defect before reigned; hence you took from us poor women our traverses and tourneys, our modest stateliness and curious slidings, and left us nothing but the new French garb of puppet hopping and setting. Lastly, poor shuttlecock[7] that was only a female invention, how have you taken it out of our hands, and made yourselves such lords and rulers over it, that though it be a very emblem of us, and our lighter despised fortunes, yet it dare now hardly come near us; nay, you keep it so imprisoned within your bed-chambers and dining rooms, amongst your pages and panders, that a poor innocent maid to give but a kick with her battledore,[8] were more than halfway to the ruin of her reputation. For this you have demolished the noble schools of horsemanship (of which many were in this city) hung up your arms to rust, glued up those swords in their scabbards that would shake all Christendom with the brandish, and entertained into your mind such softness, dullness, and effeminate niceness that it would even make *Heraclitus*[9] himself laugh against his nature to see how pulingly[1] you languish in this weak entertained sin of womanish softness. To see one of your gender either show himself (in the midst of his pride or riches) at a playhouse or public assembly; how (before he dare enter) with the Jacob's-staff of his own eyes and his pages, he takes a full survey of himself, from the highest sprig in his feather, to the lowest spangle that shines in his shoestring: how he prunes and picks himself like a hawk set a-weathering, calls every several garment to auricular[2] confession, making them utter both their mortal great stains, and their venial and less blemishes, though the mote must be much less than an atom. Then to see him pluck and tug everything into the form of the newest received fashion; and by *Durer's* rules[3] make his leg answerable to his neck; his thigh proportionable with his middle, his foot with his hand, and a world of such idle disdained foppery. To see him thus patched up with symmetry, make himself complete, and even as a circle, and lastly, cast himself among the eyes of the people (as an object of wonder) with more niceness than a virgin goes to the sheets of her first lover would make patience herself mad with anger, and cry with the poet:

> O hominum mores, O gens, O tempora dura,
> Quantus in urbe dolor; quantus in orbe dolus![4]

4. Venus, goddess of love, fell in love with the beautiful youth Adonis.
5. A brisk dance in triple time.
6. Men were thought to be dominated by dry humors and women by humid ones.
7. A small piece of cork with feathers sticking out of it, batted back and forth in the game of battledoor and shuttlecock.
8. A small racket, used to hit a shuttlecock.
9. Heraclitus was said to weep whenever he went forth in public (See Seneca, *De tranquilitate animi* 15.2).
1. In a whining tone.
2. Told privately, to the ear.
3. Albrecht Dürer (1471–1528), German painter and engraver, wrote a work on human proportions that was published after his death.
4. O customs of men, O people, O hard times / what great sadness in the city; what great fraud in the world.

Now since according to your own inference, even by the laws of nature, by the rules of religion, and the customs of all civil nations, it is necessary there be a distinct and special difference between man and woman, both in their habit and behaviors, what could we poor weak women do less (being far too weak by force to fetch back those spoils you have unjustly taken from us) than to gather up those garments you have proudly cast away, and therewith to clothe both our bodies and our minds; since no other means was left us to continue our names, and to support a difference? For to have held the way in which our forefathers first set us, or to have still embraced the civil modesty, or gentle sweetness of our soft inclinations; why, you had so far encroached upon us, and so over-bribed the world, to be deaf to any grant of restitution, that as at our creation, our whole sex was contained in man our first parent, so we should have had no other being, but in you, and your most effeminate quality. Hence we have preserved (though to our own shames) those manly things which you have forsaken, which would you again accept, and restore to us the blushes we laid by, when first we put on your masculine garments; doubt not but chaste thoughts and bashfulness will again dwell in us, and our palaces being newly gilt, trimmed, and re-edified, draw to us all the Graces, all the Muses,[5] which that you may more willingly do, and (as we of yours) grow into detestation of that deformity you have purloined, to the utter loss of your honors and reputations. Mark how the brave Italian poet,[6] even in the infancy of your abuses, most lively describes you:

About his neck a Carknet[7] rich he ware
Of precious Stones, all set in gold well tried;
His arms that erst all warlike weapons bare,
In golden bracelets wantonly were tied:
Into his ears two rings conveyed are
Of golden wire, at which on either side,
Two Indian pearls, in making like two pears,
Of passing price were pendant at his ears.

His locks bedewed with water of sweet savor,
Stood curled round in order on his head;
He had such wanton womanish behavior,
At though in valor he had ne'er been bred:
So chang'd in speech, in manners and in favor,
So from himself beyond all reason led,
By these enchantments of this amorous dame;
He was himself in nothing, but in name.

Thus you see your injury to us is of an old and inveterate continuance, having taken such strong root in your bosoms, that it can hardly be pulled up, without some offense to the soil: ours young and tender, scarce freed from the swaddling clothes, and therefore may with as much ease be lost, as it was with little difficulty found. Cast then from you our ornaments, and put on your own armors. Be men in shape, men in show, men in words, men in actions, men in counsel, men in example: then will we love and serve you; then will we hear and obey you; then will we like rich jewels hang at your

5. The graces were the three sisters, Aglaia, Thalia, and Euphrosyne, viewed as bestowers of charm and beauty; the muses were the nine daughters of Zeus and Memory who inspire poetry and the arts.

6. Ludovico Ariosto (1474–1532), whose description of Ruggiero's decadence when he is seduced by the sorceress Alcina in *Orlando Furioso* 7 is quoted here in the translation (1590) by Sir John Harington, Queen Elizabeth's godson.

7. Necklace.

ears to take our instructions, like true friends follow you through all dangers, and like careful leeches[8] pour oil into your wounds. Then shall you find delight in our words; pleasure in our faces; faith in our hearts; chastity in our thoughts, and sweetness both in our inward and outward inclinations. Comeliness shall be then our study; fear our armor, and modesty our practice: then shall we be all your most excellent thoughts can desire, and have nothing in us less than impudence and deformity.

Haec-Vir. Enough: you have both raised my eyelids, cleared my sight, and made my heart entertain both shame and delight at an instant; shame in my follies past; delight in our noble and worthy conversion. Away then from me these light vanities, the only ensigns[9] of a weak and soft nature: and come you grave and solid pieces, which arm a man with fortitude and resolution: you are too rough and stubborn for a woman's wearing, we will here change our attires, as we have changed our minds, and with our attires, our names. I will no more be *Haec-Vir*, but *Hic Vir*, nor you *Hic-Mulier*, but *Haec Mulier*. From henceforth deformity shall pack to Hell; and if at any time he hide himself upon the earth, yet it shall be with contempt and disgrace. He shall have no friend but Poverty; no favorer but Folly, nor no reward but Shame. Henceforth we will live nobly like ourselves, ever sober, ever discreet, ever worthy; true men, and true women. We will be henceforth like well-coupled doves, full of industry, full of love: I mean, not of sensual and carnal love, but heavenly and divine love, which proceeds from God, whose inexpressible nature none is able to deliver in words, since is like his dwelling, high and beyond the reach of human apprehension.

[End of Perspectives: Tracts on Women and Gender]

Thomas Dekker

1572?–1632

and

Thomas Middleton

1580?–1627

Thomas Dekker was one of the most talented and prolific of early modern dramatists, yet one of the most destitute. Though he wrote over seventy plays (many of them now lost) and more than a dozen tracts, Dekker was plagued by poverty throughout his life. In 1598, the same year that Francis Meres listed Dekker as one of the greatest English writers of tragedy, he was imprisoned for debt. The next year, he was arrested for owing money to the acting company of the Lord Chamberlain's Men. Later, he was sentenced to the King's Bench Prison from 1613 to 1619. His wife, Mary, died while he was in prison. While there, Dekker managed to publish the prose pamphlet *Villanies* (1616), the fourth edition of *Lantern and Candlelight*, to which he added descriptions of prison life.

Dekker's religious beliefs were as uncertain as his finances; he was twice indicted for recusancy—refusal to attend Church of England services. Yet he wrote many strongly Protestant works, among them *The Whore of Babylon*, a play castigating the evils of Catholic Spain and

8. Physicians.

9. Banners, signs.

celebrating the triumph of England over the Armada. He may have been avoiding church so as not to be apprehended for debt by officers of the law, who scouted Church of England services on Sundays.

Dekker began to write plays in 1593 for clients of Philip Henslowe, a theatrical entrepreneur, who paid close to six pounds per play (roughly $500 in today's purchasing power). Henslowe's *Diary* records that in one year alone, 1598, Dekker wrote fifteen plays. Jonson wrote of him in *Poetaster*, "He hath one of the most over-flowing rank wits in London."

Dekker frequently collaborated with other playwrights, including John Webster, and Shakespeare, with whom he wrote *The Play of Sir Thomas More* in 1595–1596. In 1604 Dekker worked on two plays with Thomas Middleton: *The Magnificent Entertainment*, which celebrated the accession of King James, and *The Honest Whore*, which combined a moralizing theme with a realistic depiction of London life. Then, in 1611, Dekker and Middleton cowrote *The Roaring Girl*, a romantic comedy built around the antics of the notorious London figure Moll Cutpurse. The same year, Dekker and Webster started a running debate with Jonson that began with their *Westward Ho!*, to which Jonson responded with his satire of the Puritan bourgeoisie called *Eastward Ho!*, which was in turn rebutted by Dekker and Webster's *Northward Ho!*

Dekker's work is notable for his colorful depiction of London life and his perspective—as one of their member—on the struggles of the working class and the poor. He wrote in a wide variety of dramatic genres: patriotic allegory, social satire, and romantic comedy, among others. All his work shows a reliance on the native English tradition. From the medieval mystery and morality play, Dekker took such features as the devil, allegory, moral teaching, and the simple folk as the bearers of truth. He combined these elements with the most contemporary topics, including the life of Wyatt, the defeat of the Armada, and the fortunes of Moll Cutpurse. From slang to fashion, from gender roles to class conflict, and from street crime to the venality of the middle class, Dekker's pamphlets and plays present the panorama of London with a vividness and humor that are unsurpassed in early modern English literature.

Like Dekker, Thomas Middleton was a Londoner, and although he came from a middle-class background, he was well acquainted with the London street life that they both wrote about. While Dekker made it only through grammar school, Middleton went to university and may even have studied at one of the Inns of Court. He started his writing career with verse satires, which, like Dekker's pamphlets, described the vices of London—including *Micro-Cynicon, or Six Snarling Satires* (1599). Middleton became a great but controversial success at the box office. One of his most popular plays, *A Game at Chess* (1624), was reported to the Privy Council for having "the boldness and presumption, in a rude and dishonorable fashion to represent on the stage the person of his majesty the King of Spain." Middleton was imprisoned for a brief time. Just a few years later, Middleton, like Dekker, died in poverty.

Middleton wrote for the public stage that featured the men's companies and for the more fashionable private theaters in which boy players acted. His first play, the now lost tragedy *Caesar's Fall* (1602), was commissioned by Philip Henslowe and written with John Webster. In comedy, Middleton's great collaboration was with Dekker, first on *The Honest Whore* (1604) and then on *The Roaring Girl* (1611), of which he may have been the chief author. From 1602 to 1608, Middleton wrote such witty satirical comedies as *Blurt, Master Constable*, for the Boys of Saint Paul's, and *The Family of Love*, for the Children of the Chapel Royal. Dekker may well have had a hand in both these plays. With the discontinuation of the children's companies after 1609, Middleton returned to the public stage, writing both comedies and tragedies such as *The Changeling* (1620–1621), in which a woman tries to win the man she loves but ends up as an accomplice to murder and the mistress of a murderer.

It has been said that with Middleton the great age of Elizabethan tragedy came to an end. Since T.S. Eliot drew modern attention back to Middleton as "a great recorder" of contemporary life, he has been admired mainly for his realism. But Middleton is also a great ironist and one of the finest writers of quick dialogue that turns on double meanings and innuendoes. *The*

Roaring Girl is about an actual living person, known to the audience from the streets of London and from the stage of the Fortune Theater. This comedy portrays a woman who is not only quick and witty, like Shakespeare's cross-dressing heroines, but also fiercely independent and unattached to any man, a fact that has spurred a renewal of interest in how this unusual play represents sex and gender roles.

The Roaring Girl

The Roaring Girl (1611) is unique in early modern English drama for the presentation of a notorious figure of the London streets: Mary Frith. Other works attest to her popularity: an earlier play, now lost, *Long Meg* (1594), and the anonymous jest biography *Long Meg of Westminster* (1620). Like Long Meg, the dramatic heroine Moll dresses as a man to best her male opponent in a duel. City documents and letters record the public appearances of Moll Frith. *The Consistory of London Correction Book* for 27 January 1612 cites an appearance by the real Mary Frith on the stage of the Fortune Theater in spring of 1611. And a letter of John Chamberlain recounts her public penance at Paul's Cross. Although Mary Frith had connections with London criminal world, the Star Chamber suit of 1611 attests to her help in apprehending thieves. The fictional Moll is also a type of social bandit, who not only steals from the rich to give to the poor but even uncovers greed and hypocrisy.

Drawing on the popular pamphlet literature, Middleton and Dekker wove together such elements as the cross-dressing Robin Hood, the coney-catching plot (in which a trickster fools a gullible rube), the ruses of clever wives, and canting language (a kind of street slang). The subplot in which Laxton concocts a fake legal process in an attempt to extort money from the Gallipots plays off a commonplace from rogue literature. In *A Notable Discovery of Cosenage* a trickster plays husband off against wife through a pretended lawsuit. From another popular tradition, the comic debate on the battle between the sexes, *The Batchelar's Banquet* (1603) may have provided inspiration for such devices as passing off a lover as a relative and claiming pregnancy as an excuse for capriciousness.

All these elements are part of a larger design that interweaves three plot models: New Comedy, prodigal literature, and citizen comedy. To the stock New Comedy plot of the son who is barred from marrying the woman of his choice by his disapproving father, Middleton and Dekker added the novel element of the prodigal youth doting on a notorious woman. Young Sebastian Wengrave gains his father's approval by convincing him that marriage to anyone—even the less than wealthy Mary Fitzallard—would be better than marriage to Moll. In addition to the pretense of a young man sowing his wild oats, the play also presents a subplot that turns around the fidelity of two tradesmen's wives. The stock ending in citizen comedy confirmed the chastity of the good wives, but *The Roaring Girl* adds a new twist with the wives' condemnation of their seducers' deceptions.

Many critics have assigned credit for the plot to Middleton and credit for the rogue literature elements to Dekker, but most scenes appear to have been written by both writers. This play was the last joint project of these two playwrights, and with it they succeeded in fusing their respective talents. Middleton was known for his snappy dialogue liberally laced with *double entendres;* Dekker, more of a moralist than his partner, was known for his use of popular street slang, or canting. Though Act 5, scene 1, borrows heavily from Dekker's pamphlets *The Belman of London* and *Lantern and Candlelight,* even here evidence of Middleton's influence crops up in the language. It would appear that rather than dividing up scenes between them, each edited or rewrote the other's work. This collaboration resulted in a play and a character that were more memorable than any either writer had previously produced.

If the *Roaring Girl* was once overlooked in part because of the problems posed by joint authorship, it is now enjoying a resurgence of interest because of its fascinating representation of gender, sexuality, the marketplace, and class relations. Not only does Moll's cross-dressing pose questions about sex and gender roles, but Laxton's and Goshawk's seductions of Mistresses Gallipot and Openwork portray an unsentimental view of chastity. As Moll notes, "'tis impossible to know what woman is thoroughly honest because she's ne'er thoroughly tried" (2.1). The portrayal of sex is closely related to that of the marketplace; indeed, all relationships in the play are at times reduced to a question of power: "All that live in the world are but great fish and little fish, and feed upon one another" (3.3). Rising above all this is the disturbing and indomitable Moll. On stage in seven out of eleven scenes, Moll dominates the play with her charm and wit. She exercises moral judgment without being moralistic. Moll is her own woman and her own standard: "I please myself, and care not else who loves me" (5.2). Moll Cutpurse steals the show and makes *The Roaring Girl* one of the most innovative plays in English literature.

The Roaring Girl; or, Moll Cut-Purse

Dramatis Personae

SIR ALEXANDER WENGRAVE[1]
SEBATIAN WENGRAVE, his son
SIR GUY FITZALLARD
SIR DAVY DAPPER
JACK DAPPER, his son
SIR ADAM APPLETON
SIR THOMAS LONG
SIR BEAUTEOUS GANYMEDE[2]
LORD NOLAND
GOSHAWK
LAXTON
GREENWIT
GALLIPOT, an apothecary
TILTYARD, a feather-seller
OPENWORK, a sempster° *tailor*
NEATFOOT, Sir A. Wengrave's man
GULL,° page to Jack Dapper *fool*
RALPH TRAPDOOR
TEARCAT[3]
CURTLEAX,° a sergeant *broadsword*
HANGER,° his yeoman *strap on a sword belt*
MOLL,[4] The Roaring Girl
MARY FITZALLARD, daughter to Sir Guy
MISTRESS GALLIPOT
MISTRESS TILTYARD
MISTRESS OPENWORK
Gentlemen, Cutpurses,° etc. *pickpockets*
Coachman
Porter
Tailor

1. Many of the characters' names contain puns or humorous allusions: Wengrave/Went grave, Laxton/Lack-stone (lacks land or testicles), Jack Dapper/a dapper jack (a term of mockery).
2. Ganymede, the name of Zeus's cupbearer, came to mean a young male homosexual lover.
3. "To tear a cat" means to act like a swaggering hero.
4. Moll was a common term for a prostitute as well as a nickname for Mary, a name symbolizing chastity.

Prologue

A play expected long makes the audience look
For wonders—that each scene should be a book
Composed to all perfection. Each one comes
And brings a play in's head with him; up he sums
What he would of a roaring girl have writ—
If that he finds not here, he mews at it.
Only we entreat you think our scene
Cannot speak high, the subject being but mean.
A roaring girl, whose notes till now never were,
Shall fill with laughter our vast theater:
That's all which I dare promise; tragic passion,
And such grave stuff, is this day out of fashion.
I see attention sets wide ope her gates
Of hearing, and with covetous listening waits
To know what girl this roaring girl should be—
For of that tribe are many. One is she
That roars at midnight in deep tavern bowls,
That beats the watch, and constables controls;
Another roars i' th' day-time, swears, stabs, gives braves,° *acts tough*
Yet sells her soul to the lust of fools and slaves:
Both these are suburb-roarers. Then there's besides
A civil, city-roaring girl, whose pride,
Feasting, and riding, shakes her husband's state,
And leaves him roaring through an iron grate.
None of these roaring girls is ours: she flies
With wings more lofty. Thus her character lies—
Yet what need characters, when to give a guess
Is better than the person to express?
But would you know who 'tis? Would you hear her name?—
She is called Mad Moll; her life our acts proclaim!

Scene, LONDON.

Act 1

Scene 1

[*A room in Sir Alexander Wengrave's house. Enter Mary Fitzallard disguised like a sempster,*[5] *with a case for bands, and Neatfoot with her, a napkin on his shoulder, and a trencher*[6] *in his hand, as from table.*]

NEATFOOT The young gentleman, our young master, sir Alexander's son, is it into his ears, sweet damsel, emblem[7] of fragility, you desire to have a message transported, or to be transcendent?

MARY A private word or two, sir; nothing else.

NEATFOOT You shall fructify[8] in that which you come for; your pleasure shall be satisfied to your full contentation. I will, fairest tree of generation, watch when our young master is erected, that is to say, up, and deliver him to this your most white hand.

5. Tailor. Bands: collars.
6. A shallow wooden bowl.
7. Symbol.
8. Double meanings, such as those in "fructify" (flourish/become pregnant) and "erected" (gets up/gets it up), run throughout the play.

MARY Thanks, sir.

NEATFOOT And withal certify him, that I have culled out for him, now his belly is replenished, a daintier bit or modicum than any lay upon his trencher at dinner. Hath he notion of your name, I beseech your chastity?

MARY One, sir, of whom he bespake falling bands.[9]

NEATFOOT Falling bands? it shall so be given him. If you please to venture your modesty in the hall amongst a curl-pated company of rude serving-men, and take such as they can set before you, you shall be most seriously and ingeniously[1] welcome.

MARY I have dined indeed already, sir.

NEATFOOT Or will you vouchsafe to kiss the lip of a cup of rich Orleans in the buttery amongst our waiting-women?

MARY Not now, in truth, sir.

NEATFOOT Our young master shall then have a feeling of your being here; presently it shall so be given him.

MARY I humbly thank you, sir. But that my bosom
[*Exit Neatfoot.*]
Is full of bitter sorrows, I could smile
To see this formal ape play antic tricks;
But in my breast a poisoned arrow sticks,
And smiles cannot become me. Love woven slightly,
Such as thy false heart makes, wears out as lightly;
But love being truly bred i' th' soul, like mine,
Bleeds even to death at the least wound it takes,—
The more we quench this [fire], the less it slakes:
O me!

[*Enter Sebastian Wengrave with Neatfoot.*]

SEBASTIAN A sempster speak with me, sayest thou?

NEATFOOT Yes, sir; she's there, *viva voce* to deliver her auricular confession.[2]

SEBASTIAN With me, sweetheart? what is't?

MARY I have brought home your bands, sir.

SEBASTIAN Bands?—Neatfoot.

NEATFOOT Sir?

SEBASTIAN Prithee, look in; for all the gentlemen are upon rising.

NEATFOOT Yes, sir; a most methodical attendance shall be given.

SEBASTIAN And dost hear? If my father call for me, say I am busy with a sempster.

NEATFOOT Yes, sir; he shall know it that you are busied with a needle-woman.[3]

SEBASTIAN In's ear, good Neatfoot.

NEATFOOT It shall be so given him. [*Exit.*]

SEBASTIAN Bands? You're mistaken, sweetheart, I bespake none:
When, where, I prithee? What bands? Let me see them.

MARY Yes, sir; a bond fast sealed with solemn oaths,
Subscribed unto, as I thought, with your soul;
Delivered as your deed in sight of heaven
Is this bond cancellèd? have you forgot me?

SEBASTIAN Ha! life of my life, sir Guy Fitzallard's daughter?
What has transformed my love to this strange shape?

9. Flat collar, with a play on banns of marriage and bonds of marriage contract.
1. Honestly, without reserve.
2. Telling one's sins to a priest; here a sexual confession.
3. Needle: slang for penis.

Stay; make all sure. [*Shuts doors.*] So: now speak and be brief,
Because the wolf's at door that lies in wait
To prey upon us both. Albeit mine eyes
Are blest by thine, yet this so strange disguise
Holds me with fear and wonder.

MARY Mine's a loathed sight;
Why from it are you banished else so long?

SEBASTIAN I must cut short my speech: in broken language
Thus much, sweet Moll; I must thy company shun;
I court another Moll my thoughts must run
As a horse runs that's blind round in a mill,
Out every step, yet keeping one path still.

MARY Umph! must you shun my company? in one knot
Have both our hands by th' hands of heaven been tied,
Now to be broke?[4] I thought me once your bride;
Our fathers did agree on the time when:
And must another bedfellow fill my room?

SEBASTIAN Sweet maid, let's lose no time; 'tis in heaven's book
Set down, that I must have thee; an oath we took
To keep our vows but when the knight your father
Was from mine parted, storms began to sit
Upon my covetous father's brows, which fell
From them on me. He reckoned up what gold
This marriage would draw from him; at which he swore,
To lose so much blood could not grieve him more:
He then dissuades me from thee, called thee not fair,
And asked what is she but a beggar's heir?
He scorned thy dowry of five thousand marks.[5]
If such a sum of money could be found,
And I would match with that, he'd not undo it,
Provided his bags might add nothing to it;
But vowed, if I took thee, nay, more, did swear it,
Save birth, from him I nothing should inherit.

MARY What follows then? my shipwreck?

SEBASTIAN Dearest, no
Though wildly in a labyrinth I go,
My end is to meet thee: with a side-wind
Must I now sail, else I no haven can find,
But both must sink for ever. There's a wench
Called Moll, Mad Moll, or Merry Moll; a creature
So strange in quality, a whole city takes
Note of her name and person. All that affection
I owe to thee, on her in counterfeit passion
I spend, to mad° my father; he believes *infuriate*
I doat upon this Roaring Girl, and grieves
As it becomes a father for a son
That could be so bewitched: yet I'll go on

4. Mary and Sebastian have pledged spousals *de futuro*, a contract which was often secret and the equivalent of marriage itself.

5. A small fortune. A mark equaled two-thirds of a pound.

This crooked way, sigh still for her, feign° dreams *pretend*
In which I'll talk only of her; these streams
Shall, I hope, force my father to consent
That here I anchor, rather than be rent
Upon a rock so dangerous. Art thou pleased,
Because thou seest we're waylaid, that I take
A path that's safe, though it be far about?

MARY My prayers with heaven guide thee!

SEBASTIAN Then I will on
My father is at hand; kiss, and begone!
Hours shall be watched for meetings I must now,
As men for fear, to a strange idol bow.

MARY Farewell!

SEBASTIAN I'll guide thee forth: when next we meet,
A story of Moll shall make our mirth more sweet.

[*Exeunt.*]

Scene 2

[*Enter Sir Alexander Wengrave, Sir Davy Dapper, Sir Adam Appleton, Goshawk, Laxton, and Gentlemen.*]

ALL Thanks, good sir Alexander, for our bounteous cheer!

SIR ALEXANDER Fie, fie, in giving thanks you pay too dear.

SIR DAVY When bounty spreads the table, faith, 'twere sin,
At going off if thanks should not step in.

SIR ALEXANDER No more of thanks, no more. Ay, marry, sir.
Th' inner room was too close how do you like
This parlor, gentlemen?

ALL O, passing° well! *exceedingly*

SIR ADAM What a sweet breath the air casts here, so cool!

GOSHAWK I like the prospect best.

LAXTON See how 'tis furnished!

SIR DAVY A very fair sweet room.

SIR ALEXANDER Sir Davy Dapper,
The furniture that doth adorn this room[6]
Cost many a fair grey groat[7] ere it came here;
But good things are most cheap when they're most dear.
Nay, when you look into my galleries,[8]
How bravely they're trimmed up, you all shall swear
You're highly pleased to see what's set down there:
Stories of men and women, mixed together
Fair ones with foul, like sunshine in wet weather;
Within one square[9] a thousand heads are laid,
So close that all of heads the room seems made;
As many faces there, filled with blithe looks,
Show like the promising titles of new books
Writ merrily, the readers being their own eyes,

6. This speech describes what the Fortune Theater was like.
7. Four pence.
8. Rooms for artwork or theater balconies.
9. The Fortune was built on a square plan.

Which seem to move and to give plaudities;° *applause*
And here and there, whilst with obsequious° ears *servile*
Thronged heaps° do listen, a cut-purse thrusts and leers *crowds*
With hawk's eyes for his prey; I need not show him;
By a hanging, villainous look yourselves may know him,
The face is drawn so rarely; then, sir, below
The very floor, as 'twere, waves to and fro,
And, like a floating island,[1] seems to move
Upon a sea bound in with shores above.

ALL These sights are excellent!

SIR ALEXANDER I'll show you all:
Since we are met, make our parting comical.

[*Reenter Sebastian Wengrave with Greenwit.*]

SEBASTIAN This gentleman, my friend, will take his leave, sir.

SIR ALEXANDER Ha! take his leave, Sebastian, who?

SEBASTIAN This gentleman.

SIR ALEXANDER Your love, sir, has already given me some time,
And if you please to trust my age with more,
It shall pay double interest: good sir, stay.

GREENWIT I have been too bold.

SIR ALEXANDER Not so, sir: a merry day
'Mongst friends being spent, is better than gold saved.—
Some wine, some wine! Where be these knaves I keep?

[*Reenter Neatfoot with several Servants.*]

NEATFOOT At your worshipful elbow, sir.

SIR ALEXANDER You're kissing my maids, drinking, or fast asleep.

NEATFOOT Your worship has given it us right.

SIR ALEXANDER You varlets,° stir! *knaves*
Chairs, stools, and cushions!—

[*Servants bring in wine, and place chairs, etc.*]

Prithee, sir Davy Dapper,
Make that chair thine.

SIR DAVY 'Tis but an easy gift;
And yet I thank you for it, sir: I'll take it.

SIR ALEXANDER A chair for old sir Adam Appleton!

NEATFOOT A back friend[2] to your worship.

SIR ADAM Marry, good Neatfoot,
I thank thee for't; back friends sometimes are good.

SIR ALEXANDER Pray, make that stool your perch, good master Goshawk.

GOSHAWL I stoop to your lure, sir.

SIR ALEXANDER Son Sebastian,
Take master Greenwit to you.

SEBASTIAN Sit, dear friend.

SIR ALEXANDER Nay, master Laxton—furnish master Laxton
With what he wants, a stone,—a stool, I would say,
A stool.

LAXTON I had rather stand, sir.

1. The stage.

2. A backer. Also, a pretended friend.

SIR ALEXANDER I know you had, good master Laxton so, so.
[*Exeunt Neatfoot and Servants*.]
Now here's a mess of friends; and, gentlemen,
Because time's glass shall not be running long,
I'll quicken it with a pretty tale.

SIR DAVY Good tales do well
In these bad days, where vice does so excel.

SIR ADAM Begin, Sir Alexander.

SIR ALEXANDER Last day I met
An aged man, upon whose head was scored
A debt of just so many years as these
Which I owe to my grave: the man you all know.

ALL His name, I pray you, sir?

SIR ALEXANDER Nay, you shall pardon me:
But when he saw me, with a sigh that brake,
Or seemed to break, his heart-strings, thus he spake:
O my good knight, says he (and then his eyes
Were richer even by that which made them poor,
They'd spent so many tears they had no more),
O sir, says he, you know it! for you ha' seen
Blessings to rain upon mine house and me:
Fortune, who slaves men, was my slave; her wheel
Hath spun me golden threads;[3] for, I thank heaven,
I ne'er had but one cause to curse my stars.
I ask'd him then what that one cause might be.

ALL So, sir.

SIR ALEXANDER He paused; and as we often see
A sea so much becalmed, there can be found
No wrinkle on his brow, his waves being drowned
In their own rage; but when th' imperious winds
Use strange invisible tyranny to shake
Both heaven's and earth's foundation at their noise,
The seas, swelling with wrath to part that fray,
Rise up, and are more wild, more mad than they:
Even so this good old man was by my question
Stirred up to roughness; you might see his gall[4]
Flow even in's eyes; then grew he fantastical.

SIR DAVY Fantastical? ha, ha!

SIR ALEXANDER Yes; and talked oddly.

SIR ADAM Pray, sir, proceed:
How did this old man end?

SIR ALEXANDER Marry, sir, thus:
He left his wild fit to read o'er his cards;
Yet then, though age cast snow on all his hairs,
He joyed, because, says he, the god of gold
Has been to me no niggard; that disease,
Of which all old men sicken, avarice,
Never infected me—

3. A mixed image of Fortune's Wheel with the Fates' spinning wheel.

4. Bile, resentment.

LAXTON [*Aside.*] He means not himself, I'm sure.

SIR ALEXANDER For, like a lamp
Fed with continual oil, I spend and throw
My light to all that need it, yet have still
Enough to serve myself: O but, quoth he,
Though heaven's dew fall thus on this aged tree,
I have a son that, like a wedge, doth cleave
My very heart-root!

SIR DAVY Had he such a son?

SEBASTIAN [*Aside.*] Now I do smell a fox strongly.[5]

SIR ALEXANDER Let's see; no, master Greenwit is not yet
So mellow in years as he; but as like Sebastian,
Just like my son Sebastian, such another.

SEBASTIAN [*Aside.*] How finely, like a fencer,
My father fetches his by-blows to hit me!
But if I beat you not at your own weapon
Of subtilty—

SIR ALEXANDER This son, saith he, that should be
The column and main arch unto my house,
The crutch unto my age, becomes a whirlwind
Shaking the firm foundation.

SIR ADAM 'Tis some prodigal.

SEBASTIAN [*Aside.*] Well shot, old Adam Bell!

SIR ALEXANDER No city-monster neither, no prodigal,
But sparing, wary, civil, and, though wifeless,
An excellent husband; and such a traveller,
He has more tongues in his head than some have teeth.

SIR DAVY I have but two in mine.

GOSHAWK So sparing and so wary?
What, then, could vex his father so?

SIR ALEXANDER O, a woman!

SEBASTIAN A flesh-fly, that can vex any man.

SIR ALEXANDER A scurvy woman,
On whom the passionate old man swore he doated;
A creature, saith he, nature hath brought forth
To mock the sex of woman. It is a thing
One knows not how to name; her birth began
Ere she was all made: 'tis woman more than man,
Man more than woman; and, which to none can hap,
The sun gives her two shadows to one shape;
Nay, more, let this strange thing walk, stand, or sit,
No blazing star draws more eyes after it.

SIR DAVY A monster! 'tis some monster!

SIR ALEXANDER She's a varlet.

SEBASTIAN [*Aside.*] Now is my cue to bristle.

SIR ALEXANDER A naughty pack.[6]

SEBASTIAN 'Tis false!

SIR ALEXANDER Ha, boy?

5. Smell a rat.

6. A bad person.

SEBASTIAN 'Tis false!
SIR ALEXANDER What's false? I say she's naught.
SEBASTIAN I say, that tongue
That dares speak so, but yours, sticks in the throat
Of a rank villain set yourself aside—
SIR ALEXANDER So, sir, what then?
SEBASTIAN Any here else had lied.—
[*Aside.*] I think I shall fit you.
SIR ALEXANDER Lie?
SEBASTIAN Yes.
SIR DAVY Doth this concern him?
SIR ALEXANDER Ah, sirrah-boy,
Is your blood heated? boils it? are you stung?
I'll pierce you deeper yet.—O my dear friends,
I am that wretched father! this that son,
That sees his ruin, yet headlong on doth run.
SIR ADAM Will you love such a poison?
SIR DAVY Fie, fie.
SEBASTIAN You're all mad.
SIR ALEXANDER Thou'rt sick at heart, yet feel'st it not of all these,
What gentleman but thou, knowing his disease
Mortal, would shun the cure!—O master Greenwit,
Would you to such an idol bow?
GREENWIT Not I, sir.
SIR ALEXANDER Here's master Laxton; has he mind to a woman
As thou hast?
LAXTON No, not I, sir.
SIR ALEXANDER Sir, I know it.
LAXTON Their good parts are so rare, their bad so common,
I will have nought to do with any woman.
SIR DAVY 'Tis well done, master Laxton.
SIR ALEXANDER O thou cruel boy,
Thou would'st with lust an old man's life destroy!
Because thou see'st I'm half-way in my grave,
Thou shovel'st dust upon me: would thou might'st have
Thy wish, most wicked, most unnatural!
SIR DAVY Why, sir, 'tis thought sir Guy Fitzallard's daughter
Shall wed your son Sebastian.
SIR ALEXANDER Sir Davy Dapper,
I have upon my knees wooed this fond boy
To take that virtuous maiden.
SEBASTIAN Hark you; a word, sir.
You on your knees have cursed that virtuous maiden,
And me for loving her; yet do you now
Thus baffle[7] me to my face; wear not your knees
In such entreats; give me Fitzallard's daughter.
SIR ALEXANDER I'll give thee rats-bane rather.
SEBASTIAN Well, then, you know

7. Deceive, confound.

What dish I mean to feed upon.
SIR ALEXANDER Hark, gentlemen! he swears
To have this cut-purse drab,° to spite my gall. *prostitute*
ALL Master Sebastian—
SEBASTIAN I am deaf to you all.
I'm so bewitched, so bound to my desires,
Tears, prayers, threats, nothing can quench out those fires
That burn within me. [*Exit.*]
SIR ALEXANDER [*Aside.*] Her blood shall quench it, then.—
Lose him not; O dissuade him, gentlemen!
SIR DAVY He shall be weaned, I warrant you.
SIR ALEXANDER Before his eyes
Lay down his shame, my grief, his miseries.
ALL No more, no more; away!
[*Exeunt all but Sir Alexander Wengrave.*]
SIR ALEXANDER I wash a negro,
Losing both pains and cost:[8] but take thy flight,
I'll be most near thee when I'm least in sight.
Wild buck, I'll hunt thee breathless thou shalt run on,
But I will turn thee when I'm not thought upon.—
[*Enter Trapdoor with a letter.*]
Now, sirrah, what are you? leave your ape's tricks, and speak.

TRAPDOOR A letter from my captain to your worship.

SIR ALEXANDER O, O, now I remember; 'tis to prefer thee into my service.

TRAPDOOR To be a shifter under your worship's nose of a clean trencher, when there's a good bit upon't.

SIR ALEXANDER Troth, honest fellow—Hum—ha—let me see—
[*Aside.*] This knave shall be the axe to hew that down
At which I stumble; has a face that promiseth
Much of a villain I will grind his wit,
And, if the edge prove fine, make use of it.—
Come hither, sirrah canst thou be secret, ha?

TRAPDOOR As two crafty attorneys plotting the undoing of their clients.

SIR ALEXANDER Did'st never, as thou'st walked about this town,
Hear of a wench call'd Moll, mad, merry Moll?
TRAPDOOR Moll Cutpurse, sir?
SIR ALEXANDER The same; dost thou know her, then?

TRAPDOOR As well as I know 'twill rain upon Simon and Jude's day next: I will sift all the taverns i' th' city, and drink half pots with all the water-men[9] a' th' Bankside, but, if you will, sir, I'll find her out.

SIR ALEXANDER That task is easy; do't then: hold thy hand up.
What's this? is't burnt?[1]

TRAPDOOR No, sir, no; a little singed with making fireworks.

SIR ALEXANDER There's money, spend it; that being spent, fetch more. [*Gives money.*]

TRAPDOOR O sir, that all the poor soldiers in England had such a leader! For fetching, no water-spaniel is like me.

SIR ALEXANDER This wench we speak of strays so from her kind,

8. Proverbial. See Jeremiah 13.23: "Can the black Moor change his skin? or the leopard his spots?"

9. Boatmen.

1. Branded, a common punishment for crime.

Nature repents she made her: 'tis a mermaid
Has toled° my son to shipwreck. *lured*

TRAPDOOR I'll cut her comb° for you. *put her down*

SIR ALEXANDER I'll tell out gold for thee, then. Hunt her forth,
Cast out a line hung full of silver hooks
To catch her to thy company; deep spendings
May draw her that's most chaste to a man's bosom.

TRAPDOOR The gingling of golden bells, and a good fool with a hobbyhorse, will draw all the whores i' th' town to dance in a morris.

SIR ALEXANDER Or rather, for that's best (they say sometimes
She goes in breeches), follow her as her man.

TRAPDOOR And when her breeches are off, she shall follow me.

SIR ALEXANDER Beat all thy brains to serve her.

TRAPDOOR Zounds, sir, as country wenches beat cream till butter comes.

SIR ALEXANDER Play thou the subtle spider; weave fine nets
To ensnare her very life.

TRAPDOOR Her life?

SIR ALEXANDER Yes; suck
Her heart-blood, if thou canst twist thou but cords
To catch her, I'll find law to hang her up.

TRAPDOOR Spoke like a worshipful bencher!

SIR ALEXANDER Trace all her steps at this she-fox's den
Watch what lambs enter; let me play the shepherd
To save their throats from bleeding, and cut hers.

TRAPDOOR This is the goll° shall do't. *hand*

SIR ALEXANDER Be firm, and gain me
Ever thine own this done, I entertain thee.
How is thy name?

TRAPDOOR My name, sir, is Ralph Trapdoor, honest Ralph.

SIR ALEXANDER Trapdoor, be like thy name, a dangerous step
For her to venture on; but unto me—

TRAPDOOR As fast as your sole to your boot or shoe, sir.

SIR ALEXANDER Hence, then; be little seen here as thou canst;
I'll still be at thine elbow.

TRAPDOOR The trapdoor's set.
Moll, if you budge, you're gone: this me shall crown;
A roaring boy the roaring girl puts down.

SIR ALEXANDER God-a-mercy, lose no time. [*Exeunt.*]

Act 2

Scene 1

[*Three Shops open in a rank: the first an Apothecary's shop,*[2] *the next a Feather-shop, the third a Sempster's shop; Mistress Gallipot in the first, Mistress Tiltyard in the next, Openwork and Mistress Openwork in the third. Enter Laxton, Goshawk, and Greenwit.*]

MISTRESS OPENWORK Gentlemen, what is't you lack? What is't you buy? See fine bands and ruffs, fine lawns, fine cambrics: What is't you lack, gentlemen? What is't you buy?

2. Apothecaries sold spices, medicines, and tobacco.

LAXTON Yonder's the shop.

GOSHAWK Is that she?

LAXTON Peace.

GREENWIT She that minces tobacco?

LAXTON Ay; she's a gentlewoman born, I can tell you, though it be her hard fortune now to shred Indian pot-herbs.

GOSHAWK O sir, 'tis many a good woman's fortune, when her husband turns bankrout,[3] to begin with pipes and set up again.

LAXTON And, indeed, the raising of the woman is the lifting up of the man's head at all times; if one flourish, t'other will bud as fast, I warrant ye.

GOSHAWK Come, thou'rt familiarly acquainted there, I grope[4] that.

LAXTON And you grope no better i' th' dark, you may chance lie i' th' ditch when you're drunk.

GOSHAWK Go, thou'rt a mystical lecher!

LAXTON I will not deny but my credit may take up an ounce of pure smoke.

GOSHAWK May take up an ell of pure smock! away, go! [*Aside:*] 'Tis the closest striker![5] Life, I think he commits venery forty foot deep; no man's aware on't. I, like a palpable smockster,[6] go to work so openly with the tricks of art, that I'm as apparently seen as a naked boy in a phial;[7] and were it not for a gift of treachery that I have in me, to betray my friend when he puts most trust in me—mass, yonder he is too!—and by his injury to make good my access to her, I should appear as defective in courting as a farmer's son the first day of his feather, that doth nothing at court but woo the hangings and glass windows for a month together, and some broken waiting-women for ever after. I find those imperfections in my venery, that were't not for flattery and falsehood, I should want discourse and impudence; and he that wants impudence among women is worthy to be kicked out at bed's feet. He shall not see me yet.

[*At the tobacco shop.*]

GREENWIT Troth, this is finely shred.

LAXTON O, women are the best mincers.

MISTRESS GALLIPOT 'T had been a good phrase for a cook's wife, sir.

LAXTON But 'twill serve generally, like the front of a new almanac, as thus:—calculated for the meridian of cooks' wives, but generally for all English women.

MISTRESS GALLIPOT Nay, you shall ha't, sir; I have filled it for you. [*She puts it to the fire.*]

LAXTON The pipe's in a good hand, and I wish mine always so.

GREENWIT But not to be used a' that fashion.

LAXTON O, pardon me, sir, I understand no French. I pray, be covered. Jack, a pipe of rich smoke!

GOSHAWK Rich smoke? that's sixpence a pipe, is't?

GREENWIT To me, sweet lady.

MISTRESS GALLIPOT Be not forgetful; respect my credit; seem strange: art and wit makes a fool of suspicion; pray, be wary.

LAXTON Push! I warrant you.—Come, how is't, gallants?

GREENWIT Pure and excellent.

3. Bankrupt.
4. Grasp.
5. Fornicator.
6. Go-between.
7. Abortions were considered monsters in Jacobean times and put on display in this way.

LAXTON I thought 'twas good, you were grown so silent: you are like those that love not to talk at victuals, though they make a worse noise i' th' nose than a common fiddler's 'prentice, and discourse a whole supper with snuffling.—I must speak a word with you anon.

MISTRESS GALLIPOT Make your way wisely, then.

GOSHAWK O, what else, sir? he's perfection itself; full of manners, but not an acre of ground belonging to 'em.

GREENWIT Ay, and full of form; has ne'er a good stool in's chamber.

GOSHAWK But above all, religious; he preyeth daily upon elder brothers.

GREENWIT And valiant above measure; has run three streets from a sergeant.

LAXTON Puh, puh. [*He blows tobacco in their faces.*]

GREENWIT O, puh!

GOSHAWK Ho, ho!

LAXTON So, so.

MISTRESS GALLIPOT What's the matter now, sir?

LAXTON I protest I'm in extreme want of money; if you can supply me now with any means, you do me the greatest pleasure, next to the bounty of your love, as ever poor gentleman tasted.

MISTRESS GALLIPOT What's the sum would pleasure ye, sir? though you deserve nothing less at my hands.

LAXTON Why, 'tis but for want of opportunity, thou knowest.—[*Aside:*] I put her off with opportunity still: by this light, I hate her, but for means to keep me in fashion with gallants; for what I take from her, I spend upon other wenches; bear her in hand[8] still: she has wit enough to rob her husband, and I ways enough to consume the money. —Why, how now? what, the chincough?[9]

GOSHAWK Thou hast the cowardliest trick to come before a man's face, and strangle him ere he be aware! I could find in my heart to make a quarrel in earnest.

LAXTON Pox, and thou dost—thou knowest I never use to fight with my friends—thou'lt but lose thy labor in't.—Jack Dapper!

[*Enter Jack Dapper and Gull.*]

GREENWIT Monsieur Dapper, I dive down to your ankles.

JACK DAPPER Save ye, gentlemen, all three in a peculiar salute.

GOSHAWK He were ill to make a lawyer; he despatches three at once.

LAXTON So, well said.—But is this of the same tobacco, mistress Gallipot?[1]

MISTRESS GALLIPOT The same you had at first, sir.

LAXTON I wish it no better: this will serve to drink[2] at my chamber.

GOSHAWK Shall we taste a pipe on't?

LAXTON Not of this by my troth, gentlemen, I have sworn before you.

GOSHAWK What, not Jack Dapper?

LAXTON Pardon me, sweet Jack; I'm sorry I made such a rash oath, but foolish oaths must stand: where art going, Jack?

JACK DAPPER Faith to buy one feather.

LAXTON [*Aside.*] One feather? the fool's peculiar still.

JACK DAPPER Gull.

GULL Master?

8. Keep her in expectation.
9. Whooping cough.
1. When she slips him money, he pretends that she has only given him tobacco.
2. Smoke.

JACK DAPPER Here's three halfpence for your ordinary,[3] boy; meet me an hour hence in Paul's.

GULL [*Aside*.] How? three single halfpence? life, this will scarce serve a man in sauce, a halp'orth of mustard, a halp'orth of oil, and a halp'orth of vinegar,—what's left then for the pickle herring?[4] This shows like small beer i' th' morning after a great surfeit of wine o'ernight: he could spend his three pound last night in a supper amongst girls and brave bawdyhouse[5] boys: I thought his pockets cackled not for nothing: these are the eggs of three pound, I'll go sup 'em up presently. [*Exit*.]

LAXTON Eight, nine, ten angels:[6] good wench, i'faith, and one that loves darkness well; she puts out a candle with the best tricks[7] of any drugster's wife in England: but that which mads her, I rail upon opportunity still, and take no notice on't. The other night she would needs lead me into a room with a candle in her hand to show me a naked picture, where no sooner entered, but the candle was sent of an errand: now, I not intending to understand her, but, like a puny[8] at the inns of venery, called for another light innocently; thus reward I all her cunning with simple mistaking. I know she cozens[9] her husband to keep me, and I'll keep her honest as long as I can, to make the poor man some part of amends. An honest mind of a whoremaster! how think you amongst you? What, a fresh pipe? draw in a third man?

GOSHAWK No, you're a hoarder, you engross by the ounces.

[*At the feather-shop*.]

JACK DAPPER Pooh, I like it not.

MISTRESS TILTYARD What feather is't you'd have, sir?
These are most worn and most in fashion:
Amongst the beaver gallants,[1] the stone riders,
The private stage's audience, the twelvepenny-stool gentlemen,
I can inform you 'tis the general feather.

JACK DAPPER And therefore I mislike it: tell me of general!
Now, a continual Simon and Jude's rain
Beat all your feathers as flat down as pancakes!
Show me—a—spangled feather.

MISTRESS TILTYARD O, to go a-feasting with;
You'd have it for a hench-boy,° you shall. *page*

[*At the sempster's shop*.]

OPENWORK Mass, I had quite forgot!
His honor's footman was here last night, wife;
Ha' you done with my lord's shirt?

MISTRESS OPENWORK What's that to you, sir?
I was this morning at his honor's lodging,
Ere such a snake as you crept out of your shell.

OPENWORK O, 'twas well done, good wife!

MISTRESS OPENWORK I hold it better, sir,

3. An eating house that served fixed-price meals.
4. Three halfpence will buy the sauces but not the main dish.
5. Whorehouse.
6. He counts the money Mistress Gallipot give him.
7. I.e., like a prostitute.
8. A term for a first-year student at Oxford or the Inns-of-Court.
9. Deceives.
1. Men wearing expensive beaver hats; stone-riders: riders of stallions; to sit on a stool cost sixpence.

Than if you had done't yourself.

OPENWORK Nay, so say I:

But is the countess's smock almost done, mouse?

MISTRESS OPENWORK Here lies the cambric, sir; but wants, I fear me.

OPENWORK I'll resolve you of that presently.

MISTRESS OPENWORK Heyday! O audacious groom!

Dare you presume to noble women's linen?

Keep you your yard[2] to measure shepherds' holland:

I must confine you, I see that.

[*At the tobacco-shop.*]

GOSHAWK What say you to this gear?

LAXTON I dare the arrant'st critic in tobacco

To lay one fault upon't.

[*Enter Moll in a frieze jerkin*[3] *and a black saveguard.*]

GOSHAWK Life, yonder's Moll!

LAXTON Moll! which Moll?

GOSHAWK Honest Moll.

LAXTON Prithee, let's call her.—Moll!

GOSHAWK Moll, Moll!

GREENWIT Pist, Moll!

MOLL How now? what's the matter?

GOSHAWK A pipe of good tobacco, Moll?

MOLL I cannot stay.

GOSHAWK Nay, Moll, pooh, prithee, hark; but one word, i'faith.

MOLL Well, what is't?

GREENWIT Prithee, come hither, sirrah.

LAXTON [*Aside.*] Heart, I would give but too much money to be nibbling with that wench! Life, sh'as the spirit of four great parishes, and a voice that will drown all the city! Methinks a brave captain might get all his soldiers upon her, and ne'er be beholding to a company of Mile End[4] milksops, if he could come on and come off quick enough: such a Moll were a marrow-bone[5] before an Italian;[6] he would cry *buona roba* till his ribs were nothing but bone.[7] I'll lay hard siege to her: money is that aquafortis[8] that eats into many a maidenhead; where the walls are flesh and blood, I'll ever pierce through with a golden augre.[9]

GOSHAWK Now, thy judgment, Moll? is't not good?

MOLL Yes, faith, 'tis very good tobacco.—How do you sell an ounce?—Farewell.—God b'i' you, mistress Gallipot.

GOSHAWK Why, Moll, Moll!

MOLL I cannot stay now, i'faith: I am going to buy a shag-ruff; the shop will be shut in presently.

GOSHAWK 'Tis the maddest fantasticalest girl! I never knew so much flesh and so much nimbleness put together.

2. Measuring stick; penis.
3. Man's short coat. "Saveguard": an outer petticoat to protect other clothes from the dirt.
4. Where London citizens were trained in military exercises.
5. A tasty morsel.
6. Italians were stereotyped as lustful.
7. See Florio's *A World of Words* (1598): "Buonarobba, as we say, good stuffe, a good wholesome plum-cheeked wench."
8. Nitric acid.
9. Tool for boring holes in wood.

LAXTON She slips from one company to another, like a fat eel between a Dutchman's fingers.—[*Aside*.] I'll watch my time for her.

MISTRESS GALLIPOT Some will not stick to say she is a man. And some, both man and woman.

LAXTON That were excellent: she might first cuckold the husband, and then make him do as much for the wife.

[*At the feather-shop*.]

MOLL Save you; how does mistress Tiltyard?

JACK DAPPER Moll!

MOLL Jack Dapper!

JACK DAPPER How dost, Moll?

MOLL I'll tell thee by and by; I go but to th' next shop.

JACK DAPPER Thou shalt find me here this hour about a feather.

MOLL Nay, and a feather hold you in play a whole hour, a goose will last you all the days of your life.—Let me see a good shag-ruff.

[*At the sempster's shop*.]

OPENWORK Mistress Mary, that shalt thou, i'faith, and the best in the shop.

MISTRESS OPENWORK How now? Greetings! Love-terms, with a pox, between you! Have I found out one of your haunts? I send you for hollands, and you're i' th' low countries with a mischief.[1] I'm served with good ware by th' shift; that makes it lie dead so long upon my hands: I were as good shut up shop, for when I open it I take nothing.

OPENWORK Nay, and you fall a-ringing once, the devil cannot stop you.—I'll out of the belfrey as fast as I can, Moll.

MISTRESS OPENWORK Get you from my shop!

MOLL I come to buy.

MISTRESS OPENWORK I'll sell ye nothing; I warn ye my house and shop.

MOLL You, goody[2] Openwork, you that prick out a poor living,
And sews many a bawdy skin-coat together;
Thou private pandress° between shirt and smock; *go-between*
I wish thee for a minute but a man,
Thou shouldst ne'er use more shapes; but as thou art,
I pity my revenge. Now my spleen's up,
I would not mock it willingly.—

[*Enter a Fellow, with a long rapier by his side*.]

Ha! be thankful;
Now I forgive thee.

MISTRESS OPENWORK Marry, hang thee, I never asked forgiveness in my life.

MOLL You, goodman[3] swine's face!

FELLOW What, will you murder me?

MOLL You remember, slave, how you abused me t'other night in a tavern.

FELLOW Not I, by this light!

MOLL No, but by candle-light you did: you have tricks to save your oaths; reservations have you? and I have reserved somewhat for you. [*Strikes him*.] As you like that, call for more; you know the sign again.

1. "Low countries": the Netherlands, the low-life haunts of her husband, and the lower parts of the body; "shift": evasive device, underclothing; "good ware": good merchandise, bodily wares.

2. Housewife.

3. A man with status below a gentleman.

FELLOW [*Aside*.] Pox on't, had I brought any company along with me to have borne witness on't, 'twould ne'er have grieved me; but to be struck and nobody by, 'tis my ill fortune still. Why, tread upon a worm, they say 'twill turn tail; but indeed a gentleman should have more manners. [*Exit*.]

LAXTON Gallantly performed, i'faith, Moll, and manfully! I love thee for ever for't: base rogue, had he offered but the least counter-buff, by this hand, I was prepared for him!

MOLL You prepared for him? Why should you be prepared for him? Was he any more than a man?

LAXTON No, nor so much by a yard and a handful, London measure.

MOLL Why do you speak this then? do you think I cannot ride a stone-horse,[4] unless one lead him by th' snaffle?

LAXTON Yes, and sit him bravely; I know thou canst, Moll: 'twas but an honest mistake through love, and I'll make amends for't anyway. Prithee, sweet, plump Moll, when shall thou and I go out a' town together?

MOLL Whither? to Tyburn,[5] prithee?

LAXTON Mass, that's out a' town indeed: thou hangest so many jests upon thy friends still! I mean honestly to Brainford, Staines, or Ware.[6]

MOLL What to do there?

LAXTON Nothing but be merry and lie together: I'll hire a coach with four horses.

MOLL I thought 'twould be a beastly journey. You may leave out one well; three horses will serve, if I play the jade[7] myself.

LAXTON Nay, push, thou'rt such another kicking wench! Prithee, be kind, and let's meet.

MOLL 'Tis hard but we shall meet, sir.

LAXTON Nay, but appoint the place then; there's ten angels in fair gold, Moll: you see I do not trifle with you; do but say thou wilt meet me, and I'll have a coach ready for thee.

MOLL Why, here's my hand, I'll meet you, sir.

LAXTON [*Aside*.] O good gold!—The place, sweet Moll?

MOLL It shall be your appointment.

LAXTON Somewhat near Holborn,[8] Moll.

MOLL In Gray's-Inn-Fields then.

LAXTON A match.

MOLL I'll meet you there.

LAXTON The hour?

MOLL Three.

LAXTON That will be time enough to sup at Brainford.

OPENWORK I am of such a nature, sir, I cannot endure the house when she scolds: sh'as a tongue will be heard further in a still morning than Saint Antling's bell. She rails upon me for foreign wenching, that I being a freeman must needs keep a whore i' th' suburbs, and seek to impoverish the liberties.[9] When we fall out, I trouble you still to make all whole with my wife.

GOSHAWK No trouble at all; 'tis a pleasure to me to join things together.

OPENWORK [*Aside*.] Go thy ways, I do this but to try thy honesty, Goshawk.

[*At the feather-shop*.]

4. Stallion.
5. Place of public executions.
6. Towns north of London.
7. Worn-out horse; whore.
8. The area of the law schools, such as Gray's Inn.
9. Brothels flourished in the suburbs, over which the city had no control; the liberties just beyond the city were subject to its control.

JACK DAPPER How likest thou this, Moll?

MOLL O, singularly; you're fitted now for a bunch.—[*Aside.*] He looks for all the world, with those spangled feathers, like a nobleman's bed-post. The purity of your wench would I fain try; she seems like Kent unconquered, and, I believe, as many wiles are in her. O, the gallants of these times are shallow lechers! they put not their courtship home enough to a wench: 'tis impossible to know what woman is thoroughly honest, because she's ne'er thoroughly tried; I am of that certain belief, there are more queans[1] in this town of their own making than of any man's provoking: where lies the slackness then? Many a poor soul would down, and there's nobody will push 'em:

Women are courted, but ne'er soundly tried,
As many walk in spurs that never ride.

[*At the sempster's shop.*]

MISTRESS OPENWORK O, abominable!

GOSHAWK Nay, more, I tell you in private, he keeps a whore i' th' suburbs.

MISTRESS OPENWORK O spittle[2] dealing! I came to him a gentlewoman born: I'll show you mine arms when you please, sir.

GOSHAWK [*Aside.*] I had rather see your legs, and begin that way.

MISTRESS OPENWORK 'Tis well known he took me from a lady's service, where I was well beloved of the steward: I had my Latin tongue, and a spice of the French, before I came to him; and now doth he keep a suburbian whore under my nostrils?

GOSHAWK There's ways enough to cry quit with[3] him: hark in thine ear. [*Whispers to her.*]

MISTRESS OPENWORK There's a friend worth a million!

MOLL [*Aside.*] I'll try one spear against your chastity, mistress Tiltyard, though it prove too short by the burr.[4]

[*Enter Trapdoor.*]

TRAPDOOR [*Aside.*] Mass, here she is: I'm bound already to serve her, though it be but a sluttish trick.—Bless my hopeful young mistress with long life and great limbs; send her the upper hand of all bailiffs and their hungry adherents!

MOLL How now? what art thou?

TRAPDOOR A poor ebbing gentleman, that would gladly wait for the young flood of your service.

MOLL My service? what should move you to offer your service to me, sir?

TRAPDOOR The love I bear to your heroic spirit and masculine womanhood.

MOLL So, sir! put case we should retain you to us, what parts are there in you for a gentlewoman's service?

TRAPDOOR Of two kinds, right worshipful; moveable and immoveable—moveable to run of errands, and immoveable to stand when you have occasion to use me.

MOLL What strength have you?

TRAPDOOR Strength, mistress Moll? I have gone up into a steeple, and stayed the great bell as't has been ringing; stopped a windmill going—

MOLL And never struck down yourself?

TRAPDOOR Stood as upright as I do at this present.

[*Moll trips up his heels.*]

MOLL Come, I pardon you for this; it shall be no disgrace to you: I have struck up the heels of the high German's size ere now.[5] What, not stand?

TRAPDOOR I am of that nature, where I love, I'll be at my mistress' foot to do her service.

1. Harlots, strumpets.
2. Low-class.
3. Repay.
4. A broad iron ring on the handle of a lance.
5. A tall, strong German fencer in London at that time.

MOLL Why, well said; but say your mistress should receive injury, have you the spirit of fighting in you? durst you second her?

TRAPDOOR Life, I have kept a bridge myself, and drove seven at a time before me!

MOLL Ay?

TRAPDOOR [*Aside.*] But they were all Lincolnshire bullocks, by my troth.

MOLL Well, meet me in Gray's Inn Fields between three and four this afternoon, and, upon better consideration, we'll retain you.

TRAPDOOR I humbly thank your good mistresship.—
[*Aside.*] I'll crack your neck for this kindness. [*Exit.*]

LAXTON Remember three. [*Moll meets Laxton.*]

MOLL Nay, if I fail you, hang me.

LAXTON Good wench, i'faith!

MOLL Who's this? [*Moll then meets Openwork.*]

OPENWORK 'Tis I, Moll.

MOLL Prithee, tend thy shop and prevent bastards.

OPENWORK We'll have a pint of the same wine, i'faith, Moll.
[*Exit with Moll. Bell rings.*]

GOSHAWK Hark, the bell rings! come, gentlemen. Jack Dapper, where shall's all munch?

JACK DAPPER I am for Parker's ordinary.

LAXTON He's a good guest to'm, he deserves his board; he draws all the gentlemen in a term-time thither. We'll be your followers, Jack; lead the way.—Look you, by my faith, the fool has feathered his nest well.
[*Exeunt Jack Dapper, Laxton, Goshawk, and Greenwit. Enter Gallipot, Tiltyard, and Servants, with water-spaniels and a duck.*]

TILTYARD Come, shut up your shops. Where's master Openwork?

MISTRESS GALLIPOT Nay, ask not me, master Tiltyard.

TILTYARD Where's his water-dog? puh—pist—hur—hur—pist!

GALLIPOT Come, wenches, come; we're going all to Hogsdon.[6]

MISTRESS GALLIPOT To Hogsdon, husband?

GALLIPOT Ay, to Hogsdon, pigsnie.[7]

MISTRESS GALLIPOT I'm not ready, husband.

GALLIPOT Faith, that's well—hum—pist—pist.—
[*Spits in the dog's mouth.*]
Come, mistress Openwork, you are so long!

MISTRESS OPENWORK I have no joy of my life, master Gallipot.

GALLIPOT Push, let your boy lead his water-spaniel along, and we'll show you the bravest sport at Parlous Pond.—[8] Hey, Trug, hey, Trug, hey, Trug![9] here's the best duck in England, except my wife; hey, hey, hey! fetch, fetch, fetch!—
Come let's away:
Of all the year this is the sportful'st day. [*Exeunt.*]

Scene 2

[*A Street. Enter Sebastian Wengrave.*]

SEBASTIAN If a man have a free will, where should the use
More perfect shine than in his will to love?
All creatures have their liberty in that.

6. A holiday place for apprentices.
7. A term of endearment.
8. A swimming pond, called "parlous" (perilous) because of those who drowned there.
9. Prostitute.

[*Enter behind Sir Alexander Wengrave listening.*]

Though else kept under servile yoke and fear;
The very bond-slave has his freedom there.
Amongst a world of creatures voiced and silent,
Must my desires wear fetters?—Yea, are you
So near? then I must break with my heart's truth,
Meet grief at a back way.—Well: why, suppose
The two-leaved tongues[1] of slander or of truth
Pronounce Moll loathsome; if before my love
She appear fair, what injury have I?
I have the thing I like: in all things else
Mine own eye guides me, and I find 'em prosper.
Life! what should ail it now? I know that man
Ne'er truly loves,—if he gainsay't he lies,—
That winks and marries with his father's eyes:
I'll keep mine own wide open.

[*Enter Moll and a Porter with a viol on his back.*]

SIR ALEXANDER [*Aside.*] Here's brave wilfulness!
A made match! here she comes; they met a' purpose.

PORTER Must I carry this great fiddle to your chamber, mistress Mary?

MOLL Fiddle, goodman hog-rubber?[2] Some of these porters bear so much for others, they have no time to carry wit for themselves.

PORTER To your own chamber, mistress Mary?

MOLL Who'll hear an ass speak? Whither else, goodman pageant-bearer? They're people of the worst memories!

[*Exit Porter.*]

SEBASTIAN Why, 'twere too great a burden, love, to have them
Carry things in their minds and a' their backs together.

MOLL Pardon me, sir, I thought not you so near.

SIR ALEXANDER [*Aside.*] So, so, so!

SEBASTIAN I would be nearer to thee, and in that fashion
That makes the best part of all creatures honest:
No otherwise I wish it.

MOLL Sir, I am so poor to requite you, you must look for nothing but thanks of me: I have no humor to marry; I love to lie a' both sides a' th' bed myself: and again, a' th' other side, a wife, you know, ought to be obedient, but I fear me I am too headstrong to obey; therefore I'll ne'er go about it. I love you so well, sir, for your good will, I'd be loath you should repent your bargain after; and therefore we'll ne'er come together at first. I have the head now of myself, and am man enough for a woman: marriage is but a chopping and changing, where a maiden loses one head, and has a worse i' th' place.

SIR ALEXANDER [*Aside.*] The most comfortablest answer from a roaring girl
That ever mine ears drunk in!

SEBASTIAN This were enough
Now to affright a fool for ever from thee,
When 'tis the music that I love thee for.

SIR ALEXANDER [*Aside.*] There's a boy spoils all again!

MOLL Believe it, sir,

1. Like forked tongues.

2. An abusive term for a swineherd.

I am not of that disdainful temper but I could love you faithfully.

SIR ALEXANDER [*Aside.*] A pox on you for that word! I like you not now. You're a cunning roarer, I see that already.

MOLL But sleep upon this once more, sir; you may chance shift a mind to-morrow: be not too hasty to wrong yourself; never while you live, sir, take a wife running; many have run out at heels that have done't. You see, sir, I speak against myself; and if every woman would deal with their suitor so honestly, poor younger brothers would not be so often gulled with old cozening widows,[3] that turn o'er all their wealth in trust to some kinsman, and make the poor gentleman work hard for a pension. Fare you well, sir.

SEBASTIAN Nay, prithee, one word more.

SIR ALEXANDER [*Aside.*] How do I wrong this girl! she puts him off still.

MOLL Think upon this in cold blood, sir: you make as much haste as if you were a-going upon a sturgeon voyage. Take deliberation, sir; never choose a wife as if you were going to Virginia.

SEBASTIAN And so we parted: my too-cursed fate!

SIR ALEXANDER [*Aside.*] She is but cunning, gives him longer time in't.

[*Enter Tailor.*]

TAILOR Mistress Moll, mistress Moll! so ho, ho, so ho!

MOLL There, boy, there, boy! What, dost thou go a-hawking after me with a red clout on thy finger?

TAILOR I forgot to take measure on you for your new breeches.

SIR ALEXANDER [*Aside.*] Hoyda, breeches? What, will he marry a monster with two trinkets? What age is this! If the wife go in breeches, the man must wear long coats[4] like a fool.

MOLL What fiddling's here! Would not the old pattern have served your turn?

TAILOR You change the fashion: you say you'll have the great Dutch slop,[5] mistress Mary.

MOLL Why, sir, I say so still.

TAILOR Your breeches, then, will take up a yard more.

MOLL Well, pray, look it be put in then.

TAILOR It shall stand round and full, I warrant you.

MOLL Pray, make 'em easy enough.

TAILOR I know my fault now, t'other was somewhat stiff between the legs; I'll make these open enough, I warrant you.

SIR ALEXANDER [*Aside.*] Here's good gear[6] towards! I have brought up my son to marry a Dutch slop and a French doublet; a codpiece daughter!

TAILOR So, I have gone as far as I can go.

MOLL Why, then, farewell.

TAILOR If you go presently to your chamber, mistress Mary, pray, send me the measure of your thigh by some honest body.

MOLL Well, sir, I'll send it by a porter presently. [*Exit.*]

TAILOR So you had need, it is a lusty one; both of them would make any porter's back ache in England. [*Exit.*]

SEBASTIAN I have examined the best part of man,
Reason and judgment; and in love, they tell me,
They leave me uncontrolled; he that is swayed

3. Since by law a woman's property was given over to her husband when she married, widows put their wealth in the hands of relatives to avoid having to give it over to a second husband.

4. Petticoats worn by women, idiots, and court fools.

5. Wide loose breeches.

6. Business; genitals.

By an unfeeling blood, past heat of love,
His spring-time must needs err; his watch ne'er goes right
That sets his dial by a rusty clock.

SIR ALEXANDER [*coming forward*] So; and which is that rusty clock, sir, you?

SEBASTIAN The clock at Ludgate, sir; it ne'er goes true.

SIR ALEXANDER But thou go'st falser; not thy father's cares
Can keep thee right: when that insensible work
Obeys the workman's art, lets off the hour,
And stops again when time is satisfied:
But thou runn'st on; and judgment, thy main wheel,
Beats by all stops, as if the work would break,
Begun with long pains for a minute's ruin:
Much like a suffering man brought up with care,
At last bequeathed to shame and a short prayer.

SEBASTIAN I taste you bitterer than I can deserve, sir.

SIR ALEXANDER What has bewitched thee, son? what devil or drug
Hath wrought upon the weakness of thy blood,
And betrayed all her hopes to ruinous folly?
O, wake from drowsy and enchanted shame,
Wherein thy soul sits, with a golden dream
Flattered and poisoned! I am old, my son;
O, let me prevail quickly!
For I have weightier business of mine own
Than to chide thee: I must not to my grave
As a drunkard to his bed, whereon he lies
Only to sleep, and never cares to rise:
Let me despatch in time; come no more near her.

SEBASTIAN Not honestly? not in the way of marriage?

SIR ALEXANDER What sayst thou? marriage? in what place? the Sessions-house?
And who shall give the bride, prithee? an indictment?

SEBASTIAN Sir, now ye take part with the world to wrong her.

SIR ALEXANDER Why, wouldst thou fain marry to be pointed at?
Alas, the number's great! Do not o'erburden't.
Why, as good marry a beacon on a hill,
Which all the country fix their eyes upon,
As her thy folly doats on. If thou long'st
To have the story of thy infamous fortunes
Serve for discourse in ordinaries and taverns,
Thou'rt in the way; or to confound thy name,
Keep on, thou canst not miss it; or to strike
Thy wretched father to untimely coldness,
Keep the left hand still, it will bring thee to't.
Yet, if no tears wrung from thy father's eyes,
Nor sighs that fly in sparkles from his sorrows,
Had power to alter what is wilful in thee,
Methinks her very name should fright thee from her,
And never trouble me.

SEBASTIAN Why, is the name of Moll so fatal, sir?

SIR ALEXANDER Many one, sir, where suspect is entered;
For, seek all London from one end to t'other,
More whores of that name than of any ten other.

SEBASTIAN What's that to her? Let those blush for themselves:
Can any guilt in others condemn her?
I've vow'd to love her: let all storms oppose me
That ever beat against the breast of man,
Nothing but death's black tempest shall divide us.
SIR ALEXANDER O, folly that can doat on nought but shame!
SEBASTIAN Put case, a wanton itch runs through one name
More than another; is that name the worse,
Where honesty sits possest in't? It should rather
Appear more excellent, and deserve more praise,
When through foul mists a brightness it can raise.
Why, there are of the devils honest gentlemen
And well descended, keep an open house,
And some a' th' good man's that are arrant knaves.
He hates unworthily that by rote condemns,
For the name neither saves nor yet condemns;
And for her honesty, I've made such proof on't
In several forms, so nearly watch'd her ways,
I will maintain that strict against an army,
Excepting you, my father. Here's her worst,
Sh'as a bold spirit that mingles with mankind,
But nothing else comes near it: and oftentimes
Through her apparel somewhat shames her birth;
But she is loose in nothing but in mirth:
Would all Molls were no worse!
SIR ALEXANDER [*Aside*.] This way I toil in vain, and give but aim
To infamy and ruin: he will fall;
My blessing cannot stay him: all my joys
Stand at the brink of a devouring flood,
And will be wilfully swallowed, wilfully.
But why so vain let all these tears be lost?
I'll pursue her to shame, and so all's crost. [*Exit*.]
SEBASTIAN He's gone with some strange purpose, whose effect
Will hurt me little if he shoot so wide,
To think I love so blindly: I but feed
His heart to this match, to draw on the other,
Wherein my joy sits with a full wish crowned,
Only his mood excepted, which must change
By opposite policies, courses indirect;
Plain dealing in this world takes no effect.
This mad girl I'll acquaint with my intent,
Get her assistance, make my fortunes known:
'Twixt lovers' hearts she's a fit instrument,
And has the art to help them to their own.
By her advice, for in that craft she's wise,
My love and I may meet, spite of all spies. [*Exit*.]

Act 3

Scene 1

[*Gray's Inn Fields. Enter Laxton and Coachman*.]
LAXTON Coachman.

COACHMAN Here, sir.

LAXTON There's a tester[7] more; prithee drive thy coach to the hither end of Marybone-park,[8] a fit place for Moll to get in.

COACHMAN Marybone-park, sir?

LAXTON Ay, it's in our way, thou knowest.

COACHMAN It shall be done, sir.

LAXTON Coachman.

COACHMAN Anon, sir.

LAXTON Are we fitted with good phrampel[9] jades?

COACHMAN The best in Smithfield,[1] I warrant you, sir.

LAXTON May we safely take the upper hand of any coached velvet cap, or tuftaffety[2] jacket? for they keep a vild[3] swaggering in coaches now-a-days; the highways are stopt with them.

COACHMAN My life for yours, and baffle[4] 'em too, sir; why, they are the same jades, believe it, sir, that have drawn all your famous whores to Ware.

LAXTON Nay, then they know their business; they need no more instructions.

COACHMAN They're so used to such journeys, sir, I never use whip to 'em; for if they catch but the scent of a wench once, they run like devils.

[*Exit Coachman with his whip*.]

LAXTON Fine Cerberus![5] That rogue will have the start of a thousand ones; for whilst others trot a' foot, he'll ride prancing to hell upon a coach-horse. Stay, 'tis now about the hour of her appointment, but yet I see her not. [*The clock strikes three*.] Hark! What's this? One, two, three: three by the clock at Savoy;[6] this is the hour, and Gray's Inn Fields the place, she swore she'd meet me. Ha! yonder's two Inns-a'-court[7] men with one wench, but that's not she; they walk toward Islington out of my way. I see none yet drest like her; I must look for a shag-ruff, a frieze jerken, a short sword, and a safe-guard, or I get none. Why, Moll, prithee, make haste, or the coachman will curse us anon.

[*Enter Moll, dressed as a man*.]

MOLL [*Aside*.] O, here's my gentleman! If they would keep their days as well with their mercers[8] as their hours with their harlots, no bankrupt would give seven score pound for a sergeant's place; for would you know a catchpoll[9] rightly derived, the corruption of a citizen is the generation of a sergeant. How his eye hawks for venery![1] —Come, are you ready, sir?

LAXTON Ready? for what, sir?

MOLL Do you ask that now, sir?
Why was this meeting 'pointed?

LAXTON I thought you mistook me, sir; you seem to be some young barrister;[2]
I have no suit in law, all my land's sold;
I praise heaven for't, 't has rid me of much trouble,

MOLL Then I must wake you, sir; where stands the coach?

7. Sixpence.
8. Marybone Park was frequented by prostitutes.
9. Swift, restless.
1. The worst jades came from Smithfield.
2. Taffeta with velvet stripes, a rich fabric favored by the merchant class who enjoyed showing its wealth in dress when the sumptuary laws were repealed in 1603.
3. Vile.
4. Treat contemptuously.
5. The three-headed dog guarding the gates of Hades in classical myth.
6. Hospital built by Henry VIII.
7. Law schools.
8. Dealers in costly fabric, to whom gallants were often in debt.
9. Police who arrested debtors.
1. Hunting; sexual pleasure.
2. Lawyer.

LAXTON Who's this? Moll, honest Moll?
MOLL So young, and purblind?[3]
You're an old wanton in your eyes, I see that.
LAXTON Thou'rt admirably suited for the Three Pigeons[4] at Brainford. I'll swear I knew thee not.
MOLL I'll swear you did not; but you shall know me now.
LAXTON No, not here; we shall be spied, i'faith; the coach is better: come.
MOLL Stay. [*Puts off her cloak.*]
LAXTON What, wilt thou untruss a point,[5] Moll?
MOLL Yes; here's the point [*Draws her sword.*]
That I untruss; 't has but one tag, 'twill serve though
To tie up a rogue's tongue.
LAXTON How!
MOLL There's the gold
With which you hir'd your hackney,[6] here's her pace;
She racks hard, and perhaps your bones will feel it:
Ten angels of mine own I've put to thine;
Win 'em and wear 'em.
LAXTON Hold, Moll! mistress Mary—
MOLL Draw, or I'll serve an execution on thee,
Shall lay thee up till doomsday.
LAXTON Draw upon a woman! Why, what dost mean, Moll?
MOLL To teach thy base thoughts manners: thou'rt one of those
That thinks each woman thy fond flexible whore;
If she but cast a liberal eye upon thee,
Turn back her head, she's thine; or amongst company
By chance drink first to thee, then she's quite gone,
There is no means to help her; nay, for a need,
Wilt swear unto thy credulous fellow-lechers,
That thou art more in favor with a lady
At first sight than her monkey[7] all her lifetime.
How many of our sex, by such as thou,
Have their good thoughts paid with a blasted name
That never deserved loosely, or did trip
In path of whoredom beyond cup and lip!
But for the stain of conscience and of soul,
Better had women fall into the hands
Of an act silent than a bragging nothing;
There is no mercy in't. What durst move you, sir,
To think me whorish? a name which I'd tear out
From the high German's throat, if it lay leiger[8] there
To despatch privy slanders against me.
In thee I defy all men, their worst hates
And their best flatteries, all their golden witchcrafts,
With which they entangle the poor spirits of fools,
Distressed needle-women and trade-fallen wives;

3. Completely blind.
4. A famous inn.
5. Untie the laces of the breeches; points (laces) fastened the hose to the doublet. "Untruss" also means unsheathe.
6. Horse; prostitute.
7. Pet.
8. Ambassador at a foreign court.

Fish that must needs bite, or themselves be bitten;
Such hungry things as these may soon be took
With a worm fastened on a golden hook:
Those are the lecher's food, his prey; he watches
For quarrelling wedlocks[9] and poor shifting sisters;
'Tis the best fish he takes. But why, good fisherman,
Am I thought meat for you, that never yet
Had angling rod cast towards me? 'cause, you'll say,
I'm given to sport, I'm often merry, jest:
Had mirth no kindred in the world but lust,
O shame take all her friends then! but howe'er
Thou and the baser world censure my life,
I'll send 'em word by thee, and write so much
Upon thy breast, 'cause thou shalt bear't in mind,
Tell them 'twere base to yield where I have conquered;
I scorn to prostitute myself to a man,
I that can prostitute a man to me;
And so I greet thee.

LAXTON Hear me—

MOLL Would the spirits
Of all my sland[er]ers were clasped in thine,
That I might vex an army at one time! [*They fight.*]

LOXTON I do repent me; hold!

MOLL You'll die the better Christian then.

LAXTON I do confess I have wronged thee, Moll.

MOLL Confession is but poor amends for wrong,
Unless a rope would follow.

LAXTON I ask thee pardon.

MOLL I'm your hired whore, sir!

LAXTON I yield both purse and body.

MOLL Both are mine, and now at my disposing.

LAXTON Spare my life!

MOLL I scorn to strike thee basely.

LAXTON Spoke like a noble girl, i'faith!—[*Aside.*] Heart, I think I fight with a familiar,[1] or the ghost of a fencer. Sh'as wounded me gallantly. Call you this a lecherous viage?[2] here's blood would have served me this seven year in broken heads and cut fingers; and it now runs all out together. Pox a' the Three Pigeons! I would the coach were here now to carry me to the chirurgeon's. [*Exit.*]

MOLL If I could meet my enemies one by one thus,
I might make pretty shift with 'em in time,
And make 'em know that she has wit and spirit,
May scorn to live beholding to her body for meat;
Or for apparel, like your common dame,
That makes shame get her clothes to cover shame.
Base is that mind that kneels unto her body,
As if a husband stood in awe on's wife;

9. Wives.
1. Devil's spirit.
2. Voyage.

My spirit shall be mistress of this house
As long as I have time in't.—O,
[*Enter Trapdoor.*]
Here comes my man that would be: 'tis his hour.
Faith, a good well-set fellow, if his spirit
Be answerable to his umbles;° he walks stiff, *insides*
But whether he'll stand to't stiffly, there's the point:
Has a good calf for't; and ye shall have many a woman
Choose him she means to make her head by his calf;
I do not know their tricks in't. Faith, he seems
A man without; I'll try what he's within.

TRAPDOOR She told me Gray's Inn Fields, 'twixt three and four;
I'll fit her mistress-ship with a piece of service:
I'm hired to rid the town of one mad girl.
[*Moll jostles him.*]
What a pox ails you, sir?

MOLL He begins like a gentleman.

TRAPDOOR Heart, is the field so narrow, or your eyesight—
Life, he comes back again!

MOLL Was this spoke to me, sir?

TRAPDOOR I cannot tell, sir.

MOLL Go, you're a coxcomb![3]

TRAPDOOR Coxcomb?

MOLL You're a slave!

TRAPDOOR I hope there's law for you, sir.

MOLL Yea, do you see, sir? [*Turns his hat.*]

TRAPDOOR Heart, this is no good dealing! pray, let me know what house you're of.

MOLL One of the Temple,[4] sir. [*Fillips him.*]

TRAPDOOR Mass, so methinks.

MOLL And yet sometime I lie about Chick Lane.

TRAPDOOR I like you the worse because you shift your lodging so often: I'll not meddle with you for that trick, sir.

MOLL A good shift; but it shall not serve your turn.

TRAPDOOR You'll give me leave to pass about my business, sir?

MOLL Your business? I'll make you wait on me
Before I ha' done, and glad to serve me too.

TRAPDOOR How, sir? serve you? not if there were no more men in England.

MOLL But if there were no more women in England,
I hope you'd wait upon your mistress then?

TRAPDOOR Mistress?

MOLL O, you're a tried spirit at a push, sir?

TRAPDOOR What would your worship have me do?

MOLL You a fighter!

TRAPDOOR No, I praise heaven, I had better grace and more manners.

MOLL As how, I pray, sir?

TRAPDOOR Life, 'thad been a beastly part of me to have drawn my weapons upon my mistress; all the world would a' cried shame of me for that.

MOLL Why, but you knew me not.

3. Fool.

4. A lawyer.

TRAPDOOR Do not say so, mistress; I knew you by your wide straddle, as well as if I had been in your belly.

MOLL Well, we shall try you further; i' th' mean time
We give you entertainment.

TRAPDOOR Thank your good mistress-ship.

MOLL How many suits have you?

TRAPDOOR No more suits than backs, mistress.

MOLL Well, if you deserve, I cast off this, next week,
And you may creep into't.

TRAPDOOR Thank your good worship.

MOLL Come, follow me to St. Thomas Apostle's:[5]
I'll put a livery cloak upon your back
The first thing I do.

TRAPDOOR I follow, my dear mistress. [*Exeunt*.]

Scene 2

[*Gallipot's Shop. Enter Mistress Gallipot as from supper, Gallipot following her*.]

GALLIPOT What, Pru! nay, sweet Prudence!

MISTRESS GALLIPOT What a pruing keep you! I think the baby would have a teat, it kyes[6] so. Pray, be not so fond of me, leave your city humors;[7] I'm vexed at you, to see how like a calf you come bleating after me.

GALLIPOT Nay, honey Pru, how does your rising up before all the table show, and flinging from my friends so uncivilly! Fie, Pru, fie! Come.

MISTRESS GALLIPOT Then up and ride,[8] i'faith!

GALLIPOT Up and ride? nay, my pretty Pru, that's far from my thought, duck. Why, mouse, thy mind is nibbling at something; what is't? What lies upon thy stomach?

MISTRESS GALLIPOT Such an ass as you: Hoyda, you're best turn midwife, or physician! you're a 'pothecary already, but I'm none of your drugs.

GALLIPOT Thou art a sweet drug, sweetest Pru, and the more thou art pounded,[9] the more precious.

MISTRESS GALLIPOT Must you be prying into a woman's secrets, say ye?

GALLIPOT Woman's secrets?

MISTRESS GALLIPOT What! I cannot have a qualm come upon me, but your teeth waters till your nose hang over it!

GALLIPOT It is my love, dear wife.

MISTRESS GALLIPOT Your love? Your love is all words; give me deeds: I cannot abide a man that's too fond over me,—so cookish! Thou dost not know how to handle a woman in her kind.

GALLIPOT No, Pru? why, I hope I have handled—

MISTRESS GALLIPOT Handle a fool's head of your own,—fie, fie!

GALLIPOT Ha, ha, 'tis such a wasp! It does me good now to have her sting me, little rogue!

MISTRESS GALLIPOT Now, fie, how you vex me! I cannot abide these apron husbands;[1] such cotqueans![2] You overdo your things, they become you scurvily.[3]

5. Nearby the clothes shops.
6. Cries.
7. Moods.
8. Have an erection and sexual intercourse.
9. With a sexual double meaning.
1. Husbands who are tied to their wives' apron strings.
2. Men who interfere in women's business.
3. Badly.

GALLIPOT [*Aside*.] Upon my life she breeds: heaven knows how I have strained myself to please her night and day. I wonder why we citizens should get children so fretful and untoward in the breeding, their fathers being for the most part as gentle as milch kine.[4]—Shall I leave thee, my Pru?

MISTRESS GALLIPOT Fie, fie, fie!

GALLIPOT Thou shalt not be vexed no more, pretty, kind rogue; take no cold, sweet Pru? [*Exit*.]

MISTRESS GALLIPOT As your wit has done. Now, master Laxton, show your head; what news from you? Would any husband suspect that a woman crying, *Buy any scurvy-grass*, should bring love-letters amongst her herbs to his wife? Pretty trick! Fine conveyance! Had jealousy a thousand eyes, a silly woman with scurvy-grass blinds them all.

Laxton, with bays
Crown I thy wit for this, it deserves praise:
This makes me affect thee more, this proves thee wise:
'Lack, what poor shift is love forced to devise!—

To th' point. [*Reads letter*.] O *sweet creature*—a sweet beginning!—*pardon my long absence, for thou shalt shortly be possessed with my presence: though Demopho[o]n was false to Phyllis, I will be to thee as Pan-da-rus was to Cres-sida;*[5] *though Aeneas made an ass of Dido, I will die to thee ere I do so. O sweetest creature, make much of me! for no man beneath the silver moon shall make more of a woman than I do of thee: furnish me therefore with thirty pounds; you must do it of necessity for me; I languish till I see some comfort come from thee. Protesting not to die in thy debt, but rather to live, so as hitherto I have and will,*

Thy true Laxton ever.

Alas, poor gentleman! troth, I pity him.
How shall I raise this money? thirty pound!
'Tis thirty sure, a 3 before an O;
I know his threes too well. My childbed linen,
Shall I pawn that for him? Then if my mark
Be known, I am undone; it may be thought
My husband's bankrout.° Which way shall I turn? *bankrupt*
Laxton, what with my own fears and thy wants,
I'm like a needle 'twixt two adamants.° *magnates*

[*Reenter Gallipot hastily*.]

GALLIPOT Nay, nay, wife, the women are all up—[*Aside*.] Ha! how? reading a' letters? I smell a goose, a couple of capons, and a gammon of bacon, from her mother out of the country. I hold my life—steal, steal—

MISTRESS GALLIPOT O, beshrew your heart!

GALLIPOT What letter's that? I'll see't.

[*Mistress Gallipot tears the letter*.]

MISTRESS GALLIPOT O, would thou had'st no eyes to see the downfall
Of me and of thyself! I am for ever,
For ever I'm undone!

GALLIPOT What ails my Pru?

4. Milking cows.

5. Demophoon broke his promise to return to Phyllis, and Aeneas left Dido to found Rome. Both women committed suicide. Pandarus was a go-between for Troilus and Cressida.

What paper's that thou tear'st?
MISTRESS GALLIPOT Would I could tear
My very heart in pieces! for my soul
Lies on the rack of shame, that tortures me
Beyond a woman's suffering.
GALLIPOT What means this?
MISTRESS GALLIPOT Had you no other vengeance to throw down,
But even in height of all my joys—
GALLIPOT Dear woman—
MISTRESS GALLIPOT When the full sea of pleasure and content
Seemed to flow over me?
GALLIPOT As thou desir'st
To keep me out of Bedlam,[6] tell what troubles thee!
Is not thy child at nurse fallen sick, or dead?
MISTRESS GALLIPOT O, no!
GALLIPOT Heavens bless me! are my barns and houses
Yonder at Hockley-hole consumed with fire?
I can build more, sweet Pru.
MISTRESS GALLIPOT 'Tis worse, 'tis worse!
GALLIPOT My factor broke? or is the Jonas sunk?[7]
MISTRESS GALLIPOT Would all we had were swallowed in the waves,
Rather than both should be the scorn of slaves!
GALLIPOT I'm at my wit's end.
MISTRESS GALLIPOT O my dear husband!
Where once I thought myself a fixed star,
Placed only in the heaven of thine arms,
I fear now I shall prove a wanderer.
O Laxton, Laxton! Is it then my fate
To be by thee o'erthrown?
GALLIPOT Defend me, wisdom,
From falling into frenzy! On my knees,
Sweet Pru, speak; what's that Laxton, who so heavy
Lies on thy bosom?
MISTRESS GALLIPOT I shall sure run mad!
GALLIPOT I shall run mad for company then. Speak to me;
I'm Gallipot thy husband—Pru—why, Pru
Art sick in conscience for some villanous deed
Thou wert about to act? Didst mean to rob me?
Tush, I forgive thee: hast thou on my bed
Thrust my soft pillow under another's head?
I'll wink at all faults, Pru: 'las, that's no more
Than what some neighbors near thee have done before!
Sweet honey Pru, what's that Laxton?
MISTRESS GALLIPOT O!
GALLIPOT Out with him!
MISTRESS GALLIPOT O, he's born to be my undoer!

6. Insane asylum.

7. Factor: agent, commission merchant; Jonas: a trading ship.

This hand, which thou call'st thine, to him was given,
To him was I made sure[8] i' th' sight of heaven.

GALLIPOT I never heard this thunder.

GALLIPOT Yes, yes, before
I was to thee contracted, to him I swore:
Since last I saw him, twelve months three times told
The moon hath drawn through her light silver bow;
For o'er the seas he went, and it was said,
But rumor lies, that he in France was dead;
But he's alive, O he's alive! He sent
That letter to me, which in rage I rent;
Swearing with oaths most damnably to have me,
Or tear me from this bosom: O heavens, save me!

GALLIPOT My heart will break; shamed and undone for ever!

MISTRESS GALLIPOT So black a day, poor wretch, went o'er thee never!

GALLIPOT If thou should'st wrestle with him at the law,
Thou'rt sure to fall. No odd slight? no prevention?
I'll tell him thou'rt with child.

MISTRESS GALLIPOT Umh!

GALLIPOT Or give out
One of my men was ta'en a-bed with thee.

MISTRESS GALLIPOT Umh, umh!

GALLIPOT Before I lose thee, my dear Pru,
I'll drive it to that push.

MISTRESS GALLIPOT Worse and worse still;
You embrace a mischief, to prevent an ill.

GALLIPOT I'll buy thee of him, stop his mouth with gold:
Think'st thou 'twill do?

MISTRESS GALLIPOT O me! heavens grant it would!
Yet now my senses are set more in tune.
He writ, as I remember, in his letter,
That he in riding up and down had spent,
Ere he could find me, thirty pounds: send that;
Stand not on thirty with him.

GALLIPOT Forty, Pru!
Say thou the word, 'tis done: we venture lives
For wealth, but must do more to keep our wives.
Thirty or forty, Pru?

MISTRESS GALLIPOT Thirty, good sweet;
Of an ill bargain let's save what we can:
I'll pay it him with my tears; he was a man,
When first I knew him, of a meek spirit,
All goodness is not yet dried up, I hope.

GALLIPOT He shall have thirty pound, let that stop all:
Love's sweets taste best when we have drunk down gall.

[*Enter Tiltyard, Mistress Tiltyard, Goshawk, and Mistress Openwork.*]

God's-so, our friends! come, come, smooth your cheek:
After a storm the face of heaven looks sleek.

TILTYARD Did I not tell you these turtles were together?

8. Contracted.

MISTRESS TILTYARD How dost thou, sirrah? Why, sister Gallipot—

MISTRESS OPENWORK Lord, how she's chang'd!

GOSHAWK Is your wife ill, sir?

GALLIPOT Yes, indeed, la, sir, very ill, very ill, never worse.

MISTRESS TILTYARD How her head burns! Feel how her pulses work!

MISTRESS OPENWORK Sister, lie down a little; that always does me good.

MISTRESS TILTYARD In good sadness, I find best ease in that too. Has she laid some hot thing[9] to her stomach?

MISTRESS GALLIPOT No, but I will lay something anon.

TILTYARD Come, come, fools, you trouble her.—Shall's go, master Goshawk?

GOSHAWK Yes, sweet master Tiltyard—Sirrah Rosamond, I hold my life Gallipot hath vext his wife.

MISTRESS OPENWORK She has a horrible high color indeed.

GOSHAWK We shall have your face painted with the same red soon at night, when your husband comes from his rubbers[1] in a false alley: thou wilt not believe me that his bowls run with a wrong bias.

MISTRESS OPENWORK It cannot sink into me that he feeds upon stale mutton[2] abroad, having better and fresher at home.

GOSHAWK What if I bring thee where thou shalt see him stand at rack and manger?

MISTRESS OPENWORK I'll saddle him in's kind, and spur him till he kick again.

GOSHAWK Shall thou and I ride our journey then?

MISTRESS OPENWORK Here's my hand.

GOSHAWK No more.—Come, master Tiltyard, shall we leap into the stirrups with our women, and amble home?

TILTYARD Yes, yes.—Come, wife.

MISTRESS TILTYARD In troth, sister, I hope you will do well for all this.

MISTRESS GALLIPOT I hope I shall. Farewell, good sister. Sweet master Goshawk.

GALLIPOT Welcome, brother; most kindly welcome, sir,

ALL Thanks, sir, for our good cheer.

[*Exeunt all but Gallipot and Mistress Gallipot.*]

GALLIPOT It shall be so: because a crafty knave
Shall not outreach me, nor walk by my door
With my wife arm in arm, as 'twere his whore.
I'll give him a golden coxcomb, thirty pound.
Tush, Pru, what's thirty pound? Sweet duck, look cheerly.

MISTRESS GALLIPOT Thou'rt worthy of my heart, thou buy'st it dearly.

[*Enter Laxton muffled.*[3]]

LAXTON [*Aside.*] Uds light, the tide's against me; a pox of your 'pothecaryship! O for some glister[4] to set him going! 'Tis one of Hercules' labors to tread one of these city hens, because their cocks are still crowing over them. There's no turning tail here, I must on.

MISTRESS GALLIPOT O husband, see he comes!

GALLIPOT Let me deal with him.

LAXTON Bless you, sir.

GALLIPOT Be you blest too, sir, if you come in peace.

9. With a sexual double meaning.

1. Game of cards with three rounds, with a bawdy play on "rub" and "alley." See Dekker, *O Per Se O*: "My bowls did fit her alley."

2. Slang for a whore.

3. Hiding his face.

4. Suppository, enema.

LAXTON Have you any good pudding tobacco,[5] sir?
MISTRESS GALLIPOT O, pick no quarrels, gentle sir! my husband
Is not a man of weapon, as you are;
He knows all, I have open'd all before him,
Concerning you.
LAXTON [*Aside*.] Zounds, has she shown my letters?
MISTRESS GALLIPOT Suppose my case were yours, what would you do?
At such a pinch, such batteries, such assaults
Of father, mother, kindred, to dissolve
The knot you tied, and to be bound to him;
How could you shift this storm off?
LAXTON If I know, hang me!
MISTRESS GALLIPOT Besides a story of your death was read
Each minute to me.
LAXTON [*Aside*.] What a pox means this riddling?
GALLIPOT Be wise, sir; let not you and I be tossed
On lawyers' pens; they have sharp nibs, and draw
Men's very heart-blood from them. What need you, sir,
To beat the drum of my wife's infamy,
And call your friends together, sir, to prove
Your precontract, when sh'as confessed it?
LAXTON Umh, sir,
Has she confessed it?
GALLIPOT Sh'as, 'faith, to me, sir,
Upon your letter sending.
MISTRESS GALLIPOT I have, I have.
LAXTON [*Aside*.] If I let this iron cool, call me slave.
Do you hear, you dame Prudence? think'st thou, vile woman,
I'll take these blows and wink?
MISTRESS GALLIPOT Upon my knees. [*Kneeling*.]
LAXTON Out, impudence.
GALLIPOT Good sir—
LAXTON You goatish slaves![6]
No wild fowl to cut up but mine?
GALLIPOT Alas, sir,
You make her flesh to tremble; fright her not:
She shall do reason, and what's fit.
LAXTON I'll have thee,
Wert thou more common than an hospital,
And more diseased.
GALLIPOT But one word, good sir!
LAXTON So, sir.
GALLIPOT I married her, have lien with her, and got
Two children on her body: think but on that:
Have you so beggarly an appetite,
When I upon a dainty dish have fed
To dine upon my scraps, my leavings? ha, sir?
Do I come near you now, sir?

5. Pudding tobacco was compressed in rolls.
6. Slaves to lust.

LAXTON Be-lady, you touch me!
GALLIPOT Would not you scorn to wear my clothes, sir?
LAXTON Right, sir.
GALLIPOT Then, pray, sir, wear not her; for she's a garment
So fitting for my body, I am loath
Another should put it on: you'll undo both.
Your letter, as she said, complained you had spent,
In quest of her, some thirty pound; I'll pay it:
Shall that, sir, stop this gap up 'twixt you two?
LAXTON Well, if I swallow this wrong, let her thank you:
The money being paid, sir, I am gone:
Farewell. O women, happy's he trusts none!
MISTRESS GALLIPOT Despatch him hence, sweet husband.
GALLIPOT Yes, dear wife:
Pray, sir, come in: ere master Laxton part,
Thou shalt in wine drink to him.
MISTRESS GALLIPOT With all my heart.—[*Exit Gallipot*.]
How dost thou like my wit?
LAXTON Rarely: that wile,
By which the serpent did the first woman beguile,
Did ever since all women's bosoms fill;
You're apple-eaters all, deceivers still. [*Exeunt*.]

Scene 3

[*Holborn. Enter Sir Alexander Wengrave, Sir Davy Dapper, and Sir Adam Appleton on one side, and Trapdoor on the other*.]
SIR ALEXANDER Out with your tale, sir Davy, to sir Adam:
A knave is in mine eye deep in my debt.
SIR DAVY Nay, if he be a knave, sir, hold him fast.
[*Sir Davy Dapper and Sir Adam Appleton talk apart*.]
SIR ALEXANDER Speak softly; what egg is there hatching now?
TRAPDOOR A duck's egg, sir, a duck that has eaten a frog; I have cracked the shell, and some villany or other will peep out presently: the duck that sits is the bouncing ramp,[7] that roaring girl my mistress; the drake that must tread is your son Sebastian.
SIR ALEXANDER Be quick.
TRAPDOOR As the tongue of an oyster-wench.
SIR ALEXANDER And see thy news be true.
TRAPDOOR As a barber's every Saturday night. Mad Moll—
SIR ALEXANDER Ah—
TRAPDOOR Must be let in, without knocking, at your back gate.
SIR ALEXANDER So.
TRAPDOOR Your chamber will be made bawdy.
SIR ALEXANDER Good.
TRAPDOOR She comes in a shirt of mail.
SIR ALEXANDER How? shirt of mail?
TRAPDOOR Yes, sir, or a male shirt; that's to say, in man's apparel.

7. An outspoken and outrageously bad woman or girl.

SIR ALEXANDER To my son?

TRAPDOOR Close to your son: your son and her moon will be in conjunction, if all almanacs lie not; her black saveguard is turned into a deep slop, the holes of her upper body to button-holes, her waistcoat to a doublet, her placket to the ancient seat of a codpiece, and you shall take 'em both with standing collars.[8]

SIR ALEXANDER Art sure of this?

TRAPDOOR As every throng is sure of a pick-pocket; as sure as a whore is of the clients all Michaelmas term,[9] and of the pox after the term.

SIR ALEXANDER The time of their tilting?

TRAPDOOR Three.

SIR ALEXANDER The day?

TRAPDOOR This.

SIR ALEXANDER Away; ply it, watch her.

TRAPDOOR As the devil doth for the death of a bawd; I'll watch her, do you catch her.

SIR ALEXANDER She's fast: here weave thou the nets. Hark.

TRAPDOOR They are made.

SIR ALEXANDER I told them thou didst owe me money: hold it up; maintain't.

TRAPDOOR Stiffly, as a Puritan does contention.—Pox, I owe thee not the value of a halfpenny halter.

SIR ALEXANDER Thou shalt be hanged in it ere thou 'scape so:
Varlet, I'll make thee look through a grate![1]

TRAPDOOR I'll do't presently, through a tavern grate: drawer! pish. [*Exit.*]

SIR ADAM Has the knave vexed you, sir?

SIR ALEXANDER Asked him my money,
He swears my son received it. O, that boy
Will ne'er leave heaping sorrows on my heart,
Till he has broke it quite!

SIR ADAM Is he still wild?

SIR ALEXANDER As is a Russian bear.

SIR ADAM But he has left
His old haunt with that baggage?

SIR ALEXANDER Worse still and worse;
He lays on me his shame, I on him my curse.

SIR DAVY My son, Jack Dapper, then shall run with him
All in one pasture.

SIR ADAM Proves your son bad too, sir?

SIR DAVY As villany can make him: your Sebastian
Doats but on one drab, mine on a thousand;
A noise[2] of fiddlers, tobacco, wine, and a whore,
A mercer that will let him take up more,
Dice, and a water-spaniel with a duck,—O
Bring him a-bed with these: when his purse gingles,
Roaring[3] boys follow at's tail, fencers and ningles,[4]
Beasts Adam ne'er gave name to; these horse-leeches suck

8. Saveguard: outer petticoat; deep slop: wide breeches; placket: the front part of a woman's shift; codpiece: padded covering for the penis.
9. The fall term, here with reference to the Inns of Court.
1. Prison grating.
2. Company of musicians.
3. Riotous.
4. Favorites.

My son; he being drawn dry, they all live on smoke.
SIR ALEXANDER Tobacco?
SIR DAVY Right: but I have in my brain
A windmill going that shall grind to dust
The follies of my son, and make him wise,
Or a stark fool. Pray lend me your advice.
SIR ALEXANDER, SIR ADAM That shall you, good sir Davy.
SIR DAVY Here's the springe
I ha' set to catch this woodcock in:[5] an action
In a false name, unknown to him, is entered
I' the Counter[6] to arrest Jack Dapper.
SIR ALEXANDER, SIR ADAM Ha, ha, he!
SIR DAVY Think you the Counter cannot break him?
SIR ADAM Break him?
Yes, and break's heart too, if he lie there long.
SIR DAVY I'll make him sing a counter-tenor sure.
SIR ADAM No way to tame him like it; there he shall learn
What money is indeed, and how to spend it.
SIR DAVY He's bridled there.
SIR ALEXANDER Ay, yet knows not how to mend it.
Bedlam cures not more madmen in a year
Than one of the Counters does; men pay more dear
There for their wit than anywhere: a Counter!
Why, 'tis an university, who not sees?
As scholars there, so here men take degrees,
And follow the same studies all alike.
Scholars learn first logic and rhetoric;
So does a prisoner: with fine honeyed speech
At's first coming in he doth persuade, beseech
He may be lodged with one that is not itchy,
To lie in a clean chamber, in sheets not lousy;
But when he has no money, then does he try,
By subtle logic and quaint sophistry,
To make the keepers trust him.
SIR ADAM Say they do.
SIR ALEXANDER Then he's a graduate.
SIR DAVY Say they trust him not.
SIR ALEXANDER Then is he held a freshman and a sot,
And never shall commence;[7] but being still barred,
Be expulsed from the Master's side to th' Twopenny ward,
Or else i' th' Hole beg place.
SIR ADAM When then, I pray,
Proceeds a prisoner?
SIR ALEXANDER When, money being the theme,
He can dispute with his hard creditors' hearts,

5. See *Hamlet* 1.4.115: "Springs to catch woodcocks," ways to trick the unsuspecting.
6. Debtors' prison.
7. Graduate.

And get out clear, he's then a master of arts.
Sir Davy, send your son to Wood Street college,
A gentleman can no where get more knowledge.

SIR DAVY There gallants study hard.

SIR ALEXANDER True, to get money.

SIR DAVY 'Lies by th' heels, i'faith: thanks, thanks; I ha' sent
For a couple of bears shall paw him.

SIR ADAM Who comes yonder?

SIR DAVY They look like puttocks;[8] these should be they.

[*Enter Curtleax and Hanger.*]

SIR ALEXANDER I know 'em,
They are officers; sir, we'll leave you.

SIR DAVY My good knights,
Leave me; you see I'm haunted now with sprites.[9]

SIR ALEXANDER, SIR ADAM Fare you well, sir. [*Exeunt.*]

CURTLEAX This old muzzle-chops should be he by the fellow's description.—Save you, sir.

SIR DAVY Come hither, you mad varlets; did not my man tell you I watched here for you?

CURTLEAX One in a blue coat,[1] sir, told us that in this place an old gentleman would watch for us; a thing contrary to our oath, for we are to watch for every wicked member in a city.

SIR DAVY You'll watch then for ten thousand: what's thy name, honesty?

CURTLEAX Sergeant Curtleax I, sir.

SIR DAVY An excellent name for a sergeant, Curtleax:
Sergeants indeed are weapons of the law;
When prodigal ruffians far in debt are grown,
Should not you cut them, citizens were o'erthrown.
Thou dwell'st hereby in Holborn, Curtleax?

CURTLEAX That's my circuit, sir; I conjure most in that circle.

SIR DAVY And what young toward whelp is this?

HANGER Of the same litter; his yeoman, sir; my name's Hanger.

SIR DAVY Yeoman Hanger:
One pair of shears sure cut out both your coats;[2]
You have two names most dangerous to men's throats;
You two are villanous loads on gentlemen's backs;
Dear ware this Hanger and this Curtleax!

CURTLEAX We are as other men are, sir; I cannot see but he who makes a show of honesty and religion, if his claws can fasten to his liking, he draws blood: all that live in the world are but great fish and little fish, and feed upon one another; some eat up whole men, a sergeant cares but for the shoulder of a man. They call us knaves and curs; but many times he that sets us on worries more lambs one year than we do in seven.

SIR DAVY Spoke like a noble Cerberus! is the action entered?

HANGER His name is entered in the book of unbelievers.

8. Birds of prey; sergeants.
9. Spirits.
1. Servant's dress.
2. "There was but a pair of shears between them," was a proverbial expression.

SIR DAVY What book's that?

CURTLEAX The book where all prisoners' names stand; and not one amongst forty, when he comes in, believes to come out in haste.

SIR DAVY Be as dogged to him as your office allows you to be.

BOTH O sir!

SIR DAVY You know the unthrift, Jack Dapper?

CURTLEAX Ay, ay, sir, that gull, as well as I know my yeoman.

SIR DAVY And you know his father too, sir Davy Dapper?

CURTLEAX As damned a usurer as ever was among Jews: if he were sure his father's skin would yield him any money, he would, when he dies, flea it off, and sell it to cover drums for children at Bartholomew fair.

SIR DAVY What toads are these to spit poison on a man to his face! [*Aside*.]—Do you see, my honest rascals? yonder Greyhound is the dog he hunts with; out of that tavern Jack Dapper will sally: sa, sa; give the counter; on, set upon him!

BOTH We'll charge him upo' th' back, sir.

SIR DAVY Take no bail; put mace[3] enough into his caudle; double your files, traverse your ground.

BOTH Brave, sir.

SIR DAVY Cry arm, arm, arm!

BOTH Thus, sir.

SIR DAVY There, boy, there, boy! away: look to your prey, my true English wolves; and so I vanish. [*Exit*.]

CURTLEAX Some warden of the sergeants begat this old fellow, upon my life: stand close.

HANGER Shall the ambuscado lie in one place?

CURTLEAX No; nook thou yonder. [*They retire*.]

[*Enter Moll and Trapdoor*.]

MOLL Ralph.

TRAPDOOR What says my brave captain male and female?

MOLL This Holborn is such a wrangling street!

TRAPDOOR That's because lawyers walks to and fro in't.

MOLL Here's such jostling, as if every one we met were drunk and reeled.

TRAPDOOR Stand, mistress! do you not smell carrion?

MOLL Carrion? No; yet I spy ravens.

TRAPDOOR Some poor, wind-shaken gallant will anon fall into sore labor, and these men-midwives must bring him to bed i' the Counter: there all those that are great with child with debts lie in.

MOLL Stand up.

TRAPDOOR Like your new Maypole.

HANGER Whist, whew!

CURTLEAX Hump, no.

MOLL Peeping? It shall go hard, huntsmen, but I'll spoil your game. They look for all the world like two infected malt-men coming muffled up in their cloaks in a frosty morning to London.

TRAPDOOR A course, captain; a bear comes to the stake.

[*Enter Jack Dapper and Gull*.]

MOLL It should be so, for the dogs struggle to be let loose.

HANGER Whew!

3. A spice; a sergeant's weapon.

CURTLEAX Hemp.
MOLL Hark, Trapdoor, follow your leader.
JACK DAPPER Gull
GULL Master?
JACK DAPPER Didst ever see such an ass as I am, boy?
GULL No, by my troth, sir; to lose all your money, yet have false dice of your own; why, 'tis as I saw a great fellow used t'other day; he had a fair sword and buckler, and yet a butcher dry beat him with a cudgel.
TRAPDOOR Honest servant, fly!
MOLL Fly, master Dapper! you'll be arrested else.
JACK DAPPER Run, Gull, and draw.
GULL Run, master; Gull follows you.
[*Exeunt Dapper and Gull.*]
CURTLEAX [*Moll holding him.*] I know you well enough; you're but a whore to hang upon any man!
MOLL Whores, then, are like sergeants; so now hang you.—Draw, rogue, but strike not: for a broken pate they'll keep their beds, and recover twenty marks damages.
CURTLEAX You shall pay for this rescue.—Run down Shoe Lane and meet him.
TRAPDOOR Shu! is this a rescue, gentlemen, or no?
MOLL Rescue? a pox on 'em! Trapdoor, let's away;
[*Exeunt Curtleax and Hanger.*]
I'm glad I've done perfect one good work to day.
If any gentleman be in scrivener's[4] bands,
Send but for Moll, she'll bail him by these hands.
[*Exeunt.*]

Act 4

Scene 1

[*A room in Sir Alexander Wengrave's house. Enter Sir Alexander Wengrave.*]
SIR ALEXANDER Unhappy in the follies of a son,
Led against judgment, sense, obedience,
And all the powers of nobleness and wit!
[*Enter Trapdoor.*]
O wretched father!—Now, Trapdoor, will she come?
TRAPDOOR In man's apparel, sir; I'm in her heart now,
And share in all her secrets.
SIR ALEXANDER Peace, peace, peace!
Here, take my German watch, hang't up in sight,
That I may see her hang in English[5] for't.
TRAPDOOR I warrant you for that now, next sessions rids her, sir. This watch will bring her in better than a hundred constables. [*Hangs up the watch.*]
SIR ALEXANDER Good Trapdoor, sayst thou so? Thou cheer'st my heart
After a storm of sorrow. My gold chain too;
Here, take a hundred marks in yellow links.
TRAPDOOR That will do well to bring the watch to light, sir;
And worth a thousand of your headborough's lanterns.[6]

4. Money-lender's.
5. Be hanged under English law.
6. Lanterns carried by the constable at night.

SIR ALEXANDER Place that a' the court-cupboard;[7] let it lie
Full in the view of her thief-whorish eye.
TRAPDOOR She cannot miss it, sir; I see't so plain,
That I could steal't myself. [*Places the chain.*]
SIR ALEXANDER Perhaps thou shalt too,
That or something as weighty: what she leaves
Thou shalt come closely in and filch away,
And all the weight upon her back I'll lay.
TRAPDOOR You cannot assure that, sir.
SIR ALEXANDER No? what lets it?
TRAPDOOR Being a stout girl, perhaps she'll desire pressing;[8]
Then all the weight must lie upon her belly.
SIR ALEXANDER Belly or back, I care not, so I've one.
TRAPDOOR You're of my mind for that, sir.
SIR ALEXANDER Hang up my ruff-band with the diamond at it;
It may be she'll like that best.
TRAPDOOR [*Aside.*] It's well for her, that she must have her choice; he thinks nothing too good for her. —If you hold on this mind a little longer, it shall be the first work I do to turn thief myself; 'twould do a man good to be hanged when he is so well provided for. [*Hangs up the ruff-band.*]
SIR ALEXANDER So, well said; all hangs well: would she hung so too!
The sight would please me more than all their glisterings.
O that my mysteries[9] to such straits should run,
That I must rob myself to bless my son! [*Exeunt.*]

[*Enter Sebastian Wengrave, Mary Fitzallard disguised as a page, and Moll in her male dress.*]

SEBASTIAN Thou'st done me a kind office, without touch
Either of sin or shame; our loves are honest.
MOLL I'd scorn to make such shift to bring you together else.
SEBASTIAN Now have I time and opportunity
Without all fear to bid thee welcome, love!
[*Kisses Mary.*]
MARY Never with more desire and harder venture!
MOLL How strange this shows, one man to kiss another!
SEBASTIAN I'd kiss such men to choose, Moll;
Methinks a woman's lip tastes well in a doublet.
MOLL Many an old madam[1] has the better fortune then,
Whose breaths grew stale before the fashion came:
If that will help 'em, as you think 'twill do,
They'll learn in time to pluck on the hose too.
SEBASTIAN The older they wax, Moll, troth I speak seriously,
As some have a conceit their drink tastes better
In an outlandish cup than in our own,
So methinks every kiss she gives me now
In this strange form is worth a pair of two.
Here we are safe, and furthest from the eye

7. Sideboard on which plate was displayed.
8. The loading of weights upon the accused to force a confession; intercourse.
9. Devices.
1. Prostitute.

Of all suspicion: this is my father's chamber,
Upon which floor he never steps till night:
Here he mistrusts me not, nor I his coming;
At mine own chamber he still pries unto me,
My freedom is not there at mine own finding,
Still checked and curbed; here he shall miss his purpose.

MOLL And what's your business, now you have your mind, sir?
At your great suit I promised you to come:
I pitied her for name's sake, that a Moll
Should be so crost in love, when there's so many
That owes nine lays[2] a-piece, and not so little.
My tailor fitted her; how like you his work?

SEBASTIAN So well, no art can mend it, for this purpose:
But to thy wit and help we're chief in debt,
And must live still beholding.

MOLL Any honest pity
I'm willing to bestow upon poor ringdoves.

SEBASTIAN I'll offer no worse play.

MOLL Nay, and you should, sir,
I should draw first, and prove the quicker man.

SEBASTIAN Hold, there shall need no weapon at this meeting;
But 'cause thou shalt not loose thy fury idle,
Here take this viol, run upon the guts,
And end thy quarrel singing.
[*Takes down and gives her a viol.*]

MOLL Like a swan above bridge;
For look you here's the bridge,[3] and here am I.

SEBASTIAN Hold on, sweet Moll!

MARY I've heard her much commended, sir, for one
That was ne'er taught.

MOLL I'm much beholding to 'em.
Well, since you'll needs put us together, sir,
I'll play my part as well as I can: it shall ne'er
Be said I came into a gentleman's chamber,
And let his instrument hang by the walls.

SEBASTIAN Why, well said, Moll, i'faith; it had been a shame for that gentleman then that would have let it hung still, and ne'er offered thee it.

MOLL There it should have been still then for Moll;
For though the world judge impudently of me,
I never came into that chamber yet
Where I took down the instrument myself.

SEBASTIAN Pish, let 'em prate abroad; thou'rt here where thou art known and loved; there be a thousand close dames that will call the viol an unmannerly instrument for a woman, and therefore talk broadly of thee, when you shall have them sit wider to a worse quality.

MOLL Push,
I ever fall asleep and think not of 'em, sir;
And thus I dream.

2. Wagers.

3. I.e., of the viola da gamba.

SEBASTIAN Prithee, let's hear thy dream, Moll.
MOLL [*sings*]

I dream there is a mistress,
And she lays out the money;
She goes unto her sisters,
She never comes at any.[4]

[*Reenter Sir Alexander behind.*]

She says she went to th' Burse[5] *for patterns;*
You shall find her at Saint Kathern's,[6]
And comes home with never a penny.

SEBASTIAN That's a free[7] mistress, faith!
SIR ALEXANDER Ay, ay, ay,
Like her that sings it; one of thine own choosing. [*Aside.*]
MOLL But shall I dream again? [*Sings.*]

Here comes a wench will brave ye;
Her courage was so great,
She lay with one of the navy,
Her husband lying i' the Fleet.° prison
Yet oft with him she cavilled;
I wonder what she ails;
Her husband's ship lay gravelled,° aground
When her's could hoise up sails:
Yet she began, like all my foes,
To call whore first; for so do those—
A pox of all false tails!

SEBASTIAN Marry, amen, say I!
SIR ALEXANDER [*Aside.*] So say I too.
MOLL Hang up the viol now, sir: all this while I was in a dream; one shall lie rudely then;
But being awake, I keep my legs together.
A watch? what's a' clock here?
SIR ALEXANDER [*Aside.*] Now, now she's trapt!
MOLL Between one and two; nay, then I care not. A watch and a musician are cousin-germans[8] in one thing, they must both keep time well, or there's no goodness in 'em; the one else deserves to be dashed against a wall, and t'other to have his brains knocked out with a fiddle-case.
What! a loose chain and a dangling diamond?
Here were a brave booty for an evening thief now:
There's many a younger brother would be glad
To look twice in at a window for't,
And wriggle in and out, like an eel in a sand-bag.
O, if men's secret youthful faults should judge 'em,
'Twould be the general'st execution
That e'er was seen in England!

4. Money, sexual partners, sexual fulfillment.
5. Royal Exchange.
6. The dockside district in the east end of London, notorious for its taverns.
7. Generous, loose.
8. First cousins.

There would be but few left to sing the ballads,
There would be so much work: most of our brokers
Would be chosen for hangmen; a good day for them;
They might renew their wardrobes of free cost then.

SEBASTIAN This is the roaring wench must do us good.

MARY No poison, sir, but serves us for some use;
Which is confirmed in her.

SEBASTIAN Peace, peace—
'Foot, I did hear him sure, where'er he be.

MOLL Who did you hear?

SEBASTIAN My father;
'Twas like a sigh of his: I must be wary.

SIR ALEXANDER [*Aside.*] No? wilt not be? am I alone so wretched
That nothing takes? I'll put him to his plunge[9] for't.

SEBASTIAN Life! here he comes.—Sir, I beseech you take it;
Your way of teaching does so much content me,
I'll make it four pound; here's forty shillings, sir—
I think I name it right—help me, good Moll—
Forty in hand. [*Offering money.*]

MOLL Sir, you shall pardon me:
I've more of the meanest scholar I can teach;
This pays me more than you have offered yet.

SEBASTIAN At the next quarter,
When I receive the means my father 'lows me,
You shall have t'other forty.

SIR ALEXANDER [*Aside.*] This were well now,
Were't to a man whose sorrows had blind eyes:
But mine behold his follies and untruths
With two clear glasses. [*Coming forward.*]
How now?

SEBASTIAN Sir?

SIR ALEXANDER What's he there?

SEBASTIAN You're come in good time, sir; I've a suit to you; I'd crave your present kindness.

SIR ALEXANDER What's he there.

SEBASTIAN A gentleman, a musician, sir; one of excellent fingering.

SIR ALEXANDER Ay, I think so;—[*Aside:*] I wonder how they 'scaped her.

SEBASTIAN Has the most delicate stroke, sir.

SIR ALEXANDER A stroke indeed!—[*Aside:*] I feel it at my heart.

SEBASTIAN Puts down all your famous musicians.

SIR ALEXANDER [*Aside.*] Ay, a whore may put down a hundred of 'em.

SEBASTIAN Forty shillings is the agreement, sir, between us: Now, sir, my present means mounts but to half on't.

SIR ALEXANDER And he stands upon the whole?

SEBASTIAN Ay, indeed does he, sir.

SIR ALEXANDER And will do still; he'll ne'er be in other tale.

SEBASTIAN Therefore I'd stop his mouth, sir, and I could.

9. Plunge: difficulty, straits.

SIR ALEXANDER Hum, true; there is no other way indeed;—[*Aside:*] His folly hardens; shame must needs succeed.—
Now, sir, I understand you profess music.
MOLL I'm a poor servant to that liberal science, sir.
SIR ALEXANDER Where is't you teach?
MOLL Right against Clifford's Inn.[1]
SIR ALEXANDER Hum, that's a fit place for't: you've many scholars?
MOLL And some of worth, whom I may call my masters.
SIR ALEXANDER [*Aside.*] Ay, true, a company of whoremasters.—
You teach to sing, too?
MOLL Marry, do I, sir.
SIR ALEXANDER I think you'll find an apt scholar of my son,
Especially for prick-song.
MOLL I've much hope of him.
SIR ALEXANDER [*Aside.*] I'm sorry for't, I have the less for that.—
You can play any lesson?
MOLL At first sight, sir.
SIR ALEXANDER There's a thing call'd the Witch; can you play that?
MOLL I would be sorry any one should mend me in't.
SIR ALEXANDER [*Aside.*] Ay, I believe thee; thou'st so bewitched my son,
No care will mend the work that thou hast done.
I have bethought myself, since my art fails,
I'll make her policy the art to trap her.
Here are four angels marked with holes in them
Fit for his cracked companions: gold he'll give her;
These will I make induction to her ruin,
And rid shame from my house, grief from my heart.—
Here, son, in what you take content and pleasure,
Want shall not curb you; pay the gentleman
His latter half in gold. [*Gives money.*]
SEBASTIAN I thank you, sir.
SIR ALEXANDER [*Aside.*] O may the operation on't end three;
In her life, shame in him, and grief in me! [*Exit.*]
SEBASTIAN Faith, thou shalt have 'em; 'tis my father's gift:
Never was man beguiled with better shift.
MOLL He that can take me for a male musician,
I can't choose but make him my instrument,
And play upon him. [*Exeunt.*]

Scene 2

[*Before Gallipot's Shop. Enter Mistress Gallipot and Mistress Openwork.*]

MISTRESS GALLIPOT Is, then, that bird of yours, master Goshawk, so wild?

MISTRESS OPENWORK A Goshawk? a puttock;[2] all for prey: he angles for fish, but he loves flesh better.

MISTRESS GALLIPOT Is't possible his smooth face should have wrinkles in't, and we not see them?

1. One of the Inns of Chancery, a high court.

2. Kite, bird of prey.

MISTRESS OPENWORK Possible? Why, have not many handsome legs in silk stockings villanous splay feet, for all their great roses?[3]

MISTRESS GALLIPOT Troth, sirrah, thou sayst true.

MISTRESS OPENWORK Didst never see an archer, as thou'st walked by Bunhill,[4] look a-squint when he drew his bow?

MISTRESS GALLIPOT Yes, when his arrows have fline[5] toward Islington, his eyes have shot clean contrary towards Pimlico.[6]

MISTRESS OPENWORK For all the world so does master Goshawk double with me.

MISTRESS GALLIPOT O, fie upon him: if he double once, he's not for me.

MISTRESS OPENWORK Because Goshawk goes in a shag-ruff band, with a face sticking up in't which shows like an agate set in a cramp ring,[7] he thinks I'm in love with him.

MISTRESS GALLIPOT 'Las, I think he takes his mark amiss in thee!

MISTRESS OPENWORK He has, by often beating into me, made me believe that my husband kept a whore.

MISTRESS GALLIPOT Very good.

MISTRESS OPENWORK Swore to me that my husband this very morning went in a boat, with a tilt over it, to the Three Pigeons at Brainford, and his punk with him under his tilt.

MISTRESS GALLIPOT That were wholesome.

MISTRESS OPENWORK I believed it; fell a-swearing at him, cursing of harlots; made me ready to hoise up sail and be there as soon as he.

MISTRESS GALLIPOT So, so.

MISTRESS OPENWORK And for that voyage Goshawk comes hither incontinently:[8] but, sirrah, this water-spaniel dives after no duck but me; his hope is having me at Brainford, to make me cry quack.

MISTRESS GALLIPOT Art sure of it?

MISTRESS OPENWORK Sure of it? My poor innocent Openwork came in as I was poking my ruff: presently hit I him i' the teeth with the Three Pigeons; he forswore all; I up and opened all; and now stands he in a shop hard by, like a musket on a rest,[9] to hit Goshawk i' the eye, when he comes to fetch me to the boat.

MISTRESS GALLIPOT Such another lame gelding offered to carry me through thick and thin,—Laxton, sirrah,—but I am rid of him now.

MISTRESS OPENWORK Happy is the woman can be rid of 'em all! 'Las, what are your whisking gallants to our husbands, weigh 'em rightly, man for man?

MISTRESS GALLIPOT Troth, mere shallow things.

MISTRESS OPENWORK Idle, simple things, running heads; and yet let 'em run over us never so fast, we shopkeepers, when all's done, are sure to have 'em in our pursenets[1] at length; and when they are in, lord, what simple animals they are! Then they hang the head—

MISTRESS GALLIPOT Then they droop—

MISTRESS OPENWORK Then they write letters—

MISTRESS GALLIPOT Then they cog[2]—

3. Knots of ribbons worn on the shoes.
4. Where archery matches and artillery practice were held.
5. Flown.
6. Islington: a northern suburb; Pimlico: part of Hogsdon.
7. A ring consecrated on Good Friday that was supposed to preserve the wearer against cramp.
8. Immediately.
9. A support that consisted of a wooden pole with an iron spike at the end to fix it in the ground and a piece of iron at the top to put the musket in.
1. Nets whose ends are drawn together by a string.
2. "Cog" and "ingle" both mean "to wheedle."

MISTRESS OPENWORK Then deal they underhand with us, and we must ingle with our husbands a-bed; and we must swear they are our cousins, and able to do us a pleasure at court.

MISTRESS GALLIPOT And yet, when we have done our best, all's but put into a riven dish; we are but frumped at[3] and libelled upon.

MISTRESS OPENWORK O, if it were the good Lord's will there were a law made, no citizen should trust any of 'em all!

[*Enter Goshawk.*]

MISTRESS GALLIPOT Hush, sirrah! Goshawk flutters.

GOSHAWK How now? Are you ready?

MISTRESS OPENWORK Nay, are you ready? A little thing, you see, makes us ready.

GOSHAWK Us? Why, must she make one i' the voyage?

MISTRESS OPENWORK O, by any means! Do I know how my husband will handle me?

GOSHAWK [*Aside.*] 'Foot, how shall I find water to keep these two mills going? —Well, since you'll needs be clapped under hatches, if I sail not with you both till all split,[4] hang me up at the mainyard and duck me.—[*Aside:*] It's but liquoring them both soundly, and then you shall see their cork heels fly up high,[5] like two swans when their tails are above water, and their long necks under water diving to catch gudgeons.—Come, come, oars stand ready; the tide's with us; on with those false faces; blow winds and thou shalt take thy husband casting out his net to catch fresh salmon at Brainford.

MISTRESS GALLIPOT [*Aside.*] I believe you'll eat of a cod's head of your own dressing before you reach half way thither.

[*She and Mistress Openwork mask themselves.*]

GOSHAWK So, so, follow close; pin as you go.

[*Enter Laxton muffled.*]

LAXTON Do you hear?

MISTRESS GALLIPOT Yes, I thank my ears.

LAXTON I must have a bout with your 'pothecaryship.

MISTRESS GALLIPOT At what weapon?

LAXTON I must speak with you.

MISTRESS GALLIPOT No.

LAXTON No? You shall.

MISTRESS GALLIPOT Shall? Away, souced sturgeon! Half fish, half flesh.

LAXTON Faith, gib,[6] are you spitting? I'll cut your tail, puss-cat, for this.

MISTRESS GALLIPOT 'Las, poor Laxton, I think thy tail's cut already! your worst.

LAXTON If I do not—[*Exit.*]

GOSHAWK Come, ha' you done?

[*Enter Openwork.*]

'Sfoot, Rosamond, your husband!

OPENWORK How now? Sweet master Goshawk! None more welcome;
I've wanted your embracements: when friends meet,
The music of the spheres sounds not more sweet
Than does their conference. Who's this? Rosamond?
Wife? How now, sister?

GOSHAWK Silence, if you love me!

3. Mocked.
4. Go to pieces.
5. The dramatists frequently refer to the cork heels worn by women.
6. A scold.

OPENWORK Why masked?
MISTRESS OPENWORK Does a mask grieve you, sir?
OPENWORK It does.
MISTRESS OPENWORK Then you're best get you a mumming.
GOSHAWK 'Sfoot, you'll spoil all!
MISTRESS GALLIPOT May not we cover our bare faces with masks,
As well as you cover your bald heads with hats?
OPENWORK No masks; why, they're thieves to beauty, that rob eyes
Of admiration in which true love lies.
Why are masks worn? Why good? or why desired?
Unless by their gay covers wits are fired
To read the vildest[7] looks: many bad faces,
Because rich gems are treasured up in cases,
Pass by their privilege current; but as caves
Damn misers' gold, so masks are beauties' graves.
Men ne'er meet women with such muffled eyes,
But they curse her that first did masks devise,
And swear it was some beldam.[8] Come, off with't.
MISTRESS OPENWORK I will not.
OPENWORK Good faces masked are jewels kept by sprites;
Hide none but bad ones, for they poison men's sights;
Show, then, as shopkeepers do their broidered stuff,
By owl-light; fine wares can't be open enough.
Prithee, sweet Rose, come, strike this sail.
MISTRESS OPENWORK Sail?
OPENWORK Ha!
Yes, wife, strike sail, for storms are in thine eyes.
MISTRESS OPENWORK They're here, sir, in my brows, if any rise.
OPENWORK Ha, brows?—What says she, friend? Pray, tell me why
Your two flags were advanced;[9] the comedy,
Come, what's the comedy?
MISTRESS GALLIPOT *Westward ho.*[1]
OPENWORK How?
MISTRESS OPENWORK 'Tis *Westward ho,* she says.
GOSHAWK Are you both mad?
MISTRESS OPENWORK Is't market-day at Brainford, and your ware
Not sent up yet?
OPENWORK What market-day? what ware?
MISTRESS OPENWORK A pie with three pigeons in't: 'tis drawn,
And stays your cutting up.
GOSHAWK As you regard my credit—
OPENWORK Art mad?
MISTRESS OPENWORK Yes, lecherous goat, baboon!
OPENWORK Baboon? then toss me in a blanket.
MISTRESS OPENWORK Do I it well?
MISTRESS GALLIPOT Rarely.
GOSHAWK Belike, sir, she's not well; best leave her.

7. Vilest.
8. Hag.
9. Flags were placed at the tops of theaters.
1. The boatmen's cry, and the title of a play by Webster and Dekker printed in 1607.

OPENWORK No;
I'll stand the storm now, how fierce soe'er it blow.
MISTRESS OPENWORK Did I for this lose all my friends, refuse
Rich hopes and golden fortunes, to be made
A stale[2] to a common whore?
OPENWORK This does amaze me.
MISTRESS OPENWORK O God, O God! Feed at reversion now?
A strumpet's leaving?
OPENWORK Rosamond!
GOSHAWK [*Aside*.] I sweat; would I lay in Cold Harbour![3]
MISTRESS OPENWORK Thou'st struck ten thousand daggers through my heart!
OPENWORK Not I, by heaven, sweet wife!
MISTRESS OPENWORK Go, devil, go; that which thou swear'st by damns thee!
GOSHAWK 'S heart, will you undo me?
MISTRESS OPENWORK Why stay you here? The star by which you sail
Shines yonder above Chelsea; you lose your shore;
If this moon light you, seek out your light whore.
OPENWORK Ha!
MISTRESS GALLIPOT Push, your western pug![4]
GOSHAWK Zounds, now hell roars!
MISTRESS OPENWORK With whom you tilted in a pair of oars
This very morning.
OPENWORK Oars?
MISTRESS OPENWORK At Brainford, sir.
OPENWORK Rack not my patience.—Master Goshawk,
Some slave has buzzed this into her, has he not?
I run a tilt in Brainford with a woman?
'Tis a lie!
What old bawd tells thee this? 's death, 'tis a lie!
MISTRESS OPENWORK 'Tis one who to thy face shall justify
All that I speak.
OPENWORK Ud'soul,[5] do but name that rascal!
MISTRESS OPENWORK No, sir, I will not.
GOSHAWK [*Aside*.] Keep thee there, girl, then!
OPENWORK Sister, know you this varlet?
MISTRESS GALLIPOT Yes.
OPENWORK Swear true;
Is there a rogue so low damned? a second Judas?—
A common hangman, cutting a man's throat,
Does it to his face,—bite me behind my back?
A cur dog? swear if you know this hell-hound.
MISTRESS GALLIPOT In truth, I do.
OPENWORK His name?
MISTRESS GALLIPOT Not for the world;
To have you to stab him.
GOSHAWK [*Aside*.] O brave girls, worth gold![6]

2. A lover or mistress mocked by rivals; a decoy.
3. Poor neighborhood near London Bridge.
4. Barge man working on the Thames.
5. God bless my soul.
6. "A girl worth gold" was a proverbial expression and the subtitle of Heywood's *Fair Maid of the West*.

OPENWORK A word, honest master Goshawk. [*Drawing his sword.*]
GOSHAWK What do you mean, sir?
OPENWORK Keep off, and if the devil can give a name
To this new fury, holla it through my ear,
Or wrap it up in some hid character.
I'll ride to Oxford and watch out mine eyes,
But I will hear the Brazen Head speak,[7] or else
Show me but one hair of his head or beard,
That I may sample it. If the fiend I meet
In mine own house, I'll kill him; in the street,
Or at the church-door,—there, 'cause he seeks t' untie
The knot God fastens, he deserves most to die.
MISTRESS OPENWORK My husband titles him!
OPENWORK Master Goshawk, pray, sir,
Swear to me that you know him, or know him not,
Who makes me at Brainford to take up a petticoat
Besides my wife's.
GOSHAWK By heaven, that man I know not!
MISTRESS OPENWORK Come, come, you lie!
GOSHAWK Will you not have all out?
By heaven, I know no man beneath the moon
Should do you wrong, but if I had his name,
I'd print it in text letters.
MISTRESS OPENWORK Print thine own then:
Didst not thou swear to me he kept his whore!
MISTRESS GALLIPOT And that in sinful Brainford they'd commit
That which our lips did water at, sir,—ha?
MISTRESS OPENWORK Thou spider that Hast woven thy cunning web
In mine own house t' ensnare me! hast not thou
Sucked nourishment even underneath this roof,
And turned it all to poison, spitting it
On thy friend's face, my husband, (he as 'twere sleeping),
Only to leave him ugly to mine eyes,
That they might glance on thee?
MISTRESS GALLIPOT Speak, are these lies?
GOSHAWK Mine own shame me confounds!
OPENWORK No more; he's stung.
Who'd think that in one body there could dwell
Deformity and beauty, heaven and hell?
Goodness I see is but outside; we all set
In rings of gold stones that be counterfeit:
I thought you none.
GOSHAWK Pardon me!
OPENWORK Truth I do:
This blemish grows in nature, not in you;
For man's creation stick even moles in scorn
On fairest cheeks.—Wife, nothing's perfect born.
MISTRESS OPENWORK I thought you had been born perfect.
OPENWORK What's this whole world but a gilt rotten pill?

7. In the prose tract of the *Famous Historie of Fryer Bacon* (1589) it is related how "Friar Bacon made a Brazen Head to speak, by which he would have walled England about with brass."

For at the heart lies the old core still.
I'll tell you, master Goshawk, ay, in your eye
I have seen wanton fire; and then, to try
The soundness of my judgment, I told you
I kept a whore, made you believe 'twas true,
Only to feel how your pulse beat; but find
The world can hardly yield a perfect friend.
Come, come, a trick of youth, and 'tis forgiven;
This rub put by, our love shall run more even.

MISTRESS OPENWORK You'll deal upon men's wives no more?

GOSHAWK No; you teach me
A trick for that.

MISTRESS OPENWORK Troth, do not; they'll o'erreach thee.

OPENWORK Make my house yours, sir, still.

GOSHAWK No.

OPENWORK I say you shall:
Seeing thus besieged it holds out, 'twill never fall.

[*Enter Gallipot, followed by Greenwit disguised as a Sumner; and Laxton muffled aloof off.*[8]]

OPENWORK, GOSHAWK etc. How now?

GALLIPOT With me, sir?

GREENWIT You, sir. I have gone snuffling up and down by your door this hour, to watch for you.

MISTRESS GALLIPOT What's the matter, husband?

GREENWIT I have caught a cold in my head, sir, by sitting up late in the Rose tavern; but I hope you understand my speech.

GALLIPOT So, sir.

GREENWIT I cite you by the name of Hippocrates Gallipot, and you by the name of Prudence Gallipot, to appear upon *Crastino*,—do you see?—*Crastino sancti Dunstani*,[9] this Easter term, in Bow Church.

GALLIPOT Where, sir? what says he?

GREENWIT Bow, Bow Church, to answer to a libel of precontract on the part and behalf of the said Prudence and another: you're best, sir, take a copy of the citation, 'tis but twelvepence.

OPENWORK, GALLIPOT etc. A citation!

GOSHAWK You pocky-nosed rascal, what slave fees you to this!

LAXTON [*coming forward*] Slave? I ha' nothing to do with you; do you hear, sir?

GOSHAWK Laxton, is't not? What fagary[1] is this?

GALLIPOT Trust me, I thought, sir, this storm long ago
Had been full laid, when, if you be remembered,
I paid you the last fifteen pound, besides
The thirty you had first; for then you swore—

LAXTON Tush, tush, sir, oaths,—
Truth, yet I'm loath to vex you—tell you what,
Make up the money I had an hundred pound,
And take your bellyful of her.

8. Sumner: one employed to summon people to court; aloof off: to hold aloof from.

9. May 20: the day after St. Dunstan's Day.

1. Vagary, trumped up expedition.

GALLIPOT An hundred pound?

MISTRESS GALLIPOT What, a hundred pound? he gets none: what, a hundred pound?

GALLIPOT Sweet Pru, be calm; the gentleman offers thus:
If I will make the moneys that are past
A hundred pound, he will discharge all courts,
And give his bond never to vex us more.

MISTRESS GALLIPOT A hundred pound? 'Las, take, sir, but threescore!
Do you seek my undoing?

LAXTON I'll not 'bate one sixpence.—
I'll maul you, puss, for spitting.

MISTRESS GALLIPOT Do thy worst.—
Will fourscore stop thy mouth?

LAXTON No.

MISTRESS GALLIPOT You're a slave;
Thou cheat, I'll now tear money from thy throat.—
Husband, lay hold on yonder tawny coat.[2]

GREENWIT Nay, gentlemen, seeing your women are so hot, I must lose my hair[3] in their company, I see. [*Takes off his false hair*.]

MISTRESS OPENWORK His hair sheds off, and yet he speaks not so much in the nose as he did before.

GOSHAWK He has had the better chirurgeon.—Master Greenwit, is your wit so raw as to play no better a part than a summer's?

GALLIPOT I pray, who plays *A knack to know an honest man*,[4] in this company?

MISTRESS GALLIPOT Dear husband, pardon me, I did dissemble,
Told thee I was his precontracted wife,
When letters came from him for thirty pound:
I had no shift but that.

GALLIPOT A very clean shift,
But able to make me lousy: on.

MISTRESS GALLIPOT Husband, I plucked,
When he had tempted me to think well of him,
Gelt feathers[5] from thy wings, to make him fly
More lofty.

GALLIPOT A' the top of you, wife: on.

MISTRESS GALLIPOT He having wasted them, comes now for more,
Using me as a ruffian doth his whore,
Whose sin keeps him in breath. By heaven, I vow,
Thy bed he ne'er wronged more than he does now!

GALLIPOT My bed? ha, ha! like enough; a shopboard will serve
To have a cuckold's coat cut out upon:
Of that we'll talk hereafter.—You're a villain.

LAXTON Here me but speak, sir, you shall find me none.

OPENWORK / GOSHAWK etc. Pray, sir, be patient, and hear him.

GALLIPOT I'm muzzled for biting, sir; use me how you will.

2. Apparitors and bishops' retainers wore tawny coats.
3. "So hot . . . lose my hair": a joking allusion to venereal disease.
4. Title of an anonymous comedy.
5. Golden feathers.

LAXTON The first hour that your wife was in my eye,
Myself with other gentlemen sitting by
In your shop tasting smoke, and speech being used,
That men who've fairest wives are most abused,
And hardly scape the horn, your wife maintained
That only such spots in city dames were stained
Justly but by men's slanders: for her own part,
She vowed that you had so much of her heart,
No man, by all his wit, by any wile
Never so fine-spun, should yourself beguile
Of what in her was yours.
GALLIPOT Yet, Pru, 'tis well.—
Play out your game at Irish,[6] sir: who wins?
MISTRESS OPENWORK The trial is when she comes to bearing.
LAXTON I scorned one woman thus should brave all men,
And, which more vexed me, a she-citizen;
Therefore I laid siege to her: out she held,
Gave many a brave repulse, and me compelled
With shame to sound retreat to my hot lust:
Then, seeing all base desires raked up in dust,
And that to tempt her modest ears, I swore
Ne'er to presume again: she said, her eye
Would ever give me welcome honestly;
And, since I was a gentleman, if't run low,
She would my state relieve, not to o'erthrow
Your own and hers: did so; then seeing I wrought
Upon her meekness, me she set at nought;
And yet to try if I could turn that tide,
You see what stream I strove with; but, sir, I swear
By heaven, and by those hopes men lay up there,
I neither have nor had a base intent
To wrong your bed! What's done, is merriment:
Your gold I pay back with this interest,
When I'd most power to do't, I wronged you least.
GALLIPOT If this no gullery be, sir—
OPENWORK, GOSHAWK etc. No, no, on my life!
GALLIPOT Then, sir, I am beholden—not to you, wife,—
But, master Laxton, to your want of doing
Ill, which it seems you have not.—Gentlemen,
Tarry and dine here all.
OPENWORK Brother, we've a jest,
As good as yours, to furnish out a feast.
GALLIPOT We'll crown our table with't.—Wife, brag no more
Of holding out: who most brags is most whore.
[*Exeunt.*]

6. A board game.

Act 5

Scene 1

[*A Street. Enter Jack Dapper, Moll, Sir Beauteous Ganymede, and Sir Thomas Long.*]

JACK DAPPER But, prithee, master captain Jack, be plain and perspicuous with me; was it your Meg of Westminster's[7] courage that rescued me from the Poultry puttocks[8] indeed?

MOLL The valor of my wit, I ensure you, sir, fetched you off bravely, when you were i' the forlorn hope among those desperates. Sir Beauteous Ganymede here, and sir Thomas Long, heard that cuckoo, my man Trapdoor, sing the note of your ransom from captivity.

SIR BEAUTEOUS Uds so, Moll, where's that Trapdoor?

MOLL Hanged, I think, by this time: a justice in this town, that speaks nothing but *make a mittimus, away with him to Newgate*,[9] used that rogue like a firework, to run upon a line betwixt him and me.

ALL How, how?

MOLL Marry, to lay trains of villany to blow up my life: I smelt the powder, spied what linstock gave fire to shoot against the poor captain of the galley-foist, and away slid I my man like a shovel-board shilling.[1] He struts up and down the suburbs, I think, and eats up whores, feeds upon a bawd's garbage.

SIR THOMAS Sirrah, Jack Dapper—

JACK DAPPER What sayst, Tom Long?

SIR THOMAS Thou hadst a sweet-faced boy, hail-fellow with thee, to your little Gull: how is he spent?

JACK DAPPER Troth, I whistled the poor little buzzard off a' my fist, because, when he waited upon me at the ordinaries, the gallants hit me i' the teeth still, and said I looked like a painted alderman's tomb, and the boy at my elbow like a death's head.—Sirrah Jack, Moll—

MOLL What says my little Dapper?

SIR BEAUTEOUS Come, come; walk and talk, walk and talk.

JACK DAPPER Moll and I'll be i' the midst.

MOLL These knights shall have squires' places belike then: well, Dapper, what say you?

JACK DAPPER Sirrah captain, mad Mary, the gull my own father, Dapper sir Davy, laid these London boot-halers,[2] the catchpolls, in ambush to set upon me.

ALL Your father? away, Jack!

JACK DAPPER By the tassels of this handkercher, 'tis true: and what was his warlike stratagem, think you? he thought, because a wicker cage tames a nightingale, a lousy prison could make an ass of me.

ALL A nasty plot!

JACK DAPPER Ay, as though a counter,[3] which is a park in which all the wild beasts of the city run head by head, could tame me!

MOLL Yonder comes my lord Noland.

[*Enter Lord Noland.*]

7. Meg of Westminster was celebrated in a popular tract entitled *The Life and Pranks of Long Meg of Westminster* (1582; reissued 1635). She was also the heroine of a lost play of 1594.

8. Officers, sergeants.

9. Mittimus: a warrant to commit to jail; "away with him to Newgate" was a proverbial expression for strict judges.

1. Linstock: the stick holding the gunner's match; galley foist: a long barge with oars; shovel-board shilling: a smooth coin that slipped easily, used in the game of shovel-board.

2. Slang for robbers.

3. Prison.

ALL Save you, my lord.

LORD NOLAND Well met, gentlemen all.—Good sir Beauteous Ganymede, sir Thomas Long,—and how does master Dapper?

JACK DAPPER Thanks, my lord.

MOLL No tobacco, my lord?

LORD NOLAND No, faith, Jack.

JACK DAPPER My lord Noland, will you go to Pimlico[4] with us? We are making a boon voyage to that nappy[5] land of spice-cakes.

LORD NOLAND Here's such a merry ging,[6] I could find in my heart to sail to the world's end with such company: come, gentlemen, let's on.

JACK DAPPER Here's most amorous weather, my lord.

ALL Amorous weather! [*They walk.*]

JACK DAPPER Is not amorous a good word?

[*Enter Trapdoor disguised as a poor Soldier with a patch over one eye and Tearcat all in tatters.*]

TRAPDOOR Shall we set upon the infantry, these troops of foot? Zounds, yonder comes Moll, my whorish master and mistress! would I had her kidneys between my teeth!

TEARCAT I had rather have a cow-heel.

TRAPDOOR Zounds, I am so patched up, she cannot discover me: we'll on.

TEARCAT *Alla corago*,[7] then!

TRAPDOOR Good your honors and worships, enlarge the ears of commiseration, and let the sound of a hoarse military organ-pipe penetrate your pitiful bowels, to extract out of them so many small drops of silver as may give a hard straw-bed lodging to a couple of maimed soldiers.

JACK DAPPER Where are you maimed?

TEARCAT In both our nether limbs.

MOLL Come, come, Dapper, let's give 'em something: 'las, poor men! What money have you? By my troth, I love a soldier with my soul.

SIR BEAUTEOUS Stay, stay; where have you served?

SIR THOMAS In any part of the Low Countries?

TRAPDOOR Not in the Low Countries, if it please your manhood, but in Hungary against the Turk at the siege of Belgrade.

LORD NOLAND Who served there with you, sirrah?

TRAPDOOR Many Hungarians, Moldavians, Vallachians, and Transylvanians, with some Sclavonians;[8] and retiring home, sir, the Venetian galleys took us prisoners, yet freed us, and suffered us to beg up and down the country.

JACK DAPPER You have ambled all over Italy, then?

TRAPDOOR O sir, from Venice to Roma, Vecchia, Bononia, Romagna, Bologna, Modena, Piacenza, and Tuscana, with all her cities, as Pistoia, Valteria, Mountepulchena, Arezzo; with the Siennois, and divers others.[9]

MOLL Mere rogues! put spurs to 'em once more.

JACK DAPPER Thou lookest like a strange creature, a fat butter-box, yet speakest English: what art thou?

4. The Pimlico Inn at Hogsden (Hoxton).
5. Heady, strong.
6. Gang, crowd.
7. A slang corruption of the Italian *coraggio*, courage.
8. Slavs; Transylvanians: people to the east of Austria; Moldavia: a province along the Danube under the control of the Turks in the 16th century; Wallachia: south of Moldavia, lay between the Hungarian and Turkish kingdoms.
9. All Italian cities. Bononia and Bologna are the same place; Valteria is Volterra; Montepulchena is Montepulciano; the Siennois are the people of Sienna.

TEARCAT *Ick, mine here? ick bin den ruffling Tearcat, den brave soldado; ick bin dorick all Dutchlant gereisen; der schellum das meer ine beasa ine woert gaeb, ick slaag um stroakes on tom cop; dastick den hundred touzun divel halle, frollick, mine here.*[1]

SIR BEAUTEOUS Here, here; let's be rid of their jobbering. [*About to give money.*]

MOLL Not a cross,[2] sir Beauteous—You base rogues, I have taken measure of you better than a tailor can; and I'll fit you, as you, monster with one eye, have fitted me.

TRAPDOOR Your worship will not abuse a soldier?

MOLL Soldier? Thou deservest to be hanged up by that tongue which dishonors so noble a profession: soldier? you skeldering[3] varlet! Hold, stand; there should be a trapdoor here abouts. [*Pulls off his patch.*]

TRAPDOOR The balls of these glasiers[4] of mine, mine eyes, shall be shot up and down in any hot piece of service for my invincible mistress.

JACK DAPPER I did not think there had been such knavery in black patches as now I see.[5]

MOLL O sir, he hath been brought up in the Isle of Dogs,[6] and can both fawn like a spaniel, and bite like a mastiff, as he finds occasion.

LORD NOLAND What are you, sirrah? a bird of this feather too?

TEARCAT A man beaten from the wars, sir.

SIR THOMAS I think so, for you never stood to fight.

JACK DAPPER What's thy name, fellow soldier?

TEARCAT I am called by those that have seen my valor, Tearcat.

ALL Tearcat?

MOLL A mere whip-jack,[7] and that is, in the commonwealth of rogues, a slave that can talk of sea-fight, name all your chief pirates, discover more countries to you than either the Dutch, Spanish, French, or English ever found out; yet indeed all his service is by land, and that is to rob a fair, or some such venturous exploit. Tearcat? 'foot, sirrah, I have your name, now I remember me, in my book of horners; horns for the thumb, you know how.[8]

TEARCAT No indeed, captain Moll, for I know you by sight, I am no such nipping Christian, but a maunderer upon the pad,[9] I confess; and meeting with honest Trapdoor here, whom you had cashiered from bearing arms, out at elbows, under your colors, I instructed him in the rudiments of roguery, and by my map made him sail over any country you can name, so that now he can maunder better than myself.

JACK DAPPER So, then, Trapdoor, thou art turned soldier now?

TRAPDOOR Alas, sir, now there's no wars, 'tis the safest course of life I could take!

MOLL I hope, then, you can cant, for by your cudgels, you, sirrah, are an upright man.[1]

1. Mainly in Low German: "I, my lord? I am the ruffling Tearcat, the brave soldier. I have traveled all over Deutschland. The scoundrel who gives a blow sooner than a word, I hit him with strokes on the head, to drive out a hundred thousand devils; enjoy it, my lord."
2. A piece of money marked with a cross.
3. Swindling.
4. Eyes.
5. Ornamental black patches were worn by ladies and fops.
6. A haunt of debtors and the title of a lost play by Ben Jonson.
7. There is a similar description of a "whipjacke" in Dekker's humorous pamphlet the *Belman of London* (1608).
8. "Horn-thumb": a cutpurse.
9. Cant for "beg on the high road."
1. All the cant terms used in this scene are described in the *Belman of London* and *Lantern and Candlelight*; see the excerpts on pages 1429–1432. An upright man was "a sturdy big-boned knave, that never walkes but (like a Commander) with a short truncheon in his hand, which he calls his Filchman."

TRAPDOOR As any walks the highway, I assure you.

MOLL And, Tearcat, what are you? a wild rogue, an angler, or a ruffler?[2]

TEARCAT Brother to this upright man, flesh and blood; ruffling Tearcat is my name, and a ruffler is my style, my title, my profession.

MOLL Sirrah, where's your doxy?[3] halt not with me.

ALL Doxy, Moll? what's that?

MOLL His wench.

TRAPDOOR My doxy? I have, by the salomon, a doxy that carries a kinchin mort in her slate at her back, besides my dell and my dainty wild dell, with all whom I'll tumble this next darkmans in the strommel, and drink ben bouse, and eat a fat gruntling cheat, a cackling cheat, and a quacking cheat.[4]

JACK DAPPER Here's old[5] cheating!

TRAPDOOR My doxy stays for me in a bousing ken,[6] brave captain.

MOLL He says his wench stays for him in an ale-house. You are no pure rogues!

TEARCAT Pure rogues? no, we scorn to be pure rogues; but if you come to our lib ken or our stalling ken, you shall find neither him nor me a queer cuffin.[7]

MOLL So, sir, no churl of you.

TEARCAT No, but a ben cove, a brave cove, a gentry cuffin.

LORD NOLAND Call you this canting?

JACK DAPPER Zounds, I'll give a schoolmaster half-a-crown a-week, and teach me this pedlar's French.[8]

TRAPDOOR Do but stroll, sir, half a harvest with us, sir, and you shall gabble your bellyful.

MOLL Come, you rogue, cant with me.

SIR THOMAS Well said, Moll—Cant with her, sirrah, and you shall have money, else not a penny.

TRAPDOOR I'll have a bout, if she please.

MOLL Come on, sirrah!

TRAPDOOR Ben mort, shall you and I heave a bough, mill a ken, or nip a bung, and then we'll couch a hogshead under the ruffmans, and there you shall wap with me, and I'll niggle with you.[9]

MOLL Out, you damned impudent rascal!

TRAPDOOR Cut benar whids, and hold your fambles and your stamps.[1]

LORD NOLAND Nay, nay, Moll, why art thou angry? what was his gibberish?

2. A wild rogue was "a spirit that cares not in what circle he rises, nor into the company of what Divels he falls." An angler was "a limb of an upright man, as being derived from him: their apparel in which they walk is commonly frieze jerkins and gall slops: in the daytime they beg from house to house, not so much for relief, as to spy what lies fit for their nets, which in the night following they fish for." And "the next in degree to him [the upright man] is called a ruffler: the ruffler and the upright man are so like in conditions, that you would swear them brothers: they walk with cudgels alike; they profess arms alike" (*Belman of London*).

3. Whore.

4. By the salomon: by the mass; kinchin "girls of a year or two old, which the Morts (their mothers) carry at their backs in the slates (which in the canting tongue are sheets)"; dell: "a young wench . . . but as yet not spoiled of her maidenhead. These dells are reserved for the upright men for none but they must have the first taste of them" (Dekker, *Lantern and Candlelight*). I'll tumble . . . cheat: I'll tumble this next night in the straw, and drink good drink, and eat a fat pig, a capon, and a duck.

5. Fine, rare.

6. Alehouse.

7. "Lib ken, or our stalling ken," i.e., our house to lie in or our house to receive stolen goods. "The word cone or cofe, or cuffin, signifies a man, a fellow, etc. But differs something in his property according as it meets with other words; for a gentleman is called a gentry cove, or cofe. A good fellow is a bene cofe; a churle is called a queer cuffin; queer signifies naught" (*Lantern and Candlelight*).

8. "That pedlars French or that Canting language, which is to be found among none but beggars" (*Lantern and Candlelight*).

9. In the lines that follow, Moll interprets this passage of canting. "Heave a bough": rob a booth; "mill a ken": rob a house; "nip a bung": cut a purse; "niggling," companying with a woman." See *The Canter's Dictionary*, page 1431.

1. Cut . . . stamps: speak better words and hold your hands and legs.

MOLL Marry, this, my lord, says he: *Ben mort,* good wench, *shall you and I heave a bough, mill a ken, or nip a bung?* shall you and I rob a house or cut a purse?

ALL Very good.

MOLL *And then we'll couch a hogshead under the ruffmans;* and then we'll lie under a hedge.

TRAPDOOR That was my desire, captain, as 'tis fit a soldier should lie.

MOLL *And there you shall wap with me, and I'll niggle with you,*—and that's all.

SIR BEAUTEOUS Nay, nay, Moll, what's that wap?

JACK DAPPER Nay, teach me what niggling is; I'd fain be niggling.

MOLL Wapping and niggling is all one, the rogue my man can tell you.

TRAPDOOR 'Tis fadoodling,[2] if it please you.

SIR BEAUTEOUS This is excellent! One fit more, good Moll.

MOLL Come, you rogue, sing with me.

[*Song by Moll and Tearcat.*]

A gage of ben rom-bouse
In a bousing ken of Rom-vile,
Is benar than a caster,
Peck, pennam, lap, or popler,
Which we mill in deuse a vile.
O I wud lib all the lightmans,
O I wud lib all the darkmans
By the salomon, under the ruffmans,
By the salomon, in the hartmans,
And scour the queer cramp ring,
And couch till a palliard docked my dell,
So my bousy nab might skew rom-bouse well.
Avast to the pad, let us bing;
Avast to the pad, let us bing.[3]

ALL Fine knaves, i'faith!

JACK DAPPER The grating of ten new cart-wheels, and the gruntling of five hundred hogs coming from Rumford market, cannot make a worse noise than this canting language does in my ears. Pray, my lord Noland, let's give these soldiers their pay.

SIR BEAUTEOUS Agreed, and let them march.

LORD NOLAND Here, Moll. [*Gives money.*]

MOLL Now I see that you are stalled to the rogue, and are not ashamed of your professions: look you, my lord Noland here and these gentlemen bestows upon you two two boards and a half, that's two shillings sixpence.[4]

TRAPDOOR Thanks to your lordship.

TEARCAT Thanks, heroical captain.

MOLL Away!

TRAPDOOR We shall cut ben whids[5] of your masters and mistress-ship wheresoever we come.

2. Sexual intercourse.
3. "A quart pot of good wine in an alehouse of London is better than a cloak, meat, bread, butter-milk (or whey), or porridge, which we steal in the country. O I would lie all the day, O I would lie all the night, by the mass, under the woods (or bushes), by the mass, in the stocks, and wear bolts (or fetters), and lie till a palliard [lecher] lay with my wench, so my drunken head might quaff wine well. Avast to the highway, let us hence, etc." (*Lantern and Candlelight*).
4. "Stalled to the rogue": initiated as a rogue; board: a shilling (*Lantern and Candlelight*).
5. Speak good words.

MOLL You'll maintain, sirrah, the old justice's plot to his face?
TRAPDOOR Else trine me on the cheats,[6]—hang me.
MOLL Be sure you meet me there.
TRAPDOOR Without any more maundering,[7] I'll do't.—Follow, brave Tearcat.
TEARCAT *I prae, sequor:*[8] let us go, mouse.
[*Exeunt Trapdoor and Tearcat.*]
LORD NOLAND Moll, what was in that canting song?
MOLL Troth, my lord, only a praise of good drink, the only milk which these wild beasts love to suck, and thus it was:

A rich cup of wine,
O it is juice divine!
More wholesome for the head
Than meat, drink, or bread:
To fill my drunken pate
With that, I'd sit up late;
By the heels would I lie,
Under a lowsy hedge die,
Let a slave have a pull
At my whore, so I be full
Of that precious liquor:

and a parcel of such stuff, my lord, not worth the opening.
[*Enter a Cutpurse very gallant,*[9] *with four or five others, one having a wand.*]
LORD NOLAND What gallant comes yonder?
SIR THOMAS Mass, I think I know him; 'tis one of Cumberland.
FIRST CUTPURSE Shall we venture to shuffle in amongst yon heap of gallants, and strike?[1]
SECOND CUTPURSE 'Tis a question whether there be any silver shells[2] amongst them, for all their satin outsides.
THE REST Let's try.
MOLL Pox on him, a gallant? Shadow me, I know him; 'tis one that cumbers the land indeed: if he swim near to the shore of any of your pockets, look to your purses.
LORD NOLAND / SIR BEAUTEOUS etc. Is't possible?
MOLL This brave[3] fellow is no better than a foist.
LORD NOLAND / SIR BEAUTEOUS etc. Foist! what's that?
MOLL A diver with two fingers, a pickpocket; all his train study the figging-law,[4] that's to say, cutting of purses and foisting. One of them is a nip; I took him once i' the two-penny gallery at the Fortune: then there's a cloyer, or snap, that dogs any new brother in that trade, and snaps will have half in any booty. He with the wand is both a stale, whose office is to face a man i' the streets, whilst shells are drawn by another, and then with his black conjuring rod in his hand, he, by the

6. Hang me on the gallows.
7. Muttering.
8. You first, I'll follow.
9. Well dressed.
1. Pick a purse.
2. Money.
3. Finely dressed.
4. "Figging law" is described in the *Belman of London:* "He that cuts the purse is called the *Nip*. He that is half with him is the *Snap*, or the *Cloyer*. The knife is called a *Cuttle-bung*. He that picks the pocket is called a *Foist*. He that faceth the man is the *Stale*. The taking of the purse is called *Drawing*. The spying of this villanie is called *Smoking* or *Boiling*. The purse is the *Bung*. The money the *Shels*. The act doing is called *Striking*."

nimbleness of his eye and juggling stick, will, in cheaping a piece of plate at a goldsmith's stall, make four or five rings mount from the top of his *caduceus*,[5] and, as if it were at leap-frog, they skip into his hand presently.

SECOND CUTPURSE Zounds, we are smoked!

THE REST Ha!

SECOND CUTPURSE We are boiled,[6] pox on her! see, Moll, the roaring drab!

FIRST CUTPURSE All the diseases of sixteen hospitals boil her!—Away!

MOLL Bless you, sir.

FIRST CUTPURSE And you, good sir.

MOLL Dost not ken me, man?

FIRST CUTPURSE No, trust me, sir.

MOLL Heart, there's a knight, to whom I'm bound for many favors, lost his purse at the last new play i' the Swan,[7] seven angels in't: make it good, you're best; do you see? no more.

FIRST CUTPURSE A synagogue shall be called, mistress Mary; disgrace me not; *pacus palabros*,[8] I will conjure for you: farewell. [*Exit with his companions*.]

MOLL Did not I tell you, my lord?

LORD NOLAND I wonder how thou camest to the knowledge of these nasty villains.

SIR THOMAS And why do the foul mouths of the world call thee Moll Cutpurse? a name, methinks, damned and odious.

MOLL Dare any step forth to my face and say,
I've ta'en thee doing so, Moll? I must confess,
In younger days, when I was apt to stray,
I've sat amongst such adders; seen their stings,
As any here might, and in full playhouses
Watched their quick-diving hands, to bring to shame
Such rogues, and in that stream met an ill name.
When next, my lord, you spy any one of those,
So he be in his art a scholar, question him;
Tempt him with gold to open the large book
Of his close villanies; and you yourself shall cant
Better than poor Moll can, and know more laws
Of cheaters, lifters, nips, foists, puggards, curbers,[9]
With all the devil's black-guard,[1] than it's fit
Should be discovered to a noble wit,
I know they have their orders, offices,
Circuits, and circles, unto which they're bound
To raise their own damnation in.

JACK DAPPER How dost thou know it?

MOLL As you do; I show't you, they to me show it. Suppose, my lord, you were in Venice—

LORD NOLAND Well.

MOLL If some Italian pander there would tell

5. The wand of Mercury, god of thieves.
6. Spied, found out.
7. A playhouse on the Bankside.
8. A corruption of the Spanish *pocas palabras*, "few words."
9. "The Cheating Law, or the art of winning money by false dyce: Those that practice this study call themselves Cheators, the dyce Cheaters, and the money which they purchase Cheates . . . the Curbing Law . . . teaches . . . how to hook goods out of a window . . . The Lifting Law . . . teacheth a kind of lifting of goods clean away" (*Belman of London*). "Puggards": thieves.
1. A group of attendants who were black in person, dress, or character; the kitchen-drudges who attended royal progresses.

All the close tricks of courtesans, would not you
Hearken to such a fellow?

LORD NOLAND Yes.

MOLL And here,
Being come from Venice, to a friend most dear
That were to travel thither, you'd proclaim
Your knowledge in those villanies, to save
Your friend from their quick danger: must you have
A black ill name, because ill things you know?
Good troth, my lord, I'm made Moll Cutpurse so.
How many are whores in small ruffs and still looks!
How many chaste whose names fill Slander's books!
Were all men cuckolds whom gallants in their scorns
Call so, we should not walk for goring horns.
Perhaps for my mad going some reprove me;
I please myself, and care not else who love me.

LORD NOLAND / SIR BEAUTEOUS etc. A brave mind, Moll, i'faith!

SIR THOMAS Come, my lord, shall's to the ordinary?

LORD NOLAND Ay, 'tis noon sure.

MOLL Good my lord, let not my name condemn me to you, or to the world: a fencer I hope may be called a coward; is he so for that? If all that have ill names in London were to be whipped, and to pay but twelvepence a-piece to the beadle, I would rather have his office than a constable's.

JACK DAPPER So would I, captain Moll: 'twere a sweet tickling office, i'faith. [*Exeunt.*]

Scene 2

[*A Garden attached to Sir Alexander Wengrave's House. Enter Sir Alexander Wengrave, Goshawk, Greenwit, and others.*]

SIR ALEXANDER My son marry a thief, that impudent girl,
Whom all the world stick their worst eyes upon!

GREENWIT How will your care prevent it?

GOSHAWK 'Tis impossible:
They marry close, they're gone, but none knows whither.

SIR ALEXANDER O gentlemen, when has a father's heartstrings
[*Enter Servant.*]
Held out so long from breaking?—Now what news, sir?

SEBASTIAN They were met upo' th' water an hour since, sir,
Putting in towards the Sluice.[2]

SIR ALEXANDER The Sluice? Come, gentlemen,
'Tis Lambeth works against us. [*Exit Servant.*]

GREENWIT And that Lambeth
Joins more mad matches than your six wet towns
'Twixt that and Windsor Bridge,[3] where fares lie soaking.

SIR ALEXANDER Delay no time, sweet gentlemen: to Blackfriars![4]
We'll take a pair of oars, and make after 'em.

2. A marshy riverside district, frequented by pickpockets and prostitutes.
3. Bridge over the Thames connecting Windsor with Eton.
4. A landing stage on the north side of the Thames.

[*Enter Trapdoor.*]

TRAPDOOR Your son and that bold masculine ramp[5] my mistress
Are landed now at Tower.

SIR ALEXANDER Hoyda, at Tower?

TRAPDOOR I heard it now reported.

SIR ALEXANDER Which way, gentlemen,
Shall I bestow my care? I'm drawn in pieces
Betwixt deceit and shame.

[*Enter Sir Guy Fitzallard.*]

SIR GUY Sir Alexander,
You are well met, and most rightly served;
My daughter was a scorn to you.

SIR ALEXANDER Say not so, sir.

SIR GUY A very abject she, poor gentlewoman!
Your house had been dishonored. Give you joy, sir,
Of your son's gascoyne bride![6] You'll be a grandfather shortly
To a fine crew of roaring sons and daughters;
'Twill help to stock the suburbs passing well, sir.

SIR ALEXANDER O, play not with the miseries of my heart!
Wounds should be dressed and healed, not vexed, or left
Wide open, to the anguish of the patient,
And scornful air let in; rather let pity
And advice charitably help to refresh 'em.

SIR GUY Who'd place his charity so unworthily?
Like one that gives alms to a cursing beggar:
Had I but found one spark of goodness in you
Toward my deserving child, which then grew fond
Of your son's virtues, I had eased you now;
But I perceive both fire of youth and goodness
Are raked up in the ashes of your age,
Else no such shame should have come near your house,
Nor such ignoble sorrow touch your heart.

SIR ALEXANDER If not for worth, for pity's sake assist me!

GREENWIT You urge a thing past sense; how can he help you?
All his assistance is as frail as ours:
Full as uncertain where's the place that holds 'em;
One brings us water-news; then comes another
With a full-charged mouth, like a culverin's° voice, *gun's*
And he reports the Tower: whose sounds are truest?

GOSHAWK In vain you flatter him.—Sir Alexander—

SIR GUY I flatter him? Gentlemen, you wrong me grossly.

GREENWIT He does it well, i'faith.

SIR GUY Both news are false,
Of Tower or water; they took no such way yet.

SIR ALEXANDER O strange! Hear you this, gentlemen? Yet more plunges.[7]

SIR GUY They're nearer than you think for, yet more close
Than if they were further off.

SIR ALEXANDER How am I lost

5. Wildwoman.
6. A bride who wears loose breeches.
7. Difficulties.

In these distractions!
SIR GUY For your speeches, gentlemen,
In taxing me for rashness, 'fore you all
I will engage my state to half his wealth,
Nay, to his son's revenues, which are less,
And yet nothing at all till they come from him,
That I could, if my will stuck to my power,
Prevent this marriage yet, nay, banish her
For ever from his thoughts, much more his arms.
SIR ALEXANDER Slack not this goodness, though you heap upon me
Mountains of malice and revenge hereafter!
I'd willingly resign up half my state to him,
So he would marry the meanest drudge I hire.
GREENWIT He talks impossibilities, and you believe 'em.
SIR GUY I talk no more than I know how to finish,
My fortunes else are his that dares stake with me.
The poor young gentleman I love and pity;
And to keep shame from him (because the spring
Of his affection was my daughter's first,
Till his frown blasted all), do but estate him
In those possessions which your love and care
Once pointed out for him, that he may have room
To entertain fortunes of noble birth,
Where now his desperate wants casts him upon her;
And if I do not, for his own sake chiefly,
Rid him of this disease that now grows on him,
I'll forfeit my whole state before these gentlemen.
GREENWIT Troth, but you shall not undertake such matches;
We'll persuade so much with you.
SIR ALEXANDER Here's my ring [*Gives ring.*]
He will believe this token. 'Fore these gentlemen
I will confirm it fully: all those lands
My first love 'lotted him, he shall straight possess
In that refusal.
SIR GUY If I change it not,
Change me into a beggar.
GREENWIT Are you mad, sir?
SIR GUY 'Tis done.
GOSHAWK Will you undo yourself by doing,
And show a prodigal trick in your old days?
SIR ALEXANDER 'Tis a match, gentlemen.
SIR GUY Ay, ay, sir, ay.
I ask no favor, trust to you for none;
My hope rests in the goodness of your son. [*Exit.*]
GREENWIT He holds it up well yet.
GOSHAWK Of an old knight, i'faith.
SIR ALEXANDER Curst be the time I laid his first love barren,
Wilfully barren, that before this hour
Had sprung forth fruits of comfort and of honor!
He loved a virtuous gentlewoman.
[*Enter Moll in her male dress.*]

GOSHAWK Life, here's Moll!
GREENWIT Jack?
GOSHAWK How dost thou, Jack?
MOLL How dost thou, gallant?
SIR ALEXANDER Impudence, where's my son?
MOLL Weakness, go look him.
SIR ALEXANDER Is this your wedding gown?
MOLL The man talks monthly:[8]
Hot broth and a dark chamber for the knight!
I see he'll be stark mad at our next meeting. [*Exit*.]
GOSHAWK Why, sir, take comfort now, there's no such matter,
No priest will marry her, sir, for a woman
Whiles that shape's on; and it was never known
Two men were married and conjoined in one
Your son hath made some shift to love another.
SIR ALEXANDER Whate'er she be, she has my blessing with her:
May they be rich and fruitful, and receive
Like comfort to their issue as I take
In them! Has pleased me now; marrying not this,
Through a whole world he could not choose amiss.
GREENWIT Glad you're so penitent for your former sin, sir.
GOSHAWK Say he should take a wench with her smock-dowry,
No portion with her but her lips and arms?
SIR ALEXANDER Why, who thrive better, sir? They have most blessing,
Though other have more wealth, and least repent:
Many that want most know the most content.
GREENWIT Say he should marry a kind youthful sinner?
SIR ALEXANDER Age will quench that; any offence but theft
And drunkenness, nothing but death can wipe away;
Their sins are green even when their heads are grey.
Nay, I despair not now; my heart's cheer'd, gentlemen;
No face can come unfortunately to me.—
[*Reenter Servant*.]
Now, sir, your news?
SERVANT Your son, with his fair bride,
Is near at hand.
SIR ALEXANDER Fair may their fortunes be!
GREENWIT Now you're resolved,[9] sir, it was never she.
SIR ALEXANDER I find it in the music of my heart.
[*Enter Sebastian Wengrave leading in Moll in her female dress and masked and Sir Guy Fitzallard*.]
See where they come.
GOSHAWK A proper lusty presence, sir.
SIR ALEXANDER Now has he pleased me right: I always counselled him
To choose a goodly, personable creature:
Just of her pitch was my first wife his mother.
SEBASTIAN Before I dare discover my offence,

8. Madly, at the full moon.
9. Convinced.

I kneel for pardon. [*Kneels*.]

SIR ALEXANDER My heart gave it thee
Before thy tongue could ask it:
Rise; thou hast raised my joy to greater height
Than to that seat where grief dejected it.
Both welcome to my love and care for ever!
Hide not my happiness too long; all's pardoned;
Here are our friends.—Salute her, gentlemen.

[*They unmask her*.]

ALL Heart, who's this? Moll!

SIR ALEXANDER O my reviving shame! Is't I must live
To be struck blind? Be it the work of sorrow,
Before age take't in hand!

SIR GUY Darkness and death!
Have you deceived me thus? Did I engage
My whole estate for this?

SIR ALEXANDER You asked no favor,
And you shall find as little; since my comforts
Play false with me, I'll be as cruel to thee
As grief to fathers' hearts.

MOLL Why, what's the matter with you,
'Less too much joy should make your age forgetful?
Are you too well, too happy?

SIR ALEXANDER With a vengeance!

MOLL Methinks you should be proud of such a daughter,
As good a man as your son.

SIR ALEXANDER O monstrous impudence!

MOLL You had no note before, an unmarked knight;
Now all the town will take regard on you,
And all your enemies fear you for my sake:
You may pass where you list, through crowds most thick,
And come off bravely with your purse unpicked.
You do not know the benefits I bring with me;
No cheat dares work upon you with thumb or knife,
While you've a roaring girl to your son's wife.

SIR ALEXANDER A devil rampant!

SIR GUY Have you so much charity
Yet to release me of my last rash bargain,
And I'll give in your pledge?

SIR ALEXANDER No, sir, I stand to't;
I'll work upon advantage, as all mischiefs
Do upon me.

SIR GUY Content. Bear witness all, then,
His are the lands; and so contention ends:
Here comes your son's bride 'twixt two noble friends.

[*Enter Lord Noland and Sir Beauteous Ganymede with Mary Fitzallard between them; Gallipot, Tiltyard, Openwork, and their wives*.]

MOLL Now are you gulled as you would be; thank me for't,
I'd a forefinger in't.

SEBASTIAN Forgive me, father!

Though there before your eyes my sorrow feigned,
This still was she for whom true love complained.

SIR ALEXANDER Blessings eternal, and the joys of angels,
Begin your peace here to be signed in heaven!
How short my sleep of sorrow seems now to me,
To this eternity of boundless comforts,
That finds no want but utterance and expression!
My lord, your office here appears so honorably,
So full of ancient goodness, grace, and worthiness,
I never took more joy in sight of man
Than in your comfortable presence now.

LORD NOLAND Nor I more delight in doing grace to virtue
Than in this worthy gentlewoman your son's bride,
Noble Fitzallard's daughter, to whose honor
And modest fame I am a servant vowed;
So is this knight.

SIR ALEXANDER Your loves make my joys proud.
Bring forth those deeds of land my care laid ready,
[*Exit Servant, who presently returns with deeds*.]
And which, old knight, thy nobleness may challenge,
Joined with thy daughter's virtues, whom I prize now
As dearly as that flesh I call mine own.
Forgive me, worthy gentlewoman; 'twas my blindness:
When I rejected thee, I saw thee not;
Sorrow and wilful rashness grew like films
Over the eyes of judgment; now so clear
I see the brightness of thy worth appear.

MARY Duty and love may I deserve in those!
And all my wishes have a perfect close.

SIR ALEXANDER That tongue can never err, the sound's so sweet.
Here, honest son, receive into thy hands
The keys of wealth, possession of those lands
Which my first care provided; they're thine own;
Heaven give thee a blessing with 'em! the best joys
That can in worldly shapes to man betide
Are fertile lands and a fair fruitful bride,
Of which I hope thou'rt sped.

SEBASTIAN I hope so too, sir.

MOLL Father and son, I ha' done you simple service here.

SEBASTIAN For which thou shalt not part, Moll, unrequited.

SIR ALEXANDER Thou'rt a mad girl, and yet I cannot now
Condemn thee.

MOLL Condemn me? troth, and you should, sir,
I'd make you seek out one to hang in my room:
I'd give you the slip at gallows, and cozen the people.
Heard you this jest, my lord?

LORD NOLAND What is it, Jack?

MOLL He was in fear his son would marry me,
But never dream't that I would ne'er agree.

LORD NOLAND Why, thou had'st a suitor once, Jack: when wilt marry?

MOLL Who, I, my lord? I'll tell you when, i'faith;

When you shall hear
Gallants void from sergeants' fear,
Honesty and truth unslandered,
Woman manned, but never pandered,
Cheats booted, but not coached,
Vessels older ere they're broached;
If my mind be then not varied,
Next day following I'll be married.

LORD NOLAND This sounds like doomsday.

MOLL Then were marriage best;
For if I should repent, I were soon at rest.

SIR ALEXANDER In troth thou'rt a good wench; I'm sorry now
The opinion was so hard I conceived of thee:
[*Enter Trapdoor*.]
Some wrongs I've done thee.

TRAPDOOR [*Aside*.] Is the wind there now?
'Tis time for me to kneel and confess first,
For fear it come too late, and my brains feel it.—
Upon my paws I ask you pardon, mistress!

MOLL Pardon! for what, sir? What has your rogueship done now?

TRAPDOOR I've been from time to time hired to confound you
By this old gentleman.

MOLL How?

TRAPDOOR Pray, forgive him:
But may I counsel you, you should never do't.
Many a snare t' entrap your worship's life
Have I laid privily; chains, watches, jewels;
And when he saw nothing could mount you up,
Four hollow-hearted angels he then gave you,
By which he meant to trap you, I to save you.

SIR ALEXANDER To all which shame and grief in me cry guilty.
Forgive me: now I cast the world's eyes from me,
And look upon thee freely with mine own,
I see the most of many wrongs before me,
Cast from the jaws of Envy and her people,
And nothing foul but that. I'll never more
Condemn by common voice, for that's the whore
That deceives man's opinion, mocks his trust,
Cozens his love, and makes his heart unjust.

MOLL Here be the angels, gentlemen; they were given me
As a musician: I pursue no pity;
Follow the law, and you can cuck me,[1] spare not;
Hang up my viol by me, and I care not.

SIR ALEXANDER So far I'm sorry, I'll thrice double 'em,
To make thy wrongs amends.
Come, worthy friends, my honorable lord,
Sir Beauteous Ganymede, and noble Fitzallard,

1. Set me on a cucking-stool, a punishment for scolds and shrews (women who were considered disorderly); the offender was fastened to a chair and exposed to the jeers of bystanders or ducked in water.

And you kind gentlewomen,[2] whose sparkling presence
Are glories set in marriage, beams of society,
For all your loves give lustre to my joys:
The happiness of this day shall be remembered
At the return of every smiling spring;
In my time now 'tis born; and may no sadness
Sit on the brows of men upon that day,
But as I am, so all go pleased away! [*Exeunt omnes.*]

Epilogue

A painter having drawn with curious art
The picture of a woman, every part
Limned° to the life, hung out the piece to sell. *portrayed*
People who passed along, viewing it well,
Gave several verdicts on it: some dispraised
The hair; some said the brows too high were raised;
Some hit her o'er the lips, misliked their color;
Some wished her nose were shorter; some, the eyes fuller;
Others said roses on her cheeks should grow,
Swearing they looked too pale; others cried no.
The workman still, as fault was found, did mend it,
In hope to please all: but this work being ended,
And hung open at stall, it was so vile,
So monstrous, and so ugly, all men did smile
At the poor painter's folly. Such, we doubt,
Is this our comedy: some perhaps do flout° *mock*
The plot, saying, 'tis too thin, too weak, too mean;
Some for the person will revile the scene,
And wonder that a creature of her being
Should be the subject of a poet, seeing
In the world's eye none weighs so light: others look
For all those base tricks, published in a book
Foul as his brains they flowed from, of cutpurses,
Of nips° and foists,° nasty, obscene discourses, *cutpurses/pickpockets*
As full of lies as empty of worth or wit,
For any honest ear or eye unfit.
And thus,
If we to every brain that's humorous° *fanciful*
Should fashion scenes, we, with the painter, shall,
In striving to please all, please none at all.
Yet for such faults as either the writer's wit
Or negligence of the actors do commit,
Both crave your pardons: if what both have done
Cannot full pay your expectation,
The Roaring Girl herself, some few days hence,
Shall on this stage give larger recompence.
Which mirth that you may share in, herself does woo you,
And craves this sign, your hands to beckon her to you.

2. Addressed to Mistress Gallipot and the others.

The Roaring Girl in Context
City Life

From 1400 to 1650, London grew from a small city to the second largest city in Europe, surpassed only by Paris. The population of London more than doubled from 70,000 in 1550 to 180,000 at the death of Elizabeth in 1603. Immigration from the countryside swelled the population as young single males came in search of work as laborers and apprentices. The larger workforce enabled a rise in manufacturing, especially of cloth. Increased production fed the growth of trade, created in part by the fall of Constantinople in 1453, which shifted activity from the Mediterranean to the Atlantic. England was at peace as religious wars raged in the Netherlands and France in the late sixteenth century, and London won a large share of continental trade. As its population and economy grew, London also experienced a burgeoning of culture and a rise in social problems.

Under the Tudor and Stuart reigns, London spread beyond the medieval walled city to encompass Westminster, the precinct of Court and Parliament, which expanded to become the West End of doctors, lawyers, and luxury dealers of all sorts, and the suburbs, a haven for theaters, bullbaiting and bearbaiting, pickpocketing, and prostitution. The part of London referred to as the City was the site of the guilds and the civic government and a stronghold of evangelical Protestantism. New building and development were carried on at a great rate. With the dissolution of the monasteries under Henry VIII's Reformation, many former church properties were turned into sumptuous private residences for courtiers. Indoor theater in London got its start in the 1540s, when a convent in Blackfriars was turned into a storehouse for props. One of a few religious institutions that Henry VIII had the city take over for the public welfare was the hospital of Saint Mary of Bethlehem, which became the notorious madhouse Bedlam.

A medieval city that had been dominated by the church was transformed into a center of trade. Woolen cloth was the chief export; imports ranged from silk, spices, and perfumes from the East to tobacco, sugar, and cotton from the Caribbean and North America. Joint stock companies such as the East India Company and the Virginia Company encouraged the high risks and profits of venture capitalism by financing privateering and plantation. A new architecture arose to house this commerce. Thomas Gresham, a merchant's son, built the Royal Exchange, opened by Queen Elizabeth as the commercial headquarters for London merchants. Under Charles I, the Earl of Bedford developed Covent ("convent") Garden to create arcaded housing, a Tuscan church, and a fruit and vegetable market in a piazza designed by the first great native English architect, Inigo Jones. In *Survey of London* (1598), John Stow, an environmentalist before his time, complained of the damage done to nature by the real estate boom. At the same time he celebrated the achievements of London, as did numerous mapmakers who portrayed the city's expansion over a landscape marked by the spire of Saint Paul's and by London Bridge, connecting the City's Guildhall and the Court's Whitehall with Southwark bearbaiting and theaters, all dominated by the Thames River, teeming with trading vessels.

The growth in manufacturing and trade produced an increasingly powerful city government. While the right to trade and participate as a citizen could still be inherited or bought, the chief route to citizenship was the seven-year apprenticeship in a guild. By the mid-sixteenth century, almost three-quarters of the city's adult males belonged to one of the guilds, six of which (the Mercers, Grocers, Drapers, Haberdashers, and Merchant Tailors) provided half of London's public officials. At the top of the power structure were the Lord Mayor and the Court of Alderman, who served as justices of the peace. Under these were the Court of Common Council, a legislative body with 200 representatives, elected each December by all freemen. The public pageants staged by the city government at the time of Elizabeth's corona-

Wenceslaus Hollar. *Long View of London*. 1647.

tion influenced her strongly Protestant position. The Mayor and the Common Council initially supported Charles I, but in 1642, when the King attempted to arrest dissenters from Parliament who had fled for refuge into the City, the tradesmen and apprentices of London defended the cause of Cromwell. A ring of fortifications united the City and Westminster, and London supported Cromwell's army with men and money.

A lively public culture accompanied this political and commercial activity. Theaters flourished in the suburbs outside the control of city officials. The first playhouse, the Theater, was founded in Shoreditch in 1576 by the actor James Burbage, who later built the Globe, in which Shakespeare had a tenth share. In competition with Burbage, William Henslowe, the owner of the Rose and Curtain theaters as well as many brothels, built the Fortune to the North in Aldersgate, where Middleton's and Dekker's *Roaring Girl* was performed. Not only were prostitution and plays associated with one another, but the theater was viewed as a place where disease was spread. The playhouses were shut down with each outbreak of the plague, generally during the summer months. From 1603 on, royal proclamations and statutes forbade Sunday performances, but Puritan complaints about violations of these rules show that they were not very strictly enforced. Once in power, the Puritans shut the theaters permanently in 1649; they were reopened only after the restoration of the monarchy in 1660.

The city itself was a kind of theater in which one could observe everything from the pomp of civic parades and the carnival atmosphere of the Saint Bartholomew's Day Fair to the destitution of beggars who lived on the streets—if they were not arrested for vagrancy. A popular literature of broadsides, ballads, moral tracts, and tales of rogues was published by a thriving printing industry; London had twenty-four printers in 1585 and sixty by 1659. The audience for printed tracts and stories expanded with the rise in literacy. Half of the men who were sentenced to death in early seventeenth-century Middlesex could read. Although female literacy was only at 10 percent in 1650, it rose to nearly five times that by 1690.

Rogue literature spoofed the naivete of those who were prey to the confidence scams of city slickers and celebrated the escapades of such notorious city figures as Moll Cutpurse. Like the comic drama, popular comic prose took place in shop, tavern, and marketplace in a constant interplay between civic and fictional life.

Barnabe Riche
from *My Lady's Looking Glass*[1]

It is said that Africa bringeth forth every year a new Monster,[2] the reason is, that in the deserts of that country, the wild and savage beasts that are both diverse in nature and contrary in kind will yet engender the one with the other: but England hatcheth up every month a new Monster, every week a new Sin, and every day a new Fashion: our Monsters are not bred in the Deserts, as those in Africa, but in every town and city: where they are so cheerily fostered and so daintily cherished that they multiply on heaps, by hundreds and by thousand. It were not possible for me now to set down how this monstrous generation thus hatched up by Sin hath been from time to time procreated and brought into the world, one sin still begetting another.[3]

Pride the eldest daughter of Sin was first spawned in Heaven. She was from thence expelled; but she drew after her a great dissolution of Angels. It was pride that begat Contempt in Paradise, where there was no Apple in the Garden so well pleasing to Eve as that which God had forbidden her.

It was Contempt that begot Malice. And Malice again begat Murder, when Cain killed his brother Abel.

1. Barnabe Riche (1542–1617) was a critic of the decadence of Jacobean Dublin and London. Riche ranted against the mores and politics of Catholics, the evils of "tobacco that draweth to drunkennesse," and the "gawdy attires" of women. He spent a good part of his adult life in Dublin, inveighing against what he saw as widespread corruption on every social level—from embezzlement by Protestant Archbishop Loftus (who tried to have Riche murdered) to the inflated prices of women alehouse keepers to the political dissent of Irish and English recusant Catholic gentry—that is, those who secretly defied the required conformity to the state church. Although Riche argued for such extreme measures as castration as a means to subdue the rebellious Irish, he was one of the few who stressed the need of converting the people to Protestantism. One of the great qualities of his writing for the social critic is its uncensored quality. Seemingly disparate topics are all connected in Riche's writing, as in this passage from *My Lady's Looking Glass* (1616), in which he vividly portrays the loose morality of the overpopulated city as reminiscent of the monsters of Africa.

2. "Monster" has the sense of something unnatural, as in a misshapen birth or an abortion; something beastly, partly brute and partly human; and something huge or gigantic.

3. See Milton, *Paradise Lost* 2.705–844, where Sin is described as both the daughter and the incestuous consort of Satan.

As the sons of men increased in the world, so Sin began to multiply so fast that God repented him that he had made man.

To purge the world of her abominations, the Deluge came, and all were drowned, except eight persons. After the Flood, amongst the sons of Noah the generation of the accursed Cham[4] became to be great and mighty upon the earth; at which time Sin was grown up to that strength that she began on the sudden to play the Rebel, and with a tumultuous assembly gathered together in the plains of Shinar, she began to fortify herself against Heaven.

Amongst those Giants then reigning over the face of the earth, that greedy cur Covetousness, which the Apostle termeth to the root of all evils,[5] was (amongst a number of other monstrous sins) fostered up by Ambition.

Covetousness was the first parent of Oppression, Extortion, Bribery, Usury, Fraud, Deceit, Subtlety: and that common strumpet Idolatry was a bastard born of this brood.

Idolatry had issue, the Lady Lechery, who in process of time became conversant with the Pope and his Cardinals that they procreated amongst them that loathsome sin of Buggery.

It would be a matter of impossibility for me to set down the varieties of those sins that are hatched up in these days, when so many new fashioned iniquities doth swarm both in city, town, and country that were our bodies but half so diseased with sickness as our souls be with sins, it could not be avoided, but that some strange and unheard of mortality would ensue. The time hath been men would mask their vices with cloaked dissimulation from the eye of the world, but now iniquity is set forth bare faced without any mask of pretteries[6] to hide her ugly visage.

Robert Greene
from *A Notable Discovery of Cosenage*[1]

Ah gentlemen, merchants, yeomen and farmers, let this to you all, and to every degree else, be a caveat[2] to warn you from lust, that your inordinate desire be not a mean to impoverish your purses, discredit your good names, condemn your souls, but also that your wealth got with the sweat of your brows, or left by your parents as a patrimony, shall be a prey to those cozening cross-biters.[3] Some fond men are so far in with these detestable trugs[4] that they consume what they have upon them, and find nothing but a Neapolitan favor[5] for their labor. Read the seventh of Solomon's proverbs, and there at large view the description of a shameless and impudent courtesan:[6] yet is there another kind of cross-biting which is most pestilent, and that is this. There lives about this town certain householders, yet mere shifters and cozeners,

4. The offspring of Ham, who saw his father Noah naked, were cursed. See Genesis 9.22–26.

5. Chaucer's *Pardoner's Tale* turns on this theme from 1 Timothy 6.10.

6. Prettiness. The original reads "preteires."

1. Robert Greene (1560?–1592), born in Norwich, took his B.A. and M.A. from Cambridge, then toured the Continent. After marrying and then leaving his wife, a local Norwich woman who "tried to persuade him from his wilful wickedness," he settled in London. There, he became great friends with Thomas Nashe and a great enemy of Gabriel Harvey. Whereas Nashe delighted in Greene's florid and highly rhetorical style, popularized in Lyly's *Euphues*, Harvey called him "The Ass of Euphues." Harvey despised Greene so much that he actually published scurrilous stories about him after his death. Greene died in isolation from the literary crowd and in poverty, leaving behind his mistress and his illegitimate son Fortunatus. In Greene's heyday, Nashe had praised him for the quickness of his pen: "he would have yanked a pamphlet in a night and a day as well as in a seven-year." Indeed, he was prolific, publishing twenty-eight romances and prose tracts. In one of the most popular of these, *A Notable Discovery of Cosenage*, Greene displays the tricks used by urban card sharps and pimps to hoodwink naive countrymen ("cozenage" means "cheating").

2. Caution.

3. Swindlers.

4. Prostitutes.

5. A form of syphilis.

6. See Proverbs 7.10–27, for the "woman with the attire of an harlot."

who, learning some insight in the civil law, walk abroad like paritors, summoners, and informers,[7] being none at all either in office or credit, and they go spying about where any merchant, or merchant's prentise,[8] citizen, wealthy farmer, or other of credit, either accompany with any woman familiarly, or else hath gotten some maid with child, as men's natures be prone to sin, straight they come over his fellows thus: they send for him to a tavern, and there open the matter unto him, which they have cunningly learned out, telling him he must be presented to the Arches,[9] and the citation shall be peremptorily served in his parish church. The party, afraid to have his credit cracked with the worshipful of the city and the rest of his neighbors, and grieving highly his wife should hear of it, straight takes composition with this cozener for some twenty marks, nay I heard of forty pound cross-bitten at one time, and then the cozening informer or cross-biter promiseth to wipe him out of the book and discharge him from the matter, when it was neither known nor presented: so go they to the woman and fetch her off if she be married, and though they have this gross sum yet oft times they cross-bite her for more: nay thus do they fear citizens, prentises, and farmers, that they find but any way suspicious of the like fault. The cross-biting bawds,[1] for no better can I term them, in that for lucre they conceal the sin, and smother up lust, do not only enrich themselves mightily thereby, but also discredit, hinder, and prejudice the court of the Arches, and the officers belonging to the same. There are some poor blind patches of that faculty, that have their tenements purchased and their plate on the board[2] very solemnly, who only get their gains by cross-biting, as is afore rehearsed.

Thomas Dekker
from *Lantern and Candlelight*[1]

from Chapter 1: Of Canting: How long it hath been a language; how it comes to be a language; how it is derived and by whom it is spoken.[2]

Now because a language is nothing else than heaps of words orderly woven and composed together, and that, within so narrow a circle as I have drawn to myself, it is impossible to imprint a dictionary of all the canting phrases, I will at this time not make you surfeit on too much but, as if you were walking in a garden, you shall only pluck here a flower and there another, which, as I take it, will be more delightful than if you gathered them by handfuls.

7. Paritors were summoning officers of an ecclesiastical court; summoners were officers who warn people that they have to appear in court; informers gave information against lawbreakers.

8. Apprentice.

9. The Arches, or Court of Arches, the ecclesiastical court for the province of Canterbury.

1. Panderers.

2. Silver on the table.

1. Thomas Dekker (1572?–1632), in addition to being a playwright, was a witty and colorful author of prose pamphlets, describing London street life in a kind of early modern social criticism. Most pamphleteers were following the moralistic strain of Barnabe Riche rather than the satirical vein made popular by Nashe. Indeed, a bitter, satirical, and highly topical quarrel had brought on the banning of formal verse satire by the Archbishop of Canterbury in 1599. Dekker revived the satirical style in prose pamphlets that were humorous and fantastic. He took up this genre to make some money in the wake of the closing of the theaters because of the plague of 1603. His first two pamphlets, the sardonically titled *Wonderful Year* and *Seven Deadly Sins,* were about the effects of the plague on London. Dekker's *Lantern and Candlelight* (1608), also about London street life, was so popular that it was reprinted in four different editions and, with some minor additions, under three other titles: *Villanies Discovered* (1616), *O per se—O* (1620), and *English Villanies* (1632).

2. This pamphlet tells the story of how the devil visits the earth only to find that peace and justice have fled to heaven. The only light of goodness that remains is the night watchman, or bellman, who wanders the streets of the city with his single candle. The devil finds a corrupt city in which he hears a Babel of canting, or street talk, spoken by vagabonds and beggars. Dekker's grim vision of the city is enlivened by sardonic humor and real sympathy for the poor. As he wrote in his *Work for Armourers* (1609), "God help the poor, the rich can shift."

But before I lead you into that walk, stay and hear a canter[3] in his own language making rhythms—albeit I think those charms of poesy which at the first made the barbarous tame and brought them to civility can upon these savage monsters work no such wonder. Yet this he sings, upon demand whether any of his own crew did come that way, to which he answers, "Yes," quoth he,

CANTING RHYTHMS[4]

"Enough! With boozy cove maund nase,
Tower the patring cove in the darkman case,
Docked the dell for a copper make,
His watch shall feng a prounce's nab cheat,
Cyarum, by Salmon, and thou shalt peck my jeer
In thy gan, for my watch it is nase gear,
For the bene booze my watch hath a win, etc."

This short lesson I leave to be construed by him that is desirous to try his skill in the language, which he may do by help of the following dictionary, into which way that he may more readily come, I will translate into English this broken French that follows in prose. Two canters having wrangled a while about some idle quarrel, at length growing friends thus one of them speaks to the other, viz.

A CANTER IN PROSE

Stow you, bene cofe, and cut benar whids, and bing we to Romeville to nip a bung. So shall we have lower for the boozing ken, and when we bing back to the Deuce-a-ville we will filch some duds off the ruffmans or mill the ken for a lag of duds.

THUS IN ENGLISH

Stow you, bene cofe, hold your peace, good fellow
and cut benar whids, and speak better words
and bing we to Romeville, and go we to London
to nip a bung, to cut a purse
So shall we have lower, so shall we have money
for the boozing ken, for the alehouse
and when we being back, and when we come back
to the Deuce-a-ville, into the country
we will filch some duds, we will filch some clothes
off the ruffmans, from the hedges
or mill the ken, or rob the house
for a lag of duds, for a buck[5] of clothes

Now turn to your dictionary; and because you shall not have one dish twice set before you, none of those canting words that are Englished before shall here be found, for our intent is to feast you with variety.

3. From Latin *cantus* (song, chant), canting was the street talk of thieves and beggars, who spoke in their own private language, sometimes intoned in a whining singsong.
4. These lines (untranslated by Dekker and perhaps intentionally nonsensical) come from Robert Copland's *The Highway to the Spital-House* (1536).
5. A "buck" was "a wash," the quantity of clothes washed at one time.

The Canter's Dictionary

autem, a church
autem mort, a married woman
bung, a purse
bord, a shilling
half a bord, sixpence
booze, drink
boozing ken, an alehouse
bene, good
beneship, very good
bufe, a dog
bing awast, get you hence
caster, a cloak
a commission, a shirt
chates, the gallows
to cly the jerk, to be whipped
to cut, to speak
to cut bene, to speak gently
to cut bene whids, to speak good words
to cut queer whids, to give evil language
to cant, to speak
to couch a hogshead, to lie down asleep
drawers, hosen[6]
duds, clothes
darkmans, the night
Deuce-a-ville, the country
dup the jigger, open the door
fambles, hands
fambling cheat, a ring
flag, a groat[7]
glaziers, eyes
gan, a mouth
gage, a quart pot
grannam, corn
gybe, a writing
glimmer, fire
jigger, a door
gentry mort, a gentlewoman
gentry cofe's ken, a nobleman's house
harman beck, a constable
harmans, the stocks
heave a bough, rob a booth
jark, a seal
ken, a house
lag of duds, a buck of clothes
libbege, a bed
lower, money
lap, butter, milk or whey
libken, a house to lie in
lag, water
lightmans, the day
mint, gold
a make, a halfpenny
Margery prater, a hen
maunding, asking
to mill, to steal
mill a ken, rob a house
nosegent, a nun
niggling, companying a woman
prat, a buttock
peck, meat
poplars, pottage
prancer, a horse
prigging, riding
patrico, a priest
pad, a way
quaroms, a body
ruff peck, bacon
Roger or Tib of the buttery, a goose
Romeville, London
Rome booze, wine
Rome mort, a queen
ruffmans, the woods or bushes
Ruffian, the Devil
stamps, legs
stampers, shoes
slate, a sheet
skew, a cup
Solomon, the Mass
stuling ken, a house to receive stolen goods
skipper, a barn
strommel, straw
smelling cheat, an orchard or garden
to scour the cramp-ring, to wear bolts
stalling, making or ordaining
trining, hanging
to tower, to see
win, a penny
yarum, milk

And thus have I builded up a little mint where you may coin words for your pleasure. The payment of this was a debt, for the Bellman at his farewell in his first round which he walked promised so much. If he keep not touch by tendering the due sum, he

6. Leggings or stockings.

7. A coin valued at four pence.

desires forbearance and if any that is more rich in this canting commodity will lend him any more or any better he will pay his love double. In the meantime receive this and, to give it a little more weight, you shall have a canting song wherein you may learn how this cursed generation pray or, to speak truth, curse such officers as punish them.

A Canting Song

The Ruffian cly the nab of the harman beck!
If we maund pannam, lap or ruff peck
Or poplars of yarum, he cuts "Bing to the ruffmans!"
Or else he swears by the lightmans
To put our stamps in the harmans.
The Ruffian cly the ghost of the harman beck!
If we heave a booth we cly the jerk.
If we niggle or mill a boozing ken
Or nip a bung that has but a win,
Or dup the jigger of a gentry cofe's ken,
To the queer cuffin we bing
And then to the queer ken to scour the cramp-ring,
And then to be trined on the chates in the lightmans.
The bube and Ruffian cly the harman beck and harmans!

Thus Englished

The Devil take the Constable's head!
If we beg bacon, buttermilk or bread
Or pottage, "To the hedge!" he bids us hie
Or wears "by this light!" i' th' stocks we shall lie.
The Devil haunt the Constable's ghost!
If we rob but a booth we are whipped at a post.
If an alehouse we rob or be ta'en with a whore
Or cut a purse that has just a penny and no more
Or come but stealing in at a gentleman's door,
To the Justice straight we go
And then to the gaol to be shackled, and so
To be hanged on the gallows i' th' day-time. The pox
And the Devil take the Constable and his stocks!

We have canted, I fear, too much. Let us now give ear to the Bellman and hear what he speaks in English.

Thomas Deloney
from *Thomas of Reading*[1]

How Simon's wife of Southampton, being wholly bent to pride and pleasure, requested her husband to see London, which being granted, how she got good wife Sutton of Salis-

1. Thomas Nashe wrote of Thomas Deloney (1543?–1600?), "the ballading silk-weaver of Norwich hath rhyme enough for all miracles, and wit to make a 'Garland of Good Will' . . . his Muse from the first peeping forth hath stood at livery at an ale-house wisp, never exceeding a penny a quart a day nor night." Born in London, Thomas Deloney was a silk weaver but also became a popular writer of comical and historical ballads; he also wrote broadsides on contemporary events, such as *The Queen's Visiting the Camp at Tilsburie*. Most of his works have not survived. He is best known for three prose works: *The Gentle Craft* (1597), *Jack of Newbury, the Famous and Worthy Clothier of England* (8th edition, 1619), and *Thomas of Reading, or the Six Worthy Yeomen of the West* (c. 1600). In the following selection from this last work, Deloney creates broad comedy from the fascination of a countrywoman with the marvels of shopping in the metropolis. There were numerous editions of *Thomas of Reading*, but the earliest to survive is that of 1612.

bury to go with her, who took Crab to go along with them, and how he prophesied of many things.

The clothiers[2] being all come from London, Simon's wife of Southhampton, who was with her husband very merry and pleasant, brake[3] her mind unto him in this sort.

"Good Lord husband, will you never be so kind as let me go to London with you? Shall I be penned up in Southhampton, like a parrot in a cage, or a capon in a coop? I would request no more of you in lieu of all my pains, cark[4] and care, but to have one week's time to see that fair city: what is this life if it be not mixed with some delight? And what delight is more pleasing than to see the fashions and manners of unknown places? Therefore good husband, if thou lovest me, deny not this simple request. You know I am no common gadder,[5] nor have oft troubled you with travel. God knows, this may be the last thing that ever I shall request at your hands."

"Woman," quoth he, "I would willingly satisfy your desire, but you know it is not convenient for both of us to be abroad, our charge is great, and therefore our care ought not to be small. If you will go yourself, one of my men shall go with you, and money enough you shall have in your purse: but to go with you myself, you see my business will not permit me."

"Husband," said she, "I accept your gentle offer, and it may be I shall entreat my gossip[6] Sutton to go along with me."

"I shall be glad," quoth her husband, "prepare yourself when you will."

When she had obtained this license, she sent her man Weasell to Salisbury to know of good wife Sutton if she would keep her company to London. Sutton's wife being as willing to go, as she was to request, never rested till she had gotten leave of her husband; the which when she had obtained, casting in her mind their pleasure would be small, being but they twain; thereupon the wily woman sent letter by choleric[7] Crab her man, both to Graye's wife and Fitzallen's wife, that they would meet them at Reading; who liking well of the match, consented and did so provide that they met according to promise at Reading, and from thence with Cole's wife they went all together, with each of them a man to London, each one taking up a lodging with a several friend.

When the merchants of London understood they were in town, they invited them every day home to their own houses, where they had delicate good cheer: and when they went abroad to see the commodities of the city, the merchant's wives ever bore them company, being attired most dainty and fine: which when the clothier's wives did see, it grieved their hearts they had not the like.

Now when they were brought into Cheapside, there with great wonder they beheld the shops of the goldsmiths; and on the other side, the wealthy mercers,[8] whose shops shined of all sorts of colored silks; in Watling Street, they viewed the great number of drapers[9]; in Saint Martin's, shoemakers; at Saint Nicholas church, the flesh shambles[1]; at the end of the old change, the fishmongers; in Candlewick Street the weavers; then came into the Jew's Street, where all the Jews did inhabit; then went they to Blackwell Hall, where the country clothiers did use to meet.

Afterward they proceeded, and came to Saint Paul's church, whose steeple was so high that it seemed to pierce the clouds, on the top whereof was a great and mighty weathercock of clean silver, the which notwithstanding seemed as small as a

2. Makers and sellers of woolen cloth.
3. Opened.
4. Trouble, anxiety.
5. One who wanders from place to place.
6. Friend.
7. Irascible.
8. Dealers in silks, velvets, and other expensive fabrics.
9. Cloth merchants.
1. Slaughterhouse for meat, a place where meat was sold.

sparrow to men's eyes, it stood so exceeding high, the which goodly weathercock was afterwards stolen away by a cunning cripple, who found means one night to climb up to the top of the steeple, and took it down, with the which, and a great sum of money which he had got together by begging in his lifetime, he built a gate on the Northwest side of the city, which to this day is called Cripple Gate.

From thence they went to the Tower of London, which was built by Julius Caesar, who was emperor of Rome. And there they beheld salt and wine, which had lain there ever since the Romans invaded this land, which was many years before our Savior Christ was born, the wine was grown so thick that it might have been cut like a jelly. And in that place also they saw money that was made of leather, which in ancient time went current amongst the people.

When they had to their great contentation[2] beheld all this, they repaired to their lodgings, having also a sumptuous supper ordained for them, with all delight that might be. And you shall understand that when the country weavers, which came up with their dames, saw the weavers of Candlewick Street, they had great desire presently to have some conference with them, and thus one began to challenge the other for workmanship.

Quoth Weasell, "I'll work with any of you all for a crown, take it if you dare, and he that makes his yard of cloth soonest, shall have it."

"You shall be wrought withall," said the other, "and if it were for ten crowns; but we will make this bargain, that each of us shall wind their own quills."[3]

"Content," quoth Weasell.

And so to work they went, but Weasell lost. Whereupon another of them took the matter in hand, who lost likewise: so that the London weavers triumphed against the country, casting forth diverse frumps.[4]

"Alas, poor fellows," quoth they, "your hearts are good, but your hands are ill."

"Tush, the fault was in their legs," quoth another, "pray you friend, were you not born at home?"[5]

"Why do you ask?" quoth Weasell.

"Because," said he, "the biggest place of your leg is next to your shoe."

Crab hearing this, being choleric of nature, chafed like a man of law at the bar, and he wagers with them four crowns to twain,[6] the others agreed, to work they go: but Crab conquered them all. Whereupon the London weavers were nipped in the head like birds, and had not a word to say.

"Now," saith Crab, "as we have lost nothing, so you have won nothing, and because I know ye cannot be right weavers, except you be good fellows, therefore if you will go with us, we will bestow the ale upon you."

"That is spoken like a good fellow and like a weaver," quoth the other. So along they went as it were to the sign of the red cross.

When they were set down, and had drunk well, they began merrily to prattle and to extol Crab to the skies. Whereupon Crab protested that he would come and dwell among them.

"Nay, that must not be," said a London weaver. "The king hath given us privilege, that none shall live among us, but such as serve seven years in London."

With that Crab, according to his old manner of prophesying, said thus:

2. Contentment.
3. Bobbins or spools.
4. Jeers, derisive snorts.
5. A slighting reference to the lowly origins of the provincial weavers, described as peasants with thick ankles.
6. A crown was a coin valued at five shillings; "twain": two.

"The day is very near at hand,
When as a king of this fair land
Shall privilege you more than so:
Then weavers shall in scarlet go.[7]

And to one brotherhood be brought,
The first that is in London wrought,
When other tradesmen by your fame,
Shall covet all to do the same.

Then shall you all live wondrous well,
But this one thing I shall you tell:
The day will come before the doom,
In Candlewick Street shall stand no loom.

Nor any weaver dwelling there,
But men that shall more credit bear:
For clothing shall be sore decayed,
And men undone that use that trade.

And yet the day some men shall see,
This trade again shall raised be,
When as bailiff of Sarum town,
Shall buy and purchase Bishop's down.

When there never man did sow,
Great store of goodly corn shall grow;
And woad,° that makes all colors sound *blue dye*
Shall spring upon that barren ground.

At that same day I tell you plain,
Who so alive doth then remain,
A proper maiden there shall see,
Within the town of Salisbury.

Of favor sweet, of nature kind,
With goodly eyes, and yet stark blind,
This poor blind maiden I do say,
In age shall go in rich array.

And he that takes her to his wife
Shall lead a joyful happy life,
The wealthiest clothier shall he be,
That ever was in that country.

But clothing kept as it hath been
In London never shall be seen:
For weavers then the most shall win,
That work for clothing next the skin.

7. High rank was signified by an official scarlet robe.

Till pride the commonwealth doth peel,° *exhaust*
And causeth housewives leave their wheel.° *spinning wheel*
Then poverty upon each side
Unto those workmen shall betide.

At that time, from an eagle's nest,
That proudly built in the west,
A sort shall come with cunning hand.
To bring strange weaving in this land.

And by their gains that great will fall,
They shall maintain the weaver's hall:
But long they shall not flourish so,
But folly will them overthrow.

And men shall count it mickle° shame, *much*
To bear that kind of weaver's name,
And this as sure will come to pass,
As here is ale within this glass."

When the silly souls that sat about him heard him speak in this sort, they admired and honored Crab for the same.

"Why my masters," said Weasell, "do you wonder at these words? He will tell you twenty of these tales, for which cause we call him our canvas prophet."

"His attire fits his title," said they, "and we never heard the like in our lives; and if this should be true, it would be strange."

"Doubt not but it will be true," quoth Weasell, "for I'll tell you what, he did but once see our Nick kiss Nel, and presently he powered out this rhyme.

That kiss, O Nel, God give thee joy,
Will nine months hence breed thee a boy.

"And I'll tell you what, you shall hear: we kept reckoning and it fell out as just as Jone's buttocks on a close stool, for which cause, our maids durst never kiss a man in his sight."

Upon this they broke company and went every one about his business, the London weavers to their frames and the country fellows to their dames, who after their great banqueting and merriment went every one home to their own houses, though with less money than they brought out, yet with more pride.

Especially Simon's wife of Southampton, who told the rest of her gossips that she saw no reason but that their husbands should maintain them as well as the merchants did their wives: "for I tell you what," quoth she, "we are as proper women (in my conceit) as the proudest of them all, as handsome of body, as fair of face, our legs as well made, and our feet as fine: then what reason is there (seeing our husbands are of as good wealth) but we should be as well maintained?"

"You say true, gossip," said Sutton's wife: "trust me, it made me blush, to see them brave it out so gallantly, and we to go so homely."

"But before God," said the other, "I will have my husband to buy me a London gown, or in faith he shall have little quiet."

"So shall mine," said another.

"And mine too," quoth the third.

And all of them sung the same note: so that when they came home, their husbands had no little to do.

Especially Simon, whose wife daily lay at him for London apparel, to whom he said, "Good woman, be content, let us go according to our place and ability: what will the bailiffs think, if I should prank thee up like a peacock, and thou in thy attire surpass their wives? They would either think I were mad, or else that I had more money than I could well use: consider I pray thee, good wife, that such as are in their youth wasters do prove in their age stark beggars.

"Beside that, it is enough to raise me up in the King's books:[8] for many times, men's coffers are judged by their garments. Why, we are country folks and must keep ourselves in good compass: gray russet and good homespun cloth doth best become us; I tell thee, wife, it were as undecent for us to go like Londoners as it is for Londoners to go like courtiers."

"What a coil keep you,"[9] quoth she. "Are not we God's creatures as well as Londoners? And the King's subjects, as well as they? Then finding our wealth to be as good as theirs, why should we not go as gay as Londoners? No, husband, no, here is the fault, we are kept without it, only because our husbands are not so kind as Londoners: why, man, a cobbler there keeps his wife better than the best clothier in this country: nay, I will affirm it, that the London oyster-wives, and the very kitchen-stuff criers,[1] do exceed us in their Sunday's attire: nay, more than that, I did see the water-bearer's wife which belongs to one of our merchants, come in with a tankard of water on her shoulder, and yet half a dozen gold rings on her fingers."

"You may think, wife," quoth he, "she got them not with idleness.

"But, wife, you must consider what London is, the chief and capital city of all the land, a place on the which all strangers cast their eyes. It is, wife, the King's chamber and his Majesty's royal seat: to that city repairs all nations under heaven. Therefore it is most meet and convenient that the citizens of such a city should not go in their apparel like peasants but, for the credit of our country, wear such seemly habits as do carry gravity and comeliness in the eyes of all beholders."

"But if we of the country went so," quoth she, "were it not as great credit for the land as the other?"

"Woman," quoth her husband, "it is altogether needless, and in diverse respects it may not be."

"Why then I pray you," quoth she, "let us go dwell at London."

"A word soon spoken," said her husband, "but not so easy to be performed: therefore, wife, I pray thee hold thy prating, for thy talk is foolish."

"Yea, yea, husband, your old churlish[2] conditions will never be left, you keep me here like a drudge and a droil,[3] and so you may keep your money in your purse. You care not for your credit, but before I will go so like a shepherdess, I will first go naked: and I tell you plain, I scorn it greatly that you should clap a gray gown on my back as if I had not brought you two pence. Before I was married, you swore I should have any thing that I requested, but now all is forgotten."

8. Taxation lists.
9. What a fuss you're making.
1. Hawkers, sellers of goods.
2. Grudging.
3. A servant.

And in saying this, she went in, and soon after she was so sick that needs she must go to bed: and when she was laid, she drave[4] out that night with many grievous groans, sighing and sobbing, and no rest she could take God wot.[5] And in the morning when she should rise, the good soul fell down in a swoon, which put her maidens in a great fright, who, running down to their master, cried out, "Alas, alas, our dame[6] is dead, our dame is dead."

The good man, hearing this, ran up in all haste, and there fell to rubbing and chafing of her temples, sending for *aqua vitae*, and saying, "Ah my sweet heart, speak to me, good wife, alack, alack, call in the neighbors, you queans,[7]" quoth he.

With that she lift up her head, fetching a great groan, and presently swooned again, and much ado iwis,[8] he had to keep life in her. But when she was come to herself, "How dost thou wife?" quoth he. "What wilt thou have? For God's sake, tell me if thou hast a mind to any thing, thou shalt have it."

"Away, dissembler," quoth she, "how can I believe thee? Thou hast said as much to me an hundred times, and deceived me, it is thy churlishness that hath killed my heart, never was woman matched to so unkind a man."

"Nay good wife, blame me not without cause; God knoweth how dearly I love thee."

"Love me! no, no, thou didst never carry my love but on the tip of thy tongue," quoth she, "I dare swear thou desirest nothing so much as my death, and for my part, I would to God thou hadst thy desire. But be content, I shall not trouble thee long," and with that fetching a sigh, she swooned and gave a great groan.

The man, seeing her in this case was wondrous woe. But so soon as they had recovered her he said, "O my dear wife, if any bad conceit hath engendered this sickness, let me know it; or if thou knowest any thing that may procure thy health, let me understand thereof, and I protest thou shalt have it, if it cost me all that ever I have."

"O husband," quoth she, "how may I credit your words, when for a paltry suit of apparel you denied me?"

"Well, wife, quoth he, "thou shalt have apparel or any thing else thou wilt request, if God send thee once health."

"O husband, if I may find you so kind, I shall think myself the happiest woman in the world; thy words have greatly comforted my heart, me thinketh if I had it, I could drink a good draught of Rhenish wine."

Well, wine was sent for.

"O Lord," said she, "that I had a piece of chicken, I feel my stomach desirous of some meat."

"Glad am I of that," said her husband, and so the woman within a few days after was very well.

But you shall understand that her husband was fain to dress her London-like ere he could get her quiet, neither would it please her, except the stuff were bought in Cheapside, for out of Cheapside nothing could content her, were it never so good: insomuch, that if she thought a tailor of Cheapside made not her gown, she would swear it was quite spoiled.

And having thus won her husband to her will, when the rest of the clothiers' wives heard thereof, they would be suited in the like sort too: so that ever since, the wives of Southampton, Salisbury, of Gloucester, Worcester, and Reading, went all as gallant and as brave as any Londoners' wives.

4. Drove.
5. Knows.
6. Lady.
7. Bold women, hussies.
8. Certainly.

Thomas Nashe
from *Pierce Penniless*[1]

That state or kingdom that is in league with all the world, and hath no foreign sword to vex it, is not half so strong or confirmed to endure, as that which lives every hour in fear of invasion. There is a certain waste of the people for whom there is no use, but war: and these men must have some employment still to cut them off. *Nam si foras hostem non habent, domi invenient.*[2] If they have no service abroad, they will make mutinies at home. Or if the affairs of the state be such, as cannot exhale all these corrupt excrements, it is very expedient they have some light toys to busy their heads withall, cast before them as bones to gnaw upon, which may keep them from having leisure to intermeddle with higher matters.

To this effect, the policy of plays is very necessary, howsoever some shallow-brained censurers (not the deepest searchers into the secrets of government) mightily oppugn[3] them. For whereas the afternoon being the idlest time of the day; wherein men that are their own masters (as gentlemen of the court, the inns of the court,[4] and the number of captains and soldiers about London) do wholly bestow themselves upon pleasure, and that pleasure they divide (how virtuously it skills not) either into gaming, following of harlots, drinking, or seeing a play: is it not then better (since of four extremes all the world cannot keep them but they will choose one) that they should betake them to the least, which is plays? Nay, what if I prove plays to be no extreme; but a rare exercise of virtue? First, for the subject of them (for the most part) it is borrowed out of our English chronicles, wherein our forefathers' valiant acts (that have lain long buried in rusty brass and worm-eaten books) are revived, and they themselves raised from the grave of oblivion and brought to plead their aged honors in open presence: than which, what can be a sharper reproof to these degenerate effeminate days of ours?

How would it have joyed brave Talbot (the terror of the French)[5] to think that after he had lain two hundred years in his tomb, he should triumph again on the stage, and have his bones new embalmed with the tears of ten thousand spectators at least (at several times), who, in the tragedian that represents his person, imagine they behold him fresh bleeding.

I will defend it against any collian[6] or clubfisted usurer of them all, there is no immortality can be given a man on earth like unto plays. What talk I to them of immortality, that are the only underminers of honor and do envy any man that is not sprung up by base brokery[7] like themselves? They care not if all the ancient houses

1. One of the most brilliant comic writers in the English language, Thomas Nashe (1567–1601) was a master satirist. After education at Cambridge, he came to London in 1588 to make a living as a writer. He first attracted attention for his invective against pseudo-poets and puritan reformers in *The Anatomie of Abuses* (1589). In his greatest satire *Pierce Penniless his Supplication to the Divell* (1592), Nashe exposed every kind of hypocrisy and deceit in contemporary society. This work proved a great popular success; it was reprinted six times within its first year. Among the objects of Nashe's satire was the pedantic and vindictive Gabriel Harvey, who quickly counter-attacked by portraying Nashe as a boor and an academic failure. The Harvey-Nashe pamphlet war raged on until 1599, when the Archbishop of Canterbury ordered that "all Nashe's books and Harvey's books be taken wheresoever they may be, and that none of the same books be ever printed hereafter." Nashe also wrote an entertaining parodic romance, *The Unfortunate Traveller,* whose realism has been compared to Defoe's novels. Nashe not only enjoyed the theater and befriended actors and playwrights but even cowrote the now lost play *The Isle of Dogs* with Ben Jonson. The following passage from *Pierce Penniless* shows Nashe's familiarity with the world of the theater and the realistic description that is the satirist's great skill.

2. Literally, "If they have no enemy abroad, they will find one at home."

3. Oppose.

4. The law schools of England.

5. For "fighting Talbot the terror of the French," see Shakespeare's *The First Part of King Henry VI* (1590), on Henry VI's war against France.

6. Cullion, from French *couillon,* testicle; a base person, a rascal.

7. Rascally dealing or trafficking.

were rooted out, so that, like the burgomasters of the Low-countries,[8] they might share the government amongst them as states, and be quartermasters[9] of our monarchy. All arts to them are vanity: and, if you tell them what a glorious thing it is to have Henry the Fifth represented on the stage, leading the French King prisoner, and forcing both him and the Dolphin to swear fealty, I, but (will they say) what do we get by it?[1] Respecting neither the right of fame that is due to true nobility deceased, nor what hopes of eternity are to be proposed to adventurous minds, to encourage them forward, but only their execrable lucre, and filthy unquenchable avarice.

They know when they are dead they shall not be brought upon the stage for any goodness, but in merriment of the usurer and the devil, or buying arms of the herald, who gives them the lion, without tongue, tail, or talents, because his master whom he must serve is a townsman, and a man of peace, and must not keep any quarreling beasts to annoy his honest neighbors.

In plays, all cozenages,[2] all cunning drifts overguiled with outward holiness, all strategems of war, all the cankerworms that breed on the rust of peace, are most lively anatomized: they show the ill success of treason, the fall of hasty climbers, the wretched end of usurpers, the misery of civil dissension, and how just God is evermore in punishing of murder. And to prove every one of these allegations, could I propound the circumstances of this play and that play, if I meant to handle this theme otherwise than *obiter*.[3] What should I say more? They are sour pills of reprehension, wrapt up in sweet words. Whereas some petitioners of the council against them object, they corrupt the youth of the city, and withdraw prentises from their work; they heartily wish they might be troubled with none of their youth nor their prentises; for some of them (I mean the ruder handicrafts servants) never come abroad, but they are in danger of undoing: and as for corrupting them when they come, that's false; for no play they have, encourageth any man to tumults or rebellion, but lays before such the halter and the gallows; or praiseth or approveth pride, lust, whoredom, prodigality, or drunkenness, but beats them down utterly. As for the hindrance of trades and traders of the city by them, that is an article foisted in by the vintners, alewives, and victuallers, who surmise, if there were no plays, they should have all the company that resort to them, lie boozing and beer-bathing in their houses every afternoon. Nor so, nor so, good brother bottle-ale, for there are other places besides where money can bestow itself: the sign of the smock will wipe your mouth clean: and yet I have heard ye have made her a tenant to your tap-houses. But what shall he do that hath spent himself? where shall he haunt? Faith, when dice, lust, and drunkenness, and all have dealt upon him, if there be never a play for him to go to for his penny, he sits melancholy in his chamber, devising upon felony or treason, and how he may best exalt himself by mischief.

In Augustus's time[4] (who was the patron of all witty sports) there happened a great fray in Rome about a player, insomuch as all the city was in an uproar: whereupon the emperor (after the broil was somewhat overblown) called the player before him, and asked what was the reason that a man of his quality durst presume to make such a brawl about nothing. He smilingly replied, "It is good for thee, O Caesar, that the people's heads are troubled with brawls and quarrels about us and our light matters: for otherwise they would look into thee and thy matters." Read Lipsius or any

8. Chief magistrates of Dutch towns.
9. Petty officers who steer the ship.
1. See Shakespeare's *Henry V*.
2. Tricks.
3. In passing.
4. Augustus (63 B.C.–16 A.D.) was the grandnephew of Julius Caesar and first Roman Emperor.

profane or Christian politician, and you shall find him of this opinion.[5] Our players are not as the players beyond sea, a sort of squirting bawdy comedians, that have whores and common courtesans to play women's parts, and forbear no immodest speech or unchaste action that may procure laughter;[6] but our scene is more stately furnished than ever it was in the time of Roscius,[7] our representations honorable, and full of gallant resolution, not consisting, like theirs of a pantaloon, a whore, and a zany,[8] but of emperors, kings, and princes; whose true tragedies (*Sophocleo cothurno*[9]) they do vaunt.

Not Roscius nor Aesop, those admired tragedians that have lived ever since before Christ was born, could ever perform more in action than famous Ned Allen.[1] I must accuse our poets of sloth and partiality, that they will not boast in large impressions what worthy men (above all nations) England affords. Other countries cannot have a fiddler break a string but they will put it in print, and the old Romans in the writings they published, thought scorn to use any but domestical examples of their own home-bred actors, scholars, and champions, and them they would extol to the third and fouth generation: cobblers, tinkers, fencers, none escaped them, but they mingled them all in one gallimaufry of glory.

Here I have used a like method, not of tying myself to mine own country, but by insisting in the experience of our time: and, if I ever write any thing in Latin (as I hope one day I shall), not a man of any desert here amongst us, but I will have up. Tarlton, Ned Allen, Knell, Bentley[2] shall be made known to France, Spain, and Italy: and not a part that they surmounted in, more than other, but I will there note and set down, with the manner of their habits and attire.

King James I
from *A Counterblast to Tobacco*[1]

That the manifold abuses of this vile custom of tobacco taking may the better be espied, it is fit that first you enter into consideration both of the first original thereof, and likewise of the reasons of the first entry thereof into this country. For certainly as such customs that have their first institution either from a godly, necessary, or honorable ground, and are first brought in by the means of some worthy, virtuous, and great personage, are ever, and most justly, holden in great and reverent estima-

5. Justus Lipsius (1547–1606) was a Flemish humanist who wrote on politics, edited Latin texts, and revived Stoicism.

6. Women played roles in the Renaissance Italian *commedia dell'arte,* but in Elizabethan and Jacobean times English players were all male.

7. Quintus Roscius (126–62 B.C.) was a famous Roman actor.

8. Stock *commedia dell'arte* characters: the pantaloon was a lean, foolish old man wearing pantaloons, and the zany was a servant who acted as a clown.

9. By the Sophoclean boot. Sophocles (496–c.406 B.C.), Greek tragic poet; "cothurnus," a high Greek boot worn by tragic actors.

1. A renowned English actor.

2. All English actors. Richard Tarlton (d. 1588) was well known for his jokes and jigs.

1. James I (1566–1625), the son of Mary Queen of Scots, became King of Scotland in 1567 and King of England in 1603. His tutor was the great Scots humanist George Buchanan, from whom the young prince learned a love of scholarship and literature. James wrote poetry and literary theory in addition to political works like *The True Law of Free Monarchy* (1598), an argument in favor of the divine right of kings, and *Basilikon Doron* (1599), on the art of government. Though the loose mores of his own court allowed for his affair with Robert Carr and other favorites as well as the dalliances of Carr's wife Lady Frances Howard, who "played her pranks as the toy took her in the head," James asserted a strict control over his subjects, both economically and morally. This extract from *A Counterblast to Tobacco* (1616) asserts the corrupting effects of the new import from the Americas. In his *Commisso Pro Tobacco* (1604), James had actually imposed fines on merchants who brought tobacco into England. In this text, James argued that while "the better sort" used tobacco "only as physicke to preserve health" (in fact, as a cure for venereal disease), "a number of riotous and disordered persons of mean and base condition . . . do spend most of their time in that idle vanitie to the evil and corrupting of others, and also do consume the wages that many of them do get by their labor, wherewith their families should be relieved, not caring at what price they buy that drug."

tion and account, by all wise, virtuous, and temperate spirits: So should it by the contrary, justly bring a great disgrace into that sort of customs, which having their original from base corruption and barbarity, do in like sort, make their first entry into a country, by an inconsiderate and childish affectation of novelty, as is the true case of the first invention of tobacco taking, and of the first entry thereof among us. For tobacco being a common herb, which (though under diverse names) grows almost everywhere, was first found out by some of the barbarous Indians to be a preservative or antidote against the pox,[2] a filthy disease, whereunto these barbarous people are (as all men know) very much subject, what through the uncleanly and adult constitution of their bodies, and what through the intemperate heat of their climate: so that as from them was first brought into Christendom, that most detestable disease, so from them likewise was brought this use of tobacco, as a stinking and unsavory antidote, for so corrupted and execrable a malady, the stinking suffumigation[3] whereof they yet use against that disease, making so one canker or venom to eat out another.

And now good countrymen, let us (I pray you) consider, what honor or policy can move us to imitate the barbarous and beastly manners of the wild, godless, and slavish Indians, especially in so vile and stinking a custom? Shall we that disdain to imitate the manner of our neighbor France (having the style of the first Christian kingdom) and that cannot endure the spirit of the Spaniards (their king being now comparable in largeness of dominions to the great emperor of Turkey). Shall we, I say, that have been so long civil and wealthy in peace, famous and invincible in war, fortunate in both, we that have been ever able to aid any of our neighbors (but never deafed any of their ears with any of our supplications for assistance) shall we, I say, without blushing abase ourselves so far as to imitate these beastly Indians, slaves to the Spaniards, refuse to the world, and as yet aliens from the holy covenant of God? Why do we not as well imitate them in walking naked as they do? In preferring glasses, feathers, and such toys to gold and precious stones as they do? Yea why do we not deny God and adore the devil as they do?

Now to the corrupted baseness of the first use of this tobacco, doeth very well agree the foolish and groundless first entry thereof into this kingdom. It is not so long since the first entry of this abuse amongst us here, as this present age cannot yet very well remember both the first author and the form of the first introduction of it amongst us. It was neither brought in by king, great conqueror, nor learned doctor of physic.

With the report of a great discovery for a conquest, some two or three savage men were brought in, together with the savage custom. But the pity is, the poor wild barbarous men died, but that vile barbarous custom is yet alive, yea in fresh vigor: so as it seems a miracle to me, how a custom springing from so vile a ground, and brought in by a father so generally hated, should be welcomed upon so slender a warrant. For if they that first put it in practice here, had remembered for what respect it was used by them from whence it came, I am sure they would have been loath to have taken so far the imputation of that disease upon them as they did, by using the cure thereof: For *Sanis non est opus medico*,[4] and counterpoisons are never used, but where poison is thought to precede.

---

2. Syphilis.
3. In the medical sense, having fumes (vapors) penetrate the body for a therapeutic effect.
4. It is not necessary to cure the healthy.

Ben Jonson

1572–1637

Ben Jonson's life was full of changes and contradictions. His earliest biographer, William Drummond, called him "passionately kind and angry, careless either to gain or keep, vindictive, but, if he be well answered, at himself." His father was Protestant, but Jonson turned Catholic, only to recant that conversion later; nevertheless, in his last years he called himself a "beadsman." The stepson of a bricklayer, he became Poet Laureate. He wrote poems of praise to win the patronage of king and court but also skewered their follies in satire. Though often assuming the role of moralist in his poetry and plays, Jonson admitted that as a younger man he was "given to venery" and pleaded guilty to the charge of murder. He was attached to admiring younger poets, "the tribe of Ben," yet he also enjoyed feuds, such as those with fellow dramatists Marston and Dekker. While espousing Horatian spareness and an acute sense of meter in both criticism and poetry, Jonson also had a keen ear for the colloquial language of London.

Indeed, London was one of the few constants in Jonson's turbulent career. Born in Harts-Born Lane near Charing Cross, he was buried in Poets' Corner at Westminster Abbey. Jonson portrayed the city as the world of those who lived by their wits. He dramatized literary infighting in *Every Man Out of His Humour* (1599), greedy schemes in *Volpone* (1606), intellectual confidence scams in *The Alchemist* (1610), and antitheatrical Puritan preaching in *Bartholomew Fair* (1614). The London audience at the Hope Theatre was reported to have exclaimed at a performance of *Bartholomew Fair:* "O rare Ben Jonson!"

Unlike other playwrights of his time (including Shakespeare), Jonson oversaw the publication of his plays, which appeared with his poems in the same deluxe folio volume, entitled *Works* (1616). The assertion of the dignity of popular drama surprised many of his readers, one of whom wrote, "Pray tell me Ben, where doth the mystery lurk, / What others call a play, you call a work?" That Jonson wanted his plays to be read as much as performed can be gathered from the comment printed on the title page of *Every Man Out of His Humour:* "as it was first composed by the author, Ben Jonson, containing more than hath been publicly spoken or acted."

Jonson viewed writing as his profession; he became the first poet in England to earn a living by his art. His achievement was recognized by James I, who made Jonson the first Poet Laureate of England and granted him a pension for life. Before becoming laureate, Jonson depended on a whole string of patrons. With the new Stuart king in power, Jonson was able to use his claim of Scots descent to advantage. He was supported by Esme Stuart Seigneur D'Aubigny (a cousin of King James), to whom he dedicated his first tragedy, *Sejanus* (1603). His patrons included Sir Walter Raleigh and Lady Mary Wroth, to whom he dedicated *The Alchemist*. Jonson's most important break came when he received a commission for a court masque. In 1605 he wrote *The Masque of Blackness* starring the Queen herself. To gain some idea of the extravagance of these masques, consider that in 1617, while 12,000 pounds were spent on the entire administration of Ireland, 4,000 pounds were spent on a single masque, *Pleasure Reconciled to Virtue*. The masques were lavish ventures that required costumes, music, and magnificent scenery, which was designed by Inigo Jones, who introduced the Italian invention of perspective.

If the pursuit of patronage was crucial to Jonson's advancement, his satire of politics and power repeatedly put his career and even his life at risk. In 1603 Jonson was called before the Privy Council for *Sejanus;* the charges included "popery and treason." Jonson's *Epicoene, or the Silent Woman*—which climaxes in the revelation that the silent woman is really a boy—was suppressed because it lampooned a love affair of the King's first cousin, Lady Arbella Stuart. One observer complained of the 1613 *Irish Masque at Court* that it was "no time . . . to exasperate that nation by making ridiculous." Jonson was imprisoned twice for the offense that his plays gave to the powerful—once for the now lost *The Isle of Dogs* (1597) and another time for *Eastward Ho!* (1605), in which he made fun of King James's Scots accent.

Jonson took reckless risks, whose consequences he barely managed to escape. While imprisoned for the murder of Gabriel Spencer in 1598, Jonson became a Catholic. Following his conversion, Jonson pleaded guilty to manslaughter (later calling it the result of a duel) but went free by claiming benefit of clergy. This medieval custom originally allowed clerics to be judged by the bishop's court but, by Jonson's time, permitted anyone who could translate the Latin Bible to go free. Jonson left prison with his belongings confiscated, his thumb branded for the felony, and his reputation marked by his profession of an outlaw religion. Like any other Catholic in Elizabethan England, Jonson could be fined or have his property confiscated for not attending Anglican services. Indeed, he and his wife were interrogated for their nonattendance in 1605; Jonson was also charged with being "a poet, and by fame a seducer of youth to the Popish religion." Threatened again with loss of property and another prison term, Jonson complied with the Court's order that he take instruction in Protestantism.

Not all Jonson's disputes were quite so dangerous. Like the characters in his plays, he enjoyed engaging in the game of vapors, a mock argument, drummed up for the display of wit. He not only engaged in combats of wit with Shakespeare (who acted in *Every Man Out of His Humour*), but also ridiculed Marston and Dekker in what critics call "the War of the Theaters." Jonson's *Every Man Out of His Humour* satirized Marston as a pseudo-intellectual. The same year, Jonson and Dekker collaborated on a play. Two years later, Dekker parodied Jonson as the bombastic Horace, constantly reading his work aloud and expecting praise in *Satiriomastix* (1601). The title of this play means "the whipping of the satirist," and it is full of barbs about Jonson's checkered past—both his imprisonment and his theatrical flops. Dekker called Jonson a "brown-bread mouth-stinker." Jonson responded with a "forced defense" against "base detractors and illiterate apes" in *Poetaster* (1601).

Jonson did have high regard for some of his contemporaries, as they did for him. Among these was John Donne, who wrote commendatory verses for *Volpone* and to whom Jonson wrote "Who shall doubt, Donne, whe'er I a poet be / When I dare send my epigrams to thee?" As an older man, Jonson held court at the Devil Tavern among his fellow poets as self-proclaimed *arbiter bibendi* (master of drinking), whose main object was "Not drinking much, but talking wittily." This vein of wit was carried on by Sir John Suckling's *A Session of Poets* and Herrick's *Prayer for Ben Jonson*. His servant Brome wrote an elegy for him, as did the many men of letters who contributed to *Jonsonius Virbius* ("Jonson Reborn"), the year after his death.

Jonson saw himself as a moral and poetic guide. His satire of moral depravity and intellectual delusion is hysterically funny. His plays include direct criticism of contemporary poetry and drama, contracts with the audience, and self-mockery—a foretaste of the break from realistic conventions in modernism. Jonson's comedies also persuade us that there is no reality without satire; we cannot know the world without laughing at its ridiculousness. The human foibles and obsessions portrayed in his comedies are captured in a language so vivid and oral that it has to be read aloud. Jonson's verse dazzles by concealing its art, allowing conversational words and rhythms to be perfectly wedded to poetic meters. The simplicity and restraint of his language, as in his elegy on the death of his son, are the vehicles for pure music and powerful emotion.

Volpone

Volpone was first performed in the spring of 1606 by the King's Men at the Globe Theatre on the Bankside. The King's Men, an acting troupe that included Shakespeare, produced most of Jonson's plays in the Globe, which they owned. The Globe seated some two thousand spectators of all stations—from aristocrats and prosperous merchants in the boxes to the "groundlings" who stood in the pit in front of the stage. Not only was *Volpone* a success in the public theater, but it was also performed for learned audiences at Oxford and Cambridge.

Volpone combines Jonson's unique blend of learned humanistic allusion and popular colloquial argot. The play conforms to the classical unities of place and time, taking place in Venice on a single day. Jonson drew on Erasmus's *The Praise of Folly* and translations of Lucian's dialogues, which both present mock praise, for Volpone's opening speech praising gold. Lucian had written of a childless rich old man who lived out his life playing with the various scoundrels who were trying to inherit his money. For the beastlike character of these moneygrubbing fools and his wily hero, Jonson drew on both the medieval beast fable and the Italian theatrical tradition of the improvisatory *commedia dell'arte*, with its stock figures of the old dotard and the cuckolded husband. Although the play ostensibly takes place in Italy, the commercial wealth that corrupts almost everyone in the play is as much a representation of London as of Venice. The play is not only about greed but also about manipulation and power, including the deceptive power of theater itself. As Volpone stage-manages his own supposed illness, Jonson satirizes the playwright who cons the audience into believing his illusions.

Volpone went to press in 1607 in quarto; it was published with a few changes in the 1616 folio, which is the basis of the present text. Stage directions and scene divisions have been added by the present editor to add greater clarity to the action.

Volpone; or, The Fox

Dramatis Personae[1]

Volpone, *a magnifico*	Grege (*mob*)
Mosca, *his parasite*	
Voltore, *an advocate*	Commandadori (*officers of justice*)
Corbaccio, *an old gentleman*	Mercatori (*three merchants*)
Corvino, *a merchant*	Avocatori (*four magistrates*)
Bonario, *son to Corbaccio*	Notario (*the register*)
Sir Politic Would-be, *a knight*	
Peregrine, *a gentleman traveler*	Lady Would-be, *Sir Politic's wife*
Nano, *a dwarf*	Celia, *Corvino's wife*
Castrone, *a eunuch*	
Androgyno, *a hermaphrodite*	Servitori (*servants*), two Waiting-women, etc.

The Scene, Venice

The Argument

V *olpone, childless, rich, feigns sick, despairs,*
O *ffers his state to hopes of several heirs,*
L *ies languishing: his parasite receives*
P *resents of all, assures, deludes; then weaves*
O *ther cross plots, which ope themselves, are told.*
N *ew tricks for safety are sought; they thrive: when bold,*
E *ach tempts the other again, and all are sold.*° *enslaved*

Prologue

Now, luck yet send us, and a little wit
Will serve to make our play hit;

1. The characters' names all suggest their natures: in Italian, a *volpone* is an old fox, a sly deceiver; a *magnifico* is a nobleman; a *mosca* is a fly; a *voltore* is a vulture; a *corbaccio* is a large filthy raven; a *corvino* is a crow; *bonario* means good, honest; *politic* means scheming, as in a politic Machiavellian; *peregrine* is a falcon and a traveler; an *androgyno* is a man-woman (Greek); *commendatori* are officers of the court; *mercatori* are merchants; *avocatori* are lawyers; a *notario* is a recorder; *celia* (Latin *caelica*) means heavenly.

(According to the palates of the season)
Here is rhyme, not empty of reason.
This we were bid to credit from our poet,
Whose true scope, if you would know it,
In all his poems still hath been this measure,
To mix profit with your pleasure;[2]
And not as some, whose throats their envy failing,
Cry hoarsely, All he writes is railing:° *sarcasm*
And when his plays come forth, think they can flout them,
With saying, he was a year about them.
To this there needs no lie but this his creature,
Which was two months since no feature;[3]
And though he dares give them five lives to mend it,
'Tis known, five weeks fully penned it,
From his own hand, without a co-adjutor,
Novice, journeyman, or tutor.[4]
Yet thus much I can give you as a token
Of his play's worth, no eggs are broken,
Nor quaking custards with fierce teeth affrighted,
Wherewith your rout° are so delighted; *crowd*
Nor hales he in a gull° old ends reciting, *fool*
To stop gaps in his loose writing;[5]
With such a deal of monstrous and forced action,
As might make Bethlem° a faction: *Bedlam: the madhouse*
Nor made he his play for jests stolen from each table,
But makes jests to fit his fable;
And so presents quick comedy refined,
As best critics have designed;
The laws of time, place, persons he observeth,
From no needful rule he swerveth.[6]
All gall and copperas° from his ink he draineth, *vitriol*
Only a little salt° remaineth, *wit*
Wherewith he'll rub your cheeks, till red, with laughter,
They shall look fresh a week after.

Act 1

Scene 1. *A Room in Volpone's House*

[*Enter Volpone and Mosca.*]

VOLPONE Good morning to the day; and next, my gold!—
Open the shrine, that I may see my saint.
[*Mosca withdraws the curtain, and discovers piles of gold, plate, jewels, etc.*]
Hail the world's soul, and mine! more glad than is
The teeming earth to see the longed-for sun

2. The goal of poetry according to Horace's *Ars Poetica*.
3. The proof that Jonson did not spend a year writing his plays is that *Volpone* ("his creature") did not exist two months ago.
4. A "co-adjutor" was a coauthor, while a "novice" was an apprentice; a "journeyman" was hired as the servant of a master, while a "tutor" revised another's work.
5. This play will not resort to slapstick (throwing eggs, or a custard pie in the face) or to the use of hackneyed proverbs, both popular in the Elizabethan theater.
6. The Aristotelian unities prescribed for drama by Renaissance critics included a period of 24 hours, and one location. Comic characters ("persons") were supposed to be lower- or middle-class.

Peep through the horns of the celestial Ram,[7]
Am I, to view thy splendour darkening his;
That lying here, amongst my other hoards,
Shew'st like a flame by night, or like the day
Struck out of chaos, when all darkness fled
Unto the center. O thou son of Sol,[8]
But brighter than thy father, let me kiss,
With adoration, thee, and every relic
Of sacred treasure in this blessed room.
Well did wise poets, by thy glorious name,
Title that age which they would have the best;[9]
Thou being the best of things, and far transcending
All style of joy, in children, parents, friends,
Or any other waking dream on earth:
Thy looks when they to Venus did ascribe,[1]
They should have given her twenty thousand Cupids;
Such are thy beauties and our loves! Dear saint,
Riches, the dumb god,[2] that giv'st all men tongues,
Thou canst do nought, and yet mak'st men do all things;
The price of souls;[3] even hell, with thee to boot,
Is made worth heaven. Thou art virtue, fame,
Honor, and all things else. Who can get thee,
He shall be noble valiant, honest, wise—

MOSCA And what he will, sir. Riches are in fortune
A greater good than wisdom is in nature.

VOLPONE True, my beloved Mosca. Yet I glory
More in the cunning purchase° of my wealth *gaining*
Than in the glad possession, since I gain
No common way; I use no trade, no venture;
I wound no earth with plough-shares, fat no beasts
To feed the shambles; have no mills for iron,
Oil, corn, or men, to grind them into powder:
I blow no subtle glass, expose no ships
To threat'nings of the furrow-faced sea;
I turn no monies° in the public bank, *earn no interest*
Nor usure° private. *make loans*

MOSCA No, sir, nor devour
Soft prodigals. You shall have some will swallow
A melting heir as glibly as your Dutch
Will pills of butter, and ne'er purge° for it; *empty the bowels*
Tear forth the fathers of poor families
Out of their beds, and coffin them alive
In some kind clasping prison, where their bones
May be forthcoming when the flesh is rotten:
But your sweet nature doth abhor these courses;
You loathe the widow's or the orphan's tears

7. The sun is in the Ram, or Aries, in mid-April.

8. Comparing gold to God's creation of the day out of chaos (Genesis 1), when the darkness "retreated to the underworld." Gold is the son of Sol (Latin "sun"), with a pun on sol, short for Italian coins, *soldi*.

9. The Golden Age, see Ovid, *Metamorphoses* 1.89–122.

1. "Golden" is an epithet of Venus, goddess of love.

2. The god of riches, Mammon, was called dumb, because "silence is golden."

3. Human souls were "bought with a price" (1 Corinthians 6.20) by Jesus Christ's sacrifice of his life.

Should wash your pavements, or their piteous cries
Ring in your roofs, and beat the air for vengeance.

VOLPONE Right, Mosca; I do loathe it.

MOSCA And besides, sir,
You are not like the thresher that doth stand
With a huge flail, watching a heap of corn,
And, hungry, dares not taste the smallest grain,
But feeds on mallows and such bitter herbs;
Nor like the merchant, who hath filled his vaults
With Romagnia and rich Candian wines,
Yet drinks the lees° of Lombard's vinegar:[4] *dregs*
You will lie not in straw, whilst moths and worms
Feed on your sumptuous hangings and soft beds;
You know the use of riches, and dare give now
From that bright heap, to me, your poor observer,
Or to your dwarf, or your hermaphrodite,
Your eunuch, or what other household trifle
Your pleasure allows maintenance—

VOLPONE Hold thee, Mosca, [*Gives him money*.]
Take of my hand; thou strik'st on truth in all,
And they are envious term thee parasite.
Call forth my dwarf, my eunuch, and my fool,
And let them make me sport. [*Exit Mosca*.] What should I do,
But cocker up° my genius, and live free *indulge*
To all delights my fortune calls me to?
I have no wife, no parent, child, ally,
To give my substance to; but whom I make
Must be my heir: and this makes men observe me:
This draws new clients daily to my house,
Women and men of every sex and age,
That bring me presents, send me plate, coin, jewels,
With hope that when I die (which they expect
Each greedy minute) it shall then return
Ten-fold upon them; whilst some, covetous
Above the rest, seek to engross° me whole, *monopolize*
And counter-work the one unto the other,
Contend in gifts, as they would seem in love:
All which I suffer, playing with their hopes,
And am content to coin them into profit,
And look upon their kindness, and take more,
And look on that; still bearing them in hand,° *leading them on*
Letting the cherry knock against their lips,
And draw it by their mouths, and back again.[5]—
How now!

Scene 2

[*Reenter Mosca with Nano, Androgyno, and Castrone*.]

NANO *Now, room for fresh gamesters, who do will you to know,*

4. Romagnia was a sweet Greek wine; Candian was a Cretan wine. Italian wine was considered inferior.

5. As in the game of bobbing for cherries.

They do bring you neither play nor university show;
And therefore do entreat you, that whatsoever they rehearse,
May not fare a whit the worse, for the false pace of the verse.[6]
If you wonder at this, you will wonder more ere we pass,
For know, here is enclosed the soul of Pythagoras,[7]
That juggler divine, as hereafter shall follow;
Which soul, fast and loose, sir, came first from Apollo,
And was breathed into Aethalides,[8] *Mercurius his son,*
Where it had the gift to remember all that ever was done.
From thence it fled forth, and made quick transmigration
To goldly-locked Euphorbus,[9] *who was killed in good fashion,*
At the siege of old Troy, by the cuckold of Sparta.[1]
Hermotimus was next (I find it in my charta)
To whom it did pass, where no sooner it was missing
But with one Pyrrhus of Delos it learned to go a fishing;
And thence did it enter the sophist of Greece.[2]
From Pythagore, she went into a beautiful piece,
Hight Aspasia, the meretrix;[3] *and the next toss of her*
Was again of a whore, she became a philosopher,
Crates the cynick, as it self doth relate it:
Since kings, knights, and beggars, knaves, lords, and fools gat it,
Besides ox and ass, camel, mule, goat, and brock,[4]
In all which it hath spoke, as in the cobler's cock.[5]
But I come not here to discourse of that matter,
Or his one, two, or three, or his great oath, By Quater![6]
His musics, his trigon, his golden thigh,
Or his telling how elements shift, but I
Would ask, how of late thou hast suffered translation,
And shifted thy coat in these days of reformation.

ANDROGYNO *Like one of the reformed, a fool, as you see,*
Counting all old doctrine heresie.

NANO *But not on thine own forbid meats hast thou ventured?*

ANDROGYNO *On fish, when first a Carthusian I entered.*[7]

NANO *Why, then thy dogmatical silence hath left thee?*

ANDROGYNO *Of that an obstreperous lawyer bereft me.*

NANO *O wonderful change, when sir lawyer forsook thee!*
For Pythagore's sake, what body then took thee?

ANDROGYNO *A good dull mule.*

NANO *And how! by that means*
Thou wert brought to allow of the eating of beans?[8]

ANDROGYNO *Yes.*

6. The irregular meter recalls the four-stress line of the mortality plays.

7. Nano points at Androgyno. Nano's comic story of a divine lineage imitates Diogenes Laertius's life of Pythagoras, an ancient Greek philosopher who developed the theory of the transmigration of souls.

8. Herald of the Argonauts.

9. The Trojan hero who first wounded Patroclus.

1. Menelaus, whose wife went off with Paris.

2. Pythagoras, whose biography includes Hermotimus, a prophet whose soul frequently left his body, and Pyrrhus, a fisherman of Delos.

3. Prostitute; actually Aspasia was simply Pericles' lover.

4. Badger.

5. Lucian's *Gallus* (Cock) is a comic dialogue between a cobbler and a cock that also mocks Pythagoras.

6. "By four." A reference to the Pythagorean theory of the tetrad, by which the first four numbers when added yielded the number 10. Pythagoras, known for his theories of music and geometry, was also said to have a golden thigh.

7. As a Carthusian monk, he ate fish, forbidden to the vegetarian Pythagoreans.

8. Pythagoreans were not allowed to eat beans.

NANO *But from the mule into whom didst thou pass?*
ANDROGYNO *Into a very strange beast, by some writers called an ass;*
By others, a precise, pure, illuminate brother,[9]
Of those devour flesh, and sometimes one another;
And will drop you forth a libel, or a sanctified lie,
Betwixt every spoonful of a nativity-pie.
NANO *Now quit thee, for heaven, of that profane nation,*
And gently report thy next transmigration.
ANDROGYNO *To the same that I am.*
NANO *A creature of delight,*
And, what is more than a fool, an hermaphrodite!
Now, prithee, sweet soul, in all thy variation,
Which body would'st thou choose, to keep up thy station?
ANDROGYNO *Troth, this I am in: even here would I tarry.*
NANO *'Cause here the delight of each sex thou canst vary?*
ANDROGYNO *Alas, those pleasures be stale and forsaken;*
No, 'tis your fool wherewith I am so taken,
The only one creature that I can call blessed;
For all other forms I have proved most distressed.
NANO *Spoke true, as thou wert in Pythagoras still.*
This learned opinion we celebrate will,
Fellow eunuch, as behoves us, with all our wit and art,
To dignify that whereof ourselves are so great and special a part.
VOLPONE Now, very, very pretty! Mosca, this
Was thy invention?
MOSCA If it please my patron,
Not else.
VOLPONE It doth, good Mosca.
MOSCA Then it was, sir.
[*Nano and Castrone sing.*]

Fools, they are the only nation
Worth men's envy or admiration:
Free from care of sorrow-taking,
Selves and others merry making:
All they speak or do is sterling.
Your fool he is your great man's darling,
And your ladies' sport and pleasure;
Tongue and bauble are his treasure.
E'en his face begetteth laughter,
And he speaks truth free from slaughter;
He's the grace of every feast,
And sometimes the chiefest guest;
Hath his trencher° and his stool, *dish*
When wit waits upon the fool.
O, who would not be
He, he, he? [*Knocking without.*]

9. Describing the Puritans, who called each other "brother," as nit-picking and self-righteous, Johnson mocks their aversion to the word Christmas, for which they substituted "nativity."

VOLPONE Who's that? Away! [*Exeunt Nano and Castrone.*]
Look, Mosca. Fool, begone! [*Exit Androgyno.*]
MOSCA 'Tis signior Voltore, the advocate;
I know him by his knock.
VOLPONE Fetch me my gown,
My furs and night-caps; say my couch is changing,
And let him entertain himself awhile
Without i' the gallery. [*Exit Mosca.*] Now, now, my clients
Begin their visitation! Vulture, kite,
Raven, and gorcrow, all my birds of prey,
That think me turning carcase, now they come;
I am not for them yet—
[*Reenter Mosca, with the gown, etc.*]
How now! the news?
MOSCA A piece of plate,° sir. *silver plater*
VOLPONE Of what bigness?
MOSCA Huge,
Massy, and antique, with your name inscribed,
And arms engraven.
VOLPONE Good! and not a fox
Stretched on the earth, with fine delusive sleights,
Mocking a gaping crow?[1] ha, Mosca!
MOSCA Sharp, sir.
VOLPONE Give me my furs. [*Puts on his sick dress.*]
Why dost thou laugh so, man?
MOSCA I cannot choose, sir, when I apprehend
What thoughts he has without now, as he walks:
That this might be the last gift he should give;
That this would fetch you; if you died to-day,
And gave him all, what he should be to-morrow;
What large return would come of all his ventures;
How he should worshipped be, and reverenced;
Ride with his furs and foot-cloths; waited on
By herds of fools and clients; have clear way
Made for his mule, as lettered as himself;
Be called the great and learned advocate:
And then concludes, there's nought impossible.
VOLPONE Yes, to be learned, Mosca.
MOSCA O, no: rich
Implies it. Hood an ass with reverend purple,
So you can hide his two ambitious ears,
And he shall pass for a cathedral doctor.° *of theology*
VOLPONE My caps, my caps, good Mosca. Fetch him in.
MOSCA Stay, sir; your ointment for your eyes.
VOLPONE That's true;
Dispatch,° dispatch: I long to have possession *hurry*
Of my new present.
MOSCA That, and thousands more,

1. Volpone alludes to an animal fable about a fox who played dead to trick a crow.

I hope to see you lord of.
VOLPONE Thanks, kind Mosca.
MOSCA And that, when I am lost in blended dust,
And hundred such as I am, in succession—
VOLPONE Nay, that were too much, Mosca.
MOSCA You shall live,
Still, to delude these harpies.[2]
VOLPONE Loving Mosca!
'Tis well: my pillow now, and let him enter. [*Exit Mosca.*]
Now, my feigned cough, my phthisic,° and my gout, *asthma*
My apoplexy, palsy, and catarrhs,
Help, with your forced functions, this my posture,
Wherein, this three year, I have milked their hopes.
He comes; I hear him—Uh! [*Coughing.*] uh! uh! uh! O—

Scene 3

[*Reenter Mosca, introducing Voltore, with a piece of plate.*]
MOSCA You still are what you were, sir. Only you,
Of all the rest, are he commands his love,
And you do wisely to preserve it thus,
With early visitation, and kind notes
Of your good meaning to him, which, I know,
Cannot but come most grateful. Patron! sir!
Here's signior Voltore is come—
VOLPONE [*faintly*] What say you?
MOSCA Sir, signior Voltore is come this morning
To visit you.
VOLPONE I thank him.
MOSCA And hath brought
A piece of antique plate, bought of St. Mark,° *in St. Mark's square*
With which he here presents you.
VOLPONE He is welcome.
Pray him to come more often.
MOSCA Yes.
VOLTORE What says he?
MOSCA He thanks you, and desires you see him often.
VOLPONE Mosca.
MOSCA My patron!
VOLPONE Bring him near, where is he?
I long to feel his hand.
MOSCA The plate is here, sir.
VOLTORE How fare you, sir?
VOLPONE I thank you, signior Voltore;
Where is the plate? mine eyes are bad.
VOLTORE [*putting it into his hands*] I'm sorry
To see you still thus weak.
MOSCA [*aside*] That he's not weaker.

2. Monstrous birds of vengeance; hence people who prey upon others.

VOLPONE You are too munificent.
VOLTORE No, sir; would to heaven,
I could as well give health to you, as that plate!
VOLPONE You give, sir, what you can: I thank you. Your love
Hath taste in this, and shall not be unanswered:
I pray you see me often.
VOLTORE Yes, I shall, sir.
VOLPONE Be not far from me.
MOSCA Do you observe that, sir?
VOLPONE Hearken unto me still; it will concern you.
MOSCA You are a happy man, sir; know your good.
VOLPONE I cannot now last long—
MOSCA You are his heir, sir.
VOLTORE Am I?
VOLPONE I feel me going; Uh! uh! uh! uh!
I'm sailing to my port, Uh! uh! uh! uh!
And I am glad I am so near my haven.
MOSCA Alas, kind gentleman! Well, we must all go—
VOLTORE But, Mosca—
MOSCA Age will conquer.
VOLTORE 'Pray thee, hear me:
Am I inscribed his heir for certain?
MOSCA Are you!
I do beseech you, sir, you will vouchsafe
To write me in your family. All my hopes
Depend upon your worship: I am lost,
Except the rising sun do shine on me.
VOLTORE It shall both shine and warm thee, Mosca.
MOSCA Sir,
I am a man, that hath not done your love
All the worst offices:° here I wear your keys, *duties*
See all your coffers and your caskets locked,
Keep the poor inventory of your jewels,
Your plate and monies; am your steward, sir,
Husband° your goods here. *protect*
VOLTORE But am I sole heir?
MOSCA Without a partner, sir; confirmed this morning:
The wax is warm yet, and the ink scarce dry
Upon the parchment.
VOLTORE Happy, happy me!
By what good chance, sweet Mosca?
MOSCA Your desert, sir;
I know no second cause.
VOLTORE Thy modesty
Is not to know it; well, we shall requite it.
MOSCA He ever liked your course, sir; that first took him.
I oft have heard him say how he admired
Men of your large profession, that could speak
To every cause, and things mere contraries,
Till they were hoarse again, yet all be law;

That, with most quick agility, could turn,
And re-return; could make knots, and undo them;
Give forked° counsel; take provoking gold *equivocal*
On either hand, and put it up:[3] these men,
He knew, would thrive with their humility.
And for his part, he thought he should be blest
To have his heir of such a suffering spirit,
So wise, so grave, of so perplexed a tongue,
And loud withal, that would not wag, nor scarce
Lie still, without a fee; when every word
Your worship but lets fall, is a chequin![4]—[*Knocking without.*]
Who's that? one knocks; I would not have you seen, sir.
And yet—pretend you came, and went in haste:
I'll fashion an excuse—and, gentle sir,
When you do come to swim in golden lard,
Up to the arms in honey, that your chin
Is borne up stiff with fatness of the flood,
Think on your vassal; but remember me:
I have not been your worst of clients.

VOLTORE Mosca!—

MOSCA When will you have your inventory brought, sir?
Or see a copy of the will?—Anon![5]—
I'll bring them to you, sir. Away, be gone,
Put business in your face. [*Exit Voltore.*]

VOLPONE [*springing up*] Excellent Mosca!
Come hither, let me kiss thee.

MOSCA Keep you still, sir.
Here is Corbaccio.

VOLPONE Set the plate away:
The vulture's gone, and the old raven's come!

Scene 4

MOSCA Betake you to your silence, and your sleep.
Stand there and multiply. [*Putting the plate to the rest.*]
Now, shall we see
A wretch who is indeed more impotent
Than this can feign to be; yet hopes to hop
Over his grave—
[*Enter Corbaccio.*]
Signior Corbaccio!
You're very welcome, sir.

CORBACCIO How does your patron?

MOSCA Troth, as he did, sir; no amends.

CORBACCIO What! mends he?

MOSCA No, sir: he's rather worse.

CORBACCIO That's well. Where is he?

MOSCA Upon his couch, sir, newly fall'n asleep.

3. Accept money from opposing sides and keep it.
4. A gold coin.
5. A response to the knocking at the door.

CORBACCIO Does he sleep well?
MOSCA No wink, sir, all this night.
Nor yesterday; but slumbers.° *catnaps*
CORBACCIO Good! he should take
Some counsel of physicians: I have brought him
An opiate here, from mine own doctor.
MOSCA He will not hear of drugs.
CORBACCIO Why? I myself
Stood by while it was made, saw all the ingredients:
And know it cannot but most gently work:
My life for his, 'tis but to make him sleep.
VOLPONE [*aside*] Ay, his last sleep, if he would take it.
MOSCA Sir,
He has no faith in physic.
CORBACCIO Say you, say you?
MOSCA He has no faith in physic: he does think
Most of your doctors are the greater danger,
And worse disease, to escape. I often have
Heard him protest that your physician
Should never be his heir.
CORBACCIO Not I his heir?
MOSCA Not your physician, sir.
CORBACCIO O, no, no, no,
I do not mean it.
MOSCA No, sir, nor their fees
He cannot brook: he says they flay a man,
Before they kill him.
CORBACCIO Right, I do conceive you.
MOSCA And then they do it by experiment;
For which the law not only doth absolve them,
But gives them great reward: and he is loth
To hire his death, so.
CORBACCIO It is true, they kill
With as much license as a judge.
MOSCA Nay, more;
For he but kills, sir, where the law condemns,
And these can kill him too.
CORBACCIO Ay, or me;
Or any man. How does his apoplex?
Is that strong on him still?
MOSCA Most violent.
His speech is broken and his eyes are set,
His face drawn longer than 'twas wont—
CORBACCIO How! how!
Stronger than he was wont?
MOSCA No, sir: his face
Drawn longer than 'twas wont.
CORBACCIO O, good!
MOSCA His mouth
Is ever gaping, and his eyelids hang.

CORBACCIO Good.
MOSCA A freezing numbness stiffens all his joints,
And makes the color of his flesh like lead.
CORBACCIO 'Tis good.
MOSCA His pulse beats slow and dull.
CORBACCIO Good symptoms still.
MOSCA And from his brain—
CORBACCIO I conceive you; good.
MOSCA Flows a cold sweat, with a continual rheum,
Forth the resolved corners of his eyes.
CORBACCIO Is't possible? Yet I am better, ha!
How does he with the swimming of his head?
MOSCA O, sir, 'tis past the scotomy;° he now *dizziness*
Hath lost his feeling, and hath left to snort:
You hardly can perceive him that he breathes.
CORBACCIO Excellent, excellent! sure I shall outlast him:
This makes me young again, a score of years.
MOSCA I was a coming for you, sir.
CORBACCIO Has he made his will?
What has he given me?
MOSCA No, sir.
CORBACCIO Nothing! ha?
MOSCA He has not made his will, sir.
CORBACCIO Oh, oh, oh!
What then did Voltore, the lawyer, here?
MOSCA He smelt a carcase, sir, when he but heard
My master was about his testament;
As I did urge him to it for your good—
CORBACCIO He came unto him, did he? I thought so.
MOSCA Yes, and presented him this piece of plate.
CORBACCIO To be his heir?
MOSCA I do not know, sir.
CORBACCIO True:
I know it too.
MOSCA [*aside*] By your own scale, sir.
CORBACCIO Well,
I shall prevent him, yet. See, Mosca, look,
Here, I have brought a bag of bright chequines,
Will quite weigh down his plate.
MOSCA [*taking the bag*] Yea, marry, sir.
This is true physic, this your sacred medicine;
No talk of opiates to this great elixir![6]
CORBACCIO 'Tis aurum palpabile, if not potabile.[7]
MOSCA It shall be ministered to him in his bowl.
CORBACCIO Ay, do, do, do.
MOSCA Most blessed cordial!
This will recover him.
CORBACCIO Yes, do, do, do.

6. No sedative can compete with this great medicine.
7. Material gold, if not drinkable, as the elixir was.

MOSCA I think it were not best, sir.
CORBACCIO What?
MOSCA To recover him.
CORBACCIO O, no, no, no; by no means.
MOSCA Why, sir, this
Will work some strange effect, if he but feel it.
CORBACCIO 'Tis true, therefore forbear; I'll take my venture:
Give me it again.
MOSCA At no hand; pardon me:
You shall not do yourself that wrong, sir. I
Will so advise you, you shall have it all.
CORBACCIO How?
MOSCA All, sir; 'tis your right, your own: no man
Can claim a part: 'tis yours, without a rival,
Decreed by destiny.
CORBACCIO How, how, good Mosca?
MOSCA I'll tell you, sir. This fit he shall recover.
CORBACCIO I do conceive you.
MOSCA And, on first advantage
Of his gained sense, will I re-importune him
Unto the making of his testament:
And shew him this. [*Pointing to the money.*]
CORBACCIO Good, good.
MOSCA 'Tis better yet,
If you will hear, sir.
CORBACCIO Yes, with all my heart.
MOSCA Now would I counsel you, make home with speed;
There, frame a will; whereto you shall inscribe
My master your sole heir.
CORBACCIO And disinherit
My son!
MOSCA O, sir, the better: for that color
Shall make it much more taking.[8]
CORBACCIO O, but color?
MOSCA This will, sir, you shall send it unto me.
Now when I come to inforce, as I will do,
Your cares, your watchings, and your many prayers,
Your more than many gifts, your this day's present,
And last, produce your will; where, without thought,
Or least regard, unto your proper issue,
A son so brave and highly meriting,
The stream of your diverted love hath thrown you
Upon my master, and made him your heir:
He cannot be so stupid or stone-dead,
But out of conscience and mere gratitude—
CORBACCIO He must pronounce me his?
MOSCA 'Tis true.
CORBACCIO This plot

8. If it seems that you are disinheriting your son, the trick will be more convincing.

Did I think on before.
MOSCA I do believe it.
CORBACCIO Do you not believe it?
MOSCA Yes, sir.
CORBACCIO Mine own project.
MOSCA Which, when he hath done, sir—
CORBACCIO Published me his heir?
MOSCA And you so certain to survive him—
CORBACCIO Ay.
MOSCA Being so lusty a man—
CORBACCIO 'Tis true.
MOSCA Yes, sir—
CORBACCIO I thought on that too. See, how he should be
The very organ to express my thoughts!
MOSCA You have not only done yourself a good—
CORBACCIO But multiplied it on my son.
MOSCA 'Tis right, sir.
CORBACCIO Still, my invention.
MOSCA 'Las, sir! heaven knows,
It hath been all my study, all my care,
(I e'en grow gray withal), how to work things—
CORBACCIO I do conceive, sweet Mosca.
MOSCA You are he,
For whom I labor here.
CORBACCIO Ay, do, do, do:
I'll straight about it. [*Going*.]
MOSCA Rook go with you, raven![9]
CORBACCIO I know thee honest.
MOSCA [*aside*] You do lie, sir!
CORBACCIO And—
MOSCA Your knowledge is no better than your ears, sir.
CORBACCIO I do not doubt to be a father to thee.
MOSCA Nor I to gull my brother of his blessing.[1]
CORBACCIO I may have my youth restored to me, why not?
MOSCA Your worship is a precious ass!
CORBACCIO What say'st thou?
MOSCA I do desire your worship to make haste, sir.
CORBACCIO 'Tis done, 'tis done; I go. [*Exit*.]
VOLPONE [*leaping from his couch*] O, I shall burst!
Let out my sides, let out my sides[2]
MOSCA Contain
Your flux of laughter, sir: you know this hope
Is such a bait it covers any hook.
VOLPONE O, but thy working, and thy placing it!
I cannot hold; good rascal, let me kiss thee:
I never knew thee in so rare a humor.

9. Playing on the secondary meaning of rook, a crowlike bird: cheat.
1. Mosca refers to Bonario, Corbaccio's son. Jacob robbed his brother Esau of his blessing (Genesis 27).
2. Loosen my clothes.

MOSCA Alas, sir, I but do as I am taught;
Follow your grave instructions; give them words;
Pour oil° into their ears, and send them hence. (flattery)

VOLPONE 'Tis true, 'tis true. What a rare punishment
Is avarice to itself![3]

MOSCA Ay, with our help, sir.

VOLPONE So many cares, so many maladies,
So many fears attending on old age,
Yea, death so often called on, as no wish
Can be more frequent with them, their limbs faint,
Their senses dull, their seeing, hearing, going,
All dead before them; yea, their very teeth,
Their instruments of eating, failing them:
Yet this is reckoned life! nay, here was one
Is now gone home, that wishes to live longer!
Feels not his gout, nor palsy; feigns himself
Younger by scores of years, flatters his age
With confident belying it, hopes he may,
With charms, like Aeson,[4] have his youth restored:
And with these thoughts so battens as if fate
Would be as easily cheated on as he,
And all turns air! [*Knocking within.*] Who's that there, now? a third!

MOSCA Close, to your couch again; I hear his voice:
It is Corvino, our spruce merchant.

VOLPONE [*lies down as before*] Dead.

MOSCA Another bout, sir, with your eyes. [*Anointing them.*] —Who's there?

Scene 5

[*Enter Corvino.*]
Signior Corvino! come most wished for! O,
How happy were you, if you knew it, now!

CORVINO Why? what? wherein?

MOSCA The tardy hour is come, sir.

CORVINO He is not dead?

MOSCA Not dead, sir, but as good;
He knows no man.

CORVINO How shall I do then?

MOSCA Why, sir?

CORVINO I have brought him here a pearl.

MOSCA Perhaps he has
So much remembrance left as to know you, sir:
He still calls on you; nothing but your name
Is in his mouth. Is your pearl orient,[5] sir?

CORVINO Venice was never owner of the like.

VOLPONE [*faintly*] Signior Corvino!

MOSCA Hark.

VOLPONE Signior Corvino!

MOSCA He calls you; step and give it him.—He's here, sir,

3. Seneca, *Epistle* 115.6.
4. Jason's father, restored to life by Medea's magic.
5. From the east, where the pearls were most lustrous.

And he has brought you a rich pearl.

CORVINO How do you, sir?
Tell him, it doubles the twelfth carat.

MOSCA Sir,
He cannot understand, his hearing's gone;
And yet it comforts him to see you—

CORVINO Say,
I have a diamond for him, too.

MOSCA Best shew it, sir;
Put it into his hand; 'tis only there
He apprehends:[6] he has his feeling, yet.
See how he grasps it!

CORVINO 'Las, good gentleman!
How pitiful the sight is!

MOSCA Tut! forget, sir.
The weeping of an heir should still be laughter
Under a visor.

CORVINO Why, am I his heir?

MOSCA Sir, I am sworn, I may not shew the will
Till he be dead; but here has been Corbaccio,
Here has been Voltore, here were others too,
I cannot number 'em, they were so many;
All gaping here for legacies: but I,
Taking the vantage of his naming you,
Signior Corvino, Signior Corvino, took
Paper, and pen, and ink, and there I asked him,
Whom he would have his heir? *Corvino.* Who
Should be executor? *Corvino.* And,
To any question he was silent to,
I still interpreted the nods he made,
Through weakness, for consent: and sent home th' others,
Nothing bequeathed them but to cry and curse.

CORVINO O, my dear Mosca! [*They embrace.*] Does he not perceive us?

MOSCA No more than a blind harper. He knows no man,
No face of friend, nor name of any servant,
Who 'twas that fed him last, or gave him drink:
Not those he hath begotten or brought up
Can he remember.

CORVINO Has he children?

MOSCA Bastards,
Some dozen or more, that he begot on beggars,
Gypsies, and Jews, and black-moors, when he was drunk.
Knew you not that, sir? 'Tis the common fable.[7]
The dwarf, the fool, the eunuch, are all his;
He's the true father of his family,
In all, save me:—but he has given them nothing.

CORVINO That's well, that's well! Art sure he does not hear us?

MOSCA Sure, sir! why, look you, credit your own sense. [*Shouts in Volpone's ear.*]
The pox approach and add to your diseases,

6. Playing on the Latin *apprehendere*, "to take hold of."
7. It's widely believed.

If it would send you hence the sooner, sir,
For your incontinence, it hath deserved it
Thoroughly, and thoroughly, and the plague to boot!—
You may come near, sir.—Would you would once close
Those filthy eyes of yours, that flow with slime
Like two frog-pits; and those same hanging cheeks,
Covered with hide instead of skin—Nay, help, sir—
That look like frozen dish-clouts set on end!

CORVINO [*aloud*] Or like an old smoked wall on which the rain
Ran down in streaks!

MOSCA Excellent, sir! speak out:
You may be louder yet; a culverin° *cannon*
Discharged in his ear would hardly bore it.

CORVINO His nose is like a common sewer, still running.

MOSCA 'Tis good! And what his mouth?

CORVINO A very draught.° *cesspool*

MOSCA O, stop it up—

CORVINO By no means.

MOSCA 'Pray you, let me:
Faith I could stifle him rarely with a pillow,
As well as any woman that should keep him.

CORVINO Do as you will; but I'll begone.

MOSCA Be so:
It is your presence makes him last so long.

CORVINO I pray you, use no violence.

MOSCA No, sir! why?
Why should you be thus scrupulous, pray you, sir?

CORVINO Nay, at your discretion.

MOSCA Well, good sir, begone.

CORVINO I will not trouble him now to take my pearl.

MOSCA Puh! nor your diamond. What a needless care
Is this afflicts you? Is not all here yours?
Am not I here, whom you have made your creature?
That owe my being to you?

CORVINO Grateful Mosca!
Thou art my friend, my fellow, my companion,
My partner, and shalt share in all my fortunes.

MOSCA Excepting one.

CORVINO What's that?

MOSCA Your gallant wife, sir,—[*Exit Corvino.*]
Now is he gone: we had no other means
To shoot him hence, but this.

VOLPONE My divine Mosca!
Thou hast today outgone thyself. [*Knocking within.*]—Who's there?
I will be troubled with no more. Prepare
Me music, dances, banquets, all delights;
The Turk is not more sensual in his pleasures
Than will Volpone. [*Exit Mosca.*] Let me see; a pearl!
A diamond! plate! chequines! Good morning's purchase.
Why, this is better than rob churches, yet;
Or fat, by eating, once a month, a man—

[*Reenter Mosca.*]
Who is't?
MOSCA The beauteous Lady Would-be, sir,
Wife to the English knight Sir Politic Would-be
(This is the style, sir, is directed me),
Hath sent to know how you have slept to-night,
And if you would be visited?
VOLPONE Not now:
Some three hours hence—
MOSCA I told the squire so much.
VOLPONE When I am high with mirth and wine; then, then:
'Fore heaven, I wonder at the desperate valor
Of the bold English, that they dare let loose
Their wives to all encounters!
MOSCA Sir, this knight
Had not his name for nothing, he is politic,° *devious, subtle*
And knows, howe'er his wife affect strange airs,
She hath not yet the face to be dishonest:
But had she Signior Corvino's wife's face—
VOLPONE Has she so rare a face?
MOSCA O, sir, the wonder,
The blazing star of Italy! a wench
Of the first year! a beauty ripe as harvest!
Whose skin is whiter than a swan all over
Than silver, snow, or lilies! a soft lip
Would tempt you to eternity of kissing!
And flesh that melteth in the touch to blood!
Bright as your gold, and lovely as your gold!
VOLPONE Why had not I known this before?
MOSCA Alas, sir,
Myself but yesterday discovered it.
VOLPONE How might I see her?
MOSCA O, not possible;
She's kept as warily as is your gold;
Never does come abroad, never takes air,
But at a window. All her looks are sweet,
As the first grapes or cherries, and are watched
As near as they are.
VOLPONE I must see her.
MOSCA Sir,
There is a guard of spies ten thick upon her,
All his whole household; each of which is set
Upon his fellow, and have all their charge,
When he goes out, when he comes in, examined.
VOLPONE I will go see her, though but at her window.
MOSCA In some disguise, then.
VOLPONE That is true; I must
Maintain mine own shape[8] still the same: we'll think. [*Exeunt.*]

8. Physical appearance, disguise, and theatrical role.

Act 2

Scene 1. *St. Mark's Place; a retired corner before Corvino's house*

[*Enter Sir Politic Would-be and Peregrine.*]

SIR POLITIC Sir, to a wise man, all the world's his soil:
It is not Italy, nor France, nor Europe
That must bound me, if my fates call me forth.
Yet, I protest, it is no salt desire
Of seeing countries, shifting a religion,
Nor any disaffection to the state
Where I was bred, and unto which I owe
My dearest plots,° hath brought me out; much less *ideas*
That idle, antique, stale, gray-headed project
Of knowing men's minds and manners, with Ulysses!
But a peculiar humor of my wife's,
Laid for this height of Venice, to observe,
To quote, to learn the language, and so forth—
I hope you travel, sir, with license?° *passport*

PEREGRINE Yes.

SIR POLITIC I dare the safelier converse—How long, sir,
Since you left England?

PEREGRINE Seven weeks.

SIR POLITIC So lately!
You have not been with my lord ambassador?

PEREGRINE Not yet, sir.

SIR POLITIC Pray you, what news, sir, vents our climate?[1]
I heard last night a most strange thing reported
By some of my lord's followers, and I long
To hear how 'twill be seconded.

PEREGRINE What was't, sir?

SIR POLITIC Marry, sir, of a raven[2] that should build
In a ship royal of the king's.

PEREGRINE [*aside*] This fellow,
Does he gull me, trow?[3] or is gull'd?—Your name, sir.

SIR POLITIC My name is Politic Would-be.

PEREGRINE [*aside*] O, that speaks him.—
A knight, sir?

SIR POLITIC A poor knight, sir.

PEREGRINE Your lady
Lies here in Venice, for intelligence
Of tires,° and fashions, and behavior *attire*
Among the courtesans?[4] the fine lady Would-be?

SIR POLITIC Yes, sir; the spider and the bee, ofttimes,
Suck from one flower.

PEREGRINE Good sir Politic,
I cry you mercy; I have heard much of you:
'Tis true, sir, of your raven.

SIR POLITIC On your knowledge?

1. Comes from our country.
2. A bird that bodes ill.
3. Does he try to fool me; do you think?
4. Venetian prostitutes were famously stylish.

PEREGRINE Yes, and your lion's whelping in the Tower.[5]
SIR POLITIC Another whelp!
PEREGRINE Another, sir.
SIR POLITIC Now heaven!
What prodigies be these? The fires at Berwick!
And the new star![6] These things concurring, strange,
And full of omen! Saw you those meteors?
PEREGRINE I did, sir.
SIR POLITIC Fearful! Pray you, sir, confirm me,
Were there three porpoises seen above the bridge,
As they give out?
PEREGRINE Six, and a sturgeon, sir.
SIR POLITIC I am astonished.
PEREGRINE Nay, sir, be not so;
I'll tell you a greater prodigy than these.
SIR POLITIC What should these things portend?
PEREGRINE The very day
(Let me be sure) that I put forth from London,
There was a whale discovered in the river,
As high as Woolwich, that had waited there,
Few know how many months, for the subversion
Of the Stode fleet.
SIR POLITIC Is't possible? believe it,
'Twas either sent from Spain, or the Archduke's:
Spinola's whale, upon my life, my credit![7]
Will they not leave these projects? Worthy sir,
Some other news.
PEREGRINE Faith, Stone the fool is dead,
And they do lack a tavern fool extremely.
SIR POLITIC Is Mass° Stone dead? *master*
PEREGRINE He's dead, sir; why, I hope
You thought him not immortal?—[*Aside:*] O, this knight,
Were he well known, would be a precious thing
To fit our English stage; he that should write
But such a fellow, should be thought to feign
Extremely, if not maliciously.
SIR POLITIC Stone dead!
PEREGRINE Dead.—Lord! how deeply, sir, you apprehend it?
He was no kinsman to you?
SIR POLITIC That I know of.
Well! that same fellow was an unknown fool.
PEREGRINE And yet you knew him, it seems?
SIR POLITIC I did so. Sir,
I knew him one of the most dangerous heads
Living within the state, and so I held him.
PEREGRINE Indeed, sir?

5. Lions were kept in the Tower of London.
6. Unusual northern lights had appeared over Berwick late in 1604, and a comet appeared that October.
7. Sir Politic believes the popular rumor that there was a whale sent to drown the people of London by the Spanish viceroy in the Netherlands, or by his general, Ambrosio Spinola.

SIR POLITIC While he lived, in action.
He has received weekly intelligence,
Upon my knowledge, out of the Low Countries;
For all parts of the world, in cabbages;
And those dispensed again to ambassadors,
In oranges, musk-melons, apricocks,
Lemons, pome-citrons, and such-like; sometimes
In Colchester oysters, and your Selsey cockles.

PEREGRINE You make me wonder.

SIR POLITIC Sir, upon my knowledge.
Nay, I've observed him, at your public ordinary,° *tavern*
Take his advertisement° from a traveler, *information*
A concealed statesman, in a trencher of meat;
And instantly, before the meal was done,
Convey an answer in a tooth-pick.

PEREGRINE Strange!
How could this be, sir?

SIR POLITIC Why, the meat was cut
So like his character, and so laid, as he
Must easily read the cipher.

PEREGRINE I have heard
He could not read, sir.

SIR POLITIC So 'twas given out,
In policy, by those that did employ him:
But he could read, and had your languages,
And to't,° as sound a noddle— *what's more*

PEREGRINE I have heard, sir,
That your baboons were spies, and that they were
A kind of subtle nation near to China.

SIR POLITIC Ay, ay, your Mamaluchi.[8] Faith, they had
Their hand in a French plot or two; but they
Were so extremely given to women, as
They made discovery of all; yet I
Had my advices here, on Wednesday last.
From one of their own coat they were returned,
Made their relations, as the fashion is,
And now stand fair for fresh employment.

PEREGRINE [*aside*] 'Heart!
This sir Pol will be ignorant of nothing.
It seems, sir, you know all.

SIR POLITIC Not all, sir, but
I have some general notions. I do love
To note and to observe; though I live out,
Free from the active torrent, yet I'd mark
The currents and the passages of things
For mine own private use; and know the ebbs
And flows of state.

PEREGRINE Believe it, sir, I hold
Myself in no small tie unto my fortunes

8. A military body, ruling Egypt, originally coming from Asia Minor.

For casting me thus luckily upon you,
Whose knowledge, if your bounty equal it,
May do me great assistance, in instruction
For my behavior and my bearing, which
Is yet so rude and raw.

SIR POLITIC Why, came you forth
Empty of rules for travel?

PEREGRINE Faith, I had
Some common ones, from out that vulgar° grammar, *vernacular*
Which he that cried Italian to me, taught me.

SIR POLITIC Why this it is that spoils all our brave bloods,
Trusting our hopeful gentry unto pedants,
Fellows of outside, and mere bark. You seem
To be a gentleman, of ingenuous race:°— *honorable descent*
I not profess it, but my fate hath been
To be where I have been consulted with,
In this high kind, touching some great men's sons,
Persons of blood and honor.—

Scene 2

[*Enter Mosca and Nano disguised, followed by persons with materials for erecting a Stage.*]

PEREGRINE Who be these, sir?

MOSCA Under that window, there't must be. The same.

SIR POLITIC Fellows, to mount a bank. Did your instructor
In the dear tongues never discourse to you
Of the Italian mountebanks?[9]

PEREGRINE Yes, sir.

SIR POLITIC Why,
Here you shall see one.

PEREGRINE They are quacksalvers;
Fellows that live by venting° oils and drugs. *vending*

SIR POLITIC Was that the character he gave you of them?

PEREGRINE As I remember.

SIR POLITIC Pity his ignorance.
They are the only knowing men of Europe!
Great general scholars, excellent physicians,
Most admired statesmen, profest favorites,
And cabinet counselors to the greatest princes;
The only languaged men of all the world!

PEREGRINE And I have heard they are most lewd° impostors; *ignorant*
Made all of terms and shreds; no less beliers
Of great men's favors than their own vile medicines;
Which they will utter upon monstrous oaths:
Selling that drug for two-pence, ere they part,
Which they have valued at twelve crowns before.

SIR POLITIC Sir, calumnies are answered best with silence.
Yourself shall judge.—Who is it mounts, my friends?

9. Quacks who performed on a platform (a "bank") before selling fake medicines to their audience.

MOSCA Scoto of Mantua, sir.[1]

SIR POLITIC Is't he? Nay, then
I'll proudly promise, sir, you shall behold
Another man than has been fant'sied° to you. *described*
I wonder yet, that he should mount his bank
Here in this nook, that has been wont t'appear
In face of the Piazza!—Here he comes.

[*Enter Volpone, disguised as a mountebank doctor, and followed by a crowd of people.*]

VOLPONE [*to Nano*] Mount, zany.° *fool, clown*

MOB Follow, follow, follow, follow!

SIR POLITIC See how the people follow him! he's a man
May write ten thousand crowns in bank here. Note,
[*Volpone mounts the Stage.*]
Mark but his gesture:—I do use to observe
The state he keeps in getting up.

PEREGRINE 'Tis worth it, sir.

VOLPONE *Most noble gentlemen, and my worthy patrons! It may seem strange that I, your Scoto Mantuano, who was ever wont to fix my bank in face of the public Piazza, near the shelter of the Portico to the Procuratia,*[2] *should now, after eight months' absence from this illustrious city of Venice, humbly retire myself into an obscure nook of the Piazza.*

SIR POLITIC Did not I now object the same?

PEREGRINE Peace, sir.

VOLPONE *Let me tell you: I am not, as your Lombard proverb saith, cold on my feet; or content to part with my commodities at a cheaper rate than I accustomed: look not for it. Nor that the calumnious reports of that impudent detractor and shame to our profession (Alessandro Buttone, I mean), who gave out in public I was condemned a sforzato*[3] *to the galleys, for poisoning the cardinal Bembo's——cook,*[4] *hath at all attached, much less dejected me. No, no, worthy gentlemen; to tell you true, I cannot endure to see the rabble of these ground ciarlitani,*[5] *that spread their cloaks on the pavement as if they meant to do feats of activity, and then come in lamely with their moldy tales out of Boccaccio, like stale Tabarine,*[6] *the fabulist: some of them discoursing their travels and of their tedious captivity in the Turks' galleys, when, indeed, were the truth known, they were the Christians' galleys, where very temperately they eat bread and drunk water as a wholesome penance, enjoined them by their confessors for base pilferies.*[7]

SIR POLITIC Note but his bearing and contempt of these.

VOLPONE *These turdy-facy-nasty-paty-lousy-fartical rogues, with one poor groat's-worth of unprepared antimony,*[8] *finely wrapt up in several scartoccios,*[9] *are able, very well, to kill their twenty a week, and play; yet these meager, starved spirits, who have half stopped the organs of their minds with earthy oppilations,*[1] *want not their favorers among your shrivelled salad-eating artisans, who are overjoyed that they may have their ha'f-pe'rth*[2] *of physic; though it purge them into another world, it makes no matter.*

SIR POLITIC Excellent! have you heard better language, sir?

1. A juggler and magician who had performed before Queen Elizabeth.
2. The arcade along the north side of St. Mark's square.
3. Slave.
4. Comically suppressing some term like "mistress." This tale is absurd, though; Cardinal Bembo had died 50 years before the time of the play.
5. Charlatans.
6. An Italian comedian of the previous generation.
7. Condemned criminals rowed in the Venetian galley, where they were in fact treated miserably.
8. Antimony was used as an emetic.
9. Envelopes.
1. Obstructions.
2. Half-penny worth.

VOLPONE *Well, let them go. And gentlemen, honorable gentlemen, know, that for this time, our bank, being thus removed from the clamors of the canaglia,*[3] *shall be the scene of pleasure and delight; for I have nothing to sell, little or nothing to sell.*

SIR POLITIC I told you, sir, his end.

PEREGRINE You did so, sir.

VOLPONE *I protest, I and my six servants are not able to make of this precious liquor, so fast as it is fetched away from my lodging by gentlemen of your city; strangers of the Terra-firma;*[4] *worshipful merchants; ay, and senators too: who, ever since my arrival, have detained me to their uses by their splendidous liberalities. And worthily; for what avails your rich man to have his magazines stuft with moscadelli,*[5] *or of the purest grape, when his physicians prescribe him, on pain of death, to drink nothing but water cocted with aniseeds? O, health! health! the blessing of the rich! the riches of the poor! who can buy thee at too dear a rate, since there is no enjoying this world without thee? Be not then so sparing of your purses, honorable gentlemen, as to abridge the natural course of life—*

PEREGRINE You see his end.

SIR POLITIC Ay, is't not good?

VOLPONE *For when a humid flux or catarrh, by the mutability of air, falls from your head into an arm or shoulder, or any other part, take you a ducket, or your chequin of gold, and apply to the place affected: see what good effect it can work. No, no, 'tis this blessed unguento, this rare extraction, that hath only power to disperse all malignant humors that proceed either of hot, cold, moist, or windy causes—*

PEREGRINE I would he had put in dry too.

SIR POLITIC 'Pray you, observe.

VOLPONE *To fortify the most indigest and crude stomach, ay, were it of one that, through extreme weakness, vomited blood, applying only a warm napkin to the place after the unction and fricace;*[6]*—for the vertigine in the head, putting but a drop into your nostrils, likewise behind the ears; a most sovereign and approved remedy: the mal caduco, cramps, convulsions, paralyses, epilepsies, tremor-cordia, retired nerves, ill vapors of the spleen, stopping of the liver, the stone, the strangury, hernia ventosa, iliaca passio; stops a dysenteria immediately; easeth the torsion of the small guts; and cures melancholia hypondriaca, being taken and applied according to my printed receipt.* [Pointing to his bill and his vial.] *For this is the physician, this the medicine; this counsels, this cures; this gives the direction, this works the effect; and in sum, both together may be termed an abstract of the theoric and practic in the Aesculapian*[7] *art. 'Twill cost you eight crowns. And,—Zan Fritada,*[8] *prithee sing a verse extempore in honor of it.*

SIR POLITIC How do you like him, sir?

PEREGRINE Most strangely, I!

SIR POLITIC Is not his language rare?

PEREGRINE But alchemy,
I never heard the like; or Broughton's books.[9]

[*Nano sings*.]

Had old Hippocrates or Galen,[1]
That to their books put med'cines all in,

3. The rabble.
4. The mainland.
5. A wine.
6. Anointing and rubbing in.
7. Medical.
8. Nano's stage name, Fried Fool.
9. Only alchemy and the tracts of the minor Puritan theologian Hugh Braughton are better.
1. Ancient Greek physicians.

But known this secret, they had never
(Of which they will be guilty ever)
Been murderers of so much paper,
Or wasted many a hurtless taper;
No Indian drug had e'er been famed,
Tobacco, sassafras not named;
Ne yet of guacum[2] *one small stick, sir,*
Nor Raymund Lully's great elixir.
Ne had been known the Danish Gonswart,
Or Paracelsus, with his long sword.[3]

PEREGRINE All this, yet, will not do; eight crowns is high.

VOLPONE *No more.—Gentlemen, if I had but time to discourse to you the miraculous effects of this oil, surnamed Oglio del Scoto; with the countless catalogue of those I have cured of the aforesaid and many more diseases; the patents and privileges of all the princes and commonwealths of Christendom; or but the depositions of those that appeared on my part, before the signiory of the Sanita*[4] *and most learned College of Physicians; where I was authorized, upon notice taken of the admirable virtues of my medicaments, and mine own excellency in matter of rare and unknown secrets, not only to disperse them publicly in this famous city, but in all the territories that happily joy under the government of the most pious and magnificent states of Italy. But may some other gallant fellow say, O, there be divers that make profession to have as good and as experimented receipts as yours. Indeed, very many have assayed, like apes, in imitation of that which is really and essentially in me, to make of this oil; bestowed great cost in furnices, stills, alembecks, continual fires, and preparation of the ingredients (as indeed there goes to it six hundred several simples,*[5] *besides some quality of human fat, for the conglutination, which we buy of the anatomists), but when these practitioners come to the last decoction, blow, blow, puff, puff, and all flies in fumo:*[6] *ha, ha, ha! Poor wretches! I rather pity their folly and indiscretion, than their loss of time and money; for these may be recovered by industry: but to be a fool born, is a disease incurable.*

For myself, I always from my youth have endeavored to get the rarest secrets, and book them, either in exchange, or for money. I spared not cost nor labor, where any thing was worthy to be learned. And, gentlemen, honorable gentlemen, I will undertake, by virtue of chemical art, out of the honorable hat that covers your head, to extract the four elements; that is to say, the fire, air, water, and earth, and return you your felt without burn or stain. For whilst others have been at the balloo,[7] *I have been at my book; and am now past the craggy paths of study, and come to the flowery plains of honor and reputation.*

SIR POLITIC I do assure you, sir, that is his aim.

VOLPONE But to our price—

PEREGRINE And that withal, Sir Pol.

VOLPONE *You all know, honorable gentlemen, I never valued this ampulla, or vial, at less than eight crowns; but for this time, I am content to be deprived of it for six: six crowns is the price, and less in courtesy I know you cannot offer me; take it or leave it, howsoever,*

2. Like tobacco and sassafras, New World plant products thought to have medicinal properties.
3. Raymond Lull, a 13th-century Spanish mystic philosopher, was said to have discovered the elixir of life; Paracelsus, a 16th-century German doctor, was reputed by legend to have kept medications in his sword handle.
4. Venetian medical board.
5. Separate herbs.
6. Up in smoke.
7. Balloon, a ball game.

both it and I am at your service. I ask you not as the value of the thing, for then I should demand of you a thousand crowns, so the cardinals Montalto, Farnese, the great Duke of Tuscany, my gossip, with divers other princes, have given me; but I despise money. Only to shew my affection to you honorable gentlemen and your illustrious State here, I have neglected the messages of these princes, mine own offices, framed my journey hither, only to present you with the fruits of my travels.—Tune your voices once more to the touch of your instruments, and give the honorable assembly some delightful recreation.

PEREGRINE What monstrous and most painful circumstance
Is here, to get some three or four gazettes,[8]
Some three-pence in the whole! for that 'twill come to.

[*Nano sings.*]

You that would last long, list to my song,
Make no more coil,° but buy of this oil. fuss
Would you be ever fair and young?
Stout of teeth, and strong of tongue?
Tart of palate? quick of ear?
Sharp of sight? of nostril clear?
Moist of hand? and light of foot?
Or, I will come nearer to't,
Would you live free from all diseases?
Do the act your mistress pleases,
Yet fright all aches from your bones?
Here's a medicine for the nones.° purpose

VOLPONE *Well, I am in a humor at this time to make a present of the small quantity my coffer contains; to the rich in courtesy, and to the poor for God's sake. Wherefore now mark: I asked you six crowns; and six crowns, at other times, you have paid me; you shall not give me six crowns, nor five, nor four, nor three, nor two, nor one; nor half a ducat; no, nor a moccinigo.*[9] *Sixpence it will cost you, or six hundred pound—expect no lower price, for, by the banner of my front, I will not bate a bagatine*[1]*—that I will have, only, a pledge of your loves, to carry something from amongst you, to show I am not contemned by you. Therefore, now, toss your handkerchiefs, cheerfully, cheerfully; and be advertised that the first heroic spirit that designs to grace me with a handkerchief, I will give it a little remembrance of something, beside, shall please it better, than if I had presented it with a double pistolet.*[2]

PEREGRINE Will you be that heroic spark, sir Pol?

[*Celia at a window above, throws down her handkerchief.*]

O, see! the window has prevented you.

VOLPONE *Lady, I kiss your bounty; and for this timely grace you have done your poor Scoto of Mantua, I will return you, over and above my oil, a secret of that high and inestimable nature, shall make you for ever enamored on that minute wherein your eye first descended on so mean, yet not altogether to be despised, an object. Here is a powder concealed in this paper, of which, if I should speak to the worth, nine thousand volumes were but as one page, that page as a line, that line as a word; so short is this pilgrimage of man (which some call life) to the expressing of it. Would I reflect on the price? Why, the whole world is but as an empire, that empire as a province, the province as a bank, that bank as a private purse to the purchase of it. I will only tell you: it is the powder that*

8. Venetian coins worth less than a penny.
9. Dime.
1. A fraction of a cent.
2. A Spanish coin worth close to an English pound.

made Venus a goddess (given her by Apollo), that kept her perpetually young, cleared her wrinkles, firmed her gums, filled her skin, colored her hair; from her derived to Helen, and at the sack of Troy unfortunately lost: till now, in this our age, it was as happily recovered, by a studious antiquary, out of some ruins of Asia, who sent a moiety of it to the court of France (but much sophisticated), wherewith the ladies there now color their hair. The rest at this present remains with me; extracted to a quintessence: so that wherever it but touches, in youth it perpetually preserves, in age restores the complexion; seats your teeth, did they dance like virginal jacks,[3] *firm as a wall; makes them while as ivory, that were black as—*

Scene 3

[*Enter Corvino.*]

CORVINO Spite o' the devil, and my shame! come down here;
Come down;—No house but mine to make your scene?
Signior Flaminio,[4] will you down, sir? Down?
What is my wife your Franciscina,[5] sir?
No windows on the whole Piazza here
To make your properties, but mine? But mine?
[*Beats away Volpone, Nano, etc.*]
Heart! Ere to-morrow I shall be new-christened,
And called the Pantalone di Besogniosi[6]
About the town.

PEREGRINE What should this mean, Sir Pol?

SIR POLITIC Some trick of state, believe it; I will home.

PEREGRINE It may be some design on you.

SIR POLITIC I know not,
I'll stand upon my guard.

PEREGRINE It is your best, sir.

SIR POLITIC This three weeks, all my advices, all my letters,
They have been intercepted.

PEREGRINE Indeed, sir!
Best have a care.

SIR POLITIC Nay, so I will.

PEREGRINE This knight,
I may not lose him, for my mirth, till night. [*Exeunt.*]

Scene 4. *A room in Volpone's house*

[*Enter Volpone and Mosca.*]

VOLPONE O, I am wounded!

MOSCA Where, sir?

VOLPONE Not without;
Those blows were nothing: I could bear them ever.
But angry Cupid, bolting from her eyes,
Hath shot himself into me like a flame;
Where now he flings about his burning heat,
As in a furnace an ambitious fire

3. Quills that pluck the strings of a virginal, or harpsichord.

4. A Venetian actor of Jonson's time.

5. Name of the serving girl in the Italian popular comedies (*commedia dell'arte*).

6. In the *commedia dell'arte*, an old fool and cuckold.

Whose vent is stopped. The fight is all within me.
I cannot live except thou help me, Mosca;
My liver melts, and I, without the hope
Of some soft air, from her refreshing breath,
Am but a heap of cinders.

MOSCA 'Las, good sir,
Would you had never seen her!

VOLPONE Nay, would thou
Had'st never told me of her!

MOSCA Sir, 'tis true;
I do confess I was unfortunate,
And you unhappy: but I'm bound in conscience,
No less than duty, to effect my best
To your release of torment, and I will, sir.

VOLPONE Dear Mosca, shall I hope?

MOSCA Sir, more than dear,
I will not bid you to despair of aught
With a human compass.

VOLPONE O, there spoke
My better angel. Mosca, take my keys,
Gold, plate, and jewels, all's at thy devotion;
Employ them how thou wilt; nay, coin me too:
So thou in this but crown my longings, Mosca.

MOSCA Use but your patience.

VOLPONE So I have.

MOSCA I doubt not
To bring success to your desires.

VOLPONE Nay, then,
I not repent me of my late disguise.

MOSCA If you can horn° him, sir, you need not. *cuckold*

VOLPONE True:
Besides, I never meant him for my heir.—
Is not the color of my beard and eyebrows
To make me known?

MOSCA No jot.

VOLPONE I did it well.

MOSCA So well, would I could follow you in mine
With half the happiness!—[*Aside*.] and yet I would
Escape your epilogue.

VOLPONE But were they gulled
With a belief that I was Scoto?

MOSCA Sir,
Scoto himself could hardly have distinguished!
I have not time to flatter you now; we'll part;
And as I prosper, so applaud my art. [*Exeunt*.]

Scene 5. *A room in Corvino's house*

[*Enter Corvino, with his sword in his hand, dragging in Celia*.]

CORVINO Death of mine honor, with the city's fool!
A juggling, tooth-drawing, prating mountebank!

And at a public window! Where, whilst he,
With his strained action, and his dole° of faces, *guile*
To his drug-lecture draws your itching ears,
A crew of old, unmarried, noted lechers
Stood leering up like satyrs; and you smile
Most graciously, and fan your favours forth
To give your hot spectators satisfaction!
What, was your mountebank their call? their whistle?
Or were you enamored on his copper rings,
His saffron jewel with the toad-stone in't,
Or his embroidered suit with the cope-stitch,
Made of a herse cloth?° or his old tilt-feather? *coarse fabric*
Or his starched beard? Well, you shall have him, yes!
He shall come home, and minister unto you
The fricace for the mother.[7] Or, let me see,
I think you'd rather mount; would you not mount?[8]
Why, if you'll mount, you may; yes, truly, you may:
And so you may be seen down to the foot.
Get you a cittern,° lady Vanity, *guitar*
And be a dealer with the virtuous man;
Make one: I'll but protest myself a cuckold,
And save your dowry.[9] I'm a Dutchman, I!
For, if you thought me an Italian,
You would be damned ere you did this, you whore![1]
Thou'dst tremble to imagine that the murder
Of father, mother, brother, all thy race,
Should follow as the subject of my justice.

CELIA Good sir, have patience.

CORVINO What couldst thou propose
Less to thyself, than in this heat of wrath
And stung with my dishonor, I should strike
This steel into thee, with as many stabs,
As thou wert gazed upon with goatish° eyes? *lascivious*

CELIA Alas, sir, be appeased! I could not think
My being at the window should more now
Move your impatience than at other times.

CORVINO No! not to seek and entertain a parley
With a known knave, before a multitude!
You were an actor with your handkerchief,
Which he most sweetly kissed in the receipt,
And might, no doubt, return it with a letter,
And point the place where you might meet; your sister's,
Your mother's, or your aunt's might serve the turn.

CELIA Why, dear sir, when do I make these excuses,
Or ever stir abroad, but to the church?
And that so seldom—

7. Massage for hysteria, the disease of the wandering womb.

8. Mount the stage—or the man.

9. A court that convicted a woman of adultery could grant her dowry to her husband.

1. The Dutch were stereotyped as unemotional, the Italians as intensely jealous.

CORVINO Well, it shall be less;
And thy restraint before was liberty
To what I now decree; and therefore mark me.
First, I will have this bawdy light dammed up;
And till't be done, some two or three yards off,
I'll chalk a line: o'er which if thou but chance
To set thy desperate foot, more hell, more horror,
More wild remorseless rage shall seize on thee,
Than on a conjuror that had heedless left
His circle's safety ere his devil was laid.[2]
Then here's a lock which I will hang upon thee,
And, now I think on't, I will keep thee backwards;
Thy lodging shall be backwards; thy walks backwards;
Thy prospect, all be backwards; and no pleasure
That thou shalt know but backwards. Nay, since you force
My honest nature, know, it is your own,
Being too open, makes me use you thus.
Since you will not contain your subtle nostrils
In a sweet room, but they must snuff the air
Of rank and sweaty passengers. [*Knocking within.*]—One knocks.
Away, and be not seen, pain of thy life;
Nor look toward the window: if thou dost—
Nay, stay, hear this—let me not prosper, whore,
But I will make thee an anatomy,[3]
Dissect thee mine own self, and read a lecture
Upon thee to the city, and in public.
Away!—[*Exit Celia.*]

[*Enter Servant.*]

Who's there?

SERVANT 'Tis Signior Mosca, sir.

Scene 6

CORVINO Let him come in. [*Exit Servant.*] His master's dead: there's yet
Some good to help the bad. [*Enter Mosca.*]
My Mosca, welcome!
I guess your news.

MOSCA I fear you cannot, sir.

CORVINO Is't not his death?

MOSCA Rather the contrary.

CORVINO Not his recovery?

MOSCA Yes, sir.

CORVINO I am cursed,
I am bewitched, my crosses meet to vex me.
How? how? how? how?

MOSCA Why, sir, with Scoto's oil;
Corbaccio and Voltore brought of it,
Whilst I was busy in an inner room—

2. The conjuror's magic circle was a protection against the devils that he had called forth with spells.

3. A subject of moral examination and also of dissection.

CORVINO Death! that damned mountebank; but for the law
Now, I could kill the rascal: it cannot be
His oil should have that virtue. Have not I
Known him a common rogue, come fiddling in
To the osteria° with a tumbling whore, *inn*
And, when he has done all his forced tricks, been glad
Of a poor spoonful of dead wine, with flies in't?
It cannot be. All his ingredients
Are a sheep's gall, a roasted bitch's marrow,
Some few sod earwigs, pounded caterpillars,
A little capon's grease, and fasting spittle:
I know them to a dram.

MOSCA I know not, sir;
But some on't there they poured into his ears,
Some in his nostrils, and recovered him;
Applying but the fricace.

CORVINO Pox o' that fricace!

MOSCA And since, to seem the more officious
And flatt'ring of his health, there they have had,
At extreme fees, the college of physicians
Consulting on him, how they might restore him;
Where one would have a cataplasm° of spices, *poultice*
Another a flayed ape clapped to his breast,
A third would have it a dog, a fourth an oil,
With wild cats' skins: at last, they all resolved
That to preserve him was no other means,
But some young woman must be straight sought out,
Lusty, and full of juice, to sleep by him;
And to this service, most unhappily,
And most unwillingly, am I now employed,
Which here I thought to preacquaint you with
For your advice, since it concerns you most;
Because, I would not do that thing might cross
Your ends, on whom I have my whole dependence, sir:
Yet, if I do it not, they may delate
My slackness to my patron, work me out
Of his opinion; and there all your hopes,
Ventures, or whatsoever, are all frustrate!
I do but tell you, sir. Besides, they are all
Now striving who shall first present him; therefore—
I could entreat you, briefly conclude somewhat;
Prevent them if you can.

CORVINO Death to my hopes,
This is my villainous fortune! Best to hire
Some common courtesan.

MOSCA Ay, I thought on that, sir;
But they are all so subtle, full of art—
And age again doting and flexible,
So as—I cannot tell—we may, perchance,
Light on a quean° may cheat us all. *harlot*

CORVINO 'Tis true.

MOSCA No, no: it must be one that has no tricks, sir,
Some simple thing, a creature made unto it;
Some wench you may command. Have you no kinswoman?
God's so—Think, think, think, think, think, think, think, sir.
One o' the doctors offered there his daughter.
CORVINO How!
MOSCA Yes, signior Lupo,° the physician. *wolf*
CORVINO His daughter!
MOSCA And a virgin, sir. Why, alas,
He knows the state of's body, what it is;
That nought can warm his blood, sir, but a fever;
Nor any incantation raise his spirit;
A long forgetfulness hath seized that part.
Besides sir, who shall know it? Some one or two—
CORVINO I pray thee give me leave. [*Walks aside*.] If any man
But I had this luck—The thing in't self,
I know, is nothing—Wherefore should not I
As well command my blood and my affections
As this dull doctor? In the point of honor,
The cases are all one of wife and daughter.
MOSCA [*Aside*.] I hear him coming.
CORVINO She shall do't: 'tis done.
Slight! if this doctor, who is not engaged,
Unless 't be for his counsel, which is nothing,
Offer his daughter, what should I, that am
So deeply in? I will prevent° him: Wretch! *get ahead of*
Covetous wretch!—Mosca, I have determined.
MOSCA How, sir?
CORVINO We'll make all sure. The party you wot of
Shall be mine own wife, Mosca.
MOSCA Sir, the thing.
But that I would not seem to counsel you,
I should have motioned° to you at the first: *proposed*
And make your count, you have cut all their throats.
Why, 'tis directly taking a possession!
And in his next fit, we may let him go.
'Tis but to pull the pillow from his head,
And he is throttled: it had been done before,
But for your scrupulous doubts.
CORVINO Ay, a plague on't,
My conscience fools my wit! Well, I'll be brief,
And so be thou, lest they should be before us:
Go home, prepare him, tell him with what zeal
And willingness I do it; swear it was
On the first hearing, as thou may'st do, truly,
Mine own free motion.
MOSCA Sir, I warrant you,
I'll so possess him with it that the rest
Of his starved clients shall be banished all;
And only you received. But come not, sir,
Until I send, for I have something else

To ripen for your good, you must not know't.
CORVINO But do not you forget to send now.
MOSCA Fear not. [*Exit.*]

Scene 7

CORVINO Where are you, wife? my Celia! wife!
[*Reenter Celia, weeping.*]
—What, blubbering?
Come, dry those tears. I think thou thought'st me in earnest;
Ha! by this light I talked so but to try thee:
Methinks the lightness of the occasion
Should have confirmed thee. Come, I am not jealous.
CELIA No?
CORVINO Faith I am not, I, nor never was;
It is a poor unprofitable humor.
Do not I know, if women have a will,
They'll do 'gainst all the watches of the world,[4]
And that the fiercest spies are tamed with gold?
Tut, I am confident in thee, thou shalt see't;
And see I'll give thee cause too to believe it.
Come kiss me. Go, and make thee ready, straight,
In all thy best attire, thy choicest jewels,
Put them all on, and with them thy best looks:
We are invited to a solemn feast
At old Volpone's, where it shall appear
How far I am free from jealousy or fear. [*Exeunt.*]

Act 3

Scene 1. *A street*

[*Enter Mosca.*]
MOSCA I fear, I shall begin to grow in love
With my dear self and my most prosperous parts,
They do so spring and burgeon; I can feel
A whimsy in my blood: I know not how,
Success hath made me wanton. I could skip
Out of my skin, now, like a subtle snake,
I am so limber. O! your parasite
Is a most precious thing, dropt from above,
Not bred 'mongst clods and clodpoles,° here on earth. *thick heads*
I muse, the mystery° was not made a science, *secret art*
It is so liberally professed! almost
All the wise world is little else, in nature,
But parasites or sub-parasites.—And yet,
I mean not those that have your bare town-art,
To know who's fit to feed them; have no house,
No family, no care, and therefore mold
Tales for men's ears, to bait that sense; or get
Kitchen-invention, and some stale receipts

4. Have sex no matter how well they are guarded.

To please the belly, and the groin; nor those,
With their court dog-tricks, that can fawn and fleer,° *grin falsely*
Make their revenue out of legs and faces,[1]
Echo my lord, and lick away a moth:
But your fine elegant rascal, that can rise,
And stoop, almost together, like an arrow;
Shoot through the air as nimbly as a star;
Turn short as doth a swallow; and be here,
And there, and here, and yonder, all at once;
Present to any humor, all occasion;
And change a visor,° swifter than a thought! *facial disguise*
This is the creature had the art born with him;
Toils not to learn it, but doth practise it
Out of most excellent nature: and such sparks
Are the true parasites, others but their zanies.° *clown's side-kicks*

Scene 2

[*Enter Bonario.*]
Who's this? Bonario, old Corbaccio's son?
The person I was bound to seek.—Fair sir,
You are happily met.
BONARIO That cannot be by thee.
MOSCA Why, sir?
BONARIO Nay, pray thee, know thy way, and leave me:
I would be loth to interchange discourse
With such a mate as thou art.
MOSCA Courteous sir,
Scorn not my poverty.
BONARIO Not I, by heaven;
But thou shalt give me leave to hate thy baseness.
MOSCA Baseness!
BONARIO Ay; answer me, is not thy sloth
Sufficient argument? Thy flattery?
Thy means of feeding?
MOSCA Heaven be good to me!
These imputations are too common, sir,
And easily stuck on virtue when she's poor.
You are unequal to me, and however
Your sentence may be righteous, yet you are not
That, ere you know me, thus proceed in censure;
St. Mark bear witness 'gainst you, 'tis inhuman. [*Weeps.*]
BONARIO [*aside*] What! does he weep? the sign is soft and good:
I do repent me that I was so harsh.
MOSCA 'Tis true, that, swayed by strong necessity,
I am enforced to eat my careful bread
With too much obsequy;° 'tis true, beside, *servility*
That I am fain to spin mine own poor raiment° *clothing*
Out of my mere observance,° being not born *service*

1. Bows and smiles.

To a free fortune: but that I have done
Base offices, in rending friends asunder,
Dividing families, betraying counsels,
Whispering false lies, or mining men with praises,
Trained their credulity with perjuries,
Corrupted chastity, or am in love
With mine own tender ease, but would not rather
Prove the most rugged, and laborious course,
That might redeem my present estimation,
Let me here perish, in all hope of goodness.

BONARIO [*aside*] This cannot be a personated° passion.— *pretended*
I was to blame, so to mistake thy nature;
Prithee, forgive me: and speak out thy business.

MOSCA Sir, it concerns you; and though I may seem,
At first to make a main offence in manners,
And in my gratitude unto my master,
Yet, for the pure love, which I bear all right,
And hatred of the wrong, I must reveal it.
This very hour your father is in purpose
To disinherit you—

BONARIO How!

MOSCA And thrust you forth,
As a mere stranger to his blood; 'tis true, sir,
The work no way engageth me, but, as
I claim an interest in the general state
Of goodness and true virtue, which I hear
To abound in you: and, for which mere respect,
Without a second aim, sir, I have done it.

BONARIO This tale hath lost thee much of the late trust
Thou hadst with me; it is impossible:
I know not how to lend it any thought,
My father should be so unnatural.

MOSCA It is a confidence that well becomes,
Your piety; and formed, no doubt, it is
From your own simple innocence, which makes
Your wrong more monstrous and abhorred. But, sir,
I now will tell you more. This very minute,
It is, or will be doing; and, if you
Shall be but pleased to go with me, I'll bring you,
I dare not say where you shall see, but where
Your ear shall be a witness of the deed;
Hear yourself written bastard, and profest
The common issue of the earth.

BONARIO I am amazed!

MOSCA Sir, if I do it not, draw your just sword,
And score your vengeance on my front and face:
Mark me your villain: you have too much wrong,
And I do suffer for you, sir. My heart
Weeps blood in anguish—

BONARIO Lead; I follow thee. [*Exeunt.*]

Scene 3. *A room in Volpone's house*

[*Enter Volpone*.]

VOLPONE Mosca stays long, methinks.—Bring forth your sports,
And help to make the wretched time more sweet.

[*Enter Nano, Androgyno, and Castrone*.]

NANO *Dwarf, fool, and eunuch, well met here we be.*
A question it were now, whether of us three,
Being all the known delicates° of a rich man, objects of pleasure
In pleasing him, claim the precedency can?

CASTRONE *I claim for myself.*

ANDROGYNO *And so doth the fool.*

NANO *'Tis foolish indeed: let me set you both to school.*
First for your dwarf, he's little and witty,
And every thing, as it is little, is pretty;
Else why do men say to a creature of my shape,
So soon as they see him, "It's a pretty little ape?"
And why a pretty ape, but for pleasing imitation
Of greater men's actions, in a ridiculous fashion?
Beside, this feat° body of mine doth not crave fit
Half the meat, drink, and cloth, one of your bulks will have.
Admit your fool's face be the mother of laughter,
Yet, for his brain, it must always come after:
And though that do feed him, it's a pitiful case,
His body is beholding to such a bad face. [*Knocking within.*]

VOLPONE Who's there? my couch; away! look! Nano, see:
[*Exeunt Androgyno and Castrone*.]
Give me my caps, first—go, enquire. [*Exit Nano*.]—Now, Cupid
Send it be Mosca, and with fair return!

NANO [*within*] It is the beauteous madam—

VOLPONE Would-be—is it?

NANO The same.

VOLPONE Now torment on me! Squire her in;
For she will enter, or dwell here forever.
Nay, quickly. [*Retires to his couch.*]—That my fit were past! I fear
A second hell too, that my loathing this
Will quite expel my appetite to the other:[2]
Would she were taking now her tedious leave.
Lord, how it threats me what I am to suffer!

Scene 4

[*Re-enter Nano, with Lady Politic Would-be*.]

LADY POLITIC I thank you, good sir. 'Pray you signify
Unto your patron, I am here.—This band
Shows not my neck enough.—I trouble you, sir;
Let me request you, bid one of my women
Come hither to me.—In good faith, I am dressed
Most favorably to-day! It is no matter;

2. "This" is Lady Politic; "the other" is Celia.

'Tis well enough.—
[*Enter First Waiting-woman.*]
Look, see, these petulant things,
How they have done this!
VOLPONE [*aside*] I do feel the fever
Entering in at mine ears; O, for a charm
To fright it hence!
LADY POLITIC Come nearer: is this curl
In his right place, or this? Why is this higher
Than all the rest? You have not washed your eyes, yet!
Or do they not stand even in your head?
Where is your fellow? Call her. [*Exit First Woman.*]
NANO Now, St. Mark
Deliver us! Anon, she'll beat her women,
Because her nose is red.
[*Re-enter First with Second Woman.*]
LADY POLITIC I pray you, view
This tire,° forsooth: are all things apt, or no? *headdress*
FIRST WOMAN One hair a little, here, sticks out, forsooth.
LADY POLITIC Does't so, forsooth? and where was your dear sight,
When it did so, forsooth? What now! Bird-eyed?
And you, too? 'Pray you, both approach and mend it.
Now, by that light, I muse you are not ashamed!
I, that have preached these things so oft unto you,
Read you the principles, argued all the grounds,
Disputed every fitness, every grace,
Called you to counsel of so frequent dressings—
NANO [*aside*] More carefully than of your fame or honor.
LADY POLITIC Made you acquainted, what an ample dowry
The knowledge of these things would be unto you,
Able, alone, to get you noble husbands
At your return; and you thus to neglect it!
Besides you seeing what a curious° nation *particular*
The Italians are, what will they say of me?
The English lady cannot dress herself.
Here's a fine imputation to our country!
Well, go your ways, and stay in the next room.
This fucus° was too coarse too; it's no matter.— *cosmetic*
Good sir, you'll give them entertainment?
[*Exeunt Nano and Waiting-women.*]
VOLPONE The storm comes toward me.
LADY POLITIC [*goes to the couch*] How does my Volpone?
VOLPONE Troubled with noise, I cannot sleep; I dreamt
That a strange fury entered, now, my house,
And, with the dreadful tempest of her breath,
Did cleave my roof asunder.
LADY POLITIC Believe me, and I
Had the most fearful dream, could I remember't—
VOLPONE [*aside*] Out on my fate! I have given her the occasion
How to torment me: she will tell me her's.

LADY POLITIC Me thought, the golden mediocrity, *mean*
Polite and delicate—
VOLPONE O, if you do love me,
No more: I sweat, and suffer, at the mention
Of any dream; feel how I tremble yet.
LADY POLITIC Alas, good soul! the passion of the heart.
Seed-pearl were good now, boiled with syrup of apples,
Tincture of gold, and coral, citron-pills,
Your elicampane root, myrobalanes—[3]
VOLPONE [*aside*] Ah me, I have ta'en a grass-hopper by the wing!
LADY POLITIC Burnt silk, and amber;[4] you have muscadel
Good in the house—
VOLPONE You will not drink, and part?
LADY POLITIC No, fear not that. I doubt, we shall not get
Some English saffron, half a dram would serve;
Your sixteen cloves, a little musk, dried mints,
Bugloss, and barley-meal—
VOLPONE [*aside*] She's in again!
Before I feigned diseases, now I have one.
LADY POLITIC And these applied with a right scarlet cloth.
VOLPONE [*aside*]
Another flood of words! a very torrent!
LADY POLITIC Shall I, sir, make you a poultice?
VOLPONE No, no, no,
I'm very well, you need prescribe no more.
LADY POLITIC I have a little studied physic; but now,
I'm all for music, save, in the forenoons,
An hour or two for painting. I would have
A lady, indeed, to have all, letters and arts,
Be able to discourse, to write, to paint—
But principal, as Plato holds, your music,[5]
And so does wise Pythagoras, I take it—
Is your true rapture, when there is concent *harmony*
In face, in voice, and clothes, and is, indeed,
Our sex's chiefest ornament.
VOLPONE The poet
As old in time as Plato, and as knowing,
Says, that your highest female grace is silence.[6]
LADY POLITIC Which of your poets? Petrarch, or Tasso, or Dante?
Guarini? Ariosto? Aretine?
Cieco di Hadria?[7] I have read them all.
VOLPONE [*aside*] Is every thing a cause to my destruction?
LADY POLITIC I think I have two or three of them about me.
VOLPONE [*aside*] The sun, the sea, will sooner both stand still
Than her eternal tongue! nothing can 'scape it.

3. Elicampane is a stimulant; myrobalanes is medicine for diarrhea.
4. Remedies for smallpox.
5. According to Plato's *Republic*, education in music was for men, not women.
6. Sophocles, *Ajax*, line 293.
7. Famous Italian Renaissance poets.

LADY POLITIC Here's Pastor Fido—[8]
VOLPONE [*aside*] Profess obstinate silence;
That's now my safest.
LADY POLITIC All our English writers,
I mean such as are happy in the Italian,
Will deign to steal out of this author, mainly:
Almost as much as from Montagnié.[9]
He has so modern and facile a vein,
Fitting the time, and catching the court-ear!
Your Petrarch is more passionate, yet he,
In days of sonnetting, trusted them with much.
Dante is hard, and few can understand him.
But, for a desperate wit, there's Aretine;
Only, his pictures are a little obscene—[1]
You mark me not.
VOLPONE Alas, my mind's perturbed.
LADY POLITIC Why, in such cases, we must cure ourselves,
Make use of our philosophy—
VOLPONE Oh me!
LADY POLITIC And as we find our passions do rebel,
Encounter them with reason, or divert them,
By giving scope unto some other humor
Of lesser danger: as, in politic bodies,° *governments*
There's nothing more doth overwhelm the judgment,
And cloud the understanding, than too much
Settling and fixing, and, as 'twere, subsiding
Upon one object. For the incorporating
Of these same outward things, into that part,
Which we call mental, leaves some certain faeces° *dregs*
That stop the organs, and as Plato says,
Assassinate our knowledge.
VOLPONE [*aside*] Now, the spirit
Of patience help me!
LADY POLITIC Come, in faith, I must
Visit you more a days; and make you well.
Laugh and be lusty.
VOLPONE [*aside*] My good angel save me!
LADY POLITIC There was but one sole man in all the world,
With whom I e'er could sympathize; and he
Would lie you, often, three, four hours together
To hear me speak; and be sometimes so rapt,
As he would answer me quite from the purpose,
Like you, and you are like him, just. I'll discourse,
An't be but only, sir, to bring you asleep,
How we did spend our time and loves together,
For some six years.

8. A pastoral by Guarini (1590).
9. Author of the *Essays*, which Jonson's friend John Florio had recently translated into English.
1. Aretino's "Sonnets of Lust" (*Sonnetti Lussuriosi*, 1532) were accompanied by engravings based on pornographic drawings by Giulio Romano.

VOLPONE Oh, oh, oh, oh, oh, oh!
LADY POLITIC For we were coaetanei,° and brought up— *the same age*
VOLPONE Some power, some fate, some fortune rescue me!

Scene 5

[*Enter Mosca.*]

MOSCA God save you, madam!
LADY POLITIC Good sir.
VOLPONE Mosca! welcome,
Welcome to my redemption.
MOSCA Why, sir?
VOLPONE Oh,
Rid me of this my torture, quickly, there;
My madam, with the everlasting voice:
The bells, in time of pestilence, ne'er made
Like noise, or were in that perpetual motion!
The cock-pit comes not near it. All my house,
But now, steamed like a bath with her thick breath,
A lawyer could not have been heard; nor scarce
Another woman, such a hail of words
She has let fall. For hell's sake, rid her hence.
MOSCA Has she presented?
VOLPONE O, I do not care;
I'll take her absence, upon any price,
With any loss.
MOSCA Madam—
LADY POLITIC I have brought your patron
A toy, a cap here, of mine own work.
MOSCA 'Tis well.
I had forgot to tell you, I saw your knight.
Where you would little think it.—
LADY POLITIC Where?
MOSCA Marry,
Where yet, if you make haste, you may apprehend
Rowing upon the water in a gondola
With the most cunning courtesan of Venice.
LADY POLITIC Is't true?
MOSCA Pursue them, and believe your eyes:
Leave me, to make your gift. [*Exit Lady Politic, hastily.*]
—I knew 'twould take:
For, lightly, they that use themselves most license,
Are still most jealous.
VOLPONE Mosca, hearty thanks,
For thy quick fiction, and delivery of me.
Now to my hopes, what say'st thou?
[*Re-enter Lady Politic Would-be.*]
LADY POLITIC But do you hear, sir?—
VOLPONE Again! I fear a paroxysm.
LADY POLITIC Which way
Rowed they together?

MOSCA Toward the Rialto.
LADY POLITIC I pray you lend me your dwarf.
MOSCA I pray you take him.—[*Exit Lady Politic.*]
Your hopes, sir, are like happy blossoms, fair,
And promise timely fruit, if you will stay
But the maturing; keep you at your couch,
Corbaccio will arrive straight, with the will;
When he is gone, I'll tell you more. [*Exit.*]
VOLPONE My blood,
My spirits are returned; I am alive:
And, like your wanton gamester at primero,[2]
Whose thought had whispered to him, not go less,
Methinks I lie, and draw—for an encounter.
[*The scene closes upon Volpone.*]

Scene 6. *The passage leading to Volpone's chamber*

[*Enter Mosca and Bonario.*]

MOSCA Sir, here concealed, [*shows him a closet*] you may hear all—But, pray you,
Have patience, sir; [*knocking within.*]—the same's your father knocks:
I am compelled to leave you. [*Exit.*]
BONARIO Do so.—Yet
Cannot my thought imagine this a truth. [*Goes into the closet.*]

Scene 7. *Another part of the same*

[*Enter Mosca and Corvino, Celia following.*]

MOSCA Death on me! you are come too soon, what meant you?
Did not I say, I would send?
CORVINO Yes, but I feared
You might forget it, and then they prevent us.
MOSCA [*aside*] Prevent! did e'er man haste so, for his horns?
A courtier would not ply it so, for a place.
Well, now there is no helping it, stay here;
I'll presently return. [*Crosses stage to Bonario.*]
CORVINO Where are you, Celia?
You know not wherefore I have brought you hither?
CELIA Not well, except you told me.
CORVINO Now, I will:
Hark hither. [*He leads her to one side and whispers to her.*]
MOSCA [*to Bonario*] Sir, your father hath sent word,
It will be half an hour ere he come;
And therefore, if you please to walk the while
Into that gallery—at the upper end,
There are some books to entertain the time:
And I'll take care no man shall come unto you, sir.
BONARIO Yes, I will stay there.—[aside] I do doubt this fellow. [*Exit Bonario.*]
MOSCA [*looking after him*] There; he is far enough; he can hear nothing:
And, for his father, I can keep him off.

2. A Spanish card game; "go less" means "make a smaller bet"; "lie" means "place a bet"; "draw—for an encounter" means "pick a winning card," with a sexual double meaning.

[*Mosca goes to Volpone's couch, and, sitting by him, whispers*.]
CORVINO [*to Celia*] Nay, now, there is no starting back, and therefore,
Resolve upon it; I have so decreed.
It must be done. Nor would I move't afore,
Because I would avoid all shifts and tricks
That might deny me.
CELIA Sir, let me beseech you,
Affect not these strange trials; if you doubt
My chastity, why, lock me up forever;
Make me the heir of darkness. Let me live,
Where I may please your fears, if not your trust.
CORVINO Believe it, I have no such humor, I.
All that I speak I mean; yet I'm not mad;
Nor horn-mad,[3] see you? Go to, show yourself
Obedient, and a wife.
CELIA O heaven!
CORVINO I say it,
Do so.
CELIA Was this the train?° *scheme*
CORVINO I've told you reasons;
What the physicians have set down: how much
It may concern me; what my engagements are;
My means; and the necessity of those means,
For my recovery: wherefore, if you be
Loyal, and mine, be won, respect my venture.[4]
CELIA Before your honor?
CORVINO Honor! tut, a breath:
There's no such thing in nature: a mere term
Invented to awe fools. What is my gold
The worse for touching, clothes for being looked on?
Why, this is no more. An old decrepit wretch,
That has no sense, no sinew; takes his meat
With others' fingers; only knows to gape,
When you do scald his gums; a voice, a shadow;
And, what can this man hurt you?
CELIA [*aside*] Lord! what spirit
Is this hath entered him?
CORVINO And for your fame,
That's such a jig;° as if I would go tell it, *joke*
Cry it on the Piazza! who shall know it,
But he that cannot speak it, and this fellow,
Whose lips are in my pocket? save yourself,
(If you'll proclaim't, you may,) I know no other
Should come to know it.
CELIA Are heaven and saints then nothing?
Will they be blind or stupid?
CORVINO How!
CELIA Good sir,

3. Driven mad by having been cuckolded.

4. Business transaction—i.e., his prostitution of Celia to Volpone.

Be jealous still, emulate them; and think
What hate they burn with toward every sin.
CORVINO I grant you; if I thought it were a sin,
I would not urge you. Should I offer this
To some young Frenchman, or hot Tuscan blood
That had read Aretine, conned all his prints,[5]
Knew every quirk within lust's labyrinth,
And were professed critic in lechery;
And I would look upon him, and applaud him,
This were a sin: but here, 'tis contrary,
A pious work, mere° charity for physic,° *pure/health*
And honest polity, to assure mine own.
CELIA O heaven! canst thou suffer such a change?
VOLPONE Thou art mine honor, Mosca, and my pride,
My joy, my tickling, my delight! Go bring them.
MOSCA [*advancing*] Please you draw near, sir.
CORVINO Come on, what—
You will not be rebellious? By that light—
MOSCA Sir, Signior Corvino, here, is come to see you.
VOLPONE Oh!
MOSCA And hearing of the consultation had,
So lately, for your health, is come to offer,
Or rather, sir, to prostitute—
CORVINO Thanks, sweet Mosca.
MOSCA Freely, unasked, or unintreated—
CORVINO Well.
MOSCA As the true fervent instance of his love,
His own most fair and proper wife; the beauty,
Only of price in Venice—
CORVINO 'Tis well urged.
MOSCA To be your comfortress, and to preserve you.
VOLPONE Alas, I am past, already! Pray you, thank him
For his good care and promptness; but for that,
'Tis a vain labor e'en to fight 'gainst heaven;
Applying fire to stone—uh, uh, uh, uh! [*Coughing*.]
Making a dead leaf grow again. I take
His wishes gently, though; and you may tell him,
What I have done for him: marry, my state is hopeless.
Will him to pray for me; and to use his fortune
With reverence, when he comes to't.
MOSCA Do you hear, sir?
Go to him with your wife.
CORVINO Heart of my father!
Wilt thou persist thus? come, I pray thee, come.
Thou seest 'tis nothing, Celia. By this hand,
I shall grow violent. Come, do't, I say.
CELIA Sir, kill me, rather: I will take down poison,
Eat burning coals,[6] do anything.—

5. Knew all the sexually explicit illustrations to Aretino's poems.

6. Portia, the virtuous wife of Brutus, killed herself by eating burning coals.

CORVINO Be damned!
Heart, I will drag thee hence, home, by the hair;
Cry thee a strumpet through the streets; rip up
Thy mouth unto thine ears; and slit thy nose,[7]
Like a raw rochet!°—Do not tempt me; come, *large-headed fish*
Yield, I am loth—Death! I will buy some slave
Whom I will kill, and bind thee to him, alive;[8]
And at my window hang you forth, devising
Some monstrous crime, which I, in capital letters,
Will eat into thy flesh with aquafortis,° *acid*
And burning corsives,° on this stubborn breast. *corrosives*
Now, by the blood thou hast incensed, I'll do it!
CELIA Sir, what you please, you may, I am your martyr.
CORVINO Be not thus obstinate, I have not deserved it:
Think who it is intreats you. 'Prithee, sweet;—
Good faith, thou shalt have jewels, gowns, attires,
What thou wilt think, and ask. Do but go kiss him.
Or touch him, but. For my sake.—At my suit.—
This once.—No! not! I shall remember this.
Will you disgrace me thus? Do you thirst my undoing?
MOSCA Nay, gentle lady, be advised.
CORVINO No, no.
She has watched her time. God's precious, this is scurvy,° *evil*
'Tis very scurvy; and you are—
MOSCA Nay, good sir.
CORVINO An arrant locust,[9] by heaven, a locust!
Whore, crocodile, that hast thy tears prepared,[1]
Expecting how thou'lt bid them flow—
MOSCA Nay, 'pray you, sir!
She will consider.
CELIA Would my life would serve
To satisfy—
CORVINO S'death! if she would but speak to him,
And save my reputation, it were somewhat;
But spightfully to affect my utter ruin!
MOSCA Ay, now you have put your fortune in her hands.
Why i'faith, it is her modesty, I must quit° her. *exonerate*
If you were absent, she would be more coming;
I know it: and dare undertake for her.
What woman can before her husband? 'pray you,
Let us depart, and leave her here.
CORVINO Sweet Celia,
Thou may'st redeem all, yet; I'll say no more:
If not, esteem yourself as lost. Nay, stay there.
[*Shuts the door and exits with Mosca.*]
CELIA O God, and his good angels! whither, whither,
Is shame fled human breasts? That with such ease,

7. There were cases of prostitutes being publicly mutilated in early modern Venice, although this was illegal.
8. The rapist Tarquin made similar threats to the chaste Roman heroine Lucretia.
9. A notorious devouring creature.
1. The crocodile trapped its prey with fake tears.

Men dare put off your honors, and their own?
Is that, which ever was a cause of life,
Now placed beneath the basest circumstance,
And modesty an exile made, for money?

VOLPONE [*leaping from his couch*] Ay, in Corvino, and such earth-fed minds,
That never tasted the true heaven of love.
Assure thee, Celia, he that would sell thee,
Only for hope of gain, and that uncertain,
He would have sold his part of Paradise
For ready money, had he met a cope-man.° *dealer*
Why art thou mazed to see me thus revived?
Rather applaud thy beauty's miracle;
'Tis thy great work that hath, not now alone,
But sundry times raised me, in several shapes,
And, but this morning, like a mountebank,
To see thee at thy window. Ay, before
I would have left my practice, for thy love,
In varying figures, I would have contended
With the blue Proteus, or the horned flood.[2]
Now art thou welcome.

CELIA Sir!

VOLPONE Nay, fly me not.
Nor let thy false imagination
That I was bed-rid, make thee think I am so:
Thou shalt not find it. I am, now, as fresh,
As hot, as high, and in as jovial plight,
As when, in that so celebrated scene,
At recitation of our comedy,
For entertainment of the great Valois,[3]
I acted young Antinous;[4] and attracted
The eyes and ears of all the ladies present,
To admire each graceful gesture, note, and footing. [*Sings*.][5]

Come, my Celia, let us prove,
While we can, the sports of love,
Time will not be ours for ever,
He, at length, our good will sever;
Spend not then his gifts in vain;
Suns, that set, may rise again;
But if once we lose this light,
'Tis with us perpetual night.
Why should we defer our joys?
Fame and rumor are but toys.
Cannot we delude the eyes
Of a few poor household spies?
Or his easier ears beguile,
Thus removed by our wile?—

2. Both Proteus, the sea god, and Achelous, the horned river god, transformed themselves into many different shapes.
3. The future Henry III of France visited Venice in 1574.
4. The young male lover of Emperor Hadrian, or one of Penelope's suitors in the *Odyssey*.
5. The song is based on the Latin poet Catullus's "Let us live, my Lesbia, and love."

'Tis no sin love's fruits to steal:
But the sweet thefts to reveal;
To be taken, to be seen,
These have crimes accounted been.

CELIA Some serene° blast me, or dire lightning strike — *noxious mist*
This my offending face!

VOLPONE Why droops my Celia?
Thou hast, in place of a base husband, found
A worthy lover: use thy fortune well,
With secrecy and pleasure. See, behold,
What thou art queen of; not in expectation,
As I feed others: but possessed and crowned.
See, here, a rope of pearl; and each more orient
Than that the brave Aegyptian queen[6] caroused:
Dissolve and drink them. See, a carbuncle,° — *ruby*
May put out both the eyes of our St. Mark;
A diamond, would have bought Lollia Paulina,[7]
When she came in like star-light, hid with jewels,
That were the spoils of provinces; take these,
And wear, and lose them: yet remains an ear-ring
To purchase them again, and this whole state.
A gem but worth a private patrimony,
Is nothing: we will eat such at a meal.
The heads of parrots, tongues of nightingales,
The brains of peacocks, and of ostriches,
Shall be our food: and, could we get the phoenix,
Though nature lost her kind, she were our dish.

CELIA Good sir, these things might move a mind affected
With such delights; but I, whose innocence
Is all I can think wealthy, or worth th' enjoying,
And which, once lost, I have nought to lose beyond it,
Cannot be taken with these sensual baits:
If you have conscience—

VOLPONE 'Tis the beggar's virtue;
If thou hast wisdom, hear me, Celia.
Thy baths shall be the juice of July-flowers,
Spirit of roses, and of violets,
The milk of unicorns, and panthers' breath
Gathered in bags, and mixt with Cretan wines.
Our drink shall be prepared gold and amber;
Which we will take, until my roof whirl round
With the vertigo: and my dwarf shall dance,
My eunuch sing, my fool make up the antic,
Whilst we, in changed shapes, act Ovid's tales,[8]
Thou, like Europa now, and I like Jove,
Then I like Mars, and thou like Erycine:

6. Cleopatra.
7. The Emperor Caligula's wife.
8. Ovid's *Metamorphoses* contains stories of shape changing and the pursuit of desire. The god Jupiter in the form of a bull raped Europa (*Metamorphoses* 2.858). Ericyna, from Mount Eryx in Sicily, was a name for Venus, who had an affair with Mars, god of War (*Metamorphoses* 4.171).

So, of the rest, till we have quite run through,
And wearied all the fables of the gods.
Then will I have thee in more modern forms,
Attired like some sprightly dame of France,
Brave Tuscan lady, or proud Spanish beauty;
Sometimes, unto the Persian sophy's wife;
Or the grand signior's mistress;[9] and, for change,
To one of our most artful courtesans,
Or some quick Negro, or cold Russian;
And I will meet thee in as many shapes:
Where we may so transfuse our wandering souls
Out at our lips, and score up sums of pleasures, [*Sings*.]

That the curious shall not know
How to tell them as they flow;
And the envious, when they find
What their number is, be pined.° tormented

CELIA If you have ears that will be pierced—or eyes
That can be opened—a heart that may be touched—
Or any part that yet sounds man about you—
If you have touch of holy saints—or heaven—
Do me the grace to let me 'scape—if not,
Be bountiful and kill me. You do know,
I am a creature, hither ill betrayed,
By one, whose shame I would forget it were:
If you will deign me neither of these graces,
Yet feed your wrath, sir, rather than your lust,
(It is a vice comes nearer manliness,)
And punish that unhappy crime of nature,
Which you miscall my beauty: flay my face,
Or poison it with ointments, for seducing
Your blood to this rebellion. Rub these hands,
With what may cause an eating leprosy,
E'en to my bones and marrow: any thing,
That may disfavor me, save in my honor—
And I will kneel to you, pray for you, pay down
A thousand hourly vows, sir, for your health;
Report, and think you virtuous—

VOLPONE Think me cold,
Frozen and impotent, and so report me?
That I had Nestor's hernia,[1] thou wouldst think.
I do degenerate, and abuse my nation,
To play with opportunity thus long;
I should have done the act, and then have parleyed.
Yield, or I'll force thee. [*Seizes her*.]

CELIA O! just God!

VOLPONE In vain—

BONARIO [*rushing in*] Forbear, foul ravisher, libidinous swine!

9. The Sultan of Turkey's mistress. The "Sophy" was the Shah of Persia.

1. Juvenal described the old impotent Greek warrior as having a hernia (*Satires* 6.326).

Free the forced lady, or thou diest, impostor.
But that I'm loth to snatch thy punishment
Out of the hand of justice, thou shouldst, yet,
Be made the timely sacrifice of vengeance,
Before this altar, and this dross, thy idol.—
Lady, let's quit the place, it is the den
Of villainy; fear nought, you have a guard:
And he, ere long, shall meet his just reward.
[*Exeunt Bonario and Celia.*]

VOLPONE Fall on me, roof, and bury me in ruin!
Become my grave, that wert my shelter! O!
I am unmasked, unspirited, undone,
Betrayed to beggary, to infamy—

Scene 8

[*Enter Mosca, wounded and bleeding.*]

MOSCA Where shall I run, most wretched shame of men,
To beat out my unlucky brains?

VOLPONE Here, here.
What! dost thou bleed?

MOSCA O that his well-driven sword
Had been so courteous to have cleft me down
Unto the navel, ere I lived to see
My life, my hopes, my spirits, my patron, all
Thus desperately engaged, by my error!

VOLPONE Woe on thy fortune!

MOSCA And my follies, sir.

VOLPONE Thou hast made me miserable.

MOSCA And myself, sir.
Who would have thought he would have hearkened so?

VOLPONE What shall we do?

MOSCA I know not; if my heart
Could expiate the mischance, I'd pluck it out.
Will you be pleased to hang me, or cut my throat?
And I'll requite you, sir. Let's die like Romans,
Since we have lived like Grecians.[2] [*Knocking within.*]

VOLPONE Hark! who's there?
I hear some footing; officers, the saffi,° *police*
Come to apprehend us! I do feel the brand
Hissing already at my forehead; now,
Mine ears are boring.

MOSCA To your couch, sir, you,
Make that place good, however. [*Volpone lies down, as before.*]—Guilty men
Suspect what they deserve still.
[*Enter Corbaccio.*]
Signior Corbaccio!

CORBACCIO Why, how now, Mosca?

MOSCA O, undone, amazed, sir.

2. To "die like Romans" means to commit suicide; to live "like Grecians" means to enjoy luxury.

Your son, I know not by what accident,
Acquainted with your purpose to my patron,
Touching your will, and making him your heir,
Entered our house with violence, his sword drawn
Sought for you, called you wretch, unnatural,
Vowed he would kill you.

CORBACCIO Me!

MOSCA Yes, and my patron.

CORBACCIO This act shall disinherit him indeed;
Here is the will.

MOSCA 'Tis well, sir.

CORBACCIO Right and well:
Be you as careful now for me.

[*Enter Voltore, behind.*]

MOSCA My life, sir,
Is not more tendered; I am only yours.

CORBACCIO How does he? will he die shortly, think'st thou?

MOSCA I fear
He'll outlast May.

CORBACCIO Today?

MOSCA No, last out May, sir.

CORBACCIO Could'st thou not give him a dram?

MOSCA O, by no means, sir.

CORBACCIO Nay, I'll not bid you.

VOLTORE [*coming forward*] This is a knave, I see.

MOSCA [*seeing Voltore*] How! signior Voltore! [*Aside*.] Did he hear me?

VOLTORE Parasite!

MOSCA Who's that?—O, sir, most timely welcome—

VOLTORE Scarce,
To the discovery of your tricks, I fear.
You are his, *only?* and mine also, are you not?

MOSCA Who? I, sir?

VOLTORE You, sir. What device is this
About a will?

MOSCA A plot for you, sir.

VOLTORE Come,
Put not your foists° upon me; I shall scent them. *tricks, stinks*

MOSCA Did you not hear it?

VOLTORE Yes, I hear Corbaccio
Hath made your patron there his heir.

MOSCA 'Tis true,
By my device, drawn to it by my plot,
With hope—

VOLTORE Your patron should reciprocate?
And you have promised?

MOSCA For your good, I did, sir.
Nay, more, I told his son, brought, hid him here,
Where he might hear his father pass the deed:
Being persuaded to it by this thought, sir,
That the unnaturalness, first, of the act,

And then his father's oft disclaiming in him,
(Which I did mean t'help on,) would sure enrage him
To do some violence upon his parent,
On which the law should take sufficient hold,
And you be stated in a double hope:
Truth be my comfort, and my conscience,
My only aim was to dig you a fortune
Out of these two old rotten sepulchres—

VOLTORE I cry thee mercy, Mosca.

MOSCA Worth your patience,
And your great merit, sir. And see the change!

VOLTORE Why, what success?

MOSCA Most hapless! You must help, sir.
Whilst we expected the old raven, in comes
Corvino's wife, sent hither by her husband—

VOLTORE What, with a present?

MOSCA No, sir, on visitation;
(I'll tell you how anon;) and staying long,
The youth he grows impatient, rushes forth,
Seizeth the lady, wounds me, makes her swear
(Or he would murder her, that was his vow)
To affirm my patron to have done her rape:
Which how unlike it is, you see! and hence,
With that pretext he's gone, to accuse his father,
Defame my patron, defeat you—

VOLTORE Where's her husband?
Let him be sent for straight.

MOSCA Sir, I'll go fetch him.

VOLTORE Bring him to the Scrutineo.[3]

MOSCA Sir, I will.

VOLTORE This must be stopped.

MOSCA O you do nobly, sir.
Alas, 'twas labored all, sir, for your good;
Nor was there want of counsel in the plot:
But fortune can, at any time, o'erthrow
The projects of a hundred learnèd clerks, sir.

CORBACCIO [*listening*] What's that?

VOLTORE Will't please you, sir, to go along?

[*Exit Corbaccio, followed by Voltore.*]

MOSCA Patron, go in, and pray for our success.

VOLPONE [*rising from his couch*] Need makes devotion: heaven your labor bless!
[*Exeunt.*]

Act 4

Scene 1. *A street*

[*Enter Sir Politic Would-be and Peregrine.*]

SIR POLITIC I told you, sir, it was a plot; you see
What observation is! You mentioned me

3. Law court in the Senate-house.

For some instructions: I will tell you, sir,
(Since we are met here in this height[1] of Venice,)
Some few particulars I have set down,
Only for this meridian, fit to be known
Of your crude traveler; and they are these.
I will not touch, sir, at your phrase, or clothes,
For they are old.

PEREGRINE Sir, I have better.

SIR POLITIC Pardon,
I meant, as they are themes.

PEREGRINE O, sir, proceed:
I'll slander you no more of wit, good sir.

SIR POLITIC First, for your garb,° it must be grave and serious, *behavior*
Very reserved and locked; not tell a secret
On any terms, not to your father; scarce
A fable, but with caution: make sure choice
Both of your company, and discourse; beware
You never speak a truth—

PEREGRINE How!

SIR POLITIC Not to strangers,
For those be they you must converse with most;
Others I would not know, sir, but at distance,
So as I still might be a saver[2] in them:
You shall have tricks else past upon you hourly.
And then, for your religion, profess none,
But wonder at the diversity, of all:
And, for your part, protest, were there no other
But simply the laws o' the land, you could content you,
Nic. Machiavel, and Monsieur Bodin, both
Were of this mind.[3] Then must you learn the use
And handling of your silver fork at meals,[4]
The metal of your glass; (these are main matters
With your Italian) and to know the hour
When you must eat your melons, and your figs.

PEREGRINE Is that a point of state too?

SIR POLITIC Here it is:
For your Venetian, if he see a man
Preposterous in the least, he has him straight;
He has; he strips him. I'll acquaint you, sir,
I now have lived here, 'tis some fourteen months
Within the first week of my landing here,
All took me for a citizen of Venice,
I knew the forms so well—

PEREGRINE [*aside*] And nothing else.

SIR POLITIC I had read Contarene,[5] took me a house,

1. Climate, constitution.
2. A gambling term meaning to avoid either winning or losing.
3. Niccolo Machiavelli (1469–1526) analyzed the political expediency of religion, while Jean Bodin (1530–1596) saw religious toleration as way to avoid civil war.
4. The fork, a Renaissance invention, was not yet used in early 17th century England.
5. Gasparo Contarini wrote a book on the Venetian constitution, translated as *The Commonwealth and Government of Venice* (1599).

Dealt with my Jews[6] to furnish it with moveables—
Well, if I could but find one man, one man
To mine own heart, whom I durst trust, I would—
PEREGRINE What, what, sir?
SIR POLITIC Make him rich; make him a fortune:
He should not think again. I would command it.
PEREGRINE As how?
SIR POLITIC With certain projects that I have;
Which I may not discover.° *reveal*
PEREGRINE [*aside*] If I had
But one to wager with, I would lay odds now,
He tells me instantly.
SIR POLITIC One is, and that
I care not greatly who knows, to serve the state
Of Venice with red herrings for three years,
And at a certain rate, from Rotterdam,
Where I have correspondence. There's a letter,
Sent me from one o' the States,[7] and to that purpose:
He cannot write his name, but that's his mark.
PEREGRINE He is a chandler?° *candle maker*
SIR POLITIC No, a cheesemonger.
There are some others too with whom I treat
About the same negotiation;
And I will undertake it; for, 'tis thus.
I'll do't with ease, I have cast it all; Your hoy° *small fishing boat*
Carries but three men in her, and a boy;
And she shall make me three returns a year:
So, if there come but one of three, I save;
If two, I can defalk:°—but this is now, *cut back the amount*
If my main project fail.
PEREGRINE Then you have others?
SIR POLITIC I should be loath to draw the subtle air
Of such a place, without my thousand aims.
I'll not dissemble, sir: where'er I come,
I love to be considerative; and 'tis true,
I have at my free hours thought upon
Some certain goods unto the state of Venice,
Which I do call *my Cautions*; and, sir, which
I mean, in hope of pension, to propound
To the Great Council, then unto the Forty,
So to the Ten.[8] My means are made already—
PEREGRINE By whom?
SIR POLITIC Sir, one that, though his place be obscure,
Yet he can sway, and they will hear him. He's
A commandatore.
PEREGRINE What! a common sergeant?
SIR POLITIC Sir, such as they are, put it in their mouths,

6. Borrowed money from Jews who lived in the Venetian ghetto.
7. A citizen of the United Provinces of the Netherlands; a member of the Dutch assembly, the States-General.
8. Representative assemblies of Venetian government.

What they should say, sometimes; as well as greater:
I think I have my notes to show you—[*Searching his pockets.*]

PEREGRINE Good sir.

SIR POLITIC But you shall swear unto me, on your gentry,
Not to anticipate—

PEREGRINE I, sir!

SIR POLITIC Nor reveal
A circumstance—My paper is not with me.

PEREGRINE O, but you can remember, sir.

SIR POLITIC My first is
Concerning tinder-boxes.° You must know, *match boxes*
No family is here without its box.
Now, sir, it being so portable a thing,
Put case, that you or I were ill affected
Unto the state, sir; with it in our pockets,
Might not I go into the Arsenal,[9]
Or you, come out again, and none the wiser?

PEREGRINE Except yourself, sir.

SIR POLITIC Go to, then. I therefore
Advertise to the state, how fit it were,
That none but such as were known patriots,
Sound lovers of their country, should be suffered
To enjoy them in their houses; and even those
Sealed at some office, and at such a bigness
As might not lurk in pockets.

PEREGRINE Admirable!

SIR POLITIC My next is, how to enquire, and be resolved,
By present demonstration, whether a ship,
Newly arrived from Syria, or from
Any suspected part of all the Levant,° *the Middle East*
Be guilty of the plague: and where they use
To lie out forty, fifty days, sometimes,
About the Lazaretto,[1] for their trial;
I'll save that charge and loss unto the merchant,
And in an hour clear the doubt.

PEREGRINE Indeed, sir!

SIR POLITIC Or—I will lose my labor.

PEREGRINE 'My faith, that's much.

SIR POLITIC Nay, sir, conceive me. It will cost me in onions,
Some thirty livres[2]—

PEREGRINE Which is one pound sterling.

SIR POLITIC Beside my waterworks: for this I do, sir
First, I bring in your ship 'twixt two brick walls;
But those the state shall venture: On the one
I strain me a fair tarpauling,° and in that *waterproofed canvas*
I stick my onions, cut in halves: the other
Is full of loop-holes, out at which I thrust

9. Venetian shipyard.
1. Plague hospital on an island outside Venice, where the passengers of foreign ships were held until deemed free of disease.
2. Peeled onions were used to protect the air from the plague; the livre was a French coin.

The noses of my bellows; and those bellows
I keep, with water-works, in perpetual motion,
Which is the easiest matter of a hundred.
Now, sir, your onion, which doth naturally
Attract the infection, and your bellows blowing
The air upon him, will show, instantly,
By his changed color, if there be contagion;
Or else remain as fair as at the first.
—Now it is known, 'tis nothing.

PEREGRINE You are right, sir.

SIR POLITIC I would I had my note.

PEREGRINE 'Faith, so would I:
But you have done well for once, sir.

SIR POLITIC Were I false,
Or would be made so, I could show you reasons
How I could sell this state now to the Turk,
Spite of their gallies, or their—[*Examining his papers.*]

PEREGRINE Pray you, Sir Pol.

SIR POLITIC I have them not about me.

PEREGRINE That I feared:
The're there, sir.

SIR POLITIC No, this is my diary,
Wherein I note my actions of the day.

PEREGRINE Pray you, let's see, sir. What is here? [*Reads.*] *Notandum*,[3]
A rat had gnawn my spur-leathers; notwithstanding,
I put on new, and did go forth: but first
I threw three beans over the threshold. Item,
I went and bought two tooth-picks, whereof one
I burst immediately, in a discourse
With a Dutch merchant, 'bout ragion del stato.[4]
From him I went and paid a moccinigo° *a dime*
For piecing my silk stockings; by the way
I cheapened sprats;[5] *and at St. Mark's I urined.*
'Faith these are politic notes!

SIR POLITIC Sir, I do slip
No action of my life, but thus I quote it.

PEREGRINE Believe me, it is wise!

SIR POLITIC Nay, sir, read forth.

Scene 2

[*Enter, at a distance, Lady Politic Would-be, Nano, and two Waiting-women.*]

LADY POLITIC Where should this loose knight be, trow? Sure he's housed.[6]

NANO Why, then he's fast.

LADY POLITIC Ay, he plays both[7] with me.
I pray you stay. This heat will do more harm

3. It must be noted.
4. Reasons of state, the notion that political ends justify immoral means.
5. Haggled over the price of fish.
6. Secure; involved with a courtesan.
7. Fast and loose.

To my complexion, than his heart is worth.
(I do not care to hinder, but to take him.)
How it[8] comes off! [*Rubbing her cheeks.*]
1 WOMAN My master's yonder.
LADY POLITIC Where?
2 WOMAN With a young gentleman.
LADY POLITIC That same's the party;
In man's apparel! 'Pray you, sir, jog my knight:
I will be tender to his reputation,
However he demerit.
SIR POLITIC [*seeing her*] My lady!
PEREGRINE Where?
SIR POLITIC 'Tis she indeed, sir; you shall know her. She is,
Were she not mine, a lady of that merit,
For fashion and behavior; and for beauty
I durst compare—
PEREGRINE It seems you are not jealous,
That dare commend her.
SIR POLITIC Nay, and for discourse—
PEREGRINE Being your wife, she cannot miss that.
SIR POLITIC [*introducing Peregrine*] Madam,
Here is a gentleman, pray you, use him fairly;
He seems a youth, but he is—
LADY POLITIC None?
SIR POLITIC Yes, one
Has put his face as soon into the world—
LADY POLITIC You mean, as early? But to-day?
SIR POLITIC How's this?
LADY POLITIC Why, in this habit, sir; you apprehend me:—
Well, master Would-be, this doth not become you;
I had thought the odor, sir, of your good name
Had been more precious to you; that you would not
Have done this dire massacre on your honor;
One of your gravity and rank besides!
But knights, I see, care little for the oath
They make to ladies; chiefly, their own ladies.
SIR POLITIC Now, by my spurs, the symbol of my knighthood,[9]—
PEREGRINE [*Aside.*] Lord, how his brain is humbled for an oath!
SIR POLITIC I reach you not.
LADY POLITIC Right, sir, your policy
May bear it through thus.—Sir, a word with you. [*To Peregrine.*]
I would be loth to contest publicly
With any gentlewoman, or to seem
Froward, or violent, as the courtier says;[1]
It comes too near rusticity in a lady,
Which I would shun by all means: and however

8. Her make-up.
9. A swipe at James I's bestowal of an excessively large number of knighthoods.

1. Castiglione's *Il Cortegiano* (1528), a conduct book, translated in 1561 by Hoby as *The Courtier*.

I may deserve from master Would-be, yet
T'have one fair gentlewoman thus be made
The unkind instrument to wrong another,
And one she knows not, ay, and to persèver;
In my poor judgment, is not warranted
From being a solecism[2] in our sex,
If not in manners.

PEREGRINE How is this?

SIR POLITIC Sweet madam,
Come nearer to your aim.

LADY POLITIC Marry, and will, sir.
Since you provoke me with your impudence,
And laughter of your light land-siren here,
Your Sporus,[3] your hermaphrodite—

PEREGRINE What's here?
Poetic fury, and historic storms!

SIR POLITIC The gentleman, believe it, is of worth,
And of our nation.

LADY POLITIC Ay, your White-friars nation.[4]
Come, I blush for you, master Would-be, I;
And am ashamed you should have no more forehead,° *modesty*
Than thus to be the patron, or St. George,
To a lewd harlot, a base fricatrice,° *prostitute*
A female devil, in a male outside.

SIR POLITIC Nay,
An you be such a one, I must bid adieu
To your delights. The case appears too liquid. [*Exit.*]

LADY POLITIC Ay, you may carry't clear, with your state-face!—
But for your carnival[5] concupiscence,
Who here is fled for liberty of conscience,
From furious persecution of the marshal,
Her will I dis'ple.[6]

PEREGRINE This is fine, i'faith!
And do you use this often? Is this part
Of your wit's exercise, 'gainst you have occasion?
Madam—

LADY POLITIC Go to, sir.

PEREGRINE Do you hear me, lady?
Why, if your knight have set you to beg shirts,
Or to invite me home, you might have done it
A nearer way, by far.[7]

LADY POLITIC This cannot work you
Out of my snare.

PEREGRINE Why, am I in it, then?
Indeed your husband told me you were fair.

2. An error in language use rather than in behavior, so this is itself a solecism.
3. The Roman Emperor Nero's transvestite eunuch.
4. White-frairs, a section of London frequented by prostitutes.
5. Festival characterized by sexual license and transvestism.
6. Discipline, a reference to the English marshall's public punishment of prostitutes by whipping.
7. Peregrine suggests that Sir Politic has been pimping his wife.

And so you are; only your nose inclines,
That side that's next the sun, to the queen-apple.[8]
LADY POLITIC This cannot be endured by any patience.

Scene 3

[*Enter Mosca.*]
MOSCA What is the matter, madam?
LADY POLITIC If the senate
Right not my quest in this, I will protest them
To all the world, no aristocracy.
MOSCA What is the injury, lady?
LADY POLITIC Why, the callet° *whore*
You told me of, here I have ta'en disguised.
MOSCA Who? This! What means your ladyship? The creature
I mentioned to you is apprehended now,
Before the senate; you shall see her—
LADY POLITIC Where?
MOSCA I'll bring you to her. This young gentleman,
I saw him land this morning at the port.
LADY POLITIC Is't possible! How has my judgment wandered?
Sir, I must, blushing, say to you, I have erred;
And plead your pardon.
PEREGRINE What, more changes yet!
LADY POLITIC I hope you have not the malice to remember
A gentlewoman's passion. If you stay
In Venice here, please you to use me, sir—
MOSCA Will you go, madam?
LADY POLITIC 'Pray you, sir, use me; in faith,
The more you see me, the more I shall conceive
You have forgot our quarrel.
[*Exeunt Lady Would-be, Mosca, Nano, and waiting-women.*]
PEREGRINE This is rare!
Sir Politic Would-be? No; sir Politic Bawd,° *pimp*
To bring me thus acquainted with his wife!
Well, wise Sir Pol, since you have practised thus
Upon my freshman-ship,° I'll try your salt-head,[9] *innocence*
What proof it is against a counter-plot. [*Exit.*]

Scene 4. *The Scrutineo, or Senate-House*

[*Enter Voltore, Corbaccio, Corvino, and Mosca.*]
VOLTORE Well, now you know the carriage of the business,
Your constancy is all that is required
Unto the safety of it.
MOSCA Is the lie
Safely conveyed amongst us? Is that sure?
Knows every man his burden?
CORVINO Yes.
MOSCA Then shrink not.

8. Her nose is red as an apple.

9. Lecherousness.

CORVINO But knows the advocate the truth?
MOSCA O, sir,
By no means; I devised a formal tale,
That salv'd your reputation. But be valiant, sir.
CORVINO I fear no one but him, that this his pleading
Should make him stand for a co-heir—
MOSCA Co-halter!
Hang him; we will but use his tongue, his noise,
As we do Croaker's[1] here.
CORVINO Ay, what shall he do?
MOSCA When we have done, you mean?
CORVINO Yes.
MOSCA Why, we'll think:
Sell him for mummia;[2] he's half dust already.
[*To Voltore*.] Do you not smile, to see this buffalo,
How he doth sport it with his head?[3]—[*aside*] I should,
If all were well and past.—[*To Corbaccio*.] Sir, only you
Are he that shall enjoy the crop of all,
And these not know for whom they toil.
CORBACCIO Ay, peace.
MOSCA [*Turning to Corvino*.]
But you shall eat it. [*Aside*:] Much!
[*To Voltore*.] —Worshipful sir,
Mercury sit upon your thundering tongue,
Or the French Hercules,[4] and make your language
As conquering as his club, to beat along,
As with a tempest, flat, our adversaries;
But much more yours, sir.
VOLTORE Here they come, have done.
MOSCA I have another witness, if you need, sir,
I can produce.
VOLTORE Who is it?
MOSCA Sir, I have her.

Scene 5

[*Enter Avocatori and take their seats, Bonario, Celia, Notario, Commendatori, Saffi, and other Officers of justice*.]

1 AVOCATORE The like of this the senate never heard of.
2 AVOCATORE 'Twill come most strange to them when we report it.
4 AVOCATORE The gentlewoman[5] has been ever held
Of unreproved name.
3 AVOCATORE So has the youth.[6]
4 AVOCATORE The more unnatural part that of his father.[7]
2 AVOCATORE More of the husband.[8]
1 AVOCATORE I not know to give

1. Corbaccio's, referring to the way he speaks.
2. Medicine made from mummies.
3. Enjoy the cuckold's horns on his head.
4. Mercury was the god of skill in speech; Lucian described the French Hercules as eloquent.
5. Celia.
6. Bonario.
7. Corbaccio.
8. Corvino.

His act a name, it is so monstrous!
4 AVOCATORE But the impostor,° he's a thing created *Volpone*
To exceed example!
1 AVOCATORE And all after-times!
2 AVOCATORE I never heard a true voluptuary[9]
Described, but him.
3 AVOCATORE Appear yet those were cited?
NOTARIO All but the old magnifico, Volpone.
1 AVOCATORE Why is not he here?
MOSCA Please your fatherhoods,
Here is his advocate: himself's so weak,
So feeble—
4 AVOCATORE What are you?
BONARIO His parasite,
His knave, his pandar:° I beseech the court, *procurer*
He may be forced to come, that your grave eyes
May bear strong witness of his strange impostures.
VOLTORE Upon my faith and credit with your virtues,
He is not able to endure the air.
2 AVOCATORE Bring him, however.
3 AVOCATORE We will see him.
4 AVOCATORE Fetch him.
VOLTORE Your fatherhoods' fit pleasures be obeyd;
[*Exeunt Officers*.]
But sure, the sight will rather move your pities,
Than indignation. May it please the court,
In the mean time, he may be heard in me;
I know this place most void of prejudice,
And therefore crave it, since we have no reason
To fear our truth should hurt our cause.
3 AVOCATORE Speak free.
VOLTORE Then know, most honored fathers, I must now
Discover to your strangely abused ears,
The most prodigious and most frontless° piece *shameless*
Of solid impudence, and treachery,
That ever vicious nature yet brought forth
To shame the state of Venice. This lewd woman,
That wants no artificial looks or tears
To help the visor° she has now put on, *mask*
Hath long been known a close° adulteress *secret*
To that lascivious youth there; not suspected,
I say, but known, and taken in the act
With him; and by this man, the easy husband,
Pardoned; whose timeless bounty makes him now
Stand here, the most unhappy, innocent person,
That ever man's own goodness made accused.
For these not knowing how to owe a gift
Of that dear grace, but with their shame; being placed

9. Person addicted to pleasure.

So above all powers of their gratitude,
Began to hate the benefit; and, in place
Of thanks, devise to extirp° the memory — *root out*
Of such an act: wherein I pray your fatherhoods
To observe the malice, yea, the rage of creatures
Discovered in their evils; and what heart
Such take, even from their crimes:—but that anon
Will more appear.—This gentleman, the father,
Hearing of this foul fact, with many others,
Which daily struck at his too tender ears,
And grieved in nothing more than that he could not
Preserve himself a parent, (his son's ills
Growing to that strange flood,) at last decreed
To disinherit him.

1 AVOCATORE These be strange turns!

2 AVOCATORE The young man's fame was ever fair and honest.

VOLTORE So much more full of danger is his vice,
That can beguile so under shade of virtue.
But, as I said, my honored sires, his father
Having this settled purpose, by what means
To him betrayed, we know not, and this day
Appointed for the deed; that parricide,
I cannot style him better, by confederacy° — *conspiracy*
Preparing this his paramour to be there,
Entered Volpone's house, (who was the man,
Your fatherhoods must understand, designed
For the inheritance,) there sought his father:—
But with what purpose sought he him, my lords?
I tremble to pronounce it, that a son
Unto a father, and to such a father,
Should have so foul, felonious intent!
It was to murder him: when being prevented
By his more happy absence, what then did he?
Not check his wicked thoughts; no, now new deeds,
(Mischief doth never end where it begins)
An act of horror, fathers! He dragged forth
The aged gentleman that had there lain bed-rid
Three years and more, out of his innocent couch,
Naked upon the floor, there left him; wounded
His servant in the face: and, with this strumpet
The stale° to his forged practice, who was glad — *decoy*
To be so active—(I shall here desire
Your fatherhoods to note but my collections,° — *conclusions*
As most remarkable)— thought at once to stop
His father's ends, discredit his free choice
In the old gentleman, redeem themselves,
By laying infamy upon this man,° — *Corvino*
To whom, with blushing, they should owe their lives.

1 AVOCATORE What proofs have you of this?

BONARIO Most honored fathers,

I humbly crave there be no credit given
To this man's mercenary tongue.
2 AVOCATORE Forbear.
BONARIO His soul moves in his fee.
3 AVOCATORE O, sir.
BONARIO This fellow,
For six sols° more, would plead against his Maker *coins*
1 AVOCATORE You do forget yourself.
VOLTORE Nay, nay, grave fathers,
Let him have scope: can any man imagine
That he will spare his accuser, that would not
Have spared his parent?
1 AVOCATORE Well, produce your proofs.
CELIA I would I could forget I were a creature.
VOLTORE Signior Corbaccio! [*Corbaccio comes forward.*]
4 AVOCATORE What is he?
VOLTORE The father.
2 AVOCATORE Has he had an oath?
NOTARIO Yes.
CORBACCIO What must I do now?
NOTARIO Your testimony's craved.
CORBACCIO Speak to the knave?
I'll have my mouth first stopped with earth; my heart
Abhors his knowledge: I disclaim in him.
1 AVOCATORE But for what cause?
CORBACCIO The mere portent of nature!
He is an utter stranger to my loins.
BONARIO Have they made you to this?
CORBACCIO I will not hear thee,
Monster of men, swine, goat, wolf, parricide!
Speak not, thou viper.
BONARIO Sir, I will sit down,
And rather wish my innocence should suffer,
Than I resist the authority of a father.
VOLTORE Signior Corvino! [*Corvino comes forward.*]
AVOCATORE This is strange.
1 AVOCATORE Who's this?
NOTARIO The husband.
4 AVOCATORE Is he sworn?
NOTARIO He is.
3 AVOCATORE Speak, then.
CORVINO This woman, please your fatherhoods, is a whore,
Of most hot exercise, more than a partrich,[1]
Upon record—
1 AVOCATORE No more.
CORVINO Neighs like a jennet.° *small horse*
NOTARIO Preserve the honor of the court.

1. The most lustful of birds.

CORVINO I shall,
And modesty of your most reverend ears.
And yet I hope that I may say, these eyes
Have seen her glued unto that piece of cedar,
That fine well-timbered gallant; and that here
The letters may be read, thorough the horn,
That make the story perfect.
MOSCA Excellent! sir.
CORVINO [*aside to Mosca*] There is no shame in this now, is there?
MOSCA None.
CORVINO Or if I said, I hoped that she were onward
To her damnation, if there be a hell
Greater than whore and woman; a good Catholic[2]
May make the doubt.
3 AVOCATORE His grief hath made him frantic.
1 AVOCATORE Remove him hence.
2 AVOCATORE Look to the woman. [*Celia swoons.*]
CORVINO Rare!
Prettily feigned, again!
4 AVOCATORE Stand from about her.
1 AVOCATORE Give her the air.
3 AVOCATORE [*to Mosca*] What can you say?
MOSCA My wound,
May it please your wisdoms, speaks for me, received
In aid of my good patron, when he mist
His sought-for father,[3] when that well-taught dame
Had her cue given her, to cry out, A rape!
BONARIO O most laid impudence! Fathers—
3 AVOCATORE Sir, be silent;
You had your hearing free, so must they theirs.
2 AVOCATORE I do begin to doubt the imposture here.
4 AVOCATORE This woman has too many moods.
VOLTORE Grave fathers,
She is a creature of a most profest
And prostituted lewdness.
CORVINO Most impetuous,
Unsatisfied, grave fathers!
VOLTORE May her feignings
Not take your wisdoms: but this day she baited
A stranger, a grave knight, with her loose eyes,
And more lascivious kisses. This man saw them
Together on the water, in a gondola.
MOSCA Here is the lady herself, that saw them too;
Without; who then had in the open streets
Pursued them, but for saving her knight's honor.
1 AVOCATORE Produce that lady.
2 AVOCATORE Let her come. [*Exit Mosca.*]
4 AVOCATORE These things,

2. The 1607 Quarto, printed when Jonson was still a Catholic, reads "Christian," whereas the 1616 Folio reads "Catholic."
3. Corbaccio.

They strike with wonder.
3 AVOCATORE I am turned a stone.

Scene 6

[*Reenter Mosca with Lady Would-be.*]
MOSCA Be resolute, madam.
LADY POLITIC [*pointing to Celia*] Ay, this same is she.
Out, thou chameleon[4] harlot! now thine eyes
Vie tears with the hyaena.[5] Dar'st thou look
Upon my wronged face?—I cry your pardons,
I fear I have forgettingly transgressed
Against the dignity of the court—
2 AVOCATORE No, madam.
LADY POLITIC And been exorbitant°— *excessive*
2 AVOCATORE You have not, lady.
4 AVOCATORE These proofs are strong.
LADY POLITIC Surely, I had no purpose
To scandalize your honors, or my sex's.
3 AVOCATORE We do believe it.
LADY POLITIC Surely, you may believe it.
2 AVOCATORE Madam, we do.
LADY POLITIC Indeed you may; my breeding
Is not so coarse—
4 AVOCATORE We know it.
LADY POLITIC To offend
With pertinacy—
3 AVOCATORE Lady—
LADY POLITIC Such a presence!
No surely.
1 AVOCATORE We well think it.
LADY POLITIC You may think it.
1 AVOCATORE Let her o'ercome. What witnesses have you
To make good your report?
BONARIO Our consciences.
CELIA And heaven, that never fails the innocent.
4 AVOCATORE These are no testimonies.
BONARIO Not in your courts,
Where multitude, and clamor overcomes.
1 AVOCATORE Nay, then you do wax insolent.
[*Reenter Officers, bearing Volpone on a couch.*]
VOLTORE Here, here,
The testimony comes, that will convince,
And put to utter dumbness their bold tongues:
See here, grave fathers, here's the ravisher,
The rider on men's wives, the great impostor,
The grand voluptuary! Do you not think
These limbs should affect venery?° or these eyes *lust*

4. An animal that changes colors, a symbol of fraud.

5. The hyena was known for luring its victims and then devouring them.

Covet a concubine? Pray you mark these hands;
Are they not fit to stroke a lady's breasts?—
Perhaps he doth dissemble!

BONARIO So he does.

VOLTORE Would you have him tortured?

BONARIO I would have him proved.

VOLTORE Best try him then with goads, or burning irons;
Put him to the strappado:[6] I have heard
The rack hath cured the gout; 'faith, give it him,
And help him of a malady; be courteous.
I'll undertake, before these honored fathers,
He shall have yet as many left diseases,
As she has known adulterers, or thou strumpets.—
O, my most equal hearers, if these deeds,
Acts of this bold and most exorbitant strain,
May pass with sufferance, what one citizen
But owes the forfeit of his life, yea, fame,
To him that dares traduce him? Which of you
Are safe, my honored fathers? I would ask,
With leave of your grave fatherhoods, if their plot
Have any face or color like to truth?
Or if, unto the dullest nostril here,
It smell not rank, and most abhorred slander?
I crave your care of this good gentleman,
Whose life is much endangered by their fable;
And as for them, I will conclude with this,
That vicious persons, when they're hot and fleshed
In impious acts, their constancy abounds:
Damned deeds are done with greatest confidence.

1 AVOCATORE Take them to custody, and sever them.

2 AVOCATORE 'Tis pity two such prodigies should live.

1 AVOCATORE Let the old gentleman be returned with care.
[*Exeunt Officers with Volpone.*]
I'm sorry our credulity hath wronged him.

4 AVOCATORE These are two creatures!

3 AVOCATORE I've an earthquake in me.

2 AVOCATORE Their shame, even in their cradles, fled their faces.

4 AVOCATORE [*to Voltore*]
You have done a worthy service to the state, sir,
In their discovery.

1 AVOCATORE You shall hear, ere night,
What punishment the court decrees upon them.
[*Exeunt Avocatori, Notario, and Officers with Bonario and Celia.*]

VOLTORE We thank your fatherhoods.—How like you it?

MOSCA Rare.
I'd have your tongue, sir, tipped with gold for this;
I'd have you be the heir to the whole city;
The earth I'd have want men, ere you want living:° *lack a livelihood*

6. A form of torture to extort confession in which the victim's hands were tied across his back; he was then hoisted from the ground by a pulley and let down with a jerk.

They're bound to erect your statue in St. Mark's.
Signior Corvino, I would have you go
And show yourself, that you have conquered.

CORVINO Yes.

MOSCA It was much better that you should profess
Yourself a cuckold thus, than that the other
Should have been proved.

CORVINO Nay, I considered that:
Now it is her fault.

MOSCA Then it had been yours.

CORVINO True; I do doubt this advocate still.

MOSCA I'faith
You need not, I dare ease you of that care.

CORVINO I trust thee, Mosca.

MOSCA As your own soul, sir. [*Exit Corvino.*]

CORBACCIO Mosca!

MOSCA Now for your business, sir.

CORBACCIO How! Have you business?

MOSCA Yes, yours, sir.

CORBACCIO O, none else?

MOSCA None else, not I.

CORBACCIO Be careful, then.

MOSCA Rest you with both your eyes, sir.

CORBACCIO Dispatch it.

MOSCA Instantly.

CORBACCIO And look that all,
Whatever, be put in, jewels, plate, moneys.
Household stuff, bedding, curtains.

MOSCA Curtain-rings, sir:
Only the advocate's fee must be deducted.

CORBACCIO I'll pay him now; you'll be too prodigal.

MOSCA Sir, I must tender it.

CORBACCIO Two chequines is well.

MOSCA No, six, sir.

CORBACCIO 'Tis too much.

MOSCA He talked a great while;
You must consider that, sir.

CORBACCIO Well, there's three—

MOSCA I'll give it him.

CORBACCIO Do so, and there's for thee. [*Exit.*]

MOSCA [*aside*] Bountiful bones! What horrid strange offence
Did he commit 'gainst nature, in his youth,
Worthy this age? [*To Voltore.*]—You see, sir, how I work
Unto your ends: take you no notice.

VOLTORE No,
I'll leave you. [*Exit.*]

MOSCA All is yours, the devil and all:
Good advocate!—Madam, I'll bring you home.

LADY POLITIC No, I'll go see your patron.

MOSCA That you shall not:

I'll tell you why. My purpose is to urge
My patron to reform his will; and for
The zeal you have shown to-day, whereas before
You were but third or fourth, you shall be now
Put in the first: which would appear as begged,
If you were present. Therefore—

LADY POLITIC You shall sway me. [*Exeunt*.]

Act 5

Scene 1. *A room in Volpone's house*

[*Enter Volpone*.]

VOLPONE Well, I am here, and all this brunt° is past. *crisis*
I ne'er was in dislike with my disguise
Till this fled moment: here 'twas good, in private;
But in your public,—*cave*° whilst I breathe. *watch out (Latin)*
'Fore God, my left leg 'gan to have the cramp,
And I apprehended straight some power had struck me
With a dead palsy: Well! I must be merry,
And shake it off. A many of these fears
Would put me into some villainous disease,
Should they come thick upon me: I'll prevent 'em.
Give me a bowl of lusty wine, to fright
This humor from my heart. [*Drinks*.]—Hum, hum, hum!
'Tis almost gone already; I shall conquer.
Any device, now, of rare ingenious knavery,
That would possess me with a violent laughter,
Would make me up° again. [*Drinks again*.]—So, so, so, so! *restore me*
This heat is life; 'tis blood by this time:[1]—Mosca!

Scene 2

[*Enter Mosca*.]

MOSCA How now, sir? Does the day look clear again?
Are we recovered, and wrought out of error,
Into our way, to see our path before us?
Is our trade free once more?

VOLPONE Exquisite Mosca!

MOSCA Was it not carried learnedly?

VOLPONE And stoutly:
Good wits are greatest in extremities.

MOSCA It were a folly beyond thought, to trust
Any grand act unto a cowardly spirit:
You are not taken with it enough, methinks.

VOLPONE O, more than if I had enjoyed the wench:
The pleasure of all womankind's not like it.

MOSCA Why now you speak, sir. We must here be fixed;
Here we must rest; this is our masterpiece;
We cannot think to go beyond this.

VOLPONE True,

1. Early modern medicine held that wine metabolized into blood quickly.

Thou hast played thy prize, my precious Mosca.
MOSCA Nay, sir,
To gull the court—
VOLPONE And quite divert the torrent
Upon the innocent.
MOSCA Yes, and to make
So rare a music out of discords—
VOLPONE Right.
That yet to me's the strangest, how thou hast borne it!
That these, being so divided 'mongst themselves,
Should not scent somewhat, or in me or thee,
Or doubt their own side.
MOSCA True, they will not see't.
Too much light blinds them, I think. Each of them
Is so possessed and stuffed with his own hopes,
That any thing unto the contrary,
Never so true, or never so apparent,
Never so palpable, they will resist it—
VOLPONE Like a temptation of the devil.
MOSCA Right, sir.
Merchants may talk of trade, and your great signiors
Of land that yields well; but if Italy
Have any glebe° more fruitful than these fellows, *land*
I am deceived. Did not your advocate rare?[2]
VOLPONE O—*My most honored fathers, my grave fathers,*
Under correction of your fatherhoods,
What face of truth is here? If these strange deeds
May pass, most honored fathers—I had much ado
To forbear laughing.
MOSCA It seemed to me, you sweat, sir.
VOLPONE In troth, I did a little.
MOSCA But confess, sir,
Were you not daunted?
VOLPONE In good faith, I was
A little in a mist, but not dejected;
Never, but still my self.
MOSCA I think it, sir.
Now, so truth help me, I must needs say this, sir,
And out of conscience for your advocate,
He has taken pains, in faith, sir, and deserved,
In my poor judgment, I speak it under favor,
Not to contrary you, sir, very richly—
Well—to be cozened.
VOLPONE Troth, and I think so too,
By that I heard him, in the latter end.
MOSCA O, but before, sir: had you heard him first
Draw it to certain heads, then aggravate,
Then use his vehement figures[3] —I looked still

2. Didn't Voltore do a great job as a lawyer?

3. Strong rhetoric.

When he would shift° a shirt: and, doing this — *change*
Out of pure love, no hope of gain—
VOLPONE 'Tis right.
I cannot answer him, Mosca, as I would,
Not yet; but for thy sake, at thy entreaty,
I will begin, even now—to vex them all,
This very instant.
MOSCA Good sir.
VOLPONE Call the dwarf
And eunuch forth.
MOSCA Castrone, Nano!
[*Enter Castrone and Nano.*]
NANO Here.
VOLPONE Shall we have a jig now?
MOSCA What you please, sir.
VOLPONE Go,
Straight give out about the streets, you two,
That I am dead; do it with constancy,
Sadly, do you hear? Impute it to the grief
Of this late slander. [*Exeunt Castrone and Nano.*]
MOSCA What do you mean, sir?
VOLPONE O,
I shall have instantly my vulture, crow,
Raven, come flying hither, on the news,
To peck for carrion, my she-wolf, and all,
Greedy, and full of expectation—
MOSCA And then to have it ravished from their mouths!
VOLPONE 'Tis true. I will have thee put on a gown,
And take upon thee, as thou wert mine heir:
Show them a will. Open that chest, and reach
Forth one of those that has the blanks; I'll straight
Put in thy name.
MOSCA It will be rare, sir. [*Gives him a paper.*]
VOLPONE Ay,
When they ev'n gape, and find themselves deluded—
MOSCA Yes.
VOLPONE And thou use them scurvily! Dispatch,
Get on thy gown.
MOSCA [*putting on a gown*] But what, sir, if they ask
After the body?
VOLPONE Say, it was corrupted.
MOSCA I'll say, it stunk, sir; and was fain to have it
Coffined up instantly, and sent away.
VOLPONE Any thing; what thou wilt. Hold, here's my will.
Get thee a cap, a count-book, pen and ink,
Papers afore thee; sit as thou wert taking
An inventory of parcels: I'll get up
Behind the curtain, on a stool, and hearken;
Sometime peep over, see how they do look,
With what degrees their blood doth leave their faces,

O, 'twill afford me a rare meal of laughter!
MOSCA [*putting on a cap, and setting out the table, etc.*]
Your advocate will turn stark dull upon it.
VOLPONE It will take off his oratory's edge.
MOSCA But your clarissimo,[4] old round-back, he
Will crump you like a hog-louse, with the touch.
VOLPONE And what Corvino?
MOSCA O, sir, look for him,
To-morrow morning, with a rope and dagger,
To visit all the streets; he must run mad.
My lady too, that came into the court,
To bear false witness for your worship—
VOLPONE Yes,
And kissed me 'fore the fathers, when my face
Flowed all with oils.
MOSCA And sweat, sir. Why, your gold
Is such another medicine, it dries up
All those offensive savors: it transforms
The most deformed, and restores them lovely,
As 'twere the strange poetical girdle.[5] Jove
Could not invent t' himself a shroud more subtle
To pass Acrisius' guards.[6] It is the thing
Makes all the world her grace, her youth, her beauty.
VOLPONE I think she loves me.
MOSCA Who? the lady, sir?
She's jealous° of you. *devoted to*
VOLPONE Dost thou say so? [*Knocking within.*]
MOSCA Hark,
There's some already.
VOLPONE Look.
MOSCA It is the Vulture;
He has the quickest scent.
VOLPONE I'll to my place,
Thou to thy posture. [*Goes behind the curtain.*]
MOSCA I am set.
VOLPONE But, Mosca,
Play the artificer° now, torture them rarely. *craftsman, trickster*

Scene 3

[*Enter Voltore.*]
VOLTORE How now, my Mosca?
MOSCA [*writing*] *Turkey carpets, nine—*
VOLTORE Taking an inventory! That is well.
MOSCA *Two suits of bedding, tissue*[7]*—*
VOLTORE Where's the will?
Let me read that the while.

4. A Venetian grandee, here referring to Corbaccio.
5. Venus's belt made its wearers beautiful and seductive.
6. Acrisius kept his daughter Danae in a tower protected by guards, but Zeus escaped them by coming to her in golden shower.
7. Fine fabric woven with gold and silver.

[*Enter Servants, with Corbaccio in a chair.*]

CORBACCIO So, set me down,
And get you home. [*Exeunt Servants.*]

VOLTORE Is he come now, to trouble us!

MOSCA *Of cloth of gold, two more—*

CORBACCIO Is it done, Mosca?

MOSCA *Of several velvets eight—*

VOLTORE I like his care.

CORBACCIO Dost thou not hear?

[*Enter Corvino.*]

CORVINO Ha! is the hour come, Mosca?

VOLPONE [*peeping over the curtain*] Ay, now they muster.

CORVINO What does the advocate here,
Or this Corbaccio?

CORBACCIO What do these here?

[*Enter Lady Politic Would-be.*]

LADY POLITIC Mosca!
Is his thread spun?[8]

MOSCA *Eight chests of linen—*

VOLPONE O,
My fine dame Would-be, too!

CORVINO Mosca, the will,
That I may shew it these, and rid them hence.

MOSCA *Six chests of diaper, four of damask.*[9]—There.

[*Gives them the will carelessly, over his shoulder.*]

CORBACCIO Is that the will?

MOSCA *Down-beds and bolsters—*

VOLPONE Rare!
Be busy still. Now they begin to flutter:
They never think of me. Look, see, see, see!
How their swift eyes run over the long deed,
Unto the name, and to the legacies,
What is bequeathed them there—

MOSCA *Ten suits of hangings*°— *tapestries*

VOLPONE Ay, in their garters, Mosca. Now their hopes
Are at the gasp.

VOLTORE Mosca the heir!

CORBACCIO What's that?

VOLPONE My advocate is dumb; look to my merchant,
He has heard of some strange storm, a ship is lost,
He faints; my lady will swoon. Old glazen eyes,[1]
He hath not reached his despair yet.

CORBACCIO All these
Are out of hope; I am, sure, the man. [*Takes the will.*]

CORVINO But, Mosca—

MOSCA *Two cabinets.*

CORVINO Is this in earnest?

8. The thread of life, spun and cut by the Fates.

9. Diaper is a linen fabric woven with patterns; damask is a rich silk fabric woven with designs.

1. Corbaccio wears glasses.

MOSCA *One*
Of ebony—
CORVINO Or do you but delude me?
MOSCA *The other, mother of pearl*—I am very busy.
Good faith, it is a fortune thrown upon me—
Item, one salt° *of agate*—not my seeking. *saltcellar*
LADY POLITIC. Do you hear, sir?
MOSCA *A perfumed box*—'Pray you forbear,
You see I'm troubled—*made of an onyx*—
LADY POLITIC How!
MOSCA Tomorrow or next day, I shall be at leisure
To talk with you all.
CORVINO Is this my large hope's issue?
LADY POLITIC Sir, I must have a fairer answer.
MOSCA Madam!
Marry, and shall: 'pray you, fairly quit my house.
Nay, raise no tempest with your looks; but hark you,
Remember what your ladyship offered me
To put you in an heir; go to, think on it:
And what you said e'en your best madams did
For maintenance; and why not you? Enough.
Go home, and use the poor Sir Pol, your knight, well,
For fear I tell some riddles; go, be melancholy.
[*Exit Lady Would-be.*]
VOLPONE O, my fine devil!
CORVINO Mosca, 'pray you a word.
MOSCA Lord! will you not take your dispatch hence yet?
Methinks, of all, you should have been the example.
Why should you stay here? With what thought, what promise?
Hear you; do you not know, I know you an ass,
And that you would most fain have been a wittol,[2]
If fortune would have let you? That you are
A declared cuckold, on good terms? This pearl,
You'll say, was yours? Right: this diamond?
I'll not deny't, but thank you. Much here else?
It may be so. Why, think that these good works
May help to hide your bad. I'll not betray you;
Although you be but extraordinary,
And have it only in title,[3] it sufficeth:
Go home, be melancholy too, or mad. [*Exit Corvino.*]
VOLPONE Rare Mosca! How his villainy becomes him!
VOLTORE Certain he doth delude all these for me.
CORBACCIO Mosca the heir!
VOLPONE O, his four eyes have found it.
CORBACCIO I am cozened, cheated, by a parasite slave;
Harlot, thou hast gulled me.
MOSCA Yes, sir. Stop your mouth,
Or I shall draw the only tooth is left.

2. A man who encourages the infidelity of his own wife.
3. Not a real cuckold but a seeming one.

Are not you he, that filthy covetous wretch,
With the three legs,[4] that here, in hope of prey,
Have, any time this three years, snuffed about,
With your most groveling nose, and would have hired
Me to the poisoning of my patron, sir?
Are not you he that have today in court
Professed the disinheriting of your son?
Perjured yourself? Go home, and die, and stink.
If you but croak a syllable, all comes out:
Away, and call your porters! [*Exit Corbaccio.*] Go, go, stink.

VOLPONE Excellent varlet!

VOLTORE Now, my faithful Mosca,
I find thy constancy.

MOSCA Sir!

VOLTORE Sincere.

MOSCA [*writing*] *A table*
Of porphyry—I mar'l° you'll be thus troublesome. marvel

VOLTORE Nay, leave off now, they are gone.

MOSCA Why, who are you?
What! Who did send for you? O, cry you mercy,
Reverend sir! Good faith, I am grieved for you,
That any chance of mine should thus defeat
Your (I must needs say) most deserving travails:
But I protest, sir, it was cast upon me,
And I could almost wish to be without it,
But that the will o' the dead must be observed.
Marry, my joy is that you need it not;
You have a gift, sir, (thank your education,)
Will never let you want, while there are men,
And malice, to breed causes. Would I had
But half the like, for all my fortune, sir!
If I have any suits, as I do hope,
Things being so easy and direct, I shall not,
I will make bold with your obstreperous aid,
Conceive me,—for your fee, sir. In mean time,
You that have so much law, I know have the conscience
Not to be covetous of what is mine.
Good sir, I thank you for my plate; 'twill help
To set up a young man. Good faith, you look
As you were costive;[5] best go home and purge, sir. [*Exit Voltore.*]

VOLPONE [*comes from behind the curtain*]
Bid him eat lettuce well. My witty mischief,
Let me embrace thee. O that I could now
Transform thee to a Venus!—Mosca, go,
Straight take my habit of clarissimo,[6]
And walk the streets; be seen, torment them more:
We must pursue, as well as plot. Who would
Have lost this feast?

4. Two legs and a cane.
5. Constipated.
6. By publicly wearing the clothes of a clarissimo, Mosca flouts the laws against dressing above one's rank.

MOSCA I doubt it will lose them.
VOLPONE O, my recovery shall recover all.
That I could now but think on some disguise
To meet them in, and ask them questions:
How I would vex them still at every turn!
MOSCA Sir, I can fit you.
VOLPONE Canst thou?
MOSCA Yes, I know
One o' the commandatori, sir, so like you;
Him will I straight make drunk, and bring you his habit.[7]
VOLPONE A rare disguise, and answering thy brain!
O, I will be a sharp disease unto them.
MOSCA Sir, you must look for curses—
VOLPONE Till they burst;
The Fox fares over best when he is cursed. [*Exeunt.*]

Scene 4. *A hall in Sir Politic's house*

[*Enter Peregrine disguised, and three Merchants.*]
PEREGRINE Am I enough disguised?
1 MERCHANT I warrant you.
PEREGRINE All my ambition is to fright him only.
2 MERCHANT If you could ship him away, 'twere excellent.
3 MERCHANT To Zant, or to Aleppo?[8]
PEREGRINE Yes, and have his
Adventures put i' the Book of Voyages,
And his gulled story[9] registered for truth.
Well, gentlemen, when I am in a while,
And that you think us warm in our discourse,
Know your approaches.
1 MERCHANT Trust it to our care. [*Exeunt Merchants.*]
[*Enter Waiting-woman.*]
PEREGRINE Save you, fair lady! Is Sir Pol within?
WOMAN I do not know, sir.
PEREGRINE Pray you say unto him,
Here is a merchant, upon earnest business,
Desires to speak with him.
WOMAN I will see, sir. [*Exit.*]
PEREGRINE Pray you.—
I see the family is all female here.[1]
[*Reenter Waiting-woman.*]
WOMAN He says, sir, he has weighty affairs of state,
That now require him whole; some other time
You may possess him.
PEREGRINE Pray you say again,
If those require him whole, these will exact him,
Whereof I bring him tidings. [*Exit Woman.*]—What might be

7. Volpone puts on a sergeant's uniform.
8. Zant or Zakynthos, an Ionian island, was then under Venetian rule; Aleppo is a town in Syria.
9. Story of his being tricked.
1. The family, as in Latin *familia*, refers to the household of servants.

His grave affair of state now! How to make
Bolognian sausages here in Venice, sparing
One o' the ingredients?
[*Reenter Waiting-woman.*]

WOMAN Sir, he says, he knows
By your word *tidings*, that you are no statesman,[2]
And therefore wills you stay.

PEREGRINE Sweet, pray you return him;
I have not read so many proclamations,
And studied them for words, as he has done—
But—here he deigns to come. [*Exit Woman.*]
[*Enter Sir Politic.*]

SIR POLITIC Sir, I must crave
Your courteous pardon. There hath chanced today,
Unkind disaster 'twixt my lady and me;
And I was penning my apology,
To give her satisfaction, as you came now.

PEREGRINE Sir, I am grieved I bring you worse disaster:
The gentleman you met at the port today,
That told you, he was newly arrived—

SIR POLITIC Ay, was
A fugitive punk?° *prostitute*

PEREGRINE No, sir, a spy set on you;
And he has made relation to the senate,
That you professed to him to have a plot
To sell the State of Venice to the Turk.

SIR POLITIC O me!

PEREGRINE For which, warrants are signed by this time,
To apprehend you, and to search your study
For papers—

SIR POLITIC Alas, sir, I have none, but notes
Drawn out of play-books—

PEREGRINE All the better, sir.

SIR POLITIC And some essays. What shall I do?

PEREGRINE Sir, best
Convey yourself into a sugar-chest;
Or, if you could lie round, a frail° were rare, *rush basket*
And I could send you aboard.

SIR POLITIC Sir, I but talked so,
For discourse sake merely. [*Knocking within.*]

PEREGRINE Hark! they are there.

SIR POLITIC I am a wretch, a wretch!

PEREGRINE What will you do, sir?
Have you ne'er a currant-butt° to leap into? *cask for currants*
They'll put you to the rack; you must be sudden.

SIR POLITIC Sir, I have an engine—

3 MERCHANT [*within*] Sir Politic Would-be!

2 MERCHANT [*within*] Where is he?

2. A statesman would receive intelligence rather than tidings.

SIR POLITIC That I have thought upon before time.
PEREGRINE What is it?
SIR POLITIC I shall ne'er endure the torture.
Marry, it is, sir, of a tortoise-shell,
Fitted for these extremities; pray you, sir, help me.
Here I've a place, sir, to put back my legs,
Please you to lay it on, sir, [*lies down while Peregrine places the shell upon him*]—with this cap,
And my black gloves. I'll lie, sir, like a tortoise,
'Till they are gone.
PEREGRINE And call you this an engine?
SIR POLITIC Mine own device[3]——Good sir, bid my wife's women
To burn my papers. [*Exit Peregrine.*]
[*The three Merchants rush in.*]
1 MERCHANT Where is he hid?
3 MERCHANT We must,
And will sure find him.
2 MERCHANT Which is his study?
[*Reenter Peregrine.*]
1 MERCHANT What
Are you, sir?
PEREGRINE I am a merchant, that came here
To look upon this tortoise.
3 MERCHANT How!
1 MERCHANT St. Mark!
What beast is this!
PEREGRINE It is a fish.
2 MERCHANT Come out here!
PEREGRINE Nay, you may strike him, sir, and tread upon him;
He'll bear a cart.
1 MERCHANT What, to run over him?
PEREGRINE Yes, sir.
3 MERCHANT Let's jump upon him.
2 MERCHANT Can he not go?
PEREGRINE He creeps, sir.
1 MERCHANT Let's see him creep.
PEREGRINE No, good sir, you will hurt him.
2 MERCHANT Heart, I will see him creep, or prick his guts.
3 MERCHANT Come out here!
PEREGRINE [*aside to Sir Politic*] Pray you, sir!—Creep a little.
1 MERCHANT Forth.
2 MERCHANT Yet farther.
PEREGRINE Good sir!—Creep.
2 MERCHANT We'll see his legs.
[*They pull off the shell and discover him.*]
3 MERCHANT God's so, he has garters!
1 MERCHANT Ay, and gloves!

3. Contrivance, but also an emblem, or symbol; the tortoise was an emblem of prudence.

2 MERCHANT Is this
Your fearful tortoise?
PEREGRINE [*discovering himself*] Now, Sir Pol, we are even;
For your next project I shall be prepared:
I am sorry for the funeral of your notes, sir.
1 MERCHANT 'Twere a rare motion to be seen in Fleet-street.[4]
2 MERCHANT Ay, in the Term.
1 MERCHANT Or Smithfield, in the fair.[5]
3 MERCHANT Methinks 'tis but a melancholy sight.
PEREGRINE Farewell, most politic tortoise!
[*Exeunt Peregrine and Merchants. Reenter Waiting-woman.*]
SIR POLITIC Where's my lady?
Knows she of this?
WOMAN I know not, sir.
SIR POLITIC Enquire.—
O, I shall be the fable of all feasts,
The freight of the gazetti,[6] ship-boy's tale;
And, which is worst, even talk for ordinaries.
WOMAN My lady's come most melancholy home,
And says, sir, she will straight to sea, for physic.
SIR POLITIC And I to shun this place and clime for ever,
Creeping with house on back, and think it well
To shrink my poor head in my politic shell. [*Exeunt.*]

Scene 5. *A room in Volpone's house*

[*Enter Mosca in the habit of a Clarissimo and Volpone in that of a Commendatore.*]
VOLPONE Am I then like him?
MOSCA O, sir, you are he;
No man can sever° you. *distinguish*
VOLPONE Good.
MOSCA But what am I?
VOLPONE 'Fore heaven, a brave clarissimo; thou becom'st it!
Pity thou wert not born one.
MOSCA If I hold
My made one, 'twill be well. [*Aside.*]
VOLPONE I'll go and see
What news first at the court. [*Exit.*]
MOSCA Do so. My Fox
Is out of his hole, and ere he shall reenter,
I'll make him languish in his borrowed case,° *false costume*
Except he come to composition° with me.— *financial agreement*
Androgyno, Castrone, Nano!
[*Enter Androgyno, Castrone, and Nano.*]
ALL Here.
MOSCA Go, recreate yourselves abroad; go sport.— [*Exeunt.*]

4. A rare motion was a puppet show; Fleet Street in central London was frequented by lawyers during the terms of the Inns of Court where plays were frequently performed.
5. The site of the Bartholomew Fair.
6. Gossip of the news-sheets.

So, now I have the keys, and am possessed.
Since he will needs be dead afore his time,
I'll bury him, or gain by him: I am his heir,
And so will keep me, till he share at least.
To cozen him of all, were but a cheat
Well placed; no man would construe it a sin:
Let his sport pay for't. This is called the Fox-trap.

Scene 6. *A street*

[*Enter Corbaccio and Corvino*.]
CORBACCIO They say, the court is set.
CORVINO We must maintain
Our first tale good, for both our reputations.
CORBACCIO Why, mine's no tale: my son would there have killed me.
CORVINO That's true, I had forgot: [*aside*:]—mine is, I'm sure.
But for your will, sir.
CORBACCIO Ay, I'll come upon him
For that hereafter, now his patron's dead.
[*Enter Volpone in disguise*.]
VOLPONE Signior Corvino! and Corbaccio! sir,
Much joy unto you.
CORVINO Of what?
VOLPONE The sudden good
Dropped down upon you—
CORBACCIO Where?
VOLPONE And none knows how,
From old Volpone, sir.
CORBACCIO Out, arrant knave!
VOLPONE Let not your too much wealth, sir, make you furious.
CORBACCIO Away, thou varlet!
VOLPONE Why, sir?
CORBACCIO Dost thou mock me?
VOLPONE You mock the world, sir; did you not change wills?
CORBACCIO Out, harlot!
VOLPONE O! belike you are the man.
Signior Corvino? 'faith, you carry it well;
You grow not mad withal; I love your spirit:
You are not overleavened with your fortune.
You should have some would swell now, like a wine-fat,
With such an autumn—Did he give you all, sir?
CORVINO Avoid, you rascal!
VOLPONE Troth, your wife has shown
Herself a very woman; but you are well,
You need not care, you have a good estate,
To bear it out, sir, better by this chance:
Except Corbaccio have a share.
CORBACCIO Hence, varlet.
VOLPONE You will not be aknown, sir; why, 'tis wise.
Thus do all gamesters, at all games, dissemble:

No man will seem to win. [*Exeunt Corvino and Corbaccio.*]—
Here comes my vulture,
Heaving his beak up in the air, and snuffing.

Scene 7

[*Enter Voltore.*]

VOLTORE Outstripped thus, by a parasite! a slave,
Would run on errands, and make legs° for crumbs! *bows*
Well, what I'll do—

VOLPONE The court stays for your worship.
I e'en rejoice, sir, at your worship's happiness,
And that it fell into so learned hands,
That understand the fingering—

VOLTORE What do you mean?

VOLPONE I mean to be a suitor to your worship,
For the small tenement, out of reparations,° *repair*
That, to the end of your long row of houses,
By the Piscaria:° it was, in Volpone's time, *fish market*
Your predecessor, ere he grew diseased,
A handsome, pretty, customed° bawdy-house *used by customers*
As any was in Venice, none dispraised;
But fell with him: his body and that house
Decayed together.

VOLTORE Come, sir, leave your prating.

VOLPONE Why, if your worship give me but your hand,
That I may have the refusal, I have done.
'Tis a mere toy to you, sir; candle-rents;[7]
As your learned worship knows—

VOLTORE What do I know?

VOLPONE Marry, no end of your wealth, sir; God decrease it!

VOLTORE Mistaking knave! what, mock'st thou my misfortune? [*Exit.*]

VOLPONE His blessing on your heart, sir; would 'twere more!—
Now to my first again, at the next corner. [*Exit.*]

Scene 8. *Another part of the street*

[*Enter Corbaccio and Corvino;—Mosca passes over the stage, before them.*]

CORBACCIO See, in our habit![8] see the impudent varlet!

CORVINO That I could shoot mine eyes at him like gun-stones!

[*Enter Volpone.*]

VOLPONE But is this true, sir, of the parasite?

CORBACCIO Again, to afflict us! monster!

VOLPONE In good faith, sir,
I'm heartily grieved, a beard of your grave length
Should be so overreached. I never brooked° *could stand*
That parasite's hair; methought his nose should cozen:° *cheat*
There still was somewhat in his look, did promise
The bane of a clarissimo.

7. Rents from poor properties that were only enough to buy candles with.

8. The dress reserved for members of our class.

CORBACCIO Knave—

VOLPONE Methinks

Yet you, that are so traded in the world,
A witty merchant, the fine bird, Corvino,
That have such moral emblems on your name,
Should not have sung your shame, and dropt your cheese,
To let the Fox laugh at your emptiness.

CORVINO Sirrah, you think the privilege of the place,
And your red saucy cap, that seems to me
Nailed to your jolt-head° with those two chequines,[9] *blockhead*
Can warrant your abuses; come you hither:
You shall perceive, sir, I dare beat you; approach.

VOLPONE No haste, sir, I do know your valor well,
Since you durst publish what you are, sir.

CORVINO Tarry,
I'd speak with you.

VOLPONE Sir, sir, another time—

CORVINO Nay, now.

VOLPONE O lord, sir! I were a wise man,
Would stand the fury of a distracted cuckold.

[*As he is running off, reenter Mosca.*]

CORBACCIO What, come again!

VOLPONE Upon 'em, Mosca; save me.

CORBACCIO The air's infected where he breathes.

CORVINO Let's fly him.

[*Exeunt Corvino and Corbaccio.*]

VOLPONE Excellent basilisk![1] turn upon the vulture.

Scene 9

[*Enter Voltore.*]

VOLTORE Well, flesh-fly,[2] it is summer with you now;
Your winter will come on.

MOSCA Good advocate,
Prithee not rail, nor threaten out of place thus;
Thou'lt make a solecism,[3] as madam says.
Get you a biggin[4] more, your brain breaks loose. [*Exit.*]

VOLTORE Well, sir.

VOLPONE Would you have me beat the insolent slave,
Throw dirt upon his first good clothes?

VOLTORE This same
Is doubtless some familiar.[5]

VOLPONE Sir, the court,
In troth, stays for you. I am mad, a mule
That never read Justinian,[6] should get up,

9. Coinlike buttons that were part of the commendatore's uniform.
1. Mythical reptile whose look could kill.
2. The blowfly, which lays its eggs in carrion; the meaning of Mosca's name.
3. A mistake in speech.
4. Lawyer's skullcap.
5. Household member; attending demon.
6. The Emperor Justinian drew up the Roman legal code.

And ride an advocate. Had you no quirk
To avoid gullage,° sir, by such a creature? *trickery*
I hope you do but jest; he has not done it,
'Tis but confederacy, to blind the rest.
You are the heir?

VOLTORE A strange, officious,
Troublesome knave! thou dost torment me.

VOLPONE I know—
It cannot be, sir, that you should be cozened;
'Tis not within the wit of man to do it;
You are so wise, so prudent; and 'tis fit
That wealth and wisdom still should go together. [*Exeunt.*]

Scene 10. *The Scrutineo or Senate-House*

[*Enter Avocatori, Notario, Bonario, Celia, Corbaccio, Corvino, Commendatori, Saffi, etc.*]

1 AVOCATORE Are all the parties here?

NOTARIO All but the advocate.

2 AVOCATORE And here he comes.
[*Enter Voltore and Volpone.*]

1 AVOCATORE Then bring them forth to sentence.

VOLTORE O, my most honored fathers, let your mercy
Once win upon your justice, to forgive—
I am distracted—

VOLPONE [*aside*] What will he do now?

VOLTORE O,
I know not which to address myself to first;
Whether your fatherhoods, or these innocents—

CORVINO [*aside*] Will he betray himself?

VOLTORE Whom equally
I have abused, out of most covetous ends—

CORVINO The man is mad!

CORBACCIO What's that?

CORVINO He is possessed.° *by the devil*

VOLTORE For which, now struck in conscience, here, I prostrate
Myself at your offended feet, for pardon.

1, 2 AVOCATORE Arise.

CELIA O heaven, how just thou art!

VOLPONE [*aside*] I am caught
In mine own noose—

CORVINO [*to Corbaccio*] Be constant, sir: nought now
Can help, but impudence.

1 AVOCATORE Speak forward.

COMMENDATORE Silence!

VOLTORE It is not passion in me, reverend fathers,
But only conscience, conscience, my good sires,
That makes me now tell truth. That parasite,
That knave, hath been the instrument of all.

1 AVOCATORE Where is that knave? fetch him.
VOLPONE I go. [*Exit*.]
CORVINO Grave fathers,
This man's distracted; he confessed it now:
For, hoping to be old Volpone's heir,
Who now is dead—
3 AVOCATORE How!
2 AVOCATORE Is Volpone dead?
CORVINO Dead since, grave fathers.
BONARIO O sure vengeance!
1 AVOCATORE Stay,
Then he was no deceiver?
VOLTORE O no, none:
The parasite, grave fathers.
CORVINO He does speak
Out of mere envy, 'cause the servant's made
The thing he gaped for; please your fatherhoods,
This is the truth, though I'll not justify
The other,° but he may be some-deal faulty. *Mosca*
VOLTORE Ay, to your hopes, as well as mine, Corvino:
But I'll use modesty. Pleaseth your wisdoms,
To view these certain notes, and but confer them;
As I hope favor, they shall speak clear truth.
CORVINO The devil has entered him!
BONARIO Or bides in you.
4 AVOCATORE We have done ill, by a public officer
To send for him, if he be heir.
2 AVOCATORE For whom?
4 AVOCATORE Him that they call the parasite.
3 AVOCATORE 'Tis true,
He is a man of great estate, now left.
4 AVOCATORE Go you, and learn his name, and say, the court
Entreats his presence here, but to the clearing
Of some few doubts. [*Exit Notary*.]
2 AVOCATORE This same's a labyrinth!
1 AVOCATORE Stand you unto your first report?
CORVINO My state,
My life, my fame—
BONARIO Where is it?
CORVINO Are at the stake.
1 AVOCATORE Is yours so too?
CORBACCIO The advocate's a knave,
And has a forked tongue—
2 AVOCATORE Speak to the point.
CORBACCIO So is the parasite too.
1 AVOCATORE This is confusion.
VOLTORE I do beseech your fatherhoods, read but those—[*Giving them papers*.]
CORVINO And credit nothing the false spirit hath writ:
It cannot be, but he's possessed, grave fathers. [*The scene closes*.]

Scene 11. *A street*

[*Enter Volpone.*]

VOLPONE To make a snare for mine own neck! and run
My head into it, wilfully! with laughter!
When I had newly 'scaped, was free, and clear,
Out of mere wantonness! O, the dull devil
Was in this brain of mine, when I devised it,
And Mosca gave it second; he must now
Help to sear up° this vein, or we bleed dead.— *cauterize*
[*Enter Nano, Androgyno, and Castrone.*]
How now! who let you loose? whither go you now?
What, to buy gingerbread, or to drown kitlings?

NANO Sir, master Mosca called us out of doors,
And bid us all go play, and took the keys.

ANDROGYNO Yes.

VOLPONE Did master Mosca take the keys? why so!
I'm farther in. These are my fine conceits!
I must be merry, with a mischief to me!
What a vile wretch was I, that could not bear
My fortune soberly? I must have my crotchets,
And my conundrums! Well, go you, and seek him:
His meaning may be truer than my fear.
Bid him, he straight come to me to the court;
Thither will I, and, if't be possible,
Unscrew my advocate, upon new hopes:
When I provoked him, then I lost myself. [*Exeunt.*]

Scene 12. *The Scrutineo, or Senate-House*

[*Avocatori, Bonario, Celia, Corbaccio, Corvino, Commendatori, Saffi, etc., as before.*]

1 AVOCATORE These things can ne'er be reconciled. He, here, [*Showing the papers.*]
Professeth, that the gentleman was wronged,
And that the gentlewoman was brought thither,
Forced by her husband, and there left.

VOLTORE Most true.

CELIA How ready is heaven to those that pray!

1 AVOCATORE But that
Volpone would have ravished her, he holds
Utterly false, knowing his impotence.

CORVINO Grave fathers, he's possessed; again, I say,
Possessed: nay, if there be possession, and
Obsession, he has both.[7]

3 AVOCATORE Here comes our officer.

[*Enter Volpone, still in disguise.*]

VOLPONE The parasite will straight be here, grave fathers.

4 AVOCATORE You might invent some other name, sir varlet.

3 AVOCATORE Did not the notary meet him?

7. In possession the devil controls the body from within, in obsession from without.

VOLPONE Not that I know.
4 AVOCATORE His coming will clear all.
2 AVOCATORE Yet, it is misty.
VOLTORE May't please your fatherhoods—
VOLPONE [*whispers to Voltore*]
Sir, the parasite
Willed me to tell you, that his master lives;
That you are still the man; your hopes the same;
And this was only a jest—
VOLTORE How?
VOLPONE Sir, to try
If you were firm, and how you stood affected.
VOLTORE Art sure he lives?
VOLPONE Do I live, sir?
VOLTORE O me!
I was too violent.
VOLPONE Sir, you may redeem it.
They said, you were possessed; fall down, and seem so:
I'll help to make it good. [*Voltore falls.*]—God bless the man!—
Stop your wind hard, and swell—See, see, see, see!
He vomits crooked pins! His eyes are set,
Like a dead hare's hung in a poulter's° shop! *poultry dealer*
His mouth's running away![8] Do you see, signior?
Now it is in his belly.
CORVINO Ay, the devil!
VOLPONE Now in his throat.
CORVINO Ay, I perceive it plain.
VOLPONE 'Twill out, 'twill out! Stand clear. See where it flies,
In shape of a blue toad, with a bat's wings!
Do you not see it, sir?
CORBACCIO What? I think I do.
CORVINO 'Tis too manifest.
VOLPONE Look! he comes to himself!
VOLTORE Where am I?
VOLPONE Take good heart, the worst is past, sir.
You are dispossessed.
1 AVOCATORE What accident is this!
2 AVOCATORE Sudden, and full of wonder!
3 AVOCATORE If he were
Possessed, as it appears, all this is nothing.
CORVINO He has been often subject to these fits.
1 AVOCATORE Show him that writing:—Do you know it, sir?
VOLPONE [*whispers to Voltore*] Deny it, sir, forswear it; know it not.
VOLTORE Yes, I do know it well, it is my hand;
But all that it contains is false.
BONARIO O practice!° *deceit*
2 AVOCATORE What maze is this!

8. Early modern English accounts of fraudulent exorcisms of demonic possession describe similar symptoms.

1 AVOCATORE Is he not guilty then,
Whom you there name the parasite?
VOLTORE Grave fathers,
No more than his good patron, old Volpone.
4 AVOCATORE Why, he is dead.
VOLTORE O no, my honored fathers,
He lives—
1 AVOCATORE How! lives?
VOLTORE Lives.
2 AVOCATORE This is subtler yet!
3 AVOCATORE You said he was dead.
VOLTORE Never.
3 AVOCATORE You said so.
CORVINO I heard so.
4 AVOCATORE Here comes the gentleman; make him way.
[*Enter Mosca as a clarissimo.*]
3 AVOCATORE A stool.
4 AVOCATORE [*aside*]
A proper man; and, were Volpone dead,
A fit match for my daughter.
3 AVOCATORE Give him way.
VOLPONE [*aside to Mosca*] Mosca, I was almost lost; the advocate
Had betrayed all; but now it is recovered;
All's on the hinge° again—Say, I am living. *running well*
MOSCA What busy knave is this!—Most reverend fathers,
I sooner had attended your grave pleasures,
But that my order for the funeral
Of my dear patron, did require me—
VOLPONE [*aside*] Mosca!
MOSCA Whom I intend to bury like a gentleman.
VOLPONE [*aside*] Ay, quick,° and cozen me of all *alive*
2 AVOCATORE Still stranger!
More intricate!
1 AVOCATORE And come about again!
4 AVOCATORE [*aside*] It is a match, my daughter is bestowed.
MOSCA [*aside to Volpone*] Will you give me half?
VOLPONE First, I'll be hanged.
MOSCA I know
Your voice is good, cry not so loud.
1 AVOCATORE Demand
The advocate.—Sir, did you not affirm
Volpone was alive?
VOLPONE Yes, and he is;
This gentleman told me so.—[*Aside to Mosca:*] Thou shalt have half.
MOSCA Whose drunkard is this same? Speak, some that know him:
I never saw his face.—[*Aside to Volpone:*] I cannot now
Afford it you so cheap.
VOLPONE No!
1 AVOCATORE What say you?

VOLTORE The officer told me.
VOLPONE I did, grave fathers,
And will maintain he lives, with mine own life,
And that this creature [*points to Mosca*] told me.—[*Aside*.] I was born
With all good stars my enemies.
MOSCA Most grave fathers,
If such an insolence as this must pass
Upon me, I am silent: 'twas not this
For which you sent, I hope.
2 AVOCATORE Take him away.
VOLPONE Mosca!
3 AVOCATORE Let him be whipped.
VOLPONE Wilt thou betray me?
Cozen me?
3 AVOCATORE And taught to bear himself
Toward a person of his rank.
4 AVOCATORE Away. [*The Officers seize Volpone*.]
MOSCA I humbly thank your fatherhoods.
VOLPONE [*aside*] Soft, soft. Whipped!
And lose all that I have! If I confess,
It cannot be much more.
4 AVOCATORE [*to Mosca*] Sir, are you married?
VOLPONE They'll be allied anon; I must be resolute:
The Fox shall here uncase. [*Throws off his disguise*.]
MOSCA Patron!
VOLPONE Nay, now
My ruins shall not come alone: your match
I'll hinder sure: my substance shall not glue you,
Nor screw you into a family.
MOSCA Why, patron!
VOLPONE I am Volpone, and this is my knave; [*pointing to Mosca*]
This, [*to Voltore*] his own knave; this, [*to Corbaccio*] avarice's fool;
This, [*to Corvino*] a chimera[9] of wittol, fool, and knave:
And, reverend fathers, since we all can hope
Nought but a sentence, let's not now despair it.
You hear me brief.
CORVINO May it please your fatherhoods—
COMMENDATORE Silence.
1 AVOCATORE The knot is now undone by miracle.
2 AVOCATORE Nothing can be more clear.
3 AVOCATORE Or can more prove
These innocent.
1 AVOCATORE Give them their liberty.
BONARIO Heaven could not long let such gross crimes be hid.
2 AVOCATORE If this be held the highway to get riches,
May I be poor!
3 AVOCATORE This is not the gain, but torment.

9. A fantastical creature made up of a lion's head, a goat's body, and a serpent's tail.

1 AVOCATORE These possess wealth, as sick men possess fevers,
Which trulier may be said to possess them.[1]
2 AVOCATORE Disrobe that parasite.
CORVINO AND MOSCA Most honored fathers!—
1 AVOCATORE Can you plead aught to stay the course of justice?
If you can, speak.
CORVINO AND VOLTORE We beg favor.
CELIA And mercy.
1 AVOCATORE You hurt your innocence, suing for the guilty.
Stand forth; and first the parasite. You appear
T'have been the chiefest minister, if not plotter,
In all these lewd impostures; and now, lastly,
Have with your impudence abused the court,
And habit of a gentleman of Venice,
Being a fellow of no birth or blood,[2]
For which our sentence is, first, thou be whipped;
Then live perpetual prisoner in our gallies.
VOLPONE I thank you for him.
MOSCA Bane° to thy wolvish nature! *poison*
1 AVOCATORE Deliver him to the saffi. [*Mosca is carried out.*]—
Thou, Volpone,
By blood and rank a gentleman, canst not fall
Under like censure; but our judgment on thee
Is, that thy substance all be straight confiscate
To the hospital of the Incurabili:[3]
And, since the most was gotten by imposture,
By feigning lame, gout, palsy, and such diseases,
Thou art to lie in prison, cramped with irons,
Till thou be'st sick and lame indeed.—Remove him.
[*He is taken from the Bar.*]
VOLPONE This is called mortifying of a Fox.
1 AVOCATORE Thou, Voltore, to take away the scandal
Thou hast given all worthy men of thy profession,
Art banished from their fellowship, and our state.
Corbaccio!—bring him near—We here possess
Thy son of all thy state, and confine thee
To the monastery of San Spirito;
Where, since thou knewest not how to live well here,
Thou shalt be learned° to die well. *taught*
CORBACCIO Ah! what said he?
Commendatore. You shall know anon, sir.
1 AVOCATORE Thou, Corvino, shalt
Be straight embarked from thine own house, and rowed
Round about Venice, through the grand canale,
Wearing a cap, with fair long ass's ears,
Instead of horns; and so to mount, a paper
Pinned on thy breast, to the Berlina[4]—

1. Seneca, *Epistle* 119.2.
2. Mosca's sentence is the harshest because of his class status.
3. The Venetian Hospital of Incurables, founded in 1522 for orphans, beggars, and prostitutes.
4. Pillory.

CORVINO Yes,
And have mine eyes beat out with stinking fish,
Bruised fruit, and rotten eggs—'Tis well. I am glad
I shall not see my shame yet.
1 AVOCATORE And to expiate
Thy wrongs done to thy wife, thou art to send her
Home to her father, with her dowry trebled.
And these are all your judgments.
ALL Honored fathers.—
1 AVOCATORE Which may not be revoked. Now you begin,
When crimes are done, and past, and to be punished,
To think what your crimes are: away with them.
Let all that see these vices thus rewarded,
Take heart and love to study 'em! Mischiefs feed
Like beasts, till they be fat, and then they bleed. [*Exeunt.*]
[*Volpone comes forward.*]
The seasoning of a play, is the applause.
Now, though the Fox be punished by the laws,
He yet doth hope, there is no suffering due,
For any fact which he hath done 'gainst you;
If there be, censure him; here he doubtful stands:
If not, fare jovially, and clap your hands. [*Exit.*]

On Something, That Walks Somewhere[1]

At court I met it, in clothes brave° enough, *showy*
To be a courtier; and looks grave enough,
To seem a statesman: as I near it came,
It made me a great face, I asked the name.
"A lord," it cried, "buried in flesh, and blood,
And such from whom let no man hope least good,
For I will do none; and as little ill,
For I will dare none." Good lord, walk dead still.

On My First Daughter[1]

Here lies to each her parents' ruth,° *grief*
Mary, the daughter of their youth;
Yet, all heaven's gifts, being heaven's due,
It makes the father, less, to rue.
At six months' end, she parted hence
With safety of her innocence;
Whose soul heaven's Queen (whose name she bears),
In comfort of her mother's tears,
Hath placed amongst her virgin-train;
Where, while that severed doth remain,
This grave partakes the fleshly birth;[2]
Which cover lightly, gentle earth.

1. This and the following four poems were all first printed in the collected *Works* of 1616 under the heading "Epigrams." An epigram is a short witty poem of invective or satire. Jonson's "Epigrams" include epitaphs, poems of praise, and a verse letter.

1. Probably written in the late 1590s.
2. While the soul is in heaven, the grave holds the body.

To John Donne

Donne, the delight of Phoebus,[1] and each Muse,
Who, to thy one, all other brains refuse;[2]
Whose every work, of thy most early wit
Came forth example, and remains so, yet;
Longer a-knowing than most wits do live;
And which no affection praise enough can give!
To it,[3] thy language, letters, arts, best life,
Which might with half mankind maintain a strife.
All which I meant to praise, and, yet, I would,
But leave, because I cannot as I should.

On My First Son[1]

Farewell, thou child of my right hand,[2] and joy;
My sin was too much hope of thee, loved boy.
Seven years thou wert lent to me, and I thee pay,
Exacted by thy fate, on the just day.
O, could I lose all father, now![3] For why
Will man lament the state he should envy?
To have so soon 'scaped world's and flesh's rage,
And, if no other misery, yet age?
Rest in soft peace, and, asked, say, "Here doth lie
Ben Jonson his best piece of poetry."
For whose sake, henceforth, all his vows be such,
As what he loves may never like too much.[4]

Inviting a Friend to Supper[1]

Tonight, grave sir, both my poor house and I
Do equally desire your company:
Not that we think us worthy such a guest,
But that your worth will dignify our feast
With those that come; whose grace may make that seem
Something, which else could hope for no esteem.
It is the fair acceptance, Sir, creates
The entertainment perfect, not the cates.° *food*
Yet shall you have, to rectify your palate,
An olive, capers, or some better salad
Ushering the mutton; with a short-legged hen
If we can get her, full of eggs, and then
Lemons, and wine for sauce: to these, a coney° *rabbit*
Is not to be despaired of, for our money;
And though fowl now be scarce, yet there are clerks,° *scholars*
The sky not falling, think we may have larks.

1. God of poetry.
2. The Muses give the inspiration to your brain that they deny to others.
3. In addition to your wit.
1. Benjamin, who died of the plague on his birthday in 1603.
2. In Hebrew, Benjamin means "son of the right hand; dexterous, fortunate."
3. Let go of fatherly feeling.
4. "If you wish . . . to beware of sorrows that gnaw the heart, to no man make yourself too much a comrade" (Martial 12.34, lines 8–11).
1. Based on three poems of invitation by the Roman poet Martial, 11.52, 5.78, and 10.48.

I'll tell you of more, and lie, so you will come:
Of partridge, pheasant, woodcock, of which some
May yet be there; and godwit, if we can;
Knat, rail, and ruff,° too. Howsoe'er, my man *gamebirds*
Shall read a piece of Virgil, Tacitus,
Livy, or of some better book to us,
Of which we'll speak our minds, amidst our meat;
And I'll profess no verses to repeat;
To this, if aught appear, which I not know of,
That will the pastry, not my paper, show of.[2]
Digestive cheese and fruit there sure will be;
But that, which most doth take my muse and me,
Is a pure cup of rich Canary wine,
Which is the Mermaid's,[3] now, but shall be mine:
Of which had Horace, or Anacreon tasted,
Their lives, as do their lines, till now had lasted.[4]
Tobacco, nectar, or the Thespian spring
Are all but Luther's beer to this I sing.[5]
Of this we will sup free, but moderately,
And we will have no Poley, or Parrot by;[6]
Nor shall our cups make any guilty men,
But, at our parting, we will be, as when
We innocently met. No simple word
That shall be uttered at our mirthful board
Shall make us sad next morning, or affright
The liberty, that we'll enjoy tonight.

To Penshurst[1]

Thou art not, Penshurst, built to envious show,
Of touch,° or marble; nor canst boast a row *black marble*
Of polished pillars, or a roof of gold;
Thou hast no lantern,° whereof tales are told, *turret*
Or stair, or courts; but stand'st an ancient pile,[2]
And these grudged at, art reverenced the while.
Thou joy'st in better marks, of soil, of air,
Of wood, of water; therein thou art fair.
Thou hast thy walks for health, as well as sport:
Thy mount to which the dryads° do resort, *wood nymphs*
Where Pan, and Bacchus their high feasts have made,[3]
Beneath the broad beech and the chestnut shade;
That taller tree, which of a nut was set,
At his great birth, where all the Muses met.

2. Add to this that if there is any paper, it will only be that used to keep the pastry from sticking to the pan.
3. A famous tavern in Cheapside, London.
4. Horace praised wine in Latin verse, as did Anacreon in Greek.
5. The Thespian spring, inspiration of poetry, and all these things are but Luther's beer in comparison with Canary.
6. Government spies; talkative birds.

1. First published in the 1616 *Works* in "The Forest," a title inspired by the Latin *silva* (timber), suggesting raw materials to be worked, used by classical authors for an improvised collection of poems. Penshurst was the Sidney family's house in Kent since 1552, the "great lord" (line 91) of which was Robert Sidney, Baron Sidney of Penshurst and Viscount of Lille, younger brother of Sir Philip Sidney.
2. The castle was built in 1340.
3. Pan was the god of forest, field, and pasture; Bacchus was the god of wine.

There, in the writhèd bark, are cut the names
 Of many a sylvan,° taken with his flames; *wood sprite*
And thence, the ruddy satyrs oft provoke
 The lighter fauns, to reach thy Lady's oak.[4]
Thy copse,° too, named of Gamage, thou hast there, *a small wood*
 That never fails to serve thee seasoned deer
When thou wouldst feast, or exercise thy friends.
 The lower land, that to the river bends,
Thy sheep, thy bullocks, kine° and calves do feed; *cows*
 The middle grounds thy mares and horses breed.
Each bank doth yield thee conies,° and the tops *rabbits*
 Fertile of wood, Ashour and Sydney's copse,
To crown thy open table, doth provide
 The purpled pheasant with the speckled side;
The painted partridge lies in every field,
 And, for thy mess, is willing to be killed.
And if the high-swoll'n Medway[5] fail thy dish,
 Thou hast thy ponds, that pay thee tribute fish:
Fat, agèd carps, that run into thy net.
 And pikes, now weary their own kind to eat,
As loath, the second draught, or cast to stay,
 Officiously, at first, themselves betray;
Bright eels, that emulate them, and leap on land,
 Before the fisher, or into his hand.
Then hath thy orchard fruit, thy garden flowers,
 Fresh as the air, and new as are the hours.
The early cherry, with the later plum,
 Fig, grape, and quince, each in his time doth come;
The blushing apricot and woolly peach
 Hang on thy walls, that every child may reach.
And though thy walls be of the country stone,
 They're reared with no man's ruin, no man's groan;
There's none, that dwell about them, wish them down;
 But all come in, the farmer, and the clown,° *peasant*
And no one empty-handed, to salute
 Thy lord, and lady, though they have no suit.
Some bring a capon, some a rural cake,
 Some nuts, some apples; some that think they make
The better cheeses, bring'em; or else send
 By their ripe daughters, whom they would commend
This way to husbands; and whose baskets bear
 An emblem of themselves in plum, or pear.
But what can this (more than express their love)
 Add to thy free provisions, far above
The need of such? whose liberal board doth flow
 With all that hospitality doth know!
Where comes no guest, but is allowed to eat

4. In Greek mythology the satyr with a man's body and a goat's legs was devoted to lechery. Robert Sidney's wife Barbara Gamage was said to have given birth under this oak.

5. The local river.

Without his fear, and of thy lord's own meat;
Where the same beer, and bread, and self-same wine
That is his lordship's shall be also mine,
And I not fain to sit (as some this day
At great men's tables) and yet dine away.
Here no man tells my cups; nor, standing by,
A waiter, doth my gluttony envy,
But gives me what I call, and lets me eat;
He knows below he shall find plenty of meat,
Thy tables hoard not up for the next day.
Nor, when I take my lodging, need I pray
For fire, or lights, or livery:° all is there, *provisions, food*
As if thou then wert mine, or I reigned here;
There's nothing I can wish, for which I stay.
That found King James, when, hunting late this way
With his brave son, the Prince, they saw thy fires
Shine bright on every hearth as the desires
Of thy Penates[6] had been set on flame
To entertain them; or the country came,
With all their zeal, to warm their welcome here.
What (great, I will not say, but) sudden cheer
Didst thou, then, make 'em! and what praise was heaped
On thy good lady, then, who therein reaped
The just reward of her high housewifery;
To have her linen, plate, and all things nigh,
When she was far, and not a room, but dressed
As if it had expected such a guest!
These, Penshurst, are thy praise, and yet not all.
Thy lady's noble, fruitful, chaste withall.
His children thy great lord may call his own,
A fortune, in this age, but rarely known.
They are, and have been, taught religion; thence
Their gentler spirits have sucked innocence.
Each morn and even, they are taught to pray,
With the whole household, and may every day
Read in their virtuous parents' noble parts
The mysteries of manners, arms, and arts.
Now, Penshurst, they that will proportion° thee *compare*
With other edifices, when they see
Those proud, ambitious heaps, and nothing else,
May say, their lords have built, but thy lord dwells.

Song to Celia

Drink to me only with thine eyes,
And I will pledge with mine;
Or leave a kiss but in the cup,
And I'll not look for wine.
The thirst that from the soul doth rise

6. Household gods.

Doth ask a drink divine;
But might I of Jove's nectar sup,
I would not change for thine.
I sent thee late a rosy wreath,
Not so much honoring thee
As giving it a hope that there
It could not withered be.
But thou thereon didst only breathe,
And sent'st it back on me;
Since when it grows, and smells, I swear,
Not of itself, but thee.

Queen and Huntress[1]

Queen and huntress, chaste and fair,
Now the sun is laid to sleep,
Seated in thy silver chair,
State in wonted manner keep;
Hesperus° entreats thy light, *the evening star*
Goddess excellently bright.

Earth, let not thy envious shade
Dare itself to interpose;
Cynthia's shining orb was made
Heaven to clear, when day did close.
Bless us then with wishèd sight,
Goddess excellently bright.

Lay thy bow of pearl apart,
And thy crystal-shining quiver;
Give unto the flying hart
Space to breathe, how short soever.
Thou that mak'st a day of night,
Goddess excellently bright.

To the Memory of My Beloved, the Author, Mr. William Shakespeare, and What He Hath Left Us[1]

To draw no envy, Shakespeare, on thy name,
Am I thus ample[2] to thy book, and fame,
While I confess thy writings to be such,
As neither man, nor muse, can praise too much.
'Tis true, and all men's suffrage. But these ways
Were not the paths I meant unto thy praise;
For silliest ignorance on these may light,
Which, when it sounds at best, but echoes right;
Or blind affection, which doth ne'er advance
The truth, but gropes, and urgeth all by chance;
Or crafty malice, might pretend this praise,
And think to ruin, where it seemed to raise.

1. From *Cynthia's Revels*, 5.6.1–18. Cynthia, another name for Diana, goddess of the moon and the hunt, and of chastity, an image associated with Queen Elizabeth.

1. Prefixed to the first folio of Shakespeare's plays (1623).
2. From Latin *amplus:* copious; an *amplus orator* was one who spoke richly and with dignity.

These are as some infamous bawd or whore
Should praise a matron. What could hurt her more?
But thou art proof against them, and indeed
Above the ill fortune of them, or the need.
I, therefore will begin. Soul of the age!
The applause! delight! the wonder of our stage!
My Shakespeare, rise; I will not lodge thee by
Chaucer, or Spenser, or bid Beaumont lie
A little further, to make thee a room;[3]
Thou art a monument without a tomb,
And art alive still while thy book doth live,
And we have wits to read, and praise to give.
That I not mix thee so, my brain excuses,
I mean with great, but disproportioned, Muses;
For, if I thought my judgment were of years,
I should commit thee surely with thy peers,
And tell how far thou didst our Lyly outshine,
Or sporting Kid, or Marlowe's mighty line.[4]
And though thou hadst small Latin, and less Greek,
From thence to honor thee, I would not seek
For names, but call forth thundering Aeschylus,
Euripides, and Sophocles to us,
Pacuvius, Accius, him of Cordova dead,
To life again, to hear thy buskin[5] tread
And shake a stage; or, when thy socks[6] were on,
Leave thee alone for the comparison
Of all that insolent Greece or haughty Rome
Sent forth, or since did from their ashes come.
Triumph, my Britain; thou hast one to show
To whom all scenes of Europe homage owe.
He was not of an age, but for all time!
And all the muses still were in their prime
When like Apollo he came forth to warm
Our ears, or like a Mercury to charm![7]
Nature herself was proud of his designs,
And joyed to wear the dressing of his lines,
Which were so richly spun, and woven so fit
As, since, she will vouchsafe no other wit.
The merry Greek, tart Aristophanes,
Neat Terence, witty Plautus,[8] now not please,
But antiquated, and deserted lie,
As they were not of Nature's family.
Yet must I not give Nature all; thy Art,
My gentle Shakespeare, must enjoy a part.
For though the poet's matter, Nature be,
His art doth give the fashion. And, that he,

3. Chaucer, Spenser, and Francis Beaumont were buried in Westminster Abbey; Shakespeare was buried in Stratford.

4. Lyly was an author of English prose comedies; Kyd and Marlowe were authors of English verse tragedies.

5. Boot worn by tragic actors. Jonson compares Shakespeare to tragedians of Ancient Greece (Aeschylus, Sophocles, Euripides) and Rome (Pacuvius, Accius, and "him of Cordova," Seneca).

6. Symbols of comedy.

7. Apollo and Mercury were the gods of poetry and eloquence.

8. Aristophanes was an ancient Greek comic playwright; Terence and Plautus were authors of Roman comedy.

Who casts to write a living line must sweat
  (Such as thine are) and strike the second heat
Upon the Muses' anvil: turn the same,
  And himself with it, that he thinks to frame;[9]
Or for the laurel, he may gain a scorn;
  For a good poet's made as well as born.
And such wert thou! Look how the father's face
  Lives in his issue; even so, the race
Of Shakespeare's mind, and manners brightly shines
  In his well-turnèd, and true-filèd lines:
In each of which, he seems to shake a lance,[1]
  As brandished at the eyes of ignorance.
Sweet Swan of Avon, what a sight it were
  To see thee in our waters yet appear,
And make those flights upon the banks of Thames,
  That so did take Eliza, and our James![2]
But stay, I see thee in the hemisphere
  Advanced, and made a constellation there!
Shine forth, thou star of poets, and with rage
  Or influence chide or cheer the drooping stage,[3]
Which, since thy flight from hence, hath mourned like night,
  And despairs day, but for thy volume's light.

To the Immortal Memory, and Friendship of that Noble Pair, Sir Lucius Cary and Sir H. Morison[1]

The Turne[2]

Brave infant of Saguntum, clear
Thy coming forth in that great year,
When the prodigious Hannibal did crown
His rage with razing your immortal town.[3]
Thou, looking then about,
Ere thou wert half got out,
Wise child, didst hastily return,
And mad'st thy mother's womb thine urn.
How summed° a circle[4] didst thou leave mankind *complete*
Of deepest lore, could we the center find!

The Counter-Turn

Did wiser Nature draw thee back
From out the horror of that sack,

9. See Horace, *Ars Poetica* 441: "return the ill-tuned verses to the anvil."
1. Pun on "Shake-speare."
2. Queen Elizabeth and King James.
3. Like an ancient hero, Shakespeare is given a place among the stars; as the "rage" and "influence" of the planets affect life on earth, Shakespeare affects the world of the stage.
1. Sir Lucius Cary (1610?–1643), second Viscount Falkland, son of Elizabeth Cary (author of *The Tragedy of Mariam*). He befriended Jonson and wrote an elegy on his death. Sir Henry Morison, son of Sir Richard Morison and nephew of the travel writer Fynes Morison, died on or near his twenty-first birthday.
2. "Turn," "counter-turn," and "stand" represent the Greek "strophe," "antistrophe," and "epode." Jonson's poem is the first Great Ode in English. Often in the form of an address, the ode is a dignified lyric poem, in commemoration of a person, occasion, or theme. The Greek poet Pindar wrote odes praising winners of the Olympics. His odes were sung by a chorus in a three-part scheme, which Jonson imitates here.
3. Pliny, *History* 7.3.40–42: "an infant of Saguntum . . . at once went back into the womb in the year in which the city was destroyed by Hannibal" (the great Carthaginian general in the Second Punic War).
4. Emblem of perfection.

Where shame, faith, honor, and regard of right
Lay trampled on?—the deeds of death, and night,
Urged, hurried forth, and hurled
Upon th'affrighted world?
Sword, fire, and famine, with fell fury met;
And all on utmost ruin set;
As, could they but life's miseries foresee,
No doubt all infants would return like thee.

The Stand

For, what is life, if measured by the space,
Not by the act?
Or maskèd man, if valued by his face,
Above his fact?° *deeds*
Here's one outlived his peers
And told forth fourescore years;
He vexèd time, and busied the whole state;
Troubled both foes, and friends,
But ever to no ends:
What did this stirrer, but die late?
How well at twenty had he fallen, or stood!
For three of his fourescore, he did no good.

The Turn

He entered well by virtuous parts,
Got up and thrived with honest arts:
He purchased friends, and fame, and honors then,
And had his noble name advanced with men:
But weary of that flight,
He stooped in all men's sight!
To sordid flatteries, acts of strife,
And sunk in that dead sea of life
So deep, as he did then death's waters sup;
But that the cork of title buoyed him up.

The Counter-Turn

Alas, but Morison fell young!
He never fell: thou fall'st,[5] my tongue.
He stood, a soldier to the last right end,
A perfect patriot, and a noble friend,
But most, a virtuous son.
All offices were done
By him, so ample, full, and round,
In weight, in measure, number, sound,
As, though his age imperfect might appear,
His life was of humanity the sphere.

The Stand

Go now, and tell out days summed up with fears;
And make them years;
Produce thy mass of miseries on the stage,
To swell thine age;

5. Slip, with a pun on the Latin *fallere*, to deceive, to be mistaken.

Repeat of things a throng,
To show thou hast been long,
Not lived; for life doth her great actions spell
By what was done and wrought
In season, and so brought
To light: her measures are, how well
Each syllabe° answered, and was formed, how fair; *syllable*
These make the lines of life, and that's her air.

The Turn

It is not growing like a tree
In bulk, doth make man better be;
Or standing long an oak, three hundred year,
To fall a log at last, dry, bald, and sere:
A lily of a day
Is fairer far, in May,
Although it fall and die that night;
It was the plant and flower of light.
In small proportions, we just beauty see,
And in short measures life may perfect be.

The Counter-Turn

Call, noble Lucius, then for wine,
And let thy looks with gladness shine;
Accept this garland,[6] plant it on thy head;
And think, nay know, thy Morison's not dead.
He leaped the present age,
Possessed with holy rage,
To see that bright eternal day,
Of which we priests, and poets say
Such truths, as we expect for happy men,
And there he lives with memory, and Ben

The Stand

Jonson, who sung this of him, ere he went
Himself to rest,
Or taste a part of that full joy he meant
To have expressed
In this bright asterism;° *constellation*
Where it were friendship's schism
(Were not his Lucius long with us to tarry)
To separate these twi-
Lights, the Dioscuri;[7]
And keep the one half from his Harry.
But fate doth so alternate the design,
Whilst that in heaven, this light on earth must shine.

The Turn

And shine as you exalted are;
Two names of friendship, but one star:

6. The poem itself.
7. "Twin lights": the mythical Greek brothers, Castor and Pollux. After Castor's death the twin brothers exchanged places on earth and in the underworld at regular intervals.

Of hearts the union. And those not by chance
Made, or indentured,° or leased out t' advance *contracted for*
The profits for a time.
No pleasures vain did chime,
Of rhymes, or riots, at your feasts,
Orgies of drink, or feigned protests;
But simple love of greatness, and of good;
That knits brave minds, and manners, more than blood.

The Counter-Turn

This made you first to know the why
You liked; then after, to apply
That liking; and approach so one the t'other,
Till either grew a portion of the other:
Each stylèd, by his end,
The copy of his friend.
You lived to be the great surnames
And titles by which all made claims
Unto the virtue. Nothing perfect done,
But as a Cary, or a Morison.

The Stand

And such a force the fair example had,
As they that saw
The good, and durst not practise it, were glad
That such a law
Was left yet to mankind;
Where they might read, and find
Friendship in deed was written, not in words.
And with the heart, not pen,
Of two so early° men, *youthful*
Whose lines her rolls were, and records.
Who, ere the first down bloomed on the chin,
Had sowed these fruits, and got the harvest in.

Pleasure Reconciled to Virtue

A Masque as It Was Presented at Court Before King James. 1618.[1]

The Scene was the Mountain Atlas, who had his top ending in the figure of an old man, his head and beard all hoary and frost, as if his shoulders were covered with snow; the rest wood and rock. A grove of ivy at his feet, out of which, to a wild music of cymbals, flutes, and tabors, is brought forth Comus,[2] the god of cheer or the belly, riding in triumph, his head crowned with roses and other flowers, his hair curled; they that wait upon him, crowned with ivy, their javelins done about with it; one of them going with Hercules' bowl[3] bare before him, while the rest presented him, with this

1. A masque was an entertainment performed by members of the court that included elaborate sets, dance, music, and poetry. Designed to compliment the monarch, the masque portrayed him as an ideal ruler in a moral allegory. The myth on which this masque is based is the story of Hercules' choice between pleasure and virtue, in which King James is represented as harmonizing voluptuous enjoyment and right action.

2. Allied with Dionysus, the god of wine, Comus is the god of sensual excess.

3. Hercules used the bowl that the Sun gave him as a sailing ship.

Hymn

Room, room, make room for the boucing belly,
First father of sauce and deviser of jelly,
Prime master of arts, and the giver of wit,
That found out the excellent engine, the spit,
The plough and the flail, the mill, and the hopper,
The hutch, and the bolter, the furnace and copper.
The oven, the bavin, the mawkin, and peel,
The hearth and the range, the dog and the wheel.[4]
He, he first invented both hogshead° and tun,° *cask / barrel*
The gimlet and vice, too, taught them to run.[5]
And since, with the funnel, an Hippocras bag
He's made of himself, that now he cries swag.[6]
Which shows, though the pleasure be but of four inches,
Yet he is a weezle, the gullet° that pinches, *throat*
Of any delight, and not spares from the back
Whatever, to make of the belly a sack.
Hail, hail, plump paunch! O the founder of taste
For fresh meats, or powdered, or pickle, or paste;
Devourer of broiled, baked, roasted, or sod,° *boiled*
And emptier of cups, be they even, or odd;
All which have now made thee, so wide i' the waist
As scarce with no pudding thou art to be laced;
But eating and drinking, until thou dost nod,
Thou break'st all thy girdles, and break'st forth[7] a god.

To this, the Bowl-bearer

Do you hear, my friends, to whom do you sing all this now? Pardon me only that I ask you, for I do not look for an answer; I'll answer myself. I know it is now such a time as the Saturnals[8] for all the world, that every man stands under the eaves of his own hat and sings what pleases him; that's the right and the liberty of it. Now you sing of god Comus here, the Belly-god. I say it is well, and I say it is not well. It is well, as it is a ballad, and the belly worthy of it I must needs say, and 'twere forty yards of ballad, more—as much ballad as tripe.[9] But when the belly is not edified by it, it is not well; for where did you ever read, or hear, that the belly had any ears? Come, never pump for an answer, for you are defeated. Our fellow Hunger there, that was as ancient a retainer to the belly as any of us, was turned away, for being unseasonable—not unreasonable, but unseasonable—and now is he (poor thin-gut) fain to get his living with teaching of starlings, magpies, parrots, and jackdaws, those things he would have taught the belly. Beware of dealing with the Belly; the Belly will not be talked to, especially when he is full. Then there is no venturing upon Venter,[1] then he will blow you all up; he will thunder, indeed la; some in derision call him the father of farts. But I say, he was the

4. Flail: tool for threshing corn; mill: apparatus for grinding grain; hopper: a cone through which grain is conveyed to the mill; hutch: a box for sifting grain; bolter: a sieve; bavin: bundle of light wood used in bakers' ovens; mawkin: mop for cleaning a baker's oven; peel: a baker's shovel. A dog connected to a wheel turned the roasting spit.
5. The gimlet and vice were used to tap the cask.
6. A Hippocras bag was a strainer for wine. To cry swag was to let out a hanging belly.
7. With a double meaning of fart.
8. The Roman Saturnalia was a wild festival at the end of the year, similar to Twelfth Night, part of the English Christmas season, at the celebration of which this masque was performed.
9. Edible animal intestines, and also the human stomach.
1. Belly (Latin).

first inventor of great ordinance,[2] and taught us to discharge them on festival days. Would we had a fit feast for him i'faith, to show his activity. I would have something now fetched in now to please his five senses, the throat; or the two senses, the eyes. Pardon me, for my two senses; for I that carry Hercules' bowl[3] in the service may see double by my place, for I have drunk like a frog today. I would have a tun[4] now, brought in to dance, and so many bottles about him. Ha? You look as if you would make a problem of this. Do you see? a problem: why bottles? and why a tun? and why a tun? and why bottles to dance? I say that men that drink hard and serve the belly in any place of quality (as *The Jovial Tinkers*, or *The Lusty Kindred*)[5] are living measures of drink, and can transform themselves, and do every day, to bottles or tuns when they please; and when they have done all they can, they are, as I say again (for I think I said somewhat like it afore), but moving measures of drink. And there is a piece-in-the-cellar can hold more than all they. This will I make good, if it please our new god but to give a nod; for the belly does all by signs, and I am all for the belly, the truest clock in the world to go by.

Here the first Anti-masque[6] [danced by men in the shape of bottles, tuns, etc.] after which,

HERCULES What rites are these? Breeds earth more monsters yet?
Antaeus[7] scarce is cold; what can beget
This store? and stay such contraries upon her?
Is earth so fruitful of her own dishonor?
Or 'cause his vice was inhumanity,
Hopes she, by vicious hospitality
To work an expiation first?[8] and then
(Help, Virtue) these are sponges, and not men.
Bottles? mere vessels? half a tun of paunch?
How? and the other half thrust forth in haunch?[9]
Whose feast? the belly's! Comus'! and my cup
Brought in to fill the drunken orgies up
And here abused! That was the crowned reward
Of thirsty heroes after labor hard!
Burdens and shames of nature, perish, die;
For yet you never lived, but in the sty
Of vice have wallowed, and in that swine's strife
Been buried under the offense of life.
Go, reel, and fall, under the load you make,
Till your swoll'n bowels burst with what you take.
Can this be pleasure, to extinguish man?
Or so quite change him in his figure? Can
The belly love his pain, and be content
With no delight, but what's a punishment?
These monsters plague themselves, and fitly too,
For they do suffer what and all they do.
But here must be no shelter, nor no shroud
For such: sink grove, or vanish into cloud.

2. Artillery.
3. "To carry Hercules' bowl" means to drink heavily.
4. Keg.
5. Taverns.
6. A grotesque, comic interlude.
7. Antaeus was a Libyan giant slain by Hercules.
8. Hercules assumes that Comus is another monster, like Antaeus, produced by the Earth and that Earth hopes to expiate her guilt by giving birth to one monster after another.
9. The area between the ribs and thighs.

After this, the whole grove vanished, and the whole music was discovered, sitting at the foot of the mountain, with Pleasure and Virtue seated above them. The Choir invited Hercules to rest with this

Song

Great friend and servant of the good,
Let cool a while thy heated blood,
And from thy mighty labor cease.
Lie down, lie down,
And give thy troubled spirits peace,
Whilst Virtue, for whose sake
Thou dost this godlike travail take,
May of the choicest herbage° make, *plants*
Here on this mountain bred,
A crown, a crown
For thy immortal head.

Here Hercules being laid down at their feet, the second anti-masque, which was of pygmies,[1] appeared.

1ST PYGMY Antaeus dead? And Hercules yet live!
Where is this Hercules? What would I give
To meet him, now? Meet him? Nay, three such other,
If they had hand in murder of our brother![2]
With three? with four? with ten? nay, with as many
As the name yields![3] Pray anger there by any
Whereon to feed my just revenge and soon!
How shall I kill him? Hurl him 'gainst the moon,
And break him in small portions! Give to Greece
His brain, and every tract of earth a piece!
2ND PYGMY He is yonder.
1ST Where?
3RD At the hill foot, asleep.
1ST Let one go steal his club.
2ND My charge; I'll creep.
4TH He's ours.
1ST Yes, peace.
3RD Triumph, we have him, boy.
4TH Sure, sure, he's sure.
1ST Come, let us dance for joy.

At the end of their dance they thought to surprise him, when suddenly, being awaked by the music, he roused himself, and they all ran into holes.

Song

CHOIR Wake, Hercules, awake, but heave up thy black eye,
'Tis only asked from thee to look and these will die,
Or fly.

1. In ancient Greek history, the pygmies were supposed to have been a tribe of very short people in Africa or India; the term was also used of dwarves.
2. Antaeus.
3. The Pygmies' assumption that there is more than one Hercules is a joke alluding to the many different stories about Hercules put forward by the mythographers.

Already they are fled,
Whom scorn had else left dead.

At which Mercury[4] descendeth from the hill, with a garland of poplar to crown him.

MERCURY Rest still, thou active friend of Virtue: these
Should not disturb the peace of Hercules.
Earth's worms and honor's dwarfs, at too great odds,
Prove or provoke the issue of the gods.
See here, a crown, the agèd hill hath sent thee,
My grandsire Atlas, he that did present thee
With the best sheep that in his fold were found,
Or golden fruit, on the Hesperian ground,
For rescuing his fair daughters, then the prey
Of a rude pirate, as thou cam'st this way;
And taught thee all the learning of the sphere,
And how, like him, thou mightst the heaven up-bear,
As that thy labors virtuous recompense.[5]
He, though a mountain now, hath yet the sense
Of thanking thee for more, thou being still
Constant to goodness, guardian of the hill;
Antaeus, by thee suffocated here,
And the voluptuous Comus, god of cheer,
Beat from his grove, and that defaced. But now
The time's arrived, that Atlas told thee of: how
By unaltered law, and working of the stars,
There should be a cessation of all jars° *fights*
'Twixt Virtue and her noted opposite,
Pleasure, that both should meet here, in the sight
Of Hesperus, the glory of the west,[6]
The brightest star, that from his burning crest
Lights all on this side the Atlantic seas
As far as to thy pillars Hercules.[7]
See where he shines, Justice and Wisdom placed
About his throne and those with Honor graced,
Beauty and Love. It is not with his brother
Bearing the world, but ruling such another
Is his renown.[8] Pleasure, for his delight,
Is reconciled to Virtue; and this night
Virtue brings forth twelve princes have been bred
In this rough mountain and near Atlas' head,
The hill of Knowledge; one, and chief of whom
Of the bright race of Hesperus is come,
Who shall in time the same that he is, be,
And now is only a less light than he.[9]
These now she trusts with Pleasure, and to these
She gives an entrance to the Hesperides,
Fair Beauty's garden; neither can she fear
They should grow soft or wax effeminate here,

4. The messenger god.
5. Atlas was an astronomer. His labor of holding up the heavens was taken over by Hercules so that Atlas could capture the golden apples of the Hesperides.
6. Hesperus, the brother of Atlas, was the evening star and the protector of the western isles.
7. The Pillars of Hercules are the Straits of Gibraltar.
8. Hesperus is similar to King James, who also rules "another" world: England.
9. King James's 18-year-old son Prince Charles.

Since in her sight and by her charge all's done,
Pleasure the servant, Virtue looking on.

Here the whole choir of music called the masquers forth from the lap of the mountain, which now opens with this

Song

Ope, agèd Atlas, open then thy lap,
And from thy beamy bosom, strike a light,
That men may read in thy mysterious map
All lines
And signs
Of royal education, and the right,
See how they come, and show,
That are but born to know.
Descend,
Descend,
Though pleasure lead,
Fear not to follow:
They who are bred
Within the hill
Of skill,
May safely tread
What path they will:
No ground of good is hollow.

In their descent from the hill Daedalus[1] came down before them of whom Hercules questioned Mercury.

HERCULES But Hermes, stay a little, let me pause:
Who's this that leads?
MERCURY A guide that gives them laws
To all their motions. Daedalus the wise.
HERCULES And doth in sacred harmony comprise
His precepts?
MERCURY Yes.
HERCULES They may securely prove° *experience*
Then, any labyrinth, though it be of love.

Here, while they put themselves in form, Daedalus hath his first

Song

Come on, come on, and where you go,
So interweave the curious knot,
As even th'observer scarce may know
Which lines are Pleasures, and which not.
First, figure out the doubtful way
At which, a while all youth should stay
Where she and Virtue did contend
Which should have Hercules to friend.[2]

1. Daedalus here acts as choreographer for the dance. As architect of the labyrinth, or maze, Daedalus may symbolize Inigo Jones, the set designer of the masque.
2. The story of how Hercules had to choose the arduous path of Virtue over the easy road offered to him by Vice is related by the ancient Greek author Xenophon (*Memorabilia* 2.1.21–34).

Then, as all actions of mankind.
Are but a labyrinth or maze,
So let your dances be entwined,
Yet not perplex men unto gaze;
But measured, and so numerous° too, *rhythmical*
As men may read each act you do,
And when they see the graces meet,
Admire the wisdom of your feet.

For dancing is an exercise
Not only shows the mover's wit,
But maketh the beholder wise,
As he hath power to rise to it.

The first dance.

After which Daedalus again.

Song 2

O more, and more! this was so well
As praise wants half his voice to tell;
Again yourselves compose;
And now put all the aptness on
Of figure, that proportion
Or color can disclose.

That if those silent arts were lost,
Design and picture, they might boast
From you a newer ground;
Instructed to that height'ning sense
Of dignity and reverence
In your true motions found:

Begin, begin; for look, the fair
Do longing listen to what air
You form your second touch;
That they may vent their murmuring hymns
Just to the tune you move your limbs,
And wish their own were such.

Make haste, make haste, for this
The labyrinth of Beauty is.

The second dance.

That ended, Daedalus:

Song 3

It follows now, you are to prove
The subtlest maze of all, that's love,
And if you stay too long,
The fair will think you do 'em wrong,

Go choose among—but with a mind
As gentle as the stroking wind
Runs o'er the gentler flowers.

And so let all your actions smile,
As if they meant not to beguile
The ladies, but the hours.

Grace, laughter and discourse may meet,
And yet the beauty not go less:
For what is noble should be sweet,
But not dissolved in wantonness.

Will you, that I give the law
To all your sport and sum it?
It should be such should envy draw,
But ever overcome it.

Here they danced with the ladies, and the whole revels[3] *followed; which ended, Mercury called to Daedalus in this following speech, which was after repeated in song, by two trebles, two tenors, a bass, and the whole chorus.*

Song 4

An eye of looking back were well,
Or any murmur that would tell
Your thoughts, how you were sent
And went,
To walk with Pleasure, not to dwell.

These, these are hours by Virtue spared
Herself, she being her own reward,
But she will have you know
That though
Her sports be soft, her life is hard.

You must return unto the hill,
And there advance
With labor and inhabit still
That height and crown
From whence you ever may look down
Upon triumphed Chance.

She, she it is, in darkness shines.
'Tis she that still herself refines
By her own light, to every eye,
More seen, more known, when Vice stands by.
And though a stranger here on earth,
In heaven she hath her right of birth.
There, there is Virtue's seat,
Strive to keep her your own;
'Tis only she can make you great,
Though place, here, make you known.

After which they danced their last dance, and returned into the scene, which closed, and is a mountain again, as before.

The End.

This pleased the king so well, as he would see it again; when it was presented with these additions.[4]

3. The audience, including members of the court.

4. The additions were another masque, *For the Honor of Wales*.

John Donne

1572–1631

John Donne wrote some of the most passionate love poems and most moving religious verse in the English language. Even his contemporaries wondered how one mind could express itself in such different modes. Eliciting a portrait of the artist as a split personality, Donne's letters mention the melancholic lover "Jack Donne," succeeded by the Anglican priest "Doctor Donne." Izaak Walton's *Life of Donne* (1640) portrays an earnest aspiring clergyman who wrote love poetry to his wife. Yet Donne actually wrote most of his poetry—both the love lyrics and the *Holy Sonnets*—before he entered the ministry at forty-three. An ambitious, talented, and handsome young man, Donne struggled to attain secular patronage; later he resigned himself to life in the church and, after his wife's death, came to terms with his own mortality.

Donne was born into a Catholic family. His mother was the great-niece of Sir Thomas More; she went into exile in Antwerp for a time to seek religious toleration. One of Donne's uncles was imprisoned in the Tower of London because he was a Jesuit priest. Donne wrote of his family that none "hath endured and suffered more in their persons and fortunes, for obeying the Teachers of Roman Doctrine, then it hath done." Donne and his brother Henry entered Hart Hall, Oxford, when they were just eleven and ten, young enough to be spared the required oath recognizing the Queen as head of the church. The Donne brothers later studied law at Lincoln's Inn, where Henry was arrested for harboring a priest in 1593. The priest was drawn and quartered; Henry died in Newgate prison of the plague.

Though shadowed by his brother's death, Donne's student years in London had their pleasures. Donne was distracted from studying law by "the worst voluptuousness . . . an Hydroptique immoderate desire of humane learning and languages." The young Donne was described by his friend Sir Richard Baker as "a great visitor of ladies, a great frequenter of Playes, a great writer of conceited Verses." Among these were Donne's erotic *Elegies*, including *To His Mistress Going to Bed* and *Love's Progress*, both of which were refused a license for publication in the 1633 edition of his collected verse.

Shortly after gaining a position as secretary to Sir Thomas Egerton, Lord Keeper of the Great Seal, in 1597, Donne met and fell in love with Ann More. His noble employer's niece, she was so far above Donne's station that they married secretly. When Ann's father heard the news, he asked Egerton to have Donne fired and saw to it that he was incarcerated. At this time, Donne is said to have written to Ann: "*John Donne, Ann Donne, un-done*." As a result of Donne's petition, the Court of Audience for Canterbury declared the marriage lawful; nevertheless, Ann was disinherited.

John and Ann made a love match, but their life was not easy. She bore twelve children in fifteen years, not counting miscarriages. Donne lamented the "poorness of [his] fortune and the greatness of [his] charge." After thirteen years of marriage, however, he could also still say: "we had not one another at so cheap a rate, as that we should ever be weary of one another." A few of the love poems in *Songs and Sonnets* express a mixture of bliss and hardship linked with their marriage.

Relations with friends and patrons also influenced Donne's poetry. He is said to have addressed several poems to Magdalen Herbert, mother of the poet George. Living in Mitcham near London, Donne cemented his friendship with Ben Jonson, who wrote two epigrams in praise of Donne in thanks for his Latin verses on *Volpone* (1607). Donne was also introduced to Lucy, Countess of Bedford, who asked Jonson to get her a copy of Donne's *Satires*. Donne not only addressed several verse letters to her but also enjoyed her poems. An even more generous patron was Sir Robert Drury, for the death of whose young daughter Elizabeth the poet composed A *Funeral Elegie*, the inspiration for his two *Anniversaries* (1612) on the nature of the cosmos and death.

Donne's writing from 1607 to 1611 dealt with theological and moral controversies. His *Pseudo-Martyr* (1610) argued that Catholics should take the Oath of Allegiance to the King and that resistance to him should not be glorified as a form of martyrdom. This work won him James I's advice to enter the ministry, but, still skeptical, Donne held off. He protested against sectarianism: "You know I never fettered nor imprisoned the word Religion . . . immuring it in a Rome, or a Wittenberg, or a Geneva." Donne also examined the morality of suicide in *Biathanatos* (written 1607, published 1646). His *Holy Sonnets* (some of which may have been written as early as 1608–1610) reveal an obsession with his own death and fear of damnation: "I dare not move my dim eyes any way, / Despair behind, and death before doth cast / Such terror."

Donne was plagued by professional bad luck until he became an Anglican priest. With the exception of Sir Robert Drury, Donne never found a dependable patron. His applications for secretaryships in Ireland and Virginia were unsuccessful. In search of the Earl of Somerset's patronage, Donne wrote an epithalamion for his marriage to Frances Howard and even volunteered to justify her earlier controversial divorce. Fortunately for Donne, his attempts to win a position through Somerset failed, since a year later the Earl fell from power. Giving up his long quest for secular preferment, Donne took holy orders in 1615. Once an Anglican priest, he was made a royal chaplain and received an honorary Doctorate of Divinity from Cambridge. Two years later, he became reader in divinity at his old law school Lincoln's Inn.

Prosperity was followed by tragic loss. Ann Donne died giving birth in 1617. The death of his wife turned Donne more completely toward God. His later prose viewed death from a different perspective from his earlier personal torment. Suffering from a recurring fever, he wrote *Devotions upon Emergent Occasions* (1624). In the midst of a major epidemic, at the height of his fever, distraught and sleepless, he realizes our common mortality: "never send to know for whom the bell tolls; it tolls for thee." He became a prolific and stirring preacher of sermons. Some of these, such as that urging the Company of the Virginia Plantation to spread the gospel (1622), were printed in his lifetime. One written just before his death shows confidence in God's forgiveness: "I cannot plead innocency of life, especially of my youth: But I am to be judged by a merciful God."

If Donne's life can be split into the secular and religious, his poetic sensibility cannot. His verse fuses flesh and spirit through metaphysical conceits that create fascinating connections between apparently unrelated topics. In Donne's erotic lyrics, sex excites spiritual ecstasy along with hot lust and seductive wit. Similarly, Donne's religious poems express his relation with God not as an intellectual construct but as an emotional need, articulated in intimate and even erotic language. Later ages did not always appreciate either Donne's sensuality or his intellectual extravagance; remarkably, none of his poems were included in the most important nineteenth-century anthology of poetry, Palgraves's *Golden Treasury*. Donne's fame was revived early in the twentieth century, when modernist poets, especially T. S. Eliot, took inspiration from Donne's complex mixture of immediacy and artifice, passion and subtle thought.

The Good Morrow[1]

I wonder by my troth, what thou, and I
Did, till we loved? Were we not weaned till then?
But sucked on country pleasures, childishly?
Or snorted we in the seven sleepers' den?[2]

1. Donne's love poems, written over a period of 20 years, cannot be dated with any certainty. They were first printed in 1633, scattered throughout the entire collection of poems. Then in the 1635 edition the love poems were printed as a group under the title *Songs and Sonnets*. There is no certainty that the titles were chosen by Donne.

2. Legendary cave where seven Ephesian youths were put to sleep by God to escape the persecution of Christians by the Emperor Decius (249).

'Twas so; but this, all pleasures fancies be.
If ever any beauty I did see,
Which I desired, and got, 'twas but a dream of thee.

And now good morrow to our waking souls,
Which watch not one another out of fear;
For love, all love of other sights controls,
And makes one little room, an everywhere.
Let sea-discoverers to new worlds have gone,
Let maps to others, worlds on worlds have shown,
Let us possess one world, each hath one, and is one.

My face in thine eye, thine in mine appears,
And true plain hearts do in the faces rest,
Where can we find two better hemispheres
Without sharp north, without declining west?
What ever dies, was not mixed equally;[3]
If our two loves be one, or, thou and I
Love so alike, that none do slacken, none can die.

Song

Go, and catch a falling star,
  Get with child a mandrake root,[1]
Tell me, where all past years are,
  Or who cleft the Devil's foot,
Teach me to hear mermaids singing,
Or to keep off envy's stinging,
    And find
    What wind
Serves to advance an honest mind.

If thou be borne to strange sights,
  Things invisible to see,
Ride ten thousand days and nights,[2]
  Till age snow white hairs on thee,
Thou, when thou return'st, will tell me
All strange wonders that befell thee,
    And swear
    No where
Lives a woman true, and fair.

If thou findest one, let me know,
  Such a pilgrimage were sweet;
Yet do not, I would not go,
  Though at next door we might meet,
Though she were true, when you met her,
And last, till you write your letter,
    Yet she

3. According to ancient medicine, death was caused by an imbalance of elements in the body.

1. A fork-rooted plant, resembling the human body in its form.

2. See *Faerie Queene* 3.7.56–61, where Spenser's Squire of Dames searches the country for a chaste woman.

Will be
False, ere I come, to two, or three.

The Undertaking

I have done one braver thing
Than all the Worthies did,[1]
And yet a braver thence doth spring,
Which is, to keep that hid.

It were but madness now to impart
The skill of specular stone,[2]
When he which can have learned the art
To cut it, can find none.

So, if I now should utter this,
Others (because no more
Such stuff to work upon, there is,)
Would love but as before.

But he who loveliness within
Hath found, all outward loathes,
For he who color loves, and skin,
Loves but their oldest clothes.

If, as I have, you also do
Virtue attired in woman see,
And dare love that, and say so too,
And forget the He and She;

And if this love, though placèd so,
From profane men you hide,
Which will no faith on this bestow,
Or, if they do, deride:

Then you have done a braver thing
Than all the Worthies did;
And a braver thence will spring,
Which is, to keep that hid.

The Sun Rising[1]

Busy old fool, unruly Sun,
Why dost thou thus
Through windows, and through curtains call on us?
Must to thy motions lovers' seasons run?
Saucy pedantic wretch, go chide
Late schoolboys, and sour prentices,° *apprentices*
Go tell court-huntsmen, that the king will ride,
Call country ants to harvest offices;

1. The nine great military heroes of ancient and medieval legend and history.
2. Transparent stone of ancient times, but now lost, that required great skill to cut in strips.

1. In the tradition of the alba, a love song addressing the dawn, as in Ovid's *Amores* 1.13 and Petrarch's *Canzoniere* 188.

Love, all alike, no season knows, nor clime,
Nor hours, days, months, which are the rags of time.

Thy beams, so reverend, and strong
Why shouldst thou think?
I could eclipse and cloud them with a wink,
But that I would not lose her sight so long:
If her eyes have not blinded thine,
Look, and tomorrow late, tell me,
Whether both th'Indias of spice and mine[2]
Be where thou left'st them, or lie here with me.
Ask for those kings whom thou saw'st yesterday,
And thou shalt hear, all here in one bed lay.

She is all states, and all princes, I,
Nothing else is.
Princes do but play us; compared to this,
All honor's mimic; all wealth alchemy.° *fake science*
Thou sun art half as happy as we,
In that the world's contracted thus;
Thine age asks ease, and since thy duties be
To warm the world, that's done in warming us.
Shine here to us, and thou art everywhere;
This bed thy center is, these walls, thy sphere.

The Indifferent

I can love both fair and brown,
Her whom abundance melts, and her whom want betrays,
Her who loves loneness best, and her who masks and plays,
Her whom the country formed, and whom the town,
Her who believes, and her who tries,° *questions*
Her who still weeps with spongy eyes,
And her who is dry cork, and never cries;
I can love her, and her, and you and you,
I can love any, so she be not true.

Will no other vice content you?
Will it not serve your turn to do, as did your mothers?
Or have you old vices spent, and now would find out others?
Or doth a fear, that men are true, torment you?
Oh we are not, be not you so,
Let me, and do you, twenty know.
Rob me, but bind me not, and let me go.
Must I, who came to travail,[1] thorough you
Grow your fixed subject, because you are true?

Venus heard me sigh this song,
And by love's sweetest part, variety, she swore,
She heard not this till now; and that it should be so no more.

2. The East Indies was the source of spice; the West Indies was the source of gold.

1. In three senses: to make love, to undergo hardship, to travel or move on to another woman.

She went, examined, and returned ere long,
And said, "Alas, some two or three
Poor heretics in love there be,
Which think to establish dangerous constancy.
But I have told them, 'Since you will be true,
You shall be true to them, who are false to you.'"

The Canonization[1]

For God's sake hold your tongue, and let me love,
Or° chide my palsy, or my gout, *either*
My five gray hairs, or ruined fortune flout,
With wealth your state, your mind with arts improve,
Take you a course, get you a place,
Observe his Honor, or his Grace,
Or the King's real, or his stampèd face[2]
Contemplate, what you will, approve,
So you will let me love.

Alas, alas, who's injured by my love?
What merchant's ships have my sighs drowned?
Who says my tears have overflowed his ground?
When did my colds a forward spring remove?
When did the heats which my veins fill
Add one more to the plaguy bill?[3]
Soldiers find wars, and lawyers find out still
Litigious men, which quarrels move
Though she and I do love.

Call us what you will, we are made such by love;
Call her one, me another fly,
We are tapers° too, and at our own cost die,[4] *candles*
And we in us find the eagle and the dove.
The phoenix riddle hath more wit[5]
By us; we two being one, are it.
So to one neutral thing both sexes fit,
We die and rise the same, and prove
Mysterious by this love.

We can die by it, if not live by love,
And if unfit for tombs and hearse
Our legend be, it will be fit for verse;
And if no piece of chronicle we prove,
We'll build in sonnets pretty rooms;[6]
As well a well wrought urn becomes
The greatest ashes, as half-acre tombs,
And by these hymns, all shall approve
Us canonized for love:

1. The making of saints.
2. The King's actual face or his image stamped on coins.
3. Daily list of those who have died issued during outbreaks of the plague.
4. To die is to experience orgasm.
5. The mythical bird that was burned and reborn out of its own ashes, a symbol of perfection.
6. A play on *stanza*, Italian for "room."

And thus invoke us: You whom reverend love
Made one another's hermitage;° *refuge, retreat*
You, to whom love was peace, that now is rage;
Who did the whole world's soul contract, and drove
Into the glasses° of your eyes[7] *lenses*
(So made such mirrors, and such spies,
That they did all to you epitomize)
Countries, towns, courts: beg from above
A pattern of your love!

Air and Angels

Twice or thrice had I loved thee,
Before I knew thy face or name;
So in a voice, so in a shapeless flame,
Angels affect us oft, and worshipped be;
Still when, to where thou wert, I came,
Some lovely glorious nothing I did see.[1]
But since my soul, whose child love is,
Takes limbs of flesh, and else could nothing do,
More subtle than the parent is
Love must not be, but take a body too,
And therefore what thou wert, and who,
I bid love ask, and now
That it assume thy body, I allow,
And fix itself in thy lip, eye, and brow.

Whilst thus to ballast love, I thought,
And so more steadily to have gone,
With wares which would sink admiration,
I saw, I had love's pinnace° overfraught, *light sailing ship*
Every thy hair for love to work upon
Is much too much, some fitter must be sought;
For, nor in nothing, nor in things
Extreme, and scattering bright, can love inhere;
Then as an angel, face and wings
Of air, not pure as it, yet pure doth wear,
So thy love may be my love's sphere;[2]
Just such disparity
As is twixt air and angel's purity,[3]
'Twixt women's love, and men's will ever be.

Break of Day[1]

'Tis true, 'tis day; what though it be?
Oh wilt thou therefore rise from me?

7. The lovers gazing into each other's eyes saw there a compact version or microcosm of the larger world or macrocosm.

1. A divine light shining through the body that Neoplatonists thought was the true object of desire rather than the body, which only reflected that beauty.

2. The analogy is between his love as the intelligence controlling a heavenly body and her love as the heavenly sphere, or material body.

3. Metaphysical doctrine separates being into celestial, aerial, and material. If the material lady returns his aerial love, then they will be united in a celestial union.

1. First printed, with music, in W. Corkine's *Second Book of Airs* (1612).

Why should we rise, because 'tis light?
Did we lie down, because 'twas night?
Love, which in spite of darkness brought us hither,
Should in despite of light keep us together.

Light hath no tongue, but is all eye;
If it could speak as well as spy,
This were the worst, that it could say,
That being well, I fain would stay,
And that I loved my heart and honor so,
That I would not from him, that had them, go.

Must business thee from hence remove?
Oh, that's the worst disease of love,
The poor, the foul, the false, love can
Admit, but not the busied man.
He which hath business, and makes love, does do
Such wrong, as when a married man doth woo.

A Valediction:° of Weeping

farewell

Let me pour forth
My tears before thy face, whilst I stay here,
For thy face coins them, and thy stamp° they bear, *image*
And by this mintage they are something worth,
For thus they be
Pregnant of thee;
Fruits of much grief they are, emblems° of more, *symbols*
When a tear falls, that thou falls which it bore,
So thou and I are nothing then, when on a diverse shore.

On a round ball
A workman that hath copies by, can lay
A Europe, Africa, and an Asia,
And quickly make that, which was nothing, all,[1]
So doth each tear,
Which thee doth wear,
A globe, yea world by that impression grow,
Till thy tears mixed with mine do overflow
This world, by waters sent from thee, my heaven dissolvèd so.

Oh more than moon,
Draw not up seas to drown me in thy sphere,[2]
Weep me not dead, in thine arms, but forbear
To teach the sea, what it may do too soon;
Let not the wind
Example find,
To do me more harm, than it purposeth;
Since thou and I sigh one another's breath,
Whoe'er sighs most, is cruelest, and halts the other's death.

1. The blank ball looks like a zero ("nothing") until the continents are painted on it to represent the entire world ("all").

2. An astral sphere with a power of attraction greater than the moon might draw the seas up to itself.

Love's Alchemy

Some that have deeper digged love's mine than I,
Say, where his centric° happiness doth lie: *central*
    I have loved, and got, and told,
But should I love, get, tell, till I were old,
I should not find that hidden mystery;
    Oh, 'tis imposture all:
And as no chemic° yet the elixir got,[1] *alchemist*
    But glorifies his pregnant pot,
    If by the way to him befall
Some odoriferous thing, or medicinal,
  So, lovers dream a rich and long delight,
  But get a winter-seeming summer's night.

Our ease, our thrift, our honor, and our day,
Shall we, for this vain bubble's shadow pay?
    Ends love in this, that my man,° *servant*
Can be as happy as I can; if he can
Endure the short scorn of a bridegroom's play?
    That loving wretch that swears,
'Tis not the bodies marry, but the minds,
    Which he in her angelic finds,
    Would swear as justly, that he hears,
In that day's rude hoarse minstrelsy, the spheres.[2]
  Hope not for mind in women; at their best
  Sweetness and wit, they're but mummy,[3] possessed.

The Flea[1]

Mark but this flea, and mark in this,
How little that which thou deniest me is;
It sucked me first,[2] and now sucks thee,
And in this flea, our two bloods mingled be;
Thou know'st that this cannot be said
A sin, nor shame, nor loss of maidenhead,
  Yet this enjoys before it woo,
  And pampered swells with one blood made of two,
  And this, alas, is more than we would do.

Oh stay, three lives in one flea spare,
Where we almost, nay more than married are.
This flea is you and I, and this
Our marriage bed, and marriage temple is;
Though parents grudge, and you, we are met,
And cloistered in these living walls of jet.° *black*
  Though use make you apt to kill me,
  Let not to that, self murder added be,
  And sacrilege, three sins in killing three.

1. A goal of alchemy was to produce a pure essence with the power to heal and prolong life.
2. The concentric globes that created sublime music as they revolved around the earth.
3. Medicine made from mummies; dead bodies.

1. Based on a poem attributed to Ovid, the poem plays on the belief that intercourse involved the mixing of bloods.
2. "Me it sucked first" in the 1635 edition.

Cruel and sudden, hast thou since
Purpled thy nail, in blood of innocence?
Wherein could this flea guilty be,
Except in that drop which it sucked from thee?
Yet thou triumph'st, and say'st that thou
Find'st not thy self, nor me the weaker now;
'Tis true, then learn how false, fears be;
Just so much honor, when thou yield'st to me,
Will waste, as this flea's death took life from thee.

The Bait[1]

Come live with me, and be my love,
And we will some new pleasures prove
Of golden sands, and crystal brooks,
With silken lines, and silver hooks.

There will the river whispering run
Warmed by thy eyes, more than the sun.
And there the enamored fish will stay,
Begging themselves they may betray.

When thou wilt swim in that live bath,
Each fish, which every channel hath,
Will amorously to thee swim,
Gladder to catch thee, then thou him.

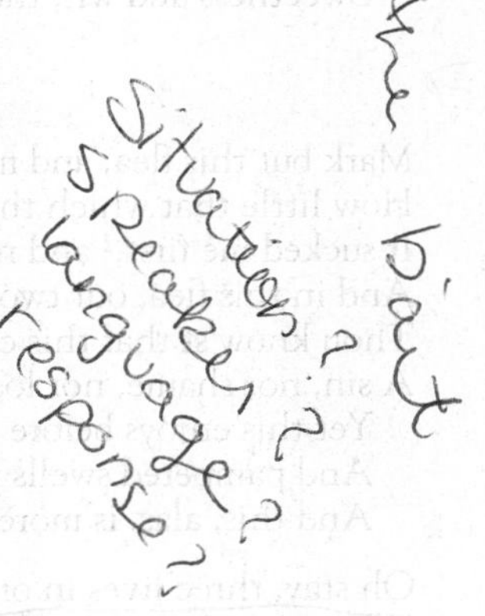

If thou, to be so seen, be'st loath,
By sun, or moon, thou darkenest both,
And if myself have leave to see,
I need not their light, having thee.

Let others freeze with angling reeds,
And cut their legs, with shells and weeds,
Or treacherously poor fish beset,
With strangling snare, or windowy net:

Let coarse bold hands, from slimy nest
The bedded fish in banks out-wrest,
Or curious traitors, sleave-silk flies[2]
Bewitch poor fishes' wandering eyes.

For thee, thou need'st no such deceit,
For thou thyself are thine own bait;
That fish, that is not catched thereby,
Alas, is wiser far than I.

The Apparition

When by thy scorn, O murderess, I am dead,
And that thou thinkst thee free

1. Parodies Marlowe's *The Passionate Shepherd to His Love* and Raleigh's *The Nymph's Reply*; see pages 1098–1100.

2. Artificial flies made from silk threads.

From all solicitation from me,
Then shall my ghost come to thy bed,
And thee, feigned vestal,° in worse arms shall see; *virgin priestess*
Then thy sick taper will begin to wink,
And he, whose thou art then, being tired before,
Will, if thou stir, or pinch to wake him, think
Thou call'st for more,
And in false sleep will from thee shrink,
And then poor aspen[1] wretch, neglected thou
Bathed in a cold quicksilver[2] sweat will lie
A verier° ghost than I; *truer*
What I will say, I will not tell thee now,
Lest that preserve thee; and since my love is spent,
I had rather thou shouldst painfully repent,
Than by my threatenings rest still innocent.

A Valediction: Forbidding Mourning[1]

As virtuous men pass mildly away,
And whisper to their souls, to go,
Whilst some of their sad friends do say,
The breath goes now, and some say, no:

So let us melt, and make no noise,
No tear-floods, nor sigh-tempests move,
'Twere profanation° of our joys *desecration*
To tell the laity[2] of our love.

Moving of th'earth brings harms and fears,
Men reckon what it did and meant,
But trepidation of the spheres,[3]
Though greater far, is innocent.

Dull sublunary[4] lovers' love
(Whose soul is sense) cannot admit
Absence, because it doth remove
Those things which elemented° it. *composed*

But we by a love, so much refined,
That our selves know not what it is,
Inter-assurèd of the mind,
Care less, eyes, lips, and hands to miss.

Our two souls therefore, which are one,
Though I must go, endure not yet
A breach, but an expansion,
Like gold to airy thinness beat.[5]

1. Trembling like an aspen leaf in the wind.
2. Liquid mercury, used to treat venereal disease.

1. In his *Life of Dr. John Donne* (1640), Walton describes the occasion as Donne's farewell to his wife before his journey to France in 1611.
2. The uninitiated.
3. Though the movement of the spheres is greater than an earthquake, we feel its effects less.
4. Under the sphere of the moon, hence sensual.
5. Gold was beaten to produce gold leaf. "Airy" suggests their love will become so fine that it will be spiritual.

If they be two, they are two so
As stiff twin compasses[6] are two,
Thy soul the fixed foot, makes no show
To move, but doth, if th' other do.

And though it in the center sit,
Yet when the other far doth roam,
It leans, and hearkens after it,
And grows erect, as that comes home.

Such wilt thou be to me, who must
Like th' other foot, obliquely run;
Thy firmness makes my circle just,° *complete*
And makes me end, where I begun.

The Ecstasy[1]

Where, like a pillow on a bed,
A pregnant bank swelled up, to rest
The violet's reclining head,[2]
Sat we two, one another's best.

Our hands were firmly cemented
With a fast balm, which thence did spring,
Our eye-beams twisted, and did thread
Our eyes, upon one double string;[3]

So to intergraft our hands, as yet
Was all the means to make us one,
And pictures in our eyes to get
Was all our propagation.[4]

As 'twixt two equal armies, Fate
Suspends uncertain victory,
Our souls (which to advance their state
Were gone out) hung 'twixt her and me.

And whilst our souls negotiate there,
We like sepulchral statues lay;
All day, the same our postures were,
And we said nothing, all the day.

If any, so by love refined,
That he soul's language understood,
And by good love were grown all mind,
Within convenient distance stood,

He (though he knew not which soul spake
Because both meant, both spake the same)

6. A common emblem of constancy amidst change.

1. From *ekstasis* (Greek) meaning passion and the withdrawal of the soul from the body. A beautiful and secluded pastoral spot was a frequent setting for love poetry.

2. The violet was an emblem of faithfulness.

3. The lovers are totally enthralled by gazing into each other's eyes.

4. The act of reflecting each other's image was called "making babies."

Might thence a new concoction[5] take,
And part far purer than he came.

This ecstasy doth unperplex,
We said, and tell us what we love,
We see by this, it was not sex,
We see, we saw not what did move:

But as all several souls contain
Mixture of things, they know not what,
Love, these mixed souls, doth mix again,
And makes both one, each this and that.

A single violet transplant,
The strength, the color, and the size,
(All which before was poor and scant)
Redoubles still, and multiplies.

When love with one another so
Interinanimates two souls,
That abler soul, which thence doth flow,
Defects of loneliness controls.

We then, who are this new soul, know,
Of what we are composed and made,
For, th' atomies° of which we grow, *components, parts*
Are souls, whom no change can invade.

But O alas, so long, so far
Our bodies why do we forbear?
They are ours, though they are not we, we are
The intelligences, they the sphere.[6]

We owe them thanks, because they thus,
Did us to us at first convey,
Yielded their forces, sense, to us,
Nor are dross° to us, but allay.° *refuse / a mixture*

On man heaven's influence works not so,
But that it first imprints the air,[7]
So soul into the soul may flow,
Though it to body first repair.

As our blood labors to beget
Spirits, as like souls as it can,
Because such fingers need to knit
That subtle knot, which makes us man:[8]

So much pure lovers' souls descend
T'affections,° and to faculties,°[9] *feelings / powers*

5. Refining of metals by heat.

6. In Aristotelian cosmology, each planet moved in a sphere (the form of its motion around the earth) and was guided by an inner spiritual force, or intelligence.

7. An angel has to put on clothes of air to be seen by men; in hermetic medicine the air mediates the influence of the stars. Just as spirits need a material medium, so souls need the union of bodies.

8. In scholastic philosophy a human being is compose[illegible] body and soul, and vapors called spirits produced [illegible] blood link the body with the soul.

9. As the blood mediates between body and soul, s[illegible] lovers' feelings mediate between flesh and spirit.

Which sense may reach and apprehend,
Else a great prince in prison lies.

To our bodies turn we then, that so
Weak men on love revealed may look;
Love's mysteries in souls do grow,
But yet the body is his book.

And if some lover, such as we,
Have heard this dialogue of one,
Let him still mark us, he shall see
Small change, when we are to bodies gone.

The Funeral

Whoever comes to shroud me, do not harm
Nor question much
That subtle wreath of hair, which crowns my arm;
The mystery, the sign you must not touch,
For 'tis my outward soul,
Viceroy to that, which then to heaven being gone,
Will leave this to control,
And keep these limbs her provinces, from dissolution.

For if the sinewy thread my brain lets fall
Through every part,
Can tie those parts, and make me one of all;[1]
These hairs which upward grew, and strength and art
Have from a better brain,
Can better do it;[2] except she meant that I
By this should know my pain,
As prisoners then are manacled when they're condemned to die.

Whate'er she meant by it, bury it with me,
For since I am
Love's martyr, it might breed idolatry,
If into others' hands these relics[3] came;
As 'twas humility
To afford to it all a soul can do,
So, 'tis some bravery,
That since you would save[4] none of me, I bury some of you.

The Relic

When my grave is broke up again
Some second guest to entertain,
(For graves have learned that woman-head[1]
To be to more than one a bed)

1. There was a theory that nerves emanating from the brain held the entire body together.
2. Her hairs coming from a better brain could better preserve his body.
3. Objects, often body parts, that served as memorials of a saint.
4. Editions from 1633 to 1669 read "have," as do some manuscripts.

1. A feminine trait, with a play on maidenhead. The reference is to the custom of burying more than one corpse in the same grave.

And he that digs it, spies
A bracelet of bright hair about the bone,
Will he not let us alone,
And think that there a loving couple lies,
Who thought that this device might be some way
To make their souls, at the last busy day,
Meet at this grave, and make a little stay?

If this fall in a time, or land,
Where misdevotion[2] doth command,
Then, he that digs us up, will bring
Us, to the Bishop, and the King,
To make us relics; then
Thou shalt be a Mary Magdalen, and I
A something else thereby;[3]
All women shall adore us, and some men;
And since at such time, miracles are sought,
I would have that age by this paper taught
What miracles we harmless lovers wrought.

First, we loved well and faithfully,
Yet knew not what we loved, nor why,
Difference of sex no more we knew,
Than our guardian angels do;
Coming and going, we
Perchance might kiss, but not between those meals;
Our hands ne'er touched the seals,
Which nature, injured by late law, sets free:[4]
These miracles we did; but now alas,
All measure, and all language, I should pass,
Should I tell what a miracle she was.

Elegy 19: To His Mistress Going to Bed[1]

Come, Madam, come, all rest my powers defy,
Until I labor, I in labor° lie. *suffering*
The foe oft-times having the foe in sight,
Is tired with standing though he never fight.
Off with that girdle,° like heaven's zone° glistering, *belt/zodiac*
But a far fairer world encompassing.
Unpin that spangled breastplate[2] which you wear,
That th'eyes of busy fools may be stopped there.
Unlace your self, for that harmonious chime,
Tells me from you, that now it is bed time.
Off with that happy busk,° which I envy, *bodice*
That still can be, and still can stand so nigh.

2. Idolatry, as in *The Second Anniversary*, where Donne calls prayers to saints "misdevotion."

3. Possibly Jesus Christ or one of Mary's lovers.

4. Nature permits a free love forbidden by human law.

1. In Latin poetry an elegy was a poem in "elegiacs" (alternating lines of dactylic hexameters and pentameters). Most of these, like Ovid's *Amores*, were about love and sex; Donne imitates Ovid's wit and eroticism. This poem was refused a license to be printed in 1633; it was first printed in *The Harmony of the Muses* (1654).

2. The stomacher, a covering for the chest worn under the bodice and covered with jewels.

Your gown going off, such beauteous state reveals,
As when from flowery meads th' hill's shadow steals.
Off with that wiry coronet and show
The hairy diadem which on you doth grow:
Now off with those shoes, and then safely tread
In this love's hallowed temple, this soft bed.
In such white robes, heaven's angels used to be
Received by men; thou angel bring'st with thee
A heaven like Mahomet's paradise;[3] and though
Ill spirits walk in white, we easily know,
By this these angels from an evil sprite,
Those set our hairs, but these our flesh upright.
  License my roving hands, and let them go,
Before, behind, between, above, below.
Oh my America! my new-found-land,
My kingdom, safliest when with one man manned,
My mine of precious stones, my empery,° *empire*
How blest I am in this discovering thee!
To enter in these bonds, is to be free;
Then where my hand is set, my seal shall be.[4]
  Full nakedness! All joys are due to thee.
As souls unbodied, bodies unclothed must be,
To taste whole joys. Gems which you women use
Are like Atlanta's balls, cast in men's views,[5]
That when a fool's eye lighteth on a gem,
His earthly soul may covet theirs, not them.
Like pictures, or like books' gay coverings made
For laymen, are all women thus arrayed;
Themselves are mystic books, which only we
(Whom their imputed grace will dignify)
Must see revealed.[6] Then since that I may know,
As liberally, as to a midwife, show
Thyself: cast all, yea, this white linen hence,
Here is no penance much less innocence.[7]
To teach thee, I am naked first; why then
What need'st thou have more covering than a man?

Holy Sonnets[1]

Divine Meditations

1

As due by many titles° I resign *legal rights*
Myself to thee, Oh God, first I was made
By thee, and for thee, and when I was decayed
Thy blood bought that, the which before was thine,

3. A heaven of sensual pleasure.

4. He has signed an agreement which he will now stamp with his seal. Also, he has put his hand where he will consummate his desire.

5. Donne changes the story of how Atalanta was distracted from racing her suitor Hippomenes when he threw three golden apples before her, which she paused to pick up.

6. The analogy is between the grace that man cannot merit from God in Calvinist doctrine and the undeserved favors women grant their lovers.

7. The 1669 edition and some manuscripts read: "There is no penance due to innocence."

1. The first twelve of the sonnets are printed in the sequence of the 1633 edition, which, according to Helen Gardner, represents Donne's order.

I am thy son, made with thyself to shine,
Thy servant, whose pains thou has still repaid,
Thy sheep, thine image, and, till I betrayed
Myself, a temple of thy Spirit divine;
Why doth the devil then usurp in me?
Why doth he steal, nay ravish that's thy right?
Except thou rise and for thine own work fight,
Oh I shall soon despair, when I do see
That thou lov'st mankind well, yet wilt not choose me,
And Satan hates me, yet is loth to lose me.

2

Oh my black soul! Now thou art summoned
By sickness, death's herald, and champion;
Thou art like a pilgrim, which abroad hath done
Treason, and durst not turn to whence he is fled,
Or like a thief, which till death's doom be read,
Wisheth himself delivered from prison;
But damned and haled° to execution, *dragged*
Wisheth that still he might be imprisoned;
Yet grace, if thou repent, thou canst not lack;
But who shall give thee that grace to begin?
Oh make thyself with holy mourning black,
And red with blushing, as thou art with sin;
Or wash thee in Christ's blood, which has this might
That being red, it dyes red souls to white.

3

This is my play's last scene, here heavens appoint
My pilgrimage's last mile; and my race
Idly, yet quickly run, hath this last pace,
My span's last inch, my minute's latest point,
And gluttonous death, will instantly unjoint
My body, and soul, and I shall sleep a space,
But my ever-waking part shall see that face,
Whose fear already shakes my every joint:
Then, as my soul, to heaven her first seat, takes flight,
And earth-borne body, in the earth shall dwell,
So, fall my sins, that all may have their right,
To where they're bred, and would press me, to hell.
Impute me righteous, thus purged of evil,[2]
For thus I leave the world, the flesh, and devil.

4

At the round earth's imagined corners, blow[3]
Your trumpets, angels, and arise, arise
From death, you numberless infinities
Of souls, and to your scattered bodies go,
All whom the flood did, and fire shall o'erthrow,[4]
All whom war, dearth, age, agues, tyrannies,

2. Protestant theology held that even when a man repented of his sins, he was still marked by the sin of Adam and needed to be made righteous by Christ's grace.

3. "I saw four angels standing on the four corners of the earth, holding the four winds of the earth" (Revelation 7.1).

4. The flood that Noah survived (Genesis 7) and the fire that will destroy the world at the last judgment (Revelation 6.11)

Despair, law, chance, hath slain, and you whose eyes,
Shall behold God, and never taste death's woe.[5]
But let them sleep, Lord, and me mourn a space,
For, if above all these, my sins abound,
'Tis late to ask abundance of thy grace,
When we are there; here on this lowly ground,
Teach me how to repent; for that's as good
As if thou'hadst sealed my pardon with thy blood.

5

If poisonous minerals, and if that tree,
Whose fruit threw death on else immortal us,
If lecherous goats, if serpents envious
Cannot be damned; alas, why should I be?
Why should intent or reason, born in me,
Make sins, else equal, in me more heinous?
And mercy being easy, and glorious
To God, in his stern wrath, why threatens he?
But who am I, that dare dispute with thee?
O God, Oh! of thine only worthy blood,
And my tears, make a heavenly Lethean[6] flood,
And drown in it my sins' black memory.
That thou remember them, some claim as debt,
I think it mercy, if thou wilt forget.

6

Death be not proud, though some have called thee
Mighty and dreadful, for thou are not so.
For, those, whom thou think'st thou dost overthrow,
Die not, poor death, nor yet canst thou kill me;
From rest and sleep, which but thy pictures be,
Much pleasure, then from thee, much more must flow,
And soonest our best men with thee do go,
Rest of their bones, and soul's delivery.
Thou art slave to fate, chance, kings, and desperate men,
And dost with poison, war, and sickness dwell,
And poppy,° or charms can make us sleep as well, *a narcotic*
And better than thy stroke; why swell'st° thou then? *grow in pride*
One short sleep past, we wake eternally,
And death shall be no more, Death thou shalt die.[7]

7

Spit in my face ye Jews, and pierce my side,
Buffet, and scoff, scourge, and crucify me,
For I have sinned, and sinned, and only he,
Who could do no iniquity, hath died:
But by my death cannot be satisfied° *atoned for*
My sins, which pass the Jews' impiety:
They killed once an inglorious[8] man, but I
Crucify him daily, being now glorified.[9]

5. The resurrection of the body (see 1 Corinthians 15.51–52).
6. Of Lethe, the river of forgetfulness in the underworld of ancient mythology.
7. "The last enemy that shall be destroyed is death" (1 Corinthians 15.26).
8. Unknown; not yet ascended into glory.
9. Every sin knowingly committed is another torture of Christ. (See Hebrews 6.6: "They crucify to themselves the Son of God afresh.")

Oh let me then, his strange love still admire:
Kings pardon, but he bore our punishment.
And Jacob came clothed in vile harsh attire
But to supplant, and with gainful intent:[1]
God clothed himself in vile man's flesh, that so
He might be weak enough to suffer woe.

8

Why are we by all creatures waited on?
Why do the prodigal elements supply
Life and food to me, being more pure than I,
Simple, and further from corruption?[2]
Why brook'st thou, ignorant horse, subjection?
Why dost thou bull, and boar so sillily
Dissemble weakness, and by one man's stroke die,[3]
Whose whole kind, you might swallow and feed upon?
Weaker I am, woe is me, and worse than you,
You have not sinned, nor need be timorous.
But wonder at a greater wonder, for to us
Created nature doth these things subdue,
But their Creator, whom sin, nor nature tied,
For us, his creatures, and his foes, hath died.

9

What if this present were the world's last night?
Mark in my heart, O soul, where thou dost dwell,
The picture of Christ crucified, and tell
Whether that countenance can thee affright,
Tears in his eyes quench the amazing light,
Blood fills his frowns, which from his pierced head fell,
And can that tongue adjudge thee unto hell,
Which prayed forgiveness for his foes' fierce spite?
No, no; but as in my idolatry[4]
I said to all my profane mistresses,
Beauty, of pity, foulness only is
A sign of rigor:[5] so I say to thee,
To wicked spirits are horrid shapes assigned,
This beauteous form assures a piteous mind.

10

Batter my heart, three-personed God;[6] for, you
As yet but knock, breathe, shine, and seek to mend;
That I may rise, and stand, o'erthrow me, and bend
Your force, to break, blow, burn and make me new.
I, like an usurped town, to another due,
Labor to admit you, but oh, to no end,
Reason your viceroy° in me, me should defend, *ruler*
But is captived, and proves weak or untrue,
Yet dearly I love you, and would be loved fain,° *willingly*

1. Jacob tricked his father Isaac into giving him his blessing by disguising himself in goatskin as his hairy brother Esau (see Genesis 27.1–36).

2. The elements are physically and morally pure, while humans are a complex mixture of all four elements, prone to decay, and moral agents, capable of sin.

3. The slaughterman's blow, and Adam's sin, causing death to all creation.

4. Erotic devotion to women.

5. Beautiful women show compassion; only ugly ones refuse their lovers.

6. The Trinity: God the Father, Son, and Holy Spirit.

But am betrothed unto your enemy,
Divorce me, untie, or break that knot again,
Take me to you, imprison me, for I
Except you enthrall me, never shall be free,
Nor ever chaste, except you ravish me.

11

Wilt thou love God, as he thee? Then digest,° *consider*
My soul, this wholesome meditation,
How God the Spirit, by angels waited on
In heaven, doth make his temple in thy breast.
The Father having begot a Son most blest,
And still begetting, (for he ne'er begun)[6]
Hath deigned to choose thee by adoption,
Coheir to his glory, and Sabbath's endless rest;
And as a robbed man, which by search doth find
His stol'n stuff sold, must lose or buy it again:
The Son of glory came down, and was slain,
Us whom he had made, and Satan stol'n, to unbind.
'Twas much, that man was made like God before,
But, that God should be made like man, much more.

12

Father, part of his double interest
Unto thy kingdom, thy Son gives to me,
His jointure° in the knotty Trinity, *joint tenancy*
He keeps, and gives me his death's conquest.
This Lamb, whose death, with life the world hath blest,
Was from the world's beginning slain, and he[7]
Hath made two wills, which with the legacy[8]
Of his and thy kingdom, do thy sons invest.
Yet such are those laws, that men argue yet
Whether a man those statutes can fulfill;
None doth, but all-healing grace and Spirit,
Revive again what law and letter kill.
Thy law's abridgement, and thy last command
Is all but love; oh let that last will stand![9]

from Devotions Upon Emergent Occasions[1]

["For whom the bell tolls"]

Nunc lento sonitu dicunt, morieris.

Now this bell tolling softly for another, says to me, Thou must die.

Perchance he for whom this bell[2] tolls may be so ill as that he knows not it tolls for him; and perchance I may think myself so much better than I am, as that they who are about me, and see my state may have caused it to toll for me, and I know not that. The Church is catholic, universal, so are all her actions; all that she does, belongs to all. When she baptises a child, that action concerns me; for that child is thereby connected to that

6. God's existence and begetting of his Son are both eternal.

7. Christ, "the Lamb slain from the foundation of the world" (Revelation 13.8).

8. Old and New Testaments.

9. "A new commandment I give unto you, that ye love one another" (John 13.34).

1. Donne wrote the *Devotions* (1624) following an illness he suffered in winter 1623. Each meditation concerns a phase of his disease.

2. The passing-bell rung slowly when a person was dying.

Head which is my Head too, and engrafted into that body,[3] whereof I am a member. And when she buries a man, that action concerns me: all mankind is of one Author, and is of one volume; when one man dies, one chapter is not torn out of the book, but translated[4] into a better language; and every chapter must be so translated. God employs several translators; some pieces are translated by age, some by sickness, some by war, some by justice; but God's hand is in every translation, and his hand shall bind up all our scattered leaves again, for that library where every book shall lie open to one another. As therefore the bell that rings to a sermon calls not upon the preacher only, but upon the congregation to come, so this bell calls us all; but how much more me, whom am brought so near the door by this sickness. There was a contention as far as a suit, (in which both piety and dignity, religion, and estimation, were mingled) which of the religious orders should ring to prayers first in the morning; and it was determined that they should ring first that rose earliest. If we understand aright the dignity of this bell that tolls for our evening prayer, we would be glad to make it ours by rising early, in that application, that it might be ours, as well as his whose indeed it is. The bell doth toll for him that thinks it doth; and though it intermit again, yet from that minute that occasion wrought upon him, he is united to God. Who casts not up his eye to the sun when it rises? but who takes off his eye from a comet when that breaks out? Who bends not his ear to any bell which upon any occasion rings? but who can remove it from that bell which is passing a piece of himself out of this world? No man is an island, entire of itself; every man is a piece of the Continent, a part of the main. If a clod be washed away by the sea, Europe is the less, as well as if a promontory were, as well as if a manor of thy friends or of thine own were Any man's death diminishes me, because I am involved in mankind; and therefore never send to know for whom the bell tolls; it tolls for thee. Neither can we call this a begging of misery or a borrowing of misery, as though we were not miserable enough of ourselves but must fetch in more from the next house in taking upon us the misery of our neighbors. Truly it were an excusable covetousness if we did; for affliction is a treasure, and scarce any man hath enough of it. No man hath affliction enough that is not matured and ripened by it, and made fit for God by that affliction. If a man carry treasure in bullion, or in a wedge of gold, and have none coined into current moneys, his treasure will not defray him as he travels. Tribulation is treasure in the nature of it, but it is not current money in the use of it, except we get nearer and nearer our home, heaven, by it. Another man may be sick too, and sick to death, and this affliction may lie in his bowels as gold in a mine and be of no use to him: but this bell that tells me of his affliction digs out and applies that gold to me, if by this consideration of another's danger I take mine own into contemplation and so secure myself by making my recourse to my God who is our only security.

from A Sermon Preached to the Honorable Company of the Virginia Plantation[1]

Beloved in him, whose kingdom, and Gospel you seek to advance, in this plantation, our Lord and Savior Christ Jesus, if you seek to establish a temporal kingdom[2]

3. United with the church.
4. From Latin *translatus,* "having been carried across."
1. This sermon was preached on November 13, 1622. It was printed three times before Donne died. The Virginia Company was founded in 1606 for the purpose of colonizing North America. In 1609 the Company split into the Virginia Company of London and the Plymouth Company. Dissension within the company arose over whether there should be martial law or a liberal form of govenment. By May 1624, when King James disbanded this corporation of private stockholders, 14,000 emigrants had been sent to Virginia.
2. The sermon interprets Acts 1.8: "But ye shall receive power, after that the Holy Ghost is come upon you, and ye shall be witnesses unto me both in Jerusalem, and in all Judea, and in Samaria, and unto the uttermost part of the earth."

there, you are not rectified, if you seek to be kings in either acceptation of the word; to be a king signifies liberty and independency, and supremacy, to be under no man, and to be a king signifies abundance, and omnisufficiency, to need no man. If those that govern there, would establish such a government, as should not depend upon this, or if those that thither, propose to themselves an exemption from laws, to live at their liberty; this is to be kings, to divest allegiance, to be under no man: and if those that adventure thither, propose to themselves present benefit, and profit, a sudden way to be rich, and an abundance of all desirable commodities from thence, this is to be sufficient of themselves, and to need no man: and to be under no man, and to need no man, are the two acceptations of being kings. Whom liberty draws to go, or present profit draws to adventure, are not yet in the right way. O, if you could once bring a catechism to be as good ware amongst them as a bugle, as a knife, as a hatchet! O, if you would be as ready to harken at the return of a ship, how many Indians were converted to Christ Jesus, as what trees, or drugs, or dyes that ship had brought, then you were in your right way, and not till then; liberty and abundance, are characters of kingdoms, and a kingdom is excluded in the Text; the Apostles were not to look for it, in their employment, nor you in this your plantation. * * *

God says to you, "No kingdom, not ease, not abundance; nay nothing at all yet; the plantation shall not discharge the charges, not defray itself yet; but yet already, now at first, it shall conduce to great uses; it shall redeem many a wretch from the jaws of death,[3] from the hands of the executioner, upon whom, perchance a small fault, or perchance a first fault, or perchance a fault heartily and sincerely repented, perchance no fault, but malice, had otherwise cast a present, and ignominious death. It shall sweep your streets, and wash your doors, from idle persons, and the children of idle persons, and employ them: and truly, if the whole country were but such a Bridewell,[4] to force idle persons to work, it has a good use. But it is already, not only a spleen, to drain the ill humors of the body, but a liver, to breed good blood; already the employment breeds mariners; already the place gives assays,[5] nay freights of marketable commodities; already it is a mark for the envy, and for the ambition of our enemies. I speak but of our doctrinal, not national enemies; as they are papists, they are sorry we have this country; and surely, twenty lectures in matter of controversy, does not so much vex them as one ship that goes, and strengthens that plantation. Neither can I recommend it to you, by any better rhetoric than their malice. They would gladly have it, and therefore let us be glad to hold it. * * *

Those amongst you, that are old now, shall pass out of this world with this great comfort, that you contributed to the beginning of that Commonwealth, and of that Church, though they live not to see the growth thereof to perfection. Apollos[6] watered, but Paul planted; he that began the work, was the greater man. And you that are young now, may live to see the enemy as much empeached by that place, and your friends, yea, children, as well accommodated in that place, as any other. You shall have made this island, which is but as the suburbs of the Old World, a bridge, a gallery to the New, to join all to that world that shall never grow old, the kingdom of heaven; you shall add persons to this kingdom, and to the kingdom of heaven, and add names to the books of our chronicles, and to the Book of Life.

To end all, as the orators which declaimed in the presence of the Roman emperors, in their panegyrics, took that way to make those emperors see, what they were

3. Many of those who were brought from England to Virginia were freed from imprisonment and execution in England by becoming indentured servants.

4. A London prison.

5. Returns of profit.

6. Paul's successor at Corinth. See 1 Corinthians 3.6.

bound to do, to say in those public orations, that those emperors had done so, (for that increased the love of the subject to the prince, to be so told, that he had done those great things, and then it conveyed a counsel into the prince to do them after). As their way was to procure things to be done, by saying they were done, so beloved I have taken a contrary way: for when I, by way of exhortation, all this while have seemed to tell you what should be done by you, I have, indeed, but told the congregation what has been done already; neither do I speak to move a wheel that stood still, but to keep the wheel in due motion; nor persuade you to begin, but to continue a good work, nor propose foreign, but your own examples, to do still, as you have done hitherto. For, for that, that which is especially in my contemplation, the conversion of the people, as I have received, so I can give this testimony, that of those persons, who have sent in moneys, and concealed their names, the greatest part, almost all, have limited their devotion, and contribution upon that point, the propagation of religion, and the conversion of the people; for the building and beautifying of the house of God, and for the instruction and education of their young children. Christ Jesus himself "is yesterday, and today, and the same forever."[7] In the advancing of his glory, be you so too, yesterday, and today, and the same forever, here; and hereafter, when time shall be no more, no more yesterday, no more today, yet forever and ever, you shall enjoy that joy, and that glory, which no ill accident can attain to diminish, or eclipse it.

Lady Mary Wroth

1586–1640

Lady Mary Wroth was born the same year that her uncle Sir Philip Sidney died in battle. Like her uncle, she wrote brilliant sonnets and an entertaining and complex prose romance, but whereas his death and writing became the stuff of myth, she died in obscurity. Appreciated by the finest poets of her time, her writing was neglected for the next 300 years; she has only recently been rediscovered as one of the most compelling women writers of her age. Her *Pamphilia to Amphilanthus*, the first Petrarchan sonnet sequence in English by a woman, was first printed in 1621 but was not reprinted until 1977. Wroth's work has finally become available outside rare book libraries, thanks to Josephine Robert's editions of Wroth's complete poems (1983) and her prose romance *The Countess of Montgomeries Urania* (1995), along with Michael Brennan's edition of her pastoral tragicomedy *Love's Victory* (1988). Recent criticism has stressed the formal complexity and variety of her poetry and prose, their creation of female subjectivity, and their relationship to her life and social context, shedding new light on one of the most emotionally powerful and stylistically innovative authors of the Jacobean period.

Mary Wroth was born into the cultivated and distinguished Sidney family. Mary and her mother, two brothers, and seven sisters lived at the family estate Penshurst in Kent. She sometimes visited her father in the Low Countries, where he commanded the English troops fighting for the Protestant cause against the Spanish. Ben Jonson sang the praises of Lady Mary's family and their way of life in *To Penshurst* (see pages 1533–1535), a place where the children not only enjoyed natural beauty—"broad beech" and "chest-nut shade"—but also learned the "mysteries of manners, arms and arts." Mary also spent a great deal of time in London with her

7. Hebrews 13.8.

aunt for whom she was named, Mary (Sidney) Herbert, Countess of Pembroke, hostess to and patron of a circle of poets that included George Chapman and Ben Jonson.

Mary found a mentor in her aunt, who herself wrote poems as well as translations of the Psalms and of Petrarch. Mary Herbert's translation of Petrarch's *Trionfo della Morte* ("Triumph of Death") portrays the poet's beloved Laura not as a passive object but as a lively and eloquent speaker. Mary Wroth's own sonnets similarly portray the woman as the suffering and desiring subject of love rather than the mute object that was common in earlier English Petrarchan poetry. Mary Wroth took the title of her *Urania* from a character in Philip Sidney's *The Countess of Pembrokes Arcadia*, whose publication had been overseen by his sister, Mary Sidney Herbert. Mary Wroth even created the character of the Queen of Naples as a fictional version of her aunt and perhaps saw *Urania* as a continuation of *Arcadia*.

When Mary married Sir Robert Wroth, Lord of Durance and Laughton House and juror for the Gunpowder Plot, she continued her close family ties with her aunt and father (yet another poet), but she also moved into the larger world of the Jacobean court. She served as Queen Anne's companion, and she became at once an observer and a center of attention in the aristocratic circle at court. In 1605, shortly after the first recorded performance of *Othello* at Whitehall, Lady Mary Wroth played in Ben Jonson's *Masque of Blackness*, in which she was presented to the court with Lady Frances Walsingham as the embodiment of gravity and dignity. Later, Wroth would deploy metaphors of darkness and night to great effect in her lyric poems.

It was in this court context that she attracted the attention of Ben Jonson, who not only wrote a poem complimenting her husband but also dedicated a sonnet and two epigrams to her. Jonson paid tribute to her as a subject and inspiration for poetry and as a powerfully moving poet in her own right. He claimed that since writing out her sonnets, he had "become / A better lover and much better poet." Dedicating his great play *The Alchemist* to her, he portrayed her as inheriting her uncle's mantle as poet: "To that Lady Most Deserving her Name and Blood, Lady Mary Wroth,"—a pun on her name, as Wroth was pronounced "worth." While she, too, punned on her married name in her poetry, Mary clung to her identity as a Sidney, using the Sidney device in her letters.

Her marriage was not particularly happy and pales in comparison with her literary friendship and love affair with her cousin William Herbert, by whom she had two illegitimate children, after she was widowed in 1614. During the years of her early widowhood she wrote the first part of her prose romance *Urania*, which was printed with *Pamphilia to Amphilanthus* in 1621. The *Urania* not only presents a fictional account of her relationship with her cousin and her parents' own happy marriage but also was read at the time as a criticism of the mores of the court. King James's courtiers, taking offense at the satire of their private lives, attacked her, prompting her to ask for the book to be removed from publication a few months after it first appeared. The early modern prejudice against women writing surfaces in Lord Denny's punning condescension to Wroth: "leave idle books alone / For wiser and worthier women have writ none."

Fortunately for us, she didn't take his advice and continued to write the second book of the *Urania*, which survives in manuscript. Indeed, no record of a warrant to recall the book survives. Her final years remain a mystery; she lived in retirement after her cousin's death. She left behind a body of poetry challenging the status quo of the court, proclaiming the suffering she had endured for love, and singing the beauty of spiritual love in a woman's voice. Imitating not only her uncle Philip's *Arcadia* but also the *Heptameron* of the French writer Marguerite de Navarre, Mary Wroth made the prose romance a complex combination of novelistic fantasy, roman à clef, and social satire. The greatest English woman writer of her age, Mary Wroth fashioned a new voice and new perspectives within literary tradition that convey the fullness and complexity of her life as woman, lover, and writer.

from **Pamphilia to Amphilanthus**[1]

1

When night's black mantle could most darkness prove,
And sleep death's image did my senses hire
From knowledge of myself, then thoughts did move
Swifter than those most swiftness need require:
In sleep, a chariot drawn by winged desire
I saw, where sat bright Venus, Queen of love,
And at her feet her son,[2] still adding fire
To burning hearts which she did hold above,
But one heart flaming more than all the rest
The goddess held, and put it to my breast.
"Dear son, now shut?"[3] said she, "thus must we win."
He her obeyed, and martyred my poor heart,
I, waking, hoped as dreams it would depart;[4]
Yet since, O me, a lover I have been.

16

Am I thus conquered? Have I lost the powers
That to withstand, which joys to ruin me?
Must I be still while it my strength devours
And captive leads me prisoner, bound, unfree?
Love first shall leave men's fant'sies to them free,[5]
Desire shall quench love's flames, spring hate sweet showers,
Love shall loose all his darts, have sight, and see
His shame, and wishings hinder happy hours.[6]
Why should we not Love's purblind° charms resist? *totally blind*
Must we be servile, doing what he list?° *wants*
No, seek some host to harbor thee: I fly
Thy babish° tricks, and freedom do profess; *childish*
But O my hurt, makes my lost heart confess
I love, and must. So farewell liberty.

17

Truly poor Night thou welcome art to me;
I love thee better in this sad attire
Than that which raiseth some men's fant'sies higher
Like painted outsides which foul inward be.[7]
I love thy grave, and saddest looks to see,
Which seems my soul, and dying heart entire,

1. The title means "From the All-loving one to the Dual Lover." First published in 1621, the sonnet sequence is here printed according to the numbering in Josephine Robert's 1983 edition.
2. Cupid. Compare the image of the chariot here with that in Petrarch's *Triumph of Love*. Also see Giordano Bruno on the symbolic meanings of Venus in Perspectives: Emblem, Metaphor, and Style, page 1605.
3. Enclose that flaming heart within Pamphilia.
4. Pamphilia's experience of love is represented as a dream vision, a symbolic narrative in which the dreamer discovers hidden truth.
5. Before I surrender to Love, Love will allow men to realize their fantasies freely.
6. Cupid blindfolded was a popular figure in Renaissance iconography.
7. Like the whitewashed sepulchers (tombs) in Matthew 23.27.

Like to the ashes of some happy fire
That flamed in joy, but quenched in misery.
I love thy count'nance,° and thy sober pace *face, expression*
Which evenly goes, and as of loving grace
To us, and me among the rest oppressed
Gives quiet, peace to my poor self alone,
And freely grants day leave when thou art gone
To give clear light to see all ill redressed.

26

When everyone to pleasing pastime hies° *goes in haste*
Some hunt, some hawk,[8] some play, while some delight
In sweet discourse, and music shows joy's might
Yet I my thoughts do far above these prize.
The joy which I take is that free from eyes
I sit, and wonder at this day-like night
So to dispose themselves, as void of right,
And leave true pleasure for poor vanities;
When others hunt, my thoughts I have in chase;
If hawk, my mind at wishèd end doth fly,
Discourse, I with my spirit talk, and cry
While others music choose as greatest grace.
O God, say I, can these fond pleasures move?
Or music be but in sweet thoughts of love?

28. Song

Sweetest love, return again,
Make not too long stay;
Killing mirth and forcing pain,
Sorrow leading way,
Let us not thus parted be,
Love and absence ne'er agree;

But since you must needs depart,
And me hapless° leave, *unlucky*
In your journey take my heart
Which will not deceive,
Yours it is, to you it flies
Joying in those lovèd eyes,

So in part, we shall not part
Though we absent be;
Time, nor place, nor greatest smart
Shall my bands make free.
Tied I am, yet think it gain,
In such knots I feel no pain.

But can I live having lost
Chiefest part of me?

8. To hunt game with hawks.

Heart is fled, and sight is crossed,
These my fortunes be;
Yet dear heart go, soon return,
As good there as here to burn.

39

Take heed mine eyes, how you your looks do cast,
Lest they betray my heart's most secret thought;
Be true unto yourselves for nothing's bought
More dear than doubt which brings a lover's fast.
Catch you all watching eyes, ere they be past,
Or take yours fixed where your best love hath sought
The pride of your desires; let them be taught
Their faults for shame, they could no truer last;
Then look, and look with joy for conquest won,
Of those that searched your hurt in double kind;
So you kept safe, let them themselves look blind;
Watch, gaze, and mark 'til they to madness run,
While you, mine eyes, enjoy full sight of love
Contented that such happinesses move.

40

False hope which feeds but to destroy, and spill° *kill*
What it first breeds; unnatural to the birth
Of thine own womb; conceiving but to kill,[9]
And plenty gives to make the greater dearth,
So tyrants do who falsely ruling earth
Outwardly grace them, and with profits fill,
Advance those who appointed are to death
To make their greater fall to please their will.
Thus shadow they their wicked vile intent,
Coloring evil with a show of good
While in fair shows their malice so is spent;
Hope kills the heart, and tyrants shed the blood.
For hope deluding brings us to the pride[1]
Of our desires the farther down to slide.

48

If ever Love had force in human breast?
If ever he could move in pensive heart?
Or if that he such power could but impart
To breed those flames whose heat brings joy's unrest,
Then look on me: I am to these addressed.
I am the soul that feels the greatest smart,
I am that heartless trunk of heart's depart,
And I, that one, by love and grief oppressed;
None ever felt the truth of Love's great miss° *need, want*
Of eyes, 'til I deprived was of bliss;
For had he seen, he must have pity showed;

9. The image is of a miscarriage or infanticide.

1. Arrogance, but also elation and pleasure.

I should not have been made this stage of woe
  Where sad disasters have their open show;
  O no, more pity he had sure bestowed.

68

My pain, still smothered in my grièved breast
  Seeks for some ease, yet cannot passage find
  To be discharged of this unwelcome guest;
  When most I strive, more fast his burdens bind,
Like to a ship, on Goodwins[2] cast by wind
  The more she strives, more deep in sand is pressed
  Till she be lost; so am I, in this kind° *way*
  Sunk and devoured, and swallowed by unrest,
Lost, shipwracked, spoiled, debarred of smallest hope
  Nothing of pleasure left; save thoughts have scope,
  Which wander may. Go then, my thoughts, and cry
Hope's perished, Love tempest-beaten, Joy lost:
  Killing Despair hath all these blessings crossed.
  Yet Faith still cries, Love will not falsify.

74. Song

Love a child is ever crying,
  Please him, and he straight is flying;
  Give him, he the more is craving,
  Never satisfied with having.

His desires have no measure,
  Endless folly is his treasure;
  What he promiseth he breaketh;
  Trust not one word that he speaketh.

He vows nothing but false matter,
  And to cozen° you he'll flatter. *trick*
  Let him gain the hand[3] he'll leave you,
  And still glory to deceive you.

He will triumph in your wailing,
  And yet cause be of your failing.
  These his virtues are, and slighter
  Are his gifts, his favors lighter.

Feathers are as firm in staying,
  Wolves no fiercer in their preying;
  As a child then leave him crying,
  Nor seek him so given to flying.

from *A Crown of Sonnets Dedicated to Love*[1]

77

In this strange labyrinth how shall I turn?
  Ways° are on all sides while the way I miss: *paths*

2. A dangerous shoal off the south eastern coast of England.
3. Let him take control.
1. The crown (Italian *corona*) is a form in which the last line of each poem is repeated as the first line of the next. The last poem of the sequence ends with the first line of the first poem.

If to the right hand, there, in love I burn;
Let me go forward, therein danger is;
If to the left, suspicion hinders bliss,
Let me turn back, shame cries I ought return,
Nor faint° though crosses with my fortunes kiss;[2] *lose heart*
Stand still is harder, although sure to mourn.[3]
Thus let me take the right, or left-hand way,
Go forward, or stand still, or back retire;
I must these doubts endure without allay° *relief*
Or help, but travail[4] find for my best hire.
Yet that which most my troubled sense doth move
Is to leave all, and take the thread of love.[5]

83

How blessed be they then, who his favors prove,
A life whereof the birth is just desire,
Breeding sweet flame which hearts invite to move
In these loved eyes which kindle Cupid's fire,
And nurse his longings with his thoughts entire,
Fixed on the heat of wishes formed by love;
Yet whereas fire destroys this doth aspire,
Increase, and foster all delights above;
Love will a painter make you, such as you
Shall able be to draw your only dear
More lovely, perfect, lasting, and more true
Than rarest workman, and to you more near.
These be the least, then all must needs confess
He that shuns love doth love himself the less.

103

My muse now happy, lay thyself to rest,
Sleep in the quiet of a faithful love,
Write you no more, but let these fant'sies move
Some other hearts, wake not to new unrest;
But if you study, be those thoughts addressed
To truth, which shall eternal goodness prove,
Enjoying of true joy, the most, and best,
The endless gain which never will remove.
Leave the discourse to Venus, and her son
To young beginners, and their brains inspire
With stories of great love, and from that fire
Get heat to write the fortunes they have won,
And thus leave off; what's past shows you can love,
Now let your constancy your honor prove.

Pamphilia.[6]

2. Though troubles embrace my luck, or fate.
3. It is more difficult to do nothing, although this is sure to make me mourn.
4. Hard work, with word play on "Travel," which occurs in the 1621 text.
5. An allusion to the myth of Ariadne, beloved of Theseus, to whom she gave a thread to unwind behind him on his path through the labyrinth so that, after slaying the Minotaur, he could retrace his steps on his way out.
6. According to the 1621 *Urania*, when Pamphilia accepts the keys to the Throne of Love, the virtue *Constancy* disappears and is transformed into Pamphilia's breast.

Robert Herrick

1591–1674

The urbane and at times pagan poet Robert Herrick might seem an unlikely candidate for rural vicar, but such were his connections that he was promoted from deacon to priest in a day. He spent most of his life as vicar of the Devonshire parish of Dean, where he wrote poetry about country customs and church liturgy. A hundred and fifty years after his death, a writer in the *Quarterly Review* was able to find people in the village who could recite from memory Herrick's *Farewell to Dean Bourn:* "I never look to see / Dean, or thy warty incivility," lines that "they said he uttered as he crossed the brook, upon being ejected from the vicarage by Cromwell." Referring to Herrick's return to the vicarage after the Restoration, these locals "added with an air of innocent triumph, 'He did see it again.'" The villagers also recalled stories of how the bachelor vicar threw his sermon at the congregation one day for their inattention and how he taught his pet pig to drink from a tankard. Many of his best poems, such as *Corinna's Going A-Maying* and *The Hock-Cart, or Harvest Home,* celebrate the landscape and the life of the country in the idealized tradition of pastoral poetry.

The son of a goldsmith in Cheapside, Herrick was apprenticed to the trade at age fourteen. After taking his B.A. from Cambridge in 1617, he returned to London, where he spent his poetic apprenticeship until he was appointed chaplain to the Duke of Buckingham in his failed expedition to aid the French Protestants of Rhé in 1627. Only a year later, Herrick moved to the vicarage at Dean, but many of his poems recount his London days, recalling the feasts frequented by Ben Jonson, whose verse "out-did the meat, out-did the frolic wine." The influence of Jonson's classical concision, wit, and urbanity can be felt in such poems as *Delight in Disorder* and his *Prayer* to the poet. While in London, Herrick also became friends with William Lawes, the court composer who wrote the music for Milton's masque *Comus*. When Lawes set Herrick's *To the Virgins to Make Much of Time* to music, this poem became one of the most popular drinking songs of the seventeenth century—often sung as a "catch," which meant that its words could be played with to produce ribald double meanings. His poems circulated in manuscript until his volume of verse was printed in 1648, with his secular poetry entitled *Hesperides* and his religious poetry entitled *Noble Numbers*. He first achieved a wide readership in the early nineteenth century with the romantic revival of interest in rural life and poetry.

The Argument of His Book[1]

I sing of brooks, of blossoms, birds, and bowers,
Of April, May, of June, and July flowers.
I sing of Maypoles, hock carts, wassails, wakes,[2]
Of bridegrooms, brides, and of their bridal cakes.
I write of youth, of love, and have access
By these, to sing of cleanly wantonness.° *carefree abandon*
I sing of dews, of rains, and piece by piece,
Of balm, of oil, of spice, and ambergris.[3]

1. All of Herrick's poems were published in 1648. The "Argument" introduces the book's themes.
2. Hock carts: harvest wagons; wassails: drinking toasts; wakes: celebrations in honor of the dedication of a parish church.
3. Secretion from the intestines of sperm whales, used to make perfume.

I sing of times trans-shifting;[4] and I write
How roses first came red, and lilies white.
I write of groves, of twilights, and I sing
The court of Mab,[5] and of the fairy king.
I write of hell; I sing (and ever shall)
Of Heaven, and hope to have it after all.

Delight in Disorder

A sweet disorder in the dress
Kindles in clothes a wantonness:
A lawn° about the shoulders thrown *scarf*
Into a fine distraction;
An erring° lace, which here and there *wandering*
Enthralls the crimson stomacher:[1]
A cuff neglectful, and thereby
Ribbons to flow confusedly:
A winning wave, deserving note,
In the tempestuous petticoat;
A carelesse shoestring, in whose tie
I see a wild civility:
Do more bewitch me, than when art
Is too precise[2] in every part.

Corinna's Going A-Maying

Get up, get up for shame! the blooming morn
Upon her wings presents the god unshorn.[1]
    See how Aurora[2] throws her fair
    Fresh-quilted colors through the air:
    Get up, sweet slug-a-bed, and see
    The dew-bespangling herb and tree.
Each flower has wept, and bowed toward the east,
Above an hour since; yet you not dressed,
    Nay! not so much as out of bed?
    When all the birds have matins° said, *morning prayer*
    And sung their thankfull hymns: 'tis sin,
    Nay, profanation° to keep in, *impiety*
Whenas a thousand virgins on this day
Spring, sooner than the lark, to fetch in May.[3]

Rise, and put on your foliage, and be seen
To come forth, like the springtime, fresh and green,
    And sweet as Flora.[4] Take no care

4. Times changing and passing; the cycle of the seasons.
5. Queen of the fairies.
1. Ornamental covering for the chest worn under the lacing of the bodice.
2. "Precise" was often used to describe the strictness of the Puritans.

1. Apollo, the sun god, whose beams are seen as his flowing locks.
2. Goddess of the dawn in Roman mythology.
3. The custom on May Day morning was to gather blossoms.
4. Ancient Italian goddess of fertility and flowers.

For jewels for your gown, or hair:
Fear not; the leaves will strew
Gems in abundance upon you;
Besides, the childhood of the day has kept,
Against you come, some orient° pearls unwept; *oriental, shining*
Come, and receive them while the light
Hangs on the dew-locks of the night,
And Titan[5] on the eastern hill
Retires himself, or else stands still
Till you come forth. Wash, dress, be brief in praying:
Few beads are best,[6] when once we go a-Maying.

Come, my Corinna, come; and coming, mark
How each field turns a street; each street a park
Made green, and trimmed with trees; see how
Devotion gives each house a bough,
Or branch: each porch, each door, ere this,
An ark, a tabernacle is,[7]
Made up of whitethorn neatly interwove;
As if here were those cooler shades of love.
Can such delights be in the street
And open fields, and we not see't?
Come, we'll abroad; and let's obey
The proclamation made for May,
And sin no more, as we have done, by staying;
But my Corinna, come, let's go a-Maying.

There's not a budding boy, or girl, this day,
But is got up, and gone to bring in May.
A deal of youth, ere this, is come
Back, and with whitethorn laden home.
Some have dispatched their cakes and cream,
Before that we have left to dream:
And some have wept, and wooed, and plighted troth,
And chose their priest, ere we can cast off sloth.
Many a green-gown has been given,
Many a kiss, both odd and even:[8]
Many a glance, too, has been sent
From out the eye, love's firmament:
Many a jest told of the keys betraying
This night, and locks picked; yet we're not a-Maying.

Come, let us go, while we are in our prime,
And take the harmless folly of the time.
We shall grow old apace, and die
Before we know our liberty.
Our life is short; and our days run
As fast away as does the sun;

5. The sun god.
6. An allusion to Catholic rosary beads.
7. The Hebrew ark of the Covenant contained the tablets of the laws; a tabernacle is an ornamental niche to hold the consecrated host.
8. Green gown . . . given: by lying in the grass. Kisses are odd and even in kissing games.

And as a vapor, or a drop of rain
Once lost, can ne'er be found again,
So when or you or I are made
A fable, song, or fleeting shade,° *soul*
All love, all liking, all delight
Lies drowned with us in endless night.
Then while time serves, and we are but decaying,
Come, my Corinna, come, let's go a-Maying.

To the Virgins, to Make Much of Time

Gather ye rosebuds while ye may,
Old time is still a-flying;[1]
And this same flower that smiles today,
Tomorrow will be dying.[2]

The glorious lamp of heaven, the sun,
The higher he's a-getting;
The sooner will his race be run,[3]
And nearer he's to setting.

That age is best, which is the first,
When youth and blood are warmer;
But being spent, the worse, and worst
Times still succeed the former.

Then be not coy, but use your time,
And while ye may, go marry;
For having lost but once your prime,
You may for ever tarry.

The Hock-Cart,[1] or Harvest Home

To the Right Honorable, Mildmay, Earl of Westmoreland[2]

Come, sons of summer, by whose toil,
We are the lords of wine and oil;
By whose tough labors, and rough hands,
We rip up first, then reap our lands.
Crowned with the ears of corn, now come,
And, to the pipe, sing harvest home.
Come forth, my Lord, and see the cart
Dressed up with all the country art.
See, here a maukin°, there a sheet, *scarecrow*
As spotlesse pure, as it is sweet,
The horses, mares, and frisking fillies,
(Clad, all, in linen, white as lilies.)
The harvest swains,° and wenches bound *young men*
For joy, to see the hock-cart crowned.

1. The Latin tag *tempus fugit* ("time flies").
2. "Dying" was also a euphemism for orgasm.
3. In Greek mythology the sun was seen as the chariot of Phoebus Apollo drawn across the sky each day as in a race.

1. Wagon carrying the last load of harvest crops.
2. The landlord, Mildmay Fane (Earl of Westmoreland), was one of Herrick's patrons.

About the cart, hear how the rout
Of rural younglings raise the shout,
Pressing before, some coming after,
Those with a shout and these with laughter.
Some blesse the cart, some kiss the sheaves;
Some prank° them up with oaken leaves: *decorate*
Some cross the fill-horse, some with great
Devotion stroke the home-borne wheat:[3]
While other rustics, less attent
To prayers, than to merriment,
Run after with their breeches rent.
 Well, on, brave boys, to your Lord's hearth,
Glittering with fire; where, for your mirth,
Ye shall see first the large and chief
Foundation of your feast, fat beef:
With upper stories, mutton, veal,
And bacon, (which makes full the meal)
With several dishes standing by,
As here a custard, there a pie,
And here all tempting frumenty.° *pudding*
And for to make the merry cheer,
If smirking° wine be wanting here, *sparkling*
There's that, which drowns all care, stout beer:
Which freely drink to your Lord's health,
Then to the plough, (the common-wealth),
Next to your flails, your fanes, your vats;[4]
Then to the maids with wheaten hats:
To the rough sickle, and crook'd sythe,
Drink, frolic boys, till all be blithe.
 Feed, and grow fat; and as ye eat,
Be mindfull, that the laboring neat[5]
As you, may have their fill of meat.
And know, besides, ye must revoke° *call back*
The patient ox unto the yoke,
And all go back unto the plow
And harrow, though they're hanged up now.
And, you must know, your Lord's word's true,
Feed him ye must, whose food fills you,
And that this pleasure is like rain,
Not sent ye for to drown your pain,
But for to make it spring again.

His Prayer to Ben Jonson[1]

When I a verse shall make,
Know I have prayed thee,

3. The fill-horse is harnessed between the shafts of the cart. Crossing the horse and kissing the sheaves of wheat were old English Catholic customs.
4. Flails: instruments for threshing; fans: used to separate wheat from chaff.
5. Cattle, whose "meat" is grain or hay.
1. The humorous conceit in this poem is of Ben Jonson as a saint in the "religion" of poetry, aiding Herrick as a saint would intercede for a sinner. Herrick pays homage to Jonson's style both in his humor and verse form.

For old religion's sake,[2]
Saint Ben to aid me.

Make the way smooth for me,
When I, thy Herrick,
Honoring thee, on my knee
Offer my lyric.

Candles I'll give to thee
And a new altar;
And thou Saint Ben shall be
Writ in my psalter.° *hymn book*

Upon Julia's Clothes

When as in silks my Julia goes,
Then, then, me thinks, how sweetly flows
That liquefaction of her clothes.
Next, when I cast mine eyes and see
That brave° vibration each way free; *splendid*
O how that glittering taketh me!

Upon His Spaniel Tracie

Now thou art dead, no eye shall ever see,
For shape and service, spaniel like to thee.
This shall my love do, give thy sad death one
Tear, that deserves of me a million.

George Herbert

1593–1633

George Herbert spent the last three years of his life as a country parson. In an age in which such a church living was often a mere sinecure, Herbert had a genuine vocation, which he chose over other paths open to him through his talent and the connections of his distinguished Welsh family. His education and vocation were most influenced by his mother Magdalene Herbert, a woman with a great appreciation for poetry and strong devotion to the Church of England. When she died in 1627, John Donne gave the funeral sermon, extolling not only her grace, wit, and charm but especially her extraordinary charity to those who suffered from the plague of 1625, among whom was Donne himself. Herbert's mother had been widowed when he was just three years old. She brought up ten children, first in Oxford and then in London, where she saw to it that they were well read in the Bible and the classics.

Herbert studied at Cambridge University, where he became Reader in Rhetoric in 1616; in 1620 he was elected Public Orator, a post that he held for eight years. He wrote poetry and delivered public addresses in Latin and worked on the Latin version of Francis Bacon's *The Advancement of Learning*. Herbert also stood for Parliament and served there in 1624, when the Virginia Company, in which many of his friends and family were stockholders, was beset by financial difficulties and ultimately dissolved by James I.

2. A reference to Jonson's Catholicism.

Though his book *The Temple,* which included all his English poems, was not published until just after his death in 1633, Herbert was already writing verse as an undergraduate in 1610, when he dedicated two sonnets to his mother that advocated religious rather than secular love as the subject for poetry. His first published poems were written in Latin, commemorating the death of Prince Henry (1612). Herbert also wrote three different collections of Latin poems during his Cambridge years: *Musae Responsoriae,* polemical poems that defended the rites of the Church of England from Puritan criticism; *Passio discerpta,* religious verse that focused on Christ's passion and death in a style reminiscent of Crashaw; and *Lucas,* a collection of brief epigrams, such as this one on pride: "Each man is earth, and the field's child. Tell me, / Will you be a sterile mountain or a fertile valley?" The sardonic and mocking tone of these epigrams may surprise a reader of his English poems, but the wit and the rhetorical finish of his Latin poetry recur in his later verse.

Herbert's poetry is some of the most complex and innovative of all English verse. In a very pared-down style, enlivened by gentle irony, Herbert produces complexity of meaning through allegory and emblem, directly or more often indirectly alluding to biblical images, events, and insights, which take on their own moral and poetic meaning in the life of the speaker and the reader. Each of his poems is a kind of spiritual event, enacting in its form, both visual and aural, the very theological experiences and beliefs—or conflict of beliefs—expressed. Herbert allows us to make the spiritual journey with him through suffering and redemption, through doubt and hope. The meaning of one of his poems unravels like a discovery, each line and stanza raising alternative possibilities and altering the meaning of the one before. His spirituality is not a matter of easy acceptance but one of struggle, portrayed with wit, logic, and passion that recall the best of Donne's verse. The humility, subtle hesitancy, and whimsical irony are Herbert's alone, as when he addresses a love poem, *The Pearl,* to God:

> I know the ways of pleasure, the sweet strains,
> The lullings and the relishes of it . . .
> My stuff is flesh, not brass; my senses live,
> And grumble oft, that they have more in me
> Then he that curbs them, being but one to five:
> Yet I love thee.

The Altar[1]

A broken ALTAR, Lord, thy servant rears,
Made of a heart, and cemented with tears:
Whole parts are as thy hand did frame;
No workman's tool has touched the same.[2]
A HEART alone
Is such a stone,
As nothing but
Thy power doth cut.
Wherefore each part
Of my hard heart
Meets in this frame,
To praise thy Name.
That, if I chance to hold my peace,
These stones to praise thee may not cease.[3]
Oh let thy blessed SACRIFICE be mine,
and sanctify this ALTAR to be thine.

1. All of Herbert's poems were published in *The Temple* (1633).

2. See Exodus 20.5, where God tells Moses: "And if thou wilt make me an altar of stone, thou shalt not build it of hewn stone: for if thou lift up thy tool upon it thou has polluted it."

3. See Luke 19.40: "I tell you that, if these should hold their peace, the stones would immediately cry out."

Redemption[1]

Having been tenant long to a rich lord,
Not thriving, I resolvèd to be bold,
And make a suit unto him, to afford
A new small-rented° lease, and cancel the old. *cheaper*

In heaven at his manor I him sought:
They told me there, that he was lately gone
About some land, which he had dearly bought
Long since on earth, to take possession.

I straight returned, and knowing his great birth,
Sought him accordingly in great resorts—
In cities, theaters, gardens, parks, and courts:
At length I heard a ragged noise and mirth

Of thieves and murderers: there I him espied,
Who straight, "Your suit is granted," said, and died.

Easter

Rise heart, thy Lord is risen. Sing his praise
Without delays,
Who takes thee by the hand, that thou likewise
With him may'st rise:
That, as his death calcinèd° thee to dust, *reduced by fire*
His life may make thee gold, and much more just.

Awake, my lute, and struggle for thy part
With all thy art.
The cross taught all wood to resound his name
Who bore the same.
His stretchèd sinews taught all strings, what key
Is best to celebrate this most high day.

Consort° both heart and lute, and twist a song *harmonize*
Pleasant and long:
Or, since all music is but three parts vied
And multiplied,[1]
Oh let thy blessed spirit bear a part,
And make up our defects with his sweet art.

I got me flowers to strew thy way;
I got me boughs off many a tree:
But thou wast up by break of day,
And brought'st thy sweets along with thee.

1. "Redemption," means deliverance from sin and comes from the Latin *redimere*, to buy back, to ransom.

1. Since music is increased by three-part harmony.

The sun arising in the east,
Though he give light, and th' east perfume,
If they should offer to contest
With thy arising, they presume.

Can there be any day but this,
Though many suns to shine endeavor?
We count three hundred, but we miss:[2]
There is but one, and that one ever.

Easter Wings[1]

Lord, who createdst man in wealth and store,[2]
Though foolishly he lost the same,
Decaying more and more,
Till he became
Most poor:
With thee
Oh let me rise
As larks, harmoniously,
And sing this day thy victories:
Then shall the fall[3] further the flight in me.

My tender age in sorrow did begin
And still with sickness and shame
Thou didst so punish sin,
That I became
Most thin.
With thee
Let me combine,
And feel this day thy victory:
For, if I imp[4] my wing on thine,
Affliction shall advance the flight in me.

Affliction (1)[1]

When first thou didst entice to thee my heart,
I thought the service brave:
So many joys I wrote down for my part,
Besides what I might have
Out of my stock of natural delights,
Augmented with thy gracious benefits.

2. We are mistaken in reckoning that there are 300-plus days in the year, since they are all but as one day when compared to the light of the Son (Christ) rising.

1. As in the first editions of Herbert, this poem is printed sideways to represent the shape of wings.

2. Plenty.

3. The human frailty of sin, as well as the speaker's own descent into sin and suffering, which Christ redeems through his rising from the dead on Easter.

4. In falconry, to insert feathers in a bird's wing.

1. Editors assign numbers to poems that Herbert gave the same title to in order to distinguish them from one another.

I lookèd on thy furniture so fine,
And made it fine to me:
Thy glorious household stuff did me entwine,
And 'tice me unto thee.
Such stars I counted mine: both heaven and earth
Paid me my wages in a world of mirth.

What pleasures could I want, whose king I served,
Where joys my fellows were?
Thus argued into hopes, my thoughts reserved
No place for grief or fear;
Therefore my sudden soul caught at the place,
And made her youth and fierceness seek thy face.

At first thou gav'st me milk and sweetness;
I had my wish and way:
My days were strawed° with flowers and happiness; *strewed*
There was no month but May.
But with my years sorrow did twist and grow,
And made a party unawares for woe.

My flesh began unto my soul in pain,[2]
Sicknesses cleave° my bones; *penetrate*
Consuming agues dwell in every vein,
And tune my breath to groans,
Sorrow was all my soul, I scarce believed,
Till grief did tell me roundly, that I lived.

When I got health, thou took'st away my life,
And more; for my friends die:
My mirth and edge was lost; a blunted knife
Was of more use than I.
Thus thin and lean without a fence or friend,
I was blown through with every storm and wind.

Whereas my birth and spirit rather took
The way that takes the town,
Thou didst betray me to a lingering book,
And wrap me in a gown.
I was entangled in the world of strife,
Before I had the power to change my life.

Yet, for I threatened often the siege to raise,
Not simpering all mine age,
Thou often did with academic praise
Melt and dissolve my rage.
I took thy sweetened pill, till I came near;
I could not go away, nor persevere.

2. The body speaks to the soul from this point on.

Yet, lest perchance I should too happy be
In my unhappiness,
Turning my purge[3] to food, thou throwest me
Into more sickness.
Thus does thy power cross-bias[4] me, not making
Thine own gift good, yet me from my ways taking.

Now I am here, what thou wilt do with me
None of my books will show:
I read, and sigh, and wish I were a tree,
For sure then I should grow
To fruit or shade; at least some bird would trust
Her household to me, and I should be just.

Yet, though thou troublest me, I must be meek;
In weakness must be stout.
Well, I will change the service, and go seek
Some other master out.
Ah my dear God! though I am clean forgot,
Let me not love thee, if I love thee not.

Prayer (1)

Prayer the church's banquet; angels' age,
God's breath in man returning to his birth;
The soul in paraphrase, heart in pilgrimage;
The Christian plummet[1] sounding heaven and earth;

Engine against th'Almighty, sinner's tower,[2]
Reversèd thunder, Christ-side-piercing spear,
The six-days world transposing in an hour;
A kind of tune, which all things hear and fear;

Softness, and peace, and joy, and love, and bliss;
Exalted manna,[3] gladness of the best;
Heaven in ordinary,[4] man well dressed,
The milky way, the bird of paradise,[5]

Church bells beyond the stars heard, the soul's blood,
The land of spices; something understood.

Jordan (1)[1]

Who says that fictions only and false hair
Become a verse? Is there in truth no beauty?
Is all good structure in a winding stair?

3. Medicine inducing evacuation of the bowels.
4. To give an inclination running counter to another.
1. A metal weight used to measure, or sound, the depth of water; figuratively, the criterion of truth.
2. A stronghold or fortress, used for purposes of defense.
3. The food that God supplied to the Jews during their wandering in the wilderness.
4. What is usual; or, a meal in a tavern.
5. A bird, found in New Guinea, known for its beautiful feathers.
1. To cross the River Jordan symbolizes entering the Promised Land.

May no lines pass, except they do their duty
Not to a true, but painted chair?

Is it no verse, except enchanted groves
And sudden arbors shadow coarse-spun lines?
Must purling° streams refresh a lover's loves? *rippling*
Must all be veiled, while he that reads, divines,[2]
Catching the sense at two removes?

Shepherds are honest people; let them sing:
Riddle who list,[3] for me, and pull for prime:[4]
I envy no man's nightingale or spring;
Nor let them punish me with loss of rhyme,
Who plainly say, *My God, My King*.

Church Monuments

While that my soul repairs to her devotion,
Here I entomb my flesh, that it betimes
May take acquaintance of this heap of dust;
To which the blast of death's incessant motion,
Fed with the exhalation of our crimes,
Drives all at last. Therefore I gladly trust

My body to this school, that it may learn
To spell his elements and find his birth
Written in dusty heraldry and lines
Which dissolution sure does best discern,
Comparing dust with dust, and earth with earth.[1]
These[2] laugh at jet and marble, put for signs

To sever the good fellowship of dust
And spoil the meeting. What shall point out them[3]
When they shall bow, and kneel, and fall down flat
To kiss those heaps, which now they have in trust?
Dear flesh, while I do pray, learn here thy stem
And true descent; that when thou shalt grow fat,

And wanton in thy cravings, thou may'st know,
That flesh is but the glass, which holds the dust
That measures all our time, which also shall
Be crumbled into dust. Mark here below
How tame these ashes are, how free from lust,
That thou may'st set thyself against thy fall.

The Windows

Lord, how can man preach thy eternal word?
He is a brittle, crazy° glass, *cracked*

2. To interpret what is obscure through magical insight or intuitive conjecture.
3. Whoever wants to may interpret.
4. Draw a lucky card, or hit upon a lucky guess.
1. An allusion to Genesis 3.19: "for dust thou art and to dust shalt thou return."
2. Dust and earth.
3. The souls that cling to "those heaps," the dust of their bodies and of the earth.

Yet in thy temple thou do him afford
This glorious and transcendent place,
To be a window, through thy grace.

But when thou dost anneal[1] in glass thy story,
Making thy life to shine within
The holy preachers, then the light and glory
More reverent grows, and does win
Which else shows watr'ish, bleak, and thin

Doctrine and life, colors and light, in one
When they combine and mingle, bring
A strong regard and awe; but speech alone
Doth vanish like a flaring thing,
And in the ear, not conscience ring.

Denial

When my devotions could not pierce
Thy silent ears;
Then was my heart broken, as was my verse:
My breast was full of tears
And disorder:

My bent thoughts, like a brittle bow,
Did fly asunder:
Each took his way; some would to pleasures go,
Some to the wars and thunder
Of alarms.

As good go anywhere, they say,
As to benumb
Both knees and heart in crying night and day,
Come, come, my God, Oh come!
But no hearing.

O that thou shouldst give dust a tongue
To cry to thee,
And then not hear it crying! All day long
My heart was in my knee,
But no hearing.

Therefore my soul lay out of sight,
Untuned, unstrung;
My feeble spirit, unable to look right,
Like a nipped bloom, hung
Discontented.

Oh cheer and tune my heartless breath,
Defer no time,
That so thy favors granting my request,
They and my mind may chime,° *ring together, agree*
And mend my rhyme.

1. To burn in colors on glass.

Virtue

Sweet day, so cool, so calm, so bright,
The bridal° of the earth and sky: *wedding*
The dew shall weep thy fall tonight,
For thou must die.

Sweet rose, whose hue, angry and brave
Bids the rash gazer wipe his eye:
Thy root is ever in its grave,
And thou must die.

Sweet spring, full of sweet days and roses,
A box where sweets° compacted lie; *pleasant fragrances*
My music shows ye have your closes,[1]
And all must die.

Only a sweet and virtuous soul,
Like seasoned timber, never gives;
But though the whole world turn to coal,[2]
Then chiefly lives.

Man

My God, I heard this day
That none doth build a stately habitation,
But he that means to dwell therein.
What house more stately hath there been,
Or can be, than is man? to[1] whose creation
All things are in decay.

For man is everything,
And more; he is a tree, yet bears more[2] fruit;
A beast, yet is, or should be more:
Reason and speech we only bring.
Parrots may thank us, if they are not mute:
They go upon the score.[3]

Man is all symmetry,
Full of proportions, one limb to another,
And all to all the world besides:
Each part may call the farthest, brother;
For head with foot has private amity,
And both with moons and tides.

Nothing hath got so far
But man hath caught and kept it as his prey.
His eyes dismount the highest star:
He is in little all the sphere.[4]

1. Cadences, indicating that Herbert wanted this poem to be sung.
2. Reduced to ashes as at the Last Judgment.
1. In comparison to.
2. An alternative reading is "no."
3. They are indebted to us.
4. See Robert Fludd's engraving of the human body as microcosm of the universe, page 1598.

Herbs gladly cure our flesh; because that they
Find their acquaintance there.

For us the winds do blow,
The earth doth rest, heav'n move, and fountains flow;
Nothing we see, but means our good,
As our delight, or as our treasure.
The whole is, either our cupboard of food,
Or cabinet of pleasure.

The stars have us to bed;
Night draws the curtain, which the sun withdraws,
Music and light attend our head.
All things unto our flesh are kind
In their descent and being; to our mind
In their ascent and cause.

Each thing is full of duty.
Waters united are our navigation,
Distinguished, our habitation;
Below, our drink; above, our meat;
Both are our cleanliness. Hath one such beauty?
Then how are all things neat?

More servants wait on man
Than he'll take notice of: in ev'ry path,
He treads down that which doth befriend him,
When sickness makes him pale and wan.
Oh mighty love! Man is one world, and hath
Another to attend him.

Since then, my God, thou hast
So brave a palace built, O dwell in it,
That it may dwell with thee at last!
Till then, afford us so much wit,
That, as the world serves us, we may serve thee,
And both thy servants be.

Jordan (2)

When first my lines of heav'nly joys made mention,
Such was their luster, they did so excel,
That I sought out quaint° words, and trim invention; *clever*
My thoughts began to burnish,° sprout, and swell, *spread out*
Curling with metaphors a plain intention,
Decking the sense, as if it were to sell.[1]

Thousands of notions in my brain did run,
Off'ring their service, if I were not sped:[2]
I often blotted what I had begun;
This was not quick° enough, and that was dead. *lively*

1. Decorating the meaning as if it were for sale.

2. Dealt with so that I was satisfied.

Nothing could seem too rich to clothe the sun,
Much less those joys which trample on his head.[3]

As flames do work and wind, when they ascend,
So did I weave my self into the sense.
But while I bustled, I might hear a friend
Whisper, "How wide° is all this long pretence! *beside the point*
There is in love a sweetness ready penn'd:
Copy out only that, and save expense."

Time

Meeting with time, "Slack thing," said I,
"Thy scythe is dull; whet it for shame."
"No marvel sir," he did reply,
"If it at length deserve some blame:
  But where one man would have me grind it,
  Twenty for one too sharp do find it."

"Perhaps some such of old did pass,[1]
Who above all things lov'd this life;
To whom thy scythe a hatchet was,
Which now is but a pruning knife.
  Christ's coming hath made man thy debtor,
  Since by thy cutting he grows better.

"And in this blessing thou art blest:
For where thou only wert before
An executioner at best,
Thou art a gard'ner now, and more,
  An usher to convey our souls
  Beyond the utmost stars and poles.

"And this is that makes life so long,
While it detains us from our God.
Ev'n pleasures here increase the wrong,
And length of days lengthen the rod.
  Who wants° the place, where God doth dwell, *lacks*
  Partakes already half of hell.

"Of what strange length must that needs be,
Which ev'n eternity excludes!"
Thus far Time heard me patiently:
Then chafing° said, "This man deludes: *getting angry*
  What do I here before his door?
  He doth not crave less time, but more."

The Collar

I struck the board,° and cried, "No more. *table*
I will abroad!

3. The sun is a symbol for Christ; the sun's head is the Son's head.

1. Herbert is the speaker in stanzas 2, 3, and 4, and the first two lines of stanza 5.

What? Shall I ever sigh and pine?
My lines and life are free; free as the road,
Loose as the wind, as large as store.° *abundance*
Shall I be still in suit?[1]
Have I no harvest but a thorn
To let me blood, and not restore
What I have lost with cordial[2] fruit?
Sure there was wine
Before my sighs did dry it; there was corn
Before my tears did drown it.
Is the year only lost to me?
Have I no bays[3] to crown it?
No flowers, no garlands gay? all blasted?
All wasted?
Not so, my heart; but there is fruit,
And thou hast hands.
Recover all thy sigh-blown age
On double pleasures: leave thy cold dispute
Of what is fit and not forsake thy cage,
Thy rope of sands,
Which petty thoughts have made, and made to thee
Good cable, to enforce and draw,
And be thy law,
While thou didst wink[4] and wouldst not see.
Away! take heed:
I will abroad.
Call in thy death's head[5] there: tie up thy fears.
He that forbears
To suit and serve his need,
Deserves his load."
But as I raved and grew more fierce and wild
At every word,
Me thoughts I heard one calling, *Child!*
And I replied, My *Lord*.

The Pulley

When God at first made man,
Having a glass of blessings standing by,
"Let us," said he "pour on him all we can:
Let the world's riches, which dispersèd lie,
Contract into a span."

So strength first made a way;
Then beauty flowed, then wisdom, honor, pleasure:
When almost all was out, God made a stay,

1. Engaged in a lawsuit.
2. Invigorating to the heart.
3. The poet's laurel wreath.
4. Shut your eyes to.
5. The skull as an emblem of human mortality.

Perceiving that alone of all his treasure
Rest in the bottom lay.[1]

"For if I should," said he,
"Bestow this jewel also on my creature,
He would adore my gifts instead of me,
And rest in Nature, not the God of Nature.
So both should losers be.

"Yet let him keep the rest,
But keep them with repining° restlessness: *complaining*
Let him be rich and weary, that at least,
If goodness lead him not, yet weariness
May toss him to my breast."

The Forerunners

The harbingers[1] are come: see, see their mark;
White is their color, and behold my head.
But must they have my brain? Must they dispark° *turn out*
Those sparkling notions, which therein were bred?
Must dullness turn me to a clod?
Yet have they left me, "Thou art still my God."

Good men ye be, to leave me my best room,
Ev'n all my heart, and what is lodged there:
I pass not, I, what of the rest become,
So "Thou art still my God," be out of fear.[2]
He will be pleasèd with that ditty;
And if I please him, I write fine and witty.

Farewell, sweet phrases, lovely metaphors:
But will ye leave me thus? when ye before
Of stews[3] and brothels only knew the doors,
Then did I wash you with my tears, and more,
Brought you to Church well-dressed and clad:
My God must have my best, ev'n all I had.

Lovely enchanting language, sugarcane,
Honey of roses, whither wilt thou fly?
Hath some fond lover 'ticed thee to thy bane?
And wilt thou leave the Church, and love a sty?
Fie, thou wilt soil thy 'broidered coat,
And hurt thy self, and him that sings the note.

Let foolish lovers, if they will love dung,
With canvas, not with arras° clothe their shame: *rich tapestry*
Let Folly speak in her own native tongue.
True Beauty dwells on high; ours is a flame

1. "Rest" in the sense of repose, or freedom from distress, and in the sense of remainder, or surplus.

1. Men sent out before a royal train to requisition lodgings by marking the doors with chalk.

2. I don't care about anything except being left with the thought that "Thou art still my God."

3. Public hot bathhouses, brothels.

But borrowed thence to light us thither:
Beauty and beauteous words should go together.

Yet if you go, I pass not; take your way.
For, "Thou art still my God" is all that ye
Perhaps with more embellishment can say,
Go, birds of spring; let winter have his fee;
Let a bleak paleness chalk the door.
So all within be livelier than before.

Love (3)

Love bade me welcome: yet my soul drew back,
Guilty of dust and sin.
But quick-eyed Love, observing me grow slack° *slow, weak*
From my first entrance in,
Drew nearer to me, sweetly questioning,
If I lacked anything.

"A guest," I answered, "worthy to be here":
Love said, "You shall be he."
"I the unkind, ungrateful? Ah my dear,
I cannot look on thee."
Love took my hand, and smiling did reply,
"Who made the eyes but I?"

"Truth Lord, but I marred them; let my shame
Go where it doth deserve."
"And know you not," says Love, "who bore the blame?"
"My dear, then I will serve."
"You must sit down," says Love, "and taste my meat."
So I did sit and eat.[1]

PERSPECTIVES

Emblem, Style, and Metaphor

The early modern period in England began at a cultural moment that was still medieval and ended at one on the verge of the modern. At the outset of the period, in the reign of Henry VIII, science was magic, symbols were biblical, and poetry was the work of makers who imitated nature; at the close of the era, with the end of the Interregnum and the Restoration, science had become more empirical, symbols had become more idiosyncratic, and poetry was the work of individual geniuses, who more than imitating nature transformed it with the unusual correspondences that they created. The in-between or liminal aspect of early modern culture helps to explain the way in which early modern art had much in common with medieval forms of representation but also began to move beyond these forms.

1. The speaker takes Communion, which symbolizes union with God.

The early modern emblem is a good example of this transitional aspect of the period's culture. Emblems were visual symbols that appeared in medieval coats of arms, illuminated manuscripts of the Bible, and church decoration. With early modern printing, books of emblems were produced that included not only the visual symbol, but also a poem and a Latin motto, either a proverb or a classical quotation. Whereas medieval iconography, or visual symbolism, was dominated largely by reference to the Bible, Renaissance iconography showed a stronger influence of classical mythology, though still often harmonized with a Christian framework. For example, the popular emblem of the phoenix, the mythological Egyptian bird that was reborn every thousand years out of its own ashes, was also a symbol of Christ. Geoffrey Whitney's use of this symbol to describe the rebirth of the town of Nantwich after a fire exemplifies the local and particular character of the early modern emblem, in contrast to the medieval symbol, which usually could be read as part of the book of the world that reflected the book of the Word, or the Bible.

More classically and (increasingly) scientifically inflected, the system of resemblances would still have made sense to a medieval audience. Early modern writers often thought in terms of a "Great Chain of Being," as the historian Arthur Lovejoy called it in 1936. This mode of thinking is well illustrated by a set of linkages made by the Italian playwright and scientist Giambattista della Porta in a treatise called *Natural Magic* (1558):

> the plant stands convenient to the brute beast, so through feeling does the brutish animal to man, who is conformable to the rest of the stars by his intelligence; these links proceed so strictly that they appear as a rope stretched from the first cause as far as the lowest and the smallest of things.

The concept of *aemulatio,* or emulation, accounts for the way in which images mirror various aspects of the world. The concept of Venus, for example, as described by Giordano Bruno, comprehends various human and cosmic qualities, including charm, beauty, natural harmony, the relationship between love and death, and "every form of pleasure." Venus's son Cupid "sets [us] on fire with his heat and enthralls with his chains," while at the same time her triumphal chariot represents wisdom and prudence. The concept of *analogia,* or analogy, expresses the relationship between the macrocosm and the microcosm in Renaissance art. Not only are human beings midway between angels and beasts, but the proportions of the human body correspond to those of the universe—a notion that is well illustrated by Robert Fludd's engraving of a human figure outstretched over the concentric circles of the Ptolemaic universe.

These conventional symbols inherited from classical and medieval culture often existed side by side with ingenious new metaphors. The symbols that allowed the world to be read as united in reference to God's word in the Bible were supplemented and even challenged by new images created by poets. For example the rood of medieval English poetry was at once a tree and the cross on which Christ died. But an early modern poet such as John Donne could shock his audience with his ingenuity by likening the sexual union of lovers to the canonization of saints. Emmanuele Tesauro's description of metaphor shows that it was the qualities of ingenuity and marvelousness that were prized in the seventeenth-century conceit, or metaphor. Whereas medieval symbols had relied on culturally accepted associations, early modern metaphors created new and unexpected associations through a transference of meaning. The term "metaphor" comes from the Greek verb *metaphorein*, which means "to transfer" or "to carry across," and this is precisely what the metaphysical conceit did: it transferred meaning from one thing to another.

Like the freshness of the poetic conceit, the simplicity and clarity of what Ben Jonson called the concise style with its brevity, pointedness, and wit characterized the new style of

Title page to volume 2 of *Utriusque cosmi, maioris scilicet et minoris, metaphysica atque technica historia,* ("Metaphysical and Technical History of both the Greater and Lesser Universe"), by Robert Fludd, 1619. After taking his degree at Oxford, Robert Fludd studied chemistry and medicine on the Continent, where he came into contact with the occult philosophy of the Rosicrucians, whose goals ranged from alchemy to moral reformation. Returning to London, he practiced medicine and published numerous works expressing his belief that science was a form of divine revelation and that all creation reflected a divinely ordered design. This engraving shows the image of a male body spread out over the cosmos as a circle, portraying the human body's perfect proportions, and their analogy to the proportions of the universe: man is a little world, the microcosm to the universe's macrocosm. The engraving also depicts the earth-centered Ptolemaic universe, the constellations and astrological signs. The innermost circles are the four bodily humors (choleric, melancholic, phlegmatic, and sanguine), and the outermost circles are the supernatural faculties of reason, intellect, and mind.

writing. Calling for a concentration on meaning rather than an abundance of ornamentation, this new style strongly influenced the development of modern English prose. The great champion of the concise or Senecan style of prose, Francis Bacon, ushered in a whole new rhythm in the English sentence and a new form known as the essay. At the very time that poets such as Donne and Marvell were using images taken from science in their poetry, Bacon was creating a new form of English prose that would help to make English the language of science that it is today.

Geoffrey Whitney
1548?–1601

Geoffrey Whitney composed one of the most important English emblem books, A *Choice of Emblems* (1586). Each emblem contains a woodcut, prefixed by a Latin motto and accompanied by verses in six-line stanzas. The book was dedicated to the Earl of Leicester and was published in Leyden, where Whitney was studying at the university. Although only twenty-three of the emblems are original and another 235 loosely or exactly copy Continental models by Alciati, Paradin, Sambucus, and Junius, Whitney gives many of the emblems a specifically English interpretation. Sometimes an emblem is used to support the politics of the Leicester court faction, who urged an active role in defending Protestants in the Low Countries. At other times, Whitney's Englishness surfaces in references to local events. For example, he applies the emblem of the phoenix to the fire of Nantwich, not far from his birthplace in Chesire, where he would retire after the death of his patron Leicester. Possibly because of the decline of the Leicester faction, Whitney's book was not republished in his lifetime. Nevertheless, his influence is seen in later Jacobean emblem books, such as Peacham's *Minerva Britanna* (London, 1612), and in decorations in domestic architecture and furnishings. Whitney's work helped to make the Continental emblem tradition known to such English poets as Shakespeare, Spenser, Donne, and Philips, whose poetry is enriched by emblematic metaphor, conjuring up both a visual image and its complex symbolic associations.

The Phoenix
Unica semper avis.[1]

To my countrymen of the Nampwiche in Cheshire.

1. "The bird that is ever unique." The picture shows a phoenix with wings outstretched rising from the flames of a fire. See Ovid, *Metamorphoses* 15, 393–407.

The Phoenix rare, with feathers fresh of hue,
Arabia's right, and sacred to the sun:
Whom, other birds with wonder seem to view,
Doth live until a thousand years be run:
Then makes a pile: which, when with sun it burns,
She flies therein, and so to ashes turns.

Whereof, behold, another Phoenix rare,
With speed doth rise most beautiful and fair:
And though for truth, this many do declare,
Yet thereunto, I mean not for to swear:
Although I know that author's witness true,
What here I write, both of the old, and new.

Which when I weighed, the new, and eke the old,
I thought upon your town destroyed with fire:
And did in mind, the new Nampwiche behold,
A spectacle for any man's desire:
Whose buildings brave, where cinders were but late,
Did represent (me thought) the Phoenix fate.

And as the old, was many hundred years,
A town of fame, before it felt that cross:
Even so, (I hope) this Wiche,[2] that now appears,
A Phoenix age shall last, and know no loss:
Which God vouchsafe, who make you thankful, all:
That see this rise, and saw the other fall.

Ben Jonson
1572–1637

Jonson's observations on style are contained in papers first found after his death by his literary executor Sir Kenelm Digby. First published in 1640, *Timber, or Discoveries*, contains not only Jonson's observations but also those of authors whose work on rhetoric and poetics he greatly admired, such as Quintilian and Horace. The following passages, based on Quintilian's *De institutione oratoria* and on Vives' *On the Proper Method of Speaking* (1532), give us insight into Jonson's approach to the process of writing, his taste in literature, and his firm conviction that an essential step in perfecting the craft of writing is to read the best authors.

For more on Jonson, see his principal listing, page 1443.

from Timber: or Discoveries

For a man to write well, there are required three necessaries: to read the best authors, observe the best speakers, and much exercise of his own style. In style to consider, what ought to be written, and after what manner; he must first think and excogitate[1] his matter, then choose his words, and examine the weight of either. Then take care in placing and ranking both matter and words, that the composition be comely; and to do this with diligence, and often. No matter how slow the style be at first, so it be

2. Originally meaning the group of buildings connected with a salt pit, "wich" was the name given to such salt-making towns as Nantwich and Northwich in Chesire.

1. Devise.

labored,[2] and accurate; seek the best, and be not glad of the froward conceits,[3] or first words, that offer themselves to us; but judge of what we invent, and order what we approve. Repeat often, what we have formerly written; which beside that it helps the consequence, and makes the juncture better, it quickens the heat of imagination, that often cools in the time of setting down, and gives it new strength, as if it grew lustier, by the going back. As we see in the contention of leaping, they jump farthest, that fetch their race largest: or, as in throwing a dart, or javelin, we force back our arms, to make our loose[4] the stronger. Yet if we have a fair gale of wind, I forbid not the steering out of our sail, so the favor of the gale deceive us not. For all that we invent doth please us in the conception, or birth, else we would never set it down. But the safest is to return to our judgment, and handle over again those things, the easiness of which might make them justly suspected. So did the best writers in their beginnings; they imposed upon themselves care, and industry; they did nothing rashly. They obtained first to write well, and then custom made it easy and a habit. By little and little their matter showed itself to them more plentifully; their words answered, their composition followed; and all, as in a well-ordered family, presented itself in the place. So that the sum of all is: Ready writing makes not good writing; but good writing brings on ready writing.

Yet, when we think we have got the faculty, it is even then good to resist it, as to give a horse a check sometimes with [a] bit, which doth not so much stop his course, as stir his mettle. Again, whither a man's genius is best able to reach, thither it should more and more contend, lift and dilate itself; as men of low stature raise themselves on their toes, and so ofttimes get even, if not eminent. Besides, as it is fit for grown and able writers to stand of themselves, and work with their own strength, to trust and endeavor by their own faculties: so it is fit for the beginner and learner to study others, and the best. For the mind, and memory are more sharply exercised in comprehending another man's things, than our own; and such as accustom themselves and are familiar with the best authors shall ever and anon find somewhat of them in themselves, and in the expression of their minds, even when they feel it not, be able to utter something like theirs, which hath an authority above their own. Nay, sometimes it is the reward of a man's study, the praise of quoting another man fitly. And though a man be more prone, and able for one kind of writing, than another, yet he must exercise all. For as in an instrument, so in style, there must be a harmony, and consent of parts.

I take this labor in teaching others, that they should not be always to be taught; and I would bring my precepts into practice. For rules are ever of less force, and value, than experiments. Yet with this purpose, rather to show the right way to those that come after, than to detect any that have slipped before by error, and I hope it will be more profitable. For men do more willingly listen, and with more favor to precept, than reprehension.[5] Among diverse opinions of an art, and most of them contrary in themselves, it is hard to make election; and therefore, though a man cannot invent new things after so many, he may do a welcome work yet to help posterity to judge rightly of the old. But arts and precepts avail nothing, except nature be beneficial, and aiding. And therefore these things are no more written to a dull disposition, than rules of husbandry to a barren soil. No precepts will profit a fool; no more than beauty will the blind, or music the deaf. As we should take care, that our style in writing, be neither dry,

2. Painstakingly worked on.
3. The initial concepts.
4. Throw.
5. Censure.

nor empty, we should look again it be not winding, or wanton with far-fetched descriptions; either is a vice. But that is worse which proceeds out of want, than that which riots out of plenty. The remedy of fruitfulness is easy, but no labor will help the contrary; I will like, and praise some things, in a young writer, which yet if he continue in, I cannot, but justly hate him for the same. There is a time to be given all things for maturity; and that even your country-husbandman can teach, who to a young plant will not put the pruning knife, because it seems to fear the iron, as not able to admit the scar. No more would I tell a green writer all his faults, lest I should make him grieve and faint, and at last despair. For nothing doth more hurt, than to make him so afraid of all things, as he can endeavor nothing. Therefore youth ought to be instructed betimes, and in the best things; for we hold those longest, we take soonest. As the first scent of a vessel lasts; and that tinct[6] the wool first receives. Therefore a master should temper his own powers, and descend to the other's infirmity. If you pour a glut of water upon a bottle, it receives little of it; but with a funnel, and by degrees, you shall fill many of them and spill little of your own; to their capacity they will all receive, and be full. And as it is fit to read the best authors to youth first, so let them be of the openest, and clearest. As Livy before Sallust,[7] Sidney before Donne; and beware of letting them taste Gower or Chaucer at first, lest falling too much in love with antiquity and, and not apprehending the weight, they grow rough and barren in language only. When their judgments are firm, and out of danger, let them read both, the old and the new: but no less take heed, that their new flowers, and sweetness do not as much corrupt, as the others dryness and squalor, if they choose not carefully. Spenser, in affecting the ancients, wrote no language.[8] Yet I would have him read for his manner; but as Virgil read Ennius.[9] The reading of Homer and Virgil is counseled by Quintilian, as the best way of informing youth, and confirming man. For besides that, the mind is raised with the height, and sublimity of such a verse, it takes spirit from the greatness of the matter, and is tincted with the best things. Tragic and lyric poetry is good too: and comic with the best, if the manners of the reader be once in safety. In the Greek poets, as also in Plautus,[1] we shall see the economy, and disposition of poems better observed than in Terence, and the latter, who thought the sole grace, and virtue of their fable, the sticking in of sentences, as ours do the forcing of jests. * * *

Custom is the most certain mistress of language, as the public stamp makes the current money.[2] But we must not be too frequent with the mint, every day coining; nor fetch words from the extreme and utmost ages, since the chief virtue of a style is perspicuity, and nothing so vicious in it as to need an interpreter. Words borrowed of antiquity do lend a kind of majesty to style, and are not without their delight sometimes. For they have the authority of years, and out of their intermission do win to themselves a kind of gracelike newness. But the eldest of the present and newest of the past language is the best. For what was the ancient language, which some men so dote upon, but the ancient custom? Yet when I name custom, I

6. Dye, color.
7. Sallust (86–c. 34 B.C.) and Livy (59 B.C.–A.D. 17), Roman historians.
8. A reference to Spenser's self-consciously archaic diction, spelling, and syntax.
9. The great epic poet Virgil (70–19 B.C.) studied but also went beyond his poetic predecessor Ennius (239–169? B.C.).
1. Plautus (254–184 B.C.) and Terence (c. 185–159 B.C.) were Roman comic playwrights.
2. The beginning of this passage is based on Quintillian, and the rest on Vives, *On the Proper Method of Speaking* (1532).

understand not the vulgar custom, for that were a precept no less dangerous to language than life, if we should speak or live after the manner of the vulgar. But that I call custom of speech which is the consent of the learned, as custom of life which is the consent of the good. Virgil was most loving of antiquity; yet how rarely doth he insert *aquai* and *pictai!*[3] Lucretius[4] is scabrous and rough in these; he seeks them, as some do Chaucerisms with us, which were better expunged and banished. Some words are to be culled out for ornament and color, as we gather flowers to strew houses or make garlands; but they are better when they grow to our style as in a meadow, where, though the mere grass and greenness delights, yet the variety of flowers doth heighten and beautify. Marry, we must not play or riot too much with them, as in paronomasias;[5] nor use too swelling or ill-sounding words, *quae per salebras altaque saxa cadunt.*[6] It is true, there is not sound but shall find some lovers, as the bitterest confections are grateful to some palates. Our composition must be more accurate in the beginning and end than in the midst, and in the end more than in the beginning; for through the midst the stream bears us. And this is attained by custom more than care or diligence. We must express readily and fully, not profusely. There is difference between a liberal and a prodigal hand. As it is a great point of art, when our matter requires it, to enlarge and veer out all sail, so to take it in and contract it is of no less praise when the argument doth ask it. Either of them hath their fitness in the place. A good man always profits by his endeavor, by his help; yea, when he is absent; nay, when he is dead, by his example and memory. So good authors in their style.

A strict and succinct style is that where you can take away nothing without loss, and that loss to be manifest. The brief style is that which expresseth much in little. The concise style, which expresseth not enough, but leaves somewhat to be understood. The abrupt style, which hath many breaches, and doth not seem to end but fall. The congruent style and harmonious fitting of parts in a sentence hath almost the fastening and force of knitting and connection, as in stones well squared, which will rise strong a great way without mortar. Periods[7] are beautiful when they are not too long, for so they have their strength too, as in a pike or javelin. As we must take the care that our words and sense be clear, so if the obscurity happen through the hearer's or the reader's want of understanding. I am not to answer for them, no more than for their not listening or marking.[8] I must neither find them ears nor mind. But a man cannot put a word so in sense but something about it will illustrate it, if the writer understand himself. For order helps much to perspicuity, as confusion hurts. *Rectitudo lucem adfert; obliquitas et circumductio offuscat.*[9] We should therefore speak what we can the nearest way, so as we keep our gait, not leap; for too short may as well not be let into the memory as too long not kept in. Whatsoever loseth the grace and clearness converts into a riddle; the obscurity is marked, but not the value. That perisheth, and is passed by, like the pearl in the fable.[1] Our style should be like a skein of silk, to be carried and found by the right thread, not ravelled and perplexed; then all is a knot, a heap.

3. Archaic forms of *aquae* (waters) and *pictae* (embroidered), that occur once each in the *Aeneid*.
4. Roman poet (c. 99–55 B.C.) who wrote *De rerum natura*.
5. Puns.
6. Martial: "Which fall on rough ground and boulders."
7. Subordinated sentences.
8. Taking to heart.
9. Vives: "Directness enlightens, shiftiness and indirection obscure matters."
1. In Plato's *Phaedrus* 3.12, a cock finds a pearl on a dunghill but simply leaves it there.

Giordano Bruno

1548–1600

Best known for having been burned at the stake as a heretic in Rome, and still suspected of having been a spy in England, the Italian philosopher Giordano Bruno was one of the great theorists of the esoteric symbolic correspondences generated by hermeticism. Sixteenth-century intellectuals believed that a work called *The Hermetic Corpus* was written by the ancient Egyptian magus Hermes Trismegistus and that its complex system of analogies linking pagan gods, planets, and their attributes with the human personality was a key to secret knowledge in astronomy, medicine, mnemonics or memory theory, and magic. Although Isaac Causabon proved in 1614 that *The Hermetic Corpus* was not an ancient Egyptian but a second-century Greek work, the philosophy that it inspired in Bruno influenced other thinkers such as the English astrologer John Dee and the German astronomer Johannes Kepler. Later, such writers as Coleridge and Joyce also had a strong interest in Bruno's work.

During his stay in England from 1583 to 1586, Bruno lectured on Copernican theory and Platonism at Cambridge and made friendships among English writers. He is said to have sung Ariosto's *Orlando Furioso* to Sir Philip Sidney while riding horseback from Oxford to London. Bruno published no fewer than six works in England. Among these, *Spaccio della bestia trionfante (The Expulsion of the Triumphant Beast)* presents ideas developed in his last work, *De imaginum compositione (On the Composition of Images, Signs, and Ideas)*, published in Frankfurt in 1591. Bruno's final book views the imagination as the means through which God communicates with humanity. Bruno sought to discover the images that could unite the multiplicity of the universe. His writing about the connections between images and words, and between painting and poetry, offers insight into how Renaissance poets conceived of the world as composed of a complex chain of analogies. His chapter on Venus shows the association of a mythological figure with many different images expressing a variety of qualities. For Bruno, as for many Renaissance poets, mythology provided not only a rich repertoire of visual symbols but also a way of creating layers of mysterious meaning in poetry.

from On the Composition of Images, Signs, and Ideas[1]

The idea, imagination, shape, designation, notation, all are the universe of God, both the work of nature and of reason. The idea is controlled by analogy with nature and reason, so that nature admirably reflects divine action, and our innate human ability to reason rivals nature. Who cannot see how nature makes so many diverse things with so few elements? Nature orders the same four elements, and under various signs, in accord with the thing formed, she drives them out of the abyss of possibility into the apex of actuality. By God, what can be easier than counting? First, since there is one, two, three and then four; second because one is not two, two is not three, three is not four. And finally because one and two make three, and one and three make four. To do this is to do everything: imagining, signifying and retaining render all things as objects that can be apprehended, and understood once apprehended, and remembered once understood.

* * *

I spoke of a certain marvelous kinship that exists among true poets, who are referred to as musicians, and that also connects true painters and true philosophers.[2] For true philosophy, music, or poetry is also painting, and true painting is also music and philosophy; and true poetry or music is a kind of divine wisdom and painting.

1. From the Dedicatory Letter. Translated by Clare Carroll.

2. From Book 1, Part 2, Chapter 20.

In other places, I have discussed how any painter naturally establishes infinite images, and how his capacity to form images creates out of sense impressions—sights and sounds—and combines them in a multiplicity of ways.

* * *

Let us relate the pleasure derived from the seven courts by viewing the image of the goddess.[3] The first image of Venus is a girl rising from the sea's foam, who, as she approaches dry land, wipes off the wetness of the sea with her dainty hands.

In her second image she appears as a naked girl whom the Hours[4] cloak in robes, and whose head they crown with a garland of flowers.

In her third image, she is a girl advancing, who produces lilies and violets in her footprints. Her accessory is a cestus,[5] in which are contained all the charms of face, word, and gesture. A prophetess carrying a willow rod follows her.[6]

The fourth image of Venus is connected with a shining chariot of amber, which is pulled by gentle swans, amorous doves, and erotic pigeons. There is a lively inner force that moves the chariot along.

In her fifth image, Venus is a queen leading a triumphal procession.[7] She holds a scepter in her right hand, and at the top of this is the image of the Sun, while in her left hand she holds a globe in the shape of the universe, decorated with stars. In the middle of this sphere Tellus appears. All applaud her divinity, which is delightful to all. In her chariot she carries a trophy, which she bears as a testament to her victory over the Parcae.[8]

In her sixth image, Venus appears as a lovely woman, with the sky above her head. She holds a poppy in her right hand and a pomegranate in her left.

In her seventh image, Venus is related to three heroic women who stand beside a shepherd with a golden apple in his hand.[9]

In the eighth image, she is with a young man slain by a boar, whom she buries.[1]

In her ninth image, she is linked with a naked boy who is marked by his bow and arrow. Shining rays stream out of his body and an atmosphere of amiability. He appears to each person variously, according to each person's own temperment. So he hits each person with his arrows in conformity to his likeness; he sets on fire with his heat and enthralls with his chains.

The last image is of a man crowned and seated on a camel, dressed in a colorful robe, carrying beside him a naked girl; a chorus of girls dance in a circle; with the blessing of Zephyrus[2] comes the court of Venus with every form of pleasure.

Conte Emmanuele Tesauro

1591–1677

The son of a poet, Emmanuele Tesauro was one of the major theorists of the *concetto*, or conceit, a defining characteristic of the metaphysical style in the poetry of Donne, Crashaw, Herbert, and Marvell. Tesauro's patron was the Duke of Savoy who sent him on many diplomatic missions and

3. From Book 2, Chapter 13.
4. The four seasons.
5. Venus's belt.
6. Either Cybele, mother of the gods, or Manto, the seer and daughter of Tiresias.
7. Venus in this aspect represents wisdom and prudence.
8. The Fates.
9. When Paris was asked to decide whether Venus, Minerva, or Juno was the most desirable goddess, he chose Venus and was granted the love of the beautiful Helen.
1. Adonis, with whom Venus fell in love.
2. The west wind.

even knighted him. In addition to his histories of Turin, Piemonte, and Italy, he also wrote poetry, tragedy, and moral philosophy. He developed the theory of metaphor in *Il Cannochiale Aristotelico* (literally "the Aristotelian telescope," translated here as *Through the Lens of Aristotle*). Written in the late 1620s and published in Turin in 1654, *Il Cannochiale* treats, as its subtitle indicates, "ideas of heroic wittiness popularly called "imprese" [heraldic devices and mottos] and of the whole symbolic aphoristic art." Heraldic devices were a daily feature of early modern life. Not only did aristocratic coats of arms feature *imprese*, but so did university insignia, guild banners, and even tavern signs. Tesauro based his concept of metaphor on Aristotle's *Rhetoric* and stressed that metaphor was a way of comprehending the correspondences, or connections, between widely disparate things. In the following excerpt from *Il Cannochiale*, Tesauro stresses the two qualities that distinguish metaphor as the greatest of all figures of speech. Metaphor is *ingegnoso*, witty or ingenious—sparking a new idea, creating a new relationship between disparate things—and *mirabile*, awesome or marvelous—inspiring a sensual impression and a feeling of wonder in the beholder.

from Through the Lens of Aristotle

And indeed at last we have arrived step by step to the highest peak of the ingenious figures, in comparison to which all the other figures described up to this point lose their value, metaphor being the most ingenious and acute, the most outlandish and wonderful, the most enjoyable and helpful, the most eloquent and fecund part of the human intellect. Most ingenious truly, because, if ingenuity consists (as we say) in tying together remote and separate notions of proposed objects, this is precisely the function of metaphor, and not of any other figure: hence, drawing the mind, no less than the word, from one genus to another, metaphor expresses one concept [*concetto*] through the means of another much different from it, finding similarity in dissimilarities. So that our author Aristotle concludes that constructing metaphors is a labor of a perspicacious and agile wit [*ingegno*]. Consequently metaphor is among the figures the most acute; since the others are formed almost grammatically and finished in the surfaces of vocabulary, but metaphor reflexively penetrates and investigates the most abstruse notions by combining them; and where those other figures clothe the concepts of words, metaphor clothes the words themselves in the concepts.

Therefore metaphor is of all others the most outlandish by the newness of ingenious accompaniment: without this novelty, ingenuity loses its glory, and the metaphor its force. So that our author advises that metaphor wants to be born only out of us, and not from anywhere else, almost like a birth, sought on loan. And out of this is born wonder, while the soul of the listener, from the overwhelming novelty, considers the acuteness of the ingenuity representing and the unexpected image of the object represented.

And if this is so full of wonder, it is also just so entertaining and delightful because from marvel delight is born, just like what you experience from unexpected combinations of scenes and from having seen many spectacles. If delight proceeds from rhetorical figures (as our author[1] teaches) from the desire of the human mind to learn new things without hard work and many things in a little space, certainly more delightful than all the other figures is metaphor: which, carrying in flight our mind from one genus to another, causes one to see one thing through another in a single word more than an object. Therefore if you say: "meadows are pleasant," you do not represent anything other than the greening of the meadows; but if you were to say: "Meadows laugh," you make me see (as you speak) the earth as an animated man, the meadow being the face, the pleasantness the happy smile. So that in a little word all these notions are transposed from different categories: earth, meadow,

1. Aristotle.

pleasantness, man, soul, smile, happiness. And reciprocally with a swift passage I observe in the human face the notions of meadows and all the relationships that pass between these and those, not observed by me at another time. And this is that swift and easy instruction from which is born delight, appearing to the mind of him who hates to see in a single word a full theater of marvels.

Richard Crashaw

1613?–1649

Richard Crashaw was one of the chief poets to introduce the Italian poëtic style of *concettismo* into English. Marked by an intense concentration of visual imagery that strove to create a striking newness and intellectual ingenuity, the conceited style provided the vehicle for Crashaw's passionate spirituality. A poet whose work is distinguished by the vividness, subtlety, and intricacy of its conceits, or metaphors, Richard Crashaw was also an artist, and twelve engravings based on his designs accompanied the third edition of his verse, published posthumously in Paris in 1652. In this same edition, two poems addressed to the Countess of Denbigh appeared for the first time. The one printed here, urging her conversion to Catholicism, had been written in 1644 in Paris, where Crashaw went to live in exile after being expelled from Peterhouse, Cambridge, whose chapel was sacked by the Puritan army. Crashaw had himself converted to Catholicism in Paris. His conversion was inspired by the Spanish mystic Saint Theresa of Avila and by his friend Nicholas Ferrar, whose religious community at Little Gidding the poet often visited. Crashaw's passionate and protean visual imagination influenced both Milton and Coleridge, and the experience of Crashaw and others at Little Gidding is alluded to in the last section of T. S. Eliot's *Four Quartets*.

Non VI.[1]

'Tis not the work of force but skill
To find the way into man's will.
'Tis love alone can hearts unlock.
Who knows the WORD, *he needs not knock.*

1. "Not by force," the motto of the emblem that introduces this poem: a heart with a hinge to the right, demonstrating that it can be opened, and a lock on the left with a scroll inscribed with letters standing for the Word of God's Law, the key to opening the heart.

To the Noblest and best of Ladies, the Countess of Denbigh

Persuading her to Resolution in Religion & to render herself without further delay into the Communion of the Catholic Church.[2]

What heaven-entreated heart is this?
Stands trembling at the gate of bliss,
Holds fast the door, yet dares not venture
Fairly to open it, and enter?
Whose definition is a doubt
Twixt life and death, twixt in and out.
Say, ling'ring fair! why comes the birth
Of your brave soul so slowly forth?
Plead your pretenses (oh you strong
In weakness!) why you choose so long
In labor of your self to lie?
Nor daring quite to live nor die.
Ah, linger not, loved soul! a slow
And late consent was a long no,
Who grants at last, long time tried
And did his best to have denied.
What magic bolts, what mystic bars,
Maintain the will in these strange wars!
What fatal yet fantastic bands
Keep the free heart from its own hands!
So when the year takes cold, we see
Poor waters their own prisoners be;
Fettered and locked up fast they lie
In a sad self-captivity.
The astonished nymphs their flood's strange fate deplore,
To see themselves their own severer shore.
  Thou that alone canst thaw this cold,
And fetch the heart from its stronghold,
Almighty Love! end this long war,
And of a meteor make a star.
Oh fix this fair Indefinite.
And 'mongst thy shafts of sovereign light
Choose out that sure decisive dart
Which has the key of this close heart,
Knows all the corners of't, and can control
The self-shut cabinet of an unsearched soul.
Oh let it be at last, love's hour!
Raise this tall trophy of thy power;
Come once the conquering way, not to confute
But kill this rebel-word, *irresolute*,
That so, in spite of all this peevish strength
Of weakness, she may write *resolved at length*,
  Unfold at length, unfold, fair flower

2. When she lost her husband, who died fighting for the King in the Civil War, Susan, Countess of Denbigh, went to live with the Queen in Paris, where she began to think about converting to Catholicism.

And use the season of love's shower.
Meet his well-meaning wounds, wise heart,
And haste to drink the wholesome dart,
That healing shaft, which heaven till now
Hath in love's quiver hid for you.
Oh dart of love! arrow of light!
Oh happy you, if it hit right,
It must not fall in vain, it must
Not mark the dry, regardless dust.
Fair one, it is your fate, and brings
Eternal worlds upon its wings.
Meet it with widespread arms; and see
Its seat your soul's just center be.
Disband dull fears; give faith the day.
To save your life, kill your delay,
It is love's siege, and sure to be
Your triumph, though his victory.
'Tis cowardice that keeps this field,
And want of courage not to yield.
Yield then, O yield, that love may win
The fort at last and let life in.
Yield quickly, lest perhaps you prove
Death's prey, before the prize of love.
This fort of your fair self, if't be not won,
He is repulsed indeed; but you are undone.

[END OF PERSPECTIVES: EMBLEM, STYLE, AND METAPHOR]

Richard Lovelace

1618–1657

In *To His Noble Friend,* Andrew Marvell portrays Richard Lovelace as an amorous and chivalrous courtier from a world destroyed by "Our Civil Wars." Marvell depicts the consternation that arose

When the beauteous ladies came to know
That their dear Lovelace was endangered so:
Lovelace that thawed the most congealèd breast
He who loved best and them defended best.

The dashing and handsome Lovelace was the last exemplar of courtly *sprezzatura* in the history of English poetry, recalling the eroticism and finesse of Wyatt and the chivalry of Sidney and Raleigh. The voluptuousness and elegance that characterized his poetry no less than the Carolinian court was destroyed by the Puritan Revolution.

Lovelace's brief life was indeed endangered more than once—all because of his allegiance to the Royalist cause. After only two years at Cambridge University, he left school to fight in the army of King Charles I, serving as senior ensign in the First Scottish expedition of 1639 and captain in the second of 1640. Both expeditions were disasters for the King's forces. Lovelace was imprisoned twice, first in 1642 for presenting an anti-Parliamentary petition from his home county Kent and again in 1648, when Marvell's patron Lord Fairfax brought the Roundhead (Puritan) army right to the doors of Lovelace's country estate. During his first stint in prison, Lovelace wrote one of his most memorable poems, *To Althea, from Prison.* Released on bail, he lived a precarious life, aiding the King's cause by selling his property and giving money to supply arms. In 1649, when he was released from prison the second time, Lovelace was reduced to selling all of his property, even his family portraits.

Lovelace is a representative of the cultural milieu of the court of Charles I, which included many poets and painters of great distinction. The regime was graced by such poets as Sir John Suckling, Thomas Carew, Abraham Cowley, and Edmund Waller, sometimes referred to as the Cavalier poets, among whom Lovelace is considered the greatest. Lovelace admired not only the works of his fellow poets but also the paintings of Rubens, Van Dyck, and Lely, which adorned the court. Lovelace was great friends with, and wrote poems praising, Lely, who designed plates for Lovelace's two books of poems, published in 1649 and 1659. Lovelace enjoyed painting and music as a gentleman amateur, the characteristic persona of a Cavalier poet. His poems express a tone of extravagant passion tempered with courtly poise achieved through lush images conveying a sensuous *joie de vivre* and a perspective of brave insouciance mixed with self-deprecating irony. His deft rhythms create songlike poems with a spontaneous grace and ease, stylistic ideals of the Cavaliers.

We know nothing about Lovelace after 1649. His brother Philip had been colonel in the King's army but survived the Interregnum to become governor of New York in 1688. Of his brother William's death on the field of battle in the Civil War, Richard had written these Stoic lines to Philip:

Iron decrees of Destiny
Are ne'er wiped out with a wet eye.
But this way you may gain the field,
Oppose but sorrow, and 'twill yield;
One gallant thorough made resolve
Doth starry influence dissolve.

To Lucasta, Going to the Wars

Tell me not, sweet, I am unkind,
  That from the nunnery
Of thy chaste breast and quiet mind
  To war and arms I fly.

True, a new mistress now I chase,
  The first foe in the field;
And with a stronger faith embrace
  A sword, a horse, a shield.

Yet this inconstancy is such
  As you too shall adore;
I could not love thee, dear, so much,
  Loved I not honor more.

1649

The Grasshopper[1]

To My Noble Friend, Mr. Charles Cotton[2]

O thou that swing'st upon the waving hair
  Of some well-fillèd oaten beard,

1. The grasshopper was associated with a carefree life.
2. Charles Cotton was a learned and literary man. This poem describes the atmosphere of Puritan rule during the Interregnum.

Drunk ev'ry night with a delicious tear
  Dropped thee from heav'n, where now th' art reared,

The joys of earth and air are thine entire,
  That with thy feet and wings dost hop and fly;
And when thy poppy[3] works thou dost retire
  To thy carved acorn-bed to lie.

Up with the day, the sun thou welcom'st then,
  Sport'st in the gilt-plats° of his beams, *golden fields*
And all these merry days mak'st merry men,
  Thyself, and melancholy streams.

But ah the sickle! golden ears are cropped,
  Ceres and Bacchus[4] bid good night;
Sharp frosty fingers all your flowers have topped,
  And what scythes spared, winds shave off quite.

Poor verdant fool! and now green ice! thy joys,
  Large and as lasting as thy perch of grass,
Bid us lay in 'gainst winter, rain, and poise° *counterbalance*
  Their floods, with an o'erflowing glass.

Thou best of men and friends! We will create
  A genuine summer in each other's breast;
And spite of this cold time and frozen fate[5]
  Thaw us a warm seat to our rest.

Our sacred hearths shall burn eternally
  As vestal flames;[6] the North Wind, he
Shall strike his frost-stretched wings, dissolve and fly
  This Etna[7] in epitome.

Dropping December shall come weeping in,
  Bewail th' usurping of his reign;
But when in showers of old Greek[8] we begin,
  Shall cry, he hath his crown[9] again!

Night as clear Hesper shall our tapers whip
  From the light casements where we play,
And the dark hag from her black mantle strip,
  And stick there everlasting day.[1]

Thus richer than untempted kings are we,
  That asking nothing, nothing need:
Though Lord of all what seas embrace; yet he
  That wants himself is poor indeed.

1649

3. A plant with narcotic powers.
4. The goddess of agriculture and the god of wine.
5. A reference to the persecution of Royalists during the rule of the Puritans.
6. The Roman Vestal Virgins attended to the eternal flame.
7. A volcano, here symbolizing the force and warmth of friendship.
8. The wine that was most prized in ancient Rome.
9. Wreath worn at a drinking party.
1. Hesperus, the morning star; casements: frames forming windows; the dark hag: Hecate, daughter of Night.

To Althea, from Prison

When love with unconfined wings
  Hovers within my gates,
And my divine Althea brings
  To whisper at the grates:
When I lie tangled in her hair
  And fettered to her eye,
The gods[1] that wanton° in the air, *play*
  Know no such liberty.

When flowing cups run swiftly round,
  With no allaying Thames,[2]
Our careless heads with roses bound,
  Our hearts with loyal flames;
When thirsty grief in wine we steep,
  When healths and draughts go free,
Fishes that tipple in the deep
  Know no such liberty.

When, like committed° linnets,° I *confined/songbirds*
  With shriller throat shall sing
The sweetness, mercy, majesty,
  And glories of my king;
When I shall voice aloud, how good
  He is, how great should be,
Enlargèd winds that curl the flood,
  Know no such liberty.

Stone walls do not a prison make,
  Nor iron bars a cage;
Minds innocent and quiet take
  That for an hermitage;° *hermit's dwelling*
If I have freedom in my love,
  And in my soul am free,
Angels alone that soar above,
  Enjoy such liberty.

1649

Love Made in the First Age: To Chloris[1]

In the nativity of time,
Chloris, it was not thought a crime
  In direct Hebrew for to woo.[2]
Now we make love, as all on fire,
Ring retrograde[3] our loud desire,
  And court in English backward too.

1. Some editions read "birds" rather than "gods."
2. River running through London; the meaning of this line is "with no water to dilute the wine."
1. "The First Age" refers to the golden age of Greek and Roman mythology, a time of idyllic plenty in which there was no need for laws or work.
2. Hebrew, which reads from right to left, was believed to have been the original language.
3. In backward or reverse direction; an imitation of notes in contrary motion.

Thrice happy was that golden age,
When compliment was construed rage,[4]
And fine words in the center hid;
When cursed *No* stained no maid's bliss,
And all discourse was summed in *Yes*,
And nought forbade, but to forbid.

Love then unstinted, love did sip,
And cherries plucked fresh from the lip,
On cheeks and roses free he fed;
Lasses like autumn plums did drop,
And lads, indifferently did crop
A flower, and a maidenhead.

Then unconfinèd each did tipple
Wine from the bunch, milk from the nipple;
Paps tractable as udders were;
Then equally the wholesome jellies
Were squeezed from olive-trees, and bellies,
Nor suits of trespass did they fear.

A fragrant bank of strawberries,
Diapered° with violet's eyes, *decorated*
Was table, tablecloth, and fare;
No palace to the clouds did swell
Each humble princess then did dwell
In the piazza[5] of her hair.

Both broken faith, and the cause of it,
All-damning gold was damned to the pit;
Their troth sealed with a clasp and kiss,
Lasted until that extreme day,
In which they smiled their souls away,
And, in each other breathed new bliss.

Because no fault, there was no tear;
No groan did grate the granting ear;
No false foul breath their delicate smell:
No serpent kiss poisoned the taste,
Each touch was naturally chaste,
And their mere sense a miracle.

Naked as their own innocence,
And unembroidered[6] from offense
They went, above poor riches, gay;
On softer than the cygnet's° down, *young swan's*
In beds they tumbled of their own;
For each within the other lay.

Thus did they live: thus did they love,
Repeating only joys above;

4. When compliments were interpreted as passionate proposals.

5. A colonnade surrounding a square.

6. Not ornamented with the trappings of authority.

And angels were, but with clothes on,
Which they would put off cheerfully,
To bathe them in the galaxy,[7]
Then gird them with the heavenly zone.[8]

Now, Chloris, miserably crave
The offered bliss you would not have;
Which evermore I must deny,
Whilst ravished with these noble dreams
And crownèd with mine own soft beams,
Enjoying of myself I lie.

1659

Henry Vaughan

1622–1695

Henry Vaughan grew up speaking Welsh among the woods and streams of Newton in the parish of Llansantffraed. He responded to the sound of his first language and to the beauty of this countryside in the music and imagery of his poetry. For example, the slope of mount Allt, on which he lived, provided a striking image: "those faint beams in which this hill is dressed,/ After the Sun's remove" The Welsh influence can be heard in his poetry's alliteration and assonance; his piling up of comparisons, as in *The Night*, is called *dyfalu* ("to liken") in Welsh poetic technique. On the title page to his second book of verse, *Olor Iscanus* ("The Swan of Usk" [a local river]), he is called a "Silurist," a member of an ancient Welsh tribe. Though his verse is written in English, Vaughan's poetry and identity were always bound up with his native land.

Henry Vaughan's Welsh childhood was followed by education at Oxford, where he studied with his twin brother Thomas, and then at the Inns of Court in London, where he began his poetic apprenticeship. An admirer of Ben Jonson's verse, Vaughan praised and imitated Jonson in his first book of poetry, *Poems with the Tenth Satyre of Juvenal Englished* (1646). The mysticism and Neoplatonism of Vaughan's best known collection of poems, *Silex Scintillans* ("The Fiery Flint") (1650), link him to the metaphysical tradition of Donne, Herbert, and Crashaw, yet his verse continued to show fondness for the wit and spareness of Jonson.

At the outbreak of the Civil War, Vaughan returned to Wales in August 1642. He worked as secretary to the Circuit Chief Justice of the Great Sessions until 1645, when he joined the company of soldiers who fought for King Charles's cause with Sir Herbert Price at Chester. The poems in *Silex Scintillans* express his anger and disappointment at the outcome of the Civil War. In *Prayer in Time of Persecution*, Vaughan rails against the Puritans for confiscating the woods of his family's estate. The 1650 Act for the Propagation of the Gospel in Wales gave a committee of Puritan commissioners the power to purge the Welsh royalist clergy. Among these was Henry's brother Thomas, who was stripped of his position and livelihood. In *The World*, Vaughan describes a "darksome statesman" reminiscent of Cromwell; and in several poems, Vaughan complains of the Puritan "zeal" that brought about regicide and persecution of the Church of England. In *Christ's Nativity*, Vaughan lamented the Puritans's prohibition of the observance of Christmas and Good Friday:

7. The Milky Way.

8. The zodiac of stars.

Shall he that came down from thence,
And here for us was slain,
Shall he be now cast off? no sense
Of all his woes remain?
Can neither Love, nor sufferings bind?
Are we all stone, and Earth?
Neither his bloody passions mind,
Nor one day bless his birth?
Alas, my God! Thy birth now here
Must not be numbered in the year.

There is even evidence in one poem, *The Proffer*, that Vaughan disdained offers of power from Cromwell's government: "I'll not stuff my story/With your Commonwealth and glory." Some time after 1650, Vaughan decided to study and practice medicine.

The 1650s were troubled years for Vaughan. During this time he grieved for the deaths of his brother Thomas and his first wife Catherine. In the preface to the second edition of *Silex Scintillans* in 1655, Vaughan refers to an illness he had suffered, which seems to have been spiritual and may even have resulted in a kind of conversion experience. In this same preface, Vaughan also praises George Herbert: "his holy life and verse gained many pious Converts of whom I am the least." Along with the Bible, Herbert's verse is the main influence on Vaughan's. The titles of twenty-six lyrics in *Silex Scintillans* are taken from Herbert's *The Temple*. Both poets describe a spiritual paradise, but while Herbert's is ineffable, Vaughan's has the physical beauty of an actual landscape. Vaughan's temple stretches beyond the pristine church architecture of Herbert's imagery to touch flowers and trees and to contemplate the stars. Vaughan's feeling for nature is unsurpassed in English verse until Wordsworth. Vaughan's intense sense of the transitoriness of natural beauty and the immanence of mortality make his verse worth contemplating and savoring.

Regeneration

A ward, and still in bonds, one day
I stole abroad;
It was high spring, and all the way
Primrosed, and hung with shade;
Yet, was it frost within,
And surly winds
Blasted my infant buds, and sin
Like clouds eclipsed my mind.

Stormed thus, I straight perceived my spring
Mere stage and show,
My walk a monstrous, mountained thing,
Roughcast with rocks, and snow;
And as a pilgrim's eye
Far from relief,
Measures the melancholy sky,
Then drops, and rains for grief,

So sighed I upwards still, at last
'Twixt steps, and falls
I reached the pinnacle, where placed
I found a pair of scales,
I took them up and laid

In th'one late pains,
The other smoke, and pleasures weighed,
But proved the heavier grains.

With that, some cried, "Away!" Straight I
Obeyed, and led
Full east, a fair, fresh field could spy;
Some called it, Jacob's bed,[1]
A virgin soil, which no
Rude feet ere trod,
Where, since he stepped there, only go
Prophets, and friends of God.

Here, I reposed; but scarce well set,
A grove descried
Of stately height, whose branches met
And mixed on every side;
I entered, and once in,
Amazed to see't,
Found all was changed, and a new spring
Did all my senses greet;

The unthrift° sun shot vital gold *spendthrift*
A thousand pieces,
And heaven its azure did unfold,
Checkered with snowy fleeces,
The air was all in spice,
And every bush
A garland wore; thus fed my eyes,
But all the ear lay hush.

Only a little fountain lent
Some use for ears,
And on the dumb shades language spent
The music of her tears;
I drew her near, and found
The cistern full
Of divers stones, some bright, and round
Others ill-shaped, and dull.

The first, pray mark, as quick as light
Danced through the flood,
But, th'last more heavy than the night
Nailed to the center stood;
I wondered much, but tired
At last with thought,
My restless eye that still desired
As strange an object brought;

It was a bank of flowers, where I descried,
Though 'twas mid-day,
Some fast asleep, others broad-eyed

1. See Genesis 28.11–19. Sleeping outdoors, Jacob had a vision of a ladder in the sky leading up to God.

And taking in the ray,
Here musing long, I heard
A rushing wind
Which still increased, but whence it stirred
Nowhere I could not find.

I turned me round, and to each shade
Dispatched an eye,
To see, if any leaf had made
Least motion, or reply;
But while I listening sought
My mind to ease
By knowing, where 'twas, or where not,
It whispered, "Where I please."[2]

"Lord," then said I, "on me one breath,
And let me die before my death!"

1650

The Retreat

Happy those early days! when I
Shined in my angel infancy.
Before I understood this place
Appointed for my second race,[1]
Or taught my soul to fancy ought
But a white, celestial thought;
When yet I had not walked above
A mile or two from my first love,
And looking back, at that short space,
Could see a glimpse of his bright face;
When on some gilded cloud, or flower
My gazing soul would dwell an hour,
And in those weaker glories spy
Some shadows of eternity;
Before I taught my tongue to wound
My conscience with a sinful sound,
Or had the black art to dispense
A several° sin to every sense, *separate*
But felt through all this fleshly dress
Bright shoots of everlastingness.
O, how I long to travel back,
And tread again that ancient track!
That I might once more reach that plain
Where first I left my glorious train,
From whence th' enlightened spirit sees
That shady city of palm trees.[2]

2. John 3.8: "The wind bloweth where it listeth, and thou hearest the sound thereof, but canst not tell whence it cometh, and whither it goeth: so is every one that is born of the Spirit." See also Genesis 2.7 for the breath of life that God breathed into humanity.

1. "Second race" implies a Platonic belief in the reincarnation of the soul and in the preexistence of the soul in the world of perfect forms.
2. The New Jerusalem, the Paradise of Heaven.

But, ah! my soul with too much stay° *hesitation*
Is drunk, and staggers in the way.
Some men a forward motion love;
But I by backward steps would move,
And when this dust falls to the urn
In that state I came, return.

1650

Silence, and Stealth of Days[1]

Silence, and stealth of days! 'tis now
Since thou art gone,
Twelve hundred hours, and not a brow[2]
But clouds hang on.
As he that in some cave's thick damp
Locked from the light,
Fixeth a solitary lamp,
To brave the night
And walking from his sun, when past
That glim'ring ray,
Cuts through the heavy mists in haste
Back to his day,[3]
So o'er fled minutes I retreat
Unto that hour
Which showed thee last, but did defeat
Thy light, and pow'r,
I search, and rack my soul to see
Those beams again,
But nothing but the snuff[4] to me
Appeareth plain;
That dark, and dead sleeps in its known
And common urn,
But those fled to their Maker's throne,
There shine, and burn;
O could I track them! but souls must
Track one the other,
And now the spirit, not the dust,
Must be thy brother.
Yet I have one Pearl[5] by whose light
All things I see,
And in the heart of earth and night,
Find Heaven and thee.

1650

The World

I saw eternity the other night,
Like a great ring of pure and endless light,

1. The poem is about the death of Vaughan's younger brother William, who died in July 1648.
2. Facial expression, but also a gallery in a coal mine, since the following lines depict the image of a miner making his way through dark mist.
3. When the miner walks a little beyond the area lit by his lamp into the dark, he then rushes back to the light.
4. The part of a candle wick burnt in order to give light; an image of his brother's body turned to dust.
5. The Bible.

All calm as it was bright;
And round beneath it, Time, in hours, days, years,
Driven by the spheres,[1]
Like a vast shadow moved, in which the world
And all her train were hurled.
The doting lover in his quaintest strain[2]
Did there complain;
Near him, his lute, his fancy, and his flights,
Wit's sour delights,
With gloves and knots,[3] the silly snares of pleasure,
Yet his dear treasure,
All scattered lay, while he his eyes did pour
Upon a flower.

The darksome statesman[4] hung with weights and woe
Like a thick midnight fog moved there so slow
He did not stay nor go;
Condemning thoughts, like sad eclipses, scowl
Upon his soul,
And clouds of crying witnesses without
Pursued him with one shout.
Yet digged the mole, and lest his ways be found,
Worked underground,
Where he did clutch his prey. But one did see
That policy:
Churches and altars fed him; perjuries
Were gnats and flies;
It rained about him blood and tears; but he
Drank them as free.

The fearful miser on a heap of rust
Sat pining all his life there, did scarce trust
His own hands with the dust;
Yet would not place° one piece above, but lives *invest*
In fear of thieves.
Thousands there were as frantic as himself,
And hugged each one his pelf:° *money*
The downright epicure placed heaven in sense,[5]
And scorned pretense;
While others, slipped into a wide excess,
Said little less;
The weaker sort slight, trivial wares enslave,
Who think them brave,° *showy*
And poor, depisèd Truth sat counting by,° *reckoning*
Their victory.

Yet some, who all this while did weep and sing,
And sing and weep, soared up into the ring;
But most would use no wing,
"O fools!" said I, "thus to prefer dark night

1. The spheres of the heavenly bodies circling the earth.
2. Most intricate melody.
3. Ties or bows worn as love tokens.
4. Possibly a reference to Cromwell.
5. An "epicure" is a person who finds the greatest good in sensual pleasure.

Before true light!
To live in grots° and caves, and hate the day caverns
Because it shows the way;
The way which from the dead and dark abode
Leads up to God,
A way where you might tread the sun and be
More bright than he!"
But as I did their madness so discuss,
One whispered thus:
"This ring the bridegroom did for none provide,
But for his bride."[6]

1650

They Are All Gone into the World of Light!

They are all gone into the world of light!
And I alone sit lingering here;
Their very memory is fair and bright,
And my sad thoughts doth clear.

It glows and glitters in my cloudy breast
Like stars upon some gloomy grove,
Or those faint beams in which this hill is dressed,
After the sun's remove.

I see them walking in an air of glory,
Whose light doth trample on my days:
My days, which are at best but dull and hoary,
Mere glimmering and decays.

O holy hope! and high humility,
High as the heavens above!
These are your walks, and you have showed them me
To kindle my cold love,

Dear, beauteous death! the jewel of the just,
Shining no where, but in the dark;
What mysteries do lie beyond thy dust,
Could man outlook that mark!

He that hath found some fledged birds nest, may know
At first sight, if the bird be flown;
But what fair well, or grove he sings in now,
That is to him unknown.

And yet, as angels in some brighter dreams
Call to the soul, when man doth sleep,
So some strange thoughts transcend our wonted themes,
And into glory peep.

If a star were confined into a tomb
Her captive flames must needs burn there;
But when the hand that locked her up, gives room,
She'll shine through all the sphere.

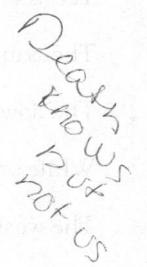

6. For the union of Christ and his Church as that between husband and wife, see Ephesians 5.23.

O Father of eternal life, and all
Created glories under thee!
Resume thy spirit from this world of thrall° *slavery*
Into true liberty.

Either disperse these mists, which blot and fill
My perspective[1] still as they pass,
Or else remove me hence unto that hill,[2]
Where I shall need no glass.

1655

The Night

John 3.2[1]

Through that pure virgin-shrine,
That sacred veil drawn o'er thy glorious noon
That men might look and live as glowworms shine,
And face the moon:
Wise Nicodemus saw such light
As made him know his God by night.

Most blest believer he!
Who in that land of darkness and blind eyes
Thy long expected healing wings could see,
When thou didst rise,
And what can never more be done,
Did at midnight speak with the Sun!

O who will tell me, where
He found thee at that dead and silent hour?
What hallowed solitary ground did bear
So rare a flower,
Within whose sacred leaves did lie
The fullness of the Deity?

No mercy-seat of gold,[2]
No dead and dusty cherub, nor carved stone,
But his own living works did my Lord hold
And lodge alone;
Where trees and herbs did watch and peep
And wonder, while the Jews did sleep.

Dear night! this world's defeat;[3]
The stop to busy fools; cares check and curb;
The day of spirits; my soul's calm retreat
Which none disturb!
Christ's progress, and his prayer time;
The hours to which high heaven doth chime;

1. Telescope; vision.
2. Sion Hill, a symbol for union with God.
1. In John 3.2, the Pharisee Nicodemus tells Jesus: "Rabbi, we know that thou art a teacher come from God: for no man can do these miracles that thou doest except God be with him."
2. God told the Israelites to build "a mercy seat of pure gold" with a cherub on either end to place above the ark (see Exodus 25.17–21).
3. This and the next stanza echo George Herbert's *Prayer (1)*; see page 1588.

God's silent, searching flight,
When my Lord's head is filled with dew, and all
His locks are wet with the clear drops of night;
His still, soft call;
His knocking time; the souls dumb watch,
When spirits their fair kindred catch.

Were all my loud, evil days
Calm and unhaunted as is thy dark tent,
Whose peace but by some angel's wing or voice
Is seldom rent;
Then I in heaven all the long year
Would keep, and never wander here.

But living where the sun
Doth all things wake, and where all mix and tire
Themselves and others, I consent and run
To ev'ry mire,° *bog*
And by this world's ill-guiding light,
Ere more then I can do by night.

There is in God (some say)
A deep, but dazzling darkness; as men here
Say it is late and dusky, because they
See not all clear;
O for that night! where I in him
Might live invisible and dim.

1655

Andrew Marvell

1621–1678

Praised by his nephew for "joining the most peculiar graces of wit and learning" and berated by his antagonist Samuel Parker for speaking the language of "boat-swains and cabin boys," Andrew Marvell left little evidence for his biographers. Most of what remains of his verse has been bequeathed to posterity by virtue of a shady banking scheme on his part and an implausible claim by his housekeeper to be "Mrs. Marvell." Though she couldn't remember the date of his death, Mary Palmer tried to prove that she was the poet's wife to get at money that her master had squirrelled away in an account for some bankrupt acquaintances. To further her claim, she saw to it that Marvell's *Miscellaneous Poems* were published in 1681. In his own name, Marvell published only a few occasional poems and a satire attacking religious intolerance and political authoritarianism.

If it is thanks to Mrs. Palmer's rummaging through the poet's papers that such exquisite poems as *To His Coy Mistress* and *The Definition of Love* saw the light of day, it is largely thanks to T. S. Eliot that modern critical attention was turned to Marvell's poetry. The Augustans and Romantics neglected him, and it was not until Eliot that such features of Marvell's verse as Latinate gravity, metaphysical wit, and muscular syntax came to be fully appreciated. For ingenious ambiguity and sheer seductive sensuousness, Marvell is one of the greatest poets of all time.

As tantalizing as the verse is, it leaves little solid evidence of what was a very private life. Marvell grew up in a house surrounded by gardens in the Yorkshire town of Hull on the Humber, where his father was the Anglican rector. There is a story that Marvell once left university for London to flirt with Catholicism, but his father made sure he returned to Cambridge and Protestantism. After his father's death, Marvell traveled in Holland, France, Italy, and Spain (1642–1647). He later tutored Mary Fairfax, daughter of Lord Fairfax of Nun-Appleton House (1650–1652), and taught William Dutton, Cromwell's ward (1653–1656). Initially recommended by Milton to serve as Assistant Latin Secretary in 1653, Marvell was first appointed Latin Secretary to the Council of State in 1657. He was elected Member of Parliament for Hull in 1659, a position he held until 1678. When Charles I returned to power, Marvell interceded on Milton's behalf and made sure his old friend and fellow poet was released from prison. Later in life, Marvell wrote satires criticizing the corruption of the Restoration regime, all but one published anonymously.

Marvell chose to keep his cards close to his chest in the ideologically volatile atmosphere of the Civil War and Restoration. A contemporary biographer remarked that Marvell "was wont to say that, he would not play the good-fellow in any man's company in whose hands he would not trust his life." He did not fight in the Civil War, since he was in Europe at the time, and as he later ambiguously maintained, "the Cause was too good to have been fought for." His strategy in dealing with change involved publicly siding with the faction in power while maintaining politically incorrect friendships and finding himself "inclinable to favor the weaker party"—whether it was a Royalist who had given his life for the King, such as Lord Hastings, or a Republican who went to prison for his convictions, such as Milton. Marvell wrote poems praising both royalists and revolutionaries. He was nothing if not tolerant.

He was also something of a chameleon, an assumer of numerous poetic personae and disguises. In *Tom May's Death,* Marvell satirized the Royalist turned Republican, here portrayed arriving in heaven drunk. Marvell equivocally praised Cromwell in *An Horatian Ode,* ironically maintaining that it was the Irish whom Cromwell had so brutally massacred who could "best affirm his praises." When he became tutor to Cromwell's ward William Dutton, Marvell wrote poems praising Cromwell in such slavishly glowing terms that the poet was made Latin Secretary to the Council of State.

The last word should go to Marvell, whose choice to translate the following chorus from Seneca's *Thyestes* shows his outlook on the vicissitudes of power:

Climb at court for me that will
Giddy favor's slippery hill;
All I seek is to lie still,
Settled in some secret nest.
In calm leisure let me rest,
And far off the public stage
Pass away my silent age.
Thus, when without noise, unknown,
I have lived out all my span,
I shall die without a groan,
An old honest countryman,
Who exposed to others' eyes,
Into his own heart ne'er pries.
Death to him's a strange surprise.

The Coronet[1]

When for the thorns with which I long, too long,
With many a piercing wound,
My Savior's head have crowned,
I seek with garlands to redress that wrong:
Through every garden, every mead,
I gather flow'rs (my fruits are only flow'rs)
Dismantling all the fragrant towers° *tall headdresses*
That once adorned my shepherdess's head.
And now when I have summed up all my store,
Thinking (so I myself deceive)
So rich a chaplet° thence to weave *wreath*
As never yet the King of Glory wore:
Alas, I find the serpent old
That, twining in his speckled breast,[2]
About the flowers disguised does fold,° *wind*
With wreaths° of fame and interest. *coils*
Ah, foolish man, that wouldst debase with them,
And mortal glory, Heaven's diadem!
But Thou who only couldst the serpent tame,
Either his slippery knots at once untie,
And disentangle all his winding snare:
Or shatter too with him my curious frame:[3]
And let these wither, so that he may die,
Though set with skill and chosen out with care:
That they, while Thou on both their spoils[4] dost tread,
May crown thy feet, that could not crown thy head.[5]

Bermudas[1]

Where the remote Bermudas ride
In th' ocean's bosom unespied,
From a small boat, that rowed along,
The list'ning winds received this song.
"What should we do but sing his praise
That led us through the watry maze,
Unto an isle so long unknown,[2]
And yet far kinder than our own?
Where he the huge sea-monsters wracks,° *shipwrecks*
That lift the deep upon their backs.
He lands us on a grassy stage,
Safe from the storms, and prelate's[3] rage.
He gave us this eternal spring,

1. Marvell's poems were first published in 1681.
2. See Spenser, *Faerie Queene* 1.11.15.
3. Ingenious structure (the chaplet).
4. Sloughing of the snake's skin; plundering.
5. See Genesis 3.15, for the prophecy that the seed of Eve will bruise the serpent's head.

1. Probably composed sometime after 1653, when Marvell was living in the house of John Oxenbridge, who had made two trips to the Bermudas. Marvell could also have known Captain John Smith's 1624 work *The General History of Virginia, New England and the Summer Isles* (as the Bermudas were called).
2. Unknown to Europeans; Juan Bermudez first came there in 1515.
3. Clergyman's, bishop's.

Which here enamels everything;
And sends the fowl to us in care,
On daily visits through the air.
He hangs in shades the orange bright,
Like golden lamps in a green night,
And does in the pom'granates close,
Jewels more rich than Ormus[4] shows.
He makes the figs our mouths to meet,
And throws the melons at our feet,
But apples° plants of such a price, *pineapples*
No tree could ever bear them twice.
With cedars, chosen by his hand,
From Lebanon, he stores the land,
And makes the hollow seas, that roar,
Proclaim the ambergris[5] on shore.
He cast (of which we rather boast)
The gospel's pearl upon our coast,
And in these rocks for us did frame
A temple, where to sound his name.
Oh let our voice his praise exalt,
Till it arrive at heaven's vault:
Which thence (perhaps) rebounding, may
Echo beyond the Mexique Bay.[6]
Thus sung they, in the English boat,
An holy and a cheerful note,
And all the way, to guide their chime,
With falling oars they kept the time.

The Nymph Complaining for the Death of Her Fawn[1]

The wanton troopers[2] riding by
Have shot my fawn, and it will die.
Ungentle men! They cannot thrive
To kill thee. Thou ne'er didst alive
Them any harm: alas, nor could
Thy death yet do them any good.
I'm sure I never wished them ill;
Nor do I for all this; nor will:
But, if my simple prayers may yet
Prevail with Heaven to forget
Thy murder, I will join my tears
Rather then fail. But, O my fears!
It cannot die so. Heaven's King
Keeps register of everything:
And nothing may we use in vain.
E'en beasts must be with justice slain,

4. Hormuz on the Persian Gulf.
5. Musky secretion of the sperm whale that is used in perfumes.
6. Gulf of Mexico.
1. Ancient Roman poets such as Catullus and Ovid had written poems on the death of pets, as did the early 16th-century English poet John Skelton in *Philip Sparrow*.
2. A term used for the Presbyterian Scots Covenanting Army that attacked England in 1640.

Else men are made their deodands.[3]
Though they should wash their guilty hands
In this warm life-blood, which doth part
From thine, and wound me to the heart,
Yet could they not be clean: their stain
Is dyed in such a purple grain.
There is not such another in
The world, to offer for their sin.
  Unconstant Sylvio, when yet
I had not found him counterfeit,
One morning (I remember well)
Tied in this silver chain and bell,
Gave it to me: nay, and I know
What he said then; I'm sure I do.
Said he, "Look how your huntsman here
Hath taught a fawn to hunt his dear."
But Sylvio soon had me beguiled.
This waxèd tame, while he grew wild,
And quite regardless of my smart,
Left me his fawn, but took his heart.
  Thenceforth I set myself to play
My solitary time away
With this: and very well content,
Could so mine idle life have spent.
For it was full of sport; and light
Of foot, and heart; and did invite
Me to its game: it seemed to bless
Itself in me. How could I less
Than love it? O I cannot be
Unkind, t' a beast that loveth me.
  Had it lived long, I do not know
Whether it too might have done so
As Sylvio did: his gifts might be
Perhaps as false or more than he.
But I am sure, for ought that I
Could in so short a time espie,
Thy Love was far more better then
The love of false and cruel men.
  With sweetest milk, and sugar, first
I it at mine own fingers nursed.
And as it grew, so every day
It waxed more white and sweet than they,
It had so sweet a breath! And oft
I blushed to see its foot more soft,
And white, (shall I say than my hand?)
Nay any lady's of the land.
  It is a wondrous thing, how fleet
'Twas on those little silver feet.

3. Otherwise, men would become forfeited objects. In early modern English law, any personal property that caused a human death had to be given up as part of the reparation for the crime.

With what a pretty skipping grace,
It oft would challenge me the race:
And when 't had left me far away,
'Twould stay, and run again, and stay.
For it was nimbler much than hinds;
And trod, as on the four winds.
  I have a garden of my own,
But so with roses overgrown,
And lilies, that you would it guess
To be a little wilderness.
And all the springtime of the year
It only lovèd to be there.
Among the beds of lilies, I
Have sought it oft, where it should lie;
Yet could not, till itself would rise,
Find it, although before mine eyes.
For, in the flaxen lilies' shade,
It like a bank of lilies laid.
Upon the roses it would feed,
Until its lips e'en seemed to bleed:
And then to me 'twould boldly trip,
And print those roses on my lip.
But all its chief delight was still
On roses thus itself to fill:
And its pure virgin limbs to fold
In whitest sheets of lilies cold.
Had it lived long, it would have been
Lilies without, roses within.
O help! O help! I see it faint:
And die as calmely as a saint.
See how it weeps. The tears do come
Sad, slowly dropping like a gum.
So weeps the wounded balsam: so
The holy frankincense doth flow.
The brotherless Heliades
Melt in such amber tears as these.[4]
  I in a golden vial will
Keep these two crystal tears; and fill
It till it do o'reflow with mine;
Then place it in Diana's[5] shrine.
  Now my sweet fawn is vanished to
Whither the swans and turtles° go: *doves*
In fair Elysium to endure,
With milk-white lambs, and ermines pure.
O do not run too fast: for I
Will but bespeak thy grave, and die.
  First my unhappy statue shall
Be cut in marble; and withal,

4. Grieving the death of their brother Phaethon, the Heliades were transformed into poplar trees which wept tears of amber.

5. Goddess of chastity and of the hunt.

Let it be weeping too:[6] but there
Th' engraver sure his art may spare;
For I so truly thee bemoan,
That I shall weep though I be stone:
Until my tears, still dropping, wear
My breast, themselves engraving there.
There at my feet shalt thou be laid,
Of purest alabaster made:
For I would have thine image be
White as I can, though not as thee.

To His Coy Mistress[1]

Had we but world enough, and time,
This coyness, Lady, were no crime.
We would sit down, and think which way
To walk, and pass our long love's day.
Thou by the Indian Ganges' side
Shouldst rubies find: I by the tide
Of Humber would complain.[2] I would
Love you ten years before the flood:
And you should if you please refuse
Till the conversion of the Jews.[3]
My vegetable love should grow
Vaster then empires, and more slow.[4]
An hundred years should go to praise
Thine eyes, and on thy forehead gaze.
Two hundred to adore each breast:
But thirty thousand to the rest.
An age at least to every part,
And the last age should show your heart.
For Lady you deserve this State;
Nor would I love at lower rate.
    But at my back I always hear
Times wingèd chariot hurrying near:
And yonder all before us lie
Deserts of vast eternity.
Thy beauty shall no more be found;
Nor, in thy marble vault, shall sound
My echoing song: then worms shall try
That long preserved virginity:
And your quaint honor turn to dust;[5]
And into ashes all my lust.
The grave's a fine and private place,

6. Niobe was turned into a weeping stone for her pride in her children.

1. A poem on the theme of *carpe diem* ("seize the day") that includes a blazon, or description of the lady from head to toe, and a logical argument: "If . . . But . . . Therefore."

2. Marvell grew up in Hull on the Humber River.

3. The end of time: the Flood occurred in the distant past, and Christians prophesied that Jews would convert to Christianity at the end of the world.

4. The "vegetable" was characterized only by growth, in contrast to the sensitive, which felt, and the rational, which could reason.

5. "Quaint honor," proud chastity. Note the pun on *queynte* (Middle English), woman's genitals.

But none, I think, do there embrace.
Now, therefore, while the youthful hue
Sits on thy skin like morning dew,[6]
And while thy willing soul transpires
At every pore with instant fires,
Now let us sport us while we may;
And now, like amorous birds of prey,
Rather at once our time devour,
Than languish in his slow-chapped° power. *slowly biting*
Let us roll all our strength, and all
Our sweetness, up into one ball:
And tear our pleasures with rough strife,
Thorough the iron gates of life.[7]
Thus, though we cannot make our sun
Stand still, yet we will make him run.[8]

The Definition of Love

My Love is of a birth as rare
As 'tis for object strange and high:
It was begotten by Despair
Upon Impossibility.

Magnanimous Despair alone
Could show me so divine a thing,
Where feeble Hope could ne'er have flown
But vainly flapped its tinsel wing.

And yet I quickly might arrive
Where my extended soul is fixed,
But Fate does iron wedges drive,
And always crowds itself betwixt.

For Fate with jealous eye does see
Two perfect loves, nor lets them close:° *unite*
Their union would her ruin be,
And her tyrannic power depose.

And therefore her decrees of steel
Us as the distant poles have placed,
(Though Love's whole world on us doth wheel)
Not by themselves to be embraced.

Unless the giddy heaven fall,
And earth some new convulsion tear;
And, us to join, the world should all
Be cramped into a planisphere.[1]

As lines (so loves) oblique[2] may well
Themselves in every angle greet:

6. In the 1681 Folio, "dew" reads "glue," and in two manuscripts the rhymes in lines 33 and 34 are "glue" and "dew."

7. One manuscript reads "grates" for "gates."

8. Joshua made the sun stand still in the war against Gibeon (see Joshua 10.12).

1. A two-dimensional map of the globe.

2. Slanting at an angle other than a right angle, and also veering away from right morals.

But ours so truly parallel,
Though infinite, can never meet.

Therefore the love which us doth bind.
But Fate so enviously debars,
Is the conjunction of the mind,
And opposition of the stars.[3]

The Mower Against Gardens

Luxurious man, to bring his vice in use,[1]
Did after him the world seduce,
And from the fields the flowers and plants allure,
Where Nature was most plain and pure.
He first enclosed within the garden's square
A dead and standing pool of air,
And a more luscious earth for them did knead,
Which stupefied them while it fed.
The pink grew then as double as his mind;[2]
The nutriment did change the kind.
With strange perfumes he did the roses taint,
And flowers themselves were taught to paint.
The tulip, white, did for complexion seek,
And learned to interline its cheek:
Its onion root they then so high did hold,
That one was for a meadow sold.[3]
Another world was searched, through oceans new,
To find the Marvel of Peru.[4]
And yet these rarities might be allowed
To man, that sovereign thing and proud,
Had he not dealt between the bark and tree,[5]
Forbidden mixtures there to see.
No plant now knew the stock from which it came;
He grafts upon the wild the tame:
That the uncertain and adult'rate fruit
Might put the palate in dispute.
His green seraglio[6] has its eunuchs too;
Lest any tyrant him outdo.
And in the cherry he does nature vex,
To procreate without a sex.[7]
'Tis all enforced; the fountain and the grot,° *grotto*
While the sweet fields do lie forgot:
Where willing Nature does to all dispense
A wild and fragrant innocence:
And fauns and fairies do the meadows till,

3. Conjunction: coming together in the same sign of the zodiac; union. Stars in opposition are diametrically opposed to one another.

1. To make current.

2. Double, both in the sense of having two blooms and being the result of sophisticated (duplicitous) thought.

3. Marvell alludes to the 17th-century lucrative trade in Dutch tulips.

4. *Mirabilis jalapa,* also known as the four-o'clock, a multi-colored flower native to tropical America.

5. An expression used to describe interfering in another's affairs, especially those of a married couple.

6. Secluded place; Turkish palace; harem.

7. To grow by grafting one strain of cherry onto another.

More by their presence than their skill.
Their statues polished by some ancient hand,
May to adorn the gardens stand:
But howsoe'er the figures do excel,
The gods themselves with us do dwell.

The Mower's Song

My mind was once the true survey
Of all these meadows fresh and gay;
And in the greenness of the grass
Did see its hopes as in a glass;° *mirror*
When Juliana came, and she,
What I do to the grass, does to my thoughts and me.[1]

But these, while I with sorrow pine,
Grew more luxuriant still and fine,
That not one blade of grass you spied,
But had a flower on either side;
When Juliana came, and she,
What I do to the grass, does to my thoughts and me.

Unthankful meadows, could you so
A fellowship so true forgo,
And in your gaudy May-games meet,[2]
While I lay trodden under feet?
When Juliana came, and she,
What I do to the grass, does to my thoughts and me.

But what you in compassion ought,
Shall now by my revenge be wrought:
And flowers, and grass, and I and all,
Will in one common ruin fall.
For Juliana comes, and she,
What I do to the grass, does to my thoughts and me.

And thus, ye meadows, which have been
Companions of my thoughts more green,
Shall now the heraldry become
With which I shall adorn my tomb;
For Juliana comes, and she,
What I do to the grass, does to my thoughts and me.

The Garden

How vainly men themselves amaze
To win the palm, the oak, or bays,[1]
And their uncessant labors see
Crowned from some single herb or tree,
Whose short and narrow-vergèd shade

1. This 12-syllable line (an alexandrine) is the only instance of a refrain in all of Marvell's poetry.
2. Festivals celebrated on May 1.

1. Vainly: arrogantly, in vain. Amaze: bewilder, go mad. The palm, the oak, or bays: prizes symbolic of military, political, and poetic excellence.

Does prudently their toils upbraid,
While all flowers and all trees do close° *unite*
To weave the garlands of repose.

Fair quiet, have I found thee here,
And innocence thy sister dear!
Mistaken long, I sought you then
In busy companies of men.
Your sacred plants, if here below,
Only among the plants will grow.
Society is all but rude,
To this delicious solitude.[2]

No white nor red[3] was ever seen
So am'rous as this lovely green.
Fond lovers, cruel as their flame,
Cut in these trees their mistress' name.
Little, alas, they know, or heed,
How far these beauties hers exceed!
Fair trees! whereso'er your barks I wound,
No name shall but your own be found.

When we have run our passion's heat,
Love hither makes his best retreat.
The gods, that mortal beauty chase,
Still in a tree did end their race.
Apollo hunted Daphne so,
Only that she might laurel grow,
And Pan did after Syrinx speed,
Not as a nymph, but for a reed.[4]

What wondrous life in this I lead!
Ripe apples drop about my head;
The luscious clusters of the vine
Upon my mouth do crush their wine;
The nectarine, and curious peach,
Into my hands themselves do reach;
Stumbling on melons, as I pass,
Insnared with flowers, I fall on grass.

Meanwhile the mind, from pleasure less,
Withdraws into its happiness:
The mind, that ocean where each kind
Does straight its own resemblance find,[5]
Yet it creates, transcending these,
Far other worlds, and other seas,

2. Compare to Katherine Philips's *A Country-life:* "Then welcome dearest solitude, / My great felicity; / Though some are pleased to call thee rude."

3. Colors used to describe the beloved's beauty.

4. As god of poetry, Apollo seeks the laurel (the bays), while Pan seeks the syrinx (pipe) of pastoral poetry. Apollo chased Daphne, who prayed to be saved from him and was transformed into a laurel tree, just as Syrinx escaped Pan's lust when she was turned into a reed.

5. It was popularly believed that animals and plants on land had counterparts in the sea. This line describes the mind as innately possessing ideas, a concept of Platonic philosophy.

Annihilating all that's made
To a green thought in a green shade.

Here at the fountain's sliding foot,
Or at some fruit-tree's mossy root,
Casting the body's vest aside,
My soul into the boughs does glide:
There like a bird it sits and sings,
Then whets and combs its silver wings;
And, till prepared for longer flight,
Waves in its plumes the various light.

Such was that happy garden-state,
While man there walked without a mate:
After a place so pure and sweet,
What other help could yet be meet!
But 'twas beyond a mortal's share
To wander solitary there:
Two paradises 'twere in one
To live in paradise alone.

How well the skillful gardener drew
Of flowers and herbs this dial new;[6]
Where from above the milder sun
Does through a fragrant zodiac run;
And, as it works, th' industrious bee
Computes its time as well as we.[7]
How could such sweet and wholesome hours
Be reckoned but with herbs and flowers!

from Upon Appleton House:
To my Lord Fairfax[1]

1

Within this sober frame expect
Work of no foreign architect,
That unto caves the quarries drew,
And forests did to pastures hew,
Who of his great design in pain
Did for a model vault° his brain, *arch*
Whose columns should so high be raised
To arch the brows that on them gazed.

2

Why should of all things man unruled
Such unproportioned dwellings build?
The beasts are by their dens expressed:
And birds contrive an equal nest;[2]

6. The garden is arranged as a floral sundial.
7. Computes its time: a pun on thyme.
1. Nun Appleton in Yorkshire was the home of Lord Fairfax, whose daughter Mary was tutored by Marvell. With the dissolution of the monasteries, the estate, which had once been a Cistercian priory, was taken over by the Fairfax family.
2. A nest in proportion to their own size.

The low-roofed tortoises do dwell
In cases fit of tortoise shell:
No creature loves an empty space;
Their bodies measure out their place.

3

But he, superfluously spread,
Demands more room alive than dead.
And in his hollow palace goes
Where winds as he themselves may lose;
What need of all this marble crust
T'impark the wanton mote of dust,
That thinks by breadth the world t'unite
Though the first builders failed in height?[3]

4

But all things are composèd here
Like Nature, orderly and near:
In which we the dimensions find
Of that more sober age and mind,
When larger-sizèd men did stoop
To enter at a narrow loop;
As practising, in doors so strait,
To strain themselves through heaven's gate.

5

And surely when the after age
Shall hither come in pilgrimage,
These sacred places to adore,
By Vere[4] and Fairfax trod before,
Men will dispute how their extent
Within such dwarfish confines went:
And some will smile at this, as well
As Romulus his bee-like cell.[5]

6

Humility alone designs
Those short but admirable lines,
By which, ungirt and unconstrained,
Things greater are in less contained.
Let others vainly strive t'immure° *enclose*
The circle in the quadrature!
These holy mathematics can
In ev'ry figure equal man.[6]

7

Yet thus the laden house does sweat,
And scarce endures the Master great:
But where he comes the swelling hall

3. The builders of the Tower of Babel failed in their attempt to make it reach heaven.
4. Lady Fairfax.
5. Romulus, founder of Rome, was said to have lived in a small hut.
6. The circle symbolized perfection, and the square symbolized virtue and justice.

Stirs, and the square grows spherical;
More by his magnitude distressed,
Then he is by its straitness pressed:
And too officiously it slights
That in itself which him delights.

8

So honor better lowness bears,
Than that unwonted greatness wears:
Height with a certain grace does bend,
But low things clownishly ascend.
And yet what needs there here excuse,
Where everything does answer use?
Where neatness nothing can condemn,
Nor pride invent what to contemn?

9

A stately frontispiece of poor
Adorns without the open door:[7]
Nor less the rooms within commends
Daily new furniture of friends.
The house was built upon the place
Only as for a mark of grace;
And for an inn to entertain
Its lord a while, but not remain.

* * *

37

When in the east the morning ray
Hangs out the colors of the day,
The bee through these known alleys hums,
Beating the *dian*° with its drums. *morning call*
Then flowers their drowsy eyelids raise,
Their silken ensigns° each displays, *banners*
And dries its pan[8] yet dank with dew,
And fills its flask[9] with odors new.

38

These, as their governor goes by,
In fragrant volleys they let fly;
And to salute their governess
Again as great a charge they press:
None for the virgin nymph;[1] for she
Seems with the flowers a flower to be.
And think so still! though not compare
With breath so sweet, or cheek so fair.

39

Well shot ye firemen! Oh how sweet,
And round your equal fires do meet,

7. The poor waiting to receive alms.
8. Part of the musket lock.
9. Powder flask.

1. Mary Fairfax, Lord Fairfax's daughter, whom Marvell was tutoring. She was between 12 and 14 at the time of the poem.

Whose shrill report no ear can tell,
But echoes to the eye and smell.
See how the flowers, as at parade,
Under their colors stand displayed:
Each regiment in order grows,
That of the tulip, pink, and rose.

40

But when the vigilant patrol
Of stars walks round about the Pole,
Their leaves, that to the stalks are curled,
Seem to their staves the ensigns furled.
Then in some flower's belovèd hut
Each bee as sentinel is shut;
And sleeps so too: but, if once stirred,
She runs you through, or asks the word.

41

Oh thou, that dear and happy isle
The garden of the world ere while,
Thou paradise of four seas,
Which heaven planted us to please,
But, to exclude the world, did guard
With watery if not flaming sword;
What luckless apple did we taste,
To make us mortal, and thee waste?

42

Unhappy! shall we never more
That sweet militia restore,
When gardens only had their towers,
And all the garrisons were flowers,
When roses only arms might bear,
And men did rosy garlands wear?
Tulips, in several colors barred,
Were then the Switzers of our Guard.[2]

43

The gardener had the soldier's place,
And his more gentle forts did trace.
The nursery of all things green
Was then the only magazine.° *storehouse*
The winter quarters were the stoves,
Where he the tender plants removes.
But war all this doth overgrow;
We ordnance° plant and powder sow. *artillery*

44

And yet their walks one on the sod
Who, had it pleasèd him and God,
Might once have made our gardens spring

2. A reference to the black, yellow, and red stripes of the papal Swiss guards.

Fresh as his own and flourishing.
But he preferred to the Cinque Ports[3]
These five imaginary forts:
And, in those half-dry trenches, spanned° *held in*
Power which the ocean might command.

45

For he did, with his utmost skill,
Ambition weed, but conscience till.
Conscience, that heaven-nursèd plant,
Which most our earthly gardens want.
A prickling leaf it bears, and such
As that which shrinks at every touch;
But flowers eternal, and divine,
That in the crowns of saints do shine.

46

The sight does from these bastions ply,
Th' invisible artillery;
And at proud Cawood Castle[4] seems
To point the battery of its beams.
As if it quarreled° in the seat *criticized*
Th' ambition of its prelate great.
But o'er the meads below it plays,
Or innocently seems to gaze.

47

And now to the abyss I pass
Of that unfathomable grass,
Where men like grasshoppers appear,
But grasshoppers are giants there:
They, in their squeaking laugh, contemn° *scorn*
Us as we walk more low than them:
And, from the precipices tall
Of the green spires, to us do call.

48

To see men through this meadow dive,
We wonder how they rise alive.
As, under water, none does know
Whether he fall through it or go.
But, as the mariners that sound,
And show upon their lead the ground,
They bring up flowers so to be seen,
And prove they've at the bottom been.

49

No scene that turns with engines strange
Does oft'ner then these meadows change.
For when the sun the grass hath vexed,
The tawny mowers enter next;

3. Five ports on the southeast coast of England.

4. Estate of the Archbishop of York.

Who seem like Israelites to be,
Walking on foot through a green sea.[5]
To them the grassy deeps divide,
And crowd a lane to either side.[6]

* * *

71

Thus I, easy philosopher,
Among the birds and trees confer:
And little now to make me wants
Or of the fowls, or of the plants.
Give me but wings as they, and I
Straight floating on the air shall fly:
Or turn me but, and you shall see
I was but an inverted tree.

72

Already I begin to call
In their most learned original:
And where I language want, my signs
The bird upon the bough divines;
And more attentive there doth sit
Than if she were with lime-twigs knit.
No leaf does tremble in the wind
Which I, returning, cannot find.

73

Out of these scattered sibyl's leaves[7]
Strange prophecies my fancy weaves:
And in one history consumes,
Like Mexique paintings, all the plumes.[8]
What Rome, Greece, Palestine, ere said
I in this light mosaic read.
Thrice happy he who, not mistook,
Hath read in Nature's mystic book.

74

And see how chance's better wit
Could with a mask my studies hit!
The oak leaves me embroider all,
Between which caterpillars crawl:
And ivy, with familiar trails,
Me licks, and clasps, and curls, and hales.
Under this antic° cope I move *fantastic*
Like some great prelate° of the grove. *bishop*

75

Then, languishing with ease, I toss
On pallets swoll'n of velvet moss;
While the wind, cooling through the boughs,

5. An allusion to the parting of the Red Sea in Exodus 14.21–31.
6. Create a crowd on either side to form a lane.
7. The Cumaean Sibyl was a prophetess who recorded her predictions on leaves.
8. Feathers used to form "Mexique paintings."

Flatters with air my panting brows.
Thanks for my rest, ye mossy banks,
And unto you cool zephyrs,° thanks, *mild west winds*
Who, as my hair, my thoughts too shed,
And winnow from the chaff my head.

76

How safe, methinks, and strong, behind
These trees have I encamped my mind;
Where beauty, aiming at the heart,
Bends in some tree its useless dart;
And where the world no certain shot
Can make, or me it toucheth not.
But I on it securely play,
And gall its horsemen all the day.

77

Bind me, ye woodbines, in your twines,
Curl me about, ye gadding vines,
And, oh, so close your circles lace,
That I may never leave this place:
But, lest your fetters prove too weak,
Ere I your silken bondage break,
Do you, O brambles, chain me too,
And courteous briars, nail me through.

78

Here in the morning tie my chain,
Where the two woods have made a lane;
While, like a guard on either side,
The trees before their Lord divide;
This, like a long and equal thread,
Betwixt two labyrinths does lead.
But, where the floods did lately drown,
There at the evening stake me down.

79

For now the waves are fallen and dried,
And now the meadows fresher dyed;
Whose grass, with moister color dashed,
Seems as green silks but newly washed.
No serpent new nor crocodile
Remains behind our little Nile;
Unless itself you will mistake,
Among these meads the only snake.

80

See in what wanton harmless folds
It everywhere the meadow holds;
And its yet muddy back doth lick,
Till as a crystal mirror slick;
Where all things gaze themselves, and doubt
If they be in it or without.

And for his shade which therein shines,
Narcissus-like, the sun too pines.[9]

81

Oh what a pleasure 'tis to hedge
My temples here with heavy sedge;
Abandoning my lazy side,
Stretched as a bank unto the tide;
Or to suspend my sliding foot
On the osier's° undermined root, *willow's*
And in its branches tough to hang,
While at my lines the fishes twang!

82

But now away my hooks, my quills,
And angles, idle utensils.
The young Maria[1] walks tonight:
Hide trifling youth thy pleasures slight.
'Twere shame that such judicious eyes
Should with such toys a man surprise;
She that already is the law
Of all her sex, her age's awe.

83

See how loose Nature, in respect
To her, itself doth recollect;
And every thing so whisht° and fine, *silent*
Starts forth with to its *bonne mine*.[2]
The sun himself, of her aware,
Seems to descend with greater care;
And lest she see him go to bed,
In blushing clouds conceals his head.

84

So when the shadows laid asleep
From underneath these banks do creep,
And on the river as it flows
With eben shuts° begin to close; *black shutters*
The modest halcyon° comes in sight, *kingfisher*
Flying betwixt the day and night;
And such an horror calm and dumb,
Admiring Nature does benumb.

85

The viscous air, wheres'e'er she fly,
Follows and sucks her azure dye;
The jellying stream compacts below,
If it might fix her shadow so;
The stupid fishes hang, as plain
As flies in crystal overta'en;
And men the silent scene assist,
Charmed with the sapphire-wingèd mist.

9. Narcissus fell in love with his own reflection in the water and, in pining for it, was turned into a flower.

1. Mary Fairfax.

2. Good appearance.

86

Maria such, and so doth hush
The world, and through the evening rush.
No new-born comet such a train
Draws through the sky, nor star new-slain.[3]
For straight those giddy rockets fail,
Which from the putrid earth exhale,
But by her flames, in heaven tried,
Nature is wholly vitrified.° *converted into glass*

87

'Tis she that to these gardens gave
That wondrous beauty which they have;
She straightness on the woods bestows;
To her the meadow sweetness owes;
Nothing could make the river be
So crystal pure but only she;
She yet more pure, sweet, straight, and fair,
Than gardens, woods, meads, rivers are.

88

Therefore what first she on them spent,
They gratefully again present:
The meadow, carpets where to tread;
The garden, flowers to crown her head;
And for a glass the limpid brook,
Where she may all her beauties look;
But, since she would not have them seen,
The wood about her draws a screen.

89

For she, to higher beauties raised,
Disdains to be for lesser praised.
She counts her beauty to converse
In all the languages as hers;
Nor yet in those herself employs
But for the wisdom, not the noise;
Nor yet that wisdom would affect,
But as 'tis heaven's dialect.

90

Blessed nymph! that couldst so soon prevent
Those trains by youth against thee meant;
Tears (watery shot that pierce the mind;)
And sighs (Love's cannon charg'd with wind;)
True praise (that breaks through all defense;)
And feigned complying innocence;
But knowing where this ambush lay,
She 'scaped the safe, but roughest way.

91

This 'tis to have been from the first
In a domestic heaven nursed,
Under the discipline severe

3. A shooting star.

Of Fairfax, and the starry Vere;
Where not one object can come nigh
But pure, and spotless as the eye;
And goodness doth itself entail
On females, if there want a male.

92

Go now fond sex that on your face
Do all your useless study place,
Nor once at vice your brows dare knit
Lest the smooth forehead wrinkled sit:
Yet your own face shall at you grin,
Thorough the black-bag of your skin;
When knowledge only could have filled
And virtue all those furrows tilled.

93

Hence she with graces more divine
Supplies beyond her sex the line;
And, like a sprig of mistletoe,
On the Fairfacian oak does grow;
Whence, for some universal good,
The priest shall cut the sacred bud;
While her glad parents most rejoice,
And make their destiny their choice.

94

Meantime, ye fields, springs, bushes, flowers,
Where yet she leads her studious hours,
(Till fate her worthily translates,
And find a Fairfax for our Thwaites)[4]
Employ the means you have by her,
And in your kind yourselves prefer;
That, as all virgins she precedes,
So you all woods, streams, gardens, meads.

95

For you Thessalian Tempe's Seat[5]
Shall now be scorned as obsolete;
Aranjuez, as less, disdain'd;
The Bel-Retiro as constrain'd;[6]
But name not the Idalian grove,[7]
For 'twas the seat of wanton love;
Much less the dead's Elysian Fields,
Yet nor to them your beauty yields.

96

'Tis not, what once it was, the world;
But a rude heap together hurled;
All negligently overthrown,
Gulfs, deserts, precipices, stone.
Your lesser world contains the same.
But in more decent order tame;

4. Piece of forest or waste land that has been cleared; also a surname.
5. A vale in Thessaly that was celebrated as a place of pleasure and love.
6. Spanish palaces known for their gardens.
7. Cyprus, a haunt of Venus.

You heaven's center, Nature's lap.
And paradise's only map.

97

But now the salmon-fishers moist
Their leathern boats begin to hoist;
And, like Antipodes in shoes,[8]
Have shod their heads in their canoes.
How tortoise-like, but not so slow,
These rational amphibii[9] go?
Let's in: for the dark hemisphere
Does now like one of them appear.

An Horatian Ode Upon Cromwell's Return from Ireland[1]

The forward youth that would appear
Must now forsake his muses dear,
Nor in the shadows sing
His numbers[2] languishing.
'Tis time to leave the books in dust,
And oil th' unusèd armor's rust:
Removing from the wall
The corslet[3] of the hall.
So restless Cromwell could not cease
In the inglorious arts of peace,
But through adventurous war
Urgèd his active star.
And, like the three-forked lightning, first
Breaking the clouds where it was nursed,
Did thorough his own side
His fiery way divide:[4]
For 'tis all one to courage high
The emulous or enemy;
And with such to enclose
Is more than to oppose.
Then burning through the air he went,
And palaces and temples rent:
And Caesar's head at last
Did through his laurels blast.[5]
'Tis madness to resist or blame
The force of angry heaven's flame:
And, if we would speak true,
Much to the man is due,
Who, from his private gardens, where
He lived reservèd and austere,

8. Like those who dwell on the opposite side of the earth.
9. The salmon fishers are amphibii because they move on both land and water.
1. Cromwell returned from his military campaign in Ireland in May 1650. After General Fairfax resigned as commander of the parliamentary army because he refused to invade Scotland, Cromwell assumed his position and attacked the Scots. This poem was printed in the 1681 edition but then was canceled from printed copies until 1776. The influence of Horace's *Odes* (especially I. 35, 37; IV. 4, 5, 14, 15) surfaces in the poised dignity of the verse and its subtly ambiguous attitude toward power.
2. Conformity to a rhythmical pattern in verse or music.
3. Defensive armor covering the upper body.
4. Cromwell's overtaking his rivals in Parliament is described as an elemental force similar to the "three-forked lightning" of Zeus.
5. Although lightning was thought not to strike the laurel (symbolizing the royal crown), Cromwell had struck down Charles I (Caesar).

As if his highest plot
To plant the bergamot,[6]
Could by industrious valor climb
To ruin the great work of Time,
And cast the kingdom old
Into another mold;
Though justice against fate complain,
And plead the ancient rights in vain:
But those do hold or break,
As men are strong or weak.
Nature, that hateth emptiness,
Allows of penetration less:[7]
And therefore must make room
Where greater spirits come.
What field of all the Civil Wars,
Where his were not the deepest scars?
And Hampton[8] shows what part
He had of wiser art,
Where, twining subtle fears with hope,
He wove a net of such a scope,
That Charles himself might chase
To Carisbrooke's narrow case:
That thence the royal actor borne,
The tragic scaffold might adorn;
While round the armèd bands
Did clap their bloody hands.
He nothing common did or mean
Upon that memorable scene:
But with his keener eye
The axe's[9] edge did try;
Nor called the gods with vulgar spite
To vindicate his helpless right,
But bowed his comely head,
Down, as upon a bed.
This was that memorable hour
Which first assured the forcèd power.
So when they did design
The Capitol's first line,
A bleeding head where they begun,
Did fright the architects to run;
And yet in that the State
Foresaw it's happy fate.[1]
And now the Irish are ashamed
To see themselves in one year tamed:[2]

6. A pear known as the "prince's pear."
7. Nature abhors not only a vacuum but even more so the penetration of one body's space by another body.
8. Hampton Court where Charles I was held captive before his execution in 1649. He had fled to Carrisbrooke Castle on the Isle of Wight, where he was betrayed to the Governor in 1647.
9. Marvell plays on the Latin "*acies*," the sharp edge of a sword, a keen glance, and the vanguard of battle.

1. In digging the foundations of the temple of Jupiter Capitolinum, the excavators found a human's head (*caput*), which was interpreted as prophesying that Rome should be the capitol of the Empire (see Livy, *Annals* I.55.6).
2. From August 1649 to his return to England in May 1650, Cromwell went on a savage military campaign that included the slaughter of Irish civilians.

So much one man can do,
That does both act and know.
They can affirm his praises best,
And have, though overcome, confessed
How good he is, how just,
And fit for highest trust.[3]
Nor yet grown stiffer with command,
But still in the Republic's hand:
How fit he is to sway
That can so well obey.[4]
He to the commons' feet presents
A kingdom, for his first year's rents:
And, what he may, forbears
His fame to make it theirs:
And has his sword and spoils ungirt,
To lay them at the public's skirt.
So when the falcon high
Falls heavy from the sky,
She, having killed, no more does search,
But on the next green bough to perch;
Where, when he first does lure,
The falconer has her sure.
What may not then our isle presume
While victory his crest does plume!
What may not others fear
If thus he crown each year!
A Caesar he ere long to Gaul,
To Italy an Hannibal,[5]
And to all states not free
Shall climactéric° be. *period of change*
The Pict no shelter now shall find
Within his particolored mind;
But from this valor sad° *severe*
Shrink underneath the plaid;[6]
Happy if in the tufted brake
The English hunter him mistake;
Nor lay his hounds in near
The Caledonian° deer. *Scottish*
But thou the wars' and fortune's son
March indefatigably on;
And for the last effect
Still keep thy sword erect:
Besides the force it has to fright
The spirits of the shady night,[7]
The same arts that did gain
A power must it maintain.

3. An example of one of the many equivocal statements in this poem; of course, the Irish did not affirm Cromwell's greatness.

4. A saying attributed to the Athenian Solon the lawgiver.

5. Neither Caesar nor Hannibal gave freedom to peoples whose countries they invaded and conquered.

6. Marvell uses "Picts" the ancient name for the Scots, creating a play on *picti* (Latin: painted) and particolored.

7. There was an ancient tradition of dead spirits being frightened by raised swords (Homer, *Odyssey* 11; Virgil, *Aeneid* 6). The dead spirits referred to here include the dead in the wars in Ireland and England, including the king.

Katherine Philips

1631–1664

Idolized as the "Matchless Orinda" in her own day, Katherine Philips is now taking her place in the history of English verse after two centuries of neglect. During her lifetime, her work circulated in manuscript among a close network of friends. The first edition of her poems appeared posthumously in 1664. The second edition of 1667 was evidently a commercial success, since it was reprinted in 1669, 1678, and 1710. The next complete edition of her poems did not appear until 1994.

John Keats esteemed Philips's *To Mrs. Mary Awbrey at Parting* as an example of "real feminine Modesty"; today, by contrast, critics praise her poems to women friends as reminiscent of the ancient Greek Sappho's erotic lyrics. By imitating Donne's love lyrics in her poems to women, Philips poetically conceives of these friendships as no less world-changing, no less ennobling and enthralling, than Donne's romantic liaisons. Some of the best poets of her own day were able to appreciate her as a fellow poet rather than as Keats's romanticized ideal woman. Marvell paid tribute to her by subtly alluding to lines of her poetry in one of his greatest poems, *The Garden*. And Henry Vaughan insisted that "No laurel grows, but for [her] brow."

Katherine Philips's work was particularly important for other women writers. Philips's lyric poetry influenced such other early modern women poets as Aphra Behn and Anne Killigrew. Yet it is impossible to pigeonhole Philips as stereotypically feminine. She wrote on public and political themes as well as personal subjects, endowing traditional genres such as the parting poem, the elegy, and the epitaph, with a particular directness and clarity all her own.

Katherine Philips was born in London to a well-to-do Presbyterian family. Her father was a prosperous merchant, and her mother was the daughter of a Fellow of the Royal College of Physicians. Philips's father was wealthy enough to invest two hundred pounds for a thousand acres in Ulster, a scheme that was begun in 1642 by the Puritan Parliament but, ironically, not realized until the Restoration, when we find Katherine in Ireland pursuing lawsuits to obtain this land. As a girl, Katherine attended Mrs. Salmon's Presbyterian School, where she learned to love poetry and began to write verses. In 1646 her widowed mother married Sir Richard Philips, and the family moved to his castle in Wales. Philips herself married Sir Richard's kinsman James Philips, and they lived together for twelve years in the small Welsh town of Cardigan when not in London, where her husband served as Member of Parliament during the Interregnum.

However Presbyterian and Cromwellian were the associations of her family and marriage, she emerged after the Restoration as a complete Anglican. Not only did she write poetry against the regicide, such as *Upon the Double Murder of King Charles*, but she became a favorite author at court. She was encouraged to write poetry by her friend "Poliarchus," Sir Charles Cotterell, Master of Ceremonies in the Court of Charles II, who showed her poems to the royal family. An Anglo-Irish nobleman, the Earl of Orrery, encouraged her to complete a translation of Corneille's *Pompey* and actually produced and had the play printed in Dublin in 1663.

Katherine Philips developed friendships that became the theme of what most critics regard as her best poems. Perhaps the most intense of these friendships was that with Mrs. Anne Owen, the Lucasia of Philips's most passionate poems, several of which echo love poems by Donne. Her friend Sir Edward Dering, whom she called "the Noble Silvander," lamented Katherine Philips's death in recounting the extraordinary accomplishment of both her poetry and her life, which had attempted

> the most generous design . . . to unite all those of her acquaintance which she found worthy or desired to make so (among which later number she was pleased to give me a place)

into one society, and by the bands of friendship to make an alliance more firm than what nature, our country or equal education can produce.

Friendship in Emblem,
or the Seal,[1]

TO MY DEAREST LUCASIA[2]

The hearts thus intermixèd speak
A love that no bold shock can break;
For joined and growing, both in one,
Neither can be disturbed alone.

That means a mutual knowledge too;
For what is't either heart can do,
Which by its panting sentinel° *guard*
It does not to the other tell?

That friendship hearts so much refines,
It nothing but itself designs:
The hearts are free from lower ends,
For each point to the other tends.

They flame, 'tis true, and several ways,
But still those flames do so much raise,
That while to either they incline
They yet are noble and divine.

From smoke or hurt those flames are free,
From grossness or mortality:
The hearts (like Moses bush presumed)[3]
Warmed and enlightened, not consumed.

The compasses that stand above
Express this great immortal Love;[4]
For friends, like them, can prove this true,
They are, and yet they are not, two.

And in their posture is expressed
Friendship's exalted interest:
Each follows where the other leans,
And what each does, the other means.

And as when one foot does stand fast,
And t'other circles seeks to cast,
The steady part does regulate
And make the wanderer's motion straight:

1. A symbolic picture, which appeared with a motto and a poem in such books as Whitney's *Choice of Emblems* (see Perspectives: Emblem, Style, and Metaphor). The central emblematic image of this poem is "the compasses" (line 21); another emblem is "those flames" (line 14).
2. Anne Owen, to whom many of Philips's poems are dedicated, was a neighbor of hers in Wales and a close friend from 1651 until Philips's death.
3. See Exodus 3.2–5 for the burning bush through which the angel of the Lord appeared to and from which God called Moses.
4. Compare the image of the compasses here to the "twin compasses" in Donne's *A Valediction: Forbidding Mourning*, pages 1559–1560.

So friends are only two in this,
T'reclaim each other when they miss:
For whose'er will grossly fall,
Can never be a friend at all.

And as that useful instrument
For even lines was ever meant;
So friendship from good angels[5] springs,
To teach the world heroic things.

As these are found out in design
To rule and measure every line;
So friendship governs actions best,
Prescribing law to all the rest.

And as in nature nothing's set
So just as lines and numbers met;
So compasses for these being made,
Do friendship's harmony persuade.

And like to them, so friends may own
Extension, not division:
Their points, like bodies, separate;
But head, like souls, knows no such fate.

And as each part so well is knit,
That their embraces ever fit:
So friends are such by destiny,
And no third can the place supply.

There needs no motto to the seal:
But that we may the mine[6] reveal
To the dull eye, it was thought fit
That friendship only should be writ.

But as there is degrees of bliss,
So there's no friendship meant by this,
But such as will transmit to fame
Lucasia's and Orinda's name.

Upon the Double Murder of King Charles

in Answer to a Libelous Rhyme Made by V. P.[1]

I think not on the state, nor am concerned
Which way soever that great helm is turned,
But as that son whose father's danger nigh
Did force his native dumbness, and untie
The fettered organs: so here is a cause

5. Guardian spirits, with puns on angels, and *angeli* (Latin), messengers.

6. A mass of gold, a store of plenty, as well as a pun on the possessive pronoun meaning "my own" and perhaps also on "mind."

1. Vavasor Powell, a Fifth Monarchist who believed that Christ's second coming was imminent, and an ardent Republican, whose verses on the murder of the king are lost. According to Philips's poem, Powell argued that Charles I had usurped God's power.

That will excuse the breach of nature's laws.[2]
Silence were now a sin: nay passion now
Wise men themselves for merit would allow.
What noble eye could see, (and careless pass)
The dying lion kicked by every ass?
Hath Charles so broke God's laws, he must not have
A quiet crown, nor yet a quiet grave?
Tombs have been sanctuaries; thieves lie here
Secure from all their penalty and fear.
Great Charles his double misery was this,
Unfaithful friends, ignoble enemies;
Had any heathen been this prince's foe,
He would have wept to see him injured so.
His title was his crime, they'd reason good
To quarrel at the right they had withstood.
He broke God's laws, and therefore he must die,
And what shall then become of thee and I?
Slander must follow treason; but yet stay,
Take not our reason with our king away.
Though you have seized upon all our defense,
Yet do not sequester° our common sense. *excommunicate, confiscate*
But I admire not at this new supply:
No bounds will hold those who at scepters fly.
Christ will be King, but I ne'er understood,
His subjects built his kingdom up with blood,
(Except their own) or that he would dispense
With his commands, though for his own defense.
Oh! to what height of horror are they come,
Who dare pull down a crown, tear up a tomb![3]

On the Third of September, 1651[1]

As when the glorious magazine of light[2]
Approaches to his canopy of night,
He with new splendor clothes his dying rays,
And double brightness to his beams conveys;
As if to brave and check his ending fate,
Puts on his highest looks in 's lowest state;
Dressed in such terror as to make us all
Be anti-Persians,[3] and adore his fall;
Then quits the world, depriving it of day,
While every herb and plant does droop away:
So when our gasping English royalty
Perceived her period now was drawing nigh,
She summons her whole strength to give one blow,

2. Breaking the prohibition against women speaking on public affairs. See Margaret Tyler, Perspectives: Tracts on Women and Gender, page 1334, for a defense of woman's ability to write about war, traditionally considered only appropriate to male authors.
3. Possibly a reference to the unearthing of the regicides' bodies.

1. Cromwell defeated Charles II at the Battle of Worcester on this date.
2. The sun; a magazine is a storehouse for gunpowder.
3. Anti-sun, since the Persians were thought to worship the sun, and anti-monarchist, possibly with reference to Darius I, the Persian king who put down many revolts during his lifetime.

To raise her self, or pull down others too.
Big with revenge and hope, she now spake more
Of terror than in many months before;
And musters her attendants, or to save
Her from, or wait upon her to the grave:
Yet but enjoyed the miserable fate
Of setting majesty, to die in state.
   Unhappy Kings! who cannot keep a throne,
Nor be so fortunate to fall alone!
Their weight sinks others: Pompey could not fly,
But half the world must bear him company;[4]
Thus captive Sampson could not life conclude,
Unless attended with a multitude.[5]
Who'd trust to greatness now, whose food is air,
Whose ruin sudden, and whose end despair?
Who would presume upon his glorious birth,
Or quarrel for a spacious share of earth,
That sees such diadems° become thus cheap, *crowns*
And heroes tumble in the common heap?
   O! give me virtue then, which sums up all,
And firmly stands when crowns and scepters fall.

To the Truly Noble, and Obliging Mrs. Anne Owen *(on My First Approaches)*[1]

Madam,
As in a triumph conquerors admit
Their meanest captives to attend on it,[2]
Who, though unworthy, have the power confessed,
And justified the yielding of the rest:
So when the busy world (in hope t'excuse
Their own surprise) your conquests do peruse,
And find my name, they will be apt to say
Your charms were blinded, or else thrown away.
There is no honor got in gaining me,
Who am a prize not worth your victory.
But this will clear you, that 'tis general
The worst applaud what is admired by all.
But I have plots in't: for the way to be
Secure of fame to all posterity,
Is to obtain the honor I pursue,
To tell the world I was subdued by you.
And since in you all wonders common are,
Your votaries° may in your virtues share, *devoted admirers*
While you by noble magic worth impart:

4. Caesar defeated Pompey at the battle of Pharsalus, where 15,000 of Pompey's men were killed. Afterward, Pompey fled to Egypt, where he was assassinated.

5. The blind Israelite hero Sampson tore down the temple at Gaza, thus killing both himself and his enemies (Judges 16).

1. Mrs. Anne Owen of Orielton, Wales, was Philips's close friend and the Lucasia of her poems; she was married to John Owen and was the heiress to the ancient seat of Presaddfed in Anglesey.

2. Here, "triumph" means military victory and the triumphal procession that announced it.

She that can conquer, can reclaim a heart.
Of this creation I shall not despair,
Since for your own sake it concerns your care:
For 'tis more honor that the world should know
You made a noble soul, than found it so.

To Mrs. Mary Awbrey at Parting[1]

I have examined, and do find,
  Of all that favor me,
There's none I grieve to leave behind
  But only, only thee.
To part with thee I needs must die,
Could parting separate thee and I.

But neither chance nor compliment
  Did element our love;
'Twas sacred sympathy was lent
  Us from the choir above.
That friendship fortune did create,
Which fears a wound from time or fate.

Our changed and mingled souls are grown
  To such acquaintance now,
That if each would assume their own,
  Alas! we know not how.
We have each other so engrossed,
That each is in the union lost.

And thus we can no absence know,
  Nor shall we be confined;
Our active souls will daily go
  To learn each other's mind.
Nay, should we never meet to sense,
Our souls would hold intelligence.[2]

Inspired with a flame divine,
  I scorn to court a stay;
For from the noble soul of thine
  I can ne'er be away.
But I shall weep when thou dost grieve;
Nor can I die whilst thou dost live.

By my own temper I shall guess
  At thy felicity,
And only like my happiness
  Because it pleaseth thee.
Our hearts at any time will tell
If thou, or I, be sick, or well.

1. Mrs. Mary Awbrey, one of Philips's classmates at Mrs. Salmon's school. Quoting the entire poem, John Keats praises it as an example of "real feminine Modesty" in a letter to J. H. Reynolds of 21 September 1817.

2. A Neoplatonic idea, that the souls would know each other not by physical contact but by spiritual communion. Compare Donne's *A Valediction: Forbidding Mourning*, pages 1559–1560.

All honor sure I must pretend,
  All that is good or great;
She that would be Rosania's[3] friend,
  Must be at least complete.
If I have any bravery,
'Tis cause I am so much of thee.

Thy leiger° soul in me shall lie, *lighter*
  And all thy thoughts reveal;
Then back again with mine shall fly,
  And thence to me shall steal.
Thus still to one another tend;
Such is the sacred name of friend.

Thus our twin souls in one shall grow,
  And teach the world new love;
Redeem the age and sex, and show
  A flame fate dares not move:
And courting death to be our friend,
Our lives together too shall end.

A dew shall dwell upon our tomb
  Of such a quality,
That fighting armies, thither come,
  Shall reconciled be.
We'll ask no epitaph, but say
  Orinda and Rosania.

To My Excellent Lucasia, on Our Friendship.

17th. July 1651[1]

I did not live until this time
  Crowned my felicity,
When I could say without a crime,
  I am not thine, but thee.
This carcass breathed, and walked, and slept,
  So that the world believed
There was a soul the motions kept;
  But they were all deceived.
For as a watch by art is wound
  To motion, such was mine:
But never had Orinda found
  A soul till she found thine;
Which now inspires, cures and supplies,
  And guides my darkened breast:
For thou art all that I can prize,
  My joy, my life, my rest.
Nor bridegroom's nor crowned conqueror's mirth
  To mine compared can be:

3. Rosania was the poetic name that Philips gave to her friend Mary Awbrey.

1. Philips met her friend Anne Owen (called Lucasia) in 1651.

They have but pieces of this earth,
I've all the world in thee.
Then let our flame still light and shine,
(And no bold fear control)
As innocent as our design,
Immortal as our soul.

The World

We falsely think it due unto our friends,
That we should grieve for their too early ends:
He that surveys the world with serious eyes,
And strips her from her gross and weak disguise,[1]
Shall find 'tis injury to mourn their fate;
He only dies untimely who dies late.
For if 'twere told to children in the womb,
To what a stage of mischief they must come;
Could they foresee with how much toil and sweat
Men court that gilded nothing, being great;
What pains they take not to be what they seem,
Rating their bliss by others' false esteem,
And sacrificing their content, to be
Guilty of grave and serious vanity;
How each condition hath its proper thorns,
And what one man admires, another scorns;
How frequently their happiness they miss,
And so far from agreeing what it is,
That the same person we can hardly find,
Who is an hour together in a mind;
Sure they would beg a period of their breath,
And what we call their birth would count their death.
Mankind is mad; for none can live alone,
Because their joys stand by comparison:
And yet they quarrel at society,
And strive to kill they know not whom, nor why.
We all live by mistake, delight in dreams,
Lost to ourselves, and dwelling in extremes;
Rejecting what we have, though ne'er so good,
And prizing what we never understood.
Compared to our boisterous inconstancy
Tempests are calm, and discords harmony.
Hence we reverse the world, and yet do find
The God that made can hardly please our mind.
We live by chance, and slip into events;
Have all of beasts except their innocence.
The soul, which no man's power can reach, a thing
That makes each woman man, each man a king,
Doth so much loose, and from its height so fall,
That some contend to have no soul at all.

1. The Platonic notion that the body is a covering for the soul.

'Tis either not observed, or at the best
By passion fought withall, by sin depressed.
Freedom of will (God's image) is forgot;
And if we know it, we improve it not.
Our thoughts, though nothing can be more our own,
Are still unguided, very seldom known.
Time 'scapes our hands as water in a sieve,
We come to die ere we begin to live.
Truth, the most suitable and noble prize,
Food of our spirits, yet neglected lies.
Errors and shadows are our choice, and we
Owe our perdition to our own decree.
If we search truth, we make it more obscure;
And when it shines, we can't the light endure.
For most men who plod on, and eat, and drink,
Have nothing less their business than to think;
And those few that enquire, how small a share
Of truth they find! how dark their notions are!
That serious evenness that calms the breast,
And in a tempest can bestow a rest,
We either not attempt, or else decline,
By every trifle snatched from our design.
(Others he must in his deceits involve,
Who is not true unto his own resolve.)
We govern not ourselves, but loose the reins,
Courting our bondage to a thousand chains;
And with as many slaveries content,
As there are tyrants ready to torment,
We live upon a rack, extended still
To one extreme, or both, but always ill.
For since our fortune is not understood,
We suffer less from bad than from the good.
The sting is better dressed and longer lasts,
As surfeits are more dangerous than fasts.
And to complete the misery to us,
We see extremes are still contiguous.
And as we run so fast from what we hate,
Like squibs on ropes,[2] to know no middle state;
So (outward storms strengthened by us) we find
Our fortune as disordered as our mind.
But that's excused by this, it doth its part;
A treacherous world befits a treacherous heart.
All ill's our own; the outward storms we loathe
Receive from us their birth, or sting, or both;
And that our vanity be past a doubt,
'Tis one new vanity to find it out.
Happy are they to whom God gives a grave,
And from themselves as from his wrath doth save.
'Tis good not to be born; but if we must,
The next good is, soon to return to dust:

2. A display of fireworks on a line.

When th'uncaged[3] soul, fled to eternity,
Shall rest, and live, and sing, and love, and see.
Here we but crawl and grope, and play and cry;[4]
Are first our own, then other's enemy:
But there shall be defaced both stain and score,
For time, and death, and sin shall be no more.[5]

The Development of English Prose

In the seventeenth century, English prose developed as a major language for both popular and learned texts. Such English prose texts as the *Geneva Bible* and Foxe's *Book of Martyrs* had been the most widely read texts of the sixteenth century. The King James Bible of 1611 brought a balanced rhythm and memorable phrasing to the language of the Church of England that would influence the poetry of the age as well. Pamphlets, both humorous and political, were popular, and the prose romance produced an early version of the entertainment that would later become the novel. Although Latin continued to be the language of academic discourse, such great philosophers as Francis Bacon and Thomas Hobbes began to use English for intellectual inquiry into science, education, and political theory. Though many of his prose works were in Latin, Milton made English an impassioned and incisive language for public debate in such prose masterpieces as *Areopagitica*, on freedom of speech, and *Reason of Church Government*, in defense of the principles of the Puritan Revolution. Even enormously learned authors such as Robert Burton could become popular authors by writing in English. Burton's *Anatomy of Melancholy*, with its meandering sentences that seem strangely fanciful to today's reader, was read as a mixture of medicine, entertainment, politics, and therapy.

Burton uses the Ciceronian, or Asian, style, which competed with the Senecan, or Attic, style in the early modern period. The Ciceronian style was characterized by *copia* (abundance), pleonasm (elegant restatement), and hypotaxis (complex sentence structure full of subordinated clauses). In contrast, the Senecan style was marked by brevity, broken rhythms, and parataxis (clauses of equal importance, which resulted in either short or loosely organized sentences). Not all authors neatly followed one or the other style. Sir Thomas Browne, for example, fuses the two in his skeptical writing, which contrasts strongly with the utopianism of Bacon. In his *Essays*, Francis Bacon was one of the first to reject the strictly Ciceronian model. The three editions of this work show Bacon refining his style for greater clarity and precision, as he strove to make English a language that could describe the material world empirically and would emphasize thought rather than style. Indeed, Bacon created the concise style that would dominate English prose even into this century, as adopted by such writing handbooks as Strunk and White's *The Elements of Style*.

Francis Bacon

1561–1626

Commenting on his one and only lyric poem, an eleventh-hour political maneuver to help reconcile the rebellious Earl of Essex and the outraged Queen Elizabeth, Francis Bacon once wrote that he had to confess himself "not to be a poet." He was, however, a great essayist. In addition to being one of the most politically powerful men of his time, Bacon was one of the

3. Free from the body.
4. See 1 Corinthians 13.11–12.
5. See Revelation 21.4.

most powerful influences on the development of English prose style. He was a master of the terse and succinct Senecan style, if still an eclectic practitioner at times of the more elaborate Ciceronianism. Bacon was also a pioneer in scientific theory. When we think of such concepts as social progress through science or the scientific method for gathering exact empirical data, we are thinking of concepts that were promoted through the writing of Francis Bacon.

If Bacon was one of the most influential men in early modern England, he was also one of the most disgraced. Little did Bacon know at the time of his former patron Essex's trial for treason in 1601 that twenty years later, he would suffer his own political fall from grace. At age sixty, he had been in every Parliament since he entered the House of Commons at age twenty-three; he had held every important legal position in the kingdom—Solicitor General, Attorney General, and finally Lord Chancellor. Charged with bribery, Bacon was fined 40,000 pounds, disqualified from holding office, and sentenced to the Tower. Although he was released from these punishments, he spent the last five years of his life largely retired from the world of power and devoted to his writing.

Bacon was the first to use the word "essay" in English, a term from the French *essayer* (to try or attempt), coined by Michel de Montaigne in 1580 to describe his skeptical and introspective prose compositions. Bacon writes about topics that admit of more than one point of view, but his end is practical rather than speculative. Indeed, in the *Essays*, Bacon faults both Montaigne and the French in general for their lack of political effectiveness. The purpose of Bacon's *Essays* is more like that of Castiglione's *Courtier* or Machiavelli's *The Prince*. In a sense, all of these are how-to books, designed to instruct the reader in the political virtue of practical wisdom.

Bacon's *Essays* appeared in three different editions: 1597, 1612, and 1625. The first edition contained only ten essays and their style was extremely terse. He added forty-eight more essays in the later editions and revised the style of his earlier essays. Thinking that his Latin works would outlast those in English, Bacon translated the *Essays* into Latin. Bacon also wrote his major philosophical work in Latin; the *Novum Organum* (1620) was the basis for his new approach to the search for knowledge. At the same time, Bacon helped to make English a language capable of philosophical and scientific expression that would ultimately overtake Latin and help to promote the democratization of knowledge that he argued for in his *Advancement of Learning* (1605). Through his works, Bacon helped to define both the prose style and the ideology of modernity.

Of Truth[1]

"What is truth?" said jesting Pilate; and would not stay for an answer.[2] Certainly there be that delight in giddiness,[3] and count it a bondage to fix a belief; affecting free-will in thinking, as well as in acting. And though the sects of philosophers of that kind[4] be gone, yet there remain certain discoursing wits[5] which are of the same veins, though there be not so much blood in them as was in those of the ancients. But it is not only the difficulty and labor which men take in finding out of truth; nor again that when it is found it imposeth upon men's thoughts; that doth bring lies in favor; but a natural though corrupt love of the lie itself. One of the later school of the Grecians examineth the matter, and is at a stand[6] to think what should be in it, that men should love lies, where neither they make for pleasure, as with poets, nor for advantage, as with the merchant; but for the lie's sake. But I cannot tell: this same truth is a naked and open daylight, that doth not show the masks and mummeries and triumphs of the world half so stately and daintily as candle-lights. Truth may perhaps come to the price of a pearl, that showeth best by day; but it will not rise to the price of a diamond or carbuncle,[7] that showeth best in varied lights. A mixture of a

1. The first essay in the 1625 edition, from which all essays here, except the 1597 *Of Studies*, are taken.
2. According to John 18.38, Pilot dismissively asks Jesus this question during his trial.
3. Unsteadiness.
4. The ancient Greek Skeptics argued that there is no certain basis from which to know the truth.
5. Rationally arguing minds.
6. Is puzzled.
7. Ruby.

lie doth ever add pleasure. Doth any man doubt, that if there were taken out of men's minds vain opinions, flattering hopes, false valuations, imaginations as one would, and the like, but it would leave the minds of a number of men poor shrunken things, full of melancholy and indisposition, and unpleasing to themselves? One of the Fathers,[8] in great severity, called poesy *vinum daemonum*[9], because it filleth the imagination; and yet it is but with the shadow of a lie. But it is not the lie that passeth through the mind, but the lie that sinketh in and settleth in it, that doth the hurt, such as we spake of before. But howsoever these things are thus in men's depraved judgments and affections, yet truth, which only doth judge itself, teacheth that the inquiry of truth, which is the love-making or wooing of it, the knowledge of truth, which is the presence of it, and the belief of truth, which is the enjoying of it, is the sovereign good of human nature. The first creature of God, in the works of the days, was the light of the sense;[1] the last was the light of reason; and his sabbath work ever since, is the illumination of his Spirit. First he breathed light upon the face of the matter or chaos; then he breathed light into the face of man; and still he breatheth and inspireth light into the face of his chosen. The poet that beautified the sect that was otherwise inferior to the rest,[2] saith yet excellently well: "It is a pleasure to stand upon the shore, and to see ships tossed upon the sea; a pleasure to stand in the window of a castle, and to see a battle and the adventures thereof below; but no pleasure is comparable to the standing upon the vantage ground of truth" (a hill not to be commanded,[3] and where the air is always clear and serene), "and to see the errors, and wanderings, and mists, and tempests, in the vale below": so always that this prospect be with pity, and not with swelling or pride. Certainly, it is heaven upon earth, to have a man's mind move in charity, rest in providence, and turn upon the poles of truth.

To pass from theological and philosophical truth, to the truth of civil business, it will be acknowledged even by those that practise it not, that clear and round dealing is the honor of man's nature, and that mixture of falsehood is like allay in coin of gold and silver, which may make the metal work the better, but it embaseth it.[4] For these winding and crooked courses are the goings of the serpent;[5] which goeth basely upon the belly, and not upon the feet. There is no vice that doth so cover a man with shame as to be found false and perfidious. And therefore Montaigne saith prettily, when he inquired the reason, why the word of the lie should be such a disgrace and such an odious charge? Saith he, "If it be well weighed, to say that a man lieth, is as much to say as that he is brave towards God and a coward towards men."[6] For a lie faces God, and shrinks from man. Surely the wickedness of falsehood and breach of faith cannot possibly be so highly expressed, as in that it shall be the last peal to call the judgments of God upon the generations of men, it being foretold, that when Christ cometh, he shall not "find faith upon the earth."[7]

Of Marriage and Single Life

He that hath wife and children hath given hostages to fortune; for they are impediments to great enterprises, either of virtue or mischief. Certainly the best works, and of greatest merit for the public, have proceeded from the unmarried or childless men,

8. Early Christian theologians.
9. Devil's wine.
1. "And God said, Let there be light" (Genesis 1.3).
2. Bacon thought that the Epicurean belief that pleasure is the greatest good was inferior. See Lucretius, *On the Nature of Things* 2.1–13.
3. Captured.
4. Debases it.
5. The devil.
6. *Essays* 2.18.
7. Luke 18.8.

which both in affection and means have married and endowed the public. Yet it were great reason that those that have children should have greatest care of future times, unto which they know they must transmit their dearest pledges. Some there are, who though they lead a single life, yet their thoughts do end with themselves, and account future times impertinences.[1] Nay, there are some other that account wife and children but as bills of charges. Nay more, there are some foolish rich covetous men that take a pride in having no children, because they may be thought so much the richer. For perhaps they have heard some talk, "Such an one is a great rich man," and another except to it, "Yea, but he hath a great charge of children"; as if it were an abatement to his riches. But the most ordinary cause of a single life is liberty, especially in certain self-pleasing and humorous[2] minds, which are so sensible of every restraint, as they will go near to think their girdles and garters to be bonds and shackles. Unmarried men are best friends, best masters, best servants, but not always best subjects, for they are light to run away, and almost all fugitives are of that condition. A single life doth well with churchmen, for charity will hardly water the ground where it must first fill a pool. It is indifferent for judges and magistrates; for if they be facile[3] and corrupt, you shall have a servant five times worse than a wife. For soldiers, I find the generals commonly in their hortatives[4] put men in mind of their wives and children; and I think the despising of marriage amongst the Turks maketh the vulgar soldier more base. Certainly wife and children are a kind of discipline of humanity; and single men, though they may be many times more charitable, because their means are less exhaust,[5] yet, on the other side, they are more cruel and hardhearted (good to make severe inquisitors), because their tenderness is not so oft called upon. Grave natures, led by custom, and therefore constant, are commonly loving husbands, as was said of Ulysses, *vetulam suam praetulit immortalitati:*[6] Chaste women are often proud and froward,[7] as presuming upon the merit of their chastity. It is one of the best bonds both of chastity and obedience in the wife, if she think her husband wise, which she will never do if she find him jealous. Wives are young men's mistresses, companions for middle age, and old men's nurses. So as a man may have a quarrel[8] to marry when he will. But yet he was reputed one of the wise men, that made answer to the question, when a man should marry: "A young man not yet, an elder man not at all."[9] It is often seen that bad husbands have very good wives; whether it be that it raiseth the price of their husband's kindness when it comes, or that the wives take a pride in their patience. But this never fails, if the bad husbands were of their own choosing, against their friend's consent; for then they will be sure to make good their own folly.

Of Superstition

It were better to have no opinion of God at all, than such an opinion as is unworthy of him. For the one is unbelief, the other is contumely:[1] and certainly superstition is the reproach of the deity. Plutarch saith well to that purpose: "Surely" (saith he) "I had rather a great deal men should say there was no such man at all as Plutarch, than that they should say that there was one Plutarch that would eat his children as soon

1. Irrelevant matters.
2. Flighty.
3. Easily led.
4. Speeches to troops before battle.
5. Used up.
6. He preferred his old wife to immortality. See *Odyssey* 5 for the story of how Odysseus chose to return home to his wife and son and accept death rather than live forever with the nymph Calypso.
7. Perverse.
8. Excuse.
9. Quoting Thales, one of the sages—unmarried—of ancient Greece.

1. Contempt.

as they were born," as the poets speak of Saturn.[2] And as the contumely is greater towards God, so the danger is greater towards men. Atheism leaves a man to sense, to philosophy, to natural piety, to laws, to reputation, all which may be guides to an outward moral virtue, though religion were not; but superstition dismounts all these, and erecteth an absolute monarchy in the minds of men. Therefore atheism did never perturb states; for it makes men wary of themselves, as looking no further: and we see the times inclined to atheism (as the time of Augustus Caesar) were civil times.[3] But superstition hath been the confusion of many states, and bringeth in a new *primum mobile,* that ravisheth all the spheres of government.[4] The master of superstition is the people; and in all superstition wise men follow fools; and arguments are fitted to practice, in a reversed order. It was gravely said by some of the prelates in the council of Trent, where the doctrine of the schoolmen bare great sway, "that the schoolmen[5] were like astronomers, which did feign eccentrics and epicycles, and such engines of orbs, to save the phaenomena; though they knew there were no such things;"[6] and in like manner, that the schoolmen had framed a number of subtle and intricate axioms and theorems, to save the practice of the church. The causes of superstition are, pleasing and sensual rites and ceremonies; excess of outward and pharisaical holiness;[7] over-great reverence of traditions, which cannot but load the church; the stratagems of prelates for their own ambition and lucre; the favoring too much of good intentions, which openeth the gate to conceits[8] and novelties; the taking an aim at divine matters by human, which cannot but breed mixture of imaginations: and, lastly, barbarous times, especially joined with calamities and disasters. Superstition, without a veil, is a deformed thing; for as it addeth deformity to an ape to be so like a man, so the similitude of superstition to religion makes it the more deformed. And as wholesome meat corrupteth to little worms, so good forms and orders corrupt into a number of petty observances. There is a superstition in avoiding superstition, when men think to do best if they go furthest from the superstition formerly received; therefore care would be had that (as it fareth in ill purgings) the good be not taken away with the bad, which commonly is done when the people is the reformer.[9]

Of Plantations[1]

Plantations are amongst ancient, primitive, and heroical works. When the world was young it begat more children; but now it is old it begets fewer: for I may justly account new plantations to be the children of former kingdoms. I like a plantation in a pure soil; that is, where people are not displanted to the end to plant in others. For else it is rather an extirpation than a plantation.[2] Planting of countries is like planting of woods; for you must make account to leese[3] almost twenty years profit, and

2. Saturn, the Roman god of time, who ate his children. Bacon refers to Plutarch's *Of Superstition*.
3. The Roman emperor Augustus's rule was peaceful. Atheism, in the early modern period could describe any belief that was not Christian or that did not agree with one's own.
4. The *primum mobile* (prime mover) controlled the motions of the other spheres.
5. Medieval scholastic philosophers.
6. "To save the phenomena" means to account for appearances. Ptolemaic astronomy, based on the mistaken geocentric theory, had many inconsistencies to explain.
7. Like the Pharisees, an ancient Jewish sect, who stressed adherence to the letter of the law and believed that this proved their spiritual superiority.
8. Fanciful notions.
9. Bacon refers to the radically antiritualistic Puritans.
1. Settlements of farmers in colonized territory. Classical and Renaissance authors discussed the pros and cons of different methods of colonization, including both armed garrisons and plantations.
2. In the 17th century, plantations of Scotts Presbyterians in the North of Ireland and of the English in North America were established on land confiscated from native inhabitants.
3. Lose.

expect your recompense in the end. For the principal thing that hath been the destruction of most plantations hath been the base and hasty drawing of profit in the first years. It is true, speedy profit is not to be neglected, as far as may stand[4] with the good of the plantation, but no further. It is a shameful and unblessed thing to take the scum of people, and wicked condemned men, to be the people with whom you plant;[5] and not only so, but it spoileth the plantation, for they will ever live like rogues, and not fall to work, but be lazy, and do mischief, and spend victuals, and be quickly weary, and then certify over[6] to their country to the discredit of the plantation. The people wherewith you plant ought to be gardeners, ploughmen, laborers, smiths, carpenters, joiners,[7] fishermen, fowlers, with some few apothecaries, surgeons, cooks, and bakers. In a country of plantation, first look about what kind of victual the country yields of itself to hand, as chestnuts, walnuts, pineapples, olives, dates, plums, cherries, wild honey, and the like, and make use of them. Then consider what victual or esculent[8] things there are, which grow speedily, and within the year; as parsnips, carrots, turnips, onions, radish, artichokes of Jerusalem, maize, and the like. For wheat, barley, and oats, they ask too much labor; but with peas and beans you may begin, both because they ask less labor, and because they serve for meat[9] as well as for bread. And of rice likewise cometh a great increase, and it is a kind of meat. Above all, there ought to be brought store of biscuit, oatmeal, flour, meal, and the like, in the beginning, till bread may be had. For beasts, or birds, take chiefly such as are least subject to diseases, and multiply fastest; as swine, goats, cocks, hens, turkeys, geese, house-doves, and the like. The victual in plantations ought to be expended almost as in a besieged town; that is, with certain allowance. And let the main part of the ground employed to gardens or corn be to a common stock; and to be laid in, and stored up, and then delivered out in proportion; besides some spots of ground that any particular person will manure[1] for his own private. Consider likewise what commodities the soil where the plantation is doth naturally yield, that they may some way help to defray the charge of the plantation, (so it be not, as was said, to the untimely prejudice of the main business,) as it hath fared with tobacco in Virginia. Wood commonly aboundeth but too much; and therefore timber is fit to be one. If there be iron ore, and streams whereupon to set the mills, iron is a brave[2] commodity, where wood aboundeth. Making of bay-salt,[3] if the climate be proper for it, would be put in experience. Growing silk likewise, if any be, is a likely commodity. Pitch and tar, where store of firs and pines are, will not fail. So drugs and sweet woods, where they are, cannot but yield great profit. Soap-ashes[4] likewise, and other things that may be thought of. But moil[5] not too much under ground; for the hope of mines is very uncertain, and useth to make the planters lazy in other things.

For government, let it be in the hands of one, assisted with some counsel; and let them have commission to exercise martial laws, with some limitation. And above all, let men make that profit of being in the wilderness, as they have God always, and his service, before their eyes. Let not the government of the plantation depend upon too many counselors and undertakers[6] in the country that planteth,

4. Accord.
5. Convicted criminals were brought to the English colonies as indentured servants.
6. Send reports home.
7. Finish carpenters.
8. Edible.
9. For a main course.
1. Enrich, cultivate.
2. Splendid.
3. Bay salt was made from evaporating seawater.
4. Ashes used in making soap.
5. Work hard.
6. The term "undertakers" was first used to describe those who held crown lands and attempted to meet the requirements for plantation in Ireland; more generally, farm managers.

but upon a temperate number; and let those be rather noblemen and gentlemen, than merchants; for they look ever to the present gain. Let there be freedom from custom,[7] till the plantation be of strength; and not only freedom from custom, but freedom to carry their commodities where they may make their best of them, except there be some special cause of caution. Cram not in people, by sending too fast company after company; but rather harken how they waste,[8] and send supplies proportionably; but so as the number may live well in the plantation, and not by surcharge[9] be in penury.

It hath been a great endangering to the health of some plantations, that they have built along the sea and rivers, in marish[1] and unwholesome grounds. Therefore, though you begin there, to avoid carriage and other like discommodities, yet build still rather upwards from the streams, than along. It concerneth likewise the health of the plantation that they have good store of salt with them, that they may use it in their victuals when it shall be necessary. If you plant where savages are, do not only entertain them with trifles and jingles, but use them justly and graciously, with sufficient guard nevertheless; and do not win their favor by helping them to invade their enemies, but for their defense it is not amiss; and send oft of them over to the country that plants, that they may see a better condition than their own, and commend it when they return. When the plantation grows to strength, then it is time to plant with women as well as with men, that the plantation may spread into generations, and not be ever pieced[2] from without. It is the sinfullest thing in the world to forsake or destitute a plantation once in forwardness; for besides the dishonor, it is the guiltiness of blood of many commiserable[3] persons.

Of Studies

[VERSION OF 1597]

Studies serve for pastimes, for ornaments and for abilities. Their chief use for pastime is in privateness and retiring; for ornament is in discourse, and for abilities is in judgment. For expert[1] men can execute, but learned men are fittest to judge or censure.

¶ To spend too much time in them is sloth, to use them too much for ornament is affectation: to make judgment wholly by their rules is the humor[2] of a scholar. ¶ They perfect nature, and are perfected by experience. ¶ Crafty men contemn[3] them, simple men admire them, wise men use them: For they teach not their own use, but that is a wisdom without them:[4] and above them won by observation. ¶ Read not to contradict, nor to believe, but to weigh and consider. ¶ Some books are to be tasted, others to be swallowed, and some few to be chewed and digested: That is, some books are to be read only in parts; others to be read, but cursorily;[5] and some few to be read wholly and with diligence and attention. ¶ Reading maketh a full man, conference[6] a ready man, and writing an exact man. And therefore if a man write little, he had need have a great memory, if he confer little, he had need have a present wit, and if he read little, he had need have much cunning, to seem to know

7. Import taxes.
8. Decline in number.
9. Overburden in population.
1. Swampy.
2. Penetrated.
3. Pitiable.
1. Experienced.
2. Fixed habit.
3. The original reads "continue," corrected by pen in the British Museum copy to "contemn."
4. Knowledge must be used outside of the books that convey it.
5. Quickly, without care.
6. Discussion.

that he doth not. ¶ Histories make men wise, Poets witty:[7] the Mathematics subtle, natural Philosophy deep: Moral grave, Logic and Rhetoric able to contend.

Of Studies

[VERSION OF 1625]

Studies serve for delight, for ornament, and for ability. Their chief use for delight is in privateness and retiring; for ornament, is in discourse; and for ability, is in the judgment and disposition of business. For expert[1] men can execute, and perhaps judge of particulars, one by one; but the general counsels, and the plots and marshalling of affairs, come best from those that are learned. To spend too much time in studies is sloth; to use them too much for ornament is affectation; to make judgment wholly by their rules is the humor[2] of a scholar. They perfect nature, and are perfected by experience; for natural abilities are like natural plants, that need pruning by study; and studies themselves do give forth directions too much at large, except they be bounded in by experience. Crafty men contemn studies, simple men admire them, and wise men use them; for they teach not their own use; but that is a wisdom without them,[3] and above them, won by observation. Read not to contradict and confute; nor to believe and take for granted; nor to find talk and discourse; but to weigh and consider. Some books are to be tasted, others to be swallowed, and some few to be chewed and digested; that is, some books are to be read only in parts; others to be read, but not curiously;[4] and some few to be read wholly, and with diligence and attention. Some books also may be read by deputy, and extracts made of them by others; but that would be only in the less important arguments, and the meaner sort of books; else distilled books are like common distilled waters,[5] flashy things. Reading maketh a full man; conference[6] a ready man; and writing an exact man. And therefore, if a man write little, he had need have a great memory; if he confer little, he had need have a present wit: and if he read little, he had need have much cunning, to seem to know that he doth not. Histories make men wise; poets witty;[7] the mathematics subtle; natural philosophy deep; moral grave; logic and rhetoric able to contend. *Abeunt studia in mores.*[8] Nay, there is no stond[9] or impediment in the wit, but may be wrought out by fit studies, like as diseases of the body may have appropriate exercises. Bowling is good for the stone and reins;[1] shooting for the lungs and breast; gentle walking for the stomach; riding for the head; and the like. So if a man's wit be wandering, let him study the mathematics; for in demonstrations, if his wit be called away never so little, he must begin again. If his wit be not apt to distinguish or find differences, let him study the schoolmen; for they are *cumini sectores*.[2] If he be not apt to beat over matters and to call up one thing to prove and illustrate another, let him study the lawyers' cases. So every defect of the mind may have a special receipt.[3]

7. Ingenious.
1. Experienced.
2. Fixed habit.
3. Knowledge must be used outside of the books that convey it.
4. With interest.
5. Ineffective herbal remedies.
6. Discussion.
7. Imaginative, ingenious.
8. Studies lead to ways of life (Ovid, *Heroides* 15.13).
9. Obstacle.
1. The gall bladder and kidneys.
2. "Dividers of cuminseed," or hair-splitters. The schoolmen are the medieval scholastic philosophers who Bacon thought were more concerned with the abstract logic of an argument than with its practical ramifications.
3. Remedy.

The King James Bible

Many earlier English translations of the Bible prepared the way for the King James Bible of 1611. As early as the late fourteenth century, the popular religious reformer John Wycliff had rendered the Latin of the Vulgate into Middle English, and in the following century the Lollards used his translation. With the Reformation, translation became both more crucial and more dangerous—crucial because one of the chief principles of the Reformation was the need for the individual to read Scripture directly; dangerous because individual readings could conflict with church authority and the authority of the state.

In the case of William Tyndale, translation of the Bible into English led to death. The first Englishman to translate the Bible directly from Hebrew and Greek in accord with humanist principles, Tyndale had to go the Continent to work on and publish his New Testament (1525–1526). When copies of it entered England, the bishops suppressed them. He then angered Henry VIII by condemning his divorce in *The Practice of Prelates* (1530). Tyndale was ultimately seized in Antwerp and burned at the stake for heresy.

Soon after Tyndale's Bible came a translation by Miles Coverdale. Then Tyndale's and Coverdale's translations were fused in the Great Bible (1540), issued as the official version in English after Henry VIII's break from Roman Catholicism. Later, the Bishop's Bible (1568), which also reworked Tyndale's translation, was meant to stand for the Elizabethan religious compromise—neither too Catholic nor too Puritan—and against the strict Calvinism of the Geneva Bible (1560). The translation of the Protestant exiles, who left England in the reign of Catholic Queen Mary in search of religious freedom, the Geneva Bible was particularly controversial because of its marginal commentary that interprets biblical history as prophetic of the judgment of God on churches, kings, and nations.

The King James Bible, or Authorized Version, of 1611 was compiled by a learned committee of forty-seven different humanist scholars and theologians, headed by Lancelot Andrews. Much of the phraseology of the Authorized Version comes from Tyndale's translation. The language of the King James Bible is distinguished by its elegant variation, its direct and memorable phrasing, and its grave and sonorous cadences. Echoes of this language can be heard throughout seventeenth-century prose and poetry, especially in Milton's *Paradise Lost*. Particularly important for Milton's great epic are the stories of the creation and fall in the second and third chapters of Genesis, here printed in their entirety.

from The King James Bible

from *Genesis*

Chapter 2

Thus the heavens and the earth were finished, and all the host of them.
2 And on the seventh day God ended his work which he had made; and he rested on the seventh day from all his work which he had made.
3 And God blessed the seventh day, and sanctified it: because that in it he had
rested from all his work which God created and made.
4 ¶These *are*[1] the generations of the heavens and of the earth when they were
created, in the day that the LORD God made the earth and the heavens,
5 And every plant of the field before it was in the earth, and every herb of the
field before it grew: for the LORD God had not caused it to rain upon the earth, and
there was not a man to till the ground.

1. Concerned to reflect the Hebrew original as accurately as possible, the translators italicize words that are needed in English but not present in Hebrew.

6 But there went up a mist from the earth, and watered the whole face of the ground.

7 And the LORD God formed man *of* the dust of the ground, and breathed into his nostrils the breath of life; and man became a living soul.

8 ¶And the LORD God planted a garden eastward in Ē´dĕn;[2] and there he put the man whom he had formed.

9 And out of the ground made the LORD God to grow every tree that is pleasant to the sight, and good for food; the tree of life also in the midst of the garden, and the tree of knowledge of good and evil.

10 And a river went out of Ē´dĕn to water the garden; and from thence it was parted, and became into four heads.

11 The name of the first *is* Pi´sŏn: that *is* it which compasseth the whole land of Hăv´ĭlăh, where *there is* gold;

12 And the gold of that land *is* good: there *is* bdellium[3] and the onyx stone.

13 And the name of the second river *is* Gi´hŏn: the same *is* it that compasseth the whole land of Ēthĭō´pĭa.

14 And the name of the third river *is* Hĭd´ĕkĕl: that *is* it which goeth toward the east of Ăssȳr´ĭă. And the fourth river *is* Eūphrā´tēs.

15 And the LORD God took the man, and put him into the garden of Ē´dĕn to dress it and to keep it.

16 And the LORD God commanded the man, saying, Of every tree of the garden thou mayest freely eat:

17 But of the tree of the knowledge of good and evil, thou shalt not eat of it: for in the day that thou eatest thereof thou shalt surely die.

18 ¶And the LORD God said, *It is* not good that the man should be alone; I will make him an help meet for him.

19 And out of the ground the LORD God formed every beast of the field, and every fowl of the air; and brought *them* unto Ăd´ăm to see what he would call them: and whatsoever Ăd´ăm called every living creature, that *was* the name thereof.

20 And Ăd´ăm gave names to all cattle, and to the fowl of the air, and to every beast of the field; but for Ăd´ăm there was not found an help meet for him.

21 And the LORD God caused a deep sleep to fall upon Ăd´ăm, and he slept: and he took one of his ribs, and closed up the flesh instead thereof;

22 And the rib, which the LORD God had taken from man, made he a woman, and brought her unto the man.

23 And Ăd´ăm said, This *is* now bone of my bones, and flesh of my flesh: she shall be called Woman, because she was taken out of Man.

24 Therefore shall a man leave his father and his mother, and shall cleave unto his wife: and they shall be one flesh.

25 And they were both naked, the man and his wife, and were not ashamed.

CHAPTER 3

Now the serpent was more subtil than any beast of the field which the LORD God had made. And he said unto the woman, Yea, hath God said, Ye shall not eat of every tree of the garden?

2 And the woman said unto the serpent, We may eat of the fruit of the trees of the garden:

2. To facilitate reading by individuals and families, the translators indicate how to pronounce all names.

3. A Latin word taken from the Greek to translate the Hebrew *b'dolakh*, a precious stone, pearl.

3 But of the fruit of the tree which *is* in the midst of the garden, God hath said, Ye shall not eat of it, neither shall ye touch it, lest ye die.

4 And the serpent said unto the woman, Ye shall not surely die:

5 For God doth know that in the day ye eat thereof, then your eyes shall be opened, and ye shall be as gods, knowing good and evil.

6 And when the woman saw that the tree *was* good for food, and that it *was* pleasant to the eyes, and a tree to be desired to make *one* wise, she took of the fruit thereof, and did eat, and gave also unto her husband with her; and he did eat.

7 And the eyes of them both were opened, and they knew that they *were* naked; and they sewed fig leaves together, and made themselves aprons.

8 And they heard the voice of the LORD God walking in the garden in the cool of the day: and Ăd′ăm and his wife hid themselves from the presence of the LORD God amongst the trees of the garden.

9 And the LORD God called unto Ăd′ăm and said unto him, Where *art* thou?

10 And he said, I heard thy voice in the garden, and I was afraid, because I *was* naked; and I hid myself.

11 And he said, Who told thee that thou *wast* naked? Hast thou eaten of the tree, whereof I commanded thee that thou shouldest not eat?

12 And the man said, The woman whom thou gavest *to be* with me, she gave me of the tree, and I did eat.

13 And the LORD God said unto the woman, What *is* this *that* thou hast done? And the woman said, The serpent beguiled me, and I did eat.

14 And the LORD God said unto the serpent, Because thou hast done this, thou *art* cursed above all cattle, and above every beast of the field; upon thy belly shalt thou go, and dust shalt thou eat all the days of thy life:

15 And I will put enmity between thee and the woman, and between thy seed and her seed; it shall bruise thy head, and thou shalt bruise his heel.

16 Unto the woman he said, I will greatly multiply thy sorrow and thy conception; in sorrow thou shalt bring forth children; and thy desire *shall be* to thy husband, and he shall rule over thee.

17 And unto Ăd′ăm he said, Because thou hast hearkened unto the voice of thy wife, and hast eaten of the tree, of which I commanded thee, saying, Thou shalt not eat of it: cursed *is* the ground for thy sake; in sorrow shalt thou eat *of* it all the days of thy life;

18 Thorns also and thistles shall it bring forth to thee; and thou shalt eat the herb of the field;

19 In the sweat of thy face shalt thou eat bread, till thou return unto the ground; for out of it wast thou taken: for dust thou *art*, and unto dust shalt thou return.

20 And Ăd′ăm called his wife's name Ēve; because she was the mother of all living.

21 Unto Ăd′ăm also and to his wife did the LORD God make coats of skins, and clothed them.

22 ¶And the LORD God said, Behold, the man is become as one of us, to know good and evil: and now, lest he put forth his hand, and take also of the tree of life, and eat, and live for ever:

23 Therefore the LORD God sent him forth from the garden of Eden, to till the ground from whence he was taken.

24 So he drove out the man; and he placed at the east of the garden of Ē′dĕn Chĕr′ūbĭms, and a flaming sword which turned every way, to keep the way of the tree of life.

Lady Mary Wroth

1586–1640

Lady Mary Wroth's *Urania* is the first work of original prose fiction by an Englishwoman. The book was first published in 1621 at a time when the controversy over women was raging and when one of the first great Continental novels, Cervantes's *Don Quixote*, had recently been translated into English by Thomas Shelton (part 1, 1612; part 2, 1620). Some of the women characters in *Urania* are not only central protagonists but also unconventional heroines who go beyond the confines of conventional gender roles. Similarly, Wroth's treatment of the romance genre in some ways exceeds the limits of the conventional romance, propelled by stereotypically feminine desire. In Book Four, for instance, English ladies simply walk away from the Prince of Florence's praises rather than swoon over them. Another bit of satire involves Pelarina, "a distressed creature in the habits of a pilgrim," who like Quixote is obsessed with an ideal of perfect love that is completely disjointed from any real love object. The first episode of the *Urania*, included here, recalls the beginning of her uncle Sir Philip Sidney's *Arcadia,* in which the shepherds mourn for Urania, yet Wroth's Urania is not a passive object but actively helps others and embarks on her own quest to discover her identity.

The text is in two parts; one part corresponds to the published version of 1621, the other to a unique manuscript in the author's hand at the Newberry Library in Chicago. The publishers entered *Urania* in the Stationer's Register in 1621; it is not clear whether or not they had the author's permission. Once in print, the book provoked attacks from powerful courtiers, who did not like to see their foibles fictionalized. In her defense, Wroth claimed that she never intended to have her work published. This may have been simply an aristocratic disclaimer against the taint of publication, but the remark may also carry a concern with the prohibition against women's publishing. Although Wroth asked for a King's warrant to recall the book, no record of such a warrant exists.

For more on Wroth, see her principal listing, page 1571.

from The Countess of Montgomery's Urania

from *Book 1*

When the spring began to appear like the welcome messenger of summer, one sweet (and in that more sweet) morning, after Aurora[1] had called all careful eyes to attend the day, forth came the fair shepherdess Urania,[2] (fair indeed; yet that far too mean a title for her, who for beauty deserved the highest style could be given by best knowing judgments). Into the mead[3] she came, where usually she drove her flocks to feed, whose leaping and wantonness showed they were proud of such a guide: But she, whose sad thoughts led her to another manner of spending her time, made her soon leave them, and follow her late begun custom; which was (while they delighted themselves) to sit under some shade, bewailing her misfortune; while they fed, to feed upon her own sorrow and tears, which at this time she began again to summon, sitting down under the shade of a well-spread beech; the ground (then blest) and the tree with full and fine leaved branches growing proud to bear and shadow such perfections. But she regarding nothing, in comparison of her woe, thus proceeded in her grief:

1. Goddess of the dawn.
2. Urania represents Susan Herbert, countess of Montgomery (1587–1629), the author's close friend. In Spenser's *Colin Clouts Come Home Again*, Urania stands for Wroth's aunt, Mary Sidney, Countess of Pembroke.
3. Meadow.

"Alas Urania," said she (the true servant to misfortune); "of any misery that can befall woman, is not this the most and greatest which thou art fallen into? Can there be any near the unhappiness of being ignorant, and that in the highest kind, not being certain of mine own estate or birth? Why was I not still continued in the belief I was, as I appear, a shepherdess, and daughter to a shepherd? My ambition then went no higher than this estate, now flies it to a knowledge; then was I contented, now perplexed. O ignorance, can thy dullness yet procure so sharp a pain? and that such a thought as makes me now aspire unto knowledge? How did I joy in this poor life being quiet? blest in the love of those I took for parents, but now by them I know the contrary, and by that knowledge, not to know myself. Miserable Urania, worse art thou now than these thy lambs; for they know their dams, while thou dost live unknown of any."

By this were others come into that mead with their flocks: but she esteeming her sorrowing thoughts her best, and choicest company, left that place, taking a little path which brought her to the further side of the plain, to the foot of the rocks, speaking as she went these lines, her eyes fixed upon the ground, her very soul turned into mourning.

Unseen, unknown, I here alone complain
   To rocks, to hills, to meadows and to springs,
Which can no help return to ease my pain,
   But back my sorrows the sad echo brings.
Thus still increasing are my woes to me,
   Doubly resounded by that moanful voice,
Which seems to second me in misery,
   And answer gives like friend of mine own choice.
Thus only she doth my companion prove,
   The others silently do offer ease:
But those that grieve, a grieving note do love;
   Pleasures to dying eyes bring but disease:
And such am I, who daily ending live,
Wailing a state which can no comfort give.

In this passion she went on, till she came to the foot of a great rock, she thinking of nothing less than ease, sought how she might ascend it; hoping there to pass away her time more peaceably with loneliness, though not to find least respite from her sorrow, which so dearly she did value, as by no means she would impart it to any. The way was hard, though by some windings making the ascent pleasing. Having attained the top, she saw under some hollow trees the entry into the rock: she fearing nothing but the continuance of her ignorance, went in; where she found a pretty room, as if that stony place had yet in pity, given leave for such perfections to come into the heart as chiefest, and most beloved place, because most loving. The place was not unlike the ancient (or the descriptions of ancient) hermitages,[4] instead of hangings, covered and lined with ivy, disdaining aught else should come there, that being in such perfection. This richness in nature's plenty made her stay to behold it, and almost grudge the pleasant fullness of content that place might have, if sensible, while she must know to taste of torments. As she was thus in passion mixed with pain, throwing her eyes as wildly as timorous lovers do for fear of discovery, she perceived a little light, and such a one, as a chink doth oft discover to our sights. She

4. Hermits' cells.

curious to see what this was, with her delicate hands put the natural ornament aside, discerning a little door, which she putting from her, passed through it into another room, like the first in all proportion; but in the midst there was a square stone, like to a pretty table, and on it a wax-candle burning; and by that a paper, which had suffered itself patiently to receive the discovering of so much of it, as presented this sonnet (as it seemed newly written) to her sight.

Here all alone in silence might I mourn:
  But how can silence be where sorrows flow?
  Sighs with complaints have poorer pains out-worn;
  But broken hearts can only true grief show.

Drops of my dearest blood shall let love know
  Such tears for her I shed, yet still do burn,
  As no spring can quench least part of my woe,
  Till this live earth, again to earth do turn.

Hateful all thought of comfort is to me,
  Despised day, let me still night possess;
  Let me all torments feel in their excess,
  And but this light[5] allow my state to see.

Which still doth waste, and wasting as this light,
Are my sad days unto eternal night.

"Alas Urania!" sighed she. "How well do these words, this place, and all agree with thy fortune? Sure poor soul thou wert here appointed to spend thy days, and these rooms ordained to keep thy tortures in; none being assuredly so matchlessly unfortunate."

Turning from the table, she discerned in the room a bed of boughs, and on it a man lying, deprived of outward sense, as she thought, and of life, as she at first did fear, which struck her into a great amazement: yet having a brave spirit, though shadowed under a mean habit, she stepped unto him, whom she found not dead, but laid upon his back, his head a little to her wards,[6] his arms folded on his breast, hair long, and beard disordered, manifesting all care; but care itself had left him: curiousness thus far afforded him, as to be perfectly discerned the most exact piece of misery; apparel he had suitable to the habitation, which was a long gray robe. This grievefull spectacle did much amaze the sweet and tender-hearted shepherdess; especially, when she perceived (as she might by the help of the candle) the tears which distilled from his eyes; who seeming the image of death, yet had this sign of worldly sorrow, the drops falling in that abundance, as if there were a kind strife among them, to rid their master first of that burdenous carriage; or else meaning to make a flood, and so drown their woeful patient in his own sorrow, who yet lay still, but then fetching a deep groan from the profoundest part of his soul, he said:

"Miserable Perissus,[7] canst thou thus live, knowing she that gave thee life is gone? Gone, O me! and with her all my joy departed. Wilt thou (unblessed creature) lie here complaining for her death, and know she died for thee? Let truth and shame make thee do something worthy of such a love, ending thy days like thyself, and one fit to be her servant. But that I must not do: then thus remain and softer storms, still

5. A candle. The story of Cleophila finding a poem atop a table in a dark cave (Philip Sidney, *Old Arcadia*) is the source for the story of Urania's finding the sonnet.

6. Toward her.

7. Lost one.

to torment thy wretched soul withall, since all are little, and too too little for such a loss. O dear Limena,[8] loving Limena, worthy Limena, and more rare, constant Limena: perfections delicately feigned to be in women were verified in thee, was such worthiness framed only to be wondered at by the best, but given as a prey to base and unworthy jealousy? When were all worthy parts joined in one, but in thee (my best Limena)? Yet all these grown subject to a creature ignorant of all but ill; like unto a fool, who in a dark cave, that hath but one way to get out, having a candle, but not the understanding what good it doth him, puts it out:[9] this ignorant wretch not being able to comprehend thy virtues, did so by thee in thy murder, putting out the world's light, and men's admiration: Limena, Limena, O my Limena."

With that he fell from complaining into such a passion, as weeping and crying were never in so woeful a perfection, as now in him; which brought as deserved a compassion from the excellent shepherdess, who already had her heart so tempered with grief, as that it was apt to take any impression that it would come to feel withall. Yet taking a brave courage to her, she stepped unto him, kneeling down by his side, and gently pulling him by the arm, she thus spake.

"Sir," said she, "having heard some part of your sorrows, they have not only made me truly pity you, but wonder at you; since if you have lost so great a treasure, you should not lie thus leaving her and your love unrevenged, suffering her murderers to live, while you lie here complaining; and if such perfections be dead in her, why make you not the phoenix[1] of your deeds live again, as to new life raised out of revenge you should take on them? Then were her end satisfied, and you deservedly accounted worthy of her favor, if she were so worthy as you say."

"If she were? O God," cried out Perissus, "what devilish spirit art thou, that thus dost come to torture me? But now I see you are a woman; and therefore not much to be marked, and less resisted: but if you know charity, I pray now practice it, and leave me who am afflicted sufficiently without your company; or if you will stay, discourse not to me."

"Neither of these will I do," said she.

"If you be then," said he, "some fury of purpose sent to vex me, use your force to the uttermost in martyring me; for never was there a fitter subject, than the heart of poor Perissus is."

"I am no fury," replied the divine Urania, "not hither come to trouble you, but by accident lighted on this place; my cruel hap[2] being such, as only the like can give me content, while the solitariness of this like cave might give me quiet, though not ease, seeking for such a one, I happened hither; and this is the true cause of my being here, though now I would use it to a better end if I might. Wherefore favor me with the knowledge of your grief; which heard, it may be I shall give you some counsel, and comfort in your sorrow."

"Cursed may I be," cried he, "if ever I take comfort, having such case of mourning: but because you are, or seem to be afflicted, I will not refuse to satisfy your demand, but tell you the saddest story that ever was rehearsed by dying man to living woman; and such a one, as I fear will fasten too much sadness in you; yet should I deny it, I were to blame, being so well known to these senseless places; as were they sensible of sorrow, they would condole, or else amazed at such cruelty, stand dumb as they do, to find that man should be so inhuman."

8. Woman of the home or threshold.
9. An allusion to the Myth of the Cave in Plato's *Republic*.
1. The mythical bird that burned and was then reborn from its ashes.
2. Fate, chance.

Thomas Hobbes
1588–1679

In an autobiographical poem that Hobbes wrote toward the end of his life, he described himself as having been born with a twin brother: fear. Born the year of the Spanish Armada, Hobbes felt that the fear of war had influenced his life. According to his friend and biographer Aubrey, Hobbes was an *enfant terrible*, having translated Euripides' *Medea* out of Greek into Latin iambics before the age of fourteen when he went to study at Magdalen Hall, Oxford. He was an incredibly well-read man and one of the great translators of his day; he produced the first (probably the greatest in English) translation of Thucydides' *The History of the Grecian War* (1628). An atmosphere that he described as "boiling hot with questions about dominion and the obedience due from subjects" affected his writing of *De Cive* (On the Citizen, 1647) in the years leading up to the Civil War. He also wrote on geometry and physics as well as on rhetoric and logic, and he tutored Margaret and William Cavendish's son, who later became Earl of Devonshire and host to his old bachelor tutor in retirement.

Best known today as the author of *Leviathan, or the Matter, Form, and Power of a Commonwealth Ecclesiastical and Civil* (1651), Hobbes was a controversial figure in his own century. Thought by many to be an atheist, he was even denounced by the University of Oxford in 1683. One of the great works of political philosophy, Hobbes's *Leviathan* imagines a social contract to explain political relations. The forceful and memorable style of this work, with its directness, clarity, and logical rigor, make it one of the masterpieces of English prose.

from Leviathan[1]

Chapter 13. Of the Natural Condition of Mankind as Concerning their Felicity, and Misery.

Nature hath made men so equal, in the faculties of the body, and mind; as that though there be found one man sometimes manifestly stronger in body, or of quicker mind than another; yet when all is reckoned together, the difference between man, and man, is not so considerable, as that one man can thereupon claim to himself any benefit, to which another may not pretend, as well as he. For as to the strength of body, the weakest has strength enough to kill the strongest, either by secret machination, or by confederacy[2] with others, that are in the same danger with himself.

And as to the faculties of the mind, setting aside the arts grounded upon words, and especially that skill of proceeding upon general, and infallible rules, called science; which very few have, and but in few things; as being not a native faculty, born with us; nor attained, as prudence, while we look after somewhat else, I find yet a greater equality amongst men, than that of strength. For prudence, is but experience; which equal time, equally bestows on all men, in those things they equally apply

1. The frontispiece to Hobbes's *Leviathan* pictures the body of a giant made up of little men, over which appears the Latin quotation: "Non est potestas super terram qui comparetur ei" (There is no power on earth to be compared with him). This line, from Job 41.33, refers to the primordial sea creature Leviathan, whom God cites as evidence of his all-creating power. The ensuing verse concludes by describing Leviathan as "king over all the sons of pride." Hobbes conceives of the secular state as both humanly constructed and the result of natural conflict.

2. Alliance.

themselves unto. That which may perhaps make such equality incredible, is but a vain conceit of one's own wisdom, which almost all men think they have in a greater degree, than the vulgar; that is, than all men but themselves, and a few others, whom by fame, or for concurring with themselves, they approve. For such is the nature of men, that howsoever they may acknowledge many others to be more witty, or more eloquent, or more learned; yet they will hardly believe there be many so wise as themselves; for they see their own wit at hand, and other men's at a distance. But this proveth rather that men are in that point equal, than unequal. For there is not ordinarily a greater sign of the equal distribution of any thing, than that every man is contented with his share.

From this equality of ability, ariseth equality of hope in the attaining of our ends. And therefore if any two men desire the same thing, which nevertheless they cannot both enjoy, they become enemies; and in the way to their end, which is principally their own conservation, and sometimes their delectation[3] only, endeavor to destroy, or subdue one another. And from hence it comes to pass, that where an invader hath no more to fear, than another man's single power; if one plant, sow, build, or possess a convenient seat, others may probably be expected to come prepared with forces united, to dispossess, and deprive him, not only of the fruit of his labor, but also of his life, or liberty. And the invader again is in the like danger of another.

And from this diffidence[4] of one another, there is no way for any man to secure himself, so reasonable, as anticipation; that is, by force, or wiles, to master the persons of all men he can, so long, till he see no other power great enough to endanger him: and this is no more than his own conservation requireth, and is generally allowed. Also because there be some, that taking pleasure in contemplating their own power in the acts of conquest, which they pursue farther than their security requires; if others, that otherwise would be glad to be at ease within modest bounds, should not by invasion increase their power, they would not be able, long time, by standing only on their defence, to subsist. And by consequence, such augmentation of dominion over men being necessary to a man's conservation, it ought to be allowed him.

Again, men have no pleasure, but on the contrary a great deal of grief, in keeping company, where there is no power able to overawe them all. For every man looketh that his companion should value him, at the same rate he sets upon himself: and upon all signs of contempt, or undervaluing, naturally endeavors, as far as he dares, (which amongst them that have no common power to keep them in quiet, is far enough to make them destroy each other), to extort a greater value from his contemners,[5] by damage; and from others, by the example.

So that in the nature of man, we find three principal causes of quarrel. First, competition; secondly, diffidence; thirdly, glory. The first, maketh men invade for gain; the second, for safety; and the third, for reputation. The first use violence, to make themselves masters of other men's persons, wives, children, and cattle; the second, to defend them; the third, for trifles, as a word, a smile, a different opinion, and any other sign of undervalue, either direct in their persons, or by reflection in their kindred, their friends, their nation, their profession, or their name.

3. Enjoyment.
4. Suspicion.
5. Scorners.

Hereby it is manifest, that during the time men live without a common power to keep them all in awe, they are in that condition which is called war; and such a war, as is of every man, against every man. For WAR, consisteth not in battle only, or the act of fighting; but in a tract of time, wherein the will to contend by battle is sufficiently known: and therefore the notion of *time*, is to be considered in the nature of war; as it is in the nature of weather. For as the nature of foul weather, lieth not in a shower or two of rain; but in an inclination thereto of many days together: so the nature of war, consisteth not in actual fighting; but in the known disposition thereto, during all the time there is no assurance to the contrary. All other time is PEACE.

Whatsoever therefore is consequent to a time of war, where every man is enemy to every man; the same is consequent to the time, wherein men live without other security, than what their own strength, and their own invention shall furnish them withal. In such condition, there is no place for industry; because the fruit thereof is uncertain: and consequently no culture of the earth; no navigation, nor use of the commodities that may be imported by sea; no commodious building; no instruments of moving, and removing, such things as require much force; no knowledge of the face of the earth; no account of time; no arts; no letters; no society; and which is worst of all, continual fear, and danger of violent death; and the life of man, solitary, poor, nasty, brutish, and short.

It may seem strange to some man, that has not well weighed these things; that nature should thus dissociate, and render men apt to invade, and destroy one another: and he may therefore, not trusting to this inference, made from the passions, desire perhaps to have the same confirmed by experience. Let him therefore consider with himself, when taking a journey, he arms himself, and seeks to go well accompanied; when going to sleep, he locks his doors; when even in his house he locks his chests; and this when he knows there be laws, and public officers, armed, to revenge all injuries shall be done him; what opinion he has of his fellow-subjects, when he rides armed; of his fellow citizens, when he locks his doors; and of his children, and servants, when he locks his chests. Does he not there as much accuse mankind by his actions, as I do by my words? But neither of us accuse man's nature in it. The desires, and other passions of man, are in themselves no sin. No more are the actions, that proceed from those passions, till they know a law that forbids them: which till laws be made they cannot know: nor can any law be made, till they have agreed upon the person that shall make it.

It may peradventure be thought, there was never such a time, nor condition of war as this; and I believe it was never generally so, over all the world: but there are many places, where they live so now. For the savage people in many places of America, except the government of small families, the concord whereof dependeth on natural lust, have no government at all; and live at this day in that brutish manner, as I said before. Howsoever, it may be perceived what manner of life there would be, where there were no common power to fear, by the manner of life, which men that have formerly lived under a peaceful government, use to degenerate into, in a civil war.

But though there had never been any time, wherein particular men were in a condition of war one against another; yet in all times, kings, and persons of sovereign authority, because of their independency, are in continual jealousies, and in the state and posture of gladiators; having their weapons pointing, and their eyes fixed on one another; that is, their forts, garrisons, and guns upon the frontiers of their kingdoms; and continual spies upon their neighbors; which is a posture of war. But because they uphold thereby, the industry of their subjects; there does not follow from it, that misery, which accompanies the liberty of particular men.

To this war of every man, against every man, this also is consequent; that nothing can be unjust. The notions of right and wrong, justice and injustice have there no place. Where there is no common power, there is no law: where no law, no injustice. Force, and fraud, are in war the two cardinal virtues. Justice, and injustice are none of the faculties neither of the body, nor mind. If they were, they might be in a man that were alone in the world, as well as his senses, and passions. They are qualities, that relate to men in society, not in solitude. It is consequent also to the same condition, that there be no propriety,[6] no dominion, no *mine* and *thine* distinct; but only that to be every man's, that he can get; and for so long, as he can keep it. And thus much for the ill condition, which man by mere nature is actually placed in; though with a possibility to come out of it, consisting partly in the passions, partly in his reason.

The passions that incline men to peace, are fear of death; desire of such things as are necessary to commodious living; and a hope by their industry to obtain them. And reason suggesteth convenient articles of peace, upon which men may be drawn to agreement. These articles, are they, which otherwise are called the Laws of Nature: whereof I shall speak more particularly, in the two following chapters.

Sir Thomas Browne

1605–1682

Coleridge described Sir Thomas Browne as "the Humorist constantly mingling with & flashing across the Philosopher." There is both a whimsical wit and a metaphysical depth to Browne's writing that make him the favorite author of Lord Peter Wimsey (the dandified detective of Dorothy Sayers's mysteries). Like Dorothy Sayers, Browne was a great lover of Dante, and like her character Wimsey, Browne was imperturbably "in England under any meridian." So modest that he was known to blush on being complimented, Browne had a gentle humor and peaceful nature that make him stand out in an age that was rife with vituperative polemics. The tact and understatement of his writing style express the equipoise between faith and reason that is the hallmark of this doctor's creed.

Browne became a public figure in 1642 with the surreptitious publication of *Religio Medici* ("A Doctor's Religion"). Having studied medicine at Oxford and Padua, Browne settled down to a medical practice and then married life in Norwich sometime after 1637. The manuscript of *Religio Medici* had at first circulated among friends; Browne wrote in the preface to the first authorized edition of 1643 that he had written the work "some seven years past . . . for my private exercise and satisfaction." Both Protestants and Catholics objected to *Religio Medici* and accused Browne of atheism. An attempt to publish the Latin translation by John Merryweather in Leyden met with rejection from the Protestant intellectual Salmasius, who asserted that it would meet with "but frowning entertainment among the ministers." The text's Paris publisher was convinced that though Browne declared himself a Protestant, he was really Roman Catholic. The papacy put the treatise on the Index Expurgatorius. The militantly Protestant Alexander Ross, who also criticized Bacon, Harvey, and Hobbes, wrote *Arcana Microcosmi* "with a refutation of Dr. Browne's Vulgar Errors" in 1652. After reading the book, one of

6. Personal property.

Browne's friends tried to convert him to Quakerism. Browne's independent-minded yet religious sensibility is best summed up in his own words: "I borrow not the rules of my religion from Rome or Geneva but the dictates of my own reason."

What Browne meant by reason, however, was not the disembodied individual rationality of the Enlightenment, but rather the cosmic reason of Platonism, one of the chief schools of philosophy at Cambridge in the mid-seventeenth century. Like Giordano Bruno, Browne had an interest in the hermetic tradition, which reconciled the occult writing of Hermes Trismegistus with Zoroastrianism, Platonism, and Christianity. Browne believed not only in the Ptolemaic universe but also in alchemy, astrology, and witchcraft. Indeed, he was even consulted to give his opinion on a case of witchcraft in 1644, at which he is recorded to have commented that "the fits were natural, but heightened by the devil's cooperating with the malice of the witches." By the same token, Browne, like Bacon, refuted the superstition of received ideas, as can be seen in his next important work, *Pseudodoxia Epidemica*, subtitled "Enquiries into Many Received Tenets and Commonly Presumed Truths, Which Examined Proved but Vulgar and Common Errors" (1646). He was also a kind of anthropologist in his *Hydriotaphia, Urn Burial* (1658), which uses the burial customs of various cultures as the basis for a profound meditation on mortality.

His family life appears to have been an unusually happy one. He and his intelligent and beautiful wife Dorothy Mileham had ten children, and if Browne's letters are any evidence, he was very devoted to them. Browne also had a great correspondence with people who wrote to him for information. One, a Lutheran minister who lived in Iceland, visited Browne in England for medical treatment. Browne seems to have been one of those who knew how to follow Voltaire's dictum that we must "cultivate our gardens." Browne's last work, *The Garden of Cyrus* (1658), exemplifies his dual interests in the natural and the metaphysical. This study treats the history of horticulture from Eden to the gardens of the Persian King Cyrus, supposedly the first person to plant the quincunx, which expressed the mystical properties of the number five.

Politically, Browne had royalist sympathies; he was eventually knighted by Charles II in 1671. As the story goes, that honor was conferred on Browne only by default, since the mayor of Norwich declined and the King wanted to knight someone. Browne's greatest honor is in the number of writers who admired his work. Coleridge, Lamb, and De Quincy wrote of the imaginative fantasy in Browne's writing. Among American authors, Melville particularly prized Browne's writing for its combination of the scientific and the transcendental. The effect of Browne's prose style is one of flowing harmony. Animated by biblical parallelism and a profound reverence for the power of the word, Browne's prose flows harmoniously while giving the illusion of spontaneous organization.

from Religio Medici
from *Part 1*

1. For my religion, though there be several circumstances that might persuade the world I have none at all, as the general scandal of my profession,[1] the natural course of my studies, the indifferency[2] of my behavior and discourse in matters of religion (neither violently defending one, nor with that common ardor and contention opposing another), yet, in despite hereof, I dare without usurpation assume the honorable style of a Christian. Not that I merely owe this title to the font,[3] my education, or the clime wherein I was born, as being bred up either to confirm those principles my parents instilled into my unwary understanding, or by a general consent proceed

1. The "scandal of his profession" was the notion that doctors were often atheists. Natural: scientific.

2. Lack of bias.

3. The baptismal font.

in the religion of my country; but that having, in my riper years and confirmed judgment, seen and examined all, I find myself obliged, by the principles of grace, and the law of mine own reason, to embrace no other name but this: neither doth herein my zeal so far make me forget the general charity I owe unto humanity, as rather to hate than pity Turks, Infidels, and (what is worse) Jews;[4] rather contenting myself to enjoy that happy style, than maligning those who refuse so glorious a title.

2. But, because the name of a Christian is become too general to express our faith, there being a geography of religion as well as lands, and every clime not only distinguished by its laws and limits, but circumscribed by its doctrines and rules of faith, to be particular, I am of that reformed new-cast religion, wherein I dislike nothing but the name;[5] of the same belief our Savior taught, the Apostles disseminated, the Fathers authorized,[6] and the Martyrs confirmed; but, by the sinister ends of princes, the ambition and avarice of prelates, and the fatal corruption of times, so decayed, impaired, and fallen from its native beauty, that it required the careful and charitable hands of these times to restore it to its primitive integrity. Now, the accidental occasion whereupon, the slender means whereby, the low and abject condition of the person by whom, so good a work was set on foot,[7] which in our adversaries beget contempt and scorn, fill me with wonder, and are the very same objections the insolent pagans first cast at Christ and his disciples.[8]

3. Yet I have not so shaken hands with those desperate resolutions[9] who had rather venture at large their decayed bottom, than bring her in to be new trimmed in the dock, who had rather promiscuously retain all, than abridge any, and obstinately be what they are, than what they have been, as to stand in diameter and sword's point with them. We have reformed from them, not against them: for, omitting those improperations[1] and terms of scurrility betwixt us, which only difference[2] our affections, and not our cause, there is between us one common name and appellation, one faith and necessary body of principles common to us both; and therefore I am not scrupulous to converse and live with them, to enter their churches in defect of ours, and either pray with them or for them. I could never perceive any rational consequence from those many texts which prohibit the children of Israel to pollute themselves with the temples of the heathens; we being all Christians, and not divided by such detested impieties as might profane our prayers, or the place wherein we make them; or that a resolved conscience may not adore her Creator anywhere, especially in places devoted to his service; where, if their devotions offend him, mine may please him; if theirs profane it, mine may hallow it. Holy water and crucifix (dangerous to the common people) deceive not my judgment, nor abuse my devotion at all. I am, I confess, naturally inclined to that which misguided zeal terms superstition: my common conversation I do acknowledge austere, my behavior full of rigor, sometimes not without morosity; yet, at my devotion I love to use the civility of my knee, my hat, and hand, with all those outward and sensible motions which may express or promote my invisible devotion. I should violate my own arm rather than a church, nor willingly deface the memory[3] of saint or martyr. At the sight of a cross, or crucifix, I can dispense with my hat, but scarce with the thought or memory of my Savior.

4. Brown thinks that it would be against charity to hate rather than pity Turks and infidels, and even worse in the case of the Jews.
5. Protestant.
6. The Church Fathers of the first few centuries of the church, in particular St. Augustine, were a major influence on the Protestant Reformation.
7. Martin Luther was the son of a miner.
8. See Mark 6.2–3: "From whence hath this man these things. . . . Is not this the carpenter, the son of Mary?"
9. Roman Catholics, whose church is described as a leaky boat.
1. Taunts.
2. Make different.
3. Memorial.

I cannot laugh at, but rather pity, the fruitless journeys of pilgrims, or contemn the miserable condition of friars; for, though misplaced in circumstances, there is something in it of devotion. I could never hear the Ave Maria bell without an elevation,[4] or think it a sufficient warrant, because they erred in one circumstance, for me to err in all,—that is, in silence and dumb contempt. Whilst, therefore, they directed their devotions to her, I offered mine to God; and rectified the errors of their prayers by rightly ordering mine own. At a solemn procession I have wept abundantly, while my consorts, blind with opposition and prejudice, have fallen into an excess of scorn and laughter. There are, questionless, both in Greek, Roman, and African churches, solemnities and ceremonies, whereof the wiser zeals do make a Christian use; and which stand condemned by us, not as evil in themselves, but as allurements and baits of superstition to those vulgar heads that look asquint on the face of truth, and those unstable judgments that cannot consist in the narrow point and center of virtue without a reel or stagger to the circumference.

4. As there were many reformers, so likewise many reformations; every country proceeding in a particular way and method, according as their national interest, together with their constitution and clime, inclined them: some angrily and with extremity; others calmly and with mediocrity, not rending, but easily dividing, the community, and leaving an honest possibility of a reconciliation; which, though peaceable spirits do desire, and may conceive that revolution of time and the mercies of God may effect, yet that judgment that shall consider the present antipathies between the two extremes, their contrarieties in condition, affection, and opinion, may, with the same hopes, expect a union in the poles of heaven.

5. But, to difference myself nearer, and draw into a lesser circle; there is no church whose every part so squares unto my conscience, whose articles, constitutions, and customs, seem so consonant unto reason, and, as it were, framed to my particular devotion, as this whereof I hold my belief—the church of England; to whose faith I am a sworn subject, and therefore, in a double obligation, subscribe unto her articles, and endeavor to observe her constitutions: whatsoever is beyond, as points indifferent, I observe according to the rules of my private reason, or the humor and fashion of my devotion; neither believing this because Luther affirmed it, nor disapproving that because Calvin hath disavouched it. I condemn not all things in the council of Trent, nor approve all in the synod of Dort.[5] In brief, where the Scripture is silent, the church is my text; where that speaks, 't is but my comment; where there is a joint silence of both, I borrow not the rules of my religion from Rome or Geneva, but from the dictates of my own reason. It is an unjust scandal of our adversaries, and a gross error in ourselves, to compute the nativity of our religion from Henry the Eighth; who, though he rejected the Pope, refused not the faith of Rome, and effected no more than what his own predecessors desired and essayed in ages past, and it was conceived the state of Venice would have attempted in our days. It is as uncharitable a point in us to fall upon those popular scurrilities and opprobrious scoffs of the bishop of Rome, to whom, as a temporal prince, we owe the duty of good language. I confess there is a cause of passion between us: by his sentence I stand excommunicated; heretic is the best language he affords me: yet can no ear witness I ever returned to him the name of antichrist, man of sin, or whore of Babylon.[6] It is the method of

4. Browne's marginalia: "A Church Bell that tolls every day at 6 and 12 of the clock, at the hearing whereof every one in what ever place soever either of house or street betakes him to his prayers, which is commonly directed to the Virgin."

5. Theological councils: for Catholicism in Trento, Italy (1545–1563) and for Calvinism in Dordrecht, Holland (1618–1619).

6. Images taken from Revelation used in Protestant polemics against Catholics.

charity to suffer without reaction: those usual satires and invectives of the pulpit may perchance produce a good effect on the vulgar, whose ears are opener to rhetoric than logic; yet do they, in no wise, confirm the faith of wiser believers, who know that a good cause needs not be patroned by passion, but can sustain itself upon a temperate dispute.

6. I could never divide myself from any man upon the difference of an opinion, or be angry with his judgment for not agreeing with me in that from which, perhaps, within a few days, I should dissent myself. I have no genius to disputes in religion; and have often thought it wisdom to decline them, especially upon a disadvantage, or when the cause of truth might suffer in the weakness of my patronage. Where we desire to be informed, 'tis good to contest with men above ourselves; but, to confirm and establish our opinions, 'tis best to argue with judgments below our own, that the frequent spoils and victories over their reasons may settle in ourselves an esteem and confirmed opinion of our own. Every man is not a proper champion for truth, nor fit to take up the gauntlet in the cause of verity: many, from the ignorance of these maxims, and an inconsiderate zeal unto truth, have too rashly charged the troops of error, and remain as trophies unto the enemies of truth. A man may be in as just possession of truth as of a city, and yet be forced to surrender; 'tis therefore far better to enjoy her with peace than to hazard her on a battle. If, therefore, there rise any doubts in my way, I do forget them, or at least defer them, till my better settled judgment and more manly reason be able to resolve them; for I perceive every man's own reason is his best Oedipus,[7] and will, upon a reasonable truce, find a way to loose those bonds wherewith the subtleties of error have enchained our more flexible and tender judgments. In philosophy, where truth seems doublefaced, there is no man more paradoxical than myself: but in divinity I love to keep the road; and, though not in an implicit, yet an humble faith, follow the great wheel of the church, by which I move; not reserving any proper poles, or motion from the epicycle[8] of my own brain. By this means I leave no gap for heresy, schisms, or errors, of which at present, I hope I shall not injure truth to say, I have no taint or tincture. I must confess my greener studies have been polluted with two or three; not any begotten in the latter centuries, but old and obsolete, such as could never have been revived but by such extravagant and irregular heads as mine. For, indeed, heresies perish not with their authors; but, like the river Arethusa,[9] though they lose their currents in one place, they rise up again in another. One general council is not able to extirpate one single heresy; it may be canceled for the present; but revolution of time, and the like aspects from heaven, will restore it, when it will flourish till it be condemned again. For, as though there were a metempsychosis,[1] and the soul of one man passed into another, opinions do find, after certain revolutions, men and minds like those that first begat them. To see ourselves again, we need not look for Plato's year;[2] every man is not only himself; there have been many Diogeneses, and as many Timons,[3] though but few of that name; men are lived over again; the world is now as it was in ages past; there was none then, but there hath been some one since, that parallels him, and is, as it were, his revived self.

7. Searcher after truth.
8. The revolving of a planet within a smaller circle within its larger orbit around the earth, a concept used by Ptolemaic astronomy to account for inconsistencies in its system, which were resolved by the simpler model of the solar system.
9. A Greek nymph who fled the sexual advances of the river god Alphaeus. She was turned into a stream but Alphaeus still pursued her. Diana rescued Arethusa by pushing the stream underground until it emerged in Sicily.
1. Transmigration of the soul.
2. Browne's marginalia: "A revolution of certain thousand years when all things should return unto their former estate and he be teaching again in his school as when he delivered this opinion."
3. Cynics and misanthropes.

from Pseudodoxia Epidemica

from *Book 1*

Chapter 1

Of the first Cause of Common Errors; the common infirmity of Human Nature

The first and father cause of common error is the common infirmity of human nature; of whose deceptible[1] condition, although, perhaps, there should not need any other eviction[2] than the frequent errors we shall ourselves commit, even in the express declarement hereof, yet shall we illustrate the same from more infallible constitutions, and persons presumed as far from us in condition as time, that is, our first and ingenerated[3] forefathers. From whom, as we derive our being, and the several wounds of constitution, so may we in some manner excuse our infirmities in the depravity of those parts, whose traductions[4] were pure in them, and their originals but once removed from God. Who, notwithstanding, (if posterity may take leave to judge of the fact, as they are assured to suffer in the punishment,) were grossly deceived in their perfection, and so weakly deluded in the clarity of their understanding, that it hath left no small obscurity in ours, how error should gain upon them.

For first, they were deceived by Satan; and that not in an invisible insinuation, but an open and discoverable apparition, that is, in the form of a serpent;[5] whereby, although there were many occasions of suspicion, and such as could not easily escape a weaker circumspection, yet did the unwary apprehension of Eve take no advantage thereof. It hath therefore seemed strange unto some, she should be deluded by a serpent, or subject her reason to a beast, which God had subjected unto hers. It hath empuzzled the enquiries of others to apprehend, and enforced them unto strange conceptions, to make out, how without fear or doubt she could discourse with such a creature, or hear a serpent speak, without suspicion of imposture. The wits of others have been so bold as to accuse her simplicity, in receiving his temptation so coldly; and, when such specious effects of the fruit were promised as to make them like gods, not to desire, at least not to wonder, he pursued not that benefit himself. And had it been their own case, would perhaps have replied, if the taste of this fruit maketh the eaters like Gods why remainest thou a beast? If it maketh us but *like* gods, we are so already. If thereby our eyes shall be opened hereafter, they are at present quick enough to discover thy deceit; and we desire them no opener to behold our own shame. If to know good and evil be our advantage, although we have free will unto both, we desire to perform but one. We know 'tis good to obey the commandment of God, but evil if we transgress it.

They were deceived by one another, and in the greatest disadvantage of delusion, that is, the stronger by the weaker: for Eve presented the fruit, and Adam received it from her. Thus the serpent was cunning enough to begin the deceit in the weaker; and the weaker of strength sufficient to consummate the fraud in the stronger. Art and fallacy was used unto her; a naked offer proved sufficient to him; so his superstruction was his ruin, and the fertility of his sleep[6] an issue of death unto him. And although the condition of sex, and posteriority of creation,[7] might somewhat extenuate the error of the woman, yet was it very strange and inexcusable in

1. Deceivable.
2. Proof.
3. Not humanly generated, Adam and Eve were created by God.
4. Transmissions of the soul from the parents to the child.
5. See Genesis 2–3, and Milton's *Paradise Lost*.
6. Eve.
7. Eve's being created after Adam.

the man: especially, if, as some affirm, he was the wisest of all men since; or if, as others have conceived, he was not ignorant of the fall of the angels, and had thereby example and punishment to deter him.

They were deceived from themselves, and their own apprehensions; for Eve either mistook, or traduced the commandment of God. "Of every tree of the garden thou mayest freely eat, but of the tree of knowledge of good and evil thou shalt not eat: for in the day thou eatest thereof, thou shalt surely die."[8] Now Eve upon the question of the serpent, returned the precept in different terms: "You shall not eat of it, neither shall you touch it, lest perhaps you die." In which delivery there were no less than two mistakes, or rather additional mendacities: for the commandment forbad not the touch of the fruit; and positively said, ye shall surely die, but she extenuating replied, *ne forte moriamini*, lest perhaps ye die. For so in the vulgar translation it runneth, and so it is expressed in the Thargum or paraphrase of Jonathan.[9] And therefore although it be said, and that very truly, that the Devil was a liar from the beginning, yet was the woman herein the first express beginner, and falsified twice, before the reply of Satan. And therefore also, to speak strictly, the sin of the fruit was not the first offence. They first transgressed the rule of their own reason, and after, the commandment of God.

They were deceived through the conduct of their senses, and by temptations from the object itself; whereby although their intellectuals[1] had not failed in the theory of truth, yet did the inservient and brutal[2] faculties control the suggestion of reason: pleasure and profit already overswaying the instructions of honesty, and sensuality perturbing the reasonable commands of virtue. For so it is delivered in the text; that when the woman saw "that the tree was good for food," and "that it was pleasant unto the eye," and "a tree to be desired to make one wise, she took of the fruit thereof and did eat."[3] Now hereby it appeareth, that Eve, before the fall, was by the same and beaten way of allurements inveigled, whereby her posterity hath been deluded ever since; that is, those three delivered by St. John, "the lust of the flesh, the lust of the eye, and the pride of life:"[4] where indeed they seemed as weakly to fail, as their debilitated posterity, ever after. Whereof, notwithstanding, some in their imperfection have resisted more powerful temptations, and in many moralities condemned the facility of their seductions.

Again, they might, for aught we know, be still deceived in the unbelief of their mortality, even after they had eat of the fruit. For, Eve observing no immediate execution of the curse, she delivered the fruit unto Adam; who after the taste thereof, perceiving himself still to live, might yet remain in doubt, whether he had incurred death; which perhaps he did not indubitably believe, until he was after convicted in the visible example of Abel. For he that would not believe the menace of God at first, it may be doubted whether, before an ocular example, he believed the curse at last. And therefore they are not without all reason, who have disputed the fact of Cain; that is, although he purposed to do mischief, whether he intended to kill his brother; or designed that, whereof he had not beheld an example in his own kind. There might be somewhat in it, that he would not have done, or desired undone, when he brake forth as desperately, as before he had done uncivilly, my iniquity is greater than can be forgiven me.[5]

8. Genesis 2.16–17.
9. The vulgar translation: the Vulgate, the Latin translation of the Bible by St. Jerome; Thargum: Aramaic translations of the Old Testament.
1. Reasoning.
2. Servile and animalistic.
3. Genesis 3.6.
4. John 2.16.
5. Genesis 4.13–14.

Some niceties I confess there are which extenuate, but many more that aggravate this delusion; which exceeding the bounds of this discourse, and perhaps our satisfaction, we shall at present pass over. And therefore whether the sin of our first parents were the greatest of any since; whether the transgression of Eve seducing did not exceed that of Adam seduced; or whether the resistibility of his reason, did not equivalence the facility of her seduction, we shall refer it to the schoolman.[6] Whether there was not in Eve as great injustice in deceiving her husband, as imprudence in being deceived herself, especially, if foretasting the fruit, her eyes were opened before his, and she knew the effect of it, before he tasted of it, we leave it unto the moralist. Whether the whole relation be not allegorical, that is, whether the temptation of the man by the woman be not the seduction of the rational and higher parts by the inferior and feminine faculties; or whether the tree in the midst of the garden, were not that part in the center of the body, in which was afterward the appointment of circumcision in males, we leave it unto the talmudist. Whether there were any policy in the devil to tempt them before the conjunction, or whether the issue, before tentation,[7] might in justice have suffered with those after, we leave it unto the lawyer. Whether Adam foreknew the advent of Christ, or the reparation of his error by his Savior; how the execution of the curse should have been ordered, if, after Eve had eaten, Adam had yet refused; whether, if they had tasted the tree of life, before that of good and evil, they had yet suffered the curse of mortality; or whether the efficacy of the one had not overpowered the penalty of the other, we leave it unto God. For he alone can truly determine these, and all things else; who, as he hath proposed the world unto our disputation, so hath he reserved many things unto his own resolution; whose determination we cannot hope from flesh, but must with reverence suspend unto that great day, whose justice shall either condemn our curiosities, or resolve our disquisitions.

Lastly, man was not only deceivable in his integrity, but the angels of light in all their clarity. He that said, he would be like the highest,[8] did err, if in some way he conceived not himself so already: but in attempting so high an effect from himself, he misunderstood the nature of God, and held a false apprehension of his own; whereby vainly attempting not only insolencies, but impossibilities, he deceived himself as low as hell. In brief, there is nothing infallible but God, who cannot possibly err. For things are really true, as they correspond unto His conception; and have so much verity, as they hold of conformity unto that intellect, in whose idea they had their first determinations.[9] And, therefore, being the rule, he cannot be irregular; nor, being truth itself, conceivably admit the impossible society of error.

from **Hydriotaphia, Urn Burial**
or a Discourse of the Sepulchral Urns lately found in Norfolk

FROM *CHAPTER 1*

In the deep discovery of the subterranean world, a shallow part would satisfy some enquirers; who, if two or three yards were open about the surface, would not care to rake the bowels of Potosi,[1] and regions towards the center. Nature hath furnished one part of the earth, and man another. The treasures of time lie high, in

6. Medieval scholastic philosopher.
7. Temptation.
8. Lucifer.
9. According to Renaissance Platonism, the idea of each thing first existed in the mind of God.
1. Browne's marginalia: "the rich mountain of Peru," a major source of silver.

urns, coins, and monuments, scarce below the roots of some vegetables. Time hath endless rarities, and shows of all varieties; which reveals old things in heaven, makes new discoveries in earth, and even earth itself a discovery. That great antiquity America lay buried for thousands of years, and a large part of the earth is still in the urn unto us.

Though if Adam were made out of an extract of the earth,[2] all parts might challenge a restitution, yet few have returned their bones far lower than they might receive them; not affecting the graves of giants, under hilly and heavy coverings, but content with less than their own depth, have wished their bones might lie soft, and the earth be light upon them. Even such as hope to rise again, would not be content with central interment, or so desperately to place their relics as to lie beyond discovery; and in no way to be seen again; which happy contrivance hath made communication with our forefathers, and left unto our view some parts, which they never beheld themselves.

Though earth hath engrossed the name, yet water[3] hath proved the smartest grave; which in forty days swallowed almost mankind, and the living creation; fishes not wholly escaping, except the salt ocean were handsomely contempered[4] by a mixture of the fresh element.

Many have taken voluminous pains to determine the state of the soul upon disunion; but men have been most fantastical in the singular contrivances of their corporal dissolution: whilst the soberest nations have rested in two ways, of simple inhumation and burning.

That carnal interment or burying was of the elder date, the old examples of Abraham and the patriarchs are sufficient to illustrate;[5] and were without competition, if it could be made out, that Adam was buried near Damascus, or Mount Calvary, according to some tradition. God himself, that buried but one, was pleased to make choice of this way, collectible from Scripture expression, and the hot contest between Satan and the archangel, about discovering the body of Moses.[6] But the practice of burning was also of great antiquity, and of no slender extent. For (not to derive the same from Hercules) noble descriptions there are hereof in the Grecian funerals of Homer, in the formal obsequies of Patroclus, and Achilles;[7] and somewhat elder in the Theban war, and solemn combustion of Meneccus, and Archemorus, contemporary unto Jair the eighth judge of Israel.[8] Confirmable also among the Trojans, from the funeral pyre of Hector, burnt before the gates of Troy: and the burning of Penthesilea the Amazonian queen:[9] and long continuance of that practice, in the inward countries of Asia; while as low as the reign of Julian,[1] we find that the king of Chionia burnt the body of his son, and interred the ashes in a silver urn.[2]

The same practice extended also far west; and, besides Herulians, Getes, and Thracians,[3] was in use with most of the Celtae, Sarmatians, Germans, Gauls, Danes, Swedes, Norwegians; not to omit some use thereof among Carthaginians and Americans. Of greater antiquity among the Romans than most opinion, or Pliny[4] seems to allow: for (beside the old table laws of burning or burying within the city,[5] of

2. There was a traditional belief that Adam was formed of dust from the four quarters of the earth.
3. The Flood; see Genesis 7.17ff.
4. Moderated.
5. Genesis 25.9.
6. Deuteronomy 34.6; Jude 9.
7. Hercules cremated Argeus; for Homer's funerals, see *Iliad* 23.161ff. and *Odyssey* 24.65ff.
8. For Meneceus and Archemorus, see Statius, *Thebaid* 12.60ff. and 6.1ff.; for Jair, see Judges 10.3–5.
9. *Iliad* 24.782ff.
1. Roman emperor (361–363).
2. Browne's marginalia: "Gumbrates King of Chionia a Country near Persia. Ammianus Marcellinus [Roman historian, c. 390]."
3. Eastern European tribe.
4. Pliny (A.D. 23–79) author of *Historia naturalis*.
5. In the Roman code of the Twelve Tables.

making the funeral fire with planed wood, or quenching the fire with wine,) Manlius the consul burnt the body of his son: Numa,[6] by special clause of his will, was not burnt but buried; and Remus was solemnly burned, according to the description of Ovid.[7]

Cornelius Sylla was not the first whose body was burned in Rome, but the first of the Cornelian family; which, being indifferently, not frequently used before; from that time spread, and became the prevalent practice. Not totally pursued in the highest run of cremation; for when even crows were funereally burnt, Poppaea the wife of Nero found a peculiar grave interment.[8] Now as all customs were founded upon some bottom of reason, so there wanted not grounds for this; according to several apprehensions of the most rational dissolution. Some being of the opinion of Thales,[9] that water was the original of all things, thought it most equal to submit unto the principle of putrefaction, and conclude in a moist relentment.[1] Others conceived it most natural to end in fire, as due unto the master principle in the composition, according to the doctrine of Heraclitus;[2] and therefore heaped up large piles, more actively to waft them toward that element, whereby they also declined a visible degeneration into worms, and left a lasting parcel of their composition.

Some apprehended a purifying virtue in fire, refining the grosser commixture, and firing out the ethereal particles so deeply immersed in it. And such as by tradition or rational conjecture held any hint of the final pyre of all things; or that this element at last must be too hard for all the rest; might conceive most naturally of the fiery dissolution. Others pretending no natural grounds, politicly declined the malice of enemies upon their buried bodies. Which consideration led Sylla unto this practice; who having thus served the body of Marius, could not but fear a retaliation upon his own; entertained after in the civil wars, and revengeful contentions of Rome.[3]

But as many nations embraced, and many left it indifferent, so others too much affected, or strictly declined this practice. The Indian Brachmans[4] seemed too great friends unto fire, who burnt themselves alive, and thought it the noblest way to end their days in fire; according to the expression of the Indian, burning himself at Athens, in his last words upon the pyre unto the amazed spectators, thus I make myself immortal.[5]

But the Chaldeans[6] the great idolaters of fire, abhorred the burning of their carcasses, as a pollution of that deity. The Persian magi declined it upon the like scruple, and being only solicitous about their bones, exposed their flesh to the prey of birds and dogs. And the Persees now in India, which expose their bodies unto vultures, and endure not so much as *feretra* or biers of wood, the proper fuel of fire, are led on with such niceties. But whether the ancient Germans, who burned their dead, held any such fear to pollute their deity of Herthus, or the earth, we have no authentic conjecture.

6. Numa, legendary King of Rome and founder of Roman religion.
7. Browne's marginalia quotes Ovid, *Fasti* 4.856 (in Latin): "At last the flame lit the funeral pyre."
8. Tacitus, *Annals* 16.6.
9. Thales (c. 636–c. 546 B.C.), Greek Milesian philosopher.
1. Putrefaction: decay; relentment: dissolution.
2. The pre-Socratic philosopher Heraclitus (c. 535–c. 475 B.C.) believed that because fire was the underlying substance of the universe, everything in the world would ultimately be consumed by fire.
3. The rivalry between the Roman generals Marius and Sulla (Sylla) over the command of the army resulted in civil war. When Sulla won, Marius fled from Rome, but he later returned to seek revenge by killing his opponents (88 B.C.).
4. The highest Hindu caste.
5. Browne's marginalia: "And therefore the Inscription of his Tomb was made accordingly." Browne's source is Nicholas of Damascus as reported by the scholar Perucci (*Pompe funebri*, 1639).
6. Inhabitants of the Tigris and Euphrates valley.

The Egyptians were afraid of fire, not as a deity, but a devouring element, mercilessly consuming their bodies, and leaving too little of them; and therefore by precious embalments, depositure in dry earths, or handsome inclosure in glasses, contrived the notablest ways of integral conservation. And from such Egyptian scruples, imbibed by Pythagoras,[7] it may be conjectured that Numa and the Pythagorical sect first waved the fiery solution.

The Scythians,[8] who swore by wind and sword, that is, by life and death, were so far from burning their bodies, that they declined all interment, and made their graves in the air: and the Ichthyophagi, or fish-eating nations about Egypt, affected the sea for their grave; thereby declining visible corruption, and restoring the debt of their bodies. Whereas the old heroes, in Homer, dreaded nothing more than water or drowning; probably upon the old opinion of the fiery substance of the soul, only extinguishable by that element; and therefore the poet emphatically implieth the total destruction in this kind of death, which happened to Ajax Oileus.[9]

The old Balearians[1] had a peculiar mode, for they used great urns and much wood, but no fire in their burials, while they bruised the flesh and bones of the dead, crowded them into urns, and laid heaps of wood upon them.[2] And the Chinese without cremation or urnal interment of their bodies, make use of trees and much burning, while they plant a pine tree by their grave, and burn great numbers of printed draughts of slaves and horses over it, civilly content with their companies *in effigy*, which barbarous nations exact unto reality.[3]

Christians abhorred this way of obsequies,[4] and though they sticked not to give their bodies to be burnt in their lives, detested that mode after death; affecting rather a depositure than absumption,[5] and properly submitting unto the sentence of God, to return not unto ashes but unto dust again, conformable unto the practice of the patriarchs, the interment of our Savior, of Peter, Paul, and the ancient martyrs. And so far at last declining promiscuous interment with Pagans, that some have suffered ecclesiastical censures, for making no scruple thereof.[6]

The Musselman believers will never admit this fiery resolution. For they hold a present trial from their black and white angels in the grave; which they must have made so hollow, that they may rise upon their knees.

The Jewish nation, though they entertained the old way of inhumation, yet sometimes admitted this practice. For the men of Jabesh burnt the body of Saul;[7] and by no prohibited practice, to avoid contagion or pollution, in time of pestilence, burnt the bodies of their friends.[8] And when they burnt not their dead bodies, yet sometimes used great burnings near and about them, deducible from the expressions concerning Jehoram, Zedechias, and the sumptuous pyre of Asa.[9] And were so little averse from Pagan burning, that the Jews lamenting the death of Caesar their friend, and revenger on Pompey,[1] frequented the place where his body was burnt for many

7. Ancient Greek philosopher who believed in the transmigration of souls.
8. People who lived on the north shore of the Black Sea who were viewed as barbarians by the Greeks.
9. Ajax, hero of Trojan War, was struck dead by lightning.
1. Natives of the Mediterranean islands Minorca and Majorca.
2. Browne's marginalia: "Diodorus Siculus [Greek historian] 5.18."
3. Browne's marginalia: "See Ramusius" (a 16th-century Venetian collector of travel literature).
4. Funeral rites.
5. Preferring to be buried rather than cremated.
6. Browne's marginalia: "Bishop Martialis, as reported by Cyprian" (Bishop of Carthage, d. 258).
7. 1 Samuel 31.12.
8. Amos 6.10.
9. Jeremiah 34.5; 2 Chronicles 16.14, 21.19.
1. Julius Caesar defeated Pompey's forces in the Roman Civil War (48 B.C.)

nights together.[2] And as they raised noble monuments and mausoleums for their own nation,[3] so they were not scrupulous in erecting some for others, according to the practice of Daniel, who left that lasting sepulchral pile in Ecbatana, for the Median and Persian kings.[4]

But even in times of subjection and hottest use,[5] they conformed not unto the Roman practice of burning; whereby the prophecy was secured concerning the body of Christ, that it should not see corruption, or a bone should not be broken;[6] which we believe was also providentially prevented, from the soldier's spear and nails that passed by the little bones both in his hands and feet; not of ordinary contrivance, that it should not corrupt on the cross, according to the laws of Roman crucifixion, or an hair of his head perish, though observable in Jewish customs, to cut the hairs of malefactors.

Nor in their long cohabitation with Egyptians, crept into a custom of their exact embalming, wherein deeply slashing the muscles, and taking out the brains and entrails, they had broken the subject[7] of so entire a resurrection, nor fully answered the types of Enoch, Elijah, or Jonah,[8] which yet to prevent or restore, was of equal facility unto that rising power, able to break the fasciations[9] and bands of death, to get clear out of the cerecloth, and an hundred pounds of ointment, and out of the sepulchre before the stone was rolled from it.

But though they embraced not this practice of burning, yet entertained they many ceremonies agreeable unto Greek and Roman obsequies. And he that observeth their funeral feasts, their lamentations at the grave, their music, and weeping mourners; how they closed the eyes of their friends, how they washed, anointed, and kissed the dead; may easily conclude these were not mere pagan civilities. But whether that mournful burthen, and treble calling out after Absalom, had any reference unto the last conclamation,[1] and triple valediction, used by other nations, we hold but a wavering conjecture.

Civilians[2] make sepulture[3] but of the law of nations, others do naturally found it and discover it also in animals. They that are so thick-skinned[4] as still to credit the story of the Phoenix, may say something for animal burning. More serious conjectures find some examples of sepulture in elephants, cranes, the sepulchral cells of pismires, and practice of bees, which civil society carrieth out their dead, and hath exequies,[5] if not interments.

Chapter 5

Now since these dead bones have already outlasted the living ones of Methuselah,[6] and in a yard under ground, and thin walls of clay, outworn all the strong and specious buildings above it; and quietly rested under the drums and tramplings of three conquests:[7] what prince can promise such diuturnity[8] unto his relics, or might not gladly say,

2. Browne's marginalia: "So Suetonius [Roman historian], *Julius* 84.5."
3. Browne's marginalia: "As that magnificent monument erected by Simon." See 1 Macabees 1.13.
4. Browne's marginalia: "'A wonderfully made work' [quoted in Greek from Josephus, *Jewish Antiquities* 10.11.7] whereof the Jewish Priest had always the custody unto Josephus his days."
5. Most violent treatment.
6. Psalms 16.10; Acts 2.31; John 19.36.
7. Substance.
8. Enoch and Elijah are prefigurations of the Resurrection in that they were assumed into heaven; Jonah was saved from the whale.
9. Bandages.
1. Shout of many together. Browne marginalia: "O Absolom, Absolom, Absolom. 1 Samuel 18.33."
2. "Experts in those things that appertain to the administration of a commonwealth." Sir Thomas Elyot, *Dictionary* (1538).
3. Burial.
4. Stupid. Browne is thinking about Alexander Ross, who defended the existence of the phoenix and the unicorn in *Arcana Microcosmi* (1651).
5. Funeral rites.
6. Said to have lived for 969 years (Genesis 5.21).
7. I.e., Anglo-Saxon, Danish, and Norman.
8. Long duration.

Sic ego componi versus in ossa velim.[9]

Time, which antiquates antiquities, and hath an art to make dust of all things, hath yet spared these minor monuments. In vain we hope to be known by open and visible conservatories,[1] when to be unknown was the means of their continuation, and obscurity their protection. If they died by violent hands, and were thrust into their urns, these bones become considerable, and some old philosophers would honor them, whose souls they conceived most pure, which were thus snatched from their bodies, and to retain a stronger propension[2] unto them; whereas they weariedly left a languishing corpse, and with faint desires of reunion. If they fell by long and aged decay, yet wrapped up in the bundle of time, they fall into indistinction,[3] and make but one blot with infants. If we begin to die when we live, and long life be but a prolongation of death, our life is a sad composition; we live with death, and die not in a moment. How many pulses made up the life of Methuselah, were work for Archimedes: common counters sum up the life of Moses his man.[4] Our days become considerable, like petty sums, by minute accumulations; where numerous fractions make up but small round numbers; and our days of a span long, make not one little finger.[5]

If the nearness of our last necessity brought a nearer conformity unto it, there were a happiness in hoary hairs, and no calamity in half senses. But the long habit of living indisposeth us for dying; when avarice makes us the sport of death, when even David grew politicly cruel, and Solomon could hardly be said to be the wisest of men.[6] But many are too early old, and before the date of age. Adversity stretcheth our days, misery makes Alcmena's nights,[7] and time hath no wings unto it. But the most tedious being is that which can unwish itself, content to be nothing, or never to have been, which was beyond the malcontent of Job, who cursed not the day of his life, but his nativity; content to have so far been, as to have a title to future being, although he had lived here but in an hidden state of life, and as it were an abortion.[8]

What song the Sirens sang, or what name Achilles assumed when he hid himself among women, though puzzling questions, are not beyond all conjecture.[9] What time the persons of these ossuaries entered the famous nations of the dead,[1] and slept with princes and counselors,[2] might admit a wide solution. But who were the proprietaries of these bones, or what bodies these ashes made up, were a question above antiquarism; not to be resolved by man, nor easily perhaps by spirits, except we consult the provincial guardians, or tutelary observators.[3] Had they made as good provision for their names, as they have done for their relics, they had not so grossly erred in the art of perpetuation. But to subsist in bones, and be but pyramidally extant, is a fallacy in duration. Vain ashes which in the oblivion of names, persons, times, and sexes, have found unto themselves a fruitless continua-

9. Thus, when naught is left of me but bones, would I be laid to rest. (Quoting the Roman elegiac poet Tibullus 3.2.26.)

1. Places to preserve things.

2. Propensity.

3. Undistinguishableness.

4. Browne's marginalia: "In the Psalm of Moses." See Psalm 90.10. The Greek mathematician Archimedes gave directions in *The Sand Reckoner* for counting the grains of sand in the universe.

5. Browne's marginalia: "According to the ancient arithmetic of the hand wherein the little finger of the right hand contracted, signified an hundred. Pierius in *Hieroglyph [1556]*."

6. Samuel 8.2 and 1 Kings 11.1.

7. Browne's marginalia: "One night as long as three," so that Zeus could have more pleasure with Alcmena, his lover and mother of Hercules.

8. Job 3.1ff.

9. The Roman emperor Tiberius tested his grammarians by asking them such questions; see the Roman historian Suetonius, *Tiberius* 70.

1. *Odyssey* 10.526; ossuaries are urns for bones.

2. Job 3.13–15.

3. See *Religio Medici* 33: "Not only whole countries, but particular persons have their tutelary and guardian angels."

tion, and only arise unto late posterity, as emblems of mortal vanities, antidotes against pride, vainglory, and madding vices. Pagan vainglories which thought the world might last for ever, had encouragement for ambition; and, finding no *Atropos*[4] unto the immortality of their names, were never damped with the necessity of oblivion. Even old ambitions had the advantage of ours, in the attempts of their vainglories, who acting early, and before the probable meridian of time,[5] have by this time found great accomplishment of their designs, whereby the ancient heroes have already outlasted their monuments, and mechanical preservations. But in this latter scene of time, we cannot expect such mummies unto our memories, when ambition may fear the prophecy of Elias,[6] and Charles the Fifth can never hope to live within two Methuselahs of Hector.[7]

And therefore, restless inquietude for the diuturnity[8] of our memories unto present considerations seems a vanity almost out of date, and superannuated piece of folly. We cannot hope to live so long in our names, as some have done in their persons. One face of Janus[9] holds no proportion unto the other. 'Tis too late to be ambitious. The great mutations of the world are acted, or time may be too short for our designs. To extend our memories by monuments, whose death we daily pray for, and whose duration we cannot hope, without injury to our expectations in the advent of the last day, were a contradiction to our beliefs. We whose generations are ordained in this setting part of time, are providentially taken off from such imaginations; and, being necessitated to eye the remaining particle of futurity, are naturally constituted unto thoughts of the next world, and cannot excusably decline the consideration of that duration, which maketh pyramids pillars of snow, and all that's past a moment.

Circles and right lines limit and close all bodies, and the mortal right lined circle[1] must conclude and shut up all. There is no antidote against the opium of time, which temporally considereth all things: our fathers find their graves in our short memories, and sadly tell us how we may be buried in our survivors. Gravestones tell truth scarce forty years.[2] Generations pass while some trees stand, and old families last not three oaks. To be read by bare inscriptions like many in Gruter,[3] to hope for eternity by enigmatical epithets or first letters of our names, to be studied by antiquaries, who we were, and have new names given us like many of the mummies,[4] are cold consolations unto the students of perpetuity, even by everlasting languages.

To be content that times to come should only know there was such a man, not caring whether they knew more of him, was a frigid ambition in Cardan;[5] disparaging his horoscopal inclination and judgment of himself. Who cares to subsist like

4. The name of the Fate who cut short human life.
5. About 1000 B.C., the supposed midpoint of the world's history.
6. Browne's marginalia: "That the world may last but six thousand years" (i.e., from 4000 B.C. to A.D. 2000).
7. "Hector's fame lasting above two lives of Methuselah" (2×969, or 1,938 years). The fame of Charles V (born 1500) can last for only 500 years before the end of the world.
8. Long duration.
9. Roman god of doorways whose temple was shut in peace and open in war.

1. Browne's marginalia: "θ The character of death." The Greek letter theta (θ) is the initial letter in *thanatos* (death).
2. Browne's marginalia: "Old one's being taken up, and other bodies laid under them."
3. Janus Gruterus, the Dutch scholar, died c. 1607.
4. Browne's note: "Which men show in several countries, giving them what names they please; and unto some the names of the old Egyptian kings out of Herodotus."
5. Girolamo Cardano (1501–1576), Italian physician and mathematician.

Hippocrates's patients, or Achilles's horses in Homer,[6] under naked nominations, without deserts and noble acts, which are the balsam of our memories, the *entelechia*[7] and soul of our subsistences? To be nameless in worthy deeds, exceeds an infamous history. The Canaanitish woman lives more happily without a name, than Herodias with one.[8] And who had not rather have been the good thief, than Pilate?

But the iniquity of oblivion blindly scattereth her poppy, and deals with the memory of men without distinction to merit of perpetuity. Who can but pity the founder of the pyramids? Herostratus lives that burnt the temple of Diana, he is almost lost that built it.[9] Time hath spared the epitaph of Adrian's horse, confounded that of himself. In vain we compute our felicities by the advantage of our good names, since bad have equal durations, and Thersites[1] is like to live as long as Agamemnon. Who knows whether the best of men be known, or whether there be not more remarkable persons forgot, than any that stand remembered in the known account of time? Without the favor of the everlasting register, the first man had been as unknown as the last, and Methuselah's long life had been his only chronicle.

Oblivion is not to be hired. The greater part must be content to be as though they had not been, to be found in the register of God, not in the record of man. Twenty seven names make up the first story before the flood, and the recorded names ever since contain not one living century. The number of the dead long exceedeth all that shall live. The night of time far surpasseth the day, and who knows when was the equinox? Every hour adds unto that current arithmetic, which scarce stands one moment. And since death must be the *Lucina*[2] of life, and even pagans could doubt, whether thus to live were to die; since our longest sun sets at right descensions, and makes but winter arches,[3] and therefore it cannot be long before we lie down in darkness, and have our light in ashes;[4] since the brother of death[5] daily haunts us with dying mementos, and time that grows old in itself, bids us hope no long duration;—diuturnity is a dream and folly of expectation.

Darkness and light divide the course of time, and oblivion shares with memory a great part even of our living beings; we slightly remember our felicities, and the smartest strokes of affliction leave but short smart upon us. Sense endureth no extremities, and sorrows destroy us or themselves. To weep into stones are fables. Afflictions induce callosities;[6] miseries are slippery, or fall like snow upon us, which notwithstanding is no unhappy stupidity. To be ignorant of evils to come, and forgetful of evils past, is a merciful provision in nature, whereby we digest the mixture of our few and evil days, and, our delivered senses not relapsing into cutting remembrances, our sorrows are not kept raw by the edge of repetitions. A great part of antiquity contented their hopes of subsistency with a

6. For Achilles's horses, see *Iliad* 16.149–52.
7. The essence of actual being according to Aristotle, *On the Soul* 312a.
8. Herodias demanded the head of John the Baptist; the Canaanite woman offered water to Christ (Matthew 14.6, 15.22).
9. For Chersiphon, who built the temple of Diana, see Pliny 36.21.

1. Obnoxious soldier who criticized Agamemnon (*Iliad* 2).
2. Roman goddess of childbirth.
3. Our longest life is but the length of a winter's day.
4. Browne's note: "According to the custom of the Jews, who place a lighted wax candle in a pot of ashes by the corps."
5. Sleep.
6. Callousness.

transmigration of their souls,—a good way to continue their memories, while, having the advantage of plural successions, they could not but act something remarkable in such variety of beings, and enjoying the fame of their passed selves, make accumulation of glory unto their last durations. Others, rather than be lost in the uncomfortable night of nothing, were content to recede into the common being, and make one particle of the public soul of all things, which was no more than to return into their unknown and divine original again. Egyptian ingenuity was more unsatisfied, contriving their bodies in sweet consistencies, to attend the return of their souls. But all was vanity, feeding the wind,[7] and folly. The Egyptian mummies, which Cambyses[8] or time hath spared, avarice now consumeth. Mummy[9] is become merchandise, Mizraim cures wounds, and Pharaoh is sold for balsams.

In vain do individuals hope for immortality, or any patent from oblivion, in preservations below the moon: men have been deceived even in their flatteries, above the sun, and studied conceits to perpetuate their names in heaven. The various cosmography of that part hath already varied the names of contrived constellations; Nimrod is lost in Orion, and Osiris in the dog-star. While we look for incorruption in the heavens, we find they are but like the earth;—durable in their main bodies, alterable in their parts; whereof, beside comets and new stars, perspectives begin to tell tales,[1] and the spots that wander about the sun, with Phaeton's favor, would make clear conviction.

There is nothing strictly immortal, but immortality. Whatever hath no beginning, may be confident of no end;—which is the peculiar of that necessary essence that cannot destroy itself;—and the highest strain of omnipotency, to be so powerfully constituted as not to suffer even from the power of itself: all others have a dependent being and within the reach of destruction. But the sufficiency of Christian immortality frustrates all earthly glory, and the quality of either state after death, makes a folly of posthumous memory. God who can only destroy our souls, and hath assured our resurrection, either of our bodies or names hath directly promised no duration. Wherein there is so much of chance, that the boldest expectants have found unhappy frustration; and to hold long subsistence, seems but a scape in oblivion. But man is a noble animal, splendid in ashes, and pompous in the grave, solemnizing nativities and deaths with equal lustre, nor omitting ceremonies of bravery in the infamy of his nature.

Life is a pure flame, and we live by an invisible sun within us. A small fire sufficeth for life, great flames seemed too little after death, while men vainly affected precious pyres, and to burn like Sardanapalus;[2] but the wisdom of funeral laws found the folly of prodigal blazes, and reduced undoing fires unto the rule of sober obsequies, wherein few could be so mean as not to provide wood, pitch, a mourner, and an urn.[3]

Five languages secured not the epitaph of Gordianus.[3] The man of God lives longer without a tomb than any by one, invisibly interred by angels, and adjudged to obscurity, though not without some marks directing human discovery. Enoch

7. Ecclesiastes 1.14.
8. Ancient Persian king who attacked Egypt.
9. Ground up, as a drug.
1. "Perspectives" (telescopes) showed that comets penetrated the region above the moon, an area that Aristotle claimed was "incorruptible."
2. Assyrian king who had his whole court buried with him.
3. Browne's note: "In Greek, Latin, Hebrew, Egyptian, Arabic, defaced by Licinus the Emperor."

and Elias,[4] without either tomb or burial, in an anomalous state of being, are the great examples of perpetuity, in their long and living memory, in strict account being still on this side death, and having a late part yet to act upon this stage of earth. If in the decretory term of the world[5] we shall not all die but be changed, according to received translation, the last day will make but few graves; at least quick resurrections will anticipate lasting sepultures. Some graves will be opened before they be quite closed, and Lazarus[6] be no wonder. When many that feared to die, shall groan that they can die but once, the dismal state is the second and living death,[7] when life puts despair on the damned; when men shall wish the coverings of mountains, not of monuments, and annihilation shall be courted.

While some have studied monuments, others have studiously declined them, and some have been so vainly boisterous, that they durst not acknowledge their graves; wherein Alaricus seems most subtle, who had a river turned to hide his bones at the bottom.[8] Even Sylla, that thought himself safe in his urn, could not prevent revenging tongues, and stones thrown at his monument. Happy are they whom privacy makes innocent, who deal so with men in this world, that they are not afraid to meet them in the next; who, when they die, make no commotion among the dead, and are not touched with that poetical taunt of Isaiah.[9]

Pyramids, arches, obelisks, were but the irregularities of vainglory, and wild enormities of ancient magnanimity. But the most magnanimous resolution rests in the Christian religion, which trampleth upon pride, and sits on the neck of ambition, humbly pursuing that infallible perpetuity, unto which all others must diminish their diameters, and be poorly seen in angles of contingency.[1]

Pious spirits who passed their days in raptures of futurity, made little more of this world, than the world that was before it, while they lay obscure in the chaos of preordination, and night of their forebeings. And if any have been so happy as truly to understand Christian annihilation, ecstasies, exolution, liquefaction, transformation, the kiss of the Spouse, gustation of God, and ingression into the divine shadow,[2] they have already had an handsome anticipation of heaven; the glory of the world is surely over, and the earth in ashes unto them.

To subsist in lasting monuments, to live in their productions, to exist in their names and predicament of chimaeras,[3] was large satisfaction unto old expectations, and made one part of their Elysiums. But all this is nothing in the metaphysics of true belief. To live indeed, is to be again ourselves, which being not only an hope, but an evidence in noble believers, 't is all one to lie in St. Innocent's churchyard,[4] as in the sands of Egypt. Ready to be any thing, in the ecstasy of being ever, and as content with six foot as the *moles* of Adrianus.[5]

> —*tabésne cadavera solvat,*
> *An rogus, haud refert.*—Lucan.[6]

4. Believed to be the "two witnesses" of Revelation 11.3ff., who would appear at the end of time.
5. I.e., the Last Judgment.
6. Raised from death by Christ (John 11).
7. Revelation 20.14, 21.8.
8. Browne's marginalia: "According to Jordandes [6th-century historian of the Goths]."
9. Browne's marginalia: "Isaiah 14.4–17."
1. Browne's marginalia: "*Angulus contingentiae*, the least of Angles."
2. Exolution: the soul's release; the Spouse: the Church; ingression into the divine shadow: echoes the Platonic philosopher Ficino, who expressed the paradox that light is the shadow of God.
3. Predicament is a term in logic, meaning that which is asserted. Chimaeras were creatures with a lion's head, a goat's body, and a serpent's tale; hence a fanciful notion or unfounded conception.
4. Browne's marginalia: "In Paris where bodies soon consume."
5. Roman mausoleum.
6. It does not matter whether the corpses are placed on the pyre or decompose (Lucan, *Civil War* 7.809–10).

Robert Burton

(1577–1640)

One of the most learned authors of his generation, Robert Burton was also one of the most popular and influential. While he spent most of his life at Oxford, where he was elected a student of Christ Church and took his Bachelor of Divinity in 1614, Burton wrote *The Anatomy of Melancholy* (1621) which went through many different editions (eight alone in the seventeenth century) and made a bundle of money for its publisher Henry Cripps. The topic was based on the ancient theory of the humors, which still dominated both medicine and personality theory in the early modern period. The sanguine humor was hot and moist and characterized a happy disposition; the choleric humor was hot and dry and characterized an angry one; the phlegmatic humor was cold and moist and characterized an impassive one; and the melancholic humor was cold and dry and signified the pensive and imaginative soul of Hamlet and so many other lovelorn sonneteers, scholars, and mystics.

An anatomy, exhaustively dissecting the topic into its parts, the book treats the full body of knowledge on the disease of melancholy with an encyclopedic thoroughness, covering the inherited wisdom of a whole gamut of ancient authors. The book is huge, a veritable brick even in paperback. It is divided into three parts: the causes and symptoms of melancholy, cures for melancholy, and love melancholy and religious melancholy. One of the liveliest parts of the book is its preface, *Democritus to the Reader*, in which Burton writes of his "silent, sedentary, solitary, private life" and of "the diseases in a commonwealth."

As this brief quotation suggests, Burton was a master of the elegant pleonasm, prolific in the elegantly varied synonym. His syntax is almost the opposite of Bacon's. Where Bacon's sentences are terse and pointed, Burton's are long and meandering. Part of the pleasure in reading this unfamiliar prose style comes from its unexpected digressions. Much loved in the author's own lifetime, Burton's *Anatomy* influenced Milton's *L'Allegro* and *Il Penseroso*. Later, Dr. Johnson wrote that *The Anatomy* was the only book that could get him out of bed two hours earlier than he was used to. Closest to Sir Thomas Browne's style in its humor, Robert Burton's *Anatomy* is a delightful read, a cure for boredom in any age.

from The Anatomy of Melancholy

[THE UTOPIA OF DEMOCRITUS][1]

Kingdoms, provinces, and politic bodies are likewise sensible and subject to this disease, as Boterus in his Politics hath proved at large.[2] "As in human bodies," saith he, "there be divers alterations proceeding from humors, so there be many diseases in a commonwealth, which do as diversely happen from several distempers," as you may easily perceive by their particular symptoms. For where you shall see the people civil, obedient to God and Princes, judicious, peaceable and quiet, rich, fortunate, and flourish, to live in peace, in unity and concord, a country well tilled, many fair built and populous cities, as old Cato said,[3] the people are neat, polite and terse, where they live well and happily, which our politicians make the chief end of a commonwealth; and which Aristotle calls a general blessing, Polybius a desirable and favor-

1. Democritus was an ancient Greek philosopher who held that all things were composed of atoms. Though melancholy by nature, he laughed at the world. Burton's purpose in his *Anatomy* is to find the cause of melancholy as Democritus searched for the cause of melancholy when he cut up beasts and looked at their insides.

2. Giovanni Botero, *De politia illustrium*, translated into English as *Of the Greatness and Magnificance of Cities* (1606).

3. Cato the Elder (234–149 B.C.) in his *De re rustica* (On Farming).

able condition, that country is free from melancholy;[4] as it was in Italy in the time of Augustus, now in China, now in many other flourishing kingdoms of Europe. But whereas you shall see many discontents, common grievances, complaints, poverty, barbarism, beggary, plagues, wars, rebellions, seditions, mutinies, contentions, idleness, riot, epicurism,[5] the land lie untilled, waste, full of bogs, fens, deserts, &c., cities decayed, base and poor towns, villages depopulated, the people squalid, ugly, uncivil; that kingdom, that country, must needs be discontent, melancholy, hath a sick body, and had need to be reformed.

Now that cannot well be effected, till the causes of these maladies be first removed, which commonly proceed from their own default, or some accidental inconvenience: as to be sited in a bad clime, too far North, sterile, in a barren place, as the desert of Libya, deserts of Arabia, places void of waters, as those of Lop and Belgian in Asia, or in a bad air, as at Alexandretta, Bantam, Pisa, Durazzo, S. John de Ullua, &c., or in danger of the sea's continual inundations, as in many places of the Low Countries, and elsewhere, or near some bad neighbors, as Hungarians to Turks, Podolians to Tartars,[6] or almost any bordering countries, they live in fear still, and by reason of hostile incursions are oftentimes left desolate. So are cities by reason of wars, fires, plagues, inundations, wild beasts, decay of trades, barred havens, the sea's violence, as Antwerp may witness of late, Syracuse of old, Brundusium in Italy, Rye & Dover with us, and many that at this day suspect the sea's fury and rage, and labor against it, as the Venetians, to their inestimable charge. But the most frequent maladies are such as proceed from themselves, as first when religion & God's service is neglected, innovated or altered, where they do not fear God, obey their Prince, where Atheism, Epicurism, Sacrilege, Simony,[7] &c., and all such impieties are freely committed, that country cannot prosper. When Abraham came to Gerar, and saw a bad land, he said, sure the fear of God was not in that place.[8] Cyprian Echovius, a Spanish Chorographer,[9] above all other Cities of Spain commends Barcino,[1] "in which there was no beggar, no man poor, &c., but all rich and in good estate, and he gives the reason, because they were more religious than their neighbors." Why was Israel so often spoiled by their enemies, led into captivity, &c., but for their idolatry, neglect of God's word, for sacrilege, even for one Achan's fault?[2] And what shall we expect that have such multitudes of Achans, Church-robbers, Simoniacal Patrons, &c.? How can they hope to flourish, that neglect divine duties, that live most part like Epicures?[3]

Other common grievances are generally noxious to a body politic; alteration of laws and customs, breaking privileges, general oppressions, seditions, &c., observed by Aristotle,[4] Bodine, Boterus, Junius, Arniseus, &c. I will only point at some of the chiefest. Confusion, ill government, which proceeds from unskillful, slothful, griping, covetous, unjust, rash, or tyrannizing magistrates, when they are fools, idiots, children, proud, wilful, partial, indiscreet, oppressors, giddy heads, tyrants, not able or unfit to manage such offices.[5] Many noble cities and flourishing kingdoms by that

4. The commonweal of Aristotle, *Politics* 3.4; see also Polybius 6 and Plato, *Laws* 5.
5. The philosophy of Epicurus, devotion to a life of ease, in which pleasure is the greatest good.
6. Podolians: inhabitants of West central Ukraine; Tartars: inhabitants of Central Asia.
7. The selling of church offices, benefices, or preferments.
8. Genesis 10.19, 20.1.
9. Cyprian Echovius, a writer of geographical description, *Deliciis Hispaniae* (1604).
1. Barcelona.
2. Achan, a Judahite who was stoned for keeping some of the spoil from Jericho. Joshua 7.1; Chronicles 2.7.
3. Those who think pleasure is the greatest good.
4. Aristotle, *Politics* 5.3.
5. A reference to *Polycraticus*, a treatise on government, by John of Salisbury, 12th-century English scholastic philosopher.

means are desolate, the whole body groans under such heads, and all the members must needs be misaffected, as at this day those goodly provinces in Asia Minor, &c., groan under the burden of a Turkish government; and those vast kingdoms of Muscovia, Russia,[6] under a tyrannizing Duke. Who ever heard of more civil and rich populous countries than those of Greece, Asia Minor, "abounding with all wealth, multitude of inhabitants, force, power, splendor, and magnificence?" and that miracle of countries, the Holy Land, that in so small a compass of ground could maintain so many towns, cities, produce so many fighting men? Egypt, another Paradise, now barbarous and desert, and almost waste, by the despotical government of an imperious Turk, sent into an intolerable slavery (one saith); not only fire and water, goods or lands, but such is their slavery, their lives and souls depend upon his insolent will and command: a tyrant that spoils all wheresoever he comes, insomuch that an historian complains, "If an old inhabitant should now see them, he would not know them, if a traveler, or stranger, it would grieve his heart to behold them." Where, as Aristotle notes, new burdens and exactions daily come upon them, like those of which Zosimus [speaks],[7] so grievous, as that men prostituted their wives, fathers their sons, for the profit of overseers, &c., they must needs be discontent, as Tully holds,[8] hence come those complaints and tears of cities, poor, miserable, rebellious, and desperate subjects, as Hippolytus[9] adds: and as a judicious countryman of ours observed not long since in a survey of that great Duchy of Tuscany, the people lived much grieved and discontent, as appeared by their manifold and manifest complainings in that kind; "that the State was like a sick body which had lately taken physic, whose humors were not yet well settled, and weakened so much by purging, that nothing was left but melancholy."

Whereas the Princes and Potentates are immoderate in lust, hypocrites, epicures, of no religion, but in show: what so brittle and unsure? what sooner subverts their estates than wandering & raging lusts on their subjects' wives, daughters, to say no worse? They that should lead the way to all virtuous actions, are the ringleaders oftentimes of all mischief and dissolute courses, and by that means their countries are plagued, "and they themselves often ruined, banished or murdered by conspiracy of their subjects,"[1] as Sardanapulus was, Dionysius Junior, Heliogabalus, Periander, Pisistratus, Tarquinius, Timocrates, Childericus, Appius Claudius, Andronicus, Galeazzo Sforza, Alexander de Medici, &c.

Whereas the Princes or great men are malicious, envious, factious, ambitious, emulators, they tear a commonwealth asunder, as so many Guelfs and Ghibellines,[2] disturb the quietness of it, and with mutual murders let it bleed to death. Our histories are too full of such barbarous inhumanities, and the miseries that issue from them.

Whereas they be like so many horse-leeches, hungry, griping, corrupt, covetous, greedy for property, ravenous as wolves (for as Tully writes, "Whoso rules is a benefit, and he who rules cattle should study their interests"), or such prefer their private before the public good (for as he said long since, "private interests always interfere with public benefits"), or whereas they be illiterate, ignorant, empirics[3] in policy, lacking in capacity, courage, & knowledge, wise only by inheritance, and in authority

6. See Dr. Giles Fletcher's *Of the Russe Common Wealth* (1591).
7. Zosimus, a strongly anti-Christian, Greek author (fl. 450), who wrote a history of the Roman empire.
8. Marcus Tullius Cicero, *Epistulae ad Atticum* 2.18.
9. Hippolytus Collibus, early modern Swiss author of *The Growth of Cities*.
1. Boterus *De Politia illustrium* 9.4.
2. The warring parties of the Pope and of the Emperor in late medieval Florence.
3. Those who draw their practice only from experience.

by birthright, favor, or for their wealth and titles; there must needs be a fault, a great defect: because, as an old philosopher affirms, such men are not always fit: "Of an infinite number few alone are Senators, and of those few fewer good, and of that small number of honest good and noble men, few that are learned, wise, discreet and sufficient, able to discharge such places;" it must needs turn to the confusion of a State.

For as the Princes are, so are the people;[4] and which Antigonus right well said of old, he that teacheth the King of Macedon, teacheth all his subjects, is a true saying still.

For Princes are the glass, the school, the book,
Where subjects' eyes do learn, do read, do look.

Shakespeare[5]

———Swiftly, in a trice,
We are corrupted by domestic vice;
When precedents of sin our great ones give,
Few are the youths that free from vice can live.

Juvenal[6]

Their examples are soonest followed, vices entertained; if they be profane, irreligious, lascivious, riotous, epicures, factious, covetous, ambitious, illiterate, so will the commons most part be idle, unthrifts, prone to lust, drunkards, and therefore poor and needy (for poverty begets sedition and villainy), upon all occasions ready to mutiny and rebel, discontent still, complaining, murmuring, grudging, apt to all outrages, thefts, treasons, murders, innovations, in debt, shifters, cozeners, outlaws, men of evil life and reputation. It was an old Politician's Aphorism, "They that are poor and bad envy rich, hate good men, abhor the present government, wish for a new, and would have all turned topsy-turvy."[7] When Catiline rebelled in Rome, he got a company of such debauched rogues together, they were his familiars and coadjutors; and such have been your rebels most part in all ages, Jack Cade, Tom Straw, Kett, and his companions.[8]

Where they be generally riotous and contentious, where there be many discords, many laws, many lawsuits, many lawyers, and many physicians, it is a manifest sign of a distempered, melancholy state, as Plato long since maintained: for where such kind of men swarm, they will make more work for themselves, and that body politic diseased, which was otherwise sound. A general mischief in these our times, an insensible plague, and never so many of them: "which are now multiplied" (saith Mat. Geraldus, a Lawyer himself,) "as so many locusts, not the parents, but the plagues of the country, & for the most part a supercilious, bad, covetous, litigious generation of men;" a purse-milking nation, a clamorous company, gowned vultures, "who live by violence and bloodshed, thieves and seminaries of discord; worse than any pollers[9] by the highway side, gold-hawks, gold-borers, money-fishers, temple thieves, market-jinglers, horrible wretches, slave-traders, &c.," that take upon them to make peace, but are indeed the very disturbers of our peace, a company of irreligious Harpies, scraping, griping catchpoles (I mean our common hungry pettifoggers; I love and honor in the mean time all good laws, and worthy lawyers, that are so many oracles

4. Cicero, *De legibus* 3.
5. Shakespeare, *The Rape of Lucrece*, 615–16.
6. Juvenal 14.31–33.
7. Sallust, *Cataline* 37.3.
8. Jack Cade led the 1450 rebellion in Kent. Robert Kett (d. 1549) led an agrarian revolt in Norfolk against the enclosure of common land for sheep grazing.
9. Robbers.

and pilots of a well-governed commonwealth), without art, without judgment, that do more harm, as Livy said, than sickness, wars, hunger, diseases; "and cause a most incredible destruction of a Commonwealth," saith Sesellius, a famous Civilian sometime in Paris. As ivy doth by an oak, embrace it so long, until it hath got the heart out of it, so do they by such places they inhabit, no counsel at all, no justice, no speech to be had, he must be fee'd still, or else he is as mute as a fish, better open an oyster without a knife. "I speak out of experience," saith Sarisburiensis,[1] "I have been a thousand times amongst them, & Charon[2] himself is more gentle than they; he is contented with his single pay, but they multiply still, they are never satisfied:" besides, they have pernicious tongues, as he terms it, they must be fee'd to say nothing, and get more to hold their peace than we can to say our best. They will speak their clients fair, and invite them to their tables, but, as he follows it, "of all injustice there is none so pernicious as that of theirs, which, when they deceive most, will seem to be honest men." They take upon them to be peacemakers, and to espouse the cause of the humble, to help them to their right, they play patron to the afflicted, but all is for their own good, that they may drain the moneybags of the rich, they plead for poor men free, but they are but as a stale to catch others. If there be no jar, they can make a jar, out of the law itself find still some quirk or other, to set them at odds, and continue causes so long, I know not how many years before the cause is heard, and when 'tis judged and determined, by reason of some tricks and errors it is as fresh to begin, after twice seven years sometimes, as it was at first; and so they prolong time, delay suits, till they have enriched themselves, and beggared their clients. And as Cato inveighed against Isocrates' scholars,[3] we may justly tax our wrangling lawyers, they do grow old in lawsuits, are so litigious & busy here on earth, that I think they will plead their clients' causes hereafter, some of them in hell. Simlerus complains, amongst the Switzers, of the Advocates in his time, that when they should make an end, they begin controversies, and "protract their causes many years, persuading them their title is good, till their patrimonies be consumed, and that they have spent more in seeking than the thing is worth, or they shall get by the recovery."[4] So he that goes to law, as the proverb is, holds a wolf by the ears, or, as a sheep in a storm runs for shelter to a briar, if he prosecute his cause he is consumed, if he surcease his suit he loseth all; what difference? They had wont, heretofore, saith Austin,[5] to end matters by common arbitrators, and so in Switzerland, (we are informed by Simlerus,) "they had some common arbitrators, or daysmen in every town, that made a friendly composition betwixt man and man; and he much wonders at their honest simplicity, that could keep peace so well, and end such great causes by that means." At Fez, in Africa, they have neither lawyers nor advocates; but if there be any controversies amongst them, both parties, plaintiff and defendant, come to their Alfakins or chief Judges, "& at once, without any further appeals or pitiful delays, the cause is heard and ended. Our forefathers, as a worthy Chorographer[6] of ours observes, had wont with a few golden crosses, and lines in verse, [to] make all conveyances, assurances. And such was the candor & integrity of succeeding ages, that a deed (as I have oft seen), to convey a whole manor, was succinctly contained

1. John of Salisbury, *Polycraticus*, 1. Prologue.
2. Mythological figure who conveyed the souls of the dead across the River Styx.
3. Plutarch, *Life of Cato* 23.
4. Simlerus, 16th century Swiss theologian and author of a history of the Helvetian Republic.
5. Saint Augustine (354–430).
6. Describer of particular regions referring to William Camden, author of *Brittania* (1586).

in some twenty lines or thereabouts; like that Schede or Scytala Laconica,[7] so much renowned of old in all contracts, which Tully so earnestly commends to Atticus,[8] Plutarch in his Lysander, Aristotle, Thucydides, Diodorus, and Suidas, approve and magnify for that Laconic brevity in this kind; and well they might, for, according to Tertullian,[9] there is much more certainty in fewer words. And so was it of old throughout: but now many skins of parchment will scarce serve turn; he that buys and sells a house, must have a house full of writings, there be so many circumstances, so many words, such tautological repetitions of all particulars (to avoid cavillation, they say), but we find, by our woeful experience, that to subtle wits it is a cause of much more contention and variance, and scarce any conveyance so accurately penned by one, which another will not find a crack in, or cavil at; if any one word be misplaced, any little error, all is disannulled. That which is law today is none tomorrow, that which is sound in one man's opinion, is most faulty to another; that, in conclusion, here is nothing amongst us but contention and confusion, we band one against another. And that which long since Plutarch complained of them in Asia, may be verified in our times. "These men here assembled, come not to sacrifice to their gods, to offer Jupiter their first fruits, or merriments to Bacchus; but a yearly disease exasperating Asia hath brought them hither, to make an end of their controversies and law suits." 'Tis a destructive rout that seek one another's ruin. Such most part are our ordinary suitors, termers, clients; new stirs every day, mistakes, errors, cavils, and at this present, as I have heard, in some one Court, I know not how many thousand causes: no person free, no title almost good, with such bitterness in following, so many slights, procrastinations, delays, forgery, such cost (for infinite sums are inconsiderately spent), violence and malice, I know not by whose fault, lawyers, clients, laws, both or all: but as Paul reprehended the Corinthians long since,[1] I may more appositely infer now: "There is a fault amongst you, & I speak it to your shame; is there not a wise man amongst you, to judge between his brethren; but that a brother goes to law with a brother?" And Christ's counsel concerning lawsuits was never so fit to be inculcated, as in this age: "Agree with thine adversary quickly," &c.[2] I could repeat many such particular grievances, which must disturb a body politic. To shut up all in brief, where good government is, prudent and wise Princes, there all things thrive and prosper, peace and happiness is in that land: where it is otherwise, all things are ugly to behold, incult,[3] barbarous, uncivil, a Paradise is turned to a wilderness. This Island amongst the rest, our next neighbors the French and Germans, may be a sufficient witness, that in a short time, by that prudent policy of the Romans, was brought from barbarism; see but what Caesar reports of us, and Tacitus of those old Germans; they were once as uncivil as they in Virginia, yet by planting of colonies and good laws, they became, from barbarous outlaws, to be full of rich and populous cities, as now they are, and most flourishing kingdoms. Even so might Virginia, and those wild Irish, have been civilized long since, if that order had been heretofore taken, which now begins, of planting colonies, &c. I have read a discourse, printed in the year 1612, "discovering the true causes why Ireland was never entirely subdued, or brought under obedience to the Crown of England, until the beginning of his Majesty's happy reign."[4] Yet if his reasons were thoroughly scanned

7. Spartan ordinance.
8. Cicero, *Epistulae ad Atticum* 10.3.
9. Roman theologian (c. A.D. 150–230).
1. 1 Corinthians 6.5–6.
2. Matthew 5.25.
3. Uncultivated, rough.
4. The author is Sir John Davies (1529–1626), Attorney General for Ireland.

by a judicious politician, I am afraid he would not altogether be approved, but that it would turn to the dishonor of our nation, to suffer it to lie so long waste. Yea, and if some travelers should see (to come nearer home) those rich United Provinces of Holland, Zealand, &c., over against us; those neat cities and populous towns, full of most industrious artificers, so much land recovered from the sea, and so painfully preserved by those artificial inventions, so wonderfully approved, as that of Bemster in Holland, so that you would find nothing equal to it or like it in the whole world, saith Bertius the Geographer, all the world cannot match it, so many navigable channels from place to place, made by men's hands, &c., and on the other side so many thousand acres of our fens lie drowned, our cities thin, and those vile, poor, and ugly to behold in respect of theirs, our trades decayed, our still running rivers stopped, and that beneficial use of transportation wholly neglected, so many havens void of ships and towns, so many parks and forests for pleasure, barren heaths, so many villages depopulated, &c., I think sure he would find some fault.

I may not deny but that this nation of ours doth bear a good name amongst foreigners, is a most noble, a most flourishing kingdom, by common consent of all Geographers, Historians, Politicians, 'tis an unique stronghold, and which Quintius in Livy said of the inhabitants of Peloponnesus, may be well applied to us, we are like so many tortoises in our shells, safely defended by an angry sea, as a wall on all sides. Our Island hath many such honorable elogiums;[5] and as a learned countryman of ours right well hath it, "Ever since the Normans' first coming into England, this country both for military matters, and all other of civility, hath been paralleled with the most flourishing kingdoms of Europe & our Christian world,"[6] a blessed, a rich country, and one of the fortunate Isles: and for some things preferred before other countries, for expert seamen, our laborious discoveries, art of navigation, true merchants, they carry the bell away from all other nations, even the Portugals and Hollanders themselves; "without all fear," saith Boterus,[7] "furrowing the ocean winter and summer, and two of their captains, with no less valor than fortune, have sailed round about the world." We have besides many particular blessings, which our neighbors want, the Gospel truly preached, Church discipline established, long peace and quietness, free from exactions, foreign fears, invasions, domestical seditions, well manured, fortified by art and nature, and now most happy in that fortunate union of England and Scotland,[8] which our forefathers have labored to effect, and desired to see. But in which we excel all others, a wise, learned, religious King, another Numa, a second Augustus, a true Josiah,[9] most worthy senators, a learned clergy, an obedient commonalty, &c. Yet amongst many roses some thistles grow, some bad weeds and enormities, which much disturb the peace of this body politic, eclipse the honor and glory of it, fit to be rooted out, and with all speed to be reformed.

Division of the Body, Humors, Spirits[1]

Of the parts of the Body, there be many divisions: the most approved is that of Laurentius,[2] out of Hippocrates: which is, into parts contained, or containing. Contained are either humors or spirits.

5. Eulogies.
6. Camden, *Brittania* (1586).
7. Giovanni Botero, an Italian political theorist.
8. Effected by James VI of Scotland's becoming James I of England.
9. Numa, founder of Roman religion; Augustus, first Roman emperor; Josiah, reformer of Jewish law.
1. Part I, Section I, Member ii, Subsection II.
2. Andreas Laurentius, 16th-century writer on anatomy; Hippocrates, Greek founder of medicine.

A humor is a liquid or fluent part of the body, comprehended in it, for the preservation of it; and is either innate or born with us, or adventitious and acquisite. The radical or innate is daily supplied by nourishment, which some call cambium, and make those secondary humors of ros and gluten to maintain it; or acquisite, to maintain these four first primary humors, coming and proceeding from the first concoction in the liver, by which means chyle[3] is excluded. Some divide them into profitable and excrementitious. But Crato[4] out of Hippocrates will have all four to be juice, and not excrements, without which no living creature can be sustained: which four, though they be comprehended in the mass of blood, yet they have their several affections, by which they are distinguished from one another, and from those adventitious, peccant, or diseased humors, as Melancthon[5] calls them.

Blood is a hot, sweet, temperate, red humor, prepared in the meseraic[6] veins, and made of the most temperate parts of the chylus in the liver, whose office is to nourish the whole body, to give it strength and color, being dispersed by the veins through every part of it. And from it spirits are first begotten in the heart, which afterwards by the arteries are communicated to the other parts.

Pituita, or phlegm, is a cold and moist humor, begotten of the colder parts of the chylus (or white juice coming out of the meat digested in the stomach) in the liver; his office is to nourish and moisten the members of the body, which, as the tongue, are moved, that they be not over dry.

Choler is hot and dry, bitter, begotten of the hotter parts of the chylus, and gathered to the gall: it helps the natural heat and senses, and serves to the expelling of excrements.

Melancholy, cold and dry, thick, black, and sour, begotten of the more feculent[7] part of nourishment, and purged from the spleen, is a bridle to the other two hot humors, blood and choler, preserving them in the blood, and nourishing the bones. These four humors have some analogy with the four elements, and to the four ages in man.

To these humors you may add serum, which is the matter of urine, & those excrementitious humors of the third concoction, sweat & tears.

Spirit is a most subtle vapor, which is expressed from the blood, and the instrument of the soul, to perform all his actions; a common tie or medium betwixt the body and the soul, as some will have it; or, as Paracelsus,[8] a fourth soul of itself. Melancthon holds the fountain of these spirits to be the heart; begotten there, and afterwards conveyed to the brain, they take another nature to them: Of these spirits there be three kinds, according to the three principal parts, brain, heart, liver; natural, vital, animal. The natural are begotten in the liver, and thence dispersed through the veins, to perform those natural actions. The vital spirits are made in the heart of the natural, which by the arteries are transported to all the other parts: if these spirits cease, then life ceaseth, as in a syncope or swooning. The animal spirits formed of the vital, brought up to the brain, and diffused by the nerves, to the subordinate members, give sense and motion to them all.

3. The white milky fluid formed by the action of the pancreatic juice and the bile on the chyme, or pulpy acid matter into which food is converted in the stomach.
4. Johann Craton, 16th-century German author of medical treatises.
5. Philip Melanchthon (1497–1560), a humanist and one of the leading figures of the Lutheran Reformation.
6. A vein of the middle belly.
7. Of the nature of feces.
8. Swiss physician, alchemist, and chemist (1493?–1541). His work was first translated into English as *One Hundred and Fourteen Experiments and Cures* (1590).

The Execution of Charles I. Seventeenth-century German print.

Perspectives

The Civil War, or the Wars of Three Kingdoms

The English Civil War arose out of citizens' revolutionary demands for their rights and those of their legislature, and out of England's attempt to dominate Ireland and Scotland. The armed conflicts that arose from the demand for political self-determination in every part of the British Isles would have consequences for centuries to come. During the period from 1639 to 1651, war raged not only in England but also in Ireland, Scotland, and Wales; hence, historians now prefer to call this period of conflict the Wars of Three Kingdoms. The origins of the conflict in England were between Parliament and a King who had an absolutist style of governing. Charles I reigned without Parliament from 1629 to 1640, a period referred to as the "Eleven Years' Tyranny." He also imposed unpopular heavy taxes in the form of ship money levies to build up the fleet. Even more controversial was his imposition of Anglican worship and episcopal authority on Puritans and Presbyterians, who felt that such ritual was tantamount to Roman Catholicism. The King placed two Anglican bishops on the court of Star Chamber, who used the arbitrary power of this body to enforce unpopular religious practices.

When the King decided to impose an Anglican liturgy on the Scottish Kirk in 1639, riots broke out in Edinburgh, and Scottish Lowlanders united in a National Covenant against English interference. In 1639 and 1640, Scottish military uprisings necessitated Charles I's recalling Parliament to ask for financial aid. The Parliament was already angered by the eleven-year shutdown by the King, his imposition of taxes without its consent, and his support for Archbishop Laud, whom Parliament viewed as too dictatorial and too high church, shutting out both Puritans (who elected their ministers and disdained Catholic sacraments) and Presbyterians (who favored central church government but not Anglo-Catholic authority or ritual). When Parliament refused after three weeks to grant the King's request for money, the King decided to dissolve the "Short Parliament." In the wake of the dissolution of Parliament, soldiers went on rampages against churches, smashing stained glass windows and altar rails that smacked to them of Roman Catholicism. In some places, soldiers mutinied against their aristocratic commanders.

When the Scots defeated the King's army in the fall of 1640, he had to recall Parliament to petition for more funds. Led by John Pym, the "Long Parliament" seized the opportunity to criticize the King. It passed a Bill of Attainder, condemning to death as a traitor the general of the King's army, Viscount Strafford, who had been accused of instigating the war against Scotland and of suggesting that an Irish Catholic army could be used against England. No proof of guilt was necessary, only assent from the House of Lords and the King. Despite the King's reluctance, the combined opposition of the House of Commons and armed mobs in London in the spring of 1641 pressured him into signing Strafford's death warrant.

That fall two rebellions broke out in Ireland—one organized by Catholic Irish gentry, another arising more spontaneously among the native Gaelic Irish in Ulster against Scots and English settlers who had dispossessed them of their land. Pym blamed the unrest on the King and his Catholic court. Although there was terrible violence, especially in the popular uprisings, the English press wildly exaggerated the extent of the bloodshed, claiming a figure for Protestant deaths in the North of Ireland that was greater than the number of Protestants then living in the whole country. Pym, the leader of the House of Commons, moved that Parliament should offer no help in repressing Irish rebellion unless Charles agreed to dismiss his guilty counselors. The next day, Oliver Cromwell moved that the Parliament empower the Puritan Earl of Essex to head the English militia. Attacks on the King became stronger: his irresponsibility and violation of the security and rights of the people mandated Parliament's wresting power from him. On May 12, Archbishop Laud was executed. Although the King made some concessions, by January 1642 he decided to impeach Pym, four other members of Commons, and one from the House of Lords for treason. However, the accused were safely hidden in the City, and the King left London, not to return until he was put on trial and beheaded six years later. Just on the eve of the outbreak of the war, the "Gentlewomen and Tradesmen's Wives of London" presented their petition to Parliament, complaining against Archbishop Laud's Anglicanism and the threat of violence from Ireland. The first part of the English Civil War (1642–1646), arising from the disputes between Parliament and the King, culminated in the victory of Parliament's New Model Army, headed by Sir Thomas Fairfax.

With the King defeated by the combined forces of the New Model Army and the Scots Covenanters in 1646, new conflicts arose between the army and the Parliament. Closely tied to the army, the Levellers, led by John Lilburne, agitated for a fundamental revision of the constitution: a single representative body, universal suffrage for men, and the abolition of monarchy and noble privilege. Colonel Ludlow, a leader of the republicans, opposed any negotiations with the King and petitioned Parliament to reform the constitution and to put the King on trial. When the House of Commons refused to listen to the army and continued to negotiate with the King, Colonels Ludlow, Ireton, and Pride purged Parliament, placing forty-five members under arrest and prohibiting another 186 from entering the House. This Rump Parliament set up a high court to try the King. On 27 January 1649, Charles I was condemned to death as a tyrant and traitor who had shed the blood of his people. John Bradshaw, President of the Court, proclaimed that the King was subject to the law and the law proceeded from Parliament. Arising out of these events came both the King's own memoir, *Eikon Basilike* ("the

Peter Paul Rubens. *Peace and War.* 1630. One of the greatest painters of the Flemish school, Rubens grew up in Antwerp, where he married and set up his studio. After the death of his wife in 1626, he entered the diplomatic service, traveling to Spain to negotiate a treaty between Philip IV and England in 1628. Idolized and knighted in London, Rubens painted *Peace and War* for Charles I to commemorate the English-Spanish peace treaty of 1629–30. Charles later walked to his death through the Banqueting Hall under a ceiling Rubens painted. *Peace and War* optimistically represents both the court of Charles I at its zenith and the hope for European peace that would be dashed ten years later. The painting is charged with movement. A satyr grasps the fruits of peace, while to the right, Minerva, goddess of wisdom, drives out Mars, god of war, and the fury Allecto. At the center, Peace extends her full breast to the baby Plutus, god of riches.

Royal Image"), ghostwritten and published after his execution by John Gauden, and Milton's militantly republican response *Eikonoklastes* ("Image-Breaker").

In the last stage of the civil war, the dead king's son, Charles II, attempted to regain power through Irish and Scottish aid. In Ireland the Marquis of Ormonde led a coalition of royalists that secured the support of Irish troops for the King in exchange for the free exercise of Catholicism. Before Charles II could land in Dublin, the English sent troops there to put down the uprising. Cromwell slaughtered many at the siege of Drogheda; his campaign throughout Munster killed many civilians. In the aftermath of Cromwell's conquest, what remained of an Irish intelligentsia was either exiled or killed off, and large numbers of native inhabitants were either thrown off their land onto poorer farming land in western Ireland or sent into indentured servitude in the Caribbean. Following policies begun by Elizabeth and James, Cromwell granted Irish land to English settlers. The late events of the war in Ireland are represented here by one of Cromwell's letters from his campaign in Ireland, and by *John O'Dwyer of the Glenn*, a translation of one of the many Irish-language laments for the devastation of the Cromwellian conquest.

In Scotland, Charles II found allies among Presbyterian Covenanters, infuriated with the English Parliament for executing a Scottish monarch, and in the Marquis of Montrose, who recruited the Highland clans. When the Covenanters met with Charles II for the Treaty of Breda in Holland, they imposed on him a promise to reestablish Presbyterianism as the religion of both England and Scotland, to reinstate the Scottish Parliament, and to repudiate his pledges to Ormonde and Montrose. When Charles landed in Scotland, he learned that Montrose, most loyal of all royalists, had been hanged and quartered as a traitor. The political intrigue of Argyle against Montrose can be seen in the Earl of Clarendon's account of Montrose's death. The Covenanters, fighting for Scotland rather than for the King, were defeated by Cromwell at Dunbar. The Scots' losses were so huge that Scottish royalism was revived for one last battle between the King's Cavaliers and Cromwell's Roundheads. Facing Cromwell's army at Worcester in 1651, the forces of Scots and English royalists were vastly outnumbered and easily defeated. Charles II escaped to France, where he remained until the Restoration. Two years later, Cromwell became Lord Protector of the Commonwealth.

John Gauden
1605–1662

John Gauden wrote the most influential account of the royalist cause, *Eikon Basilike* ("Royal Portrait"), advance copies of which were sold on the day of Charles I's execution in 1649. Although Gauden at first sided with Parliament and the Presbyterians, he did not agree to the abolition of the bishops. In 1647 supporters of Charles I, then confined at Hampton Court by Parliament, sought Gauden's help to revise the King's meditations for publication. When the manuscript was complete, Gauden showed it to the King, who hesitated about having it published under his name. Meanwhile, the King was preoccupied first by his attempts to escape and then by his confinement, trial, and execution. When Royston first printed the book in January 1649, he believed that King Charles was the author. Just months later, William Duggard published another edition based on a manuscript that had been revised by the King; Gauden's authorship remained publically unknown until 1690.

Throughout the interregnum, Gauden managed to keep his deanery at Brockton by conforming to Presbyterianism. With the Restoration in 1660, he was made Bishop of Exeter. In letters to Sir Edward Hyde, Gauden admitted his authorship and complained that his reward had not been sufficient. He was then promoted to the bishopric of Worcester, just a year before his death.

Eikon Basilike was written to influence public opinion and to guide the Prince of Wales, who waited in exile to regain his father's throne. A collection of meditations written in a lofty style, *Eikon Basilike* justified the King's views and evoked sympathy for his plight. The emblematic frontispiece shows the King in a saintly light—kneeling in prayer. Admirers of the work called it "most charitable, most heavenly" and "most pious, most ravishing." By the end of 1649, thirty-five editions had been printed in England. The most important of these, that of March 1649, added the King's prayers, the Prince of Wales's letter to his father, and an epitaph on the King's death. An English-language edition was published in Ireland in 1649, and twenty foreign language editions were published on the Continent for the English community in exile as well as their European supporters.

The text aroused both support and criticism. Parliament had the printer Duggard arrested but released him when he produced a license to publish the book. Parliament prohibited the further sale of the book in May 1649, but by the end of 1649, five clandestine editions and two responses had appeared. *The Princely Pellican* explained how Charles had come to write the book, and *Eikon Alethine* attacked it as a fraud. Milton wrote his own rebuttal in *Eikonoklastes*, a savagely satirical prosecution of the King. *Eikonoklastes* merely went through two editions, showing that it could not compete in popularity with *Eikon Basilike*.

from **Eikon Basilike**

from *Chapter 4. Upon the Insolency of the Tumults*

I never thought anything, except our sins, more ominously presaging all these mischiefs which have followed, than those tumults in London and Westminster soon after the convening of this Parliament which were not like a storm at sea, (which yet wants not its terror,) but like an earthquake, shaking the very foundation of all; than which nothing in the world hath more of horror.

As it is one of the most convincing arguments that there is a God, while His power sets bounds to the raging of the sea, so it is no less that He restrains the madness of the people. Nor does anything portend more God's displeasure against a nation than when He suffers the confluence and clamors of the vulgar to pass all boundaries of laws and reverence to authority.

Which those tumults did to so high degrees of insolence, that they spared not to invade the honor and freedom of the two Houses, menacing, reproaching, shaking, yea, and assaulting some members of both Houses as they fancied or disliked them; nor did they forbear most rude and unseemly deportments, both in contemptuous words and actions, to myself and my court.

Nor was this a short fit or two of shaking, as an ague, but a quotidian fever, always increasing to higher inflammations, impatient of any mitigation, restraint, or remission.

First, they must be a guard against those fears which some men scared themselves and others withal; when, indeed, nothing was more to be feared, and less to be used by wise men, than those tumultuary confluxes of mean and rude people who are taught first to petition, then to protect, then to dictate, at last to command and overawe the Parliament.

All obstructions of Parliament, that is, all freedom of differing in votes, and debating matters with reason and candor, must be taken away with these tumults. By these must the Houses be purged, and all rotten members (as they pleased to count them) cast out; by these the obstinacy of men, resolved to discharge their consciences, must be subdued; by these all factious, seditious, and schismatical proposals against government, ecclesiastical or civil, must be backed and abetted till they prevailed.

Generally, whoever had most mind to bring forth confusion and ruin upon Church and State used the midwifery of those tumults, whose riot and impatience was such as they would not stay the ripening and season of counsels, or fair production of acts, in the order, gravity, and deliberateness befitting a Parliament, but ripped up with barbarous cruelty, and forcibly cut out abortive notes, such as their inviters and encouragers most fancied.

Yea, so enormous and detestable were their outrages, that no sober man could be without infinite shame and sorrow to see them so tolerated and connived at by some, countenanced, encouraged, and applauded by others.

What good man had not rather want anything he most desired for the public good, than obtain it by such unlawful and irreligious means? But men's passions and God's directions seldom agree; violent designs and motions must have suitable engines; such as too much attend their own ends, seldom confine themselves to God's means. Force must crowd in what reason will not lead.

Who were the chief demagogues and patrons of tumults, to send for them, to flatter and embolden them, to direct and tune their clamorous importunities, some men yet living are too conscious to pretend ignorance. God in His due time will let these see that those were no fit means to be used for attaining His ends.

But as it is no strange thing for the sea to rage when strong winds blow upon it, so neither for multitudes to become insolent when they have men of some reputation for parts and piety to set them on.

That which made their rudeness most formidable was, that many complaints being made, and messages sent by myself and some of both Houses yet no order for redress could be obtained with any vigor and efficacy proportionable to the malignity of that now far-spread disease and predominant mischief.

Such was some men's stupidity, that they feared no inconvenience; others' petulancy, that they joyed to see their betters shamefully outraged and abused, while they knew their only security consisted in vulgar flattery, so insensible were they of mine or the two Houses common safety and honors.

Nor could ever any order be obtained impartially to examine, censure, and punish the known boutefeus[1] and impudent incendiaries, who boasted of the influence they had, and used to convoke those tumults as their advantages served.

Yea some, who should have been wiser statesmen, owned them as friends, commending their courage, zeal, and industry, which to sober men could seem no better than that of the devil, who goes about seeking whom he may deceive and devour.

I confess, when I found such a deafness, that no declaration from the bishops, who were first foully insolenced and assaulted, nor yet from other lords and gentlemen of honor, nor yet from myself, could take place for the due repression of these tumults, and securing not only our freedom in Parliament, but our very persons in the streets; I thought myself not bound by my presence to provoke them to higher boldness and contempts; I hoped by my withdrawing[2] to give time both for the ebbing of their tumultuous fury, and others regaining some degrees of modesty and sober sense.

Some may interpret it as an effect of pusillanimity[3] in any man, for popular terrors, to desert his public station; but I think it is hardiness beyond true valor for a wise man to set himself against the breaking in of a sea, which to resist at present threatens imminent danger, but to withdraw gives it space to spend its fury, and gains a fitter time to repair the breach. Certainly a gallant man had rather fight to great disadvantages for number and place in the field in an orderly way, than scuffle with an undisciplined rabble.

Some suspected and affirmed that I meditated a war, when I went from Whitehall only to redeem my person and conscience from violence: God knows I did not then think of a war. Nor will any prudent man conceive that I would, by so many former and some after acts, have so much weakened myself if I had purposed to engage in a war, which to decline by all means I denied myself in so many particulars. It is evident I had then no army to fly unto for protection and vindication.

Who can blame me, or any other, for withdrawing ourselves from the daily baitings of the tumults, not knowing whether their fury and discontent might not fly so high as to worry and tear those in pieces whom as yet they but played with in their paws? God, who is my sole judge, is my witness in heaven that I never had any thoughts of my going from my house at Whitehall if I could have had but any reasonable fair quarter. I was resolved to bear much, and did so; but I did not think myself bound to prostitute the majesty of my place and person, the safety of my wife and

1. Firebrands.
2. Charles decided to flee from London on the night of 10 January 1642, in response to rioting that erupted as a result of his failed attempts to arrest the five opposition leaders in the House of Commons. Charles returned to Whitehall only as a prisoner just before his execution.
3. Cowardice.

children, to those who are prone to insult most when they have objects and opportunity most capable of their rudeness and petulancy.

But this business of the tumults, whereof some have given already an account to God, others yet living know themselves desperately guilty, time and the guilt of many has so smothered up and buried, that I think it best to leave it as it is; only I believe the just avenger of all disorders will in time make those men and that city see their sin in the glass of their punishment. It is more than an even lay, that they may one day see themselves punished by that way they offended.

Had this Parliament, as it was in its first election and constitution, sat full and free, the members of both Houses, being left to their freedom of voting, as in all reason, honor, and religion they should have been, I doubt not but things would have been so carried as would have given no less good content to all good men than they wished or expected.

For I was resolved to hear reason in all things, and to consent to it as far as I could comprehend it; but as swine are to gardens and orderly plantations, so are tumults to Parliaments, and plebeian concourses to public counsels, turning all into disorders and sordid confusions.

I am prone sometimes to think that had I called this Parliament to any other place in England, as I might opportunely enough have done, the sad consequences in all likelihood, with God's blessing, might have been prevented. A Parliament would have been welcome in any place; no place afforded such confluence of various and vicious humors as that where it was unhappily convened. But we must leave all to God, who orders our disorders, and magnifies His wisdom most when our follies and miseries are most discovered.

John Milton

1608–1674

With the popularity of the royalist tract *Eikon Basilike* after the execution of Charles I, the new Puritan government needed to find someone to defend its cause against the growing support for the King. The Puritans found their man in the newly appointed Secretary for Foreign Tongues to the Council of State, John Milton. In *Eikonoklastes* ("Image Breaker"), Milton focused his attack on the arguments of *Eikon Basilike* more than on its authorship. He doubted whether the King wrote his own defense, but he chose to concentrate on a chapter-by-chapter refutation of the book's account of history—in terms of both events and the perspective on them. Milton also revealed that one the prayers attributed to the King was really Pamela's prayer from Sir Philip Sidney's prose romance *Arcadia*. For the Puritan Milton this was a shocking piece of paganism and plagiarism by one who presented himself as pious. Milton's language in *Eikonoklastes* is iconoclastic—mocking and sarcastic, marked by invective and sharply stinging *ad hominem* argument. One royalist called *Eikonoklastes* a "blackguardly book" in which Milton "blows his viper's breath upon those immortal devotions." Some royalists even viewed Milton's blindness as God's punishment for his having attacked the King. Shortly after the Restoration of Charles II in 1660 the House of Commons ordered the burning of *Eikonoklastes* and had Milton arrested. He was imprisoned for several months before being released through the aid of his friend Andrew Marvell. *Eikonklastes* was first published in October 1649; the second and final edition in Milton's lifetime appeared in 1650.

For more about Milton, see his principal listing, page 1729.

from Eikonoklastes

from *Chapter 1. Upon the King's Calling This Last Parliament*

"The odium and offenses which some men's rigor, or remissness in church and state had contracted upon his government, he resolved to have expiated with better laws and regulations." And yet the worst of misdemeanors committed by the worst of all his favorites, in the height of their dominion, whether acts of rigor or remissness, he hath from time to time continued, owned, and taken upon himself by public declarations, as often as the clergy, or any other of his instruments felt themselves overburdened with the people's hatred. And who knows not the superstitious rigor of his Sunday's chapel, and the licentious remissness of his Sunday's theater;[1] accompanied with that reverend statute for dominical jigs and maypoles,[2] published in his own name, and derived from the example of his father James? Which testifies all that rigor in superstition, all that remissness in religion to have issued out originally from his own house, and from his own authority.

Much rather then may those general miscarriages in State, his proper sphere, be imputed to no other person chiefly than to himself. And which of all those oppressive acts, or impositions did he ever disclaim or disavow, till the fatal awe of this Parliament hung ominously over him. Yet here he smoothly seeks to wipe off all the envy of his evil government upon his substitutes, and under-officers: and promises, though much too late, what wonders he purposed to have done in the reforming of religion—a work wherein all his undertakings heretofore declare him to have had little or no judgment. Neither could his breeding, or his course of life acquaint him with a thing so spiritual. Which may well assure us what kind of reformation we could expect from him; either some politic form of an imposed religion, or else perpetual vexation, and persecution to all those that complied not with such a form.

The like amendment he promises in State; not a step further "than his reason and conscience told him was fit to be desired"; wishing "he had kept within those bounds, and not suffered his own judgment to have been overborne in some things," of which things one was the Earl of Strafford's execution.[3] And what signifies all this, but that still his resolution was the same, to set up an arbitrary government of his own; and that all Britain was to be tied and chained to the conscience, judgment, and reason of one man; as if those gifts had been only his peculiar and prerogative, entailed upon him with his fortune to be a king? When as doubtless no man so obstinate, or so much a tyrant, but professes to be guided by that which he calls his reason, and his judgment, though never so corrupted; and pretends also his conscience. In the meanwhile, for any Parliament or the whole nation to have either reason, judgment, or conscience, by this rule was altogether in vain, if it thwarted the king's will; which was easy for him to call by any other more plausible name. He himself hath

1. While observers such as the Spanish ambassador noted Charles's sincere piety, Milton considered traditional ritual "superstitious" ironically linking it to irreligious theater life. Like the Puritans, Milton abhorred Sunday theater performances, and in *Of Reformation* he attacked the bishops for promoting "gaming, jigging, wassailing, and mixed dancing" on Sundays.

2. The *Book of Sports* (1633) forbade bearbaiting and bullbaiting on Sundays, but also rebuked the Puritans for condemning other forms of recreation such as dancing and archery.

3. Thomas Wentworth, Earl of Strafford, was executed in May 1641. Charles had recalled Strafford from the Lord Deputyship in Ireland to help with the war against the Scots Covenanters. Parliament accused Wentworth of planning to use the Irish army to suppress the King's opponents in Scotland and England. Even though Strafford was successfully defended against the charges, Charles signed his death warrant, fearing retaliation against himself and the Queen for their part in a plot to rescue Strafford.

many times acknowledged to have no right over us but by law; and by the same law to govern us: but law in a free nation hath been ever public reason, the enacted reason of a Parliament; which he denying to enact, denies to govern us by that which ought to be our law; interposing his own private reason, which to us is no law. And thus we find these fair and specious promises, made upon the experience of many hard sufferings, and his most mortified retirements, being thoroughly sifted, to contain nothing in them much different from his former practices, so cross, and so averse to all his Parliaments, and both the nations of this island. What fruits they could in likelihood have produced in his restorement, is obvious to any prudent foresight.

And this is the substance of his first section, till we come to the devout of it, modeled into the form of a private psalter. Which they who so much admire, either for the matter or the manner, may as well admire the archbishop's late breviary,[4] and many other as good *Manuals,* and *Handmaids of Devotion,* the lip-work of every prelatical liturgist, clapped together, and quilted out of Scripture phrase, with as much ease, and as little need of Christian diligence, or judgment, as belongs to the compiling of any ordinary and salable piece of English divinity, that the shops value. But he who from such a kind of psalmistry, or any other verbal devotion, without the pledge and earnest of suitable deeds, can be persuaded of a zeal, and true righteousness in the person, hath much yet to learn; and knows not that the deepest policy of a tyrant hath been ever to counterfeit religious. And Aristotle in his *Politics,* hath mentioned that special craft among twelve other tyrannical sophisms.[5] Neither want we examples. Andronicus Comnenus the Byzantine Emperor, though a most cruel tyrant, is reported by Nicetas[6] to have been a constant reader of Saint Paul's Epistles; and by continual study had so incorporated the phrase and style of that transcendent apostle into all his familiar letters, that the imitation seemed to vie with the original. Yet this availed not to deceive the people of that empire; who notwithstanding his saint's vizard, tore him to pieces for his tyranny.

From stories of this nature both ancient and modern which abound, the poets also, and some English, have been in this point so mindful of decorum, as to put never more pious words in the mouth of any person, than of a tyrant. I shall not instance an abstruse author, wherein the King might be less conversant, but one whom we well know was the closet companion of these his solitudes, William Shakespeare, who introduces the person of Richard the Third, speaking in as high a strain of piety, and mortification, as is uttered in any passage of this book, and sometimes to the same sense and purpose with some words in this place, "I intended," saith he, "not only to oblige my friends but mine enemies." The like saith Richard, Act 2. Scene 1,

I do not know that Englishman alive
With whom my soul is any jot at odds,
More than the infant that is born tonight;
I thank my God for my humility.

Other stuff of this sort may be read throughout the whole tragedy, wherein the poet used not much license in departing from the truth of history, which delivers him a deep dissembler, not of his affections only, but of religion.

4. Milton's name for Archbishop Laud's *Prayer Book,* which the Puritans hated because of its similarity to Roman Catholic ritual.

5. See Aristotle, *Politics* 5.9.15, for the notion that care in religious ritual is a device of tyrants.

6. A 12th-century historian who recorded the cruelty of Comnenus's reign (1183–1185).

from *Chapter 4. Upon the Insolency of the Tumults*

And that the King was so emphatical and elaborate on this theme against tumults, and expressed with such a vehemence his hatred of them, will redound less perhaps, than he was aware, to the commendation of his government. For besides that in good governments they happen seldomest, and rise not without cause, if they prove extreme and pernicious, they were never counted so to monarchy, but to monarchical tyranny; and extremes one with another are at most antipathy. If then the King so extremely stood in fear of tumults, the inference will endanger him to be the other extreme. Thus far the occasion of this discourse against tumults; now to the discourse itself, voluble enough, and full of sentence,[1] but that, for the most part, either specious rather than solid, or to his cause nothing pertinent.

"He never thought any thing more to presage the mischiefs that ensued, than those tumults." Then was his foresight but short, and much mistaken. Those tumults were but the mild effects of an evil and injurious reign; not signs of mischiefs to come, but seeking relief for mischiefs past; those signs were to be read more apparent in his rage and purposed revenge of those free expostulations, and clamors of the people against his lawless government. "Not any thing," saith he, "portends more God's displeasure against a nation than when he suffers the clamors of the vulgar to pass all bounds of law & reverence to authority." It portends rather his displeasure against a tyrannous King, whose proud throne he intends to overturn by that contemptible vulgar; the sad cries and oppressions of whom his royalty regarded not. As for that supplicating people they did no hurt either to law or authority, but stood for it rather in the Parliament against whom they feared would violate it.

That "they invaded the honor and freedom of the two Houses," is his own officious accusation, not seconded by the Parliament, who had they seen cause, were themselves best able to complain. And if they "shook & menaced" any, they were such as had more relation to the Court, than to the Commonwealth; enemies, not patrons of the people. But if their petitioning unarmed were an invasion of both Houses, what was his entrance into the House of Commons, besetting it with armed men, in what condition then was the honor, and freedom of that House?

"They forbore not rude deportments, contemptuous words and actions to himself and his Court."

It was more wonder, having heard what treacherous hostility he had designed against the city, and his whole kingdom, that they forbore to handle him as people in their rage have handled tyrants heretofore for less offenses.

"They were not a short ague, but a fierce quotidian fever:" He indeed may best say it, who most felt it; for the shaking was within him; and it shook him by his own description "worse than a storm, worse then an earthquake, Belshazzar's Palsy."[2] Had not worse fears, terrors, and envies made within him that commotion, how could a multitude of his subjects, armed with no other weapon then petitions, have shaken all his joints with such a terrible ague. Yet that the Parliament should entertain the least fear of bad intentions from him or his party, he endures not; but would persuade

1. Significance, meaning.

2. In *Of Reformation*, Milton compares the feasting of Anglican bishops to that of Belshazzar in his palace in Babylon on the eve of the fall of the city to the Medes and Persians. When King Belshazzar saw the mysterious writing on the wall that foretold his doom, "the joints of his loins were loosed, and his knees smote one against another" (Daniel 5.6).

us that "men scare themselves and others without cause;" for he thought fear would be to them a kind of armor, and his design was, if it were possible, to disarm all, especially of a wise fear and suspicion; for that he knew would find weapons.

He goes on therefore with vehemence to repeat the mischiefs done by these tumults. "They first petitioned, then protected, dictate next, and lastly overawe the Parliament. They removed obstructions, they purged the Houses, cast out rotten members." If there were a man of iron, such as Talus, by our poet Spenser, is feigned to be the page of Justice, who with his iron flail could do all this, and expeditiously, without those deceitful forms and circumstances of law, worse than ceremonies in religion; I say God send it down, whether by one Talus, or by a thousand.[3]

"But they subdued the men of conscience in Parliament, backed and abetted all seditious and schismatical proposals against government ecclesiastical and civil."

Now we may perceive the root of his hatred whence it springs. It was not the King's grace or princely goodness, but this iron flail the people, that drove the bishops out of their baronies, out of their cathedrals, out of the Lord's house, out of their copes and surplices, and all those papistical innovations,[4] threw down the High Commission and Star Chamber, gave us a triennial Parliament, and what we most desired;[5] in revenge whereof he now so bitterly inveighs against them; these are those seditious and scismatical proposals, then by him condescended to, as acts of grace, now of another name; which declares him, touching matters of Church and State, to have been no other man in the deepest of his solitude, than he was before at the highest of his sovereignty.

But this was not the worst of these tumults, they played the hasty "midwives," and "would not stay the ripening, but went straight to ripping up, and forcibly cut out abortive votes."

They would not stay perhaps the Spanish demurring, and putting off such wholesome acts and counsels, as the politic cabin at Whitehall had no mind to. But all this is complained here as done to the Parliament, and yet we heard not the Parliament at that time complain of any violence from the people, but from him. Wherefore intrudes he to plead the cause of Parliament against the people, while the Parliament was pleading their own cause against him; and against him were forced to seek refuge of the people? 'Tis plain then that those confluxes and resorts interrupted not the Parliament, nor by them were thought tumultuous, but by him only and his court faction.

"But what good Man had not rather want any thing he most desired for the public good, then attain it by such unlawful and irreligious means;" as much as to say, had not rather sit still and let his country be tyrannized, then that the people, finding no other remedy, should stand up like men and demand their rights and liberties. This is the artificialest piece of fineness to persuade men into slavery that the wit of court could have invented. But hear how much better the moral of this lesson would befit the teacher. What good man had not rather want a boundless and arbitrary power, and those fine flowers of the crown, called prerogatives, then for them to use force and perpetual vexation to his faithful subjects, nay to wade for them through blood and civil war? So that

3. Talus is the iron flail who ruthlessly cuts down all who oppose Artegal, the Knight of Justice, in Spenser's *Faerie Queene* 5, much of which is about the subjugation of Ireland by England.

4. Milton refers to the London petition calling for the abolition of the bishops' power, introduced into Parliament in December 1640, that resulted in their exclusion from the House of Lords.

5. The High Commission, the highest ecclesiastical court, investigated such matters as heresy, recusancy, and any writing against the Book of Common Prayer; Parliament abolished it on July 5, 1641. The Star Chamber was also abolished because it was viewed as a special tool of government favoring the special right of the sovereign above all other persons and the common law. A triennial Parliament is a parliament convened every three years.

this and the whole bundle of those following sentences may be applied better to the convincement of his own violent courses, then of those pretended tumults.

"Who were the chief demagogues to send for those tumults, some alive are not ignorant." Setting aside the affrightment of this goblin word; for the King by his leave cannot coin English as he could money, to be current (and tis believed this wording was above his known style and orthography, and accuses the whole composure to be conscious of some other author)[6] yet if the people "were sent for, emboldened and directed" by those "demagogues," who, saving his Greek, were good patriots, and by his own confession "Men of some repute for parts and piety," it helps well to assure us there was both urgent cause, and the less danger of their coming.

"Complaints were made, yet no redress could be obtained." The Parliament also complained of what danger they sat in from another party, and demanded of him a guard, but it was not granted. What marvel then if it cheered them to see some store of their friends, and in the Roman not the pettifogging sense, their clients so near about them; a defense due by nature both from whom it was offered, and to whom; as due as to their parents; though the Court stormed, and fretted to see such honor given to them, who were then best fathers of the Commonwealth. And both the Parliament and people complained, and demanded justice for those assaults, if not murders done at his own doors, by that crew of rufflers, but he, instead of doing justice on them, justified and abetted them in what they did, as in his public "Answer to a Petition from the City" may be read. Neither is it slightly to be passed over, that in the very place where blood was first drawn in this cause, as the beginning of all that followed, there was his own blood shed by the executioner. According to that sentence of divine justice, "In the place where dogs licked the blood of Naboth, shall dogs lick thy blood, even thine."

From hence he takes occasion to excuse that improvident and fatal error of his absenting from the Parliament. "When he found that no declaration of the bishops could take place against those tumults." Was that worth his considering, that foolish and self-undoing declaration of twelve cypher bishops, who were immediately appeached of treason for that audacious declaring?[7] The bishops peradventure were now and then pulled by the rochets,[8] and deserved another kind of pulling; but what amounted this to "the fear of his own person in the streets"? Did he not the very next day after his irruption into the House of Commons, than which nothing had more exasperated the people, go in his coach unguarded into the city? did he receive the least affront, much less violence in any of the streets, but rather humble demeanors, and supplications? Hence may be gathered, that however in his own guiltiness he might have justly feared, yet that he knew the people so full of awe and reverence to his person, as to dare commit himself single among the thickest of them, at a time when he had most provoked them. Besides in Scotland they had handled the Bishops in a more robustious manner; Edinburgh had been full of tumults,[9] two armies from thence had entered England against him;[1] yet after all this, he was not fearful, but very forward to take so long a journey to Edinburgh;[2] which argues first, as did also his rendition afterward to the Scotch Army,[3] that to England he continued still, as he was indeed, a stranger, and full of diffidence; to the Scots

6. Milton believed that Charles I could not have written *Eikon Basilike* because such passages as this one showed a word choice and style different from Charles's.
7. The Bishops' Exclusion Bill was Parliament's reaction to the assertion by 12 bishops that any legislation passed by the House of Lords when the bishops were absent was void.
8. Vestments.
9. When Charles attempted to force the Book of Common Prayer on the Scottish churches, the people rioted.
1. The first Scottish war ended with the Treaty of Berwick in June 1639, the second with the Treaty of Ripon in October 1640.
2. Charles went to Edinburgh in 1641, hoping to pit the Covenanters against their opponents.
3. Charles surrendered himself to the Scottish army commanders in May 1646.

only a native King,[4] in his confidence, though not in his dealing towards them. It shows us next beyond doubting, that all this his fear of tumults was but a mere color and occasion taken of his resolved absence from the Parliament, for some other end not difficult to be guessed. And those instances wherein valor is not to be questioned for not "scuffling with the sea, or an undisciplined rabble," are but subservient to carry on the solemn jest of his fearing tumults: if they discover not withall, the true reason why he departed; only to turn his slashing at the court gate, to slaughtering "in the field"; his disorderly bickering, to an orderly invading: which was nothing else but a more orderly disorder.

"Some suspected and affirmed, that he meditated a War when he went first from Whitehall." And they were not the worst heads that did so, nor did "any of his former acts weaken him" to that, as he alleges for himself, or if they had, they clear him only for the time of passing them, not for what ever thoughts might come after into his mind. Former actions of improvidence or fear, not with him unusual, cannot absolve him of all after meditations.

He goes on protesting his "no intention to have left Whitehall," had these horrid tumults given him but "fair quarter," as if he himself, his wife and children had been in peril. But to this enough hath been answered.

"Had this Parliament as it was in its first election," namely, with the Lord and Baron Bishops, "sat full and free," he doubts not but all had gone well. What warrant this of his to us? Whose not doubting was all good men's greatest doubt.

"He was resolved to hear reason, and to consent so far as he could comprehend." A hopeful resolution; what if his reason were found by oft experience to comprehend nothing beyond his own advantages, was this a reason fit to be intrusted with the common good of three nations?

"But," saith he, "as swine are to gardens, so are tumults to Parliaments." This the Parliament, had they found it so, could best have told us. In the meanwhile, who knows not that one great hog may do as much mischief in a garden, as many little swine.[5]

"He was sometimes prone to think that had he called this last Parliament to any other place in England, the sad consequences might have been prevented." But change of air changes not the mind. Was not his first Parliament at Oxford dissolved after two subsidies given him, and no justice received? Was not his last in the same place, where they sat with as much freedom, as much quiet from tumults, as they could desire, a Parliament both in his account, and their own, consisting of all his friends, that fled after him, and suffered for him, and yet by him nicknamed, and cashiered for a "mongrel Parliament that vexed his Queen with their base and mutinous motions," as his cabinet letter tells us?[6] Whereby the world may see plainly, that no shifting of place, no sifting of members to his own mind, no number, no paucity, no freedom from tumults, could ever bring his arbitrary wilfulness, and tyrannical designs to brook the least shape or similitude, the least counterfeit of a Parliament.

Finally instead of praying for his people as a good King should do, he prays to be delivered from them, as "from wild beasts, inundations, and raging seas, that had overborne all loyalty, modesty, laws, justice, and religion." God save the people from such intercessors.

4. Charles was born in Scotland, and he made special appeals to the Scots to be their king in both 1641 and 1646.

5. Milton may echo the identification of the hog with Henry VIII for his failure to carry out a thorough and consistent reformation in Anthony Gilby's *An Admonition to England and Scotland to Call Them to Repentance* (Geneva, 1558).

6. Charles called an opposition Parliament that met in Oxford in January 22, 1644, and that he ordered closed after disagreement with them. This Parliament first attempted a peaceful settlement with the Westminster Parliament and then declared it guilty of treason. The King called it his "mongrel Parliament."

The Petition of Gentlewomen and Tradesmen's Wives

A month after the King tried to have the five chief members of Parliament arrested, two petitions were presented to the Commons by "Gentlewomen and Tradesmen's Wives" of London. In the first of these, dated 1 February 1642, the women complained about the lack of trade, which caused great want and blamed the "opposition of some bishops or lords" for the neglect of the women's earlier petitions. In the second petition, reprinted here, the women complain about threats to the security of the state posed by the bishops and Catholic lords in the House of Lords, the still not yet executed Archbishop Laud, and the Catholic Mass. From the London women's vantage point, the 1641 rebellion of the Catholics in Ireland demonstrated the risk to Puritans of attacks from Catholics (indistinguishable from Anglicans) within England. The violence unleashed by the more spontaneous and popular revolts in Ireland had been luridly portrayed and grossly exaggerated in the English press. Nevertheless, the Catholic revolt did bring much bloodshed, which increased with the Protestant retaliation. Interestingly, some of the Irish uprisings were led by women, a fact that would not have made any difference to the London women, even if they had known it.

The chief terms of the petition, like the chief terms of the Wars of the Three Kingdoms, were religious. Archbishop Laud is attacked here, but the King is not. Even the women's justification of their right to approach Parliament with a petition is articulated in religious terms. They argue that women are the same as men in Christ's eyes and that women have suffered as much religious persecution as men. If these women argue that women are equal to men, it is mainly insofar as they are believers in the Puritan practice of religion. Delegated by his fellow members to make a reply, Pym publicly reassured the women that their petition had been read and that they would receive "satisfaction . . . to [their] just and lawful desires." The next day, the House of Lords passed a bill excluding the Bishops, and so Parliament met at least one of the women petitioners' demands.

A True Copy of the Petition of the Gentlewomen and Tradesmen's Wives, In and About the City of London[1]

Delivered to the Honorable, the Knights, Citizens, and Burgesses of the House of Commons in Parliament, the 4th of February, 1642

Together with their several reasons why their sex ought thus to petition, as well as the men; and the manner how both their petition and reasons was delivered.

Likewise the answer which the Honorable Assembly sent to them by Mr. Pym,[2] as they stood at the house door.

To the Honorable Knights, Citizens and Burgesses,[3] of the House of Commons assembled in Parliament. The most humble Petition of the Gentlewomen, Tradesmen's Wives, and many others of the female sex, all inhabitants of the city of London, and the suburbs thereto.

With lowest submission showing,

1. Printed in the *Parliamentary History* ii.1074.
2. John Pym (1583?–1643) was a strong Puritan opponent of episcopacy and a leader of the House of Commons, one of the five members whom Charles I unsuccessfully attempted to have arrested in 1642.
3. Members of Parliament representing boroughs or corporate towns.

That we also with all thankful humility acknowledging the unwearied pains, care and great charge, besides hazard of health and life, which you the noble worthies of this honorable and renowned assembly have undergone, for the safety both of church and commonwealth, for a long time already past; for which not only we your humble petitioners, and all well affected in this kingdom, but also all other good Christians are bound now and at all times acknowledge; yet notwithstanding that many worthy deeds have been done by you, great danger and fear do still attend us, and will, as long as Popish Lords and superstitious bishops are suffered to have their voice in the House of Peers, and that accursed and abominable idol of the Mass suffered in the kingdom, and that archenemy[4] of our prosperity and reformation lieth in the Tower, yet not receiving his deserved punishment.

All these under correction, gives us great cause to suspect that God is angry with us, and to be the chief causes why your pious endeavors for a further reformation proceedeth not with that success as you desire, and is most earnestly prayed for of all that wish well to true religion, and the flourishing estate both of king and kingdom; the insolencies of the papists and their abettors, raiseth a just fear and suspicion of sowing sedition, and breaking out into bloody persecution in this kingdom, as they have done in Ireland, the thoughts of which sad and barbarous events maketh our tender hearts to melt within us, forcing us humbly to petition to this honorable assembly, to make safe provision for yourselves and us, before it be too late.

And whereas we, whose hearts have joined cheerfully with all those petitions which have been exhibited unto you in the behalf of the purity of religion, and the liberty of our husbands' persons and estates, recounting ourselves to have an interest in the common privileges with them, do with the same confidence assure ourselves to find the same gracious acceptance with you, for easing of those grievances, which in regard of our frail condition, do more nearly concern us, and do deeply terrify our souls: our domestical dangers with which this kingdom is so much distressed, especially growing on us from those treacherous and wicked attempts already are such as we find ourselves to have as deep a share as any other.

We cannot but tremble at the very thoughts of the horrid and hideous facts which modesty forbids us now to name, occasioned by the bloody wars in Germany,[5] his Majesty's late Northern Army, how often did it affright our hearts, whilst their violence began to break out so furiously upon the persons of those whose husbands or parents were not able to rescue: we wish we had no cause to speak of those insolencies, and savage usage and unheard-of rapes, exercised upon our sex in Ireland, and have we not just cause to fear they will prove the forerunners of our ruin, except Almighty God by the wisdom and care of this Parliament be pleased to succor us, our husbands and children, which are as dear and tender unto us as the lives and blood of our hearts, to see them murdered and mangled and cut in pieces before our eyes, to see our children dashed against the stones, and the mothers' milk mingled with the infants' blood, running down the streets, to see our houses on flaming fire over our heads: oh how dreadful would this be?[6] We thought it misery enough (though nothing to that we have just cause to fear) but few years since for some of our sex, by

4. Archbishop Laud (1573–1645), who enforced forms of worship that were Anglican High Church, or similar to Roman Catholicism, and promoted church government by Anglican bishops. His policies and support for Charles I won Laud impeachment in 1642; in 1643 he was condemned to death by the Commons.

5. The Thirty Years War (1618–1648) was a European-wide war fought mainly in Germany between Protestant opponents to Hapsburg rule and Catholic supporters of the Holy Roman Empire.

6. While there was violence on both sides, woodcuts of the Irish rebellions in the English press sensationalized the violence of Catholics against Protestant settlers by depicting the murder of infants and attacks upon women.

unjust divisions from their bosom comforts, to be rendered in a manner widows, and the children fatherless, husbands were imprisoned from the society of their wives, even against the laws of God and nature, and little infants suffered in their fathers' banishments: thousands of our dearest friends have been compelled to fly from Episcopal persecutions into desert places amongst wild beasts, there finding more favor than in their native soil, and in the midst of all their sorrows such hath the pity of the Prelates[7] been, that our cries could never enter into their ears or hearts, not yet through multitudes of obstructions could never have access or come nigh to those royal mercies of our most gracious sovereign, which we confidently hope would have relieved us: but after all these pressures ended, we humbly signify that our present fears are, that unless the bloodthirsty faction of the Papists and Prelates be hindered in their designs, ourselves here in England as well as they in Ireland, shall be exposed to the misery which is more intolerable than that which is already past, as namely to the rage not of men alone, but of devils incarnate (as we may so say), besides the thralldom of our souls and consciences in matters concerning God, which of all things are most dear unto us.

Now the remembrance of all these fearful accidents aforementioned do strongly move us from the example of the woman of Tekoa (II Samuel 14.2–20)[8] to fall submissively at the feet of his Majesty, our dread sovereign, and cry Help, oh King, help oh ye the noble Worthies now sitting in Parliament: And we humbly beseech you, that you will be a means to his Majesty and the House of Peers, that they will be pleased to take our heartbreaking grievances into timely consideration, and to add strength and encouragement to your noble endeavors, and further that you would move his Majesty with our humble requests, that he would be graciously pleased according to the example of the good King Asa,[9] to purge both the court and kingdom of that great idolatrous service of the Mass, which is tolerated in the Queen's court, this sin (as we conceive) is able to draw down a greater curse upon the whole kingdom than all your noble and pious endeavors can prevent, which was the cause that the good and pious King Asa would not suffer idolatry in his own mother, whose example if it shall please his Majesty's gracious goodness to follow, in putting down Popery and idolatry both in great and small, in court and in the kingdom throughout, to subdue the Papists and their abettors, and by taking away the power of the Prelates, whose government by long and woeful experience we have found to be against the liberty of our conscience and the freedom of the Gospel, and the sincere profession and practice thereof, then shall our fears be removed, and we may expect that God will pour down his blessings in abundance both upon his Majesty, and upon this Honorable Assembly, and upon the whole land.

For which your new petitioners shall pray affectionately.

The reasons follow.

It may be thought strange and unbeseeming our sex to show ourselves by way of petition to this Honorable Assembly: but the matter being rightly considered, of the right and interest we have in the common and public cause of the church, it will, as we conceive (under correction) be found a duty commanded and required.

7. Churchmen, bishops.

8. The wise woman of Tekoa went before King David and urged him to act mercifully toward his son Absalom. King David had been failing to act decisively against rape and murder within his own household.

9. Charles I is asked to banish Catholics and the Mass just as King Asa banished sodomites and idolatry in 1 Kings 15.8–12.

First, because Christ hath purchased us at as dear a rate as he hath done men, and therefore requireth the like obedience for the same mercy as of men.

Secondly, because in the free enjoying of Christ in his own laws, and a flourishing estate of the church and commonwealth, consisteth the happiness of women as well as men.

Thirdly, because women are sharers in the common calamities that accompany both church and commonwealth, when oppression is exercised over the church or kingdom wherein they live; and an unlimited power have been given to Prelates to exercise authority over the consciences of women, as well as men, witness Newgate, Smithfield,[1] and other places of persecution, wherein women as well as men have felt the smart of their fury.

Neither are we left without example in scripture, for when the state of the church, in the time of King Ahasuerus, was by the bloody enemies thereof sought to be utterly destroyed, we find that Esther the Queen and her maids fasted and prayed, and that Esther petitioned to the King in the behalf of the church:[2] and though she enterprised this duty with the hazard of her own life, being contrary to the law to appear before the King before she were sent for, yet her love to the church carried her through all difficulties, to the performance of that duty.

On which grounds we are emboldened to present our humble petition unto this Honorable Assembly, not weighing the reproaches which may and are by many cast upon us, who (not well weighing the premises) scoff and deride our good intent. We do it not out of any self-conceit, or pride of heart, as seeking to equal ourselves with men, either in authority or wisdom: But according to our places to discharge that duty we owe to God, and the cause of the church, as far as lieth in us, following herein the example of the men which have gone in this duty before us.

A relation of the manner how it was delivered, with their answer, sent by Mr. Pym.

This petition, with their reasons, was delivered the 4th of Feb. 1641/2, by Mrs. Anne Stagg, a gentlewoman and brewer's wife, and many others with her of like rank and quality, which when they had delivered it, after some time spent in reading of it, the Honorable Assembly sent them an answer by Mr. Pym, which was performed in this manner.

Mr. Pym came to the Commons door, and called for the women, and spake unto them in these words: Good women, your petition and the reasons have been read in the house; and is very thankfully accepted of, and is come in a seasonable time: You shall (God willing) receive from us all the satisfaction which we can possibly give to your just and lawful desires. We entreat you to repair to your houses, and turn your petition which you have delivered here into prayers at home for us; for we have been, are and shall be (to our utmost power) ready to relieve you, your husbands, and children, and to perform the trust committed unto us towards God, our King and country, as becometh faithful Christians and loyal subjects.

1. Persecutions at Smithfield and Newgate.

2. The Jewish Esther became the Queen of Ahasuerus and saved the Jews from Haman, who planned to massacre the Jews; see the Book of Esther and also *Esther Hath Hang'd Haman* in Perspectives: Tracts on Women and Gender, page 1344.

John Lilburne
1614?–1657

John Lilburne was one of the most tireless political reformers of the Civil War in England. His pamphlets against the Anglican Church in 1638 got him arrested and brought before the Star Chamber (the secret royal tribunal that judged and punished without a jury). Lilburne seized the opportunity to question the court's procedures by refusing to incriminate himself. With Cromwell's help in the House of Commons, Lilburne was released from prison and became a lieutenant in the Parliamentary army (1642–45), from which he resigned in objection to Presbyterianism as the state religion. Examined several times by the House of Commons for his criticisms of its policies and members, Lilburne became the chief exponent of the Levellers, derisively called such because of their egalitarianism. The Levellers wanted fundamental changes in the government, including universal suffrage, freedom of speech and religion, freedom from exorbitant taxation, care of the poor and aged, and trial by jury. Though a convinced antimonarchist, Lilburne even protested against the condemnation of Charles I without a proper trial.

The House of Commons rejected Leveller reforms in January 1648. This defeat, combined with Lilburne's fear that the Levellers would be brought to trial for their dissent, provoked his speech to Commons in February. This speech was published as *England's New Chains Discovered*. The first part (a selection from which is reprinted here) reviews the Levellers' concerns, and the second part criticizes the members of Parliament, who condemned Lilburne's speech as seditious. Lilburne went on to publish tracts criticizing Cromwell, monopolies, and enclosures but was ordered into exile by Parliament in 1652 only for attacking his uncle's business enemy, Sir Arthur Hesilrige, as a man "fit to be spewed out of all human society." In 1653, Lilburne returned to England in defiance of Cromwell and was arrested on arrival. His plight aroused popular petitions in his favor, and he was finally acquitted. Nevertheless, the government would not let him go free. Having converted to Quakerism, he died in confinement just a year before the death of Cromwell.

from England's New Chains Discovered

or, The serious apprehensions of a part of the People, in behalf of the Commonwealth; (being Presenters, Promoters, and Approvers of the Large Petition of September 11. 1648.)

Presented to the Supreme Authority of England, the Representers of the people in Parliament assembled.

By Lieut. Col. John Lilburn, and divers other Citizens of London, and Borough of Southwark; February 26. 1648. Whereunto his speech delivered at the Bar is annexed.

Since you have done the nation so much right, and yourselves so much honor as to declare that the people (under God) are the original of all just powers; and given us thereby fair grounds to hope, that you really intend their freedom and prosperity; yet the way thereunto being frequently mistaken, and through haste or error of judgment, those who mean the best, are many times misled so far to the prejudice of those that trust them, as to leave them in a condition nearest to bondage, when they have thought they had brought them into a way of freedom. And since woeful experience hath manifested this to be a truth, there seemeth no small reason that you should seriously lay to heart what at present we have to offer, for discovery and prevention of so great a danger.

And because we have been the first movers in and concerning an Agreement of the People,[1] as the most proper and just means for the settling the long and tedious distractions of this nation, occasioned by nothing more, than the uncertainty of our government; and since there hath been an Agreement prepared and presented by some officers of the army to this honorable House,[2] as what they thought requisite to be agreed unto by the people (you approving thereof) we shall in the first place deliver our apprehensions thereupon.

That an Agreement between those that trust, and those who are trusted, hath appeared a thing acceptable to this honorable House, his Excellency, and the officers of the army, is as much to our rejoicing, as we conceive it just in itself, and profitable for the Commonwealth,[3] and cannot doubt but that you will protect those of the people, who have no ways forfeited their birthright, in their proper liberty of taking this, or any other, as God and their own considerations[4] shall direct them.

Which we the rather mention, for that many particulars in the Agreement before you, are upon serious examination thereof, dissatisfactory to most of those who are very earnestly desirous of an Agreement, and many very material things seem to be wanting therein, which may be supplied in another: As

1. They are now much troubled there should be any intervals between the ending of this Representative, and the beginning of the next as being desirous that this present Parliament that hath lately done so great things in so short a time, tending to their liberties, should sit; until with certainty and safety they can see them delivered into the hands of another Representative, rather than to leave them (though never so small a time) under the dominion of a Council of State; a Constitution of a new and unexperienced nature, and which they fear, as the case now stands, may design to perpetuate their power, and to keep off Parliaments for ever.

2. They now conceive no less danger, in that it is provided that Parliaments for the future are to continue but 6 months, and a Council of State 18. In which time, if they should prove corrupt, having command of all forces by sea and land, they will have great opportunities to make themselves absolute and unaccountable: And because this is a danger, than which there cannot well be a greater; they generally incline to Annual Parliaments, bounded and limited as reason shall devise, not dissolvable, but to be continued or adjourned as shall seem good in their discretion, during that year, but no longer; and then to dissolve of course, and give way to those who shall be chosen immediately to succeed them, and in the intervals of their adjournments, to entrust an ordinary Committee of their own members, as in other cases limited and bounded with express instructions, and accountable to the next session, which will avoid all those dangers feared from a Council of State, as at present this is constituted.

3. They are not satisfied with the clause, wherein it is said, that the power of the Representatives shall extend to the erecting and abolishing of Courts of Justice; since the alteration of the usual way of trials by twelve sworn men of the neighborhood, may be included therein: a constitution so equal and just in itself, as that they conceive it ought to remain unalterable. Neither is it clear what is meant by these

1. The Levellers published their proposals for "An Agreement of the People" in *Foundations of Freedom* (15 December 1648). The beginning of this speech complains about how the government has betrayed the principles set forth in the Leveller "Agreement."
2. *An Agreement Prepared for the People of England* was submitted to Parliament on January 20, 1649.
3. Commonwealth, meaning both public good and body politic, and specifically the republican government established in England between the execution of Charles I in 1649 and the Restoration in 1660.
4. Attentive thoughts.

words, (viz.) That the Representatives have the highest final judgment. They conceiving that their authority in these cases, is only to make laws, rules, and directions for other courts and persons assigned by law for the execution thereof; unto which every member of the Commonwealth, as well those of the Representative, as others, should be alike subject; it being likewise unreasonable in itself, and an occasion of much partiality, injustice, and vexation to the people, that the law-makers should be law-executors.[5]

4. Although it doth provide that in the laws hereafter to be made, no person by virtue of any tenure, grant, charter, patent, degree, or birth, shall be privileged from subjection thereunto, or from being bound thereby, as well as others. Yet doth it not null and make void those present protections by law, or otherwise; nor leave all persons, as well Lords as others, alike liable in person and estate, as in reason and conscience they ought to be.[6]

5. They are very much unsatisfied with what is expressed as a reserve from the Representative, in matters of religion, as being very obscure, and full of perplexity, that ought to be most plain and clear; there having occurred no greater trouble to the nation about any thing than by the intermeddling of Parliaments in matters of religion.[7]

6. They seem to conceive it absolutely necessary, that there be in their agreement, a reserve from ever having any kingly government, and a bar against restoring the House of Lords, both which are wanting in the agreement which is before you.

7. They seem to be resolved to take away all known and burdensome grievances, as tithes,[8] that great oppression of the country's industry and hindrance of tillage: excise, and customs, those secret thieves, and robbers, drainers of the poor and middle sort of people, and the greatest obstructers of trade, surmounting all the prejudices of ship money, patents, and projects,[9] before this Parliament: also to take away all monopolizing companies of merchants, the hinderers and decayers of clothing and cloth-working, dying, and the like useful professions; by which thousands of poor people might be set at work, that are now ready to starve, were merchandising restored to its due and proper freedom: they conceive likewise that the three grievances before mentioned, (viz.) monopolizing companies, excise, and customs, do exceedingly prejudice shipping and navigation, and consequently discourage seamen, and mariners, and which have had no small influence upon the late unhappy revolts which have so much endangered the nation, and so much advantaged your enemies. They also incline to direct a more equal and less burdensome way for levying monies for the future, those other forementioned being so chargeable in the receipt, as that the very stipends and allowance to the officers attending thereupon would defray a very great part of the charge of the army; whereas now they engender and support a corrupt interest. They also have in mind to take away all imprisonment of disabled men, for debt; and to provide some effectual course to enforce all that are able to a

5. Lilburne is calling for a clear distinction between the power of the House of Commons to legislate and the power of the Courts to interpret the law.

6. The Commonwealth did not thoroughly abolish the privileges of the landed classes and so did not provide a government in which all classes would be treated equally under the law.

7. Lilburne criticizes the Commons for not completely separating Church and State, which he sees as a major danger, since the King's imposition of the rituals of the Anglican Church was one of the reasons the English Civil War was fought.

8. The tenth part of the annual produce of agriculture, due as payment for the Church.

9. "Ship money" was an ancient tax levied in time of war on maritime cities, which was revived by Charles I and applied to inland counties as well; patents were the sole right or license to sell or deal in a commodity; and projects were plans or schemes, here especially those by the government to get money.

speedy payment, and not suffer them to be sheltered in prisons, where they live in plenty, whilst their creditors are undone. They have also in mind to provide work, and comfortable maintenance for all sorts of poor, aged, and impotent people, and to establish some more speedy, less troublesome and chargeable way for deciding of controversies in law, whole families having been ruined by seeking right in the ways yet in being. All which, though of greatest and most immediate concernment to the people, are yet omitted in their Agreement before you.

These and the like are their intentions in what they purpose for an Agreement of the people, as being resolved (so far as they are able) to lay an impossibility upon all whom they shall hereafter trust, of ever wronging the Commonwealth in any considerable measure, without certainty of ruining themselves, and as conceiving it to be an improper tedious, and unprofitable thing for the people, to be ever running after their Representatives with petitions for redress of such grievances as may at once be removed by themselves, or to depend for these things so essential to their happiness and freedom, upon the uncertain judgments of several Representatives, the one being apt to renew what the other hath taken away.

Oliver Cromwell
1599–1658

Cromwell's brutal conquest of Ireland (1649–1650) was the culmination of a long military, political, and religiously zealous career and the turning point in his rise to the position of Lord Protector. He had risen steadily in the Parliamentary Army, serving in the early days of the Civil War as captain of a troop of horses and finally becoming the chief of the New Model Army. Not only did he have a genius for military strategy but he was one of those who "never stirred from their troops . . . but fought to the last minute." He and his men were both called "Ironsides" in tribute to their indomitability. As a member of Parliament, he argued vigorously for the Puritan cause, and when Parliament was purged of Presbyterians in 1649, Cromwell's power and that of his fellow Congregationalists or Independents increased. At the trial of Charles I in January 1649, Cromwell adamantly demanded execution. Afterward, when the new Commonwealth was set up, one of Parliament's first charges was to send Cromwell to subdue Ireland, where Irish Royalists and Rebels, once pitted against each other, had formed a coalition and were gaining ground.

Cromwell's treatment of the Irish tested the limits of the principles of the Puritan Revolution and left a legacy of devastation. Although Cromwell was a strong member of the English Parliament, he helped to bring about the abolition of both Irish and Scottish Parliaments with his military defeats of both kingdoms. In September 1644, Cromwell urged the Presbyterian Parliament to guarantee liberty of conscience to the Independents among his troops, but when the Catholics of New Ross, Ireland, called for similar toleration in October 1649, Cromwell refused them: "if by liberty of conscience, you mean a liberty to exercise the Mass, I judge it best to use plain dealing, and to let you know, where the Parliament of England have power, that will not be allowed of." Indeed during Cromwell's rule in England, only Jews and non-Anglican Protestants were tolerated. Furthermore, Cromwell escalated the policy (begun under Elizabeth and James) of giving lands confiscated from native Irish inhabitants to English colonists. The massacre of Drogheda—including civilians as well as troops—made the Irish remember Cromwell as cruel. In the following letter of September 17, 1649, Cromwell presents his troops' massacre of the people of Drogheda as "the righteous judgment of God." The same religious conviction that had made him and his New Model Army such valiant defenders of English liberty was used to justify Irish slaughter.

Cromwell also used his letters to keep Parliament informed of his progress, to ask for further supplies, and to promote his political power. He was to go on to defeat the Scots in 1650. Ultimately, his power grew to such an extent that in 1657 he became Lord Protector, assuming the pomp and trappings of royalty. When his son Richard succeeded him at his death in September 1658, it seemed as if Oliver Cromwell's rule had led to a new monarchy. His son proved a weak successor, and the Commonwealth was restored in May 1659, only to collapse with the Restoration of 1660. If Cromwell's participation in parliamentary politics and the New Model Army contributed to the cause of republican liberty, his conquest of Ireland marked one of the bleakest chapters in the English colonization of Ireland.

from Letters from Ireland

Relating the Several Great Success It Hath Pleased God to Give Unto the Parliament's Forces There, in the Taking of Drogheda, Trym, Dundalk, Carlingford, and the Nury . . . .

For the Honorable *William Lenthal* Esq;
Speaker of the Parliament of *England*

Sir,

Your army[1] being safely arrived at Dublin, and the enemy endeavoring to draw all his forces together about Trym and Tecroghan[2] (as my intelligence gave me); from whence endeavors were used by the Marquis of Ormonde, to draw Owen Roe O'Neal with his forces to his assistance, but with what success I cannot yet learn.[3] I resolved after some refreshment taken for our weather beaten men and horses, and accommodations for a march, to take the field; and accordingly upon Friday the thirtieth of August last, rendezvoused with eight regiments of foot, and six of horse, and some troops of dragoons, three miles on the north side of Dublin; the design was, to endeavor the regaining of Drogheda,[4] or tempting the enemy, upon his hazard of the loss of that place, to fight. Your army came before the town upon Monday following, where having pitched, as speedy course as could be was taken to frame our batteries,[5] which took up the more time, because divers of the battering guns were on shipboard. Upon Monday the ninth of this instant, the batteries began to play; whereupon I sent Sir Arthur Ashton the then Governor a summons, to deliver the town to the use of the Parliament of England; to the which I received no satisfactory answer, but proceeded that day to beat down the steeple of the church on the south side of the town, and to beat down a tower not far from the same place, which you will discern by the card[6] enclosed. Our guns not being able to do much that day, it was resolved to endeavor to do our utmost the next day to make breaches[7] assaultable, and by the help of God to storm them. The places pitched upon, were that part of the town wall next a church, called St. Marie's, which was the rather chosen, because we did hope that if we did enter and possess that church, we should be the better able to keep it against their horse and foot, until we could make way for the entrance of our horse,

1. The letter is addressed to Parliament from the commander of the parliamentary army, hence "your army."
2. A town and townland in County Meath, northwest of Dublin.
3. James Butler, Earl of Ormonde, represented Charles I in Ireland throughout the 1640s. At first opposed to the Catholic Confederation led by Owen Roe O'Neill (c. 1590–1649), Ormonde joined forces with O'Neill against the incursion of Cromwell's army.
4. Drogheda (Droichead átha, "Bridge of the ford"), a city in County Louth, was under royalist command when Cromwell arrived there on 2 September 1649.
5. Platforms on which artillery was mounted.
6. Chart, map.
7. Gaps in fortifications.

which we did not conceive that any part of the town would afford the like advantage for that purpose with this. The batteries planted were two, one was for that part of the wall against the east end of the said church, the other against the wall on the south side; being somewhat long in battering, the enemy made six retrenchments, three of them from the said church to Duleek Gate, and three from the east end of the church to the town wall, and so backward. The guns after some two or three hundred shot, beat down the corner tower, and opened two reasonable good breaches in the east and south wall. Upon Tuesday the tenth of this instant, about five of the clock in the evening, we began the storm, and after some hot dispute, we entered about seven or eight hundred men, the enemy disputing it very stiffly with us; and indeed through the advantages of the place, and the courage God was pleased to give the defenders, our men were forced to retreat quite out of the breach, not without some considerable loss; Colonel Cassel being there shot in the head, whereof he presently died, and divers soldiers and officers doing their duty, killed and wounded. There was a tenalia[8] to flanker the south wall of the town, between Duleek Gate, and the corner tower before mentioned, which our men entered, wherein they found some forty or fifty of the enemy, which they put to the sword, and this they held; but it being without[9] the wall, and the sallyport[1] through the wall into that tenalia being choked up with some of the enemy which were killed in it, it proved of no use for our entrance into the town that way.

Although our men that stormed the breaches were forced to recoil, as before is expressed, yet being encouraged to recover their loss, they made a second attempt, wherein God was pleased to animate them, that they got ground of the enemy, and by the goodness of God, forced him to quit his entrenchments; and after a very hot dispute, the enemy having both horse and foot, and we only foot within the wall, the enemy gave ground, and our men became masters; but of their retrenchments and the church, which indeed although they made our entrance the more difficult, yet they proved of excellent use to us, so that the enemy could not annoy us with their horse, but thereby we had advantage to make good the ground, that so we might let in our own horse, which accordingly was done, though with much difficulty; the enemy retreated divers of them into the Mill-Mount, a place very strong and of difficult access, being exceeding high, having a good graft[2] and strongly pallisadoed;[3] the Governor Sir Arthur Ashton and divers considerable officers being there, our men getting up to them, were ordered by me to put them all to the sword; and indeed being in the heat of action, I forbade them to spare any that were in arms in the town, and I think that night they put to the sword about two thousand men, divers of the officers and soldiers being fled over the bridge into the other part of the town, where about one hundred of them possessed St. Peter's church steeple, some the west gate, and others, a round strong tower next the gate, called St. Sunday's. These being summoned to yield to mercy, refused; whereupon I ordered the steeple of St. Peter's church to be fired, where one of them was heard to say in the midst of the flames, "God damn me, God confound me, I burn, I burn." The next day the other two towers were summoned,[4] in one of which was about six or seven score, but they refused to yield themselves; and we knowing that hunger must compel them, set only good guards to secure them from running away, until their stomachs were come down.

8. A low fortification to protect the wall from the side.
9. Outside.
1. An opening for troops to pass through.
2. Ditch, moat.
3. Defended with a strong fence of pointed stakes.
4. Called to surrender.

From one of the said towers, notwithstanding their condition, they killed and wounded some of our men; when they submitted, their officers were knocked on the head, and every tenth man of the soldiers killed, and the rest shipped for the Barbados;[5] the soldiers in the other tower were all spared, as to their lives only, and shipped likewise for the Barbados. I am persuaded that this is a righteous judgment of God upon these barbarous wretches, who have imbrued their hands in so much innocent blood, and that it will tend to prevent the effusion of blood for the future, which are the satisfactory grounds to such actions, which otherwise cannot but work remorse and regret.

The officers and soldiers of this garrison were the flower of all their army; and their great expectation was that our attempting this place would put fair to ruin us; they being confident of the resolution of their men, and the advantage of the place; if we had divided our force into two quarters, to have besieged the north town and the south town, we could not have had such a correspondency between the two parts of our army, but that they might have chosen to have brought their army, and have fought with which part they pleased, and at the same time have made a sally with two thousand men upon us, and have left their walls manned, they having in the town the numbers specified in this inclosed, by some say near four thousand. Since this great mercy vouchsafed to us, I sent a party of horse and dragoons to Dundalk, which the enemy quitted, and we are possessed of; as also another castle they deserted between Trym and Drogheda, upon the Boynes.[6] I sent a party of horse and dragoons to a house within five miles of Trym, there being then in Trym some Scots companies which the Lord of Ards[7] brought to assist the Lord of Ormonde; but upon the news of Drogheda they ran away, leaving their great guns behind them, which we also have possessed. And now give me leave to say how it comes to pass that this work is wrought. It was set upon some of our hearts, that a great thing should be done, not by power, or might, but by the Spirit of God; and is it not so clear? That which caused your men to storm so courageously, it was the Spirit of God, who gave your men courage, and took it away again, and gave the enemy courage, and took it away again, and gave your men courage again, and therewith this happy success; and therefore it is good that God alone have all the glory.

It is remarkable, that these people at the first set up the Mass in some places of the town that had been monasteries; but afterwards grew so insolent, that the last Lord's day before the Storm,[8] the Protestants were thrust out of the great church, called St. Peter's, and they had public Mass there; and in this very place near one thousand of them were put to the sword, flying thither for safety: I believe all their friars were knocked on the head promiscuously, but two, the one of which was Father Peter Taaff (Brother to the Lord Taaff)[9] whom the Soldiers took the next day, and made an end of; the other was taken in the round tower, under the repute of lieutenant, and when he understood the officers in that tower had no quarter, he confessed he was a friar, but that did not save him. A great deal of loss in this business, fell upon Col. Hewson, Col. Cassel, and Colonel Ewers' regiments; Colonel Ewers having two field-officers in his regiment shot, Colonel Cassel and a captain of his

5. In the Cromwellian period in Ireland, not only men captured in battle but also women and children were sent into indentured servitude to English colonies in the Caribbean.

6. The Boyne River.

7. Hugh Montgomery (c. 1623–1663), 3rd Viscount of Ards.

8. I.e., Cromwell's attack on the town.

9. Theobald, 2nd Viscount Taaff (d. 1677). An uncle of Lord Taaff, Lucas was forced to surrender New Ross to Cromwell in October 1649.

regiment slain, Colonel Hewson's captain-lieutenant slain; I do not think we lost one hundred men upon the place, though many be wounded. I most humbly pray, the Parliament will be pleased this army may be maintained, and that a consideration may be had of them, and of the carrying on of the affairs here, as may give a speedy issue to this work, to which there seems to be a marvelous fair opportunity offered by God. And although it may seem very chargeable to the State of England to maintain so great a force, yet surely to stretch a little for the present, in following God's Providence, in hope the charge will not be long, I trust it will not be thought by any (that have no irreconcilable or malicious principles) unfit for me to move for a constant supply, which in humane probability, as to outward means, is most likely to hasten and perfect this work; and indeed, if God please to finish it here, as he hath done in England, the war is like to pay itself. We keep the field much, our tents sheltering us from the wet and cold, but yet the country sickness overtakes many, and therefore we desire recruits, and some fresh regiments of foot may be sent us; for it is easily conceived by what the garrisons already drink up, what our field army will come to, if God shall give more garrisons into our hands. Craving pardon for this great trouble, I rest,

Your most humble Servant,

Dublin, Sept. 17. 1649 O. CROMWELL

John O'Dwyer of the Glenn

c. 1651

John O'Dwyer of the Glenn (*Seán O'Duibhir an Ghleanna*) is one of the most beautiful popular Irish-language songs commemorating the war against the Cromwellian conquest of Ireland and its aftermath. According to James Hardiman, who collected this song in his *Irish Minstrelsy, or Bardic Remains of Ireland* (1831), John O'Dwyer was "a distinguished officer who commanded in the Counties of Waterford and Tipperary in 1651." The poem is listed under the heading "Jacobite Relics," which places it in a long tradition of support for the Stuart kings, which began with the celebration of the accession of James I in elite bardic poetry and continued into the eighteenth century with support for Bonnie Prince Charlie in popular ballads.

The imagery of the natural world in *John O'Dwyer of the Glenn* symbolizes the state of Ireland. The lyric begins with a pastoral idyll, as the speaker describes awakening in the morning to the sound of birds singing. The intrusion of a fox signals the advent of war, and a sad old woman who stands by the side of the road reckoning her geese evokes Ireland weeping for those she has lost. Some of the geese (*geidh*), here referred to as "that prowler's spoil," died in battle; others, like the "wild geese" (*geidh fiádháin*) who left Ireland after the defeat of the Gaelic chiefs in 1603, fled to the Continent. John O'Dwyer and his men were said by Hardiman to have embarked for Spain.

The translation here is that of Thomas Furlong as printed in Hardiman's *Irish Minstrelsy.* The song originated in County Tipperary in the mid-seventeenth century, and there are more verses in Irish. It is still sung in both English and Irish. The best edition of the Irish text is that edited by Padraig de Brún and Breandán O Buachalla in *Nua-Dhuanaire* (1971), which also contains poems by such mid-seventeenth-century Irish poets as Piaras Feiritéar and Dáibhí O Bruadair.

John O'Dwyer of the Glenn

Blithe the bright dawn found me,
Rest with strength had crown'd me,

Sweet the birds sung round me,
    Sport was all their toil.
The horn its clang was keeping,
Forth the fox was creeping,
Round each dame stood weeping,
    O'er that prowler's spoil.
Hark, the foe is calling,
Fast the woods are falling,
Scenes and sights appalling
    Mark the wasted soil.[1]

War and confiscation
Curse the fallen nation;
Gloom and desolation
    Shade the lost land o'er.
Chill the winds are blowing,
Death aloft is going;
Peace or hope seems growing
    For our race no more.
Hark the foe is calling,
Fast the woods are falling,
Scenes and sights appalling
    Throng our blood-stained shore.

Where's my goat to cheer me,[2]
Now it plays not near me;
Friends no more can hear me;
    Strangers round me stand.
Nobles once high-hearted,
From their homes have parted,
Scatter'd, scar'd and started
    By a base-born band.
Hark the foe is calling,
Fast the woods are falling;
Scenes and sights appalling
    Thicken round the land.

Oh! that death had found me
And in darkness bound me,
Ere each object round me
    Grew so sweet, so dear.
Spots that once were cheering,
Girls beloved endearing,
Friends from whom I'm steering,
    Take this parting tear.
Hark, the foe is calling,
Fast the woods are falling;
Scenes and sights appalling
    Plague and haunt me here.

1. The falling woods are the old Irish families who have been thrown off their land, and the "wasted soil" is the country after war.

2. The goat stands for both Charles II in exile and the defeated Irish lords.

The Story of Alexander Agnew

Alexander Agnew is seen by contemporary Scots writers such as Booker Prize–winning novelist James Kelman as something of a hero. An unrepentant freethinker, Agnew was the first man in Scots history publicly to deny the existence of God. Offending the Presbyterian laws of Scotland, Agnew was found guilty of blasphemy and hanged. The following journalistic account of his trial gives the sense of a man being driven to greater and greater levels of vitriolic sarcasm by the nitpicking detail of his Presbyterian examiners. Since the story begins with his refusing to go to church, saying, "Hang God, God was hanged long since," the ninth count against him—that he refused to say grace—seems oddly anticlimactic.

The story was printed in *Mercurius Politicus*, a pamphlet founded by Marchamont Needham in June 1650. In 1649, Parliament had had Needham arrested for the royalist *Mercurius Pragmaticus*, a pamphlet he had been editing since 1647, and ordered John Milton to examine Needham on his political views. Less than a year after his brush with the law, Needham reemerged as the editor of *Mercurius Politicus, the Common-Wealth of England Stated . . . With a Discourse of Excellencie of a Free-State, above a Kingly-Government*. Needham's editorial style has been described as slangy, even reminiscent of Dekker's canting. For example, in Needham's first sentence in *Mercurius Politicus* 15, he refers to the Scots Prebyterians as "our gown'd Granado's." Needham clearly had it in for the Scots, whose independence he and his pamphlet's republican English audience saw as one of the greatest obstacles to the Commonwealth.

The Story of Alexander Agnew; or Jock of Broad Scotland[1]

Alexander Agnew, commonly called Jock of broad Scotland, being accused; forasmuch as by the Divine Law of Almighty God, and Acts of Parliament of this nation, the committers of the horrid crime of blasphemy are punished by death; nevertheless, in plain contempt of the said Laws and Acts of Parliament, the said Alexander Agnew uttered heinous and grievous blasphemies against the Omnipotent and Almighty God; and second and third persons of the Trinity, as the same is set down in diverse articles in manner following; to wit,

First, the said Alexander being desired to go to church answered, "Hang God, God was hanged long since." What had he to do with God? He had nothing to do with God. Secondly, he answered, he was nothing in God's common,[2] God gave him nothing, and he was no more obliged to God than to the Devil, and God was very greedy. Thirdly, when he was desired to seek anything in God's name, he said he would never seek anything for God's sake, and that it was neither God nor the Devil that gave the fruits of the ground, the wives of the country gave him his meat. Fourthly, being asked, wherein he believed, answered, he believed in white meal, water, and salt. Fifthly, being asked how many persons were in the Godhead, answered there was only one person in the Godhead who made all, but for Christ he was not God, because he was made, and came into the world after it was made, and died as other men, being nothing but a mere man.

Sixthly, he declared that he knew not whether God or the Devil had the greater power, but he thought the Devil had the greatest, "And when I die," said he, "let God and the Devil strive for my soul, and let him that is strongest take it." Seventhly, he denied there was a holy Ghost, or knew there was a Spirit, and denied he was a

1. From *Mercurius Politicus*, 3 July 1656.

2. Community.

sinner or needed mercy. Eighthly, he denied he was a sinner and that he scorned to seek God's mercy. Ninthly, he ordinarily mocked all exercise of God's worship, and invocation on his name, in derision saying, "Pray you to your God and I will pray to mine when I think time." And when he was desired by some to give thanks for his meat, he said, "Take a sackful of prayers to the mill and shell them, and grind them and take your breakfast of them." To others he said, "I will give you a twopence, and pray until a bowl of meal and one stone[3] of butter fall down from heaven through the house rigging to you." To others he said when bread and cheese was given him, and was laid on the ground by him, he said, "If I leave this, I will long cry to God before he give it me again." To others he said, "Take a bannock[4] and break it in two, and lay down the one half thereof, and ye will long pray to God before he put the other half to it again."

Tenthly, being posed whether or not he knew God or Christ, he answered, he had never had any profession, nor never would; he never had any religion, nor never would: also that there was no God nor Christ, and that he never received anything from God but from nature, which he said ever reigned, and ever would, and that to speak of God and their persons was an idle thing, and that he would never name such names, for he had shaken his cap of these things long since, and he denied that a man has a soul, or that there is a heaven or a hell, or that the Scriptures are the word of God. Concerning Christ he said, that he heard of such a man, but for the second person of the Trinity, he had been the second person of the Trinity, if the ministers had not put him in prison, and that he was no more obliged to God nor the Devil. And these aforesaid blasphemies are not rarely or seldom uttered by him, but frequently and ordinarily in several places where he resorted, to the entangling, deluding, and seducing of the common people: through the committing of which blasphemies he hath contravened the tenor of the said Laws and Acts of Parliament and incurred the pain of death mentioned therein, which ought to be inflicted upon him with all rigor, in manner specified in the indictment.

Which indictment being put to the knowledge of an assize,[5] the said Alexander Agnew called Jock of broad Scotland, was by the said assize, all in one voice, by the mouth of William Carlile, late baily[6] of Dumfrize their chancellor[7] found guilty of the crime of blasphemy mentioned in his indictment. For which the commissioners ordained him upon Wednesday, 21 May 1656, betwixt 2 and 4 hours in the afternoon to be taken to the ordinary place of execution for the burgh of Dumfrize, and there to be hanged on a gibbet while he be dead, and all his movable goods to be escheat.[8]

Edward Hyde, Earl of Clarendon

1609–1674

Bound up in the politics of his day, Edward Hyde was also often at odds with the powerful. From a long line of lawyers, he was neither noble nor wealthy by birth but rose to power through the law. Hyde played the observer in his roles as scholar, legislator, and diplomat. At law school at the Middle Temple in 1627 he complained that the whole country was a "sea of wine, and women, and quarrels, and gaming." A member of a humanist circle surrounding Sir Lucius Cary, Secretary

3. Fourteen pounds.
4. In Scotland and the North of England, a large round loaf of bread.
5. In Scotland, a trial by jury.
6. In Scotland, the chief magistrate of a county who functions as a sheriff.
7. In Scotland, the foreman of a jury.
8. Forfeited to the state.

of State under Charles I, Clarendon found them too naive about the realities of power. Entering Parliament in 1640, Hyde initially supported Parliament's curbs on royal absolutism, such as the impeachment of the King's man in Ireland, the Earl of Strafford. Later, however, fearing that parliamentary radicalism was a threat to the English constitution, Clarendon sided with the King. Serving Charles I closely throughout the 1640s by urging compromise with Parliament rather than war, Clarendon was no more comfortable among the King's followers than among the Parliamentarians. After the execution of Charles I, Clarendon was hired by Charles II in exile only when all other policies had been tried and failed. After the Restoration he held the position of Lord Chancellor until he was removed from power by Charles II's rakish courtiers, who resented his political ethos of moderation and tradition. Exiled in disgrace, he wrote the final version of *The History of the Rebellion and Civil Wars in England*, published a quarter century after his death (1702–1704).

Ironic detachment in tension with partisanship characterizes the history as it does his life. Strangely enough, neither his autobiography nor his history contains an account of how he abandoned the Parliamentarians for Charles I. Yet his scathing criticism of those who crossed the royalists—Presbyterians, Scots, Irish, Independents—reveals a private audience of like-minded royalists among family and friends. At times, Clarendon's irony escalates to sarcasm, as in his comments on the Scottish nobleman Argyle in the following account of the death of the great Scots military hero Montrose. Montrose's support of Charles I had thwarted Argyle's rise to power in Scotland. When Montrose returned to Scotland in 1649 as Charles II's Lieutenant General, Argyle succeeded in having him arrested on charges of heresy. A vacillating Charles II did not intervene, and Montrose was executed with theatrical brutality. As Martine Brownley has commented, there are "no unalloyed heroes or villains" in Clarendon's history, and so Montrose is portrayed in understated terms, and the narrative does not shrink from revealing Charles II's betrayal of his old ally. Clarendon's style eschews high rhetoric and opts for a middle style in a syntax uniting periods in a loose linear fashion. The poised detachment and sober gravity of his style produce the kind of authority that caused the German historian Ranke to say of Clarendon's *History of the Rebellion*: "the view of the event in England itself and in the educated world generally . . . has been determined by the book."

from True Historical Narrative of the Rebellion

[The Death of Montrose]

Permission was then given to him[1] to speak; and without the least trouble in his countenance, or disorder, upon all the indignities he had suffered, he told them, since the King had owned them so far as to treat with them, he had appeared before them with reverence, and bareheaded, which otherwise he would not have done: that he had done nothing of which he was ashamed, or had cause to repent; that the first Covenant he had taken,[2] and complied with it, and with them who took it, as long as the ends for which it was ordained were observed; but when he discovered, which was now evident to all the world, that private and particular men designed to satisfy their own ambition and interest, instead of considering the public benefit, and that under the pretence of reforming some errors in religion they resolved to abridge and take away the King's just power and lawful authority, he had withdrawn himself from that engagement: that for the League and Covenant,[3] he had never taken it, and therefore could not break it; and it was now too apparent to the whole Christian world what monstrous mischiefs it had produced: that when, under color of it, an army from Scotland had invaded England in assistance of the rebellion that was then against their lawful King, he had, by his

1. Montrose.
2. Montrose had sworn to the National Covenant of 1638, a pact drawn up by the Scots Presbyterians to drive out Anglicanism and the innovations of Archbishop Laud, particularly the English Book of Common Prayer.
3. The Solemn League and Covenant (1643) was an Anglo-Scottish alliance to establish a state Presbyterian Church in Scotland and Ireland and to pledge military aid against the King, both funding for the Scots Presbyterian forces in Ulster and the entrance of these forces into England.

majesty's command, received a commission from him to raise forces in Scotland, that he might thereby divert them from the other odious prosecution: that he had executed that commission with the obedience and duty that he owed to the King, and in all the circumstances of it had proceeded like a gentleman, and had never suffered any blood to be shed but in the heat of the battle; and that he saw many persons there whose lives he had saved: when the King commanded him, he laid down his arms, and withdrew out of the kingdom, which they could not have compelled him to have done. He said he was now again entered into the kingdom by his majesty's command and with his authority; and what success soever it might have pleased God to have given him, he would always have obeyed any command he should have received from him. He advised them to consider well of the consequence before they proceeded against him, and that all his actions might be examined and judged by the laws of the land, or those of nations.

As soon as he had ended his discourse he was ordered to withdraw, and after a short space was again brought in, and told by the Chancellor that he was on the morrow, being the one and twentieth of May 1650, to be carried to Edinborough cross, and there to be hanged upon a gallows thirty foot high, for the space of three hours, and then to be taken down, and his head to be cut off upon a scaffold, and hanged on Edinborough tollbooth, and his legs and arms to be hanged up in other public towns of the kingdom, and his body to be buried at the place where he was to be executed, except the Kirk should take off his excommunication, and then his body might be buried in the common place of burial. He desired that he might say somewhat to them, but was not suffered, and so was carried back to the prison.

That he might not enjoy any ease or quiet during the short remainder of his life, their ministers came presently to insult over him with all the reproaches imaginable, pronounced his damnation, and assured him that the judgment he was the next day to undergo was but an easy prologue to that which he was to undergo afterward. And after many such barbarities, they offered to intercede for him to the Kirk upon his repentance, and to pray with him; but he too well understood the form of their common prayers in those cases to be only the most virulent and insolent imprecations against the persons of those they prayed against ("Lord, vouchsafe yet to touch the obdurate heart of this proud incorrigible sinner, this wicked, perjured, traitorous, and profane person, who refuses to hearken to the voice of thy Kirk," and the like charitable expressions), and therefore he desired them to spare their pains, and to leave him to his own devotions. He told them that they were a miserable, deluded, and deluding people; and would shortly bring that poor nation under the most insupportable servitude ever people had submitted to. He told them he was prouder to have his head set upon the place it was appointed to be, than he could have been to have had his picture hung in the King's bedchamber: that he was so far from being troubled that his four limbs were to be hanged in four cities of the kingdom, that he heartily wished that he had flesh enough to be sent to every city in Christendom, as a testimony of the cause for which he suffered.

The next day they executed every part and circumstance of that barbarous sentence with all the inhumanity imaginable; and he bore it with all the courage and magnanimity, and the greatest piety, that a good Christian could manifest. He magnified the virtue, courage, and religion of the last King, exceedingly commended the justice and goodness and understanding of the present King, and prayed that they might not betray him as they had done his father. When he had ended all he meant to say, and was expecting to expire, they had yet one scene more to act of their tyranny. The hangman brought the book that had been published of his truly heroic actions whilst he had commanded in that kingdom, which book was tied in a small cord that was put about his neck. The marquis smiled at this new instance of their malice, and thanked them for it; and said he was pleased that it should be there, and was prouder of wearing it than ever he had been of the Garter;[4] and so renewing some devout ejaculations, he patiently endured the last act of the executioner.

Soon after, the officers who had been taken with him, Sir William Hurry, Sir Francis Hay, and many others of as good families as any in the kingdom, were executed, to the number of thirty or forty, in several quarters of the kingdom; many of them being suffered to be beheaded. There was one whom they thought fit to save, one Colonel Whitford; who, when he was brought to die, said, he knew the reason why he was put to death, which was only because he had killed Dorislaus at the Hague, who was one of those who had murdered the last King. One of the magistrates, who were present to see the execution, caused it to be suspended, till he presently informed the council what the man had said; and they thought fit to avoid the reproach, and so preserved the gentleman, who was not before known to have had a hand in that action.

Thus died the gallant Marquis of Montrose, after he had given as great a testimony of loyalty and courage as a subject can do, and performed as wonderful actions in several battles, upon as great inequality of numbers and as great disadvantages in respect of arms and other preparations for war, as hath been performed in this age. He was a gentleman of a very ancient extraction, many of whose ancestors had exercised the highest charges under the King in that kingdom, and had been allied to the Crown itself. He was of very good parts, which were improved by a good education: he had always a great emulation, or rather a great contempt, of the Marquis of Argyle (as he was too apt to contemn those he did not love), who wanted nothing but honesty and courage to be a very extraordinary man, having all other good talents in a great degree. He was in his nature fearless of danger, and never declined any enterprise for the difficulty of going through with it, but exceedingly affected those which seemed desperate to other men and did believe somewhat to be in him[self] which other men were not acquainted with, which made him live more easily towards those who were, or were willing to be, inferior to him, and towards whom he exercised wonderful civility and generosity, than with his superiors or equals. He was naturally jealous, and suspected those who did not concur with him in the way not to mean so well as he. He was not without vanity, but his virtues were much superior, and he well deserved to have his memory preserved and celebrated amongst the most illustrious persons of the age in which he lived.

The King received an account and information of all these particulars before he embarked from Holland, without any other apology for the affront and indignity to himself than that they assured him that the proceeding against the late Marquis of Montrose had been for his service. They who were most displeased with Argyle and his faction were not sorry for this inhuman and monstrous prosecution; which at the same time must render him the more odious, and had rid them of an enemy that they thought would have been more dangerous to them; and they persuaded the King, who was enough afflicted with the news and all the circumstances of it, that he might sooner take revenge upon that people by a temporary complying with them and going to them, than by staying away and absenting himself, which would invest them in an absolute dominion in that kingdom, and give them power to corrupt or destroy all those who yet remained faithful to him, and were ready to spend their lives in his service: and so he pursued his former resolution and embarked for Scotland.

[END OF PERSPECTIVES: THE CIVIL WAR, OR THE WARS OF THREE KINGDOMS]

4. The Order of the Garter is the oldest and most important order of knighthood in England, instituted by Edward III (c. 1346).

John Milton

1608–1674

While writing *Paradise Lost,* Milton would rise early to begin composing poetry; when his secretary arrived late, the old blind man would complain, "I want to be milked." Prodigious in his memory and ingenuity, austere in his frugality and discipline, Milton devoted his life to learning, politics, and art. He put his eloquence at the service of the Puritan Revolution, which brought on the beheading of a king and the institution of a republican commonwealth. Milton entered controversies on divorce and freedom of the press. He showed courage in defending the Puritan republic when he could have lost his life for doing so. Radical, scholar, sage—Milton is above all the great epic poet of England.

Milton's life was marked by a passionate devotion to his religious, political, and artistic ideals, a devotion that ran in his family. Milton's father was said to have been disinherited for his Protestantism by his own father, who was Roman Catholic. When the Civil War broke out, Milton sided with Cromwell while his brother fought for the King. The oldest of three children in a prosperous middle-class family, young John read Virgil, Ovid, and Livy; he especially loved "our sage and serious Spenser," whom he called "a better teacher than Aquinas." Milton later wrote that from the age of twelve he "hardly ever gave up reading for bed till midnight." After his first year at Christ's College, Cambridge, the poet was expelled. While in exile, Milton excoriated academia: "How wretchedly suited that place is to the worshippers of Phoebus! It is disgusting to be constantly subjected to the threats of a rough tutor and to other indignities my spirit cannot endure." Returning to Cambridge, he took his B.A. in 1629 and his M.A. in 1632. On vacations during these years he wrote two of his most musical lyrics, the erotic *L'Allegro* and the Platonic *Il Penseroso.* After leaving university, Milton lived with his parents in Berkshire, where he wrote *Lycidas,* a haunting elegy for the early death of his Cambridge friend Edward King, and *Comus,* a masque for the prominent noble Egerton family at Ludlow Castle.

After his mother's death in 1638, Milton traveled to Europe. He stayed longest in Italy, where his poems were greatly admired by the Florentine literati, who welcomed him into their academies. He later reflected that it was in Italy that he first sensed his vocation as an epic poet, hoping to "perhaps leave something so written, as they should not willingly let it die." Visiting Rome, Naples, and Venice, Milton collected Monteverdi's music, which he would later sing and play. He also met the famed astronomer Galileo, the censorship of whose works Milton would later protest. Concerned about political turmoil in England, he returned home at the outbreak of the Civil War.

From 1640 to 1660, Milton devoted himself to "the cause of real and substantial liberty," by which he meant religious, domestic, and civil liberties. Defending religious liberty, he decried Anglican hierarchy and ritualism—"the new vomited paganism of sensual idolatry"—in a series of tracts, including *Of Reformation* (1641) and *The Reason of Church Government* (1642).

That same year, Milton married seventeen-year-old Mary Powell, who came from a royalist Oxfordshire family. After only a month, she left Milton alone to his "philosophical" life for a more sociable one at home. Troubled by the unhappiness of his marriage, Milton wrote four treatises on divorce, for which he was publicly condemned. He argued that incompatibility should be grounds for divorce, that both husband and wife should be allowed to remarry, and that to maintain otherwise was contrary to reason and scripture. According to his nephew, whom Milton tutored during this time, he was interested in marrying another woman but by 1645 was reunited with Mary. They had a daughter soon afterward. They were joined for several years by Mary's family, who had lost their estate in the Civil War.

Along with "the true conception of marriage," Milton's concept of domestic liberty included "the sound education of children, and freedom of thought and speech." In *Of Education* (1644), opposing strictly vocational instruction, Milton called for the study of languages, rhetoric, poetry, philosophy, and science, the goal of which was "to perform justly, skillfully and magnanimously all of the offices both private and public of peace and war." In *Areopagitica* (1644), Milton fought against censorship before publication but counseled control of printed texts posing political or religious danger. In the 1640s, Milton steered a course midway between the religious conformity demanded by the once dissenting Presbyterians and the complete separation of church and state advocated by such radicals as Roger Williams, who ultimately went to America in search of greater toleration.

After Oliver Cromwell defeated the Royalists and the King was tried and executed by order of the "Rump" parliament purged of dissenters, Milton wrote *The Tenure of Kings and Magistrates* (1649) to argue that subjects could justly overthrow a tyrant. This tract won him the job of Latin Secretary to the Council of State, handling all correspondence to foreign governments. After the beheading of Charles I in 1649, *Eikon Basilike*, "the Royal Image" appeared, pieced together from the King's papers by his chaplain John Gauden. To counteract sympathy for the King's cause that this work might elicit, Milton wrote a chapter-by-chapter refutation of it entitled *Eikonoklastes*, or *Image-Breaker* (1649). Milton also defended Cromwell's government in three Latin works that were in some measure self-defenses: *First* and *Second Defense of the English People* (1651, 1654) and *Defense of Himself* (1656).

His eyes weakened by the strain of so much writing, Milton went blind. His wife Mary died, leaving three daughters and one son. The boy died soon after, in May 1652. That same month, Milton wrote a sonnet exhorting the Lord General Cromwell to "Help us to save free conscience from the paw of hireling wolves," a reference to ministers who wanted to exclude dissenters from a unified established church. Sounding the cry for liberty again in *Avenge, O Lord these Slaughtered Saints* (1655), Milton lamented the massacre of Italian Protestants. One of Milton's most beautiful and best-known sonnets, *Me thought I saw my late espoused saint*, is said to be about his second wife, Katherine Woodcock, who, after just two years of marriage, died following the birth of her child in 1558.

Cromwell died the same year, and his son Richard's succession to power began a period of political confusion. Milton continued to write political tracts, now even more radical in arguing for universal education and freedom from allegiance to *any* established church and against the abuse of church positions for money. In *De Doctrina Christiana* (written 1655–1660, published 1823), Milton set forth his individualistic theology; he was convinced that no one should be required to attend church and that everyone should interpret scripture in his own way. Committed to the cause of the republic even after the Restoration of Charles II, Milton published *The Ready and Easy Way to Establish a Free Commonwealth* in 1660. Shortly after its appearance, Milton went into hiding. The House of Commons ordered the burning of *Eikonoklastes* and had Milton arrested. He was held in prison for several months. For a time threatened with heavy fines and even death by hanging, Milton was finally released through the aid of his friend Andrew Marvell.

In the aftermath of the Restoration, Milton lived in obscurity and desolation. On the anniversary of Charles I's execution, Cromwell's body was dug up and hanged. More than a few of Milton's friends were either executed or forced into exile. The republic to which he had devoted his life's work had been defeated. Amid this experience of defeat, he worked on *Paradise Lost*, with its themes of fall, damnation, war in heaven, and future redemption for an erring humanity.

While writing his epic, he was much helped by the companionship and housekeeping of his young and amiable third wife Elizabeth Minshull, whom he married in 1663. Young pupils, secretaries, and his daughters read to him in many languages (some of which they didn't understand). The Miltons lived frugally on the money that he had saved from his salary as Latin Secretary (1649–1659). Milton had begun writing *Paradise Lost* by 1658–1659, but he only completed the first edition for publication in 1667. First conceiving of this work as a drama, he had written a soliloquy for the rebellious Lucifer in 1642, which later appeared near the opening of the epic's fourth book. Milton explained that he had put off writing *Paradise Lost* because it was "a work to be raised . . . by devout prayer to that eternal Spirit who can enrich with all utterance and knowledge."

In the last ten years of his life, Milton also wrote *Paradise Regained* (1671), a short epic about the temptation of Christ, based on the model of the Book of Job. Published in the same year was *Samson Agonistes*, a verse tragedy about the Biblical hero, who, betrayed by his lover Delilah, brought down destruction on himself as well as his enemies. In 1673 he published an expanded edition of his *Poems* (1645), to which he added his translations of the Psalms. Finally, in 1674, all twelve books of *Paradise Lost* as we know it were published. That same year, Milton died in a fit of gout and was buried in Saint Giles Cripplegate alongside his father.

Milton combined the traditional erudition of a Renaissance poet with the committed politics of a Puritan radical, both of which contributed to his crowning achievement, *Paradise Lost*. Milton draws on the Bible, Homer, Virgil, and Dante to create his own original sound and story. The vivid sensual imagery of *L'Allegro*, echoing Shakespeare and Spenser, suggests the pastoral idyll of Adam and Eve in Paradise. The intellectual rebelliousness of his prose works inflects the epic's dramatic embodiment of such problems as the origin of evil, sin, and death. Like *Samson Agonistes*, *Paradise Lost* reaches humanity's psychological depths: arrogance, despair, revenge, self-destruction, desire, and self-knowledge. Most of all, *Paradise Lost* dramatizes human wayfaring in the face of the Fall, not unlike Milton's own heroic perseverance in writing his epic after the loss of the world he had helped to create.

L'Allegro[1]

Hence loathèd Melancholy
　Of Cerberus,[2] and blackest midnight born,
In Stygian cave forlorn.
　'Mongst horrid shapes, and shreiks, and sights unholy,
Find out some uncouth° cell, *unknown*
　Where brooding darkness spreads his jealous wings,
And the night-raven[3] sings;
　There under ebon shades, and low-brow'd rocks,
As ragged as thy Locks,
　In dark Cimmerian[4] desert ever dwell.
But come thou goddess fair and free,
In Heaven yclept° Euphrosyne, *called*
And by men, heart-easing Mirth,
Whom lovely Venus at a birth
With two sister Graces more
To ivy-crownèd Bacchus bore;[5]
Or whether (as some sager sing)
The frolic wind that breathes the spring,
Zephyr with Aurora playing,
As he met her once a-Maying,[6]

1. The happy person. This and the companion poem *Il Penseroso* (the pensive one) were composed around 1631; they were first published in 1645.
2. For the underworld cave of the three-headed dog Cerberus, see Virgil, *Aeneid* 6.418. Milton makes Cerberus and Night the parents of Melancholy, which is the subject of *Il Penseroso*.
3. Ominous bird.
4. The Cimmerians lived at the extreme limit of the known world (see *Odyssey* 11.13–22).
5. The Graces: Euphrosyne (Mirth), Aglaia (Brightness), and Thalia (Bloom). Servius's commentary to the *Aeneid* makes Venus and Bacchus their parents.
6. Milton invented this parentage of the Graces by Aurora, the dawn, and Zephyr, the west wind.

There on beds of violets blue,
And fresh-blown roses washed in dew,
Filled her with thee a daughter fair,
So buxom,° blithe, and debonair. *yielding*
Haste thee nymph, and bring with thee
Jest and youthful Jollity,
Quips and cranks,° and wanton wiles, *jests*
Nods, and becks, and wreathèd smiles,
Such as hang on Hebe's[7] cheek,
And love to live in dimple sleek;
Sport that wrinkled Care derides,
And Laughter holding both his sides.
Come, and trip it as you go
On the light fantastic toe,
And in thy right hand lead with thee,
The mountain nymph, sweet Liberty;
And if I give thee honor due,
Mirth, admit me of thy crew
To live with her, and live with thee,
In unreprovèd pleasures free;
To hear the lark begin his flight,
And singing startle the dull night,
From his watch-tower in the skies,
Till the dappled dawn doth rise;
Then to come in spite of sorrow,
And at my window bid good morrow,
Through the sweetbriar, or the vine,
Or the twisted eglantine.° *honey-suckle*
While the cock with lively din,
Scatters the rear of darkness thin,
And to the stack, or the barn door,
Stoutly struts his dames before,
Oft listening how the hounds and horn
Cheerly rouse the slumbring morn,
From the side of some hoar° hill, *grey with mist*
Through the high wood echoing shrill.
Sometime walking not unseen
By hedge-row elms, on hillocks green,
Right against the eastern gate,
Where the great sun begins his state,° *progress*
Robed in flames, and amber light,
The clouds in thousand liveries dight,° *dressed*
While the plowman near at hand,
Whistles ore the furrowed land,
And the milkmaid singeth blithe,
And the mower whets his scythe,
And every shepherd tells his tale
Under the hawthorn in the dale.
Straight mine eye hath caught new pleasures

7. Goddess of youth and daughter of Zeus and Hera.

Whilst the landscape round it measures,
Russet lawns, and fallows° gray, *plowed lands*
Where the nibling flocks do stray,
Mountains on whose barren breast
The laboring clouds do often rest;
Meadows trim with daisies pied,° *variegated*
Shallow brooks, and rivers wide.
Towers and battlements it sees
Bosomed high in tufted trees,
Where perhaps some beauty lies,
The cynosure[8] of neighboring eyes.
Hard by, a cottage chimney smokes
From betwixt two agèd oaks,
Where Corydon and Thyrsis met,
Are at their savory dinner set
Of herbs, and other country messes,
Which the neat-handed Phyllis dresses;
And then in haste her bower she leaves,
With Thestylis[9] to bind the sheaves;
Or if the earlier season lead
To the tanned haycock° in the mead, *heaps of hay*
Sometimes with secure delight
The upland hamlets will invite,
When the merry bells ring round,
And the jocond rebecks° sound *fiddles*
To many a youth, and many a maid,
Dancing in the checkered shade;
And young and old come forth to play
On a sunshine holiday,
Till the livelong daylight fail,
Then to the spicy nut-brown ale,
With stories told of many a feat,
How fairy Mab[1] the junkets° eat, *cream cheeses*
She was pinched, and pulled she said,
And by the friar's lantern led
Tells how the drudging goblin sweat,
To earn his cream-bowl duly set,
When in one night, ere glimpse of morn,
His shadowy flail hath threshed the corn
That ten day-laborers could not end;
Then lies him down the lubber fiend.[2]
And stretched out all the chimney's length,
Basks at the fire his hairy strength;
And crop-full out of doors he flings,
Ere the first cock his matin rings.
Thus done the tales, to bed they creep,
By whispering winds soon lulled asleep.

8. The North Star, here meaning, the center of attention.
9. The shepherds' names are common in Renaissance pastoral.
1. Queen of the fairies, and the topic of Mercutio's famous speech (*Romeo and Juliet* 1.4.54–95).
2. Slaving demon, like Robin Goodfellow called "lob of spirits" in *Midsummer Night's Dream* 2.1.16.

Towered cities please us then,
And the busy hum of men,
Where throngs of knights and barons bold,
In weeds° of peace high triumphs° hold, *clothes/tournaments*
With store of ladies, whose bright eyes
Rain influence,[3] and judge the prize,
Of wit, or arms, while both contend
To win her grace, whom all commend.
There let Hymen[4] oft appear
In saffron robe, with taper clear,
And pomp, and feast, and revelry,
With mask, and antique pageantry;
Such sights as youthful poets dream
On summer eves by haunted stream.
Then to the well-trod stage anon,
If Jonson's learned sock[5] be on,
Or sweetest Shakespeare fancy's child,
Warble his native wood-notes wild,
And ever against eating cares
Lap me in soft Lydian airs,[6]
Married to immortal verse
Such as the meeting soul may pierce
In notes, with many a winding bout
Of linkèd sweetness long drawn out,
With wanton heed and giddy cunning,
The melting voice through mazes running,
Untwisting all the chains that tie
The hidden soul of harmony.
That Orpheus' self may heave his head
From golden slumber on a bed
Of heaped Elysian flowers, and hear
Such strains as would have won the ear
Of Pluto, to have quite set free
His half regained Eurydice.[7]
These delights, if thou canst give,
Mirth with thee, I mean to live.[8]

Il Penseroso[1]

Hence vain deluding joys,
  The brood of Folly without father bred,
How little you bestead,° *help*
  Or fill the fixèd mind with all your toys;
Dwell in some idle brain,

3. In astrology, the process by which an etherial fluid emanating from the stars ruled human fate.
4. Roman wedding god.
5. Low-heeled slipper of the comic actor in ancient Greece and Rome.
6. Plato considered the Lydian mode to be morally corrupting and loose; others found it a source of relaxed enjoyment.
7. When Orpheus attempted to rescue his wife Eurydice from Hades, he lost her by violating the command that he not look back to see if she were behind him.
8. The concluding lines recall the final couplet of Marlowe's lyric *The Passionate Shepherd to His Love:* "If these delights thy mind may move, / Then live with me, and be my love."
1. The pensive one.

And fancies fond with gaudy shapes possess,
As thick and numberless
As the gay motes that people the sunbeams,
Or likest hovering dreams,
The fickle pensioners° of Morpheus'[2] train. *guards*
But hail thou Goddess, sage and holy,
Hail divinest Melancholy,
Whose saintly visage is too bright
To hit° the sense of human sight, *fit*
And therefore to our weaker view,
O'er laid with black staid Wisdom's hue;[3]
Black, but such as in esteem,
Prince Memnon's sister[4] might beseem,
Or that starred Ethiope Queen[5] that strove
To set her beauties praise above
The sea nymphs, and their powers offended.
Yet thou art higher far descended,
Thee bright-haired Vesta[6] long of yore,
To solitary Saturn bore;
His daughter she (in Saturn's reign
Such mixture was not held a stain)[7]
Oft in glimmering bowers, and glades
He met her, and in secret shades
Of woody Ida's inmost grove,
While yet there was no fear of Jove.
Come pensive nun, devout and pure,
Sober, steadfast, and demure,
All in a robe of darkest grain,
Flowing with majestic train,
And sable° stole of cypress lawn,° *dark / fine linen*
Over thy decent shoulders drawn.
Come, but keep thy wonted state,
With even step, and musing gait,
And looks commercing with the skies,
Thy rapt soul sitting in thine eyes:
There held in holy passion still,
Forget thyself to marble,[8] till
With a sad leaden downward cast,
Thou fix them on the earth as fast.
And join with thee calm Peace, and Quiet,
Spare Fast, that oft with gods doth diet,
And hears the Muses in a ring,
Ay round about Jove's altar sing.
And add to these retired leisure;

2. God of dreams and son of Sleep.
3. Melancholy was governed by the black bile in the body and manifested itself in a black face.
4. The Ethiopian Prince Memnon (*Odyssey* 11.521) had a sister named Himera (Greek, "light of day").
5. Cassiopea was turned into a constellation because she boasted that she was more beautiful than the Nereids.
6. Milton makes Vesta a mother; by tradition, she was a virgin, daughter of Saturn, and goddess of the hearth.
7. The Golden Age was a time of plenty and sexual freedom.
8. Turning to stone through grief comes from the story of Niobe.

That in trim gardens takes his pleasure;
But first, and chiefest, with thee bring
Him that yon soars on golden wing,
Guiding the fiery-wheelèd throne,[9]
The cherub Contemplation;[1]
And the mute Silence hist° along, *a call*
'Less Philomel[2] will deign a song,
In her sweetest, saddest plight,
Smoothing the rugged brow of night,
While Cynthia[3] checks her dragon yoke,
Gently o'er th'accustomed oak;
Sweet bird that shunn'st the noise of folly,
Most musical, most melancholy!
Thee chantress oft the woods among,
I woo to hear thy evensong;
And missing thee, I walk unseen
On the dry smooth-shaven green,
To behold the wandring moon,
Riding near her highest noon,
Like one that had been led astray
Through the heaven's wide pathless way;
And oft, as if her head she bowed,
Stooping through a fleecy cloud.
Oft on a plat° of rising ground, *plot*
I hear the far-off curfew sound,
Over some wide-watered shore,
Swinging slow with sullen roar;
Or if the air will not permit,
Some still removèd place will fit,
Where glowing embers through the room
Teach light to counterfeit a gloom,
Far from all resort of mirth,
Save the cricket on the hearth,
Or the bellman's drowsy charm,[4]
To bless the doors from nightly harm;
Or let my lamp at midnight hour,
Be seen in some high lonely tower,
Where I may oft out-watch the Bear,[5]
With thrice great Hermes,[6] or unsphere[7]
The spirit of Plato to unfold
What worlds, or what vast regions hold
The immortal mind that hath forsook
Her mansion in this fleshly nook;
And of those demons that are found

9. See Ezekiel 1.4–6.
1. The angel Cherubim contemplate God.
2. The nightingale (Greek).
3. The moon goddess, another name for Hecate; for her dragons, see Ovid, *Metamorphoses* 7.218–19.
4. The night-watchman, or bellman, cries out the hours in a chant, or charm (from *carmen*, Latin for song).
5. The constellation of the Great Bear, which never sets, symbolizes perfection.
6. Hermes Trismegistus was believed to be the author of the Hermetica, texts of esoteric neoplatonism and magic. See Giordano Bruno in Perspectives: Emblem, Style, and Metaphor, page 1604.
7. To remove from the eternal sphere and make reappear on earth.

In fire, air, flood, or under ground,
Whose power hath a true consent
With planet, or with element.
Sometime let gorgeous Tragedy
In scepter'd pall° come sweeping by, *robe*
Presenting Thebes, or Pelops line,
Or the tale of Troy divine.[8]
Or what (though rare) of later age
Ennobled hath the buskined stage.[9]
But, O sad virgin, that thy power
Might raise Musaeus[1] from his bower,
Or bid the soul of Orpheus[2] sing
Such notes as warbled to the string,
Drew iron tears down Pluto's cheek,
And made Hell grant what Love did seek.
Or call up him[3] that left half told
The story of Cambuscan bold,
Of Camball, and of Algarsife,
And who had Canace to wife,
That owned the virtuous° ring and glass, *magical*
And of the wondrous horse of brass,
On which the Tartar king did ride;
And if aught else, great bards beside,[4]
In sage and solemn tunes have sung,
Of tourneys and of trophies hung;
Of forests, and enchantments drear,
Where more is meant then meets the ear.
Thus, Night, oft see me in thy pale career,
Till civil-suited Morn appear,
Not tricked and frounced[5] as she was wont,
With the Attic boy[6] to hunt,
But kerchiefed in a comely cloud,
While rocking winds are piping loud,
Or ushered with a shower still,° *quiet*
When the gust hath blown his fill,
Ending on the rustling leaves,
With minute drops from off the eaves.
And when the sun begins to fling
His flaring beams, me, Goddess, bring
To archèd walks of twilight groves,
And shadows brown that Sylvan[7] loves
Of pine, or monumental oak,
Where the rude ax with heavèd stroke.

8. Thebes was the birthplace of Oedipus, tragic hero of Sophocles' *Oedipus Rex*. Pelops's descendants Agamemnon and Orestes are the subject of Aeschylus' tragedy *Oresteia*. Troy was the city destroyed by the Trojan War, the tragic consequences of which are the subject of Euripides' *The Trojan Women*.
9. The high boots of tragic actors. Compare *L'Allegro* line 132.
1. Prophet and poet, who studied with the mythic bard Orpheus.
2. See *L'Allegro* 145–50.
3. Chaucer; the "story" is the unfinished *Squire's Tale*.
4. Lines 116–20 refer to Spenser's allegorical *Faerie Queene*.
5. Richly attired and wearing ringlets.
6. Cephalus, beloved of Aurora, who met him while he was hunting. (See Ovid, *Metamorphoses* 7.700–13.)
7. Roman god of the forest.

Was never heard the nymphs to daunt,
Or fright them from their hallowed haunt.
There in close covert by some brook,
Where no prophaner eye may look,
Hide me from day's garish eye,
While the bee with honeyed thigh,
That at her flowery work doth sing,
And the waters murmuring
With such consort° as they keep, *musical harmony*
Entice the dewy-feathered sleep;
And let some strange mysterious dream
Wave at his wings in airy stream
Of lively portraiture displayed,
Softly on my eye-lids laid.
And as I wake, sweet music breathe
Above, about, or underneath,
Sent by some spirit to mortals good,
Or th'unseen genius° of the wood. *presiding local god*
But let my due feet never fail
To walk the studious cloisters° pale, *enclosure*
And love the high embowèd° roof, *arched*
With antic pillars massy proof,° *impenetrability*
And storied[8] windows richly dight,° *decorated*
Casting a dim religious light.
There let the pealing organ blow
To the full voiced choir below,
In service high, and anthems clear,
As may with sweetness, through mine ear,
Dissolve me into ecstasies,
And bring all heaven before mine eyes.
And may at last my weary age
Find out the peaceful hermitage,
The hairy gown and mossy cell,
Where I may sit and rightly spell° *find out about*
Of every star that heaven doth shew,
And every herb that sips the dew,
Till old experience do attain
To something like prophetic strain.
These pleasures Melancholy give,
And I with thee will choose to live.[9]

Lycidas

In this Monody[1] the Author bewails a learned Friend,[2] unfortunately drowned in his passage from Chester on the Irish Seas, 1637. And by occasion foretells the ruin of our corrupted Clergy then in their height.

8. With stories from the Bible.
9. See *L'Allegro* 151–52.
1. A mournful song sung by one voice. *Lycidas* is a pastoral elegy, a lament for the dead through language evoking nature and the rural life of shepherds. The first *Idyll* of Theocritus and Virgil's fifth *Eclogue* are classical precedents for *Lycidas*. Shelley's *Adonais* and Arnold's *Thyrsis* are later examples of this form.
2. Edward King, who attended Cambridge when Milton did, and drowned 10 August 1637. He had planned to enter the clergy and had written some Latin poems.

Yet once more, O ye laurels, and once more
Ye myrtles brown, with ivy[3] never sear,° *withered*
I come to pluck your berries harsh and crude,° *unripe*
And with forced fingers rude,
Shatter your leaves before the mellowing year.
Bitter constraint, and sad occasion dear,
Compels me to disturb your season due:
For Lycidas is dead, dead ere his prime,[4]
Young Lycidas, and hath not left his peer:
Who would not sing for Lycidas? he knew
Himself to sing, and build the lofty rhyme.
He must not float upon his watery bier
Unwept, and welter° to the parching wind, *writhe*
Without the meed° of some melodious tear.° *recompense/elegy*
Begin then, sisters of the sacred well,[5]
That from beneath the seat of Jove doth spring,
Begin, and somewhat loudly sweep the string.
Hence with denial vain, and coy excuse,
So may some gentle Muse
With lucky words favor my destined urn,
And as he passes turn,
And bid fair peace be to my sable° shrowd. *black*
For we were nursed upon the self-same hill,
Fed the same flock; by fountain, shade, and rill.
Together both, ere the high lawns appeared
Under the opening eyelids of the morn,
We drove a field, and both together heard
What time the grayfly[6] winds her sultry horn,
Battening° our flocks with the fresh dews of night, *fattening*
Oft till the star that rose, at evening, bright,
Toward heaven's descent had sloped his westering wheel.
Meanwhile the rural ditties were not mute,
Tempered to th' oaten flute,
Rough satyrs danced, and fauns with cloven heel,
From the glad sound would not be absent long,
And old Damaetas[7] lov'd to hear our song.
But O the heavy change, now thou art gone,
Now thou art gone, and never must return!
Thee shepherd, thee the woods, and desert caves,
With wild thyme and the gadding° vine o'ergrown, *wandering*
And all their echoes mourn.
The willows, and the hazle copses green,
Shall now no more be seen,
Fanning their joyous leaves to thy soft lays.
As killing as the canker° to the rose, *cankerworm*
Or taint-worm[8] to the weanling herds that graze,

3. Laurels . . . myrtles . . . ivy: the leaves used to crown respectively poets, lovers, and scholars.
4. King ("Lycidas") was 25 when he died.
5. Sisters: the nine muses; well: Aganippe, on Mount Helicon, where there was an altar to Jove.
6. Name used to designate various kinds of insect.
7. "Damaetas" is etymologically derived from the Greek verb meaning "to tame"; thus a tutor is meant.
8. An intestinal worm that can kill newly weaned calves.

Or frost to flowers, that their gay wardrop wear,
When first the white thorn blows;
Such, Lycidas, thy loss to shepherd's ear.
Where were ye nymphs when the remorseless deep
Closed o'er the head of your loved Lycidas?
For neither were ye playing on the steep
Where your old Bards, the famous Druids,° lie, *pagan Celtic priests*
Nor on the shaggy top of Mona[9] high,
Nor yet where Deva spreads her wizard stream:
Ay me, I fondly dream!
Had ye been there—for what could that have done?
What could the Muse[1] herself that Orpheus bore,
The Muse her self for her inchanting son
Whom universal nature did lament,
When by the rout that made the hideous roar
His gory visage down the stream was sent,
Down the swift Hebrus to the Lesbian shore.[2]
Alas! What boots° it with incessant care *avails*
To tend the homely slighted shepherd's trade,
And strictly meditate the thankless Muse,
Were it not better done as others use,
To sport with Amaryllis in the shade,
Or with the tangles of Neaera's hair?[3]
Fame is the spur that the clear spirit doth raise
(That last infirmity of noble mind)
To scorn delights, and live laborious days;
But the fair guerdon° when we hope to find, *reward*
And think to burst out into sudden blaze,
Comes the blind Fury[4] with th'abhorred shears,
And slits the thin spun life. "But not the praise,"
Phoebus replied, and touched my trembling ears;[5]
"Fame is no plant that grows on mortal soil,
Nor in the glistering foil[6]
Set off to the world, nor in broad rumor lies,
But lives and spreds aloft by those pure eyes,
And perfet witness of all-judging Jove;
As he pronounces lastly on each deed,
Of so much fame in heaven expect thy meed."
O Fountain Arethuse, and thou honored flood,
Smooth-sliding Mincius, crowned with vocal reeds,
That strain I heard was of a higher mood.[7]
But now my oat proceeds,

9. The island of Anglesey; Deva: the river Dee, viewed as magical and prophetic by the inhabitants.

1. Calliope, Orpheus' mother.

2. Ovid, *Metamorphoses*, 11.1–55, relates how Orpheus was torn to pieces by the Thracian women and how his severed head floated down the Hebrus and was carried across to the island of Lesbos.

3. Amaryllis symbolizes erotic poetry (Virgil, *Eclogues* 2.14–5; Neaera: see *Eclogues* 3.3.

4. Atropos, one of the Fates, who cut the thread of life spun by her sisters.

5. Echoing Virgil, *Eclogues* 6.3–4: "the Cynthian plucked my ear and warned me."

6. A reflecting leaf of gold or silver placed under a precious stone.

7. The "higher mood" is the lofty tone of Phoebus' speech. The invocation to the river Arethuse (in Sicily) and the Mincius (Virgil's native river) marks a return to pastoral.

And listens to the herald of the sea
That came in Neptune's plea.[8]
He asked the waves, and asked the felon° winds, *savage*
"What hard mishap hath doomed this gentle swain?"
And questioned every gust of rugged wings
That blows from off each beakèd promontory;
They knew not of his story,
And sage Hippotades[9] their answer brings,
That not a blast was from his dungeon strayed,
The air was calm, and on the level brine,
Sleek Panope[1] with all her sisters played.
It was that fatal and perfidious bark,
Built in th' eclipse,° and rigged with curses dark, *period of evil omen*
That sunk so low that sacred head of thine.
 Next Camus,[2] reverend sire, went footing slow,
His mantle hairy, and his bonnet sedge,[3]
Inwrought with figures dim, and on the edge
Like to that sanguine flower inscribed with woe.[4]
"Ah! who hath reft (quoth he) my dearest pledge?"° *child*
Last came, and last did go,
The Pilot of the Galilean lake,[5]
Two massy keys he bore of metals twain,
(The golden opes, the iron shuts amain°) *vehemently*
He shook his mitered[6] locks, and stern bespake,
"How well could I have spared for thee, young swain,
Enow° of such as for their bellies' sake, *enough*
Creep and intrude, and climb into the fold?[7]
Of other care they little reckoning make,
Than how to scramble at the shearer's feast,
And shove away the worthy bidden guest.
Blind mouths![8] that scarce themselves know how to hold
A sheep-hook, or have learned aught else the least
That to the faithfull herdman's art belongs!
What recks it them?[9] What need they? They are sped;° *satisfied*
And when they list,° their lean and flashy° songs *please/insipid*
Grate on their scrannel° pipes of wretched straw, *feeble*
The hungry sheep look up, and are not fed,
But swoln with wind, and the rank mist they draw,
Rot inwardly, and foul contagion spread.
Besides what the grim woolf[1] with privy° paw *secret, hidden*
Daily devours apace, and nothing said,
But that two-handed engine at the door,

8. The herald Triton came to defend Neptune from blame for King's death.
9. God of winds, son of Hippotes.
1. One of the 50 Nereids (sea nymphs), mentioned by Virgil, *Aeneid* 5.240.
2. The River Cam, representing Cambridge University.
3. "Hairy" refers to the fur of the academic gown; "sedge" is a rushlike plant growing near water.
4. The hyacinth; see Ovid, *Metamorphoses* 10.214–6: "the flower bore the marks AI AI, letters of lamentation."
5. St. Peter bearing the keys of heaven given to him by Christ (Matthew 16.19).
6. Wearing a bishop's headdress.
7. See John 10.1: "He that entereth not by the door into the sheepfold, but climbeth up some other way, the same is a thief and a robber."
8. Milton's charge against the greed of the clergy.
9. What business is it of theirs?
1. The Roman Catholic Church.

Stands ready to smite once, and smite no more."[2]
   Return Alpheus,[3] the dread voice is past,
That shrunk thy streams; return Sicilian muse,
And call the vales, and bid them hither cast
Their bells, and flowerets of a thousand hues.
Ye valleys low where the mild whispers use,° *often go*
Of shades and wanton winds, and gushing brooks,
On whose fresh lap the swart star[4] sparely looks,
Throw hither all your quaint enameled eyes,
That on the green turf suck the honeyed showers,
And purple all the ground with vernal flowers.
Bring the rathe° primrose that forsaken dies. *early*
The tufted crow-toe,° and pale jessamine,° *hyacinth/jasmine*
The white pink, and the pansie freaked° with jet, *adorned*
The glowing violet.
The musk-rose, and the well attired woodbine,
With cowslips wan° that hang the pensive head, *pale*
And every flower that sad embroidery wears:
Bid amaranthus[5] all his beauty shed,
And daffadillies fill their cups with tears,
To strew the laureate hearse where Lycid lies.
For so to interpose a little ease,
Let our frail thoughts dally with false surmise.[6]
Ay me! whilst thee the shores, and sounding seas
Wash far away, where'er thy bones are hurled,
Whether beyond the stormy Hebrides[7]
Where thou perhaps under the whelming tide
Visit'st the bottom of the monstrous world;
Or whether thou to our moist° vows denied, *tearful*
Sleep'st by the fable of Bellerus[8] old,
Where the great vision of the guarded mount
Looks toward Namancos and Bayona's hold;[9]
Look homeward angel° now, and melt with ruth.° *Michael/pity*
And, O ye dolphins, waft the haples youth.[1]
   Weep no more, woeful shepherds weep no more,
For Lycidas your sorrow is not dead,
Sunk though he be beneath the wat'ry floor,
So sinks the day-star° in the ocean bed, *the sun*
And yet anon repairs his drooping head,
And tricks° his beams, and with new spangled ore,° *arrays/gold*
Flames in the forehead of the morning sky:
So Lycidas sunk low, but mounted high,
Through the dear might of him[2] that walked the waves

2. Indicates that the corrupted clergy will be punished; see 1 Samuel 26.8.
3. The Arcadian hunter, who pursued Arethusa, the nymph he loved, under the sea to Sicily.
4. The Dog-star, Sirius. Its rising brings on the dog-days of heat.
5. The eternal flower (see *Paradise Lost,* 3.353–7).
6. The surmise is false since King's body drowned and will have no hearse.
7. Islands off the northwest coast of Scotland.
8. A giant of Bellerium, the Latin name for Land's End.
9. Namancos: an ancient name for a district in northwestern Spain; Bayona: a fortress town about 50 miles south of Cape Finisterre. The two names represent the threat of Spanish Catholicism, against which St. Michael guards England.
1. The dolphin is a symbol of Christ; waft: convey by water.
2. Christ, who walks on the sea in Matthew 14.25–6.

Where other groves, and other streams along,
With nectar pure his oozy lock's he laves,[3]
And hears the unexpressive nuptial[4] song,
In the blest kingdoms meek of joy and love.
There entertain him all the saints above,
In solemn troops, and sweet societies
That sing, and singing in their glory move,
And wipe the tears for ever from his eyes.[5]
Now Lycidas the shepherds weep no more;
Henceforth thou art the genius° of the shore, *local deity*
In thy large recompense, and shalt be good
To all that wander in that perilous flood.
  Thus sang the uncouth° swain to th' oaks and rills, *unknown*
While the still morn went out with sandals gray,
He touched the tender stops of various quills,[6]
With eager thought warbling his Doric° lay: *pastoral*
And now the sun had stretched out all the hills,[7]
And now was dropped into the western bay;
At last he rose, and twitch'd his mantle blue:[8]
Tomorrow to fresh woods, and pastures new.

1638

How Soon Hath Time

How soon hath time the subtle thief of youth,
  Stol'n on his wing my three and twentieth year![1]
  My hasting days fly on with full career,° *speed*
  But my late spring no bud or blossom shew'th.
Perhaps my semblance° might deceive the truth, *appearance*
  That I to manhood am arrived so near,
  And inward ripeness doth much less appear,
  That some more timely-happy spirits[2] endu'th.° *gives, endows*
Yet be it less or more, or soon or slow,
  It shall be still° in strictest measure even,° *always/level with*
  To that same lot, however mean or high,
Toward which Time leads me, and the will of Heaven;
  All is, if I have grace to use it so,
  As ever in my great task Master's° eye. *God's*

On the New Forcers of Conscience Under the Long Parliament[1]

Because you have thrown off your prelate Lord,[2]
  And with stiff vows renounced his liturgy[3]

3. The brooks in Eden run with nectar, *Paradise Lost* 4.240; oozy: slimy from contact with the sea.
4. Relating to the marriage of the Lamb, or Christ, to the Church (Revelation 19.7).
5. See Revelation 7.17: "God shall wipe away all tears from their eyes"; see also Revelation 21.4.
6. Stops are the finger-holes in the pipes; quills are the hollow reeds of the shepherd's pipe.
7. The setting sun had shone over the hills and lengthened their shadows.
8. Blue is the traditional symbol of hope.
1. Written when Milton was 23, this sonnet was published in 1645.
2. Those individuals of Milton's age who have already achieved success.
1. Written c. 1646, but printed in 1673.
2. Refers to the abolishment of episcopacy in England in September 1646.
3. The House of Commons forbade the use of the *Book of Common Prayer* in August 1645.

To seize the widowed whore Plurality[4]
From them whose sin ye envied, not abhored,
Dare ye for this adjure° the civil sword — entreat
To force our consciences that Christ set free,[5]
And ride us with a classic hierarchy[6]
Taught ye by meer A. S. and Rutherford?[7]
Men whose life, learning, faith and pure intent
Would have been held in high esteem with Paul
Must now be named and printed heretics
By shallow Edwards[8] and Scotch what d'ye call:
But we do hope to find out all your tricks,
Your plots and packing worse then those of Trent[9]
That so the Parliament
May with their wholsome and preventive shears
Clip your phylacteries,[1] though balk° your ears,[2] — stop short of
And succor our just fears
When they shall read this clearly in your charge
New presbyter is but *old priest* writ large.[3]

To the Lord General Cromwell

Cromwell, our chief of men, who through a cloud[1]
Not of war only, but detractions rude,
Guided by faith and matchless fortitude
To peace and truth thy glorious way hast ploughed,
And on the neck of crownèd Fortune[2] proud
Hast reard° God's trophies and his work pursued, — raised, erected
While Darwen stream[3] with blood of Scotts imbrued,° — stained
And Dunbarr field[4] resounds thy praises loud,
And Worester's laureate wreath;[5] yet much remains
To conquer still; peace hath her victories
No less renownd than war, new foes arise

4. The practice of holding more than one living identified with episcopacy but subsequently supported by the Presbyterian system.
5. Milton complains of the Westminster Assembly's attempt to impose Presbyterianism by force.
6. Parliament resolved that the English congregations were to be grouped in Presbyteries or "Classes," which could impose rules after the Scottish pattern.
7. A. S.: Dr. Adam Stewart, Scottish Presbyterian controversialist; Rutherford: Samuel Rutherford, author of pamphlets in defense of Presbyterianism.
8. Thomas Edwards, author of *Antapologia,* advocating strict Presbyterianism, and *Gangraena* (1646), which included a denunciation of Milton's views on divorce.
9. Comparing the overwhelming Presbyterian predominance in the Assembly to the anti-protestant Roman Catholic Council of Trent (1545–1563).
1. Small leather boxes containing scriptural texts worn by Jews as a mark of obedience. Christ in Matthew 23.5 uses the phrase "make broad their phylacteries" in the sense "vaunt their own righteousness."
2. William Prynne, who had attacked one of the Bishops in print, actually did have both of his ears cut off. Milton's manuscript of this poem contains the line: "Crop ye as close as marginal P—'s ears."
3. "Priest" is etymologically a contracted form of Latin "presbyter" (an elder). The Presbyterians now appeared as dictatorial as the bishops had been.
1. In Virgil, Aeneas prevails through the "war-cloud" of battle as he conquers Italy (*Aeneid* 10.809).
2. Refers to Charles I and to his successor, whose army Cromwell defeated at Worcester after he had been crowned king in Scotland on 1 January 1651. This poem was written in 1652 but not published until 1694.
3. Near Preston, where, on 17–19 August 1648, Cromwell routed the invading Scottish army.
4. At Dunbar, on 3 September 1650, after being virtually surrounded, Cromwell routed the Scottish army.
5. At Worcester, on 3 September 1651, Cromwell virtually annihilated Charles II's Royalist Scottish army.

Threatening to bind our souls with secular chains:
Help us to save free conscience from the paw
Of hireling wolves whose gospel is their maw.

On the Late Massacre in Piedmont[1]

Avenge O Lord thy slaughtered saints, whose bones
Lie scattered on the Alpine mountains cold,[2]
Even them who kept thy truth so pure of old
When all our Fathers worshiped stocks and stones,[3]
Forget not: in thy book[4] record their groans
Who were thy sheep and in their ancient fold
Slain by the bloody Piemontese that rolled
Mother with infant down the rocks. Their moans
The vales redoubled to the hills, and they
To Heaven. Their martyred blood and ashes sow
O'er all th' Italian fields where still doth sway
The triple tyrant:[5] that from these may grow
A hundred-fold,[6] who having learnt thy way
Early may fly the Babylonian[7] woe.

When I Consider How My Light Is Spent[1]

When I consider how my light is spent,
Ere half my days, in this dark world and wide,
And that one talent which is death to hide,[2]
Lodged with me useless, though my soul more bent
To serve therewith my Maker, and present
My true account, lest he returning chide,
Doth God exact day-labor, light denied,
I fondly° ask; but Patience to prevent *foolishly*
That murmur, soon replies, "God doth not need
Either man's work or his own gifts,[3] who best
Bear his mild yoke,[4] they serve him best, his state
Is kingly. Thousands at his bidding speed
And post o'er land and ocean without rest:
They also serve who only stand and wait."

1. The poem protests the persecution of Protestants in northern Italy in 1655.
2. See Luke 18.7: "shall not God avenge his own elect," and Psalms 141.7: "Our bones are scattered at the grave's mouth."
3. Gods of wood and stone.
4. See Revelation 5.1: "I saw in the right hand of him that sat on the throne a book."
5. The Pope with his three-tiered crown.
6. Lines 10–13 combine the parable of the sower (Matthew 13.3–23) with the legend of Cadmus, in which an army of warriors sprouts from the sowing of a dragon's teeth.
7. The Puritans used the corrupt Babylon of Revelation as a symbol for the Roman Catholic Church.

1. Probably written around 1652, as Milton's blindness became complete.
2. In the parable of the talents, Jesus tells of a servant who is given a talent (a large sum of money) to keep for his master. He buries the money; his master condemns him for not having invested it wisely. Matthew 25.14–30.
3. See Job 22.2.
4. See Matthew 11.30: "My yoke is easy."

Methought I Saw My Late Espoused Saint[1]

Methought I saw my late espousèd saint° *soul in heaven*
Brought to me like Alcestis[2] from the grave,
Whom Jove's great son to her glad husband gave,
Rescued from death by force though pale and faint.
Mine as whom washed from spot of child-bed taint,
Purification in the old Law[3] did save,
And such, as yet once more I trust to have
Full sight of her in Heaven without restraint,
Came vested all in white, pure as her mind:
Her face was veiled, yet to my fancied sight,
Love, sweetness, goodness, in her person shined
So clear, as in no face with more delight,
But O, as to embrace me she enclined,
I waked, she fled, and day brought back my night.[4]

Areopagitica

The title *Areopagitica* refers to the Areopagus, the ancient Athenian Council of State. Milton wrote *Areopagitica* to criticize the Parliamentary Ordinance of June 14, 1643 "to prevent and suppress the licence of printing." Although *Areopagitica* was unlicensed, Milton made the bold move of affixing his name to the title page, which made no mention of the printer. Also on the title page are these lines from Euripides' *Suppliant Women* (436–441):

> There is true Liberty when free born men
> Having to advise the public may speak free,
> Which he who can and will, deserv'd high praise,
> Who neither can nor will, may hold his peace;
> What can be juster in a state than this?

from Areopagitica[1]

A Speech of Mr. John Milton for the Liberty of Unlicensed Printing, to the Parliament of England

* * * Good and evil we know in the field of this world grow up together almost inseparably; and the knowledge of good is so involved and interwoven with the knowledge of evil, and in so many cunning resemblances hardly to be discerned, that those confused seeds which were imposed on Psyche as an incessant labor to cull out and sort

1. The date of composition is placed at 1658; the poem appears as the last sonnet in the 1673 edition.
2. In Euripides' *Alcestis* she gives her life for her husband Admetus, but Hercules ("Jove's great son") wrestles with death and brings her back from the grave.
3. According to Leviticus 12.4–8, after bearing a female child, a woman shall be unclean "two weeks, as in her separation: and she shall continue in the blood of her purifying threescore and six days" (i.e., during this period "she shall touch no hallowed thing, nor come into the sanctuary"). Some critics construe this line as evidence that the sonnet is about the death of Milton's second wife Katherine Woodcock, who died three months after childbirth in 1658.
4. In Virgil, Aeneas sees the ghost of his wife Creusa amid the ruins of Troy; when he tries to embrace her, "she withdrew into thin air . . . most like a winged dream" (*Aeneid* 2.791–794).

1. The Areopagus was the seat of the Council of State, organized as a judicial tribunal by Solon in the sixth century B.C. The Athenian orator Isocrates argues for its renewal in his *Areopagiticus*.

asunder, were not more intermixed.[2] It was from out the rind of one apple tasted, that the knowledge of good and evil, as two twins cleaving together, leaped forth into the world. And perhaps this is that doom which Adam fell into of knowing good and evil, that is to say, of knowing good by evil.[3]

As therefore the state of man now is, what wisdom can there be to choose, what continence to forbear without the knowledge of evil? He that can apprehend and consider vice with all her baits and seeming pleasures, and yet abstain, and yet distinguish, and yet prefer that which is truly better, he is the true wayfaring[4] Christian. I cannot praise a fugitive and cloistered virtue, unexercised and unbreathed, that never sallies out and sees her adversary, but slinks out of the race where that immortal garland is to be run for, not without dust and heat. Assuredly we bring not innocence into the world, we bring impurity much rather: that which purifies us is trial, and trial is by what is contrary. That virtue therefore which is but a youngling in the contemplation of evil, and knows not the utmost that vice promises to her followers, and rejects it, is but a blank virtue, not a pure; her whiteness is but an excremental[5] whiteness; which was the reason why our sage and serious poet Spenser, whom I dare be known to think a better teacher than Scotus or Aquinas, describing true temperance under the person of Guyon, brings him in with his palmer through the cave of Mammon and the bower of earthly bliss, that he might see and know, and yet abstain.[6]

Since therefore, the knowledge and survey of vice is in this world so necessary to the constituting of human virtue, and the scanning of error to the confirmation of truth, how can we more safely and with less danger scout into the regions of sin and falsity than by reading all manner of tractates and hearing all manner of reason? And this is the benefit which may be had of books promiscuously read.

But of the harm that may result hence, three kinds are usually reckoned. First is feared the infection that may spread; but then all human learning and controversy in religious points must remove out of the world, yea the Bible itself; for that ofttimes relates blasphemy not nicely,[7] it describes the carnal sense of wicked men not unelegantly, it brings in holiest men passionately murmuring against providence through all the arguments of Epicurus;[8] in other great disputes it answers dubiously and darkly to the common reader; and ask a Talmudist what ails the modesty of his marginal Keri, that Moses and all the prophets cannot persuade him to pronounce the textual Chetiv.[9] For these causes we all know the Bible itself put by the papist into the first rank of prohibited books. The ancientest fathers must be next removed, as Clement of Alexandria, and that Eusebian book of Evangelic preparation transmitting our ears through a hoard of heathenish obscenities to receive the Gospel. Who finds not that Irenaeus, Epiphanius, Jerome,[1] and others discover more heresies than they well confute, and that oft for heresy which is the truer opinion?[2]

2. Furious over her son Cupid's love for Psyche, Venus ordered Psyche to sort out a huge mass of seeds, but the ants, sympathizing with her plight, sorted them for her. See Apuleius, *Golden Ass* 4–6.

3. See *Paradise Lost* 4.222: "Knowledge of Good bought dear by knowing ill."

4. The original reads "warfaring," but in several copies this is corrected by hand to "wayfaring."

5. Superficial.

6. Duns Scotus and Thomas Aquinas here represent types of the scholastic theologian. For the cave of Mammon, see *The Faerie Queene* 2.7 (the Palmer is not with Guyon in Mammon's Cave); the "Bower of Bliss," 2.12.

7. Delicately.

8. The Greek philosopher who propounded a morality based on pleasure.

9. Talmudist: a student of the Talmud, the Jewish commentaries on the Bible; Keri: marginal emendations of rabbinical scholars on the Chetiv, the text of the Bible.

1. Early apologists of Christianity: St. Clement of Alexandria (2nd century) and Eusebius, who describes pagan depravity to promote faith in Christianity, as do St. Irenaeus (2nd century), Epiphanius (4th century), and St. Jerome (early 5th century).

2. Milton goes on to argue that the effect of books depends upon the teacher, who, if really good, needs no books. Milton stresses the role of the reader: A wise person can find something instructive in even the worst books.

* * *

Impunity and remissness, for certain, are the bane of a commonwealth; but here the great art lies, to discern in what the law is to bid restraint and punishment, and in what things persuasion only is to work. If every action which is good or evil in man at ripe years, were to be under pittance and prescription and compulsion, what were virtue but a name, what praise could be then due to well-doing, what gramercy[3] to be sober, just, or continent?

Many there be that complain of divine providence for suffering Adam to transgress. Foolish tongues! when God gave him reason, he gave him freedom to choose, for reason is but choosing; he had been else a mere artificial Adam, such an Adam as he is in the motions.[4] We ourselves esteem not of that obedience, or love, or gift, which is of force. God therefore left him free, set before him a provoking object, ever almost in his eyes; herein consisted his merit, herein the right of his reward, the praise of his abstinence. Wherefore did he create passions within us, pleasures round about us, but that these rightly tempered are the very ingredients of virtue? They are not skilful considerers of human things who imagine to remove sin by removing the matter of sin. For, besides that it is a huge heap increasing under the very act of diminishing, though some part of it may for a time be withdrawn from some persons, it cannot from all, in such a universal thing as books are; and when this is done, yet the sin remains entire. Though ye take from a covetous man all his treasure, he has yet one jewel left—ye cannot bereave him of his covetousness. Banish all objects of lust, shut up all youth into the severest discipline that can be exercised in any hermitage, ye cannot make them chaste that came not thither so: such great care and wisdom is required to the right managing of this point.

Suppose we could expel sin by this means; look how much we thus expel of sin, so much we expel of virtue: for the matter of them both is the same; remove that, and ye remove them both alike. This justifies the high providence of God, who, though he command us temperance, justice, continence, yet pours out before us, even to a profuseness, all desirable things, and gives us minds that can wander beyond all limit and satiety. Why should we then affect a rigor contrary to the manner of God and of nature, by abridging or scanting those means which books freely permitted are, both to the trial of virtue and the exercise of truth?[5]

* * *

And lest some should persuade ye, Lords and Commons, that these arguments of learned men's discouragement at this your Order are mere flourishes, and not real, I could recount what I have seen and heard in other countries where this kind of inquisition tyrannizes; when I have sat among their learned men, for that honor I had, and been counted happy to be born in such a place of philosophic freedom as they supposed England was, while themselves did nothing but bemoan the servile condition into which learning amongst them was brought; that this was it which had damped the glory of Italian wits; that nothing had been there written now these many years but flattery and fustian. There it was that I found and visited the famous Galileo, grown old, a prisoner to the Inquisition[6] for thinking in astronomy otherwise

3. Thanks.
4. Puppet shows. For this statement about Adam, see *Paradise Lost* 3.103–28, page 1802.
5. Milton argues that no intelligent person will be willing to take on the job of censorship and that an unintelligent person would be prone to commit serious errors. In addition to giving power to stupid people, censorship would actually encourage people to read banned books and to adhere to the perverse opinions expressed in such books.
6. In 1633 the great Italian astronomer Galileo was tried by the Inquisition at Rome and forced to abjure his earlier assertion that his findings confirmed the Copernican heliocentric theory of the universe. He was under house arrest in Florence when Milton visited there in 1638–39.

than the Franciscan and Dominican licensers thought. And though I knew that England then was groaning loudest under the prelatical yoke, nevertheless I took it as a pledge of future happiness that other nations were so persuaded of her liberty.

Yet was it beyond my hope that those worthies were then breathing in her air, who should be her leaders to such a deliverance as shall never be forgotten by any revolution of time that this world hath to finish. When that was once begun, it was as little in my fear, that what words of complaint I heard among learned men of other parts uttered against the Inquisition, the same I should hear by as learned men at home uttered in time of Parliament against an order of licensing; and that so generally, that when I had disclosed myself a companion of their discontent, I might say, if without envy, that he whom an honest quaestorship had endeared to the Sicilians, was not more by them importuned against Verres,[7] than the favorable opinion which I had among many who honor ye, and are known and respected by ye, loaded me with entreaties and persuasions that I would not despair to lay together that which just reason should bring into my mind toward the removal of an undeserved thraldom upon learning.

That this is not, therefore, the disburdening of a particular fancy, but the common grievance of all those who had prepared their minds and studies above the vulgar pitch to advance truth in others, and from others to entertain it, thus much may satisfy. And in their name I shall for neither friend nor foe conceal what the general murmur is; that if it come to inquisitioning again and licensing, and that we are so timorous of ourselves and so suspicious of all men as to fear each book and the shaking of every leaf, before we know what the contents are; if some who but of late were little better than silenced from preaching, shall come now to silence us from reading, except what they please, it cannot be guessed what is intended by some but a second tyranny over learning; and will soon put it out of controversy that bishops and presbyters are the same to us both name and thing.

* * *

But I am certain that a state governed by the rules of justice and fortitude, or a church built and founded upon the rock of faith and true knowledge, cannot be so pusillanimous.[8] While things are yet not constituted in religion, that freedom of writing should be restrained by a discipline imitated from the prelates, and learnt by them from the Inquisition, to shut us up all again into the breast of a licenser, must needs give cause of doubt and discouragement to all learned and religious men. Who cannot but discern the fineness of this politic drift, and who are the contrivers: that while bishops were to be baited down, then all presses might be open; it was the people's birthright and privilege in time of parliament, it was the breaking forth of light.

But now, the bishops abrogated and voided out of the church, as if our reformation sought no more but to make room for others into their seats under another name, the episcopal arts begin to bud again; the cruse[9] of truth must run no more oil; liberty of printing must be enthralled again under a prelatical commission of twenty, the privilege of the people nullified; and, which is worse, the freedom of learning must groan again, and to her old fetters: all this the parliament yet sitting. Although their own late arguments and defenses against the prelates might remember them that this obstructing violence meets for the most part with an event utterly opposite to the end which it drives at; instead of suppressing sects and

7. Cicero exposed the corruption of Verres' government in 75 B.C.

8. Mean-spirited, cowardly.

9. Small vessel; see 1 Kings 17.12–16.

schisms, it raises them and invests them with a reputation: "The punishing of wits enhances their authority," saith the Viscount St. Albans,[1] "and a forbidden writing is thought to be a certain spark of truth that flies up in the faces of them who seek to tread it out."

This Order, therefore, may prove a nursing mother to sects, but I shall easily show how it will be a stepdame to Truth; and first by disenabling us to the maintenance of what is known already.

Well knows he who uses to consider, that our faith and knowledge thrives by exercise, as well as our limbs and complexion. Truth is compared in scripture to a streaming fountain;[2] if her waters flow not in a perpetual progression, they sicken into a muddy pool of conformity and tradition. A man may be a heretic in the truth; and if he believe things only because his pastor says so, or the Assembly so determines, without knowing other reason, though his belief be true, yet the very truth he holds becomes his heresy. There is not any burden that some would gladlier post off to another than the charge and care of their religion. There be, who knows not that there be, of protestants and professors who live and die in as arrant an implicit faith, as any lay papist of Loreto.[3]

A wealthy man addicted to his pleasure and to his profits, finds religion to be a traffic so entangled, and of so many piddling accounts, that of all mysteries[4] he cannot skill to keep a stock going upon that trade. What should he do? Fain he would have the name to be religious, fain he would bear up with his neighbors in that. What does he, therefore, but resolves to give over toiling, and to find himself out some factor to whose care and credit he may commit the whole managing of his religious affairs; some Divine of note and estimation that must be. To him he adheres, resigns the whole warehouse of his religion with all the locks and keys into his custody; and indeed makes the very person of that man his religion; esteems his associating with him a sufficient evidence and commendatory of his own piety. So that a man may say his religion is now no more within himself, but is become a dividual movable,[5] and goes and comes near him, according as that good man frequents the house. He entertains him, gives him gifts, feasts him, lodges him. His religion comes home at night, prays, is liberally supped, and sumptuously laid to sleep, rises, is saluted, and after the malmsey, or some well spiced brewage, and better breakfasted than he[6] whose morning appetite would have gladly fed on green figs between Bethany and Jerusalem, his religion walks abroad at eight, and leaves his kind entertainer in the shop trading all day without his religion.

Another sort there be, who, when they hear that all things shall be ordered, all things regulated and settled, nothing written but what passes through the customhouse of certain publicans[7] that have the tonnaging and the poundaging of all free-spoken truth, will straight give themselves up into your hands, make 'em and cut 'em out what religion ye please. There be delights, there be recreations and jolly pastimes that will fetch the day about from sun to sun, and rock the tedious year as in a delightful dream. What need they torture their heads with that which others have taken so strictly and so unalterably into their own purveying? These are the fruits which a dull ease and cessation of our knowledge will bring forth among the people.

1. Sir Francis Bacon, *An Advertisement Touching the Controversies of the Church of England*.
2. See Psalms 85.11.
3. Professors: those who profess religion; Loreto: a Catholic shrine supposed to have been transported to Italy from the Holy Land.
4. Trades, crafts.
5. A separate piece of property.
6. For this description of Christ, see Mark 11.12–14.
7. Tax collectors.

How goodly, and how to be wished, were such an obedient unanimity as this, what a fine conformity would it starch us all into! Doubtless a staunch and solid piece of framework, as any January could freeze together.[8]

* * *

Truth indeed came once into the world with her divine Master, and was a perfect shape most glorious to look on. But when he ascended, and his apostles after him were laid asleep, then straight arose a wicked race of deceivers, who, as that story goes of the Egyptian Typhon with his conspirators, how they dealt with the good Osiris, took the virgin Truth, hewed her lovely form into a thousand pieces, and scattered them to the four winds.[9] From that time ever since, the sad friends of Truth, such as durst appear, imitating the careful search that Isis made for the mangled body of Osiris, went up and down gathering up limb by limb still as they could find them. We have not yet found them all, Lords and Commons, nor ever shall do, till her Master's second coming. He shall bring together every joint and member, and shall mold them into an immortal feature of loveliness and perfection. Suffer not these licensing prohibitions to stand at every place of opportunity, forbidding and disturbing them that continue seeking, that continue to do our obsequies to the torn body of our martyred saint.

We boast our light; but if we look not wisely on the sun itself, it smites us into darkness. Who can discern those planets that are oft combust, and those stars of brightest magnitude that rise and set with the sun, until the opposite motion of their orbs bring them to such a place in the firmament, where they may be seen evening or morning. The light which we have gained, was given us, not to be ever staring on, but by it to discover onward things more remote from our knowledge. It is not the unfrocking of a priest, the unmitering of a bishop, and the removing him from off the Presbyterian shoulders that will make us a happy nation; no, if other things as great in the church, and in the rule of life both economical and political, be not looked into and reformed, we have looked so long upon the blaze that Zwinglius[1] and Calvin hath beaconed up to us, that we are stark blind.

There be who perpetually complain of schisms and sects, and make it such a calamity that any man dissents from their maxims. It is their own pride and ignorance which causes the disturbing, who neither will hear with meekness, nor can convince, yet all must be suppressed which is not found in their syntagma.[2] They are the troublers, they are the dividers of unity, who neglect and permit not others to unite those dissevered pieces which are yet wanting to the body of Truth. To be still searching what we know not by what we know, still closing up truth to truth as we find it (for all her body is homogeneal[3] and proportional), this is the golden rule in theology as well as in arithmetic, and makes up the best harmony in a church; not the forced and outward union of cold and neutral and inwardly divided minds.

Lords and Commons of England, consider what nation it is whereof ye are, and whereof ye are the governors; a nation not slow and dull, but of a quick, ingenious, and piercing spirit, acute to invent, subtle and sinewy to discourse, not beneath the reach of any point the highest that human capacity can soar to. Therefore the studies of learning in her deepest sciences have been so ancient and so eminent among us that writers of good antiquity and ablest judgment have been persuaded that even the

8. Milton goes on to argue that censorship will make the clergy lazy and will hinder the Reformation's goal of seeking truth.

9. Typhon tore apart and scattered Osiris's body, and his wife Isis and son Horus collected it. The interpretation here is based on Plutarch's allegory in *Isis and Osiris*.

1. Ulrich Zwingli (1484–1531), the Protestant reformer of Zurich.

2. Systematic doctrinal treatise.

3. Homogeneous.

school of Pythagoras and the Persian wisdom took beginning from the old philosophy of this island.[4] And that wise and civil Roman, Julius Agricola, who governed once here for Caesar, preferred the natural wits of Britain before the labored studies of the French.[5] Nor is it for nothing that the grave and frugal Transylvanian[6] sends out yearly from as far as the mountainous borders of Russia and beyond the Hercynian wilderness,[7] not their youth, but their staid men to learn our language and our theologic arts.

Yet that which is above all this, the favor and the love of Heaven, we have great argument to think in a peculiar manner propitious and propending towards us. Why else was this nation chosen before any other, that out of her as out of Sion should be proclaimed and sounded forth the first tidings and trumpet of reformation to all Europe? And had it not been the obstinate perverseness of our prelates against the divine and admirable spirit of Wycliffe[8] to suppress him as a schismatic and innovator, perhaps neither the Bohemian Huss and Jerome,[9] no, nor the name of Luther, or of Calvin, had been ever known; the glory of reforming all our neighbors had been completely ours. But now, as our obdurate clergy have with violence demeaned the matter, we are become hitherto the latest and the backwardest scholars of whom God offered to have made us the teachers.

Now once again by all concurrence of signs, and by the general instinct of holy and devout men, as they daily and solemnly express their thoughts, God is decreeing to begin some new and great period in his Church, even to the reforming of reformation itself. What does he then but reveal himself to his servants, and, as his manner is, first to his Englishmen? I say as his manner is, first to us, though we mark not the method of his counsels and are unworthy. Behold now this vast city, a city of refuge, the mansion house of liberty, encompassed and surrounded with his protection. The shop of war hath not there more anvils and hammers waking, to fashion out the plates and instruments of armed justice in defense of beleaguered Truth, than there be pens and heads there, sitting by their studious lamps, musing, searching, revolving new notions and ideas wherewith to present, as with their homage and their fealty, the approaching reformation; others as fast reading, trying all things, assenting to the force of reason and convincement.

What could a man require more from a nation so pliant and so prone to seek after knowledge? What wants there to such a towardly[1] and pregnant soul but wise and faithful laborers to make a knowing people, a nation of prophets, of sages, and of worthies? We reckon more than five months yet to harvest; there need not be five weeks, had we but eyes to lift up; the fields are white already. Where there is much desire to learn, there of necessity will be much arguing, much writing, many opinions; for opinion in good men is but knowledge in the making. Under these fantastic terrors of sect and schism, we wrong the earnest and zealous thirst after knowledge and understanding which God hath stirred up in this city.

What some lament of, we rather should rejoice at, should rather praise this pious forwardness among men, to reassume the ill-deputed care of their religion into their own hands again. A little generous prudence, a little forbearance of one another, and

4. For the connection between the Druids and Zoroastrian and Pythagorean philosophy, see Pliny, *Natural History* 30.2.
5. See Tacitus, *Agricola* 21.
6. Seventeenth-century Transylvania was Protestant and independent.
7. South central Germany.
8. English Protestants viewed John Wycliff (1320?–84) as the initiator of the Reformation in England.
9. Jerome of Prague (c. 1365–1416), a disciple of Wycliff, and John Huss of Bohemia (1373–1415).
1. Promising.

some grain of charity might win all these diligences to join and unite into one general and brotherly search after truth; could we but forego this prelatical tradition of crowding free consciences and Christian liberties into canons and precepts of men. I doubt not, if some great and worthy stranger should come among us, wise to discern the mold and temper of a people, and how to govern it, observing the high hopes and aims, the diligent alacrity of our extended thoughts and reasonings in the pursuance of truth and freedom, but that he would cry out as Pyrrhus did, admiring the Roman docility and courage, "If such were my Epirots, I would not despair the greatest design that could be attempted to make a church or kingdom happy."[2]

Yet these are the men cried out against for schismatics and sectaries;[3] as if, while the temple of the Lord was building, some cutting, some squaring the marble, others hewing the cedars, there should be a sort of irrational men who could not consider there must be many schisms and many dissections made in the quarry and in the timber, ere the house of God can be built. And when every stone is laid artfully together, it cannot be united into a continuity, it can but be contiguous in this world; neither can every piece of the building be of one form; nay rather the perfection consists in this, that out of many moderate varieties and brotherly dissimilitudes that are not vastly disproportional, arises the goodly and the graceful symmetry that commends the whole pile and structure.

Let us, therefore, be more considerate builders, more wise in spiritual architecture, when great reformation is expected. For now the time seems come, wherein Moses, the great prophet, may sit in heaven rejoicing to see that memorable and glorious wish of his fulfilled, when not only our seventy elders, but all the Lord's people, are become prophets.

* * *

Methinks I see in my mind a noble and puissant nation rousing herself like a strong man after sleep, and shaking her invincible locks. Methinks I see her as an eagle muing[4] her mighty youth, and kindling her undazzled eyes at the full midday beam; purging and unscaling her long-abused sight at the fountain itself of heavenly radiance; while the whole noise of timorous and flocking birds, with those also that love the twilight, flutter about, amazed at what she means, and in their envious gabble would prognosticate a year of sects and schisms.

What should ye do then, should ye suppress all this flowery crop of knowledge and new light sprung up and yet springing daily in this city? Should ye set an oligarchy of twenty engrossers[5] over it, to bring a famine upon our minds again, when we shall know nothing but what is measured to us by their bushel? Believe it, Lords and Commons, they who counsel ye to such a suppressing, do as good as bid ye suppress yourselves; and I will soon show how.

* * *

And now the time in special is, by privilege, to write and speak what may help to the further discussing of matters in agitation. The temple of Janus with his two controversal faces might now not unsignificantly be set open.[6] And though all the winds of doctrine were let loose to play upon the earth, so Truth be in the field, we do injuriously by licensing and prohibiting to misdoubt her strength. Let her and Falsehood grapple; who ever knew Truth put to the worse, in a free and open encounter. Her

2. King Pyrrhus of Epirus defeated the Romans at Hereclea in 280 B.C.
3. Dividers of the church.
4. Renewing.
5. Monopolists.
6. The Roman god Janus's head had two faces looking in opposite directions. During times of war the gates of Janus were open.

confuting is the best and surest suppressing. He who hears what praying there is for light and clearer knowledge to be sent down among us, would think of other matters to be constituted beyond the discipline of Geneva, framed and fabriced already to our hands.[7]

Yet when the new light which we beg for shines in upon us, there be who envy and oppose, if it come not first in at their casements. What a collusion[8] is this, whenas we are exhorted by the wise man to use diligence, to seek for wisdom as for hidden treasures[9] early and late, that another order shall enjoin us to know nothing but by statute. When a man hath been laboring the hardest labor in the deep mines of knowledge, hath furnished out his findings in all their equipage, drawn forth his reasons as it were a battle ranged, scattered and defeated all objections in his way, calls out his adversary into the plain, offers him the advantage of wind and sun, if he please, only that he may try the matter by dint of argument; for his opponents then to skulk, to lay ambushments, to keep a narrow bridge of licensing where the challenger should pass, though it be valor enough in soldiership, is but weakness and cowardice in the wars of Truth.

For who knows not that Truth is strong, next to the Almighty. She needs no policies, nor stratagems, nor licensings to make her victorious—those are the shifts and the defenses that error uses against her power. Give her but room, and do not bind her when she sleeps, for then she speaks not true, as the old Proteus did, who spake oracles only when he was caught and bound,[1] but then rather she turns herself into all shapes except her own, and perhaps tunes her voice according to the time, as Micaiah did before Ahab,[2] until she be adjured into her own likeness.

Yet is it not impossible that she may have more shapes than one. What else is all that rank of things indifferent, wherein Truth may be on this side, or on the other, without being unlike herself? What but a vain shadow else is the abolition of those ordinances, that handwriting nailed to the cross;[3] what great purchase is this Christian liberty which Paul so often boasts of? His doctrine is, that he who eats, or eats not, regards a day, or regards it not, may do either to the Lord.[4] How many other things might be tolerated in peace and left to conscience, had we but charity, and were it not the chief stronghold of our hypocrisy to be ever judging one another. I fear yet this iron yoke of outward conformity hath left a slavish print upon our necks; the ghost of a linen decency[5] yet haunts us. We stumble and are impatient at the least dividing of one visible congregation from another, though it be not in fundamentals; and through our forwardness to suppress, and our backwardness to recover any enthralled piece of truth out of the gripe of custom, we care not to keep truth separated from truth, which is the fiercest rent and disunion of all. We do not see that while we still affect by all means a rigid external formality, we may as soon fall again into a gross conforming stupidity, a stark and dead congealment of "wood, and hay, and stubble"[6] forced and frozen together, which is more to the sudden degenerating of a church than many subdichotomies[7] of petty schisms.

Not that I can think well of every light separation, or that all in a church is to be expected "gold and silver and precious stones."[8] It is not possible for man to sever the wheat from the tares, the good fish from the other fry; that must be the angels' min-

7. Discipline of Geneva: Calvinism; fabriced: fabricated.
8. Secret agreement for purposes of trickery; ambiguity in words or reasoning.
9. The wise man is Solomon; see Proverbs 8.11 and Matthew 13.44.
1. The story of Proteus is in *Odyssey* 384–93.
2. 1 Kings 22.
3. Colossians 2.14.
4. Romans 14.1–13.
5. A reference to the controversy over ecclesiastical vestments.
6. See 1 Corinthians 3.12.
7. Inconsequential divisions.
8. 1 Corinthians 3.12.

istry at the end of mortal things.[9] Yet if all cannot be of one mind,—as who looks they should be?—this doubtless is more wholesome, more prudent, and more Christian, that many be tolerated, rather than all compelled. I mean not tolerated popery and open superstition, which, as it extirpates all religions and civil supremacies, so itself should be extirpate, provided first that all charitable and compassionate means be used to win and regain the weak and the misled; that also which is impious or evil absolutely, either against faith or manners, no law can possibly permit, that intends not to unlaw itself; but those neighboring differences, or rather indifferences, are what I speak of, whether in some point of doctrine or of discipline, which though they may be many, yet need not interrupt "the unity of spirit," if we could but find among us the "bond of peace."[1]

In the meanwhile, if any one would write and bring his helpful hand to the slow-moving reformation which we labor under, if truth have spoken to him before others, or but seemed at least to speak, who hath so bejesuited us that we should trouble that man with asking license to do so worthy a deed? And not consider this, that if it come to prohibiting, there is not aught more likely to be prohibited than truth itself; whose first appearance to our eyes bleared and dimmed with prejudice and custom, is more unsightly and unplausible than many errors, even as the person is of many a great man slight and contemptible to see to. And what do they tell us vainly of new opinions, when this very opinion of theirs, that none must be heard but whom they like, is the worst and newest opinion of all others; and is the chief cause why sects and schisms do so much abound, and true knowledge is kept at distance from us; besides yet a greater danger which is in it. For when God shakes a kingdom with strong and healthful commotions to a general reforming, it is not untrue that many sectaries and false teachers are then busiest in seducing; but yet more true it is that God then raises to his own work men of rare abilities and more than common industry, not only to look back and revise what hath been taught heretofore, but to gain further and go on some new enlightened steps in the discovery of truth.

Paradise Lost

Paradise Lost is about devastating loss attended by redemption. The reader's knowledge of the Fall creates a sense of tragic inevitability. And Satan, no less than Adam and Eve, appears in all the psychological complexity and verbal grandeur of a tragic hero. Indeed, there is even a manuscript in which Milton outlined the story as a tragedy. In that version, "Lucifer's contriving Adam's ruin" is Act 3. Following epic tradition, Milton places this part of the action at the forefront of his poem, beginning *in medias res*.

So powerful is Milton's opening portrayal of Satan that the Romantic poets thought Satan was the hero of the poem. Focusing on the first two books, the romantic reading sees him as a dynamic rebel. From a Renaissance point of view, Satan is more like an Elizabethan hero-villain, with his many soliloquies and his tortured psychology of brilliance twisted toward evil. Only in Book 9, however, does Milton say, "I now must change these notes to tragic," thereby signaling that he is about to narrate the fall of Adam and Eve. From this point on the poem follows Adam and Eve's tragic movement from sin to despair to the recognition of sin and the need for repentance. Adam and Eve's learning through suffering and the prophecy of the Son's redemption of sin make this a story of gain as well as loss, on the order of Aeschylean tragedy.

Like all epics, *Paradise Lost* is encyclopedic, combining many different genres. To read this poem is to have an education in everything from literary history to astronomy. Milton draws on a vast wealth of reading, with the Bible as his main source—not only Genesis, but

9. Matthew 13.24.

1. Ephesians 4.3.

also Exodus, the Prophets, Revelation, Saint Paul, and especially the Psalms, which he had translated. Milton also makes great use of biblical commentary from rabbinical, patristic, and contemporary sources. Early on, Milton had envisaged a poem about the Arthurian legend, and his choice of the nonmartial, seemingly unheroic biblical story of Adam and Eve marks a bold departure from epic tradition. While Spenser's *Faerie Queene* is Milton's most important vernacular model, among epic poets his closest affinity is with Virgil and Dante, both of whom had written of the underworld; Dante especially devoted himself to humanity's free choice of sin. Like Dante, Milton creates his poem as a microcosm of the natural universe. His ideal vision of the world before the Fall is one where day and night are equal and the sun is always in the same sign of the zodiac, an image that embodies in poetic astronomy the world of simplicity and perfection that humans have lost through sin. Milton does not choose between the earth-centered Ptolemaic and the heliocentric Copernican systems but presents both as alternative explanations for the order of the universe.

Although we know nothing about the order in which the parts of the poem were composed, we do know that Milton typically composed at night or in the early morning. Sometimes he lay awake unable to write a line; at others he was seized "with a certain impetus and *oestro*" [frenzy]. He would dictate forty lines from memory and then reduce them to half that number. According to his nephew, the poem was written from 1658 to 1663.

The one extant manuscript of the poem, which contains the first book, reveals that Milton revised for punctuation and spelling. There were two editions in Milton's lifetime, both printed by Samuel Simmons. The first edition, *Paradise Lost: A poem in ten books*, was printed in six different issues in 1667, 1668, and 1669. From the fourth issue of the poem on, such paratexts as "The Printer to Reader," "The Argument" (which stood altogether), and Milton's note on the verse appear. With the second octave edition of 1674, Milton divided Books 7 and 10 into two books each to create twelve books in all. Prefaced by dedicatory Latin verses, one of which was by his old friend Andrew Marvell, this 1674 edition, which appeared in the year of Milton's death, is the basis for the present text.

from PARADISE LOST[1]

Book 1

The Argument

This first Book proposes, first in brief, the whole Subject, *Man's disobedience, and the loss thereupon of Paradise wherein he was plac't:* Then touches *the prime cause of his fall, the Serpent, or rather* Satan *in the Serpent; who revolting from God, and drawing to his side many Legions of Angels, was by the command of God driven out of Heaven with all his Crew into the great Deep.* Which action past over, the Poem hastes into the midst of things,[2] presenting *Satan with his Angels now fallen into Hell,* describ'd here, *not in the Centre* (for Heaven and Earth may be suppos'd as yet not made, certainly not yet accurst) *but in a place of utter darkness, fitliest call'd* Chaos: *Here Satan with his Angels lying on the burning Lake, thunder-struck and astonisht, after a certain space recovers, as from confusion, calls up him who next in Order and Dignity lay by him; they confer of thir miserable fall.* Satan *awakens all his Legions, who lay till then in the same manner confounded; They rise, thir Numbers, array of Battle, thir chief Leaders nam'd, according to the Idols known afterwards in* Canaan *and the Countries adjoining. To these Satan directs his Speech, comforts them with hope yet of regaining Heaven, but tells them lastly of a new World and new kind of Creature to be created, according to an ancient Prophecy or report*

1. Our text is taken, and the notes are adapted, from John Carey and Alastair Fowler, eds., *The Poems of John Milton.*

2. Following Horace's rule that the epic should plunge "*in medias res.*"

in Heaven; for that Angels were long before this visible Creation, was the opinion of many ancient Fathers. *To find out the truth of this Prophecy, and what to determine thereon he refers to a full Council. What his Associates thence attempt.* Pandemonium *the Palace of* Satan *rises, suddenly built out of the Deep: The infernal Peers there sit in Council.*

Of Man's First Disobedience, and the Fruit
Of that Forbidden Tree, whose mortal[3] taste
Brought Death into the World, and all our woe,[4]
With loss of *Eden,* till one greater Man[5]
Restore us, and regain the blissful Seat,
Sing Heav'nly Muse,[6] that on the secret top
Of *Oreb,* or of *Sinai,* didst inspire
That Shepherd, who first taught the chosen Seed,[7]
In the Beginning how the Heav'ns and Earth
Rose out of *Chaos:* Or if *Sion* Hill[8]
Delight thee more, and *Siloa's* Brook[9] that flow'd
Fast° by the Oracle of God; I thence — *close*
Invoke thy aid to my advent'rous Song,
That with no middle flight intends to soar
Above th' *Aonian* Mount,[1] while it pursues
Things unattempted yet in Prose or Rhyme.[2]
And chiefly Thou O Spirit, that dost prefer
Before all Temples th' upright heart and pure,[3]
Instruct me, for Thou know'st; Thou from the first
Wast present, and with mighty wings outspread
Dove-like satst brooding on the vast Abyss
And mad'st it pregnant:[4] What in me is dark
Illumine, what is low raise and support;
That to the highth of this great Argument° — *theme*
I may assert Eternal Providence,
And justify[5] the ways of God to men.
Say first, for Heav'n hides nothing from thy view
Nor the deep Tract of Hell, say first what cause
Mov'd our Grand[6] Parents in that happy State,

3. "Death-bringing" (Latin *mortalis*) but also "to mortals."

4. This definition of the first sin follows Calvin's Catechism.

5. Christ, in Pauline theology the second Adam (see Romans 5.19). The people and events referred to in these lines have a typological connection, i.e., the Christian interpretation of the Old Testament as a prefiguration of the New.

6. Rhetorically, lines 1–49 are the *invocatio,* consisting of an address to the Muse, and the *principium* that states the whole scope of the poem's action. The "Heavenly Muse," later addressed as the muse of astronomy Urania (7.1), is here identified with the Holy Spirit of the Bible, which inspires Moses.

7. The "Shepherd" is Moses, who was granted the vision of the burning bush on Mount Oreb (Exodus 3) and received the Law, either on Mount Oreb (Deuteronomy 4.10) or on its lower part, Mount Sinai (Exodus 19.20). Moses, the first Jewish writer, taught "the chosen seed," the children of Israel, about the beginning of the world in Genesis.

8. The sanctuary, a place of ceremonial song but also (Isaiah 2.3) of oracular pronouncements.

9. A spring immediately west of Mount Zion and beside Calvary, often used as a symbol of the operation of the Holy Ghost.

1. Helicon, sacred to the Muses.

2. Ironically translating Ariosto's boast in the invocation to *Orlando Furioso*.

3. The Spirit is the voice of God, which inspired the Hebrew prophets.

4. Identifying the Spirit present at the creation (Genesis 1.2) with the Spirit in the form of a dove that descended on Jesus at the beginning of his ministry (John 1.32). Vast: large; deserted (Latin *vastus*).

5. Does not mean merely "demonstrate logically" but has its biblical meaning and implies spiritual rather than rational understanding.

6. Implies not only greatness, but also inclusiveness of generality or parentage.

Favor'd of Heav'n so highly, to fall off
From thir Creator, and transgress his Will
For° one restraint, Lords of the World besides?° *because of/otherwise*
Who first seduc'd them to that foul revolt?
Th' infernal Serpent;[7] hee it was, whose guile
Stirr'd up with Envy and Revenge, deceiv'd
The Mother of Mankind; what time his Pride
Had cast him out from Heav'n, with all his Host
Of Rebel Angels, by whose aid aspiring
To set himself in Glory above his Peers,
He trusted to have equall'd the most High,[8]
If he oppos'd; and with ambitious aim
Against the Throne and Monarchy of God
Rais'd impious War in Heav'n and Battle proud
With vain attempt. Him the Almighty Power
Hurl'd headlong flaming from th' Ethereal Sky[9]
With hideous ruin and combustion down
To bottomless perdition, there to dwell
In Adamantine Chains[1] and penal Fire,
Who durst defy th' Omnipotent to Arms.
Nine times the Space that measures Day and Night[2]
To mortal men, hee with his horrid crew
Lay vanquisht, rolling in the fiery Gulf
Confounded though immortal: But his doom
Reserv'd him to more wrath; for now the thought
Both of lost happiness and lasting pain
Torments him; round he throws his baleful° eyes *evil, suffering*
That witness'd huge affliction and dismay
Mixt with obdúrate° pride and steadfast hate: *unyielding*
At once as far as Angels' ken° he views *power of vision*
The dismal° Situation waste and wild, *dreadful, sinister*
A Dungeon horrible, on all sides round
As one great Furnace flam'd, yet from those flames
No light, but rather darkness visible
Serv'd only to discover sights of woe,[3]
Regions of sorrow, doleful shades, where peace
And rest can never dwell, hope never comes
That comes to all;[4] but torture without end
Still urges,° and a fiery Deluge, fed *presses*
With ever-burning Sulphur unconsum'd:

7. "That old serpent, called the Devil, and Satan" (Revelation 12.9) both because Satan entered the body of a serpent to tempt Eve and because his nature is guileful and dangerous to humans.
8. Satan's crime was not his aspiring "above his peers" but aspiring "To set himself in [divine] Glory." Numerous verbal echoes relate lines 40–48 to the biblical accounts of the fall and binding of Lucifer, in 2 Peter 2.4, Revelation 20.1–2, and Isaiah 14.12–15: "Thou hast said . . . I will exalt my throne above the stars of God . . . I will be like the most High. Yet thou shalt be brought down to hell."
9. Mingling an allusion to Luke 10.18, "I beheld Satan as lightning fall from heaven," with one to Homer, *Iliad* 1.591, Hephaistos "hurled from the ethereal threshold."
1. 2 Peter 2.4; "God spared not the angels that sinned, but . . . delivered them into chains of darkness."
2. The devils fall for the same number of days that the Titans fall from heaven when overthrown by the Olympian gods (see Hesiod, *Theogony* 664–735).
3. See the account of the land of the dead in Job 10.22: "the light is as darkness."
4. The phrase echoes Dante's *Inferno*: "All hope abandon, ye who enter here."

Such place Eternal Justice had prepar'd
For those rebellious, here thir Prison ordained
In utter° darkness, and thir portion set *complete, outer*
As far remov'd from God and light of Heav'n
As from the Center thrice to th' utmost Pole.[5]
O how unlike the place from whence they fell!
There the companions of his fall, o'erwhelm'd
With Floods and Whirlwinds of tempestuous fire,
He soon discerns, and welt'ring by his side
One next himself in power, and next in crime,
Long after known in *Palestine*, and nam'd
Beëlzebub.[6] To whom th' Arch-Enemy,
And thence in Heav'n call'd Satan,[7] with bold words
Breaking the horrid silence thus began.[8]
 If thou beest hee; But O how fall'n! how chang'd
From him, who in the happy Realms of Light
Cloth'd with transcendent brightness didst outshine
Myriads though bright:[9] If he whom mutual league,
United thoughts and counsels, equal hope,
And hazard in the Glorious Enterprise,
Join'd with me once, now misery hath join'd
In equal ruin: into what Pit thou seest
From what highth fall'n, so much the stronger prov'd
He with his Thunder: and till then who knew
The force of those dire Arms? yet not for those,
Nor what the Potent Victor in his rage
Can else inflict, do I repent or change,
Though chang'd in outward luster; that fixt mind
And high disdain, from sense of injur'd merit,
That with the mightiest rais'd me to contend,
And to the fierce contention brought along
Innumerable force of Spirits arm'd
That durst dislike his reign, and mee preferring,
His utmost power with adverse power oppos'd
In dubious Battle on the Plains of Heav'n,
And shook his throne.[1] What though the field be lost?
All is not lost; the unconquerable Will,
And study° of revenge, immortal hate, *pursuit*
And courage never to submit or yield:
And what is else not to be overcome?

5. Milton refers to the Ptolemaic universe in which the earth is at the center of ten concentric spheres. Milton draws attention to the numerical proportion, heaven-earth:earth-hell—i.e., earth divides the interval between heaven and hell in the proportion that Neoplatonists believed should be maintained between reason and concupiscence.

6. Hebrew, "Lord of the flies"; Matthew 12.24, "the prince of the devils."

7. Hebrew, "enemy." After his rebellion, Satan's "former name" (Lucifer) was no longer used (5.658).

8. Rhetorically, the opening of the action proper. The 41-line speech beginning here, the first speech in the book, exactly balances the last, which also is spoken by Satan and also consists of 41 lines (1.622–662).

9. The break in grammatical concord (between "him" and "didst") reflects Satan's doubt whether Beelzebub is present and so whether second-person forms are appropriate.

1. The Son's chariot, not Satan's armies, shakes heaven to its foundations, as we learn in Book 6. Throughout the present passage, Satan sees himself as the hero of a pagan epic.

That Glory[2] never shall his wrath or might
Extort from me. To bow and sue for grace
With suppliant knee, and deify his power
Who from the terror of this Arm so late
Doubted° his Empire, that were low indeed, *feared for*
That were an ignominy and shame beneath
This downfall; since by Fate the strength of Gods
And this Empyreal substance cannot fail,[3]
Since through experience of this great event
In Arms not worse, in foresight much advanc't,
We may with more successful hope resolve
To wage by force or guile eternal War
Irreconcilable to our grand Foe,
Who now triúmphs, and in th' excess of joy
Sole reigning holds the Tyranny of Heav'n.[4]
 So spake th' Apostate Angel, though in pain,
Vaunting aloud, but rackt with deep despair:
And him thus answer'd soon his bold Compeer.° *comrade*
 O Prince, O Chief of many Throned Powers,
That led th' imbattl'd Seraphim[5] to War
Under thy conduct, and in dreadful deeds
Fearless, endanger'd Heav'n's perpetual King;
And put to proof his high Supremacy,
Whether upheld by strength, or Chance, or Fate;[6]
Too well I see and rue the dire event,
That with sad overthrow and foul defeat
Hath lost us Heav'n, and all this mighty Host
In horrible destruction laid thus low,
As far as Gods and Heav'nly Essences
Can perish: for the mind and spirit remains
Invincible, and vigor soon returns,
Though all our Glory extinct, and happy state
Here swallow'd up in endless misery.
But what if he our Conqueror (whom I now
Of force° believe Almighty, since no less *necessarily*
Than such could have o'erpow'rd such force as ours)
Have left us this our spirit and strength entire
Strongly to suffer and support our pains,
That we may so suffice° his vengeful ire, *satisfy*
Or do him mightier service as his thralls
By right of War, whate'er his business be
Here in the heart of Hell to work in Fire,
Or do his Errands in the gloomy Deep;
What can it then avail though yet we feel
Strength undiminisht, or eternal being

2. Either "the glory of overcoming me" or "my glory of will."
3. Implying not only that as angels they are immortal, but also that the continuance of their strength is assured by fate.
4. An obvious instance of the devil's bias.
5. The traditional nine orders of angels are seraphim, cherubim, thrones, dominions, virtues, powers, principalities, archangels, and angels, but Milton does not use these terms systematically.
6. The main powers recognized in the devils' ideology. God's power rests on a quality that does not occur to Beelzebub: goodness.

To undergo eternal punishment?[7]
Whereto with speedy words th' Arch-fiend repli'd.
Fall'n Cherub, to be weak is miserable
Doing or Suffering: but of this be sure,
To do aught good never will be our task,
But ever to do ill our sole delight,
As being the contrary to his high will
Whom we resist.[8] If then his Providence
Out of our evil seek to bring forth good,
Our labor must be to pervert that end,
And out of good still to find means of evil;
Which oft-times may succeed, so as perhaps
Shall grieve him, if I fail not, and disturb
His inmost counsels from thir destin'd aim.
But see the angry Victor hath recall'd
His Ministers of vengeance and pursuit
Back to the Gates of Heav'n: the Sulphurous Hail
Shot after us in storm, o'erblown hath laid° *subdued*
The fiery Surge, that from the Precipice
Of Heav'n receiv'd us falling, and the Thunder,
Wing'd with red Lightning and impetuous rage,
Perhaps hath spent his shafts, and ceases now
To bellow through the vast and boundless Deep.
Let us not slip° th' occasion, whether scorn, *lose*
Or satiate fury yield it from our Foe.
Seest thou yon dreary Plain, forlorn and wild,
The seat of desolation, void of light,
Save what the glimmering of these livid flames
Casts pale and dreadful? Thither let us tend
From off the tossing of these fiery waves,
There rest, if any rest can harbor there,
And reassembling our afflicted° Powers, *downcast*
Consult how we may henceforth most offend° *harm*
Our Enemy, our own loss how repair,
How overcome this dire Calamity,
What reinforcement we may gain from Hope,
If not what resolution from despair.
Thus Satan talking to his nearest Mate
With Head up-lift above the wave, and Eyes
That sparkling blaz'd, his other Parts besides
Prone on the Flood, extended long and large
Lay floating many a rood,° in bulk as huge *six to eight yards*
As whom the Fables name of monstrous size,
Titanian, or *Earth-born*, that warr'd on *Jove*,
Briareos or *Typhon*,[9] whom the Den

7. Existing eternally, merely so that our punishment may also be eternal.

8. This fundamental disobedience and disorientation make Satan's heroic virtue into the corresponding excess of vice. Lines 163–165 look forward to 12.470–78 and Adam's wonder at the astonishing reversal whereby God will turn the Fall into an occasion for good.

9. The serpent-legged *Briareos* was a Titan, the serpent-headed *Typhon* (Typhoeus) a Giant. Each was a son of Earth; each fought against Jupiter; and each was eventually confined beneath Aetna (see lines 232–37). Typhon was so powerful that when he first made war on the Olympians, they had to resort to metamorphoses to escape (Ovid, *Metamorphoses* 5.325–31 and 346–58).

By ancient *Tarsus*[1] held, or that Sea-beast
Leviathan,[2] which God of all his works
Created hugest that swim th' Ocean stream:
Him haply slumb'ring on the *Norway* foam
The Pilot of some small night-founder'd° Skiff, *sunk in night*
Deeming some Island, oft, as Seamen tell,
With fixed Anchor in his scaly rind
Moors by his side under the Lee, while Night
Invests° the Sea, and wished Morn delays: *wraps*
So stretcht out huge in length the Arch-fiend lay
Chain'd on the burning Lake, nor ever thence
Had ris'n or heav'd his head, but that the will
And high permission of all-ruling Heaven
Left him at large to his own dark designs,
That with reiterated crimes he might
Heap on himself damnation, while he sought
Evil to others, and enrag'd might see
How all his malice serv'd but to bring forth
Infinite goodness, grace and mercy shown
On Man by him seduc't, but on himself
Treble confusion, wrath and vengeance pour'd.
Forthwith upright he rears from off the Pool
His mighty Stature; on each hand the flames
Driv'n backward slope thir pointing spires, and roll'd
In billows, leave i' th' midst a horrid° Vale. *bristling*
Then with expanded wings he steers his flight
Aloft, incumbent[3] on the dusky Air
That felt unusual weight, till on dry Land
He lights, if it were Land that ever burn'd
With solid, as the Lake with liquid fire
And such appear'd in hue;[4] as when the force
Of subterranean wind transports a Hill
Torn from *Pelorus*,[5] or the shatter'd side
Of thund'ring *AEtna,* whose combustible
And fuell'd entrails thence conceiving Fire,
Sublim'd[6] with Mineral fury,[7] aid the Winds,
And leave a singed bottom all involv'd° *wreathed*
With stench and smoke: Such resting found the sole
Of unblest feet. Him follow'd his next Mate,
Both glorying to have scap't the *Stygian*[8] flood
As Gods, and by thir own recover'd strength,
Not by the sufferance of supernal Power.
Is this the Region, this the Soil, the Clime,
Said then the lost Arch-Angel, this the seat
That we must change° for Heav'n, this mournful gloom *exchange*

1. The biblical Tarsus was the capital of Cilicia, and both Pindar and Aeschylus describe Typhon's habitat as a Cilician cave or "den."
2. The monster of Job 41, identified in Isaiah's prophecy of judgement as "the crooked serpent" (Isaiah 27.1) but also sometimes thought of as a whale.
3. Pressing with his weight.
4. In the 17th century, "hue" referred to surface appearance and texture as well as color.
5. Pelorus and Aetna are volcanic mountains in Sicily.
6. Converted directly from solid to vapor by volcanic heat in such a way as to resolidify on cooling.
7. Disorder of minerals, or subterranean disorder.
8. Of the River Styx—i.e., hellish.

For that celestial light? Be it so, since he
Who now is Sovran can dispose and bid
What shall be right: fardest° from him is best *farthest*
Whom reason hath equall'd, force hath made supreme
Above his equals. Farewell happy Fields
Where Joy for ever dwells: Hail horrors, hail
Infernal world, and thou profoundest Hell
Receive thy new Possessor: One who brings
A mind not to be chang'd by Place or Time.
The mind is its own place, and in itself
Can make a Heav'n of Hell, a Hell of Heav'n.[9]
What matter where, if I be still the same,
And what I should be, all but less than hee
Whom Thunder hath made greater? Here at least
We shall be free; th' Almighty hath not built
Here for his envy, will not drive us hence:
Here we may reign secure, and in my choice
To reign is worth ambition[1] though in Hell:
Better to reign in Hell, than serve in Heav'n.
But wherefore let we then our faithful friends,
Th' associates and copartners of our loss
Lie thus astonisht on th' oblivious Pool,[2]
And call them not to share with us their part
In this unhappy Mansion: or once more
With rallied Arms to try what may be yet
Regain'd in Heav'n, or what more lost in Hell?
  So *Satan* spake, and him *Beëlzebub*
Thus answer'd. Leader of those Armies bright,
Which but th' Omnipotent none could have foiled,
If once they hear that voice, thir liveliest pledge
Of hope in fears and dangers, heard so oft
In worst extremes, and on the perilous edge° *front line*
Of battle when it rag'd, in all assaults
Thir surest signal, they will soon resume
New courage and revive, though now they lie
Groveling and prostrate on yon Lake of Fire,
As we erewhile, astounded and amaz'd;
No wonder, fall'n such a pernicious highth.
  He scarce had ceas't when the superior Fiend
Was moving toward the shore; his ponderous shield
Ethereal temper,[3] massy, large and round,
Behind him cast; the broad circumference
Hung on his shoulders like the Moon, whose Orb
Through Optic Glass the *Tuscan* Artist[4] views
At Ev'ning from the top of *Fesole*,

9. The view that heaven and hell are states of mind was held by Amaury de Bene, a medieval heretic often cited in 17th-century accounts of atheism.
1. Worth striving for (Latin *ambitio*). Satan refers not merely to a mental state but also to an active effort that is the price of power.
2. The pool attended by forgetfulness.
3. Tempered in celestial fire.
4. Galileo, who looked through a telescope ("optic glass"), had been placed under house arrest by the Inquisition near Florence, which is in the "Valdarno" or the Valley of the Arno, overlooked by the hills of "Fesole" or Fiesole.

Or in *Valdarno*, to descry new Lands,
Rivers or Mountains in her spotty Globe.
His Spear, to equal which the tallest Pine
Hewn on *Norwegian* hills, to be the Mast
Of some great Ammiral,° were but a wand, *flagship*
He walkt with to support uneasy steps
Over the burning Marl,° not like those steps *ground*
On Heaven's Azure, and the torrid Clime
Smote on him sore besides, vaulted with Fire;
Nathless° he so endur'd, till on the Beach *nevertheless*
Of that inflamed Sea, he stood and call'd
His Legions, Angel Forms, who lay intrans't
Thick as Autumnal Leaves that strow the Brooks
In *Vallombrosa*, where th' *Etrurian* shades
High overarch't imbow'r;[5] or scatter'd sedge
Afloat, when with fierce Winds *Orion* arm'd
Hath vext the Red-Sea Coast,[6] whose waves o'erthrew
Busiris and his *Memphian* Chivalry,
While with perfidious hatred they pursu'd
The Sojourners of *Goshen*, who beheld
From the safe shore thir floating Carcasses
And broken Chariot Wheels;[7] so thick bestrown
Abject and lost lay these, covering the Flood,
Under amazement of thir hideous change.
He call'd so loud, that all the hollow Deep
Of Hell resounded. Princes, Potentates,
Warriors, the Flow'r of Heav'n, once yours, now lost,
If such astonishment as this can seize
Eternal spirits; or have ye chos'n this place
After the toil of Battle to repose
Your wearied virtue,° for the ease you find *strength*
To slumber here, as in the Vales of Heav'n?
Or in this abject posture have ye sworn
To adore the Conqueror? who now beholds
Cherub and Seraph rolling in the Flood
With scatter'd Arms and Ensigns,° till anon *battle flags*
His swift pursuers from Heav'n Gates discern
Th' advantage, and descending tread us down
Thus drooping, or with linked Thunderbolts
Transfix us to the bottom of this Gulf.
Awake, arise, or be for ever fall'n.
They heard, and were abasht, and up they sprung
Upon the wing; as when men wont to watch

5. See Isaiah 34.4: "and all their host shall fall down, as the leaf falleth off from the vine, and as a falling fig from the fig tree." Fallen leaves were an enduring simile for the numberless dead; see Homer, *Iliad* 6.146; Virgil, *Aeneid* 6.309; Dante, *Inferno* 3.112. Milton adds an actual locality, Vallombrosa, again near Florence.

6. Commentators on Job 9.9 and Amos 5.8 interpreted the creation of Orion as a symbol of God's power to raise tempests and floods to execute his judgments. Thus Milton's transition to the Egyptians overwhelmed by God's judgment in lines 306–11 is a natural one. The Hebrew name for the Red Sea was "Sea of Sedge."

7. Contrary to his promise, the Pharaoh with his Memphian (i.e., Egyptian) charioteers pursued the Israelites—who had been in captivity in Goshen—across the Red Sea. The Israelites passed over safely; but the Egyptians' chariot wheels were broken (Exodus 14.25), and the rising sea engulfed them and cast their corpses on the shore.

On duty, sleeping found by whom they dread,
Rouse and bestir themselves ere well awake.
Nor did they not perceive the evil plight
In which they were, or the fierce pains not feel;
Yet to thir General's Voice they soon obey'd
Innumerable. As when the potent Rod
Of *Amram's* Son[8] in *Egypt's* evil day
Wav'd round the Coast, up call'd a pitchy cloud
Of *Locusts,* warping° on the Eastern Wind, *floating*
That o'er the Realm of impious *Pharaoh* hung
Like Night, and darken'd all the Land of *Nile:*
So numberless were those bad Angels seen
Hovering on wing under the Cope° of Hell *canopy*
'Twixt upper, nether, and surrounding Fires;
Till, as a signal giv'n, th' uplifted Spear
Of thir great Sultan waving to direct
Thir course, in even balance down they light
On the firm brimstone, and fill all the Plain;
A multitude, like which the populous North
Pour'd never from her frozen loins, to pass
Rhene or the *Danaw,* when her barbarous Sons
Came like a Deluge on the South, and spread
Beneath *Gibraltar* to the *Lybian* sands.[9]
Forthwith from every Squadron and each Band
The Heads and Leaders thither haste where stood
Thir great Commander; Godlike shapes and forms
Excelling human, Princely Dignities,
And Powers that erst in Heaven sat on Thrones;
Though of thir Names in heav'nly Records now
Be no memorial, blotted out and ras'd
By thir Rebellion, from the Books of Life.[1]
Nor had they yet among the Sons of *Eve*
Got them new Names, till wand'ring o'er the Earth,
Through God's high sufferance for the trial of man,
By falsities and lies the greatest part
Of Mankind they corrupted to forsake
God thir Creator, and th' invisible
Glory of him that made them, to transform
Oft to the Image of a Brute, adorn'd
With gay Religions° full of Pomp and Gold, *ceremonies*
And Devils to adore for Deities:[2]
Then were they known to men by various Names,
And various Idols through the Heathen World.
Say, Muse, thir Names then known, who first, who last,
Rous'd from the slumber on that fiery Couch,
At thir great Emperor's call, as next in worth

8. Moses, who used his rod to bring down on the Egyptians a plague of locusts (Exodus 10.12–15).
9. The barbarian invasions of Rome began with crossings of the Rhine ("Rhene") and Danube ("Danaw") Rivers and spread to North Africa.
1. See Revelation 3.5 ("He that overcometh . . . I will not blot out his name out of the book of life") and Exodus 32.32–3.
2. The catalogue of gods here is an epic convention.

Came singly where he stood on the bare strand,
While the promiscuous crowd stood yet aloof?
The chief were those who from the Pit of Hell
Roaming to seek thir prey on earth, durst fix
Thir Seats long after next the Seat of God,
Thir Altars by his Altar, Gods ador'd
Among the Nations round, and durst abide
Jehovah thund'ring out of *Sion*, thron'd
Between the Cherubim; yea, often plac'd
Within his Sanctuary itself thir Shrines,
Abominations; and with cursed things
His holy Rites, and solemn Feasts profan'd,
And with thir darkness durst affront his light.
First *Moloch*,[3] horrid King besmear'd with blood
Of human sacrifice, and parents' tears,
Though for the noise of Drums and Timbrels° loud *tambourines*
Thir children's cries unheard, that pass'd through fire
To his grim Idol. Him the *Ammonite*
Worshipt in *Rabba* and her wat'ry Plain,
In *Argob* and in *Basan*, to the stream
Of utmost *Arnon*.[4] Nor content with such
Audacious neighborhood, the wisest heart
Of *Solomon*[5] he led by fraud to build
His Temple right against the Temple of God
On that opprobrious Hill,[6] and made his Grove
The pleasant Valley of *Hinnom*, *Tophet* thence
And black *Gehenna* call'd, the Type of Hell.[7]
Next *Chemos*,[8] th' obscene dread of *Moab's* Sons,
From *Aroar* to *Nebo*, and the wild
Of Southmost *Abarim*; in *Hesebon*
And *Horonaim*, *Seon's* Realm, beyond
The flow'ry Dale of *Sibma* clad with Vines,
And *Eleale* to th' *Asphaltic* Pool.[9]
Peor[1] his other Name, when he entic'd
Israel in *Sittim* on thir march from *Nile*

3. Satan gathers twelve disciples: Moloch, Chemos, Baalim, Ashtaroth, Astoreth, Thammuz, Dagon, Rimmon, Osiris, Isis, Horus, and Belial. The literal meaning of *Moloch* is "king."

4. Though ostensibly magnifying Moloch's empire, these lines look forward to his eventual defeat; for Rabba, the Ammonite royal city, is best known for its capture by David after his repentance (2 Samuel 12), while the Israelite conquest of the regions of Argob and Basan, as far as the boundary river Arnon, is recalled by Moses as particularly crushing (Deuteronomy 3.1–13).

5. Solomon's wives drew him into idolatry (1 Kings 11.5–7); but the "high places that were before Jerusalem . . . on the right hand of the mount of corruption which Solomon . . . had builded for Ashtoreth the abomination of the Zidonians, and for Chemosh the abomination of the Moabites, and Milcom the abomination of the children of Ammon" were later destroyed by Josiah (2 Kings 23.13–14).

6. The Mount of Olives, because of Solomon's idolatry called "mount of corruption." Throughout the poem, Solomon functions as a type both of Adam and of Christ.

7. To abolish sacrifice to Moloch, Josiah "defiled Topheth, which is in the valley of the children of Hinnom" (2 Kings 23.10). Gehenna, for "Valley of Hinnom," is used in Matthew 10.28 as a name for hell.

8. "The abomination of Moab," associated with the neighboring god Moloch in 1 Kings 11.7.

9. Most of these places are named in Numbers 32 as the formerly Moabite inheritance assigned by Moses to the tribes of Reuben and Gad. Numbers 21.25–30 rejoices at the Israelite capture of Hesebon (Heshbon), a Moabite city which had been taken by the Amorite King Seon, or Sihon. Heshbon, Horonaim, "the vine of Sibmah," and Elealeh all figure in Isaiah's sad prophecy of the destruction of Moab (Isaiah 15.5, 16.8f). The Asphaltic Pool is the Dead Sea.

1. For the story of Peor, see Numbers 25.1–3 and Hosea 9.10.

To do him wanton rites, which cost them woe.[2]
Yet thence his lustful Orgies he enlarg'd
Even to that Hill of scandal, by the Grove
Of *Moloch* homicide, lust hard by hate;
Till good *Josiah*[3] drove them thence to Hell.
With these came they, who from the bord'ring flood
Of old *Euphrates*[4] to the Brook that parts
Egypt from *Syrian* ground, had general Names
Of *Baalim* and *Ashtaroth*,[5] those male,
These Feminine. For Spirits when they please
Can either Sex assume, or both; so soft
And uncompounded is thir Essence pure,
Not ti'd or manacl'd with joint or limb,
Nor founded on the brittle strength of bones,
Like cumbrous flesh; but in what shape they choose
Dilated° or condens't, bright or obscure, *expanded*
Can execute thir aery purposes,
And works of love or enmity fulfil.
For those the Race of *Israel* oft forsook
Thir living strength,[6] and unfrequented left
His righteous Altar, bowing lowly down
To bestial Gods; for which thir heads as low
Bow'd down in Battle, sunk before the Spear
Of despicable foes. With these in troop
Came *Astoreth*, whom the *Phoenicians* call'd
Astarte, Queen of Heav'n, with crescent Horns;[7]
To whose bright Image nightly by the Moon
Sidonian Virgins paid thir Vows and Songs,
In *Sion* also not unsung, where stood
Her Temple on th' offensive Mountain, built
By that uxorious King, whose heart though large,
Beguil'd by fair Idolatresses, fell
To Idols foul. *Thammuz*[8] came next behind,
Whose annual wound in *Lebanon* allur'd
The *Syrian* Damsels to lament his fate
In amorous ditties all a Summer's day,
While smooth *Adonis* from his native Rock
Ran purple to the Sea, suppos'd with blood
Of *Thammuz* yearly wounded: the Love-tale
Infected *Sion*'s daughters with like heat,

2. A plague that killed 24,000 (Numbers 25.9).
3. Always a favorite with the Reformers because of his destruction of idolatrous images.
4. An area stretching from the northeast limit of Syria to the southwest limit of Canaan, the river Besor.
5. Baal is the general name for most idols; the Phoenician and Canaanite sun gods were collectively called Baalim (plural form). Astartes (Ishtars) were manifestations of the moon goddess.
6. See 1 Samuel 15.29: "Strength of Israel," a formulaic periphrasis for Jehovah.
7. The image of Astoreth or Astarte, the Sidonian (Phoenician) moon goddess and Venus, was the statue of a woman with the head of a bull above her head with horns resembling the crescent moon. "Queen of heaven": from Jeremiah 44.17–19.
8. The lover of Astarte. His identification with Adonis was based on St. Jerome's commentary on the passage in Ezekiel 8.14, drawn on by Milton in lines 454–456. The Syrian festival of Tammuz was celebrated after the summer solstice; the slaying of the young god by a boar was mourned as a symbol of the southward withdrawal of the sun and the death of vegetation. Each year when the River Adonis became discolored with red mud, it was regarded as a renewed sign of the god's wound.

Whose wanton passions in the sacred Porch
Ezekiel saw, when by the Vision led
His eye survey'd the dark Idolatries
Of alienated *Judah*. Next came one
Who mourn'd in earnest, when the Captive Ark
Maim'd his brute Image, head and hands lopt off
In his own Temple, on the grunsel° edge, *threshold*
Where he fell flat, and sham'd his Worshippers:
Dagon his Name, Sea Monster, upward Man
And downward Fish:[9] yet had his Temple high
Rear'd in *Azotus*, dreaded through the Coast
Of *Palestine*, in *Gath* and *Ascalon*,
And *Accaron* and *Gaza's* frontier bounds.[1]
Him follow'd *Rimmon*, whose delightful Seat
Was fair *Damascus*, on the fertile Banks
Of *Abbana* and *Pharphar*, lucid streams.[2]
He also against the house of God was bold:
A Leper once he lost and gain'd a King,
Ahaz his sottish Conqueror, whom he drew
God's Altar to disparage and displace
For one of *Syrian* mode, whereon to burn
His odious off'rings, and adore the Gods
Whom he had vanquisht.[3] After these appear'd
A crew who under Names of old Renown,
Osiris, *Isis*, *Orus* and thir Train
With monstrous shapes and sorceries abus'd° *deceived*
Fanatic *Egypt* and her Priests, to seek
Thir wand'ring Gods disguis'd in brutish forms
Rather than human.[4] Nor did *Israel* scape
Th' infection when thir borrow'd Gold compos'd
The Calf in *Oreb:*[5] and the Rebel King[6]
Doubl'd that sin in *Bethel* and in *Dan*,
Lik'ning his Maker to the Grazed Ox,[7]
Jehovah, who in one Night when he pass'd
From *Egypt* marching, equall'd with one stroke
Both her first born and all her bleating Gods.[8]

9. When the Philistines put the ark of the Lord, which they had captured, into the temple of Dagon, "on the morrow morning, behold, Dagon was fallen upon his face to the ground . . . and the head of Dagon and both the palms of his hands were cut off upon the threshold" (1 Samuel 5.4).

1. Divine vengeance on these Philistine cities is prophesied in Zephaniah 2.4.

2. When Elisha told Naaman that his leprosy would be cured if he washed in the Jordan, the Syrian was at first angry (2 Kings 5.12: "Are not Abana and Pharpar, rivers of Damascus, better than all the waters of Israel?") but then humbled himself and was cured.

3. After engineering the overthrow of Damascus by the Assyrians, the sottish (foolish) King Ahaz became interested in the cult of Rimmon and had an altar of the Syrian type put in the temple of the Lord (2 Kings 16.9–17).

4. Milton alludes to the myth of the Olympian gods fleeing from the Giant Typhoeus into Egypt and hiding in bestial forms (Ovid, *Metamorphoses* 5.319–31) afterward worshipped by the Egyptians.

5. Perhaps the most familiar of all Israelite apostasies was their worship of "a calf in Horeb" (Psalms 106.19) made by Aaron while Moses was away receiving the tables of the Law (Exodus 32).

6. Jeroboam, who led the revolt of the ten tribes of Israel against Rehoboam, Solomon's successor; he "doubled" Aaron's sin, since he made "two calves of gold," placing one in Bethel and the other in Dan (1 Kings 12.28–9).

7. "Thus they changed their glory into the similitude of an ox that eateth grass" (Psalms 106.20).

8. At the passover, Jehovah smote all the Egyptian firstborn, "both man and beast" (Exodus 12.12); presumably, this stroke would extend to their sacred animals.

Belial came last,[9] than whom a Spirit more lewd
Fell not from Heaven, or more gross to love
Vice for itself: To him no Temple stood
Or Altar smok'd; yet who more oft than hee
In Temples and at Altars, when the Priest
Turns Atheist, as did *Ely's* Sons, who fill'd
With lust and violence the house of God.[1]
In Courts and Palaces he also Reigns
And in luxurious Cities, where the noise
Of riot ascends above thir loftiest Tow'rs,
And injury and outrage: And when Night
Darkens the Streets, then wander forth the Sons
Of *Belial*, flown° with insolence and wine.[2] *swollen*
Witness the Streets of *Sodom*, and that night
In *Gibeah*, when the hospitable door
Expos'd a Matron to avoid worse rape.[3]
These were the prime in order and in might;
The rest were long to tell, though far renown'd,
Th' *Ionian* Gods,[4] of *Javan's* Issue held
Gods, yet confest later than Heav'n and Earth
Thir boasted Parents; *Titan* Heav'n's first born
With his enormous° brood, and birthright seiz'd *monstrous*
By younger *Saturn*, he from mightier *Jove*
His own and *Rhea's* Son like measure found;
So *Jove* usurping reign'd: these first in *Crete*
And *Ida* known,[5] thence on the Snowy top
Of cold *Olympus* rul'd the middle Air
Thir highest Heav'n; or on the *Delphian* Cliff,[6]
Or in *Dodona*, and through all the bounds
Of *Doric* Land;° or who with *Saturn* old *Greece*
Fled over *Adria* to th' *Hesperian* Fields,
And o'er the *Celtic* roam'd the utmost Isles.[7]
All these and more came flocking; but with looks
Downcast and damp,° yet such wherein appear'd *depressed*
Obscure some glimpse of joy, to have found thir chief
Not in despair, to have found themselves not lost
In loss itself; which on his count'nance cast
Like doubtful hue: but he his wonted pride
Soon recollecting,° with high words, that bore *recovering*
Semblance of worth, not substance, gently rais'd
Thir fainting courage, and dispell'd thir fears.

9. Belial comes last, both because he had no local cult and because in the poem he is "timorous and slothful" (2.117). Properly, "Belial" is an abstract noun meaning "iniquity."

1. The impiety and fornication of Ely's sons are described in 1 Samuel 2.12–24.

2. The Puritans referred to their enemies as the Sons of Belial.

3. See Genesis 19 and Judges 19.

4. The Ionian Greeks were held by some to be the issue of Javan the son of Japhet the son of Noah, on the basis of the Septuagint version of Genesis 10.

5. Jove was born and secretly reared on Mount Ida, in Crete.

6. Delphi was famed as the site of the Pythian oracle of Apollo, but cults of Ge, Poseidon, and Artemis were also celebrated there.

7. After Saturn's downfall he fled across the Adriatic Sea (Adria) to Italy (Hesperian Fields), France (the Celtic), and the British Isles (Utmost Isles).

Then straight commands that at the warlike sound
Of Trumpets loud and Clarions° be uprear'd *shrill trumpets*
His mighty Standard; that proud honor claim'd
Azazel as his right, a Cherub tall:[8]
Who forthwith from the glittering Staff unfurl'd
Th' Imperial Ensign, which full high advanc't
Shone like a Meteor streaming to the Wind
With Gems and Golden lustre rich imblaz'd,[9]
Seraphic arms and Trophies: all the while
Sonorous metal blowing Martial sounds:
At which the universal Host upsent
A shout that tore Hell's Concave,° and beyond *vault*
Frighted the Reign of *Chaos* and old Night.[1]
All in a moment through the gloom were seen
Ten thousand Banners rise into the Air
With Orient° Colors waving: with them rose *brilliant*
A Forest huge of Spears: and thronging Helms
Appear'd, and serried° Shields in thick array *locked together*
Of depth immeasurable: Anon they move
In perfect *Phalanx*[2] to the *Dorian*° mood *solemn*
Of Flutes and soft Recorders; such as rais'd
To highth of noblest temper Heroes old
Arming to Battle, and instead of rage
Deliberate valor breath'd, firm and unmov'd
With dread of death to flight or foul retreat,
Nor wanting power to mitigate and swage° *assuage*
With solemn touches, troubl'd thoughts, and chase
Anguish and doubt and fear and sorrow and pain
From mortal or immortal minds. Thus they
Breathing united force with fixed thought
Mov'd on in silence to soft Pipes that charm'd
Thir painful steps o'er the burnt soil; and now
Advanc't in view they stand, a horrid° Front *bristling*
Of dreadful length and dazzling Arms, in guise
Of Warriors old with order'd Spear and Shield,
Awaiting what command thir mighty Chief
Had to impose: He through the armed Files
Darts his experienc't eye, and soon traverse° *across*
The whole Battalion views, thir order due,
Thir visages and stature as of Gods;
Thir number last he sums. And now his heart
Distends with pride, and hard'ning in his strength
Glories: For never since created man,[3]
Met such imbodied° force, as nam'd with these *united*
Could merit more than that small infantry

8. Azazel was one of the chief fallen angels who are the object of God's wrath in the apocryphal apocalypse The Book of Enoch. For the healing of the earth he is bound and cast into the same wilderness where the scapegoat was led (Enoch 10.4–8).

9. Adorned with heraldic devices.

1. Chaos and Night, rulers of the region of unformed matter between Heaven and Hell.

2. A square battle formation.

3. Since humanity was created.

Warr'd on by Cranes:[4] though all the Giant brood
Of *Phlegra* with th' Heroic Race were join'd
That fought at *Thebes* and *Ilium*, on each side
Mixt with auxiliar Gods;[5] and what resounds
In Fable or *Romance* of *Uther's* Son° *King Arthur*
Begirt with *British* and *Armoric*[6] Knights;
And all who since, Baptiz'd or Infidel
Jousted in *Aspramont* or *Montalban*,
Damasco, or *Marocco*, or *Trebisond*,
Or whom *Biserta* sent from *Afric* shore
When *Charlemain* with all his Peerage fell
By *Fontarabbia*.[7] Thus far these beyond
Compare of mortal prowess, yet observ'd° *obeyed*
Thir dread commander: he above the rest
In shape and gesture proudly eminent
Stood like a Tow'r; his form had yet not lost
All her Original brightness, nor appear'd
Less than Arch-Angel ruin'd, and th' excess
Of Glory obscur'd: As when the Sun new ris'n
Looks through the Horizontal misty Air
Shorn of his Beams, or from behind the Moon
In dim Eclipse disastrous twilight sheds
On half the Nations, and with fear of change
Perplexes Monarchs.[8] Dark'n'd so, yet shone
Above them all th' Arch-Angel: but his face
Deep scars of Thunder had intrencht, and care
Sat on his faded cheek, but under Brows
Of dauntless courage, and considerate° Pride *deliberate*
Waiting revenge: cruel his eye, but cast
Signs of remorse and passion to behold
The fellows of his crime, the followers rather
(Far other once beheld in bliss) condemn'd
For ever now to have thir lot in pain,
Millions of Spirits for his fault amerc't° *deprived*
Of Heav'n, and from Eternal Splendors flung
For his revolt, yet faithful how they stood,
Thir Glory wither'd. As when Heaven's Fire
Hath scath'd the Forest Oaks, or Mountain Pines,
With singed top thir stately growth though bare
Stands on the blasted Heath. He now prepar'd
To speak; whereat thir doubl'd Ranks they bend

4. When compared with the Devil's, any army would seem no bigger than pygmies ("that small infantry"), who were portrayed by Pliny as tiny men who fought with canes.

5. To amplify the heroic stature of the angels, Milton mentions a series of armies that had been thought worthy of epic treatment only to dismiss them. The Giants, who fought with the Olympians at Phlegra, join with the heroes of Thebes and Troy (Ilium).

6. From Brittany.

7. Aspramont was a castle near Nice, and Montalban was the castle of Rinaldo; these castles figure in Ariosto's *Orlando Furioso* and the romances concerned with chivalric wars between Christians and Saracens. Milton would know late versions of the Charlemagne legend. Charlemagne's whole rearguard, led by Roland, one of the 12 peers or paladins, was massacred at Roncesvalles, about 40 miles from Fontarabbia (Fuenterrabia).

8. The comparison is ironically double-edged, for the ominous solar eclipse presages not only disaster for creation but also the doom of the godlike ruler for whom the sun was a traditional symbol.

From wing to wing, and half enclose him round
With all his Peers: attention held them mute.
Thrice he assay'd, and thrice in spite of scorn,
Tears such as Angels weep, burst forth: at last
Words interwove with sighs found out thir way.
  O Myriads of immortal Spirits, O Powers
Matchless, but with th' Almighty, and that strife
Was not inglorious, though th' event° was dire, *result*
As this place testifies, and this dire change
Hateful to utter: but what power of mind
Foreseeing or presaging, from the Depth
Of knowledge past or present, could have fear'd
How such united force of Gods, how such
As stood like these, could ever know repulse?
For who can yet believe, though after loss,
That all these puissant° Legions, whose exíle *powerful*
Hath emptied Heav'n, shall fail to re-ascend
Self-rais'd, and repossess thir native seat?
For mee be witness all the Host of Heav'n,
If counsels different, or danger shunn'd
By me, have lost our hopes. But he who reigns
Monarch in Heav'n, till then as one secure
Sat on his Throne, upheld by old repute,
Consent or custom, and his Regal State
Put forth at full, but still his strength conceal'd,
Which tempted our attempt, and wrought our fall.
Henceforth his might we know, and know our own
So as not either to provoke, or dread
New War, provok't; our better part remains
To work in close° design, by fraud or guile *secret*
What force effected not: that he no less
At length from us may find, who overcomes
By force, hath overcome but half his foe.
Space may produce new Worlds; whereof so rife° *common*
There went a fame° in Heav'n that he ere long *rumor*
Intended to create, and therein plant
A generation, whom his choice regard
Should favor equal to the Sons of Heaven:
Thither, if but to pry, shall be perhaps
Our first eruption, thither or elsewhere:
For this Infernal Pit shall never hold
Celestial Spirits in Bondage, nor th' Abyss
Long under darkness cover. But these thoughts
Full Counsel must mature: Peace is despair'd,
For who can think Submission? War then, War
Open or understood, must be resolv'd.
  He spake: and to confirm his words, out-flew
Millions of flaming swords, drawn from the thighs
Of mighty Cherubim; the sudden blaze
Far round illumin'd hell: highly they rag'd

Against the Highest, and fierce with grasped Arms
Clash'd on thir sounding shields the din of war,
Hurling defiance toward the Vault of Heav'n.
There stood a Hill not far whose grisly top
Belch'd fire and rolling smoke; the rest entire
Shone with a glossy scurf, undoubted sign
That in his womb was hid metallic Ore,
The work of Sulphur.[9] Thither wing'd with speed
A numerous Brígad° hasten'd. As when bands *brigade*
Of Píoners° with Spade and Pickax arm'd *engineers*
Forerun the Royal Camp, to trench a Field,
Or cast a Rampart. *Mammon*[1] led them on,
Mammon, the least erected° Spirit that fell *elevated*
From Heav'n, for ev'n in Heav'n his looks and thoughts
Were always downward bent, admiring more
The riches of Heav'n's pavement, trodd'n Gold,
Than aught divine or holy else enjoy'd
In vision beatific: by him first
Men also, and by his suggestion taught,
Ransack'd the Center, and with impious hands
Rifl'd the bowels of thir mother Earth
For Treasures better hid. Soon had his crew
Op'n'd into the Hill a spacious wound
And digg'd out ribs of Gold. Let none admire° *wonder*
That riches grow in Hell; that soil may best
Deserve the precious bane. And here let those
Who boast in mortal things, and wond'ring tell
Of *Babel,* and the works of *Memphian* Kings,[2]
Learn how thir greatest Monuments of Fame,
And Strength and Art are easily outdone
By Spirits reprobate, and in an hour
What in an age they with incessant toil
And hands innumerable scarce perform.
Nigh on the Plain in many cells prepar'd,
That underneath had veins of liquid fire
Sluic'd° from the Lake, a second multitude *led by channels*
With wondrous Art founded the massy Ore,
Severing each kind, and scumm'd the Bullion dross:
A third as soon had form'd within the ground
A various mould, and from the boiling cells
By strange conveyance fill'd each hollow nook:
As in an Organ from one blast of wind
To many a row of Pipes the sound-board breathes.
Anon out of the earth a Fabric huge

9. The traditional physiognomy of the fiend is in Milton's hell displaced onto the landscape. It is a dead or corrupt body imaged as scurf (i.e., scales, crust), belching, ransacked womb, bowels, entrails, and ribs.

1. In Matthew 6.24 and Luke 16.13, "Mammon" is an abstract noun meaning wealth, but later it was used as the name of "the prince of this world" (John 12.31). Medieval and Renaissance tradition often associated Mammon with Plutus, the Greek god of riches.

2. The Tower of Babel was built by the ambitious Nimrod. The works of Memphian kings, the Pyramids, were regarded as memorials of vanity.

Rose like an Exhalation,[3] with the sound
Of Dulcet Symphonies and voices sweet,
Built like a Temple, where *Pilasters*° round *columns*
Were set, and Doric pillars overlaid
With Golden Architrave; nor did there want
Cornice or Frieze, with bossy° Sculptures grav'n; *embossed*
The Roof was fretted° Gold. Not *Babylon*,[4] *patterned*
Nor great *Alcairo* such magnificence
Equall'd in all thir glories,[5] to inshrine
Belus[6] or *Serapis*[7] thir Gods, or seat
Thir Kings, when *Egypt* with *Assyria* strove
In wealth and luxury. Th' ascending pile
Stood fixt her stately highth, and straight the doors
Op'ning thir brazen folds discover wide
Within, her ample spaces, o'er the smooth
And level pavement: from the arched roof
Pendant by subtle Magic many a row
Of Starry Lamps and blazing Cressets[8] fed
With *Naphtha* and *Asphaltus*[9] yielded light
As from a sky. The hasty multitude
Admiring enter'd, and the work some praise
And some the Architect: his hand was known
In Heav'n by many a Tow'red structure high,
Where Scepter'd Angels held thir residence,
And sat as Princes, whom the supreme King
Exalted to such power, and gave to rule,
Each in his Hierarchy, the Orders bright.
Nor was his name unheard or unador'd
In ancient *Greece*; and in *Ausonian* land
Men call'd him *Mulciber*;[1] and how he fell
From Heav'n, they fabl'd, thrown by angry *Jove*
Sheer o'er the Crystal Battlements: from Morn
To Noon he fell, from Noon to dewy Eve,
A Summer's day; and with the setting Sun
Dropt from the Zenith like a falling Star,
On *Lemnos* th' *Aegean* Isle:[2] thus they relate,
Erring; for he with this rebellious rout

3. Pandaemonium rises to music, since in the Renaissance it was believed that musical proportions governed the forms of architecture.

4. An ironic allusion to Ovid's description of the Palace of the Sun built by Mulciber (*Metamorphoses* 2. 1–4). Pandaemonium has a classical design, complete in every respect, like that of the ancient (but still surviving) gilt-roofed Pantheon, the most admired building of Milton's time. Doric is the oldest and simplest order of Greek architecture.

5. In traditional biblical exegesis, Babylon, a place of proud iniquity, was often a figure of Antichrist or of hell. Memphis (modern Cairo) was the most splendid city of heathen Egypt.

6. Bel, the Babylonian Baal; see lines 421–423n and Jeremiah 51.44: "I will punish Bel in Babylon."

7. An Egyptian deity.

8. Basketlike lamps.

9. *Naphtha* is an oily constituent of asphalt (asphaltus).

1. The Greek god Hephaistos, in Latin *Mulciber* or Vulcan, presided over all arts, such as metal-working, that required the use of fire. He built all the palaces of the gods. "Ausonian land" is the old Greek name for Italy. Milton emulates Homer's description of the daylong fall of Hephaistos (*Iliad* 1.591–95) and then deflates it in the casual but commanding dismissal of 2.746–48.

2. In Homer (*Iliad* 2.87–90) the Achaians going to a council are compared to bees, as are the Carthaginians; in Virgil (*Aeneid* 1.430–436). Milton also glances at Virgil's mock-epic account of the ideal social organization of the hive (*Georgics* 4.149–227).

Fell long before; nor aught avail'd him now
To have built in Heav'n high Tow'rs; nor did he scape
By all his Engines, but was headlong sent
With his industrious crew to build in hell.
Meanwhile the winged Heralds by command
Of Sovran power, with awful Ceremony
And Trumpets' sound throughout the Host proclaim
A solemn Council forthwith to be held
At *Pandaemonium*, the high Capitol
Of Satan and his Peers: thir summons call'd
From every Band and squared Regiment
By place or choice the worthiest; they anon
With hunderds and with thousands trooping came
Attended: all access was throng'd, the Gates
And Porches wide, but chief the spacious Hall
(Though like a cover'd field, where Champions bold
Wont ride in arm'd, and at the Soldan's° chair *Sultan's*
Defi'd the best of *Paynim*° chivalry *pagan*
To mortal combat or career with Lance)
Thick swarm'd, both on the ground and in the air,
Brusht with the hiss of rustling wings. As Bees
In spring time, when the Sun with *Taurus*[3] rides,
Pour forth thir populous youth about the Hive
In clusters; they among fresh dews and flowers
Fly to and fro, or on the smoothed Plank,
The suburb of thir Straw-built Citadel,
New rubb'd with Balm, expatiate° and confer *debate*
Thir State affairs. So thick the aery crowd
Swarm'd and were strait'n'd; till the Signal giv'n,
Behold a wonder! they but now who seem'd
In bigness to surpass Earth's Giant Sons
Now less than smallest Dwarfs, in narrow room
Throng numberless, like that Pigmean Race
Beyond the *Indian* Mount, or Faery Elves,
Whose midnight Revels, by a Forest side
Or Fountain some belated Peasant sees,
Or dreams he sees, while over-head the Moon
Sits Arbitress, and nearer to the Earth
Wheels her pale course;[4] they on thir mirth and dance
Intent, with jocund Music charm his ear;
At once with joy and fear his heart rebounds.
Thus incorporeal Spirits to smallest forms
Reduc'd thir shapes immense, and were at large,
Though without number still amidst the Hall
Of that infernal Court. But far within
And in thir own dimensions like themselves

3. In Milton's time the sun entered the second sign of the zodiac in mid-April, according to the Julian calendar.
4. Echoing *A Midsummer Night's Dream* 2.1.28f and 141. "The moon / Sits arbitress" because the moon-goddess was queen of faery.

The great Seraphic Lords and Cherubim
In close° recess and secret conclave[5] sat *secret*
A thousand Demi-Gods on golden seats,
Frequent° and full. After short silence then *crowded*
And summons read, the great consult began.

The End of the First Book.

Book 2

The Argument

The Consultation begun, Satan *debates whether another Battle be to be hazarded for the recovery of Heaven: some advise it, others dissuade: A third proposal is preferr'd, mention'd before by* Satan, *to search the truth of that Prophecy or Tradition in Heaven concerning another world, and another kind of creature equal or not much inferior to themselves, about this time to be created: Thir doubt who shall be sent on this difficult search:* Satan *thir chief undertakes alone the voyage, is honor'd and applauded. The Council thus ended, the rest betake them several ways and to several employments, as thir inclinations lead them, to entertain the time till* Satan *return. He passes on his Journey to Hell Gates, finds them shut, and who sat there to guard them, by whom at length they are op'n'd, and discover*[1] *to him the great Gulf between Hell and Heaven; with what difficulty he passes through, directed by* Chaos, *the Power of that place, to the sight of this new World which he sought.*

High on a Throne of Royal State,[2] which far
Outshone the wealth of *Ormus* and of *Ind*,[3]
Or where the gorgeous East with richest hand
Show'rs on her Kings *Barbaric* Pearl and Gold,
Satan exalted sat, by merit rais'd
To that bad eminence; and from despair
Thus high uplifted beyond hope, aspires
Beyond thus high, insatiate to pursue
Vain War with Heav'n, and by success° untaught *result*
His proud imaginations thus display'd.
Powers and Dominions,[4] Deities of Heav'n,
For since no deep within her gulf can hold
Immortal vigor, though opprest and fall'n,
I give not Heav'n for lost. From this descent
Celestial Virtues rising, will appear
More glorious and more dread than from no fall
And trust themselves to fear no second fate:
Mee though just right and the fixt Laws of Heav'n
Did first create your Leader, next, free choice,
With what besides, in Counsel or in Fight,
Hath been achiev'd of merit, yet this loss

5. "Conclave" could refer to any assembly in secret session but already had the specifically ecclesiastical meaning on which Milton's satire here depends.
1. Disclose.
2. Compare Spenser's description of the bright throne of the Phaethonlike Lucifera, embodiment of pride in *The Faerie Queene* 1.4.8, page 778.
3. India. Ormus, an island town in the Persian Gulf, was famous as a jewel market.
4. Two angelic orders mentioned by St. Paul in Colossians 1.16.

Thus far at least recover'd, hath much more
Establisht in a safe unenvied Throne
Yielded with full consent. The happier state
In Heav'n, which follows dignity, might draw
Envy from each inferior; but who here
Will envy whom the highest place exposes
Foremost to stand against the Thunderer's aim[5]
Your bulwark, and condemns to greatest share
Of endless pain? where there is then no good
For which to strive, no strife can grow up there
From Faction; for none sure will claim in Hell
Precedence, none, whose portion is so small
Of present pain, that with ambitious mind
Will covet more. With this advantage then
To union, and firm Faith, and firm accord,
More than can be in Heav'n, we now return
To claim our just inheritance of old,
Surer to prosper than prosperity
Could have assur'd us; and by what best way,
Whether of open War or covert guile,
We now debate; who can advise, may speak.
He ceas'd, and next him *Moloch*, Scepter'd King
Stood up, the strongest and the fiercest Spirit
That fought in Heav'n; now fiercer by despair:
His trust was with th' Eternal to be deem'd
Equal in strength, and rather than be less
Car'd not to be at all; with that care lost
Went all his fear: of God, or Hell, or worse
He reck'd° not, and these words thereafter spake. *cared*
My sentence° is for open War: Of Wiles, *opinion*
More unexpert,° I boast not: them let those *inexperienced*
Contrive who need, or when they need, not now.
For while they sit contriving, shall the rest,
Millions that stand in Arms, and longing wait
The Signal to ascend, sit ling'ring here
Heav'n's fugitives, and for thir dwelling place
Accept this dark opprobrious Den of shame,
The Prison of his Tyranny who Reigns
By our delay? no, let us rather choose
Arm'd with Hell flames and fury[6] all at once
O'er Heav'n's high Tow'rs to force resistless way,
Turning our Tortures into horrid Arms
Against the Torturer; when to meet the noise
Of his Almighty Engine[7] he shall hear
Infernal Thunder, and for Lightning see
Black fire and horror shot with equal rage
Among his Angels; and his Throne itself

5. By identifying him with thunder, the attribute of Jupiter, Satan reduces God to a mere Olympian tyrant.
6. The violent yoking of concrete and abstract words is one of the most characteristic figures of Milton's style.
7. Machine of war, probably here referring to the Messiah's chariot or perhaps to his thunder.

Mixt with *Tartarean* Sulphur, and strange fire,[8]
His own invented Torments. But perhaps
The way seems difficult and steep to scale
With upright wing against a higher foe.
Let such bethink them, if the sleepy drench[9]
Of that forgetful Lake benumb not still,
That in our proper motion we ascend
Up to our native seat: descent and fall
To us is adverse. Who but felt of late
When the fierce Foe hung on our brok'n Rear
Insulting,° and pursu'd us through the Deep, *assaulting, exulting*
With what compulsion and laborious flight
We sunk thus low? Th' ascent is easy then;
Th' event° is fear'd; should we again provoke *outcome*
Our stronger, some worse way his wrath may find
To our destruction: if there be in Hell
Fear to be worse destroy'd: what can be worse
Than to dwell here, driv'n out from bliss, condemn'd
In this abhorred deep to utter woe;
Where pain of unextinguishable fire
Must exercise° us without hope of end *afflict*
The Vassals[1] of his anger, when the Scourge
Inexorably, and the torturing hour
Calls us to Penance? More destroy'd than thus
We should be quite abolisht and expire.
What fear we then? what doubt we to incense
His utmost ire? which to the highth enrag'd,
Will either quite consume us, and reduce
To nothing this essential,° happier far *essence*
Than miserable to have eternal being:
Or if our substance be indeed Divine,
And cannot cease to be, we are at worst
On this side nothing;[2] and by proof we feel
Our power sufficient to disturb his Heav'n,
And with perpetual inroads to Alarm,
Though inaccessible, his fatal Throne:
Which if not Victory is yet Revenge.
  He ended frowning, and his look denounc'd
Desperate revenge, and Battle dangerous
To less than Gods. On th' other side up rose
Belial, in act more graceful and humane;
A fairer person lost not Heav'n; he seem'd
For dignity compos'd and high exploit:
But all was false and hollow; though his Tongue
Dropt Manna, and could make the worse appear

8. In the classical underworld, Tartarus was the place of the guilty. For "strange fire" see Leviticus 10.1–2: "Nadab and Abihu, the sons of Aaron . . . offered strange fire before the Lord, which he commanded them not. And there went out fire from the Lord, and devoured them."
9. A draught of medicine for an animal.
1. Servants, slaves. Also an allusion to Romans 9.22: "What if God, willing to show his wrath, and to make his power known, endured with much longsuffering the vessels of wrath fitted to destruction . . . ?"
2. Already we are in the worst condition possible, short of being nothing, being annihilated.

The better reason,[3] to perplex and dash
Maturest Counsels: for his thoughts were low;
To vice industrious, but to Nobler deeds
Timorous and slothful: yet he pleas'd the ear,
And with persuasive accent thus began.
  I should be much for open War, O Peers,
As not behind in hate; if what was urg'd
Main reason to persuade immediate War,
Did not dissuade me most, and seem to cast
Ominous conjecture on the whole success:
When he who most excels in fact° of Arms, *feat*
In what he counsels and in what excels
Mistrustful, grounds his courage on despair
And utter dissolution, as the scope
Of all his aim, after some dire revenge.
First, what Revenge? the Tow'rs of Heav'n are fill'd
With Armed watch, that render all access
Impregnable; oft on the bordering Deep
Encamp thir Legions, or with obscure[4] wing
Scout far and wide into the Realm of night,
Scorning surprise. Or could we break our way
By force, and at our heels all Hell should rise
With blackest Insurrection, to confound
Heav'n's purest Light, yet our great Enemy
All incorruptible would on his Throne
Sit unpolluted, and th' Ethereal mould
Incapable of stain would soon expel
Her mischief, and purge off the baser fire
Victorious.[5] Thus repuls'd, our final hope
Is flat° despair: we must exasperate *absolute*
Th' Almighty Victor to spend all his rage,
And that must end us, that must be our cure,
To be no more; sad cure; for who would lose,
Though full of pain, this intellectual being,
Those thoughts that wander through Eternity,
To perish rather, swallow'd up and lost
In the wide womb of uncreated night,
Devoid of sense and motion? and who knows,
Let this be good,[6] whether our angry Foe
Can give it, or will ever? how he can
Is doubtful; that he never will is sure.
Will he, so wise, let loose at once his ire,
Belike° through impotence, or unaware, *no doubt*
To give his Enemies thir wish, and end
Them in his anger, whom his anger saves
To punish endless? wherefore cease we then?

3. This was the claim of the Greek Sophists, who taught their students how to use rhetoric to win an argument.
4. "Obscure" is stressed on the first syllable here.
5. Criticizing Moloch's proposal to mix God's throne with sulphur (lines 68–9) and shoot "black fire" among his angels. This "baser fire" Belial contrasts with the "ethereal" (derived from ether, the fifth and purest element) fire of the throne.
6. Suppose it is good to be destroyed.

Say they who counsel War, we are decreed,
Reserv'd and destin'd to Eternal woe;
Whatever doing, what can we suffer more,
What can we suffer worse? is this then worst,
Thus sitting, thus consulting, thus in Arms?
What when we fled amain,° pursu'd and strook° *headlong/struck*
With Heav'n's afflicting Thunder, and besought
The Deep to shelter us? this Hell then seem'd
A refuge from those wounds: or when we lay
Chain'd on the burning Lake? that sure was worse.
What if the breath that kindl'd those grim fires
Awak'd should blow them into sevenfold rage
And plunge us in the flames? or from above
Should intermitted vengeance arm again
His red right hand to plague us? what if all
Her° stores were op'n'd, and this Firmament *Hell's*
Of Hell should spout her Cataracts of Fire,
Impendent° horrors, threat'ning hideous fall *threatening*
One day upon our heads; while we perhaps
Designing or exhorting glorious war,
Caught in a fiery Tempest shall be hurl'd
Each on his rock transfixt, the sport and prey
Of racking whirlwinds, or for ever sunk
Under yon boiling Ocean, wrapt in Chains;
There to converse with everlasting groans,
Unrespited, unpitied, unrepriev'd,
Ages of hopeless end; this would be worse.
War therefore, open or conceal'd, alike
My voice dissuades; for what can force or guile
With him, or who deceive his mind, whose eye
Views all things at one view? he from Heav'n's highth
All these our motions° vain, sees and derides; *schemes*
Not more Almighty to resist our might
Than wise to frustrate all our plots and wiles.
Shall we then live thus vile, the race of Heav'n
Thus trampl'd, thus expell'd to suffer here
Chains and these Torments? better these than worse
By my advice; since fate inevitable
Subdues us, and Omnipotent Decree,
The Victor's will. To suffer, as to do,
Our strength is equal, nor the Law unjust
That so ordains: this was at first resolv'd,
If we were wise, against so great a foe
Contending, and so doubtful what might fall.
I laugh, when those who at the Spear are bold
And vent'rous, if that fail them, shrink and fear
What yet they know must follow, to endure
Exile, or ignominy, or bonds, or pain,
The sentence of thir Conqueror: This is now
Our doom; which if we can sustain and bear,
Our Supreme Foe in time may much remit

His anger, and perhaps thus far remov'd
Not mind us not offending, satisfi'd
With what is punisht; whence these raging fires
Will slack'n, if his breath stir not thir flames.
Our purer essence then will overcome
Thir noxious vapor, or enur'd° not feel, *accustomed*
Or chang'd at length, and to the place conform'd
In temper[7] and in nature, will receive
Familiar the fierce heat, and void of pain;
This horror will grow mild, this darkness light,[8]
Besides what hope the never-ending flight
Of future days may bring, what chance, what change
Worth waiting, since our present lot appears
For happy though but ill, for ill not worst,[9]
If we procure not to ourselves more woe.
Thus *Belial* with words cloth'd in reason's garb
Counsell'd ignoble ease, and peaceful sloth,
Not peace: and after him thus *Mammon* spake.
Either to disinthrone the King of Heav'n
We war, if war be best, or to regain
Our own right lost: him to unthrone we then
May hope, when everlasting Fate shall yield
To fickle Chance, and *Chaos* judge the strife:
The former vain to hope argues as vain
The latter: for what place can be for us
Within Heav'n's bound, unless Heav'n's Lord supreme
We overpower? Suppose he should relent
And publish Grace to all, on promise made
Of new Subjection; with what eyes could we
Stand in his presence humble, and receive
Strict Laws impos'd, to celebrate his Throne
With warbl'd Hymns, and to his Godhead sing
Forc't Halleluiahs;[1] while he Lordly sits
Our envied Sovran, and his Altar breathes
Ambrosial[2] Odors and Ambrosial Flowers,
Our servile offerings. This must be our task
In Heav'n, this our delight; how wearisome
Eternity so spent in worship paid
To whom we hate. Let us not then pursue
By force impossible, by leave obtain'd
Unácceptable, though in Heav'n, our state
Of splendid vassalage, but rather seek
Our own good from ourselves, and from our own
Live to ourselves, though in this vast recess,
Free, and to none accountable, preferring

7. Temperament, the mixture or adjustment of humors. Thus the phrase means "adjusted psychologically and physically to the new environment."

8. Easy to bear, and illumination.

9. Though as far as happiness is concerned, the devils are but ill off, as far as evil is concerned, they could be worse.

1. The word "hallelujah" (Hebrew, "praise Jehovah") occurred in so many psalms that it came to mean a song of praise to God.

2. Fragrant and perfumed, immortal. Ambrosia was the fabled food or drink of the gods.

Hard liberty before the easy yoke
Of servile Pomp.[3] Our greatness will appear
Then most conspicuous, when great things of small,
Useful of hurtful, prosperous of adverse
We can create, and in what place soe'er
Thrive under evil, and work ease out of pain
Through labor and endurance. This deep world
Of darkness do we dread? How oft amidst
Thick clouds and dark doth Heav'n's all-ruling Sire
Choose to reside, his Glory unobscur'd,
And with the Majesty of darkness round
Covers his Throne; from whence deep thunders roar
Must'ring thir rage, and Heav'n resembles Hell?
As he our darkness, cannot we his Light
Imitate when we please? This Desert soil
Wants not her hidden lustre, Gems and Gold;
Nor want we skill or art, from whence to raise
Magnificence; and what can Heav'n show more?
Our torments also may in length of time
Become our Elements, these piercing Fires
As soft as now severe, our temper chang'd
Into their temper;[4] which must needs remove
The sensible of pain.[5] All things invite
To peaceful Counsels, and the settl'd State
Of order, how in safety best we may
Compose° our present evils, with regard *order*
Of what we are and where, dismissing quite
All thoughts of War; ye have what I advise.
He scarce had finisht, when such murmur fill'd
Th' Assembly, as when hollow Rocks retain
The sound of blust'ring winds, which all night long
Had rous'd the Sea, now with hoarse cadence lull
Sea-faring men o'erwatcht, whose Bark by chance
Or Pinnace anchors in a craggy Bay
After the Tempest: Such applause was heard
As *Mammon* ended, and his Sentence° pleas'd, *opinion*
Advising peace: for such another Field
They dreaded worse than Hell: so much the fear
Of Thunder and the Sword of *Michaël*[6]
Wrought still within them; and no less desire
To found this nether Empire, which might rise
By policy,[7] and long process of time,
In emulation opposite to Heav'n.

3. In *Samson Agonistes* 271, Samson condemns those who are fonder of "bondage with ease than strenuous liberty." The antithesis is from the Roman historian, Sallust, who assigns it to an opponent of the dictator Sulla. See also Jesus' words in Matthew 11.28–30: "Come unto me. . . . For my yoke is easy."

4. Milton alludes to an idea of St. Augustine's, that the devils are bound to tormenting fires as if to bodies (*City of God*, 21.10).

5. The part of pain apprehended through the senses.

6. In the war in Heaven, Michael's two-handed sword felled "squadrons at once" and wounded even Satan. "Michael" here has three syllables.

7. Statesmanship, often in a bad sense, implying Machiavellian strategems. "Process" is stressed on the second syllable.

Which when *Beëlzebub*[8] perceiv'd, than whom,
Satan except, none higher sat, with grave
Aspect he rose, and in his rising seem'd
A Pillar of State; deep on his Front° engraven *forehead*
Deliberation sat and public care;
And Princely counsel in his face yet shone,
Majestic though in ruin: sage he stood
With *Atlantean*[9] shoulders fit to bear
The weight of mightiest Monarchies; his look
Drew audience and attention still as Night
Or Summer's Noon-tide air, while thus he spake.
Thrones and Imperial Powers, off-spring of Heav'n,
Ethereal Virtues; or these Titles now
Must we renounce, and changing style be call'd
Princes of Hell? for so the popular vote
Inclines, here to continue, and build up here
A growing Empire; doubtless; while we dream,
And know not that the King of Heav'n hath doom'd
This place our dungeon, not our safe retreat
Beyond his Potent arm, to live exempt
From Heav'n's high jurisdiction, in new League
Banded against his Throne, but to remain
In strictest bondage, though thus far remov'd,
Under th' inevitable curb, reserv'd
His captive multitude: For he, be sure,
In highth or depth, still first and last will Reign
Sole King, and of his Kingdom lose no part
By our revolt, but over Hell extend
His Empire, and with Iron Sceptre rule
Us here, as with his Golden those in Heav'n.
What° sit we then projecting peace and war? *why*
War hath determin'd[1] us, and foil'd with loss
Irreparable; terms of peace yet none
Voutsaf't[2] or sought; for what peace will be giv'n
To us enslav'd, but custody severe,
And stripes, and arbitrary punishment
Inflicted? and what peace can we return,
But to our power[3] hostility and hate,
Untam'd reluctance,° and revenge though slow, *resistance*
Yet ever plotting how the Conqueror least
May reap his conquest, and may least rejoice
In doing what we most in suffering feel?[4]
Nor will occasion want, nor shall we need
With dangerous expedition to invade

8. Satan's closest associate.
9. Worthy of Atlas, who was forced by Jupiter to carry the heavens on his shoulders as a punishment for his part in the rebellion of the Titans.
1. Finished, but the context also activates a subsidiary meaning, "war has given us a settled aim."
2. "Vouchsafed": granted; Milton's spelling, "Voutsaf't," indicates the 17th-century pronunciation he preferred.
3. To the limit of our power.
4. How God may get the least happiness from our pain. Beelzebub portrays God as similar in his motives to the devils.

Heav'n, whose high walls fear no assault or Siege,
Or ambush from the Deep. What if we find
Some easier enterprise? There is a place
(If ancient and prophetic fame in Heav'n
Err not) another World, the happy seat
Of some new Race call'd *Man,* about this time
To be created like to us, though less
In power and excellence, but favor'd more
Of him who rules above;[5] so was his will
Pronounc'd among the Gods, and by an Oath,
That shook Heav'n's whole circumference, confirm'd.[6]
Thither let us bend all our thoughts, to learn
What creatures there inhabit, of what mould,
Or substance, how endu'd,° and what thir Power, *gifted*
And where thir weakness, how attempted° best, *attacked*
By force or subtlety: Though Heav'n be shut,
And Heav'n's high Arbitrator sit secure
In his own strength, this place may lie expos'd
The utmost border of his Kingdom, left
To their defense who hold it: here perhaps
Some advantageous act may be achiev'd
By sudden onset, either with Hell fire
To waste his whole Creation, or possess
All as our own, and drive as we were driven,
The puny° habitants, or if not drive, *weak*
Seduce them to our Party, that thir God
May prove thir foe, and with repenting hand
Abolish his own works. This would surpass
Common revenge, and interrupt his joy
In our Confusion, and our Joy upraise
In his disturbance; when his darling Sons
Hurl'd headlong to partake with us,[7] shall curse
Thir frail Original,° and faded bliss, *author*
Faded so soon. Advise if this be worth
Attempting, or to sit in darkness here
Hatching vain Empires. Thus *Beëlzebub*
Pleaded his devilish Counsel, first devis'd
By *Satan,* and in part propos'd: for whence,
But from the Author of all ill could Spring
So deep a malice, to confound the race
Of mankind in one root,[8] and Earth with Hell
To mingle and involve, done all to spite
The great Creator? But thir spite still serves
His glory to augment. The bold design
Pleas'd highly those infernal States,[9] and joy

5. The creation of humanity was the subject of a public oath by God, but the time of the creation was the subject of a rumor only ("it is not for you to know the times or season," Acts 1.7).
6. See Isaiah 13.12–3: "I will make a man more precious than fine gold. . . . Therefore I will shake the Heavens."
7. Share in our condition; also, take sides with us.
8. Adam, the root of the genealogical tree of man.
9. Estates of the realm, people of rank and authority.

Sparkl'd in all thir eyes; with full assent
They vote: whereat his speech he thus renews.
Well have ye judg'd, well ended long debate,
Synod[1] of Gods, and like to what ye are,
Great things resolv'd, which from the lowest deep
Will once more lift us up, in spite of Fate,
Nearer our ancient Seat; perhaps in view
Of those bright confines, whence with neighboring Arms
And opportune excursion we may chance
Re-enter Heav'n; or else in some mild Zone
Dwell not unvisited of Heav'n's fair Light
Secure, and at the bright'ning Orient beam
Purge off this gloom; the soft delicious Air,
To heal the scar of these corrosive Fires
Shall breathe her balm. But first whom shall we send
In search of this new world, whom shall we find
Sufficient? who shall tempt° with wand'ring feet *venture upon*
The dark unbottom'd infinite Abyss
And through the palpable obscure[2] find out
His uncouth° way, or spread his aery flight *unknown*
Upborne with indefatigable wings
Over the vast abrupt,[3] ere he arrive
The happy Isle; what strength, what art can then
Suffice, or what evasion bear him safe
Through the strict Senteries° and Stations thick *sentries*
Of Angels watching round? Here he had need
All circumspection, and wee now no less
Choice in our suffrage;[4] for on whom we send,
The weight of all and our last hope relies.
This said, he sat; and expectation held
His look suspense, awaiting who appear'd
To second, or oppose, or undertake
The perilous attempt; but all sat mute,
Pondering the danger with deep thoughts; and each
In other's count'nance read his own dismay
Astonisht: none among the choice and prime
Of those Heav'n-warring Champions could be found
So hardy as to proffer° or accept *offer*
Alone the dreadful voyage; till at last
Satan, whom now transcendent glory rais'd
Above his fellows, with Monarchal pride
Conscious of highest worth, unmov'd thus spake.
O Progeny of Heav'n, Empyreal Thrones,
With reason hath deep silence and demur° *delay*
Seiz'd us, though undismay'd: long is the way
And hard, that out of Hell leads up to light;

1. A meeting of councillors.
2. See Exodus 10.21: "The Lord said unto Moses, Stretch out thine hand toward heaven, that there may be darkness over the land of Egypt, even darkness which may be felt."
3. The adjective (precipitous, broken off) is here used as a noun and refers to the abyss between hell and heaven.
4. Care in our vote (to elect him).

Our prison strong, this huge convex° of Fire, *vault*
Outrageous to devour, immures us round
Ninefold, and gates of burning Adamant
Barr'd over us prohibit all egress.
These past, if any pass, the void profound
Of unessential° Night receives him next *empty*
Wide gaping, and with utter loss of being
Threatens him, plung'd in that abortive gulf.
If thence he scape into whatever world,
Or unknown Region, what remains him less
Than[5] unknown dangers and as hard escape.
But I should ill become this Throne, O Peers,
And this Imperial Sov'ranty, adorn'd
With splendor, arm'd with power, if aught propos'd
And judg'd of public moment, in the shape
Of difficulty or danger could deter
Mee from attempting. Wherefore do I assume
These Royalties, and not refuse to Reign,
Refusing[6] to accept as great a share
Of hazard as of honor, due alike
To him who Reigns, and so much to him due
Of hazard more, as he above the rest
High honor'd sits? Go therefore mighty Powers.
Terror of Heav'n, though fall'n; intend° at home, *consider*
While here shall be our home, what best may ease
The present misery, and render Hell
More tolerable; if there be cure or charm
To respite° or deceive, or slack the pain *rest*
Of this ill Mansion: intermit no watch
Against a wakeful Foe, while I abroad
Through all the Coasts of dark destruction seek
Deliverance for us all: this enterprise
None shall partake with me. Thus saying rose
The Monarch, and prevented all reply,
Prudent, lest from his resolution rais'd° *encouraged*
Others among the chief might offer now
(Certain to be refus'd) what erst they fear'd;
And so refus'd might in opinion stand
His Rivals, winning cheap the high repute
Which he through hazard huge must earn. But they
Dreaded not more th' adventure than his voice
Forbidding; and at once with him they rose;
Thir rising all at once was as the sound
Of Thunder heard remote. Towards him they bend
With awful° reverence prone; and as a God *respectful*
Extol him equal to the highest in Heav'n:
Nor fail'd they to express how much they prais'd,
That for the general safety he despis'd
His own: for neither do the Spirits damn'd

5. What awaits him except.

6. If I refuse.

Lose all thir virtue; lest bad men should boast[7]
Thir specious° deeds on earth, which glory excites, *pretending*
Or close° ambition varnisht o'er with zeal. *secret*
Thus they thir doubtful consultations dark
Ended rejoicing in their matchless Chief:
As when from mountain tops the dusky clouds
Ascending, while the North wind sleeps, o'erspread
Heav'n's cheerful face, the low'ring Element
Scowls o'er the dark'n'd lantskip° Snow, or show'r; *landscape*
If chance the radiant Sun with farewell sweet
Extend his ev'ning beam, the fields revive,
The birds thir notes renew, and bleating herds
Attest thir joy, that hill and valley rings.
O shame to men! Devil with Devil damn'd
Firm concord holds, men only disagree
Of Creatures rational, though under hope
Of heavenly Grace; and God proclaiming peace,
Yet live in hatred, enmity, and strife
Among themselves, and levy cruel wars,
Wasting the Earth, each other to destroy:
As if (which might induce us to accord)
Man had not hellish foes anow° besides, *enough*
That day and night for his destruction wait.
    The *Stygian* Council thus dissolv'd; and forth
In order came the grand infernal Peers:
Midst came thir mighty Paramount,° and seem'd *ruler*
Alone th' Antagonist of Heav'n, nor less
Than Hell's dread Emperor with pomp Supreme,[8]
And God-like imitated State; him round
A Globe° of fiery Seraphim inclos'd *band*
With bright imblazonry,° and horrent° Arms. *heraldry/bristling*
Then of thir Session ended they bid cry
With Trumpet's regal sound the great result:
Toward the four winds four speedy Cherubim
Put to thir mouths the sounding Alchymy[9]
By Herald's voice explain'd: the hollow Abyss
Heard far and wide, and all the host of Hell
With deaf'ning shout, return'd them loud acclaim.
Thence more at ease thir minds and somewhat rais'd° *encouraged*
By false presumptuous hope, the ranged powers[1]
Disband, and wand'ring, each his several way
Pursues, as inclination or sad choice
Leads him perplext, where he may likeliest find
Truce to his restless thoughts, and entertain
The irksome hours, till this great Chief return.
Part on the Plain, or in the Air sublime° *uplifted*
Upon the wing, or in swift Race contend,

7. So that men ought not to boast.

8. Lines 510–520 may portray the English mob's easy gullibility and their passion (which Milton detested) for the regalia of monarchy.

9. Trumpets made of the alloy brass, associated with alchemy.

1. Armies drawn up in ranks.

As at th' *Olympian* Games or *Pythian* fields;[2]
Part curb thir fiery Steeds, or shun the Goal
With rapid wheels, or fronted Brígads form.
As when to warn proud Cities war appears
Wag'd in the troubl'd Sky, and Armies rush
To Battle in the Clouds, before each Van
Prick forth the Aery Knights, and couch thir spears
Till thickest Legions close; with feats of Arms
From either end of Heav'n the welkin° burns. *sky*
Others with vast *Typhoean*[3] rage more fell
Rend up both Rocks and Hills, and ride the Air
In whirlwind; Hell scarce holds the wild uproar.
As when *Alcides* from *Oechalia* Crown'd
With conquest, felt th' envenom'd robe, and tore
Through pain up by the roots *Thessalian* Pines,
And *Lichas* from the top of *Oeta* threw
Into th' *Euboic* Sea.[4] Others more mild,
Retreated in a silent valley, sing
With notes Angelical to many a Harp
Thir own Heroic deeds and hapless fall
By doom of Battle; and complain that Fate
Free Virtue should enthrall to Force or Chance.
Thir Song was partial,° but the harmony *prejudiced*
(What could it less when Spirits immortal sing?)
Suspended° Hell, and took with ravishment *enthralled*
The thronging audience. In discourse more sweet
(For Eloquence the Soul, Song charms the Sense,)
Others apart sat on a Hill retir'd,
In thoughts more elevate, and reason'd high
Of Providence, Foreknowledge, Will, and Fate,
Fixt Fate, Free will, Foreknowledge absolute,
And found no end, in wand'ring mazes lost.
Of good and evil much they argu'd then,
Of happiness and final misery,
Passion and Apathy, and glory and shame,
Vain wisdom all, and false Philosophie:[5]
Yet with a pleasing sorcery could charm
Pain for a while or anguish, and excite
Fallacious hope, or arm th' obdured° breast *hardened*
With stubborn patience as with triple steel.
Another part in Squadrons and gross° Bands, *dense*
On bold adventure to discover wide
That dismal World, if any Clime perhaps

2. Epic models for lines 528–569 include the sports of the Myrmidons during Achilles' absence from the war (Homer, *Iliad* 2.774ff.), the Greek funeral games of *Iliad* 23 and the Trojan of *Aeneid* 5, and the amusements of the blessed dead in Virgil's Elysium (*Aeneid* 6.642–59). To "shun the goal" (line 531) is to drive a chariot as close as possible around a post without touching it.

3. Like that of Typhon, the hundred-headed Titan. A pun, for "typhon" was also an English word meaning "whirlwind."

4. "Alcides" (Hercules) returning as victor from "Oechalia" (Ovid, *Metamorphoses* 9.136) put on a ritual robe that had inadvertently been soaked by his wife in corrosive poison. Mad with pain, he blamed his friend Lichas, who had brought the robe, and hurled him far into the "Euboic" (Euboean) Sea.

5. Directed against Stoicism, the most formidable ethical challenge to Christianity; "apathy," or complete freedom from passion, was a Stoic ideal.

Might yield them easier habitation, bend
Four ways thir flying March, along the Banks
Of four infernal Rivers that disgorge
Into the burning Lake thir baleful° streams;[6] *evil*
Abhorred *Styx* the flood of deadly hate,
Sad *Acheron* of sorrow, black and deep;
Cocytus, nam'd of lamentation loud
Heard on the rueful stream; fierce *Phlegeton*
Whose waves of torrent fire inflame with rage.
Far off from these a slow and silent stream,
Lethe the River of Oblivion rolls
Her wat'ry Labyrinth, whereof who drinks,
Forthwith his former state and being forgets,
Forgets both joy and grief, pleasure and pain.
Beyond this flood a frozen Continent
Lies dark and wild, beat with perpetual storms
Of Whirlwind and dire Hail, which on firm land
Thaws not, but gathers heap, and ruin seems
Of ancient pile; all else deep snow and ice,
A gulf profound as that *Serbonian* Bog[7]
Betwixt *Damiata* and Mount *Casius* old,
Where Armies whole have sunk: the parching° Air *withering*
Burns frore,° and cold performs th' effect of Fire. *frozen*
Thither by harpy-footed Furies hal'd,[8]
At certain revolutions all the damn'd
Are brought: and feel by turns the bitter change
Of fierce extremes, extremes by change more fierce,
From Beds of raging Fire to starve° in Ice *stifle*
Thir soft Ethereal warmth, and there to pine
Immovable, infixt, and frozen round,
Periods of time, thence hurried back to fire.
They ferry over this *Lethean* Sound
Both to and fro, thir sorrow to augment,
And wish and struggle, as they pass, to reach
The tempting stream, with one small drop to lose
In sweet forgetfulness all pain and woe,
All in one moment, and so near the brink;
But Fate withstands, and to oppose th' attempt
Medusa[9] with *Gorgonian* terror guards
The Ford, and of itself the water flies
All taste of living wight, as once it fled
The lip of *Tantalus.*[1] Thus roving on
In confus'd march forlorn, th' advent'rous Bands

6. This description of the four rivers of hell takes its broad outline from Virgil's (*Aeneid* 6), Dante's *Inferno* 14, and Spenser's *Faerie Queene* 2.7.56ff. Milton adds the detail of confluence in the "burning lake." The epithet or description attached to each river translates its Greek name (e.g., "Styx" means hateful).

7. Serbonis, a lake bordered by quicksands on the Egyptian coast.

8. Milton combines the hook-clawed Harpies of Dante and Virgil with the ancient Greek Furies, daughters of Acheron and Night and agencies of divine vengeance.

9. One of the Gorgons, mythical sisters with snakes for hair, whose look turned the beholder into stone.

1. In Homer's hell, Tantalus is tormented by thirst, standing in a pool that recedes whenever he tries to drink (*Odyssey* 11.582–92).

With shudd'ring horror pale, and eyes aghast
View'd first thir lamentable lot, and found
No rest: through many a dark and dreary Vale
They pass'd, and many a Region dolorous,
O'er many a Frozen, many a Fiery Alp,
Rocks, Caves, Lakes, Fens, Bogs, Dens, and shades of death,
A Universe of death, which God by curse
Created evil, for evil only good,
Where all life dies, death lives, and Nature breeds,
Perverse, all monstrous, all prodigious things,
Abominable, inutterable, and worse
Than Fables yet have feign'd, or fear conceiv'd,
Gorgons and *Hydras*, and *Chimeras* dire.[2]
Meanwhile the Adversary of God and Man,
Satan with thoughts inflam'd of highest design,
Puts on swift wings, and towards the Gates of Hell
Explores his solitary flight; sometimes
He scours the right hand coast, sometimes the left,
Now shaves with level wing the Deep, then soars
Up to the fiery concave tow'ring high.
As when far off at Sea a Fleet descri'd
Hangs in the Clouds, by *Equinoctial* Winds
Close sailing from *Bengala*, or the Isles
Of *Ternate* and *Tidore*, whence Merchants bring
Thir spicy Drugs:[3] they on the Trading Flood
Through the wide *Ethiopian* to the Cape
Ply stemming nightly toward the Pole. So seem'd
Far off the flying Fiend: at last appear
Hell bounds high reaching to the horrid Roof,
And thrice threefold the Gates; three folds were Brass,
Three Iron, three of Adamantine Rock,
Impenetrable, impal'd° with circling fire, *enclosed*
Yet unconsum'd. Before the Gates there sat
On either side a formidable shape;
The one seem'd Woman to the waist, and fair,[4]
But ended foul in many a scaly fold
Voluminous and vast, a Serpent arm'd
With mortal° sting: about her middle round *death-dealing*
A cry of Hell Hounds never ceasing bark'd
With wide *Cerberean* mouths full loud, and rung
A hideous Peal:[5] yet, when they list, would creep,
If aught disturb'd thir noise, into her womb,
And kennel there, yet there still bark'd and howl'd
Within unseen. Far less abhorr'd than these

2. The Hydra was many-headed, and the Chimeras breathed flame.
3. In Milton's time there was increased trade with "Bengala" (Bengal) and "Ternate" and "Tidore" (two of the "spice islands," or Moluccas). The spice ships would cross the "Ethiopian" Sea (the Indian Ocean) before rounding the Cape of Good Hope.
4. The nearest analogue to Milton's Sin is probably Spenser's Errour, who is half serpent and half woman, has a "mortal sting," and swallows her young (*The Faerie Queene* 1.1.14–16, pages 748–749). The serpent of sin that tempted Adam and Eve was traditionally portrayed as having a woman's head or bust.
5. There is a whole "cry" (pack) of hounds, because one sin engenders many consequences, sometimes hidden. Cerberus was the many-headed dog who guarded Hades.

Vex'd *Scylla* bathing in the Sea that parts
Calabria from the hoarse *Trinacrian* shore:[6]
Nor uglier follow the Night-Hag,[7] when call'd
In secret, riding through the Air she comes
Lur'd with the smell of infant blood, to dance
With *Lapland* Witches, while the laboring Moon
Eclipses at thir charms. The other shape,
If shape it might be call'd that shape had none
Distinguishable in member, joint, or limb,
Or substance might be call'd that shadow seem'd,
For each seem'd either; black it stood as Night,
Fierce as ten Furies, terrible as Hell,
And shook a dreadful Dart;[8] what seem'd his head
The likeness of a Kingly Crown had on.
Satan was now at hand, and from his seat
The Monster moving onward came as fast,
With horrid strides; Hell trembled as he strode.
Th' undaunted Fiend what this might be admir'd,° *wondered*
Admir'd, not fear'd; God and his Son except,
Created thing naught valu'd he nor shunn'd;
And with disdainful look thus first began.
  Whence and what are thou, execrable shape,
That dar'st, though grim and terrible, advance
Thy miscreated Front athwart my way
To yonder Gates? through them I mean to pass,
That be assured, without leave askt of thee:
Retire, or taste thy folly, and learn by proof,° *experience*
Hell-born, not to contend with Spirits of Heav'n.
  To whom the Goblin full of wrath repli'd:
Art thou that Traitor Angel, art thou hee,
Who first broke peace in Heav'n and Faith, till then
Unbrok'n, and in proud rebellious Arms
Drew after him the third part of Heav'n's Sons
Conjur'd[9] against the Highest, for which both Thou
And they outcast from God, are here condemn'd
To waste Eternal days in woe and pain?
And reck'n'st thou thyself with Spirits of Heav'n,
Hell-doom'd, and breath'st defiance here and scorn,
Where I reign King, and to enrage thee more,
Thy King and Lord? Back to thy punishment,
False fugitive, and to thy speed add wings,
Lest with a whip of Scorpions I pursue
Thy ling'ring, or with one stroke of this Dart
Strange horror seize thee, and pangs unfelt before.

6. Circe, jealous of the nymph Scylla, changed her lower parts into a knot of "gaping dogs' heads, such as a Cerberus might have" (Ovid, *Metamorphoses* 14.50–74). Later Scylla was again transformed, into a dangerous rock between "Trinacria" (Sicily) and Calabria. In the medieval moralized Ovid, she became a symbol of lust or of sin.

7. Hecate, whose charms were used by Circe in her spell against Scylla. Milton may allude here to the hellish yeth hounds, which, according to popular superstition, followed the queen of darkness across the sky in pursuit of the souls of the damned.

8. The "dreadful dart" was a traditional attribute of Death, signifying his sharpness and suddenness.

9. Sworn together in conspiracy; bewitched.

So spake the grisly terror, and in shape,
So speaking and so threat'ning, grew tenfold
More dreadful and deform: on th' other side
Incens't with indignation *Satan* stood
Unterrifi'd, and like a Comet burn'd,
That fires the length of *Ophiucus*[1] huge
In th' Artic Sky, and from his horrid hair
Shakes Pestilence and War. Each at the Head
Levell'd his deadly aim; thir fatal hands
No second stroke intend, and such a frown
Each cast at th' other, as when two black Clouds
With Heav'n's Artillery fraught, come rattling on
Over the *Caspian*, then stand front to front
Hov'ring a space, till Winds the signal blow
To join thir dark Encounter in mid air:
So frown'd the mighty Combatants, that Hell
Grew darker at thir frown, so matcht they stood;
For never but once more was either like
To meet so great a foe:[2] and now great deeds
Had been achiev'd, whereof all Hell had rung,
Had not the Snaky Sorceress that sat
Fast by Hell Gate, and kept the fatal Key,
Ris'n, and with hideous outcry rush'd between.
O Father, what intends thy hand, she cri'd,
Against thy only Son?[3] What fury O Son,
Possesses thee to bend that mortal Dart
Against thy Father's head? and know'st for whom;
For him who sits above and laughs the while
At thee ordain'd his drudge, to execute
Whate'er his wrath, which he calls Justice, bids,
His wrath which one day will destroy ye both.
She spake, and at her words the hellish Pest
Forbore, then these to her *Satan* return'd:
So strange thy outcry, and thy words so strange
Thou interposest, that my sudden hand
Prevented spares to tell thee yet by deeds
What it intends; till first I know of thee,
What thing thou art, thus double-form'd, and why
In this infernal Vale first met thou call'st
Me Father, and that Phantasm call'st my Son?
I know thee not, nor ever saw till now
Sight more detestable than him and thee.
T' whom thus the Portress of Hell Gate repli'd:[4]
Hast thou forgot me then, and do I seem

1. The comet referred to here may be a magnificent one that appeared in 1618 in the constellation *Ophiuchus*. In his diary, John Evelyn held it responsible for the Thirty Years' War. Ophiuchus (Serpent Bearer) is also chosen to allude to Satan's later transformation into a serpent.

2. When Christ destroys "him that had the power of death, that is, the devil" (Hebrews 2.14), as well as "the last enemy . . . death" (1 Corinthians 15.26).

3. The allegory whereby Sin is daughter of Satan and mother of Death is from St. Basil's *Hexameron*.

4. Sin's office is an allegorical statement of the idea that access to hell is by sinning.

Now in thine eye so foul, once deem'd so fair
In Heav'n, when at th' Assembly, and in sight
Of all the Seraphim with thee combin'd
In bold conspiracy against Heav'n's King,
All on a sudden miserable pain
Surpris'd thee, dim thine eyes, and dizzy swum
In darkness, while thy head flames thick and fast
Threw forth, till on the left side op'ning wide,
Likest to thee in shape and count'nance bright,
Then shining heav'nly fair, a Goddess arm'd
Out of thy head I sprung:[5] amazement seiz'd
All th' Host of Heav'n; back they recoil'd afraid
At first, and call'd me *Sin*, and for a Sign
Portentous held me; but familiar grown,
I pleas'd, and with attractive graces won
The most averse, thee chiefly, who full oft
Thyself in me thy perfect image viewing
Becam'st enamor'd, and such joy thou took'st
With me in secret, that my womb conceiv'd
A growing burden. Meanwhile War arose,
And fields were fought in Heav'n: wherein remain'd
(For what could else) to our Almighty Foe
Clear Victory, to our part loss and rout
Through all the Empyrean: down they fell
Driv'n headlong from the Pitch° of Heaven, down *summit*
Into this Deep, and in the general fall
I also; at which time this powerful Key
Into my hand was giv'n, with charge to keep
These Gates for ever shut, which none can pass
Without my op'ning. Pensive here I sat
Alone, but long I sat not, till my womb
Pregnant by thee, and now excessive grown
Prodigious motion felt and rueful throes.
At last this odious offspring whom thou seest
Thine own begotten, breaking violent way
Tore through my entrails, that with fear and pain
Distorted, all my nether shape thus grew
Transform'd: but he my inbred enemy
Forth issu'd, brandishing his fatal Dart
Made to destroy: I fled, and cri'd out *Death;*
Hell trembl'd at the hideous Name, and sigh'd
From all her Caves, and back resounded *Death*.
I fled, but he pursu'd (though more, it seems,
Inflam'd with lust than rage) and swifter far,
Mee overtook his mother all dismay'd,
And in embraces forcible and foul
Ingend'ring with me, of that rape begot

5. The circumstances of Sin's birth recall the ancient myth about Athena springing fully formed from the head of Zeus. It is thus presented as a parody of God's generation of the Son, since Minerva's birth had traditionally been allegorized by theologians in that sense.

These yelling Monsters that with ceasless cry
Surround me, as thou saw'st, hourly conceiv'd
And hourly born, with sorrow infinite
To me, for when they list, into the womb
That bred them they return, and howl and gnaw
My Bowels, thir repast; then bursting forth
Afresh with conscious terrors vex° me round, *harass*
That rest or intermission none I find.[6]
Before mine eyes in opposition sits
Grim *Death* my Son and foe, who sets them on,
And me his Parent would full soon devour
For want of other prey, but that he knows
His end with mine involv'd; and knows that I
Should prove a bitter Morsel, and his bane,
Whenever that shall be; so Fate pronounc'd.
But thou O Father, I forewarn thee, shun
His deadly arrow; neither vainly hope
To be invulnerable in those bright Arms,
Though temper'd heav'nly, for that mortal dint,
Save he who reigns above, none can resist.[7]
    She finish'd, and the subtle Fiend his lore
Soon learn'd, now milder, and thus answer'd smooth.
Dear Daughter, since thou claim'st me for thy Sire,
And my fair Son here show'st me, the dear pledge
Of dalliance had with thee in Heav'n, and joys
Then sweet, now sad to mention, through dire change
Befall'n us unforeseen, unthought of, know
I come no enemy, but to set free
From out this dark and dismal house of pain,
Both him and thee, and all the heav'nly Host
Of Spirits that in our just pretenses arm'd
Fell with us from on high: from them I go
This uncouth° errand sole, and one for all *strange*
Myself expose, with lonely steps to tread
Th' unfounded° deep, and through the void immense *bottomless*
To search with wand'ring quest a place foretold
Should be, and, by concurring signs, ere now
Created vast and round, a place of bliss
In the Purlieus° of Heav'n, and therein plac't *outskirts*
A race of upstart Creatures, to supply
Perhaps our vacant room, though more remov'd,
Lest Heav'n surcharg'd° with potent multitude *too full*
Might hap to move new broils: Be this or aught
Than this more secret now design'd, I haste
To know, and this once known, shall soon return,
And bring ye to the place where Thou and Death
Shall dwell at ease, and up and down unseen

6. Here Sin's offspring appear to symbolize the pangs of guilt or fear. "Conscious terrors" are terrors of guilty knowledge.

7. "Dint," stroke given with a weapon. Only God is immune to death.

Wing silently the buxom° Air, imbalm'd[8] *unresisting*
With odors; there ye shall be fed and fill'd
Immeasurably, all things shall be your prey.
He ceas'd, for both seem'd highly pleas'd, and Death
Grinn'd horrible a ghastly smile, to hear
His famine° should be fill'd, and blest his maw *hunger*
Destin'd to that good hour: no less rejoic'd
His mother bad, and thus bespake her Sire.
The key of this infernal Pit by due,
And by command of Heav'n's all-powerful King
I keep, by him forbidden to unlock
These Adamantine Gates; against all force
Death ready stands to interpose his dart,
Fearless to be o'ermatcht by living might.
But what owe I to his commands above
Who hates me, and hath hither thrust me down
Into this gloom of *Tartarus* profound,
To sit in hateful Office here confin'd,
Inhabitant of Heav'n, and heav'nly-born,
Here in perpetual agony and pain,
With terrors and with clamors compasst round
Of mine own brood, that on my bowels feed:
Thou art my Father, thou my Author, thou
My being gav'st me; whom should I obey
But thee, whom follow? thou wilt bring me soon
To that new world of light and bliss, among
The Gods who live at ease, where I shall Reign
At thy right hand voluptuous, as beseems
Thy daughter and thy darling, without end.[9]
Thus saying, from her side the fatal Key,
Sad instrument of all our woe, she took;[1]
And towards the Gate rolling her bestial train,
Forthwith the huge Portcullis high up drew,
Which but herself not all the *Stygian* powers
Could once have mov'd; then in the key-hole turns
Th' intricate wards,[2] and every Bolt and Bar
Of massy Iron or solid Rock with ease
Unfast'ns: on a sudden op'n fly
With impetuous recoil and jarring sound
Th' infernal doors, and on thir hinges grate
Harsh Thunder, that the lowest bottom shook
Of *Erebus*.[3] She op'n'd, but to shut
Excell'd her power; the Gates wide op'n stood,
That with extended wings a Banner'd Host
Under spread Ensigns marching might pass through
With Horse and Chariots rankt in loose array;

8. Balmy, rendered resistent to decay.
9. Parodying the Nicene creed ("on the right hand of the Father . . . [Christ] whose kingdom shall have no end"). In Sin's fantasy she enjoys glory like Christ's. Satan, Sin, and Death form a complete anti-Trinity.
1. "Sad instrument" may stand in apposition to "she" as well as to "key"; it could mean "a person made use of by another, for the accomplishment of a purpose."
2. The incisions in a key's bit.
3. Classical name for Hell.

So wide they stood, and like a Furnace mouth
Cast forth redounding° smoke and ruddy flame. *surging*
Before thir eyes in sudden view appear
The secrets of the hoary deep, a dark
Illimitable Ocean without bound,
Without dimension, where length, breadth, and highth,
And time and place are lost; where eldest *Night*
And *Chaos*, Ancestors of Nature, hold
Eternal Anarchy, amidst the noise
Of endless wars, and by confusion stand.
For hot, cold, moist, and dry, four Champions fierce
Strive here for Maistry, and to Battle bring
Thir embryon Atoms;[4] they around the flag
Of each his Faction, in thir several Clans,
Light-arm'd or heavy, sharp, smooth, swift or slow,
Swarm populous, unnumber'd as the Sands
Of *Barca* or *Cyrene's* torrid soil,[5]
Levied° to side with warring Winds, and poise *enlisted*
Thir lighter wings. To whom these most adhere,
Hee rules a moment; *Chaos* Umpire sits,
And by decision more imbroils the fray
By which he Reigns: next him high Arbiter
Chance governs all. Into this wild Abyss,
The Womb of nature and perhaps her Grave,
Of neither Sea, nor Shore, nor Air, nor Fire,
But all these in thir pregnant causes mixt
Confus'dly, and which thus must ever fight,
Unless th' Almighty Maker them ordain
His dark materials to create more Worlds,
Into this wild Abyss the wary fiend
Stood on the brink of Hell and look'd a while,
Pondering his Voyage: for no narrow frith° *channel*
He had to cross. Nor was his ear less peal'd° *dinned*
With noises loud and ruinous (to compare
Great things with small) than when *Bellona*[6] storms,
With all her battering Engines bent to rase
Some Capital City; or less than if this frame
Of Heav'n were falling, and these Elements
In mutiny had from her Axle torn
The steadfast Earth. At last his Sail-broad Vans° *wings*
He spreads for flight, and in the surging smoke
Uplifted spurns the ground, thence many a League
As in a cloudy Chair ascending rides
Audacious, but that seat soon failing, meets
A vast vacuity: all unawares

4. In works such as Hesiod's *Theogony* and Boccaccio's *De genealogiis*, Chaos and Night were made "ancestors" of nature. Milton's description of the strife between contrary qualities that preceded the emergence of the cosmos is close to Ovid's account of the primeval chaos in which "cold things strove with hot, moist with dry, soft with hard, weightless with heavy" (*Metamorphoses* 1.19ff.).

5. "Barca," an ancient city of Cyrenaica, of which "Cyrene" was the capital.

6. Goddess of war, here a metonymy for war itself.

Flutt'ring his pennons° vain plumb down he drops *wings*
Ten thousand fadom° deep, and to this hour *fathoms*
Down had been falling, had not by ill chance
The strong rebuff of some tumultuous cloud
Instinct° with Fire and Nitre hurried him *inflamed*
As many miles aloft: that fury stay'd,
Quencht in a Boggy *Syrtis*, neither Sea,[7]
Nor good dry Land, nigh founder'd on he fares,
Treading the crude consistence, half on foot,
Half flying;[8] behoves him now both Oar and Sail.
As when a Gryfon through the Wilderness
With winged course o'er Hill or moory Dale,
Pursues the *Arimaspian*, who by stealth
Had from his wakeful custody purloin'd
The guarded Gold: So eagerly the fiend
O'er bog or steep, through strait, rough, dense, or rare,
With head, hands, wings, or feet pursues his way,
And swims or sinks, or wades, or creeps, or flies:
At length a universal hubbub wild
Of stunning sounds and voices all confus'd
Borne through the hollow dark assaults his ear
With loudest vehemence: thither he plies,
Undaunted to meet there whatever power
Or Spirit of the nethermost Abyss
Might in that noise reside, of whom to ask
Which way the nearest coast of darkness lies
Bordering on light; when straight behold the Throne
Of *Chaos*, and his dark Pavilion spread
Wide on the wasteful Deep; with him Enthron'd
Sat Sable-vested *Night*, eldest of things,
The Consort of his Reign; and by them stood
Orcus and *Ades*, and the dreaded name
Of *Demogorgon*;[9] *Rumor* next and *Chance*,
And *Tumult* and *Confusion* all imbroil'd,
And *Discord* with a thousand various mouths.
    T' whom *Satan* turning boldly, thus. Ye Powers
And Spirits of this nethermost Abyss,
Chaos and *ancient Night*, I come no Spy,
With purpose to explore or to disturb
The secrets of your Realm, but by constraint
Wand'ring this darksome Desert, as my way
Lies through your spacious Empire up to light,

7. The Syrtes were two huge and proverbially dangerous shifting sandbanks off the North African shore.

8. Spenser's dragon of evil is similarly described as "halfe flying, and halfe footing in his hast" (*The Faerie Queene* 1.11.8). The legend of "gold-guarding griffins" in Scythia, from whom the one-eyed Arimaspi steal, was often retold out of Herodotus (3.116) and Pliny (*Natural History* 7.10). The griffin (a composite monster: half eagle, half lion) is appropriate here partly because it was subdued by the sun god Apollo, as Satan will be by Christ.

9. In general, this court of personifications resembles Virgil's halls of Pluto (*Aeneid* 6.268–81), though the only member common to both is Discord. Milton's Demogorgon is from Boccaccio's *De genealogiis deorum*, in which he comes first of all the dark gods. Among his brood are Night, Tartarus, Erebus, the serpent Python, Litigium (cf. Milton's Tumult and Discord), and Fama (Milton's Rumor). Orcus and Ades are Latin and Greek names of Pluto, god of hell.

Alone, and without guide, half lost, I seek
What readiest path leads where your gloomy bounds
Confine with° Heav'n; or if some other place *border on*
From your Dominion won, th' Ethereal King
Possesses lately, thither to arrive
I travel this profound,° direct my course; *deep pit*
Directed, no mean recompence it brings
To your behoof, if I that Region lost,
All usurpation thence expell'd, reduce
To her original darkness and your sway
(Which is my present journey) and once more
Erect the Standard there of *ancient Night;*
Yours be th' advantage all, mine the revenge.
   Thus *Satan;* and him thus the Anarch[1] old
With falt'ring speech and visage incompos'd° *disordered*
Answer'd. I know thee, stranger, who thou art,
That mighty leading Angel, who of late
Made head against Heav'n's King, though overthrown.
I saw and heard, for such a numerous Host
Fled not in silence through the frighted deep
With ruin upon ruin, rout on rout,
Confusion worse confounded; and Heav'n Gates
Pour'd out by millions her victorious Bands
Pursuing. I upon my Frontiers here
Keep residence; if all I can will serve,
That little which is left so to defend,
Encroacht on still through our intestine broils
Weak'ning the Sceptre of old *Night:* first Hell
Your dungeon stretching far and wide beneath;
Now lately Heaven and Earth, another World
Hung o'er my Realm, link'd in a golden Chain
To that side Heav'n from whence your Legions fell:
If that way be your walk, you have not far;
So much the nearer danger; go and speed;
Havoc and spoil and ruin are my gain.
   He ceas'd; and *Satan* stay'd not to reply,
But glad that now his Sea should find a shore,
With fresh alacrity and force renew'd
Springs upward like a Pyramid of fire
Into the wild expanse, and through the shock
Of fighting Elements, on all sides round
Environ'd wins his way; harder beset
And more endanger'd, than when *Argo* pass'd
Through *Bosporus* betwixt the justling° Rocks:[2] *jostling*
Or when *Ulysses* on the Larboard shunn'd
Charybdis, and by th' other whirlpool steer'd.[3]

1. Chaos, ruler or antiruler of the "eternal anarchy" (line 896).

2. When Jason and the Argonauts sailed through the Bosporus (Straits of Constantinople) en route to Colchis, their boat, the *Argo*, narrowly escaped destruction between the Symplegades, the clashing or "jostling" rocks. See Apollonius Rhodius, *Argonautica* 2.317, 552–611.

3. Homer tells how Odysseus followed Circe's advice in avoiding Charybdis and sailing close by Scylla ("the other whirlpool") in his passage through the Straits of Messina between Sicily and Italy (*Odyssey* 12).

So he with difficulty and labor hard
Mov'd on, with difficulty and labor hee;
But hee once past, soon after when man fell,
Strange alteration! Sin and Death amain° *without delay*
Following his track, such was the will of Heav'n,
Pav'd after him a broad and beat'n way
Over the dark Abyss, whose boiling Gulf
Tamely endur'd a Bridge of wondrous length
From Hell continu'd reaching th' utmost Orb
Of this frail World; by which the Spirits perverse
With easy intercourse pass to and fro
To tempt or punish mortals, except whom
God and good Angels guard by special grace.
But now at last the sacred influence
Of light appears, and from the walls of Heav'n
Shoots far into the bosom of dim Night
A glimmering dawn; here Nature first begins
Her fardest° verge, and *Chaos* to retire *farthest*
As from her outmost works a brok'n foe
With tumult less and with less hostile din,
That *Satan* with less toil, and now with ease
Wafts on the calmer wave by dubious light
And like a weather-beaten Vessel holds° *remains in*
Gladly the Port, though Shrouds and Tackle torn;
Or in the emptier waste, resembling Air,
Weighs his spread wings, at leisure to behold
Far off th' Empyreal Heav'n, extended wide
In circuit, undetermin'd square or round,[4]
With Opal Tow'rs and Battlements adorn'd
Of living° Sapphire, once his native Seat; *unshaped*
And fast by hanging in a golden Chain[5]
This pendant world, in bigness as a Star
Of smallest Magnitude close by the Moon.
Thither full fraught with mischievous revenge,
Accurst, and in a cursed hour he hies.

The End of the Second Book.

from Book 3

The Argument

God *sitting on his Throne sees* Satan *flying towards this world, then newly created; shows him to the Son who sat at his right hand; foretells the success of* Satan *in perverting mankind; clears his own Justice and Wisdom from all imputation, having created Man free and able enough to have withstood his Tempter; yet declares his purpose of grace towards him, in regard he fell not of his own malice, as did* Satan, *but by him seduc't. The Son of God renders praises to his Father for the manifestation of his gra-*

4. So wide that it was impossible to tell whether the boundary was rectilinear or curved.

5. Homer's Zeus asserts his transcendence by claiming that if a golden chain were lowered from Heaven, he could draw up by it all the other gods, together with the earth and the sea, and hang them from a pinnacle of Olympus (*Iliad* 8.18–27). Milton interprets this chain as "the universal concord and sweet union of all things which Pythagoras poetically figures as harmony" (*Prolusion* 2), thus accepting a philosophical and literary tradition that runs from Plato through Boethius, Chaucer, and Spenser.

cious purpose towards Man; but God again declares, that Grace cannot be extended towards Man without the satisfaction of divine Justice; Man hath offended the majesty of God by aspiring to Godhead, and therefore with all his Progeny devoted to death must die, unless some one can be found sufficient to answer for his offense, and undergo his Punishment. The Son of God freely offers himself a Ransom for Man: the Father accepts him, ordains his incarnation, pronounces his exaltation above all Names in Heaven and Earth; commands all the Angels to adore him; they obey, and hymning to thir Harps in full Choir, celebrate the Father and the Son. Meanwhile Satan *alights upon the bare convex of this World's outermost Orb; where wand'ring he first finds a place since call'd The Limbo of Vanity; what persons and things fly up thither; thence comes to the Gate of Heaven, describ'd ascending by stairs, and the waters above the Firmament that flow about it: His passage thence to the Orb of the Sun; he finds there* Uriel *the Regent of that Orb, but first changes himself into the shape of a meaner Angel; and pretending a zealous desire to behold the new Creation and Man whom God had plac't there, inquires of him the place of his habitation, and is directed; alights first on Mount* Niphates.

Hail holy Light, offspring of Heav'n first-born,
Or of th' Eternal Coeternal beam
May I express thee unblam'd?! since God is Light,
And never but in unapproached Light
Dwelt from Eternity, dwelt then in thee,
Bright effluence° of bright essence increate.[2] *radiance*
Or hear'st thou rather[3] pure Ethereal stream,
Whose Fountain who shall tell? before the Sun,
Before the Heavens thou wert, and at the voice
Of God, as with a Mantle didst invest° *cover*
The rising world of waters dark and deep,
Won from the void° and formless infinite.[4] *chaos*
Thee I revisit now with bolder wing,
Escap't the *Stygian* Pool, though long detain'd
In that obscure sojourn, while in my flight
Through utter and through middle darkness borne[5]
With other notes than to th' *Orphean* Lyre
I sung of *Chaos* and *Eternal Night*,
Taught by the heav'nly Muse° to venture down *Urania*
The dark descent, and up to reascend,
Though hard and rare:[6] thee I revisit safe,
And feel thy sovran vital Lamp; but thou

1. The light of the invocation has been interpreted as the Son of God, as physical light, and as the principal image of God and the divine emanation itself, according to the Platonic system. Milton proposes three images or forms of address, "offspring," "beam," and "stream," each of which associates the divine Light or Wisdom with a different aspect of deity. The blame could attach only to using the second name, "co-eternal beam"; it is this name that is justified by the implicit appeal to scriptural authority.

2. "God is Light," from 1 John 1.5. God "only hath immortality, dwelling in the light which no man can approach unto" (1 Timothy 6.16). "Essence increate," the uncreated divine essence. In the physics and metaphysics of Milton's time, light was regarded as an "accident" (quality), not a body or substance.

3. Do you prefer to be called.

4. See Genesis 1.1–5.

5. The "Stygian pool" and the "utter" (outer) darkness are hell; the "middle darkness" is chaos.

6. Alluding to the "fable of Orpheus, whom they faigne to have recovered his Euridice from Hell with his Musick, that is, Truth and Equity from darkenesse of Barbarisme and Ignorance with his profound and excellent Doctrines; but, that in the way to the upper-earth, she was lost againe" (Henry Reynolds, *Mythomystes*). "Other notes," because Milton, unlike Orpheus, claims not to have lost his Eurydice.

Revisit'st not these eyes, that roll in vain
To find thy piercing ray, and find no dawn;
So thick a drop serene[7] hath quencht thir Orbs,
Or dim suffusion° veil'd. Yet not the more *cataract*
Cease I to wander where the Muses haunt
Clear Spring, or shady Grove, or Sunny Hill,
Smit with the love of sacred Song;[8] but chief
Thee *Sion*[9] and the flow'ry Brooks beneath
That wash thy hallow'd feet, and warbling flow,
Nightly I visit: nor sometimes forget
Those other two equall'd with me in Fate,
So were I equall'd with them in renown,
Blind *Thamyris* and blind *Maeonides*,
And *Tiresias* and *Phineus* Prophets old.[1]
Then feed on thoughts, that voluntary move
Harmonious numbers;° as the wakeful Bird[2] *rhythmic measure*
Sings darkling,° and in shadiest Covert hid *in the dark*
Tunes her nocturnal Note. Thus with the Year
Seasons return, but not to me returns
Day, or the sweet approach of Ev'n or Morn,
Or sight of vernal bloom, or Summer's Rose,
Or flocks, or herds, or human face divine;
But cloud instead, and ever-during dark
Surrounds me, from the cheerful ways of men
Cut off, and for the Book of knowledge[3] fair
Presented with a Universal blanc° *blank*
Of Nature's works to me expung'd and ras'd,° *erased*
And wisdom at one entrance quite shut out.
So much the rather thou Celestial Light
Shine inward, and the mind through all her powers
Irradiate, there plant eyes, all mist from thence
Purge and disperse, that I may see and tell
Of things invisible to mortal sight.
  Now had th' Almighty Father from above,
From the pure Empyrean where he sits
High Thron'd above all highth, bent down his eye,
His own works and their works at once to view:
About him all the Sanctities of Heaven
Stood thick as Stars, and from his sight receiv'd
Beatitude past utterance; on his right
The radiant image of his Glory sat,
His only Son; On Earth he first beheld

7. Literally translating *gutta serena*, the medical term for the form of blindness from which Milton suffered.
8. An allusion to Virgil's prayer that "smitten with a great love" of the Muses, he may be shown by them the secrets of nature (*Georgics* 2.475–489).
9. The mountain of scriptural inspiration.
1. Thamyris was a Thracian poet who fell in love with the Muses and challenged them to a contest in which the loser was to give the winner whatever he wanted. The Muses, having won, took Thamyris's eyes and his lyre. Maeonides was Homer's surname; the contrast between his outward blindness and inner vision was a commonplace. In *De Idea Platonica*, Milton writes of Tiresias that his "very blindness gave him boundless light." The Thracian king Phineus lost his sight because he had become too good a prophet.
2. The nightingale. The soul of Thamyris passed into a nightingale.
3. The Book of Nature.

Our two first Parents, yet the only two
Of mankind, in the happy Garden plac't,
Reaping immortal fruits of joy and love,
Uninterrupted joy, unrivall'd love
In blissful solitude; he then survey'd
Hell and the Gulf between, and *Satan* there
Coasting the wall of Heav'n on this side Night
In the dun° Air sublime,° and ready now *dusky/aloft*
To stoop with wearied wings, and willing feet
On the bare outside of this World, that seem'd
Firm land imbosom'd without Firmament,[4]
Uncertain which, in Ocean or in Air.
Him God beholding from his prospect high,
Wherein past, present, future he beholds,
Thus to his only Son foreseeing spake.
  Only begotten Son, seest thou what rage
Transports our adversary, whom no bounds
Prescrib'd, no bars of Hell, nor all the chains
Heapt on him there, nor yet the main Abyss
Wide interrupt° can hold; so bent he seems *divided*
On desperate revenge, that shall redound
Upon his own rebellious head. And now
Through all restraint broke loose he wings his way
Not far off Heav'n, in the Precincts of light,
Directly towards the new created World,
And Man there plac't, with purpose to assay° *test*
If him by force he can destroy, or worse,
By some false guile pervert; and shall pervert;
For Man will heark'n to his glozing° lies, *flattering*
And easily transgress the sole Command,[5]
Sole pledge of his obedience: So will fall
Hee and his faithless Progeny: whose fault?
Whose but his own? ingrate, he had of mee
All he could have; I made him just and right,
Sufficient to have stood, though free to fall.
Such I created all th' Ethereal Powers
And Spirits, both them who stood and them who fail'd;
Freely they stood who stood, and fell who fell.
Not free, what proof could they have giv'n sincere
Of true allegiance, constant Faith or Love,
Where only what they needs must do, appear'd,
Not what they would? what praise could they receive?
What pleasure I from such obedience paid,
When Will and Reason (Reason also is choice)
Useless and vain, of freedom both despoil'd,
Made passive both, had serv'd necessity,
Not mee. They therefore as to right belong'd,
So were created, nor can justly accuse

4. The firmament or atmosphere, being inside the shell of the universe that Satan stands on, is invisible to him.

5. I.e., not to taste the fruit of the forbidden tree.

Thir maker, or thir making, or thir Fate;
As if Predestination over-rul'd
Thir will, dispos'd by absolute Decree
Or high foreknowledge; they themselves decreed
Thir own revolt, not I: if I foreknew,
Foreknowledge had no influence on their fault,
Which had no less prov'd certain unforeknown.
So without least impulse or shadow of Fate,
Or aught by me immutably foreseen,
They trespass, Authors to themselves in all
Both what they judge and what they choose; for so
I form'd them free, and free they must remain,
Till they enthrall themselves: I else must change
Thir nature, and revoke the high Decree
Unchangeable, Eternal, which ordain'd
Thir freedom: they themselves ordain'd thir fall.
The first sort[6] by thir own suggestion° fell, *temptation*
Self-tempted, self-deprav'd: Man falls deceiv'd
By th' other first: Man therefore shall find grace,
The other none: in Mercy and Justice both,
Through Heav'n and Earth, so shall my glory excel,
But Mercy first and last shall brightest shine.
Thus while God spake, ambrosial fragrance fill'd
All Heav'n, and in the blessed Spirits elect[7]
Sense of new joy ineffable diffus'd:
Beyond compare the Son of God was seen
Most glorious, in him all his Father shone
Substantially express'd, and in his face
Divine compassion visibly appear'd,
Love without end, and without measure Grace,
Which uttering thus he to his Father spake.
O Father, gracious was that word which clos'd
Thy sovran° sentence, that Man should find grace; *sovereign*
For which both Heav'n and Earth shall high extol
Thy praises, with th' innumerable sound
Of Hymns and sacred Songs, wherewith thy Throne
Encompass'd shall resound thee ever blest.
For should Man finally be lost, should Man
Thy creature late so lov'd, thy youngest Son
Fall circumvented thus by fraud, though join'd
With his own folly? that be from thee far,
That far be from thee, Father, who art Judge
Of all things made, and judgest only right.
Or shall the Adversary[8] thus obtain
His end, and frustrate thine, shall he fulfil
His malice, and thy goodness bring to naught,
Or proud return though to his heavier doom,

6. Satan and the rebel angels.
7. The "elect angels" of 1 Timothy 5.21, explained in Milton's *De doctrina* 1.9 as angels "who have not revolted."
8. The literal meaning of "Satan."

Yet with revenge accomplish't and to Hell
Draw after him the whole Race of mankind,
By him corrupted? or wilt thou thyself
Abolish thy Creation, and unmake,
For him, what for thy glory thou hast made?
So should thy goodness and thy greatness both
Be question'd and blasphem'd without defense.
  To whom the great Creator thus repli'd.
O Son, in whom my Soul hath chief delight,[9]
Son of my bosom, Son who art alone
My word, my wisdom, and effectual might,
All hast thou spok'n as my thoughts are, all
As my Eternal purpose hath decreed:
Man shall not quite be lost, but sav'd who will,
Yet not of will in him, but grace in me
Freely voutsaf't;° once more I will renew *vouchsafed*
His lapsed° powers, though forfeit and enthrall'd *decayed*
By sin to foul exorbitant desires;
Upheld by me, yet once more he shall stand
On even ground against his mortal foe,
By me upheld, that he may know how frail
His fall'n condition is, and to me owe
All his deliv'rance, and to none but me.
Some I have chosen of peculiar grace
Elect above the rest; so is my will:[1]
The rest shall hear me call, and oft be warn'd
Thir sinful state, and to appease betimes
Th' incensed Deity while offer'd grace
Invites; for I will clear thir senses dark,
What may suffice, and soft'n stony hearts
To pray, repent, and bring obedience due.
To Prayer, repentance, and obedience due,
Though but endeavor'd with sincere intent,
Mine ear shall not be slow, mine eye not shut.
And I will place within them as a guide
My Umpire *Conscience*, whom if they will hear,
Light after light well us'd they shall attain,
And to the end persisting, safe arrive.
This my long sufferance and my day of grace
They who neglect and scorn, shall never taste;
But hard be hard'n'd, blind be blinded more,
That they may stumble on, and deeper fall;
And none but such from mercy I exclude.
But yet all is not done; Man disobeying,

9. Echoing Mark 1.11, the words out of the heavens at Jesus' baptism: "Thou art my beloved Son, in whom I am well pleased."

1. In *De doctrina* 1.4, Milton sets out an Arminian position, explicitly opposed to the Calvinist, on such doctrines as predestination, election, and reprobation, and he could be regarded as doing something similar here (lines 173–202); e.g., his God seems to make salvation depend on humans' will to avail themselves of grace, or on "prayer, repentance, and obedience" (line 191), whereas Calvinists regarded humans as incapable of contributing in any way to their own salvation. By the term "elect," Milton usually means no more than "whoever believes and continues in the faith."

Disloyal breaks his fealty, and sins
Against the high Supremacy of Heav'n,
Affecting° God-head, and so losing all, *seeking*
To expiate his Treason hath naught left,
But to destruction sacred and devote,° *dedicated*
He with his whole posterity must die,
Die hee or Justice must; unless for him
Some other able, and as willing, pay
The rigid satisfaction, death for death.[2]
Say Heav'nly Powers, where shall we find such love,
Which of ye will be mortal[3] to redeem
Man's mortal crime, and just th' unjust to save,
Dwells in all Heaven charity° so dear? *compassionate love*
  He ask'd, but all the Heav'nly Choir stood mute,
And silence was in Heav'n: on man's behalf
Patron or Intercessor none appear'd,
Much less that durst upon his own head draw
The deadly forfeiture, and ransom set.[4]
And now without redemption all mankind
Must have been lost, adjudg'd to Death and Hell
By doom° severe, had not the Son of God, *judgment*
In whom the fulness dwells of love divine,
His dearest mediation thus renew'd.
  Father, thy word is past,[5] man shall find grace;
And shall grace not find means, that finds her way,
The speediest of thy winged messengers,
To visit all thy creatures, and to all
Comes unprevented,° unimplor'd, unsought? *unanticipated*
Happy for man, so coming; he her aid
Can never seek, once dead in sins and lost;
Atonement for himself or offering meet,
Indebted and undone, hath none to bring:
Behold mee then, mee for him, life for life
I offer, on mee let thine anger fall;
Account mee man; I for his sake will leave
Thy bosom, and this glory next to thee
Freely put off, and for him lastly die
Well pleas'd, on me let Death wreck all his rage;
Under his gloomy power I shall not long
Lie vanquisht; thou hast giv'n me to possess
Life in myself for ever, by thee I live,[6]
Though now to Death I yield, and am his due
All that of me can die, yet that debt paid,
Thou wilt not leave me in the loathsome grave
His prey, nor suffer my unspotted Soul

2. Note that human death is here regarded by God not as a punishment, but as a "satisfaction" for the treason. See *De doctrina* 1.16: "The satisfaction of Christ is the complete reparation made by him . . . by the fulfilment of the Law, and payment of the required price for all mankind."

3. Is willing to be subject to death.

4. Put down the ransom price (by giving his own life).

5. Your word of honor is pledged.

6. See John 5.26: "As the Father hath life in himself: so hath he given to the Son to have life in himself."

For ever with corruption there to dwell;
But I shall rise Victorious, and subdue
My vanquisher, spoil'd of his vaunted spoil;
Death his death's wound shall then receive, and stoop
Inglorious, of his mortal sting disarm'd.[7]
I through the ample Air in Triumph high
Shall lead Hell Captive maugre° Hell, and show *despite*
The powers of darkness bound. Thou at the sight
Pleas'd, out of Heaven shalt look down and smile,
While by thee rais'd I ruin all my Foes,
Death last, and with his Carcass glut the Grave:[8]
Then with the multitude of my redeem'd
Shall enter Heav'n long absent, and return,
Father, to see thy face, wherein no cloud
Of anger shall remain, but peace assur'd,
And reconcilement; wrath shall be no more
Thenceforth, but in thy presence Joy entire.
  His words here ended, but his meek aspéct
Silent yet spake, and breath'd immortal love
To mortal men, above which only shone
Filial obedience: as a sacrifice
Glad to be offer'd, he attends° the will *awaits*
Of his great Father. Admiration seiz'd
All Heav'n, what this might mean, and whither tend
Wond'ring; but soon th' Almighty thus repli'd:
  O thou in Heav'n and Earth the only peace
Found out for mankind under wrath, O thou
My sole complacence! well thou know'st how dear
To me are all my works, nor Man the least
Though last created, that for him I spare
Thee from my bosom and right hand, to save,
By losing thee a while, the whole Race lost.
Thou therefore whom thou only canst redeem,
Thir Nature also to thy Nature join;
And be thyself Man among men on Earth,
Made flesh, when time shall be, of Virgin seed,
By wondrous birth: Be thou in *Adam's* room° *place*
The Head of all mankind, though *Adam's* Son.
As in him perish all men, so in thee
As from a second root shall be restor'd,
As many as are restor'd, without thee none.[9]
His crime makes guilty all his Sons, thy merit
Imputed shall absolve them who renounce
Thir own both righteous and unrighteous deeds,[1]

7. See 1 Corinthians 15.55–6: "O death, where is thy sting? O grave, where is thy victory? The sting of death is sin; and the strength of sin is the law."
8. Alludes to 1 Corinthians 15.26: "The last enemy that shall be destroyed is death."
9. See 1 Corinthians 15.22: "As in Adam all die, even so in Christ shall all be made alive."
1. See *De doctrina* 1.22: "As therefore our sins are imputed to Christ, so the merits or righteousness of Christ are imputed to us through faith." If one simply renounced dependence on "righteous" deeds, one would be justified by faith alone; but for the "living faith"—faith issuing in works—that Milton believes necessary, one has to renounce (in a different sense) "unrighteous" deeds.

And live in thee transplanted, and from thee
Receive new life. So Man, as is most just,
Shall satisfy for Man, be judg'd and die,
And dying rise, and rising with him raise
His Brethren, ransom'd with his own dear life.
So Heav'nly love shall outdo Hellish hate,
Giving to death, and dying to redeem,
So dearly to redeem what Hellish hate
So easily destroy'd, and still destroys
In those who, when they may, accept not grace.
Nor shalt thou by descending to assume
Man's Nature, lessen or degrade thine own.
Because thou hast, though Thron'd in highest bliss
Equal to God, and equally enjoying
God-like fruition, quitted[2] all to save
A world from utter loss, and hast been found
By Merit more than Birthright Son of God,
Found worthiest to be so by being Good,
Far more than Great or High; because in thee
Love hath abounded more than Glory abounds,
Therefore thy Humiliation shall exalt
With thee thy Manhood also to this Throne;
Here shalt thou sit incarnate, here shalt Reign
Both God and Man, Son both of God and Man,
Anointed[3] universal King; all Power
I give thee, reign for ever, and assume
Thy Merits; under thee as Head Supreme
Thrones, Princedoms, Powers, Dominions I reduce:
All knees to thee shall bow, of them that bide
In Heaven, or Earth, or under Earth in Hell;
When thou attended gloriously from Heav'n
Shalt in the Sky appear, and from thee send
The summoning Arch-Angels to proclaim
Thy dread Tribunal: forthwith from all Winds
The living, and forthwith the cited° dead *summoned*
Of all past Ages to the general Doom° *judgment*
Shall hast'n, such a peal shall rouse thir sleep.
Then all thy Saints° assembl'd, thou shalt judge *elect*
Bad men and Angels, they arraign'd shall sink
Beneath thy Sentence; Hell, her numbers full,
Thenceforth shall be for ever shut. Meanwhile
The World shall burn, and from her ashes spring
New Heav'n and Earth, wherein the just shall dwell
And after all thir tribulations long
See golden days, fruitful of golden deeds,
With Joy and Love triumphing, and fair Truth.[4]
Then thou thy regal Sceptre shalt lay by,
For regal Sceptre then no more shall need,

2. A pun, since "quitted" meant "redeemed, remitted" as well as "left."

3. The "Anointed" in Hebrew is the Messiah.

4. The burning of Earth is based on 2 Peter 3.12ff.

God shall be All in All. But all ye Gods,° *angels*
Adore him, who to compass all this dies,
Adore the Son, and honor him as mee.
No sooner had th' Almighty ceas't, but all
The multitude of Angels with a shout
Loud as from numbers without number, sweet
As from blest voices, uttering joy, Heav'n rung
With Jubilee, and loud Hosannas fill'd
Th' eternal Regions: lowly reverent
Towards either Throne they bow, and to the ground
With solemn adoration down they cast
Thir Crowns inwove with Amarant and Gold,
Immortal Amarant,[5] a Flow'r which once
In Paradise, fast by the Tree of Life
Began to bloom, but soon for man's offense
To Heav'n remov'd where first it grew, there grows,
And flow'rs aloft shading the Fount of Life,
And where the river of Bliss through midst of Heav'n
Rolls o'er *Elysian* Flow'rs her Amber stream;[6]
With these that never fade the Spirits elect
Bind thir resplendent locks inwreath'd with beams,
Now in loose Garlands thick thrown off, the bright
Pavement that like a Sea of Jasper shone
Impurpl'd with Celestial Roses smil'd.
Then Crown'd again thir gold'n Harps they took,
Harps ever tun'd, that glittering by thir side
Like Quivers hung, and with Preamble sweet
Of charming symphony they introduce
Thir sacred Song, and waken raptures high;
No voice exempt,° no voice but well could join *debarred*
Melodious part, such concord is in Heav'n.
Thee Father first they sung Omnipotent,
Immutable, Immortal, Infinite,[7]
Eternal King; thee Author of all being,
Fountain of Light, thyself invisible
Amidst the glorious brightness where thou sit'st
Thron'd inaccessible, but° when thou shad'st *except*
The full blaze of thy beams, and through a cloud
Drawn round about thee like a radiant Shrine,
Dark with excessive bright thy skirts appear,
Yet dazzle Heav'n, that brightest Seraphim
Approach not, but with both wings veil thir eyes.
Thee next they sang of all Creation first,
Begotten Son, Divine Similitude,
In whose conspicuous count'nance, without cloud
Made visible, th' Almighty Father shines,

5. "Amaranth" in Greek means "unwithering"; a purple flower that was a "symbol of immortality"; the amarantine crown was an ancient pagan symbol of untroubled tranquillity and health.
6. Allusion to Virgil, *Aeneid* 6.656–59, the description of spirits chanting in chorus beside the Eridanus, in the Elysian fields; "amber" was a standard of purity or clarity.
7. Line 373 is transplanted in its entirety from Sylvester's translation of Du Bartas's poem on creation.

Whom else no Creature can behold;[8] on thee
Impresst th' effulgence of his Glory abides,
Transfus'd on thee his ample Spirit rests.
Hee Heav'n of Heavens and all the Powers therein
By thee created, and by thee threw down
Th' aspiring Dominations:° thou that day *rebel angels*
Thy Father's dreadful Thunder didst not spare,
Nor stop thy flaming Chariot wheels, that shook
Heav'n's everlasting Frame, while o'er the necks
Thou drov'st of warring Angels disarray'd.
Back from pursuit thy Powers with loud acclaim
Thee only extoll'd, Son of thy Father's might,
To execute fierce vengeance on his foes:
Not so on Man; him through their malice fall'n,
Father of Mercy and Grace, thou didst not doom° *judge*
So strictly, but much more to pity incline:
No sooner did thy dear and only Son
Perceive thee purpos'd not to doom frail Man
So strictly, but much more to pity inclin'd,[9]
Hee to appease thy wrath, and end the strife
Of Mercy and Justice in thy face discern'd,
Regardless of the Bliss wherein hee sat
Second to thee, offer'd himself to die
For man's offense. O unexampl'd love,
Love nowhere to be found less than Divine!
Hail Son of God, Savior of Men, thy Name
Shall be the copious matter of my Song
Henceforth, and never shall my Harp thy praise
Forget, nor from thy Father's praise disjoin.
  Thus they in Heav'n, above the starry Sphere,
Thir happy hours in joy and hymning spent.
Meanwhile upon the firm opacous Globe
Of this round World, whose first convex divides
The luminous inferior Orbs, enclos'd
From *Chaos* and th' inroad of Darkness old,[1]
Satan alighted walks: a Globe far off
It seem'd, now seems a boundless Continent
Dark, waste, and wild, under the frown of Night
Starless expos'd, and ever-threat'ning storms
Of *Chaos* blust'ring round, inclement sky;
Save on that side which from the wall of Heav'n,
Though distant far, some small reflection gains
Of glimmering air less vext° with tempest loud: *tossed about*
Here walk'd the Fiend at large in spacious field.
As when a Vultur on *Imaus* bred,
Whose snowy ridge the roving *Tartar* bounds,

8. See John 1.18 and 14.9.

9. Most editors say that "but" or "than" has to be supplied before "He" (line 406). However, if "much more to pity inclined" refers to the Son, the "but" immediately preceding is available for the main clause.

1. The "starry Sphere," is either the sphere of the fixed stars or, more loosely, the stars and planets together. The stars are enclosed within the *primum mobile* or "first convex" (sphere). Both heaven and chaos lie outside that opaque ("opacous") shell.

Dislodging from a Region scarce of prey
To gorge the flesh of Lambs or yeanling Kids
On Hills where Flocks are fed, flies toward the Springs
Of *Ganges* or *Hydaspes*, *Indian* streams;
But in his way lights on the barren Plains
Of *Sericana*, where *Chineses* drive
With Sails and Wind thir cany Waggons light:
So on this windy Sea of Land, the Fiend
Walk'd up and down alone bent on his prey,[2]
Alone, for other Creature in this place
Living or lifeless to be found was none,
None yet, but store hereafter from the earth
Up hither like Aereal vapors flew
Of all things transitory and vain, when Sin
With vanity had fill'd the works of men:[3]
Both all things vain, and all who in vain things
Built thir fond hopes of Glory or lasting fame,
Or happiness in this or th' other life;
All who have thir reward on Earth, the fruits
Of painful Superstition and blind Zeal,
Naught seeking but the praise of men, here find
Fit retribution, empty as thir deeds;
All th' unaccomplisht works of Nature's hand,
Abortive, monstrous, or unkindly mixt,
Dissolv'd on Earth, fleet hither, and in vain,
Till final dissolution, wander here,
Not in the neighboring Moon, as some have dream'd;
Those argent Fields more likely habitants,
Translated Saints,[4] or middle Spirits hold
Betwixt th' Angelical and Human kind:
Hither of ill-join'd Sons and Daughters born
First from the ancient World those Giants came
With many a vain exploit, though then renown'd:[5]
The builders next of *Babel* on the Plain
Of *Sennaar*, and still with vain design
New *Babels*, had they wherewithal, would build:[6]
Others came single; he who to be deem'd
A God, leap'd fondly into *AEtna* flames,
Empedocles, and hee who to enjoy
Plato's Elysium, leap'd into the Sea,

2. The simile compares the vulture's journey to Satan's. One journey is from Imaus, (a mountain range said to run through Afghanistan), to the rivers of India; the other is from the "frozen continent" (2.587) of Tartarus, which did not keep Satan from roving, to Eden with its rivers. The "barren plains of Sericana" correspond to the *primum mobile* because both are stopping places and in both the elements are confused. (The Chinese use sails, the means of propulsion for ships, on their land vehicles; and the *primum mobile* is a "sea of land.")

3. In *Orlando Furioso* 34.73ff., a passage from which Milton quotes in *Of Reformation*, Ariosto tells how Astolfo searches for his lost wits in a Limbo of Vanity on the moon.

4. Probably such as Enoch (Genesis 5.24) and Elijah (2 Kings 2).

5. The first group of fools are the Giants, "mighty men . . . of renown," born of the misunion of "sons of God" with "daughters of men" (Genesis 6.4).

6. At 12.45–47 the builders of Babel are said to have formed their "vain design" out of a desire for fame. "New Babels" suggests the New Babylon of anti-Papist propaganda.

Cleombrotus,[7] and many more too long,
Embryos, and Idiots, Eremites and Friars
White, Black and Grey, with all thir trumpery.[8]
Here Pilgrims roam, that stray'd so far to seek
In *Golgotha*[9] him dead, who lives in Heav'n;
And they who to be sure of Paradise
Dying put on the weeds of *Dominic*,
Or in *Franciscan* think to pass disguis'd;[1]
They pass the Planets seven, and pass the fixt,
And that Crystalline Sphere whose balance weighs
The Trepidation talkt, and that first mov'd;[2]
And now Saint *Peter* at Heav'n's Wicket seems
To wait them with his Keys, and now at foot
Of Heav'n's ascent they lift thir Feet, when lo
A violent cross wind from either Coast
Blows them transverse ten thousand Leagues awry
Into the devious Air; then might ye see
Cowls, Hoods and Habits with thir weares tost
And flutter'd into Rags, then Reliques, Beads,
Indulgences, Dispenses,[3] Pardons, Bulls,
The sport of Winds: all these upwhirl'd aloft
Fly o'er the backside of the World far off
Into a *Limbo*° large and broad, since call'd *empty region*
The Paradise of Fools, to few unknown
Long after, now unpeopl'd and untrod;
All this dark Globe the Fiend found as he pass'd,
And long he wander'd, till at last a gleam
Of dawning light turn'd thither-ward in haste
His travell'd steps; far distant he descries
Ascending by degrees magnificent
Up to the wall of Heaven a Structure high,
At top whereof, but far more rich appear'd
The work as of a Kingly Palace Gate
With Frontispiece[4] of Diamond and Gold
Imbellisht; thick with sparkling orient° Gems *brilliant*
The Portal shone, inimitable on Earth
By Model, or by shading Pencil drawn.
The Stairs were such as whereon *Jacob* saw
Angels ascending and descending, bands

7. Empedocles and Cleombrotus were not associated by classical writers but occur together in Lactantius' chapter on "Pythagoreans and Stoics who, Believing in the Immortality of the Soul, Foolishly Persuade a Voluntary Death" (*Divinae Institutiones* 3.18). Cleombrotus drowned himself after an unwise reading of Plato's *Phaedo*; Empedocles' motive was to conceal his own mortality.

8. Milton here satirizes a Catholic tradition that consigned cretins and unbaptized infants to a much debated *limbo infantum*. The friars were specified by robe color; "white" meant Carmelite, "black" Dominican, and "grey" Franciscan. The contemptuous juxtaposition of all three colors ridicules the importance assigned to external trappings. "Eremites" were Order of Friars Hermits.

9. The hill where Christ was crucified and buried.

1. Compare *Inferno* 27.67–84, in which Dante tells how Guido da Montefeltro hoped to get into heaven by virtue of Franciscan robes but found to his cost that absolution without repentance is vain.

2. In order of proximity to earth, the spheres passed are the seven planetary spheres; the eighth sphere, containing the "fixed" stars; the ninth, "crystalline sphere"; and the tenth sphere, the "first moved" or *primum mobile*.

3. A "dispense" or dispensation was an exemption from a solemn obligation by licence of an ecclesiastical dignitary, especially the Pope.

4. A decorated entrance or a pediment over the gate.

Of Guardians bright, when he from *Esau* fled
To *Padan-Aram* in the field of *Luz*,
Dreaming by night under the open Sky,
And waking cri'd, *This is the Gate of Heav'n.*[5]
Each Stair mysteriously° was meant,[6] nor stood symbolically
There always, but drawn up to Heav'n sometimes
Viewless, and underneath a bright Sea flow'd
Of Jasper, or of liquid Pearl, whereon
Who after came from Earth, sailing arriv'd,
Wafted by Angels, or flew o'er the Lake
Rapt in a Chariot drawn by fiery Steeds.
The Stairs were then let down, whether to dare
The Fiend by easy ascent, or aggravate
His sad exclusion from the doors of Bliss.
Direct against which op'n'd from beneath,
Just o'er the blissful seat of Paradise,
A passage down to th' Earth, a passage wide,
Wider by far than that of after-times
Over Mount *Sion*, and, though that were large,
Over the *Promis'd Land* to God so dear,
By which, to visit oft those happy Tribes,
On high behests his Angels to and fro
Pass'd frequent, and his eye with choice° regard careful
From *Paneas* the fount of *Jordan's* flood
To *Beërsaba*,[7] where the *Holy Land*
Borders on *Egypt* and th' *Arabian* shore;
So wide the op'ning seem'd, where bounds were set
To darkness, such as bound the Ocean wave.
Satan from hence now on the lower stair
That scal'd by steps of Gold to Heaven Gate
Looks down with wonder at the sudden view
Of all this World at once. As when a Scout
Through dark and desert ways with peril gone
All night; at last by break of cheerful dawn
Obtains° the brow of some high-climbing Hill, reaches
Which to his eye discovers unaware
The goodly prospect of some foreign land
First seen, or some renown'd Metropolis
With glistering Spires and Pinnacles adorn'd,
Which now the Rising Sun gilds with his beams.
Such wonder seiz'd, though after Heaven seen,
The Spirit malign, but much more envy seiz'd
At sight of all this World beheld so fair.[8] * * *

5. The unregenerate Jacob was terrified by the vision of a ladder reaching to heaven just after he had cheated Esau out of his father's blessing (Genesis 27–8). The experience awed him into belief and a vow to the Lord.

6. Jacob's ladder had been identified with Homer's golden chain linking the universe to Jupiter. Each "stair," or step, could be interpreted as a spiritual stage extending "from the supreme God even to the bottomest dregs of the universe."

7. "Paneas," is a later Greek name for Dan—not the city of Dan but the spring of the same name, "the easternmost fountain of Jordan." Beersaba was the southern limit of Canaan, as Dan was the northern.

8. Seeing the archangel Uriel, Satan now disguises himself as a cherub and asks the way to Eden. Uriel directs him, not realizing who he is—"For neither Man nor Angel can discern / Hypocrisy, the only evil that walks / Invisible, except to God alone" (lines 682–5).

from Book 4

The Argument

Satan *now in prospect of* Eden, *and nigh the place where he must now attempt the bold enterprise which he undertook alone against God and Man, falls into many doubts with himself, and many passions, fear, envy, and despair; but at length confirms himself in evil, journeys on to Paradise, whose outward prospect and situation is described, overleaps the bounds, sits in the shape of a Cormorant on the Tree of Life, as highest in the Garden to look about him. The Garden describ'd;* Satan's *first sight of* Adam *and* Eve; *his wonder at thir excellent form and happy state, but with resolution to work thir fall; overhears thir discourse, thence gathers that the Tree of Knowledge was forbidden them to eat of, under penalty of death; and thereon intends to found his Temptation, by seducing them to transgress: then leaves them a while, to know further of thir state by some other means. Meanwhile* Uriel *descending on a Sun-beam warns* Gabriel, *who had in charge the Gate of Paradise, that some evil spirit had escap'd the Deep, and past at Noon by his Sphere in the shape of a good Angel down to Paradise, discovered after by his furious gestures in the Mount.* Gabriel *promises to find him ere morning. Night coming on,* Adam *and* Eve *discourse of going to thir rest: thir Bower describ'd; thir Evening worship.* Gabriel *drawing forth his Bands of Night-watch to walk the round of Paradise, appoints two strong Angels to* Adam's *Bower, lest the evil spirit should be there doing some harm to* Adam *or* Eve *sleeping; there they find him at the ear of Eve, tempting her in a dream, and bring him, though unwilling, to* Gabriel; *by whom question'd, he scornfully answers, prepares resistance, but hinder'd by a Sign from Heaven, flies out of Paradise.*

O for that warning voice, which he who saw
Th' *Apocalypse*, heard cry in Heav'n aloud,
Then when the Dragon, put to second rout,
Came furious down to be reveng'd on men,
Woe to the inhabitants on Earth![1] that now,
While time was, our first Parents had been warn'd
The coming of thir secret foe, and scap'd
Haply so scap'd his mortal snare; for now
Satan, now first inflam'd with rage, came down,
The Tempter ere th' Accuser of man-kind,
To wreck° on innocent frail man his loss — *avenge*
Of that first Battle, and his flight to Hell:
Yet not rejoicing in his speed, though bold,
Far off and fearless, nor with cause to boast,
Begins his dire attempt, which nigh the birth
Now rolling, boils in his tumultuous breast,
And like a devilish Engine back recoils
Upon himself; horror and doubt distract
His troubl'd thoughts, and from the bottom stir
The Hell within him, for within him Hell
He brings, and round about him, nor from Hell
One step no more than from himself can fly
By change of place: Now conscience wakes despair

1. The *Apocalypse* of St. John relates a vision of a second battle in heaven between Michael and "the Dragon," Satan.

That slumber'd, wakes the bitter memory
Of what he was, what is, and what must be
Worse; of worse deeds worse sufferings must ensue.
Sometimes towards *Eden* which now in his view
Lay pleasant,[2] his griev'd look he fixes sad,
Sometimes towards Heav'n and the full-blazing Sun,
Which now sat high in his Meridian Tow'r:
Then much revolving, thus in sighs began.
   O thou that with surpassing Glory crown'd,
Look'st from thy sole Dominion like the God
Of this new World; at whose sight all the Stars
Hide thir diminisht heads; to thee I call,
But with no friendly voice, and add thy name
O Sun, to tell thee how I hate thy beams
That bring to my remembrance from what state
I fell, how glorious once above thy Sphere;
Till Pride and worse Ambition threw me down
Warring in Heav'n against Heav'n's matchless King:[3]
Ah wherefore! he deserv'd no such return
From me, whom he created what I was
In that bright eminence, and with his good
Upbraided none;[4] nor was his service hard.
What could be less than to afford him praise,
The easiest recompense, and pay him thanks,
How due! yet all his good prov'd ill in me,
And wrought but malice; lifted up so high
I sdein'd° subjection, and thought one step higher *disdained*
Would set me highest, and in a moment quit° *pay off*
The debt immense of endless gratitude,
So burdensome, still paying, still to owe;
Forgetful what from him I still receiv'd,
And understood not that a grateful mind
By owing owes not, but still pays, at once
Indebted and discharg'd; what burden then?[5]
O had his powerful Destiny ordain'd
Me some inferior Angel, I had stood
Then happy; no unbounded hope had rais'd
Ambition. Yet why not? some other Power
As great might have aspir'd, and me though mean
Drawn to his part; but other Powers as great
Fell not, but stand unshak'n, from within
Or from without, to all temptations arm'd.
Hadst thou the same free Will and Power to stand?
Thou hadst: whom hast thou then or what to accuse,
But Heav'n's free Love dealt equally to all?

2. The etymological meaning of "Eden" is "pleasure, delight."

3. According to Edward Phillips, lines 32–41 were shown to him and some others "before the Poem was begun," when Milton intended to write a tragedy on the Fall.

4. Demanded no return for his benefits; see James 1.5.

5. Simply by owning an obligation gratefully, one ceases to owe it.

Be then his Love accurst, since love or hate,
To me alike, it deals eternal woe.
Nay curs'd be thou; since against his thy will
Chose freely what it now so justly rues.
Me miserable! which way shall I fly
Infinite wrath, and infinite despair?
Which way I fly is Hell; myself am Hell;
And in the lowest deep a lower deep
Still threat'ning to devour me opens wide,
To which the Hell I suffer seems a Heav'n.
O then at last relent: is there no place
Left for Repentance, none for Pardon left?
None left but by submission; and that word
Disdain forbids me, and my dread of shame
Among the Spirits beneath, whom I seduc'd
With other promises and other vaunts
Than to submit, boasting I could subdue
Th' Omnipotent. Ay me, they little know
How dearly I abide that boast so vain,
Under what torments inwardly I groan:
While they adore me on the Throne of Hell,
With Diadem and Sceptre high advanc'd
The lower still I fall, only Supreme
In misery; such joy Ambition finds.
But say I could repent and could obtain
By Act of Grace[6] my former state; how soon
Would highth recall high thoughts, how soon unsay
What feign'd submission swore: ease would recant
Vows made in pain, as violent and void.
For never can true reconcilement grow
Where wounds of deadly hate have pierc'd so deep:
Which would but lead me to a worse relapse,
And heavier fall: so should I purchase dear
Short intermission bought with double smart.
This knows my punisher; therefore as far
From granting hee, as I from begging peace:
All hope excluded thus, behold instead
Of us out-cast, exil'd, his new delight,
Mankind created, and for him this World.
So farewell Hope, and with Hope farewell Fear,
Farewell Remorse: all Good to me is lost;
Evil be thou my Good; by thee at least
Divided Empire with Heav'n's King I hold
By thee, and more than half perhaps will reign;
As Man ere long, and this new World shall know.
    Thus while he spake, each passion dimm'd his face,
Thrice chang'd with pale, ire, envy and despair,

6. By concession of favor, not of right; often used for a formal pardon by Parliament.

Which marr'd his borrow'd visage, and betray'd
Him counterfeit, if any eye beheld.
For heav'nly minds from such distempers foul
Are ever clear. Whereof hee soon aware,
Each perturbation smooth'd with outward calm,
Artificer° of fraud; and was the first *inventor*
That practis'd falsehood under saintly show,
Deep malice to conceal, couch't° with revenge: *hidden*
Yet not anough had practis'd to deceive
Uriel once warn'd; whose eye pursu'd him down
The way he went, and on th' *Assyrian* mount° *Niphates*
Saw him disfigur'd, more than could befall
Spirit of happy sort: his gestures fierce
He mark'd and mad demeanor, then alone,
As he suppos'd, all unobserv'd, unseen.
So on he fares, and to the border comes
Of *Eden,* where delicious Paradise,
Now nearer, Crowns with her enclosure green,
As with a rural mound the champaign° head *unenclosed, level*
Of a steep wilderness, whose hairy sides
With thicket overgrown, grotesque and wild,
Access deni'd; and over head up grew
Insuperable highth of loftiest shade,
Cedar, and Pine, and Fir, and branching Palm,
A Silvan Scene, and as the ranks ascend
Shade above shade, a woody Theatre
Of stateliest view. Yet higher than thir tops
The verdurous wall of Paradise up sprung:
Which to our general Sire° gave prospect large *Adam*
Into his nether Empire neighboring round.
And higher than that Wall a circling row
Of goodliest Trees loaden with fairest Fruit,
Blossoms and Fruits at once of golden hue
Appear'd, with gay enamell'd° colors mixt: *lustrous*
On which the Sun more glad impress'd his beams
Than in fair Evening Cloud, or humid Bow,° *rainbow*
When God hath show'r'd the earth; so lovely seem'd
That Lantskip:° And of pure now purer air *landscape*
Meets his approach, and to the heart inspires
Vernal delight and joy, able to drive
All sadness but despair: now gentle gales
Fanning thir odoriferous wings dispense
Native perfúmes, and whisper whence they stole
Those balmy spoils. As when to them who sail
Beyond the *Cape* of *Hope,* and now are past
Mozambic,[7] off at Sea North-East winds blow
Sabean[8] Odors from the spicy shore

7. Mozambique, a Portuguese colony on the east coast of Africa; the trade route lay between Mozambique and Madagascar.

8. Of Saba or Sheba (now Yemen). Milton draws on the description of "Araby the blest"—"Arabia felix"— in Diodorus Siculus 3.46.

Of *Araby* the blest, with such delay
Well pleas'd they slack thir course, and many a League
Cheer'd with the grateful smell old Ocean smiles.
So entertain'd those odorous sweets the Fiend
Who came thir bane, though with them better pleas'd
Than *Asmodeus* with the fishy fume,
That drove him, though enamor'd, from the Spouse
Of *Tobit's* Son, and with a vengeance sent
From *Media* post to *Egypt,* there fast bound.[9]
  Now to th' ascent of that steep savage° Hill *wild*
Satan had journey'd on, pensive and slow;
But further way found none, so thick entwin'd,
As one continu'd brake, the undergrowth
Of shrubs and tangling bushes had perplext
All path of Man or Beast that pass'd that way:
One Gate there only was, and that look'd East
On th' other side: which when th' arch-felon saw
Due entrance he disdain'd, and in contempt,
At one slight bound high overleap'd all bound
Of Hill or highest Wall, and sheer within
Lights on his feet. As when a prowling Wolf,
Whom hunger drives to seek new haunt for prey,
Watching where Shepherds pen thir Flocks at eve
In hurdl'd Cotes° amid the field secure, *shelters*
Leaps o'er the fence with ease into the Fold:
Or as a Thief bent to unhoard the cash
Of some rich Burgher, whose substantial doors,
Cross-barr'd and bolted fast, fear no assault,
In at the window climbs, or o'er the tiles:
So clomb° this first grand Thief into God's Fold: *climbed*
So since into his Church lewd Hirelings[1] climb.
Thence up he flew, and on the Tree of Life,
The middle Tree and highest there that grew,
Sat like a Cormorant;[2] yet not true Life
Thereby regain'd, but sat devising Death
To them who liv'd; nor on the virtue thought
Of that life-giving Plant, but only us'd
For prospect,° what well us'd had been the pledge *lookout*
Of immortality. So little knows
Any, but God alone, to value right
The good before him, but perverts best things
To worst abuse, or to thir meanest use.
Beneath him with new wonder now he views
To all delight of human sense expos'd
In narrow room Nature's whole wealth, yea more,

9. The apocryphal book Tobit relates the story of Tobit's son Tobias, who was sent into Media on an errand and there married Sara. Sara had previously been given to seven men, but all were killed by the jealous spirit Asmodeus before their marriages could be consummated. By the advice of Raphael, however, Tobias succeeded by creating a fishy smoke to drive away the devil Asmodeus.

1. Wicked men motivated only by material gain.

2. A voracious sea bird, often used to describe greedy clergy.

A Heaven on Earth: for blissful Paradise
Of God the Garden was, by him in the East
Of *Eden* planted; *Eden* stretch'd her Line
From *Auran* Eastward to the Royal Tow'rs
Of Great *Seleucia*, built by *Grecian* Kings,
Or where the Sons of *Eden* long before
Dwelt in *Telassar:*[3] in this pleasant soil
His far more pleasant Garden God ordain'd;
Out of the fertile ground he caus'd to grow
All Trees of noblest kind for sight, smell, taste;
And all amid them stood the Tree of Life,
High eminent, blooming Ambrosial Fruit
Of vegetable Gold; and next to Life
Our Death the Tree of Knowledge grew fast by,
Knowledge of Good bought dear by knowing ill.[4]
Southward through *Eden* went a River large,
Nor chang'd his course, but through the shaggy hill
Pass'd underneath ingulft, for God had thrown
That Mountain as his Garden mould high rais'd
Upon the rapid current, which through veins
Of porous Earth with kindly° thirst up-drawn, *natural*
Rose a fresh Fountain, and with many a rill
Water'd the Garden;[5] thence united fell
Down the steep glade, and met the nether Flood,
Which from his darksome passage now appears,
And now divided into four main Streams,
Runs diverse, wand'ring many a famous Realm
And Country whereof here needs no account,
But rather to tell how, if Art could tell,
How from that Sapphire Fount the crisped° Brooks, *wavy*
Rolling on Orient Pearl and sands of Gold,
With mazy error° under pendant shades *wandering*
Ran Nectar, visiting each plant, and fed
Flow'rs worthy of Paradise which not nice° Art *careful*
In Beds and curious Knots, but Nature boon° *bounteous*
Pour'd forth profuse on Hill and Dale and Plain,
Both where the morning Sun first warmly smote
The open field, and where the unpierc't shade
Imbrown'd° the noontide Bow'rs: Thus was this place, *darkened*
A happy rural seat of various view:
Groves whose rich Trees wept odorous Gums and Balm,
Others whose fruit burnisht with Golden Rind
Hung amiable,° *Hesperian* Fables true,[6] *lovely*
If true, here only, and of delicious taste:

3. Auran was an eastern boundary of the land of Israel. Great Seleucia was built by Alexander's general Seleucus Nicator as a seat of government for his Syrian empire. The mention of Telassar prophesies war in Eden; see 2 Kings 14.11ff., where Telassar is an instance of lands destroyed utterly.

4. See Genesis 2.9.

5. See Genesis 2.10.

6. Golden fruit like the legendary apples of the western islands, the Hesperides.

Betwixt them Lawns, or level Downs, and Flocks
Grazing the tender herb, were interpos'd,
Or palmy hillock, or the flow'ry lap
Of some irriguous° Valley spread her store, *well-watered*
Flow'rs of all hue, and without Thorn the Rose:[7]
Another side, umbrageous° Grots and Caves *shady*
Of cool recess, o'er which the mantling Vine
Lays forth her purple Grape, and gently creeps
Luxuriant; meanwhile murmuring waters fall
Down the slope hills, disperst, or in a Lake,
That to the fringed Bank with Myrtle crown'd,
Her crystal mirror holds, unite thir streams.
The Birds thir choir apply;° airs, vernal airs,[8] *practice*
Breathing the smell of field and grove, attune
The trembling leaves, while Universal *Pan*[9]
Knit with the *Graces* and the *Hours* in dance
Led on th' Eternal Spring.[1] Not that fair field
Of *Enna*, where *Proserpin* gath'ring flow'rs
Herself a fairer Flow'r by gloomy *Dis*
Was gather'd, which cost *Ceres* all that pain
To seek her through the world;[2] nor that sweet Grove
Of *Daphne* by *Orontes*, and th' inspir'd
Castalian Spring[3] might with this Paradise
Of *Eden* strive; nor that *Nyseian* Isle
Girt with the River *Triton*, where old *Cham*,
Whom Gentiles *Ammon* call and *Lybian Jove*,
Hid *Amalthea* and her Florid° Son, *ruddy-complexioned*
Young *Bacchus*, from his Stepdame *Rhea's* eye;[4]
Nor where *Abassin* Kings thir issue Guard,
Mount *Amara*, though this by some suppos'd
True Paradise under the *Ethiop* Line
By *Nilus* head, enclos'd with shining Rock,
A whole day's journey high,[5] but wide remote
From this *Assyrian* Garden, where the Fiend
Saw undelighted all delight, all kind
Of living Creatures new to sight and strange:
Two of far nobler shape erect and tall,
Godlike erect, with native Honor clad
In naked Majesty seem'd Lords of all,

7. The thornless rose was used to symbolize the sinless state of humanity before the Fall; or the state of grace.

8. Breezes and melodies.

9. Pan (Greek for "all") was a symbol of universal nature.

1. Neoplatonists thought the triadic pattern of their dance expressed the movement underlying all natural generation.

2. The rape of Proserpina by Dis, the king of hell, was located in *Enna* by Ovid (*Fasti* 4.420ff.). The search for her made the world barren, and even when she was found, she was restored to Ceres—and fruitfulness to the world—only for half the year.

3. The grove called "Daphne" beside the River Orontes, near Antioch, had an Apolline oracle and a stream named after the famous Castalian spring of Parnassus.

4. Ammon, King of Libya, had an illicit affair with a maiden Amaltheia, who gave birth to a marvelous son Dionysus (Bacchus). To protect mother and child from the jealousy of his wife Rhea, Ammon hid them on Nysa, an island near modern Tunis. The identifications of Ammon with the Libyan Jupiter and with Noah's son Ham were widely accepted.

5. Milton takes his description of Mount Amara from Peter Heylyn's *Cosmographie* 4.64.

And worthy seem'd, for in thir looks Divine
The image of thir glorious Maker shone,[6]
Truth, Wisdom, Sanctitude severe and pure,
Severe, but in true filial freedom plac't;
Whence true autority in men; though both
Not equal, as thir sex not equal seem'd;
For contemplation hee and valor form'd,
For softness shee and sweet attractive Grace,
Hee for God only, shee for God in him:[7]
His fair large Front° and Eye sublime° declar'd *forehead/uplifted*
Absolute rule; and Hyacinthine Locks
Round from his parted forelock manly hung
Clust'ring, but not beneath his shoulders broad:
Shee as a veil down to the slender waist
Her unadorned golden tresses wore
Dishevell'd, but in wanton ringlets wav'd
As the Vine curls her tendrils, which impli'd
Subjection, but requir'd with gentle sway,
And by her yielded, by him best receiv'd,
Yielded with coy° submission, modest pride, *modest*
And sweet reluctant amorous delay.
Nor those mysterious parts were then conceal'd,
Then was not guilty shame: dishonest shame
Of Nature's works, honor dishonorable,
Sin-bred, how have ye troubl'd all mankind
With shows instead, mere shows of seeming pure,
And banisht from man's life his happiest life,
Simplicity and spotless innocence.
So pass'd they naked on, nor shunn'd the sight
Of God or Angel, for they thought no ill:
So hand in hand they pass'd, the loveliest pair
That ever since in love's imbraces met,
Adam the goodliest man of men since born
His Sons, the fairest of her Daughters *Eve*.
Under a tuft of shade that on a green
Stood whispering soft, by a fresh Fountain side
They sat them down, and after no more toil
Of thir sweet Gard'ning labor than suffic'd
To recommend cool *Zephyr*,[8] and made ease
More easy, wholesome thirst and appetite
More grateful, to thir Supper Fruits they fell,
Nectarine Fruits which the compliant boughs
Yielded them, side-long as they sat recline° *lying down*
On the soft downy Bank damaskt with flow'rs:
The savory pulp they chew, and in the rind
Still as they thirsted scoop the brimming stream;

6. See Genesis 1.27: "God created man in his own image."

7. See 1 Corinthians 11.3: "The head of every man is Christ; and the head of the woman is the man; and the head of Christ is God."

8. The west wind.

Nor gentle purpose,° nor endearing smiles *conversation*
Wanted,° nor youthful dalliance as beseems *lacked*
Fair couple, linkt in happy nuptial League,
Alone as they. About them frisking play'd
All Beasts of th' Earth, since wild, and of all chase
In Wood or Wilderness, Forest or Den;
Sporting the Lion ramp'd,° and in his paw *reared up*
Dandl'd the Kid; Bears, Tigers, Ounces,° Pards° *lynxes/leopards*
Gamboll'd before them, th' unwieldy Elephant
To make them mirth us'd all his might, and wreath'd
His Lithe Proboscis; close the Serpent sly
Insinuating,[9] wove with Gordian twine[1]
His braided train, and of his fatal guile
Gave proof unheeded; others on the grass
Coucht, and now fill'd with pasture gazing sat,
Or Bedward ruminating;[2] for the Sun
Declin'd was hasting now with prone career
To th' Ocean Isles,[3] and in th' ascending Scale
Of Heav'n the Stars that usher Evening rose:
When *Satan* still in gaze, as first he stood,
Scarce thus at length fail'd speech recover'd sad.
O Hell! what do mine eyes with grief behold,
Into our room of bliss thus high advanc't
Creatures of other mould, earth-born perhaps,
Not Spirits, yet to heav'nly Spirits bright
Little inferior; whom my thoughts pursue
With wonder, and could love, so lively shines
In them Divine resemblance, and such grace
The hand that form'd them on thir shape hath pour'd.
Ah gentle pair, yee little think how nigh
Your change approaches, when all these delights
Will vanish and deliver ye to woe,
More woe, the more your taste is now of joy;
Happy, but for so happy ill secur'd
Long to continue, and this high seat your Heav'n
Ill fenc't for Heav'n to keep out such a foe
As now is enter'd; yet no purpos'd foe
To you whom I could pity thus forlorn
Though I unpitied: League with you I seek,
And mutual amity so strait,° so close, *intimate*
That I with you must dwell, or you with me
Henceforth; my dwelling haply may not please
Like this fair Paradise, your sense, yet such
Accept your Maker's work; he gave it me,
Which I as freely give; Hell shall unfold,[4]

9. Penetrating by sinuous ways.
1. Coil, convolution, as difficult to undo as the Gordian knot, which it took the hero Alexander to cut.
2. Chewing the cud before going to rest.
3. The Azores.
4. A blasphemous echo of Matthew 10.8 ("freely ye have received, freely give").

To entertain you two, her widest Gates,
And send forth all her Kings; there will be room,
Not like these narrow limits, to receive
Your numerous offspring; if no better place,
Thank him who puts me loath to this revenge
On you who wrong me not for him who wrong'd.
And should I at your harmless innocence
Melt, as I do, yet public reason[5] just,
Honor and Empire with revenge enlarg'd,
By conquering this new World, compels me now
To do what else though damn'd I should abhor.
So spake the Fiend, and with necessity,
The Tyrant's plea, excus'd his devilish deeds.
Then from his lofty stand on that high Tree
Down he alights among the sportful Herd
Of those fourfooted kinds, himself now one,
Now other, as thir shape serv'd best his end
Nearer to view his prey, and unespi'd
To mark what of thir state he more might learn
By word or action markt: about them round
A Lion now he stalks with fiery glare,
Then as a Tiger, who by chance hath spi'd
In some Purlieu° two gentle Fawns at play, *edge of a forest*
Straight couches close, then rising changes oft
His couchant watch, as one who chose his ground
Whence rushing he might surest seize them both
Gript in each paw: when *Adam* first of men
To first of women *Eve* thus moving speech,
Turn'd him° all ear to hear new utterance flow. *Satan*
Sole partner and sole part of all these joys,[6]
Dearer thyself than all; needs must the Power
That made us, and for us this ample World
Be infinitely good, and of his good
As liberal and free as infinite,
That rais'd us from the dust and plac't us here
In all this happiness, who at his hand
Have nothing merited, nor can perform
Aught whereof hee hath need, hee who requires
From us no other service than to keep
This one, this easy charge, of all the Trees
In Paradise that bear delicious fruit
So various, not to taste that only Tree
Of Knowledge, planted by the Tree of Life,[7]
So near grows Death to Life, whate'er Death is,
Some dreadful thing no doubt; for well thou know'st
God hath pronounc't it death to taste that Tree,

5. Reason of state, a perversion of the Ciceronian principle (*Laws* 3.3.8) that the good of the people is the supreme law.

6. The first "sole" means "only"; the second, "unrivalled."

7. See Genesis 2.16ff.

The only sign of our obedience left
Among so many signs of power and rule
Conferr'd upon us, and Dominion giv'n
Over all other Creatures that possess
Earth, Air, and Sea.[8] Then let us not think hard
One easy prohibition, who enjoy
Free leave so large to all things else, and choice
Unlimited of manifold delights:
But let us ever praise him, and extol
His bounty, following our delightful task
To prune these growing Plants, and tend these Flow'rs,
Which were it toilsome, yet with thee were sweet.
To whom thus Eve repli'd. O thou for whom
And from whom I was form'd flesh of thy flesh,[9]
And without whom am to no end, my Guide
And Head, what thou hast said is just and right.[1]
For wee to him indeed all praises owe,
And daily thanks, I chiefly who enjoy
So far the happier Lot, enjoying thee
Preëminent by so much odds,° while thou *advantage*
Like consort to thyself canst nowhere find.
That day I oft remember, when from sleep
I first awak't, and found myself repos'd
Under a shade on flow'rs, much wond'ring where
And what I was, whence thither brought, and how.
Not distant far from thence a murmuring sound
Of waters issu'd from a Cave and spread
Into a liquid Plain, then stood unmov'd
Pure as th' expanse of Heav'n; I thither went
With unexperienc't thought, and laid me down
On the green bank, to look into the clear
Smooth Lake, that to me seem'd another Sky.
As I bent down to look, just opposite,
A Shape within the wat'ry gleam appear'd
Bending to look on me, I started back,
It started back, but pleas'd I soon return'd,
Pleas'd it return'd as soon with answering looks
Of sympathy and love; there I had fixt
Mine eyes till now, and pin'd with vain desire,[2]
Had not a voice thus warn'd me, What thou seest,
What there thou seest fair Creature is thyself,
With thee it came and goes: but follow me,
And I will bring thee where no shadow stays° *awaits*

8. See Genesis 1.28: "God said unto them . . . have dominion over the fish of the sea, and over the fowl of the air, and over every living thing that moveth upon the earth."

9. See 1 Corinthians 11.9: "Neither was the man created for the woman; but the woman for the man." See Genesis 2.23.

1. See 1 Corinthians 11.3: "The head of every man is Christ; and the head of the woman is the man; and the head of Christ is God."

2. Alluding to Ovid's story of the proud youth Narcissus, who was punished for his scornfulness by being made to fall in love with his own reflection in a pool.

Thy coming, and thy soft imbraces, hee
Whose image thou art, him thou shalt enjoy
Inseparably thine, to him shalt bear
Multitudes like thyself, and thence be call'd
Mother of human Race: what could I do,
But follow straight, invisibly thus led?
Till I espi'd thee, fair indeed and tall,
Under a Platan, yet methought less fair,
Less winning soft, less amiably mild,
Than that smooth wat'ry image; back I turn'd,
Thou following cri'd'st aloud, Return fair *Eve,*
Whom fli'st thou? whom thou fli'st, of him thou art,
His flesh, his bone; to give thee being I lent
Out of my side to thee, nearest my heart
Substantial Life, to have thee by my side
Henceforth an individual° solace dear; *inseparable*
Part of my Soul I seek thee, and thee claim
My other half: with that thy gentle hand
Seiz'd mine, I yielded, and from that time see
How beauty is excell'd by manly grace
And wisdom, which alone is truly fair.
  So spake our general Mother, and with eyes
Of conjugal attraction unreprov'd,° *innocent*
And meek surrender, half imbracing lean'd
On our first Father, half her swelling Breast
Naked met his under the flowing Gold
Of her loose tresses hid: hee in delight
Both of her Beauty and submissive Charms
Smil'd with superior Love, as *Jupiter*
On *Juno* smiles, when he impregns° the Clouds *impregnates*
That shed *May* Flowers; and press'd her Matron lip
With kisses pure: aside the Devil turn'd
For envy, yet with jealous leer malign
Ey'd them askance, and to himself thus plain'd.° *complained*
  Sight hateful, sight tormenting! thus these two
Imparadis't in one another's arms
The happier *Eden,* shall enjoy thir fill
Of bliss on bliss, while I to Hell am thrust,
Where neither joy nor love, but fierce desire,
Among our other torments not the least,
Still unfulfill'd with pain of longing pines;° *troubles*
Yet let me not forget what I have gain'd
From thir own mouths; all is not theirs it seems:
One fatal Tree there stands of Knowledge call'd,
Forbidden them to taste: Knowledge forbidd'n?
Suspicious, reasonless. Why should thir Lord
Envy them that? can it be sin to know,
Can it be death? and do they only stand
By Ignorance, is that thir happy state,
The proof of thir obedience and thir faith?

O fair foundation laid whereon to build
Thir ruin! Hence I will excite thir minds
With more desire to know, and to reject
Envious commands, invented with design
To keep them low whom Knowledge might exalt
Equal with Gods; aspiring to be such,
They taste and die: what likelier can ensue?
But first with narrow search I must walk round
This Garden, and no corner leave unspi'd;
A chance but chance[3] may lead where I may met
Some wand'ring Spirit of Heav'n, by Fountain side,
Or in thick shade retir'd, from him to draw
What further would be learnt. Live while ye may,
Yet happy pair; enjoy, till I return,
Short pleasures, for long woes are to succeed.
  So saying, his proud step he scornful turn'd,
But with sly circumspection, and began
Through wood, through waste, o'er hill, o'er dale his roam.
Meanwhile in utmost Longitude,[4] where Heav'n
With Earth and Ocean meets, the setting Sun
Slowly descended, and with right aspect
Against the eastern Gate of Paradise
Levell'd his ev'ning Rays: it was a Rock
Of Alablaster,° pil'd up to the Clouds, *alabaster*
Conspicuous far, winding with one ascent
Accessible from Earth, one entrance high;
The rest was craggy cliff, that overhung
Still as it rose, impossible to climb.[5]
Betwixt these rocky Pillars *Gabriel*[6] sat
Chief of th' Angelic Guards, awaiting night;
About him exercis'd Heroic Games
Th' unarmed Youth of Heav'n, but nigh at hand
Celestial Armory, Shields, Helms, and Spears
Hung high with Diamond flaming, and with Gold.
Thither came *Uriel*, gliding through the Even
On a Sun-beam, swift as a shooting Star
In *Autumn* thwarts° the night, when vapors fir'd *crosses*
Impress the Air, and shows the Mariner
From what point of his Compass to beware
Impetuous winds:[7] he thus began in haste.
  Gabriel, to thee thy course by Lot hath giv'n
Charge and strict watch that to this happy place
No evil thing approach or enter in;
This day at highth of Noon came to my Sphere
A Spirit, zealous, as he seem'd, to know

3. An accident and an opportunity.
4. The farthest west.
5. A possible source is the paradise of Mount Amara in Heylyn's *Cosmographie*.
6. "Strength of God," one of the four archangels ruling the corners of the world.
7. Shooting stars were thought to be a sign of storm because in falling they were thrust down by winds.

More of th' Almighty's works, and chiefly Man
God's latest Image: I describ'd° his way *observed*
Bent all on speed, and markt his Aery Gait;
But in the Mount that lies from *Eden* North,
Where he first lighted, soon discern'd his looks
Alien from Heav'n, with passions foul obscur'd:
Mine eye pursu'd him still, but under shade
Lost sight of him; one of the banisht crew
I fear, hath ventur'd from the Deep, to raise
New troubles; him thy care must be to find.
To whom the winged Warrior thus return'd:
Uriel,[8] no wonder if thy perfect sight,
Amid the Sun's bright circle where thou sitst,
See far and wide: in at this Gate none pass
The vigilance here plac't, but such as come
Well known from Heav'n; and since Meridian hour
No Creature thence: if Spirit of other sort,
So minded, have o'erleapt these earthy bounds
On purpose, hard thou know'st it to exclude
Spiritual substance with corporeal bar.
But if within the circuit of these walks
In whatsoever shape he lurk, of whom
Thou tell'st, by morrow dawning I shall know.
So promis'd hee, and *Uriel* to his charge
Return'd on that bright beam, whose point now rais'd
Bore him slope downward to the Sun now fall'n
Beneath th' *Azores;* whither the prime Orb,
Incredible how swift, had thither roll'd
Diurnal,° or this less volúbil[9] Earth *in one day*
By shorter flight to th' East, had left him there
Arraying with reflected Purple and Gold
The Clouds that on his Western Throne attend:[1]
Now came still Ev'ning on, and Twilight gray
Had in her sober Livery all things clad;
Silence accompanied, for Beast and Bird,
They to thir grassy Couch, these to thir Nests
Were slunk, all but the wakeful Nightingale;
She all night long her amorous descant sung;
Silence was pleas'd: now glow'd the Firmament
With living Sapphires: *Hesperus*[2] that led
The starry Host, rode brightest, till the Moon
Rising in clouded Majesty, at length
Apparent Queen unveil'd her peerless light,
And o'er the dark her Silver Mantle threw.
When *Adam* thus to *Eve:* Fair Consort, th' hour
Of night, and all things now retir'd to rest
Mind us of like repose, since God hath set

8. "Light of God."
9. Capable of ready rotation on its axis.
1. The appearance of sunset can be regarded as caused either by orbital motion of the sun about the earth or by the earth's rotation (a lesser movement).
2. The evening star.

Labor and rest, as day and night to men
Successive, and the timely dew of sleep
Now falling with soft slumbrous weight inclines
Our eye-lids; other Creatures all day long
Rove idle unimploy'd, and less need rest;
Man hath his daily work of body or mind
Appointed, which declares his Dignity,
And the regard of Heav'n on all his ways;
While other Animals unactive range,
And of thir doings God takes no account.
Tomorrow ere fresh Morning streak the East
With first approach of light, we must be ris'n,
And at our pleasant labor, to reform
Yon flow'ry Arbors, yonder Alleys green,
Our walk at noon, with branches overgrown,
That mock our scant manuring,° and require *cultivating*
More hands than ours to lop thir wanton growth:
Those Blossoms also, and those dropping Gums,
That lie bestrown unsightly and unsmooth,
Ask riddance, if we mean to tread with ease;
Meanwhile, as Nature wills, Night bids us rest.
  To whom thus *Eve* with perfect beauty adorn'd.
My Author° and Disposer, what thou bidd'st *origin, creator*
Unargu'd I obey; so God ordains,
God is thy Law, thou mine: to know no more
Is woman's happiest knowledge and her praise.
With thee conversing I forget all time,
All seasons and thir change, all please alike.[3]
Sweet is the breath of morn, her rising sweet,
With charm° of earliest Birds; pleasant the Sun *song*
When first on this delightful Land he spreads
His orient Beams, on herb, tree, fruit, and flow'r,
Glist'ring with dew; fragrant the fertile earth
After soft showers; and sweet the coming on
Of grateful Ev'ning mild, then silent Night
With this her solemn Bird and this fair Moon,
And these the Gems of Heav'n, her starry train:
But neither breath of Morn when she ascends
With charm of earliest Birds, nor rising Sun
On this delightful land, nor herb, fruit, flow'r,
Glist'ring with dew, nor fragrance after showers,
Nor grateful Ev'ning mild, nor silent Night
With this her solemn Bird, nor walk by Moon,
Or glittering Star-light without thee is sweet.
But wherefore all night long shine these, for whom
This glorious sight, when sleep hath shut all eyes?
  To whom our general Ancestor repli'd.
Daughter of God and Man, accomplish't *Eve*,

3. Time of day; not "seasons of the year," since it is still eternal spring.

Those have thir course to finish, round the Earth,
By morrow Ev'ning, and from Land to Land
In order, though to Nations yet unborn,
Minist'ring light prepar'd, they set and rise;
Lest total darkness should by Night regain
Her old possession, and extinguish life
In Nature and all things, which these soft fires
Not only enlighten, but with kindly heat
Of various influence foment and warm,
Temper or nourish, or in part shed down
Thir stellar virtue on all kinds that grow
On Earth, made hereby apter to receive
Perfection from the Sun's more potent Ray.[4]
These then, though unbeheld in deep of night,
Shine not in vain, nor think, though men were none,
That Heav'n would want spectators, God want praise;
Millions of spiritual Creatures walk the Earth
Unseen, both when we wake, and when we sleep:
All these with ceaseless praise his works behold
Both day and night: how often from the steep
Of echoing Hill or Thicket have we heard
Celestial voices to the midnight air,
Sole, or responsive each to other's note
Singing thir great Creator: oft in bands
While they keep watch, or nightly rounding walk,
With Heav'nly touch of instrumental sounds
In full harmonic number join'd, thir songs
Divide the night, and lift our thoughts to Heaven.
Thus talking hand in hand alone they pass'd
On to thir blissful Bower; it was a place
Chos'n by the sovran Planter, when he fram'd
All things to man's delightful use; the roof
Of thickest covert was inwoven shade
Laurel and Myrtle, and what higher grew
Of firm and fragrant leaf; on either side
Acanthus, and each odorous bushy shrub
Fenc'd up the verdant wall; each beauteous flow'r,
Iris all hues, Roses, and Jessamin° *jasmine*
Rear'd high thir flourisht heads between, and wrought
Mosaic; underfoot the Violet,
Crocus, and Hyacinth with rich inlay
Broider'd the ground, more color'd than with stone
Of costliest Emblem:[5] other Creature here

4. In Neoplatonic astrology, Sol was said to accomplish the generation of new life by acting through each of the other planets in turn; their function was only to modulate his influence or to select from his complete spectrum of virtues. After the Fall, the influence of the stars becomes less "kindly" (benign; natural).

5. Any ornament of inlaid work; the other sense of "emblem" (pictorial symbol) also operates here, to draw attention to the emblematic properties of the flowers (the humility of the violet, prudence of the hyacinth, amiability of the jasmine, etc.). The bower as a whole is an emblem of true married love.

Beast, Bird, Insect, or Worm durst enter none;
Such was thir awe of Man. In shadier Bower
More sacred and sequester'd, though but feign'd,
Pan or *Silvanus* never slept, nor Nymph,
Nor *Faunus* haunted.[6] Here in close recess
With Flowers, Garlands, and sweet-smelling Herbs
Espoused *Eve* deckt first her Nuptial Bed,
And heav'nly Choirs the Hymenaean° sung, [*wedding hymn*]
What day the genial° Angel to our Sire [*nuptial, generative*]
Brought her in naked beauty more adorn'd,
More lovely than *Pandora,* whom the Gods
Endow'd with all thir gifts, and O too like
In sad event, when to the unwiser Son
Of *Japhet* brought by *Hermes,* she ensnar'd
Mankind with her fair looks, to be aveng'd
On him who had stole *Jove's* authentic fire.[7]
   Thus at thir shady Lodge arriv'd, both stood,
Both turn'd, and under op'n Sky ador'd
The God that made both Sky, Air, Earth and Heav'n
Which they beheld, the Moon's resplendent Globe
And starry Pole:° Thou also mad'st the Night, [*sky*]
Maker Omnipotent, and thou the Day,
Which we in our appointed work imploy'd
Have finisht happy in our mutual help
And mutual love, the Crown of all our bliss
Ordain'd by thee, and this delicious place
For us too large, where thy abundance wants
Partakers, and uncropt falls to the ground.
But thou hast promis'd from us two a Race
To fill the Earth, who shall with us extol
Thy goodness infinite, both when we wake,
And when we seek, as now, thy gift of sleep.
   This said unanimous, and other Rites
Observing none, but adoration pure
Which God likes best, into thir inmost bower
Handed they went; and eas'd the putting off
These troublesome disguises which wee wear,
Straight side by side were laid, nor turn'd I ween
Adam from his fair Spouse, nor *Eve* the Rites
Mysterious of connubial Love refus'd:

6. Pan, Silvanus, and Faunus were confused, for all were represented as half man, half goat. Pan was a symbol of fecundity; Silvanus, god of woods, symbolized gardens and limits; Faunus, the Roman Pan, a wood god, and the father of satyrs, was an emblem of concupiscence.

7. Milton has followed Charles Estienne's version of the myth: "Pandora . . . is feigned by Hesiod the first woman—made by Vulcan at Jupiter's command— . . . she was called Pandora, either because she was 'endowed with all [the gods'] gifts,' or because she was endowed with gifts by all." She was "sent with a closed casket to Epimetheus, since Jupiter wanted revenge on the human race for the boldness of Prometheus, who had stolen fire from heaven and taken it . . . down to earth; and that Epimetheus received her and opened the casket, which contained every kind of evil, so that it filled the world with diseases and calamaties." Prometheus and Epimetheus were sons of Iapetus, the Titan son of Coelus and Terra. Milton identifies Iapetus with Iaphet (Noah's son).

Whatever Hypocrites austerely talk
Of purity and place and innocence,
Defaming as impure what God declares
Pure, and commands to some, leaves free to all.
Our Maker bids increase,[8] who bids abstain
But our Destroyer, foe to God and Man?
Hail wedded Love, mysterious Law, true source
Of human offspring, sole propriety
In Paradise of all things common else.
By thee adulterous lust was driv'n from men
Among the bestial herds to range, by thee
Founded in Reason, Loyal, Just, and Pure,
Relations dear, and all the Charities° *affections*
Of Father, Son, and Brother first were known.
Far be it, that I should write thee sin or blame,
Or think thee unbefitting holiest place,
Perpetual Fountain of Domestic sweets,
Whose bed is undefil'd and chaste pronounc't,[9]
Present, or past, as Saints and Patriarchs us'd.
Here Love his golden shafts imploys,[1] here lights
His constant Lamp, and waves his purple wings,
Reigns here and revels; not in the bought smile
Of Harlots, loveless, joyless, unindear'd,
Casual fruition, nor in Court Amours,
Mixt Dance, or wanton Mask, or Midnight Ball,
Or Serenate, which the starv'd Lover sings
To his proud fair, best quitted with disdain.
These lull'd by Nightingales imbracing slept,
And on thir naked limbs the flow'ry roof
Show'r'd Roses, which the Morn repair'd.° Sleep on, *made up for*
Blest pair; and O yet happiest if ye seek
No happier state, and know to know no more.[2]
  Now had night measur'd with her shadowy Cone
Half way up Hill this vast Sublunar Vault,[3]
And from thir Ivory Port the Cherubim
Forth issuing at th' accustom'd hour stood arm'd
To thir night watches in warlike Parade,
When *Gabriel* to his next in power thus spake.
  Uzziel,[4] half these draw off, and coast the South
With strictest watch; these other wheel the North;
Our circuit meets full West. As flame they part
Half wheeling to the Shield, half to the Spear.[5]

8. See Genesis 1.28.
9. See Hebrews 13.4: "Marriage is honourable in all, and the bed undefiled."
1. Cupid's "golden shafts" were sharp and gleaming and kindled love, while those of lead were blunt and put love to flight (Ovid, *Metamorphoses* 1.468–471).
2. Either "know that it is best not to seek new knowledge (by eating the forbidden fruit)" or "know how to limit your experience to the state of innocence."
3. The earth's shadow is a cone that appears to circle around it in diametrical opposition to the sun. When the axis of the cone reaches the meridian, it is midnight; but here it is only "Half way up," so the time is nine o'clock.
4. "Uzziel" (Strength of God) occurs in the Bible as an ordinary human name (e.g., Exodus 6.18), and so does "Zephon" (Searcher of Secrets: Numbers 26.15). "Ithuriel" (Discovery of God) is not from the Bible.
5. "Shield" for "left" and "spear" for "right" were ancient military terms.

From these, two strong and subtle Spirits he call'd
That near him stood, and gave them thus in charge.
Ithuriel and *Zephon*, with wing'd speed
Search through this Garden, leave unsearcht no nook,
But chiefly where those two fair Creatures Lodge,
Now laid perhaps asleep secure° of harm. *careless*
This Ev'ning from the Sun's decline arriv'd
Who tells of some infernal Spirit seen
Hitherward bent (who could have thought?) escap'd
The bars of Hell, on errand bad no doubt:
Such where ye find, seize fast, and hither bring.
So saying, on he led his radiant Files,
Dazzling the Moon; these to the Bower direct
In search of whom they sought: him there they found
Squat like a Toad, close at the ear of *Eve*;
Assaying by his Devilish art to reach
The Organs of her Fancy, and with them forge
Illusions as he list, Phantasms° and Dreams, *illusions*
Or if, inspiring venom, he might taint
Th' animal spirits[6] that from pure blood arise
Like gentle breaths from Rivers pure, thence raise
At least distemper'd,° discontented thoughts, *vexed*
Vain hopes, vain aims, inordinate desires
Blown up with high conceits ingend'ring pride.
Him thus intent *Ithuriel* with his Spear
Touch'd lightly; for no falsehood can endure
Touch of Celestial temper, but returns
Of force to its own likeness: up he starts
Discover'd and surpris'd. As when a spark
Lights on a heap of nitrous[7] Powder, laid
Fit for the Tun[8] some Magazin to store
Against° a rumor'd War, the Smutty grain *preparing for*
With sudden blaze diffus'd, inflames the Air:
So started up in his own shape the Fiend.
Back stepp'd those two fair Angels half amaz'd
So sudden to behold the grisly King;
Yet thus, unmov'd with fear, accost him soon.
Which of those rebel Spirits adjudg'd to Hell
Com'st thou, escap'd thy prison, and transform'd,
Why satst thou like an enemy in wait
Here watching at the head of these that sleep?
Know ye not then said *Satan*, fill'd with scorn,
Know ye not mee?[9] * * *

6. Spirits in this sense were fine vapors, regarded by some as a medium between body and soul, by others as a separate soul. Animal spirits (Latin *anima*, soul) ascended to the brain and issued through the nerves to impart motion to the body. Local movement of the animal spirits could also produce imaginative apparitions, by which angels were thought to affect the human mind.

7. Mixed with niter (potassium nitrate or saltpeter, an ingredient in gunpowder) to form an explosive.

8. In proper condition for casking, ready for use.

9. Ithuriel and Zephon take Satan to Gabriel, who orders him to return to Hell. Satan rises up to fight the assembled angels—"His Stature reacht the Sky, and on his Crest / Sat horror Plum'd"—but then God displays scales in heaven, showing victory tilting to Gabriel, and Satan flees.

from Book 5

The Argument

Morning approacht, Eve *relates to* Adam *her troublesome dream; he likes it not, yet comforts her: They come forth to thir day labors: Thir Morning Hymn at the Door of thir Bower. God to render Man inexcusable sends* Raphael *to admonish him of his obedience, of his free estate, of his enemy near at hand; who he is, and why his enemy, and whatever else may avail* Adam *to know.* Raphael *comes down to Paradise, his appearance describ'd, his coming discern'd by* Adam *afar off sitting at the door of his Bower; he goes out to meet him, brings him to his lodge, entertains him with the choicest fruits of Paradise got together by* Eve; *thir discourse at Table:* Raphael *performs his message, minds* Adam *of his state and of his enemy; relates at* Adam's *request who that enemy is, and how he came to be so, beginning from his first revolt in Heaven, and the occasion thereof; how he drew his Legions after him to the parts of the North, and there incited them to rebel with him, persuading all but only* Abdiel *a Seraph, who in Argument dissuades and opposes him, then forsakes him.*

Now Morn her rosy steps in th' Eastern Clime
Advancing, sow'd the Earth with Orient Pearl,
When *Adam* wak't, so custom'd, for his sleep
Was Aery light, from pure digestion bred,
And temperate vapors bland, which th' only sound
Of leaves and fuming rills, *Aurora's* fan,
Lightly dispers'd, and the shrill Matin° Song *morning*
Of Birds on every bough;[1] so much the more
His wonder was to find unwak'n'd *Eve*
With Tresses discompos'd, and glowing Cheek,
As through unquiet rest: hee on his side
Leaning half-rais'd, with looks of cordial Love
Hung over her enamor'd, and beheld
Beauty, which whether waking or asleep,
Shot forth peculiar° graces; then with voice *distinctive*
Mild, as when *Zephyrus*[2] on *Flora* breathes,
Her hand soft touching, whisper'd thus. Awake
My fairest, my espous'd, my latest found,
Heav'n's last best gift, my ever new delight,
Awake, the morning shines, and the fresh field
Calls us; we lose the prime,[3] to mark how spring
Our tended Plants, how blows° the Citron Grove, *blossoms*
What drops the Myrrh, and what the balmy Reed,
How Nature paints her colors, how the Bee
Sits on the Bloom extracting liquid sweet.[4]
Such whispering wak'd her, but with startl'd eye
On *Adam*, whom imbracing, thus she spake.
O Sole in whom my thoughts find all repose,
My Glory, my Perfection, glad I see

1. The "only" (mere) sound of leaves, water, and birds was enough to rouse Adam. The fan of Aurora, the goddess of morning, is the leaves.
2. The west wind. Zephyrus's sweet breath was supposed to produce flowers, as was that of his wife, the flower-goddess Flora.
3. The first hour of the day.
4. For lines 18–25, see Song of Solomon 2.10–13 and 7.12.

Thy face, and Morn return'd, for I this Night,
Such night till this I never pass'd, have dream'd,
If dream'd, not as I oft am wont, of thee,
Works of day past, or morrow's next design,
But of offense and trouble, which my mind
Knew never till this irksome night; methought
Close at mine ear one call'd me forth to walk
With gentle voice, I thought it thine; it said,
Why sleep'st thou *Eve?* now is the pleasant time,
The cool, the silent, save where silence yields
To the night-warbling Bird, that now awake
Tunes sweetest his love-labor'd song; now reigns
Full Orb'd the Moon, and with more pleasing light
Shadowy sets off the face of things; in vain,
If none regard; Heav'n wakes with all his eyes,
Whom to behold but thee, Nature's desire,
In whose sight all things joy, with ravishment
Attracted by thy beauty still to gaze.
I rose as at thy call, but found thee not;
To find thee I directed then my walk;
And on, methought, alone I pass'd through ways
That brought me on a sudden to the Tree
Of interdicted Knowledge: fair it seem'd,
Much fairer to my Fancy than by day:
And as I wond'ring lookt, beside it stood
One shap'd and wing'd like one of those from Heav'n
By us oft seen; his dewy locks distill'd
Ambrosia;[5] on that Tree he also gaz'd;
And O fair Plant, said he, with fruit surcharg'd,
Deigns none to ease thy load and taste thy sweet,
Nor God, nor Man; is Knowledge so despis'd?
Or envy, or what reserve[6] forbids to taste?
Forbid who will, none shall from me withhold
Longer thy offer'd good, why else set here?
This said he paus'd not, but with vent'rous Arm
He pluckt, he tasted; mee damp horror chill'd
At such bold words voucht with a deed so bold:
But he thus overjoy'd, O Fruit Divine,
Sweet of thyself, but much more sweet thus cropt,
Forbidd'n here, it seems, as only fit
For Gods, yet able to make Gods of Men:
And why not Gods of Men, since good, the more
Communicated, more abundant grows,
The Author not impair'd, but honor'd more?
Here, happy Creature, fair Angelic *Eve,*
Partake thou also; happy though thou art,
Happier thou may'st be, worthier canst not be:
Taste this, and be henceforth among the Gods

5. The fabled anointing oil of the gods.

6. Limitation, restriction, or knowledge kept secret on the part of God; but perhaps also inhibition, self-restraint on the part of humans.

Thyself a Goddess, not to Earth confin'd,
But sometimes in the Air, as wee, sometimes
Ascend to Heav'n, by merit thine, and see
What life the Gods live there, and such live thou.
So saying, he drew nigh, and to me held,
Even to my mouth of that same fruit held part
Which he had pluckt; the pleasant savory smell[7]
So quick'n'd appetite, that I, methought,
Could not but taste. Forthwith up to the Clouds
With him I flew, and underneath beheld
The Earth outstretcht immense, a prospect wide
And various: wond'ring at my flight and change
To this high exaltation; suddenly
My Guide was gone, and I, methought, sunk down,
And fell asleep; but O how glad I wak'd
To find this but a dream! Thus *Eve* her Night
Related, and thus *Adam* answer'd sad.° *gravely*
Best Image of myself and dearer half,
The trouble of thy thoughts this night in sleep
Affects me equally; nor can I like
This uncouth° dream, of evil sprung I fear; *strange*
Yet evil whence? in thee can harbor none,
Created pure. But know that in the Soul
Are many lesser Faculties that serve
Reason as chief; among these Fancy next
Her office holds; of all external things,
Which the five watchful Senses represent,
She forms Imaginations, Aery shapes,
Which Reason joining or disjoining, frames
All what we affirm or what deny, and call
Our knowledge or opinion; then retires
Into her private Cell when Nature rests.[8]
Oft in her absence mimic Fancy wakes
To imitate her; but misjoining shapes,
Wild work produces oft, and most in dreams,
Ill matching words and deeds long past or late.
Some such resemblances methinks I find
Of our last Ev'ning's talk,[9] in this thy dream,
But with addition strange; yet be not sad.
Evil into the mind of God[1] or Man
May come and go, so unapprov'd, and leave
No spot or blame behind: Which gives me hope
That what in sleep thou didst abhor to dream,
Waking thou never wilt consent to do.

7. The fruit has an appetizing, fragrant scent, but "savory" could also mean "spiritually edifying."

8. For the psychology involved here, see Burton, *Anatomy of Melancholy* 1.1.2.7: "Phantasy, or imagination . . . is an inner sense which doth more fully examine the species perceived by common sense, of things present or absent. . . . In time of sleep this faculty is free, and many times conceives strange, stupend, absurd shapes . . . it is subject and governed by reason, or at least should be."

9. Their discussion of the prohibition of the Tree of Knowledge (4.421ff.).

1. Probably "angel." But Milton (if not Adam) may also intend a reference to the doctrine that God's omniscience extends to evil.

Be not disheart'n'd then, nor cloud those looks
That wont to be more cheerful and serene
Than when fair Morning first smiles on the World,
And let us to our fresh imployments rise
Among the Groves, the Fountains, and the Flow'rs
That open now thir choicest bosom'd° smells *hidden*
Reserv'd from night, and kept for thee in store.
So cheer'd he his fair Spouse, and she was cheer'd,
But silently a gentle tear let fall
From either eye, and wip'd them with her hair;
Two other precious drops that ready stood,
Each in thir crystal sluice, hee ere they fell
Kiss'd as the gracious signs of sweet remorse
And pious awe, that fear'd to have offended.
So all was clear'd, and to the Field they haste.
But first from under shady arborous roof,
Soon as they forth were come to open sight
Of day-spring,° and the Sun, who scarce up risen *daybreak*
With wheels yet hov'ring o'er the Ocean brim,
Shot parallel to the earth his dewy ray,
Discovering in wide Lantskip° all the East *landscape*
Of Paradise and *Eden's* happy Plains,
Lowly they bow'd adoring, and began
Thir Orisons,° each Morning duly paid *prayers*
In various style, for neither various style
Nor holy rapture wanted they to praise
Thir Maker, in fit strains pronounct or sung
Unmeditated, such prompt eloquence
Flow'd from thir lips, in Prose or numerous Verse,
More tuneable° than needed Lute or Harp *tuneful*
To add more sweetness, and they thus began.[2]
These are thy glorious works, Parent of good,
Almighty, thine this universal Frame,[3]
Thus wondrous fair; thyself how wondrous then!
Unspeakable, who sit'st above these Heavens
To us invisible or dimly seen
In these thy lowest works, yet these declare
Thy goodness beyond thought, and Power Divine:
Speak yee who best can tell, ye Sons of Light,
Angels, for yee behold him, and with songs
And choral symphonies, Day without Night,
Circle his Throne rejoicing, yee in Heav'n;
On Earth join all ye Creatures to extol
Him first, him last, him midst, and without end.
Fairest of Stars,[4] last in the train of Night,
If better thou belong not to the dawn,

2. The hymn (lines 153–208) is based on Psalms 148 and on the Canticle *Benedicite, omnia opera* (in the 1549 *Book of Common Prayer*).
3. Used of heaven, earth, or the universe regarded as structures fabricated by God.
4. The planet Venus rises in the east just before sunrise and is known as the morning star.

Sure pledge of day, that crown'st the smiling Morn
With thy bright Circlet, praise him in thy Sphere
While day arises, that sweet hour of Prime.
Thou Sun, of this great World both Eye and Soul,[5]
Acknowledge him thy Greater, sound his praise
In thy eternal course, both when thou climb'st,
And when high Noon hast gain'd, and when thou fall'st.
Moon, that now meet'st the orient Sun, now fli'st
With the fixt Stars, fixt in thir Orb that flies,
And yee five other wand'ring Fires that move
In mystic Dance not without Song,[6] resound
His praise, who out of Darkness call'd up Light.
Air, and ye Elements the eldest birth
Of Nature's Womb, that in quaternion run
Perpetual Circle, multiform, and mix
And nourish all things, let your ceaseless change
Vary to our great Maker still new praise.
Ye Mists and Exhalations that now rise
From Hill or steaming Lake, dusky or grey,
Till the Sun paint your fleecy skirts with Gold,
In honor to the World's great Author rise,
Whether to deck with Clouds th' uncolor'd sky,
Or wet the thirsty Earth with falling showers,
Rising or falling still advance his praise.
His praise ye Winds, that from four Quarters blow,
Breathe soft or loud; and wave your tops, ye Pines,
With every Plant, in sign of Worship wave.
Fountains and yee, that warble, as ye flow,
Melodious murmurs, warbling tune his praise.
Join voices all ye living Souls; ye Birds,
That singing up to Heaven Gate ascend,
Bear on your wings and in your notes his praise;
Yee that in Waters glide, and yee that walk
The Earth, and stately tread, or lowly creep;
Witness if I be silent, Morn or Even,
To Hill, or Valley, Fountain, or fresh shade
Made vocal by my Song, and taught his praise.
Hail universal Lord, be bounteous still
To give us only good; and if the night
Have gather'd aught of evil or conceal'd,
Disperse it, as now light dispels the dark.
    So pray'd they innocent, and to thir thoughts
Firm peace recover'd soon and wonted calm.
On to thir morning's rural work they haste
Among sweet dews and flow'rs; where any row

5. The metaphor of the sun as an eye implied a connection between seeing and understanding and hence an identification of the sun with the creative word. The sun is "soul" of the world in the sense that it gives life.

6. The music of the spheres, inaudible now to fallen humans' gross hearing. The elements are a form of the quaternion, or tetrad, a group of four regarded as one: air, earth, fire, and water. For the transformation of the elements into one another, see *Cicero, De natura deorum* 2.33.

Of Fruit-trees overwoody reach'd too far
Thir pamper'd boughs, and needed hands to check
Fruitless imbraces: or they led the Vine
To wed her Elm; she spous'd about him twines
Her marriageable arms, and with her brings
Her dow'r th' adopted Clusters, to adorn
His barren leaves. Them thus imploy'd beheld
With pity Heav'n's high King, and to him call'd
  Raphael, the sociable Spirit, that deign'd
To travel with *Tobias*, and secur'd
His marriage with the seven-times-wedded Maid.
Raphael, said hee, thou hear'st what stir on Earth
Satan from Hell scap't through the darksome Gulf
Hath rais'd in Paradise, and how disturb'd
This night the human pair, how he designs
In them at once to ruin all mankind.
Go therefore, half this day as friend with friend
Converse with *Adam*, in what Bow'r or shade
Thou find'st him from the heat of Noon retir'd,
To respite his day-labor with repast,
Or with repose; and such discourse bring on,
As may advise him of his happy state,
Happiness in his power left free to will,
Left to his own free Will, his Will though free,
Yet mutable; whence warn him to beware
He swerve not too secure:[7] tell him withal
His danger, and from whom, what enemy
Late fall'n himself from Heaven, is plotting now
The fall of others from like state of bliss;
By violence, no, for that shall be withstood,
But by deceit and lies; this let him know,
Lest wilfully transgressing he pretend
Surprisal, unadmonisht, unforewarn'd.[8]

* * *

Meanwhile our Primitive great Sire, to meet
His god-like Guest, walks forth, without more train
Accompanied than with his own complete
Perfections; in himself was all his state,° *dignity*
More solemn than the tedious pomp that waits
On Princes, when thir rich Retinue long
Of Horses led, and Grooms besmear'd with Gold
Dazzles the crowd, and sets them all agape.
Nearer his presence *Adam* though not aw'd,
Yet with submiss° approach and reverence meek, *submissive*
As to a superior Nature, bowing low,
  Thus said. Native of Heav'n, for other place
None can than Heav'n such glorious shape contain;
Since by descending from the Thrones above,

7. To be careful not to err through overconfidence.

8. Raphael now flies to Eden to see Adam.

Those happy places thou hast deign'd a while
To want,° and honor these, voutsafe with us *miss*
Two only, who yet by sovran gift possess
This spacious ground, in yonder shady Bow'r
To rest, and what the Garden choicest bears
To sit and taste, till this meridian heat
Be over, and the Sun more cool decline.
Whom thus the Angelic Virtue answer'd mild.
Adam, I therefore came, nor art thou such
Created, or such place hast here to dwell,
As may not oft invite, though Spirits of Heav'n
To visit thee; lead on then where thy Bow'r
O'ershades; for these mid-hours, till Ev'ning rise
I have at will. So to the Silvan Lodge
They came, that like *Pomona's* Arbor smil'd
With flow'rets deck't and fragrant smells; but *Eve*
Undeckt, save with herself more lovely fair
Than Wood-Nymph,[9] or the fairest Goddess feign'd
Of three that in Mount *Ida* naked strove,[1]
Stood to entertain her guest from Heav'n; no veil
Shee needed, Virtue-proof, no thought infirm
Alter'd her cheek. On whom the Angel *Hail*
Bestow'd, the holy salutation us'd
Long after to blest *Mary*, second *Eve*.
Hail Mother of Mankind, whose fruitful Womb
Shall fill the World more numerous with thy Sons
Than with these various fruits the Trees of God
Have heap'd this Table. Rais'd of grassy turf
Thir Table was, and mossy seats had round,
And on her ample Square from side to side
All *Autumn* pil'd, though *Spring* and *Autumn* here
Danc'd hand in hand. A while discourse they hold;
No fear lest Dinner cool; when thus began
Our Author.° Heav'nly stranger, please to taste *ancestor*
These bounties which our Nourisher, from whom
All perfet good unmeasur'd out, descends,
To us for food and for delight hath caus'd
The Earth to yield; unsavory food perhaps
To spiritual Natures; only this I know,
That one Celestial Father gives to all.
To whom the Angel. Therefore what he gives
(Whose praise be ever sung) to man in part
Spiritual, may of purest Spirits be found
No ingrateful food:[2] and food alike those pure
Intelligential substances[3] require

9. The Roman wood-nymph Pomona presided over gardens and especially fruit trees.

1. The three goddesses Juno, Minerva, and Venus all claimed the apple of Strife, inscribed TO THE FAIREST, and the mortal Paris, famed for his wisdom, was appointed arbiter. The judgment of Paris was delivered on Mount Ida, where the goddesses appeared before him naked and without ornament.

2. Food acceptable to the angels ("purest spirits") because acceptable to humans ("in part spiritual").

3. Intellectual beings.

As doth your Rational; and both contain
Within them every lower faculty
Of sense, whereby they hear, see, smell, touch, taste,
Tasting concoct, digest, assimilate,
And corporeal to incorporeal turn.[4]
For know, whatever was created, needs
To be sustain'd and fed; of Elements
The grosser feeds the purer, Earth the Sea,
Earth and the Sea feed Air, the Air those Fires
Ethereal, and as lowest first the Moon;
Whence in her visage round those spots, unpurg'd
Vapors not yet into her substance turn'd.
Nor doth the Moon no nourishment exhale[5]
From her moist Continent to higher Orbs.
The Sun that light imparts to all, receives
From all his alimental° recompense *nutritive*
In humid exhalations, and at Even
Sups with the Ocean:[6] though in Heav'n the Trees
Of life ambrosial fruitage bear, and vines
Yield Nectar, though from off the boughs each Morn
We brush mellifluous° Dews, and find the ground *sweetly flowing*
Cover'd with pearly grain:[7] yet God hath here
Varied his bounty so with new delights,
As may compare with Heaven; and to taste
Think not I shall be nice.° So down they sat, *overrefined*
And to thir viands fell, nor seemingly[8]
The Angel, nor in mist, the common gloss
Of Theologians, but with keen dispatch
Of real hunger, and concoctive heat
To transubstantiate;[9] what redounds,° transpires *remains in excess*
Through Spirits with ease; nor wonder; if by fire
Of sooty coal the Empiric Alchemist
Can turn, or holds it possible to turn
Metals of drossiest Ore to perfet Gold
As from the Mine. Meanwhile at Table *Eve*
Minister'd naked, and thir flowing cups
With pleasant liquors crown'd: O innocence
Deserving Paradise! if ever, then,
Then had the Sons of God° excuse to have been *angels*
Enamour'd at that sight; but in those hearts
Love unlibidinous reign'd, nor jealousy

4. Physiological theory distinguished three stages of digestion: the "first concoction," or digestion in the stomach ("concoct"); the "second concoction," or conversion to blood ("digest"); and the "third concoction," or secretion ("assimilate").

5. The ancient theory was that vapors drawn up to the moon from the earth caused lunar spots. Galileo explained them as landscape features, a theory used above at lines 287–291.

6. This version of the Great Chain of Being was held by Stoics and Epicureans and was also popular in Milton's own time with mystical and alchemic Platonists such as Robert Fludd.

7. Manna, the "corn of heaven."

8. Refers to the Docetist theories about angelic appearances, devised to explain away the awkwardly materialistic accounts of angels in the Bible (e.g., at Genesis 18.8, "they did eat"). The Reformers on the whole rejected such evasions.

9. Transubstantiation is the Roman Catholic doctrine that the bread and wine of the Eucharist become the body and blood of Christ so "transubstantiate" contrasts sharply with the direct concrete simplicity of "keen . . . hunger."

Was understood, the injur'd Lover's Hell.
  Thus when with meats and drinks they had suffic't,
Not burd'n'd Nature, sudden mind arose
In *Adam,* not to let th' occasion pass
Given him by this great Conference to know
Of things above his World, and of thir being
Who dwell in Heav'n, whose excellence he saw
Transcend his own so far, whose radiant forms
Divine effulgence, whose high Power so far
Exceeded human, and his wary speech
Thus to th' Empyreal° Minister he fram'd. *heavenly*
  Inhabitant with God, now know I well
Thy favor, in this honor done to Man,
Under whose lowly roof thou hast voutsaf't
To enter, and these earthly fruits to taste,
Food not of Angels, yet accepted so,
As that more willingly thou couldst not seem
At Heav'n's high feasts to have fed: yet what compare?
  To whom the winged Hierarch repli'd.
O *Adam,* one Almighty is, from whom
All things proceed, and up to him return,
If not deprav'd from good, created all
Such to perfection, one first matter all,
Indu'd with various forms, various degrees
Of substance, and in things that live, of life;[1]
But more refin'd, more spiritous, and pure,
As nearer to him plac't or nearer tending
Each in thir several active Spheres assign'd,
Till body up to spirit work, in bounds
Proportion'd to each kind. So from the root
Springs lighter the green stalk, from thence the leaves
More aery, last the bright consummate° flow'r *perfected*
Spirits odorous breathes: flow'rs and thir fruit
Man's nourishment, by gradual scale sublim'd° *raised*
To vital spirits aspire, to animal,
To intellectual, give both life and sense,[2]
Fancy° and understanding, whence the Soul *imagination*
Reason receives, and reason is her being,
Discursive, or Intuitive; discourse
Is oftest yours, the latter most is ours,
Differing but in degree, of kind the same.[3]
Wonder not then, what God for you saw good
If I refuse not, but convert, as you,
To proper substance; time may come when men

1. Raphael's world picture is characterized by a cyclic movement of emanation and return that marks it as Platonic, just as does the notion of successive degrees of spirituousness. The plant simile explains the notion of a scale of being from vegetable to animal, human, and angelic natures.
2. "Vital spirits" were fine pure fluids, given off by the blood of the heart and sustaining life; "animal spirits" had their seat in the brain and controlled sensation and voluntary motion.
3. The distinction between the "intuitive," simple undifferentiated operation of the contemplating intellect and the "discursive" or ratiocinative, piecemeal operation of the intellect working in conjunction with the reason goes back ultimately to Plato.

With Angels may participate, and find
No inconvenient Diet, nor too light Fare:
And from these corporal nutriments perhaps
Your bodies may at last turn all to spirit,
Improv'd by tract of time, and wing'd ascend
Ethereal, as wee, or may at choice
Here or in Heav'nly Paradises dwell;
If ye be found obedient, and retain
Unalterably firm his love entire
Whose progeny you are. Meanwhile enjoy
Your fill what happiness this happy state
Can comprehend, incapable of more.
   To whom the Patriarch of mankind repli'd:
O favorable Spirit, propitious guest,
Well hast thou taught the way that might direct
Our knowledge, and the scale of Nature set
From centre to circumference, whereon
In contemplation of created things
By steps we may ascend to God.[4] But say,
What meant that caution join'd, *if ye be found*
Obedient? can we want obedience then
To him, or possibly his love desert
Who form'd us from the dust, and plac'd us here
Full to the utmost measure of what bliss
Human desires can seek or apprehend?
   To whom the Angel. Son of Heav'n and Earth,
Attend: That thou art happy, owe to God;
That thou continu'st such, owe to thyself,
That is, to thy obedience; therein stand.
This was that caution giv'n thee; be advis'd.
God made thee perfet, not immutable;
And good he made thee, but to persevere
He left it in thy power, ordain'd thy will
By nature free, not over-rul'd by Fate
Inextricable, or strict necessity;
Our voluntary service he requires,
Not our necessitated, such with him
Finds no acceptance, nor can find, for how
Can hearts, not free, be tri'd whether they serve
Willing or no, who will but what they must
By Destiny, and can no other choose?
Myself and all th' Angelic Host that stand
In sight of God enthron'd, our happy state
Hold, as you yours, while our obedience holds;
On other surety none; freely we serve,
Because we freely love, as in our will
To love or not; in this we stand or fall:
And some are fall'n, to disobedience fall'n,

4. In the scale or ladder of nature, Adam refers to the Platonic ascent from image to universal, up the hierarchic grades of existence.

And so from Heav'n to deepest Hell; O fall
From what high state of bliss into what woe!
To whom our great Progenitor. Thy words
Attentive, and with more delighted ear
Divine instructor, I have heard, than when
Cherubic Songs by night from neighboring Hills
Aereal Music send: nor knew I not
To be both will and deed created free;
Yet that we never shall forget to love
Our maker, and obey him whose command
Single, is yet so just, my constant thoughts
Assur'd me and still assure: though what thou tell'st
Hath past in Heav'n, some doubt within me move,
But more desire to hear, if thou consent,
The full relation, which must needs be strange,
Worthy of Sacred silence to be heard;
And we have yet large day, for scarce the Sun
Hath finisht half his journey, and scarce begins
His other half in the great Zone of Heav'n.
Thus *Adam* made request, and *Raphaël*
After short pause assenting, thus began.[5] * * *

Book 6

The Argument

Raphael *continues to relate how* Michael *and* Gabriel *were sent forth to Battle against* Satan *and his* Angels. *The first fight describ'd:* Satan *and his Powers retire under Night: He calls a Council, invents devilish Engines, which in the second day's Fight put* Michael *and his* Angels *to some disorder; but they at length pulling up Mountains overwhelm'd both the force and Machines of* Satan: *Yet the Tumult not so ending, God on the third day sends* Messiah *his Son for whom he had reserv'd the glory of the Victory: Hee in the Power of his Father coming to the place, and causing all his Legions to stand still on either side, with his Chariot and Thunder driving into the midst of his Enemies, pursues them unable to resist towards the wall of Heaven; which opening they leap down with horror and confusion in the place of punishment prepar'd for them in the Deep:* Messiah *returns with triumph to his Father.*

from Book 7

The Argument

Raphael *at the request of* Adam *relates how and wherefore this world was first created; that God, after the expelling of Satan and his Angels out of Heaven, declar'd his pleasure to create another World and other Creatures to dwell therein; sends his Son with Glory and attendance of Angels to perform the work of Creation in six days: the Angels celebrate with Hymns the performance thereof, and his reascension into Heaven.*

5. Raphael's account of the war in heaven continues to the end of Book 6. It is one of the two long "episodes," or inset narrations, that conclude the two halves of the poem (the other is at the end of Book 11).

[The Invocation]

Descend from Heav'n *Urania*,[1] by that name
If rightly thou art call'd, whose Voice divine
Following, above th' *Olympian* Hill I soar,
Above the flight of *Pegasean* wing.[2]
The meaning, not the Name I call: for thou
Nor of the Muses nine, nor on the top
Of old *Olympus* dwell'st, but Heav'nly born,
Before the Hills appear'd, or Fountain flow'd,
Thou with Eternal Wisdom didst converse,
Wisdom thy Sister, and with her didst play
In presence of th' Almighty Father, pleas'd
With thy Celestial Song. Up led by thee
Into the Heav'n of Heav'ns I have presum'd,
An Earthly Guest, and drawn Empyreal Air,
Thy temp'ring;[3] with like safety guided down
Return me to my Native Element:
Lest from this flying Steed unrein'd, (as once
Bellerophon, though from a lower Clime)
Dismounted, on th' *Aleian* Field I fall
Erroneous° there to wander and forlorn.[4] *wandering, erring*
Half yet remains unsung, but narrower bound
Within the visible Diurnal Sphere;
Standing on Earth, not rapt° above the Pole,[5] *entranced*
More safe I Sing with mortal voice, unchang'd
To hoarse or mute, though fall'n on evil days,
On evil days though fall'n, and evil tongues;
In darkness, and with dangers compast round,
And solitude;[6] yet not alone, while thou
Visit'st my slumbers Nightly, or when Morn
Purples the East: still govern thou my Song,
Urania, and fit audience find, though few.
But drive far off the barbarous dissonance
Of *Bacchus* and his Revellers, the Race
Of that wild Rout that tore the *Thracian* Bard
In *Rhodope*, where Woods and Rocks had Ears
To rapture, till the savage clamor drown'd
Both Harp and Voice;[7] nor could the Muse defend
Her Son. So fail not thou, who thee implores:
For thou art Heavn'ly, shee an empty dream. * * *

1. Only in this invocation is the Muse ever named. *Urania* was the Muse of Astronomy. Milton's denial that his Urania is one "of the Muses nine" directs attention to a more recent, single Muse. Since Du Bartas's *Uranie*, the name had been used for the Christian Muse of the divine poetry movement.
2. The winged horse Pegasus was an emblem for the inspired poet.
3. The air of the "first region" (3.562–64) was fatal to mortals.
4. When Bellerephon tried to fly to heaven on Pegasus, Jupiter sent an insect to sting the horse and throw the rider. Bellerephon fell on the Aleian plain and wandered blind and lonely until his death.
5. Either the celestial pole or a synecdoche for the sky.
6. The obfuscated syntax conceals an allusion to Milton's dangerous situation during the persecutions that immediately followed the Restoration.
7. Orpheus as a type of the inspired poet. The myth of his dismemberment by Thracian women during orgies of Bacchus seems to have focused some of Milton's deepest fears. Rhodope was a mountain range in Thrace. In Ovid, *Metamorphoses* 11.1–60, the "woods and rocks" mourned Orpheus's loss, though they were the instruments of his murder.

from Book 8

The Argument

Adam *inquires concerning celestial Motions, is doubtfully answer'd, and exhorted to search rather things more worthy of knowledge:* Adam *assents, and still desirous to detain* Raphael, *relates to him what he remember'd since his own Creation, his placing in Paradise, his talk with* God *concerning solitude and fit society, his first meeting and Nuptials with* Eve, *his discourse with the Angel thereupon; who after admonitions repeated departs.*

To whom thus Adam clear'd of doubt, repli'd.
How fully hast thou satisfi'd me, pure
Intelligence° of Heav'n, Angel serene, *spirit*
And freed from intricacies, taught to live
The easiest way, nor with perplexing thoughts
To interrupt the sweet of Life, from which
God hath bid dwell far off all anxious cares,
And not molest us, unless we ourselves
Seek them with wand'ring thoughts, and notions vain.
But apt the Mind or Fancy is to rove
Uncheckt, and of her roving is no end;
Till warn'd, or by experience taught, she learn
That not to know at large of things remote
From use, obscure and subtle, but to know
That which before us lies in daily life,
Is the prime Wisdom; what is more, is fume,° *smoke*
Or emptiness, or fond impertinence,° *foolish irrelevance*
And renders us in things that most concern
Unpractic'd, unprepar'd, and still to seek.
Therefore from this high pitch let us descend
A lower flight, and speak of things at hand
Useful, whence haply mention may arise
Of something not unseasonable to ask
By sufferance,° and thy wonted favor deign'd. *permission*
Thee I have heard relating what was done
Ere my remembrance: now hear mee relate
My Story, which perhaps thou hast not heard;
And Day is yet not spent; till then thou seest
How subtly to detain thee I devise,
Inviting thee to hear while I relate,
Fond, were it not in hope of thy reply:
For while I sit with thee, I seem in Heav'n,
And sweeter thy discourse is to my ear
Than Fruits of Palm-tree pleasantest to thirst
And hunger both, from labor, at the hour
Of sweet repast; they satiate, and soon fill,
Though pleasant, but thy words with Grace Divine
Imbu'd, bring to thir sweetness no satiety.
To whom thus *Raphael* answer'd heav'nly meek.
Nor are thy lips ungraceful, Sire of men,
Nor tongue ineloquent; for God on thee
Abundantly his gifts hath also pour'd

Inward and outward both, his image fair:
Speaking or mute all comeliness and grace
Attends thee, and each word, each motion forms.
Nor less think wee in Heav'n of thee on Earth
Than of our fellow servant, and inquire
Gladly into the ways of God with Man:
For God we see hath honor'd thee, and set
On Man his Equal Love: say therefore on;
For I that Day was absent, as befell,
Bound on a voyage uncouth° and obscure, *unfamiliar*
Far on excursion toward the Gates of Hell;
Squar'd in full Legion (such command we had)
To see that none thence issu'd forth a spy,
Or enemy, while God was in his work,
Lest hee incenst at such eruption bold,
Destruction with Creation might have mixt.
Not that they durst without his leave attempt,
But us he sends upon his high behests
For state,° as Sovran King, and to enure *ceremony*
Our prompt obedience. Fast we found, fast shut
The dismal Gates, and barricado'd strong;
But long ere our approaching heard within
Noise, other than the sound of Dance or Song,
Torment, and loud lament, and furious rage.
Glad we return'd up to the coasts of Light
Ere Sabbath Ev'ning: so we had in charge.
But thy relation now; for I attend,
Pleas'd with thy words no less than thou with mine.
So spake the Godlike Power, and thus our Sire.
For man to tell how human Life began
Is hard; for who himself beginning knew?
Desire with thee still longer to converse
Induc'd me. As new wak't from soundest sleep
Soft on the flow'ry herb I found me laid
In Balmy Sweat, which with his Beams the Sun
Soon dri'd, and on the reeking moisture fed.
Straight toward Heav'n my wond'ring Eyes I turn'd,
And gaz'd a while the ample Sky, till rais'd
By quick instinctive motion up I sprung,
As thitherward endeavoring, and upright
Stood on my feet; about me round I saw
Hill, Dale, and shady Woods, and sunny Plains,
And liquid Lapse of murmuring Streams; by these,
Creatures that liv'd, and mov'd, and walk'd, or flew,
Birds on the branches warbling; all things smil'd,
With fragrance and with joy my heart o'erflow'd.
Myself I then perus'd, and Limb by Limb
Survey'd, and sometimes went,° and sometimes ran *walked*
With supple joints, as lively vigor led:
But who I was, or where, or from what cause,
Knew not; to speak I tri'd, and forthwith spake,

My Tongue obey'd and readily could name
Whate'er I saw. Thou Sun, said I, fair Light,
And thou enlight'n'd Earth, so fresh and gay,
Ye Hills and Dales, ye Rivers, Woods, and Plains
And ye that live and move, fair Creatures, tell,
Tell, if ye saw, how came I thus, how here?
Not of myself; by some great Maker then,
In goodness and in power preëminent;
Tell me, how may I know him, how adore,
From whom I have that thus I move and live,[1]
And feel that I am happier than I know.
While thus I call'd, and stray'd I knew not whither,
From where I first drew Air, and first beheld
This happy Light, when answer none return'd,
On a green shady Bank profuse of Flow'rs
Pensive I sat me down; there gentle sleep
First found me, and with soft oppression seiz'd
My drowsed sense, untroubl'd, though I thought
I then was passing to my former state
Insensible, and forthwith to dissolve:
When suddenly stood at my Head a dream,
Whose inward apparition gently mov'd
My fancy to believe I yet had being,
And liv'd: One came, methought, of shape Divine,
And said, thy Mansion° wants thee, *Adam,* rise, *home*
First Man, of Men innumerable ordain'd
First Father, call'd by thee I come thy Guide
To the Garden of bliss, thy seat prepar'd.[2]
So saying, by the hand he took me rais'd,
And over Fields and Waters, as in Air
Smooth sliding without step, last led me up
A woody Mountain; whose high top was plain,
A Circuit wide, enclos'd, with goodliest Trees
Planted, with Walks, and Bowers, that what I saw
Of Earth before scarce pleasant seem'd. Each Tree
Load'n with fairest Fruit, that hung to the Eye
Tempting, stirr'd in me sudden appetite
To pluck and eat; whereat I wak'd, and found
Before mine Eyes all real, as the dream
Had lively shadow'd: Here had new begun
My wand'ring, had not hee who was my Guide
Up hither, from among the Trees appear'd,
Presence Divine. Rejoicing, but with awe,
In adoration at his feet I fell
Submiss:° he rear'd me, and Whom thou sought'st I am,[3] *submissive*
Said mildly, Author of all this thou seest

1. See St. Paul's Mars' hill sermon on the Unknown God, Acts 17.28: "For in him we live, and move, and have our being."
2. See Genesis 2.8 and 2.15.
3. See Exodus 3.14: "I AM THAT I AM. . . . Thus shalt thou say unto the children of Israel, I AM hath sent me unto you."

Above, or round about thee or beneath.
This Paradise I give thee, count it thine
To Till and keep, and of the Fruit to eat:
Of every Tree that in the Garden grows
Eat freely with glad heart; fear here no dearth:[4]
But of the Tree whose operation brings
Knowledge of good and ill, which I have set
The Pledge of thy Obedience and thy Faith,
Amid the Garden by the Tree of Life,
Remember what I warn thee, shun to taste,
And shun the bitter consequence: for know,
The day thou eat'st thereof, my sole command
Transgrest, inevitably thou shalt die;
From that day mortal, and this happy State
Shalt lose, expell'd from hence into a World
Of woe and sorrow. Sternly he pronounc'd
The rigid interdiction,° which resounds *prohibition*
Yet dreadful in mine ear, though in my choice
Not to incur; but soon his clear aspect
Return'd and gracious purpose° thus renew'd. *discourse*
Not only these fair bounds, but all the Earth
To thee and to thy Race I give; as Lords
Possess it, and all things that therein live,
Or live in Sea, or Air, Beast, Fish, and Fowl.[5]
In sign whereof each Bird and Beast behold
After thir kinds; I bring them to receive
From thee thir Names, and pay thee fealty
With low subjection; understand the same
Of Fish within thir wat'ry residence,
Not hither summon'd, since they cannot change
Thir Element to draw the thinner Air.
As thus he spake, each Bird and Beast behold
Approaching two and two, These cow'ring low
With blandishment, each Bird stoop'd on his wing.
I nam'd them, as they pass'd, and understood
Thir Nature, with such knowledge God endu'd
My sudden apprehension: but in these
I found not what methought I wanted still;
And to the Heav'nly vision thus presum'd.

O by what Name, for thou above all these,
Above mankind, or aught than mankind higher,
Surpassest far my naming, how may I
Adore thee, Author of this Universe,
And all this good to man, for whose well being
So amply, and with hands so liberal
Thou hast provided all things: but with mee
I see not who partakes. In solitude
What happiness, who can enjoy alone,
Or all enjoying, what contentment find?

4. See Genesis 2.15ff.

5. See Genesis 1.28.

Thus I presumptuous; and the vision bright,
As with a smile more bright'n'd, thus repli'd.
What call'st thou solitude? is not the Earth
With various living creatures, and the Air
Replenisht, and all these at thy command
To come and play before thee; know'st thou not
Thir language and thir ways? They also know,[6]
And reason not contemptibly; with these
Find pastime, and bear rule; thy Realm is large.
So spake the Universal Lord, and seem'd
So ordering. I with leave of speech implor'd,
And humble deprecation thus repli'd.
Let not my words offend thee, Heav'nly Power,
My Maker, be propitious while I speak.
Hast thou not made me here thy substitute,
And these inferior far beneath me set?
Among unequals what society
Can sort,° what harmony or true delight? *agree*
Which must be mutual, in proportion due
Giv'n and receiv'd; but in disparity
The one intense, the other still remiss
Cannot well suit with either, but soon prove
Tedious alike:[7] Of fellowship I speak
Such as I seek, fit to participate
All rational delight, wherein the brute
Cannot be human consort; they rejoice
Each with thir kind, Lion with Lioness;
So fitly them in pairs thou hast combin'd;
Much less can Bird with Beast, or Fish with Fowl
So well converse, nor with the Ox the Ape;
Worse then can Man with Beast, and least of all.
Whereto th' Almighty answer'd, not displeas'd.
A nice and subtle happiness I see
Thou to thyself proposest, in the choice
Of thy Associates, *Adam*, and wilt taste
No pleasure, though in pleasure, solitary.
What think'st thou then of mee, and this my State,
Seem I to thee sufficiently possest
Of happiness, or not? who am alone
From all Eternity, for none I know
Second to mee or like, equal much less.
How have I then with whom to hold converse
Save with the Creatures which I made, and those
To me inferior, infinite descents
Beneath what other Creatures are to thee?
He ceas'd, I lowly answer'd. To attain
The highth and depth of thy Eternal ways
All human thoughts come short, Supreme of things;

6. It was a widespread Jewish belief that before the Fall, Adam understood the language of the beasts. The original language was usually supposed to have been Hebrew, but sometimes Syriac, Greek, or Aramaic.

7. In a stringed instrument the strings should bear a due ratio of length and frequency. But the human string is too strained ("intense") and therefore high in pitch, while the animal string is too "remiss," i.e., low in pitch.

Thou in thyself art perfet, and in thee
Is no deficience found; not so is Man,
But in degree, the cause of his desire
By conversation with his like to help,
Or solace his defects. No need that thou
Shouldst propagate, already infinite;
And through all numbers absolute, though One;[8]
But Man by number is to manifest
His single imperfection, and beget
Like of his like, his Image multipli'd,
In unity defective, which requires
Collateral love, and dearest amity.
Thou in thy secrecy although alone,
Best with thyself accompanied, seek'st not
Social communication, yet so pleas'd,
Canst raise thy Creature to what highth thou wilt
Of Union or Communion, deifi'd;
I by conversing cannot these erect
From prone, nor in thir ways complacence° find. *source of pleasure*
Thus I embold'n'd spake, and freedom us'd
Permissive, and acceptance found, which gain'd
This answer from the gracious voice Divine.
  Thus far to try thee, *Adam*, I was pleas'd,
And find thee knowing not of Beasts alone,
Which thou hast rightly nam'd, but of thyself,
Expressing well the spirit within thee free,
My Image, not imparted to the Brute,
Whose fellowship therefore unmeet for thee
Good reason was thou freely shouldst dislike,
And be so minded still; I, ere thou spak'st,
Knew it not good for Man to be alone,
And no such company as then thou saw'st
Intended thee, for trial only brought,
To see how thou couldst judge of fit and meet:
What next I bring shall please thee, be assur'd,
Thy likeness, thy fit help, thy other self,
Thy wish, exactly to thy heart's desire.
  Hee ended, or I heard no more, for now
My earthly° by his Heav'nly overpower'd, *earthly nature*
Which it had long stood under, strain'd to the highth
In that celestial Colloquy sublime,
As with an object that excels the sense,
Dazzl'd and spent, sunk down, and sought repair
Of sleep, which instantly fell on me, call'd
By Nature as in aid, and clos'd mine eyes.[9]
Mine eyes he clos'd, but op'n left the Cell
Of Fancy my internal sight, by which
Abstract° as in a trance methought I saw, *withdrawn*
Though sleeping, where I lay, and saw the shape

8. The divine monad contains all other numbers and is therefore complete and perfect through them all. The monad is like God because it is the fountain and origin of all numbers, as God is the origin of created being.

9. For lines 452–486, see Genesis 2.21ff.

Still glorious before whom awake I stood;
Who stooping op'n'd my left side, and took
From thence a Rib, with cordial spirits warm,
And Life-blood streaming fresh; wide was the wound,
But suddenly with flesh fill'd up and heal'd:
The Rib he form'd and fashion'd with his hands;
Under his forming hands a Creature grew,
Manlike, but different sex, so lovely fair,
That what seem'd fair in all the World, seem'd now
Mean, or in her summ'd up, in her contain'd
And in her looks, which from that time infus'd
Sweetness into my heart, unfelt before,
And into all things from her Air inspir'd
The spirit of love and amorous delight.
Shee disappear'd, and left me dark, I wak'd
To find her, or for ever to deplore
Her loss, and other pleasures all abjure:
When out of hope, behold her, not far off,
Such as I saw her in my dream, adorn'd
With what all Earth or Heaven could bestow
To make her amiable: On she came,
Led by her Heav'nly Maker, though unseen,
And guided by his voice, nor uninform'd
Of nuptial Sanctity and marriage Rites:
Grace was in all her steps, Heav'n in her Eye,
In every gesture dignity and love.
I overjoy'd could not forbear aloud.° *saying aloud*
    This turn hath made amends; thou hast fulfill'd
Thy words, Creator bounteous and benign,
Giver of all things fair, but fairest this
Of all thy gifts, nor enviest. I now see
Bone of my Bone, Flesh of my Flesh, my Self
Before me; Woman is her Name, of Man
Extracted; for this cause he shall forgo
Father and Mother, and to his Wife adhere;
And they shall be one Flesh, one Heart, one Soul.[1]
    She heard me thus, and though divinely brought,
Yet Innocence and Virgin Modesty,
Her virtue and the conscience° of her worth, *consciousness*
That would be woo'd, and not unsought be won,
Not obvious, not obtrusive, but retir'd,
The more desirable, or to say all,
Nature herself, though pure of sinful thought,
Wrought in her so, that seeing me, she turn'd;
I follow'd her, she what was Honor knew,
And with obsequious° Majesty approv'd *compliant*
My pleaded reason. To the Nuptial Bow'r
I led her blushing like the Morn: all Heav'n,
And happy Constellations on that hour
Shed thir selectest influence; the Earth

1. See *Genesis* 3.23ff. The biblical expression "one flesh" is replaced by the familiar Platonic tripartite division into parts.

Gave sign of gratulation,° and each Hill; *joy*
Joyous the Birds; fresh Gales and gentle Airs
Whisper'd it to the Woods, and from thir wings
Flung Rose, flung Odors from the spicy Shrub,
Disporting, till the amorous Bird of Night[2]
Sung Spousal, and bid haste the Ev'ning Star
On his Hill top, to light the bridal Lamp.
Thus I have told thee all my State, and brought
My Story to the sum of earthly bliss
Which I enjoy, and must confess to find
In all things else delight indeed, but such
As us'd or not, works in the mind no change,
Nor vehement desire, these delicacies
I mean of Taste, Sight, Smell, Herbs, Fruits, and Flow'rs,
Walks, and the melody of Birds; but here
Far otherwise, transported I behold,
Transported touch; here passion first I felt,
Commotion strange, in all enjoyments else
Superior and unmov'd, here only weak
Against the charm of Beauty's powerful glance.
Or° Nature fail'd in mee, and left some part *either*
Not proof enough such Object to sustain,
Or from my side subducting,° took perhaps *subtracting*
More than enough; at least on her bestow'd
Too much of Ornament, in outward show
Elaborate, of inward less exact.° *perfect*
For well I understand in the prime end
Of Nature her th' inferior, in the mind
And inward Faculties, which most excel,
In outward also her resembling less
His Image who made both, and less expressing
The character of that Dominion giv'n
O'er other Creatures; yet when I approach
Her loveliness, so absolute she seems
And in herself complete, so well to know
Her own, that what she wills to do or say,
Seems wisest, virtuousest, discreetest, best;
All higher knowledge in her presence falls
Degraded, Wisdom in discourse with her
Loses discount'nanc't, and like folly shows;
Authority and Reason on her wait,
As one intended first, not after made
Occasionally;° and to consummate all, *accidentally*
Greatness of mind and nobleness thir seat
Build in her loveliest, and create an awe
About her, as a guard Angelic plac't.
To whom the Angel with contracted brow.
  Accuse not Nature, she hath done her part;
Do thou but thine, and be not diffident° *mistrustful*
Of Wisdom, she deserts thee not, if thou

2. The nightingale; see 5.40–41, page 1833.

Dismiss not her, when most thou need'st her nigh,
By attribúting overmuch to things
Less excellent, as thou thyself perceiv'st.
For what admir'st thou, what transports thee so,
An outside? fair no doubt, and worthy well
Thy cherishing, thy honoring, and thy love,
Not thy subjection: weigh with her thyself;
Then value: Oft-times nothing profits more
Than self-esteem, grounded on just and right
Well manag'd; of that skill the more thou know'st,
The more she will acknowledge thee her Head,[3]
And to realities yield all her shows;
Made so adorn for thy delight the more,
So awful, that with honor thou may'st love
Thy mate, who sees when thou art seen least wise.
But if the sense of touch whereby mankind
Is propagated seem such dear delight
Beyond all other, think the same voutsaf't
To Cattle and each Beast; which would not be
To them made common and divulg'd, if aught
Therein enjoy'd were worthy to subdue
The Soul of Man, or passion in him move.
What higher in her society thou find'st
Attractive, human, rational, love still;
In loving thou dost well, in passion not,
Wherein true Love consists not; Love refines
The thoughts, and heart enlarges, hath his seat
In Reason, and is judicious, is the scale[4]
By which to heav'nly Love thou may'st ascend,
Not sunk in carnal pleasure, for which cause
Among the Beasts no Mate for thee was found.[5]
To whom thus half abash't *Adam* repli'd.[6]
Neither her out-side form'd so fair, nor aught
In procreation common to all kinds
(Though higher of the genial° Bed by far, *nuptial*
And with mysterious reverence I deem)
So much delights me, as those graceful acts,
Those thousand decencies that daily flow
From all her words and actions, mixt with Love
And sweet compliance, which declare unfeign'd
Union of Mind, or in us both one Soul;
Harmony to behold in wedded pair
More grateful than harmonious sound to the ear.

3. Alludes to 1 Corinthians 11.3: "The head of every man is Christ; and the head of the woman is the man; and the head of Christ is God."
4. The Neoplatonic ladder of love.
5. Raphael here expounds the very familiar Neoplatonic distinction between divine or celestial love, human or terrestrial love, and bestial love. The first (Milton's "heavenly love") is the love of the contemplative, belonging to mind alone. The second ("true love") is the force that drives humans to propagate the earthly image of divine beauty but may also, in its ideal form, lead them to the first. The third ("sunk . . . pleasure") is experienced by humans who stoop to debauchery.
6. The conversation of Raphael and Adam does in some respects resemble a debate between Heavenly Love and Human Love in which the angel/human distinction is intensified into an antithesis.

Yet these subject not; I to thee disclose
What inward thence I feel, not therefore foil'd,° *overcome*
Who meet with various objects, from the sense
Variously representing; yet still free
Approve the best, and follow what I approve.
To Love thou blam'st me not, for Love thou say'st
Leads up to Heav'n, is both the way and guide;
Bear with me then, if lawful what I ask;
Love not the heav'nly Spirits, and how thir Love
Express they, by looks only, or do they mix
Irradiance, virtual or immediate touch?
To whom the Angel with a smile that glow'd
Celestial rosy red, Love's proper hue,
Answer'd. Let it suffice thee that thou know'st
Us happy, and without Love no happiness.
Whatever pure thou in the body enjoy'st
(And pure thou wert created) we enjoy
In eminence, and obstacle find none
Of membrance, joint, or limb, exclusive bars:
Easier than Air with Air, if Spirits embrace,
Total they mix, Union of Pure with Pure
Desiring; nor restrain'd conveyance need
As Flesh to mix with Flesh, or Soul with Soul.
But I can now no more; the parting Sun
Beyond the Earth's green Cape and verdant Isles
Hesperian sets, my Signal to depart.[7]
Be strong, live happy, and love, but first of all
Him whom to love is to obey, and keep
His great command; take heed lest Passion sway
Thy Judgment to do aught, which else free Will
Would not admit; thine and of all thy Sons
The weal or woe in thee is plac't; beware.
I in thy persevering shall rejoice,
And all the Blest: stand fast; to stand or fall
Free in thine own Arbitrement it lies.
Perfet within, no outward aid require;
And all temptation to transgress repel.
So saying, he arose; whom *Adam* thus
Follow'd with benediction. Since to part,
Go heavenly Guest, Ethereal Messenger,
Sent from whose sovran goodness I adore.
Gentle to me and affable hath been
Thy condescension, and shall be honor'd ever
With grateful Memory: thou to mankind
Be good and friendly still, and oft return.
So parted they, the Angel up to Heav'n
From the thick shade, and *Adam* to his Bow'r.

The End of the Eighth Book.

7. Where the sun sets "beneath the Azores." Here the "green Cape" is Cape Verde, and the "verdant Isles" are the Cape Verde Islands.

Book 9

The Argument

Satan *having compast the Earth, with meditated guile returns as a mist by Night into Paradise, enters into the Serpent sleeping.* Adam *and* Eve *in the Morning go forth to thir labors, which* Eve *proposes to divide in several places, each laboring apart:* Adam *consents not, alleging the danger, lest that Enemy, of whom they were forewarn'd, should attempt her found alone:* Eve *loath to be thought not circumspect or firm enough, urges her going apart, the rather desirous to make trial of her strength;* Adam *at last yields: The Serpent finds her alone; his subtle approach, first gazing, then speaking, with much flattery extolling* Eve *above all other Creatures.* Eve *wond'ring to hear the Serpent speak, asks how he attain'd to human speech and such understanding not till now; the Serpent answers, that by tasting of a certain Tree in the Garden he attain'd both to Speech and Reason, till then void of both:* Eve *requires him to bring her to that Tree, and finds it to be the Tree of Knowledge forbidden: The Serpent now grown bolder, with many wiles and arguments induces her at length to eat; she pleas'd with the taste deliberates awhile whether to impart thereof to* Adam *or not, at last brings him of the Fruit, relates what persuaded her to eat thereof:* Adam *at first amaz'd, but perceiving her lost, resolves through vehemence[1] of love to perish with her; and extenuating[2] the trespass, eats also of the Fruit: The effects thereof in them both; they seek to cover thir nakedness; then fall to variance and accusation of one another.*

No more of talk where God or Angel Guest
With Man, as with his Friend, familiar us'd
To sit indulgent, and with him partake
Rural repast, permitting him the while
Venial° discourse unblam'd: I now must change *permissible*
Those Notes to Tragic; foul distrust, and breach
Disloyal on the part of Man, revolt,
And disobedience: On the part of Heav'n
Now alienated, distance and distaste,
Anger and just rebuke, and judgment giv'n,
That brought into this World a world of woe,
Sin and her shadow Death, and Misery
Death's Harbinger: Sad task, yet argument
Not less but more Heroic than the wrath
Of stern *Achilles* on his Foe pursu'd
Thrice Fugitive about *Troy* Wall; or rage
Of *Turnus* for *Lavinia* disespous'd,
Or *Neptune's* ire or *Juno's*, that so long
Perplex'd the *Greek* and *Cytherea's* Son;[3]
If answerable° style I can obtain *equal, accountable*
Of my Celestial Patroness,[4] who deigns
Her nightly visitation unimplor'd,

1. The root meaning of Latin "vehementia" is mindlessness.
2. Carrying further, drawing out.
3. Achilles is "stern" in his "wrath" because he refused any covenant with Hector, and Turnus dies fighting Aeneas for the hand of Lavinia, whereas Messiah, more heroically, is not implacable in his anger. He issued his sole commandment "sternly" (8.333); but when it is disobeyed, he works for reconciliation. Similarly, God's anger is distinguished from "Neptune's ire" and "Juno's" (which merely "perplexed" Odysseus and Aeneas) in that it is expressed in justice rather than in victimization.
4. The heavenly Muse, Urania. Both ancient and modern epics had always had war, or at least fighting, as a principal ingredient. (So has *Paradise Lost,* in the first half of the poem; but in the second half this subject is transcended.) Milton now glances unfavorably at the typical matter of the romantic epic.

And dictates to me slumb'ring, or inspires
Easy my unpremeditated Verse:
Since first this Subject for Heroic Song
Pleas'd me long choosing, and beginning late;
Not sedulous by Nature to indite
Wars, hitherto the only Argument
Heroic deem'd, chief maistry to dissect
With long and tedious havoc fabl'd Knights
In Battles feign'd; the better fortitude
Of Patience and Heroic Martyrdom
Unsung; or to describe Races and Games,
Or tilting Furniture, emblazon'd Shields,
Impreses[5] quaint, Caparisons[6] and Steeds;
Bases and tinsel Trappings, gorgeous Knights
At Joust and Tournament; then marshall'd Feast
Serv'd up in Hall with Sewers,° and Seneschals;° *waiters/stewards*
The skill of Artifice or Office mean,
Not that which justly gives Heroic name
To Person or to Poem.[7] Mee of these
Nor skill'd nor studious, higher Argument
Remains, sufficient of itself to raise
That name,[8] unless an age too late, or cold
Climate, or Years damp my intended wing
Deprest; and much they may, if all be mine,
Not Hers who brings it nightly to my Ear.
The Sun was sunk, and after him the Star
Of *Hesperus*,° whose Office is to bring *the planet Venus*
Twilight upon the Earth, short Arbiter
Twixt Day and Night, and now from end to end
Night's Hemisphere had veil'd the Horizon round:
When *Satan* who late fled before the threats
Of *Gabriel* out of *Eden*,[9] now improv'd° *intensified*
In meditated fraud and malice, bent
On Man's destruction, maugre what might hap
Of heavier on himself,[1] fearless return'd.
By Night he fled, and at Midnight return'd
From compassing the Earth, cautious of day,
Since *Uriel* Regent of the Sun descri'd
His entrance, and forewarn'd the Cherubim
That kept thir watch; thence full of anguish driv'n,
The space of seven continu'd Nights he rode
With darkness, thrice the Equinoctial Line
He circl'd, four times cross'd the Car of Night
From Pole to Pole, traversing each Colure;[2]
On th'eighth return'd, and on the Coast averse
From entrance or Cherubic Watch, by stealth

5. Heraldic devices, often with accompanying mottos.
6. Ornamented coverings spread over the saddle of a horse.
7. Artifice implies mechanic or applied art. It is beneath the dignity of epic to teach etiquette and social ceremony and heraldry.
8. The name of epic.
9. I.e., at the end of Book 4, a week earlier.
1. Despite the danger of heavier punishment.
2. By keeping to earth's shadow, Satan contrives to experience a whole week of darkness. The two colures were great circles, intersecting at right angels at the poles and dividing the equinoctial circle (the equator) into four equal parts.

Found unsuspected way. There was a place,
Now not, though Sin, not Time, first wrought the change,
Where *Tigris* at the foot of Paradise
Into a Gulf shot under ground, till part
Rose up a Fountain by the Tree of Life;
In with the River sunk, and with it rose
Satan involv'd in rising Mist, then sought
Where to lie hid; Sea he had searcht and Land
From *Eden* over *Pontus*, and the Pool
Maeotis, up beyond the River *Ob*;[3]
Downward as far Antarctic; and in length
West from *Orontes* to the Ocean barr'd
At *Darien*, thence to the Land where flows
Ganges and *Indus*:[4] thus the Orb he roam'd
With narrow search; and with inspection deep
Consider'd every Creature, which of all
Most opportune might serve his Wiles, and found
The Serpent subtlest Beast of all the Field.[5]
Him after long debate, irresolute° *undecided*
Of thoughts revolv'd, his final sentence° chose *judgment*
Fit Vessel, fittest Imp° of fraud, in whom *offshoot*
To enter, and his dark suggestions hide
From sharpest sight: for in the wily Snake,
Whatever sleights none would suspicious mark,
As from his wit and native subtlety
Proceeding, which in other Beasts observ'd
Doubt° might beget of Diabolic pow'r *suspicion*
Active within beyond the sense of brute.
Thus he resolv'd, but first from inward grief
His bursting passion into plaints thus pour'd:
O Earth, how like to Heav'n, if not preferr'd
More justly, Seat worthier of Gods, as built
With second thoughts, reforming what was old!
For what God after better worse would build?
Terrestrial Heav'n, danc't round by other Heav'ns
That shine, yet bear thir bright officious Lamps,
Light above Light, for thee alone, as seems,
In thee concentring all thir precious beams
Of sacred influence:[6] As God in Heav'n
Is Centre, yet extends to all, so thou
Centring receiv'st from all those Orbs; in thee,
Not in themselves, all thir known virtue appears
Productive in Herb, Plant, and nobler birth
Of Creatures animate with gradual life
Of Growth, Sense, Reason, all summ'd up in Man.[7]

3. In his north-south circles, Satan passed Pontus (the Black Sea), the "pool / Maeotis" (the Sea of Azov), and the Siberian River Ob, which flows north into the Gulf of Ob and from there into the Arctic Ocean.

4. In his westward circling of the equinoctial line, he crossed the Syrian River Orontes, then the Pacific ("peaceful") "Ocean barred" by the Isthmus of Darien (Panama) and India.

5. See Genesis 3.1.

6. The case for an earth-centered universe, put at 8.86–114 by Raphael, is now put by Satan.

7. "Growth, sense, reason" are the activities of the vegetable, animal, and rational souls, respectively, in humans.

With what delight could I have walkt thee round,
If I could joy in aught, sweet interchange
Of Hill and Valley, Rivers, Woods and Plains,
Now Land, now Sea, and Shores with Forest crown'd,
Rocks, Dens, and Caves; but I in none of these
Find place or refuge; and the more I see
Pleasures about me, so much more I feel
Torment within me, as from the hateful siege° *conflict*
Of contraries; all good to me becomes
Bane,° and in Heav'n much worse would be my state. *poison*
But neither here seek I, no nor in Heav'n
To dwell, unless by maistring Heav'n's Supreme;
Nor hope to be myself less miserable
By what I seek, but others to make such
As I, though thereby worse to me redound:
For only in destroying I find ease
To my relentless thoughts; and him destroy'd,
Or won to what may work his utter loss,
For whom all this was made, all this will soon
Follow, as to him linkt in weal or woe,
In woe then: that destruction wide may range:[8]
To mee shall be the glory sole among
Th'infernal Powers, in one day to have marr'd
What he *Almight* styl'd, six Nights and Days
Continu'd making, and who knows how long
Before had been contriving, though perhaps
Not longer than since I in one Night freed
From servitude inglorious well nigh half
Th' Angelic Name, and thinner left the throng
Of his adorers: hee to be aveng'd,
And to repair his numbers thus impair'd,
Whether such virtue° spent of old now fail'd *power*
More Angels to Create, if they at least
Are his Created, or to spite us more,
Determin'd to advance into our room
A Creature form'd of Earth, and him endow,
Exalted from so base original,
With Heav'nly spoils, our spoils; What he decreed
He effected; Man he made, and for him built
Magnificent this World, and Earth his seat,
Him Lord pronounc'd, and, O indignity!
Subjected to his service Angel wings,
And flaming Ministers to watch and tend
Thir earthy Charge: Of these the vigilance
I dread, and to elude, thus wrapt in mist
Of midnight vapor glide obscure, and pry
In every Bush and Brake, where hap may find
The Serpent sleeping, in whose mazy folds
To hide me, and the dark intent I bring.
O foul descent! that I who erst contended

8. The created cosmos will follow humans to destruction.

With Gods to sit the highest, am now constrain'd
Into a Beast, and mixt with bestial slime,
This essence to incarnate and imbrute,
That to the highth of Deity aspir'd;
But what will not Ambition and Revenge
Descend to? who aspires must down as low
As high he soar'd, obnoxious° first or last *exposed*
To basest things. Revenge, at first though sweet,
Bitter ere long back on itself recoils;
Let it, I reck not, so it light well aim'd,
Since higher I fall short, on him who next
Provokes my envy, this new Favorite
Of Heav'n, this Man of Clay, Son of despite,
Whom us the more to spite his Maker rais'd
From dust: spite then with spite is best repaid.
So saying, through each Thicket Dank or Dry,
Like a black mist low creeping, he held on
His midnight search, where soonest he might find
The Serpent: him fast sleeping soon he found
In Labyrinth of many a round self-roll'd,
His head the midst, well stor'd with subtle wiles:
Not yet in horrid Shade or dismal Den,
Nor nocent° yet, but on the grassy Herb *harmful, guilty*
Fearless unfear'd he slept: in at his Mouth
The Devil enter'd, and his brutal sense,
In heart or head, possessing soon inspir'd
With act intelligential; but his sleep
Disturb'd not, waiting close° th' approach of Morn. *concealed*
Now whenas sacred Light began to dawn
In *Eden* on the humid Flow'rs, that breath'd
Thir morning incense, when all things that breathe,
From th' Earth's great Altar send up silent praise
To the Creator, and his Nostrils fill
With grateful Smell, forth came the human pair
And join'd thir vocal Worship to the Choir
Of Creatures wanting voice; that done, partake
The season, prime for sweetest Scents and Airs:
Then cómmune how that day they best may ply
Thir growing work: for much thir work outgrew
The hands' dispatch of two Gard'ning so wide.
And *Eve* first to her Husband thus began.
Adam, well may we labor still to dress
This Garden, still to tend Plant, Herb and Flow'r,
Our pleasant task enjoin'd, but till more hands
Aid us, the work under our labor grows,
Luxurious by restraint; what we by day
Lop overgrown, or prune, or prop, or bind,
One night or two with wanton growth derides
Tending to wild. Thou therefore now advise
Or hear what to my mind first thoughts present,
Let us divide our labors, thou where choice
Leads thee, or where most needs, whether to wind

The Woodbine round this Arbor, or direct
The clasping Ivy where to climb, while I
In yonder Spring of Roses intermixt
With Myrtle, find what to redress till Noon:
For while so near each other thus all day
Our task we choose, what wonder if so near
Looks intervene and smiles, or object new
Casual discourse draw on, which intermits
Our day's work brought to little, though begun
Early, and th' hour of Supper comes unearn'd.
  To whom mild answer *Adam* thus return'd.
Sole *Eve*, Associate sole, to me beyond
Compare above all living Creatures dear,
Well hast thou motion'd,° well thy thoughts imploy'd *proposed*
How we might best fulfil the work which here
God hath assign'd us, nor of me shalt pass
Unprais'd: for nothing lovelier can be found
In Woman, than to study household good,
And good works in her Husband to promote.
Yet not so strictly hath our Lord impos'd
Labor, as to debar us when we need
Refreshment, whether food, or talk between,
Food of the mind, or this sweet intercourse
Of looks and smiles, for smiles from Reason flow,
To brute deni'd, and are of Love the food,
Love not the lowest end of human life.
For not to irksome toil, but to delight
He made us, and delight to Reason join'd.
These paths and Bowers doubt not but our joint hands
Will keep from Wilderness with ease, as wide
As we need walk, till younger hands ere long
Assist us: But if much converse perhaps
Thee satiate, to short absence I could yield.
For solitude sometimes is best society,
And short retirement urges sweet return.
But other doubt possesses me, lest harm
Befall thee sever'd from me; for thou know'st
What hath been warn'd us, what malicious Foe
Envying our happiness, and of his own
Despairing, seeks to work us woe and shame
By sly assault; and somewhere nigh at hand
Watches, no doubt, with greedy hope to find
His wish and best advantage, us asunder,
Hopeless to circumvent us join'd, where each
To other speedy aid might lend at need;
Whether his first design be to withdraw
Our fealty from God, or to disturb
Conjugal Love, than which perhaps no bliss
Enjoy'd by us excites his envy more;
Or this, or worse,[9] leave not the faithful side

9. Whether this or worse (be his first design).

That gave thee being, still shades thee and protects.
The Wife, where danger or dishonor lurks,
Safest and seemliest by her Husband stays,
Who guards her, or with her the worst endures.
   To whom the Virgin° Majesty of *Eve*, *chaste, innocent*
As one who loves, and some unkindness meets,
With sweet austere composure thus repli'd.
   Offspring of Heav'n and Earth, and all Earth's Lord,
That such an Enemy we have, who seeks
Our ruin, both by thee inform'd I learn,
And from the parting Angel over-heard
As in a shady nook I stood behind,
Just then return'd at shut of Ev'ning Flow'rs.
But that thou shouldst my firmness therefore doubt
To God or thee, because we have a foe
May tempt it, I expected not to hear.
His violence thou fear'st not, being such,
As wee, not capable of death or pain,
Can either not receive, or can repel.
His fraud is then thy fear, which plain infers
Thy equal fear that my firm Faith and Love
Can by his fraud be shak'n or seduc't;
Thoughts, which how found they harbor in thy breast,
Adam, misthought of her to thee so dear?
   To whom with healing words *Adam* repli'd.
Daughter of God and Man, immortal *Eve*,
For such thou art, from sin and blame entire:° *free*
Not diffident° of thee do I dissuade *mistrustful*
Thy absence from my sight, but to avoid
Th' attempt itself, intended by our Foe.
For hee who tempts, though in vain, at least asperses° *falsely charges*
The tempted with dishonor foul, suppos'd
Not incorruptible of Faith, not proof
Against temptation: thou thyself with scorn
And anger wouldst resent the offer'd wrong,
Though ineffectual found: misdeem not then,
If such affront I labor to avert
From thee alone, which on us both at once
The Enemy, though bold, will hardly dare,
Or daring, first on mee th' assault shall light.
Nor thou his malice and false guile contemn;
Subtle he needs must be, who could seduce
Angels, nor think superfluous others' aid.
I from the influence of thy looks receive
Access° in every Virtue, in thy sight *increase*
More wise, more watchful, stronger, if need were
Of outward strength; while shame, thou looking on,
Shame to be overcome or over-reacht
Would utmost vigor raise, and rais'd unite.
Why shouldst not thou like sense within thee feel
When I am present, and thy trial choose
With me, best witness of thy Virtue tri'd.

So spake domestic *Adam* in his care
And Matrimonial Love; but *Eve*, who thought
Less° attribúted to her Faith sincere, *too little*
Thus her reply with accent sweet renew'd.
If this be our condition, thus to dwell
In narrow circuit strait'n'd by a Foe,
Subtle or violent, we not endu'd
Single with like defense, wherever met,
How are we happy, still in fear of harm?
But harm precedes not sin: only our Foe
Tempting affronts us with his foul esteem
Of our integrity: his foul esteem
Sticks no dishonor on our Front,° but turns *forehead*
Foul on himself; then wherefore shunn'd or fear'd
By us? who rather double honor gain
From his surmise prov'd false, find peace within,
Favor from Heav'n, our witness from th' event.
And what is Faith, Love, Virtue unassay'd
Alone, without exterior help sustain'd?
Let us not then suspect our happy State
Left so imperfet by the Maker wise,
As not secure to single or combin'd.
Frail is our happiness, if this be so,
And *Eden* were no Eden[1] thus expos'd.
To whom thus Adam fervently repli'd.
O Woman, best are all things as the will
Of God ordain'd them, his creating hand
Nothing imperfet or deficient left
Of all that he Created, much less Man,
Or aught that might his happy State secure,
Secure from outward force; within himself
The danger lies, yet lies within his power:
Against his will he can receive no harm.
But God left free the Will, for what obeys
Reason, is free, and Reason he made right,
But bid her well beware, and still erect,[2]
Lest by some fair appearing good surpris'd
She dictate false, and misinform the Will
To do what God expressly hath forbid.
Not then mistrust, but tender love enjoins,
That I should mind thee oft, and mind thou me.
Firm we subsist, yet possible to swerve,
Since Reason not impossibly may meet
Some specious object by the Foe suborn'd,
And fall into deception unaware,
Not keeping strictest watch, as she was warn'd.
Seek not temptation then, which to avoid
Were better, and most likely if from mee
Thou sever not: Trial will come unsought.
Wouldst thou approve° thy constancy, approve *demonstrate*

1. I.e., no pleasure, the literal Hebrew meaning of "Eden."

2. Always attentive, but also with a glance at upright.

First thy obedience; th' other who can know,
Not seeing thee attempted, who attest?
But if thou think, trial unsought may find
Us both securer° than thus warn'd thou seem'st, *more careless*
Go; for thy stay, not free, absents thee more;
Go in thy native innocence, rely
On what thou hast of virtue, summon all,
For God towards thee hath done his part, do thine.
  So spake the Patriarch of Mankind, but *Eve*
Persisted, yet submiss, though last, repli'd.
  With thy permission then, and thus forewarn'd
Chiefly by what thy own last reasoning words
Touch'd only, that our trial, when least sought,
May find us both perhaps far less prepar'd,
The willinger I go, nor much expect
A Foe so proud will first the weaker seek;
So bent, the more shall shame him his repulse.
Thus saying, from her Husband's hand her hand
Soft she withdrew, and like a Wood-Nymph light,
Oread or *Dryad*, or of *Delia's* Train,[3]
Betook her to the Groves, but *Delia's* self
In gait surpass'd and Goddess-like deport,
Though not as shee with Bow and Quiver arm'd,
But with such Gard'ning Tools as Art yet rude,
Guiltless° of fire had form'd, or Angels brought.[4] *innocent, ignorant*
To Pales, or Pomona, thus adorn'd,
Likest she seem'd, Pomona when she fled
Vertumnus, or to *Ceres* in her Prime,
Yet Virgin of *Proserpina* from *Jove*.[5]
Her long and ardent look his Eye pursu'd
Delighted, but desiring more her stay.
Oft he to her his charge of quick return
Repeated, shee to him as oft engag'd
To be return'd by Noon amid the Bow'r,
And all things in best order to invite
Noontide repast, or Afternoon's repose.
O much deceiv'd, much failing, hapless *Eve*,
Of thy presum'd return! event perverse!
Thou never from that hour in Paradise
Found'st either sweet repast, or sound repose;
Such ambush hid among sweet Flow'rs and Shades
Waited with hellish rancor imminent
To intercept thy way, or send thee back
Despoil'd of Innocence, of Faith, of Bliss.
For now, and since first break of dawn the Fiend,
Mere° Serpent in appearance, forth was come, *plain*
And on his Quest, where likeliest he might find

3. Oreads, were mountain nymphs, such as attended on Diana; dryads were wood nymphs. Neither class of nymphs were immortal.

4. Only as a result of the Fall did it become necessary for humans to have some means of warming themselves. There may also be an allusion to the fire stolen from heaven by Prometheus.

5. Pales was the Roman goddess of pastures; Pomona was the nymph or goddess of fruit trees, seduced by the disguised Vertumnus; Ceres was the goddess of corn and agriculture who bore Proserpina to Jove.

The only two of Mankind, but in them
The whole included Race, his purpos'd prey.
In Bow'r and Field he sought, where any tuft
Of Grove or Garden-Plot more pleasant lay,
Thir tendance° or Plantation for delight, *object of care*
By Fountain or by shady Rivulet,
He sought them both, but wish'd his hap° might find *chance*
Eve separate, he wish'd, but not with hope
Of what so seldom chanc'd, when to his wish,
Beyond his hope, *Eve* separate he spies,
Veil'd in a Cloud of Fragrance, where she stood,
Half spi'd, so thick the Roses bushing round
About her glow'd, oft stooping to support
Each Flow'r of slender stalk, whose head though gay
Carnation, Purple, Azure, or speckt with Gold,
Hung drooping unsustain'd, them she upstays
Gently with Myrtle band, mindless the while,
Herself, though fairest unsupported Flow'r,
From her best prop so far, and storm so nigh.[6]
Nearer he drew, and many a walk travers'd
Of stateliest Covert, Cedar, Pine, or Palm,
Then voluble and bold, now hid, now seen
Among thick-wov'n Arborets and Flow'rs
Imborder'd on each Bank, the hand° of *Eve:* *handiwork*
Spot more delicious than those Gardens feign'd
Or of reviv'd *Adonis*, or renown'd
Alcinoüs, host of old *Laertes'* Son,
Or that, not Mystic, where the Sapient King
Held dalliance with his fair *Egyptian* Spouse.[7]
Much hee the Place admir'd, the Person more.
As one who long in populous City pent,
Where Houses thick and Sewers annoy the Air,
Forth issuing on a Summer's Morn to breathe
Among the pleasant Villages and Farms
Adjoin'd, from each thing met conceives delight,
The smell of Grain, or tedded° Grass, or Kine,° *mown/cows*
Or Dairy, each rural sight, each rural sound;
If chance with Nymphlike step fair Virgin pass,
What pleasing seem'd, for her now pleases more,
She most, and in her look sums all Delight.
Such Pleasure took the Serpent to behold
This Flow'ry Plat,° the sweet recess of *Eve* *piece of ground*
Thus early, thus alone; her Heav'nly form
Angelic, but more soft, and Feminine,
Her graceful Innocence, her every Air
Of gesture or least action overaw'd
His Malice, and with rapine sweet bereav'd

6. See 4.270, page 1819, where Proserpina (and by implication Eve) was "Herself a fairer flower" when she was carried off by the king of hell.

7. "The sapient king" was Solomon (*Song of Solomon* 6.2). Milton alludes to Spenser's addition to the myth of Adonis, that Venus keeps Adonis hidden in a secret garden (*The Faerie Queene* 3.6). "Laertes' son" was Odysseus; much-traveled as he was, he marveled when he saw the Garden of Alcinoüs (Homer, *Odyssey* 7).

His fierceness of the fierce intent it brought:
That space the Evil one abstracted stood
From his own evil, and for the time remain'd
Stupidly good, of enmity disarm'd,
Of guile, of hate, of envy, of revenge;
But the hot Hell that always in him burns,
Though in mid Heav'n, soon ended his delight,
And tortures him now more, the more he sees
Of pleasure not for him ordain'd: then soon
Fierce hate he recollects, and all his thoughts
Of mischief, gratulating,° thus excites. *rejoicing*
Thoughts, whither have ye led me, with what sweet
Compulsion thus transported to forget
What hither brought us, hate, not love, nor hope
Of Paradise for Hell, hope here to taste
Of pleasure, but all pleasure to destroy,
Save what is in destroying, other joy
To me is lost. Then let me not let pass
Occasion which now smiles, behold alone
The Woman, opportune° to all attempts, *exposed*
Her Husband, for I view far round, not nigh,
Whose higher intellectual more I shun,
And strength, of courage haughty, and of limb
Heroic built, though of terrestrial mould,° *formed of earth*
Foe not informidable, exempt from wound,
I not; so much hath Hell debas'd, and pain
Infeebl'd me, to what I was in Heav'n.
Shee fair, divinely fair, fit Love for Gods,
Not terrible, though terror be in Love
And beauty, not approacht by stronger hate,
Hate stronger, under show of Love well feign'd,
The way which to her ruin now I tend.
So spake the Enemy of Mankind, enclos'd
In Serpent, Inmate bad, and toward *Eve*
Address'd his way, not with indented wave,
Prone on the ground, as since, but on his rear,
Circular base of rising folds, that tow'r'd
Fold above fold a surging Maze, his Head
Crested aloft, and Carbuncle his Eyes;[8]
With burnisht Neck of verdant Gold, erect
Amidst his circling Spires,° that on the grass *coils*
Floated redundant:° pleasing was his shape, *abundant to excess*
And lovely, never since of Serpent kind
Lovelier, not those that in *Illyria* chang'd
Hermione and *Cadmus*, or the God
In *Epidaurus;*[9] nor to which transform'd
Ammonian Jove, or *Capitoline* was seen,
Hee with *Olympias*, this with her who bore

8. "Carbuncle" or reddish eyes denoted rage.
9. Cadmus was turned into a serpent first; only after he had embraced his wife Hermione (Harmonia) in his new form did she too change (Ovid, *Metamorphoses* 4.572–603). Aesculapius, the god of healing, once changed into a serpent to help the Romans in that form (Ovid, *Metamorphoses* 15.626–744).

Scipio the highth of Rome.[1] With tract oblique
At first, as one who sought access, but fear'd
To interrupt, side-long he works his way.
As when a Ship by skilful Steersman wrought
Nigh River's mouth or Foreland, where the Wind
Veers oft, as oft so steers, and shifts her Sail;
So varied hee, and of his tortuous Train
Curl'd many a wanton wreath in sight of *Eve*,
To lure her Eye; shee busied heard the sound
Of rustling Leaves, but minded not, as us'd
To such disport before her through the Field,
From every Beast, more duteous at her call,
Than at *Circean* call the Herd disguis'd.[2]
Hee bolder now, uncall'd before her stood;
But as in gaze admiring: Oft he bow'd
His turret Crest, and sleek enamell'd Neck,
Fawning, and lick'd the ground whereon she trod.
His gentle dumb expression turn'd at length
The Eye of *Eve* to mark his play; he glad
Of her attention gain'd, with Serpent Tongue
Organic, or impulse of vocal Air,
His fraudulent temptation thus began.
    Wonder not, sovran Mistress, if perhaps
Thou canst, who are sole Wonder, much less arm
Thy looks, the Heav'n of mildness, with disdain,
Displeas'd that I approach thee thus, and gaze
Insatiate, I thus single, nor have fear'd
Thy awful brow, more awful thus retir'd.
Fairest resemblance of thy Maker fair,
Thee all things living gaze on, all things thine
By gift, and thy Celestial Beauty adore
With ravishment beheld, there best beheld
Where universally admir'd: but here
In this enclosure wild, these Beasts among,
Beholders rude, and shallow to discern
Half what in thee is fair, one man except,
Who sees thee? (and what is one?) who shouldst be seen
A Goddess among Gods, ador'd and serv'd
By Angels numberless, thy daily Train.
    So gloz'd° the Tempter, and his Proem° tun'd; *flattered/prelude*
Into the Heart of *Eve* his words made way,
Though at the voice much marvelling; at length
Not unamaz'd she thus in answer spake.
    What may this mean? Language of Man pronounc't
By Tongue of Brute, and human sense exprest?[3]
The first at least of these I thought deni'd
To Beasts, whom God on thir Creation-Day

1. Jupiter Ammon, the "Lybian Jove," as a serpent mated with Olympias to father Alexander the Great, just as the Roman Jupiter, Capitolinus, took the form of a snake to father the great general Scipio.
2. Homer's Circe changed men into beasts who surprised Odysseus's company by fawning on them like dogs (*Odyssey* 10.212–219).
3. Milton is unusually favorable to Eve in making her ask the serpent how it came by its voice. The Eve of Scriptural exegesis, by contrast, is carried away by the words and makes no inquiry into their source.

Created mute to all articulate sound;
The latter I demur,° for in thir looks *hesitate about*
Much reason, and in thir actions oft appears.
Thee, Serpent, subtlest beast of all the field
I knew, but not with human voice endu'd;
Redouble then this miracle, and say,
How cam'st thou speakable of mute,[4] and how
To me so friendly grown above the rest
Of brutal kind, that daily are in sight?
Say, for such wonder claims attention due.
  To whom the guileful Tempter thus repli'd.
Empress of this fair World, resplendent *Eve*,
Easy to mee it is to tell thee all
What thou command'st and right thou should'st be obey'd:
I was at first as other Beasts that graze
The trodden Herb, of abject° thoughts and low, *mean-spirited*
As was my food, nor aught but food discern'd
Or Sex, and apprehended nothing high:
Till on a day roving the field, I chanc'd
A goodly Tree far distant to behold
Loaden with fruit of fairest colors mixt,
Ruddy and Gold: I nearer drew to gaze;
When from the boughs a savory odor blown,
Grateful to appetite, more pleas'd my sense
Than smell of sweetest Fennel, or the Teats
Of Ewe or Goat dropping with Milk at Ev'n,
Unsuckt of Lamb or Kid, that tend thir play.
To satisfy the sharp desire I had
Of tasting those fair Apples, I resolv'd
Not to defer; hunger and thirst at once,
Powerful persuaders, quick'n'd at the scent
Of that alluring fruit, urg'd me so keen.
About the mossy Trunk I wound me soon,
For high from ground the branches would require
Thy utmost reach or *Adam's:* Round the Tree
All other Beasts that saw, with like desire
Longing and envying stood, but could not reach.
Amid the Tree now got, where plenty hung
Tempting so nigh, to pluck and eat my fill
I spar'd not, for such pleasure till that hour
At Feed or Fountain never had I found.
Sated at length, ere long I might perceive
Strange alteration in me, to degree
Of Reason in my inward Powers, and Speech
Wanted not long, though to this shape retain'd.
Thenceforth to Speculations high or deep
I turn'd my thoughts, and with capacious mind
Consider'd all things visible in Heav'n,
Or Earth, or Middle, all things fair and good;
But all that fair and good in thy Divine

4. How did you become capable of speech from being dumb?

Semblance, and in thy Beauty's heav'nly Ray
United I beheld; no Fair° to thine *beauty*
Equivalent or second, which compell'd
Mee thus, though importune perhaps, to come
And gaze, and worship thee of right declar'd
Sovran of Creatures, universal Dame.
So talk'd the spirited[5] sly Snake; and *Eve*,
Yet more amaz'd unwary thus repli'd.
Serpent, thy overpraising leaves in doubt
The virtue° of that Fruit, in thee first prov'd: *power*
But say, where grows the Tree, from hence how far?
For many are the Trees of God that grow
In Paradise, and various, yet unknown
To us, in such abundance lies our choice,
As leaves a greater store of Fruit untoucht,
Still hanging incorruptible, till men
Grow up to thir provision, and more hands
Help to disburden Nature of her Birth.
To whom the wily Adder, blithe and glad.
Empress, the way is ready, and not long,
Beyond a row of Myrtles, on a Flat,
Fast by a Fountain, one small Thicket past
Of blowing° Myrrh and Balm; if thou accept *blooming*
My conduct,° I can bring thee thither soon. *guidance*
Lead then, said Eve. Hee leading swiftly roll'd
In tangles, and made intricate seem straight,
To mischief swift. Hope elevates, and joy
Bright'ns his Crest, as when a wand'ring Fire,
Compact° of unctuous vapor, which the Night *made up*
Condenses, and the cold invirons round,
Kindl'd through agitation to a Flame,
Which oft, they say, some evil Spirit attends,
Hovering and blazing with delusive Light,
Misleads th' amaz'd Night-wanderer from his way
To Bogs and Mires, and oft through Pond or Pool,
There swallow'd up and lost, from succor far.
So glister'd the dire Snake, and into fraud
Led *Eve* our credulous Mother, to the Tree
Of prohibition, root of all our woe;
Which when she saw, thus to her guide she spake.
Serpent, we might have spar'd our coming hither,
Fruitless to mee, though Fruit be here to excess,
The credit of whose virtue rest with thee,
Wondrous indeed, if cause of such effects.
But of this Tree we may not taste nor touch;
God so commanded, and left that Command
Sole Daughter of his voice;[6] the rest, we live
Law to ourselves, our Reason is our Law.
To whom the Tempter guilefully repli'd.
Indeed? hath God then said that of the Fruit

5. Endowed with an animating spirit, stirred up; also energetic, enterprising, possessed by a spirit.

6. A Hebraism for "voice sent from heaven."

Of all these Garden Trees ye shall not eat,
Yet Lords declar'd of all in Earth or Air?[7]
To whom thus *Eve* yet sinless. Of the Fruit
Of each Tree in the Garden we may eat,
But of the Fruit of this fair Tree amidst
The Garden, God hath said, Ye shall not eat
Thereof, nor shall ye touch it, lest ye die.
She scarce had said, though brief, when now more bold
The Tempter, but with show of Zeal and Love
To Man, and indignation at his wrong,
New part puts on, and as to passion mov'd,
Fluctuates disturb'd, yet comely, and in act
Rais'd, as of some great matter to begin.
As when of old some Orator renown'd
In *Athens* or free *Rome*, where Eloquence
Flourish'd, since mute, to some great cause addrest,
Stood in himself collected, while each part,
Motion, each act won audience ere the tongue,
Sometimes in highth began, as no delay
Of Preface brooking through his Zeal of Right.[8]
So standing, moving, or to highth upgrown
The Tempter all impassion'd thus began.
O Sacred, Wise, and Wisdom-giving Plant,
Mother of Science,° Now I feel thy Power *knowledge*
Within me clear, not only to discern
Things in thir Causes, but to trace the ways
Of highest Agents, deem'd however wise.
Queen of this Universe, do not believe
Those rigid threats of Death; ye shall not Die:
How should ye? by the Fruit? it gives you Life
To° Knowledge: By the Threat'ner? look on mee, *in addition to*
Mee who have touch'd and tasted, yet both live,
And life more perfet have attain'd than Fate
Meant mee, by vent'ring higher than my Lot.
Shall that be shut to Man, which to the Beast
Is open? or will God incense his ire
For such a petty Trespass, and not praise
Rather your dauntless virtue, whom the pain
Of Death denounc't, whatever thing Death be,
Deterr'd not from achieving what might lead
To happier life, knowledge of Good and Evil;
Of good, how just? of evil, if what is evil
Be real, why not known, since easier shunn'd?[9]
God therefore cannot hurt ye, and be just;
Not just, not God; not fear'd then, nor obey'd:
Your fear itself of Death removes the fear.
Why then was this forbid? Why but to awe,

7. Lines 655–58 closely follow Genesis. 3.1.

8. This simile blends oratorical, theatrical, and theological meanings. Thus "part" means "part of the body," "dramatic role," and "moral act"; "motion" means "gesture," "mime" (or "puppet-show"), and "instigation, persuasive force, inclination"; "act" means "action," "performance of a play," and "the accomplished deed itself."

9. If the knowledge is good, how is it just to prohibit it? Here occurs the most egregious logical fallacy in speech. (For evil to be "shunned," it is not at all necessary that it should be "known" in the sense of being experienced.)

Why but to keep ye low and ignorant,
His worshippers; he knows that in the day
Ye Eat thereof, your Eyes that seem so clear,
Yet are but dim, shall perfetly be then
Op'n'd and clear'd, and ye shall be as Gods,
Knowing both Good and Evil as they know.[1]
That ye should be as Gods, since I as Man,
Internal Man,[2] is but proportion meet,
I of brute human, thee of human Gods.
So ye shall die perhaps, by putting off
Human, to put on Gods, death to be wisht,
Though threat'n'd, which no worse than this can bring.[3]
And what are Gods that Man may not become
As they, participating° God-like food? *sharing*
The Gods are first, and that advantage use
On our belief, that all from them proceeds;
I question it, for this fair Earth I see,
Warm'd by the Sun, producing every kind,
Them nothing: If they° all things, who enclos'd *if they produce*
Knowledge of Good and Evil in this Tree,
That who so eats thereof, forthwith attains
Wisdom without their leave? and wherein lies
Th' offense, that Man should thus attain to know?
What can your knowledge hurt him, or this Tree
Impart against his will if all be his?
Or is it envy, and can envy dwell
In heav'nly breasts?[4] these, these and many more
Causes import° your need of this fair Fruit. *suggest*
Goddess humane, reach then, and freely taste.
He ended, and his words replete with guile
Into her heart too easy entrance won:
Fixt on the Fruit she gaz'd, which to behold
Might tempt alone, and in her ears the sound
Yet rung of his persuasive words, impregn'd° *impregnated*
With Reason, to her seeming, and with Truth;
Meanwhile the hour of Noon drew on, and wak'd
An eager appetite, rais'd by the smell
So savory of that Fruit, which with desire,
Inclinable now grown to touch or taste,
Solicited her longing eye;[5] yet first
Pausing a while, thus to herself she mus'd.
Great are thy Virtues, doubtless, best of Fruits,
Though kept from Man, and worthy to be admir'd,
Whose taste, too long forborne, at first assay
Gave elocution to the mute, and taught
The Tongue not made for Speech to speak thy praise:[6]

1. See Genesis 3.5.
2. The serpent's pretence is that his "inward powers" are human.
3. Satan offers a travesty of Christian mortification and death to sin; see *Colossians* 3.1–15: "ye have put off the old man with his deeds; And have put on the new man, which is renewed in knowledge after the image of him that created him."
4. See Virgil, *Aeneid* 1.11; Satan is inviting Eve to participate in a pagan epic, complete with machinery of jealous gods.
5. For lines 735–43, see Genesis 3.6.
6. Eve has trusted Satan's account of the fruit and consequently argues from false premises, such as its magical power.

Thy praise hee also who forbids thy use,
Conceals not from us, naming thee the Tree
Of Knowledge, knowledge both of good and evil;
Forbids us then to taste, but his forbidding
Commends thee more, while it infers the good
By thee communicated, and our want:
For good unknown, sure is not had, or had
And yet unknown, is as not had at all.
In plain° then, what forbids he but to know, *plainly*
Forbids us good, forbids us to be wise?
Such prohibitions bind not. But if Death
Bind us with after-bands, what profits then
Our inward freedom? In the day we eat
Of this fair Fruit, our doom is, we shall die.
How dies the Serpent? hee hath eat'n and lives,
And knows, and speaks, and reasons, and discerns,
Irrational till then. For us alone
Was death invented? or to us deni'd
This intellectual food, for beasts reserv'd?
For Beasts it seems: yet that one Beast which first
Hath tasted, envies not, but brings with joy
The good befall'n him, Author unsuspect,[7]
Friendly to man, far from deceit or guile.
What fear I then, rather what know to fear[8]
Under this ignorance of Good and Evil,
Of God or Death, of Law or Penalty?
Here grows the Cure of all, this Fruit Divine,
Fair to the Eye, inviting to the Taste,
Of virtue° to make wise: what hinders then *power*
To reach, and feed at once both Body and Mind?
So saying, her rash hand in evil hour
Forth reaching to the Fruit, she pluck'd, she eat:° *ate*
Earth felt the wound, and Nature from her seat
Sighing through all her Works gave signs of woe,
That all was lost. Back to the Thicket slunk
The guilty Serpent, and well might, for *Eve*,
Intent now wholly on her taste, naught else
Regarded, such delight till then, as seem'd,
In Fruit she never tasted, whether true
Or fancied so, through expectation high
Of knowledge, nor was God-head from her thought.[9]
Greedily she ingorg'd without restraint,
And knew not eating Death:[1] Satiate at length,
And hight'n'd as with Wine, jocund and boon,° *jolly*
Thus to herself she pleasingly began.
O Sovran, virtuous, precious of all Trees
In Paradise, of operation blest
To Sapience,[2] hitherto obscur'd, infam'd,° *defamed*

7. Eve means "informant not subject to suspicion."
8. What fear I, then—or rather (since I'm not allowed to know anything) what do I know that is to be feared?
9. She expected to achieve godhead.
1. She knew not that she was eating death; "she was unaware, while she ate death" or even "she 'knew'; not eating (immediate) death."
2. "Sapience" is derived from Latin *sapientia* (discernment, taste) and ultimately from *sapere* (to taste).

And thy fair Fruit let hang, as to no end
Created; but henceforth my early care,
Not without Song, each Morning, and due praise
Shall tend thee, and the fertile burden ease
Of thy full branches offer'd free to all;
Till dieted by thee I grow mature
In knowledge, as the Gods who all things know;
Though others[3] envy what they cannot give;
For had the gift been theirs, it had not here
Thus grown. Experience, next to thee I owe,
Best guide; not following thee, I had remain'd
In ignorance, thou op'n'st Wisdom's way,
And giv'st access, though secret she retire.
And I perhaps am secret; Heav'n is high,
High and remote to see from thence distinct
Each thing on Earth; and other care perhaps
May have diverted from continual watch
Our great Forbidder, safe with all his Spies
About him. But to *Adam* in what sort
Shall I appear? shall I to him make known
As yet my change, and give him to partake
Full happiness with mee, or rather not.
But keep the odds of Knowledge in my power
Without Copartner? so to add what wants
In Female Sex, the more to draw his Love,
And render me more equal, and perhaps,
A thing not undesirable, sometime
Superior: for inferior who is free?
This may be well: but what if God have seen,
And Death ensue? then I shall be no more,
And *Adam* wedded to another *Eve*,
Shall live with her enjoying, I extinct;
A death to think. Confirm'd then I resolve,
Adam shall share with me in bliss or woe:
So dear I love him, that with him all deaths
I could endure, without him live no life.

So saying, from the Tree her step she turn'd,
But first low Reverence done, as to the power
That dwelt within, whose presence had infus'd
Into the plant sciential[4] sap, deriv'd
From Nectar, drink of Gods. *Adam* the while
Waiting desirous her return, had wove
Of choicest Flow'rs a Garland to adorn
Her Tresses, and her rural labors crown,
As Reapers oft are wont thir Harvest Queen.
Great joy he promis'd to his thoughts, and new
Solace in her return, so long delay'd;
Yet oft his heart, divine° of something ill, *prophet*
Misgave him; hee the falt'ring measure[5] felt;
And forth to meet her went, the way she took

3. I.e., God. Eve's language is now full of lapses in logic and evasions in theology.

4. Endowed with knowledge.

5. The rhythm of his own heart.

That Morn when first they parted; by the Tree
Of Knowledge he must pass; there he her met,
Scarce from the Tree returning; in her hand
A bough of fairest fruit that downy smil'd,
New gather'd, and ambrosial smell diffus'd.
To him she hasted, in her face excuse
Came Prologue, and Apology to prompt,[6]
Which with bland words at will she thus addrest.
 Hast thou not wonder'd, *Adam,* at my stay?
Thee I have misst, and thought it long, depriv'd
Thy presence, agony of love till now
Not felt, nor shall be twice, for never more
Mean I to try, what rash untri'd I sought,
The pain of absence from thy sight. But strange
Hath been the cause, and wonderful to hear:
This Tree is not as we are told, a Tree
Of danger tasted,° nor to evil unknown *if tasted*
Op'ning the way, but of Divine effect
To open Eyes, and make them Gods who taste;
And hath been tasted such: the Serpent wise,
Or not restrain'd as wee, or not obeying,
Hath eat'n of the fruit, and is become,
Not dead, as we are threat'n'd, but thenceforth
Endu'd with human voice and human sense,
Reasoning to admiration, and with mee
Persuasively hath so prevail'd, that I
Have also tasted, and have also found
Th' effects to correspond, opener mine Eyes,
Dim erst, dilated Spirits, ampler Heart,
And growing up to Godhead; which for thee
Chiefly I sought, without thee can despise.
For bliss, as thou hast part, to me is bliss,
Tedious, unshar'd with thee, and odious soon.
Thou therefore also taste, that equal Lot
May join us, equal Joy, as equal Love;
Lest thou not tasting, different degree[7]
Disjoin us, and I then too late renounce
Deity for thee, when Fate will not permit.
 Thus *Eve* with Count'nance blithe her story told;
But in her Cheek distemper[8] flushing glow'd.
On th' other side, *Adam,* soon as he heard
The fatal Trespass done by *Eve,* amaz'd,
Astonied° stood and Blank, while horror chill *stunned*
Ran through his veins, and all his joints relax'd;
From his slack hand the Garland wreath'd for *Eve,*
Down dropp'd, and all the faded Roses shed:
Speechless he stood and pale, till thus at length
First to himself he inward silence broke.

6. The expression on Eve's face is visible in advance as she approaches and so is like the prologue-speaker of a play. But it also remains on her face as she speaks, to help out her words, and so is like the prompter of the play. The actor prompted is apology, i.e., justification or defense personified.

7. Differing position in the scale of creatures.

8. A disordered condition due to disturbance of the temperament of the bodily humors.

O fairest of Creation, last and best
Of all God's Works, Creature in whom excell'd
Whatever can to sight or thought be form'd,
Holy, divine, good, amiable, or sweet!
How art thou lost, how on a sudden lost,
Defac't, deflow'r'd, and now to death devote?° *given over*
Rather how hast thou yielded to transgress
The strict forbiddance, how to violate
The sacred Fruit forbidd'n! some cursed fraud
Of Enemy hath beguil'd thee, yet unknown,
And mee with thee hath ruin'd, for with thee
Certain my resolution is to Die;
How can I live without thee, how forgo
Thy sweet Converse and Love so dearly join'd,
To live again in these wild Woods forlorn?
Should God create another *Eve*, and I
Another Rib afford, yet loss of thee
Would never from my heart; no no, I feel
The Link of Nature draw me: Flesh of Flesh,
Bone of my Bone thou art, and from thy State
Mine never shall be parted, bliss or woe.
So having said, as one from sad dismay
Recomforted, and after thoughts disturb'd
Submitting to what seem'd remediless,
Thus in calm mood his Words to *Eve* he turn'd.
Bold deed thou hast presum'd, advent'rous *Eve*,
And peril great provok't, who thus hath dar'd
Had it been only coveting to Eye
That sacred Fruit, sacred° to abstinence, *devoted*
Much more to taste it under ban to touch.
But past who can recall, or done undo?
Not God Omnipotent, nor Fate; yet so
Perhaps thou shalt not Die, perhaps the Fact° *crime, deed*
Is not so heinous now, foretasted Fruit,
Profan'd first by the Serpent, by him first
Made common and unhallow'd ere our taste;
Nor yet on him found deadly, he yet lives,
Lives, as thou said'st, and gains to live as Man
Higher degree of Life, inducement strong
To us, as likely tasting to attain
Proportional ascent, which cannot be
But to be Gods, or Angels Demi-gods.
Nor can I think that God, Creator wise,
Though threat'ning, will in earnest so destroy
Us his prime Creatures, dignifi'd so high,
Set over all his Works, which in our Fall,
For us created, needs with us must fail,
Dependent made; so God shall uncreate,
Be frustrate, do, undo, and labor lose,
Not well conceiv'd of God, who though his Power
Creation could repeat, yet would be loath
Us to abolish, lest the Adversary

Triumph and say; Fickle their State whom God
Most Favors, who can please him long? Mee first
He ruin'd, now Mankind; whom will he next?
Matter of scorn, not to be given the Foe.
However I with thee have fixt my Lot,
Certain to undergo like doom;[9] if Death
Consort with thee, Death is to mee as Life;
So forcible within my heart I feel
The Bond of Nature draw me to my own,
My own in thee, for what thou art is mine;
Our State cannot be sever'd, we are one,
One Flesh; to lose thee were to lose myself.
So *Adam,* and thus *Eve* to him repli'd.
O glorious trial of exceeding Love,
Illustrious evidence, example high!
Ingaging me to emulate, but short
Of thy perfection, how shall I attain,
Adam, from whose dear side I boast me sprung,
And gladly of our Union hear thee speak,
One Heart, one Soul in both; whereof good proof
This day affords, declaring thee resolv'd,
Rather than Death or aught than Death more dread
Shall separate us, linkt in Love so dear,
To undergo with mee one Guilt, one Crime,
If any be, of tasting this fair Fruit,
Whose virtue, for of good still good proceeds,
Direct, or by occasion[1] hath presented
This happy trial of thy Love, which else
So eminently never had been known.
Were it I thought Death menac't would ensue
This my attempt, I would sustain alone
The worst, and not persuade thee, rather die
Deserted, than oblige° thee with a fact *make liable*
Pernicious to thy Peace, chiefly assur'd
Remarkably so late of thy so true,
So faithful Love unequall'd; but I feel
Far otherwise th' event,° nor Death, but Life *result*
Augmented, op'n'd Eyes, new Hopes, new Joys,
Taste so Divine, that what of sweet before
Hath toucht my sense, flat seems to this, and harsh.
On my experience, *Adam,* freely taste,
And fear of Death deliver to the Winds.
So saying, she embrac'd him, and for joy
Tenderly wept, much won that he his Love
Had so ennobl'd, as of choice to incur
Divine displeasure for her sake, or Death.
In recompense (for such compliance bad
Such recompense best merits) from the bough
She gave him of that fair enticing Fruit
With liberal hand: he scrupl'd not to eat

9. Three separate meanings are possible: judgment, irrevocable destiny, and death.

1. I.e., directly or indirectly.

Against his better knowledge, not deceiv'd,
But fondly overcome with Female charm.[2]
Earth trembl'd from her entrails, as again
In pangs, and Nature gave a second groan,
Sky low'r'd, and muttering Thunder, some sad drops
Wept at completing of the mortal Sin
Original;[3] while *Adam* took no thought,
Eating his fill, nor *Eve* to iterate
Her former trespass fear'd, the more to soothe
Him with her lov'd society, that now
As with new Wine intoxicated both
They swim in mirth, and fancy that they feel
Divinity within them breeding wings
Wherewith to scorn the Earth: but that false Fruit
Far other operation first display'd,
Carnal desire inflaming, hee on *Eve*
Began to cast lascivious Eyes, she him
As wantonly repaid; in Lust they burn:
Till *Adam* thus 'gan *Eve* to dalliance move.
Eve, now I see thou are exact of taste,
And elegant, of Sapience[4] no small part,
Since to each meaning savor[5] we apply,
And Palate call judicious; I the praise
Yield thee, so well this day thou hast purvey'd.° *provided*
Much pleasure we have lost, while we abstain'd
From this delightful Fruit, nor known till now
True relish, tasting; if such pleasure be
In things to us forbidden, it might be wish'd,
For this one Tree had been forbidden ten.
But come, so well refresh't, now let us play,
As meet is, after such delicious Fare;
For never did thy Beauty since the day
I saw thee first and wedded thee, adorn'd
With all perfections, so inflame my sense
With ardor to enjoy thee, fairer now
Than ever, bounty of this virtuous Tree.[6]
So said he, and forbore not glance or toy° *caress*
Of amorous intent, well understood
Of° *Eve*, whose Eye darted contagious Fire. *by*
Her hand he seiz'd, and to a shady bank,
Thick overhead with verdant roof imbowr'd
He led her nothing loath; Flow'rs were the Couch,
Pansies, and Violets, and Asphodel,
And Hyacinth, Earth's freshest softest lap.
There they thir fill of Love and Love's disport
Took largely, of thir mutual guilt the Seal,

2. See 1 Timothy 2.14: "And Adam was not deceived, but the woman being deceived was in the transgression."

3. The only occurrence in *Paradise Lost* of the term "Original Sin." In his *De doctrina* (1.11) where Milton defines Original Sin as "the sin which is common to all men, that which our first parents, and in them all their posterity committed, when, casting off their obedience to God, they tasted the fruit of the forbidden tree."

4. Wisdom, from Latin *sapere*, to taste.

5. Tastiness, understanding.

6. See Homer, *Iliad*. 14, where Hera, bent on deceiving Zeus, comes to him wearing Aphrodite's belt and seems more charming to him than ever before.

The solace of thir sin, till dewy sleep
Oppress'd them, wearied with thir amorous play.
Soon as the force of that fallacious Fruit,
That with exhilarating vapor bland° *pleasing*
About thir spirits had play'd, and inmost powers
Made err, was now exhal'd, and grosser sleep
Bred of unkindly fumes,[7] with conscious dreams
Encumber'd, now had left them, up they rose
As from unrest, and each the other viewing,
Soon found thir Eyes how op'n'd, and thir minds
How dark'n'd;[8] innocence, that as a veil
Had shadow'd them from knowing ill, was gone,
Just confidence, and native righteousness,
And honor from about them, naked left
To guilty shame: hee cover'd, but his Robe
Uncover'd more. So rose the *Danite* strong
Herculean Samson from the Harlot-lap
Of *Philistean Dalilah*, and wak'd
Shorn of his strength, They destitute and bare
Of all thir virtue:[9] silent, and in face
Confounded long they sat, as struck'n mute,
Till *Adam*, though not less than *Eve* abasht,
At length gave utterance to these words constrain'd.
  O *Eve*, in evil hour thou didst give ear
To that false Worm, of whomsoever taught
To counterfeit Man's voice, true in our Fall,
False in our promis'd Rising; since our Eyes
Op'n'd we find indeed, and find we know
Both Good and Evil, Good lost, and Evil got,
Bad Fruit of Knowledge, if this be to know,
Which leaves us naked thus, of Honor void,
Of Innocence, of Faith, of Purity,
Our wonted Ornaments now soil'd and stain'd,
And in our Faces evident the signs
Of foul concupiscence; whence evil store;
Even shame, the last of evils; of the first
Be sure then. How shall I behold the face
Henceforth of God or Angel, erst with joy
And rapture so oft beheld? those heav'nly shapes
Will dazzle now this earthly, with thir blaze
Insufferably bright. O might I here
In solitude live savage, in some glade
Obscur'd, where highest Woods impenetrable
To Star or Sun-light, spread thir umbrage broad,
And brown as Evening: Cover me ye Pines,
Ye Cedars, with innumerable boughs
Hide me, where I may never see them more.
But let us now, as in bad plight, devise
What best may for the present serve to hide

7. Unnatural vapors or exhalations rising from the stomach to the brain.

8. See Genesis 3.7: "The eyes of them both were opened, and they knew that they were naked."

9. See Judges 16 for the story of Samson's betrayal by Delilah.

The Parts of each from other, that seem most
To shame obnoxious,° and unseemliest seen, *exposed*
Some Tree whose broad smooth Leaves together sew'd,
And girded on our loins, may cover round
Those middle parts, that this new comer, Shame,
There sit not, and reproach us as unclean.[1]
 So counsell'd hee, and both together went
Into the thickest Wood, there soon they chose
The Figtree,[2] not that kind for Fruit renown'd,
But such as at this day to *Indians* known
In *Malabar* or *Decan* spreads her Arms
Branching so broad and long, that in the ground
The bended Twigs take root, and Daughters grow
About the Mother Tree, a Pillar'd shade
High overarch't, and echoing Walks between;
There oft the *Indian* Herdsman shunning heat
Shelters in cool, and tends his pasturing Herds
At Loopholes cut through thickest shade: Those Leaves
They gather'd, broad as Amazonian Targe,° *shield*
And with what skill they had, together sew'd,
To gird thir waist, vain Covering if to hide
Thir guilt and dreaded shame; O how unlike
To that first naked Glory. Such of late
Columbus found th' *American* so girt
With feather'd Cincture,° naked else and wild *belt*
Among the Trees on Isles and woody Shores.
Thus fenc't, and as they thought, thir shame in part
Cover'd, but not at rest or ease of Mind,
They sat them down to weep, nor only Tears
Rain'd at thir Eyes, but high Winds worse within
Began to rise, high Passions, Anger, Hate,
Mistrust, Suspicion, Discord, and shook sore
Thir inward State of Mind, calm Region once
And full of Peace, now toss't and turbulent:
For Understanding rul'd not, and the Will
Heard not her lore, both in subjection now
To sensual Appetite, who from beneath
Usurping over sovran Reason claim'd
Superior sway: From thus distemper'd breast,
Adam, estrang'd in look and alter'd style,
Speech intermitted thus to *Eve* renew'd.
 Would thou hadst heark'n'd to my words, and stay'd
With me, as I besought thee, when that strange
Desire of wand'ring this unhappy Morn,
I know not whence possess'd thee; we had then
Remain'd still happy, not as now, despoil'd
Of all our good, sham'd, naked, miserable.
Let none henceforth seek needless cause to approve° *give proof of*
The Faith they owe;[3] when earnestly they seek
Such proof, conclude, they then begin to fail.

1. See Genesis 3.7.
2. Milton's description of the banyan or Indian fig comes from Gerard's *Herball* (1597).
3. Be under obligation to render or possess.

To whom soon mov'd with touch of blame thus *Eve*.
What words have past thy Lips,[4] *Adam* severe,
Imput'st thou that to my default, or will
Of wand'ring, as thou call'st it, which who knows
But might as ill have happ'n'd thou being by,
Or to thyself perhaps: hadst thou been there,
Or here th' attempt, thou couldst not have discern'd
Fraud in the Serpent, speaking as he spake;
No ground of enmity between us known,
Why hee should mean me ill, or seek to harm.
Was I to have never parted from thy side?
As good have grown there still a lifeless Rib.
Being as I am, why didst not thou the Head[5]
Command me absolutely not to go,
Going into such danger as thou said'st?
Too facile° then thou didst not much gainsay, *permissive*
Nay, didst permit, approve, and fair dismiss.
Hadst thou been firm and fixt in thy dissent,
Neither had I transgress'd, nor thou with mee.
To whom then first incenst Adam repli'd.
Is this the Love, is this the recompense
Of mine to thee, ingrateful *Eve*, express't
Immutable° when thou wert lost, not I, *unchangeable*
Who might have liv'd and joy'd immortal bliss,
Yet willingly chose rather Death with thee:
And am I now upbraided, as the cause
Of thy transgressing? not enough severe,
It seems, in thy restraint: what could I more?
I warn'd thee, I admonish'd thee, foretold
The danger, and the lurking Enemy
That lay in wait; beyond this had been force,
And force upon free Will hath here no place.
But confidence then bore thee on, secure
Either to meet no danger, or to find
Matter of glorious trial; and perhaps
I also err'd in overmuch admiring
What seem'd in thee so perfet, that I thought
No evil durst attempt thee, but I rue
That error now, which is become my crime,
And thou th' accuser. Thus it shall befall
Him who to worth in Woman overtrusting
Lets her Will rule; restraint she will not brook,
And left to herself, if evil thence ensue,
Shee first his weak indulgence will accuse.
Thus they in mutual accusation spent
The fruitless hours, but neither self-condemning,
And of thir vain contést appear'd no end.

The End of the Ninth Book.

4. Echoes Odysseus's disapproval of a speech of Agamemnon's (*Iliad* 14.83).
5. Alludes to 1 Corinthians 11.3: "The head of every man is Christ; and the head of the woman is the man; and the head of Christ is God."

Book 10

The Argument

Man's *transgression known, the Guardian Angels forsake Paradise, and return up to Heaven to approve thir vigilance, and are approv'd,* God *declaring that the entrance of* Satan *could not be by them prevented. He sends his Son to judge the Transgressors, who descends and gives Sentence accordingly; then in pity clothes them both, and reascends.* Sin *and* Death *sitting till then at the Gates of Hell, by wondrous sympathy feeling the success of* Satan *in this new World, and the sin by Man there committed, resolve to sit no longer confin'd in Hell, but to follow* Satan *thir Sire up to the place of Man: To make the way easier from Hell to this World to and fro, they pave a broad Highway or Bridge over Chaos, according to the Track that* Satan *first made; then preparing for Earth, they meet him proud of his success returning to Hell; thir mutual gratulation.* Satan *arrives at* Pandemonium, *in full assembly relates with boasting his success against Man; instead of applause is entertained with a general hiss by all his audience, transform'd with himself also suddenly into Serpents, according to his doom giv'n in Paradise; then deluded with a show of the forbidden Tree springing up before them, they greedily reaching to take of the Fruit, chew dust and bitter ashes. The proceedings of* Sin *and* Death; God *foretells the final Victory of his Son over them, and the renewing of all things; but for the present commands his Angels to make several alterations in the Heavens and Elements.* Adam *more and more perceiving his fall'n condition heavily bewails, rejects the condolement of* Eve; *she persists and at length appeases him: then to evade the Curse likely to fall on thir Offspring, proposes to* Adam *violent ways, which he approves not, but conceiving better hope, puts her in mind of the late Promise made them, that her Seed should be reveng'd on the Serpent, and exhorts her with him to seek Peace of the offended Deity, by repentance and supplication.*

Meanwhile the heinous and despiteful act
Of *Satan* done in Paradise, and how
Hee in the Serpent had perverted *Eve*,
Her Husband shee, to taste the fatal fruit,
Was known in Heav'n;[1] for what can scape the Eye
Of God All-seeing, or deceive his Heart
Omniscient, who in all things wise and just,
Hinder'd not *Satan* to attempt the mind
Of Man, with strength entire, and free will arm'd,
Complete to have discover'd and repulst
Whatever wiles of Foe or seeming Friend.
For still they knew, and ought to have still remember'd
The high Injunction not to taste that Fruit,
Whoever tempted; which they not obeying,
Incurr'd, what could they less, the penalty,
And manifold[2] in sin, deserv'd to fall.
Up into Heav'n from Paradise in haste
Th' Angelic Guards ascended, mute and sad

1. Rhetorically, lines 1–16 function both as *principium*, stating the subject of the book, and as *initium*, introducing the first scene. They also sum up the theological content of Book 3, which will receive specific application in the present book, in the exchanges between the Father and the Son (lines 34–84) and between the Son and Adam (lines 124ff.). Note the structural symmetry whereby the divine decrees of the third book are balanced by those of the third last.

2. Multiplied; alluding to Psalms 38.19: "they that hate me wrongfully are multiplied."

For Man, for of his state by this they knew,
Much wond'ring how the subtle Fiend had stol'n
Entrance unseen. Soon as th' unwelcome news
From Earth arriv'd at Heaven Gate, displeas'd
All were who heard, dim sadness did not spare
That time Celestial visages, yet mixt
With pity, violated not thir bliss.
About the new-arriv'd, in multitudes
Th' ethereal People ran, to hear and know
How all befell: they towards the Throne Supreme
Accountable made haste to make appear
With righteous plea, thir utmost vigilance,
And easily approv'd; when the most High
Eternal Father from his secret Cloud,
Amidst in Thunder utter'd thus his voice.
  Assembl'd Angels, and ye Powers return'd
From unsuccessful charge, be not dismay'd,
Nor troubl'd at these tidings from the Earth,
Which your sincerest care could not prevent,
Foretold so lately what would come to pass,
When first this Tempter cross'd the Gulf from Hell.
I told ye then he should prevail and speed° *succeed*
On his bad Errand, Man should be seduc't
And flatter'd out of all, believing lies
Against his Maker; no Decree of mine
Concurring to necessitate his Fall,
Or touch with lightest moment of impulse
His free Will, to her own inclining left
In even scale.[3] But fall'n he is, and now
What rests, but that the mortal Sentence pass
On his transgression. Death denounc't that day,
Which he presumes already vain and void,
Because not yet inflicted, as he fear'd,
By some immediate stroke; but soon shall find
Forbearance no acquittance ere day end.
Justice shall not return as bounty scorn'd.
But whom send I to judge them? whom but thee
Vicegerent Son, to thee I have transferr'd
All Judgment, whether in Heav'n, or Earth, or Hell.
Easy it may be seen that I intend
Mercy colleague with Justice, sending thee
Man's Friend, his Mediator, his design'd
Both Ransom and Redeemer voluntary,
And destin'd Man himself to judge Man fall'n.[4]
  So spake the Father, and unfolding bright
Toward the right hand his Glory, on the Son

3. "Moment" is a term applied to the smallest increment that could affect the equilibrium of a balance. If man had been protected from the tempter, then there would have been real interference with the free action of the scales of justice.

4. The double syntax—line 62 can be read as either "himself a man, destined to judge man" (primary) or "destined to judge man himself, man fallen"—mimes the close identification of Christ with humanity.

Blaz'd forth unclouded Deity; he full
Resplendent all his Father manifest
Express'd, and thus divinely answer'd mild.
   Father Eternal, thine is to decree,
Mine both in Heav'n and Earth to do thy will
Supreme, that thou in mee thy Son belov'd
May'st ever rest well pleas'd.[5] I go to judge
On Earth these thy transgressors, but thou know'st,
Whoever judg'd, the worst on mee must light,
When time shall be, for so I undertook
Before thee; and not repenting, this obtain
Of right, that I may mitigate thir doom
On me deriv'd, yet I shall temper so
Justice with Mercy, as may illustrate most
Them fully satisfied, and thee appease.
Attendance none shall need, nor Train, where none
Are to behold the Judgment, but the judg'd,
Those two; the third[6] best absent is condemn'd,
Convict° by flight, and Rebel to all Law: *convicted*
Conviction to the Serpent none belongs.[7]
   Thus saying, from his radiant Seat he rose
Of high collateral° glory: him Thrones and Powers, *side by side*
Princedoms, and Dominations ministrant
Accompanied to Heaven Gate, from whence
Eden and all the Coast in prospect lay.
Down he descended straight; the speed of Gods
Time counts not, though with swiftest minutes wing'd.
Now was the Sun in Western cadence° low[8] *falling*
From Noon, and gentle Airs due at thir hour
To fan the Earth now wak'd, and usher in
The Ev'ning cool, when he from wrath more cool
Came the mild Judge and Intercessor both
To sentence Man: the voice of God they heard
Now walking in the Garden, by soft winds
Brought to thir Ears, while day declin'd, they heard,
And from his presence hid themselves among
The thickest Trees, both Man and Wife, till God
Approaching, thus to Adam call'd aloud.
   Where art thou *Adam*, wont with joy to meet
My coming seen far off? I miss thee here,
Not pleas'd, thus entertain'd with solitude,
Where obvious duty erewhile appear'd unsought:
Or come I less conspicuous, or what change
Absents thee, or what chance detains? Come forth.
He came, and with him *Eve*, more loath, though first
To offend, discount'nanc't both, and discompos'd;
Love was not in thir looks, either to God

5. Echoing Matthew 3.17.
6. Satan.
7. "Conviction" has both the legal sense (proof of guilt) and the theological (the condition of being convinced of sin).
8. Lines 92–123 follow Genesis 3.8–11.

Or to each other, but apparent guilt,
And shame, and perturbation, and despair,
Anger, and obstinacy, and hate, and guile.
Whence *Adam* falt'ring long, thus answer'd brief.
I heard thee in the Garden, and of thy voice
Afraid, being naked, hid myself. To whom
The gracious Judge without revile repli'd.
My voice thou oft hast heard, and hast not fear'd,
But still rejoic't, how is it now become
So dreadful to thee? that thou art naked, who
Hath told thee? hast thou eaten of the Tree
Whereof I gave thee charge thou shouldst not eat?
To whom thus *Adam* sore beset repli'd.
O Heav'n! in evil strait this day I stand
Before my Judge, either to undergo
Myself the total Crime, or to accuse
My other self, the partner of my life;
Whose failing, while her Faith to me remains,
I should conceal, and not expose to blame
By my complaint; but strict necessity
Subdues me, and calamitous constraint,
Lest on my head both sin and punishment,
However insupportable, be all
Devolv'd;[9] though should I hold my peace, yet thou
Wouldst easily detect what I conceal.
This Woman whom thou mad'st to be my help,
And gav'st me as thy perfet gift, so good,
So fit, so acceptable, so Divine,
That from her hand I could suspect no ill,
And what she did, whatever in itself,
Her doing seem'd to justify the deed;
Shee gave me of the Tree, and I did eat.[1]
To whom the sovran Presence thus repli'd.
Was shee thy God, that her thou didst obey
Before his voice, or was shee made thy guide,
Superior, or but equal, that to her
Thou didst resign thy Manhood, and the Place
Wherein God set thee above her made of thee,
And for thee, whose perfection far excell'd
Hers in all real° dignity:[2] Adorn'd *regal*
She was indeed, and lovely to attract
Thy Love, not thy Subjection, and her Gifts
Were such as under Government well seem'd,
Unseemly to bear rule, which was thy part° *role*
And person,° hadst thou known thyself aright. *character*
So having said, he thus to Eve in few:
Say Woman, what is this which thou hast done?

9. Caused to fall upon.
1. See Genesis 3.12.
2. See 1 Corinthians 11.8ff.: "For the man is not of the woman; but the woman of the man. Neither was the man created for the woman; but the woman for the man."

To whom sad *Eve* with shame nigh overwhelm'd,
Confessing soon, yet not before her Judge
Bold or loquacious, thus abasht repli'd.
The Serpent me beguil'd and I did eat.[3]
Which when the Lord God heard, without delay
To Judgment he proceeded on th' accus'd
Serpent though brute, unable to transfer
The Guilt on him who made him instrument
Of mischief, and polluted from the end
Of his Creation; justly then accurst,
As vitiated in Nature: more to know
Concern'd not Man (since he no further knew)
Nor alter'd his offense; yet God at last
To Satan first in sin his doom appli'd,
Though in mysterious° terms, judg'd as then best: *mystical*
And on the Serpent thus his curse let fall.
Because thou hast done this, thou art accurst
Above all Cattle, each Beast of the Field;
Upon thy Belly groveling thou shalt go,
And dust shalt eat all the days of thy Life.
Between Thee and the Woman I will put
Enmity, and between thine and her Seed;
Her Seed shall bruise thy head, thou bruise his heel.[4]
So spake this Oracle, then verifi'd
When *Jesus* son of *Mary* second *Eve*,
Saw Satan fall like Lightning down from Heav'n,[5]
Prince of the Air; then rising from his Grave
Spoil'd Principalities and Powers, triumpht
In open show, and with ascension bright
Captivity led captive through the Air,[6]
The Realm itself of Satan long usurpt,
Whom he shall tread at last under our feet;[7]
Ev'n hee who now foretold his fatal bruise,
And to the Woman thus his Sentence turn'd.
Thy sorrow I will greatly multiply
By thy Conception; Children thou shalt bring
In sorrow forth, and to thy Husband's will
Thine shall submit, hee over thee shall rule.
On *Adam* last thus judgment he pronounc'd.
Because thou hast heark'n'd to the voice of thy Wife,
And eaten of the Tree concerning which
I charg'd thee, saying: Thou shalt not eat thereof,
Curs'd is the ground for thy sake, thou in sorrow
Shalt eat thereof all the days of thy Life;[8]
Thorns also and Thistles it shall bring thee forth
Unbid, and thou shalt eat th' Herb of the Field,

3. Repeating Genesis 3.13.
4. See Genesis 3.14ff.
5. "I beheld Satan as lightning fall from heaven" (Luke 10.18).
6. Psalms 68.18: "Thou hast ascended on high, thou hast led captivity captive": applied to Christ in Ephesians 4.8.
7. See Romans 16.20: "And the God of peace shall bruise Satan under your feet shortly."
8. See Genesis 3.17.

In the sweat of thy Face shalt thou eat Bread,
Till thou return unto the ground, for thou
Out of the ground wast taken, know thy Birth,
For dust thou art, and shalt to dust return.[9]
So judg'd he Man, both Judge and Savior sent,
And th' instant stroke of Death denounc't that day
Remov'd far off;[1] then pitying how they stood
Before him naked to the air, that now
Must suffer change, disdain'd not to begin
Thenceforth the form of servant to assume,[2]
As when he wash'd his servants' feet, so now
As Father of his Family he clad
Thir nakedness with Skins of Beasts, or slain,
Or as the Snake with youthful Coat repaid;
And thought not much to clothe his Enemies:
Nor hee thir outward only with the Skins
Of Beasts, but inward nakedness, much more
Opprobrious, with his Robe of righteousness,
Arraying cover'd from his Father's sight.
To him with swift ascent he up return'd,
Into his blissful bosom reassum'd
In glory as of old, to him appeas'd
All, though all-knowing, what had past with Man
Recounted, mixing intercession sweet.[3]

* * *

Th' other way *Satan* went down
The Causey° to Hell Gate; on either side — causeway
Disparted *Chaos* over-built exclaim'd,
And with rebounding surge the bars assail'd,
That scorn'd his indignation: through the Gate,
Wide open and unguarded, *Satan* pass'd,
And all about found desolate; for those
Appointed to sit there,[4] had left thir charge,
Flown to the upper World; the rest were all
Far to th'inland retir'd, about the walls
Of *Pandaemonium*, City and proud seat
Of *Lucifer*, so by allusion call'd,
Of that bright Star to *Satan* paragon'd.° — compared
There kept thir Watch the Legions, while the Grand
In Council sat, solicitous° what chance — anxious
Might intercept thir Emperor sent, so hee
Departing gave command, and they observ'd.
As when the Tartar from his *Russian* Foe
By *Astracan*[5] over the Snowy Plains
Retires, or *Bactrian* Sophi[6] from the horns

9. See Genesis 3.18–9.
1. Christ removes the fear that physical death will follow the eating of the fruit on the same day.
2. See Phillipians. 2.7: "made himself of no reputation, and took upon him the form of a servant, and was made in the likeness of men."
3. Sin and Death now pave a highway across Chaos from Hell to earth. Satan meets them and sends them on to dwell on earth; he heads home to Hell.
4. Sin and Death.
5. Astracan, or Astrakhan, was a Tartar kingdom and capital city near the outh of the Volga.
6. Persian king.

Of *Turkish* Crescent,[7] leaves all waste beyond
The Realm of *Aladule,*[8] in his retreat
To *Tauris* or *Casbeen:*[9] So these the late
Heav'n-banisht Host, left desert utmost Hell
Many a dark League, reduc't in careful Watch
Round thir Metropolis, and now expecting
Each hour their great adventurer from the search
Of Foreign Worlds: he through the midst unmark't,
In show Plebeian Angel militant
Of lowest order, pass't; and from the door
Of that *Plutonian*[1] Hall, invisible
Ascended his high Throne, which under state° *canopy*
Of richest texture spread, at th' upper end
Was plac't in regal lustre. Down a while
He sat, and round about him saw unseen:
At last as from a Cloud his fulgent head
And shape Star-bright appear'd, or brighter, clad
With what permissive glory since his fall
Was left him, or false glitter: All amaz'd
At that so sudden blaze the Stygian throng
Bent thir aspect, and whom they wish'd beheld,
Thir mighty Chief return'd: loud was th' acclaim:
Forth rush'd in haste the great consulting Peers,
Rais'd from thir dark *Divan,*[2] and with like joy
Congratulant approach'd him, who with hand
Silence, and with these words attention won.
  Thrones, Dominations, Princedoms, Virtues, Powers,
For in possession such, not only of right,
I call ye and declare ye now, return'd
Successful beyond hope, to lead ye forth
Triumphant out of this infernal Pit
Abominable, accurst, the house of woe,
And Dungeon of our Tyrant: Now possess,
As Lords, a spacious World, to our native Heaven
Little inferior, by my adventure hard
With peril great achiev'd. Long were to tell
What I have done, what suffer'd, with what pain
Voyag'd th' unreal, vast, unbounded deep
Of horrible confusion, over which
By Sin and Death a broad way now is pav'd
To expedite your glorious march; but I
Toil'd out my úncouth° passage, forc't to ride *strange*
Th' untractable Abyss, plung'd in the womb
Of unoriginal° *Night* and *Chaos* wild, *uncreated*
That jealous of thir secrets fiercely oppos'd
My journey strange, with clamorous uproar

7. Refers not only to the Turkish ensign, but also to their battle formations.
8. Greater Armenia.
9. Tauris (modern Tabriz) is in the extreme northwest of Persia; Casbeen, or Kazvin, is north of Teheran.
1. Pertaining to Pluto, ruler of the classical underworld.
2. Turkish council of state.

Protesting Fate supreme; thence how I found
The new created World, which fame in Heav'n
Long had foretold, a Fabric wonderful
Of absolute perfection, therein Man
Plac't in a Paradise, by our exile
Made happy: Him by fraud I have seduc'd
From his Creator, and the more to increase
Your wonder, with an Apple; he thereat
Offended, worth your laughter, hath giv'n up
Both his beloved Man and all his World,
To Sin and Death a prey, and so to us,
Without our hazard, labor, or alarm,
To range in, and to dwell, and over Man
To rule, as over all he should have rul'd.
True is, mee also he hath judg'd, or rather
Mee not, but the brute Serpent in whose shape
Man I deceiv'd: that which to mee belongs,
Is enmity, which he will put between
Mee and Mankind; I am to bruise his heel;
His Seed, when is not set, shall bruise my head:
A World who would not purchase with a bruise,
Or much more grievous pain? Ye have th' account
Of my performance: What remains, ye Gods,
But up and enter now into full bliss.
　So having said, a while he stood, expecting
Thir universal shout and high applause
To fill his ear, when contrary he hears
On all sides, from innumerable tongues
A dismal universal hiss, the sound
Of public scorn; he wonder'd, but not long
Had leisure, wond'ring at himself now more;
His Visage drawn he felt to sharp and spare,
His Arms clung to his Ribs, his Legs entwining
Each other, till supplanted° down he fell　　*tripped*
A monstrous Serpent on his Belly prone,[3]
Reluctant,° but in vain: a greater power　　*resisting*
Now rul'd him, punisht in the shape he sinn'd,
According to his doom: he would have spoke,
But hiss for hiss return'd with forked tongue
To forked tongue, for now were all transform'd
Alike, to Serpents all as accessories
To his bold Riot: dreadful was the din
Of hissing through the Hall, thick swarming now
With complicated° monsters, head and tail,　　*compound*
Scorpion and Asp, and *Amphisbaena* dire,
Cerastes horn'd, *Hydrus*, and *Ellops* drear,
And *Dipsas*[4] (not so thick swarm'd once the Soil

3. See the metamorphosis of Cadmus in Ovid, *Metamorphoses* 4.572–603, and the mutual interchange of serpentine forms in Dante's canto of the thieves, *Inferno* 25.

4. The amphisbaena is a serpent with a head at either end. The cerastes has four horns on its head. The hydrus is a water snake. The ellops, though sometimes identified as the swordfish, is mentioned as a serpent in Pliny, *Natural History* 32.5. The dipsas causes raging thirst by its bite.

Bedropt with blood of *Gorgon*, or the Isle
Ophiusa) but still greatest hee the midst,[5]
Now Dragon grown, larger than whom the Sun
Ingender'd in the *Pythian* Vale on slime,
Huge *Python*, and his Power no less he seem'd
Above the rest still to retain;[6] they all
Him follow'd issuing forth to th' open Field,
Where all yet left of that revolted Rout
Heav'n-fall'n, in station stood or just array,
Sublime° with expectation when to see *uplifted*
In Triumph issuing forth thir glorious Chief;
They saw, but other sight instead, a crowd
Of ugly Serpents; horror on them fell,
And horrid sympathy; for what they saw,
They felt themselves now changing; down thir arms,
Down fell both Spear and Shield, down they as fast,
And the dire hiss renew'd, and the dire form
Catcht by Contagion, like in punishment,
As in thir crime. Thus was th' applause they meant,
Turn'd to exploding hiss, triumph to shame
Cast on themselves from thir own mouths. There stood
A Grove hard by, sprung up with this thir change,
His will who reigns above, to aggravate
Thir penance, laden with fair Fruit, like that
Which grew in Paradise, the bait of *Eve*
Us'd by the Tempter: on that prospect strange
Thir earnest eyes they fix'd, imagining
For one forbidden Tree a multitude
Now ris'n, to work them furder° woe or shame; *further*
Yet parcht with scalding thirst and hunger fierce,
Though to delude them sent, could not abstain,
But on they roll'd in heaps, and up the Trees
Climbing, sat thicker than the snaky locks
That curl'd *Megaera:*[7] greedily they pluck'd
The Fruitage fair to sight, like that which grew
Near that bituminous Lake where *Sodom* flam'd;[8]
This more delusive, not the touch, but taste
Deceiv'd; they fondly thinking to allay
Thir appetite with gust,° instead of Fruit *taste*
Chew'd bitter Ashes, which th' offended taste
With spattering noise rejected: oft they assay'd,
Hunger and thirst constraining, drugg'd° as oft, *nauseated*
With hatefullest disrelish writh'd thir jaws
With soot and cinders fill'd; so oft they fell
Into the same illusion, not as Man

5. When Perseus was bringing back the severed head of Medusa, drops of blood fell to earth and became serpents. "Ophiusa" means literally "full of serpents"; a name anciently given to several islands, including Rhodes and one of the Balearic group.

6. For the birth of Python from the slime remaining after the flood, see Ovid, *Metamorphoses* 1.438–440. Python was slain by Apollo. Satan's dragon shape is that of the "old dragon" of Christian apocalypse; see Revelation 12.9: "the great dragon was cast out, that old serpent, called the Devil, and Satan."

7. One of the Furies, often described as snaky-haired.

8. The allusion is to Josephus, *Wars* 4.8.4, where it is said that traces still remain of the divine fire that burnt Sodom, such as tasty-looking fruits that turned to ashes when plucked.

Whom they triumph'd, once lapst. Thus were they plagu'd
And worn with Famine long, and ceaseless hiss,
Till thir lost shape, permitted, they resum'd,
Yearly enjoin'd, some say, to undergo
This annual humbling certain number'd days,
To dash thir pride, and joy for Man seduc't.
However some tradition they dispers'd
Among the Heathen of thir purchase got,
And Fabl'd how the Serpent, whom they call'd
Ophion with *Eurynome*, the wide-
Encroaching *Eve* perhaps, had first the rule
Of high *Olympus*, thence by Saturn driv'n
And Ops, ere yet *Dictaean Jove* was born.[9]
Meanwhile in Paradise the hellish pair
Too soon arriv'd, *Sin* there in power before,
Once actual, now in body, and to dwell
Habitual habitant; behind her *Death*
Close following pace for pace, not mounted yet
On his pale Horse:[1] to whom *Sin* thus began.
  Second of *Satan* sprung, all conquering *Death*,
What think'st thou of our Empire now, though earn'd
With travail difficult, not better far
Than still at Hell's dark threshold to have sat watch,
Unnam'd, undreaded, and thyself half starv'd?
  Whom thus the Sin-born Monster answer'd soon.
To mee, who with eternal Famine pine,
Alike is Hell, or Paradise, or Heaven,
There best, where most with ravin I may meet;
Which here, though plenteous, all too little seems
To stuff this Maw, this vast unhide-bound Corpse.
  To whom th' incestuous Mother thus repli'd.
Thou therefore on these Herbs, and Fruits, and Flow'rs
Feed first, on each Beast next, and Fish, and Fowl,
No homely morsels, and whatever thing
The Scythe of Time mows down, devour unspar'd,
Till I in Man residing through the Race,
His thoughts, his looks, words, actions all infect,
And season him thy last and sweetest prey.
  This said, they both betook them several ways,
Both to destroy, or unimmortal make
All kinds, and for destruction to mature
Sooner or later; which th' Almighty seeing
From his transcendent Seat the Saints among,
To those bright Orders utter'd thus his voice.
  See with what heat these Dogs of Hell advance
To waste and havoc° yonder World, which I — *devastate*
So fair and good created, and had still
Kept in that state, had not the folly of Man

9. Ophion and Eurynome ruled Olympus until the one yielded to Cronos (Saturn) and the other to Rhea (Ops). Their two successors then ruled the Titans, while Zeus lived in the Dictaean cave. See Apollonius Rhodius, *Argonautica* 1.503–9.

1. See Revelation 6.8: "I looked, and behold a pale horse: and his name that sat on him was Death, and Hell followed with him."

Let in these wasteful Furies, who impute
Folly to mee, so doth the Prince of Hell
And his Adherents, that with so much ease
I suffer them to enter and possess
A place so heav'nly, and conniving seem
To gratify my scornful Enemies,
That laugh, as if transported with some fit
Of Passion, I to them had quitted° all, *yielded*
At random yielded up to their misrule;
And know not that I call'd and drew them thither
My Hell-hounds, to lick up the draff° and filth *refuse*
Which man's polluting Sin with taint hath shed
On what was pure, till cramm'd and gorg'd, nigh burst
With suckt and glutted offal, at one sling
Of thy victorious Arm, well-pleasing Son,
Both *Sin*, and *Death*, and yawning *Grave* at last
Through *Chaos* hurl'd, obstruct the mouth of Hell
For ever, and seal up his ravenous Jaws.
Then Heav'n and Earth renew'd shall be made pure
To sanctity that shall receive no stain:
Till then the Curse pronounc't on both precedes.[2]

* * *

Thus began
Outrage from lifeless things; but Discord first
Daughter of Sin, among th' irrational,
Death introduc'd through fierce antipathy:
Beast now with Beast gan war, and Fowl with Fowl,
And Fish with Fish; to graze the Herb all leaving,
Devour'd each other; nor stood much in awe
Of Man, but fled him, or with count'nance grim
Glar'd on him passing: these were from without
The growing miseries, which *Adam* saw
Already in part, though hid in gloomiest shade,
To sorrow abandon'd, but worse felt within,
And in a troubl'd Sea of passion tost,
Thus to disburd'n sought with sad complaint.
O miserable of happy! is this the end
Of this new glorious World, and mee so late
The Glory of that Glory, who now become
Accurst of blessed, hide me from the face
Of God, whom to behold was then my highth
Of happiness: yet well, if here would end
The misery, I deserv'd it, and would
My own deservings; but this will not serve;
All that I eat or drink, or shall beget,
Is propagated curse.[3] O voice once heard
Delightfully, *Increase and multiply*,[4]

2. See Genesis 3.17: "Cursed is the ground for thy sake." God next commands the angels to make the earth turn on its axis and so cause the change of seasons, and to disrupt the order of the planets, making their effect on the world negative as well as positive.

3. Handed down from one generation to another. Food prolongs life and thus extends the curse, while begetting children hands it on. Note also that eating and sex are jointly the concerns of the concupiscible faculty, which was often regarded as the special field of operation of concupiscence or the "body of sin."

4. See Genesis 1.28.

Now death to hear! for what can I increase
Or multiply, but curses on my head?
Who of all Ages to succeed, but feeling
The evil on him brought by me, will curse
My Head; Ill fare our Ancestor impure,
For this we may thank *Adam;* but his thanks
Shall be the execration; so besides
Mine own that bide upon me, all from mee
Shall with a fierce reflux on mee redound,° *overflow, come back*
On mee as on thir natural centre light
Heavy, though in thir place. O fleeting joys
Of Paradise, dear bought with lasting woes!
Did I request thee, Maker, from my Clay
To mould me Man, did I solicit thee
From darkness to promote me, or here place
In this delicious Garden? as my Will
Concurr'd not to my being, it were but right
And equal° to reduce me to my dust, *just*
Desirous to resign, and render back
All I receiv'd, unable to perform
Thy terms too hard, by which I was to hold
The good I sought not. To the loss of that,
Sufficient penalty, why hast thou added
The sense of endless woes? inexplicable
Thy Justice seems; yet to say truth, too late
I thus contest; then should have been refus'd
Those terms whatever, when they were propos'd:
Thou didst accept them; wilt thou enjoy the good,
Then cavil the conditions? and though God
Made thee without thy leave, what if thy Son
Prove disobedient, and reprov'd, retort,
Wherefore didst thou beget me? I sought it not:
Wouldst thou admit for his contempt of thee
That proud excuse? yet him not thy election,° *choice*
But Natural necessity begot.
God made thee of choice his own, and of his own
To serve him, thy reward was of his grace,
Thy punishment then justly is at his Will.
Be it so, for I submit, his doom° is fair, *judgment*
That dust I am, and shall to dust return:[5]
O welcome hour whenever! why delays
His hand to execute what his Decree
Fix'd on this day? why do I overlive,
Why am I mockt with death, and length'n'd out
To deathless pain? How gladly would I meet
Mortality my sentence, and be Earth
Insensible, how glad would lay me down
As in my Mother's lap![6] There I should rest
And sleep secure; his dreadful voice no more
Would Thunder in my ears, no fear of worse

5. Alluding to Genesis 3.19.

6. Adam's lament echoes Job 3.

To mee and to my offspring would torment me
With cruel expectation. Yet one doubt
Pursues me still, lest all I cannot die,
Lest that pure breath of Life, the Spirit of Man
Which God inspir'd, cannot together perish
With this corporeal Clod; then in the Grave,
Or in some other dismal place, who knows
But I shall die a living Death? O thought
Horrid, if true! yet why? it was but breath
Of Life that sinn'd; what dies but what had life
And sin? the Body properly hath neither.
All of me then shall die:[7] let this appease
The doubt, since human reach no further knows.
For though the Lord of all be infinite,
Is his wrath also? be it, Man is not so,
But mortal doom'd. How can he exercise
Wrath without end on Man whom Death must end?
Can he make deathless Death? that were to make
Strange contradiction, which to God himself
Impossible is held, as Argument
Of weakness, not of Power. Will he draw out,
For anger's sake, finite to infinite
In punisht Man, to satisfy his rigor
Satisfi'd never; that were to extend
His Sentence beyond dust and Nature's Law,
By which all Causes else according still
To the reception of thir matter act,
Not to th' extent of thir own Sphere.[8] But say
That Death be not one stroke, as I suppos'd,
Bereaving sense, but endless misery
From this day onward, which I feel begun
Both in me, and without me, and so last
To perpetuity; Ay me, that fear
Comes thund'ring back with dreadful revolution
On my defenseless head; both Death and I
Am found Eternal, and incorporate° both, *united, embodied*
Nor I on my part single, in mee all
Posterity stands curst:[9] Fair Patrimony
That I must leave ye, Sons; O were I able
To waste it all myself, and leave ye none!
So disinherited how would ye bless
Me now your Curse! Ah, why should all mankind
For one man's fault thus guiltless be condemn'd,
If guiltless? But from me what can proceed,
But all corrupt, both Mind and Will deprav'd,

7. Adam's question is like Milton's in *De doctrina* 1.13: "What could be more absurd than that the mind, which is the part principally offending, should escape the threatened death; and that the body alone, to which immortality was equally allotted, before death came into the world by sin, should pay the penalty of sin by undergoing death, though not implicated in the transgression?" Milton's belief in the joint extinction and joint resurrection of man's body and mind was not an eccentric heresy but good biblical theology.

8. Adam tries to comfort himself with an argument drawn from medieval philosophy. Here Adam means that God would be going beyond a natural law, that any agent acts according to the powers of what receives its action, not according to its own powers.

9. Not only are Death and I double, two in one, but so also am I, since I am both myself and my descendants.

Not to do only, but to will the same
With me? how can they then acquitted stand
In sight of God? Him after all Disputes
Forc't I absolve: all my evasions vain
And reasonings, though through Mazes, lead me still
But to my own conviction:[1] first and last
On mee, mee only, as the source and spring
Of all corruption, all the blame lights due;
So might the wrath. Fond wish! couldst thou support
That burden heavier than the Earth to bear,
Than all the World much heavier, though divided
With that bad Woman? Thus what thou desir'st,
And what thou fear'st, alike destroys all hope
Of refuge, and concludes thee miserable
Beyond all past example and futúre,
To *Satan* only like both crime and doom.
O Conscience, into what Abyss of fears
And horrors hast thou driv'n me; out of which
I find no way, from deep to deeper plung'd!
Thus *Adam* to himself lamented loud
Through the still Night, not now, as ere man fell,
Wholesome and cool and mild, but with black Air
Accompanied, with damps and dreadful gloom,
Which to his evil Conscience represented
All things with double terror: On the ground
Outstretcht he lay, on the cold ground, and oft
Curs'd his Creation, Death as oft accus'd
Of tardy execution, since denounc't
The day of his offense. Why comes not Death,
Said he, with one thrice àcceptable stroke
To end me? Shall Truth fail to keep her word,
Justice Divine not hast'n to be just?
But Death comes not at call, Justice Divine
Mends not her slowest pace for prayers or cries.
O Woods, O Fountains, Hillocks, Dales and Bow'rs,
With other echo late I taught your Shades
To answer, and resound far other Song.
Whom thus afflicted when sad Eve beheld,
Desolate where she sat, approaching nigh,
Soft words to his fierce passion she assay'd:
But her with stern regard he thus repell'd.
Out of my sight, thou Serpent, that name best
Befits thee with him leagu'd, thyself as false
And hateful; nothing wants, but that thy shape,
Like his, and color Serpentine may show
Thy inward fraud, to warn all Creatures from thee
Henceforth; lest that too heav'nly form, pretended[2]
To hellish falsehood, snare them. But for thee
I had persisted happy, had not thy pride

1. Adam at last reaches full conviction of his sin; but being unable yet to pass to contrition, the next stage of repentance, he falls instead into despair. The present passage should be compared with Satan's similar fall into conscience-stricken despair at 4.86–113.
2. Stretched in front as a covering serving as a mask.

And wand'ring vanity, when least was safe,
Rejected my forewarning, and disdain'd
Not to be trusted, longing to be seen
Though by the Devil himself, him overweening
To over-reach, but with the Serpent meeting
Fool'd and beguil'd, by him thou, I by thee,
To trust thee from my side, imagin'd wise,
Constant, mature, proof against all assaults,
And understood not all was but a show
Rather than solid virtue, all but a Rib
Crooked by nature, bent, as now appears,
More to the part sinister[3] from me drawn,
Well if thrown out, as supernumerary
To my just number found. O why did God,
Creator wise, that peopl'd highest Heav'n
With Spirits Masculine, create at last
This novelty on Earth, this fair defect
Of Nature, and not fill the World at once
With Men as Angels without Feminine,
Or find some other way to generate
Mankind?[4] this mischief had not then befall'n,
And more that shall befall, innumerable
Disturbances on Earth through Female snares,
And strait conjunction with this Sex: for either
He never shall find out fit Mate, but such
As some misfortune brings him, or mistake,
Or whom he wishes most shall seldom gain
Through her perverseness, but shall see her gain'd
By a far worse, or if she love, withheld
By Parents, or his happiest choice too late
Shall meet, already linkt and Wedlock-bound
To a fell° Adversary, his hate or shame: *bitter*
Which infinite calamity shall cause
To Human life, and household peace confound.
He added not, and from her turn'd, but *Eve*
Not so repulst, with Tears that ceas'd not flowing,
And tresses all disorder'd, at his feet
Fell humble, and imbracing them, besought
His peace, and thus proceeded in her plaint.
Forsake me not thus, *Adam*, witness Heav'n
What love sincere, and reverence in my heart
I bear thee, and unweeting° have offended, *unintentionally*
Unhappily deceiv'd; thy suppliant
I beg, and clasp thy knees; bereave me not,
Whereon I live, thy gentle looks, thy aid,
Thy counsel in this uttermost distress,
My only strength and stay: forlorn of thee,
Whither shall I betake me, where subsist?

3. Left; also corrupt, evil, base. The notion that woman is formed from a bent rib, and therefore crooked, had appeared in tracts like Swetnam's *The Arraignment of Lewd, Idle, Froward, and Inconstant Women* (page 1335).

4. Another ancient piece of antifeminism; see Euripides, *Hippolytus* 616ff. Aristotle had said in the *De generatione* that the female is a defective male.

While yet we live, scarce one short hour perhaps,
Between us two let there be peace, both joining,
As join'd in injuries, one enmity
Against a Foe by doom express assign'd us,
That cruel Serpent: On me exercise not
Thy hatred for this misery befall'n,
On me already lost, mee than thyself
More miserable; both have sinn'd, but thou
Against God only, I against God and thee,
And to the place of judgment will return,
There with my cries importune Heaven, that all
The sentence from thy head remov'd may light
On me, sole cause to thee of all this woe,
Mee mee only just object of his ire.
  She ended weeping, and her lowly plight,
Immovable till peace obtain'd from fault
Acknowledg'd and deplor'd,[5] in *Adam* wrought
Commiseration; soon his heart relented
Towards her, his life so late and sole delight,
Now at his feet submissive in distress,
Creature so fair his reconcilement seeking,
His counsel whom she had displeas'd, his aid;
As one disarm'd, his anger all he lost,
And thus with peaceful words uprais'd her soon.
  Unwary, and too desirous, as before,
So now of what thou know'st not, who desir'st
The punishment all on thyself; alas,
Bear thine own first, ill able to sustain
His full wrath whose thou feel'st as yet least part,
And my displeasure bear'st so ill. If Prayers
Could alter high Decrees, I to that place
Would speed before thee, and be louder heard,
That on my head all might be visited,
Thy frailty and infirmer Sex forgiv'n,
To me committed and by me expos'd.
But rise, let us no more contend, nor blame
Each other, blam'd enough elsewhere,[6] but strive
In offices of Love, how we may light'n
Each other's burden in our share of woe;
Since this day's Death denounc't, if aught I see,
Will prove no sudden, but a slow-pac't evil,
A long day's dying to augment our pain,
And to our Seed (O hapless Seed!) deriv'd.
  To whom thus *Eve*, recovering heart, repli'd.
Adam, by sad experiment I know
How little weight my words with thee can find,
Found so erroneous, thence by just event° *consequence*
Found so unfortunate; nevertheless,

5. Eve cannot be moved from Adam's feet until he forgives her.

6. Either "heaven" or the "place of judgment" of line 932.

Restor'd by thee, vile as I am, to place
Of new acceptance, hopeful to regain
Thy Love, the sole contentment of my heart
Living or dying, from thee I will not hide
What thoughts in my unquiet breast are ris'n,
Tending to some relief of our extremes,
Or end, though sharp and sad, yet tolerable,
As in our evils, and of easier choice.
If care of our descent° perplex° us most, *descendants / torment*
Which must be born to certain woe, devour'd
By Death at last, and miserable it is
To be to other cause of misery,
Our own begott'n, and of our Loins to bring
Into this cursed World a woeful Race,
That after wretched Life must be at last
Food for so foul a Monster, in thy power
It lies, yet ere Conception to prevent
The Race unblest, to being yet unbegot.
Childless thou art, Childless remain: So Death
Shall be deceiv'd his glut, and with us two
Be forc'd to satisfy his Rav'nous Maw.
But if thou judge it hard and difficult,
Conversing, looking, loving, to abstain
From Love's due Rites, Nuptial embraces sweet,
And with desire to languish without hope,[7]
Before the present object° languishing *Eve*
With like desire, which would be misery
And torment less than none of what we dread,
Then both ourselves and Seed at once to free
From what we fear for both, let us make short,
Let us seek Death, or he not found, supply
With our own hands his Office on ourselves;
Why stand we longer shivering under fears,
That show no end but Death, and have the power,
Of many ways to die the shortest choosing,
Destruction with destruction to destroy.
  She ended here, or vehement despair
Broke off the rest; so much of Death her thoughts
Had entertain'd, as dy'd her Cheeks with pale.
But *Adam* with such counsel nothing sway'd,
To better hopes his more attentive mind
Laboring had rais'd, and thus to *Eve* replied.
  Eve, thy contempt of life and pleasure seems
To argue in thee something more sublime
And excellent than what thy mind contemns;
But self-destruction therefore sought, refutes
That excellence thought in thee, and implies,
Not thy contempt, but anguish and regret
For loss of life and pleasure overlov'd.

7. See Dante, *Inferno* 4.42, "without hope we live in desire."

Or if thou covet death, as utmost end
Of misery, so thinking to evade
The penalty pronounc't, doubt not but God
Hath wiselier arm'd his vengeful ire than so
To be forestall'd; much more I fear lest Death
So snatcht will not exempt us from the pain
We are by doom to pay; rather such acts
Of contumacy° will provoke the Highest *contempt*
To make death in us live: Then let us seek
Some safer resolution, which methinks
I have in view, calling to mind with heed
Part of our Sentence, that thy Seed shall bruise
The Serpent's head; piteous amends, unless
Be meant, whom I conjecture, our grand Foe
Satan, who in the Serpent hath contriv'd
Against us this deceit: to crush his head
Would be revenge indeed; which will be lost
By death brought on ourselves, or childless days
Resolv'd, as thou proposest; so our Foe
Shall 'scape his punishment ordain'd, and wee
Instead shall double ours upon our heads.
No more be mention'd then of violence
Against ourselves, and wilful barrenness,
That cuts us off from hope, and savors only
Rancor and pride, impatience and despite,
Reluctance° against God and his just yoke *resistance*
Laid on our Necks. Remember with what mild
And gracious temper he both heard and judg'd
Without wrath or reviling; wee expected
Immediate dissolution, which we thought
Was meant by Death that day, when lo, to thee
Pains only in Child-bearing were foretold,
And bringing forth, soon recompens't with joy,
Fruit of thy Womb: On mee the Curse aslope
Glanc'd on the ground, with labor I must earn
My bread;[8] what harm? Idleness had been worse;
My labor will sustain me; and lest Cold
Or Heat should injure us, his timely care
Hath unbesought provided, and his hands
Cloth'd us unworthy, pitying while he judg'd;
How much more, if we pray him, will his ear
Be open, and his heart to pity incline,[9]
And teach us further by what means to shun
Th' inclement Seasons, Rain, Ice, Hail and Snow,
Which now the Sky with various Face begins
To show us in this Mountain, while the Winds
Blow moist and keen, shattering the graceful locks
Of these fair spreading Trees; which bids us seek

8. Referring to Christ's words at lines 201–5.

9. Biblical diction; see Psalms 24.4, 119.36, 112; and 1 Peter 3.12.

Some better shroud,° some better warmth to cherish — *shelter*
Our Limbs benumb'd, ere this diurnal Star[1]
Leave cold the Night, how we his gather'd beams
Reflected, may with matter sere foment,[2]
Or by collision of two bodies grind
The Air attrite° to Fire, as late the Clouds — *ground down*
Justling° or pusht with Winds rude in thir shock — *jostling*
Tine° the slant Lightning, whose thwart flame driv'n down — *ignite*
Kindles the gummy bark of Fir or Pine,
And sends a comfortable heat from far,
Which might supply° the Sun: such Fire to use, — *take the place of*
And what may else be remedy or cure
To evils which our own misdeeds have wrought,
Hee will instruct us praying, and of Grace
Beseeching him, so as we need not fear
To pass commodiously this life, sustain'd
By him with many comforts, till we end
In dust, our final rest and native home.
What better can we do, than to the place
Repairing where he judg'd us, prostrate fall
Before him reverent, and there confess
Humbly our faults, and pardon beg, with tears
Watering the ground, and with our sighs the Air
Frequenting,° sent from hearts contrite, in sign — *filling*
Of sorrow unfeign'd, and humiliation meek.[3]
Undoubtedly he will relent and turn
From his displeasure; in whose look serene,
When angry most he seem'd and most severe,
What else but favor, grace, and mercy shone?
  So spake our Father penitent, nor Eve
Felt less remorse: they forthwith to the place
Repairing where he judg'd them prostrate fell
Before him reverent, and both confess'd
Humbly thir faults, and pardon begg'd, with tears
Watering the ground, and with thir sighs the Air
Frequenting, sent from hearts contrite, in sign
Of sorrow unfeign'd, and humiliation meek.[4]
  The End of the Tenth Book.

Book 11

The Argument

The Son of God present to his Father the Prayers of our first Parents now repenting, and intercedes for them: God accepts them, but declares that they must no longer abide in Paradise; sends Michael *with a Band of Cherubim to dispossess them; but first to reveal to*

1. The sun.
2. Cherish; but alluding also to Latin *fomes* (tinder). Adam envisages making fire: focusing the sun's rays onto dry combustibles ("matter sere") with a parabolic mirror.
3. Having passed on from conviction of sin Adam, now "contrite" (line 1103), is ready for confession, the third stage of repentance. An allusion to the Penitential Psalm: "The sacrifices of God are a broken spirit: a broken and a contrite heart, O God, thou wilt not despise" (Psalms 51.17).
4. Repeating lines 1086–92, modulated into narrative discourse (only the last two verses remain identical).

Adam *future things;* Michael's *coming down.* Adam *shows to* Eve *certain ominous signs; he discerns* Michael's *approach, goes out to meet him: the Angel denounces thir departure.* Eve's *Lamentation.* Adam *pleads, but submits: The Angel leads him up to a high Hill, sets before him in vision what shall happ'n till the Flood.*

Book 12

The Argument

The Angel Michael *continues from the Flood to relate what shall succeed; then, in the mention of* Abraham, *comes by degrees to explain, who that Seed of the Woman shall be, which was promised* Adam *and* Eve *in the Fall; his Incarnation, Death, Resurrection, and Ascension; the state of the Church till his second Coming.* Adam *greatly satisfied and recomforted by these Relations and Promises descends the Hill with* Michael; *wakens* Eve, *who all this while had slept, but with gentle dreams compos'd to quietness of mind and submission.* Michael *in either hand leads them out of Paradise, the fiery Sword waving behind them, and the Cherubim taking thir Stations to guard the Place.*

As one who in his journey bates° at Noon, *pauses*
Though bent on speed, so here the Arch-Angel paus'd
Betwixt the world destroy'd and world restor'd,
If *Adam* aught perhaps might interpose;
Then with transition sweet new Speech resumes.
Thus thou hast seen one World begin and end;
And Man as from a second stock proceed.[1]
Much thou hast yet to see, but I perceive
Thy mortal sight to fail; objects divine
Must needs impair and weary human sense:
Henceforth what is to come I will relate,
Thou therefore give due audience, and attend.
This second source of Men, while yet but few,
And while the dread of judgment past remains
Fresh in thir minds, fearing the Deity,
With some regard to what is just and right
Shall lead thir lives, and multiply apace,
Laboring° the soil, and reaping plenteous crop, *tilling*
Corn, wine and oil; and from the herd or flock,
Oft sacrificing Bullock, Lamb, or Kid,
With large Wine-offerings pour'd, and sacred Feast,
Shall spend thir days in joy unblam'd, and dwell
Long time in peace by Families and Tribes
Under paternal rule; till one shall rise[2]
Of proud ambitious heart, who not content
With fair equality, fraternal state,
Will arrogate Dominion undeserv'd

1. "Stock," an ambiguity, refers not only to the literal replacement of one source of the human line of descent (Adam) by another (Noah), but also to the grafting of mankind onto the stem of Christ, according to the Pauline allegory of regeneration (Romans 11). The covenant with Noah was a type of the New Covenant.

2. Nimrod is not connected with the builders of the Tower in Genesis 10.8. The connection is made, however, in Josephus, *Antiquities* 1.4.2ff., where we also learn that Nimrod "changed the government into tyranny."

Over his brethren, and quite dispossess
Concord and law of Nature from the Earth;[3]
Hunting (and Men not Beasts shall be his game)
With War and hostile snare such as refuse
Subjection to his Empire tyrannous:[4]
A mighty Hunter thence he shall be styl'd
Before the Lord, as in despite of Heav'n,
Or from Heav'n claiming second Sovranty;[5]
And from Rebellion shall derive his name,
Though of Rebellion others he accuse.
Hee with a crew, whom like Ambition joins
With him or under him to tyrannize,
Marching from *Eden* towards the West, shall find
The Plain, wherein a black bituminous gurge° *whirlpool*
Boils out from under ground, the mouth of Hell;
Of Brick, and of that stuff they cast to build
A City and Tow'r, whose top may reach to Heav'n;[6]
And get themselves a name, lest far disperst
In foreign Lands thir memory be lost,
Regardless whether good or evil fame.[7]
But God who oft descends to visit men
Unseen, and through thir habitations walks
To mark thir doings, them beholding soon,
Comes down to see thir City, ere the Tower
Obstruct Heav'n Tow'rs, and in derision sets
Upon thir Tongues a various Spirit to rase
Quite out thir Native Language, and instead
To sow a jangling noise of words unknown:
Forthwith a hideous gabble rises loud
Among the Builders; each to other calls
Not understood, till hoarse, and all in rage,
As mockt they storm;[8] great laughter was in Heav'n
And looking down, to see the hubbub strange
And hear the din; thus was the building left
Ridiculous, and the work Confusion nam'd.[9]
  Whereto thus *Adam* fatherly displeas'd.
O execrable Son so to aspire
Above his Brethren, to himself assuming
Authority usurpt, from God not giv'n:
He gave us only over Beast, Fish, Fowl
Dominion absolute; that right we hold

3. In *The Tenure of Kings and Magistrates,* Milton denies the natural right of kings and insists that their power is committed to them in trust by the people.
4. See *Eikonoklastes:* "The Bishops could have told him, that 'Nimrod,' the first that hunted after Faction is reputed, by ancient Tradition, the first that founded monarchy; whence it appeares that to hunt after Faction is more properly the Kings Game."
5. "Before the Lord," Genesis 10.9; Milton takes it in a constitutional sense; see *The Tenure:* "To say Kings are accountable to none but God, is the overturning of all Law."
6. The materials of the Tower—brick with bitumen as mortar—are specified in Genesis 11.3.
7. See Genesis 11.4.
8. In the 17th century it was generally believed that the separation of language into distinct individual languages had its beginning at the confusion of tongues at Babel.
9. See Genesis 11.9, "Therefore is the name of it called Babel"; marginal gloss: "that is, Confusion."

By his donation; but Man over men
He made not Lord; such title to himself
Reserving, human left from human free.
But this Usurper his encroachment proud
Stays not on Man; to God his Tower intends
Siege and defiance: Wretched man! what food
Will he convey up thither to sustain
Himself and his rash Army, where thin Air
Above the Clouds will pine his entrails gross,
And famish him of breath, if not of Bread?
   To whom thus *Michael.* Justly thou abhorr'st
That Son, who on the quiet state of men
Such trouble brought, affecting to subdue
Rational Liberty;[1] yet know withal,
Since thy original lapse, true Liberty
Is lost, which always with right Reason dwells
Twinn'd, and from her hath no dividual° being: *separate*
Reason in man obscur'd, or not obey'd,
Immediately inordinate desires
And upstart Passions catch the Government
From Reason, and to servitude reduce
Man till then free. Therefore since hee permits
Within himself unworthy Powers to reign
Over free Reason, God in Judgment just
Subjects him from without to violent Lords;
Who oft as undeservedly enthral
His outward freedom: Tyranny must be,
Though to the Tyrant thereby no excuse.
Yet sometimes Nations will decline so low
From virtue, which is reason, that no wrong,
But Justice, and some fatal curse annext
Deprives them of thir outward liberty,
Thir inward lost:[2] * * *
   So spake th' Arch-Angel *Michaël,* then paus'd,
As at the World's great period;[3] and our Sire
Replete with joy and wonder thus repli'd.
   O goodness infinite, goodness immense![4]
That all this good of evil shall produce,
And evil turn to good; more wonderful
Than that which by creation first brought forth
Light out of darkness! full of doubt I stand,
Whether I should repent me now of sin

1. Lines 80–101 recall the regicide tracts and follow St. Augustine's *City of God* 19.15, where we read that the derivation of servitude, whose mother is sin, is the "first cause of man's subjection to man: which notwithstanding comes not to pass but by the direction of the highest, in whom is no injustice." For the connection between psychological and political enslavement, see 9.1127–31.

2. Michael goes on to describe the history of Israel, from Abraham to King David, then tells of the birth of the Messiah, who will crush Satan and defeat Sin and Death.

3. This is Michael's second pause; the first was at 12.2. The three divisions of Adam's instruction are meant to correspond to "three drops" of the well of life placed in his eyes (11.416). Here the pause is compared with the world's period the dawning of the present age, from the first to the second coming of Christ.

4. The Final Cause or end of the Fall: a greater "glory" for God and an opportunity for him to show his surpassing love through the sacrifice of Christ.

By mee done and occasion'd, or rejoice
Much more, that much more good thereof shall spring,
To God more glory, more good will to Men
From God, and over wrath grace shall abound.[5]
But say, if our deliverer up to Heav'n
Must reascend, what will betide the few
His faithful, left among th' unfaithful herd,
The enemies of truth; who then shall guide
His people, who defend? will they not deal
Worse with his followers than with him they dealt?
   Be sure they will, said th' Angel; but from Heav'n
Hee to his own a Comforter will send,[6]
The promise of the Father, who shall dwell
His Spirit within them, and the Law of Faith
Working through love, upon thir hearts shall write,[7]
To guide them in all truth, and also arm
With spiritual Armor, able to resist
Satan's assaults, and quench his fiery darts,[8]
What Man can do against them, not afraid,
Though to the death, against such cruelties
With inward consolations recompens't,
And oft supported so as shall amaze
Thir proudest persecutors: for the Spirit
Pour'd first on his Apostles, whom he sends
To evangelize the Nations, then on all
Baptiz'd, shall them with wondrous gifts endue° *endow*
To speak all Tongues, and do all Miracles,
As did thir Lord before them. Thus they win
Great numbers of each Nation to receive
With joy the tidings brought from Heav'n: at length
Thir Ministry perform'd, and race well run,
Thir doctrine and thir story written left,
They die; but in thir room, as they forewarn,
Wolves shall succeed for teachers, grievous Wolves,[9]
Who all the sacred mysteries of Heav'n
To thir own vile advantages shall turn
Of lucre and ambition, and the truth
With superstitions and traditions taint,
Left only in those written Records pure,
Though not but by the Spirit understood.[1]
Then shall they seek to avail themselves of names,
Places and titles, and with these to join
Secular power, though feigning still to act
By spiritual, to themselves appropriating

5. See Romans 5.20 ("where sin abounded, grace did much more abound") and 2 Corinthians 4.15.
6. The Holy Spirit. See John 14.18 and 15.26.
7. See Galations 5.6: "faith which worketh by love."
8. Alluding to the allegory in Ephesians 6.16: "Above all, taking the shield of faith, wherewith ye shall be able to quench all the fiery darts of the wicked."
9. "For I know this, that after my departing shall grievous wolves enter in among you, not sparing the flock" (Acts 20.29). See the simile comparing Satan to a wolf in the fold, at 4.183–87; see also *Lycidas* 113ff, page 1741.
1. It was an important article of Protestant belief that in doctrinal matters the ultimate arbiter is individual conscience rather than mere authority.

The Spirit of God, promis'd alike and giv'n
To all Believers;[2] and from that pretense,
Spiritual Laws by carnal° power shall force *worldly*
On every conscience; Laws which none shall find
Left them inroll'd, or what the Spirit within
Shall on the heart engrave.[3] What will they then
But force the Spirit of Grace itself, and bind
His consort Liberty; what, but unbuild
His living Temples, built by Faith to stand,[4]
Thir own Faith not another's: for on Earth
Who against Faith and Conscience can be heard
Infallible?[5] yet many will presume:
Whence heavy persecution shall arise
On all who in the worship persevere
Of Spirit and Truth; the rest, far greater part,
Will deem in outward Rites and specious forms
Religion satisfi'd; Truth shall retire
Bestuck with sland'rous darts, and works of Faith
Rarely be found: so shall the World go on,
To good malignant, to bad men benign,
Under her own weight groaning, till the day
Appear of respiration[6] to the just,
And vengeance to the wicked, at return
Of him so lately promis'd to thy aid,
The Woman's seed, obscurely then foretold,
Now amplier known thy Saviour and thy Lord,
Last in the Clouds from Heav'n to be reveal'd
In glory of the Father, to dissolve
Satan with his perverted World, then raise
From the conflagrant° mass, purg'd and refin'd, *burning*
New Heav'ns, new Earth, Ages of endless date
Founded in righteousness and peace and love,
To bring forth fruits Joy and eternal Bliss.
He ended; and thus *Adam* last repli'd.
How soon hath thy prediction, Seer blest,
Measur'd this transient World, the Race of time,
Till time stand fixt: beyond is all abyss,
Eternity, whose end no eye can reach.
Greatly instructed I shall hence depart,
Greatly in peace of thought, and have my fill
Of knowledge, what this Vessel can contain;
Beyond which was my folly to aspire.
Henceforth I learn, that to obey is best,

2. The corruption of the Church through its pursuit of "secular power" is a subject Milton had dealt with in *Of Reformation*. In *De doctrina* 1.30 he condemns the enforcement of obedience to human opinions or authority.

3. The wolves will enforce laws written neither in Scripture nor in the individual conscience.

4. See 1 Corinthians 3.17: "The temple of God is holy, which temple ye are."

5. Even though the doctrine of papal infallibility was not formally adapted until 1870, there can be no doubt that Rome is Milton's main target here. In *A Treatise of Civil Power* he writes that the "Pope assumes infallibility over conscience and scripture."

6. Opportunity for breathing again; rest.

And love with fear the only God, to walk
As in his presence, ever to observe
His providence, and on him sole depend,
Merciful over all his works, with good
Still overcoming evil, and by small
Accomplishing great things, by things deem'd weak
Subverting worldly strong, and worldly wise
By simply meek; that suffering for Truth's sake
Is fortitude to highest victory,
And to the faithful Death the Gate of Life;
Taught this by his example whom I now
Acknowledge my Redeemer ever blest.
  To whom thus also th' Angel last repli'd:
This having learnt, thou hast attain'd the sum
Of wisdom; hope no higher, though all the Stars
Thou knew'st by name, and all th' ethereal Powers,
All secrets of the deep, all Nature's works,
Or works of God in Heav'n, Air, Earth, or Sea,
And all the riches of this World enjoy'dst,
And all the rule, one Empire; only add
Deeds to thy knowledge answerable, add Faith,
Add Virtue, Patience, Temperance, add Love,
By name to come call'd Charity, the soul
Of all the rest:[7] then wilt thou not be loath
To leave this Paradise, but shalt possess
A paradise within thee, happier far.
Let us descend now therefore from this top
Of Speculation;[8] for the hour precise
Exacts our parting hence; and see the Guards,
By mee encampt on yonder Hill, expect
Thir motion,[9] at whose Front a flaming Sword,
In signal of remove, waves fiercely round;
We may no longer stay: go, waken *Eve;*
Her also I with gentle Dreams have calm'd
Portending good, and all her spirits compos'd
To meek submission: thou at season fit
Let her with thee partake what thou hast heard,
Chiefly what may concern her Faith to know,
The great deliverance by her Seed to come
(For by the Woman's Seed)[1] on all Mankind,
That ye may live, which will be many days,[2]
Both in one Faith unanimous though sad,
With cause for evils past, yet much more cheer'd
With meditation on the happy end.

7. Compare 2 Peter 1.5–7: "Add to your faith virtue; and to virtue knowledge; and to knowledge temperance; and to temperance patience; and to patience godliness; and to godliness brotherly kindness; and to brotherly kindness charity."

8. Vantage point but also height of theological speculation.

9. Await deployment, marching orders.

1. Alluding to the birth of Jesus.

2. Adam lived to be 930 years of age (Genesis 5.5).

He ended, and they both descend the Hill;
Descended, *Adam* to the Bow'r where *Eve*
Lay sleeping ran before, but found her wak't;
And thus with words not sad she him receiv'd.
Whence thou return'st, and whither went'st, I know;
For God is also in sleep, and Dreams advise,
Which he hath sent propitious, some great good
Presaging, since with sorrow and heart's distress
Wearied I fell asleep: but now lead on;
In mee is no delay; with thee to go,
Is to stay here; without thee here to stay,
Is to go hence unwilling; thou to mee
Art all things under Heav'n, all places thou,
Who for my wilful crime art banisht hence.[3]
This further consolation yet secure
I carry hence; though all by mee is lost,
Such favor I unworthy am voutsaf't,
By mee the Promis'd Seed shall all restore.
So spake our Mother *Eve*, and *Adam* heard
Well pleas'd, but answer'd not; for now too nigh
Th' Arch-Angel stood, and from the other Hill
To thir fixt Station, all in bright array
The Cherubim descended; on the ground
Gliding meteorous,° as Ev'ning Mist *meteoric*
Ris'n from a River o'er the marish° glides, *marsh*
And gathers ground fast at the Laborer's heel
Homeward returning. High in Front advanc't,
The brandisht Sword of God before them blaz'd
Fierce as a Comet; which with torrid heat,
And vapor as the *Libyan* Air adust,° *scorched*
Began to parch that temperate Clime; whereat
In either hand the hast'ning Angel caught
Our ling'ring Parents, and to th' Eastern Gate
Led them direct, and down the Cliff as fast
To the subjected° Plain; then disappear'd. *underlying*
They looking back, all th' Eastern side beheld
Of Paradise, so late thir happy seat,
Wav'd over by that flaming Brand,[4] the Gate
With dreadful Faces throng'd and fiery Arms:
Some natural tears they dropp'd, but wip'd them soon;
The World was all before them, where to choose
Thir place of rest, and Providence thir guide:[5]
They hand in hand with wand'ring steps and slow,
Through *Eden* took thir solitary way.

The End

3. Eve has assimilated Michael's exhortation at 11.292: "where [Adam] abides, think there thy native soil." There is also a resonance with Eve's song at 4.635–56 (every time of day is pleasing with Adam, none is pleasing without him).

4. See Genesis. 3.24: "a flaming sword which turned every way."

5. Note that "Providence" can be the object of "choose": decisions of faith lie ahead.

Samson Agonistes

Milton's readers knew Samson as the hero in Judges 13–16, whose strength Delila destroys by cutting his hair. Samson's Philistine enemies then blind him and set him to turn a millstone. When they bring him out to mock him during a feast in honor of their god Dagon, Samson prays to God for strength, and pulls down the pillars upholding the palace roof; he and several thousand Philistines are killed. The epithet "Agonistes" in Milton's title expresses Milton's reshaping of the biblical myth as tragedy, since "Agonistes" (from *agon*, Greek for combat) means "in struggle, under trial." Milton's Samson not only struggles with his external enemies—the Philistines, Delila, and a giant named Harapha—but with himself.

Though a "closet" drama rather than one intended to be staged, Milton's *Samson* is a work of profound psychological complexity, and Milton's reworking of his biblical material highlights the poem's tragic mystery. In the Bible, Samson's father Manoa does not plan to ransom his son as he does in Milton's work. Manoa's belief that he can save his son's life, along with the prophetic realization that Samson has regained his strength so that God might "use him further yet in some great service," strike notes of tragic irony. Milton also deepens the sense of Samson's part in his own downfall as a tragic hero. In speaking to his father, Milton's Samson accepts his suffering as a just punishment for breaking his vow as a Nazarite never to drink wine or cut his hair.

Milton's portrayal of Dalila is similarly complex. Milton makes her Samson's wife rather than his mistress, as she is in the Bible. The poet intensifies both her treachery and Samson's love for her. When she begs Samson's forgiveness for having betrayed him to save her country, she pleads jealousy as the cause. In contrast to the Chorus's view that she is "a manifest serpent by her sting" and "wanton, whose distrustful eye / Was fixed upon reward," Samson takes the full responsibility for his downfall upon himself: "she was not the prime cause / But I myself."

Like Greek tragedy, Milton's play works simultaneously on psychological, political, and spiritual levels. Many critics have seen the tragedy as related to Milton's own personal and public struggles—his blindness as well as his imprisonment following the Restoration. The poem may also allude to political conflicts, as in Harapha's arrogant challenge of Samson, which has been construed as reminiscent of the dueling challenges of the Cavaliers, who fought for the King and disdained the Puritans. Through defeating Harapha, Samson regains a faith in himself that leads to his final victory in suicide. Though suicide was seen as a sin by Christianity, Milton makes Samson's self-destruction at once an act of fate and of spiritual redemption. As in Greek tragedy, the *daimon* or spirit from within Samson ineluctably overtakes him—"self killed / Not willingly, but tangled in the fold / Of dire necessity." As in Christian resurrection, Samson is spiritually reborn like the phoenix: "His fiery virtue roused / From under ashes into sudden flame." The phoenix image defies any one explanation. "Like that self-begotten bird," Samson paradoxically arises triumphant in his own destruction.

Though some critics have argued that Milton may have begun *Samson Agonistes* as early as the 1640s, the text was first published along with *Paradise Regained* in 1671. Our text and notes are adapted from John Carey and Alastair Fowler, eds., *The Poems of John Milton*.

Samson Agonistes

a Dramatic Poem

Of That Sort of Dramatic Poem Which Is Called Tragedy

Tragedy, as it was anciently composed, hath been ever held the gravest, moralest, and most profitable of all other Poems: therefore said by Aristotle to be of power by raising pity and fear, or terror, to purge the mind of those and such like passions, that is to temper and reduce them to just measure with a kind of delight, stirred up by reading or seeing those passions well imitated. Nor is Nature wanting in her own effects to make good his assertion: for so in Physic things of melancholic hue and quality are used against melancholy, sour against sour, salt to remove salt humours. Hence Philosophers and other gravest Writers, as Cicero, Plutarch and others, frequently cite out of Tragic Poets, both to adorn and illustrate their discourse. The Apostle Paul himself thought it not unworthy to insert a verse of Euripides into the Text of Holy Scripture, I Cor. 15.33, and Paraeus,[1] commenting on the Revelation, divides the whole Book as a Tragedy, into Acts distinguisht each by a Chorus of Heavenly Harpings and Song between. Heretofore Men in highest dignity have laboured not a little to be thought able to compose a Tragedy. Of that honour Dionysius[2] the elder was no less ambitious, than before of his attaining to the Tyranny. Augustus Caesar also had begun his *Ajax*, but unable to please his own judgment with what he had begun, left it unfinisht. Seneca[3] the Philosopher is by some thought the Author of those Tragedies (at lest the best of them) that go under that name. Gregory Nazianzen,[4] a Father of the Church, thought it not unbeseeming the sanctity of his person to write a Tragedy, which he entitled *Christ suffering*. This is mentioned to vindicate Tragedy from the small esteem, or rather infamy, which in the account of many it undergoes at this day with other common Interludes; hap'ning through the Poet's error of intermixing Comic stuff with Tragic sadness and gravity; or introducing trivial and vulgar persons, which by all judicious hath been counted absurd; and brought in without discretion, corruptly to gratify the people. And though ancient Tragedy use no Prologue,[5] yet using sometimes, in case of self-defence, or explanation, that which Martial[6] calls an Epistle; in behalf of this Tragedy coming forth after the ancient manner, much different from what among us passes for best, thus much beforehand may be Epistled; that *Chorus* is here introduced after the Greek manner, not ancient only but modern, and still in use among the Italians. In the modelling therefore of this Poem, with good reason, the Ancients and Italians[7] are rather followed, as of much more authority and fame. The measure of Verse used in the Chorus is of all sorts, called by the Greeks Monostrophic, or rather Apolelymenon, without regard had to Strophe, Antistrophe or Epode,[8] which were a kind of Stanzas framed only for the Music then used with the Chorus that sung; not essential to the Poem, and therefore not material; or being divided into Stanzas or Pauses, they may be called Allaeostropha. Division into Act and Scene referring chiefly to the Stage (to which this work never was intended) is here omitted.

It suffices if the whole Drama be found not produc't beyond the fifth Act. Of the style and uniformity, and that commonly called the Plot, whether intricate or explicit, which is nothing indeed but such economy[9] or disposition of the fable as may

1. David Paraeus, a German Calvinist whose *Commentary on Romans* (1609) was publicly burned by the universities of Oxford and Cambridge. Milton here refers to his work *On the Divine Apocalypse* (1618).
2. Tyrant of Syracuse (431–367 B.C.).
3. Lucius Annaeus Seneca (3 B.C.–A.D. 65). The doubt as to his authorship of his ten tragedies is due to a mistake of Sidonius Apollinaris, *Carmen* 9.230–38, who distinguishes between Seneca the philosopher and Seneca the tragedian.
4. Bishop of Constantinople (A.D. 325?–390?).
5. Milton uses the term "prologue" in its modern sense (a preliminary address to the audience), not in Aristotle's sense (the part of a tragedy that precedes the entrance of the chorus).
6. Martial notes that tragedies and comedies may need epistles since "they cannot speak for themselves" (*Epigrams* 2).
7. Tasso's *Aminta* and Guarini's *Pastor Fido*, for example, both have a chorus, as did 16th-century Italian tragic drama frequently.
8. Apolelymenon: Greek "freed" (i.e., from the restraint of any firm stanza pattern). In Greek drama the strophe was a stanza sung by the chorus as it moved from right to left, and the antistrophe corresponded exactly to the strophe in structure, as it moved in the opposite direction. The concluding epode was sung standing still. Milton says that if his choruses do seem at times to divide into stanzas, then they should be called "allaeostropha" (Greek: "of irregular strophes").
9. "Intricate . . . explicit": Aristotle, *Poetics* 6, divides plots into two classes, simple and complex; "which is nothing indeed," i.e., the plot is merely the management ("economy") of the events: the "putting together of the incidents," as Aristotle calls it.

stand best with verisimilitude and decorum; they only will best judge who are not unacquainted with Aeschylus,[1] Sophocles, and Euripides, the three Tragic Poets unequalled yet by any, and the best rule to all who endeavor to write Tragedy. The circumscription of time wherein the whole Drama begins and ends, is according to ancient rule,[2] and best example, within the space of 24 hours.

The Argument

SAMSON made captive, blind, and now in the prison at Gaza, there to labor as in a common workhouse, on a Festival day, in the general cessation from labor, comes forth into the open air, to a place nigh, somewhat retired there to sit a while and bemoan his condition. Where he happens at length to be visited by certain friends and equals of his tribe, which make the Chorus, who seek to comfort him what they can; then by his old father, Manoa, who endeavours the like, and withal tells him his purpose to procure his liberty by ransom; lastly, that this feast was proclaimed by the Philistines as a day of thanksgiving for their deliverance from the hands of Samson, which yet more troubles him. Manoa then departs to prosecute his endeavor with the Philistian Lords for Samson's redemption; who in the mean while is visited by other persons; and lastly by a public Officer to require his coming to the feast before the Lords and People, to play or show his strength in their presence; he at first refuses, dismissing the public Officer with absolute denial to come; at length persuaded inwardly that this was from God, he yields to go along with him, who came now the second time with great threatenings to fetch him; the Chorus yet remaining on the place, Manoa returns full of joyful hope, to procure ere long his Son's deliverance: in the midst of which discourse an Hebrew comes in haste confusedly at first; and afterward more distinctly relating the catastrophe, what Samson had done to the Philistines, and by accident to himself; wherewith the tragedy ends.

The Persons

SAMSON
MANOA, *the father of Samson*
DALILA, *his wife*
HARAPHA OF GATH
PUBLIC OFFICER
MESSENGER
CHORUS OF DANITES

THE SCENE BEFORE THE PRISON IN GAZA

SAMSON A little onward lend thy guiding hand
To these dark steps, a little further on;[3]
For yonder bank hath choice of sun or shade,
There I am wont to sit, when any chance
Relieves me from my task of servile toil,
Daily in the common prison else enjoined me,
Where I a prisoner chained, scarce freely draw
The air imprisoned also, close and damp,
Unwholsome draught: but here I feel amends,
The breath of Heaven fresh-blowing, pure and sweet,
With day-spring[4] born; here leave me to respire.
This day a solemn feast the people hold

1. Milton is unusual among 17th-century scholars in ranking Aeschylus with Sophocles and Euripides.
2. "The unity of time," Aristotle, *Poetics* 5.
3. See Sophocles, *Oedipus at Colonus*, where Oedipus is led forward by Antigone, and Euripides, *Phoenician Maidens* 834–35, where Tiresias asks his daughter to lead him on and says she is as eyes to his "blind feet." In Sidney's *Arcadia* 2.10.3, the blinded King of Paphlagonia complains that there is no one to "lend [him] a hande to guide [his] dark steps."
4. Daybreak; see Luke 1.78: "The day-spring from on high hath visited us."

To Dagon[5] their sea-idol, and forbid
Laborious works, unwillingly this rest
Their superstition yields me; hence with leave
Retiring from the popular noise, I seek
This unfrequented place to find some ease,
Ease to the body some, none to the mind
From restless thoughts, that like a deadly swarm
Of hornets armed, no sooner found alone,
But rush upon me thronging, and present
Times past, what once I was, and what am now.
O wherefore was my birth from heaven foretold
Twice[6] by an angel, who at last in sight
Of both my parents all in flames ascended
From off the altar, where an offering burned,
As in a fiery column charioting
His godlike presence, and from some great act
Or benefit revealed to Abraham's race?
Why was my breeding ordered and prescribed
As of a person separate to God,[7]
Designed for great exploits; if I must die
Betrayed, captived, and both my eyes put out,
Made of my enemies the scorn and gaze;
To grind in brazen fetters under task
With this heaven-gifted strength? O glorious strength
Put to the labor of a beast, debas't
Lower then bondslave! Promise was that I
Should Israel from Philistian yoke deliver;[8]
Ask for this great deliverer now, and find him
Eyeless in gaza at the mill with slaves,
Himself in bonds under Philistian yoke;
Yet stay, let me not rashly call in doubt
Divine prediction; what if all foretold
Had been fulfilled but through mine own default,
Whom have I to complain of but myself?
Who this high gift of strength committed to me,
In what part lodged, how easily bereft me,
Under the seal of silence could not keep,
But weakly to a woman must reveal it,
O'ercome with importunity and tears.
O impotence of mind, in body strong![9]
But what is strength without a double share
Of wisdom, vast, unwieldy, burdensom,[1]
Proudly secure, yet liable to fall
By weakest suttleties, not made to rule,
But to subserve where wisdom bears command.

5. National deity of the Philistines, presented in *Paradise Lost* 1.462–3 as half-man, half-fish (the name is possibly derived from Hebrew *dag*, "fish").
6. First to his mother alone (Judges 13.3–5) and later to both parents (Judges 13.10–20).
7. "Nazarite" is derived from Hebrew *nazar*, "to separate oneself." The angel says to Samson's mother "The child shall be a Nazarite unto God" (Judges 13.7).
8. See Judges 13.5: "He shall begin to deliver Israel out of the hand of the Philistines."
9. Samson's weak-mindedness is unique to Milton.
1. See Horace, *Odes* 3.4.65: "Brute force bereft of wisdom falls to ruin by its own weight."

God, when he gave me strength, to show withal
How slight the gift was, hung it in my hair.
But peace, I must not quarrel with the will
Of highest dispensation, which herein
Happ'ly had ends above my reach to know:
Suffices that to me strength is my bane,
And proves the sourse of all my miseries;
So many, and so huge, that each apart
Would ask a life to wail, but chief of all,
O loss of sight, of thee I most complain!
Blind among enemies, O worse then chains,
Dungeon, or beggery, or decrepit age!
Light the prime work of God to me is extinct,
And all her various objects of delight
Annulled, which might in part my grief have eased,
Inferior to the vilest now become
Of man or worm; the vilest here excel me,
They creep, yet see, I dark in light exposed
To daily fraud, contempt, abuse and wrong,
Within doors, or without, still° as a fool, *always*
In power of others, never in my own;
Scarce half I seem to live, dead more then half.
O dark, dark, dark, amid the blaze of noon,
Irrecoverably dark, total eclipse
Without all hope of day!
O first created beam, and thou great Word,
Let there be light, and light was over all;[2]
Why am I thus bereaved thy prime decree?
The sun to me is dark
And silent as the moon,[3]
When she deserts the night
Hid in her vacant interlunar cave.
Since light so necessary is to life,
And almost life itself, if it be true
That light is in the soul,
She all in every part;[4] why was the sight
To such a tender ball as th' eye confined?
So obvious° and so easie to be quench't, *exposed*
And not as feeling through all parts diffused,
That she might look at will through every pore?
Then had I not been thus exiled from light;
As in the land of darkness yet in light,
To live a life half dead, a living death,
And buried; but O yet more miserable!
My self my sepulcher, a moving grave,
Buried, yet not exempt
By privilege of death and burial
From worst of other evils, pains and wrongs,

2. See Genesis 1.3.

3. Silent: not shining; vacant: Milton thinks of the moon at leisure (Latin *vacare*) resting in a cave.

4. The theory that the soul is diffused throughout the body; see Augustine, *De Trinitate* 6.6: "The soul . . . in any body, is both all in the whole, and all in every part."

But made hereby obnoxious° more *liable to*
To all the miseries of life,
Life in captivity
Among inhuman foes.
But who are these? for with joint pace I hear
The tread of many feet stearing this way;
Perhaps my enemies who come to stare
At my affliction, and perhaps to insult,
Their daily practice to afflict me more.

CHORUS This, this is he; softly a while,
Let us not break in upon him;
O change beyond report, thought, or belief!
See how he lies at random, carelessly diffused,
With languish't head unpropt,
As one past hope, abandoned,
And by himself given over;
In slavish habit, ill-fitted weeds
O'er worn and soiled;
Or do my eyes misrepresent? Can this be he,
That heroic, that renowned,
Irresistible Samson? whom unarmed
No strength of man, or fiercest wild beast could withstand;
Who tore the lion, as the lion tears the kid,[5]
Ran on embattled armies clad in iron,
And weaponless himself,
Made arms ridiculous, useless the forgery° *forging*
Of brazen shield and spear, the hammered cuirass,
Chalybean[6] tempered steel, and frock of mail
Adamantean proof;[7]
But safest he who stood aloof,
When insupportably° his foot advanc't, *irresistibly*
In scorn of their proud arms and warlike tools,
Spurned them to death by troops. The bold Ascalonite[8]
Fled from his lion° ramp,° old warriors turned *lionlike / rearing up*
Their plated° backs under his heel; *armored*
Or groveling soiled their crested helmets in the dust.
Then with what trivial weapon came to hand,
The jaw of a dead ass, his sword of bone,[9]
A thousand foreskins[1] fell, the flower of Palestine,
In Ramath-lechi[2] famous to this day:
Then by main force pulled up, and on his shoulders bore
The gates of Azza, post, and massie bar
Up to the hill by Hebron, seat of giants old,[3]

5. See Judges 14.6: "And he rent him [the young lion] as he would have rent a kid."

6. See Virgil, *Georgics* 1.58: "the naked Chalybes give us iron." They were famous metal workers.

7. "Adamant" (Latin *adamas*) was the name applied to the hardest known substance—at first steel, later diamond; "proof armor" was considered to be impenetrable.

8. Ascalon was one of the five main cities of the Philistines. In Judges 14.19, Samson goes down to Ascalon and kills 30 men there.

9. In Judges 15.15–6, Samson finds the jawbone of an ass and kills 1,000 men with it.

1. Uncircumcised Philistines.

2. The name of the city means "the lifting up" or "casting away of the jawbone."

3. This exploit is narrated in Judges 16.3. "Azza" is a variant form of Gaza; "Hebron" was the city of Arba (Joshua 14.15), father of Anak, 15.13–4, whose children, the Anakim, were giants (Numbers 13.33).

No journey of a Sabbath day, and loaded so;
Like whom° the Gentiles feign to bear up heav'n. *Atlas*
Which shall I first bewail,
Thy bondage or lost sight,
Prison within Prison
Inseparably dark?
Thou art become (O worst imprisonment!)
The dungeon of thyself; thy soul
(Which men enjoying sight oft without cause complain)[4]
Imprisoned now indeed,
In real darkness of the body dwells,
Shut up from outward light
To incorporate with gloomy night;
For inward light alas
Puts forth no visual beam.° *beam of eyesight*
O mirror of our fickle state,
Since man on earth unparalleled!
The rarer thy example stands,
By how much from the top of wondrous glory,
Strongest of mortal men,
To lowest pitch of abject fortune thou art fallen.
For him I reckon not in high estate
Whom long descent of birth
Or the sphere of fortune raises;
But thee whose strength, while virtue was her mate,
Might have subdued the earth,
Universally crowned with highest praises.

SAMSON I hear the sound of words, their sense the air
Dissolves unjointed e'er it reach my ear.

CHORUS He speaks, let us draw nigh. Matchless in might,
The glory late of Israel, now the grief;
We come thy friends and neighbours not unknown
From Eshtaol and Zora's fruitful vale[5]
To visit or bewail thee, or if better,
Counsel or consolation we may bring,
Salve to thy sores, apt words have power to suage
The tumors of a troubled mind,
And are as balm to festered wounds.

SAMSON Your coming, friends, revives me, for I learn
Now of my own experience, not by talk,
How counterfeit a coin they are who friends
Bear in their superscription° (of the most *the stamp on a coin*
I would be understood) in prosperous days
They swarm, but in adverse withdraw their head
Not to be found, though sought. Yee see, O friends,
How many evils have enclosed me round;
Yet that which was the worst now least afflicts me,
Blindness, for had I sight, confused with shame,

4. I.e., men often complain that the soul is imprisoned in the body.

5. Samson was born at Zora (Judges 13.2) and buried between Zora and Eshtaol (Judges 16.31). These towns lay "in the valley" and are ascribed to both Judah and Dan (Joshua 15.33 and 19.41).

How could I once look up, or heave the head,
Who like a foolish pilot have shipwrack't,
My vessel trusted to me from above,
Gloriously rigged; and for a word, a tear,
Fool, have divulged the secret gift of God
To a deceitful woman: tell me, friends,
Am I not sung and proverbed[6] for a fool
In every street, do they not say, "How well
Are come upon him his deserts?" Yet why?
Immeasurable strength they might behold
In me, of wisdom nothing more then mean;° *average*
This with the other should, at least, have paired,
These two proportioned ill drove me transverse.° *sideways*

CHORUS Tax not divine disposal, wisest men
Have erred, and by bad women been deceived;
And shall again, pretend they ne'er so wise.
Deject not then so overmuch thyself,
Who hast of sorrow thy full load besides;
Yet truth to say, I oft have heard men wonder
Why thou shouldst wed Philistian women rather
Then of thine own tribe fairer, or as fair,
At least of thy own nation, and as noble.

SAMSON The first I saw at Timna, and she pleased
Me, not my Parents, that I sought to wed,
The daughter of an infidel: they knew not
That what I motioned was of God; I knew
From intimate impulse, and therefore urged
The marriage on; that by occasion hence
I might begin Israel's deliverance,
The work to which I was divinely called;[7]
She proving false,[8] the next I took to wife
(O that I never had! fond wish too late!)
Was in the vale of Sorec,[9] Dalila,
That specious° monster, my accomplished snare. *falsely attractive*
I thought it lawful from my former act,
And the same end; still watching to oppress
Israel's oppressours: of what now I suffer
She was not the prime cause, but I myself,
Who vanquished with a peal[1] of words (O weakness!)
Gave up my fort of silence to a woman.

CHORUS In seeking just occasion to provoke
The Philistine, thy country's enemy,

6. See Psalms 69.11: "I became a proverb to them," and Job 30.9: "and now am I their song, yea, I am their byword."

7. In lines 219–26, Milton follows the account in Judges 14.1–4 exactly, except in the detail of Samson's "intimate impulse," which is not found in Judges; the reason Samson gives there for the match is "that she pleaseth me well."

8. In Judges 14.5–20 she extracts from Samson the answer to the riddle he has set the young men of Timna and tells it to them. Her father then gives her to Samson's "companion, whom he had used as his friend," meaning groomsman; the Samson of Judges was not married to Dalila.

9. See Judges 16.4: "He loved a woman in the valley of Sorek."

1. An artillery term. A peal of guns was used as a salute or sign of rejoicing; the guns were not weapons of attack when pealing.

Thou never wast remiss, I bear thee witness:
Yet Israel still serves with all his sons.
SAMSON That fault I take not on me, but transfer
On Israel's governours, and heads of tribes,
Who seeing those great acts which God had done
Singly by me against their conquerors
Acknowledged not, or not at all considered
Deliverance offered: I on th' other side
Used no ambition[2] to commend my deeds,
The deeds themselves, though mute, spoke loud the doer;
But they persisted deaf, and would not seem
To count them things worth notice, till at length
Their lords the Philistines with gathered powers
Entered Judea seeking me, who then
Safe to the rock of Etham was retired,
Not flying, but fore-casting in what place
To set upon them, what advantaged best;[3]
Meanwhile the men of Judah to prevent
The harrass of their land, beset me round;[4]
I willingly on some conditions came[5]
Into their hands, and they as gladly yield me
To the uncircumcised a welcome prey,
Bound with two cords; but cords to me were threads
Touched with the flame: on their whole host I flew
Unarmed, and with a trivial weapon felled
Their choicest youth; they only lived who fled.[6]
Had Judah that day joined, or one whole tribe,
They had by this° possessed the towers of Gath,[7] *by this time*
And lorded over them whom now they serve;
But what more oft in nations grown corrupt,
And by their vices brought to servitude,
Then to love bondage more than liberty,[8]
Bondage with ease than strenuous liberty;
And to despise, or envy, or suspect
Whom God hath of his special favor raised
As their deliverer; if he aught begin,
How frequent° to desert him, and at last *accustomed*
To heap ingratitude on worthiest deeds?
CHORUS Thy words to my remembrance bring
How Succoth and the Fort of Penuel
Their great deliverer contemned,
The matchless Gideon[9] in pursuit

2. In the sense of Latin *ambitio,* which means "walking about to solicit votes or applause."
3. In Judges 15, Samson burns the Philistines' standing corn. They, in revenge, burn his wife and her father (Judges 15.5–6); he smites them "hip and thigh with a great slaughter" and goes to dwell "in the top of the rock Etam" (Judges 15.8). "Then the Philistines went up, and pitched in Judah" (Judges 15.9).
4. See Judges 15.11–12.
5. Judges 15.12: "Swear unto me, that ye will not fall upon me yourselves."
6. See Judges 15.13–16.
7. A city of Philistia.
8. See Matthew 11.28–30, where Jesus says, "Come unto me. . . . For my yoke is easy."
9. See Judges 8.5–9, where Gideon, pursuing Zebah and Zalmunna, kings of Midian, asks for bread for his 300 followers from Succoth and Penuel but is refused; "Madian" is the Vulgate form of Midian.

Of Madian and her vanquished kings:
And how ingrateful Ephraim
Had dealt with Jephtha,[1] who by argument,
Not worse then by his shield and spear
Defended Israel from the Ammonite,
Had not his prowess quelled their pride
In that sore battle when so many died
Without reprieve adjudged to death,
For want of well pronouncing Shibboleth.[2]

SAMSON Of such examples add me to the roll,[3]
Me easily indeed mine° may neglect, *my people*
But God's proposed deliverance not so.

CHORUS Just are the ways of God,
And justifiable to men;
Unless there be who think not God at all,
If any be, they walk obscure;
For of such doctrine never was there school,
But the heart of the fool,[4]
And no man therein doctor but himself.
Yet more there be who doubt his ways not just,
As to his own edicts, found contradicting,
Then give the reins to wandering thought,
Regardless of his glory diminution;
Till by their own perplexities involved
They ravel° more, still less resolved, *become entangled*
But never find self-satisfying solution.
As if they would confine th' interminable,
And tie him to his own prescript,
Who made our laws to bind us, not himself,
And hath full right to exempt
Whom so it pleases him by choice
From national obstriction,[5] without taint
Of sin, or legal debt;° *duty to Mosaic law*
For with his own laws he can best dispense.
He would not else who never wanted means,
Nor in respect of the enemy just cause
To set his people free,
Have prompted this heroic Nazarite,
Against his vow of strictest purity,[6]
To seek in marriage that fallacious bride,
Unclean, unchaste.

1. See Judges 11.12–33 and 12.1–4, where the Ephraimites refuse to help Jephtha against the Ammonites, whom he first refutes in argument and then defeats in battle.
2. Judges 12.5–6; Ephraimites had a distinctive dialect. When they deny their identity in order to escape punishment, Jephtha asks them to say the word "shibboleth" (ear of corn), which they can only pronounce as "sibboleth," thereby giving themselves away.
3. Gideon and Jephtha were considered saints like Samson and for the same reason. See Hebrews 11.32.
4. See Psalms 14.1: "The fool hath said in his heart, There is no God."
5. Obstruction; the obligation referred to is recorded in Deuteronomy 7.1–3, which, however, does not prohibit marriage specifically with Philistines.
6. Celibacy was not included in the Nazarite vow (Numbers 6.1–21), and marriage with Gentiles was not impurity until after the reformation of Ezra.

Down Reason then, at least vain reasonings down,
Though Reason here aver
That moral verdict quits° her of unclean: *acquits*
Unchaste was subsequent,[7] her stain not his.
But see here comes thy reverend sire
With careful step, locks white as down,
Old Manoah: advise
Forthwith how thou ought'st to receive him.

SAMSON Ay me, another inward grief awaked,
With mention of that name renews th' assault.

MANOA Brethren and men of Dan, for such ye seem,
Though in this uncouth° place; if old respect, *unknown*
As I suppose, towards your once gloried friend,
My son now captive, hither hath informed
Your younger feet, while mine cast back with age
Came lagging after; say if he be here.

CHORUS As signal° now in low dejected state, *remarkable*
As erst in highest, behold him where he lies.

MANOA O miserable change! Is this the man,
That invincible Samson, far renowned,
The dread of Israel's foes, who with a strength
Equivalent to angels walked their streets,
None offering fight; who single combatant
Duelled their armies ranked in proud array,
Himself an army, now unequal match
To save himself against a coward armed
At one spear's length. O ever failing trust
In mortal strength! And oh, what not in man
Deceivable and vain! Nay, what thing good
Prayed for, but often proves our woe, our bane?
I prayed for children, and thought barrenness
In wedlock a reproach; I gained a son,
And such a son as all men hailed me happy;
Who would be now a father in my stead?
O wherefore did God grant me my request,
And as a blessing with such pomp adorned?
Why are his gifts desirable, to tempt
Our earnest prayers, then given with solemn hand
As graces, draw a scorpion's tail behind?
For this did the angel twice descend? for this
Ordained thy nurture holy, as of a plant;
Select, and sacred, glorious for a while,
The miracle of men: then in an hour
Ensnared, assaulted, overcome, led bound,
Thy foes' derision, captive, poor, and blind
Into a dungeon thrust, to work with slaves?
Alas, methinks whom God hath chosen once
To worthiest deeds, if he through frailty err,

7. The woman of Timna was unclean only in a legal sense, as a Gentile, and her unchastity took place afterward ("was subsequent"); see Judges 14.20: "Samson's wife was given to his companion."

He should not so o'erwhelm, and as a thrall
Subject him to so foul indignities,
Be it but for honor's sake of former deeds.

SAMSON Appoint not heavenly disposition, father,
Nothing of all these evils hath befallen me
But justly; I myself have brought them on,
Sole author I, sole cause: if aught seem vile,
As vile hath been my folly, who have profaned[8]
The mystery of God given me under pledge
Of vow, and have betrayed it to a woman,
A Canaanite,[9] my faithless enemy.
This well I knew, nor was at all surprised,
But warned by oft experience: did not she
Of Timna first betray me,[1] and reveal
The secret wrested from me in her highth
Of nuptial love profest, carrying it straight
To them who had corrupted her, my spies
And rivals? In this other was there found
More faith? who also in her prime of love,
Spousal embraces, vitiated° with gold,[2] *corrupted*
Though offered only, by the scent conceived
Her spurious first-born; treason against me?
Thrice[3] she assayed with flattering prayers and sighs,
And amorous reproaches[4] to win from me
My capital[5] secret, in what part my strength
Lay stored, in what part summed, that she might know:
Thrice I deluded her, and turned to sport
Her importunity, each time perceiving
How openly, and with what impudence
She purposed to betray me, and (which was worse
Than undissembled hate) with what contempt
She sought to make me traitor to myself;
Yet the fourth time, when mustering all her wiles,
With blandished parlies,° feminine assaults, *flattering words*
Tongue-batteries, she surceased not day nor night
To storm me over-watched,° and wearied out. *kept awake*
At times when men seek most repose and rest,
I yielded, and unlocked her all my heart,
Who with a grain of manhood well resolved
Might easily have shook off all her snares:
But foul effeminacy held me yoked
Her bond-slave; O indignity, O blot
To honor and religion! Servile mind
Rewarded well with servile punishment!
The base degree to which I now am fallen,

8. Published (Latin *profanus*, "outside the temple," hence "public").
9. The Philistines were immigrants into Canaan from Caphtor. See Amos 9.7.
1. See line 227.
2. See Judges 16.5: "And we will give thee every one of us eleven hundred pieces of silver."
3. See Judges 16.6–14.
4. See Judges 16.15: "How canst thou say, I love thee, when thine heart is not with me?"
5. A pun: "most important," and also "pertaining to the head" (Latin *caput*).

These rags, this grinding, is not yet so base
As was my former servitude, ignoble,
Unmanly, ignominious, infamous,
True slavery, and that blindness worse then this,
That saw not how degenerately I served.

MANOA I cannot praise thy marriage choices, son,
Rather approved them not; but thou didst plead
Divine impulsion prompting how thou might'st
Find some occasion to infest° our foes. *harass*
I state[6] not that; this I am sure; our foes
Found soon occasion thereby to make thee
Their captive, and their triumph; thou the sooner
Temptation found'st, or over-potent charms
To violate the sacred trust of silence
Deposited within thee; which to have kept
Tacit, was in thy power; true; and thou bear'st
Enough and more the burden of that fault:
Bitterly hast thou paid, and still art paying
That rigid score.° A worse thing yet remains: *account of a debt*
This day the Philistines a popular feast
Here celebrate in Gaza; and proclaim
Great pomp, and sacrifice, and praises loud
To Dagon, as their God who hath delivered
Thee, Samson, bound and blind into their hands,
Them[7] out of thine, who slew'st them many a slain.
So Dagon shall be magnified, and God,
Besides whom is not God, compared with idols,
Disglorified, blasphemed, and had in scorn
By th' Idolatrous rout amidst their wine;
Which to have come to pass by means of thee,
Samson, of all thy sufferings think the heaviest,
Of all reproach the most with shame that ever
Could have befallen thee and thy father's house.

SAMSON Father, I do acknowledge and confess
That I this honor, I this pomp have brought
To Dagon, and advanced his praises high
Among the heathen round; to God have brought
Dishonor, obloquy, and oped the mouths
Of idolists° and atheists; have brought scandal *idolaters*
To Israel, diffidence of God, and doubt
In feeble hearts, propense° enough before *inclined*
To waver, or fall off and join with idols;
Which is my chief affliction, shame and sorrow,
The anguish of my soul, that suffers not
Mine eye to harbor sleep, or thoughts to rest.
This only hope relieves me, that the strife
With me hath end; all the contést is now
'Twixt God and Dagon; Dagon hath presumed,
Me overthrown, to enter lists° with God, *competition*

6. "Assign a value to, have an opinion upon."

7. An imitation of a Latin dative: "to them."

His deity comparing and preferring
Before the God of Abraham. He, be sure,
Will not connive,° or linger, thus provoked, *stay dormant*
But will arise and his great name assert:
Dagon must stoop, and shall ere long receive
Such a discomfit,° as shall quite despoil him *defeat*
Of all these boasted trophies won on me,
And with confusion blank° his worshippers. *nonplus*

MANOA With cause this hope relieves thee, and these words
I as a prophecy receive: for God,
Nothing more certain, will not long defer
To vindicate the glory of his name
Against all competition, nor will long
Endure it, doubtful whether God be Lord,
Or Dagon. But for thee what shall be done?
Thou must not in the meanwhile here forgot
Lie in this miserable loathsome plight
Neglected. I already have made way
To some Philistian lords, with whom to treat
About thy ransom:[8] well they may by this
Have satisfied their utmost of revenge
By pains and slaveries, worse than death inflicted
On thee, who now no more canst do them harm.

SAMSON Spare that proposal, father, spare the trouble
Of that solicitation; let me here,
As I deserve, pay on my punishment;
And expiate, if possible, my crime,
Shameful garrulity. To have revealed
Secrets of men, the secrets of a friend,
How heinous had the fact been, how deserving
Contempt and scorn of all, to be excluded
All friendship, and avoided as a blab,
The mark of fool set on his front? But I
God's counsel have not kept, his holy secret
Presumptuously have published, impiously,
Weakly at least, and shamefully: A sin
That Gentiles in their parables condemn[9]
To their abyss and horrid pains confined.

MANOA Be penitent and for thy fault contrite,
But act not in thy own affliction, son,
Repent the sin, but if the punishment
Thou canst avoid, self-preservation bids;
Or th' execution leave to high disposal,
And let another hand, not thine, exact
Thy penal forfeit from thyself;[1] perhaps
God will relent, and quit thee all his debt;[2]

8. Having Manoa sue with the Philistines for the release of his son is a Miltonic innovation to the story.
9. Alluding to the myth of Tantalus, who was placed in Hades for revealing the secrets of the gods.
1. See Augustine, *De Doctrina* 2.8: "The love of man towards himself consists in loving himself next to God . . . Opposed to this is, first, a perverse hatred of self . . . In this class are to be reckoned those who lay violent hands on themselves."
2. Remit all your debt to him ("thee" is a dative).

Who evermore approves and more accepts
(Best pleased with humble and filial submission)
Him who imploring mercy sues for life,
Then who self-rigorous chooses death as due;
Which argues over-just,[3] and self-displeased
For self-offence, more than for God offended.
Reject not then what offered means, who knows
But God hath set before us, to return thee
Home to thy country and his sacred house,
Where thou mayst bring thy offerings, to avert
His further ire, with prayers and vows renewed.

SAMSON His pardon I implore; but as for life,
To what end should I seek it? When in strength
All mortals I excelled, and great in hopes
With youthful courage and magnanimous thoughts
Of birth from heaven foretold and high exploits,
Full of divine instinct, after some proof
Of acts indeed heroic, far beyond
The sons of Anak,[4] famous now and blazed,° *published*
Fearless of danger, like a petty God
I walked about admired of all and dreaded
On hostile ground, none daring my affront.
Then swollen with pride into the snare I fell
Of fair fallacious looks, venereal trains,° *sexual snares*
Softned with pleasure and voluptuous life;
At length to lay my head and hallowed pledge
Of all my strength in the lascivious lap[5]
Of a deceitful concubine who shore[6] me
Like a tame wether,° all my precious fleece, *castrated sheep*
Then turned me out ridiculous, despóiled,
Shaven, and disarmed among my enemies.

CHORUS Desire of wine and all delicious drinks,[7]
Which many a famous warrior overturns,
Thou couldst repress, nor did the dancing ruby
Sparkling, outpoured, the flavor or the smell,
Or taste that cheers the heart of Gods and men,[8]
Allure thee from the cool Crystálline stream.

SAMSON Wherever fountain or fresh current flowed
Against[9] the eastern ray, translucent, pure,
With touch etheral of heavens fiery rod
I drank, from the clear milky[1] juice allaying
Thirst, and refreshed; nor envied them the grape
Whose heads that turbulent liquor fills with fumes.

CHORUS O madness, to think use of strongest wines

3. Proves a man just to excess.
4. Giants; see line 148.
5. See Judges 16.19: "She made him sleep upon her knees."
6. Shaved. In Judges 16.19, Dalila calls for a man to shave Samson's head; here, she apparently does it herself.
7. As a Nazarite, Samson vowed to abstain from strong drink, Numbers 6.3.
8. See Judges 9.13: "wine, which cheereth God and man."
9. In the direction of. In Ezekiel 47.8–9 the waters that flow eastward are said to have life-giving powers.
1. The concept is of earth as mother; possibly Milton recalls Song of Solomon 5.12: "doves by the rivers of water, washed with milk," where the last phrase can be translated as "splashed by the milky water."

And strongest drinks our chief support of health,
When God with these forbidden made choice to rear
His mighty champion, strong above compare,
Whose drink was only from the liquid° brook. *transparent*
SAMSON But what availed this temperance, not complete
Against another object more enticing?
What boots it° at one gate to make defence, *what use is it*
And at another to let in the foe
Effeminately vanquished? by which means,
Now blind, disheartened, shamed, dishonored, quelled,
To what can I be useful, wherein serve
My nation, and the work from heaven imposed,
But to sit idle on the houshold hearth,
A burdenous drone; to visitants a gaze° *object gazed at*
Or pitied object, these redundant° locks *abounding*
Robustious° to no purpose clustering down, *robust*
Vain monument of strength; till length of years
And sedentary numbness craze° my limbs *weaken*
To a contemptible old age obscure.
Here rather let me drudge and earn my bread,
Till vermin or the draff° of servile food *pig-swill*
Consume me, and oft-invocated death
Hasten the welcome end of all my pains.
MANOA Wilt thou then serve the Philistines with that gift
Which was expressly given thee to annoy° them? *molest*
Better at home lie bed-rid, not only idle,
Inglorious, unemployed, with age out-worn.
But God who caused a fountain at thy prayer
From the dry ground to spring, thy thirst to allay
After the brunt of battle,[2] can as easy
Cause light again within thy eyes to spring,
Wherewith to serve him better then thou hast;
And I persuade me so; why else this strength
Miraculous yet remaining in those locks?
His might continues in thee not for naught,
Nor shall his wondrous gifts be frustrate thus.
SAMSON All otherwise to me my thoughts portend,
That these dark orbs no more shall treat with light,
Nor th' other light of life continue long,
But yield to double darkness nigh at hand:
So much I feel my genial[3] spirits droop,
My hopes all flat,° nature within me seems *overthrown*
In all her functions weary of herself;
My race of glory run, and race of shame,
And I shall shortly be with them that rest.[4]
MANOA Believe not these suggestions which proceed

2. See Judges 15.19: "But God clave an hollow place that was in the jaw [or "in Lehi"], and there came water thereout."
3. Pertaining to genius or natural disposition.
4. In lines 581–98, Milton seems to have remembered the exchange between Jason and Phineus in Apollonius Rhodius, *Argonautica* 2.438–48.

From anguish of the mind and humors black,[5]
That mingle with thy fancy.° I however *imagination*
Must not omit a Father's timely care
To prosecute° the means of thy deliverance *persist in*
By ransom or how else: meanwhile be calm,
And healing words from these thy friends admit.

SAMSON O that torment should not be confined
To the body's wounds and sores
With maladies innumerable
In heart, head, breast, and reins;° *kidneys*
But must secret passage find
To th' inmost mind,
There exercise all his fierce accidents,° *symptoms*
And on her purest spirits prey,
As on entrails, joints, and limbs,
With answerable° pains, but more intense, *corresponding*
Though void of corporal sense.
My griefs not only pain me
As a lingring disease,
But finding no redress, ferment and rage,
Nor less than wounds immedicable
Rankle, and fester, and gangrene,
To black mortification.° *decay*
Thoughts, my tormenters, armed with deadly stings
Mangle my apprehensive° tenderest parts, *sensitive*
Exasperate,° exulcerate,° and raise *worsen / infect*
Dire inflammation which no cooling herb
Or medicinal liquor can assuage,
Nor breath of vernal air from snowy alp.
Sleep hath forsook and given me o'er
To death's benumbing opium as my only cure.
Thence faintings, swoonings of despair,
And sense of heaven's desertion.
I was his nursling once and choice delight,
His destined from the womb,
Promised by heavenly message twice descending.
Under his special eye
Abstemious I grew up and thrived amain;
He led me on to mightiest deeds
Above the nerve° of mortal arm *muscle*
Against the uncircumcised, our enemies.
But now hath cast me off as never known,
And to those cruel enemies,
Whom I by his appointment° had provok't, *command*
Left me all helpless with th' irreparable loss
Of sight, reserved alive to be repeated° *spoken of as*
The subject of their cruelty or scorn.
Nor am I in the list of them that hope;

5. The black humor was melancholy (black bile).

Hopeless are all my evils, all remediless;
This one prayer yet remains, might I be heard,
No long petition: speedy death,
The close of all my miseries, and the balm.
CHORUS Many are the sayings of the wise
In antient and in modern books enrolled;
Extolling patience as the truest fortitude;
And to the bearing well of all calamities,
All chances incident to man's frail life[6]
Consolatories° writ *writings of comfort*
With studied argument, and much persuasion sought[7]
Lenient of grief and anxious thought,[8]
But with th' afflicted in his pangs their sound
Little prevails, or rather seems a tune,
Harsh, and of dissonant mood from his complaint,
Unless he feel within
Some source of consolation from above;
Secret refreshings, that repair his strength,
And fainting spirits uphold.
God of our Fathers, what is man![9]
That thou towards him with hand so various,
Or might I say contrarious,° *opposed*
Temper'st thy providence through his short course,
Not evenly, as thou rulest
The angelic orders and inferiour creatures mute,
Irrational and brute.
Nor do I name of men the common rout,
That wandring loose about
Grow up and perish, as the summer fly,
Heads without name no more rememberd,
But such as thou hast solemnly elected,
With gifts and graces eminently adorned
To some great work, thy glory,
And people's safety, which in part they effect:
Yet toward these thus dignified, thou oft
Amidst their height of noon,
Changest thy countenance, and thy hand with no regard
Of highest favors past
From thee on them, or them to thee of service.
Nor only dost degrade them, or remit
To life obscured, which were a fair dismission,° *dismissal*
But throw'st them lower than thou didst exalt them high,
Unseemly falls in human eye,
Too grievous for the trespass or omission,
Oft leav'st them to the hostile sword
Of heathen and profane, their carcasses

6. Echoing Shakespeare's *Timon of Athens* 5.1.203–5: "With other incident throes / That nature's fragile vessel doth sustain / In life's uncertain voyage."
7. Persuasion painstakingly constructed.
8. Tending to soothe; see Horace, *Epistles* 1.1.34: "There are words and sayings with which you may soothe the pain."
9. See Psalms 8.4: "What is man, that thou art mindful of him?"

To dogs and fowls a prey, or else captívéd:[1]
Or to the unjust tribunals, under change of times,
And condemnation of the ingrateful multitude.
If these they scape, perhaps in poverty
With sickness and disease thou bow'st them down,
Painful diseases and deformed,
In crude° old age; *premature*
Though not disordinate,° yet causless suffering *immoderate*
The punishment of dissolute days, in fine,
Just or unjust, alike seem miserable,
For oft alike, both come to evil end.
  So deal not with this once thy glorious champion,
The image of thy strength, and mighty minister.
What do I beg? how hast thou dealt already?
Behold him in this state calamitous, and turn
His labors, for thou canst, to peaceful end.
  But who is this, what thing of sea or land?
Femal of sex it seems,
That so bedeckt, ornate, and gay,
Comes this way sailing
Like a stately ship
Of Tarsus,[2] bound for th' Isles
Of Javan or Gadier[3]
With all her bravery on, and tackle trim,
Sails filled, and streamers waving,
Courted by all the winds that hold them play,° *move them*
An amber scent of odorous perfume
Her harbinger, a damsel train behind;
Some rich Philistian matron she may seem,
And now at nearer view, no other certain
Than Dalila thy wife.

SAMSON My wife, my traitress, let her not come near me.

CHORUS Yet on she moves, now stands and eyes thee fixed,
About t' have spoke, but now, with head declined
Like a fair flower surcharged with dew, she weeps
And words addressed seem into tears dissolved,
Wetting the borders of her silken veil:
But now again she makes address° to speak. *prepares*

DALILA With doubtful feet and wavering resolution
I came, still dreading thy displeasure, Samson,
Which to have merited, without excuse
I cannot but acknowledge; yet if tears
May expiate° (though the fact° more evil drew *make amends for/deed*
In the perverse event° than I foresaw) *outcome*
My penance hath not slackened, though my pardon
No way assured. But conjugal affection
Prevailing over fear, and timerous doubt

1. Echoing Homer, *Iliad* 1.4–5: the dead in the Trojan war are "made a spoil for dogs and all manner of birds."
2. The biblical phrase "ships of Tarshish" (i.e., probably Tartessus in southern Spain) is found in Isaiah 23.1, 14 and Psalm 48.7.
3. Ionian isles. Javan, son of Japhet (Genesis 10.2) and grandson of Noah, was the supposed ancestor of the Ionians. "Gadire" is Cadiz, on the southern coast of Spain.

Hath led me on desirous to behold
Once more thy face, and know of thy estate.
If aught in my ability may serve
To lighten what thou suffer'st, and appease
Thy mind with what amends is in my power,
Though late, yet in some part to recompense
My rash but more unfortunate misdeed.

SAMSON Out, out Hyaena;[4] these are thy wonted arts,
And arts of every woman false like thee,
To break all faith, all vows, deceive, betray,
Then as repentant to submit, beseech,
And reconcilement move with feigned remorse,
Confess, and promise wonders in her change,
Not truly penitent, but chief to try
Her husband, how far urged his patience bears,
His virtue or weakness which way to assail:
Then with more cautious and instructed skill
Again transgresses, and again submits;
That wisest and best men full oft beguiled
With goodness principled not to reject
The penitent, but ever to forgive,
Are drawn to wear out miserable days,
Entangled with a poisonous bosom snake,
If not by quick destruction soon cut off
As I by thee, to ages an example.

DALILA Yet hear me, Samson; not that I endeavor
To lessen or extenuate my offence,
But that on th' other side if it be weighed
By itself, with aggravations° not surcharged, *exaggerations*
Or else with just allowance counterpoised,
I may, if possible, thy pardon find
The easier towards me, or thy hatred less.
First granting, as I do, it was a weakness
In me, but incident to all our sex,
Curiosity, inquisitive, importune
Of secrets,[5] then with like infirmity
To publish them, both common female faults:
Was it not weakness also to make known
For importunity, that is for naught,
Wherein consisted all thy strength and safety?
To what I did thou show'dst me first the way.
But I to enemies revealed, and should not.
Nor shouldst thou have trusted that to womans frailty
E'er I to thee, thou to thyself wast cruel.[6]
Let weakness then with weakness come to parle° *talk*

4. According to Pliny 8.44, the hyena is believed to contain within itself both sexes, to imitate the human voice and thus lure men out to devour them, and to be the only animal that digs up graves to get at the bodies of the dead. Magicians, he says (28.27), believe that it has magical powers and can deprive human beings of their senses. All these attributes help to give point to Samson's abuse. See also Jonson, *Volpone* 4.6.3: "now, thine eyes / Vie tears with the hyaena."

5. Irksomely persistent in discovering secrets.

6. See Shakespeare, Sonnet 1: "to thy sweet self too cruel" (page 1169).

So near related, or the same of kind,
Thine forgive mine; that men may censure thine
The gentler, if severely thou exact not
More strength from me than in thyself was found.
And what if Love, which thou interpret'st hate,
The jealousy of love, powerful of sway
In human hearts, nor less in mine towards thee,
Caused what I did? I saw thee mutable
Of fancy, feared lest one day thou wouldst leave me
As her at Timna, sought by all means therefore
How to endear and hold thee to me firmest:
No better way I saw than by importuning
To learn thy secrets, get into my power
Thy key of strength and safety: thou wilt say,
Why then revealed? I was assured by those
Who tempted me, that nothing was designed
Against thee but safe custody, and hold:[7]
That made for me,° I knew that liberty *was to my advantage*
Would draw thee forth to perilous enterprises,
While I at home sat full of cares and fears
Wailing thy absence in my widowed bed;
Here I should still enjoy thee day and night
Mine and love's prisoner, not the Philistines',
Whole to myself, unhazarded abroad,
Fearless at home of partners in my love.
These reasons in Love's law have passed for good,
Though fond and reasonless to some perhaps;
And love hath oft, well meaning, wrought much woe,
Yet always pity or pardon hath obtained.
Be not unlike all others, not austere
As thou art strong, inflexible as steel.
If thou in strength all mortals dost exceed,
In uncompassionate anger do not so.

SAMSON How cunningly the sorceress displays
Her own transgressions, to upbraid me mine!
That malice not repentance brought thee hither,
By this appears: I gave, thou say'st, th' example,
I led the way; bitter reproach, but true,
I to myself was false ere thou to me,
Such pardon therefore as I give my folly,
Take to thy wicked deed: which when thou seest
Impartial, self-severe, inexorable,
Thou wilt renounce thy seeking, and much rather
Confess it feigned; weakness is thy excuse,
And I believe it, weakness to resist
Philistian gold: if weakness may excuse,
What murderer, what traitor, parricide,
Incestuous, sacrilegious, but may plead it?
All wickedness is weakness: that plea therefore

7. In Judges 16.5 the Lords of the Philistines say to Dalila: "Entice him . . . that we may bind him to afflict him."

With God or man will gain thee no remission.
But love constrained thee; call it furious rage
To satisfy thy lust: love seeks to have love;
My love how couldst thou hope, who tookst the way
To raise in me inexpiable hate,
Knowing, as needs I must, by thee betrayed?
In vain thou striv'st to cover shame with shame,
Or by evasions thy crime uncover'st more.

DALILA Since thou determin'st weakness for no plea
In man or woman, though to thy own condemning,
Hear what assaults I had, what snares besides,
What sieges girt me round, ere I consented;
Which might have awed the best resolved of men,
The constantest to have yielded without blame.
It was not gold, as to my charge thou lay'st,
That wrought with me: thou know'st the magistrates
And princes of my country came in person,
Solicited, commanded, threatened, urged,
Adjured by all the bonds of civil duty
And of religion, pressed how just it was,
How honorable, how glorious to entrap
A common enemy, who had destroyed
Such numbers of our nation: and the priest[8]
Was not behind, but ever at my ear,
Preaching how meritorious with the gods
It would be to ensnare an irreligious
Dishonorer of Dagon: what had I
To oppose against such powerful arguments?
Only my love of thee held long debate;
And combated in silence all these reasons
With hard contest: at length that grounded maxim
So rife and celebrated in the mouths
Of wisest men; that to the public good
Private respects must yield; with grave authority
Took full possession of me and prevailed;
Virtue, as I thought, truth, duty so enjoining.

SAMSON I thought where all thy circling wiles would end;
In feigned religion, smooth hypocrisy.
But had thy love, still odiously pretended,
Been, as it ought, sincere, it would have taught thee
Far other reasonings, brought forth other deeds.
I before all the daughters of my tribe
And of my nation chose thee from among
My enemies, loved thee, as too well thou knew'st,
Too well, unbosomed all my secrets to thee,
Not out of levity, but over-powered
By thy request, who could deny thee nothing;[9]
Yet now am judged an enemy. Why then

8. No priest is mentioned in the biblical account.

9. Echoes *Othello* 3.3.76: "I will deny thee nothing," and 5.2.351, where Othello says he "lov'd not wisely, but too well" (pages 1217 and 1260).

Didst thou at first receive me for thy husband?
Then, as since then, thy country's foe professed:
Being once a wife, for me thou wast to leave
Parents and country; nor was I their subject,
Nor under their protection but my own,
Thou mine, not theirs: if aught against my life
Thy country sought of thee, it sought unjustly,
Against the law of nature, law of nations,[1]
No more thy country, but an impious crew
Of men conspiring to uphold their state
By worse then hostile deeds, violating the ends
For which our country is a name so dear;
Not therefore to be obeyed. But zeal moved thee;
To please thy gods thou didst it; gods unable
To acquit themselves and prosecute their foes
But by ungodly deeds, the contradiction
Of their own deity, Gods cannot be:
Less therefore to be pleased, obeyed, or feared,
These false pretexts and varnished colors° failing, *specious excuses*
Bare in thy guilt how foul must thou appear?

DALILA In argument with men a woman ever
Goes by the worse, whatever be her cause.

SAMSON For want of words no doubt, or lack of breath,
Witness when I was worried with thy peals.[2]

DALILA I was a fool, too rash, and quite mistaken
In what I thought would have succeeded best.
Let me obtain forgiveness of thee, Samson,
Afford me place to show what recompense
Towards thee I intend for what I have misdone,
Misguided; only what remains past cure
Bear not too sensibly,° nor still insist *feel not too acutely*
To afflict thyself in vain: though sight be lost,
Life yet hath many solaces, enjoyed
Where other senses want not their delights
At home in leisure and domestic ease,
Exempt from many a care and chance to which
Eye-sight exposes daily men abroad.
I to the lords will intercede, not doubting
Their favorable ear, that I may fetch thee
From forth this loathsome prison-house, to abide
With me, where my redoubled love and care
With nursing diligence, to me glad office,
May ever tend about thee to old age
With all things grateful cheered, and so supplied,
That what by me thou hast lost thou least shalt miss.

SAMSON No, no, of my condition take no care;
It fits not; thou and I long since are twain;
Nor think me so unwary or accurst

1. Echoes *Troilus and Cressida* 2.2.184–5: "these moral laws / Of nature and of nations."

2. See line 235.

To bring my feet again into the snare
Where once I have been caught; I know thy trains° *snares*
Though dearly to my cost, thy gins° and toils;° *traps / harassment*
Thy fair enchanted cup and warbling charms[3]
No more on me have power, their force is nulled,
So much of adder's wisdom I have learned
To fence my ear against thy sorceries.[4]
If in my flower of youth and strength, when all men
Loved, honoured, feared me, thou alone could hate me
Thy husband, slight me, sell me, and forgo me;
How wouldst thou use me now, blind, and thereby
Deceiveable, in most things as a child
Helpless, thence easily contemned, and scorned,
And last neglected? How wouldst thou insult
When I must live uxorious to thy will
In perfet thraldom, how again betray me,
Bearing my words and doings to the lords
To gloss upon, and censuring, frown or smile?
This gaol° I count the house of liberty *jail*
To thine whose doors my feet shall never enter.

DALILA Let me approach at least, and touch thy hand.

SAMSON Not for thy life, lest fierce remembrance wake
My sudden rage to tear thee joint by joint.
At distance I forgive thee, go with that;
Bewail thy falsehood, and the pious works
It hath brought forth to make thee memorable
Among illustrious women, faithful wives:
Cherish thy hastened widowhood with the gold
Of matrimonial treason: so farewell.

DALILA I see thou art implacable, more deaf
To prayers, than winds and seas, yet winds to seas
Are reconciled at length, and sea to shore:
Thy anger, unappeasable, still rages,
Eternal tempest never to be calmed.
Why do I humble thus myself, and suing
For peace, reap nothing but repulse and hate?
Bid go with evil omen and the brand
Of infamy upon my name denounced?
To mix with thy concernments I desist
Henceforth, nor too much disapprove my own.
Fame if not double-faced is double-mouthed,[5]
And with contrary blast proclaims most deeds,
On both his wings, one black, th' other white,
Bears greatest names in his wild airy flight.
My name perhaps among the circumcised

3. Alludes to the Circe story (*Odyssey* 10).
4. The proverb "As deaf as an adder" originated in Psalm 58.4: "They are like the deaf adder that stoppeth her ears."
5. No source has been found for Milton's representation of Fame as male, double-mouthed, and with one wing black and one wing white. In Chaucer's *House of Fame* (1571–1582, 1637), Fame employs Aeolus, god of winds, as trumpeter, and he has two trumpets, one golden, "Clear Laud," and the other black, "Slander."

In Dan,[6] in Judah, and the bordering tribes,
To all posterity may stand defamed,
With malediction mentioned, and the blot
Of falsehood most unconjugal traduced.
But in my country where I most desire,
In Ekron, Gaza, Asdod, and in Gath[7]
I shall be named among the famousest
Of women, sung at solemn festivals,
Living and dead recorded, who to save
Her country from a fierce destroyer, chose
Above the faith of wedlock-bands, my tomb
With odors° visited and annual flowers. *from burnt spices*
Not less renowned than in Mount Ephraim,
Jael, who with inhospitable guile
Smote Sisera sleeping through the temples nailed.[8]
Nor shall I count it heinous to enjoy
The public marks of honor and reward
Conferred upon me, for the piety
Which to my country I was judged to have shown.
At this who ever envies or repines
I leave him to his lot, and like my own.[9]

CHORUS She's gone, a manifest serpent by her sting
Discovered in the end, till now concealed.

SAMSON So let her go; God sent her to debase me,
And aggravate my folly who committed
To such a viper his most sacred trust
Of secrecy, my safety, and my life.

CHORUS Yet beauty, though injurious, hath strange power,
After offense returning, to regain
Love once possessed, nor can be easily
Repulsed, without much inward passion felt
And secret sting of amorous remorse.

SAMSON Love-quarrels oft in pleasing concord end,
Not wedlock-treachery endangering life.

CHORUS It is not virtue, wisdom, valor, wit,
Strength, comeliness of shape, or amplest merit
That woman's love can win or long inherit;° *hold*
But what it is, hard is to say,
Harder to hit,
(Which way soever men refer it)
Much like thy riddle,[1] Samson, in one day
Or seven, though one should musing sit;
If any of these or all, the Timnian bride

6. Samson's tribe.
7. Four of the five chief Philistine cities.
8. In Judges 4.21, Jael, Heber's wife, kills Sisera, the Canaanite general, by driving a nail into his temples as he sleeps after taking refuge in her tent from Barak and the Israelites. Jael's praises are sung (Judges 5.24) by Barak and by the prophetess Deborah, who lived (Judges 4.5) in Mount Ephraim.
9. See Sophocles, *Ajax* 1038–39: "If there be any in whose mind this wins no favor, let him hold to his own thoughts, as I hold to mine."
1. See Judges 14.8–14: Samson, finding that bees have made honey in the carcass of the lion he killed, sets the 30 companions a riddle, "Out of the eater came forth meat, and out of the strong came forth sweetness," and gives them seven days to solve it.

Had not so soon preferred
Thy paranymph,[2] worthless to thee compared,
Successor in thy bed,
Nor both° so loosely disallied *both wives*
Their nuptials, nor this last so treacherously
Had shorn the fatal harvest of thy head.
Is it for that such outward ornament
Was lavished on their sex, that inward gifts
Were left for haste unfinished, judgment scant,
Capacity not raised to apprehend
Or value what is best
In choice, but oftest to affect the wrong?
Or was too much of self-love mixed,
Of constancy no root infixed,
That either they love nothing, or not long?
  Whate'er it be, to wisest men and best
Seeming at first all heavenly under virgin veil,
Soft, modest, meek, demure,
Once joined, the contrary she proves,[3] a thorn[4]
Intestine°, far within defensive arms *domestic*
A cleaving[5] mischief, in his way to virtue
Adverse and turbulent, or by her charms
Draws him awry enslaved
With dotage, and his sense depraved
To folly and shameful deeds which ruin ends.
What pilot so expert but needs must wreck
Embarked with such a steers-mate at the helm?
  Favored of Heaven who finds
One virtuous rarely found,
That in domestic good combines:
Happy that house! his way to peace is smooth:[6]
But virtue which breaks through all opposition,
And all temptation can remove,
Most shines and most is acceptable above.
  Therefore God's universal law
Gave to the man despotic power
Over his female in due awe,
Nor from that right to part an hour,
Smile she or lour:
So shall he least confusion draw
On his whole life, not swayed
By female usurpation, nor dismayed.
  But had we best retire, I see a storm?
SAMSON Fair days have oft contracted wind and rain.

2. Groomsman. In Judges 14.20, Samson's wife is given to his groomsman; see line 227.
3. In the *Doctrine and Discipline of Divorce,* Milton says that "The sobrest and best govern'd men are least practiz'd in these affairs; and who knows not that the bashful mutenes of a virgin may oft-times hide all the unlivelines and naturall sloth which is really unfit for conversation."
4. See 2 Corinthians 12.7: "a thorn in the flesh."
5. Perhaps a reference to the poisoned shirt sent to Hercules by Deianira in hope of regaining his love (Sophocles, *Trachiniae*); see Euripides, *Orestes* 605–606: "Women were born to mar the lives of men / Ever, unto their surer overthrow."
6. See Proverbs 31.10–28.

CHORUS But this another kind of tempest brings.
SAMSON Be less abstruse, my riddling days[7] are past.
CHORUS Look now for no enchanting voice, nor fear
The bait of honeyed words; a rougher tongue
Draws hitherward, I know him by his stride,
The giant Harapha[8] of Gath, his look
Haughty as is his pile° high-built and proud. *frame*
Comes he in peace? What wind hath blown him hither
I less conjecture than when first I saw
The sumptuous Dalila floating this way:
His habit carries peace, his brow defiance.
SAMSON Or peace or not, alike to me he comes.
CHORUS His fraught° we soon shall know, he now arrives. *cargo*
HARAPHA I come not, Samson, to condole thy chance,
As these perhaps, yet wish it had not been,
Though for no friendly intent. I am of Gath;
Men call me Harapha, of stock renowned
As Og or Anak and the Emims old
That Kiriathaim held,[9] thou knowst me now
If thou at all art known.° Much I have heard *knowledgeable*
Of thy prodigious might and feats performed
Incredible to me, in this displeased,
That I was never present on the place
Of those encounters where we might have tried
Each other's force in camp or listed° field: *open or enclosed*
And now am come to see of whom such noise
Hath walked about, and each limb to survey,
If thy appearance answer loud report.
SAMSON The way to know were not to see but taste.° *try*
HARAPHA Dost thou already single° me; I thought *challenge*
Gyves° and the mill had tamed thee; O that fortune *chains*
Had brought me to the field where thou art famed
To have wrought such wonders with an Ass's jaw;
I should have forced thee soon with other arms,
Or left thy carcass where the ass lay thrown:
So had the glory of prowess been recovered
To Palestine, won by a Philistine
From the unforeskinned race, of whom thou bear'st
The highest name for valiant acts, that honor
Certain to have won by mortal duel from thee,
I lose, prevented by thy eyes put out.
SAMSON Boast not of what thou wouldst have done, but do
What then thou would'st; thou seest it in thy hand.
HARAPHA To combat with a blind man I disdain,

7. See lines 1016–17.

8. Milton has invented this giant, a Philistine whose sons were slain by David and his servants (an allusion to 2 Samuel 21.20). The name "Harapha" translates as "the giant."

9. "Og," see Deuteronomy 3.2: "Only Og king of Bashan remained of the remnant of the giants"; "Anak," see Numbers 13.33: "And there we saw the giants, the sons of Anak . . . and we were in our own sight as grasshoppers"; "Emims . . . Kiriathaim," see Deuteronomy 2.10–11: "The Emims dwelt therein . . . Which also were accounted giants," and Genesis 14.5: "the Emims in Shaveh ["the plain of"] Kiriathaim."

And thou hast need much washing to be touched.
SAMSON Such usage as your honorable lords
Afford me assassinated° and betrayed, *wounded by treachery*
Who durst not with their whole united powers
In fight withstand me single and unarmed,
Nor in the house with chamber ambushes
Close-banded durst attack me, no not sleeping,
Till they had hired a woman with their gold
Breaking her marriage faith to circumvent me.
Therefore without feigned shifts let be assigned
Some narrow place enclosed, where sight may give thee,
Or rather flight, no great advantage on me;
Then put on all thy gorgeous arms, thy helmet
And brigandine of brass, thy broad habergeon,
Vant-brass and greaves, and gauntlet, add thy spear
A weaver's beam, and seven-times-folded shield,[1]
I only with an oaken staff will meet thee,
And raise such outcries on thy clattered iron,
Which long shall not withhold me from thy head,
That in a little time while breath remains thee,
Thou oft shalt wish thy self at Gath to boast
Again in safety what thou wouldst have done
To Samson, but shalt never see Gath more.
HARAPHA Thou durst not thus disparage glorious arms
Which greatest heroes have in battle worn,
Their ornament and safety, had not spells
And black enchantments, some magician's art
Armed thee or charmed thee strong, which thou from heaven
Feignd'st at thy birth was given thee in thy hair,
Where strength can least abide, though all thy hairs
Were bristles ranged like those that ridge the back
Of chaf't° wild boars, or ruffled porcupines. *angered*
SAMSON I know no spells, use no forbidden arts;
My trust is in the living God who gave me
At my nativity this strength, diffused
No less through all my sinews, joints and bones,
Then thine, while I preserved these locks unshorn,
The pledge of my unviolated vow.
For proof hereof, if Dagon be thy god,
Go to his temple, invocate his aid
With solemnest devotion, spread before him
How highly it concerns his glory now
To frustrate and dissolve these magic spells,
Which I to be the power of Israel's God
Avow, and challenge Dagon to the test,
Offering to combat thee, his champion bold,
With th' utmost of his godhead seconded:

1. Brigandine: body armor of metal rings or plates sewn on canvas or leather; habergeon: sleeveless coat of mail; vantbrace: armor for the fore-arm; weaver's beam: the wooden roller in a loom on which the warp is wound before weaving, and the similar roller on which the cloth is wound as it is woven—(see 1 Samuel 17.7, of Goliath: "the staff of his spear was like a weaver's beam"); shield: see the shield of Ajax (*Iliad* 7.220), made of seven layers of bull's hide.

Then thou shalt see, or rather to thy sorrow
Soon feel, whose God is strongest, thine or mine.

HARAPHA Presume not on thy God, whate'er he be,
Thee he regards not, owns not, hath cut off
Quite from his people, and delivered up
Into thy enemies' hand, permitted them
To put out both thine eyes, and fettered send thee
Into the common prison, there to grind
Among the slaves and asses, thy comrades,
As good for nothing else, no better service
With those thy boist'rous locks, no worthy match
For valor to assail, nor by the sword
Of noble warrior, so to stain his honor,
But by the barber's razor best subdued.

SAMSON All these indignities, for such they are
From thine,° these evils I deserve and more, *thy people*
Acknowledge them from God inflicted on me
Justly, yet despair not of his final pardon
Whose ear is ever open; and his eye
Gracious to re-admit the suppliant;
In confidence whereof I once again
Defy thee to the trial of mortal fight,
By combat to decide whose god is God,
Thine or whom I with Israel's sons adore.

HARAPHA Fair honor that thou dost thy God, in trusting
He will accept thee to defend his cause,
A murderer, a revolter, and a robber.

SAMSON Tongue-doughty giant, how dost thou prove me these?

HARAPHA Is not thy nation subject to our lords?
Their magistrates confest it, when they took thee
As a league-breaker and delivered bound
Into our hands:[2] for hadst thou not committed
Notorious murder on those thirty men
At Askalon, who never did thee harm,
Then like a robber stripd'st them of their robes?[3]
The Philistines, when thou hadst broke the league,
Went up with armed powers thee only seeking,
To others did no violence nor spoil.

SAMSON Among the daughters of the Philistines
I chose a wife, which argued me no foe;
And in your city held my nuptial feast:
But your ill-meaning politician lords,
Under pretense of bridal friends and guests,
Appointed to await me thirty spies,[4]
Who threatening cruel death constrained the bride

2. See lines 259–64.

3. See Judges 14.19. Samson had wagered "thirty change of garments" that his "companions" would not be able to solve his riddle. They extracted the answer from his wife, so he killed 30 men at Ascalon and took their clothes to be able to pay the wager.

4. There is nothing in Judges to support this claim that the 30 "companions" were spies. However, Josephus, *Antiquities* 5.8, says, "now the people of Timnath, out of dread of the young man's strength, gave him during the time of the wedding feast . . . thirty of the most stout of their youth, in pretence to be his companions, but in reality to be a guard upon him, that he might not attempt to give them any disturbance."

To wring from me and tell to them my secret,
That solved the riddle which I had proposed.
When I perceived all set on enmity,
As on my enemies, wherever chanced,
I used hostility, and took their spoil
To pay my underminers in their coin.[5]
My nation was subjected to your lords.
It was the force of conquest; force with force
Is well ejected when the conquered can.
But I a private person, whom my country
As a league-breaker gave up bound, presumed
Single rebellion and did hostile acts.
I was no private but a person raised
With strength sufficient and command from heaven
To free my Country; if their servile minds
Me their deliverer sent would not receive,
But to their masters gave me up for nought,
Th' unworthier they; whence to this day they serve.
I was to do my part from heaven assigned,
And had performed it if my known offense
Had not disabled me, not all your force:
These shifts refuted, answer thy appellant° *challenger*
Though by his blindness maimed for high attempts,
Who now defies thee thrice[6] to single fight,
As a petty enterprise of small enforce.° *effort*

HARAPHA With thee a man condemned, a slave enrolled,
Due by the law to capital punishment?
To fight with thee no man of arms will deign.

SAMSON Camest thou for this, vain boaster, to survey me,
To descant on my strength, and give thy verdict?
Come nearer, part not hence so slight informed;
But take good heed my hand survey not thee.

HARAPHA O Baal-zebub! can my ears unused[7]
Hear these dishonors, and not render death?

SAMSON No man withholds thee, nothing from thy hand
Fear I incurable; bring up thy van,° *vanguard*
My heels are fettered, but my fist is free.

HARAPHA This insolence other kind of answer fits.

SAMSON Go, baffled° coward, lest I run upon thee, *disgraced*
Though in these chains, bulk without spirit vast,
And with one buffet lay thy structure low,
Or swing thee in the air, then dash thee down
To the hazard of thy brains and shattered sides.

HARAPHA By Astaroth[8] ere long thou shalt lament
These braveries in irons loaden on thee.

CHORUS His Giantship is gone somewhat crestfallen,

5. They threatened to kill to win a wager; he killed to pay it; underminers: secret assailants.
6. Previously at lines 1151 and 1175.
7. Baal-zebub: God of the flies; a Philistine idol, with temple at Ekron, 2 Kings 1.2. Unused: not used to hearing "dishonors."
8. The plural form of Astareth, supreme goddess of the Phoenicians representing fertility and passion; identical with the Syrian Astarte.

Stalking with less unconscionable° strides, *excessive*
And lower looks, but in a sultry chafe.
SAMSON I dread him not, nor all his giant-brood,
Though fame divulge him father of five sons
All of gigantic size, Goliah chief.[9]
CHORUS He will directly to the lords, I fear,
And with malicious counsel stir them up
Some way or other yet further to afflict thee.
SAMSON He must allege some cause, and offered fight
Will not dare mention, lest a question rise
Whether he durst accept the offer or not,
And that he durst not plain enough appeared.
Much more affliction then already felt
They cannot well impose, nor I sustain;
If they intend advantage of my labors
The work of many hands, which earns my keeping
With no small profit daily to my owners.
But come what will, my deadliest foe will prove
My speediest friend, by death to rid me hence,
The worst that he can give, to me the best.
Yet so it may fall out, because their end
Is hate, not help to me, it may with mine
Draw their own ruin who attempt the deed.
CHORUS Oh how comely it is[1] and how reviving
To the Spirits of just men long opprest!
When God into the hands of their deliverer
Puts invincible might
To quell the mighty of the earth, th' oppressor,
The brute and boist'rous force of violent men
Hardy and industrious to support
Tyrannic power, but raging to pursue
The righteous and all such as honor truth;
He all their ammunition° *military supplies*
And feats of war defeats
With plain heroic magnitude of mind
And celestial vigor armed,
Their armories and magazines contemns,
Renders them useless, while
With winged expedition
Swift as the lightning glance he executes
His errand on the wicked, who surprised
Lose their defence distracted and amazed.
But patience is more oft the exercise
Of saints, the trial of their fortitude,
Making them each his own deliverer,
And victor over all
That tryranny or fortune can inflict,
Either of these is in thy lot,

9. See 2 Samuel 21.16–22.

1. See Ecclesiasticus 25.4–5: "O how comely a thing is judgment . . . O how comely is the wisdom of old men!"

Samson, with might endued
Above the sons of men; but sight bereaved
May chance to number thee with those
Whom patience finally must crown.
This idol's day hath bin to thee no day of rest,
Laboring thy mind
More than the working day thy hands,
And yet perhaps more trouble is behind.
For I descry this way
Some other tending, in his hand
A scepter or quaint° staff he bears, *elaborate*
Comes on amain, speed in his look.
By his habit I discern him now
A public officer, and now at hand.
His message will be short and voluble.° *straightforward*

OFFICER Hebrews, the prisoner Samson here I seek.

CHORUS His manacles remark° him, there he sits. *distinguish*

OFFICER Samson, to thee our lords thus bid me say;
This day to Dagon is a solemn feast,
With sacrifices, triumph, pomp, and games;
Thy strength they know surpassing human rate,
And now some public proof thereof require
To honor this great feast and great assembly;
Rise therefore with all speed and come along,
Where I will see thee heartened and fresh clad
To appear as fits before th' illustrious lords.

SAMSON Thou knowst I am an Hebrew, therefore tell them,
Our law forbids[2] at their religious rites
My presence; for that cause I cannot come.

OFFICER This answer, be assured, will not content them.

SAMSON Have they not sword-players, and every sort
Of gymnic° artists, wrestlers, riders, runners, *gymnastic*
Juglers and dancers, antics,° mummers,° mimics, *clowns/mimes*
But they must pick me out with shackles tired,
And over-labored at their public mill,
To make them sport with blind activity?
Do they not seek occasion of new quarrels
On my refusal to distress me more,
Or make a game of my calamities?
Return the way thou camest, I will not come.

OFFICER Regard thyself, this will offend them highly.

SAMSON My self? My conscience and internal peace.
Can they think me so broken, so debased
With corporal servitude, that my mind ever
Will condescend to such absurd commands?
Although their drudge, to be their fool or jester,
And in my midst of sorrow and heart-grief
To show them feats and play before their god,
The worst of all indignities, yet on me

2. See Exodus 20.4–5, 23.24.

Joined° with extreme contempt? I will not come. *charged*
OFFICER My message was imposed on me with speed,
Brooks no delay: is this thy resolution?
SAMSON So take it with what speed thy message needs.
OFFICER I am sorry what this stoutness° will produce. *pride*
SAMSON Perhaps thou shalt have cause to sorrow indeed.
CHORUS Consider, Samson; matters now are strained
Up to the height, whether to hold or break;
He's gone, and who knows how he may report
Thy words by adding fuel to the flame?
Expect another message more imperious,
More lordly thundering than thou well wilt bear.
SAMSON Shall I abuse this consecrated gift
Of strength, again returning with my hair
After my great transgression, so requite
Favor renewed, and add a greater sin
By prostituting holy things to idols;
A Nazarite in place abominable
Vaunting my strength in honor to their Dagon?
Besides, how vile, contemptible, ridiculous,
What act more execrably unclean, profane?
CHORUS Yet with this strength thou serv'st the Philistines,
Idolatrous, uncircumcised, unclean.
SAMSON Not in their idol-worship, but by labor
Honest and lawful to deserve my food
Of those who have me in their civil power.
CHORUS Where the heart joins not, outward acts defile not.[3]
SAMSON Where outward force constrains, the sentence° holds *maxim*
But who constrains me to the temple of Dagon,
Not dragging? the Philistian lords command.
Commands are no constraints. If I obey them,
I do it freely; venturing to displease
God for the fear of man, and man prefer,
Set God behind: which in his jealousy[4]
Shall never, unrepented, find forgiveness.
Yet that he may dispense with° me or thee *grant pardon to*
Present in temples at idolatrous rites
For some important cause, thou needst not doubt.
CHORUS How thou wilt here come off° surmounts my reach. *escape*
SAMSON Be of good courage, I begin to feel
Some rousing motions in me which dispose
To something extraordinary my thoughts.
I with this messenger will go along,
Nothing to do, be sure, that may dishonor
Our law, or stain my vow of Nazarite.
If there be aught of presage in the mind,
This day will be remarkable in my life

3. See Aristotle, *Ethics* 3.1.1: "It is only voluntary actions for which praise and blame are given; those that are involuntary are condoned, and sometimes even pitied."

4. See Exodus 20.5: "I the Lord thy God am a jealous God."

By some great act, or of my days the last.[5]
CHORUS In time thou hast resolved, the man returns.
OFFICER Samson, this second message from our lords
To thee I am bid say. Art thou our slave,
Our captive, at the public mill our drudge,
And dar'st thou at our sending and command
Dispute thy coming? Come without delay;
Or we shall find such engines to assail
And hamper thee, as thou shalt come of force,
Though thou wert firmlier fastened than a rock.
SAMSON I could be well content to try their art,
Which to no few of them would prove pernicious.
Yet knowing their advantages too many,
Because they shall not trail me through their streets
Like a wild beast, I am content to go.
Masters' commands come with a power resistless
To such as owe them absolute subjection;
And for a life who will not change his purpose?
(So mutable are all the ways of men.)
Yet this be sure, in nothing to comply
Scandalous or forbidden in our law.
OFFICER I praise thy resolution, doff these links:
By this compliance thou wilt win the lords
To favor, and perhaps to set thee free.
SAMSON Brethren farewell, your company along
I will not wish, lest it perhaps offend them
To see me girt with friends; and how the sight
Of me as of a common enemy,
So dreaded once, may now exasperate them
I know not. Lords are lordliest in their wine;
And the well-feasted priest then soonest fired
With zeal, if aught religion seem concerned:
No less the people on their holy-days
Impetuous, insolent, unquenchable;[6]
Happen what may, of me expect to hear
Nothing dishonorable, impure, unworthy
Our God, our law, my nation, or myself,
The last of me or no I cannot warrant.
CHORUS Go, and the Holy One
Of Israel be thy guide
To what may serve his glory best, and spread his name
Great among the heathen round:
Send thee the angel of thy birth, to stand
Fast by thy side, who from thy father's field
Rode up in flames after his message told
Of thy conception,[7] and be now a shield

5. Milton is perhaps indebted to Sophocles, *Trachiniae* 1169–73, where Heracles realizes that the oracle that foretold release from his labors meant death to him, not final prosperity.

6. See Horace, *Ars Poetica* 224: "The spectator, after the rites had been observed, was drunk and in a lawless mood."

7. See line 24ff.

Of fire; that spirit that first rusht on thee
In the camp of Dan[8]
Be efficacious in thee now at need.
For never was from heaven imparted
Measure of strength so great to mortal seed,
As in thy wond'rous actions hath been seen.
But wherefore comes old Manoa in such haste
With youthful steps? much livelier then erewhile
He seems: supposing here to find his son,
Or of him bringing to us some glad news?

MANOA Peace with you brethren; my inducement hither
Was not at present here to find my son,
By order of the lords new parted hence
To come and play before them at their feast.
I heard all as I came, the city rings
And numbers thither flock, I had no will,
Lest I should see him forced to things unseemly.
But that which moved my coming now, was chiefly
To give ye part with me what hope I have
With good success° to work his liberty. *outcome*

CHORUS That hope would much rejoice us to partake
With thee; say, reverend sire, we thirst to hear.

MANOA I have attempted° one by one the lords *sought to influence*
Either at home, or through the high street passing,
With supplication prone° and father's tears *prostrated*
To accept of ransom for my son their prisoner,
Some much averse I found and wondrous harsh,
Contemptuous, proud, set on revenge and spite;
That part most reverenced Dagon and his priests,
Others more moderate seeming, but their aim
Private reward, for which both god and state
They easily would set to sale, a third
More generous far and civil, who confessed
They had enough revenged, having reduced
Their foe to misery beneath their fears,
The rest was magnanimity to remit,
If some convenient ransom were proposed.
What noise or shout was that? it tore the sky.

CHORUS Doubtless the people shouting to behold
Their once great dread, captive, and blind before them,
Or at some proof of strength before them shown.

MANOA His ransom, if my whole inheritance
May compass it, shall willingly be paid
And numbered down: much rather I shall choose
To live the poorest in my tribe, than richest,
And he in that calamitous prison left.
No, I am fixed not to part hence without him.
For his redemption all my patrimony,
If need be, I am ready to forgo

8. See Judges 13.25, also 14.6: "the Spirit of the Lord came mightily upon him."

And quit: not wanting him, I shall want nothing.
CHORUS Fathers are wont to lay up for their sons,
Thou for thy son art bent to lay out all;
Sons wont to nurse their parents in old age,
Thou in old age carest how to nurse thy son
Made older then thy age through eyesight lost.
MANOA It shall be my delight to tend his eyes,
And view him sitting in the house, enobled
With all those high exploits by him achieved,
And on his shoulders waving down those locks,
That of a nation armed the strength contained:
And I persuade me God had not permitted
His strength again to grow up with his hair
Garrisoned round about him like a camp
Of faithful soldiery, were not his purpose
To use him further yet in some great service,
Not to sit idle with so great a gift
Useless, and thence ridiculous about him.
And since his strength with eyesight was not lost,
God will restore him eyesight to his strength.
CHORUS Thy hopes are not ill founded, nor seem vain
Of his delivery, and thy joy thereon
Conceived, agreeable to a father's love,
In both which we, as next° participate. *of kin*
MANOA I know your friendly minds and—O what noise!
Mercy of heaven, what hideous noise was that!
Horribly loud unlike the former shout.
CHORUS Noise call you it or universal groan
As if the whole inhabitation perished,
Blood, death, and deathful deeds are in that noise,
Ruin, destruction at the utmost point.
MANOA Of ruin indeed methought I heard the noise,
Oh it continues, they have slain my son.
CHORUS Thy Son is rather slaying them, that outcry
From slaughter of one foe could not ascend.
MANOA Some dismal accident it needs must be;
What shall we do, stay here or run and see?
CHORUS Best keep together here, lest running thither
We unawares run into danger's mouth.[9]
This evil on the Philistines is fallen,
From whom could else a general cry be heard?
The sufferers then will scarce molest us here,
From other hands we need not much to fear.
What if his eyesight (for to Israel's God
Nothing is hard) by miracle restored,
He now be dealing dole[1] among his foes,
And over heaps of slaughtered walk his way?
MANOA That were a joy presumptuous to be thought.
CHORUS Yet God hath wrought things as incredible

9. There is a similarly hesitant chorus in Euripides, *Hippolytus* 782–85.

1. A pun; "dole" means "that which is dealt" and also "grief, pain."

For his people of old; what hinders now?
MANOA He can, I know, but doubt to think he will;
Yet Hope would fain subscribe, and tempts belief.
A little stay will bring some notice hither.
CHORUS Of good or bad so great, of bad the sooner;
For evil news rides post, while good news baits.° *travels slowly*
And to our wish I see one hither speeding,
An Hebrew, as I guess, and of our tribe.
MESSENGER O whither shall I run, or which way fly
The sight of this so horrid spectacle
Which erst my eyes beheld and yet behold;
For dire imagination still persues me.
But providence or instinct of nature seems,
Or reason though disturbed, and scarse consulted
To have guided me aright, I know not how,
To thee first reverend Manoa, and to these
My Countrymen, whom here I knew remaining,
As at some distance from the place of horror,
So in the sad event too much concerned.
MANOA The accident was loud, and here before thee
With rueful cry, yet what it was we hear not,
No preface needs, thou seest we long to know.
MESSENGER It would burst forth, but I recover breath
And sense distract, to know well what I utter.
MANOA Tell us the sum, the circumstance defer.
MESSENGER Gaza yet stands, but all her sons are fallen,
All in a moment overwhelmed and fallen.
MANOA Sad, but thou knowst to Israelites not saddest
The desolation of a hostile city.
MESSENGER Feed on that first, there may in grief be surfeit.[2]
MANOA Relate by whom.
MESSENGER By Samson.
MANOA That still lessens
The sorrow, and converts it nigh to joy.
MESSENGER Ah, Manoa, I refrain, too suddenly
To utter what will come at last too soon;
Lest evil tidings with too rude irruption° *bursting in*
Hitting thy aged ear should pierce too deep.
MANOA Suspense in news is torture, speak them out.
MESSENGER Then take the worst in brief: Samson is dead.[3]
MANOA The worst indeed, O all my hope's defeated
To free him hence! but death who sets all free
Hath paid his ransom now and full discharge.
What windy° joy this day had I conceived *vain*
Hopeful of his delivery, which now proves
Abortive as the first-born bloom of spring
Nipped with the lagging rear of winter's frost.[4]

2. Echoes Shakespeare's *Two Gentlemen of Verona* 3.1.220–1: "O, I have fed upon this woe already, / And now excess of it will make me surfeit."
3. See the announcement of Orestes' death in Sophocles, *Electra* 673: "In short, Orestes is dead."
4. Echoing *Love's Labour's Lost* 1.1.100–101: "An envious-sneaping frost, / That bites the first born infants of the spring."

Yet ere I give the rains to grief, say first,
How died he? death to life is crown or shame.
All by him fell, thou say'st, by whom fell he,
What glorious hand gave Samson his death's wound?

MESSENGER Unwounded of his enemies he fell.

MANOA Wearied with slaughter then, or how? Explain.

MESSENGER By his own hands.

MANOA Self-violence? What cause
Brought him so soon at variance with himself
Among his foes?

MESSENGER Inevitable cause
At once both to destroy and be destroyed;
The edifice where all were met to see him
Upon their heads and on his own he pulled.

MANOA O lastly over-strong against thy self!
A dreadful way thou took'st to thy revenge.
More than enough we know; but while things yet
Are in confusion, give us if thou canst,
Eye-witness of what first or last was done,
Relation more particular and distinct.

MESSENGER Occasions° drew me early to this city, *business*
And as the gates I entered with sun-rise,
The morning trumpets festival proclaimed
Through each high street: little° I had dispatched *little business*
When all abroad was rumored that this day
Samson should be brought forth to show the people
Proof of his mighty strength in feats and games;
I sorrowed at his captive state, but minded
Not to be absent at that spectacle.
The building was a spacious theatre
Half round on two main pillars vaulted high,
With seats where all the lords and each degree
Of sort, might sit in order to behold,
The other side was open, where the throng
On banks° and scaffolds under sky might stand;[5] *benches*
I among these aloof obscurely stood.
The feast and noon grew high, and sacrifice
Had filled their hearts with mirth, high cheer, and wine,
When to their sports they turned. Immediately
Was Samson as a public servant brought,
In their state livery clad; before him pipes
And timbrels, on each side went armed guards,
Both horse and foot before him and behind
Archers, and slingers, cataphracts° and spears.° *soldiers / spearsmen*
At sight of him the people with a shout
Rifted the air clamoring their god with praise,
Who had made their dreadful enemy their thrall.
He patient but undaunted where they led him,
Came to the place, and what was set before him
Which without help of eye, might be assayed,

5. See Judges 16.27, where the building is called a "house" and has 3,000 men and women on the roof.

To heave, pull, draw, or break, he still performed
All with incredible, stupendious force,
None daring to appear antagonist.
At length for intermission sake they led him
Between the pillars; he his guide requested
(For so from such as nearer stood we heard)
As overtired to let him lean a while
With both his arms on those two massy pillars
That to the arched roof gave main support.[6]
He unsuspicious led him; which when Samson
Felt in his arms, with head a while inclined,
And eyes fast fixed he stood, as one who prayed,[7]
Or some great matter in his mind revolved.
At last with head erect thus cried aloud,
"Hitherto, Lords, what your commands imposed
I have performed, as reason was, obeying,
Not without wonder or delight beheld.
Now of my own accord such other trial
I mean to show you of my strength, yet greater;
As with amaze° shall strike all who behold." *confusion*
This uttered, straining all his nerves he bowed,
As with the force of winds and waters pent,
When mountains tremble, those two massy pillars
With horrible convulsion to and fro
He tugged, he shook, till down they came and drew
The whole roof after them, with burst of thunder
Upon the heads of all who sat beneath,
Lords, ladies, captains, councellors, or priests,
Their choice nobility and flower, not only
Of this but each Philistian city round
Met from all parts to solemnize this feast.
Samson with these immixed, inevitably
Pulled down the same destruction on himself;
The vulgar° only scaped who stood without.[8] *commoners*

CHORUS O dearly-bought revenge, yet glorious!
Living or dying thou hast fulfilled
The work for which thou wast foretold
To Israel, and now liest victorious
Among thy slain self-killed
Not willingly, but tangled in the fold
Of dire necessity, whose law in death conjoined
Thee with thy slaughtered foes in number more
Then all thy life had slain before.[9]

SEMICHORUS While their hearts were jocund and sublime,° *exalted*
Drunk with idolatry, drunk with wine,
And fat regorged° of bulls and goats, *reswallowed*

6. See Judges 16.26: "And Samson said unto the lad that held him by the hand, Suffer me that I may feel the pillars whereupon the house standeth, that I may lean upon them."
7. In Judges 16.30, Samson prays: "Let me [Hebrew: "my soul"] die with the Philistines." The speech, with its suicidal implications, was one of the major obstacles to those who wished to regard Samson as a saint. In the Scholastic period his suicide was excused as the prompting of the Holy Ghost.
8. Not found in the scriptural account (Judges 16.30).
9. See Judges 16.30: "The dead which he slew at his death were more than they which he slew in his life."

Chaunting their idol, and preferring
Before our living Dread who dwells
In Silo[1] his bright sanctuary:
Among them he a spirit of frenzy sent,
Who hurt their minds,
And urged them on with mad desire
To call in haste for their destroyer;
They only set on sport and play
Unweetingly importuned
Their own destruction to come speedy upon them.
So fond° are mortal men *foolish*
Fallen into wrath divine,
As their own ruin on themselves to invite,
Insensate left, or to sense reprobate,[2]
And with blindness internal struck.

SEMICHORUS But he though blind of sight,
Despised and thought extinguished quite,
With inward eyes illuminated
His fiery virtue roused
From under ashes into sudden flame,
And as an evening dragon° came, *huge python*
Assailant on the perched roosts,
And nests in order ranged
Of tame villatic° fowl; but as an eagle *farmyard*
His cloudless thunder bolted on their heads.
So virtue given for lost,
Depressed, and overthrown, as seemed,
Like that self-begotten bird[3]
In the Arabian woods embossed,° *sheltered*
That no second knows nor third,[4]
And lay erewhile a holocaust,[5]
From out her ashy womb now teemed,° *delivered*
Revives, reflourishes, then vigorous most
When most unactive deemed,
And though her body die, her fame survives,
A secular° bird, ages of lives. *centuries-long*

MANOA Come, come, no time for lamentation now,
Nor much more cause; Samson hath quit himself
Like Samson, and heroicly hath finished
A life heroic, on his enemies
Fully revenged, hath left them years of mourning,
And lamentation to the sons of Caphtor[6]
Through all Philistian bounds. To Israel
Honour hath left, and freedom, let but them
Find courage to lay hold on this occasion,

1. Where the ark remained from the time of Joshua until "the people sent to Shiloh, that they might bring from thence the ark of the covenant" (1 Samuel 4.4).

2. Either left senseless, or left to a reprobate sense; see Romans 1.28: "God gave them over to a reprobate mind."

3. The Phoenix, a symbol of resurrection. See Geoffrey Whitney, *The Phoenix,* in Perspectives: Emblem, Style and Metaphor, page 1599.

4. Only one phoenix lives at a time.

5. A thing wholly consumed by fire.

6. The Philistines; see line 380.

To himself and father's house eternal fame;
And which is best and happiest yet, all this
With God not parted from him, as was feared,
But favoring and assisting to the end.
Nothing is here for tears, nothing to wail
Or knock the breast, no weakness, no contempt,
Dispraise, or blame, nothing but well and fair,
And what may quiet us in a death so noble.
Let us go find the body where it lies
Soaked in his enemies' blood, and from the stream
With lavers° pure and cleansing herbs wash off *washbasins*
The clotted gore. I with what speed° the while *what speed I can*
(Gaza is not in plight to say us nay)
Will send for all my kindred, all my friends
To fetch him hence and solemnly attend
With silent obsequy° and funeral train *burial rite*
Home to his father's house:[7] there will I build him
A monument, and plant it round with shade
Of laurel ever green, and branching palm,
With all his trophies hung, and acts enrolled
In copious legend, or sweet lyric song.
Thither shall all the valiant youth resort,
And from his memory inflame their breasts
To matchless valor, and adventures high:
The virgins also shall on feastful days
Visit his tomb with flowers, only bewailing
His lot unfortunate in nuptial choice,
From whence captivity and loss of eyes.

CHORUS All is best, though we oft doubt,
What th' unsearchable dispose
Of highest wisdom brings about,
And ever best found in the close.[8]
Oft he seems to hide his face,[9]
But unexpectedly returns
And to his faithful champion hath in place° *at hand*
Bore witness gloriously; whence Gaza mourns
And all that band them to resist
His uncontrollable intent,
His servants he with new acquist° *acquisition*
Of true experience from this great event
With peace and consolation hath dismissed,
And calm of mind all passion spent.[1]

The End.

7. See Judges 16.31: "Then his brethren and all the house of his father came down, and took him, and brought him up, and buried him."

8. See the closing chorus of Euripides, *Alcestis* 1160–64: "Manifold things unhoped-for the gods to accomplishment bring . . . So fell this marvelous thing." The same chorus is used at the end of *Andromache*, *Bacchae*, *Helen*, and in *Medea* (with a different first line: "All dooms be of Zeus in Olympus: 'tis his to reveal them").

9. See Psalm 104.29: "Thou hidest thy face, they are troubled" (also Psalm 30.7 and 27.9).

1. The poem ends in the rhyme scheme of a sonnet, which is noteworthy considering Milton's argument on "The Verse" prefacing *Paradise Lost*: "Rime being no necessary Adjunct or true Ornament of Poem or good Verse . . . , but the Invention of a barbarous Age, to set off wretched matter and lame meter."

PERSPECTIVES

Spiritual Self-Reckonings

As the title of this section suggests, autobiographical writing in early modern England was tied to religious experience, the individual, and the act of reckoning. Just as the Civil War was fought largely over religious differences, so allegiance to a particular interpretation of Christianity, usually tied to a specific institution and set of beliefs and practices, was one of the chief shapers of identity in the seventeenth century. All the accounts in this section relate a life as lived from the perspective of belief—from Elizabeth Cary's conversion to Catholicism to John Bunyan's Puritan salvation by grace, from Anna Trapnel's ecstatic visions to the preacher Ralph Josselin's sober reflections on his daily blessings. The fictional Robinson Crusoe experiences a dramatic conversion on being saved from death by drowning, just as Alice Thornton renews her trust in salvation every time she recovers from the sickness brought on by the death of a child or a near-fatal labor.

The status of the self is necessarily qualified by religion; it is impossible to speak of self-knowledge in isolation from knowledge of God in this period. The selves that are described in these accounts are shaped by the literary forms their narratives take. In the case of Elizabeth Cary, Lady Falkland, her daughter chose to tell her story as a kind of spiritual biography, in which all the events, even including her quarrels with Calvinist theology in youth, tend to converge on the moment of her conversion. In some sense the mother's story may also be a way for the daughter, a Benedictine nun as well as a convert to Catholicism, to witness her own religious experience. For Anna Trapnel the life story takes the form of a testimonial that relates her trial for witchcraft, a drama of persecution from which she emerges triumphant in her reliance on God. Diarists such as Alice Thornton and Ralph Josselin also rely on God as they struggle with their daily trials. Among these is often the struggle for life itself, as in the pregnancies and labors of Alice Thornton and of Ralph Josselin's wife. With Bunyan and Defoe, autobiography is fictionalized as both travel novel and salvational allegory. Both heroes are on journeys; both journeys, according to the authors, have allegorical significance.

The other major influence on these life stories is the rise of a certain way of accounting for material experience—that of time and of money. Reckoning entails counting, calculating, and recording. The journals of Alice Thornton and Ralph Josselin record dates. In his journal, Robinson Crusoe keeps a strict record of the number of days since his shipwreck. If Ralph Josselin reckons his capital in gains and debits, he also reckons his blessings to shore himself up against his losses. Similarly, Robinson Crusoe takes stock of himself by writing a ledger of his spiritual goods and evils. The language of credit gains importance toward the close of the century. As England becomes not just the battleground of saints, as it was in the Civil War, but the seat of empire, as it develops as a world trader and a colonial power, the "self" expresses itself in relation to Lady Credit as well as the Lord.

The Lady Falkland: Her Life

The Lady Falkland: Her Life is the first known biography of an Englishwoman by a woman. The text survives in a manuscript located in the Archives of the Département du Nord in Lille, France, a collection that contains documents from the Benedictine monastery of Our Blessed Lady of Consolation in Cambray, where four of Elizabeth Cary's six daughters became Benedictine nuns. Donald Foster has connected the italic hand of the manuscript with Anne Cary, who was born in 1615 and entered the convent in 1639. However, Margaret Ferguson and Barry Weller argue that Lucy Cary cannot be ruled out as possible author, since her obituary makes reference to the "Life of Lady Falkland," written by "one who knew her well."

The passage reprinted here, from the first half of the biography, highlights Elizabeth Cary's intellectual precociousness, theological questioning, obedience to her husband, devotion to her children, and, above all, her strong spiritual life despite her many trials. One of the most palpable expressions of Cary's spirituality was her philanthropy in Ireland. When her husband was Lord Deputy there (1622–29), Elizabeth set up a trade school to help poor children. In a characteristically seventeenth-century God-centered view of life, Cary, according to her daughter, viewed the failure of the enterprise as God's punishment for the forced conversion of the children from Catholicism to Protestantism. Although the selection here stops short of Cary's own conversion from Protestantism to Catholicism, her daughter writes from the perspective of that change as the defining event of her mother's spiritual life.

from The Lady Falkland Her Life, by one of Her Daughters

Her mother's name was Elizabeth Symondes. She was their only child. She was christened Elizabeth. She learnt to read very soon and loved it much. When she was but four or five year old they put her to learn French, which she did about five weeks and, not profiting at all, gave it over. After, of herself, without a teacher, whilst she was a child, she learnt French, Spanish, Italian, which she always understood very perfectly. She learnt Latin in the same manner (without being taught) and understood it perfectly when she was young, and translated the Epistles of Seneca out of it into English; after having long discontinued it, she was much more imperfect in it, so as a little afore her death, translating some (intending to have done it all had she lived) of Blosius[1] out of Latin, she was fain to help herself somewhat with the Spanish translation. Hebrew she likewise, about the same time, learnt with very little teaching; but for many year neglecting it, she lost it much; yet not long before her death, she again beginning to use it, could in the Bible understand well, in which she was most perfectly well read. She then learnt also, of a Transylvanian, his language, but never finding any use of it, forgot it entirely. She was skilful and curious in working,[2] ⟨but⟩ never having been helped by anybody; those that knew her would never have believed she knew how to hold a needle unless they had seen it.

Being once present when she was ⟨about⟩ ten year old, when a poor old woman was brought before her father for a witch, and, being accused for having bewitched two or 3 to death, the witness not being found convincing, her father asked the woman what she said for herself? She falling down before him trembling and weeping, confessed all to be true, desiring him to be good to her and she would mend. Then he asking her particularly, did you bewitch such a one to death? she answered yes. He asked her how she did it? One of her accusers, preventing her, said, "Did not you send your familiar in the shape of a black dog, a hare or a ⟨toad?⟩ cat, and he finding him asleep, licked his hand, or breathed on him, or stepped over him, and he presently came home sick and languished away?" She, quaking, begging pardon, acknowledged all, and the same of each particular accusation, with a several manner of doing it. Then the standers-by said, what would they have more than her own confession? But the child, seeing the poor woman in so terrible a fear, and in so simple a manner confess all, thought fear had made her idle,[3] so she whispered her father and desired him to ask her whether she had bewitched to death Mr John Symondes of such a place

1. Louis de Blois (1506–66), Benedictine mystic and author of devotional works such as *Institutio Spiritualis* ("Spiritual Instruction") and *Consolatio Pusillanimium* ("Comfort for the Fainthearted").

2. Needleworking. In the next phrase and onward, angle brackets indicate likely readings of illegible words in the manuscript.

3. Delirious.

(her uncle that was one of the standers-by). He did so, to which she said yes, just as she had done to the rest, promising to do so no more if they would have pity on her. He asked how she did it? She told one of her former stories; then (all the company laughing) he asked her what she ailed to say so? told her the man was alive, and stood there. She cried, "Alas, sir, I knew him not, I said so because you asked me." Then he, "Are you no witch then?" ⟨(says he)⟩ "No, God knows," says she, "I know no more what belongs to it than the child newborn." "Nor did you never see the devil?" She answered, "No, God bless me, never in all my life." Then he examined her what she meant to confess all this, if it were false? She answered they had threatened her if she would not confess, and said, if she would, she should have mercy showed her—which she said with such simplicity that (the witness brought against her being of little force, and her own confession appearing now to be of less) she was easily believed innocent, and [ac]quitted.

She having neither brother nor sister, nor other companion of her age, spent her whole time in reading; to which she gave herself so much that she frequently read all night; so as her mother was fain to forbid her servants to let her have candles, which command they turned to their own profit, and let themselves be hired by her to let her have them, selling them to her at half a crown apiece, so was she bent to reading; and she not having money so free, was to owe it them, and in this fashion was she in debt a hundred pound afore she was twelve year old, which with two hundred more ⟨afore⟩ for the like bargains and promises she paid on her wedding day; this will not seem strange to those that knew her well. When she was twelve year old, her father (who loved much to have her read, and she as much to please him) gave her Calvin's *Institutions*[4] and bid her read it, against which she made so many objections, and found in him so many contradictions, and with all of them she still went to her father, that he said, "This girl hath a spirit averse from Calvin."

At fifteen year old, her father married her to one Sir Harry Cary (son to Sir Edward Cary of Barkhamsteed in Harfordshire), then Master of the Jewel House to Queen Elizabeth. He married her only for being an heir, for he had no acquaintance with her (she scarce ever having spoke to him) and she was nothing handsome, though then very fair. The first year or more she lived at her own father's; her husband about that time went into Holland, leaving her ⟨there⟩ still with her own friends.[5] He, in the time they had been married, had been for the most part at the court or his father's house, from her, and ⟨so⟩ had heard her speak little, and those letters he had received from her had been indited by others, by her mother's appointment, so he knew her then very little.

Soon after his being gone, his mother must needs have her to her, and, her friends not being able to satisfy the mother-in-law with any excuse, were fain to send her; though her husband had left her with them till his return, knowing his own mother well, and desiring (though he did not care for his wife) to have her be where she should be best content. Her mother-in-law having her, and being one that loved much to be humored, and finding her not to apply herself to it, used her very hardly, so far, as at last, to confine her to her chamber; which seeing she little cared for, but entertained herself with reading, the mother-in-law took away all her books, with command to have no more brought her; then she set herself to make verses. There was only two in the whole house (besides her own servants) that ever came to see

4. *Institutes of the Christian Religion* (1536) defines the central doctrines of Calvinist theology, including moral election and predestination for redemption.
5. Relatives.

her, which they did by stealth: one of her husband's sisters and a gentlewoman that waited on her mother-in-law. (To the first of them, she always, all her life after, showed herself a very true friend in all occasions wheresoever she was able ⟨to⟩; of the other (being gone from her mother-in-law's service) she never gave over to take care till she died, she [the gentlewoman] having continual recourse to her when she had need, who ever provided her places with her children or friends, and helped her in the meantime.) But her husband returning (who had been taken prisoner in the Low Countries by the Spaniards, and carried prisoner into Spain, where he was kept a year whilst his father was raising his ransom),[6] all this was soon at an end, he being much displeased to see her so used.

In his absence he had received some letters from her, since she came from her mother, which seemed to him to be in a very different style from the former, which he had thought to have been her own. These he liked much, but believed some other did them, till, having examined her about it and found the contrary, he grew better acquainted with her and esteemed her more. From this time she writ many things for her private recreation, on several subjects, and occasions, all in verse (out of which she scarce ever writ anything that was not translations). One of them was after stolen out of that sister-in-law's (her friend's) chamber and printed, but by her own procurement was called in. Of all she then writ, that which was said to be the best was the life of Tamberlaine in verse.[7]

She continued to read much, and when she was about twenty year old, through reading, she grew into much doubt of her religion. The first occasion of it was reading a Protestant book much esteemed, called Hooker's *Ecclesiastical Polity*.[8] It seemed to her, he left her hanging in the air, for having brought her so far (which she thought he did very reasonably), she saw not how, nor at what, she could stop, till she returned to the church from whence they were come. This was more confirmed in her by a brother of her husband's returning out of Italy, with a good opinion of Catholic religion. His wit, judgment and ⟨company⟩ conversation she was much pleased withal. He was a great reader of the Fathers, especially St Augustine, whom he affirmed to be of the religion of the Church of Rome. He persuaded her to read the Fathers also (what she had read till then having been for the most part poetry and history, except Seneca, and some other such, whose Epistles it is probable she translated afore she left her father's house, because the only copy of it was found by her son in her father's study)—which she did upon his persuasion, all that she could meet with in French, Spanish or Italian. It may be she might then read some in Latin, but for many year only in the others.

Her distrust of her religion increased by reading them, so far as that at two several times she refused to go to church for a long while together. The first time she satisfied herself she might continue as she was, having a great mind to do so. The second time, going much to the house of a Protestant bishop,[9] which was frequented by many of the learnedest of their divines (out of the number of whose chaplains, those of the King's were frequently chosen, and some of their greatest bishops), she there grew acquaint[ed] with many of them, making great account of them, and using them with much respect (being ever more inclined to do so to any for their learning and

6. Spanish troops captured Henry Cary in October 1605, when he was fighting with a joint English-Dutch force.
7. Tamerlane (1336–1405), the Mongol military leader whose conquests are the subject of Christopher Marlowe's *Tamberlaine the Great*, Parts I and II (1587–1588).
8. Richard Hooker wrote *Of the Laws of Ecclesiastical Polity* (Books 1–4, 1593; Book 5, 1597) to defend the bishops of the Church of England.
9. Richard Neile, dean of Westminster (1605) and archbishop of York (1631).

worth, than for their greatness of quality, and she had learnt in the Fathers, and histories of former Christian times to bear a high reverence to the dignity they pretended to). By them she was persuaded she might lawfully remain as she was, she never making question for all that but that to be in the Roman Church were infinitely better and securer. Thus (from the first) she remained about two and twenty year, flattering herself with good intentions. She was in the house of the same bishop divers times present at the examination of such beginners, or receivers, of new opinions, as were by them esteemed heretics, where some (strangers to her), wondering to see her, asked the bishop how he durst trust that young lady to be there? who answered, he would warrant she would never be in danger to be an heretic, so much honor and adherence did she ever render to authority, where she ⟨conceived⟩ imagined it to be, much more where she knew it to be.

She was married seven year without any child; after, had eleven born alive.[1] When she had some children, she and her husband went to keep house by themselves, where she, taking the care of her family, which at first was but little, did seem to show herself capable of what she would apply herself to. She was very careful and diligent in the disposition of the affairs of her house of all sorts; and she herself would work hard, together with her women and her maids, curious pieces of work, teaching them and directing all herself; nor was her care of her children less, to whom she was so much a mother that she nursed them all herself, but only her eldest son[2] (whom her father took from her to live with him from his birth), and she taught 3 or 4 of the eldest. After, having other occasions to divert her, she left that to others, of whose care long experience might make her confident, for she never changed her servants about them, and whilst she was with them she was careful nothing in that kind might be wanting.

Her first care was (whether by herself or others) to have them soon inclined to the knowledge, love, and esteem of all moral virtue; and to have them according to their capacities instructed in the principles of Christianity, not in manner of a catechism (which would have instructed them in the particular Protestant doctrines, of the truth of which she was little satisfied), but in a manner more apt to make an impression in them (than things learnt by rote and not understood), as letting them know, when they loved anything, that they were to love God more than it; that he made it, and them, and all things; they must love him, and honor him, more than their father; he gave them their father, he sent them every good thing, and made it for them; the King was his servant, he made all kings, and gave them their kingdom[s?].

* * *

Being once like to die, whilst she had but two or 3 children, and those very little, that her care of them might not die with her, she writ (directed to her two eldest, a daughter and a son) a letter of some sheets of paper (to be given them when they were come to a more capable age), full of such moral precepts as she judged most proper for them, and such effect had this care of hers in the mind of her eldest daughter (for the forming of whose spirit and her instruction (though she were of a good nature) she had taken extraordinary pains, and ever found her again the most dutiful and best loving of all her children), that being married afore she was thirteen year old, and going then to live in the house of her mother-in-law (in which she yielded a great obedience to her father's will) where she lived till her death (which was

1. She had five sons and six daughters.

2. Lucius Cary (1610–1643), second Viscount Falkland, about whom Ben Jonson wrote in the *Cary-Morison Ode* (page 1538).

between sixteen and seventeen year old, in childbed of her first child), she being exceedingly beloved by her mother-in-law and all her family, her own mother asked her what she had done to gain all their affections in so great a degree? She said, indeed, she knew not anything that she did, unless that she had been careful to observe, as exactly as she could, the rule she had given her, when she took her leave of her at her first going from her: that wheresoever conscience and reason would permit her, she should prefer the will of another before her own.

Neither did she neglect to have those that were of a bigness capable of it (whilst she was with them) learn all those things that might be fit for them. She always thought it a most misbecoming thing in a mother to make herself more her business than her children and, whilst she had care of herself, to neglect them. Her doing was most contrary to this, being excessive in all that concerned their clothes or recreation, and she that never (not in her youth) could take care or delight in her own fineness, could apply herself to have too much care and take pleasure in theirs.

To her husband she bore so much respect that she taught her children, as a duty, to love him better than herself; and, though she saw it was a lesson they could learn without teaching, and that all but her eldest son did it in a very high degree, it never lessened her love or kindness to any of them. He was very absolute, and though she had a strong will, she had learnt to make it obey his. The desire to please him ⟨would⟩ had power to make her do that, that others would have scarce believed possible for her: as taking care of her house in all things (to which she could have no inclination but what his will gave her); the applying herself to use and love work;[3] and, being most fearful of a horse, both before and after, she did (he loving hunting and desiring to have her a good horsewoman) for many year ride so much, and so desperately, as if she had no fear but much delight in it; and so she had, to see him pleased, and did really make herself love it as long as that lasted. But after (as before) she neither had the courage, nor the skill, to sit upon a horse; ⟨and he left to desire it, after her having had a fall from her horse (leaping a hedge and ditch being with child of her fourth child, when she was taken up for dead though both she and her child did well), she being continually after as long as she lived with him either with child or giving suck⟩.

Dressing was all her life a torture to her, yet because he would have it so, she willingly supported it, all the while she lived with him, in her younger days, even to tediousness; but all that ever she could do towards it, was to have those about her that could do it well, and to take order that it should be done, and then endure the trouble; for though she was very careful it should be so, she was not able to attend to it all, nor ever was her mind the least engaged in it, but her women were fain to walk round the room after her (which was her custom) while she was seriously thinking on some other business, and pin on her things and braid her hair; and while she writ or read, curl her hair and dress her head; and it did sufficiently appear how alone for his will she did undergo the trouble by the extraordinary great carelessness she had of herself after he was angry with her, from which time she never went out of plain black, frieze or coarse stuff, or cloth.

Where his interest was concerned, she seemed not able to have any consideration of her own; which amongst other things, she showed in this: a considerable part of her jointure[4] (which upon her marriage had been made sufficiently good) having been reassumed to the crown, to which it had formerly belonged, a greater part of it (being all that remained, but some very small thing) she did on his occasions consent

3. Needlework.

4. The holding of property for a wife to be granted her in widowhood.

to have mortgaged; which act of hers did so displease her own father that he disinherited her upon it, putting before her, her two eldest (and then only) sons, tying his estate on the eldest and, in case he failed,[5] on the second. She showed herself always no less ready to avoid whatsoever might displease him. Of this all her life she gave many proofs; and after she was a Catholic, when he would neither speak to her nor see her, she forbore things most ordinarily done by all, and which she did much delight in, for hearing from some other that he seemed to dislike it; and where she did but apprehend it would not please him, she would not do the least thing, though on good occasion; so as she seemed to prefer nothing but religion and her duty to God before his will. The rules which she did, in some things she writ (and in her opinions), seem to think fit to be held in this, did displease many as overstrict. She did always much disapprove ⟨a⟩ the practice ⟨with⟩ of satisfying oneself with their conscience being free from fault, not forbearing all that might have the least show, ⟨of unfit⟩ or suspicion, of uncomeliness, or unfitness; what she thought to be required in this she expressed in this motto (which she caused [to be inscribed] in her daughter's wedding ring): be and seem.

In this time she had some occasions of trouble, which afflicted her so much as twice to put her into so deep melancholy ⟨(while she was with child of her 2[d] and 4th child) that she lost the perfect use of her reason, and was in much danger of her life. She had ground for the beginning of her apprehensions, but she giving full way to them (which were always apt to go as far as she would let them), they arrived so far as to be plain distractedness. It is like she at first gave the more way to it at those times, thinking her husband would then be most sensible of her trouble, knowing he was extraordinary careful of her when she was with child or gave suck, as being a most tenderly loving father.⟩ One of these times for fourteen days together she eat nor drunk nothing in the world, but only a little beer with a toast, yet without touching the toast, so as being great with child and quick, the child left to stir, and she became as flat as if she had not been with child at all. Yet after, coming out of her melancholy, the child and she did well.

From this time she seemed so far to have overcome all sadness that she was scarce ever subject to it on any occasion (but only once), but always looked on the best side of everything, and what good every accident brought with it. Her greatest sign of sadness (after) was sleeping, which she was used to say she could do when she would, and then had most will to when she had occasion to have sad thoughts waking; which she much sought to avoid, and it seemed could (for the most part) do it, when she gave herself to it; and she could well divert others in occasions of trouble, having sometimes with her conversation much lightened the grief of some, suddenly, in that which touched them nearliest. This occasion of her own trouble being past, she did so far pardon the causers of it as to some of them she showed herself a most faithful and constant friend, to others so careful a provider and reliever in their necessities that she was by some (that knew her but afar off, and were not witness of what she had suffered) thought almost guilty of their faults.

She continued the care of her house till, her husband being made Controller of the King's Household, she came to live frequently at his lodgings at court; and her father-in-law dying, their family being increased, she put it into the hands of others. She continued her opinion of religion, and bore a great and high reverence to our Blessed Lady, to whom, being with child of her last daughter[6] (and still a Protestant) she offered up that child, promising if it were a girl it should (in devotion to her) bear

5. Died without a male heir.

6. Mary Cary, born c. 1621.

her name, and that as much as was in her power, she would endeavor to have it be a nun. Whilst she yet gave suck to the same child, she went into Ireland,[7] with her lord and all her children, except her eldest daughter (who, just before her going, was married into Scotland). Being there, she had much affection to that nation, and was very desirous to have made use of ⟨her⟩ what power she had on any occasion in their behalf, as also in that of any Catholics. She there learnt to read Irish in an Irish Bible; but it being very hard (so as she could scarce find one that could teach it) and few books in it, she quickly lost what she had learnt.

Here chiefly the desire of the benefit and commodity of that nation set her upon a great design. It was to bring up the use of all trades in that country, which is fain to be beholding to others for the smallest commodities. To this end she procured some of each kind to come from those other places where those trades are exercised (as several sorts of linen and woolen weavers, dyers, all sorts of spinners, and knitters, hatters, lace makers, and many other trades) at the very beginning; and for this purpose she took of beggar children (with which that country swarms) more than 8 score prentices, refusing none above seven year old, and taking some less. These were disposed to their several masters and mistresses to learn those trades they were thought most fit for, the least amongst them being set to something, as making points, tags, buttons, or lace, or some other thing. They were parted in their several rooms and houses, where they exercised their trades, many rooms being filled with little boys or girls, sitting all round at work; besides those that were bigger, for trades needing more understanding and strength. She brought it to that pass that they there made broadcloth so fine and good (of Irish wool, and spun and weaved and dyed and dressed there) that her Lord, being Deputy, wore it.

Yet it came to nothing; which she imputed to a judgment of God on her, because the overseers made all those poor children go to church; and she had great losses by fire and water (which she judged extraordinary, others but casual).[8] Her workhouse, with all that was in it, much cloth and much materials, was burnt; her fulling mills carried away; and much of her things spoiled with water—all which when she was a Catholic she took to be the punishment of God for the children's going to church, and that therefore her business did not succeed. But others thought it rather that she was better at contriving than executing, and that too many things were undertaken at the very first, and that she was fain (having little choice) to employ either those that had little skill in the matters they dealt in, or less honesty, and so she was extremely cozened,[9] which she was most easily, though she were not a little suspicious in her nature; but chiefly the ill order she took for paying money in this (as in all other occasions). Having the worst memory, in such things, in the world, and wholly trusting to it (or them she dealt with), and never keeping any account of what she did, she was most subject to pay the same thing often (as she hath had it confessed to her, by some, that they have (in a small matter) made her pay them the same thing five times in five days). Neither would she suffer herself to be undeceived by them that stood by and saw her do it frequently; rather suspecting they said it out of dislike of her designs, and to divert her from them; and the same unwillingness she had to see she was cozened, in all things on which she was set with such violence (as she was on all the things she undertook, which were many), which violence in all

7. Henry Cary's tenure as Lord Deputy of Ireland (1622–1629) was characterized by such policies as the suppression of the Roman Catholic clergy and continued colonization.

8. She thought these events were due to God's anger while others saw them as accidents.

9. Tricked or deceived.

occasions made her ever subject to necessities (even when she had most), and made her continually pawn and sell anything she had (though it were a thing she should need (almost) within an hour after) to procure what she had a mind to at the present: the same violence made her subject to make great promises to those that assisted her in those things which, being many, could not always be performed. It made her, too, to acknowledge small things, done at the instants she desired them, so great (and without regarding to whom it was) that, if it chanced to be to such as would claim a requital according to the acknowledgment (and not the worth of the thing), at a greater distance, looking on it with truer eyes, what she had said could not always be stood to.

About these works, after the beginning of them, her lord seemed often displeased with her; yet rather with the manner of ordering it than the thing itself, which she knew not how to mend. It would have been in his power easily to have made her give over; but she conceived what he showed in it was rather not to engage his own credit in the success of it, than that he desired to have her leave it; and in this she after saw herself not deceived; for, some letters of his, to others, came after to her hands, where she saw he highly praised that for which he had often chidden her, and that he affirmed it would have been to the exceeding great benefit of that kingdom, could it have been well prosecuted.

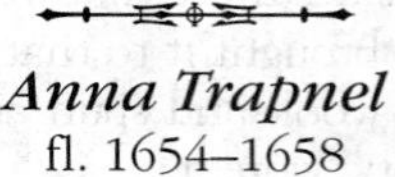

Anna Trapnel
fl. 1654–1658

During the English Civil War, some 300 women publicly testified to their visions. Among them one of the most outspoken was Anna Trapnel, whose prophecies (either written by her or transcribed from her testimony) were published in *The Cry of a Stone* (1654), *Strange and Wonderful Newes from White-Hall* (1654), *Anna Trapnel's Report and Plea* (1654), *A Legacy for Saints* (1654), and A *Voice for the King of Saints* (1658). Anna first discovered her power of prophecy while listening to a sermon the day after her mother's death. Inspired by visions and by Scripture, Anna was a Fifth Monarchist, belonging to a radical Puritan group who believed that Jesus was about to return to reign on earth. Supporters of the overthrow of Charles I, they turned against Cromwell when he set himself up as Lord Protector in Charles's place. Trapnel's excited spontaneous performances—a mixture of prophecy, trances, visions, and songs—drew large audiences and brought on the wrath of the government. She was charged with witchcraft and sentenced to prison for almost six months. When she was brought to trial, the authorities tried to silence her, but she spoke out, calling on the crowds outside to witness that it was God who spoke through her. In her remarks "To the Reader," she indicates that the civil and religious authorities viewed her behavior as madness and witchcraft. Such charges against her, including that she was "a monster or some ill-shaped creature" rather than "a woman like others that were modest and civil," necessitated her going into print. Her *Report and Plea* (1654), from which the following excerpt is taken, is an autobiography that contains several different forms—the narrative of events, political argument, and even the drama of her interrogation in court. At the close of her text she triumphantly reports that she had effectively convinced her audience that "this woman is no witch."

from Anna Trapnel's Report and Plea

Then the Lord made his rivers flow, which soon broke down the banks of an ordinary capacity, and extraordinarily mounted my spirits into a praying and singing frame, and so they remained till morning light, as I was told, for I was not capable of that.

But when I had done, and was a while silent, I came to speak weakly to those about me, saying, "I must go to bed, for I am very weak"; and the men and women went away, and my friend that tended me, and some other maids, helped me to bed, where I lay till the afternoon, they said, silent. And that time I had a vision of the minister's wife stirring against me; and she was presented to me as one enviously bent against me, calling that falsity which she understood not. And I saw the clergyman and the jurors contriving an indictment against me, and I saw myself stand before them; in a vision I saw this. And I sang with much courage, and told them I feared not them nor their doings, for that I had not deserved such usage.

But while I was singing praises to the Lord for his love to me, the justices sent their constable to fetch me, who came and said he must have me with him. And he pulled, and called me, they said that were by, but I was not capable thereof. They said he was greatly troubled how to have me to his master; they told him he had better obey God than man. And his hand shook, they said, while he was pulling me. Then some went to the justices to tell them I could not come. But they would not be pacified. Some offered to be bound for my appearance next day, if I were in a capacity, but this was refused. They would have me out of my bed, unless some would take their oaths that it would endanger my life to be taken out of my bed, which none could do, without they had loved to take false oaths, like some others in those parts. Then a friend persuaded them to see whether they could put me out of that condition, and told them I was never known to be put out of it; so they came. Justice Launce, now a Parliament-man, was one of them, I was told. These justices that came to fetch me out of my bed, they made a great tumult, them and their followers, in the house, and some came upstairs crying "A witch! A witch!", making a great stir on the stairs. And a poor honest man rebuking such that said so, he was tumbled downstairs and beaten too, by one of the justices' followers. And the justices made a great noise in putting out of my chamber where I lay many of my friends; and they said if my friends would not take me up, they would have some should take me up. One of my friends told them that they must fetch their silk gowns to do it then, for the poor would not do it. And they threatened much, but the Lord overruled them. They caused my eyelids to be pulled up, for they said I held them fast, because I would deceive the people; they spake to this purpose. One of the justices pinched me by the nose, and caused my pillow to be pulled from under my head, and kept pulling me, and calling me; but I heard none of all this stir and bustle. Neither did I hear Mr. Welstead, which I was told called to the rulers, saying, "a whip will fetch her up"; and he stood at the chamber door talking against me, and said, "She speaks nonsense." The women said, "Hearken, for you cannot hear, there is such a noise"; then he listened, and said, "Now she hears me speak, she speaks sense." And this clergyman durst not come till the rulers came, for then, they say, the witches can have no power over them: so that one depends upon another, rulers upon clergy, and clergy upon rulers.

And again, after they had made all the fury appear that the Lord permitted them to vent against me, they then went away, saying, "She will fall in a trance when we shall at any time call for her." The Lord kept me this day from their cruelty, which they had a good mind further to have let out against me. And that witch-trier woman of that town, some would fain have had come with her great pin which she used to thrust into witches to try them, but the Lord my God in whom I trust delivered me from their malice, making good that word to me in the Psalms,[1] "The rage of man

1. Psalm 76.10.

shall turn to thy praise, and the remnant of rages thou wilt restrain." Then further, to tell you how the Lord carried me in singing and prayer after they were gone two hours, as I was told, and then I came to myself; and being all alone, I blessed God for that quiet still day that I had. And the gentlewoman of the house coming into the chamber, I said, "Have I lain alone all this day? I have had a sweet day." She replied, and said, did not I hear the justices there, and the uproar that was in my chamber? I said, "No." Then she told me how they dealt by her house, bringing in their followers, and what a noise they made. Then another friend asked me whether I did not hear that stir. I said, "No." They wondered, and so did I when I heard the relation, which is much more than I will write, for I don't take delight to stir in such puddles, it's no pleasant work to me. But that truth engageth me to let the world know what men have acted against the pourings-out of the spirit in a dispensation beyond their understanding; they hearkened not to scripture advice, which would not have any judge that they know not.

After that day's tumult, at night many came to catch at my words. And it was very probable that the rulers sent some to watch for what could be had further against me. And there were two women, that they had got their names, who had promised them to swear against me, and of this I shall further speak when I come to it. But now I am telling of what passed that night mentioned: many people spake much to me, asking me questions, the which the Lord helped me to answer. And my friends kept most part of that night in prayer on my behalf. And many watched what they said in prayer, for there were listeners under the window, which fain would have had something to have informed against them. There was great endeavoring to have found a bill of indictment against Captain Langdon, but they could not; they could not vent their spleen, though they to the utmost desired it, the Lord would not let them have their evil desires herein. For though they in this would have brought him into contempt, yet they endeavored this that so I might want a surety, and then they had what they desired, which was to have cast me into the jail. But to leave that, and to tell you that I had the presence of the Lord with me that night abundantly, and my sleep was sweeter than at other times. My sister Langdon lay with me that night, and in the morning she told me that she could not sleep all night for thinking of my going to the sessions that day. She told me she wondered I could sleep so soundly all night. I told her I never had a sweeter night in my life, and as for my going before the rulers, I was no whit afraid or thoughtful, for I had cast my care upon the Lord, which I was persuaded would speak for me. Therefore I was not troubled nor afraid, for the Lord said to me, "Fear not, be not dismayed, I am thy God, and will stand by thee."[2]

Then I rose up, and prepared to go before them at sessions-house; and walking out in the garden before I went, I was thinking what I should say before the justices. But I was taken off from my own thoughts quickly, through the word, "Take no heed what thou shalt say; being brought before them for the Lord Christ's sake, he will give thee words. Dost thou know what they will ask thee? Therefore look to the Lord, who will give thee answers suitable to what shall be required of thee." So I was resolved to cast myself upon the Lord and his teaching. And though I had heard how the form of bills run, and of that word "Not guilty," according to the form of the bill, yet I said, "I shall not remember to say thus, if the Lord don't bid me say so; and if he bids me, I will say it." And this I thought, I would be nothing, the Lord should have all the praise, it being his due. So I went, the officer coming for me; and as I went

2. Isaiah 41.10.

along the street, I had followed me abundance of all manner of people, men and women, boys and girls, which crowded after me. And some pulled me by the arms, and stared me in the face, making wry faces at me, and saying, "How do you now? How is it with you now?" And thus they mocked and derided at me as I went to the sessions. But I was never in such a blessed self-denying lamb-like frame of spirit in my life as then; I had such lovely apprehensions of Christ's sufferings, and of that scripture which saith, "He went as a sheep, dumb before the shearers, he opened not his mouth; and when reviled, he reviled not again."[3] The Lord kept me also, so that I went silent to the sessions-house, which was much thronged with people: some said the sessions-house was never so filled since it was a sessions-house. So that I was a gazing-stock for all sorts of people, but I praise the Lord, this did not daunt me, nor a great deal more that I suffered that day, for the eternal grace of Jehovah surrounded me, and kept me from harm. So way was made for me to draw near to the table, which stood lower than the justices; and round the table sat the lawyers and others that attended them, and I with my friends that went with me stood by the lawyers, and the justices leaned over a rail, which railed them in together. Only I espied a clergyman at their elbow, who helped to make up their indictment, so that he could not be absent, though his pulpit wanted him, it being a fast-day, set apart by authority, which he broke without any scruple that so he might keep close to the work of accusation. But though he and the witch-trying woman looked steadfastly in my face, it did no way dismay me, nor the grim fierce looks of the justices did not daunt me, for as soon as I beheld them I remembered a dear friend to Christ, who smiled in the face of a great man that looked fiercely on him, and sat as a judge to condemn him for the testimony of Jesus; but this servant of the Lord looked cheerfully all the time of his accusations charged upon him. So I thinking upon that posture of his before those that acted against him, I begged the same cheerfulness, and I had the same courage to look my accusers in the face, which was no carnal boldness, though they called it so.

And when I came before them, Lobb, being the mouth of the court, as he was foreman of the jury he represented the whole court, and he first demanded my name, and I told him. And he said, "Anna Trapnel, here is a bill of indictment to be read, for you to give your answer concerning." Then Justice Lobb said, "Read the bill," so it was read to me; and Lobb said, "Are you guilty, or not?" I had no word to say at the present, but the Lord said to me, "Say 'not guilty,' according to the form of the bill." So I spoke it as from the Lord, who knew I was not guilty of such an indictment. Then said Lobb, "Traverse the bill to the next assizes";[4] so that was done. Then Lobb said I must enter into bond for my appearance at the next assizes, unto which I agreed. Then they demanded sureties, so I desired Captain Langdon and Major Bawden to be my sureties, unto which they were willing. So there were two recognizances drawn, one for my appearance, and the other bound me to the good behavior; and I was entered into both the recognizances £300, and my sureties as much, to both the recognizances. And this being done, they whispered a while, and I thought they had done with me at that time. So they had, if they had gone according to true law, which was not to have brought their interrogatories then; but the report was that I would discover myself to be a witch when I came before the justices, by having never a word to answer for myself, for it used to be so among the witches, they could not

3. Isaiah 53.7; 1 Peter 2.23.

4. Carry the case over to the next court session; Trapnel is next ordered to pledge a large sum (guaranteed by two wealthy friends) to ensure that she will reappear for the trial.

speak before the magistrates, and so they said it would be with me. But the Lord quickly defeated them herein, and caused many to be of another mind. Then Lobb said, "Tender her the book which was written from something said at Whitehall," so the book was reached out to me, and Justice Lobb said, "What say you to that book? Will you own it? Is it yours?"

A. T. "I am not careful to answer you in that matter."

Then they said, "She denies her book." Then they whispered with those behind them. Then spake Justice Lobb again, and said, "Read a vision of the horns out of the book," so that was read. Then Justice Lobb said, "What say you to this? Is this yours?"

A. T. "I am not careful to answer you in that matter, touching the whole book. As I told you before, so I say again. For what was spoken was at Whitehall, at a place of concourse of people, and near a council I suppose wise enough to call me into question if I offended, and unto them I appeal." But though it was said I appealed unto Caesar and unto Caesar should I go, yet I have not been brought before him which is called Caesar; so much by the by. Again, I said I supposed they had not power to question me for that which was spoke in another county; they said yea, that they had. Then the book was put by, and they again whispered.

Then Justice Lobb asked me about my coming into that country, how it came to pass that I came into that country.

I answered I came as others did that were minded to go into the country.

Lobb. "But why did you come into this country?"

A. T. "Why might not I come here, as well as into another country?"

Lobb. "But you have no lands, nor livings, nor acquaintance to come to in this country."

A. T. "What though I had not? I am a single person, and why may I not be with my friends anywhere?"

Lobb. "I understand you are not married."

A. T. "Then having no hindrance, why may not I go where I please, if the Lord so will?"

Then spoke Justice Launce, "But did not some desire you to come down?" And this Lobb asked me too, but I told them I would accuse none, I was there to answer as to what they should charge my own particular with.

Launce said, "Pray, Mistress, tell us what moved you to come such a journey?"

A. T. "The Lord gave me leave to come, asking of him leave, whitherever I went. I used still to pray for his direction in all I do, and so I suppose ought you," I said.

Justice Launce. "But pray tell us, what moved you to come such a journey?"

A. T. "The Lord moved me, and gave me leave."

Launce. "But had you not some extraordinary impulses of spirit that brought you down? Pray tell us what those were."

A. T. "When you are capable of extraordinary impulses of spirit, I will tell you; but I suppose you are not in a capacity now," for I saw how deridingly he spoke. And for answering him thus, he said I was one of a bold spirit, but he soon took me down: so himself said. But some said it took them down, for the Lord carried me so to speak, that they were in a hurry and confusion and sometimes would speak all together, that I was going to say, "What, are you like women, all speakers and no hearers?" But I said thus, "What, do you speak all at a time? I cannot answer all, when speaking at once. I appeal to the civilest of you," and I directed my speech to Justice Lobb, who spake very moderately, and gave me a civil answer, saying, "You are not acquainted with the manner of the court, which is to give in their sayings."

A. T. "But I cannot answer all at once. Indeed I do not know the manner of the court, for I never was before any till now."

Justice Lobb. "You prophesy against Truro."

A. T. "Indeed I pray against the sins of the people of Truro, and for their souls' welfare. Are you angry for that?"

Lobb. "But you must not judge authority, but pray for them, and not speak so suspiciously of them," and more to this purpose he spoke to me.

A. T. "I will take up your word, in which you said I was not to judge. You said well, for so saith the scripture, 'Who art thou that judgest another man's servant? To his own master he standeth or falleth; yea, he shall be holden up, for God is able to make him stand.'[5] But you have judged me, and never heard me speak: you have not dealt so well by me as Agrippa dealt by Paul. Though Agrippa was an heathen, he would have Paul speak before he gave in his judgment concerning him."[6]

Justice Tregagle. "Oh, you are a dreamer!"

A. T. "So they called Joseph, therefore I wonder not that you call me so."[7]

Justice Selye said, "You knew we were with you yesterday."

A. T. "I did not."

Justice Selye. "He which is the major said you will not say so."

A. T. "I will speak it, being it's truth."

He said, "Call the women that will witness they heard you say you knew we were with you." And he pulled out a writing, and named their names, calling to some to fetch them.

A. T. "You may suborn false witnesses against me, for they did so against Christ." And I said, "Produce your witnesses."

Justice Selye. "We shall have them for you at next assizes."

They put it off long enough, because one was fallen in a swoon before she got out of the house where she dwelt; and the other was come into the sessions-house. And Mrs Grose, a gentlewoman of the town, standing by her that was their false witness, said, "Wilt thou take an oath thus? Take heed what thou dost, it's a dangerous thing to take a false oath." And she ran out of the sessions-house; this was credibly reported. And here ended their witnesses that they had procured against me as to that. There was a soldier that smiled to hear how the Lord carried me along in my speech, and Justice Selye called to the jailer to take him away, saying he laughed at the court. He thought him to be one of my friends, and for his cheerful looking the jailer had like to have had him. Then I said, "Scripture speaks of such who 'make a man an offender for a word,'[8] but you make a man an offender for a look." They greatly bustled, as if they would have taken him away; but this was quickly squashed, their heat as to this lasted not long. In the meantime, the other, Selye, was talking to Major Bawden, wondering such a man as he, who had been so well reputed for a judicious, sober, understanding man, should hearken to me; many words were used to him to that purpose. I said, "Why may not he and others try all things, and hold fast that which is best?" But they still cast grim looks on me. And they had a saying to Major Bawden, and to Captain Langdon then, whom they derided in a letter sent from Truro by some of their learned court, which wrote that Captain Langdon and Major Bawden stood up and made a learned defence. They had indeed such learning from the spirit of wisdom and of a sound mind, which the jurors and their companions

5. Romans 14.4.
6. Acts 25–26.
7. Genesis 37.5–11.
8. Isaiah 29.21.

were not able to contend against, their speech and whole deportment was so humble and self-denying, and so seasoned with the salt of grace,[9] which their flashy unsavory spirits could not endure. Those that are raised from the dunghill and set on thrones cannot sit there without vaunting and showing their fool's coat of many colors, as envy, and pride, and vainglory; these and other colors they show, which delights not King Jesus nor his followers. Justice Lobb told me I made a disturbance in the town. I asked wherein. He said by drawing so many people after me. I said, "How did I draw them?" He said I set open my chamber doors and my windows for people to hear.

A. T. "That's a very unlikely thing, that I should do so, for I prayed the maid to lock my chamber door when I went to bed, and I did not rise in the night sure to open it." I said, "Why may not I pray with many people in the room, as well as your professing woman that prays before men and women, she knowing them to be there; but I know not that there is anybody in the room when I pray. And if you indict one for praying, why not another? Why are you so partial in your doings?"

Justice Lobb. "But you don't pray so, as others."

A. T. "I pray in my chamber."

Justice Trevill. "Your chamber!"

A. T. "Yea, that it's my chamber while I am there, through the pleasure of my friends."

They used more words to me, sometimes slighting and mockingly they spoke, and sometimes seeming to advise me to take heed how I spoke and prayed so again. Many such kind of words Justice Trevill used, and Justice Lobb. And one thing I omitted in telling you when I told you how I answered Justice Launce: I should have told you how I said to him, if he would know what the ordinary impulse of spirit was that I had to bring me into that country, I would tell him. So I related the scriptures, as that in the Psalms, and in the prophet Isaiah, how the presence and spirit of the Lord should be with me, and he would uphold me and strengthen me with the right hand of his righteousness.[1] He answered such impulse was common, they hoped they had that, they were not ignorant of such impulse of spirit; much to this effect was spoken. I seeing they were very willing to be gone, I said, "Have you done with me?" Answer was I might now go away. But I said, "Pray, what is it to break the good behavior you have bound me over to? I know not what you may make a breaking of it: is it a breaking the good behavior to pray and sing?" Justice Trevill said no, so I did it at the habitation where I abode. "It's well," said I, "you will give me leave it shall be anywhere." I said, "I will leave one word with you, and that is this: a time will come when you and I shall appear before the great judge of the tribunal seat of the most high, and then I think you will hardly be able to give an account for this day's work before the Lord, at that day of true judgment." Said Tregagle, "Take you no care for us." So they were willing to have no more discourse with me.

And as I went in the crowd, many strangers were very loving and careful to help me out of the crowd; and the rude multitude said, "Sure this woman is not witch, for she speaks many good words, which the witches could not." And thus the Lord made the rude rabble to justify his appearance. For in all that was said by me, I was nothing, the Lord put all in my mouth, and told me what I should say, and that from the written word, he put it in my memory and mouth; so that I will have nothing ascribed to me, but all honor and praise given to him whose right it is, even to Jehovah, who is the king that lives for ever. I have left out some things that I thought were not so

9. Colossians 4.6.

1. Psalm 139.7–10; Isaiah 29.21.

material to be written; and what I have written of this, it's to declare as much as is convenient to take off those falsities and contrary reports that are abroad concerning my sufferings, some making it worse than it was, and some saying it was little or nothing. Now to inform all people's judgments, I have thought it meet to offer this relation to the world's view, and with as much covering as I can of saints' weaknesses herein, praying the Lord to forgive them; and as for the Lord's enemies, that he would confound them; but as for my enemies, I still pray.

Alice Thornton

fl. 1645–1662

Alice Thornton wrote three volumes of an autobiography, spanning the years 1629 to 1660. From a royalist family, she tells in the early part of her story how her mother protected herself and her daughter from Scots soldiers who wanted to be quartered in their home. When one Captain Innis demanded that he have Alice in marriage, her mother hid her and paid another family to house him. The threat of rape in wartime was a real one, and when Alice learned that Captain Innis planned to kidnap her, she never ventured out of the house. The two passages printed here are from the decade after the Civil War, during her married life, in which the dangers she suffered were mainly due to the perils of reproduction. Her perspective is at once religious and biological. Images and allusions from the Bible as well as a belief in salvation color her narrative. At the same time, Mrs. Thornton depicts her physical suffering in the most graphic and realistic detail. Most married women of the early modern period were pregnant during most of their adult lives, and they often died in childbirth, as did their infants. Even if the mother survived labor, her risk of sickness was great. Alice Thornton relates her ordeal following her first two labors and expresses thanks to God for helping her through the sicknesses that followed.

from Book of Remembrances

Meditations upon my deliverance of my first child;
and of the great sickness followed for three quarters of a year;
August 6, 1652, lasted till May 2, 1653

About seven weeks after I married it pleased God to give me the blessing of conception. The first quarter I was exceeding sickly in breeding, till I was with quick child; after which I was very strong and healthy, I bless God, only much hotter than formerly, as is usual in such cases from a natural cause, insomuch that my nose bled much when I was about half gone, by reason of the increase of heat. Being helped more forward in the distemper by the extreme heat of the weather at that time, when the extreme great eclipse of the sun was in its height, and a great and total eclipse fell out this year 1652. At which time I was big with child, and the sight of it much affrighted me, it being so dark in the morning that [one] could not see to eat his breakfast without a candle. But this did amaze me much, and I could not refrain going out into the garden and look on the eclipse in water, discovering the power of God so great to a miracle, who did withdraw His light from our sun so totally that the sky was dark, and stars appeared, and a cold storm for a time did possess the earth. Which dreadful change did put me into most serious and deep consideration of the day of judgment which would come as sudden and as certainly upon all the earth as this eclipse fell out, which caused me to desire and beg of His Majesty that He would prepare me for this great day in repentance, faith, and a holy life, for the judgments of God was just and certain upon all sins and sinners. O prepare me, O God, for all Thy dispensations and trials in this world, and make me ready and prepared with oil in my lamp, as the wise virgins, against the coming of the sweet Bridegroom of my soul.

About a month after, Mr. Thornton desired and his relations that I should go to see them both at Crathorne, Buttercrambe, York, and at Hull and Beverley, at Burn Park where his mother lived then . . . and by God's mercy did I go to all those places where his friends lived, and [was] most kindly received and entertained. I bless God who gave me favor in the eyes of my husband's friends. When I came to Hull, Dr. Witty would have had me advised to be let blood. . . . In my return home by Newton when I saw the old house the remains of it, as I was in the great chamber, the door into a little room was so low as I got a great knock on my forehead which struck me down, and I fell with the force of the blow, at which my husband was troubled. But I recovering my astonishment (because he should not be too much concerned), smiled, said I hoped I was not much worse, but said I had taken possession, which made him smile, and said it was to my hurt, and indeed so it was many ways. For in my going homeward he carried me to that place of the great rocks and cliffs which is called Whitson Cliff. . . . But this my husband would not have had me go down this way, but by Ampleford, about, and plain way, but for Mr. Bradley, who told him it would not do me no hurt, because his wife went down that way and was no worse. However, the effect to me was contrary, for I being to go to my cousin Ascough's, she did admire that I came that way, and wished I might get safe home. It was indeed the good pleasure of my God to bring me safe home to my dear mother's house, Hipswell.

But my dangerous journey the effects of it did soon appear on me, and Dr. Witty's words came true. For as soon as I got home I fell into the most dreadful sickness that ever any creature could possibly be saved out of, and by a strong and putrid fever, which was on me eleven days before Dr. Witty came from Hull, had so putrefied my whole blood that both myself and poor infant was like to go. . . . The more particular description of this great and long-lasting sickness I have related in my first book of my Life, and with the miraculous deliverance was towards me in all that time. Mr. Thornton had a desire that I should visit his friends, in which I freely joined, his mother living about fifty miles from Hipswell, and all at Newton and Buttercrambe. In my passage thither I sweat exceedingly, and was much inclining to be feverish wanting not eight weeks of my time, so that Dr. Witty said that I should go near to fall into a fever, or some desperate sickness, if I did not cool my blood, by taking some away, and if I had stayed but two days longer, I had followed his advice. In his return home from Newton, his own estate, I was carried over Hambleton towards Sir William Ascough's house, where I passed down on foot a very high wall betwixt Hudhill and Whitson Cliff, which is above a mile steep down, and indeed so bad that I could not scarce tread the narrow steps, which was exceeding bad for me in that condition, and sore to endure, the way so straight and none to lead me but my maid [Susan Gosling], which could scarce make shift to get down herself, all our company being gone down before. Each step did very much strain me, being so big with child, nor could I have got down if I had not then been in my full strength and nimble on foot. But, I bless God, I got down safe at last, though much tired, and hot and weary, finding myself not well, but troubled with pains after my walk. Mr. Thornton would not have brought me that way if he had known it so dangerous, and I was a stranger in that place; but he was advised by some to go that way before we came down the hill.

This was the first occasion which brought me a great deal of misery, and killed my sweet infant in my womb. For I continued ill in pain by fits upon this journey, and within a fortnight fell into a desperate fever at Hipswell. Upon which my old doctor, Mr. Mahum, was called, but could do little towards the cure, because of being with child. I was willing to be ordered by him, but said I found it absolutely necessary to be let blood if they would save my life, but I was freely willing to resign my will to God's, if He saw fit for me, to spare my life, yet to live with my husband; but still with subserviency to my Heavenly Father. Nor was I wanting to supplicate my God for direction what to do, either for life or death. I had very often and frequent impressions to desire the latter before the former, finding no true joy in this life, but I confess also that which moved me to use all means for my recovery, in regard of the great sorrow of my dear and aged mother and my dear husband took for me, far exceeding my deserts, made me more willing to save my life for them, and that I might render praises to my God in the land of the living. But truly, I found my heart still did cleave to my Maker that I never found myself more desirous of a change to be delivered from this wicked world and body of sin and death, desiring to be dissolved and to be with Christ. Therefore endured I all the rigors and extremity of my sickness with such a share of patience as my God gave me.

As for my friends, they were so much concerned for me that, upon the importunity of my husband, although I was brought indeed very weak and desperately ill about eleventh day of my sickness, I did let him send for Dr. Witty, if it were not too late. The doctor came post the next day, when he found me very weak, and durst not let me blood that night, but gave me cordials, etc., till the next day, and if I got but one hour's rest that night, he would do it the morning following. That night the two doctors had a dispute about the letting me blood. Mr. Mahum was against it, and Dr. Witty for it; but I soon decided that dispute, and told them, if they would save my life, I must bleed. So the next day I had six or seven ounces taken which was turned very bad by my sickness, but I found a change immediately in my sight, which was exceeding dim before, and then I see as well as ever clearly, and my strength began a little to return; these things I relate that I may set forth the mercy of my ever-gracious God, who had blessed the means in such manner. Who can sufficiently extol his Majesty for his boundless mercies to me his weak creature, for from that time I was better, and he had hopes of my life.

The doctor stayed with me seven days during my sickness; my poor infant within me was greatly forced with violent motions perpetually, till it grew so weak that it had left stirring, and about the 27th of August I found myself in great pains as it were the colic, after which I began to be in travail, and about the next day at night I was delivered of a goodly daughter, who lived not so long as that we could get a minister to baptize it, though we presently sent for one. This my sweet babe and first child departed this life half an hour after its birth, being received, I hope, into the arms of Him that gave it. She was buried that night, being Friday, the 27th of August, 1652, at Easby Church.

The effects of this fever remained by several distempers successively, first, after the miscarriage I fell into a most terrible shaking ague, lasting one quarter of a year, by fits each day twice, in much violency, so that the sweat was great with faintings, being thereby weakened till I could not stand or go. The hair on my head came off, my nails of my fingers and toes came off, my teeth did shake, and ready to come out and grew black. After the ague left me, upon a medicine of London treacle, I fell into the jaundice, which vexed me very hardly one full quarter and a half more. I finding Dr. Witty's judgment true, that it would prove a chronical[1] distemper; but blessed be the Lord, upon great and many means used and all remedies, I was at length cured of all distempers and weaknesses, which, from its beginning, had lasted three quarters of a year full out. Thus had I a sad entertainment and beginning of my change of life, the comforts thereof being turned into much discomforts and weaknesses, but still I was upheld by an Almighty Power, therefore will I praise the Lord my God. Amen.

Upon the birth of my second child and daughter, born at Hipswell on the 3rd of January in the year 1654.

Alice Thornton, my second child, was born at Hipswell near Richmond in Yorkshire the 3rd day of January, 1654, baptized the 5th of the same. Witnesses, my mother the Lady Wandesforde, my uncle Mr. Major Norton, and my cousin York his daughter, at Hipswell, by Mr. Michell Siddall, minister then of Caterick.

It was the pleasure of God to give me but a weak time after my daughter Alice her birth, and she had many preservations from death in the first year, being one night delivered from being overlaid by her nurse, who laid in my dear mother's chamber a good while. One night my mother was writing pretty late, and she heard my dear child make a groaning troublesomely, and stepping immediately to nurse's bedside she saw the nurse fallen asleep, with her breast in the child's mouth, and lying over the child; at which she, being affrighted, pulled the nurse suddenly off from her, and so preserved my dear child from being smothered . * * *

After I was delivered [of her third child, Elizabeth], and in my weary bed and very weak, it fell out that my little daughter Alice, being then newly weaned, and about a year old, being asleep in one cradle and the young infant [Elizabeth] in another, she fell into a most desperate fit, of the convulsions as supposed to be, her breath stopped, grew black in her face, which sore frighted her maid Jane Flouer. She took her up immediately, and with the help of the midwife, Jane Rimer, to open her teeth and to bring her to life again.

But still, afterwards, no sooner that she was out of one fit but fell into another fit, and the remedies could be by my dear mother and aunt Norton could scarce keep her alive, she having at least twenty fits; all friends expecting when she should have died. But I lying the next chamber to her and did hear her, when she came out of them, to give great shrieks and suddenly, that it frighted me extremely, and all the time of this poor child's illness I myself was at death's door by the extreme excess of those, upon the fright and terror came upon me, so great floods that I was spent, and my breath lost, my strength departed from me, and I could not speak for faintings, and dispirited so that my dear mother and aunt and friends did not expect my life, but overcome with sorrow for me. Nor durst they tell me in what a condition my dear Naly [Alice's nickname] was in her fits, lest grief for her, added to my own extremity, with loss of blood, might have extinguished my miserable life: but removing her in her cradle into the Blue Parlor, a great way off me, lest I hearing her sad shrieks should renew my sorrows. These extremities did so lessen my milk, that though I began to recruit strength, yet I must be subject to the changes of my condition. After my dear Naly was in most miraculous mercy restored to me the next day, and recruited my strength; within a fortnight I recovered my milk, and was overjoyed to give my sweet Betty suck, which I did, and

1. Chronic, lasting a long time.

began to recover to a miracle, blessed be my great and gracious Lord God, who remembered mercy towards me.

Ralph Josselin
1616–1683

Vicar of an Essex parish, Ralph Josselin kept a diary for forty-two years; it became one of the most substantial diaries of the century. It included an extensive annual accounting of his finances, recorded each March at the start of the church year, followed by three or four entries each week describing events—"God's dealings." Financial language pervades Josselin's reckonings of his financial dealings and his spiritual debts alike, as he strives to improve both his material and his spiritual well-being.

from Diary

Nov: 18: God good to me, and mine in manifold outward mercies, but I find such a vanity in my spirit that boweth down my soul, yet this trouble is my hope for surely there is the spirit stirring against the flesh, but when shall Christ so strengthen me that I shall in his grace be more than a conqueror.

19: We killed a good hog, which proved neat and clean, a mercy to be observed, at night a violent wind and snow which covered the earth die 20.[1] so that we gave our cattle meat twice in the day, having begun to give once a day ever since octob. 29.

21. Received in a little wood from Sprigs marsh, its a mercy when God is our own to have any thing to call our own.

Nov: 25. The season somewhat more winterly then formerly. I observe how apt we are to account a harsh time the hardest we ever felt and a mild the best, letting slip out of our mind what was formerly, and very commonly not eying God that giveth both, God good to me in many mercies, a zeal in me in preaching the word, Lord warm their souls in the love, and embracement of the truth as it is in Jesus.

* * *

March. 24: A sad season for wet, yet some sow their oats. God good to me and mine in mercies, Bettie more quiet in nights then formerly. Mr. H. very ill which is a great trouble to me. Lord bear up my heart to thee, that nothing may overset my soul; God good to me in the word, awakening my heart unto him, the Lord stablish me in his fear, prayed earnestly for fair weather, this evening was the most hopeful and clear I have seen of many for which mercy I praise the Lord, but the next morning wet as formerly Lord be not angry with the prayers of thy people.

27. Rid[2] to choose Knights of the shire, we lost it, and my heart quiet, the Lord liveth and reigneth and if he put his own servants and things on suffering his will be done. Went on to London. returned safe.

30. with a vain heart, Lord be my help, and stir up my soul to endeavor it.

March. 31. My dear friend Mr R. H. under a visible distraction, the Lord in infinite mercy raise him up again. When I come to view my expenses I find I have laid out 233li. 9s. 6d. ob.[3] I have received in all receipts whatsoever only. 146. 16. 0. but my stock which I valued last year at. 25li. is worth now about. 55li. so though I have

1. On the twentieth day.
2. Rode.
3. 233 pounds, 9 shillings, 6 pence, "ob," short for Latin *obolus*, a halfpenny.

laid out. 87. 6. 5. ob more then received yet on the whole matter I am not abated in my stock above. 50li. and in lieu of that I am sure I have laid out. above 80li. on the house on the green.

My roll of debts as in the blew book are 80li. about. owing unto me. ——— 167. 10. 0

I have in cash towards my building about 50li. and my uncle Shepheard being dead, I have a meadow befalls my wife worth about. 50li. more, which when it cometh into my hand I shall value.

Yet God even in outward things is good to me, Lord make me upright before thee in all my ways, I humbly entreat thee and continue thy kindness to me, and all that fear thy name.

April. 1. 2. 3. I sew oats on lay, and other land. Lord command a blessing for my hope is in thee. went towards London on Mr H. account, a sad providence, oh Lord melt my bowels, accept my praises for my family's health, reason, return to them in favor: die. 6. I came home, God with me in the journey.

Ap: 7. The season very good, springing. God merciful to me in many outward mercies, but sensible I am my heart is out of frame, the Lord sanctify my thoughts, help me to watch over them, the Lord command mercy for me and mine in Christ Jesus, I had but little time for my sermons this day, Lord help me to trust thee but not for any thing to neglect any opportunities

God gave an answer to prayer in the season from March 27. yet, so that men are at work on all hands for their employment.

Daniel Defoe

1660–1731

Son of a butcher, Daniel Defoe was one of the most prolific and influential English journalists and novelists, publishing 566 separate works. His rise to fame was fraught with financial and political crises. A merchant and trader, Defoe speculated in land and overseas ventures, risking such enormous sums of capital that by 1692 he owed his creditors seventeen thousand pounds. After a short stint running a brick and tile factory, Defoe turned to political writing and journalism to pay his debts. His many works included propaganda for William III, and two important essays on the capitalist economy, *An Essay Upon Public Credit* and—a subject he knew all too well—*An Essay upon Loans* (1710).

His literary career began at the age of fifty-nine with *The Life and Strange Surprizing Adventures of Robinson Crusoe, Mariner of York* (1719). This became Part One of a trilogy, followed by *The Farther Adventures of Robinson Crusoe* (1719) and in 1720 by *The Serious Reflections of . . . Robinson Crusoe*. The story is about a young man who rebels against his father by sailing the high seas rather than following the "middle life" at home. After a series of adventures, Crusoe becomes a planter in Brazil and finally, en route to Africa to buy slaves, he is shipwrecked on an island off the northeast coast of South America, where he lives alone for twenty-eight years. A fascinating mixture of fiction and fact, Defoe's novel had its immediate source in the popular story of Alexander Selkirk, a Scottish sailor marooned from 1704 to 1709 on an island 300 miles west of Chile, as related in Captain Woodes Rogers's *Cruising Voyage Round the World* (1712).

Defoe plays with the factual status of his fiction by maintaining in the preface that the story was "a just history of fact," yet later, accused of being a liar, he explained in his *Serious Reflections* (1720) that the novel was an allegory of his own life. One can find plenty of parallels between Defoe's life and Crusoe's and between the form of the novel and autobiography. In the first-person narrative, Crusoe portrays himself as a self-destructive risk taker—"the wilful agent of my own miseries" thanks to a "rash and immoderate desire of rising faster." Commenting on his reckless love of danger is the voice of a sober inward-looking Presbyterian, who attempts to control all this chaos in whatever way he can. Once shipwrecked, Crusoe begins the process of taking stock of himself by reckoning his spiritual credits and debits, by keeping track of time and writing a journal of his experiences. While money is no longer valuable to him—"O drug . . . what art thou good for?" he says to the thirty-six pounds he finds in the shipwreck—his assets are expressed in terms of capital, as if they could be reckoned as pluses and minuses in a financial accounting.

For more on Defoe, see his principal listing, page 2289.

from The Life and Strange and Surprizing Adventures of Robinson Crusoe, of York, Mariner

I now began to consider seriously my condition, and the circumstance I was reduced to, and I drew up the state of my affairs in writing, not so much to leave them to any that were to come after me, for I was like to have but few heirs, as to deliver my thoughts from daily poring upon them, and afflicting my mind; and as my reason began now to master my despondency, I began to comfort my self as well as I could, and to set the good against the evil, that I might have something to distinguish my case from worse, and I stated it very impartially, like debtor and creditor, the comforts I enjoyed, against the miseries I suffered, thus,

Evil.	**Good.**
I am cast upon a horrible desolate island, void of all hope of recovery.	But I am alive, and not drowned as all my ship's company was.
I am singled out and separated, as it were, from all the World to be miserable.	But I am singled out too from all the ship's crew to be spared from death; and he that miraculously saved me from death, can deliver me from this condition.
I am divided from mankind, a solitaire, one banished from humane society.	But I am not starved and perishing on a barren place, affording no sustenance.
I have not clothes to cover me.	But I am in a hot climate, where if I had clothes I could hardly wear them.
I am without any defence or means to resist any violence of man or beast.	But I am cast on an island, where I see no wild beasts to hurt me, as I saw on the coast of Africa: And what if I had been shipwrecked there?
I have no soul to speak to, or relieve me.	But God wonderfully sent the ship in near enough to the shore, that I have gotten out so many necessary things as will either supply my wants, or enable me to supply my self even as long as I live.

Upon the whole, here was an undoubted testimony, that there was scarce any condition in the world so miserable, but there was something *negative* or something *positive* to be thankful for in it; and let this stand as a direction from the experience of the most miserable of all conditions in this world, that we may always find in it something to comfort our selves from, and to set in the description of good and evil, on the credit side of the accompt.

John Bunyan
1628–1688

Born at Elstow near Bedford in 1628, John Bunyan was descended from a family of small farmers, or yeomen, who had fallen on hard times. His father was forced to become a traveling tinker, a mender of pots and household utensils. As a child, Bunyan learned to read and write at a grammar school. At the age of sixteen he joined the local militia to fight on the parliamentary side in the Civil War. Some time around 1648, Bunyan underwent a crisis of faith. He was plagued with doubts about his faith and fear of damnation. This ordeal ultimately led to his conversion. Bunyan became a Noncomformist preacher and set out to spread the good news of the Bible to others. With the Restoration of Charles II and the Church of England, Bunyan was arrested for preaching. Refusing to conform to the Church of England and to stop his Nonconformist preaching, he spent first twelve years in prison and then another six months. While in prison for this second short stay, Bunyan wrote *The Pilgrim's Progress* (1678), the great classic of Puritan literature. A dream vision, the allegorical journey of the protagonist Christian begins with his falling asleep in a "den," which is designated in the margin of the text as "the gaol" (jail). Christian is both a kind of everyman and a representative of Bunyan himself. Christian's experiences symbolically relate the crises of Bunyan's life—his falling into despair, figured as the Slough of Despond, and his temptation by the things of this world, portrayed as Vanity Fair. The most popular book of its time and for long afterward a favorite text of English Protestant missionaries around the world, *Pilgrim's Progress* presents the myth of life as a war between the forces of good and evil, light and darkness, God and the devil, in a powerful and symbolically complex narrative of spiritual despair, struggle with temptation, longing for salvation, and redemption through dependence on God's grace.

from The Pilgrim's Progress from This World to That Which Is to Come.

The Author's Apology for His Book

When at the first I took my pen in hand
Thus for to write, I did not understand
That I at all should make a little book
In such a mode; nay, I had undertook
To make another, which when almost done,
Before I was aware, I this begun.
And thus it was: I writing of the way
And race of saints, in this our Gospel-day,
Fell suddenly into an allegory
About their journey, and the way to glory,
In more than twenty things which I set down;
This done, I twenty more had in my crown,
And they again began to multiply,
Like sparks that from the coals of fire do fly.
Nay then, thought I, if that you breed so fast,
I'll put you by yourselves, lest you at last

Should prove *ad infinitum*, and eat out
The book that I already am about.
 Well, so I did; but yet I did not think
To show to all the world my pen and ink
In such a mode; I only thought to make
I knew not what: nor did I undertake
Thereby to please my neighbor; no, not I,
I did it mine own self to gratify.
 Neither did I but vacant seasons spend
In this my scribble: nor did I intend
But to divert myself in doing this,
From worser thoughts which make me do amiss.
 Thus I set pen to paper with delight,
And quickly had my thoughts in black and white.
For, having now my method by the end,
Still as I pulled, it came; and so I penned
It down, until it came at last to be
For length and breadth the bigness which you see.
 Well, when I had thus put mine ends together,
I showed them others, that I might see whether
They would condemn them, or them justify:
And some said, "Let them live"; some, "Let them die."
Some said, "John, print it"; others said, "Not so."
Some said, "It might do good" others said, "No."
 Now was I in a strait, and did not see
Which was the best thing to be done by me:
At last I thought, since you are thus divided,
I print it will, and so the case decided.
 For, thought I, some I see would have it done,
Though others in that channel do not run.
To prove then who advised for the best,
Thus I thought fit to put it to the test.
 I further thought, if now I did deny
Those that would have it thus, to gratify,
I did not know, but hinder them I might,
Of that which would to them be great delight.
 For those which were not for its coming forth,
I said to them, Offend you I am loth;° *unwilling*
Yet since your brethren pleased with it be,
Forbear to judge, till you do further see.
 If that thou wilt not read, let it alone;
Some love the meat, some love to pick the bone:
Yea, that I might them better palliate,
I did too with them thus expostulate.
 May I not write in such a style as this?
In such a method too, and yet not miss
Mine end, thy good? why may it not be done?
Dark clouds bring waters, when the bright bring none;
Yea, dark or bright, if they their silver drops
Cause to descend, the earth, by yielding crops
Gives praise to both, and carpeth not at either,

But treasures up the fruit they yield together;
Yea, so commixes both, that in her fruit
None can distinguish this from that, they suit
Her well, when hungry, but if she be full
She spews out both, and makes their blessings null.
You see the ways the fisherman doth take
To catch the fish, what engines doth he make?
Behold! how he engageth all his wits
Also his snares, lines, angles, hooks, and nets.
Yet fish there be, that neither hook, nor line,
Nor snare, nor net, nor engine can make thine;
They must be groped for, and be tickled too,
Or they will not be catched, whate'er you do.
How doth the fowler seek to catch his game
By divers means, all which one cannot name?
His gun, his nets, his lime-twigs, light, and bell:
He creeps, he goes, he stands; yea who can tell
Of all his postures? Yet there's none of these
Will make him master of what fowls he please.
Yea, he must pipe, and whistle to catch *this*,
Yet if he does so, *that* bird he will miss.
If that a pearl may in a toad's head dwell,
And may be found too in an oyster-shell;
If things that promise nothing do contain
What better is than gold, who will disdain,
That have an inkling of it, there to look,
That they may find it? Now my little book
(Though void of all those paintings that may make
It with this or the other man to take)
Is not without those things that do excel,
What do in brave but empty notions dwell.
Well, yet I am not fully satisfied,
That this your book will stand, when soundly tried.
Why, what's the matter? "It is dark." What tho'?
"But it is feigned."° What of that I trow?° *invented / suppose*
Some men, by feigning words as dark as mine,
Make truth to spangle, and its rays to shine.
"But they want solidness." Speak man thy mind.
"They drowned the weak; metaphors make us blind."
Solidity, indeed becomes the pen
Of him that writeth things divine to men;
But must I needs want solidness, because
By metaphors I speak? Were not God's laws,
His Gospel-laws, in olden time held forth
By types, shadows, and metaphors? Yet loth
Will any sober man be to find fault
With them, lest he be found for to assault
The highest wisdom. No, he rather stoops,
And seeks to find out what by pins and loops,
By calves, and sheep, by heifers, and by rams,
By birds, and herbs, and by the blood of lambs,

God speaketh to him: and happy is he
That finds the light and grace that in them be.
 Be not too forward therefore to conclude
That I want solidness, that I am rude:
All things solid in show not solid be;
All things in parables despise not we
Lest things most hurtful lightly we receive;
And things that good are, of our souls bereave.
 My dark and cloudy words they do but hold
The truth, as cabinets enclose the gold.
 The prophets used much by metaphors
To set forth truth; yea, who so considers
Christ, his Apostles too, shall plainly see,
That truths to this day in such mantles° be. *cloaks, coverings*
 Am I afraid to say that Holy Writ,
Which for its style and phrase puts down all wit,
Is everywhere so full of all these things,
(Dark figures, allegories), yet there springs
From that same book that lustre, and those rays
Of light, that turns our darkest nights to days.
 Come, let my carper to his life now look,
And find there darker lines than in my book
He findeth any, Yea, and let him know
That in his best things there are worse lines too.
 May we but stand before impartial men,
To his poor one, I dare adventure ten,
That they will take my meaning in these lines
Far better than his lies in silver shrines.
Come, truth, although in swaddling-clouts, I find
Informs the judgment, rectifies the mind,
Pleases the understanding, makes the will
Submit; the memory too it doth fill
With what doth our imagination please,
Likewise, it tends our troubles to appease.
 Sound words I know Timothy is to use,
And old wives' fables he is to refuse,
But yet grave Paul him nowhere doth forbid
The use of parables; in which lay hid
That gold, those pearls, and precious stones that were
Worth digging for, and that with greatest care.
 Let me add one word more. O man of God!
Art thou offended? Dost thou wish I had
Put forth my matter in another dress,
Or that I had in things been more express?
Three things let me propound, then I submit
To those that are my betters, (as is fit).
 1. I find not that I am denied the use
Of this my method, so I no abuse
Put on the words, things, readers, or be rude
In handling figure, or similitude,
In application; but, all that I may,

Seek the advance of Truth this or that way.
Denied, did I say? Nay, I have leave
(Example too, and that from them that have
God better pleased, by their words or ways
Than any man that breatheth nowadays),
Thus to express my mind, thus to declare
Things unto thee, that excellentest are.
  2. I find that men (as high as trees) will write
Dialogue-wise; yet no man doth them slight
For writing so: Indeed if they abuse
Truth, cursed be they, and the craft they use
To that intent; but yet let truth be free
To make her sallies upon thee and me,
Which way it pleases God. For who knows how,
Better than he that taught us first to plow,
To guide our Mind and Pens for his design?
And he makes base things usher in divine.
  3. I find that Holy Writ in many places
Hath semblance with this method, where the cases
Do call for one thing, to set forth another;
Use it I may then, and yet nothing smother
Truth's golden beams: nay, by this method may
Make it cast forth its rays as light as day.
  And now, before I do put up my pen,
I'll show the profit of my book, and then
Commit both thee and it unto that hand
That pulls the strong down, and makes weak ones stand.
  This book it chalketh out before thine eyes
The man that seeks the everlasting prize;
It shows you whence he comes, whither he goes,
What he leaves undone, also what he does:
It also shows you how he runs and runs,
Till he unto the Gate of Glory comes.
  It shows too who set out for life amain,
As if the lasting Crown they would obtain:
Here also you may see the reason why
They lose their labor, and like fools do die.
  This book will make a traveler of thee,
If by its counsel thou wilt ruled be;
It will direct thee to the Holy Land,
If thou wilt its directions understand:
Yea, it will make the slothful active be;
The blind also delightful things to see.
  Art thou for something rare and profitable?
Wouldst thou see a truth within a fable?
Art thou forgetful? Wouldest thou remember
From New-year's-day to the last of December?
Then read my fancies, they will stick like burrs,
And may be to the helpless, comforters.
  This Book is writ in such a dialect
As may the minds of listless men affect:
It seems a novelty, and yet contains

Nothing but sound and honest Gospel strains.
Wouldst thou divert thyself from melancholy?
Wouldst thou be pleasant, yet be far from folly?
Wouldst thou read riddles, and their explanation?
Or else be drowned in thy contemplation?
Dost thou love picking meat? Or wouldst thou see
A man i' th' clouds, and hear him speak to thee?
Wouldst thou be in a dream, and yet not sleep?
Or wouldst thou in a moment laugh and weep?
Wouldest thou lose thyself, and catch no harm,
And find thyself again without a charm?
Wouldst read thyself, and read thou know'st not what,
And yet know whether thou art blest or not,
By reading the same lines? O then come hither,
And lay my book, thy head and heart together.

JOHN BUNYAN.

[THE SLOUGH OF DESPOND[1] AND MR. WORLDLY WISDOM]

Now I saw in my dream, that just as they had ended this talk, they drew near to a very miry Slough, that was in the midst of the plain; and they being heedless did both fall suddenly into the bog. The name of the slough was Despond. Here, therefore, they wallowed for a time, being grievously bedaubed with the dirt; and Christian, because of the burden that was on his back, began to sink in the mire.

Pli. Then said Pliable, Ah, neighbor Christian, where are you now?

Chr. Truly, said Christian, I do not know.

Pli. At that Pliable began to be offended, and angrily said to his fellow, Is this the happiness you have told me all this while of? If we have such ill speed at our first setting out, what may we expect 'twixt this and our journey's end? May I get out again with my life, you shall possess the brave country alone for me. And with that he gave a desperate struggle or two, and got out of the mire on that side of the slough which was next to his own house: so away he went, and Christian saw him no more.

Wherefore Christian was left to tumble in the Slough of Despond alone: but still he endeavored to struggle to that side of the slough that was still further from his own house, and next to the wicket-gate; the which he did, but could not get out, because of the burden that was upon his back: but I beheld in my dream, that a man came to him, whose name was Help, and asked him what he did there?

Chr. Sir, said Christian, I was bid go this way by a man called *Evangelist*; who directed me also to yonder gate, that I might escape the wrath to come; and as I was going thither, I fell in here.

Help. But why did you not look for the steps?

Chr. Fear followed me so hard, that I fled the next way, and fell in.

Help. Then said he, Give me thy hand. So he gave him his hand, and he drew him out, and set him upon sound ground, and bid him go on his way.

Then I stepped to him that pluckt him out, and said, Sir, wherefore (since over this place is the way from the City of Destruction to yonder gate), is it that this plat[2] is not mended, that poor travelers might go thither with more security? And he said unto me, This miry Slough is such a place as cannot be mended; it is the descent

1. "Slough" rhymes with "cow." "Despond" means dejection, loss of hope.

2. Piece of ground.

whither the scum and filth that attends conviction for sin doth continually run, and therefore it is called the Slough of Despond; for still as the sinner is awakened about his lost condition, there ariseth in his soul many fears and doubts, and discouraging apprehensions, which all of them get together, and settle in this place: And this is the reason of the badness of this ground.

It is not the pleasure of the King that this place should remain so bad. His laborers also have, by the direction of His Majesty's surveyors, been for above these sixteen hundred years employed about this patch of ground, if perhaps it might have been mended. Yea, and to my knowledge, saith he, here hath been swallowed up at least twenty thousand cart-loads, yea, millions of wholesome instructions, that have at all seasons been brought from all places of the King's dominions, and they that can tell say they are the best materials to make good ground of the place. If so be it might have been mended, but it is the Slough of Despond still, and so will be when they have done what they can.

True, there are by the direction of the lawgiver, certain good and substantial steps,[3] placed even through the very midst of this Slough; but at such time as this place doth much spew out its filth, as it doth against change of weather, these steps are hardly seen; or if they be, men through the dizziness of their heads, step besides; and then they are bemired to purpose, notwithstanding the steps be there; but the ground is good when they are once got in at the gate.

[Vanity Fair][4]

Then I saw in my dream, that when they were got out of the wilderness, they presently saw a town before them, and the name of that town is Vanity; and at the town there is a Fair kept, called Vanity Fair: it is kept all the year long; it beareth the name of Vanity Fair, because the town where 'tis kept is lighter than Vanity; and also because all that is there sold, or that cometh thither, is vanity. As is the saying of the wise, "All that cometh is vanity."[5]

This fair is no new erected business, but a thing of ancient standing; I will show you the original of it.

Almost five thousand years agone, there were pilgrims walking to the Caelestial City, as these two honest persons are; and Beelzebub, Apollyon, and Legion,[6] with their Companions, perceiving by the path that the Pilgrims made, that their way to the City lay through this Town of Vanity, they contrived here to set up a Fair; a Fair wherein should be sold of all sorts of Vanity, and that it should last all the year long: therefore at this Fair are all such merchandise sold, as houses, lands, trades, places, honors, preferments, titles, countries, kingdoms, lusts, pleasures, and delights of all sorts, as whores, bawds, wives, husbands, children, masters, servants, lives, blood, bodies, souls, silver, gold, pearls, precious stones, and what not.

And moreover, at this Fair there is at all times to be seen jugglings, cheats, games, plays, fools, apes, knaves, and rogues, and that of all sorts.

Here are to be seen too, and that for nothing, thefts, murders, adulteries, false-swearers, and that of a blood-red color.

And as in other fairs of less moment, there are the several rows and streets under their proper names, where such and such wares are vended; so here likewise you have the proper places, rows, streets (*viz.* countries and kingdoms) where the wares of this

3. The steps are promises of forgiveness and acceptance through a life of faith in Christ.
4. From the image of a local fair, Bunyan creates a symbol of the emptiness and material worldliness that tempt the Christian.
5. Ecclesiastes 1.2, 1.14; 2.11, 2.17; Isaiah 40.17.
6. Beelzebub, the prince of demons (Matthew 12.24); Apollyon, "the angel of the bottomless pit" (Revelation 9.11); Legion, the "unclean spirit" (Mark 5.9).

Fair are soonest to be found: Here is the Britain Row, the French Row, the Italian Row, the Spanish Row, the German Row, where several sorts of vanities are to be sold. But as in other fairs, some one commodity is as the chief of all the fair, so the ware of Rome and her Merchandise is greatly promoted in this Fair; only our English nation, with some others, have taken a dislike thereat.

Now, as I said, the way to the Caelestial City lies just through this Town where this lusty Fair is kept; and he that will go to the City, and yet not go through this town, must needs go out of the World. The Prince of Princes himself, when here, went through this Town to his own Country, and that upon a Fair-day too; yea, and as I think, it was Beelzebub, the chief lord of this Fair, that invited him to buy of his vanities: yea, would have made him Lord of the Fair, would he but have done him reverence as he went through the town. Yea, because he was such a person of honor, Beelzebub had him from street to street, and showed him all the kingdoms of the world in a little time, that he might (if possible) allure that Blessed One to cheapen and buy some of his vanities. But he had no mind to the merchandise, and therefore left the town, without laying out so much as one farthing upon these vanities. This Fair therefore is an ancient thing, of long standing, and a very great Fair.

Now these pilgrims, as I said, must needs go through this Fair: well, so they did: but behold, even as they entered into the Fair, all the people in the Fair were moved, and the town itself as it were in a hubbub about them; and that for several reasons: for,

First, the pilgrims were clothed with such kind of raiment as was diverse from the raiment of any that traded in that Fair. The people therefore of the Fair made a great gazing upon them: Some said they were fools, some they were bedlams,[7] and some they are outlandish-men.

Secondly, and as they wondered at their Apparel, so they did likewise at their speech; for few could understand what they said: they naturally spoke the language of Canaan,[8] but they that kept the Fair were the men of this world; so that, from one end of the Fair to the other, they seemed barbarians each to the other.

Thirdly, but that which did not a little amuse the merchandisers was, that these pilgrims set very light by all their wares, they cared not so much as to look upon them; and if they called upon them to buy, they would put their fingers in their ears, and cry, "Turn away mine eyes from beholding vanity," and look upwards, signifying that their trade and traffic was in Heaven.[9]

One chanced mockingly, beholding the carriages of the men, to say unto them, What will ye buy? But they, looking gravely upon him, answered, "We buy the Truth."[1] At that there was an occasion taken to despise the men the more; some mocking, some taunting, some speaking reproachfully, and some calling upon others to smite them. At last things came to an hubbub and great stir in the Fair, insomuch that all order was confounded. Now was word presently brought to the great one of the Fair, who quickly came down and deputed some of his most trusty friends to take these men into examination, about whom the Fair was almost overturned. So the men were brought to examination; and they that sat upon them,[2] asked them whence they came, whither they went, and what they did there in such an unusual garb? The men told them that they were pilgrims and strangers in the world, and that they were going to their own country, which was the heavenly Jerusalem;[3] and that they had given none occasion to

7. Mad people from Bedlam, the Hospital of St. Mary of Bethlehem, which was made an insane asylum in 1647. In 1 Corinthians 2.7 St. Paul says that Christian wisdom looks like folly to worldly observers.

8. The Promised Land in the Bible.

9. Psalm 119.37; Philippians 3.19, 3.20.

1. Proverbs 23.23.

2. Questioned them.

3. Hebrews 11.13–16.

the men of the town, nor yet to the merchandisers, thus to abuse them, and to let[4] them in their journey, except it was for that, when one asked them what they would buy, they said they would buy the truth. But they that were appointed to examine them did not believe them to be any other than bedlams and mad, or else such as came to put all things into a confusion in the Fair. Therefore they took them and beat them, and besmeared them with dirt, and then put them into the cage, that they might be made a spectacle to all the men of the Fair. There therefore they lay for some time, and were made the objects of any man's sport, or malice, or revenge, the great one of the Fair laughing still at all that befell them. But the men being patient, and not rendering railing for railing, but contrariwise blessing, and giving good words for bad, and kindness for injuries done, some men in the Fair that were more observing, and less prejudiced than the rest, began to check and blame the baser sort for their continual abuses done by them to the men; they therefore in angry manner let fly at them again, counting them as bad as the men in the cage, and telling them that they seemed confederates, and should be made partakers of their misfortunes. The other replied, that for aught they could see, the men were quiet, and sober, and intended nobody any harm; and that there were many that traded in their Fair that were more worthy to be put into the cage, yea, and pillory[5] too, than were the men that they had abused. Thus, after divers words had passed on both sides, (the men behaving themselves all the while very wisely and soberly before them) they fell to some blows among themselves, and did harm one to another. Then were these two poor men brought before their examiners again, and there charged as being guilty of the late hubbub that had been in the Fair. So they beat them pitifully and hanged irons upon them, and led them in chains up and down the Fair, for an example and a terror to others, lest any should further speak in their behalf, or join themselves unto them. But Christian and Faithful behaved themselves yet more wisely, and received the ignominy and shame that was cast upon them, with so much meekness and patience, that it won to their side (though but few in comparison of the rest) several of the men in the Fair. This put the other party yet into a greater rage, insomuch that they concluded the death of these two men. Wherefore they threatened, that the cage nor irons should serve their turn, but that they should die, for the abuse they had done, and for deluding the men of the Fair.

Behold Vanity Fair; the Pilgrims there
Are chained and stoned beside;
Even so it was, our Lord passed here,
And on Mount Calvary died.

Then were they remanded to the cage again, until further order should be taken with them. So they put them in, and made their feet fast in the stocks.

Here also they called again to mind what they had heard from their faithful friend Evangelist, and were the more confirmed in their way and sufferings, by what he told them would happen to them. They also now comforted each other, that whose lot it was to suffer, even he should have the best on't; therefore each man secretly wished that he might have that preferment: but committing themselves to the allwise dispose of Him that ruleth all things, with much content they abode in the condition in which they were, until they should be otherwise disposed of.

[END OF PERSPECTIVES: SPIRITUAL SELF-RECKONINGS]

4. Hinder.
5. A wooden framework with holes through which the head and the hands of the offender were placed, in which state he or she was subjected to the public hurling verbal abuse and such objects as rotten vegetables.

POLITICAL AND RELIGIOUS ORDERS

One political order that cannot be ignored by readers of British literature and history is the monarchy, since it provides the terms by which historical periods are even today divided up. Thus much of the nineteenth century is often spoken of as the "Victorian" age or period, after Queen Victoria (reigned 1837–1901), and the writing of the period is given the name Victorian literature. By the same token, writing of the period 1559–1603 is often called "Elizabethan" after Elizabeth I, and that of 1901–1910 "Edwardian" after Edward VII. This system however is based more on convention than logic, since few would call the history (or literature) of late twentieth-century Britain "Elizabethan" any more than they would call the history and literature of the eighteenth century "Georgian," though four king Georges reigned between 1714 and 1820. Where other, better terms exist these are generally adopted.

As these notes suggest, however, it is still common to think of British history in terms of the dates of the reigning monarch, even though the political influence of the monarchy has been strictly limited since the seventeenth century. Thus, where an outstanding political figure has emerged it is he or she who tends to name the period of a decade or longer; for the British, for example, the 1980s was the decade of "Thatcherism" as for Americans it was the period of "Reaganomics." The monarchy, though, still provides a point of common reference and has up to now shown a remarkable historical persistence, transforming itself as occasion dictates to fit new social circumstances. Thus, while most of the other European monarchies disappeared early in the twentieth century, if they had not already done so, the British institution managed to transform itself from imperial monarchy, a role adopted in the nineteenth century, to become the head of a welfare state and member of the European Union. Few of the titles gathered by Queen Victoria, such as Empress of India, remain to Elizabeth II (reigns 1952–), whose responsibilities now extend only to the British Isles with some vestigial role in Australia, Canada, and New Zealand among other places.

The monarchy's political power, like that of the aristocracy, has been successively diminished over the past several centuries, with the result that today both monarch and aristocracy have only formal authority. This withered state of today's institutions, however, should not blind us to the very real power they wielded in earlier centuries. Though the medieval monarch King John had famously been obliged to recognize the rule of law by signing the Magna Carta ("Great Charter") in 1215, thus ending arbitrary rule, the sixteenth- and seventeenth-century English monarchs still officially ruled by "divine right" and were under no obligation to attend to the wishes of Parliament. Charles I in the 1630s reigned mostly without summoning a parliament, and the concept of a "constitutional monarchy," being one whose powers were formally bound by statute, was introduced only when King William agreed to the Declaration of Right in 1689. This document, together with the contemporaneous Bill of Rights, while recognizing that sovereignty still rests in the monarch, formally transferred executive and legislative powers to Parliament. Bills still have to receive Royal Assent, though this was last denied by Queen Anne in 1707; the monarch still holds "prerogative" powers, though these, which include the appointment of certain officials, the dissolution of Parliament and so on, are, in practice wielded by the prime minister. Further information on the political character of various historical periods can be found in the period introductions.

Political power in Britain is thus held by the prime minister and his or her cabinet, members of which are also members of the governing party in the House of Commons. As long as the government is able to command a majority in the House of Commons, sometimes by a coalition of several parties but more usually by the absolute majority of one, it both makes the laws and carries them out. The situation is therefore very different from the American doctrine of the "Separation of Powers," in which Congress is independent of the President and can even be controlled by the opposing party. The British state of affairs has led to the office of prime minister being compared to that of an "elected dictatorship" with surprising frequency over the past several hundred years.

British government is bicameral, having both an upper and a lower house. Unlike other bicameral systems, however, the upper house, the House of Lords, is not elected, its membership being largely hereditary. Membership can come about in four main ways: (1) by birth, (2) by appointment by the current prime minister often in consultation with the Leader of the Opposition, (3) by virtue of holding a senior position in the judiciary, and (4) by being a bishop of the Established Church (the Church of England). In the House of Commons, the lower house, the particular features of the British electoral system have meant that there are never more than two large parties, one of which is in power. These are, together, "Her Majesty's Government and Opposition." Local conditions in Northern Ireland and Scotland have meant that these areas sometimes send members to Parliament in London who are members neither of the Conservative nor of the Labour parties; in general, however, the only other group in the Commons is the small Liberal Party.

Taking these categories in turn, all members of the hereditary aristocracy (the "peerage") have a seat in the House of Lords. The British aristocracy, unlike those of other European countries, was never formally dispossessed of political power (for example by a revolution), and though their influence is now limited, nevertheless all holders of hereditary title—dukes, marquesses, earls, viscounts and barons, in that order of precedence—sit in the Lords. Some continue to do political work and may be members of the Government or of the Opposition, though today it would be considered unusual for a senior member of government to sit in the House of Lords. The presence of the hereditary element in the Lords tends to give the institution a conservative tone, though the presence of the other members ensures this is by no means always the case. Secondly there are "life peers," who are created by the monarch on the prime minister's recommendation under legislation dating from 1958. They are generally individuals who have distinguished themselves in one field or another; retiring senior politicians from the Commons are generally elevated to the Lords, for example, as are some senior civil servants, diplomats, business and trade union leaders, academics, figures in the arts, retiring archbishops, and members of the military. Some of these take on formal political responsibilities and others do not. Finally, senior members of the judiciary sit in the Lords as Law Lords, while senior members of the Church of England hierarchy also sit in the Lords and frequently intervene in political matters. It has been a matter of some controversy whether senior members of other religious denominations, or religions, should also sit in the House of Lords. Within the constitution (by the Parliament Act of 1911 and other acts) the powers of the House of Lords are limited mostly to the amendment and delay of legislation; from time to time the question of its reform or abolition is raised.

In addition, there are minor orders of nobility that should be mentioned. A baronet is a holder of a hereditary title, but he is not a member of the peerage; the style is Sir (followed by his first and last names), Baronet (usually abbreviated as Bart. or Bt.). A knight is a member of one of the various orders of British knighthood, the oldest of which dates back to the Middle Ages (the Order of the Garter), the majority to the eighteenth or nineteenth centuries (the Order of the Thistle, the Bath, Saint Michael, and Saint George, etc.). The title is nonhereditary and is given for various services; it is marked by various initials coming after the name. K.C.B., for example, stands for "Knight Commander of the Bath," and there are many others.

In the House of Commons itself, the outstanding feature is the dominance of the party system. Party labels, such as "Whigs" and "Tories," were first used from the late seventeenth century, when groups of members began to form opposing factions in a Parliament now freed of much of the power of the king. The "Tories," for example, a name now used to refer to the modern Conservative Party, were originally members of that faction that supported James II (exiled in 1689); the word "Tory" comes from the Irish (Gaelic) for outlaw or thief. The "Whigs," on the other hand, supported the constitutional reforms associated with the 1689 Glorious Revolution; the word "whig" is obscurely related to the idea of regicide. The Whig faction largely dominated the political history of the eighteenth century, though the electorate was too small, and politics too controlled by the patronage of the great aristocratic families, for much of a party system to develop. It was only in the middle decades of the nineteenth century that the familiar party system in parliament and the associated electioneering organization in the country at large came into being. The Whigs were replaced by the Liberal Party around the mid-century, as the Liberals were to be replaced by the Labour Party in the early decades of the twentieth century; the Tories had become firm Conservatives by the time of Lord Derby's administrations in the mid-nineteenth century.

The party system has always been fertile ground for a certain amount of parliamentary theater, and it has fostered the emergence of some powerful personalities. Whereas the eighteenth-century Whig prime minister Sir Robert Walpole owed his authority to a mixture of personal patronage and the power made available through the alliances of powerful families, nineteenth-century figures such as Benjamin Disraeli (Conservative prime minister 1868, 1874–1880) and William Ewart Gladstone (Liberal prime minister 1868–1874; 1880–1885; 1885; 1892–1894), were at the apex of their respective party machines. Disraeli, theatrical, personable and with a keen eye for publicity (he was, among other things, a close personal friend of Queen Victoria), formed a great contrast to the massive moral appeals of his parliamentary opponent Gladstone. One earlier figure, William Pitt (1759–1806), prime minister at twenty-four and leader of the country during the French Revolution and earlier Napoleonic wars, stands comparison with these in the historical record; of twentieth-century political figures, David Lloyd-George, Liberal prime minister during World War I, and Winston Churchill, Conservative, during World War II, deserve special mention.

Though political power in the United Kingdom now rests with Parliament at Westminster in London, this has not always been the only case. Wales, which is now formally a principality within the political construction "England and Wales," was conquered by the English toward the end of the thirteenth century—too early for indigenous representative institutions to have fallen into place. Scotland, on the other hand, which from 1603 was linked with England under a joint monarchy but only became part of the same political entity with the Act of Union in 1707, did develop discrete institutions. Recent votes in both Scotland and Wales are leading toward greater local legislative control over domestic issues in both Scotland and Wales. Many Scottish institutions—for example, the legal and educational systems—are substantially different from those of England, which is not true in the case of Wales. The Church of Scotland in particular has no link with the Church of England, having been separately established in 1690 on a Presbyterian basis; this means that authority in the Scottish church is vested in elected pastors and lay elders and not in an ecclesiastical hierarchy of priests and bishops. But the most vexed of the relationships within the union has undoubtedly been that between England and Ireland.

There has been an English presence in Ireland from the Middle Ages on, and this became dominant in the later sixteenth century when English policy was deliberately to conquer and colonize the rest of the country. The consequence of this policy, however, was that an Irish Protestant "Ascendancy" came to rule over a largely dispossessed Catholic Irish peasantry; in 1689 at the Battle of the Boyne this state of affairs was made permanent, as Irish Catholic support for the exiled and Catholic-sympathizing James II was routed by the invading troops of the new Protestant king, William III. An Irish parliament met in Dublin, but this was restricted to Protestants; the Church of Ireland was the established Protestant church in a country where most of the population was Catholic. Irish political representation was shifted to Westminster by Pitt in 1800 under the formal Act of Union with Ireland; the Church of Ireland was disestablished by Gladstone later in the century. In the twentieth century, continuing agitation in the Catholic south of the country first for Home Rule and subsequently for independence from Britain—agitation that had been a feature of almost the whole nineteenth century at greater or lesser levels of intensity—led to the establishment first of the Irish Free State (1922) and later of the Republic (1948). In the Protestant North of the country, a local parliament met from 1922 within the common framework of the United Kingdom, but this was suspended in 1972 and representation returned to Westminster, as renewed violence in the province threatened local institutions. In Northern Ireland several hundred years of conflict between Protestants, who form the majority of the population in the province, and Catholics have led to continuing political problems.

Since the Reformation in the sixteenth century Britain has officially been a Protestant country with a national church headed by the monarch. This "Established Church," the Church of England or Anglican Church, has its own body of doctrine in the Thirty-Nine Articles and elsewhere, its own order of services in the Book of Common Prayer, and its own translation of the Bible (the "Authorized Version"), commissioned by James I (reigned 1603–1625) as Head of the Church. There is an extensive ecclesiastical hierarchy and a worldwide communion that includes the American Episcopalian Church.

The Reformation in England was not an easy business, and it has certain negative consequences even today. Some of these have been touched upon above in the case of Ireland. Those professing Roman Catholicism were excluded from political office and suffered other penalties until 1829, and a Catholic hierarchy parallel to that of the Church of England only came into being in Britain in the later nineteenth century. Though many of the restrictions on Roman Catholics enacted by Act of Parliament at the end of the seventeenth century were considerably softened in the course of the eighteenth, nevertheless they were very real.

English Protestantism, however, is far from being all of a piece. As early as the sixteenth century, many saw the substitution of the King's authority and that of the national ecclesiastical hierarchy for that of the Pope to be no genuine Protestant Reformation, which they thought demanded local autonomy and individual judgment. In the seventeenth century many "dissenting" or "Non-Conformist" Protestant sects thus grew up or gathered strength (many becoming "Puritans"), and these rejected the authority of the national church and its bishops and so the authority of the king. They had a brief moment of freedom during the Civil War and the Commonwealth (1649–1660) following the execution of Charles I, when there was a flowering of sects from Baptists and Quakers, which still exist today, to Ranters, Shakers, Anabaptists, Muggletonians, etc., which in the main do not (except for some sects in the United States). The monarchy and the Church were decisively reestablished in 1660, but subsequent legislation, most importantly the Act of Toleration (1689), suspended laws against dissenters on certain conditions.

Religious dissent or nonconformity remained powerful social movements over the following centuries and received new stimulus from the "New Dissenting" revivalist movements of the eighteenth century (particularly Methodism, though there was also a growth in the Congregationalist and Baptist churches). By the nineteenth century, the social character and geographical pattern of English dissent had been established: religious nonconformity was a feature of the new working classes brought into being by the Industrial Revolution in the towns of the Midlands and North of England. Anglicanism, which was associated with the pre-industrial traditional order, was rejected also by many among the rising bourgeoisie and lower middle classes; almost every major English novel of the mid-nineteenth century and beyond is written against a background of religious nonconformity or dissent, which had complex social and political meanings. Nonconformity was also a particular feature of Welsh society.

Under legislation enacted by Edward I in 1290, the Jews were expelled from England, and there were few of them in the country until the end of the seventeenth century, when well-established Jewish communities began to appear in London (the medieval legislation was repealed under the Commonwealth in the 1650s). Restrictions on Jews holding public office continued until the mid-nineteenth century, and at the end of the century large Jewish communities were formed in many English cities by refugees from Central and Eastern European anti-Semitism.

Britain today is a multicultural country and significant proportions of the population, many of whom came to Britain from former British Empire territories, profess Hinduism or Islam, among other religions. The United Kingdom has been a member of the European Union since the early 1970s, and this has further loosened ties between Britain and former empire territories or dominions, many of which are still linked to Britain by virtue of the fact that the British monarch is Head of the "Commonwealth," an organization to which many of them belong. In some cases, the British monarch is also Head of State. Most importantly, however, British membership of the European Union has meant that powers formerly held by the national parliament have been transferred either to the European Parliament in Strasbourg, France, or to the European Commission, the executive agency in Brussels, Belgium, or, in the case of judicial review and appeal, to the European Court of Justice. This process seems set to generate tensions in Britain for some years to come.

David Tresilian

English Monarchs

Before the Norman conquest (1066), these included:

Alfred the Great	871–899
Edmund I	940–946
Ethelred the Unready	948–1016
Edward the Confessor	1042–1066
Harold II	1066

The following monarchs are divided by the dynasty ("House") to which they belong:

Normandy

William I the Conqueror	1066–1087
William II, Rufus	1087–1100
Henry I	1100–1135

Blois

Stephen	1135–1154

Plantagenet

Henry II	1154–1189
Richard I "Coeur de Lion"	1189–1199
John	1199–1216
Henry III	1216–1272
Edward I	1272–1307
Edward II	1307–1327
Edward III	1327–1377
Richard II	1377–1400

Lancaster

Henry IV	1399–1413
Henry V	1413–1422
Henry VI	1422–1471

York

Edward IV	1461–1483
Edward V	1483
Richard III	1483–1485

Tudor

Henry VII	1485–1509
Henry VIII	1509–1547
Edward VI	1547–1553
Mary I	1553–1558
Elizabeth I	1558–1603

Kings of England and of Scotland:

Stuart

James I (James VI of Scotland)	1603–1625
Charles I	1625–1649

Commonwealth (Republic)

Council of State	1649–1653
Oliver Cromwell, Lord Protector	1653–1658
Richard Cromwell	1658–1660

Stuart

Charles II	1660–1685
James II	1685–1688
(Interregnum 1688–1689)	
William III and Mary II	1685–1701 (Mary dies 1694)
Anne	1702–1714

Hanover

George I	1714–1727
George II	1727–1760
George III	1760–1820
George IV	1820–1830
William IV	1830–1837
Victoria	1837–1901

Saxe-Coburg and Gotha

Edward VII	1901–1910

Windsor

George V	1910–1936
Edward VIII	1936
George VI	1936–1952
Elizabeth II	1952–

MONEY, WEIGHTS, AND MEASURES

The possibility of confusion by the British monetary system has considerably decreased since 1971, when decimalization of the currency took place. There are now 100 pence to a pound (worth about $1.60 in the late 1990s). Prior to this date the currency featured a gallery of other units as well. These coins—shillings, crowns, half-crowns, florins, threepenny-bits, and farthings—were contemporary survivals of the currency's historical development. As such they had a familiar presence in the culture, which was reflected in the slang terms used to refer to them in the spoken language. At least one of these terms, that of a "quid" for a pound, is still in use today.

The old currency divided the pound into 20 shillings, each of which contained 12 pence. There were, therefore, 240 pence in 1 pound. Five shillings made a crown, a half-crown was 2½ shillings, and a florin was 2 shillings; there was also a sixpence, a threepenny-bit, and a farthing (a quarter of a penny). In slang, a shilling was a "bob," a sixpence a "tanner," and a penny a "copper." Sums were written as, for example, £12. 6s. 6d. or £12/6/6 (12 pounds, 6 shillings, and 6 pence; the "d." stands for "denarius," from the Latin). Figures up to £5 were often expressed in shillings alone: the father of the novelist D. H. Lawrence, for instance, who was a coal miner, was paid around 35 shillings a week at the beginning of the twentieth century—i.e., 1 pound and 15 shillings, or £1/15/–. At this time two gold coins were also still in circulation, the sovereign (£1) and the half-sovereign (10s.), which had been the principal coins of the nineteenth century; the largest silver coin was the half-crown (2 / 6). Later all coins were composed either of copper or an alloy of copper and nickel. The guinea was £1/1/– (1 pound and 1 shilling, or 21 shillings); though the actual coin had not been minted since the beginning of the nineteenth century, the term was still used well into the twentieth to price luxury items and to pay professional fees.

The number of dollars that a pound could buy has fluctuated with British economic fortunes. The current figure has been noted above; in 1912 it was about $5.00. To get a sense of how much the pound was worth to those who used it as an everyday index of value, however, we have to look at what it could buy within the system in which it was used. To continue the Lawrence example, a coal miner may have been earning 35 shillings a week in the early years of the twentieth century, but of this he would have to have paid six shillings as rent on the family house; his son, by contrast, could command a figure of £300 as a publisher's advance on his novel *The Rainbow* (pub. 1915), a sum which alone would have placed him somewhere in the middle class. In *A Room of One's Own* (1928) Virginia Woolf recommended the figure of £500 a year as necessary if a woman were to write; at today's values this would be worth around £25,000 ($41,000)—considerably more than the pay of, for example, a junior faculty member at a British university, either then or now.

In earlier periods an idea of the worth of the currency, being the relation between wages and prices, can similarly be established by taking samples from across the country at specific dates. Toward the end of the seventeenth century, for example, Poor Law records tell us that a family of five could be considered to subsist on an annual income of £13/14/–, which included £9/14/– spent on food. At the same time an agricultural laborer earned around £15/12/– annually, while at the upper end of the social scale, the aristocracy dramatically recovered and increased their wealth in the period after the restoration of the monarchy in 1660. By 1672 the early industrialist Lord Wharton was realizing an annual profit of £3,200 on his lead mine and smelting plant in the north of England; landed aristocratic families such as the Russells, sponsors of the 1689 Glorious Revolution and later dukes of Bedford, were already worth £10,000 a year in 1660. Such details allow us to form some idea of the value of the £10 the poet John Milton received for *Paradise Lost* (pub. 1667), as well as to see the great wealth that went into building the eighteenth-century estates that now dot the English countryside.

By extending the same method to the analysis of wage-values during the Industrial Revolution over a century and a half later, the economic background to incidents of public disorder in the period, such as the 1819 "Peterloo Massacre," can be reconstructed, as can the background to the poems of Wordsworth, for example, many of which concern vagrancy and the lives of the rural poor. Thus the essayist William Cobbett calculated in the 1820s that £1/4/– a week was needed to support a family of five, though actual average earnings were less than half this sum. By contrast, Wordsworth's projection of "a volume which consisting of 160 pages might be sold at 5 shillings" (1806)—part of the negotiations for his *Poems in Two Volumes* (1807)—firmly establishes the book as a luxury item. Jane Austen's contemporaneous novel *Mansfield Park* (1814), which gives many details about the economic affairs of the English rural gentry, suggests that at least £1000 a year is a desirable income.

Today's pound sterling, though still cited on the international exchanges with the dollar, the deutsche mark, and the yen, decisively lost to the dollar after World War I as the central currency in the international system. At present it seems highly likely that, with some other European national currencies, it will shortly cease to exist as the currency unit of the European Union is adopted as a single currency in the constituent countries of the Union.

British weights and measures present less difficulty to American readers since the vast inertia permeating industry and commerce following the separation of the United States from Britain prevented the reform of American weights and measures along metric lines, which had taken place where the monetary system was concerned. Thus the British "Imperial" system, with some minor local differences, was in place in both countries until decimalization of the British system began in stages from the early 1970s on. Today all British weights and measures, with the exception of road signs, which still generally give distances in miles, are metric in order to bring Britain into line with European Union standards. Though it is still possible to hear especially older people measuring area in acres and not in hectares, distances in miles and not in kilometers, or feet and yards and not centimeters and meters, weight in pounds and ounces and not in grams and kilograms, and temperature in Fahrenheit and not in centigrade, etc., it is becoming increasingly uncommon. Measures of distance that might be found in older texts—such as the league (three miles, but never in regular use), the furlong (220 yards), and the ell (45 inches)—are now all obsolete; the only measure still heard in current use is the stone (14 pounds), and this is generally used for body weight.

David Tresilian

LITERARY AND CULTURAL TERMS*

Absolutism. In criticism, the belief in irreducible, unchanging values of form and content that underlie the tastes of individuals and periods and arise from the stability of an absolute hierarchical order.

Accent. Stress or emphasis on a syllable, as opposed to the syllable's length of duration, its quantity. *Metrical accent* denotes the metrical pattern (⌣ –) to which writers fit and adjust accented words and rhetorical emphases, keeping the meter as they substitute word-accented feet and tune their rhetoric.

Accentual Verse. Verse with lines established by counting accents only, without regard to the number of unstressed syllables. This was the dominant form of verse in English until the time of Chaucer.

Acrostic. Words arranged, frequently in a poem or puzzle, to disclose a hidden word or message when the correct combination of letters is read in sequence.

Aestheticism. Devotion to beauty. The term applies particularly to a 19th-century literary and artistic movement celebrating beauty as independent from morality, and praising form above content; art for art's sake.

Aesthetics. The study of the beautiful; the branch of philosophy concerned with defining the nature of art and establishing criteria of judgment.

Alexandrine. A six-foot iambic pentameter line.

Allegorical Meaning. A secondary meaning of a narrative in addition to its primary meaning or literal meaning.

Allegory. A story that suggests another story. The first part of this word comes from the Greek *allos,* "other." An allegory is present in literature whenever it is clear that the author is saying, "By this I also mean that." In practice, allegory appears when a progression of events or images suggests a translation of them into conceptual language. Allegory is thus a technique of aligning imaginative constructs, mythological or poetic, with conceptual or moral models. During the Romantic era a distinction arose between allegory and symbol. With Coleridge, symbol took precedence: "an allegory is but a translation of abstract notions into picture-language," but "a symbol always partakes of the reality which it makes intelligible."

Alliteration. "Adding letters" (Latin *ad* + *littera,* "letter"). Two or more words, or accented syllables, chime on the same initial letter (*l*ost *l*ove *a*lone; *a*fter *a*pple-picking) or repeat the same consonant.

Alliterative Revival. The outburst of alliterative verse that occurred in the second half of the 14th century in west and northwest England.

Alliterative Verse. Verse using alliteration on stressed syllables for its fundamental structure.

Allusion. A meaningful reference, direct or indirect, as when William Butler Yeats writes, "Another Troy must rise and set," calling to mind the whole tragic history of Troy.

Amplification. A restatement of something more fully and in more detail, especially in oratory, poetry, and music.

Analogy. A comparison between things similar in a number of ways; frequently used to explain the unfamiliar by the familiar.

Anapest. A metrical foot: ⌣ ⌣ –.

Anaphora. The technique of beginning successive clauses or lines with the same word.

*Adapted from *The Harper Handbook to Literature* by Northrop Frye, Sheridan Baker, George Perkins, and Barbara M. Perkins, 2d edition (Longman, 1997).

Anatomy. Greek for "a cutting up": a dissection, analysis, or systematic study. The term was popular in titles in the 16th and 17th centuries.

Anglo-Norman (Language). The language of upper-class England after the Norman Conquest in 1066.

Anglo-Saxon. The people, culture, and language of three neighboring tribes—Jutes, Angles, and Saxons—who invaded England, beginning in 449, from the lower part of Denmark's Jutland Peninsula. The Angles, settling along the eastern seaboard of central and northern England, developed the first literate culture of any Germanic people. Hence England (Angle-land) became the dominant term.

Antagonist. In Greek drama, the character who opposes the protagonist, or hero: therefore, any character who opposes another. In some works, the antagonist is clearly the villain (Iago in *Othello*), but in strict terminology an antagonist is merely an opponent and may be in the right.

Anthropomorphism. The practice of giving human attributes to animals, plants, rivers, winds, and the like, or to such entities as Grecian urns and abstract ideas.

Antithesis. (1) A direct contrast or opposition. (2) The second phase of dialectical argument, which considers the opposition—the three steps being *thesis, antithesis, synthesis*. (3) A rhetorical figure sharply contrasting ideas in balanced parallel structures.

Aphorism. A pithy saying of known authorship, as distinguished from a folk proverb.

Apology. A justification, as in Sir Philip Sidney's *The Apology for Poetry* (1595).

Apostrophe. (Greek, "a turning away"). An address to an absent or imaginary person, a thing, or a personified abstraction.

Archaism. An archaic or old-fashioned word or expression—for example, *o'er, ere,* or *darkling*.

Archetype. (1) The first of a genre, like Homer's *Iliad,* the first heroic epic. (2) A natural symbol imprinted in human consciousness by experience and literature, like dawn symbolizing hope or an awakening; night, death or repose.

Assonance. Repetition of middle vowel sounds: *fight, hive; pane, make*. Assonance, most effective on stressed syllables, is often found within a line of poetry; less frequently it substitutes for end rhyme.

Aubade. Dawn song, from French *aube*, for dawn. The aubade originated in the Middle Ages as a song sung by a lover greeting the dawn, ordinarily expressing regret that morning means parting.

Avant-Garde. Experimental, innovative, at the forefront of a literary or artistic trend or movement. The term is French for *vanguard,* the advance unit of an army. It frequently suggests a struggle with tradition and convention.

Ballad. A narrative poem in short stanzas, with or without music. The term derives by way of French *ballade* from Latin *ballare*, "to dance," and once meant a simple song of any kind, lyric or narrative, especially one to accompany a dance. As ballads evolved, most lost their association with dance, although they kept their strong rhythms. Modern usage distinguishes three major kinds: the anonymous *traditional ballad* (popular ballad or *folk ballad*), transmitted orally; the *broadside ballad,* printed and sold on single sheets; and the *literary ballad* (or art ballad), a sophisticated imitation of the traditional ballad.

Ballad Stanza. The name for common meter as found in ballads: a quatrain in iambic meter, alternating tetrameter and trimeter lines, usually rhyming *abcb*.

Bard. An ancient Celtic singer of the culture's lore in epic form; a poetic term for any poet.

Baroque. (1) A richly ornamented style in architecture and art. Founded in Rome by Frederigo Barocci about 1550, and characterized by swirling allegorical frescoes on ceilings and walls, it flourished throughout Europe until 1700. (2) A chromatic musical style with strict forms containing similar exuberant ornamentation, flourishing from 1600 to 1750. In literature, Richard Crashaw's bizarre imagery and the conceits and rhythms of John Donne and other metaphysical poets are sometimes called baroque, sometimes mannerist.

Some literary historians designate a Baroque Age from 1580 to 1680, between the Renaissance and the Enlightenment.

Bathos. (1) A sudden slippage from the sublime to the ridiculous. (2) Any anticlimax. (3) Sentimental pathos. (4) Triteness or dullness.

Blank Verse. Unrhymed iambic pentameter. *See also* Meter. In the 1540s Henry Howard, earl of Surrey, seems to have originated it in English as the equivalent of Virgil's unrhymed dactylic hexameter. In *Gorboduc* (1561), Thomas Sackville and Thomas Norton introduced blank verse into the drama, whence it soared with Marlowe and Shakespeare in the 1590s. Milton forged it anew for the epic in *Paradise Lost* (1667).

Bloomsbury Group. An informal social and intellectual group associated with Bloomsbury, a London residential district near the British Museum, from about 1904 until the outbreak of World War II. Virginia Woolf was a principal member. With her husband, Leonard Woolf, she established the Hogarth Press, which published works by many of their friends. The group was loosely knit, but famed, especially in the 1920s, for its exclusiveness, aestheticism, and social and political freethinking.

Broadside. A sheet of paper printed on one side only. Broadsides containing a ballad, a tract, a criminal's gallows speech, a scurrilous satire, and the like were once commonly sold on the streets like newspapers.

Burden. (1) A refrain or set phrase repeated at intervals throughout a song or poem. (2) A bass accompaniment, the "load" carried by the melody, the origin of the term.

Burlesque. (1) A ridicule, especially on the stage, treating the lofty in low style, or the low in grandiose style. (2) A bawdy vaudeville, with obscene clowning and stripteasing.

Caesura. A pause in a metrical line, indicated by punctuation, momentarily suspending the beat (from Latin "a cutting off"). Caesuras are *masculine* at the end of a foot, and *feminine* in mid-foot.

Canon. The writings accepted as forming a part of the Bible, of the works of an author, or of a body of literature. Shakespeare's canon consists of works he wrote, which may be distinguished from works attributed to him but written by others. The word derives from Greek *kanon*, "rod" or "rule," and suggests authority. Canonical authors and texts are those taught most frequently, noncanonical are those rarely taught, and in between are disputed degrees of canonicity for authors considered minor or marginalized.

Canto. A major division in a long poem. The Italian expression is from Latin *cantus*, "song," a section singable in one sitting.

Caricature. Literary cartooning, depicting characters with exaggerated physical traits such as huge noses and bellies, short stature, squints, tics, humped backs, and so forth. Sir Thomas Browne seems to have introduced the term into English in 1682 from the Italian *caricatura*.

Catalog. In literature, an enumeration of ancestors, of ships, of warriors, of a woman's beauties, and the like; a standard feature of the classical epic.

Celtic Revival. In the 18th century, a groundswell of the Romantic movement in discovering the power in ancient, primitive poetry, particularly Welsh and Scottish Gaelic, as distinct from that of the classics.

Chiasmus. A rhetorical balance created by the inversion of one of two parallel phrases or clauses; from the Greek for a "placing crosswise," as in the Greek letter χ (chi).

Chronicle. A kind of history, with the emphasis on *time* (Greek *chronos*). Events are described in order as they occurred. The chronicles of the Middle Ages provided material for later writers and serve now as important sources of knowledge about the period. Raphael Holinshed's *Chronicle* (1577) is especially famous as the immediate source of much of Shakespeare's knowledge of English history.

Chronicle Play. A play dramatizing historical events, as from a chronicle. Chronicle plays tend to stress time order, presenting the reign of a king, for example, with much emphasis on pageantry and little on the unity of action and dramatic conflict necessary for a tragedy.

Classical Literature. (1) The literature of ancient Greece and Rome. (2) Later literature reflecting the qualities of classical Greece or Rome. *See also*, Classicism; Neoclassicism. (3) The classic literature of any time or place, as, for example, classical American literature or classical Japanese literature.

Classicism. A principle in art and conduct reflecting the ethos of ancient Greece and Rome: balance, form, proportion, propriety, dignity, simplicity, objectivity, rationality, restraint, unity rather than diversity. In English literature, classicism emerged with Erasmus (1466–1536) and his fellow humanists. In the Restoration and 18th century, classicism, or neoclassicism, expressed society's deep need for balance and restraint after the shattering Civil War and Puritan commonwealth. Classicism continued in the 19th century, after the Romantic period, particularly in the work of Matthew Arnold. T. E. Hulme, Ezra Pound, and T. S. Eliot expressed it for the 20th century.

Cliché. An overused expression, once clever or metaphorical but now trite and timeworn.

Closed Couplet. The heroic couplet, especially when the thought and grammar are complete in the two iambic pentameter lines.

Closet Drama. A play written for reading in the "closet," or private study. Closet dramas were usually in verse, like Percy Shelley's *Prometheus Unbound* (1820) and Robert Browning's *Pippa Passes* (1841).

Cockney. A native of the East End of central London. The term originally meant "cocks' eggs," a rural term of contempt for city softies and fools. Cockneys are London's ingenious street peddlers, speaking a dialect rich with an inventive rhyming slang, dropping and adding aitches.

Comedy. One of the typical literary structures, originating as a form of drama and later extending into prose fiction and other genres as well. Comedy, as Susanne Langer says, is the image of Fortune; tragedy, the image of Fate. Each sorts out for attention the different facts of life. Comedy sorts its pleasures. It pleases our egos and endows our dreams, stirring at once two opposing impulses, our vindictive lust for superiority and our wishful drive for success and happiness ever after. The dark impulse stirs the pleasure of laughter; the light, the pleasure of wish fulfillment.

Comedy of Humors. Comedy based on the ancient physiological theory that a predominance of one of the body's four fluids (humors) produces a comically unbalanced personality: (1) blood—sanguine, hearty, cheerful, amorous; (2) phlegm—phlegmatic, sluggish; (3) choler (yellow bile)—angry, touchy; (4) black bile—melancholic.

Comedy of Manners. Suave, witty, and risqué, satire of upper-class manners and immorals, particularly that of Restoration masters like George Etherege and William Congreve.

Common Meter. The ballad stanza as found in hymns and other poems: a quatrain (four-line stanza) in iambic meter, alternating tetrameter and trimeter, rhyming *abcb* or *abab*.

Complaint. A lyric poem, popular in the Middle Ages and the Renaissance, complaining of unrequited love, a personal situation, or the state of the world.

Conceit. Any fanciful, ingenious expression or idea, but especially one in the form of an extended metaphor.

Concordia Discors. "Discordant harmony," a phrase expressing for the 18th century the harmonious diversity of nature, a pleasing balance of opposites.

Concrete Poetry. Poetry that attempts a concrete embodiment of its idea, expressing itself physically apart from the meaning of the words. A recent relative of the much older *shaped poem*, the concrete poem places heavy emphasis on the picture and less on the words, so that the visual experience may be more interesting than the linguistic.

Connotation. The ideas, attitudes, or emotions associated with a word in the mind of speaker or listener, writer or reader. It is contrasted with the *denotation*, the thing the word stands for, the dictionary definition, an objective concept without emotional coloring.

Consonance. (1) Repetition of inner or end consonant sounds, as, for example, the *r* and *s* sounds from Gerard Manley Hopkins's *God's Grandeur*: "broods with warm breast." (2) In a broader sense, a generally pleasing combination of sounds or ideas; things that sound well together.

Couplet. A pair of rhymed metrical lines, usually in iambic tetrameter or pentameter. Sometimes the two lines are of different length.

Covenanters. Scottish Presbyterians who signed a covenant in 1557 as a "godly band" to stand together to resist the Anglican church and the English establishment.

Cynghanedd. A complex medieval Welsh system of rhyme, alliteration, and consonance, to which Gerard Manley Hopkins alluded to describe his interplay of euphonious sounds, actually to be heard in any rich poet, as in the Welsh Dylan Thomas: "The force that through the green fuse drives the flower / Drives my green age."

Dactyl. A three-syllable metrical foot: – ⌣ ⌣. It is the basic foot of dactylic hexameter, the six-foot line of Greek and Roman epic poetry.

Dactylic Hexameter. The classical or heroic line of the epic. A line based on six dactylic feet, with spondees substituted, and always ending – ⌣⌣ | – –.

Dead Metaphor. A metaphor accepted without its figurative picture: "a jacket," for the paper around a book, with no mental picture of the human coat that prompted the original metaphor.

Decasyllabic. Having ten syllables. An iambic pentameter line is decasyllabic.

Deconstruction. The critical dissection of a literary text's statements, ambiguities, and structure to expose its hidden contradictions, implications, and fundamental instability of meaning. Jacques Derrida originated deconstruction in *Of Grammatology* (1967) and *Writing and Difference* (1967). Because no understanding of any text is stable, as each new reading is subject to the deconstruction of any meaning it appears to have established, it follows that criticism can be a kind of game, either playful or serious, as each critic ingeniously deconstructs the meanings established by others.

Decorum. Propriety, fitness, the quality of being appropriate. George Puttenham, in his *Arte of English Poesie* (1589), chides a translator of Virgil for his indecorum of having Aeneas "trudge," like a beggar, from Troy.

Defamiliarization. Turning the familiar to the strange by disrupting habitual ways of perceiving things. Derived from the thought of Victor Shklovsky and other Russian formalists, the idea is that art forces us to see things differently as we view them through the artist's sensibility, not our own.

Deism. A rational philosophy of religion, beginning with the theories of Lord Herbert of Cherbury, the "Father of Deism," in his *De Veritate* (1624). Deists generally held that God, the supreme Artisan, created a perfect clock of a universe, withdrew, and left it running, not to return to intervene in its natural works or the life of humankind; that the Bible is a moral guide, but neither historically accurate nor divinely authentic; and that reason guides human beings to virtuous conduct.

Denotation. The thing that a word stands for, the dictionary definition, an objective concept without emotional coloring. It is contrasted with the *connotation*, ideas, attitudes, or emotions associated with the word in the mind of user or hearer.

Dénouement. French for "unknotting": the unraveling of plot threads toward the end of a play, novel, or other narrative.

Determinism. The philosophical belief that events are shaped by forces beyond the control of human beings.

Dialect. A variety of language belonging to a particular time, place, or social group, as, for example, an 18th-century cockney dialect, a New England dialect, or a coal miner's dialect. A language other than one's own is for the most part unintelligible without study or translation; a dialect other than one's own can generally be understood, although pronunciation, vocabulary, and syntax seem strange.

Dialogue. Conversation between two or more persons, as represented in prose fiction, drama, or essays, as opposed to *monologue*, the speech of one person. Good dialogue characterizes each speaker by idiom and attitude as it advances the dramatic conflict. The dialogue as a form of speculative exposition, or dialectical argument, is often less careful to distinguish the diction and character of the speakers.

Diatribe. Greek for "a wearing away": a bitter and abusive criticism or invective, often lengthy, directed against a person, institution, or work.

Diction. Word choice in speech or writing, an important element of style.

Didactic. Greek for "teaching": instructive, or having the qualities of a teacher. Since ancient times, literature has been assumed to have two functions, instruction and entertainment, with sometimes one and sometimes the other dominant. Literature intended primarily for instruction or containing an important moralistic element is didactic.

Dirge. A lamenting funeral song.

Discourse. (1) A formal discussion of a subject. (2) The conventions of communication associated with specific areas, in usages such as "poetic discourse," "the discourse of the novel," or "historical discourse."

Dissenter. A term arising in the 1640s for a member of the clergy or a follower who dissented from the forms of the established Anglican church, particularly Puritans. Dissenters generally came from the lower middle classes, merchants who disapproved of aristocratic frivolity and ecclesiastical pomp.

Dissonance. (1) Harsh and jarring sound; discord. It is frequently an intentional effect, as in the poems of Robert Browning. (2) Occasionally a term for half rhyme or slant rhyme.

Distich. A couplet, or pair of rhymed metrical lines.

Dithyramb. A frenzied choral song and dance to honor Dionysus, Greek god of wine and the power of fertility. Any irregular, impassioned poetry may be called *dithyrambic*. The irregular ode also evolved from the dithyramb.

Doggerel. (1) Trivial verse clumsily aiming at meter, usually tetrameter. (2) Any verse facetiously low and loose in meter and rhyme.

Domesday Book. The recorded census and survey of landholders that William the Conqueror ordered in 1085; from "Doomsday," the Last Judgment.

Dramatic Irony. A character in drama or fiction unknowingly says or does something in ironic contrast to what the audience or reader knows or will learn.

Dramatic Monologue. A monologue in verse. A speaker addresses a silent listener, revealing, in dramatic irony, things about himself or herself of which the speaker is unaware.

Eclogue. A short poem, usually a pastoral, and often in the form of a dialogue or soliloquy. During the Renaissance, in the works of Spenser and others, the eclogue became a major form of verse, with shepherds exchanging verses of love, lament, or eulogy.

Edition. The form in which a book is published, including its physical qualities and its content. A *first edition* is the first form of a book, printed and bound; a *second edition* is a later form, usually with substantial changes in content. Between the two, there may be more than one printing or impression of the first edition, sometimes with minor corrections. The term *edition* also refers to the format of a book. For example, an *illustrated edition* or a *two-volume edition* may be identical in verbal content to one without pictures or bound in a single volume.

Edwardian Period (1901–1914). From the death of Queen Victoria to the outbreak of World War I, named for the reign of Victoria's son, Edward VII (1901–1910), a period generally reacting against Victorian propriety and convention.

Elegiac Stanza. An iambic pentameter quatrain rhyming *abab*. Taking its name from Thomas Gray's *Elegy Written in a Country Churchyard* (1751), it is identical to the heroic quatrain.

Elegy. Greek for "lament": a poem on death or on a serious loss; characteristically a sustained

Elision. Latin for "striking out": the omission or slurring of an unstressed vowel at the end of a word to bring a line of poetry closer to a prescribed metrical pattern, as in John Milton's *Lycidas*: "Tempered to th'oaten flute." *See also* Meter; Syncope.

Elizabethan Drama. English drama of the reign of Elizabeth I (1558–1603). Strictly speaking, drama from the reign of James I (1603–1625) belongs to the Jacobean period and that from the reign of Charles I (1625–1642) to the Caroline period, but the term *Elizabethan* is sometimes extended to include works of later reigns, before the closing of the theaters in 1642.

Elizabethan Period (1558–1603). The years marked by the reign of Elizabeth I; the "Golden Age of English Literature," especially as exemplified by the lyric poetry and dramas of Christopher Marlowe, Edmund Spenser, Sir Philip Sidney, and William Shakespeare, as well as the early Ben Jonson and John Donne.

Ellipsis. The omission of words for rhetorical effect: "*Drop dead*" for "You drop dead."

Emblem. (1) A didactic pictorial and literary form consisting of a word or phrase (*mot* or *motto*), a symbolic woodcut or engraving, and a brief moralistic poem (*explicatio*). Collections of emblems in book form were popular in the 16th and 17th centuries. (2) A type or symbol.

Emendation. A change made in a literary text to remove faults that have appeared through tampering or by errors in reading, transcription, or printing from the manuscript.

Empathy. Greek for "feeling with": identification with the feelings or passions of another person, natural creature, or even an inanimate object conceived of as possessing human attributes. Empathy suggests emotional identification, whereas sympathy may be largely an intellectual appreciation of another's situation.

Emphasis. Stress placed on words, phrases, or ideas to show their importance, by *italics*, **boldface**, and punctuation "!!!"; by figurative language, meter, and rhyme; or by strategies of rhetoric, like climactic order, contrast, repetition, and position.

Empiricism. Greek for "experience": the belief that all knowledge comes from experience, that human understanding of general truth can be founded only on observation of particulars. Empiricism is basic to the scientific method and to literary naturalism. It is opposed to rationalism, which discovers truth through reason alone, without regard to experience.

Enclosed Rhyme. A couplet, or pair of rhyming lines, enclosed in rhyming lines to give the pattern *abba*.

Encomium. Originally a Greek choral song in praise of a hero; later, any formal expression of praise, in verse or prose.

End Rhyme. Rhyme at the end of a line of verse (the usual placement), as distinguished from *initial rhyme*, at the beginning, or *internal rhyme*, within the line.

Enjambment. Run-on lines in which grammatical sense runs from one line of poetry to the next without pause or punctuation. The opposite of an end-stopped line.

Enlightenment. A philosophical movement in the 17th and 18th centuries, particularly in France, characterized by the conviction that reason could achieve all knowledge, supplant organized religion, and ensure progress toward happiness and perfection.

Envoy (or **Envoi**). A concluding stanza, generally shorter than the earlier stanzas of a poem, giving a brief summary of theme, address to a prince or patron, or return to a refrain.

Epic. A long narrative poem, typically a recounting of history or legend or of the deeds of a national hero. During the Renaissance, critical theory emphasized two assumptions: (1) the encyclopedic knowledge needed for major poetry, and (2) an aristocracy of genres, according to which epic and tragedy, because they deal with heroes and ruling-class figures, were reserved for major poets. Romanticism revived both the long mythological poem and the verse romance, but the prestige of the encyclopedic epic still lingered. In his autobiographical poem *The Prelude*, Wordsworth self-consciously internalized the heroic argument of the epic.

Epic Simile. Sometimes called a *Homeric simile*: an extended simile, comparing one thing with another by lengthy description of the second, often beginning with "as when" and concluding with "so" or "such."

Epicurean. Often meaning hedonistic (*see also* Hedonism), devoted to sensual pleasure and ease. Actually, Epicurus (c. 341–270 B.C.) was a kind of puritanical Stoic, recommending detachment from pleasure and pain to avoid life's inevitable suffering, hence advocating serenity as the highest happiness, intellect over the senses.

Epigram. (1) A brief poetic and witty couching of a home truth. (2) An equivalent statement in prose.

Epigraph. (1) An inscription on a monument or building. (2) A quotation or motto heading a book or chapter.

Epilogue. (1) A poetic address to the audience at the end of a play. (2) The actor performing the address. (3) Any similar appendage to a literary work, usually describing what happens to the characters in the future.

Epiphany. In religious tradition, the revelation of a divinity. James Joyce adapted the term to signify a moment of profound or spiritual revelation, when even the stroke of a clock or a noise in the street brings sudden illumination, and "its soul, its whatness leaps to us from the vestment of its appearance." For Joyce, art was an epiphany.

Episode. An incident in a play or novel; a continuous event in action and dialogue. Originally the term referred to a section in Greek tragedy between two choric songs.

Episodic Structure. In narration, the incidental stringing of one episode upon another, as in *Don Quixote* or *Moll Flanders*, in which one episode follows another with no necessary causal connection or plot.

Epistle. (1) A letter, usually a formal or artistic one, like Saint Paul's Epistles in the New Testament, or Horace's verse *Epistles*, widely imitated in the late 17th and 18th centuries, most notably by Alexander Pope. (2) A dedication in a prefatory epistle to a play or book.

Epitaph. (1) An inscription on a tombstone or monument memorializing the person, or persons, buried there. (2) A literary epigram or brief poem epitomizing the dead.

Epithalamium (or **Epithalamion**). A lyric ode honoring a bride and groom.

Epithet. A term characterizing a person or thing: e.g., *Richard the Lion-Hearted*.

Epitome. (1) A summary, an abridgment, an abstract. (2) One that supremely represents an entire class.

Essay. A literary composition on a single subject; usually short, in prose, and nonexhaustive. The word derives from French *essai* "an attempt," first used in the modern sense by Michel de Montaigne, whose *Essais* (1580–1588) are classics of the genre. Francis Bacon's *Essays* (1597) brought the term and form to English.

Estates. The "three estates of the realm," recognized from feudal times onward: the clergy (Lords Spiritual), the nobility (Lords Temporal), and the burghers (the Commons). In *Heroes and Hero-Worship*, Thomas Carlyle says that Edmund Burke (member of Parliament from 1766 to 1794) added to Parliament's three estates "the Reporters' Gallery" where "sat a fourth Estate more important than they all" (Lecture V). The Fourth Estate is now the press and other media.

Eulogy. A speech or composition of praise, especially of a deceased person.

Euphemism. Greek for "good speech": an attractive substitute for a harsh or unpleasant word or concept; figurative language or circumlocution substituting an indirect or oblique reference for a direct one.

Euphony. Melodious sound, the opposite of cacophony. A major feature of verse, but also a consideration in prose, euphony results from smooth-flowing meter or sentence rhythm as well as attractive sounds.

Euphuism. An artificial, highly elaborate affected style that takes its name from John Lyly's *Euphues: The Anatomy of Wit* (1578). Euphuism is characterized by the heavy use of rhetorical devices such as balance and antithesis, by much attention to alliteration and other sound patterns, and by learned allusion.

Excursus. (1) A lengthy discussion of a point, appended to a literary work. (2) A long digression.

Exegesis. (1) A detailed analysis, explanation, and interpretation of a difficult text, especially the Bible. (2) A rhetorical figure, also called *explicatio,* which clarifies a thought.

Exemplum. Latin for "example": a story used to illustrate a moral point. *Exempla* were a characteristic feature of medieval sermons. Chaucer's *Pardoner's Tale* and *Nun's Priest's Tale* are famous secular examples.

Existentialism. A philosophy centered on individual existence as unique and unrepeatable, hence rejecting the past for present existence and its unique dilemmas. Existentialism rose to prominence in the 1930s and 1940s, particularly in France after World War II in the work of Jean-Paul Sartre.

Expressionism. An early 20th-century movement in art and literature, best understood as a reaction against conventional realism and naturalism, and especially as a revolt against conventional society. The expressionist looked inward for images, expressing in paint, on stage, or in prose or verse a distorted, nightmarish version of reality, things dreamed about rather than actually existing.

Eye Rhyme. A rhyme of words that look but do not sound the same: *one, stone; word, lord; teak, break.*

Fable. (1) A short, allegorical story in verse or prose, frequently of animals, told to illustrate a moral. (2) The story line or plot of a narrative or drama. (3) Loosely, any legendary or fabulous account.

Falling Meter. A meter beginning with a stress, running from heavy to light.

Farce. A wildly comic play, mocking dramatic and social conventions, frequently with satiric intent.

Feminine Ending. An extra unstressed syllable at the end of a metrical line, usually iambic.

Feminine Rhyme. A rhyme of both the stressed and the unstressed syllables of one feminine ending with another.

Feudalism. The political and social system prevailing in Europe from the ninth century until the 1400s. It was a system of independent holdings (*feud* is Germanic for "estate") in which autonomous lords pledged fealty and service to those more powerful in exchange for protection, as did villagers to the neighboring lord of the manor.

Fiction. An imagined creation in verse, drama, or prose. Fiction is a thing made, an invention. It is distinguished from nonfiction by its essentially imaginative nature, but elements of fiction appear in fundamentally nonfictional constructions such as essays, biographies, autobiographies, and histories. Fictional anecdotes and illustrations abound in the works of politicians, business leaders, the clergy, philosophers, and scientists. Although any invented person, place, event, or condition is a fiction, the term is now most frequently used to mean "prose fiction," as distinct from verse or drama.

Figurative Language. Language that is not literal, being either metaphorical or rhetorically patterned.

Figure of Speech. An expression extending language beyond its literal meaning, either pictorially through metaphor, simile, allusion, and the like, or rhetorically through repetition, balance, antithesis, and the like. A figure of speech is also called a *trope.*

Fin de Siècle. "The end of the century," especially the last decade of the 19th. The term, acquired with the French influence of the symbolists Stéphane Mallarmé and Charles Baudelaire, connotes preciosity and decadence.

First-Person Narration. Narration by a character involved in a story.

Flyting. Scottish for "scolding": a form of invective, or violent verbal assault, in verse; traditional in Scottish literature, possibly Celtic in origin. Typically, two poets exchange scurrilous and often exhaustive abuse.

Folio. From Latin for "leaf." (1) A sheet of paper, folded once. (2) The largest of the book sizes, made from standard printing sheets, folded once before trimming and binding.

Folk Song. A song forming part of the folklore of a community. Like the folktale and the legend, a folk song is a traditional creative expression, characteristically shaped by oral tradition into the form in which it is later recorded in manuscript or print.

Folktale. A story forming part of the folklore of a community, generally less serious than the stories called *myths*. In preliterate societies, virtually all narratives were either myths or folktales: oral histories of real wars, kings, heroes, great families, and the like accumulating large amounts of legendary material.

Foot. The metrical unit; in English, an accented syllable with accompanying light syllable or syllables.

Foreshadowing. The technique of suggesting or prefiguring a development in a literary work before it occurs.

Formula. A plot outline or set of characteristic ingredients used in the construction of a literary work or applied to a portion of one. Formula fiction is written to the requirements of a particular market, usually undistinguished by much imagination or originality in applying the formula.

Foul Copy. A manuscript that has been used for printing, bearing the marks of the proofreader, editor, and printer, as well as, frequently, the author's queries and comments.

Four Elements. In ancient and medieval cosmology, earth, air, fire, and water—the four ultimate, exclusive, and eternal constituents that, according to Empedocles (c. 493–c. 433 B.C.) made up the world.

Four Senses of Interpretation. A mode of medieval criticism in which a work is examined for four kinds of meaning. The *literal meaning* is related to fact or history. The *moral* or *tropological meaning* is the lesson of the work as applied to individual behavior. The *allegorical meaning* is the particular story in its application to people generally, with emphasis on their beliefs. The *anagogical meaning* is its spiritual or mystical truth, its universal significance. After the literal, each of the others represents a broader form of what is usually called allegory, moving from individual morality to social organization to God.

Fourteeners. Lines of 14 syllables—7 iambic feet, popular with the Elizabethans.

Frame Narrative. A narrative enclosing one or more separate stories. Characteristically, the frame narrative is created as a vehicle for the stories it contains.

Free Verse. French *vers libre;* poetry free of traditional metrical and stanzaic patterns.

Genre. A term often applied loosely to the larger forms of literary convention, roughly analogous to "species" in biology. The Greeks spoke of three main genres of poetry—lyric, epic, and drama. Within each major genre, there are subgenres. In written forms dominated by prose, for example, there is a broad distinction between works of fiction (e.g., the novel) and thematic works (e.g., the essay). Within the fictional category, we note a distinction between novel and romance, and other forms such as satire and confession. The object of making these distinctions in literary tradition is not simply to classify but to judge authors in terms of the conventions they themselves chose.

Georgian. (1) Pertaining to the reigns of the four Georges—1714–1830, particularly the reigns of the first three, up to the close of the 18th century. (2) The literature written during the early years (1910–1914) of the reign of George V.

Georgic. A poem about farming and annual rural labors, after Virgil's *Georgics*.

Gloss. An explanation (from Greek *glossa* "tongue, language"); originally, Latin synonyms in the margins of Greek manuscripts and vernacular synonyms in later manuscripts as scribes gave the reader some help.

Glossary. A list of words, with explanations or definitions. A glossary is ordinarily a partial dictionary, appended to the end of a book to explain technical or unfamiliar terms.

Gothic. Originally, pertaining to the Goths, then to any Germanic people. Because the Goths began warring with the Roman empire in the 3rd century A.D., eventually sacking Rome itself, the term later became a synonym for "barbaric," which the 18th century next applied to anything medieval, of the Dark Ages.

Gothic Novel. A type of fiction introduced and named by Horace Walpole's *Castle of Otranto, A Gothic Story* (1764). Walpole introduced supernatural terror, with a huge mysterious helmet, portraits that walk abroad, and statues with nosebleeds. Matthew Gregory Lewis, "Monk Lewis," added sexual depravity to the murderous supernatural mix (*The Monk*, 1796). Mary Shelley's *Frankenstein* (1818) transformed the Gothic into moral science fiction.

Grotesque. Anything unnaturally distorted, ugly, ludicrous, fanciful, or bizarre; especially, in the 19th century, literature exploiting the abnormal.

Hedonism. A philosophy that sees pleasure as the highest good.

Hegelianism. The philosophy of G. W. F. Hegel (1770–1831), who developed the system of thought known as Hegelian dialectic, in which a given concept, or *thesis*, generates its opposite, or *antithesis*, and from the interaction of the two arises a *synthesis*. The synthesis then forms a thesis for a new cycle. Hegelian dialectic suggests that history is not static but contains a rational progression, an idea influential on many later thinkers.

Heroic Couplet. The closed and balanced iambic pentameter couplet typical of the heroic plays of John Dryden; hence, any closed couplet.

Heroic Quatrain. A stanza in four lines of iambic pentameter, rhyming *abab* (*see also* Meter). Also known as the *heroic stanza* and the *elegiac stanza*.

Hexameter. Six-foot lines.

Historicism. (1) Historical relativism. (2) An approach to literature that emphasizes its historical environment, the climate of ideas, belief, and literary conventions surrounding and influencing the writer.

Homily. A religious discourse or sermon, especially one emphasizing practical spiritual or moral advice.

Hubris. From Greek *hybris*, "pride": prideful arrogance or insolence of the kind that causes the tragic hero to ignore the warnings that might turn aside the action that leads to disaster.

Humors. The *cardinal humors* of ancient medical theory: blood, phlegm, yellow bile (choler), black bile (melancholy). From ancient times until the 19th century, the humors were believed largely responsible for health and disposition. Hippocrates (c. 460–c. 370 B.C.) thought an imbalance produced illness. Galen (c. A.D. 130–300) suggested that character types are produced by dominance of fluids: *sanguine*, or kindly, cheerful, amorous; *phlegmatic*, or sluggish, unresponsive; *choleric*, or quick-tempered; and *melancholic*, or brooding, dejected. In literature, especially during the early modern period, characters were portrayed according to the humors that dominated them, as in the comedy of humors.

Hyperbole. Overstatement to make a point, as when a parent tells a child "I've told you a thousand times."

Iambus (or Iamb). A metrical foot: ⏑ –.

Idealism. (1) In philosophy and ethics, an emphasis on ideas and ideals, as opposed to the sensory emphasis of materialism. (2) Literary idealism follows from philosophical precepts, emphasizing a world in which the most important reality is a spiritual or transcendent truth not always reflected in the world of sense perception.

Idyll. A short poem of rustic pastoral serenity.

Image. A concrete picture, either literally descriptive, as in "Red roses covered the white wall," or figurative, as in "She is a rose," each carrying a sensual and emotive connotation. A figurative image may be an analogy, metaphor, simile, personification, or the like.

Impressionism. A literary style conveying subjective impressions rather than objective reality, taking its name from the movement in French painting in the mid-19th century, notably in the works of Manet, Monet, and Renoir. The Imagists represented impressionism in poetry; in fiction, writers like Virginia Woolf and James Joyce.

Industrial Revolution. The accelerated change, beginning in the 1760s, from an agricultural-shopkeeping society, using hand tools, to an industrial-mechanized one.

Influence. The apparent effect of literary works on subsequent writers and their work, as in Robert Browning's influence on T. S. Eliot.

Innuendo. An indirect remark or gesture, especially one implying something derogatory; an insinuation.

Interlocking Rhyme. Rhyme between stanzas; a word unrhymed in one stanza is used as a rhyme for the next, as in terza rima: *aba bcb cdc* and so on.

Internal Rhyme. Rhyme within a line, rather than at the beginning (*initial rhyme*) or end (*end rhyme*); also, rhyme matching sounds in the middle of a line with sounds at the end.

Intertextuality. (1) The relations between one literary text and others it evokes through such means as quotation, paraphrase, allusion, parody, and revision. (2) More broadly, the relations between a given text and all other texts, the potentially infinite sum of knowledge within which any text has its meaning.

Inversion. A reversal of sequence or position, as when the normal order of elements within a sentence is inverted for poetic or rhetorical effect.

Irony. In general, irony is the perception of a clash between appearance and reality, between *seems* and *is*, or between *ought* and *is*. The myriad shadings of irony seem to fall into three categories: (1) *Verbal irony*—saying something contrary to what it means; the appearance is what the words say, the reality is their contrary meaning. (2) *Dramatic irony*—saying or doing something while unaware of its ironic contrast with the whole truth; named for its frequency in drama, dramatic irony is a verbal irony with the speaker's awareness erased. (3) *Situational irony*—events turning to the opposite of what is expected or what should be. The ironic situation turns the speaker's unknowing words ironic. Situational irony is the essence of both comedy and tragedy: the young lovers run into the worst possible luck, until everything clears up happily; the most noble spirits go to their death, while the featherheads survive.

Italian Sonnet (or **Petrarchan Sonnet**). A sonnet composed of an octave and sestet, rhyming *abbaabba cdecde* (or *cdcdcd* or some variant, without a closing couplet).

Italic (or **Italics**). Type slanting upward to the right. *This sentence is italic*.

Jacobean Period (1603–1625). The reign of James I, *Jacobus* being the Latin for "James." A certain skepticism and even cynicism seeped into Elizabethan joy. The Puritans and the court party, the Cavaliers, grew more antagonistic. But it was in the Jacobean period that Shakespeare wrote his greatest tragedies and tragi-comedies, and Ben Jonson did his major work.

Jargon. (1) Language peculiar to a trade or calling, as, for example, the jargon of astronauts, lawyers, or literary critics. (2) Confused or confusing language. This kind of jargon does not communicate to anybody.

Jeremiad. A lament or complaint, especially one enumerating transgressions and predicting destruction of a people, of the kind found in the Book of Jeremiah.

Juvenilia. Youthful literary products.

Kenning. A compound figurative metaphor, a circumlocution, in Old English and Old Norse poetry: hronrād, "whale-road," for the sea.

Lament. A grieving poem, an elegy, in Anglo-Saxon or Renaissance times. *Deor's Lament* (c. 980) records the actual grief of a scop, or court poet, at being displaced in his lord's hall.

Lampoon. A satirical, personal ridicule in verse or prose. The term probably derives from the French *lampons*, "Let's guzzle," a refrain in 17th-century drinking songs.

Lay (or **Lai**). (1) A ballad or related metrical romance originating with the Breton lay of French Brittany and retaining some of its Celtic magic and folklore.

Lexicon. A word list, a vocabulary, a dictionary.

Libretto. "The little book" (Italian): the text of an opera, cantata, or other musical drama.

Litany. A prayer with phrases spoken or sung by a leader alternated with responses from congregation or choir. *The Litany* is a group of such prayers in the Book of Common Prayer.

Literal. According to the letter (of the alphabet): the precise, plain meaning of a word or phrase in its simplest, original sense, considered apart from its sense as a metaphor or other figure of speech. Literal language is the opposite of figurative language.

Literature. Strictly defined, anything written. Therefore the oral culture of a people—its folklore, folk songs, folktales, and so on—is not literature until it is written down. The movies are not literature except in their printed scripts. By the same strict meaning, historical records, telephone books, and the like are all literature because they are written in letters of the alphabet, although they are not taught as literature in schools. In contrast to this strict, literal meaning, literature has come to be equated with *creative writing* or works of the imagination: chiefly poetry, prose fiction, and drama.

Lollards. From Middle Dutch, literally, "mumblers": a derisive term applied to the followers of John Wyclif (c. 1328–1384), the reformer behind the Wyclif Bible (1385), the first in English. Lollards preached against the abuses of the medieval church, setting up a standard of poverty and individual service as against wealth and hierarchical privilege.

Lyric. A poem, brief and discontinuous, emphasizing sound and pictorial imagery rather than narrative or dramatic movement.

Macaronic Verse. (1) Strictly, verse mixing words in a writer's native language with endings, phrases, and syntax of another language, usually Latin or Greek, creating a comic or burlesque effect. (2) Loosely, any verse mingling two or more languages.

Mannerism, Mannerist. (1) In architecture and painting, a style elongating and distorting human figures and spaces, deliberately confusing scale and perspective. (2) Literary or artistic affectation; a stylistic quality produced by excessively peculiar, ornamental, or ingenious devices.

Manners. Social behavior. In usages like comedy of manners and novel of manners, the term suggests an examination of the behavior, morals, and values of a particular time, place, or social class.

Manuscript. Literally, "written by hand": any handwritten document, as, for example, a letter or diary; also, a work submitted for publication.

Marginalia. Commentary, references, or other material written by a reader in the margins of a manuscript or book.

Masculine Ending. The usual iambic ending, on the accented foot: ⌣ –.

Masculine Rhyme. The most common rhyme in English, on the last syllable of a line.

Masque. An allegorical, poetic, and musical dramatic spectacle popular in the English courts and mansions of the 16th and early 17th centuries. Figures from mythology, history, and romance mingled in a pastoral fantasy with fairies, fauns, satyrs, and witches, as masked amateurs from the court (including kings and queens) participated in dances and scenes.

Materialism. In philosophy, an emphasis upon the material world as the ultimate reality. Its opposite is *idealism*. Thomas Hobbes was an early materialist in 17th-century England. In the 19th century, materialism had evolved into naturalism, which emerged as an especially materialistic form of realism.

Melodrama. A play with dire ingredients—the mortgage foreclosed, the daughter tied to the railroad tracks—but with a happy ending. The typical emotions produced here result in romantic tremors, pity, and terror.

Menippean Satire. Satire on pedants, bigots, rapacious professional people, and other persons or institutions perceiving the world from a single framework. The focus is on intellectual limitations and mental attitudes. Typical ingredients include a rambling narrative; unusual settings; displays of erudition; and long digressions.

Metaphor. Greek for "transfer" (*meta* and *trans* meaning "across"; *phor* and *fer* meaning "carry"): to carry something across. Hence a metaphor treats something as if it were something else. Money becomes a *nest egg;* a sandwich, a *submarine*.

Metaphysical Poetry. Seventeenth-century poetry of wit and startling extended metaphor.

Meter. The measured pulse of poetry. English meters derive from four Greek and Roman quantitative meters (*see* also Quantitative Verse), which English stresses more sharply, although the patterns are the same. The unit of each pattern is the *foot*, containing one stressed syllable and one or two light ones. *Rising meter* goes from light to heavy; *falling meter*, from heavy to light. One meter—iambic—has dominated English poetry, with the three others lending an occasional foot, for variety, and producing a few poems.

Rising Meters

Iambic: ⏑ – (the iambus)
Anapestic: ⏑⏑ – (the anapest)

Falling Meters

Trochaic: – ⏑ (the trochee)
Dactylic: – ⏑⏑ (the dactyl)

The number of feet in a line also gives the verse a name:

1 foot: monometer
2 feet: dimeter
3 feet: trimeter
4 feet: tetrameter
5 feet: pentameter
6 feet: hexameter
7 feet: heptameter

All meters show some variations, and substitutions of other kinds of feet, but three variations in iambic writing are virtually standard:

Inverted foot: – ⏑ (a trochee)
Spondee: – –
Ionic double foot: ⏑⏑ – –

The *pyrrhic foot* of classical meters, two light syllables (⏑⏑), lives in the English line only in the Ionic double foot, although some prosodists scan a relatively light iambus as pyrrhic.

Examples of meters and scansion:

Iambic Tetrameter

An-ni- | hil-a- | ting all | that's made |
To a | green thought | in a | green shade. |

Andrew Marvell, "The Garden"

Iambic Tetrameter
(with two inverted feet)

Close to | the sun | in lone- | ly lands, |
Ringed with | the az- | ure world, | he stands. |

Alfred, Lord Tennyson, "The Eagle"

Iambic Pentameter

Love's not | Time's fool, | though ros- | y lips | and cheeks |
Within | his bend- | ing sick- | le's com- | pass come |

William Shakespeare, Sonnet 116

When to | the ses- | sions of | sweet si- | lent thought |

William Shakespeare, Sonnet 30

Anapestic Tetrameter

(trochees substituted)
The pop- | lars are felled; | farewell | to the shade |
And the whis- | pering sound | of the cool | colonnade |

William Cowper, "The Popular Field"

Trochaic Tetrameter

Tell me | not in | mournful | numbers |

Henry Wadsworth Longfellow, "A Psalm of Life"

Dactylic Hexameter

This is the | forest prim- | eval. The | murmuring | pines and the | hemlocks |
Bearded with | moss . . . .

Henry Wadsworth Longfellow, "Evangeline"

Metonymy. "Substitute naming." A figure of speech in which an associated idea stands in for the actual item: "The *pen* is mightier than the *sword*" for "Literature and propaganda accomplish more and survive longer than warfare," or "The *White House* announced" for "The President announced." *See also* synecdoche.

Metrics. The analysis and description of meter; also called *prosody*.

Middle English. The language of England from the middle of the 12th century to approximately 1500. English began to lose its inflectional endings and accepted many French words into its vocabulary, especially terms associated with the new social, legal, and governmental structures (*baron, judge, jury, marshal, parliament, prince*), and those in common use by the French upper classes (*mansion, chamber, veal, beef*).

Mimesis. A term meaning "imitation." It has been central to literary criticism since Aristotle's *Poetics*. The ordinary meaning of *imitation* as creating a resemblance to something else is clearly involved in Aristotle's definition of dramatic plot as *mimesis praxeos*, the imitation of an action. But there are many things that a work of literature may imitate, and hence many contexts of imitation. Works of literature may imitate other works of literature: this is the aspect of literature that comes into such conceptions as convention and genre. In a larger sense, every work of literature imitates, or finds its identity in, the entire "world of words," in Wallace Stevens's phrase, the sense of the whole of reality as potentially literary, as finding its end in a book, as Stéphane Mallarmé says.

Miracle Play. A medieval play based on a saint's life or story from the Bible.

Miscellany. A collection of various things. A literary miscellany is therefore a book collecting varied works, usually poems by different authors, a kind of anthology. The term is applied especially to the many books of this kind that appeared in the Elizabethan period.

Mock Epic. A poem in epic form and manner ludicrously elevating some trivial subject to epic grandeur.

Modernism. A collective term, generally associated with the first half of the 20th century, for various aesthetic and cultural attempts to place a "modern" face on experience. Modernism arose from a sense that the old ways were worn out. The new century opened with broad social, philosophical, religious, and cultural discussion and reform. For creative artists, the challenges of the new present meant that art became subject to change in every way, that the content, forms, and techniques inherited from the 19th century existed to be challenged, broken apart, and re-formed.

Monodrama. (1) A play with one character. (2) A closet drama or dramatic monologue.

Monody. (1) A Greek ode for one voice. (2) An elegiac lament, a dirge, in poetic soliloquy.

Monologue. (1) A poem or story in the form of a soliloquy. (2) Any extended speech.

Motif (or **Motive**). (1) A recurrent thematic element—word, image, symbol, object, phrase, action. (2) A conventional incident, situation, or device like the unknown knight of mysterious origin and low degree in the romance, or the baffling riddle in fairy tales.

Muse. The inspirer of poetry, on whom the poet calls for assistance. In Greek mythology the Muses were the nine daughters of Zeus and Mnemosyne ("Memory") presiding over the arts and sciences.

Mystery Play. Medieval religious drama; eventually performed in elaborate cycles of plays acted on pageant wagons or stages throughout city streets, with different guilds of artisans and merchants responsible for each.

Mysticism. A spiritual discipline in which sensory experience is expunged and the mind is devoted to deep contemplation and the reaching of a transcendental union with God.

Myth. From Greek *mythos,* "plot" or "narrative." The verbal culture of most if not all human societies began with stories, and certain stories have achieved a distinctive importance as being connected with what the society feels it most needs to know: stories illustrating the society's religion, history, class structure, or the origin of peculiar features of the natural environment.

Narrative Poem. One that tells a story, particularly the epic, metrical romance, and shorter narratives, like the ballad.

Naturalism. (1) Broadly, according to nature. In this sense, naturalism is opposed to idealism, emphasizing things accessible to the senses in this world in contrast to permanent or spiritual truths presumed to lie outside it. (2) More specifically, a literary movement of the late 19th century; an extension of realism, naturalism was a reaction against the restrictions inherent in the realistic emphasis on the ordinary, as naturalists insisted that the extraordinary is real, too.

Neoclassical Period. Generally, the span of time from the restoration of Charles II to his father's throne in 1660 until the publication of William Wordsworth and Samuel Taylor Coleridge's *Lyrical Ballads* (1798). Writers hoped to revive something like the classical Pax Romana, an era of peace and literary excellence.

Neologism. A word newly coined or introduced into a language, or a new meaning given to an old word.

New Criticism. An approach to criticism prominent in the United States after the publication of John Crowe Ransom's *New Criticism* (1941). Generally, the New Critics were agreed that a poem or story should be considered an organic unit, with each part working to support the whole. They worked by close analysis, considering the text as the final authority, and were distrustful, though not wholly neglectful, of considerations brought from outside the text, as, for example, from biography or history.

New Historicism. A cross-disciplinary approach fostered by the rise of feminist and multicultural studies as well as a renewed emphasis on historical perspective. Associated in particular with work on the early modern and the romantic periods in the United States and England, the approach emphasizes analysis of the relationship between history and literature, viewing writings in both fields as "texts" for study. New Historicism has tended to note political influences on literary and historical texts, to illuminate the role of the writer against the backdrop of social customs and assumptions, and to view history as changeable and interconnected instead of as a linear progressive evolution.

Nocturne. A night piece; writing evocative of evening or night.

Nominalism. In the Middle Ages, the belief that universals have no real being, but are only names, their existence limited to their presence in the minds and language of humans. This belief was opposed to the beliefs of medieval realists, who held that universals have an independent existence, at least in the mind of God.

Norman Conquest. The period of English history in which the Normans consolidated their hold on England after the defeat of the Saxon King Harold by William, Duke of Normandy, in 1066. French became the court language and Norman lords gained control of English lands, but Anglo-Saxon administrative and judicial systems remained largely in place.

Novel. The extended prose fiction that arose in the 18th century to become a major literary expression of the modern world. The term comes from the Italian *novella*, the short "new" tale of intrigue and moral comeuppance most eminently disseminated by Boccaccio's *Decameron* (1348–1353). The terms *novel* and *romance*, from the French *roman*, competed interchangeably for most of the 18th century.

Novella. (1) Originally, a short tale. (2) In modern usage, a term sometimes used interchangeably with short novel or for a fiction of middle length, between a short story and a novel. See Novel, above.

Octave. (1) The first unit in an Italian sonnet: eight lines of iambic pentameter, rhyming *abbaabba*. *See also* Meter. (2) A stanza in eight lines.

Octavo (Abbreviated 8vo). A book made from sheets folded to give signatures of eight leaves (16 pages), a book of average size.

Octet. An octastich or octave.

Octosyllabic. Eight-syllable.

Ode. A long, stately lyric poem in stanzas of varied metrical pattern.

Old English. The language brought to England, beginning in 449, by the Jute, Angle, and Saxon invaders from Denmark; the language base from which modern English evolved.

Old English Literature. The literature of England from the Anglo-Saxon invasion of the mid-5th century until the beginning of the Middle English period in the mid-12th century.

Omniscient Narrative. A narrative account untrammeled by constraints of time or space. An omniscient narrator perspective knows about the external and internal realities of characters as well as incidents unknown to them, and can interpret motivation and meaning.

Onomatopoeia. The use of words formed or sounding like what they signify—*buzz, crack, smack, whinny*—especially in an extensive capturing of sense by sound.

Orientalism. A term denoting Western portrayals of Oriental culture. In literature it refers to a varied body of work beginning in the 18th century that described for Western readers the history, language, politics, and culture of the area east of the Mediterranean.

Oxford Movement. A 19th-century movement to reform the Anglican church according to the high-church and more nearly Catholic ideals and rituals of the later 17th-century church.

Oxymoron. A pointed stupidity: *oxy*, "sharp," plus *moron*. One of the great ironic figures of speech—for example, "a fearful joy," or Milton's "darkness visible."

Paleography. The study and interpretation of ancient handwriting and manuscript styles.

Palimpsest. A piece of writing on secondhand vellum, parchment, or other surface carrying traces of erased previous writings.

Panegyric. A piece of writing in praise of a person, thing, or achievement.

Pantheism. A belief that God and the universe are identical, from the Greek words *pan* ("all") and *theos* ("god"). God is all; all is God.

Pantomime. A form of drama presented without words, in a dumb show.

Parable. (1) A short tale, such as those of Jesus in the gospels, encapsulating a moral or religious lesson. (2) Any saying, figure of speech, or narrative in which one thing is expressed in terms of another.

Paradox. An apparently untrue or self-contradictory statement or circumstance that proves true upon reflection or when examined in another light.

Paraphrase. A rendering in other words of the sense of a text or passage, as of a poem, essay, short story, or other writing.

Parody. Originally, "a song sung beside" another. From this idea of juxtaposition arose the two basic elements of parody, comedy and criticism. As comedy, parody exaggerates or distorts the prominent features of style or content in a work. As criticism, it mimics the work, borrowing words or phrases or characteristic turns of thought in order to highlight weaknesses of conception or expression.

Passion Play. Originally a play based on Christ's Passion; later, one including both Passion and Resurrection. Such plays began in the Middle Ages, performed from the 13th century onward, often as part of the pageants presented for the feast of Corpus Christi.

Pastiche. A literary or other artistic work created by assembling bits and pieces from other works.

Pastoral. From Latin *pastor*, a shepherd. The first pastoral poet was Theocritus, a Greek of the 3rd century B.C. The pastoral was especially popular in Europe from the 14th through the 18th centuries, with some fine examples still written in England in the 19th century. The pastoral mode is self-reflexive. Typically the poet echoes the conventions of earlier pastorals in order to put "the complex into the simple," as William Empson observed in *Some Versions of Pastoral* (1935). The poem is not really about shepherds, but about the complex society the poet and readers inhabit.

Pathetic Fallacy. The attribution of animate or human characteristics to nature, as, for example, when rocks, trees, or weather are portrayed as reacting in sympathy to human feelings or events.

Pathos. The feeling of pity, sympathy, tenderness, compassion, or sorrow evoked by someone or something that is helpless.

Pedantry. Ostentatious book learning: an accusation frequently hurled in scholarly disagreements.

Pentameter. A line of five metrical feet. (*See* Meter.)

Peripeteia (or **Peripetia, Peripety**). A sudden change in situation in a drama or fiction, a reversal of luck for good or ill.

Periphrasis. The practice of talking around the point; a wordy restatement; a circumlocution.

Peroration. (1) The summative conclusion of a formal oration. (2) Loosely, a grandiloquent speech.

Persona. A mask (in Latin); in poetry and fiction, the projected speaker or narrator of the work—that is, a mask for the actual author.

Personification. The technique of treating abstractions, things, or animals as persons. A kind of metaphor, personification turns abstract ideas, like love, into a physical beauty named Venus, or conversely, makes dumb animals speak and act like humans.

Petrarchan Sonnet. Another name for an Italian sonnet.

Philology. The study of ancient languages and literatures; also more broadly interpreted from its basic meaning, "love of the word," to include all literary studies. In the 19th century, the field of historical linguistics.

Phoneme. In linguistics, the smallest distinguishable unit of sound. Different for each language, phonemes are defined by determining which differences in sound function to signal a difference in meaning.

Phonetics. (1) The study of speech sounds and their production, transmission, and reception. (2) The phonetic system of a particular language. (3) Symbols used to represent speech sounds.

Picaresque Novel. A novel chronicling the adventures of a rogue (Spanish: *picaro*), typically presented as an autobiography, episodic in structure and panoramic in its coverage of time and place.

Picturesque, The. A quality in landscape, and in idealized landscape painting, admired in the second half of the 18th century and featuring crags, flaring and blasted trees, a torrent or winding stream, ruins, and perhaps a quiet cottage and cart, with contrasting light and shadow. It was considered an aesthetic mean between the poles of Edmund Burke's *A Philosophical Inquiry into the Sublime and the Beautiful* (1756).

Plagiarism. Literary kidnapping (Latin *plagiarius*, "kidnapper")—the seizing and presenting as one's own the ideas or writings of another.

Plain Style. The straightforward, unembellished style of preaching favored by 17th-century Puritans as well as by reformers within the Anglican church, as speaking God's word directly from the inspired heart as opposed to the high style of aristocratic oratory and courtliness, the vehicle of subterfuge. Plain style was simultaneously advocated for scientific accuracy by the Royal Society.

Platonism. Any reflection of Plato's philosophy, particularly the belief in the eternal reality of ideal forms, of which the diversities of the physical world are but transitory shadows.

Poetics. The theory, art, or science of poetry. Poetics is concerned with the nature and function of poetry and with identifying and explaining its types, forms, and techniques.

Poet Laureate. Since the 17th century, a title conferred by the monarch on English poets. At first, the laureate was required to write poems to commemorate special occasions, such as royal birthdays, national celebrations, and the like, but since the early 19th century the appointment has been for the most part honorary.

Poetry. Imaginatively intense language, usually in verse. Poetry is a form of fiction—"the supreme fiction," said Wallace Stevens. It is distinguished from other fictions by the compression resulting from its heavier use of figures of speech and allusion and, usually, by the music of its patterns of sounds.

Postmodernism. A term first used in relation to literature in the late 1940s by Randall Jarrell and John Berryman to proclaim a new sensibility arising to challenge the reigning assumptions and practices of modernism. The attitudes and literary devices of the modernists—stream of consciousness, for example—had taken on the patina of tradition. For many of the postmodernists, disillusionment seemed to have reached its fullest measure. Life had little meaning, art less, and a neat closure to expectations raised by the artist seemed impossible. Intruding into one's own fiction to ponder its powers became a hallmark of the 1960s and 1970s.

Poststructuralism. A mode of literary criticism and thought centered on Jacques Derrida's concept of deconstruction. Structuralists see language as the paradigm for all structures. Poststructuralists see language as based on differences—hence the analytical deconstruction of what seemed an immutable system. What language expresses is already absent. Poststructuralism challenges the New Criticism, which seeks a truth fixed within the "verbal icon," the text, in W. K. Wimsatt's term. Poststructuralism invites interpretations through the spaces left by the way words operate.

Pragmatism. In philosophy, the idea that the value of a belief is best judged by the acts that follow from it—its practical results.

Preciosity. Since the 19th century, a term for an affected or overingenious refinement of language.

Predestination. The belief that an omniscient God, at the Creation, destined all subsequent events, particularly, in Calvinist belief, the election for salvation and the damnation of individual souls.

Pre-Raphaelite. Characteristic of a small but influential group of mid-19th-century painters who hoped to recapture the spiritual vividness they saw in medieval painting before Raphael (1483–1520).

Presbyterianism. John Calvin's organization of ecclesiastical governance not by bishops representing the pope but by elders representing the congregation.

Proscenium. Originally, in Greece, the whole acting area ("in front of the scenery"); now, that part of the stage projecting in front of the curtain.

Prose. Ordinary writing patterned on speech, as distinct from verse.

Prose Poetry. Prose rich in cadenced and poetic effects like alliteration, assonance, consonance, and the like, and in imagery.

Prosody. The analysis and description of meters; metrics (*see also* Meter). Linguists apply the term to the study of patterns of accent in a language.

Protagonist. The leading character in a play or story; originally the leader of the chorus in the agon ("contest") of Greek drama, faced with the antagonist, the opposition.

Pseudonym. A fictitious name adopted by an author for public use, like George Eliot (Mary Ann/Marian Evans), and George Orwell (Eric Arthur Blair).

Psychoanalytic Criticism. A form of criticism that uses the insights of Freudian psychology to illuminate a work.

Ptolemaic Universe. The universe as perceived by Ptolemy, a Greco-Egyptian astronomer of the 2nd century A.D., whose theories were dominant until the Renaissance produced the Copernican universe. In Ptolemy's system, the universe was world-centered, with the sun, moon, planets, and stars understood as rotating around the earth in a series of concentric spheres, producing as they revolved the harmonious "music of the spheres."

Puritanism. A Protestant movement arising in the mid-16th century with the Reformation in England. Theocracy—the individual and the congregation governed directly under God through Christ—became primary, reflected in the centrality of the Scriptures and their exposition, direct confession through prayer and public confession to the congregation rather than through priests, and the direct individual experience of God's grace.

Quadrivium. The more advanced four of the seven liberal arts as studied in medieval universities: arithmetic, geometry, astronomy, and music.

Quantitative Verse. Verse that takes account of the quantity of the syllables (whether they take a long or short time to pronounce) rather than their stress patterns.

Quarto (Abbreviated 4to, 4o). A book made from sheets folded twice, giving signatures of four leaves (eight pages). Many of Shakespeare's plays were first printed individually in quarto editions, designated First Quarto, Second Quarto, etc.

Quatrain. A stanza of four lines, rhymed or unrhymed. With its many variations, it is the most common stanzaic form in English.

Rationalism. The theory that reason, rather than revelation or authority, provides knowledge, truth, the choice of good over evil, and an adequate understanding of God and the universe.

Reader-Response Theory. A form of criticism that arose during the 1970s; it postulates the essential active involvement of the reader with the text and focuses on the effect of the process of reading on the mind.

Realism (in literature). The faithful representation of life. Realism carries the conviction of true reports of phenomena observable by others.

Realism (in philosophy). (1) In the Middle Ages, the belief that universal concepts possess real existence apart from particular things and the human mind. They exist either as entities like Platonic forms or as concepts in the mind of God. Medieval realism was opposed to nominalism. (2) In later epistemology, the belief that things exist apart from our perception of them. In this sense, realism is opposed to idealism, which locates all reality in our minds.

Recension. (1) A process of editorial revision based on an examination of the various versions and sources of a literary text. (2) The text produced as a result of reconciling variant readings.

Recto. The right-hand page of an open book; the front of a leaf as opposed to the *verso* or back of a leaf.

Redaction. (1) A revised version. (2) A rewriting or condensing of an older work.

Refrain. A set phrase, or chorus, recurring throughout a song or poem, usually at the end of a stanza or other regular interval.

Relativism. The philosophical belief that nothing is absolute, that values are relative to circumstances. In criticism, relativism is either personal or historical.

Revenge Tragedy. The popular Elizabethan mode, initiated by Thomas Kyd's *Spanish Tragedy* (c. 1586), wherein the hero must revenge a ruler's murder of father, son, or lover.

Reversal. The thrilling change of luck for the protagonist at the last moment in comedy or tragedy—the *peripeteia,* which Aristotle first described in his *Poetics,* along with the discovery that usually sparks it.

Rhetoric. From Greek *rhetor*, "orator": the art of persuasion in speaking or writing. Since ancient times, rhetoric has been understood by some as a system of persuasive devices divorced from considerations of the merits of the case argued.

Rhetorical Figure. A figure of speech employing stylized patterns of word order or meaning for purposes of ornamentation or persuasion.

Rhetorical Question. A question posed for rhetorical effect, usually with a self-evident answer.

Rhyme (sometimes **Rime,** an older spelling). The effect created by matching sounds at the ends of words. The functions of rhyme are essentially four: pleasurable, mnemonic, structural, and rhetorical. Like meter and figurative language, rhyme provides a pleasure derived from fulfillment of a basic human desire to see similarity in dissimilarity, likeness with a difference.

Rhyme Royal. A stanza of seven lines of iambic pentameter, rhyming *ababbcc* (*see also* Meter).

Rhythm. The measured flow of repeated sound patterns, as, for example, the heavy stresses of accentual verse, the long and short syllables of quantitative verse, the balanced syntactical arrangements of parallelism in either verse or prose.

Romance. A continuous narrative in which the emphasis is on what happens in the plot, rather than on what is reflected from ordinary life or experience. Thus a central element in romance is adventure; at its most primitive, romance is an endless sequence of adventures.

Romanticism. A term describing qualities that colored most elements of European and American intellectual life in the late 18th and early 19th centuries, from literature, art, and music, through architecture, landscape gardening, philosophy, and politics. Within the social, political, and intellectual structures of society, the Romantics stressed the separateness of the person, celebrated individual perception and imagination, and embraced nature as a model for harmony in society and art. Their view was an egalitarian one, stressing the value of expressive abilities common to all, inborn rather than developed through training.

Roundheads. Adherents of the Parliamentary, or Puritan, party in the English Civil War, so called from their short haircuts, as opposed to the fashionable long wigs of the Cavaliers, supporters of King Charles I.

Rubric. From Latin *rubrica,* "red earth" (for coloring): in a book or manuscript, a heading, marginal notation, or other section distinguished for special attention by being printed in red ink or in distinctive type.

Run-on Line. A line of poetry whose sense does not stop at the end, with punctuation, but runs on to the next line.

Satire. Poking corrective ridicule at persons, types, actions, follies, mores, and beliefs.

Scop. An Anglo-Saxon bard, or court poet, a kind of poet laureate.

Semiotics. In anthropology, sociology, and linguistics, the study of signs, including words, other sounds, gestures, facial expressions, music, pictures, and other signals used in communication.

Senecan Tragedy. The bloody and bombastic tragedies of revenge inspired by Seneca's nine closet dramas, which had been discovered in Italy in the mid-16th century and soon thereafter translated into English.

Sensibility. Sensitive feeling, emotion. The term arose early in the 18th century to denote the tender undercurrent of feeling in the neoclassical period, continuing through Jane Austen's *Sense and Sensibility* (1811) and afterward.

Sequel. A literary work that explores later events in the lives of characters introduced elsewhere.

Serial. A narration presented in segments separated by time. Novels by Charles Dickens and other 19th-century writers were first serialized in magazines.

Seven Liberal Arts. The subjects studied in medieval universities, consisting of the *trivium* (grammar, logic, and rhetoric), for the B.A., and the *quadrivium* (arithmetic, geometry, astronomy, and music), for the M.A.

Shakespearean Sonnet (or English Sonnet). A sonnet in three quatrains and a couplet, rhyming *abab cdcd efef gg.*

Signified, Signifier. In structural linguistics, the *signified* is the idea in mind when a word is used, an entity separate from the *signifier,* the word itself.

Simile. A metaphor stating the comparison by use of *like, as,* or *as if*.

Slang. The special vocabulary of a class or group of people (as, for example, truck drivers, jazz musicians, salespeople, drug dealers), generally considered substandard, low, or offensive when measured against formal, educated usage.

Sonnet. A verse form of 14 lines, in English characteristically in iambic pentameter and most often in one of two rhyme schemes: the *Italian* (or *Petrarchan*) or *Shakespearean* (or *English*). An Italian sonnet is composed of an octave, rhyming *abbaabba,* and a sestet, rhyming *cdecde* or *cdcdcd,* or in some variant pattern, but with no closing couplet. A Shakespearean sonnet has three quatrains and a couplet, and rhymes *abab cdcd efef gg.* In both types, the content tends to follow the formal outline suggested by rhyme linkage, giving two divisions to the thought of an Italian sonnet and four to a Shakespearean one.

Sonnet Sequence. A group of sonnets thematically unified to create a longer work, although generally, unlike the stanza, each sonnet so connected can also be read as a meaningful separate unit.

Spondee. A metrical foot of two long, or stressed, syllables: – –.

Sprung Rhythm. Gerard Manley Hopkins's term to describe his variations of iambic meter to avoid the "same and tame." His feet, he said, vary from one to four syllables, with one stress per foot, on the first syllable.

Stanza. A term derived from an Italian word for "room" or "stopping place" and used, loosely, to designate any grouping of lines in a separate unit in a poem: a verse paragraph. More strictly, a stanza is a grouping of a prescribed number of lines in a given meter, usually with a particular rhyme scheme, repeated as a unit of structure. Poems in stanzas provide an instance of the aesthetic pleasure in repetition with a difference that also underlies the metrical and rhyming elements of poetry.

Stereotype. A character representing generalized racial or social traits repeated as typical from work to work, with no individualizing traits.

Stichomythia. Dialogue in alternate lines, favored in Greek tragedy and by Seneca and his imitators among the Elizabethans—including William Shakespeare.

Stock Characters. Familiar types repeated in literature to become symbolic of a particular genre, like the strong, silent hero of the western or the hard-boiled hero of the detective story.

Stoicism. (1) Generally, fortitude, repression of feeling, indifference to pleasure or pain. (2) Specifically, the philosophy of the Stoics, who, cultivating endurance and self-control, restrain passions such as joy and grief that place them in conflict with nature's dictates.

Stress. In poetry, the accent or emphasis given to certain syllables, indicated in scansion by a *macron* (–). In a trochee, for example, the stress falls on the first syllable: *sūmmĕr*. *See also* Meter.

Structuralism. The study of social organizations and myths, of language, and of literature as structures. Each part is significant only as it relates to others in the total structure, with nothing meaningful by itself.

Structural Linguistics. Analysis and description of the grammatical structures of a spoken language.

Sublime. In literature, a quality attributed to lofty or noble ideas, grand or elevated expression, or (the ideal of sublimity) an inspiring combination of thought and language. In nature or art, it is a quality, as in a landscape or painting, that inspires awe or reverence.

Subplot. A sequence of events subordinate to the main story in a narrative or dramatic work.

Syllabic Verse. Poetry in which meter has been set aside and the line is controlled by a set number of syllables, regardless of stress.

Symbol. Something standing for its natural qualities in another context, with human meaning added: an eagle, standing for the soaring imperious dominance of Rome.

Symbolism. Any use of symbols, especially with a theoretical commitment, as when the French Symbolists of the 1880s and 1890s stressed, in Stéphane Mallarmé's words, not the thing but the effect, the subjective emotion implied by the surface rendering.

Snycopation. The effect produced in verse or music when two stress patterns play off against one another.

Synecdoche. The understanding of one thing by another—a kind of metaphor in which a part stands for the whole, or the whole for a part: *a hired hand* meaning "a laborer."

Synesthesia. Greek for "perceiving together": close association or confusion of sense impressions. The result is essentially a metaphor, transferring qualities of one sense to another, as in common phrases like "blue note" and "cold eye."

Synonyms. Words in the same language denoting the same thing, usually with different connotations: *female, woman, lady, dame; male, masculine, macho*.

Synopsis. A summary of a play, a narrative, or an argument.

Tenor and **Vehicle.** I. A. Richards's terms for the two aspects of metaphor, *tenor* being the actual thing projected figuratively in the *vehicle*. "She [tenor] is a rose [vehicle]."

Tercet (or **Triplet**). A verse unit of three lines, sometimes rhymed, sometimes not.

Terza Rima. A verse form composed of tercets with interlocking rhyme (*aba bcb cdc,* and so on), usually in iambic pentameter. Invented by Dante for his *Divine Comedy*.

Third-Person Narration. A method of storytelling in which someone who is not involved in the story, but stands somewhere outside it in space and time, tells of the events.

Topos. A commonplace, from Greek *topos* (plural *topoi*), "place." (1) A topic for argument, remembered by the classical system of placing it, in the mind's eye, in a place within a building and then proceeding mentally from one place to the next. (2) A rhetorical device, similarly remembered as a commonplace.

Tragedy. Fundamentally, a serious fiction involving the downfall of a hero or heroine. As a literary form, a basic mode of drama. Tragedy often involves the theme of isolation, in which a hero, a character of greater than ordinary human importance, becomes isolated from the community. Then there is the theme of the violation and reestablishment of order, in which the neutralizing of the violent act may take the form of revenge. Finally, a character may embody a passion too great for the cosmic order to tolerate, such as the passion of sexual love. Renaissance tragedy seems to be essentially a mixture of the heroic and the ironic. It tends to center on heroes who, though they cannot be of divine parentage in Christianized Western Europe, are still of titanic importance, with an articulateness and social authority beyond anything in our normal experience.

Tragic Irony. The essence of tragedy, in which the most noble and most deserving person, because of the very grounds of his or her excellence, dies in defeat. *See also* Irony.

Tragicomedy. (1) A tragedy with happy ending, frequently with penitent villain and romantic setting, disguises, and discoveries.

Travesty. Literally a "cross-dressing": a literary work so clothed, or presented, as to appear ludicrous; a grotesque image or likeness.

Trivium. The first three of the seven liberal arts as studied in medieval universities: grammar, logic, and rhetoric (including oratory).

Trochee. A metrical foot going – ⌣.

Trope. Greek *tropos* for "a turn": a word or phrase turned from its usual meaning to an unusual one; hence, a figure of speech, or an expression turned beyond its literal meaning.

Type. (1) A literary genre. (2) One of the type characters. (3) A symbol or emblem. (4) In theology and literary criticism, an event in early Scriptures or literatures that is seen as prefiguring an event in later Scriptures or in history or literature generally.

Type Characters. Individuals endowed with traits that mark them more distinctly as representatives of a type or class than as standing apart from a type: the typical doctor or rakish aristocrat, for example. Type characters are the opposite of individualized characters.

Typology. The study of types. Typology springs from a theory of literature or history that recognizes events as duplicated in time.

Utopia. A word from two Greek roots (*outopia,* meaning "no place," and *eutopia,* meaning "good place"), pointing to the idea that a utopia is a nonexistent land of social perfection.

Verisimilitude (*vraisemblance* in French). The appearance of actuality.

Verso. The left-hand page of an open book; the back of a leaf of paper.

Vice. A stock character from the medieval morality play, a mischief-making tempter.

Vignette. (1) A brief, subtle, and intimate literary portrait, named for *vignette* portraiture, which is unbordered, shading off into the surrounding color at the edges, with features delicately rendered. (2) A short essay, sketch, or story, usually fewer than five hundred words.

Villanelle. One of the French verse forms, in five tercets, all rhyming *aba,* and a quatrain, rhyming *abaa.* The entire first and third lines are repeated alternately as the final lines of tercets 2, 3, 4, and 5, and together to conclude the quatrain.

Virgule. A "little rod"—the diagonal mark or slash used to indicate line ends in poetry printed continuously in running prose.

Vulgate. (1) A people's common vernacular language (Latin *vulgus,* "common people"). (2) The Vulgate Bible, translated by St. Jerome c. 383–405; the official Roman Catholic Bible.

Wit and **Humor.** *Wit* is intellectual acuity; *humor,* an amused indulgence of human deficiencies. Wit now denotes the acuity that produces laughter. It originally meant mere understanding, then quickness of understanding, then, beginning in the 17th century, quick perception coupled with creative fancy. Humor (British *humour,* from the four bodily humors) was simply a disposition, usually eccentric. In the 18th century, *humour* came to mean a laughable eccentricity and then a kindly amusement at such eccentricity.

Zeugma. The technique of using one word to yoke two or more others for ironic or amusing effect, achieved when at least one of the yoked is a misfit, as in Alexander Pope's "lose her Heart, or Necklace, at a Ball."

BIBLIOGRAPHY

Bibliographies • *English Literary Renaissance*, 1971 to present. • Alfred Harbage, ed., S. Schoenbaum rev., *Annals of English Drama, 975–1700*, 3 vols. • *New Cambridge Bibliography of English Literature, 600–1600*, 1969. • S. A. and D. R. Tannenbaum, eds., *Elizabethan Bibliographies*, 10 vols., 1967.

Guides to Research • A. R. Braunmuller and Michael Hattaway, *The Cambridge Companion to English Renaissance Drama*, 1990. • Douglas Bush, *English Literature in the Earlier Seventeenth Century 1600–1660*, 1962. • C. S. Lewis, *English Literature in the Sixteenth Century*, 1954. • A. W. Ward and A. R. Waller, eds., *The Cambridge History of English Literature*, 15 vols., vols. 3–6, 1909.

Drama, Poetry, and Prose • David Bevington, *Tudor Drama and Politics*, 1968. • Rebecca Bushnell, *Tragedies of Tyrants*, 1990. • Jonathan Dollimore, *Radical Tragedy. Religion, Ideology and Power in the Drama of Shakespeare and His Contemporaries*, 1985. • Martin Elsky, *Authorizing Words: Speech, Writing and Print in the Renaissance*, 1989. • Anne Ferry, *"The Inward Language": Sonnets of Wyatt, Sidney, Shakespeare and Donne*, 1983. • Ernest B. Gilman, *Iconoclasm and Poetry in the English Reformation*, 1986. • Stephen Greenblatt, *Renaissance Self-Fashioning*, 1980. • Thomas M. Greene, *The Light in Troy: Imitation and Discovery in Renaissance Poetry*, 1982. • Andrew Gurr, *Playgoing in Shakespeare's London*, 1987. • Peter Herman, ed., *Rethinking the Henrician Age: Essays on Early Tudor Texts and Contexts*, 1994. • John King, *English Reformation Literature: The Tudor Origins of the Protestant Tradition*, 1982. • Janel Mueller, *The Native Tongue and the Word: Developments in English Prose Style, 1380–1580*, 1984. • Steven Mullaney, *The Place of the Stage: License, Place and Power in Renaissance England*, 1988. • David Norbrook, *Poetry and Politics in the English Renaissance*, 1984. • Stephen Orgel, *The Illusion of Power: Political Theater in the English Renaissance*, 1971. • Patricia Parker, *Inescapable Romance*, 1979. • David Quint, *Epic and Empire*, 1993. • Wayne Rebhorn, *The Emperor of Men's Minds: Literature and the Renaissance Discourse of Rhetoric*, 1995. • Rosemund Tuve, *Elizabethan and Metaphysical Imagery*, 1947.

History, Religion, and Political Thought • Glenn Burgess, *Absolute Monarchy and the Stuart Constitution*, 1996. • Patrick Collinson, *The Elizabethan Puritan Movement*, 1967. • John Guy, *Tudor England*, 1988. • Richard Helgerson, *Forms of Nationhood: The Elizabethan Writing of England*, 1992. • F. J. Levy, *Tudor Historical Thought*, 1967. • Annabel Patterson, *Reading Holinshed's Cronicles*, 1994. • Linda Levy Peck, ed., *The Mental World of the Jacobean Court*, 1991. • Conrad Russell, *The Crisis of Parliaments: English History 1509–1660*, 1971. • Quentin Skinner, *The Foundations of Modern Political Thought*, 2 vols., 1978. • J. P. Sommerville, *Politics and Ideology in England, 1608–1640*, 1986. • D. W. Woolf, *The Idea of History in Early Stuart England*, 1990.

Humanism • Douglas Bush, *The Renaissance and English Humanism*, 1939. • William Kerrigan and Gordon Braden, *The Idea of the Renaissance*, 1989. • Arthur Kinney, *Humanist Poetics*, 1986. • Charles Schmitt and Quentin Skinner, eds., *The Cambridge History of Renaissance Philosophy*, 1988.

Science and Exploration • David Cressy, *Coming Over: Migration and Communication between England and New England in the Seventeenth Century*, 1987. • Stephen Greenblatt, *Marvelous Possessions: The Wonder of the New World*, 1991. • Stephen Greenblatt, ed., *New World Encounters*, 1993. • Jeffrey Knapp, *An Empire Nowhere: England, America, and Literature from* Utopia *to* The Tempest, 1995. • Thomas Laqueur, *Making Sex: Body and Gender from the Greeks to Freud*, 1990. • Frank Lestrigant, *Mapping the Renaissance World*, 1991. • Wayne Shumaker, *The Occult Sciences in the Renaissance*, 1972. • Nancy G. Siraisi, *Medieval and Early Renaissance Science*, 1990. • Keith Thomas, *Religion and the Decline of Magic*, 1971.

Social Settings and Gender Roles • Susan Dwyer Amussen, *An Ordered Society: Gender and Class* *in Early Modern England*, 1988. • Elaine V. Beilin, *Redeeming Eve: Women Writers of the English Renaissance*, 1987. • Alan Bray, *Homosexuality in Renaissance England*, 1982. • Anthony Fletcher, *Gender, Sex, and Subordination in England, 1500–1800*, 1995. • Kim F. Hall, *Things of Darkness: Economies of Race and Gender in Early Modern England*, 1995. • Margo Hendricks and Patricia Parker, eds., *Women, "Race" and Writing in the Early Modern Period*, 1994. • Daniel Javitch, *Poetry and Courtliness in Renaissance England*, 1976. • Constance Jordan, *Renaissance Feminism: Literary Texts and Political Models*, 1990. • Peter Laslett, *The World We Have Lost—Further Explored*, 1983. • Barbara Kiefer Lewalski, *Writing Women in Jacobean England*, 1993. • Ian Maclean, *The Renaissance Notion of Woman*, 1980. • Lawrence Manley, *Literature and Culture in Early Modern London*, 1995. • Steve Rappaport, *Worlds within Worlds: Structures of Life in Sixteenth-Century London*, 1989. • Bruce R. Smith, *Homosexual Desire in Shakespeare's England: A Cultural Poetics*, 1991. • Lawrence Stone, *The Family, Sex, and Marriage, 1500–1800*, 1965. • Linda Woodbridge, *Women and the English Renaissance: Literature and the Nature of Womankind, 1540–1640*, 1984.

Perspectives: The Civil War, or the Wars of Three Kingdoms • Texts. • Thomas Carlyle, ed., *Oliver Cromwell's Letters and Speeches: With Elucidations*, 2 vols., 1904. • Pádraig De Brún, Breandán O Buachalla, and Tomás O Concheanainn, eds., *Nua-Dhuanaire*, vol. 1., 1971. • "John O'Dwyer of the Glenn" in *Irish Mistrelsy or the Bardic Remains of Ireland*, ed. James Hardiman, 2 vols., 1831. • Philip A. Knachel, ed., *Eikon Basilike*, 1966. • John Lilburne, *Englands New Chains Discoverd. The Leveller Tracts, 1647–1653*, ed. Godfrey Davies Haller, 1944. • W. Dunn Macray, ed., *History of the Rebellion and Civil Wars in England: Begun in the Year 1641 by Edward, Earl of Clarendon*, 1888. • "The Petition of the Gentlewomen and Tradesmen's Wives" in *English Women's Voices 1540–1700*, ed. Charlotte F. Otten, 1992.

Criticism and History. • Martyn Bennett, *The Civil Wars in Britain and Ireland: 1638–1651*, 1997. • Martyn Bennett, *The English Civil War: 1640–1649*, 1995. • Christopher Hill, *The World Turned Upside Down: Radical Ideas During the English Revolution*, 1972. • Jane Ohlmeyer, ed., *Ireland from Independence to Occupation, 1641–1660*, 1995. • Nigel Smith, *Literature and Revolution in England, 1640–1660*, 1994. • Keith Thomas, "Women and the Civil War Sects," *Past and Present*, 1958.

Perspectives: Emblem, Style, and Metaphor • Editions. • Giordano Bruno, *De Imaginum, Signorum & Idearum Compositione*, 1591. • Dick Higgins, ed., Giordano Bruno, *On the Composition of Images, Signs and Ideas*, trans. Charles Doria, 1991. • L. C. Martin, ed., *The Poems English, Latin and Greek of Richard Crashaw*, 1927. • Henry Green, ed., A Choice of Emblemes *by Geoffrey Whitney*, 1967. • Ezio Raimondi, ed., *Emanuele Tesauro, Il Cannocchiale Aristotelico*, 1978. • James D. Redwine, ed., *Ben Jonson's Literary Criticism*, 1970.

Criticism. • Michael Bath, *Speaking Pictures: English Emblem Books and Renaissance Culture*, 1993. • Joan F. Bennett, *Five Metaphysical Poets: Donne, Herbert, Vaughan, Crashaw, Marvell*, 1964. • Michel Foucault, "The Prose of the World," in *The Order of Things*, 1970. • Rosemary Freeman, *English Emblem Books*, 1948. • John Manning, "Whitney's *Choice of Emblemes*: A Reassessment," *Renaissance Studies*, vol. 4, no. 2, 1990. • Mario Praz, *The Flaming Heart*, 1958. • Ezio Raimondi, *Letteratura Barocca*, 1961. • John R. Roberts, *New Perspectives on the Life and Art of Richard Crashaw*, 1990. • George Walton Williams, *Image and Symbol in the Sacred Poetry of Richard Crashaw*, 1963. • Frances Yates, *Giordano Bruno and the Hermetic Tradition*, 1964.

Perspectives: Government and Self-Government • Editions. • Roger Ascham, *The Schoolmaster*, 1570, ed. Lawrence Ryan. • Baldassare Castiglione, *The Book of the Courtier*, trans. Sir Thomas Hoby, 1966. • Sir Thomas Elyot, *The Book Named the Governor*, ed. S. E. Lehmberg, 1963. • Sir Thomas Elyot, *The Defence of Good Women*, ed. Edwin Johnson Howard, 1940. • John Foxe, *The Acts and Monuments of John Foxe*, ed. Stephen Cattley, 8 vols., 1843–1847, repr. 1965. • Richard Hooker, *The Folger Library Edition of the Works of Richard Hooker*, ed. W. Speed Hill, 8 vols, 1977. • James VI and I, *Political Writings*, ed. Johann P. Sommerville, 1994. • Richard Mulcaster, *Elementarie*, ed. E. T. Compagnac, 1925. • Thomas Russell, ed., *The Works of the English Reformers: William Tyndale and John Frith*, 3 vols., 1831. • Juan Luis Vives, *The Instruction of a Christen Woman*, trans. Richard Hyrde, 1540.

Perspectives: Spiritual Self-Reckonings • Editions. • John Bunyan, *The Pilgrim's Progress*, ed. J. B. Wharey, 1928. • Daniel Defoe, *The Life and Strange and Surprizing Adventures of Robinson Crusoe of York*, ed. Donald Crowley, 1972. • Margaret Ferguson and Barry Weller, eds., The Tragedy of Mariam: The Fair Queen of Jewry *with* The Lady Falkland: Her Life by One of Her Daughters, 1994. • Alan MacFarlane, ed., *The Diary of Ralph Josselin*, 1976. • Charlotte F. Otten, ed., *English Women's Voices 1540–1700*, 1992.

Criticism. • Paul Delany, *British Autobiography in the Seventeenth Century*, 1969. • Thomas H. Luxon, *Literal Figures: Puritan Allegory and the Reformation Crisis in Representation*, 1995. • Phyllis Mack, "Women as Prophets During the English Civil War," *Feminist Studies*, vol. 8 (Spring), 1982. • Mary Beth Rose, "Gender, Genre, and History: Seventeenth-Century English Women and the Art of Autobiography," in *Women in the Middle Ages and Renaissance: Literary and Historical Perspectives*, ed. Mary Beth Rose, 1986. • Sandra Sherman, *Finance and Fictionality in the Early Eighteenth Century: Accounting for Defoe*, 1996. • Stuart Sherman, *Telling Time: Clocks and Calendars, Secrecy and Self Recording in English Diurnal Form*, 1997.

Perspectives: Tracts on Women and Gender • Editions. • Desiderius Erasmus, *A Ryght Frutefull Epistle Devised in Laude and Praise of Matrimony*, trans. Richard Tavernour, 1534. • *Haec Vir: Or, The Womanish Man*, 1620. • *Hic Mulier: Or The Man-Woman*, 1620. • Barbara Kiefer Lewalski, ed., *The Polemics and Poems of Rachel Speght*, 1996. • Randall Martin, *Women Writers in Renaissance England*, 1997. • Charlotte F. Otten, ed., *English Women's Voices, 1540–1700*, 1992. • Barnabe Riche, *My Ladies Looking-Glasse*, 1616. • Simon Shepherd, ed., *The Women's Sharp Revenge: Five Women's Pamphlets from the Renaissance*, 1985. • Esther Soweram, *Ester Hath Hang'd Haman*, 1617. • Rachel Speght, *A Mouzell for Melastomus*, 1617. • Joseph Swetnam, *The Araignment of Lewde, Idle, Froward, and Unconstant Women*, 1615. • Betty Travitsky, ed., *The Paradise of Women: Writings by Englishwomen of the Renaissance*, 1981. • Margaret Tyler, *The Mirrour of Princely Deedes and Knighthood, Book I*, 1578.

Criticism. • Elaine Beilin, *Redeeming Eve: Women Writers of the English Renaissance*, 1987. • Ann Rosalind Jones, "Counterattacks on 'the Bayter of Women': Three Pamphleteers of the Early Seventeenth Century," in *The Renaissance Englishwoman in Print*, eds. Anne Hazelcorn and Betty Travitsky, 1990. • Constance Jordan, *Renaissance Feminism: Literary Texts and Political Models*, 1990. • Barbara Kiefer Lewalski, *Writing Women in Jacobean England*, 1993. • R. Valerie Lucas, "Hic Mulier: The Female Transvestite in Early Modern England," *Renaissance and Reformation*, vol. XXIV, no. 1, 1988. • Megan Matchinske, "Legislating 'Middle-Class' Morality in the Marriage Market: Ester Sowernam's, *Ester Hath Hang'd Haman*," *English Literary Renaissance*, vol. 24, no. 1, 1994. • Linda Woodbridge, *Women and the English Renaissance: Literature and the Nature of Womankind, 1540–1620*, 1986.

Francis Bacon • Editions. • John Pitcher, ed., *The Essays*, 1985. • Robert Leslie Ellis Spedding and Douglas Denon Heath, eds., *The Works of Francis Bacon (English and Latin)*, 14 vols., 1857–1874. • Brian Vickers, ed., *Selections*, 1996. • Sidney Warhaft, ed., *Selections*, 1986.

Biography. • Catherine Drinker Bowen, *Francis Bacon: The Temper of a Man*, 1963. • Jonathan L. Marwil, *The Trials of Counsel: Francis Bacon in 1621*, 1976. • Anthony Quinton, *Francis Bacon*, 1980. • Charles Williams, *Bacon*, 1933.

Criticism. • John C. Briggs, *Francis Bacon and the Rhetoric of Nature*, 1989. • Lisa Jardine, *Francis Bacon: Discovery and the Art of Discourse*, 1974. • Brian Vickers, *Francis Bacon and Renaissance Prose*, 1968.

Our Text. • Robert Leslie Ellis Spedding and Douglas Denon Heath, eds., *The Works of Francis Bacon (English and Latin)*, 14 vols., 1857–1874.

Richard Barnfield • Editions. • George Klawitter, ed., *Complete Poems*, 1990.

Criticism. • Alan Bray, *Homosexual Desire in Shakespeare's England*, 1982. • Gregory W. Bredbeck, *Sodomy and Interpretation: Marlowe to Milton*, 1991. • Bruce R. Smith, *Homosexual Desire in Shakespeare's England: A Cultural Poetics*, 1991.

The King James Bible • Elizabeth W. Cleaveland, *A Study of Tindale's* Genesis, *Compared with the* Genesis *of Coverdale and of the Authorized Version*, 1911, repr. 1972. • S. L. Greenslade, ed., *The Cambridge History of the*

Bible, vol. 3, *The West from the Reformation to the Present Day*, 1963. • John Ray Knott, *The Sword of the Spirit: Puritan Responses to the Bible*, 1980. • David Norton, *A History of the Bible as Literature*, 1993. • H. Wheeler Robinson, *The Bible in Its Ancient and English Versions*, 1954.

Sir Thomas Browne • Editions. • L. C. Martin, ed., Religio Medici *and Other Works*, 1964. • C. A. Patrides, ed., *Thomas Browne: The Major Works*, 1977. • Robin Robbins, ed., *Pseudodoxia Epidemica*, 1981. • James Winny, ed., *Religio Medici*, 1963.

Biography. • Joan Bennett, *Sir Thomas Browne*, 1962. • Dennis G. Donovan, *Sir Thomas Browne and Robert Burton: A Reference Guide*, 1981. • Frank L. Huntley, *Sir Thomas Browne: A Biographical and Critical Study*, 1962. • Jonathan F. S. Post, *Sir Thomas Browne*, 1987.

Criticism. • Roberta F. Brinkley, ed., *Coleridge on the Seventeenth Century*, 1955. • Howard Marchitello, *Narrative and Meaning in Early Modern England: Browne's Skull and Other Histories*, 1997. • Leonard Nathanson, *The Strategy of Truth*, 1967. • C. A. Patrides, ed., *Approaches to Sir Thomas Browne: The Ann Arbor Tercentenary Lectures and Essays*, 1982. • Sharon Cadman Seelig, *Generating Texts: The Progeny of Seventeenth-Century Prose*, 1996. • Victoria Silver, "Liberal Theology and Sir Thomas Browne's 'Soft and Flexible Discourse'," *English Literary Renaissance*, vol. 20, no. 1 (Winter), 1990.

Robert Burton • Editions. • Thomas C. Faulkner, Nicholas K. Kiessling, and Rhonda L. Blair, eds., *The Anatomy of Melancholy*, 1989. • Holbrook Jackson, ed., *Anatomy of Melancholy*, 1932.

Biography. • Michael O'Connell, *Robert Burton*, 1986.

Criticism. • Lawrence Babb, *Sanity in Bedlam*, 1959. • Ruth A. Fox, *The Tangled Chain: The Structure of Disorder in The Anatomy of Melancholy*, 1976. • Martin Heusser, *The Gilded Pill: A Study of the Reader-Writer Relationship in Robert Burton's* Anatomy of Melancholy, 1987. • Devon Hodges, *Renaissance Fictions of Anatomy*, 1985. • Raymond Klibanksy, Erwin Panofksky, and Fritz Saxl, *Saturn and Melancholy*, 1964. • Patricia Vicari, *The View from Minerva's Tower: Learning and Imagination in* The Anatomy of Melancholy, 1989.

Our Text. • Floyd Dell and Paul Jordan-Smith, eds., The Anatomy of Melancholy: *Now for the First Time with the Latin Given Completely in an All-English Text*, 1927.

Elizabeth Cary, Lady Falkland • Editions. • A. C. Dunstan and W. W. Greg, eds., *Elizabeth Cary*. The Tragedy of Mariam. *Facsimile of the 1613 Edition*, 1914. • Margaret Ferguson and Barry Weller, eds., The Tragedy of Mariam: The Fair Queen of Jewry *with* The Lady Falkland: Her Life by One of Her Daughters, 1994.

Biography. • Virginia Blain, Patricia Clements, and Isobel Grundy, eds., *The Feminist Companion to Literature in English: Women Writers from the Middle Ages to the Present*, 1990. • Kenneth Murdock, *The Sun at Noon: Three Biographical Sketches*, 1939.

Criticism. • Elaine Beilin, "Elizabeth Cary and *The Tragedie of Mariam*," *Papers on Language and Literature*, vol. 16, no. 1 (Winter), 1980. • Dympna Callaghan, "Re-reading, *The Tragedie of Mariam, the Faire Queene of Jewry*," in *Women, "Race," Writing in the Early Modern Period*, eds. Margo Hendricks and Patricia Parker, 1994. • Margaret Ferguson, "Running on With Almost Public Voice: The Case of 'E.C.'," *Tradition and the Talents of Women*, ed. Florence Howe, 1991. • Margaret Ferguson, "The Spectre of Resistance," *Staging the Renaissance: Reinterpretations of Elizabethan and Jacobean Drama*, eds. David Kastan and Peter Stallybrass, 1991. • Tina Krontiris, *Oppositional Voices: Women as Writers and Translators of Literature in the English Renaissance*, 1992. • Maureen Quilligan, "Staging Gender: William Shakespeare and Elizabeth Cary," *Sexuality and Gender in Early Modern Europe: Institutions, Texts, Images*, ed. James Grantham Turner, 1993. • Laurie J. Shannon, "*The Tragedie of Mariam:* Cary's Critique of the Terms of Founding Social Discourses," *English Literary Renaissance*, vol. 24, no. 1 (Winter), 1994. • Betty Travitsky, "The *Feme Covert* in Elizabeth Cary's *Mariam*," *Ambiguous Realities: Women in the Middle Ages and Renaissance*, eds. Carole Levin and Jeanie Watson, 1987.

Our Text. • A. C. Dunstan and W. W. Greg, eds., *Elizabeth Cary*. The Tragedy of Mariam. *Facsimile of the 1613 Edition*, 1914.

Thomas Dekker and Thomas Middleton • Editions. • Fredson Bowers, ed., *The Dramatic Works of Thomas Dekker*, 1953–1961. • A. H. Bullen, ed., *Works*, 1885–1886. • Havelock

Ellis, ed., *Thomas Middleton*, 1887–1890. • Paul Mulholland, ed., *The Roaring Girl*, 1987.

Biography. • Doris Ray Adler, *Thomas Dekker: A Reference Guide*, 1983. • Norman A. Brittin, *Thomas Middleton*, 1972. • George R. Price, *Thomas Dekker*, 1969. • Sara Jayne Steen, *Thomas Middleton: A Reference Guide*, 1984.

Criticism. • Jane Baston, "Rehabilitating Moll's Subversion in *The Roaring Girl*," *Studies in English Literature*, vol. 37, no. 2 (Spring), 1997. • Swapan Chakravorty, *Society and Politics in the Plays of Thomas Middleton*, 1996. • Larry Champion, *Thomas Dekker and the Traditions of English Drama*, 1985. • Viviana Comensoli, "Play-Making, Domestic Conduct, and the Multiple Plot in *The Roaring Girl*," *Studies in English Literature*, vol. 27, no. 2 (Spring), 1987. • Marjorie Garber, "The Logic of the Transvestite: *The Roaring Girl*," in *Staging the Renaissance: Reinterpretations of Elizabethan and Jacobean Drama*, David Scott Kastan and Peter Stallybrass, eds., 1991. • David M. Holmes, *The Art of Thomas Middleton*, 1970. • Jo E. Miller, "Women and the Market in *The Roaring Girl*," *Renaissance and Reformation*, vol. 14, no. 1 (Winter), 1990. • Mary Beth Rose, "Women in Men's Clothing: Apparel and Social Stability in *The Roaring Girl*," *English Literary Renaissance*, vol. 14, no. 3 (Autumn), 1984. • Paul Edward Yachnin, *Stage-Wrights: Shakespeare, Jonson, Middleton and the Making of Theatrical Value*, 1997. • Susan Zimmerman, ed., *Erotic Politics: Desire on the Renaissance Stage*, 1992.

Our Text. • A. H. Bullen, ed., *Works*, 1885–1886.

***The Roaring Girl* in Context: City Life** • Editions. • James Craigie and Alexander Law, eds., *Minor Prose Works of King James VI and I*, 1982. • Robert Greene, *A Notable Discovery of Cosenage*, 1591, ed. G. B. Harrison, 1923. • Arthur Kinney, ed., *Rogues, Vagabonds, and Sturdy Beggars: A New Gallery of Tudor and Early Stuart Rogue Literature*, 1990. • Francis Oscar Mann, ed., *The Works of Thomas Deloney*, 1912. • E. D. Pendry, ed., *Thomas Dekker:* The Wonderful Year; The Gulls's Horn-Book; Penny-Wise and Pound Foolish: English Villainies Discovered by Lantern and Candlelight *and Selected Writings*, 1967. • Barnabe Riche, My *Ladies Looking-Glasse*, 1616. • Stanley Wells, ed., *Thomas Nashe: Selected Writings*, 1964. • F. P. Wilson, ed., *The Works of Thomas Nashe, Edited from the Original Texts by Ronald B. McKerrow*, 1958.

Criticism. • Lorna Hutson, *Thomas Nashe in Context*, 1989. • Virginia L. MacDonald, "Robert Greene's Innovative Contributions to Prose Fiction in A *Notable Discovery*," *Shakespeare-Jarbuch*, vol. 117, 1981. • David Margolies, *Novel and Society in Elizabethan England*, 1985. • John Simons, *Realistic Romance: The Prose Fiction of Thomas Deloney*, 1983. • David L. Smith, Richard Strier, and David Bevington, eds., *The Theatrical City: Culture, Theatre, and Politics in London*, 1995. • Frederick Oswin Waage, *Thomas Dekker's Pamphlets, 1603–1609, and Jacobean Popular Literature*, 1977.

John Donne • Editions. • John Carey, ed., *John Donne: Selected Poetry*, 1996. • Helen Gardner, ed., *John Donne: The Divine Poems*, 1952. • Helen Gardner, ed., *John Donne: The Elegies and The Songs and Sonnets*, 1965. • H. J. C. Grierson, ed., *The Poems of John Donne*, 1912. • G. R. Peter and Evelyn Simpson, eds., *Sermons*, 10 vols., 1953–1962. • Neil Rhodes, ed., *Prose Works: Selections*, 1987. • A. J. Smith, ed., *John Donne: The Complete English Poems*, 1971. • Gary A. Stringer, ed., *The Variorum Edition of the Poetry of John Donne*, 1995.

Biography. • R. C. Bald, *John Donne: A Life*. 1970. • John Carey, *John Donne: Life, Mind and Art*, 1981. • Izaac Walton, *Life of Dr. John Donne*, ed. G. Saintsbury, 1927. • Frank J. Warnke, *John Donne*, 1987.

Criticism. • James S. Baumlin, *John Donne and the Rhetorics of Renaissance Discourse*, 1991. • Harold Bloom, ed., *John Donne and the Seventeenth-Century Metaphysical Poets*, 1986. • Cleanth Brooks, *The Well Wrought Urn*, 1949. • Meg Lotta Brown, *Donne and the Politics of Conscience*, 1995. • Naresh Chandra, *John Donne and Metaphysical Poetry*, 1990. • Denis Flynn, *John Donne and the Ancient Catholic Nobility*, 1995. • T. S. Eliot, *The Varieties of Metaphysical Poetry*, ed. Ronald Schuchard, 1993. • Barbara L. Estrin, *Laura: Uncovering Gender and Genre in Wyatt, Donne, and Marvell*, 1994. • Pierre Legouis, *Donne the Craftsman*, 1928. • Arthur F. Marotti, ed., *Critical Essays on John Donne*, 1994. • Arthur Marotti, *John Donne, a Coterie Poet*, 1986. • Murray Roston, *The Soul of Wit*, 1974. • A. J. Smith, ed., *John Donne: The Critical Heritage*, 1975–1996. • A. J. Smith, ed., *John Donne: Essays in Celebration*, 1972. • Helen Wilcox, Richard Todd, and Alasdair MacDonald, eds., *Sacred and Profane: Secular and Devotional Interplay in Early Modern British Literature*, 1996.

• William Zunder, *The Poetry of John Donne: Literature and Culture in the Elizabethan and Jacobean Period*, 1982.

Our Texts. • Helen Gardner, ed., *John Donne: The Divine Poems*, 1952. • H. J. C. Grierson, ed., *The Poems of John Donne*, 1912. • G. R. Peter and Evelyn Simpson, eds., *Sermons*, 10 vols., 1953–1962. • J. Sparrow, ed., *Devotions Upon Emergent Occasions*, 1923.

Queen Elizabeth I • Editions. • Leicester Bradner, ed., *The Poems of Elizabeth I*, 1964. • Caroline Pemberton, ed., *Queen Elizabeth's Englishings of Boethius,* De Consolatione Philosophiae, *A.D. 1593*, 1889, repr. 1973.

Biography. • Christopher Haigh, *Elizabeth I*, 1988. • Christopher Hibbert, *Elizabeth I: Genius of the Golden Age*, 1991. • Wallace MacCaffrey, *Elizabeth I*, 1993. • J. E. Neale, *Queen Elizabeth I*, 1934. • Maria Perry, *The Word of a Prince: The Life of Elizabeth from Contemporary Documents*, 1990.

Criticism. • Marie Axton, *The Queen's Two Bodies: Drama and Elizabethan Succession*, 1977. • Philippa Berry, *Of Chastity and Power: Elizabethan Literature and the Unmarried Queen*, 1989. • Susan Frye, *Elizabeth I: The Competition for Representation*, 1993. • Helen Hackett, *Virgin Mother, Maiden Queen: Elizabeth I and the Cult of the Virgin Mary*, 1995. • Lisa Hopkins, *Queen Elizabeth and Her Court*, 1990. • J. E. Neale, *Elizabeth and Her Parliaments*, 2 vols., 1953 • Frances Yates, *Astraea: The Imperial Theme*, 1973.

George Gascoigne • Editions. • John Cunliffe, ed., *The Complete Works*, 2 vols., 1907, 1910. • C. T. Prouty, ed., *A Hundreth Sundrie Flowres*, 1942.

Biography. • Ronald Johnson, *George Gascoigne*, 1972.

Criticism. • E. Jane Hedley, "Allegoria: Gascoigne's Master Trope," *English Literary Renaissance*, vol. 11, 1981. • Richard Helgerson, *Elizabethan Prodigals*, 1976. • Richard C. McCoy, "Gascoigne's 'Poemata Castrata': The Wages of Courtly Success." *Criticism*, vol. 27, 1985. • C. T. Prouty, *George Gascoigne, Elizabethan Courtier, Soldier, and Poet*, 1942, repr. 1966.

Edmund Spenser • Editions. • Edwin A. Greenlaw et al., eds., *The Works of Edmund Spenser, a Variorum Edition*, 10 vols., 1932–1949. • A. C. Hamilton, ed., *The Faerie Queene*, 1980. • William Oram et al., eds., *The Yale Edition of the Shorter Poems of Edmund Spenser*, 1989. • Thomas P. Roche, Jr. and C. Patrick O'Donell, eds., *Edmund Spenser:* The Faerie Queene, 1981. • J. C. Smith and E. De Selincourt, eds., *Complete Poetical Works*, 1970.

Biography. • Judith H. Anderson, Donald Cheney, and David A. Richardson, eds., *Spenser's Life and the Subject of Biography*, 1996. • Patrick Cheney, *Spenser's Famous Flight: A Renaissance Idea of a Literary Career*, 1993. • Richard Rambuss, *Spenser's Secret Career*, 1993.

Criticism. • Paul Alpers, *The Poetry of* The Faerie Queene, 1967. • Harry Berger, *The Allegorical Temper*, 1957. • Harry Berger, *Revisionary Play: Studies in the Spenserian Dynamics*, 1988. • Patricia Coughlan, ed., *Spenser and Ireland: An Interdisciplinary Perspective*, 1989. • Jonathan Goldberg, *Endlesse Worke: Spenser and the Structures of Discourse*, 1981. • Kenneth Gross, *Spenserian Poetics: Idolatry, Iconoclasm, and Magic*, 1985. • John Guillory, *Poetic Authority: Spenser, Milton, and Literary History*, 1983. • A .C. Hamilton, *The Spenser Encyclopedia*, 1990. • John N. King, *Spenser's Poetry and the Reformation Tradition*, 1990. • Theresa M. Krier, *Gazing on Secret Sights: Spenser, Classical Imitation, and the Decorums of Vision*, 1990. • Isabel G. MacCaffrey, *Spenser's Allegory: The Anatomy of the Imagination*, 1976. • David Lee Miller, *The Poem's Two Bodies: The Poetics of the 1590* Faerie Queene, 1988. • James Nohrnberg, *The Analogy of* The Faerie Queene, 1976. • Thomas P. Roche, Jr., *The Kindly Flame: A Study of the Third and Fourth Books of Spenser's* Faerie Queene, 1964. • John Rooks, *Love's Courtly Ethic in* The Faerie Queene: *From Garden to Wilderness*, 1992. • David R. Shore, *Spenser and the Poetics of Pastoral*, 1985. • Kathleen Williams, *Spenser's World of Glass: A Reading of* The Faerie Queene, 1966.

George Herbert • Editions. • Mario Di Cesare, ed., *George Herbert and the Seventeenth-Century Religious Poets*, 1978. • F. E. Hutchinson, ed., *The Works of George Herbert*, 1941. • C. A. Patrides, ed., *The English Poems of George Herbert*, 1974.

Biography. • Amy M. Charles, *Life of George Herbert*, 1977. • Stanley Stewart, *George Herbert*, 1986.

Criticism. • Stanley Fish, *The Living Temple: George Herbert and Catechizing*, 1978. • Barbara Leah Harman, *Costly Monuments: Representations of the Self in George Herbert's Poetry*,

1982. • Seamus Heaney, *The Redress of Poetry*, 1990. • Christopher Hodgkins, *Authority, Church, and Society in George Herbert: Return to the Middle Way*, 1993 • C. A. Patrides, ed., *George Herbert: The Critical Heritage*, 1983. • Terry Sherwood, *Herbert's Prayerful Art*, 1989. • Marion White Singleton, *God's Courtier: Configuring a Different Grace in George Herbert's Temple*, 1987. • J. H. Summers, *George Herbert: His Religion and Art*, 1954. • Rosemond Tuve, *A Reading of George Herbert*, 1952. • Helen Vendler, *The Poetry of George Herbert*, 1975.

Mary Herbert, Countess of Pembroke • Editions. • J. C. A. Rathmell, *The Psalms of Sir Philip Sidney and the Countess of Pembroke*, 1963. • G. F. Waller, *Poems, etc.*, 1977.

Biography. • Margaret P. Hannay, *Philip's Phoenix*, 1990.

Criticism. • Anne M. Haselkorn and Betty Travitsky, eds., *The Renaissance Englishwoman in Print: Counterbalancing the Canon*, 1990. • Mary Ellen Lamb, *Gender and Authorship in the Sidney Circle*, 1990. • Gary Waller, *Mary Sidney, Countess of Pembroke: A Critical Study of Her Writings and Literary Milieu*, 1979.

Robert Herrick • Editions. • L. C. Martin, ed., *Poetical Works*, 1956. • J. Max Patrick, ed., *Complete Poetry*, 1963.

Biography. • Roger B. Rollin, *Robert Herrick*, 1966. • George Walton Scott, *Robert Herrick*, 1974.

Criticism. • Robert Deming, *Ceremony and Art*, 1974. • A. Leigh Deneef, *"This Poetick Liturgy": Robert Herrick's Ceremonial Mode*, 1974. • Leah Marcus, *The Politics of Mirth: Jonson, Herrick, Milton, Marvell, and the Defense of Old Holiday Pastimes*, 1986. • Roger B. Rollin and J. Max Patrick, eds., *"Trust To Good Verses": Herrick Tercentenary Essays*, 1978. • L. E. Semler, "Robert Herrick, the Human Figure, and the English Mannerist Aesthetic," *Studies in English Literature*, vol. 35, no. 1 (Winter), 1995.

Thomas Hobbes • Editions. • C. P. MacPherson, ed., *Hobbes:* Leviathan, 1968. • Sir William Molesworth, ed., *Thomas Hobbes: English Works*, 11 vols., 1839–1845.

Biography. • Miriam Reik, *The Golden Lands of Thomas Hobbes*, 1977. • Arnold Rogow, *Thomas Hobbes: Radical in the Service of Reaction*, 1986.

Criticism. • Charles Cantalupo, *A Literary Leviathan:* Thomas Hobbes' Masterpiece of Language, 1991. • R. G. Collingwood, The New Leviathan *or Man, Civilization, and Barbarism*, ed. David Boucher. 1992. • David Johnston, *The Rhetoric of* Leviathan: *Thomas Hobbes and the Politics of Cultural Transformation*, 1986. • Samuel I. Mintz, *The Hunting of* Leviathan: *Seventeenth-Century Reaction to the Materialism and Moral Philosophy of Thomas Hobbes*, 1962. • Michael Oakeshott, *Hobbes on Civil Association*, 1975.

Henry Howard, Earl of Surrey • Editions. • Emrys Jones, ed., *Henry Howard, Earl of Surrey: Poems*, 1964.

Biography. • William Sessions, *Henry Howard, Earl of Surrey*, 1986.

Criticism. • Leonard Forster, *The Icy Fire: Five Studies in European Petrarchanism*, 1969. • Susanne Woods, *Natural Emphasis: English Versification from Chaucer to Dryden*, 1984, c1985.

Ben Jonson • Editions. • Robert Adams, ed., *Ben Jonson's Plays and Masques*, 1979. • Ian Donaldson, ed., *Ben Jonson*, 1985. • C. H. Herford, Percy Simspon, and Evelyn Simpson, eds., *The Works of Ben Jonson*, 11 vols., 1925–1952. • Stephen Orgel, ed., *Complete Masques*, 1969. • Helen Ostovich, ed., *Jonson, Four Comedies*, 1997.

Biography. • David Riggs, *Ben Jonson: A Life*, 1989. • George E. Rowe, *Distinguishing Jonson*, 1988.

Criticism. • Richard Burt, *Licensed by Authority: Ben Jonson and the Discourses of Censorship*, 1993. • Ian Donaldson, *The World Upside Down*, 1970. • Jonathan Haynes, *The Social Relations of Jonson's Theater*, 1992. • Richard Helgerson, *Self-Crowned Laureates*, 1983. • James Hirsh, ed., *New Perspectives on Ben Jonson*, 1997. • G. B. Jackson, *Vision and Judgment in Ben Jonson's Drama*, 1968. • Alexander Leggatt, *Ben Jonson, His Vision and His Art*, 1981. • Katharine Eisaman Maus, *Ben Jonson and the Roman Frame of Mind*, 1984. • David C. McPherson, *Shakespeare, Jonson and the Myth of Venice*, 1990. • Rosalind Miles, *Ben Jonson, His Craft and Art*, 1990. • Stephen Orgel, *The Jonsonian Masque*, 1965. • Stephen Orgel and Roy Strong, *Inigo Jones: The Theatre of the Stuart Court*, 1973. • E. B. Patridge, *The Broken Compass*, 1958. • William W. E.

Slights, *Ben Jonson and the Art of Secrecy*, 1994. John Gordon Sweeney, *Jonson and the Psychology of the Public Theater*, 1985. • Robert N. Watson, *Ben Jonson's Parodic Strategy*, 1987. • Don E. Wayne, *Penshurst: The Semiotics of Place and the Poetics of History*, 1984.

Our Text. • C. H. Herford, Percy Simspon, and Eveyln Simpson, eds., *The Works of Ben Jonson*, 11 vols., 1925–1952.

Aemilia Lanyer • Editions. • A. L. Rowse, ed., *The Poems of Shakespeare's Dark Lady:* Salve Deus Rex Judaeorum, 1979. • Susanne Woods, ed., *The Poems of Aemilia Lanyer:* Salve Deus Rex Judaeorum, 1993.

Criticism. • Barbara Kiefer Lewalski, *Writing Women in Jacobean England*, 1993. • Lisa Schnell, "'So Great a Diffrence Is There in Degree': Aemilia Lanyer and the Aims of Feminist Criticism," *Modern Language Quarterly*, vol. 57, no. 1, 1996.

Richard Lovelace • Editions. • C. H. Wilkinson, ed., *The Poems of Richard Lovelace*, 1925.

Biography. • Manfred Weidhorn, *Richard Lovelace*, 1970.

Criticism. • Raymond A. Anselment, "'Stone Walls' and 'Iron Bars': Richard Lovelace and the Conventions of Seventeenth-Century Prison Literature," *Renaissance and Reformation*, vol. 17, no. 1 (Winter), 1993. • Cyril Hughes Hartmann, *The Cavalier Spirit and Its Influence on the Life and Work of Richard Lovelace*, 1970. • Earl Miner, *The Cavalier Mode from Jonson to Cotton*, 1971. • Sharon Cadman Seelig, "My Curious Hand or Eye: The Wit of Richard Lovelace," *The Wit of Seventeenth-Century Poetry*, eds. Claude J. Summers and Ted-Larry Pebworth, 1995. • Claude J. Summers and Ted-Larry Pebworth, eds., *Classic and Cavalier: Essays on Jonson and the Sons of Ben*, 1982. • Geoffrey Walton, "The Cavalier Poets," *The New Pelican Guide to English Literature III: From Donne to Marvell*, ed. Boris Ford, 1982.

Our Text. • C. H. Wilkinson, ed., *The Poems of Richard Lovelace*, 1925.

Andrew Marvell • Editions. • Elizabeth Story Donno, ed., *The Complete Poems*, 1985. • Frank Kermode and Keith Walker, eds., *Poems. Selections*, 1994. • M. Margoliouth, ed., *Poems and Letters*, 1927, rev. Pierre Legouis and E. E. Duncan-Jones, 1971.

Biography. • John Dixon Hunt, *Andrew Marvell: His Life and Writings*, 1978. • Patsy Griffin, *The Modest Ambition of Andrew Marvell: A Study of Marvell and His Relation to Lovelace, Fairfax, Cromwell, and Milton*, 1995. • Thomas Wheeler, *Andrew Marvell Revisited*, 1996.

Criticism. • Philip Brockbank, *Approaches to Marvell*, ed. C. A. Patrides, 1978. • Warren L. Chernaik, *The Poet's Time: Politics and Religion in the Work of Andrew Marvell*, 1983. • Rosalie Colie, *My Echoing Song*, 1970. • Conal Condren and A. D. Cousins, eds., *The Political Identity of Andrew Marvell*, 1990. • Patrick Cullen, *Spenser, Marvell, and Renaissance Pastoral*, 1970. • E. S. Donno, ed., *Andrew Marvell: The Critical Heritage*, 1978. • Annabel Patterson, *Marvell and the Civic Crown*, 1978. • Allan Pritchard, "Marvell's 'The Garden': A Restoration Poem?" *Studies in English Literature*, vol. 23, no. 3 (Summer), 1983. • Robert Wilcher, *Andrew Marvell*, 1985.

Our Text. • M. Margoliouth, ed., *Poems and Letters*, 1927.

Christopher Marlowe • Editions. • David Bevington and Eric Rasmussen, eds., Doctor Faustus *A-and B-Texts (1604, 1616): Christopher Marlowe and his Collaborator and Revisers*, 1993. • Fredson Bowers, *The Complete Works of Christopher Marlowe*, 2 vols., 1981. • Stephen Orgel, *The Complete Poems and Translations of Christopher Marlowe*, 1971.

Biography. • John Bakeless, *The Tragicall History of Christopher Marlowe*, 2 vols., 1942. • Charles Nicholl, *The Reckoning: The Murder of Christopher Marlowe*, 1992.

Criticism. • C. L. Barber, *Creating Elizabethan Tragedy: The Theater of Marlowe and Kyd*, 1988. • Douglas Cole, *Suffering and Evil in the Plays of Christopher Marlowe*, 1962. • Roma Gill, *The Plays of Christopher Marlowe*, 1971. • Darryll Grantley and Peter Roberts, eds., *Christopher Marlowe and English Renaissance Culture*, 1996. • Clark Hulse, *Metamorphic Verse: The Elizabethan Minor Epic*, 1981. • William Keach, *Elizabethan Erotic Narratives*, 1977. • Harry Levin, *The Overreacher: A Study of Christopher Marlowe*, 1952. • Simon Shepherd, *Marlowe and the Politics of Elizabethan Theater*, 1986. • Vivien Thomas and William Tydeman, eds., *Christopher Marlowe: The Plays and Their Sources*, 1994.

John Milton • Editions. • John Carey and Alastair Fowler, eds., *The Poems of John Milton*,

1968. • Alastair Fowler, ed., *John Milton:* Paradise Lost, 1968. • Merritt Y. Hughes, ed., *Complete Poetry and Major Prose*, 1957. • C. A. Patrides, ed., *John Milton: Selected Prose*, 1985. • F. A. Patterson et al., eds., *The Works of John Milton*, 1931–1938. • Don M. Wolfe, ed., *The Complete Prose Works of John Milton*, 1953–1982.

Biography. • Douglas Bush, *John Milton*, 1964. • Joseph M. French, *The Life Records of John Milton*, 1949–1958. • W. R. Parker, *Milton: A Biography*, 1968. • A. N. Wilson, *The Life of John Milton*, 1983.

Criticism. • Arthur Barker, *Milton and the Puritan Dilemma, 1641–1660*, 1942. • Joan S. Bennett, *Reviving Liberty: Radical Christian Humanism in Milton's Great Poems*, 1989. • Lana Cable, *Carnal Rhetoric: Milton's Iconoclasm and the Poetics of Desire*, 1995. • Dennis Danielson, ed., *The Cambridge Companion to Milton*, 1989. • Mario Di Cesare, ed., *Milton in Italy*, 1991. • William Empson, *Milton's God*, 1965. • Stanley Fish, *Surprised by Sin: The Argument of* Paradise Lost, 1971. • Christopher Hill, *Milton and the English Revolution*, 1977. • Frank Kermode, *The Living Milton*, 1960. • Barbara K. Lewalski, Paradise Lost *and the Rhetoric of Literary Forms*, 1985. • C. S. Lewis, *A Preface to* Paradise Lost, 1942. • David Lowenstein and James Grantham Turner, *Politics, Poetics, and Hermeneutics in Milton's Prose*, 1990. • Kristin McColgan and Charles Durham, eds., *Arenas of Conflict: Milton and the Unfettered Mind*, 1996. • Marjorie Nicolson, *John Milton: A Reader's Guide to His Poetry*, 1963. • Mary Nyquist and Margaret Ferguson, eds., *Remembering Milton: Essays on the Texts and Traditions*, 1988. • W. R. Parker, *Milton's Debt to Greek Tragedy in* Samson Agonistes, 1937. • Annabel Patterson, ed., *John Milton*, 1992. • Maureen Quilligan, *Milton's Spenser: The Politics of Reading*, 1983. • Mary Ann Radzinowicz, *Toward* Samson Agonistes, 1978. • B. Rajan, Paradise Lost *and the Seventeenth-Century Reader*, 1962. • John Rogers, *The Matter of Revolution: Science, Poetry and Politics in the Age of Milton*, 1996. • John P. Rumrich, *Milton Unbound: Controversy and Reinterpretation*, 1996. • John T. Shawcross, *John Milton: The Self and the World*, 1993. • John Steadman, *Epic and Tragic Structure in* Paradise Lost, 1976. • Paul Stevens, *Imagination and the Presence of Shakespeare in* Paradise Lost, 1985. • Joseph Summers, *The Muse's Method: An Introduction to* Paradise Lost, 1962. • Joseph Wittreich, *Interpreting* Samson Agonistes, 1986.

Our Text. • Merrit Y. Hughes, ed., *Complete Poetry and Major Prose*, 1957.

Annotations Based On. • John Carey and Alastair Fowler, eds., *The Poems of John Milton*, 1968. • Alastair Fowler, ed., *John Milton: Paradise Lost*, 1968.

Sir Thomas More • Editions. • *The Yale Edition of the Complete Works of St. Thomas More*, vols. 2–6, 8–15, 1963–1984. • George M. Logan and Robert M. Adams, eds., *Utopia*, 1989. • Edward Surtz and J. H. Hexter, eds., *Utopia*, 1964.

Biography. • Alistair Fox, *Thomas More: History and Providence*, 1983. • Richard Marius, *Thomas More: A Biography*, 1984. • Louis L. Martz, *Thomas More: The Search for the Inner Man*, 1990.

Criticism. • Alistair Fox, Utopia: *An Elusive Vision*, 1993. • J. H. Hexter, *More's* Utopia: *Biography of an Idea*, 1952, rev. 1965. • Robbin S. Johnson, *More's* Utopia: *Ideal and Illusion*, 1969. • George M. Logan, *The Meaning of More's* Utopia, 1983.

Katherine Philips • Editions. • George Saintsbury, ed., *Minor Poets of the Caroline Period*, 1905. • Patrick Thomas, ed., *The Collected Works of Katherine Philips:* The Matchless Orinda, 1993.

Biography. • Philip Webster Souers, *The Matchless Orinda*, 1931. • Patrick Thomas, *Katherine Philips* (Orinda), 1988.

Criticism. • Harriette Andreadis, "The Sapphic-Platonics of Katherine Philips, 1632–1664," *Signs*, vol. 15, no. 1 (Autumn), 1989. • Celia A. Easton, "Excusing the Breach of Nature's Laws: The Discourse of Denial and Disguise in Katherine Philips' Friendship Poetry," *Restoration Studies in English Literary Culture*, 1660–1700, vol. 14, no. 1 (Spring), 1990. • Elizabeth Hageman, "Katherine Philips: *The Matchless Orinda*," in Katharina M. Wilson, ed., *Women Writers of the Renaissance and Reformation*, 1987. • Claudia A. Limbert, "The Poetry of Katherine Philips: Holographs, Manuscripts, and Early Printed Texts," *Philological Quarterly*, vol. 70, no. 2 (Spring), 1991. • Dorothy Mermin, "Women Becoming Poets: Katherine Philips, Aphra Behn, Anne Finch," *English Literary History*, vol. 57, no. 2 (Summer), 1990. • Ellen Moody, "Orinda, Rosania, Lucasia et Aliae: Towards a New Edition of the Works of

Katherine Philips," *Philological Quarterly*, vol. 66, no. 3 (Summer), 1987. • Arlene Stiebel, "Subversive Sexuality: Masking the Erotic in Poems by Katherine Philips and Aphra Behn," *Renaissance Discourses of Desire*, eds. Claude J. Summers and Ted Larry Pebworth, 1993.

Our Text. • Katherine Philips, *Poems by the Most Deservedly Admired Mrs. Katherine Philips The Matchless Orinda*, 1669.

Sir Walter Raleigh • Editions. • A. M. C. Latham, ed., *Poems*, 1950. • William Oldys and Thomas Birch, eds., *The Works of Sir Walter Raleigh*, 8 vols., 1829, repr. 1968.

Biography. • Willard Wallace, *Sir Walter Raleigh*, 1959.

Criticism. • Philip Edwards, *Sir Walter Ralegh*, 1953, repr. 1976. • Stephen J. Greenblatt, *Sir Walter Ralegh: The Renaissance Man and His Roles*, 1973. • David B. Quinn, *Ralegh and the British Empire*, 1947, repr. 1962. • E. A. Strathmann, *Sir Walter Ralegh: A Study in Elizabethan Skepticism*, 1951.

***The Discovery* in Context: Voyage Literature** • Editions. • Arthur Barlow, in Richard Hakluyt, *The Principal Navigations, Voyages, Traffiques, and Discoveries of the English Nation*, 8 vols., 1907. • Richard Hakluyt, *Divers Voyages Touching the Discoverie of America*, 1580. • Thomas Hariot, *Briefe and True Report of the Newfoundland Land of Virginia*, 1580; facs., 1931. • René Landonnière in Richard Hakluyt, *The Principal Navigations, Voyages, Traffiques, and Discoveries of the English Nation*, 8 vols., 1907. • Michel de Montaigne, *Essays*, trans. John Florio, 3 vols., 1910, repr. 1928.

William Shakespeare, *Othello* • Editions. • David Bevington, ed., *The Complete Works of Shakespeare*, 1992. • Alvin Kernan, ed., *The Tragedy of Othello, the Moor of Venice*, 1965. • Norman Sanders, *Othello*, 1984. • Alice Walker and John Dover Wilson, eds., *Othello*, 1969.

Criticism. • Jane Adamson, Othello *as Tragedy: Some Problems of Judgment and Feeling*, 1980. • James R. Aubrey, "Race and the Spectacle of the Monstrous in *Othello*," *Clio*, vol. 22, no. 3 (Spring), 1993. • John Bayley, "Love and Identity," *The Characters of Love: A Study in the Literature of Personality*, 1960. • Anthony Gerard Barthelemy, ed., *Critical Essays on Shakespeare's* Othello, 1994. • Lynda E. Boose, "Othello's Handkerchief: 'The Recognizance and Pledge of Love'," *English Literary Renaissance*, vol. 5, 1975. • A. C. Bradley, "*Othello*," in *Shakespearean Tragedy*, 1904. • Stanley Cavell, "Literature as Knowledge of the Outsider," *The Claim of Reason: Wittgenstein, Scepticism, Morality and Tragedy*, 1979. • Helen Gardner, "The Noble Moor," *Proceedings of the British Academy*, vol. 41, 1956 (for 1955). • Harley Granville-Barker, "Preface to *Othello*," *Prefaces to Shakespeare*, vol. II, 1946–1947. • Stephen Greenblatt, "The Improvisation of Power," *Renaissance Self-Fashioning*, 1980. • Kim Hall, "Beauty and the Beast of Whiteness: Teaching Race and Gender," *Shakespeare Quarterly*, vol. 47, no. 4 (Winter), 1996. • Margo Hendricks and Patricia Parker, eds., *Women, "Race," and Writing in the Early Modern Period*, 1994. • Eldred Jones, *Othello's Countrymen: The African in English Renaissance Drama*, 1965. • Carol Thomas Neely, "Women and Men in *Othello*: 'What Should Such a Fool / Do With So Good a Woman?'" in *The Woman's Part: Feminist Criticism of Shakespeare*, eds. Carolyn Ruth Swift Lenz, Gayle Greene, and Carol Thomas Neely, 1980. • Martin Orkin, "*Othello* and the 'Plain Face' of Racism," *Shakespeare Quarterly*, vol. 38, 1987. • Marvin Rosenberg, *The Masks of* Othello: *The Search for the Identity of Othello, Iago and Desdemona by Three Centuries of Actors and Critics*, 1961. • Virginia Mason Vaughan, Othello: *A Contextual History*, 1994.

Our Text. • David Bevington, ed., *The Complete Works of Shakespeare*, 1992.

***Othello* in Context: Ethnography and the Literature of Travel and Colonization** • Editions. • Edward Arber, ed., *The First Three English Books on America*, 1885, repr. 1971. • Richard Eden, *The Decades of the New World ... Written in ... Latin ... by Peter Martyr*, 1555. • Robert Brown, ed., *The History and Description of Africa ... Written by Al-Hassan Ibn-Mohammed Al Wezaz Al-Fasi ... Done into English in the Year 1600, by John Pory*, 3 vols., 1896. • Henry Morley, ed., *Ireland Under Elizabeth and James the First, Described by Edmund Spenser, Sir John Davies and Fynes Moryson*, 1890. • Andrew Hadfield and Willy Maley, eds., A View of the State of Ireland: *From the First Printed Edition (1633)*, 1997. • Pliny the younger, *The History of the World. Commonly Called the Naturall Historie of C. Plinius Secundus. Translated into English by Philemon Hol-*

land, 1601. • Philip L. Barbour, ed., *The Complete Works of Captain John Smith*, 1986.

Criticism. • Emily C. Bartels, "Making More of the Moor: Aaron, Othello, and Renaissance Refashioning of Race," *Shakespeare Quarterly*, vol. 41, no. 4 (Winter), 1990. • Rosalind R. Johnson, "The African Presence in Shakespearean Drama: Parallels Between Othello and the Historical Leo Africanus," *Journal of African Civilizations*, vol. 7, no. 2, 1985. • Eldred D. Jones, *The Elizabethan Image of Africa*, 1971.

Sir Philip Sidney • Editions. • Katherine Duncan-Jones, ed., *The Countess of Pembroke's* Arcadia (The Old Arcadia), 1985. • Katherine Duncan-Jones and Jan van Dorsten, eds., *Miscellaneous Prose of Sir Philip Sidney*, 1973. • Maurice Evans, ed., *The Countess of Pembroke's* Arcadia, 1977. • Albert Feuillerat, ed., *The Complete Works*, 4 vols., 1922–1926. • Robert Kimbrough, ed., *Sir Philip Sidney: Selected Prose and Poetry*, 1983. • William Ringler, ed., *Poetry*, 1962. • Jean Robertson, *The Countess of Pembroke's* Arcadia (The Old Arcadia), 1973. • J. A Van Dorsten, ed., *A Defence of Poetry*, 1966.

Biography. • John Buxton, *Sir Philip Sidney and the English Renaissance*, 1964. • Katharine Duncan-Jones, *Sir Philip Sidney, Courtier Poet*, 1991. • A. C. Hamilton, *Sir Philip Sidney: A Study of His Life and Works*, 1977. • James M. Osborn, *Young Philip Sidney, 1572–1577*, 1972.

Criticism. • Dorothy Connell, *Sir Philip Sidney: The Maker's Mind*, 1977. • David Kalstone, *Sidney's Poetry: Contexts and Interpretations*, 1965. • Dennis Kay, ed., *Sir Philip Sidney: An Anthology of Modern Criticism*, 1987. • Arthur F. Kinney, ed., *Sidney in Retrospect: Selections from English Literary Renaissance*, 1988. • Jon S. Lawry, *Sidney's Two Arcadias; Pattern and Proceeding*, 1972. • Richard C. McCoy, *Sir Philip Sidney: Rebellion in Arcadia*, 1978. • Gary F. Waller and Michael D. Moore, *Sir Philip Sidney and the Interpretation of Renaissance Culture: A Collection of Critical and Scholarly Essays*, 1984. • Andrew D. Weiner, *Sir Philip Sidney and the Poetics of Protestantism: A Study of Contexts*, 1978.

***The Apology* in Context: The Art of Poetry** • Editions. • Samuel Daniel, *A Defence of Ryme*, ed. G. B. Harrison, 1966. • George Gascoigne, *The Complete Works*, ed. John Cunliffe, 2 vols., 1907, 1910. • Stephen Gosson, *The School of Abuse*, ed. Edward Arber, 1869. • George Puttenham, *The Arte of English Poesie*, eds. Gladys Dodge Willcock and Alice Walker, 1970.

Criticism. • Peter C. Herman, *Squitter-Wits and Muse-Haters: Sidney, Spenser, Milton and Renaissance Antipoetic Sentiment*, 1996.

John Skelton • Editions. • Robert S. Kinsman, ed., *Poems*, 1969. • John Scattergood, ed., *Complete English Poems*, 1983.

Biography. • Nan Cooke Carpenter, *John Skelton*, 1967.

Criticism. • Stanley Fish, *John Skelton's Poetry*, 1965. • Richard Halpern, *The Poetics of Primitive Accumulation: English Renaissance Culture and the Genealogy of Capital*, 1991. • Arthur F. Kinney, *John Skelton: Priest as Poet, Seasons of Discovery*, 1987. • Greg Walker, *John Skelton and the Politics of the 1520s*, 1988.

Henry Vaughan • Editions. • French Fogle, ed., *The Complete Poetry of Henry Vaughan*, 1964. • Alan Rudrum, ed., *The Complete Poems of Henry Vaughan*, 1976.

Biography. • F. E. Hutchinson, *Henry Vaughan, a Life and Interpretation*, 1947.

Criticism. • Thomas O. Calhoun, *Henry Vaughan: The Achievement of Silex Scintillans*, 1981. • Elizabeth Holmes, *Henry Vaughan and the Hermetic Philosophy*, 1932. • E. C. Pettet, *Of Paradise and Light*, 1960. • Jonathan Post, *The Unfolding Vision*, 1982. • Alan Rudrum, *Essential Articles for the Study of Henry Vaughan*, 1987. • Noel K. Thomas, *Henry Vaughan: Poet of Revelation*, 1986.

Our Text. • L. C. Martin, *Works*, 1957.

Isabella Whitney • Editions. • Michael David Felder, *The Poems of Isabella Whitney: A Critical Edition*.

Criticism. • Elaine V. Beilin, "Writing Public Poetry: Humanism and the Woman Writer," *Modern Language Quarterly*, vol. 51, 1990. • Ann Rosalind Jones, "Nets and Bridles: Early Modern Conduct Books and Sixteenth-Century Women's Lyrics," *The Ideology of Conduct: Essays on Literature and the History of Sexuality*, eds. Nancy Armstrong and Leonard Tennenhouse, 1987. • Wendy Wall, "Isabella Whitney and the Female Legacy," *English Literary History*, vol. 58, 1991.

Lady Mary Wroth • Editions. • R. E. Pritchard, ed., *Poems: A Modernized Edition*, 1996. • Josephine A. Roberts, ed., *The Poems of Lady Mary Wroth*, 1983. • Josephine A. Roberts, ed., *The First Part of the Countess of Montgomery's* Urania *by Lady Mary Wroth*, 1995. • G. F. Waller, ed., *Pamphilia to Amphilanthus*, 1977.

Biography. • Kim Walker, *Women Writers of the English Renaissance*, 1996.

Criticism. • Naomi J. Miller, *Changing the Subject: Mary Wroth and the Figurations of Gender in Early Modern England*, 1996. • Naomi J. Miller and Gary Waller, eds., *Reading Mary Wroth: Representing Alternatives in Early Modern England*, 1991. • May Nelson Paulissen, *The Love Sonnets of Lady Mary Wroth: A Critical Introduction*, 1982. • Gary Waller, *The Sidney Family Romance: Mary Wroth, William Herbert, and the Early Modern Construction of Gender*, 1993. • Anne Hazelcorn and Betty Travitsky, eds., *The Renaissance Englishwoman in Print*, 1990.

Sir Thomas Wyatt • Editions. • Kenneth Muir and Patricia Thomson, *Collected Poems of Sir Thomas Wyatt*, 1693. • Richard Harrier, *The Canon of Sir Thomas Wyatt's Poetry*, 1975.

Biography. • Stephen Foley, *Sir Thomas Wyatt*, 1990.

Criticism. • Jonathan Crewe, *Trials of Authorship: Anterior Forms and Poetic Reconstruction from Wyatt to Shakespeare*, 1990. • Barbara Estrin, *Laura: Uncovering Gender and Genre in Wyatt, Donne and Marvell*, 1994. • Thomas M. Greene, *The Light in Troy: Imitation and Discovery in Renaissance Poetry*, 1982.

INDEX